TheStreet Ratings' Guide to Exchange-Traded Funds

TheStreet Ratings' Guide to Exchange-Traded Funds

A Quarterly Compilation of Investment Ratings and Analyses Covering ETFs and Other Closed-End Mutual Funds

Winter 2012-13

GREY HOUSE PUBLISHING

TheStreet, Inc.
14 Wall Street, 15th Floor
New York, NY 10005
800-289-9222

The Street Ratings

Published by Grey House Publishing, Inc. located at 4919 Route 22, Amenia, NY, 12501; telephone 518-789-8700. Grey House Publishing neither guarantees the accuracy of the data contained herein nor assumes any responsibility for errors, omissions or discrepancies. Grey House Publishing accepts no payment for listing; inclusion in the publication of any organization agency, institution, publication, service or individual does not imply endorsement of the publisher.

Grey House
Publishing

4919 Route 22
PO Box 56
Amenia, NY 12501-0056

Edition No. 39, Winter 2012-13

ISBN: 978-1-61925-019-2
ISSN: 2158-6101

Contents

Introduction

Appendix

* Includes other Closed-End Funds

Terms and Conditions

This Document is prepared strictly for the confidential use of our customer(s). It has been provided to you at your specific request. It is not directed to, or intended for distribution to or use by, any person or entity who is a citizen or resident of or located in any locality, state, country or other jurisdiction where such distribution, publication, availability or use would be contrary to law or regulation or which would subject TheStreet or its affiliates to any registration or licensing requirement within such jurisdiction.

No part of the analysts' compensation was, is, or will be, directly or indirectly, related to the specific recommendations or views expressed in this research report.

This Document is not intended for the direct or indirect solicitation of business. TheStreet, Inc. and its affiliates disclaims any and all liability to any person or entity for any loss or damage caused, in whole or in part, by any error (negligent or otherwise) or other circumstances involved in, resulting from or relating to the procurement, compilation, analysis, interpretation, editing, transcribing, publishing and/or dissemination or transmittal of any information contained herein.

TheStreet has not taken any steps to ensure that the securities or investment vehicle referred to in this report are suitable for any particular investor. The investment or services contained or referred to in this report may not be suitable for you and it is recommended that you consult an independent investment advisor if you are in doubt about such investments or investment services. Nothing in this report constitutes investment, legal, accounting or tax advice or a representation that any investment or strategy is suitable or appropriate to your individual circumstances or otherwise constitutes a personal recommendation to you.

The ratings and other opinions contained in this Document must be construed solely as statements of opinion from TheStreet, Inc., and not statements of fact. Each rating or opinion must be weighed solely as a factor in your choice of an institution and should not be construed as a recommendation to buy, sell or otherwise act with respect to the particular product or company involved.

Past performance should not be taken as an indication or guarantee of future performance, and no representation or warranty, expressed or implied, is made regarding future performance. Information, opinions and estimates contained in this report reflect a judgment at its original date of publication and are subject to change without notice. TheStreet offers a notification service for rating changes on companies you specify. For more information call 1-800-289-9222 or visit www.thestreet.com/ratings. The price, value and income from any of the securities or financial instruments mentioned in this report can fall as well as rise.

This Document and the information contained herein is copyrighted by TheStreet, Inc. Any copying, displaying, selling, distributing or otherwise delivering of this information or any part of this Document to any other person, without the express written consent of TheStreet, Inc. except by a reviewer or editor who may quote brief passages in connection with a review or a news story, is prohibited.

Welcome to TheStreet Ratings
Guide to Exchange-Traded Funds

With the growing popularity of mutual fund investing, consumers need a reliable source to help them track and evaluate the performance of their mutual fund holdings. Plus, they need a way of identifying and monitoring other funds as potential new investments. Unfortunately, the hundreds of performance and risk measures available – multiplied by the vast number of mutual fund investments on the market today – can make this a daunting task for even the most sophisticated investor.

TheStreet Investment Ratings simplify the evaluation process. We condense all of the available mutual fund data into a single composite opinion of each fund's risk-adjusted performance. This allows you to instantly identify those funds that have historically done well and those that have underperformed the market. While there is no guarantee of future performance, TheStreet Investment Ratings provide a solid framework for making informed investment decisions.

TheStreet Ratings' Mission Statement

TheStreet Ratings' mission is to empower consumers, professionals, and institutions with high quality advisory information for selecting or monitoring a financial services company or financial investment.

In doing so, TheStreet Ratings will adhere to the highest ethical standards by maintaining our independent, unbiased outlook and approach to advising our customers.

Why rely on TheStreet Ratings?

TheStreet Ratings provides financial strength ratings evaluating the financial stability of insurance companies and banks in addition to TheStreet Investment Ratings. Our goal is to provide fair, objective information to help professionals and consumers alike make educated purchasing decisions.

At TheStreet Ratings, objectivity and total independence are never compromised. We never take a penny from rated companies for issuing our ratings, and we publish them without regard for the companies' preferences. TheStreet's ratings are more frequently reviewed and updated than any other ratings, so you can be sure that the information you receive is accurate and current.

Our rating scale, from A to E, is easy to understand as follows:

	Rating	Description
Top 10% of funds	A	Excellent
Next 20% of funds	B	Good
Middle 40% of funds	C	Fair
Next 20% of funds	D	Weak
Bottom 10% of funds	E	Very Weak

In addition, a plus or minus sign designates that a fund is in the top third or bottom third of funds with the same letter grade.

Thank you for your trust and purchase of this Guide. If you have any comments, or wish to review other products from TheStreet Ratings, please call 1-800-289-9222 or visit www.thestreetratings.com. We look forward to hearing from you.

How to Use This Guide

The purpose of the *Guide to Exchange-Traded Funds* is to provide investors with a reliable source of investment ratings and analyses on a timely basis. We realize that past performance is an important factor to consider when making the decision to purchase shares in a mutual fund. The ratings and analyses in this Guide can make that evaluation easier when you are considering ETF and other closed-end:

- growth funds

- sector or international funds

- municipal bond funds

- corporate bond funds

- or other ETFs and closed-end funds

However, this Guide does not include open-end mutual funds since they represent a whole separate class of investments with unique risk profiles and performance expectations. For information on open-end equity funds, refer to *TheStreet Ratings' Guide to Stock Mutual Funds*. And if you are interested in open-end bond or money market funds, refer to *TheStreet Ratings' Guide to Bond and Money Market Mutual Funds*.

The rating for a particular fund indicates our opinion regarding that fund's past risk-adjusted performance. When evaluating a specific mutual fund, we recommend you follow these steps:

Step 1   **Confirm the fund name and ticker symbol.** To ensure you evaluate the correct mutual fund, verify the fund's exact name and ticker symbol as it was given to you in its prospectus or appears on your account statement. Many funds have similar names, so you want to make sure the fund you look up is really the one you are interested in evaluating.

Step 2   **Check the fund's Investment Rating.** Turn to Section I, the Index of Exchange-Traded Funds, and locate the fund you are evaluating. This section contains all ETFs and other closed-end mutual funds analyzed by TheStreet Ratings, including those that did not receive a Investment Rating. All funds are listed in alphabetical order by the name of the fund with the ticker symbol following the name for additional verification. Once you have located your specific fund, the first column after the ticker symbol shows its Investment Rating. Turn to *About TheStreet Investment Ratings* on page 7 for information about what this rating means.

Step 3   **Analyze the supporting data.** Following TheStreet Investment Rating are some of the various measures we have used in rating the fund. Refer to the Section I introduction (beginning on page 15) to see what each of these factors measures. In most cases, lower rated funds will have a low performance rating and/or a low risk rating (i.e., high volatility). Bear in mind, however, that TheStreet Investment Rating is the result of a complex computer-generated analysis which cannot be reproduced using only the data provided here.

When looking to identify a mutual fund that achieves your specific investing goals, we recommend the following:

Step 4   **View the top-performing funds.** If your priority is to achieve the highest return, regardless of the amount of risk, turn to Section V which lists the ETFs and other closed-end mutual funds with the best financial performance. Keep in mind that past performance alone is not always a true indicator of the future since these funds have already experienced a run up in price and could be due for a correction.

Step 5   **View the top-rated funds by fund type.** If you are looking to invest in a particular type of mutual fund (e.g., corporate high-yield bond or emerging market), turn to Section VI, Top-Rated ETFs and Other Closed-End Mutual Funds by Fund Type. There you will find the ETFs and other closed-end mutual funds with the highest performance rating in each category. Please be careful to also consider the risk component when selecting a fund from one of these lists.

Step 6   **Refer back to Section I.** Once you have identified a particular fund that interests you, refer back to Section I, the Index of ETFs and Other Closed-End Mutual Funds, for a more thorough analysis.

Always remember:

Step 7   **Read our warnings and cautions.** In order to use TheStreet Investment Ratings most effectively, we strongly recommend you consult the Important Warnings and Cautions listed on page 11. These are more than just "standard disclaimers." They are very important factors you should be aware of before using this Guide.

Step 8   **Stay up to date.** Periodically review the latest TheStreet Investment Ratings for the funds that you own to make sure they are still in line with your investment goals and level of risk tolerance. For information on how to acquire follow-up reports on a particular mutual fund, call 1-800-289-9222 or visit www.thestreetratings.com.

Data Source: Thomson Wealth Management
1455 Research Boulevard
Rockville, MD 20850

Date of data analyzed: December 31, 2012

About TheStreet Investment Ratings

TheStreet Investment Ratings represent a completely independent, unbiased opinion of a mutual fund's historical risk-adjusted performance. Each fund's rating is based on two primary components:

Primary Component #1   A fund's **Performance Rating** is based on its total return to shareholders over a period of up to three years, including share price appreciation and distributions to shareholders. This total return figure is stated net of the expenses and fees charged by the fund.

This adjusted return is then weighted to give more recent performance a slightly greater emphasis. Thus, two mutual funds may have provided identical returns to their shareholders over the last three years, but the one with the better performance in the last 12 months will receive a slightly higher performance rating.

Primary Component #2   The **Risk Rating** is based on the level of volatility in the fund's monthly returns, also over a period of up to three years. We use several statistical measures – standard deviation, semi-deviation and a drawdown factor – as our barometer of volatility. Funds with more volatility relative to other mutual funds are considered riskier, and thus receive a lower risk rating. By contrast, funds with very stable returns are considered less risky and receive a higher risk rating. In addition to considering the fund's volatility, the risk rating also considers the fund's discount/premium as compared to its historical average, as well as an assessment of the valuation and quality of the fund's holdings.

Note that none of the mutual funds listed in this publication have received a risk rating in the A (Excellent) range. This is because all closed-end mutual fund investments, by their very nature, involve at least some degree of risk.

Rarely will you ever find a mutual fund that has both a very high Performance Rating plus, at the same time, a very high Risk Rating. Therefore, the funds that receive the highest overall Investment Ratings are those that attain the ideal combination of both primary components. There is always a tradeoff between risk and reward.

Keep in mind that while TheStreet Investment Ratings use the same rating scale as TheStreet Financial Strength Ratings of financial institutions, the two ratings have totally independent meanings. TheStreet Financial Strength Ratings assess the *future* financial stability of an insurer or bank as a way of helping investors place their money with a financially sound company and minimize the risk of loss. These ratings are derived without regard to the performance of the individual investments offered by the insurance companies, banks, or thrifts.

On the other hand, TheStreet Investment Ratings employ a ranking system to evaluate both safety and performance. Based on these measures, funds are divided into percentiles, and an individual performance rating and a risk rating are assigned to each fund. Then these measures are combined to derive a fund's composite percentile ranking. Finally, TheStreet Investment Ratings are assigned to their corresponding percentile rankings as shown on page 3.

How Our Ratings Differ From Those of Other Services

Balanced approach: TheStreet Investment Ratings are designed to meet the needs of aggressive *as well as* conservative investors. We realize that your investment goals can be different from those of other investors based upon your age, income, and tolerance for risk. Therefore, our ratings balance a fund's performance against the amount of risk it poses to identify those funds that have achieved the optimum mix of both factors. Some of these top funds have achieved excellent returns with only average risk. Others have achieved average returns with only moderate risk. Whatever your personal preferences, we can help you identify a top notch fund that meets your investing style.

Other investment rating firms give a far greater weight to performance and insufficient consideration to risk. In effect, they bet too heavily on a rising market and do not give enough consideration to the risk of a decline. While performance is obviously a very important factor to consider, we believe that the riskiness of a fund is also very important. Therefore, we weigh these two components more equally when assigning TheStreet Investment Ratings.

But we don't stop there. We also assign a separate performance rating and risk rating to each fund so you can focus on the component that is most important to you.

Easy to use: Unlike those of other services, TheStreet Investment Ratings are extremely intuitive and easy to use. Our rating scale (A to E) is easily understood by members of the general public based on their familiarity with school grades. So, there are no stars to count and no numbering systems to interpret.

More funds: *TheStreet Ratings Guide to Exchange-Traded Funds* tracks more closed-end mutual funds than any other publication – with updates that come out more frequently than those of other rating agencies. We've included more than 1,500 funds in this edition, all of which are updated every three months.

Recency: Recognizing that every fund's performance is going to have its peaks and valleys, superior long-term performance is a major consideration in TheStreet Investment Ratings. Even so, we do not give a fund a top rating solely because it did well 10 or 15 years ago. Times change and the top performing funds in the current economic environment are often very different from those of a decade ago. Thus, our ratings are designed to keep you abreast of the best funds available *today* and in the *near future,* not the distant past.

Thoroughness: One of the unique characteristics of closed-end funds is that they often trade either above (premium) or below (discount) their net asset value (NAV). Our ratings not only consider performance and risk factors of each fund, but we also evaluate the current premium or discount of each fund as compared to its historical average. This evaluation is factored into the overall rating and can help investors identify funds that may be overvalued or undervalued.

What Our Ratings Mean

A   **Excellent**. The mutual fund has an excellent track record for maximizing performance while minimizing risk, thus delivering the best possible combination of total return on investment and reduced volatility. It has made the most of the recent economic environment to maximize risk-adjusted returns compared to other mutual funds. While past performance is just an indication – not a guarantee – we believe this fund is among the most likely to deliver superior performance relative to risk in the future.

B   **Good.** The mutual fund has a good track record for balancing performance with risk. Compared to other mutual funds, it has achieved above-average returns given the level of risk in its underlying investments. While the risk-adjusted performance of any mutual fund is subject to change, we believe that this fund has proven to be a good investment in the recent past.

C   **Fair.** In the trade-off between performance and risk, the mutual fund has a track record which is about average. It is neither significantly better nor significantly worse than most other mutual funds. With some funds in this category, the total return may be better than average, but this can be misleading since the higher return was achieved with higher than average risk. With other funds, the risk may be lower than average, but the returns are also lower. In short, based on recent history, there is no particular advantage to investing in this fund.

D   **Weak.** The mutual fund has underperformed the universe of other funds given the level of risk in its underlying investments, resulting in a weak risk-adjusted performance. Thus, its investment strategy and/or management has not been attuned to capitalize on the recent economic environment. While the risk-adjusted performance of any mutual fund is subject to change, we believe that this fund has proven to be a bad investment over the recent past.

E   **Very Weak.** The mutual fund has significantly underperformed most other funds given the level of risk in its underlying investments, resulting in a very weak risk-adjusted performance. Thus, its investment strategy and/or management has done just the opposite of what was needed to maximize returns in the recent economic environment. While the risk-adjusted performance of any mutual fund is subject to change, we believe this fund has proven to be a very bad investment in the recent past.

+   **The plus sign** is an indication that the fund is in the top third of its letter grade.

-   **The minus sign** is an indication that the fund is in the bottom third of its letter grade.

U   **Unrated.** The mutual fund is unrated because it is too new to make a reliable assessment of its risk-adjusted performance.

Important Warnings and Cautions

1. **A rating alone cannot tell the whole story.** Please read the explanatory information contained here, in the section introductions and in the appendix. It is provided in order to give you an understanding of our rating methodology as well as to paint a more complete picture of a mutual fund's strengths and weaknesses.

2. **Investment ratings shown in this Guide were current as of the publication date.** In the meantime, the rating may have been updated based on more recent data. TheStreet Ratings offers a notification service for ratings changes on companies that you specify. For more information call 1-800-289-9222 or visit www.thestreet.com/ratings.

3. **When deciding to buy or sell shares in a specific mutual fund, your decision must be based on a wide variety of factors in addition to TheStreet Investment Rating.** These include any charges you may incur from switching funds, to what degree it meets your long-term planning needs, and what other choices are available to you.

4. **TheStreet Investment Ratings represent our opinion of a mutual fund's past risk-adjusted performance.** As such, a high rating means we feel that the mutual fund has performed very well for its shareholders compared to other closed-end mutual funds. A high rating is not a guarantee that a fund will continue to perform well, nor is a low rating a prediction of continued weak performance. TheStreet Investment Ratings are not deemed to be a recommendation concerning the purchase or sale of any mutual fund.

5. **A mutual fund's individual performance is not the only factor in determining its rating.** Since TheStreet Investment Ratings are based on performance relative to other funds, it is possible for a fund's rating to be upgraded or downgraded based strictly on the improved or deteriorated performance of other funds.

6. **All funds that have the same TheStreet Investment Rating should be considered to be essentially equal from a risk/reward perspective.** This is true regardless of any differences in the underlying numbers which might appear to indicate greater strengths.

7. **Our rating standards are more consumer-oriented than those used by other rating agencies.** We make more conservative assumptions as we attempt to identify those funds that have historically provided superior returns with only little or moderate risk.

8. **We are an independent rating agency and do not depend on the cooperation of the managers operating the mutual funds we rate.** Our data are derived, for the most part, from price quotes obtained and documented on the open market. This is supplemented by information collected from the mutual fund prospectuses and regulatory filings. Although we seek to maintain an open line of communication with the mutual fund managers, we do not grant them the right to stop or influence publication of the ratings. This policy stems from the fact that this Guide is designed for the information of the consumer.

9. **This Guide does not cover open-end funds.** Because open-end funds represent a whole separate class of investments with unique risk profiles and performance expectations, they are available in separate publications. Please see our *Guide to Stock Mutual Funds* and our *Guide to Bond and Money Market Mutual Funds* for our analyses of open-end mutual funds.

Section I

Index of ETFs and Other Closed-End Funds

An analysis of all rated and unrated

Exchange-Traded Funds and

Other Closed-End Mutual Funds.

Funds are listed in alphabetical order.

Section I Contents

Left Pages

1. Fund Type

The mutual fund's peer category based on an analysis of its investment portfolio.

COH	Corporate – High Yield	HL	Health
COI	Corporate – Inv. Grade	IN	Income
EM	Emerging Market	LP	Loan Participation
EN	Energy/Natural Resources	MTG	Mortgage
FS	Financial Services	MUH	Municipal – High Yield
FO	Foreign	MUN	Municipal – National
GEI	General – Inv. Grade	MUS	Municipal – Single State
GEN	General Bond	PM	Precious Metals
GL	Global	USA	U.S. Gov. – Agency
GR	Growth	UT	Utilities
GI	Growth and Income		

A blank fund type means that the mutual fund has not yet been categorized.

2. Fund Name

The name of the mutual fund as stated in its prospectus, which can sometimes differ slightly from the name that the company uses for advertising. If you cannot find the particular mutual fund you are interested in, or if you have any doubts regarding the precise name, verify the information with your broker or on your account statement. Also, use the fund's ticker symbol for confirmation. (See column 3.)

3. Ticker Symbol

The unique alphabetic symbol used for identifying and trading a specific mutual fund. No two funds can have the same ticker symbol.

4. Overall Investment Rating

Our overall rating is measured on a scale from A to E based on each fund's risk-adjusted performance. Please see page 10 for specific descriptions of each letter grade. Also, refer to page 7 for information on how our ratings are derived. Most important, when using this rating, please be sure to consider the warnings beginning on page 11 regarding the ratings' limitations and the underlying assumptions.

5.	**Price**	Closing price of the fund on the date shown.

| 6. | **52-Week High** | Highest price at which the fund has traded in the last 52 weeks. |

| 7. | **52-Week Low** | Lowest price at which the fund has traded in the last 52 weeks. |

| 8. | **Performance Rating/Points** | A letter grade rating based solely on the mutual fund's financial performance over the trailing three years, without any consideration for the amount of risk the fund poses. Like the overall Investment Rating, the Performance Rating is measured on a scale from A to E for ease of interpretation. The points score indicates where the Performance Rating falls on a scale of 0 to 10. |

| 9. | **3-Month Total Return** | The total return the fund has provided to investors over the preceding 13 weeks. This total return figure is computed based on the fund's dividend distributions and share price appreciation/depreciation during the period, net of the expenses and fees it imposes on its shareholders. The 3-Month Total Return shown here is not annualized. |

| 10. | **6-Month Total Return** | The total return the fund has provided investors over the preceding 26 weeks, not annualized. |

| 11. | **1-Year Total Return** | The total return the fund has provided investors over the preceding 52 weeks. |

| 12. | **1-Year Total Return Percentile** | The fund's percentile rank based on its one-year performance compared to that of all other closed-end funds in existence for at least one year. A score of 99 is the best possible, indicating that the fund outperformed 99% of the closed-end mutual funds. Zero is the worst possible percentile score. |

| 13. | **3-Year Total Return** | The total annual return the fund has provided investors over the preceding 156 weeks. |

| 14. | **3-Year Total Return Percentile** | The fund's percentile rank based on its three-year performance compared to that of all other closed-end funds in existence for at least three years. A score of 99 is the best possible, indicating that the fund outperformed 99% of the closed-end mutual funds. Zero is the worst possible percentile score. |

| 15. | **5-Year Total Return** | The total annual return the fund has provided investors over the preceding 260 weeks. |

| 16. | **5-Year Total Return Percentile** | The fund's percentile rank based on its five-year performance compared to that of all other closed-end funds in existence for at least five years. A score of 99 is the best possible, indicating that the fund outperformed 99% of the closed-end mutual funds. Zero is the worst possible percentile score. |

<u>*Right Pages*</u>

1. Dividend Yield   Most recent quarterly dividend to fund investors annualized, expressed as a percent of the fund's current share price. The dividend yield of a fund can have little correlation to the amount of dividends the fund has received from its underlying investments. Rather, dividend distributions are based on a fund's need to pass earnings from both dividends and gains on the sale of investments along to shareholders. Thus, these dividend distributions are included as a part of the fund's total return.

Keep in mind that dividend income may be taxed at a different rate than capital gains depending on your income tax bracket.

2. Expense Ratio   The expense ratio is taken directly from each fund's annual report with no further calculation. It indicates the percentage of the fund's assets that are deducted each fiscal year to cover its expenses, although for practical purposes, it is actually accrued daily. Typical fund expenses include management fees and other costs incurred by the fund. Brokerage costs incurred by the fund to buy or sell shares of the underlying securities are not included in the expense ratio.

If a mutual fund's net assets are small, its expense ratio can be quite high because the fund must cover its expenses from a smaller asset base. Conversely, as the net assets of the fund grow, the expense percentage should ideally diminish since the expenses are being spread across a larger asset base.

Funds with higher expense ratios are generally less attractive since the expense ratio represents a hurdle that must be met before the investment becomes profitable to its shareholders. Since a fund's expenses affect its total return though, they are already factored into its TheStreet Investment Rating.

3. Risk Rating/Points   A letter grade rating based solely on the mutual fund's risk as determined by its monthly performance volatility over the trailing three years. The risk rating does not take into consideration the overall financial performance the fund has achieved or the total return it has provided to its shareholders. Like the overall Investment Rating, the Risk Rating is measured on a scale from A to E for ease of interpretation. The points score indicates where the Risk Rating falls on a scale of 0 to 10.

| 4. | **Standard Deviation** | A statistical measure of the amount of volatility in a fund's monthly performance over the last trailing 36 months. In absolute terms, standard deviation provides a historical measure of a fund's deviation from its mean, or average, monthly total return over the period. |

A high standard deviation indicates a high degree of volatility in the past, which usually means you should expect to see a high degree of volatility in the future as well. This translates into higher risk since a large negative swing could easily become a sizable loss in the event you need to liquidate your shares.

| 5. | **Beta** | The level of correlation between the fund's monthly performance over the last trailing 36 months and the performance of its investment category as a whole. |

A beta of 1.00 means that the fund's returns have matched those of the index one for one during the stock market's ups and downs. A beta of 1.10 means that on average the fund has outperformed the index by 10% during rising markets and underperformed it by 10% during falling markets. Conversely, a beta of 0.85 means that the fund has typically performed 15% worse than the overall market during up markets and 15% better during down markets.

| 6. | **Average Duration** | Expressed in years, duration is a measure of a bond fund's sensitivity to interest rate fluctuations, or its level of interest rate risk. |

The longer a fund's duration, the more sensitive the fund is to shifts in interest rates. For example, a fund with a duration of eight years is twice as sensitive to a change in rates as a fund with a four year duration.

| 7. | **NAV** | The fund's net asset value (NAV) as of the date indicated. A fund's NAV is computed by dividing the value of the fund's asset holdings, less accrued fees and expenses, by the number of its shares outstanding. |

Because a closed-end fund's shares trade on an exchange and the price is based on investor demand, the fund may trade at a price higher or lower than its NAV.

| 8. | **Net Assets** | The total value (stated in millions of dollars) of all of the fund's asset holdings including stocks, bonds, cash, and other financial instruments, less accrued expenses and fees. |

Larger funds have the advantage of being able to spread their expenses over a greater asset base so that the effect per share is lessened. On the other hand, if a fund becomes too large, it can be more difficult for the fund manager to buy and sell investments for the benefit of shareholders.

9.	Premium/ Discount	A comparison of the fund's price to its NAV as of the date indicated. The premium (+) or discount (-) indicates the percentage the shares are trading above or below the fund's NAV per share.

If the price is above the fund's NAV, the fund is said to be trading at a premium. If the price is lower than the fund's NAV, the fund is trading at a discount.

10.	1-Year Average Premium/ Discount	The average of the fund's premium/discount over the preceding year.

It can be useful to compare the fund's current premium/discount to its one-year average. If the fund is currently trading at a premium/discount that is lower/higher than its one-year average, then there has been less demand for the fund in more recent times than over the past year. Conversely, if the fund is currently trading at a premium/discount that is higher/lower than its one-year average, this indicates that there has been greater demand for the fund in more recent times than over the past year.

11.	Weighted Average Price-to-Earnings	The average of the price-to-earnings (P/E) ratios for the equity securities of the fund, where larger holdings are weighted more heavily than smaller holdings. A high P/E multiple indicates that investors have high expectations for future growth of the securities of that fund.

Compare this number to that of funds of the same type to get a feel for whether the equity securities of the fund might be overvalued or undervalued.

12.	Cash %	The percentage of the fund's assets held in cash or money market funds as of the last reporting period. Investments in this area will tend to hamper the fund's returns while adding to its stability during market swings.

13.	Stocks %	The percentage of the fund's assets held in common or preferred stocks as of the last reporting period. Since stocks are inherently riskier investments than the other categories, it is common for funds invested primarily or exclusively in stocks to receive a lower risk rating.

14.	Bonds %	The percentage of the fund's assets held in bonds as of the last reporting period. This category includes corporate bonds, municipal bonds, and government bonds such as T-bills and T-bonds.

15.	Other %	The percentage of the fund's assets invested as of the last reporting period in other types of financial instruments such as convertible securities, options, and warrants.

16. Portfolio Turnover Ratio

The average annual portion of the fund's holdings that have been moved from one specific investment to another over the past three years. This indicates the amount of buying and selling the fund manager engages in. A portfolio turnover ratio of 100% signifies that on average, the entire value of the fund's assets is turned over once during the course of a year.

A high portfolio turnover ratio has implications for shareholders since the fund is required to pass all realized earnings along to shareholders each year. Thus a high portfolio turnover ratio will result in higher annual distributions for shareholders, effectively increasing their annual taxable income. In contrast, a low turnover ratio means a higher level of unrealized gains that will not be taxable until you sell your shares in the fund.

17. Manager Quality Percentile

The manager quality percentile is based on a ranking of the fund's alpha, a statistical measure representing the difference between a fund's actual returns and its expected performance given its level of risk. Fund managers who have been able to exceed the fund's statistically expected performance receive a high percentile rank with 99 representing the highest possible score. At the other end of the spectrum, fund managers who have actually detracted from the fund's expected performance receive a low percentile rank with 0 representing the lowest possible score.

18. Manager Tenure

The number of years the current manager has been managing the fund. Since fund managers who deliver substandard returns are usually replaced, a long tenure is usually a good sign that shareholders are satisfied that the fund is achieving its stated objectives.

Fund Type	Fund Name	Ticker Symbol	Overall Investment Rating	PRICE Price As of 12/31/12	52 Week High	52 Week Low	PERFORMANCE Perform-ance Rating/Pts	3 Mo	6 Mo	1Yr/Pct	Annualized 3Yr/Pct	Annualized 5Yr/Pct
GI	*2x Levered CS Mrg Arb Lq Idx	CSMB	D-	18.18	27.08	17.32	E+ / 0.9	-0.22	-0.49	-7.14 / 9	--	--
GL	*Accuvest Global Long Short ETF	AGLS	C-	22.38	22.79	20.54	C- / 3.4	4.60	4.65	6.93 / 28		
GL	*Accuvest Global Opportunities ET	ACCU	U	28.25	N/A	N/A	U /	9.58	18.37	--		
GI	*AlphaClone Alternative Alpha ETF	ALFA	U	27.90	N/A	N/A	U /	4.37	12.20			
EN	*Alps Alerian MLP ETF	AMLP	C	15.95	17.19	15.20	C- / 3.3	1.99	5.34	7.44 / 29	--	
IN	*Alps Equal Sector Weight ETF	EQL	C	39.89	41.18	35.77	C / 5.0	3.38	9.38	15.06 / 48	11.13 / 53	
GL	*Alps Jefferies / TR/J CRB Gl Cm	CRBQ	D	44.72	48.49	38.90	D+ / 2.3	3.44	11.37	5.35 / 24	2.89 / 23	
IN	*Alps Sector Dividend Dogs ETF	SDOG	U	26.48	N/A	N/A	U /	4.22	10.32	--		
GI	*Arrow Dow Jones Global Yield ETF	GYLD	U	26.21	N/A	N/A	U /	4.46	13.63	--		
GR	*Barclays ETN + VEQTOR ETN	VQT	D-	129.27	137.85	125.74	D / 2.0	0.69	2.17	2.25 / 19	--	
FO	*BLDRS Asia 50 ADR Index	ADRA	D+	26.18	27.43	21.62	D+ / 2.8	13.67	17.33	15.88 / 52	2.50 / 21	-0.01 / 19
FO	*BLDRS Developed Mkts 100 ADR Ind	ADRD	C-	21.03	21.82	17.28	C- / 4.1	11.24	20.35	20.69 / 73	3.54 / 24	-1.50 / 15
EM	*BLDRS Emerging Market 50 ADR Ind	ADRE	D	40.22	44.48	35.00	D / 1.8	5.57	11.70	4.38 / 23	0.11 / 15	-1.17 / 16
FO	*BLDRS Europe Select ADR Index	ADRU	D+	20.83	21.60	17.05	C- / 3.4	9.91	22.17	21.85 / 76	3.95 / 26	-1.84 / 14
GR	*Brclys ETN+ Inv S&P500 VIX STF E	XXV	D	37.82	38.05	33.77	C- / 4.0	0.75	3.03	12.74 / 41	--	
IN	*Brclys ETN+ Lg C Lv S&P500 TR ET	BXUC	C	167.93	184.96	138.69	B+ / 8.7	5.83	15.85	28.37 / 89	19.72 / 88	
IN	*Brclys ETN+InvS&P500 VIX STF ETN	IVOP	B	35.44	36.37	24.90	A+ / 9.7	--	--	47.46 / 98	--	
IN	*C-Tracks ETN Citi Volatility Idx	CVOL	E-	29.70	239.10	23.67	E- / 0.0	-39.02	-70.60	-90.16 / 0	--	
GI	*Cambria Global Tactical ETF Fund	GTAA	C	24.31	25.12	22.99	C- / 4.0	4.08	6.57	8.40 / 31	--	
GI	*Cohen & Steers Global Realty Maj	GRI	B-	39.25	41.36	33.41	B / 7.6	8.46	12.83	29.99 / 91	14.11 / 69	
GEI	*Columbia Core Bond Strategy	GMTB	C-	52.90	55.63	51.87	D / 1.8	-2.53	0.72	4.41 / 23	--	
GR	*Columbia Growth Equity Strategy	RPX	C-	30.46	35.90	27.00	C- / 4.2	3.76	--	17.75 / 61	10.09 / 48	
MUN	*Columbia Intermediate Muni Bd St	GMMB	C-	54.40	81.43	51.53	D+ / 2.6	0.34	1.71	4.02 / 26	--	
GR	*Columbia Large-Cap Growth Eq Str	RWG	C	29.85	34.25	26.10	C / 4.7	10.23	20.74	16.92 / 58	8.90 / 42	
GR	*Consumer Discretionary Sel Sec S	XLY	B+	47.44	48.95	40.41	B+ / 8.4	6.35	13.16	23.04 / 80	19.54 / 87	12.42 / 78
GR	*Consumer Staples Select Sector S	XLP	C+	34.90	36.59	31.84	C / 5.3	1.34	3.56	15.23 / 49	13.53 / 66	8.78 / 64
EN	*Credit Suisse Cushing 30 MLP ETN	MLPN	D	24.10	26.56	22.10	C- / 4.1	1.74	9.17	8.36 / 31	--	
GR	*Credit Suisse L/S Liq Idx ETN	CSLS	D-	22.36	23.26	21.31	D / 1.9	-0.42	3.05	2.06 / 18	--	
GR	*Credit Suisse Merger Arb Lq Id E	CSMA	D-	19.65	20.86	19.16	D- / 1.1	-0.31	-0.40	-3.72 / 11	--	--
GI	*db-X 2010 Target Date Fund	TDD	D+	21.40	24.20	19.94	D- / 1.2	3.32	2.83	-7.67 / 9	-1.23 / 13	-0.81 / 17
GI	*db-X 2020 Target Date Fund	TDH	C-	22.30	23.79	20.54	D+ / 2.4	4.97	7.97	3.57 / 22	4.04 / 26	1.44 / 25
GI	*db-X 2030 Target Date Fund	TDN	C+	21.47	22.89	19.03	C / 5.2	7.47	15.89	19.79 / 70	8.73 / 42	2.60 / 30
GI	*db-X 2040 Target Date Fund	TDV	C-	20.95	23.99	19.36	C- / 4.0	0.84	8.05	18.06 / 63	8.46 / 40	2.00 / 27
GI	*db-X In-Target Date Fund	TDX	D+	24.50	27.55	20.82	D- / 1.5	2.96	7.47	-2.54 / 12	0.30 / 16	0.72 / 21
FO	*DBX MSCI Brazil Currency-Hedged	DBBR	B-	20.12	24.71	19.10	B- / 7.2	12.12	19.67	4.78 / 23	--	
FO	*DBX MSCI Canada Currency-Hedged	DBCN	U	22.89	24.00	20.47	U /	--	--	--	--	
FO	*DBX MSCI EAFE Currency-Hedged Eq	DBEF	A+	22.06	33.07	20.11	A / 9.5	15.58	19.47	19.21 / 68	--	
EM	*DBX MSCI Emg Mkt Currency-Hedged	DBEM	C+	22.84	35.00	20.38	B / 7.9	8.58	14.32	13.10 / 42	--	
FO	*DBX MSCI Japan Currency-Hedged E	DBJP	U	26.35	27.65	20.20	U /	--	21.97	--		
GI	*Direxion All Cap Insider Sentime	KNOW	B+	43.64	47.10	37.11	B / 8.0	6.77	15.33	13.71 / 44	--	
GL	*Direxion Daily 20+ Yr Treas Bear	TYBS	D-	26.45	30.89	25.30	D- / 1.2	1.98	5.56	-6.44 / 10	--	
USA	*Direxion Daily 20+ Yr Treas Bear	TMV	E-	54.24	87.28	45.98	E- / 0.2	5.38	12.85	-18.14 / 5	-44.44 / 1	
USA	*Direxion Daily 20+ Yr Treas Bull	TMF	C+	71.81	92.50	52.84	A- / 9.2	-9.23	-19.59	-1.79 / 12	33.30 / 99	
GL	*Direxion Daily 7-10 Yr Treas Br	TYNS	D+	32.93	35.22	32.37	D- / 1.1	0.09	--	-4.85 / 11	--	
USA	*Direxion Daily 7-10 Yr Trs Bear	TYO	E+	22.98	29.66	22.10	E / 0.4	1.08	0.86	-13.93 / 7	-27.46 / 3	
USA	*Direxion Daily 7-10 Yr Trs Bull	TYD	B+	85.82	89.67	70.75	B+ / 8.7	-3.72	-5.20	6.67 / 27	27.23 / 99	
IN	*Direxion Daily Basic Mat Bull 3x	MATL	C-	29.33	33.50	19.84	A+ / 9.8	23.61	40.06	20.43 / 72	--	
FO	*Direxion Daily China Bear 3x ETF	YANG	E-	10.45	19.49	8.90	E- / 0.1	-27.74	-43.28	-40.43 / 2	-37.71 / 2	
FO	*Direxion Daily China Bull 3x ETF	YINN	E-	18.70	26.29	12.50	E+ / 0.8	28.05	49.75	7.58 / 29	-17.61 / 5	
PM	*Direxion Daily Gold Miners Bear	DUST	E	31.50	78.54	22.04	D / 1.8	45.88	-26.63	-5.88 / 10	--	
PM	*Direxion Daily Gold Miners Bull	NUGT	E-	11.00	27.01	7.70	E- / 0.1	-35.10	11.27	-54.60 / 1	--	
HL	*Direxion Daily Healthcare Bull 3	CURE	A-	52.92	61.06	36.62	A+ / 9.9	10.86	31.88	66.44 / 99	--	

I. Index of ETFs and Other Closed-End Funds

Incl. in Returns		RISK				NET ASSETS		VALUATION			ASSET					FUND MANAGER	
Dividend Yield %	Expense Ratio	Risk Rating/ Pts	3 Year Standard Deviation	Beta	Avg Dura-tion	NAV as of 12/31/12	Total $(Mil)	Premium / Discount As of 12/31/12	1 Year Average	Wtd Avg P/E	Cash %	Stocks %	Bonds %	Other %	Portfolio Turnover Ratio	Manager Quality Pct	Manager Tenure (Years)
0.00	N/A	C / 5.2	N/A	N/A	N/A	18.51	21	-1.78	-0.19	N/A	0	0	0	100	N/A	12	2
0.00	1.50	B- / 7.9	N/A	N/A	N/A	22.45	24	-0.31	0.06	N/A	0	100	0	0	751	86	3
1.19	N/A	U /	N/A	N/A	N/A	28.62	17	-1.29	N/A	N/A	0	0	0	0	N/A	N/A	1
0.43	N/A	U /	N/A	N/A	N/A	29.11	3	-4.16	N/A	N/A	0	0	0	100	N/A	N/A	1
6.42	0.85	B+ / 9.0	N/A	N/A	N/A	16.71	4,449	-4.55	0.06	N/A	0	100	0	100	N/A	N/A	1
3.16	0.34	B / 8.3	14.4	0.93	N/A	41.16	78	-3.09	0.01	N/A	0	100	0	0	6	51	2
1.76	0.65	C+ / 6.9	23.7	1.04	N/A	46.23	74	-3.27	-0.11	N/A	0	100	0	0	2	55	4
5.03	N/A	U /	N/A	N/A	N/A	27.50	70	-3.71	N/A	N/A	0	100	0	0	9	40	2
13.92	N/A	U /	N/A	N/A	N/A	26.42	27	-0.79	N/A	N/A	0	0	0	100	N/A	N/A	1
0.00	N/A	C+ / 5.6	N/A	N/A	N/A	130.40	364	-0.87	-0.01	N/A	0	0	0	100	N/A	22	3
1.86	0.30	B- / 7.4	19.2	0.88	N/A	26.93	29	-2.79	-0.33	N/A	0	99	0	1	11	50	N/A
5.95	0.30	B- / 7.2	20.9	1.03	N/A	21.79	47	-3.49	-0.31	54.5	0	99	0	1	6	43	N/A
2.81	0.30	B- / 7.1	22.3	0.96	N/A	41.14	324	-2.24	-0.09	N/A	0	99	0	1	8	21	N/A
5.05	0.30	B- / 7.1	22.3	1.08	N/A	21.55	14	-3.34	-0.14	54.5	0	99	0	1	4	41	N/A
0.00	N/A	C / 4.9	N/A	N/A	N/A	38.07	5	-0.66	-0.05	N/A	0	0	0	100	N/A	82	N/A
0.00	N/A	C- / 4.2	29.8	1.89	N/A	180.75	19	-7.09	0.01	N/A	0	0	0	100	N/A	29	4
0.00	N/A	C / 5.5	N/A	N/A	N/A	36.36	2	-2.53	-0.14	N/A	0	0	0	100	N/A	97	2
0.00	N/A	D / 1.9	N/A	N/A	N/A	23.59	N/A	25.90	0.16	N/A	0	0	0	100	N/A	N/A	N/A
2.30	0.99	B / 8.7	N/A	N/A	N/A	24.84	64	-2.13	-0.20	N/A	33	56	11	0	475	36	N/A
22.77	0.55	C+ / 6.9	18.1	1.05	N/A	39.69	70	-1.11	0.19	99.3	0	100	0	0	1	67	2
2.55	0.35	B+ / 9.6	N/A	N/A	N/A	52.76	5	0.27	0.83	N/A	9	0	90	1	89	68	2
1.15	0.89	B- / 7.6	20.6	0.88	N/A	32.03	2	-4.90	-1.30	N/A	0	100	0	0	75	43	2
1.91	0.35	B / 8.9	N/A	N/A	N/A	54.78	8	-0.69	2.50	N/A	0	0	100	0	5	89	3
0.16	0.89	B- / 7.5	19.0	1.01	N/A	32.14	8	-7.13	-1.63	N/A	0	99	0	1	35	26	2
2.58	0.18	B- / 7.9	17.4	1.06	N/A	48.90	3,743	-2.99	N/A	52.9	0	100	0	0	5	83	15
4.56	0.18	B+ / 9.0	9.7	0.50	N/A	35.89	5,531	-2.76	N/A	25.8	0	100	0	0	12	85	15
4.07	N/A	C / 5.0	N/A	N/A	N/A	25.73	303	-6.34	0.09	N/A	0	0	0	100	N/A	35	3
0.00	N/A	C / 5.4	N/A	N/A	N/A	22.26	21	0.45	-0.10	N/A	0	0	0	100	N/A	22	3
0.00	N/A	C / 5.5	N/A	N/A	N/A	19.89	75	-1.21	-0.21	N/A	0	0	0	100	N/A	17	N/A
0.91	0.65	B / 8.9	7.5	0.13	3.4	24.08	10	-11.13	-7.42	49.2	26	15	57	2	65	33	4
2.67	0.65	B / 8.7	9.9	0.57	3.6	24.61	29	-9.39	-6.66	58.6	0	62	36	2	55	34	4
4.80	0.65	B / 8.3	13.2	0.76	15.3	23.64	32	-9.18	-6.43	58.7	0	84	14	2	40	47	4
4.67	0.65	B- / 7.8	16.0	0.98	15.5	23.04	27	-9.07	-1.55	58.6	0	95	4	1	34	32	4
1.16	0.65	B / 8.8	9.0	0.34	3.3	27.09	11	-9.56	-6.67	56.8	27	27	44	2	59	31	4
4.28	1.13	B- / 7.8	N/A	N/A	N/A	20.51	4	-1.90	0.10	N/A	1	97	0	2	34	9	2
5.50	1.04	U /	N/A	N/A	N/A	23.02	5	-0.56	0.12	N/A	0	97	0	3	17	58	2
2.71	0.57	B / 8.0	N/A	N/A	N/A	22.61	14	-2.43	-0.02	N/A	0	95	0	5	14	87	2
3.04	1.19	C / 5.5	N/A	N/A	N/A	23.06	5	-0.95	0.94	N/A	0	93	0	7	19	53	2
3.97	1.03	U /	N/A	N/A	N/A	26.96	5	-2.26	0.36	N/A	0	96	0	4	16	72	2
0.61	N/A	B / 8.0	N/A	N/A	N/A	45.19	4	-3.43	-0.12	N/A	0	100	0	0	N/A	14	2
0.00	0.65	C+ / 6.4	N/A	N/A	N/A	27.10	3	-2.40	-0.01	N/A	100	0	0	0	N/A	8	2
0.00	0.94	D+ / 2.4	48.5	-3.84	N/A	55.86	300	-2.90	0.02	N/A	100	0	0	0	N/A	10	N/A
0.10	0.95	C / 5.3	45.1	3.59	N/A	69.37	25	3.52	-0.02	N/A	24	0	75	1	128	9	N/A
0.00	0.65	B / 8.5	N/A	N/A	N/A	32.99	2	-0.18	0.05	N/A	100	0	0	0	N/A	17	2
0.00	0.95	C / 4.4	18.8	-1.42	N/A	23.28	49	-1.29	0.02	N/A	100	0	0	0	N/A	8	5
0.00	0.95	B- / 7.8	18.1	1.37	N/A	84.40	4	1.68	-0.02	N/A	15	0	84	1	536	89	5
0.00	N/A	D / 2.0	N/A	N/A	N/A	33.11	3	-11.42	-0.06	N/A	0	99	0	1	N/A	6	2
0.00	0.95	D / 1.9	71.9	-2.66	N/A	9.13	8	14.46	-0.18	N/A	100	0	0	0	N/A	2	4
0.00	0.95	D / 1.9	78.0	3.05	N/A	20.96	77	-10.78	0.16	N/A	0	100	0	0	19	3	4
0.00	0.95	D / 2.2	N/A	N/A	N/A	35.14	33	-10.36	0.23	N/A	100	0	0	0	N/A	20	3
0.00	0.95	D / 1.9	N/A	N/A	N/A	10.22	464	7.63	-0.03	N/A	0	100	0	0	N/A	N/A	3
0.03	0.95	C+ / 6.9	N/A	N/A	N/A	60.78	5	-12.93	0.01	N/A	75	24	0	1	N/A	95	2

* Denotes ETF Fund, N/A denotes number is not available

Data as of December 31, 2012

I. Index of ETFs and Other Closed-End Funds

99 Pct = Best
0 Pct = Worst

Fund Type	Fund Name	Ticker Symbol	Overall Investment Rating	PRICE Price As of 12/31/12	52 Week High	52 Week Low	Performance Rating/Pts		3 Mo	6 Mo	1Yr/Pct	3Yr/Pct	5Yr/Pct
EM	*Direxion Daily India Bull 3X	INDL	D	20.14	33.66	12.90	C+	6.0	0.83	26.66	2.97 / 20	--	--
FO	*Direxion Daily Latin Amer Bull 3	LBJ	E-	74.14	112.42	52.05	E+	0.7	20.14	25.90	1.19 / 16	-18.23 / 5	--
GR	*Direxion Daily Mid Cap Bear 3X	MIDZ	E-	16.41	29.03	14.45	E-	0.0	-25.06	-35.17	-48.52 / 1	-49.62 / 0	--
GR	*Direxion Daily Mid Cap Bull 3X	MIDU	C-	37.66	45.66	28.44	A+	9.7	26.40	40.02	54.09 / 99	27.74 / 99	--
GR	*Direxion Daily Nat Gas Rel Bear	GASX	E-	17.30	32.36	11.19	E	0.5	21.99	-18.19	-25.86 / 4	--	--
GR	*Direxion Daily Nat Gas Rel Bull	GASL	E-	19.98	47.65	16.56	E-	0.1	-26.85	-7.56	-36.84 / 2	--	--
GR	*Direxion Daily Real Estate Bear	DRV	E-	20.70	37.49	19.15	E-	0.0	-15.33	-11.76	-48.85 / 1	-60.74 / 0	--
GR	*Direxion Daily Real Estate Bull	DRN	C-	77.50	86.35	53.12	A+	9.8	14.10	5.64	57.28 / 99	39.96 / 99	--
GR	*Direxion Daily Retail Bull 3X	RETL	A+	99.26	121.20	62.27	A+	9.9	1.13	17.88	84.71 / 99	--	--
GI	*Direxion Daily Russia Bear 3x	RUSS	E-	14.85	45.90	13.65	E-	0.0	-22.37	-46.57	-54.83 / 1	--	--
FO	*Direxion Daily Russia Bull 3x	RUSL	C-	36.77	60.33	17.88	A	9.5	16.72	42.43	2.68 / 19	--	--
IN	*Direxion Daily Semiconductor Bea	SOXS	E-	32.84	55.07	28.16	E-	0.0	-30.41	-40.76	-41.32 / 2	--	--
IN	*Direxion Daily Semiconductor Bul	SOXL	C-	26.89	46.00	20.45	A+	9.6	29.93	37.25	2.76 / 20	-55.56 / 0	--
GR	*Direxion Daily Small Cap Bear 3x	TZA	E-	13.50	24.66	11.92	E-	0.0	-22.71	-32.65	-49.42 / 1	-41.74 / 1	--
GR	*Direxion Daily Small Cap Bull 3x	TNA	C-	63.96	71.77	41.55	A	9.4	21.31	31.13	43.44 / 98	16.04 / 77	--
GR	*Direxion Daily Technology Bear 3	TECS	E-	9.36	14.75	7.52	E-	0.1	-2.81	-21.53	-41.82 / 2	-41.74 / 1	--
GR	*Direxion Daily Technology Bull 3	TECL	D	48.73	68.50	40.18	C+	6.3	-3.98	12.98	30.36 / 91	12.51 / 61	--
GR	*Direxion Daily Total Market Bear	TOTS	U	31.32	35.77	29.99	U		-3.89	-10.23	--	--	--
GL	*Direxion Developed Markets Bear	DPK	E-	16.82	38.06	15.69	E-	0.1	-27.69	-45.07	-53.99 / 1	-38.79 / 1	--
GL	*Direxion Developed Markets Bull	DZK	E+	44.95	47.94	23.77	C-	3.5	31.69	60.55	59.68 / 99	-6.88 / 8	--
GL	*Direxion Emerging Markets Bear 3	EDZ	E-	9.02	19.50	8.45	E-	0.1	-24.15	-41.94	-49.14 / 1	-42.88 / 1	--
GL	*Direxion Emerging Markets Bull 3	EDC	E-	109.28	121.00	62.56	D-	1.2	25.09	49.50	33.47 / 94	-13.62 / 6	--
EN	*Direxion Energy Bear 3x Shares	ERY	E-	7.82	14.99	6.66	E-	0.1	-10.15	-34.20	-36.27 / 2	-48.07 / 0	--
EN	*Direxion Energy Bull 3x Shares	ERX	E+	48.48	61.75	31.25	C-	3.9	3.32	31.36	12.68 / 40	7.01 / 35	--
FS	*Direxion Financial Bear 3x Share	FAZ	E-	15.11	32.79	13.11	E-	0.1	-24.95	-40.42	-58.56 / 0	-46.78 / 0	--
FS	*Direxion Financial Bull 3x Share	FAS	C-	119.92	136.95	67.79	A-	9.0	25.35	50.67	80.74 / 99	0.30 / 16	--
IN	*Direxion NASDAQ-100 Eq Weighted	QQQE	U	37.95	N/A	N/A	U		6.54	12.16	--	--	--
GR	*Direxion S&P 500 Bear 3X Shares	SPXS	E-	16.91	27.06	15.25	E-	0.1	-13.01	-28.40	-43.62 / 2	-42.51 / 1	--
GR	*Direxion S&P 500 Bull 3X Shares	SPXL	C+	87.65	96.83	62.00	A	9.5	9.50	27.96	46.04 / 98	21.16 / 91	--
GI	*Direxion S&P DRRC 1500 Vol Respo	VSPR	U	42.31	N/A	N/A	U		--	11.10	--	--	--
GI	*Direxion S&P DRRC 500 Vol Respon	VSPY	U	43.86	N/A	N/A	U		2.17	9.87	--	--	--
FS	*Direxion S&P LATAM 40 DRRC Vol R	VLAT	U	39.86	N/A	N/A	U		--	9.47	--	--	--
GL	*EGShares Basic Materials GEMS ET	LGEM	C-	14.71	17.70	12.66	C+	6.3	9.88	13.21	7.54 / 29	--	--
FO	*EGShares Beyond BRICs ETF	BBRC	U	21.58	N/A	N/A	U		5.52	--	--	--	--
FO	*EGShares Brazil Infrastructure E	BRXX	D+	21.00	25.38	20.03	D+	2.7	4.74	5.29	2.51 / 19	--	--
FO	*EGShares China Infrastructure ET	CHXX	B	19.63	20.65	14.56	A+	9.8	22.41	26.11	30.62 / 92	--	--
GL	*EGShares Consumer Goods GEMS ETF	GGEM	B	23.82	24.11	19.23	B	8.1	--	14.80	19.24 / 68	--	--
GL	*EGShares COnsumer Services GEMS	VGEM	B+	22.14	22.50	17.83	A	9.3	11.60	15.97	20.89 / 73	--	--
EM	*EGShares Em Mkts Metals&Mining E	EMT	E-	14.50	17.99	12.44	E+	0.9	9.36	13.67	-2.59 / 12	-8.66 / 7	--
FO	*EGShares Emer Mrkts Dom Demand E	EMDD	U	22.07	N/A	N/A	U		8.10	--	--	--	--
EM	*EGShares Emerging Markets Cons E	ECON	B+	26.64	27.06	21.55	A-	9.0	7.32	16.93	19.39 / 69	--	--
EM	*EGShares Emerging Markets Core E	EMCR	U	21.07	N/A	N/A	U		--	--	--	--	--
EM	*EGShares Energy GEMS ETF	OGEM	E+	24.18	26.62	20.17	D+	2.3	5.05	14.90	8.68 / 32	1.97 / 20	--
FS	*EGShares Financials GEMS ETF	FGEM	D-	21.75	22.62	16.90	C-	3.2	14.28	24.58	21.18 / 74	2.63 / 22	--
EM	*EGShares GEMS Composite ETF	AGEM	E+	23.51	24.63	19.47	D	2.1	7.54	14.97	10.83 / 36	0.24 / 16	--
HL	*EGShares Health Care GEMS ETF	HGEM	A-	22.32	22.66	17.18	A	9.5	2.53	18.34	28.15 / 89	--	--
GI	*EGShares India Consumer ETF	INCO	B+	24.32	25.19	16.25	A+	9.9	8.08	33.43	44.13 / 98	--	--
FO	*EGShares India Infrastructure ET	INXX	C-	14.57	16.74	11.44	C+	6.4	1.16	13.30	12.92 / 41	--	--
FO	*EGShares India Small Cap ETF	SCIN	C-	14.84	16.78	11.62	B	7.8	2.67	13.85	16.78 / 57	--	--
GL	*EGShares Industrials GEMS ETF	IGEM	B+	20.67	21.27	15.82	A+	9.7	13.40	23.63	29.56 / 90	--	--
GI	*EGShares Low Vol Em Mkts Div ETF	HILO	B+	20.29	21.23	17.58	B	8.2	10.93	13.73	13.68 / 44	--	--
GR	*EGShares Technology GEMS ETF	QGEM	U	16.77	19.57	15.10	U		2.95	9.09	--	--	--

* Denotes ETF Fund, N/A denotes number is not avail

www.thestreetratings.

Incl. in Returns		RISK				NET ASSETS		VALUATION			ASSET					FUND MANAGER	
Dividend Yield %	Expense Ratio	Risk Rating/ Pts	Standard Deviation (3 Year)	Beta (3 Year)	Avg Dura-tion	NAV as of 12/31/12	Total $(Mil)	Premium / Discount As of 12/31/12	1 Year Average	Wtd Avg P/E	Cash %	Stocks %	Bonds %	Other %	Portfolio Turnover Ratio	Manager Quality Pct	Manager Tenure (Years)
0.00	0.95	D / 2.1	N/A	N/A	N/A	20.76	28	-2.99	0.08	N/A	67	32	0	1	N/A	1	3
0.10	0.95	D / 1.9	81.8	3.35	N/A	81.22	33	-8.72	-0.10	N/A	60	39	0	1	102	2	4
0.00	0.95	D+ / 2.4	51.5	-3.09	N/A	14.66	14	11.94	-0.01	N/A	100	0	0	0	N/A	2	4
0.00	1.10	D / 1.9	57.9	3.46	N/A	42.14	38	-10.63	-0.08	N/A	73	26	0	1	63	10	4
0.00	0.95	D / 2.1	N/A	N/A	N/A	16.02	3	7.99	-0.05	N/A	100	0	0	0	N/A	99	3
0.00	0.95	D / 1.9	N/A	N/A	N/A	21.37	29	-6.50	N/A	N/A	42	57	0	1	17	N/A	3
0.00	0.95	D / 1.9	56.6	-2.77	N/A	19.39	19	6.76	N/A	N/A	100	0	0	0	N/A	1	4
0.00	0.95	D / 1.9	61.1	3.17	N/A	82.52	109	-6.08	-0.02	N/A	72	27	0	1	4	37	4
0.00	0.95	B- / 7.9	N/A	N/A	N/A	105.12	10	-5.57	0.13	N/A	65	34	0	1	1	98	3
0.00	0.95	D / 1.9	N/A	N/A	N/A	14.94	6	-0.60	-0.19	N/A	100	0	0	0	N/A	98	2
0.00	0.95	D / 1.9	N/A	N/A	N/A	36.09	26	1.88	0.02	N/A	54	45	0	1	98	N/A	2
0.00	0.95	D / 1.9	N/A	N/A	N/A	28.20	26	16.45	-0.05	N/A	100	0	0	0	N/A	97	3
0.00	0.95	D / 1.9	N/A	N/A	N/A	30.92	97	-13.03	-0.08	N/A	59	40	0	1	69	N/A	3
0.00	0.96	D / 1.9	63.1	-3.61	N/A	12.02	682	12.31	-0.01	N/A	100	0	0	0	N/A	2	5
0.00	0.95	D+ / 2.4	69.0	3.97	N/A	71.12	732	-10.07	-0.08	N/A	90	9	0	1	305	4	5
0.00	0.95	D+ / 2.3	58.6	-3.28	N/A	8.63	27	8.46	N/A	N/A	100	0	0	0	N/A	7	5
0.00	0.95	D / 1.9	62.8	3.56	N/A	52.00	139	-6.29	-0.05	N/A	71	28	0	1	3	4	4
0.00	0.65	U /	N/A	N/A	N/A	30.04	6	4.26	0.16	N/A	100	0	0	0	N/A	66	2
0.00	0.95	D / 2.2	60.9	-2.80	N/A	15.75	11	6.79	0.02	N/A	100	0	0	0	N/A	2	5
0.00	0.99	D / 2.1	70.2	3.25	N/A	47.79	27	-5.94	N/A	N/A	54	46	0	0	116	6	5
0.00	0.95	D / 1.9	74.9	-2.96	N/A	8.90	88	1.35	-0.04	N/A	100	0	0	0	187	1	N/A
0.00	0.95	D / 1.9	81.3	3.39	N/A	110.00	351	-0.65	-0.03	N/A	82	17	0	1	187	4	8
0.00	0.95	D / 1.9	69.8	-2.84	N/A	7.08	74	10.45	-0.04	N/A	100	0	0	1	N/A	2	5
0.00	0.95	D / 2.1	76.0	3.09	N/A	53.14	265	-8.77	-0.01	N/A	60	39	0	1	37	6	5
0.00	0.95	D / 2.0	59.7	-2.75	N/A	13.18	575	14.64	-0.02	N/A	100	0	0	0	N/A	2	5
0.00	0.95	D / 1.9	66.8	3.12	N/A	136.10	1,135	-11.89	-0.06	N/A	84	15	0	1	N/A	2	5
1.65	N/A	U /	N/A	N/A	N/A	40.38	2	-6.02	N/A	N/A	0	0	0	100	1	5	5
0.00	0.95	D+ / 2.7	46.6	-2.88	N/A	15.27	168	10.74	N/A	N/A	100	0	0	0	N/A	N/A	1
0.00	0.95	C- / 4.1	51.1	3.16	N/A	96.30	219	-8.98	-0.09	N/A	87	12	0	1	N/A	4	5
0.96	N/A	U /	N/A	N/A	N/A	44.17	4	-4.21	N/A	N/A	0	0	0	100	116	9	5
1.14	N/A	U /	N/A	N/A	N/A	44.48	4	-1.39	N/A	N/A	0	0	0	100	N/A	N/A	1
0.18	N/A	U /	N/A	N/A	N/A	40.22	4	-0.90	N/A	N/A	0	0	0	100	N/A	N/A	1
4.14	0.85	C / 5.5	N/A	N/A	N/A	14.77	4	-0.41	0.67	N/A	0	99	0	1	N/A	N/A	1
1.49	N/A	U /	N/A	N/A	N/A	21.50	7	0.37	N/A	N/A	0	0	0	100	21	5	2
3.93	0.88	B- / 7.0	N/A	N/A	N/A	21.13	74	-0.62	-0.01	N/A	0	0	0	100	N/A	N/A	1
1.21	0.85	C / 5.4	N/A	N/A	N/A	19.91	12	-1.41	-0.13	N/A	1	98	0	1	30	13	3
0.99	0.85	B- / 7.7	N/A	N/A	N/A	23.96	2	-0.58	-0.31	N/A	1	98	0	1	12	94	3
0.31	0.85	B- / 7.1	N/A	N/A	N/A	22.16	2	-0.09	-0.15	N/A	0	99	0	1	50	45	4
2.95	0.85	D / 2.2	31.5	1.31	N/A	14.76	10	-1.76	0.01	N/A	0	99	0	1	51	76	4
1.13	N/A	U /	N/A	N/A	N/A	22.10	2	-0.14	N/A	N/A	0	99	0	1	10	9	4
0.40	0.85	B- / 7.6	N/A	N/A	N/A	26.49	477	0.57	0.23	N/A	0	0	0	100	N/A	N/A	1
1.15	N/A	U /	N/A	N/A	N/A	21.22	2	-0.71	N/A	N/A	0	0	0	100	3	84	3
2.37	0.85	C- / 3.4	26.5	1.10	N/A	24.35	8	-0.70	-0.18	N/A	0	0	0	100	N/A	N/A	1
1.91	0.85	C- / 3.2	28.9	1.10	N/A	22.31	5	-2.51	-0.41	N/A	2	97	0	1	19	31	4
1.47	0.75	C- / 3.3	23.6	1.00	N/A	23.56	15	-0.21	-0.04	N/A	0	99	0	1	25	16	4
0.17	0.85	B- / 7.3	N/A	N/A	N/A	22.12	3	0.90	-0.06	N/A	1	99	0	0	10	23	4
0.00	0.89	C+ / 6.7	N/A	N/A	N/A	23.65	2	2.83	0.48	N/A	0	99	0	1	26	93	4
1.27	0.85	C / 4.7	N/A	N/A	N/A	14.50	58	0.48	-0.21	N/A	0	100	0	0	104	92	1
0.69	0.85	C- / 4.1	N/A	N/A	N/A	14.97	25	-0.87	0.14	N/A	0	100	0	0	23	22	N/A
0.94	0.85	C+ / 6.8	N/A	N/A	N/A	20.74	2	-0.34	-0.09	N/A	0	99	0	1	125	62	N/A
0.06	0.85	B- / 7.8	N/A	N/A	N/A	20.20	82	0.45	0.25	N/A	0	99	0	1	70	90	4
0.08	0.85	U /	N/A	N/A	N/A	17.48	1	-4.06	-0.07	N/A	0	99	0	1	21	7	4

Denotes ETF Fund, N/A denotes number is not available

I. Index of ETFs and Other Closed-End Funds

Fund Type	Fund Name	Ticker Symbol	Overall Investment Rating	Price As of 12/31/12	52 Week High	52 Week Low	Performance Rating/Pts	3 Mo	6 Mo	1Yr/Pct	Annualized 3Yr/Pct	Annualized 5Yr/Pct
GL	*EGShares Telecom GEMS ETF	TGEM	C+	20.22	21.06	17.57	C+ / 6.0	3.26	9.41	13.20 / 42	--	--
UT	*EGShares Utilities GEMS ETF	UGEM	D	17.13	19.52	15.95	D+ / 2.6	1.48	-0.08	7.59 / 29	--	--
EN	*ELEMENTS MLCX Biofuels Tot Ret	FUE	D-	11.20	14.02	9.65	C- / 3.0	-8.30	-11.27	6.15 / 26	9.67 / 46	--
EN	*ELEMENTS MLCX Grains Idx Tot Ret	GRU	D-	7.17	8.62	5.81	C- / 3.2	-9.28	-9.58	20.82 / 73	10.00 / 47	--
EN	*ELEMENTS RIC Energy Total Return	RJN	E+	6.54	7.52	5.46	D / 1.7	-1.89	7.86	-2.80 / 11	1.89 / 19	-9.19 / 5
EN	*ELEMENTS RIC Index Agri Total Re	RJA	D-	9.06	10.11	8.01	D+ / 2.3	-4.26	-5.74	2.84 / 20	5.86 / 32	-4.53 / 9
EN	*ELEMENTS RIC Index Total Return	RJI	D-	8.62	9.62	7.53	D / 2.1	-1.93	3.59	0.81 / 15	3.90 / 26	-4.14 / 9
EN	*ELEMENTS RIC Metals Total Return	RJZ	D-	10.73	11.94	9.14	D / 1.9	0.43	9.60	0.84 / 16	1.86 / 19	2.09 / 27
EN	*Energy Select Sector SPDR	XLE	C-	71.42	77.35	61.11	C- / 3.8	1.97	11.32	7.99 / 30	9.34 / 44	3.07 / 32
PM	*ETFS Physical Asian Gold Shares	AGOL	D+	166.25	178.86	152.64	D / 1.8	-5.02	5.17	2.19 / 19	--	--
PM	*ETFS Physical Palladium Shares	PALL	C+	69.22	71.54	54.78	B / 8.1	10.23	20.21	9.27 / 33	--	--
PM	*ETFS Physical Platinum Shares	PPLT	C-	151.36	171.46	136.01	C / 4.6	-1.43	13.84	8.82 / 32	--	--
PM	*ETFS Physical PM Basket Shares	GLTR	D	92.81	105.21	83.78	D / 2.0	-5.98	7.83	2.22 / 19	--	--
GL	*ETFS Physical Silver Shares	SIVR	C-	30.06	37.10	25.92	C+ / 6.3	-9.18	11.54	2.52 / 19	17.89 / 82	--
PM	*ETFS Physical Swiss Gold Shares	SGOL	C	165.16	177.43	151.53	C / 4.3	-5.31	4.49	1.10 / 16	13.26 / 64	--
PM	*ETFS Physical WM Basket Shares	WITE	D	50.76	59.69	44.32	C- / 3.0	-4.97	12.62	4.99 / 24	--	--
PM	*FactorShares Gold Bull S&P 500 B	FSG	E+	20.88	30.17	18.66	E- / 0.2	-18.12	-12.83	-32.13 / 3	--	--
GI	*FactorShares Oil Bull S&P 500 Be	FOL	E-	9.69	21.33	8.47	E- / 0.1	-11.14	-20.05	-53.93 / 1	--	--
GI	*FactorShares S&P 500 Bull Tbd Be	FSE	E	10.95	15.59	9.12	D- / 1.0	3.03	--	-7.34 / 9	--	--
GR	*FactorShares Tbd Bull S&P 500 Be	FSA	E	19.40	29.93	17.48	E- / 0.1	--	-33.57	-40.23 / 2	--	--
GR	*Fidelity Nasdaq Comp Tracker Sto	ONEQ	C	118.41	127.00	107.45	C / 5.3	3.16	8.17	16.58 / 55	11.92 / 58	6.93 / 5
FS	*Financial Select Sector SPDR	XLF	C	16.39	17.17	13.30	C / 5.1	8.91	17.59	26.16 / 86	6.21 / 33	-5.65 /
HL	*First Trust AMEX Biotechnology	FBT	B-	45.95	49.05	36.57	B+ / 8.3	7.54	10.16	31.41 / 92	17.93 / 83	15.17 / 9
FO	*First Trust AsiaPac Ex-Jpn Alpha	FPA	B+	27.94	28.47	21.83	A / 9.5	8.81	21.84	22.14 / 77	--	--
FO	*First Trust Australia AlphaDEX	FAUS	U	31.40	N/A	N/A	U /	11.10	--	--	--	--
FO	*First Trust BICK Index	BICK	C	25.33	28.30	21.12	B- / 7.3	9.80	18.12	7.65 / 29	--	--
FO	*First Trust Brazil AlphaDEX	FBZ	D	23.83	29.21	20.99	D+ / 2.4	1.88	9.25	-0.58 / 13	--	--
FO	*First Trust Canada AlphaDEX	FCAN	U	31.83	N/A	N/A	U /	6.44	18.90	--	--	--
IN	*First Trust CBOE S&P500 VIXTail	VIXH	U	19.49	N/A	N/A	U /	0.59	--	--	--	--
FO	*First Trust China AlphaDEX	FCA	B	25.13	26.47	18.71	A+ / 9.8	22.91	29.95	29.58 / 90	--	--
IN	*First Trust Consumer Dis AlphaDE	FXD	B-	22.60	23.39	19.78	B- / 7.1	7.00	15.66	15.72 / 51	15.97 / 77	9.52 /
IN	*First Trust Consumer Stap AlphaD	FXG	B-	25.33	26.20	21.42	C+ / 6.2	10.14	11.25	12.81 / 41	14.31 / 70	9.62 /
FO	*First Trust Dev Mkt Ex-US AlphaD	FDT	B+	44.27	44.99	35.60	A- / 9.0	9.79	19.74	16.75 / 57	--	--
FO	*First Trust DevMkt exUS SC Alpha	FDTS	U	30.23	N/A	N/A	U /	12.16	22.53	--	--	--
GL	*First Trust DJ Glb Sel Div Idx F	FGD	C	24.22	24.92	20.81	C / 4.9	6.14	13.77	19.30 / 69	8.63 / 41	2.69 /
GR	*First Trust Dow Jones Internet I	FDN	C+	38.97	40.92	32.64	B+ / 8.6	10.27	18.78	25.60 / 85	18.36 / 84	13.14 /
GR	*First Trust Dow Jones Sel Micro	FDM	C	22.83	23.60	19.71	C / 4.9	7.16	9.51	15.05 / 48	10.03 / 47	4.94 /
EM	*First Trust EM Small Cap AlphaDE	FEMS	U	34.52	N/A	N/A	U /	29.21	--	--	--	--
EM	*First Trust Emerg Mkt AlphaDEX	FEM	B+	26.39	28.98	21.39	A / 9.4	12.13	19.62	19.13 / 68	--	--
EN	*First Trust Energy AlphaDEX	FXN	D+	19.85	22.07	16.07	C- / 3.0	4.52	16.22	6.89 / 28	5.85 / 32	0.65 /
FO	*First Trust Europe AlphaDEX	FEP	A-	26.20	39.05	20.18	A+ / 9.7	11.80	28.86	24.40 / 83	--	--
FS	*First Trust Financial AlphaDEX	FXO	C+	15.67	16.44	13.47	C+ / 6.0	8.20	13.44	21.27 / 74	10.99 / 53	5.18
GI	*First Trust FTSE EPRA/NAREIT Glb	FFR	C+	39.37	40.22	32.72	B- / 7.2	7.67	11.67	28.61 / 89	13.21 / 64	2.84
FO	*First Trust Germany AlphaDEX	FGM	U	33.52	N/A	N/A	U /	14.50	29.33	--	--	--
HL	*First Trust Health Care AlphaDEX	FXH	B	32.57	34.30	27.95	B- / 7.2	4.77	11.26	22.85 / 79	15.26 / 73	11.27
IN	*First Trust Industrials AlphaDEX	FXR	C	19.43	20.27	16.75	C / 5.1	11.29	17.34	13.70 / 44	10.78 / 52	5.60
IN	*First Trust ISE Chindia Index Fu	FNI	D	20.95	22.93	17.40	D+ / 2.6	10.10	21.14	14.51 / 47	1.90 / 19	-0.11
GL	*First Trust ISE Cloud Computing	SKYY	B+	19.87	21.63	17.06	A- / 9.1	9.35	18.09	18.50 / 65	--	--
GL	*First Trust ISE Glb Eng & Constr	FLM	D+	42.28	44.00	32.98	C- / 3.4	12.28	23.03	18.58 / 65	4.28 / 27	--
EN	*First Trust ISE Glb Wind Energy	FAN	E+	6.94	8.68	5.45	E+ / 0.6	16.10	26.92	-1.56 / 13	-20.08 / 4	--
PM	*First Trust ISE Global Copper Id	CU	C	30.32	35.70	23.69	B+ / 8.4	13.39	29.76	3.02 / 21	--	--
PM	*First Trust ISE Global Platinum	PLTM	E+	14.77	21.57	12.80	D / 1.9	17.23	14.45	-16.60 / 6	--	--

* Denotes ETF Fund, N/A denotes number is not aval

Incl. in Returns		RISK				NET ASSETS		VALUATION			ASSET					FUND MANAGER	
			3 Year		Avg Dura-tion			Premium / Discount		Wtd Avg P/E					Portfolio Turnover Ratio		
Dividend Yield %	Expense Ratio	Risk Rating/ Pts	Standard Deviation	Beta		NAV as of 12/31/12	Total $(Mil)	As of 12/31/12	1 Year Average		Cash %	Stocks %	Bonds %	Other %		Manager Quality Pct	Manager Tenure (Years)
3.06	0.85	B- / 7.9	N/A	N/A	N/A	20.48	4	-1.27	0.13	N/A	0	99	0	1	18	29	4
1.68	0.87	C+ / 6.9	N/A	N/A	N/A	17.28	2	-0.87	-0.32	N/A	0	99	0	1	27	89	4
0.00	0.75	C / 4.5	31.0	0.70	N/A	11.30	2	-0.88	-1.12	N/A	0	0	0	100	N/A	64	5
0.00	0.75	C / 4.5	32.9	0.69	N/A	7.06	16	1.56	0.07	N/A	0	0	0	100	N/A	64	5
0.00	0.75	C / 4.3	24.2	0.90	N/A	6.59	53	-0.76	0.06	N/A	0	0	0	100	N/A	17	6
0.00	0.75	C- / 4.1	23.4	0.61	N/A	9.03	303	0.33	-0.04	N/A	0	0	0	100	N/A	42	6
0.00	0.75	C / 4.4	20.9	0.78	N/A	8.65	511	-0.35	N/A	N/A	0	0	0	100	N/A	26	6
0.00	0.75	C / 4.3	24.1	0.79	N/A	10.78	58	-0.46	-0.11	N/A	0	0	0	100	N/A	24	6
2.08	0.18	B- / 7.3	23.8	1.04	N/A	73.64	6,770	-3.01	N/A	18.7	0	100	0	0	5	52	15
0.00	0.39	B / 8.0	N/A	N/A	N/A	164.46	83	1.09	-0.14	N/A	0	0	0	100	N/A	57	2
0.00	0.60	C+ / 6.4	N/A	N/A	N/A	68.11	498	1.63	0.11	N/A	0	0	0	100	N/A	69	3
0.00	0.60	C+ / 6.9	N/A	N/A	N/A	159.68	770	-5.21	0.25	N/A	0	0	0	100	N/A	60	3
0.00	0.60	C+ / 6.8	N/A	N/A	N/A	92.88	202	-0.08	0.27	N/A	0	0	0	100	N/A	44	N/A
0.00	0.30	C / 4.9	43.9	0.99	N/A	30.35	551	-0.96	0.53	N/A	0	0	0	100	N/A	96	4
0.00	0.39	B / 8.1	18.8	0.91	N/A	163.60	1,930	0.95	0.15	N/A	0	0	0	100	N/A	60	4
0.00	0.60	C / 5.4	N/A	N/A	N/A	51.82	38	-2.05	0.37	N/A	0	0	0	100	N/A	39	3
0.00	2.85	C / 4.4	N/A	N/A	N/A	18.88	6	10.59	-0.05	N/A	99	0	0	1	N/A	3	2
0.00	5.96	D+ / 2.9	N/A	N/A	N/A	9.26	2	4.64	0.10	N/A	100	0	0	0	N/A	N/A	2
0.00	7.12	D+ / 2.5	N/A	N/A	N/A	11.22	1	-2.41	0.15	N/A	94	0	0	6	N/A	1	2
0.00	5.26	C- / 3.9	N/A	N/A	N/A	17.52	2	10.73	-0.11	N/A	0	0	0	100	N/A	41	2
2.77	0.35	B- / 7.1	18.3	1.16	N/A	122.80	178	-3.57	-0.03	105.5	0	100	0	0	13	38	9
2.54	0.18	B- / 7.2	21.2	1.05	N/A	17.11	9,237	-4.21	-0.01	21.6	0	100	0	0	8	36	15
0.00	0.60	C+ / 6.3	26.2	1.15	N/A	48.75	239	-5.74	0.02	101.2	0	99	0	1	13	76	7
0.62	0.80	C+ / 6.8	N/A	N/A	N/A	28.07	14	-0.46	0.35	N/A	0	100	0	0	91	75	2
7.90	N/A	U /	N/A	N/A	N/A	31.98	3	-1.81	N/A	N/A	0	90	0	10	N/A	N/A	1
0.61	0.64	C+ / 5.9	N/A	N/A	N/A	25.87	48	-2.09	-0.17	N/A	0	98	0	2	55	15	3
1.78	0.82	C+ / 6.4	N/A	N/A	N/A	23.51	6	1.36	0.28	N/A	0	99	0	1	50	8	2
2.77	N/A	U /	N/A	N/A	N/A	32.52	8	-2.12	N/A	N/A	0	94	0	6	N/A	N/A	1
2.85	N/A	U /	N/A	N/A	N/A	19.82	3	-1.66	N/A	N/A	0	0	0	100	N/A	N/A	1
1.06	0.80	C+ / 5.8	N/A	N/A	N/A	25.67	2	-2.10	0.23	N/A	0	99	0	1	61	94	2
2.17	0.70	B- / 7.8	20.8	1.23	N/A	23.36	493	-3.25	N/A	42.3	0	100	0	0	98	65	6
2.70	0.70	B / 8.8	12.3	0.65	N/A	26.07	398	-2.84	0.01	25.3	0	99	0	1	126	83	6
1.91	0.80	B- / 7.5	N/A	N/A	N/A	44.78	92	-1.14	0.42	N/A	0	100	0	0	103	42	2
7.16	N/A	U /	N/A	N/A	N/A	31.41	2	-3.76	N/A	N/A	0	0	0	100	N/A	N/A	1
5.01	0.60	B / 8.1	17.8	0.85	N/A	24.70	231	-1.94	0.31	20.0	0	100	0	0	21	79	6
0.00	0.60	C+ / 5.8	20.1	1.19	N/A	40.89	558	-4.70	-0.01	184.8	0	100	0	0	14	69	7
4.04	0.60	B- / 7.2	22.7	1.36	N/A	23.46	41	-2.69	-0.06	25.8	0	99	0	1	7	24	8
1.41	N/A	U /	N/A	N/A	N/A	35.76	2	-3.47	N/A	N/A	0	0	0	100	N/A	N/A	1
0.36	0.80	B- / 7.1	N/A	N/A	N/A	26.79	129	-1.49	0.43	N/A	0	100	0	0	78	54	2
1.45	0.70	C+ / 6.7	29.3	1.24	N/A	20.40	76	-2.70	-0.01	16.8	0	99	0	1	90	24	6
0.29	0.80	B- / 7.2	N/A	N/A	N/A	26.48	31	-1.06	0.77	N/A	0	100	0	0	55	53	2
2.71	0.70	B- / 7.7	17.5	0.86	N/A	16.42	197	-4.57	0.01	27.5	0	99	0	1	93	74	6
0.62	0.60	B- / 7.0	19.2	1.13	N/A	39.65	102	-0.71	0.20	94.7	0	99	0	1	8	56	6
2.81	N/A	U /	N/A	N/A	N/A	34.14	5	-1.82	N/A	N/A	1	98	0	1	N/A	N/A	1
0.76	0.70	B / 8.3	14.1	0.77	N/A	34.09	644	-4.46	0.01	41.8	0	99	0	1	109	82	6
3.08	0.70	B- / 7.4	20.8	1.25	N/A	20.20	132	-3.81	0.04	28.4	0	99	0	1	97	31	6
0.05	0.60	C+ / 6.1	28.3	1.43	N/A	22.19	66	-5.59	-0.14	78.8	0	99	0	1	16	9	6
0.00	0.60	B- / 7.6	N/A	N/A	N/A	20.81	78	-4.52	0.02	N/A	0	0	0	100	28	28	2
0.50	0.70	C+ / 6.5	25.0	1.16	N/A	43.79	19	-3.45	-0.16	N/A	0	99	0	1	10	53	5
0.73	0.60	C / 4.9	28.5	0.93	N/A	7.59	19	-8.56	-0.68	43.6	0	99	0	1	57	3	5
1.32	0.70	C / 4.6	N/A	N/A	N/A	31.91	47	-4.98	-0.22	N/A	0	100	0	0	46	22	3
0.23	0.70	C- / 3.6	N/A	N/A	N/A	15.75	9	-6.22	-0.02	N/A	0	99	0	1	64	4	3

				PRICE				PERFORMANCE						
	99 Pct = Best 0 Pct = Worst		Overall Investment Rating	Price As of 12/31/12	52 Week		Perform-ance Rating/Pts		% Total Return Through 12/31/12			Annualized		
Fund Type	Fund Name	Ticker Symbol			High	Low			3 Mo	6 Mo	1Yr/Pct	3Yr/Pct	5Yr/Pct	
IN	*First Trust ISE Water Index Fund	FIW	B	26.02	26.98	20.97	B / 7.6	11.49	18.10	25.92 / 85	13.29 / 64	7.62 / 58
IN	*First Trust ISE-Revere Natural G	FCG	D-	15.68	19.62	14.11	E+ / 0.9	-9.00	0.18	-7.33 / 9	-4.16 / 10	-4.64 / 9
FO	*First Trust Japan AlphaDEX	FJP	D	36.33	40.25	34.01	D- / 1.5	2.24	1.22	-0.97 / 13	--	--
GR	*First Trust Large Cap Gro AlphaD	FTC	C	29.88	30.94	26.84	C / 4.7	5.55	9.90	11.76 / 38	10.44 / 50	3.18 / 33
IN	*First Trust Large Cap Val AlphaD	FTA	C+	30.48	31.56	25.87	C+ / 6.2	6.27	15.38	16.64 / 56	12.36 / 60	7.84 / 59
FO	*First Trust Latin America AlphaD	FLN	C+	27.16	29.69	22.75	B / 7.6	6.81	16.96	11.18 / 37	--	--
GI	*First Trust Lrg Cap Core AlphaDE	FEX	C+	30.65	31.63	26.62	C+ / 5.6	6.08	13.01	14.61 / 47	11.67 / 56	5.87 / 48
IN	*First Trust Materials AlphaDEX	FXZ	C+	25.80	27.02	21.25	C+ / 6.7	13.90	20.18	20.07 / 71	13.10 / 64	9.11 / 66
GR	*First Trust Mega Cap AlphaDEX	FMK	C+	18.93	20.05	16.93	C+ / 6.2	5.17	13.09	10.13 / 35	--	--
GR	*First Trust Mid Cap Core AlphaDE	FNX	C+	36.88	38.60	31.79	C+ / 6.5	8.57	11.95	14.87 / 47	13.84 / 68	9.90 / 69
GR	*First Trust Mid Cap Growth Alpha	FNY	B-	20.63	21.50	18.41	C+ / 6.2	7.09	9.55	11.40 / 37	--	--
GR	*First Trust Mid Cap Val AlphaDEX	FNK	A-	21.58	22.87	18.45	B+ / 8.5	8.39	13.37	17.45 / 60	--	--
IN	*First Trust Morningstar Div Lead	FDL	B-	18.46	19.80	17.08	C / 5.4	0.06	2.28	12.90 / 41	14.05 / 69	5.16 / 45
GR	*First Trust Multi Cap Grth Alpha	FAD	C	32.73	33.92	23.69	C / 5.1	6.24	9.35	12.03 / 39	12.15 / 59	5.08 / 44
IN	*First Trust Multi Cap Val AlphaD	FAB	B-	32.78	34.06	27.71	C+ / 6.5	7.88	14.85	16.63 / 55	13.09 / 64	9.81 / 69
IN	*First Trust MultiAsst Dvsfd Inc	MDIV	U	19.89	N/A	N/A	U /	3.39	--	--	--	--
GR	*First Trust NASD Cln Edge Smt Gd	GRID	D	29.23	30.78	24.33	D / 2.1	6.84	17.17	19.52 / 69	-1.00 / 13	--
IN	*First Trust NASDAQ ABA Community	QABA	D+	25.54	27.13	23.18	D+ / 2.7	1.10	3.00	8.78 / 32	5.57 / 31	--
GL	*First Trust NASDAQ CEA Smartphon	FONE	B	25.10	28.03	20.73	B+ / 8.7	16.70	22.56	7.56 / 29	--	--
IN	*First Trust NASDAQ Cln Edg US Li	QCLN	D-	9.29	12.01	8.14	E+ / 0.7	16.82	12.47	-2.08 / 12	-13.65 / 6	-15.53 / 4
GL	*First Trust NASDAQ Global Auto	CARZ	B+	29.12	30.28	22.00	A+ / 9.8	23.14	30.66	26.04 / 85	--	--
IN	*First Trust NASDAQ Tech Div Idx	TDIV	U	19.32	N/A	N/A	U /	6.12	--	--	--	--
GR	*First Trust NASDAQ-100 Equal Wei	QQEW	C+	26.13	27.28	23.40	C+ / 5.7	7.55	12.96	14.59 / 47	11.75 / 57	7.12 / 55
IN	*First Trust NASDAQ-100 Ex-Tech S	QQXT	C+	24.65	25.79	21.95	C+ / 6.5	6.59	12.07	18.85 / 67	13.42 / 66	6.53 / 52
GR	*First Trust NASDAQ-100-Technolog	QTEC	C-	25.85	28.97	23.33	C- / 4.0	8.60	13.72	8.66 / 32	9.16 / 44	7.77 / 58
EN	*First Trust North Am Energy Infr	EMLP	U	20.83	N/A	N/A	U /	2.19	4.83	--	--	--
IN	*First Trust S&P REIT Index Fund	FRI	B-	17.75	18.55	15.65	B- / 7.3	4.67	2.60	18.74 / 66	18.17 / 84	7.17 / 56
GR	*First Trust Small Cap Core Alpha	FYX	C+	34.12	35.42	29.03	C+ / 6.5	8.25	11.87	15.20 / 49	13.80 / 68	9.06 / 66
GR	*First Trust Small Cap Gro AlphaD	FYC	B	21.30	24.73	18.86	B- / 7.1	5.91	9.57	15.12 / 48	--	--
GR	*First Trust Small Cap Val AlphaD	FYT	A-	22.38	23.31	18.50	B+ / 8.4	9.98	14.93	15.26 / 49	--	--
FO	*First Trust South Korea AlphaDEX	FKO	B+	26.83	27.45	20.97	A- / 9.2	8.95	20.59	18.28 / 64	--	--
FO	*First Trust STOXX European Sel D	FDD	D	12.31	12.80	10.60	D+ / 2.5	3.81	13.87	15.79 / 51	0.23 / 16	-10.34 / 5
IN	*First Trust Strategic Value Inde	FDV	C	24.88	26.36	21.26	C / 5.0	6.76	18.34	16.05 / 53	10.25 / 48	5.79 / 48
FO	*First Trust Switz AlphaDEX	FSZ	U	32.41	N/A	N/A	U /	10.31	24.34	--	--	--
GR	*First Trust Technology AlphaDEX	FXL	D+	21.68	23.99	19.41	C- / 3.7	8.29	12.74	7.83 / 30	8.31 / 39	5.36 / 46
FO	*First Trust UK AlphaDEX	FKU	U	33.90	N/A	N/A	U /	8.15	22.30	--	--	--
GR	*First Trust US IPO Index Fund	FPX	A-	30.90	32.31	25.03	B+ / 8.8	13.44	20.44	31.61 / 93	17.71 / 82	9.57 / 68
UT	*First Trust Utilities AlphaDEX	FXU	C	17.98	19.42	16.81	C- / 3.1	-2.90	3.65	5.84 / 25	8.47 / 40	3.98 / 37
GR	*First Trust Value Line 100 Fund	FVL	C-	13.26	14.17	11.65	C- / 4.1	5.97	9.77	8.12 / 31	9.99 / 47	-1.93 / 14
GI	*First Trust Value Line Dividend	FVD	C+	17.30	17.78	15.85	C / 5.2	3.67	7.02	13.66 / 43	12.58 / 61	7.40 / 57
GI	*First Trust Value Line Equity Al	FVI	D+	18.90	20.20	16.97	C- / 3.0	3.33	12.54	9.90 / 34	5.71 / 32	3.75 / 36
EM	*FlexShares MS EM Fact Tilt Idx	TLTE	U	53.98	N/A	N/A	U /	8.84	--	--	--	--
GL	*FlexShares Ready Access Var Inc	RAVI	U	74.99	N/A	N/A	U /	--	--	--	--	--
USA	*FlexShs iB 3Y Tgt Dur TIPS Idx	TDTT	C-	25.52	25.90	25.10	D / 1.9	0.21	0.93	2.94 / 20	--	--
USA	*FlexShs iB 5Y Tgt Dur TIPS Idx	TDTF	C	26.30	26.78	25.28	D+ / 2.3	0.04	1.46	5.31 / 24	--	--
EN	*FlexShs Morningstar Gl Upstream	GUNR	C	35.62	37.32	30.62	C / 4.9	4.03	11.99	7.60 / 29	--	--
IN	*FlexShs Morningstar US Mkt Fac T	TILT	A-	59.72	62.17	52.62	B / 7.9	5.59	11.51	16.96 / 58	--	--
FO	*FlexShs MS Dev Mkts exUS Fctrs T	TLTD	U	52.81	N/A	N/A	U /	9.89	--	--	--	--
GI	*Global Alpha & Beta ETF	RRGR	U	25.79	N/A	N/A	U /	3.01	--	--	--	--
GL	*Global Echo ETF	GIVE	U	51.63	N/A	N/A	U /	1.70	4.15	--	--	--
FO	*Global X Brazil Consumer ETF	BRAQ	B	20.27	20.50	14.96	A+ / 9.7	4.12	27.48	26.72 / 87	--	--
FO	*Global X Brazil Financials ETF	BRAF	D+	13.26	17.00	11.36	C / 4.6	5.95	19.53	0.40 / 15	--	--

| Incl. in Returns | | RISK | | | | NET ASSETS | | VALUATION | | | ASSET | | | | | FUND MANAGER | |
Dividend Yield %	Expense Ratio	Risk Rating/ Pts	3 Year Standard Deviation	Beta	Avg Dura-tion	NAV as of 12/31/12	Total $(Mil)	Premium / Discount As of 12/31/12	1 Year Average	Wtd Avg P/E	Cash %	Stocks %	Bonds %	Other %	Portfolio Turnover Ratio	Manager Quality Pct	Manager Tenure (Years)
0.55	0.60	B- / 7.6	19.0	1.17	N/A	26.96	73	-3.49	-0.03	52.0	0	99	0	1	9	51	6
0.09	0.60	C+ / 6.6	28.3	1.43	N/A	16.04	388	-2.24	N/A	17.6	0	100	0	0	27	7	6
1.67	0.80	B / 8.0	N/A	N/A	N/A	35.60	2	2.05	0.06	N/A	0	100	0	0	52	11	2
1.63	0.70	B- / 7.7	16.6	1.03	N/A	30.82	117	-3.05	-0.02	60.5	0	99	0	0	52	11	2
1.91	0.70	B / 8.2	16.6	1.05	N/A	31.38	279	-2.87	0.04	18.5	0	99	0	1	162	40	6
0.63	0.81	C+ / 6.8	N/A	N/A	N/A	27.18	9	-0.07	0.52	N/A	0	100	0	0	88	58	6
1.86	0.70	B / 8.0	16.4	1.05	N/A	31.57	345	-2.91	0.02	33.1	0	100	0	0	73	15	2
3.49	0.70	B- / 7.0	23.7	1.40	N/A	26.78	204	-3.66	-0.01	38.6	0	99	0	1	95	49	6
1.83	0.70	B / 8.2	N/A	N/A	N/A	19.86	10	-4.68	-0.03	N/A	0	99	0	1	92	33	6
1.21	0.70	B- / 7.7	18.9	1.17	N/A	38.20	301	-3.46	0.02	35.9	0	99	0	1	164	13	2
0.95	0.70	B / 8.6	N/A	N/A	N/A	21.39	17	-3.55	0.13	N/A	0	99	0	1	94	56	6
1.35	0.70	B / 8.4	N/A	N/A	N/A	22.30	10	-3.23	0.21	N/A	0	99	0	1	166	28	2
4.46	0.45	B+ / 9.2	10.6	0.50	N/A	18.92	546	-2.43	0.03	20.5	0	99	0	1	100	37	2
1.17	0.70	B- / 7.5	17.5	1.07	N/A	33.85	31	-3.31	0.02	63.8	0	99	0	1	22	86	16
1.76	0.70	B / 8.1	17.7	1.12	N/A	33.78	56	-2.96	0.02	20.8	0	99	0	1	155	46	6
4.27	N/A	U /	N/A	N/A	N/A	20.57	66	-3.31	N/A	N/A	0	99	0	1	90	57	6
0.91	0.70	C+ / 6.7	22.6	1.28	N/A	30.93	13	-5.50	-0.39	N/A	0	0	0	100	N/A	N/A	1
0.68	0.60	B- / 7.0	21.3	1.18	N/A	26.29	9	-2.85	0.02	N/A	0	100	0	0	46	8	4
1.33	0.70	B- / 7.2	N/A	N/A	N/A	26.14	11	-3.98	-0.37	N/A	0	99	0	1	9	18	4
0.93	0.60	C / 5.4	29.1	1.65	N/A	9.91	14	-6.26	-0.23	36.9	0	99	0	1	35	13	2
0.69	0.70	C+ / 6.6	N/A	N/A	N/A	29.99	7	-2.90	0.17	N/A	0	100	0	0	7	3	6
5.13	N/A	U /	N/A	N/A	N/A	20.17	50	-4.21	N/A	N/A	0	99	0	1	17	90	2
1.57	0.60	B- / 7.6	18.8	1.17	N/A	27.18	85	-3.86	0.03	64.3	0	0	0	100	N/A	N/A	N/A
1.98	0.60	B- / 7.5	16.6	1.01	N/A	25.68	42	-4.01	-0.05	85.3	0	99	0	1	12	35	7
0.65	0.60	B- / 7.6	22.1	1.32	N/A	26.99	106	-4.22	-0.03	43.0	0	99	0	1	14	64	7
2.67	N/A	U /	N/A	N/A	N/A	21.62	124	-3.65	N/A	N/A	0	99	0	1	8	18	7
1.81	0.50	B- / 7.6	18.6	1.03	N/A	18.12	403	-2.04	0.01	66.8	0	0	0	100	N/A	N/A	1
1.55	0.70	B- / 7.6	20.3	1.24	N/A	35.21	164	-3.10	0.03	44.4	0	99	0	1	3	81	6
0.70	0.70	B / 8.5	N/A	N/A	N/A	22.08	10	-3.53	0.10	N/A	0	99	0	1	101	52	6
1.37	0.70	B / 8.3	N/A	N/A	N/A	23.03	25	-2.82	0.08	N/A	0	99	0	1	162	38	2
0.92	0.80	C+ / 6.8	N/A	N/A	N/A	26.55	3	1.05	-0.01	N/A	0	100	0	0	103	24	2
2.25	0.60	C+ / 6.8	20.5	0.95	N/A	12.43	18	-0.97	0.52	N/A	0	96	0	4	42	63	2
2.61	0.65	B- / 7.8	19.3	1.18	N/A	26.31	33	-5.44	-0.09	22.5	0	99	0	1	31	29	N/A
1.82	N/A	U /	N/A	N/A	N/A	33.59	5	-3.51	N/A	N/A	0	99	0	1	47	26	7
0.59	0.70	C+ / 6.9	22.6	1.33	N/A	22.46	138	-3.47	-0.01	63.2	0	99	0	1	N/A	N/A	1
2.68	N/A	U /	N/A	N/A	N/A	34.51	7	-1.77	N/A	N/A	0	99	0	1	101	17	6
1.28	0.60	B / 8.0	18.0	1.11	N/A	32.20	21	-4.04	-0.02	N/A	0	99	0	1	N/A	N/A	1
2.74	0.70	B+ / 9.0	11.1	0.89	N/A	18.18	140	-1.10	-0.02	24.4	0	99	0	1	27	77	7
1.89	0.70	B- / 7.1	22.5	1.35	N/A	13.82	46	-4.05	-0.08	35.7	0	99	0	1	72	53	6
3.46	0.70	B / 8.8	11.9	0.75	N/A	17.73	508	-2.43	0.07	23.4	0	99	0	1	116	20	10
3.45	0.70	B- / 7.7	16.7	0.99	N/A	19.98	4	-5.41	-0.12	37.1	0	99	0	1	27	75	10
0.39	N/A	U /	N/A	N/A	N/A	54.19	20	-0.39	N/A	N/A	0	0	0	100	104	20	7
0.69	N/A	U /	N/A	N/A	N/A	75.01	8	-0.03	N/A	N/A	0	0	0	100	N/A	N/A	1
0.56	0.20	B+ / 9.9	N/A	N/A	N/A	25.45	720	0.28	0.23	N/A	0	0	0	100	N/A	N/A	1
0.75	0.20	B+ / 9.9	N/A	N/A	N/A	26.16	385	0.54	0.12	N/A	0	0	0	100	55	71	2
1.03	0.48	B / 8.1	N/A	N/A	N/A	36.24	604	-1.71	0.34	N/A	0	0	0	100	60	79	2
1.11	0.27	B+ / 9.1	N/A	N/A	N/A	61.78	154	-3.33	0.11	N/A	0	0	0	100	5	78	2
0.86	N/A	U /	N/A	N/A	N/A	53.59	20	-1.46	N/A	N/A	0	0	0	100	15	43	2
1.26	N/A	U /	N/A	N/A	N/A	26.71	1	-3.44	N/A	N/A	0	0	0	100	N/A	N/A	1
0.00	N/A	U /	N/A	N/A	N/A	52.09	5	-0.88	N/A	N/A	0	0	0	100	N/A	N/A	1
1.21	0.77	C+ / 6.1	N/A	N/A	N/A	20.19	24	0.40	-0.13	N/A	0	100	0	0	31	86	3
3.75	0.77	C+ / 5.8	N/A	N/A	N/A	13.58	4	-2.36	-0.26	N/A	0	90	0	10	10	8	3

* Denotes ETF Fund, N/A denotes number is not available

I. Index of ETFs and Other Closed-End Funds

Fund Type	Fund Name	Ticker Symbol	Overall Investment Rating	Price As of 12/31/12	52 Week High	52 Week Low	Performance Rating/Pts	3 Mo	6 Mo	1Yr/Pct	3Yr/Pct	5Yr/Pct
FO	*Global X Brazil Mid Cap ETF	BRAZ	C-	15.61	18.19	13.90	C / 4.9	4.19	10.48	8.42 / 31	--	--
FO	*Global X Canada Preferred ETF	CNPF	C-	14.65	15.85	13.74	D+ / 2.8	0.52	4.90	5.85 / 26		--
FO	*Global X China Consumer ETF	CHIQ	D-	14.87	16.23	11.86	D / 1.7	12.22	20.45	8.63 / 32	-2.29 / 11	
EN	*Global X China Energy ETF	CHIE	D	14.50	15.35	11.83	D+ / 2.7	16.90	25.25	11.42 / 37	1.55 / 18	--
FS	*Global X China Financials ETF	CHIX	D	13.66	14.35	10.07	C- / 4.1	24.78	32.91	32.91 / 94	2.33 / 21	--
FO	*Global X China Industrials ETF	CHII	D-	12.45	13.50	9.23	D / 2.1	24.91	30.67	25.46 / 84	-5.45 / 9	
FO	*Global X China Materials ETF	CHIM	C+	8.77	10.47	6.85	A / 9.5	21.07	28.61	8.46 / 31	--	--
PM	*Global X Copper Miners ETF	COPX	C	13.02	15.82	10.34	B+ / 8.3	11.81	31.10	2.17 / 19	--	--
GL	*Global X Fertilizers/Potash ETF	SOIL	B-	14.04	14.79	11.50	B+ / 8.3	7.74	14.59	15.92 / 52	--	--
FO	*Global X FTSE Andean 40 ETF	AND	C+	14.58	15.56	13.19	B- / 7.4	7.60	8.49	15.73 / 51	--	--
FO	*Global X FTSE Argentina 20 ETF	ARGT	E+	8.55	12.08	7.57	D- / 1.0	3.94	16.49	-18.48 / 5	--	
GL	*Global X FTSE ASEAN 40 ETF	ASEA	C+	17.04	17.30	14.45	B- / 7.1	3.91	8.69	16.74 / 57	--	--
FO	*Global X FTSE Greece 20 ETF	GREK	C+	18.06	19.93	8.78	A+ / 9.9	17.63	65.55	48.10 / 98	--	--
GL	*Global X FTSE Nordic Region ETF	GXF	C+	19.54	20.42	15.06	B- / 7.1	12.09	24.93	32.53 / 94	8.51 / 41	--
FO	*Global X FTSE Norway 30 ETF	NORW	B	15.25	15.95	11.70	A+ / 9.6	5.08	20.93	26.06 / 86	--	--
GL	*Global X Gold Explorers ETF	GLDX	E	7.32	12.75	6.83	E / 0.4	-10.20	4.83	-30.83 / 3	--	--
EN	*Global X Junior Miners ETF	JUNR	D	9.29	12.38	8.00	C / 4.5	-3.99	20.26	5.56 / 25	--	--
GR	*Global X Lithium ETF	LIT	D-	14.36	17.45	12.96	D / 1.9	1.20	5.99	-1.17 / 13	--	--
EN	*Global X MLP ETF	MLPA	U	14.53	N/A	N/A	U /	1.28	5.44	--	--	--
FO	*Global X NASDAQ China Tech ETF	QQQC	D	14.23	16.18	12.31	D / 1.6	10.05	16.72	7.99 / 30	-2.21 / 11	--
GI	*Global X Permanent ETF	PERM	U	25.63	N/A	N/A	U /	-0.41	3.09	--	--	--
PM	*Global X Pure Gold Miners ETF	GGGG	E+	10.48	14.29	9.33	E / 0.4	-16.34	2.13	-20.59 / 5	--	--
PM	*Global X Silver Miners ETF	SIL	D+	22.65	26.62	16.54	C / 4.4	-7.20	27.19	2.33 / 19	--	--
GL	*Global X Social Media Index ETF	SOCL	D+	12.94	16.00	11.81	C- / 3.5	6.51	4.05	6.67 / 28	--	--
GL	*Global X SuperDividend ETF	SDIV	B	22.10	22.98	19.60	B / 8.2	6.67	12.07	17.79 / 61	--	--
GL	*Global X SuperIncome Preferred E	SPFF	U	14.92	N/A	N/A	U /	1.64	--	--	--	--
GI	*Global X Top Guru Holdings Idx E	GURU	U	17.41	N/A	N/A	U /	10.77	23.00	--	--	--
GL	*Global X Uranium ETF	URA	E-	6.51	10.98	5.73	E / 0.5	-2.57	-5.85	-22.62 / 5	--	--
FO	*Global X/InterBolsa FTSE Col 20	GXG	C-	22.24	23.16	18.92	B / 7.6	7.83	11.41	20.96 / 73	16.17 / 77	--
GI	*GreenHaven Continuous Commodity	GCC	D	28.83	32.36	26.53	D / 1.7	-4.40	-1.13	-4.65 / 11	3.06 / 23	
GR	*GS Cnct S&P GSCI Enh Cmd TR Str	GSC	D	47.97	54.63	41.20	D / 1.9	-2.83	3.77	-2.41 / 12	3.51 / 24	-4.90 /
IN	*Guggenheim 2x S&P 500 ETF	RSU	B	51.45	55.46	40.69	B+ / 8.8	6.42	18.93	33.20 / 94	18.65 / 85	0.10 / 2
FO	*Guggenheim ABC High Dividend ETF	ABCS	D	19.15	24.05	17.56	D+ / 2.3	4.11	5.17	0.57 / 15	--	--
GL	*Guggenheim Airline ETF	FAA	C+	34.91	37.93	27.25	B- / 7.4	26.46	19.81	39.02 / 97	5.76 / 32	
FO	*Guggenheim Australian Dollar Sha	FXA	C-	104.15	108.85	93.95	C- / 3.2	3.50	4.35	5.21 / 24	8.14 / 39	7.21 /
COI	*Guggenheim BltShs 2013 Corp Bd E	BSCD	C-	20.80	20.98	20.77	D- / 1.5	-0.29	0.16	1.10 / 16	--	--
COI	*Guggenheim BltShs 2014 Corp Bd E	BSCE	C-	21.27	21.38	20.95	D / 2.0	0.23	1.28	3.29 / 21	--	--
COI	*Guggenheim BltShs 2015 Corp Bd E	BSCF	C	21.80	21.93	21.15	D+ / 2.4	0.35	2.30	5.30 / 24	--	--
COI	*Guggenheim BltShs 2016 Corp Bd E	BSCG	C	22.22	22.36	21.31	D+ / 2.7	0.37	2.91	9.03 / 33	--	--
COI	*Guggenheim BltShs 2017 Corp Bd E	BSCH	C	22.82	22.98	21.54	C- / 3.2	0.35	3.93	1.18 / 16	-1.92 / 12	-1.92 /
IN	*Guggenheim BRIC ETF	EEB	D	36.02	42.02	32.00	D- / 1.4	7.09	12.32	4.88 / 23	-0.56 / 14	-3.52 /
FO	*Guggenheim British Pound Sterlin	FXB	D+	160.71	161.35	151.96	D- / 1.4	0.19	3.33	4.00 / 22	1.53 / 18	1.07 /
FO	*Guggenheim Canadian Dollar Shs	FXC	C-	100.14	102.96	95.30	D / 1.8	-0.49	3.14	-3.91 / 11	-1.33 / 12	-3.63 /
EN	*Guggenheim Canadian Energy Inc E	ENY	D-	15.52	18.53	13.70	D- / 1.2	-5.58	8.92	18.55 / 65	3.42 / 24	
FO	*Guggenheim China All-Cap ETF	YAO	D+	25.54	26.56	20.92	C- / 3.2	14.16	23.47	57.22 / 99	12.72 / 62	3.14 /
GI	*Guggenheim China Real Estate ETF	TAO	B	22.85	24.08	15.60	A / 9.3	21.15	30.29	28.51 / 89	-1.27 / 12	
FO	*Guggenheim China Small Cap ETF	HAO	D-	23.99	25.67	18.41	D+ / 2.8	23.72	28.32	12.58 / 40	-2.61 / 11	
FO	*Guggenheim China Technology ETF	CQQQ	D-	22.32	25.05	18.88	D / 1.8	14.74	20.23	0.14 / 14	--	
GI	*Guggenheim Chinese Renminbi Shs	FXCH	C-	79.80	82.00	77.00	D / 1.7	1.57	1.97	11.55 / 38	13.83 / 68	7.01
IN	*Guggenheim Defensive Equity ETF	DEF	B-	28.57	30.14	26.92	C / 5.4	1.93	4.19	3.13 / 21	6.64 / 34	
GEI	*Guggenheim Enhanced Core Bond ET	GIY	C-	51.75	53.22	51.10	D+ / 2.6	-0.89	-0.39	1.69 / 17	0.51 / 16	
GR	*Guggenheim Enhanced Sh Bd ETF	GSY	C-	50.05	50.18	49.54	D- / 1.5	0.48	0.83			

* Denotes ETF Fund, N/A denotes number is not avail

www.thestreetratings.

Incl. in Returns		RISK				NET ASSETS		VALUATION			ASSET				FUND MANAGER		
			3 Year					Premium / Discount									
Dividend Yield %	Expense Ratio	Risk Rating/ Pts	Standard Deviation	Beta	Avg Dura-tion	NAV as of 12/31/12	Total $(Mil)	As of 12/31/12	1 Year Average	Wtd Avg P/E	Cash %	Stocks %	Bonds %	Other %	Portfolio Turnover Ratio	Manager Quality Pct	Manager Tenure (Years)
2.90	0.69	C+ / 6.4	N/A	N/A	N/A	15.92	19	-1.95	-0.30	N/A	0	100	0	0	17	14	3
4.31	0.58	B / 8.4	N/A	N/A	N/A	14.76	15	-0.75	0.20	N/A	0	0	0	100	19	52	2
1.12	0.65	C+ / 5.7	27.9	0.96	N/A	15.26	186	-2.56	0.03	N/A	0	99	0	1	11	18	4
1.75	0.65	C+ / 6.4	24.7	0.86	N/A	15.16	5	-4.35	-0.24	N/A	0	99	0	1	6	17	4
2.73	0.65	C / 5.2	34.8	1.07	N/A	13.96	7	-2.15	-0.36	N/A	0	99	0	1	7	15	4
1.30	0.65	C / 4.8	37.0	1.23	N/A	13.11	5	-5.03	-0.07	N/A	0	99	0	1	11	12	4
1.53	0.65	C / 4.5	N/A	N/A	N/A	9.47	3	-7.39	0.18	N/A	0	99	0	1	5	8	3
3.29	0.65	C / 4.4	N/A	N/A	N/A	13.76	31	-5.38	-0.11	N/A	0	100	0	0	18	18	3
1.15	0.69	C+ / 6.5	N/A	N/A	N/A	14.81	29	-5.20	-0.03	N/A	0	100	0	0	14	33	2
1.78	0.72	B- / 7.1	N/A	N/A	N/A	15.00	9	-2.80	-0.26	N/A	0	99	0	1	11	75	2
1.05	0.75	C / 4.4	N/A	N/A	N/A	9.08	3	-5.84	-0.16	N/A	0	99	0	1	15	1	2
2.20	0.65	B- / 7.3	N/A	N/A	N/A	16.84	38	1.19	0.37	N/A	0	99	0	1	7	84	2
0.13	0.66	C / 4.4	N/A	N/A	N/A	18.96	23	-4.75	1.00	N/A	0	99	0	1	13	4	2
2.53	0.50	C+ / 6.4	26.5	1.26	N/A	20.26	27	-3.55	-0.08	N/A	0	99	0	1	4	76	4
2.81	0.50	C+ / 6.2	N/A	N/A	N/A	15.60	56	-2.24	-0.03	N/A	0	99	0	1	13	44	3
4.92	0.65	C- / 3.1	N/A	N/A	N/A	7.39	39	-0.95	0.32	N/A	0	100	0	0	23	1	3
12.12	0.75	C / 4.3	N/A	N/A	N/A	9.37	3	-0.85	-0.16	N/A	0	100	0	0	77	65	2
2.42	0.75	C / 5.3	N/A	N/A	N/A	14.94	66	-3.88	-0.52	N/A	0	100	0	0	22	3	3
7.37	N/A	U /	N/A	N/A	N/A	15.19	23	-4.34	N/A	N/A	0	0	0	100	N/A	N/A	1
0.56	0.65	C+ / 6.2	25.0	0.95	N/A	14.99	3	-5.07	-0.70	N/A	1	98	0	1	55	21	4
0.97	N/A	U /	N/A	N/A	N/A	25.25	14	1.50	N/A	N/A	0	0	0	100	N/A	N/A	1
0.13	0.59	C / 5.3	N/A	N/A	N/A	10.24	4	2.34	0.38	N/A	0	99	0	1	12	4	2
0.89	0.65	C / 5.2	N/A	N/A	N/A	22.40	350	1.12	-0.01	N/A	0	99	0	1	14	24	3
0.84	0.65	B- / 7.0	N/A	N/A	N/A	13.92	12	-7.04	-0.31	N/A	0	0	0	100	52	5	2
16.47	0.58	B- / 7.6	N/A	N/A	N/A	22.67	193	-2.51	0.50	N/A	0	100	0	0	21	94	2
13.71	N/A	U /	N/A	N/A	N/A	15.10	7	-1.19	N/A	N/A	0	0	0	100	N/A	N/A	1
2.30	N/A	U /	N/A	N/A	N/A	18.18	2	-4.24	N/A	N/A	0	0	0	100	N/A	N/A	1
1.90	0.69	D+ / 2.6	N/A	N/A	N/A	6.81	133	-4.41	0.25	N/A	0	99	0	1	37	1	3
2.02	0.78	C- / 3.3	21.0	0.65	N/A	22.22	179	0.09	0.15	N/A	1	98	0	1	17	95	4
0.00	1.04	B- / 7.3	17.5	0.78	N/A	28.83	475	0.00	-0.05	N/A	100	0	0	0	N/A	22	5
0.00	N/A	B- / 7.1	22.6	1.16	N/A	48.17	N/A	-0.42	N/A	N/A	0	0	0	100	N/A	14	6
1.46	0.71	C+ / 6.5	31.8	2.03	N/A	54.95	52	-6.37	-0.09	50.2	16	83	0	1	6	24	6
6.48	0.65	C+ / 6.4	N/A	N/A	N/A	19.31	10	-0.83	0.09	N/A	0	100	0	0	95	7	2
0.00	0.70	C+ / 6.3	25.3	0.60	N/A	37.79	17	-7.62	-0.07	N/A	0	92	0	8	50	69	3
2.36	0.40	B / 8.5	14.6	0.65	N/A	105.58	583	-1.35	-0.02	N/A	100	0	0	0	N/A	82	7
1.27	0.24	B+ / 9.9	N/A	N/A	N/A	20.84	159	-0.19	0.20	N/A	0	0	100	0	4	60	3
1.58	0.24	B+ / 9.9	N/A	N/A	N/A	21.24	178	0.14	0.35	N/A	0	0	100	0	3	59	3
1.93	0.24	B+ / 9.8	N/A	N/A	N/A	21.80	166	0.00	0.37	N/A	0	0	100	0	1	64	3
2.11	0.24	B+ / 9.7	N/A	N/A	N/A	22.21	159	0.05	0.37	N/A	0	0	100	0	5	65	3
2.31	0.24	B+ / 9.7	N/A	N/A	N/A	22.80	181	0.09	0.43	N/A	0	0	100	0	3	70	3
2.64	0.64	C+ / 6.5	25.0	1.37	N/A	36.80	321	-2.12	-0.07	N/A	0	100	0	0	10	7	3
0.00	0.40	B / 8.9	8.9	0.35	N/A	159.45	64	0.79	0.04	N/A	100	0	0	0	N/A	39	7
0.13	0.40	B+ / 9.0	8.7	0.39	N/A	101.09	499	-0.94	-0.04	N/A	100	0	0	0	N/A	55	7
3.25	0.70	C+ / 6.3	29.0	1.19	N/A	15.77	76	-1.59	-0.32	14.3	0	99	0	1	81	13	3
2.20	0.70	C+ / 6.4	26.0	1.00	N/A	26.07	55	-2.03	-0.30	N/A	0	99	0	1	12	38	3
1.70	0.70	C+ / 6.0	32.6	1.40	N/A	23.52	80	-2.85	0.02	N/A	0	100	0	0	14	20	3
1.31	0.75	C / 4.3	30.7	1.11	N/A	24.91	302	-3.69	0.19	155.0	0	100	0	0	35	20	3
1.91	0.70	C+ / 5.6	29.4	1.15	N/A	24.07	18	-7.27	-0.37	N/A	0	99	0	1	43	16	3
0.00	N/A	B+ / 9.8	N/A	N/A	N/A	80.55	4	-0.93	0.47	N/A	0	0	0	100	N/A	55	2
2.61	0.65	B+ / 9.2	9.3	0.52	N/A	29.41	67	-2.86	-0.01	23.9	0	82	0	18	27	84	3
2.32	0.27	B+ / 9.4	5.1	0.85	N/A	51.76	5	-0.02	-0.09	N/A	0	0	100	0	296	61	5
1.89	0.26	B+ / 9.9	0.4	N/A	3.6	50.12	225	-0.14	-0.02	N/A	55	0	43	2	7	56	2

* Denotes ETF Fund, N/A denotes number is not available

				PRICE			PERFORMANCE						
	99 Pct = Best 0 Pct = Worst		Overall Investment Rating	Price As of 12/31/12	52 Week		Perform- ance Rating/Pts		% Total Return Through 12/31/12				
					High	Low			3 Mo	6 Mo	1Yr/Pct	Annualized	
Fund Type	Fund Name	Ticker Symbol										3Yr/Pct	5Yr/Pct
FO	*Guggenheim Euro Shares	FXE	D	130.96	134.26	119.73	D- / 1.3		2.84	8.74	4.77 / 23	-2.60 / 11	-1.45 / 15
GL	*Guggenheim Frontier Markets ETF	FRN	D+	19.76	21.85	18.60	D+ / 2.9		4.62	6.57	11.24 / 37	4.50 / 28	--
IN	*Guggenheim Insider Sentiment ETF	NFO	C+	34.75	36.31	29.89	C+ / 6.0		6.65	12.78	16.27 / 54	12.45 / 61	8.78 / 64
FO	*Guggenheim Intl Multi-Asset Inc	HGI	D+	16.84	18.27	14.76	D+ / 2.5		6.70	13.26	9.79 / 34	2.86 / 22	-0.30 / 18
IN	*Guggenheim Inverse 2x S&P 500 ET	RSW	E	22.10	29.57	20.50	E / 0.3		-8.09	-19.15	-30.56 / 3	-27.61 / 3	-24.00 / 2
FO	*Guggenheim Japanese Yen Trust	FXY	D+	113.03	129.36	109.66	D- / 1.0		-12.21	-11.32	-14.10 / 6	0.23 / 15	3.26 / 34
GR	*Guggenheim Mid-Cap Core ETF	CZA	B-	33.75	35.37	29.92	C+ / 6.8		6.26	11.30	16.92 / 58	14.75 / 72	9.55 / 67
EM	*Guggenheim MSCI EAFE Eq Weight E	EWEF	B+	38.56	39.87	32.22	A / 9.3		9.82	18.25	20.61 / 72	--	--
EM	*Guggenheim MSCI Em Mkt Eq Weight	EWEM	C+	35.73	37.50	29.71	B / 8.1		8.20	15.28	13.69 / 44	--	--
IN	*Guggenheim Multi-Asset Income ET	CVY	C+	21.92	23.28	20.06	C+ / 5.9		4.34	9.97	15.56 / 50	13.43 / 66	7.84 / 59
IN	*Guggenheim Raymond James SB1 Eq	RYJ	C+	23.47	24.45	20.10	C+ / 6.5		7.76	11.33	15.64 / 51	13.89 / 68	10.09 / 70
IN	*Guggenheim Russ Top 50 Mega Cap	XLG	C	102.98	109.46	93.41	C / 4.4		1.00	6.83	17.01 / 58	10.20 / 48	3.60 / 35
GR	*Guggenheim Russell 1000 Eq Wght	EWRI	B+	34.52	36.23	30.37	B+ / 8.3		7.12	13.35	16.66 / 56	--	--
GR	*Guggenheim Russell 2000 Eq Wght	EWRS	C+	32.10	33.89	28.79	C+ / 6.8		5.93	9.83	13.77 / 44	--	--
GR	*Guggenheim Russell MC Eq Wght ET	EWRM	B+	35.19	36.43	29.89	B+ / 8.3		7.73	13.67	16.88 / 57	--	--
GR	*Guggenheim S&P 500 Eq WgCon Dsc	RCD	B	56.42	58.21	49.04	B / 7.8		5.61	13.34	20.84 / 73	17.13 / 80	12.65 / 79
GR	*Guggenheim S&P 500 Eq WgCon St E	RHS	B-	69.18	71.37	62.39	C+ / 6.1		3.65	6.77	16.18 / 54	14.59 / 71	10.07 / 70
EN	*Guggenheim S&P 500 Eq Wght Engy	RYE	D+	63.85	69.93	53.26	C- / 3.6		1.73	14.24	8.20 / 31	8.60 / 41	3.19 / 33
FS	*Guggenheim S&P 500 Eq Wght Finl	RYF	C+	29.16	30.66	24.42	C+ / 6.6		8.39	17.69	25.08 / 84	10.73 / 51	-0.56 / 18
GR	*Guggenheim S&P 500 Eq Wght HC ET	RYH	B-	78.39	82.52	68.90	C+ / 6.6		5.93	12.18	22.02 / 76	12.90 / 63	8.77 / 64
GR	*Guggenheim S&P 500 Eq Wght Ind E	RGI	C+	59.03	62.57	50.85	C+ / 6.2		10.87	17.63	15.47 / 50	13.13 / 64	6.66 / 53
GR	*Guggenheim S&P 500 Eq Wght Mat E	RTM	C	64.79	67.80	54.08	C / 4.8		10.33	16.44	14.12 / 45	10.06 / 47	8.57 / 63
GR	*Guggenheim S&P 500 Eq Wght Tech	RYT	C-	55.27	59.23	48.78	C / 4.4		8.87	16.51	13.02 / 41	9.27 / 44	6.40 / 51
UT	*Guggenheim S&P 500 Eq Wght Util	RYU	C+	57.47	61.64	53.00	C / 4.7		-1.30	3.88	14.01 / 45	12.63 / 61	5.28 / 45
IN	*Guggenheim S&P 500 Equal Wght	RSP	C+	53.32	55.15	46.03	C+ / 6.3		6.63	13.46	17.68 / 61	12.64 / 62	7.26 / 56
GR	*Guggenheim S&P 500 Pure Growth	RPG	C+	49.28	51.25	43.87	C+ / 6.5		5.65	9.93	15.59 / 51	14.58 / 71	9.28 / 67
IN	*Guggenheim S&P 500 Pure Value	RPV	B+	34.20	35.47	26.79	B / 8.0		10.59	23.75	23.82 / 81	14.15 / 69	7.52 / 57
IN	*Guggenheim S&P Gl Div Opps Idx E	LVL	D+	13.14	14.46	11.41	D+ / 2.5		8.04	14.85	9.42 / 33	2.57 / 21	0.85 / 22
EN	*Guggenheim S&P Global Water Idx	CGW	C	22.24	22.86	19.16	C / 5.2		7.09	13.50	21.16 / 74	8.74 / 42	2.82 / 31
GR	*Guggenheim S&P Mid Cap 400 Eq Wg	EWMD	A	32.56	33.91	28.33	B+ / 8.6		8.66	13.91	17.80 / 61	--	--
GR	*Guggenheim S&P Mid Cap 400 Pure	RFV	C+	36.93	38.90	31.01	C+ / 6.1		10.29	16.08	18.25 / 64	10.79 / 52	8.23 / 61
GR	*Guggenheim S&P Mid Cap 400 Pure	RFG	B	91.26	95.72	78.98	B- / 7.5		7.73	12.59	15.86 / 52	17.18 / 80	13.96 / 85
GR	*Guggenheim S&P Sm Cap 600 Eq Wgh	EWSM	A	32.92	34.32	29.22	B+ / 8.5		7.15	11.46	19.87 / 70	--	--
GR	*Guggenheim S&P Sm Cap 600 Pure G	RZG	B-	55.82	58.53	49.94	B- / 7.0		7.32	9.48	16.06 / 53	15.93 / 76	10.38 / 71
GR	*Guggenheim S&P Sm Cap 600 Pure V	RZV	C+	43.21	45.90	34.36	C+ / 6.9		10.37	17.78	20.39 / 72	12.10 / 58	10.43 / 71
GL	*Guggenheim Shipping ETF	SEA	C+	16.10	19.37	14.40	B+ / 8.6		13.85	12.13	15.74 / 51	--	--
EN	*Guggenheim Solar ETF	TAN	E	15.64	38.70	12.60	E / 0.3		31.10	21.27	-30.07 / 3	-39.25 / 1	--
IN	*Guggenheim Spin-Off ETF	CSD	A-	29.64	30.94	23.85	B / 8.2		8.70	13.66	26.96 / 87	16.82 / 79	6.83 / 54
FO	*Guggenheim Swedish Krona	FXS	D+	153.14	154.04	136.26	D+ / 2.5		3.77	9.27	9.23 / 33	3.81 / 26	0.77 / 21
FO	*Guggenheim Swiss Franc	FXF	D+	107.46	110.49	98.83	D / 2.2		2.03	7.17	3.80 / 22	3.55 / 24	3.60 / 35
GL	*Guggenheim Timber ETF	CUT	C	20.44	21.39	15.16	C / 5.3		18.23	29.25	26.46 / 86	7.34 / 36	2.42 / 29
GR	*Guggenheim Wilshire 4500 Comp ET	WXSP	B	32.57	34.13	29.36	B / 7.8		--	14.42	17.92 / 62	--	--
IN	*Guggenheim Wilshire MicroCap ETF	WMCR	C-	18.48	19.35	16.14	C / 4.8		3.97	8.05	20.97 / 73	9.35 / 44	1.24 / 24
GI	*Guggenheim Wilshire US REIT ETF	WREI	B-	36.10	37.84	32.27	C+ / 6.6		3.86	2.01	19.83 / 70	--	--
GR	*Guggenheim Wilshire5000 Tot Mkt	WFVK	B+	31.45	32.95	28.28	B / 8.0		3.75	11.84	18.19 / 63	--	--
GL	*Guggenheim Yuan Bond ETF	RMB	C-	24.86	25.69	23.16	D- / 1.4		-0.99	0.73	0.60 / 15	--	--
COH	*Guggenhm BltShs 2013 HY Corp Bd	BSJD	C	25.80	26.04	25.25	D+ / 2.7		0.92	2.69	6.78 / 28	--	--
COH	*Guggenhm BltShs 2014 HY Corp Bd	BSJE	C+	26.48	26.64	25.40	C- / 3.8		2.27	4.57	10.11 / 35	--	--
COH	*Guggenhm BltShs 2015 HY Corp Bd	BSJF	C+	26.60	26.74	25.22	C / 4.5		2.70	6.07	11.15 / 37	--	--
COH	*Guggenhm BltShs 2016 HY Corp Bd	BSJG	U	26.23	N/A	N/A	U /		3.24	7.36			
COH	*Guggenhm BltShs 2017 HY Corp Bd	BSJH	U	26.38	N/A	N/A	U /		3.06	7.43			
COH	*Guggenhm BltShs 2018 HY Corp Bd	BSJI	U	26.15	N/A	N/A	U /		3.73	7.60			

* Denotes ETF Fund, N/A denotes number is not available

www.thestreetratings.com

| Incl. in Returns | | RISK | | | | NET ASSETS | | VALUATION | | | ASSET | | | | | FUND MANAGER | |
Dividend Yield %	Expense Ratio	Risk Rating/ Pts	3 Year Standard Deviation	Beta	Avg Dura-tion	NAV as of 12/31/12	Total $(Mil)	Premium/Discount As of 12/31/12	1 Year Average	Wtd Avg P/E	Cash %	Stocks %	Bonds %	Other %	Portfolio Turnover Ratio	Manager Quality Pct	Manager Tenure (Years)
0.00	0.40	B / 8.2	12.4	0.53	N/A	132.44	222	-1.12	0.03	N/A	100	0	0	0	N/A	23	8
3.07	0.70	B- / 7.2	20.0	0.70	N/A	20.37	156	-2.99	0.45	N/A	0	100	0	0	30	68	3
1.74	0.65	B- / 7.6	20.7	1.28	N/A	36.25	96	-4.14	-0.02	28.6	0	100	0	0	89	33	3
3.11	0.70	B- / 7.6	20.0	0.97	N/A	17.28	119	-2.55	0.30	5.7	0	100	0	0	73	41	3
0.00	0.71	C- / 3.8	30.1	-1.91	N/A	20.54	36	7.59	N/A	N/A	100	0	0	0	N/A	11	6
0.00	0.40	B / 8.7	9.4	-0.10	N/A	110.08	125	2.68	-0.04	N/A	100	0	0	0	N/A	68	5
1.23	0.65	B / 8.1	15.5	0.97	N/A	35.00	47	-3.57	0.10	37.9	0	86	0	14	63	70	3
2.70	0.56	B- / 7.0	N/A	N/A	N/A	40.01	12	-3.62	-0.54	N/A	1	98	0	1	15	64	N/A
1.06	0.59	C+ / 6.0	N/A	N/A	N/A	36.33	14	-1.65	-0.18	N/A	3	96	0	1	25	41	N/A
5.82	0.65	B / 8.5	12.5	0.78	N/A	22.82	794	-3.94	0.09	26.2	0	95	0	5	113	76	3
0.35	0.75	B- / 7.6	20.1	1.25	N/A	24.41	102	-3.85	0.04	29.7	0	94	0	6	63	43	3
2.72	0.20	B / 8.0	14.6	0.94	N/A	106.30	567	-3.12	0.01	57.4	0	99	0	1	6	47	N/A
2.72	0.41	B- / 7.8	N/A	N/A	N/A	36.19	39	-4.61	-0.04	N/A	0	99	0	1	13	35	N/A
4.08	0.41	B- / 7.3	N/A	N/A	N/A	33.80	13	-5.03	-0.04	N/A	0	99	0	1	20	13	N/A
2.46	0.41	B- / 7.8	N/A	N/A	N/A	36.40	53	-3.32	0.01	N/A	0	99	0	1	14	53	N/A
2.55	0.50	B- / 7.9	19.7	1.20	N/A	58.11	43	-2.91	-0.04	44.5	0	99	0	1	11	73	N/A
3.97	0.50	B / 8.9	10.7	0.59	N/A	70.98	42	-2.54	0.03	25.8	0	99	0	1	8	85	N/A
1.52	0.50	C+ / 6.9	27.7	1.18	N/A	65.90	29	-3.11	-0.07	20.8	0	99	0	1	13	39	N/A
2.98	0.50	B- / 7.5	20.5	1.01	N/A	30.55	13	-4.55	-0.07	21.8	0	99	0	1	10	69	N/A
1.06	0.50	B / 8.2	13.7	0.79	N/A	82.23	63	-4.67	N/A	48.3	0	99	0	1	8	74	N/A
3.18	0.50	B- / 7.7	19.2	1.17	N/A	61.41	18	-3.88	-0.04	30.5	0	99	0	1	7	69	N/A
2.57	0.50	B- / 7.3	22.8	1.36	N/A	67.17	29	-3.54	-0.08	27.8	0	99	0	1	8	23	N/A
1.56	0.50	B- / 7.2	21.4	1.30	N/A	57.58	92	-4.01	-0.03	65.0	0	99	0	1	11	19	N/A
4.01	0.50	B+ / 9.2	10.2	0.90	N/A	59.12	38	-2.79	-0.04	23.5	0	99	0	1	10	71	N/A
2.11	0.40	B- / 7.9	17.3	1.11	N/A	55.07	2,697	-3.18	-0.01	36.4	0	99	0	1	9	54	N/A
1.19	0.35	B- / 7.2	18.6	1.15	N/A	51.13	328	-3.62	N/A	92.1	0	99	0	1	34	60	N/A
1.71	0.35	B / 8.0	19.5	1.19	N/A	35.26	108	-3.01	-0.01	15.2	0	99	0	1	34	65	N/A
4.20	0.65	B- / 7.1	19.2	1.10	N/A	13.52	51	-2.81	0.06	N/A	0	100	0	0	91	14	3
2.03	0.70	B / 8.0	16.8	0.61	N/A	22.67	206	-1.90	-0.16	42.8	0	100	0	0	31	71	3
2.17	0.41	B / 8.8	N/A	N/A	N/A	33.77	3	-3.58	0.01	N/A	0	0	0	100	11	42	N/A
2.95	0.35	B- / 7.7	20.4	1.24	N/A	38.28	37	-3.53	0.05	18.8	0	99	0	1	42	34	N/A
1.93	0.35	B- / 7.8	19.2	1.11	N/A	94.16	534	-3.08	-0.01	57.5	0	99	0	1	41	77	N/A
2.56	0.41	B / 8.8	N/A	N/A	N/A	34.10	2	-3.46	-0.09	N/A	0	0	0	100	14	40	N/A
2.87	0.35	B- / 7.5	18.5	1.12	N/A	58.41	73	-4.43	N/A	65.6	0	99	0	1	42	69	N/A
2.89	0.35	B- / 7.2	25.9	1.52	N/A	44.66	71	-3.25	-0.03	23.4	0	99	0	1	44	28	N/A
2.09	0.65	C / 5.1	N/A	N/A	N/A	17.22	27	-6.50	-0.10	N/A	0	100	0	0	43	22	5
9.10	0.70	C- / 3.6	53.9	1.56	N/A	18.89	47	-17.20	-0.09	2.4	0	100	0	0	49	N/A	3
0.26	0.65	B / 8.5	15.0	0.90	N/A	30.28	65	-2.11	0.17	5.8	0	100	0	0	77	83	3
0.55	0.40	B / 8.1	14.3	0.63	N/A	153.76	69	-0.40	N/A	N/A	100	0	0	0	N/A	63	7
0.00	0.40	B / 8.0	13.8	0.50	N/A	107.81	339	-0.32	0.01	N/A	100	0	0	0	N/A	65	7
1.24	0.70	B- / 7.0	23.4	1.03	N/A	21.27	196	-3.90	0.23	17.1	0	100	0	0	56	67	3
1.75	0.18	B- / 7.5	N/A	N/A	N/A	34.15	7	-4.63	-0.03	44.4	0	100	0	0	15	43	3
1.11	0.50	B- / 7.2	21.7	1.32	N/A	19.33	13	-4.40	-0.28	33.6	0	100	0	0	58	20	3
3.29	0.32	B / 8.0	N/A	N/A	N/A	37.03	18	-2.51	N/A	N/A	0	100	0	0	13	76	3
2.07	0.12	B / 8.1	N/A	N/A	N/A	32.61	6	-3.56	0.25	47.1	0	100	0	0	5	42	3
1.79	0.65	B+ / 9.7	N/A	N/A	N/A	25.59	5	-2.85	0.09	N/A	0	0	0	100	54	63	2
4.42	0.42	B+ / 9.6	N/A	N/A	N/A	25.80	198	0.00	0.37	N/A	0	0	100	0	50	40	2
4.98	0.42	B+ / 9.6	N/A	N/A	N/A	26.52	190	-0.15	0.38	N/A	0	0	100	0	56	41	3
5.91	0.42	B+ / 9.4	N/A	N/A	N/A	26.66	336	-0.23	0.37	N/A	0	0	100	0	70	32	3
5.31	N/A	U /	N/A	N/A	N/A	26.36	44	-0.49	N/A	N/A	0	0	0	100	N/A	N/A	1
5.55	N/A	U /	N/A	N/A	N/A	26.54	21	-0.60	N/A	N/A	0	0	0	100	N/A	N/A	1
5.29	N/A	U /	N/A	N/A	N/A	26.38	29	-0.87	N/A	N/A	0	0	0	100	N/A	N/A	1

Denotes ETF Fund, N/A denotes number is not available

Fund Type	Fund Name	Ticker Symbol	Overall Investment Rating	Price As of 12/31/12	52 Week High	52 Week Low	Performance Rating/Pts		3 Mo	6 Mo	1Yr/Pct	3Yr/Pct	5Yr/Pct
COI	*Guggenhm BulletShs 2018 Corp Bd	BSCI	U	21.12	N/A	N/A	U	/	0.29	4.54	--	--	--
COI	*Guggenhm BulletShs 2019 Corp Bd	BSCJ	U	21.04	N/A	N/A	U	/	0.63	4.27	--	--	--
COI	*Guggenhm BulletShs 2020 Corp Bd	BSCK	U	21.29	N/A	N/A	U	/	0.49	4.36	--	--	--
HL	*Health Care Select Sector SPDR	XLV	C+	39.88	41.88	35.38	C+	/ 5.6	4.19	10.69	20.36 / 72	11.23 / 54	5.90 / 49
GL	*Huntington EcoLogical Strategy E	HECO	U	26.17	N/A	N/A	U	/	4.92	10.31	--	--	--
IN	*Huntington US Eq Rotation Strat	HUSE	U	26.20	N/A	N/A	U	/	3.13	--	--	--	--
GR	*Industrial Select Sector SPDR	XLI	C	37.90	39.26	33.08	C+	/ 5.6	8.04	13.67	12.73 / 41	12.74 / 62	4.95 / 43
FO	*iPath Asian & Gulf Curncy Reval	PGD	D-	50.61	51.88	48.32	D-	/ 1.4	-0.27	1.77	0.98 / 16	0.36 / 16	--
GR	*iPath CBOE S&P 500 BuyWrite Idx	BWV	C-	51.92	54.79	48.81	D+	/ 2.4	-1.20	-0.32	4.84 / 23	5.43 / 31	2.63 / 30
EN	*iPath Cptl Glbl Carbon Tot Ret E	GRN	E-	7.82	13.98	6.98	E-	/ 0.2	-33.80	-33.81	-29.17 / 4	-33.88 / 2	--
EN	*iPath DJ UBS Agri Tot Ret Sub	JJA	D-	55.14	67.18	48.01	D+	/ 2.7	-8.14	-11.84	6.87 / 28	8.29 / 39	-1.73 / 14
EN	*iPath DJ UBS Almin Tot Ret Sub	JJU	E	24.18	29.39	21.69	E+	/ 0.8	3.16	5.99	-9.37 / 8	-9.21 / 7	--
EN	*iPath DJ UBS Cocoa Tot Ret Sub	NIB	E	30.30	37.04	27.46	E+	/ 0.6	-5.05	0.49	-1.13 / 13	-15.52 / 5	--
EN	*iPath DJ UBS Coffee Tot Ret Sub	JO	E-	32.37	57.08	31.70	E+	/ 0.7	-9.50	-23.18	-38.91 / 2	-4.97 / 9	--
EN	*iPath DJ UBS Copper Total Ret Su	JJC	E+	45.99	51.41	41.70	D-	/ 1.3	-1.58	3.85	-1.87 / 12	-0.08 / 15	0.09 / 20
EN	*iPath DJ UBS Cotton Tot Ret Sub	BAL	E+	49.14	61.61	41.24	C-	/ 3.4	4.95	3.05	-16.47 / 6	11.96 / 58	--
EN	*iPath DJ UBS Energy Tot Ret Sub	JJE	E	17.12	20.07	14.80	E+	/ 0.7	-9.17	2.96	-9.98 / 8	-13.29 / 6	-20.22 / 3
EN	*iPath DJ UBS Grains Tot Ret	JJG	D	52.93	64.92	41.87	C-	/ 3.7	-9.63	-10.38	24.61 / 83	11.82 / 57	-3.07 / 11
EN	*iPath DJ UBS Ind Me Tot Ret Sub	JJM	E+	34.87	40.26	31.23	D-	/ 1.0	1.69	5.89	-4.88 / 10	-5.00 / 9	-5.28 / 8
EN	*iPath DJ UBS Lead Tot Ret Sub	LD	E+	56.32	59.12	42.77	D-	/ 1.4	5.61	21.71	11.16 / 37	-4.11 / 10	--
EN	*iPath DJ UBS Live Stk TR Sub	COW	D-	28.53	31.09	26.70	D-	/ 1.2	0.54	1.23	-5.81 / 10	-0.90 / 13	-9.18 / 6
EN	*iPath DJ UBS Nkl Tot Ret Sub	JJN	E	24.10	31.88	21.40	D-	/ 1.0	1.62	7.22	-12.54 / 7	-3.74 / 10	-11.41 / 4
EN	*iPath DJ UBS Ntrl Gas Tot Ret Su	GAZ	E-	2.69	6.90	2.60	E-	/ 0.1	-19.39	-18.65	-21.07 / 5	-42.93 / 1	-44.34 / 0
EN	*iPath DJ UBS Platinum Tot Ret Su	PGM	E+	34.80	40.55	31.20	D-	/ 1.3	-1.89	13.96	7.74 / 30	-2.53 / 11	--
EN	*iPath DJ UBS Precious Mtls Tot R	JJP	D	89.23	100.25	81.88	C	/ 4.4	-7.05	5.48	0.10 / 14	13.83 / 68	--
EN	*iPath DJ UBS Softs Tot Ret Sub	JJS	E	53.00	72.44	51.34	D-	/ 1.0	-4.08	-15.67	-24.35 / 4	1.22 / 18	--
EN	*iPath DJ UBS Sugar Tot Ret Sub	SGG	E	70.35	94.85	65.81	E+	/ 0.8	-5.21	-19.43	-17.39 / 6	-4.11 / 10	--
EN	*iPath DJ UBS Tin Tot Ret Sub	JJT	D	53.86	60.95	39.14	C+	/ 6.1	15.52	36.05	18.00 / 62	10.26 / 49	--
GR	*iPath DJ-UBS Commodity Index Tot	DJP	D	41.35	45.52	37.27	D-	/ 1.2	-5.88	-1.51	-2.02 / 12	-0.51 / 14	-6.43 / 7
USA	*iPath ETN US Treasury 5Yr Bear E	DFVS	E+	38.26	44.83	37.17	E+	/ 0.9	--	--	-6.79 / 10	--	--
FO	*iPath EUR/USD Exch Rate ETN	ERO	D	51.97	51.97	46.62	D-	/ 1.2	2.83	8.08	3.00 / 20	-2.89 / 10	-1.48 / 15
GR	*iPath GBP/USD Exchange Rate ETN	GBB	D+	43.03	45.99	41.18	D-	/ 1.3	--	3.00	4.25 / 23	-0.80 / 13	-3.38 / 10
FO	*iPath GEMS Asia 8 ETN	AYT	D-	48.20	50.00	44.40	D	/ 1.8	5.35	3.73	3.54 / 21	1.28 / 18	--
GI	*iPath GEMS Index ETN	JEM	D-	42.50	45.07	40.86	D	/ 1.7	3.21	--	6.17 / 26	0.31 / 16	--
FO	*iPath JPY/USD Exchange Rate ETN	JYN	D+	71.94	77.35	64.51	D-	/ 1.0	-13.58	--	-15.52 / 6	-0.39 / 14	2.91 / 31
EM	*iPath Long Enh MSCI Em Mkt Idx E	EMLB	C-	108.98	154.99	72.00	A	/ 9.5	25.69	--	25.63 / 85	--	--
IN	*iPath Long Ext Rus 2000 TR Idx E	RTLA	C-	75.46	82.67	51.07	A+	/ 9.8	16.98	25.52	43.34 / 98	--	--
IN	*iPath Long Ext S&P 500 TR Idx ET	SFLA	C	85.71	91.95	63.61	A+	/ 9.7	--	22.02	41.26 / 97	--	--
EM	*iPath MSCI India Index ETN	INP	D-	59.33	62.35	45.38	D	/ 1.7	2.49	16.61	18.28 / 64	-2.89 / 10	-7.27 / 7
GL	*iPath Optimized Currency Carry E	ICI	C-	46.88	48.99	44.96	D	/ 1.6	1.18	-0.88	1.96 / 18	0.82 / 17	--
IN	*iPath Pure Beta Agriculture ETN	DIRT	D-	47.35	54.90	40.08	D	/ 2.0	-6.79	-6.67	12.89 / 41	--	--
IN	*iPath Pure Beta Aluminum ETN	FOIL	E+	34.53	39.30	31.81	E+	/ 0.9	1.41	--	-9.98 / 8	--	--
IN	*iPath Pure Beta Broad Commodity	BCM	D-	44.62	48.05	39.76	D-	/ 1.3	-3.98	1.84	0.37 / 15	--	--
IN	*iPath Pure Beta Cocoa ETN	CHOC	E	33.58	41.90	31.00	E+	/ 0.9	-5.34	0.53	-4.83 / 11	--	--
IN	*iPath Pure Beta Coffee ETN	CAFE	E-	21.23	37.05	21.03	E-	/ 0.2	-7.46	-20.28	-37.51 / 2	--	--
GI	*iPath Pure Beta Copper ETN	CUPM	E+	40.62	44.45	37.11	D-	/ 1.4	--	--	0.56 / 15	--	--
IN	*iPath Pure Beta Cotton ETN	CTNN	U	29.49	38.61	25.95	U	/	2.97	6.05	--	--	--
IN	*iPath Pure Beta Crude Oil ETN	OLEM	E+	38.48	47.96	33.99	E+	/ 0.8	0.08	3.38	-12.49 / 7	--	--
IN	*iPath Pure Beta Grains ETN	WEET	D	50.44	59.10	40.84	C-	/ 4.0	--	-6.37	19.74 / 70	--	--
IN	*iPath Pure Beta Lead ETN	LEDD	C-	43.98	43.98	32.79	B	/ 7.6	4.16	20.73	10.28 / 35	--	--
IN	*iPath Pure Beta Nickel ETN	NINI	E	32.57	40.82	29.03	E+	/ 0.7	--	--	-13.07 / 7	--	--
PM	*iPath Pure Beta Precious Metals	BLNG	U	51.03	58.80	46.21	U	/	--	7.28	--	--	--

Incl. in Returns		RISK				NET ASSETS		VALUATION			ASSET					FUND MANAGER	
Dividend Yield %	Expense Ratio	Risk Rating/Pts	3 Year Standard Deviation	Beta	Avg Dura-tion	NAV as of 12/31/12	Total $(Mil)	Premium/Discount As of 12/31/12	1 Year Average	Wtd Avg P/E	Cash %	Stocks %	Bonds %	Other %	Portfolio Turnover Ratio	Manager Quality Pct	Manager Tenure (Years)
2.05	N/A	U /	N/A	N/A	N/A	21.10	32	0.09	N/A	N/A	0	0	0	100	N/A	N/A	1
1.17	N/A	U /	N/A	N/A	N/A	21.05	19	-0.05	N/A	N/A	0	0	0	100	N/A	N/A	1
2.76	N/A	U /	N/A	N/A	N/A	21.16	16	0.61	N/A	N/A	0	0	0	100	N/A	N/A	1
2.20	0.18	B / 8.4	11.6	0.61	N/A	41.73	5,571	-4.43	-0.01	47.1	0	100	0	0	5	77	15
1.02	N/A	U /	N/A	N/A	N/A	27.40	8	-4.49	N/A	N/A	0	0	0	100	N/A	N/A	1
1.22	N/A	U /	N/A	N/A	N/A	27.44	8	-4.52	N/A	N/A	0	0	0	100	N/A	N/A	1
2.96	0.18	B- / 7.7	19.6	1.21	N/A	39.10	3,878	-3.07	N/A	25.3	0	100	0	0	8	52	15
0.31	N/A	C+ / 5.8	4.1	0.13	N/A	50.97	3	-0.71	-0.72	N/A	0	0	0	100	N/A	46	5
0.00	0.75	B / 8.6	12.1	0.70	N/A	53.39	10	-2.75	-0.21	N/A	0	0	0	100	N/A	30	6
0.00	0.75	D / 1.9	47.5	0.24	N/A	7.57	4	3.30	-7.58	N/A	0	0	0	100	N/A	2	5
0.00	0.75	C / 4.3	29.0	0.71	N/A	54.73	68	0.75	N/A	N/A	0	0	0	100	N/A	53	6
0.00	0.75	C- / 3.5	24.3	0.70	N/A	24.43	7	-1.02	-0.11	N/A	0	0	0	100	N/A	9	5
0.00	0.75	D+ / 2.9	32.0	0.65	N/A	30.62	28	-1.05	-0.01	N/A	0	0	0	100	N/A	5	5
0.00	0.75	D / 2.1	32.7	0.45	N/A	34.49	8	-6.15	0.05	N/A	0	0	0	100	N/A	13	5
0.00	0.75	C- / 3.8	30.7	1.03	N/A	46.04	130	-0.11	-0.02	N/A	0	0	0	100	N/A	14	6
0.00	0.75	D / 2.1	38.9	0.73	N/A	49.32	23	-0.36	0.06	N/A	0	0	0	100	N/A	71	5
0.00	0.75	C- / 3.4	21.4	0.73	N/A	17.16	11	-0.23	-0.08	N/A	0	0	0	100	N/A	6	6
0.00	0.75	C / 4.4	33.9	0.78	N/A	52.24	57	1.32	0.01	N/A	0	0	0	100	N/A	65	6
0.00	0.75	C- / 3.8	28.5	0.95	N/A	34.77	50	0.29	N/A	N/A	0	0	0	100	N/A	10	6
0.00	0.75	C- / 3.8	37.0	1.00	N/A	55.59	14	1.31	-0.11	N/A	0	0	0	100	N/A	10	5
0.00	0.75	C / 4.9	14.1	0.06	N/A	28.00	110	1.89	0.08	N/A	0	0	0	100	N/A	50	6
0.00	0.75	D+ / 2.9	37.6	1.14	N/A	24.39	15	-1.19	-0.05	N/A	0	0	0	100	N/A	9	6
0.00	0.75	D / 1.9	48.3	0.66	N/A	2.35	208	14.47	37.98	N/A	0	0	0	100	N/A	1	6
0.00	0.75	C- / 4.2	24.9	0.72	N/A	36.88	103	-5.64	0.20	N/A	0	0	0	100	N/A	13	5
0.00	0.75	C / 4.7	24.5	0.40	N/A	88.83	8	0.45	-0.10	N/A	0	0	0	100	N/A	92	5
0.00	0.75	C- / 3.2	26.3	0.52	N/A	53.56	5	-1.05	-0.10	N/A	0	0	0	100	N/A	29	5
0.00	0.75	D+ / 2.5	45.6	0.47	N/A	68.97	27	2.00	0.07	N/A	0	0	0	100	N/A	19	5
0.00	0.75	D+ / 2.9	34.5	0.94	N/A	57.26	2	-5.94	-0.13	N/A	0	0	0	100	N/A	64	5
0.00	0.75	B- / 7.0	19.5	0.94	N/A	41.03	1,897	0.78	0.03	N/A	0	100	0	0	N/A	13	7
0.00	N/A	C / 4.8	N/A	N/A	N/A	38.50	2	-0.62	0.44	N/A	0	0	0	100	N/A	16	2
0.00	0.40	B / 8.1	13.3	0.55	N/A	51.72	8	0.48	-0.43	N/A	0	0	0	100	N/A	23	6
0.00	0.40	B / 8.8	9.8	0.26	N/A	42.90	2	0.30	-0.08	N/A	0	0	0	100	N/A	30	6
0.75	N/A	C / 5.5	6.7	0.25	N/A	48.46	20	-0.54	-0.10	N/A	0	0	0	100	N/A	62	5
3.89	N/A	C / 5.1	11.8	0.63	N/A	43.15	1	-1.51	-0.40	N/A	0	0	0	100	N/A	23	5
0.00	0.40	B+ / 9.1	8.7	-0.09	N/A	65.46	11	9.90	0.07	N/A	0	0	0	100	N/A	78	6
0.00	N/A	D+ / 2.5	N/A	N/A	N/A	104.88	3	3.91	-1.99	N/A	0	0	0	100	N/A	88	N/A
0.00	N/A	D / 2.1	N/A	N/A	N/A	83.26	7	-9.37	-0.03	N/A	0	0	0	100	N/A	18	N/A
0.00	N/A	C- / 3.4	N/A	N/A	N/A	91.95	4	-6.79	-0.38	N/A	0	0	0	100	N/A	25	N/A
0.00	0.89	C+ / 5.7	31.4	1.17	N/A	59.72	1,059	-0.65	0.30	N/A	0	0	0	100	N/A	15	7
0.00	0.65	B+ / 9.5	4.9	0.12	N/A	47.40	27	-1.10	-0.05	N/A	0	0	0	100	N/A	56	5
0.00	N/A	C / 4.7	N/A	N/A	N/A	46.85	3	1.07	-0.11	N/A	0	0	0	100	N/A	65	2
0.00	N/A	C- / 3.8	N/A	N/A	N/A	34.35	1	0.52	-0.33	N/A	0	0	0	100	N/A	9	2
0.00	N/A	C / 4.8	N/A	N/A	N/A	43.79	22	1.90	-0.01	N/A	0	0	0	100	N/A	10	2
0.00	N/A	C- / 3.5	N/A	N/A	N/A	33.90	3	-0.94	-0.29	N/A	0	0	0	100	N/A	12	2
0.00	N/A	D+ / 2.3	N/A	N/A	N/A	22.62	2	-6.15	-0.06	N/A	0	0	0	100	N/A	1	2
0.00	N/A	C / 4.6	N/A	N/A	N/A	41.56	3	-2.26	-0.15	N/A	0	0	0	100	N/A	12	2
0.00	N/A	U /	N/A	N/A	N/A	29.44	1	0.17	-0.06	N/A	0	0	0	100	N/A	1	2
0.00	N/A	C / 4.6	N/A	N/A	N/A	39.11	2	-1.61	N/A	N/A	0	0	0	100	N/A	2	2
0.00	N/A	C / 4.5	N/A	N/A	N/A	49.46	3	1.98	-0.23	N/A	0	0	0	100	N/A	85	2
0.00	N/A	C- / 3.6	N/A	N/A	N/A	42.53	1	3.41	-0.77	N/A	0	0	0	100	N/A	93	2
0.00	N/A	C- / 3.5	N/A	N/A	N/A	32.26	1	0.96	-0.18	N/A	0	0	0	100	N/A	4	2
0.00	N/A	U /	N/A	N/A	N/A	49.97	2	2.12	-0.34	N/A	0	0	0	100	N/A	58	2

Denotes ETF Fund, N/A denotes number is not available

Fund Type	Fund Name	Ticker Symbol	Overall Investment Rating	Price As of 12/31/12	52 Week High	52 Week Low	Performance Rating/Pts	3 Mo	6 Mo	1Yr/Pct	3Yr/Pct	5Yr/Pct
											Annualized	
PM	*iPath Pure Beta S&P GW ETN	SBV	U	41.99	N/A	N/A	U /	--	--	--	--	--
IN	*iPath Pure Beta Softs ETN	GRWN	E	32.65	43.93	31.60	E / 0.4	--	-14.27	-26.52 / 4	--	--
GI	*iPath Pure Beta Sugar ETN	SGAR	E	43.69	55.84	41.43	E / 0.4	-2.90	-15.65	-18.07 / 5	--	--
GL	*iPath S&P 500 Dynamic VIX ETN	XVZ	E+	46.04	60.06	43.34	E / 0.3	-12.96	-21.76	-22.83 / 4	--	--
IN	*iPath S&P 500 VIX Mid-Trm Futr E	VXZ	E-	27.95	58.27	25.31	E- / 0.2	-19.77	-38.50	-55.82 / 0	-28.99 / 3	--
IN	*iPath S&P 500 VIX Sm-Trm Futr ET	VXX	E-	31.81	125.92	26.45	E- / 0.0	-25.21	-50.45	-78.99 / 0	-61.73 / 0	--
EN	*iPath S&P GSCI Crude Oil TotRet	OIL	D-	21.79	28.08	18.82	E+ / 0.9	0.13	4.50	-11.55 / 7	-4.21 / 10	-15.80 / 4
GR	*iPath S&P GSCI Total Return ETN	GSP	D	33.28	37.47	28.57	D / 1.8	-3.01	4.33	-1.47 / 13	2.62 / 22	-8.51 / 6
EN	*iPath Seasonal Natural Gas ETN	DCNG	U	29.03	32.25	24.91	U /	-9.26	3.78	--	--	--
USA	*iPath US Treas 10Yr Bear ETN	DTYS	E	26.75	35.88	24.84	E+ / 0.9	3.80	4.36	-13.91 / 7	--	--
USA	*iPath US Treas 10Yr Bull ETN	DTYL	D-	71.70	73.16	62.77	D / 1.7	-1.94	-2.29	4.87 / 23	--	--
USA	*iPath US Treas 2Yr Bear ETN	DTUS	E+	40.51	42.72	39.50	D- / 1.2	-0.37	-0.07	-1.39 / 13	--	--
USA	*iPath US Treas Flattener ETN	FLAT	D-	62.48	65.27	55.87	D- / 1.5	-2.75	-2.88	4.88 / 24	--	--
USA	*iPath US Treas Lng Bd Bear ETN	DLBS	E+	28.54	37.18	25.22	D / 1.9	5.86	11.51	-7.97 / 9	--	--
USA	*iPath US Treas Lng Bd Bull ETN	DLBL	D-	70.33	73.01	61.54	D- / 1.2	-2.59	-5.55	2.89 / 20	--	--
USA	*iPath US Treas Steepen ETN	STPP	E+	35.12	42.99	33.73	E+ / 0.9	3.75	3.60	-11.46 / 8	--	--
FO	*IQ Australia Small Cap ETF	KROO	C	21.57	24.50	18.18	C+ / 6.9	7.91	19.77	5.96 / 26	--	--
FO	*IQ Canada Small Cap ETF	CNDA	D-	23.15	29.07	20.83	D / 1.8	-1.24	14.18	-5.59 / 10	--	--
GL	*IQ Global Agribusiness SmCp ETF	CROP	B	25.58	26.39	22.21	B / 8.0	7.68	12.03	15.65 / 51	--	--
GL	*IQ Global Oil Small Cap ETF	IOIL	C+	16.75	19.21	14.30	B / 7.7	6.49	16.81	12.19 / 39	--	--
EN	*IQ Global Resources ETF	GRES	C-	30.42	30.69	25.82	C- / 3.0	6.52	15.27	6.66 / 27	5.81 / 32	--
GL	*IQ Hedge Macro Tracker ETF	MCRO	C-	27.40	28.60	26.51	D / 1.8	-0.48	1.82	3.80 / 22	1.70 / 19	--
PM	*IQ Hedge Market Neutral Tracker	QMN	U	25.08	N/A	N/A	U /	--	--	--	--	--
GL	*IQ Hedge Multi-Strategy Tracker	QAI	C-	27.81	29.45	27.06	D / 1.9	0.03	2.17	3.22 / 21	2.03 / 20	--
GL	*IQ Merger Arbitrage ETF	MNA	D+	25.16	26.71	22.20	D- / 1.4	1.32	2.18	1.24 / 16	-0.08 / 15	--
IN	*IQ Real Return ETF	CPI	C-	26.32	27.53	25.85	D / 1.7	-0.58	0.44	1.25 / 16	1.90 / 19	--
GI	*IQ US Real Estate SmCp ETF	ROOF	A	22.48	24.06	18.10	A+ / 9.7	9.43	16.18	36.39 / 96	--	--
GL	*iShares 10+ Year Credit Bond	CLY	C+	62.67	64.11	56.89	C / 4.4	-0.88	2.66	11.29 / 37	11.91 / 58	--
GEI	*iShares 2013 S&P AMT-Free Muni S	MUAB	C-	50.72	51.39	50.17	D- / 1.3	-0.30	-0.07	-0.16 / 14	--	--
GEI	*iShares 2014 S&P AMT-Free Muni S	MUAC	C-	51.68	56.78	50.74	D- / 1.5	0.08	0.76	0.51 / 15	--	--
GEI	*iShares 2015 S&P AMT-Free Muni S	MUAD	C-	53.23	54.50	52.94	D / 1.6	0.06	0.51	1.18 / 16	--	--
GEI	*iShares 2016 S&P AMT-Free Muni S	MUAE	C-	53.56	80.47	53.05	D / 1.6	-0.01	0.36	1.43 / 17	--	--
GEI	*iShares 2017 S&P AMT-Free Muni S	MUAF	C-	55.29	56.26	54.53	D / 1.7	-0.11	1.00	1.85 / 18	--	--
COI	*iShares Aaa-A Rated Corporate Bo	QLTA	U	52.27	N/A	N/A	U /	-0.29	2.05	--	--	--
FO	*iShares Asia/Pacific Dividend 30	DVYA	U	54.29	N/A	N/A	U /	3.56	13.13	--	--	--
COI	*iShares B-Ca Rated Corporate Bon	QLTC	U	52.18	N/A	N/A	U /	4.06	7.21	--	--	--
COI	*iShares Baa - Ba Rated Corporate	QLTB	U	52.50	N/A	N/A	U /	2.52	6.24	--	--	--
USA	*iShares Barclays 0-5 Year TIPS B	STIP	C-	103.08	104.33	102.05	D / 1.7	0.09	1.04	1.79 / 18	--	--
COI	*iShares Barclays 1-3 Year Credit	CSJ	C-	105.48	105.92	104.00	D / 1.9	0.34	1.63	2.94 / 20	2.39 / 21	3.41 / 34
USA	*iShares Barclays 1-3Yr Treasury	SHY	C-	84.42	84.60	84.18	D / 1.6	0.06	0.12	0.25 / 14	1.14 / 18	1.91 / 26
USA	*iShares Barclays 10-20 Yr Treasu	TLH	C	134.86	140.83	125.73	C- / 3.4	-1.45	-2.83	2.83 / 20	10.48 / 50	7.90 / 59
USA	*iShares Barclays 20+Yr Treasury	TLT	C	121.18	132.22	109.69	C- / 4.2	-2.70	-6.01	1.84 / 18	13.66 / 67	8.72 / 64
USA	*iShares Barclays 3-7 Yr Treasury	IEI	C	123.22	123.97	120.02	D+ / 2.3	-0.15	0.10	1.58 / 17	5.05 / 29	4.89 / 43
USA	*iShares Barclays 7-10Yr Treasury	IEF	C	107.49	109.89	101.77	C- / 3.1	-0.74	-1.18	3.01 / 20	8.67 / 41	6.88 / 54
USA	*iShares Barclays Agency Bond	AGZ	C-	113.30	114.45	111.90	D / 2.0	-0.23	0.13	1.29 / 17	3.17 / 23	--
COI	*iShares Barclays CMBS Bond	CMBS	U	51.75	N/A	N/A	U /	0.75	3.83	--	--	--
COI	*iShares Barclays Credit Bond Fd	CFT	C	113.16	114.84	108.56	C- / 3.1	-0.07	2.50	7.42 / 29	7.91 / 38	6.82 / 54
GEI	*iShares Barclays GNMA Bond	GNMA	U	50.11	N/A	N/A	U /	-0.57	-0.34	--	--	--
USA	*iShares Barclays Govt/Credit Bd	GBF	C	114.87	116.99	111.77	D+ / 2.5	-0.41	0.25	3.29 / 21	5.81 / 32	5.42 / 47
COI	*iShares Barclays Intrm Credit Bd	CIU	C	111.29	112.11	107.08	D+ / 2.7	0.26	2.79	7.00 / 28	6.18 / 33	5.93 / 49
GEI	*iShares Barclays Intrm Govt/Crdt	GVI	C	112.41	113.13	107.01	D / 2.2	-0.07	0.79	3.15 / 21	4.47 / 28	4.57 / 43
MTG	*iShares Barclays MBS Bond	MBB	C-	107.99	109.46	107.47	D / 2.2	-0.31	0.05	1.71 / 17	4.12 / 26	4.88 / 43

99 Pct = Best
0 Pct = Worst

* Denotes ETF Fund, N/A denotes number is not available

Incl. in Returns Dividend Yield %	Expense Ratio	RISK Risk Rating/ Pts	3 Year Standard Deviation	Beta	Avg Dura-tion	NET ASSETS NAV as of 12/31/12	Total $(Mil)	VALUATION Premium/Discount As of 12/31/12	1 Year Average	Wtd Avg P/E	Cash %	Stocks %	Bonds %	Other %	Portfolio Turnover Ratio	Manager Quality Pct	Manager Tenure (Years)
0.00	N/A	U /	N/A	N/A	N/A	42.00	1	-0.02	N/A	N/A	0	0	0	100	N/A	N/A	2
0.00	N/A	C- / 3.4	N/A	N/A	N/A	32.40	1	0.77	-0.10	N/A	0	0	0	100	N/A	3	2
0.00	N/A	C- / 3.8	N/A	N/A	N/A	42.92	3	1.79	-0.20	N/A	0	0	0	100	N/A	2	2
0.00	N/A	C / 4.6	N/A	N/A	N/A	43.86	267	4.97	-0.06	N/A	0	0	0	100	N/A	6	2
0.00	0.89	D / 1.9	37.6	-1.86	N/A	25.51	29	9.56	-0.15	N/A	0	0	0	100	N/A	9	4
0.00	0.89	D / 1.9	75.2	-3.77	N/A	26.26	665	21.13	-0.14	N/A	0	0	0	100	N/A	1	4
0.00	0.75	C+ / 5.9	30.6	1.08	N/A	22.27	564	-2.16	0.11	N/A	0	0	0	100	N/A	8	7
0.00	0.75	B- / 7.1	22.6	1.19	N/A	33.35	79	-0.21	0.13	N/A	0	0	0	100	N/A	13	7
0.00	N/A	U /	N/A	N/A	N/A	28.85	49	0.62	-0.37	N/A	0	0	0	100	N/A	11	3
0.00	N/A	D+ / 2.5	N/A	N/A	N/A	27.39	106	-2.34	-0.04	N/A	0	0	0	100	N/A	11	3
0.00	N/A	C / 5.1	N/A	N/A	N/A	70.68	6	1.44	-0.02	N/A	0	0	0	100	N/A	79	3
0.00	N/A	C / 4.7	N/A	N/A	N/A	40.31	15	0.50	0.04	N/A	0	0	0	100	N/A	39	3
0.00	N/A	C / 5.2	N/A	N/A	N/A	61.77	21	1.15	N/A	N/A	0	0	0	100	N/A	77	3
0.00	N/A	D+ / 2.6	N/A	N/A	N/A	29.53	23	-3.35	-0.04	N/A	0	0	0	100	N/A	31	3
0.00	N/A	C / 5.0	N/A	N/A	N/A	68.54	3	2.61	-0.24	N/A	0	0	0	100	N/A	70	3
0.00	N/A	C- / 3.5	N/A	N/A	N/A	36.00	8	-2.44	-0.03	N/A	0	0	0	100	N/A	13	3
1.82	0.69	C / 5.4	N/A	N/A	N/A	22.03	14	-2.09	0.13	N/A	0	100	0	0	42	11	2
3.76	0.69	C+ / 5.7	N/A	N/A	N/A	23.90	20	-3.14	-0.38	N/A	0	100	0	0	37	5	2
1.40	0.75	B- / 7.8	N/A	N/A	N/A	26.02	37	-1.69	-0.06	N/A	0	100	0	0	26	73	2
1.80	0.75	C+ / 5.9	N/A	N/A	N/A	17.45	3	-4.01	-0.10	N/A	0	100	0	0	10	14	2
1.20	0.75	B- / 7.8	15.1	0.55	N/A	30.17	76	0.83	0.06	52.9	0	100	0	0	178	66	2
1.77	0.75	B+ / 9.2	7.2	0.29	N/A	27.25	38	0.55	0.05	N/A	1	98	0	1	108	62	4
1.52	N/A	U /	N/A	N/A	N/A	25.27	8	-0.75	N/A	N/A	0	0	0	100	N/A	N/A	1
1.11	0.75	B+ / 9.6	4.8	0.20	N/A	27.92	315	-0.39	0.08	N/A	0	81	0	19	90	63	5
0.19	0.75	B+ / 9.1	6.0	0.19	N/A	25.21	12	-0.20	-0.10	N/A	0	100	0	0	365	45	2
0.06	0.48	B+ / 9.9	1.8	0.01	N/A	26.39	41	-0.27	0.03	N/A	0	100	0	0	62	64	2
3.62	0.69	B- / 7.5	N/A	N/A	N/A	23.48	17	-4.26	0.10	N/A	1	98	0	1	11	96	2
4.50	0.20	B+ / 9.4	7.0	0.26	N/A	61.92	448	1.21	0.58	N/A	1	0	96	3	9	92	3
0.67	0.30	B+ / 9.9	N/A	N/A	N/A	50.70	38	0.04	0.03	N/A	0	0	100	0	1	53	3
0.64	0.30	B+ / 9.7	N/A	N/A	N/A	51.57	49	0.21	0.33	N/A	0	0	100	0	1	56	3
0.96	0.30	B+ / 9.8	N/A	N/A	N/A	53.12	53	0.21	0.47	N/A	1	0	98	1	2	50	3
1.18	0.30	B+ / 9.7	N/A	N/A	N/A	53.50	51	0.11	0.49	N/A	0	0	100	0	1	45	3
1.35	0.30	B+ / 9.4	N/A	N/A	N/A	55.33	66	-0.07	0.45	N/A	0	0	100	0	4	30	3
1.91	0.15	U /	N/A	N/A	N/A	51.77	317	0.97	N/A	N/A	0	0	0	100	10	N/A	1
6.02	N/A	U /	N/A	N/A	N/A	54.31	24	-0.04	N/A	N/A	0	0	0	100	N/A	N/A	N/A
7.17	0.55	U /	N/A	N/A	N/A	52.81	10	-1.19	N/A	N/A	0	0	0	100	N/A	N/A	1
.40	0.30	U /	N/A	N/A	N/A	52.79	16	-0.55	N/A	N/A	0	0	0	100	N/A	N/A	1
.71	0.20	B+ / 9.9	N/A	N/A	N/A	103.08	428	0.00	0.11	N/A	0	0	100	0	10	67	3
.56	0.20	B+ / 9.8	1.4	0.26	3.6	105.42	9,225	0.06	0.14	N/A	0	0	98	2	4	55	3
.30	0.15	B+ / 9.9	0.8	0.03	3.5	84.42	8,045	0.00	0.02	N/A	0	0	100	0	47	60	3
.11	0.15	B+ / 9.1	8.7	0.71	15.6	133.58	609	0.96	0.07	N/A	0	0	100	0	6	65	3
.66	0.15	B / 8.4	14.8	1.23	15.6	119.42	3,193	1.47	0.12	N/A	0	0	100	0	9	35	3
.61	0.15	B+ / 9.7	3.2	0.18	4.7	123.05	3,097	0.14	0.04	N/A	0	0	100	0	23	72	3
.68	0.15	B+ / 9.5	6.0	0.46	6.4	106.76	4,406	0.68	0.05	N/A	0	0	100	0	30	73	3
.12	0.20	B+ / 9.9	1.7	0.10	4.7	113.34	426	-0.04	0.12	N/A	0	0	100	0	34	66	3
.97	0.25	U /	N/A	N/A	N/A	51.93	52	-0.35	N/A	N/A	0	0	0	100	1	N/A	1
.82	0.20	B+ / 9.5	3.8	1.01	8.5	113.09	1,405	0.06	0.41	N/A	0	0	98	2	4	48	3
.76	0.25	U /	N/A	N/A	N/A	49.79	20	0.64	N/A	N/A	0	0	0	100	383	N/A	1
.15	0.20	B+ / 9.7	3.2	0.22	6.8	114.88	190	-0.01	0.33	N/A	0	0	98	2	9	73	3
.08	0.20	B+ / 9.7	2.9	0.71	4.7	111.02	5,340	0.24	0.26	N/A	1	0	97	2	3	56	3
.94	0.20	B+ / 9.8	2.2	0.86	4.6	112.19	955	0.20	0.21	N/A	2	0	96	2	7	47	3
.03	0.25	B+ / 9.7	1.8	0.99	14.5	108.09	6,519	-0.09	0.06	N/A	0	0	97	3	222	49	3

Denotes ETF Fund, N/A denotes number is not available

I. Index of ETFs and Other Closed-End Funds

				PRICE			PERFORMANCE					
	99 Pct = Best 0 Pct = Worst		**Overall Investment Rating**	**Price As of 12/31/12**	**52 Week**		**Perform-ance Rating/Pts**	**% Total Return Through 12/31/12**				
											Annualized	
Fund Type	**Fund Name**	**Ticker Symbol**			High	Low		3 Mo	6 Mo	1Yr/Pct	3Yr/Pct	5Yr/Pct
USA	*iShares Barclays Short Treasury	SHV	C-	110.26	110.26	110.05	D- / 1.3	0.03	0.03	0.02 / 14	0.07 / 15	0.55 / 21
USA	*iShares Barclays TIPS Bond	TIP	C	121.41	123.44	116.49	C- / 3.1	-0.13	0.88	5.46 / 25	8.13 / 39	6.19 / 50
USA	*iShares Barclays US Treasury Bon	GOVT	U	25.16	N/A	N/A	U /	-0.52	-0.87	--	--	--
IN	*iShares Cohen & Steers Realty Ma	ICF	B	78.54	82.90	71.03	B- / 7.5	4.07	1.23	16.69 / 56	18.87 / 86	6.79 / 53
GL	*iShares Core Long-Term US Bond E	ILTB	C+	63.78	66.49	57.85	C- / 4.2	-2.06	-1.64	6.72 / 28	12.29 / 60	--
EM	*iShares Core MSCI EAFE	IEFA	U	50.85	N/A	N/A	U /	--	--	--	--	--
EM	*iShares Core MSCI Emerging Marke	IEMG	U	52.20	N/A	N/A	U /	--	--	--	--	--
EM	*iShares Core MSCI Total Intl Sto	IXUS	U	51.91	N/A	N/A	U /	--	--	--	--	--
GR	*iShares Core S&P 500 ETF	IVV	C	143.14	148.74	127.57	C / 5.2	3.78	9.80	16.64 / 56	11.31 / 54	4.38 / 40
GR	*iShares Core S&P Mid-Cap ETF	IJH	B-	101.70	106.06	88.22	C+ / 6.9	8.84	13.07	18.23 / 64	13.95 / 69	8.49 / 62
GR	*iShares Core S&P Small-Cap ETF	IJR	C+	78.10	80.98	67.75	C+ / 6.7	7.71	10.78	16.46 / 55	14.53 / 71	8.24 / 61
IN	*iShares Core S&P Tot US Stk Mkt	ITOT	C	64.94	67.21	57.68	C / 5.3	4.25	10.15	16.72 / 56	11.49 / 55	4.74 / 42
USA	*iShares Core Short Term US Bond	ISTB	U	100.09	N/A	N/A	U /	--	--	--	--	--
GEI	*iShares Core Total US Bond Mkt E	AGG	C	111.08	112.71	108.84	D+ / 2.4	-0.30	0.50	3.26 / 21	5.49 / 31	5.26 / 45
GL	*iShares Diversified Alternatives	ALT	C-	50.65	51.33	48.35	D / 1.6	1.67	1.65	3.28 / 21	0.33 / 16	--
FO	*iShares DJ Intl Select Dividend	IDV	C	33.67	34.48	27.60	C / 5.1	8.31	17.50	22.58 / 78	7.31 / 36	1.26 / 24
IN	*iShares DJ Select Dividend	DVY	C+	57.24	59.08	53.44	C / 5.4	2.70	5.10	12.63 / 40	13.60 / 66	4.23 / 38
IN	*iShares DJ Transportation	IYT	C	94.35	99.76	85.83	C / 4.7	11.36	7.58	8.99 / 32	11.29 / 54	7.36 / 57
IN	*iShares DJ US Aerospace & Def Id	ITA	C	68.25	70.63	59.69	C / 5.1	7.76	11.96	12.55 / 40	10.53 / 50	4.49 / 40
IN	*iShares DJ US Basic Material	IYM	D+	69.31	73.76	60.25	C- / 3.2	7.25	14.16	5.88 / 26	6.78 / 35	2.98 / 31
FS	*iShares DJ US Broker-Dealers Idx	IAI	D	23.63	26.26	19.75	D / 2.0	14.36	18.86	17.23 / 59	-2.15 / 11	-9.05 / 6
IN	*iShares DJ US Consumer Goods	IYK	B-	74.99	77.84	68.73	C+ / 6.0	5.13	8.47	15.43 / 50	13.67 / 67	8.06 / 60
IN	*iShares DJ US Consumer Services	IYC	B+	86.80	89.53	73.30	B / 8.1	4.97	11.19	24.62 / 83	18.50 / 84	11.05 / 73
EN	*iShares DJ US Energy	IYE	C-	40.84	44.26	35.25	C- / 3.6	2.34	10.78	7.75 / 30	8.85 / 42	2.60 / 30
FS	*iShares DJ US Financial Sector	IYF	C	60.70	63.68	50.42	C / 5.3	8.36	15.54	25.29 / 84	7.56 / 37	-3.17 / 11
FS	*iShares DJ US Financial Services	IYG	C	59.31	62.46	46.74	C / 5.1	10.43	20.62	29.73 / 91	4.67 / 28	-5.23 / 8
HL	*iShares DJ US Healthcare	IYH	C+	83.51	87.66	73.53	C+ / 5.7	3.56	10.32	21.45 / 75	11.62 / 56	6.45 / 51
HL	*iShares DJ US HealthCare Provide	IHF	C	68.45	70.98	59.04	C / 4.8	1.03	6.90	15.86 / 52	11.35 / 54	2.59 / 30
IN	*iShares DJ US Home Cons Idx	ITB	B+	21.16	22.63	13.00	A+ / 9.7	15.22	30.93	69.50 / 99	21.15 / 91	9.55 / 67
IN	*iShares DJ US Index	IYY	C	71.64	74.14	63.60	C / 5.3	4.37	10.24	16.80 / 57	11.49 / 55	4.87 / 43
IN	*iShares DJ US Industrial	IYJ	C+	73.33	75.90	62.96	C+ / 6.4	8.12	14.53	15.34 / 49	13.10 / 64	5.17 / 45
IN	*iShares DJ US Insurance Idx	IAK	C	32.99	34.63	28.34	C / 5.4	6.21	15.57	19.08 / 67	9.77 / 46	-3.07 / 11
HL	*iShares DJ US Medical Devices Id	IHI	C-	67.60	71.15	60.12	C / 4.9	6.51	10.07	18.76 / 66	9.32 / 44	4.48 / 40
EN	*iShares DJ US Oil & Gas Exp & Pr	IEO	D+	63.54	71.95	52.01	C- / 3.0	4.06	13.27	6.29 / 27	6.20 / 33	2.42 / 18
EN	*iShares DJ US Oil Equip & Svcs	IEZ	D	51.01	60.25	42.08	D+ / 2.8	5.02	14.89	3.36 / 21	5.42 / 31	-0.24 / 18
HL	*iShares DJ US Pharmaceuticals	IHE	B-	85.02	92.37	76.75	C+ / 6.7	0.85	4.18	18.29 / 64	16.92 / 80	12.90 / 80
IN	*iShares DJ US Real Estate	IYR	B-	64.67	68.26	57.83	B- / 7.4	5.25	4.06	19.70 / 70	17.69 / 82	7.23 / 56
FS	*iShares DJ US Regional Banks	IAT	D+	24.43	26.68	21.73	C- / 3.0	0.87	5.52	12.77 / 41	5.78 / 32	-3.33 / 11
GR	*iShares DJ US Technology	IYW	D+	70.72	78.98	65.94	C- / 3.4	-0.65	4.59	10.94 / 36	8.73 / 42	6.46 / 52
IN	*iShares DJ US Telecommunications	IYZ	C+	24.26	26.25	20.66	C / 5.2	-0.71	9.63	19.22 / 68	11.70 / 56	3.00 / 32
UT	*iShares DJ US Utilities	IDU	C	86.36	93.97	83.28	C- / 3.2	-1.36	-2.50	5.85 / 25	9.28 / 44	1.79 / 25
COI	*iShares Emerging Markets Corpora	CEMB	U	53.65	N/A	N/A	U /	1.14	6.80	--	--	--
EM	*iShares Emerging Markets Hi Yld	EMHY	U	55.71	N/A	N/A	U /	4.37	11.31	--	--	--
GL	*iShares Emerging Mkts Lcl Cur Bo	LEMB	B-	53.86	54.26	48.11	C / 5.5	3.52	8.85	11.82 / 38	--	--
COI	*iShares Financials Sector Bond	MONY	U	53.09	N/A	N/A	U /	1.98	6.73	--	--	--
COI	*iShares Floating Rate Note	FLOT	C-	50.59	50.80	49.12	D / 2.2	0.47	1.60	4.00 / 22	--	--
FO	*iShares FTSE China 25	FXI	D	40.45	41.97	31.62	D+ / 2.8	13.19	26.40	15.01 / 48	1.77 / 19	-2.88 / 12
FO	*iShares FTSE China Index	FCHI	D+	49.65	51.50	39.71	C- / 3.4	14.57	25.39	18.96 / 67	3.72 / 25	--
FO	*iShares FTSE Dev Sm Cap ex-North	IFSM	C	36.26	37.50	30.18	C / 5.1	11.15	21.07	22.98 / 79	5.88 / 33	1.07 / 23
GI	*iShares FTSE EPRA/NAREIT Asia In	IFAS	B	33.67	34.27	25.66	B+ / 8.4	12.66	24.63	42.71 / 98	11.60 / 56	1.02 / 22
GI	*iShares FTSE EPRA/NAREIT Dev RE	IFGL	C	33.13	33.82	26.20	B- / 7.5	9.74	19.45	36.15 / 96	10.54 / 51	0.67 / 21
GI	*iShares FTSE EPRA/NAREIT Europe	IFEU	C	30.75	31.57	24.34	C+ / 6.0	9.66	17.69	34.75 / 95	6.63 / 34	-2.08 / 13

Incl. in Returns		RISK	3 Year			NET ASSETS		VALUATION Premium / Discount			ASSET					FUND MANAGER	
Dividend Yield %	Expense Ratio	Risk Rating/ Pts	Standard Deviation	Beta	Avg Dura-tion	NAV as of 12/31/12	Total $(Mil)	As of 12/31/12	1 Year Average	Wtd Avg P/E	Cash %	Stocks %	Bonds %	Other %	Portfolio Turnover Ratio	Manager Quality Pct	Manager Tenure (Years)
0.01	0.13	B+ / 9.9	0.1	N/A	N/A	110.22	2,579	0.04	0.01	N/A	6	0	92	2	96	52	3
0.05	0.20	B+ / 9.7	4.4	0.13	8.2	121.19	22,285	0.18	0.10	N/A	0	0	99	1	6	84	3
0.78	0.15	U /	N/A	N/A	N/A	25.09	146	0.28	N/A	N/A	0	0	0	100	2	N/A	1
3.39	0.35	B- / 7.6	18.8	1.02	N/A	80.02	2,705	-1.85	-0.01	64.5	0	99	0	1	16	83	5
3.49	0.20	B+ / 9.2	8.6	0.04	N/A	62.76	206	1.63	0.29	N/A	1	0	98	1	11	93	3
2.01	N/A	U /	N/A	N/A	N/A	51.53	279	-1.32	N/A	N/A	0	0	0	100	N/A	N/A	1
0.19	N/A	U /	N/A	N/A	N/A	52.13	261	0.13	N/A	N/A	0	0	0	100	N/A	N/A	1
1.99	N/A	U /	N/A	N/A	N/A	51.92	66	-0.02	N/A	N/A	0	0	0	100	N/A	N/A	1
2.60	0.09	B / 8.0	15.3	1.00	N/A	147.81	34,912	-3.16	-0.01	50.0	0	99	0	1	5	N/A	5
2.30	0.20	B- / 7.7	18.2	1.13	N/A	105.55	13,558	-3.65	N/A	39.0	0	99	0	1	14	60	5
3.05	0.20	B- / 7.5	19.3	1.20	N/A	80.73	8,091	-3.26	N/A	49.3	0	99	0	1	18	59	5
2.45	0.20	B / 8.0	15.7	1.01	N/A	67.05	435	-3.15	-0.07	49.2	0	99	0	1	5	52	5
0.46	N/A	U /	N/A	N/A	N/A	100.16	25	-0.07	N/A	N/A	0	0	0	100	N/A	N/A	1
2.49	0.20	B+ / 9.8	2.5	1.04	10.1	110.80	15,336	0.25	0.10	N/A	0	0	0	100	N/A	N/A	1
0.00	1.02	B+ / 9.4	4.8	0.07	N/A	50.72	51	-0.14	-0.15	N/A	0	0	99	1	46	47	3
2.40	0.50	B- / 7.5	21.8	1.06	N/A	34.33	1,426	-1.92	0.35	17.9	0	0	0	100	N/A	55	N/A
3.85	0.40	B / 8.9	11.5	0.69	N/A	58.54	10,372	-2.22	N/A	21.1	0	99	0	1	28	72	5
1.19	0.47	B- / 7.6	20.0	1.09	N/A	99.42	594	-5.10	N/A	32.2	0	99	0	1	16	81	5
4.40	0.47	B- / 7.9	17.4	1.04	N/A	69.64	79	-2.00	-0.05	43.7	0	99	0	1	25	37	5
2.89	0.47	C+ / 6.9	26.3	1.52	N/A	71.57	534	-3.16	-0.01	24.6	0	99	0	1	16	56	5
0.54	0.47	C+ / 6.7	24.0	1.13	N/A	24.93	45	-5.21	-0.04	19.0	2	97	0	1	11	14	5
2.88	0.47	B / 8.8	11.3	0.67	N/A	77.80	394	-3.61	N/A	30.3	0	99	0	1	20	11	5
3.11	0.47	B / 8.1	15.7	0.96	N/A	89.52	334	-3.04	N/A	52.3	0	99	0	1	6	80	5
1.81	0.47	B- / 7.4	22.9	1.00	N/A	42.34	817	-3.54	0.01	18.3	0	99	0	1	5	83	5
2.33	0.47	B- / 7.4	20.0	1.00	N/A	63.52	615	-4.44	-0.01	28.2	0	99	0	1	8	47	5
0.18	0.47	B- / 7.0	23.4	1.15	N/A	62.21	353	-4.66	-0.01	20.6	0	99	0	1	6	46	5
1.85	0.47	B / 8.3	12.0	0.65	N/A	87.39	706	-4.44	N/A	50.0	0	99	0	1	4	25	5
2.44	0.47	B- / 7.9	17.8	0.92	N/A	69.86	226	-2.02	0.01	29.0	0	99	0	1	7	76	5
0.48	0.47	C+ / 6.4	29.1	1.43	N/A	22.20	1,628	-4.68	N/A	9.9	0	100	0	0	23	69	5
2.70	0.20	B- / 7.9	15.8	1.03	N/A	74.06	609	-3.27	-0.02	49.4	0	100	0	0	10	80	5
0.46	0.47	B- / 7.6	19.8	1.24	N/A	75.70	689	-3.13	-0.02	28.9	0	99	0	1	5	50	5
3.63	0.47	B- / 7.8	18.7	1.12	N/A	34.49	79	-4.35	-0.04	15.1	2	97	0	1	6	49	5
1.39	0.47	B- / 7.0	17.6	0.96	N/A	70.93	274	-4.69	-0.03	95.9	0	99	0	1	11	31	5
0.93	0.47	C+ / 6.8	28.1	1.18	N/A	65.47	315	-2.95	-0.01	17.8	0	99	0	1	20	40	5
0.84	0.47	C+ / 6.2	34.0	1.40	N/A	53.82	324	-5.22	-0.02	24.0	0	99	0	1	13	24	5
1.90	0.47	B / 8.0	12.5	0.62	N/A	90.16	349	-5.70	N/A	87.4	0	99	0	1	13	19	5
4.89	0.47	B- / 7.7	17.3	0.98	N/A	66.54	4,591	-2.81	0.01	59.7	0	99	0	1	18	87	5
0.25	0.47	B- / 7.3	22.4	0.96	N/A	25.35	174	-3.63	-0.01	10.5	0	100	0	0	14	80	5
1.55	0.47	C+ / 6.9	19.6	1.17	N/A	72.32	1,514	-2.21	-0.01	123.8	0	99	0	1	7	52	5
3.54	0.47	B / 8.2	16.3	0.85	N/A	24.77	479	-2.06	-0.03	16.1	0	99	0	1	6	24	5
3.04	0.47	B+ / 9.2	9.5	0.92	N/A	87.68	838	-1.51	-0.01	20.4	1	98	0	1	25	58	5
2.75	0.60	U /	N/A	N/A	N/A	53.23	27	0.79	N/A	N/A	0	0	0	100	6	56	5
3.23	0.65	U /	N/A	N/A	N/A	55.22	198	0.89	N/A	N/A	0	0	0	100	N/A	N/A	1
4.16	0.60	B+ / 9.1	N/A	N/A	N/A	53.23	381	1.18	1.45	N/A	0	0	0	100	N/A	N/A	1
2.96	0.30	U /	N/A	N/A	N/A	52.82	11	0.51	N/A	N/A	0	0	0	100	23	90	2
0.93	0.20	B+ / 9.9	N/A	N/A	N/A	50.42	403	0.34	0.36	N/A	0	0	0	100	5	N/A	1
0.43	0.74	C+ / 6.5	25.2	0.92	N/A	40.83	8,478	-0.93	0.04	N/A	0	0	0	100	11	72	2
1.10	0.74	C+ / 6.6	23.9	0.87	N/A	50.48	34	-1.64	-0.19	N/A	0	99	0	1	21	29	5
3.37	0.50	B- / 7.5	22.1	1.06	N/A	37.22	29	-2.58	0.34	0.3	0	99	0	1	6	44	5
5.84	0.48	B- / 7.1	22.3	1.16	N/A	33.76	36	-0.27	0.18	N/A	0	99	0	1	25	68	5
3.14	0.48	C+ / 5.6	20.8	1.14	N/A	33.13	1,546	0.00	0.30	357.4	0	99	0	1	11	39	5
2.59	0.48	C+ / 6.6	25.5	1.30	N/A	30.91	14	-0.52	0.47	N/A	0	99	0	1	13	19	5

* Denotes ETF Fund, N/A denotes number is not available

Index of ETFs and Other Closed-End Funds

Fund Type	Fund Name	Ticker Symbol	Overall Investment Rating	PRICE Price As of 12/31/12	52 Week High	52 Week Low	PERFORMANCE Performance Rating/Pts	3 Mo	6 Mo	1Yr/Pct	Annualized 3Yr/Pct	5Yr/Pct
GI	*iShares FTSE EPRA/NAREIT NA Idx	IFNA	C+	47.17	50.06	42.84	B- / 7.2	3.46	3.53	18.22 / 63	17.88 / 82	7.82 / 59
IN	*iShares FTSE NAREIT Indl/Off Idx	FNIO	C	28.73	30.48	25.77	C / 5.0	3.02	5.16	19.09 / 67	11.13 / 53	0.42 / 21
IN	*iShares FTSE NAREIT Mtge+Capped	REM	C+	13.67	15.65	12.85	C+ / 5.8	4.27	7.39	26.26 / 86	11.10 / 53	-1.21 / 16
IN	*iShares FTSE NAREIT Real Estate	FTY	B	39.82	41.95	35.76	B- / 7.5	4.84	3.22	19.33 / 69	18.58 / 85	8.41 / 62
IN	*iShares FTSE NAREIT Residential	REZ	B+	48.47	51.11	43.89	B / 8.2	6.52	1.01	16.69 / 56	21.25 / 92	11.45 / 75
IN	*iShares FTSE NAREIT Retail Idx	RTL	B+	35.08	37.20	29.24	B+ / 8.7	2.82	5.05	27.54 / 88	22.92 / 94	6.92 / 54
GL	*iShares Glbl ex USD Hi Yld Corp	HYXU	U	54.14	N/A	N/A	U /	9.46	21.27	--	--	--
GL	*iShares Global High Yield Corp B	GHYG	U	52.69	N/A	N/A	U /	5.64	10.45	--	--	--
GL	*iShares Global Inflation-Linked	GTIP	B	54.08	54.63	48.75	C+ / 6.0	6.15	10.10	11.11 / 36	--	--
PM	*iShares Gold Trust	IAU	D-	16.28	17.48	14.91	C / 4.3	-5.33	4.52	1.25 / 16	13.37 / 65	13.04 / 81
GL	*iShares High Dividend Equity	HDV	C+	58.79	62.04	54.27	C / 4.5	1.37	2.71	14.15 / 45	--	--
COH	*iShares iBoxx $ High Yld Corp Bo	HYG	C-	93.35	94.52	86.36	C / 4.4	3.84	7.19	13.60 / 43	10.08 / 48	8.19 / 60
COI	*iShares iBoxx $ Inves Grade Corp	LQD	C	120.99	123.20	114.00	C- / 3.5	-0.43	3.34	9.98 / 34	9.47 / 45	7.72 / 58
COI	*iShares Industrials Sector Bond	ENGN	U	51.75	N/A	N/A	U /	-1.18	1.79	--	--	--
GL	*iShares Internat Inflation-Link	ITIP	B	51.29	51.79	45.07	B- / 7.1	4.38	13.23	13.28 / 42	--	--
EM	*iShares JPMorgan USD Emg Mkts Bo	EMB	C+	122.79	124.43	108.31	C / 4.6	0.08	5.81	17.25 / 59	11.17 / 53	9.07 / 66
GR	*iShares Morningstar Large Core	JKD	C+	82.04	84.69	72.62	C / 5.5	4.84	9.90	18.05 / 63	11.51 / 55	4.96 / 43
GR	*iShares Morningstar Large Growth	JKE	C	76.50	81.15	67.86	C / 5.0	1.76	7.40	18.50 / 65	11.12 / 53	5.31 / 46
IN	*iShares Morningstar Large Value	JKF	C	64.47	67.37	57.58	C / 4.4	3.11	10.49	14.06 / 45	9.60 / 45	1.43 / 24
GR	*iShares Morningstar Mid Core	JKG	B	98.60	102.78	86.00	B- / 7.3	8.22	13.52	18.12 / 63	15.27 / 73	8.41 / 62
GR	*iShares Morningstar Mid Growth	JKH	C+	106.95	110.70	93.70	C+ / 6.2	6.07	10.96	15.47 / 50	13.52 / 66	5.13 / 44
GR	*iShares Morningstar Mid Value	JKI	C+	82.35	85.56	70.80	C+ / 6.1	7.07	16.19	18.04 / 62	11.50 / 55	6.64 / 53
GI	*iShares Morningstar MltAsst Inc	IYLD	U	26.17	N/A	N/A	U /	1.26	3.55	--	--	--
GR	*iShares Morningstar Small Core	JKJ	C	95.27	99.15	83.31	C+ / 6.0	8.48	11.18	16.66 / 56	12.33 / 60	8.31 / 61
GR	*iShares Morningstar Small Growth	JKK	C+	93.85	98.28	82.18	C+ / 6.6	5.74	9.58	15.44 / 50	14.98 / 72	6.97 / 54
GR	*iShares Morningstar Small Value	JKL	C+	90.76	94.49	77.32	C+ / 6.7	7.76	12.96	18.71 / 66	13.47 / 66	10.17 / 70
FO	*iShares MSCI AC Asia xJapan SC I	AXJS	U	55.54	N/A	N/A	U /	9.19	--	--	--	--
GL	*iShares MSCI ACW Minimum Vol Ind	ACWV	C+	55.63	57.89	51.79	C / 4.6	2.71	4.99	12.41 / 40	--	--
EN	*iShares MSCI ACWI ex US Enrgy Id	AXEN	D+	53.92	62.73	48.13	C- / 3.1	2.33	11.52	1.84 / 18	--	--
FS	*iShares MSCI ACWI ex US Fn Sctr	AXFN	B+	23.40	24.75	18.30	A+ / 9.7	--	27.35	33.40 / 94	--	--
HL	*iShares MSCI ACWI ex US HlthCre	AXHE	A+	65.41	68.32	55.49	A / 9.3	5.65	15.88	24.29 / 82	--	--
FO	*iShares MSCI ACWI ex US Index	ACWX	C-	41.88	42.74	34.76	C- / 3.7	9.62	17.48	18.92 / 67	3.32 / 24	--
FO	*iShares MSCI ACWI ex US Indsl In	AXID	B-	55.86	57.99	48.10	B / 7.7	13.96	--	19.19 / 68	--	--
PM	*iShares MSCI ACWI ex US Mtls Ind	AXMT	C	54.92	59.40	45.50	B- / 7.4	10.61	20.20	5.84 / 25	--	--
EM	*iShares MSCI ACWI ex US TS Index	AXTE	D+	51.37	55.50	48.60	D+ / 2.4	0.95	--	6.53 / 27	--	--
UT	*iShares MSCI ACWI ex US Utl Sct	AXUT	D+	41.26	46.00	37.70	D+ / 2.8	2.06	6.64	3.85 / 22	--	--
GL	*iShares MSCI ACWI Index Fund	ACWI	C-	48.08	49.32	41.06	C- / 4.2	6.72	14.13	17.86 / 62	6.70 / 35	--
FO	*iShares MSCI ACWI xUS Cnsmr Dis	AXDI	B+	66.77	68.03	55.35	A- / 9.1	--	20.22	22.69 / 78	--	--
FO	*iShares MSCI ACWI xUS Cnsmr Stp	AXSL	A-	71.04	73.13	60.24	B / 8.2	--	13.50	20.43 / 72	--	--
FO	*iShares MSCI All Cntry Asia ex J	AAXJ	C-	60.52	61.94	49.08	C- / 3.9	9.49	18.08	19.73 / 70	4.13 / 27	--
FO	*iShares MSCI All Cntry Asia IT I	AAIT	U	27.69	N/A	N/A	U /	11.37	10.94	--	--	--
FO	*iShares MSCI All Peru Capped Idx	EPU	C+	45.88	47.70	38.69	B / 7.7	9.55	16.13	21.53 / 75	15.53 / 75	--
FO	*iShares MSCI Australia	EWA	C-	25.14	25.87	20.35	C / 4.3	9.62	20.97	20.88 / 73	7.39 / 37	4.25 / 38
FO	*iShares MSCI Australia Sm Cap In	EWAS	U	24.38	N/A	N/A	U /	--	19.71	--	--	--
FO	*iShares MSCI Austria Inv Mkt	EWO	D	18.19	18.55	12.94	D+ / 2.9	17.20	34.58	35.72 / 95	-2.18 / 11	-7.48 / 6
FO	*iShares MSCI Belgium Cp Inv Mkt	EWK	C	13.85	14.05	10.64	C+ / 6.4	11.07	25.55	38.55 / 97	5.28 / 30	-4.55 / 9
FO	*iShares MSCI Brazil	EWZ	D-	55.94	70.74	48.27	D- / 1.0	5.43	10.95	-5.20 / 10	-5.74 / 9	-1.02 / 17
FO	*iShares MSCI Brazil Small Cap In	EWZS	B	27.80	29.03	21.49	A / 9.5	5.42	26.47	21.15 / 74	--	--
FO	*iShares MSCI BRIC	BKF	D	40.84	44.48	33.62	D / 1.8	8.81	17.59	10.32 / 35	-1.72 / 12	-3.02 / 12
FO	*iShares MSCI Canada	EWC	D+	28.40	29.63	24.43	D+ / 2.9	3.80	14.32	9.44 / 33	4.88 / 29	2.29 / 28
FO	*iShares MSCI Canada Small Cap In	EWCS	U	23.59	N/A	N/A	U /	-0.39	14.61	--	--	--
FO	*iShares MSCI Chile Inv Market	ECH	D	63.24	69.60	57.58	D+ / 2.7	4.54	5.30	10.29 / 35	4.19 / 27	10.51 / 72

99 Pct = Best
0 Pct = Worst

% Total Return Through 12/31/12

* Denotes ETF Fund, N/A denotes number is not available

www.thestreetratings.com

Incl. in Returns		RISK				NET ASSETS		VALUATION			ASSET					FUND MANAGER	
Dividend Yield %	Expense Ratio	Risk Rating/ Pts	3 Year Standard Deviation	Beta	Avg Dura-tion	NAV as of 12/31/12	Total $(Mil)	Premium / Discount As of 12/31/12	1 Year Average	Wtd Avg P/E	Cash %	Stocks %	Bonds %	Other %	Portfolio Turnover Ratio	Manager Quality Pct	Manager Tenure (Years)
3.54	0.48	B- / 7.3	17.1	0.93	N/A	48.78	22	-3.30	0.13	94.7	0	99	0	1	9	80	5
3.11	0.48	B- / 7.3	20.9	1.14	N/A	29.61	10	-2.97	-0.08	46.0	0	99	0	1	15	34	5
13.48	0.48	B / 8.1	11.8	0.60	N/A	14.60	862	-6.37	0.06	10.5	0	97	0	3	79	68	5
3.65	0.48	B- / 7.9	16.6	0.94	N/A	40.88	70	-2.59	0.01	59.5	0	99	0	1	19	83	5
3.12	0.48	B- / 7.9	17.0	0.77	N/A	49.45	257	-1.98	0.02	70.4	0	99	0	1	28	91	5
4.79	0.48	B- / 7.7	18.3	1.01	N/A	35.69	23	-1.71	N/A	63.7	0	99	0	1	24	90	5
7.42	0.40	U /	N/A	N/A	N/A	55.11	27	-1.76	N/A	N/A	0	0	0	100	N/A	N/A	1
6.11	0.40	U /	N/A	N/A	N/A	53.17	37	-0.90	N/A	N/A	0	0	0	100	1	N/A	1
3.92	0.40	B+ / 9.2	N/A	N/A	N/A	53.65	16	0.80	-1.07	N/A	0	0	0	100	9	90	2
0.00	0.25	D / 1.9	18.9	0.92	N/A	16.12	11,645	0.99	0.15	N/A	0	0	0	100	N/A	60	8
3.48	0.40	B+ / 9.4	N/A	N/A	N/A	60.68	2,136	-3.11	0.02	N/A	0	99	0	1	28	89	2
6.49	0.50	B- / 7.7	9.3	1.19	13.9	94.08	15,972	-0.78	0.45	N/A	1	0	97	2	12	29	3
3.59	0.15	B+ / 9.4	5.3	1.38	9.8	120.75	25,350	0.20	0.43	N/A	0	0	97	3	3	35	3
2.53	0.30	U /	N/A	N/A	N/A	51.06	15	1.35	N/A	N/A	0	0	0	100	2	N/A	1
5.24	0.40	B / 8.7	N/A	N/A	N/A	50.74	66	1.08	0.85	N/A	0	0	0	100	20	93	2
3.82	0.60	B / 8.9	7.3	0.66	11.1	121.17	6,903	1.34	0.55	N/A	2	0	96	2	15	88	3
2.75	0.20	B / 8.4	14.2	0.92	N/A	84.67	287	-3.11	-0.03	24.0	0	99	0	1	33	60	5
2.39	0.25	B- / 7.1	17.4	1.10	N/A	78.94	448	-3.09	-0.03	111.9	0	99	0	1	28	39	5
3.16	0.25	B / 8.2	14.8	0.93	N/A	66.68	245	-3.31	-0.01	16.9	0	99	0	1	30	47	5
1.77	0.25	B- / 7.8	17.8	1.13	N/A	102.43	158	-3.74	-0.03	38.1	0	99	0	1	53	67	5
2.03	0.30	B- / 7.8	17.9	1.09	N/A	110.48	161	-3.20	-0.03	49.7	0	99	0	1	45	59	5
3.01	0.30	B- / 7.9	17.0	1.08	N/A	85.49	99	-3.67	-0.02	24.2	0	99	0	1	50	46	5
2.13	N/A	U /	N/A	N/A	N/A	26.46	86	-1.10	N/A	N/A	0	0	0	100	N/A	N/A	1
3.34	0.25	B- / 7.2	21.2	1.30	N/A	98.84	134	-3.61	-0.06	47.5	0	99	0	1	62	35	5
3.42	0.30	B- / 7.1	20.3	1.26	N/A	97.46	89	-3.70	-0.01	75.6	0	99	0	1	68	54	5
3.95	0.30	B- / 7.7	19.2	1.19	N/A	93.83	209	-3.27	-0.01	24.4	0	99	0	1	52	54	5
1.00	N/A	U /	N/A	N/A	N/A	56.99	3	-2.54	N/A	N/A	0	0	0	100	N/A	N/A	1
2.92	0.23	B+ / 9.5	N/A	N/A	N/A	56.66	648	-1.82	0.55	N/A	0	0	0	100	22	80	2
2.59	0.48	C+ / 6.6	N/A	N/A	N/A	55.54	5	-2.92	-0.11	N/A	0	99	0	1	6	26	3
4.76	0.48	C+ / 6.6	N/A	N/A	N/A	23.98	1	-2.42	0.13	N/A	0	99	0	1	5	65	3
1.18	0.48	B / 8.4	N/A	N/A	N/A	67.22	10	-2.69	0.48	N/A	0	99	0	1	10	78	3
1.92	0.34	B- / 7.4	20.8	1.02	N/A	42.61	1,276	-1.71	0.19	31.7	0	99	0	1	9	47	5
1.28	0.48	B- / 7.0	N/A	N/A	N/A	58.15	3	-3.94	-0.44	N/A	0	99	0	1	6	94	3
1.90	0.48	C+ / 5.9	N/A	N/A	N/A	55.76	3	-1.51	-0.69	N/A	0	99	0	1	5	74	3
2.95	0.48	B- / 7.9	N/A	N/A	N/A	52.47	3	-2.10	0.03	N/A	0	99	0	1	11	29	3
2.89	0.48	B- / 7.0	N/A	N/A	N/A	42.32	6	-2.50	0.13	N/A	0	99	0	1	9	76	3
1.98	0.34	B- / 7.5	18.5	0.90	N/A	49.15	3,262	-2.18	0.07	46.5	0	99	0	1	6	72	5
1.62	0.48	B- / 7.1	N/A	N/A	N/A	67.37	3	-0.89	-0.31	N/A	0	99	0	1	8	91	3
1.36	0.48	B / 8.6	N/A	N/A	N/A	72.02	4	-1.36	0.18	N/A	0	99	0	1	5	88	3
1.79	0.69	C+ / 6.9	22.7	0.99	N/A	60.54	2,128	-0.03	0.10	N/A	0	99	0	1	26	58	5
3.69	0.11	U /	N/A	N/A	N/A	27.87	3	-0.65	N/A	N/A	0	0	0	100	5	N/A	1
2.34	0.51	C+ / 6.7	26.0	0.69	N/A	47.35	510	-3.10	-0.11	58.0	0	99	0	1	10	92	4
7.12	0.53	C+ / 6.6	27.2	1.21	N/A	25.41	2,388	-1.06	0.07	N/A	0	94	0	6	9	73	5
0.44	0.59	U /	N/A	N/A	N/A	24.76	1	-1.53	N/A	N/A	1	83	0	16	10	N/A	1
0.77	0.52	C / 5.4	31.4	1.42	N/A	18.49	121	-1.62	0.07	N/A	1	98	0	1	13	20	5
0.30	0.53	C+ / 6.6	22.8	1.03	N/A	14.00	57	-1.07	0.13	N/A	0	99	0	1	19	67	5
0.69	0.53	C+ / 6.2	30.1	1.25	N/A	56.42	9,304	-0.85	-0.04	N/A	0	98	0	2	7	12	5
2.36	0.61	C+ / 6.1	N/A	N/A	N/A	27.84	55	-0.14	-0.16	N/A	0	91	0	9	67	76	3
0.16	0.69	C+ / 6.4	26.8	1.14	N/A	41.19	773	-0.85	-0.11	N/A	0	99	0	1	32	19	5
2.65	0.53	B- / 7.5	19.3	0.82	N/A	29.10	4,733	-2.41	-0.10	34.4	0	99	0	1	5	62	5
3.90	0.59	U /	N/A	N/A	N/A	24.15	2	-2.32	N/A	N/A	0	93	0	7	18	N/A	1
0.10	0.61	C+ / 6.4	25.6	0.82	N/A	65.16	548	-2.95	-0.18	N/A	0	99	0	1	48	71	5

Denotes ETF Fund, N/A denotes number is not available

41

Fund Type	Fund Name	Ticker Symbol	Overall Investment Rating	PRICE Price As of 12/31/12	52 Week High	52 Week Low	PERFORMANCE Perform-ance Rating/Pts	3 Mo	6 Mo	1Yr/Pct	Annualized 3Yr/Pct	5Yr/Pct
	99 Pct = Best											
	0 Pct = Worst											
FO	*iShares MSCI China Index	MCHI	B	48.54	50.14	38.70	A+ / 9.6	13.39	24.02	20.53 / 72	--	--
FO	*iShares MSCI China Small Cap Ind	ECNS	B-	41.09	44.28	31.20	A+ / 9.8	28.69	30.03	31.87 / 93	--	--
FO	*iShares MSCI Denmark CpInv Mkt I	EDEN	U	31.98	N/A	N/A	U /	11.17	24.83	--	--	--
FO	*iShares MSCI EAFE	EFA	C-	56.86	58.11	46.53	C- / 4.1	10.34	18.88	21.12 / 74	3.74 / 25	-1.15 / 16
FO	*iShares MSCI EAFE Growth	EFG	C-	60.04	60.97	49.97	C- / 3.9	8.52	16.03	19.10 / 67	4.62 / 28	-0.71 / 17
FO	*iShares MSCI EAFE Minimum Vol Id	EFAV	B-	54.68	55.78	47.69	C+ / 5.7	2.06	7.99	13.87 / 44	--	--
FO	*iShares MSCI EAFE Small Cap Idx	SCZ	C	40.71	42.08	33.93	C / 5.5	11.04	20.54	22.33 / 78	7.12 / 36	1.89 / 26
FO	*iShares MSCI EAFE Value	EFV	C-	48.64	50.32	39.22	C- / 4.2	11.57	21.72	23.23 / 80	2.70 / 22	-1.62 / 15
EM	*iShares MSCI EM Cons Discrt Sect	EMDI	U	52.55	N/A	N/A	U /	4.29	14.86	--	--	--
EM	*iShares MSCI EM Eastern Europe	ESR	D-	27.06	29.40	21.41	D+ / 2.3	6.31	16.31	16.28 / 54	0.42 / 16	--
EM	*iShares MSCI EM Engy Sector Cp I	EMEY	U	43.60	N/A	N/A	U /	--	12.85	--	--	--
FO	*iShares MSCI Em Mkts Lat Amer In	EEML	U	52.42	N/A	N/A	U /	8.74	16.53	--	--	--
EM	*iShares MSCI Emerg Markets Divid	DVYE	U	57.01	N/A	N/A	U /	8.53	14.88	--	--	--
EM	*iShares MSCI Emerging Markets	EEM	D+	44.35	45.33	36.57	D+ / 2.9	8.44	16.29	15.33 / 49	3.76 / 25	1.58 / 25
EM	*iShares MSCI Emg Markets Value I	EVAL	U	50.88	N/A	N/A	U /	7.44	13.95	--	--	--
EM	*iShares MSCI Emg Mkts Asia Index	EEMA	U	57.59	N/A	N/A	U /	10.17	18.84	--	--	--
EM	*iShares MSCI Emg Mkts EMEA Index	EEME	U	56.78	N/A	N/A	U /	7.69	--	--	--	--
EM	*iShares MSCI Emg Mkts Finls Sctr	EMFN	B+	27.65	29.82	21.10	A+ / 9.7	16.81	22.38	28.09 / 88	--	--
EM	*iShares MSCI Emg Mkts Growth Ind	EGRW	U	56.95	N/A	N/A	U /	9.77	17.73	--	--	--
EM	*iShares MSCI Emg Mkts Matl Sctr	EMMT	C+	21.18	23.33	17.57	B+ / 8.3	12.23	18.07	10.46 / 35	--	--
EM	*iShares MSCI Emg Mkts Min Vol In	EEMV	A	60.56	62.22	50.99	B+ / 8.7	6.71	12.43	20.57 / 72	--	--
EM	*iShares MSCI Emg Mkts Sm Cap Ind	EEMS	B+	47.30	50.25	40.33	A / 9.3	10.35	18.62	20.19 / 71	--	--
FO	*iShares MSCI EMU	EZU	D	33.46	34.28	24.77	D+ / 2.9	12.82	30.02	27.79 / 88	-0.15 / 15	-5.31 / 8
FS	*iShares MSCI Europ Finls Sctr Id	EUFN	B-	19.80	21.05	13.57	A+ / 9.9	18.67	42.66	44.74 / 98	--	--
FS	*iShares MSCI Far East Finls Sctr	FEFN	U	26.72	27.86	21.32	U /	14.58	--	--	--	--
FO	*iShares MSCI Finland Cp Inv Mkt	EFNL	U	26.18	N/A	N/A	U /	16.03	35.06	--	--	--
FO	*iShares MSCI France	EWQ	D	23.59	23.86	17.83	D+ / 2.6	12.17	26.93	27.06 / 87	-0.54 / 14	-3.79 / 10
FO	*iShares MSCI Frontier 100 Index	FM	U	27.62	N/A	N/A	U /	6.57	--	--	--	--
FO	*iShares MSCI Germany	EWG	C	24.70	25.12	18.44	C+ / 6.4	10.10	28.02	31.89 / 93	6.29 / 33	-2.12 / 13
FO	*iShares MSCI Germany Small Cap I	EWGS	U	30.65	N/A	N/A	U /	12.66	27.55	--	--	--
PM	*iShares MSCI Gl Sel M&MP	PICK	U	22.64	N/A	N/A	U /	12.39	21.05	--	--	--
GL	*iShares MSCI Global Agri Pro	VEGI	U	26.97	N/A	N/A	U /	7.57	13.86	--	--	--
EN	*iShares MSCI Global Engy Pro	FILL	U	23.39	N/A	N/A	U /	0.79	10.26	--	--	--
PM	*iShares MSCI Global Gold Miners	RING	U	19.29	N/A	N/A	U /	-13.05	3.72	--	--	--
PM	*iShares MSCI Global Silver Miner	SLVP	U	21.69	N/A	N/A	U /	-5.69	22.36	--	--	--
FO	*iShares MSCI Hong Kong	EWH	B-	19.42	20.10	15.48	B- / 7.5	10.99	21.51	30.54 / 91	11.23 / 54	3.17 / 33
FO	*iShares MSCI Hong Kong Sm Cap In	EWHS	U	26.67	N/A	N/A	U /	14.78	--	--	--	--
FO	*iShares MSCI India Index	INDA	U	26.23	N/A	N/A	U /	3.65	16.42	--	--	--
FO	*iShares MSCI India Small Cap Ind	SMIN	U	25.61	N/A	N/A	U /	2.64	16.10	--	--	--
FO	*iShares MSCI Indonesia Inv Mkt I	EIDO	D	30.26	32.06	25.70	D- / 1.5	-2.58	3.25	0.47 / 15	--	--
FO	*iShares MSCI Irlnd Capd Inv Mkt	EIRL	A	25.09	25.71	18.87	A+ / 9.8	13.66	27.08	37.24 / 96	--	--
FO	*iShares MSCI Israel Capped Inv M	EIS	D-	41.90	44.57	35.11	D- / 1.1	4.34	17.12	6.01 / 26	-6.06 / 8	--
FO	*iShares MSCI Italy	EWI	D-	13.45	14.33	9.21	D / 1.6	15.86	36.43	26.57 / 86	-7.79 / 8	-11.18 / 4
FO	*iShares MSCI Japan	EWJ	D	9.75	10.21	8.64	D / 2.0	11.42	8.99	10.21 / 35	-0.12 / 15	-3.02 / 12
FO	*iShares MSCI Japan Small Cap	SCJ	C-	44.39	47.17	40.92	D+ / 2.6	8.10	5.21	6.72 / 28	4.52 / 28	1.30 / 24
IN	*iShares MSCI KLD 400 Social Idx	DSI	C	51.74	53.45	46.68	C- / 4.2	4.36	9.78	13.81 / 44	8.84 / 42	4.40 / 40
GL	*iShares MSCI Kokusai Index	TOK	C-	42.69	43.98	37.00	C- / 4.2	4.59	11.64	17.13 / 59	7.66 / 37	2.13 / 27
FO	*iShares MSCI Malaysia	EWM	C+	15.13	15.33	13.47	C+ / 5.9	3.57	7.55	13.75 / 44	14.36 / 70	6.42 / 51
FO	*iShares MSCI Mexico Inv Market	EWW	B	70.53	73.70	53.49	B+ / 8.4	10.18	18.64	36.35 / 96	14.89 / 72	9.27 / 67
FO	*iShares MSCI Netherlands Inv Mar	EWN	C-	20.51	21.08	15.68	C / 4.7	11.68	25.95	29.11 / 90	2.42 / 21	-1.56 / 15
FO	*iShares MSCI New Zealand Inv Mk	ENZL	A+	34.58	35.68	27.86	A+ / 9.7	7.86	22.25	34.74 / 95	--	--
FO	*iShares MSCI Norway Cp Inv Mkt I	ENOR	U	29.10	N/A	N/A	U /	6.69	21.47	--	--	--

Incl. in Returns		RISK					NET ASSETS		VALUATION			ASSET					FUND MANAGER	
Dividend Yield %	Expense Ratio	Risk Rating/ Pts	3 Year		Avg Dura-tion	NAV as of 12/31/12	Total $(Mil)	Premium / Discount		Wtd Avg P/E	Cash %	Stocks %	Bonds %	Other %	Portfolio Turnover Ratio	Manager Quality Pct	Manager Tenure (Years)
			Standard Deviation	Beta				As of 12/31/12	1 Year Average								
0.38	0.61	C+ / 6.3	N/A	N/A	N/A	48.86	831	-0.65	0.25	N/A	0	99	0	1	8	84	2
2.18	0.61	C / 5.2	N/A	N/A	N/A	42.77	22	-3.93	-0.26	N/A	0	99	0	1	33	91	3
0.31	0.53	U /	N/A	N/A	N/A	33.51	3	-4.57	N/A	N/A	0	99	0	1	12	N/A	1
2.14	0.34	B- / 7.3	20.6	1.02	N/A	57.82	38,815	-1.66	0.15	47.8	0	99	0	1	5	52	5
1.60	0.40	B- / 7.3	20.4	1.00	N/A	60.75	1,376	-1.17	0.14	47.8	0	99	0	1	26	62	5
1.83	0.20	B+ / 9.0	N/A	N/A	N/A	54.93	211	-0.46	0.55	N/A	0	0	0	100	25	54	2
3.70	0.40	B- / 7.7	21.2	1.02	N/A	41.73	1,619	-2.44	0.16	0.3	0	99	0	1	16	74	5
2.37	0.40	C+ / 6.9	21.6	1.06	N/A	49.97	1,614	-2.66	0.25	N/A	0	99	0	1	27	40	5
2.21	0.68	U /	N/A	N/A	N/A	52.13	3	0.81	N/A	N/A	0	0	0	100	54	N/A	1
1.27	0.69	C / 5.3	33.5	1.35	N/A	26.94	17	0.45	0.07	N/A	0	99	0	1	8	25	4
1.03	0.68	U /	N/A	N/A	N/A	43.78	2	-0.41	N/A	N/A	0	0	0	100	29	N/A	1
1.78	0.49	U /	N/A	N/A	N/A	52.64	5	-0.42	N/A	N/A	0	0	0	100	3	N/A	1
1.11	N/A	U /	N/A	N/A	N/A	56.05	64	1.71	N/A	N/A	0	0	0	100	N/A	N/A	1
0.10	0.68	C+ / 6.8	24.7	1.07	N/A	44.33	48,190	0.05	0.18	55.6	0	99	0	1	15	41	5
3.11	0.49	U /	N/A	N/A	N/A	50.78	10	0.20	N/A	N/A	0	0	0	100	12	N/A	1
2.01	0.49	U /	N/A	N/A	N/A	57.51	23	0.14	N/A	N/A	0	0	0	100	3	N/A	1
3.41	0.49	U /	N/A	N/A	N/A	56.44	6	0.60	N/A	N/A	0	0	0	100	5	N/A	1
0.40	0.69	C+ / 6.6	N/A	N/A	N/A	27.49	4	0.58	0.44	N/A	0	99	0	1	2	94	3
4.52	0.49	U /	N/A	N/A	N/A	56.54	3	0.73	N/A	N/A	0	0	0	100	12	N/A	1
2.74	0.69	C+ / 5.9	N/A	N/A	N/A	21.62	5	-2.04	-0.59	N/A	0	99	0	1	5	14	5
1.27	0.25	B / 8.7	N/A	N/A	N/A	60.41	847	0.25	0.43	N/A	0	0	0	100	31	88	2
6.63	0.69	B- / 7.3	N/A	N/A	N/A	48.82	9	-3.11	N/A	N/A	0	0	0	100	32	69	2
0.13	0.53	C+ / 6.1	28.2	1.34	N/A	34.13	2,195	-1.96	0.11	47.8	0	99	0	1	7	20	5
1.70	0.48	C / 5.2	N/A	N/A	N/A	20.88	33	-5.17	0.14	N/A	0	99	0	1	8	18	3
3.78	0.48	U /	N/A	N/A	N/A	26.68	1	0.15	N/A	N/A	0	99	0	1	7	82	3
0.37	N/A	U /	N/A	N/A	N/A	27.40	1	-4.45	N/A	N/A	0	99	0	1	N/A	N/A	1
0.96	0.53	C+ / 6.0	28.1	1.31	N/A	23.79	448	-0.84	0.09	N/A	0	99	0	1	6	22	5
0.00	N/A	U /	N/A	N/A	N/A	27.88	17	-0.93	N/A	N/A	0	0	0	100	N/A	N/A	1
2.35	0.53	C+ / 6.2	29.1	1.35	N/A	25.06	3,992	-1.44	0.06	47.8	0	99	0	1	4	55	5
0.82	0.59	U /	N/A	N/A	N/A	31.98	8	-4.16	N/A	N/A	0	99	0	1	10	N/A	1
1.71	0.39	U /	N/A	N/A	N/A	22.69	254	-0.22	N/A	N/A	0	0	0	100	1	N/A	1
1.21	0.38	U /	N/A	N/A	N/A	27.62	11	-2.35	N/A	N/A	0	0	0	100	6	N/A	1
2.92	0.39	U /	N/A	N/A	N/A	24.23	5	-3.47	N/A	N/A	0	0	0	100	5	N/A	1
1.29	0.39	U /	N/A	N/A	N/A	18.96	29	1.74	N/A	N/A	0	0	0	100	11	N/A	1
2.46	0.39	U /	N/A	N/A	N/A	21.97	2	-1.27	N/A	N/A	0	0	0	100	9	N/A	1
1.36	0.53	B- / 7.1	22.1	0.89	N/A	19.83	3,002	-2.07	0.08	N/A	0	96	0	4	11	84	5
0.27	0.59	U /	N/A	N/A	N/A	27.33	1	-2.41	N/A	N/A	0	95	0	5	9	N/A	1
0.22	0.67	U /	N/A	N/A	N/A	26.05	67	0.69	N/A	N/A	0	99	0	1	4	N/A	1
2.59	0.74	U /	N/A	N/A	N/A	25.80	5	-0.74	N/A	N/A	0	99	0	1	6	N/A	1
0.49	0.61	C+ / 6.8	N/A	N/A	N/A	30.13	387	0.43	-0.50	N/A	0	100	0	0	8	13	5
0.74	0.53	B- / 7.3	N/A	N/A	N/A	25.16	35	-0.28	0.57	N/A	0	96	0	4	21	93	3
2.55	0.61	C+ / 5.9	23.7	0.91	N/A	43.22	80	-3.05	-0.19	N/A	0	99	0	1	20	14	5
0.92	0.53	C / 4.6	34.4	1.55	N/A	14.25	384	-5.61	0.16	N/A	0	99	0	1	14	8	5
2.07	0.53	B- / 7.5	16.1	0.60	N/A	9.79	5,156	-0.41	0.12	N/A	0	99	0	1	3	46	5
3.44	0.53	B / 8.3	13.6	0.41	N/A	44.34	40	0.11	-0.15	N/A	0	99	0	1	9	78	5
2.47	0.50	B / 8.2	14.9	0.96	N/A	53.46	166	-3.22	-0.02	42.5	0	99	0	1	9	35	5
2.33	0.25	B- / 7.7	17.3	0.82	N/A	43.87	636	-2.69	0.31	48.6	0	99	0	1	5	77	5
1.93	0.53	B- / 7.8	17.5	0.68	N/A	15.24	971	-0.72	0.07	N/A	0	99	0	1	24	93	5
0.49	0.53	B- / 7.3	22.9	0.95	N/A	73.37	1,929	-3.87	0.08	N/A	0	99	0	1	10	90	5
0.35	0.53	C+ / 6.5	24.8	1.17	N/A	21.01	148	-2.38	0.08	N/A	0	100	0	0	10	34	5
5.47	0.53	B- / 7.8	N/A	N/A	N/A	35.36	157	-2.21	0.10	N/A	0	99	0	1	12	96	3
0.96	0.53	U /	N/A	N/A	N/A	30.00	9	-3.00	N/A	N/A	0	100	0	0	7	N/A	1

Denotes ETF Fund, N/A denotes number is not available

Data as of December 31, 2012

I. Index of ETFs and Other Closed-End Funds

Fund Type	Fund Name	Ticker Symbol	Overall Investment Rating	PRICE Price As of 12/31/12	52 Week High	52 Week Low	PERFORMANCE Perform-ance Rating/Pts	% Total Return Through 12/31/12 3 Mo	6 Mo	1Yr/Pct	Annualized 3Yr/Pct	5Yr/Pct
	99 Pct = Best *0 Pct = Worst*											
FO	*iShares MSCI Pacific ex-Japan	EPP	C	47.14	48.19	38.02	C+ / 5.8	9.23	19.62	23.59 / 81	8.34 / 39	4.39 / 40
FO	*iShares MSCI Philipps Invst Mkt	EPHE	A	34.55	36.29	25.25	A+ / 9.8	15.54	20.76	45.19 / 98	--	--
FO	*iShares MSCI Poland Invstbl Mkt	EPOL	B-	29.62	29.88	20.26	A+ / 9.8	11.29	30.20	39.88 / 97	--	--
FO	*iShares MSCI Russia Capped Index	ERUS	C-	23.65	26.75	18.82	C+ / 6.8	6.12	13.66	10.94 / 36	--	--
FO	*iShares MSCI Singapore	EWS	C	13.69	13.92	11.32	C / 5.5	5.79	10.28	24.38 / 83	9.79 / 46	6.37 / 51
FO	*iShares MSCI Singapore Sm Cp Ind	EWSS	U	29.99	N/A	N/A	U /	10.99	27.20	--	--	--
FO	*iShares MSCI South Africa	EZA	C-	71.58	71.72	60.38	C / 5.1	9.41	10.47	14.86 / 47	10.03 / 47	6.63 / 53
FO	*iShares MSCI South Korea	EWY	C-	63.35	65.00	50.93	C / 5.1	10.82	19.96	19.04 / 67	9.46 / 45	2.75 / 31
FO	*iShares MSCI Spain	EWP	E+	30.26	32.92	19.73	D / 1.7	19.41	44.96	16.00 / 53	-6.66 / 8	-5.31 / 8
FO	*iShares MSCI Sweden	EWD	C	30.20	30.68	23.67	B- / 7.0	11.62	20.02	25.22 / 84	10.96 / 53	5.91 / 49
FO	*iShares MSCI Switzerland	EWL	C+	26.80	28.01	21.69	C+ / 6.9	10.52	24.01	27.51 / 88	9.37 / 44	4.84 / 43
FO	*iShares MSCI Taiwan	EWT	D+	13.62	13.95	11.46	D+ / 2.9	7.24	16.31	14.96 / 48	3.64 / 25	2.35 / 28
FO	*iShares MSCI Thailand Inv Market	THD	B+	82.49	84.24	60.80	A+ / 9.6	9.59	18.28	39.82 / 97	26.94 / 99	--
FO	*iShares MSCI Turkey Inv Market	TUR	B-	66.78	69.38	43.36	A- / 9.1	18.93	32.62	68.00 / 99	8.64 / 41	--
FO	*iShares MSCI UK Small Cap Index	EWUS	U	30.55	N/A	N/A	U /	7.94	22.17	--	--	--
FO	*iShares MSCI United Kingdom	EWU	C-	17.94	18.32	15.22	C- / 4.1	6.31	12.65	17.92 / 62	6.50 / 34	0.19 / 20
IN	*iShares MSCI USA	EUSA	B	30.68	31.71	27.46	B / 7.7	4.09	11.97	16.85 / 57	--	--
GR	*iShares MSCI USA ESG Select Soc	KLD	C	59.33	62.14	54.58	C- / 4.1	4.40	9.40	11.30 / 37	9.03 / 43	4.22 / 38
IN	*iShares MSCI USA Minimum Vol Idx	USMV	B-	29.04	30.29	26.87	C / 4.8	2.29	3.60	14.08 / 45	--	--
GL	*iShares MSCI World Index	URTH	U	56.11	N/A	N/A	U /	5.13	13.68	--	--	--
HL	*iShares Nasdaq Biotechnology	IBB	B-	137.22	148.54	111.75	B+ / 8.6	2.79	10.77	30.12 / 91	20.43 / 89	12.68 / 79
IN	*iShares NYSE 100	NY	C	66.21	69.08	58.91	C / 4.6	3.37	10.17	15.84 / 52	9.84 / 46	2.58 / 30
IN	*iShares NYSE Composite	NYC	C	76.69	79.49	66.52	C / 4.7	6.50	13.84	17.11 / 59	8.28 / 39	2.39 / 28
IN	*iShares PHLX SOX Semicon Sector	SOXX	D+	52.04	60.32	47.02	C- / 3.2	10.20	13.44	6.31 / 27	6.29 / 34	2.81 / 31
GR	*iShares Russell 1000	IWB	C+	79.15	81.87	70.25	C / 5.4	4.32	10.42	16.95 / 58	11.47 / 55	4.68 / 41
GR	*iShares Russell 1000 Growth	IWF	C	65.49	68.45	59.53	C / 5.2	3.23	8.40	15.83 / 52	11.89 / 57	5.81 / 48
IN	*iShares Russell 1000 Value	IWD	C+	72.82	75.39	63.14	C / 5.5	5.35	12.23	17.84 / 61	10.94 / 52	3.35 / 34
GR	*iShares Russell 2000	IWM	C+	84.32	87.69	72.94	C+ / 6.1	7.31	10.88	16.69 / 56	12.85 / 62	6.98 / 55
GR	*iShares Russell 2000 Growth	IWO	C	95.31	99.70	83.12	C+ / 6.2	6.76	9.68	15.53 / 50	13.78 / 68	7.15 / 55
GR	*iShares Russell 2000 Value	IWN	C+	75.51	78.38	64.92	C+ / 5.9	7.97	12.14	17.97 / 62	11.74 / 56	6.75 / 53
IN	*iShares Russell 3000	IWV	C+	84.68	87.48	74.95	C / 5.4	4.55	10.34	16.89 / 57	11.59 / 56	4.78 / 42
GR	*iShares Russell 3000 Growth	IWZ	C	53.41	55.72	48.41	C / 5.2	3.43	8.44	15.74 / 51	11.92 / 58	5.87 / 48
IN	*iShares Russell 3000 Value	IWW	C+	95.35	98.71	82.60	C / 5.5	5.56	12.23	17.89 / 62	10.95 / 52	3.56 / 35
GR	*iShares Russell Micro Cap	IWC	C	52.32	54.70	45.56	C+ / 5.8	5.65	8.36	19.38 / 69	12.08 / 58	4.34 / 39
GR	*iShares Russell Mid Cap	IWR	C+	113.10	117.20	98.48	C+ / 6.5	6.82	12.91	17.22 / 59	13.38 / 65	6.78 / 53
GR	*iShares Russell Mid Cap Growth	IWP	C+	62.80	65.10	55.60	C+ / 6.2	6.36	11.44	15.39 / 49	13.35 / 65	6.45 / 52
GR	*iShares Russell Mid Cap Value	IWS	B-	50.24	51.98	43.06	C+ / 6.6	7.09	14.12	18.68 / 66	13.31 / 65	6.80 / 54
GR	*iShares Russell Top 200 Growth	IWY	C+	34.71	36.73	31.60	C / 4.8	1.87	7.09	15.92 / 52	11.32 / 54	--
IN	*iShares Russell Top 200 Idx	IWL	C	32.50	34.23	29.72	C / 4.9	3.20	9.27	16.98 / 58	10.61 / 51	--
IN	*iShares Russell Top 200 Value Id	IWX	C	31.17	32.35	27.39	C / 4.8	4.43	11.40	17.41 / 60	9.58 / 45	--
GR	*iShares S&P 100	OEF	C	64.69	68.07	58.25	C / 4.8	2.36	8.49	16.75 / 57	10.72 / 51	3.82 / 37
GR	*iShares S&P 500 Growth	IVW	C	75.74	79.72	68.81	C / 5.1	2.25	7.45	16.04 / 53	11.90 / 57	6.06 / 50
IN	*iShares S&P 500 Value	IVE	C+	66.39	68.65	57.66	C / 5.3	5.33	12.50	17.10 / 59	10.54 / 50	2.49 / 29
GI	*iShares S&P Aggressive Allocatio	AOA	C	37.17	38.10	33.11	C / 4.8	5.31	10.35	15.48 / 50	9.82 / 46	--
FO	*iShares S&P Asia 50 Index	AIA	C	48.15	49.46	39.04	C+ / 5.8	9.90	20.55	21.84 / 76	8.45 / 40	4.21 / 38
MUS	*iShares S&P CA AMT-Free Muni Bon	CMF	C	115.30	120.00	110.64	C- / 3.9	0.39	2.53	5.23 / 30	6.82 / 50	5.54 / 62
GI	*iShares S&P Conservative Allocat	AOK	C	30.58	30.91	29.33	D+ / 2.7	1.68	3.89	6.57 / 27	5.70 / 32	--
FO	*iShares S&P Dev ex-US Property	WPS	C+	36.31	36.83	28.35	B / 7.8	9.76	20.80	38.20 / 96	11.11 / 53	1.12 / 23
GL	*iShares S&P Emerging Mkts Infr	EMIF	C-	34.24	35.11	29.34	C / 4.3	8.44	10.76	20.15 / 71	6.84 / 35	--
FO	*iShares S&P Europe 350	IEV	C-	39.30	40.44	31.25	C / 4.5	10.28	22.54	24.73 / 83	3.78 / 25	-1.79 / 14
GL	*iShares S&P Gl Cons Staples Sect	KXI	C+	73.63	76.04	65.21	C+ / 5.6	3.02	7.40	19.05 / 67	12.46 / 61	7.75 / 58
GL	*iShares S&P Glb Infrastructure	IGF	C-	35.71	36.59	31.97	C- / 3.1	3.93	8.32	13.81 / 44	5.05 / 29	-1.15 / 16

* Denotes ETF Fund, N/A denotes number is not available

Dividend Yield %	Expense Ratio	Risk Rating/ Pts	Standard Deviation	Beta	Avg Dura-tion	NAV as of 12/31/12	Total $(Mil)	As of 12/31/12	1 Year Average	Wtd Avg P/E	Cash %	Stocks %	Bonds %	Other %	Portfolio Turnover Ratio	Manager Quality Pct	Manager Tenure (Years)
4.69	0.50	C+ / 6.9	24.7	1.11	N/A	47.67	3,799	-1.11	0.09	N/A	0	99	0	1	7	77	5
0.24	0.61	B- / 7.5	N/A	N/A	N/A	35.83	218	-3.57	0.14	N/A	0	100	0	0	25	98	3
4.25	0.61	C / 4.8	N/A	N/A	N/A	29.04	185	2.00	0.21	N/A	2	97	0	1	15	84	3
0.38	0.61	C / 5.1	N/A	N/A	N/A	23.61	206	0.17	0.36	N/A	0	99	0	1	16	9	3
5.06	0.53	B- / 7.1	22.6	0.93	N/A	13.71	1,521	-0.15	0.11	N/A	0	97	0	3	3	82	5
40.97	0.59	U /	N/A	N/A	N/A	30.66	6	-2.19	N/A	N/A	1	50	0	49	4	N/A	1
3.14	0.61	C+ / 6.9	27.0	1.02	N/A	68.40	534	4.65	0.10	N/A	0	98	0	2	4	86	5
0.58	0.61	C+ / 6.3	28.6	1.20	N/A	62.92	3,345	0.68	-0.02	N/A	0	99	0	1	12	82	5
4.81	0.53	C / 4.4	36.0	1.48	N/A	32.09	242	-5.70	0.03	N/A	0	99	0	1	17	9	5
3.03	0.53	C+ / 6.2	28.1	1.29	N/A	30.59	366	-1.27	0.05	N/A	0	100	0	0	7	84	5
2.36	0.53	B- / 7.4	19.4	0.88	N/A	27.95	699	-4.11	0.08	N/A	0	99	0	1	7	79	5
1.99	0.61	B- / 7.0	22.8	0.98	N/A	13.62	2,694	0.00	0.21	N/A	0	99	0	1	22	55	5
1.01	0.61	C+ / 6.9	27.4	0.93	N/A	82.48	789	0.01	0.25	N/A	0	99	0	1	12	97	5
1.52	0.61	C / 5.4	31.4	1.08	N/A	68.80	768	-2.94	0.17	N/A	0	99	0	1	9	80	5
4.33	0.59	U /	N/A	N/A	N/A	31.57	3	-3.23	N/A	N/A	0	99	0	1	12	N/A	1
2.82	0.53	B- / 7.4	21.1	1.02	N/A	18.28	1,424	-1.86	0.27	N/A	0	99	0	1	7	70	5
2.71	0.15	B / 8.1	N/A	N/A	N/A	31.66	150	-3.10	-0.05	49.8	0	99	0	1	6	50	3
2.60	0.50	B / 8.1	15.4	0.99	N/A	61.53	173	-3.58	-0.03	46.3	0	99	0	1	20	34	5
0.28	0.15	B+ / 9.8	N/A	N/A	N/A	29.96	752	-3.07	0.09	N/A	0	99	0	1	30	76	2
2.99	0.24	U /	N/A	N/A	N/A	57.41	6	-2.26	N/A	N/A	0	0	0	100	3	N/A	1
0.30	0.48	C+ / 6.4	16.9	0.87	N/A	145.45	2,146	-5.66	0.02	149.2	0	99	0	1	19	88	5
2.86	0.20	B / 8.3	14.3	0.92	N/A	69.17	53	-4.28	0.01	25.1	0	99	0	1	10	44	5
0.31	0.25	B / 8.0	16.7	1.07	N/A	79.47	62	-3.50	-0.03	30.0	0	99	0	1	11	28	5
1.44	0.48	B- / 7.4	24.4	1.36	N/A	54.66	216	-4.79	-0.02	25.5	0	99	0	1	27	12	5
2.73	0.15	B / 8.0	15.6	1.02	N/A	81.74	6,546	-3.17	-0.02	49.3	0	99	0	1	6	51	5
2.52	0.20	B- / 7.6	15.9	1.02	N/A	67.56	16,907	-3.06	N/A	78.4	0	99	0	1	19	53	5
2.86	0.20	B / 8.2	15.8	1.02	N/A	75.32	14,536	-3.32	-0.01	20.7	0	99	0	1	21	48	5
3.45	0.20	B- / 7.3	20.7	1.28	N/A	87.41	15,997	-3.54	-0.02	47.1	0	99	0	1	21	38	5
3.29	0.25	B- / 7.0	21.1	1.30	N/A	99.32	3,915	-4.04	-0.02	74.2	0	99	0	1	37	42	5
4.11	0.25	B- / 7.5	20.4	1.26	N/A	78.03	4,260	-3.23	-0.01	25.2	0	99	0	1	32	34	5
2.78	0.20	B- / 7.9	15.8	1.03	N/A	87.43	3,661	-3.15	-0.01	49.2	0	99	0	1	6	50	5
2.36	0.25	B- / 7.6	16.1	1.04	N/A	55.16	363	-3.17	-0.01	78.2	0	99	0	1	20	51	5
3.01	0.25	B / 8.1	16.0	1.03	N/A	98.65	367	-3.35	-0.02	21.0	0	99	0	1	21	47	5
3.66	0.60	B- / 7.3	22.2	1.34	N/A	54.32	461	-3.68	-0.05	34.9	0	99	0	1	31	31	5
2.91	0.20	B- / 7.9	17.4	1.11	N/A	116.89	6,524	-3.24	-0.01	34.4	0	99	0	1	13	59	5
2.59	0.25	B- / 7.7	18.2	1.14	N/A	64.90	3,289	-3.24	-0.01	47.2	0	99	0	1	29	54	5
3.07	0.25	B- / 7.9	17.1	1.09	N/A	51.91	3,907	-3.22	N/A	24.7	0	99	0	1	27	62	5
2.48	0.20	B / 8.5	15.1	0.97	N/A	35.81	352	-3.07	N/A	N/A	0	99	0	1	18	50	4
6.88	0.15	B / 8.4	14.1	0.91	N/A	33.60	52	-3.27	-0.01	N/A	0	99	0	1	7	51	4
2.97	0.20	B / 8.0	15.4	0.98	N/A	32.31	80	-3.53	-0.03	N/A	0	99	0	1	24	40	4
2.83	0.20	B / 8.0	14.9	0.97	N/A	66.88	3,940	-3.27	-0.01	53.0	0	99	0	1	7	50	5
2.43	0.18	B- / 7.8	15.1	0.97	N/A	78.18	6,644	-3.12	-0.01	73.6	0	99	0	1	23	57	5
2.95	0.18	B / 8.1	16.0	1.03	N/A	68.59	4,831	-3.21	-0.02	20.4	0	99	0	1	22	44	5
2.98	0.11	B / 8.1	15.4	0.99	N/A	38.08	106	-2.39	0.03	N/A	0	99	0	1	12	43	5
1.98	0.50	B- / 7.1	21.7	0.94	N/A	48.02	227	0.27	0.04	N/A	0	99	0	1	8	79	5
2.83	0.25	B+ / 9.1	6.1	1.51	10.0	115.81	282	-0.44	0.55	N/A	0	0	100	0	6	30	N/A
3.97	0.11	B+ / 9.8	3.7	0.23	N/A	30.80	116	-0.71	0.01	N/A	0	21	78	1	12	74	5
0.43	0.48	C+ / 5.6	20.5	0.96	N/A	36.45	233	-0.38	0.14	329.7	0	99	0	1	8	85	5
1.50	0.72	C+ / 6.9	21.8	0.91	N/A	34.96	131	-2.06	0.09	N/A	0	98	0	2	14	77	4
1.20	0.60	C+ / 6.9	23.9	1.17	N/A	40.24	1,201	-2.34	0.12	47.8	0	99	0	1	7	42	5
2.84	0.48	B / 8.9	11.8	0.49	N/A	75.09	440	-1.94	0.02	25.6	0	99	0	1	4	90	5
4.39	0.48	B / 8.2	16.0	0.77	N/A	36.00	357	-0.81	N/A	21.0	0	99	0	1	16	70	5

* Denotes ETF Fund, N/A denotes number is not available

Fund Type	Fund Name	Ticker Symbol	Overall Investment Rating	PRICE Price As of 12/31/12	52 Week High	52 Week Low	PERFORMANCE Perform-ance Rating/Pts	3 Mo	6 Mo	1Yr/Pct	Annualized 3Yr/Pct	5Yr/Pct
	99 Pct = Best 0 Pct = Worst									% Total Return Through 12/31/12		
GL	*iShares S&P Glb Timber & Forestr	WOOD	C-	45.10	46.67	34.25	C / 4.5	16.13	23.38	22.86 / 79	6.83 / 35	--
GR	*iShares S&P Global 100	IOO	C-	63.96	66.12	55.23	C- / 4.2	8.13	16.09	17.86 / 62	5.71 / 32	0.97 / 22
EN	*iShares S&P Global Clean Energy	ICLN	E+	7.17	10.48	6.13	E / 0.4	15.56	12.73	-11.82 / 7	-27.66 / 3	--
GL	*iShares S&P Global Cons Disc	RXI	B	61.71	63.44	51.92	B / 7.6	10.72	17.26	24.68 / 83	13.64 / 67	7.39 / 57
EN	*iShares S&P Global Energy	IXC	D+	38.25	42.19	33.56	D+ / 2.5	1.41	9.82	5.33 / 24	4.63 / 28	1.03 / 22
FS	*iShares S&P Global Financials	IXG	C	45.66	47.66	35.12	C / 5.4	13.09	26.12	32.05 / 93	3.30 / 24	-5.08 / 8
HL	*iShares S&P Global Healthcare	IXJ	C+	64.50	67.34	56.06	C+ / 5.7	4.80	12.57	21.92 / 76	10.59 / 51	5.41 / 46
GL	*iShares S&P Global Industrials	EXI	C-	54.89	56.71	46.77	C / 4.5	10.19	16.75	16.08 / 53	8.93 / 43	2.30 / 28
GL	*iShares S&P Global Materials	MXI	D	62.45	66.52	52.50	D+ / 2.3	8.54	17.19	7.07 / 28	1.64 / 19	-0.14 / 19
EN	*iShares S&P Global Nuclear	NUCL	D	31.93	35.89	29.57	D- / 1.1	2.16	5.53	3.89 / 22	-4.92 / 9	--
GL	*iShares S&P Global Technology	IXN	D+	67.31	71.87	60.18	C- / 3.9	3.16	9.77	16.08 / 53	7.64 / 37	4.70 / 42
GL	*iShares S&P Global Telecom	IXP	C-	57.17	62.07	54.13	C- / 3.4	1.24	2.77	12.60 / 40	8.22 / 39	0.94 / 22
UT	*iShares S&P Global Utilities	JXI	D+	41.23	43.56	39.37	D- / 1.4	-0.67	0.91	5.86 / 26	-0.62 / 14	-5.05 / 9
GI	*iShares S&P Growth Allocation	AOR	C	33.97	34.53	31.26	C- / 3.6	3.59	7.46	11.64 / 38	7.71 / 38	--
IN	*iShares S&P GSCI Commodity-Index	GSG	D	32.79	36.72	28.30	D- / 1.5	-3.01	4.08	-1.79 / 12	1.15 / 18	-8.57 / 6
EM	*iShares S&P India Nifty 50	INDY	D	24.97	26.17	19.39	D / 1.9	1.79	13.69	17.19 / 59	-0.94 / 13	--
COI	*iShares S&P Intl Preferred Stock	IPFF	B	27.10	27.86	24.24	C+ / 6.1	3.76	10.11	12.72 / 40	--	--
FO	*iShares S&P Latin American 40	ILF	D	43.84	49.54	38.88	D / 2.0	7.19	9.79	5.14 / 24	1.10 / 17	3.24 / 33
GR	*iShares S&P Mid Cap 400 Growth	IJK	B-	114.41	119.74	100.32	B- / 7.3	8.44	13.11	17.85 / 62	15.38 / 74	9.27 / 67
GR	*iShares S&P Mid Cap 400 Value	IJJ	C+	88.14	91.57	75.65	C+ / 6.4	9.20	13.02	18.72 / 66	12.49 / 61	7.68 / 58
GI	*iShares S&P Moderate Allocation	AOM	C	31.73	32.11	29.93	C- / 3.0	2.60	5.50	8.65 / 32	6.08 / 33	--
EN	*iShares S&P NA Natural Resource	IGE	D+	38.16	42.73	33.05	D+ / 2.5	1.11	12.13	2.92 / 20	4.92 / 29	1.15 / 23
GR	*iShares S&P NA Tech-Multimedia N	IGN	D	28.14	31.75	22.71	D+ / 2.7	13.77	26.45	4.25 / 23	2.68 / 22	1.06 / 22
GR	*iShares S&P NA Technology Sector	IGM	C-	67.46	71.72	61.29	C / 4.5	4.01	10.40	15.30 / 49	9.65 / 45	6.72 / 53
IN	*iShares S&P NA Technology-Softwa	IGV	C-	63.03	66.73	55.83	C+ / 5.7	5.96	11.40	17.72 / 61	11.65 / 56	7.25 / 56
MUN	*iShares S&P Natl AMT-Free Muni B	MUB	C	110.64	114.52	107.25	C- / 3.6	1.16	3.18	4.56 / 28	6.23 / 45	5.26 / 60
MUS	*iShares S&P NY AMT-Free Muni Bon	NYF	C	111.52	116.35	108.00	C- / 3.6	0.84	2.52	5.65 / 32	6.14 / 45	5.29 / 60
MUN	*iShares S&P Sh Tm Ntl AMT-Fr Mun	SUB	C-	106.23	107.97	105.26	D / 1.8	0.12	0.37	0.04 / 14	1.64 / 21	--
GR	*iShares S&P Small Cap 600 Growth	IJT	C+	84.04	87.45	74.72	B- / 7.0	7.46	9.39	16.37 / 54	15.69 / 76	8.48 / 62
GR	*iShares S&P Small Cap 600 Value	IJS	C+	80.91	83.89	68.42	C+ / 6.4	7.87	11.99	16.69 / 56	13.40 / 66	7.94 / 59
GI	*iShares S&P Target Date 2010 Ind	TZD	C	32.96	33.35	31.12	C- / 3.2	2.48	5.51	9.59 / 34	7.04 / 36	--
GI	*iShares S&P Target Date 2015 Ind	TZE	C	34.13	34.82	31.58	C- / 3.5	3.19	7.19	10.43 / 35	7.75 / 38	--
GI	*iShares S&P Target Date 2020 Ind	TZG	C	34.99	35.63	31.92	C- / 3.7	3.87	8.39	11.96 / 39	7.89 / 38	--
GI	*iShares S&P Target Date 2025 Ind	TZI	C	35.33	36.23	32.15	C- / 3.9	4.32	9.19	12.98 / 41	8.39 / 40	--
GI	*iShares S&P Target Date 2030 Ind	TZL	C	35.78	36.79	32.33	C- / 4.2	4.64	10.66	14.18 / 45	8.61 / 41	--
GI	*iShares S&P Target Date 2035 Ind	TZO	C	35.80	36.82	32.27	C / 4.4	5.24	10.42	15.14 / 48	8.95 / 43	--
GI	*iShares S&P Target Date 2040 Ind	TZV	C	36.30	37.25	32.15	C / 4.5	5.68	10.52	15.79 / 51	9.02 / 43	--
GL	*iShares S&P Target Date 2045 Ind	TZW	B+	28.05	28.89	24.81	B / 7.9	5.20	13.44	15.80 / 51	--	--
GL	*iShares S&P Target Date 2050 Ind	TZY	B+	27.95	32.85	24.85	B / 8.0	4.67	13.18	16.60 / 55	--	--
GI	*iShares S&P Target Date Ret Inco	TGR	C	31.45	31.94	30.27	D+ / 2.9	1.81	3.84	7.60 / 29	6.50 / 34	--
IN	*iShares S&P USPreferred Stock	PFF	C	39.62	40.26	37.23	C- / 4.0	2.11	6.51	15.27 / 49	9.10 / 43	6.19 / 50
GL	*iShares S&P/Citigroup 1-3 Year I	ISHG	D+	97.02	101.13	90.01	D- / 1.4	0.05	5.60	1.15 / 16	-0.29 / 14	--
GL	*iShares S&P/Citigroup Intl Treas	IGOV	C-	102.93	105.80	96.30	D / 2.2	0.47	6.20	8.55 / 31	2.33 / 21	--
FO	*iShares S&P/Topix 150	ITF	D+	42.45	44.03	37.04	D / 2.2	14.19	11.79	12.71 / 40	0.13 / 15	-2.87 / 12
PM	*iShares Silver Trust	SLV	C-	29.37	36.44	25.34	C+ / 6.3	-9.15	11.50	2.29 / 19	17.77 / 82	12.96 / 80
COI	*iShares Utilities Sector Bond	AMPS	U	51.60	N/A	N/A	U /	-2.46	-0.77	--	--	--
EN	*JPMorgan Alerian MLP Idx ETN	AMJ	C	38.46	41.68	34.98	B- / 7.0	1.45	5.85	10.78 / 36	17.74 / 82	--
GR	*JPMorgan Dbl Short 10 Year Trs E	DSXJ	E-	28.00	43.49	27.10	E- / 0.2	--	-29.56	-34.50 / 3	--	--
GR	*Madrona Domestic ETF	FWDD	B+	27.80	40.89	23.49	B+ / 8.5	7.41	14.68	17.09 / 59	--	--
GL	*Madrona Global Bond ETF	FWDB	C	26.55	30.22	25.20	C- / 3.1	1.07	3.90	7.64 / 29	--	--
FO	*Madrona International ETF	FWDI	B+	24.03	26.00	19.17	A / 9.5	11.32	21.78	19.96 / 71	--	--
GL	*Market Vector RVE Hard Asst Prd	HAP	D+	35.85	38.43	30.87	D+ / 2.5	4.94	13.16	7.09 / 28	3.66 / 25	--

* Denotes ETF Fund, N/A denotes number is not available

Incl. in Returns		RISK				NET ASSETS		VALUATION			ASSET					FUND MANAGER	
			3 Year		Avg	NAV as		Premium / Discount		Wtd					Portfolio	Manager	Manager
Dividend Yield %	Expense Ratio	Risk Rating/ Pts	Standard Deviation	Beta	Dura-tion	of 12/31/12	Total $(Mil)	As of 12/31/12	1 Year Average	Avg P/E	Cash %	Stocks %	Bonds %	Other %	Turnover Ratio	Quality Pct	Tenure (Years)
0.09	0.48	B- / 7.1	20.4	0.89	N/A	46.40	227	-2.80	0.13	22.2	0	99	0	1	21	72	5
4.43	0.40	B- / 7.9	18.3	1.13	N/A	65.91	1,054	-2.96	0.01	22.1	0	99	0	1	4	18	5
1.55	0.48	C / 4.4	35.7	1.12	N/A	7.63	26	-6.03	-0.01	25.0	0	99	0	1	58	1	5
1.43	0.48	B- / 7.8	18.2	0.83	N/A	63.28	163	-2.48	0.10	50.9	0	99	0	1	9	90	5
2.45	0.48	B- / 7.4	23.0	0.99	N/A	39.36	991	-2.82	-0.03	16.9	0	99	0	1	3	26	5
1.83	0.48	B- / 7.0	23.7	1.11	N/A	47.38	220	-3.63	0.01	21.1	0	99	0	1	6	22	5
1.62	0.48	B / 8.3	12.3	0.63	N/A	67.13	573	-3.92	-0.01	46.8	0	99	0	1	6	72	5
2.03	0.48	B- / 7.5	20.4	0.94	N/A	56.35	153	-2.59	-0.04	25.1	0	99	0	1	6	81	5
1.95	0.48	C+ / 6.6	26.4	1.19	N/A	63.04	486	-0.94	0.12	58.1	0	99	0	1	9	32	5
2.20	0.48	C+ / 6.8	18.7	0.67	N/A	32.80	9	-2.65	-0.44	43.0	0	99	0	1	50	11	5
1.47	0.48	C+ / 6.7	19.2	0.84	N/A	68.83	484	-2.21	-0.03	122.7	0	99	0	1	6	76	5
3.99	0.48	B / 8.6	14.0	0.59	N/A	58.76	475	-2.71	0.15	22.3	0	99	0	1	13	77	5
3.56	0.48	B / 8.4	12.8	0.91	N/A	41.32	235	-0.22	0.16	19.7	0	99	0	1	6	15	5
2.96	0.11	B / 8.8	9.7	0.63	N/A	34.52	153	-1.59	0.04	N/A	0	57	42	1	5	61	5
0.00	0.80	B- / 7.3	21.6	1.13	N/A	33.00	1,168	-0.64	-0.32	N/A	0	100	0	0	N/A	13	7
0.37	0.92	C+ / 6.0	29.6	1.13	N/A	24.91	358	0.24	0.34	N/A	0	99	0	1	28	21	4
3.53	N/A	B+ / 9.1	N/A	N/A	N/A	27.11	123	-0.04	0.31	N/A	0	0	0	100	N/A	72	2
1.00	0.50	C+ / 6.9	24.9	1.08	N/A	45.12	1,603	-2.84	-0.02	52.8	0	99	0	1	22	25	5
1.76	0.25	B- / 7.7	18.3	1.12	N/A	118.89	3,117	-3.77	-0.01	49.3	0	99	0	1	35	67	5
2.88	0.25	B- / 7.6	18.5	1.16	N/A	91.34	2,254	-3.50	-0.01	28.7	0	99	0	1	33	47	5
3.21	0.11	B+ / 9.3	6.3	0.40	N/A	32.08	146	-1.09	0.02	N/A	0	32	67	1	9	66	5
2.34	0.48	B- / 7.1	24.0	1.02	N/A	39.15	1,745	-2.53	N/A	30.1	0	99	0	1	8	26	5
6.35	0.48	C+ / 6.6	26.6	1.50	N/A	29.01	254	-3.00	-0.01	34.6	0	99	0	1	33	10	5
1.60	0.48	B- / 7.3	19.2	1.18	N/A	69.77	494	-3.31	-0.01	93.8	0	99	0	1	9	25	5
0.42	0.48	C+ / 5.9	20.2	1.16	N/A	65.50	641	-3.77	0.01	185.0	0	99	0	1	10	35	5
2.68	0.25	B+ / 9.4	5.4	1.38	9.6	111.36	3,476	-0.65	0.65	N/A	0	0	98	2	5	29	3
2.78	0.25	B+ / 9.4	5.1	1.14	10.9	111.97	128	-0.40	0.61	N/A	0	0	98	2	6	39	3
0.79	0.25	B+ / 9.9	1.2	0.24	N/A	106.33	621	-0.09	0.26	N/A	2	0	96	2	20	52	3
2.75	0.25	B- / 7.4	18.6	1.13	N/A	87.20	1,606	-3.62	-0.01	63.4	0	99	0	1	43	68	5
3.04	0.25	B- / 7.6	20.5	1.26	N/A	83.16	1,904	-2.71	N/A	36.1	0	99	0	1	30	46	5
4.94	0.11	B+ / 9.3	7.6	0.41	N/A	33.22	5	-0.78	-0.05	N/A	0	43	55	2	20	70	5
3.27	0.11	B / 8.9	9.7	0.59	N/A	34.71	15	-1.67	-0.02	N/A	0	54	44	2	23	61	5
3.23	0.11	B / 8.8	10.4	0.66	N/A	35.55	26	-1.58	0.08	N/A	0	64	34	2	20	60	5
3.21	0.11	B / 8.6	12.3	0.78	N/A	36.15	20	-2.27	0.03	N/A	0	72	26	2	26	48	5
3.12	0.11	B / 8.5	12.9	0.77	N/A	36.59	18	-2.21	0.04	N/A	0	78	20	2	21	42	5
3.11	0.11	B / 8.2	14.6	0.91	N/A	36.75	13	-2.59	0.12	N/A	0	83	15	2	21	41	5
3.05	0.11	B / 8.0	15.7	0.98	N/A	37.16	22	-2.31	0.03	N/A	0	86	12	2	19	36	5
3.00	0.11	B / 8.6	N/A	N/A	N/A	28.80	4	-2.60	0.02	N/A	0	0	0	100	17	65	2
2.90	0.11	B / 8.5	N/A	N/A	N/A	28.90	6	-3.29	0.02	N/A	0	0	0	100	15	55	2
4.30	0.11	B+ / 9.6	4.8	0.28	N/A	31.90	8	-1.41	0.07	N/A	0	30	67	3	18	73	5
7.87	0.48	B / 8.9	8.7	0.37	N/A	40.18	10,747	-1.39	0.07	95.6	2	0	0	98	16	81	5
6.29	0.35	B / 8.5	9.6	1.07	N/A	97.20	204	-0.19	0.48	N/A	2	0	95	3	57	25	3
7.54	0.35	B / 8.8	9.0	1.05	N/A	102.62	365	0.30	0.17	N/A	1	0	96	3	35	41	3
2.34	0.50	B- / 7.4	16.6	0.63	N/A	42.49	72	-0.09	-0.44	N/A	0	99	0	1	4	48	5
0.00	0.50	C / 4.9	44.0	1.72	N/A	29.67	9,707	-1.01	0.51	N/A	0	0	0	100	N/A	22	7
5.15	0.30	U /	N/A	N/A	N/A	51.30	10	0.58	N/A	N/A	0	0	0	100	3	N/A	1
6.97	N/A	C / 5.1	13.4	0.45	N/A	41.32	4,869	-6.92	0.13	N/A	0	0	0	100	N/A	91	4
0.00	N/A	D+ / 2.7	N/A	N/A	N/A	39.00	N/A	-28.21	-3.51	N/A	0	0	0	100	N/A	1	N/A
5.46	1.25	B- / 7.9	N/A	N/A	N/A	28.24	15	-1.56	-0.19	N/A	1	97	0	2	40	48	2
5.31	0.95	B+ / 9.8	N/A	N/A	N/A	26.54	23	0.04	0.07	N/A	6	0	89	5	12	86	2
5.23	1.25	C+ / 6.7	N/A	N/A	N/A	24.60	15	-2.32	-0.23	N/A	1	98	0	1	110	38	2
5.38	0.52	B- / 7.0	23.5	1.06	N/A	36.93	122	-2.92	-0.12	42.6	0	99	0	1	4	47	5

Denotes ETF Fund, N/A denotes number is not available

Fund Type	Fund Name	Ticker Symbol	Overall Investment Rating	PRICE Price As of 12/31/12	52 Week High	52 Week Low	PERFORMANCE Perform-ance Rating/Pts	3 Mo	6 Mo	1Yr/Pct	Annualized 3Yr/Pct	Annualized 5Yr/Pct
FO	*Market Vectors Africa Index ETF	AFK	C-	31.35	32.19	26.65	C- / 3.8	2.86	16.09	22.68 / 78	4.71 / 29	--
GL	*Market Vectors Agribusiness ETF	MOO	C-	52.76	55.00	43.43	C- / 3.6	8.76	13.42	11.78 / 38	7.43 / 37	2.90 / 31
IN	*Market Vectors Bank and Brokerag	RKH	B	45.73	83.12	34.14	A+ / 9.8	15.52	31.39	31.01 / 92	--	--
IN	*Market Vectors Biotech ETF	BBH	B	53.50	57.42	39.89	A+ / 9.8	5.59	18.60	42.75 / 98	--	--
FO	*Market Vectors Brazil Small-Cap	BRF	D	42.62	47.44	33.99	D+ / 2.5	5.05	22.66	10.45 / 35	2.17 / 20	--
MUN	*Market Vectors CEF Muni Inc ETF	XMPT	A+	28.30	30.26	25.88	B+ / 8.6	3.21	5.99	15.31 / 81	--	--
FO	*Market Vectors China ETF	PEK	C	36.50	39.62	29.00	C+ / 6.8	9.66	13.61	9.00 / 32	--	--
FO	*Market Vectors Chinese RMB USD E	CNY	C-	41.62	42.54	40.15	D / 1.7	0.78	1.77	1.84 / 18	1.03 / 17	--
EN	*Market Vectors Coal ETF	KOL	E+	25.14	37.40	21.49	E+ / 0.7	3.81	9.52	-22.64 / 4	-12.07 / 6	--
GL	*Market Vectors Colombia ETF	COLX	B+	19.81	20.42	17.20	B+ / 8.9	11.99	13.15	18.42 / 65	--	--
FO	*Market Vectors Double Long Euro	URR	D-	27.00	30.13	19.08	E+ / 0.8	0.39	--	1.32 / 17	-9.01 / 7	--
FO	*Market Vectors Double Shrt Euro	DRR	D-	43.15	52.25	41.63	D- / 1.1	-6.27	-16.89	-11.69 / 7	0.51 / 16	--
EM	*Market Vectors Egypt Index ETF	EGPT	C+	13.08	15.97	10.27	A+ / 9.6	-7.22	13.26	39.59 / 97	--	--
GL	*Market Vectors EM Lcl Curr Bnd E	EMLC	B	27.45	27.53	24.07	B- / 7.1	4.41	8.93	16.43 / 54	--	--
EM	*Market Vectors Emg Mkts Hi Yld B	HYEM	U	26.97	N/A	N/A	U /	5.44	10.45	--	--	--
IN	*Market Vectors Environment Svc E	EVX	C-	50.97	53.59	44.47	C- / 3.6	8.38	11.83	11.69 / 38	7.55 / 37	3.28 / 34
GEI	*Market Vectors FA Hi Yld Bd ETF	ANGL	U	26.80	N/A	N/A	U /	5.41	11.35	--	--	--
GL	*Market Vectors Gaming ETF	BJK	B	35.45	38.14	29.31	B+ / 8.5	16.74	26.82	26.54 / 86	17.62 / 81	--
FO	*Market Vectors Germany SmallCap	GERJ	B	22.91	24.55	17.98	A+ / 9.7	11.94	27.53	30.79 / 92	--	--
EN	*Market Vectors Global Alt Enrgy	GEX	E+	11.04	13.11	9.14	E+ / 0.6	17.47	21.45	3.66 / 22	-21.16 / 4	-22.69 / 3
PM	*Market Vectors Gold Miners ETF	GDX	D-	46.39	57.94	39.08	D- / 1.1	-11.24	8.37	-15.17 / 6	-0.80 / 13	-0.82 / 17
FO	*Market Vectors Gulf States Idx E	MES	C-	20.25	21.51	18.73	C- / 3.6	6.23	10.07	14.48 / 47	6.36 / 34	--
MUH	*Market Vectors Hi-Yld Mun Idx ET	HYD	B	32.84	33.57	30.32	C+ / 6.1	1.76	4.49	14.47 / 77	8.70 / 66	--
FO	*Market Vectors India Small-Cap E	SCIF	D	11.12	14.07	8.98	C / 4.9	4.65	9.35	9.08 / 33	--	--
FO	*Market Vectors Indian Rupee USD	INR	D	36.75	39.89	34.01	D- / 1.2	-3.04	--	1.72 / 17	-1.73 / 12	--
FO	*Market Vectors Indonesia Idx ETF	IDX	D-	28.64	30.90	24.20	C- / 3.1	-1.62	3.62	-1.76 / 12	9.41 / 45	--
FO	*Market Vectors Indonesia SC ETF	IDXJ	U	14.50	N/A	N/A	U /	1.64	-8.94	--	--	--
MUN	*Market Vectors Interm Muni Idx E	ITM	C+	23.64	24.50	22.48	C- / 4.0	0.84	2.69	5.23 / 30	7.01 / 52	5.85 / 65
GL	*Market Vectors Intl Hi Yld Bond	IHY	U	27.14	N/A	N/A	U /	7.11	17.48	--	--	--
COI	*Market Vectors Invest Grade FR E	FLTR	C	24.72	25.09	22.97	C- / 3.1	1.05	4.02	8.14 / 31	--	--
PM	*Market Vectors Junior Gold Mnrs	GDXJ	E+	19.80	30.55	17.38	E+ / 0.9	-12.68	13.27	-20.49 / 5	-4.17 / 10	--
FO	*Market Vectors Lat Am SC Index E	LATM	B-	24.41	27.15	20.40	B+ / 8.9	5.97	23.44	15.21 / 49	--	--
GEI	*Market Vectors LatAm Aggrgte Bd	BONO	B	26.15	26.63	23.71	C+ / 6.5	4.13	7.58	15.41 / 50	--	--
MUN	*Market Vectors Long Muni Index E	MLN	C+	20.12	20.93	19.03	C / 4.9	1.12	3.53	8.34 / 41	8.14 / 61	--
IN	*Market Vectors Mstr Wide Moat Rs	MOAT	U	22.21	N/A	N/A	U /	8.62	15.73	--	--	--
MTG	*Market Vectors Mtge REIT Income	MORT	A+	25.18	28.43	23.54	A- / 9.1	5.58	9.16	26.96 / 87	--	--
IN	*Market Vectors Oil Services ETF	OIH	D-	38.63	130.98	32.54	C / 4.5	3.90	13.41	5.73 / 25	--	--
IN	*Market Vectors Pharmaceutical ET	PPH	B-	39.73	73.80	36.05	B / 7.9	4.83	10.64	18.04 / 62	--	--
EM	*Market Vectors Poland ETF	PLND	D-	22.47	23.45	16.00	D+ / 2.9	11.50	29.01	35.16 / 95	-1.04 / 13	--
MUN	*Market Vectors Pre-Refnded Muni	PRB	C-	25.36	25.70	25.10	D / 1.9	0.07	0.65	1.58 / 19	1.81 / 22	--
COI	*Market Vectors Prfrd Secs ex Fin	PFXF	U	20.49	N/A	N/A	U /	2.11	--	--	--	--
EM	*Market Vectors Renminbi Bond ETF	CHLC	C-	25.53	26.15	24.82	D- / 1.5	0.34	-0.66	1.27 / 17	--	--
IN	*Market Vectors Retail ETF	RTH	C+	43.83	119.17	38.07	B- / 7.4	1.75	6.95	20.32 / 71	--	--
FO	*Market Vectors Russia ETF	RSX	D-	29.90	33.74	23.12	D / 1.6	6.21	15.81	9.61 / 34	-2.52 / 11	-7.46 / 6
FO	*Market Vectors Russia SmallCap E	RSXJ	E+	15.24	19.00	13.29	D- / 1.3	0.45	7.67	-6.32 / 10	--	--
IN	*Market Vectors Semiconductor ETF	SMH	U	32.33	N/A	N/A	U /	13.53	13.82	--	--	--
MUN	*Market Vectors Short Muni Index	SMB	C-	17.68	25.54	17.51	D / 2.2	0.02	0.80	1.85 / 20	2.79 / 27	--
EN	*Market Vectors Solar Energy ETF	KWT	E	35.83	85.20	27.46	E / 0.3	33.15	25.08	-29.44 / 3	-39.94 / 1	--
IN	*Market Vectors Steel Index ETF	SLX	D-	48.69	58.54	40.18	D- / 1.0	13.42	14.01	-2.75 / 12	-7.12 / 8	-5.20 / 8
GL	*Market Vectors Uranium+Nuc Engy	NLR	D-	13.76	17.67	12.96	E+ / 0.8	1.87	5.48	-4.67 / 11	-9.64 / 7	-10.83 / 5
FO	*Market Vectors Vietnam ETF	VNM	D-	18.00	21.28	15.35	D- / 1.4	24.46	11.68	33.41 / 94	-7.93 / 8	--
GR	*Materials Select Sector SPDR	XLB	C-	37.54	39.18	32.59	C- / 3.6	8.20	13.88	10.61 / 36	7.71 / 37	3.57 / 35

99 Pct = Best
0 Pct = Worst

Incl. in Returns Dividend Yield %	Expense Ratio	RISK Risk Rating/ Pts	3 Year Standard Deviation	Beta	Avg Dura-tion	NET ASSETS NAV as of 12/31/12	Total $(Mil)	VALUATION Premium/Discount As of 12/31/12	1 Year Average	Wtd Avg P/E	ASSET Cash %	Stocks %	Bonds %	Other %	Portfolio Turnover Ratio	FUND MANAGER Manager Quality Pct	Manager Tenure (Years)
3.39	0.78	B- / 7.6	21.2	0.87	N/A	31.09	85	0.84	0.12	9.5	0	99	0	1	11	70	5
1.84	0.54	B- / 7.2	23.9	1.01	N/A	54.82	5,667	-3.76	-0.07	51.2	0	99	0	1	6	74	6
1.88	0.35	C+ / 6.0	N/A	N/A	N/A	47.96	33	-4.65	0.01	N/A	0	0	0	100	1	62	2
0.03	0.35	C+ / 6.1	N/A	N/A	N/A	56.75	147	-5.73	0.05	N/A	0	0	0	100	1	98	2
1.45	0.59	C / 5.4	33.0	1.15	N/A	42.29	553	0.78	-0.11	N/A	0	92	0	8	45	32	4
6.11	0.40	B+ / 9.2	N/A	N/A	N/A	29.66	16	-4.59	0.11	N/A	0	0	0	100	3	27	2
0.00	0.72	C+ / 6.2	N/A	N/A	N/A	32.55	33	12.14	5.64	N/A	100	0	0	0	N/A	86	3
0.00	0.55	B+ / 9.9	2.7	0.07	N/A	41.48	27	0.34	-0.07	N/A	0	0	0	100	N/A	59	5
1.69	0.59	C / 4.9	38.3	1.40	N/A	25.40	235	-1.02	-0.05	19.2	0	100	0	0	12	5	5
1.68	0.75	B- / 7.3	N/A	N/A	N/A	20.10	3	-1.44	0.80	N/A	0	97	0	3	18	92	2
0.00	0.65	C+ / 6.4	24.7	1.02	N/A	27.48	5	-1.75	-0.93	N/A	0	0	0	100	N/A	11	5
0.00	0.65	C+ / 6.3	25.6	-1.06	N/A	42.00	28	2.74	-0.02	N/A	0	0	0	100	N/A	80	5
7.13	0.94	C- / 4.2	N/A	N/A	N/A	13.11	36	-0.23	-0.56	N/A	0	100	0	0	27	95	3
3.98	0.47	B / 8.4	N/A	N/A	N/A	27.29	927	0.59	0.53	N/A	0	0	0	100	21	95	3
5.56	N/A	U /	N/A	N/A	N/A	27.07	21	-0.37	N/A	N/A	0	0	0	100	N/A	N/A	1
1.55	0.55	B- / 7.8	16.1	0.91	N/A	52.65	21	-3.19	-0.16	55.9	0	99	0	1	1	34	7
6.55	N/A	U /	N/A	N/A	N/A	27.18	11	-1.40	N/A	N/A	0	0	0	100	N/A	N/A	1
3.90	0.65	B- / 7.2	25.8	1.08	N/A	37.82	61	-6.27	-0.33	40.8	0	99	0	1	19	93	5
2.68	0.55	C+ / 6.0	N/A	N/A	N/A	23.44	5	-2.26	0.01	N/A	0	100	0	0	19	95	2
1.88	0.62	C / 4.7	28.8	0.95	N/A	11.65	46	-5.24	-0.46	43.5	0	99	0	1	13	3	6
1.00	0.52	C / 5.1	28.6	1.18	N/A	45.36	9,406	2.27	-0.03	145.2	0	100	0	0	5	8	7
2.99	0.98	B- / 7.9	16.9	0.52	N/A	21.46	10	-5.64	-1.81	N/A	0	100	0	0	9	66	5
5.30	0.35	B+ / 9.1	5.3	1.16	N/A	33.06	1,044	-0.67	0.21	N/A	1	0	98	1	18	61	5
0.12	0.85	C- / 3.3	N/A	N/A	N/A	11.21	81	-0.80	0.37	N/A	0	100	0	0	26	16	3
0.00	0.55	B / 8.2	11.6	0.41	N/A	37.32	7	-1.53	-0.77	N/A	0	0	0	100	N/A	31	5
1.78	0.59	C / 4.5	27.4	0.98	N/A	28.43	405	0.74	-0.42	N/A	0	100	0	0	11	88	4
2.46	N/A	U /	N/A	N/A	N/A	15.50	2	-6.45	N/A	N/A	0	94	0	6	N/A	N/A	1
2.43	0.24	B+ / 9.4	5.4	1.38	6.6	23.74	690	-0.42	0.17	N/A	1	0	98	1	7	35	6
5.79	N/A	U /	N/A	N/A	N/A	27.56	19	-1.52	N/A	N/A	0	0	0	100	N/A	N/A	1
0.83	0.19	B+ / 9.4	N/A	N/A	N/A	24.77	7	-0.20	-1.04	N/A	0	0	0	100	14	71	2
3.79	0.55	C- / 4.1	39.2	1.54	N/A	20.19	2,537	-1.93	0.17	N/A	0	99	0	1	14	4	4
4.47	0.63	C+ / 5.9	N/A	N/A	N/A	25.36	14	-3.75	-0.30	N/A	0	90	0	10	18	21	2
4.13	0.49	B / 8.9	N/A	N/A	N/A	25.88	8	1.04	0.49	N/A	0	0	0	100	11	97	2
3.83	0.24	B+/ 9.0	6.9	1.76	9.3	20.34	120	-1.08	0.11	N/A	1	0	98	1	22	29	5
0.92	N/A	U /	N/A	N/A	N/A	23.07	115	-3.73	N/A	N/A	0	0	0	100	N/A	N/A	1
2.39	0.40	B / 8.8	N/A	N/A	N/A	27.01	79	-6.78	0.12	N/A	0	0	0	100	8	80	2
1.04	0.35	D / 1.9	N/A	N/A	N/A	40.67	1,283	-5.02	-0.02	N/A	0	0	0	100	2	6	2
3.39	0.35	B- / 7.1	N/A	N/A	N/A	41.64	164	-4.59	N/A	N/A	0	0	0	100	N/A	65	2
3.65	0.60	C / 4.8	36.4	1.45	N/A	22.39	32	0.36	0.16	N/A	0	99	0	1	6	18	4
4.49	0.24	B+ / 9.7	2.5	0.56	N/A	25.47	36	-0.43	-0.11	N/A	1	0	98	1	40	38	5
3.55	N/A	U /	N/A	N/A	N/A	20.72	100	-1.11	N/A	N/A	0	0	0	100	N/A	N/A	1
3.29	0.39	B+ / 9.7	N/A	N/A	N/A	26.13	5	-2.30	0.15	N/A	0	0	0	100	11	63	2
4.93	0.35	C+ / 6.3	N/A	N/A	N/A	44.55	34	-1.62	0.02	N/A	0	0	0	100	N/A	88	2
2.44	0.62	C / 5.0	35.1	1.47	N/A	29.89	1,634	0.03	0.14	N/A	0	100	0	0	29	21	6
2.02	0.67	C / 4.8	N/A	N/A	N/A	15.12	8	0.79	0.35	N/A	0	99	0	1	30	3	2
2.36	0.35	U /	N/A	N/A	N/A	33.87	294	-4.55	N/A	N/A	0	0	0	100	N/A	N/A	2
4.45	0.20	B+ / 9.7	2.4	0.55	4.2	17.74	177	-0.34	0.19	N/A	0	0	100	0	23	43	5
3.68	0.65	C- / 3.6	54.5	1.59	N/A	44.32	11	-19.16	0.32	2.4	0	99	0	1	23	N/A	5
2.21	0.55	C+ / 5.9	35.4	1.92	N/A	49.11	154	-0.86	-0.05	10.5	0	100	0	0	4	4	7
4.59	0.60	C+ / 5.7	26.0	1.06	N/A	14.26	79	-3.51	-0.01	12.7	0	99	0	1	29	10	6
2.04	0.73	C / 4.9	29.0	0.72	N/A	19.23	287	-6.40	0.89	N/A	3	96	0	1	23	10	4
3.51	0.18	B- / 7.1	23.5	1.39	N/A	39.00	2,446	-3.74	N/A	41.6	0	100	0	0	12	17	15

Denotes ETF Fund, N/A denotes number is not available

Fund Type	Fund Name	Ticker Symbol	Overall Investment Rating	PRICE Price As of 12/31/12	52 Week High	52 Week Low	PERFORMANCE Perform-ance Rating/Pts	3 Mo	6 Mo	1Yr/Pct	Annualized 3Yr/Pct	5Yr/Pct
GI	*Meidell Tactical Advantage ETF	MATH	C+	25.93	27.45	24.48	C- / 4.0	6.10	6.91	7.08 / 28	--	--
EN	*Mk Vectors Unconv O&G ETF	FRAK	U	22.76	N/A	N/A	U /	-1.32	11.88	--	--	--
GR	*Morgan Stanley Technology ETF	MTK	C-	68.37	71.93	60.10	C / 5.0	8.08	15.82	18.18 / 63	8.16 / 39	6.16 / 50
GR	*Mrkt Vectors Rare Earth/Str Met	REMX	E+	13.16	18.63	11.79	E+ / 0.9	7.35	3.43	-15.70 / 6	--	--
GR	*Nuveen Diversified Commodity	CFD	D	19.97	24.98	19.16	D / 1.7	-3.26	1.70	2.93 / 20	--	--
FO	*Pax MSCI EAFE ESG Index ETF	EAPS	B+	24.51	25.70	19.59	A- / 9.1	9.84	17.51	18.41 / 65	--	--
GR	*Pax MSCI North America ESG Idx E	NASI	C+	29.62	31.23	27.01	C+ / 6.1	4.27	9.38	13.02 / 41	--	--
COH	*Peritus High Yield ETF	HYLD	B	50.07	50.74	48.00	C+ / 6.3	3.83	7.66	15.04 / 48	--	--
COI	*PIMCO 0-5 Year Hi Yield Corp Bd	HYS	B-	103.43	104.58	97.72	C / 5.0	3.35	6.83	11.95 / 38	--	--
USA	*PIMCO 1-3 Year US Treasury Idx E	TUZ	C-	50.85	51.13	50.85	D / 1.6	0.17	0.19	0.28 / 14	1.20 / 18	--
USA	*PIMCO 1-5 Year US TIPS Index ETF	STPZ	C-	54.06	54.45	53.29	D / 2.1	0.22	1.16	2.01 / 18	3.32 / 24	--
USA	*PIMCO 15 Plus Year US TIPS Idx E	LTPZ	C+	71.65	74.36	64.29	C / 5.3	-0.31	0.23	9.54 / 34	14.46 / 71	--
USA	*PIMCO 25+ Year Zero Coupon US Tr	ZROZ	C+	109.12	126.85	94.50	C+ / 6.5	-4.57	-10.56	0.81 / 15	20.20 / 89	--
USA	*PIMCO 3-7 Year US Treasury Idx E	FIVZ	C-	81.36	82.61	80.11	D+ / 2.3	-0.22	-0.10	1.53 / 17	4.99 / 29	--
USA	*PIMCO 7-15 Year US Treasury Idx	TENZ	C	86.82	89.46	82.89	C- / 3.0	-1.18	-1.54	2.51 / 19	8.64 / 41	--
GL	*PIMCO Australia Bond Index ETF	AUD	C	104.36	106.67	95.41	C- / 3.5	2.09	4.56	8.97 / 32	--	--
USA	*PIMCO Broad US TIPS Index ETF	TIPZ	C	61.20	62.32	58.25	C- / 3.1	-0.16	0.93	5.62 / 25	8.52 / 41	--
USA	*PIMCO Broad US Treasury Index ET	TRSY	C-	106.66	111.08	102.18	D- / 1.4	-1.52	--	1.64 / 17	--	--
USA	*PIMCO Build America Bond ETF	BABZ	C-	55.00	59.17	53.37	D+ / 2.8	0.73	0.53	8.46 / 31	--	--
GL	*PIMCO Canada Bond Index ETF	CAD	C-	105.58	108.90	101.10	D+ / 2.4	-0.58	2.77	5.64 / 25	--	--
COI	*PIMCO Enhanced Short Maturity ET	MINT	C-	101.48	101.60	100.24	D / 1.7	0.27	0.81	2.31 / 19	1.49 / 18	--
GL	*PIMCO Germany Bond Index ETF	BUND	C	102.50	102.82	93.00	C- / 3.0	3.52	--	8.40 / 31	--	--
GL	*PIMCO Global Adv Infl-Link Bond	ILB	U	54.35	N/A	N/A	U /	1.76	8.06	--	--	--
MUN	*PIMCO Intermediate Municipal Bd	MUNI	C	54.37	56.08	52.90	C- / 3.3	0.79	2.12	4.22 / 27	5.52 / 40	--
MUN	*PIMCO Short Term Muncipal Bond E	SMMU	C-	50.42	54.80	50.13	D- / 1.5	-0.23	0.02	0.68 / 16	--	--
COI	*PIMCO Total Return Exchange-Trad	BOND	U	109.05	N/A	N/A	U /	1.28	4.29	--	--	--
USA	*PowerShares 1-30 Laddered Treasu	PLW	C	32.60	34.13	30.62	C- / 3.2	-1.33	-2.96	2.02 / 18	9.61 / 45	7.06 / 55
GI	*PowerShares Act US Real Estate	PSR	B	56.83	59.48	50.95	B / 7.7	5.39	2.16	17.47 / 60	19.25 / 87	--
GI	*PowerShares Active Low Dur Fd	PLK	C-	25.25	25.69	25.20	D / 1.6	0.04	-0.04	0.20 / 14	1.03 / 17	--
GR	*PowerShares Active Mega-Cap Fd	PMA	C	28.84	30.42	26.18	C / 4.7	2.26	8.99	13.66 / 44	10.96 / 53	--
IN	*PowerShares Aerospace & Defense	PPA	C	20.94	21.66	17.89	C / 5.0	8.90	16.05	16.71 / 56	8.17 / 39	2.99 / 32
USA	*PowerShares Build America Bond	BAB	C+	30.24	30.94	28.40	C / 4.6	1.15	1.94	9.09 / 33	12.68 / 62	--
IN	*PowerShares Buyback Achievers	PKW	B-	29.80	30.85	26.74	C+ / 6.3	4.18	10.18	15.47 / 50	14.44 / 70	8.11 / 60
IN	*PowerShares CEF Inc Composite Po	PCEF	B	25.14	26.12	23.50	C+ / 6.7	2.68	8.26	16.55 / 55	--	--
GL	*PowerShares Chinese YDS Bd	DSUM	C+	24.79	25.50	23.64	C- / 3.8	3.57	6.33	8.09 / 30	--	--
IN	*PowerShares Cleantech Portfolio	PZD	D	23.12	24.68	19.48	D / 2.1	12.61	18.06	8.58 / 32	-0.36 / 14	-3.54 / 10
GI	*PowerShares Convertible Secs Por	CVRT	C	23.84	24.85	21.50	C / 4.4	1.30	8.64	10.02 / 34	--	--
GL	*PowerShares DB 3x German Bd Fut	BUNT	D-	34.64	35.82	28.52	D / 1.6	-2.61	-5.70	6.89 / 28	--	--
GL	*PowerShares DB 3x Inv Jpnese Gvt	JGBD	D-	18.63	22.08	17.65	D- / 1.0	-0.48	-0.48	-5.74 / 10	--	--
GL	*PowerShares DB 3x Itn Trs B Fut	ITLT	C+	30.05	32.62	15.47	A+ / 9.9	25.96	63.13	119.41 / 99	--	--
USA	*PowerShares DB 3x Lg 25+ Yr Tr E	LBND	E+	47.22	58.56	34.41	E+ / 0.7	-8.25	-16.96	0.62 / 15	--	--
GI	*PowerShares DB 3x Lng USD I Fut	UUPT	E+	20.00	23.70	19.08	E / 0.5	-1.05	-14.67	-12.94 / 7	--	--
USA	*PowerShares DB 3x Sh 25+ Yr Tr E	SBND	E	7.47	11.37	6.08	D / 1.7	7.08	17.71	-14.24 / 6	--	--
GI	*PowerShares DB 3x Sht USD I Fut	UDNT	D	17.71	19.58	14.98	C / 5.1	0.34	15.60	8.06 / 30	--	--
GR	*PowerShares DB Agri Double Long	DAG	E	11.79	14.86	8.64	D- / 1.5	-11.57	-15.55	9.55 / 34	4.25 / 27	--
GR	*PowerShares DB Agri Double Sht	AGA	E-	13.03	23.90	11.95	E / 0.4	8.87	5.71	-26.22 / 4	-25.49 / 4	--
IN	*PowerShares DB Agriculture Fund	DBA	D	27.95	30.87	25.70	D- / 1.5	-3.94	-5.64	-2.97 / 11	2.09 / 20	-5.03 / 9
GR	*PowerShares DB Agriculture Long	AGF	D-	20.00	22.69	16.47	D / 2.1	-5.78	-6.01	9.20 / 33	5.05 / 30	--
GR	*PowerShares DB Agriculture Sht E	ADZ	E	21.34	26.60	18.51	E+ / 0.7	6.14	2.78	-13.23 / 7	-12.68 / 6	--
IN	*PowerShares DB Base Metals Fund	DBB	D-	19.28	21.62	17.28	D- / 1.0	1.71	5.07	-3.84 / 11	-5.41 / 9	-2.93 / 12
PM	*PowerShares DB Base Metals Sht E	BOS	E+	20.34	23.05	18.57	D- / 1.0	-5.02	-8.88	-2.92 / 11	-2.79 / 11	--
PM	*PowerShares DB Base Mtls Dbl Lg	BDD	E-	10.82	14.10	9.00	E+ / 0.7	2.68	13.42	-10.92 / 8	-15.22 / 5	--

Incl. in Returns		RISK				NET ASSETS		VALUATION			ASSET					FUND MANAGER	
Dividend Yield %	Expense Ratio	Risk Rating/ Pts	3 Year Standard Deviation	Beta	Avg Dura-tion	NAV as of 12/31/12	Total $(Mil)	Premium/Discount As of 12/31/12	1 Year Average	Wtd Avg P/E	Cash %	Stocks %	Bonds %	Other %	Portfolio Turnover Ratio	Manager Quality Pct	Manager Tenure (Years)
0.90	1.35	B+ / 9.3	N/A	N/A	N/A	26.53	7	-2.26	0.48	N/A	14	85	0	1	817	28	2
1.15	N/A	U /	N/A	N/A	N/A	23.29	16	-2.28	N/A	N/A	0	0	0	100	N/A	N/A	1
1.31	0.50	C+ / 6.5	21.3	1.29	N/A	71.02	164	-3.73	-0.05	119.4	0	100	0	0	21	18	13
1.72	0.57	C- / 3.8	N/A	N/A	N/A	13.39	175	-1.72	-0.13	N/A	0	97	0	3	18	2	3
8.71	1.63	C+ / 6.3	N/A	N/A	N/A	21.37	197	-6.55	-4.51	N/A	0	0	0	100	N/A	8	3
1.79	0.55	B- / 7.4	N/A	N/A	N/A	24.63	13	-0.49	0.76	N/A	4	95	0	1	7	67	2
2.48	0.50	B / 8.3	N/A	N/A	N/A	30.94	12	-4.27	0.37	N/A	0	99	0	1	7	48	3
10.28	1.35	B+ / 9.0	N/A	N/A	N/A	50.77	177	-1.38	0.15	N/A	9	0	90	1	80	69	N/A
5.57	0.55	B+ / 9.6	N/A	N/A	N/A	103.94	792	-0.49	0.20	N/A	0	0	0	100	33	91	2
0.32	0.09	B+ / 9.9	0.7	0.03	N/A	50.90	122	-0.10	-0.02	N/A	5	0	95	0	8	59	4
0.55	0.20	B+ / 9.9	2.2	-0.06	N/A	54.05	993	0.02	-0.01	N/A	25	0	75	0	31	77	4
0.98	0.20	B+ / 9.1	9.5	0.44	N/A	71.24	156	0.58	0.01	N/A	1	0	99	0	11	88	4
3.96	0.15	B- / 7.1	26.8	2.15	N/A	107.06	101	1.92	-0.20	N/A	0	0	100	0	14	16	4
1.37	0.15	B+ / 9.7	3.1	0.18	N/A	81.22	22	0.17	-0.03	N/A	1	0	99	0	37	72	4
1.52	0.15	B+ / 9.3	6.2	0.45	N/A	86.03	16	0.92	-0.02	N/A	2	0	98	0	15	73	4
4.02	0.45	B+ / 9.3	N/A	N/A	N/A	105.01	40	-0.62	0.16	N/A	0	0	0	100	37	85	2
1.25	0.20	B+ / 9.7	4.5	0.16	N/A	61.00	137	0.33	N/A	N/A	10	0	90	0	6	84	4
1.46	0.15	B+ / 9.6	N/A	N/A	N/A	104.39	19	2.17	0.21	N/A	0	0	0	100	211	67	3
4.15	0.45	B+ / 9.3	N/A	N/A	N/A	54.67	42	0.60	-0.01	N/A	0	0	0	100	71	87	2
2.96	0.45	B+ / 9.6	N/A	N/A	N/A	105.58	30	0.00	0.20	N/A	0	0	0	100	91	75	2
1.19	0.35	B+ / 9.9	0.6	0.06	N/A	101.52	2,169	-0.04	0.01	N/A	6	0	94	0	229	60	4
1.02	0.45	B+ / 9.2	N/A	N/A	N/A	102.08	3	0.41	-0.16	N/A	0	0	0	100	130	84	2
1.06	N/A	U /	N/A	N/A	N/A	53.86	110	0.91	N/A	N/A	0	0	0	100	N/A	N/A	1
2.16	0.35	B+ / 9.7	3.3	0.82	N/A	54.61	204	-0.44	0.05	N/A	2	0	98	0	11	53	2
0.98	0.35	B+ / 9.9	N/A	N/A	N/A	50.44	58	-0.04	0.02	N/A	0	0	100	0	17	56	2
1.98	N/A	U /	N/A	N/A	N/A	109.26	3,871	-0.19	N/A	N/A	0	0	0	100	N/A	N/A	1
3.10	0.25	B+ / 9.2	8.4	0.71	13.4	32.35	167	0.77	0.06	N/A	4	0	95	1	2	60	6
3.49	0.80	B- / 7.8	17.8	0.98	N/A	58.52	17	-2.89	0.02	64.7	0	100	0	0	17	82	5
1.13	0.29	B+ / 9.9	1.2	-0.03	2.8	25.39	8	-0.55	-0.24	N/A	15	0	84	1	31	63	4
4.29	0.75	B / 8.2	15.4	0.96	N/A	30.12	6	-4.25	0.04	46.6	0	99	0	1	22	49	5
2.48	0.66	B- / 7.9	17.6	1.06	N/A	21.49	46	-2.56	-0.09	29.6	0	100	0	0	25	31	6
4.73	0.28	B+ / 9.3	6.7	0.47	N/A	30.10	1,124	0.47	0.10	N/A	3	0	96	1	15	84	4
2.53	0.71	B / 8.5	14.0	0.89	N/A	30.80	214	-3.25	0.07	31.3	0	99	0	1	32	76	6
7.83	0.50	B / 8.6	N/A	N/A	N/A	26.02	394	-3.38	0.09	N/A	0	100	0	0	10	79	3
3.30	N/A	B+ / 9.8	N/A	N/A	N/A	24.90	36	-0.44	0.63	N/A	0	0	0	100	N/A	87	2
0.57	0.67	C+ / 6.8	23.2	1.37	N/A	24.14	66	-4.23	-0.41	41.6	0	99	0	1	27	8	6
2.85	0.35	B / 8.6	N/A	N/A	N/A	24.58	10	-3.01	-0.65	N/A	0	0	0	100	8	20	2
0.00	N/A	C / 5.4	N/A	N/A	N/A	32.57	N/A	6.36	N/A	N/A	0	0	0	100	N/A	96	2
0.00	N/A	C / 5.5	N/A	N/A	N/A	19.49	N/A	-4.41	-2.89	N/A	0	0	0	100	N/A	19	2
0.00	N/A	C- / 3.8	N/A	N/A	N/A	24.33	N/A	23.51	6.18	N/A	0	0	0	100	N/A	99	2
0.00	N/A	C / 4.8	N/A	N/A	N/A	45.31	N/A	4.22	0.01	N/A	0	0	0	100	N/A	14	3
0.00	N/A	C / 5.1	N/A	N/A	N/A	19.76	N/A	1.21	-0.16	N/A	0	0	0	100	N/A	96	2
0.00	N/A	D / 1.9	N/A	N/A	N/A	7.77	N/A	-3.86	-0.15	N/A	0	0	0	100	N/A	23	3
0.00	N/A	C- / 4.0	N/A	N/A	N/A	17.82	N/A	-0.62	-0.04	N/A	0	0	0	100	N/A	5	2
0.00	0.75	C- / 3.0	53.5	1.43	N/A	11.25	87	4.80	0.75	N/A	0	0	0	100	N/A	12	5
0.00	0.75	D / 1.9	52.8	-1.46	N/A	13.78	4	-5.44	8.21	N/A	0	0	0	100	N/A	7	5
0.00	0.92	B- / 7.5	17.3	0.60	N/A	27.72	1,661	0.83	-0.04	N/A	0	0	0	100	N/A	25	N/A
0.00	0.75	C / 4.6	27.3	0.80	N/A	19.70	5	1.52	0.43	N/A	0	0	0	100	N/A	27	5
0.00	0.75	D+ / 2.7	26.3	-0.78	N/A	21.75	3	-1.89	0.69	N/A	0	0	0	100	N/A	24	5
0.00	0.77	C+ / 6.5	27.5	1.37	N/A	19.00	310	1.47	-0.03	N/A	0	0	0	100	N/A	6	N/A
0.00	0.75	C- / 3.9	27.0	-0.55	N/A	20.33	3	0.05	-0.27	N/A	0	0	0	100	N/A	82	5
0.00	0.75	D+ / 2.4	57.9	1.24	N/A	10.60	23	2.08	-0.07	N/A	0	0	0	100	N/A	3	5

* Denotes ETF Fund, N/A denotes number is not available

Index of ETFs and Other Closed-End Funds

Fund Type	Fund Name	Ticker Symbol	Overall Investment Rating	PRICE Price As of 12/31/12	52 Week High	52 Week Low	PERFORMANCE Performance Rating/Pts	% Total Return Through 12/31/12 3 Mo	6 Mo	1Yr/Pct	Annualized 3Yr/Pct	5Yr/Pct
PM	*PowerShares DB Base Mtls Dbl Sh	BOM	E-	11.87	15.89	10.50	E+ / 0.7	-6.54	-16.34	-7.88 / 9	-8.93 / 7	--
GR	*PowerShares DB Commodity Double	DEE	E-	26.50	38.64	24.00	E / 0.5	7.20	-10.19	-2.42 / 12	-19.48 / 4	--
GR	*PowerShares DB Commodity Double	DYY	E+	9.21	13.79	6.97	D / 2.1	-3.31	6.45	-3.30 / 11	4.00 / 26	-2.24 / 13
GR	*PowerShares DB Commodity Idx Tra	DBC	D+	27.78	29.93	24.12	D / 2.2	-3.36	3.33	1.10 / 16	4.22 / 27	--
GR	*PowerShares DB Commodity Short E	DDP	E+	30.70	64.00	26.91	E+ / 0.8	-5.47	-8.13	-0.83 / 13	-7.92 / 8	--
GR	*PowerShares DB Crude Oil Dbl Sh	DTO	E-	44.69	61.11	32.64	E+ / 0.6	-2.61	-13.70	3.62 / 22	-15.01 / 5	--
GR	*PowerShares DB Crude Oil Long ET	OLO	E+	12.72	15.97	11.13	D- / 1.2	0.70	4.43	-8.37 / 9	-0.93 / 13	--
GR	*PowerShares DB Crude Oil Short E	SZO	E+	43.41	50.32	36.42	D- / 1.0	-1.07	-5.19	4.67 / 23	-4.62 / 9	-3.23 / 11
EN	*PowerShares DB Energy Fund	DBE	D	27.94	31.47	23.39	D / 2.0	-2.87	7.93	-0.99 / 13	2.97 / 23	0.34 / 21
IN	*PowerShares DB G10 Currency Harv	DBV	C-	26.15	26.74	23.34	D+ / 2.8	5.86	8.18	10.43 / 35	3.77 / 25	--
GL	*PowerShares DB German Bond Fut E	BUNL	D-	23.93	24.93	22.49	D / 1.9	0.50	-0.62	3.55 / 21	--	--
PM	*PowerShares DB Gold Double Lg ET	DGP	C-	52.03	61.54	44.22	B- / 7.5	-10.74	7.85	-1.29 / 13	22.20 / 93	--
PM	*PowerShares DB Gold Double Sht E	DZZ	E-	4.47	5.39	3.89	E / 0.4	11.17	-10.12	-8.11 / 9	-29.85 / 3	11.55 / 75
PM	*PowerShares DB Gold Fund	DGL	C-	57.35	62.24	52.88	C- / 3.8	-5.65	4.00	-0.02 / 14	12.06 / 58	--
PM	*PowerShares DB Gold Short ETN	DGZ	E	11.81	12.95	11.02	E+ / 0.6	5.41	-4.96	-3.34 / 11	-14.98 / 6	--
GL	*PowerShares DB Inv Jpnese Gvt Bd	JGBS	D-	19.54	21.74	19.13	D- / 1.2	-0.56	0.06	-1.95 / 12	--	--
GL	*PowerShares DB Itn Trs B Fut ETN	ITLY	B-	23.84	24.55	18.77	A+ / 9.6	--	18.63	31.28 / 92	--	--
GL	*PowerShares DB Japanese GvBd Fut	JGBL	D-	20.81	20.97	20.10	D- / 1.5	0.14	0.10	0.77 / 15	--	--
EN	*PowerShares DB Oil Fund	DBO	D-	25.94	32.06	22.62	D- / 1.2	0.50	4.98	-8.57 / 9	-0.97 / 13	-4.18 / 9
PM	*PowerShares DB Precious Metals F	DBP	C-	57.09	63.62	50.18	C- / 4.2	-6.46	5.30	0.21 / 14	13.05 / 63	11.82 / 76
PM	*PowerShares DB Silver Fund	DBS	D+	52.35	65.44	45.06	C+ / 5.8	-9.67	11.37	1.53 / 17	16.82 / 79	11.87 / 76
USA	*PowerShares DB US Deflation ETN	DEFL	D-	46.77	50.93	46.41	E+ / 0.9	--	--	-7.51 / 9	--	--
GR	*PowerShares DB US Dollar Bearish	UDN	D+	27.21	27.64	25.80	D- / 1.4	0.07	4.72	2.94 / 20	-0.71 / 14	-0.18 / 19
GR	*PowerShares DB US Dollar Bullish	UUP	D+	21.81	23.14	21.57	D- / 1.1	-0.41	-5.19	-4.44 / 11	-1.53 / 12	-1.60 / 15
USA	*PowerShares DB US Inflation ETN	INFL	D	51.33	53.70	48.56	D+ / 2.4	--	4.22	4.32 / 23	--	--
IN	*PowerShares Div Achievers	PFM	C+	16.16	16.80	14.93	C / 5.1	2.43	6.62	13.95 / 45	12.28 / 59	4.33 / 39
FO	*PowerShares DWA Dev Mkt Tech Lea	PIZ	D+	20.14	20.60	16.31	C- / 3.9	7.20	19.13	19.18 / 68	4.19 / 27	-0.02 / 19
EM	*PowerShares DWA Emg Mkts Tech Le	PIE	C-	18.59	19.43	15.58	C / 4.6	7.69	12.46	16.22 / 54	8.30 / 39	-3.30 / 11
IN	*PowerShares DWA Sm Cap Tech Lead	DWAS	U	26.49	N/A	N/A	U	7.85	--	--	--	--
IN	*PowerShares DWA Technical Leader	PDP	B-	27.92	28.79	24.60	C+ / 6.9	5.12	8.91	18.12 / 63	15.44 / 75	4.28 / 38
FS	*PowerShares Dynamic Banking Port	PJB	D+	13.31	14.47	10.62	D+ / 2.8	-0.44	4.63	12.67 / 40	5.27 / 30	-1.79 / 14
IN	*PowerShares Dynamic Basic Materi	PYZ	B	40.45	43.64	32.51	B+ / 8.5	14.65	20.91	24.47 / 83	16.67 / 79	9.19 / 66
HL	*PowerShares Dynamic Biotech&Geno	PBE	D+	22.84	24.84	20.57	C / 4.7	1.63	2.71	14.24 / 46	12.18 / 59	6.01 / 49
IN	*PowerShares Dynamic Bldg & Cons	PKB	B+	17.41	19.15	11.90	A / 9.4	15.05	29.28	41.98 / 97	18.58 / 84	5.46 / 47
IN	*PowerShares Dynamic Consumer Dis	PEZ	C+	29.74	31.03	25.64	C+ / 6.4	1.77	8.02	17.08 / 59	15.41 / 74	8.66 / 63
IN	*PowerShares Dynamic Consumer Sta	PSL	C+	33.22	34.74	28.71	C / 5.4	3.34	5.33	13.52 / 43	13.46 / 66	7.98 / 60
EN	*PowerShares Dynamic Energy	PXI	B-	42.89	45.20	34.57	B / 7.8	6.94	17.73	16.26 / 54	18.10 / 83	7.81 / 59
EN	*PowerShares Dynamic Enrg Exp & P	PXE	B	26.97	28.10	20.46	B+ / 8.7	7.85	21.95	24.36 / 82	19.40 / 87	5.95 / 49
FS	*PowerShares Dynamic Financial	PFI	C+	21.15	22.30	17.92	C+ / 5.8	5.52	14.45	20.09 / 71	10.76 / 52	1.15 / 23
IN	*PowerShares Dynamic Food & Bever	PBJ	C+	19.91	20.55	18.81	C+ / 5.6	4.28	3.74	9.53 / 34	14.54 / 71	7.15 / 55
HL	*PowerShares Dynamic Hlthcare	PTH	C	32.82	34.86	29.20	C / 5.5	2.61	5.78	18.86 / 67	12.62 / 61	3.28 / 34
IN	*PowerShares Dynamic Industrials	PRN	B	31.82	33.47	27.04	B / 7.8	13.11	16.94	18.81 / 66	15.30 / 74	5.81 / 48
IN	*PowerShares Dynamic Insurance	PIC	B-	17.60	18.52	14.99	B- / 7.1	7.60	17.30	23.08 / 80	12.86 / 62	5.42 / 46
GR	*PowerShares Dynamic Large Cap Gr	PWB	C+	18.93	19.56	16.41	C+ / 5.7	4.48	9.90	21.29 / 74	11.42 / 55	4.24 / 38
IN	*PowerShares Dynamic Large Cap Va	PWV	C+	21.85	22.62	19.20	C+ / 6.0	4.10	11.00	17.96 / 62	12.90 / 63	6.85 / 54
IN	*PowerShares Dynamic Leisure&Ente	PEJ	A-	22.95	24.38	19.28	B+ / 8.8	6.73	11.20	25.82 / 85	21.77 / 92	13.01 / 81
IN	*PowerShares Dynamic MagniQuant	PIQ	C+	27.05	28.32	23.75	C+ / 6.1	6.49	12.31	18.77 / 66	12.29 / 60	4.72 / 42
GR	*PowerShares Dynamic Market	PWC	C+	48.78	50.72	41.67	C+ / 6.0	7.19	11.48	22.57 / 78	11.31 / 54	3.19 / 33
IN	*PowerShares Dynamic Media	PBS	B-	16.69	17.25	13.50	B- / 7.5	4.20	17.96	26.49 / 86	14.43 / 70	7.39 / 57
GR	*PowerShares Dynamic Networking	PXQ	C-	25.33	28.95	22.35	C / 5.0	10.29	13.37	2.93 / 20	12.41 / 60	11.66 / 76
EN	*PowerShares Dynamic Oil & Gas Sv	PXJ	D	20.34	22.81	16.10	C- / 3.3	8.22	19.05	6.34 / 27	6.46 / 34	-2.07 / 13
GR	*PowerShares Dynamic OTC Portfoli	PWO	D+	48.10	52.06	45.18	C- / 3.3	4.19	4.89	8.38 / 31	7.72 / 38	1.86 / 26

* Denotes ETF Fund, N/A denotes number is not available

www.thestreetratings.com

Dividend Yield %	Expense Ratio	Risk Rating/Pts	Std Deviation (3 Yr)	Beta (3 Yr)	Avg Duration	NAV as of 12/31/12	Total $(Mil)	Prem/Disc as of 12/31/12	1 Year Average	Wtd Avg P/E	Cash %	Stocks %	Bonds %	Other %	Portfolio Turnover Ratio	Manager Quality Pct	Manager Tenure (Years)
0.00	0.75	D / 2.2	56.0	-1.09	N/A	12.24	2	-3.02	-0.19	N/A	0	0	0	100	N/A	81	5
0.00	0.75	D / 2.1	41.8	-1.92	N/A	27.79	6	-4.64	0.23	N/A	0	0	0	100	N/A	35	5
0.00	0.75	C- / 3.1	50.1	2.26	N/A	9.07	43	1.54	0.81	N/A	0	0	0	100	N/A	6	5
0.00	0.87	B- / 7.5	20.1	1.05	N/A	27.55	6,608	0.83	0.03	N/A	0	0	0	100	N/A	18	N/A
0.00	0.75	C- / 3.7	36.0	-1.18	N/A	29.89	10	2.71	10.83	N/A	0	0	0	100	N/A	80	5
0.00	0.75	D / 2.1	58.6	-2.76	N/A	42.90	97	4.17	-0.02	N/A	0	0	0	100	N/A	95	5
0.00	0.75	C- / 3.9	26.3	1.35	N/A	12.98	15	-2.00	-0.09	N/A	0	0	0	100	N/A	8	5
0.00	0.75	C- / 3.9	27.2	-1.34	N/A	42.46	14	2.24	-0.09	N/A	0	0	0	100	N/A	91	5
0.00	0.77	B- / 7.1	23.2	0.87	N/A	28.05	140	-0.39	0.02	N/A	0	0	0	100	N/A	21	N/A
0.00	0.79	B / 8.9	11.2	0.65	N/A	26.58	345	-1.62	-0.03	N/A	0	0	0	100	N/A	29	N/A
0.00	N/A	C+ / 5.8	N/A	N/A	N/A	23.89	N/A	0.17	-0.15	N/A	65	0	0	35	N/A	78	2
0.00	N/A	C- / 3.9	39.0	1.85	N/A	51.20	N/A	1.62	0.02	N/A	0	0	0	100	N/A	29	5
0.00	N/A	D / 1.9	39.9	-1.87	N/A	4.55	N/A	-1.76	-0.07	N/A	0	0	0	100	N/A	11	5
0.00	0.76	B / 8.1	18.9	0.92	N/A	56.89	517	0.81	0.01	N/A	0	0	0	100	N/A	49	N/A
0.00	N/A	C- / 3.0	18.9	-0.92	N/A	11.90	N/A	-0.76	-0.04	N/A	0	0	0	100	N/A	23	5
0.00	N/A	C+ / 5.8	N/A	N/A	N/A	18.68	N/A	4.60	3.21	N/A	0	0	0	100	N/A	34	2
0.00	N/A	C / 5.3	N/A	N/A	N/A	32.51	N/A	-26.67	-4.23	N/A	0	0	0	100	N/A	98	2
0.00	N/A	C+ / 5.9	N/A	N/A	N/A	20.72	N/A	0.43	0.11	N/A	0	0	0	100	N/A	66	2
0.00	0.77	C+ / 6.2	27.3	1.02	N/A	26.35	775	-1.56	-0.02	N/A	0	0	0	100	N/A	12	N/A
0.00	0.77	B- / 7.5	23.4	1.10	N/A	56.73	354	0.63	N/A	N/A	0	0	0	100	N/A	38	N/A
0.00	0.76	C / 4.8	44.8	1.76	N/A	52.28	62	0.13	0.04	N/A	0	0	0	100	N/A	19	N/A
0.00	N/A	C+ / 5.6	N/A	N/A	N/A	46.62	N/A	0.32	0.01	N/A	0	0	0	100	N/A	10	2
0.00	0.80	B / 8.8	9.5	0.47	N/A	27.29	93	-0.29	N/A	N/A	100	0	0	0	N/A	22	N/A
0.00	0.81	B / 8.4	9.4	-0.46	N/A	21.73	689	0.37	-0.03	N/A	1	0	0	99	N/A	71	N/A
0.00	N/A	C+ / 5.7	N/A	N/A	N/A	51.26	N/A	0.14	0.19	N/A	0	0	0	100	N/A	85	2
3.08	0.60	B / 8.8	11.3	0.71	N/A	16.68	255	-3.12	-0.02	29.2	0	99	0	1	20	76	6
1.62	0.80	C+ / 6.8	24.2	1.14	N/A	20.43	101	-1.42	0.15	40.1	0	100	0	0	54	57	6
0.33	0.90	C+ / 6.9	25.2	1.03	N/A	18.71	239	-0.64	0.15	N/A	0	100	0	0	42	75	6
2.00	N/A	U /	N/A	N/A	N/A	27.83	12	-4.81	N/A	N/A	0	0	0	100	N/A	N/A	1
1.88	0.65	B- / 7.8	17.0	1.04	N/A	28.74	721	-2.85	0.03	57.9	0	0	0	100	96	74	6
2.27	0.65	B- / 7.3	20.5	0.92	N/A	13.86	10	-3.97	-0.17	11.2	0	100	0	0	120	38	6
3.67	0.65	C+ / 6.8	26.1	1.55	N/A	42.43	71	-4.67	N/A	38.2	0	99	0	1	78	37	6
0.00	0.63	C+ / 5.8	19.1	1.06	N/A	24.32	127	-6.09	-0.16	202.7	0	99	0	1	53	48	6
0.93	0.63	B- / 7.1	26.2	1.48	N/A	17.96	66	-3.06	-0.03	22.0	0	100	0	0	72	63	6
2.30	0.65	B- / 7.9	19.9	1.14	N/A	30.31	31	-1.88	0.03	41.3	0	100	0	0	88	71	6
4.24	0.65	B / 8.7	11.5	0.66	N/A	34.19	33	-2.84	-0.05	37.2	0	100	0	0	35	80	6
2.90	0.65	B- / 7.1	25.6	1.07	N/A	44.45	114	-3.51	-0.05	18.5	0	100	0	0	107	85	6
5.49	0.65	B- / 7.1	26.7	1.11	N/A	27.89	65	-3.30	-0.03	10.7	0	100	0	0	94	87	6
2.25	0.65	B- / 7.9	17.7	0.86	N/A	22.03	19	-3.99	-0.05	21.4	0	100	0	0	102	72	6
2.78	0.63	B / 8.8	11.0	0.55	N/A	20.50	103	-2.88	-0.06	27.5	0	99	0	1	134	85	6
1.99	0.65	B- / 7.1	15.9	0.89	N/A	34.37	50	-4.51	-0.02	99.6	0	100	0	0	99	67	6
4.61	0.65	B- / 7.4	21.6	1.28	N/A	33.28	29	-4.39	-0.13	22.8	0	100	0	0	129	54	6
2.69	0.63	B- / 7.9	16.6	1.01	N/A	18.44	8	-4.56	-0.08	28.9	0	99	0	1	87	54	6
2.54	0.61	B- / 7.6	17.0	1.07	N/A	19.55	188	-3.17	-0.04	63.3	0	99	0	1	64	43	6
2.93	0.59	B / 8.5	14.3	0.91	N/A	22.56	460	-3.15	-0.01	20.2	0	99	0	1	41	67	6
0.77	0.63	B / 8.0	20.0	1.14	N/A	24.03	59	-4.49	N/A	28.6	0	100	0	0	90	86	6
3.58	0.65	B- / 7.6	20.6	1.27	N/A	28.34	16	-4.55	-0.09	32.9	0	100	0	0	110	31	6
3.90	0.60	B- / 7.6	18.0	1.13	N/A	50.67	132	-3.73	-0.04	35.1	0	100	0	0	133	37	6
1.55	0.63	B- / 7.4	21.8	1.32	N/A	17.22	85	-3.08	0.01	37.6	0	100	0	0	89	44	6
0.24	0.63	C+ / 6.9	26.5	1.49	N/A	26.03	39	-2.69	-0.10	48.1	0	100	0	0	84	27	6
0.13	0.63	C+ / 6.0	34.9	1.44	N/A	21.41	113	-5.00	-0.08	26.3	0	99	0	1	70	19	6
3.95	0.60	B- / 7.1	19.5	1.17	N/A	49.88	22	-3.57	-0.06	79.0	0	100	0	0	99	21	6

Denotes ETF Fund, N/A denotes number is not available

Fund Type	Fund Name	Ticker Symbol	Overall Investment Rating	Price As of 12/31/12	52 Week High	52 Week Low	Performance Rating/Pts	3 Mo	6 Mo	1Yr/Pct	3Yr/Pct	5Yr/Pct
	99 Pct = Best / 0 Pct = Worst									% Total Return Through 12/31/12 — Annualized		
HL	*PowerShares Dynamic Pharmaceutic	PJP	B+	34.53	36.78	28.50	A / 9.3	6.72	11.15	28.77 / 90	25.51 / 98	16.42 / 94
IN	*PowerShares Dynamic Retail	PMR	B	25.22	26.64	22.63	B- / 7.2	2.44	2.79	14.43 / 46	18.09 / 83	13.79 / 85
IN	*PowerShares Dynamic Semiconducto	PSI	D	14.40	16.32	12.88	D+ / 2.7	12.90	7.28	3.68 / 22	5.02 / 29	1.00 / 22
GR	*PowerShares Dynamic Software	PSJ	C-	27.14	28.24	23.26	C / 4.9	2.78	8.12	21.13 / 74	10.07 / 48	10.25 / 71
GR	*PowerShares Dynamic Technology	PTF	D+	26.17	27.96	23.78	C- / 3.9	7.13	11.46	15.18 / 49	6.78 / 35	3.46 / 35
UT	*PowerShares Dynamic Utilities	PUI	C	17.31	18.05	16.02	C- / 3.7	0.98	3.76	12.42 / 40	9.34 / 44	2.87 / 31
EM	*PowerShares Emg Mkts Infrastruct	PXR	D	43.21	45.40	35.60	D+ / 2.5	12.63	19.64	15.10 / 48	1.15 / 18	--
EM	*PowerShares Emrg Mkt Sovereign D	PCY	B-	31.45	31.58	26.72	C+ / 5.8	0.88	7.91	21.90 / 76	13.01 / 63	10.09 / 70
FS	*PowerShares Financial Preferred	PGF	C	18.28	18.70	16.91	C / 4.4	1.56	4.81	16.96 / 58	10.33 / 49	4.99 / 44
FO	*PowerShares FTSE RAFI Asia Pac E	PAF	C+	57.17	58.49	44.94	C+ / 6.7	11.28	22.58	24.02 / 82	9.68 / 46	6.16 / 50
FO	*PowerShares FTSE RAFI DM exUS Sm	PDN	D+	23.50	24.75	19.31	C- / 3.8	11.78	19.93	19.68 / 70	5.98 / 33	4.71 / 42
FO	*PowerShares FTSE RAFI Dvlp Mkt e	PXF	D+	36.45	37.58	29.21	D+ / 2.8	11.56	21.15	20.24 / 71	1.81 / 19	-1.02 / 17
EM	*PowerShares FTSE RAFI Emg Mkts	PXH	D	22.82	24.20	19.01	D+ / 2.3	7.54	16.02	10.98 / 36	1.51 / 18	1.80 / 26
IN	*PowerShares FTSE RAFI US 1000	PRF	C+	62.43	64.63	53.96	C+ / 5.8	5.91	12.85	17.73 / 61	11.92 / 58	6.33 / 51
IN	*PowerShares FTSE RAFI US 1500 Sm	PRFZ	C+	69.54	72.72	59.29	C+ / 6.5	8.65	12.93	18.31 / 64	12.88 / 63	10.35 / 71
COH	*PowerShares Fundamental High Yie	PHB	C-	19.25	19.50	18.25	C- / 3.7	2.49	5.76	11.36 / 37	8.89 / 42	3.66 / 36
GR	*PowerShares Fundamental Pure Lg	PXLC	C+	26.64	27.96	24.89	C / 5.0	3.88	10.02	14.44 / 46	10.94 / 52	4.32 / 39
GR	*PowerShares Fundamental Pure Lg	PXLG	B	22.47	24.70	20.39	C+ / 6.6	1.48	7.57	17.52 / 60	--	--
GR	*PowerShares Fundamental Pure Lg	PXLV	A	21.86	23.80	18.29	B+ / 8.9	6.63	16.58	19.60 / 69	--	--
GR	*PowerShares Fundamental Pure Md	PXMC	C+	26.92	27.78	23.59	C / 5.5	5.93	13.03	14.68 / 47	11.33 / 54	4.32 / 39
GR	*PowerShares Fundamental Pure Md	PXMG	C+	23.09	23.92	19.91	C+ / 6.2	8.99	13.01	14.82 / 47	12.76 / 62	2.83 / 31
GR	*PowerShares Fundamental Pure Md	PXMV	C+	17.82	18.61	15.08	C+ / 6.2	7.57	16.05	19.97 / 71	11.23 / 54	4.40 / 40
GR	*PowerShares Fundamental Pure Sm	PXSG	C	17.93	18.65	15.76	C+ / 6.1	6.71	11.89	14.63 / 47	13.33 / 65	4.38 / 40
GR	*PowerShares Fundamental Pure Sm	PXSV	C+	17.47	18.15	14.46	B- / 7.0	9.55	14.41	20.93 / 73	13.37 / 65	6.72 / 53
GR	*PowerShares Fundamental Pure Sm	PXSC	C	24.26	25.48	21.70	C+ / 5.8	8.23	10.06	15.82 / 51	12.18 / 59	4.60 / 41
COI	*PowerShares Fundmntl Inv Gr Corp	PFIG	C	25.69	26.24	24.92	D / 2.2	-0.27	1.38	5.04 / 24	--	--
EN	*PowerShares Gb Nuclear Energy Po	PKN	D	15.80	17.91	14.20	D- / 1.3	4.15	8.10	4.03 / 22	-2.52 / 11	--
PM	*PowerShares Glb Gold & Precious	PSAU	E+	37.08	46.07	29.53	D- / 1.1	-9.93	10.81	-12.62 / 7	-1.00 / 13	--
GL	*PowerShares Global Agriculture P	PAGG	D+	30.73	31.84	25.80	C- / 3.5	7.23	12.16	13.55 / 43	5.21 / 30	--
EN	*PowerShares Global Clean Energy	PBD	E+	7.89	10.06	6.71	E+ / 0.6	14.70	18.48	-0.36 / 13	-19.16 / 4	-18.69 / 3
EN	*PowerShares Global Coal Portfoli	PKOL	D-	19.76	28.06	17.65	E+ / 0.7	2.92	6.69	-19.65 / 5	-11.57 / 7	--
IN	*PowerShares Global Listed Priv E	PSP	C+	10.12	10.61	8.00	B- / 7.5	14.70	23.05	31.96 / 93	9.74 / 46	-5.75 / 7
GL	*PowerShares Global Steel Portfol	PSTL	D-	14.57	17.94	12.04	E+ / 0.8	17.63	14.81	-3.95 / 11	-11.99 / 7	--
EN	*PowerShares Global Water Portfol	PIO	D	18.01	18.39	15.65	D+ / 2.9	7.68	14.37	16.46 / 55	1.02 / 17	-1.22 / 16
EN	*PowerShares Global Wind Energy P	PWND	E+	5.63	7.74	4.65	E / 0.5	16.17	26.46	-5.23 / 10	-25.32 / 4	--
GL	*PowerShares Golden Dragon China	PGJ	D-	19.16	22.91	16.70	D- / 1.1	8.24	12.30	-1.34 / 13	-5.19 / 9	-5.83 / 7
IN	*PowerShares High Yld Eq Div Ach	PEY	C+	9.41	9.85	8.90	C / 4.6	2.06	5.19	9.52 / 34	12.11 / 58	0.20 / 20
GL	*PowerShares Ibbotson Altv Comp	PTO	C-	11.62	12.00	10.33	D+ / 2.6	1.82	7.33	8.10 / 31	4.14 / 27	--
FO	*PowerShares India Portfolio	PIN	D-	18.36	20.92	15.44	D- / 1.1	0.96	9.94	7.30 / 29	-6.03 / 8	--
MUN	*PowerShares Insured CA Mun Bond	PWZ	C+	25.26	30.91	24.47	C- / 4.2	1.08	2.80	7.22 / 36	7.08 / 52	4.66 / 56
MUN	*PowerShares Insured National Mun	PZA	C+	25.75	26.40	24.53	C / 4.6	1.45	3.48	7.77 / 38	7.70 / 57	5.10 / 59
MUN	*PowerShares Insured NY Mun Bond	PZT	C	24.57	25.41	23.93	C- / 3.8	0.77	1.90	5.66 / 32	6.65 / 48	4.17 / 51
GL	*PowerShares International Corp B	PICB	B+	29.61	29.78	26.12	B / 7.8	3.34	11.96	17.65 / 61	--	--
FO	*PowerShares Intl Dividend Ach	PID	C	15.83	16.33	13.60	C / 4.3	7.23	12.64	14.78 / 47	7.66 / 37	1.01 / 22
IN	*PowerShares KBW Bank	KBWB	A+	26.27	27.59	20.90	A / 9.4	6.84	16.70	24.09 / 82	--	--
IN	*PowerShares KBW Capital Markets	KBWC	A	32.72	36.15	28.64	A / 9.3	--	23.55	22.28 / 77	--	--
GI	*PowerShares KBW High Div Yield F	KBWD	C+	23.15	25.06	21.15	C+ / 5.6	3.08	3.89	15.91 / 52	--	--
IN	*PowerShares KBW Insurance	KBWI	U	42.66	45.44	36.72	U /	7.36	--	--	--	--
FO	*PowerShares KBW International Fn	KBWX	U	22.95	24.03	18.71	U /	--	30.51	--	--	--
IN	*PowerShares KBW Premium Yld Eq R	KBWY	A	28.10	29.54	23.70	A / 9.4	6.78	11.55	27.82 / 88	--	--
GR	*PowerShares KBW Prop & Casualty	KBWP	U	29.73	31.26	25.93	U /	4.21	11.52	--	--	--
IN	*PowerShares KBW Regional Banking	KBWR	C	27.35	29.69	25.10	C- / 3.4	2.23	2.80	9.33 / 33	--	--

Incl. in Returns Dividend Yield %	Expense Ratio	RISK Risk Rating/Pts	3 Year Standard Deviation	Beta	Avg Duration	NET ASSETS NAV as of 12/31/12	Total $(Mil)	VALUATION Premium/Discount As of 12/31/12	1 Year Average	Wtd Avg P/E	ASSET Cash %	Stocks %	Bonds %	Other %	Portfolio Turnover Ratio	FUND MANAGER Manager Quality Pct	Manager Tenure (Years)
4.32	0.63	B- / 7.1	13.1	0.70	N/A	36.53	316	-5.47	0.03	146.7	0	100	0	0	23	95	6
7.47	0.63	B / 8.2	18.5	0.99	N/A	25.17	53	0.20	-0.04	29.9	0	99	0	1	111	85	6
1.07	0.63	C+ / 6.7	27.8	1.58	N/A	14.84	16	-2.96	-0.03	37.0	0	100	0	0	57	10	6
0.00	0.63	C+ / 6.8	17.9	1.05	N/A	28.13	45	-3.52	-0.04	109.4	0	99	0	1	100	35	6
1.45	0.65	C+ / 6.8	22.3	1.36	N/A	27.44	29	-4.63	-0.10	85.0	0	100	0	0	108	14	6
3.69	0.63	B / 8.8	10.6	0.85	N/A	17.74	38	-2.42	-0.16	21.8	0	100	0	0	71	59	6
1.40	0.75	C+ / 6.2	30.2	1.30	N/A	44.13	101	-2.08	-0.20	32.8	0	99	0	1	10	25	5
4.44	0.50	B / 8.9	7.9	0.65	12.2	31.18	3,033	0.87	0.05	N/A	1	0	98	1	5	90	6
7.60	0.66	B / 8.8	9.9	0.32	N/A	18.59	1,720	-1.67	0.08	N/A	0	0	0	100	6	88	6
6.26	0.80	C+ / 6.7	25.2	1.13	N/A	57.62	65	-0.78	-0.01	N/A	0	99	0	1	12	81	N/A
4.87	0.75	C+ / 6.6	19.6	0.94	N/A	23.87	63	-1.55	-0.29	103.5	0	99	0	1	25	70	6
3.03	0.75	B- / 7.0	23.5	1.14	N/A	37.47	301	-2.72	0.18	22.8	0	99	0	1	15	32	6
1.39	0.85	C+ / 6.7	23.6	1.02	N/A	22.90	384	-0.35	0.16	N/A	0	99	0	1	28	29	6
3.04	0.39	B / 8.1	16.4	1.06	N/A	64.54	1,479	-3.27	0.02	26.1	0	99	0	1	6	55	6
3.68	0.39	B- / 7.3	21.6	1.33	N/A	72.03	487	-3.46	-0.02	42.2	0	99	0	1	15	36	6
4.89	0.50	B / 8.1	6.5	0.83	5.0	19.46	845	-1.08	-0.01	N/A	1	0	98	1	9	48	6
3.32	0.43	B / 8.5	14.0	0.88	N/A	27.93	25	-4.62	-0.06	23.5	0	99	0	1	58	54	6
2.22	0.39	B / 8.5	N/A	N/A	N/A	23.35	6	-3.77	0.05	N/A	0	99	0	1	3	65	2
3.07	0.39	B / 8.1	N/A	N/A	N/A	22.64	6	-3.45	-0.01	N/A	0	100	0	0	2	58	2
3.28	0.43	B / 8.0	17.1	1.07	N/A	27.76	17	-3.03	-0.02	34.8	0	99	0	1	83	45	6
1.64	0.43	B- / 7.4	20.2	1.21	N/A	23.90	75	-3.39	-0.07	48.4	0	99	0	1	75	42	6
3.61	0.43	B / 8.0	16.8	1.04	N/A	18.57	27	-4.04	-0.13	17.0	0	99	0	1	83	44	6
0.70	0.48	C+ / 6.9	20.1	1.20	N/A	18.64	27	-3.81	-0.12	81.6	0	99	0	1	189	47	6
4.24	0.43	B- / 7.5	21.2	1.29	N/A	18.05	45	-3.21	-0.13	20.4	0	99	0	1	109	40	6
2.59	0.43	B- / 7.5	20.0	1.22	N/A	25.50	13	-4.86	-0.21	42.0	0	99	0	1	97	34	6
3.48	0.22	B+ / 9.9	N/A	N/A	N/A	25.68	33	0.04	0.38	N/A	0	0	0	100	N/A	56	2
4.87	0.75	C+ / 6.8	22.6	0.84	N/A	16.39	10	-3.60	-0.48	35.7	0	99	0	1	11	13	5
0.52	0.75	C / 4.7	28.1	1.14	N/A	36.12	37	2.66	-0.17	162.9	0	99	0	1	11	9	5
1.48	0.75	B- / 7.0	25.1	1.05	N/A	31.84	109	-3.49	-0.28	56.9	0	99	0	1	17	65	5
2.10	0.75	C / 4.9	30.1	1.04	N/A	8.52	57	-7.39	-0.58	41.7	0	100	0	0	26	3	5
4.37	0.75	C / 5.4	34.0	1.27	N/A	20.14	9	-1.89	0.11	13.6	0	99	0	1	27	5	5
3.85	0.71	C+ / 6.0	26.0	1.55	N/A	10.55	301	-4.08	0.03	N/A	0	100	0	0	88	20	5
3.61	0.75	C+ / 5.8	32.5	1.40	N/A	14.90	2	-2.21	-0.53	6.5	0	99	0	1	21	7	5
1.05	0.75	C+ / 6.6	19.8	0.72	N/A	18.37	197	-1.96	-0.38	86.8	0	99	0	1	70	22	6
2.26	0.75	C / 4.9	28.8	0.94	N/A	6.39	9	-11.89	-0.72	15.2	0	99	0	1	34	2	5
2.03	0.69	C+ / 5.9	25.3	1.00	N/A	20.15	197	-4.91	-0.13	63.6	0	99	0	1	23	13	6
3.23	0.60	B+ / 9.1	11.1	0.64	N/A	9.68	276	-2.79	-0.02	17.5	0	99	0	1	35	79	6
2.74	0.25	B / 8.4	14.6	0.63	N/A	11.78	8	-1.36	-0.34	N/A	0	100	0	0	5	71	5
1.88	0.80	C+ / 6.0	27.4	0.95	N/A	18.63	407	-1.45	0.08	N/A	0	100	0	0	39	14	5
3.66	0.28	B+ / 9.3	5.4	1.38	14.5	25.42	72	-0.63	0.08	N/A	2	0	97	1	4	36	6
3.90	0.28	B+ / 9.3	5.6	1.46	14.2	25.88	982	-0.50	0.07	N/A	2	0	97	1	11	36	6
3.72	0.28	B+ / 9.3	5.3	1.36	16.0	24.78	69	-0.85	0.06	N/A	3	0	96	1	37	33	6
2.98	0.50	B / 8.7	N/A	N/A	N/A	29.63	133	-0.07	0.17	N/A	0	0	100	0	4	94	3
1.81	0.55	B / 8.0	16.6	0.81	N/A	16.29	738	-2.82	0.09	36.2	0	99	0	1	33	78	6
1.33	0.15	B / 8.6	N/A	N/A	N/A	27.28	39	-3.70	-0.03	N/A	0	0	0	100	2	82	2
5.41	0.12	B- / 7.8	N/A	N/A	N/A	35.32	2	-7.36	-0.07	N/A	0	0	0	100	3	11	2
3.82	0.35	B / 8.4	N/A	N/A	N/A	24.27	169	-4.61	0.11	N/A	0	100	0	0	12	74	3
4.59	0.06	U /	N/A	N/A	N/A	45.43	2	-6.10	-0.16	N/A	0	100	0	0	3	33	2
2.96	0.40	U /	N/A	N/A	N/A	23.96	1	-4.22	-0.09	N/A	0	100	0	0	2	86	3
5.53	0.35	B- / 7.7	N/A	N/A	N/A	28.96	30	-2.97	0.16	N/A	0	99	0	1	38	92	3
3.07	0.35	U /	N/A	N/A	N/A	30.78	3	-3.41	-0.02	N/A	0	99	0	1	2	96	3
3.88	0.05	B+ / 9.2	N/A	N/A	N/A	28.47	21	-3.93	-0.09	N/A	0	0	0	100	1	28	2

Denotes ETF Fund, N/A denotes number is not available

Fund Type	Fund Name	Ticker Symbol	Overall Investment Rating	Price As of 12/31/12	52 Week High	52 Week Low	Performance Rating/Pts	3 Mo	6 Mo	1Yr/Pct	3Yr/Pct	5Yr/Pct
GR	*PowerShares Lux Nanotech	PXN	D-	5.96	6.87	5.41	E+ / 0.7	3.74	-1.79	0.71 / 15	-14.95 / 6	-13.88 / 4
FO	*PowerShares MENA Frontier Countr	PMNA	D	10.83	11.74	9.96	D- / 1.3	1.20	3.50	11.96 / 38	-2.43 / 11	--
IN	*PowerShares Mrnngstr StockInv Co	PYH	C+	23.25	24.26	19.97	C / 5.3	5.22	12.88	18.90 / 67	10.13 / 48	-0.64 / 18
IN	*PowerShares NASDAQ Internet Port	PNQI	B-	41.46	43.38	35.62	B+ / 8.4	5.92	15.62	22.28 / 77	19.47 / 87	--
GEI	*PowerShares Preferred Port	PGX	C+	14.68	14.93	13.85	C- / 4.0	1.45	4.63	13.12 / 42	9.96 / 47	--
GR	*PowerShares QQQ	QQQ	C	65.13	70.58	58.49	C+ / 6.0	1.44	7.05	17.07 / 59	14.59 / 71	8.92 / 65
GI	*PowerShares RiverFront Tact Bal	PAO	C-	12.58	13.18	6.46	C- / 3.3	5.40	9.36	12.78 / 41	5.57 / 31	--
GI	*PowerShares RiverFront Tact Gr &	PCA	C	13.24	13.58	11.83	C- / 3.5	4.70	7.91	12.56 / 40	6.76 / 35	--
IN	*PowerShares S&P 500 BuyWrite Por	PBP	C-	19.65	21.35	19.01	D+ / 2.9	-0.83	1.01	5.20 / 24	7.29 / 36	3.35 / 34
IN	*Powershares S&P 500 High Beta Po	SPHB	B+	21.92	23.46	17.36	A- / 9.1	10.88	23.08	14.61 / 47	--	--
COH	*PowerShares S&P 500 High Dividen	SPHD	U	24.39	N/A	N/A	U /	--	--	--	--	--
IN	*PowerShares S&P 500 High Quality	SPHQ	B-	15.72	16.24	14.22	C+ / 6.5	4.62	9.31	15.42 / 50	14.94 / 72	1.64 / 25
GR	*Powershares S&P 500 Low Vol Port	SPLV	C+	27.68	28.66	25.57	C / 4.5	1.98	3.26	13.46 / 43	--	--
EM	*PowerShares S&P EM High Beta	EEHB	U	23.85	N/A	N/A	U /	14.64	28.76	--	--	--
EM	*PowerShares S&P EM Low Vol	EELV	U	28.85	N/A	N/A	U /	7.73	10.28	--	--	--
FO	*PowerShares S&P Intl Dev Hi Beta	IDHB	U	25.30	N/A	N/A	U /	17.20	--	--	--	--
FO	*PowerShares S&P Intl Dev High Qu	IDHQ	C-	17.33	17.83	14.37	C / 4.3	7.10	17.52	23.03 / 80	5.23 / 30	-0.95 / 17
FO	*PowerShares S&P Intl Dev Low Vol	IDLV	U	28.10	N/A	N/A	U /	2.67	7.39	--	--	--
GR	*PowerShares S&P SC Cnsmr Discr	PSCD	B+	32.98	34.40	28.07	A- / 9.1	6.54	14.55	23.09 / 80	--	--
GR	*PowerShares S&P SC Cnsmr Staples	PSCC	C+	34.44	36.71	30.75	C / 4.9	2.88	2.08	14.97 / 48	--	--
GR	*PowerShares S&P SC Energy	PSCE	D	33.64	40.50	27.98	C- / 3.1	3.58	10.46	2.20 / 19	--	--
GR	*PowerShares S&P SC Financials	PSCF	B-	30.89	32.39	27.43	B- / 7.1	5.65	5.83	17.63 / 61	--	--
GR	*PowerShares S&P SC Health Care	PSCH	C+	35.35	38.14	31.68	C+ / 6.2	4.34	3.64	17.04 / 58	--	--
GR	*PowerShares S&P SC Industrials	PSCI	B+	32.03	33.55	26.46	A / 9.5	13.49	18.78	20.37 / 72	--	--
GR	*PowerShares S&P SC Information T	PSCT	B	30.69	32.28	26.86	B / 8.2	12.54	14.73	12.31 / 39	--	--
GR	*PowerShares S&P SC Materials	PSCM	B+	31.49	33.79	24.94	B+ / 8.8	15.13	--	25.18 / 84	--	--
GR	*PowerShares S&P SC Utilities	PSCU	D+	29.56	36.08	28.14	D- / 1.5	-2.15	-2.17	3.67 / 22	--	--
LP	*PowerShares Senior Loan	BKLN	C	24.98	25.20	23.63	C- / 3.7	2.07	5.18	9.36 / 33	--	--
MUH	*PowerShares VRDO Tax-Free Weekly	PVI	C-	24.99	25.00	24.93	D- / 1.4	0.01	-0.05	0.13 / 14	0.33 / 16	1.08 / 25
IN	*PowerShares Water Resources	PHO	C	20.75	21.55	16.90	C+ / 5.9	12.00	18.30	23.06 / 80	8.55 / 41	3.74 / 36
EN	*PowerShares Wilder Clean Energy	PBW	E+	4.08	6.48	3.46	E / 0.4	9.52	3.74	-20.14 / 5	-24.84 / 4	-26.28 / 2
EN	*PowerShares WilderHill Progr Ene	PUW	D	25.58	27.50	21.70	D+ / 2.6	7.71	12.99	12.24 / 39	3.16 / 23	1.57 / 25
GR	*PowerShares Zacks Micro Cap	PZI	C	11.83	12.38	10.25	C / 5.0	8.25	11.81	19.79 / 70	8.57 / 41	-0.22 / 19
GL	*Precidian Maxis Nikkei 225 Index	NKY	B+	14.45	14.84	12.71	B / 7.9	12.35	10.83	13.48 / 43	--	--
GEI	*ProShares 30 Year TIPS TSY Sprea	RINF	U	40.71	N/A	N/A	U /	3.84	8.92	--	--	--
IN	*ProShares Credit Suisse 130/30	CSM	C	65.83	68.46	56.84	C / 5.1	3.16	10.41	18.27 / 64	10.64 / 51	--
GL	*ProShares German Sovereign Sub S	GGOV	U	41.61	N/A	N/A	U /	1.00	--	--	--	--
GL	*ProShares Hedge Replication ETF	HDG	C-	39.89	42.57	37.35	D+ / 2.5	2.55	3.79	3.63 / 22	--	--
IN	*ProShares RAFI Long/Short	RALS	C-	38.82	40.00	34.51	D+ / 2.4	2.27	7.64	0.83 / 16	--	--
USA	*ProShares Short 20+ Year Treas	TBF	D-	29.38	34.03	27.62	E+ / 0.6	2.07	4.81	-5.00 / 10	-15.89 / 5	--
GEI	*ProShares Short 30 Yr TIPS TSY S	FINF	U	36.30	N/A	N/A	U /	--	-9.02	--	--	--
GEI	*ProShares Short 7-10 Year Treasu	TBX	D	32.42	35.01	31.89	D- / 1.1	0.71	0.59	-4.37 / 11	--	--
GR	*ProShares Short Basic Materials	SBM	D-	33.75	40.81	32.26	E / 0.5	-7.91	-14.42	-10.36 / 8	--	--
GR	*ProShares Short Dow30	DOG	D-	34.40	38.58	33.38	E+ / 0.6	-2.45	-7.56	-12.31 / 7	-13.35 / 6	-10.30 / 5
GI	*ProShares Short Euro	EUFX	U	37.64	N/A	N/A	U /	-1.17	-6.74	--	--	--
FS	*ProShares Short Financials	SEF	D-	28.39	35.83	26.82	E / 0.5	-8.57	-14.86	-23.32 / 4	-14.10 / 6	--
FO	*ProShares Short FTSE China 25	YXI	D-	35.50	47.11	33.89	E / 0.3	-13.11	-23.31	-19.26 / 5	--	--
GEI	*ProShares Short High Yield	SJB	D	32.15	37.18	31.74	E / 0.5	-4.39	-8.08	-14.63 / 6	--	--
COI	*ProShares Short Inv Grade Corp	IGS	D	31.90	35.99	31.65	E+ / 0.7	0.34	-4.29	-10.86 / 8	--	--
FS	*ProShares Short KBW Regional Ban	KRS	D-	43.91	50.45	41.41	E+ / 0.7	-2.54	-3.97	-13.08 / 7	--	--
GR	*ProShares Short Midcap 400	MYY	D-	25.35	30.11	24.37	E / 0.5	-8.81	-12.73	-18.29 / 5	-17.36 / 5	-15.82 / 4
FO	*ProShares Short MSCI EAFE	EFZ	D-	41.51	53.76	40.64	E+ / 0.6	-10.02	-17.40	-20.76 / 5	-10.34 / 7	-9.28 / 5

* Denotes ETF Fund, N/A denotes number is not available

www.thestreetratings.com

| Incl. in Returns | | RISK | 3 Year | | Avg Dura-tion | NET ASSETS | | VALUATION | | Wtd Avg P/E | ASSET | | | | Portfolio Turnover Ratio | FUND MANAGER | |
Dividend Yield %	Expense Ratio	Risk Rating/ Pts	Standard Deviation	Beta		NAV as of 12/31/12	Total $(Mil)	Premium / Discount As of 12/31/12	1 Year Average		Cash %	Stocks %	Bonds %	Other %		Manager Quality Pct	Manager Tenure (Years)
0.30	0.70	C+ / 5.9	24.9	1.40	N/A	6.38	20	-6.58	-0.24	31.3	0	99	0	1	55	3	6
1.75	0.70	B- / 7.6	14.3	0.57	N/A	11.10	16	-2.43	-0.75	N/A	0	99	0	1	49	23	5
1.56	0.50	B / 8.2	15.6	0.94	N/A	24.27	14	-4.20	-0.16	35.3	0	99	0	1	3	47	6
0.10	0.60	C+ / 6.3	21.8	1.20	N/A	43.40	48	-4.47	-0.05	126.6	0	99	0	1	23	74	5
6.38	0.50	B+ / 9.4	5.8	0.24	N/A	14.89	2,149	-1.41	0.15	N/A	0	0	0	100	16	87	5
2.25	0.20	B- / 7.1	17.9	1.09	N/A	67.26	30,417	-3.17	N/A	119.3	0	100	0	0	29	63	N/A
4.55	0.25	B- / 7.9	14.3	0.88	N/A	12.95	16	-2.86	-0.33	N/A	0	100	0	0	62	27	5
5.90	0.25	B / 8.7	9.6	0.60	N/A	13.50	15	-1.93	-0.25	N/A	0	100	0	0	57	55	5
8.19	0.75	B / 8.2	12.0	0.65	N/A	19.97	275	-1.60	0.17	50.1	0	100	0	0	58	48	6
1.69	0.25	B- / 7.2	N/A	N/A	N/A	22.78	119	-3.78	0.01	N/A	0	99	0	1	17	14	2
6.01	N/A	U /	N/A	N/A	N/A	25.16	28	-3.06	N/A	N/A	0	0	0	100	N/A	N/A	1
2.49	0.50	B / 8.6	13.8	0.86	N/A	16.20	176	-2.96	-0.01	28.4	0	99	0	1	14	77	6
4.58	0.25	B+ / 9.7	N/A	N/A	N/A	28.38	3,092	-2.47	0.03	N/A	0	100	0	0	12	79	2
2.63	0.29	U /	N/A	N/A	N/A	24.47	2	-2.53	N/A	N/A	0	0	0	100	12	N/A	1
1.09	0.29	U /	N/A	N/A	N/A	28.79	88	0.21	N/A	N/A	0	0	0	100	14	N/A	1
3.70	0.25	U /	N/A	N/A	N/A	25.69	2	-1.52	N/A	N/A	0	0	0	100	5	N/A	1
2.59	0.75	B- / 7.5	22.3	1.07	N/A	17.56	19	-1.31	-0.28	17.2	0	100	0	0	76	64	6
5.44	0.25	U /	N/A	N/A	N/A	28.13	22	-0.11	N/A	N/A	0	0	0	100	4	N/A	1
6.72	0.29	B- / 7.4	N/A	N/A	N/A	34.04	63	-3.11	-0.04	N/A	0	99	0	1	4	82	3
3.92	0.29	B / 8.7	N/A	N/A	N/A	35.24	28	-2.27	0.02	N/A	0	100	0	0	2	56	3
1.48	0.29	C+ / 5.7	N/A	N/A	N/A	34.75	30	-3.19	-0.10	N/A	0	100	0	0	23	3	3
6.68	0.29	B- / 7.8	N/A	N/A	N/A	31.75	74	-2.71	-0.11	N/A	0	99	0	1	6	73	3
0.77	0.29	B- / 7.9	N/A	N/A	N/A	36.96	110	-4.36	-0.08	N/A	0	100	0	0	17	24	3
6.26	0.29	B- / 7.2	N/A	N/A	N/A	33.48	24	-4.33	-0.05	N/A	0	100	0	0	4	70	3
1.88	0.29	B- / 7.0	N/A	N/A	N/A	31.89	85	-3.76	-0.08	N/A	0	99	0	1	8	18	3
3.12	0.29	B- / 7.2	N/A	N/A	N/A	33.79	6	-6.81	-0.09	N/A	0	99	0	1	5	63	3
9.89	0.29	B / 8.9	N/A	N/A	N/A	30.27	28	-2.35	-0.08	N/A	0	100	0	0	2	20	3
4.68	0.65	B+ / 9.6	N/A	N/A	N/A	25.14	1,499	-0.64	0.40	N/A	0	0	0	100	20	87	2
0.05	0.25	B+ / 9.9	0.2	N/A	0.5	25.00	275	-0.04	-0.03	N/A	6	0	93	1	34	55	6
0.80	0.62	C+ / 6.8	21.0	1.29	N/A	21.56	824	-3.76	-0.09	78.1	0	99	0	1	44	21	6
1.99	0.70	C / 4.5	32.0	1.13	N/A	4.38	123	-6.85	-0.19	38.7	0	99	0	1	46	2	6
1.19	0.71	C+ / 6.7	25.6	1.03	N/A	26.55	37	-3.65	-0.12	30.7	0	99	0	1	36	21	6
4.15	0.70	B- / 7.1	24.8	1.51	N/A	12.35	29	-4.21	-0.24	24.7	0	99	0	1	67	16	6
1.59	0.50	B / 8.3	N/A	N/A	N/A	14.45	193	0.00	0.10	N/A	0	0	0	100	N/A	92	2
1.01	0.75	U /	N/A	N/A	N/A	41.08	4	-0.90	N/A	N/A	0	0	0	100	136	N/A	1
0.94	0.95	B / 8.1	16.1	1.04	N/A	67.94	76	-3.11	-0.05	N/A	0	97	0	3	73	43	3
1.43	0.45	U /	N/A	N/A	N/A	42.44	4	-1.96	N/A	N/A	0	0	0	100	22	N/A	1
0.13	0.95	B+ / 9.4	N/A	N/A	N/A	40.34	22	-1.12	0.09	N/A	0	0	0	100	158	34	1
1.60	0.95	B / 8.7	N/A	N/A	N/A	38.91	12	-0.23	-0.18	N/A	0	0	0	100	56	64	N/A
0.00	0.95	C+ / 5.9	15.0	-1.25	N/A	29.76	781	-1.28	-0.11	N/A	9	0	0	91	N/A	33	3
2.36	0.75	U /	N/A	N/A	N/A	36.26	4	0.11	N/A	N/A	0	0	0	100	123	N/A	1
0.00	0.95	B / 8.4	N/A	N/A	N/A	32.54	15	-0.37	-0.03	N/A	0	0	0	100	123	N/A	1
0.00	0.95	C+ / 5.7	N/A	N/A	N/A	32.71	7	3.18	-0.03	N/A	2	0	0	98	N/A	69	2
0.00	0.95	C+ / 6.6	13.4	-0.86	N/A	33.39	261	3.02	-0.02	N/A	8	0	0	92	N/A	74	2
0.00	N/A	U /	N/A	N/A	N/A	38.01	4	-0.97	N/A	N/A	0	0	0	100	N/A	22	4
0.00	0.95	C+ / 6.3	19.4	-0.96	N/A	27.22	70	4.30	N/A	N/A	20	0	0	80	N/A	N/A	1
0.00	0.95	C+ / 6.3	N/A	N/A	N/A	34.63	9	2.51	0.01	N/A	23	0	0	77	N/A	16	2
0.00	0.95	B- / 7.8	N/A	N/A	N/A	31.75	40	1.26	-0.02	N/A	0	0	0	100	N/A	14	3
0.00	0.95	B / 8.3	N/A	N/A	N/A	31.89	5	0.03	0.26	N/A	0	0	0	100	N/A	8	2
0.00	0.95	C / 5.5	N/A	N/A	N/A	42.42	4	3.51	-0.18	N/A	0	0	0	100	N/A	65	2
0.00	0.95	C+ / 5.8	17.7	-1.11	N/A	24.40	19	3.89	-0.04	N/A	0	0	0	100	N/A	81	2
0.00	0.95	C+ / 6.4	20.0	-0.98	N/A	40.70	134	1.99	-0.01	N/A	11	0	0	89	N/A	16	4

* Denotes ETF Fund, N/A denotes number is not available

Fund Type	Fund Name	Ticker Symbol	Overall Investment Rating	PRICE Price As of 12/31/12	52 Week High	52 Week Low	PERFORMANCE Perform-ance Rating/Pts	3 Mo	6 Mo	1Yr/Pct	3Yr/Pct	5Yr/Pct
			99 Pct = Best 0 Pct = Worst						% Total Return Through 12/31/12		Annualized	
EM	*ProShares Short MSCI Emg Mkts	EUM	D-	26.68	33.86	26.12	E+ / 0.6	-8.53	-15.67	-17.45 / 6	-11.45 / 7	-18.18 / 3
IN	*ProShares Short Oil and Gas	DDG	D-	32.08	38.97	29.79	E+ / 0.6	-3.55	-11.52	-11.48 / 7	-14.72 / 6	--
GR	*ProShares Short QQQ	PSQ	D-	25.57	29.82	23.95	E / 0.5	-2.25	-8.10	-17.51 / 6	-17.17 / 5	-15.21 / 4
GI	*ProShares Short Real Estate	REK	D-	28.00	33.61	26.13	E / 0.5	-5.65	-5.29	-19.29 / 5	--	--
GR	*ProShares Short Russell 2000	RWM	E+	24.32	29.30	23.33	E / 0.5	-7.80	-11.52	-18.17 / 5	-18.50 / 5	-17.06 / 3
GR	*ProShares Short S&P500	SH	D-	34.03	39.37	32.88	E+ / 0.6	-4.19	-9.99	-16.33 / 6	-13.89 / 6	-10.52 / 5
GR	*ProShares Short Small Cap 600	SBB	E+	20.97	25.27	19.00	E / 0.4	-8.31	-11.36	-17.81 / 5	-19.06 / 5	-16.74 / 3
GI	*ProShares Short VIX Sh-Tm Fut ET	SVXY	C	65.45	79.35	29.36	A+ / 9.9	13.44	54.02	164.27 / 99	--	--
IN	*ProShares Ult Telecommunications	LTL	B	58.58	68.07	42.70	B+ / 8.8	-2.14	18.49	37.61 / 96	19.59 / 88	--
USA	*ProShares Ultra 20+ Year Treasur	UBT	E+	69.53	81.35	55.60	E+ / 0.8	-6.31	-13.36	0.39 / 15	--	--
USA	*ProShares Ultra 7-10 Year Treasu	UST	E+	56.75	58.60	49.94	D / 1.6	-1.84	-2.84	4.73 / 23	--	--
GI	*ProShares Ultra Australian Dolla	GDAY	U	42.45	N/A	N/A	U /	--	--	--	--	--
IN	*ProShares Ultra Basic Materials	UYM	D-	36.68	42.10	27.73	C- / 3.2	14.10	27.88	7.04 / 28	4.40 / 28	-10.12 / 5
IN	*ProShares Ultra Consumer Goods	UGE	A	94.10	102.95	78.99	A / 9.4	7.24	16.16	29.99 / 91	25.65 / 98	11.17 / 74
IN	*ProShares Ultra Consumer Service	UCC	A-	78.44	85.81	56.06	A+ / 9.8	9.25	25.48	52.14 / 99	35.36 / 99	14.45 / 88
IN	*ProShares Ultra DJ-UBS Commodity	UCD	E+	23.93	29.55	20.51	E+ / 0.8	-14.05	-6.11	-7.97 / 9	-4.82 / 9	--
EN	*ProShares Ultra DJ-UBS Crude Oil	UCO	E	29.32	49.86	23.13	E+ / 0.6	-1.17	5.46	-25.69 / 4	-14.21 / 6	--
EN	*ProShares Ultra DJ-UBS Natural G	BOIL	E-	39.24	85.80	29.35	E- / 0.0	-33.67	-17.62	-51.80 / 1	--	--
GR	*ProShares Ultra Dow30	DDM	B-	70.23	76.30	58.85	B / 8.1	3.21	13.19	21.02 / 74	18.74 / 85	2.22 / 28
FO	*ProShares Ultra Euro	ULE	D-	24.32	25.80	20.50	D- / 1.1	5.19	17.39	7.81 / 30	-6.72 / 8	--
FS	*ProShares Ultra Financials	UYG	C+	67.81	74.11	46.29	B+ / 8.4	16.46	31.70	51.91 / 99	7.65 / 37	-24.31 / 2
FO	*ProShares Ultra FTSE China 25	XPP	D-	62.37	67.00	38.30	C- / 3.3	27.50	57.80	27.68 / 88	-2.15 / 11	--
PM	*ProShares Ultra Gold	UGL	C	85.26	102.48	73.50	B- / 7.0	-11.05	7.25	-2.60 / 12	20.99 / 91	--
HL	*ProShares Ultra Health Care	RXL	B+	83.83	92.11	64.43	A / 9.3	6.41	20.38	44.11 / 98	20.46 / 89	7.21 / 56
COH	*ProShares Ultra High Yield	UJB	A+	50.37	51.53	40.78	A / 9.3	7.11	13.68	25.48 / 85	--	--
IN	*ProShares Ultra Industrials	UXI	C+	54.60	58.84	40.19	A- / 9.0	16.71	29.59	28.53 / 89	20.77 / 90	0.15 / 20
COI	*ProShares Ultra Invest Grade Cor	IGU	B	55.58	57.07	46.50	C+ / 6.0	-1.92	5.29	19.16 / 68	--	--
FS	*ProShares Ultra KBW Regional Ban	KRU	D	45.21	53.50	37.43	C / 4.9	5.06	2.56	13.34 / 43	--	--
GR	*ProShares Ultra MidCap 400	MVV	B	74.05	80.26	55.60	A / 9.5	17.53	25.91	34.56 / 95	21.99 / 93	5.77 / 47
FO	*ProShares Ultra MSCI Brazil	UBR	E+	70.24	112.00	53.20	D / 1.8	10.11	19.47	-16.02 / 6	--	--
IN	*ProShares Ultra MSCI EAFE	EFO	C+	78.88	82.53	51.08	A+ / 9.9	20.41	39.39	40.38 / 97	--	--
EM	*ProShares Ultra MSCI Emerging Mk	EET	D-	85.62	89.15	57.99	D+ / 2.7	16.80	33.13	26.98 / 87	-1.45 / 12	--
FO	*ProShares Ultra MSCI Europe	UPV	C+	33.44	35.48	20.21	A+ / 9.9	21.21	47.35	50.40 / 99	--	--
FO	*ProShares Ultra MSCI Japan	EZJ	D-	60.62	65.26	46.55	D / 1.7	24.10	17.13	17.55 / 60	-4.80 / 9	--
FO	*ProShares Ultra MSCI Mex Invest	UMX	C+	49.02	62.73	28.69	A+ / 9.9	21.08	--	74.42 / 99	--	--
FO	*ProShares Ultra MSCI Pacific ex-	UXJ	C+	37.92	39.54	23.43	A+ / 9.9	18.31	42.07	44.88 / 98	--	--
HL	*ProShares Ultra Nasdaq Biotech	BIB	C	57.97	69.59	39.63	A+ / 9.9	4.34	20.65	62.43 / 99	--	--
EN	*ProShares Ultra Oil and Gas	DIG	D	45.73	53.40	34.07	C / 4.6	3.61	20.31	10.97 / 36	10.31 / 49	-8.98 / 6
GR	*ProShares Ultra QQQ	QLD	C-	54.81	64.36	44.64	A / 9.3	2.06	12.90	32.54 / 94	25.27 / 97	8.85 / 64
IN	*ProShares Ultra Real Estate	URE	B	69.09	74.57	52.83	A+ / 9.6	10.36	7.26	40.33 / 97	30.24 / 99	-9.85 / 5
GR	*ProShares Ultra Rus Mid Cap Grow	UKW	B-	53.08	57.50	42.50	A- / 9.0	10.93	20.49	26.71 / 86	20.58 / 90	2.03 / 27
GR	*ProShares Ultra Rus Mid Cap Valu	UVU	B	42.95	45.93	31.95	A- / 9.2	--	29.58	35.71 / 95	20.79 / 90	2.50 / 29
IN	*ProShares Ultra Russell 3000	UWC	B-	100.12	101.01	74.80	B+ / 8.6	6.81	18.45	31.58 / 93	17.85 / 82	--
GR	*ProShares Ultra Russell1000 Grow	UKF	B-	62.41	68.59	52.72	B+ / 8.5	3.77	14.97	28.14 / 89	19.06 / 86	3.32 / 34
IN	*ProShares Ultra Russell1000 Valu	UVG	B	35.35	38.28	28.39	B+ / 8.8	7.33	25.93	34.37 / 94	16.76 / 79	-3.05 / 11
GR	*ProShares Ultra Russell2000	UWM	C+	45.52	49.31	33.65	A- / 9.0	14.49	21.35	31.48 / 93	18.47 / 84	1.35 / 24
GR	*ProShares Ultra Russell2000 Grow	UKK	C+	50.13	54.29	37.90	B+ / 8.9	13.93	18.00	27.52 / 88	19.52 / 87	1.55 / 25
IN	*ProShares Ultra Russell2000 Valu	UVT	C+	33.21	35.80	24.23	B+ / 8.7	13.33	23.22	33.80 / 94	15.65 / 75	0.14 / 20
GR	*ProShares Ultra S&P500	SSO	B-	60.35	64.27	47.31	B+ / 8.7	6.66	19.05	32.03 / 93	18.21 / 84	0.01 / 20
IN	*ProShares Ultra Semiconductors	USD	D-	30.25	46.46	25.40	D / 1.9	18.99	6.42	-8.80 / 9	2.04 / 20	-5.46 / 8
EN	*ProShares Ultra Silver	AGQ	E+	44.10	74.65	34.45	C- / 3.0	-19.20	18.38	-6.80 / 10	9.91 / 47	--
GR	*ProShares Ultra SmallCap 600	SAA	B-	54.60	58.87	40.96	A / 9.3	14.72	20.98	31.00 / 92	22.10 / 93	4.62 / 41

* Denotes ETF Fund, N/A denotes number is not available

Incl. in Returns Dividend Yield %	Expense Ratio	RISK Risk Rating/ Pts	3 Year Standard Deviation	Beta	Avg Dura-tion	NET ASSETS NAV as of 12/31/12	Total $(Mil)	VALUATION Premium/Discount As of 12/31/12	1 Year Average	Wtd Avg P/E	Cash %	Stocks %	Bonds %	Other %	Portfolio Turnover Ratio	Manager Quality Pct	Manager Tenure (Years)
0.00	0.95	C+/ 6.1	24.0	-1.03	N/A	26.58	214	0.38	N/A	N/A	14	0	0	86	N/A	17	4
0.00	0.95	C+/ 5.7	21.5	-1.23	N/A	30.86	5	3.95	-0.11	N/A	13	0	0	87	N/A	30	2
0.00	0.95	C+/ 5.6	17.4	-1.06	N/A	24.72	184	3.44	-0.01	N/A	10	0	0	90	N/A	17	4
0.00	0.95	C+/ 5.9	N/A	N/A	N/A	27.20	28	2.94	-0.07	N/A	0	0	0	100	N/A	13	2
0.00	0.95	C / 5.5	20.2	-1.24	N/A	23.39	437	3.98	0.02	N/A	7	0	0	93	N/A	17	4
0.00	0.89	C+/ 6.4	15.0	-0.98	N/A	32.91	1,850	3.40	N/A	N/A	3	0	0	97	N/A	24	3
0.00	0.95	C / 5.4	19.0	-1.17	N/A	20.36	16	3.00	-0.09	N/A	2	0	0	98	N/A	15	3
0.00	N/A	D+/ 2.5	N/A	N/A	N/A	77.87	79	-15.95	0.19	N/A	0	0	0	100	N/A	97	2
0.21	0.95	C+/ 6.9	33.6	1.64	N/A	61.81	5	-5.23	0.16	16.1	22	45	0	33	178	30	2
0.07	0.95	C / 4.4	N/A	N/A	N/A	67.31	14	3.30	0.19	N/A	1	63	0	36	203	19	3
0.02	0.95	C / 4.3	N/A	N/A	N/A	56.02	741	1.30	0.09	N/A	14	0	9	77	146	73	3
0.00	N/A	U /	N/A	N/A	N/A	42.43	4	0.05	N/A	N/A	0	0	0	100	N/A	N/A	1
0.92	0.95	C / 4.4	55.3	3.09	N/A	39.19	157	-6.40	-0.04	24.6	10	41	0	49	28	4	2
0.85	0.95	B-/ 7.9	24.2	1.40	N/A	103.59	15	-9.16	-0.16	30.7	18	57	0	25	3	83	2
0.22	0.95	B-/ 7.1	31.8	1.90	N/A	83.76	12	-6.35	0.08	52.3	34	25	0	41	163	89	2
0.00	0.95	C / 4.5	38.4	1.83	N/A	24.19	6	-1.07	-0.85	N/A	0	100	0	0	N/A	4	N/A
0.00	0.98	D+/ 2.8	58.9	2.01	N/A	30.48	495	-3.81	N/A	N/A	0	100	0	0	N/A	2	N/A
0.00	N/A	D / 1.9	N/A	N/A	N/A	38.16	73	2.83	-0.04	N/A	0	0	0	100	N/A	N/A	N/A
0.50	0.95	C+/ 6.8	28.2	1.78	N/A	74.85	217	-6.17	N/A	N/A	41	48	0	11	30	34	6
0.00	0.95	C+/ 6.3	25.2	1.05	N/A	24.86	5	-2.17	-0.14	N/A	0	0	100	0	N/A	12	N/A
1.39	0.95	C / 5.1	42.1	2.04	N/A	73.79	755	-8.10	-0.05	28.2	0	99	0	1	26	16	2
0.00	0.95	C-/ 3.6	52.0	1.86	N/A	64.18	44	-2.82	-0.01	N/A	80	0	0	20	N/A	11	4
0.00	0.95	C+/ 5.9	38.9	1.84	N/A	83.59	364	2.00	0.24	P/E	0	0	0	100	N/A	25	N/A
0.71	0.95	B-/ 7.2	24.3	1.30	N/A	91.74	44	-8.62	-0.06	50.0	0	99	0	1	3	79	2
0.00	0.95	B / 8.2	N/A	N/A	N/A	51.64	5	-2.46	-0.04	N/A	34	0	0	66	N/A	7	2
0.18	0.95	C / 5.5	41.5	2.52	N/A	58.33	21	-6.39	-0.09	28.9	0	99	0	1	9	18	2
0.00	0.95	B+/ 9.2	N/A	N/A	N/A	55.70	6	-0.22	0.13	N/A	15	0	0	85	N/A	27	2
2.82	0.95	C-/ 3.8	N/A	N/A	N/A	48.18	2	-6.16	0.04	N/A	0	63	22	15	49	7	2
0.06	0.95	C+/ 5.7	38.2	2.32	N/A	79.48	644	-6.83	-0.02	39.0	0	100	0	0	143	24	3
0.00	0.95	D+/ 2.6	N/A	N/A	N/A	71.38	14	-1.60	0.01	N/A	23	0	0	77	N/A	1	3
0.00	0.95	C / 4.4	43.6	2.49	N/A	82.45	12	-4.33	-0.11	N/A	51	0	0	49	145	4	4
0.00	0.95	C-/ 3.8	50.8	2.14	N/A	85.98	43	-0.42	-0.02	N/A	39	14	0	47	163	12	4
0.00	0.95	C-/ 3.7	N/A	N/A	N/A	35.46	8	-5.70	-0.04	N/A	47	0	0	53	N/A	41	4
0.00	0.95	C / 5.1	33.7	1.22	N/A	62.00	18	-2.23	-0.11	N/A	12	0	0	88	N/A	20	4
0.00	0.95	C / 4.6	N/A	N/A	N/A	53.10	3	-7.68	-0.25	N/A	36	0	0	64	N/A	98	3
0.00	0.95	C-/ 4.0	N/A	N/A	N/A	38.97	4	-2.69	-0.10	N/A	50	0	0	50	N/A	75	3
0.00	0.95	D+/ 2.6	N/A	N/A	N/A	65.03	38	-10.86	-0.03	N/A	21	59	0	20	39	97	2
0.21	0.95	C-/ 4.2	48.0	2.03	N/A	49.08	192	-6.83	-0.01	N/A	0	99	0	1	23	16	2
0.15	0.95	D+/ 2.8	37.4	2.22	N/A	58.48	671	-6.28	-0.01	119.3	0	100	0	0	6	33	4
0.50	0.95	C+/ 6.0	36.5	2.02	N/A	73.01	350	-5.37	-0.02	59.7	0	99	0	1	11	75	2
0.00	0.95	C+/ 5.8	38.3	2.32	N/A	57.81	8	-8.18	-0.04	47.1	0	99	0	1	39	18	4
0.21	0.95	C+/ 6.1	36.3	2.20	N/A	46.31	7	-7.26	-0.33	24.7	0	99	0	1	30	26	4
0.00	0.95	C+/ 6.0	36.8	2.27	N/A	100.46	5	-0.34	-0.08	N/A	0	99	0	1	75	19	6
0.18	0.95	C+/ 6.2	33.6	2.05	N/A	67.70	14	-7.81	-0.25	78.6	0	100	0	0	20	22	4
0.35	0.95	C+/ 6.5	34.0	2.11	N/A	38.57	5	-8.35	-0.21	20.7	0	99	0	1	43	17	4
0.02	0.95	C / 5.1	43.6	2.61	N/A	48.97	127	-7.05	-0.02	47.1	0	99	0	1	29	12	4
0.00	0.95	C / 4.8	44.5	2.65	N/A	54.11	11	-7.36	-0.11	73.9	0	99	0	1	80	12	4
0.68	0.95	C / 5.5	42.8	2.55	N/A	35.43	10	-6.27	-0.08	25.2	31	42	0	27	36	11	4
0.74	0.91	C+/ 6.4	31.9	2.03	N/A	64.19	1,279	-5.98	-0.04	50.1	0	99	0	1	3	23	3
0.80	0.95	C / 4.9	48.0	2.52	N/A	33.21	39	-8.91	-0.03	N/A	0	99	0	1	16	3	2
0.00	0.95	D / 1.9	99.2	2.15	N/A	44.80	746	-1.56	0.96	N/A	0	0	0	100	N/A	26	N/A
0.03	0.95	C / 5.5	40.8	2.45	N/A	58.37	21	-6.46	-0.09	49.2	0	99	0	1	13	19	3

* Denotes ETF Fund, N/A denotes number is not available

Fund Type	Fund Name	Ticker Symbol	Overall Investment Rating	Price As of 12/31/12	52 Week High	52 Week Low	Performance Rating/Pts	3 Mo	6 Mo	1Yr/Pct	Annualized 3Yr/Pct	5Yr/Pct
GR	*ProShares Ultra Technology	ROM	D+	70.01	89.58	61.22	C / 4.8	-2.68	6.88	17.88 / 62	11.75 / 57	3.89 / 37
UT	*ProShares Ultra Utilities	UPW	C+	54.01	63.57	50.45	C / 5.3	-3.96	-6.38	8.98 / 32	15.55 / 75	-2.78 / 12
GI	*ProShares Ultra VIX Sh-Tm Fut ET	UVXY	E-	20.90	565.20	14.13	E- / 0.0	-52.70	-81.16	-97.51 / 0	--	--
FO	*ProShares Ultra Yen	YCL	D	28.28	37.13	26.54	E+ / 0.8	-22.74	-21.74	-27.05 / 4	-0.93 / 13	--
GEI	*ProShares UltraPro 10 Year TIPS	UINF	U	38.59	N/A	N/A	U /	0.79	--	--	--	--
GR	*ProShares UltraPro Dow30	UDOW	C	54.82	61.71	42.15	A+ / 9.6	4.05	19.12	30.56 / 92	--	--
GI	*ProShares UltraPro Financials	FINU	U	55.17	N/A	N/A	U /	24.50	--	--	--	--
GR	*ProShares UltraPro MidCap400	UMDD	C-	84.85	95.49	56.31	A+ / 9.9	26.19	39.13	51.19 / 99	--	--
GR	*ProShares UltraPro QQQ	TQQQ	C-	51.69	66.00	39.00	A+ / 9.8	2.07	18.08	47.95 / 98	--	--
GR	*ProShares UltraPro Russell2000	URTY	C-	71.13	80.15	46.16	A+ / 9.9	21.62	31.80	45.22 / 98	--	--
IN	*ProShares UltraPro S&P500	UPRO	C-	87.86	97.02	61.69	A+ / 9.6	9.86	28.42	48.56 / 98	22.26 / 94	--
GR	*ProShares UltraPro Short Dow30	SDOW	E	68.47	98.12	62.41	E- / 0.2	-7.91	-21.99	-34.23 / 3	--	--
GI	*ProShares UltraPro Short Financi	FINZ	U	26.26	N/A	N/A	U /	-23.62	--	--	--	--
GR	*ProShares UltraPro Short MidCap4	SMDD	E-	36.87	63.70	32.33	E- / 0.0	-24.95	-35.03	-48.24 / 1	--	--
GR	*ProShares UltraPro Short QQQ	SQQQ	E-	40.55	68.20	33.93	E- / 0.1	-8.31	-24.52	-47.23 / 1	--	--
GR	*ProShares UltraPro Short S&P500	SPXU	E-	37.86	60.40	34.13	E- / 0.1	-12.95	-28.17	-43.52 / 2	-41.50 / 1	--
GR	*ProShares UltraPro Shrt Russell2	SRTY	E-	33.74	61.29	29.75	E- / 0.0	-22.71	-32.58	-49.17 / 1	--	--
USA	*ProShares UltraPro Sht 20+ Yr Tr	TTT	U	17.35	N/A	N/A	U /	5.81	13.47	--	--	--
IN	*ProShares UltraShort 20+ Year Tr	TBT	E	63.45	86.20	56.32	E / 0.4	4.12	9.33	-10.91 / 8	-30.70 / 3	--
GEI	*ProShares UltraShort 3-7 Yr Trea	TBZ	D	31.94	34.72	31.42	D- / 1.0	-0.28	-0.61	-4.91 / 10	--	--
IN	*ProShares UltraShort 7-10 Year T	PST	D-	27.60	32.31	26.85	E / 0.5	0.87	1.16	-8.39 / 9	-18.88 / 5	--
IN	*ProShares UltraShort Basic Mater	SMN	E-	53.77	79.44	49.50	E / 0.3	-15.85	-27.73	-21.94 / 5	-31.56 / 2	-39.30 / 1
IN	*ProShares UltraShort Consumer Go	SZK	E+	62.39	82.36	59.06	E / 0.3	-9.32	-16.51	-27.84 / 4	-28.65 / 3	-23.90 / 2
IN	*ProShares UltraShort Consumer Se	SCC	E	39.00	60.26	36.22	E- / 0.2	-11.12	-21.72	-40.22 / 2	-37.41 / 2	-34.13 / 1
IN	*ProShares UltraShort DJ-UBS Com	CMD	E+	51.64	68.00	45.00	E+ / 0.8	11.80	-1.39	-4.22 / 11	-10.02 / 7	--
EN	*ProShares UltraShort DJ-UBS Cr O	SCO	E	40.44	61.04	30.74	E / 0.5	-3.87	-16.14	1.26 / 17	-18.25 / 5	--
IN	*ProShares UltraShort DJ-UBS Nat	KOLD	E-	25.41	61.63	18.00	D- / 1.1	32.36	-11.47	-14.01 / 6	--	--
GR	*ProShares UltraShort Dow 30	DXD	E+	47.78	60.44	44.95	E / 0.4	-5.19	-14.96	-23.78 / 4	-26.53 / 4	-23.74 / 2
FO	*ProShares UltraShort Euro	EUO	D-	19.01	23.04	18.50	D- / 1.1	-6.06	-16.64	-12.02 / 7	0.16 / 15	--
FS	*ProShares UltraShort Financials	SKF	E	33.54	54.59	30.60	E- / 0.2	-16.48	-27.81	-42.43 / 2	-30.26 / 3	-43.11 / 0
FO	*ProShares UltraShort FTSE China	FXP	E	17.58	32.35	16.27	E / 0.3	-24.94	-42.16	-37.35 / 2	-26.75 / 4	-47.66 / 0
EN	*ProShares UltraShort Gold	GLL	E	62.60	78.84	55.04	E / 0.4	9.58	-11.64	-11.64 / 7	-31.04 / 2	--
HL	*ProShares UltraShort Health Care	RXD	E+	56.06	78.72	50.22	E / 0.3	-7.87	-20.39	-36.15 / 2	-27.07 / 3	-22.54 / 3
IN	*ProShares UltraShort Industrials	SIJ	E	27.63	40.48	24.58	E- / 0.2	-16.53	-26.85	-31.41 / 3	-34.12 / 2	-30.06 / 1
GR	*ProShares UltraShort MidCap 400	MZZ	E	25.31	36.14	23.30	E- / 0.2	-17.05	-24.36	-34.17 / 3	-34.55 / 2	-34.82 / 1
FO	*ProShares UltraShort MSCI Brazil	BZQ	E	63.59	94.13	48.36	E+ / 0.6	-12.03	-23.81	-5.17 / 10	-13.19 / 6	--
FO	*ProShares UltraShort MSCI EAFE	EFU	E	16.47	27.97	15.18	E / 0.4	-19.27	-32.23	-38.66 / 2	-23.93 / 4	-25.61 / 2
EM	*ProShares UltraShort MSCI Emg Mk	EEV	E	21.18	34.85	20.31	E / 0.3	-16.38	-29.48	-33.78 / 3	-26.47 / 4	-45.05 / 0
FO	*ProShares UltraShort MSCI Europe	EPV	E	26.10	49.47	24.75	E- / 0.2	-19.67	-37.66	-46.89 / 1	-33.55 / 2	--
FO	*ProShares UltraShort MSCI Japan	EWV	E+	29.01	40.51	27.55	E / 0.5	-21.27	-19.64	-25.20 / 4	-12.64 / 6	-16.97 / 3
FO	*ProShares UltraShort MSCI Mex In	SMK	E-	24.81	46.97	22.72	E- / 0.1	-19.80	-32.58	-53.40 / 1	-39.05 / 1	--
FO	*ProShares UltraShort MSCI PXJ	JPX	E	30.19	51.30	28.32	E- / 0.2	-16.15	-32.91	-40.10 / 2	-31.91 / 2	--
HL	*ProShares UltraShort Nasdaq Biot	BIS	E	66.33	114.68	57.53	E- / 0.1	-8.59	-23.16	-47.85 / 1	--	--
EN	*ProShares UltraShort Oil & Gas	DUG	E	21.04	31.08	18.67	E / 0.3	-6.47	-22.00	-22.81 / 4	-30.84 / 3	-35.59 / 1
GR	*ProShares UltraShort QQQ	QID	E	29.65	41.03	26.15	E / 0.3	-5.04	-16.23	-33.29 / 3	-33.61 / 2	-32.97 / 1
IN	*ProShares UltraShort Real Estate	SRS	E	24.26	35.35	22.62	E- / 0.1	-11.17	-10.09	-35.57 / 2	-41.30 / 1	-58.70 / 0
GR	*ProShares UltraShort Russell 300	TWQ	E	46.22	61.58	42.57	E / 0.3	-6.46	-21.83	-32.31 / 3	-29.13 / 3	--
GR	*ProShares UltraShort Russell MC	SJL	E	32.04	46.39	30.20	E / 0.3	-13.86	--	-33.61 / 3	-32.94 / 2	-33.15 / 1
GR	*ProShares UltraShort Russell1000	SFK	E	54.05	69.68	49.39	E / 0.3	-7.12	-18.55	-29.96 / 3	-28.84 / 3	-25.52 / 2
GR	*ProShares UltraShort Russell2000	TWM	E	25.35	37.21	23.29	E- / 0.2	-15.27	-22.30	-34.57 / 2	-37.55 / 2	-38.19 / 1
GR	*ProShares UltraShort Russell2000	SKK	E	24.12	34.12	21.90	E- / 0.2	-14.11	-19.53	-33.36 / 3	-38.60 / 1	-36.70 / 1
GR	*ProShares UltraShort S&P500	SDS	E	54.11	73.04	50.63	E / 0.3	-8.40	-19.25	-30.65 / 3	-27.77 / 3	-25.09 / 2

Incl. in Returns		RISK	3 Year		Avg Dura-tion	NET ASSETS		VALUATION			ASSET				Portfolio Turnover Ratio	FUND MANAGER	
Dividend Yield %	Expense Ratio	Risk Rating/ Pts	Standard Deviation	Beta		NAV as of 12/31/12	Total $(Mil)	Premium / Discount As of 12/31/12	1 Year Average	Wtd Avg P/E	Cash %	Stocks %	Bonds %	Other %		Manager Quality Pct	Manager Tenure (Years)
0.00	0.95	C / 5.4	41.2	2.38	N/A	73.60	74	-4.88	-0.03	124.1	0	99	0	1	4	9	2
2.17	0.95	B / 8.3	19.6	1.85	N/A	56.18	16	-3.86	-0.15	20.4	0	99	0	1	4	31	2
0.00	N/A	D / 1.9	N/A	N/A	N/A	13.92	73	50.14	-0.19	N/A	0	0	0	100	N/A	N/A	2
0.00	0.95	B- / 7.3	18.5	-0.20	N/A	26.62	4	6.24	-0.11	N/A	0	0	0	100	N/A	N/A	2
0.16	N/A	U /	N/A	N/A	N/A	40.22	4	-4.05	N/A	N/A	0	0	0	100	N/A	71	N/A
0.15	0.95	C- / 3.1	N/A	N/A	N/A	59.78	47	-8.30	-0.03	25.0	0	0	0	100	N/A	N/A	1
0.37	N/A	U /	N/A	N/A	N/A	63.38	3	-12.95	N/A	N/A	0	100	0	0	29	8	4
0.00	0.95	D / 2.1	N/A	N/A	N/A	94.18	26	-9.91	-0.07	N/A	0	0	0	100	N/A	N/A	1
0.00	0.95	D / 1.9	N/A	N/A	N/A	56.78	318	-8.96	-0.01	N/A	1	98	0	1	115	33	3
0.03	0.95	D / 1.9	N/A	N/A	N/A	79.38	68	-10.39	-0.05	N/A	0	100	0	0	21	6	3
0.04	0.95	D / 1.9	49.5	3.07	N/A	96.72	366	-9.16	-0.05	N/A	20	64	0	16	93	10	3
0.00	0.95	C- / 3.1	N/A	N/A	N/A	62.40	82	9.73	-0.02	N/A	1	99	0	0	90	10	3
0.00	N/A	U /	N/A	N/A	N/A	22.52	1	16.61	N/A	N/A	0	0	0	100	N/A	58	3
0.00	0.95	D / 2.2	N/A	N/A	N/A	32.91	6	12.03	0.01	N/A	4	0	0	96	N/A	N/A	1
0.00	0.95	D / 2.2	N/A	N/A	N/A	36.57	134	10.88	0.07	N/A	0	0	0	100	N/A	5	3
0.00	0.93	D+ / 2.8	45.5	-2.82	N/A	34.18	462	10.77	-0.01	N/A	0	0	0	100	N/A	23	4
0.00	0.95	D / 1.9	N/A	N/A	N/A	30.07	61	12.20	0.01	N/A	0	0	0	100	N/A	5	3
0.00	N/A	U /	N/A	N/A	N/A	18.03	23	-3.77	N/A	N/A	0	0	0	100	N/A	8	3
0.00	0.92	C- / 3.6	30.9	1.54	N/A	65.16	2,902	-2.62	-0.21	N/A	0	0	0	100	N/A	N/A	1
0.00	0.95	B / 8.5	N/A	N/A	N/A	32.17	5	-0.71	-0.21	N/A	8	0	0	92	N/A	1	5
0.00	0.95	C+ / 5.9	12.1	0.56	N/A	27.94	293	-1.22	-0.09	N/A	15	0	0	85	N/A	68	2
0.00	0.95	D+ / 2.7	52.9	-2.90	N/A	50.19	30	7.13	0.01	N/A	2	0	0	98	N/A	4	5
0.00	0.95	C- / 4.2	22.8	-1.32	N/A	59.29	2	5.23	0.01	N/A	0	0	0	100	N/A	15	2
0.00	0.95	C- / 3.6	30.4	-1.82	N/A	36.46	6	6.97	-0.03	N/A	0	0	0	100	N/A	6	2
0.00	0.95	C / 5.0	37.0	-1.73	N/A	54.45	3	-5.16	-0.41	N/A	0	0	0	100	N/A	4	2
0.00	0.99	C- / 3.7	56.9	-1.93	N/A	38.80	85	4.23	-0.04	N/A	0	0	0	100	N/A	83	N/A
0.00	N/A	D / 1.9	N/A	N/A	N/A	25.55	13	-0.55	0.01	N/A	0	0	0	100	N/A	46	N/A
0.00	0.95	C- / 4.1	27.0	-1.69	N/A	44.96	272	6.27	-0.01	N/A	22	0	0	78	N/A	8	N/A
0.00	0.95	C+ / 6.5	24.7	-1.03	N/A	18.59	531	2.26	-0.02	N/A	0	0	0	100	N/A	10	4
0.00	0.95	C- / 3.3	39.5	-1.89	N/A	30.74	169	9.11	0.01	N/A	55	0	0	45	N/A	78	N/A
0.00	0.95	C- / 3.0	50.9	-1.73	N/A	16.95	112	3.72	-0.05	N/A	9	0	0	91	N/A	5	2
0.00	0.95	C- / 3.4	38.5	-0.35	N/A	63.62	94	-1.60	-0.29	N/A	0	0	0	100	N/A	5	4
0.00	0.95	C- / 4.2	23.2	-1.21	N/A	50.38	5	11.27	0.06	N/A	12	0	0	88	N/A	2	N/A
0.00	0.95	C- / 3.6	39.5	-2.37	N/A	25.85	7	6.89	0.04	N/A	0	0	0	100	N/A	7	2
0.00	0.95	C- / 4.0	35.7	-2.16	N/A	23.53	25	7.56	0.02	N/A	0	0	0	100	N/A	7	2
0.00	0.95	D+ / 2.8	61.3	-2.36	N/A	62.23	14	2.19	-0.01	N/A	8	0	0	92	N/A	6	6
0.00	0.95	C- / 3.4	40.1	-1.91	N/A	15.82	11	4.11	-0.04	N/A	25	0	0	75	N/A	28	4
0.00	0.95	D+ / 3.0	48.9	-2.02	N/A	21.04	49	0.67	-0.02	N/A	0	0	0	100	N/A	6	4
0.00	0.95	C- / 3.1	46.7	-2.16	N/A	24.78	85	5.33	0.02	N/A	0	0	0	100	N/A	5	4
0.00	0.95	C / 5.3	30.7	-1.15	N/A	28.16	11	3.02	0.02	N/A	6	0	0	94	N/A	3	4
0.00	0.95	C- / 3.0	43.7	-1.70	N/A	22.69	1	9.34	0.13	N/A	0	0	0	100	N/A	10	4
0.00	0.95	C- / 3.4	46.6	-2.01	N/A	28.56	2	5.71	0.17	N/A	18	0	0	82	N/A	2	4
0.00	0.95	C- / 3.4	N/A	N/A	N/A	58.66	5	13.08	0.06	N/A	0	0	0	100	N/A	3	4
0.00	0.95	C- / 3.1	45.6	-1.92	N/A	19.48	58	8.01	-0.01	N/A	7	0	0	93	N/A	2	2
0.00	0.95	C- / 4.2	35.4	-2.08	N/A	27.67	377	7.16	-0.02	N/A	22	0	0	78	N/A	6	2
0.00	0.95	C- / 4.2	34.8	-1.84	N/A	22.93	109	5.80	N/A	N/A	4	0	0	96	N/A	7	6
0.00	0.95	C- / 3.7	32.3	-2.00	N/A	42.53	1	8.68	0.17	N/A	24	0	0	76	N/A	3	2
0.00	0.95	C- / 4.0	35.9	-2.10	N/A	30.20	1	6.09	0.59	N/A	0	0	0	100	N/A	11	4
0.00	0.95	C- / 3.8	32.3	-2.01	N/A	49.16	2	9.95	0.03	N/A	0	0	0	100	N/A	7	4
0.00	0.95	C- / 3.4	41.1	-2.44	N/A	23.45	264	8.10	-0.02	N/A	14	0	0	86	N/A	12	4
0.00	0.95	C- / 3.4	42.4	-2.49	N/A	22.01	7	9.59	-0.15	N/A	0	0	0	100	N/A	5	4
0.00	0.89	C- / 3.8	30.1	-1.91	N/A	50.67	1,561	6.79	N/A	N/A	0	0	0	100	N/A	11	3

* Denotes ETF Fund, N/A denotes number is not available

Data as of December 31, 2012

I. Index of ETFs and Other Closed-End Funds

Fund Type	Fund Name	Ticker Symbol	Overall Investment Rating	Price As of 12/31/12	52 Week High	52 Week Low	Performance Rating/Pts	3 Mo	6 Mo	1Yr/Pct	3Yr/Pct	5Yr/Pct
	99 Pct = Best 0 Pct = Worst									% Total Return Through 12/31/12	Annualized	
IN	*ProShares UltraShort Semiconduct	SSG	E	41.56	50.08	32.01	E / 0.4	-19.55	-14.15	-10.12 / 8	-26.64 / 4	-32.81 / 1
EN	*ProShares UltraShort Silver	ZSL	E-	50.07	74.98	38.61	E- / 0.0	15.40	-28.16	-28.31 / 4	-60.50 / 0	--
GR	*ProShares UltraShort SmallCap 60	SDD	E-	25.80	37.35	23.92	E- / 0.2	-15.02	-21.44	-33.79 / 3	-37.91 / 1	-36.96 / 1
GR	*ProShares UltraShort Technology	REW	E+	37.00	47.65	30.98	E / 0.4	-1.43	-12.86	-26.81 / 4	-26.76 / 4	-29.69 / 2
IN	*ProShares UltraShort Telecomncti	TLL	E+	29.19	42.81	25.50	E / 0.3	-1.94	-23.01	-34.52 / 3	-29.39 / 3	
GR	*ProShares UltraShort TIPS	TPS	D	25.57	29.54	24.90	E+ / 0.7	0.27	-2.27	-11.71 / 7	--	
UT	*ProShares UltraShort Utilities	SDP	D-	29.74	34.45	26.13	E / 0.4	1.39	0.32	-15.41 / 6	-22.97 / 4	-17.34 / 3
FO	*ProShares UltraShort Yen	YCS	D	50.77	53.87	39.95	D+ / 2.4	28.69	25.20	31.05 / 92	-4.32 / 9	--
GI	*ProShares UltraSht Australian Dl	CROC	U	37.74	N/A	N/A	U /	-6.96	--	--	--	--
GL	*ProShares USD Covered Bond	COBO	U	101.92	N/A	N/A	U /	0.40	1.35	--		
GEI	*ProShares VIX Mid-Term Futures E	VIXM	E	34.22	71.30	31.04	E- / 0.0	-19.87	-38.28	-55.69 / 1	--	--
GEI	*ProShares VIX Short-Term Futures	VIXY	E-	17.01	67.01	14.18	E- / 0.0	-25.05	-50.05	-78.89 / 0	--	--
LP	*Pyxis iBoxx Senior Loan ETF	SNLN	U	20.14	N/A	N/A	U /	--	--	--	--	--
GL	*QAM Equity Hedge ETF	QEH	U	25.49	N/A	N/A	U /	3.38	--	--	--	--
GR	*QuantShares US Market Neutral Si	SIZ	C-	25.12	27.14	24.11	D / 1.6	3.06	--	-0.30 / 13	--	--
IN	*QuantShares US Market Neutral Va	CHEP	D+	24.57	27.47	23.12	D- / 1.5	3.57	4.44	-4.30 / 11	--	--
GR	*QuantShares US Mkt Neut Anti-Bet	BTAL	D	22.04	24.92	20.53	E+ / 0.7	-7.09	-12.75	-5.78 / 10	--	--
GR	*QuantShares US Mkt Neutral Momen	MOM	D	24.42	27.33	22.51	E+ / 0.7	-3.17	-7.47	-7.01 / 9	--	--
GR	*Ranger Equity Bear ETF	HDGE	D-	18.28	25.50	17.58	E- / 0.2	-15.36	-25.83	-24.95 / 4	--	--
EM	*RBS China Trendpilot ETN	TCHI	U	25.17	N/A	N/A	U /	8.37	11.34	--	--	--
GL	*RBS Global Big Pharma ETN	DRGS	C+	29.57	31.17	26.08	B / 7.9	4.77	11.08	17.67 / 61	--	--
EN	*RBS Gold Trendpilot ETN	TBAR	D-	29.38	31.48	28.21	D- / 1.1	-5.69	0.24	0.14 / 14	--	--
IN	*RBS NASDAQ 100 Trendpilot ETN	TNDQ	D-	27.51	30.61	26.18	D / 2.0	-1.25	-1.33	5.98 / 26	--	--
GL	*RBS Oil Trendpilot ETN	TWTI	E+	22.99	29.90	21.63	E+ / 0.6	-5.76	-9.89	-11.36 / 8	--	--
EN	*RBS Rogers Enhanced Agriculture	RGRA	U	23.96	N/A	N/A	U /	--	--	--	--	--
EN	*RBS Rogers Enhanced Commodity ET	RGRC	U	24.75	N/A	N/A	U /	--	--	--	--	--
EN	*RBS Rogers Enhanced Energy ETN	RGRE	U	24.77	N/A	N/A	U /	--	--	--	--	--
IN	*RBS US Large Cap Alternator ETN	ALTL	U	26.04	N/A	N/A	U /	2.11	--	--	--	--
GR	*RBS US Large Cap Trendpilot ETN	TRND	B	27.70	28.60	24.37	C+ / 6.9	3.37	9.42	15.90 / 52	--	--
GR	*RBS US Mid Cap Trendpilot ETN	TRNM	C	24.78	25.73	21.48	B / 8.0	8.50	12.83	14.97 / 48	--	--
IN	*RevenueShares ADR Fund	RTR	D+	35.29	37.16	29.22	D+ / 2.7	10.97	19.85	14.74 / 47	2.12 / 20	--
FS	*RevenueShares Financials Sector	RWW	C	32.04	33.69	25.00	C+ / 5.9	9.82	24.38	31.49 / 93	6.00 / 33	--
GR	*RevenueShares Large Cap Fund	RWL	C+	26.92	27.84	23.36	C+ / 5.7	5.58	12.80	18.30 / 64	11.42 / 55	--
GR	*RevenueShares Mid Cap Fund	RWK	C+	32.08	33.60	27.82	C+ / 6.9	13.15	16.07	17.09 / 59	12.49 / 61	--
IN	*RevenueShares Navellier OA A100	RWV	C	39.66	41.65	36.36	C / 4.4	2.06	8.21	14.00 / 45	10.34 / 49	--
GR	*RevenueShares Small Cap Fund	RWJ	C+	37.44	38.98	31.06	B- / 7.0	9.16	14.30	16.99 / 58	14.08 / 69	--
IN	*Rockledge SectorSAM ETF	SSAM	U	24.87	N/A	N/A	U /	-1.00	0.05	--	--	--
GL	*Russell Equity ETF	ONEF	B	29.14	30.26	25.39	B / 8.0	--	14.25	18.94 / 67	--	--
FO	*Schwab Emerging Markets Equity E	SCHE	B+	26.39	26.95	21.78	A- / 9.0	10.77	19.36	16.40 / 54	--	--
FO	*Schwab International Equity ETF	SCHF	C	27.10	27.86	22.13	C / 5.0	12.71	22.02	23.10 / 80	4.85 / 29	--
FO	*Schwab Intl Small-Cap Equity ETF	SCHC	B	27.05	27.94	22.42	A+ / 9.7	12.76	23.96	24.30 / 82	--	--
USA	*Schwab Intmdt-Term US Treasury E	SCHR	C-	54.08	54.68	52.29	D / 1.6	-0.30	-0.27	1.96 / 18	--	--
USA	*Schwab Short-Term US Treas ETF	SCHO	C-	50.49	50.61	50.34	D- / 1.4	0.05	0.14	0.25 / 14	--	--
GEN	*Schwab US Aggregate Bond ETF	SCHZ	C-	52.34	53.12	50.96	D / 1.8	-0.53	0.29	2.77 / 20	--	--
IN	*Schwab US Broad Market ETF	SCHB	C+	34.41	35.58	30.51	C+ / 5.8	5.31	11.24	17.97 / 62	12.12 / 59	--
GI	*Schwab US Dividend Equity ETF	SCHD	B+	28.34	29.32	26.13	C+ / 6.4	3.87	7.55	15.37 / 49	--	--
IN	*Schwab US Large-Cap ETF	SCHX	C+	33.89	35.12	30.22	C+ / 5.7	4.95	11.02	17.79 / 61	11.81 / 57	--
GR	*Schwab US Large-Cap Growth ETF	SCHG	C+	34.15	35.72	30.64	C / 5.5	4.68	10.79	17.77 / 61	11.62 / 56	--
IN	*Schwab US Large-Cap Value ETF	SCHV	C+	31.83	32.94	28.43	C+ / 5.7	5.15	11.28	17.53 / 60	11.78 / 57	--
GR	*Schwab US Mid-Cap ETF	SCHM	B+	27.87	28.95	24.00	B+ / 8.8	9.03	14.74	18.38 / 64	--	--
GI	*Schwab US REIT ETF	SCHH	B-	30.64	32.10	27.22	B- / 7.0	5.51	2.81	19.50 / 69	--	--
GR	*Schwab US Small-Cap ETF	SCHA	B-	38.12	39.76	32.58	B- / 7.2	8.97	13.27	19.62 / 69	14.50 / 71	--

* Denotes ETF Fund, N/A denotes number is not available

www.thestreetratings.com

Dividend Yield %	Expense Ratio	Risk Rating / Pts	Standard Deviation	Beta	Avg Dura-tion	NAV as of 12/31/12	Total $(Mil)	P/D As of 12/31/12	1 Year Average	Wtd Avg P/E	Cash %	Stocks %	Bonds %	Other %	Portfolio Turnover Ratio	Manager Quality Pct	Manager Tenure (Years)
0.00	0.95	C- / 3.5	46.9	-2.41	N/A	37.59	11	10.56	-0.01	N/A	7	0	0	93	N/A	38	2
0.00	0.95	D / 1.9	83.2	-1.74	N/A	48.36	106	3.54	-1.08	N/A	0	0	0	100	N/A	N/A	N/A
0.00	0.95	C- / 3.4	38.6	-2.29	N/A	24.23	8	6.48	-0.09	N/A	18	0	0	82	N/A	5	3
0.00	0.95	C- / 4.2	39.1	-2.24	N/A	35.20	13	5.11	-0.03	N/A	6	0	0	94	N/A	18	2
0.00	0.95	C / 4.5	32.9	-1.60	N/A	26.74	2	9.16	0.22	N/A	0	0	0	100	N/A	10	2
0.00	0.95	B- / 7.4	N/A	N/A	N/A	25.82	4	-0.97	N/A	N/A	0	0	0	100	N/A	7	2
0.00	0.95	C+ / 5.8	20.1	-1.89	N/A	28.39	3	4.76	0.02	N/A	3	0	0	97	N/A	16	2
0.00	0.95	C+ / 6.5	18.9	0.21	N/A	53.62	401	-5.32	-0.01	N/A	0	0	0	100	N/A	15	N/A
0.00	N/A	U /	N/A	N/A	N/A	36.67	4	2.92	N/A	N/A	0	0	0	100	N/A	N/A	1
0.93	N/A	U /	N/A	N/A	N/A	101.92	13	0.00	N/A	N/A	0	0	0	100	N/A	N/A	1
0.00	0.85	C- / 3.6	N/A	N/A	N/A	31.28	37	9.40	-0.16	N/A	0	0	0	100	N/A	N/A	2
0.00	0.85	D / 1.9	N/A	N/A	N/A	14.07	148	20.90	-0.13	N/A	0	0	0	100	N/A	N/A	2
8.90	N/A	U /	N/A	N/A	N/A	20.17	32	-0.15	N/A	N/A	0	0	0	100	N/A	N/A	1
0.88	N/A	U /	N/A	N/A	N/A	26.01	4	-2.00	N/A	N/A	0	0	0	100	N/A	N/A	1
0.00	0.99	B+ / 9.5	N/A	N/A	N/A	25.14	5	-0.08	-0.24	N/A	0	0	0	100	128	36	2
0.00	0.99	B+ / 9.1	N/A	N/A	N/A	24.74	4	-0.69	-0.09	N/A	0	0	0	100	83	27	2
0.00	0.99	B / 8.1	N/A	N/A	N/A	21.41	17	2.94	-0.04	N/A	0	0	0	100	117	82	2
0.00	0.99	B / 8.6	N/A	N/A	N/A	24.78	1	-1.45	-0.31	N/A	0	0	0	100	179	94	2
0.00	1.69	C+ / 6.2	N/A	N/A	N/A	17.73	219	3.10	0.05	N/A	12	88	0	0	756	19	N/A
0.00	N/A	U /	N/A	N/A	N/A	26.42	N/A	-4.73	N/A	N/A	0	0	0	100	N/A	N/A	1
0.00	N/A	C+ / 5.7	N/A	N/A	N/A	30.85	4	-4.15	0.02	N/A	0	0	0	100	N/A	76	2
0.00	N/A	C / 5.0	N/A	N/A	N/A	28.97	26	1.42	0.14	N/A	0	0	0	100	N/A	75	2
0.00	N/A	C / 5.3	N/A	N/A	N/A	27.69	N/A	-0.65	0.13	N/A	0	0	0	100	N/A	16	2
0.00	N/A	C / 4.8	N/A	N/A	N/A	23.02	9	-0.13	-0.17	N/A	0	0	0	100	N/A	6	2
0.00	N/A	U /	N/A	N/A	N/A	23.75	N/A	0.88	N/A	N/A	0	0	0	100	N/A	N/A	1
0.00	N/A	U /	N/A	N/A	N/A	24.74	N/A	0.04	N/A	N/A	0	0	0	100	N/A	N/A	1
0.00	N/A	U /	N/A	N/A	N/A	25.16	N/A	-1.55	N/A	N/A	0	0	0	100	N/A	N/A	1
0.00	N/A	U /	N/A	N/A	N/A	26.63	N/A	-2.22	N/A	N/A	0	0	0	100	N/A	N/A	1
0.00	N/A	B / 8.5	N/A	N/A	N/A	28.53	70	-2.91	0.08	N/A	0	0	0	100	N/A	45	3
0.00	N/A	C / 4.7	N/A	N/A	N/A	25.70	33	-3.58	-0.05	N/A	0	0	0	100	N/A	30	2
3.84	0.49	C+ / 6.9	22.1	1.32	N/A	36.39	27	-3.02	-0.10	N/A	1	98	0	1	35	12	N/A
1.98	0.49	C+ / 6.6	24.2	1.18	N/A	33.56	10	-4.53	-0.16	N/A	0	99	0	1	26	30	5
2.66	0.49	B / 8.1	16.0	1.03	N/A	27.80	151	-3.17	-0.04	28.8	0	99	0	1	29	52	5
1.84	0.54	B- / 7.6	23.0	1.27	N/A	33.58	105	-4.47	-0.06	30.3	0	99	0	1	55	36	5
1.20	0.60	B- / 7.8	19.3	1.08	N/A	41.36	8	-4.11	-0.12	N/A	0	100	0	0	154	31	N/A
2.02	0.54	B- / 7.5	22.0	1.35	N/A	38.67	122	-3.18	-0.03	32.5	0	99	0	1	48	43	5
0.00	N/A	U /	N/A	N/A	N/A	25.11	1	-0.96	N/A	N/A	0	0	0	100	N/A	N/A	1
6.90	0.35	B- / 7.8	N/A	N/A	N/A	29.84	3	-2.35	-0.06	N/A	0	100	0	0	6	82	3
4.22	0.25	C+ / 6.9	N/A	N/A	N/A	26.36	694	0.11	0.38	N/A	0	97	0	3	9	62	3
5.34	0.13	B- / 7.5	20.9	1.03	N/A	27.45	979	-1.28	0.55	28.2	0	97	0	3	8	61	4
5.99	0.35	C+ / 6.0	N/A	N/A	N/A	27.53	205	-1.74	0.48	126.9	0	93	0	7	25	77	3
0.94	0.12	B+ / 9.7	N/A	N/A	N/A	53.97	217	0.20	N/A	N/A	0	0	100	0	33	62	3
0.29	0.12	B+ / 9.9	N/A	N/A	N/A	50.53	250	-0.08	N/A	N/A	1	0	98	1	52	52	3
1.98	0.10	B+ / 9.9	N/A	N/A	N/A	52.27	388	0.13	0.18	N/A	0	0	100	0	92	40	2
5.96	0.06	B / 8.1	15.8	1.03	N/A	35.52	1,335	-3.13	0.03	N/A	0	99	0	1	5	56	4
7.29	N/A	B+ / 9.6	N/A	N/A	N/A	29.20	575	-2.95	0.04	N/A	0	99	0	1	N/A	69	2
5.93	0.08	B / 8.1	15.4	1.01	N/A	35.03	1,018	-3.25	0.01	N/A	1	99	0	0	4	55	4
4.89	0.13	B / 8.0	17.3	1.11	N/A	35.36	528	-3.42	0.03	N/A	0	99	0	1	8	42	4
7.45	0.13	B / 8.2	14.1	0.91	N/A	32.90	420	-3.25	0.04	N/A	0	99	0	1	8	63	4
5.36	0.13	B- / 7.5	N/A	N/A	N/A	28.87	293	-3.46	0.05	N/A	0	99	0	1	19	64	2
6.85	0.13	B- / 7.9	N/A	N/A	N/A	31.26	373	-1.98	0.03	N/A	0	99	0	1	3	83	2
7.36	0.13	B- / 7.4	20.5	1.28	N/A	39.46	707	-3.40	0.04	N/A	1	98	0	1	12	54	4

* Denotes ETF Fund, N/A denotes number is not available

Fund Type	Fund Name	Ticker Symbol	Overall Investment Rating	Price As of 12/31/12	52 Week High	52 Week Low	Performance Rating/Pts	3 Mo	6 Mo	1Yr/Pct	3Yr/Pct	5Yr/Pct
										% Total Return Through 12/31/12	Annualized	
GEI	*Schwab US TIPS ETF	SCHP	C-	58.30	59.29	55.50	D / 2.2	-0.11	0.86	5.44 / 25	--	--
FS	*SP Bank ETF	KBE	D+	23.83	25.06	20.15	C- / 3.3	5.60	13.41	17.30 / 60	3.79 / 25	-6.30 / 7
FS	*SP Capital Markets ETF	KCE	C-	34.11	36.26	28.35	C / 4.3	14.76	20.67	26.88 / 87	1.96 / 20	-6.45 / 7
IN	*SP Insurance ETF	KIE	C	44.00	46.12	37.90	C+ / 5.9	7.46	15.16	22.93 / 79	10.08 / 48	1.41 / 24
FS	*SP Regional Banking ETF	KRE	C-	27.97	30.08	24.80	C- / 3.8	3.57	5.59	12.58 / 40	8.84 / 42	0.33 / 21
USA	*SPDR Barclays 1-3 Month T-Bill E	BIL	C-	45.81	45.83	45.80	D- / 1.3	-0.02	-0.04	-0.04 / 14	-0.03 / 15	0.27 / 20
GEI	*SPDR Barclays Aggregate Bond ETF	LAG	C	58.77	59.44	57.16	D+ / 2.4	-0.06	0.48	3.48 / 21	5.19 / 30	5.16 / 45
GI	*SPDR Barclays Conv Sec ETF	CWB	C	40.30	41.26	36.08	C- / 3.9	5.39	13.04	14.25 / 46	6.78 / 35	--
GI	*SPDR Barclays Em Mkt Local Bond	EBND	C+	32.29	33.01	29.53	C+ / 5.8	3.30	8.44	13.19 / 42	--	--
COH	*SPDR Barclays High Yield Bond ET	JNK	C-	40.71	41.25	37.51	C / 4.5	4.07	7.87	14.40 / 46	10.05 / 47	7.98 / 60
GEI	*SPDR Barclays Int Term Crp Bond	ITR	C	34.82	35.17	33.42	D+ / 2.8	0.06	2.69	7.25 / 29	6.53 / 34	--
USA	*SPDR Barclays Int Tr Treas ETF	ITE	C-	60.72	61.69	60.15	D / 2.1	-0.05	-0.04	1.31 / 17	3.91 / 26	4.00 / 37
COI	*SPDR Barclays Intl Corporate Bd	IBND	B+	35.40	36.39	31.20	B- / 7.3	3.55	12.37	15.22 / 49	--	--
GL	*SPDR Barclays Intl Treasury Bd E	BWX	C-	61.01	61.94	58.19	D / 2.2	-1.17	3.73	6.27 / 27	3.57 / 24	3.96 / 37
COI	*SPDR Barclays Invest Grade Flrt	FLRN	C-	30.66	45.60	30.00	D / 2.1	1.07	1.86	3.04 / 21	--	--
COI	*SPDR Barclays Iss Sco Corp Bond	CBND	C	32.58	33.22	31.30	D+ / 2.8	0.37	2.91	7.08 / 28	--	--
USA	*SPDR Barclays LongTerm Treasury	TLO	C	70.11	75.73	64.18	C- / 3.9	-2.41	-5.30	1.83 / 18	12.50 / 61	8.57 / 63
GEI	*SPDR Barclays LongTrm Corp Bond	LWC	C	41.14	42.76	37.67	C- / 3.8	-1.91	1.51	9.21 / 33	10.57 / 51	--
MTG	*SPDR Barclays Mortg Backed Bond	MBG	C-	27.31	28.96	27.20	D / 2.1	-0.31	-0.14	1.76 / 18	3.71 / 25	--
COH	*SPDR Barclays Short Term HiYld B	SJNK	U	30.55	N/A	N/A	U /	2.99	6.35	--	--	--
COI	*SPDR Barclays Sht Trm Corp Bond	SCPB	C-	30.72	30.87	30.29	D / 2.0	0.38	1.64	2.97 / 20	2.68 / 22	--
USA	*SPDR Barclays Sht Trm Treasury E	SST	C-	30.17	31.37	29.77	D- / 1.5	0.03	0.36	0.77 / 15	--	--
GL	*SPDR Barclays ST Intl Treas Bd E	BWZ	D+	36.65	37.45	34.91	D / 1.7	-0.88	4.21	2.84 / 20	1.02 / 17	--
USA	*SPDR Barclays TIPS ETF	IPE	C	60.72	61.70	57.84	C- / 3.3	-0.13	0.80	6.31 / 27	8.92 / 43	6.56 / 52
COI	*SPDR BofA Merrill Lynch CrOvr Co	XOVR	U	26.64	N/A	N/A	U /	1.21	5.11	--	--	--
EM	*SPDR BofA Merrill Lynch Em Mkt C	EMCD	U	31.69	N/A	N/A	U /	2.92	5.78	--	--	--
GL	*SPDR DB Intl Gvt Inflation Pt Bo	WIP	C	63.54	64.03	57.01	C- / 3.6	3.20	10.48	14.58 / 47	6.70 / 34	--
IN	*SPDR DJ REIT ETF	RWR	B	72.97	76.81	65.14	B / 7.6	4.58	1.93	18.20 / 63	18.69 / 85	7.84 / 59
GR	*SPDR DJ Total Market ETF	TMW	C+	106.26	110.00	94.57	C / 5.4	4.29	10.45	16.66 / 56	11.52 / 56	4.99 / 44
GI	*SPDR DJ Wilshire Glb Real Est ET	RWO	B	42.12	42.84	35.50	B- / 7.4	6.49	8.31	25.71 / 85	15.26 / 73	--
FO	*SPDR DJ Wilshire Intl Real Estat	RWX	C	41.35	42.97	32.94	B / 7.7	8.51	16.77	35.27 / 95	12.37 / 60	1.46 / 25
GR	*SPDR DJ Wilshire Large Cap ETF	ELR	C+	66.40	69.04	60.11	C / 5.2	3.49	9.81	17.04 / 58	11.39 / 55	4.75 / 42
GR	*SPDR DJ Wilshire Mid Cap ETF	EMM	C+	66.09	68.75	57.68	C+ / 6.7	8.24	14.03	17.25 / 59	13.68 / 67	8.42 / 62
GR	*SPDR Dow Jones Industrial Averag	DIA	C	130.58	136.48	120.19	C / 4.4	1.91	6.99	11.31 / 37	11.18 / 54	5.23 / 45
FO	*SPDR Euro STOXX 50 ETF	FEZ	D	34.66	35.64	25.29	D+ / 2.7	13.80	32.21	27.78 / 88	-1.14 / 13	-5.47 / 8
GL	*SPDR FTSE/Macquarie Glob Infr 10	GII	C-	40.26	41.66	37.70	D / 2.2	1.00	2.83	8.22 / 31	2.31 / 21	-3.22 / 11
GL	*SPDR Global Dow ETF	DGT	D+	56.18	58.16	47.94	D+ / 2.7	9.23	16.78	16.63 / 55	2.59 / 22	-1.68 / 15
PM	*SPDR Gold Shares	GLD	C	162.02	174.07	148.53	C / 4.3	-5.29	4.49	1.13 / 16	13.26 / 64	13.00 / 81
GL	*SPDR MSCI ACWI ex-US ETF	CWI	C-	32.19	32.79	26.69	C- / 3.7	9.30	17.47	18.18 / 63	3.60 / 25	-0.20 / 19
GL	*SPDR MSCI ACWI IMI ETF	ACIM	U	49.75	N/A	N/A	U /	3.69	11.99	--	--	--
MUN	*SPDR Nuveen Barclays Bld Amr Bd	BABS	B-	61.55	64.71	57.20	C+ / 5.6	2.19	1.67	10.82 / 56	--	--
MUN	*SPDR Nuveen Barclays CA Muni Bd	CXA	C+	24.18	25.57	23.41	C / 4.7	1.09	2.98	7.23 / 37	7.93 / 59	5.98 / 66
MUN	*SPDR Nuveen Barclays Muni Bond E	TFI	C	24.24	25.01	23.32	C- / 3.7	0.99	2.71	5.24 / 30	6.35 / 46	5.23 / 60
MUN	*SPDR Nuveen Barclays NY Muni Bd	INY	C	23.95	25.48	23.19	C- / 3.9	1.73	3.34	6.68 / 35	6.56 / 48	5.40 / 61
MUN	*SPDR Nuveen Barclays ST Muni Bd	SHM	C-	24.31	24.62	24.21	D / 1.9	-0.07	0.39	1.07 / 17	1.93 / 23	2.89 / 40
COH	*SPDR Nuveen S&P Hi Yld Muni Bd E	HYMB	B+	58.00	59.60	53.13	C+ / 6.5	3.32	6.42	16.79 / 57	--	--
GEI	*SPDR Nuveen S&P VRDO Muni Bond E	VRD	C-	29.88	30.04	29.65	D- / 1.4	-0.18	-0.14	-0.26 / 13	0.38 / 16	--
FO	*SPDR Russell/Nomura PRIME Japan	JPP	D+	37.10	39.50	33.12	D / 2.2	11.69	9.85	9.02 / 32	1.02 / 17	-2.04 / 14
FO	*SPDR Russell/Nomura Small Cap Ja	JSC	C-	42.35	44.67	38.61	D+ / 2.6	8.62	5.11	6.26 / 27	4.93 / 29	3.07 / 32
GR	*SPDR S&P 400 Mid Cap Growth ETF	MDYG	B-	85.22	88.72	74.99	B- / 7.0	8.47	14.44	17.83 / 61	14.18 / 69	9.23 / 66
GR	*SPDR S&P 400 Mid Cap Value ETF	MDYV	C+	59.85	62.11	51.71	C+ / 6.3	7.96	12.82	18.88 / 67	12.29 / 59	7.13 / 55
GR	*SPDR S&P 500 ETF	SPY	C	142.41	148.11	127.14	C / 5.2	3.66	9.71	16.70 / 56	11.26 / 54	4.42 / 40

99 Pct = Best
0 Pct = Worst

* Denotes ETF Fund, N/A denotes number is not available

| Incl. in Returns | | RISK | | | | NET ASSETS | | VALUATION | | | ASSET | | | | | FUND MANAGER | |
Dividend Yield %	Expense Ratio	Risk Rating/ Pts	3 Year Standard Deviation	Beta	Avg Dura-tion	NAV as of 12/31/12	Total $(Mil)	Premium / Discount As of 12/31/12	1 Year Average	Wtd Avg P/E	Cash %	Stocks %	Bonds %	Other %	Portfolio Turnover Ratio	Manager Quality Pct	Manager Tenure (Years)
1.31	0.14	B+ / 9.7	N/A	N/A	N/A	58.10	571	0.34	0.08	N/A	0	0	99	1	103	38	3
3.47	0.35	C+ / 6.9	24.0	1.10	N/A	24.76	1,679	-3.76	-0.02	10.5	0	100	0	0	55	32	8
7.76	0.36	C+ / 6.7	24.1	1.16	N/A	36.25	20	-5.90	-0.05	22.9	0	100	0	0	64	15	8
4.06	0.35	B- / 7.3	20.6	1.22	N/A	46.01	143	-4.37	N/A	26.0	0	100	0	0	62	30	8
3.27	0.35	B- / 7.3	24.5	1.09	N/A	28.96	1,147	-3.42	0.01	11.0	0	100	0	0	44	63	N/A
0.00	0.14	B+ / 9.9	0.1	N/A	N/A	45.81	1,297	0.00	N/A	N/A	0	0	99	1	619	50	N/A
1.57	0.13	B+ / 9.7	2.8	1.11	N/A	58.50	622	0.46	N/A	N/A	0	0	99	1	428	41	N/A
11.22	0.40	B / 8.3	11.5	0.70	N/A	41.08	918	-1.90	0.05	N/A	0	0	0	100	17	45	N/A
15.52	0.50	B / 8.7	N/A	N/A	N/A	32.19	151	0.31	0.86	N/A	2	0	97	1	18	68	N/A
6.33	0.40	B- / 7.3	9.5	1.28	7.8	41.07	12,502	-0.88	0.24	N/A	0	0	99	1	38	26	N/A
2.84	0.15	B+ / 9.7	3.2	0.81	N/A	34.64	350	0.52	0.54	N/A	0	0	99	1	15	66	N/A
1.54	0.14	B+ / 9.8	2.6	0.16	4.4	60.70	170	0.03	-0.06	N/A	0	0	99	1	35	67	N/A
1.64	0.55	B / 8.7	N/A	N/A	N/A	35.36	116	0.11	0.38	N/A	0	0	99	1	42	95	N/A
2.81	0.50	B+ / 9.3	8.5	1.08	7.3	60.47	1,975	0.89	0.23	N/A	0	0	99	1	38	53	N/A
1.21	0.15	B+ / 9.6	N/A	N/A	N/A	30.49	15	0.56	0.81	N/A	0	0	100	0	5	27	N/A
3.15	0.16	B+ / 9.9	N/A	N/A	N/A	32.55	29	0.09	0.70	N/A	0	0	99	1	17	50	N/A
2.57	0.14	B / 8.7	12.4	1.04	15.6	69.30	42	1.17	0.05	N/A	0	0	99	1	22	46	N/A
4.38	0.15	B+ / 9.0	8.1	2.43	N/A	41.08	128	0.15	0.59	N/A	0	0	99	1	21	26	N/A
0.22	0.20	B+ / 9.6	3.4	1.36	N/A	27.25	36	0.22	N/A	N/A	0	0	99	1	1,489	33	N/A
6.94	N/A	U /	N/A	N/A	N/A	30.60	622	-0.16	N/A	N/A	0	0	0	100	N/A	N/A	N/A
1.25	0.23	B+ / 9.9	1.3	0.24	N/A	30.70	1,723	0.07	0.32	N/A	0	0	99	1	17	57	N/A
0.74	0.12	B+ / 9.9	N/A	N/A	N/A	30.14	3	0.10	0.02	N/A	0	0	0	100	24	58	N/A
0.01	0.35	B / 8.7	8.8	0.82	N/A	36.69	257	-0.11	0.12	N/A	1	0	98	1	116	36	N/A
0.31	0.19	B+ / 9.7	4.6	0.15	8.6	60.50	772	0.36	0.01	N/A	0	0	99	1	23	85	N/A
4.48	N/A	U /	N/A	N/A	N/A	26.40	16	0.91	N/A	N/A	0	0	0	100	N/A	N/A	N/A
5.50	N/A	U /	N/A	N/A	N/A	31.95	16	-0.81	N/A	N/A	0	0	0	100	N/A	N/A	N/A
4.58	0.50	B / 8.8	10.7	1.09	N/A	63.34	1,427	0.32	0.18	N/A	0	0	99	1	40	72	N/A
3.52	0.25	B- / 7.6	18.5	1.02	N/A	74.39	1,892	-1.91	N/A	67.1	0	100	0	0	7	82	N/A
2.60	0.20	B / 8.0	15.7	1.02	N/A	110.03	431	-3.43	-0.05	46.5	0	100	0	0	3	51	13
6.70	0.50	B- / 7.8	18.2	1.07	N/A	42.43	685	-0.73	0.29	N/A	0	100	0	0	8	71	5
15.52	0.59	C+ / 5.6	20.9	0.96	N/A	41.21	3,453	0.34	0.25	175.5	0	100	0	0	11	88	N/A
2.72	0.20	B / 8.2	14.3	0.92	N/A	69.05	43	-3.84	-0.04	49.8	0	100	0	0	4	58	7
2.75	0.25	B- / 7.6	18.7	1.17	N/A	68.60	76	-3.66	-0.03	40.6	0	100	0	0	20	54	8
3.79	0.17	B / 8.5	13.6	0.88	N/A	134.69	10,923	-3.05	N/A	25.0	0	100	0	0	5	61	N/A
2.09	0.29	C+ / 5.7	29.3	1.37	N/A	35.48	1,305	-2.31	0.16	N/A	0	100	0	0	9	17	11
2.52	0.59	B / 8.6	12.8	0.56	N/A	40.35	60	-0.22	-0.07	22.3	0	99	0	1	10	50	N/A
2.30	0.50	B- / 7.5	18.1	0.88	N/A	58.03	89	-3.19	-0.14	38.3	0	99	0	1	11	38	8
0.00	0.40	B / 8.1	18.9	0.92	N/A	160.49	72,239	0.95	0.14	N/A	0	0	0	100	N/A	59	9
2.72	0.34	B- / 7.3	20.7	1.02	N/A	32.66	368	-1.44	-0.11	30.8	0	100	0	0	8	51	N/A
2.72	0.25	U /	N/A	N/A	N/A	52.25	5	-4.78	N/A	N/A	0	99	0	1	N/A	N/A	1
4.15	0.35	B+ / 9.0	N/A	N/A	N/A	60.96	105	0.97	-0.07	N/A	0	0	99	1	112	53	N/A
2.85	0.20	B+ / 9.0	7.4	1.80	8.6	24.44	100	-1.06	-0.06	N/A	1	0	98	1	14	26	N/A
2.65	0.23	B+ / 9.3	5.3	1.37	8.1	24.37	1,217	-0.53	-0.16	N/A	0	0	99	1	17	32	N/A
2.85	0.20	B+ / 9.2	6.3	1.51	8.4	24.14	31	-0.79	0.03	N/A	0	0	99	1	24	28	N/A
1.05	0.20	B+ / 9.8	1.7	0.35	3.2	24.32	1,614	-0.04	-0.01	N/A	0	0	100	0	23	49	N/A
4.58	0.45	B+ / 9.8	N/A	N/A	N/A	58.71	193	-1.21	-0.01	N/A	0	0	88	12	24	95	N/A
0.05	0.21	B+ / 9.9	0.6	-0.03	N/A	30.01	12	-0.43	-0.24	N/A	0	0	99	1	92	57	N/A
2.24	0.50	B- / 7.5	15.7	0.61	N/A	37.42	15	-0.86	-0.03	N/A	0	100	0	0	1	45	N/A
2.13	0.55	B / 8.4	13.7	0.39	N/A	42.33	61	0.05	-0.19	N/A	0	100	0	0	1	78	N/A
1.61	0.25	B- / 7.7	18.6	1.15	N/A	88.35	68	-3.54	0.04	49.3	0	100	0	0	33	61	N/A
3.40	0.25	B- / 7.7	17.8	1.12	N/A	62.11	24	-3.64	0.03	28.7	0	100	0	0	28	45	8
2.87	0.09	B / 8.0	15.3	1.00	N/A	147.07	123,001	-3.17	-0.01	50.1	0	100	0	0	4	52	N/A

* Denotes ETF Fund, N/A denotes number is not available

Fund Type	Fund Name	Ticker Symbol	Overall Investment Rating	PRICE Price As of 12/31/12	52 Week High	52 Week Low	PERFORMANCE Perform-ance Rating/Pts		% Total Return Through 12/31/12 3 Mo	6 Mo	1Yr/Pct	Annualized 3Yr/Pct	5Yr/Pct
	99 Pct = Best 0 Pct = Worst												
GR	*SPDR S&P 500 Growth ETF	SPYG	C	65.56	68.90	59.60	C	5.2	2.18	7.57	15.99 / 53	12.20 / 59	6.49 / 52
IN	*SPDR S&P 500 Value ETF	SPYV	C+	71.79	74.43	62.93	C	5.4	5.35	12.50	17.94 / 62	10.76 / 52	2.70 / 30
GR	*SPDR S&P 600 Small Cap ETF	SLY	C+	75.11	78.15	65.50	C+	6.7	7.61	10.59	16.46 / 55	14.56 / 71	9.12 / 66
GR	*SPDR S&P 600 Small Cap Growth ET	SLYG	B-	126.35	131.64	112.88	B-	7.1	7.51	9.38	16.70 / 56	15.91 / 76	9.64 / 68
GR	*SPDR S&P 600 Small Cap Value ETF	SLYV	C+	77.01	80.29	65.63	C+	6.3	7.15	11.83	16.90 / 57	13.08 / 64	8.84 / 64
IN	*SPDR S&P Aerospace & Defense ETF	XAR	A+	62.80	66.15	55.02	B+	8.7	8.95	16.08	17.14 / 59	--	--
HL	*SPDR S&P Biotech ETF	XBI	B-	87.91	96.67	72.15	B+	8.4	3.66	4.93	29.71 / 91	20.18 / 89	10.40 / 71
FO	*SPDR S&P BRIC 40 ETF	BIK	D	24.40	26.58	20.27	D+	2.5	8.87	18.73	9.81 / 34	2.07 / 20	-0.31 / 18
FO	*SPDR S&P China ETF	GXC	D+	74.09	76.79	60.00	C-	3.2	13.59	23.29	18.11 / 63	3.54 / 24	0.80 / 21
IN	*SPDR S&P Dividend ETF	SDY	C+	58.16	60.01	53.01	C	5.5	4.65	9.91	14.33 / 46	12.30 / 60	7.56 / 58
EM	*SPDR S&P Emerg Middle East&Afric	GAF	C-	73.91	74.25	63.46	C	4.3	8.46	10.58	16.43 / 54	7.62 / 37	5.10 / 44
EM	*SPDR S&P Emerging Asia Pacific E	GMF	D+	77.49	79.45	64.14	C-	3.2	8.87	17.60	15.56 / 50	4.80 / 29	2.43 / 29
EM	*SPDR S&P Emerging Europe ETF	GUR	D	43.95	45.49	33.33	C-	3.4	8.51	20.87	21.40 / 75	1.00 / 17	-5.16 / 8
EM	*SPDR S&P Emerging Latin America	GML	D	74.30	82.62	64.40	D	2.0	6.94	11.42	6.48 / 27	0.65 / 16	3.39 / 34
EM	*SPDR S&P Emerging Markets ETF	GMM	D+	67.22	69.38	55.95	C-	3.0	8.51	15.85	14.50 / 47	4.06 / 26	2.04 / 29
GI	*SPDR S&P Emg Markets Dividend ET	EDIV	C-	47.18	54.72	41.35	C	4.8	9.93	11.31	4.30 / 23	--	--
GL	*SPDR S&P Emg Markets Sm Cap ETF	EWX	D+	46.64	48.39	38.58	C-	3.9	10.03	16.11	25.12 / 84	2.73 / 22	--
EN	*SPDR S&P Glbl Natural Resources	GNR	C-	51.56	55.86	44.15	C	4.7	5.56	13.36	5.16 / 24	--	--
HL	*SPDR S&P Health Care Equipment E	XHE	B-	54.90	61.27	50.12	B-	7.1	3.61	5.33	19.17 / 68	--	--
HL	*SPDR S&P Health Care Services ET	XHS	A+	66.30	70.03	54.19	A-	9.2	7.12	12.25	24.71 / 83	--	--
IN	*SPDR S&P Homebuilders ETF	XHB	A-	26.60	28.03	18.35	A+	9.6	13.13	28.99	52.39 / 99	22.76 / 94	11.72 / 76
EM	*SPDR S&P International Div ETF	DWX	D	48.11	51.73	40.32	D+	2.4	10.21	15.10	13.40 / 43	1.57 / 19	--
GL	*SPDR S&P International Mid Cap E	MDD	C-	28.69	29.41	23.83	C	4.9	10.18	17.70	19.82 / 70	6.75 / 35	--
FO	*SPDR S&P International Small Cap	GWX	C	28.45	29.41	24.12	C	4.6	10.02	17.87	18.55 / 65	6.27 / 33	1.86 / 26
IN	*SPDR S&P Metals & Mining ETF	XME	D-	45.13	57.06	37.10	E+	0.9	3.10	12.62	-11.36 / 8	-5.57 / 9	-4.07 / 9
GR	*SPDR S&P MidCap 400 ETF	MDY	C+	185.71	193.28	160.69	C+	6.8	8.70	12.86	17.70 / 61	13.77 / 68	8.40 / 61
EN	*SPDR S&P Oil & Gas Equip & Serv	XES	D+	34.62	40.12	27.71	C-	3.3	8.91	17.29	5.58 / 25	6.61 / 34	1.14 / 23
IN	*SPDR S&P Oil & Gas Expl & Prod	XOP	C-	54.08	61.82	5.90	C-	4.2	1.59	13.41	7.85 / 30	10.27 / 49	4.50 / 41
HL	*SPDR S&P Pharmaceuticals ETF	XPH	C+	55.91	62.43	51.87	C+	6.3	-0.52	2.12	14.43 / 46	16.15 / 77	13.63 / 84
IN	*SPDR S&P Retail ETF	XRT	B+	62.38	65.47	52.85	B+	8.6	2.24	7.79	21.55 / 75	22.25 / 94	18.04 / 97
EM	*SPDR S&P Russia	RBL	C-	29.11	33.21	23.27	C+	6.1	5.12	14.13	9.23 / 33	--	--
EM	*SPDR S&P SC Emerging Asia Pac ET	GMFS	U	41.86	N/A	N/A	U		11.13	16.38		--	--
IN	*SPDR S&P Semiconductor ETF	XSD	D	45.07	54.23	38.66	D+	2.3	15.07	13.34	1.95 / 18	2.01 / 20	4.79 / 42
GR	*SPDR S&P Software & Services ETF	XSW	A	62.39	67.34	55.21	B+	8.3	5.49	12.79	18.88 / 67	--	--
GR	*SPDR S&P Telecom ETF	XTL	B-	45.20	47.70	38.54	B	7.9	5.97	21.40	10.03 / 34	--	--
UT	*SPDR S&P Transportation ETF	XTN	B+	53.78	74.93	44.55	A	9.4	14.75	15.05	21.40 / 75	--	--
GL	*SPDR S&P WORLD EX-US ETF	GWL	C-	25.33	25.98	20.78	C-	4.2	10.22	18.80	21.29 / 74	4.36 / 28	-0.59 / 18
GL	*SPDR SP Intl Con Disc Sect ETF	IPD	C+	30.32	30.95	24.85	C+	6.7	14.23	20.80	25.38 / 84	9.11 / 43	--
GL	*SPDR SP Intl Con Stap Sect ETF	IPS	C+	35.67	36.20	30.50	C+	5.6	4.34	11.63	22.46 / 78	10.63 / 51	--
EN	*SPDR SP Intl Energy Sector ETF	IPW	D	24.96	28.15	21.81	D	2.0	3.15	11.36	6.14 / 26	0.99 / 17	--
FS	*SPDR SP Intl Finl Sector ETF	IPF	D+	19.33	20.15	14.45	C-	3.1	--	--	35.80 / 96	2.26 / 21	--
HL	*SPDR SP Intl Health Care ETF	IRY	C+	35.81	36.87	29.63	C+	5.7	5.14	16.50	22.07 / 77	9.67 / 46	--
GL	*SPDR SP Intl Industrial ETF	IPN	C-	26.35	27.13	21.94	C-	3.6	12.60	20.00	19.30 / 69	5.18 / 30	--
GL	*SPDR SP Intl Materials Sec ETF	IRV	D	24.87	26.99	20.39	D	2.0	8.33	18.85	6.21 / 26	-0.11 / 15	--
GL	*SPDR SP Intl Tech Sector ETF	IPK	D+	27.11	27.63	21.63	C-	3.7	18.13	24.76	23.98 / 82	3.81 / 26	--
GL	*SPDR SP Intl Telecom Sect ETF	IST	D+	22.00	23.95	20.37	D+	2.6	3.59	4.78	9.23 / 33	4.12 / 27	--
UT	*SPDR SP Intl Utils Sector ETF	IPU	D	16.73	17.68	14.50	D-	1.1	2.32	8.58	8.09 / 30	-5.75 / 8	--
FS	*SPDR SP Mortgage Finance ETF	KME	D+	42.70	44.84	34.81	C	4.7	7.15	18.90	35.02 / 95	3.37 / 24	--
GI	*SPDR SSgA Global Allocation ETF	GAL	U	30.97	N/A	N/A	U		4.74	9.93	--	--	--
GI	*SPDR SSgA Income Allocation ETF	INKM	U	30.90	N/A	N/A	U		3.41	6.61	--	--	--
GI	*SPDR SSgA Multi Asset Real Retur	RLY	U	30.64	N/A	N/A	U		2.40	8.71	--	--	--
FO	*SPDR STOXX Europe 50 ETF	FEU	D+	33.62	35.98	27.27	C-	3.5	8.43	19.15	21.10 / 74	2.18 / 20	-2.74 / 12

* Denotes ETF Fund, N/A denotes number is not available

www.thestreetratings.com

| Incl. in Returns | | RISK | | | | NET ASSETS | | VALUATION | | | ASSET | | | | | FUND MANAGER | |
Dividend Yield %	Expense Ratio	Risk Rating/ Pts	3 Year Standard Deviation	Beta	Avg Duration	NAV as of 12/31/12	Total $(Mil)	Premium/Discount As of 12/31/12	1 Year Average	Wtd Avg P/E	Cash %	Stocks %	Bonds %	Other %	Portfolio Turnover Ratio	Manager Quality Pct	Manager Tenure (Years)
2.38	0.20	B- / 7.8	15.4	0.99	N/A	67.65	216	-3.09	-0.01	73.8	0	100	0	0	21	59	13
3.48	0.20	B / 8.1	15.6	1.00	N/A	74.35	115	-3.44	0.02	20.4	0	100	0	0	25	47	8
3.04	0.20	B- / 7.5	20.1	1.24	N/A	77.60	229	-3.21	0.08	49.2	0	100	0	0	13	57	8
2.71	0.25	B- / 7.4	19.8	1.22	N/A	131.10	164	-3.62	-0.02	63.3	0	100	0	0	37	66	13
3.47	0.25	B- / 7.6	20.6	1.26	N/A	79.70	132	-3.38	-0.01	36.0	0	100	0	0	34	43	13
3.59	0.35	B+ / 9.1	N/A	N/A	N/A	65.81	13	-4.57	-0.01	N/A	0	100	0	0	23	62	N/A
0.22	0.35	C+ / 6.5	21.7	1.08	N/A	95.47	629	-7.92	0.03	121.8	0	100	0	0	61	81	N/A
1.80	0.50	C+ / 6.6	25.1	1.07	N/A	24.81	320	-1.65	-0.01	N/A	0	100	0	0	13	30	N/A
0.88	0.59	C+ / 6.4	24.8	0.94	N/A	75.31	1,067	-1.62	0.11	72.8	0	100	0	0	10	44	N/A
4.01	0.35	B / 8.7	12.3	0.76	N/A	59.99	9,399	-3.05	N/A	23.5	0	100	0	0	94	73	8
3.15	0.59	B- / 7.2	23.5	0.89	N/A	71.47	95	3.41	-0.09	N/A	0	100	0	0	7	78	N/A
2.24	0.60	B- / 7.0	22.4	0.97	N/A	78.45	482	-1.22	-0.04	56.7	0	100	0	0	7	53	N/A
3.52	0.60	C / 5.4	31.9	1.28	N/A	44.19	95	-0.54	0.02	N/A	0	100	0	0	6	29	N/A
1.71	0.59	C+ / 6.7	26.8	1.13	N/A	75.82	111	-2.00	-0.08	55.5	0	100	0	0	7	21	N/A
2.31	0.59	B- / 7.0	23.0	1.00	N/A	67.62	159	-0.59	0.10	54.8	0	99	0	1	11	46	N/A
2.47	0.61	B- / 7.1	N/A	N/A	N/A	47.05	358	0.28	0.28	N/A	0	100	0	0	134	9	N/A
2.97	0.66	C+ / 5.9	25.5	1.08	N/A	47.91	875	-2.65	0.28	92.3	0	99	0	1	22	40	N/A
1.83	0.40	C+ / 6.7	N/A	N/A	N/A	52.66	490	-2.09	0.22	N/A	2	97	0	1	18	70	N/A
1.01	0.35	B / 8.1	N/A	N/A	N/A	58.13	20	-5.56	-0.04	N/A	0	100	0	0	42	20	N/A
3.05	0.35	B / 8.9	N/A	N/A	N/A	68.63	13	-3.40	-0.02	N/A	0	100	0	0	25	49	N/A
1.18	0.35	B- / 7.1	27.1	1.46	N/A	27.78	2,206	-4.25	-0.01	20.6	0	100	0	0	46	80	N/A
3.59	0.45	C+ / 6.4	23.0	0.90	N/A	49.35	1,147	-2.51	0.23	N/A	0	100	0	0	127	32	N/A
3.77	0.45	B- / 7.1	20.2	0.99	N/A	29.38	34	-2.35	-0.19	N/A	0	100	0	0	28	74	N/A
3.46	0.59	B- / 7.6	20.9	0.99	N/A	29.18	694	-2.50	0.14	18.0	0	100	0	0	2	71	N/A
1.85	0.35	C+ / 5.6	34.2	1.80	N/A	45.34	1,004	-0.46	-0.02	18.6	0	100	0	0	32	5	N/A
1.32	0.25	B- / 7.7	18.8	1.17	N/A	192.43	10,617	-3.49	-0.01	39.0	0	100	0	0	18	57	N/A
1.21	0.35	C+ / 6.3	32.1	1.34	N/A	36.30	277	-4.63	N/A	28.7	0	100	0	0	30	23	N/A
2.37	0.35	C+ / 6.7	29.4	1.54	N/A	56.06	722	-3.53	0.02	19.4	0	100	0	0	42	20	N/A
1.74	0.35	B- / 7.3	13.8	0.71	N/A	59.11	308	-5.41	N/A	120.1	0	100	0	0	31	85	N/A
3.71	0.35	B / 8.0	20.3	1.14	N/A	63.11	536	-1.16	-0.01	44.5	0	100	0	0	39	88	N/A
4.68	0.59	C / 5.3	N/A	N/A	N/A	29.21	37	-0.34	0.12	N/A	0	100	0	0	11	9	N/A
4.16	N/A	U /	N/A	N/A	N/A	43.58	2	-3.95	N/A	N/A	0	0	0	100	N/A	N/A	1
1.30	0.35	C+ / 6.8	26.3	1.45	N/A	46.90	34	-3.90	-0.02	32.9	0	100	0	0	36	8	N/A
2.63	0.35	B / 8.9	N/A	N/A	N/A	65.25	13	-4.38	-0.02	N/A	0	100	0	0	32	23	N/A
9.90	0.35	C+ / 6.8	N/A	N/A	N/A	46.49	5	-2.77	-0.04	N/A	0	0	0	100	50	10	N/A
2.16	0.35	B- / 7.1	N/A	N/A	N/A	56.79	14	-5.30	-0.08	N/A	0	100	0	0	25	97	N/A
2.08	0.34	B- / 7.3	20.8	1.02	N/A	25.81	460	-1.86	0.27	40.8	0	100	0	0	8	57	N/A
4.92	0.51	B- / 7.5	20.7	0.97	N/A	30.82	6	-1.62	0.13	N/A	0	100	0	0	5	81	N/A
1.03	0.50	B / 8.6	14.7	0.66	N/A	35.91	19	-0.67	0.20	19.6	0	100	0	0	2	86	N/A
4.54	0.50	B- / 7.3	24.2	0.99	N/A	25.46	11	-1.96	-0.41	14.0	0	100	0	0	6	15	N/A
10.48	0.50	B- / 7.0	23.8	1.00	N/A	19.86	6	-2.67	-0.13	17.7	0	100	0	0	6	22	N/A
1.77	0.50	B / 8.2	14.1	0.70	N/A	36.84	30	-2.80	0.10	47.8	1	98	0	1	14	63	N/A
7.88	0.50	B- / 7.4	20.1	0.97	N/A	26.91	7	-2.08	-0.06	25.8	1	98	0	1	11	67	N/A
4.11	0.50	C+ / 5.9	27.5	1.24	N/A	25.19	10	-1.27	-0.32	83.8	0	100	0	0	1	25	N/A
1.87	0.50	C+ / 6.7	22.1	1.01	N/A	27.26	12	-0.55	-0.26	83.0	0	99	0	1	6	61	N/A
3.49	0.50	B- / 7.6	17.0	0.74	N/A	22.62	25	-2.74	0.38	33.2	0	100	0	0	3	54	N/A
3.38	0.50	B- / 7.2	17.5	0.74	N/A	16.67	27	0.36	0.36	23.8	0	100	0	0	8	11	N/A
4.80	0.35	C+ / 5.9	23.3	0.94	N/A	44.93	4	-4.96	-0.02	N/A	0	100	0	0	91	29	N/A
4.92	N/A	U /	N/A	N/A	N/A	31.52	14	-1.74	N/A	N/A	0	0	0	100	N/A	N/A	1
5.42	N/A	U /	N/A	N/A	N/A	31.33	50	-1.37	N/A	N/A	0	0	0	100	N/A	N/A	1
4.13	N/A	U /	N/A	N/A	N/A	30.91	55	-0.87	N/A	N/A	0	0	0	100	N/A	N/A	1
1.90	0.29	C+ / 6.9	23.3	1.13	N/A	34.31	45	-2.01	0.47	N/A	0	100	0	0	6	30	11

* Denotes ETF Fund, N/A denotes number is not available

Fund Type	Fund Name	Ticker Symbol	Overall Investment Rating	PRICE Price As of 12/31/12	52 Week High	52 Week Low	PERFORMANCE Performance Rating/Pts	% Total Return Through 12/31/12 3 Mo	6 Mo	1Yr/Pct	Annualized 3Yr/Pct	5Yr/Pct
IN	*SPDR Wells Fargo Preferred Stk E	PSK	C	44.98	46.59	43.50	C- / 3.5	0.77	3.16	11.16 / 37	8.90 / 42	--
GI	*Star Global Buy Write ETF	VEGA	U	24.75	N/A	N/A	U /	0.84	--	--	--	--
GL	*Stream S&P Dynamic Roll Glbl Com	BNPC	U	27.54	N/A	N/A	U /	-3.33	4.94	--	--	--
GL	*Sustainable North Ame Oil Sands	SNDS	U	21.99	N/A	N/A	U /	4.60	15.33	--	--	--
GR	*Technology Select Sector SPDR	XLK	C-	28.85	31.74	26.14	C / 4.4	-0.53	5.72	15.41 / 49	11.01 / 53	6.66 / 53
GL	*Teucrium Agricultural Fund	TAGS	U	48.44	N/A	N/A	U /	-8.47	-19.59	--	--	--
GR	*Teucrium Corn	CORN	D	44.32	52.69	35.24	D / 1.6	-8.47	-8.41	12.25 / 39	--	--
GR	*Teucrium Natural Gas	NAGS	E+	11.58	13.54	10.11	E+ / 0.6	-12.97	-5.31	-8.20 / 9	--	--
GL	*Teucrium Soybean	SOYB	D	24.07	28.85	21.10	D- / 1.2	-8.65	-10.40	10.95 / 36	--	--
GL	*Teucrium Sugar	CANE	D-	17.84	24.66	16.96	E / 0.4	-2.97	-14.88	-23.01 / 4	--	--
GL	*Teucrium Wheat	WEAT	D	21.32	28.30	18.01	E+ / 0.6	-12.88	-14.08	-1.64 / 12	--	--
GI	*Teucrium WTI Crude Oil	CRUD	D-	39.53	48.81	35.77	E+ / 0.8	-1.07	2.81	-11.36 / 8	--	--
IN	*TrimTabs Float Shrink ETF	TTFS	B	33.89	37.00	30.60	C+ / 6.5	3.16	8.42	15.40 / 49	--	--
IN	*UBS AG FI Enhanced BC Growth ETN	FBG	U	28.06	N/A	N/A	U /	5.51	15.97	--	--	--
IN	*UBS E Tracs Alerian MLP Infrast	MLPI	D	32.54	35.55	29.77	C- / 3.9	1.65	7.27	9.04 / 33	--	--
GR	*UBS E Tracs CMCI Agriculture TR	UAG	D	28.82	33.00	25.16	C- / 3.2	-5.58	-8.22	5.69 / 25	10.33 / 49	--
GR	*UBS E Tracs CMCI Food Tr	FUD	D-	28.03	31.63	23.25	C- / 3.1	-5.36	-7.19	6.16 / 26	9.25 / 44	--
GR	*UBS E Tracs CMCI Gold TR	UBG	D	44.34	48.61	40.02	C- / 3.7	-6.47	3.72	0.11 / 14	11.89 / 57	--
GR	*UBS E Tracs CMCI Industrial Meta	UBM	E+	19.77	22.15	17.77	D- / 1.2	1.66	6.59	-2.55 / 12	-2.48 / 11	--
GR	*UBS E Tracs CMCI Livestock Tr	UBC	D-	19.68	21.84	18.83	D- / 1.2	-0.77	-2.76	-8.20 / 9	0.74 / 17	--
GR	*UBS E Tracs CMCI Silver TR	USV	D	41.96	52.56	36.91	C / 5.5	-11.83	10.11	0.86 / 16	16.59 / 78	--
GR	*UBS E Tracs CMCI Total Return	UCI	D-	22.06	24.68	19.53	D / 2.0	-2.78	1.94	0.92 / 16	3.59 / 24	--
GL	*UBS E TRACS DJ Com Idx 246 Blnd	BLND	U	24.86	N/A	N/A	U /	-5.54	0.82	--	--	--
IN	*UBS E Tracs DJ-UBS Comm Idx Tot	DJCI	E+	26.03	28.53	23.75	D- / 1.2	-5.67	-1.52	-2.48 / 12	-0.37 / 14	--
GR	*UBS E Tracs Long Platinum ETN	PTM	E+	17.59	23.98	15.61	D- / 1.3	-7.27	12.65	-0.64 / 13	-1.24 / 12	--
EN	*UBS E-TRACS 2x Levd Lng Alerian	MLPL	C+	38.55	45.93	32.63	B+ / 8.8	5.19	16.69	19.74 / 70	--	--
GR	*UBS E-TRACS 2x Levd Long WF BDC	BDCL	C+	26.06	28.06	17.82	A+ / 9.9	11.21	25.19	60.83 / 99	--	--
EN	*UBS E-TRACS Alerian MLP Index ET	AMU	U	24.25	N/A	N/A	U /	1.40	--	--	--	--
EN	*UBS E-TRACS Alerian Nat Gas MLP	MLPG	D-	28.56	31.64	27.14	D+ / 2.6	-0.93	5.25	5.17 / 24	--	--
GR	*UBS E-TRACS Internet IPO ETN	EIPO	E+	13.90	17.74	12.20	D- / 1.1	3.16	0.55	-6.55 / 10	--	--
GR	*UBS E-TRACS Mnth 2xLevd Itr IPO	EIPL	E-	25.36	52.76	18.56	E+ / 0.9	6.62	--	-11.04 / 8	--	--
IN	*UBS E-TRACS Mnth Pay 2xL DJ SDI	DVYL	U	27.45	N/A	N/A	U /	3.68	8.46	--	--	--
IN	*UBS E-TRACS MnthPay 2xL S&P Div	SDYL	U	28.99	N/A	N/A	U /	6.53	18.69	--	--	--
GL	*UBS E-TRACS Mo 2x Lvgd ISE SSD I	SSDL	U	20.37	63.10	17.17	U /	--	8.35	--	--	--
FO	*UBS E-TRACS Mo Py 2x Levd DJ Int	RWXL	U	32.31	N/A	N/A	U /	16.87	--	--	--	--
GL	*UBS E-TRACS Mo Py 2x Levd Mort R	MORL	U	24.45	N/A	N/A	U /	--	--	--	--	--
GL	*UBS E-TRACS Monthly 2X LISE CCTR	LSKY	C+	36.00	43.64	26.47	A+ / 9.7	--	36.17	31.94 / 93	--	--
GR	*UBS E-TRACS Nat Gas Ft Contango	GASZ	D-	28.87	32.50	27.19	D+ / 2.4	4.78	-0.21	3.99 / 22	--	--
GR	*UBS E-TRACS Oil Fut Contago ETN	OILZ	U	24.96	25.80	23.99	U /	-0.40	0.97	--	--	--
PM	*UBS E-TRACS S&P 500 Gold Hedged	SPGH	C	50.99	57.43	43.53	B / 7.9	-1.61	17.43	17.25 / 59	--	--
GR	*UBS E-TRACS Wells Fargo BDC Inde	BDCS	C+	25.12	26.45	20.76	A / 9.4	5.70	12.41	27.58 / 88	--	--
EN	*UBS E-TRACS Wells Fargo MLP Inde	MLPW	D+	28.71	29.65	25.24	C / 4.6	2.15	7.41	10.98 / 36	--	--
IN	*UBS ETRACS FsherGartman Rsk Off	OFF	E+	20.65	27.64	19.46	E / 0.5	-2.38	-12.93	-17.38 / 6	--	--
IN	*UBS ETRACS FsherGartman Rsk On E	ONN	D+	27.60	29.80	22.44	C / 5.0	-1.02	10.10	12.06 / 39	--	--
EN	*United States 12 Month Oil Fund	USL	D-	39.67	48.28	34.68	D- / 1.3	-0.15	4.06	-8.27 / 9	0.38 / 16	-4.84 / 9
GL	*United States Agriculture Index	USAG	U	25.59	N/A	N/A	U /	-7.72	-7.74	--	--	--
EN	*United States Brent Oil Fund	BNO	C-	82.07	89.07	63.14	C- / 3.7	-1.11	13.18	5.90 / 26	--	--
IN	*United States Commodity Index	USCI	D	58.63	64.54	55.29	D- / 1.0	-3.79	-2.14	-2.73 / 12	--	--
IN	*United States Copper Index	CPER	D+	25.01	28.25	23.07	D / 1.7	-2.81	6.17	-0.11 / 14	--	--
EN	*United States Gasoline Fund LP	UGA	C+	58.44	62.13	45.13	C+ / 6.8	-3.99	11.25	15.34 / 49	16.73 / 79	--
EN	*United States Heating Oil Fund	UHN	D+	33.73	37.48	28.16	D+ / 2.8	-6.58	7.34	-2.32 / 12	7.88 / 38	--
GI	*United States Metal Index	USMI	U	31.07	N/A	N/A	U /	-3.03	9.25	--	--	--

Incl. in Returns Dividend Yield %	Expense Ratio	Risk Rating/ Pts	3 Year Standard Deviation	3 Year Beta	Avg Dura-tion	NAV as of 12/31/12	Total $(Mil)	Premium/Discount As of 12/31/12	Premium/Discount 1 Year Average	Wtd Avg P/E	Cash %	Stocks %	Bonds %	Other %	Portfolio Turnover Ratio	Manager Quality Pct	Manager Tenure (Years)
7.60	0.45	B+ / 9.1	6.7	0.25	N/A	45.47	321	-1.08	0.13	N/A	3	0	0	97	69	83	N/A
2.70	N/A	U /	N/A	N/A	N/A	24.76	14	-0.04	N/A	N/A	0	0	0	100	N/A	N/A	1
0.00	N/A	U /	N/A	N/A	N/A	27.69	18	-0.54	N/A	N/A	0	0	0	100	N/A	N/A	1
3.32	N/A	U /	N/A	N/A	N/A	23.16	1	-5.05	N/A	N/A	0	0	0	100	N/A	N/A	1
2.32	0.18	B- / 7.2	17.4	1.06	N/A	29.61	8,284	-2.57	-0.01	109.4	0	100	0	0	5	37	15
0.00	N/A	U /	N/A	N/A	N/A	47.50	N/A	1.98	N/A	N/A	0	0	0	100	N/A	N/A	1
0.00	2.55	C+ / 6.6	N/A	N/A	N/A	43.80	38	1.19	-0.01	N/A	0	0	0	100	N/A	19	3
0.00	N/A	C / 4.6	N/A	N/A	N/A	11.46	5	1.05	-0.11	N/A	0	0	0	100	N/A	13	2
0.00	N/A	B / 8.0	N/A	N/A	N/A	23.45	7	2.64	-0.05	N/A	0	0	0	100	N/A	65	2
0.00	N/A	C+ / 6.6	N/A	N/A	N/A	17.70	2	0.79	0.37	N/A	0	0	0	100	N/A	3	2
0.00	N/A	B / 8.1	N/A	N/A	N/A	20.48	4	4.10	0.01	N/A	0	0	0	100	N/A	15	2
0.00	N/A	C+ / 6.2	N/A	N/A	N/A	40.07	2	-1.35	-0.02	N/A	0	0	0	100	N/A	3	2
0.63	0.99	B / 8.8	N/A	N/A	N/A	35.30	11	-3.99	-0.12	N/A	0	0	0	100	201	38	2
0.00	N/A	U /	N/A	N/A	N/A	29.59	140	-5.17	N/A	N/A	0	0	0	100	N/A	N/A	1
3.94	N/A	C / 5.3	N/A	N/A	N/A	34.41	499	-5.43	N/A	N/A	0	0	0	100	N/A	14	3
0.00	0.65	C / 4.5	26.3	0.86	N/A	28.51	3	1.09	-0.20	N/A	0	0	0	100	N/A	45	5
0.00	0.65	C / 4.6	23.4	0.81	N/A	27.63	6	1.45	-0.02	N/A	0	0	0	100	N/A	47	5
0.00	0.30	C / 5.0	18.3	0.13	N/A	43.98	5	0.82	-0.10	N/A	0	0	0	100	N/A	93	5
0.00	0.65	C- / 4.1	25.5	1.25	N/A	19.99	4	-1.10	-0.12	N/A	0	0	0	100	N/A	9	5
0.00	0.65	C / 4.8	11.8	-0.02	N/A	19.37	8	1.60	-0.08	N/A	0	0	0	100	N/A	71	5
0.00	0.40	C- / 3.0	44.3	1.23	N/A	42.54	4	-1.36	-0.36	N/A	0	0	0	100	N/A	81	5
0.00	0.65	C / 4.6	19.3	1.06	N/A	22.00	12	0.27	0.04	N/A	0	0	0	100	N/A	17	5
0.00	N/A	U /	N/A	N/A	N/A	24.86	10	0.00	N/A	N/A	0	0	0	100	N/A	N/A	N/A
0.00	N/A	C- / 4.2	19.6	0.93	N/A	25.94	70	0.35	-0.10	N/A	0	0	0	100	N/A	13	4
0.00	0.65	C- / 4.0	29.2	1.18	N/A	18.62	66	-5.53	3.28	N/A	0	0	0	100	N/A	10	5
8.42	N/A	C / 4.6	N/A	N/A	N/A	42.87	128	-10.08	-0.07	N/A	0	0	0	100	N/A	26	3
7.04	N/A	C- / 4.2	N/A	N/A	N/A	27.33	74	-4.65	-0.03	N/A	0	0	0	100	N/A	98	2
3.50	N/A	U /	N/A	N/A	N/A	26.03	34	-6.84	N/A	N/A	0	0	0	100	N/A	N/A	1
4.50	N/A	C / 5.1	N/A	N/A	N/A	29.74	26	-3.97	-0.08	N/A	0	0	0	100	N/A	32	3
0.00	N/A	C- / 4.2	N/A	N/A	N/A	14.80	6	-6.08	-0.34	N/A	0	0	0	100	N/A	4	2
0.00	N/A	D / 1.9	N/A	N/A	N/A	28.03	2	-9.53	-1.34	N/A	0	0	0	100	N/A	N/A	2
6.92	N/A	U /	N/A	N/A	N/A	28.62	11	-4.09	N/A	N/A	0	0	0	100	N/A	N/A	1
5.10	N/A	U /	N/A	N/A	N/A	30.69	12	-5.54	N/A	N/A	0	0	0	100	N/A	N/A	1
0.00	N/A	U /	N/A	N/A	N/A	22.58	8	-9.79	-0.90	N/A	0	0	0	100	N/A	N/A	2
2.08	N/A	U /	N/A	N/A	N/A	32.86	13	-1.67	N/A	N/A	0	0	0	100	N/A	N/A	1
2.56	N/A	U /	N/A	N/A	N/A	26.52	32	-7.81	N/A	N/A	0	0	0	100	N/A	N/A	1
0.00	N/A	C- / 3.8	N/A	N/A	N/A	39.37	14	-8.56	-0.03	N/A	0	0	0	100	N/A	7	2
0.00	N/A	C / 5.2	N/A	N/A	N/A	28.94	12	-0.24	0.02	N/A	0	0	0	100	N/A	48	2
0.00	N/A	U /	N/A	N/A	N/A	24.94	10	0.08	-0.03	N/A	0	0	0	100	N/A	25	2
0.00	N/A	C / 4.8	N/A	N/A	N/A	53.14	19	-4.05	-0.10	N/A	0	0	0	100	N/A	91	3
3.53	N/A	C / 4.7	N/A	N/A	N/A	25.70	21	-2.26	-0.02	N/A	0	0	0	100	N/A	94	2
3.80	N/A	C / 5.2	N/A	N/A	N/A	29.52	11	-2.74	-0.13	N/A	0	0	0	100	N/A	84	N/A
0.00	N/A	C / 4.7	N/A	N/A	N/A	20.07	12	2.89	-0.01	N/A	0	0	0	100	N/A	94	2
0.00	N/A	C / 4.8	N/A	N/A	N/A	28.39	11	-2.78	-0.01	N/A	0	0	0	100	N/A	6	2
0.00	0.77	C+ / 6.4	26.2	0.97	N/A	40.29	100	-1.54	-0.06	N/A	91	0	0	9	N/A	14	6
0.00	N/A	U /	N/A	N/A	N/A	25.15	3	1.75	N/A	N/A	0	0	0	100	N/A	N/A	1
0.00	0.94	B- / 7.6	N/A	N/A	N/A	81.85	45	0.27	0.03	N/A	0	0	0	100	N/A	78	N/A
0.00	1.15	B- / 7.7	N/A	N/A	N/A	58.21	485	0.72	0.04	N/A	0	0	0	100	N/A	10	N/A
0.00	N/A	B / 8.1	N/A	N/A	N/A	25.47	3	-1.81	-0.12	N/A	0	0	0	100	N/A	6	2
0.00	0.84	B- / 7.3	26.2	0.81	N/A	57.90	64	0.93	0.05	N/A	91	0	0	9	N/A	88	N/A
0.00	0.90	B- / 7.4	24.1	0.85	N/A	33.50	7	0.69	0.03	N/A	100	0	0	0	N/A	44	5
0.00	N/A	U /	N/A	N/A	N/A	26.62	3	16.72	N/A	N/A	0	0	0	100	N/A	N/A	1

Denotes ETF Fund, N/A denotes number is not available

I. Index of ETFs and Other Closed-End Funds

Fund Type	Fund Name	Ticker Symbol	Overall Investment Rating	Price As of 12/31/12	52 Week High	52 Week Low	Performance Rating/Pts	3 Mo	6 Mo	1Yr/Pct	Annualized 3Yr/Pct	Annualized 5Yr/P
EN	*United States Natural Gas Fund	UNG	E	18.90	23.92	14.25	E- / 0.2	-19.17	-4.54	-17.46 / 6	-38.86 / 1	-42.85 /
EN	*United States Oil Fund	USO	D-	33.37	42.30	29.02	D- / 1.0	0.18	4.22	-10.74 / 8	-3.92 / 10	-13.79 /
EN	*United States Short Oil Fund	DNO	D-	37.88	45.47	32.32	D- / 1.0	-0.32	-6.15	4.90 / 24	-5.53 / 9	--
EN	*US 12 Month Natural Gas Fund	UNL	E	17.24	20.26	14.91	E / 0.3	-13.29	-3.58	-11.66 / 7	-32.38 / 2	--
UT	*Utilities Select Sector SPDR	XLU	C	34.92	38.54	33.85	C- / 3.1	-1.90	-3.10	5.64 / 25	8.99 / 43	1.84 /
IN	*Vanguard Consumer Discret ETF	VCR	B+	75.87	78.61	64.34	B+ / 8.5	6.97	14.93	23.94 / 82	19.81 / 88	12.24 /
IN	*Vanguard Consumer Staples ETF	VDC	C+	87.91	93.43	80.24	C / 5.4	1.74	4.05	15.59 / 51	13.65 / 67	8.98 /
GR	*Vanguard Div Appreciation ETF	VIG	C+	59.57	61.51	54.09	C / 5.1	4.54	9.54	14.16 / 45	11.34 / 54	5.97 /
EN	*Vanguard Energy ETF	VDE	C-	102.26	112.08	88.79	C- / 3.5	2.18	10.51	6.58 / 27	8.54 / 41	2.89 /
GR	*Vanguard Extended Market Index E	VXF	C+	60.50	63.21	52.20	C+ / 6.9	8.43	13.34	18.78 / 66	13.87 / 68	7.79 /
USA	*Vanguard Extnd Durtn Trea Idx ET	EDV	C+	116.00	138.53	104.97	C+ / 6.4	-4.00	-9.52	1.38 / 17	19.69 / 88	10.82 /
FS	*Vanguard Financials ETF	VFH	C	34.10	35.61	28.35	C / 5.5	8.34	15.23	25.33 / 84	8.02 / 38	-2.71 /
FO	*Vanguard FTSE All-Wld ex-US S/C	VSS	C-	90.89	93.57	75.51	C / 4.9	9.44	19.11	21.70 / 76	6.11 / 33	--
FO	*Vanguard FTSE All-World ex-US ET	VEU	C-	45.75	46.63	37.54	C- / 4.1	9.71	18.61	19.73 / 70	4.24 / 27	-0.17 /
EM	*Vanguard FTSE Emerging Markets E	VWO	D+	44.53	45.54	36.94	C- / 3.1	8.90	16.63	15.78 / 51	4.64 / 28	1.29 /
GL	*Vanguard Global ex-US RE I Fd ET	VNQI	A	55.03	55.82	42.36	A+ / 9.8	11.79	21.86	40.47 / 97	--	--
GR	*Vanguard Growth ETF	VUG	C	71.18	74.49	63.72	C+ / 5.7	3.42	9.74	17.58 / 61	12.38 / 60	6.32 /
HL	*Vanguard HealthCare Index ETF	VHT	C+	71.67	75.54	62.95	C+ / 5.9	4.06	10.22	21.78 / 76	12.12 / 59	6.77 /
IN	*Vanguard High Dividend Yield ETF	VYM	C+	49.38	51.47	45.00	C / 5.3	2.39	7.34	14.52 / 47	12.87 / 63	5.05 /
IN	*Vanguard Industrials Index ETF	VIS	C+	71.25	73.99	61.45	C+ / 6.4	8.91	14.94	15.01 / 48	12.92 / 63	4.63 /
GR	*Vanguard Info Tech Ind ETF	VGT	C-	69.11	75.85	63.26	C- / 4.2	1.13	7.06	13.91 / 45	9.94 / 47	7.20 /
GEI	*Vanguard Intermediate Term Bond	BIV	C	88.25	90.71	81.05	C- / 3.1	-0.10	1.45	6.13 / 26	8.39 / 40	7.15 /
COI	*Vanguard Intm-Term Corp Bd Idx E	VCIT	C	87.66	88.84	82.67	C- / 3.5	0.28	3.67	10.02 / 34	9.19 / 44	--
USA	*Vanguard Intm-Term Govt Bd Idx E	VGIT	C-	65.41	97.97	64.17	D+ / 2.4	-0.25	-0.15	1.96 / 18	5.80 / 32	--
GR	*Vanguard Large Cap ETF	VV	C	65.16	67.61	58.05	C / 5.3	4.08	10.21	16.77 / 57	11.46 / 55	4.73 /
GEI	*Vanguard Long Term Bd Idx ETF	BLV	C+	93.87	99.66	87.23	C / 4.4	-1.44	-0.88	7.10 / 28	12.84 / 62	9.61
COI	*Vanguard Long-Term Corp Bd Idx E	VCLT	C+	91.70	98.99	83.90	C / 4.5	-2.06	2.05	10.39 / 35	12.48 / 61	-
USA	*Vanguard Long-Term Govt Bd Idx E	VGLT	C	75.30	82.00	69.11	C- / 3.8	-2.37	-4.98	2.03 / 18	12.28 / 59	-
IN	*Vanguard Materials ETF	VAW	C-	84.21	88.10	71.63	C / 4.8	8.99	15.91	13.21 / 42	10.26 / 49	4.68
IN	*Vanguard Mega Cap 300 ETF	MGC	C	48.83	50.90	43.68	C / 5.1	3.38	9.59	16.81 / 57	11.05 / 53	4.33
GR	*Vanguard Mega Cap 300 Growth ETF	MGK	C	55.46	58.39	49.54	C / 5.4	2.59	9.04	18.08 / 63	12.03 / 58	6.33
IN	*Vanguard Mega Cap 300 Value ETF	MGV	C	42.67	44.22	37.89	C / 4.8	4.19	10.14	15.83 / 52	10.08 / 48	2.15
GR	*Vanguard Mid Cap ETF	VO	C+	82.44	85.43	71.81	C+ / 6.3	7.19	12.84	16.17 / 53	12.95 / 63	6.53
GR	*Vanguard Mid Cap Growth ETF	VOT	C+	68.58	71.30	60.32	C+ / 6.4	7.02	12.63	15.64 / 51	13.53 / 66	5.40
GR	*Vanguard Mid Cap Value Index ETF	VOE	C+	58.81	61.10	50.89	C+ / 6.0	7.41	13.15	16.69 / 56	12.24 / 59	7.42
MTG	*Vanguard Mort-Backed Secs Idx ET	VMBS	C-	52.20	53.00	51.75	D / 2.1	-0.52	0.09	1.73 / 17	4.10 / 26	-
FO	*Vanguard MSCI EAFE ETF	VEA	D	35.23	36.03	28.75	C- / 4.1	10.24	18.93	20.86 / 73	3.81 / 26	-0.92
FO	*Vanguard MSCI Europe ETF	VGK	D+	48.84	50.09	38.47	C / 4.9	10.28	22.38	25.59 / 85	4.57 / 28	-1.26
FO	*Vanguard MSCI Pacific Fund ETF	VPL	C-	53.39	54.56	45.75	C- / 3.4	10.83	13.32	15.88 / 52	3.45 / 24	0.12
IN	*Vanguard REIT ETF	VNQ	B	65.80	69.20	58.64	B / 7.6	4.95	2.69	19.22 / 68	18.86 / 86	8.86
GR	*Vanguard Russell 1000 Gro Idx ET	VONG	B	67.12	70.18	61.03	C+ / 6.8	3.12	9.02	16.06 / 53	--	
GR	*Vanguard Russell 1000 Index ETF	VONE	B	65.21	67.44	58.23	B / 7.6	4.20	10.26	17.38 / 60	--	
GR	*Vanguard Russell 1000 Val Index	VONV	B+	63.35	65.86	55.23	B / 8.2	5.43	12.43	18.23 / 64	--	
GR	*Vanguard Russell 2000 Gro Idx ET	VTWG	B	69.11	72.17	60.04	B / 7.8	7.52	10.26	16.25 / 54	--	
GR	*Vanguard Russell 2000 Idx ETF	VTWO	B	67.00	69.55	58.60	B / 8.0	7.40	10.47	16.75 / 57	--	
GR	*Vanguard Russell 2000 Val Index	VTWV	B	64.62	67.41	55.87	B+ / 8.3	6.78	11.59	18.18 / 63	--	
GR	*Vanguard Russell 3000 Index ETF	VTHR	B	65.22	67.69	58.20	B / 7.7	4.39	11.53	16.91 / 57	--	
GR	*Vanguard S&P 500 Val Indx ETF	VOOV	B+	63.61	65.89	55.44	B / 8.2	5.30	12.90	17.89 / 62	--	
GR	*Vanguard S&P Mid-Cap 400 Gro ETF	IVOG	A-	69.97	73.15	61.39	B+ / 8.8	9.22	13.84	18.78 / 66	--	
GR	*Vanguard S&P Mid-Cap 400 Index E	IVOO	B+	68.07	70.98	59.35	B+ / 8.6	8.76	12.93	18.42 / 65	--	
GR	*Vanguard S&P Mid-Cap 400 Value E	IVOV	B+	65.63	68.35	57.24	B+ / 8.8	9.21	14.23	18.81 / 66	--	
GR	*Vanguard S&P SC 600 G Indx ETF	VIOG	B	71.64	74.72	63.96	B / 7.7	7.70	9.34	16.50 / 55	--	

99 Pct = Best
0 Pct = Worst

* Denotes ETF Fund, N/A denotes number is not ava

| Incl. in Returns | | RISK | | | | NET ASSETS | | VALUATION | | | ASSET | | | | | FUND MANAGER | |
Dividend Yield %	Expense Ratio	Risk Rating/ Pts	Standard Deviation	Beta	Avg Dura-tion	NAV as of 12/31/12	Total $(Mil)	As of 12/31/12	1 Year Average	Wtd Avg P/E	Cash %	Stocks %	Bonds %	Other %	Portfolio Turnover Ratio	Manager Quality Pct	Manager Tenure (Years)
0.00	0.96	C- / 3.4	38.1	0.24	N/A	18.73	1,175	0.91	-0.05	N/A	100	0	0	0	N/A	1	N/A
0.00	0.65	C+ / 6.1	28.9	1.02	N/A	34.04	1,200	-1.97	0.01	N/A	64	0	0	36	N/A	9	7
0.00	0.85	C+ / 6.2	28.2	-1.00	N/A	37.18	13	1.88	-0.01	N/A	0	0	0	100	N/A	76	4
0.00	0.92	C- / 4.1	23.3	0.15	N/A	16.61	43	3.79	0.06	N/A	0	0	0	100	N/A	2	N/A
4.58	0.18	B+ / 9.1	9.7	0.94	N/A	35.39	5,458	-1.33	-0.02	19.6	0	100	0	0	4	51	15
1.52	0.14	B- / 7.9	18.5	1.13	N/A	78.35	573	-3.17	0.03	50.8	0	100	0	0	6	82	3
2.95	0.14	B+ / 9.0	9.8	0.51	N/A	90.51	1,203	-2.87	0.01	27.7	0	100	0	0	7	85	3
3.34	0.10	B / 8.4	12.8	0.82	N/A	61.47	12,040	-3.09	0.01	30.6	0	100	0	0	7	66	7
1.95	0.14	B- / 7.3	23.7	1.03	N/A	105.80	1,881	-3.35	0.01	18.3	0	100	0	0	12	45	3
3.23	0.10	B- / 7.5	19.5	1.22	N/A	62.84	1,401	-3.72	0.01	44.9	0	100	0	0	11	59	16
4.13	0.12	B- / 7.7	24.3	1.97	N/A	113.61	177	2.10	0.27	N/A	0	0	100	0	47	19	6
3.46	0.14	B- / 7.4	20.4	1.02	N/A	35.48	851	-3.89	0.02	24.3	0	99	0	1	7	51	3
4.29	0.27	C+ / 6.1	22.3	1.06	N/A	92.53	1,067	-1.77	0.51	114.8	0	99	0	1	23	69	4
2.39	0.17	B- / 7.3	21.3	1.05	N/A	46.38	7,830	-1.36	0.26	33.7	0	99	0	1	8	55	5
2.02	0.19	C+ / 6.8	24.4	1.06	1.7	44.75	56,969	-0.49	0.10	55.7	0	99	0	1	8	49	5
8.49	0.34	B- / 7.3	N/A	N/A	N/A	55.08	423	-0.09	0.41	N/A	0	99	0	1	5	97	3
2.37	0.10	B- / 7.6	16.4	1.06	N/A	73.52	8,447	-3.18	N/A	79.6	0	100	0	0	17	55	19
1.67	0.14	B / 8.4	12.2	0.67	N/A	75.06	1,014	-4.52	0.04	51.0	0	98	0	2	9	77	9
3.99	0.11	B / 8.7	12.8	0.81	1.7	50.87	4,231	-2.93	0.03	21.6	0	99	0	1	20	74	7
2.09	0.14	B- / 7.6	20.2	1.25	N/A	73.50	516	-3.06	-0.01	27.6	0	100	0	0	6	48	3
1.21	0.14	B- / 7.0	19.4	1.19	N/A	71.02	2,484	-2.69	0.04	116.9	0	99	0	1	6	28	3
3.00	0.10	B+ / 9.5	4.1	1.64	6.1	87.85	4,368	0.46	0.28	N/A	0	0	99	1	79	41	5
3.15	0.12	B+ / 9.7	4.3	1.12	N/A	87.43	3,223	0.26	0.58	N/A	0	0	0	100	69	52	4
1.45	0.12	B+ / 9.6	3.9	0.25	N/A	65.30	126	0.17	0.05	N/A	1	0	98	1	51	72	4
2.84	0.10	B / 8.0	15.6	1.02	N/A	67.36	3,560	-3.27	N/A	49.2	0	100	0	0	6	51	9
4.15	0.10	B+ / 9.1	8.6	3.04	17.5	93.18	832	0.74	0.28	N/A	1	0	98	1	52	21	5
4.42	0.12	B+ / 9.2	7.9	1.88	N/A	91.51	1,164	0.21	0.74	N/A	0	0	0	100	71	28	4
2.73	0.12	B / 8.7	12.4	1.04	N/A	74.51	81	1.06	0.09	N/A	0	0	0	100	46	44	4
1.87	0.14	B- / 7.1	24.0	1.42	N/A	87.49	700	-3.75	0.01	42.3	0	100	0	0	7	22	3
3.09	0.12	B / 8.0	15.2	0.99	N/A	50.42	454	-3.15	0.02	51.5	0	100	0	0	19	50	6
2.80	0.12	B- / 7.6	16.2	1.04	N/A	57.25	780	-3.13	0.02	84.9	0	100	0	0	16	53	3
3.25	0.12	B / 8.2	15.0	0.96	N/A	44.15	431	-3.35	0.03	18.0	0	99	0	1	17	45	4
2.80	0.10	B- / 7.8	17.8	1.13	N/A	85.21	3,829	-3.25	N/A	36.4	0	99	0	1	15	55	15
1.36	0.10	B- / 7.7	19.1	1.18	N/A	71.06	1,165	-3.49	-0.01	46.9	0	100	0	0	32	51	7
3.84	0.10	B / 8.0	16.8	1.07	N/A	60.86	1,123	-3.37	0.02	27.7	0	100	0	0	32	55	7
0.51	0.12	B+ / 9.8	1.9	1.04	N/A	52.13	289	0.13	0.20	N/A	0	0	0	100	529	48	4
2.95	0.11	C / 5.4	20.9	1.03	N/A	35.90	10,213	-1.87	0.21	210.3	0	99	0	1	1	51	5
1.60	0.13	C / 5.1	24.0	1.17	N/A	49.90	4,379	-2.12	0.15	208.4	0	100	0	0	4	49	5
3.61	0.14	B- / 7.7	16.8	0.78	N/A	53.98	1,599	-1.09	0.02	N/A	0	99	0	1	3	65	16
4.84	0.10	B- / 7.6	18.3	1.01	N/A	67.18	14,609	-2.05	N/A	66.5	0	99	0	1	10	83	17
2.65	0.15	B / 8.4	N/A	N/A	N/A	69.25	83	-3.08	-0.04	N/A	0	99	0	1	25	43	3
2.90	0.12	B / 8.2	N/A	N/A	N/A	67.46	176	-3.34	-0.06	N/A	0	99	0	1	36	51	3
3.19	0.15	B / 8.1	N/A	N/A	N/A	65.75	47	-3.65	N/A	N/A	0	100	0	0	29	67	3
1.63	0.20	B- / 7.4	N/A	N/A	N/A	71.94	47	-3.93	-0.02	N/A	0	100	0	0	51	25	3
1.56	0.15	B- / 7.5	N/A	N/A	N/A	69.52	164	-3.62	-0.05	N/A	0	100	0	0	35	38	3
1.92	0.20	B- / 7.5	N/A	N/A	N/A	67.09	19	-3.68	0.07	N/A	0	100	0	0	40	37	3
2.44	0.15	B / 8.2	N/A	N/A	N/A	67.64	39	-3.58	-0.05	N/A	0	100	0	0	20	46	3
2.58	0.15	B / 8.0	N/A	N/A	N/A	65.74	63	-3.24	0.02	N/A	0	100	0	0	20	64	3
1.39	0.20	B- / 7.9	N/A	N/A	N/A	72.67	97	-3.72	0.03	N/A	0	100	0	0	26	68	3
1.07	0.15	B- / 7.8	N/A	N/A	N/A	70.64	101	-3.64	0.04	N/A	0	99	0	1	13	69	3
1.64	0.20	B- / 7.6	N/A	N/A	N/A	68.21	10	-3.78	0.06	N/A	0	99	0	1	31	64	3
1.14	0.20	B- / 7.9	N/A	N/A	N/A	74.48	14	-3.81	0.03	N/A	0	100	0	0	45	44	3

* Denotes ETF Fund, N/A denotes number is not available

I. Index of ETFs and Other Closed-End Funds

Fund Type	Fund Name	Ticker Symbol	Overall Investment Rating	Price As of 12/31/12	52 Week High	52 Week Low	Performance Rating/Pts	3 Mo	6 Mo	1Yr/Pct	3Yr/Pct	5Yr/Pct
GR	*Vanguard S&P SC 600 Indx ETF	VIOO	B	70.25	72.76	61.10	B / 8.1	8.05	10.79	16.69 / 56	--	--
GR	*Vanguard S&P SC 600 Val Indx ETF	VIOV	B+	69.17	71.63	58.48	B+ / 8.3	7.98	11.98	17.30 / 60	--	--
GEI	*Vanguard Short-Term Bd Idx ETF	BSV	C-	80.99	81.51	80.67	D / 1.9	0.15	0.72	1.94 / 18	2.69 / 22	3.42 / 34
COI	*Vanguard Short-Term Crp Bd Idx E	VCSH	C	80.33	80.77	78.17	D+ / 2.3	0.27	2.14	5.34 / 24	4.22 / 27	--
USA	*Vanguard Short-Term Gvt Bd Idx E	VGSH	C-	60.89	61.46	60.75	D / 1.6	0.10	0.20	0.46 / 15	1.16 / 18	--
GR	*Vanguard Small Cap ETF	VB	C+	80.90	84.14	69.43	C+ / 6.9	7.93	11.99	18.62 / 65	14.23 / 70	8.63 / 63
GR	*Vanguard Small Cap Growth ETF	VBK	C+	89.03	92.55	76.10	B- / 7.2	7.71	11.80	18.40 / 65	15.49 / 75	8.95 / 65
GR	*Vanguard Small Cap Value ETF	VBR	C+	72.65	75.52	62.59	C+ / 6.4	8.00	12.08	18.68 / 66	12.95 / 63	8.21 / 61
GEI	*Vanguard ST Inf Prot Sec Idx ETF	VTIP	U	50.12	N/A	N/A	U /	--	--	--	--	--
IN	*Vanguard Telecom Serv ETF	VOX	C+	70.01	76.52	60.96	C / 5.3	-0.45	6.58	18.47 / 65	12.58 / 61	5.11 / 44
GEI	*Vanguard Total Bond Market ETF	BND	C	84.03	85.36	82.59	D+ / 2.4	-0.27	0.54	3.45 / 21	5.59 / 31	5.40 / 46
GL	*Vanguard Total Intl Stock Index	VXUS	B+	46.96	47.97	38.83	A- / 9.2	9.98	18.42	19.12 / 68	--	--
GI	*Vanguard Total Stock Market ETF	VTI	C+	73.28	75.91	64.94	C / 5.5	4.54	10.43	17.04 / 58	11.85 / 57	5.21 / 45
EM	*Vanguard Total World Stock ETF	VT	C-	49.42	50.79	42.19	C / 4.4	7.20	14.74	18.18 / 63	7.05 / 36	--
UT	*Vanguard Utilities Index ETF	VPU	C	75.30	84.92	72.64	C- / 3.4	-1.11	-2.08	6.67 / 27	9.62 / 45	2.42 / 29
IN	*Vanguard Value ETF	VTV	C	58.80	60.93	51.97	C / 5.0	4.72	10.74	15.96 / 52	10.48 / 50	3.17 / 33
GL	*VelocityShares 2x Long Platinum	LPLT	E+	44.43	60.12	33.55	D / 1.8	-13.41	16.54	-0.20 / 13	--	--
GL	*VelocityShares 3x Inv Nat Gas ET	DGAZ	U	20.59	N/A	N/A	U /	48.03	-33.07	--	--	--
GL	*VelocityShares 3x Inverse Crude	DWTI	U	47.86	N/A	N/A	U /	-7.79	-25.33	--	--	--
GL	*VelocityShares 3x Inverse Gold E	DGLD	E	41.24	58.50	34.25	E+ / 0.6	15.04	-16.33	-17.35 / 6	--	--
GL	*VelocityShares 3x Inverse Silver	DSLV	E-	26.91	51.71	18.99	E- / 0.1	19.97	-40.23	-44.91 / 1	--	--
GL	*VelocityShares 3x Long Crude ETN	UWTI	U	28.70	N/A	N/A	U /	-4.24	2.52	--	--	--
GL	*VelocityShares 3x Long Gold ETN	UGLD	E+	41.86	57.42	34.10	E+ / 0.8	-16.80	9.89	-7.11 / 9	--	--
GL	*VelocityShares 3x Long Nat Gas E	UGAZ	U	21.87	N/A	N/A	U /	-49.98	-30.15	--	--	--
GL	*VelocityShares 3x Long Silver ET	USLV	E-	26.11	65.13	18.80	E / 0.5	-29.86	24.44	-21.10 / 5	--	--
IN	*VelocityShares Daily 2x VIX S-T	TVIX	E-	9.34	247.90	6.54	E- / 0.0	-54.80	-81.89	-97.36 / 0	--	--
IN	*VelocityShares Dly 2x VIX Med-T	TVIZ	E-	11.48	54.85	9.49	E- / 0.0	-38.05	-64.26	-82.86 / 0	--	--
GEI	*VelocityShares Dly Invs VIX M-T	ZIV	B	23.77	26.02	12.89	A+ / 9.9	21.01	55.10	99.69 / 99	--	--
GI	*VelocityShares Dly Invs VIX ST E	XIV	C-	16.57	20.14	7.32	A+ / 9.9	14.04	55.40	168.59 / 99	--	--
GL	*VelocityShares TM 3x Inv Brnt Cr	DOIL	U	35.22	N/A	N/A	U /	-0.27	-42.67	--	--	--
GL	*VelocityShares TM 3x Lng Brnt Cr	UOIL	U	42.49	N/A	N/A	U /	-9.38	28.88	--	--	--
GI	*VelocityShares VIX Medium-Term E	VIIZ	E-	38.65	79.21	35.31	E- / 0.0	-22.36	-39.94	-54.85 / 1	--	--
GI	*VelocityShares VIX Short-Term ET	VIIX	E-	17.19	67.41	14.30	E- / 0.0	-25.24	-50.45	-79.00 / 0	--	--
GL	*WCM/BNY Mellon Focused Gro ADR E	AADR	B+	30.74	32.30	27.23	B+ / 8.5	9.34	16.04	15.42 / 50	--	--
GL	*WisdomTree Asia Local Debt	ALD	C	52.55	58.88	49.79	C- / 3.1	2.06	4.76	6.66 / 27	--	--
FO	*WisdomTree Asia Pacific ex-Japan	AXJL	C	69.06	70.27	57.09	C / 5.2	8.20	15.83	20.13 / 71	8.40 / 40	4.04 / 37
FO	*WisdomTree Australia and NZ Debt	AUNZ	D+	22.74	24.49	20.86	D+ / 2.4	2.78	4.03	8.73 / 32	3.03 / 23	--
FO	*WisdomTree Australia Divide	AUSE	C-	58.17	60.43	48.00	C / 4.5	12.81	22.64	22.23 / 77	7.35 / 36	5.21 / 45
FO	*WisdomTree China Div ex Financia	CHXF	U	55.53	N/A	N/A	U /	10.01	--	--	--	--
FO	*WisdomTree Commodity Country Equ	CCXE	C-	31.83	32.65	26.89	C / 4.6	7.95	15.33	18.54 / 65	7.33 / 36	3.00 / 32
FO	*WisdomTree DEFA	DWM	C-	46.47	47.61	38.01	C- / 4.0	9.81	17.92	21.28 / 74	3.78 / 25	-1.29 / 16
FO	*WisdomTree DEFA Equity Income	DTH	D+	40.43	41.60	33.09	C- / 3.8	9.08	18.69	20.80 / 73	3.23 / 23	-2.19 / 13
IN	*WisdomTree Dividend Ex-Financial	DTN	B	55.58	57.62	50.38	C+ / 6.6	3.38	8.89	13.44 / 43	15.88 / 76	6.85 / 54
FO	*WisdomTree Dr Brazilian Real Fun	BZF	D	18.91	21.65	17.74	D / 2.2	1.34	2.43	-6.51 / 10	5.29 / 30	--
FO	*WisdomTree Dr Chinese Yuan Fund	CYB	C-	25.53	25.88	25.00	D / 2.0	1.73	3.02	2.33 / 19	2.64 / 22	--
GL	*WisdomTree Dr Commodity Curr Fun	CCX	D	21.48	22.03	19.60	D+ / 2.9	2.13	5.02	5.43 / 25	--	--
FO	*WisdomTree Dr Emerg Curr Fd	CEW	D+	21.09	21.35	19.29	D+ / 2.3	2.12	5.32	5.84 / 25	2.98 / 23	--
FO	*WisdomTree Dr Indian Rupee Fund	ICN	D	21.09	23.16	19.41	D- / 1.3	-3.35	4.30	1.30 / 17	-0.70 / 14	--
IN	*WisdomTree Earnings 500 Fund	EPS	C+	49.36	51.36	44.10	C / 5.2	3.87	10.27	15.60 / 51	11.37 / 55	4.60 / 41
EM	*WisdomTree EM Corporate Bond	EMCB	U	80.85	N/A	N/A	U /	2.00	8.37	--	--	--
EM	*WisdomTree Emg Mkts Eqty Inc Fd	DEM	C-	57.19	59.43	49.09	C- / 3.8	7.22	14.64	12.48 / 40	7.99 / 38	7.46 / 57
EM	*WisdomTree Emg Mkts Local Debt F	ELD	C+	53.46	54.03	47.99	C+ / 5.6	3.91	7.56	12.93 / 41	--	--

99 Pct = Best
0 Pct = Worst

* Denotes ETF Fund, N/A denotes number is not available

www.thestreetratings.com

Incl. in Returns		RISK				NET ASSETS		VALUATION			ASSET					FUND MANAGER	
Dividend Yield %	Expense Ratio	Risk Rating/ Pts	Standard Deviation	Beta	Avg Dura-tion	NAV as of 12/31/12	Total $(Mil)	As of 12/31/12	1 Year Average	Wtd Avg P/E	Cash %	Stocks %	Bonds %	Other %	Portfolio Turnover Ratio	Manager Quality Pct	Manager Tenure (Years)
1.45	0.15	B- / 7.8	N/A	N/A	N/A	72.52	48	-3.13	0.03	N/A	0	100	0	0	12	44	3
1.31	0.20	B- / 7.7	N/A	N/A	N/A	71.04	17	-2.63	-0.04	N/A	0	100	0	0	29	39	3
1.40	0.10	B+ / 9.8	1.3	0.48	4.6	80.94	9,274	0.06	0.08	N/A	0	0	99	1	55	52	8
1.97	0.12	B+ / 9.9	2.0	0.42	N/A	80.13	4,649	0.25	0.35	N/A	0	0	0	100	65	60	4
0.24	0.12	B+ / 9.9	0.8	0.03	N/A	60.87	226	0.03	0.03	N/A	0	0	0	100	72	60	4
3.67	0.10	B- / 7.4	20.3	1.27	N/A	83.79	4,491	-3.45	0.01	49.3	0	99	0	1	13	50	22
2.06	0.10	B- / 7.0	21.1	1.31	N/A	92.31	2,101	-3.55	N/A	75.2	0	99	0	1	34	56	9
5.16	0.10	B- / 7.6	19.6	1.22	N/A	75.11	2,170	-3.28	0.03	30.2	0	100	0	0	35	45	15
0.62	N/A	U /	N/A	N/A	N/A	50.03	55	0.18	N/A	N/A	0	0	0	100	N/A	N/A	1
3.53	0.14	B / 8.6	14.5	0.73	N/A	71.50	485	-2.08	0.01	18.7	0	100	0	0	28	71	9
2.39	0.10	B+ / 9.8	2.4	1.01	10.1	83.78	17,721	0.30	0.13	N/A	0	0	99	1	72	49	21
2.71	0.17	B- / 7.2	N/A	N/A	N/A	47.66	1,066	-1.47	0.29	40.9	0	99	0	1	2	58	5
2.97	0.05	B- / 7.9	16.0	1.04	1.7	75.75	23,383	-3.26	0.01	49.2	0	99	0	1	3	52	19
2.25	0.21	B- / 7.4	18.5	0.76	N/A	50.57	1,560	-2.27	0.17	59.9	0	100	0	0	19	73	5
4.24	0.14	B+ / 9.2	9.5	0.92	N/A	76.44	1,130	-1.49	0.02	20.6	0	97	0	3	5	59	3
3.33	0.10	B / 8.2	15.1	0.97	N/A	60.84	6,758	-3.35	0.01	19.6	0	100	0	0	19	48	19
0.00	N/A	C- / 3.7	N/A	N/A	N/A	45.24	3	-1.79	-0.35	N/A	0	0	0	100	N/A	5	2
0.00	N/A	U /	N/A	N/A	N/A	20.55	10	0.19	N/A	N/A	0	0	0	100	N/A	N/A	1
0.00	N/A	U /	N/A	N/A	N/A	45.02	2	6.31	N/A	N/A	0	0	0	100	N/A	N/A	1
0.00	N/A	C- / 3.5	N/A	N/A	N/A	42.04	6	-1.90	-0.02	N/A	0	0	0	100	N/A	21	2
0.00	N/A	D / 1.9	N/A	N/A	N/A	26.46	17	1.70	-0.17	N/A	0	0	0	100	N/A	4	2
0.00	N/A	U /	N/A	N/A	N/A	30.47	5	-5.81	N/A	N/A	0	0	0	100	N/A	N/A	1
0.00	N/A	C- / 3.7	N/A	N/A	N/A	40.76	42	2.70	0.07	N/A	0	0	0	100	N/A	7	2
0.00	N/A	U /	N/A	N/A	N/A	20.81	59	5.09	N/A	N/A	0	0	0	100	N/A	N/A	1
0.00	N/A	D / 2.2	N/A	N/A	N/A	25.98	121	0.50	0.15	N/A	0	0	0	100	N/A	1	2
0.00	N/A	D / 1.9	N/A	N/A	N/A	6.05	118	54.38	8.42	N/A	0	0	0	100	N/A	N/A	3
0.00	N/A	D / 1.9	N/A	N/A	N/A	9.61	2	19.46	-0.31	N/A	0	0	0	100	N/A	N/A	3
0.00	N/A	C / 5.3	N/A	N/A	N/A	25.85	16	-8.05	0.27	N/A	0	0	0	100	N/A	99	3
0.00	N/A	D / 1.9	N/A	N/A	N/A	19.74	347	-16.06	-0.03	N/A	0	0	0	100	N/A	97	3
0.00	N/A	U /	N/A	N/A	N/A	37.38	1	-5.78	N/A	N/A	0	0	0	100	N/A	N/A	1
0.00	N/A	U /	N/A	N/A	N/A	43.02	1	-1.23	N/A	N/A	0	0	0	100	N/A	N/A	1
0.00	N/A	D / 1.9	N/A	N/A	N/A	35.38	5	9.24	-0.39	N/A	0	0	0	100	N/A	1	3
0.00	N/A	D / 1.9	N/A	N/A	N/A	14.20	14	21.06	0.03	N/A	0	0	0	100	N/A	N/A	3
0.55	1.25	B- / 7.8	N/A	N/A	N/A	32.23	7	-4.62	-0.02	N/A	3	96	0	1	16	45	N/A
13.74	0.55	B+ / 9.1	N/A	N/A	N/A	52.90	457	-0.66	0.09	N/A	0	0	0	100	35	81	2
2.27	0.48	B- / 7.2	21.0	0.96	N/A	69.23	92	-0.25	0.17	N/A	0	100	0	0	60	80	5
2.83	0.45	B- / 7.8	14.2	0.43	N/A	22.91	63	-0.74	0.27	N/A	100	0	0	0	9	64	5
1.42	0.58	C+ / 6.7	25.4	1.15	N/A	60.30	69	-3.53	0.20	N/A	0	100	0	0	68	67	5
0.00	N/A	U /	N/A	N/A	N/A	55.86	30	-0.59	N/A	N/A	0	0	0	100	N/A	N/A	1
2.85	0.58	B- / 7.2	26.2	1.21	N/A	32.47	27	-1.97	-0.28	18.2	0	100	0	0	116	70	5
2.83	0.48	B- / 7.1	20.9	1.03	N/A	47.41	418	-1.98	0.36	N/A	0	100	0	0	27	51	N/A
3.24	0.58	C+ / 6.9	22.3	1.07	N/A	41.31	184	-2.13	0.31	N/A	0	100	0	0	32	37	5
4.97	0.38	B / 8.9	12.1	0.75	N/A	57.13	1,081	-2.71	0.07	20.0	0	100	0	0	38	84	5
0.00	0.45	C+ / 5.8	18.3	0.62	N/A	19.06	61	-0.79	-0.15	N/A	0	0	75	25	N/A	67	5
0.78	0.45	B+ / 9.8	3.4	0.10	N/A	25.74	240	-0.82	-0.11	N/A	0	0	72	28	8	67	5
0.00	0.55	C+ / 6.6	N/A	N/A	N/A	21.59	24	-0.51	-0.18	N/A	0	0	0	100	N/A	27	3
0.00	0.55	B / 8.2	10.9	0.47	N/A	21.19	272	-0.47	-0.11	N/A	100	0	0	0	N/A	63	4
0.00	0.45	B- / 7.0	11.5	0.45	N/A	21.21	15	-0.57	0.06	N/A	20	0	79	1	N/A	35	5
2.83	0.28	B / 8.2	14.4	0.93	N/A	51.16	57	-3.52	0.01	40.8	0	100	0	0	16	57	5
3.92	N/A	U /	N/A	N/A	N/A	80.75	96	0.12	N/A	N/A	0	0	0	100	N/A	N/A	1
1.41	0.63	B- / 7.1	21.3	0.90	N/A	56.81	4,866	0.67	0.52	N/A	0	100	0	0	37	79	5
0.44	0.55	B / 8.6	N/A	N/A	N/A	53.44	1,498	0.04	0.19	N/A	5	0	94	1	43	92	3

Denotes ETF Fund, N/A denotes number is not available

				PRICE			PERFORMANCE					
99 Pct = Best *0 Pct = Worst*			Overall Investment Rating	Price As of 12/31/12	52 Week		Perform-ance Rating/Pts	% Total Return Through 12/31/12			Annualized	
Fund Type	Fund Name	Ticker Symbol			High	Low		3 Mo	6 Mo	1Yr/Pct	3Yr/Pct	5Yr/Pct
EM	*WisdomTree Emg Mkts SmCap Div Fd	DGS	C	49.44	51.05	41.51	C / 5.5	9.44	17.83	21.30 / 74	8.20 / 39	6.97 / 55
GI	*WisdomTree Equity Income Fund	DHS	B	45.80	48.33	42.70	C+ / 6.2	1.70	4.30	14.10 / 45	15.60 / 75	4.32 / 39
FO	*WisdomTree Euro Debt	EU	D+	22.27	24.37	18.20	D / 2.1	1.50	19.01	12.79 / 41	0.07 / 15	--
FO	*WisdomTree Europe Hedged Equity	HEDJ	C	47.67	48.77	39.83	C- / 4.0	12.25	14.16	20.60 / 72	4.28 / 27	--
FO	*WisdomTree Europe Small Cap Div	DFE	C+	41.08	42.81	31.40	B / 7.7	15.66	33.27	34.63 / 95	7.93 / 38	1.31 / 24
GL	*WisdomTree Global Equity Income	DEW	C-	43.27	44.26	36.54	C- / 4.1	5.97	13.47	18.19 / 63	6.46 / 34	-0.80 / 17
GL	*WisdomTree Global ex-US Growth	DNL	D+	52.94	53.73	42.87	C- / 3.3	9.05	15.74	15.71 / 51	5.32 / 31	4.40 / 40
FO	*WisdomTree Global ex-US Real Est	DRW	C+	29.97	31.50	24.32	B+ / 8.4	10.71	20.62	36.67 / 96	14.45 / 71	1.24 / 24
UT	*WisdomTree Global ex-US Utilitie	DBU	D	18.40	19.30	15.93	D- / 1.5	5.68	9.84	8.64 / 32	-1.76 / 12	-6.53 / 7
EN	*WisdomTree Global Natural Resour	GNAT	D	24.54	27.00	20.81	D / 2.1	5.12	14.54	5.89 / 26	1.17 / 18	-0.11 / 19
GI	*WisdomTree Global Real Return Fu	RRF	D+	47.79	48.99	43.90	D / 1.8	2.38	--	1.78 / 18	--	--
FO	*WisdomTree India Earnings Fund	EPI	D-	19.37	21.59	15.41	D- / 1.3	4.49	14.80	15.27 / 49	-4.31 / 10	--
FO	*WisdomTree Intl Div Ex-Financial	DOO	D+	41.90	42.92	35.01	D+ / 2.9	7.68	15.26	14.99 / 48	3.86 / 26	-2.44 / 13
FO	*WisdomTree Intl LargeCap Dividen	DOL	C-	44.93	45.86	36.66	C- / 3.6	8.58	17.46	19.66 / 69	3.17 / 23	-1.72 / 14
FO	*WisdomTree Intl MidCap Dividend	DIM	C	50.29	51.66	40.82	C / 5.0	11.74	20.93	23.49 / 80	5.34 / 31	0.94 / 22
FO	*WisdomTree Intl Small Cap Divide	DLS	C+	52.13	53.69	42.00	C+ / 6.8	14.34	24.53	26.39 / 86	8.45 / 40	2.36 / 28
FO	*WisdomTree Japan Hedged Equity	DXJ	D+	36.88	38.60	30.07	D+ / 2.6	24.68	20.14	23.92 / 81	-1.10 / 13	-2.33 / 13
FO	*WisdomTree Japan SmallCap Div Fd	DFJ	C-	43.70	45.68	39.91	C- / 3.0	7.33	4.81	7.40 / 29	5.33 / 31	3.01 / 32
GI	*WisdomTree LargeCap Dividend Fun	DLN	C+	53.64	55.82	49.12	C / 5.5	2.64	6.93	14.25 / 46	13.32 / 65	4.28 / 38
IN	*WisdomTree LargeCap Value Fund	EZY	C-	44.65	47.03	36.06	C- / 4.1	0.05	6.24	11.55 / 38	10.52 / 50	3.15 / 33
GR	*WisdomTree Mgd Futures Strategy	WDTI	D	40.30	45.48	39.32	E+ / 0.8	--	0.10	-10.74 / 8	--	--
GR	*WisdomTree MidCap Dividend Fund	DON	B-	57.41	59.65	51.07	C+ / 6.6	6.40	10.38	16.25 / 54	14.67 / 72	9.07 / 66
GR	*WisdomTree MidCap Earnings Fund	EZM	B	62.38	65.00	52.28	B- / 7.5	10.46	16.63	17.84 / 61	15.06 / 73	11.19 / 74
FO	*WisdomTree Middle East Dividend	GULF	C-	14.99	44.20	13.43	C- / 4.1	7.00	13.05	13.59 / 43	7.19 / 36	--
GR	*WisdomTree SmallCap Dividend Fd	DES	B-	50.95	52.82	44.67	C+ / 6.6	6.03	9.40	18.12 / 63	14.49 / 71	8.55 / 63
GR	*WisdomTree SmallCap Earnings Fun	EES	C+	56.71	59.03	49.17	C+ / 5.9	7.37	10.19	14.06 / 45	13.08 / 64	11.33 / 75
IN	*WisdomTree Total Dividend	DTD	C+	53.79	55.91	49.03	C+ / 5.6	3.13	7.39	14.48 / 46	13.52 / 66	5.01 / 44
IN	*WisdomTree Total Earnings Fund	EXT	C+	50.39	52.65	45.30	C / 5.4	4.44	10.42	15.90 / 52	11.66 / 56	5.30 / 45
GL	*Yorkville High Income MLP ETF	YMLP	U	17.43	N/A	N/A	U /	-0.93	3.02		--	--
GL	Aberdeen Asia-Pacific Income Fund	FAX	C+	7.74	8.01	7.16	C / 5.3	1.68	5.82	12.62 / 40	13.38 / 65	13.61 / 84
FO	Aberdeen Australia Equity Fund	IAF	D+	10.44	11.21	9.31	C- / 3.9	6.66	13.11	21.74 / 76	5.15 / 30	5.38 / 46
FO	Aberdeen Chile Fund	CH	D	15.09	19.43	13.74	C- / 3.7	4.85	3.90	5.23 / 24	10.13 / 48	12.13 / 77
EM	Aberdeen Emerging Mkt Tele & Infr	ETF	B-	21.50	21.95	17.15	C+ / 6.7	6.64	17.19	24.99 / 84	11.55 / 56	1.95 / 27
GL	Aberdeen Global Income Fund	FCO	C+	14.22	15.35	12.92	C / 5.2	2.76	6.06	8.45 / 31	13.66 / 67	14.14 / 86
EM	Aberdeen Indonesia Fund	IF	B	11.67	14.23	11.53	B / 8.0	5.83	11.57	18.78 / 66	19.05 / 86	12.91 / 86
FO	Aberdeen Israel Fund	ISL	D	13.10	14.34	11.35	D / 2.0	9.18	19.34	8.85 / 32	-0.60 / 14	-2.72 / 12
FO	Aberdeen Latin America Equity Fund	LAQ	C	36.24	38.27	30.00	C+ / 6.0	13.38	22.57	22.29 / 77	10.96 / 52	8.99 / 65
IN	Adams Express Company	ADX	C	10.59	11.57	9.95	C / 4.3	2.98	9.87	17.43 / 60	8.85 / 42	3.58 / 35
GI	Advent Claymore Cnv Sec & Inc	AVK	C-	16.12	17.09	14.64	C / 4.3	0.80	12.27	13.66 / 43	9.68 / 46	3.28 / 34
GL	Advent Claymore Enhanced Gr & Inc	LCM	D+	9.10	10.14	8.61	D+ / 2.9	4.22	8.72	13.30 / 42	3.66 / 25	2.06 / 27
GI	Advent/Claymore Gbl Con Sec & Inc	AGC	D	6.48	7.06	6.06	D+ / 2.4	5.16	10.58	12.71 / 40	0.82 / 17	-4.28 / 9
GI	AGIC Convertible & Income Fund	NCV	C-	8.69	9.96	8.09	C / 4.5	1.93	6.57	13.04 / 42	11.03 / 53	7.84 / 59
GI	AGIC Convertible & Income Fund II	NCZ	C-	7.93	9.03	7.37	C- / 4.2	0.62	6.02	13.72 / 44	10.36 / 49	6.16 / 50
IN	AGIC Equity & Convertible Income F	NIE	C-	16.64	18.07	15.77	C- / 3.4	1.44	8.11	12.13 / 39	7.34 / 36	3.90 / 37
GL	AGIC Global Equity & Conv Inc Fund	NGZ	D+	13.49	14.79	12.05	C- / 3.3	5.97	13.93	14.45 / 46	4.20 / 27	2.22 / 28
FO	AGIC Intl & Premium Strategy Fund	NAI	D-	9.70	11.92	8.70	D / 1.6	7.98	2.70	16.26 / 54	-1.79 / 12	-0.69 / 17
MUS	Alliance CA Municipal Income Fund	AKP	B+	14.65	17.24	13.91	B- / 7.1	-3.12	-5.85	8.84 / 43	13.02 / 89	7.97 / 78
MUS	Alliance NY Municipal Income Fund	AYN	C	14.37	16.08	14.22	C- / 4.1	-4.46	-3.15	0.91 / 17	8.90 / 67	7.38 / 75
GL	AllianceBernstein Global High Inc	AWF	B	15.65	16.29	14.02	B / 7.9	8.21	14.00	24.71 / 83	15.90 / 76	16.74 / 95
GL	AllianceBernstein Income Fund	ACG	C	8.10	8.83	8.06	C- / 4.1	2.84	6.39	13.28 / 42	9.66 / 45	8.12 / 60
MUN	AllianceBernstein Nat Muni Inc Fun	AFB	A+	15.55	16.68	13.94	A- / 9.1	5.80	9.98	19.71 / 91	14.21 / 93	10.59 / 94
GL	Alpine Global Dynamic Div Fd	AGD	E+	5.23	6.34	4.80	E+ / 0.9	-3.48	5.46	13.20 / 42	-7.67 / 8	-9.18 / 5

* Denotes ETF Fund, N/A denotes number is not available

www.thestreetratings.com

Dividend Yield %	Expense Ratio	Risk Rating/ Pts	Standard Deviation	Beta	Avg Dura-tion	NAV as of 12/31/12	Total $(Mil)	As of 12/31/12	1 Year Average	Wtd Avg P/E	Cash %	Stocks %	Bonds %	Other %	Portfolio Turnover Ratio	Manager Quality Pct	Manager Tenure (Years)
1.54	0.63	C+/6.6	23.3	0.99	N/A	49.86	1,192	-0.84	0.55	N/A	0	100	0	0	53	74	5
3.34	0.38	B+/9.0	11.0	0.62	N/A	47.28	536	-3.13	0.13	20.7	0	100	0	0	22	86	5
10.89	0.35	B-/7.5	16.4	0.62	N/A	22.64	5	-1.63	-3.43	N/A	49	0	50	1	26	32	5
1.22	0.58	B/8.2	12.9	0.57	N/A	48.18	35	-1.06	0.89	N/A	0	100	0	0	42	64	4
2.58	0.58	C+/6.5	25.0	1.18	N/A	42.28	34	-2.84	0.68	N/A	0	100	0	0	58	75	5
2.94	0.58	B-/7.8	18.4	0.88	N/A	44.10	99	-1.88	0.49	19.4	0	100	0	0	25	69	5
1.58	0.58	C+/6.7	22.9	1.06	N/A	52.64	68	0.57	0.06	69.0	0	100	0	0	28	64	5
16.32	0.58	C/5.3	22.7	1.03	N/A	30.33	108	-1.19	0.07	197.3	0	100	0	0	43	89	5
2.82	0.58	B-/7.5	19.1	1.00	N/A	18.48	37	-0.43	0.05	22.9	0	100	0	0	66	13	5
2.18	0.58	C+/6.8	27.6	1.07	N/A	24.73	28	-0.77	-0.04	18.6	0	100	0	0	99	17	5
2.25	0.60	B/8.8	N/A	N/A	N/A	48.58	5	-1.63	-2.27	N/A	0	100	0	0	N/A	62	2
0.50	0.76	C/5.5	30.7	1.08	N/A	19.58	1,232	-1.07	0.37	N/A	0	0	0	100	32	16	5
2.69	0.58	B-/7.1	20.5	0.98	N/A	42.68	347	-1.83	0.28	N/A	0	100	0	0	28	47	5
2.64	0.48	B-/7.1	21.2	1.04	N/A	45.66	199	-1.60	0.37	N/A	0	100	0	0	23	43	5
1.08	0.38	B-/7.1	21.0	1.03	N/A	51.47	105	-2.29	-0.07	N/A	0	100	0	0	29	61	5
2.42	0.38	B-/7.5	19.3	0.91	N/A	53.25	484	-2.10	0.32	N/A	0	100	0	0	31	81	5
1.89	0.48	B-/7.2	18.1	0.56	N/A	38.09	1,223	-3.18	0.24	N/A	0	100	0	0	41	32	5
1.66	0.58	B/8.6	13.5	0.36	N/A	43.59	177	0.25	0.15	N/A	0	100	0	0	36	81	5
1.87	0.28	B/8.7	12.5	0.79	N/A	55.30	1,240	-3.00	0.07	24.3	0	100	0	0	14	75	5
2.74	0.38	B-/7.8	17.5	1.08	N/A	45.52	29	-1.91	-0.05	53.2	0	100	0	0	62	41	5
0.00	0.95	B-/7.8	N/A	N/A	N/A	40.64	117	-0.84	-0.06	N/A	0	0	0	100	N/A	12	2
3.33	0.38	B/8.2	15.1	0.96	N/A	59.51	391	-3.53	0.12	26.7	0	100	0	0	29	72	5
3.04	0.38	B-/7.7	18.7	1.16	N/A	64.46	165	-3.23	0.08	38.4	0	100	0	0	38	64	5
6.68	0.88	B/8.0	14.6	0.50	N/A	15.59	12	-3.85	-0.55	N/A	0	100	0	0	37	75	N/A
4.10	0.38	B/8.0	17.1	1.05	N/A	52.47	402	-2.90	0.18	23.9	0	100	0	0	31	68	5
4.22	0.38	B-/7.6	19.7	1.20	N/A	58.62	156	-3.26	0.11	38.1	0	100	0	0	41	49	5
2.00	0.28	B/8.6	12.8	0.82	N/A	55.48	266	-3.05	0.07	24.4	0	100	0	0	15	75	5
3.02	0.28	B/8.1	14.8	0.96	N/A	52.56	48	-4.13	0.03	40.8	0	100	0	0	12	53	5
9.30	N/A	U/	N/A	N/A	N/A	18.56	98	-6.09	N/A	N/A	0	0	0	100	N/A	N/A	1
5.43	1.49	B/8.6	13.2	0.93	N/A	7.80	1,952	-0.77	0.94	N/A	0	0	99	1	72	90	N/A
2.01	1.34	C+/6.6	28.1	1.20	N/A	10.21	230	2.25	5.97	N/A	0	92	0	8	30	56	N/A
3.73	1.90	C/5.4	33.5	1.10	N/A	15.61	142	-3.33	2.54	N/A	0	100	0	0	1	85	4
1.14	1.50	B/8.3	17.4	0.73	N/A	24.17	165	-11.05	-11.42	38.1	2	97	0	1	50	86	N/A
5.91	2.13	B/8.5	15.0	0.75	12.2	13.97	122	1.79	1.90	N/A	0	0	99	1	76	90	N/A
1.86	1.44	B-/7.3	22.6	0.82	N/A	12.96	116	-9.95	-9.48	N/A	0	100	0	0	44	95	N/A
1.33	1.68	C+/6.7	21.7	0.87	N/A	15.90	60	-17.61	-13.34	38.1	3	94	0	3	3	26	N/A
2.11	1.20	C+/6.6	26.4	1.10	N/A	40.93	264	-11.46	-9.30	N/A	1	98	0	1	6	79	4
1.89	0.68	B-/7.7	17.2	1.09	N/A	12.85	1,125	-17.59	-14.12	44.8	4	95	0	1	28	27	27
6.99	1.58	C+/6.7	18.0	0.92	7.7	18.21	413	-11.48	-7.19	14.0	8	1	23	68	93	49	10
9.23	2.11	C+/6.7	16.1	0.63	6.2	10.97	145	-17.05	-10.35	56.3	1	17	18	64	121	51	6
8.70	1.99	C+/6.0	19.9	0.92	8.0	7.61	239	-14.85	-8.99	13.9	1	0	14	85	125	16	6
2.43	1.30	B-/7.2	20.3	1.07	N/A	8.67	627	0.23	9.11	N/A	3	0	46	51	17	42	10
2.86	1.33	B-/7.4	17.9	0.96	N/A	7.86	473	0.89	10.49	N/A	3	0	46	51	18	52	10
6.73	1.09	B-/7.5	16.6	0.96	5.1	19.69	417	-15.49	-10.60	46.3	3	69	0	28	67	27	N/A
8.90	1.29	B-/7.2	19.2	0.82	4.9	15.42	104	-12.52	-10.45	44.5	2	79	0	19	63	54	N/A
1.34	1.34	C+/5.9	21.4	0.90	N/A	10.83	103	-10.43	-1.57	N/A	0	98	0	2	17	17	N/A
5.14	1.30	B/8.8	10.8	1.92	9.6	15.14	120	-3.24	3.72	N/A	1	0	98	1	14	42	N/A
4.29	1.44	B+/9.0	11.0	1.86	10.0	14.92	70	-3.69	3.02	N/A	2	0	97	1	15	30	N/A
0.82	0.98	B-/7.7	14.9	0.77	17.4	15.63	1,267	0.13	2.60	22.6	0	0	98	2	26	93	21
5.93	0.65	B+/9.1	5.6	0.16	N/A	8.91	2	-9.09	-9.12	N/A	1	0	98	1	36	86	26
5.98	1.13	B/8.8	9.2	1.72	10.7	15.20	409	2.30	3.24	N/A	0	0	100	0	10	59	N/A
7.66	1.39	C/4.6	36.7	1.31	N/A	5.11	143	2.35	7.59	46.9	0	100	0	0	299	9	7

Denotes ETF Fund, N/A denotes number is not available

Fund Type	Fund Name	Ticker Symbol	Overall Investment Rating	PRICE Price As of 12/31/12	52 Week High	52 Week Low	PERFORMANCE Perform-ance Rating/Pts	3 Mo	6 Mo	1Yr/Pct	3Yr/Pct Annualized	5Yr/Pct Annualized
	99 Pct = Best									% Total Return Through 12/31/12		
	0 Pct = Worst											
GI	Alpine Global Premier Properties F	AWP	B	7.28	7.74	5.55	B+ / 8.8	5.81	24.48	51.27 / 99	13.65 / 67	1.21 / 23
GL	Alpine Total Dynamic Dividend Fund	AOD	E+	4.03	4.84	3.71	E+ / 0.8	-1.35	6.28	7.99 / 30	-11.03 / 7	-9.51 / 5
MTG	American Income Fund	MRF	C+	8.37	8.80	7.61	C+ / 6.6	3.22	12.88	21.42 / 75	13.67 / 67	11.03 / 73
MUN	American Municipal Income Portfoli	XAA	A	15.77	19.08	14.05	B+ / 8.9	6.39	8.65	21.48 / 94	13.00 / 89	12.11 / 98
MTG	American Select Portfolio	SLA	C	10.93	11.47	9.96	C / 4.4	0.54	8.10	17.50 / 60	9.72 / 46	9.58 / 68
MTG	American Strat Inc Portfolio	ASP	C	11.45	12.48	10.71	C- / 4.1	-0.97	3.04	15.12 / 48	10.64 / 51	11.88 / 76
MTG	American Strat Inc Portfolio II	BSP	C-	8.82	9.24	7.98	C- / 3.7	2.61	6.65	20.45 / 72	6.59 / 34	6.32 / 50
MTG	American Strat Inc Portfolio III	CSP	C-	7.49	7.72	6.50	C- / 3.4	0.56	9.01	21.53 / 75	5.13 / 30	2.21 / 28
LP	Apollo Senior Floating Rate Fd Inc	AFT	B+	18.77	20.09	16.65	B / 8.2	-0.23	8.97	23.59 / 81	--	--
PM	ASA Gold & Precious Metals Ltd	ASA	E	21.53	29.38	20.60	E+ / 0.9	-6.66	4.88	-17.80 / 5	-3.98 / 10	-0.22 / 18
FO	Asia Pacific Fund	APB	D+	10.82	11.16	8.97	D+ / 2.5	8.62	15.88	13.03 / 41	1.92 / 20	-0.98 / 17
FO	Asia Tigers Fund	GRR	D-	12.59	15.00	12.00	D / 2.2	10.98	16.65	22.72 / 79	-1.55 / 12	-1.73 / 14
LP	Avenue Income Credit Strategies	ACP	A-	18.17	18.98	15.82	A+ / 9.6	8.30	19.83	25.54 / 85	--	--
GL	Babson Capital Glb Sht Dur Hi Yiel	BGH	U	23.77	N/A	N/A	U /	--	--	--	--	--
GI	Bancroft Fund Ltd.	BCV	C-	16.40	17.11	15.33	C- / 3.5	3.94	8.68	11.58 / 38	7.18 / 36	2.96 / 31
MUN	BlackRock Build America Bond	BBN	B	22.87	24.17	20.37	C+ / 6.9	1.12	1.77	13.97 / 75	--	--
MUS	BlackRock CA Muni 2018 Income Trus	BJZ	C+	16.21	17.13	15.24	C / 4.7	1.16	3.94	3.00 / 23	8.43 / 63	7.02 / 72
MUS	BlackRock CA Municipal Income Trus	BFZ	A+	16.34	17.51	14.35	A / 9.5	4.47	11.58	22.89 / 95	16.94 / 98	9.14 / 86
GEI	BlackRock Core Bond Trust	BHK	B-	14.90	16.25	13.08	C+ / 6.1	-0.77	5.09	17.36 / 60	15.58 / 75	11.88 / 76
COH	BlackRock Corporate High Yield Fun	COY	C	7.74	8.29	6.60	C+ / 5.9	3.06	7.22	19.92 / 70	13.31 / 65	14.57 / 89
COH	BlackRock Corporate High Yield III	CYE	C+	7.57	8.16	7.04	C+ / 6.5	0.72	7.81	20.51 / 72	15.07 / 73	14.78 / 89
COH	BlackRock Corporate High Yield V	HYV	C+	12.56	13.58	11.40	B- / 7.0	2.10	6.38	20.08 / 71	16.43 / 78	14.71 / 89
COH	BlackRock Corporate High Yield VI	HYT	C+	12.39	13.37	11.31	C+ / 6.8	1.72	8.11	21.72 / 76	15.45 / 75	14.23 / 87
IN	BlackRock Credit Alloc Inc Tr IV	BTZ	B	13.73	14.44	12.36	C+ / 6.6	2.25	7.95	22.18 / 77	14.60 / 71	5.89 / 48
COH	BlackRock Debt Strategies Fund Inc	DSU	B+	4.30	4.62	3.86	B- / 7.4	7.42	10.53	22.22 / 77	15.43 / 74	6.06 / 49
LP	BlackRock Defined Opp Credit Trust	BHL	C+	14.18	14.66	12.85	C / 5.3	4.67	9.11	18.06 / 63	11.28 / 54	--
EN	BlackRock EcoSolutions Investment	BQR	D	8.39	10.41	7.59	D+ / 2.5	4.38	9.19	13.17 / 42	1.64 / 19	-2.08 / 13
EN	BlackRock Energy & Resources	BGR	D+	23.55	28.00	20.89	D+ / 2.5	2.22	10.14	2.75 / 20	5.00 / 29	4.33 / 39
GI	BlackRock Enhanced Capital and Inc	CII	D+	12.42	13.89	11.80	D+ / 2.9	1.24	4.12	11.02 / 36	5.72 / 32	5.36 / 46
IN	BlackRock Enhanced Equity Div	BDJ	D+	7.18	7.73	6.83	D+ / 2.6	0.33	6.11	12.61 / 40	3.98 / 26	3.12 / 32
USA	BlackRock Enhanced Government	EGF	C-	15.63	16.17	15.02	D+ / 2.3	1.55	4.61	7.24 / 29	3.33 / 24	5.72 / 47
MUS	BlackRock FL Muni 2020 Term Tr	BFO	B+	15.64	16.34	14.87	B- / 7.1	1.34	3.53	9.70 / 48	11.40 / 81	8.59 / 82
LP	BlackRock Floating Rate Inc Strat	FRA	C	15.15	15.49	13.51	C / 5.1	5.15	10.77	22.18 / 77	9.41 / 45	8.47 / 62
LP	BlackRock Floating Rt Income	BGT	C	15.05	15.80	13.33	C+ / 5.6	2.27	10.73	22.71 / 79	11.23 / 54	8.89 / 65
GL	BlackRock Global Opportunities Eq	BOE	D	13.20	16.03	11.92	D+ / 2.6	3.63	10.59	13.65 / 43	1.81 / 19	2.21 / 28
HL	BlackRock Health Sciences Trust	BME	C+	28.02	31.01	26.17	B- / 7.4	9.20	13.98	22.56 / 78	14.24 / 70	10.51 / 72
COH	BlackRock High Income Shares	HIS	B+	2.36	2.52	2.04	B- / 7.4	1.42	5.64	21.72 / 76	17.94 / 83	14.54 / 88
COH	BlackRock High Yield Trust	BHY	C	7.37	8.37	6.64	C+ / 5.9	-1.30	1.35	19.15 / 68	15.56 / 75	13.01 / 81
GEI	BlackRock Income Opportunity Trust	BNA	C+	11.34	12.10	10.15	C / 5.3	-1.96	5.49	16.45 / 55	13.66 / 67	10.06 / 70
MTG	BlackRock Income Trust	BKT	C	7.35	7.74	7.07	C- / 3.5	-4.25	-0.67	5.06 / 24	10.46 / 50	10.51 / 71
FO	BlackRock Intl Grth and Inc Tr	BGY	D-	7.35	8.49	6.72	D / 2.1	6.15	13.82	16.50 / 55	-0.53 / 14	-0.23 / 18
MUN	BlackRock Investment Qual Muni Tr	BKN	A	16.34	17.43	14.78	B+ / 8.7	1.25	5.58	14.87 / 79	14.89 / 94	9.36 / 89
GEN	BlackRock Limited Duration Income	BLW	B-	18.17	18.97	16.38	B- / 7.2	7.08	9.43	21.54 / 75	15.21 / 73	11.38 / 75
MUN	BlackRock Long Term Muni Adv	BTA	A	12.59	13.59	11.25	A- / 9.0	3.57	6.56	18.14 / 88	15.62 / 96	8.54 / 82
MUS	BlackRock MD Muni Bond Trust	BZM	C+	16.17	20.21	15.28	C+ / 6.4	-4.39	-4.59	5.59 / 32	12.09 / 85	6.46 / 69
MUN	BlackRock Muni 2020 Term Trust	BKK	B+	16.70	17.27	15.42	B- / 7.1	3.08	7.18	13.78 / 74	9.99 / 74	8.67 / 83
MUS	BlackRock Muni Bond Invt Trust	BIE	A+	17.18	17.99	14.90	A- / 9.0	2.32	7.28	17.68 / 87	15.80 / 96	9.07 / 85
MUN	BlackRock Muni Interm Duration	MUI	A+	16.63	17.88	14.73	A- / 9.1	4.10	7.98	15.74 / 82	15.93 / 97	10.75 / 95
MUS	BlackRock Muni NY Interm Duration	MNE	A+	15.44	16.53	14.10	B+ / 8.8	1.59	7.78	15.95 / 83	14.72 / 94	9.46 / 89
MUN	BlackRock MuniAssets Fund	MUA	A-	13.92	14.61	12.04	B / 8.1	4.62	9.00	17.37 / 86	10.97 / 79	8.04 / 78
MUN	BlackRock Municipal 2018 Income Tr	BPK	B-	16.56	17.48	15.81	C+ / 5.6	0.28	2.77	7.94 / 39	9.37 / 70	8.27 / 80
MUN	BlackRock Municipal Bond Trust	BBK	A+	17.00	19.00	15.26	A- / 9.1	5.12	3.98	18.70 / 90	15.95 / 97	10.67 / 94

Incl. in Returns		RISK				NET ASSETS		VALUATION			ASSET					FUND MANAGER	
Dividend Yield %	Expense Ratio	Risk Rating/ Pts	3 Year Standard Deviation	Beta	Avg Dura-tion	NAV as of 12/31/12	Total $(Mil)	Premium / Discount As of 12/31/12	1 Year Average	Wtd Avg P/E	Cash %	Stocks %	Bonds %	Other %	Portfolio Turnover Ratio	Manager Quality Pct	Manager Tenure (Years)
8.24	1.29	C+ / 6.8	25.3	1.38	N/A	8.18	759	-11.00	-9.18	51.1	0	100	0	0	67	39	6
16.38	1.35	C / 4.7	30.3	1.08	N/A	4.62	1,134	-12.77	-7.82	45.1	0	100	0	0	367	8	6
6.81	1.25	B- / 7.1	9.5	0.45	12.4	8.67	80	-3.46	-4.40	N/A	0	0	100	0	260	90	N/A
5.90	1.32	B / 8.5	11.5	1.97	11.9	15.86	91	-0.57	1.79	N/A	0	0	100	0	12	37	N/A
6.86	1.95	B / 8.2	9.1	0.95	12.4	12.16	128	-10.12	-10.34	N/A	2	0	86	12	44	78	N/A
6.81	1.93	B / 8.1	9.8	1.19	16.0	12.60	55	-9.13	-8.53	N/A	0	0	99	1	18	80	N/A
6.46	2.00	B- / 7.9	8.5	0.09	15.4	10.27	163	-14.12	-14.31	N/A	0	0	100	0	31	80	N/A
6.01	2.11	B- / 7.5	9.3	0.05	11.8	8.14	175	-7.99	-11.93	N/A	0	0	100	0	52	80	N/A
14.70	3.24	B- / 7.8	N/A	N/A	N/A	18.99	284	-1.16	-0.04	N/A	0	0	0	100	42	99	N/A
6.50	0.76	D+ / 2.8	24.9	1.01	N/A	23.63	455	-8.89	-7.98	60.8	0	99	0	1	4	7	N/A
0.00	2.15	B- / 7.1	24.0	1.01	N/A	12.31	121	-12.10	-10.15	N/A	0	99	0	1	137	31	9
0.16	2.36	C / 5.2	22.2	0.81	N/A	13.66	57	-7.83	-8.49	N/A	1	94	0	5	42	27	N/A
7.93	2.50	B- / 7.3	N/A	N/A	N/A	19.07	127	-4.72	-3.24	N/A	0	0	81	19	56	97	N/A
4.23	N/A	U /	N/A	N/A	N/A	24.71	487	-3.80	N/A	N/A	0	0	0	100	N/A	N/A	N/A
4.76	1.10	B / 8.2	12.3	0.70	5.3	19.79	98	-17.13	-13.83	N/A	2	0	0	98	43	46	17
6.92	1.09	B / 8.5	N/A	N/A	N/A	23.41	1,368	-2.31	-3.08	N/A	0	0	100	0	7	66	N/A
4.26	0.95	B+ / 9.4	5.8	0.59	6.2	15.84	101	2.34	3.39	N/A	0	0	100	0	10	77	7
5.71	1.46	B / 8.4	11.1	2.35	13.2	16.53	520	-1.15	-0.21	N/A	1	0	98	1	30	41	7
0.63	0.94	B / 8.8	8.1	2.17	N/A	15.31	411	-2.68	-1.48	N/A	2	0	95	3	290	61	N/A
7.91	1.26	B- / 7.1	10.8	0.59	5.1	7.75	258	-0.13	4.19	19.7	0	6	90	4	32	82	7
5.61	1.44	B- / 7.1	11.6	1.12	5.1	7.87	282	-3.81	3.04	31.6	1	6	87	6	33	70	7
7.87	1.42	B- / 7.1	11.6	1.09	5.1	13.16	417	-4.56	2.37	19.8	1	5	87	7	61	73	N/A
5.35	1.51	B- / 7.2	11.2	1.08	5.4	12.84	436	-3.50	2.75	19.4	1	5	86	8	61	68	7
7.43	1.09	B / 8.8	9.3	0.26	N/A	15.41	722	-10.90	-8.03	N/A	0	0	80	20	54	91	2
0.33	1.39	B / 8.6	11.5	1.01	N/A	4.35	453	-1.15	1.14	N/A	0	2	95	3	31	72	4
8.17	1.91	B / 8.2	10.5	-165.10	4.5	14.39	127	-1.46	-2.88	N/A	0	1	98	1	53	98	N/A
8.55	1.40	C+ / 6.3	23.5	0.67	N/A	9.50	117	-11.68	-3.20	49.5	0	100	0	0	86	25	6
6.88	1.15	B- / 7.1	24.0	0.96	N/A	26.62	843	-11.53	-5.49	28.6	0	100	0	0	111	23	N/A
9.66	0.93	B- / 7.8	15.0	0.74	N/A	14.20	612	-12.54	-7.95	20.1	0	100	0	0	190	28	1
7.80	1.14	B- / 7.9	14.2	0.68	N/A	8.42	576	-14.73	-11.13	21.9	0	100	0	0	231	27	3
4.99	1.46	B+ / 9.1	4.7	0.11	N/A	16.03	178	-2.50	-4.97	N/A	6	0	90	4	59	63	N/A
4.30	1.06	B+ / 9.3	6.4	1.18	7.7	16.13	89	-3.04	-1.83	N/A	0	0	99	1	32	69	7
6.61	1.67	B- / 7.5	17.1	-284.49	4.4	15.25	277	-0.66	-0.79	N/A	0	0	98	2	53	99	4
6.94	1.60	B- / 7.6	15.2	-172.54	4.7	14.62	330	2.94	1.94	N/A	0	1	98	1	89	98	4
9.45	1.09	C+ / 6.2	21.0	0.88	N/A	15.48	1,114	-14.73	-8.48	58.2	0	100	0	0	253	41	4
7.62	1.13	B- / 7.1	17.6	0.88	N/A	28.96	203	-3.25	-0.21	86.3	0	100	0	0	226	66	8
4.34	1.54	B / 8.6	11.3	1.15	5.1	2.32	124	1.72	3.34	N/A	2	1	91	6	63	77	N/A
7.25	2.01	B- / 7.2	12.1	1.23	5.1	7.59	47	-2.90	3.98	29.9	5	2	89	4	59	56	N/A
6.03	0.90	B / 8.7	7.5	1.80	11.2	11.96	408	-5.18	-4.27	N/A	3	0	94	3	285	68	N/A
6.61	0.97	B+ / 9.6	4.5	1.40	N/A	7.67	508	-4.17	-4.76	N/A	1	0	99	1	487	75	25
9.14	1.10	C / 4.6	21.4	0.82	N/A	8.60	959	-14.53	-9.73	161.0	0	100	0	0	217	23	N/A
6.20	1.26	B / 8.4	12.1	2.13	12.6	16.29	263	0.31	3.89	N/A	2	0	97	1	47	54	7
2.98	1.05	B- / 7.4	11.5	-0.09	6.8	17.79	642	2.14	2.90	12.7	2	1	95	2	54	95	6
5.92	1.42	B / 8.3	11.4	2.38	14.8	12.84	163	-1.95	1.67	N/A	0	0	99	1	26	40	N/A
4.64	1.60	B- / 7.9	17.9	1.75	13.9	15.73	32	2.80	13.82	N/A	11	0	88	1	30	40	7
4.48	0.99	B+ / 9.4	6.3	0.96	7.0	16.76	331	-0.36	-0.23	N/A	0	0	100	0	18	73	7
5.45	2.12	B / 8.6	11.9	2.27	14.3	17.09	56	0.53	-0.12	N/A	0	0	100	0	36	57	N/A
6.01	1.88	B / 8.8	10.3	2.09	9.6	16.59	617	0.24	1.64	N/A	2	0	97	1	27	57	7
4.86	1.81	B+ / 9.1	8.9	1.94	9.8	15.98	67	-3.38	-2.24	N/A	2	0	97	1	27	58	10
7.69	0.77	B / 8.6	7.8	1.72	13.6	14.19	482	-1.90	-1.34	N/A	2	0	97	1	28	48	N/A
6.78	0.82	B+ / 9.3	5.6	0.79	6.9	16.08	255	2.99	5.11	N/A	1	0	98	1	17	76	7
6.05	1.64	B / 8.4	12.5	2.24	11.9	16.95	176	0.29	3.74	N/A	1	0	98	1	46	50	7

Denotes ETF Fund, N/A denotes number is not available

Fund Type	Fund Name	Ticker Symbol	Overall Investment Rating	PRICE Price As of 12/31/12	52 Week High	52 Week Low	PERFORMANCE Perform- ance Rating/Pts		% Total Return Through 12/31/12 3 Mo	6 Mo	1Yr/Pct	Annualized 3Yr/Pct	5Yr/Pct
MUS	BlackRock Municipal Income Inv Qly	BAF	A-	16.40	17.49	14.52	B+	8.6	2.95	7.24	13.96 / 75	14.38 / 93	11.00 / 96
MUS	BlackRock Municipal Income Invt Tr	BBF	A	15.87	16.76	13.89	A-	9.1	4.05	4.67	20.61 / 93	15.43 / 96	9.30 / 87
MUN	BlackRock Municipal Income Quality	BYM	A+	16.20	17.47	14.34	A	9.4	6.26	10.27	22.96 / 95	15.38 / 96	10.27 / 92
MUN	BlackRock Municipal Income Trust	BFK	A	15.52	16.79	13.85	B+	8.6	1.24	3.91	17.48 / 87	14.71 / 94	9.51 / 89
MUN	BlackRock Municipal Income Trust I	BLE	A+	16.21	17.64	14.52	A-	9.0	3.70	8.10	18.50 / 89	15.19 / 95	10.06 / 91
MUN	BlackRock Municipal Target Term	BTT	U	23.36	N/A	N/A	U		-0.85	--	--	--	--
MUN	BlackRock MuniEnhanced Fund	MEN	A-	12.29	13.65	10.92	B+	8.4	2.29	4.89	15.42 / 81	13.68 / 91	10.28 / 91
MUS	BlackRock MuniHoldings CA Qly	MUC	A+	16.34	18.45	14.29	A	9.5	3.51	9.49	18.55 / 89	17.93 / 99	11.85 / 98
MUN	BlackRock MuniHoldings Fund	MHD	A+	18.36	19.99	16.20	A+	9.6	5.38	9.14	23.49 / 96	17.52 / 99	13.13 / 99
MUN	BlackRock MuniHoldings Fund II	MUH	A+	16.64	18.52	14.83	A-	9.2	3.00	8.32	18.29 / 89	16.54 / 97	12.35 / 99
MUS	BlackRock MuniHoldings Inv Quality	MFL	A+	16.10	17.20	13.85	A-	9.2	5.00	8.86	20.17 / 92	15.59 / 96	12.22 / 98
MUS	BlackRock MuniHoldings New York Ql	MHN	A	16.15	17.10	14.70	B+	8.7	4.38	8.81	14.81 / 79	13.80 / 91	11.23 / 96
MUS	BlackRock MuniHoldings NJ Qly	MUJ	A+	16.67	17.37	14.76	B+	8.7	4.34	10.83	15.67 / 82	13.38 / 90	10.71 / 95
MUN	BlackRock MuniHoldings Quality	MUS	A-	15.10	17.12	13.36	B+	8.6	0.96	7.73	16.30 / 84	14.33 / 93	11.63 / 97
MUN	BlackRock MuniHoldings Quality II	MUE	A	15.08	16.23	13.08	A-	9.0	5.89	9.50	16.37 / 84	14.55 / 94	11.96 / 98
MUN	BlackRock MuniVest Fund	MVF	A+	11.03	12.29	9.66	A-	9.2	3.73	10.08	19.23 / 90	15.19 / 95	11.68 / 98
MUN	BlackRock MuniVest Fund II	MVT	A+	17.51	18.49	15.39	A-	9.2	3.19	7.68	20.33 / 92	16.07 / 97	12.83 / 99
MUS	BlackRock MuniYield AZ Fund	MZA	A	15.34	16.55	13.54	B+	8.6	4.58	2.55	17.05 / 86	14.29 / 93	9.23 / 87
MUS	BlackRock MuniYield CA Fund	MYC	A+	16.93	17.91	14.75	A	9.4	1.50	8.87	18.07 / 88	17.83 / 99	11.78 / 98
MUS	BlackRock MuniYield California Qly	MCA	A+	16.43	17.19	14.21	A	9.5	4.08	11.38	21.56 / 94	17.78 / 99	11.33 / 97
MUN	BlackRock MuniYield Fund	MYD	A+	16.37	17.90	14.31	A	9.4	3.92	8.42	21.19 / 94	16.92 / 98	11.05 / 96
MUS	BlackRock MuniYield Inv Quality	MFT	A+	15.70	16.91	13.58	A-	9.1	1.07	10.84	19.34 / 91	15.41 / 96	11.74 / 98
MUS	BlackRock MuniYield Invt Fund	MYF	A+	16.87	18.15	14.24	A+	9.6	5.53	10.42	22.37 / 95	17.94 / 99	12.79 / 99
MUS	BlackRock MuniYield Michigan Qly	MIY	A+	15.65	17.02	14.19	B+	8.9	1.93	10.40	16.13 / 83	15.07 / 95	10.68 / 95
MUS	BlackRock MuniYield Michigan Qly I	MYM	A-	14.35	15.80	13.55	B+	8.3	--	6.06	7.37 / 37	14.48 / 94	9.69 / 90
MUS	BlackRock MuniYield New Jersey Qly	MJI	A-	16.23	17.41	15.02	B+	8.3	-0.26	5.03	14.92 / 79	14.00 / 92	10.67 / 94
MUS	BlackRock MuniYield New York Qly	MYN	A	15.10	16.30	13.39	B+	8.9	3.29	8.36	14.52 / 78	15.35 / 96	9.69 / 90
MUS	BlackRock MuniYield NJ Fund	MYJ	A	16.60	18.25	14.88	B+	8.5	-0.33	6.88	17.84 / 87	13.90 / 92	10.51 / 94
MUS	BlackRock MuniYield PA Qly	MPA	A	16.35	17.42	15.12	B+	8.4	2.18	8.09	9.29 / 46	14.12 / 92	10.06 / 91
MUN	BlackRock MuniYield Quality Fund	MQY	A+	17.64	18.54	14.72	A	9.4	4.83	12.20	20.98 / 93	15.80 / 96	12.39 / 99
MUN	BlackRock MuniYield Quality Fund I	MQT	A	14.44	16.34	12.91	B+	8.9	3.29	7.19	15.56 / 81	15.29 / 95	11.57 / 97
MUN	BlackRock MuniYield Quality III	MYI	A	15.30	16.54	13.50	A-	9.0	4.41	8.33	16.08 / 83	15.23 / 95	10.18 / 92
MUS	BlackRock New York Muni Inc Qly	BSE	A	16.11	17.28	14.39	B+	8.5	2.33	5.94	15.21 / 80	14.22 / 93	8.71 / 83
MUS	BlackRock NJ Muni Bond Trust	BLJ	B+	17.00	19.18	15.04	B+	8.6	-1.03	3.04	17.89 / 88	15.03 / 95	7.07 / 73
MUS	BlackRock NJ Municipal Income Trus	BNJ	A	17.05	18.63	15.32	A-	9.0	0.10	8.34	19.94 / 92	15.55 / 96	7.65 / 76
MUS	BlackRock NY Muni 2018 Income Trus	BLH	C	16.05	17.40	15.75	C-	3.3	1.90	2.62	2.53 / 22	5.76 / 42	5.52 / 62
MUS	BlackRock NY Muni Bond Trust	BQH	B+	16.57	17.27	15.36	B	7.7	4.45	7.12	14.97 / 80	10.82 / 79	6.26 / 68
MUS	BlackRock NY Municipal Income Tr I	BFY	B+	16.00	17.51	15.23	B-	7.4	-0.47	0.88	9.29 / 46	12.48 / 87	9.41 / 88
MUS	BlackRock NY Municipal Income Trus	BNY	A-	16.51	17.28	15.15	B	8.0	4.74	3.02	14.77 / 79	12.17 / 85	7.39 / 75
MUS	BlackRock PA Strategic Muni Tr	BPS	A	15.21	16.48	14.24	A-	9.1	5.74	9.60	15.53 / 81	15.45 / 96	8.56 / 82
IN	BlackRock Real Asset Equity Trust	BCF	D	10.26	12.70	9.17	D	1.8	1.48	5.16	1.20 / 16	1.72 / 19	1.94 / 26
IN	BlackRock Res & Commdty Strat Trus	BCX	D	12.82	16.31	12.41	D	2.2	-3.71	5.75	4.08 / 23	--	--
GL	BlackRock S&P Qual Rkg Glob Eq Mgd	BQY	C-	12.24	13.90	11.04	C-	3.7	1.46	5.37	11.23 / 37	9.26 / 44	4.19 / 38
COH	BlackRock Senior High Income Fund	ARK	B	4.20	4.55	3.80	B-	7.3	3.68	8.25	22.94 / 79	16.18 / 77	5.95 / 49
COH	BlackRock Strategic Bond Trust	BHD	B+	14.59	16.07	12.96	B	7.8	5.79	11.93	28.00 / 88	15.88 / 76	14.34 / 88
MUN	BlackRock Strategic Municipal Tr	BSD	A+	14.84	16.49	13.13	A-	9.2	0.72	8.04	18.55 / 89	16.32 / 97	8.17 / 79
GL	BlackRock Utility & Infrastructure	BUI	D+	17.89	20.44	16.83	D-	1.4	-1.79	-0.95	2.36 / 19	--	--
MUS	BlackRock VA Muni Bond Trust	BHV	C+	19.31	22.91	18.39	C+	6.4	2.05	8.66	7.26 / 37	10.01 / 74	7.04 / 72
LP	Blackstone / GSO Lng-Sht Credit In	BGX	B-	18.75	19.73	17.32	C+	6.5	0.64	8.37	16.94 / 58	--	--
COH	Blackstone / GSO Strategic Credit	BGB	U	18.55	N/A	N/A	U		-1.49	--	--	--	--
LP	Blackstone/GSO Sr Floating Rate Tr	BSL	B+	20.33	20.90	18.30	B	7.8	5.40	11.29	16.98 / 58	--	--
GI	Boulder Growth&Income Fund	BIF	C	6.33	6.75	5.58	C	4.7	5.71	14.35	20.65 / 72	7.57 / 37	-2.65 / 12

I. Index of ETFs and Other Closed-End Funds

Incl. in Returns		RISK				NET ASSETS		VALUATION			ASSET					FUND MANAGER	
Dividend Yield %	Expense Ratio	Risk Rating/ Pts	3 Year Standard Deviation	Beta	Avg Dura-tion	NAV as of 12/31/12	Total $(Mil)	Premium/Discount As of 12/31/12	1 Year Average	Wtd Avg P/E	Cash %	Stocks %	Bonds %	Other %	Portfolio Turnover Ratio	Manager Quality Pct	Manager Tenure (Years)
5.01	1.49	B / 8.2	12.7	2.64	13.6	16.78	145	-2.26	-0.99	N/A	1	0	98	1	51	26	N/A
5.47	1.99	B / 8.2	11.1	2.32	14.3	16.12	107	-1.55	0.04	N/A	2	0	97	1	39	42	7
5.78	1.46	B / 8.2	12.4	2.30	13.3	16.16	425	0.25	1.44	N/A	1	0	98	1	17	33	N/A
6.28	1.45	B / 8.4	11.6	2.28	13.7	15.36	648	1.04	3.88	N/A	1	0	98	1	17	43	7
6.93	1.48	B / 8.4	10.8	2.30	13.8	16.24	377	-0.18	3.15	N/A	2	0	97	1	24	36	7
3.81	N/A	U /	N/A	N/A	N/A	23.95	1,678	-2.46	N/A	N/A	0	0	0	100	N/A	N/A	1
5.66	1.70	B / 8.6	12.4	2.44	13.0	12.62	357	-2.61	-1.21	N/A	1	0	98	1	22	28	24
5.80	1.39	B / 8.6	10.8	2.08	13.6	16.49	671	-0.91	-0.64	N/A	2	0	97	1	46	66	15
7.52	1.41	B / 8.7	11.3	1.98	14.2	18.07	244	1.60	3.24	N/A	1	0	98	1	19	70	N/A
9.27	1.37	B / 8.5	11.8	2.41	13.9	16.88	183	-1.42	1.38	N/A	1	0	98	1	18	40	N/A
5.70	1.80	B / 8.5	10.7	1.99	14.1	16.17	603	-0.43	-0.23	N/A	5	0	94	1	44	61	N/A
5.73	1.87	B / 8.4	10.9	2.18	14.1	15.61	485	3.46	2.00	N/A	2	0	97	1	14	44	N/A
5.33	1.78	B / 8.7	9.4	1.73	11.9	16.57	352	0.60	-1.72	N/A	1	0	98	1	17	66	N/A
5.88	1.41	B / 8.3	13.3	2.57	14.3	15.41	190	-2.01	1.13	N/A	4	0	95	1	30	26	N/A
5.67	1.46	B / 8.3	14.1	2.49	14.2	15.39	341	-2.01	-0.21	N/A	5	0	94	1	36	25	N/A
6.42	1.51	B / 8.8	11.2	2.23	14.5	10.73	679	2.80	4.59	N/A	0	0	100	0	11	43	25
6.60	1.41	B / 8.6	11.2	1.88	14.2	16.66	331	5.10	5.84	N/A	0	0	100	0	13	71	14
5.44	1.96	B / 8.7	9.6	1.65	12.6	15.24	69	0.66	1.30	N/A	3	0	96	1	26	72	20
5.60	1.64	B / 8.7	12.3	2.35	14.3	17.14	361	-1.23	-0.95	N/A	2	0	97	1	48	58	21
5.55	1.61	B / 8.6	10.6	2.31	14.0	16.72	571	-1.73	-2.52	N/A	2	0	97	1	34	57	21
7.21	1.53	B / 8.5	10.5	2.06	13.7	15.98	703	2.44	3.64	N/A	1	0	98	1	19	66	N/A
5.43	1.58	B / 8.7	11.1	1.93	13.9	15.99	133	-1.81	-1.02	N/A	5	0	94	1	43	60	N/A
5.62	1.66	B / 8.8	10.3	2.00	14.5	16.52	222	2.12	1.78	N/A	1	0	98	1	34	74	N/A
5.87	1.72	B / 8.6	11.1	2.34	12.6	16.25	295	-3.69	-1.60	N/A	0	0	99	1	19	34	21
5.77	1.71	B / 8.6	12.2	2.21	13.0	15.20	183	-5.59	-2.34	N/A	0	0	99	1	19	41	21
5.84	1.70	B / 8.6	11.1	1.94	12.7	16.38	145	-0.92	0.93	N/A	1	0	98	1	21	54	N/A
5.64	1.65	B / 8.4	10.5	2.30	14.1	15.02	595	0.53	-0.85	N/A	2	0	97	1	17	50	21
5.66	1.60	B / 8.7	10.3	2.11	13.4	16.97	241	-2.18	-0.43	N/A	4	0	95	1	23	41	N/A
5.43	1.65	B / 8.7	10.1	1.52	13.2	16.70	191	-2.10	-2.04	N/A	2	0	97	1	23	73	21
5.47	1.46	B / 8.4	11.9	2.47	12.9	16.85	495	4.69	1.98	N/A	1	0	98	1	25	41	21
5.78	1.31	B / 8.4	12.3	2.80	13.2	14.67	317	-1.57	0.13	N/A	1	0	98	1	20	24	N/A
5.87	1.56	B / 8.4	11.0	2.26	12.8	15.45	1,036	-0.97	0.38	N/A	1	0	98	1	18	46	21
5.33	1.82	B / 8.5	13.2	2.35	13.8	15.56	101	3.53	2.94	N/A	0	0	99	1	24	31	7
5.15	1.59	B- / 7.7	16.1	2.63	12.5	16.80	39	1.19	4.64	N/A	5	0	94	1	25	23	7
5.71	1.46	B / 8.3	12.8	2.42	12.8	16.25	123	4.92	7.48	N/A	0	0	96	1	20	42	7
4.84	0.95	B+ / 9.2	6.8	1.01	7.3	15.74	57	1.97	4.42	N/A	2	0	97	1	29	35	7
5.22	2.20	B / 8.7	8.8	1.70	15.2	16.61	46	-0.24	1.34	N/A	1	0	98	1	45	39	N/A
5.78	1.95	B / 8.7	9.5	1.75	14.8	16.20	80	-1.23	4.18	N/A	1	0	98	1	25	46	7
5.45	1.49	B / 8.8	8.6	1.76	14.6	15.63	200	5.63	6.69	N/A	1	0	98	1	24	51	7
6.53	1.71	B / 8.2	12.2	2.64	13.7	15.52	31	-2.00	0.29	N/A	1	0	98	1	34	25	7
8.64	1.09	C+ / 6.6	24.8	1.37	N/A	11.25	712	-8.80	-3.17	27.9	0	100	0	0	79	11	7
9.05	1.13	C+ / 5.8	N/A	N/A	N/A	15.01	784	-14.59	-8.01	N/A	22	78	0	0	27	7	2
8.17	1.19	B / 8.1	16.0	0.68	N/A	13.68	82	-10.53	-7.31	23.5	0	100	0	0	97	81	3
13.43	1.26	B / 8.6	11.0	0.85	5.3	4.34	239	-3.23	0.41	N/A	0	1	96	3	31	79	4
7.53	1.45	B / 8.4	9.1	0.67	9.8	14.83	4	-1.62	1.14	12.7	2	1	93	4	47	83	6
5.98	1.55	B / 8.5	10.9	1.99	14.4	15.25	105	-2.69	0.66	N/A	3	0	96	1	30	63	7
8.11	N/A	B / 8.7	N/A	N/A	N/A	20.10	331	-11.00	-4.90	N/A	0	0	0	100	N/A	28	2
5.28	1.64	B- / 7.8	16.3	1.98	14.1	16.78	26	15.08	22.11	N/A	1	0	98	1	23	24	7
6.91	1.78	B / 8.3	N/A	N/A	N/A	19.16	230	-2.14	-0.78	N/A	0	0	99	1	104	98	2
5.05	N/A	U /	N/A	N/A	N/A	19.37	856	-4.23	N/A	N/A	0	0	0	100	N/A	N/A	1
6.49	2.79	B / 8.3	N/A	N/A	N/A	19.44	285	4.58	1.81	N/A	6	0	0	94	N/A	N/A	1
2.21	2.84	B / 8.0	14.3	0.74	N/A	8.67	187	-26.99	-21.67	N/A	7	88	1	4	1	36	41

* Denotes ETF Fund, N/A denotes number is not available

Data as of December 31, 2012

I. Index of ETFs and Other Closed-End Funds

				PRICE			PERFORMANCE					
99 Pct = Best 0 Pct = Worst										% Total Return Through 12/31/12		
			Overall	Price	52 Week		Perform-					Annualized
Fund Type	Fund Name	Ticker Symbol	Investment Rating	As of 12/31/12	High	Low	ance Rating/Pts	3 Mo	6 Mo	1Yr/Pct	3Yr/Pct	5Yr/Pct
IN	Boulder Total Return Fund	BTF	B-	18.04	19.10	15.28	B- / 7.3	5.47	14.52	23.88 / 81	14.28 / 70	1.47 / 25
GL	Brookfield Gl Lstd Infr Inc Fd	INF	B	20.06	20.84	17.25	B / 7.7	5.30	7.59	19.21 / 68	--	--
GI	Calamos Convertible Opport&Income	CHI	C	11.94	12.98	11.29	C- / 4.0	2.80	5.68	15.95 / 52	8.98 / 43	7.17 / 56
GI	Calamos Convertible&High Income	CHY	C	12.15	12.97	11.52	C / 4.3	4.58	5.17	12.17 / 39	10.34 / 49	8.66 / 63
GL	Calamos Global Dynamic Income Fd	CHW	C+	8.35	8.89	7.56	C+ / 6.0	4.53	8.46	26.76 / 87	11.38 / 55	3.79 / 36
GI	Calamos Global Total Return Fund	CGO	C-	13.74	15.46	12.23	C- / 3.3	5.90	12.47	9.27 / 33	6.84 / 35	5.41 / 46
GI	Calamos Strategic Total Return Fun	CSQ	C+	9.81	10.48	8.64	C+ / 6.9	3.35	11.29	28.40 / 89	13.07 / 63	4.17 / 38
FO	Canadian General Investments Ltd	T.CGI	D	15.75	17.88	14.51	D+ / 2.8	5.13	12.62	4.07 / 22	5.63 / 31	-3.67 / 10
GL	Canadian World Fund Limited	T.CWF	D-	3.45	3.99	3.05	D / 1.9	4.17	11.11	-0.85 / 13	1.47 / 18	-8.00 / 6
GI	CBRE Clarion Global Real Estate In	IGR	B+	8.86	9.35	7.06	B+ / 8.6	5.01	15.68	36.06 / 96	17.61 / 81	1.29 / 24
FO	Central Europe & Russia Fund	CEE	D+	33.92	35.82	27.00	C / 4.8	8.96	19.53	22.89 / 79	5.68 / 31	-1.68 / 15
PM	Central Fund of Canada	CEF	C-	21.03	24.46	18.49	C / 4.8	-7.40	9.80	1.86 / 18	14.14 / 69	13.52 / 84
PM	Central Gold-Trust	GTU	C-	62.78	69.10	56.77	C- / 3.7	-5.79	3.87	-0.57 / 13	11.87 / 57	13.34 / 83
GR	Central Securities	CET	C-	19.98	22.27	18.76	C- / 3.0	3.57	4.09	0.70 / 15	7.90 / 38	3.80 / 36
FO	China Fund	CHN	D	21.41	24.25	20.60	C- / 3.6	14.02	15.22	19.44 / 69	2.28 / 21	4.67 / 41
EN	ClearBridge Energy MLP Fund Inc	CEM	B-	23.03	25.02	20.46	C+ / 6.8	3.87	10.03	14.80 / 47	--	--
EN	ClearBridge Energy MLP Oppty Fd In	EMO	B-	20.70	22.25	17.99	B- / 7.1	2.83	10.86	15.96 / 52	--	--
IN	ClearBridge Engy MLP To Rtn Fd Inc	CTR	U	19.04	N/A	N/A	U /	0.82	1.64	--	--	--
GI	Clough Global Allocation Fund	GLV	C-	13.70	14.33	12.18	C- / 3.8	7.46	12.61	19.25 / 68	4.97 / 29	1.14 / 23
GL	Clough Global Equity Fund	GLQ	C	13.00	13.72	11.40	C / 4.8	8.58	18.48	22.30 / 78	6.18 / 33	2.51 / 29
GL	Clough Global Opportunities Fund	GLO	C	11.74	12.45	10.19	C / 4.9	9.25	18.47	24.12 / 82	5.88 / 32	2.70 / 30
GL	Cohen & Steers Closed-End Opp Fd	FOF	C	12.42	13.29	11.77	C / 4.6	2.76	10.31	14.30 / 46	10.19 / 48	5.10 / 44
GL	Cohen & Steers Global Inc Builder	INB	C-	10.32	11.34	9.42	C / 4.5	1.56	8.96	23.61 / 81	8.37 / 40	3.45 / 35
GL	Cohen Steers Ltd Dur Pref and Inc	LDP	U	25.04	N/A	N/A	U /	3.34	--	--	--	--
IN	Cohen&Steers Dividend Majors	DVM	B-	13.84	15.62	12.44	B- / 7.3	0.47	4.55	19.01 / 67	18.69 / 85	5.83 / 48
UT	Cohen&Steers Infrastructure Fund	UTF	B+	18.75	19.49	15.63	B / 8.0	6.90	15.60	26.40 / 86	15.68 / 76	3.54 / 35
GI	Cohen&Steers Quality Income Realty	RQI	B+	10.16	11.22	8.78	A / 9.4	2.65	2.41	27.83 / 88	28.55 / 99	3.95 / 37
IN	Cohen&Steers REIT& Preferred Incom	RNP	A-	16.99	18.33	14.65	A / 9.4	6.14	8.74	29.34 / 90	27.64 / 99	9.88 / 69
IN	Cohen&Steers Sel Preferred & Incom	PSF	A+	26.76	28.68	22.95	A+ / 9.7	6.98	18.36	35.33 / 95	--	--
GI	Cohen&Steers Total Return Realty	RFI	A-	14.72	15.50	11.90	A / 9.5	13.85	17.33	30.01 / 91	25.32 / 97	13.44 / 83
GR	Columbia Seligman Prem Tech Gro	STK	D	14.51	19.00	12.86	D / 1.6	3.17	0.26	3.36 / 21	0.13 / 15	--
IN	Cornerstone Progressive Return Fun	CFP	D	5.01	7.15	4.69	D+ / 2.7	0.87	10.85	9.30 / 33	4.76 / 29	-0.34 / 18
IN	Cornerstone Strategic Value Fund	CLM	D-	6.00	8.06	5.77	D- / 1.3	-9.29	0.30	18.31 / 64	-1.87 / 12	-0.35 / 18
IN	Cornerstone Total Return Fund	CRF	D-	5.36	7.15	5.25	D- / 1.1	-9.36	-2.70	13.65 / 43	-3.51 / 10	-4.06 / 10
COH	Credit Suisse Asset Mgmt Income	CIK	B+	4.03	4.11	3.51	B- / 7.4	5.22	11.38	21.64 / 75	16.02 / 77	14.27 / 87
COH	Credit Suisse High Yield Bond Fund	DHY	B-	3.20	3.33	2.88	C+ / 6.1	0.77	8.65	23.25 / 80	13.32 / 65	13.39 / 83
IN	Cushing Renaissance	SZC	U	22.69	N/A	N/A	U /	-3.16	--	--	--	--
USA	Cushing Royalty & Income Fund	SRF	U	18.99	N/A	N/A	U /	-0.17	-2.63	--	--	--
COI	Cutwater Select Income	CSI	B-	19.65	20.84	17.43	C / 5.1	0.16	6.29	12.22 / 39	13.10 / 64	9.44 / 67
GL	Delaware Enhanced Glb Div & Inc Fd	DEX	C-	11.60	13.06	10.15	C / 4.5	7.09	5.12	13.91 / 45	10.20 / 48	8.37 / 61
MUS	Delaware Inv CO Muni Inc	VCF	B+	15.12	16.31	13.85	B- / 7.4	5.10	2.60	18.40 / 89	9.94 / 73	5.62 / 63
GI	Delaware Inv Div & Inc	DDF	B-	7.92	8.44	7.19	B- / 7.3	4.08	12.15	23.98 / 82	15.33 / 74	8.25 / 58
MUS	Delaware Inv MN Muni Inc Fund II	VMM	A+	15.22	15.80	13.60	B+ / 8.5	3.58	6.42	18.67 / 90	12.84 / 88	8.25 / 79
MUN	Delaware Inv Nat Muni Inc	VFL	A-	14.03	15.13	12.71	B / 7.9	3.22	8.67	16.37 / 84	10.79 / 78	7.55 / 75
GI	Dividend and Income Fund Inc	DNI	D+	13.50	14.76	12.60	C- / 3.2	-2.43	7.47	14.20 / 45	6.71 / 35	-2.15 / 13
UT	DNP Select Income Fund Inc	DNP	C-	9.47	11.60	8.78	C- / 3.6	3.30	-8.76	-3.42 / 11	12.13 / 59	7.50 / 57
GEI	DoubleLine Opportunistic Credit Fd	DBL	U	27.00	N/A	N/A	U /	3.03	7.97	--	--	--
IN	Dow 30 Enhanced Premium & Income F	DPO	C	10.73	11.45	9.72	C / 4.3	2.31	4.38	15.35 / 49	10.48 / 50	6.38 / 51
IN	Dow 30 Premium & Dividend Income	DPD	C-	13.25	14.46	12.45	C- / 3.0	1.20	6.03	11.62 / 38	5.53 / 31	5.77 / 47
COH	Dreyfus High Yield Strategies Fund	DHF	C-	4.12	4.70	3.75	C+ / 5.6	0.77	0.84	5.62 / 25	15.64 / 75	15.54 / 91
MUN	Dreyfus Municipal Income	DMF	A-	10.43	13.00	9.43	B+ / 8.4	-0.06	3.30	15.70 / 82	14.53 / 94	12.03 / 98
MUN	Dreyfus Strategic Muni Bond Fund	DSM	A+	9.36	9.90	8.15	A- / 9.0	2.93	9.09	18.76 / 90	14.99 / 95	10.67 / 94

I. Index of ETFs and Other Closed-End Funds

		RISK				NET ASSETS		VALUATION			ASSET					FUND MANAGER	
Incl. in Returns		Risk Rating/ Pts	3 Year		Avg Dura-tion	NAV as of 12/31/12	Total $(Mil)	Premium / Discount		Wtd Avg P/E	Cash %	Stocks %	Bonds %	Other %	Portfolio Turnover Ratio	Manager Quality Pct	Manager Tenure (Years)
Dividend Yield %	Expense Ratio		Standard Deviation	Beta				As of 12/31/12	1 Year Average								
0.00	2.12	B- / 7.7	18.0	0.90	N/A	24.04	234	-24.96	-20.95	N/A	5	93	1	1	3	68	20
6.98	N/A	B- / 7.5	N/A	N/A	N/A	22.38	166	-10.37	-7.48	N/A	0	0	0	100	N/A	87	2
9.55	1.55	B / 8.2	12.6	0.67	7.1	12.69	827	-5.91	-0.26	N/A	4	1	58	37	44	62	11
8.40	1.61	B / 8.0	13.8	0.69	7.2	13.32	918	-8.78	-3.78	N/A	5	1	64	30	42	72	10
8.91	1.93	B- / 7.5	20.5	0.93	N/A	9.61	535	-13.11	-9.21	N/A	4	59	19	18	43	84	6
8.73	1.90	B- / 7.6	15.3	0.82	5.7	14.41	120	-4.65	-0.84	55.0	3	44	21	32	89	40	8
8.56	1.93	B- / 7.7	17.6	1.07	7.7	10.86	1,568	-9.67	-6.86	30.0	1	54	21	24	30	55	9
1.52	3.57	C / 4.9	17.7	0.58	N/A	22.32	288	-29.44	-27.61	46.6	1	98	0	1	27	70	25
0.00	3.04	C / 4.4	16.0	0.51	N/A	5.40	20	-36.11	-33.14	94.9	4	95	0	1	19	36	N/A
11.78	1.03	B- / 7.5	21.4	1.11	N/A	9.62	950	-7.90	-8.40	48.6	0	74	0	26	2	85	7
4.33	1.11	C / 5.4	30.7	1.36	N/A	38.44	506	-11.76	-9.59	N/A	0	100	0	0	33	70	N/A
0.05	0.30	B- / 7.0	29.5	1.26	N/A	20.50	5,621	2.59	4.19	N/A	1	0	0	99	N/A	28	7
0.00	0.35	B- / 7.7	21.9	1.00	N/A	61.40	1,130	2.25	3.23	N/A	1	0	0	99	N/A	32	10
5.41	0.66	B- / 7.8	16.2	0.94	N/A	25.15	556	-20.56	-17.65	33.1	0	99	0	1	2	35	40
1.72	1.01	C+ / 5.9	21.6	0.85	N/A	23.02	660	-6.99	-8.92	N/A	7	92	0	1	20	45	1
6.43	1.71	B / 8.1	N/A	N/A	N/A	23.66	1,363	-2.66	3.20	N/A	0	99	0	1	14	83	N/A
6.47	1.66	B / 8.0	N/A	N/A	N/A	20.76	568	-0.29	1.06	N/A	0	0	0	100	4	93	N/A
6.83	N/A	U /	N/A	N/A	N/A	20.22	734	-5.84	N/A	N/A	0	0	0	100	N/A	N/A	1
8.76	3.05	B- / 7.3	17.1	1.00	6.0	16.38	170	-16.36	-13.81	48.1	5	77	17	1	192	21	9
8.92	3.43	B- / 7.3	18.9	0.84	5.1	15.54	277	-16.34	-14.36	47.4	8	74	15	3	183	68	8
9.20	3.61	B- / 7.3	18.8	0.80	5.6	13.79	716	-14.87	-13.99	48.1	8	66	23	3	193	70	7
8.37	0.95	B / 8.4	12.3	0.48	N/A	14.28	354	-13.03	-8.28	80.6	0	45	43	12	82	85	N/A
10.85	2.01	B- / 7.2	19.9	0.89	N/A	11.58	246	-10.88	-7.67	N/A	0	95	0	5	56	77	N/A
2.54	N/A	U /	N/A	N/A	N/A	26.16	N/A	-4.28	N/A	N/A	0	0	0	100	N/A	N/A	1
6.65	0.96	B- / 7.6	21.0	1.16	N/A	15.22	187	-9.07	-5.91	52.0	0	99	0	1	28	76	8
7.68	2.09	B / 8.3	19.0	1.18	24.9	21.03	1,609	-10.84	-8.85	27.4	0	77	0	23	25	74	9
7.09	1.84	B- / 7.0	25.2	1.36	29.3	11.18	1,191	-9.12	-4.66	71.7	0	81	0	19	33	91	N/A
7.06	1.72	B- / 7.5	19.6	1.09	22.1	18.82	738	-9.72	-5.81	71.0	0	46	0	54	52	94	10
6.51	1.78	B / 8.7	N/A	N/A	N/A	27.72	271	-3.46	0.72	N/A	1	0	6	93	48	97	N/A
5.98	0.95	B- / 7.4	23.1	1.12	N/A	13.22	129	11.35	2.89	N/A	0	82	0	18	72	92	N/A
12.75	1.10	B- / 7.0	17.0	0.77	N/A	15.66	261	-7.34	-3.00	N/A	0	100	0	0	71	16	N/A
21.89	1.45	C / 5.5	23.9	0.78	N/A	4.83	78	3.73	16.53	N/A	1	98	0	1	113	19	6
22.18	1.40	C / 4.9	28.4	0.76	N/A	5.76	87	4.17	19.23	59.6	0	99	0	1	20	11	12
21.85	1.76	C / 5.0	27.4	0.67	N/A	5.14	36	4.28	18.70	58.4	0	99	0	1	21	12	N/A
7.89	0.73	B / 8.5	12.2	1.02	N/A	3.82	185	5.50	4.51	N/A	0	0	96	4	32	74	N/A
9.94	2.00	B / 8.6	11.6	0.54	N/A	3.11	212	2.89	6.77	N/A	0	0	99	1	66	87	N/A
0.44	N/A	U /	N/A	N/A	N/A	24.94	N/A	-9.02	N/A	P/E	0	0	0	100	N/A	N/A	1
10.53	N/A	U /	N/A	N/A	N/A	19.84	194	-4.28	N/A	N/A	0	0	0	100	N/A	N/A	1
5.39	0.74	B+ / 9.6	5.4	0.55	12.0	21.42	218	-8.26	-4.93	N/A	0	0	99	1	20	86	8
7.76	2.09	C+ / 6.9	20.4	0.70	20.1	12.46	176	-6.90	-0.95	91.0	6	46	44	4	29	84	6
4.56	0.73	B+ / 9.0	8.7	1.29	13.6	15.63	73	-3.26	-1.19	N/A	0	0	100	0	64	60	9
7.95	1.57	B- / 7.8	14.7	0.79	21.6	9.04	76	-12.39	-6.33	27.5	1	53	32	14	17	73	7
4.53	0.70	B+ / 9.4	5.6	1.15	12.3	15.46	172	-1.55	-2.68	N/A	0	0	100	0	44	78	10
4.70	0.99	B+ / 9.0	8.4	1.64	13.6	15.21	63	-7.76	-5.44	N/A	0	0	100	0	101	37	10
12.09	2.57	B- / 7.2	16.6	0.85	5.0	16.03	93	-15.78	-11.95	23.9	6	40	51	3	5	31	2
8.24	1.84	B / 8.1	13.2	0.41	N/A	8.45	2,052	12.07	26.18	N/A	0	71	25	4	8	84	17
26.14	1.30	U /	N/A	N/A	N/A	25.00	366	8.00	N/A	N/A	0	0	0	100	11	N/A	N/A
8.13	1.01	B- / 7.9	17.0	0.89	N/A	11.68	306	-8.13	-5.64	24.9	5	94	0	1	3	44	2
8.03	1.00	B / 8.2	15.5	0.84	N/A	14.71	174	-9.93	-6.69	25.0	0	100	0	0	6	27	2
10.19	1.90	C+ / 6.2	12.9	1.20	4.6	4.07	282	1.23	13.08	N/A	0	0	99	1	58	61	N/A
6.04	1.27	B / 8.6	12.1	1.81	10.7	10.42	204	0.10	4.18	N/A	0	0	100	0	11	66	4
6.09	1.09	B / 8.7	10.9	1.55	11.6	9.07	431	3.20	3.98	N/A	0	0	100	0	7	75	12

* Denotes ETF Fund, N/A denotes number is not available

Fund Type	Fund Name	Ticker Symbol	Overall Investment Rating	PRICE			PERFORMANCE					
				Price As of 12/31/12	52 Week		Perform-ance Rating/Pts	% Total Return Through 12/31/12			Annualized	
					High	Low		3 Mo	6 Mo	1Yr/Pct	3Yr/Pct	5Yr/Pct
MUN	Dreyfus Strategic Municipals	LEO	A	9.55	10.26	8.52	B+ / 8.8	2.86	10.42	16.97 / 86	14.00 / 92	10.68 / 94
MUN	DTF Tax Free Income	DTF	B+	16.82	19.15	16.06	B / 7.6	-0.79	5.75	11.16 / 59	12.19 / 85	10.01 / 91
UT	Duff & Phelps Global Utility Incom	DPG	D+	16.87	19.78	16.53	D / 1.9	-0.62	-0.60	4.66 / 23	--	--
GEI	Duff & Phelps Utilities & Crp Bd T	DUC	C-	12.26	12.78	11.51	C- / 3.3	0.45	2.21	9.35 / 33	8.52 / 41	10.89 / 73
GL	DWS Global High Income Fund	LBF	B	8.78	9.22	7.61	B- / 7.5	4.70	13.21	26.80 / 87	14.82 / 72	10.19 / 70
GL	DWS High Income Opportunities Fund	DHG	C+	15.16	16.49	14.16	C+ / 6.8	0.83	5.68	20.46 / 72	16.37 / 78	0.19 / 20
COH	DWS High Income Trust	KHI	B-	10.20	11.02	9.13	C+ / 6.7	2.99	6.32	12.73 / 40	16.66 / 79	12.05 / 77
GL	DWS Multi-Market Income Trust	KMM	C+	10.44	11.37	9.57	B- / 7.0	0.85	5.76	16.06 / 53	17.17 / 80	15.92 / 93
MUN	DWS Municipal Income Trust	KTF	A+	14.39	15.53	12.63	A / 9.3	5.03	6.65	18.72 / 90	16.63 / 98	14.72 / 99
GL	DWS Strategic Income Fund	KST	B-	14.26	15.19	12.75	B- / 7.0	0.98	4.35	19.74 / 70	17.46 / 81	14.36 / 88
MUN	DWS Strategic Municipal Inc Tr	KSM	A-	14.55	16.39	13.36	B / 8.2	0.75	2.67	14.13 / 76	13.95 / 92	14.88 / 99
GR	Eagle Capital Growth Fund	GRF	C+	7.10	7.61	6.05	C+ / 5.8	7.16	10.92	14.60 / 47	12.64 / 61	3.79 / 36
MUS	Eaton Vance CA Muni Bond	EVM	C+	12.14	13.55	11.62	C / 5.5	1.88	3.96	5.29 / 31	9.33 / 70	4.44 / 54
MUS	Eaton Vance CA Muni Bond II	EIA	A+	14.10	16.07	11.89	A+ / 9.6	10.76	16.84	27.57 / 97	16.50 / 97	9.23 / 87
MUS	Eaton Vance CA Muni Inc Tr	CEV	A-	14.27	15.09	12.90	B+ / 8.3	2.99	7.34	16.62 / 85	12.75 / 88	7.89 / 77
IN	Eaton Vance Enhanced Eqty Inc	EOI	D+	10.66	11.33	10.04	D+ / 2.8	2.89	10.32	18.28 / 64	2.37 / 21	2.21 / 28
IN	Eaton Vance Enhanced Eqty Inc II	EOS	D	10.44	11.30	9.98	D+ / 2.7	0.91	7.96	14.39 / 46	3.24 / 23	2.55 / 29
LP	Eaton Vance Floating Rate Income T	EFT	B	17.04	17.81	14.65	B / 7.8	12.09	16.18	29.64 / 90	13.38 / 65	9.95 / 69
GEN	Eaton Vance Limited Duration Incom	EVV	C	16.66	17.38	15.26	C+ / 5.6	3.02	8.55	19.59 / 69	12.09 / 58	11.90 / 77
MUS	Eaton Vance MA Muni Bond	MAB	B	15.90	17.99	14.78	B- / 7.3	2.69	6.81	14.35 / 77	10.29 / 76	8.36 / 80
MUS	Eaton Vance MA Muni Inc Tr	MMV	B-	15.26	16.94	14.05	C+ / 6.4	-1.64	3.04	9.39 / 46	10.59 / 78	9.15 / 86
MUS	Eaton Vance MI Muni Bond	MIW	C+	14.40	17.55	14.14	C / 5.4	-3.03	-1.97	7.93 / 39	9.90 / 73	8.17 / 79
MUS	Eaton Vance MI Muni Inc Tr	EMI	A	13.80	14.87	12.90	B+ / 8.5	3.81	7.25	14.79 / 79	13.32 / 90	8.95 / 85
MUN	Eaton Vance Muni Bond Fund	EIM	B+	13.99	15.25	12.34	B / 7.9	2.06	7.76	17.80 / 87	10.94 / 79	6.38 / 69
MUN	Eaton Vance Muni Bond II	EIV	C+	13.32	14.95	13.10	C / 5.4	3.76	4.79	2.62 / 22	9.26 / 70	6.66 / 70
MUN	Eaton Vance Municipal Inc Tr	EVN	A+	13.77	14.52	12.83	A- / 9.1	2.77	6.96	20.45 / 93	15.65 / 96	9.22 / 86
MUN	Eaton Vance National Municipal Opp	EOT	B-	22.14	25.30	20.08	C+ / 6.8	-2.83	4.91	14.04 / 75	10.97 / 79	--
MUS	Eaton Vance NJ Muni Bond	EMJ	B+	16.24	16.59	13.62	B / 8.1	4.50	10.09	20.89 / 93	9.98 / 74	7.18 / 73
MUS	Eaton Vance NJ Muni Inc Tr	EVJ	B+	15.10	16.99	13.18	B / 7.6	-0.89	10.04	17.70 / 87	10.49 / 77	10.01 / 91
MUS	Eaton Vance NY Muni Bond	ENX	C+	13.93	15.86	13.18	C / 5.2	0.09	5.25	10.82 / 56	8.01 / 60	5.82 / 65
MUS	Eaton Vance NY Muni Bond II	NYH	B-	13.37	15.20	13.10	C+ / 6.3	3.94	6.93	7.30 / 37	9.86 / 73	6.41 / 69
MUS	Eaton Vance NY Muni Inc Tr	EVY	A+	15.64	16.29	13.37	A- / 9.1	7.56	9.58	18.28 / 88	14.38 / 93	9.26 / 87
MUS	Eaton Vance OH Muni Bond	EIO	B-	14.08	19.23	13.26	C+ / 6.7	0.48	-0.32	14.47 / 77	11.01 / 80	7.77 / 77
MUS	Eaton Vance OH Muni Inc Tr	EVO	A	16.45	18.49	14.11	A- / 9.0	2.33	12.03	21.03 / 94	14.20 / 92	10.99 / 96
MUS	Eaton Vance PA Muni Bond	EIP	B	15.40	16.80	13.59	B / 7.6	1.07	6.02	19.36 / 91	10.52 / 77	8.50 / 81
MUS	Eaton Vance PA Muni Inc Tr	EVP	A-	14.46	15.37	13.40	B / 8.1	2.22	9.43	16.84 / 85	11.60 / 82	8.89 / 84
IN	Eaton Vance Risk Mgd Div Eq Inc	ETJ	D	10.43	11.01	9.86	D- / 1.3	2.45	10.38	13.70 / 44	-3.91 / 10	1.89 / 26
LP	Eaton Vance Senior Floating Rate	EFR	C	15.97	16.90	14.76	C+ / 5.7	7.93	12.23	20.69 / 73	10.35 / 49	9.61 / 68
LP	Eaton Vance Senior Income Trust	EVF	B-	7.54	7.94	6.46	C+ / 6.6	2.95	13.58	26.89 / 87	12.43 / 60	9.18 / 66
GL	Eaton Vance Sh Dur Diversified Inc	EVG	C	17.31	17.87	16.20	C- / 3.8	1.82	6.45	12.78 / 41	8.93 / 43	8.70 / 63
GL	Eaton Vance Tax Adv Glob Div Inc	ETG	C+	13.58	14.86	12.40	C+ / 6.8	9.90	18.14	26.59 / 86	10.64 / 51	0.88 / 22
GL	Eaton Vance Tax Adv Global Div Opp	ETO	C+	20.09	21.05	16.65	C+ / 6.4	8.37	20.32	28.34 / 89	9.02 / 43	1.76 / 25
IN	Eaton Vance Tax Advantage Div Inc	EVT	C+	16.50	17.72	14.84	C+ / 6.0	4.13	13.67	24.30 / 82	11.06 / 53	2.15 / 27
IN	Eaton Vance Tax Mgd Buy Write Opp	ETV	C-	12.50	13.40	11.55	C- / 4.1	2.50	8.64	19.07 / 67	8.02 / 38	8.07 / 60
IN	Eaton Vance Tax Mgd Div Eqty Inc	ETY	D+	9.37	9.89	8.51	C- / 3.2	4.70	14.64	20.65 / 73	2.29 / 21	3.52 / 35
IN	Eaton Vance Tax-Managed Buy-Write	ETB	C-	14.03	16.29	12.47	C- / 3.9	0.57	12.85	22.80 / 79	6.27 / 33	8.69 / 63
GL	Eaton Vance Tax-Mgd Gbl Div Eq Inc	EXG	D+	8.81	9.34	7.78	C- / 3.6	7.03	18.27	22.42 / 78	2.87 / 22	2.65 / 30
MUN	Eaton Vance Tx Adv Bd&Option Str	EXD	A	17.67	18.49	16.33	A- / 9.2	1.96	6.12	18.88 / 90	--	--
GL	Eaton Vance Tx Mgd Glb Buy Wrt Opp	ETW	D+	10.69	11.57	10.04	C- / 3.6	3.56	12.46	18.77 / 66	5.13 / 30	4.81 / 43
GI	Ellsworth Fund Ltd	ECF	C-	7.14	7.50	6.61	C- / 3.5	2.98	7.12	10.10 / 35	7.98 / 38	3.59 / 35
HL	Engex	EGX	E+	2.06	3.23	1.55	D / 2.1	44.19	1.22	31.91 / 93	-5.19 / 9	-18.20 / 3
IN	Equus Total Return	EQS	D-	2.36	2.69	1.81	E+ / 0.8	9.05	-3.78	12.09 / 39	-12.00 / 7	-15.61 / 4

Dividend Yield %	Expense Ratio	Risk Rating/ Pts	Standard Deviation	Beta	Avg Dura-tion	NAV as of 12/31/12	Total $(Mil)	As of 12/31/12	1 Year Average	Wtd Avg P/E	Cash %	Stocks %	Bonds %	Other %	Portfolio Turnover Ratio	Manager Quality Pct	Manager Tenure (Years)
6.16	1.19	B / 8.4	11.0	1.88	12.0	9.33	542	2.36	4.29	N/A	0	0	100	0	10	58	4
0.44	1.23	B / 8.7	10.4	2.07	13.0	17.35	138	-3.05	0.60	N/A	2	0	97	1	6	31	N/A
8.30	N/A	B- / 7.9	N/A	N/A	N/A	19.42	704	-13.13	-4.55	N/A	0	0	0	100	N/A	53	2
6.85	1.78	B / 8.7	8.4	2.05	7.6	11.86	324	3.37	4.06	N/A	0	0	100	0	7	23	17
5.64	2.22	B- / 7.8	11.3	0.91	6.2	9.93	63	-11.58	-9.80	N/A	4	0	96	0	89	89	N/A
8.23	2.08	B- / 7.0	13.2	0.41	4.6	16.49	270	-8.07	-0.88	N/A	0	0	100	0	36	95	3
7.47	1.73	B / 8.0	15.0	1.27	N/A	10.20	154	0.00	5.59	N/A	2	0	98	0	21	62	15
8.85	1.63	B- / 7.2	13.0	0.72	5.0	10.50	238	-0.57	5.87	N/A	1	0	99	0	21	94	N/A
5.84	1.14	B / 8.6	11.3	2.25	10.6	14.37	536	0.14	4.36	N/A	0	0	100	0	24	44	N/A
7.99	2.03	B- / 7.6	10.4	0.44	5.0	14.62	63	-2.46	2.07	N/A	1	0	99	0	22	95	N/A
6.35	1.26	B / 8.6	9.3	1.73	12.0	14.24	150	2.18	8.40	N/A	0	0	100	0	21	62	15
0.60	1.31	B / 8.3	21.1	0.69	N/A	7.86	24	-9.67	-12.43	N/A	5	94	0	1	16	77	N/A
5.39	1.73	B / 8.1	14.4	2.89	12.6	13.16	282	-7.75	-2.23	N/A	0	0	100	0	27	14	11
5.46	1.50	B / 8.2	13.1	2.78	11.8	13.57	52	3.91	1.85	N/A	0	0	100	0	15	28	11
5.72	1.80	B / 8.5	11.0	2.21	11.6	14.28	100	-0.07	1.14	N/A	0	0	100	0	8	42	14
9.73	1.15	B- / 7.1	15.8	0.84	N/A	12.68	504	-15.93	-13.04	55.6	0	96	0	4	35	16	9
10.06	1.11	C+ / 6.8	17.3	0.81	N/A	12.25	589	-14.78	-12.12	80.3	0	96	0	4	24	15	8
6.27	1.86	B / 8.1	14.3	-247.42	4.7	16.11	582	5.77	2.68	N/A	0	0	0	100	38	99	9
7.51	1.71	B- / 7.7	9.0	0.47	4.8	16.82	1,942	-0.95	-0.92	N/A	1	0	66	33	42	88	10
5.28	1.55	B / 8.4	13.2	2.53	13.5	15.95	28	-0.31	3.31	N/A	0	0	100	0	2	15	3
5.21	1.85	B / 8.6	11.2	1.72	12.5	15.75	42	-3.11	0.22	N/A	0	0	100	0	8	39	3
5.55	1.54	B / 8.4	14.2	1.52	12.8	15.11	23	-4.70	3.90	N/A	0	0	100	0	19	45	11
5.57	1.91	B / 8.7	9.7	2.06	12.4	14.91	31	-7.44	-5.69	N/A	0	0	100	0	8	39	14
5.47	1.78	B / 8.3	12.9	2.60	10.8	14.29	961	-2.10	-0.57	N/A	0	0	100	0	17	21	3
5.68	1.65	B / 8.6	11.7	2.37	13.0	13.52	134	-1.48	6.86	N/A	0	0	100	0	16	18	9
6.82	2.09	B / 8.5	11.1	2.07	13.5	12.98	277	6.09	12.52	N/A	0	0	100	0	14	60	14
4.83	0.91	B / 8.3	10.9	2.08	N/A	22.93	331	-3.45	0.14	N/A	0	0	100	0	10	33	4
4.80	1.51	B / 8.3	12.7	1.53	9.6	14.84	38	9.43	4.45	N/A	0	0	100	0	16	59	3
5.22	1.84	B / 8.4	11.4	2.38	12.2	14.53	65	3.92	3.97	N/A	0	0	100	0	10	21	3
4.94	1.65	B / 8.3	13.2	2.36	11.6	14.56	230	-4.33	0.79	N/A	0	0	100	0	17	15	8
5.14	1.64	B / 8.4	13.7	2.35	11.9	14.02	36	-4.64	2.28	N/A	0	0	100	0	18	17	8
5.82	1.87	B / 8.6	10.9	2.29	13.9	15.09	80	3.64	3.14	N/A	0	0	100	0	12	33	14
5.48	1.36	B / 8.2	16.3	2.15	11.5	14.04	35	0.28	8.53	N/A	0	0	100	0	12	29	8
5.06	1.79	B / 8.2	14.1	1.73	12.4	15.39	42	6.89	3.34	N/A	0	0	100	0	5	68	8
5.67	1.37	B / 8.3	13.7	2.45	12.2	14.58	43	5.62	5.95	N/A	0	0	100	0	11	20	6
5.59	1.90	B / 8.7	10.3	1.80	12.5	14.40	38	0.42	1.07	N/A	0	0	100	0	6	36	6
10.70	1.09	C+ / 6.6	8.9	0.23	N/A	12.23	922	-14.72	-14.15	53.2	0	100	0	0	103	18	6
6.99	1.73	B- / 7.5	18.0	-196.88	4.8	15.75	503	1.40	2.43	N/A	0	0	0	100	49	99	10
9.23	2.24	B / 8.4	11.7	-189.93	4.8	7.40	263	1.89	-0.16	N/A	3	1	7	89	38	99	15
5.72	1.89	B / 8.6	7.3	0.07	14.2	17.90	336	-3.30	-4.07	N/A	0	0	73	27	35	88	8
9.06	1.55	B- / 7.5	21.3	0.95	8.8	15.56	1,097	-12.72	-5.82	40.1	1	80	0	19	95	79	9
8.06	1.57	B- / 7.2	21.3	0.99	N/A	23.52	304	-14.58	-12.33	36.1	1	77	0	22	95	78	9
7.82	1.68	B- / 7.7	18.3	1.11	12.8	19.19	1,333	-14.02	-8.98	29.9	1	68	0	31	94	33	10
10.63	1.09	B- / 7.2	14.5	0.66	N/A	14.09	897	-11.28	-10.77	81.7	0	100	0	0	2	34	8
10.80	1.07	C+ / 6.5	15.8	0.88	N/A	11.27	1,652	-16.86	-13.94	55.0	0	100	0	0	63	15	7
9.24	1.14	B- / 7.3	18.8	0.69	N/A	15.26	371	-8.06	-8.34	48.5	0	100	0	0	5	30	8
11.08	1.05	C+ / 6.5	19.1	0.81	N/A	10.57	3,122	-16.65	-13.86	55.6	0	100	0	0	53	36	6
9.62	1.43	B / 8.0	N/A	N/A	N/A	18.23	195	-3.07	-4.11	N/A	21	0	78	1	59	92	3
10.93	1.08	C+ / 6.9	17.6	0.68	N/A	12.59	1,318	-15.09	-13.35	74.9	0	100	0	0	3	48	8
4.20	1.10	B- / 7.6	12.3	0.71	5.4	8.65	114	-17.46	-13.74	22.2	2	6	0	92	39	45	27
0.00	4.69	D+ / 2.7	59.2	1.14	N/A	4.02	5	-48.76	-24.42	N/A	0	96	0	4	25	6	N/A
0.00	N/A	C / 5.4	31.6	0.95	N/A	3.33	38	-29.13	-34.50	N/A	0	12	59	29	N/A	6	21

* Denotes ETF Fund, N/A denotes number is not available

Fund Type	Fund Name	Ticker Symbol	Overall Investment Rating	Price As of 12/31/12	52 Week High	52 Week Low	Performance Rating/Pts	3 Mo	6 Mo	1Yr/Pct	3Yr/Pct	5Yr/Pct
	99 Pct = Best 0 Pct = Worst									% Total Return Through 12/31/12 / Annualized		
IN	F&C/Claymore Preferred Sec Inc Fun	FFC	A+	19.55	20.74	17.24	B+ / 8.9	2.99	13.00	25.83 / 85	23.07 / 95	15.56 / 91
IN	F&C/Claymore Total Return Fund	FLC	A+	20.14	21.42	18.30	B+ / 8.9	2.98	12.21	25.26 / 84	23.05 / 95	15.84 / 93
USA	Federated Enhanced Treasury Income	FTT	D	14.18	16.00	14.11	D / 2.1	0.75	1.95	2.73 / 19	--	--
MUN	Federated Prem Intermediate Muni	FPT	B-	14.61	16.21	14.19	C+ / 6.1	-0.05	3.70	11.95 / 64	9.79 / 72	9.89 / 91
MUN	Federated Premier Muni Income	FMN	B	15.99	17.59	14.51	C+ / 6.9	-2.29	1.98	14.56 / 78	11.51 / 82	10.62 / 94
EN	Fiduciary/Claymore MLP Opp	FMO	C+	21.77	24.45	20.05	C+ / 6.2	3.54	3.16	13.92 / 45	15.40 / 74	9.47 / 67
FS	Financial Trends Fund	DHFT	B+	11.44	12.24	9.17	B+ / 8.9	11.60	24.02	38.91 / 97	16.59 / 78	3.08 / 32
FS	First Opportunity Fund	FOFI	C-	7.69	8.00	6.32	C- / 4.0	1.83	7.29	23.22 / 80	7.32 / 36	-3.28 / 11
LP	First Tr Senior Floating Rte Inc I	FCT	B	15.17	16.08	13.70	B- / 7.1	5.10	11.56	18.93 / 67	15.41 / 74	7.30 / 56
FS	First Tr Specialty Finance &Fin Op	FGB	B+	7.80	8.63	6.71	A- / 9.1	8.43	17.84	36.89 / 96	19.96 / 88	6.26 / 50
GL	First Trust Active Dividend Inc Fd	FAV	D-	7.55	8.80	7.00	E+ / 0.9	-2.45	5.62	3.39 / 21	-6.41 / 8	-0.18 / 19
EN	First Trust Energy Income and Gro	FEN	B+	30.65	33.22	27.45	B / 8.0	9.27	3.29	20.42 / 72	19.11 / 86	16.16 / 93
EN	First Trust Energy Infrastructure	FIF	A+	21.15	22.88	19.53	B+ / 8.5	8.65	11.65	18.49 / 65	--	--
IN	First Trust Enhanced Equity Income	FFA	C	11.84	12.46	10.90	C / 4.6	2.73	9.35	18.78 / 66	9.50 / 45	6.36 / 51
GL	First Trust High Income Long/Short	FSD	B+	18.12	18.97	16.10	B+ / 8.7	1.84	8.20	26.83 / 87	--	--
MTG	First Trust Mortgage Income Fund	FMY	C-	17.66	20.64	16.99	C- / 3.6	-5.87	0.16	5.39 / 25	10.89 / 52	12.18 / 77
GEN	First Trust Strategic High Inc II	FHY	B	16.60	18.08	15.11	B- / 7.3	-1.38	4.01	23.33 / 80	17.98 / 83	-1.71 / 15
GL	First Trust/Aberdeen Emerg Opp Fd	FEO	B+	22.05	23.64	18.19	B+ / 8.6	8.56	20.99	34.77 / 95	16.35 / 78	14.38 / 88
GL	First Trust/Aberdeen Glob Opp Inc	FAM	B-	17.85	18.70	15.89	C+ / 6.4	2.94	8.45	23.80 / 81	13.56 / 66	12.45 / 78
IN	Flaherty&Crumrine Preferred Inc Op	PFO	A-	11.22	12.67	10.72	B+ / 8.3	2.46	6.84	13.33 / 42	21.92 / 93	12.62 / 79
IN	Flaherty&Crumrine Preferred Income	PFD	B+	13.63	16.10	13.29	B / 7.9	-1.20	6.87	10.13 / 35	21.07 / 91	13.44 / 83
GEI	Fort Dearborn Inc. Secs.	FDI	B+	16.54	17.63	15.76	B- / 7.3	1.05	4.57	15.56 / 50	18.11 / 83	13.39 / 83
IN	Foxby Corp	FXBY	D+	1.45	1.70	1.25	D+ / 2.8	-3.90	-5.73	14.59 / 47	7.48 / 37	-11.54 / 4
GEN	Franklin Templeton Ltd Duration In	FTF	B-	14.37	15.39	12.88	C+ / 6.6	3.65	8.36	21.69 / 76	14.36 / 70	13.33 / 82
GI	Franklin Universal Trust	FT	C+	7.06	7.56	4.65	C+ / 6.3	0.15	4.80	18.11 / 63	15.77 / 76	10.45 / 71
GI	Gabelli Convertible&Income Sec Fun	GCV	C-	5.33	6.05	4.95	C- / 3.3	1.19	6.55	13.58 / 43	6.68 / 34	3.78 / 36
IN	Gabelli Dividend & Income Trust	GDV	C+	16.18	17.13	14.43	C+ / 6.6	2.74	11.66	16.51 / 55	14.90 / 72	6.15 / 50
IN	Gabelli Equity Trust	GAB	B	5.58	6.01	5.02	B / 8.1	9.14	14.31	26.90 / 87	16.52 / 78	6.35 / 51
UT	Gabelli Global Utility&Income Trus	GLU	C	20.88	21.85	19.13	C- / 3.3	0.96	5.51	9.13 / 33	8.06 / 39	5.80 / 48
HL	Gabelli Healthcare & WellnessRx Tr	GRX	A	8.62	9.62	7.32	B+ / 8.8	7.71	18.77	39.31 / 97	16.98 / 80	11.00 / 73
GL	Gabelli Multimedia Trust	GGT	B+	7.85	8.40	6.40	A / 9.5	12.58	26.05	41.73 / 97	21.05 / 91	3.81 / 37
UT	Gabelli Utility Trust	GUT	D	6.16	8.30	6.06	D- / 1.2	-10.75	-11.32	-4.99 / 10	1.11 / 17	4.90 / 43
PM	GAMCO Global Gold Nat ResandIncome	GGN	D	12.80	16.65	11.83	D / 2.1	-3.22	8.37	-0.15 / 14	3.25 / 23	-3.39 / 10
EN	GAMCO Nat Res Gold & Income Trust	GNT	D	13.66	16.89	13.31	C- / 3.0	-5.38	5.13	10.33 / 35	--	--
GL	GDL Fund	GDL	D+	11.42	12.84	11.09	D+ / 2.3	0.48	2.50	7.24 / 29	3.86 / 26	4.30 / 39
GR	General American Investors	GAM	C	27.82	29.72	25.71	C / 5.3	4.76	11.84	18.78 / 66	10.37 / 49	1.92 / 26
EM	Global High Income Fund	GHI	C	12.92	13.81	11.54	C+ / 5.7	1.94	9.45	16.98 / 58	13.08 / 64	8.98 / 65
GL	Global Income Fund	GIFD	C	3.69	4.40	3.63	C / 4.5	2.18	5.11	16.70 / 56	10.53 / 50	7.42 / 57
FO	Greater China Fund	GCH	D+	12.88	13.38	9.85	D+ / 2.6	14.53	26.43	25.37 / 84	-0.85 / 13	-1.05 / 16
GEI	Guggenheim Build America Bd Mgd Du	GBAB	C+	22.95	24.41	20.61	C / 5.0	0.40	4.02	15.44 / 50	--	--
IN	Guggenheim Enhanced Equity Income	GPM	C-	8.20	9.68	7.92	C / 4.5	-0.26	-0.61	17.20 / 59	12.26 / 59	2.44 / 29
IN	Guggenheim Enhanced Equity Strateg	GGE	C+	16.66	17.96	15.61	C+ / 5.7	2.36	6.34	15.84 / 52	13.92 / 68	-20.50 / 3
IN	Guggenheim Equal Weight Enh Eq Inc	GEQ	D+	17.73	20.01	17.34	D / 1.8	-7.43	-0.45	7.80 / 30	--	--
GI	Guggenheim Strategic Opportunities	GOF	A-	21.50	23.17	19.73	B+ / 8.3	3.02	11.10	21.67 / 75	20.14 / 89	17.46 / 97
HL	H&Q Healthcare Investors	HQH	B	17.31	18.77	14.87	A / 9.3	5.28	13.85	36.56 / 96	24.16 / 96	10.96 / 73
HL	H&Q Life Sciences Investors	HQL	B	14.50	15.84	12.28	A / 9.5	5.61	11.48	37.86 / 96	27.58 / 99	12.77 / 80
GEN	Helios Advantage Income Fund Inc	HAV	A	8.65	9.45	7.90	B / 8.2	1.12	5.88	22.30 / 78	21.10 / 91	-1.04 / 16
GEN	Helios High Income Fund Inc	HIH	B+	8.36	9.15	7.58	B / 7.6	4.24	3.35	20.30 / 71	18.71 / 85	-1.96 / 14
COH	Helios High Yield Fund	HHY	A-	10.12	11.04	9.42	B / 8.0	-0.14	8.16	13.30 / 42	20.75 / 90	14.03 / 86
GEN	Helios Multi Sector High Income	HMH	A-	6.04	6.56	5.45	B / 7.6	0.17	5.75	21.81 / 76	19.11 / 87	-7.41 / 6
GEN	Helios Strategic Income Fund Inc	HSA	B	6.32	6.66	5.59	B / 7.8	6.21	9.89	26.56 / 86	16.53 / 78	-5.60 / 7
MTG	Helios Total Return Fund Inc	HTR	C	23.62	25.79	6.07	C+ / 5.6	-0.97	1.44	16.15 / 53	15.06 / 72	7.84 / 59

Dividend Yield %	Expense Ratio	Risk Rating/ Pts	Standard Deviation	Beta	Avg Duration	NAV as of 12/31/12	Total $(Mil)	Premium / Discount As of 12/31/12	1 Year Average	Wtd Avg P/E	Cash %	Stocks %	Bonds %	Other %	Portfolio Turnover Ratio	Manager Quality Pct	Manager Tenure (Years)
15.53	1.68	B / 8.9	11.2	0.38	22.9	19.33	747	1.14	5.56	9.2	1	0	4	95	17	96	10
13.17	2.02	B / 8.9	11.0	0.27	N/A	20.55	182	-2.00	3.78	N/A	1	0	6	93	15	96	10
6.18	1.02	B- / 7.5	N/A	N/A	N/A	15.81	151	-10.31	-9.76	N/A	1	0	98	1	19	81	N/A
4.97	1.15	B / 8.6	12.0	2.43	7.5	14.96	103	-2.34	3.08	N/A	0	0	100	0	13	17	11
5.67	1.14	B / 8.5	10.3	1.77	12.5	15.73	94	1.65	6.16	N/A	0	0	100	0	11	37	11
7.11	2.04	B- / 7.9	16.3	0.51	N/A	21.90	499	-0.59	7.23	43.5	0	100	0	0	9	89	9
0.10	1.61	B- / 7.7	23.7	1.08	N/A	12.31	45	-7.07	-7.60	9.5	10	89	0	1	24	86	N/A
0.00	1.05	B / 8.0	15.4	0.61	N/A	10.23	267	-24.83	-23.28	N/A	1	97	0	2	59	75	3
6.92	1.88	B / 8.3	12.1	-166.01	N/A	15.04	367	0.86	1.31	N/A	0	0	0	100	63	99	N/A
8.46	1.84	B- / 7.4	21.0	0.75	N/A	8.38	102	-6.92	-2.49	29.5	0	100	0	0	12	93	N/A
9.54	1.50	C+ / 5.9	20.4	0.72	N/A	8.83	70	-14.50	-10.12	39.6	0	100	0	0	535	14	N/A
6.39	2.26	B / 8.5	13.1	0.40	N/A	30.64	385	0.03	5.23	30.1	0	100	0	0	13	93	N/A
6.24	N/A	B+ / 9.2	N/A	N/A	N/A	22.53	375	-6.13	-5.78	N/A	0	0	0	100	N/A	94	2
7.60	1.21	B- / 7.8	17.3	1.00	N/A	13.74	262	-13.83	-11.02	40.5	0	100	0	0	39	37	N/A
7.65	2.09	B- / 7.7	N/A	N/A	N/A	19.78	642	-8.39	-2.80	N/A	0	1	95	4	18	97	N/A
9.51	2.23	B- / 7.2	10.9	0.21	16.7	17.93	75	-1.51	9.41	N/A	0	0	100	0	47	87	N/A
8.67	2.35	B / 8.6	12.5	0.76	6.6	17.52	131	-5.25	2.18	N/A	0	0	99	1	49	92	N/A
2.42	1.68	B- / 7.6	19.6	0.76	6.6	23.88	108	-7.66	-6.91	N/A	0	43	56	1	51	91	N/A
8.74	2.09	B / 8.2	12.2	1.09	8.7	18.34	303	-2.67	-1.11	N/A	0	0	100	0	21	89	N/A
20.27	2.14	B / 8.6	14.5	0.37	N/A	11.33	124	-0.97	9.57	N/A	1	0	3	96	16	96	N/A
18.49	2.10	B / 8.3	16.2	0.28	N/A	13.68	135	-0.37	14.48	N/A	1	0	3	96	17	96	N/A
4.23	0.67	B / 8.9	8.0	1.36	N/A	17.11	157	-3.33	-5.09	N/A	0	0	95	5	175	89	N/A
0.69	2.63	B- / 7.4	19.9	0.61	N/A	2.18	5	-33.49	-27.05	90.1	2	97	0	1	11	82	8
6.93	1.15	B / 8.5	12.6	-0.44	N/A	14.32	370	0.35	1.31	N/A	1	0	98	1	302	96	N/A
6.46	2.46	B- / 7.8	9.9	0.42	5.1	7.65	188	-7.71	-3.94	17.7	0	28	71	1	19	90	22
9.01	1.99	B- / 7.5	16.7	0.83	6.4	5.79	100	-7.94	-2.56	22.7	19	54	0	27	10	32	24
5.93	1.34	B / 8.0	18.9	1.14	1.0	19.26	1,923	-15.99	-10.95	24.3	4	94	0	2	8	63	10
10.04	1.45	B- / 7.6	19.0	1.10	0.3	5.83	1,293	-4.29	0.55	34.3	0	99	0	1	6	72	27
5.75	1.30	B+ / 9.0	10.5	0.66	0.1	20.83	63	0.24	2.12	21.4	3	95	0	2	3	72	9
31.67	2.22	B / 8.3	16.2	0.83	N/A	9.81	96	-12.13	-13.08	35.5	6	94	0	0	66	83	N/A
10.19	2.34	C+ / 6.9	21.3	0.91	N/A	8.59	135	-8.61	-7.90	50.7	6	93	0	1	14	95	19
9.95	1.61	C+ / 6.6	28.7	0.55	0.1	5.58	231	10.39	33.95	23.5	0	98	0	2	1	18	14
11.25	1.23	C+ / 6.2	25.0	0.79	0.2	13.41	1,223	-4.55	4.09	71.8	2	90	4	4	15	15	8
12.30	1.17	C+ / 6.1	N/A	N/A	N/A	14.08	311	-2.98	4.62	N/A	0	0	0	100	38	89	2
11.21	4.89	B / 8.1	8.7	0.30	0.6	13.34	294	-14.39	-12.79	40.4	56	42	0	2	336	66	6
0.61	1.51	B- / 7.6	19.8	1.25	N/A	33.78	915	-17.64	-14.63	44.9	0	100	0	0	3	28	N/A
7.40	1.44	B- / 7.4	19.0	1.32	10.2	13.78	281	-6.24	-3.18	N/A	8	0	90	2	71	88	N/A
28.46	1.96	B / 8.0	10.8	0.53	N/A	4.82	37	-23.44	-19.61	56.4	0	56	41	3	103	85	N/A
0.79	1.80	B- / 7.1	23.8	0.95	N/A	13.58	282	-5.15	-8.08	55.2	5	94	0	1	51	21	N/A
7.05	1.36	B+ / 9.2	N/A	N/A	N/A	23.57	409	-2.63	-2.36	N/A	0	0	97	3	7	75	N/A
11.71	1.71	B- / 7.4	19.1	1.03	N/A	9.19	178	-10.77	-4.43	N/A	0	100	0	0	367	43	N/A
7.50	2.23	B- / 7.7	20.0	1.01	N/A	19.24	90	-13.41	-11.04	N/A	0	100	0	0	267	30	N/A
9.87	N/A	B / 8.5	N/A	N/A	N/A	19.06	168	-6.98	-2.89	N/A	0	0	0	100	N/A	35	2
9.45	2.55	B / 8.5	11.9	0.17	20.5	20.47	207	5.03	7.95	N/A	7	10	73	10	112	96	6
6.24	1.43	C+ / 6.3	16.4	0.81	N/A	19.61	465	-11.73	-6.86	165.0	7	82	0	11	44	93	9
6.21	1.75	C+ / 6.2	16.5	0.80	N/A	15.87	208	-8.63	-3.92	196.0	5	84	0	11	41	96	21
8.67	2.48	B+ / 9.0	11.2	-1.06	5.9	9.45	58	-8.47	-0.85	N/A	0	1	99	0	29	98	2
8.61	2.70	B / 8.8	11.7	-0.80	5.9	8.98	41	-6.90	0.89	N/A	0	1	99	0	29	97	2
0.08	2.21	B / 8.8	13.2	1.33	6.0	10.57	67	-4.26	2.75	N/A	1	1	98	0	24	74	N/A
8.44	2.63	B+ / 9.2	9.2	-0.10	5.9	6.51	46	-7.22	-2.10	N/A	0	1	99	0	30	97	2
7.59	2.69	B- / 7.8	8.8	0.32	7.8	7.09	39	-10.86	-8.73	20.7	0	4	96	0	36	93	2
9.65	1.88	B- / 7.0	N/A	1.96	15.8	25.35	245	-6.82	0.48	N/A	0	0	100	0	26	80	N/A

* Denotes ETF Fund, N/A denotes number is not available

www.thestreetratings.com

Data as of December 31, 2012

Fund Type	Fund Name	Ticker Symbol	Overall Investment Rating	Price As of 12/31/12	52 Week High	52 Week Low	Performance Rating/Pts	3 Mo	6 Mo	1Yr/Pct	3Yr/Pct	5Yr/Pct
FO	Herzfeld Caribbean Basin Fund	CUBA	C+	7.64	8.14	6.40	C+ / 5.9	11.77	18.76	25.99 / 85	7.88 / 38	3.41 / 34
FO	India Fund	IFN	E+	20.91	24.27	18.43	D- / 1.0	1.92	14.91	14.13 / 45	-8.09 / 8	-8.34 / 6
GL	ING Asia Pacific High Div Eq Inc F	IAE	C-	15.72	17.46	13.90	C / 4.7	9.46	18.19	19.27 / 68	6.49 / 34	3.14 / 33
EM	ING Emerging Markets High Div Eqty	IHD	B	14.63	16.44	12.82	A+ / 9.6	13.75	16.09	23.70 / 81	--	--
GL	ING Global Advantage and Premium O	IGA	C-	11.35	12.06	10.31	C- / 4.2	6.44	12.30	21.71 / 76	6.03 / 33	3.68 / 36
GL	ING Gobal Equity Dividend Premium	IGD	D+	8.67	9.62	7.87	D+ / 2.6	4.53	10.11	16.04 / 53	1.56 / 19	1.13 / 23
GR	ING Infrastructure Indus & Mtrls	IDE	C+	16.39	19.05	14.70	B / 7.7	5.67	11.55	16.34 / 54	--	--
GL	ING International High Div Eq Inc	IID	D+	9.64	10.80	7.98	C- / 3.7	9.19	10.71	20.14 / 71	4.71 / 29	4.55 / 41
LP	ING Prime Rate Trust	PPR	C+	6.21	6.45	5.26	C+ / 6.3	6.57	13.75	27.65 / 88	10.54 / 50	7.61 / 58
EN	ING Risk Managed Nat Resources Fun	IRR	D	10.34	12.68	9.73	E+ / 0.9	-4.55	2.87	2.58 / 19	-5.82 / 8	1.95 / 27
MUN	Invesco Municipal Income Opp Tr	OIA	A	7.32	8.02	6.45	B+ / 8.9	3.29	8.21	19.81 / 91	14.08 / 92	7.47 / 75
MUN	Invesco Quality Municipal Income T	IQI	B	13.70	15.07	12.97	B- / 7.0	-1.82	-1.03	10.23 / 51	11.99 / 84	8.83 / 84
MUN	Invesco Value Municipal Income Tr	IIM	B+	16.81	17.89	15.03	B / 7.7	4.93	3.84	4.89 / 29	12.98 / 88	10.45 / 93
MUN	Invesco Van Kampen Adv Muni Inc II	VKI	A-	13.15	14.26	12.21	B / 8.2	-0.48	7.46	14.35 / 77	13.30 / 89	8.56 / 82
GEI	Invesco Van Kampen Bond	VBF	C	21.34	22.67	19.13	C- / 4.0	-0.17	2.19	16.57 / 55	10.03 / 47	10.54 / 72
MUS	Invesco Van Kampen CA Val Muni Inc	VCV	B+	13.74	14.57	12.67	B / 8.0	3.14	0.74	11.69 / 62	13.13 / 89	5.70 / 64
LP	Invesco Van Kampen Dynamic Cred Op	VTA	C+	12.48	13.09	10.81	C+ / 5.7	1.95	13.07	27.92 / 88	9.80 / 46	6.61 / 52
COH	Invesco Van Kampen High Inc Tr II	VLT	B	17.25	19.04	16.09	B / 7.6	5.49	8.81	21.82 / 76	17.34 / 81	10.10 / 70
MUN	Invesco Van Kampen Muni Opp	VMO	B+	14.59	15.89	14.02	B- / 7.4	-0.48	3.55	12.98 / 71	12.25 / 86	8.37 / 80
MUN	Invesco Van Kampen Muni Trust	VKQ	B	14.40	15.76	13.42	B- / 7.3	1.13	3.28	12.73 / 69	11.74 / 83	7.19 / 74
MUS	Invesco Van Kampen PA Val Muni Inc	VPV	A+	15.30	17.02	13.74	A- / 9.0	5.52	7.84	18.95 / 90	14.54 / 94	10.50 / 93
LP	Invesco Van Kampen Senior Inc Tr	VVR	B	5.18	5.37	4.40	B- / 7.5	8.04	14.99	28.71 / 90	13.74 / 68	3.78 / 36
MUN	Invesco Van Kampen Tr Fr Inv Gr Mu	VGM	B+	15.22	16.37	14.31	B / 7.9	-0.41	7.37	13.01 / 71	12.61 / 87	9.11 / 85
MUS	Invesco Van Kampen Tr Fr Inv NY Mu	VTN	A	16.59	17.40	14.73	B+ / 8.7	3.26	9.85	17.09 / 86	13.31 / 90	10.25 / 92
GI	J Hancock Hedged Eqty & Inc Fd	HEQ	C	15.26	16.74	14.32	C / 4.7	0.98	4.58	13.90 / 44	--	--
GEI	J Hancock Income Securities Tr	JHS	B-	16.34	17.47	14.71	C+ / 6.3	2.27	5.89	21.32 / 75	14.33 / 70	13.80 / 85
GEI	J Hancock Investors Trust	JHI	B	22.57	24.95	19.53	C+ / 6.6	-0.68	-2.01	13.20 / 42	17.55 / 81	17.15 / 96
IN	J Hancock Preferred Inc	HPI	B+	21.91	25.81	20.18	B- / 7.4	3.14	3.38	13.73 / 44	18.69 / 85	11.99 / 77
IN	J Hancock Preferred Income II	HPF	B+	21.66	23.80	20.11	B- / 7.4	0.18	5.38	16.78 / 57	18.26 / 84	11.85 / 76
IN	J Hancock Preferred Income III	HPS	B	18.75	20.30	17.31	C+ / 6.8	-0.80	4.07	19.36 / 69	17.27 / 80	9.79 / 69
GL	J Hancock Tax Adv Glb Shlr Yield	HTY	C-	11.84	14.25	11.16	C- / 4.1	-0.80	6.32	11.56 / 38	10.64 / 51	8.35 / 61
IN	J Hancock Tax Advantage Div Income	HTD	B+	18.04	19.62	16.76	B / 7.6	-1.86	2.49	12.77 / 41	20.29 / 89	12.42 / 78
FO	Japan Equity Fund	JEQ	D+	5.57	5.89	4.83	D+ / 2.9	20.03	16.03	15.58 / 50	2.34 / 21	-2.36 / 13
FO	Japan Smaller Cap Fund Inc.	JOF	D	7.20	7.99	6.71	D- / 1.4	9.00	3.16	0.81 / 15	-0.65 / 14	-1.39 / 15
FO	JF China Region Fund	JFC	D+	14.00	14.50	11.45	C- / 3.8	12.92	19.37	22.51 / 78	1.91 / 20	0.41 / 21
FS	John Hancock Financial Opptys	BTO	B-	17.60	19.16	15.03	B / 8.2	7.89	17.87	32.66 / 94	15.20 / 73	4.00 / 37
IN	John Hancock Premium Dividend	PDT	B+	13.57	15.32	11.47	B- / 7.2	-0.75	-2.47	9.51 / 34	19.76 / 88	15.80 / 92
EN	Kayne Anderson Energy Tot Ret	KYE	C-	24.59	29.43	23.32	C / 4.3	-3.31	2.34	3.21 / 21	12.93 / 63	9.72 / 68
EN	Kayne Anderson Engy Development Co	KED	A	0.00	27.80	21.15	A / 9.3	-4.44	10.75	30.56 / 91	27.89 / 99	10.80 / 72
IN	Kayne Anderson Midstream/Energy	KMF	A+	28.75	31.68	24.19	A+ / 9.6	5.49	18.52	30.41 / 91	--	--
EN	Kayne Anderson MLP Inv Co	KYN	B	29.47	33.10	27.25	B- / 7.3	3.67	6.70	12.10 / 39	18.38 / 84	9.85 / 69
FO	Korea Equity Fund	KEF	C-	9.22	10.16	8.20	C+ / 5.9	6.73	20.81	12.17 / 39	13.10 / 64	3.04 / 32
FO	Korea Fund	KF	C-	41.26	42.30	34.58	C / 4.3	9.11	17.77	14.36 / 46	8.80 / 42	0.62 / 21
FO	Latin American Discovery Fund	LDF	D	15.59	17.10	13.30	D+ / 2.5	11.68	17.02	11.78 / 38	1.99 / 20	1.88 / 26
GL	Lazard Global Total Return&Income	LGI	C	15.09	15.64	12.96	C+ / 5.6	8.03	16.68	24.78 / 83	8.31 / 39	3.62 / 36
GL	Lazard World Div&Inc Fd	LOR	B	12.55	13.35	10.40	B / 8.1	12.60	22.75	30.82 / 92	13.01 / 63	4.36 / 39
GL	Legg Mason BW Global Income Opps	BWG	U	20.26	N/A	N/A	U /	5.13	12.87	--	--	--
IN	Liberty All-Star Equity Fund	USA	C	4.77	5.01	4.21	C / 5.2	4.16	12.17	17.40 / 60	10.57 / 51	3.09 / 32
IN	Liberty All-Star Growth Fund	ASG	C	4.06	4.43	3.65	C+ / 6.2	4.14	10.42	15.70 / 51	14.18 / 69	4.88 / 43
GI	LMP Capital and Income Fund Inc	SCD	B+	13.47	14.67	12.14	B+ / 8.4	5.03	14.22	24.25 / 82	19.70 / 88	5.07 / 44
LP	LMP Corporate Loan Fund Inc	TLI	B-	12.92	13.66	11.31	C+ / 6.4	1.47	9.48	20.40 / 72	14.26 / 70	9.17 / 66
GI	LMP Real Estate Income Fund Inc	RIT	B+	10.97	12.08	9.51	B+ / 8.8	3.78	14.07	30.01 / 91	21.45 / 92	9.03 / 65

* Denotes ETF Fund, N/A denotes number is not available

www.thestreetratings.com

| Incl. in Returns | | RISK | | | | NET ASSETS | | VALUATION | | | ASSET | | | | | FUND MANAGER | |
Dividend Yield %	Expense Ratio	Risk Rating/ Pts	Standard Deviation	Beta	Avg Dura-tion	NAV as of 12/31/12	Total $(Mil)	Premium/Discount As of 12/31/12	1 Year Average	Wtd Avg P/E	Cash %	Stocks %	Bonds %	Other %	Portfolio Turnover Ratio	Manager Quality Pct	Manager Tenure (Years)
0.00	2.68	B / 8.2	17.8	0.71	N/A	8.97	29	-14.83	-10.14	15.7	1	98	0	1	15	77	19
0.72	1.26	C / 4.8	27.6	0.91	N/A	23.81	899	-12.18	-11.28	N/A	2	97	0	1	31	12	N/A
9.03	1.49	C+ / 6.6	26.9	1.05	N/A	15.82	207	-0.63	2.13	N/A	0	99	0	1	123	46	6
9.84	1.41	C+ / 6.1	N/A	N/A	N/A	14.72	320	-0.61	-0.60	N/A	0	100	0	0	61	76	2
9.87	1.00	B- / 7.4	13.5	0.53	N/A	12.72	232	-10.77	-7.66	45.0	0	99	0	1	135	68	8
11.63	1.14	B- / 7.0	16.9	0.65	N/A	9.83	977	-11.80	-5.88	19.8	4	95	0	1	90	37	8
9.88	1.21	C+ / 6.6	N/A	N/A	N/A	18.27	394	-10.29	-5.29	N/A	0	98	0	2	22	27	3
9.59	1.26	C+ / 6.9	22.8	0.97	N/A	9.69	82	-0.52	4.20	21.7	1	98	0	1	94	56	6
6.55	2.20	B- / 8.0	15.2	-223.92	N/A	5.98	851	3.85	-0.02	N/A	0	0	0	100	81	99	13
10.83	1.22	C+ / 6.8	16.0	0.49	N/A	11.61	299	-10.94	-6.05	23.2	0	100	0	0	28	12	7
5.74	0.73	B / 8.5	10.0	1.98	12.7	7.52	353	-2.66	-1.00	N/A	0	0	100	0	6	47	N/A
6.03	1.14	B / 8.7	9.5	1.81	10.2	14.25	334	-3.86	1.03	N/A	0	0	100	0	9	46	N/A
5.35	1.09	B / 8.5	12.9	2.29	9.4	16.75	344	0.36	0.37	N/A	0	0	100	0	16	32	N/A
6.48	1.58	B / 8.7	10.8	1.76	10.0	13.07	578	0.61	3.44	N/A	0	0	98	2	7	58	11
4.36	0.57	B / 8.7	9.2	1.15	N/A	20.93	242	1.96	1.08	N/A	1	0	98	1	41	75	3
5.76	1.70	B / 8.4	12.5	2.59	10.3	13.79	652	-0.36	3.09	N/A	0	0	97	3	6	24	11
7.21	2.09	B / 8.0	12.9	-253.73	4.6	13.08	938	-4.59	-3.91	N/A	0	0	0	100	53	99	3
8.07	1.93	B / 8.1	15.6	1.31	N/A	17.56	136	-1.77	3.78	N/A	0	0	99	1	26	56	N/A
6.58	1.63	B / 8.7	11.2	1.55	9.9	14.55	493	0.27	5.20	N/A	0	0	97	3	8	58	11
6.36	1.46	B / 8.4	12.9	2.00	10.6	14.58	570	-1.23	3.17	N/A	0	0	97	3	5	33	22
5.88	1.49	B / 8.5	13.9	2.24	11.2	15.54	367	-1.54	0.36	N/A	0	0	98	2	5	38	11
7.07	1.93	B / 8.3	14.3	-188.48	4.7	5.13	899	0.97	-1.29	N/A	1	0	3	96	45	99	N/A
6.54	1.52	B / 8.8	9.2	1.50	10.4	15.20	823	0.13	3.14	N/A	0	0	99	1	4	61	16
6.08	1.63	B / 8.8	9.7	1.94	10.4	15.93	310	4.14	3.28	N/A	0	0	100	0	3	48	6
4.40	N/A	B- / 7.4	N/A	N/A	N/A	18.01	241	-15.27	-10.73	N/A	7	92	0	1	N/A	28	2
7.55	1.56	B / 8.7	11.3	0.86	25.1	15.89	170	2.83	4.49	62.9	1	2	94	3	71	89	7
8.84	1.62	B / 8.7	13.4	0.37	N/A	20.65	164	9.30	17.59	N/A	5	1	89	5	45	95	7
7.67	1.74	B / 8.9	13.1	0.15	N/A	22.26	572	-1.57	3.86	N/A	3	1	1	95	18	96	11
7.76	1.75	B / 8.8	13.6	0.33	N/A	22.12	466	-2.08	2.90	N/A	3	2	3	92	19	94	11
7.82	1.73	B / 8.8	14.2	0.38	N/A	19.32	598	-2.95	1.85	N/A	4	0	3	93	16	92	10
10.81	1.28	B- / 7.8	17.7	0.46	N/A	11.80	115	0.34	5.41	21.8	2	96	0	2	95	81	6
6.55	1.56	B / 8.8	13.6	0.58	N/A	20.20	690	-10.69	-7.21	21.1	0	61	0	39	16	93	N/A
1.16	1.38	B- / 7.4	17.3	0.65	N/A	6.32	87	-11.87	-10.76	N/A	0	99	0	1	59	56	7
0.00	1.15	B- / 7.3	17.4	0.46	N/A	8.22	234	-12.41	-12.83	N/A	0	79	0	21	16	36	N/A
0.74	1.89	C+ / 6.6	25.0	1.03	N/A	15.86	82	-11.73	-11.95	N/A	0	99	0	1	67	30	8
6.73	1.37	C+ / 6.9	24.7	1.14	N/A	19.40	298	-9.28	-8.12	N/A	1	96	0	3	23	79	7
6.12	1.87	B / 8.9	14.4	0.32	N/A	14.44	660	-6.02	-0.97	22.2	2	33	0	65	13	95	8
7.81	4.30	B- / 7.2	20.3	0.59	4.6	26.46	884	-7.07	1.86	36.7	0	87	13	0	58	79	8
5.03	3.90	B / 8.0	18.6	0.20	N/A	0.00	238		4.98	N/A	0	82	18	0	68	98	N/A
6.16	2.90	B / 8.5	N/A	N/A	N/A	30.22	562	-4.86	-3.70	N/A	0	84	16	0	74	89	N/A
9.33	4.90	B / 8.2	15.8	0.33	4.5	29.26	2,030	0.72	8.03	37.6	0	100	0	0	22	91	9
0.00	1.90	C / 5.4	25.0	0.98	N/A	10.05	121	-8.26	-9.26	N/A	1	92	0	7	75	89	8
0.00	1.12	C+ / 6.4	26.1	1.04	N/A	45.32	388	-8.96	-8.77	N/A	0	97	0	3	43	80	N/A
1.56	1.41	C+ / 6.3	26.4	1.13	N/A	17.66	126	-11.72	-8.94	89.4	0	100	0	0	20	26	11
5.88	1.54	B- / 7.6	19.4	0.90	N/A	17.81	149	-15.27	-11.97	27.2	0	67	32	1	33	78	N/A
6.35	1.97	B- / 7.4	20.6	0.95	N/A	14.74	87	-14.86	-11.66	29.6	1	71	27	1	46	86	N/A
6.19	N/A	U /	N/A	N/A	N/A	22.19	460	-8.70	N/A	N/A	0	0	0	100	N/A	N/A	1
6.71	1.06	B- / 7.2	21.1	1.29	N/A	5.55	943	-14.05	-11.69	55.9	2	97	0	1	25	29	N/A
6.90	1.45	C+ / 6.2	19.3	1.11	N/A	4.69	130	-13.43	-9.17	129.8	3	96	0	1	15	63	27
8.31	1.59	B / 8.0	15.4	0.89	N/A	14.93	240	-9.78	-5.62	N/A	12	75	12	1	33	83	N/A
6.73	1.94	B / 8.4	12.3	-274.97	4.6	13.00	125	-0.62	-1.31	N/A	0	0	0	100	32	99	N/A
6.56	1.68	B- / 7.8	19.1	1.05	N/A	12.48	37	-12.10	-8.87	51.2	0	61	0	39	26	85	N/A

I. Index of ETFs and Other Closed-End Funds

99 Pct = Best
0 Pct = Worst

Fund Type	Fund Name	Ticker Symbol	Overall Investment Rating	Price As of 12/31/12	52 Week High	52 Week Low	Performance Rating/Pts	3 Mo	6 Mo	1Yr/Pct	3Yr/Pct	5Yr/Pct
MUS	MA Health & Education Tax-Exempt T	MHE	A-	14.85	16.69	13.77	B / 8.0	-2.34	3.12	7.83 / 39	14.03 / 92	11.32 / 97
GL	Macquarie Global Infr Total Return	MGU	C+	19.07	20.12	16.16	C+ / 6.6	6.29	14.86	22.67 / 78	12.30 / 60	-0.09 / 19
GL	Macquarie/FTG Infr/ Util Div&Inc	MFD	B-	15.25	16.48	13.48	C+ / 6.7	2.94	7.07	19.15 / 68	15.70 / 76	-1.24 / 16
IN	Madison Covered Call & Equity Stra	MCN	D+	7.62	8.30	7.04	D+ / 2.9	1.70	7.73	12.61 / 40	4.44 / 28	4.21 / 38
IN	Madison Strategic Sector Premium	MSP	C-	11.09	12.06	10.45	C- / 3.4	2.61	9.09	13.30 / 42	6.76 / 35	5.72 / 47
GEI	MainStay DefinedTerm Muncipal Opp	MMD	U	20.39	N/A	N/A	U /	4.51	4.70	--	--	--
MUN	Managed Duration Investment Grd Mu	MZF	B+	15.30	16.77	14.36	B / 8.1	-1.91	2.59	13.41 / 72	13.55 / 91	11.97 / 98
GL	Managed High Yield Plus Fund	HYF	C-	2.14	2.39	1.93	C- / 4.1	0.73	2.88	11.65 / 38	11.02 / 53	2.48 / 29
FO	Mexico Equity & Income Fund	MXE	A+	14.25	15.73	10.25	A+ / 9.7	19.92	31.62	54.56 / 99	26.13 / 98	11.30 / 74
FO	Mexico Fund	MXF	A	29.02	31.39	21.69	A+ / 9.7	16.17	30.89	52.02 / 99	22.55 / 94	12.25 / 78
MUS	MFS CA Muni	CCA	B	12.13	12.77	10.83	B- / 7.2	0.98	4.53	14.70 / 78	10.89 / 79	7.22 / 74
GEI	MFS Charter Income Trust	MCR	B-	10.12	10.53	9.25	C+ / 5.9	3.45	10.47	20.27 / 71	12.43 / 60	12.53 / 79
GL	MFS Government Markets Income Trus	MGF	C-	6.85	7.55	6.49	D+ / 2.3	-5.13	-0.26	3.16 / 21	5.18 / 30	7.08 / 55
MUH	MFS High Inc Muni Tr	CXE	B+	5.46	6.08	5.14	B / 8.1	2.92	2.29	13.57 / 73	13.30 / 89	8.67 / 83
MUH	MFS High Yield Muni Trust	CMU	B+	4.86	5.52	4.51	B / 7.8	2.87	2.44	13.58 / 73	12.54 / 87	8.82 / 84
COH	MFS Interm High Inc	CIF	B	3.07	3.29	2.82	B- / 7.2	2.70	6.50	18.70 / 66	17.51 / 81	13.06 / 81
GL	MFS Intermediate Income Trust	MIN	C-	6.44	7.03	6.06	D+ / 2.9	-0.94	1.94	10.74 / 36	6.88 / 35	9.54 / 67
GL	MFS InterMkt Inc Tr I	CMK	C	8.79	9.27	8.04	C- / 3.7	-0.98	6.78	13.16 / 42	8.93 / 43	9.23 / 66
MUN	MFS Invst Gr Muni Tr	CXH	B-	10.46	11.69	9.88	C+ / 6.2	-1.98	-3.47	12.75 / 69	11.55 / 82	8.58 / 82
GEN	MFS Multimarket Income Trust	MMT	C+	7.28	7.41	6.71	C / 4.9	1.11	6.07	16.09 / 53	11.91 / 57	13.22 / 82
MUN	MFS Municipal Income Trust	MFM	B+	7.62	8.34	6.99	B- / 7.5	-0.15	4.47	14.98 / 80	11.65 / 83	10.15 / 92
GI	MFS Special Value Trust	MFV	C	6.91	7.93	6.45	C / 5.2	-3.40	8.19	19.18 / 68	12.54 / 61	11.42 / 75
MUS	Minnesota Municipal Inc Portfolio	MXA	B	17.17	18.75	15.46	C+ / 6.3	-1.56	3.42	11.14 / 59	10.72 / 78	13.03 / 99
MUS	Minnesota Municipal Income Fund II	MXN	B+	16.15	18.70	15.10	B- / 7.1	6.40	-2.65	10.79 / 55	11.41 / 81	11.80 / 98
GEI	Montgomery Street Inc. Sec.	MTS	C+	16.90	17.38	15.39	C / 4.7	3.37	9.76	16.75 / 57	10.05 / 47	5.95 / 49
FO	Morgan Stanley Asia Pacific Fund	APF	D+	14.98	15.58	12.46	C- / 3.1	13.24	16.00	14.90 / 48	4.35 / 28	2.05 / 27
FO	Morgan Stanley China A Share Fund	CAF	D	24.05	24.98	17.68	C- / 3.2	24.62	26.53	23.62 / 81	1.07 / 17	1.22 / 23
FO	Morgan Stanley Eastern Europe	RNE	D+	17.13	17.60	13.20	C- / 3.4	6.60	18.26	23.08 / 80	1.55 / 18	-8.56 / 6
EM	Morgan Stanley Emerging Markets	MSF	C-	15.50	16.27	12.90	C- / 3.9	9.14	15.27	19.93 / 71	4.51 / 28	1.04 / 22
EM	Morgan Stanley Emerging Mkts Debt	MSD	B-	11.95	12.43	10.33	C+ / 6.9	4.16	10.89	25.75 / 85	13.70 / 67	13.10 / 81
EM	Morgan Stanley Emg Mkts Dom Debt	EDD	C+	16.84	17.52	14.28	C+ / 6.6	6.81	10.86	19.69 / 70	13.71 / 68	9.39 / 6
GEN	Morgan Stanley Income Sec	ICB	C	18.46	19.49	17.17	C- / 3.6	-0.79	2.41	10.77 / 36	10.03 / 47	8.85 / 6
FO	Morgan Stanley India Inv Fund	IIF	D-	18.53	18.95	13.96	D / 1.9	5.81	20.57	22.96 / 79	-2.71 / 11	-5.44 /
IN	Nasdaq Premium Income & Growth Fun	QQQX	C+	15.17	16.48	13.45	B- / 7.0	4.13	8.51	25.68 / 85	14.47 / 71	11.07 / 7
MUS	Neuberger Berman CA Inter Muni Fun	NBW	B+	15.50	17.12	14.59	B- / 7.2	-1.84	-1.35	9.73 / 48	12.38 / 86	9.19 / 8
COH	Neuberger Berman High Yield Strat	NHS	C-	13.90	15.29	12.45	C+ / 5.6	-2.21	1.81	13.14 / 42	14.81 / 72	15.85 / 9
MUN	Neuberger Berman Intermediate Muni	NBH	A+	16.18	17.56	14.50	B+ / 8.4	3.94	4.55	13.07 / 71	13.89 / 92	11.10 / 9
MUS	Neuberger Berman NY Int Muni	NBO	B	15.21	16.59	14.05	B- / 7.3	0.05	1.86	9.79 / 48	11.98 / 84	9.59 / 8
GI	Neuberger Berman Real Est Secs Inc	NRO	A-	4.59	4.88	3.84	B+ / 8.9	3.46	8.26	31.62 / 93	22.92 / 94	-1.07 / 1
COH	New America High Income Fund	HYB	B	10.45	12.25	9.46	B / 7.7	3.12	10.07	22.82 / 79	17.82 / 82	17.51 / 9
FO	New Germany Fund	GF	B	15.58	16.29	12.57	B+ / 8.9	14.69	29.71	38.58 / 97	14.21 / 69	6.29 / 5
GEN	NexPoint Credit Strategies Fund	HCF	C-	6.64	7.56	6.00	C / 4.3	2.06	12.31	16.40 / 54	8.57 / 41	-3.48 / 1
GI	NFJ Dividend Interest & Premium St	NFJ	C-	15.60	18.21	14.65	C- / 3.8	0.93	2.95	6.22 / 27	10.65 / 51	2.57 / 1
MUN	Nuveen AMT-Fr Muni Income	NEA	C+	14.84	15.95	13.86	C+ / 5.8	0.90	5.34	10.47 / 53	8.97 / 68	6.86 /
MUN	Nuveen AMT-Free Municipal Value	NUW	C+	17.63	19.36	16.03	C+ / 6.2	1.13	5.35	10.37 / 52	9.70 / 72	--
MUS	Nuveen AZ Div Adv Muni	NFZ	B+	14.98	15.92	13.32	B / 8.1	1.66	3.98	15.74 / 82	13.05 / 89	7.93 /
MUS	Nuveen AZ Div Adv Muni Fund 2	NKR	B+	15.59	16.36	13.97	B / 7.7	2.58	2.58	15.73 / 82	11.84 / 84	8.26 /
MUS	Nuveen AZ Div Adv Muni Fund 3	NXE	A-	14.77	15.36	13.42	B / 8.0	1.93	4.56	16.56 / 85	12.02 / 84	8.10 /
MUS	Nuveen AZ Prem Inc Muni	NAZ	B-	15.33	16.18	13.86	C+ / 6.5	2.32	1.90	13.79 / 74	9.98 / 74	9.43 /
MUN	Nuveen Build America Bond Fund	NBB	B-	21.18	21.96	19.14	C+ / 5.9	2.71	2.67	10.44 / 53	--	--
GEI	Nuveen Build America Bond Oppty Fd	NBD	C-	21.66	22.41	20.20	D+ / 2.8	2.01	2.65	6.45 / 27	--	--
MUS	Nuveen CA AMT-Free Municipal Incom	NKX	B+	14.73	16.42	13.90	B / 7.9	-0.03	2.56	12.09 / 65	12.99 / 88	6.80 /

* Denotes ETF Fund, N/A denotes number is not availa

www.thestreetratings.c

Incl. in Returns Dividend Yield %	Expense Ratio	Risk Rating/ Pts	3 Year Standard Deviation	Beta	Avg Dura-tion	NAV as of 12/31/12	Total $(Mil)	Premium/Discount As of 12/31/12	1 Year Average	Wtd Avg P/E	Cash %	Stocks %	Bonds %	Other %	Portfolio Turnover Ratio	Manager Quality Pct	Manager Tenure (Years)
5.05	1.50	B / 8.8	11.5	1.17	14.7	14.48	34	2.56	6.84	N/A	1	0	98	1	17	83	N/A
6.71	2.22	B- / 7.8	21.7	0.96	N/A	22.31	326	-14.52	-10.97	27.5	0	100	0	0	35	86	N/A
9.18	2.25	B- / 7.9	20.3	0.89	N/A	16.50	123	-7.58	-2.61	31.4	0	76	0	24	79	92	N/A
9.45	1.36	B- / 7.5	15.9	0.95	N/A	8.84	166	-13.80	-11.02	39.3	0	100	0	0	33	19	N/A
9.38	0.97	B- / 7.9	14.5	0.82	N/A	13.12	74	-15.47	-12.74	37.2	0	100	0	0	34	30	8
3.76	N/A	U /	N/A	N/A	N/A	20.25	553	0.69	N/A	N/A	0	0	0	100	N/A	N/A	1
6.08	1.36	B / 8.5	10.8	2.15	12.2	15.39	105	-0.58	3.19	N/A	0	0	100	0	15	37	10
8.41	1.46	B- / 7.3	19.5	0.86	16.5	2.28	131	-6.14	1.16	N/A	1	0	98	1	50	90	4
0.00	1.57	B / 8.0	21.1	0.80	16.6	16.85	87	-15.43	-11.28	33.1	1	97	1	1	277	97	23
1.08	1.42	B- / 7.5	23.0	0.96	N/A	32.20	339	-9.88	-7.81	24.6	1	98	0	1	25	96	N/A
4.95	1.41	B / 8.3	12.9	2.31	11.4	12.81	33	-5.31	-1.18	N/A	3	0	97	0	12	24	6
6.34	0.98	B / 8.8	8.5	0.44	18.0	10.53	546	-3.89	-3.50	N/A	0	0	99	1	26	87	9
7.29	0.79	B / 8.6	8.5	0.07	11.8	6.79	227	0.88	0.56	N/A	10	0	90	0	12	78	N/A
5.93	1.45	B / 8.6	10.7	1.91	N/A	5.57	164	-1.97	6.00	N/A	0	0	100	0	8	48	6
5.93	1.33	B / 8.6	10.5	1.63	12.4	5.00	132	-2.80	6.45	N/A	1	0	99	0	7	58	6
2.12	1.74	B / 8.7	12.8	1.11	N/A	3.19	62	-3.76	2.80	N/A	0	1	98	1	20	49	6
8.22	0.71	B / 8.5	9.1	0.21	N/A	6.19	746	4.04	3.58	N/A	0	0	100	0	16	84	11
5.15	1.12	B / 8.9	5.7	0.41	10.6	9.54	100	-7.86	-8.02	N/A	0	0	100	0	24	86	6
5.28	1.21	B / 8.6	10.9	2.13	11.2	10.82	119	-3.33	3.07	N/A	0	0	100	0	8	31	6
6.59	1.12	B / 8.5	8.4	0.31	19.7	7.77	564	-6.31	-4.85	N/A	0	0	100	0	49	49	N/A
5.83	1.42	B / 8.6	10.2	1.57	12.8	7.56	271	0.79	5.30	N/A	1	0	99	0	22	62	20
9.83	1.39	B- / 7.8	14.4	0.36	N/A	7.02	46	-1.57	4.82	N/A	2	25	73	0	53	81	N/A
5.17	1.42	B / 8.8	11.5	1.76	9.9	16.25	67	5.66	8.48	N/A	0	0	100	0	6	54	N/A
4.83	2.45	B+ / 9.0	10.6	0.93	12.4	15.83	23	2.02	7.42	N/A	0	0	99	1	11	70	N/A
6.86	0.71	B+ / 9.5	5.5	0.81	N/A	18.47	185	-8.50	-9.16	N/A	15	0	85	0	154	78	N/A
0.67	1.22	B- / 7.1	20.3	0.93	N/A	17.44	302	-14.11	-10.90	N/A	5	94	0	1	25	57	N/A
0.00	2.13	C+ / 5.8	29.9	0.95	N/A	23.09	491	4.16	-7.37	N/A	0	99	0	1	77	24	N/A
0.26	2.01	C+ / 6.3	29.3	1.34	N/A	19.47	68	-12.02	-10.86	N/A	4	94	0	2	17	34	17
0.53	1.50	B- / 7.3	22.5	0.97	N/A	17.48	263	-11.33	-9.71	60.8	3	96	0	1	22	44	22
6.03	1.12	B / 8.2	12.6	0.98	9.8	13.03	286	-8.29	-8.16	N/A	0	0	99	1	19	89	11
5.94	2.16	B- / 7.6	20.9	1.53	N/A	18.62	1,283	-9.56	-6.73	N/A	0	0	100	0	64	87	6
3.74	0.63	B+ / 9.0	6.7	0.87	17.3	19.80	177	-6.77	-4.56	N/A	1	0	98	1	61	79	5
0.00	1.34	C / 5.2	28.2	1.03	N/A	20.69	378	-10.44	-10.86	71.2	3	96	0	1	49	20	19
7.96	1.04	B- / 7.0	18.0	1.00	N/A	15.67	260	-3.19	-1.67	116.7	0	100	0	0	51	53	2
5.26	1.29	B+ / 9.1	9.4	1.32	6.8	15.84	83	-2.15	2.73	N/A	2	0	97	1	16	68	N/A
7.77	1.68	C+ / 6.4	17.9	1.72	5.7	14.45	253	-3.81	3.10	N/A	0	0	100	0	100	25	8
5.19	1.05	B+ / 9.1	8.8	1.42	7.6	16.04	278	0.87	3.81	N/A	2	0	97	1	23	71	N/A
5.13	1.29	B / 8.6	12.6	1.84	7.7	15.01	73	1.33	4.00	N/A	4	0	95	1	16	39	N/A
5.23	2.21	B- / 7.9	17.3	0.91	N/A	5.40	257	-15.00	-12.27	N/A	0	58	0	42	19	91	N/A
7.42	1.10	B / 8.2	13.8	1.19	N/A	10.67	321	-2.06	3.14	N/A	0	0	96	4	32	70	N/A
8.13	1.17	C+ / 6.4	28.7	1.29	N/A	18.32	263	-14.96	-10.22	47.8	0	100	0	0	6	89	N/A
6.33	3.15	B- / 7.6	15.7	-1.38	4.9	7.62	443	-12.86	-10.40	12.8	0	10	28	62	52	96	N/A
1.54	0.97	B- / 7.7	17.1	0.98	6.3	17.55	1,644	-11.11	-4.90	16.6	4	71	0	25	23	49	N/A
5.50	2.01	B / 8.6	9.9	2.08	12.1	15.47	327	-4.07	-1.46	N/A	11	0	89	0	2	22	7
4.56	0.71	B / 8.3	12.0	2.46	N/A	17.79	213	-0.90	1.91	N/A	2	0	92	6	1	18	4
4.89	3.47	B / 8.4	12.1	1.89	11.0	15.47	24	-3.17	-3.09	N/A	3	0	96	1	11	51	2
4.93	2.94	B+ / 9.0	7.8	1.64	10.9	15.82	38	-1.45	-1.95	N/A	2	0	97	1	8	60	2
4.71	3.48	B+ / 9.0	7.7	1.74	11.4	15.30	47	-3.46	-3.82	N/A	6	0	93	1	6	54	2
5.01	1.82	B / 8.4	11.8	1.55	11.6	15.41	68	-0.52	0.63	N/A	3	0	96	1	8	64	2
6.29	1.05	B / 8.8	N/A	N/A	N/A	22.19	566	-4.55	-4.91	N/A	8	0	91	1	18	57	N/A
6.01	0.97	B+ / 9.3	N/A	N/A	N/A	23.35	163	-7.24	-6.74	N/A	18	0	81	1	7	20	N/A
5.23	1.65	B / 8.4	12.4	2.49	11.8	15.53	641	-5.15	-0.47	N/A	4	0	90	6	12	24	11

Denotes ETF Fund, N/A denotes number is not available

Fund Type	Fund Name	Ticker Symbol	Overall Investment Rating	PRICE Price As of 12/31/12	52 Week High	52 Week Low	PERFORMANCE Perform-ance Rating/Pts		% Total Return Through 12/31/12 3 Mo	6 Mo	1Yr/Pct	Annualized 3Yr/Pct	5Yr/Pct
MUS	Nuveen CA Div Adv Muni	NAC	A+	16.10	16.58	13.67	A	9.4	4.26	9.55	19.95 / 92	17.04 / 98	10.81 / 95
MUS	Nuveen CA Div Adv Muni 2	NVX	A-	15.61	17.27	14.27	B	8.2	0.40	6.31	13.60 / 73	13.41 / 90	10.27 / 92
MUS	Nuveen CA Div Adv Muni 3	NZH	A-	14.34	14.96	13.04	B	8.0	2.28	6.54	13.52 / 73	12.38 / 86	8.26 / 79
MUS	Nuveen CA Inv Quality Muni	NQC	A	15.68	17.28	14.35	B+	8.8	-1.18	5.53	16.49 / 84	15.90 / 97	10.90 / 95
MUS	Nuveen CA Muni Market Opportunity	NCO	A+	16.34	17.40	14.15	A	9.5	5.71	9.96	23.30 / 96	16.96 / 98	11.26 / 97
MUS	Nuveen CA Muni Value	NCA	B-	10.03	10.90	9.17	C+	5.9	-1.48	0.01	14.63 / 78	9.93 / 73	7.24 / 74
MUS	Nuveen CA Performance Plus Muni	NCP	A+	16.26	16.82	14.09	A	9.4	2.54	9.12	16.94 / 85	17.51 / 98	11.06 / 96
MUS	Nuveen CA Prem Inc Muni	NCU	A+	15.46	16.82	14.08	A-	9.2	1.45	8.59	16.22 / 84	16.97 / 98	10.72 / 95
MUS	Nuveen CA Quality Inc Muni	NUC	A+	17.35	18.00	15.25	A+	9.6	5.75	11.88	20.94 / 93	17.52 / 99	12.56 / 99
MUS	Nuveen CA Select Quality Muni	NVC	A+	16.64	17.62	14.79	A	9.4	3.55	10.44	20.28 / 92	16.55 / 98	12.54 / 99
MUS	Nuveen CA Select Tax-Free Inc Port	NXC	A-	15.21	16.29	14.01	B	7.9	-0.22	5.95	15.53 / 81	12.27 / 86	7.54 / 75
MUN	Nuveen California Municipal Value	NCB	B	16.29	17.23	15.20	B-	7.3	3.52	1.87	15.25 / 80	10.81 / 78	--
IN	Nuveen Core Equity Alpha Fund	JCE	C+	13.35	14.37	12.70	C+	5.9	0.65	8.40	17.19 / 59	14.12 / 69	7.55 / 58
GI	Nuveen Credit Strategies Income	JQC	B+	9.65	10.02	8.32	B	8.1	3.59	10.25	30.00 / 91	17.80 / 82	8.54 / 62
MUS	Nuveen CT Prem Inc Muni	NTC	C+	14.32	14.80	13.78	C	4.3	2.86	3.71	8.43 / 41	6.69 / 49	6.53 / 69
MUN	Nuveen Div Adv Muni	NAD	A-	15.48	16.33	13.92	B+	8.4	2.96	7.82	15.89 / 83	12.99 / 88	9.99 / 91
MUN	Nuveen Div Adv Muni 3	NZF	B	15.09	16.29	14.12	B-	7.2	0.66	4.82	11.93 / 64	11.47 / 81	8.50 / 81
MUN	Nuveen Div Adv Muni Income	NVG	B	15.35	16.30	14.17	C+	6.9	2.51	5.93	10.96 / 57	10.42 / 77	9.28 / 87
GL	Nuveen Diversified Currency Opp	JGT	D+	12.87	13.77	11.98	D+	2.8	0.78	9.94	16.13 / 53	2.89 / 22	4.44 / 40
GI	Nuveen Diversified Dividend&Income	JDD	B	11.60	12.93	10.65	B-	7.4	1.91	7.92	24.13 / 82	16.78 / 79	8.52 / 62
MUN	Nuveen Dividend Advantage Muni 2	NXZ	B	15.22	16.54	14.07	C+	6.5	1.88	3.64	11.97 / 65	10.10 / 75	7.17 / 73
GI	Nuveen Energy MLP Total Return Fun	JMF	D+	17.70	19.02	15.89	C-	3.4	1.41	3.26	10.00 / 34	--	--
GEI	Nuveen EnhancedMunicipal Value	NEV	B-	16.10	17.02	14.32	C+	6.7	5.06	7.87	23.56 / 81	14.06 / 69	--
IN	Nuveen Equity Premium & Growth Fun	JPG	C	12.93	13.80	12.11	C	5.0	3.16	8.92	19.72 / 70	10.30 / 49	5.53 / 47
IN	Nuveen Equity Premium Advantage	JLA	C-	11.90	12.91	11.18	C-	3.9	1.65	6.38	16.58 / 55	8.51 / 40	6.13 / 50
IN	Nuveen Equity Premium Income Fund	JPZ	C-	11.83	12.80	11.27	C-	4.0	1.31	6.70	18.79 / 66	8.43 / 40	6.03 / 49
IN	Nuveen Equity Premium Opportunity	JSN	C-	12.07	12.91	11.17	C-	3.8	0.36	7.32	16.58 / 55	8.09 / 39	5.67 / 47
LP	Nuveen Floating Rate Income Fund	JFR	C+	12.19	12.87	10.86	C+	6.5	4.10	10.72	22.55 / 78	13.40 / 66	9.94 / 69
LP	Nuveen Floating Rate Income Opp	JRO	C+	12.25	13.08	11.23	C+	5.9	3.56	11.12	19.92 / 70	12.32 / 60	10.72 / 72
MUS	Nuveen GA Div Adv Muni Fund 2	NKG	B-	14.85	15.59	13.78	C+	6.3	3.55	5.53	8.01 / 39	9.95 / 74	8.07 / 78
GL	Nuveen Global Income Oppportunitie	JGG	C-	14.02	14.94	13.68	D+	2.5	1.61	3.45	10.39 / 35	3.68 / 25	5.84 / 48
GL	Nuveen Global Value Opportunities	JGV	D	14.91	17.87	13.38	D	2.0	3.85	12.44	0.36 / 14	1.74 / 19	5.78 / 47
MUN	Nuveen Investment Quality Muni Fun	NQM	A	16.03	17.68	14.92	B+	8.6	3.03	4.92	13.94 / 75	14.43 / 93	10.15 / 92
MUS	Nuveen MA AMT/F Muni Income	NGX	D+	13.82	15.69	13.66	D+	2.4	-1.38	-1.91	6.77 / 35	3.40 / 30	4.36 / 63
MUS	Nuveen MA Div Adv Muni	NMB	C+	14.96	15.88	13.57	C	5.2	-0.35	2.61	11.07 / 58	8.71 / 66	7.07 / 73
MUS	Nuveen MA Prem Inc Muni	NMT	C+	14.82	15.98	14.00	C	4.9	-2.14	2.74	9.86 / 49	8.57 / 64	7.95 / 78
MUS	Nuveen MD Prem Inc Muni Fund	NMY	C+	15.20	16.43	14.39	C	5.4	1.23	-0.47	5.25 / 30	9.70 / 72	8.71 / 83
MUS	Nuveen MI Quality Inc Muni	NUM	A-	15.31	16.54	14.23	B	8.1	-0.04	4.10	13.83 / 74	13.65 / 91	9.64 / 90
MUS	Nuveen MO Prem Inc Muni	NOM	B	16.00	18.30	15.61	B-	7.1	2.17	3.72	11.60 / 61	11.19 / 80	8.90 / 84
MTG	Nuveen Mortgage Opportunity Term	JLS	B+	27.22	29.19	21.85	B+	8.3	6.63	20.74	39.78 / 97	13.86 / 68	--
MTG	Nuveen Mortgage Opportunity Term 2	JMT	A+	27.18	29.11	21.51	A+	9.8	5.67	20.20	41.29 / 97	--	--
MUN	Nuveen Muni Advantage	NMA	B	15.21	16.16	13.94	B-	7.5	3.23	5.63	14.21 / 76	10.80 / 78	9.29 / 87
MUH	Nuveen Muni High Income Opport	NMZ	A-	14.10	14.49	11.98	B+	8.6	3.41	9.24	21.21 / 94	12.30 / 86	6.73 / 71
MUH	Nuveen Muni High Income Opport 2	NMD	A	13.42	14.05	11.33	A-	9.1	6.97	9.35	25.58 / 97	12.94 / 88	6.55 / 70
MUN	Nuveen Muni Income	NMI	B-	12.15	12.95	10.93	C+	6.2	0.98	3.22	12.26 / 67	9.82 / 73	8.43 / 80
MUN	Nuveen Muni Market Opportunity	NMO	B	14.66	15.36	13.22	B-	7.3	3.31	6.09	13.65 / 74	10.51 / 77	8.78 / 84
MUN	Nuveen Muni Opportunity	NIO	B+	15.33	16.04	14.00	B	7.8	3.68	6.82	12.26 / 67	11.79 / 83	9.11 / 86
MUN	Nuveen Muni Value	NUV	C+	10.25	10.67	9.37	C	4.8	1.82	2.35	10.80 / 55	7.53 / 56	7.30 / 74
MUS	Nuveen NC Prem Inc Muni	NNC	C	15.11	16.16	14.74	C	4.4	2.06	4.11	5.46 / 31	7.49 / 55	8.17 / 79
MUN	Nuveen New Jersey Municipal Value	NJV	A	17.14	18.03	15.24	B+	8.5	8.01	8.06	18.51 / 89	11.68 / 83	--
MUN	Nuveen New York Municipal Value 2	NYV	B-	15.66	16.60	14.61	C+	6.0	-0.22	3.42	15.41 / 81	8.90 / 67	--
MUS	Nuveen NJ Div Adv Muni	NXJ	A-	15.34	16.74	13.96	B	8.2	-2.21	5.11	17.73 / 87	13.53 / 90	9.89 / 91

* Denotes ETF Fund, N/A denotes number is not available

www.thestreetratings.com

Dividend Yield %	Expense Ratio	Risk Rating/ Pts	Standard Deviation	Beta	Avg Duration	NAV as of 12/31/12	Total $(Mil)	As of 12/31/12	1 Year Average	Wtd Avg P/E	Cash %	Stocks %	Bonds %	Other %	Portfolio Turnover Ratio	Manager Quality Pct	Manager Tenure (Years)
5.52	1.64	B / 8.5	9.7	2.08	12.4	15.86	364	1.51	-0.43	N/A	9	0	90	1	8	67	11
5.77	2.23	B / 8.7	9.5	2.13	12.4	16.35	236	-4.53	-1.04	N/A	9	0	90	1	13	36	11
5.61	2.56	B / 8.7	9.8	1.84	12.8	14.69	347	-2.38	-1.00	N/A	8	0	91	1	13	52	11
5.89	1.63	B / 8.6	11.2	2.47	12.3	16.15	216	-2.91	1.87	N/A	8	0	91	1	9	34	11
5.88	1.73	B / 8.7	10.4	2.05	12.2	16.52	131	-1.09	0.53	N/A	10	0	89	1	10	59	11
5.05	0.65	B / 8.8	8.4	1.31	11.7	10.44	261	-3.93	-0.37	N/A	2	0	97	1	11	52	11
5.83	1.55	B / 8.6	9.6	2.12	12.5	16.04	205	1.37	1.23	N/A	9	0	90	1	5	68	11
5.43	2.16	B / 8.7	10.5	2.17	12.4	15.95	90	-3.07	-1.56	N/A	10	0	89	1	8	58	11
5.88	1.61	B / 8.4	11.5	2.43	12.0	16.64	362	4.27	3.28	N/A	8	0	91	1	5	49	11
5.99	1.64	B / 8.4	11.2	2.31	12.5	16.62	364	0.12	2.43	N/A	10	0	89	1	16	49	11
4.50	0.42	B+ / 9.0	7.7	1.31	9.8	15.73	94	-3.31	-1.32	N/A	3	0	96	1	11	69	21
5.19	0.76	B / 8.6	8.4	1.64	N/A	17.50	56	-6.91	-3.79	N/A	5	0	94	1	3	39	N/A
8.09	1.05	B- / 7.8	16.3	0.92	N/A	15.12	222	-11.71	-7.35	53.5	0	95	0	5	67	65	N/A
7.17	1.86	B / 8.4	12.4	0.62	4.1	9.96	1,388	-3.11	-4.24	53.4	5	36	0	59	156	90	10
5.17	3.08	B+ / 9.1	6.7	1.40	12.0	15.37	82	-6.83	-6.46	N/A	3	0	93	4	11	34	N/A
6.07	2.02	B / 8.6	10.1	2.24	10.1	16.19	565	-4.39	-2.95	N/A	3	0	91	6	15	29	11
5.38	1.46	B / 8.7	10.0	1.89	11.8	16.09	587	-6.22	-2.48	N/A	1	0	91	8	30	40	7
5.51	1.84	B+ / 9.0	7.7	1.68	11.0	16.27	448	-5.65	-3.78	N/A	1	0	93	6	7	35	7
9.25	1.06	B- / 7.8	14.3	1.16	3.2	14.91	606	-13.68	-11.63	N/A	8	0	91	1	41	43	N/A
8.62	1.92	B / 8.0	15.8	0.75	10.7	12.73	240	-8.88	-3.85	44.1	3	0	0	97	26	85	10
5.28	1.75	B / 8.7	10.0	1.79	12.4	16.23	427	-6.22	-2.10	N/A	3	0	93	4	40	32	N/A
7.14	1.78	B- / 7.3	N/A	N/A	N/A	18.05	410	-1.94	2.39	N/A	0	99	0	1	46	15	N/A
6.19	1.17	B / 8.3	10.4	2.17	N/A	15.93	269	1.07	2.12	N/A	0	0	84	16	33	55	3
8.66	0.96	B / 8.1	11.9	0.64	N/A	14.63	232	-11.62	-10.05	47.5	0	99	0	1	4	63	N/A
9.55	0.99	B- / 7.5	11.7	0.54	N/A	13.52	347	-11.98	-10.59	79.5	1	99	0	0	3	61	N/A
9.16	0.90	B- / 7.9	12.1	0.61	N/A	13.31	508	-11.12	-9.07	47.9	3	96	0	1	2	82	N/A
9.25	0.88	B- / 7.8	12.0	0.57	N/A	13.22	874	-8.70	-8.45	62.1	0	99	0	1	5	59	N/A
7.85	1.72	B / 8.0	14.2	-240.79	4.6	12.25	572	-0.49	-0.17	N/A	5	2	6	87	57	99	N/A
9.87	1.65	B- / 7.9	15.4	-235.78	4.6	12.21	370	0.33	1.74	N/A	3	1	8	88-	85	99	6
4.90	2.95	B / 8.7	11.0	1.42	11.7	14.90	67	-0.34	0.08	N/A	1	0	96	3	11	57	6
8.42	1.06	B / 8.3	8.0	0.36	11.5	15.67	145	-10.53	-6.72	N/A	10	0	88	2	36	57	N/A
7.78	1.16	B- / 7.1	15.8	0.56	6.2	16.28	325	-8.42	-6.77	22.3	24	53	11	12	92	49	5
6.16	1.50	B / 8.6	10.8	2.31	10.7	16.66	536	-3.78	0.05	N/A	2	0	89	9	12	36	N/A
4.17	3.16	B / 8.3	11.4	1.89	14.1	14.95	41	-7.56	-1.79	N/A	4	0	93	3	14	15	N/A
4.57	3.09	B / 8.4	11.4	1.75	13.0	15.58	30	-3.98	-2.64	N/A	2	0	89	9	8	30	N/A
5.48	3.03	B / 8.7	9.7	1.79	12.8	15.53	74	-4.57	-1.48	N/A	3	0	94	3	12	31	N/A
5.05	2.91	B / 8.8	9.5	1.61	11.1	15.67	167	-3.00	-0.70	N/A	2	0	94	4	7	38	2
5.80	1.75	B / 8.9	8.6	1.77	11.3	16.36	187	-6.42	-3.19	N/A	1	0	96	3	6	60	6
4.58	2.95	B / 8.4	13.9	1.42	11.9	14.80	34	8.11	16.37	N/A	1	0	97	2	13	30	N/A
7.60	1.44	B / 8.2	11.4	-1.73	N/A	27.62	347	-1.45	2.77	N/A	7	0	93	0	23	97	N/A
7.62	1.58	B / 8.3	N/A	N/A	N/A	27.92	105	-2.65	1.68	N/A	17	0	82	1	35	98	N/A
6.22	2.01	B / 8.4	11.3	2.10	10.5	15.82	627	-3.86	-1.65	N/A	3	0	91	6	14	27	11
6.53	1.40	B / 8.1	11.1	1.72	13.0	13.59	323	3.75	3.52	N/A	2	0	88	10	32	58	10
6.48	1.61	B / 8.2	10.5	1.73	12.3	13.18	199	1.82	0.86	N/A	6	0	80	14	17	66	N/A
4.85	0.77	B / 8.7	8.2	1.39	11.8	11.72	88	3.67	5.40	N/A	3	0	92	5	16	50	N/A
5.48	2.10	B / 8.5	9.6	2.17	10.7	15.38	623	-4.68	-2.67	N/A	2	0	94	4	14	27	11
5.71	1.63	B / 8.8	8.9	1.75	11.8	15.99	1,405	-4.13	-3.48	N/A	1	0	92	7	10	45	7
4.74	0.65	B+ / 9.0	5.9	1.34	12.1	10.35	1,915	-0.97	0.68	N/A	2	0	94	4	10	39	26
4.73	3.28	B / 8.8	8.7	1.39	11.0	15.43	97	-2.07	0.75	N/A	1	0	96	3	13	35	6
4.76	0.85	B / 8.6	9.4	1.46	N/A	16.92	26	1.30	-0.49	N/A	1	0	96	3	20	61	N/A
4.29	0.75	B / 8.7	8.5	1.48	N/A	16.42	38	-4.63	-2.45	N/A	1	0	92	7	10	38	N/A
4.54	2.52	B / 8.5	10.5	2.22	9.9	16.15	101	-5.02	-1.92	N/A	1	0	97	2	15	34	2

* Denotes ETF Fund, N/A denotes number is not available

					PRICE			PERFORMANCE						
	99 Pct = Best 0 Pct = Worst			Overall	Price As of 12/31/12	52 Week		Perform-ance Rating/Pts		% Total Return Through 12/31/12			Annualized	
Fund Type	Fund Name	Ticker Symbol		Investment Rating		High	Low			3 Mo	6 Mo	1Yr/Pct	3Yr/Pct	5Yr/Pct
MUS	Nuveen NJ Div Adv Muni Fund 2	NUJ		A-	16.34	17.48	13.94	B+ / 8.8		3.55	5.16	20.32 / 92	13.81 / 91	10.35 / 93
MUS	Nuveen NJ Investment Quality Muni	NQJ		B+	15.30	16.35	13.97	B / 7.7		0.10	3.96	15.01 / 80	12.37 / 86	9.86 / 90
MUS	Nuveen NJ Prem Inc Muni	NNJ		A+	16.53	17.87	14.58	B+ / 8.8		0.99	9.95	18.59 / 89	14.32 / 93	10.92 / 96
MUS	Nuveen NY AMT/Fr Muni Income	NRK		B	15.10	16.03	13.84	C+ / 6.8		2.95	5.80	12.63 / 69	9.82 / 73	7.31 / 74
MUS	Nuveen NY Div Adv Muni	NAN		A-	15.29	16.49	14.02	B / 7.8		0.64	6.40	13.05 / 71	12.43 / 87	8.92 / 85
MUS	Nuveen NY Div Adv Muni 2	NXK		B+	15.01	15.91	14.15	B / 7.6		1.40	5.87	12.65 / 69	12.07 / 84	8.76 / 84
MUS	Nuveen NY Div Adv Muni Income	NKO		B	14.87	16.07	14.30	C+ / 6.7		1.18	1.79	9.31 / 46	11.06 / 80	8.43 / 81
MUS	Nuveen NY Investment Quality Muni	NQN		B	15.46	16.14	14.49	C+ / 6.7		2.27	3.25	5.39 / 31	11.22 / 80	8.94 / 85
MUS	Nuveen NY Muni Value	NNY		C+	10.30	10.90	9.61	C / 4.6		0.22	2.69	8.58 / 42	7.99 / 59	7.58 / 76
MUS	Nuveen NY Performance Plus Muni	NNP		A	16.47	17.76	14.85	B+ / 8.5		2.36	8.89	14.67 / 78	13.34 / 90	10.26 / 92
MUS	Nuveen NY Prem Inc Muni	NNF		B	15.81	17.86	14.87	B- / 7.0		-1.74	1.11	6.73 / 35	12.29 / 86	9.33 / 88
MUS	Nuveen NY Quality Inc Muni	NUN		B+	15.19	16.38	14.50	B- / 7.2		2.94	4.74	7.03 / 36	11.79 / 83	9.04 / 85
MUS	Nuveen NY Select Quality Muni	NVN		B+	15.66	16.58	14.57	B / 7.9		4.03	6.80	10.12 / 50	12.37 / 86	9.79 / 90
MUS	Nuveen NY Select Tax-Free Inc Port	NXN		B	15.27	15.96	13.69	C+ / 6.1		3.48	4.69	11.36 / 60	8.92 / 68	7.15 / 73
MUS	Nuveen OH Div Adv Muni	NXI		A	16.31	18.00	14.79	B+ / 8.5		5.00	9.37	15.85 / 83	12.45 / 87	10.68 / 95
MUS	Nuveen OH Div Adv Muni 2	NBJ		A-	15.89	17.67	14.40	B / 8.2		2.30	7.66	19.59 / 91	11.48 / 81	9.54 / 89
MUS	Nuveen OH Div Adv Muni Fund 3	NVJ		B+	16.84	17.88	14.96	B / 7.7		3.89	9.11	15.66 / 82	10.34 / 76	9.60 / 89
MUS	Nuveen OH Quality Inc Muni	NUO		A+	19.05	20.09	16.05	A / 9.3		5.05	12.76	23.39 / 96	14.25 / 93	12.75 / 99
MUS	Nuveen PA Div Adv Muni	NXM		B+	15.04	15.98	13.71	B- / 7.5		-0.83	5.80	14.04 / 75	11.70 / 83	8.68 / 83
MUS	Nuveen PA Div Adv Muni Fund 2	NVY		B+	15.02	16.46	13.91	B- / 7.4		1.09	4.67	13.61 / 73	11.53 / 82	8.22 / 79
MUS	Nuveen PA Investment Quality Muni	NQP		A	15.64	16.83	14.52	B / 8.2		1.13	3.62	11.78 / 63	13.66 / 91	10.29 / 93
MUS	Nuveen PA Prem Inc Muni 2	NPY		A	15.08	15.81	13.40	B+ / 8.5		3.32	6.82	15.55 / 81	13.78 / 91	10.33 / 93
MUN	Nuveen Pennsylvania Municipal Valu	NPN		C+	15.75	16.68	14.85	C / 5.2		5.10	7.09	10.52 / 54	6.75 / 50	--
MUN	Nuveen Performance Plus Muni	NPP		A	16.17	17.47	14.62	B+ / 8.4		3.72	7.20	14.39 / 77	13.20 / 89	10.85 / 95
GL	Nuveen Preferred and Income Term	JPI		U	24.55	N/A	N/A	U /		0.69	--	--	--	--
GI	Nuveen Preferref Income Opps	JPC		A-	9.71	10.10	7.96	B+ / 8.4		2.13	9.64	34.75 / 95	18.80 / 85	8.31 / 61
MUN	Nuveen Prem Inc Muni	NPI		A-	14.97	15.94	13.75	B / 8.1		2.55	5.75	14.30 / 76	12.66 / 87	9.30 / 87
MUN	Nuveen Prem Inc Muni 4	NPT		A	14.11	15.02	12.62	B+ / 8.6		4.47	7.98	16.10 / 83	13.56 / 91	11.15 / 96
MUN	Nuveen Prem Inc Muni Oppty	NPX		A-	14.27	15.49	12.95	B / 8.0		3.55	5.87	13.91 / 75	12.08 / 84	9.69 / 90
MUN	Nuveen Premier Muni Inc	NPF		B+	14.92	15.81	14.08	B / 7.8		0.81	5.17	10.10 / 50	12.70 / 87	9.56 / 89
MUN	Nuveen Premier Muni Oppty	NIF		B-	15.34	16.73	14.43	C+ / 6.2		3.00	1.94	3.73 / 25	10.82 / 78	9.68 / 90
MUN	Nuveen Premium Income Muni 2	NPM		B+	15.20	16.12	14.07	B / 7.8		2.97	4.09	12.05 / 65	12.30 / 86	9.23 / 86
MUN	Nuveen Quality Inc Muni	NQU		B+	15.26	16.40	14.17	B / 7.7		3.60	4.68	13.68 / 74	11.71 / 83	9.25 / 87
MUN	Nuveen Quality Municipal	NQI		B	14.97	16.03	13.64	C+ / 6.7		0.19	6.00	12.12 / 66	10.39 / 77	8.54 / 82
IN	Nuveen Quality Preferred Income	JTP		B+	8.67	9.01	7.84	B- / 7.3		1.97	5.42	18.54 / 65	18.00 / 83	4.08 / 38
IN	Nuveen Quality Preferred Income 2	JPS		B	9.46	9.87	8.07	B- / 7.2		0.64	5.30	24.95 / 84	16.83 / 79	5.71 / 47
IN	Nuveen Quality Preferred Income 3	JHP		B	8.89	9.50	8.05	B- / 7.2		0.30	7.78	20.64 / 72	17.36 / 81	4.69 / 42
GL	Nuveen Real Asset Income and Growt	JRI		U	18.67	N/A	N/A	U /		1.48	10.41		--	--
GI	Nuveen Real Estate Inc Fund	JRS		B	10.48	12.00	9.50	B / 7.9		-3.06	3.49	15.95 / 52	20.72 / 90	7.35 / 57
MUN	Nuveen Select Maturities Muni	NIM		C-	10.39	11.37	10.08	D+ / 2.6		-2.17	0.81	1.44 / 19	4.57 / 36	6.79 / 71
MUN	Nuveen Select Quality Muni	NQS		B+	15.83	16.74	14.41	B / 7.8		1.59	7.10	12.45 / 68	12.20 / 85	9.67 / 90
MUN	Nuveen Select T-F Inc Portf	NXP		C	14.93	17.69	13.89	C- / 4.0		0.04	4.46	8.74 / 43	6.43 / 46	6.86 / 72
MUN	Nuveen Select T-F Inc Portf 2	NXQ		C	14.09	15.34	13.03	C- / 3.5		-2.30	1.37	11.52 / 61	5.53 / 40	6.65 / 70
MUN	Nuveen Select Tax-Free Inc 3	NXR		C	14.62	16.34	13.67	C- / 4.0		-2.51	3.13	11.25 / 60	6.59 / 48	7.75 / 77
GI	Nuveen Short Duration Credit Oppty	JSD		A	19.95	21.39	18.02	B / 8.1		3.02	9.57	21.15 / 74	--	--
LP	Nuveen Sr Inc	NSL		C	7.31	7.94	6.63	C / 5.0		3.52	10.06	20.65 / 72	9.68 / 46	9.03 / 65
IN	Nuveen Tax-Advant Tot Ret Strat Fd	JTA		C	10.51	11.75	9.55	C / 4.9		4.44	14.27	17.86 / 62	9.06 / 43	-2.31 / 13
GI	Nuveen Tax-Advantaged Dividend Grt	JTD		A-	14.50	15.35	12.47	B+ / 8.7		8.23	18.21	28.18 / 89	18.68 / 85	8.93 / 65
MUS	Nuveen TX Quality Inc Muni	NTX		C	15.84	17.44	15.43	C- / 3.9		-2.21	-1.15	3.75 / 25	7.65 / 57	9.55 / 89
MUS	Nuveen VA Premium Income Municipal	NPV		C	15.55	18.10	15.35	C- / 4.2		-0.99	-3.59	4.95 / 29	8.34 / 62	8.49 / 81
COH	Pacholder High Yield Fund	PHF		C+	8.87	10.13	7.90	B- / 7.0		-1.50	5.94	13.51 / 43	17.62 / 81	15.21 / 91
MTG	PCM Fund	PCM		A+	12.02	12.60	10.57	A- / 9.0		3.16	11.23	24.67 / 83	24.45 / 96	16.99 / 96

Incl. in Returns		RISK				NET ASSETS		VALUATION			ASSET					FUND MANAGER	
Dividend Yield %	Expense Ratio	Risk Rating/ Pts	3 Year Standard Deviation	3 Year Beta	Avg Dura-tion	NAV as of 12/31/12	Total $(Mil)	Premium/Discount As of 12/31/12	Premium/Discount 1 Year Average	Wtd Avg P/E	Cash %	Stocks %	Bonds %	Other %	Portfolio Turnover Ratio	Manager Quality Pct	Manager Tenure (Years)
4.41	2.52	B / 8.2	14.1	1.87	11.7	15.71	69	4.01	3.43	N/A	0	0	98	2	9	61	N/A
5.29	1.61	B / 8.6	9.8	1.91	11.3	15.84	313	-3.41	-0.83	N/A	3	0	95	2	9	47	N/A
5.15	1.64	B / 8.6	9.4	1.44	11.2	16.32	171	1.29	1.32	N/A	1	0	97	2	10	74	N/A
4.53	2.82	B+ / 9.0	7.7	1.48	14.1	15.29	54	-1.24	-2.39	N/A	1	0	96	3	15	46	N/A
4.94	2.37	B / 8.9	8.5	1.82	12.0	16.02	149	-4.56	-3.92	N/A	4	0	88	8	9	50	N/A
5.19	2.32	B / 8.9	8.4	1.78	11.8	15.85	104	-5.30	-4.17	N/A	3	0	90	7	10	47	N/A
5.25	1.68	B+ / 9.0	8.3	1.58	14.0	15.65	126	-4.98	-3.20	N/A	1	0	93	6	21	51	N/A
5.36	1.59	B / 8.8	10.1	1.85	11.9	15.78	279	-2.03	-2.42	N/A	2	0	90	8	12	43	N/A
3.85	0.65	B+ / 9.1	7.2	1.42	12.0	10.37	158	-0.68	-0.27	N/A	1	0	97	2	10	37	N/A
5.37	1.64	B+ / 9.0	8.8	1.64	11.6	16.72	253	-1.50	-1.20	N/A	2	0	89	9	11	62	N/A
5.28	1.70	B / 8.8	10.0	1.92	12.8	16.09	134	-1.74	-0.23	N/A	5	0	87	8	13	42	N/A
5.53	1.58	B / 8.9	10.1	1.85	13.6	15.77	379	-3.68	-2.62	N/A	1	0	92	7	19	40	N/A
5.56	1.59	B / 8.7	9.7	1.96	13.1	16.16	378	-3.09	-2.65	N/A	2	0	92	6	12	38	N/A
4.28	0.50	B+ / 9.1	7.8	1.53	12.1	14.83	57	2.97	0.16	N/A	1	0	96	3	19	42	N/A
4.78	3.07	B / 8.6	11.5	2.10	12.0	16.27	68	0.25	0.36	N/A	2	0	96	2	8	32	6
4.91	3.22	B / 8.7	10.2	1.95	11.9	16.00	49	-0.69	-0.46	N/A	1	0	96	3	9	40	6
4.70	3.42	B / 8.5	11.0	2.25	11.3	16.30	35	3.31	1.21	N/A	3	0	96	1	10	27	6
5.04	1.79	B / 8.8	9.1	1.39	11.5	17.67	171	7.81	4.66	N/A	2	0	97	1	6	71	N/A
5.03	2.55	B / 8.6	9.8	1.94	11.5	15.91	51	-5.47	-4.66	N/A	2	0	97	1	20	39	N/A
5.59	2.47	B / 8.7	10.0	1.70	11.8	15.58	57	-3.59	-2.03	N/A	5	0	94	1	11	53	N/A
5.68	1.63	B / 8.9	9.0	1.72	10.8	16.24	254	-3.69	-1.01	N/A	7	0	92	1	18	62	N/A
5.57	1.59	B / 8.8	8.9	1.84	11.2	15.49	236	-2.65	-3.58	N/A	5	0	94	1	8	59	N/A
4.04	0.86	B / 8.6	7.9	1.53	N/A	16.46	20	-4.31	-4.83	N/A	5	0	94	1	11	28	N/A
5.71	1.62	B / 8.7	9.9	1.97	10.1	16.80	893	-3.75	-1.72	N/A	4	0	95	1	10	41	11
6.61	N/A	U /	N/A	N/A	N/A	25.52	569	-3.80	N/A	N/A	0	0	0	100	N/A	N/A	1
6.52	1.86	B / 8.4	12.3	0.66	30.2	10.46	915	-7.17	-4.06	8.5	6	36	57	1	100	91	N/A
6.77	1.66	B / 8.8	9.2	1.58	11.3	15.50	900	-3.42	-1.36	N/A	9	0	90	1	9	59	7
6.78	1.99	B / 8.6	9.9	1.79	11.7	14.57	566	-3.16	-0.95	N/A	7	0	92	1	11	54	N/A
6.21	1.80	B / 8.7	10.1	2.07	12.4	14.91	506	-4.29	-2.29	N/A	2	0	91	7	20	32	N/A
6.63	1.55	B / 8.8	9.0	2.08	9.5	15.68	287	-4.85	-2.26	N/A	9	0	90	1	10	34	N/A
6.63	1.65	B / 8.3	14.1	2.46	10.5	16.11	287	-4.78	-0.57	N/A	9	0	90	1	8	20	7
6.76	1.48	B / 8.8	8.2	1.86	11.0	16.01	1,040	-5.06	-2.55	N/A	7	0	92	1	8	42	16
6.94	1.92	B / 8.7	9.0	1.99	11.3	16.22	781	-5.92	-1.91	N/A	5	0	94	1	16	33	11
6.85	1.66	B / 8.5	10.1	2.09	11.1	15.51	545	-3.48	-1.67	N/A	2	0	91	7	18	27	N/A
6.92	1.83	B / 8.9	12.1	0.28	13.7	9.13	557	-5.04	-1.10	20.4	8	0	0	92	21	95	N/A
6.98	1.80	B / 8.6	12.8	0.42	16.1	9.67	1,097	-2.17	-0.52	20.4	11	0	0	89	19	93	N/A
7.02	1.84	B / 8.5	13.5	0.43	16.3	9.40	209	-5.43	-0.53	20.4	13	0	0	87	23	92	N/A
8.33	N/A	U /	N/A	N/A	N/A	20.56	199	-9.19	N/A	N/A	0	0	0	100	N/A	N/A	1
6.78	1.93	B- / 7.4	19.1	0.93	10.6	10.70	306	-2.06	6.28	70.0	0	66	0	34	28	87	N/A
6.41	0.62	B / 8.6	10.3	1.52	9.2	10.66	130	-2.53	2.17	N/A	1	0	98	1	17	21	N/A
6.54	1.53	B / 8.5	9.8	2.07	10.8	16.01	491	-1.12	1.18	N/A	7	0	92	1	13	37	11
6.35	0.31	B / 8.7	8.8	1.65	10.2	15.13	241	-1.32	2.86	N/A	1	0	98	1	19	22	14
6.67	0.35	B / 8.7	7.8	1.59	10.9	14.42	246	-2.29	0.55	N/A	2	0	97	1	20	23	14
6.60	0.38	B / 8.7	9.0	1.51	10.4	15.02	188	-2.66	1.54	N/A	1	0	98	1	16	23	14
6.90	1.75	B / 8.9	N/A	N/A	N/A	19.77	195	0.91	-0.04	N/A	0	0	0	100	62	92	2
6.41	1.82	B / 8.0	14.0	-128.18	4.6	7.29	232	0.27	1.61	N/A	2	1	7	90	64	98	14
6.37	2.03	B / 8.0	18.3	0.90	0.7	12.21	156	-13.92	-8.89	18.7	7	68	0	25	20	40	9
6.17	1.87	B / 8.3	14.4	0.80	8.7	15.62	196	-7.17	-6.36	33.9	4	72	1	23	50	86	N/A
6.62	2.40	B+ / 9.0	8.6	1.35	11.1	15.88	152	-0.25	5.93	N/A	2	0	97	1	7	39	N/A
6.88	2.78	B / 8.5	11.0	2.04	10.8	15.65	141	-0.64	5.26	N/A	5	0	94	1	12	19	N/A
6.47	1.16	B- / 7.4	14.0	0.86	31.9	8.73	106,346	1.60	10.15	N/A	0	0	100	0	28	83	N/A
6.76	2.64	B / 8.8	12.1	-0.06	N/A	11.57	118	3.89	8.27	N/A	1	0	97	2	3	98	12

Denotes ETF Fund, N/A denotes number is not available

				PRICE			PERFORMANCE					
99 Pct = Best 0 Pct = Worst			Overall Investment Rating	Price As of 12/31/12	52 Week		Perform-ance Rating/Pts	% Total Return Through 12/31/12			Annualized	
Fund Type	Fund Name	Ticker Symbol			High	Low		3 Mo	6 Mo	1Yr/Pct	3Yr/Pct	5Yr/Pc
EN	Petroleum and Resources Corp.	PEO	D+	23.92	27.26	22.07	C- / 3.3	1.03	9.83	7.74 / 29	7.70 / 37	1.43 / 2
MUS	PIMCO CA Municipal Income Fund	PCQ	A+	15.93	17.10	13.26	A+ / 9.6	8.60	5.56	24.29 / 96	17.46 / 98	8.79 / 8
MUS	PIMCO CA Municipal Income Fund II	PCK	A+	10.59	11.23	9.61	A / 9.3	3.82	6.34	21.87 / 94	16.47 / 97	3.12 / 4
MUS	PIMCO CA Municipal Income Fund III	PZC	A+	11.28	11.92	9.75	A- / 9.2	3.07	5.27	22.38 / 95	16.10 / 97	3.45 / 4
COH	PIMCO Corporate and Income Oppty	PTY	A	19.41	20.85	17.11	A- / 9.2	6.55	15.52	30.62 / 92	24.05 / 96	20.98 / 9
COH	PIMCO Corporate and ncome Strategy	PCN	B+	17.65	19.17	15.49	B+ / 8.7	4.42	14.53	27.45 / 87	20.62 / 90	17.26 / 9
GL	PIMCO Dynamic Income	PDI	U	29.24	N/A	N/A	U /	11.88	23.17		--	--
GL	PIMCO Global StocksPLUS&Inc	PGP	C+	17.83	22.42	15.35	C+ / 6.6	5.33	4.94	16.99 / 58	15.79 / 76	19.39 / 9
COH	PIMCO High Income Fund	PHK	C-	10.48	14.32	9.88	C / 5.1	-1.28	-7.03	7.74 / 30	14.96 / 72	14.83 / 8
GL	Pimco Income Opportunity Fund	PKO	A	29.12	30.61	25.71	B+ / 8.9	4.58	14.07	28.12 / 89	21.87 / 93	16.15 / 9
LP	PIMCO Income Strategy Fund	PFL	B	12.74	13.57	10.78	B+ / 8.3	7.01	16.76	35.82 / 96	15.40 / 74	8.40 / 8
LP	PIMCO Income Strategy Fund II	PFN	B+	11.05	11.95	9.52	B+ / 8.5	8.33	17.41	36.21 / 96	16.34 / 78	6.87 / 8
MUN	PIMCO Municipal Income Fund	PMF	A+	15.70	16.81	13.93	A- / 9.1	0.65	7.51	17.24 / 86	16.64 / 98	8.87 / 8
MUN	PIMCO Municipal Income Fund II	PML	A+	13.16	13.88	11.46	A- / 9.2	4.83	6.79	21.57 / 94	15.06 / 95	5.40 / 8
MUN	PIMCO Municipal Income Fund III	PMX	A+	12.33	13.45	11.20	B+ / 8.9	1.03	7.20	18.28 / 88	15.31 / 95	5.17 / 8
MUS	PIMCO NY Muni Income Fund	PNF	A-	12.28	13.01	10.55	B+ / 8.3	2.52	5.06	15.24 / 80	13.36 / 90	6.34 / 8
MUS	PIMCO NY Municipal Income Fund II	PNI	A+	12.78	14.73	11.50	B+ / 8.9	2.74	7.17	21.17 / 94	14.50 / 94	5.72 / 8
MUS	PIMCO NY Municipal Income Fund III	PYN	A	10.63	11.02	9.24	B+ / 8.3	3.35	5.08	16.44 / 84	12.91 / 88	2.09 / 8
MTG	PIMCO Strategic Glob Gov Fund	RCS	C+	11.35	12.82	10.00	C+ / 5.9	3.44	4.98	15.59 / 50	14.63 / 71	16.21 / 8
GL	Pioneer Diversified High Income Tr	HNW	C+	20.08	22.14	18.56	C+ / 6.9	2.78	7.82	18.33 / 64	16.21 / 77	13.90 / 8
LP	Pioneer Floating Rate Trust	PHD	C+	13.27	14.37	12.24	C+ / 5.8	2.71	9.52	18.29 / 64	12.80 / 62	6.33 / 8
GL	Pioneer High Income Trust	PHT	C	15.92	18.82	14.55	C+ / 5.7	0.45	1.48	4.77 / 23	15.91 / 76	16.71 / 8
MUH	Pioneer Municipal High Income Adv	MAV	A+	15.47	16.34	14.00	A / 9.3	3.34	9.00	18.62 / 90	16.94 / 98	11.36 / 8
MUH	Pioneer Municipal High Income Trus	MHI	A+	15.79	16.84	14.10	A / 9.3	5.43	11.97	20.52 / 93	15.03 / 95	11.53 / 8
COH	Prudential Sht Dur Hi Yield Fd Inc	ISD	U	18.92	N/A	N/A	U /	0.40	1.98	--	--	--
GEN	Putnam High Income Securities	PCF	D+	7.95	8.62	7.34	C- / 3.5	0.34	3.83	11.05 / 36	8.96 / 43	8.72 / 8
MUN	Putnam Managed Muni Inc Tr	PMM	A	8.06	8.60	7.24	A- / 9.0	1.32	7.72	19.05 / 90	15.20 / 95	10.54 / 8
GEN	Putnam Master Intermediate Inc Tr	PIM	D	5.06	5.27	4.56	D / 2.2	1.04	3.56	9.48 / 34	2.51 / 21	5.09 / 8
MUN	Putnam Muni Opp Tr	PMO	A-	12.95	14.01	11.91	B / 8.2	2.47	5.05	14.76 / 79	13.04 / 89	10.30 / 8
GEN	Putnam Premier Income Trust	PPT	D	5.46	5.90	5.18	D+ / 2.7	-2.50	3.18	12.10 / 39	5.70 / 31	7.45 / 8
UT	Reaves Utility Income Trust	UTG	C+	23.82	28.22	22.00	C+ / 5.8	-1.04	-2.80	3.95 / 22	17.13 / 80	9.57 / 8
GI	RENN Global Entrepreneurs Fund Inc	RCG	E+	1.42	2.21	1.26	E / 0.5	7.86	-9.58	-10.12 / 8	-16.89 / 5	-23.48 / 8
GI	RMR Real Estate Income	RIF	C+	18.21	19.13	13.72	B / 7.9	8.86	15.98	47.66 / 98	10.34 / 49	-5.54 / 8
GR	Royce Focus Trust	FUND	D+	6.60	7.44	5.94	C- / 3.2	6.93	14.54	11.86 / 38	5.81 / 32	2.67 / 8
GR	Royce Micro-Cap Trust	RMT	C+	9.45	9.95	8.25	C+ / 6.7	9.94	11.82	18.30 / 64	13.38 / 65	5.32 / 8
GR	Royce Value Trust	RVT	C+	13.42	14.40	11.87	C+ / 6.9	11.37	15.14	16.88 / 57	13.30 / 65	4.66 / 8
IN	Salient Midstream and MLP Fund	SMM	U	0.00	N/A	N/A	U /	0.86	0.66		--	--
EN	Salient MLP & Energy Infrastructur	SMF	C	0.00	26.99	23.31	C / 4.3	1.54	2.65	13.79 / 44	--	--
FO	Singapore Fund	SGF	C	13.98	14.37	11.42	C+ / 6.0	7.13	13.88	29.60 / 90	9.22 / 44	4.62 / 8
IN	Source Capital	SOR	C+	52.22	55.36	45.55	B- / 7.2	10.95	14.25	19.78 / 70	14.00 / 69	7.23 / 8
MUN	Special Opportunities Fund	SPE	B	15.01	16.38	14.23	C+ / 6.3	6.24	10.53	11.86 / 64	7.41 / 55	8.31 / 8
EM	Stone Harbor Emg Markets Income	EDF	A-	24.76	25.60	22.03	B+ / 8.7	5.27	11.93	21.77 / 76	--	--
GL	Stone Harbor Emg Markets Total Inc	XEDIX	U	24.52	N/A	N/A	U /	--	--	--	--	--
GL	Strategic Global Income Fund	SGL	B-	10.97	11.48	10.10	B- / 7.1	2.49	8.45	17.39 / 60	16.91 / 79	14.25 / 8
FO	Swiss Helvetia Fund	SWZ	C-	11.29	11.78	9.60	C / 5.0	7.32	16.86	16.97 / 58	8.41 / 40	-0.37 / 8
FO	Taiwan Fund	TWN	D+	16.34	17.72	14.15	C- / 3.5	3.66	12.21	13.97 / 45	6.13 / 33	1.58 / 8
GI	TCW Strategic Income Fund	TSI	A	5.36	5.89	4.80	A- / 9.2	3.36	15.69	28.58 / 89	24.58 / 97	23.35 / 8
FO	Templeton Dragon Fund	TDF	C	28.44	29.35	24.63	C / 5.4	13.09	21.56	17.06 / 58	10.42 / 50	9.61 / 8
EM	Templeton Emerging Markets Fd	EMF	D	20.00	21.56	16.28	D / 2.2	11.64	19.64	10.51 / 36	-0.16 / 14	4.31 / 8
EM	Templeton Emerging Markets Income	TEI	B-	17.31	17.99	14.52	B- / 7.4	5.68	11.79	22.22 / 77	15.55 / 75	16.23 / 8
GL	Templeton Global Income Fd	GIM	C-	9.44	10.19	8.82	C- / 3.5	2.87	6.02	5.35 / 24	9.12 / 44	11.81 / 8
FO	Templeton Russia&East European Fun	TRF	E+	14.63	18.11	12.67	E+ / 0.8	-2.14	9.05	5.16 / 24	-9.47 / 7	-10.85 / 8

| Incl. in Returns | | RISK | | | | NET ASSETS | | VALUATION | | | ASSET | | | | | FUND MANAGER | |
| Dividend Yield % | Expense Ratio | Risk Rating/ Pts | 3 Year | | Avg Dura-tion | NAV as of 12/31/12 | Total $(Mil) | Premium / Discount | | Wtd Avg P/E | Cash % | Stocks % | Bonds % | Other % | Portfolio Turnover Ratio | Manager Quality Pct | Manager Tenure (Years) |
			Standard Deviation	Beta				As of 12/31/12	1 Year Average								
3.01	0.70	B- / 7.3	23.8	1.02	N/A	28.86	710	-17.12	-13.18	18.5	3	97	0	0	11	33	3
5.80	1.36	B / 8.3	13.1	2.28	14.4	14.60	254	9.11	8.32	N/A	0	0	100	0	9	61	2
7.08	1.44	B / 8.7	10.3	2.11	13.2	9.14	273	15.86	19.12	N/A	1	0	98	1	25	64	2
6.38	1.34	B / 8.6	12.9	2.07	14.7	10.36	225	8.88	9.33	N/A	0	0	100	0	10	65	2
26.46	1.12	B- / 7.8	18.2	1.41	N/A	16.91	1,046	14.78	19.68	N/A	0	0	94	6	12	83	N/A
15.84	1.30	B- / 7.9	16.3	1.47	N/A	16.29	515	8.35	15.87	N/A	11	0	84	5	32	66	N/A
24.21	N/A	U /	N/A	N/A	N/A	30.06	1,311	-2.73	N/A	N/A	0	0	0	100	N/A	N/A	N/A
12.34	2.71	C+ / 6.8	23.9	0.75	N/A	14.03	129	27.08	67.14	N/A	1	0	98	1	90	87	8
13.96	1.16	C+ / 6.8	20.4	1.74	N/A	8.49	960	23.44	60.34	N/A	3	0	95	2	24	16	N/A
24.55	2.44	B / 8.4	12.9	0.61	N/A	28.71	360	1.43	7.21	N/A	0	0	94	6	194	96	6
32.65	1.85	B- / 7.6	15.9	-227.70	N/A	12.32	283	3.41	7.15	N/A	28	0	72	0	23	99	N/A
58.82	1.48	B / 8.1	13.9	-138.62	N/A	10.68	598	3.46	4.88	N/A	35	0	65	0	17	98	4
6.21	1.28	B / 8.5	11.0	1.67	14.5	13.82	327	13.60	17.21	N/A	4	0	96	0	18	78	2
5.93	1.19	B / 8.5	12.6	2.43	14.7	12.48	722	5.45	6.77	N/A	8	0	92	0	26	44	2
6.81	1.27	B / 8.8	10.4	1.54	13.9	11.23	357	9.80	15.53	N/A	8	0	92	0	25	77	2
5.57	1.37	B / 8.6	11.5	2.17	13.7	12.07	87	1.74	4.85	N/A	7	0	93	0	21	33	2
6.23	1.45	B / 8.5	10.6	2.06	14.3	11.76	124	8.67	11.24	N/A	9	0	91	0	18	42	2
5.93	1.64	B / 8.7	11.1	2.01	14.5	9.71	54	9.47	8.80	N/A	0	0	100	0	16	53	2
32.64	1.55	B / 8.4	15.4	4.47	13.1	9.59	377	18.35	23.53	N/A	2	0	97	1	147	19	8
1.16	2.04	B- / 7.2	14.0	0.28	23.9	20.32	161	-1.18	4.75	N/A	3	0	96	1	24	94	N/A
6.78	1.58	B / 8.1	15.4	-218.30	4.2	13.17	315	0.76	1.27	N/A	0	5	8	87	20	99	N/A
10.36	1.05	B- / 7.4	12.4	0.53	22.4	13.97	380	13.96	29.07	9.0	0	0	93	7	24	93	N/A
7.37	1.36	B / 8.4	10.6	1.87	15.4	13.80	300	12.10	15.38	N/A	2	0	97	1	15	76	N/A
7.85	1.08	B / 8.4	9.5	1.58	13.8	14.85	318	6.33	8.47	N/A	2	0	97	1	11	71	N/A
7.77	N/A	U /	N/A	N/A	N/A	19.33	635	-2.12	N/A	N/A	0	0	0	100	N/A	N/A	1
5.89	0.93	B- / 7.0	14.0	-0.50	14.2	8.69	141	-8.52	-1.06	8.6	2	2	40	56	36	94	N/A
5.79	1.03	B / 8.4	9.1	1.58	12.0	8.14	424	-0.98	1.23	N/A	1	0	98	1	17	73	24
6.17	0.96	C+ / 6.2	10.2	0.79	12.0	5.58	356	-9.32	-5.80	22.9	0	0	100	0	157	32	19
5.18	0.99	B / 8.7	9.0	1.97	10.6	13.59	556	-4.71	-1.59	N/A	1	0	98	1	21	44	11
5.71	0.88	C+ / 6.0	13.4	0.87	17.0	5.96	818	-8.39	-4.55	22.9	0	0	100	0	153	50	21
6.61	1.93	B / 8.7	15.0	0.78	4.4	25.03	545	-4.83	2.54	24.0	1	97	0	2	34	88	9
0.00	5.25	C / 4.7	32.9	0.60	N/A	2.55	10	-44.31	-33.26	N/A	1	87	0	12	7	4	19
6.81	1.86	C+ / 5.6	23.7	1.21	N/A	21.44	153,779	-15.07	-16.23	N/A	3	97	0	0	331	25	N/A
10.30	1.34	B- / 7.2	22.9	1.29	N/A	7.81	149	-15.49	-12.57	34.4	13	86	0	1	11	17	17
5.50	1.50	B- / 7.3	22.7	1.35	N/A	11.31	293	-16.45	-12.76	46.7	11	88	0	1	13	38	20
7.15	0.68	B- / 7.0	23.8	1.44	N/A	16.00	992	-16.13	-12.62	38.6	6	93	0	1	13	29	27
6.05	N/A	U /	N/A	N/A	N/A	0.00	188		N/A	N/A	0	0	0	100	N/A	N/A	1
7.13	N/A	B / 8.3	N/A	N/A	N/A	0.00	151		2.75	N/A	0	0	0	100	N/A	94	2
1.13	1.83	C+ / 6.5	24.6	0.93	N/A	15.60	138	-10.38	-9.94	N/A	0	95	0	5	76	78	2
1.34	0.98	B- / 7.2	21.2	1.24	5.0	60.89	472	-14.24	-11.15	24.0	4	89	4	3	12	49	17
5.00	1.61	B+ / 9.1	9.7	-0.62	6.5	17.77	115	-15.53	-9.80	317.7	10	0	89	1	30	89	N/A
8.00	1.76	B / 8.0	N/A	N/A	N/A	24.65	335	0.45	3.57	N/A	0	0	0	100	57	95	N/A
4.55	N/A	U /	N/A	N/A	N/A	25.29	239	-3.04	N/A	N/A	0	0	0	100	N/A	N/A	1
4.83	1.16	B- / 7.9	13.1	1.10	7.8	11.66	203	-5.92	-5.66	N/A	3	0	96	1	74	91	N/A
0.94	1.46	C+ / 6.5	19.0	0.85	N/A	13.70	362	-17.59	-12.33	N/A	0	96	0	4	17	73	17
0.00	1.61	C+ / 6.9	24.6	0.91	N/A	18.44	155	-11.39	-8.22	N/A	0	95	0	5	75	69	N/A
1.38	1.39	B / 8.2	10.5	0.39	14.8	5.71	253	-6.13	-2.22	N/A	0	0	89	11	10	96	N/A
2.01	1.33	B- / 7.3	19.5	0.72	N/A	32.16	1,090	-11.57	-10.59	62.3	0	99	0	1	1	81	19
1.44	1.37	C+ / 6.5	27.8	1.19	N/A	21.99	348	-9.05	-7.77	N/A	0	80	0	20	2	25	22
6.04	1.15	B- / 7.4	15.3	1.02	6.1	16.06	759	7.78	3.74	N/A	4	0	95	1	17	92	N/A
3.08	0.75	B- / 7.7	16.5	1.28	N/A	9.21	1,209	2.50	4.26	N/A	5	0	94	1	39	75	25
1.08	1.59	C / 5.1	31.4	1.29	N/A	16.35	102	-10.52	-8.91	N/A	16	82	0	2	8	11	18

* Denotes ETF Fund, N/A denotes number is not available

				PRICE			PERFORMANCE					
	99 Pct = Best 0 Pct = Worst			Price	52 Week		Perform-ance	% Total Return Through 12/31/12				
			Overall	As of							Annualized	
Fund Type	Fund Name	Ticker Symbol	Investment Rating	12/31/12	High	Low	Rating/Pts	3 Mo	6 Mo	1Yr/Pct	3Yr/Pct	5Yr/Pct
FO	Thai Capital Fund	TF	B-	12.11	13.07	8.86	A+ / 9.7	15.30	28.83	49.86 / 98	28.26 / 99	15.14 / 90
FO	Thai Fund	TTF	A+	19.95	20.99	12.65	A+ / 9.8	16.85	30.78	69.21 / 99	36.28 / 99	19.11 / 99
GI	The Cushing MLP Total Return Fund	SRV	D	7.17	10.65	6.95	D- / 1.4	-8.70	-5.53	-9.87 / 8	3.53 / 24	-3.44 / 10
GI	The Denali Fund Inc.	DNY	C+	16.22	17.21	13.65	C+ / 6.1	5.57	17.30	23.62 / 81	10.54 / 51	5.91 / 49
FO	The European Equity Fund	EEA	C	7.03	7.31	5.64	C+ / 5.8	11.40	24.73	34.49 / 95	4.51 / 28	-3.58 / 10
FO	The New Ireland Fund	IRL	B-	9.10	10.50	6.90	B- / 7.5	10.11	29.18	35.49 / 95	8.65 / 41	-2.48 / 12
EN	Tortoise Energy Capital	TYY	C	0.00	30.11	23.89	C+ / 6.9	4.57	12.61	16.30 / 54	15.21 / 73	10.47 / 71
GL	Tortoise Energy Independence Fund	NDP	U	0.00	N/A	N/A	U /	-4.55	--	--	--	--
EN	Tortoise Energy Infrastr Corp	TYG	C	0.00	42.79	36.17	C+ / 5.8	0.67	2.65	5.90 / 26	15.88 / 76	12.84 / 80
GR	Tortoise MLP Fund Inc	NTG	C-	0.00	27.49	22.87	C- / 3.0	2.09	4.41	6.14 / 26	--	--
EN	Tortoise North American Energy	TYN	C	0.00	27.77	22.81	C / 5.5	5.27	10.97	16.38 / 54	11.62 / 56	10.71 / 72
EN	Tortoise Pipeline & Enrgy Fund Inc	TTP	B	0.00	26.28	21.82	C+ / 6.8	2.31	12.74	13.89 / 44	--	--
EN	Tortoise Power and Energy Inf Fund	TPZ	B	0.00	26.69	23.21	C+ / 6.8	5.25	7.84	9.55 / 34	17.06 / 80	--
GL	Transamerica Income Shares	TAI	C	23.24	26.35	21.34	C- / 4.2	-1.24	-0.91	13.72 / 44	11.99 / 58	11.49 / 75
IN	Tri-Continental Corporation	TY	B-	16.05	16.86	14.51	B- / 7.0	4.44	10.26	18.59 / 65	15.56 / 75	3.02 / 32
FO	Turkish Investment Fund	TKF	B-	16.64	18.46	11.50	B+ / 8.7	17.36	26.94	53.41 / 99	10.07 / 47	1.93 / 26
GL	Virtus Global Multi-Sector Income	VGI	U	18.90	N/A	N/A	U /	2.58	9.24	--	--	--
GI	Virtus Total Return	DCA	A+	3.87	4.15	3.32	A / 9.4	6.53	13.52	26.28 / 86	27.38 / 99	-3.14 / 11
GL	Wells Fargo Avtg Global Div Oppty	EOD	D+	7.57	9.33	6.89	D+ / 2.3	-5.03	4.99	13.62 / 43	2.99 / 23	-1.41 / 15
COH	Wells Fargo Avtg Income Oppty	EAD	C-	10.07	11.88	9.21	C / 4.6	-0.01	5.52	11.48 / 37	12.06 / 58	11.30 / 74
GL	Wells Fargo Avtg Multi-Sector Inc	ERC	C+	16.17	16.88	14.65	C+ / 5.7	0.74	9.45	19.18 / 68	12.87 / 62	12.13 / 77
UT	Wells Fargo Avtg Utilities&High In	ERH	D	11.18	12.43	10.29	D- / 1.3	-2.15	3.54	5.97 / 26	-1.60 / 12	-6.74 / 7
EM	Western Asset Emerging Market Debt	ESD	B+	21.80	22.84	18.90	B- / 7.5	4.13	9.81	24.80 / 83	16.24 / 77	13.89 / 85
EM	Western Asset Emerging Mkts Inc	EMD	C+	15.32	16.70	13.37	C+ / 6.1	-3.24	7.56	22.25 / 77	14.65 / 71	13.11 / 82
GL	Western Asset Global Corp Def Oppt	GDO	B-	20.75	23.75	18.37	C+ / 5.6	4.36	10.48	22.16 / 77	10.90 / 52	--
GL	Western Asset Global High Income	EHI	B-	13.78	14.12	12.39	B- / 7.2	2.09	8.21	19.75 / 70	16.91 / 80	14.07 / 86
GL	Western Asset Global Partners Inc	GDF	C	12.65	14.05	11.51	C / 4.7	-1.39	8.10	11.39 / 37	12.02 / 58	15.60 / 92
GL	Western Asset High Inc Fd II	HIX	C	9.66	10.76	8.85	C / 4.8	-0.65	4.87	13.92 / 45	12.68 / 62	14.44 / 88
COH	Western Asset High Income Fund	HIF	C	9.41	10.14	8.52	C- / 4.0	2.75	5.94	14.98 / 48	9.17 / 44	11.87 / 76
COH	Western Asset High Income Opp Inc.	HIO	C+	6.44	6.84	4.72	C+ / 5.7	3.66	8.47	17.36 / 60	12.71 / 62	14.18 / 86
COH	Western Asset High Yld Def Opp	HYI	C	18.33	19.97	17.28	C / 4.8	0.82	2.10	16.05 / 53	--	--
GEI	Western Asset Income Fund	PAI	C+	14.82	16.39	13.34	C / 4.4	-2.70	6.76	17.35 / 60	10.94 / 52	8.15 / 60
GL	Western Asset Inflation Mgmt	IMF	C	18.79	19.20	17.57	C- / 3.3	-0.90	3.34	8.10 / 30	8.76 / 42	6.55 / 52
MUN	Western Asset Intermediate Muni	SBI	B+	10.58	11.18	9.52	B- / 7.5	1.80	4.64	14.89 / 79	11.27 / 81	9.32 / 88
COH	Western Asset Managed High Income	MHY	C	6.17	6.77	5.75	C / 4.7	2.80	5.34	13.71 / 44	11.52 / 56	13.27 / 82
MUN	Western Asset Managed Municipals	MMU	A+	14.37	16.42	12.72	B+ / 8.9	5.59	7.89	18.73 / 90	14.08 / 92	13.66 / 99
MTG	Western Asset Mtge Defined Oppty	DMO	A+	24.21	26.99	19.70	A+ / 9.8	4.76	22.79	46.13 / 98	--	--
MUN	Western Asset Municipal Defined Op	MTT	B	23.06	25.23	21.14	B- / 7.0	3.77	4.78	14.02 / 75	10.03 / 74	--
MUH	Western Asset Municipal High Inc	MHF	C+	7.92	9.27	7.39	C / 5.4	-1.29	3.28	10.45 / 53	9.21 / 69	8.45 / 81
MUN	Western Asset Municipal Partners	MNP	A+	17.22	18.32	15.05	A- / 9.2	3.08	7.75	19.70 / 91	16.43 / 97	11.89 / 98
GEI	Western Asset Premier Bond Fund	WEA	B-	15.54	16.88	14.43	C+ / 6.8	0.43	6.46	9.83 / 34	17.58 / 81	15.23 / 91
GL	Western Asset Var Rt Strat Fd	GFY	B-	17.76	18.95	14.95	B- / 7.5	4.21	13.55	30.70 / 92	13.93 / 69	8.63 / 63
EM	Western Asset Worldwide Inc Fd	SBW	C+	15.12	16.59	13.51	C+ / 5.8	-1.41	7.88	20.75 / 73	13.68 / 67	12.05 / 77
USA	Western Asset/Claymore Inf-Link O&	WIW	C	13.20	13.58	12.66	D+ / 2.9	0.51	1.26	7.11 / 28	7.16 / 36	6.62 / 52
USA	Western Asset/Claymore Inf-Link S&	WIA	C-	13.11	13.40	12.57	D+ / 2.5	-0.20	1.14	6.30 / 27	5.33 / 31	5.81 / 48
COI	Western Asst Invst Grade Define Op	IGI	C+	23.05	24.89	20.77	C / 5.5	1.04	8.53	16.57 / 55	13.04 / 63	--
IN	Zweig Fund	ZF	C-	12.16	13.24	11.28	C- / 3.4	1.36	8.26	10.78 / 36	7.72 / 38	3.50 / 35
GI	Zweig Total Return Fund	ZTR	D+	12.31	13.24	11.88	D+ / 2.6	2.71	8.01	11.71 / 38	3.25 / 23	3.83 / 37

I. Index of ETFs and Other Closed-End Funds

Column groups: **RISK** (Incl. in Returns: Dividend Yield %, Expense Ratio; Risk Rating/Pts; 3 Year: Standard Deviation, Beta; Avg Duration) · **NET ASSETS** (NAV as of 12/31/12, Total $(Mil)) · **VALUATION** (Premium/Discount: As of 12/31/12, 1 Year Average; Wtd Avg P/E) · **ASSET** (Cash %, Stocks %, Bonds %, Other %) · Portfolio Turnover Ratio · **FUND MANAGER** (Manager Quality Pct, Manager Tenure (Years))

Dividend Yield %	Expense Ratio	Risk Rating / Pts	Std Dev (3 Yr)	Beta (3 Yr)	Avg Duration	NAV as of 12/31/12	Total $(Mil)	Prem/Disc As of 12/31/12	Prem/Disc 1 Yr Avg	Wtd Avg P/E	Cash %	Stocks %	Bonds %	Other %	Portfolio Turnover Ratio	Mgr Quality Pct	Mgr Tenure (Yrs)
0.00	2.32	C / 5.1	24.8	0.75	N/A	12.80	41	-5.39	-7.59	N/A	2	97	0	1	51	97	N/A
1.66	1.39	B- / 7.8	25.2	0.80	N/A	23.34	271	-14.52	-12.77	N/A	5	94	0	1	10	98	5
12.55	5.07	C+ / 6.7	19.0	0.71	4.8	6.64	216	7.98	25.23	41.2	0	90	9	1	73	31	N/A
0.00	2.64	B- / 7.8	16.8	0.82	N/A	21.37	75	-24.10	-19.58	N/A	26	65	0	9	7	48	N/A
8.65	1.75	C+ / 6.4	25.5	1.19	N/A	8.16	73	-13.85	-9.99	N/A	0	100	0	0	53	39	N/A
0.00	2.22	B- / 7.4	22.8	0.91	N/A	10.77	54	-15.51	-12.29	N/A	0	94	0	6	23	80	4
5.87	4.01	C+ / 6.3	18.3	0.61	N/A	0.00	485		2.91	29.5	0	100	0	0	4	87	8
4.87	N/A	U /	N/A	N/A	N/A	0.00	N/A		N/A	N/A	0	0	0	100	N/A	N/A	1
5.96	3.40	C+ / 6.6	16.2	0.59	N/A	0.00	907		13.52	31.0	0	100	0	0	5	87	9
6.78	2.34	B- / 7.8	N/A	N/A	N/A	0.00	1,086		2.79	N/A	0	100	0	0	4	21	N/A
6.17	1.90	C+ / 6.9	11.9	0.33	N/A	0.00	150		-0.10	31.7	0	100	0	0	8	87	6
6.69	2.33	B / 8.6	N/A	N/A	N/A	0.00	238		-3.33	N/A	0	100	0	0	8	87	2
5.96	1.73	B / 8.3	12.2	0.36	N/A	0.00	176		-3.77	N/A	0	0	0	100	12	87	N/A
5.16	0.78	B / 8.6	13.3	0.25	N/A	23.18	140	0.26	3.03	N/A	2	97	0	1	8	91	N/A
4.74	0.59	B / 8.1	17.3	1.10	5.1	19.28	1,148	-16.75	-14.38	45.9	2	0	90	8	33	92	N/A
1.37	1.18	C+ / 5.9	29.1	1.05	N/A	19.89	113	-16.34	-10.95	N/A	0	99	0	1	38	69	3
6.69	N/A	U /	N/A	N/A	N/A	20.41	229	-7.40	N/A	N/A	5	94	0	1	29	79	16
6.46	1.90	B / 8.2	24.3	1.13	17.3	4.48	115	-13.62	-11.51	26.0	0	0	0	100	N/A	N/A	1
11.10	1.08	B- / 7.3	18.3	0.68	N/A	8.29	405	-8.69	-2.58	13.9	6	70	7	17	18	91	N/A
9.18	1.03	B- / 7.3	12.4	1.17	6.3	10.08	684	-0.10	5.32	N/A	4	60	0	36	93	46	N/A
7.42	1.24	B / 8.7	11.0	0.55	7.6	17.30	715	-6.53	-5.54	N/A	5	0	94	1	25	46	N/A
8.05	1.20	C+ / 6.5	21.1	0.48	5.5	11.93	108	-6.29	-0.11	24.0	1	0	98	1	78	91	N/A
6.61	1.03	B / 8.6	11.5	0.75	10.9	22.35	654	-2.46	-4.19	N/A	9	52	28	11	48	22	9
6.66	1.25	B / 8.1	14.1	1.08	10.6	15.78	423	-2.92	-2.95	N/A	0	0	99	1	7	93	N/A
2.44	1.40	B / 8.9	10.6	0.69	N/A	21.05	291	-1.43	-1.80	N/A	3	0	96	1	19	90	N/A
8.39	1.50	B- / 7.7	11.9	0.73	10.1	14.06	395	-1.99	0.22	12.7	3	0	96	1	16	84	N/A
9.01	1.53	B- / 7.5	16.7	0.75	17.4	12.60	188	0.40	6.99	N/A	4	0	95	1	33	94	N/A
9.94	1.51	B- / 7.9	11.7	0.57	13.4	9.43	756	2.44	13.16	12.7	3	0	96	1	37	90	N/A
7.59	1.18	B / 8.5	11.4	0.76	N/A	9.79	48	-3.88	2.13	N/A	3	0	96	1	45	91	N/A
7.73	0.88	B- / 7.6	11.1	1.09	14.8	6.45	473	-0.16	4.33	N/A	3	0	97	0	36	61	7
9.17	0.89	B- / 7.9	N/A	N/A	N/A	19.43	417	-5.66	3.17	N/A	3	0	96	1	53	45	7
4.66	0.75	B+ / 9.0	9.2	0.31	23.5	15.11	135	-1.92	1.06	N/A	0	0	99	1	53	16	N/A
2.93	0.78	B+ / 9.5	5.4	0.10	N/A	20.08	141	-6.42	-8.29	N/A	0	0	99	1	45	88	N/A
4.54	0.92	B+ / 9.1	7.4	1.15	8.1	10.53	145	0.47	0.57	N/A	4	0	95	1	26	89	7
7.78	0.92	B- / 7.6	11.5	0.97	15.0	6.24	283	-1.12	5.27	N/A	4	0	96	0	7	73	N/A
5.43	0.90	B / 8.7	11.3	1.68	N/A	14.46	595	-0.62	3.21	N/A	3	0	97	0	24	57	N/A
7.43	2.24	B / 8.5	N/A	N/A	N/A	24.70	197	-1.98	3.69	N/A	1	0	98	1	12	59	21
4.37	0.68	B / 8.7	9.0	1.56	N/A	23.29	272	-0.99	3.05	N/A	1	0	98	1	13	98	N/A
5.00	0.68	B / 8.7	10.8	1.87	13.6	8.21	164	-3.53	2.68	N/A	0	0	99	1	1	37	N/A
4.88	1.16	B / 8.7	10.2	2.08	11.7	16.87	160	2.07	1.92	N/A	0	0	100	0	10	26	N/A
8.11	1.10	B / 8.3	11.0	0.31	14.0	15.06	163	3.19	14.05	N/A	4	0	95	1	7	62	N/A
4.90	1.20	B- / 7.5	9.5	0.15	11.0	18.89	123	-5.98	-4.98	N/A	0	0	99	1	14	94	N/A
6.67	1.29	B / 8.2	12.8	1.00	14.2	16.14	201	-6.32	-5.41	N/A	0	0	99	1	18	92	N/A
2.79	0.70	B+ / 9.6	5.3	0.05	N/A	14.90	897	-11.41	-10.83	N/A	0	0	91	9	8	88	N/A
2.68	0.72	B+ / 9.5	6.4	0.07	N/A	14.70	423	-10.82	-10.58	N/A	0	0	92	8	40	82	N/A
4.99	0.80	B / 8.9	9.3	1.10	N/A	22.66	230	1.72	3.47	N/A	0	0	99	1	34	79	9
7.01	1.13	B- / 7.6	15.7	0.91	N/A	14.13	314	-13.94	-11.53	58.6	14	81	3	2	40	35	10
7.99	0.92	B / 8.1	8.6	0.40	5.8	14.28	508	-13.80	-12.26	47.4	24	44	30	2	33	36	10

* Denotes ETF Fund, N/A denotes number is not available

Data as of December 31, 2012

Section II

Analysis of
ETFs and Other
Closed-End Funds

A summary analysis of all

Exchange-Traded Funds and

Other Closed-End Mutual Funds

receiving a TheStreet Investment Rating.

Funds are listed in alphabetical order.

Section II Contents

1. **Fund Name**

   The name of the mutual fund as stated in its prospectus, which can sometimes differ slightly from the name that the company uses for advertising. If you cannot find the paritcular mutual fund you are interested in, or if you have any doubts regarding the precise name, verify the information with your broker or on your account statement. Also, use the fund's ticker symbol for confirmation.

2. **Ticker Symbol**

   The unique alphabetic symbol used for identifying and trading a specific mutual fund. No two funds can have the same ticker symbol.

3. **Investment Rating**

   Our overall rating is measured on a scale from A to E based on each fund's risk-adjusted performance. Please see page 10 for specific descriptions of each letter grade. Also refer to page 7 for information on how our ratings are derived. Most important, when using this rating, please be sure to consider the warnings beginning on page 11 regarding the ratings' limitations and the underlying assumptions.

4. **Fund Family**

   The umbrella group of mutual funds to which the fund belongs.

5. **Fund Type**

   The mutual fund's peer category based on an analysis of its investment portfolio.

COH	Corporate – High Yield	HL	Health
COI	Corporate – Inv. Grade	IN	Income
EM	Emerging Market	LP	Loan Participation
EN	Energy/Natural Resources	MTG	Mortgage
FS	Financial Services	MUH	Municipal – High Yield
FO	Foreign	MUN	Municipal – National
GEI	General – Inv. Grade	MUS	Municipal – Single State
GEN	General Bond	PM	Precious Metals
GL	Global	USA	U.S. Gov. – Agency
GR	Growth	UT	Utilities
GI	Growth and Income		

   A blank fund type means that the mutual fund has not yet been categorized.

6. **Inception Date**

   The date on which the fund began.

7. **Major Rating Factors**

   A synopsis of the key ratios and sub-factors that have most influenced the rating of a particular mutual fund, including an examination of the fund's performance, risk, and managerial performance. There may be additional factors which have influenced the rating but do not appear due to space limitations.

How to Read the Annualized Total Return Graph

The annualized total return graph provides a clearer picture of a fund's yearly financial performance. In addition to the solid line denoting the fund's calendar year returns for the last six years, the graph also shows the yearly return for a benchmark index for easy comparison using a dotted line. The S&P 500 Composite Index is used for ETFs and other closed-end mutual funds that are primarily invested in stocks. One of two indexes is shown for funds with the majority of their assets held in bonds. Municipal bond funds display the Lehman Brothers Municipals Index, and other bond funds will show the Lehman Brothers Aggregate Bond Index.

The top of the shaded area of the graph denotes the average returns for all funds within the same fund type. If the solid line falls into the shaded area, that means that the fund has performed below the average for its type.

How to Read the Historical Data Table

Data Date:
The quarter-end or year-end as of date used for evaluating the mutual fund.

Price:
The fund's share price as of the date indicated. A fund's price is determined by investor demand. The fund may trade at a price higher or lower than its net asset value (NAV).

Risk Rating/Pts:
A letter grade rating based solely on the mutual fund's risk as determined by its monthly performance volatility over the trailing three years. Pts are rating points where 0=worst and 10=best.

Data Date	Investment Rating	Net Assets ($Mil)	Price	Performance Rating/Pts	Total Return Y-T-D	Risk Rating/Pts
12-12	B+	126.6	8.91	A- / 9.2	52.38%	C+ / 6.0
2011	C+	178.56	7.43	C+ / 5.7	2.57%	C+ / 6.1
2010	B+	86.42	19.76	B / 7.8	8.78%	C+ / 6.8
2009	B	87.35	14.30	C / 5.4	4.71%	B / 8.3
2008	D+	284.1	6.90	C- / 3.2	5.19%	C / 4.6

Investment Rating:
Our overall opinion of the fund's risk-adjusted performance at the specified time period.

Net Assets $(Mil):
The total value of all of the fund's asset holdings (in millions) including stocks, bonds, cash, and other financial instruments, less accrued expenses and fees.

Performance Rating/Pts:
A letter grade rating based solely on the mutual fund's return to shareholders over the trailing three years, without any consideration for the amount of risk the fund poses. Pts are rating points where 0=worst and 10=best

Total Return Y-T-D:
The fund's total return to shareholders since the beginning of the calendar year specified.

---

*2x Levered CS Mrg Arb Lq Idx (CSMB)   D-   Weak

Fund Family: Credit Suisse Asset Management LLC
Fund Type: Growth and Income
Inception Date: March 7, 2011

Data Date	Investment Rating	Net Assets ($Mil)	Price	Performance Rating/Pts	Total Return Y-T-D	Risk Rating/Pts
12-12	D-	20.90	18.18	E+ / 0.9	0.94%	C / 5.2

Major Rating Factors:
Very poor performance is the major factor driving the D- (Weak) TheStreet.com Investment Rating for *2x Levered CS Mrg Arb Lq Idx. The fund currently has a performance rating of E+ (Very Weak) based on an annualized return of 0.00% over the last three years and a total return of 0.94% year to date 2012.

The fund's risk rating is currently C (Fair). It carries a beta of 0.00, meaning the fund's expected move will be 0.0% for every 10% move in the market. Volatility, as measured by both the semi-deviation and a drawdown factor, is considered average. As of December 31, 2012, *2x Levered CS Mrg Arb Lq Idx traded at a discount of 1.78% below its net asset value, which is better than its one-year historical average discount of .19%.

This fund has been team managed for 2 years and currently receives a manager quality ranking of 12 (0=worst, 99=best). This fund offers an average level of risk but investors looking for strong performance will be frustrated.

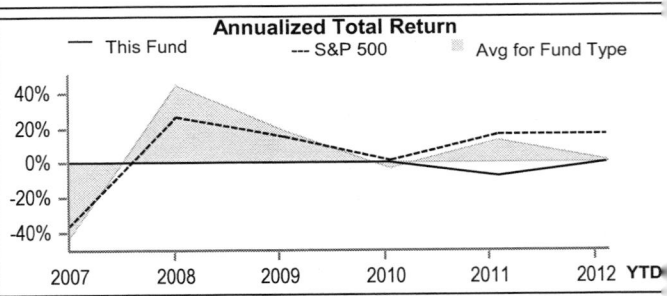

*Accuvest Global Long Short ETF (AGLS)   C-   Fair

Fund Family: AdvisorShares Investments LLC
Fund Type: Global
Inception Date: July 9, 2010

Data Date	Investment Rating	Net Assets ($Mil)	Price	Performance Rating/Pts	Total Return Y-T-D	Risk Rating/Pts
12-12	C-	23.92	22.38	C- / 3.4	0.63%	B- / 7.9

Major Rating Factors: Middle of the road best describes *Accuvest Global Long Short ETF whose TheStreet.com Investment Rating is currently a C- (Fair). The fund currently has a performance rating of C- (Fair) based on an annualized return of 0.00% year to date 2012. Factored into the performance evaluation is an expense ratio of 1.50% (average).

The fund's risk rating is currently B- (Good). It carries a beta of 0.00, meaning the fund's expected move will be 0.0% for every 10% move in the market. Volatility, as measured by both the semi-deviation and a drawdown factor, is considered low. As of December 31, 2012, *Accuvest Global Long Short ETF traded at a discount of .31% below its net asset value, which is better than its one-year historical average premium of .06%.

David A. Houle has been running the fund for 3 years and currently receives a manager quality ranking of 86 (0=worst, 99=best). If you desire an average level of risk, then this fund may be an option.

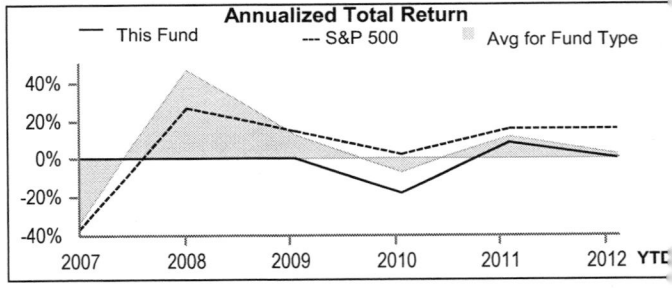

*Alps Alerian MLP ETF (AMLP)   C   Fair

Fund Family: ALPS Advisors Inc
Fund Type: Energy/Natural Resources
Inception Date: August 25, 2010

Data Date	Investment Rating	Net Assets ($Mil)	Price	Performance Rating/Pts	Total Return Y-T-D	Risk Rating/Pts
12-12	C	4,449.10	15.95	C- / 3.3	4.89%	B+ / 9.0
2011	B-	1,989.90	16.62	C+ / 6.0	0.60%	B+ / 9.2

Major Rating Factors: Middle of the road best describes *Alps Alerian MLP ETF whose TheStreet.com Investment Rating is currently a C (Fair). The fund currently has a performance rating of C- (Fair) based on an annualized return of 0.00% over the last three years and a total return of 4.89% year to date 2012. Factored into the performance evaluation is an expense ratio of 0.85% (very low).

The fund's risk rating is currently B+ (Good). It carries a beta of 0.00, meaning the fund's expected move will be 0.0% for every 10% move in the market. Volatility, as measured by both the semi-deviation and a drawdown factor, is considered very low. As of December 31, 2012, *Alps Alerian MLP ETF traded at a discount of 4.55% below its net asset value, which is better than its one-year historical average premium of .06%.

Michael Akins has been running the fund for 2 years and currently receives a manager quality ranking of 51 (0=worst, 99=best). If you desire an average level of risk, then this fund may be an option.

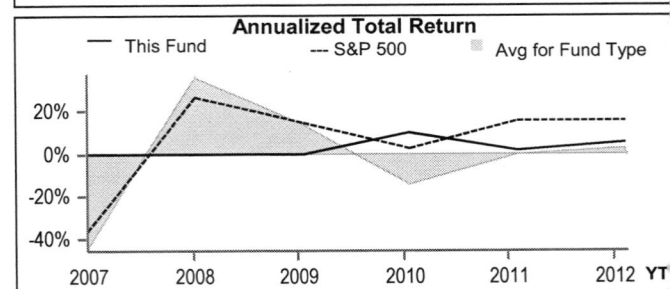

*Alps Equal Sector Weight ETF (EQL)

C   Fair

Fund Family: ALPS Advisors Inc
Fund Type: Income
Inception Date: July 7, 2009

Major Rating Factors: Middle of the road best describes *Alps Equal Sector Weight ETF whose TheStreet.com Investment Rating is currently a C (Fair). The fund currently has a performance rating of C (Fair) based on an annualized return of 11.13% over the last three years and a total return of 3.23% year to date 2012. Factored into the performance evaluation is an expense ratio of 0.34% (very low).

The fund's risk rating is currently B (Good). It carries a beta of 0.93, meaning that its performance tracks fairly well with that of the overall stock market. Volatility, as measured by both the semi-deviation and a drawdown factor, is considered low. As of December 31, 2012, *Alps Equal Sector Weight ETF traded at a discount of 3.09% below its net asset value, which is better than its one-year historical average premium of .01%.

Daniel Franciscus has been running the fund for 4 years and currently receives a manager quality ranking of 55 (0=worst, 99=best). If you desire an average level of risk, then this fund may be an option.

Data Date	Investment Rating	Net Assets ($Mil)	Price	Performance Rating/Pts	Total Return Y-T-D	Risk Rating/Pts
12-12	C	77.80	39.89	C / 5.0	3.23%	B / 8.3
2011	C-	62.30	35.60	D+ / 2.9	1.46%	B / 8.4
2010	A+	53.00	35.36	A- / 9.1	14.85%	B- / 7.9

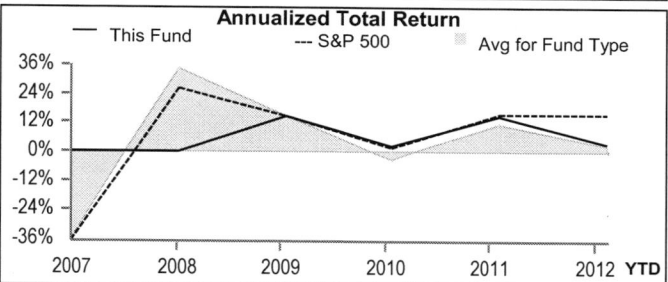

*Alps Jefferies / TR/J CRB Gl Cm (CRBQ)

D   Weak

Fund Family: ALPS Advisors Inc
Fund Type: Global
Inception Date: September 21, 2009

Major Rating Factors:
Disappointing performance is the major factor driving the D (Weak) TheStreet.com Investment Rating for *Alps Jefferies / TR/J CRB Gl Cm. The fund currently has a performance rating of D+ (Weak) based on an annualized return of 2.89% over the last three years and a total return of 3.17% year to date 2012. Factored into the performance evaluation is an expense ratio of 0.65% (very low).

The fund's risk rating is currently C+ (Fair). It carries a beta of 1.04, meaning that its performance tracks fairly well with that of the overall stock market. Volatility, as measured by both the semi-deviation and a drawdown factor, is considered low. As of December 31, 2012, *Alps Jefferies / TR/J CRB Gl Cm traded at a discount of 3.27% below its net asset value, which is better than its one-year historical average discount of .11%.

Michael Akins has been running the fund for 2 years and currently receives a manager quality ranking of 40 (0=worst, 99=best). This fund offers only a moderate level of risk but investors looking for strong performance are still waiting.

Data Date	Investment Rating	Net Assets ($Mil)	Price	Performance Rating/Pts	Total Return Y-T-D	Risk Rating/Pts
12-12	D	73.90	44.72	D+ / 2.3	3.17%	C+ / 6.9
2011	D	83.50	42.54	D- / 1.3	3.35%	B- / 7.1
2010	A+	111.00	49.58	A / 9.5	16.98%	B- / 7.3

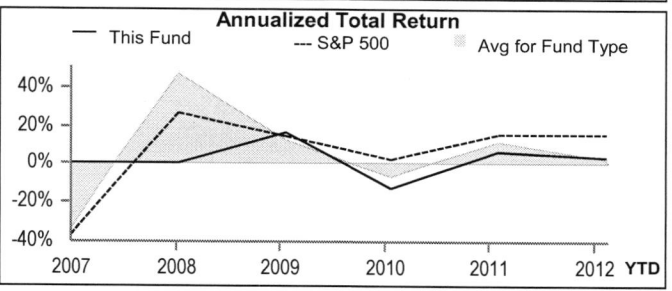

*Barclays ETN + VEQTOR ETN (VQT)

D-   Weak

Fund Family: Barclays Bank PLC
Fund Type: Growth
Inception Date: August 31, 2010

Major Rating Factors:
Disappointing performance is the major factor driving the D- (Weak) TheStreet.com Investment Rating for *Barclays ETN + VEQTOR ETN. The fund currently has a performance rating of D (Weak) based on an annualized return of 0.00% over the last three years and a total return of 0.91% year to date 2012.

The fund's risk rating is currently C+ (Fair). It carries a beta of 0.00, meaning the fund's expected move will be 0.0% for every 10% move in the market. Volatility, as measured by both the semi-deviation and a drawdown factor, is considered low. As of December 31, 2012, *Barclays ETN + VEQTOR ETN traded at a discount of .87% below its net asset value, which is better than its one-year historical average discount of .01%.

This fund has been team managed for 3 years and currently receives a manager quality ranking of 22 (0=worst, 99=best). This fund offers only a moderate level of risk but investors looking for strong performance are still waiting.

Data Date	Investment Rating	Net Assets ($Mil)	Price	Performance Rating/Pts	Total Return Y-T-D	Risk Rating/Pts
12-12	D-	364.20	129.27	D / 2.0	0.91%	C+ / 5.6
2011	C	192.50	125.97	C+ / 6.8	0.73%	C+ / 5.8

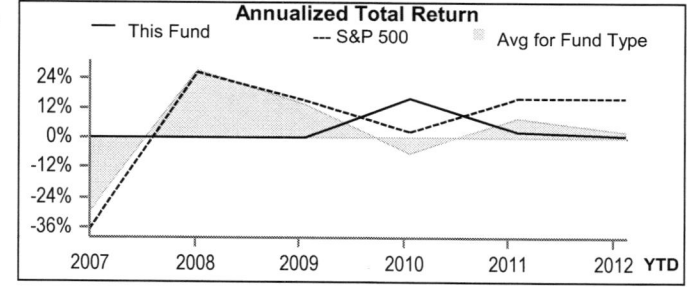

*BLDRS Asia 50 ADR Index (ADRA)

D+   **Weak**

Fund Family: Bank of New York Mellon
Fund Type: Foreign
Inception Date: November 13, 2002

Major Rating Factors:
Disappointing performance is the major factor driving the D+ (Weak) TheStreet.com Investment Rating for *BLDRS Asia 50 ADR Index. The fund currently has a performance rating of D+ (Weak) based on an annualized return of 2.50% over the last three years and a total return of 2.21% year to date 2012. Factored into the performance evaluation is an expense ratio of 0.30% (very low).

The fund's risk rating is currently B- (Good). It carries a beta of 0.88, meaning the fund's expected move will be 8.8% for every 10% move in the market. Volatility, as measured by both the semi-deviation and a drawdown factor, is considered low. As of December 31, 2012, *BLDRS Asia 50 ADR Index traded at a discount of 2.79% below its net asset value, which is better than its one-year historical average discount of .33%.

Alan L. Supple currently receives a manager quality ranking of 50 (0=worst, 99=best). This fund offers only a moderate level of risk but investors looking for strong performance are still waiting.

Data Date	Investment Rating	Net Assets ($Mil)	Price	Performance Rating/Pts	Total Return Y-T-D	Risk Rating/Pts
12-12	D+	29.10	26.18	D+ / 2.8	2.21%	B- / 7.4
2011	D+	29.40	22.43	D+ / 2.7	2.85%	B- / 7.6
2010	C-	50.10	28.66	C- / 3.9	14.13%	C / 5.1
2009	D+	65.75	25.72	D+ / 2.7	31.01%	C / 5.2

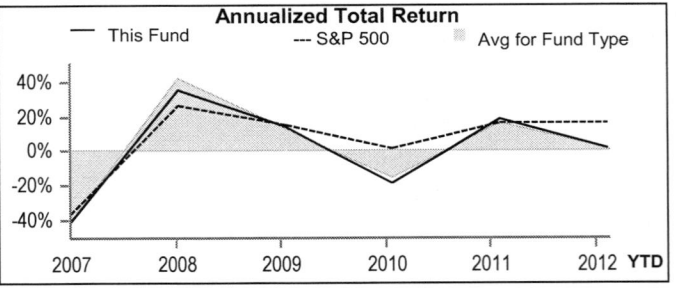

*BLDRS Developed Mkts 100 ADR Ind (ADRD)

C-   **Fair**

Fund Family: Bank of New York Mellon
Fund Type: Foreign
Inception Date: November 13, 2002

Major Rating Factors: Middle of the road best describes *BLDRS Developed Mkts 100 ADR Ind whose TheStreet.com Investment Rating is currently a C- (Fair). The fund currently has a performance rating of C- (Fair) based on an annualized return of 3.54% over the last three years and a total return of 3.61% year to date 2012. Factored into the performance evaluation is an expense ratio of 0.30% (very low).

The fund's risk rating is currently B- (Good). It carries a beta of 1.03, meaning that its performance tracks fairly well with that of the overall stock market. Volatility, as measured by both the semi-deviation and a drawdown factor, is considered low. As of December 31, 2012, *BLDRS Developed Mkts 100 ADR Ind traded at a discount of 3.49% below its net asset value, which is better than its one-year historical average discount of .31%.

Alan L. Supple currently receives a manager quality ranking of 43 (0=worst, 99=best). If you desire an average level of risk, then this fund may be an option.

Data Date	Investment Rating	Net Assets ($Mil)	Price	Performance Rating/Pts	Total Return Y-T-D	Risk Rating/Pts
12-12	C-	46.60	21.03	C- / 4.1	3.61%	B- / 7.2
2011	D+	55.10	18.69	D+ / 2.4	0.02%	B- / 7.4
2010	D-	76.20	21.45	D- / 1.4	3.96%	C / 4.8
2009	D+	76.03	21.44	D / 2.2	26.46%	C+ / 5.6

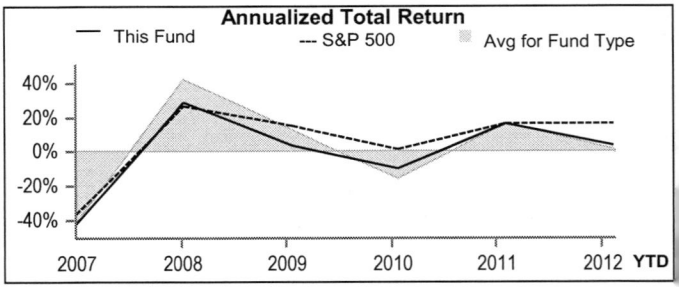

*BLDRS Emerging Market 50 ADR Ind (ADRE)

D   **Weak**

Fund Family: Bank of New York Mellon
Fund Type: Emerging Market
Inception Date: November 13, 2002

Major Rating Factors:
Disappointing performance is the major factor driving the D (Weak) TheStreet.com Investment Rating for *BLDRS Emerging Market 50 ADR Ind. The fund currently has a performance rating of D (Weak) based on an annualized return of 0.11% over the last three years and a total return of 2.29% year to date 2012. Factored into the performance evaluation is an expense ratio of 0.30% (very low).

The fund's risk rating is currently B- (Good). It carries a beta of 0.96, meaning that its performance tracks fairly well with that of the overall stock market. Volatility, as measured by both the semi-deviation and a drawdown factor, is considered low. As of December 31, 2012, *BLDRS Emerging Market 50 ADR Ind traded at a discount of 2.24% below its net asset value, which is better than its one-year historical average discount of .09%.

Alan L. Supple currently receives a manager quality ranking of 21 (0=worst, 99=best). This fund offers only a moderate level of risk but investors looking for strong performance are still waiting.

Data Date	Investment Rating	Net Assets ($Mil)	Price	Performance Rating/Pts	Total Return Y-T-D	Risk Rating/Pts
12-12	D	323.70	40.22	D / 1.8	2.29%	B- / 7.1
2011	C-	405.80	38.07	C- / 4.0	2.50%	B- / 7.3
2010	D+	674.10	48.15	C- / 3.8	11.58%	C / 4.5
2009	C+	627.30	44.13	B- / 7.3	57.25%	C / 4.8

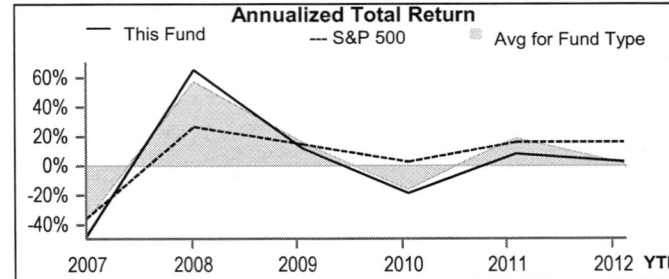

*BLDRS Europe Select ADR Index (ADRU)

D+ **Weak**

Fund Family: Bank of New York Mellon
Fund Type: Foreign
Inception Date: November 13, 2002

Major Rating Factors: *BLDRS Europe Select ADR Index receives a TheStreet.com Investment Rating of D+ (Weak). The fund currently has a performance rating of C- (Fair) based on an annualized return of 3.95% over the last three years and a total return of 3.60% year to date 2012. Factored into the performance evaluation is an expense ratio of 0.30% (very low).

The fund's risk rating is currently B- (Good). It carries a beta of 1.08, meaning that its performance tracks fairly well with that of the overall stock market. Volatility, as measured by both the semi-deviation and a drawdown factor, is considered low. As of December 31, 2012, *BLDRS Europe Select ADR Index traded at a discount of 3.34% below its net asset value, which is better than its one-year historical average discount of .14%.

Alan L. Supple currently receives a manager quality ranking of 41 (0=worst, 99=best). If you desire an average level of risk, then this fund may be an option.

Data Date	Investment Rating	Net Assets ($Mil)	Price	Perfor-mance Rating/Pts	Total Return Y-T-D	Risk Rating/Pts
12-12	D+	13.60	20.83	C- / 3.4	3.60%	B- / 7.1
2011	D+	14.80	18.63	D+ / 2.6	-0.64%	B- / 7.0
2010	D-	22.90	20.82	D- / 1.0	1.77%	C / 5.0
2009	D+	19.73	21.31	D+ / 2.5	28.00%	C / 5.4

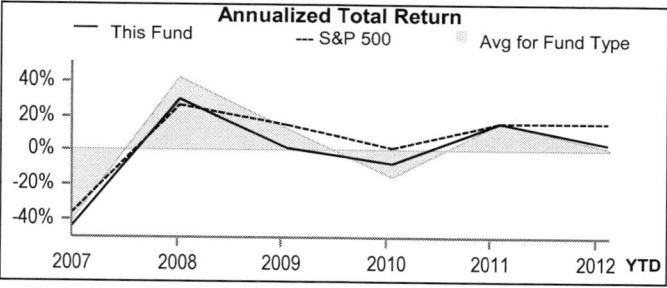

*Brclys ETN+ Inv S&P500 VIX STF E (XXV)

D **Weak**

Fund Family: Barclays Bank PLC
Fund Type: Growth
Inception Date: July 20, 2010

Major Rating Factors: *Brclys ETN+ Inv S&P500 VIX STF E receives a TheStreet.com Investment Rating of D (Weak). The fund currently has a performance rating of C- (Fair) based on an annualized return of 0.00% over the last three years and a total return of 0.58% year to date 2012.

The fund's risk rating is currently C (Fair). It carries a beta of 0.00, meaning the fund's expected move will be 0.0% for every 10% move in the market. Volatility, as measured by both the semi-deviation and a drawdown factor, is considered average. As of December 31, 2012, *Brclys ETN+ Inv S&P500 VIX STF E traded at a discount of .66% below its net asset value, which is better than its one-year historical average discount of .05%.

This team managed and currently receives a manager quality ranking of 82 (0=worst, 99=best). If you desire an average level of risk, then this fund may be an option.

Data Date	Investment Rating	Net Assets ($Mil)	Price	Perfor-mance Rating/Pts	Total Return Y-T-D	Risk Rating/Pts
12-12	D	4.60	37.82	C- / 4.0	0.58%	C / 4.9
2011	D-	14.70	33.00	D+ / 2.3	1.79%	C / 5.0

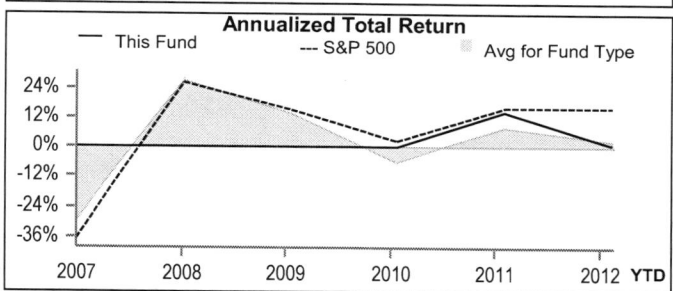

*Brclys ETN+ Lg C Lv S&P500 TR ET (BXUC)

C **Fair**

Fund Family: Barclays Bank PLC
Fund Type: Income
Inception Date: November 17, 2009

Major Rating Factors: Strong performance is the major factor driving the C (Fair) TheStreet.com Investment Rating for *Brclys ETN+ Lg C Lv S&P500 TR ET. The fund currently has a performance rating of B+ (Good) based on an annualized return of 19.72% over the last three years and a total return of 7.53% year to date 2012.

The fund's risk rating is currently C- (Fair). It carries a beta of 1.89, meaning it is expected to move 18.9% for every 10% move in the market. Volatility, as measured by both the semi-deviation and a drawdown factor, is considered average. As of December 31, 2012, *Brclys ETN+ Lg C Lv S&P500 TR ET traded at a discount of 7.09% below its net asset value, which is better than its one-year historical average premium of .01%.

This fund has been team managed for 4 years and currently receives a manager quality ranking of 29 (0=worst, 99=best). If you desire an average level of risk and strong performance, then this fund is a good option.

Data Date	Investment Rating	Net Assets ($Mil)	Price	Perfor-mance Rating/Pts	Total Return Y-T-D	Risk Rating/Pts
12-12	C	18.70	167.93	B+ / 8.7	7.53%	C- / 4.2
2011	D	14.30	135.64	C- / 3.9	2.71%	C / 4.3
2010	B+	12.70	130.79	A+ / 9.7	27.35%	C- / 3.8

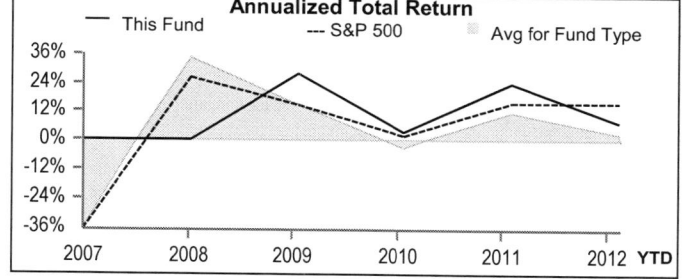

*Brclys ETN+InvS&P500 VIX STF ETN (IVOP) — B Good

Fund Family: Barclays Bank PLC
Fund Type: Income
Inception Date: September 16, 2011

Major Rating Factors:
Exceptional performance is the major factor driving the B (Good) TheStreet.com Investment Rating for *Brclys ETN+InvS&P500 VIX STF ETN. The fund currently has a performance rating of A+ (Excellent) based on an annualized return of 0.00% over the last three years and a total return of 2.40% year to date 2012.

The fund's risk rating is currently C (Fair). It carries a beta of 0.00, meaning the fund's expected move will be 0.0% for every 10% move in the market. Volatility, as measured by both the semi-deviation and a drawdown factor, is considered average. As of December 31, 2012, *Brclys ETN+InvS&P500 VIX STF ETN traded at a discount of 2.53% below its net asset value, which is better than its one-year historical average discount of .14%.

This fund has been team managed for 2 years and currently receives a manager quality ranking of 97 (0=worst, 99=best). If you desire an average level of risk and strong performance, then this fund is a good option.

Data Date	Investment Rating	Net Assets ($Mil)	Price	Performance Rating/Pts	Total Return Y-T-D	Risk Rating/Pts
12-12	B	1.80	35.44	A+ / 9.7	2.40%	C / 5.5

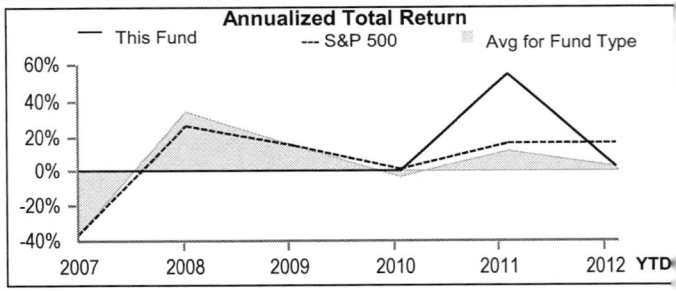

*C-Tracks ETN Citi Volatility Idx (CVOL) — E- Very Weak

Fund Family: Citi Fund Management Inc
Fund Type: Income
Inception Date: November 15, 2010

Major Rating Factors: *C-Tracks ETN Citi Volatility Idx has adopted a very risky asset allocation strategy and currently receives an overall TheStreet.com Investment Rating of E- (Very Weak). The fund has a high level of volatility, as measured by both semi-deviation and drawdown factors. It carries a beta of 0.00, meaning the fund's expected move will be 0.0% for every 10% move in the market. As of December 31, 2012, *C-Tracks ETN Citi Volatility Idx traded at a premium of 25.90% above its net asset value, which is worse than its one-year historical average premium of .16%. Unfortunately, the high level of risk (D, Weak) failed to pay off as investors endured very poor performance.

The fund's performance rating is currently E- (Very Weak). It has registered an annualized return of 0.00% over the last three years but is down -20.13% year to date 2012.

This is team managed and currently receives a manager quality ranking of 0 (0=worst, 99=best). If you can tolerate very high levels of risk in the hope of improved future returns, holding this fund may be an option.

Data Date	Investment Rating	Net Assets ($Mil)	Price	Performance Rating/Pts	Total Return Y-T-D	Risk Rating/Pts
12-12	E-	0.00	29.70	E- / 0	-20.13%	D / 1.9
2011	E-	0.00	28.41	E- / 0	-13.60%	D / 2.1

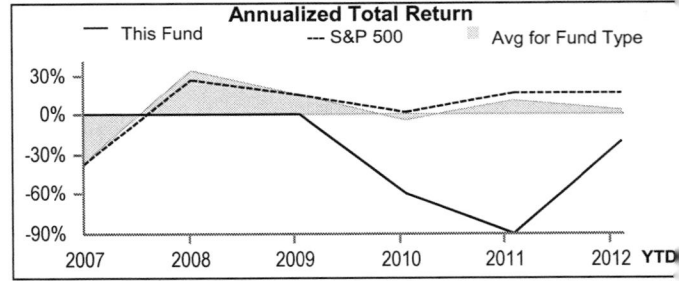

*Cambria Global Tactical ETF Fund (GTAA) — C Fair

Fund Family: AdvisorShares Investments LLC
Fund Type: Growth and Income
Inception Date: October 25, 2010

Major Rating Factors: Middle of the road best describes *Cambria Global Tactical ETF Fund whose TheStreet.com Investment Rating is currently a C (Fair). The fund currently has a performance rating of C- (Fair) based on an annualized return of 0.00% over the last three years and a total return of 2.29% year to date 2012. Factored into the performance evaluation is an expense ratio of 0.99% (low).

The fund's risk rating is currently B (Good). It carries a beta of 0.00, meaning the fund's expected move will be 0.0% for every 10% move in the market. Volatility, as measured by both the semi-deviation and a drawdown factor, is considered low. As of December 31, 2012, *Cambria Global Tactical ETF Fund traded at a discount of 2.13% below its net asset value, which is better than its one-year historical average discount of .20%.

Mebane T. Faber currently receives a manager quality ranking of 36 (0=worst, 99=best). If you desire an average level of risk, then this fund may be an option.

Data Date	Investment Rating	Net Assets ($Mil)	Price	Performance Rating/Pts	Total Return Y-T-D	Risk Rating/Pts
12-12	C	63.60	24.31	C- / 4.0	2.29%	B / 8.7
2011	D+	140.70	23.49	D- / 1.2	-0.64%	B / 8.8

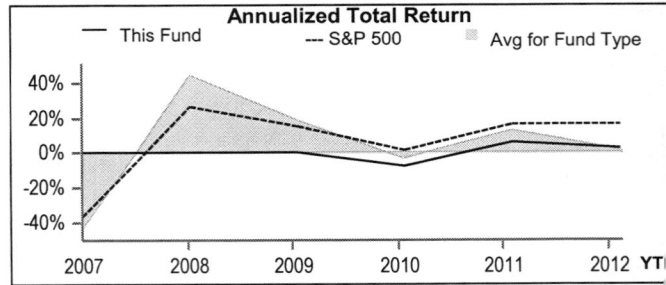

*Cohen & Steers Global Realty Maj (GRI)

B-   Good

Fund Family: ALPS Advisors Inc
Fund Type: Growth and Income
Inception Date: May 7, 2008

Major Rating Factors: Strong performance is the major factor driving the B- (Good) TheStreet.com Investment Rating for *Cohen & Steers Global Realty Maj. The fund currently has a performance rating of B (Good) based on an annualized return of 14.11% over the last three years and a total return of 1.56% year to date 2012. Factored into the performance evaluation is an expense ratio of 0.55% (very low).

The fund's risk rating is currently C+ (Fair). It carries a beta of 1.05, meaning that its performance tracks fairly well with that of the overall stock market. Volatility, as measured by both the semi-deviation and a drawdown factor, is considered low. As of December 31, 2012, *Cohen & Steers Global Realty Maj traded at a discount of 1.11% below its net asset value, which is better than its one-year historical average premium of .19%.

Michael Akins has been running the fund for 2 years and currently receives a manager quality ranking of 67 (0=worst, 99=best). If you desire only a moderate level of risk and strong performance, then this fund is an excellent option.

Data Date	Investment Rating	Net Assets ($Mil)	Price	Perfor-mance Rating/Pts	Total Return Y-T-D	Risk Rating/Pts
12-12	B-	70.30	39.25	B / 7.6	1.56%	C+ / 6.9
2011	C-	50.50	32.59	C / 4.6	-0.25%	C+ / 6.3
2010	B+	40.90	35.86	A- / 9.2	20.75%	C / 4.5
2009	B-	5.01	31.43	B+ / 8.7	30.67%	C- / 4.0

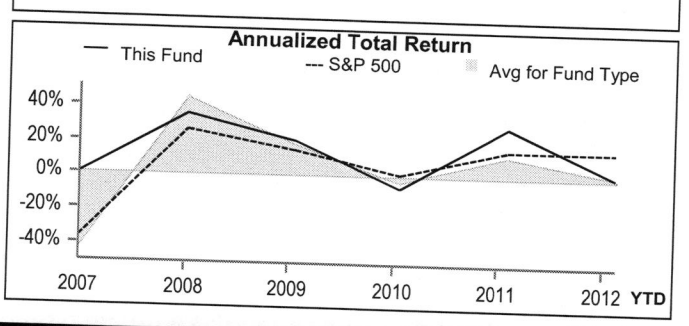

Annualized Total Return

*Columbia Core Bond Strategy (GMTB)

C-   Fair

Fund Family: Columbia Management Inv Advisers LL
Fund Type: General - Investment Grade
Inception Date: January 29, 2010

Major Rating Factors:
Disappointing performance is the major factor driving the C- (Fair) TheStreet.com Investment Rating for *Columbia Core Bond Strategy. The fund currently has a performance rating of D (Weak) based on an annualized return of 0.00% over the last three years and a total return of -0.02% year to date 2012. Factored into the performance evaluation is an expense ratio of 0.35% (very low).

The fund's risk rating is currently B+ (Good). It carries a beta of 0.00, meaning the fund's expected move will be 0.0% for every 10% move in the market. Volatility, as measured by both the semi-deviation and a drawdown factor, is considered very low. As of December 31, 2012, *Columbia Core Bond Strategy traded at a premium of .27% above its net asset value, which is better than its one-year historical average premium of .83%.

Orhan Imer has been running the fund for 2 years and currently receives a manager quality ranking of 68 (0=worst, 99=best). This fund offers only a moderate level of risk but investors looking for strong performance are still waiting.

Data Date	Investment Rating	Net Assets ($Mil)	Price	Perfor-mance Rating/Pts	Total Return Y-T-D	Risk Rating/Pts
12-12	C-	5.30	52.90	D / 1.8	-0.02%	B+ / 9.6

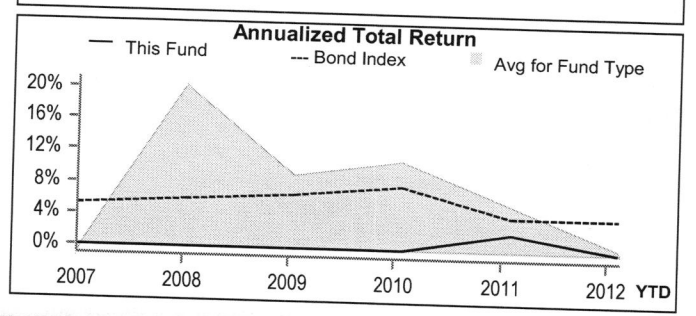

Annualized Total Return

*Columbia Growth Equity Strategy (RPX)

C-   Fair

Fund Family: Columbia Management Inv Advisers LL
Fund Type: Growth
Inception Date: October 2, 2009

Major Rating Factors: Middle of the road best describes *Columbia Growth Equity Strategy whose TheStreet.com Investment Rating is currently a C- (Fair). The fund currently has a performance rating of C- (Fair) based on an annualized return of 10.09% over the last three years and a total return of 4.56% year to date 2012. Factored into the performance evaluation is an expense ratio of 0.89% (low).

The fund's risk rating is currently B- (Good). It carries a beta of 0.88, meaning the fund's expected move will be 8.8% for every 10% move in the market. Volatility, as measured by both the semi-deviation and a drawdown factor, is considered low. As of December 31, 2012, *Columbia Growth Equity Strategy traded at a discount of 4.90% below its net asset value, which is better than its one-year historical average discount of 1.30%.

Colin Moore has been running the fund for 2 years and currently receives a manager quality ranking of 43 (0=worst, 99=best). If you desire an average level of risk, then this fund may be an option.

Data Date	Investment Rating	Net Assets ($Mil)	Price	Perfor-mance Rating/Pts	Total Return Y-T-D	Risk Rating/Pts
12-12	C-	1.50	30.46	C- / 4.2	4.56%	B- / 7.6
2011	D+	1.30	28.00	D / 1.7	-5.11%	B- / 7.7
2010	A+	4.70	31.22	B+ / 8.8	12.99%	B / 8.1

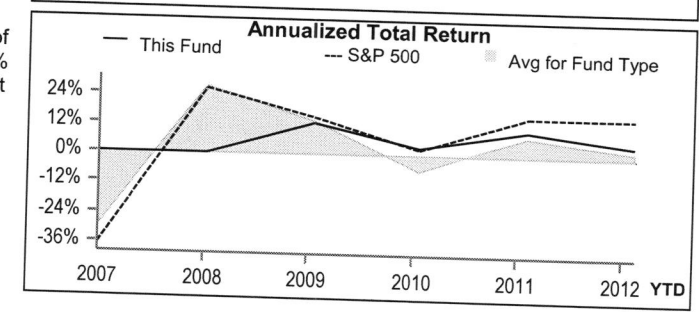

Annualized Total Return

* Denotes ETF Fund

*Columbia Intermediate Muni Bd St (GMMB)

C- **Fair**

Fund Family: Columbia Management Inv Advisers LL
Fund Type: Municipal - National
Inception Date: January 29, 2010

Major Rating Factors:
Disappointing performance is the major factor driving the C- (Fair) TheStreet.com Investment Rating for *Columbia Intermediate Muni Bd St. The fund currently has a performance rating of D+ (Weak) based on an annualized return of 0.00% over the last three years and a total return of 0.11% year to date 2012. Factored into the performance evaluation is an expense ratio of 0.35% (very low).

The fund's risk rating is currently B (Good). It carries a beta of 0.00, meaning the fund's expected move will be 0.0% for every 10% move in the market. Volatility, as measured by both the semi-deviation and a drawdown factor, is considered low. As of December 31, 2012, *Columbia Intermediate Muni Bd St traded at a discount of .69% below its net asset value, which is better than its one-year historical average premium of 2.50%.

Dawn Daggy-Mangerson has been running the fund for 3 years and currently receives a manager quality ranking of 89 (0=worst, 99=best). This fund offers only a moderate level of risk but investors looking for strong performance are still waiting.

Data Date	Investment Rating	Net Assets ($Mil)	Price	Performance Rating/Pts	Total Return Y-T-D	Risk Rating/Pts
12-12	C-	8.20	54.40	D+ / 2.6	0.11%	B / 8.9
2011	B	5.30	53.03	C+ / 6.8	0.73%	B+ / 9.3

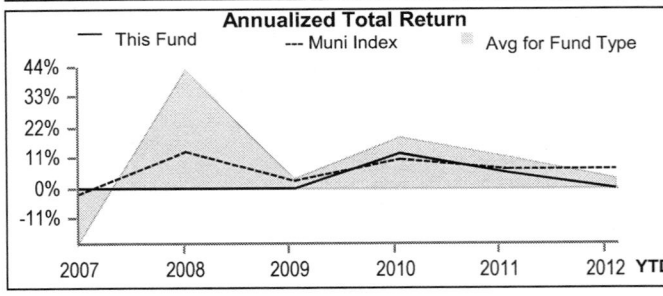

Annualized Total Return

*Columbia Large-Cap Growth Eq Str (RWG)

C **Fair**

Fund Family: Columbia Management Inv Advisers LL
Fund Type: Growth
Inception Date: October 2, 2009

Major Rating Factors: Middle of the road best describes *Columbia Large-Cap Growth Eq Str whose TheStreet.com Investment Rating is currently a C (Fair). The fund currently has a performance rating of C (Fair) based on an annualized return of 8.90% over the last three years and a total return of 7.50% year to date 2012. Factored into the performance evaluation is an expense ratio of 0.89% (low).

The fund's risk rating is currently B- (Good). It carries a beta of 1.01, meaning that its performance tracks fairly well with that of the overall stock market. Volatility, as measured by both the semi-deviation and a drawdown factor, is considered low. As of December 31, 2012, *Columbia Large-Cap Growth Eq Str traded at a discount of 7.13% below its net asset value, which is better than its one-year historical average discount of 1.63%.

Colin Moore has been running the fund for 2 years and currently receives a manager quality ranking of 26 (0=worst, 99=best). If you desire an average level of risk, then this fund may be an option.

Data Date	Investment Rating	Net Assets ($Mil)	Price	Performance Rating/Pts	Total Return Y-T-D	Risk Rating/Pts
12-12	C	7.60	29.85	C / 4.7	7.50%	B- / 7.5
2011	D	8.00	26.26	D- / 1.2	0.04%	B- / 7.8
2010	A+	9.30	30.90	A- / 9.0	14.11%	B / 8.2

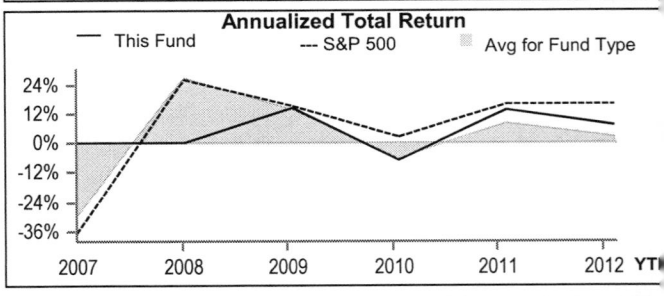

Annualized Total Return

*Consumer Discretionary Sel Sec S (XLY)

B+ **Good**

Fund Family: SSgA Funds Management Inc
Fund Type: Growth
Inception Date: December 16, 1998

Major Rating Factors: Strong performance is the major factor driving the B+ (Good) TheStreet.com Investment Rating for *Consumer Discretionary Sel Sec S. The fund currently has a performance rating of B+ (Good) based on an annualized return of 19.54% over the last three years and a total return of 3.02% year to date 2012. Factored into the performance evaluation is an expense ratio of 0.18% (very low).

The fund's risk rating is currently B- (Good). It carries a beta of 1.06, meaning that its performance tracks fairly well with that of the overall stock market. Volatility, as measured by both the semi-deviation and a drawdown factor, is considered low. As of December 31, 2012, *Consumer Discretionary Sel Sec S traded at a discount of 2.99% below its net asset value.

John A. Tucker has been running the fund for 15 years and currently receives a manager quality ranking of 83 (0=worst, 99=best). If you desire only a moderate level of risk and strong performance, then this fund is an excellent option.

Data Date	Investment Rating	Net Assets ($Mil)	Price	Performance Rating/Pts	Total Return Y-T-D	Risk Rating/Pts
12-12	B+	3,743.20	47.44	B+ / 8.4	3.02%	B- / 7.9
2011	B	2,487.80	39.02	B / 7.7	2.64%	B- / 7.8
2010	B+	2,478.90	37.41	B / 8.0	27.50%	C+ / 5.9
2009	D+	1,268.30	29.77	D+ / 2.7	33.81%	C+ / 5.8

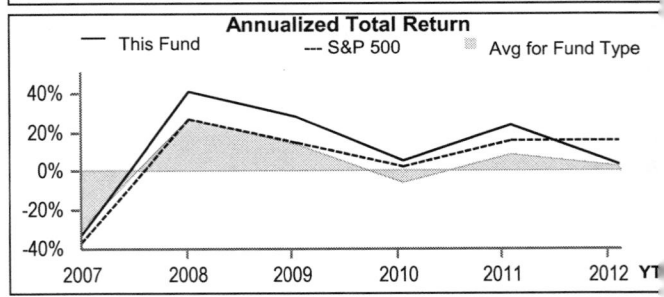

Annualized Total Return

*Consumer Staples Select Sector S (XLP)

C+   **Fair**

Fund Family: SSgA Funds Management Inc
Fund Type: Growth
Inception Date: December 16, 1998

Major Rating Factors: Middle of the road best describes *Consumer Staples Select Sector S whose TheStreet.com Investment Rating is currently a C+ (Fair). The fund currently has a performance rating of C (Fair) based on an annualized return of 13.53% over the last three years and a total return of 2.92% year to date 2012. Factored into the performance evaluation is an expense ratio of 0.18% (very low).

The fund's risk rating is currently B+ (Good). It carries a beta of 0.50, meaning the fund's expected move will be 5.0% for every 10% move in the market. Volatility, as measured by both the semi-deviation and a drawdown factor, is considered very low. As of December 31, 2012, *Consumer Staples Select Sector S traded at a discount of 2.76% below its net asset value.

John A. Tucker has been running the fund for 15 years and currently receives a manager quality ranking of 85 (0=worst, 99=best). If you desire an average level of risk, then this fund may be an option.

Data Date	Investment Rating	Net Assets ($Mil)	Price	Performance Rating/Pts	Total Return Y-T-D	Risk Rating/Pts
12-12	C+	5,530.70	34.90	C / 5.3	2.92%	B+ / 9.0
2011	B-	5,836.70	32.49	C+ / 5.9	-1.02%	B / 8.6
2010	B-	3,104.00	29.31	C+ / 5.9	13.81%	B- / 7.3
2009	C	1,885.36	26.47	C- / 3.9	12.61%	B- / 7.4

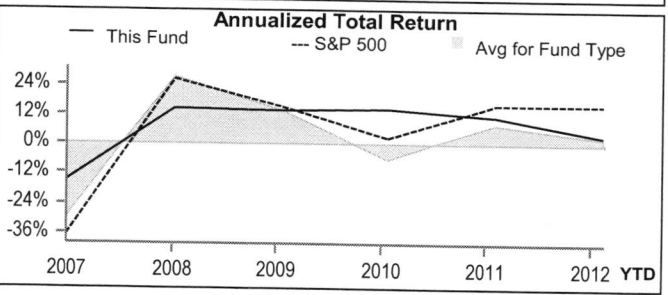

*Credit Suisse Cushing 30 MLP ETN (MLPN)

D   **Weak**

Fund Family: Credit Suisse Asset Management LLC
Fund Type: Energy/Natural Resources
Inception Date: April 13, 2010

Major Rating Factors: *Credit Suisse Cushing 30 MLP ETN receives a TheStreet.com Investment Rating of D (Weak). The fund currently has a performance rating of C- (Fair) based on an annualized return of 0.00% over the last three years and a total return of 6.72% year to date 2012.

The fund's risk rating is currently C (Fair). It carries a beta of 0.00, meaning the fund's expected move will be 0.0% for every 10% move in the market. Volatility, as measured by both the semi-deviation and a drawdown factor, is considered average. As of December 31, 2012, *Credit Suisse Cushing 30 MLP ETN traded at a discount of 6.34% below its net asset value, which is better than its one-year historical average premium of .09%.

This fund has been team managed for 3 years and currently receives a manager quality ranking of 35 (0=worst, 99=best). If you desire an average level of risk, then this fund may be an option.

Data Date	Investment Rating	Net Assets ($Mil)	Price	Performance Rating/Pts	Total Return Y-T-D	Risk Rating/Pts
12-12	D	303.10	24.10	C- / 4.1	6.72%	C / 5.0
2011	C-	0.00	24.95	C / 5.4	2.12%	C / 5.1

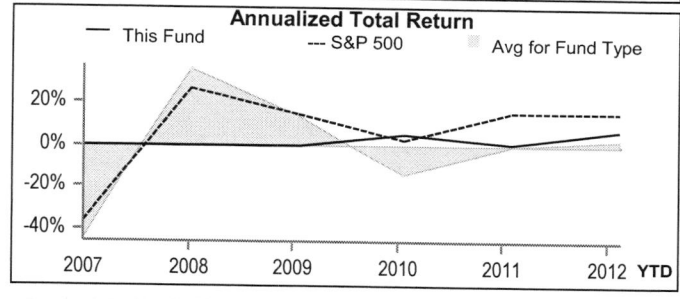

*Credit Suisse L/S Liq Idx ETN (CSLS)

D-   **Weak**

Fund Family: Credit Suisse Asset Management LLC
Fund Type: Growth
Inception Date: February 19, 2010

Major Rating Factors:
Disappointing performance is the major factor driving the D- (Weak) TheStreet.com Investment Rating for *Credit Suisse L/S Liq Idx ETN. The fund currently has a performance rating of D (Weak) based on an annualized return of 0.00% over the last three years and a total return of -0.68% year to date 2012.

The fund's risk rating is currently C (Fair). It carries a beta of 0.00, meaning the fund's expected move will be 0.0% for every 10% move in the market. Volatility, as measured by both the semi-deviation and a drawdown factor, is considered average. As of December 31, 2012, *Credit Suisse L/S Liq Idx ETN traded at a premium of .45% above its net asset value, which is worse than its one-year historical average discount of .10%.

This fund has been team managed for 3 years and currently receives a manager quality ranking of 22 (0=worst, 99=best). This fund offers an average level of risk but investors looking for strong performance will be frustrated.

Data Date	Investment Rating	Net Assets ($Mil)	Price	Performance Rating/Pts	Total Return Y-T-D	Risk Rating/Pts
12-12	D-	21.10	22.36	D / 1.9	-0.68%	C / 5.4
2011	D-	32.30	21.65	D / 1.7	0.14%	C / 5.4

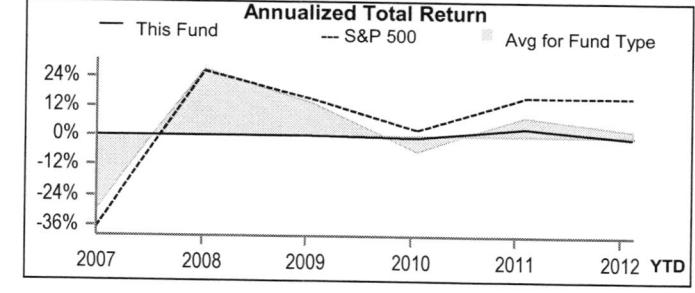

*Credit Suisse Merger Arb Lq Id E (CSMA)

D-   Weak

Fund Family: Credit Suisse Asset Management LLC
Fund Type: Growth
Inception Date: October 1, 2010

Major Rating Factors:
Disappointing performance is the major factor driving the D- (Weak) TheStreet.com Investment Rating for *Credit Suisse Merger Arb Lq Id E. The fund currently has a performance rating of D- (Weak) based on an annualized return of 0.00% over the last three years and a total return of 0.20% year to date 2012.

The fund's risk rating is currently C (Fair). It carries a beta of 0.00, meaning the fund's expected move will be 0.0% for every 10% move in the market. Volatility, as measured by both the semi-deviation and a drawdown factor, is considered average. As of December 31, 2012, *Credit Suisse Merger Arb Lq Id E traded at a discount of 1.21% below its net asset value, which is better than its one-year historical average discount of .21%.

This is team managed and currently receives a manager quality ranking of 17 (0=worst, 99=best). This fund offers an average level of risk but investors looking for strong performance will be frustrated.

Data Date	Investment Rating	Net Assets ($Mil)	Price	Performance Rating/Pts	Total Return Y-T-D	Risk Rating/Pts
12-12	D-	74.60	19.65	D- / 1.1	0.20%	C / 5.5
2011	D	94.40	21.00	D / 2.1	-2.53%	C+ / 5.8

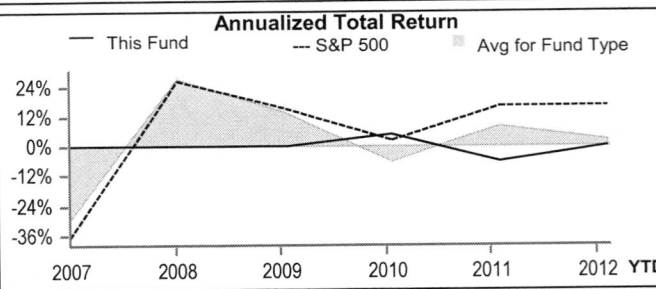

Annualized Total Return

*db-X 2010 Target Date Fund (TDD)

D+   Weak

Fund Family: DBX Strategic Advisors LLC
Fund Type: Growth and Income
Inception Date: October 1, 2007

Major Rating Factors:
Disappointing performance is the major factor driving the D+ (Weak) TheStreet.com Investment Rating for *db-X 2010 Target Date Fund. The fund currently has a performance rating of D- (Weak) based on an annualized return of -1.23% over the last three years and a total return of 0.47% year to date 2012. Factored into the performance evaluation is an expense ratio of 0.65% (very low).

The fund's risk rating is currently B (Good). It carries a beta of 0.13, meaning the fund's expected move will be 1.3% for every 10% move in the market. Volatility, as measured by both the semi-deviation and a drawdown factor, is considered low. As of December 31, 2012, *db-X 2010 Target Date Fund traded at a discount of 11.13% below its net asset value, which is better than its one-year historical average discount of 7.42%.

Glenn S. Davis has been running the fund for 4 years and currently receives a manager quality ranking of 33 (0=worst, 99=best). This fund offers only a moderate level of risk but investors looking for strong performance are still waiting.

Data Date	Investment Rating	Net Assets ($Mil)	Price	Performance Rating/Pts	Total Return Y-T-D	Risk Rating/Pts
12-12	D+	9.60	21.40	D- / 1.2	0.47%	B / 8.9
2011	C	14.10	23.19	D+ / 2.7	1.25%	B+ / 9.5
2010	C-	14.10	22.74	D+ / 2.3	2.54%	B- / 7.7
2009	C+	17.69	22.82	C- / 4.1	5.70%	B- / 7.8

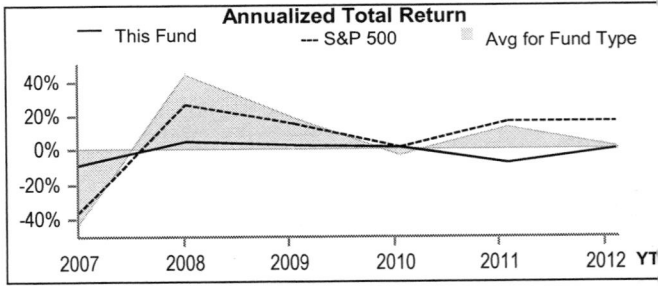

Annualized Total Return

*db-X 2020 Target Date Fund (TDH)

C-   Fair

Fund Family: DBX Strategic Advisors LLC
Fund Type: Growth and Income
Inception Date: October 1, 2007

Major Rating Factors:
Disappointing performance is the major factor driving the C- (Fair) TheStreet.com Investment Rating for *db-X 2020 Target Date Fund. The fund currently has a performance rating of D+ (Weak) based on an annualized return of 4.04% over the last three years and a total return of 2.24% year to date 2012. Factored into the performance evaluation is an expense ratio of 0.65% (very low).

The fund's risk rating is currently B (Good). It carries a beta of 0.57, meaning the fund's expected move will be 5.7% for every 10% move in the market. Volatility, as measured by both the semi-deviation and a drawdown factor, is considered low. As of December 31, 2012, *db-X 2020 Target Date Fund traded at a discount of 9.39% below its net asset value, which is better than its one-year historical average discount of 6.66%.

Glenn S. Davis has been running the fund for 4 years and currently receives a manager quality ranking of 34 (0=worst, 99=best). This fund offers only a moderate level of risk but investors looking for strong performance are still waiting.

Data Date	Investment Rating	Net Assets ($Mil)	Price	Performance Rating/Pts	Total Return Y-T-D	Risk Rating/Pts
12-12	C-	29.00	22.30	D+ / 2.4	2.24%	B / 8.7
2011	C	36.00	22.01	C- / 3.4	1.27%	B / 8.7
2010	C-	40.80	22.18	C- / 3.1	8.50%	C+ / 6.8
2009	C+	37.14	20.93	C+ / 5.9	9.83%	C+ / 6.9

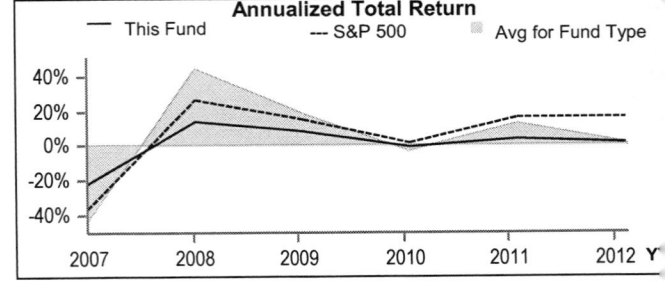

Annualized Total Return

*db-X 2030 Target Date Fund (TDN)

C+   **Fair**

Fund Family: DBX Strategic Advisors LLC
Fund Type: Growth and Income
Inception Date: October 1, 2007

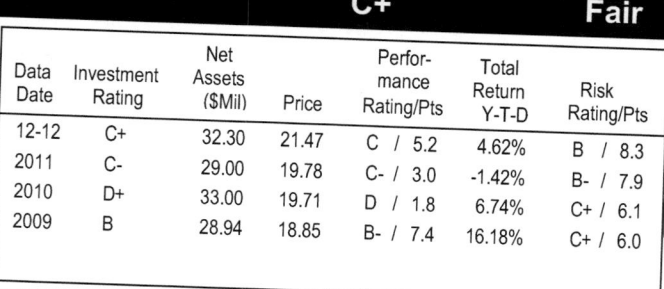

Data Date	Investment Rating	Net Assets ($Mil)	Price	Performance Rating/Pts	Total Return Y-T-D	Risk Rating/Pts
12-12	C+	32.30	21.47	C / 5.2	4.62%	B / 8.3
2011	C-	29.00	19.78	C- / 3.0	-1.42%	B- / 7.9
2010	D+	33.00	19.71	D / 1.8	6.74%	C+ / 6.1
2009	B	28.94	18.85	B- / 7.4	16.18%	C+ / 6.0

Major Rating Factors: Middle of the road best describes *db-X 2030 Target Date Fund whose TheStreet.com Investment Rating is currently a C+ (Fair). The fund currently has a performance rating of C (Fair) based on an annualized return of 8.73% over the last three years and a total return of 4.62% year to date 2012. Factored into the performance evaluation is an expense ratio of 0.65% (very low).

The fund's risk rating is currently B (Good). It carries a beta of 0.76, meaning the fund's expected move will be 7.6% for every 10% move in the market. Volatility, as measured by both the semi-deviation and a drawdown factor, is considered low. As of December 31, 2012, *db-X 2030 Target Date Fund traded at a discount of 9.18% below its net asset value, which is better than its one-year historical average discount of 6.43%.

Glenn S. Davis has been running the fund for 4 years and currently receives a manager quality ranking of 47 (0=worst, 99=best). If you desire an average level of risk, then this fund may be an option.

Annualized Total Return
— This Fund --- S&P 500 ▨ Avg for Fund Type

*db-X 2040 Target Date Fund (TDV)

C-   **Fair**

Fund Family: DBX Strategic Advisors LLC
Fund Type: Growth and Income
Inception Date: October 1, 2007

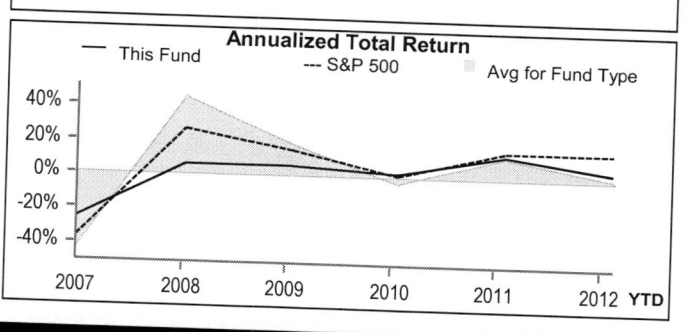

Data Date	Investment Rating	Net Assets ($Mil)	Price	Performance Rating/Pts	Total Return Y-T-D	Risk Rating/Pts
12-12	C-	26.90	20.95	C- / 4.0	3.48%	B- / 7.8
2011	C-	27.60	19.50	C- / 3.7	-1.03%	B- / 7.8
2010	D+	32.30	19.61	D / 2.2	10.09%	C+ / 5.8
2009	B+	27.65	18.14	B / 7.8	21.30%	C+ / 5.8

Major Rating Factors: Middle of the road best describes *db-X 2040 Target Date Fund whose TheStreet.com Investment Rating is currently a C- (Fair). The fund currently has a performance rating of C- (Fair) based on an annualized return of 8.46% over the last three years and a total return of 3.48% year to date 2012. Factored into the performance evaluation is an expense ratio of 0.65% (very low).

The fund's risk rating is currently B- (Good). It carries a beta of 0.98, meaning that its performance tracks fairly well with that of the overall stock market. Volatility, as measured by both the semi-deviation and a drawdown factor, is considered low. As of December 31, 2012, *db-X 2040 Target Date Fund traded at a discount of 9.07% below its net asset value, which is better than its one-year historical average discount of 1.55%.

Glenn S. Davis has been running the fund for 4 years and currently receives a manager quality ranking of 32 (0=worst, 99=best). If you desire an average level of risk, then this fund may be an option.

Annualized Total Return
— This Fund --- S&P 500 ▨ Avg for Fund Type

*db-X In-Target Date Fund (TDX)

D+   **Weak**

Fund Family: DBX Strategic Advisors LLC
Fund Type: Growth and Income
Inception Date: October 1, 2007

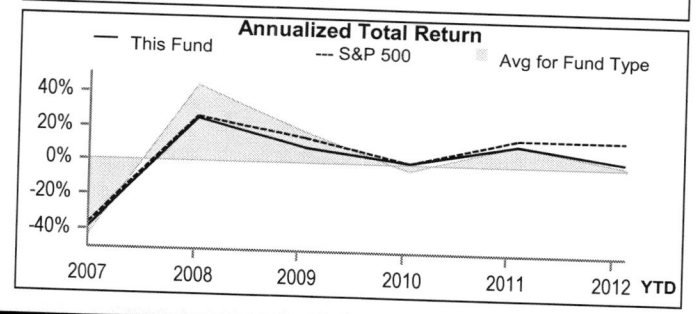

Data Date	Investment Rating	Net Assets ($Mil)	Price	Performance Rating/Pts	Total Return Y-T-D	Risk Rating/Pts
12-12	D+	10.70	24.50	D- / 1.5	0.04%	B / 8.8
2011	C-	15.40	25.91	D+ / 2.3	-3.13%	B+ / 9.3
2010	C	15.60	24.76	D+ / 2.6	1.45%	B / 8.6
2009	B	24.40	24.79	C / 4.4	8.95%	B / 8.9

Major Rating Factors:
Disappointing performance is the major factor driving the D+ (Weak) TheStreet.com Investment Rating for *db-X In-Target Date Fund. The fund currently has a performance rating of D- (Weak) based on an annualized return of 0.30% over the last three years and a total return of 0.04% year to date 2012. Factored into the performance evaluation is an expense ratio of 0.65% (very low).

The fund's risk rating is currently B (Good). It carries a beta of 0.34, meaning the fund's expected move will be 3.4% for every 10% move in the market. Volatility, as measured by both the semi-deviation and a drawdown factor, is considered low. As of December 31, 2012, *db-X In-Target Date Fund traded at a discount of 9.56% below its net asset value, which is better than its one-year historical average discount of 6.67%.

Glenn S. Davis has been running the fund for 4 years and currently receives a manager quality ranking of 31 (0=worst, 99=best). This fund offers only a moderate level of risk but investors looking for strong performance are still waiting.

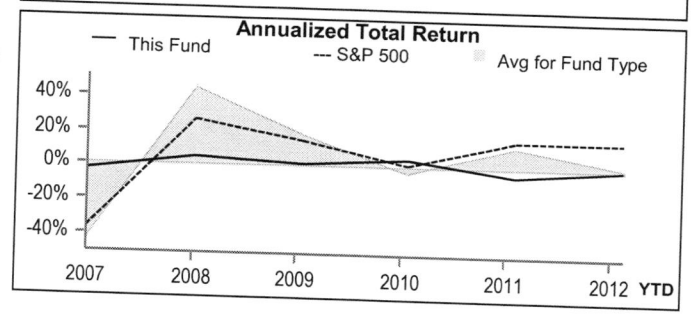

Annualized Total Return
— This Fund --- S&P 500 ▨ Avg for Fund Type

*DBX MSCI Brazil Currency-Hedged (DBBR)

B- **Good**

Fund Family: DBX Advisors LLC
Fund Type: Foreign
Inception Date: June 9, 2011

Data Date	Investment Rating	Net Assets ($Mil)	Price	Performance Rating/Pts	Total Return Y-T-D	Risk Rating/Pts
12-12	B-	4.20	20.12	B- / 7.2	2.14%	B- / 7.8

Major Rating Factors: Strong performance is the major factor driving the B- (Good) TheStreet.com Investment Rating for *DBX MSCI Brazil Currency-Hedged. The fund currently has a performance rating of B- (Good) based on an annualized return of 0.00% over the last three years and a total return of 2.14% year to date 2012. Factored into the performance evaluation is an expense ratio of 1.13% (low).

The fund's risk rating is currently B- (Good). It carries a beta of 0.00, meaning the fund's expected move will be 0.0% for every 10% move in the market. Volatility, as measured by both the semi-deviation and a drawdown factor, is considered low. As of December 31, 2012, *DBX MSCI Brazil Currency-Hedged traded at a discount of 1.90% below its net asset value, which is better than its one-year historical average premium of .10%.

Dino Bourdos has been running the fund for 2 years and currently receives a manager quality ranking of 9 (0=worst, 99=best). If you desire only a moderate level of risk and strong performance, then this fund is an excellent option.

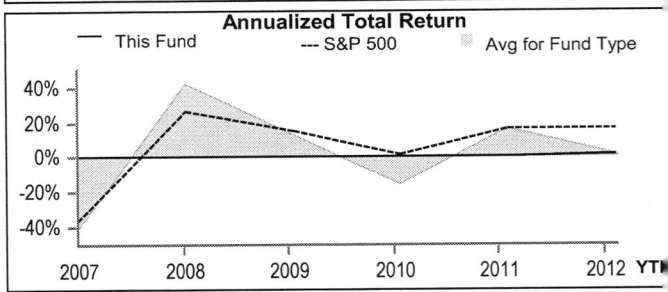

*DBX MSCI EAFE Currency-Hedged Eq (DBEF)

A+ **Excellent**

Fund Family: DBX Advisors LLC
Fund Type: Foreign
Inception Date: June 9, 2011

Data Date	Investment Rating	Net Assets ($Mil)	Price	Performance Rating/Pts	Total Return Y-T-D	Risk Rating/Pts
12-12	A+	14.30	22.06	A / 9.5	5.94%	B / 8.0

Major Rating Factors:
Exceptional performance is the major factor driving the A+ (Excellent) TheStreet.com Investment Rating for *DBX MSCI EAFE Currency-Hedged Eq. The fund currently has a performance rating of A (Excellent) based on an annualized return of 0.00% over the last three years and a total return of 5.94% year to date 2012. Factored into the performance evaluation is an expense ratio of 0.57% (very low).

The fund's risk rating is currently B (Good). It carries a beta of 0.00, meaning the fund's expected move will be 0.0% for every 10% move in the market. Volatility, as measured by both the semi-deviation and a drawdown factor, is considered low. As of December 31, 2012, *DBX MSCI EAFE Currency-Hedged Eq traded at a discount of 2.43% below its net asset value, which is better than its one-year historical average discount of .02%.

Dino Bourdos has been running the fund for 2 years and currently receives a manager quality ranking of 87 (0=worst, 99=best). If you desire only a moderate level of risk and strong performance, then this fund is an excellent option.

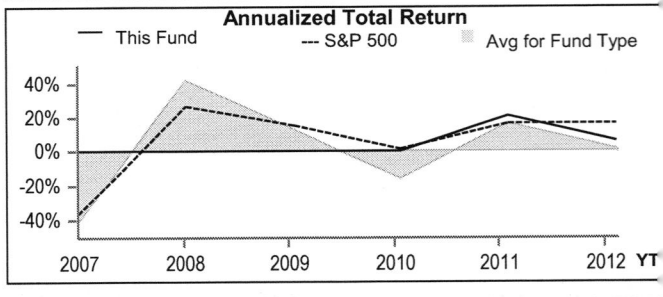

*DBX MSCI Emg Mkt Currency-Hedged (DBEM)

C+ **Fair**

Fund Family: DBX Advisors LLC
Fund Type: Emerging Market
Inception Date: June 9, 2011

Data Date	Investment Rating	Net Assets ($Mil)	Price	Performance Rating/Pts	Total Return Y-T-D	Risk Rating/Pts
12-12	C+	4.50	22.84	B / 7.9	2.22%	C / 5.5

Major Rating Factors: Strong performance is the major factor driving the C+ (Fair) TheStreet.com Investment Rating for *DBX MSCI Emg Mkt Currency-Hedged. The fund currently has a performance rating of B (Good) based on an annualized return of 0.00% over the last three years and a total return of 2.22% year to date 2012. Factored into the performance evaluation is an expense ratio of 1.19% (average).

The fund's risk rating is currently C (Fair). It carries a beta of 0.00, meaning the fund's expected move will be 0.0% for every 10% move in the market. Volatility, as measured by both the semi-deviation and a drawdown factor, is considered average. As of December 31, 2012, *DBX MSCI Emg Mkt Currency-Hedged traded at a discount of .95% below its net asset value, which is better than its one-year historical average premium of .94%.

Dino Bourdos has been running the fund for 2 years and currently receives a manager quality ranking of 53 (0=worst, 99=best). If you desire an average level of risk and strong performance, then this fund is a good option.

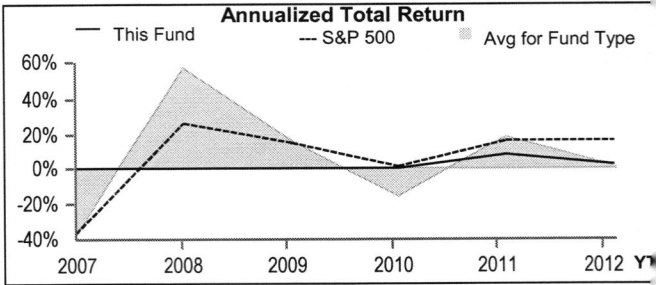

*Direxion All Cap Insider Sentime (KNOW)

B+   **Good**

Fund Family: Rafferty Asset Management LLC
Fund Type: Growth and Income
Inception Date: December 8, 2011

Major Rating Factors: Strong performance is the major factor driving the B+ (Good) TheStreet.com Investment Rating for *Direxion All Cap Insider Sentime. The fund currently has a performance rating of B (Good) based on an annualized return of 0.00% over the last three years and a total return of 3.05% year to date 2012.

The fund's risk rating is currently B (Good). It carries a beta of 0.00, meaning the fund's expected move will be 0.0% for every 10% move in the market. Volatility, as measured by both the semi-deviation and a drawdown factor, is considered low. As of December 31, 2012, *Direxion All Cap Insider Sentime traded at a discount of 3.43% below its net asset value, which is better than its one-year historical average discount of .12%.

Paul Brigandi has been running the fund for 2 years and currently receives a manager quality ranking of 14 (0=worst, 99=best). If you desire only a moderate level of risk and strong performance, then this fund is an excellent option.

Data Date	Investment Rating	Net Assets ($Mil)	Price	Performance Rating/Pts	Total Return Y-T-D	Risk Rating/Pts
12-12	B+	4.40	43.64	B / 8.0	3.05%	B / 8.0

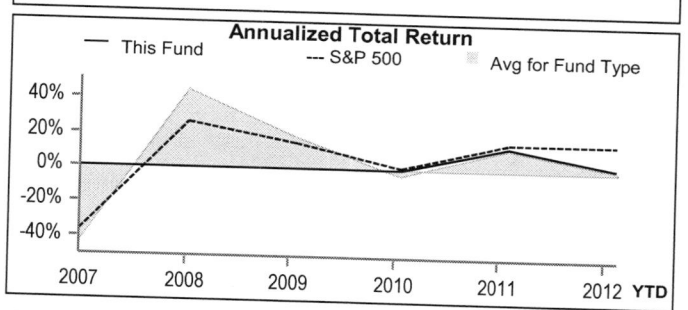

*Direxion Daily 20+ Yr Treas Bear (TYBS)

D-   **Weak**

Fund Family: Rafferty Asset Management LLC
Fund Type: Global
Inception Date: March 23, 2011

Major Rating Factors:
Disappointing performance is the major factor driving the D- (Weak) TheStreet.com Investment Rating for *Direxion Daily 20+ Yr Treas Bear. The fund currently has a performance rating of D- (Weak) based on an annualized return of 0.00% over the last three years and a total return of 3.29% year to date 2012. Factored into the performance evaluation is an expense ratio of 0.65% (very low).

The fund's risk rating is currently C+ (Fair). It carries a beta of 0.00, meaning the fund's expected move will be 0.0% for every 10% move in the market. Volatility, as measured by both the semi-deviation and a drawdown factor, is considered low. As of December 31, 2012, *Direxion Daily 20+ Yr Treas Bear traded at a discount of 2.40% below its net asset value, which is better than its one-year historical average discount of .01%.

Paul Brigandi has been running the fund for 2 years and currently receives a manager quality ranking of 8 (0=worst, 99=best). This fund offers only a moderate level of risk but investors looking for strong performance are still waiting.

Data Date	Investment Rating	Net Assets ($Mil)	Price	Performance Rating/Pts	Total Return Y-T-D	Risk Rating/Pts
12-12	D-	2.70	26.45	D- / 1.2	3.29%	C+ / 6.4

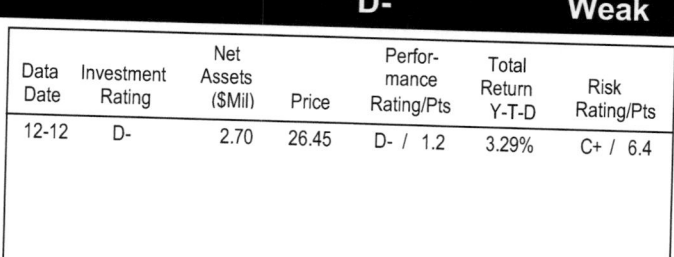

*Direxion Daily 20+ Yr Treas Bear (TMV)

E-   **Very Weak**

Fund Family: Rafferty Asset Management LLC
Fund Type: US Government/Agency
Inception Date: April 16, 2009

Major Rating Factors: *Direxion Daily 20+ Yr Treas Bear has adopted a risky asset allocation strategy and currently receives an overall TheStreet.com Investment Rating of E- (Very Weak). The fund has an above average level of volatility, as measured by both semi-deviation and drawdown factors. It carries a beta of -3.84, meaning the fund's expected move will be -38.4% for every 10% move in the market. As of December 31, 2012, *Direxion Daily 20+ Yr Treas Bear traded at a discount of 2.90% below its net asset value, which is better than its one-year historical average premium of .02%. Unfortunately, the high level of risk (D+, Weak) failed to pay off as investors endured very poor performance.

The fund's performance rating is currently E- (Very Weak). It has registered an annualized return of -44.44% over the last three years and is up 2.99% year to date 2012. Factored into the performance evaluation is an expense ratio of 0.94% (low).

Paul Brigandi currently receives a manager quality ranking of 10 (0=worst, 99=best). If you can tolerate high levels of risk in the hope of improved future returns, holding this fund may be an option.

Data Date	Investment Rating	Net Assets ($Mil)	Price	Performance Rating/Pts	Total Return Y-T-D	Risk Rating/Pts
12-12	E-	299.50	54.24	E- / 0.2	2.99%	D+ / 2.4
2011	E-	258.60	67.96	E- / 0	6.18%	D+ / 2.6
2010	E+	303.90	43.21	E+ / 0.7	-36.69%	C- / 3.5

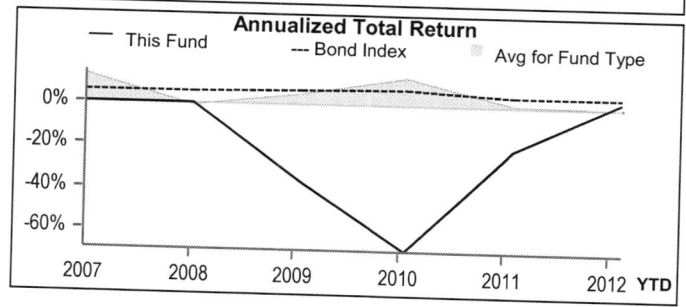

*Direxion Daily 20+ Yr Treas Bull (TMF)   C+   Fair

Fund Family: Rafferty Asset Management LLC
Fund Type: US Government/Agency
Inception Date: April 16, 2009

Major Rating Factors:
Exceptional performance is the major factor driving the C+ (Fair) TheStreet.com Investment Rating for *Direxion Daily 20+ Yr Treas Bull. The fund currently has a performance rating of A- (Excellent) based on an annualized return of 33.30% over the last three years and a total return of -3.31% year to date 2012. Factored into the performance evaluation is an expense ratio of 0.95% (low).

The fund's risk rating is currently C (Fair). It carries a beta of 3.59, meaning it is expected to move 35.9% for every 10% move in the market. Volatility, as measured by both the semi-deviation and a drawdown factor, is considered average. As of December 31, 2012, *Direxion Daily 20+ Yr Treas Bull traded at a premium of 3.52% above its net asset value, which is worse than its one-year historical average discount of .02%.

Paul Brigandi currently receives a manager quality ranking of 9 (0=worst, 99=best). If you desire an average level of risk and strong performance, then this fund is a good option.

Data Date	Investment Rating	Net Assets ($Mil)	Price	Performance Rating/Pts	Total Return Y-T-D	Risk Rating/Pts
12-12	C+	25.30	71.81	A- / 9.2	-3.31%	C / 5.3
2011	B-	42.90	71.52	A+ / 9.9	-6.21%	C / 5.2
2010	D-	19.30	34.45	D- / 1.1	19.49%	C / 5.0

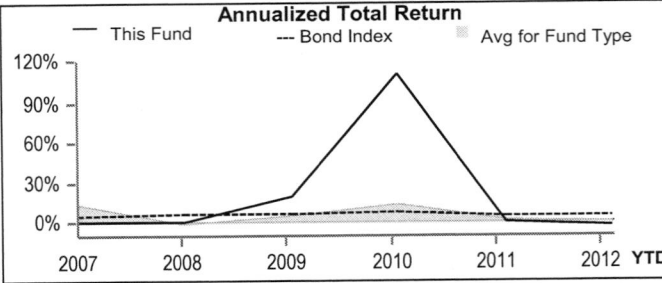

Annualized Total Return

*Direxion Daily 7-10 Yr Treas Br (TYNS)   D+   Weak

Fund Family: Rafferty Asset Management LLC
Fund Type: Global
Inception Date: March 23, 2011

Major Rating Factors:
Disappointing performance is the major factor driving the D+ (Weak) TheStreet.com Investment Rating for *Direxion Daily 7-10 Yr Treas Br. The fund currently has a performance rating of D- (Weak) based on an annualized return of 0.00% over the last three years and a total return of 0.15% year to date 2012. Factored into the performance evaluation is an expense ratio of 0.65% (very low).

The fund's risk rating is currently B (Good). It carries a beta of 0.00, meaning the fund's expected move will be 0.0% for every 10% move in the market. Volatility, as measured by both the semi-deviation and a drawdown factor, is considered low. As of December 31, 2012, *Direxion Daily 7-10 Yr Treas Br traded at a discount of .18% below its net asset value, which is better than its one-year historical average premium of .05%.

Paul Brigandi has been running the fund for 2 years and currently receives a manager quality ranking of 17 (0=worst, 99=best). This fund offers only a moderate level of risk but investors looking for strong performance are still waiting.

Data Date	Investment Rating	Net Assets ($Mil)	Price	Performance Rating/Pts	Total Return Y-T-D	Risk Rating/Pts
12-12	D+	1.60	32.93	D- / 1.1	0.15%	B / 8.5

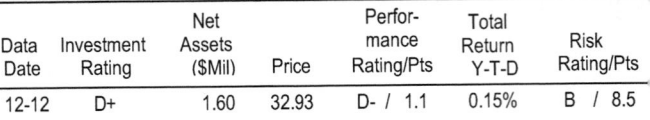

Annualized Total Return

*Direxion Daily 7-10 Yr Trs Bear (TYO)   E+   Very Weak

Fund Family: Rafferty Asset Management LLC
Fund Type: US Government/Agency
Inception Date: April 16, 2009

Major Rating Factors:
Very poor performance is the major factor driving the E+ (Very Weak) TheStreet.com Investment Rating for *Direxion Daily 7-10 Yr Trs Bear. The fund currently has a performance rating of E (Very Weak) based on an annualized return of -27.46% over the last three years and a total return of 1.64% year to date 2012. Factored into the performance evaluation is an expense ratio of 0.95% (low).

The fund's risk rating is currently C (Fair). It carries a beta of -1.42, meaning the fund's expected move will be -14.2% for every 10% move in the market. Volatility, as measured by both the semi-deviation and a drawdown factor, is considered average. As of December 31, 2012, *Direxion Daily 7-10 Yr Trs Bear traded at a discount of 1.29% below its net asset value, which is better than its one-year historical average premium of .02%.

Milu E. Komer has been running the fund for 5 years and currently receives a manager quality ranking of 8 (0=worst, 99=best). This fund offers an average level of risk but investors looking for strong performance will be frustrated.

Data Date	Investment Rating	Net Assets ($Mil)	Price	Performance Rating/Pts	Total Return Y-T-D	Risk Rating/Pts
12-12	E+	49.20	22.98	E / 0.4	1.64%	C / 4.4
2011	E+	57.30	27.38	E- / 0.2	1.35%	C / 4.5
2010	D-	68.40	45.84	E+ / 0.6	-28.62%	C+ / 5.6

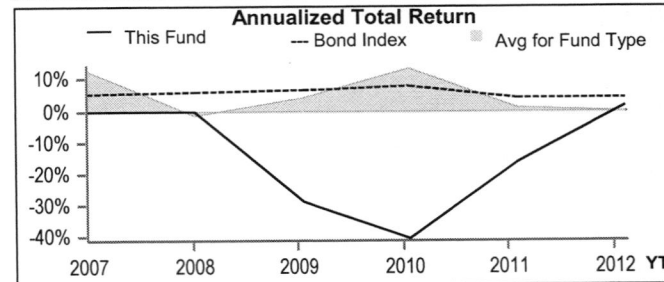

Annualized Total Return

*Direxion Daily 7-10 Yr Trs Bull (TYD)

B+   **Good**

Fund Family: Rafferty Asset Management LLC
Fund Type: US Government/Agency
Inception Date: April 16, 2009

Major Rating Factors: Strong performance is the major factor driving the B+ (Good) TheStreet.com Investment Rating for *Direxion Daily 7-10 Yr Trs Bull. The fund currently has a performance rating of B+ (Good) based on an annualized return of 27.23% over the last three years and a total return of -2.88% year to date 2012. Factored into the performance evaluation is an expense ratio of 0.95% (low).

The fund's risk rating is currently B- (Good). It carries a beta of 1.37, meaning it is expected to move 13.7% for every 10% move in the market. Volatility, as measured by both the semi-deviation and a drawdown factor, is considered low. As of December 31, 2012, *Direxion Daily 7-10 Yr Trs Bull traded at a premium of 1.68% above its net asset value, which is worse than its one-year historical average discount of .02%.

Milu E. Komer has been running the fund for 5 years and currently receives a manager quality ranking of 89 (0=worst, 99=best). If you desire only a moderate level of risk and strong performance, then this fund is an excellent option.

Data Date	Investment Rating	Net Assets ($Mil)	Price	Performance Rating/Pts	Total Return Y-T-D	Risk Rating/Pts
12-12	B+	4.30	85.82	B+ / 8.7	-2.88%	B- / 7.8
2011	A-	3.90	77.87	A+ / 9.9	-1.71%	B- / 7.6
2010	A	10.90	54.11	B+ / 8.5	28.71%	C+ / 6.9

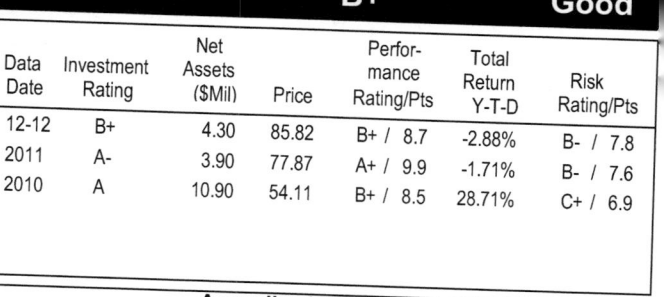

*Direxion Daily Basic Mat Bull 3x (MATL)

C-   **Fair**

Fund Family: Rafferty Asset Management LLC
Fund Type: Income
Inception Date: June 15, 2011

Major Rating Factors: *Direxion Daily Basic Mat Bull 3x has adopted a very risky asset allocation strategy and currently receives an overall TheStreet.com Investment Rating of C- (Fair). The fund has shown a high level of volatility, as measured by both semi-deviation and drawdown factors. It carries a beta of 0.00, meaning the fund's expected move will be 0.0% for every 10% move in the market. As of December 31, 2012, *Direxion Daily Basic Mat Bull 3x traded at a discount of 11.42% below its net asset value, which is better than its one-year historical average discount of .06%. The high level of risk (D, Weak) did however, reward investors with excellent performance.

The fund's performance rating is currently A+ (Excellent). It has registered an annualized return of 0.00% over the last three years and is up 12.66% year to date 2012.

Paul Brigandi has been running the fund for 2 years and currently receives a manager quality ranking of 6 (0=worst, 99=best). If you are comfortable owning a very high risk investment, this fund may be an option.

Data Date	Investment Rating	Net Assets ($Mil)	Price	Performance Rating/Pts	Total Return Y-T-D	Risk Rating/Pts
12-12	C-	3.00	29.33	A+ / 9.8	12.66%	D / 2.0

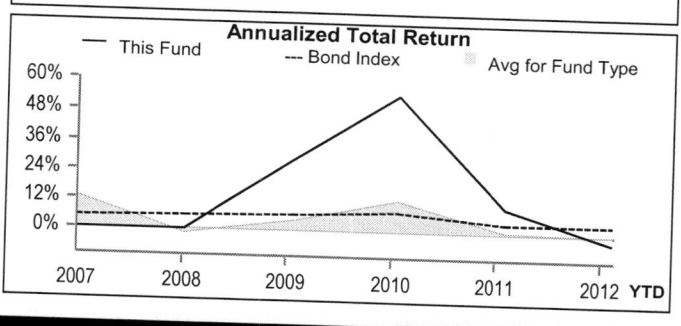

*Direxion Daily China Bear 3x ETF (YANG)

E-   **Very Weak**

Fund Family: Rafferty Asset Management LLC
Fund Type: Foreign
Inception Date: December 3, 2009

Major Rating Factors: *Direxion Daily China Bear 3x ETF has adopted a very risky asset allocation strategy and currently receives an overall TheStreet.com Investment Rating of E- (Very Weak). The fund has a high level of volatility, as measured by both semi-deviation and drawdown factors. It carries a beta of -2.66, meaning the fund's expected move will be -26.6% for every 10% move in the market. As of December 31, 2012, *Direxion Daily China Bear 3x ETF traded at a premium of 14.46% above its net asset value, which is worse than its one-year historical average discount of .18%. Unfortunately, the high level of risk (D, Weak) failed to pay off as investors endured very poor performance.

The fund's performance rating is currently E- (Very Weak). It has registered an annualized return of -37.71% over the last three years and is down -12.34% year to date 2012. Factored into the performance evaluation is an expense ratio of 0.95% (low).

Paul Brigandi has been running the fund for 4 years and currently receives a manager quality ranking of 2 (0=worst, 99=best). If you can tolerate very high levels of risk in the hope of improved future returns, holding this fund may be an option.

Data Date	Investment Rating	Net Assets ($Mil)	Price	Performance Rating/Pts	Total Return Y-T-D	Risk Rating/Pts
12-12	E-	7.80	10.45	E- / 0.1	-12.34%	D / 1.9
2011	E+	12.40	19.01	D+ / 2.4	-8.89%	D / 2.1
2010	E-	11.90	18.41	E- / 0.1	-56.32%	D / 1.9

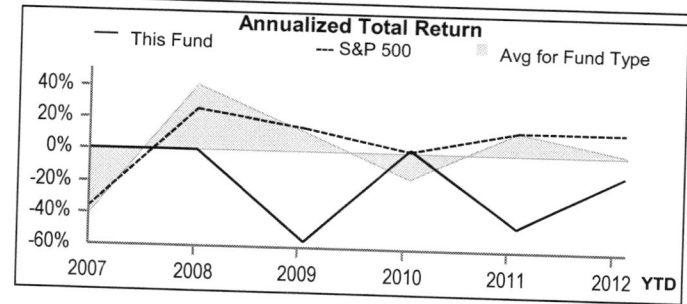

*Direxion Daily China Bull 3x ETF (YINN)

E-   **Very Weak**

Fund Family: Rafferty Asset Management LLC
Fund Type: Foreign
Inception Date: December 3, 2009

Data Date	Investment Rating	Net Assets ($Mil)	Price	Perfor-mance Rating/Pts	Total Return Y-T-D	Risk Rating/Pts
12-12	E-	76.90	18.70	E+ / 0.8	12.67%	D / 1.9
2011	E-	35.90	16.37	E- / 0	6.29%	D / 1.9
2010	A-	65.50	43.51	A+ / 9.6	25.05%	C / 4.9

Major Rating Factors: *Direxion Daily China Bull 3x ETF has adopted a very risky asset allocation strategy and currently receives an overall TheStreet.com Investment Rating of E- (Very Weak). The fund has a high level of volatility, as measured by both semi-deviation and drawdown factors. It carries a beta of 3.05, meaning it is expected to move 30.5% for every 10% move in the market. As of December 31, 2012, *Direxion Daily China Bull 3x ETF traded at a discount of 10.78% below its net asset value, which is better than its one-year historical average premium of .16%. Unfortunately, the high level of risk (D, Weak) failed to pay off as investors endured very poor performance.

The fund's performance rating is currently E+ (Very Weak). It has registered an annualized return of -17.61% over the last three years and is up 12.67% year to date 2012. Factored into the performance evaluation is an expense ratio of 0.95% (low).

Paul Brigandi has been running the fund for 4 years and currently receives a manager quality ranking of 3 (0=worst, 99=best). If you can tolerate very high levels of risk in the hope of improved future returns, holding this fund may be an option.

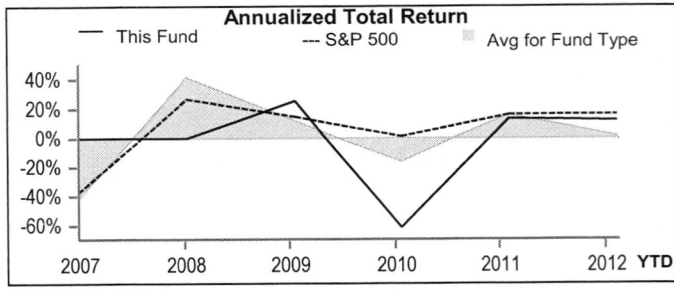

*Direxion Daily Gold Miners Bear (DUST)

E   **Very Weak**

Fund Family: Rafferty Asset Management LLC
Fund Type: Precious Metals
Inception Date: December 8, 2010

Data Date	Investment Rating	Net Assets ($Mil)	Price	Perfor-mance Rating/Pts	Total Return Y-T-D	Risk Rating/Pts
12-12	E	32.90	31.50	D / 1.8	11.24%	D / 2.2
2011	E+	6.40	42.60	D- / 1.2	-13.66%	C / 4.3

Major Rating Factors: *Direxion Daily Gold Miners Bear has adopted a very risky asset allocation strategy and currently receives an overall TheStreet.com Investment Rating of E (Very Weak). The fund has a high level of volatility, as measured by both semi-deviation and drawdown factors. It carries a beta of 0.00, meaning the fund's expected move will be 0.0% for every 10% move in the market. As of December 31, 2012, *Direxion Daily Gold Miners Bear traded at a discount of 10.36% below its net asset value, which is better than its one-year historical average premium of .23%. Unfortunately, the high level of risk (D, Weak) failed to pay off as investors endured poor performance.

The fund's performance rating is currently D (Weak). It has registered an annualized return of 0.00% over the last three years and is up 11.24% year to date 2012. Factored into the performance evaluation is an expense ratio of 0.95% (low).

Paul Brigandi has been running the fund for 3 years and currently receives a manager quality ranking of 20 (0=worst, 99=best). If you can tolerate very high levels of risk in the hope of improved future returns, holding this fund may be an option.

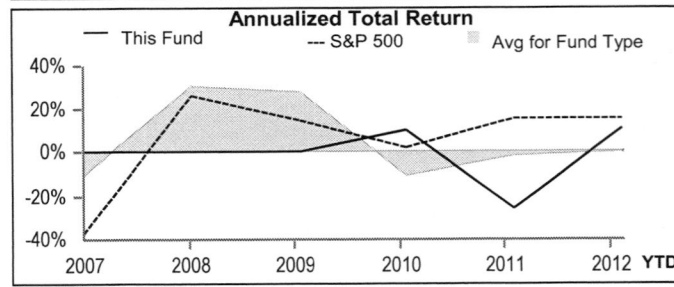

*Direxion Daily Gold Miners Bull (NUGT)

E-   **Very Weak**

Fund Family: Rafferty Asset Management LLC
Fund Type: Precious Metals
Inception Date: December 8, 2010

Data Date	Investment Rating	Net Assets ($Mil)	Price	Perfor-mance Rating/Pts	Total Return Y-T-D	Risk Rating/Pts
12-12	E-	464.20	11.00	E- / 0.1	-7.55%	D / 1.9
2011	E	90.60	19.57	E- / 0.2	10.42%	D+ / 2.9

Major Rating Factors: *Direxion Daily Gold Miners Bull has adopted a very risky asset allocation strategy and currently receives an overall TheStreet.com Investment Rating of E- (Very Weak). The fund has a high level of volatility, as measured by both semi-deviation and drawdown factors. It carries a beta of 0.00, meaning the fund's expected move will be 0.0% for every 10% move in the market. As of December 31, 2012, *Direxion Daily Gold Miners Bull traded at a premium of 7.63% above its net asset value, which is worse than its one-year historical average discount of .03%. Unfortunately, the high level of risk (D, Weak) failed to pay off as investors endured very poor performance.

The fund's performance rating is currently E- (Very Weak). It has registered an annualized return of 0.00% over the last three years but is down -7.55% year to date 2012. Factored into the performance evaluation is an expense ratio of 0.95% (low).

Paul Brigandi has been running the fund for 3 years and currently receives a manager quality ranking of 0 (0=worst, 99=best). If you can tolerate very high levels of risk in the hope of improved future returns, holding this fund may be an option.

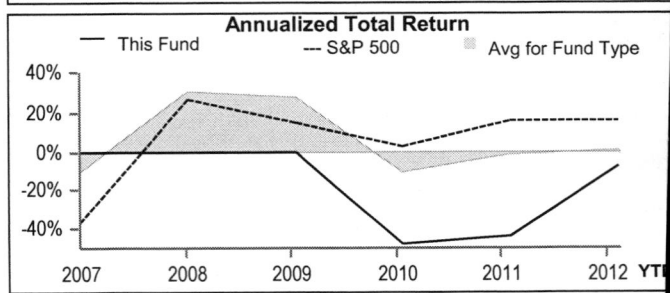

*Direxion Daily Healthcare Bull 3 (CURE)

A-   **Excellent**

Fund Family: Rafferty Asset Management LLC
Fund Type: Health
Inception Date: June 15, 2011

Data Date	Investment Rating	Net Assets ($Mil)	Price	Performance Rating/Pts	Total Return Y-T-D	Risk Rating/Pts
12-12	A-	5.30	52.92	A+ / 9.9	15.00%	C+ / 6.9

Major Rating Factors:
Exceptional performance is the major factor driving the A- (Excellent) TheStreet.com Investment Rating for *Direxion Daily Healthcare Bull 3. The fund currently has a performance rating of A+ (Excellent) based on an annualized return of 0.00% over the last three years and a total return of 15.00% year to date 2012. Factored into the performance evaluation is an expense ratio of 0.95% (low).

The fund's risk rating is currently C+ (Fair). It carries a beta of 0.00, meaning the fund's expected move will be 0.0% for every 10% move in the market. Volatility, as measured by both the semi-deviation and a drawdown factor, is considered low. As of December 31, 2012, *Direxion Daily Healthcare Bull 3 traded at a discount of 12.93% below its net asset value, which is better than its one-year historical average premium of .01%.

Paul Brigandi has been running the fund for 2 years and currently receives a manager quality ranking of 95 (0=worst, 99=best). If you desire only a moderate level of risk and strong performance, then this fund is an excellent option.

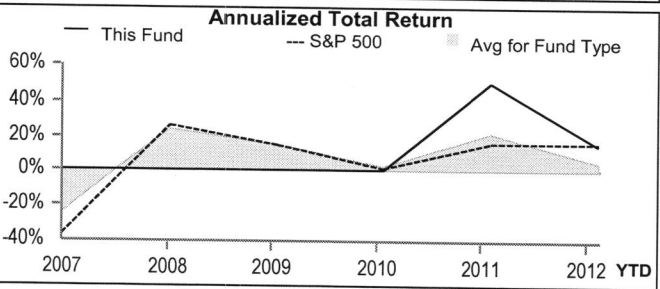

Annualized Total Return

*Direxion Daily India Bull 3X (INDL)

D   **Weak**

Fund Family: Rafferty Asset Management LLC
Fund Type: Emerging Market
Inception Date: March 11, 2010

Data Date	Investment Rating	Net Assets ($Mil)	Price	Performance Rating/Pts	Total Return Y-T-D	Risk Rating/Pts
12-12	D	28.20	20.14	C+ / 6.0	3.13%	D / 2.1
2011	E-	10.70	16.52	E- / 0	10.17%	D+ / 2.4

Major Rating Factors: *Direxion Daily India Bull 3X has adopted a very risky asset allocation strategy and currently receives an overall TheStreet.com Investment Rating of D (Weak). The fund has a high level of volatility, as measured by both semi-deviation and drawdown factors. It carries a beta of 0.00, meaning the fund's expected move will be 0.0% for every 10% move in the market. As of December 31, 2012, *Direxion Daily India Bull 3X traded at a discount of 2.99% below its net asset value, which is better than its one-year historical average premium of .08%. Unfortunately, the high level of risk (D, Weak) has only provided investors with average performance.

The fund's performance rating is currently C+ (Fair). It has registered an annualized return of 0.00% over the last three years and is up 3.13% year to date 2012. Factored into the performance evaluation is an expense ratio of 0.95% (low).

Paul Brigandi has been running the fund for 3 years and currently receives a manager quality ranking of 1 (0=worst, 99=best). If you are comfortable owning a very high risk investment, then this fund may be an option.

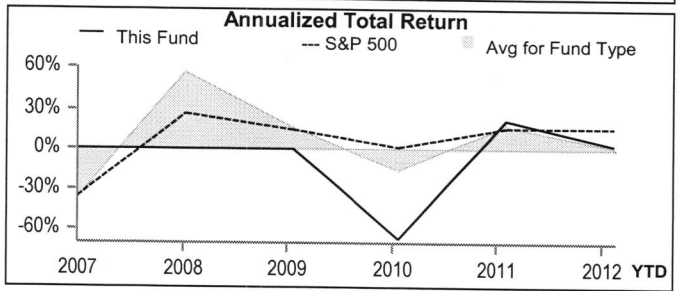

Annualized Total Return

*Direxion Daily Latin Amer Bull 3 (LBJ)

E-   **Very Weak**

Fund Family: Rafferty Asset Management LLC
Fund Type: Foreign
Inception Date: December 3, 2009

Data Date	Investment Rating	Net Assets ($Mil)	Price	Performance Rating/Pts	Total Return Y-T-D	Risk Rating/Pts
12-12	E-	32.80	74.14	E+ / 0.7	9.18%	D / 1.9
2011	E-	43.00	72.83	E- / 0.1	3.60%	D / 1.9
2010	B	44.80	40.60	A+ / 9.8	25.82%	C- / 3.4

Major Rating Factors: *Direxion Daily Latin Amer Bull 3 has adopted a very risky asset allocation strategy and currently receives an overall TheStreet.com Investment Rating of E- (Very Weak). The fund has a high level of volatility, as measured by both semi-deviation and drawdown factors. It carries a beta of 3.35, meaning it is expected to move 33.5% for every 10% move in the market. As of December 31, 2012, *Direxion Daily Latin Amer Bull 3 traded at a discount of 8.72% below its net asset value, which is better than its one-year historical average discount of .10%. Unfortunately, the high level of risk (D, Weak) failed to pay off as investors endured very poor performance.

The fund's performance rating is currently E+ (Very Weak). It has registered an annualized return of -18.23% over the last three years and is up 9.18% year to date 2012. Factored into the performance evaluation is an expense ratio of 0.95% (low).

Paul Brigandi has been running the fund for 4 years and currently receives a manager quality ranking of 2 (0=worst, 99=best). If you can tolerate very high levels of risk in the hope of improved future returns, holding this fund may be an option.

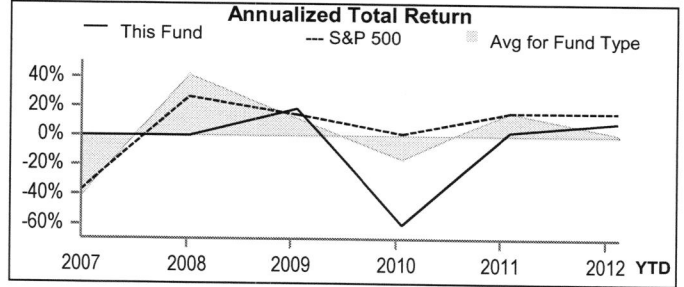

Annualized Total Return

*Direxion Daily Mid Cap Bear 3X (MIDZ)   E-   Very Weak

Fund Family: Rafferty Asset Management LLC
Fund Type: Growth
Inception Date: January 8, 2009

Data Date	Investment Rating	Net Assets ($Mil)	Price	Perfor-mance Rating/Pts	Total Return Y-T-D	Risk Rating/Pts
12-12	E-	13.60	16.41	E- / 0	-10.60%	D+ / 2.4
2011	E-	16.40	31.13	E / 0.3	-3.89%	D / 1.9
2010	E-	12.40	9.36	E- / 0	-62.04%	D- / 1.0

Major Rating Factors: *Direxion Daily Mid Cap Bear 3X has adopted a risky asset allocation strategy and currently receives an overall TheStreet.com Investment Rating of E- (Very Weak). The fund has an above average level of volatility, as measured by both semi-deviation and drawdown factors. It carries a beta of -3.09, meaning the fund's expected move will be -30.9% for every 10% move in the market. As of December 31, 2012, *Direxion Daily Mid Cap Bear 3X traded at a premium of 11.94% above its net asset value, which is worse than its one-year historical average discount of .01%. Unfortunately, the high level of risk (D+, Weak) failed to pay off as investors endured very poor performance.

The fund's performance rating is currently E- (Very Weak). It has registered an annualized return of -49.62% over the last three years and is down -10.60% year to date 2012. Factored into the performance evaluation is an expense ratio of 0.95% (low).

Paul Brigandi has been running the fund for 4 years and currently receives a manager quality ranking of 2 (0=worst, 99=best). If you can tolerate high levels of risk in the hope of improved future returns, holding this fund may be an option.

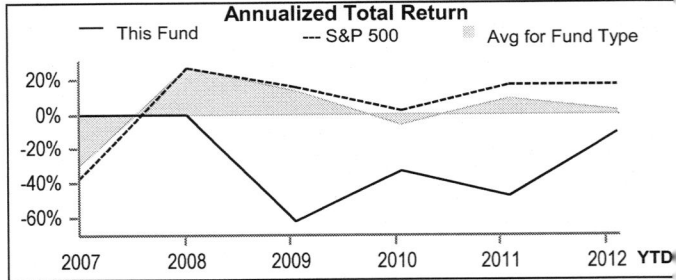

*Direxion Daily Mid Cap Bull 3X (MIDU)   C-   Fair

Fund Family: Rafferty Asset Management LLC
Fund Type: Growth
Inception Date: January 8, 2009

Data Date	Investment Rating	Net Assets ($Mil)	Price	Perfor-mance Rating/Pts	Total Return Y-T-D	Risk Rating/Pts
12-12	C-	37.90	37.66	A+ / 9.7	11.76%	D / 1.9
2011	E-	56.70	31.44	E+ / 0.8	4.55%	D / 1.9
2010	C	52.20	47.61	A+ / 9.9	75.27%	D- / 1.1

Major Rating Factors: *Direxion Daily Mid Cap Bull 3X has adopted a very risky asset allocation strategy and currently receives an overall TheStreet.com Investment Rating of C- (Fair). The fund has shown a high level of volatility, as measured by both semi-deviation and drawdown factors. It carries a beta of 3.46, meaning it is expected to move 34.6% for every 10% move in the market. As of December 31, 2012, *Direxion Daily Mid Cap Bull 3X traded at a discount of 10.63% below its net asset value, which is better than its one-year historical average discount of .08%. The high level of risk (D, Weak) did however, reward investors with excellent performance.

The fund's performance rating is currently A+ (Excellent). It has registered an annualized return of 27.74% over the last three years and is up 11.76% year to date 2012. Factored into the performance evaluation is an expense ratio of 1.10% (low).

Paul Brigandi has been running the fund for 4 years and currently receives a manager quality ranking of 10 (0=worst, 99=best). If you are comfortable owning a very high risk investment, this fund may be an option.

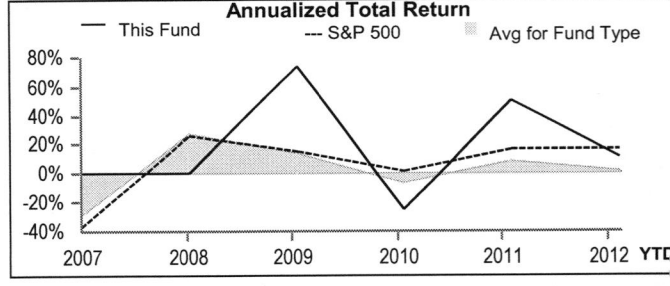

*Direxion Daily Nat Gas Rel Bear (GASX)   E-   Very Weak

Fund Family: Rafferty Asset Management LLC
Fund Type: Growth
Inception Date: July 14, 2010

Data Date	Investment Rating	Net Assets ($Mil)	Price	Perfor-mance Rating/Pts	Total Return Y-T-D	Risk Rating/Pts
12-12	E-	2.60	17.30	E / 0.5	-7.34%	D / 2.1
2011	E-	2.90	19.11	E / 0.4	-8.18%	D+ / 2.3

Major Rating Factors: *Direxion Daily Nat Gas Rel Bear has adopted a very risky asset allocation strategy and currently receives an overall TheStreet.com Investment Rating of E- (Very Weak). The fund has a high level of volatility, as measured by both semi-deviation and drawdown factors. It carries a beta of 0.00, meaning the fund's expected move will be 0.0% for every 10% move in the market. As of December 31, 2012, *Direxion Daily Nat Gas Rel Bear traded at a premium of 7.99% above its net asset value, which is worse than its one-year historical average discount of .05%. Unfortunately, the high level of risk (D, Weak) failed to pay off as investors endured very poor performance.

The fund's performance rating is currently E (Very Weak). It has registered an annualized return of 0.00% over the last three years but is down -7.34% year to date 2012. Factored into the performance evaluation is an expense ratio of 0.95% (low).

Paul Brigandi has been running the fund for 3 years and currently receives a manager quality ranking of 99 (0=worst, 99=best). If you can tolerate very high levels of risk in the hope of improved future returns, holding this fund may be an option.

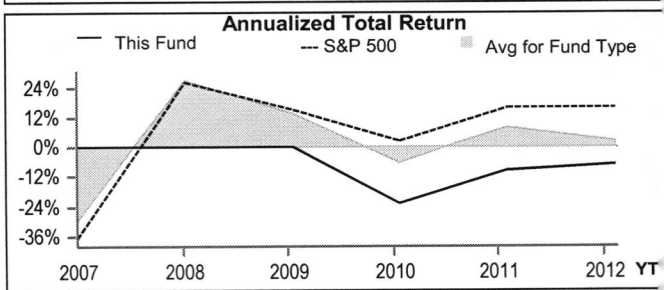

*Direxion Daily Nat Gas Rel Bull (GASL)

E-   Very Weak

Fund Family: Rafferty Asset Management LLC
Fund Type: Growth
Inception Date: July 14, 2010

Major Rating Factors: *Direxion Daily Nat Gas Rel Bull has adopted a very risky asset allocation strategy and currently receives an overall TheStreet.com Investment Rating of E- (Very Weak). The fund has a high level of volatility, as measured by both semi-deviation and drawdown factors. It carries a beta of 0.00, meaning the fund's expected move will be 0.0% for every 10% move in the market. As of December 31, 2012, *Direxion Daily Nat Gas Rel Bull traded at a discount of 6.50% below its net asset value. Unfortunately, the high level of risk (D, Weak) failed to pay off as investors endured very poor performance.

The fund's performance rating is currently E- (Very Weak). It has registered an annualized return of 0.00% over the last three years and is up 7.16% year to date 2012. Factored into the performance evaluation is an expense ratio of 0.95% (low).

Paul Brigandi has been running the fund for 3 years and currently receives a manager quality ranking of 0 (0=worst, 99=best). If you can tolerate very high levels of risk in the hope of improved future returns, holding this fund may be an option.

Data Date	Investment Rating	Net Assets ($Mil)	Price	Performance Rating/Pts	Total Return Y-T-D	Risk Rating/Pts
12-12	E-	29.00	19.98	E- / 0.1	7.16%	D / 1.9
2011	E	9.90	39.53	E+ / 0.6	7.46%	D+ / 2.7

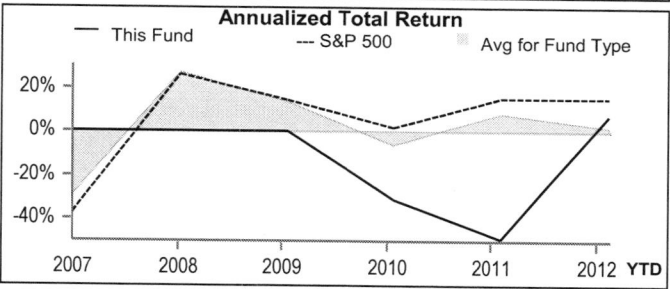

*Direxion Daily Real Estate Bear (DRV)

E-   Very Weak

Fund Family: Rafferty Asset Management LLC
Fund Type: Growth
Inception Date: July 16, 2009

Major Rating Factors: *Direxion Daily Real Estate Bear has adopted a very risky asset allocation strategy and currently receives an overall TheStreet.com Investment Rating of E- (Very Weak). The fund has a high level of volatility, as measured by both semi-deviation and drawdown factors. It carries a beta of -2.77, meaning the fund's expected move will be -27.7% for every 10% move in the market. As of December 31, 2012, *Direxion Daily Real Estate Bear traded at a premium of 6.76% above its net asset value. Unfortunately, the high level of risk (D, Weak) failed to pay off as investors endured very poor performance.

The fund's performance rating is currently E- (Very Weak). It has registered an annualized return of -60.74% over the last three years and is down -6.15% year to date 2012. Factored into the performance evaluation is an expense ratio of 0.95% (low).

Paul Brigandi has been running the fund for 4 years and currently receives a manager quality ranking of 1 (0=worst, 99=best). If you can tolerate very high levels of risk in the hope of improved future returns, holding this fund may be an option.

Data Date	Investment Rating	Net Assets ($Mil)	Price	Performance Rating/Pts	Total Return Y-T-D	Risk Rating/Pts
12-12	E-	19.30	20.70	E- / 0	-6.15%	D / 1.9
2011	E-	26.70	38.86	E- / 0	0.72%	D / 1.9
2010	E-	55.50	18.01	E- / 0	-71.73%	D- / 1.3

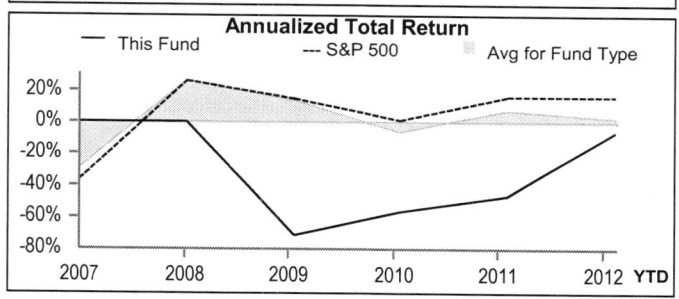

*Direxion Daily Real Estate Bull (DRN)

C-   Fair

Fund Family: Rafferty Asset Management LLC
Fund Type: Growth
Inception Date: July 16, 2009

Major Rating Factors: *Direxion Daily Real Estate Bull has adopted a very risky asset allocation strategy and currently receives an overall TheStreet.com Investment Rating of C- (Fair). The fund has shown a high level of volatility, as measured by both semi-deviation and drawdown factors. It carries a beta of 3.17, meaning it is expected to move 31.7% for every 10% move in the market. As of December 31, 2012, *Direxion Daily Real Estate Bull traded at a discount of 6.08% below its net asset value, which is better than its one-year historical average discount of .02%. The high level of risk (D, Weak) did however, reward investors with excellent performance.

The fund's performance rating is currently A+ (Excellent). It has registered an annualized return of 39.96% over the last three years and is up 6.41% year to date 2012. Factored into the performance evaluation is an expense ratio of 0.95% (low).

Paul Brigandi has been running the fund for 4 years and currently receives a manager quality ranking of 37 (0=worst, 99=best). If you are comfortable owning a very high risk investment, this fund may be an option.

Data Date	Investment Rating	Net Assets ($Mil)	Price	Performance Rating/Pts	Total Return Y-T-D	Risk Rating/Pts
12-12	C-	108.70	77.50	A+ / 9.8	6.41%	D / 1.9
2011	D-	118.50	51.57	C / 5.2	-1.36%	D / 1.9
2010	C	170.20	56.82	A+ / 9.9	63.42%	D- / 1.0

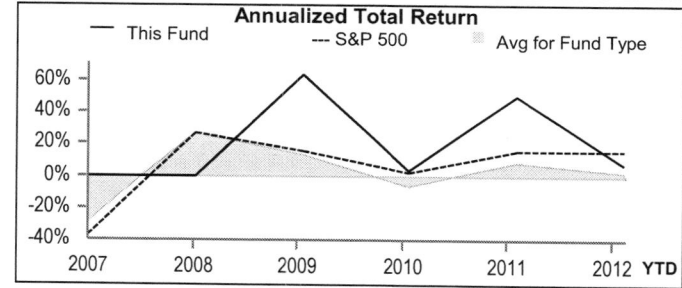

*Direxion Daily Retail Bull 3X (RETL)

A+   Excellent

Fund Family: Rafferty Asset Management LLC
Fund Type: Growth
Inception Date: July 14, 2010

Data Date	Investment Rating	Net Assets ($Mil)	Price	Performance Rating/Pts	Total Return Y-T-D	Risk Rating/Pts
12-12	A+	10.00	99.26	A+ / 9.9	5.91%	B- / 7.9
2011	C+	5.90	59.11	C+ / 5.9	2.47%	B / 8.4

Major Rating Factors:
Exceptional performance is the major factor driving the A+ (Excellent) TheStreet.com Investment Rating for *Direxion Daily Retail Bull 3X. The fund currently has a performance rating of A+ (Excellent) based on an annualized return of 0.00% over the last three years and a total return of 5.91% year to date 2012. Factored into the performance evaluation is an expense ratio of 0.95% (low).

The fund's risk rating is currently B- (Good). It carries a beta of 0.00, meaning the fund's expected move will be 0.0% for every 10% move in the market. Volatility, as measured by both the semi-deviation and a drawdown factor, is considered low. As of December 31, 2012, *Direxion Daily Retail Bull 3X traded at a discount of 5.57% below its net asset value, which is better than its one-year historical average premium of .13%.

Paul Brigandi has been running the fund for 3 years and currently receives a manager quality ranking of 98 (0=worst, 99=best). If you desire only a moderate level of risk and strong performance, then this fund is an excellent option.

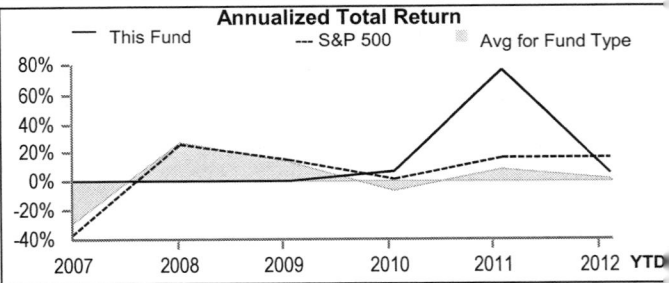

*Direxion Daily Russia Bear 3x (RUSS)

E-   Very Weak

Fund Family: Rafferty Asset Management LLC
Fund Type: Growth and Income
Inception Date: May 25, 2011

Data Date	Investment Rating	Net Assets ($Mil)	Price	Performance Rating/Pts	Total Return Y-T-D	Risk Rating/Pts
12-12	E-	5.90	14.85	E- / 0	0.74%	D / 1.9

Major Rating Factors: *Direxion Daily Russia Bear 3x has adopted a very risky asset allocation strategy and currently receives an overall TheStreet.com Investment Rating of E- (Very Weak). The fund has a high level of volatility, as measured by both semi-deviation and drawdown factors. It carries a beta of 0.00, meaning the fund's expected move will be 0.0% for every 10% move in the market. As of December 31, 2012, *Direxion Daily Russia Bear 3x traded at a discount of .60% below its net asset value, which is better than its one-year historical average discount of .19%. Unfortunately, the high level of risk (D, Weak) failed to pay off as investors endured very poor performance.

The fund's performance rating is currently E- (Very Weak). It has registered an annualized return of 0.00% over the last three years and is up 0.74% year to date 2012. Factored into the performance evaluation is an expense ratio of 0.95% (low).

Paul Brigandi has been running the fund for 2 years and currently receives a manager quality ranking of 98 (0=worst, 99=best). If you can tolerate very high levels of risk in the hope of improved future returns, holding this fund may be an option.

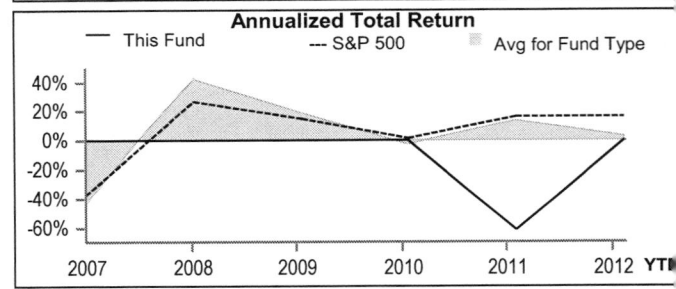
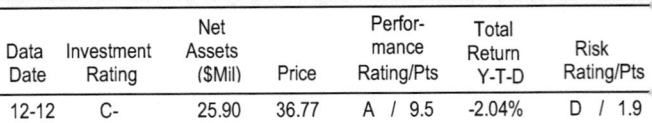

*Direxion Daily Russia Bull 3x (RUSL)

C-   Fair

Fund Family: Rafferty Asset Management LLC
Fund Type: Foreign
Inception Date: May 25, 2011

Data Date	Investment Rating	Net Assets ($Mil)	Price	Performance Rating/Pts	Total Return Y-T-D	Risk Rating/Pts
12-12	C-	25.90	36.77	A / 9.5	-2.04%	D / 1.9

Major Rating Factors: *Direxion Daily Russia Bull 3x has adopted a very risky asset allocation strategy and currently receives an overall TheStreet.com Investment Rating of C- (Fair). The fund has shown a high level of volatility, as measured by both semi-deviation and drawdown factors. It carries a beta of 0.00, meaning the fund's expected move will be 0.0% for every 10% move in the market. As of December 31, 2012, *Direxion Daily Russia Bull 3x traded at a premium of 1.88% above its net asset value, which is worse than its one-year historical average premium of .02%. The high level of risk (D, Weak) did however, reward investors with excellent performance.

The fund's performance rating is currently A (Excellent). It has registered an annualized return of 0.00% over the last three years but is down -2.04% year to date 2012. Factored into the performance evaluation is an expense ratio of 0.95% (low).

Paul Brigandi has been running the fund for 2 years and currently receives a manager quality ranking of 0 (0=worst, 99=best). If you are comfortable owning a very high risk investment, this fund may be an option.

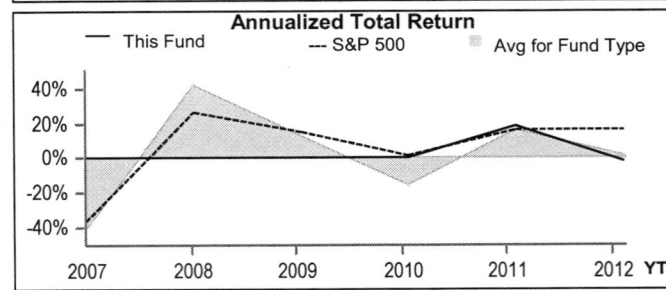

*Direxion Daily Semiconductor Bea (SOXS)

E- **Very Weak**

Fund Family: Rafferty Asset Management LLC
Fund Type: Income
Inception Date: March 11, 2010

Major Rating Factors: *Direxion Daily Semiconductor Bea has adopted a very risky asset allocation strategy and currently receives an overall TheStreet.com Investment Rating of E- (Very Weak). The fund has a high level of volatility, as measured by both semi-deviation and drawdown factors. It carries a beta of 0.00, meaning the fund's expected move will be 0.0% for every 10% move in the market. As of December 31, 2012, *Direxion Daily Semiconductor Bea traded at a premium of 16.45% above its net asset value, which is worse than its one-year historical average discount of .05%. Unfortunately, the high level of risk (D, Weak) failed to pay off as investors endured very poor performance.

The fund's performance rating is currently E- (Very Weak). It has registered an annualized return of 0.00% over the last three years but is down -14.16% year to date 2012. Factored into the performance evaluation is an expense ratio of 0.95% (low).

Paul Brigandi has been running the fund for 3 years and currently receives a manager quality ranking of 97 (0=worst, 99=best). If you can tolerate very high levels of risk in the hope of improved future returns, holding this fund may be an option.

Data Date	Investment Rating	Net Assets ($Mil)	Price	Perfor-mance Rating/Pts	Total Return Y-T-D	Risk Rating/Pts
12-12	E-	26.40	32.84	E- / 0	-14.16%	D / 1.9
2011	E-	17.00	56.94	E / 0.4	-8.87%	D / 1.9

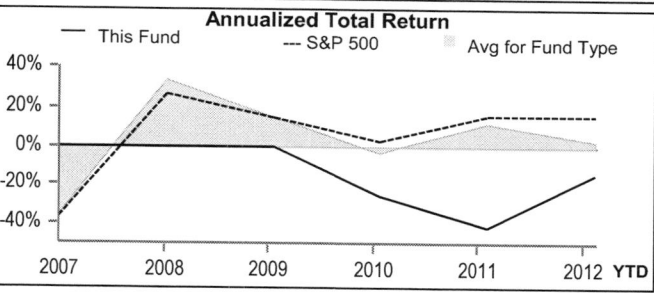

*Direxion Daily Semiconductor Bul (SOXL)

C- **Fair**

Fund Family: Rafferty Asset Management LLC
Fund Type: Income
Inception Date: March 11, 2010

Major Rating Factors: *Direxion Daily Semiconductor Bul has adopted a very risky asset allocation strategy and currently receives an overall TheStreet.com Investment Rating of C- (Fair). The fund has shown a high level of volatility, as measured by both semi-deviation and drawdown factors. It carries a beta of 0.00, meaning the fund's expected move will be 0.0% for every 10% move in the market. As of December 31, 2012, *Direxion Daily Semiconductor Bul traded at a discount of 13.03% below its net asset value, which is better than its one-year historical average discount of .08%. The high level of risk (D, Weak) did however, reward investors with excellent performance.

The fund's performance rating is currently A+ (Excellent). It has registered an annualized return of 0.00% over the last three years and is up 15.10% year to date 2012. Factored into the performance evaluation is an expense ratio of 0.95% (low).

Paul Brigandi has been running the fund for 3 years and currently receives a manager quality ranking of 0 (0=worst, 99=best). If you are comfortable owning a very high risk investment, this fund may be an option.

Data Date	Investment Rating	Net Assets ($Mil)	Price	Perfor-mance Rating/Pts	Total Return Y-T-D	Risk Rating/Pts
12-12	C-	97.10	26.89	A+ / 9.6	15.10%	D / 1.9
2011	E-	109.20	25.96	E- / 0.1	9.01%	D / 1.9

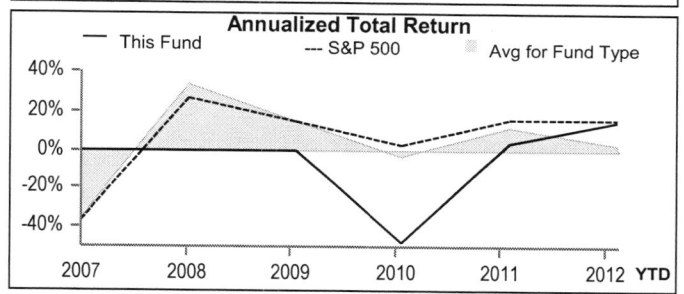

*Direxion Daily Small Cap Bear 3x (TZA)

E- **Very Weak**

Fund Family: Rafferty Asset Management LLC
Fund Type: Growth
Inception Date: November 5, 2008

Major Rating Factors: *Direxion Daily Small Cap Bear 3x has adopted a very risky asset allocation strategy and currently receives an overall TheStreet.com Investment Rating of E- (Very Weak). The fund has a high level of volatility, as measured by both semi-deviation and drawdown factors. It carries a beta of -3.61, meaning the fund's expected move will be -36.1% for every 10% move in the market. As of December 31, 2012, *Direxion Daily Small Cap Bear 3x traded at a premium of 12.31% above its net asset value, which is worse than its one-year historical average discount of .01%. Unfortunately, the high level of risk (D, Weak) failed to pay off as investors endured very poor performance.

The fund's performance rating is currently E- (Very Weak). It has registered an annualized return of -55.56% over the last three years and is down -10.79% year to date 2012. Factored into the performance evaluation is an expense ratio of 0.96% (low).

Paul Brigandi has been running the fund for 5 years and currently receives a manager quality ranking of 2 (0=worst, 99=best). If you can tolerate very high levels of risk in the hope of improved future returns, holding this fund may be an option.

Data Date	Investment Rating	Net Assets ($Mil)	Price	Perfor-mance Rating/Pts	Total Return Y-T-D	Risk Rating/Pts
12-12	E-	681.70	13.50	E- / 0	-10.79%	D / 1.9
2011	E-	741.80	26.48	E- / 0	-3.88%	D / 1.9
2010	E-	635.20	15.61	E- / 0	-68.34%	D- / 1.0
2009	E-	199.35	9.86	E- / 0	-78.57%	D- / 1.1

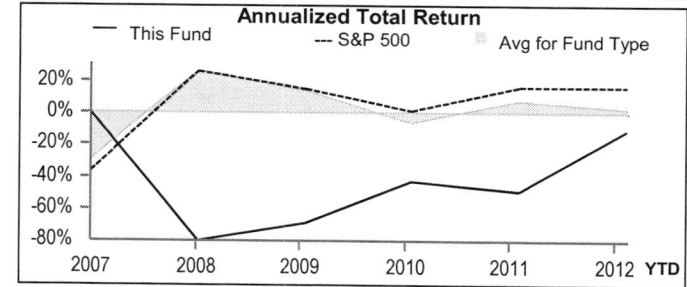

*Direxion Daily Small Cap Bull 3x (TNA)   C-   Fair

Fund Family: Rafferty Asset Management LLC
Fund Type: Growth
Inception Date: November 5, 2008

Data Date	Investment Rating	Net Assets ($Mil)	Price	Performance Rating/Pts	Total Return Y-T-D	Risk Rating/Pts
12-12	C-	732.10	63.96	A / 9.4	10.88%	D+ / 2.4
2011	D-	1,027.30	44.84	C / 4.3	3.84%	D / 2.2
2010	B+	565.00	72.43	A+ / 9.9	69.80%	C- / 3.7
2009	C+	219.09	42.74	A+ / 9.6	35.68%	C- / 3.0

Major Rating Factors: *Direxion Daily Small Cap Bull 3x has adopted a risky asset allocation strategy and currently receives an overall TheStreet.com Investment Rating of C- (Fair). The fund has shown an above average level of volatility, as measured by both semi-deviation and drawdown factors. It carries a beta of 3.97, meaning it is expected to move 39.7% for every 10% move in the market. As of December 31, 2012, *Direxion Daily Small Cap Bull 3x traded at a discount of 10.07% below its net asset value, which is better than its one-year historical average discount of .08%. The high level of risk (D+, Weak) did however, reward investors with excellent performance.

The fund's performance rating is currently A (Excellent). It has registered an annualized return of 16.04% over the last three years and is up 10.88% year to date 2012. Factored into the performance evaluation is an expense ratio of 0.95% (low).

Paul Brigandi has been running the fund for 5 years and currently receives a manager quality ranking of 4 (0=worst, 99=best). If you are comfortable owning a high risk investment, this fund may be an option.

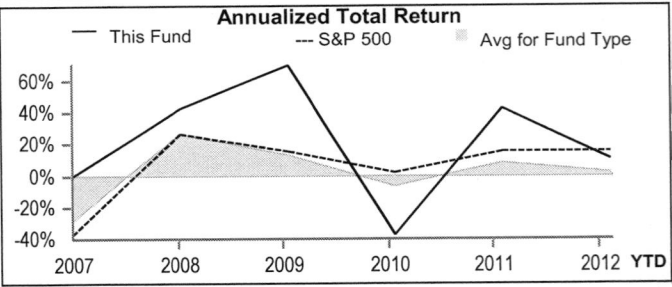

*Direxion Daily Technology Bear 3 (TECS)   E-   Very Weak

Fund Family: Rafferty Asset Management LLC
Fund Type: Growth
Inception Date: December 17, 2008

Data Date	Investment Rating	Net Assets ($Mil)	Price	Performance Rating/Pts	Total Return Y-T-D	Risk Rating/Pts
12-12	E-	26.70	9.36	E- / 0.1	-7.69%	D+ / 2.3
2011	E-	32.00	16.30	E- / 0	-8.22%	D / 1.9
2010	E-	44.50	23.91	E- / 0	-45.29%	D- / 1.0
2009	E-	9.69	8.74	E- / 0	-84.58%	D- / 1.1

Major Rating Factors: *Direxion Daily Technology Bear 3 has adopted a risky asset allocation strategy and currently receives an overall TheStreet.com Investment Rating of E- (Very Weak). The fund has an above average level of volatility, as measured by both semi-deviation and drawdown factors. It carries a beta of -3.28, meaning the fund's expected move will be -32.8% for every 10% move in the market. As of December 31, 2012, *Direxion Daily Technology Bear 3 traded at a premium of 8.46% above its net asset value. Unfortunately, the high level of risk (D+, Weak) failed to pay off as investors endured very poor performance.

The fund's performance rating is currently E- (Very Weak). It has registered an annualized return of -41.74% over the last three years and is down -7.69% year to date 2012. Factored into the performance evaluation is an expense ratio of 0.95% (low).

Paul Brigandi has been running the fund for 5 years and currently receives a manager quality ranking of 7 (0=worst, 99=best). If you can tolerate high levels of risk in the hope of improved future returns, holding this fund may be an option.

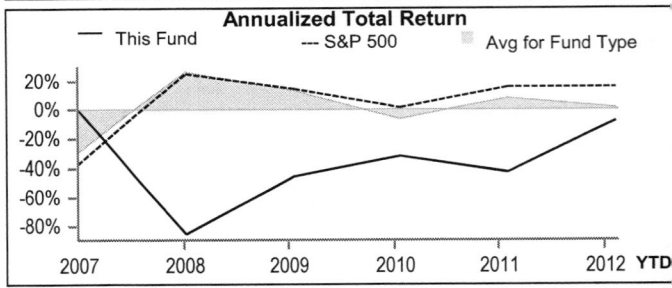

*Direxion Daily Technology Bull 3 (TECL)   D   Weak

Fund Family: Rafferty Asset Management LLC
Fund Type: Growth
Inception Date: December 17, 2008

Data Date	Investment Rating	Net Assets ($Mil)	Price	Performance Rating/Pts	Total Return Y-T-D	Risk Rating/Pts
12-12	D	138.60	48.73	C+ / 6.3	6.61%	D / 1.9
2011	C-	178.80	36.45	A+ / 9.9	8.50%	D / 1.9
2010	C	208.60	45.50	A+ / 9.8	21.21%	D- / 1.0
2009	A+	41.33	157.96	A+ / 9.9	203.65%	B- / 7.3

Major Rating Factors: *Direxion Daily Technology Bull 3 has adopted a very risky asset allocation strategy and currently receives an overall TheStreet.com Investment Rating of D (Weak). The fund has a high level of volatility, as measured by both semi-deviation and drawdown factors. It carries a beta of 3.56, meaning it is expected to move 35.6% for every 10% move in the market. As of December 31, 2012, *Direxion Daily Technology Bull 3 traded at a discount of 6.29% below its net asset value, which is better than its one-year historical average discount of .05%. Unfortunately, the high level of risk (D, Weak) has only provided investors with average performance.

The fund's performance rating is currently C+ (Fair). It has registered an annualized return of 12.51% over the last three years and is up 6.61% year to date 2012. Factored into the performance evaluation is an expense ratio of 0.95% (low).

Paul Brigandi has been running the fund for 4 years and currently receives a manager quality ranking of 4 (0=worst, 99=best). If you are comfortable owning a very high risk investment, then this fund may be an option.

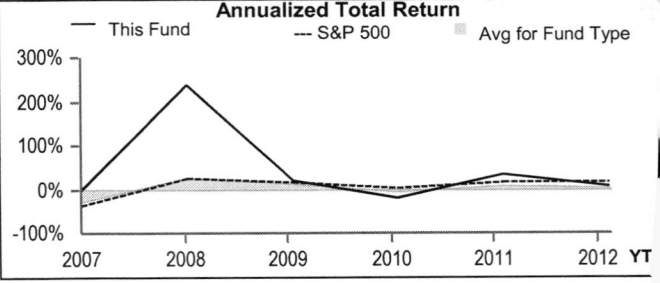

*Direxion Developed Markets Bear (DPK)

E-   **Very Weak**

Fund Family: Rafferty Asset Management LLC
Fund Type: Global
Inception Date: December 17, 2008

Major Rating Factors: *Direxion Developed Markets Bear has adopted a very risky asset allocation strategy and currently receives an overall TheStreet.com Investment Rating of E- (Very Weak). The fund has a high level of volatility, as measured by both semi-deviation and drawdown factors. It carries a beta of -2.80, meaning the fund's expected move will be -28.0% for every 10% move in the market. As of December 31, 2012, *Direxion Developed Markets Bear traded at a premium of 6.79% above its net asset value, which is worse than its one-year historical average premium of .02%. Unfortunately, the high level of risk (D, Weak) failed to pay off as investors endured very poor performance.

The fund's performance rating is currently E- (Very Weak). It has registered an annualized return of -38.79% over the last three years and is down -6.36% year to date 2012. Factored into the performance evaluation is an expense ratio of 0.95% (low).

Paul Brigandi has been running the fund for 5 years and currently receives a manager quality ranking of 2 (0=worst, 99=best). If you can tolerate very high levels of risk in the hope of improved future returns, holding this fund may be an option.

Data Date	Investment Rating	Net Assets ($Mil)	Price	Performance Rating/Pts	Total Return Y-T-D	Risk Rating/Pts
12-12	E-	10.80	16.82	E- / 0.1	-6.36%	D / 2.2
2011	E-	17.00	34.75	E- / 0.2	1.27%	D / 1.9
2010	E-	15.20	8.22	E- / 0.1	-46.41%	D- / 1.0
2009	E-	4.91	15.34	E- / 0	-73.28%	D- / 1.1

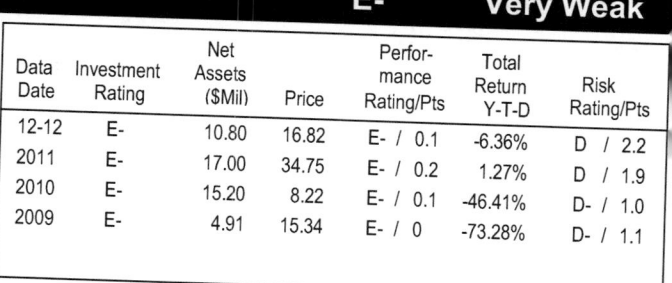

*Direxion Developed Markets Bull (DZK)

E+   **Very Weak**

Fund Family: Rafferty Asset Management LLC
Fund Type: Global
Inception Date: December 17, 2008

Major Rating Factors: *Direxion Developed Markets Bull has adopted a very risky asset allocation strategy and currently receives an overall TheStreet.com Investment Rating of E+ (Very Weak). The fund has a high level of volatility, as measured by both semi-deviation and drawdown factors. It carries a beta of 3.25, meaning it is expected to move 32.5% for every 10% move in the market. As of December 31, 2012, *Direxion Developed Markets Bull traded at a discount of 5.94% below its net asset value. Unfortunately, the high level of risk (D, Weak) has only provided investors with average performance.

The fund's performance rating is currently C- (Fair). It has registered an annualized return of -6.88% over the last three years and is up 6.47% year to date 2012. Factored into the performance evaluation is an expense ratio of 0.99% (low).

Adam Gould has been running the fund for 5 years and currently receives a manager quality ranking of 6 (0=worst, 99=best). If you are comfortable owning a very high risk investment, then this fund may be an option.

Data Date	Investment Rating	Net Assets ($Mil)	Price	Performance Rating/Pts	Total Return Y-T-D	Risk Rating/Pts
12-12	E+	27.00	44.95	C- / 3.5	6.47%	D / 2.1
2011	E	19.70	30.35	D- / 1.1	-2.67%	D+ / 2.3
2010	C+	23.50	67.07	A+ / 9.8	11.84%	D+ / 2.5
2009	B	5.92	72.94	A+ / 9.6	41.40%	C- / 3.9

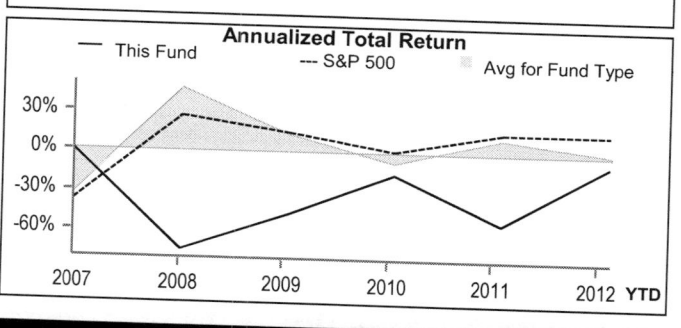

*Direxion Emerging Markets Bear 3 (EDZ)

E-   **Very Weak**

Fund Family: Rafferty Asset Management LLC
Fund Type: Global
Inception Date: December 17, 2008

Major Rating Factors: *Direxion Emerging Markets Bear 3 has adopted a very risky asset allocation strategy and currently receives an overall TheStreet.com Investment Rating of E- (Very Weak). The fund has a high level of volatility, as measured by both semi-deviation and drawdown factors. It carries a beta of -2.96, meaning the fund's expected move will be -29.6% for every 10% move in the market. As of December 31, 2012, *Direxion Emerging Markets Bear 3 traded at a premium of 1.35% above its net asset value, which is worse than its one-year historical average discount of .04%. Unfortunately, the high level of risk (D, Weak) failed to pay off as investors endured very poor performance.

The fund's performance rating is currently E- (Very Weak). It has registered an annualized return of -42.88% over the last three years and is down -1.44% year to date 2012. Factored into the performance evaluation is an expense ratio of 0.95% (low).

David A. Plecha currently receives a manager quality ranking of 1 (0=worst, 99=best). If you can tolerate very high levels of risk in the hope of improved future returns, holding this fund may be an option.

Data Date	Investment Rating	Net Assets ($Mil)	Price	Performance Rating/Pts	Total Return Y-T-D	Risk Rating/Pts
12-12	E-	88.20	9.02	E- / 0.1	-1.44%	D / 1.9
2011	E-	125.90	19.69	E- / 0	-3.00%	D / 1.9
2010	E-	87.20	20.29	E- / 0	-59.34%	D- / 1.0
2009	E-	19.06	4.99	E- / 0	-91.17%	D- / 1.1

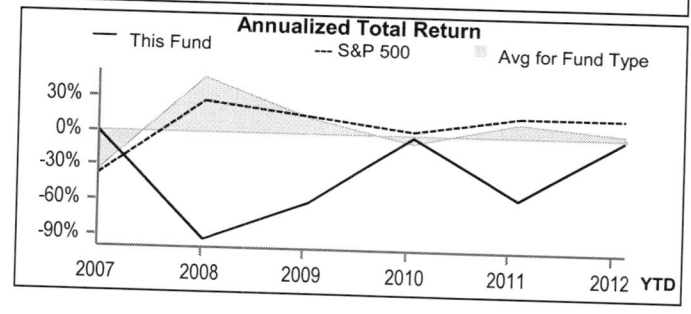

II. Analysis of ETFs and Other Closed-End Funds

*Direxion Emerging Markets Bull 3 (EDC)

E-   Very Weak

Fund Family: Rafferty Asset Management LLC
Fund Type: Global
Inception Date: December 17, 2008

Major Rating Factors: *Direxion Emerging Markets Bull 3 has adopted a very risky asset allocation strategy and currently receives an overall TheStreet.com Investment Rating of E- (Very Weak). The fund has a high level of volatility, as measured by both semi-deviation and drawdown factors. It carries a beta of 3.39, meaning it is expected to move 33.9% for every 10% move in the market. As of December 31, 2012, *Direxion Emerging Markets Bull 3 traded at a discount of .65% below its net asset value, which is better than its one-year historical average discount of .03%. Unfortunately, the high level of risk (D, Weak) failed to pay off as investors endured poor performance.

The fund's performance rating is currently D- (Weak). It has registered an annualized return of -13.62% over the last three years and is up 0.70% year to date 2012. Factored into the performance evaluation is an expense ratio of 0.95% (low).

Paul Brigandi has been running the fund for 8 years and currently receives a manager quality ranking of 4 (0=worst, 99=best). If you can tolerate very high levels of risk in the hope of improved future returns, holding this fund may be an option.

Data Date	Investment Rating	Net Assets ($Mil)	Price	Perfor-mance Rating/Pts	Total Return Y-T-D	Risk Rating/Pts
12-12	E-	351.40	109.28	D- / 1.2	0.70%	D / 1.9
2011	E	369.70	74.61	D / 1.9	2.16%	D / 1.9
2010	C	426.80	41.31	A+ / 9.8	24.29%	D- / 1.0
2009	A+	63.36	134.35	A+ / 9.9	166.37%	C+ / 5.7

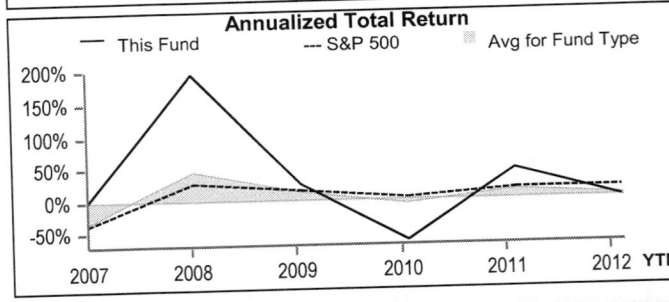

Annualized Total Return

*Direxion Energy Bear 3x Shares (ERY)

E-   Very Weak

Fund Family: Rafferty Asset Management LLC
Fund Type: Energy/Natural Resources
Inception Date: November 6, 2008

Major Rating Factors: *Direxion Energy Bear 3x Shares has adopted a very risky asset allocation strategy and currently receives an overall TheStreet.com Investment Rating of E- (Very Weak). The fund has a high level of volatility, as measured by both semi-deviation and drawdown factors. It carries a beta of -2.84, meaning the fund's expected move will be -28.4% for every 10% move in the market. As of December 31, 2012, *Direxion Energy Bear 3x Shares traded at a premium of 10.45% above its net asset value, which is worse than its one-year historical average discount of .04%. Unfortunately, the high level of risk (D, Weak) failed to pay off as investors endured very poor performance.

The fund's performance rating is currently E- (Very Weak). It has registered an annualized return of -48.07% over the last three years and is down -9.46% year to date 2012. Factored into the performance evaluation is an expense ratio of 0.95% (low).

Paul Brigandi has been running the fund for 5 years and currently receives a manager quality ranking of 2 (0=worst, 99=best). If you can tolerate very high levels of risk in the hope of improved future returns, holding this fund may be an option.

Data Date	Investment Rating	Net Assets ($Mil)	Price	Perfor-mance Rating/Pts	Total Return Y-T-D	Risk Rating/Pts
12-12	E-	73.70	7.82	E- / 0.1	-9.46%	D / 1.9
2011	E-	94.90	11.31	E- / 0	-5.66%	D / 1.9
2010	E-	50.60	22.55	E- / 0	-60.02%	D- / 1.1
2009	E-	37.07	11.28	E- / 0	-65.40%	D / 1.6

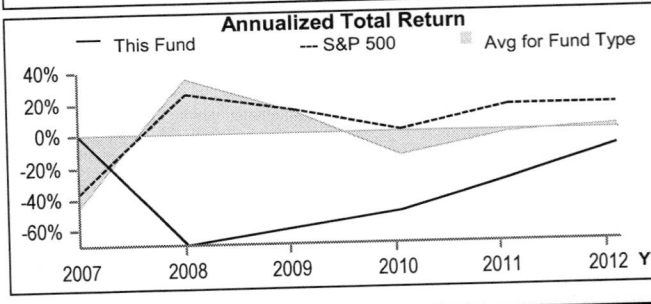

Annualized Total Return

*Direxion Energy Bull 3x Shares (ERX)

E+   Very Weak

Fund Family: Rafferty Asset Management LLC
Fund Type: Energy/Natural Resources
Inception Date: November 6, 2008

Major Rating Factors: *Direxion Energy Bull 3x Shares has adopted a very risky asset allocation strategy and currently receives an overall TheStreet.com Investment Rating of E+ (Very Weak). The fund has a high level of volatility, as measured by both semi-deviation and drawdown factors. It carries a beta of 3.09, meaning it is expected to move 30.9% for every 10% move in the market. As of December 31, 2012, *Direxion Energy Bull 3x Shares traded at a discount of 8.77% below its net asset value, which is better than its one-year historical average discount of .01%. Unfortunately, the high level of risk (D, Weak) has only provided investors with average performance.

The fund's performance rating is currently C- (Fair). It has registered an annualized return of 7.01% over the last three years and is up 9.63% year to date 2012. Factored into the performance evaluation is an expense ratio of 0.95% (low).

Paul Brigandi has been running the fund for 5 years and currently receives a manager quality ranking of 6 (0=worst, 99=best). If you are comfortable owning a very high risk investment, then this fund may be an option.

Data Date	Investment Rating	Net Assets ($Mil)	Price	Perfor-mance Rating/Pts	Total Return Y-T-D	Risk Rating/P
12-12	E+	264.80	48.48	C- / 3.9	9.63%	D / 2.
2011	E+	384.20	46.85	C- / 3.9	4.97%	D / 2.
2010	B	241.40	58.45	A+ / 9.9	48.98%	C- / 3.
2009	B-	130.44	39.68	B+ / 8.8	-0.04%	C- / 3

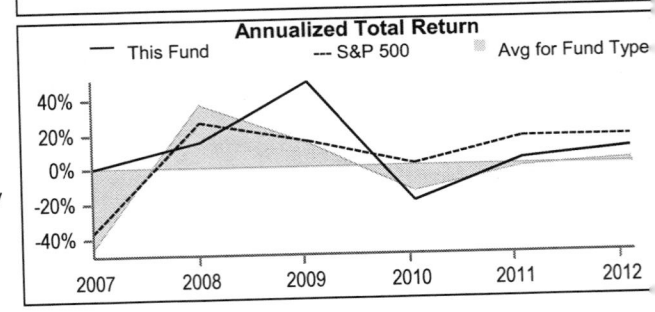

Annualized Total Return

* Denotes ETF Fund

*Direxion Financial Bear 3x Share (FAZ)

E-   Very Weak

Fund Family: Rafferty Asset Management LLC
Fund Type: Financial Services
Inception Date: November 6, 2008

Major Rating Factors: *Direxion Financial Bear 3x Share has adopted a very risky asset allocation strategy and currently receives an overall TheStreet.com Investment Rating of E- (Very Weak). The fund has a high level of volatility, as measured by both semi-deviation and drawdown factors. It carries a beta of -2.75, meaning the fund's expected move will be -27.5% for every 10% move in the market. As of December 31, 2012, *Direxion Financial Bear 3x Share traded at a premium of 14.64% above its net asset value, which is worse than its one-year historical average discount of .02%. Unfortunately, the high level of risk (D, Weak) failed to pay off as investors endured very poor performance.

The fund's performance rating is currently E- (Very Weak). It has registered an annualized return of -46.78% over the last three years and is down -12.78% year to date 2012. Factored into the performance evaluation is an expense ratio of 0.95% (low).

Paul Brigandi has been running the fund for 5 years and currently receives a manager quality ranking of 2 (0=worst, 99=best). If you can tolerate very high levels of risk in the hope of improved future returns, holding this fund may be an option.

Data Date	Investment Rating	Net Assets ($Mil)	Price	Performance Rating/Pts	Total Return Y-T-D	Risk Rating/Pts
12-12	E-	574.80	15.11	E- / 0.1	-12.78%	D / 2.0
2011	E-	823.80	37.35	E- / 0	-7.32%	D / 1.9
2010	E-	971.50	9.45	E- / 0	-51.36%	D- / 1.0
2009	E-	1,433.17	19.43	E- / 0	-94.34%	D- / 1.1

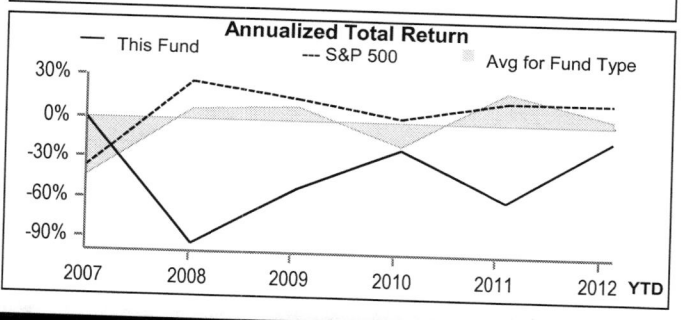

*Direxion Financial Bull 3x Share (FAS)

C-   Fair

Fund Family: Rafferty Asset Management LLC
Fund Type: Financial Services
Inception Date: November 6, 2008

Major Rating Factors: *Direxion Financial Bull 3x Share has adopted a very risky asset allocation strategy and currently receives an overall TheStreet.com Investment Rating of C- (Fair). The fund has shown a high level of volatility, as measured by both semi-deviation and drawdown factors. It carries a beta of 3.12, meaning it is expected to move 31.2% for every 10% move in the market. As of December 31, 2012, *Direxion Financial Bull 3x Share traded at a discount of 11.89% below its net asset value, which is better than its one-year historical average discount of .06%. The high level of risk (D, Weak) did however, reward investors with excellent performance.

The fund's performance rating is currently A- (Excellent). It has registered an annualized return of 0.30% over the last three years and is up 13.42% year to date 2012. Factored into the performance evaluation is an expense ratio of 0.95% (low).

Paul Brigandi has been running the fund for 5 years and currently receives a manager quality ranking of 5 (0=worst, 99=best). If you are comfortable owning a very high risk investment, this fund may be an option.

Data Date	Investment Rating	Net Assets ($Mil)	Price	Performance Rating/Pts	Total Return Y-T-D	Risk Rating/Pts
12-12	C-	1,135.20	119.92	A- / 9.0	13.42%	D / 1.9
2011	E-	1,391.00	64.87	E+ / 0.6	7.13%	D / 1.9
2010	C	1,921.20	27.84	A+ / 9.6	12.75%	D- / 1.0
2009	D	1,072.79	74.13	C / 4.6	-42.39%	D- / 1.2

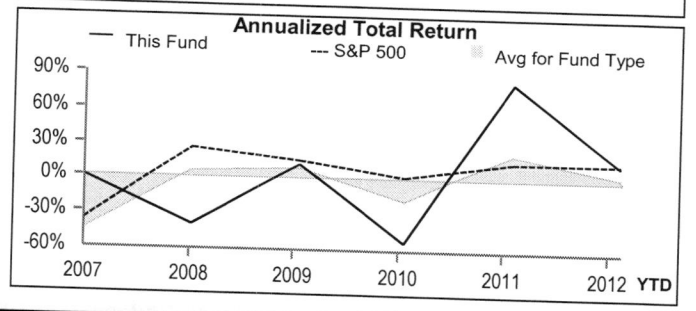

*Direxion S&P 500 Bear 3X Shares (SPXS)

E-   Very Weak

Fund Family: Rafferty Asset Management LLC
Fund Type: Growth
Inception Date: November 5, 2008

Major Rating Factors: *Direxion S&P 500 Bear 3X Shares has adopted a risky asset allocation strategy and currently receives an overall TheStreet.com Investment Rating of E- (Very Weak). The fund has an above average level of volatility, as measured by both semi-deviation and drawdown factors. It carries a beta of -2.88, meaning the fund's expected move will be -28.8% for every 10% move in the market. As of December 31, 2012, *Direxion S&P 500 Bear 3X Shares traded at a premium of 10.74% above its net asset value. Unfortunately, the high level of risk (D+, Weak) failed to pay off as investors endured very poor performance.

The fund's performance rating is currently E- (Very Weak). It has registered an annualized return of -42.51% over the last three years and is down -9.82% year to date 2012. Factored into the performance evaluation is an expense ratio of 0.95% (low).

Paul Brigandi has been running the fund for 5 years and currently receives a manager quality ranking of 4 (0=worst, 99=best). If you can tolerate high levels of risk in the hope of improved future returns, holding this fund may be an option.

Data Date	Investment Rating	Net Assets ($Mil)	Price	Performance Rating/Pts	Total Return Y-T-D	Risk Rating/Pts
12-12	E-	167.90	16.91	E- / 0.1	-9.82%	D+ / 2.7
2011	E-	155.90	29.53	E- / 0.1	-5.25%	D / 2.1
2010	E-	194.00	8.77	E- / 0	-48.74%	D- / 1.0
2009	E-	364.97	17.11	E- / 0	-67.89%	D- / 1.2

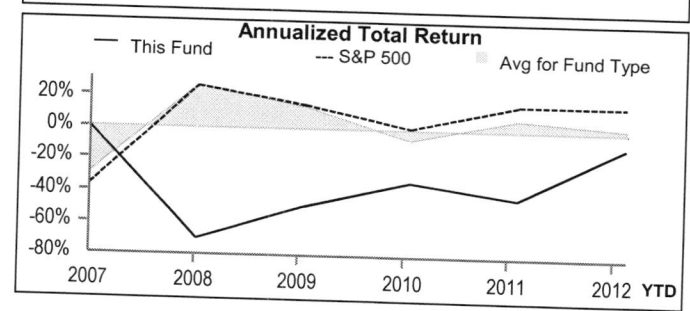

* Denotes ETF Fund

*Direxion S&P 500 Bull 3X Shares (SPXL)   C+   Fair

Fund Family: Rafferty Asset Management LLC
Fund Type: Growth
Inception Date: November 5, 2008

Major Rating Factors:
Exceptional performance is the major factor driving the C+ (Fair) TheStreet.com Investment Rating for *Direxion S&P 500 Bull 3X Shares. The fund currently has a performance rating of A (Excellent) based on an annualized return of 21.16% over the last three years and a total return of 9.95% year to date 2012. Factored into the performance evaluation is an expense ratio of 0.95% (low).

The fund's risk rating is currently C- (Fair). It carries a beta of 3.16, meaning it is expected to move 31.6% for every 10% move in the market. Volatility, as measured by both the semi-deviation and a drawdown factor, is considered average. As of December 31, 2012, *Direxion S&P 500 Bull 3X Shares traded at a discount of 8.98% below its net asset value, which is better than its one-year historical average discount of .09%.

Paul Brigandi has been running the fund for 5 years and currently receives a manager quality ranking of 9 (0=worst, 99=best). If you desire an average level of risk and strong performance, then this fund is a good option.

Data Date	Investment Rating	Net Assets ($Mil)	Price	Perfor-mance Rating/Pts	Total Return Y-T-D	Risk Rating/Pts
12-12	C+	219.20	87.65	A / 9.5	9.95%	C- / 4.1
2011	C-	307.50	60.84	B / 7.7	5.13%	C- / 4.1
2010	A-	235.20	71.50	A+ / 9.9	39.78%	C / 4.6
2009	B+	284.63	52.51	A+ / 9.8	50.44%	C- / 4.2

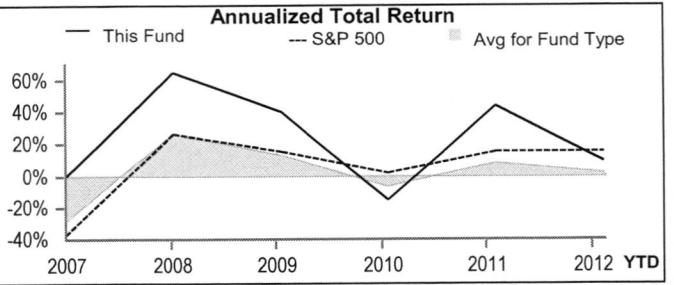

Annualized Total Return

*EGShares Basic Materials GEMS ET (LGEM)   C-   Fair

Fund Family: ALPS Advisors Inc
Fund Type: Global
Inception Date: June 23, 2011

Major Rating Factors: Middle of the road best describes *EGShares Basic Materials GEMS ET whose TheStreet.com Investment Rating is currently a C- (Fair). The fund currently has a performance rating of C+ (Fair) based on an annualized return of 0.00% over the last three years and a total return of 2.04% year to date 2012. Factored into the performance evaluation is an expense ratio of 0.85% (very low).

The fund's risk rating is currently C (Fair). It carries a beta of 0.00, meaning the fund's expected move will be 0.0% for every 10% move in the market. Volatility, as measured by both the semi-deviation and a drawdown factor, is considered average. As of December 31, 2012, *EGShares Basic Materials GEMS ET traded at a discount of .41% below its net asset value, which is better than its one-year historical average premium of .67%.

Richard C. Kang has been running the fund for 2 years and currently receives a manager quality ranking of 5 (0=worst, 99=best). If you desire an average level of risk, then this fund may be an option.

Data Date	Investment Rating	Net Assets ($Mil)	Price	Perfor-mance Rating/Pts	Total Return Y-T-D	Risk Rating/Pts
12-12	C-	3.50	14.71	C+ / 6.3	2.04%	C / 5.5

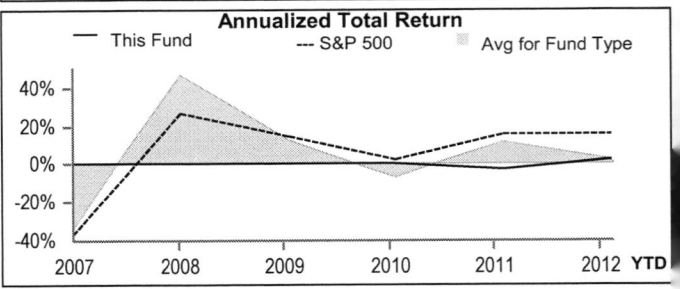

Annualized Total Return

*EGShares Brazil Infrastructure E (BRXX)   D+   Weak

Fund Family: ALPS Advisors Inc
Fund Type: Foreign
Inception Date: February 24, 2010

Major Rating Factors:
Disappointing performance is the major factor driving the D+ (Weak) TheStreet.com Investment Rating for *EGShares Brazil Infrastructure E. The fund currently has a performance rating of D+ (Weak) based on an annualized return of 0.00% over the last three years and a total return of 1.05% year to date 2012. Factored into the performance evaluation is an expense ratio of 0.88% (low).

The fund's risk rating is currently B- (Good). It carries a beta of 0.00, meaning the fund's expected move will be 0.0% for every 10% move in the market. Volatility, as measured by both the semi-deviation and a drawdown factor, is considered low. As of December 31, 2012, *EGShares Brazil Infrastructure E traded at a discount of .62% below its net asset value, which is better than its one-year historical average discount of .01%.

Richard C. Kang has been running the fund for 3 years and currently receives a manager quality ranking of 13 (0=worst, 99=best). This fund offers only a moderate level of risk but investors looking for strong performance are still waiting.

Data Date	Investment Rating	Net Assets ($Mil)	Price	Perfor-mance Rating/Pts	Total Return Y-T-D	Risk Rating/Pts
12-12	D+	73.70	21.00	D+ / 2.7	1.05%	B- / 7.0
2011	D	65.70	20.53	D- / 1.2	1.07%	B- / 7.1

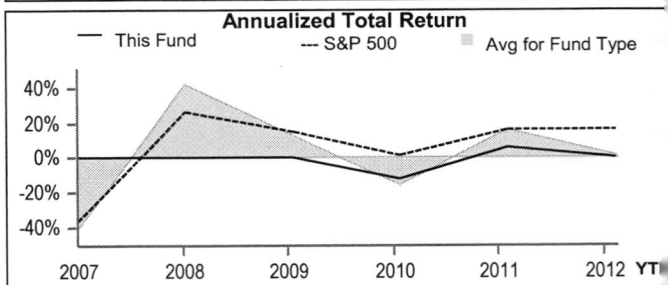

Annualized Total Return

*EGShares China Infrastructure ET (CHXX)

B   **Good**

Fund Family: ALPS Advisors Inc
Fund Type: Foreign
Inception Date: February 17, 2010

Major Rating Factors:

Exceptional performance is the major factor driving the B (Good) TheStreet.com Investment Rating for *EGShares China Infrastructure ET. The fund currently has a performance rating of A+ (Excellent) based on an annualized return of 0.00% over the last three years and a total return of 2.85% year to date 2012. Factored into the performance evaluation is an expense ratio of 0.85% (very low).

The fund's risk rating is currently C (Fair). It carries a beta of 0.00, meaning the fund's expected move will be 0.0% for every 10% move in the market. Volatility, as measured by both the semi-deviation and a drawdown factor, is considered average. As of December 31, 2012, *EGShares China Infrastructure ET traded at a discount of 1.41% below its net asset value, which is better than its one-year historical average discount of .13%.

Richard C. Kang has been running the fund for 3 years and currently receives a manager quality ranking of 94 (0=worst, 99=best). If you desire an average level of risk and strong performance, then this fund is a good option.

Data Date	Investment Rating	Net Assets ($Mil)	Price	Performance Rating/Pts	Total Return Y-T-D	Risk Rating/Pts
12-12	B	11.90	19.63	A+ / 9.8	2.85%	C / 5.4
2011	E+	12.20	15.16	E / 0.5	-2.18%	C / 5.5

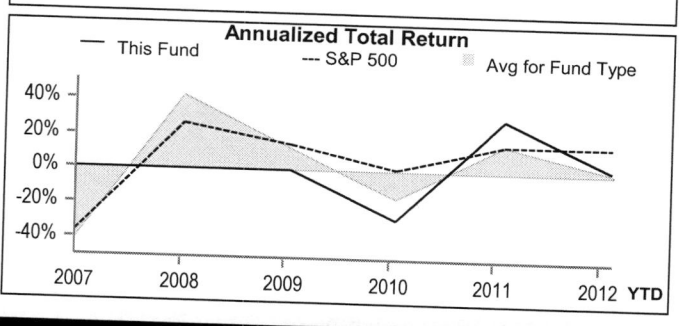

*EGShares Consumer Goods GEMS ETF (GGEM)

B   **Good**

Fund Family: ALPS Advisors Inc
Fund Type: Global
Inception Date: June 23, 2011

Major Rating Factors: Strong performance is the major factor driving the B (Good) TheStreet.com Investment Rating for *EGShares Consumer Goods GEMS ETF. The fund currently has a performance rating of B (Good) based on an annualized return of 0.00% over the last three years and a total return of 0.00% year to date 2012. Factored into the performance evaluation is an expense ratio of 0.85% (very low).

The fund's risk rating is currently B- (Good). It carries a beta of 0.00, meaning the fund's expected move will be 0.0% for every 10% move in the market. Volatility, as measured by both the semi-deviation and a drawdown factor, is considered low. As of December 31, 2012, *EGShares Consumer Goods GEMS ETF traded at a discount of .58% below its net asset value, which is better than its one-year historical average discount of .31%.

Richard C. Kang has been running the fund for 4 years and currently receives a manager quality ranking of 45 (0=worst, 99=best). If you desire only a moderate level of risk and strong performance, then this fund is an excellent option.

Data Date	Investment Rating	Net Assets ($Mil)	Price	Performance Rating/Pts	Total Return Y-T-D	Risk Rating/Pts
12-12	B	2.30	23.82	B / 8.1	0.00%	B- / 7.7

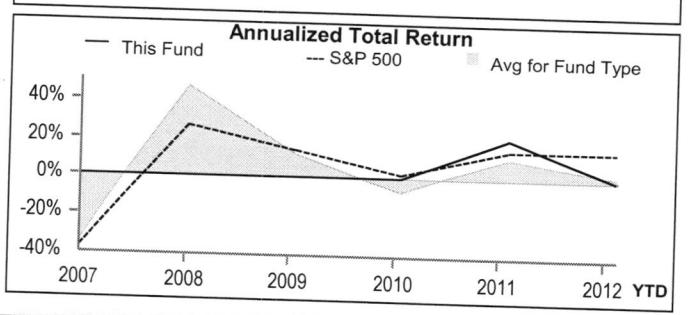

*EGShares COnsumer Services GEMS (VGEM)

B+   **Good**

Fund Family: ALPS Advisors Inc
Fund Type: Global
Inception Date: June 23, 2011

Major Rating Factors:

Exceptional performance is the major factor driving the B+ (Good) TheStreet.com Investment Rating for *EGShares COnsumer Services GEMS. The fund currently has a performance rating of A (Excellent) based on an annualized return of 0.00% over the last three years and a total return of 0.09% year to date 2012. Factored into the performance evaluation is an expense ratio of 0.85% (very low).

The fund's risk rating is currently B- (Good). It carries a beta of 0.00, meaning the fund's expected move will be 0.0% for every 10% move in the market. Volatility, as measured by both the semi-deviation and a drawdown factor, is considered low. As of December 31, 2012, *EGShares COnsumer Services GEMS traded at a discount of .09% below its net asset value, which is worse than its one-year historical average discount of .15%.

Richard C. Kang has been running the fund for 4 years and currently receives a manager quality ranking of 76 (0=worst, 99=best). If you desire only a moderate level of risk and strong performance, then this fund is an excellent option.

Data Date	Investment Rating	Net Assets ($Mil)	Price	Performance Rating/Pts	Total Return Y-T-D	Risk Rating/Pts
12-12	B+	2.10	22.14	A / 9.3	0.09%	B- / 7.1

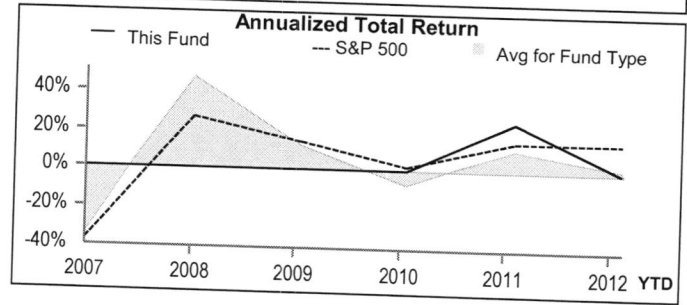

*EGShares Em Mkts Metals&Mining E (EMT)

E-   **Very Weak**

Fund Family: ALPS Advisors Inc
Fund Type: Emerging Market
Inception Date: May 21, 2009

Data Date	Investment Rating	Net Assets ($Mil)	Price	Performance Rating/Pts	Total Return Y-T-D	Risk Rating/Pts
12-12	E-	9.70	14.50	E+ / 0.9	2.14%	D / 2.2
2011	E-	13.10	14.42	E / 0.4	2.64%	D+ / 2.3
2010	C	24.80	23.40	A / 9.5	19.31%	D / 1.6

Major Rating Factors: *EGShares Em Mkts Metals&Mining E has adopted a very risky asset allocation strategy and currently receives an overall TheStreet.com Investment Rating of E- (Very Weak). The fund has a high level of volatility, as measured by both semi-deviation and drawdown factors. It carries a beta of 1.31, meaning it is expected to move 13.1% for every 10% move in the market. As of December 31, 2012, *EGShares Em Mkts Metals&Mining E traded at a discount of 1.76% below its net asset value, which is better than its one-year historical average premium of .01%. Unfortunately, the high level of risk (D, Weak) failed to pay off as investors endured very poor performance.

The fund's performance rating is currently E+ (Very Weak). It has registered an annualized return of -8.66% over the last three years and is up 2.14% year to date 2012. Factored into the performance evaluation is an expense ratio of 0.85% (very low).

Richard C. Kang has been running the fund for 4 years and currently receives a manager quality ranking of 9 (0=worst, 99=best). If you can tolerate very high levels of risk in the hope of improved future returns, holding this fund may be an option.

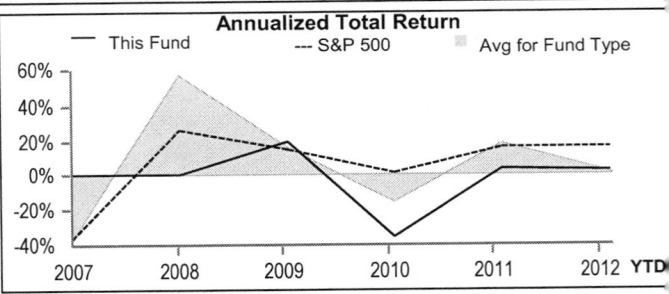

*EGShares Emerging Markets Cons E (ECON)

B+   **Good**

Fund Family: ALPS Advisors Inc
Fund Type: Emerging Market
Inception Date: September 14, 2010

Data Date	Investment Rating	Net Assets ($Mil)	Price	Performance Rating/Pts	Total Return Y-T-D	Risk Rating/Pts
12-12	B+	476.60	26.64	A- / 9.0	-0.38%	B- / 7.6
2011	D	293.90	21.98	D- / 1.5	0.00%	B- / 7.7

Major Rating Factors:
Exceptional performance is the major factor driving the B+ (Good) TheStreet.com Investment Rating for *EGShares Emerging Markets Cons E. The fund currently has a performance rating of A- (Excellent) based on an annualized return of 0.00% over the last three years and a total return of -0.38% year to date 2012. Factored into the performance evaluation is an expense ratio of 0.85% (very low).

The fund's risk rating is currently B- (Good). It carries a beta of 0.00, meaning the fund's expected move will be 0.0% for every 10% move in the market. Volatility, as measured by both the semi-deviation and a drawdown factor, is considered low. As of December 31, 2012, *EGShares Emerging Markets Cons E traded at a premium of .57% above its net asset value, which is worse than its one-year historical average premium of .23%.

Richard C. Kang has been running the fund for 3 years and currently receives a manager quality ranking of 84 (0=worst, 99=best). If you desire only a moderate level of risk and strong performance, then this fund is an excellent option.

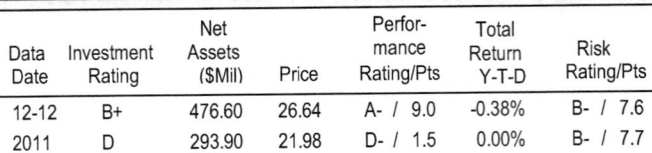
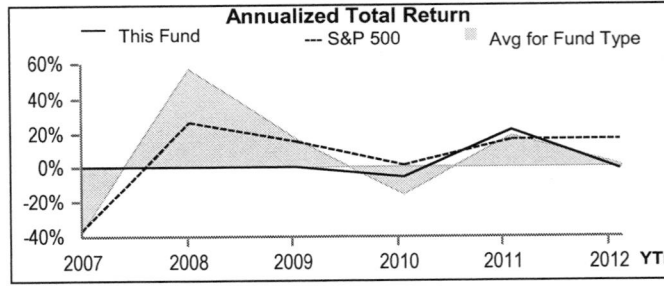

*EGShares Energy GEMS ETF (OGEM)

E+   **Very Weak**

Fund Family: ALPS Advisors Inc
Fund Type: Emerging Market
Inception Date: May 21, 2009

Data Date	Investment Rating	Net Assets ($Mil)	Price	Performance Rating/Pts	Total Return Y-T-D	Risk Rating/Pts
12-12	E+	8.20	24.18	D+ / 2.3	0.95%	C- / 3.4
2011	E+	13.10	21.64	D- / 1.0	3.42%	C- / 3.8
2010	B	9.90	27.27	A- / 9.2	16.79%	C- / 3.7

Major Rating Factors:
Disappointing performance is the major factor driving the E+ (Very Weak) TheStreet.com Investment Rating for *EGShares Energy GEMS ETF. The fund currently has a performance rating of D+ (Weak) based on an annualized return of 1.97% over the last three years and a total return of 0.95% year to date 2012. Factored into the performance evaluation is an expense ratio of 0.85% (very low).

The fund's risk rating is currently C- (Fair). It carries a beta of 1.10, meaning it is expected to move 11.0% for every 10% move in the market. Volatility, as measured by both the semi-deviation and a drawdown factor, is considered average. As of December 31, 2012, *EGShares Energy GEMS ETF traded at a discount of .70% below its net asset value, which is better than its one-year historical average discount of .18%.

Richard C. Kang has been running the fund for 4 years and currently receives a manager quality ranking of 31 (0=worst, 99=best). This fund offers an average level of risk but investors looking for strong performance will be frustrated.

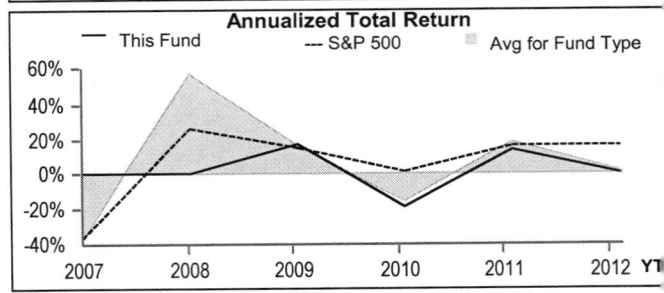

*EGShares Financials GEMS ETF (FGEM)

Fund Family: ALPS Advisors Inc
Fund Type: Financial Services
Inception Date: September 16, 2009

| | D- | | | | Weak |

Major Rating Factors: *EGShares Financials GEMS ETF receives a TheStreet.com Investment Rating of D- (Weak). The fund currently has a performance rating of C- (Fair) based on an annualized return of 2.63% over the last three years and a total return of 2.21% year to date 2012. Factored into the performance evaluation is an expense ratio of 0.85% (very low).

The fund's risk rating is currently C- (Fair). It carries a beta of 1.10, meaning it is expected to move 11.0% for every 10% move in the market. Volatility, as measured by both the semi-deviation and a drawdown factor, is considered average. As of December 31, 2012, *EGShares Financials GEMS ETF traded at a discount of 2.51% below its net asset value, which is better than its one-year historical average discount of .41%.

Richard C. Kang has been running the fund for 4 years and currently receives a manager quality ranking of 16 (0=worst, 99=best). If you desire an average level of risk, then this fund may be an option.

Data Date	Investment Rating	Net Assets ($Mil)	Price	Performance Rating/Pts	Total Return Y-T-D	Risk Rating/Pts
12-12	D-	5.20	21.75	C- / 3.2	2.21%	C- / 3.2
2011	E	2.70	17.57	E+ / 0.7	1.20%	C- / 3.1
2010	C+	12.20	24.86	B / 8.2	11.18%	C- / 3.6

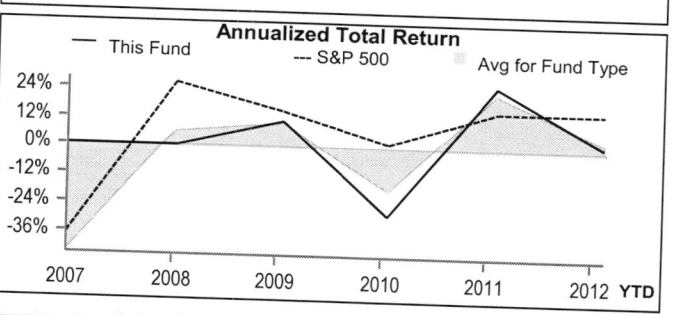

*EGShares GEMS Composite ETF (AGEM)

Fund Family: ALPS Advisors Inc
Fund Type: Emerging Market
Inception Date: July 22, 2009

| | E+ | | | | Very Weak |

Major Rating Factors:
Disappointing performance is the major factor driving the E+ (Very Weak) TheStreet.com Investment Rating for *EGShares GEMS Composite ETF. The fund currently has a performance rating of D (Weak) based on an annualized return of 0.24% over the last three years and a total return of 0.44% year to date 2012. Factored into the performance evaluation is an expense ratio of 0.75% (very low).

The fund's risk rating is currently C- (Fair). It carries a beta of 1.00, meaning that its performance tracks fairly well with that of the overall stock market. Volatility, as measured by both the semi-deviation and a drawdown factor, is considered average. As of December 31, 2012, *EGShares GEMS Composite ETF traded at a discount of .21% below its net asset value, which is better than its one-year historical average discount of .04%.

Richard C. Kang has been running the fund for 4 years and currently receives a manager quality ranking of 23 (0=worst, 99=best). This fund offers an average level of risk but investors looking for strong performance will be frustrated.

Data Date	Investment Rating	Net Assets ($Mil)	Price	Performance Rating/Pts	Total Return Y-T-D	Risk Rating/Pts
12-12	E+	14.50	23.51	D / 2.1	0.44%	C- / 3.3
2011	E+	16.60	20.63	E+ / 0.9	2.03%	C- / 3.5
2010	C+	28.10	26.90	B+ / 8.7	10.75%	C- / 3.6

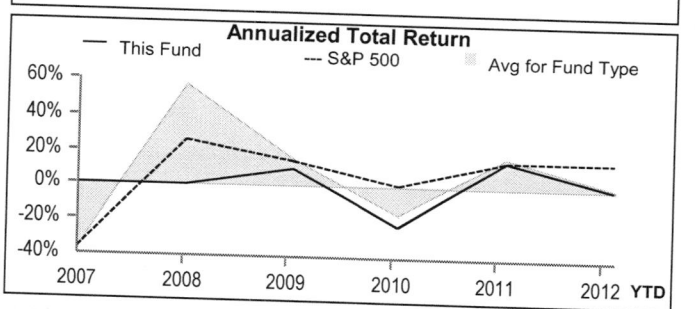

*EGShares Health Care GEMS ETF (HGEM)

Fund Family: ALPS Advisors Inc
Fund Type: Health
Inception Date: June 23, 2011

| | A- | | | | Excellent |

Major Rating Factors:
Exceptional performance is the major factor driving the A- (Excellent) TheStreet.com Investment Rating for *EGShares Health Care GEMS ETF. The fund currently has a performance rating of A (Excellent) based on an annualized return of 0.00% over the last three years and a total return of -0.43% year to date 2012. Factored into the performance evaluation is an expense ratio of 0.85% (very low).

The fund's risk rating is currently B- (Good). It carries a beta of 0.00, meaning the fund's expected move will be 0.0% for every 10% move in the market. Volatility, as measured by both the semi-deviation and a drawdown factor, is considered low. As of December 31, 2012, *EGShares Health Care GEMS ETF traded at a premium of .90% above its net asset value, which is worse than its one-year historical average discount of .06%.

Richard C. Kang has been running the fund for 4 years and currently receives a manager quality ranking of 93 (0=worst, 99=best). If you desire only a moderate level of risk and strong performance, then this fund is an excellent option.

Data Date	Investment Rating	Net Assets ($Mil)	Price	Performance Rating/Pts	Total Return Y-T-D	Risk Rating/Pts
12-12	A-	3.20	22.32	A / 9.5	-0.43%	B- / 7.3

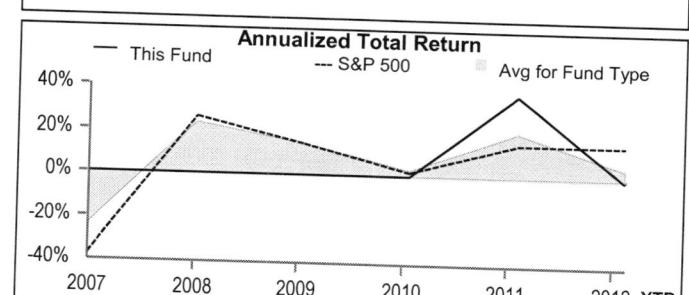

---

*EGShares India Consumer ETF (INCO)   B+   Good

Fund Family: ALPS Advisors Inc
Fund Type: Growth and Income
Inception Date: August 10, 2011

Data Date	Investment Rating	Net Assets ($Mil)	Price	Performance Rating/Pts	Total Return Y-T-D	Risk Rating/Pts
12-12	B+	2.40	24.32	A+ / 9.9	-1.03%	C+ / 6.7

Major Rating Factors:
Exceptional performance is the major factor driving the B+ (Good) TheStreet.com Investment Rating for *EGShares India Consumer ETF. The fund currently has a performance rating of A+ (Excellent) based on an annualized return of 0.00% over the last three years and a total return of -1.03% year to date 2012. Factored into the performance evaluation is an expense ratio of 0.89% (low).

The fund's risk rating is currently C+ (Fair). It carries a beta of 0.00, meaning the fund's expected move will be 0.0% for every 10% move in the market. Volatility, as measured by both the semi-deviation and a drawdown factor, is considered low. As of December 31, 2012, *EGShares India Consumer ETF traded at a premium of 2.83% above its net asset value, which is worse than its one-year historical average premium of .48%.

Richard C. Kang has been running the fund for 1 year and currently receives a manager quality ranking of 92 (0=worst, 99=best). If you desire only a moderate level of risk and strong performance, then this fund is an excellent option.

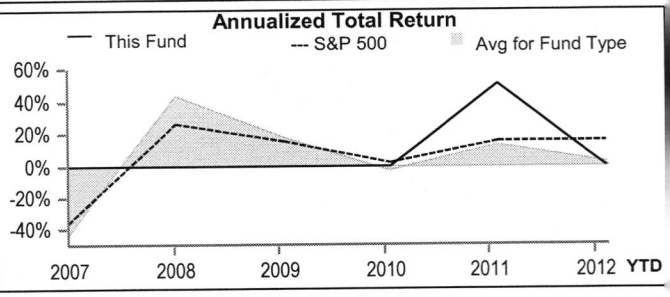

---

*EGShares India Infrastructure ET (INXX)   C-   Fair

Fund Family: ALPS Advisors Inc
Fund Type: Foreign
Inception Date: August 11, 2010

Data Date	Investment Rating	Net Assets ($Mil)	Price	Performance Rating/Pts	Total Return Y-T-D	Risk Rating/Pts
12-12	C-	58.00	14.57	C+ / 6.4	-0.21%	C / 4.7
2011	E+	48.60	11.60	E- / 0.1	3.10%	C / 4.8

Major Rating Factors: Middle of the road best describes *EGShares India Infrastructure ET whose TheStreet.com Investment Rating is currently a C- (Fair). The fund currently has a performance rating of C+ (Fair) based on an annualized return of 0.00% over the last three years and a total return of -0.21% year to date 2012. Factored into the performance evaluation is an expense ratio of 0.85% (very low).

The fund's risk rating is currently C (Fair). It carries a beta of 0.00, meaning the fund's expected move will be 0.0% for every 10% move in the market. Volatility, as measured by both the semi-deviation and a drawdown factor, is considered average. As of December 31, 2012, *EGShares India Infrastructure ET traded at a premium of .48% above its net asset value, which is worse than its one-year historical average discount of .21%.

Richard C. Kang currently receives a manager quality ranking of 22 (0=worst, 99=best). If you desire an average level of risk, then this fund may be an option.

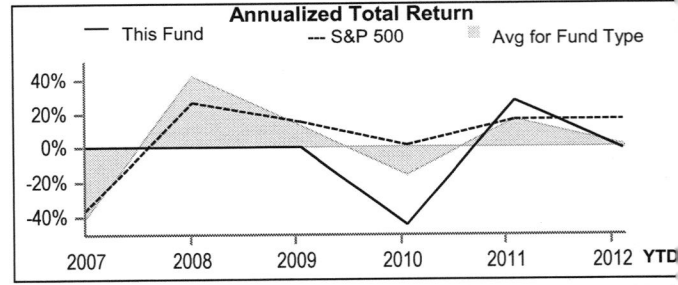

---

*EGShares India Small Cap ETF (SCIN)   C-   Fair

Fund Family: ALPS Advisors Inc
Fund Type: Foreign
Inception Date: July 7, 2010

Data Date	Investment Rating	Net Assets ($Mil)	Price	Performance Rating/Pts	Total Return Y-T-D	Risk Rating/Pts
12-12	C-	24.90	14.84	B / 7.8	0.36%	C- / 4.1
2011	E	17.00	11.18	E- / 0	4.11%	C- / 4.1

Major Rating Factors: Strong performance is the major factor driving the C- (Fair) TheStreet.com Investment Rating for *EGShares India Small Cap ETF. The fund currently has a performance rating of B (Good) based on an annualized return of 0.00% over the last three years and a total return of 0.36% year to date 2012. Factored into the performance evaluation is an expense ratio of 0.85% (very low).

The fund's risk rating is currently C- (Fair). It carries a beta of 0.00, meaning the fund's expected move will be 0.0% for every 10% move in the market. Volatility, as measured by both the semi-deviation and a drawdown factor, is considered average. As of December 31, 2012, *EGShares India Small Cap ETF traded at a discount of .87% below its net asset value, which is better than its one-year historical average premium of .14%.

Richard C. Kang currently receives a manager quality ranking of 62 (0=worst, 99=best). If you desire an average level of risk and strong performance, then this fund is a good option.

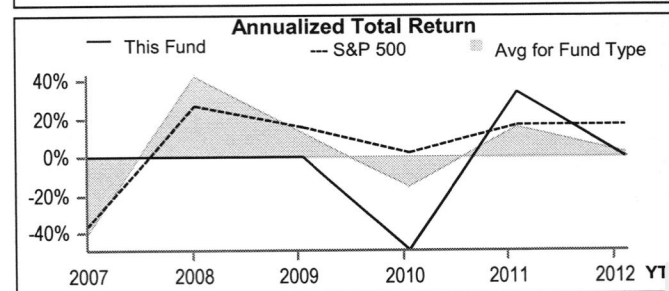

---

*EGShares Industrials GEMS ETF (IGEM)

B+   **Good**

Fund Family: ALPS Advisors Inc
Fund Type: Global
Inception Date: June 23, 2011

Major Rating Factors:
Exceptional performance is the major factor driving the B+ (Good) TheStreet.com Investment Rating for *EGShares Industrials GEMS ETF. The fund currently has a performance rating of A+ (Excellent) based on an annualized return of 0.00% over the last three years and a total return of 1.09% year to date 2012. Factored into the performance evaluation is an expense ratio of 0.85% (very low).

The fund's risk rating is currently C+ (Fair). It carries a beta of 0.00, meaning the fund's expected move will be 0.0% for every 10% move in the market. Volatility, as measured by both the semi-deviation and a drawdown factor, is considered low. As of December 31, 2012, *EGShares Industrials GEMS ETF traded at a discount of .34% below its net asset value, which is better than its one-year historical average discount of .09%.

Richard C. Kang has been running the fund for 4 years and currently receives a manager quality ranking of 90 (0=worst, 99=best). If you desire only a moderate level of risk and strong performance, then this fund is an excellent option.

Data Date	Investment Rating	Net Assets ($Mil)	Price	Performance Rating/Pts	Total Return Y-T-D	Risk Rating/Pts
12-12	B+	1.90	20.67	A+ / 9.7	1.09%	C+ / 6.8

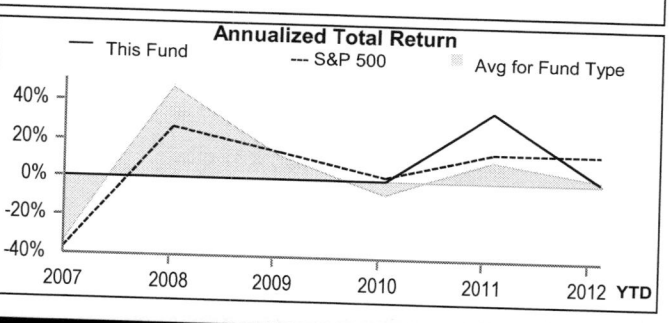

*EGShares Low Vol Em Mkts Div ETF (HILO)

B+   **Good**

Fund Family: ALPS Advisors Inc
Fund Type: Growth and Income
Inception Date: August 4, 2011

Major Rating Factors: Strong performance is the major factor driving the B+ (Good) TheStreet.com Investment Rating for *EGShares Low Vol Em Mkts Div ETF. The fund currently has a performance rating of B (Good) based on an annualized return of 0.00% over the last three years and a total return of -0.05% year to date 2012. Factored into the performance evaluation is an expense ratio of 0.85% (very low).

The fund's risk rating is currently B- (Good). It carries a beta of 0.00, meaning the fund's expected move will be 0.0% for every 10% move in the market. Volatility, as measured by both the semi-deviation and a drawdown factor, is considered low. As of December 31, 2012, *EGShares Low Vol Em Mkts Div ETF traded at a premium of .45% above its net asset value, which is worse than its one-year historical average premium of .25%.

Richard C. Kang has been running the fund for 2 years and currently receives a manager quality ranking of 26 (0=worst, 99=best). If you desire only a moderate level of risk and strong performance, then this fund is an excellent option.

Data Date	Investment Rating	Net Assets ($Mil)	Price	Performance Rating/Pts	Total Return Y-T-D	Risk Rating/Pts
12-12	B+	81.90	20.29	B / 8.2	-0.05%	B- / 7.8

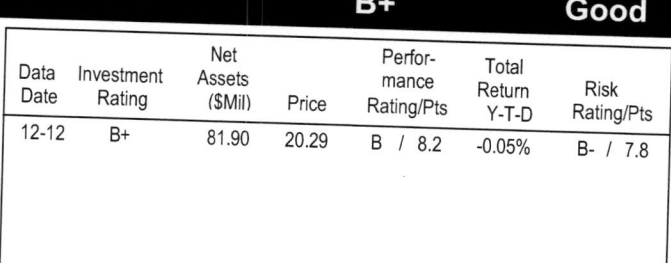

*EGShares Telecom GEMS ETF (TGEM)

C+   **Fair**

Fund Family: ALPS Advisors Inc
Fund Type: Global
Inception Date: June 23, 2011

Major Rating Factors: Middle of the road best describes *EGShares Telecom GEMS ETF whose TheStreet.com Investment Rating is currently a C+ (Fair). The fund currently has a performance rating of C+ (Fair) based on an annualized return of 0.00% over the last three years and a total return of 0.46% year to date 2012. Factored into the performance evaluation is an expense ratio of 0.85% (very low).

The fund's risk rating is currently B- (Good). It carries a beta of 0.00, meaning the fund's expected move will be 0.0% for every 10% move in the market. Volatility, as measured by both the semi-deviation and a drawdown factor, is considered low. As of December 31, 2012, *EGShares Telecom GEMS ETF traded at a discount of 1.27% below its net asset value, which is better than its one-year historical average premium of .13%.

Richard C. Kang has been running the fund for 4 years and currently receives a manager quality ranking of 29 (0=worst, 99=best). If you desire an average level of risk, then this fund may be an option.

Data Date	Investment Rating	Net Assets ($Mil)	Price	Performance Rating/Pts	Total Return Y-T-D	Risk Rating/Pts
12-12	C+	4.00	20.22	C+ / 6.0	0.46%	B- / 7.9

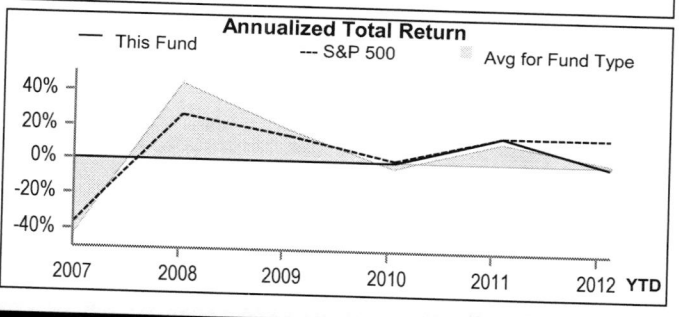

*EGShares Utilities GEMS ETF (UGEM)

D   **Weak**

Fund Family: ALPS Advisors Inc
Fund Type: Utilities
Inception Date: June 23, 2011

Data Date	Investment Rating	Net Assets ($Mil)	Price	Performance Rating/Pts	Total Return Y-T-D	Risk Rating/Pts
12-12	D	1.70	17.13	D+ / 2.6	0.47%	C+ / 6.9

Major Rating Factors:
Disappointing performance is the major factor driving the D (Weak) TheStreet.com Investment Rating for *EGShares Utilities GEMS ETF. The fund currently has a performance rating of D+ (Weak) based on an annualized return of 0.00% over the last three years and a total return of 0.47% year to date 2012. Factored into the performance evaluation is an expense ratio of 0.87% (low).

The fund's risk rating is currently C+ (Fair). It carries a beta of 0.00, meaning the fund's expected move will be 0.0% for every 10% move in the market. Volatility, as measured by both the semi-deviation and a drawdown factor, is considered low. As of December 31, 2012, *EGShares Utilities GEMS ETF traded at a discount of .87% below its net asset value, which is better than its one-year historical average discount of .32%.

Richard C. Kang has been running the fund for 4 years and currently receives a manager quality ranking of 89 (0=worst, 99=best). This fund offers only a moderate level of risk but investors looking for strong performance are still waiting.

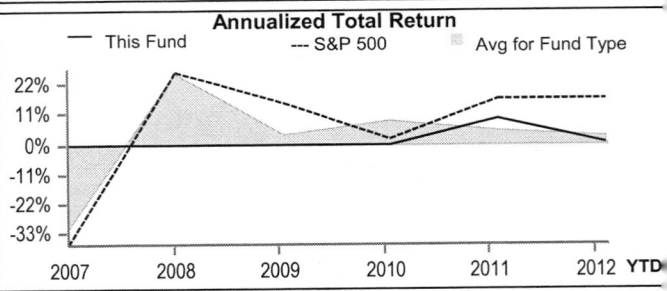

*ELEMENTS MLCX Biofuels Tot Ret (FUE)

D-   **Weak**

Fund Family: Swedish Export Credit Corporation
Fund Type: Energy/Natural Resources
Inception Date: February 5, 2008

Data Date	Investment Rating	Net Assets ($Mil)	Price	Performance Rating/Pts	Total Return Y-T-D	Risk Rating/Pts
12-12	D-	1.86	11.20	C- / 3.0	-2.00%	C / 4.5
2011	D	2.40	10.80	C- / 3.9	-2.78%	C / 4.6
2010	C+	2.50	11.35	A+ / 9.7	27.82%	D+ / 2.6
2009	C	1.59	8.50	B / 8.1	25.00%	D+ / 2.8

Major Rating Factors: *ELEMENTS MLCX Biofuels Tot Ret receives a TheStreet.com Investment Rating of D- (Weak). The fund currently has a performance rating of C- (Fair) based on an annualized return of 9.67% over the last three years and a total return of -2.00% year to date 2012. Factored into the performance evaluation is an expense ratio of 0.75% (very low).

The fund's risk rating is currently C (Fair). It carries a beta of 0.70, meaning the fund's expected move will be 7.0% for every 10% move in the market. Volatility, as measured by both the semi-deviation and a drawdown factor, is considered average. As of December 31, 2012, *ELEMENTS MLCX Biofuels Tot Ret traded at a discount of .88% below its net asset value, which is worse than its one-year historical average discount of 1.12%.

This fund has been team managed for 5 years and currently receives a manager quality ranking of 64 (0=worst, 99=best). If you desire an average level of risk, then this fund may be an option.

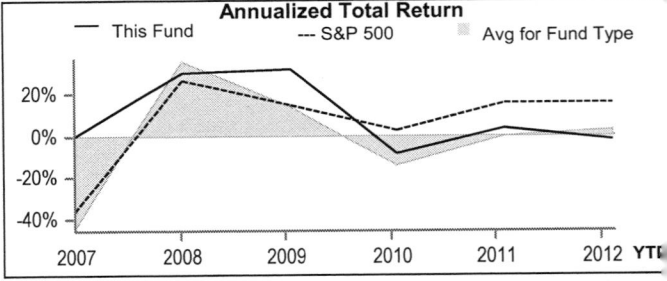

*ELEMENTS MLCX Grains Idx Tot Ret (GRU)

D-   **Weak**

Fund Family: Swedish Export Credit Corporation
Fund Type: Energy/Natural Resources
Inception Date: February 5, 2008

Data Date	Investment Rating	Net Assets ($Mil)	Price	Performance Rating/Pts	Total Return Y-T-D	Risk Rating/Pts
12-12	D-	15.58	7.17	C- / 3.2	-1.20%	C / 4.5
2011	E+	17.90	6.25	D / 1.6	-1.84%	C- / 4.0
2010	C+	18.50	7.24	A+ / 9.7	27.24%	D / 2.2
2009	E	5.37	5.71	D / 1.8	-11.88%	D+ / 2.6

Major Rating Factors: *ELEMENTS MLCX Grains Idx Tot Ret receives a TheStreet.com Investment Rating of D- (Weak). The fund currently has a performance rating of C- (Fair) based on an annualized return of 10.00% over the last three years and a total return of -1.20% year to date 2012. Factored into the performance evaluation is an expense ratio of 0.75% (very low).

The fund's risk rating is currently C (Fair). It carries a beta of 0.69, meaning the fund's expected move will be 6.9% for every 10% move in the market. Volatility, as measured by both the semi-deviation and a drawdown factor, is considered average. As of December 31, 2012, *ELEMENTS MLCX Grains Idx Tot Ret traded at a premium of 1.56% above its net asset value, which is worse than its one-year historical average premium of .07%.

This fund has been team managed for 5 years and currently receives a manager quality ranking of 64 (0=worst, 99=best). If you desire an average level of risk, then this fund may be an option.

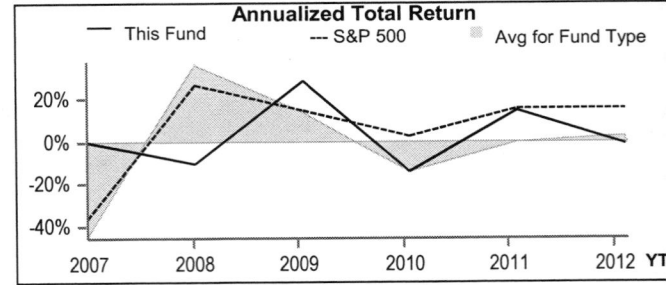

*ELEMENTS RIC Energy Total Return (RJN)

Fund Family: Swedish Export Credit Corporation
Fund Type: Energy/Natural Resources
Inception Date: October 17, 2007

E+   Very Weak

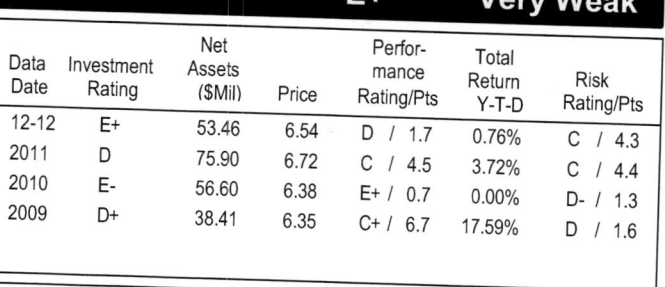

Data Date	Investment Rating	Net Assets ($Mil)	Price	Performance Rating/Pts	Total Return Y-T-D	Risk Rating/Pts
12-12	E+	53.46	6.54	D / 1.7	0.76%	C / 4.3
2011	D	75.90	6.72	C / 4.5	3.72%	C / 4.4
2010	E-	56.60	6.38	E+ / 0.7	0.00%	D- / 1.3
2009	D+	38.41	6.35	C+ / 6.7	17.59%	D / 1.6

Major Rating Factors:

Disappointing performance is the major factor driving the E+ (Very Weak) TheStreet.com Investment Rating for *ELEMENTS RIC Energy Total Return. The fund currently has a performance rating of D (Weak) based on an annualized return of 1.89% over the last three years and a total return of 0.76% year to date 2012. Factored into the performance evaluation is an expense ratio of 0.75% (very low).

The fund's risk rating is currently C (Fair). It carries a beta of 0.90, meaning that its performance tracks fairly well with that of the overall stock market. Volatility, as measured by both the semi-deviation and a drawdown factor, is considered average. As of December 31, 2012, *ELEMENTS RIC Energy Total Return traded at a discount of .76% below its net asset value, which is better than its one-year historical average premium of .06%.

This fund has been team managed for 6 years and currently receives a manager quality ranking of 17 (0=worst, 99=best). This fund offers an average level of risk but investors looking for strong performance will be frustrated.

*ELEMENTS RIC Index Agri Total Re (RJA)

Fund Family: Swedish Export Credit Corporation
Fund Type: Energy/Natural Resources
Inception Date: October 17, 2007

D-   Weak

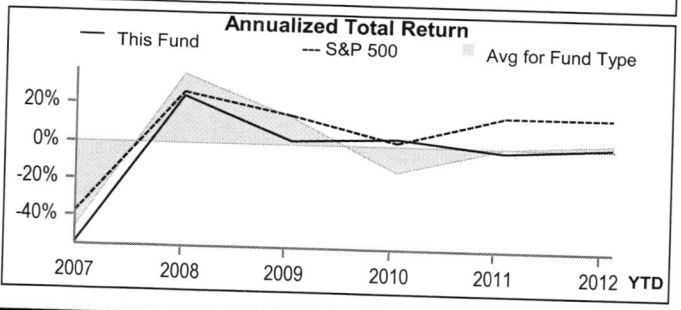

Data Date	Investment Rating	Net Assets ($Mil)	Price	Performance Rating/Pts	Total Return Y-T-D	Risk Rating/Pts
12-12	D-	302.91	9.06	D+ / 2.3	-0.22%	C- / 4.1
2011	D-	420.40	8.95	D / 2.1	-0.56%	C / 4.5
2010	C-	408.50	10.67	C+ / 6.8	34.05%	D+ / 2.6
2009	D+	244.95	7.94	C+ / 5.6	4.75%	D+ / 2.8

Major Rating Factors:

Disappointing performance is the major factor driving the D- (Weak) TheStreet.com Investment Rating for *ELEMENTS RIC Index Agri Total Re. The fund currently has a performance rating of D+ (Weak) based on an annualized return of 5.86% over the last three years and a total return of -0.22% year to date 2012. Factored into the performance evaluation is an expense ratio of 0.75% (very low).

The fund's risk rating is currently C- (Fair). It carries a beta of 0.61, meaning the fund's expected move will be 6.1% for every 10% move in the market. Volatility, as measured by both the semi-deviation and a drawdown factor, is considered average. As of December 31, 2012, *ELEMENTS RIC Index Agri Total Re traded at a premium of .33% above its net asset value, which is worse than its one-year historical average discount of .04%.

This fund has been team managed for 6 years and currently receives a manager quality ranking of 42 (0=worst, 99=best). This fund offers an average level of risk but investors looking for strong performance will be frustrated.

*ELEMENTS RIC Index Total Return (RJI)

Fund Family: Swedish Export Credit Corporation
Fund Type: Energy/Natural Resources
Inception Date: October 17, 2007

D-   Weak

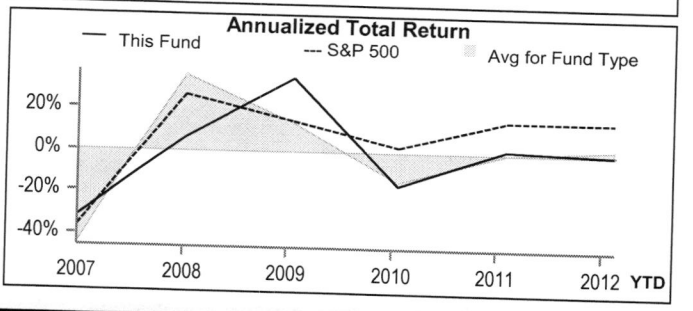

Data Date	Investment Rating	Net Assets ($Mil)	Price	Performance Rating/Pts	Total Return Y-T-D	Risk Rating/Pts
12-12	D-	510.91	8.62	D / 2.1	0.46%	C / 4.4
2011	D	666.30	8.51	C- / 3.8	1.88%	C / 4.6
2010	E+	566.30	9.16	D+ / 2.5	16.24%	D / 2.1
2009	C-	303.18	7.84	B / 7.8	21.74%	D+ / 2.3

Major Rating Factors:

Disappointing performance is the major factor driving the D- (Weak) TheStreet.com Investment Rating for *ELEMENTS RIC Index Total Return. The fund currently has a performance rating of D (Weak) based on an annualized return of 3.90% over the last three years and a total return of 0.46% year to date 2012. Factored into the performance evaluation is an expense ratio of 0.75% (very low).

The fund's risk rating is currently C (Fair). It carries a beta of 0.78, meaning the fund's expected move will be 7.8% for every 10% move in the market. Volatility, as measured by both the semi-deviation and a drawdown factor, is considered average. As of December 31, 2012, *ELEMENTS RIC Index Total Return traded at a discount of .35% below its net asset value.

This fund has been team managed for 6 years and currently receives a manager quality ranking of 26 (0=worst, 99=best). This fund offers an average level of risk but investors looking for strong performance will be frustrated.

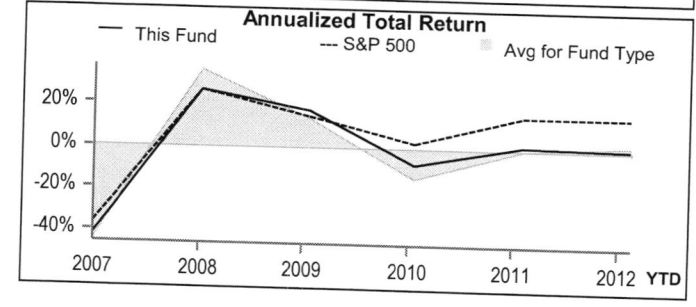

* Denotes ETF Fund

*ELEMENTS RIC Metals Total Return (RJZ)

D-   **Weak**

Fund Family: Swedish Export Credit Corporation
Fund Type: Energy/Natural Resources
Inception Date: October 17, 2007

Major Rating Factors:
Disappointing performance is the major factor driving the D- (Weak) TheStreet.com Investment Rating for *ELEMENTS RIC Metals Total Return. The fund currently has a performance rating of D (Weak) based on an annualized return of 1.86% over the last three years and a total return of 0.37% year to date 2012. Factored into the performance evaluation is an expense ratio of 0.75% (very low).

The fund's risk rating is currently C (Fair). It carries a beta of 0.79, meaning the fund's expected move will be 7.9% for every 10% move in the market. Volatility, as measured by both the semi-deviation and a drawdown factor, is considered average. As of December 31, 2012, *ELEMENTS RIC Metals Total Return traded at a discount of .46% below its net asset value, which is better than its one-year historical average discount of .11%.

This fund has been team managed for 6 years and currently receives a manager quality ranking of 24 (0=worst, 99=best). This fund offers an average level of risk but investors looking for strong performance will be frustrated.

Data Date	Investment Rating	Net Assets ($Mil)	Price	Performance Rating/Pts	Total Return Y-T-D	Risk Rating/Pts
12-12	D-	57.91	10.73	D / 1.9	0.37%	C / 4.3
2011	D+	46.30	10.15	C / 4.8	1.03%	C / 4.6
2010	C	57.20	12.25	B / 8.1	23.36%	D+ / 2.5
2009	C+	46.75	9.90	A+ / 9.6	64.45%	D+ / 2.7

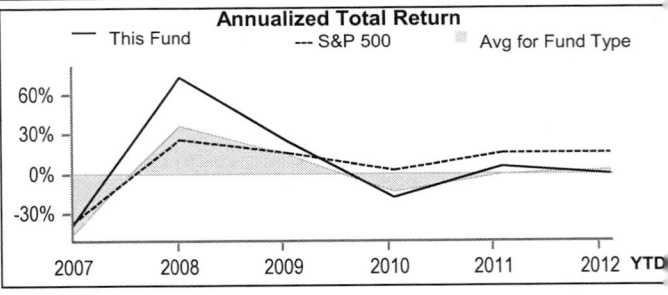

*Energy Select Sector SPDR (XLE)

C-   **Fair**

Fund Family: SSgA Funds Management Inc
Fund Type: Energy/Natural Resources
Inception Date: December 16, 1998

Major Rating Factors: Middle of the road best describes *Energy Select Sector SPDR whose TheStreet.com Investment Rating is currently a C- (Fair). The fund currently has a performance rating of C- (Fair) based on an annualized return of 9.34% over the last three years and a total return of 3.07% year to date 2012. Factored into the performance evaluation is an expense ratio of 0.18% (very low).

The fund's risk rating is currently B- (Good). It carries a beta of 1.04, meaning that its performance tracks fairly well with that of the overall stock market. Volatility, as measured by both the semi-deviation and a drawdown factor, is considered low. As of December 31, 2012, *Energy Select Sector SPDR traded at a discount of 3.01% below its net asset value.

John A. Tucker has been running the fund for 15 years and currently receives a manager quality ranking of 52 (0=worst, 99=best). If you desire an average level of risk, then this fund may be an option.

Data Date	Investment Rating	Net Assets ($Mil)	Price	Performance Rating/Pts	Total Return Y-T-D	Risk Rating/Pts
12-12	C-	6,770.20	71.42	C- / 3.8	3.07%	B- / 7.3
2011	C	6,717.60	69.13	C / 5.3	1.89%	B- / 7.1
2010	C	8,385.10	68.25	C / 5.1	21.81%	C+ / 5.6
2009	C-	5,219.00	57.01	C- / 4.1	16.02%	C+ / 5.9

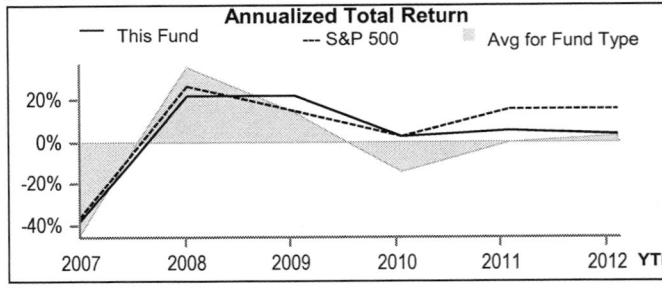

*ETFS Physical Asian Gold Shares (AGOL)

D+   **Weak**

Fund Family: ETF Securities USA LLC
Fund Type: Precious Metals
Inception Date: January 11, 2011

Major Rating Factors:
Disappointing performance is the major factor driving the D+ (Weak) TheStreet.com Investment Rating for *ETFS Physical Asian Gold Shares. The fund currently has a performance rating of D (Weak) based on an annualized return of 0.00% over the last three years and a total return of -0.71% year to date 2012. Factored into the performance evaluation is an expense ratio of 0.39% (very low).

The fund's risk rating is currently B (Good). It carries a beta of 0.00, meaning the fund's expected move will be 0.0% for every 10% move in the market. Volatility, as measured by both the semi-deviation and a drawdown factor, is considered low. As of December 31, 2012, *ETFS Physical Asian Gold Shares traded at a premium of 1.09% above its net asset value, which is worse than its one-year historical average discount of .14%.

This fund has been team managed for 2 years and currently receives a manager quality ranking of 57 (0=worst, 99=best). This fund offers only a moderate level of risk but investors looking for strong performance are still waiting.

Data Date	Investment Rating	Net Assets ($Mil)	Price	Performance Rating/Pts	Total Return Y-T-D	Risk Rating/Pts
12-12	D+	82.60	166.25	D / 1.8	-0.71%	B / 8.0

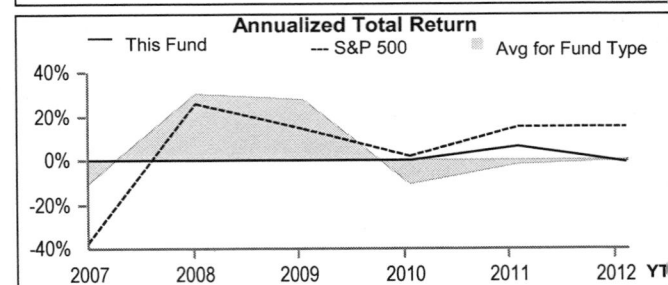

*ETFS Physical Palladium Shares (PALL)

C+　　　　**Fair**

Fund Family: ETF Securities USA LLC
Fund Type: Precious Metals
Inception Date: January 7, 2010

Data Date	Investment Rating	Net Assets ($Mil)	Price	Performance Rating/Pts	Total Return Y-T-D	Risk Rating/Pts
12-12	C+	497.80	69.22	B / 8.1	-0.33%	C+ / 6.4
2011	D-	373.90	64.57	E+ / 0.8	-5.68%	C+ / 6.6

Major Rating Factors: Strong performance is the major factor driving the C+ (Fair) TheStreet.com Investment Rating for *ETFS Physical Palladium Shares. The fund currently has a performance rating of B (Good) based on an annualized return of 0.00% over the last three years and a total return of -0.33% year to date 2012. Factored into the performance evaluation is an expense ratio of 0.60% (very low).

The fund's risk rating is currently C+ (Fair). It carries a beta of 0.00, meaning the fund's expected move will be 0.0% for every 10% move in the market. Volatility, as measured by both the semi-deviation and a drawdown factor, is considered low. As of December 31, 2012, *ETFS Physical Palladium Shares traded at a premium of 1.63% above its net asset value, which is worse than its one-year historical average premium of .11%.

This fund has been team managed for 3 years and currently receives a manager quality ranking of 69 (0=worst, 99=best). If you desire only a moderate level of risk and strong performance, then this fund is an excellent option.

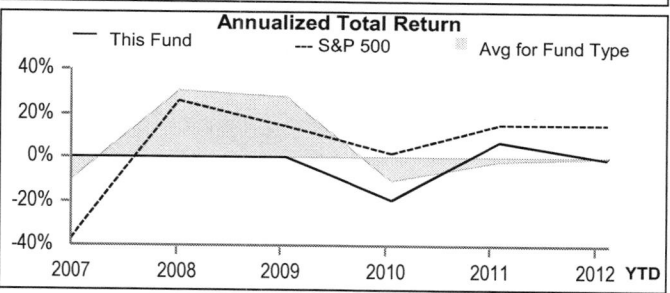

*ETFS Physical Platinum Shares (PPLT)

C-　　　　**Fair**

Fund Family: ETF Securities USA LLC
Fund Type: Precious Metals
Inception Date: January 7, 2010

Data Date	Investment Rating	Net Assets ($Mil)	Price	Performance Rating/Pts	Total Return Y-T-D	Risk Rating/Pts
12-12	C-	770.40	151.36	C / 4.6	5.83%	C+ / 6.9
2011	D-	607.30	137.82	E+ / 0.7	0.54%	B- / 7.0

Major Rating Factors: Middle of the road best describes *ETFS Physical Platinum Shares whose TheStreet.com Investment Rating is currently a C- (Fair). The fund currently has a performance rating of C (Fair) based on an annualized return of 0.00% over the last three years and a total return of 5.83% year to date 2012. Factored into the performance evaluation is an expense ratio of 0.60% (very low).

The fund's risk rating is currently C+ (Fair). It carries a beta of 0.00, meaning the fund's expected move will be 0.0% for every 10% move in the market. Volatility, as measured by both the semi-deviation and a drawdown factor, is considered low. As of December 31, 2012, *ETFS Physical Platinum Shares traded at a discount of 5.21% below its net asset value, which is better than its one-year historical average premium of .25%.

This fund has been team managed for 3 years and currently receives a manager quality ranking of 60 (0=worst, 99=best). If you desire an average level of risk, then this fund may be an option.

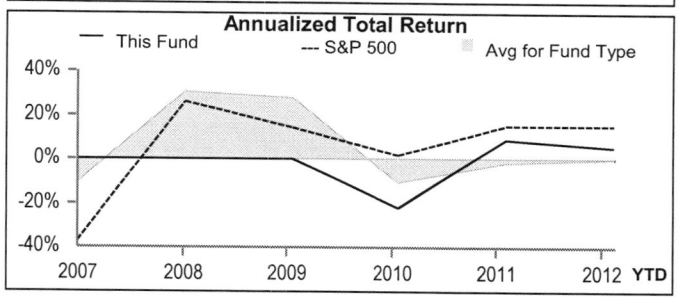

*ETFS Physical PM Basket Shares (GLTR)

D　　　　**Weak**

Fund Family: ETF Securities USA LLC
Fund Type: Precious Metals
Inception Date: October 21, 2010

Data Date	Investment Rating	Net Assets ($Mil)	Price	Performance Rating/Pts	Total Return Y-T-D	Risk Rating/Pts
12-12	D	202.20	92.81	D / 2.0	0.12%	C+ / 6.8
2011	D	0.00	86.25	D / 1.9	3.81%	C+ / 6.6

Major Rating Factors:
Disappointing performance is the major factor driving the D (Weak) TheStreet.com Investment Rating for *ETFS Physical PM Basket Shares. The fund currently has a performance rating of D (Weak) based on an annualized return of 0.00% over the last three years and a total return of 0.12% year to date 2012. Factored into the performance evaluation is an expense ratio of 0.60% (very low).

The fund's risk rating is currently C+ (Fair). It carries a beta of 0.00, meaning the fund's expected move will be 0.0% for every 10% move in the market. Volatility, as measured by both the semi-deviation and a drawdown factor, is considered low. As of December 31, 2012, *ETFS Physical PM Basket Shares traded at a discount of .08% below its net asset value, which is better than its one-year historical average premium of .27%.

This is team managed and currently receives a manager quality ranking of 44 (0=worst, 99=best). This fund offers only a moderate level of risk but investors looking for strong performance are still waiting.

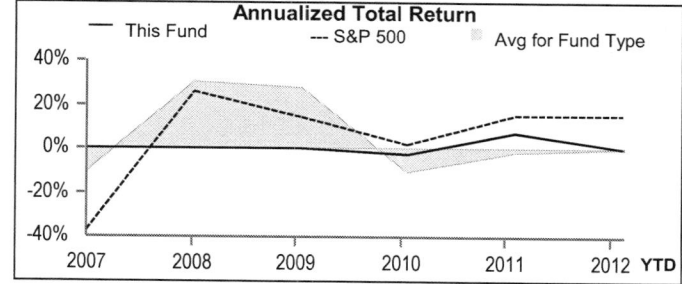

*ETFS Physical Silver Shares (SIVR)   C-   Fair

Fund Family: ETF Securities USA LLC
Fund Type: Global
Inception Date: July 20, 2009

Major Rating Factors: Middle of the road best describes *ETFS Physical Silver Shares whose TheStreet.com Investment Rating is currently a C- (Fair). The fund currently has a performance rating of C+ (Fair) based on an annualized return of 17.89% over the last three years and a total return of 0.33% year to date 2012. Factored into the performance evaluation is an expense ratio of 0.30% (very low).

The fund's risk rating is currently C (Fair). It carries a beta of 0.99, meaning that its performance tracks fairly well with that of the overall stock market. Volatility, as measured by both the semi-deviation and a drawdown factor, is considered average. As of December 31, 2012, *ETFS Physical Silver Shares traded at a discount of .96% below its net asset value, which is better than its one-year historical average premium of .53%.

This fund has been team managed for 4 years and currently receives a manager quality ranking of 96 (0=worst, 99=best). If you desire an average level of risk, then this fund may be an option.

Data Date	Investment Rating	Net Assets ($Mil)	Price	Performance Rating/Pts	Total Return Y-T-D	Risk Rating/Pts
12-12	C-	551.30	30.06	C+ / 6.3	0.33%	C / 4.9
2011	D-	534.30	27.52	D- / 1.1	3.52%	C / 5.2
2010	A+	391.80	30.73	A+ / 9.9	82.16%	B / 8.4

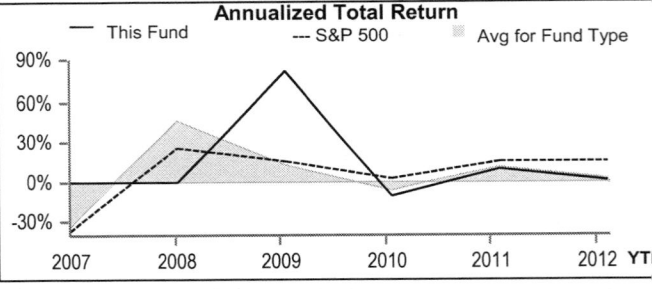

Annualized Total Return

*ETFS Physical Swiss Gold Shares (SGOL)   C   Fair

Fund Family: ETF Securities USA LLC
Fund Type: Precious Metals
Inception Date: September 8, 2009

Major Rating Factors: Middle of the road best describes *ETFS Physical Swiss Gold Shares whose TheStreet.com Investment Rating is currently a C (Fair). The fund currently has a performance rating of C (Fair) based on an annualized return of 13.26% over the last three years and a total return of -0.61% year to date 2012. Factored into the performance evaluation is an expense ratio of 0.39% (very low).

The fund's risk rating is currently B (Good). It carries a beta of 0.91, meaning that its performance tracks fairly well with that of the overall stock market. Volatility, as measured by both the semi-deviation and a drawdown factor, is considered low. As of December 31, 2012, *ETFS Physical Swiss Gold Shares traded at a premium of .95% above its net asset value, which is worse than its one-year historical average premium of .15%.

This fund has been team managed for 4 years and currently receives a manager quality ranking of 60 (0=worst, 99=best). If you desire an average level of risk, then this fund may be an option.

Data Date	Investment Rating	Net Assets ($Mil)	Price	Performance Rating/Pts	Total Return Y-T-D	Risk Rating/Pts
12-12	C	1,930.10	165.16	C / 4.3	-0.61%	B / 8.1
2011	C+	1,677.40	154.93	C / 5.3	3.40%	B / 8.2
2010	A+	1,087.70	141.39	A / 9.3	29.23%	B / 8.4

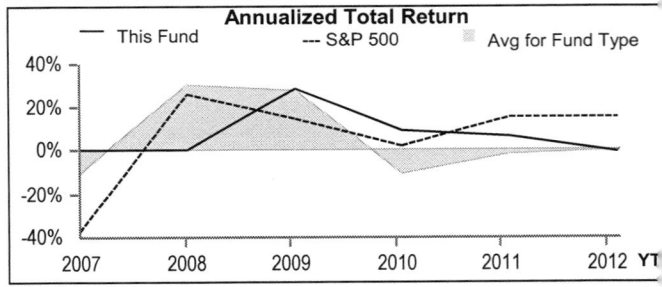

Annualized Total Return

*ETFS Physical WM Basket Shares (WITE)   D   Weak

Fund Family: ETF Securities USA LLC
Fund Type: Precious Metals
Inception Date: December 2, 2010

Major Rating Factors: *ETFS Physical WM Basket Shares receives a TheStreet.com Investment Rating of D (Weak). The fund currently has a performance rating of C- (Fair) based on an annualized return of 0.00% over the last three years and a total return of 1.99% year to date 2012. Factored into the performance evaluation is an expense ratio of 0.60% (very low).

The fund's risk rating is currently C (Fair). It carries a beta of 0.00, meaning the fund's expected move will be 0.0% for every 10% move in the market. Volatility, as measured by both the semi-deviation and a drawdown factor, is considered average. As of December 31, 2012, *ETFS Physical WM Basket Shares traded at a discount of 2.05% below its net asset value, which is better than its one-year historical average premium of .37%.

This fund has been team managed for 3 years and currently receives a manager quality ranking of 39 (0=worst, 99=best). If you desire an average level of risk, then this fund may be an option.

Data Date	Investment Rating	Net Assets ($Mil)	Price	Performance Rating/Pts	Total Return Y-T-D	Risk Rating/Pts
12-12	D	37.60	50.76	C- / 3.0	1.99%	C / 5.4
2011	E+	39.80	46.69	E+ / 0.9	1.62%	C / 5.1

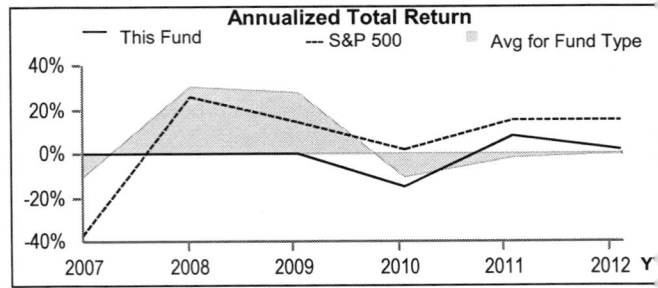

Annualized Total Return

*FactorShares Gold Bull S&P 500 B (FSG)

| | | E+ | Very Weak |

Fund Family: Factor Capital Management LLC
Fund Type: Precious Metals
Inception Date: February 22, 2011

Data Date	Investment Rating	Net Assets ($Mil)	Price	Performance Rating/Pts	Total Return Y-T-D	Risk Rating/Pts
12-12	E+	6.30	20.88	E- / 0.2	-9.87%	C / 4.4

Major Rating Factors:
Very poor performance is the major factor driving the E+ (Very Weak) TheStreet.com Investment Rating for *FactorShares Gold Bull S&P 500 B. The fund currently has a performance rating of E- (Very Weak) based on an annualized return of 0.00% over the last three years and a total return of -9.87% year to date 2012. Factored into the performance evaluation is an expense ratio of 2.85% (high).

The fund's risk rating is currently C (Fair). It carries a beta of 0.00, meaning the fund's expected move will be 0.0% for every 10% move in the market. Volatility, as measured by both the semi-deviation and a drawdown factor, is considered average. As of December 31, 2012, *FactorShares Gold Bull S&P 500 B traded at a premium of 10.59% above its net asset value, which is worse than its one-year historical average discount of .05%.

This fund has been team managed for 2 years and currently receives a manager quality ranking of 3 (0=worst, 99=best). This fund offers an average level of risk but investors looking for strong performance will be frustrated.

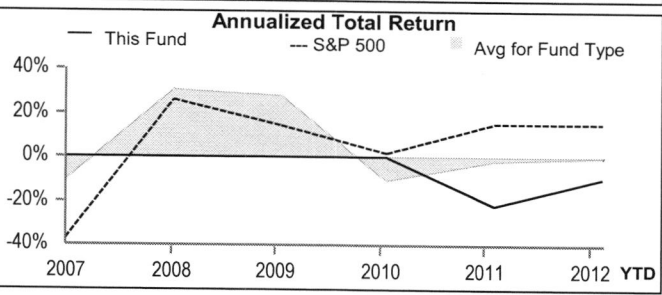

*FactorShares Oil Bull S&P 500 Be (FOL)

| | | E- | Very Weak |

Fund Family: Factor Capital Management LLC
Fund Type: Growth and Income
Inception Date: February 22, 2011

Data Date	Investment Rating	Net Assets ($Mil)	Price	Performance Rating/Pts	Total Return Y-T-D	Risk Rating/Pts
12-12	E-	1.90	9.69	E- / 0.1	-4.54%	D+ / 2.9

Major Rating Factors: *FactorShares Oil Bull S&P 500 Be has adopted a risky asset allocation strategy and currently receives an overall TheStreet.com Investment Rating of E- (Very Weak). The fund has an above average level of volatility, as measured by both semi-deviation and drawdown factors. It carries a beta of 0.00, meaning the fund's expected move will be 0.0% for every 10% move in the market. As of December 31, 2012, *FactorShares Oil Bull S&P 500 Be traded at a premium of 4.64% above its net asset value, which is worse than its one-year historical average premium of .10%. Unfortunately, the high level of risk (D+, Weak) failed to pay off as investors endured very poor performance.

The fund's performance rating is currently E- (Very Weak). It has registered an annualized return of 0.00% over the last three years but is down -4.54% year to date 2012. Factored into the performance evaluation is an expense ratio of 5.96% (high).

This fund has been team managed for 2 years and currently receives a manager quality ranking of 0 (0=worst, 99=best). If you can tolerate high levels of risk in the hope of improved future returns, holding this fund may be an option.

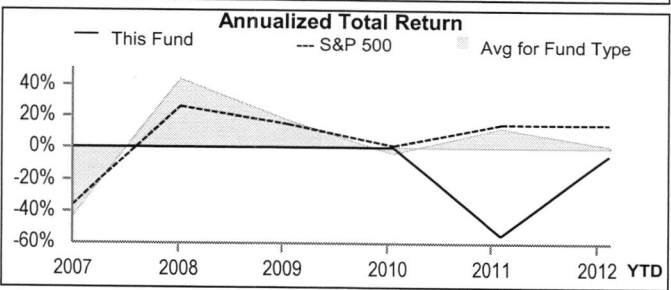

*FactorShares S&P 500 Bull Tbd Be (FSE)

| | | E | Very Weak |

Fund Family: Factor Capital Management LLC
Fund Type: Growth and Income
Inception Date: February 22, 2011

Data Date	Investment Rating	Net Assets ($Mil)	Price	Performance Rating/Pts	Total Return Y-T-D	Risk Rating/Pts
12-12	E	1.00	10.95	D- / 1.0	2.56%	D+ / 2.5

Major Rating Factors: *FactorShares S&P 500 Bull Tbd Be has adopted a risky asset allocation strategy and currently receives an overall TheStreet.com Investment Rating of E (Very Weak). The fund has an above average level of volatility, as measured by both semi-deviation and drawdown factors. It carries a beta of 0.00, meaning the fund's expected move will be 0.0% for every 10% move in the market. As of December 31, 2012, *FactorShares S&P 500 Bull Tbd Be traded at a discount of 2.41% below its net asset value, which is better than its one-year historical average premium of .15%. Unfortunately, the high level of risk (D+, Weak) failed to pay off as investors endured poor performance.

The fund's performance rating is currently D- (Weak). It has registered an annualized return of 0.00% over the last three years and is up 2.56% year to date 2012. Factored into the performance evaluation is an expense ratio of 7.12% (high).

This fund has been team managed for 2 years and currently receives a manager quality ranking of 1 (0=worst, 99=best). If you can tolerate high levels of risk in the hope of improved future returns, holding this fund may be an option.

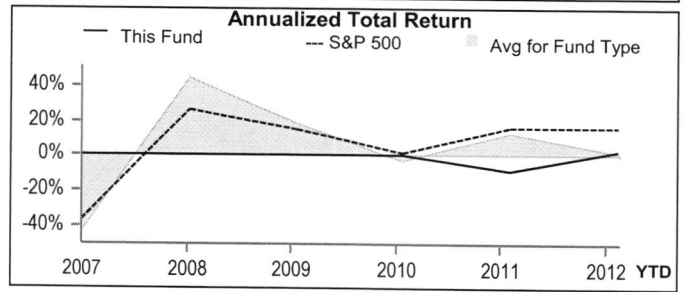

*FactorShares Tbd Bull S&P 500 Be (FSA)

E   **Very Weak**

Fund Family: Factor Capital Management LLC
Fund Type: Growth
Inception Date: February 22, 2011

Data Date	Investment Rating	Net Assets ($Mil)	Price	Performance Rating/Pts	Total Return Y-T-D	Risk Rating/Pts
12-12	E	2.00	19.40	E- / 0.1	-9.85%	C- / 3.9

Major Rating Factors: Very poor performance is the major factor driving the E (Very Weak) TheStreet.com Investment Rating for *FactorShares Tbd Bull S&P 500 Be. The fund currently has a performance rating of E- (Very Weak) based on an annualized return of 0.00% over the last three years and a total return of -9.85% year to date 2012. Factored into the performance evaluation is an expense ratio of 5.26% (high).

The fund's risk rating is currently C- (Fair). It carries a beta of 0.00, meaning the fund's expected move will be 0.0% for every 10% move in the market. Volatility, as measured by both the semi-deviation and a drawdown factor, is considered average. As of December 31, 2012, *FactorShares Tbd Bull S&P 500 Be traded at a premium of 10.73% above its net asset value, which is worse than its one-year historical average discount of .11%.

This fund has been team managed for 2 years and currently receives a manager quality ranking of 41 (0=worst, 99=best). This fund offers an average level of risk but investors looking for strong performance will be frustrated.

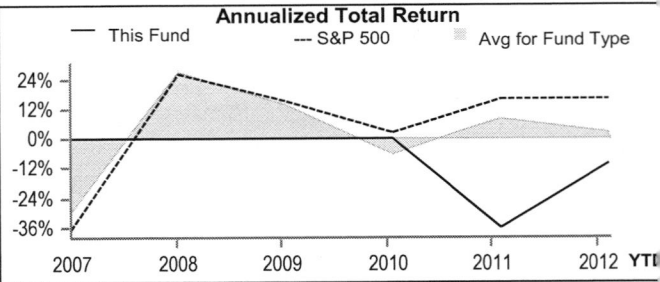

Annualized Total Return

*Fidelity Nasdaq Comp Tracker Sto (ONEQ)

C   **Fair**

Fund Family: Fidelity Management & Research Comp
Fund Type: Growth
Inception Date: September 25, 2003

Data Date	Investment Rating	Net Assets ($Mil)	Price	Performance Rating/Pts	Total Return Y-T-D	Risk Rating/Pts
12-12	C	178.40	118.41	C / 5.3	3.63%	B- / 7.1
2011	C+	154.00	103.02	C+ / 6.4	2.39%	B- / 7.2
2010	C+	156.80	104.77	C+ / 6.3	17.79%	C / 5.5
2009	C-	90.90	89.60	C- / 4.2	39.92%	C+ / 5.6

Major Rating Factors: Middle of the road best describes *Fidelity Nasdaq Comp Tracker Sto whose TheStreet.com Investment Rating is currently a C (Fair). The fund currently has a performance rating of C (Fair) based on an annualized return of 11.92% over the last three years and a total return of 3.63% year to date 2012. Factored into the performance evaluation is an expense ratio of 0.35% (very low).

The fund's risk rating is currently B- (Good). It carries a beta of 1.16, meaning it is expected to move 11.6% for every 10% move in the market. Volatility, as measured by both the semi-deviation and a drawdown factor, is considered low. As of December 31, 2012, *Fidelity Nasdaq Comp Tracker Sto traded at a discount of 3.57% below its net asset value, which is better than its one-year historical average discount of .03%.

Patrick J. Waddell has been running the fund for 9 years and currently receives a manager quality ranking of 38 (0=worst, 99=best). If you desire an average level of risk, then this fund may be an option.

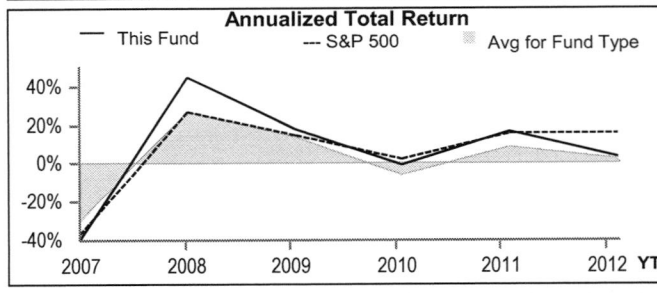

Annualized Total Return

*Financial Select Sector SPDR (XLF)

C   **Fair**

Fund Family: SSgA Funds Management Inc
Fund Type: Financial Services
Inception Date: December 16, 1998

Data Date	Investment Rating	Net Assets ($Mil)	Price	Performance Rating/Pts	Total Return Y-T-D	Risk Rating/Pts
12-12	C	9,237.20	16.39	C / 5.1	4.39%	B- / 7.2
2011	D	5,373.30	13.00	D+ / 2.7	3.04%	C+ / 6.6
2010	D-	7,470.50	15.95	E+ / 0.8	11.91%	C- / 4.1
2009	E+	7,494.11	14.40	E+ / 0.6	16.19%	C- / 4.2

Major Rating Factors: Middle of the road best describes *Financial Select Sector SPDR whose TheStreet.com Investment Rating is currently a C (Fair). The fund currently has a performance rating of C (Fair) based on an annualized return of 6.21% over the last three years and a total return of 4.39% year to date 2012. Factored into the performance evaluation is an expense ratio of 0.18% (very low).

The fund's risk rating is currently B- (Good). It carries a beta of 1.05, meaning that its performance tracks fairly well with that of the overall stock market. Volatility, as measured by both the semi-deviation and a drawdown factor, is considered low. As of December 31, 2012, *Financial Select Sector SPDR traded at a discount of 4.21% below its net asset value, which is better than its one-year historical average discount of .01%.

John A. Tucker has been running the fund for 15 years and currently receives a manager quality ranking of 36 (0=worst, 99=best). If you desire an average level of risk, then this fund may be an option.

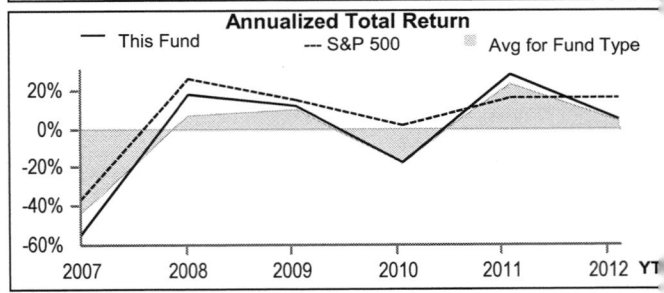

Annualized Total Return

*First Trust AMEX Biotechnology (FBT)

B-   Good

Fund Family: First Trust Advisors LP
Fund Type: Health
Inception Date: June 19, 2006

Major Rating Factors: Strong performance is the major factor driving the B- (Good) TheStreet.com Investment Rating for *First Trust AMEX Biotechnology. The fund currently has a performance rating of B+ (Good) based on an annualized return of 17.93% over the last three years and a total return of 6.16% year to date 2012. Factored into the performance evaluation is an expense ratio of 0.60% (very low).

The fund's risk rating is currently C+ (Fair). It carries a beta of 1.15, meaning it is expected to move 11.5% for every 10% move in the market. Volatility, as measured by both the semi-deviation and a drawdown factor, is considered low. As of December 31, 2012, *First Trust AMEX Biotechnology traded at a discount of 5.74% below its net asset value, which is better than its one-year historical average premium of .02%.

Stan Ueland has been running the fund for 7 years and currently receives a manager quality ranking of 76 (0=worst, 99=best). If you desire only a moderate level of risk and strong performance, then this fund is an excellent option.

Data Date	Investment Rating	Net Assets ($Mil)	Price	Performance Rating/Pts	Total Return Y-T-D	Risk Rating/Pts
12-12	B-	239.40	45.95	B+ / 8.3	6.16%	C+ / 6.3
2011	C	183.00	32.66	C+ / 5.8	6.52%	C+ / 6.2
2010	A	201.20	39.11	A- / 9.1	36.94%	C+ / 6.0
2009	C+	60.38	28.56	C+ / 6.9	42.94%	C+ / 6.2

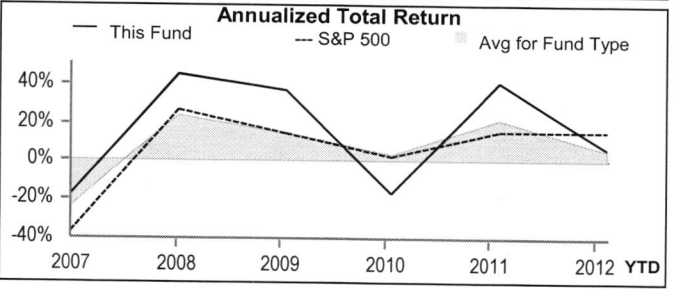

*First Trust AsiaPac Ex-Jpn Alpha (FPA)

B+   Good

Fund Family: First Trust Advisors LP
Fund Type: Foreign
Inception Date: April 18, 2011

Major Rating Factors:
Exceptional performance is the major factor driving the B+ (Good) TheStreet.com Investment Rating for *First Trust AsiaPac Ex-Jpn Alpha. The fund currently has a performance rating of A (Excellent) based on an annualized return of 0.00% over the last three years and a total return of 0.57% year to date 2012. Factored into the performance evaluation is an expense ratio of 0.80% (very low).

The fund's risk rating is currently C+ (Fair). It carries a beta of 0.00, meaning the fund's expected move will be 0.0% for every 10% move in the market. Volatility, as measured by both the semi-deviation and a drawdown factor, is considered low. As of December 31, 2012, *First Trust AsiaPac Ex-Jpn Alpha traded at a discount of .46% below its net asset value, which is better than its one-year historical average premium of .35%.

Jonathan Erickson has been running the fund for 2 years and currently receives a manager quality ranking of 75 (0=worst, 99=best). If you desire only a moderate level of risk and strong performance, then this fund is an excellent option.

Data Date	Investment Rating	Net Assets ($Mil)	Price	Performance Rating/Pts	Total Return Y-T-D	Risk Rating/Pts
12-12	B+	13.80	27.94	A / 9.5	0.57%	C+ / 6.8

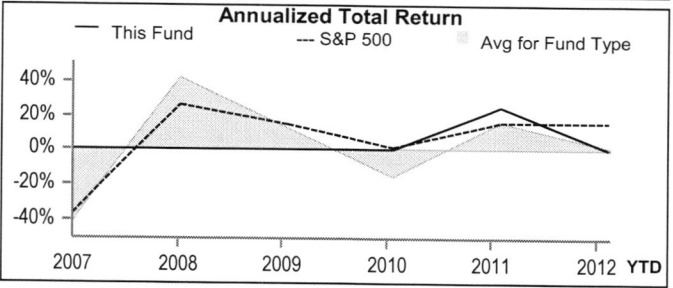

*First Trust BICK Index (BICK)

C   Fair

Fund Family: First Trust Advisors LP
Fund Type: Foreign
Inception Date: April 12, 2010

Major Rating Factors: Strong performance is the major factor driving the C (Fair) TheStreet.com Investment Rating for *First Trust BICK Index. The fund currently has a performance rating of B- (Good) based on an annualized return of 0.00% over the last three years and a total return of 2.05% year to date 2012. Factored into the performance evaluation is an expense ratio of 0.64% (very low).

The fund's risk rating is currently C+ (Fair). It carries a beta of 0.00, meaning the fund's expected move will be 0.0% for every 10% move in the market. Volatility, as measured by both the semi-deviation and a drawdown factor, is considered low. As of December 31, 2012, *First Trust BICK Index traded at a discount of 2.09% below its net asset value, which is better than its one-year historical average discount of .17%.

Jonathan Erickson has been running the fund for 3 years and currently receives a manager quality ranking of 15 (0=worst, 99=best). If you desire only a moderate level of risk and strong performance, then this fund is an excellent option.

Data Date	Investment Rating	Net Assets ($Mil)	Price	Performance Rating/Pts	Total Return Y-T-D	Risk Rating/Pts
12-12	C	48.20	25.33	B- / 7.3	2.05%	C+ / 5.9
2011	D-	43.30	22.68	E / 0.5	2.07%	C+ / 6.0

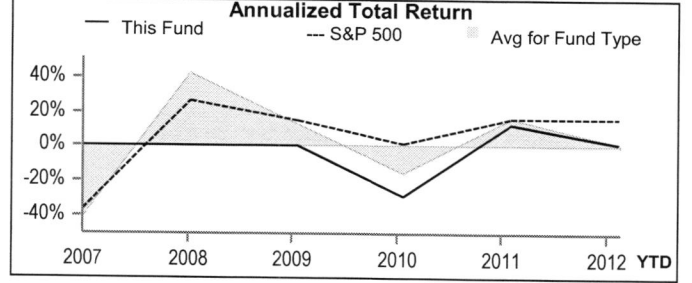

*First Trust Brazil AlphaDEX (FBZ)

D   **Weak**

Fund Family: First Trust Advisors LP
Fund Type: Foreign
Inception Date: April 18, 2011

Data Date	Investment Rating	Net Assets ($Mil)	Price	Perfor-mance Rating/Pts	Total Return Y-T-D	Risk Rating/Pts
12-12	D	5.90	23.83	D+ / 2.4	-1.11%	C+ / 6.4

Major Rating Factors:
Disappointing performance is the major factor driving the D (Weak) TheStreet.com Investment Rating for *First Trust Brazil AlphaDEX. The fund currently has a performance rating of D+ (Weak) based on an annualized return of 0.00% over the last three years and a total return of -1.11% year to date 2012. Factored into the performance evaluation is an expense ratio of 0.82% (very low).

The fund's risk rating is currently C+ (Fair). It carries a beta of 0.00, meaning the fund's expected move will be 0.0% for every 10% move in the market. Volatility, as measured by both the semi-deviation and a drawdown factor, is considered low. As of December 31, 2012, *First Trust Brazil AlphaDEX traded at a premium of 1.36% above its net asset value, which is worse than its one-year historical average premium of .28%.

Jonathan Erickson has been running the fund for 2 years and currently receives a manager quality ranking of 8 (0=worst, 99=best). This fund offers only a moderate level of risk but investors looking for strong performance are still waiting.

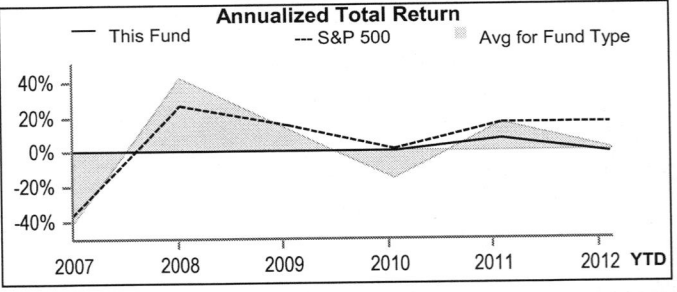
Annualized Total Return

---

*First Trust China AlphaDEX (FCA)

B   **Good**

Fund Family: First Trust Advisors LP
Fund Type: Foreign
Inception Date: April 18, 2011

Data Date	Investment Rating	Net Assets ($Mil)	Price	Perfor-mance Rating/Pts	Total Return Y-T-D	Risk Rating/Pts
12-12	B	2.30	25.13	A+ / 9.8	3.98%	C+ / 5.8

Major Rating Factors:
Exceptional performance is the major factor driving the B (Good) TheStreet.com Investment Rating for *First Trust China AlphaDEX. The fund currently has a performance rating of A+ (Excellent) based on an annualized return of 0.00% over the last three years and a total return of 3.98% year to date 2012. Factored into the performance evaluation is an expense ratio of 0.80% (very low).

The fund's risk rating is currently C+ (Fair). It carries a beta of 0.00, meaning the fund's expected move will be 0.0% for every 10% move in the market. Volatility, as measured by both the semi-deviation and a drawdown factor, is considered low. As of December 31, 2012, *First Trust China AlphaDEX traded at a discount of 2.10% below its net asset value, which is better than its one-year historical average premium of .23%.

Jonathan Erickson has been running the fund for 2 years and currently receives a manager quality ranking of 94 (0=worst, 99=best). If you desire only a moderate level of risk and strong performance, then this fund is an excellent option.

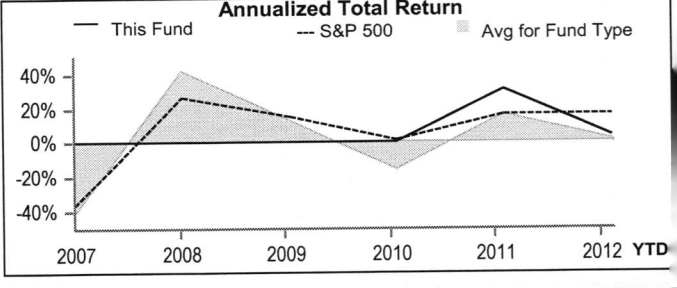
Annualized Total Return

---

*First Trust Consumer Dis AlphaDE (FXD)

B-   **Good**

Fund Family: First Trust Advisors LP
Fund Type: Income
Inception Date: May 8, 2007

Data Date	Investment Rating	Net Assets ($Mil)	Price	Perfor-mance Rating/Pts	Total Return Y-T-D	Risk Rating/Pts
12-12	B-	493.20	22.60	B- / 7.1	3.27%	B- / 7.8
2011	B	461.80	19.84	B / 7.9	1.26%	B- / 7.8
2010	B	401.00	19.78	B / 8.2	32.01%	C / 5.1
2009	A	6.39	15.06	A / 9.3	51.60%	C / 5.3

Major Rating Factors: Strong performance is the major factor driving the B- (Good) TheStreet.com Investment Rating for *First Trust Consumer Dis AlphaDE. The fund currently has a performance rating of B- (Good) based on an annualized return of 15.97% over the last three years and a total return of 3.27% year to date 2012. Factored into the performance evaluation is an expense ratio of 0.70% (very low).

The fund's risk rating is currently B- (Good). It carries a beta of 1.23, meaning it is expected to move 12.3% for every 10% move in the market. Volatility, as measured by both the semi-deviation and a drawdown factor, is considered low. As of December 31, 2012, *First Trust Consumer Dis AlphaDE traded at a discount of 3.25% below its net asset value.

Daniel J. Lindquist has been running the fund for 6 years and currently receives a manager quality ranking of 65 (0=worst, 99=best). If you desire only a moderate level of risk and strong performance, then this fund is an excellent option.

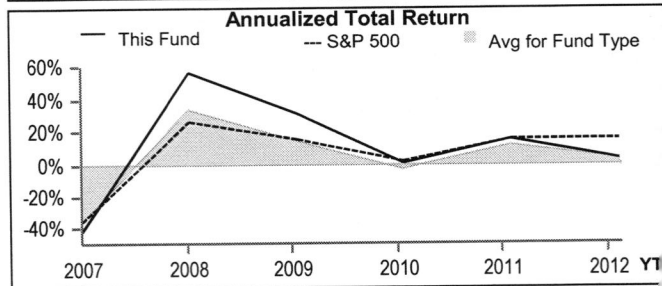
Annualized Total Return

*First Trust Consumer Stap AlphaD (FXG)

B-   **Good**

Fund Family: First Trust Advisors LP
Fund Type: Income
Inception Date: May 8, 2007

Major Rating Factors: *First Trust Consumer Stap AlphaD receives a TheStreet.com Investment Rating of B- (Good). The fund currently has a performance rating of C+ (Fair) based on an annualized return of 14.31% over the last three years and a total return of 2.92% year to date 2012. Factored into the performance evaluation is an expense ratio of 0.70% (very low).

The fund's risk rating is currently B (Good). It carries a beta of 0.65, meaning the fund's expected move will be 6.5% for every 10% move in the market. Volatility, as measured by both the semi-deviation and a drawdown factor, is considered low. As of December 31, 2012, *First Trust Consumer Stap AlphaD traded at a discount of 2.84% below its net asset value, which is better than its one-year historical average premium of .01%.

Daniel J. Lindquist has been running the fund for 6 years and currently receives a manager quality ranking of 83 (0=worst, 99=best). If you desire an average level of risk, then this fund may be an option.

Data Date	Investment Rating	Net Assets ($Mil)	Price	Performance Rating/Pts	Total Return Y-T-D	Risk Rating/Pts
12-12	B-	398.30	25.33	C+ / 6.2	2.92%	B / 8.8
2011	B-	206.70	23.65	C+ / 6.7	-0.63%	B / 8.4
2010	B+	33.70	21.10	B- / 7.0	19.75%	C+ / 6.9
2009	A+	9.02	17.82	B / 8.0	24.83%	C+ / 6.9

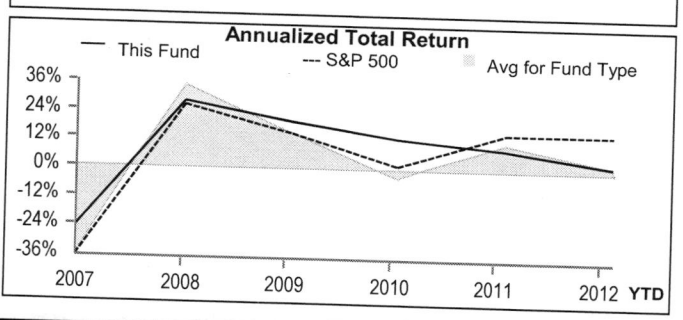

*First Trust Dev Mkt Ex-US AlphaD (FDT)

B+   **Good**

Fund Family: First Trust Advisors LP
Fund Type: Foreign
Inception Date: April 18, 2011

Major Rating Factors:
Exceptional performance is the major factor driving the B+ (Good) TheStreet.com Investment Rating for *First Trust Dev Mkt Ex-US AlphaD. The fund currently has a performance rating of A- (Excellent) based on an annualized return of 0.00% over the last three years and a total return of 1.63% year to date 2012. Factored into the performance evaluation is an expense ratio of 0.80% (very low).

The fund's risk rating is currently B- (Good). It carries a beta of 0.00, meaning the fund's expected move will be 0.0% for every 10% move in the market. Volatility, as measured by both the semi-deviation and a drawdown factor, is considered low. As of December 31, 2012, *First Trust Dev Mkt Ex-US AlphaD traded at a discount of 1.14% below its net asset value, which is better than its one-year historical average premium of .42%.

Jonathan Erickson has been running the fund for 2 years and currently receives a manager quality ranking of 42 (0=worst, 99=best). If you desire only a moderate level of risk and strong performance, then this fund is an excellent option.

Data Date	Investment Rating	Net Assets ($Mil)	Price	Performance Rating/Pts	Total Return Y-T-D	Risk Rating/Pts
12-12	B+	92.30	44.27	A- / 9.0	1.63%	B- / 7.5

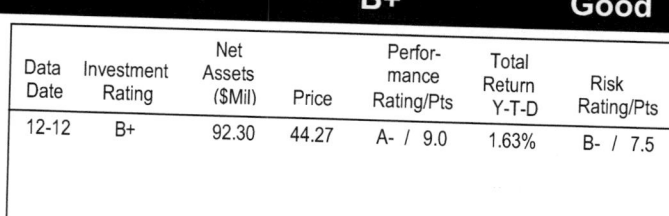

*First Trust DJ Glb Sel Div Idx F (FGD)

C   **Fair**

Fund Family: First Trust Advisors LP
Fund Type: Global
Inception Date: November 21, 2007

Major Rating Factors: Middle of the road best describes *First Trust DJ Glb Sel Div Idx F whose TheStreet.com Investment Rating is currently a C (Fair). The fund currently has a performance rating of C (Fair) based on an annualized return of 8.63% over the last three years and a total return of 2.48% year to date 2012. Factored into the performance evaluation is an expense ratio of 0.60% (very low).

The fund's risk rating is currently B (Good). It carries a beta of 0.85, meaning the fund's expected move will be 8.5% for every 10% move in the market. Volatility, as measured by both the semi-deviation and a drawdown factor, is considered low. As of December 31, 2012, *First Trust DJ Glb Sel Div Idx F traded at a discount of 1.94% below its net asset value, which is better than its one-year historical average premium of .31%.

Jonathan Erickson has been running the fund for 6 years and currently receives a manager quality ranking of 79 (0=worst, 99=best). If you desire an average level of risk, then this fund may be an option.

Data Date	Investment Rating	Net Assets ($Mil)	Price	Performance Rating/Pts	Total Return Y-T-D	Risk Rating/Pts
12-12	C	231.40	24.22	C / 4.9	2.48%	B / 8.1
2011	C+	124.60	21.97	C+ / 6.3	-1.09%	B- / 7.9
2010	D	59.80	23.67	D+ / 2.9	12.56%	C / 5.0
2009	A	28.79	22.04	A / 9.4	58.09%	C / 5.1

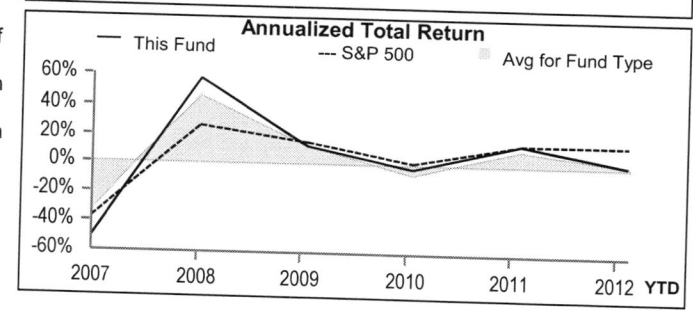

*First Trust Dow Jones Internet I (FDN)

| | C+ | Fair |

Fund Family: First Trust Advisors LP
Fund Type: Growth
Inception Date: June 19, 2006

Major Rating Factors: Strong performance is the major factor driving the C+ (Fair) TheStreet.com Investment Rating for *First Trust Dow Jones Internet I. The fund currently has a performance rating of B+ (Good) based on an annualized return of 18.36% over the last three years and a total return of 5.00% year to date 2012. Factored into the performance evaluation is an expense ratio of 0.60% (very low).

The fund's risk rating is currently C+ (Fair). It carries a beta of 1.19, meaning it is expected to move 11.9% for every 10% move in the market. Volatility, as measured by both the semi-deviation and a drawdown factor, is considered low. As of December 31, 2012, *First Trust Dow Jones Internet I traded at a discount of 4.70% below its net asset value, which is better than its one-year historical average discount of .01%.

Stan Ueland has been running the fund for 7 years and currently receives a manager quality ranking of 69 (0=worst, 99=best). If you desire only a moderate level of risk and strong performance, then this fund is an excellent option.

Data Date	Investment Rating	Net Assets ($Mil)	Price	Performance Rating/Pts	Total Return Y-T-D	Risk Rating/Pts
12-12	C+	557.90	38.97	B+ / 8.6	5.00%	C+ / 5.8
2011	C+	519.70	32.30	B / 8.1	1.11%	C+ / 6.2
2010	B-	589.50	34.32	B+ / 8.7	36.72%	C- / 4.0
2009	C+	33.65	25.13	B- / 7.3	73.19%	C / 4.6

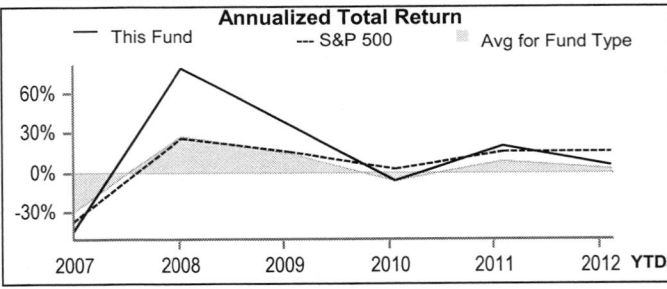

*First Trust Dow Jones Sel Micro (FDM)

| | C | Fair |

Fund Family: First Trust Advisors LP
Fund Type: Growth
Inception Date: September 27, 2005

Major Rating Factors: Middle of the road best describes *First Trust Dow Jones Sel Micro whose TheStreet.com Investment Rating is currently a C (Fair). The fund currently has a performance rating of C (Fair) based on an annualized return of 10.03% over the last three years and a total return of 2.58% year to date 2012. Factored into the performance evaluation is an expense ratio of 0.60% (very low).

The fund's risk rating is currently B- (Good). It carries a beta of 1.36, meaning it is expected to move 13.6% for every 10% move in the market. Volatility, as measured by both the semi-deviation and a drawdown factor, is considered low. As of December 31, 2012, *First Trust Dow Jones Sel Micro traded at a discount of 2.69% below its net asset value, which is better than its one-year historical average discount of .06%.

Jonathan Erickson has been running the fund for 8 years and currently receives a manager quality ranking of 24 (0=worst, 99=best). If you desire an average level of risk, then this fund may be an option.

Data Date	Investment Rating	Net Assets ($Mil)	Price	Performance Rating/Pts	Total Return Y-T-D	Risk Rating/Pts
12-12	C	41.30	22.83	C / 4.9	2.58%	B- / 7.2
2011	C-	52.30	20.08	C / 4.5	1.84%	B- / 7.0
2010	C+	153.00	22.15	C+ / 6.9	25.58%	C+ / 5.7
2009	D	14.44	17.71	D- / 1.5	20.02%	C / 5.4

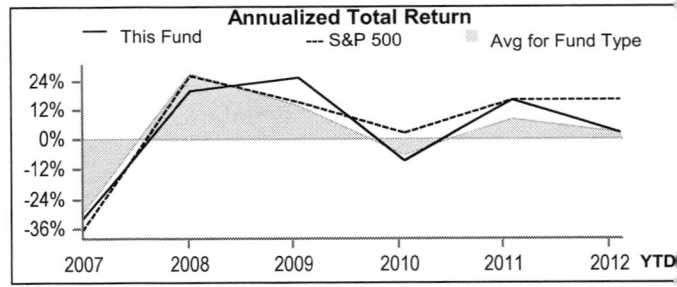

*First Trust Emerg Mkt AlphaDEX (FEM)

| | B+ | Good |

Fund Family: First Trust Advisors LP
Fund Type: Emerging Market
Inception Date: April 18, 2011

Major Rating Factors:
Exceptional performance is the major factor driving the B+ (Good) TheStreet.com Investment Rating for *First Trust Emerg Mkt AlphaDEX. The fund currently has a performance rating of A (Excellent) based on an annualized return of 0.00% over the last three years and a total return of 2.24% year to date 2012. Factored into the performance evaluation is an expense ratio of 0.80% (very low).

The fund's risk rating is currently B- (Good). It carries a beta of 0.00, meaning the fund's expected move will be 0.0% for every 10% move in the market. Volatility, as measured by both the semi-deviation and a drawdown factor, is considered low. As of December 31, 2012, *First Trust Emerg Mkt AlphaDEX traded at a discount of 1.49% below its net asset value, which is better than its one-year historical average premium of .43%.

Jonathan Erickson has been running the fund for 2 years and currently receives a manager quality ranking of 54 (0=worst, 99=best). If you desire only a moderate level of risk and strong performance, then this fund is an excellent option.

Data Date	Investment Rating	Net Assets ($Mil)	Price	Performance Rating/Pts	Total Return Y-T-D	Risk Rating/Pts
12-12	B+	129.20	26.39	A / 9.4	2.24%	B- / 7.1

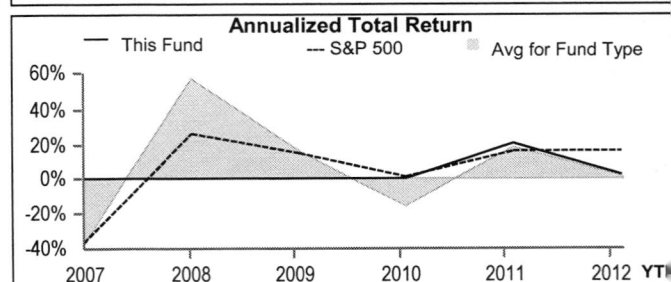

*First Trust Energy AlphaDEX (FXN)

D+ **Weak**

Fund Family: First Trust Advisors LP
Fund Type: Energy/Natural Resources
Inception Date: May 8, 2007

Major Rating Factors: *First Trust Energy AlphaDEX receives a TheStreet.com Investment Rating of D+ (Weak). The fund currently has a performance rating of C- (Fair) based on an annualized return of 5.85% over the last three years and a total return of 2.77% year to date 2012. Factored into the performance evaluation is an expense ratio of 0.70% (very low).

The fund's risk rating is currently C+ (Fair). It carries a beta of 1.24, meaning it is expected to move 12.4% for every 10% move in the market. Volatility, as measured by both the semi-deviation and a drawdown factor, is considered low. As of December 31, 2012, *First Trust Energy AlphaDEX traded at a discount of 2.70% below its net asset value, which is better than its one-year historical average discount of .01%.

Daniel J. Lindquist has been running the fund for 6 years and currently receives a manager quality ranking of 24 (0=worst, 99=best). If you desire an average level of risk, then this fund may be an option.

Data Date	Investment Rating	Net Assets ($Mil)	Price	Performance Rating/Pts	Total Return Y-T-D	Risk Rating/Pts
12-12	D+	76.30	19.85	C- / 3.0	2.77%	C+ / 6.7
2011	C	90.80	19.31	C+ / 6.0	3.00%	C+ / 6.6
2010	C	86.60	21.17	C+ / 5.9	27.63%	C / 4.3
2009	B+	9.53	16.69	A- / 9.2	40.63%	C / 4.6

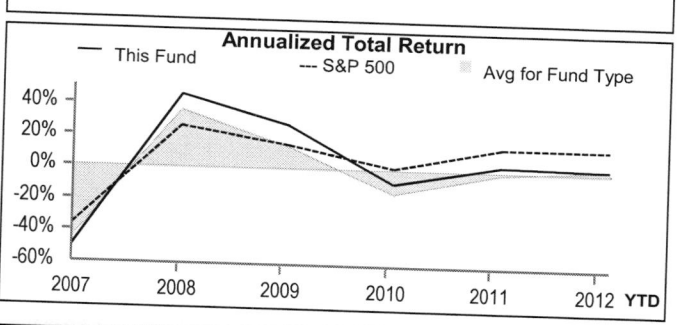

*First Trust Europe AlphaDEX (FEP)

A- **Excellent**

Fund Family: First Trust Advisors LP
Fund Type: Foreign
Inception Date: April 18, 2011

Major Rating Factors:
Exceptional performance is the major factor driving the A- (Excellent) TheStreet.com Investment Rating for *First Trust Europe AlphaDEX. The fund currently has a performance rating of A+ (Excellent) based on an annualized return of 0.00% over the last three years and a total return of 1.95% year to date 2012. Factored into the performance evaluation is an expense ratio of 0.80% (very low).

The fund's risk rating is currently B- (Good). It carries a beta of 0.00, meaning the fund's expected move will be 0.0% for every 10% move in the market. Volatility, as measured by both the semi-deviation and a drawdown factor, is considered low. As of December 31, 2012, *First Trust Europe AlphaDEX traded at a discount of 1.06% below its net asset value, which is better than its one-year historical average premium of .77%.

Jonathan Erickson has been running the fund for 2 years and currently receives a manager quality ranking of 53 (0=worst, 99=best). If you desire only a moderate level of risk and strong performance, then this fund is an excellent option.

Data Date	Investment Rating	Net Assets ($Mil)	Price	Performance Rating/Pts	Total Return Y-T-D	Risk Rating/Pts
12-12	A-	30.80	26.20	A+ / 9.7	1.95%	B- / 7.2

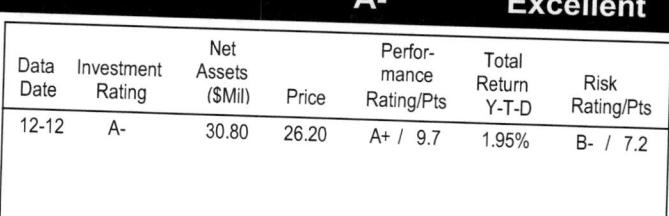

*First Trust Financial AlphaDEX (FXO)

C+ **Fair**

Fund Family: First Trust Advisors LP
Fund Type: Financial Services
Inception Date: May 8, 2007

Major Rating Factors: Middle of the road best describes *First Trust Financial AlphaDEX whose TheStreet.com Investment Rating is currently a C+ (Fair). The fund currently has a performance rating of C+ (Fair) based on an annualized return of 10.99% over the last three years and a total return of 4.85% year to date 2012. Factored into the performance evaluation is an expense ratio of 0.70% (very low).

The fund's risk rating is currently B- (Good). It carries a beta of 0.86, meaning the fund's expected move will be 8.6% for every 10% move in the market. Volatility, as measured by both the semi-deviation and a drawdown factor, is considered low. As of December 31, 2012, *First Trust Financial AlphaDEX traded at a discount of 4.57% below its net asset value, which is better than its one-year historical average premium of .01%.

Daniel J. Lindquist has been running the fund for 6 years and currently receives a manager quality ranking of 74 (0=worst, 99=best). If you desire an average level of risk, then this fund may be an option.

Data Date	Investment Rating	Net Assets ($Mil)	Price	Performance Rating/Pts	Total Return Y-T-D	Risk Rating/Pts
12-12	C+	196.90	15.67	C+ / 6.0	4.85%	B- / 7.7
2011	C	77.80	13.19	C / 4.9	1.67%	B- / 7.3
2010	C-	330.00	14.61	C / 4.9	19.25%	C / 5.1
2009	B+	8.30	12.42	B+ / 8.7	30.64%	C / 5.0

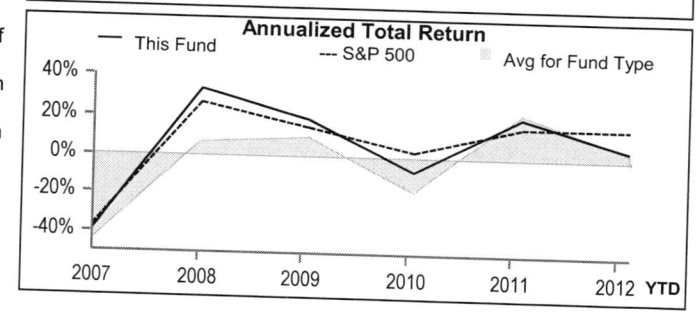

*First Trust FTSE EPRA/NAREIT Glb (FFR)

C+   **Fair**

Fund Family: First Trust Advisors LP
Fund Type: Growth and Income
Inception Date: August 27, 2007

Major Rating Factors: Strong performance is the major factor driving the C+ (Fair) TheStreet.com Investment Rating for *First Trust FTSE EPRA/NAREIT Glb. The fund currently has a performance rating of B- (Good) based on an annualized return of 13.21% over the last three years and a total return of 1.42% year to date 2012. Factored into the performance evaluation is an expense ratio of 0.60% (very low).

The fund's risk rating is currently B- (Good). It carries a beta of 1.13, meaning it is expected to move 11.3% for every 10% move in the market. Volatility, as measured by both the semi-deviation and a drawdown factor, is considered low. As of December 31, 2012, *First Trust FTSE EPRA/NAREIT Glb traded at a discount of .71% below its net asset value, which is better than its one-year historical average premium of .20%.

Daniel J. Lindquist has been running the fund for 6 years and currently receives a manager quality ranking of 56 (0=worst, 99=best). If you desire only a moderate level of risk and strong performance, then this fund is an excellent option.

Data Date	Investment Rating	Net Assets ($Mil)	Price	Performance Rating/Pts	Total Return Y-T-D	Risk Rating/Pts
12-12	C+	101.80	39.37	B- / 7.2	1.42%	B- / 7.0
2011	C-	71.70	32.00	C / 4.6	-0.37%	C+ / 6.1
2010	D	59.20	34.93	C- / 3.1	19.23%	C- / 4.2
2009	B-	15.24	30.52	B+ / 8.8	33.85%	C- / 4.1

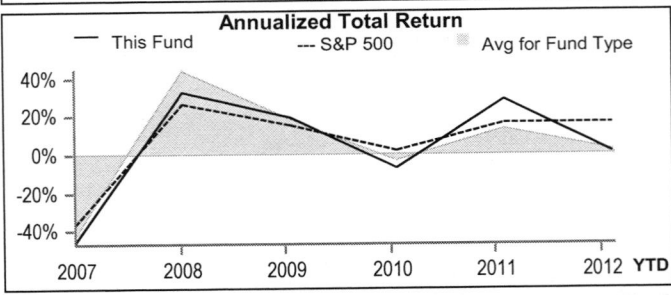

*First Trust Health Care AlphaDEX (FXH)

B   **Good**

Fund Family: First Trust Advisors LP
Fund Type: Health
Inception Date: May 8, 2007

Major Rating Factors: Strong performance is the major factor driving the B (Good) TheStreet.com Investment Rating for *First Trust Health Care AlphaDEX. The fund currently has a performance rating of B- (Good) based on an annualized return of 15.26% over the last three years and a total return of 4.82% year to date 2012. Factored into the performance evaluation is an expense ratio of 0.70% (very low).

The fund's risk rating is currently B (Good). It carries a beta of 0.77, meaning the fund's expected move will be 7.7% for every 10% move in the market. Volatility, as measured by both the semi-deviation and a drawdown factor, is considered low. As of December 31, 2012, *First Trust Health Care AlphaDEX traded at a discount of 4.46% below its net asset value, which is better than its one-year historical average premium of .01%.

Daniel J. Lindquist has been running the fund for 6 years and currently receives a manager quality ranking of 82 (0=worst, 99=best). If you desire only a moderate level of risk and strong performance, then this fund is an excellent option.

Data Date	Investment Rating	Net Assets ($Mil)	Price	Performance Rating/Pts	Total Return Y-T-D	Risk Rating/Pts
12-12	B	644.00	32.57	B- / 7.2	4.82%	B / 8.3
2011	B	401.20	27.12	B- / 7.5	1.70%	B- / 7.8
2010	A-	59.00	25.69	B / 7.6	19.02%	C+ / 6.8
2009	A+	15.02	21.61	A / 9.3	48.93%	C+ / 6.8

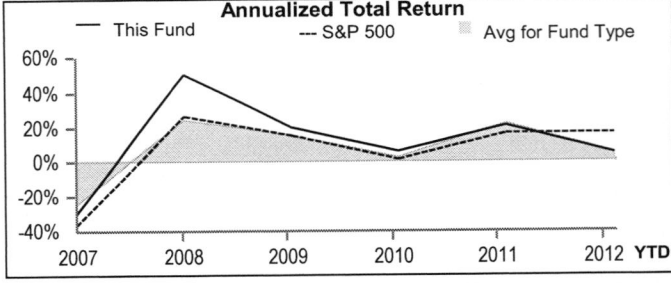

*First Trust Industrials AlphaDEX (FXR)

C   **Fair**

Fund Family: First Trust Advisors LP
Fund Type: Income
Inception Date: May 8, 2007

Major Rating Factors: Middle of the road best describes *First Trust Industrials AlphaDEX whose TheStreet.com Investment Rating is currently a C (Fair). The fund currently has a performance rating of C (Fair) based on an annualized return of 10.78% over the last three years and a total return of 3.96% year to date 2012. Factored into the performance evaluation is an expense ratio of 0.70% (very low).

The fund's risk rating is currently B- (Good). It carries a beta of 1.25, meaning it is expected to move 12.5% for every 10% move in the market. Volatility, as measured by both the semi-deviation and a drawdown factor, is considered low. As of December 31, 2012, *First Trust Industrials AlphaDEX traded at a discount of 3.81% below its net asset value, which is better than its one-year historical average premium of .04%.

This fund has been team managed for 6 years and currently receives a manager quality ranking of 31 (0=worst, 99=best). If you desire an average level of risk, then this fund may be an option.

Data Date	Investment Rating	Net Assets ($Mil)	Price	Performance Rating/Pts	Total Return Y-T-D	Risk Rating/Pts
12-12	C	132.30	19.43	C / 5.1	3.96%	B- / 7.4
2011	C	54.20	17.17	C+ / 5.8	2.27%	B- / 7.2
2010	C	43.20	18.48	C+ / 6.2	26.08%	C / 4.3
2009	A-	5.41	14.75	A- / 9.1	39.18%	C / 5.1

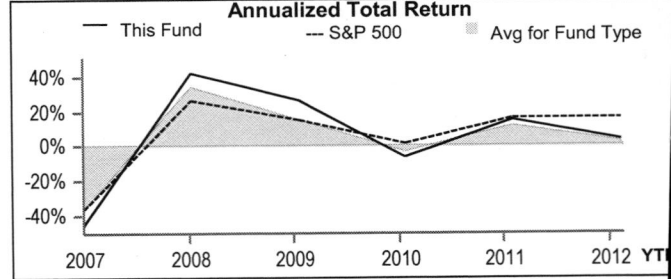

*First Trust ISE Chindia Index Fu (FNI)

	D	**Weak**

Fund Family: First Trust Advisors LP
Fund Type: Income
Inception Date: May 8, 2007

Major Rating Factors:
Disappointing performance is the major factor driving the D (Weak) TheStreet.com Investment Rating for *First Trust ISE Chindia Index Fu. The fund currently has a performance rating of D+ (Weak) based on an annualized return of 1.90% over the last three years and a total return of 5.82% year to date 2012. Factored into the performance evaluation is an expense ratio of 0.60% (very low).

The fund's risk rating is currently C+ (Fair). It carries a beta of 1.43, meaning it is expected to move 14.3% for every 10% move in the market. Volatility, as measured by both the semi-deviation and a drawdown factor, is considered low. As of December 31, 2012, *First Trust ISE Chindia Index Fu traded at a discount of 5.59% below its net asset value, which is better than its one-year historical average discount of .14%.

Jonathan Erickson has been running the fund for 6 years and currently receives a manager quality ranking of 9 (0=worst, 99=best). This fund offers only a moderate level of risk but investors looking for strong performance are still waiting.

Data Date	Investment Rating	Net Assets ($Mil)	Price	Performance Rating/Pts	Total Return Y-T-D	Risk Rating/Pts
12-12	D	66.10	20.95	D+ / 2.6	5.82%	C+ / 6.1
2011	D+	79.30	18.15	C / 4.3	3.31%	C+ / 5.9
2010	D	176.30	25.02	C- / 3.7	18.17%	C- / 4.1
2009	C+	67.11	21.34	A+ / 9.6	71.88%	D+ / 2.9

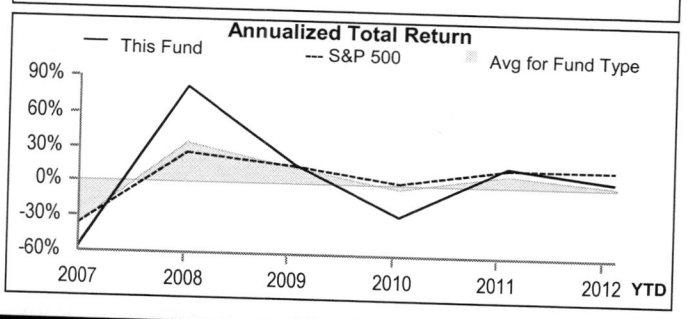

*First Trust ISE Cloud Computing (SKYY)

	B+	**Good**

Fund Family: First Trust Advisors LP
Fund Type: Global
Inception Date: July 6, 2011

Major Rating Factors:
Exceptional performance is the major factor driving the B+ (Good) TheStreet.com Investment Rating for *First Trust ISE Cloud Computing. The fund currently has a performance rating of A- (Excellent) based on an annualized return of 0.00% over the last three years and a total return of 4.78% year to date 2012. Factored into the performance evaluation is an expense ratio of 0.60% (very low).

The fund's risk rating is currently B- (Good). It carries a beta of 0.00, meaning the fund's expected move will be 0.0% for every 10% move in the market. Volatility, as measured by both the semi-deviation and a drawdown factor, is considered low. As of December 31, 2012, *First Trust ISE Cloud Computing traded at a discount of 4.52% below its net asset value, which is better than its one-year historical average premium of .02%.

Jonathan Erickson has been running the fund for 2 years and currently receives a manager quality ranking of 28 (0=worst, 99=best). If you desire only a moderate level of risk and strong performance, then this fund is an excellent option.

Data Date	Investment Rating	Net Assets ($Mil)	Price	Performance Rating/Pts	Total Return Y-T-D	Risk Rating/Pts
12-12	B+	77.50	19.87	A- / 9.1	4.78%	B- / 7.6

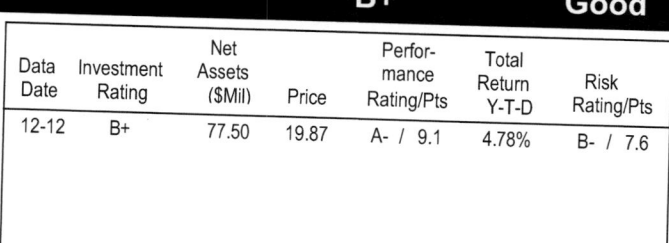

*First Trust ISE Glb Eng & Constr (FLM)

	D+	**Weak**

Fund Family: First Trust Advisors LP
Fund Type: Global
Inception Date: October 13, 2008

Major Rating Factors: *First Trust ISE Glb Eng & Constr receives a TheStreet.com Investment Rating of D+ (Weak). The fund currently has a performance rating of C- (Fair) based on an annualized return of 4.28% over the last three years and a total return of 3.48% year to date 2012. Factored into the performance evaluation is an expense ratio of 0.70% (very low).

The fund's risk rating is currently C+ (Fair). It carries a beta of 1.16, meaning it is expected to move 11.6% for every 10% move in the market. Volatility, as measured by both the semi-deviation and a drawdown factor, is considered low. As of December 31, 2012, *First Trust ISE Glb Eng & Constr traded at a discount of 3.45% below its net asset value, which is better than its one-year historical average discount of .16%.

Jonathan Erickson has been running the fund for 5 years and currently receives a manager quality ranking of 53 (0=worst, 99=best). If you desire an average level of risk, then this fund may be an option.

Data Date	Investment Rating	Net Assets ($Mil)	Price	Performance Rating/Pts	Total Return Y-T-D	Risk Rating/Pts
12-12	D+	19.10	42.28	C- / 3.4	3.48%	C+ / 6.5
2011	D	25.30	36.03	D+ / 2.3	0.70%	C+ / 6.7
2010	A	37.90	44.71	A / 9.4	17.63%	C+ / 6.6
2009	A	35.78	38.64	B / 7.6	22.86%	C+ / 6.8

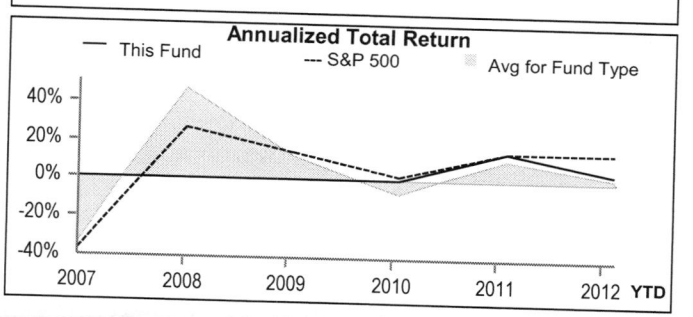

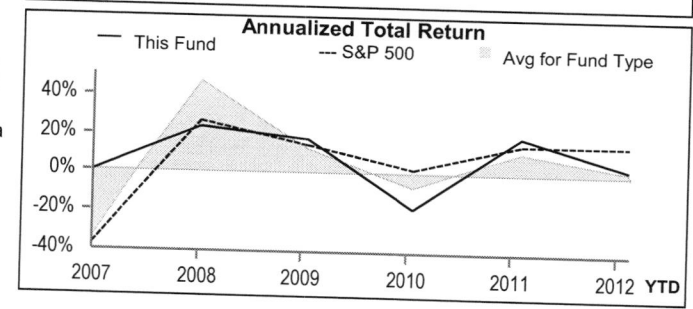

* Denotes ETF Fund

*First Trust ISE Glb Wind Energy (FAN)   E+   Very Weak

Fund Family: First Trust Advisors LP
Fund Type: Energy/Natural Resources
Inception Date: June 16, 2008

Data Date	Investment Rating	Net Assets ($Mil)	Price	Performance Rating/Pts	Total Return Y-T-D	Risk Rating/Pts
12-12	E+	19.40	6.94	E+ / 0.6	9.51%	C / 4.9
2011	D-	29.20	7.92	D- / 1.0	-1.64%	C / 5.5
2010	E+	51.80	10.25	E / 0.5	-31.11%	C- / 3.8
2009	C-	100.85	15.02	C+ / 5.9	19.40%	C- / 3.6

Major Rating Factors:
Very poor performance is the major factor driving the E+ (Very Weak) TheStreet.com Investment Rating for *First Trust ISE Glb Wind Energy. The fund currently has a performance rating of E+ (Very Weak) based on an annualized return of -20.08% over the last three years and a total return of 9.51% year to date 2012. Factored into the performance evaluation is an expense ratio of 0.60% (very low).

The fund's risk rating is currently C (Fair). It carries a beta of 0.93, meaning that its performance tracks fairly well with that of the overall stock market. Volatility, as measured by both the semi-deviation and a drawdown factor, is considered average. As of December 31, 2012, *First Trust ISE Glb Wind Energy traded at a discount of 8.56% below its net asset value, which is better than its one-year historical average discount of .68%.

Jonathan Erickson has been running the fund for 5 years and currently receives a manager quality ranking of 3 (0=worst, 99=best). This fund offers an average level of risk but investors looking for strong performance will be frustrated.

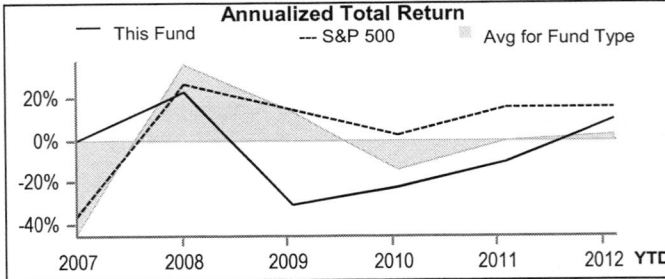

*First Trust ISE Global Copper Id (CU)   C   Fair

Fund Family: First Trust Advisors LP
Fund Type: Precious Metals
Inception Date: March 11, 2010

Data Date	Investment Rating	Net Assets ($Mil)	Price	Performance Rating/Pts	Total Return Y-T-D	Risk Rating/Pts
12-12	C	47.10	30.32	B+ / 8.4	5.16%	C / 4.6
2011	E+	51.30	29.29	E / 0.5	2.90%	C / 4.9

Major Rating Factors: Strong performance is the major factor driving the C (Fair) TheStreet.com Investment Rating for *First Trust ISE Global Copper Id. The fund currently has a performance rating of B+ (Good) based on an annualized return of 0.00% over the last three years and a total return of 5.16% year to date 2012. Factored into the performance evaluation is an expense ratio of 0.70% (very low).

The fund's risk rating is currently C (Fair). It carries a beta of 0.00, meaning the fund's expected move will be 0.0% for every 10% move in the market. Volatility, as measured by both the semi-deviation and a drawdown factor, is considered average. As of December 31, 2012, *First Trust ISE Global Copper Id traded at a discount of 4.98% below its net asset value, which is better than its one-year historical average discount of .22%.

Jonathan Erickson has been running the fund for 3 years and currently receives a manager quality ranking of 22 (0=worst, 99=best). If you desire an average level of risk and strong performance, then this fund is a good option.

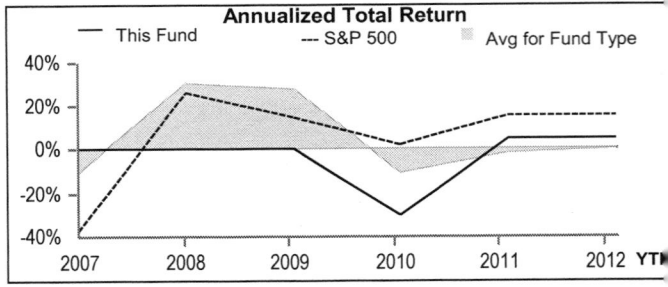

*First Trust ISE Global Platinum (PLTM)   E+   Very Weak

Fund Family: First Trust Advisors LP
Fund Type: Precious Metals
Inception Date: March 11, 2010

Data Date	Investment Rating	Net Assets ($Mil)	Price	Performance Rating/Pts	Total Return Y-T-D	Risk Rating/Pts
12-12	E+	8.90	14.77	D / 1.9	7.11%	C- / 3.6
2011	E+	7.20	17.84	E- / 0.1	4.20%	C / 4.7

Major Rating Factors:
Disappointing performance is the major factor driving the E+ (Very Weak) TheStreet.com Investment Rating for *First Trust ISE Global Platinum. The fund currently has a performance rating of D (Weak) based on an annualized return of 0.00% over the last three years and a total return of 7.11% year to date 2012. Factored into the performance evaluation is an expense ratio of 0.70% (very low).

The fund's risk rating is currently C- (Fair). It carries a beta of 0.00, meaning the fund's expected move will be 0.0% for every 10% move in the market. Volatility, as measured by both the semi-deviation and a drawdown factor, is considered average. As of December 31, 2012, *First Trust ISE Global Platinum traded at a discount of 6.22% below its net asset value, which is better than its one-year historical average discount of .02%.

Jonathan Erickson has been running the fund for 3 years and currently receives a manager quality ranking of 4 (0=worst, 99=best). This fund offers an average level of risk but investors looking for strong performance will be frustrated.

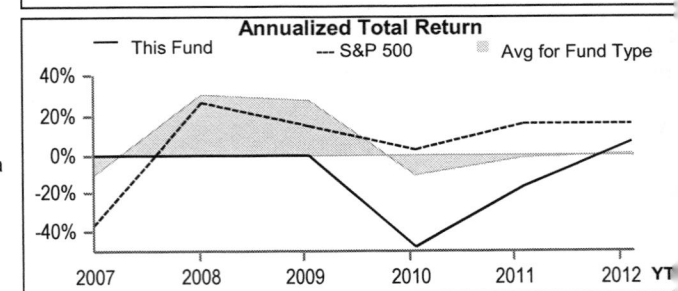

*First Trust ISE Water Index Fund (FIW)

B   **Good**

Fund Family: First Trust Advisors LP
Fund Type: Income
Inception Date: May 8, 2007

Major Rating Factors: Strong performance is the major factor driving the B (Good) TheStreet.com Investment Rating for *First Trust ISE Water Index Fund. The fund currently has a performance rating of B (Good) based on an annualized return of 13.29% over the last three years and a total return of 3.65% year to date 2012. Factored into the performance evaluation is an expense ratio of 0.60% (very low).

The fund's risk rating is currently B- (Good). It carries a beta of 1.17, meaning it is expected to move 11.7% for every 10% move in the market. Volatility, as measured by both the semi-deviation and a drawdown factor, is considered low. As of December 31, 2012, *First Trust ISE Water Index Fund traded at a discount of 3.49% below its net asset value, which is better than its one-year historical average discount of .03%.

Jonathan Erickson has been running the fund for 6 years and currently receives a manager quality ranking of 51 (0=worst, 99=best). If you desire only a moderate level of risk and strong performance, then this fund is an excellent option.

Data Date	Investment Rating	Net Assets ($Mil)	Price	Performance Rating/Pts	Total Return Y-T-D	Risk Rating/Pts
12-12	B	72.80	26.02	B / 7.6	3.65%	B- / 7.6
2011	C-	58.00	20.77	C- / 4.2	1.76%	C+ / 6.7
2010	C+	53.10	22.17	C+ / 6.2	19.90%	C / 5.4
2009	B-	32.94	18.63	B / 7.6	17.77%	C / 5.3

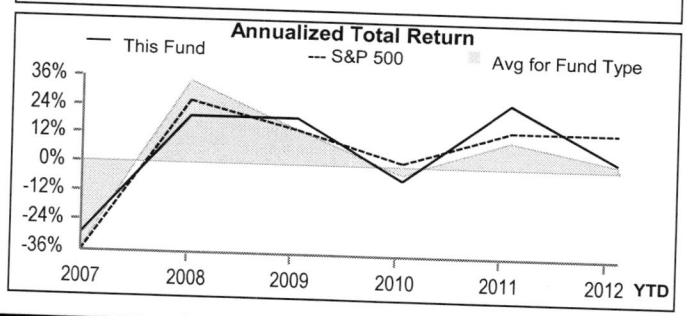

*First Trust ISE-Revere Natural G (FCG)

D-   **Weak**

Fund Family: First Trust Advisors LP
Fund Type: Income
Inception Date: May 8, 2007

Major Rating Factors:
Very poor performance is the major factor driving the D- (Weak) TheStreet.com Investment Rating for *First Trust ISE-Revere Natural G. The fund currently has a performance rating of E+ (Very Weak) based on an annualized return of -4.16% over the last three years and a total return of 2.23% year to date 2012. Factored into the performance evaluation is an expense ratio of 0.60% (very low).

The fund's risk rating is currently C+ (Fair). It carries a beta of 1.43, meaning it is expected to move 14.3% for every 10% move in the market. Volatility, as measured by both the semi-deviation and a drawdown factor, is considered low. As of December 31, 2012, *First Trust ISE-Revere Natural G traded at a discount of 2.24% below its net asset value.

Jonathan Erickson has been running the fund for 6 years and currently receives a manager quality ranking of 7 (0=worst, 99=best). This fund offers only a moderate level of risk but investors looking for strong performance are still waiting.

Data Date	Investment Rating	Net Assets ($Mil)	Price	Performance Rating/Pts	Total Return Y-T-D	Risk Rating/Pts
12-12	D-	387.90	15.68	E+ / 0.9	2.23%	C+ / 6.6
2011	C-	346.50	18.19	C / 4.5	2.53%	C+ / 6.7
2010	D	396.90	19.68	C- / 3.4	12.23%	C / 4.5
2009	B+	85.84	17.59	A- / 9.2	40.85%	C / 4.7

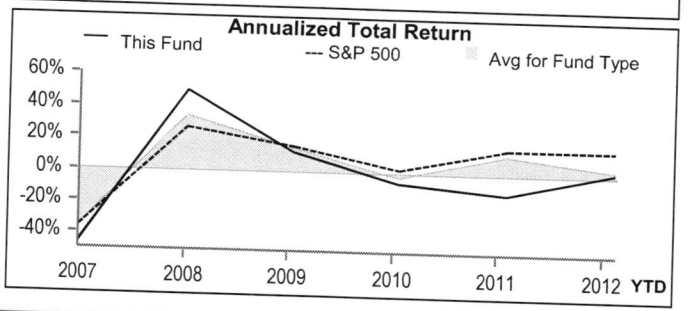

*First Trust Japan AlphaDEX (FJP)

D   **Weak**

Fund Family: First Trust Advisors LP
Fund Type: Foreign
Inception Date: April 18, 2011

Major Rating Factors:
Disappointing performance is the major factor driving the D (Weak) TheStreet.com Investment Rating for *First Trust Japan AlphaDEX. The fund currently has a performance rating of D- (Weak) based on an annualized return of 0.00% over the last three years and a total return of -0.39% year to date 2012. Factored into the performance evaluation is an expense ratio of 0.80% (very low).

The fund's risk rating is currently B (Good). It carries a beta of 0.00, meaning the fund's expected move will be 0.0% for every 10% move in the market. Volatility, as measured by both the semi-deviation and a drawdown factor, is considered low. As of December 31, 2012, *First Trust Japan AlphaDEX traded at a premium of 2.05% above its net asset value, which is worse than its one-year historical average premium of .06%.

Jonathan Erickson has been running the fund for 2 years and currently receives a manager quality ranking of 11 (0=worst, 99=best). This fund offers only a moderate level of risk but investors looking for strong performance are still waiting.

Data Date	Investment Rating	Net Assets ($Mil)	Price	Performance Rating/Pts	Total Return Y-T-D	Risk Rating/Pts
12-12	D	1.80	36.33	D- / 1.5	-0.39%	B / 8.0

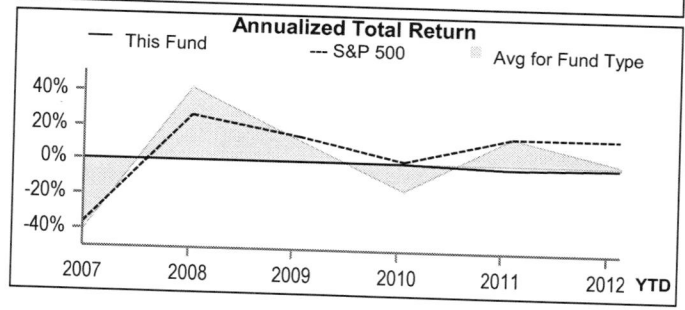

* Denotes ETF Fund

*First Trust Large Cap Gro AlphaD (FTC)

C   **Fair**

Fund Family: First Trust Advisors LP
Fund Type: Growth
Inception Date: May 8, 2007

Major Rating Factors: Middle of the road best describes *First Trust Large Cap Gro AlphaD whose TheStreet.com Investment Rating is currently a C (Fair). The fund currently has a performance rating of C (Fair) based on an annualized return of 10.44% over the last three years and a total return of 3.06% year to date 2012. Factored into the performance evaluation is an expense ratio of 0.70% (very low).

The fund's risk rating is currently B- (Good). It carries a beta of 1.03, meaning that its performance tracks fairly well with that of the overall stock market. Volatility, as measured by both the semi-deviation and a drawdown factor, is considered low. As of December 31, 2012, *First Trust Large Cap Gro AlphaD traded at a discount of 3.05% below its net asset value, which is better than its one-year historical average discount of .02%.

Daniel J. Lindquist has been running the fund for 6 years and currently receives a manager quality ranking of 40 (0=worst, 99=best). If you desire an average level of risk, then this fund may be an option.

Data Date	Investment Rating	Net Assets ($Mil)	Price	Performance Rating/Pts	Total Return Y-T-D	Risk Rating/Pts
12-12	C	116.50	29.88	C / 4.7	3.06%	B- / 7.7
2011	C	125.10	27.48	C / 5.1	1.06%	B- / 7.6
2010	C	82.50	28.48	C / 5.1	23.63%	C+ / 5.7
2009	A-	13.96	23.17	B+ / 8.5	26.59%	C+ / 5.8

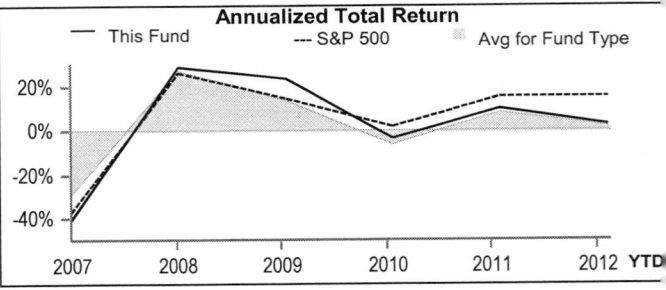

Annualized Total Return

*First Trust Large Cap Val AlphaD (FTA)

C+   **Fair**

Fund Family: First Trust Advisors LP
Fund Type: Income
Inception Date: May 8, 2007

Major Rating Factors: Middle of the road best describes *First Trust Large Cap Val AlphaD whose TheStreet.com Investment Rating is currently a C+ (Fair). The fund currently has a performance rating of C+ (Fair) based on an annualized return of 12.36% over the last three years and a total return of 2.89% year to date 2012. Factored into the performance evaluation is an expense ratio of 0.70% (very low).

The fund's risk rating is currently B (Good). It carries a beta of 1.05, meaning that its performance tracks fairly well with that of the overall stock market. Volatility, as measured by both the semi-deviation and a drawdown factor, is considered low. As of December 31, 2012, *First Trust Large Cap Val AlphaD traded at a discount of 2.87% below its net asset value, which is better than its one-year historical average premium of .04%.

Daniel J. Lindquist has been running the fund for 6 years and currently receives a manager quality ranking of 58 (0=worst, 99=best). If you desire an average level of risk, then this fund may be an option.

Data Date	Investment Rating	Net Assets ($Mil)	Price	Performance Rating/Pts	Total Return Y-T-D	Risk Rating/Pts
12-12	C+	278.90	30.48	C+ / 6.2	2.89%	B / 8.2
2011	C+	184.90	26.45	C+ / 6.4	1.89%	B- / 7.8
2010	C+	92.50	26.45	C+ / 6.5	18.69%	C+ / 5.7
2009	A	18.14	22.60	B+ / 8.9	36.27%	C+ / 5.6

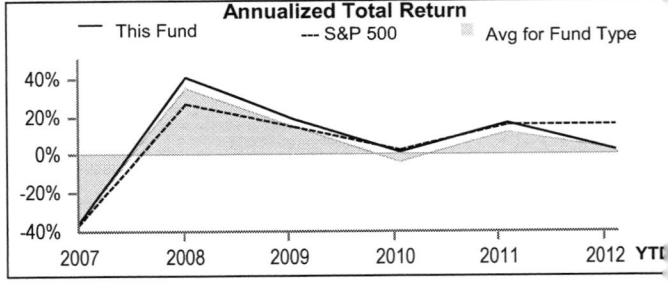

Annualized Total Return

*First Trust Latin America AlphaD (FLN)

C+   **Fair**

Fund Family: First Trust Advisors LP
Fund Type: Foreign
Inception Date: April 18, 2011

Major Rating Factors: Strong performance is the major factor driving the C+ (Fair) TheStreet.com Investment Rating for *First Trust Latin America AlphaD. The fund currently has a performance rating of B (Good) based on an annualized return of 0.00% over the last three years and a total return of 1.40% year to date 2012. Factored into the performance evaluation is an expense ratio of 0.81% (very low).

The fund's risk rating is currently C+ (Fair). It carries a beta of 0.00, meaning the fund's expected move will be 0.0% for every 10% move in the market. Volatility, as measured by both the semi-deviation and a drawdown factor, is considered low. As of December 31, 2012, *First Trust Latin America AlphaD traded at a discount of .07% below its net asset value, which is better than its one-year historical average premium of .52%.

Jonathan Erickson has been running the fund for 2 years and currently receives a manager quality ranking of 15 (0=worst, 99=best). If you desire only a moderate level of risk and strong performance, then this fund is an excellent option.

Data Date	Investment Rating	Net Assets ($Mil)	Price	Performance Rating/Pts	Total Return Y-T-D	Risk Rating/Pts
12-12	C+	9.30	27.16	B / 7.6	1.40%	C+ / 6.8

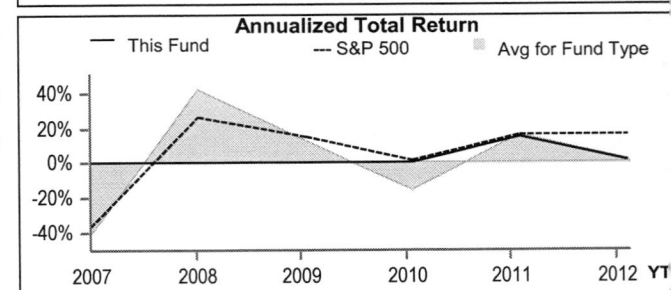

Annualized Total Return

*First Trust Lrg Cap Core AlphaDE (FEX)

C+   **Fair**

Fund Family: First Trust Advisors LP
Fund Type: Growth and Income
Inception Date: May 8, 2007

Major Rating Factors: Middle of the road best describes *First Trust Lrg Cap Core AlphaDE whose TheStreet.com Investment Rating is currently a C+ (Fair). The fund currently has a performance rating of C+ (Fair) based on an annualized return of 11.67% over the last three years and a total return of 2.87% year to date 2012. Factored into the performance evaluation is an expense ratio of 0.70% (very low).

The fund's risk rating is currently B (Good). It carries a beta of 1.05, meaning that its performance tracks fairly well with that of the overall stock market. Volatility, as measured by both the semi-deviation and a drawdown factor, is considered low. As of December 31, 2012, *First Trust Lrg Cap Core AlphaDE traded at a discount of 2.91% below its net asset value, which is better than its one-year historical average premium of .02%.

Daniel J. Lindquist has been running the fund for 6 years and currently receives a manager quality ranking of 49 (0=worst, 99=best). If you desire an average level of risk, then this fund may be an option.

Data Date	Investment Rating	Net Assets ($Mil)	Price	Performance Rating/Pts	Total Return Y-T-D	Risk Rating/Pts
12-12	C+	344.70	30.65	C+ / 5.6	2.87%	B / 8.0
2011	C+	267.70	27.17	C+ / 6.1	1.58%	B- / 7.9
2010	C+	128.00	27.58	C+ / 5.9	20.67%	C+ / 5.8
2009	A	13.72	23.08	B+ / 8.7	32.18%	C+ / 5.9

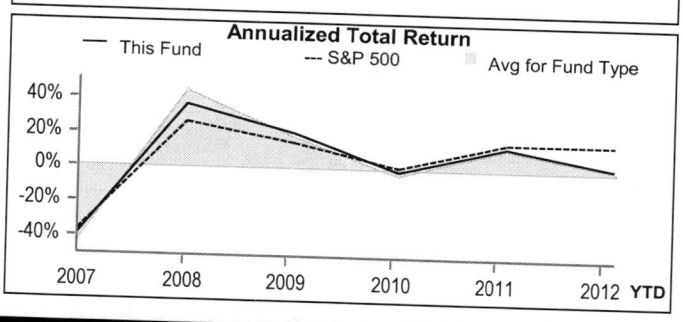

---

*First Trust Materials AlphaDEX (FXZ)

C+   **Fair**

Fund Family: First Trust Advisors LP
Fund Type: Income
Inception Date: May 8, 2007

Major Rating Factors: Middle of the road best describes *First Trust Materials AlphaDEX whose TheStreet.com Investment Rating is currently a C+ (Fair). The fund currently has a performance rating of C+ (Fair) based on an annualized return of 13.10% over the last three years and a total return of 3.88% year to date 2012. Factored into the performance evaluation is an expense ratio of 0.70% (very low).

The fund's risk rating is currently B- (Good). It carries a beta of 1.40, meaning it is expected to move 14.0% for every 10% move in the market. Volatility, as measured by both the semi-deviation and a drawdown factor, is considered low. As of December 31, 2012, *First Trust Materials AlphaDEX traded at a discount of 3.66% below its net asset value, which is better than its one-year historical average discount of .01%.

Daniel J. Lindquist has been running the fund for 6 years and currently receives a manager quality ranking of 33 (0=worst, 99=best). If you desire an average level of risk, then this fund may be an option.

Data Date	Investment Rating	Net Assets ($Mil)	Price	Performance Rating/Pts	Total Return Y-T-D	Risk Rating/Pts
12-12	C+	203.90	25.80	C+ / 6.7	3.88%	B- / 7.0
2011	C+	121.10	21.23	B- / 7.0	4.00%	B- / 7.1
2010	C+	417.20	23.76	B / 7.6	28.28%	C / 4.7
2009	A	9.92	18.84	A / 9.4	53.07%	C / 5.0

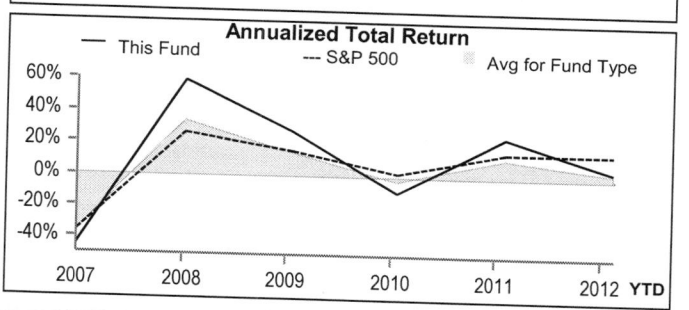

---

*First Trust Mega Cap AlphaDEX (FMK)

C+   **Fair**

Fund Family: First Trust Advisors LP
Fund Type: Growth
Inception Date: May 11, 2011

Major Rating Factors: Middle of the road best describes *First Trust Mega Cap AlphaDEX whose TheStreet.com Investment Rating is currently a C+ (Fair). The fund currently has a performance rating of C+ (Fair) based on an annualized return of 0.00% over the last three years and a total return of 4.97% year to date 2012. Factored into the performance evaluation is an expense ratio of 0.70% (very low).

The fund's risk rating is currently B (Good). It carries a beta of 0.00, meaning the fund's expected move will be 0.0% for every 10% move in the market. Volatility, as measured by both the semi-deviation and a drawdown factor, is considered low. As of December 31, 2012, *First Trust Mega Cap AlphaDEX traded at a discount of 4.68% below its net asset value, which is better than its one-year historical average discount of .03%.

Daniel J. Lindquist has been running the fund for 2 years and currently receives a manager quality ranking of 13 (0=worst, 99=best). If you desire an average level of risk, then this fund may be an option.

Data Date	Investment Rating	Net Assets ($Mil)	Price	Performance Rating/Pts	Total Return Y-T-D	Risk Rating/Pts
12-12	C+	9.50	18.93	C+ / 6.2	4.97%	B / 8.2

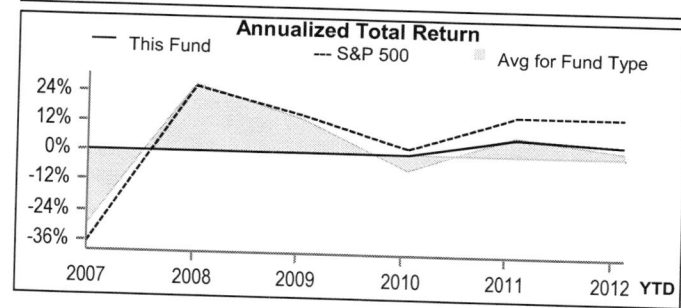

* Denotes ETF Fund

*First Trust Mid Cap Core AlphaDE (FNX)

C+   **Fair**

Fund Family: First Trust Advisors LP
Fund Type: Growth
Inception Date: May 8, 2007

Major Rating Factors: Middle of the road best describes *First Trust Mid Cap Core AlphaDE whose TheStreet.com Investment Rating is currently a C+ (Fair). The fund currently has a performance rating of C+ (Fair) based on an annualized return of 13.84% over the last three years and a total return of 3.65% year to date 2012. Factored into the performance evaluation is an expense ratio of 0.70% (very low).

The fund's risk rating is currently B- (Good). It carries a beta of 1.17, meaning it is expected to move 11.7% for every 10% move in the market. Volatility, as measured by both the semi-deviation and a drawdown factor, is considered low. As of December 31, 2012, *First Trust Mid Cap Core AlphaDE traded at a discount of 3.46% below its net asset value, which is better than its one-year historical average premium of .02%.

Daniel J. Lindquist has been running the fund for 6 years and currently receives a manager quality ranking of 56 (0=worst, 99=best). If you desire an average level of risk, then this fund may be an option.

Data Date	Investment Rating	Net Assets ($Mil)	Price	Performance Rating/Pts	Total Return Y-T-D	Risk Rating/Pts
12-12	C+	301.10	36.88	C+ / 6.5	3.65%	B- / 7.7
2011	B-	244.70	32.62	B- / 7.3	1.47%	B- / 7.8
2010	B+	151.20	32.51	B / 7.8	26.64%	C+ / 5.7
2009	A+	8.80	25.80	A- / 9.1	46.78%	C+ / 6.0

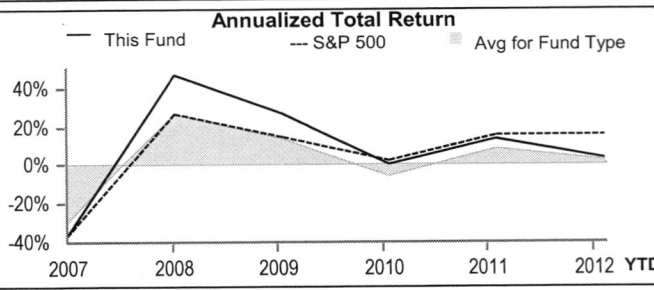

*First Trust Mid Cap Growth Alpha (FNY)

B-   **Good**

Fund Family: First Trust Advisors LP
Fund Type: Growth
Inception Date: April 19, 2011

Major Rating Factors: *First Trust Mid Cap Growth Alpha receives a TheStreet.com Investment Rating of B- (Good). The fund currently has a performance rating of C+ (Fair) based on an annualized return of 0.00% over the last three years and a total return of 3.80% year to date 2012. Factored into the performance evaluation is an expense ratio of 0.70% (very low).

The fund's risk rating is currently B (Good). It carries a beta of 0.00, meaning the fund's expected move will be 0.0% for every 10% move in the market. Volatility, as measured by both the semi-deviation and a drawdown factor, is considered low. As of December 31, 2012, *First Trust Mid Cap Growth Alpha traded at a discount of 3.55% below its net asset value, which is better than its one-year historical average premium of .13%.

Daniel J. Lindquist has been running the fund for 2 years and currently receives a manager quality ranking of 28 (0=worst, 99=best). If you desire an average level of risk, then this fund may be an option.

Data Date	Investment Rating	Net Assets ($Mil)	Price	Performance Rating/Pts	Total Return Y-T-D	Risk Rating/Pts
12-12	B-	16.50	20.63	C+ / 6.2	3.80%	B / 8.6

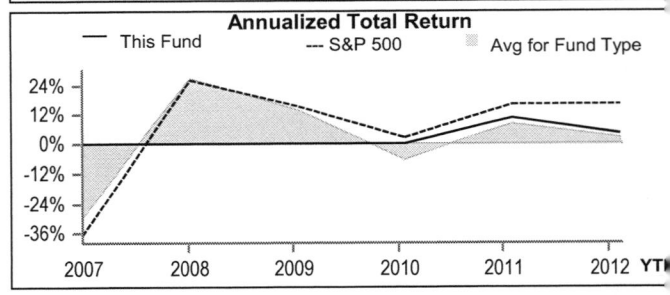

*First Trust Mid Cap Val AlphaDEX (FNK)

A-   **Excellent**

Fund Family: First Trust Advisors LP
Fund Type: Growth
Inception Date: April 19, 2011

Major Rating Factors:
Strong performance is the major factor driving the A- (Excellent) TheStreet.com Investment Rating for *First Trust Mid Cap Val AlphaDEX. The fund currently has a performance rating of B+ (Good) based on an annualized return of 0.00% over the last three years and a total return of 3.46% year to date 2012. Factored into the performance evaluation is an expense ratio of 0.70% (very low).

The fund's risk rating is currently B (Good). It carries a beta of 0.00, meaning the fund's expected move will be 0.0% for every 10% move in the market. Volatility, as measured by both the semi-deviation and a drawdown factor, is considered low. As of December 31, 2012, *First Trust Mid Cap Val AlphaDEX traded at a discount of 3.23% below its net asset value, which is better than its one-year historical average premium of .21%.

Daniel J. Lindquist has been running the fund for 2 years and currently receives a manager quality ranking of 37 (0=worst, 99=best). If you desire only a moderate level of risk and strong performance, then this fund is an excellent option.

Data Date	Investment Rating	Net Assets ($Mil)	Price	Performance Rating/Pts	Total Return Y-T-D	Risk Rating/Pts
12-12	A-	9.70	21.58	B+ / 8.5	3.46%	B / 8.4

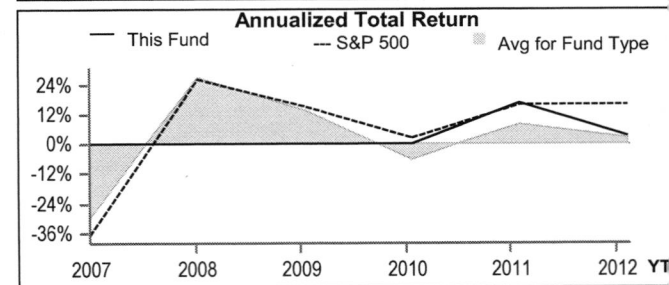

*First Trust Morningstar Div Lead (FDL)

B-   **Good**

Fund Family: First Trust Advisors LP
Fund Type: Income
Inception Date: March 9, 2006

Major Rating Factors: *First Trust Morningstar Div Lead receives a TheStreet.com Investment Rating of B- (Good). The fund currently has a performance rating of C (Fair) based on an annualized return of 14.05% over the last three years and a total return of 2.49% year to date 2012. Factored into the performance evaluation is an expense ratio of 0.45% (very low).

The fund's risk rating is currently B+ (Good). It carries a beta of 0.50, meaning the fund's expected move will be 5.0% for every 10% move in the market. Volatility, as measured by both the semi-deviation and a drawdown factor, is considered very low. As of December 31, 2012, *First Trust Morningstar Div Lead traded at a discount of 2.43% below its net asset value, which is better than its one-year historical average premium of .03%.

Jonathan Erickson has been running the fund for 16 years and currently receives a manager quality ranking of 86 (0=worst, 99=best). If you desire an average level of risk, then this fund may be an option.

Data Date	Investment Rating	Net Assets ($Mil)	Price	Performance Rating/Pts	Total Return Y-T-D	Risk Rating/Pts
12-12	B-	545.50	18.46	C / 5.4	2.49%	B+ / 9.2
2011	C+	447.00	17.58	C+ / 6.2	-1.14%	B- / 7.4
2010	C-	143.30	15.94	C- / 3.5	16.19%	C / 5.4
2009	D-	40.48	14.27	D- / 1.1	12.02%	C / 5.3

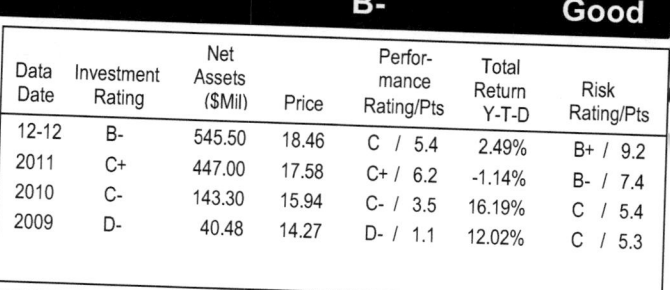

*First Trust Multi Cap Grth Alpha (FAD)

C   **Fair**

Fund Family: First Trust Advisors LP
Fund Type: Growth
Inception Date: May 8, 2007

Major Rating Factors: Middle of the road best describes *First Trust Multi Cap Grth Alpha whose TheStreet.com Investment Rating is currently a C (Fair). The fund currently has a performance rating of C (Fair) based on an annualized return of 12.15% over the last three years and a total return of 3.24% year to date 2012. Factored into the performance evaluation is an expense ratio of 0.70% (very low).

The fund's risk rating is currently B- (Good). It carries a beta of 1.07, meaning that its performance tracks fairly well with that of the overall stock market. Volatility, as measured by both the semi-deviation and a drawdown factor, is considered low. As of December 31, 2012, *First Trust Multi Cap Grth Alpha traded at a discount of 3.31% below its net asset value, which is better than its one-year historical average premium of .02%.

Daniel J. Lindquist has been running the fund for 6 years and currently receives a manager quality ranking of 46 (0=worst, 99=best). If you desire an average level of risk, then this fund may be an option.

Data Date	Investment Rating	Net Assets ($Mil)	Price	Performance Rating/Pts	Total Return Y-T-D	Risk Rating/Pts
12-12	C	31.10	32.73	C / 5.1	3.24%	B- / 7.5
2011	C+	25.40	29.94	C+ / 6.0	0.69%	B- / 7.5
2010	C+	18.10	30.27	C+ / 6.4	25.14%	C+ / 5.6
2009	A-	5.20	24.26	B+ / 8.6	30.89%	C+ / 5.7

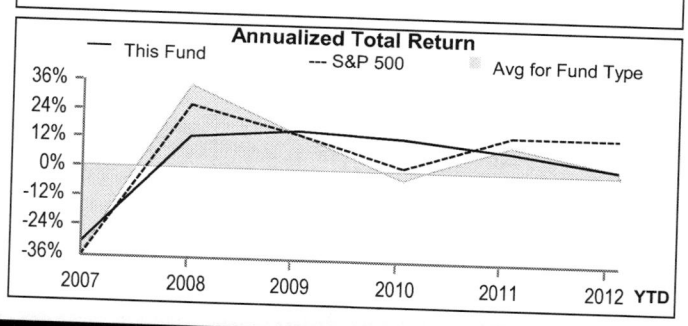

*First Trust Multi Cap Val AlphaD (FAB)

B-   **Good**

Fund Family: First Trust Advisors LP
Fund Type: Income
Inception Date: May 8, 2007

Major Rating Factors: *First Trust Multi Cap Val AlphaD receives a TheStreet.com Investment Rating of B- (Good). The fund currently has a performance rating of C+ (Fair) based on an annualized return of 13.09% over the last three years and a total return of 3.03% year to date 2012. Factored into the performance evaluation is an expense ratio of 0.70% (very low).

The fund's risk rating is currently B (Good). It carries a beta of 1.12, meaning it is expected to move 11.2% for every 10% move in the market. Volatility, as measured by both the semi-deviation and a drawdown factor, is considered low. As of December 31, 2012, *First Trust Multi Cap Val AlphaD traded at a discount of 2.96% below its net asset value, which is better than its one-year historical average premium of .02%.

Daniel J. Lindquist has been running the fund for 6 years and currently receives a manager quality ranking of 57 (0=worst, 99=best). If you desire an average level of risk, then this fund may be an option.

Data Date	Investment Rating	Net Assets ($Mil)	Price	Performance Rating/Pts	Total Return Y-T-D	Risk Rating/Pts
12-12	B-	55.70	32.78	C+ / 6.5	3.03%	B / 8.1
2011	B-	39.70	28.48	B- / 7.1	1.82%	B- / 7.8
2010	B	25.70	28.69	B- / 7.3	22.42%	C+ / 5.7
2009	A+	10.10	23.75	A- / 9.1	48.31%	C+ / 5.6

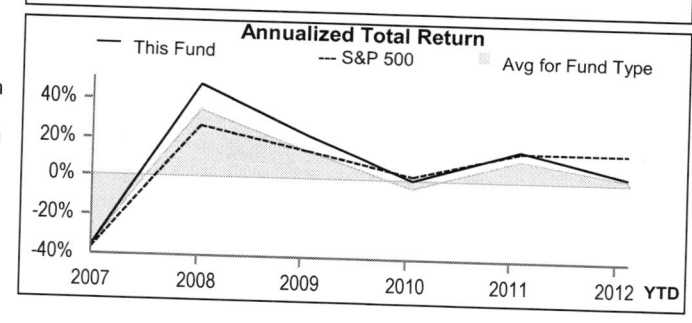

* Denotes ETF Fund

*First Trust NASD Cln Edge Smt Gd (GRID) — D Weak

Fund Family: First Trust Advisors LP
Fund Type: Growth
Inception Date: November 16, 2009

Major Rating Factors:
Disappointing performance is the major factor driving the D (Weak) TheStreet.com Investment Rating for *First Trust NASD Cln Edge Smt Gd. The fund currently has a performance rating of D (Weak) based on an annualized return of -1.00% over the last three years and a total return of 5.30% year to date 2012. Factored into the performance evaluation is an expense ratio of 0.70% (very low).

The fund's risk rating is currently C+ (Fair). It carries a beta of 1.28, meaning it is expected to move 12.8% for every 10% move in the market. Volatility, as measured by both the semi-deviation and a drawdown factor, is considered low. As of December 31, 2012, *First Trust NASD Cln Edge Smt Gd traded at a discount of 5.50% below its net asset value, which is better than its one-year historical average discount of .39%.

Jonathan Erickson has been running the fund for 4 years and currently receives a manager quality ranking of 8 (0=worst, 99=best). This fund offers only a moderate level of risk but investors looking for strong performance are still waiting.

Data Date	Investment Rating	Net Assets ($Mil)	Price	Performance Rating/Pts	Total Return Y-T-D	Risk Rating/Pts
12-12	D	13.30	29.23	D / 2.1	5.30%	C+ / 6.7
2011	D-	14.90	24.93	E+ / 0.7	0.32%	C+ / 6.7
2010	B-	28.60	31.77	C+ / 6.5	-1.06%	B- / 7.2

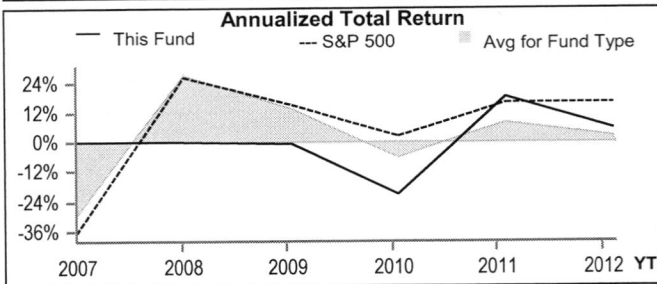

*First Trust NASDAQ ABA Community (QABA) — D+ Weak

Fund Family: First Trust Advisors LP
Fund Type: Income
Inception Date: June 29, 2009

Major Rating Factors:
Disappointing performance is the major factor driving the D+ (Weak) TheStreet.com Investment Rating for *First Trust NASDAQ ABA Community. The fund currently has a performance rating of D+ (Weak) based on an annualized return of 5.57% over the last three years and a total return of 2.76% year to date 2012. Factored into the performance evaluation is an expense ratio of 0.60% (very low).

The fund's risk rating is currently B- (Good). It carries a beta of 1.18, meaning it is expected to move 11.8% for every 10% move in the market. Volatility, as measured by both the semi-deviation and a drawdown factor, is considered low. As of December 31, 2012, *First Trust NASDAQ ABA Community traded at a discount of 2.85% below its net asset value, which is better than its one-year historical average premium of .02%.

Cynthia J. Clemson has been running the fund for 4 years and currently receives a manager quality ranking of 18 (0=worst, 99=best). This fund offers only a moderate level of risk but investors looking for strong performance are still waiting.

Data Date	Investment Rating	Net Assets ($Mil)	Price	Performance Rating/Pts	Total Return Y-T-D	Risk Rating/Pts
12-12	D+	8.90	25.54	D+ / 2.7	2.76%	B- / 7.0
2011	D+	12.60	22.96	D+ / 2.7	4.14%	B- / 7.1
2010	A	10.00	25.05	B+ / 8.7	11.73%	C+ / 6.9

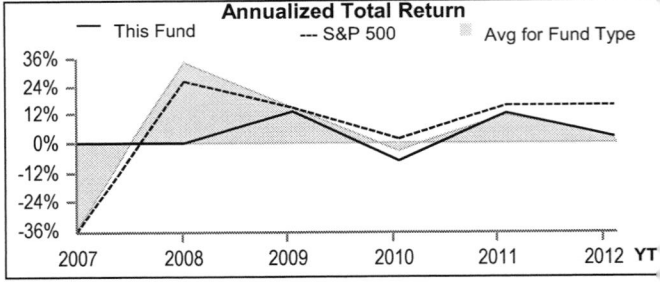

*First Trust NASDAQ CEA Smartphon (FONE) — B Good

Fund Family: First Trust Advisors LP
Fund Type: Global
Inception Date: February 17, 2011

Major Rating Factors: Strong performance is the major factor driving the B (Good) TheStreet.com Investment Rating for *First Trust NASDAQ CEA Smartphon. The fund currently has a performance rating of B+ (Good) based on an annualized return of 0.00% over the last three years and a total return of 3.82% year to date 2012. Factored into the performance evaluation is an expense ratio of 0.70% (very low).

The fund's risk rating is currently B- (Good). It carries a beta of 0.00, meaning the fund's expected move will be 0.0% for every 10% move in the market. Volatility, as measured by both the semi-deviation and a drawdown factor, is considered low. As of December 31, 2012, *First Trust NASDAQ CEA Smartphon traded at a discount of 3.98% below its net asset value, which is better than its one-year historical average discount of .37%.

Jonathan Erickson has been running the fund for 2 years and currently receives a manager quality ranking of 13 (0=worst, 99=best). If you desire only a moderate level of risk and strong performance, then this fund is an excellent option.

Data Date	Investment Rating	Net Assets ($Mil)	Price	Performance Rating/Pts	Total Return Y-T-D	Risk Rating/Pts
12-12	B	11.40	25.10	B+ / 8.7	3.82%	B- / 7.2

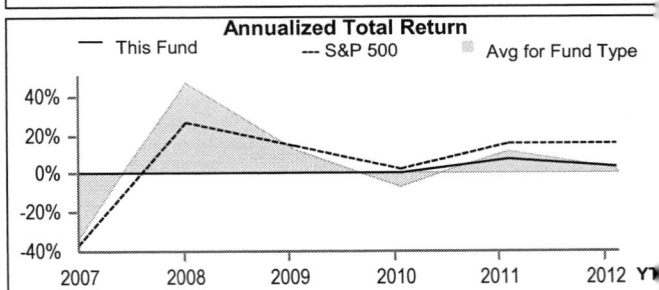

*First Trust NASDAQ Cln Edg US Li (QCLN)

D-   **Weak**

Fund Family: First Trust Advisors LP
Fund Type: Income
Inception Date: February 8, 2007

Major Rating Factors:
Very poor performance is the major factor driving the D- (Weak) TheStreet.com Investment Rating for *First Trust NASDAQ Cln Edg US Li. The fund currently has a performance rating of E+ (Very Weak) based on an annualized return of -13.65% over the last three years and a total return of 6.14% year to date 2012. Factored into the performance evaluation is an expense ratio of 0.60% (very low).

The fund's risk rating is currently C (Fair). It carries a beta of 1.65, meaning it is expected to move 16.5% for every 10% move in the market. Volatility, as measured by both the semi-deviation and a drawdown factor, is considered average. As of December 31, 2012, *First Trust NASDAQ Cln Edg US Li traded at a discount of 6.26% below its net asset value, which is better than its one-year historical average discount of .23%.

Jonathan Erickson has been running the fund for 6 years and currently receives a manager quality ranking of 3 (0=worst, 99=best). This fund offers an average level of risk but investors looking for strong performance will be frustrated.

Data Date	Investment Rating	Net Assets ($Mil)	Price	Performance Rating/Pts	Total Return Y-T-D	Risk Rating/Pts
12-12	D-	13.70	9.29	E+ / 0.7	6.14%	C / 5.4
2011	D-	20.70	9.59	D- / 1.1	2.10%	C+ / 5.7
2010	E+	36.10	16.42	E+ / 0.7	2.18%	C- / 4.0
2009	C+	38.05	16.07	B+ / 8.5	34.59%	C- / 3.8

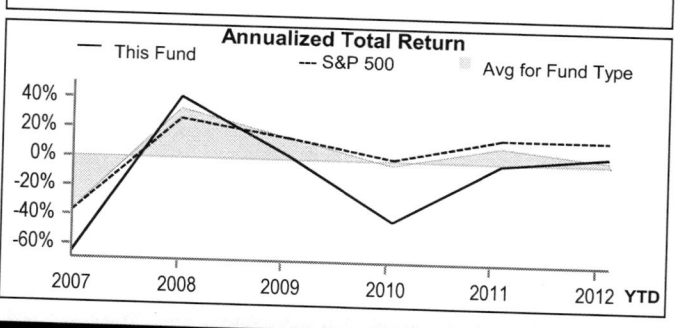

*First Trust NASDAQ Global Auto (CARZ)

B+   **Good**

Fund Family: First Trust Advisors LP
Fund Type: Global
Inception Date: May 9, 2011

Major Rating Factors:
Exceptional performance is the major factor driving the B+ (Good) TheStreet.com Investment Rating for *First Trust NASDAQ Global Auto. The fund currently has a performance rating of A+ (Excellent) based on an annualized return of 0.00% over the last three years and a total return of 3.98% year to date 2012. Factored into the performance evaluation is an expense ratio of 0.70% (very low).

The fund's risk rating is currently C+ (Fair). It carries a beta of 0.00, meaning the fund's expected move will be 0.0% for every 10% move in the market. Volatility, as measured by both the semi-deviation and a drawdown factor, is considered low. As of December 31, 2012, *First Trust NASDAQ Global Auto traded at a discount of 2.90% below its net asset value, which is better than its one-year historical average premium of .17%.

Jonathan Erickson has been running the fund for 2 years and currently receives a manager quality ranking of 90 (0=worst, 99=best). If you desire only a moderate level of risk and strong performance, then this fund is an excellent option.

Data Date	Investment Rating	Net Assets ($Mil)	Price	Performance Rating/Pts	Total Return Y-T-D	Risk Rating/Pts
12-12	B+	7.30	29.12	A+ / 9.8	3.98%	C+ / 6.6

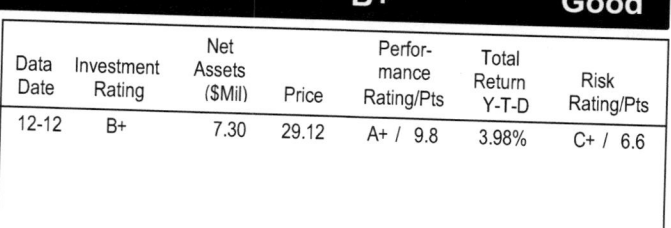

*First Trust NASDAQ-100 Equal Wei (QQEW)

C+   **Fair**

Fund Family: First Trust Advisors LP
Fund Type: Growth
Inception Date: April 19, 2006

Major Rating Factors: Middle of the road best describes *First Trust NASDAQ-100 Equal Wei whose TheStreet.com Investment Rating is currently a C+ (Fair). The fund currently has a performance rating of C+ (Fair) based on an annualized return of 11.75% over the last three years and a total return of 4.21% year to date 2012. Factored into the performance evaluation is an expense ratio of 0.60% (very low).

The fund's risk rating is currently B- (Good). It carries a beta of 1.17, meaning it is expected to move 11.7% for every 10% move in the market. Volatility, as measured by both the semi-deviation and a drawdown factor, is considered low. As of December 31, 2012, *First Trust NASDAQ-100 Equal Wei traded at a discount of 3.86% below its net asset value, which is better than its one-year historical average premium of .03%.

Jonathan Erickson has been running the fund for 7 years and currently receives a manager quality ranking of 35 (0=worst, 99=best). If you desire an average level of risk, then this fund may be an option.

Data Date	Investment Rating	Net Assets ($Mil)	Price	Performance Rating/Pts	Total Return Y-T-D	Risk Rating/Pts
12-12	C+	84.80	26.13	C+ / 5.7	4.21%	B- / 7.6
2011	B-	73.50	22.95	C+ / 6.9	2.66%	B- / 7.7
2010	C+	76.00	23.72	C+ / 6.9	20.10%	C / 5.5
2009	C	22.94	19.75	C / 4.6	53.21%	C+ / 5.6

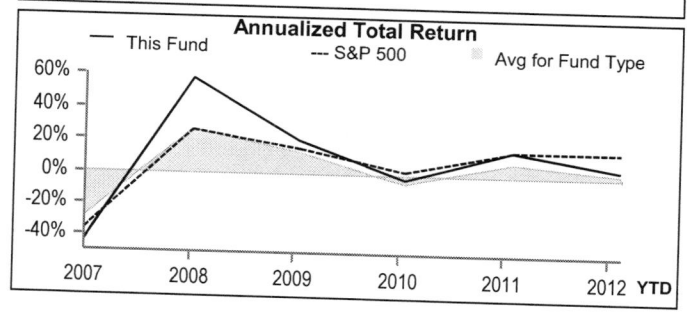

* Denotes ETF Fund

*First Trust NASDAQ-100 Ex-Tech S (QQXT)   C+   Fair

Fund Family: First Trust Advisors LP
Fund Type: Income
Inception Date: February 8, 2007

Major Rating Factors: Middle of the road best describes *First Trust NASDAQ-100 Ex-Tech S whose TheStreet.com Investment Rating is currently a C+ (Fair). The fund currently has a performance rating of C+ (Fair) based on an annualized return of 13.42% over the last three years and a total return of 4.22% year to date 2012. Factored into the performance evaluation is an expense ratio of 0.60% (very low).

The fund's risk rating is currently B- (Good). It carries a beta of 1.01, meaning that its performance tracks fairly well with that of the overall stock market. Volatility, as measured by both the semi-deviation and a drawdown factor, is considered low. As of December 31, 2012, *First Trust NASDAQ-100 Ex-Tech S traded at a discount of 4.01% below its net asset value, which is better than its one-year historical average discount of .05%.

Jonathan Erickson has been running the fund for 7 years and currently receives a manager quality ranking of 64 (0=worst, 99=best). If you desire an average level of risk, then this fund may be an option.

Data Date	Investment Rating	Net Assets ($Mil)	Price	Performance Rating/Pts	Total Return Y-T-D	Risk Rating/Pts
12-12	C+	42.00	24.65	C+ / 6.5	4.22%	B- / 7.5
2011	C+	30.20	20.78	C+ / 6.3	2.60%	B- / 7.7
2010	C+	22.20	21.10	C+ / 5.7	19.48%	C+ / 5.7
2009	A	6.35	17.66	B+ / 8.9	40.33%	C+ / 5.8

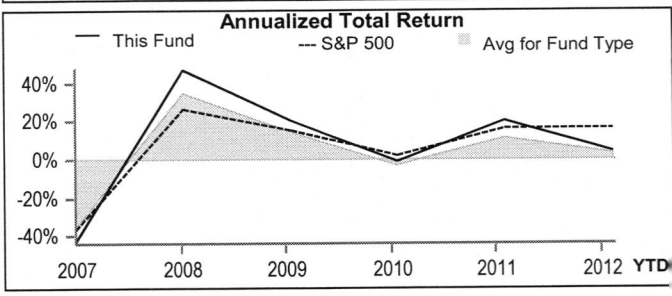

*First Trust NASDAQ-100-Technolog (QTEC)   C-   Fair

Fund Family: First Trust Advisors LP
Fund Type: Growth
Inception Date: April 19, 2006

Major Rating Factors: Middle of the road best describes *First Trust NASDAQ-100-Technolog whose TheStreet.com Investment Rating is currently a C- (Fair). The fund currently has a performance rating of C- (Fair) based on an annualized return of 9.16% over the last three years and a total return of 4.36% year to date 2012. Factored into the performance evaluation is an expense ratio of 0.60% (very low).

The fund's risk rating is currently B- (Good). It carries a beta of 1.32, meaning it is expected to move 13.2% for every 10% move in the market. Volatility, as measured by both the semi-deviation and a drawdown factor, is considered low. As of December 31, 2012, *First Trust NASDAQ-100-Technolog traded at a discount of 4.22% below its net asset value, which is better than its one-year historical average discount of .03%.

Jonathan Erickson has been running the fund for 7 years and currently receives a manager quality ranking of 18 (0=worst, 99=best). If you desire an average level of risk, then this fund may be an option.

Data Date	Investment Rating	Net Assets ($Mil)	Price	Performance Rating/Pts	Total Return Y-T-D	Risk Rating/Pts
12-12	C-	106.00	25.85	C- / 4.0	4.36%	B- / 7.6
2011	B-	149.70	24.12	B / 7.6	2.65%	B- / 7.6
2010	B+	453.40	25.71	B / 8.0	21.22%	C / 5.5
2009	B-	21.30	21.21	B- / 7.2	73.54%	C+ / 5.7

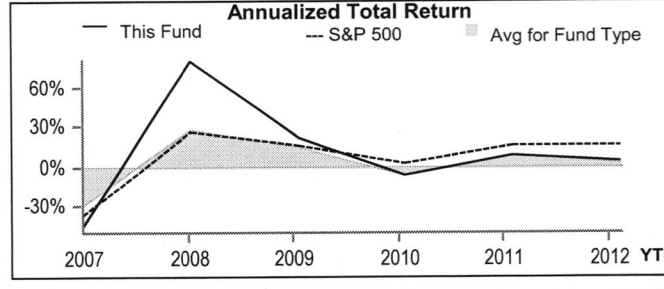

*First Trust S&P REIT Index Fund (FRI)   B-   Good

Fund Family: First Trust Advisors LP
Fund Type: Income
Inception Date: May 8, 2007

Major Rating Factors: Strong performance is the major factor driving the B- (Good) TheStreet.com Investment Rating for *First Trust S&P REIT Index Fund. The fund currently has a performance rating of B- (Good) based on an annualized return of 18.17% over the last three years and a total return of 1.97% year to date 2012. Factored into the performance evaluation is an expense ratio of 0.50% (very low).

The fund's risk rating is currently B- (Good). It carries a beta of 1.03, meaning that its performance tracks fairly well with that of the overall stock market. Volatility, as measured by both the semi-deviation and a drawdown factor, is considered low. As of December 31, 2012, *First Trust S&P REIT Index Fund traded at a discount of 2.04% below its net asset value, which is better than its one-year historical average premium of .01%.

Jonathan Erickson has been running the fund for 6 years and currently receives a manager quality ranking of 81 (0=worst, 99=best). If you desire only a moderate level of risk and strong performance, then this fund is an excellent option.

Data Date	Investment Rating	Net Assets ($Mil)	Price	Performance Rating/Pts	Total Return Y-T-D	Risk Rating/Pts
12-12	B-	402.90	17.75	B- / 7.3	1.97%	B- / 7.6
2011	C+	325.00	15.49	B / 7.7	-0.45%	C+ / 6.4
2010	C	71.10	14.65	B- / 7.0	27.73%	C- / 4.2
2009	B	4.44	11.72	A- / 9.2	30.49%	C- / 4.2

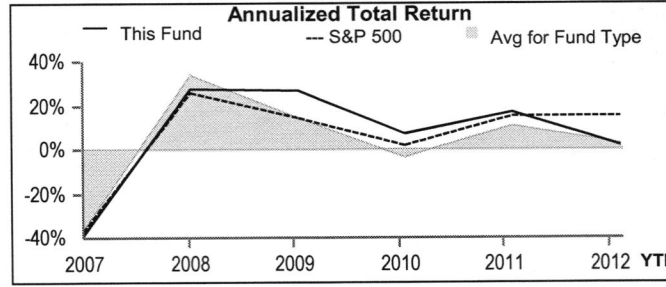

*First Trust Small Cap Core Alpha (FYX)

C+   **Fair**

Fund Family: First Trust Advisors LP
Fund Type: Growth
Inception Date: May 8, 2007

Major Rating Factors: Middle of the road best describes *First Trust Small Cap Core Alpha whose TheStreet.com Investment Rating is currently a C+ (Fair). The fund currently has a performance rating of C+ (Fair) based on an annualized return of 13.80% over the last three years and a total return of 3.14% year to date 2012. Factored into the performance evaluation is an expense ratio of 0.70% (very low).

The fund's risk rating is currently B- (Good). It carries a beta of 1.24, meaning it is expected to move 12.4% for every 10% move in the market. Volatility, as measured by both the semi-deviation and a drawdown factor, is considered low. As of December 31, 2012, *First Trust Small Cap Core Alpha traded at a discount of 3.10% below its net asset value, which is better than its one-year historical average premium of .03%.

Daniel J. Lindquist has been running the fund for 6 years and currently receives a manager quality ranking of 52 (0=worst, 99=best). If you desire an average level of risk, then this fund may be an option.

Data Date	Investment Rating	Net Assets ($Mil)	Price	Performance Rating/Pts	Total Return Y-T-D	Risk Rating/Pts
12-12	C+	163.70	34.12	C+ / 6.5	3.14%	B- / 7.6
2011	B-	125.60	29.91	C+ / 6.9	1.47%	B- / 7.5
2010	B	82.50	30.08	B / 7.8	27.35%	C / 5.5
2009	B+	8.31	23.72	B+ / 8.5	34.43%	C / 5.5

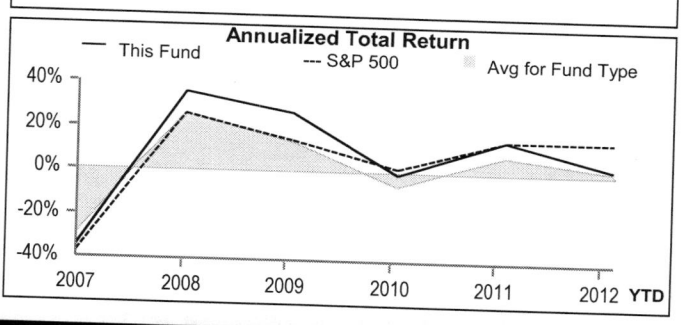

Annualized Total Return

---

*First Trust Small Cap Gro AlphaD (FYC)

B   **Good**

Fund Family: First Trust Advisors LP
Fund Type: Growth
Inception Date: April 19, 2011

Major Rating Factors: Strong performance is the major factor driving the B (Good) TheStreet.com Investment Rating for *First Trust Small Cap Gro AlphaD. The fund currently has a performance rating of B- (Good) based on an annualized return of 0.00% over the last three years and a total return of 3.80% year to date 2012. Factored into the performance evaluation is an expense ratio of 0.70% (very low).

The fund's risk rating is currently B (Good). It carries a beta of 0.00, meaning the fund's expected move will be 0.0% for every 10% move in the market. Volatility, as measured by both the semi-deviation and a drawdown factor, is considered low. As of December 31, 2012, *First Trust Small Cap Gro AlphaD traded at a discount of 3.53% below its net asset value, which is better than its one-year historical average premium of .10%.

Daniel J. Lindquist has been running the fund for 2 years and currently receives a manager quality ranking of 38 (0=worst, 99=best). If you desire only a moderate level of risk and strong performance, then this fund is an excellent option.

Data Date	Investment Rating	Net Assets ($Mil)	Price	Performance Rating/Pts	Total Return Y-T-D	Risk Rating/Pts
12-12	B	9.60	21.30	B- / 7.1	3.80%	B / 8.5

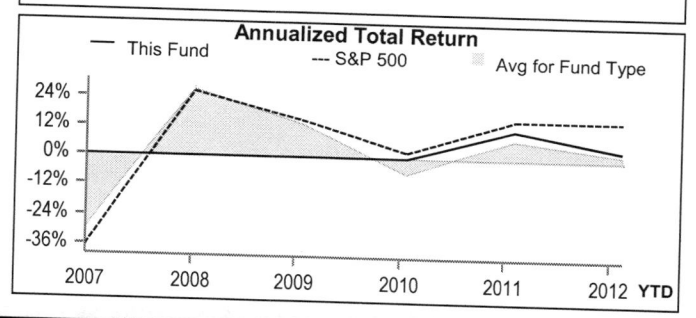

Annualized Total Return

---

*First Trust Small Cap Val AlphaD (FYT)

A-   **Excellent**

Fund Family: First Trust Advisors LP
Fund Type: Growth
Inception Date: April 19, 2011

Major Rating Factors:
Strong performance is the major factor driving the A- (Excellent) TheStreet.com Investment Rating for *First Trust Small Cap Val AlphaD. The fund currently has a performance rating of B+ (Good) based on an annualized return of 0.00% over the last three years and a total return of 3.13% year to date 2012. Factored into the performance evaluation is an expense ratio of 0.70% (very low).

The fund's risk rating is currently B (Good). It carries a beta of 0.00, meaning the fund's expected move will be 0.0% for every 10% move in the market. Volatility, as measured by both the semi-deviation and a drawdown factor, is considered low. As of December 31, 2012, *First Trust Small Cap Val AlphaD traded at a discount of 2.82% below its net asset value, which is better than its one-year historical average premium of .08%.

Daniel J. Lindquist has been running the fund for 2 years and currently receives a manager quality ranking of 24 (0=worst, 99=best). If you desire only a moderate level of risk and strong performance, then this fund is an excellent option.

Data Date	Investment Rating	Net Assets ($Mil)	Price	Performance Rating/Pts	Total Return Y-T-D	Risk Rating/Pts
12-12	A-	24.60	22.38	B+ / 8.4	3.13%	B / 8.3

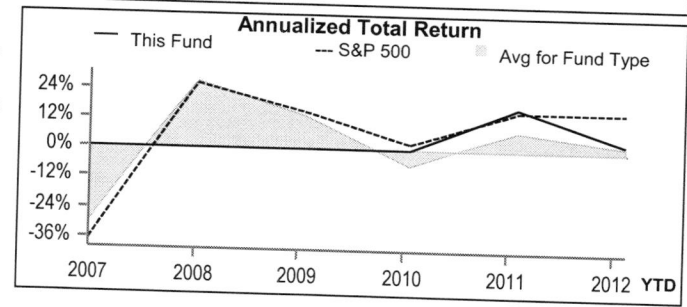

Annualized Total Return

* Denotes ETF Fund

*First Trust South Korea AlphaDEX (FKO)   B+   Good

Fund Family: First Trust Advisors LP
Fund Type: Foreign
Inception Date: April 18, 2011

Major Rating Factors:
Exceptional performance is the major factor driving the B+ (Good) TheStreet.com Investment Rating for *First Trust South Korea AlphaDEX. The fund currently has a performance rating of A- (Excellent) based on an annualized return of 0.00% over the last three years and a total return of -0.67% year to date 2012. Factored into the performance evaluation is an expense ratio of 0.80% (very low).

The fund's risk rating is currently C+ (Fair). It carries a beta of 0.00, meaning the fund's expected move will be 0.0% for every 10% move in the market. Volatility, as measured by both the semi-deviation and a drawdown factor, is considered low. As of December 31, 2012, *First Trust South Korea AlphaDEX traded at a premium of 1.05% above its net asset value, which is worse than its one-year historical average discount of .01%.

Jonathan Erickson has been running the fund for 2 years and currently receives a manager quality ranking of 63 (0=worst, 99=best). If you desire only a moderate level of risk and strong performance, then this fund is an excellent option.

Data Date	Investment Rating	Net Assets ($Mil)	Price	Performance Rating/Pts	Total Return Y-T-D	Risk Rating/Pts
12-12	B+	2.60	26.83	A- / 9.2	-0.67%	C+ / 6.8

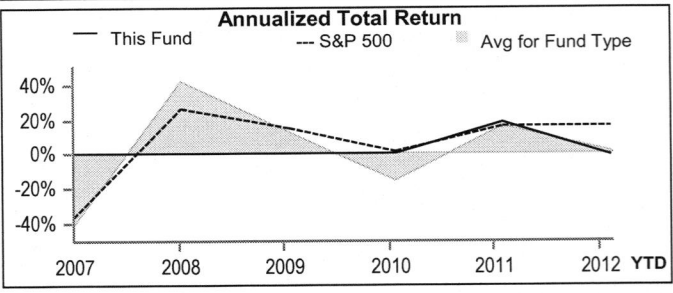

*First Trust STOXX European Sel D (FDD)   D   Weak

Fund Family: First Trust Advisors LP
Fund Type: Foreign
Inception Date: August 27, 2007

Major Rating Factors:
Disappointing performance is the major factor driving the D (Weak) TheStreet.com Investment Rating for *First Trust STOXX European Sel D. The fund currently has a performance rating of D+ (Weak) based on an annualized return of 0.23% over the last three years and a total return of 1.54% year to date 2012. Factored into the performance evaluation is an expense ratio of 0.60% (very low).

The fund's risk rating is currently C+ (Fair). It carries a beta of 0.95, meaning that its performance tracks fairly well with that of the overall stock market. Volatility, as measured by both the semi-deviation and a drawdown factor, is considered low. As of December 31, 2012, *First Trust STOXX European Sel D traded at a discount of .97% below its net asset value, which is better than its one-year historical average premium of .52%.

Daniel J. Lindquist currently receives a manager quality ranking of 29 (0=worst, 99=best). This fund offers only a moderate level of risk but investors looking for strong performance are still waiting.

Data Date	Investment Rating	Net Assets ($Mil)	Price	Performance Rating/Pts	Total Return Y-T-D	Risk Rating/Pts
12-12	D	18.20	12.31	D+ / 2.5	1.54%	C+ / 6.8
2011	D+	9.90	11.86	D / 2.2	-3.74%	B- / 7.4
2010	E+	9.60	13.69	E+ / 0.6	1.93%	C- / 3.7
2009	C+	8.33	14.05	B+ / 8.5	31.16%	C- / 3.7

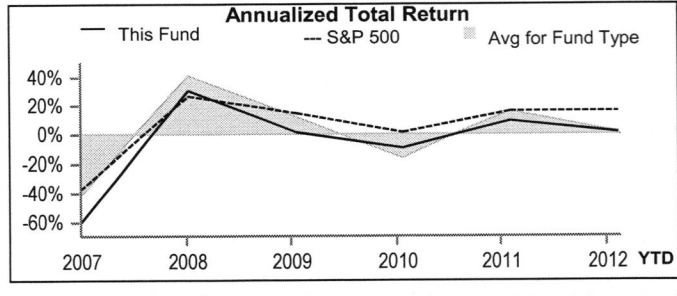

*First Trust Strategic Value Inde (FDV)   C   Fair

Fund Family: First Trust Advisors LP
Fund Type: Income
Inception Date: July 6, 2006

Major Rating Factors: Middle of the road best describes *First Trust Strategic Value Inde whose TheStreet.com Investment Rating is currently a C (Fair). The fund currently has a performance rating of C (Fair) based on an annualized return of 10.25% over the last three years and a total return of 5.63% year to date 2012. Factored into the performance evaluation is an expense ratio of 0.65% (very low).

The fund's risk rating is currently B- (Good). It carries a beta of 1.18, meaning it is expected to move 11.8% for every 10% move in the market. Volatility, as measured by both the semi-deviation and a drawdown factor, is considered low. As of December 31, 2012, *First Trust Strategic Value Inde traded at a discount of 5.44% below its net asset value, which is better than its one-year historical average discount of .09%.

Jonathan Erickson has been running the fund for 7 years and currently receives a manager quality ranking of 26 (0=worst, 99=best). If you desire an average level of risk, then this fund may be an option.

Data Date	Investment Rating	Net Assets ($Mil)	Price	Performance Rating/Pts	Total Return Y-T-D	Risk Rating/Pts
12-12	C	32.70	24.88	C / 5.0	5.63%	B- / 7.8
2011	C	31.60	21.85	C / 5.3	3.02%	B- / 7.9
2010	C	36.60	22.91	C / 5.1	13.81%	C+ / 6.1
2009	C	38.35	20.52	C- / 4.2	35.14%	C+ / 6.2

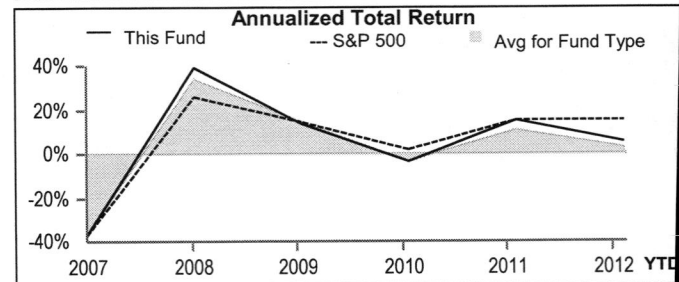

*First Trust Technology AlphaDEX (FXL)

D+ **Weak**

Fund Family: First Trust Advisors LP
Fund Type: Growth
Inception Date: May 8, 2007

Major Rating Factors: *First Trust Technology AlphaDEX receives a TheStreet.com Investment Rating of D+ (Weak). The fund currently has a performance rating of C- (Fair) based on an annualized return of 8.31% over the last three years and a total return of 3.58% year to date 2012. Factored into the performance evaluation is an expense ratio of 0.70% (very low).

The fund's risk rating is currently C+ (Fair). It carries a beta of 1.33, meaning it is expected to move 13.3% for every 10% move in the market. Volatility, as measured by both the semi-deviation and a drawdown factor, is considered low. As of December 31, 2012, *First Trust Technology AlphaDEX traded at a discount of 3.47% below its net asset value, which is better than its one-year historical average discount of .01%.

Daniel J. Lindquist has been running the fund for 6 years and currently receives a manager quality ranking of 17 (0=worst, 99=best). If you desire an average level of risk, then this fund may be an option.

Data Date	Investment Rating	Net Assets ($Mil)	Price	Performance Rating/Pts	Total Return Y-T-D	Risk Rating/Pts
12-12	D+	138.10	21.68	C- / 3.7	3.58%	C+ / 6.9
2011	C+	188.30	20.04	C+ / 6.5	2.69%	B- / 7.2
2010	C+	119.10	22.70	B- / 7.2	26.64%	C / 4.8
2009	A	12.37	17.93	A / 9.5	60.38%	C / 5.0

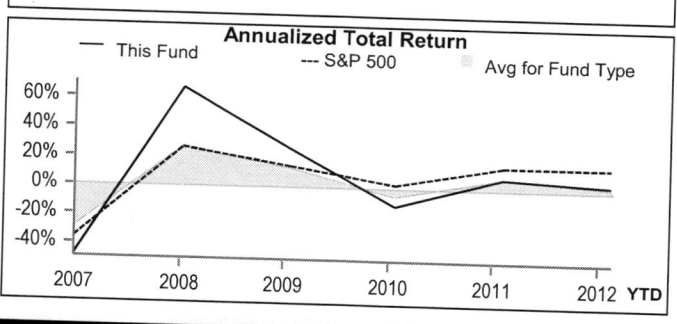

Annualized Total Return — This Fund, --- S&P 500, Avg for Fund Type

*First Trust US IPO Index Fund (FPX)

A- **Excellent**

Fund Family: First Trust Advisors LP
Fund Type: Growth
Inception Date: April 12, 2006

Major Rating Factors:
Strong performance is the major factor driving the A- (Excellent) TheStreet.com Investment Rating for *First Trust US IPO Index Fund. The fund currently has a performance rating of B+ (Good) based on an annualized return of 17.71% over the last three years and a total return of 4.37% year to date 2012. Factored into the performance evaluation is an expense ratio of 0.60% (very low).

The fund's risk rating is currently B (Good). It carries a beta of 1.11, meaning it is expected to move 11.1% for every 10% move in the market. Volatility, as measured by both the semi-deviation and a drawdown factor, is considered low. As of December 31, 2012, *First Trust US IPO Index Fund traded at a discount of 4.04% below its net asset value, which is better than its one-year historical average discount of .02%.

Jonathan Erickson has been running the fund for 7 years and currently receives a manager quality ranking of 77 (0=worst, 99=best). If you desire only a moderate level of risk and strong performance, then this fund is an excellent option.

Data Date	Investment Rating	Net Assets ($Mil)	Price	Performance Rating/Pts	Total Return Y-T-D	Risk Rating/Pts
12-12	A-	21.30	30.90	B+ / 8.8	4.37%	B / 8.0
2011	B-	15.60	23.97	C+ / 6.6	1.38%	B / 8.2
2010	C	15.30	23.51	C / 5.2	18.17%	C / 5.1
2009	D+	8.75	20.10	C- / 4.1	41.66%	C / 4.5

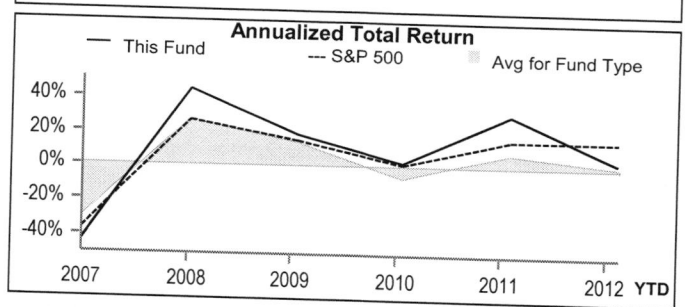

Annualized Total Return — This Fund, --- S&P 500, Avg for Fund Type

*First Trust Utilities AlphaDEX (FXU)

C **Fair**

Fund Family: First Trust Advisors LP
Fund Type: Utilities
Inception Date: May 8, 2007

Major Rating Factors: Middle of the road best describes *First Trust Utilities AlphaDEX whose TheStreet.com Investment Rating is currently a C (Fair). The fund currently has a performance rating of C- (Fair) based on an annualized return of 8.47% over the last three years and a total return of 1.17% year to date 2012. Factored into the performance evaluation is an expense ratio of 0.70% (very low).

The fund's risk rating is currently B+ (Good). It carries a beta of 0.89, meaning the fund's expected move will be 8.9% for every 10% move in the market. Volatility, as measured by both the semi-deviation and a drawdown factor, is considered very low. As of December 31, 2012, *First Trust Utilities AlphaDEX traded at a discount of 1.10% below its net asset value, which is better than its one-year historical average discount of .02%.

Daniel J. Lindquist has been running the fund for 6 years and currently receives a manager quality ranking of 53 (0=worst, 99=best). If you desire an average level of risk, then this fund may be an option.

Data Date	Investment Rating	Net Assets ($Mil)	Price	Performance Rating/Pts	Total Return Y-T-D	Risk Rating/Pts
12-12	C	140.30	17.98	C- / 3.1	1.17%	B+ / 9.0
2011	C+	331.30	17.93	C / 4.9	-1.56%	B / 8.4
2010	C	39.70	16.53	C- / 3.6	10.47%	C+ / 6.8
2009	A	13.66	15.40	B / 7.9	18.95%	C+ / 6.6

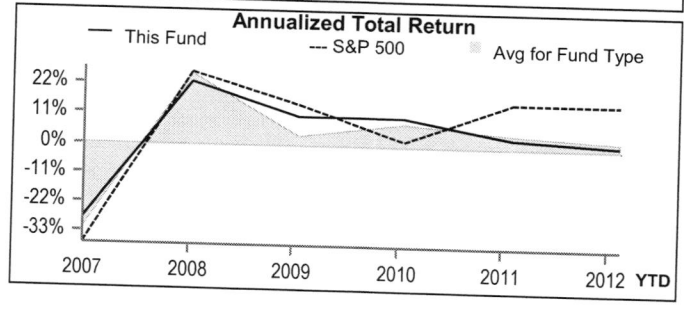

Annualized Total Return — This Fund, --- S&P 500, Avg for Fund Type

* Denotes ETF Fund

*First Trust Value Line 100 Fund (FVL)

C-　　　**Fair**

Fund Family: First Trust Advisors LP
Fund Type: Growth
Inception Date: June 12, 2003

Major Rating Factors: Middle of the road best describes *First Trust Value Line 100 Fund whose TheStreet.com Investment Rating is currently a C- (Fair). The fund currently has a performance rating of C- (Fair) based on an annualized return of 9.99% over the last three years and a total return of 3.96% year to date 2012. Factored into the performance evaluation is an expense ratio of 0.70% (very low).

The fund's risk rating is currently B- (Good). It carries a beta of 1.35, meaning it is expected to move 13.5% for every 10% move in the market. Volatility, as measured by both the semi-deviation and a drawdown factor, is considered low. As of December 31, 2012, *First Trust Value Line 100 Fund traded at a discount of 4.05% below its net asset value, which is better than its one-year historical average discount of .08%.

Jonathan Erickson has been running the fund for 10 years and currently receives a manager quality ranking of 20 (0=worst, 99=best). If you desire an average level of risk, then this fund may be an option.

Data Date	Investment Rating	Net Assets ($Mil)	Price	Performance Rating/Pts	Total Return Y-T-D	Risk Rating/Pts
12-12	C-	45.60	13.26	C- / 4.1	3.96%	B- / 7.1
2011	C-	55.50	12.39	C- / 4.1	3.00%	B- / 7.2
2010	D	88.40	13.52	D+ / 2.6	28.27%	C / 5.2
2009	D-	63.08	10.54	D- / 1.3	11.77%	C / 4.9

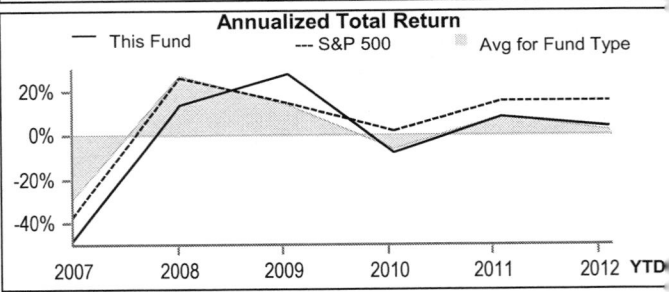
Annualized Total Return

*First Trust Value Line Dividend (FVD)

C+　　　**Fair**

Fund Family: First Trust Advisors LP
Fund Type: Growth and Income
Inception Date: August 19, 2003

Major Rating Factors: Middle of the road best describes *First Trust Value Line Dividend whose TheStreet.com Investment Rating is currently a C+ (Fair). The fund currently has a performance rating of C (Fair) based on an annualized return of 12.58% over the last three years and a total return of 2.54% year to date 2012. Factored into the performance evaluation is an expense ratio of 0.70% (very low).

The fund's risk rating is currently B (Good). It carries a beta of 0.75, meaning the fund's expected move will be 7.5% for every 10% move in the market. Volatility, as measured by both the semi-deviation and a drawdown factor, is considered low. As of December 31, 2012, *First Trust Value Line Dividend traded at a discount of 2.43% below its net asset value, which is better than its one-year historical average premium of .07%.

Jonathan Erickson has been running the fund for 10 years and currently receives a manager quality ranking of 75 (0=worst, 99=best). If you desire an average level of risk, then this fund may be an option.

Data Date	Investment Rating	Net Assets ($Mil)	Price	Performance Rating/Pts	Total Return Y-T-D	Risk Rating/Pts
12-12	C+	508.10	17.30	C / 5.2	2.54%	B / 8.8
2011	C+	366.40	16.01	C / 5.4	-0.25%	B / 8.1
2010	C+	218.50	15.09	C+ / 5.7	16.07%	C+ / 6.5
2009	C-	121.90	13.38	D+ / 2.3	16.74%	C+ / 6.4

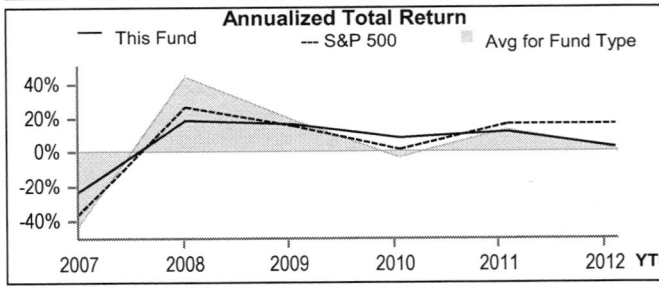
Annualized Total Return

*First Trust Value Line Equity AI (FVI)

D+　　　**Weak**

Fund Family: First Trust Advisors LP
Fund Type: Growth and Income
Inception Date: December 5, 2006

Major Rating Factors: *First Trust Value Line Equity AI receives a TheStreet.com Investment Rating of D+ (Weak). The fund currently has a performance rating of C- (Fair) based on an annualized return of 5.71% over the last three years and a total return of 5.21% year to date 2012. Factored into the performance evaluation is an expense ratio of 0.70% (very low).

The fund's risk rating is currently B- (Good). It carries a beta of 0.99, meaning that its performance tracks fairly well with that of the overall stock market. Volatility, as measured by both the semi-deviation and a drawdown factor, is considered low. As of December 31, 2012, *First Trust Value Line Equity AI traded at a discount of 5.41% below its net asset value, which is better than its one-year historical average discount of .12%.

Jonathan Erickson has been running the fund for 7 years and currently receives a manager quality ranking of 20 (0=worst, 99=best). If you desire an average level of risk, then this fund may be an option.

Data Date	Investment Rating	Net Assets ($Mil)	Price	Performance Rating/Pts	Total Return Y-T-D	Risk Rating/Pts
12-12	D+	3.90	18.90	C- / 3.0	5.21%	B- / 7.7
2011	C	6.40	18.23	C / 4.3	0.49%	B- / 7.7
2010	C+	7.10	20.35	C+ / 6.0	19.25%	C+ / 6.0
2009	C-	5.43	17.34	C- / 3.8	35.37%	C+ / 6.1

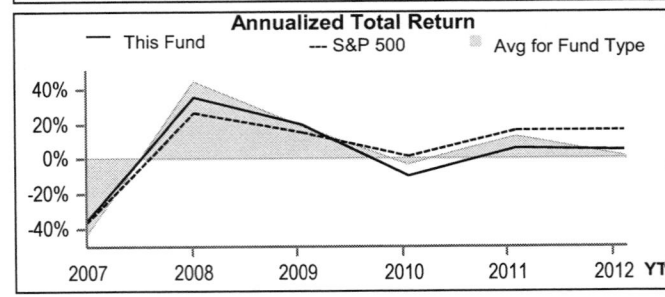
Annualized Total Return

*FlexShs iB 3Y Tgt Dur TIPS Idx (TDTT)

Fund Family: Northern Trust Investments Inc
Fund Type: US Government/Agency
Inception Date: September 19, 2011

C-   **Fair**

Major Rating Factors:
Disappointing performance is the major factor driving the C- (Fair) TheStreet.com Investment Rating for *FlexShs iB 3Y Tgt Dur TIPS Idx. The fund currently has a performance rating of D (Weak) based on an annualized return of 0.00% over the last three years and a total return of -0.16% year to date 2012. Factored into the performance evaluation is an expense ratio of 0.20% (very low).

The fund's risk rating is currently B+ (Good). It carries a beta of 0.00, meaning the fund's expected move will be 0.0% for every 10% move in the market. Volatility, as measured by both the semi-deviation and a drawdown factor, is considered very low. As of December 31, 2012, *FlexShs iB 3Y Tgt Dur TIPS Idx traded at a premium of .28% above its net asset value, which is worse than its one-year historical average premium of .23%.

Brandon P. Ferguson has been running the fund for 2 years and currently receives a manager quality ranking of 71 (0=worst, 99=best). This fund offers only a moderate level of risk but investors looking for strong performance are still waiting.

Data Date	Investment Rating	Net Assets ($Mil)	Price	Performance Rating/Pts	Total Return Y-T-D	Risk Rating/Pts
12-12	C-	719.80	25.52	D / 1.9	-0.16%	B+ / 9.9

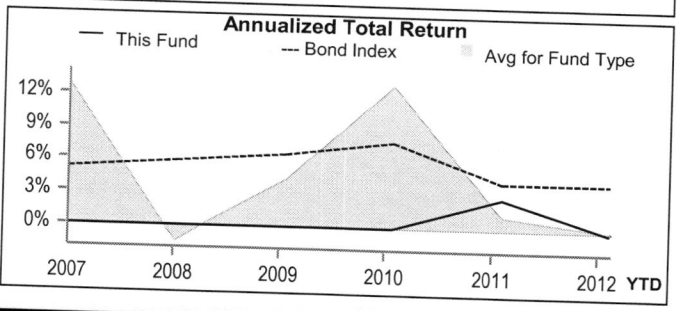

*FlexShs iB 5Y Tgt Dur TIPS Idx (TDTF)

Fund Family: Northern Trust Investments Inc
Fund Type: US Government/Agency
Inception Date: September 19, 2011

C   **Fair**

Major Rating Factors:
Disappointing performance is the major factor driving the C (Fair) TheStreet.com Investment Rating for *FlexShs iB 5Y Tgt Dur TIPS Idx. The fund currently has a performance rating of D+ (Weak) based on an annualized return of 0.00% over the last three years and a total return of -0.42% year to date 2012. Factored into the performance evaluation is an expense ratio of 0.20% (very low).

The fund's risk rating is currently B+ (Good). It carries a beta of 0.00, meaning the fund's expected move will be 0.0% for every 10% move in the market. Volatility, as measured by both the semi-deviation and a drawdown factor, is considered very low. As of December 31, 2012, *FlexShs iB 5Y Tgt Dur TIPS Idx traded at a premium of .54% above its net asset value, which is worse than its one-year historical average premium of .12%.

Brandon P. Ferguson has been running the fund for 2 years and currently receives a manager quality ranking of 79 (0=worst, 99=best). This fund offers only a moderate level of risk but investors looking for strong performance are still waiting.

Data Date	Investment Rating	Net Assets ($Mil)	Price	Performance Rating/Pts	Total Return Y-T-D	Risk Rating/Pts
12-12	C	384.80	26.30	D+ / 2.3	-0.42%	B+ / 9.9

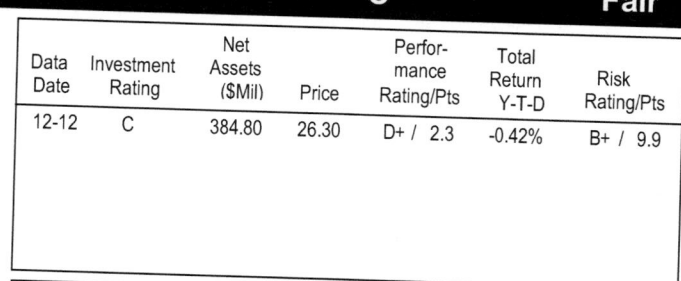

*FlexShs Morningstar Gl Upstream (GUNR)

Fund Family: Northern Trust Investments Inc
Fund Type: Energy/Natural Resources
Inception Date: September 16, 2011

C   **Fair**

Major Rating Factors: Middle of the road best describes *FlexShs Morningstar Gl Upstream whose TheStreet.com Investment Rating is currently a C (Fair). The fund currently has a performance rating of C (Fair) based on an annualized return of 0.00% over the last three years and a total return of 2.05% year to date 2012. Factored into the performance evaluation is an expense ratio of 0.48% (very low).

The fund's risk rating is currently B (Good). It carries a beta of 0.00, meaning the fund's expected move will be 0.0% for every 10% move in the market. Volatility, as measured by both the semi-deviation and a drawdown factor, is considered low. As of December 31, 2012, *FlexShs Morningstar Gl Upstream traded at a discount of 1.71% below its net asset value, which is better than its one-year historical average premium of .34%.

Chad M. Rakvin has been running the fund for 2 years and currently receives a manager quality ranking of 78 (0=worst, 99=best). If you desire an average level of risk, then this fund may be an option.

Data Date	Investment Rating	Net Assets ($Mil)	Price	Performance Rating/Pts	Total Return Y-T-D	Risk Rating/Pts
12-12	C	604.20	35.62	C / 4.9	2.05%	B / 8.1

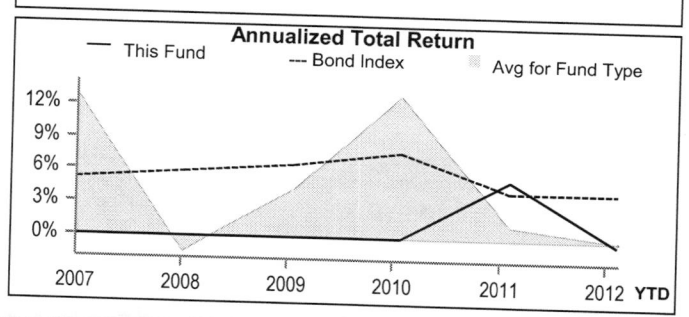

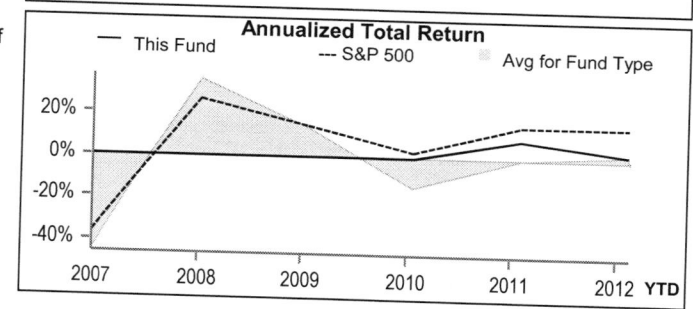

* Denotes ETF Fund

*FlexShs Morningstar US Mkt Fac T (TILT)

A-   **Excellent**

Fund Family: Northern Trust Investments Inc
Fund Type: Income
Inception Date: September 16, 2011

Data Date	Investment Rating	Net Assets ($Mil)	Price	Perfor-mance Rating/Pts	Total Return Y-T-D	Risk Rating/Pts
12-12	A-	153.90	59.72	B / 7.9	3.47%	B+ / 9.1

Major Rating Factors:
Strong performance is the major factor driving the A- (Excellent) TheStreet.com Investment Rating for *FlexShs Morningstar US Mkt Fac T. The fund currently has a performance rating of B (Good) based on an annualized return of 0.00% over the last three years and a total return of 3.47% year to date 2012. Factored into the performance evaluation is an expense ratio of 0.27% (very low).

The fund's risk rating is currently B+ (Good). It carries a beta of 0.00, meaning the fund's expected move will be 0.0% for every 10% move in the market. Volatility, as measured by both the semi-deviation and a drawdown factor, is considered very low. As of December 31, 2012, *FlexShs Morningstar US Mkt Fac T traded at a discount of 3.33% below its net asset value, which is better than its one-year historical average premium of .11%.

Chad M. Rakvin has been running the fund for 2 years and currently receives a manager quality ranking of 43 (0=worst, 99=best). If you desire only a moderate level of risk and strong performance, then this fund is an excellent option.

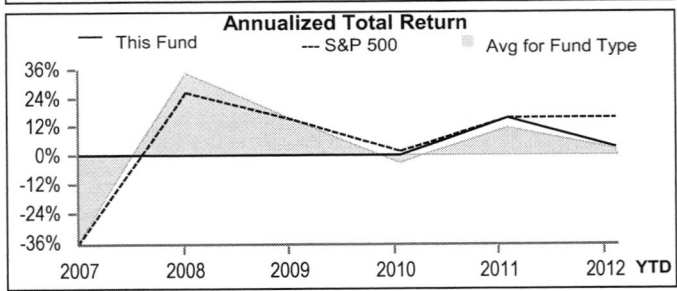

Annualized Total Return

*Global X Brazil Consumer ETF (BRAQ)

B   **Good**

Fund Family: Global X Management Company LLC
Fund Type: Foreign
Inception Date: July 7, 2010

Data Date	Investment Rating	Net Assets ($Mil)	Price	Perfor-mance Rating/Pts	Total Return Y-T-D	Risk Rating/Pts
12-12	B	24.20	20.27	A+ / 9.7	-0.60%	C+ / 6.1
2011	D-	27.00	15.08	E+ / 0.8	1.95%	C+ / 6.1

Major Rating Factors:
Exceptional performance is the major factor driving the B (Good) TheStreet.com Investment Rating for *Global X Brazil Consumer ETF. The fund currently has a performance rating of A+ (Excellent) based on an annualized return of 0.00% over the last three years and a total return of -0.60% year to date 2012. Factored into the performance evaluation is an expense ratio of 0.77% (very low).

The fund's risk rating is currently C+ (Fair). It carries a beta of 0.00, meaning the fund's expected move will be 0.0% for every 10% move in the market. Volatility, as measured by both the semi-deviation and a drawdown factor, is considered low. As of December 31, 2012, *Global X Brazil Consumer ETF traded at a premium of .40% above its net asset value, which is worse than its one-year historical average discount of .13%.

Bruno Del Ama has been running the fund for 3 years and currently receives a manager quality ranking of 86 (0=worst, 99=best). If you desire only a moderate level of risk and strong performance, then this fund is an excellent option.

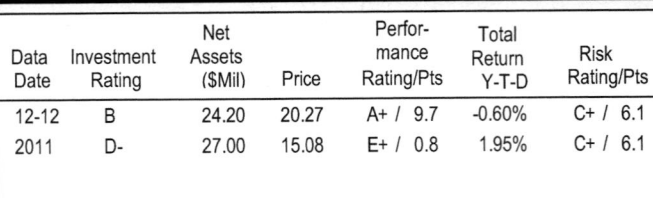

Annualized Total Return

*Global X Brazil Financials ETF (BRAF)

D+   **Weak**

Fund Family: Global X Management Company LLC
Fund Type: Foreign
Inception Date: July 28, 2010

Data Date	Investment Rating	Net Assets ($Mil)	Price	Perfor-mance Rating/Pts	Total Return Y-T-D	Risk Rating/Pts
12-12	D+	4.00	13.26	C / 4.6	1.73%	C+ / 5.8
2011	D-	5.20	13.03	D- / 1.3	5.14%	C+ / 6.3

Major Rating Factors: *Global X Brazil Financials ETF receives a TheStreet.com Investment Rating of D+ (Weak). The fund currently has a performance rating of C (Fair) based on an annualized return of 0.00% over the last three years and a total return of 1.73% year to date 2012. Factored into the performance evaluation is an expense ratio of 0.77% (very low).

The fund's risk rating is currently C+ (Fair). It carries a beta of 0.00, meaning the fund's expected move will be 0.0% for every 10% move in the market. Volatility, as measured by both the semi-deviation and a drawdown factor, is considered low. As of December 31, 2012, *Global X Brazil Financials ETF traded at a discount of 2.36% below its net asset value, which is better than its one-year historical average discount of .26%.

Bruno Del Ama has been running the fund for 3 years and currently receives a manager quality ranking of 8 (0=worst, 99=best). If you desire an average level of risk, then this fund may be an option.

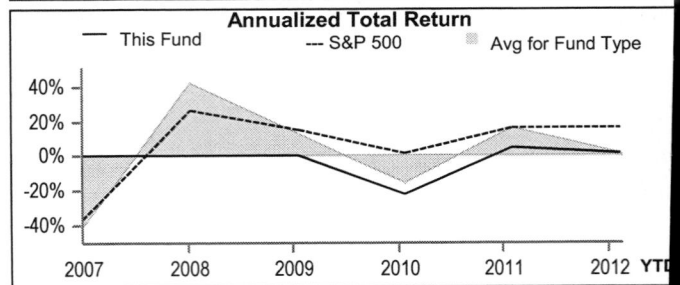

Annualized Total Return

*Global X Brazil Mid Cap ETF (BRAZ)

Fund Family: Global X Management Company LLC
Fund Type: Foreign
Inception Date: June 21, 2010

| | | C- | | | Fair | |

Major Rating Factors: Middle of the road best describes *Global X Brazil Mid Cap ETF whose TheStreet.com Investment Rating is currently a C- (Fair). The fund currently has a performance rating of C (Fair) based on an annualized return of 0.00% over the last three years and a total return of 1.41% year to date 2012. Factored into the performance evaluation is an expense ratio of 0.69% (very low).

The fund's risk rating is currently C+ (Fair). It carries a beta of 0.00, meaning the fund's expected move will be 0.0% for every 10% move in the market. Volatility, as measured by both the semi-deviation and a drawdown factor, is considered low. As of December 31, 2012, *Global X Brazil Mid Cap ETF traded at a discount of 1.95% below its net asset value, which is better than its one-year historical average discount of .30%.

Bruno Del Ama has been running the fund for 3 years and currently receives a manager quality ranking of 14 (0=worst, 99=best). If you desire an average level of risk, then this fund may be an option.

Data Date	Investment Rating	Net Assets ($Mil)	Price	Performance Rating/Pts	Total Return Y-T-D	Risk Rating/Pts
12-12	C-	18.80	15.61	C / 4.9	1.41%	C+ / 6.4
2011	D-	20.70	14.23	D- / 1.0	2.24%	C+ / 6.4

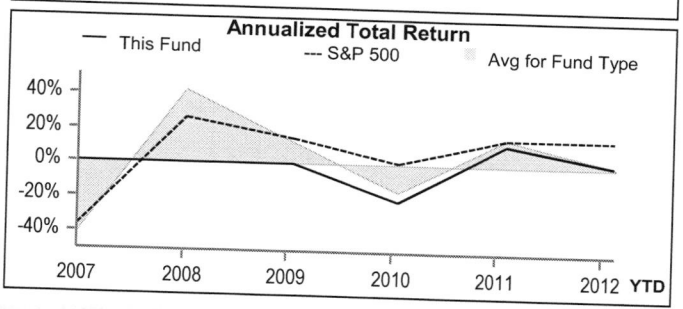

*Global X Canada Preferred ETF (CNPF)

Fund Family: Global X Management Company LLC
Fund Type: Foreign
Inception Date: May 24, 2011

| | | C- | | | Fair | |

Major Rating Factors:
Disappointing performance is the major factor driving the C- (Fair) TheStreet.com Investment Rating for *Global X Canada Preferred ETF. The fund currently has a performance rating of D+ (Weak) based on an annualized return of 0.00% over the last three years and a total return of 0.96% year to date 2012. Factored into the performance evaluation is an expense ratio of 0.58% (very low).

The fund's risk rating is currently B (Good). It carries a beta of 0.00, meaning the fund's expected move will be 0.0% for every 10% move in the market. Volatility, as measured by both the semi-deviation and a drawdown factor, is considered low. As of December 31, 2012, *Global X Canada Preferred ETF traded at a discount of .75% below its net asset value, which is better than its one-year historical average premium of .20%.

Bruno Del Ama has been running the fund for 2 years and currently receives a manager quality ranking of 52 (0=worst, 99=best). This fund offers only a moderate level of risk but investors looking for strong performance are still waiting.

Data Date	Investment Rating	Net Assets ($Mil)	Price	Performance Rating/Pts	Total Return Y-T-D	Risk Rating/Pts
12-12	C-	15.30	14.65	D+ / 2.8	0.96%	B / 8.4

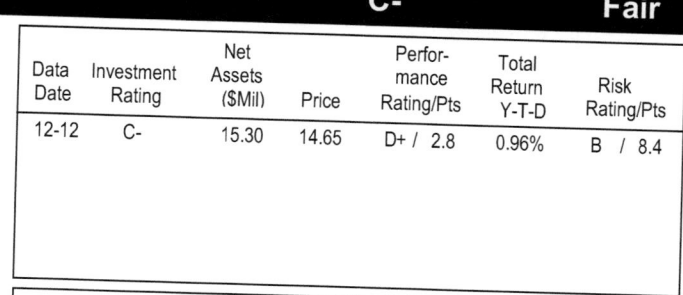

*Global X China Consumer ETF (CHIQ)

Fund Family: Global X Management Company LLC
Fund Type: Foreign
Inception Date: November 30, 2009

| | | D- | | | Weak | |

Major Rating Factors:
Disappointing performance is the major factor driving the D- (Weak) TheStreet.com Investment Rating for *Global X China Consumer ETF. The fund currently has a performance rating of D (Weak) based on an annualized return of -2.29% over the last three years and a total return of 3.83% year to date 2012. Factored into the performance evaluation is an expense ratio of 0.65% (very low).

The fund's risk rating is currently C+ (Fair). It carries a beta of 0.96, meaning that its performance tracks fairly well with that of the overall stock market. Volatility, as measured by both the semi-deviation and a drawdown factor, is considered low. As of December 31, 2012, *Global X China Consumer ETF traded at a discount of 2.56% below its net asset value, which is better than its one-year historical average premium of .03%.

Bruno Del Ama has been running the fund for 4 years and currently receives a manager quality ranking of 18 (0=worst, 99=best). This fund offers only a moderate level of risk but investors looking for strong performance are still waiting.

Data Date	Investment Rating	Net Assets ($Mil)	Price	Performance Rating/Pts	Total Return Y-T-D	Risk Rating/Pts
12-12	D-	186.30	14.87	D / 1.7	3.83%	C+ / 5.7
2011	D-	119.20	13.71	E+ / 0.6	-0.51%	C+ / 5.8
2010	B-	165.00	18.09	C+ / 6.0	9.64%	B- / 7.5

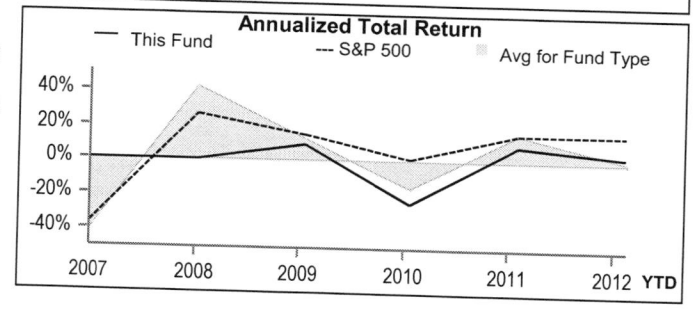

* Denotes ETF Fund

*Global X China Energy ETF (CHIE)

D   **Weak**

Fund Family: Global X Management Company LLC
Fund Type: Energy/Natural Resources
Inception Date: December 15, 2009

Major Rating Factors:
Disappointing performance is the major factor driving the D (Weak) TheStreet.com Investment Rating for *Global X China Energy ETF. The fund currently has a performance rating of D+ (Weak) based on an annualized return of 1.55% over the last three years and a total return of 4.76% year to date 2012. Factored into the performance evaluation is an expense ratio of 0.65% (very low).

The fund's risk rating is currently C+ (Fair). It carries a beta of 0.86, meaning the fund's expected move will be 8.6% for every 10% move in the market. Volatility, as measured by both the semi-deviation and a drawdown factor, is considered low. As of December 31, 2012, *Global X China Energy ETF traded at a discount of 4.35% below its net asset value, which is better than its one-year historical average discount of .24%.

Bruno Del Ama has been running the fund for 4 years and currently receives a manager quality ranking of 17 (0=worst, 99=best). This fund offers only a moderate level of risk but investors looking for strong performance are still waiting.

Data Date	Investment Rating	Net Assets ($Mil)	Price	Performance Rating/Pts	Total Return Y-T-D	Risk Rating/Pts
12-12	D	5.10	14.50	D+ / 2.7	4.76%	C+ / 6.4
2011	D-	3.90	13.01	D- / 1.1	1.80%	C+ / 6.4
2010	A	7.10	15.75	B / 8.1	5.07%	B- / 7.5

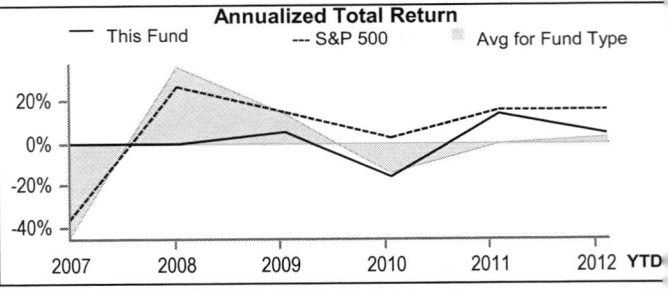

Annualized Total Return

*Global X China Financials ETF (CHIX)

D   **Weak**

Fund Family: Global X Management Company LLC
Fund Type: Financial Services
Inception Date: December 10, 2009

Major Rating Factors: *Global X China Financials ETF receives a TheStreet.com Investment Rating of D (Weak). The fund currently has a performance rating of C- (Fair) based on an annualized return of 2.33% over the last three years and a total return of 3.22% year to date 2012. Factored into the performance evaluation is an expense ratio of 0.65% (very low).

The fund's risk rating is currently C (Fair). It carries a beta of 1.07, meaning that its performance tracks fairly well with that of the overall stock market. Volatility, as measured by both the semi-deviation and a drawdown factor, is considered average. As of December 31, 2012, *Global X China Financials ETF traded at a discount of 2.15% below its net asset value, which is better than its one-year historical average discount of .36%.

Bruno Del Ama has been running the fund for 4 years and currently receives a manager quality ranking of 15 (0=worst, 99=best). If you desire an average level of risk, then this fund may be an option.

Data Date	Investment Rating	Net Assets ($Mil)	Price	Performance Rating/Pts	Total Return Y-T-D	Risk Rating/Pts
12-12	D	6.70	13.66	C- / 4.1	3.22%	C / 5.2
2011	E+	14.00	10.39	E+ / 0.8	-2.30%	C / 5.2
2010	D+	67.40	13.35	D- / 1.2	-6.58%	B- / 7.4

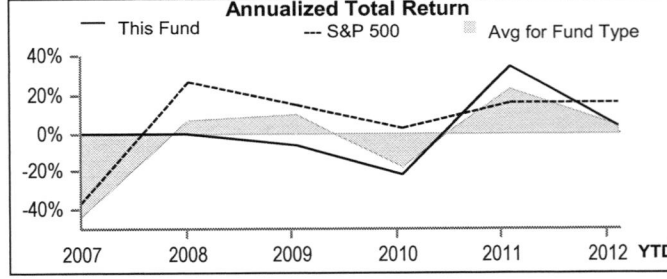

Annualized Total Return

*Global X China Industrials ETF (CHII)

D-   **Weak**

Fund Family: Global X Management Company LLC
Fund Type: Foreign
Inception Date: November 30, 2009

Major Rating Factors:
Disappointing performance is the major factor driving the D- (Weak) TheStreet.com Investment Rating for *Global X China Industrials ETF. The fund currently has a performance rating of D (Weak) based on an annualized return of -5.45% over the last three years and a total return of 5.88% year to date 2012. Factored into the performance evaluation is an expense ratio of 0.65% (very low).

The fund's risk rating is currently C (Fair). It carries a beta of 1.23, meaning it is expected to move 12.3% for every 10% move in the market. Volatility, as measured by both the semi-deviation and a drawdown factor, is considered average. As of December 31, 2012, *Global X China Industrials ETF traded at a discount of 5.03% below its net asset value, which is better than its one-year historical average discount of .07%.

Bruno Del Ama has been running the fund for 4 years and currently receives a manager quality ranking of 12 (0=worst, 99=best). This fund offers an average level of risk but investors looking for strong performance will be frustrated.

Data Date	Investment Rating	Net Assets ($Mil)	Price	Performance Rating/Pts	Total Return Y-T-D	Risk Rating/Pts
12-12	D-	4.90	12.45	D / 2.1	5.88%	C / 4.8
2011	E+	4.10	10.28	E / 0.4	-2.52%	C / 4.8
2010	A	10.70	16.40	B / 8.0	6.01%	B- / 7.6

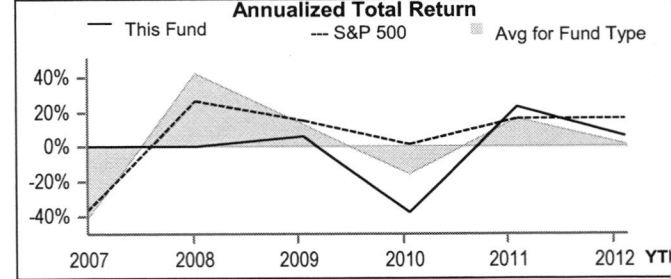

Annualized Total Return

*Global X China Materials ETF (CHIM)

C+ **Fair**

Fund Family: Global X Management Company LLC
Fund Type: Foreign
Inception Date: January 12, 2010

Major Rating Factors:
Exceptional performance is the major factor driving the C+ (Fair) TheStreet.com Investment Rating for *Global X China Materials ETF. The fund currently has a performance rating of A (Excellent) based on an annualized return of 0.00% over the last three years and a total return of 8.89% year to date 2012. Factored into the performance evaluation is an expense ratio of 0.65% (very low).

The fund's risk rating is currently C (Fair). It carries a beta of 0.00, meaning the fund's expected move will be 0.0% for every 10% move in the market. Volatility, as measured by both the semi-deviation and a drawdown factor, is considered average. As of December 31, 2012, *Global X China Materials ETF traded at a discount of 7.39% below its net asset value, which is better than its one-year historical average premium of .18%.

Bruno Del Ama has been running the fund for 3 years and currently receives a manager quality ranking of 8 (0=worst, 99=best). If you desire an average level of risk and strong performance, then this fund is a good option.

Data Date	Investment Rating	Net Assets ($Mil)	Price	Performance Rating/Pts	Total Return Y-T-D	Risk Rating/Pts
12-12	C+	2.70	8.77	A / 9.5	8.89%	C / 4.5
2011	E+	2.20	8.71	E- / 0.2	-2.08%	C / 5.0

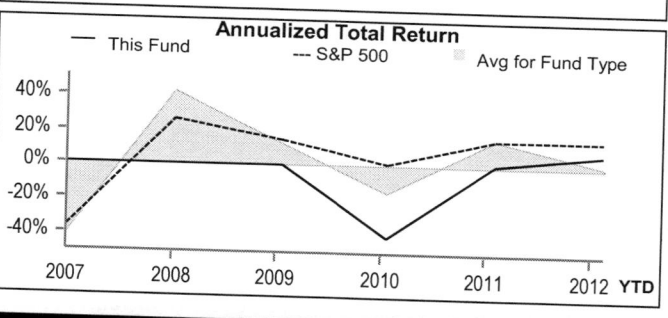

*Global X Copper Miners ETF (COPX)

C **Fair**

Fund Family: Global X Management Company LLC
Fund Type: Precious Metals
Inception Date: April 19, 2010

Major Rating Factors: Strong performance is the major factor driving the C (Fair) TheStreet.com Investment Rating for *Global X Copper Miners ETF. The fund currently has a performance rating of B+ (Good) based on an annualized return of 0.00% over the last three years and a total return of 5.86% year to date 2012. Factored into the performance evaluation is an expense ratio of 0.65% (very low).

The fund's risk rating is currently C (Fair). It carries a beta of 0.00, meaning the fund's expected move will be 0.0% for every 10% move in the market. Volatility, as measured by both the semi-deviation and a drawdown factor, is considered average. As of December 31, 2012, *Global X Copper Miners ETF traded at a discount of 5.38% below its net asset value, which is better than its one-year historical average discount of .11%.

Bruno Del Ama has been running the fund for 3 years and currently receives a manager quality ranking of 18 (0=worst, 99=best). If you desire an average level of risk and strong performance, then this fund is a good option.

Data Date	Investment Rating	Net Assets ($Mil)	Price	Performance Rating/Pts	Total Return Y-T-D	Risk Rating/Pts
12-12	C	31.20	13.02	B+ / 8.3	5.86%	C / 4.4
2011	E+	38.00	12.84	E+ / 0.7	3.74%	C / 4.7

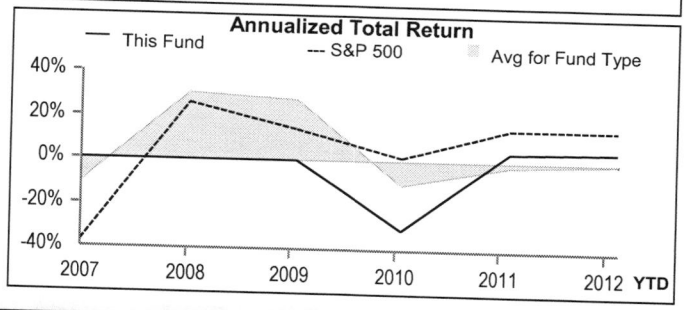

*Global X Fertilizers/Potash ETF (SOIL)

B- **Good**

Fund Family: Global X Management Company LLC
Fund Type: Global
Inception Date: May 26, 2011

Major Rating Factors: Strong performance is the major factor driving the B- (Good) TheStreet.com Investment Rating for *Global X Fertilizers/Potash ETF. The fund currently has a performance rating of B+ (Good) based on an annualized return of 0.00% over the last three years and a total return of 5.34% year to date 2012. Factored into the performance evaluation is an expense ratio of 0.69% (very low).

The fund's risk rating is currently C+ (Fair). It carries a beta of 0.00, meaning the fund's expected move will be 0.0% for every 10% move in the market. Volatility, as measured by both the semi-deviation and a drawdown factor, is considered low. As of December 31, 2012, *Global X Fertilizers/Potash ETF traded at a discount of 5.20% below its net asset value, which is better than its one-year historical average discount of .03%.

Bruno Del Ama has been running the fund for 2 years and currently receives a manager quality ranking of 33 (0=worst, 99=best). If you desire only a moderate level of risk and strong performance, then this fund is an excellent option.

Data Date	Investment Rating	Net Assets ($Mil)	Price	Performance Rating/Pts	Total Return Y-T-D	Risk Rating/Pts
12-12	B-	28.70	14.04	B+ / 8.3	5.34%	C+ / 6.5

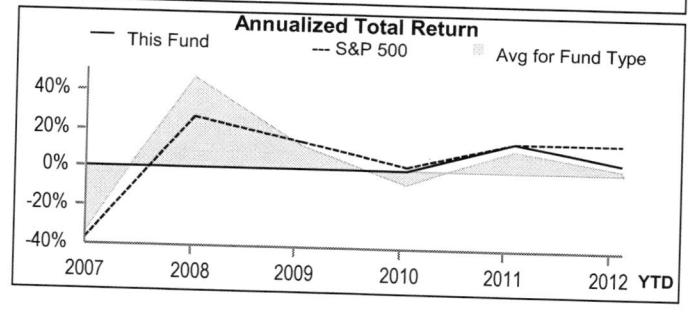

* Denotes ETF Fund

*Global X FTSE Andean 40 ETF (AND)

C+   Fair

Fund Family: Global X Management Company LLC
Fund Type: Foreign
Inception Date: February 2, 2011

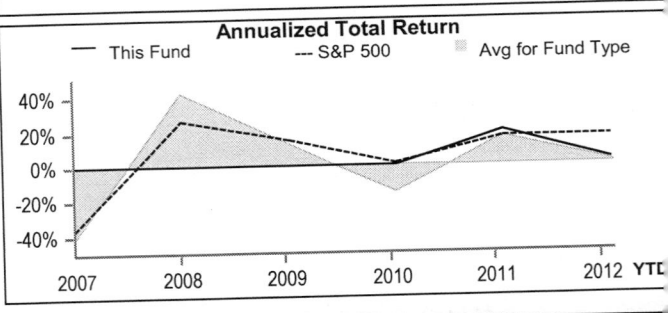

Data Date	Investment Rating	Net Assets ($Mil)	Price	Performance Rating/Pts	Total Return Y-T-D	Risk Rating/Pts
12-12	C+	8.70	14.58	B- / 7.4	3.15%	B- / 7.1

Major Rating Factors: Strong performance is the major factor driving the C+ (Fair) TheStreet.com Investment Rating for *Global X FTSE Andean 40 ETF. The fund currently has a performance rating of B- (Good) based on an annualized return of 0.00% over the last three years and a total return of 3.15% year to date 2012. Factored into the performance evaluation is an expense ratio of 0.72% (very low).

The fund's risk rating is currently B- (Good). It carries a beta of 0.00, meaning the fund's expected move will be 0.0% for every 10% move in the market. Volatility, as measured by both the semi-deviation and a drawdown factor, is considered low. As of December 31, 2012, *Global X FTSE Andean 40 ETF traded at a discount of 2.80% below its net asset value, which is better than its one-year historical average discount of .26%.

Bruno Del Ama has been running the fund for 2 years and currently receives a manager quality ranking of 75 (0=worst, 99=best). If you desire only a moderate level of risk and strong performance, then this fund is an excellent option.

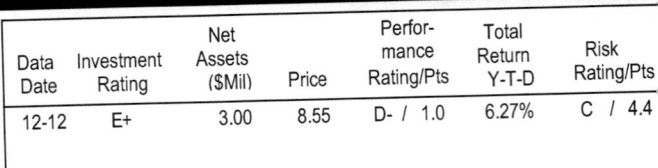

Annualized Total Return

— This Fund   --- S&P 500   ▓ Avg for Fund Type

*Global X FTSE Argentina 20 ETF (ARGT)

E+   Very Weak

Fund Family: Global X Management Company LLC
Fund Type: Foreign
Inception Date: March 3, 2011

Data Date	Investment Rating	Net Assets ($Mil)	Price	Performance Rating/Pts	Total Return Y-T-D	Risk Rating/Pts
12-12	E+	3.00	8.55	D- / 1.0	6.27%	C / 4.4

Major Rating Factors:
Disappointing performance is the major factor driving the E+ (Very Weak) TheStreet.com Investment Rating for *Global X FTSE Argentina 20 ETF. The fund currently has a performance rating of D- (Weak) based on an annualized return of 0.00% over the last three years and a total return of 6.27% year to date 2012. Factored into the performance evaluation is an expense ratio of 0.75% (very low).

The fund's risk rating is currently C (Fair). It carries a beta of 0.00, meaning the fund's expected move will be 0.0% for every 10% move in the market. Volatility, as measured by both the semi-deviation and a drawdown factor, is considered average. As of December 31, 2012, *Global X FTSE Argentina 20 ETF traded at a discount of 5.84% below its net asset value, which is better than its one-year historical average discount of .16%.

Bruno Del Ama has been running the fund for 2 years and currently receives a manager quality ranking of 1 (0=worst, 99=best). This fund offers an average level of risk but investors looking for strong performance will be frustrated.

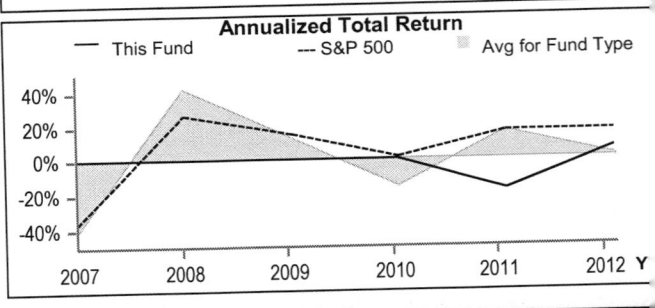

Annualized Total Return

— This Fund   --- S&P 500   ▓ Avg for Fund Type

*Global X FTSE ASEAN 40 ETF (ASEA)

C+   Fair

Fund Family: Global X Management Company LLC
Fund Type: Global
Inception Date: February 16, 2011

Data Date	Investment Rating	Net Assets ($Mil)	Price	Performance Rating/Pts	Total Return Y-T-D	Risk Rating/Pts
12-12	C+	37.70	17.04	B- / 7.1	-0.47%	B- / 7.

Major Rating Factors: Strong performance is the major factor driving the C+ (Fair) TheStreet.com Investment Rating for *Global X FTSE ASEAN 40 ETF. The fund currently has a performance rating of B- (Good) based on an annualized return of 0.00% over the last three years and a total return of -0.47% year to date 2012. Factored into the performance evaluation is an expense ratio of 0.65% (very low).

The fund's risk rating is currently B- (Good). It carries a beta of 0.00, meaning the fund's expected move will be 0.0% for every 10% move in the market. Volatility, as measured by both the semi-deviation and a drawdown factor, is considered low. As of December 31, 2012, *Global X FTSE ASEAN 40 ETF traded at a premium of 1.19% above its net asset value, which is worse than its one-year historical average premium of .37%.

Bruno Del Ama has been running the fund for 2 years and currently receives a manager quality ranking of 84 (0=worst, 99=best). If you desire only a moderate level of risk and strong performance, then this fund is an excellent option.

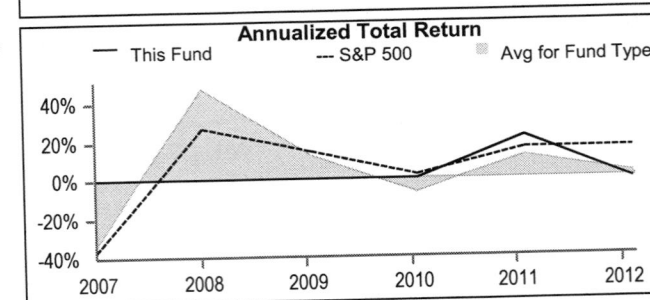

Annualized Total Return

— This Fund   --- S&P 500   ▓ Avg for Fund Type

*Global X FTSE Greece 20 ETF (GREK)

C+   **Fair**

Fund Family: Global X Management Company LLC
Fund Type: Foreign
Inception Date: December 7, 2011

Major Rating Factors:
Exceptional performance is the major factor driving the C+ (Fair) TheStreet.com Investment Rating for *Global X FTSE Greece 20 ETF. The fund currently has a performance rating of A+ (Excellent) based on an annualized return of 0.00% over the last three years and a total return of 6.48% year to date 2012. Factored into the performance evaluation is an expense ratio of 0.66% (very low).

The fund's risk rating is currently C (Fair). It carries a beta of 0.00, meaning the fund's expected move will be 0.0% for every 10% move in the market. Volatility, as measured by both the semi-deviation and a drawdown factor, is considered average. As of December 31, 2012, *Global X FTSE Greece 20 ETF traded at a discount of 4.75% below its net asset value, which is better than its one-year historical average premium of 1.00%.

Bruno Del Ama has been running the fund for 2 years and currently receives a manager quality ranking of 4 (0=worst, 99=best). If you desire an average level of risk and strong performance, then this fund is a good option.

Data Date	Investment Rating	Net Assets ($Mil)	Price	Performance Rating/Pts	Total Return Y-T-D	Risk Rating/Pts
12-12	C+	22.70	18.06	A+ / 9.9	6.48%	C / 4.4

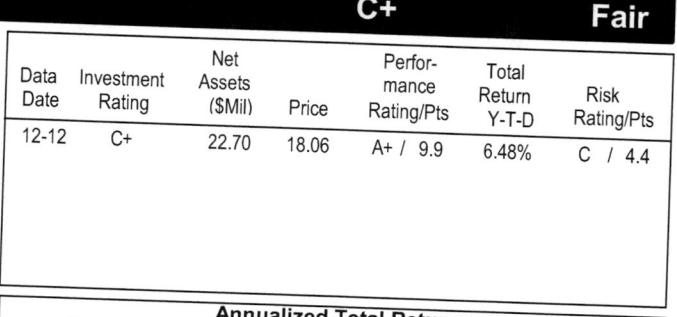

*Global X FTSE Nordic Region ETF (GXF)

C+   **Fair**

Fund Family: Global X Management Company LLC
Fund Type: Global
Inception Date: August 19, 2009

Major Rating Factors: Strong performance is the major factor driving the C+ (Fair) TheStreet.com Investment Rating for *Global X FTSE Nordic Region ETF. The fund currently has a performance rating of B- (Good) based on an annualized return of 8.51% over the last three years and a total return of 4.34% year to date 2012. Factored into the performance evaluation is an expense ratio of 0.50% (very low).

The fund's risk rating is currently C+ (Fair). It carries a beta of 1.26, meaning it is expected to move 12.6% for every 10% move in the market. Volatility, as measured by both the semi-deviation and a drawdown factor, is considered low. As of December 31, 2012, *Global X FTSE Nordic Region ETF traded at a discount of 3.55% below its net asset value, which is better than its one-year historical average discount of .08%.

Bruno Del Ama has been running the fund for 4 years and currently receives a manager quality ranking of 76 (0=worst, 99=best). If you desire only a moderate level of risk and strong performance, then this fund is an excellent option.

Data Date	Investment Rating	Net Assets ($Mil)	Price	Performance Rating/Pts	Total Return Y-T-D	Risk Rating/Pts
12-12	C+	27.30	19.54	B- / 7.1	4.34%	C+ / 6.4
2011	D-	22.20	15.64	E+ / 0.9	0.80%	C+ / 6.7
2010	A+	18.20	20.08	A / 9.4	25.42%	B- / 7.5

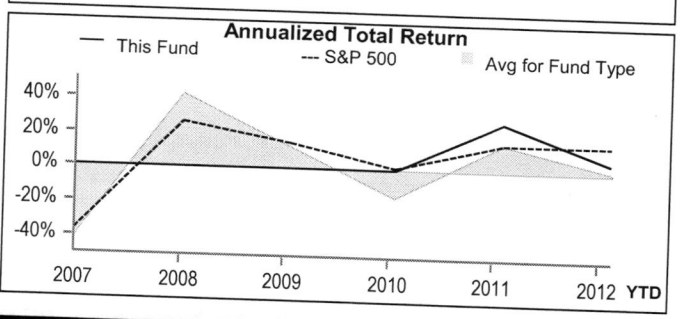

*Global X FTSE Norway 30 ETF (NORW)

B   **Good**

Fund Family: Global X Management Company LLC
Fund Type: Foreign
Inception Date: November 9, 2010

Major Rating Factors:
Exceptional performance is the major factor driving the B (Good) TheStreet.com Investment Rating for *Global X FTSE Norway 30 ETF. The fund currently has a performance rating of A+ (Excellent) based on an annualized return of 0.00% over the last three years and a total return of 2.30% year to date 2012. Factored into the performance evaluation is an expense ratio of 0.50% (very low).

The fund's risk rating is currently C+ (Fair). It carries a beta of 0.00, meaning the fund's expected move will be 0.0% for every 10% move in the market. Volatility, as measured by both the semi-deviation and a drawdown factor, is considered low. As of December 31, 2012, *Global X FTSE Norway 30 ETF traded at a discount of 2.24% below its net asset value, which is better than its one-year historical average discount of .03%.

Bruno Del Ama has been running the fund for 3 years and currently receives a manager quality ranking of 44 (0=worst, 99=best). If you desire only a moderate level of risk and strong performance, then this fund is an excellent option.

Data Date	Investment Rating	Net Assets ($Mil)	Price	Performance Rating/Pts	Total Return Y-T-D	Risk Rating/Pts
12-12	B	55.70	15.25	A+ / 9.6	2.30%	C+ / 6.2
2011	D-	44.00	12.54	D- / 1.0	0.40%	C+ / 6.2

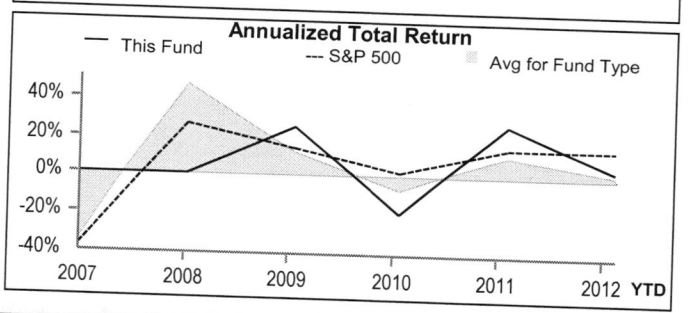

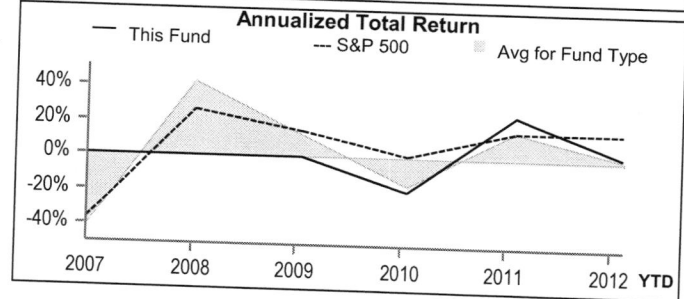

		E			Very Weak

*Global X Gold Explorers ETF (GLDX)

Fund Family: Global X Management Company LLC
Fund Type: Global
Inception Date: November 3, 2010

Data Date	Investment Rating	Net Assets ($Mil)	Price	Perfor-mance Rating/Pts	Total Return Y-T-D	Risk Rating/Pts
12-12	E	39.30	7.32	E / 0.4	1.08%	C- / 3.1
2011	E+	24.00	10.75	E / 0.4	2.05%	C / 4.3

Major Rating Factors: Very poor performance is the major factor driving the E (Very Weak) TheStreet.com Investment Rating for *Global X Gold Explorers ETF. The fund currently has a performance rating of E (Very Weak) based on an annualized return of 0.00% over the last three years and a total return of 1.08% year to date 2012. Factored into the performance evaluation is an expense ratio of 0.65% (very low).

The fund's risk rating is currently C- (Fair). It carries a beta of 0.00, meaning the fund's expected move will be 0.0% for every 10% move in the market. Volatility, as measured by both the semi-deviation and a drawdown factor, is considered average. As of December 31, 2012, *Global X Gold Explorers ETF traded at a discount of .95% below its net asset value, which is better than its one-year historical average premium of .32%.

Bruno Del Ama has been running the fund for 3 years and currently receives a manager quality ranking of 1 (0=worst, 99=best). This fund offers an average level of risk but investors looking for strong performance will be frustrated.

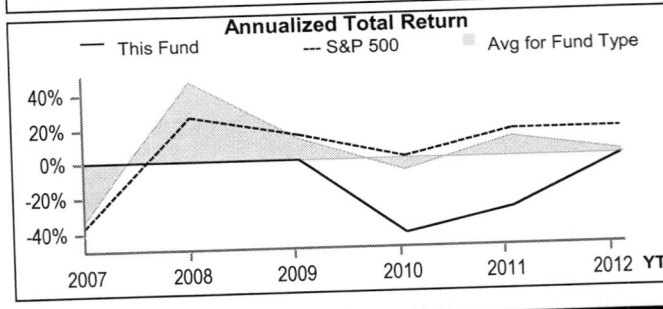

Annualized Total Return

		D			Weak

*Global X Junior Miners ETF (JUNR)

Fund Family: Global X Management Company LLC
Fund Type: Energy/Natural Resources
Inception Date: March 16, 2011

Data Date	Investment Rating	Net Assets ($Mil)	Price	Perfor-mance Rating/Pts	Total Return Y-T-D	Risk Rating/Pts
12-12	D	2.70	9.29	C / 4.5	1.60%	C / 4.3

Major Rating Factors: *Global X Junior Miners ETF receives a TheStreet.com Investment Rating of D (Weak). The fund currently has a performance rating of C (Fair) based on an annualized return of 0.00% over the last three years and a total return of 1.60% year to date 2012. Factored into the performance evaluation is an expense ratio of 0.75% (very low).

The fund's risk rating is currently C (Fair). It carries a beta of 0.00, meaning the fund's expected move will be 0.0% for every 10% move in the market. Volatility, as measured by both the semi-deviation and a drawdown factor, is considered average. As of December 31, 2012, *Global X Junior Miners ETF traded at a discount of .85% below its net asset value, which is better than its one-year historical average discount of .16%. Bruno Del Ama has been running the fund for 2 years and currently receives a manager quality ranking of 65 (0=worst, 99=best). If you desire an average level of risk, then this fund may be an option.

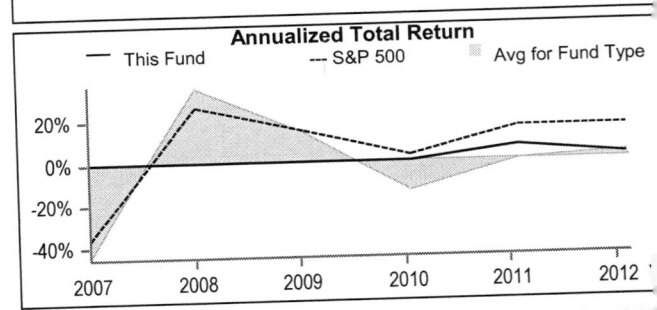

Annualized Total Return

		D-			Wea

*Global X Lithium ETF (LIT)

Fund Family: Global X Management Company LLC
Fund Type: Growth
Inception Date: July 22, 2010

Data Date	Investment Rating	Net Assets ($Mil)	Price	Perfor-mance Rating/Pts	Total Return Y-T-D	Risk Rating/
12-12	D-	66.40	14.36	D / 1.9	3.48%	C /
2011	E+	86.70	14.33	E / 0.5	4.05%	C /

Major Rating Factors:
Disappointing performance is the major factor driving the D- (Weak) TheStreet.com Investment Rating for *Global X Lithium ETF. The fund currently has a performance rating of D (Weak) based on an annualized return of 0.00% over the last three years and a total return of 3.48% year to date 2012. Factored into the performance evaluation is an expense ratio of 0.75% (very low).

The fund's risk rating is currently C (Fair). It carries a beta of 0.00, meaning the fund's expected move will be 0.0% for every 10% move in the market. Volatility, as measured by both the semi-deviation and a drawdown factor, is considered average. As of December 31, 2012, *Global X Lithium ETF traded at a discount of 3.88% below its net asset value, which is better than its one-year historical average discount of .52%.

Bruno Del Ama has been running the fund for 3 years and currently receives a manager quality ranking of 3 (0=worst, 99=best). This fund offers an average level of risk but investors looking for strong performance will be frustrated.

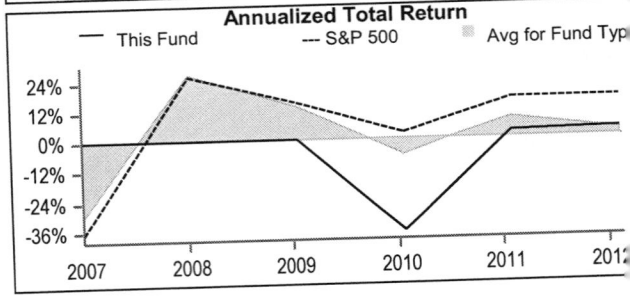

Annualized Total Return

*Global X NASDAQ China Tech ETF (QQQC)

D   **Weak**

Fund Family: Global X Management Company LLC
Fund Type: Foreign
Inception Date: December 8, 2009

Major Rating Factors:
Disappointing performance is the major factor driving the D (Weak) TheStreet.com Investment Rating for *Global X NASDAQ China Tech ETF. The fund currently has a performance rating of D (Weak) based on an annualized return of -2.21% over the last three years and a total return of 5.97% year to date 2012. Factored into the performance evaluation is an expense ratio of 0.65% (very low).

The fund's risk rating is currently C+ (Fair). It carries a beta of 0.95, meaning that its performance tracks fairly well with that of the overall stock market. Volatility, as measured by both the semi-deviation and a drawdown factor, is considered low. As of December 31, 2012, *Global X NASDAQ China Tech ETF traded at a discount of 5.07% below its net asset value, which is better than its one-year historical average discount of .70%.

Bruno Del Ama has been running the fund for 4 years and currently receives a manager quality ranking of 21 (0=worst, 99=best). This fund offers only a moderate level of risk but investors looking for strong performance are still waiting.

Data Date	Investment Rating	Net Assets ($Mil)	Price	Performance Rating/Pts	Total Return Y-T-D	Risk Rating/Pts
12-12	D	2.80	14.23	D / 1.6	5.97%	C+ / 6.2
2010	A	4.90	16.50	B+ / 8.3	8.34%	B- / 7.7

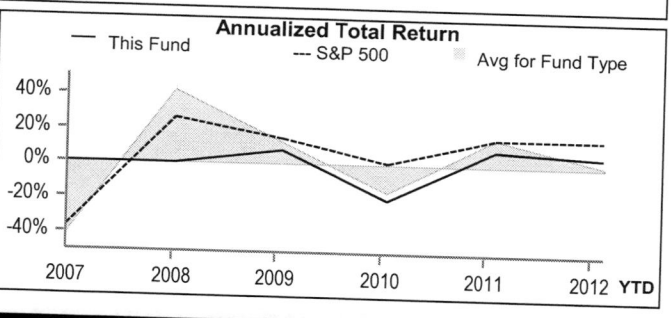

*Global X Pure Gold Miners ETF (GGGG)

E+   **Very Weak**

Fund Family: Global X Management Company LLC
Fund Type: Precious Metals
Inception Date: March 14, 2011

Major Rating Factors:
Very poor performance is the major factor driving the E+ (Very Weak) TheStreet.com Investment Rating for *Global X Pure Gold Miners ETF. The fund currently has a performance rating of E (Very Weak) based on an annualized return of 0.00% over the last three years and a total return of -2.39% year to date 2012. Factored into the performance evaluation is an expense ratio of 0.59% (very low).

The fund's risk rating is currently C (Fair). It carries a beta of 0.00, meaning the fund's expected move will be 0.0% for every 10% move in the market. Volatility, as measured by both the semi-deviation and a drawdown factor, is considered average. As of December 31, 2012, *Global X Pure Gold Miners ETF traded at a premium of 2.34% above its net asset value, which is worse than its one-year historical average premium of .38%.

Bruno Del Ama has been running the fund for 2 years and currently receives a manager quality ranking of 4 (0=worst, 99=best). This fund offers an average level of risk but investors looking for strong performance will be frustrated.

Data Date	Investment Rating	Net Assets ($Mil)	Price	Performance Rating/Pts	Total Return Y-T-D	Risk Rating/Pts
12-12	E+	4.20	10.48	E / 0.4	-2.39%	C / 5.3

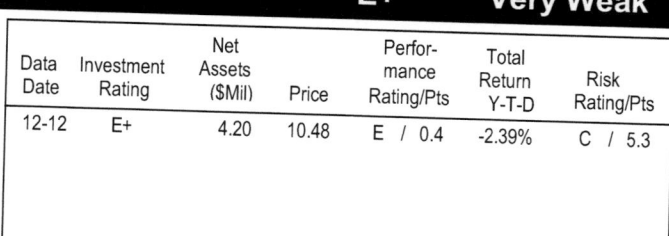

*Global X Silver Miners ETF (SIL)

D+   **Weak**

Fund Family: Global X Management Company LLC
Fund Type: Precious Metals
Inception Date: April 19, 2010

Major Rating Factors: *Global X Silver Miners ETF receives a TheStreet.com Investment Rating of D+ (Weak). The fund currently has a performance rating of C (Fair) based on an annualized return of 0.00% over the last three years and a total return of -1.06% year to date 2012. Factored into the performance evaluation is an expense ratio of 0.65% (very low).

The fund's risk rating is currently C (Fair). It carries a beta of 0.00, meaning the fund's expected move will be 0.0% for every 10% move in the market. Volatility, as measured by both the semi-deviation and a drawdown factor, is considered average. As of December 31, 2012, *Global X Silver Miners ETF traded at a premium of 1.12% above its net asset value, which is worse than its one-year historical average discount of .01%.

Bruno Del Ama has been running the fund for 3 years and currently receives a manager quality ranking of 24 (0=worst, 99=best). If you desire an average level of risk, then this fund may be an option.

Data Date	Investment Rating	Net Assets ($Mil)	Price	Performance Rating/Pts	Total Return Y-T-D	Risk Rating/Pts
12-12	D+	349.90	22.65	C / 4.4	-1.06%	C / 5.2
2011	D-	314.10	21.12	D- / 1.2	3.91%	C+ / 6.1

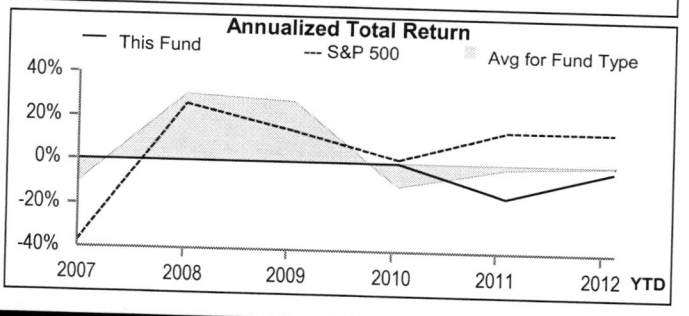

* Denotes ETF Fund

*Global X Social Media Index ETF (SOCL)

D+ **Weak**

Fund Family: Global X Management Company LLC
Fund Type: Global
Inception Date: November 14, 2011

Major Rating Factors: *Global X Social Media Index ETF receives a TheStreet.com Investment Rating of D+ (Weak). The fund currently has a performance rating of C- (Fair) based on an annualized return of 0.00% over the last three years and a total return of 6.96% year to date 2012. Factored into the performance evaluation is an expense ratio of 0.65% (very low).

The fund's risk rating is currently B- (Good). It carries a beta of 0.00, meaning the fund's expected move will be 0.0% for every 10% move in the market. Volatility, as measured by both the semi-deviation and a drawdown factor, is considered low. As of December 31, 2012, *Global X Social Media Index ETF traded at a discount of 7.04% below its net asset value, which is better than its one-year historical average discount of .31%.

Bruno Del Ama has been running the fund for 2 years and currently receives a manager quality ranking of 5 (0=worst, 99=best). If you desire an average level of risk, then this fund may be an option.

Data Date	Investment Rating	Net Assets ($Mil)	Price	Performance Rating/Pts	Total Return Y-T-D	Risk Rating/Pts
12-12	D+	11.60	12.94	C- / 3.5	6.96%	B- / 7.0

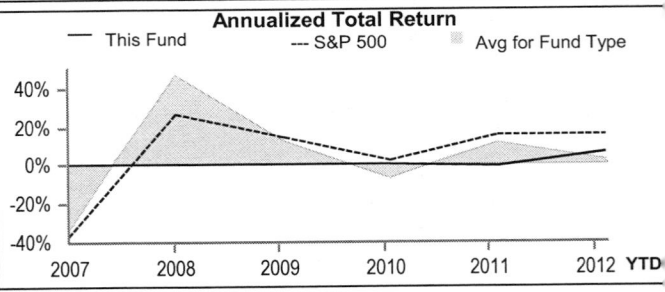

*Global X SuperDividend ETF (SDIV)

B **Good**

Fund Family: Global X Management Company LLC
Fund Type: Global
Inception Date: June 8, 2011

Major Rating Factors: Strong performance is the major factor driving the B (Good) TheStreet.com Investment Rating for *Global X SuperDividend ETF. The fund currently has a performance rating of B (Good) based on an annualized return of 0.00% over the last three years and a total return of 3.03% year to date 2012. Factored into the performance evaluation is an expense ratio of 0.58% (very low).

The fund's risk rating is currently B- (Good). It carries a beta of 0.00, meaning the fund's expected move will be 0.0% for every 10% move in the market. Volatility, as measured by both the semi-deviation and a drawdown factor, is considered low. As of December 31, 2012, *Global X SuperDividend ETF traded at a discount of 2.51% below its net asset value, which is better than its one-year historical average premium of .50%.

Bruno Del Ama has been running the fund for 2 years and currently receives a manager quality ranking of 94 (0=worst, 99=best). If you desire only a moderate level of risk and strong performance, then this fund is an excellent option.

Data Date	Investment Rating	Net Assets ($Mil)	Price	Performance Rating/Pts	Total Return Y-T-D	Risk Rating/Pts
12-12	B	192.90	22.10	B / 8.2	3.03%	B- / 7.6

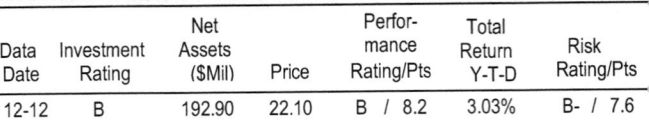

*Global X Uranium ETF (URA)

E- **Very Weak**

Fund Family: Global X Management Company LLC
Fund Type: Global
Inception Date: November 3, 2010

Major Rating Factors: *Global X Uranium ETF has adopted a risky asset allocation strategy and currently receives an overall TheStreet.com Investment Rating of E- (Very Weak). The fund has an above average level of volatility, as measured by both semi-deviation and drawdown factors. It carries a beta of 0.00, meaning the fund's expected move will be 0.0% for every 10% move in the market. As of December 31, 2012, *Global X Uranium ETF traded at a discount of 4.41% below its net asset value, which is better than its one-year historical average premium of .25%. Unfortunately, the high level of risk (D+, Weak) failed to pay off as investors endured very poor performance.

The fund's performance rating is currently E (Very Weak). It has registered an annualized return of 0.00% over the last three years and is up 5.53% year to date 2012. Factored into the performance evaluation is an expense ratio of 0.69% (very low).

Bruno Del Ama has been running the fund for 3 years and currently receives a manager quality ranking of 1 (0=worst, 99=best). If you can tolerate high levels of risk in the hope of improved future returns, holding this fund may be an option.

Data Date	Investment Rating	Net Assets ($Mil)	Price	Performance Rating/Pts	Total Return Y-T-D	Risk Rating/Pts
12-12	E-	133.00	6.51	E / 0.5	5.53%	D+ / 2.6
2011	E-	164.00	8.15	E- / 0.1	3.44%	D+ / 2.3

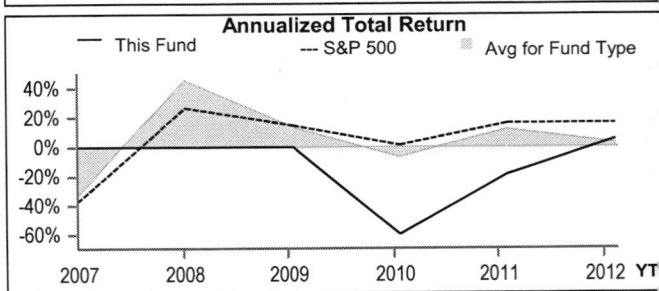

*Global X/InterBolsa FTSE Col 20 (GXG)

C-   **Fair**

Fund Family: Global X Management Company LLC
Fund Type: Foreign
Inception Date: February 5, 2009

Major Rating Factors: Strong performance is the major factor driving the C- (Fair) TheStreet.com Investment Rating for *Global X/InterBolsa FTSE Col 20. The fund currently has a performance rating of B (Good) based on an annualized return of 16.17% over the last three years and a total return of 0.72% year to date 2012. Factored into the performance evaluation is an expense ratio of 0.78% (very low).

The fund's risk rating is currently C- (Fair). It carries a beta of 0.65, meaning the fund's expected move will be 6.5% for every 10% move in the market. Volatility, as measured by both the semi-deviation and a drawdown factor, is considered average. As of December 31, 2012, *Global X/InterBolsa FTSE Col 20 traded at a premium of .09% above its net asset value, which is better than its one-year historical average premium of .15%.

Bruno Del Ama has been running the fund for 4 years and currently receives a manager quality ranking of 95 (0=worst, 99=best). If you desire an average level of risk and strong performance, then this fund is a good option.

Data Date	Investment Rating	Net Assets ($Mil)	Price	Performance Rating/Pts	Total Return Y-T-D	Risk Rating/Pts
12-12	C-	179.30	22.24	B / 7.6	0.72%	C- / 3.3
2011	E+	121.60	17.82	D- / 1.2	3.48%	C- / 3.6
2010	A+	170.40	42.53	A+ / 9.6	50.18%	B- / 7.9

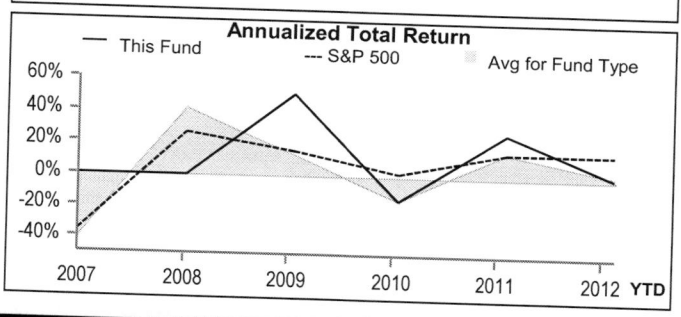

*GreenHaven Continuous Commodity (GCC)

D   **Weak**

Fund Family: Greenhaven Commodity Services LLC
Fund Type: Growth and Income
Inception Date: January 24, 2008

Major Rating Factors:
Disappointing performance is the major factor driving the D (Weak) TheStreet.com Investment Rating for *GreenHaven Continuous Commodity. The fund currently has a performance rating of D (Weak) based on an annualized return of 3.06% over the last three years and a total return of 0.21% year to date 2012. Factored into the performance evaluation is an expense ratio of 1.04% (low).

The fund's risk rating is currently B- (Good). It carries a beta of 0.78, meaning the fund's expected move will be 7.8% for every 10% move in the market. Volatility, as measured by both the semi-deviation and a drawdown factor, is considered average. As of December 31, 2012, *GreenHaven Continuous Commodity traded at a price exactly equal to its net asset value, which is worse than its one-year historical average discount of .05%.

Greenhaven Commodity Services has been running the fund for 5 years and currently receives a manager quality ranking of 22 (0=worst, 99=best). This fund offers only a moderate level of risk but investors looking for strong performance are still waiting.

Data Date	Investment Rating	Net Assets ($Mil)	Price	Performance Rating/Pts	Total Return Y-T-D	Risk Rating/Pts
12-12	D	474.60	28.83	D / 1.7	0.21%	B- / 7.3
2011	C-	581.20	29.92	C- / 3.4	0.77%	B / 8.1
2010	A	442.10	32.95	A / 9.5	25.19%	C+ / 5.7
2009	B+	143.21	26.32	B / 7.8	18.83%	C+ / 5.8

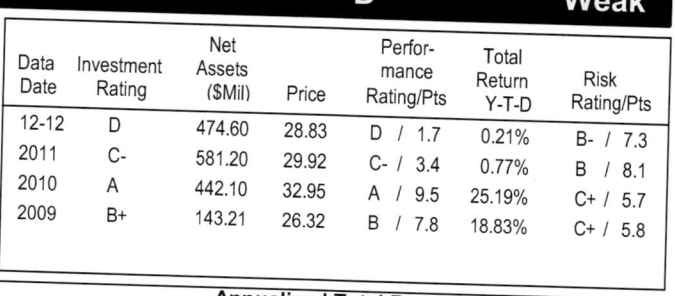

*GS Cnct S&P GSCI Enh Cmd TR Str (GSC)

D   **Weak**

Fund Family: Goldman Sachs & Co/GSAM
Fund Type: Growth
Inception Date: July 31, 2007

Major Rating Factors:
Disappointing performance is the major factor driving the D (Weak) TheStreet.com Investment Rating for *GS Cnct S&P GSCI Enh Cmd TR Str. The fund currently has a performance rating of D (Weak) based on an annualized return of 3.51% over the last three years and a total return of 0.41% year to date 2012.

The fund's risk rating is currently B- (Good). It carries a beta of 1.16, meaning it is expected to move 11.6% for every 10% move in the market. Volatility, as measured by both the semi-deviation and a drawdown factor, is considered low. As of December 31, 2012, *GS Cnct S&P GSCI Enh Cmd TR Str traded at a discount of .42% below its net asset value.

This fund has been team managed for 6 years and currently receives a manager quality ranking of 14 (0=worst, 99=best). This fund offers only a moderate level of risk but investors looking for strong performance are still waiting.

Data Date	Investment Rating	Net Assets ($Mil)	Price	Performance Rating/Pts	Total Return Y-T-D	Risk Rating/Pts
12-12	D	0.00	47.97	D / 1.9	0.41%	B- / 7.1
2011	C-	0.00	48.88	C- / 4.2	2.19%	B- / 7.4
2010	D-	0.00	48.82	D- / 1.4	10.33%	C / 4.4
2009	C+	0.00	44.25	B- / 7.5	20.70%	C / 4.8

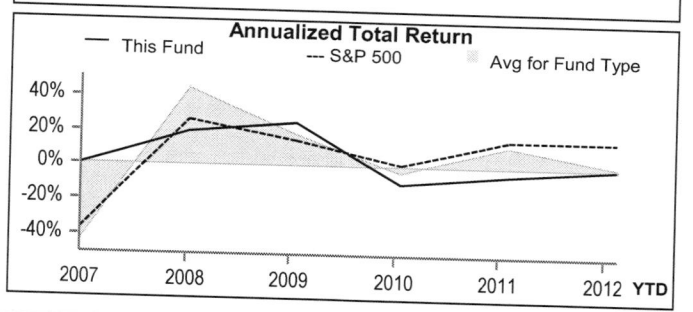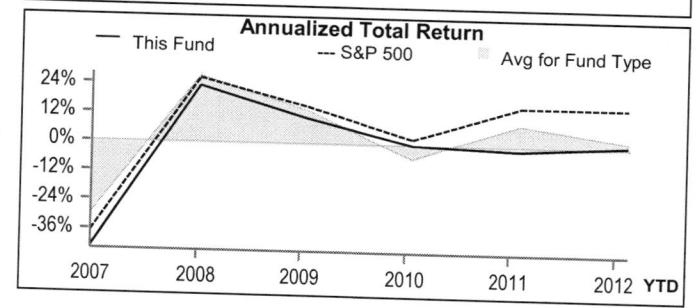

* Denotes ETF Fund

*Guggenheim 2x S&P 500 ETF (RSU)

B **Good**

Fund Family: Guggenheim Investments
Fund Type: Income
Inception Date: November 5, 2007

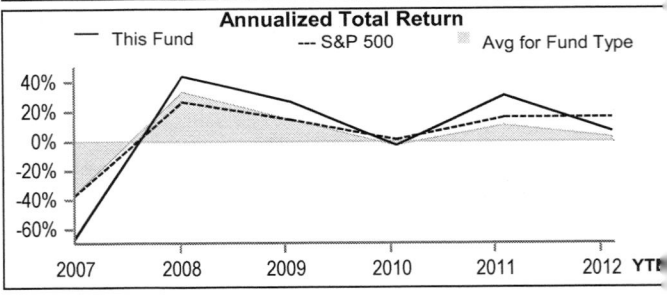

Data Date	Investment Rating	Net Assets ($Mil)	Price	Perfor-mance Rating/Pts	Total Return Y-T-D	Risk Rating/Pts
12-12	B	51.60	51.45	B+ / 8.8	6.51%	C+ / 6.5
2011	C+	73.50	39.66	B- / 7.4	3.28%	C+ / 6.3
2010	D-	90.40	41.10	D / 1.6	27.31%	C- / 3.5
2009	B-	146.78	32.62	A / 9.4	38.23%	C- / 3.5

Major Rating Factors: Strong performance is the major factor driving the B (Good) TheStreet.com Investment Rating for *Guggenheim 2x S&P 500 ETF. The fund currently has a performance rating of B+ (Good) based on an annualized return of 18.65% over the last three years and a total return of 6.51% year to date 2012. Factored into the performance evaluation is an expense ratio of 0.71% (very low).

The fund's risk rating is currently C+ (Fair). It carries a beta of 2.03, meaning it is expected to move 20.3% for every 10% move in the market. Volatility, as measured by both the semi-deviation and a drawdown factor, is considered low. As of December 31, 2012, *Guggenheim 2x S&P 500 ETF traded at a discount of 6.37% below its net asset value, which is better than its one-year historical average discount of .09%.

Michael Dellapa has been running the fund for 6 years and currently receives a manager quality ranking of 24 (0=worst, 99=best). If you desire only a moderate level of risk and strong performance, then this fund is an excellent option.

*Guggenheim ABC High Dividend ETF (ABCS)

D **Weak**

Fund Family: Guggenheim Funds Investment Advisor
Fund Type: Foreign
Inception Date: June 8, 2011

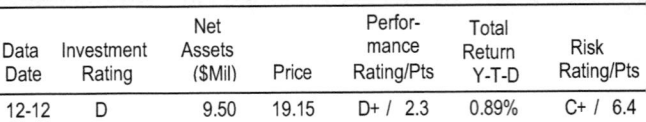

Data Date	Investment Rating	Net Assets ($Mil)	Price	Perfor-mance Rating/Pts	Total Return Y-T-D	Risk Rating/Pts
12-12	D	9.50	19.15	D+ / 2.3	0.89%	C+ / 6.4

Major Rating Factors:
Disappointing performance is the major factor driving the D (Weak) TheStreet.com Investment Rating for *Guggenheim ABC High Dividend ETF. The fund currently has a performance rating of D+ (Weak) based on an annualized return of 0.00% over the last three years and a total return of 0.89% year to date 2012. Factored into the performance evaluation is an expense ratio of 0.65% (very low).

The fund's risk rating is currently C+ (Fair). It carries a beta of 0.00, meaning the fund's expected move will be 0.0% for every 10% move in the market. Volatility, as measured by both the semi-deviation and a drawdown factor, is considered low. As of December 31, 2012, *Guggenheim ABC High Dividend ETF traded at a discount of .83% below its net asset value, which is better than its one-year historical average premium of .09%.

Saroj Kanuri has been running the fund for 2 years and currently receives a manager quality ranking of 7 (0=worst, 99=best). This fund offers only a moderate level of risk but investors looking for strong performance are still waiting.

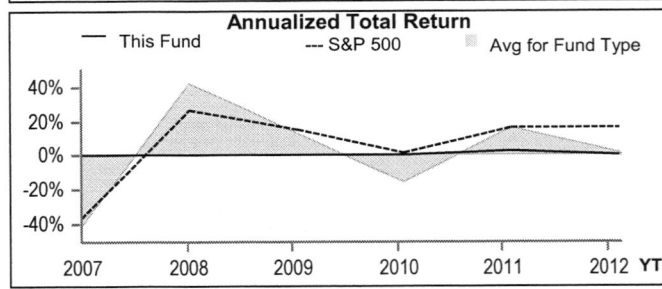

*Guggenheim Airline ETF (FAA)

C+ **Fair**

Fund Family: Guggenheim Funds Investment Advisor
Fund Type: Global
Inception Date: January 26, 2009

Data Date	Investment Rating	Net Assets ($Mil)	Price	Perfor-mance Rating/Pts	Total Return Y-T-D	Risk Rating/Pts
12-12	C+	17.40	34.91	B- / 7.4	8.29%	C+ / 6.3
2011	D-	14.50	26.25	E / 0.5	0.76%	C+ / 5.9
2010	A	37.60	39.56	A / 9.4	29.54%	C+ / 6.5

Major Rating Factors: Strong performance is the major factor driving the C+ (Fair) TheStreet.com Investment Rating for *Guggenheim Airline ETF. The fund currently has a performance rating of B- (Good) based on an annualized return of 5.76% over the last three years and a total return of 8.29% year to date 2012. Factored into the performance evaluation is an expense ratio of 0.70% (very low).

The fund's risk rating is currently C+ (Fair). It carries a beta of 0.60, meaning the fund's expected move will be 6.0% for every 10% move in the market. Volatility, as measured by both the semi-deviation and a drawdown factor, is considered low. As of December 31, 2012, *Guggenheim Airline ETF traded at a discount of 7.62% below its net asset value, which is better than its one-year historical average discount of .07%.

Saroj Kanuri has been running the fund for 3 years and currently receives a manager quality ranking of 69 (0=worst, 99=best). If you desire only a moderate level of risk and strong performance, then this fund is an excellent option.

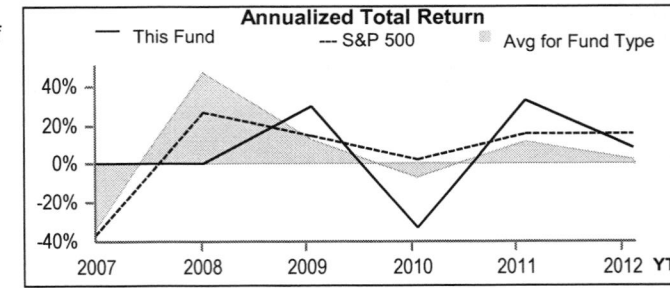

*Guggenheim Australian Dollar Sha (FXA)

C-   **Fair**

Fund Family: Guggenheim Investments
Fund Type: Foreign
Inception Date: June 26, 2006

Major Rating Factors: Middle of the road best describes *Guggenheim Australian Dollar Sha whose TheStreet.com Investment Rating is currently a C- (Fair). The fund currently has a performance rating of C- (Fair) based on an annualized return of 8.14% over the last three years and a total return of 1.39% year to date 2012. Factored into the performance evaluation is an expense ratio of 0.40% (very low).

The fund's risk rating is currently B (Good). It carries a beta of 0.65, meaning the fund's expected move will be 6.5% for every 10% move in the market. Volatility, as measured by both the semi-deviation and a drawdown factor, is considered low. As of December 31, 2012, *Guggenheim Australian Dollar Sha traded at a discount of 1.35% below its net asset value, which is better than its one-year historical average discount of .02%.

This fund has been team managed for 7 years and currently receives a manager quality ranking of 82 (0=worst, 99=best). If you desire an average level of risk, then this fund may be an option.

Data Date	Investment Rating	Net Assets ($Mil)	Price	Perfor-mance Rating/Pts	Total Return Y-T-D	Risk Rating/Pts
12-12	C-	582.50	104.15	C- / 3.2	1.39%	B / 8.5
2011	B-	784.40	102.62	C+ / 5.8	0.03%	B / 8.7
2010	B+	735.50	102.66	B / 7.7	18.23%	C+ / 6.4
2009	C+	557.97	90.07	C+ / 5.9	29.41%	C+ / 6.8

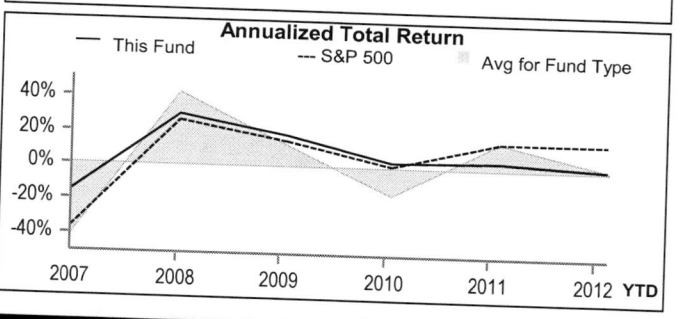

*Guggenheim BltShs 2013 Corp Bd E (BSCD)

C-   **Fair**

Fund Family: Guggenheim Funds Investment Advisor
Fund Type: Corporate - Investment Grade
Inception Date: June 7, 2010

Major Rating Factors:
Disappointing performance is the major factor driving the C- (Fair) TheStreet.com Investment Rating for *Guggenheim BltShs 2013 Corp Bd E. The fund currently has a performance rating of D- (Weak) based on an annualized return of 0.00% over the last three years and a total return of 0.00% year to date 2012. Factored into the performance evaluation is an expense ratio of 0.24% (very low).

The fund's risk rating is currently B+ (Good). It carries a beta of 0.00, meaning the fund's expected move will be 0.0% for every 10% move in the market. Volatility, as measured by both the semi-deviation and a drawdown factor, is considered very low. As of December 31, 2012, *Guggenheim BltShs 2013 Corp Bd E traded at a discount of .19% below its net asset value, which is better than its one-year historical average premium of .20%.

Saroj Kanuri has been running the fund for 3 years and currently receives a manager quality ranking of 60 (0=worst, 99=best). This fund offers only a moderate level of risk but investors looking for strong performance are still waiting.

Data Date	Investment Rating	Net Assets ($Mil)	Price	Perfor-mance Rating/Pts	Total Return Y-T-D	Risk Rating/Pts
12-12	C-	159.30	20.80	D- / 1.5	0.00%	B+ / 9.9
2011	C	111.40	20.72	D / 2.2	0.24%	B+ / 9.9

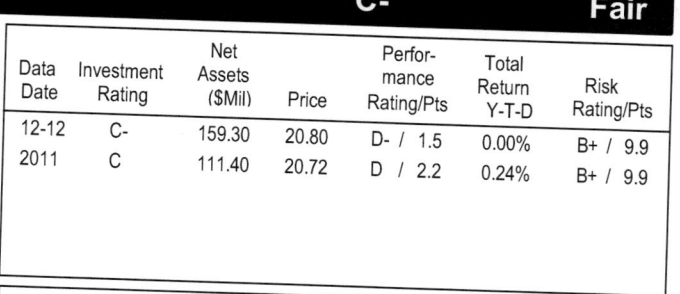

*Guggenheim BltShs 2014 Corp Bd E (BSCE)

C-   **Fair**

Fund Family: Guggenheim Funds Investment Advisor
Fund Type: Corporate - Investment Grade
Inception Date: June 7, 2010

Major Rating Factors:
Disappointing performance is the major factor driving the C- (Fair) TheStreet.com Investment Rating for *Guggenheim BltShs 2014 Corp Bd E. The fund currently has a performance rating of D (Weak) based on an annualized return of 0.00% over the last three years and a total return of 0.09% year to date 2012. Factored into the performance evaluation is an expense ratio of 0.24% (very low).

The fund's risk rating is currently B+ (Good). It carries a beta of 0.00, meaning the fund's expected move will be 0.0% for every 10% move in the market. Volatility, as measured by both the semi-deviation and a drawdown factor, is considered very low. As of December 31, 2012, *Guggenheim BltShs 2014 Corp Bd E traded at a premium of .14% above its net asset value, which is better than its one-year historical average premium of .35%.

Saroj Kanuri has been running the fund for 3 years and currently receives a manager quality ranking of 59 (0=worst, 99=best). This fund offers only a moderate level of risk but investors looking for strong performance are still waiting.

Data Date	Investment Rating	Net Assets ($Mil)	Price	Perfor-mance Rating/Pts	Total Return Y-T-D	Risk Rating/Pts
12-12	C-	178.30	21.27	D / 2.0	0.09%	B+ / 9.9
2011	C	96.30	20.90	D+ / 2.4	0.00%	B+ / 9.9

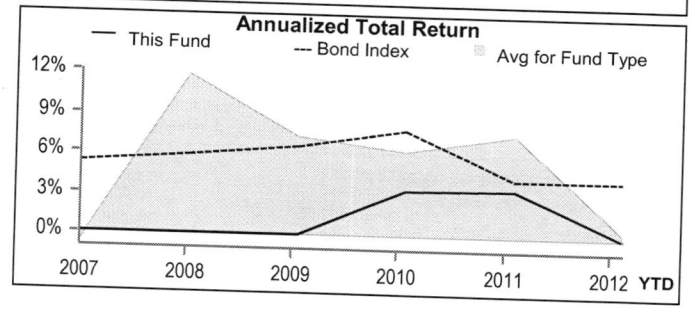

* Denotes ETF Fund

*Guggenheim BltShs 2015 Corp Bd E (BSCF)

C   **Fair**

Fund Family: Guggenheim Funds Investment Advisor
Fund Type: Corporate - Investment Grade
Inception Date: June 7, 2010

Data Date	Investment Rating	Net Assets ($Mil)	Price	Performance Rating/Pts	Total Return Y-T-D	Risk Rating/Pts
12-12	C	166.40	21.80	D+ / 2.4	0.14%	B+ / 9.8
2011	C	68.80	21.00	D+ / 2.5	-0.10%	B+ / 9.8

Major Rating Factors:
Disappointing performance is the major factor driving the C (Fair) TheStreet.com Investment Rating for *Guggenheim BltShs 2015 Corp Bd E. The fund currently has a performance rating of D+ (Weak) based on an annualized return of 0.00% over the last three years and a total return of 0.14% year to date 2012. Factored into the performance evaluation is an expense ratio of 0.24% (very low).

The fund's risk rating is currently B+ (Good). It carries a beta of 0.00, meaning the fund's expected move will be 0.0% for every 10% move in the market. Volatility, as measured by both the semi-deviation and a drawdown factor, is considered very low. As of December 31, 2012, *Guggenheim BltShs 2015 Corp Bd E traded at a price exactly equal to its net asset value, which is better than its one-year historical average premium of .37%.

Saroj Kanuri has been running the fund for 3 years and currently receives a manager quality ranking of 64 (0=worst, 99=best). This fund offers only a moderate level of risk but investors looking for strong performance are still waiting.

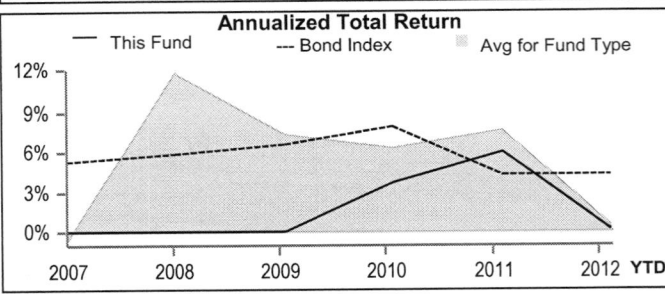

*Guggenheim BltShs 2016 Corp Bd E (BSCG)

C   **Fair**

Fund Family: Guggenheim Funds Investment Advisor
Fund Type: Corporate - Investment Grade
Inception Date: June 7, 2010

Data Date	Investment Rating	Net Assets ($Mil)	Price	Performance Rating/Pts	Total Return Y-T-D	Risk Rating/Pts
12-12	C	159.40	22.22	D+ / 2.7	0.27%	B+ / 9.7
2011	C	66.30	21.26	D+ / 2.9	-0.02%	B+ / 9.8

Major Rating Factors:
Disappointing performance is the major factor driving the C (Fair) TheStreet.com Investment Rating for *Guggenheim BltShs 2016 Corp Bd E. The fund currently has a performance rating of D+ (Weak) based on an annualized return of 0.00% over the last three years and a total return of 0.27% year to date 2012. Factored into the performance evaluation is an expense ratio of 0.24% (very low).

The fund's risk rating is currently B+ (Good). It carries a beta of 0.00, meaning the fund's expected move will be 0.0% for every 10% move in the market. Volatility, as measured by both the semi-deviation and a drawdown factor, is considered very low. As of December 31, 2012, *Guggenheim BltShs 2016 Corp Bd E traded at a premium of .05% above its net asset value, which is better than its one-year historical average premium of .37%.

Saroj Kanuri has been running the fund for 3 years and currently receives a manager quality ranking of 65 (0=worst, 99=best). This fund offers only a moderate level of risk but investors looking for strong performance are still waiting.

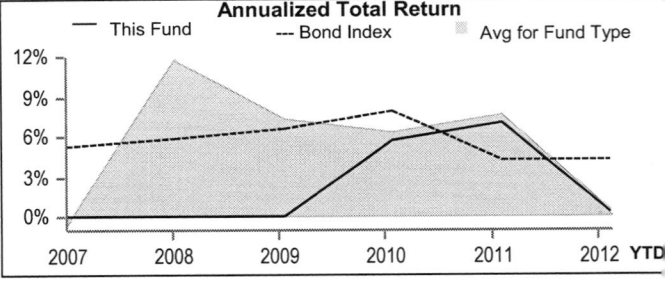

*Guggenheim BltShs 2017 Corp Bd E (BSCH)

C   **Fair**

Fund Family: Guggenheim Funds Investment Advisor
Fund Type: Corporate - Investment Grade
Inception Date: June 7, 2010

Data Date	Investment Rating	Net Assets ($Mil)	Price	Performance Rating/Pts	Total Return Y-T-D	Risk Rating/Pts
12-12	C	181.10	22.82	C- / 3.2	0.22%	B+ / 9.7
2011	C	53.90	21.32	C- / 3.0	0.07%	B+ / 9.8

Major Rating Factors: Middle of the road best describes *Guggenheim BltShs 2017 Corp Bd E whose TheStreet.com Investment Rating is currently a C (Fair). The fund currently has a performance rating of C- (Fair) based on an annualized return of 0.00% over the last three years and a total return of 0.22% year to date 2012. Factored into the performance evaluation is an expense ratio of 0.24% (very low).

The fund's risk rating is currently B+ (Good). It carries a beta of 0.00, meaning the fund's expected move will be 0.0% for every 10% move in the market. Volatility, as measured by both the semi-deviation and a drawdown factor, is considered very low. As of December 31, 2012, *Guggenheim BltShs 2017 Corp Bd E traded at a premium of .09% above its net asset value, which is better than its one-year historical average premium of .43%.

Saroj Kanuri has been running the fund for 3 years and currently receives a manager quality ranking of 70 (0=worst, 99=best). If you desire an average level of risk, then this fund may be an option.

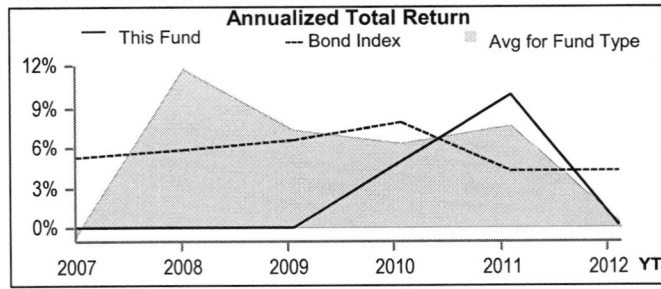

*Guggenheim BRIC ETF (EEB)

D **Weak**

Fund Family: Guggenheim Funds Investment Advisor
Fund Type: Income
Inception Date: September 21, 2006

Major Rating Factors:

Disappointing performance is the major factor driving the D (Weak) TheStreet.com Investment Rating for *Guggenheim BRIC ETF. The fund currently has a performance rating of D- (Weak) based on an annualized return of -1.92% over the last three years and a total return of 2.17% year to date 2012. Factored into the performance evaluation is an expense ratio of 0.64% (very low).

The fund's risk rating is currently C+ (Fair). It carries a beta of 1.37, meaning it is expected to move 13.7% for every 10% move in the market. Volatility, as measured by both the semi-deviation and a drawdown factor, is considered low. As of December 31, 2012, *Guggenheim BRIC ETF traded at a discount of 2.12% below its net asset value, which is better than its one-year historical average discount of .07%.

Saroj Kanuri has been running the fund for 3 years and currently receives a manager quality ranking of 7 (0=worst, 99=best). This fund offers only a moderate level of risk but investors looking for strong performance are still waiting.

Data Date	Investment Rating	Net Assets ($Mil)	Price	Performance Rating/Pts	Total Return Y-T-D	Risk Rating/Pts
12-12	D	320.50	36.02	D- / 1.4	2.17%	C+ / 6.5
2011	C-	418.90	35.03	C / 4.6	2.80%	B- / 7.0
2010	D	1,054.70	46.14	C- / 3.5	10.49%	C- / 4.2
2009	C+	753.72	42.46	B / 8.1	73.91%	C / 4.3

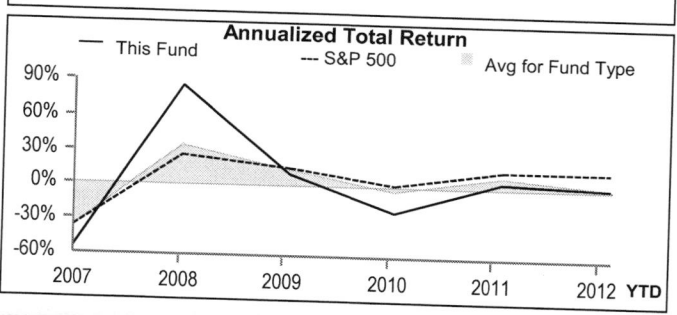

*Guggenheim British Pound Sterlin (FXB)

D+ **Weak**

Fund Family: Guggenheim Investments
Fund Type: Foreign
Inception Date: June 26, 2006

Major Rating Factors:

Disappointing performance is the major factor driving the D+ (Weak) TheStreet.com Investment Rating for *Guggenheim British Pound Sterlin. The fund currently has a performance rating of D- (Weak) based on an annualized return of -0.56% over the last three years and a total return of -0.81% year to date 2012. Factored into the performance evaluation is an expense ratio of 0.40% (very low).

The fund's risk rating is currently B (Good). It carries a beta of 0.35, meaning the fund's expected move will be 3.5% for every 10% move in the market. Volatility, as measured by both the semi-deviation and a drawdown factor, is considered low. As of December 31, 2012, *Guggenheim British Pound Sterlin traded at a premium of .79% above its net asset value, which is worse than its one-year historical average premium of .04%.

This fund has been team managed for 7 years and currently receives a manager quality ranking of 39 (0=worst, 99=best). This fund offers only a moderate level of risk but investors looking for strong performance are still waiting.

Data Date	Investment Rating	Net Assets ($Mil)	Price	Performance Rating/Pts	Total Return Y-T-D	Risk Rating/Pts
12-12	D+	64.30	160.71	D- / 1.4	-0.81%	B / 8.9
2011	C-	92.50	154.10	D / 1.9	-0.70%	B / 8.8
2010	D+	124.50	155.77	D- / 1.0	-3.33%	B- / 7.1
2009	C-	157.26	161.13	D / 1.6	11.30%	B- / 7.3

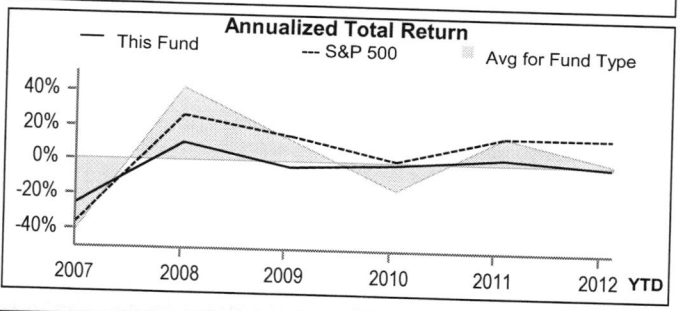

*Guggenheim Canadian Dollar Shs (FXC)

C- **Fair**

Fund Family: Guggenheim Investments
Fund Type: Foreign
Inception Date: June 26, 2006

Major Rating Factors:

Disappointing performance is the major factor driving the C- (Fair) TheStreet.com Investment Rating for *Guggenheim Canadian Dollar Shs. The fund currently has a performance rating of D (Weak) based on an annualized return of 1.53% over the last three years and a total return of 0.89% year to date 2012. Factored into the performance evaluation is an expense ratio of 0.40% (very low).

The fund's risk rating is currently B+ (Good). It carries a beta of 0.39, meaning the fund's expected move will be 3.9% for every 10% move in the market. Volatility, as measured by both the semi-deviation and a drawdown factor, is considered very low. As of December 31, 2012, *Guggenheim Canadian Dollar Shs traded at a discount of .94% below its net asset value, which is better than its one-year historical average discount of .04%.

This fund has been team managed for 7 years and currently receives a manager quality ranking of 55 (0=worst, 99=best). This fund offers only a moderate level of risk but investors looking for strong performance are still waiting.

Data Date	Investment Rating	Net Assets ($Mil)	Price	Performance Rating/Pts	Total Return Y-T-D	Risk Rating/Pts
12-12	C-	499.40	100.14	D / 1.8	0.89%	B+ / 9.0
2011	C-	576.20	97.62	D+ / 2.5	-0.83%	B+ / 9.0
2010	C	590.50	99.54	C- / 3.0	4.97%	B- / 7.4
2009	C+	489.42	94.85	C / 4.6	15.22%	B- / 7.5

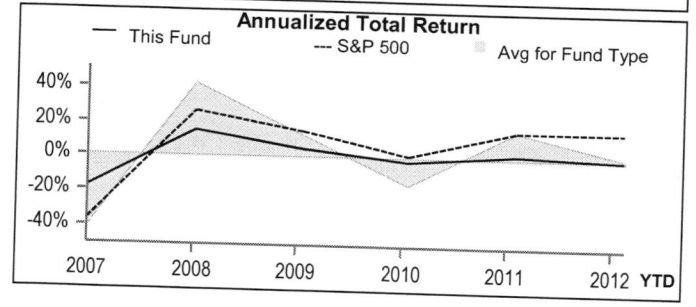

*Guggenheim Canadian Energy Inc E (ENY)

D-   **Weak**

Fund Family: Guggenheim Funds Investment Advisor
Fund Type: Energy/Natural Resources
Inception Date: July 3, 2007

Major Rating Factors:
Disappointing performance is the major factor driving the D- (Weak) TheStreet.com Investment Rating for *Guggenheim Canadian Energy Inc E. The fund currently has a performance rating of D- (Weak) based on an annualized return of -1.33% over the last three years and a total return of 0.97% year to date 2012. Factored into the performance evaluation is an expense ratio of 0.70% (very low).

The fund's risk rating is currently C+ (Fair). It carries a beta of 1.19, meaning it is expected to move 11.9% for every 10% move in the market. Volatility, as measured by both the semi-deviation and a drawdown factor, is considered low. As of December 31, 2012, *Guggenheim Canadian Energy Inc E traded at a discount of 1.59% below its net asset value, which is better than its one-year historical average discount of .32%.

Saroj Kanuri has been running the fund for 3 years and currently receives a manager quality ranking of 13 (0=worst, 99=best). This fund offers only a moderate level of risk but investors looking for strong performance are still waiting.

Data Date	Investment Rating	Net Assets ($Mil)	Price	Perfor-mance Rating/Pts	Total Return Y-T-D	Risk Rating/Pts
12-12	D-	75.60	15.52	D- / 1.2	0.97%	C+ / 6.3
2011	C-	114.70	16.85	C / 5.0	1.42%	C+ / 6.4
2010	D	97.90	20.15	C- / 4.0	22.45%	C- / 3.6
2009	B+	37.79	16.98	A / 9.4	50.27%	C / 4.3

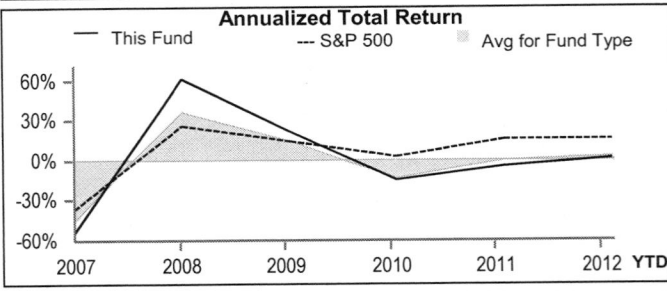

Annualized Total Return

---

*Guggenheim China All-Cap ETF (YAO)

D+   **Weak**

Fund Family: Guggenheim Funds Investment Advisor
Fund Type: Foreign
Inception Date: October 19, 2009

Major Rating Factors: *Guggenheim China All-Cap ETF receives a TheStreet.com Investment Rating of D+ (Weak). The fund currently has a performance rating of C- (Fair) based on an annualized return of 3.42% over the last three years and a total return of 2.66% year to date 2012. Factored into the performance evaluation is an expense ratio of 0.70% (very low).

The fund's risk rating is currently C+ (Fair). It carries a beta of 1.00, meaning that its performance tracks fairly well with that of the overall stock market. Volatility, as measured by both the semi-deviation and a drawdown factor, is considered low. As of December 31, 2012, *Guggenheim China All-Cap ETF traded at a discount of 2.03% below its net asset value, which is better than its one-year historical average discount of .30%.

Saroj Kanuri has been running the fund for 3 years and currently receives a manager quality ranking of 38 (0=worst, 99=best). If you desire an average level of risk, then this fund may be an option.

Data Date	Investment Rating	Net Assets ($Mil)	Price	Perfor-mance Rating/Pts	Total Return Y-T-D	Risk Rating/Pts
12-12	D+	55.30	25.54	C- / 3.2	2.66%	C+ / 6.4
2011	D-	53.80	21.35	E+ / 0.8	0.76%	C+ / 6.5
2010	A	84.10	27.16	B / 8.1	8.81%	B- / 7.9

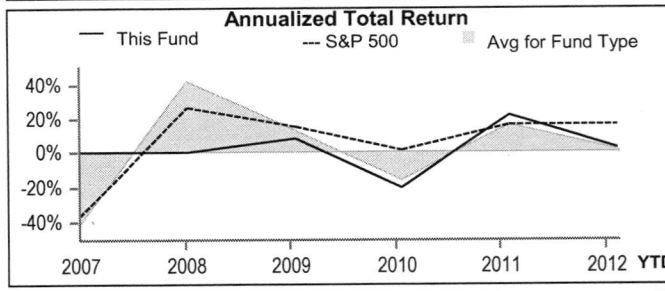

Annualized Total Return

---

*Guggenheim China Real Estate ETF (TAO)

B   **Good**

Fund Family: Guggenheim Funds Investment Advisor
Fund Type: Growth and Income
Inception Date: December 18, 2007

Major Rating Factors:
Exceptional performance is the major factor driving the B (Good) TheStreet.com Investment Rating for *Guggenheim China Real Estate ETF. The fund currently has a performance rating of A (Excellent) based on an annualized return of 12.72% over the last three years and a total return of 4.03% year to date 2012. Factored into the performance evaluation is an expense ratio of 0.70% (very low).

The fund's risk rating is currently C+ (Fair). It carries a beta of 1.40, meaning it is expected to move 14.0% for every 10% move in the market. Volatility, as measured by both the semi-deviation and a drawdown factor, is considered low. As of December 31, 2012, *Guggenheim China Real Estate ETF traded at a discount of 2.85% below its net asset value, which is better than its one-year historical average premium of .02%.

Saroj Kanuri has been running the fund for 3 years and currently receives a manager quality ranking of 20 (0=worst, 99=best). If you desire only a moderate level of risk and strong performance, then this fund is an excellent option.

Data Date	Investment Rating	Net Assets ($Mil)	Price	Perfor-mance Rating/Pts	Total Return Y-T-D	Risk Rating/Pts
12-12	B	79.60	22.85	A / 9.3	4.03%	C+ / 6.0
2011	D	17.90	14.64	C- / 3.2	0.07%	C+ / 6.1
2010	D-	65.40	19.94	D / 2.0	10.10%	C- / 4.0
2009	B	39.80	18.15	A / 9.3	68.65%	C- / 4.2

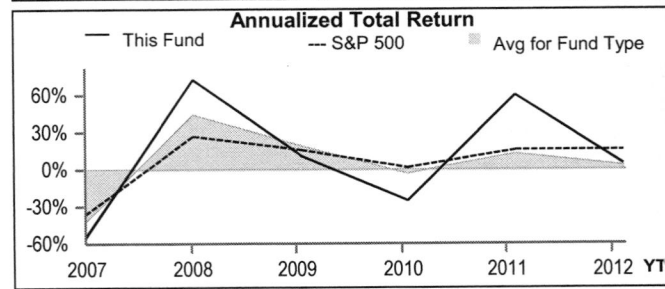

Annualized Total Return

*Guggenheim China Small Cap ETF (HAO)

D-   **Weak**

Fund Family: Guggenheim Funds Investment Advisor
Fund Type: Foreign
Inception Date: January 30, 2008

Major Rating Factors:

Disappointing performance is the major factor driving the D- (Weak) TheStreet.com Investment Rating for *Guggenheim China Small Cap ETF. The fund currently has a performance rating of D+ (Weak) based on an annualized return of -1.27% over the last three years and a total return of 5.09% year to date 2012. Factored into the performance evaluation is an expense ratio of 0.75% (very low).

The fund's risk rating is currently C (Fair). It carries a beta of 1.11, meaning it is expected to move 11.1% for every 10% move in the market. Volatility, as measured by both the semi-deviation and a drawdown factor, is considered average. As of December 31, 2012, *Guggenheim China Small Cap ETF traded at a discount of 3.69% below its net asset value, which is better than its one-year historical average premium of .19%.

Saroj Kanuri has been running the fund for 3 years and currently receives a manager quality ranking of 20 (0=worst, 99=best). This fund offers an average level of risk but investors looking for strong performance will be frustrated.

Data Date	Investment Rating	Net Assets ($Mil)	Price	Performance Rating/Pts	Total Return Y-T-D	Risk Rating/Pts
12-12	D-	302.20	23.99	D+ / 2.8	5.09%	C / 4.3
2011	D-	142.00	19.30	C- / 3.2	-1.55%	C / 4.4
2010	B-	438.70	30.06	B+ / 8.9	15.32%	C- / 3.7
2009	B	62.94	26.33	A+ / 9.8	88.42%	C- / 3.5

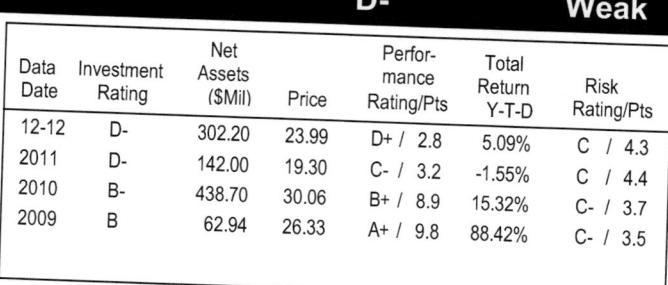

Annualized Total Return

*Guggenheim China Technology ETF (CQQQ)

D-   **Weak**

Fund Family: Guggenheim Funds Investment Advisor
Fund Type: Foreign
Inception Date: December 8, 2009

Major Rating Factors:

Disappointing performance is the major factor driving the D- (Weak) TheStreet.com Investment Rating for *Guggenheim China Technology ETF. The fund currently has a performance rating of D (Weak) based on an annualized return of -2.61% over the last three years and a total return of 8.06% year to date 2012. Factored into the performance evaluation is an expense ratio of 0.70% (very low).

The fund's risk rating is currently C+ (Fair). It carries a beta of 1.15, meaning it is expected to move 11.5% for every 10% move in the market. Volatility, as measured by both the semi-deviation and a drawdown factor, is considered low. As of December 31, 2012, *Guggenheim China Technology ETF traded at a discount of 7.27% below its net asset value, which is better than its one-year historical average discount of .37%.

Saroj Kanuri has been running the fund for 3 years and currently receives a manager quality ranking of 16 (0=worst, 99=best). This fund offers only a moderate level of risk but investors looking for strong performance are still waiting.

Data Date	Investment Rating	Net Assets ($Mil)	Price	Performance Rating/Pts	Total Return Y-T-D	Risk Rating/Pts
12-12	D-	17.60	22.32	D / 1.8	8.06%	C+ / 5.6
2011	D-	21.60	20.43	E+ / 0.6	-0.10%	C+ / 5.8
2010	A	37.10	27.58	B / 8.0	7.08%	B- / 7.4

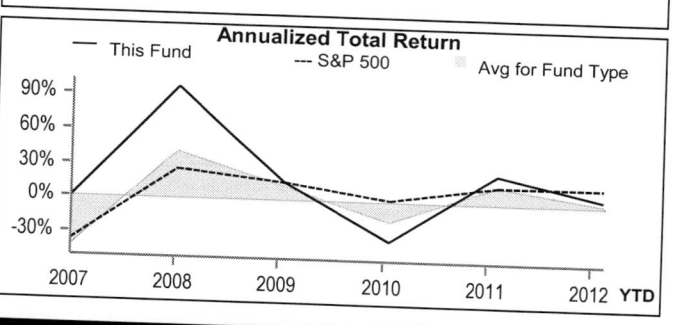

Annualized Total Return

*Guggenheim Chinese Renminbi Shs (FXCH)

C-   **Fair**

Fund Family: Guggenheim Investments
Fund Type: Growth and Income
Inception Date: September 29, 2011

Major Rating Factors:

Disappointing performance is the major factor driving the C- (Fair) TheStreet.com Investment Rating for *Guggenheim Chinese Renminbi Shs. The fund currently has a performance rating of D (Weak) based on an annualized return of 0.00% over the last three years and a total return of 0.56% year to date 2012.

The fund's risk rating is currently B+ (Good). It carries a beta of 0.00, meaning the fund's expected move will be 0.0% for every 10% move in the market. Volatility, as measured by both the semi-deviation and a drawdown factor, is considered very low. As of December 31, 2012, *Guggenheim Chinese Renminbi Shs traded at a discount of .93% below its net asset value, which is better than its one-year historical average premium of .47%.

Joseph Arruda has been running the fund for 2 years and currently receives a manager quality ranking of 55 (0=worst, 99=best). This fund offers only a moderate level of risk but investors looking for strong performance are still waiting.

Data Date	Investment Rating	Net Assets ($Mil)	Price	Performance Rating/Pts	Total Return Y-T-D	Risk Rating/Pts
12-12	C-	4.00	79.80	D / 1.7	0.56%	B+ / 9.8

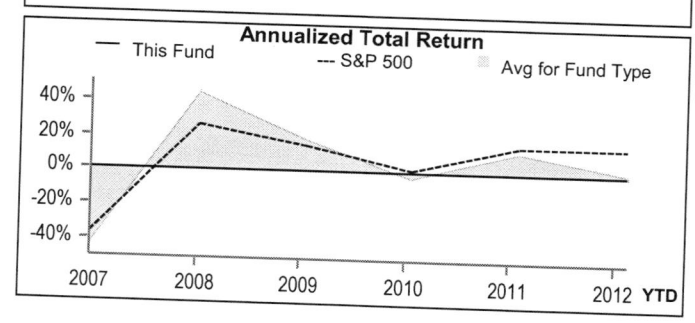

Annualized Total Return

*Guggenheim Defensive Equity ETF (DEF)

B-   **Good**

Fund Family: Guggenheim Funds Investment Advisor
Fund Type: Income
Inception Date: December 15, 2006

Major Rating Factors: *Guggenheim Defensive Equity ETF receives a TheStreet.com Investment Rating of B- (Good). The fund currently has a performance rating of C (Fair) based on an annualized return of 13.83% over the last three years and a total return of 2.85% year to date 2012. Factored into the performance evaluation is an expense ratio of 0.65% (very low).

The fund's risk rating is currently B+ (Good). It carries a beta of 0.52, meaning the fund's expected move will be 5.2% for every 10% move in the market. Volatility, as measured by both the semi-deviation and a drawdown factor, is considered very low. As of December 31, 2012, *Guggenheim Defensive Equity ETF traded at a discount of 2.86% below its net asset value, which is better than its one-year historical average discount of .01%.

Saroj Kanuri has been running the fund for 3 years and currently receives a manager quality ranking of 84 (0=worst, 99=best). If you desire an average level of risk, then this fund may be an option.

Data Date	Investment Rating	Net Assets ($Mil)	Price	Performance Rating/Pts	Total Return Y-T-D	Risk Rating/Pts
12-12	B-	67.10	28.57	C / 5.4	2.85%	B+ / 9.2
2011	B-	47.60	27.34	C+ / 6.6	-0.84%	B / 8.5
2010	C+	19.60	24.53	C / 5.4	18.77%	C+ / 6.0
2009	C-	15.52	20.86	D+ / 2.5	19.95%	C+ / 6.3

Annualized Total Return

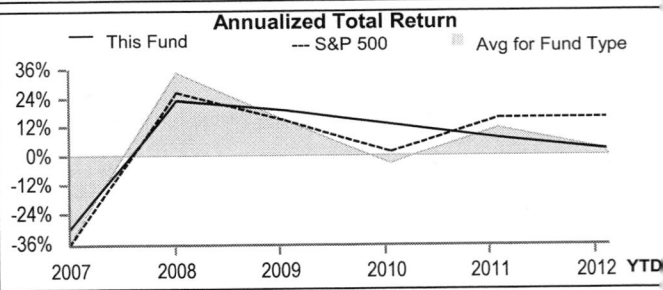

*Guggenheim Enhanced Core Bond ET (GIY)

C-   **Fair**

Fund Family: Guggenheim Funds Investment Advisor
Fund Type: General - Investment Grade
Inception Date: February 12, 2008

Major Rating Factors:
Disappointing performance is the major factor driving the C- (Fair) TheStreet.com Investment Rating for *Guggenheim Enhanced Core Bond ET. The fund currently has a performance rating of D+ (Weak) based on an annualized return of 6.64% over the last three years and a total return of -0.29% year to date 2012. Factored into the performance evaluation is an expense ratio of 0.27% (very low).

The fund's risk rating is currently B+ (Good). It carries a beta of 0.85, meaning the fund's expected move will be 8.5% for every 10% move in the market. Volatility, as measured by both the semi-deviation and a drawdown factor, is considered very low. As of December 31, 2012, *Guggenheim Enhanced Core Bond ET traded at a discount of .02% below its net asset value, which is worse than its one-year historical average discount of .09%.

David C. Kwan has been running the fund for 5 years and currently receives a manager quality ranking of 61 (0=worst, 99=best). This fund offers only a moderate level of risk but investors looking for strong performance are still waiting.

Data Date	Investment Rating	Net Assets ($Mil)	Price	Performance Rating/Pts	Total Return Y-T-D	Risk Rating/Pts
12-12	C-	5.20	51.75	D+ / 2.6	-0.29%	B+ / 9.4
2011	C	5.20	51.81	C- / 3.8	-0.86%	B / 8.9
2010	B-	10.40	51.71	C / 4.3	8.30%	B / 8.2
2009	B	5.04	49.00	C / 5.3	11.22%	B / 8.4

Annualized Total Return

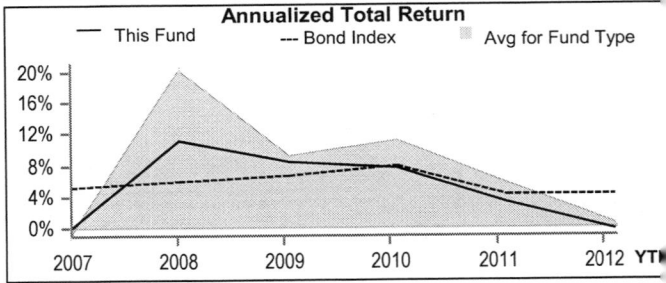

*Guggenheim Enhanced Sh Bd ETF (GSY)

C-   **Fair**

Fund Family: Guggenheim Funds Investment Advisor
Fund Type: Growth
Inception Date: February 12, 2008

Major Rating Factors:
Disappointing performance is the major factor driving the C- (Fair) TheStreet.com Investment Rating for *Guggenheim Enhanced Sh Bd ETF. The fund currently has a performance rating of D- (Weak) based on an annualized return of 0.51% over the last three years and a total return of 0.08% year to date 2012. Factored into the performance evaluation is an expense ratio of 0.26% (very low).

The fund's risk rating is currently B+ (Good). It carries a beta of 0.00, meaning the fund's expected move will be 0.0% for every 10% move in the market. Volatility, as measured by both the semi-deviation and a drawdown factor, is considered very low. As of December 31, 2012, *Guggenheim Enhanced Sh Bd ETF traded at a discount of .14% below its net asset value, which is better than its one-year historical average discount of .02%.

Anne Walsh has been running the fund for 2 years and currently receives a manager quality ranking of 56 (0=worst, 99=best). This fund offers only a moderate level of risk but investors looking for strong performance are still waiting.

Data Date	Investment Rating	Net Assets ($Mil)	Price	Performance Rating/Pts	Total Return Y-T-D	Risk Rating/Pts
12-12	C-	225.30	50.05	D- / 1.5	0.08%	B+ / 9.9
2011	C-	14.90	49.66	D / 2.0	-0.02%	B+ / 9.9
2010	C	5.00	49.77	D / 2.2	-0.17%	B+ / 9.0
2009	C	9.97	49.86	D / 1.9	0.06%	B+ / 9.1

Annualized Total Return

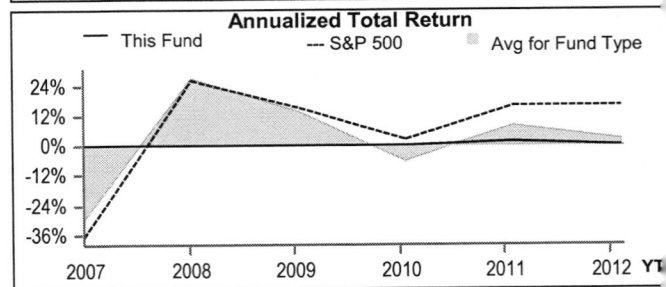

*Guggenheim Euro Shares (FXE)

D **Weak**

Fund Family: Guggenheim Investments
Fund Type: Foreign
Inception Date: December 9, 2005

Major Rating Factors:

Disappointing performance is the major factor driving the D (Weak) TheStreet.com Investment Rating for *Guggenheim Euro Shares. The fund currently has a performance rating of D- (Weak) based on an annualized return of -2.60% over the last three years and a total return of 1.07% year to date 2012. Factored into the performance evaluation is an expense ratio of 0.40% (very low).

The fund's risk rating is currently B (Good). It carries a beta of 0.53, meaning the fund's expected move will be 5.3% for every 10% move in the market. Volatility, as measured by the semi-deviation and a drawdown factor, is considered low. As of December 31, 2012, *Guggenheim Euro Shares traded at a discount of 1.12% below its net asset value, which is better than its one-year historical average premium of .03%.

This fund has been team managed for 8 years and currently receives a manager quality ranking of 23 (0=worst, 99=best). This fund offers only a moderate level of risk but investors looking for strong performance are still waiting.

Data Date	Investment Rating	Net Assets ($Mil)	Price	Performance Rating/Pts	Total Return Y-T-D	Risk Rating/Pts
12-12	D	222.40	130.96	D- / 1.3	1.07%	B / 8.2
2011	D+	278.00	128.92	D / 1.6	-1.71%	B / 8.2
2010	D+	354.10	133.09	D- / 1.5	-6.87%	B- / 7.2
2009	C	616.52	142.91	C- / 3.5	3.32%	B- / 7.9

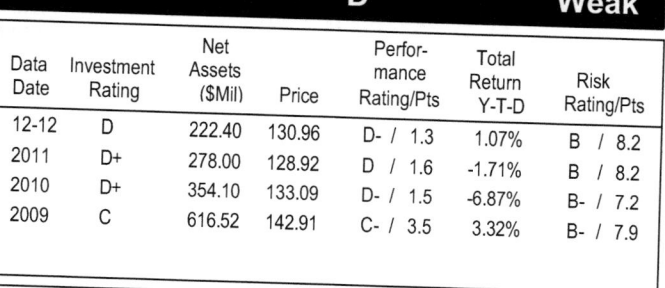

*Guggenheim Frontier Markets ETF (FRN)

D+ **Weak**

Fund Family: Guggenheim Funds Investment Advisor
Fund Type: Global
Inception Date: June 12, 2008

Major Rating Factors:

Disappointing performance is the major factor driving the D+ (Weak) TheStreet.com Investment Rating for *Guggenheim Frontier Markets ETF. The fund currently has a performance rating of D+ (Weak) based on an annualized return of 4.50% over the last three years and a total return of 3.64% year to date 2012. Factored into the performance evaluation is an expense ratio of 0.70% (very low).

The fund's risk rating is currently B- (Good). It carries a beta of 0.70, meaning the fund's expected move will be 7.0% for every 10% move in the market. Volatility, as measured by both the semi-deviation and a drawdown factor, is considered low. As of December 31, 2012, *Guggenheim Frontier Markets ETF traded at a discount of 2.99% below its net asset value, which is better than its one-year historical average premium of .45%.

Saroj Kanuri has been running the fund for 3 years and currently receives a manager quality ranking of 68 (0=worst, 99=best). This fund offers only a moderate level of risk but investors looking for strong performance are still waiting.

Data Date	Investment Rating	Net Assets ($Mil)	Price	Performance Rating/Pts	Total Return Y-T-D	Risk Rating/Pts
12-12	D+	156.10	19.76	D+ / 2.9	3.64%	B- / 7.2
2011	C-	121.20	18.14	C / 4.4	1.93%	B- / 7.3
2010	B+	242.00	24.44	A+ / 9.6	33.59%	C / 4.5
2009	B+	15.07	18.35	A- / 9.0	50.14%	C / 4.7

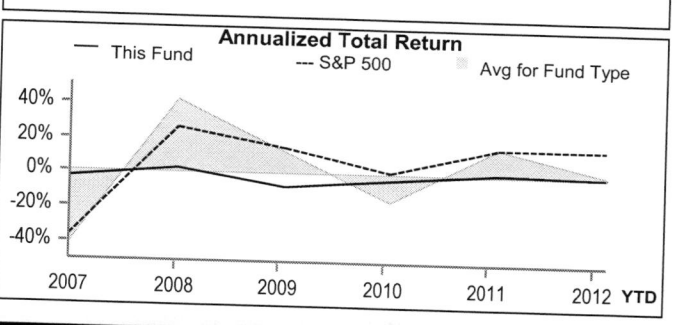

*Guggenheim Insider Sentiment ETF (NFO)

C+ **Fair**

Fund Family: Guggenheim Funds Investment Advisor
Fund Type: Income
Inception Date: September 21, 2006

Major Rating Factors: Middle of the road best describes *Guggenheim Insider Sentiment ETF whose TheStreet.com Investment Rating is currently a C+ (Fair). The fund currently has a performance rating of C+ (Fair) based on an annualized return of 12.45% over the last three years and a total return of 4.28% year to date 2012. Factored into the performance evaluation is an expense ratio of 0.65% (very low).

The fund's risk rating is currently B- (Good). It carries a beta of 1.28, meaning it is expected to move 12.8% for every 10% move in the market. Volatility, as measured by both the semi-deviation and a drawdown factor, is considered low. As of December 31, 2012, *Guggenheim Insider Sentiment ETF traded at a discount of 4.14% below its net asset value, which is better than its one-year historical average discount of .02%.

Saroj Kanuri has been running the fund for 3 years and currently receives a manager quality ranking of 33 (0=worst, 99=best). If you desire an average level of risk, then this fund may be an option.

Data Date	Investment Rating	Net Assets ($Mil)	Price	Performance Rating/Pts	Total Return Y-T-D	Risk Rating/Pts
12-12	C+	96.00	34.75	C+ / 6.0	4.28%	B- / 7.6
2011	C+	97.00	30.79	C+ / 6.8	2.50%	B- / 7.5
2010	B	127.00	32.65	B / 7.9	25.48%	C / 5.4
2009	C	56.46	25.91	C+ / 5.8	45.07%	C / 5.5

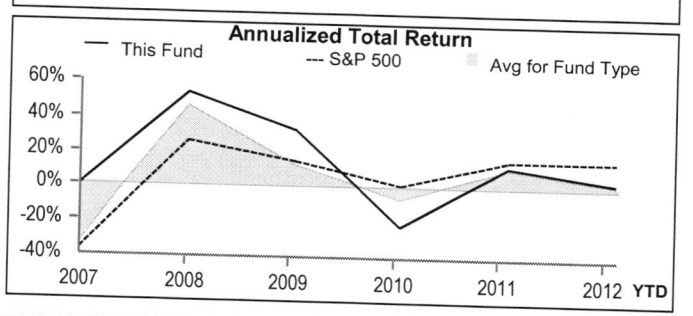

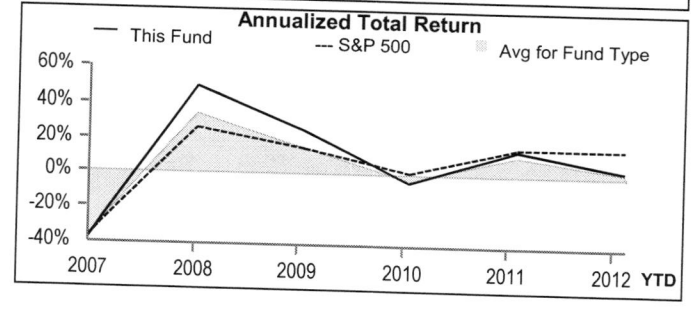

* Denotes ETF Fund

*Guggenheim Intl Multi-Asset Inc (HGI)

D+   **Weak**

Fund Family: Guggenheim Funds Investment Advisor
Fund Type: Foreign
Inception Date: July 11, 2007

Major Rating Factors:
Disappointing performance is the major factor driving the D+ (Weak) TheStreet.com Investment Rating for *Guggenheim Intl Multi-Asset Inc. The fund currently has a performance rating of D+ (Weak) based on an annualized return of 2.86% over the last three years and a total return of 2.67% year to date 2012. Factored into the performance evaluation is an expense ratio of 0.70% (very low).

The fund's risk rating is currently B- (Good). It carries a beta of 0.97, meaning that its performance tracks fairly well with that of the overall stock market. Volatility, as measured by both the semi-deviation and a drawdown factor, is considered low. As of December 31, 2012, *Guggenheim Intl Multi-Asset Inc traded at a discount of 2.55% below its net asset value, which is better than its one-year historical average premium of .30%.

Saroj Kanuri has been running the fund for 3 years and currently receives a manager quality ranking of 41 (0=worst, 99=best). This fund offers only a moderate level of risk but investors looking for strong performance are still waiting.

Data Date	Investment Rating	Net Assets ($Mil)	Price	Perfor- mance Rating/Pts	Total Return Y-T-D	Risk Rating/Pts
12-12	D+	118.90	16.84	D+ / 2.5	2.67%	B- / 7.6
2011	C-	85.70	16.22	C- / 4.2	0.49%	B- / 7.3
2010	C-	80.30	19.24	C- / 3.8	12.13%	C / 5.4
2009	B	14.31	17.90	A- / 9.1	45.77%	C / 4.5

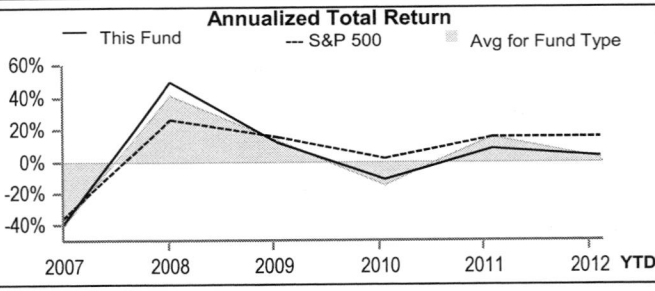

*Guggenheim Inverse 2x S&P 500 ET (RSW)

E   **Very Weak**

Fund Family: Guggenheim Investments
Fund Type: Income
Inception Date: November 5, 2007

Major Rating Factors: Very poor performance is the major factor driving the E (Very Weak) TheStreet.com Investment Rating for *Guggenheim Inverse 2x S&P 500 ET. The fund currently has a performance rating of E (Very Weak) based on an annualized return of -27.61% over the last three years and a total return of -6.97% year to date 2012. Factored into the performance evaluation is an expense ratio of 0.71% (very low).

The fund's risk rating is currently C- (Fair). It carries a beta of -1.91, meaning the fund's expected move will be -19.1% for every 10% move in the market. Volatility, as measured by both the semi-deviation and a drawdown factor, is considered average. As of December 31, 2012, *Guggenheim Inverse 2x S&P 500 ET traded at a premium of 7.59% above its net asset value.

Michael Dellapa has been running the fund for 6 years and currently receives a manager quality ranking of 11 (0=worst, 99=best). This fund offers an average level of risk but investors looking for strong performance will be frustrated.

Data Date	Investment Rating	Net Assets ($Mil)	Price	Perfor- mance Rating/Pts	Total Return Y-T-D	Risk Rating/Pts
12-12	E	36.30	22.10	E / 0.3	-6.97%	C- / 3.8
2011	E	51.60	31.20	E / 0.5	-3.08%	C- / 3.4
2010	E	67.50	38.53	E / 0.4	-31.79%	D+ / 2.9
2009	E	97.55	56.49	E- / 0.2	-47.15%	C- / 4.0

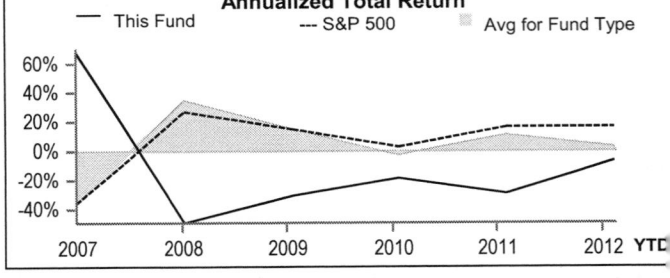

*Guggenheim Japanese Yen Trust (FXY)

D+   **Weak**

Fund Family: Guggenheim Investments
Fund Type: Foreign
Inception Date: February 13, 2007

Major Rating Factors:
Disappointing performance is the major factor driving the D+ (Weak) TheStreet.com Investment Rating for *Guggenheim Japanese Yen Trust. The fund currently has a performance rating of D- (Weak) based on an annualized return of 0.23% over the last three years and a total return of -2.75% year to date 2012. Factored into the performance evaluation is an expense ratio of 0.40% (very low).

The fund's risk rating is currently B (Good). It carries a beta of -0.10, meaning the fund's expected move will be -1.0% for every 10% move in the market. Volatility, as measured by both the semi-deviation and a drawdown factor, is considered low. As of December 31, 2012, *Guggenheim Japanese Yen Trust traded at a premium of 2.68% above its net asset value, which is worse than its one-year historical average discount of .04%.

David C. Kwan has been running the fund for 5 years and currently receives a manager quality ranking of 68 (0=worst, 99=best). This fund offers only a moderate level of risk but investors looking for strong performance are still waiting.

Data Date	Investment Rating	Net Assets ($Mil)	Price	Perfor- mance Rating/Pts	Total Return Y-T-D	Risk Rating/Pts
12-12	D+	124.80	113.03	D- / 1.0	-2.75%	B / 8.7
2011	C	729.50	127.93	C- / 3.1	-0.03%	B+ / 9.0
2010	A	207.20	121.75	B- / 7.4	14.20%	B / 8.2
2009	C	553.53	106.61	D / 1.7	-1.09%	B / 8.5

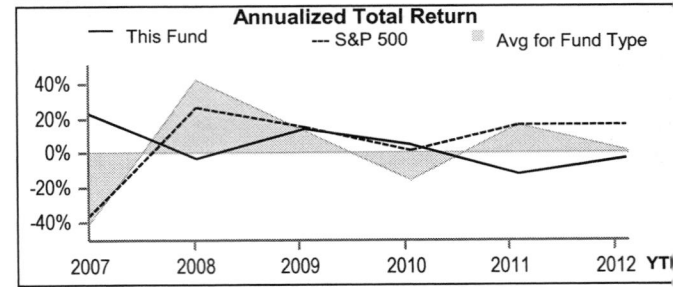

*Guggenheim Mid-Cap Core ETF (CZA)

B-   **Good**

Fund Family: Guggenheim Funds Investment Advisor
Fund Type: Growth
Inception Date: April 2, 2007

Major Rating Factors: *Guggenheim Mid-Cap Core ETF receives a TheStreet.com Investment Rating of B- (Good). The fund currently has a performance rating of C+ (Fair) based on an annualized return of 14.75% over the last three years and a total return of 3.82% year to date 2012. Factored into the performance evaluation is an expense ratio of 0.65% (very low).

The fund's risk rating is currently B (Good). It carries a beta of 0.97, meaning that its performance tracks fairly well with that of the overall stock market. Volatility, as measured by both the semi-deviation and a drawdown factor, is considered low. As of December 31, 2012, *Guggenheim Mid-Cap Core ETF traded at a discount of 3.57% below its net asset value, which is better than its one-year historical average premium of .10%.

Saroj Kanuri has been running the fund for 3 years and currently receives a manager quality ranking of 70 (0=worst, 99=best). If you desire an average level of risk, then this fund may be an option.

Data Date	Investment Rating	Net Assets ($Mil)	Price	Performance Rating/Pts	Total Return Y-T-D	Risk Rating/Pts
12-12	B-	47.30	33.75	C+ / 6.8	3.82%	B / 8.1
2011	B-	26.70	29.75	B- / 7.1	0.91%	B / 8.0
2010	B+	11.50	28.75	B- / 7.1	22.60%	C+ / 6.4
2009	A	4.13	23.61	B+ / 8.9	40.07%	C+ / 5.7

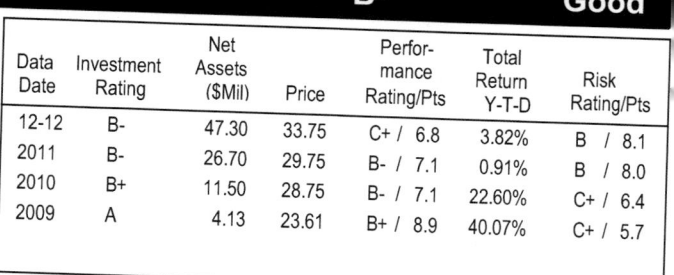

Annualized Total Return

---

*Guggenheim MSCI EAFE Eq Weight E (EWEF)

B+   **Good**

Fund Family: Guggenheim Investments
Fund Type: Emerging Market
Inception Date: December 3, 2010

Major Rating Factors:
Exceptional performance is the major factor driving the B+ (Good) TheStreet.com Investment Rating for *Guggenheim MSCI EAFE Eq Weight E. The fund currently has a performance rating of A (Excellent) based on an annualized return of 0.00% over the last three years and a total return of 3.37% year to date 2012. Factored into the performance evaluation is an expense ratio of 0.56% (very low).

The fund's risk rating is currently B- (Good). It carries a beta of 0.00, meaning the fund's expected move will be 0.0% for every 10% move in the market. Volatility, as measured by both the semi-deviation and a drawdown factor, is considered low. As of December 31, 2012, *Guggenheim MSCI EAFE Eq Weight E traded at a discount of 3.62% below its net asset value, which is better than its one-year historical average discount of .54%.

Adrian G.W. Duffy currently receives a manager quality ranking of 64 (0=worst, 99=best). If you desire only a moderate level of risk and strong performance, then this fund is an excellent option.

Data Date	Investment Rating	Net Assets ($Mil)	Price	Performance Rating/Pts	Total Return Y-T-D	Risk Rating/Pts
12-12	B+	11.60	38.56	A / 9.3	3.37%	B- / 7.0
2011	D	10.30	34.20	E+ / 0.9	-0.26%	B- / 7.0

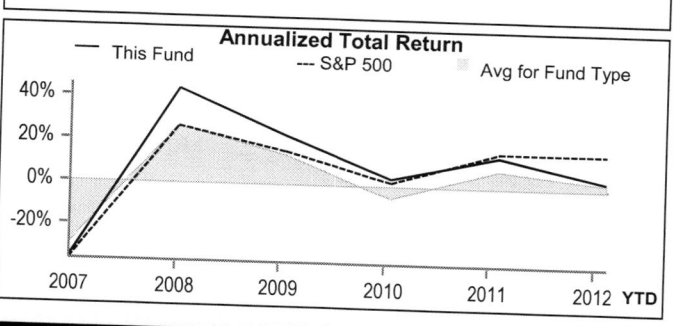

Annualized Total Return

---

*Guggenheim MSCI Em Mkt Eq Weight (EWEM)

C+   **Fair**

Fund Family: Guggenheim Investments
Fund Type: Emerging Market
Inception Date: December 3, 2010

Major Rating Factors: Strong performance is the major factor driving the C+ (Fair) TheStreet.com Investment Rating for *Guggenheim MSCI Em Mkt Eq Weight. The fund currently has a performance rating of B (Good) based on an annualized return of 0.00% over the last three years and a total return of 0.96% year to date 2012. Factored into the performance evaluation is an expense ratio of 0.59% (very low).

The fund's risk rating is currently C+ (Fair). It carries a beta of 0.00, meaning the fund's expected move will be 0.0% for every 10% move in the market. Volatility, as measured by both the semi-deviation and a drawdown factor, is considered low. As of December 31, 2012, *Guggenheim MSCI Em Mkt Eq Weight traded at a discount of 1.65% below its net asset value, which is better than its one-year historical average discount of .18%.

Adrian G.W. Duffy currently receives a manager quality ranking of 41 (0=worst, 99=best). If you desire only a moderate level of risk and strong performance, then this fund is an excellent option.

Data Date	Investment Rating	Net Assets ($Mil)	Price	Performance Rating/Pts	Total Return Y-T-D	Risk Rating/Pts
12-12	C+	14.20	35.73	B / 8.1	0.96%	C+ / 6.0
2011	D-	12.30	30.97	E+ / 0.7	0.65%	C+ / 5.7

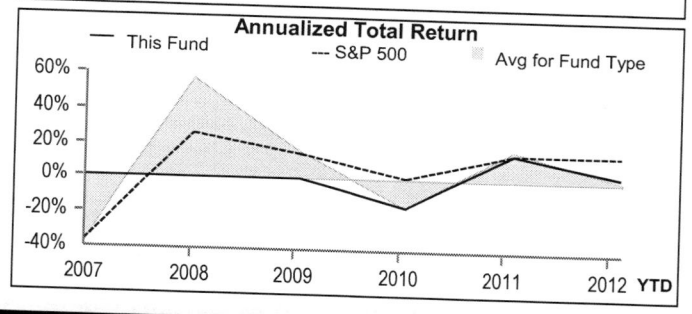

Annualized Total Return

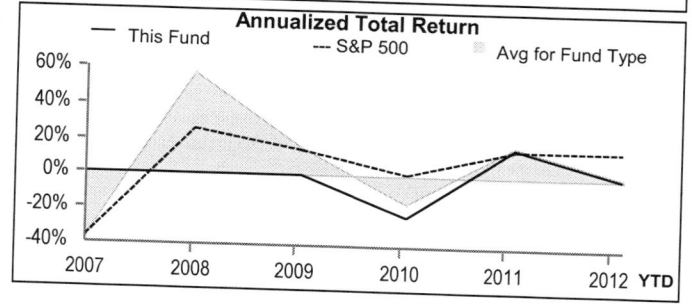

* Denotes ETF Fund

*Guggenheim Multi-Asset Income ET (CVY)

C+   Fair

Fund Family: Guggenheim Funds Investment Advisor
Fund Type: Income
Inception Date: September 21, 2006

Major Rating Factors: Middle of the road best describes *Guggenheim Multi-Asset Income ET whose TheStreet.com Investment Rating is currently a C+ (Fair). The fund currently has a performance rating of C+ (Fair) based on an annualized return of 13.43% over the last three years and a total return of 4.20% year to date 2012. Factored into the performance evaluation is an expense ratio of 0.65% (very low).

The fund's risk rating is currently B (Good). It carries a beta of 0.78, meaning the fund's expected move will be 7.8% for every 10% move in the market. Volatility, as measured by both the semi-deviation and a drawdown factor, is considered low. As of December 31, 2012, *Guggenheim Multi-Asset Income ET traded at a discount of 3.94% below its net asset value, which is better than its one-year historical average premium of .09%.

Saroj Kanuri has been running the fund for 3 years and currently receives a manager quality ranking of 76 (0=worst, 99=best). If you desire an average level of risk, then this fund may be an option.

Data Date	Investment Rating	Net Assets ($Mil)	Price	Performance Rating/Pts	Total Return Y-T-D	Risk Rating/Pts
12-12	C+	794.00	21.92	C+ / 5.9	4.20%	B / 8.5
2011	B	474.80	20.45	B- / 7.5	1.22%	B / 8.0
2010	C	358.70	20.07	C+ / 5.7	16.98%	C / 4.9
2009	D+	121.12	17.92	C- / 3.2	45.19%	C / 5.3

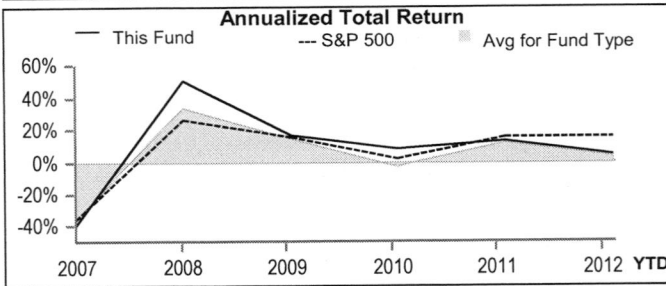

*Guggenheim Raymond James SB1 Eq (RYJ)

C+   Fair

Fund Family: Guggenheim Funds Investment Advisor
Fund Type: Income
Inception Date: May 19, 2006

Major Rating Factors: Middle of the road best describes *Guggenheim Raymond James SB1 Eq whose TheStreet.com Investment Rating is currently a C+ (Fair). The fund currently has a performance rating of C+ (Fair) based on an annualized return of 13.89% over the last three years and a total return of 4.09% year to date 2012. Factored into the performance evaluation is an expense ratio of 0.75% (very low).

The fund's risk rating is currently B- (Good). It carries a beta of 1.25, meaning it is expected to move 12.5% for every 10% move in the market. Volatility, as measured by both the semi-deviation and a drawdown factor, is considered low. As of December 31, 2012, *Guggenheim Raymond James SB1 Eq traded at a discount of 3.85% below its net asset value, which is better than its one-year historical average premium of .04%.

Saroj Kanuri has been running the fund for 3 years and currently receives a manager quality ranking of 43 (0=worst, 99=best). If you desire an average level of risk, then this fund may be an option.

Data Date	Investment Rating	Net Assets ($Mil)	Price	Performance Rating/Pts	Total Return Y-T-D	Risk Rating/Pts
12-12	C+	101.50	23.47	C+ / 6.5	4.09%	B- / 7.6
2011	B-	82.50	20.53	B- / 7.3	2.43%	B- / 7.6
2010	B-	63.40	21.03	B / 8.1	27.45%	C / 4.6
2009	C	39.56	16.51	C+ / 6.1	98.92%	C / 4.7

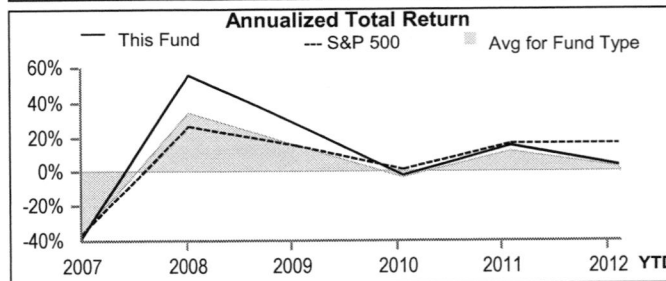

*Guggenheim Russ Top 50 Mega Cap (XLG)

C   Fair

Fund Family: Guggenheim Investments
Fund Type: Income
Inception Date: May 4, 2005

Major Rating Factors: Middle of the road best describes *Guggenheim Russ Top 50 Mega Cap whose TheStreet.com Investment Rating is currently a C (Fair). The fund currently has a performance rating of C (Fair) based on an annualized return of 10.20% over the last three years and a total return of 3.19% year to date 2012. Factored into the performance evaluation is an expense ratio of 0.20% (very low).

The fund's risk rating is currently B (Good). It carries a beta of 0.94, meaning that its performance tracks fairly well with that of the overall stock market. Volatility, as measured by both the semi-deviation and a drawdown factor, is considered low. As of December 31, 2012, *Guggenheim Russ Top 50 Mega Cap traded at a discount of 3.12% below its net asset value, which is better than its one-year historical average premium of .01%.

Adrian G.W. Duffy currently receives a manager quality ranking of 47 (0=worst, 99=best). If you desire an average level of risk, then this fund may be an option.

Data Date	Investment Rating	Net Assets ($Mil)	Price	Performance Rating/Pts	Total Return Y-T-D	Risk Rating/Pts
12-12	C	566.80	102.98	C / 4.4	3.19%	B / 8.0
2011	C	461.20	91.31	C / 4.8	1.91%	B- / 7.9
2010	D+	331.20	89.50	D+ / 2.4	9.32%	C+ / 6.2
2009	D+	307.38	83.59	D / 1.8	16.90%	C+ / 6.2

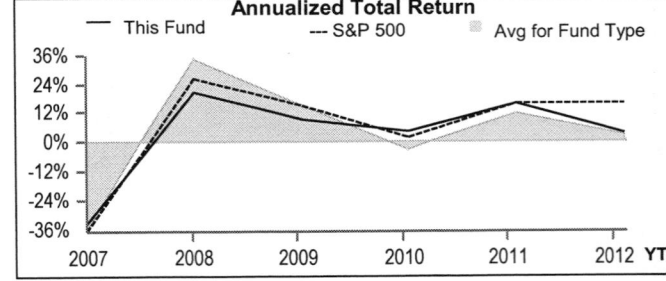

*Guggenheim Russell 1000 Eq Wght (EWRI)

B+   **Good**

Fund Family: Guggenheim Investments
Fund Type: Growth
Inception Date: December 3, 2010

Major Rating Factors: Strong performance is the major factor driving the B+ (Good) TheStreet.com Investment Rating for *Guggenheim Russell 1000 Eq Wght. The fund currently has a performance rating of B+ (Good) based on an annualized return of 0.00% over the last three years and a total return of 4.76% year to date 2012. Factored into the performance evaluation is an expense ratio of 0.41% (very low).

The fund's risk rating is currently B- (Good). It carries a beta of 0.00, meaning the fund's expected move will be 0.0% for every 10% move in the market. Volatility, as measured by both the semi-deviation and a drawdown factor, is considered low. As of December 31, 2012, *Guggenheim Russell 1000 Eq Wght traded at a discount of 4.61% below its net asset value, which is better than its one-year historical average discount of .04%.

Adrian G.W. Duffy currently receives a manager quality ranking of 35 (0=worst, 99=best). If you desire only a moderate level of risk and strong performance, then this fund is an excellent option.

Data Date	Investment Rating	Net Assets ($Mil)	Price	Performance Rating/Pts	Total Return Y-T-D	Risk Rating/Pts
12-12	B+	38.50	34.52	B+ / 8.3	4.76%	B- / 7.8
2011	D+	35.30	30.70	D+ / 2.3	1.82%	B- / 7.8

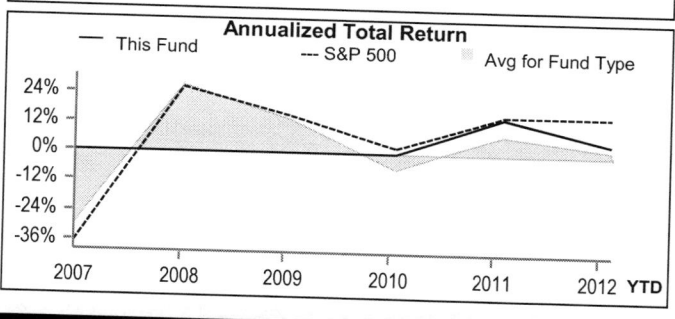

*Guggenheim Russell 2000 Eq Wght (EWRS)

C+   **Fair**

Fund Family: Guggenheim Investments
Fund Type: Growth
Inception Date: December 3, 2010

Major Rating Factors: Middle of the road best describes *Guggenheim Russell 2000 Eq Wght whose TheStreet.com Investment Rating is currently a C+ (Fair). The fund currently has a performance rating of C+ (Fair) based on an annualized return of 0.00% over the last three years and a total return of 5.02% year to date 2012. Factored into the performance evaluation is an expense ratio of 0.41% (very low).

The fund's risk rating is currently B- (Good). It carries a beta of 0.00, meaning the fund's expected move will be 0.0% for every 10% move in the market. Volatility, as measured by both the semi-deviation and a drawdown factor, is considered low. As of December 31, 2012, *Guggenheim Russell 2000 Eq Wght traded at a discount of 5.03% below its net asset value, which is better than its one-year historical average discount of .04%.

Adrian G.W. Duffy currently receives a manager quality ranking of 13 (0=worst, 99=best). If you desire an average level of risk, then this fund may be an option.

Data Date	Investment Rating	Net Assets ($Mil)	Price	Performance Rating/Pts	Total Return Y-T-D	Risk Rating/Pts
12-12	C+	13.10	32.10	C+ / 6.8	5.02%	B- / 7.3
2011	D	17.60	29.36	D / 1.6	1.37%	B- / 7.3

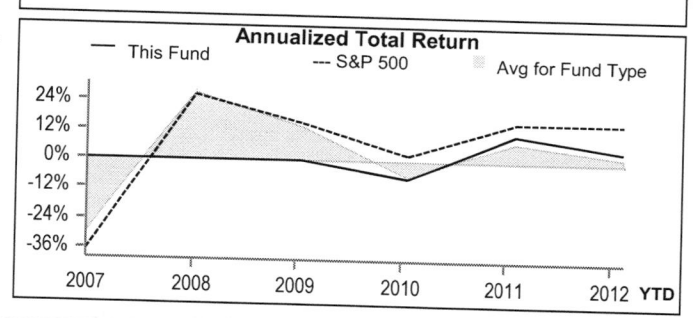

*Guggenheim Russell MC Eq Wght ET (EWRM)

B+   **Good**

Fund Family: Guggenheim Investments
Fund Type: Growth
Inception Date: December 3, 2010

Major Rating Factors: Strong performance is the major factor driving the B+ (Good) TheStreet.com Investment Rating for *Guggenheim Russell MC Eq Wght ET. The fund currently has a performance rating of B+ (Good) based on an annualized return of 0.00% over the last three years and a total return of 3.50% year to date 2012. Factored into the performance evaluation is an expense ratio of 0.41% (very low).

The fund's risk rating is currently B- (Good). It carries a beta of 0.00, meaning the fund's expected move will be 0.0% for every 10% move in the market. Volatility, as measured by both the semi-deviation and a drawdown factor, is considered low. As of December 31, 2012, *Guggenheim Russell MC Eq Wght ET traded at a discount of 3.32% below its net asset value, which is better than its one-year historical average premium of .01%.

Adrian G.W. Duffy currently receives a manager quality ranking of 53 (0=worst, 99=best). If you desire only a moderate level of risk and strong performance, then this fund is an excellent option.

Data Date	Investment Rating	Net Assets ($Mil)	Price	Performance Rating/Pts	Total Return Y-T-D	Risk Rating/Pts
12-12	B+	52.80	35.19	B+ / 8.3	3.50%	B- / 7.8
2011	D+	49.20	30.78	D / 2.2	1.69%	B- / 7.7

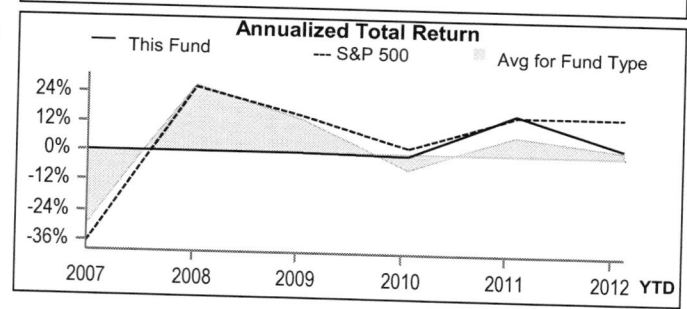

* Denotes ETF Fund

*Guggenheim S&P 500 Eq WgCon Dsc (RCD)

B   **Good**

Fund Family: Guggenheim Investments
Fund Type: Growth
Inception Date: November 1, 2006

Major Rating Factors: Strong performance is the major factor driving the B (Good) TheStreet.com Investment Rating for *Guggenheim S&P 500 Eq WgCon Dsc. The fund currently has a performance rating of B (Good) based on an annualized return of 17.13% over the last three years and a total return of 2.95% year to date 2012. Factored into the performance evaluation is an expense ratio of 0.50% (very low).

The fund's risk rating is currently B- (Good). It carries a beta of 1.20, meaning it is expected to move 12.0% for every 10% move in the market. Volatility, as measured by both the semi-deviation and a drawdown factor, is considered low. As of December 31, 2012, *Guggenheim S&P 500 Eq WgCon Dsc traded at a discount of 2.91% below its net asset value, which is better than its one-year historical average discount of .04%.

Adrian G.W. Duffy currently receives a manager quality ranking of 73 (0=worst, 99=best). If you desire only a moderate level of risk and strong performance, then this fund is an excellent option.

Data Date	Investment Rating	Net Assets ($Mil)	Price	Performance Rating/Pts	Total Return Y-T-D	Risk Rating/Pts
12-12	B	42.50	56.42	B / 7.8	2.95%	B- / 7.9
2011	B	26.00	47.32	B / 8.2	2.07%	B- / 7.7
2010	B+	27.50	45.86	B+ / 8.3	26.07%	C / 5.3
2009	C-	5.36	36.76	C- / 3.9	56.80%	C / 5.2

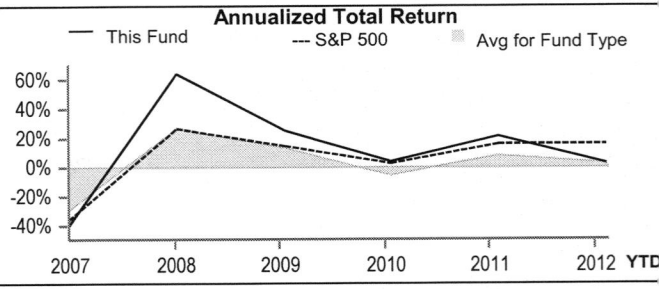

*Guggenheim S&P 500 Eq WgCon St E (RHS)

B-   **Good**

Fund Family: Guggenheim Investments
Fund Type: Growth
Inception Date: November 1, 2006

Major Rating Factors: *Guggenheim S&P 500 Eq WgCon St E receives a TheStreet.com Investment Rating of B- (Good). The fund currently has a performance rating of C+ (Fair) based on an annualized return of 14.59% over the last three years and a total return of 2.50% year to date 2012. Factored into the performance evaluation is an expense ratio of 0.50% (very low).

The fund's risk rating is currently B (Good). It carries a beta of 0.59, meaning the fund's expected move will be 5.9% for every 10% move in the market. Volatility, as measured by both the semi-deviation and a drawdown factor, is considered low. As of December 31, 2012, *Guggenheim S&P 500 Eq WgCon St E traded at a discount of 2.54% below its net asset value, which is better than its one-year historical average premium of .03%.

Adrian G.W. Duffy currently receives a manager quality ranking of 85 (0=worst, 99=best). If you desire an average level of risk, then this fund may be an option.

Data Date	Investment Rating	Net Assets ($Mil)	Price	Performance Rating/Pts	Total Return Y-T-D	Risk Rating/Pts
12-12	B-	41.50	69.18	C+ / 6.1	2.50%	B / 8.9
2011	B	28.40	63.25	C+ / 6.6	-0.95%	B / 8.7
2010	A-	14.30	57.22	B- / 7.3	17.03%	B- / 7.1
2009	C+	8.06	49.92	C / 4.8	26.18%	B- / 7.2

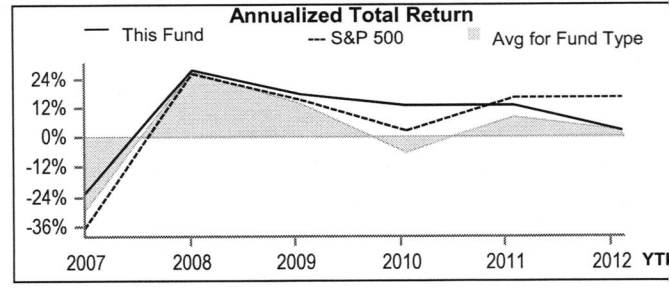

*Guggenheim S&P 500 Eq Wght Engy (RYE)

D+   **Weak**

Fund Family: Guggenheim Investments
Fund Type: Energy/Natural Resources
Inception Date: November 1, 2006

Major Rating Factors: *Guggenheim S&P 500 Eq Wght Engy receives a TheStreet.com Investment Rating of D+ (Weak). The fund currently has a performance rating of C- (Fair) based on an annualized return of 8.60% over the last three years and a total return of 2.96% year to date 2012. Factored into the performance evaluation is an expense ratio of 0.50% (very low).

The fund's risk rating is currently C+ (Fair). It carries a beta of 1.18, meaning it is expected to move 11.8% for every 10% move in the market. Volatility, as measured by both the semi-deviation and a drawdown factor, is considered low. As of December 31, 2012, *Guggenheim S&P 500 Eq Wght Engy traded at a discount of 3.11% below its net asset value, which is better than its one-year historical average discount of .07%.

Adrian G.W. Duffy currently receives a manager quality ranking of 39 (0=worst, 99=best). If you desire an average level of risk, then this fund may be an option.

Data Date	Investment Rating	Net Assets ($Mil)	Price	Performance Rating/Pts	Total Return Y-T-D	Risk Rating/Pts
12-12	D+	29.00	63.85	C- / 3.6	2.96%	C+ / 6.9
2011	C+	33.80	61.61	C+ / 6.6	2.39%	C+ / 6.9
2010	C	22.00	62.84	C+ / 6.0	26.08%	C / 4.9
2009	C	5.55	50.24	C+ / 6.1	38.51%	C / 5.2

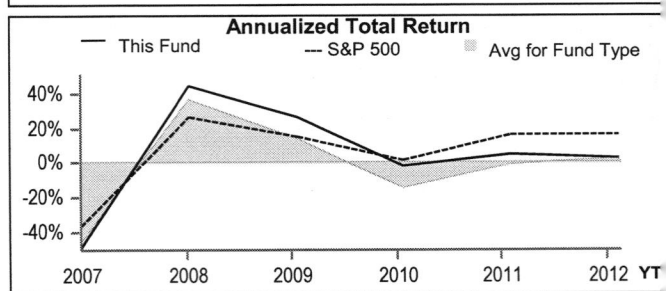

*Guggenheim S&P 500 Eq Wght Finl (RYF)

C+   **Fair**

Fund Family: Guggenheim Investments
Fund Type: Financial Services
Inception Date: November 1, 2006

Major Rating Factors: Middle of the road best describes *Guggenheim S&P 500 Eq Wght Finl whose TheStreet.com Investment Rating is currently a C+ (Fair). The fund currently has a performance rating of C+ (Fair) based on an annualized return of 10.73% over the last three years and a total return of 4.93% year to date 2012. Factored into the performance evaluation is an expense ratio of 0.50% (very low).

The fund's risk rating is currently B- (Good). It carries a beta of 1.01, meaning that its performance tracks fairly well with that of the overall stock market. Volatility, as measured by both the semi-deviation and a drawdown factor, is considered low. As of December 31, 2012, *Guggenheim S&P 500 Eq Wght Finl traded at a discount of 4.55% below its net asset value, which is better than its one-year historical average discount of .07%.

Adrian G.W. Duffy currently receives a manager quality ranking of 69 (0=worst, 99=best). If you desire an average level of risk, then this fund may be an option.

Data Date	Investment Rating	Net Assets ($Mil)	Price	Performance Rating/Pts	Total Return Y-T-D	Risk Rating/Pts
12-12	C+	13.20	29.16	C+ / 6.6	4.93%	B- / 7.5
2011	C-	15.60	23.99	C- / 4.1	2.88%	C+ / 6.9
2010	D-	18.10	27.84	D / 1.8	22.41%	C / 4.3
2009	E+	8.91	23.03	E+ / 0.7	32.97%	C / 4.3

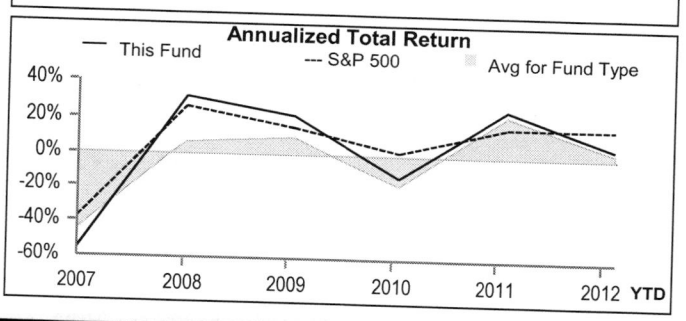

*Guggenheim S&P 500 Eq Wght HC ET (RYH)

B-   **Good**

Fund Family: Guggenheim Investments
Fund Type: Growth
Inception Date: November 1, 2006

Major Rating Factors: *Guggenheim S&P 500 Eq Wght HC ET receives a TheStreet.com Investment Rating of B- (Good). The fund currently has a performance rating of C+ (Fair) based on an annualized return of 12.90% over the last three years and a total return of 4.85% year to date 2012. Factored into the performance evaluation is an expense ratio of 0.50% (very low).

The fund's risk rating is currently B (Good). It carries a beta of 0.79, meaning the fund's expected move will be 7.9% for every 10% move in the market. Volatility, as measured by both the semi-deviation and a drawdown factor, is considered low. As of December 31, 2012, *Guggenheim S&P 500 Eq Wght HC ET traded at a discount of 4.67% below its net asset value.

Adrian G.W. Duffy currently receives a manager quality ranking of 74 (0=worst, 99=best). If you desire an average level of risk, then this fund may be an option.

Data Date	Investment Rating	Net Assets ($Mil)	Price	Performance Rating/Pts	Total Return Y-T-D	Risk Rating/Pts
12-12	B-	63.00	78.39	C+ / 6.6	4.85%	B / 8.2
2011	C+	46.60	66.44	C+ / 6.3	2.14%	B / 8.1
2010	C+	50.30	62.81	C+ / 6.1	10.67%	C+ / 6.7
2009	C+	37.51	56.96	C+ / 5.8	34.99%	C+ / 6.8

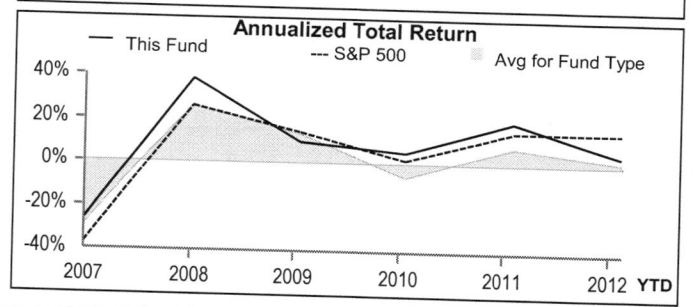

*Guggenheim S&P 500 Eq Wght Ind E (RGI)

C+   **Fair**

Fund Family: Guggenheim Investments
Fund Type: Growth
Inception Date: November 1, 2006

Major Rating Factors: Middle of the road best describes *Guggenheim S&P 500 Eq Wght Ind E whose TheStreet.com Investment Rating is currently a C+ (Fair). The fund currently has a performance rating of C+ (Fair) based on an annualized return of 13.13% over the last three years and a total return of 4.15% year to date 2012. Factored into the performance evaluation is an expense ratio of 0.50% (very low).

The fund's risk rating is currently B- (Good). It carries a beta of 1.17, meaning it is expected to move 11.7% for every 10% move in the market. Volatility, as measured by both the semi-deviation and a drawdown factor, is considered low. As of December 31, 2012, *Guggenheim S&P 500 Eq Wght Ind E traded at a discount of 3.88% below its net asset value, which is better than its one-year historical average discount of .04%.

Adrian G.W. Duffy currently receives a manager quality ranking of 69 (0=worst, 99=best). If you desire an average level of risk, then this fund may be an option.

Data Date	Investment Rating	Net Assets ($Mil)	Price	Performance Rating/Pts	Total Return Y-T-D	Risk Rating/Pts
12-12	C+	17.80	59.03	C+ / 6.2	4.15%	B- / 7.7
2011	C+	13.00	52.03	C+ / 5.6	2.18%	B- / 7.6
2010	C+	48.70	54.21	C+ / 6.5	26.13%	C / 5.5
2009	C-	11.91	43.56	C- / 3.5	29.62%	C+ / 5.9

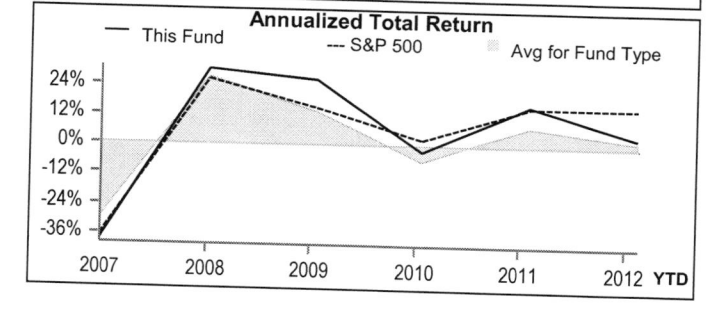

* Denotes ETF Fund

*Guggenheim S&P 500 Eq Wght Mat E (RTM)   C   Fair

Fund Family: Guggenheim Investments
Fund Type: Growth
Inception Date: November 1, 2006

Major Rating Factors: Middle of the road best describes *Guggenheim S&P 500 Eq Wght Mat E whose TheStreet.com Investment Rating is currently a C (Fair). The fund currently has a performance rating of C (Fair) based on an annualized return of 10.06% over the last three years and a total return of 3.69% year to date 2012. Factored into the performance evaluation is an expense ratio of 0.50% (very low).

The fund's risk rating is currently B- (Good). It carries a beta of 1.36, meaning it is expected to move 13.6% for every 10% move in the market. Volatility, as measured by both the semi-deviation and a drawdown factor, is considered low. As of December 31, 2012, *Guggenheim S&P 500 Eq Wght Mat E traded at a discount of 3.54% below its net asset value, which is better than its one-year historical average discount of .08%.

Adrian G.W. Duffy currently receives a manager quality ranking of 23 (0=worst, 99=best). If you desire an average level of risk, then this fund may be an option.

Data Date	Investment Rating	Net Assets ($Mil)	Price	Performance Rating/Pts	Total Return Y-T-D	Risk Rating/Pts
12-12	C	29.20	64.79	C / 4.8	3.69%	B- / 7.3
2011	C+	33.70	56.17	B- / 7.1	3.43%	B- / 7.3
2010	B	40.90	63.00	B / 7.9	23.12%	C / 5.4
2009	B-	5.60	52.73	B- / 7.0	61.99%	C+ / 5.7

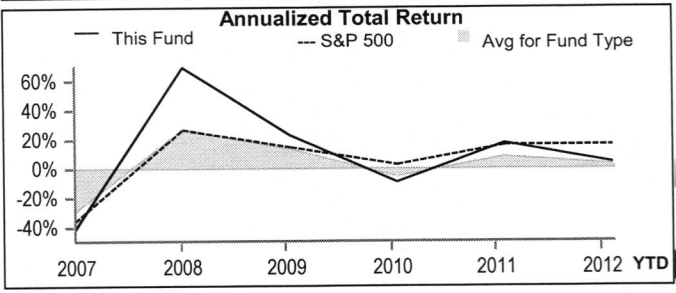

*Guggenheim S&P 500 Eq Wght Tech (RYT)   C-   Fair

Fund Family: Guggenheim Investments
Fund Type: Growth
Inception Date: November 1, 2006

Major Rating Factors: Middle of the road best describes *Guggenheim S&P 500 Eq Wght Tech whose TheStreet.com Investment Rating is currently a C- (Fair). The fund currently has a performance rating of C (Fair) based on an annualized return of 9.27% over the last three years and a total return of 4.18% year to date 2012. Factored into the performance evaluation is an expense ratio of 0.50% (very low).

The fund's risk rating is currently B- (Good). It carries a beta of 1.30, meaning it is expected to move 13.0% for every 10% move in the market. Volatility, as measured by both the semi-deviation and a drawdown factor, is considered low. As of December 31, 2012, *Guggenheim S&P 500 Eq Wght Tech traded at a discount of 4.01% below its net asset value, which is better than its one-year historical average discount of .03%.

Adrian G.W. Duffy currently receives a manager quality ranking of 19 (0=worst, 99=best). If you desire an average level of risk, then this fund may be an option.

Data Date	Investment Rating	Net Assets ($Mil)	Price	Performance Rating/Pts	Total Return Y-T-D	Risk Rating/Pts
12-12	C-	91.50	55.27	C / 4.4	4.18%	B- / 7.2
2011	C+	102.40	49.99	C+ / 6.5	1.66%	B- / 7.4
2010	B-	102.30	53.77	B- / 7.0	17.89%	C / 5.4
2009	C	8.25	45.75	C / 4.8	69.07%	C / 5.5

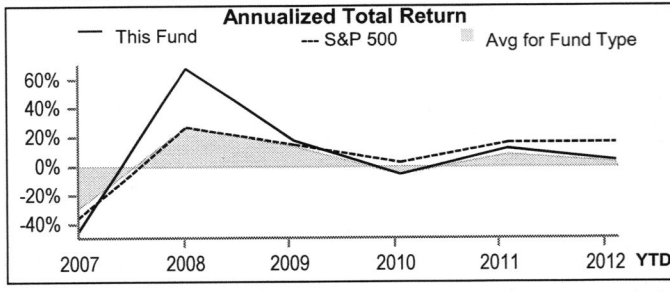

*Guggenheim S&P 500 Eq Wght Util (RYU)   C+   Fair

Fund Family: Guggenheim Investments
Fund Type: Utilities
Inception Date: November 1, 2006

Major Rating Factors: Middle of the road best describes *Guggenheim S&P 500 Eq Wght Util whose TheStreet.com Investment Rating is currently a C+ (Fair). The fund currently has a performance rating of C (Fair) based on an annualized return of 12.63% over the last three years and a total return of 2.65% year to date 2012. Factored into the performance evaluation is an expense ratio of 0.50% (very low).

The fund's risk rating is currently B+ (Good). It carries a beta of 0.90, meaning that its performance tracks fairly well with that of the overall stock market. Volatility, as measured by both the semi-deviation and a drawdown factor, is considered very low. As of December 31, 2012, *Guggenheim S&P 500 Eq Wght Util traded at a discount of 2.79% below its net asset value, which is better than its one-year historical average discount of .04%.

Adrian G.W. Duffy currently receives a manager quality ranking of 71 (0=worst, 99=best). If you desire an average level of risk, then this fund may be an option.

Data Date	Investment Rating	Net Assets ($Mil)	Price	Performance Rating/Pts	Total Return Y-T-D	Risk Rating/Pts
12-12	C+	37.70	57.47	C / 4.7	2.65%	B+ / 9.2
2011	C+	33.30	55.53	C / 4.9	-2.36%	B / 8.8
2010	C-	20.40	51.10	C- / 3.3	12.70%	C+ / 6.7
2009	C-	5.70	47.10	C- / 3.0	20.77%	C+ / 6.7

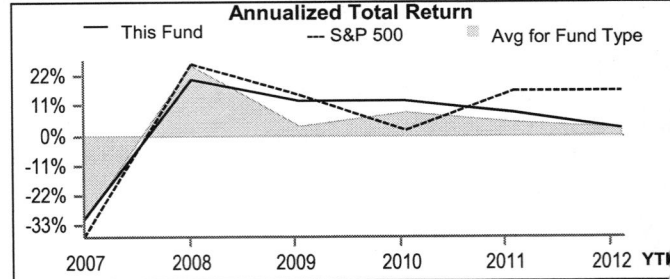

*Guggenheim S&P 500 Equal Wght (RSP)

C+   **Fair**

Fund Family: Guggenheim Investments
Fund Type: Income
Inception Date: April 24, 2003

Major Rating Factors: Middle of the road best describes *Guggenheim S&P 500 Equal Wght whose TheStreet.com Investment Rating is currently a C+ (Fair). The fund currently has a performance rating of C+ (Fair) based on an annualized return of 12.64% over the last three years and a total return of 3.36% year to date 2012. Factored into the performance evaluation is an expense ratio of 0.40% (very low).

The fund's risk rating is currently B- (Good). It carries a beta of 1.11, meaning it is expected to move 11.1% for every 10% move in the market. Volatility, as measured by both the semi-deviation and a drawdown factor, is considered low. As of December 31, 2012, *Guggenheim S&P 500 Equal Wght traded at a discount of 3.18% below its net asset value, which is better than its one-year historical average discount of .01%.

Adrian G.W. Duffy currently receives a manager quality ranking of 54 (0=worst, 99=best). If you desire an average level of risk, then this fund may be an option.

Data Date	Investment Rating	Net Assets ($Mil)	Price	Performance Rating/Pts	Total Return Y-T-D	Risk Rating/Pts
12-12	C+	2,696.80	53.32	C+ / 6.3	3.36%	B- / 7.9
2011	C+	2,640.10	46.28	C+ / 6.5	1.73%	B- / 7.8
2010	C+	3,181.20	47.31	C+ / 6.6	21.39%	C+ / 5.7
2009	C-	890.08	39.53	C- / 3.4	39.81%	C+ / 5.7

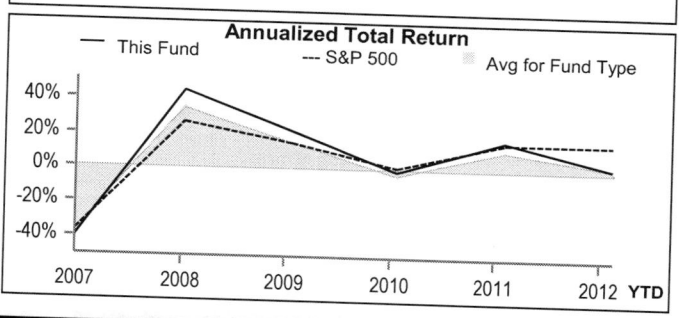

*Guggenheim S&P 500 Pure Growth (RPG)

C+   **Fair**

Fund Family: Guggenheim Investments
Fund Type: Growth
Inception Date: March 1, 2006

Major Rating Factors: Middle of the road best describes *Guggenheim S&P 500 Pure Growth whose TheStreet.com Investment Rating is currently a C+ (Fair). The fund currently has a performance rating of C+ (Fair) based on an annualized return of 14.58% over the last three years and a total return of 3.75% year to date 2012. Factored into the performance evaluation is an expense ratio of 0.35% (very low).

The fund's risk rating is currently B- (Good). It carries a beta of 1.15, meaning it is expected to move 11.5% for every 10% move in the market. Volatility, as measured by both the semi-deviation and a drawdown factor, is considered low. As of December 31, 2012, *Guggenheim S&P 500 Pure Growth traded at a discount of 3.62% below its net asset value.

Adrian G.W. Duffy currently receives a manager quality ranking of 60 (0=worst, 99=best). If you desire an average level of risk, then this fund may be an option.

Data Date	Investment Rating	Net Assets ($Mil)	Price	Performance Rating/Pts	Total Return Y-T-D	Risk Rating/Pts
12-12	C+	328.20	49.28	C+ / 6.5	3.75%	B- / 7.2
2011	C+	257.40	43.24	B- / 7.2	2.00%	B- / 7.0
2010	B	197.00	43.25	B / 7.8	26.91%	C / 5.3
2009	C	31.22	34.23	C / 4.5	43.07%	C+ / 5.8

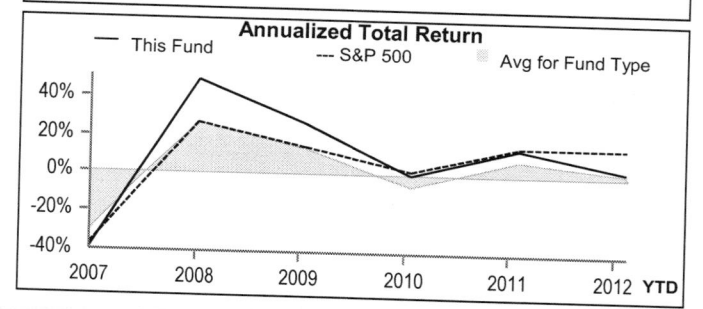

*Guggenheim S&P 500 Pure Value (RPV)

B+   **Good**

Fund Family: Guggenheim Investments
Fund Type: Income
Inception Date: March 1, 2006

Major Rating Factors: Strong performance is the major factor driving the B+ (Good) TheStreet.com Investment Rating for *Guggenheim S&P 500 Pure Value. The fund currently has a performance rating of B (Good) based on an annualized return of 14.15% over the last three years and a total return of 3.19% year to date 2012. Factored into the performance evaluation is an expense ratio of 0.35% (very low).

The fund's risk rating is currently B (Good). It carries a beta of 1.19, meaning it is expected to move 11.9% for every 10% move in the market. Volatility, as measured by both the semi-deviation and a drawdown factor, is considered low. As of December 31, 2012, *Guggenheim S&P 500 Pure Value traded at a discount of 3.01% below its net asset value, which is better than its one-year historical average discount of .01%.

Adrian G.W. Duffy currently receives a manager quality ranking of 65 (0=worst, 99=best). If you desire only a moderate level of risk and strong performance, then this fund is an excellent option.

Data Date	Investment Rating	Net Assets ($Mil)	Price	Performance Rating/Pts	Total Return Y-T-D	Risk Rating/Pts
12-12	B+	107.70	34.20	B / 8.0	3.19%	B / 8.0
2011	C+	77.80	27.81	C+ / 6.8	1.97%	B- / 7.1
2010	C	62.90	28.59	C+ / 6.1	22.52%	C / 4.7
2009	D+	13.85	23.65	C- / 3.1	47.44%	C / 4.9

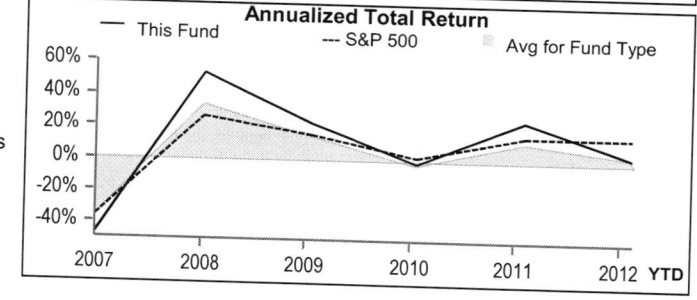

* Denotes ETF Fund

*Guggenheim S&P Gl Div Opps Idx E (LVL)

D+ **Weak**

Fund Family: Guggenheim Funds Investment Advisor
Fund Type: Income
Inception Date: June 25, 2007

Major Rating Factors:
Disappointing performance is the major factor driving the D+ (Weak) TheStreet.com Investment Rating for *Guggenheim S&P Gl Div Opps Idx E. The fund currently has a performance rating of D+ (Weak) based on an annualized return of 2.57% over the last three years and a total return of 3.73% year to date 2012. Factored into the performance evaluation is an expense ratio of 0.65% (very low).

The fund's risk rating is currently B- (Good). It carries a beta of 1.10, meaning it is expected to move 11.0% for every 10% move in the market. Volatility, as measured by both the semi-deviation and a drawdown factor, is considered low. As of December 31, 2012, *Guggenheim S&P Gl Div Opps Idx E traded at a discount of 2.81% below its net asset value, which is better than its one-year historical average premium of .06%.

Saroj Kanuri has been running the fund for 3 years and currently receives a manager quality ranking of 14 (0=worst, 99=best). This fund offers only a moderate level of risk but investors looking for strong performance are still waiting.

Data Date	Investment Rating	Net Assets ($Mil)	Price	Performance Rating/Pts	Total Return Y-T-D	Risk Rating/Pts
12-12	D+	50.70	13.14	D+ / 2.5	3.73%	B- / 7.1
2011	C	53.00	13.25	C / 5.1	0.15%	B- / 7.5
2010	D	27.20	14.80	D+ / 2.4	6.00%	C- / 4.1
2009	B+	5.54	14.90	A / 9.5	59.39%	C / 4.6

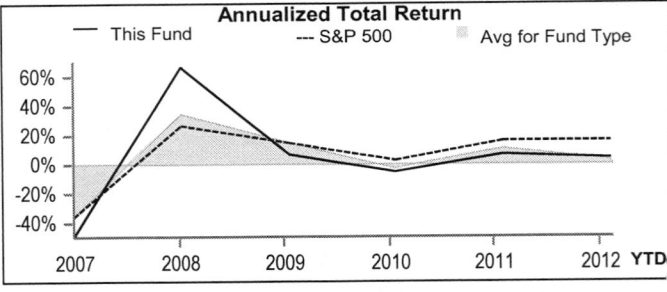

*Guggenheim S&P Global Water Idx (CGW)

C **Fair**

Fund Family: Guggenheim Funds Investment Advisor
Fund Type: Energy/Natural Resources
Inception Date: May 14, 2007

Major Rating Factors: Middle of the road best describes *Guggenheim S&P Global Water Idx whose TheStreet.com Investment Rating is currently a C (Fair). The fund currently has a performance rating of C (Fair) based on an annualized return of 8.74% over the last three years and a total return of 2.00% year to date 2012. Factored into the performance evaluation is an expense ratio of 0.70% (very low).

The fund's risk rating is currently B (Good). It carries a beta of 0.61, meaning the fund's expected move will be 6.1% for every 10% move in the market. Volatility, as measured by both the semi-deviation and a drawdown factor, is considered low. As of December 31, 2012, *Guggenheim S&P Global Water Idx traded at a discount of 1.90% below its net asset value, which is better than its one-year historical average discount of .16%.

Saroj Kanuri has been running the fund for 3 years and currently receives a manager quality ranking of 71 (0=worst, 99=best). If you desire an average level of risk, then this fund may be an option.

Data Date	Investment Rating	Net Assets ($Mil)	Price	Performance Rating/Pts	Total Return Y-T-D	Risk Rating/Pts
12-12	C	206.40	22.24	C / 5.2	2.00%	B / 8.0
2011	D+	179.80	18.74	C- / 3.8	0.21%	C+ / 6.1
2010	D+	220.00	20.77	C- / 3.6	14.46%	C / 4.9
2009	B-	178.94	18.42	B+ / 8.3	27.62%	C / 4.7

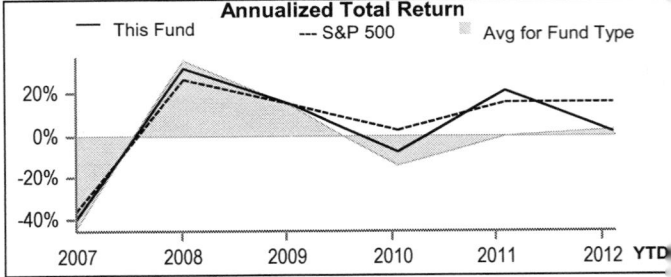

*Guggenheim S&P Mid Cap 400 Eq Wg (EWMD)

A **Excellent**

Fund Family: Guggenheim Investments
Fund Type: Growth
Inception Date: August 2, 2011

Major Rating Factors:
Strong performance is the major factor driving the A (Excellent) TheStreet.com Investment Rating for *Guggenheim S&P Mid Cap 400 Eq Wg. The fund currently has a performance rating of B+ (Good) based on an annualized return of 0.00% over the last three years and a total return of 3.65% year to date 2012. Factored into the performance evaluation is an expense ratio of 0.41% (very low).

The fund's risk rating is currently B (Good). It carries a beta of 0.00, meaning the fund's expected move will be 0.0% for every 10% move in the market. Volatility, as measured by both the semi-deviation and a drawdown factor, is considered low. As of December 31, 2012, *Guggenheim S&P Mid Cap 400 Eq Wg traded at a discount of 3.58% below its net asset value, which is better than its one-year historical average premium of .01%.

Adrian G.W. Duffy currently receives a manager quality ranking of 42 (0=worst, 99=best). If you desire only a moderate level of risk and strong performance, then this fund is an excellent option.

Data Date	Investment Rating	Net Assets ($Mil)	Price	Performance Rating/Pts	Total Return Y-T-D	Risk Rating/Pts
12-12	A	3.30	32.56	B+ / 8.6	3.65%	B / 8.8

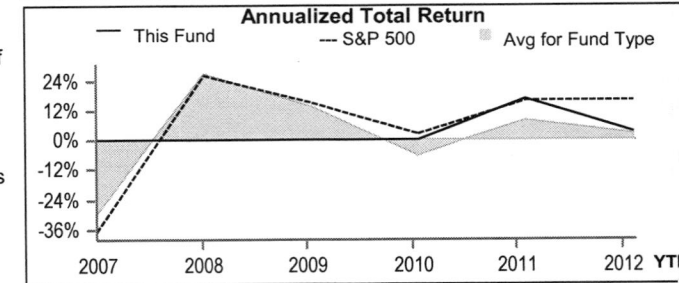

*Guggenheim S&P Mid Cap 400 Pure (RFV)

C+   **Fair**

Fund Family: Guggenheim Investments
Fund Type: Growth
Inception Date: March 1, 2006

Major Rating Factors: Middle of the road best describes *Guggenheim S&P Mid Cap 400 Pure whose TheStreet.com Investment Rating is currently a C+ (Fair). The fund currently has a performance rating of C+ (Fair) based on an annualized return of 10.79% over the last three years and a total return of 3.57% year to date 2012. Factored into the performance evaluation is an expense ratio of 0.35% (very low).

The fund's risk rating is currently B- (Good). It carries a beta of 1.24, meaning it is expected to move 12.4% for every 10% move in the market. Volatility, as measured by both the semi-deviation and a drawdown factor, is considered low. As of December 31, 2012, *Guggenheim S&P Mid Cap 400 Pure traded at a discount of 3.53% below its net asset value, which is better than its one-year historical average premium of .05%.

Adrian G.W. Duffy currently receives a manager quality ranking of 34 (0=worst, 99=best). If you desire an average level of risk, then this fund may be an option.

Data Date	Investment Rating	Net Assets ($Mil)	Price	Performance Rating/Pts	Total Return Y-T-D	Risk Rating/Pts
12-12	C+	37.00	36.93	C+ / 6.1	3.57%	B- / 7.7
2011	B-	39.60	31.66	C+ / 6.9	2.37%	B- / 7.5
2010	B-	45.90	34.01	B- / 7.5	22.34%	C / 5.0
2009	C-	8.36	28.11	C / 4.4	54.62%	C / 5.1

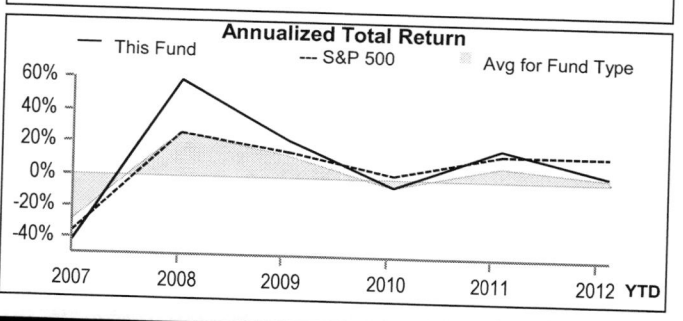

*Guggenheim S&P Mid Cap 400 Pure (RFG)

B   **Good**

Fund Family: Guggenheim Investments
Fund Type: Growth
Inception Date: March 1, 2006

Major Rating Factors: Strong performance is the major factor driving the B (Good) TheStreet.com Investment Rating for *Guggenheim S&P Mid Cap 400 Pure. The fund currently has a performance rating of B- (Good) based on an annualized return of 17.18% over the last three years and a total return of 3.21% year to date 2012. Factored into the performance evaluation is an expense ratio of 0.35% (very low).

The fund's risk rating is currently B- (Good). It carries a beta of 1.11, meaning it is expected to move 11.1% for every 10% move in the market. Volatility, as measured by both the semi-deviation and a drawdown factor, is considered low. As of December 31, 2012, *Guggenheim S&P Mid Cap 400 Pure traded at a discount of 3.08% below its net asset value, which is better than its one-year historical average discount of .01%.

Adrian G.W. Duffy currently receives a manager quality ranking of 77 (0=worst, 99=best). If you desire only a moderate level of risk and strong performance, then this fund is an excellent option.

Data Date	Investment Rating	Net Assets ($Mil)	Price	Performance Rating/Pts	Total Return Y-T-D	Risk Rating/Pts
12-12	B	534.00	91.26	B- / 7.5	3.21%	B- / 7.8
2011	B	514.80	78.48	B / 8.0	1.58%	B- / 7.6
2010	B+	477.40	78.35	B+ / 8.7	34.84%	C / 4.8
2009	C+	19.05	58.17	C+ / 6.8	53.85%	C+ / 6.2

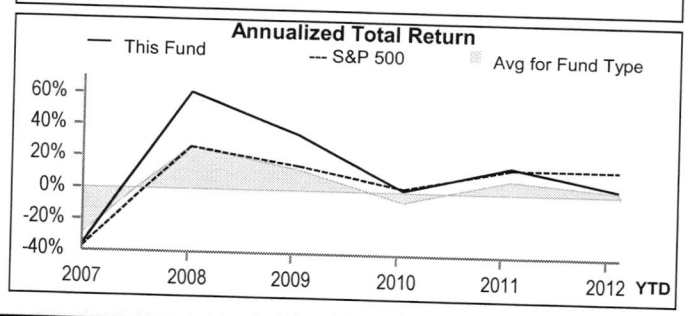

*Guggenheim S&P Sm Cap 600 Eq Wgh (EWSM)

A   **Excellent**

Fund Family: Guggenheim Investments
Fund Type: Growth
Inception Date: August 2, 2011

Major Rating Factors:
Strong performance is the major factor driving the A (Excellent) TheStreet.com Investment Rating for *Guggenheim S&P Sm Cap 600 Eq Wgh. The fund currently has a performance rating of B+ (Good) based on an annualized return of 0.00% over the last three years and a total return of 3.81% year to date 2012. Factored into the performance evaluation is an expense ratio of 0.41% (very low).

The fund's risk rating is currently B (Good). It carries a beta of 0.00, meaning the fund's expected move will be 0.0% for every 10% move in the market. Volatility, as measured by both the semi-deviation and a drawdown factor, is considered low. As of December 31, 2012, *Guggenheim S&P Sm Cap 600 Eq Wgh traded at a discount of 3.46% below its net asset value, which is better than its one-year historical average discount of .09%.

Adrian G.W. Duffy currently receives a manager quality ranking of 40 (0=worst, 99=best). If you desire only a moderate level of risk and strong performance, then this fund is an excellent option.

Data Date	Investment Rating	Net Assets ($Mil)	Price	Performance Rating/Pts	Total Return Y-T-D	Risk Rating/Pts
12-12	A	1.70	32.92	B+ / 8.5	3.81%	B / 8.8

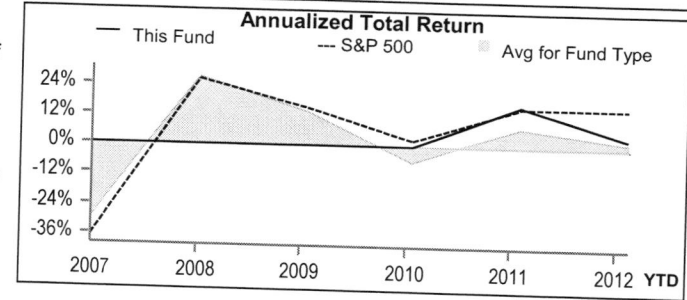

* Denotes ETF Fund

*Guggenheim S&P Sm Cap 600 Pure G (RZG)   B-   Good

Fund Family: Guggenheim Investments
Fund Type: Growth
Inception Date: March 1, 2006

Major Rating Factors: Strong performance is the major factor driving the B- (Good) TheStreet.com Investment Rating for *Guggenheim S&P Sm Cap 600 Pure G. The fund currently has a performance rating of B- (Good) based on an annualized return of 15.93% over the last three years and a total return of 4.55% year to date 2012. Factored into the performance evaluation is an expense ratio of 0.35% (very low).

The fund's risk rating is currently B- (Good). It carries a beta of 1.12, meaning it is expected to move 11.2% for every 10% move in the market. Volatility, as measured by both the semi-deviation and a drawdown factor, is considered low. As of December 31, 2012, *Guggenheim S&P Sm Cap 600 Pure G traded at a discount of 4.43% below its net asset value.

Adrian G.W. Duffy currently receives a manager quality ranking of 69 (0=worst, 99=best). If you desire only a moderate level of risk and strong performance, then this fund is an excellent option.

Data Date	Investment Rating	Net Assets ($Mil)	Price	Performance Rating/Pts	Total Return Y-T-D	Risk Rating/Pts
12-12	B-	72.60	55.82	B- / 7.0	4.55%	B- / 7.5
2011	C+	55.10	50.21	B- / 7.0	-0.08%	C+ / 6.7
2010	B+	26.30	47.88	B / 8.0	28.38%	C / 5.3
2009	C-	5.77	37.42	C- / 3.6	34.23%	C+ / 5.7

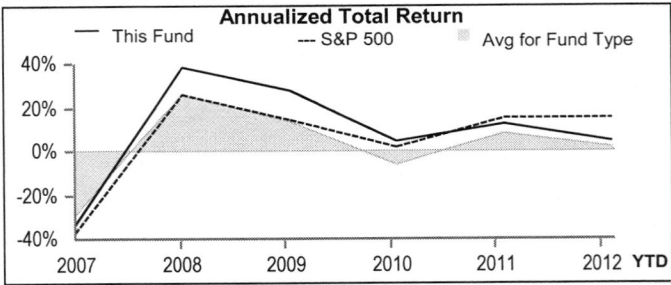

*Guggenheim S&P Sm Cap 600 Pure V (RZV)   C+   Fair

Fund Family: Guggenheim Investments
Fund Type: Growth
Inception Date: March 1, 2006

Major Rating Factors: Middle of the road best describes *Guggenheim S&P Sm Cap 600 Pure V whose TheStreet.com Investment Rating is currently a C+ (Fair). The fund currently has a performance rating of C+ (Fair) based on an annualized return of 12.10% over the last three years and a total return of 3.38% year to date 2012. Factored into the performance evaluation is an expense ratio of 0.35% (very low).

The fund's risk rating is currently B- (Good). It carries a beta of 1.52, meaning it is expected to move 15.2% for every 10% move in the market. Volatility, as measured by both the semi-deviation and a drawdown factor, is considered low. As of December 31, 2012, *Guggenheim S&P Sm Cap 600 Pure V traded at a discount of 3.25% below its net asset value, which is better than its one-year historical average discount of .03%.

Adrian G.W. Duffy currently receives a manager quality ranking of 28 (0=worst, 99=best). If you desire an average level of risk, then this fund may be an option.

Data Date	Investment Rating	Net Assets ($Mil)	Price	Performance Rating/Pts	Total Return Y-T-D	Risk Rating/Pts
12-12	C+	71.30	43.21	C+ / 6.9	3.38%	B- / 7.2
2011	C+	63.20	36.08	B- / 7.0	1.43%	C+ / 6.3
2010	B	106.20	39.40	B+ / 8.4	28.57%	C / 4.4
2009	D	23.71	30.81	D+ / 2.9	59.83%	C / 4.5

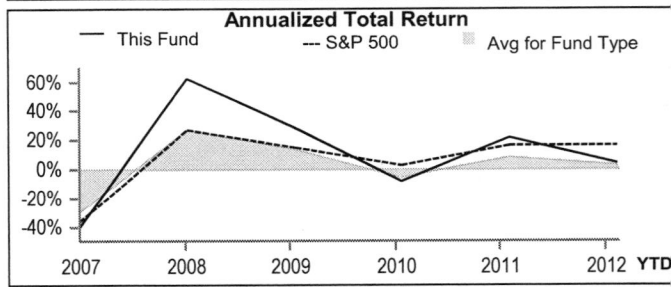

*Guggenheim Shipping ETF (SEA)   C+   Fair

Fund Family: Guggenheim Funds Investment Advisor
Fund Type: Global
Inception Date: June 11, 2010

Major Rating Factors: Strong performance is the major factor driving the C+ (Fair) TheStreet.com Investment Rating for *Guggenheim Shipping ETF. The fund currently has a performance rating of B+ (Good) based on an annualized return of 0.00% over the last three years and a total return of 7.33% year to date 2012. Factored into the performance evaluation is an expense ratio of 0.65% (very low).

The fund's risk rating is currently C (Fair). It carries a beta of 0.00, meaning the fund's expected move will be 0.0% for every 10% move in the market. Volatility, as measured by both the semi-deviation and a drawdown factor, is considered average. As of December 31, 2012, *Guggenheim Shipping ETF traded at a discount of 6.50% below its net asset value, which is better than its one-year historical average discount of .10%.

Saroj Kanuri has been running the fund for 5 years and currently receives a manager quality ranking of 22 (0=worst, 99=best). If you desire an average level of risk and strong performance, then this fund is a good option.

Data Date	Investment Rating	Net Assets ($Mil)	Price	Performance Rating/Pts	Total Return Y-T-D	Risk Rating/Pts
12-12	C+	27.20	16.10	B+ / 8.6	7.33%	C / 5.1
2011	E+	34.10	14.88	E- / 0.2	0.94%	C / 5.1

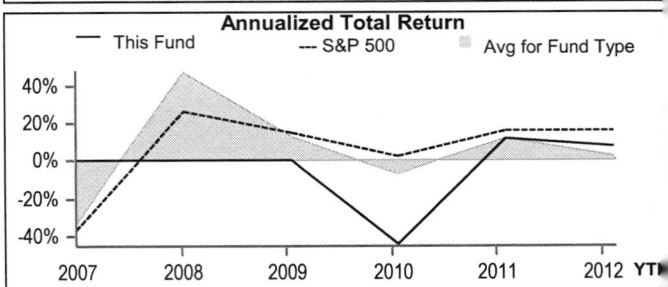

*Guggenheim Solar ETF (TAN)

Fund Family: Guggenheim Funds Investment Advisor
Fund Type: Energy/Natural Resources
Inception Date: April 15, 2008

E   Very Weak

Major Rating Factors: Very poor performance is the major factor driving the E (Very Weak) TheStreet.com Investment Rating for *Guggenheim Solar ETF. The fund currently has a performance rating of E (Very Weak) based on an annualized return of -39.25% over the last three years and a total return of 21.23% year to date 2012. Factored into the performance evaluation is an expense ratio of 0.70% (very low).

The fund's risk rating is currently C- (Fair). It carries a beta of 1.56, meaning it is expected to move 15.6% for every 10% move in the market. Volatility, as measured by both the semi-deviation and a drawdown factor, is considered average. As of December 31, 2012, *Guggenheim Solar ETF traded at a discount of 17.20% below its net asset value, which is better than its one-year historical average discount of .09%.

Saroj Kanuri has been running the fund for 3 years and currently receives a manager quality ranking of 0 (0=worst, 99=best). This fund offers an average level of risk but investors looking for strong performance will be frustrated.

Data Date	Investment Rating	Net Assets ($Mil)	Price	Performance Rating/Pts	Total Return Y-T-D	Risk Rating/Pts
12-12	E	47.30	15.64	E / 0.3	21.23%	C- / 3.6
2011	E	59.30	2.47	E / 0.4	3.64%	C- / 3.7
2010	E	142.70	7.30	E / 0.5	-28.64%	D+ / 2.8
2009	C-	166.57	10.25	C+ / 6.2	10.57%	D+ / 2.7

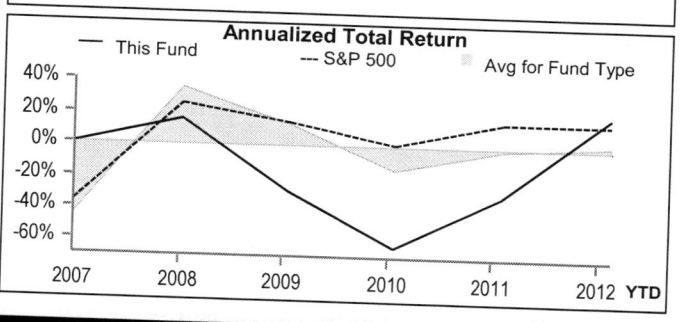

*Guggenheim Spin-Off ETF (CSD)

Fund Family: Guggenheim Funds Investment Advisor
Fund Type: Income
Inception Date: December 15, 2006

A-   Excellent

Major Rating Factors:
Strong performance is the major factor driving the A- (Excellent) TheStreet.com Investment Rating for *Guggenheim Spin-Off ETF. The fund currently has a performance rating of B (Good) based on an annualized return of 16.82% over the last three years and a total return of 2.19% year to date 2012. Factored into the performance evaluation is an expense ratio of 0.65% (very low).

The fund's risk rating is currently B (Good). It carries a beta of 0.90, meaning that its performance tracks fairly well with that of the overall stock market. Volatility, as measured by both the semi-deviation and a drawdown factor, is considered low. As of December 31, 2012, *Guggenheim Spin-Off ETF traded at a discount of 2.11% below its net asset value, which is better than its one-year historical average premium of .17%.

Saroj Kanuri has been running the fund for 3 years and currently receives a manager quality ranking of 83 (0=worst, 99=best). If you desire only a moderate level of risk and strong performance, then this fund is an excellent option.

Data Date	Investment Rating	Net Assets ($Mil)	Price	Performance Rating/Pts	Total Return Y-T-D	Risk Rating/Pts
12-12	A-	65.30	29.64	B / 8.2	2.19%	B / 8.5
2011	B+	29.30	23.52	B / 8.0	1.19%	B / 8.4
2010	C-	15.90	22.78	C / 4.4	21.35%	C / 4.8
2009	C-	8.07	18.76	C / 4.3	65.69%	C / 5.0

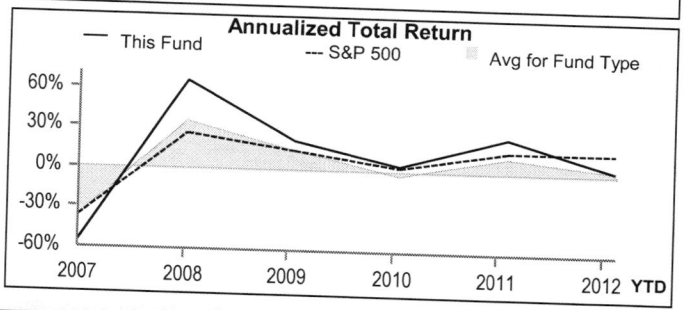

*Guggenheim Swedish Krona (FXS)

Fund Family: Guggenheim Investments
Fund Type: Foreign
Inception Date: June 26, 2006

D+   Weak

Major Rating Factors:
Disappointing performance is the major factor driving the D+ (Weak) TheStreet.com Investment Rating for *Guggenheim Swedish Krona. The fund currently has a performance rating of D+ (Weak) based on an annualized return of 3.81% over the last three years and a total return of 0.58% year to date 2012. Factored into the performance evaluation is an expense ratio of 0.40% (very low).

The fund's risk rating is currently B (Good). It carries a beta of 0.63, meaning the fund's expected move will be 6.3% for every 10% move in the market. Volatility, as measured by both the semi-deviation and a drawdown factor, is considered low. As of December 31, 2012, *Guggenheim Swedish Krona traded at a discount of .40% below its net asset value.

This fund has been team managed for 7 years and currently receives a manager quality ranking of 63 (0=worst, 99=best). This fund offers only a moderate level of risk but investors looking for strong performance are still waiting.

Data Date	Investment Rating	Net Assets ($Mil)	Price	Performance Rating/Pts	Total Return Y-T-D	Risk Rating/Pts
12-12	D+	68.90	153.14	D+ / 2.5	0.58%	B / 8.1
2011	C-	87.10	144.57	D+ / 2.6	-0.89%	B / 8.5
2010	C-	51.80	148.96	D+ / 2.7	7.00%	C+ / 6.6
2009	C-	34.29	139.35	D+ / 2.9	8.89%	B- / 7.0

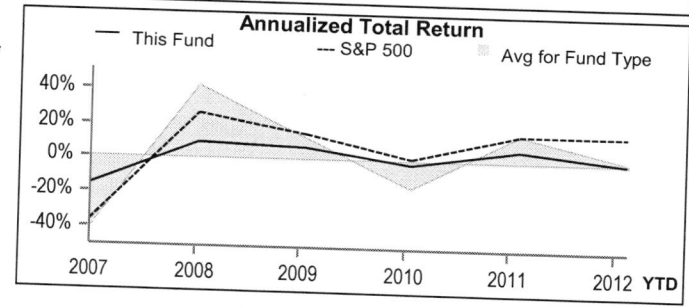

* Denotes ETF Fund

*Guggenheim Swiss Franc (FXF)

D+ **Weak**

Fund Family: Guggenheim Investments
Fund Type: Foreign
Inception Date: June 26, 2006

Major Rating Factors:
Disappointing performance is the major factor driving the D+ (Weak) TheStreet.com Investment Rating for *Guggenheim Swiss Franc. The fund currently has a performance rating of D (Weak) based on an annualized return of 3.55% over the last three years and a total return of 0.16% year to date 2012. Factored into the performance evaluation is an expense ratio of 0.40% (very low).

The fund's risk rating is currently B (Good). It carries a beta of 0.50, meaning the fund's expected move will be 5.0% for every 10% move in the market. Volatility, as measured by both the semi-deviation and a drawdown factor, is considered low. As of December 31, 2012, *Guggenheim Swiss Franc traded at a discount of .32% below its net asset value, which is better than its one-year historical average premium of .01%.

This fund has been team managed for 7 years and currently receives a manager quality ranking of 65 (0=worst, 99=best). This fund offers only a moderate level of risk but investors looking for strong performance are still waiting.

Data Date	Investment Rating	Net Assets ($Mil)	Price	Performance Rating/Pts	Total Return Y-T-D	Risk Rating/Pts
12-12	D+	338.50	107.46	D / 2.2	0.16%	B / 8.0
2011	C-	427.70	105.10	D+ / 2.4	-1.62%	B / 8.4
2010	B-	393.60	106.25	C+ / 6.3	10.54%	B- / 7.7
2009	C+	352.07	96.12	C- / 4.0	4.08%	B / 8.1

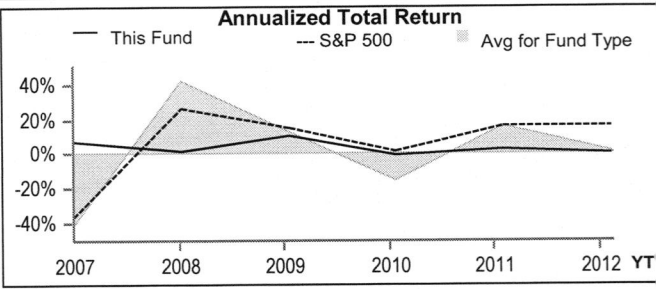

*Guggenheim Timber ETF (CUT)

C **Fair**

Fund Family: Guggenheim Funds Investment Advisor
Fund Type: Global
Inception Date: November 9, 2007

Major Rating Factors: Middle of the road best describes *Guggenheim Timber ETF whose TheStreet.com Investment Rating is currently a C (Fair). The fund currently has a performance rating of C (Fair) based on an annualized return of 7.34% over the last three years and a total return of 4.55% year to date 2012. Factored into the performance evaluation is an expense ratio of 0.70% (very low).

The fund's risk rating is currently B- (Good). It carries a beta of 1.03, meaning that its performance tracks fairly well with that of the overall stock market. Volatility, as measured by both the semi-deviation and a drawdown factor, is considered low. As of December 31, 2012, *Guggenheim Timber ETF traded at a discount of 3.90% below its net asset value, which is better than its one-year historical average premium of .23%.

Saroj Kanuri has been running the fund for 3 years and currently receives a manager quality ranking of 67 (0=worst, 99=best). If you desire an average level of risk, then this fund may be an option.

Data Date	Investment Rating	Net Assets ($Mil)	Price	Performance Rating/Pts	Total Return Y-T-D	Risk Rating/Pts
12-12	C	195.70	20.44	C / 5.3	4.55%	B- / 7.0
2011	C-	103.60	16.54	C- / 3.8	1.09%	B- / 7.1
2010	C-	142.80	20.63	C- / 3.8	17.21%	C / 5.2
2009	A-	45.92	17.96	A- / 9.2	46.77%	C / 5.0

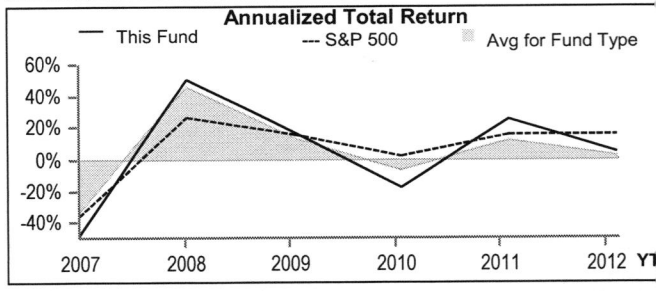

*Guggenheim Wilshire 4500 Comp ET (WXSP)

B **Good**

Fund Family: Guggenheim Funds Investment Advisor
Fund Type: Growth
Inception Date: March 8, 2010

Major Rating Factors: Strong performance is the major factor driving the B (Good) TheStreet.com Investment Rating for *Guggenheim Wilshire 4500 Comp ET. The fund currently has a performance rating of B (Good) based on an annualized return of 0.00% over the last three years and a total return of 4.79% year to date 2012. Factored into the performance evaluation is an expense ratio of 0.18% (very low).

The fund's risk rating is currently B- (Good). It carries a beta of 0.00, meaning the fund's expected move will be 0.0% for every 10% move in the market. Volatility, as measured by both the semi-deviation and a drawdown factor, is considered low. As of December 31, 2012, *Guggenheim Wilshire 4500 Comp ET traded at a discount of 4.63% below its net asset value, which is better than its one-year historical average discount of .03%.

Saroj Kanuri has been running the fund for 3 years and currently receives a manager quality ranking of 43 (0=worst, 99=best). If you desire only a moderate level of risk and strong performance, then this fund is an excellent option.

Data Date	Investment Rating	Net Assets ($Mil)	Price	Performance Rating/Pts	Total Return Y-T-D	Risk Rating/Pts
12-12	B	6.60	32.57	B / 7.8	4.79%	B- / 7.5

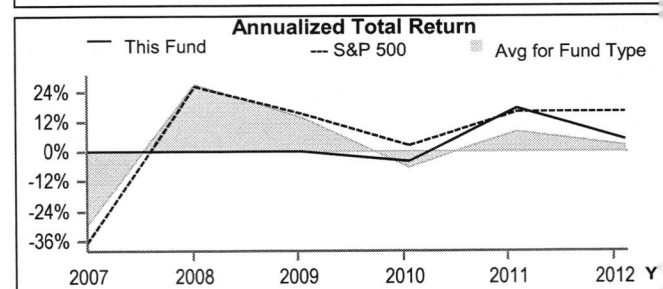

*Guggenheim Wilshire MicroCap ETF (WMCR)

C-   **Fair**

Fund Family: Guggenheim Funds Investment Advisor
Fund Type: Income
Inception Date: September 21, 2006

Data Date	Investment Rating	Net Assets ($Mil)	Price	Performance Rating/Pts	Total Return Y-T-D	Risk Rating/Pts
12-12	C-	12.90	18.48	C / 4.8	4.49%	B- / 7.2
2011	D+	13.80	15.25	C- / 3.1	2.62%	B- / 7.1
2010	C-	39.90	19.14	C / 5.0	24.27%	C / 5.2
2009	E+	3.56	15.45	E+ / 0.9	18.46%	C- / 3.5

Major Rating Factors: Middle of the road best describes *Guggenheim Wilshire MicroCap ETF whose TheStreet.com Investment Rating is currently a C- (Fair). The fund currently has a performance rating of C (Fair) based on an annualized return of 9.35% over the last three years and a total return of 4.49% year to date 2012. Factored into the performance evaluation is an expense ratio of 0.50% (very low).

The fund's risk rating is currently B- (Good). It carries a beta of 1.32, meaning it is expected to move 13.2% for every 10% move in the market. Volatility, as measured by both the semi-deviation and a drawdown factor, is considered low. As of December 31, 2012, *Guggenheim Wilshire MicroCap ETF traded at a discount of 4.40% below its net asset value, which is better than its one-year historical average discount of .28%.

Saroj Kanuri has been running the fund for 3 years and currently receives a manager quality ranking of 20 (0=worst, 99=best). If you desire an average level of risk, then this fund may be an option.

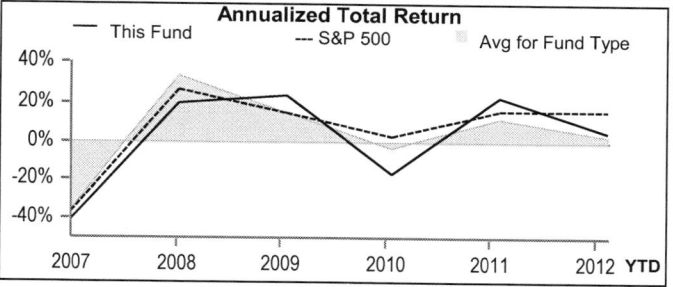

*Guggenheim Wilshire US REIT ETF (WREI)

B-   **Good**

Fund Family: Guggenheim Funds Investment Advisor
Fund Type: Growth and Income
Inception Date: March 8, 2010

Data Date	Investment Rating	Net Assets ($Mil)	Price	Performance Rating/Pts	Total Return Y-T-D	Risk Rating/Pts
12-12	B-	18.20	36.10	C+ / 6.6	2.49%	B / 8.0
2011	C	8.00	31.97	C- / 4.0	-0.69%	B / 8.0

Major Rating Factors: *Guggenheim Wilshire US REIT ETF receives a TheStreet.com Investment Rating of B- (Good). The fund currently has a performance rating of C+ (Fair) based on an annualized return of 0.00% over the last three years and a total return of 2.49% year to date 2012. Factored into the performance evaluation is an expense ratio of 0.32% (very low).

The fund's risk rating is currently B (Good). It carries a beta of 0.00, meaning the fund's expected move will be 0.0% for every 10% move in the market. Volatility, as measured by both the semi-deviation and a drawdown factor, is considered low. As of December 31, 2012, *Guggenheim Wilshire US REIT ETF traded at a discount of 2.51% below its net asset value.

Saroj Kanuri has been running the fund for 3 years and currently receives a manager quality ranking of 76 (0=worst, 99=best). If you desire an average level of risk, then this fund may be an option.

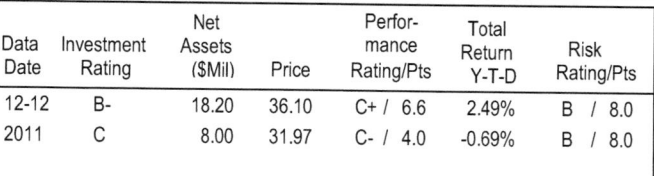
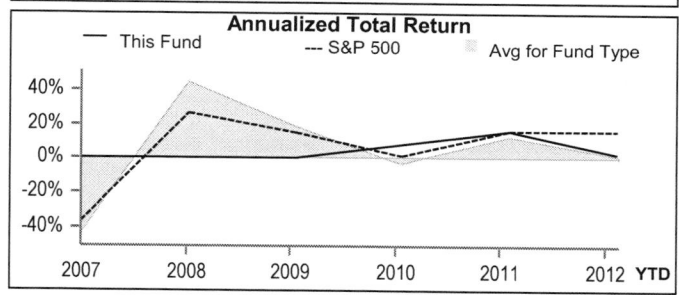

*Guggenheim Wilshire5000 Tot Mkt (WFVK)

B+   **Good**

Fund Family: Guggenheim Funds Investment Advisor
Fund Type: Growth
Inception Date: March 8, 2010

Data Date	Investment Rating	Net Assets ($Mil)	Price	Performance Rating/Pts	Total Return Y-T-D	Risk Rating/Pts
12-12	B+	6.30	31.45	B / 8.0	4.13%	B / 8.1
2011	C-	5.50	27.82	D+ / 2.6	1.69%	B / 8.3

Major Rating Factors: Strong performance is the major factor driving the B+ (Good) TheStreet.com Investment Rating for *Guggenheim Wilshire5000 Tot Mkt. The fund currently has a performance rating of B (Good) based on an annualized return of 0.00% over the last three years and a total return of 4.13% year to date 2012. Factored into the performance evaluation is an expense ratio of 0.12% (very low).

The fund's risk rating is currently B (Good). It carries a beta of 0.00, meaning the fund's expected move will be 0.0% for every 10% move in the market. Volatility, as measured by both the semi-deviation and a drawdown factor, is considered low. As of December 31, 2012, *Guggenheim Wilshire5000 Tot Mkt traded at a discount of 3.56% below its net asset value, which is better than its one-year historical average premium of .25%.

Saroj Kanuri has been running the fund for 3 years and currently receives a manager quality ranking of 42 (0=worst, 99=best). If you desire only a moderate level of risk and strong performance, then this fund is an excellent option.

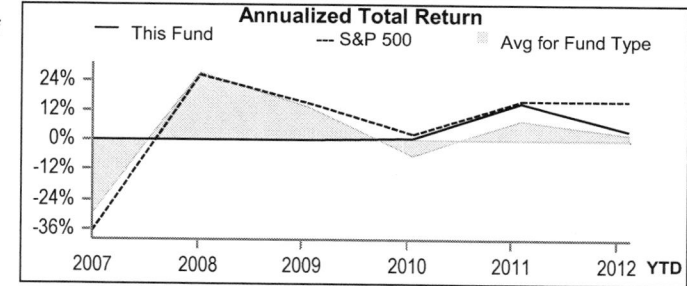

*Guggenheim Yuan Bond ETF (RMB)

C-   Fair

Fund Family: Guggenheim Funds Investment Advisor
Fund Type: Global
Inception Date: September 22, 2011

Data Date	Investment Rating	Net Assets ($Mil)	Price	Perfor-mance Rating/Pts	Total Return Y-T-D	Risk Rating/Pts
12-12	C-	5.10	24.86	D- / 1.4	0.16%	B+ / 9.7

Major Rating Factors:
Disappointing performance is the major factor driving the C- (Fair) TheStreet.com Investment Rating for *Guggenheim Yuan Bond ETF. The fund currently has a performance rating of D- (Weak) based on an annualized return of 0.00% over the last three years and a total return of 0.16% year to date 2012. Factored into the performance evaluation is an expense ratio of 0.65% (very low).

The fund's risk rating is currently B+ (Good). It carries a beta of 0.00, meaning the fund's expected move will be 0.0% for every 10% move in the market. Volatility, as measured by both the semi-deviation and a drawdown factor, is considered very low. As of December 31, 2012, *Guggenheim Yuan Bond ETF traded at a discount of 2.85% below its net asset value, which is better than its one-year historical average premium of .09%.

Shaw-Yann Ho has been running the fund for 2 years and currently receives a manager quality ranking of 63 (0=worst, 99=best). This fund offers only a moderate level of risk but investors looking for strong performance are still waiting.

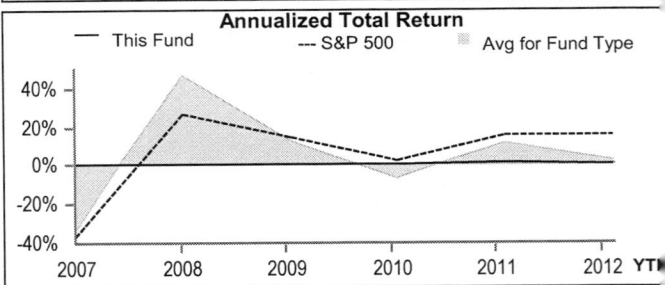

Annualized Total Return
— This Fund   --- S&P 500   Avg for Fund Type

*Guggenhm BltShs 2013 HY Corp Bd (BSJD)

C   Fair

Fund Family: Guggenheim Funds Investment Advisor
Fund Type: Corporate - High Yield
Inception Date: January 24, 2011

Data Date	Investment Rating	Net Assets ($Mil)	Price	Perfor-mance Rating/Pts	Total Return Y-T-D	Risk Rating/Pts
12-12	C	197.70	25.80	D+ / 2.7	0.00%	B+ / 9.6

Major Rating Factors:
Disappointing performance is the major factor driving the C (Fair) TheStreet.com Investment Rating for *Guggenhm BltShs 2013 HY Corp Bd. The fund currently has a performance rating of D+ (Weak) based on an annualized return of 0.00% over the last three years and a total return of 0.00% year to date 2012. Factored into the performance evaluation is an expense ratio of 0.42% (very low).

The fund's risk rating is currently B+ (Good). It carries a beta of 0.00, meaning the fund's expected move will be 0.0% for every 10% move in the market. Volatility, as measured by both the semi-deviation and a drawdown factor, is considered very low. As of December 31, 2012, *Guggenhm BltShs 2013 HY Corp Bd traded at a price exactly equal to its net asset value, which is better than its one-year historical average premium of .37%.

Saroj Kanuri has been running the fund for 2 years and currently receives a manager quality ranking of 40 (0=worst, 99=best). This fund offers only a moderate level of risk but investors looking for strong performance are still waiting.

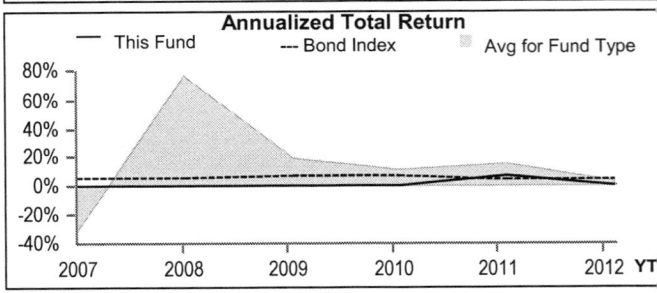

Annualized Total Return
— This Fund   --- Bond Index   Avg for Fund Type

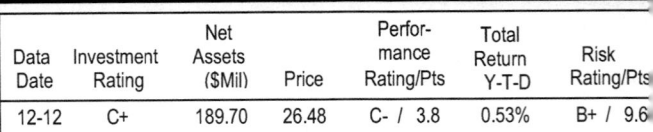

*Guggenhm BltShs 2014 HY Corp Bd (BSJE)

C+   Fair

Fund Family: Guggenheim Funds Investment Advisor
Fund Type: Corporate - High Yield
Inception Date: January 24, 2011

Data Date	Investment Rating	Net Assets ($Mil)	Price	Perfor-mance Rating/Pts	Total Return Y-T-D	Risk Rating/Pts
12-12	C+	189.70	26.48	C- / 3.8	0.53%	B+ / 9.6

Major Rating Factors: Middle of the road best describes *Guggenhm BltShs 2014 HY Corp Bd whose TheStreet.com Investment Rating is currently a C+ (Fair). The fund currently has a performance rating of C- (Fair) based on an annualized return of 0.00% over the last three years and a total return of 0.53% year to date 2012. Factored into the performance evaluation is an expense ratio of 0.42% (very low).

The fund's risk rating is currently B+ (Good). It carries a beta of 0.00, meaning the fund's expected move will be 0.0% for every 10% move in the market. Volatility, as measured by both the semi-deviation and a drawdown factor, is considered very low. As of December 31, 2012, *Guggenhm BltShs 2014 HY Corp Bd traded at a discount of .15% below its net asset value, which is better than its one-year historical average premium of .38%.

Saroj Kanuri has been running the fund for 3 years and currently receives a manager quality ranking of 41 (0=worst, 99=best). If you desire an average level of risk, then this fund may be an option.

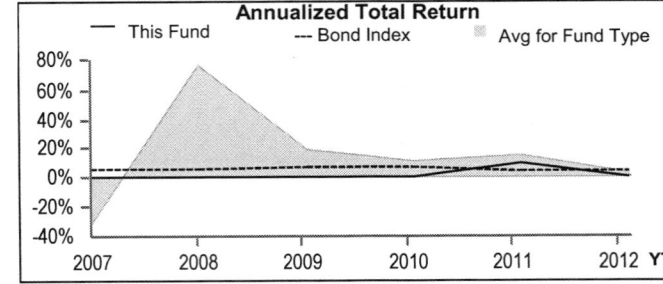

Annualized Total Return
— This Fund   --- Bond Index   Avg for Fund Type

*Guggenhm BltShs 2015 HY Corp Bd (BSJF)

C+   **Fair**

Fund Family: Guggenheim Funds Investment Advisor
Fund Type: Corporate - High Yield
Inception Date: January 24, 2011

Major Rating Factors: Middle of the road best describes *Guggenhm BltShs 2015 HY Corp Bd whose TheStreet.com Investment Rating is currently a C+ (Fair). The fund currently has a performance rating of C (Fair) based on an annualized return of 0.00% over the last three years and a total return of 0.53% year to date 2012. Factored into the performance evaluation is an expense ratio of 0.42% (very low).

The fund's risk rating is currently B+ (Good). It carries a beta of 0.00, meaning the fund's expected move will be 0.0% for every 10% move in the market. Volatility, as measured by both the semi-deviation and a drawdown factor, is considered very low. As of December 31, 2012, *Guggenhm BltShs 2015 HY Corp Bd traded at a discount of .23% below its net asset value, which is better than its one-year historical average premium of .37%.

Saroj Kanuri has been running the fund for 3 years and currently receives a manager quality ranking of 32 (0=worst, 99=best). If you desire an average level of risk, then this fund may be an option.

Data Date	Investment Rating	Net Assets ($Mil)	Price	Performance Rating/Pts	Total Return Y-T-D	Risk Rating/Pts
12-12	C+	335.60	26.60	C / 4.5	0.53%	B+ / 9.4

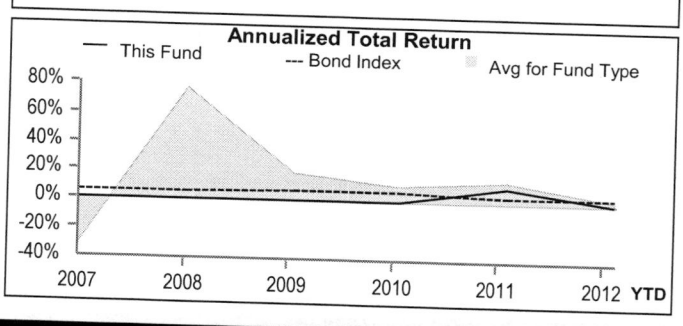

*Health Care Select Sector SPDR (XLV)

C+   **Fair**

Fund Family: SSgA Funds Management Inc
Fund Type: Health
Inception Date: December 16, 1998

Major Rating Factors: Middle of the road best describes *Health Care Select Sector SPDR whose TheStreet.com Investment Rating is currently a C+ (Fair). The fund currently has a performance rating of C+ (Fair) based on an annualized return of 11.23% over the last three years and a total return of 4.74% year to date 2012. Factored into the performance evaluation is an expense ratio of 0.18% (very low).

The fund's risk rating is currently B (Good). It carries a beta of 0.61, meaning the fund's expected move will be 6.1% for every 10% move in the market. Volatility, as measured by both the semi-deviation and a drawdown factor, is considered low. As of December 31, 2012, *Health Care Select Sector SPDR traded at a discount of 4.43% below its net asset value, which is better than its one-year historical average discount of .01%.

John A. Tucker has been running the fund for 15 years and currently receives a manager quality ranking of 77 (0=worst, 99=best). If you desire an average level of risk, then this fund may be an option.

Data Date	Investment Rating	Net Assets ($Mil)	Price	Performance Rating/Pts	Total Return Y-T-D	Risk Rating/Pts
12-12	C+	5,571.00	39.88	C+ / 5.6	4.74%	B / 8.4
2011	C	3,400.80	34.69	C / 4.9	1.27%	B / 8.2
2010	C-	2,705.80	31.50	D+ / 2.5	3.32%	C+ / 6.9
2009	C-	1,979.59	31.07	C- / 3.2	17.10%	C+ / 6.8

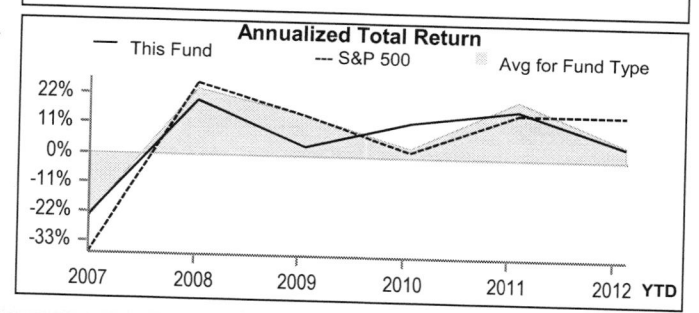

*Industrial Select Sector SPDR (XLI)

C   **Fair**

Fund Family: SSgA Funds Management Inc
Fund Type: Growth
Inception Date: December 16, 1998

Major Rating Factors: Middle of the road best describes *Industrial Select Sector SPDR whose TheStreet.com Investment Rating is currently a C (Fair). The fund currently has a performance rating of C+ (Fair) based on an annualized return of 12.74% over the last three years and a total return of 3.14% year to date 2012. Factored into the performance evaluation is an expense ratio of 0.18% (very low).

The fund's risk rating is currently B- (Good). It carries a beta of 1.21, meaning it is expected to move 12.1% for every 10% move in the market. Volatility, as measured by both the semi-deviation and a drawdown factor, is considered low. As of December 31, 2012, *Industrial Select Sector SPDR traded at a discount of 3.07% below its net asset value.

John A. Tucker has been running the fund for 15 years and currently receives a manager quality ranking of 52 (0=worst, 99=best). If you desire an average level of risk, then this fund may be an option.

Data Date	Investment Rating	Net Assets ($Mil)	Price	Performance Rating/Pts	Total Return Y-T-D	Risk Rating/Pts
12-12	C	3,878.20	37.90	C+ / 5.6	3.14%	B- / 7.7
2011	C	2,711.00	33.75	C+ / 5.8	2.49%	B- / 7.3
2010	C	3,744.30	34.87	C+ / 5.8	27.85%	C / 5.4
2009	D+	2,010.29	27.79	D / 2.2	17.67%	C+ / 5.7

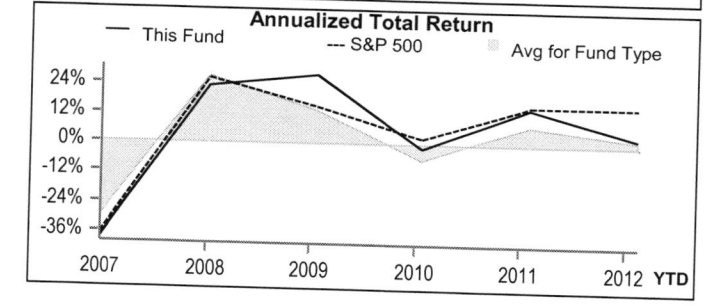

* Denotes ETF Fund

*iPath Asian & Gulf Curncy Reval (PGD)   D-   Weak

Fund Family: Barclays Bank PLC
Fund Type: Foreign
Inception Date: February 5, 2008

Major Rating Factors:

Disappointing performance is the major factor driving the D- (Weak) TheStreet.com Investment Rating for *iPath Asian & Gulf Curncy Reval. The fund currently has a performance rating of D- (Weak) based on an annualized return of 0.36% over the last three years and a total return of 0.26% year to date 2012.

The fund's risk rating is currently C+ (Fair). It carries a beta of 0.13, meaning the fund's expected move will be 1.3% for every 10% move in the market. Volatility, as measured by both the semi-deviation and a drawdown factor, is considered low. As of December 31, 2012, *iPath Asian & Gulf Curncy Reval traded at a discount of .71% below its net asset value, which is worse than its one-year historical average discount of .72%.

This fund has been team managed for 5 years and currently receives a manager quality ranking of 46 (0=worst, 99=best). This fund offers only a moderate level of risk but investors looking for strong performance are still waiting.

Data Date	Investment Rating	Net Assets ($Mil)	Price	Performance Rating/Pts	Total Return Y-T-D	Risk Rating/Pts
12-12	D-	2.80	50.61	D- / 1.4	0.26%	C+ / 5.8
2011	D-	4.00	50.20	D / 2.0	0.22%	C+ / 5.9
2010	D+	4.00	51.21	C- / 3.7	0.85%	C / 4.9
2009	C	0.00	50.78	C- / 3.1	1.63%	B / 8.1

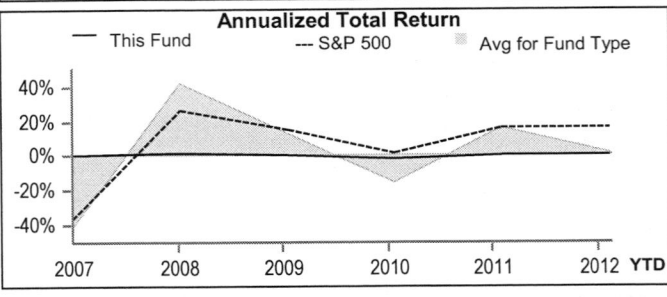

Annualized Total Return

*iPath CBOE S&P 500 BuyWrite Idx (BWV)   C-   Fair

Fund Family: Barclays Bank PLC
Fund Type: Growth
Inception Date: May 22, 2007

Major Rating Factors:

Disappointing performance is the major factor driving the C- (Fair) TheStreet.com Investment Rating for *iPath CBOE S&P 500 BuyWrite Idx. The fund currently has a performance rating of D+ (Weak) based on an annualized return of 5.43% over the last three years and a total return of 2.72% year to date 2012. Factored into the performance evaluation is an expense ratio of 0.75% (very low).

The fund's risk rating is currently B (Good). It carries a beta of 0.70, meaning the fund's expected move will be 7.0% for every 10% move in the market. Volatility, as measured by both the semi-deviation and a drawdown factor, is considered low. As of December 31, 2012, *iPath CBOE S&P 500 BuyWrite Idx traded at a discount of 2.75% below its net asset value, which is better than its one-year historical average discount of .21%.

This fund has been team managed for 6 years and currently receives a manager quality ranking of 30 (0=worst, 99=best). This fund offers only a moderate level of risk but investors looking for strong performance are still waiting.

Data Date	Investment Rating	Net Assets ($Mil)	Price	Performance Rating/Pts	Total Return Y-T-D	Risk Rating/Pts
12-12	C-	10.45	51.92	D+ / 2.4	2.72%	B / 8.6
2011	C+	18.80	50.40	C / 4.7	0.63%	B / 8.7
2010	C-	16.70	47.83	D+ / 2.8	4.80%	C+ / 6.4
2009	A	10.45	45.64	B / 8.1	23.72%	C+ / 6.7

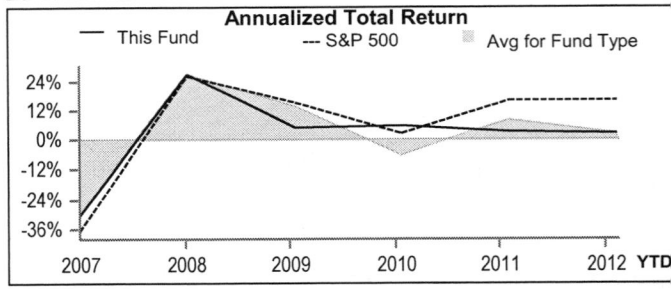

Annualized Total Return

*iPath Cptl Glbl Carbon Tot Ret E (GRN)   E-   Very Weak

Fund Family: Barclays Bank PLC
Fund Type: Energy/Natural Resources
Inception Date: June 24, 2008

Major Rating Factors: *iPath Cptl Glbl Carbon Tot Ret E has adopted a very risky asset allocation strategy and currently receives an overall TheStreet.com Investment Rating of E- (Very Weak). The fund has a high level of volatility, as measured by both semi-deviation and drawdown factors. It carries a beta of 0.24, meaning the fund's expected move will be 2.4% for every 10% move in the market. As of December 31, 2012, *iPath Cptl Glbl Carbon Tot Ret E traded at a premium of 3.30% above its net asset value, which is worse than its one-year historical average discount of 7.58%. Unfortunately, the high level of risk (D, Weak) failed to pay off as investors endured very poor performance.

The fund's performance rating is currently E- (Very Weak). It has registered an annualized return of -33.88% over the last three years and is down -10.69% year to date 2012. Factored into the performance evaluation is an expense ratio of 0.75% (very low).

This fund has been team managed for 5 years and currently receives a manager quality ranking of 2 (0=worst, 99=best). If you can tolerate very high levels of risk in the hope of improved future returns, holding this fund may be an option.

Data Date	Investment Rating	Net Assets ($Mil)	Price	Performance Rating/Pts	Total Return Y-T-D	Risk Rating/Pts
12-12	E-	4.10	7.82	E- / 0.2	-10.69%	D / 1.9
2011	E-	1.20	10.34	E / 0.4	3.97%	D / 1.9
2010	E+	3.80	25.54	D+ / 2.4	11.67%	D- / 1.4
2009	D-	4.10	22.87	E / 0.5	-20.86%	C+ / 5.7

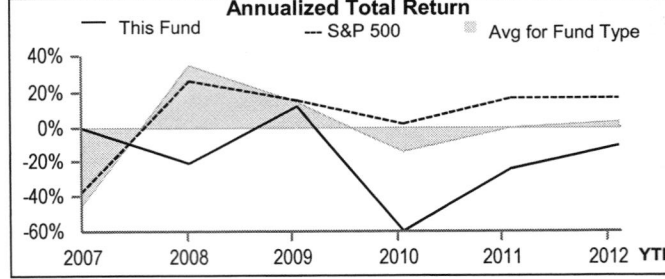

Annualized Total Return

*iPath DJ UBS Agri Tot Ret Sub (JJA)

D- **Weak**

Fund Family: Barclays Bank PLC
Fund Type: Energy/Natural Resources
Inception Date: October 23, 2007

Major Rating Factors:
Disappointing performance is the major factor driving the D- (Weak) TheStreet.com Investment Rating for *iPath DJ UBS Agri Tot Ret Sub. The fund currently has a performance rating of D+ (Weak) based on an annualized return of 8.29% over the last three years and a total return of -0.54% year to date 2012. Factored into the performance evaluation is an expense ratio of 0.75% (very low).

The fund's risk rating is currently C (Fair). It carries a beta of 0.71, meaning the fund's expected move will be 7.1% for every 10% move in the market. Volatility, as measured by both the semi-deviation and a drawdown factor, is considered average. As of December 31, 2012, *iPath DJ UBS Agri Tot Ret Sub traded at a premium of .75% above its net asset value.

This fund has been team managed for 6 years and currently receives a manager quality ranking of 53 (0=worst, 99=best). This fund offers an average level of risk but investors looking for strong performance will be frustrated.

Data Date	Investment Rating	Net Assets ($Mil)	Price	Performance Rating/Pts	Total Return Y-T-D	Risk Rating/Pts
12-12	D-	68.43	55.14	D+ / 2.7	-0.54%	C / 4.3
2011	D-	135.50	53.42	D+ / 2.8	-1.10%	C / 4.6
2010	C	142.20	63.07	B / 8.2	38.40%	D+ / 2.6
2009	C-	68.43	45.57	B- / 7.0	12.08%	D+ / 2.9

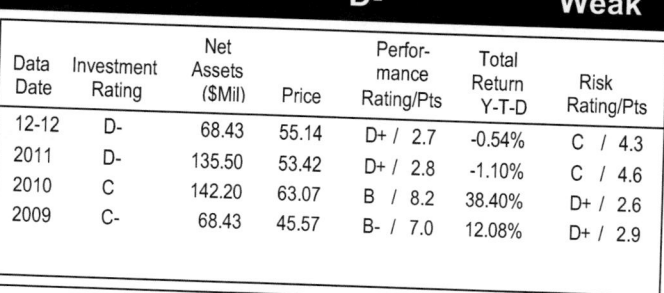

*iPath DJ UBS Almin Tot Ret Sub (JJU)

E **Very Weak**

Fund Family: Barclays Bank PLC
Fund Type: Energy/Natural Resources
Inception Date: June 24, 2008

Major Rating Factors: Very poor performance is the major factor driving the E (Very Weak) TheStreet.com Investment Rating for *iPath DJ UBS Almin Tot Ret Sub. The fund currently has a performance rating of E+ (Very Weak) based on an annualized return of -9.21% over the last three years and a total return of 0.90% year to date 2012. Factored into the performance evaluation is an expense ratio of 0.75% (very low).

The fund's risk rating is currently C- (Fair). It carries a beta of 0.70, meaning the fund's expected move will be 7.0% for every 10% move in the market. Volatility, as measured by both the semi-deviation and a drawdown factor, is considered average. As of December 31, 2012, *iPath DJ UBS Almin Tot Ret Sub traded at a discount of 1.02% below its net asset value, which is better than its one-year historical average discount of .11%.

This fund has been team managed for 5 years and currently receives a manager quality ranking of 9 (0=worst, 99=best). This fund offers an average level of risk but investors looking for strong performance will be frustrated.

Data Date	Investment Rating	Net Assets ($Mil)	Price	Performance Rating/Pts	Total Return Y-T-D	Risk Rating/Pts
12-12	E	6.79	24.18	E+ / 0.8	0.90%	C- / 3.5
2011	E+	4.50	25.30	D / 1.6	1.54%	C- / 4.2
2010	C	11.60	33.10	B+ / 8.5	4.48%	D / 2.1
2009	C	6.79	31.68	A- / 9.0	32.55%	D+ / 2.4

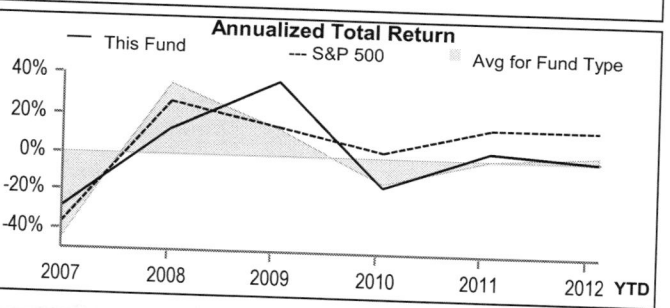

*iPath DJ UBS Cocoa Tot Ret Sub (NIB)

E **Very Weak**

Fund Family: Barclays Bank PLC
Fund Type: Energy/Natural Resources
Inception Date: June 24, 2008

Major Rating Factors: *iPath DJ UBS Cocoa Tot Ret Sub has adopted a risky asset allocation strategy and currently receives an overall TheStreet.com Investment Rating of E (Very Weak). The fund has an above average level of volatility, as measured by both semi-deviation and drawdown factors. It carries a beta of 0.65, meaning the fund's expected move will be 6.5% for every 10% move in the market. As of December 31, 2012, *iPath DJ UBS Cocoa Tot Ret Sub traded at a discount of 1.05% below its net asset value, which is better than its one-year historical average discount of .01%. Unfortunately, the high level of risk (D+, Weak) failed to pay off as investors endured very poor performance.

The fund's performance rating is currently E+ (Very Weak). It has registered an annualized return of -15.52% over the last three years and is up 1.06% year to date 2012. Factored into the performance evaluation is an expense ratio of 0.75% (very low).

This fund has been team managed for 5 years and currently receives a manager quality ranking of 5 (0=worst, 99=best). If you can tolerate high levels of risk in the hope of improved future returns, holding this fund may be an option.

Data Date	Investment Rating	Net Assets ($Mil)	Price	Performance Rating/Pts	Total Return Y-T-D	Risk Rating/Pts
12-12	E	27.73	30.30	E+ / 0.6	1.06%	D+ / 2.9
2011	E	17.60	28.75	E+ / 0.9	-4.70%	C- / 3.1
2010	E+	15.20	43.18	D- / 1.1	-11.66%	C- / 3.6
2009	C+	27.73	48.88	B+ / 8.3	25.98%	C- / 3.8

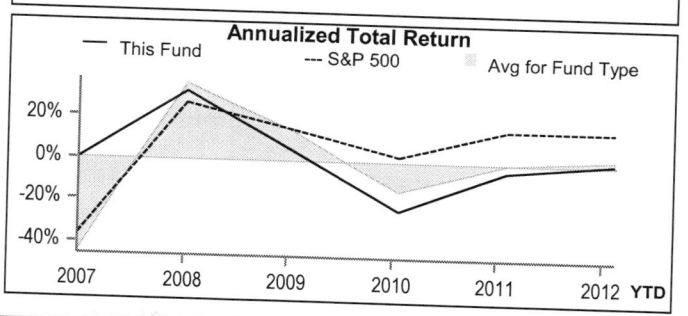

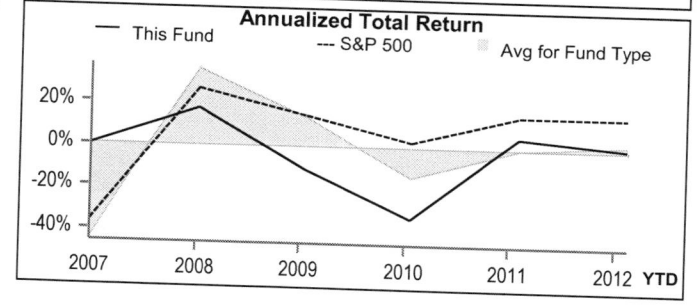

* Denotes ETF Fund

*iPath DJ UBS Coffee Tot Ret Sub (JO)

E-   Very Weak

Fund Family: Barclays Bank PLC
Fund Type: Energy/Natural Resources
Inception Date: June 24, 2008

Data Date	Investment Rating	Net Assets ($Mil)	Price	Performance Rating/Pts	Total Return Y-T-D	Risk Rating/Pts
12-12	E-	7.89	32.37	E+ / 0.7	6.58%	D / 2.1
2011	D	25.70	56.52	C- / 3.7	-3.59%	C- / 4.2
2010	B	34.50	64.03	A+ / 9.8	65.37%	C- / 3.5
2009	C-	7.89	38.72	C / 5.4	10.44%	C- / 3.7

Major Rating Factors: *iPath DJ UBS Coffee Tot Ret Sub has adopted a very risky asset allocation strategy and currently receives an overall TheStreet.com Investment Rating of E- (Very Weak). The fund has a high level of volatility, as measured by both semi-deviation and drawdown factors. It carries a beta of 0.45, meaning the fund's expected move will be 4.5% for every 10% move in the market. As of December 31, 2012, *iPath DJ UBS Coffee Tot Ret Sub traded at a discount of 6.15% below its net asset value, which is better than its one-year historical average premium of .05%. Unfortunately, the high level of risk (D, Weak) failed to pay off as investors endured very poor performance.

The fund's performance rating is currently E+ (Very Weak). It has registered an annualized return of -4.97% over the last three years and is up 6.58% year to date 2012. Factored into the performance evaluation is an expense ratio of 0.75% (very low).

This fund has been team managed for 5 years and currently receives a manager quality ranking of 13 (0=worst, 99=best). If you can tolerate very high levels of risk in the hope of improved future returns, holding this fund may be an option.

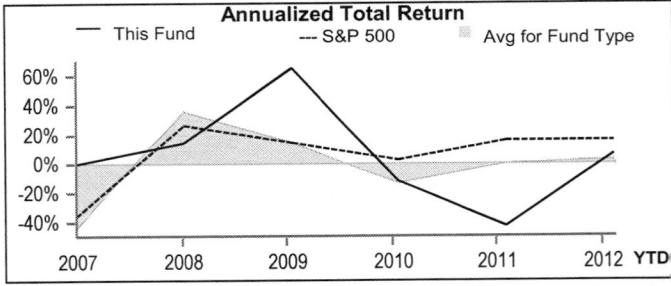

Annualized Total Return

*iPath DJ UBS Copper Total Ret Su (JJC)

E+   Very Weak

Fund Family: Barclays Bank PLC
Fund Type: Energy/Natural Resources
Inception Date: October 23, 2007

Data Date	Investment Rating	Net Assets ($Mil)	Price	Performance Rating/Pts	Total Return Y-T-D	Risk Rating/Pts
12-12	E+	130.36	45.99	D- / 1.3	0.22%	C- / 3.8
2011	D+	127.80	44.04	C+ / 6.4	-0.57%	C- / 4.0
2010	C	252.40	59.10	B+ / 8.6	29.04%	D / 1.8
2009	C+	130.36	45.80	A+ / 9.9	122.44%	D / 2.0

Major Rating Factors:
Disappointing performance is the major factor driving the E+ (Very Weak) TheStreet.com Investment Rating for *iPath DJ UBS Copper Total Ret Su. The fund currently has a performance rating of D- (Weak) based on an annualized return of -0.08% over the last three years and a total return of 0.22% year to date 2012. Factored into the performance evaluation is an expense ratio of 0.75% (very low).

The fund's risk rating is currently C- (Fair). It carries a beta of 1.03, meaning that its performance tracks fairly well with that of the overall stock market. Volatility, as measured by both the semi-deviation and a drawdown factor, is considered average. As of December 31, 2012, *iPath DJ UBS Copper Total Ret Su traded at a discount of .11% below its net asset value, which is better than its one-year historical average discount of .02%.

This fund has been team managed for 6 years and currently receives a manager quality ranking of 14 (0=worst, 99=best). This fund offers an average level of risk but investors looking for strong performance will be frustrated.

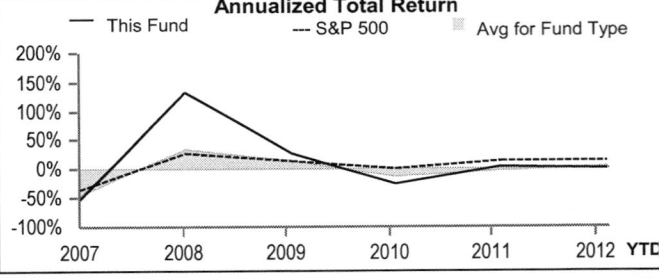

Annualized Total Return

*iPath DJ UBS Cotton Tot Ret Sub (BAL)

E+   Very Weak

Fund Family: Barclays Bank PLC
Fund Type: Energy/Natural Resources
Inception Date: June 24, 2008

Data Date	Investment Rating	Net Assets ($Mil)	Price	Performance Rating/Pts	Total Return Y-T-D	Risk Rating/Pts
12-12	E+	22.72	49.14	C- / 3.4	0.53%	D / 2.1
2011	D+	45.50	56.46	C+ / 6.6	3.67%	C- / 3.1
2010	B-	56.40	73.05	A+ / 9.9	96.21%	D+ / 2.7
2009	C	22.72	37.23	B+ / 8.5	29.90%	D+ / 2.9

Major Rating Factors: *iPath DJ UBS Cotton Tot Ret Sub has adopted a very risky asset allocation strategy and currently receives an overall TheStreet.com Investment Rating of E+ (Very Weak). The fund has a high level of volatility, as measured by both semi-deviation and drawdown factors. It carries a beta of 0.73, meaning the fund's expected move will be 7.3% for every 10% move in the market. As of December 31, 2012, *iPath DJ UBS Cotton Tot Ret Sub traded at a discount of .36% below its net asset value, which is better than its one-year historical average premium of .06%. Unfortunately, the high level of risk (D, Weak) has only provided investors with average performance.

The fund's performance rating is currently C- (Fair). It has registered an annualized return of 11.96% over the last three years and is up 0.53% year to date 2012. Factored into the performance evaluation is an expense ratio of 0.75% (very low).

This fund has been team managed for 5 years and currently receives a manager quality ranking of 71 (0=worst, 99=best). If you are comfortable owning a very high risk investment, then this fund may be an option.

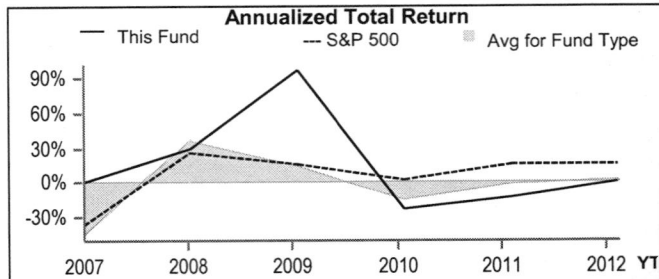

Annualized Total Return

*iPath DJ UBS Energy Tot Ret Sub (JJE)

Fund Family: Barclays Bank PLC
Fund Type: Energy/Natural Resources
Inception Date: October 23, 2007

E   Very Weak

Major Rating Factors: Very poor performance is the major factor driving the E (Very Weak) TheStreet.com Investment Rating for *iPath DJ UBS Energy Tot Ret Sub. The fund currently has a performance rating of E+ (Very Weak) based on an annualized return of -13.29% over the last three years and a total return of -0.47% year to date 2012. Factored into the performance evaluation is an expense ratio of 0.75% (very low).

The fund's risk rating is currently C- (Fair). It carries a beta of 0.73, meaning the fund's expected move will be 7.3% for every 10% move in the market. Volatility, as measured by both the semi-deviation and a drawdown factor, is considered average. As of December 31, 2012, *iPath DJ UBS Energy Tot Ret Sub traded at a discount of .23% below its net asset value, which is better than its one-year historical average discount of .08%.

This fund has been team managed for 6 years and currently receives a manager quality ranking of 6 (0=worst, 99=best). This fund offers an average level of risk but investors looking for strong performance will be frustrated.

Data Date	Investment Rating	Net Assets ($Mil)	Price	Performance Rating/Pts	Total Return Y-T-D	Risk Rating/Pts
12-12	E	10.54	17.12	E+ / 0.7	-0.47%	C- / 3.4
2011	E+	19.00	19.15	D- / 1.2	3.13%	C- / 4.0
2010	E-	15.60	23.21	E / 0.5	-11.92%	D- / 1.2
2009	E	10.54	26.35	D / 1.6	-9.42%	D- / 1.5

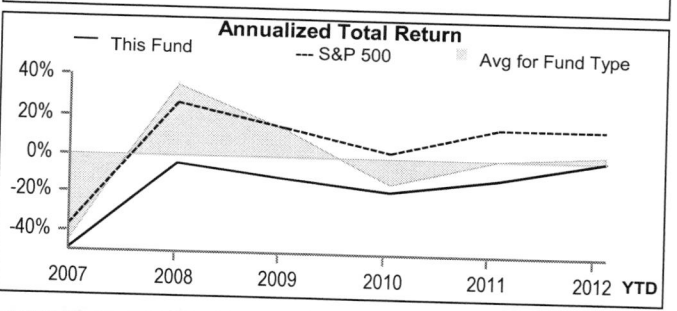

*iPath DJ UBS Grains Tot Ret (JJG)

Fund Family: Barclays Bank PLC
Fund Type: Energy/Natural Resources
Inception Date: October 23, 2007

D   Weak

Major Rating Factors: *iPath DJ UBS Grains Tot Ret receives a TheStreet.com Investment Rating of D (Weak). The fund currently has a performance rating of C- (Fair) based on an annualized return of 11.82% over the last three years and a total return of -0.89% year to date 2012. Factored into the performance evaluation is an expense ratio of 0.75% (very low).

The fund's risk rating is currently C (Fair). It carries a beta of 0.78, meaning the fund's expected move will be 7.8% for every 10% move in the market. Volatility, as measured by both the semi-deviation and a drawdown factor, is considered average. As of December 31, 2012, *iPath DJ UBS Grains Tot Ret traded at a premium of 1.32% above its net asset value, which is worse than its one-year historical average premium of .01%.

This fund has been team managed for 6 years and currently receives a manager quality ranking of 65 (0=worst, 99=best). If you desire an average level of risk, then this fund may be an option.

Data Date	Investment Rating	Net Assets ($Mil)	Price	Performance Rating/Pts	Total Return Y-T-D	Risk Rating/Pts
12-12	D	57.16	52.93	C- / 3.7	-0.89%	C / 4.4
2011	D-	166.80	45.03	D / 1.8	-1.57%	C / 4.4
2010	D+	190.60	53.09	C+ / 5.9	29.87%	D+ / 2.4
2009	D	57.16	40.89	C / 4.4	-2.67%	D+ / 2.7

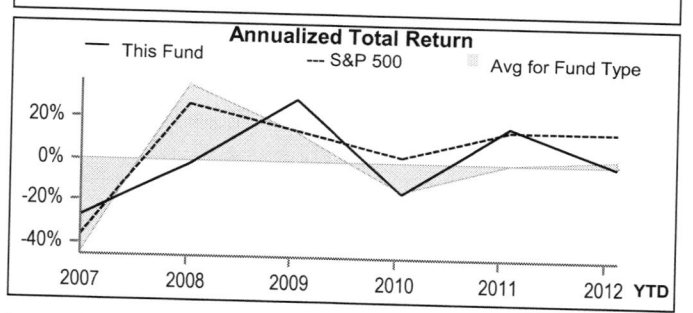

*iPath DJ UBS Ind Me Tot Ret Sub (JJM)

Fund Family: Barclays Bank PLC
Fund Type: Energy/Natural Resources
Inception Date: October 23, 2007

E+   Very Weak

Major Rating Factors:
Disappointing performance is the major factor driving the E+ (Very Weak) TheStreet.com Investment Rating for *iPath DJ UBS Ind Me Tot Ret Sub. The fund currently has a performance rating of D- (Weak) based on an annualized return of -5.00% over the last three years and a total return of 0.14% year to date 2012. Factored into the performance evaluation is an expense ratio of 0.75% (very low).

The fund's risk rating is currently C- (Fair). It carries a beta of 0.95, meaning that its performance tracks fairly well with that of the overall stock market. Volatility, as measured by both the semi-deviation and a drawdown factor, is considered average. As of December 31, 2012, *iPath DJ UBS Ind Me Tot Ret Sub traded at a premium of .29% above its net asset value.

This fund has been team managed for 6 years and currently receives a manager quality ranking of 10 (0=worst, 99=best). This fund offers an average level of risk but investors looking for strong performance will be frustrated.

Data Date	Investment Rating	Net Assets ($Mil)	Price	Performance Rating/Pts	Total Return Y-T-D	Risk Rating/Pts
12-12	E+	49.69	34.87	D- / 1.0	0.14%	C- / 3.8
2011	D-	31.50	34.70	C- / 3.4	0.58%	C- / 4.1
2010	D	71.70	46.87	C+ / 5.8	15.59%	D / 1.9
2009	C+	49.69	40.55	A+ / 9.7	72.92%	D / 2.1

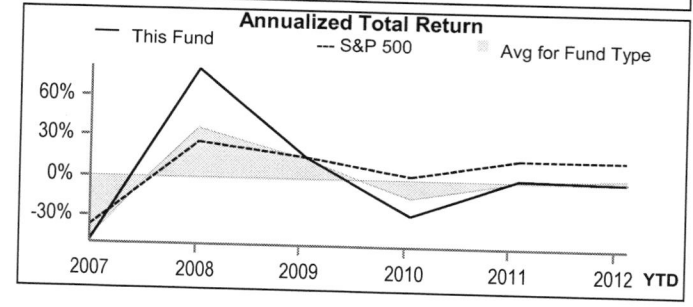

* Denotes ETF Fund

*iPath DJ UBS Lead Tot Ret Sub (LD)

E+ **Very Weak**

Fund Family: Barclays Bank PLC
Fund Type: Energy/Natural Resources
Inception Date: June 24, 2008

Data Date	Investment Rating	Net Assets ($Mil)	Price	Performance Rating/Pts	Total Return Y-T-D	Risk Rating/Pts
12-12	E+	13.63	56.32	D- / 1.4	-0.75%	C- / 3.8
2011	D-	4.20	49.05	C- / 3.5	1.43%	C- / 4.2
2010	C+	6.70	64.98	A / 9.3	3.22%	D / 2.2
2009	C+	13.63	62.95	A+ / 9.9	110.54%	D+ / 2.5

Major Rating Factors:
Disappointing performance is the major factor driving the E+ (Very Weak) TheStreet.com Investment Rating for *iPath DJ UBS Lead Tot Ret Sub. The fund currently has a performance rating of D- (Weak) based on an annualized return of -4.11% over the last three years and a total return of -0.75% year to date 2012. Factored into the performance evaluation is an expense ratio of 0.75% (very low).

The fund's risk rating is currently C- (Fair). It carries a beta of 1.00, meaning that its performance tracks fairly well with that of the overall stock market. Volatility, as measured by both the semi-deviation and a drawdown factor, is considered average. As of December 31, 2012, *iPath DJ UBS Lead Tot Ret Sub traded at a premium of 1.31% above its net asset value, which is worse than its one-year historical average discount of .11%.

This fund has been team managed for 5 years and currently receives a manager quality ranking of 10 (0=worst, 99=best). This fund offers an average level of risk but investors looking for strong performance will be frustrated.

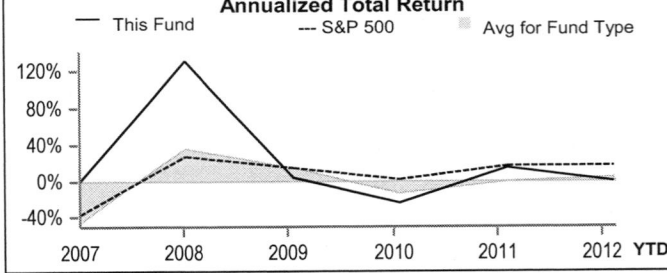

*iPath DJ UBS Live Stk TR Sub (COW)

D- **Weak**

Fund Family: Barclays Bank PLC
Fund Type: Energy/Natural Resources
Inception Date: October 23, 2007

Data Date	Investment Rating	Net Assets ($Mil)	Price	Performance Rating/Pts	Total Return Y-T-D	Risk Rating/Pts
12-12	D-	110.42	28.53	D- / 1.2	-1.61%	C / 4.9
2011	D-	99.20	29.76	D- / 1.5	-0.38%	C / 4.8
2010	E+	65.00	30.75	E+ / 0.8	9.20%	D+ / 2.9
2009	E	110.42	28.16	E+ / 0.7	-19.08%	C- / 3.0

Major Rating Factors:
Disappointing performance is the major factor driving the D- (Weak) TheStreet.com Investment Rating for *iPath DJ UBS Live Stk TR Sub. The fund currently has a performance rating of D- (Weak) based on an annualized return of -0.90% over the last three years and a total return of -1.61% year to date 2012. Factored into the performance evaluation is an expense ratio of 0.75% (very low).

The fund's risk rating is currently C (Fair). It carries a beta of 0.06, meaning the fund's expected move will be 0.6% for every 10% move in the market. Volatility, as measured by both the semi-deviation and a drawdown factor, is considered average. As of December 31, 2012, *iPath DJ UBS Live Stk TR Sub traded at a premium of 1.89% above its net asset value, which is worse than its one-year historical average premium of .08%.

This fund has been team managed for 6 years and currently receives a manager quality ranking of 50 (0=worst, 99=best). This fund offers an average level of risk but investors looking for strong performance will be frustrated.

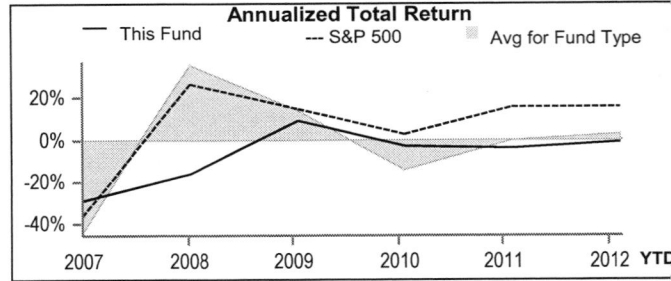

*iPath DJ UBS Nkl Tot Ret Sub (JJN)

E **Very Weak**

Fund Family: Barclays Bank PLC
Fund Type: Energy/Natural Resources
Inception Date: October 23, 2007

Data Date	Investment Rating	Net Assets ($Mil)	Price	Performance Rating/Pts	Total Return Y-T-D	Risk Rating/Pts
12-12	E	14.87	24.10	D- / 1.0	1.62%	D+ / 2.9
2011	D-	8.00	26.68	C- / 3.2	-0.45%	C- / 3.5
2010	E+	18.30	36.65	C- / 3.0	32.12%	D- / 1.5
2009	C	14.87	27.74	B+ / 8.5	40.10%	D / 1.7

Major Rating Factors: *iPath DJ UBS Nkl Tot Ret Sub has adopted a risky asset allocation strategy and currently receives an overall TheStreet.com Investment Rating of E (Very Weak). The fund has an above average level of volatility, as measured by both semi-deviation and drawdown factors. It carries a beta of 1.14, meaning it is expected to move 11.4% for every 10% move in the market. As of December 31, 2012, *iPath DJ UBS Nkl Tot Ret Sub traded at a discount of 1.19% below its net asset value, which is better than its one-year historical average discount of .05%. Unfortunately, the high level of risk (D+, Weak) failed to pay off as investors endured poor performance.

The fund's performance rating is currently D- (Weak). It has registered an annualized return of -3.74% over the last three years and is up 1.62% year to date 2012. Factored into the performance evaluation is an expense ratio of 0.75% (very low).

This fund has been team managed for 6 years and currently receives a manager quality ranking of 9 (0=worst, 99=best). If you can tolerate high levels of risk in the hope of improved future returns, holding this fund may be an option.

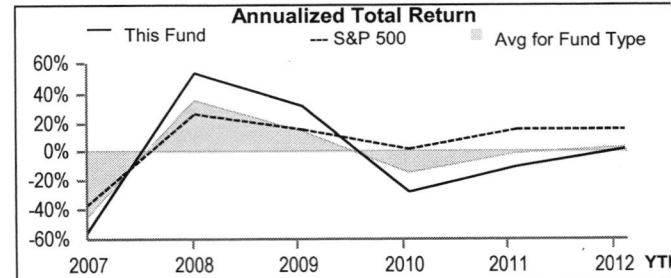

*iPath DJ UBS Ntrl Gas Tot Ret Su (GAZ)

E-   Very Weak

Fund Family: Barclays Bank PLC
Fund Type: Energy/Natural Resources
Inception Date: October 23, 2007

Major Rating Factors: *iPath DJ UBS Ntrl Gas Tot Ret Su has adopted a very risky asset allocation strategy and currently receives an overall TheStreet.com Investment Rating of E- (Very Weak). The fund has a high level of volatility, as measured by both semi-deviation and drawdown factors. It carries a beta of 0.66, meaning the fund's expected move will be 6.6% for every 10% move in the market. As of December 31, 2012, *iPath DJ UBS Ntrl Gas Tot Ret Su traded at a premium of 14.47% above its net asset value, which is better than its one-year historical average premium of 37.98%. Unfortunately, the high level of risk (D, Weak) failed to pay off as investors endured very poor performance.

The fund's performance rating is currently E- (Very Weak). It has registered an annualized return of -42.93% over the last three years and is down -1.11% year to date 2012. Factored into the performance evaluation is an expense ratio of 0.75% (very low).

This fund has been team managed for 6 years and currently receives a manager quality ranking of 1 (0=worst, 99=best). If you can tolerate very high levels of risk in the hope of improved future returns, holding this fund may be an option.

Data Date	Investment Rating	Net Assets ($Mil)	Price	Performance Rating/Pts	Total Return Y-T-D	Risk Rating/Pts
12-12	E-	208.19	2.69	E- / 0.1	-1.11%	D / 1.9
2011	E-	56.10	3.77	E- / 0.1	0.27%	D / 1.9
2010	E-	119.30	8.05	E- / 0.2	-43.63%	D- / 1.0
2009	E-	208.19	14.28	E / 0.3	-54.29%	D- / 1.1

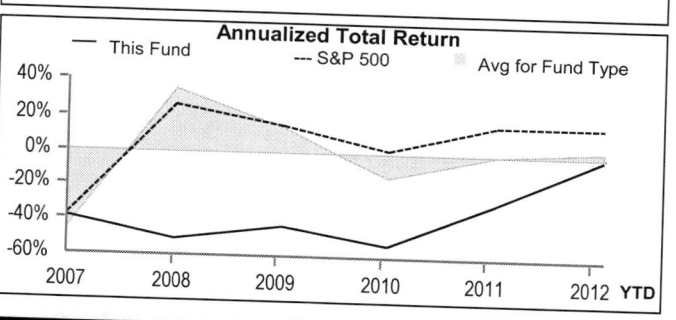

*iPath DJ UBS Platinum Tot Ret Su (PGM)

E+   Very Weak

Fund Family: Barclays Bank PLC
Fund Type: Energy/Natural Resources
Inception Date: June 24, 2008

Major Rating Factors:
Disappointing performance is the major factor driving the E+ (Very Weak) TheStreet.com Investment Rating for *iPath DJ UBS Platinum Tot Ret Su. The fund currently has a performance rating of D- (Weak) based on an annualized return of -2.53% over the last three years and a total return of 6.01% year to date 2012. Factored into the performance evaluation is an expense ratio of 0.75% (very low).

The fund's risk rating is currently C- (Fair). It carries a beta of 0.72, meaning the fund's expected move will be 7.2% for every 10% move in the market. Volatility, as measured by both the semi-deviation and a drawdown factor, is considered average. As of December 31, 2012, *iPath DJ UBS Platinum Tot Ret Su traded at a discount of 5.64% below its net asset value, which is better than its one-year historical average premium of .20%.

This fund has been team managed for 5 years and currently receives a manager quality ranking of 13 (0=worst, 99=best). This fund offers an average level of risk but investors looking for strong performance will be frustrated.

Data Date	Investment Rating	Net Assets ($Mil)	Price	Performance Rating/Pts	Total Return Y-T-D	Risk Rating/Pts
12-12	E+	103.49	34.80	D- / 1.3	6.01%	C- / 4.2
2011	D-	30.80	32.03	D+ / 2.7	1.58%	C / 4.3
2010	C-	78.00	41.85	B+ / 8.4	8.59%	D / 1.6
2009	A+	103.49	38.54	A+ / 9.6	63.51%	C / 5.4

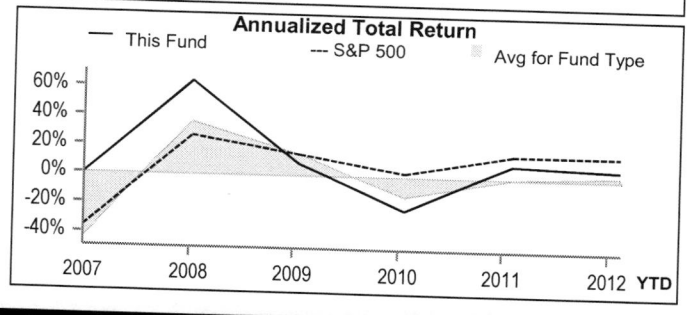

*iPath DJ UBS Precious Mtls Tot R (JJP)

D   Weak

Fund Family: Barclays Bank PLC
Fund Type: Energy/Natural Resources
Inception Date: June 24, 2008

Major Rating Factors: *iPath DJ UBS Precious Mtls Tot R receives a TheStreet.com Investment Rating of D (Weak). The fund currently has a performance rating of C (Fair) based on an annualized return of 13.83% over the last three years and a total return of -0.42% year to date 2012. Factored into the performance evaluation is an expense ratio of 0.75% (very low).

The fund's risk rating is currently C (Fair). It carries a beta of 0.40, meaning the fund's expected move will be 4.0% for every 10% move in the market. Volatility, as measured by both the semi-deviation and a drawdown factor, is considered average. As of December 31, 2012, *iPath DJ UBS Precious Mtls Tot R traded at a premium of .45% above its net asset value, which is worse than its one-year historical average discount of .10%.

This fund has been team managed for 5 years and currently receives a manager quality ranking of 92 (0=worst, 99=best). If you desire an average level of risk, then this fund may be an option.

Data Date	Investment Rating	Net Assets ($Mil)	Price	Performance Rating/Pts	Total Return Y-T-D	Risk Rating/Pts
12-12	D	8.23	89.23	C / 4.4	-0.42%	C / 4.7
2011	C	73.20	84.32	B / 7.8	4.17%	C / 4.8
2010	B+	28.40	81.64	A+ / 9.7	41.91%	C- / 3.7
2009	C+	8.23	57.53	B+ / 8.3	29.43%	C- / 3.9

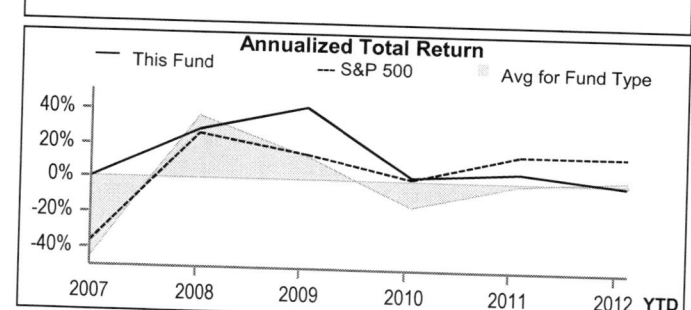

* Denotes ETF Fund

*iPath DJ UBS Softs Tot Ret Sub (JJS)   E   Very Weak

Fund Family: Barclays Bank PLC
Fund Type: Energy/Natural Resources
Inception Date: June 24, 2008

Major Rating Factors:
Disappointing performance is the major factor driving the E (Very Weak) TheStreet.com Investment Rating for *iPath DJ UBS Softs Tot Ret Sub. The fund currently has a performance rating of D- (Weak) based on an annualized return of 1.22% over the last three years and a total return of 0.62% year to date 2012. Factored into the performance evaluation is an expense ratio of 0.75% (very low).

The fund's risk rating is currently C- (Fair). It carries a beta of 0.52, meaning the fund's expected move will be 5.2% for every 10% move in the market. Volatility, as measured by both the semi-deviation and a drawdown factor, is considered average. As of December 31, 2012, *iPath DJ UBS Softs Tot Ret Sub traded at a discount of 1.05% below its net asset value, which is better than its one-year historical average discount of .10%.

This fund has been team managed for 5 years and currently receives a manager quality ranking of 29 (0=worst, 99=best). This fund offers an average level of risk but investors looking for strong performance will be frustrated.

Data Date	Investment Rating	Net Assets ($Mil)	Price	Performance Rating/Pts	Total Return Y-T-D	Risk Rating/Pts
12-12	E	4.67	53.00	D- / 1.0	0.62%	C- / 3.2
2011	C-	17.40	69.30	C+ / 6.0	-1.30%	C / 4.5
2010	B+	43.50	81.05	A+ / 9.9	58.86%	C- / 3.6
2009	B-	4.67	51.02	A- / 9.0	43.60%	C- / 3.8

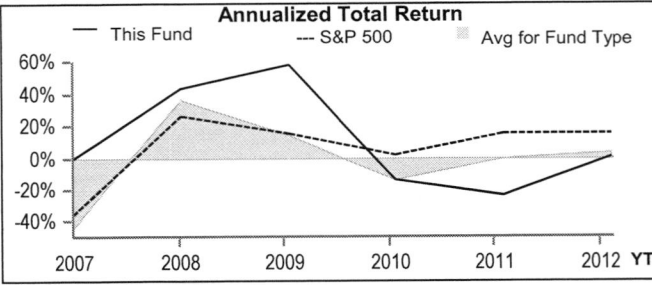

Annualized Total Return

*iPath DJ UBS Sugar Tot Ret Sub (SGG)   E   Very Weak

Fund Family: Barclays Bank PLC
Fund Type: Energy/Natural Resources
Inception Date: June 24, 2008

Major Rating Factors: *iPath DJ UBS Sugar Tot Ret Sub has adopted a risky asset allocation strategy and currently receives an overall TheStreet.com Investment Rating of E (Very Weak). The fund has an above average level of volatility, as measured by both semi-deviation and drawdown factors. It carries a beta of 0.47, meaning the fund's expected move will be 4.7% for every 10% move in the market. As of December 31, 2012, *iPath DJ UBS Sugar Tot Ret Sub traded at a premium of 2.00% above its net asset value, which is worse than its one-year historical average premium of .07%. Unfortunately, the high level of risk (D+, Weak) failed to pay off as investors endured very poor performance.

The fund's performance rating is currently E+ (Very Weak). It has registered an annualized return of -4.11% over the last three years and is down -1.92% year to date 2012. Factored into the performance evaluation is an expense ratio of 0.75% (very low).

This fund has been team managed for 5 years and currently receives a manager quality ranking of 19 (0=worst, 99=best). If you can tolerate high levels of risk in the hope of improved future returns, holding this fund may be an option.

Data Date	Investment Rating	Net Assets ($Mil)	Price	Performance Rating/Pts	Total Return Y-T-D	Risk Rating/Pts
12-12	E	26.55	70.35	E+ / 0.8	-1.92%	D+ / 2.5
2011	D	32.90	81.80	C+ / 6.6	-0.56%	D+ / 2.7
2010	C+	81.10	93.55	A+ / 9.9	25.07%	D+ / 2.4
2009	B+	26.55	74.80	A+ / 9.8	82.62%	C- / 4.0

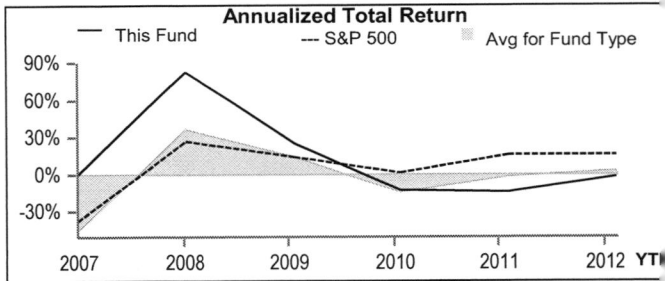

Annualized Total Return

*iPath DJ UBS Tin Tot Ret Sub (JJT)   D   Weak

Fund Family: Barclays Bank PLC
Fund Type: Energy/Natural Resources
Inception Date: June 24, 2008

Major Rating Factors: *iPath DJ UBS Tin Tot Ret Sub has adopted a risky asset allocation strategy and currently receives an overall TheStreet.com Investment Rating of D (Weak). The fund has an above average level of volatility, as measured by both semi-deviation and drawdown factors. It carries a beta of 0.94, meaning that its performance tracks fairly well with that of the overall stock market. As of December 31, 2012, *iPath DJ UBS Tin Tot Ret Sub traded at a discount of 5.94% below its net asset value, which is better than its one-year historical average discount of .13%. Unfortunately, the high level of risk (D+, Weak) has only provided investors with average performance.

The fund's performance rating is currently C+ (Fair). It has registered an annualized return of 10.26% over the last three years and is up 7.35% year to date 2012. Factored into the performance evaluation is an expense ratio of 0.75% (very low).

This fund has been team managed for 5 years and currently receives a manager quality ranking of 64 (0=worst, 99=best). If you are comfortable owning a high risk investment, then this fund may be an option.

Data Date	Investment Rating	Net Assets ($Mil)	Price	Performance Rating/Pts	Total Return Y-T-D	Risk Rating/Pts
12-12	D	1.74	53.86	C+ / 6.1	7.35%	D+ / 2.9
2011	D	7.50	43.71	C / 4.5	3.48%	C- / 3.3
2010	C+	33.40	63.37	A+ / 9.8	58.74%	D+ / 2.4
2009	C+	1.74	39.92	A- / 9.2	55.39%	D+ / 2.7

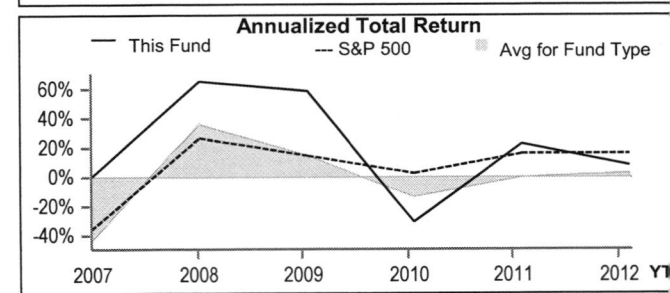

Annualized Total Return

*iPath DJ-UBS Commodity Index Tot (DJP)

Fund Family: Barclays Bank PLC
Fund Type: Growth
Inception Date: June 6, 2006

D   **Weak**

Major Rating Factors:

Disappointing performance is the major factor driving the D (Weak) TheStreet.com Investment Rating for *iPath DJ-UBS Commodity Index Tot. The fund currently has a performance rating of D- (Weak) based on an annualized return of -0.51% over the last three years and a total return of -0.46% year to date 2012. Factored into the performance evaluation is an expense ratio of 0.75% (very low).

The fund's risk rating is currently B- (Good). It carries a beta of 0.94, meaning that its performance tracks fairly well with that of the overall stock market. Volatility, as measured by both the semi-deviation and a drawdown factor, is considered low. As of December 31, 2012, *iPath DJ-UBS Commodity Index Tot traded at a premium of .78% above its net asset value, which is worse than its one-year historical average premium of .03%.

This fund has been team managed for 7 years and currently receives a manager quality ranking of 13 (0=worst, 99=best). This fund offers only a moderate level of risk but investors looking for strong performance are still waiting.

Data Date	Investment Rating	Net Assets ($Mil)	Price	Performance Rating/Pts	Total Return Y-T-D	Risk Rating/Pts
12-12	D	1,897.33	41.35	D- / 1.2	-0.46%	B- / 7.0
2011	D+	2,581.80	42.24	D+ / 2.4	0.76%	B- / 7.7
2010	D	2,854.70	49.12	C- / 3.0	16.23%	C / 4.9
2009	D+	1,897.33	42.26	D+ / 2.5	16.26%	C / 5.3

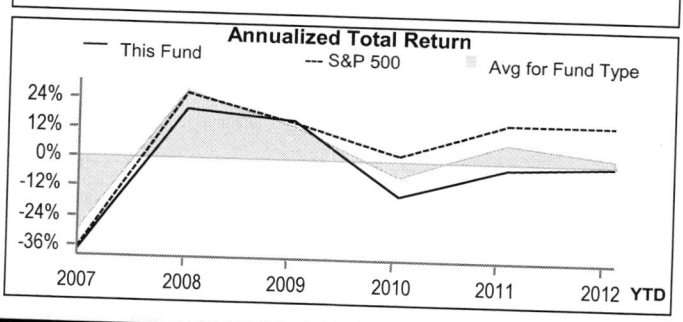

*iPath ETN US Treasury 5Yr Bear E (DFVS)

Fund Family: Barclays Bank PLC
Fund Type: US Government/Agency
Inception Date: July 11, 2011

E+   **Very Weak**

Major Rating Factors:

Very poor performance is the major factor driving the E+ (Very Weak) TheStreet.com Investment Rating for *iPath ETN US Treasury 5Yr Bear E. The fund currently has a performance rating of E+ (Very Weak) based on an annualized return of 0.00% over the last three years and a total return of 0.89% year to date 2012.

The fund's risk rating is currently C (Fair). It carries a beta of 0.00, meaning the fund's expected move will be 0.0% for every 10% move in the market. Volatility, as measured by both the semi-deviation and a drawdown factor, is considered average. As of December 31, 2012, *iPath ETN US Treasury 5Yr Bear E traded at a discount of .62% below its net asset value, which is better than its one-year historical average premium of .44%.

This fund has been team managed for 2 years and currently receives a manager quality ranking of 16 (0=worst, 99=best). This fund offers an average level of risk but investors looking for strong performance will be frustrated.

Data Date	Investment Rating	Net Assets ($Mil)	Price	Performance Rating/Pts	Total Return Y-T-D	Risk Rating/Pts
12-12	E+	1.70	38.26	E+ / 0.9	0.89%	C / 4.8

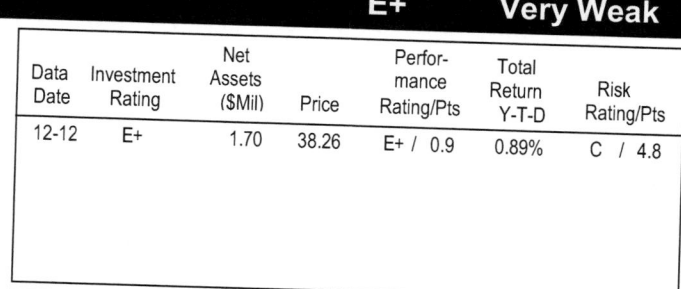

*iPath EUR/USD Exch Rate ETN (ERO)

Fund Family: Barclays Bank PLC
Fund Type: Foreign
Inception Date: May 8, 2007

D   **Weak**

Major Rating Factors:

Disappointing performance is the major factor driving the D (Weak) TheStreet.com Investment Rating for *iPath EUR/USD Exch Rate ETN. The fund currently has a performance rating of D- (Weak) based on an annualized return of -2.89% over the last three years and a total return of -1.42% year to date 2012. Factored into the performance evaluation is an expense ratio of 0.40% (very low).

The fund's risk rating is currently B (Good). It carries a beta of 0.55, meaning the fund's expected move will be 5.5% for every 10% move in the market. Volatility, as measured by both the semi-deviation and a drawdown factor, is considered low. As of December 31, 2012, *iPath EUR/USD Exch Rate ETN traded at a premium of .48% above its net asset value, which is worse than its one-year historical average discount of .43%.

This fund has been team managed for 6 years and currently receives a manager quality ranking of 23 (0=worst, 99=best). This fund offers only a moderate level of risk but investors looking for strong performance are still waiting.

Data Date	Investment Rating	Net Assets ($Mil)	Price	Performance Rating/Pts	Total Return Y-T-D	Risk Rating/Pts
12-12	D	8.45	51.97	D- / 1.2	-1.42%	B / 8.1
2011	D+	4.80	50.34	D / 1.8	0.74%	B / 8.1
2010	D+	6.40	51.77	D- / 1.5	-7.50%	C+ / 6.8
2009	C-	8.45	55.97	D+ / 2.8	4.17%	B- / 7.2

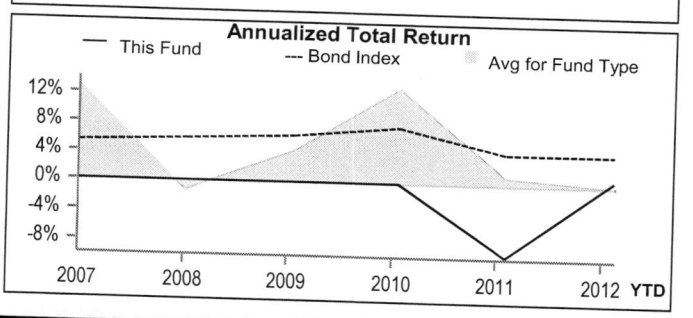

* Denotes ETF Fund

*iPath GBP/USD Exchange Rate ETN (GBB)   D+   Weak

Fund Family: Barclays Bank PLC
Fund Type: Growth
Inception Date: May 8, 2007

Major Rating Factors:
Disappointing performance is the major factor driving the D+ (Weak) TheStreet.com
Investment Rating for *iPath GBP/USD Exchange Rate ETN. The fund currently has
a performance rating of D- (Weak) based on an annualized return of -0.80% over the
last three years and a total return of -0.30% year to date 2012. Factored into the
performance evaluation is an expense ratio of 0.40% (very low).

The fund's risk rating is currently B (Good). It carries a beta of 0.26, meaning the
fund's expected move will be 2.6% for every 10% move in the market. Volatility, as
measured by both the semi-deviation and a drawdown factor, is considered low. As of
December 31, 2012, *iPath GBP/USD Exchange Rate ETN traded at a premium
of .30% above its net asset value, which is worse than its one-year historical average
discount of .08%.

This fund has been team managed for 6 years and currently receives a manager
quality ranking of 30 (0=worst, 99=best). This fund offers only a moderate level of risk
but investors looking for strong performance are still waiting.

Data Date	Investment Rating	Net Assets ($Mil)	Price	Performance Rating/Pts	Total Return Y-T-D	Risk Rating/Pts
12-12	D+	1.78	43.03	D- / 1.3	-0.30%	B / 8.8
2011	C-	2.50	41.43	D+ / 2.3	2.85%	B / 8.7
2010	D	6.80	41.40	E+ / 0.9	-3.77%	C+ / 6.5
2009	C	1.78	43.02	C- / 3.6	9.35%	C+ / 6.9

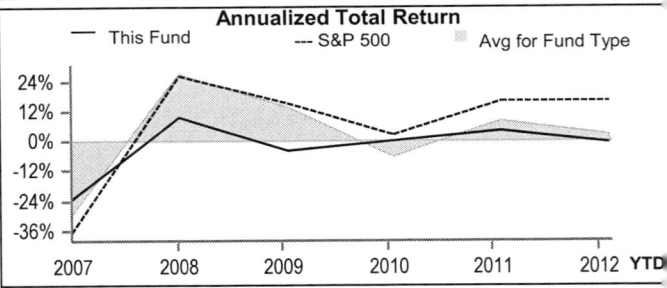

*iPath GEMS Asia 8 ETN (AYT)   D-   Weak

Fund Family: Barclays Bank PLC
Fund Type: Foreign
Inception Date: April 2, 2008

Major Rating Factors:
Disappointing performance is the major factor driving the D- (Weak) TheStreet.com
Investment Rating for *iPath GEMS Asia 8 ETN. The fund currently has a
performance rating of D (Weak) based on an annualized return of 1.28% over the last
three years and a total return of 0.52% year to date 2012.

The fund's risk rating is currently C (Fair). It carries a beta of 0.25, meaning the
fund's expected move will be 2.5% for every 10% move in the market. Volatility, as
measured by both the semi-deviation and a drawdown factor, is considered average.
As of December 31, 2012, *iPath GEMS Asia 8 ETN traded at a discount of .54%
below its net asset value, which is better than its one-year historical average discount
of .10%.

This fund has been team managed for 5 years and currently receives a manager
quality ranking of 62 (0=worst, 99=best). This fund offers an average level of risk but
investors looking for strong performance will be frustrated.

Data Date	Investment Rating	Net Assets ($Mil)	Price	Performance Rating/Pts	Total Return Y-T-D	Risk Rating/Pts
12-12	D-	19.70	48.20	D / 1.8	0.52%	C / 5.5
2011	D-	18.40	47.01	D / 2.2	0.68%	C+ / 5.6
2010	C+	10.00	48.99	C+ / 6.5	6.79%	C / 4.9

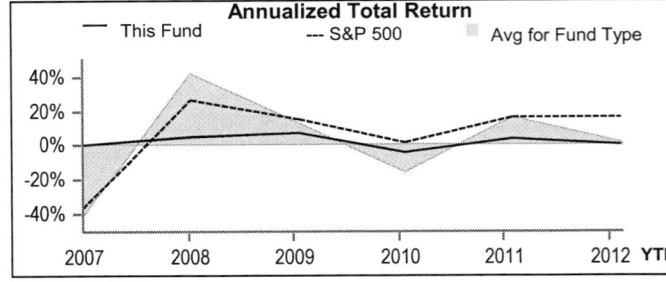

*iPath GEMS Index ETN (JEM)   D-   Weak

Fund Family: Barclays Bank PLC
Fund Type: Growth and Income
Inception Date: February 1, 2008

Major Rating Factors:
Disappointing performance is the major factor driving the D- (Weak) TheStreet.com
Investment Rating for *iPath GEMS Index ETN. The fund currently has a performance
rating of D (Weak) based on an annualized return of 0.31% over the last three years
and a total return of 0.71% year to date 2012.

The fund's risk rating is currently C (Fair). It carries a beta of 0.63, meaning the
fund's expected move will be 6.3% for every 10% move in the market. Volatility, as
measured by both the semi-deviation and a drawdown factor, is considered average.
As of December 31, 2012, *iPath GEMS Index ETN traded at a discount of 1.51%
below its net asset value, which is better than its one-year historical average discount
of .40%.

Barclays Capital has been running the fund for 5 years and currently receives a
manager quality ranking of 23 (0=worst, 99=best). This fund offers an average level
of risk but investors looking for strong performance will be frustrated.

Data Date	Investment Rating	Net Assets ($Mil)	Price	Performance Rating/Pts	Total Return Y-T-D	Risk Rating/Pts
12-12	D-	1.40	42.50	D / 1.7	0.71%	C / 5.1
2011	D-	1.40	42.00	D / 2.1	-0.48%	C / 5.3
2010	C	4.10	46.50	B- / 7.4	6.69%	C- / 3.7
2009	D+	0.00	44.65	C- / 4.0	14.42%	C- / 3.9

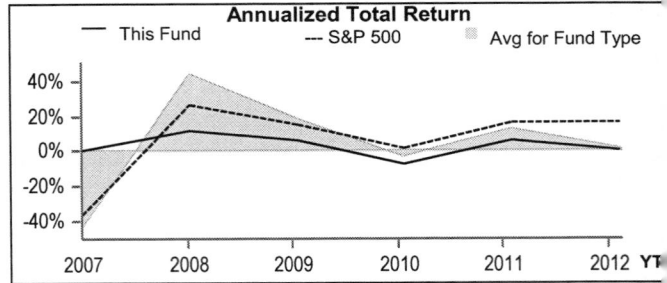

*iPath JPY/USD Exchange Rate ETN (JYN)

D+ **Weak**

Fund Family: Barclays Bank PLC
Fund Type: Foreign
Inception Date: May 8, 2007

Major Rating Factors:
Disappointing performance is the major factor driving the D+ (Weak) TheStreet.com Investment Rating for *iPath JPY/USD Exchange Rate ETN. The fund currently has a performance rating of D- (Weak) based on an annualized return of -0.39% over the last three years and a total return of -10.33% year to date 2012. Factored into the performance evaluation is an expense ratio of 0.40% (very low).

The fund's risk rating is currently B+ (Good). It carries a beta of -0.09, meaning the fund's expected move will be -0.9% for every 10% move in the market. Volatility, as measured by both the semi-deviation and a drawdown factor, is considered very low. As of December 31, 2012, *iPath JPY/USD Exchange Rate ETN traded at a premium of 9.90% above its net asset value, which is worse than its one-year historical average premium of .07%.

This fund has been team managed for 6 years and currently receives a manager quality ranking of 78 (0=worst, 99=best). This fund offers only a moderate level of risk but investors looking for strong performance are still waiting.

Data Date	Investment Rating	Net Assets ($Mil)	Price	Performance Rating/Pts	Total Return Y-T-D	Risk Rating/Pts
12-12	D+	11.27	71.94	D- / 1.0	-10.33%	B+ / 9.1
2011	C	20.00	76.45	C- / 3.1	-0.12%	B+ / 9.0
2010	B	8.90	72.80	B- / 7.3	14.09%	C+ / 5.9
2009	D+	11.27	63.81	D / 1.7	-1.31%	C+ / 6.3

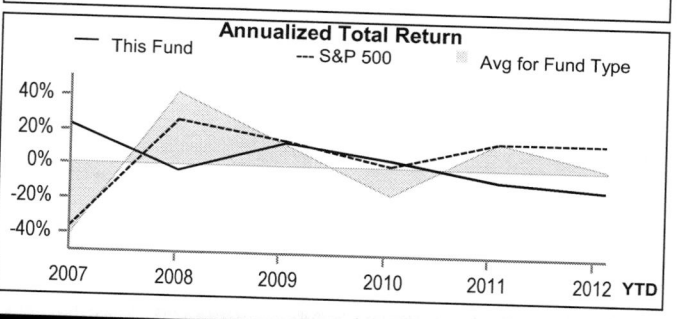

*iPath Long Enh MSCI Em Mkt Idx E (EMLB)

C- **Fair**

Fund Family: Barclays Bank PLC
Fund Type: Emerging Market
Inception Date: November 29, 2010

Major Rating Factors: *iPath Long Enh MSCI Em Mkt Idx E has adopted a risky asset allocation strategy and currently receives an overall TheStreet.com Investment Rating of C- (Fair). The fund has shown an above average level of volatility, as measured by both semi-deviation and drawdown factors. It carries a beta of 0.00, meaning the fund's expected move will be 0.0% for every 10% move in the market. As of December 31, 2012, *iPath Long Enh MSCI Em Mkt Idx E traded at a premium of 3.91% above its net asset value, which is worse than its one-year historical average discount of 1.99%. The high level of risk (D+, Weak) did however, reward investors with excellent performance.

The fund's performance rating is currently A (Excellent). It has registered an annualized return of 0.00% over the last three years and is up 2.36% year to date 2012.

This is team managed and currently receives a manager quality ranking of 88 (0=worst, 99=best). If you are comfortable owning a high risk investment, this fund may be an option.

Data Date	Investment Rating	Net Assets ($Mil)	Price	Performance Rating/Pts	Total Return Y-T-D	Risk Rating/Pts
12-12	C-	3.40	108.98	A / 9.5	2.36%	D+ / 2.5
2011	C	2.40	71.71	A+ / 9.9	62.52%	D+ / 2.7

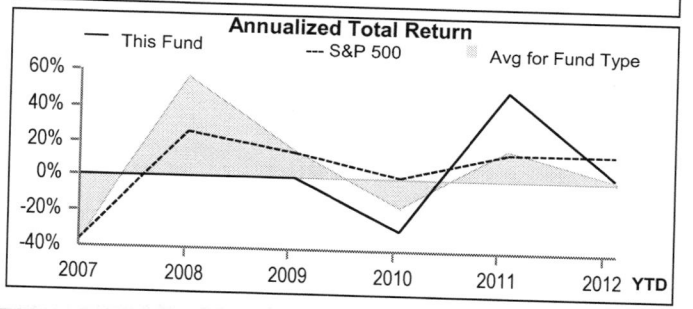

*iPath Long Ext Rus 2000 TR Idx E (RTLA)

C- **Fair**

Fund Family: Barclays Bank PLC
Fund Type: Income
Inception Date: November 29, 2010

Major Rating Factors: *iPath Long Ext Rus 2000 TR Idx E has adopted a very risky asset allocation strategy and currently receives an overall TheStreet.com Investment Rating of C- (Fair). The fund has shown a high level of volatility, as measured by both semi-deviation and drawdown factors. It carries a beta of 0.00, meaning the fund's expected move will be 0.0% for every 10% move in the market. As of December 31, 2012, *iPath Long Ext Rus 2000 TR Idx E traded at a discount of 9.37% below its net asset value, which is better than its one-year historical average discount of .03%. The high level of risk (D, Weak) did however, reward investors with excellent performance.

The fund's performance rating is currently A+ (Excellent). It has registered an annualized return of 0.00% over the last three years and is up 9.45% year to date 2012.

This is team managed and currently receives a manager quality ranking of 18 (0=worst, 99=best). If you are comfortable owning a very high risk investment, this fund may be an option.

Data Date	Investment Rating	Net Assets ($Mil)	Price	Performance Rating/Pts	Total Return Y-T-D	Risk Rating/Pts
12-12	C-	6.60	75.46	A+ / 9.8	9.45%	D / 2.1
2011	E+	4.50	53.45	D+ / 2.7	2.81%	D+ / 2.3

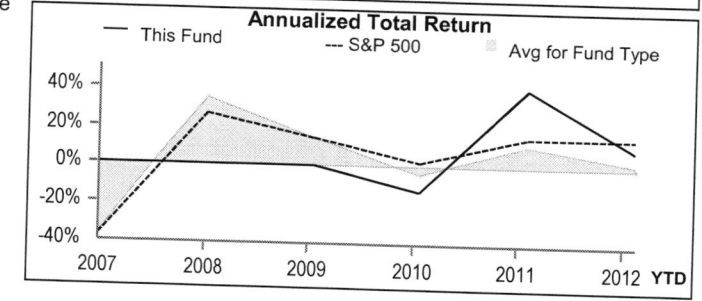

* Denotes ETF Fund

*iPath Long Ext S&P 500 TR Idx ET (SFLA)

C   **Fair**

Fund Family: Barclays Bank PLC
Fund Type: Income
Inception Date: November 29, 2010

Major Rating Factors:
Exceptional performance is the major factor driving the C (Fair) TheStreet.com Investment Rating for *iPath Long Ext S&P 500 TR Idx ET. The fund currently has a performance rating of A+ (Excellent) based on an annualized return of 0.00% over the last three years and a total return of 7.05% year to date 2012.

The fund's risk rating is currently C- (Fair). It carries a beta of 0.00, meaning the fund's expected move will be 0.0% for every 10% move in the market. Volatility, as measured by both the semi-deviation and a drawdown factor, is considered average. As of December 31, 2012, *iPath Long Ext S&P 500 TR Idx ET traded at a discount of 6.79% below its net asset value, which is better than its one-year historical average discount of .38%.

This is team managed and currently receives a manager quality ranking of 25 (0=worst, 99=best). If you desire an average level of risk and strong performance, then this fund is a good option.

Data Date	Investment Rating	Net Assets ($Mil)	Price	Performance Rating/Pts	Total Return Y-T-D	Risk Rating/Pts
12-12	C	3.60	85.71	A+ / 9.7	7.05%	C- / 3.4
2011	D	5.20	61.42	C / 5.0	4.60%	C- / 3.6

Annualized Total Return

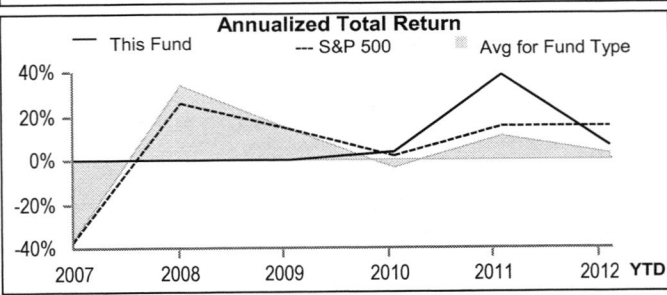

*iPath MSCI India Index ETN (INP)

D-   **Weak**

Fund Family: Barclays Bank PLC
Fund Type: Emerging Market
Inception Date: December 19, 2006

Major Rating Factors:
Disappointing performance is the major factor driving the D- (Weak) TheStreet.com Investment Rating for *iPath MSCI India Index ETN. The fund currently has a performance rating of D (Weak) based on an annualized return of -2.89% over the last three years and a total return of 0.79% year to date 2012. Factored into the performance evaluation is an expense ratio of 0.89% (low).

The fund's risk rating is currently C+ (Fair). It carries a beta of 1.17, meaning it is expected to move 11.7% for every 10% move in the market. Volatility, as measured by both the semi-deviation and a drawdown factor, is considered low. As of December 31, 2012, *iPath MSCI India Index ETN traded at a discount of .65% below its net asset value, which is better than its one-year historical average premium of .30%.

This fund has been team managed for 7 years and currently receives a manager quality ranking of 15 (0=worst, 99=best). This fund offers only a moderate level of risk but investors looking for strong performance are still waiting.

Data Date	Investment Rating	Net Assets ($Mil)	Price	Performance Rating/Pts	Total Return Y-T-D	Risk Rating/Pts
12-12	D-	1,058.84	59.33	D / 1.7	0.79%	C+ / 5.7
2011	D	454.00	46.62	C- / 3.4	3.56%	C+ / 5.9
2010	D-	1,154.20	77.66	D / 2.1	21.23%	C- / 3.4
2009	C	1,058.84	64.06	B / 7.8	91.11%	C- / 3.6

Annualized Total Return

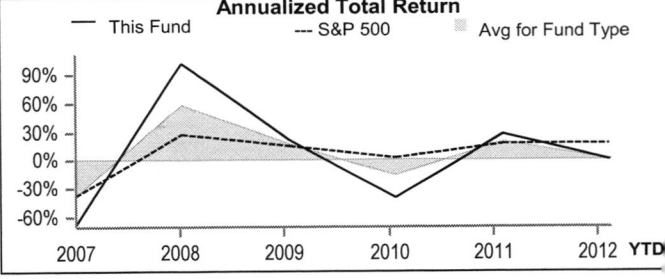

*iPath Optimized Currency Carry E (ICI)

C-   **Fair**

Fund Family: Barclays Bank PLC
Fund Type: Global
Inception Date: January 31, 2008

Major Rating Factors:
Disappointing performance is the major factor driving the C- (Fair) TheStreet.com Investment Rating for *iPath Optimized Currency Carry E. The fund currently has a performance rating of D (Weak) based on an annualized return of 0.82% over the last three years and a total return of 0.75% year to date 2012. Factored into the performance evaluation is an expense ratio of 0.65% (very low).

The fund's risk rating is currently B+ (Good). It carries a beta of 0.12, meaning the fund's expected move will be 1.2% for every 10% move in the market. Volatility, as measured by both the semi-deviation and a drawdown factor, is considered very low. As of December 31, 2012, *iPath Optimized Currency Carry E traded at a discount of 1.10% below its net asset value, which is better than its one-year historical average discount of .05%.

This fund has been team managed for 5 years and currently receives a manager quality ranking of 56 (0=worst, 99=best). This fund offers only a moderate level of risk but investors looking for strong performance are still waiting.

Data Date	Investment Rating	Net Assets ($Mil)	Price	Performance Rating/Pts	Total Return Y-T-D	Risk Rating/Pts
12-12	C-	27.19	46.88	D / 1.6	0.75%	B+ / 9.5
2011	C-	87.30	46.10	D+ / 2.3	0.48%	B+ / 9.6
2010	B	22.90	46.98	C / 4.7	3.07%	B / 8.2
2009	C+	27.19	45.58	C- / 3.5	4.76%	B / 8.4

Annualized Total Return

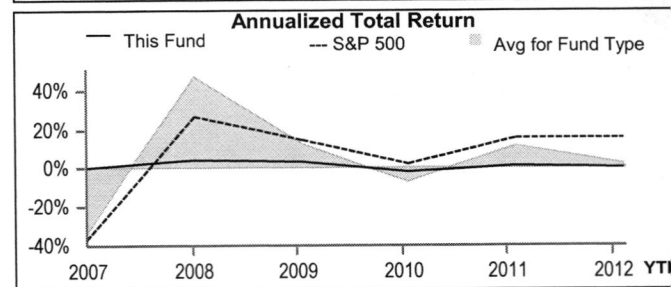

*iPath Pure Beta Agriculture ETN (DIRT)

Fund Family: Barclays Bank PLC
Fund Type: Income
Inception Date: April 20, 2011

D-   **Weak**

Major Rating Factors:
Disappointing performance is the major factor driving the D- (Weak) TheStreet.com Investment Rating for *iPath Pure Beta Agriculture ETN. The fund currently has a performance rating of D (Weak) based on an annualized return of 0.00% over the last three years and a total return of -1.08% year to date 2012.

The fund's risk rating is currently C (Fair). It carries a beta of 0.00, meaning the fund's expected move will be 0.0% for every 10% move in the market. Volatility, as measured by both the semi-deviation and a drawdown factor, is considered average. As of December 31, 2012, *iPath Pure Beta Agriculture ETN traded at a premium of 1.07% above its net asset value, which is worse than its one-year historical average discount of .11%.

This fund has been team managed for 2 years and currently receives a manager quality ranking of 65 (0=worst, 99=best). This fund offers an average level of risk but investors looking for strong performance will be frustrated.

Data Date	Investment Rating	Net Assets ($Mil)	Price	Perfor-mance Rating/Pts	Total Return Y-T-D	Risk Rating/Pts
12-12	D-	3.20	47.35	D / 2.0	-1.08%	C / 4.7

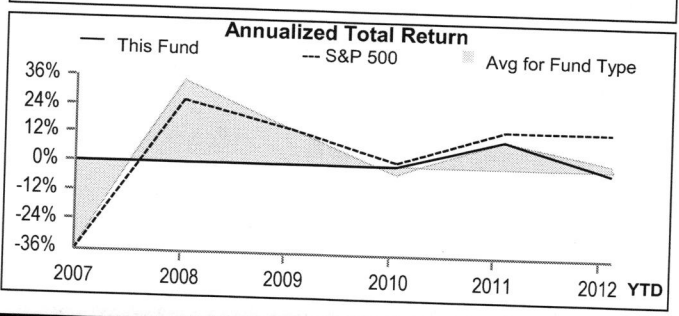

*iPath Pure Beta Aluminum ETN (FOIL)

Fund Family: Barclays Bank PLC
Fund Type: Income
Inception Date: April 20, 2011

E+   **Very Weak**

Major Rating Factors:
Very poor performance is the major factor driving the E+ (Very Weak) TheStreet.com Investment Rating for *iPath Pure Beta Aluminum ETN. The fund currently has a performance rating of E+ (Very Weak) based on an annualized return of 0.00% over the last three years and a total return of -0.17% year to date 2012.

The fund's risk rating is currently C- (Fair). It carries a beta of 0.00, meaning the fund's expected move will be 0.0% for every 10% move in the market. Volatility, as measured by both the semi-deviation and a drawdown factor, is considered average. As of December 31, 2012, *iPath Pure Beta Aluminum ETN traded at a premium of .52% above its net asset value, which is worse than its one-year historical average discount of .33%.

This fund has been team managed for 2 years and currently receives a manager quality ranking of 9 (0=worst, 99=best). This fund offers an average level of risk but investors looking for strong performance will be frustrated.

Data Date	Investment Rating	Net Assets ($Mil)	Price	Perfor-mance Rating/Pts	Total Return Y-T-D	Risk Rating/Pts
12-12	E+	1.40	34.53	E+ / 0.9	-0.17%	C- / 3.8

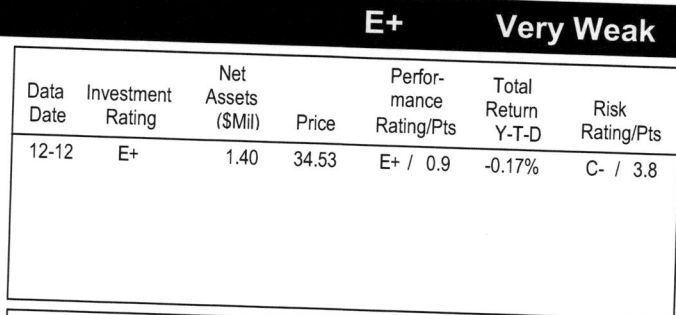

*iPath Pure Beta Broad Commodity (BCM)

Fund Family: Barclays Bank PLC
Fund Type: Income
Inception Date: April 20, 2011

D-   **Weak**

Major Rating Factors:
Disappointing performance is the major factor driving the D- (Weak) TheStreet.com Investment Rating for *iPath Pure Beta Broad Commodity. The fund currently has a performance rating of D- (Weak) based on an annualized return of 0.00% over the last three years and a total return of -1.55% year to date 2012.

The fund's risk rating is currently C (Fair). It carries a beta of 0.00, meaning the fund's expected move will be 0.0% for every 10% move in the market. Volatility, as measured by both the semi-deviation and a drawdown factor, is considered average. As of December 31, 2012, *iPath Pure Beta Broad Commodity traded at a premium of 1.90% above its net asset value, which is worse than its one-year historical average discount of .01%.

This fund has been team managed for 2 years and currently receives a manager quality ranking of 10 (0=worst, 99=best). This fund offers an average level of risk but investors looking for strong performance will be frustrated.

Data Date	Investment Rating	Net Assets ($Mil)	Price	Perfor-mance Rating/Pts	Total Return Y-T-D	Risk Rating/Pts
12-12	D-	21.50	44.62	D- / 1.3	-1.55%	C / 4.8

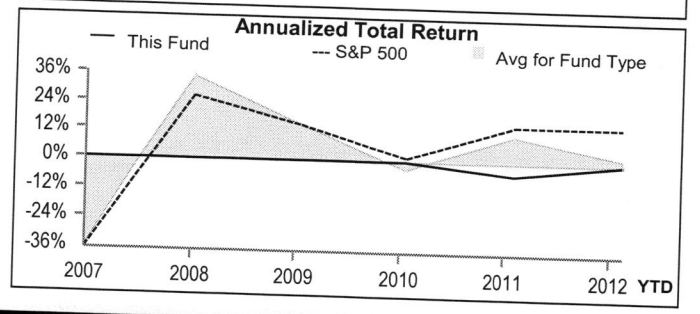
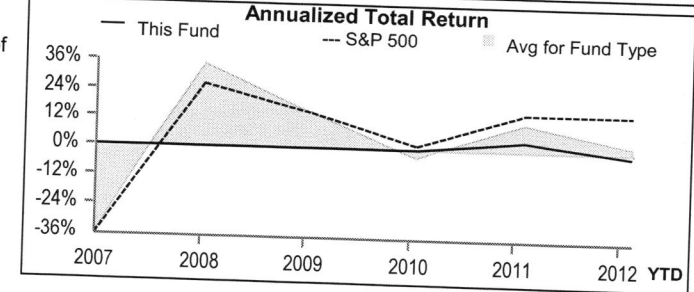

* Denotes ETF Fund

*iPath Pure Beta Cocoa ETN (CHOC)
E   Very Weak

Fund Family: Barclays Bank PLC
Fund Type: Income
Inception Date: April 20, 2011

Data Date	Investment Rating	Net Assets ($Mil)	Price	Performance Rating/Pts	Total Return Y-T-D	Risk Rating/Pts
12-12	E	3.00	33.58	E+ / 0.9	0.83%	C- / 3.5

Major Rating Factors: Very poor performance is the major factor driving the E (Very Weak) TheStreet.com Investment Rating for *iPath Pure Beta Cocoa ETN. The fund currently has a performance rating of E+ (Very Weak) based on an annualized return of 0.00% over the last three years and a total return of 0.83% year to date 2012.

The fund's risk rating is currently C- (Fair). It carries a beta of 0.00, meaning the fund's expected move will be 0.0% for every 10% move in the market. Volatility, as measured by both the semi-deviation and a drawdown factor, is considered average. As of December 31, 2012, *iPath Pure Beta Cocoa ETN traded at a discount of .94% below its net asset value, which is better than its one-year historical average discount of .29%.

This fund has been team managed for 2 years and currently receives a manager quality ranking of 12 (0=worst, 99=best). This fund offers an average level of risk but investors looking for strong performance will be frustrated.

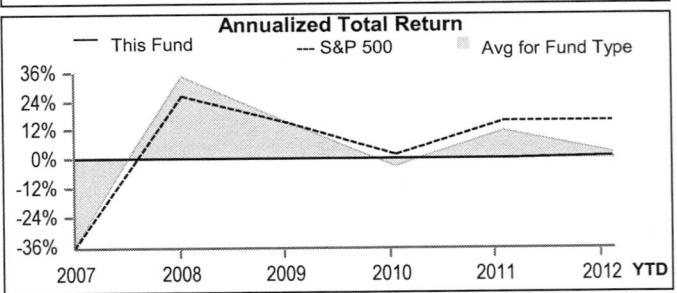

*iPath Pure Beta Coffee ETN (CAFE)
E-   Very Weak

Fund Family: Barclays Bank PLC
Fund Type: Income
Inception Date: April 20, 2011

Data Date	Investment Rating	Net Assets ($Mil)	Price	Performance Rating/Pts	Total Return Y-T-D	Risk Rating/Pts
12-12	E-	2.00	21.23	E- / 0.2	6.24%	D+ / 2.3

Major Rating Factors: *iPath Pure Beta Coffee ETN has adopted a risky asset allocation strategy and currently receives an overall TheStreet.com Investment Rating of E- (Very Weak). The fund has an above average level of volatility, as measured by both semi-deviation and drawdown factors. It carries a beta of 0.00, meaning the fund's expected move will be 0.0% for every 10% move in the market. As of December 31, 2012, *iPath Pure Beta Coffee ETN traded at a discount of 6.15% below its net asset value, which is better than its one-year historical average discount of .06%. Unfortunately, the high level of risk (D+, Weak) failed to pay off as investors endured very poor performance.

The fund's performance rating is currently E- (Very Weak). It has registered an annualized return of 0.00% over the last three years and is up 6.24% year to date 2012.

This fund has been team managed for 2 years and currently receives a manager quality ranking of 1 (0=worst, 99=best). If you can tolerate high levels of risk in the hope of improved future returns, holding this fund may be an option.

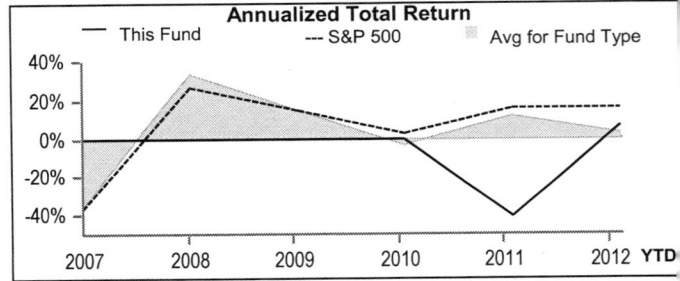

*iPath Pure Beta Copper ETN (CUPM)
E+   Very Weak

Fund Family: Barclays Bank PLC
Fund Type: Growth and Income
Inception Date: April 20, 2011

Data Date	Investment Rating	Net Assets ($Mil)	Price	Performance Rating/Pts	Total Return Y-T-D	Risk Rating/Pts
12-12	E+	2.80	40.62	D- / 1.4	2.26%	C / 4.6

Major Rating Factors:
Disappointing performance is the major factor driving the E+ (Very Weak) TheStreet.com Investment Rating for *iPath Pure Beta Copper ETN. The fund currently has a performance rating of D- (Weak) based on an annualized return of 0.00% over the last three years and a total return of 2.26% year to date 2012.

The fund's risk rating is currently C (Fair). It carries a beta of 0.00, meaning the fund's expected move will be 0.0% for every 10% move in the market. Volatility, as measured by both the semi-deviation and a drawdown factor, is considered average. As of December 31, 2012, *iPath Pure Beta Copper ETN traded at a discount of 2.26% below its net asset value, which is better than its one-year historical average discount of .15%.

This fund has been team managed for 2 years and currently receives a manager quality ranking of 12 (0=worst, 99=best). This fund offers an average level of risk but investors looking for strong performance will be frustrated.

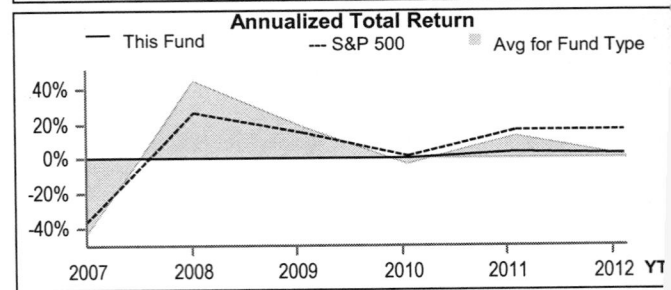

*iPath Pure Beta Crude Oil ETN (OLEM)

Fund Family: Barclays Bank PLC
Fund Type: Income
Inception Date: April 20, 2011

E+   Very Weak

Major Rating Factors:
Very poor performance is the major factor driving the E+ (Very Weak) TheStreet.com Investment Rating for *iPath Pure Beta Crude Oil ETN. The fund currently has a performance rating of E+ (Very Weak) based on an annualized return of 0.00% over the last three years and a total return of 1.83% year to date 2012.

The fund's risk rating is currently C (Fair). It carries a beta of 0.00, meaning the fund's expected move will be 0.0% for every 10% move in the market. Volatility, as measured by both the semi-deviation and a drawdown factor, is considered average. As of December 31, 2012, *iPath Pure Beta Crude Oil ETN traded at a discount of 1.61% below its net asset value.

This fund has been team managed for 2 years and currently receives a manager quality ranking of 2 (0=worst, 99=best). This fund offers an average level of risk but investors looking for strong performance will be frustrated.

Data Date	Investment Rating	Net Assets ($Mil)	Price	Performance Rating/Pts	Total Return Y-T-D	Risk Rating/Pts
12-12	E+	2.10	38.48	E+ / 0.8	1.83%	C / 4.6

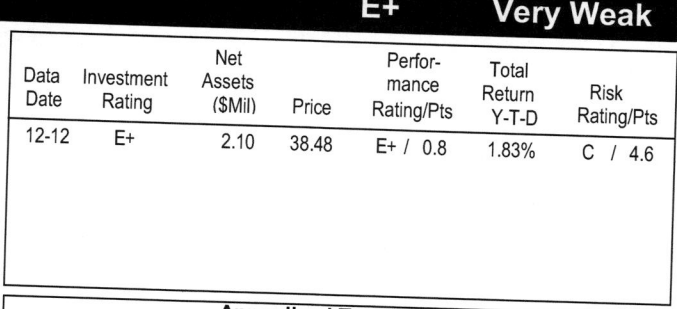

*iPath Pure Beta Grains ETN (WEET)

Fund Family: Barclays Bank PLC
Fund Type: Income
Inception Date: April 20, 2011

D   Weak

Major Rating Factors: *iPath Pure Beta Grains ETN receives a TheStreet.com Investment Rating of D (Weak). The fund currently has a performance rating of C- (Fair) based on an annualized return of 0.00% over the last three years and a total return of -2.12% year to date 2012.

The fund's risk rating is currently C (Fair). It carries a beta of 0.00, meaning the fund's expected move will be 0.0% for every 10% move in the market. Volatility, as measured by both the semi-deviation and a drawdown factor, is considered average. As of December 31, 2012, *iPath Pure Beta Grains ETN traded at a premium of 1.98% above its net asset value, which is worse than its one-year historical average discount of .23%.

This fund has been team managed for 2 years and currently receives a manager quality ranking of 85 (0=worst, 99=best). If you desire an average level of risk, then this fund may be an option.

Data Date	Investment Rating	Net Assets ($Mil)	Price	Performance Rating/Pts	Total Return Y-T-D	Risk Rating/Pts
12-12	D	2.80	50.44	C- / 4.0	-2.12%	C / 4.5

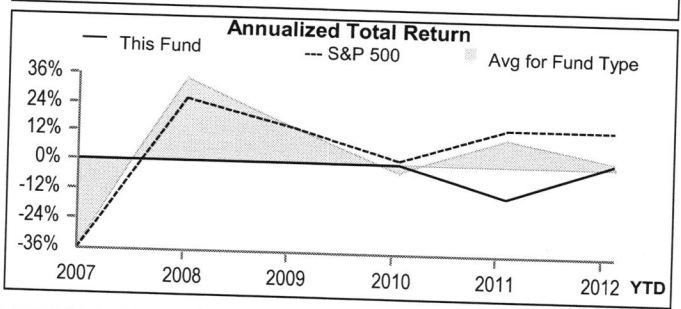

*iPath Pure Beta Lead ETN (LEDD)

Fund Family: Barclays Bank PLC
Fund Type: Income
Inception Date: April 20, 2011

C-   Fair

Major Rating Factors: Strong performance is the major factor driving the C- (Fair) TheStreet.com Investment Rating for *iPath Pure Beta Lead ETN. The fund currently has a performance rating of B (Good) based on an annualized return of 0.00% over the last three years and a total return of -3.87% year to date 2012.

The fund's risk rating is currently C- (Fair). It carries a beta of 0.00, meaning the fund's expected move will be 0.0% for every 10% move in the market. Volatility, as measured by both the semi-deviation and a drawdown factor, is considered average. As of December 31, 2012, *iPath Pure Beta Lead ETN traded at a premium of 3.41% above its net asset value, which is worse than its one-year historical average discount of .77%.

This fund has been team managed for 2 years and currently receives a manager quality ranking of 93 (0=worst, 99=best). If you desire an average level of risk and strong performance, then this fund is a good option.

Data Date	Investment Rating	Net Assets ($Mil)	Price	Performance Rating/Pts	Total Return Y-T-D	Risk Rating/Pts
12-12	C-	0.70	43.98	B / 7.6	-3.87%	C- / 3.6

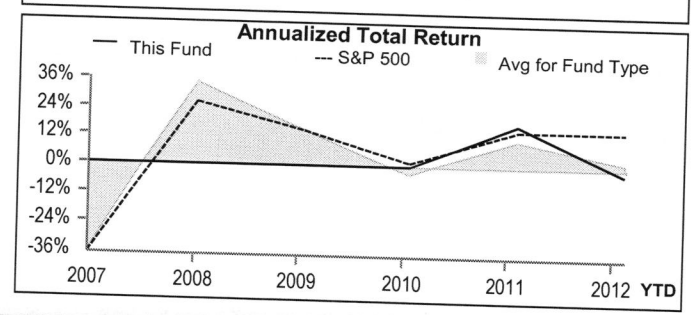
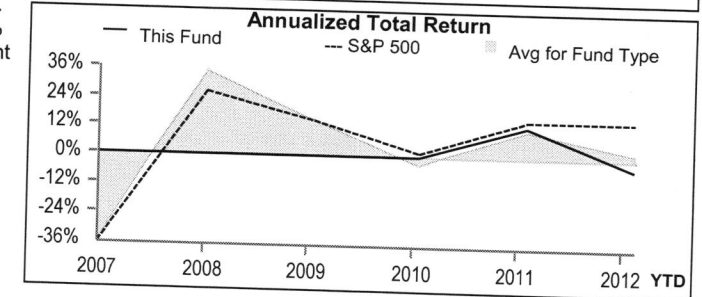

*iPath Pure Beta Nickel ETN (NINI)   E   Very Weak

Fund Family: Barclays Bank PLC
Fund Type: Income
Inception Date: April 20, 2011

Data Date	Investment Rating	Net Assets ($Mil)	Price	Performance Rating/Pts	Total Return Y-T-D	Risk Rating/Pts
12-12	E	1.40	32.57	E+ / 0.7	-0.92%	C- / 3.5

Major Rating Factors: Very poor performance is the major factor driving the E (Very Weak) TheStreet.com Investment Rating for *iPath Pure Beta Nickel ETN. The fund currently has a performance rating of E+ (Very Weak) based on an annualized return of 0.00% over the last three years and a total return of -0.92% year to date 2012.

The fund's risk rating is currently C- (Fair). It carries a beta of 0.00, meaning the fund's expected move will be 0.0% for every 10% move in the market. Volatility, as measured by both the semi-deviation and a drawdown factor, is considered average. As of December 31, 2012, *iPath Pure Beta Nickel ETN traded at a premium of .96% above its net asset value, which is worse than its one-year historical average discount of .18%.

This fund has been team managed for 2 years and currently receives a manager quality ranking of 4 (0=worst, 99=best). This fund offers an average level of risk but investors looking for strong performance will be frustrated.

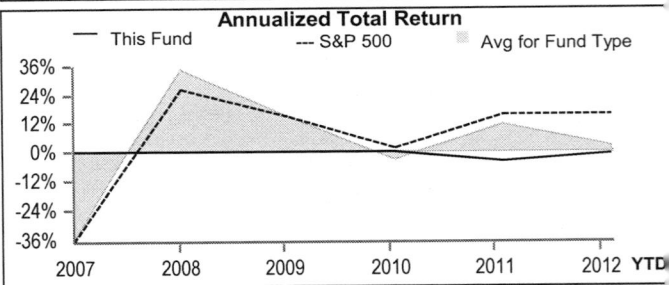

*iPath Pure Beta Softs ETN (GRWN)   E   Very Weak

Fund Family: Barclays Bank PLC
Fund Type: Income
Inception Date: April 20, 2011

Data Date	Investment Rating	Net Assets ($Mil)	Price	Performance Rating/Pts	Total Return Y-T-D	Risk Rating/Pts
12-12	E	0.90	32.65	E / 0.4	-0.46%	C- / 3.4

Major Rating Factors: Very poor performance is the major factor driving the E (Very Weak) TheStreet.com Investment Rating for *iPath Pure Beta Softs ETN. The fund currently has a performance rating of E (Very Weak) based on an annualized return of 0.00% over the last three years and a total return of -0.46% year to date 2012.

The fund's risk rating is currently C- (Fair). It carries a beta of 0.00, meaning the fund's expected move will be 0.0% for every 10% move in the market. Volatility, as measured by both the semi-deviation and a drawdown factor, is considered average. As of December 31, 2012, *iPath Pure Beta Softs ETN traded at a premium of .77% above its net asset value, which is worse than its one-year historical average discount of .10%.

This fund has been team managed for 2 years and currently receives a manager quality ranking of 3 (0=worst, 99=best). This fund offers an average level of risk but investors looking for strong performance will be frustrated.

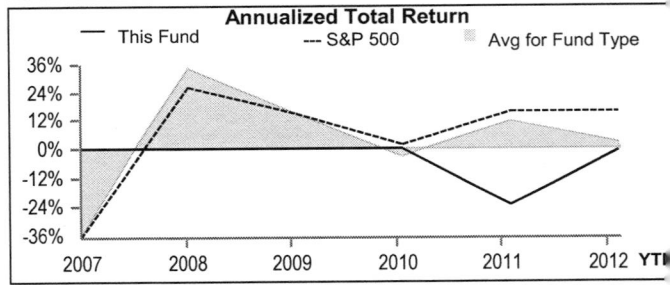

*iPath Pure Beta Sugar ETN (SGAR)   E   Very Weak

Fund Family: Barclays Bank PLC
Fund Type: Growth and Income
Inception Date: April 20, 2011

Data Date	Investment Rating	Net Assets ($Mil)	Price	Performance Rating/Pts	Total Return Y-T-D	Risk Rating/Pts
12-12	E	2.70	43.69	E / 0.4	-2.06%	C- / 3.8

Major Rating Factors: Very poor performance is the major factor driving the E (Very Weak) TheStreet.com Investment Rating for *iPath Pure Beta Sugar ETN. The fund currently has a performance rating of E (Very Weak) based on an annualized return of 0.00% over the last three years and a total return of -2.06% year to date 2012.

The fund's risk rating is currently C- (Fair). It carries a beta of 0.00, meaning the fund's expected move will be 0.0% for every 10% move in the market. Volatility, as measured by both the semi-deviation and a drawdown factor, is considered average. As of December 31, 2012, *iPath Pure Beta Sugar ETN traded at a premium of 1.79% above its net asset value, which is worse than its one-year historical average discount of .20%.

This fund has been team managed for 2 years and currently receives a manager quality ranking of 2 (0=worst, 99=best). This fund offers an average level of risk but investors looking for strong performance will be frustrated.

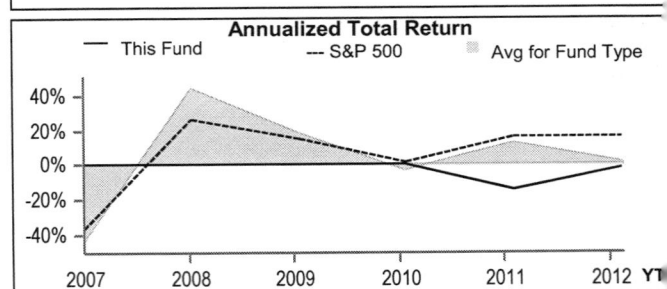

*IPath S&P 500 Dynamic VIX ETN (XVZ)

E+   Very Weak

Fund Family: Barclays Bank PLC
Fund Type: Global
Inception Date: August 17, 2011

Major Rating Factors:
Very poor performance is the major factor driving the E+ (Very Weak) TheStreet.com Investment Rating for *IPath S&P 500 Dynamic VIX ETN. The fund currently has a performance rating of E (Very Weak) based on an annualized return of 0.00% over the last three years and a total return of -5.13% year to date 2012.

The fund's risk rating is currently C (Fair). It carries a beta of 0.00, meaning the fund's expected move will be 0.0% for every 10% move in the market. Volatility, as measured by both the semi-deviation and a drawdown factor, is considered average. As of December 31, 2012, *IPath S&P 500 Dynamic VIX ETN traded at a premium of 4.97% above its net asset value, which is worse than its one-year historical average discount of .06%.

This fund has been team managed for 2 years and currently receives a manager quality ranking of 6 (0=worst, 99=best). This fund offers an average level of risk but investors looking for strong performance will be frustrated.

Data Date	Investment Rating	Net Assets ($Mil)	Price	Performance Rating/Pts	Total Return Y-T-D	Risk Rating/Pts
12-12	E+	266.60	46.04	E / 0.3	-5.13%	C / 4.6

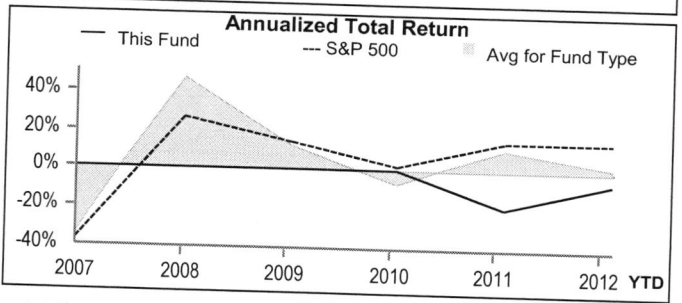

*IPath S&P 500 VIX Mid-Trm Futr E (VXZ)

E-   Very Weak

Fund Family: Barclays Bank PLC
Fund Type: Income
Inception Date: January 29, 2009

Major Rating Factors: *IPath S&P 500 VIX Mid-Trm Futr E has adopted a very risky asset allocation strategy and currently receives an overall TheStreet.com Investment Rating of E- (Very Weak). The fund has a high level of volatility, as measured by both semi-deviation and drawdown factors. It carries a beta of -1.86, meaning the fund's expected move will be -18.6% for every 10% move in the market. As of December 31, 2012, *IPath S&P 500 VIX Mid-Trm Futr E traded at a premium of 9.56% above its net asset value, which is worse than its one-year historical average discount of .15%. Unfortunately, the high level of risk (D, Weak) failed to pay off as investors endured very poor performance.

The fund's performance rating is currently E- (Very Weak). It has registered an annualized return of -28.99% over the last three years and is down -8.84% year to date 2012. Factored into the performance evaluation is an expense ratio of 0.89% (low).

This fund has been team managed for 4 years and currently receives a manager quality ranking of 9 (0=worst, 99=best). If you can tolerate very high levels of risk in the hope of improved future returns, holding this fund may be an option.

Data Date	Investment Rating	Net Assets ($Mil)	Price	Performance Rating/Pts	Total Return Y-T-D	Risk Rating/Pts
12-12	E-	28.95	27.95	E- / 0.2	-8.84%	D / 1.9
2011	E	186.50	60.66	D- / 1.5	-4.86%	D+ / 2.4
2010	E	702.60	65.76	E / 0.3	-14.43%	D+ / 2.9

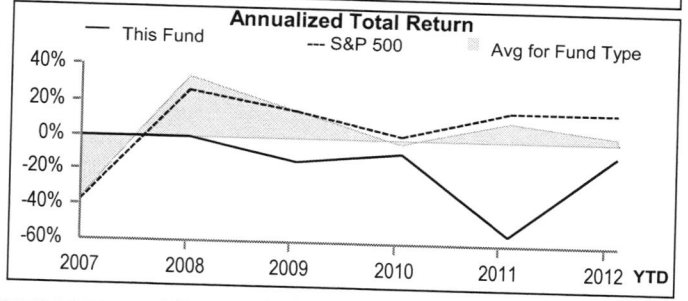

*IPath S&P 500 VIX Sm-Trm Futr ET (VXX)

E-   Very Weak

Fund Family: Barclays Bank PLC
Fund Type: Income
Inception Date: January 29, 2009

Major Rating Factors: *IPath S&P 500 VIX Sm-Trm Futr ET has adopted a very risky asset allocation strategy and currently receives an overall TheStreet.com Investment Rating of E- (Very Weak). The fund has a high level of volatility, as measured by both semi-deviation and drawdown factors. It carries a beta of -3.77, meaning the fund's expected move will be -37.7% for every 10% move in the market. As of December 31, 2012, *IPath S&P 500 VIX Sm-Trm Futr ET traded at a premium of 21.13% above its net asset value, which is worse than its one-year historical average discount of .14%. Unfortunately, the high level of risk (D, Weak) failed to pay off as investors endured very poor performance.

The fund's performance rating is currently E- (Very Weak). It has registered an annualized return of -61.73% over the last three years and is down -16.82% year to date 2012. Factored into the performance evaluation is an expense ratio of 0.89% (low).

This fund has been team managed for 4 years and currently receives a manager quality ranking of 1 (0=worst, 99=best). If you can tolerate very high levels of risk in the hope of improved future returns, holding this fund may be an option.

Data Date	Investment Rating	Net Assets ($Mil)	Price	Performance Rating/Pts	Total Return Y-T-D	Risk Rating/Pts
12-12	E-	664.55	31.81	E- / 0	-16.82%	D / 1.9
2011	E+	791.90	35.53	C- / 3.2	-9.23%	D / 1.9
2010	E-	1,994.20	37.61	E- / 0	-72.40%	D- / 1.0

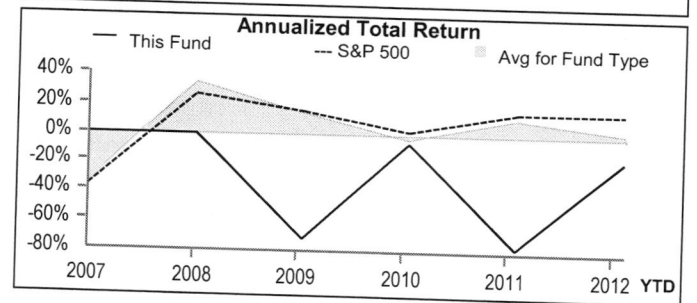

* Denotes ETF Fund

*iPath S&P GSCI Crude Oil TotRet (OIL)

D-   **Weak**

Fund Family: Barclays Bank PLC
Fund Type: Energy/Natural Resources
Inception Date: August 15, 2006

Major Rating Factors:

Very poor performance is the major factor driving the D- (Weak) TheStreet.com Investment Rating for *iPath S&P GSCI Crude Oil TotRet. The fund currently has a performance rating of E+ (Very Weak) based on an annualized return of -4.21% over the last three years and a total return of 2.25% year to date 2012. Factored into the performance evaluation is an expense ratio of 0.75% (very low).

The fund's risk rating is currently C+ (Fair). It carries a beta of 1.08, meaning that its performance tracks fairly well with that of the overall stock market. Volatility, as measured by both the semi-deviation and a drawdown factor, is considered low. As of December 31, 2012, *iPath S&P GSCI Crude Oil TotRet traded at a discount of 2.16% below its net asset value, which is better than its one-year historical average premium of .11%.

This fund has been team managed for 7 years and currently receives a manager quality ranking of 8 (0=worst, 99=best). This fund offers only a moderate level of risk but investors looking for strong performance are still waiting.

Data Date	Investment Rating	Net Assets ($Mil)	Price	Performance Rating/Pts	Total Return Y-T-D	Risk Rating/Pts
12-12	D-	564.45	21.79	E+ / 0.9	2.25%	C+ / 5.9
2011	D+	436.60	25.12	C- / 3.6	3.11%	C+ / 6.4
2010	E	643.90	25.61	E+ / 0.6	-1.04%	D+ / 2.4
2009	E	564.45	25.88	D- / 1.0	3.07%	C- / 3.1

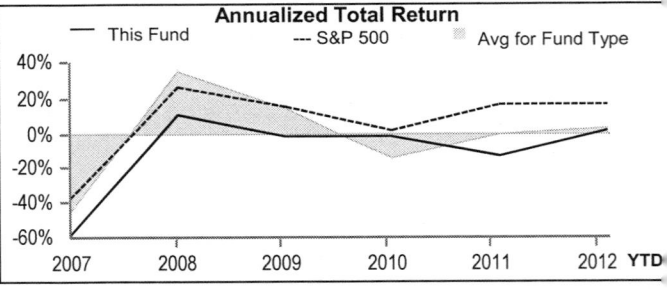

---

*iPath S&P GSCI Total Return ETN (GSP)

D   **Weak**

Fund Family: Barclays Bank PLC
Fund Type: Growth
Inception Date: June 6, 2006

Major Rating Factors:

Disappointing performance is the major factor driving the D (Weak) TheStreet.com Investment Rating for *iPath S&P GSCI Total Return ETN. The fund currently has a performance rating of D (Weak) based on an annualized return of 2.62% over the last three years and a total return of 0.58% year to date 2012. Factored into the performance evaluation is an expense ratio of 0.75% (very low).

The fund's risk rating is currently B- (Good). It carries a beta of 1.19, meaning it is expected to move 11.9% for every 10% move in the market. Volatility, as measured by both the semi-deviation and a drawdown factor, is considered low. As of December 31, 2012, *iPath S&P GSCI Total Return ETN traded at a discount of .21% below its net asset value, which is better than its one-year historical average premium of .13%.

This fund has been team managed for 7 years and currently receives a manager quality ranking of 13 (0=worst, 99=best). This fund offers only a moderate level of risk but investors looking for strong performance are still waiting.

Data Date	Investment Rating	Net Assets ($Mil)	Price	Performance Rating/Pts	Total Return Y-T-D	Risk Rating/Pts
12-12	D	79.00	33.28	D / 1.8	0.58%	B- / 7.1
2011	C-	97.60	33.75	C- / 3.6	2.49%	B- / 7.4
2010	E+	102.50	34.23	E+ / 0.9	8.36%	C- / 3.5
2009	D-	79.00	31.59	D- / 1.5	9.54%	C- / 4.1

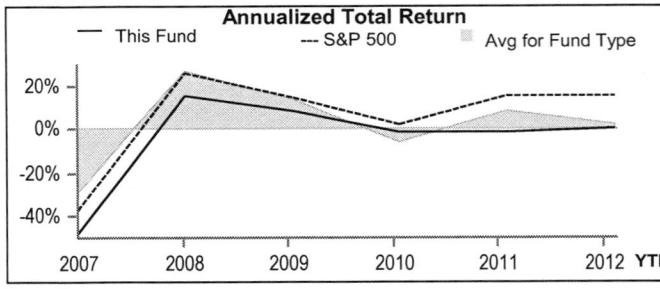

---

*iPath US Treas 10Yr Bear ETN (DTYS)

E   **Very Weak**

Fund Family: Barclays Bank PLC
Fund Type: US Government/Agency
Inception Date: August 9, 2010

Major Rating Factors: *iPath US Treas 10Yr Bear ETN has adopted a risky asset allocation strategy and currently receives an overall TheStreet.com Investment Rating of E (Very Weak). The fund has an above average level of volatility, as measured by both semi-deviation and drawdown factors. It carries a beta of 0.00, meaning the fund's expected move will be 0.0% for every 10% move in the market. As of December 31, 2012, *iPath US Treas 10Yr Bear ETN traded at a discount of 2.34% below its net asset value, which is better than its one-year historical average discount of .04%. Unfortunately, the high level of risk (D+, Weak) failed to pay off as investors endured very poor performance.

The fund's performance rating is currently E+ (Very Weak). It has registered an annualized return of 0.00% over the last three years and is up 2.09% year to date 2012.

This fund has been team managed for 3 years and currently receives a manager quality ranking of 11 (0=worst, 99=best). If you can tolerate high levels of risk in the hope of improved future returns, holding this fund may be an option.

Data Date	Investment Rating	Net Assets ($Mil)	Price	Performance Rating/Pts	Total Return Y-T-D	Risk Rating/Pts
12-12	E	106.20	26.75	E+ / 0.9	2.09%	D+ / 2.5
2011	E	40.60	32.26	E / 0.3	1.92%	C- / 3.5

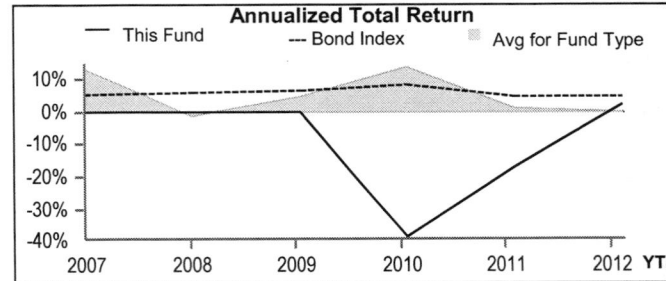

---

*iPath US Treas 10Yr Bull ETN (DTYL)

D-   **Weak**

Fund Family: Barclays Bank PLC
Fund Type: US Government/Agency
Inception Date: August 9, 2010

Major Rating Factors:
Disappointing performance is the major factor driving the D- (Weak) TheStreet.com Investment Rating for *iPath US Treas 10Yr Bull ETN. The fund currently has a performance rating of D (Weak) based on an annualized return of 0.00% over the last three years and a total return of -1.42% year to date 2012.

The fund's risk rating is currently C (Fair). It carries a beta of 0.00, meaning the fund's expected move will be 0.0% for every 10% move in the market. Volatility, as measured by both the semi-deviation and a drawdown factor, is considered average. As of December 31, 2012, *iPath US Treas 10Yr Bull ETN traded at a premium of 1.44% above its net asset value, which is worse than its one-year historical average discount of .02%.

This fund has been team managed for 3 years and currently receives a manager quality ranking of 79 (0=worst, 99=best). This fund offers an average level of risk but investors looking for strong performance will be frustrated.

Data Date	Investment Rating	Net Assets ($Mil)	Price	Performance Rating/Pts	Total Return Y-T-D	Risk Rating/Pts
12-12	D-	5.70	71.70	D / 1.7	-1.42%	C / 5.1
2011	B-	4.80	66.75	A+ / 9.8	-1.14%	C / 5.2

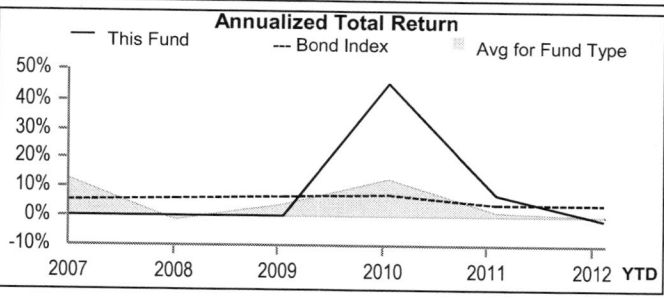

*iPath US Treas 2Yr Bear ETN (DTUS)

E+   **Very Weak**

Fund Family: Barclays Bank PLC
Fund Type: US Government/Agency
Inception Date: August 9, 2010

Major Rating Factors:
Disappointing performance is the major factor driving the E+ (Very Weak) TheStreet.com Investment Rating for *iPath US Treas 2Yr Bear ETN. The fund currently has a performance rating of D- (Weak) based on an annualized return of 0.00% over the last three years and a total return of -0.43% year to date 2012.

The fund's risk rating is currently C (Fair). It carries a beta of 0.00, meaning the fund's expected move will be 0.0% for every 10% move in the market. Volatility, as measured by both the semi-deviation and a drawdown factor, is considered average. As of December 31, 2012, *iPath US Treas 2Yr Bear ETN traded at a premium of .50% above its net asset value, which is worse than its one-year historical average premium of .04%.

This fund has been team managed for 3 years and currently receives a manager quality ranking of 39 (0=worst, 99=best). This fund offers an average level of risk but investors looking for strong performance will be frustrated.

Data Date	Investment Rating	Net Assets ($Mil)	Price	Performance Rating/Pts	Total Return Y-T-D	Risk Rating/Pts
12-12	E+	15.10	40.51	D- / 1.2	-0.43%	C / 4.7
2011	D-	13.00	41.51	D- / 1.1	-0.39%	C / 5.0

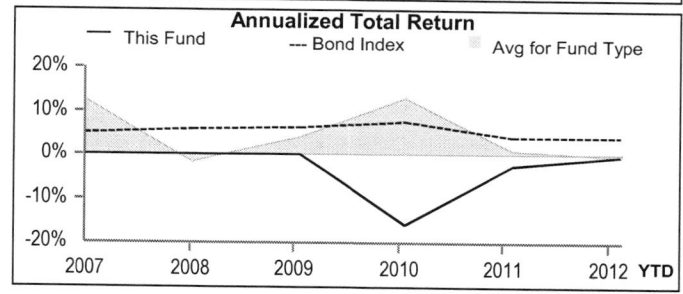

*iPath US Treas Flattener ETN (FLAT)

D-   **Weak**

Fund Family: Barclays Bank PLC
Fund Type: US Government/Agency
Inception Date: August 9, 2010

Major Rating Factors:
Disappointing performance is the major factor driving the D- (Weak) TheStreet.com Investment Rating for *iPath US Treas Flattener ETN. The fund currently has a performance rating of D- (Weak) based on an annualized return of 0.00% over the last three years and a total return of -1.62% year to date 2012.

The fund's risk rating is currently C (Fair). It carries a beta of 0.00, meaning the fund's expected move will be 0.0% for every 10% move in the market. Volatility, as measured by both the semi-deviation and a drawdown factor, is considered average. As of December 31, 2012, *iPath US Treas Flattener ETN traded at a premium of 1.15% above its net asset value.

This fund has been team managed for 3 years and currently receives a manager quality ranking of 77 (0=worst, 99=best). This fund offers an average level of risk but investors looking for strong performance will be frustrated.

Data Date	Investment Rating	Net Assets ($Mil)	Price	Performance Rating/Pts	Total Return Y-T-D	Risk Rating/Pts
12-12	D-	20.70	62.48	D- / 1.5	-1.62%	C / 5.2
2011	C+	49.80	58.33	B+ / 8.4	-1.13%	C / 5.3

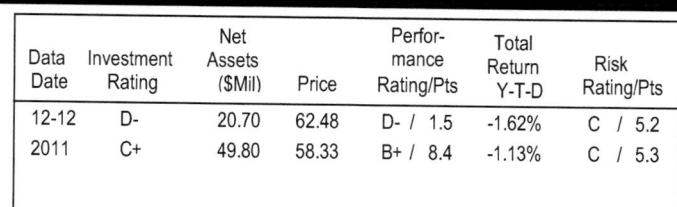

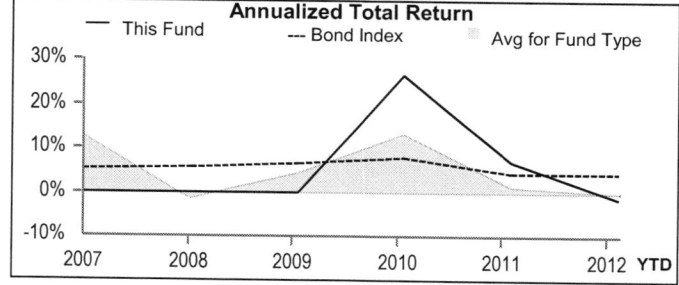

*iPath US Treas Lng Bd Bear ETN (DLBS)

E+ **Very Weak**

Fund Family: Barclays Bank PLC
Fund Type: US Government/Agency
Inception Date: August 9, 2010

Major Rating Factors: *iPath US Treas Lng Bd Bear ETN has adopted a risky asset allocation strategy and currently receives an overall TheStreet.com Investment Rating of E+ (Very Weak). The fund has an above average level of volatility, as measured by both semi-deviation and drawdown factors. It carries a beta of 0.00, meaning the fund's expected move will be 0.0% for every 10% move in the market. As of December 31, 2012, *iPath US Treas Lng Bd Bear ETN traded at a discount of 3.35% below its net asset value, which is better than its one-year historical average discount of .04%. Unfortunately, the high level of risk (D+, Weak) failed to pay off as investors endured poor performance.

The fund's performance rating is currently D (Weak). It has registered an annualized return of 0.00% over the last three years and is up 3.22% year to date 2012.

This fund has been team managed for 3 years and currently receives a manager quality ranking of 31 (0=worst, 99=best). If you can tolerate high levels of risk in the hope of improved future returns, holding this fund may be an option.

Data Date	Investment Rating	Net Assets ($Mil)	Price	Performance Rating/Pts	Total Return Y-T-D	Risk Rating/Pts
12-12	E+	22.60	28.54	D / 1.9	3.22%	D+ / 2.6
2011	E	18.80	31.97	E / 0.3	5.20%	C- / 3.4

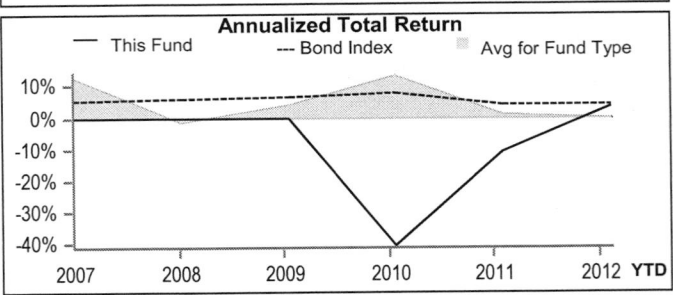

Annualized Total Return

---

*iPath US Treas Lng Bd Bull ETN (DLBL)

D- **Weak**

Fund Family: Barclays Bank PLC
Fund Type: US Government/Agency
Inception Date: August 9, 2010

Major Rating Factors:
Disappointing performance is the major factor driving the D- (Weak) TheStreet.com Investment Rating for *iPath US Treas Lng Bd Bull ETN. The fund currently has a performance rating of D- (Weak) based on an annualized return of 0.00% over the last three years and a total return of -3.26% year to date 2012.

The fund's risk rating is currently C (Fair). It carries a beta of 0.00, meaning the fund's expected move will be 0.0% for every 10% move in the market. Volatility, as measured by both the semi-deviation and a drawdown factor, is considered average. As of December 31, 2012, *iPath US Treas Lng Bd Bull ETN traded at a premium of 2.61% above its net asset value, which is worse than its one-year historical average discount of .24%.

This fund has been team managed for 3 years and currently receives a manager quality ranking of 70 (0=worst, 99=best). This fund offers an average level of risk but investors looking for strong performance will be frustrated.

Data Date	Investment Rating	Net Assets ($Mil)	Price	Performance Rating/Pts	Total Return Y-T-D	Risk Rating/Pts
12-12	D-	3.00	70.33	D- / 1.2	-3.26%	C / 5.0
2011	B-	10.70	66.82	A+ / 9.9	-1.65%	C / 5.1

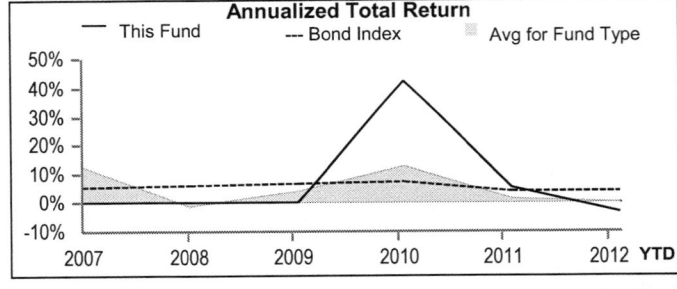

Annualized Total Return

---

*iPath US Treas Steepen ETN (STPP)

E+ **Very Weak**

Fund Family: Barclays Bank PLC
Fund Type: US Government/Agency
Inception Date: August 9, 2010

Major Rating Factors:
Very poor performance is the major factor driving the E+ (Very Weak) TheStreet.com Investment Rating for *iPath US Treas Steepen ETN. The fund currently has a performance rating of E+ (Very Weak) based on an annualized return of 0.00% over the last three years and a total return of 2.48% year to date 2012.

The fund's risk rating is currently C- (Fair). It carries a beta of 0.00, meaning the fund's expected move will be 0.0% for every 10% move in the market. Volatility, as measured by both the semi-deviation and a drawdown factor, is considered average. As of December 31, 2012, *iPath US Treas Steepen ETN traded at a discount of 2.44% below its net asset value, which is better than its one-year historical average discount of .03%.

This fund has been team managed for 3 years and currently receives a manager quality ranking of 13 (0=worst, 99=best). This fund offers an average level of risk but investors looking for strong performance will be frustrated.

Data Date	Investment Rating	Net Assets ($Mil)	Price	Performance Rating/Pts	Total Return Y-T-D	Risk Rating/Pts
12-12	E+	7.80	35.12	E+ / 0.9	2.48%	C- / 3.5
2011	E+	2.50	40.21	E+ / 0.7	1.42%	C / 4.4

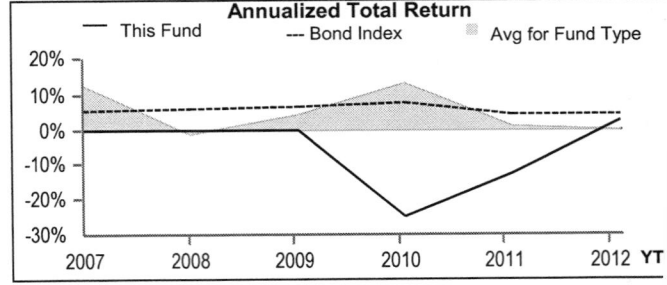

Annualized Total Return

*IQ Australia Small Cap ETF (KROO)

C   **Fair**

Fund Family: IndexIQ Advisors LLC
Fund Type: Foreign
Inception Date: March 22, 2010

Major Rating Factors: Middle of the road best describes *IQ Australia Small Cap ETF whose TheStreet.com Investment Rating is currently a C (Fair). The fund currently has a performance rating of C+ (Fair) based on an annualized return of 0.00% over the last three years and a total return of 2.50% year to date 2012. Factored into the performance evaluation is an expense ratio of 0.69% (very low).

The fund's risk rating is currently C (Fair). It carries a beta of 0.00, meaning the fund's expected move will be 0.0% for every 10% move in the market. Volatility, as measured by both the semi-deviation and a drawdown factor, is considered average. As of December 31, 2012, *IQ Australia Small Cap ETF traded at a discount of 2.09% below its net asset value, which is better than its one-year historical average premium of .13%.

Julie S. Abbett has been running the fund for 2 years and currently receives a manager quality ranking of 11 (0=worst, 99=best). If you desire an average level of risk, then this fund may be an option.

Data Date	Investment Rating	Net Assets ($Mil)	Price	Performance Rating/Pts	Total Return Y-T-D	Risk Rating/Pts
12-12	C	13.80	21.57	C+ / 6.9	2.50%	C / 5.4
2011	D-	15.10	20.15	E+ / 0.8	1.30%	C+ / 5.6

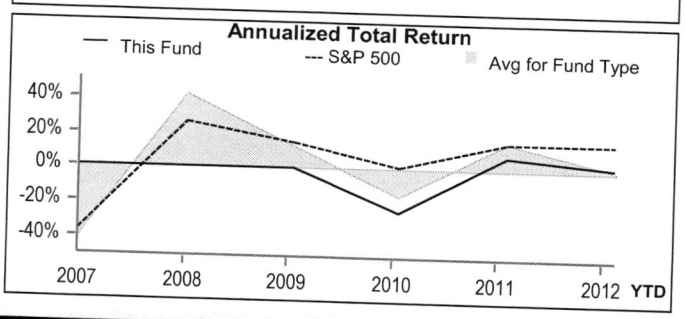

*IQ Canada Small Cap ETF (CNDA)

D-   **Weak**

Fund Family: IndexIQ Advisors LLC
Fund Type: Foreign
Inception Date: March 22, 2010

Major Rating Factors:
Disappointing performance is the major factor driving the D- (Weak) TheStreet.com Investment Rating for *IQ Canada Small Cap ETF. The fund currently has a performance rating of D (Weak) based on an annualized return of 0.00% over the last three years and a total return of 2.68% year to date 2012. Factored into the performance evaluation is an expense ratio of 0.69% (very low).

The fund's risk rating is currently C+ (Fair). It carries a beta of 0.00, meaning the fund's expected move will be 0.0% for every 10% move in the market. Volatility, as measured by both the semi-deviation and a drawdown factor, is considered low. As of December 31, 2012, *IQ Canada Small Cap ETF traded at a discount of 3.14% below its net asset value, which is better than its one-year historical average discount of .38%.

Julie S. Abbett has been running the fund for 2 years and currently receives a manager quality ranking of 5 (0=worst, 99=best). This fund offers only a moderate level of risk but investors looking for strong performance are still waiting.

Data Date	Investment Rating	Net Assets ($Mil)	Price	Performance Rating/Pts	Total Return Y-T-D	Risk Rating/Pts
12-12	D-	19.80	23.15	D / 1.8	2.68%	C+ / 5.7
2011	D-	31.80	25.33	E+ / 0.9	3.14%	C+ / 6.2

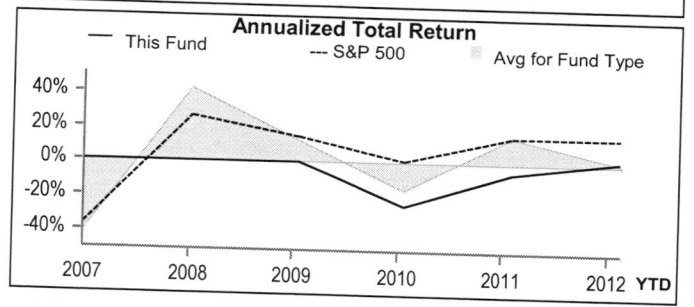

*IQ Global Agribusiness SmCp ETF (CROP)

B   **Good**

Fund Family: IndexIQ Advisors LLC
Fund Type: Global
Inception Date: March 21, 2011

Major Rating Factors: Strong performance is the major factor driving the B (Good) TheStreet.com Investment Rating for *IQ Global Agribusiness SmCp ETF. The fund currently has a performance rating of B (Good) based on an annualized return of 0.00% over the last three years and a total return of 2.23% year to date 2012. Factored into the performance evaluation is an expense ratio of 0.75% (very low).

The fund's risk rating is currently B- (Good). It carries a beta of 0.00, meaning the fund's expected move will be 0.0% for every 10% move in the market. Volatility, as measured by both the semi-deviation and a drawdown factor, is considered low. As of December 31, 2012, *IQ Global Agribusiness SmCp ETF traded at a discount of 1.69% below its net asset value, which is better than its one-year historical average discount of .06%.

Julie S. Abbett has been running the fund for 2 years and currently receives a manager quality ranking of 73 (0=worst, 99=best). If you desire only a moderate level of risk and strong performance, then this fund is an excellent option.

Data Date	Investment Rating	Net Assets ($Mil)	Price	Performance Rating/Pts	Total Return Y-T-D	Risk Rating/Pts
12-12	B	36.90	25.58	B / 8.0	2.23%	B- / 7.8

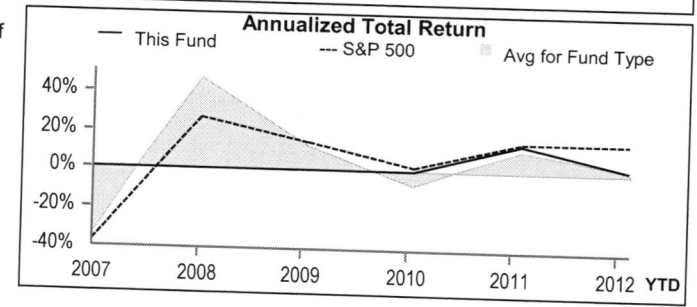

*IQ Global Oil Small Cap ETF (IOIL)

C+ **Fair**

Fund Family: IndexIQ Advisors LLC
Fund Type: Global
Inception Date: May 4, 2011

Major Rating Factors: Strong performance is the major factor driving the C+ (Fair) TheStreet.com Investment Rating for *IQ Global Oil Small Cap ETF. The fund currently has a performance rating of B (Good) based on an annualized return of 0.00% over the last three years and a total return of 4.66% year to date 2012. Factored into the performance evaluation is an expense ratio of 0.75% (very low).

The fund's risk rating is currently C+ (Fair). It carries a beta of 0.00, meaning the fund's expected move will be 0.0% for every 10% move in the market. Volatility, as measured by both the semi-deviation and a drawdown factor, is considered low. As of December 31, 2012, *IQ Global Oil Small Cap ETF traded at a discount of 4.01% below its net asset value, which is better than its one-year historical average discount of .10%.

Julie S. Abbett has been running the fund for 2 years and currently receives a manager quality ranking of 14 (0=worst, 99=best). If you desire only a moderate level of risk and strong performance, then this fund is an excellent option.

Data Date	Investment Rating	Net Assets ($Mil)	Price	Performance Rating/Pts	Total Return Y-T-D	Risk Rating/Pts
12-12	C+	2.60	16.75	B / 7.7	4.66%	C+ / 5.9

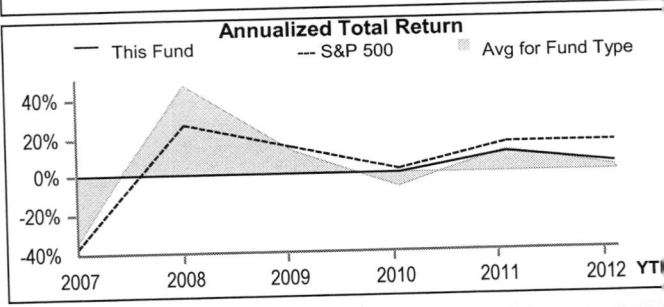

Annualized Total Return

*IQ Global Resources ETF (GRES)

C- **Fair**

Fund Family: IndexIQ Advisors LLC
Fund Type: Energy/Natural Resources
Inception Date: October 26, 2009

Major Rating Factors: Middle of the road best describes *IQ Global Resources ETF whose TheStreet.com Investment Rating is currently a C- (Fair). The fund currently has a performance rating of C- (Fair) based on an annualized return of 5.81% over the last three years and a total return of -0.46% year to date 2012. Factored into the performance evaluation is an expense ratio of 0.75% (very low).

The fund's risk rating is currently B- (Good). It carries a beta of 0.55, meaning the fund's expected move will be 5.5% for every 10% move in the market. Volatility, as measured by both the semi-deviation and a drawdown factor, is considered low. As of December 31, 2012, *IQ Global Resources ETF traded at a premium of .83% above its net asset value, which is worse than its one-year historical average premium of .06%.

Julie S. Abbett has been running the fund for 2 years and currently receives a manager quality ranking of 66 (0=worst, 99=best). If you desire an average level of risk, then this fund may be an option.

Data Date	Investment Rating	Net Assets ($Mil)	Price	Performance Rating/Pts	Total Return Y-T-D	Risk Rating/Pts
12-12	C-	76.10	30.42	C- / 3.0	-0.46%	B- / 7.8
2011	D	61.70	28.02	D- / 1.5	2.00%	B- / 7.2
2010	A+	42.50	31.83	A / 9.3	23.38%	B / 8.3

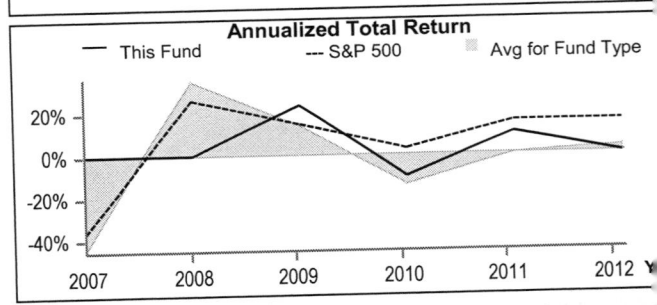

Annualized Total Return

*IQ Hedge Macro Tracker ETF (MCRO)

C- **Fai**

Fund Family: IndexIQ Advisors LLC
Fund Type: Global
Inception Date: June 8, 2009

Major Rating Factors:
Disappointing performance is the major factor driving the C- (Fair) TheStreet.com Investment Rating for *IQ Hedge Macro Tracker ETF. The fund currently has a performance rating of D (Weak) based on an annualized return of 1.70% over the last three years and a total return of -0.56% year to date 2012. Factored into the performance evaluation is an expense ratio of 0.75% (very low).

The fund's risk rating is currently B+ (Good). It carries a beta of 0.29, meaning the fund's expected move will be 2.9% for every 10% move in the market. Volatility, as measured by both the semi-deviation and a drawdown factor, is considered very low. As of December 31, 2012, *IQ Hedge Macro Tracker ETF traded at a premium of .55% above its net asset value, which is worse than its one-year historical average premium of .05%.

Denise Krisko has been running the fund for 4 years and currently receives a manager quality ranking of 62 (0=worst, 99=best). This fund offers only a moderate level of risk but investors looking for strong performance are still waiting.

Data Date	Investment Rating	Net Assets ($Mil)	Price	Performance Rating/Pts	Total Return Y-T-D	Risk Rating/P
12-12	C-	38.30	27.40	D / 1.8	-0.56%	B+ / 9
2011	C-	32.90	26.27	D / 1.6	0.80%	B+ / 9
2010	B	24.70	27.54	C / 5.5	4.88%	B /

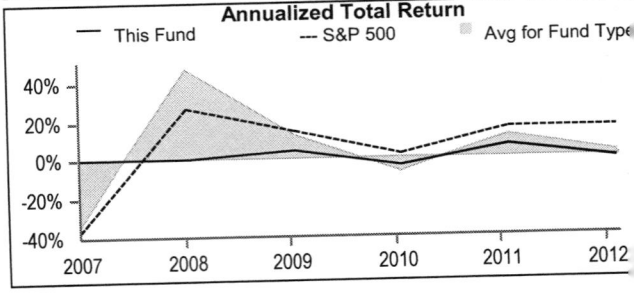

Annualized Total Return

*IQ Hedge Multi-Strategy Tracker (QAI)

Fund Family: IndexIQ Advisors LLC
Fund Type: Global
Inception Date: March 24, 2009

C-	Fair

Major Rating Factors:

Disappointing performance is the major factor driving the C- (Fair) TheStreet.com Investment Rating for *IQ Hedge Multi-Strategy Tracker. The fund currently has a performance rating of D (Weak) based on an annualized return of 2.03% over the last three years and a total return of 0.32% year to date 2012. Factored into the performance evaluation is an expense ratio of 0.75% (very low).

The fund's risk rating is currently B+ (Good). It carries a beta of 0.20, meaning the fund's expected move will be 2.0% for every 10% move in the market. Volatility, as measured by both the semi-deviation and a drawdown factor, is considered very low. As of December 31, 2012, *IQ Hedge Multi-Strategy Tracker traded at a discount of .39% below its net asset value, which is better than its one-year historical average premium of .08%.

Donald J. Mulvihill has been running the fund for 5 years and currently receives a manager quality ranking of 63 (0=worst, 99=best). This fund offers only a moderate level of risk but investors looking for strong performance are still waiting.

Data Date	Investment Rating	Net Assets ($Mil)	Price	Performance Rating/Pts	Total Return Y-T-D	Risk Rating/Pts
12-12	C-	314.80	27.81	D / 1.9	0.32%	B+ / 9.6
2011	C-	177.40	27.08	D / 2.0	0.37%	B+ / 9.6
2010	B	123.30	27.41	C- / 4.2	2.57%	B / 8.8

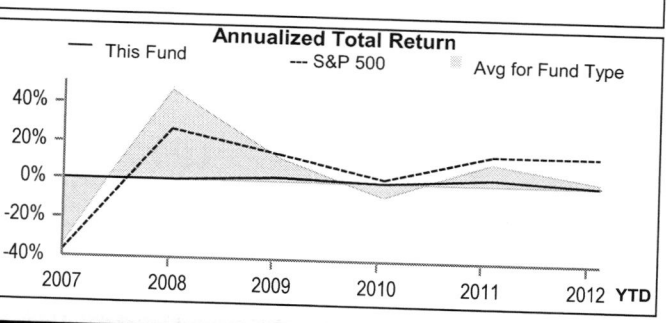

*IQ Merger Arbitrage ETF (MNA)

Fund Family: IndexIQ Advisors LLC
Fund Type: Global
Inception Date: November 16, 2009

D+	Weak

Major Rating Factors:

Disappointing performance is the major factor driving the D+ (Weak) TheStreet.com Investment Rating for *IQ Merger Arbitrage ETF. The fund currently has a performance rating of D- (Weak) based on an annualized return of -0.08% over the last three years and a total return of 0.16% year to date 2012. Factored into the performance evaluation is an expense ratio of 0.75% (very low).

The fund's risk rating is currently B+ (Good). It carries a beta of 0.19, meaning the fund's expected move will be 1.9% for every 10% move in the market. Volatility, as measured by both the semi-deviation and a drawdown factor, is considered very low. As of December 31, 2012, *IQ Merger Arbitrage ETF traded at a discount of .20% below its net asset value, which is better than its one-year historical average discount of .10%.

Julie S. Abbett has been running the fund for 2 years and currently receives a manager quality ranking of 45 (0=worst, 99=best). This fund offers only a moderate level of risk but investors looking for strong performance are still waiting.

Data Date	Investment Rating	Net Assets ($Mil)	Price	Performance Rating/Pts	Total Return Y-T-D	Risk Rating/Pts
12-12	D+	12.40	25.16	D- / 1.4	0.16%	B+ / 9.1
2011	C-	24.80	24.58	D / 2.0	1.55%	B+ / 9.2
2010	C-	23.60	24.70	D- / 1.1	-3.05%	B / 8.6

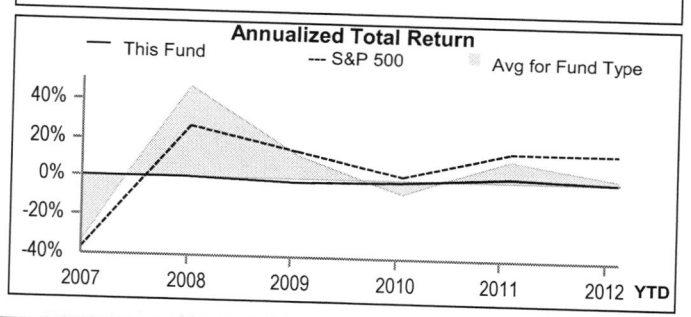

*IQ Real Return ETF (CPI)

Fund Family: IndexIQ Advisors LLC
Fund Type: Income
Inception Date: October 26, 2009

C-	Fair

Major Rating Factors:

Disappointing performance is the major factor driving the C- (Fair) TheStreet.com Investment Rating for *IQ Real Return ETF. The fund currently has a performance rating of D (Weak) based on an annualized return of 1.90% over the last three years and a total return of 0.23% year to date 2012. Factored into the performance evaluation is an expense ratio of 0.48% (very low).

The fund's risk rating is currently B+ (Good). It carries a beta of 0.01, meaning the fund's expected move will be 0.1% for every 10% move in the market. Volatility, as measured by both the semi-deviation and a drawdown factor, is considered very low. As of December 31, 2012, *IQ Real Return ETF traded at a discount of .27% below its net asset value, which is better than its one-year historical average premium of .03%.

Julie S. Abbett has been running the fund for 2 years and currently receives a manager quality ranking of 64 (0=worst, 99=best). This fund offers only a moderate level of risk but investors looking for strong performance are still waiting.

Data Date	Investment Rating	Net Assets ($Mil)	Price	Performance Rating/Pts	Total Return Y-T-D	Risk Rating/Pts
12-12	C-	40.80	26.32	D / 1.7	0.23%	B+ / 9.9
2011	C	33.70	26.00	D+ / 2.6	-0.16%	B+ / 9.9
2010	C+	12.70	25.48	C- / 3.2	1.57%	B / 8.3

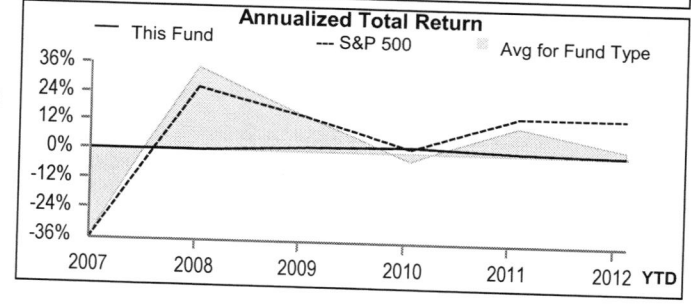

* Denotes ETF Fund

*IQ US Real Estate SmCp ETF (ROOF)   A   Excellent

Fund Family: IndexIQ Advisors LLC
Fund Type: Growth and Income
Inception Date: June 13, 2011

Data Date	Investment Rating	Net Assets ($Mil)	Price	Performance Rating/Pts	Total Return Y-T-D	Risk Rating/Pts
12-12	A	16.90	22.48	A+ / 9.7	4.66%	B- / 7.5

Major Rating Factors:
Exceptional performance is the major factor driving the A (Excellent) TheStreet.com Investment Rating for *IQ US Real Estate SmCp ETF. The fund currently has a performance rating of A+ (Excellent) based on an annualized return of 0.00% over the last three years and a total return of 4.66% year to date 2012. Factored into the performance evaluation is an expense ratio of 0.69% (very low).

The fund's risk rating is currently B- (Good). It carries a beta of 0.00, meaning the fund's expected move will be 0.0% for every 10% move in the market. Volatility, as measured by both the semi-deviation and a drawdown factor, is considered low. As of December 31, 2012, *IQ US Real Estate SmCp ETF traded at a discount of 4.26% below its net asset value, which is better than its one-year historical average premium of .10%.

Julie S. Abbett has been running the fund for 2 years and currently receives a manager quality ranking of 96 (0=worst, 99=best). If you desire only a moderate level of risk and strong performance, then this fund is an excellent option.

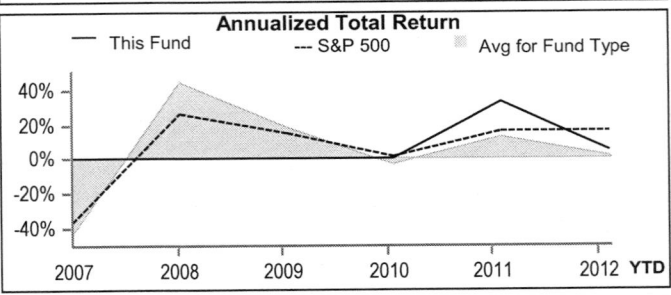
Annualized Total Return

*iShares 10+ Year Credit Bond (CLY)   C+   Fair

Fund Family: BlackRock Fund Advisors
Fund Type: Global
Inception Date: December 8, 2009

Data Date	Investment Rating	Net Assets ($Mil)	Price	Performance Rating/Pts	Total Return Y-T-D	Risk Rating/Pts
12-12	C+	448.30	62.67	C / 4.4	-0.35%	B+ / 9.4
2011	B	340.40	59.02	C+ / 6.6	-0.63%	B+ / 9.5
2010	B	15.80	52.98	C+ / 6.4	10.72%	B / 8.7

Major Rating Factors: Middle of the road best describes *iShares 10+ Year Credit Bond whose TheStreet.com Investment Rating is currently a C+ (Fair). The fund currently has a performance rating of C (Fair) based on an annualized return of 11.91% over the last three years and a total return of -0.35% year to date 2012. Factored into the performance evaluation is an expense ratio of 0.20% (very low).

The fund's risk rating is currently B+ (Good). It carries a beta of 0.26, meaning the fund's expected move will be 2.6% for every 10% move in the market. Volatility, as measured by both the semi-deviation and a drawdown factor, is considered very low. As of December 31, 2012, *iShares 10+ Year Credit Bond traded at a premium of 1.21% above its net asset value, which is worse than its one-year historical average premium of .58%.

Scott F. Radell has been running the fund for 3 years and currently receives a manager quality ranking of 92 (0=worst, 99=best). If you desire an average level of risk, then this fund may be an option.

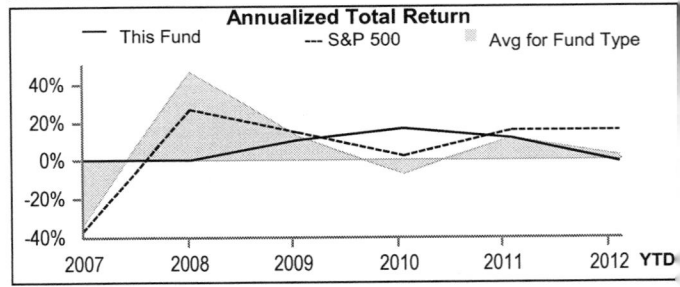
Annualized Total Return

*iShares 2013 S&P AMT-Free Muni S (MUAB)   C-   Fair

Fund Family: BlackRock Fund Advisors
Fund Type: General - Investment Grade
Inception Date: January 7, 2010

Data Date	Investment Rating	Net Assets ($Mil)	Price	Performance Rating/Pts	Total Return Y-T-D	Risk Rating/Pts
12-12	C-	38.00	50.72	D- / 1.3	-0.35%	B+ / 9.9
2011	C	33.10	50.77	D / 2.2	0.35%	B+ / 9.9

Major Rating Factors:
Disappointing performance is the major factor driving the C- (Fair) TheStreet.com Investment Rating for *iShares 2013 S&P AMT-Free Muni S. The fund currently has a performance rating of D- (Weak) based on an annualized return of 0.00% over the last three years and a total return of -0.35% year to date 2012. Factored into the performance evaluation is an expense ratio of 0.30% (very low).

The fund's risk rating is currently B+ (Good). It carries a beta of 0.00, meaning the fund's expected move will be 0.0% for every 10% move in the market. Volatility, as measured by both the semi-deviation and a drawdown factor, is considered very low. As of December 31, 2012, *iShares 2013 S&P AMT-Free Muni S traded at a premium of .04% above its net asset value, which is worse than its one-year historical average premium of .03%.

Scott F. Radell has been running the fund for 3 years and currently receives a manager quality ranking of 53 (0=worst, 99=best). This fund offers only a moderate level of risk but investors looking for strong performance are still waiting.

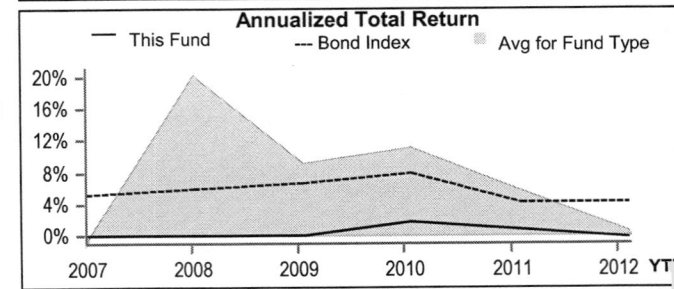
Annualized Total Return

*iShares 2014 S&P AMT-Free Muni S (MUAC)

C- | **Fair**

Fund Family: BlackRock Fund Advisors
Fund Type: General - Investment Grade
Inception Date: January 7, 2010

Major Rating Factors:

Disappointing performance is the major factor driving the C- (Fair) TheStreet.com Investment Rating for *iShares 2014 S&P AMT-Free Muni S. The fund currently has a performance rating of D- (Weak) based on an annualized return of 0.00% over the last three years and a total return of 0.05% year to date 2012. Factored into the performance evaluation is an expense ratio of 0.30% (very low).

The fund's risk rating is currently B+ (Good). It carries a beta of 0.00, meaning the fund's expected move will be 0.0% for every 10% move in the market. Volatility, as measured by both the semi-deviation and a drawdown factor, is considered very low. As of December 31, 2012, *iShares 2014 S&P AMT-Free Muni S traded at a premium of .21% above its net asset value, which is better than its one-year historical average premium of .33%.

Scott F. Radell has been running the fund for 3 years and currently receives a manager quality ranking of 56 (0=worst, 99=best). This fund offers only a moderate level of risk but investors looking for strong performance are still waiting.

Data Date	Investment Rating	Net Assets ($Mil)	Price	Performance Rating/Pts	Total Return Y-T-D	Risk Rating/Pts
12-12	C-	48.90	51.68	D- / 1.5	0.05%	B+ / 9.7
2011	C	33.40	51.67	D+ / 2.8	0.08%	B+ / 9.8

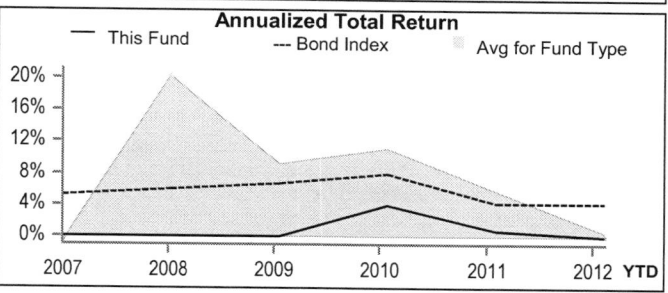

*iShares 2015 S&P AMT-Free Muni S (MUAD)

C- | **Fair**

Fund Family: BlackRock Fund Advisors
Fund Type: General - Investment Grade
Inception Date: January 7, 2010

Major Rating Factors:

Disappointing performance is the major factor driving the C- (Fair) TheStreet.com Investment Rating for *iShares 2015 S&P AMT-Free Muni S. The fund currently has a performance rating of D (Weak) based on an annualized return of 0.00% over the last three years and a total return of 0.30% year to date 2012. Factored into the performance evaluation is an expense ratio of 0.30% (very low).

The fund's risk rating is currently B+ (Good). It carries a beta of 0.00, meaning the fund's expected move will be 0.0% for every 10% move in the market. Volatility, as measured by both the semi-deviation and a drawdown factor, is considered very low. As of December 31, 2012, *iShares 2015 S&P AMT-Free Muni S traded at a premium of .21% above its net asset value, which is better than its one-year historical average premium of .47%.

Scott F. Radell has been running the fund for 3 years and currently receives a manager quality ranking of 50 (0=worst, 99=best). This fund offers only a moderate level of risk but investors looking for strong performance are still waiting.

Data Date	Investment Rating	Net Assets ($Mil)	Price	Performance Rating/Pts	Total Return Y-T-D	Risk Rating/Pts
12-12	C-	53.00	53.23	D / 1.6	0.30%	B+ / 9.8
2011	C	34.30	53.10	C- / 3.2	-0.04%	B+ / 9.8

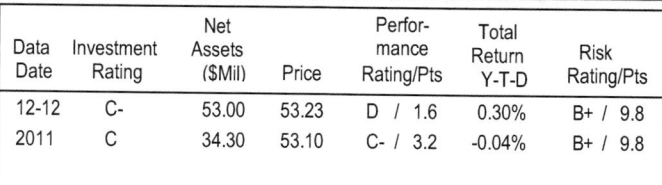
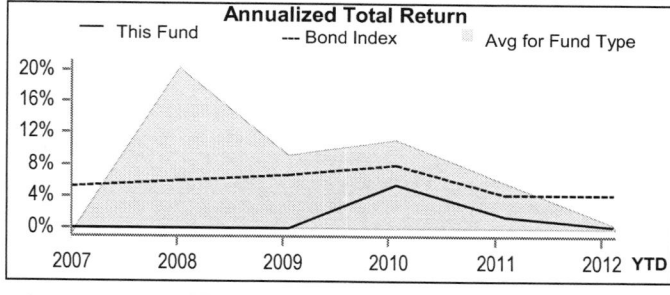

*iShares 2016 S&P AMT-Free Muni S (MUAE)

C- | **Fair**

Fund Family: BlackRock Fund Advisors
Fund Type: General - Investment Grade
Inception Date: January 7, 2010

Major Rating Factors:

Disappointing performance is the major factor driving the C- (Fair) TheStreet.com Investment Rating for *iShares 2016 S&P AMT-Free Muni S. The fund currently has a performance rating of D (Weak) based on an annualized return of 0.00% over the last three years and a total return of 0.26% year to date 2012. Factored into the performance evaluation is an expense ratio of 0.30% (very low).

The fund's risk rating is currently B+ (Good). It carries a beta of 0.00, meaning the fund's expected move will be 0.0% for every 10% move in the market. Volatility, as measured by both the semi-deviation and a drawdown factor, is considered very low. As of December 31, 2012, *iShares 2016 S&P AMT-Free Muni S traded at a premium of .11% above its net asset value, which is better than its one-year historical average premium of .49%.

Scott F. Radell has been running the fund for 3 years and currently receives a manager quality ranking of 45 (0=worst, 99=best). This fund offers only a moderate level of risk but investors looking for strong performance are still waiting.

Data Date	Investment Rating	Net Assets ($Mil)	Price	Performance Rating/Pts	Total Return Y-T-D	Risk Rating/Pts
12-12	C-	50.70	53.56	D / 1.6	0.26%	B+ / 9.7
2011	C+	26.50	53.26	C- / 3.9	0.04%	B+ / 9.8

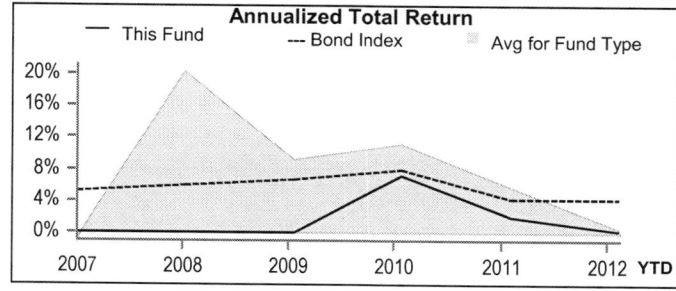

*iShares 2017 S&P AMT-Free Muni S (MUAF)

C-   Fair

Fund Family: BlackRock Fund Advisors
Fund Type: General - Investment Grade
Inception Date: January 7, 2010

Data Date	Investment Rating	Net Assets ($Mil)	Price	Performance Rating/Pts	Total Return Y-T-D	Risk Rating/Pts
12-12	C-	66.10	55.29	D / 1.7	0.52%	B+ / 9.4
2011	C+	35.50	54.96	C / 4.4	0.15%	B+ / 9.5

Major Rating Factors:
Disappointing performance is the major factor driving the C- (Fair) TheStreet.com Investment Rating for *iShares 2017 S&P AMT-Free Muni S. The fund currently has a performance rating of D (Weak) based on an annualized return of 0.00% over the last three years and a total return of 0.52% year to date 2012. Factored into the performance evaluation is an expense ratio of 0.30% (very low).

The fund's risk rating is currently B+ (Good). It carries a beta of 0.00, meaning the fund's expected move will be 0.0% for every 10% move in the market. Volatility, as measured by both the semi-deviation and a drawdown factor, is considered very low. As of December 31, 2012, *iShares 2017 S&P AMT-Free Muni S traded at a discount of .07% below its net asset value, which is better than its one-year historical average premium of .45%.

Scott F. Radell has been running the fund for 3 years and currently receives a manager quality ranking of 30 (0=worst, 99=best). This fund offers only a moderate level of risk but investors looking for strong performance are still waiting.

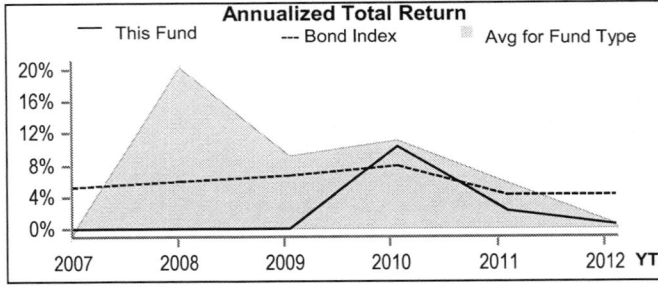

Annualized Total Return

*iShares Barclays 0-5 Year TIPS B (STIP)

C-   Fair

Fund Family: BlackRock Fund Advisors
Fund Type: US Government/Agency
Inception Date: December 1, 2010

Data Date	Investment Rating	Net Assets ($Mil)	Price	Performance Rating/Pts	Total Return Y-T-D	Risk Rating/Pts
12-12	C-	427.60	103.08	D / 1.7	0.04%	B+ / 9.9
2011	C	244.50	102.01	D+ / 2.6	0.42%	B+ / 9.9

Major Rating Factors:
Disappointing performance is the major factor driving the C- (Fair) TheStreet.com Investment Rating for *iShares Barclays 0-5 Year TIPS B. The fund currently has a performance rating of D (Weak) based on an annualized return of 0.00% over the last three years and a total return of 0.04% year to date 2012. Factored into the performance evaluation is an expense ratio of 0.20% (very low).

The fund's risk rating is currently B+ (Good). It carries a beta of 0.00, meaning the fund's expected move will be 0.0% for every 10% move in the market. Volatility, as measured by both the semi-deviation and a drawdown factor, is considered very low. As of December 31, 2012, *iShares Barclays 0-5 Year TIPS B traded at a price exactly equal to its net asset value, which is better than its one-year historical average premium of .11%.

Scott F. Radell has been running the fund for 3 years and currently receives a manager quality ranking of 67 (0=worst, 99=best). This fund offers only a moderate level of risk but investors looking for strong performance are still waiting.

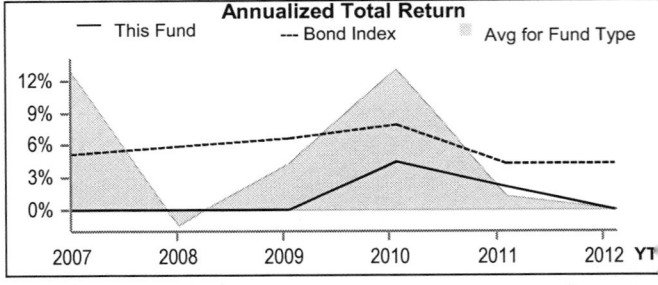

Annualized Total Return

*iShares Barclays 1-3 Year Credit (CSJ)

C-   Fair

Fund Family: BlackRock Fund Advisors
Fund Type: Corporate - Investment Grade
Inception Date: January 5, 2007

Data Date	Investment Rating	Net Assets ($Mil)	Price	Performance Rating/Pts	Total Return Y-T-D	Risk Rating/Pts
12-12	C-	9,225.10	105.48	D / 1.9	0.22%	B+ / 9.8
2011	C	8,835.10	104.20	D+ / 2.5	0.04%	B+ / 9.9
2010	B	7,219.20	104.28	C / 4.3	2.88%	B / 8.8
2009	B-	3,228.95	103.96	C- / 4.1	7.26%	B / 8.9

Major Rating Factors:
Disappointing performance is the major factor driving the C- (Fair) TheStreet.com Investment Rating for *iShares Barclays 1-3 Year Credit. The fund currently has a performance rating of D (Weak) based on an annualized return of 2.39% over the last three years and a total return of 0.22% year to date 2012. Factored into the performance evaluation is an expense ratio of 0.20% (very low).

The fund's risk rating is currently B+ (Good). It carries a beta of 0.26, meaning the fund's expected move will be 2.6% for every 10% move in the market. Volatility, as measured by both the semi-deviation and a drawdown factor, is considered very low. As of December 31, 2012, *iShares Barclays 1-3 Year Credit traded at a premium of .06% above its net asset value, which is better than its one-year historical average premium of .14%.

Scott F. Radell has been running the fund for 3 years and currently receives a manager quality ranking of 55 (0=worst, 99=best). This fund offers only a moderate level of risk but investors looking for strong performance are still waiting.

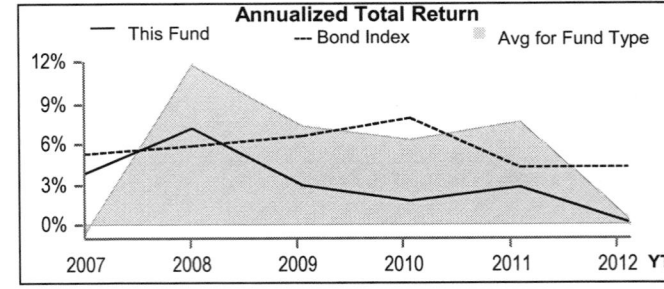

Annualized Total Return

*iShares Barclays 1-3Yr Treasury (SHY)

C- **Fair**

Fund Family: BlackRock Fund Advisors
Fund Type: US Government/Agency
Inception Date: July 22, 2002

Major Rating Factors:
Disappointing performance is the major factor driving the C- (Fair) TheStreet.com Investment Rating for *iShares Barclays 1-3Yr Treasury. The fund currently has a performance rating of D (Weak) based on an annualized return of 1.14% over the last three years and a total return of 0.01% year to date 2012. Factored into the performance evaluation is an expense ratio of 0.15% (very low).

The fund's risk rating is currently B+ (Good). It carries a beta of 0.03, meaning the fund's expected move will be 0.3% for every 10% move in the market. Volatility, as measured by both the semi-deviation and a drawdown factor, is considered very low. As of December 31, 2012, *iShares Barclays 1-3Yr Treasury traded at a price exactly equal to its net asset value, which is better than its one-year historical average premium of .02%.

Scott F. Radell has been running the fund for 3 years and currently receives a manager quality ranking of 60 (0=worst, 99=best). This fund offers only a moderate level of risk but investors looking for strong performance are still waiting.

Data Date	Investment Rating	Net Assets ($Mil)	Price	Performance Rating/Pts	Total Return Y-T-D	Risk Rating/Pts
12-12	C-	8,044.90	84.42	D / 1.6	0.01%	B+ / 9.9
2011	C	10,905.40	84.50	D / 2.2	-0.05%	B+ / 9.9
2010	B-	8,102.10	83.98	C- / 3.6	2.28%	B+ / 9.1
2009	C+	7,187.00	82.96	C- / 3.2	0.89%	B+ / 9.2

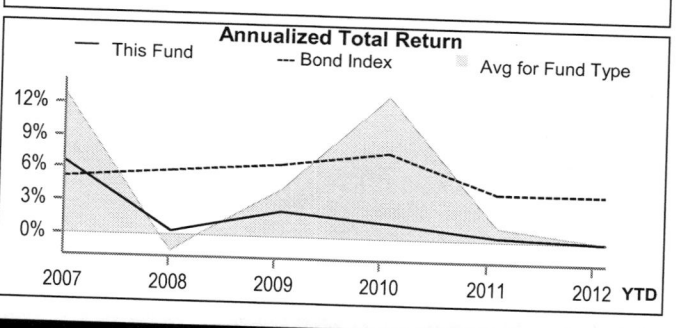

*iShares Barclays 10-20 Yr Treasu (TLH)

C **Fair**

Fund Family: BlackRock Fund Advisors
Fund Type: US Government/Agency
Inception Date: January 5, 2007

Major Rating Factors: Middle of the road best describes *iShares Barclays 10-20 Yr Treasu whose TheStreet.com Investment Rating is currently a C (Fair). The fund currently has a performance rating of C- (Fair) based on an annualized return of 10.48% over the last three years and a total return of -0.81% year to date 2012. Factored into the performance evaluation is an expense ratio of 0.15% (very low).

The fund's risk rating is currently B+ (Good). It carries a beta of 0.71, meaning the fund's expected move will be 7.1% for every 10% move in the market. Volatility, as measured by both the semi-deviation and a drawdown factor, is considered very low. As of December 31, 2012, *iShares Barclays 10-20 Yr Treasu traded at a premium of .96% above its net asset value, which is worse than its one-year historical average premium of .07%.

Scott F. Radell has been running the fund for 3 years and currently receives a manager quality ranking of 65 (0=worst, 99=best). If you desire an average level of risk, then this fund may be an option.

Data Date	Investment Rating	Net Assets ($Mil)	Price	Performance Rating/Pts	Total Return Y-T-D	Risk Rating/Pts
12-12	C	609.00	134.86	C- / 3.4	-0.81%	B+ / 9.1
2011	C+	505.20	132.93	C / 4.5	-0.98%	B / 8.9
2010	B	248.10	112.70	C / 4.6	9.71%	B / 8.4
2009	C-	243.39	106.47	E+ / 0.9	-6.98%	B / 8.6

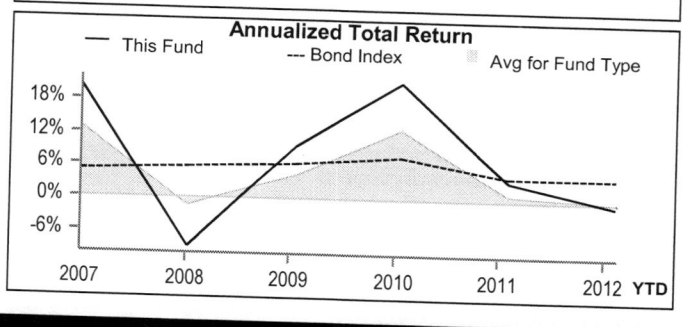

*iShares Barclays 20+Yr Treasury (TLT)

C **Fair**

Fund Family: BlackRock Fund Advisors
Fund Type: US Government/Agency
Inception Date: July 22, 2002

Major Rating Factors: Middle of the road best describes *iShares Barclays 20+Yr Treasury whose TheStreet.com Investment Rating is currently a C (Fair). The fund currently has a performance rating of C- (Fair) based on an annualized return of 13.66% over the last three years and a total return of -1.10% year to date 2012. Factored into the performance evaluation is an expense ratio of 0.15% (very low).

The fund's risk rating is currently B (Good). It carries a beta of 1.23, meaning it is expected to move 12.3% for every 10% move in the market. Volatility, as measured by both the semi-deviation and a drawdown factor, is considered low. As of December 31, 2012, *iShares Barclays 20+Yr Treasury traded at a premium of 1.47% above its net asset value, which is worse than its one-year historical average premium of .12%.

Scott F. Radell has been running the fund for 3 years and currently receives a manager quality ranking of 35 (0=worst, 99=best). If you desire an average level of risk, then this fund may be an option.

Data Date	Investment Rating	Net Assets ($Mil)	Price	Performance Rating/Pts	Total Return Y-T-D	Risk Rating/Pts
12-12	C	3,193.10	121.18	C- / 4.2	-1.10%	B / 8.4
2011	C+	3,382.10	121.25	C / 5.4	-2.08%	B- / 7.9
2010	C+	2,726.90	94.12	C- / 3.4	9.06%	B / 8.0
2009	C	2,202.01	89.89	D / 2.0	-19.74%	B / 8.2

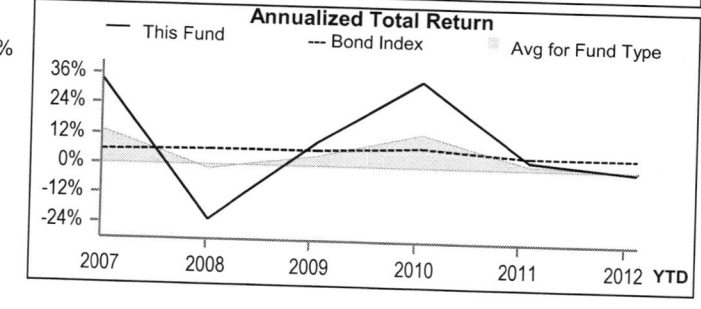

* Denotes ETF Fund

*iShares Barclays 3-7 Yr Treasury (IEI)   C   Fair

Fund Family: BlackRock Fund Advisors
Fund Type: US Government/Agency
Inception Date: January 5, 2007

Data Date	Investment Rating	Net Assets ($Mil)	Price	Performance Rating/Pts	Total Return Y-T-D	Risk Rating/Pts
12-12	C	3,096.70	123.22	D+ / 2.3	-0.06%	B+ / 9.7
2011	C	2,816.00	122.04	C- / 3.0	-0.11%	B+ / 9.7
2010	B+	1,308.00	114.65	C / 4.6	6.32%	B+ / 9.0
2009	C	805.43	110.16	D / 1.7	-1.05%	B+ / 9.2

Major Rating Factors:

Disappointing performance is the major factor driving the C (Fair) TheStreet.com Investment Rating for *iShares Barclays 3-7 Yr Treasury. The fund currently has a performance rating of D+ (Weak) based on an annualized return of 5.05% over the last three years and a total return of -0.06% year to date 2012. Factored into the performance evaluation is an expense ratio of 0.15% (very low).

The fund's risk rating is currently B+ (Good). It carries a beta of 0.18, meaning the fund's expected move will be 1.8% for every 10% move in the market. Volatility, as measured by both the semi-deviation and a drawdown factor, is considered very low. As of December 31, 2012, *iShares Barclays 3-7 Yr Treasury traded at a premium of .14% above its net asset value, which is worse than its one-year historical average premium of .04%.

Scott F. Radell has been running the fund for 3 years and currently receives a manager quality ranking of 72 (0=worst, 99=best). This fund offers only a moderate level of risk but investors looking for strong performance are still waiting.

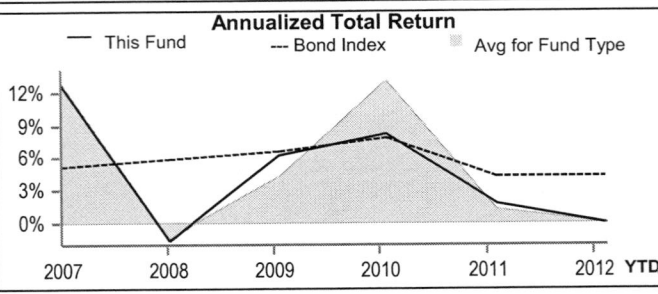
Annualized Total Return

*iShares Barclays 7-10Yr Treasury (IEF)   C   Fair

Fund Family: BlackRock Fund Advisors
Fund Type: US Government/Agency
Inception Date: July 22, 2002

Data Date	Investment Rating	Net Assets ($Mil)	Price	Performance Rating/Pts	Total Return Y-T-D	Risk Rating/Pts
12-12	C	4,405.80	107.49	C- / 3.1	-0.54%	B+ / 9.5
2011	C	4,795.30	105.57	C- / 3.8	-0.54%	B+ / 9.2
2010	B+	3,039.30	93.82	C / 4.9	9.37%	B / 8.6
2009	C+	2,564.75	88.60	C- / 3.4	-5.21%	B / 8.9

Major Rating Factors: Middle of the road best describes *iShares Barclays 7-10Yr Treasury whose TheStreet.com Investment Rating is currently a C (Fair). The fund currently has a performance rating of C- (Fair) based on an annualized return of 8.67% over the last three years and a total return of -0.54% year to date 2012. Factored into the performance evaluation is an expense ratio of 0.15% (very low).

The fund's risk rating is currently B+ (Good). It carries a beta of 0.46, meaning the fund's expected move will be 4.6% for every 10% move in the market. Volatility, as measured by both the semi-deviation and a drawdown factor, is considered very low. As of December 31, 2012, *iShares Barclays 7-10Yr Treasury traded at a premium of .68% above its net asset value, which is worse than its one-year historical average premium of .05%.

Scott F. Radell has been running the fund for 3 years and currently receives a manager quality ranking of 73 (0=worst, 99=best). If you desire an average level of risk, then this fund may be an option.

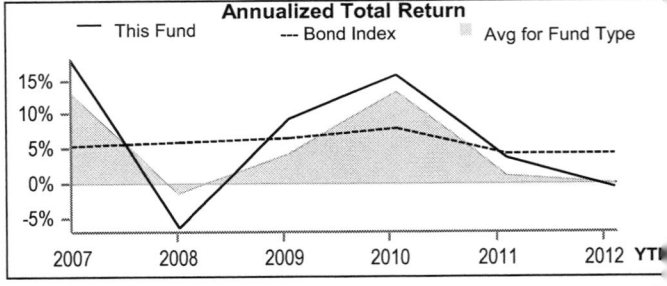
Annualized Total Return

*iShares Barclays Agency Bond (AGZ)   C-   Fair

Fund Family: BlackRock Fund Advisors
Fund Type: US Government/Agency
Inception Date: November 5, 2008

Data Date	Investment Rating	Net Assets ($Mil)	Price	Performance Rating/Pts	Total Return Y-T-D	Risk Rating/Pts
12-12	C-	425.60	113.30	D / 2.0	0.03%	B+ / 9.9
2011	C	360.50	112.95	D+ / 2.6	-0.26%	B+ / 9.9
2010	B-	361.40	109.52	C- / 3.4	3.75%	B+ / 9.1
2009	C	215.78	107.57	D+ / 2.4	2.08%	B+ / 9.2

Major Rating Factors:

Disappointing performance is the major factor driving the C- (Fair) TheStreet.com Investment Rating for *iShares Barclays Agency Bond. The fund currently has a performance rating of D (Weak) based on an annualized return of 3.17% over the last three years and a total return of 0.03% year to date 2012. Factored into the performance evaluation is an expense ratio of 0.20% (very low).

The fund's risk rating is currently B+ (Good). It carries a beta of 0.10, meaning the fund's expected move will be 1.0% for every 10% move in the market. Volatility, as measured by both the semi-deviation and a drawdown factor, is considered very low. As of December 31, 2012, *iShares Barclays Agency Bond traded at a discount of .04% below its net asset value, which is better than its one-year historical average premium of .12%.

Scott F. Radell has been running the fund for 3 years and currently receives a manager quality ranking of 66 (0=worst, 99=best). This fund offers only a moderate level of risk but investors looking for strong performance are still waiting.

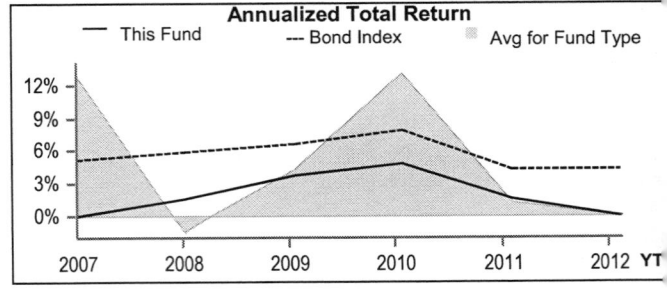
Annualized Total Return

*iShares Barclays Credit Bond Fd (CFT)

C   **Fair**

Fund Family: BlackRock Fund Advisors
Fund Type: Corporate - Investment Grade
Inception Date: January 5, 2007

Major Rating Factors: Middle of the road best describes *iShares Barclays Credit Bond Fd whose TheStreet.com Investment Rating is currently a C (Fair). The fund currently has a performance rating of C- (Fair) based on an annualized return of 7.91% over the last three years and a total return of 0.25% year to date 2012. Factored into the performance evaluation is an expense ratio of 0.20% (very low).

The fund's risk rating is currently B+ (Good). It carries a beta of 1.01, meaning that its performance tracks fairly well with that of the overall stock market. Volatility, as measured by both the semi-deviation and a drawdown factor, is considered very low. As of December 31, 2012, *iShares Barclays Credit Bond Fd traded at a premium of .06% above its net asset value, which is better than its one-year historical average premium of .41%.

Scott F. Radell has been running the fund for 3 years and currently receives a manager quality ranking of 48 (0=worst, 99=best). If you desire an average level of risk, then this fund may be an option.

Data Date	Investment Rating	Net Assets ($Mil)	Price	Performance Rating/Pts	Total Return Y-T-D	Risk Rating/Pts
12-12	C	1,405.20	113.16	C- / 3.1	0.25%	B+ / 9.5
2011	C+	1,043.90	108.96	C- / 4.0	-0.57%	B+ / 9.3
2010	B	727.30	104.13	C / 5.3	8.43%	B / 8.1
2009	B	379.52	100.53	C / 4.8	11.31%	B / 8.4

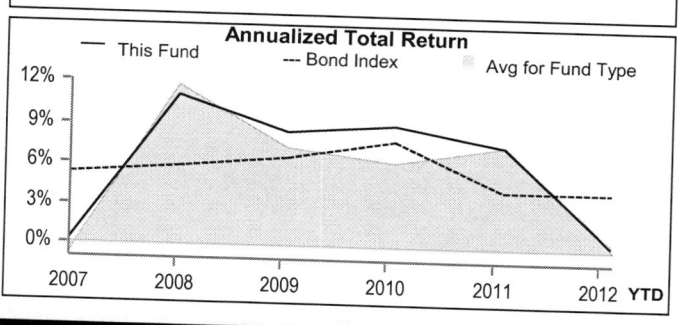

*iShares Barclays Govt/Credit Bd (GBF)

C   **Fair**

Fund Family: BlackRock Fund Advisors
Fund Type: US Government/Agency
Inception Date: January 5, 2007

Major Rating Factors:
Disappointing performance is the major factor driving the C (Fair) TheStreet.com Investment Rating for *iShares Barclays Govt/Credit Bd. The fund currently has a performance rating of D+ (Weak) based on an annualized return of 5.81% over the last three years and a total return of 0.08% year to date 2012. Factored into the performance evaluation is an expense ratio of 0.20% (very low).

The fund's risk rating is currently B+ (Good). It carries a beta of 0.22, meaning the fund's expected move will be 2.2% for every 10% move in the market. Volatility, as measured by both the semi-deviation and a drawdown factor, is considered very low. As of December 31, 2012, *iShares Barclays Govt/Credit Bd traded at a discount of .01% below its net asset value, which is better than its one-year historical average premium of .33%.

Scott F. Radell has been running the fund for 3 years and currently receives a manager quality ranking of 73 (0=worst, 99=best). This fund offers only a moderate level of risk but investors looking for strong performance are still waiting.

Data Date	Investment Rating	Net Assets ($Mil)	Price	Performance Rating/Pts	Total Return Y-T-D	Risk Rating/Pts
12-12	C	190.20	114.87	D+ / 2.5	0.08%	B+ / 9.7
2011	C+	113.10	113.83	C- / 3.5	-0.12%	B+ / 9.7
2010	B	129.00	107.39	C / 4.5	5.72%	B / 8.8
2009	C+	126.09	104.86	C- / 3.0	3.49%	B+ / 9.0

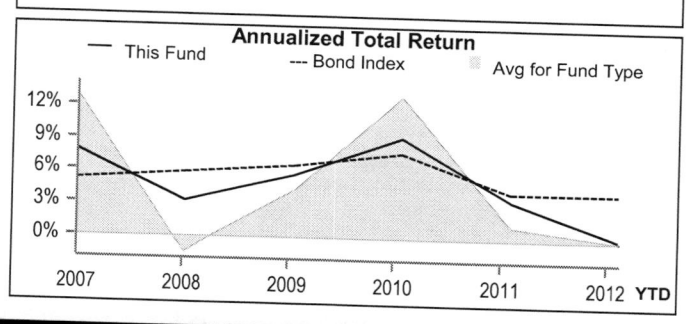

*iShares Barclays Intrm Credit Bd (CIU)

C   **Fair**

Fund Family: BlackRock Fund Advisors
Fund Type: Corporate - Investment Grade
Inception Date: January 5, 2007

Major Rating Factors:
Disappointing performance is the major factor driving the C (Fair) TheStreet.com Investment Rating for *iShares Barclays Intrm Credit Bd. The fund currently has a performance rating of D+ (Weak) based on an annualized return of 6.18% over the last three years and a total return of -0.08% year to date 2012. Factored into the performance evaluation is an expense ratio of 0.20% (very low).

The fund's risk rating is currently B+ (Good). It carries a beta of 0.71, meaning the fund's expected move will be 7.1% for every 10% move in the market. Volatility, as measured by both the semi-deviation and a drawdown factor, is considered very low. As of December 31, 2012, *iShares Barclays Intrm Credit Bd traded at a premium of .24% above its net asset value, which is better than its one-year historical average premium of .26%.

Scott F. Radell has been running the fund for 3 years and currently receives a manager quality ranking of 56 (0=worst, 99=best). This fund offers only a moderate level of risk but investors looking for strong performance are still waiting.

Data Date	Investment Rating	Net Assets ($Mil)	Price	Performance Rating/Pts	Total Return Y-T-D	Risk Rating/Pts
12-12	C	5,339.90	111.29	D+ / 2.7	-0.08%	B+ / 9.7
2011	C	4,475.90	107.18	C- / 3.5	-0.05%	B+ / 9.6
2010	B	2,950.70	105.18	C / 5.2	6.84%	B / 8.4
2009	B	1,625.94	102.71	C / 4.9	10.60%	B / 8.6

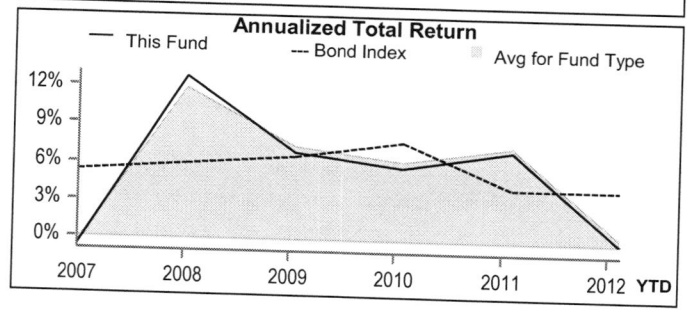

*iShares Barclays Intrm Govt/Crdt (GVI)

C   **Fair**

Fund Family: BlackRock Fund Advisors
Fund Type: General - Investment Grade
Inception Date: January 5, 2007

Major Rating Factors:

Disappointing performance is the major factor driving the C (Fair) TheStreet.com Investment Rating for *iShares Barclays Intrm Govt/Crdt. The fund currently has a performance rating of D (Weak) based on an annualized return of 4.47% over the last three years and a total return of -0.01% year to date 2012. Factored into the performance evaluation is an expense ratio of 0.20% (very low).

The fund's risk rating is currently B+ (Good). It carries a beta of 0.86, meaning the fund's expected move will be 8.6% for every 10% move in the market. Volatility, as measured by both the semi-deviation and a drawdown factor, is considered very low. As of December 31, 2012, *iShares Barclays Intrm Govt/Crdt traded at a premium of .20% above its net asset value, which is better than its one-year historical average premium of .21%.

Scott F. Radell has been running the fund for 3 years and currently receives a manager quality ranking of 47 (0=worst, 99=best). This fund offers only a moderate level of risk but investors looking for strong performance are still waiting.

Data Date	Investment Rating	Net Assets ($Mil)	Price	Performance Rating/Pts	Total Return Y-T-D	Risk Rating/Pts
12-12	C	955.10	112.41	D / 2.2	-0.01%	B+ / 9.8
2011	C	686.70	111.29	D+ / 2.9	-0.21%	B+ / 9.8
2010	B+	538.40	107.88	C / 4.5	5.47%	B / 8.9
2009	C+	357.64	105.26	D+ / 2.9	2.81%	B+ / 9.0

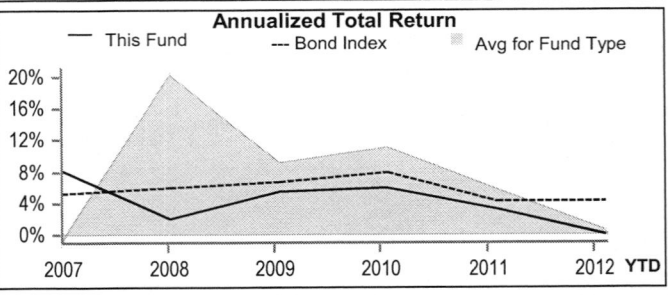

*iShares Barclays MBS Bond (MBB)

C-   **Fair**

Fund Family: BlackRock Fund Advisors
Fund Type: Mortgage
Inception Date: March 13, 2007

Major Rating Factors:

Disappointing performance is the major factor driving the C- (Fair) TheStreet.com Investment Rating for *iShares Barclays MBS Bond. The fund currently has a performance rating of D (Weak) based on an annualized return of 4.12% over the last three years and a total return of 0.05% year to date 2012. Factored into the performance evaluation is an expense ratio of 0.25% (very low).

The fund's risk rating is currently B+ (Good). It carries a beta of 0.99, meaning that its performance tracks fairly well with that of the overall stock market. Volatility, as measured by both the semi-deviation and a drawdown factor, is considered very low. As of December 31, 2012, *iShares Barclays MBS Bond traded at a discount of .09% below its net asset value, which is better than its one-year historical average premium of .06%.

Scott F. Radell has been running the fund for 3 years and currently receives a manager quality ranking of 49 (0=worst, 99=best). This fund offers only a moderate level of risk but investors looking for strong performance are still waiting.

Data Date	Investment Rating	Net Assets ($Mil)	Price	Performance Rating/Pts	Total Return Y-T-D	Risk Rating/Pts
12-12	C-	6,518.70	107.99	D / 2.2	0.05%	B+ / 9.7
2011	C	4,057.40	108.07	C- / 3.1	0.03%	B+ / 9.7
2010	B+	2,224.20	105.58	C / 5.1	5.58%	B / 8.9
2009	C+	1,646.02	105.98	C- / 3.4	4.73%	B+ / 9.0

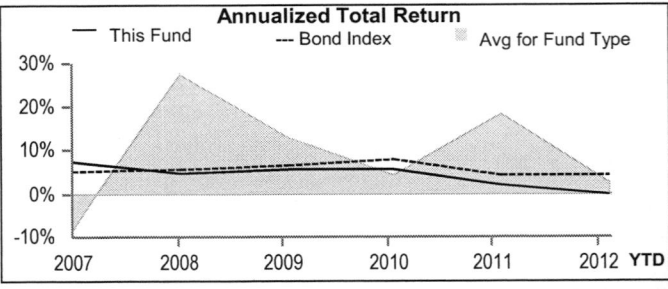

*iShares Barclays Short Treasury (SHV)

C-   **Fair**

Fund Family: BlackRock Fund Advisors
Fund Type: US Government/Agency
Inception Date: January 5, 2007

Major Rating Factors:

Disappointing performance is the major factor driving the C- (Fair) TheStreet.com Investment Rating for *iShares Barclays Short Treasury. The fund currently has a performance rating of D- (Weak) based on an annualized return of 0.07% over the last three years and a total return of -0.02% year to date 2012. Factored into the performance evaluation is an expense ratio of 0.13% (very low).

The fund's risk rating is currently B+ (Good). It carries a beta of 0.00, meaning the fund's expected move will be 0.0% for every 10% move in the market. Volatility, as measured by both the semi-deviation and a drawdown factor, is considered very low. As of December 31, 2012, *iShares Barclays Short Treasury traded at a premium of .04% above its net asset value, which is worse than its one-year historical average premium of .01%.

Scott F. Radell has been running the fund for 3 years and currently receives a manager quality ranking of 52 (0=worst, 99=best). This fund offers only a moderate level of risk but investors looking for strong performance are still waiting.

Data Date	Investment Rating	Net Assets ($Mil)	Price	Performance Rating/Pts	Total Return Y-T-D	Risk Rating/Pts
12-12	C-	2,579.10	110.26	D- / 1.3	-0.02%	B+ / 9.9
2011	C-	2,589.70	110.23	D / 2.0	-0.01%	B+ / 9.9
2010	C+	4,000.20	110.24	D+ / 2.5	0.12%	B+ / 9.1
2009	C	1,785.08	110.19	D / 1.9	0.32%	B+ / 9.2

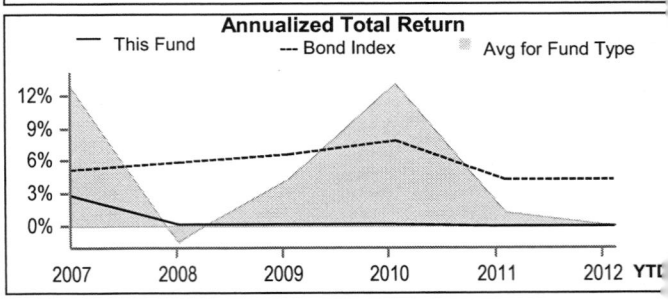

*iShares Barclays TIPS Bond (TIP)

C   **Fair**

Fund Family: BlackRock Fund Advisors
Fund Type: US Government/Agency
Inception Date: December 4, 2003

Major Rating Factors: Middle of the road best describes *iShares Barclays TIPS Bond whose TheStreet.com Investment Rating is currently a C (Fair). The fund currently has a performance rating of C- (Fair) based on an annualized return of 8.13% over the last three years and a total return of -0.12% year to date 2012. Factored into the performance evaluation is an expense ratio of 0.20% (very low).

The fund's risk rating is currently B+ (Good). It carries a beta of 0.13, meaning the fund's expected move will be 1.3% for every 10% move in the market. Volatility, as measured by both the semi-deviation and a drawdown factor, is considered very low. As of December 31, 2012, *iShares Barclays TIPS Bond traded at a premium of .18% above its net asset value, which is worse than its one-year historical average premium of .10%.

Scott F. Radell has been running the fund for 3 years and currently receives a manager quality ranking of 84 (0=worst, 99=best). If you desire an average level of risk, then this fund may be an option.

Data Date	Investment Rating	Net Assets ($Mil)	Price	Performance Rating/Pts	Total Return Y-T-D	Risk Rating/Pts
12-12	C	22,284.70	121.41	C- / 3.1	-0.12%	B+ / 9.7
2011	C+	22,164.20	116.69	C / 4.4	0.58%	B+ / 9.7
2010	B-	19,351.30	107.52	C / 4.5	6.14%	B / 8.3
2009	B-	15,405.47	103.90	C / 4.4	11.03%	B / 8.5

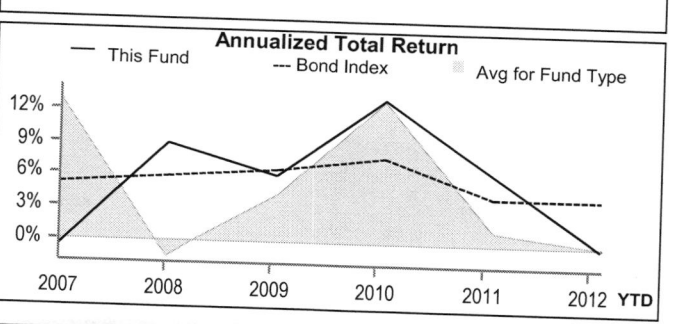

*iShares Cohen & Steers Realty Ma (ICF)

B   **Good**

Fund Family: BlackRock Fund Advisors
Fund Type: Income
Inception Date: January 29, 2001

Major Rating Factors: Strong performance is the major factor driving the B (Good) TheStreet.com Investment Rating for *iShares Cohen & Steers Realty Ma. The fund currently has a performance rating of B- (Good) based on an annualized return of 18.87% over the last three years and a total return of 1.82% year to date 2012. Factored into the performance evaluation is an expense ratio of 0.35% (very low).

The fund's risk rating is currently B- (Good). It carries a beta of 1.02, meaning that its performance tracks fairly well with that of the overall stock market. Volatility, as measured by both the semi-deviation and a drawdown factor, is considered low. As of December 31, 2012, *iShares Cohen & Steers Realty Ma traded at a discount of 1.85% below its net asset value, which is better than its one-year historical average discount of .01%.

Diane Hsiung has been running the fund for 5 years and currently receives a manager quality ranking of 83 (0=worst, 99=best). If you desire only a moderate level of risk and strong performance, then this fund is an excellent option.

Data Date	Investment Rating	Net Assets ($Mil)	Price	Performance Rating/Pts	Total Return Y-T-D	Risk Rating/Pts
12-12	B	2,705.30	78.54	B- / 7.5	1.82%	B- / 7.6
2011	C+	2,315.40	70.22	B / 7.8	-0.57%	C+ / 6.1
2010	C	2,212.70	65.72	B- / 7.1	29.14%	C- / 3.9
2009	E+	1,124.21	52.52	D- / 1.2	28.36%	C- / 3.9

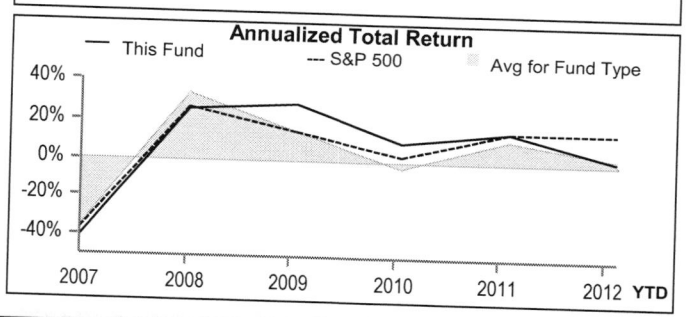

*iShares Core Long-Term US Bond E (ILTB)

C+   **Fair**

Fund Family: BlackRock Fund Advisors
Fund Type: Global
Inception Date: December 8, 2009

Major Rating Factors: Middle of the road best describes *iShares Core Long-Term US Bond E whose TheStreet.com Investment Rating is currently a C+ (Fair). The fund currently has a performance rating of C- (Fair) based on an annualized return of 12.29% over the last three years and a total return of -1.32% year to date 2012. Factored into the performance evaluation is an expense ratio of 0.20% (very low).

The fund's risk rating is currently B+ (Good). It carries a beta of 0.04, meaning the fund's expected move will be 0.4% for every 10% move in the market. Volatility, as measured by both the semi-deviation and a drawdown factor, is considered very low. As of December 31, 2012, *iShares Core Long-Term US Bond E traded at a premium of 1.63% above its net asset value, which is worse than its one-year historical average premium of .29%.

Scott F. Radell has been running the fund for 3 years and currently receives a manager quality ranking of 93 (0=worst, 99=best). If you desire an average level of risk, then this fund may be an option.

Data Date	Investment Rating	Net Assets ($Mil)	Price	Performance Rating/Pts	Total Return Y-T-D	Risk Rating/Pts
12-12	C+	206.30	63.78	C- / 4.2	-1.32%	B+ / 9.2
2011	B+	24.30	60.74	B / 7.6	-1.47%	B+ / 9.3
2010	B	15.60	52.27	C / 4.3	9.17%	B / 8.5

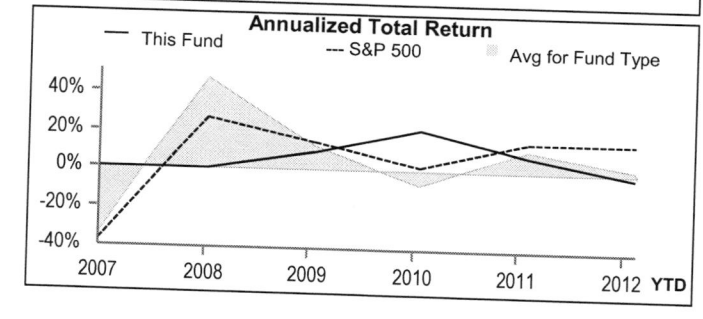

* Denotes ETF Fund

*iShares Core S&P 500 ETF (IVV)

C **Fair**

Fund Family: BlackRock Fund Advisors
Fund Type: Growth
Inception Date: May 15, 2000

Major Rating Factors: Middle of the road best describes *iShares Core S&P 500 ETF whose TheStreet.com Investment Rating is currently a C (Fair). The fund currently has a performance rating of C (Fair) based on an annualized return of 11.31% over the last three years and a total return of 3.30% year to date 2012. Factored into the performance evaluation is an expense ratio of 0.09% (very low).

The fund's risk rating is currently B (Good). It carries a beta of 1.00, meaning that its performance tracks fairly well with that of the overall stock market. Volatility, as measured by both the semi-deviation and a drawdown factor, is considered low. As of December 31, 2012, *iShares Core S&P 500 ETF traded at a discount of 3.16% below its net asset value, which is better than its one-year historical average discount of .01%.

Diane Hsiung has been running the fund for 5 years and currently receives a manager quality ranking of 0 (0=worst, 99=best). If you desire an average level of risk, then this fund may be an option.

Data Date	Investment Rating	Net Assets ($Mil)	Price	Performance Rating/Pts	Total Return Y-T-D	Risk Rating/Pts
12-12	C	34,911.50	143.14	C / 5.2	3.30%	B / 8.0
2011	C+	26,208.70	125.96	C / 5.3	1.83%	B- / 7.9
2010	C-	25,763.50	126.25	C- / 3.9	15.11%	C+ / 6.0
2009	D+	20,494.00	111.81	D / 2.2	22.60%	C+ / 6.1

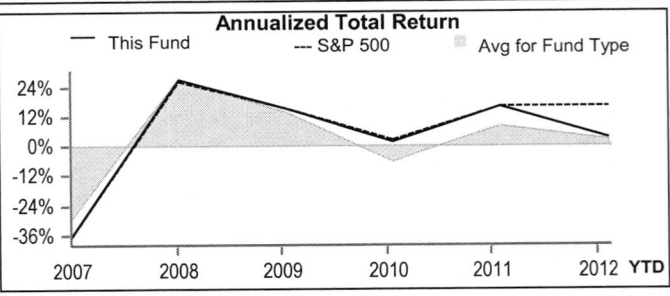

*iShares Core S&P Mid-Cap ETF (IJH)

B- **Good**

Fund Family: BlackRock Fund Advisors
Fund Type: Growth
Inception Date: May 22, 2000

Major Rating Factors: *iShares Core S&P Mid-Cap ETF receives a TheStreet.com Investment Rating of B- (Good). The fund currently has a performance rating of C+ (Fair) based on an annualized return of 13.95% over the last three years and a total return of 3.74% year to date 2012. Factored into the performance evaluation is an expense ratio of 0.20% (very low).

The fund's risk rating is currently B- (Good). It carries a beta of 1.13, meaning it is expected to move 11.3% for every 10% move in the market. Volatility, as measured by both the semi-deviation and a drawdown factor, is considered low. As of December 31, 2012, *iShares Core S&P Mid-Cap ETF traded at a discount of 3.65% below its net asset value.

Diane Hsiung has been running the fund for 5 years and currently receives a manager quality ranking of 60 (0=worst, 99=best). If you desire an average level of risk, then this fund may be an option.

Data Date	Investment Rating	Net Assets ($Mil)	Price	Performance Rating/Pts	Total Return Y-T-D	Risk Rating/Pts
12-12	B-	13,558.40	101.70	C+ / 6.9	3.74%	B- / 7.7
2011	C+	9,297.30	87.61	C+ / 6.4	1.48%	B- / 7.7
2010	B	9,360.60	90.69	B- / 7.4	26.73%	C+ / 5.7
2009	C-	6,099.88	72.41	C- / 3.8	34.21%	C+ / 6.0

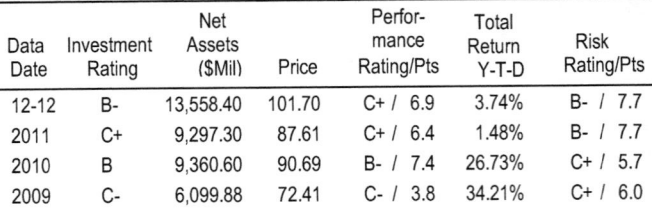

*iShares Core S&P Small-Cap ETF (IJR)

C+ **Fair**

Fund Family: BlackRock Fund Advisors
Fund Type: Growth
Inception Date: May 22, 2000

Major Rating Factors: Middle of the road best describes *iShares Core S&P Small-Cap ETF whose TheStreet.com Investment Rating is currently a C+ (Fair). The fund currently has a performance rating of C+ (Fair) based on an annualized return of 14.53% over the last three years and a total return of 3.32% year to date 2012. Factored into the performance evaluation is an expense ratio of 0.20% (very low).

The fund's risk rating is currently B- (Good). It carries a beta of 1.20, meaning it is expected to move 12.0% for every 10% move in the market. Volatility, as measured by both the semi-deviation and a drawdown factor, is considered low. As of December 31, 2012, *iShares Core S&P Small-Cap ETF traded at a discount of 3.26% below its net asset value.

Diane Hsiung has been running the fund for 5 years and currently receives a manager quality ranking of 59 (0=worst, 99=best). If you desire an average level of risk, then this fund may be an option.

Data Date	Investment Rating	Net Assets ($Mil)	Price	Performance Rating/Pts	Total Return Y-T-D	Risk Rating/Pts
12-12	C+	8,090.60	78.10	C+ / 6.7	3.32%	B- / 7.5
2011	C+	6,915.20	68.30	C+ / 6.4	1.29%	B- / 7.5
2010	B	6,785.10	68.47	B- / 7.3	26.61%	C+ / 5.7
2009	D+	4,901.74	54.72	D+ / 2.5	23.80%	C+ / 5.8

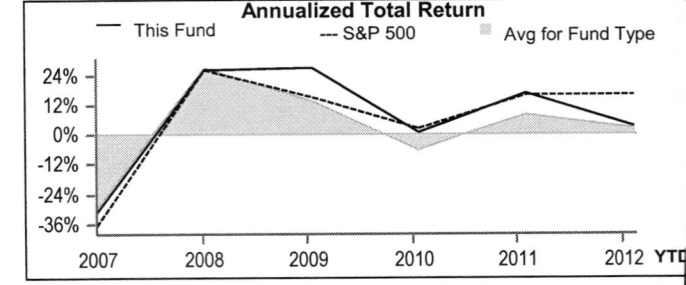

*iShares Core S&P Tot US Stk Mkt (ITOT)

C   **Fair**

Fund Family: BlackRock Fund Advisors
Fund Type: Income
Inception Date: January 20, 2004

Major Rating Factors: Middle of the road best describes *iShares Core S&P Tot US Stk Mkt whose TheStreet.com Investment Rating is currently a C (Fair). The fund currently has a performance rating of C (Fair) based on an annualized return of 11.49% over the last three years and a total return of 3.27% year to date 2012. Factored into the performance evaluation is an expense ratio of 0.20% (very low).

The fund's risk rating is currently B (Good). It carries a beta of 1.01, meaning that its performance tracks fairly well with that of the overall stock market. Volatility, as measured by both the semi-deviation and a drawdown factor, is considered low. As of December 31, 2012, *iShares Core S&P Tot US Stk Mkt traded at a discount of 3.15% below its net asset value, which is better than its one-year historical average discount of .07%.

Diane Hsiung has been running the fund for 5 years and currently receives a manager quality ranking of 52 (0=worst, 99=best). If you desire an average level of risk, then this fund may be an option.

Data Date	Investment Rating	Net Assets ($Mil)	Price	Perfor-mance Rating/Pts	Total Return Y-T-D	Risk Rating/Pts
12-12	C	434.80	64.94	C / 5.3	3.27%	B / 8.0
2011	C+	299.60	57.17	C / 5.3	1.45%	B- / 7.9
2010	D+	323.40	57.25	C- / 4.2	16.24%	C- / 3.7
2009	D-	290.33	50.14	D / 2.2	23.36%	C- / 4.2

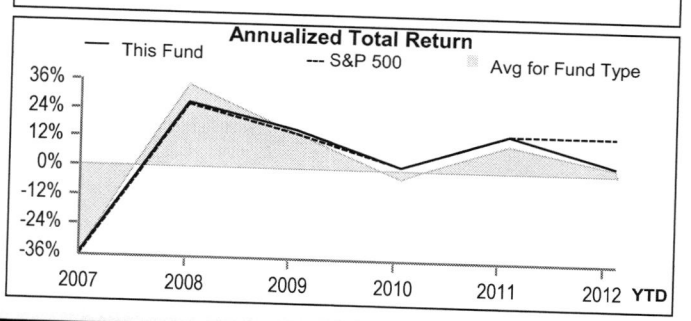

---

*iShares Core Total US Bond Mkt E (AGG)

C   **Fair**

Fund Family: BlackRock Fund Advisors
Fund Type: General - Investment Grade
Inception Date: September 22, 2003

Major Rating Factors:
Disappointing performance is the major factor driving the C (Fair) TheStreet.com Investment Rating for *iShares Core Total US Bond Mkt E. The fund currently has a performance rating of D+ (Weak) based on an annualized return of 5.49% over the last three years and a total return of -0.21% year to date 2012. Factored into the performance evaluation is an expense ratio of 0.20% (very low).

The fund's risk rating is currently B+ (Good). It carries a beta of 1.04, meaning that its performance tracks fairly well with that of the overall stock market. Volatility, as measured by both the semi-deviation and a drawdown factor, is considered very low. As of December 31, 2012, *iShares Core Total US Bond Mkt E traded at a premium of .25% above its net asset value, which is worse than its one-year historical average premium of .10%.

Scott F. Radell has been running the fund for 3 years and currently receives a manager quality ranking of 47 (0=worst, 99=best). This fund offers only a moderate level of risk but investors looking for strong performance are still waiting.

Data Date	Investment Rating	Net Assets ($Mil)	Price	Perfor-mance Rating/Pts	Total Return Y-T-D	Risk Rating/Pts
12-12	C	15,335.80	111.08	D+ / 2.4	-0.21%	B+ / 9.8
2011	C+	14,146.60	110.25	C- / 3.4	-0.12%	B+ / 9.8
2010	B+	11,219.50	105.75	C / 4.8	6.38%	B / 8.9
2009	C+	10,290.01	103.19	C- / 3.6	3.64%	B+ / 9.0

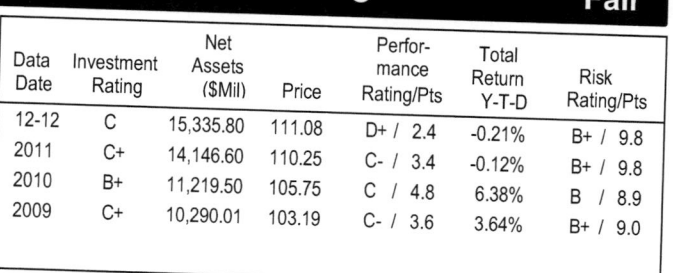

---

*iShares Diversified Alternatives (ALT)

C-   **Fair**

Fund Family: BlackRock Fund Advisors
Fund Type: Global
Inception Date: October 6, 2009

Major Rating Factors:
Disappointing performance is the major factor driving the C- (Fair) TheStreet.com Investment Rating for *iShares Diversified Alternatives. The fund currently has a performance rating of D (Weak) based on an annualized return of 0.33% over the last three years and a total return of -0.42% year to date 2012. Factored into the performance evaluation is an expense ratio of 1.02% (low).

The fund's risk rating is currently B+ (Good). It carries a beta of 0.07, meaning the fund's expected move will be 0.7% for every 10% move in the market. Volatility, as measured by both the semi-deviation and a drawdown factor, is considered very low. As of December 31, 2012, *iShares Diversified Alternatives traded at a discount of .14% below its net asset value, which is worse than its one-year historical average discount of .15%.

Alan Mason currently receives a manager quality ranking of 55 (0=worst, 99=best). This fund offers only a moderate level of risk but investors looking for strong performance are still waiting.

Data Date	Investment Rating	Net Assets ($Mil)	Price	Perfor-mance Rating/Pts	Total Return Y-T-D	Risk Rating/Pts
12-12	C-	50.80	50.65	D / 1.6	-0.42%	B+ / 9.4
2011	C-	87.90	48.75	D- / 1.5	0.39%	B+ / 9.5
2010	C+	110.90	50.55	C- / 3.3	1.61%	B+ / 9.0

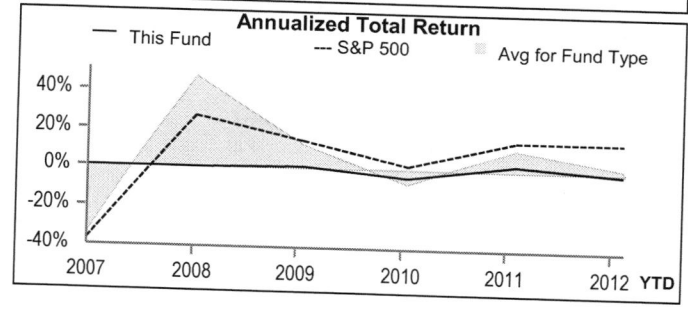

* Denotes ETF Fund

*iShares DJ Intl Select Dividend (IDV)

C   **Fair**

Fund Family: BlackRock Fund Advisors
Fund Type: Foreign
Inception Date: June 11, 2007

Major Rating Factors: Middle of the road best describes *iShares DJ Intl Select Dividend whose TheStreet.com Investment Rating is currently a C (Fair). The fund currently has a performance rating of C (Fair) based on an annualized return of 7.31% over the last three years and a total return of 2.32% year to date 2012. Factored into the performance evaluation is an expense ratio of 0.50% (very low).

    The fund's risk rating is currently B- (Good). It carries a beta of 1.06, meaning that its performance tracks fairly well with that of the overall stock market. Volatility, as measured by both the semi-deviation and a drawdown factor, is considered low. As of December 31, 2012, *iShares DJ Intl Select Dividend traded at a discount of 1.92% below its net asset value, which is better than its one-year historical average premium of .35%.

    Diane Hsiung has been running the fund for 5 years and currently receives a manager quality ranking of 72 (0=worst, 99=best). If you desire an average level of risk, then this fund may be an option.

Data Date	Investment Rating	Net Assets ($Mil)	Price	Performance Rating/Pts	Total Return Y-T-D	Risk Rating/Pts
12-12	C	1,426.10	33.67	C / 5.1	2.32%	B- / 7.5
2011	C+	698.80	29.69	C+ / 5.6	-0.77%	B- / 7.7
2010	D	347.20	33.64	D+ / 2.6	11.82%	C / 4.9
2009	A-	52.03	31.42	A / 9.4	57.77%	C / 4.9

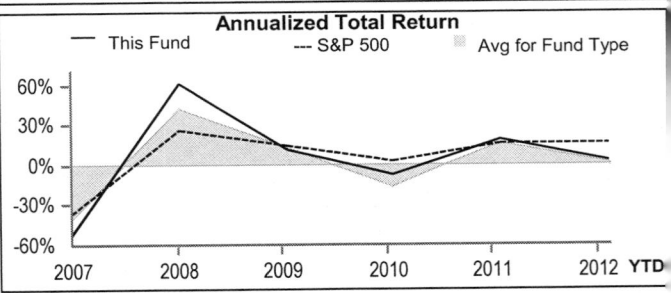

*iShares DJ Select Dividend (DVY)

C+   **Fair**

Fund Family: BlackRock Fund Advisors
Fund Type: Income
Inception Date: November 3, 2003

Major Rating Factors: Middle of the road best describes *iShares DJ Select Dividend whose TheStreet.com Investment Rating is currently a C+ (Fair). The fund currently has a performance rating of C (Fair) based on an annualized return of 13.60% over the last three years and a total return of 2.32% year to date 2012. Factored into the performance evaluation is an expense ratio of 0.40% (very low).

    The fund's risk rating is currently B (Good). It carries a beta of 0.69, meaning the fund's expected move will be 6.9% for every 10% move in the market. Volatility, as measured by both the semi-deviation and a drawdown factor, is considered low. As of December 31, 2012, *iShares DJ Select Dividend traded at a discount of 2.22% below its net asset value.

    Diane Hsiung has been running the fund for 5 years and currently receives a manager quality ranking of 81 (0=worst, 99=best). If you desire an average level of risk, then this fund may be an option.

Data Date	Investment Rating	Net Assets ($Mil)	Price	Performance Rating/Pts	Total Return Y-T-D	Risk Rating/Pts
12-12	C+	10,371.70	57.24	C / 5.4	2.32%	B / 8.9
2011	C+	9,548.00	53.77	C+ / 5.8	-0.17%	B- / 7.6
2010	C-	6,011.90	49.86	C- / 3.3	17.79%	C+ / 5.7
2009	D-	2,961.00	43.91	D- / 1.1	9.19%	C / 5.4

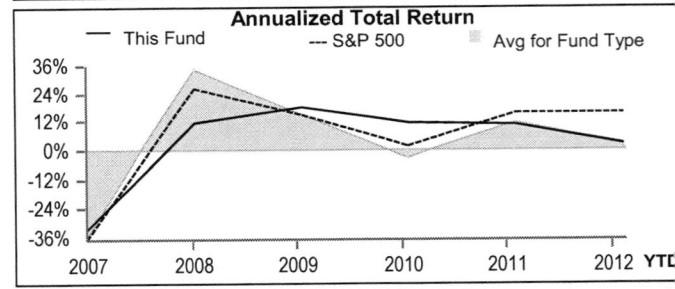

*iShares DJ Transportation (IYT)

C   **Fair**

Fund Family: BlackRock Fund Advisors
Fund Type: Income
Inception Date: October 6, 2003

Major Rating Factors: Middle of the road best describes *iShares DJ Transportation whose TheStreet.com Investment Rating is currently a C (Fair). The fund currently has a performance rating of C (Fair) based on an annualized return of 11.29% over the last three years and a total return of 5.34% year to date 2012. Factored into the performance evaluation is an expense ratio of 0.47% (very low).

    The fund's risk rating is currently B- (Good). It carries a beta of 1.09, meaning that its performance tracks fairly well with that of the overall stock market. Volatility, as measured by both the semi-deviation and a drawdown factor, is considered low. As of December 31, 2012, *iShares DJ Transportation traded at a discount of 5.10% below its net asset value.

    Diane Hsiung has been running the fund for 5 years and currently receives a manager quality ranking of 37 (0=worst, 99=best). If you desire an average level of risk, then this fund may be an option.

Data Date	Investment Rating	Net Assets ($Mil)	Price	Performance Rating/Pts	Total Return Y-T-D	Risk Rating/Pts
12-12	C	594.40	94.35	C / 4.7	5.34%	B- / 7.6
2011	C	411.70	89.47	C / 5.0	0.94%	B- / 7.2
2010	B+	673.20	92.32	B / 8.0	26.74%	C / 5.5
2009	C-	261.45	73.82	C- / 3.0	15.27%	C+ / 5.9

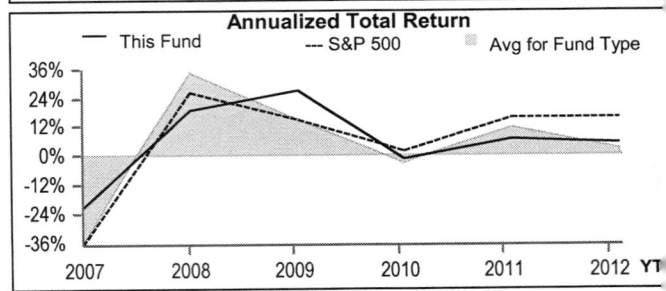

*iShares DJ US Aerospace & Def Id (ITA)

C **Fair**

Fund Family: BlackRock Fund Advisors
Fund Type: Income
Inception Date: May 1, 2006

Major Rating Factors: Middle of the road best describes *iShares DJ US Aerospace & Def Id whose TheStreet.com Investment Rating is currently a C (Fair). The fund currently has a performance rating of C (Fair) based on an annualized return of 10.53% over the last three years and a total return of 2.02% year to date 2012. Factored into the performance evaluation is an expense ratio of 0.47% (very low).

The fund's risk rating is currently B- (Good). It carries a beta of 1.04, meaning that its performance tracks fairly well with that of the overall stock market. Volatility, as measured by both the semi-deviation and a drawdown factor, is considered low. As of December 31, 2012, *iShares DJ US Aerospace & Def Id traded at a discount of 2.00% below its net asset value, which is better than its one-year historical average discount of .05%.

Diane Hsiung has been running the fund for 5 years and currently receives a manager quality ranking of 56 (0=worst, 99=best). If you desire an average level of risk, then this fund may be an option.

Data Date	Investment Rating	Net Assets ($Mil)	Price	Performance Rating/Pts	Total Return Y-T-D	Risk Rating/Pts
12-12	C	78.50	68.25	C / 5.1	2.02%	B- / 7.9
2011	C	106.90	61.19	C / 5.2	1.08%	B- / 7.5
2010	D+	147.10	58.85	C- / 3.4	16.60%	C / 5.5
2009	C-	132.14	50.96	C- / 3.7	20.90%	C+ / 5.7

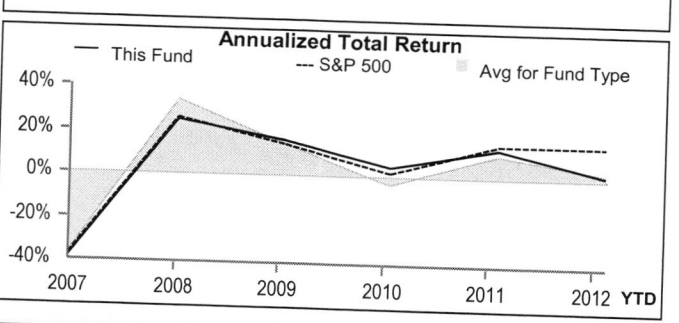

*iShares DJ US Basic Material (IYM)

D+ **Weak**

Fund Family: BlackRock Fund Advisors
Fund Type: Income
Inception Date: June 12, 2000

Major Rating Factors: *iShares DJ US Basic Material receives a TheStreet.com Investment Rating of D+ (Weak). The fund currently has a performance rating of C- (Fair) based on an annualized return of 6.78% over the last three years and a total return of 3.20% year to date 2012. Factored into the performance evaluation is an expense ratio of 0.47% (very low).

The fund's risk rating is currently C+ (Fair). It carries a beta of 1.52, meaning it is expected to move 15.2% for every 10% move in the market. Volatility, as measured by both the semi-deviation and a drawdown factor, is considered low. As of December 31, 2012, *iShares DJ US Basic Material traded at a discount of 3.16% below its net asset value, which is better than its one-year historical average discount of .01%.

Diane Hsiung has been running the fund for 5 years and currently receives a manager quality ranking of 14 (0=worst, 99=best). If you desire an average level of risk, then this fund may be an option.

Data Date	Investment Rating	Net Assets ($Mil)	Price	Performance Rating/Pts	Total Return Y-T-D	Risk Rating/Pts
12-12	D+	533.80	69.31	C- / 3.2	3.20%	C+ / 6.9
2011	C+	530.50	64.30	C+ / 6.4	3.45%	C+ / 6.9
2010	C+	1,114.50	77.46	B- / 7.5	31.02%	C / 4.7
2009	C+	402.11	59.91	B- / 7.1	57.73%	C / 5.1

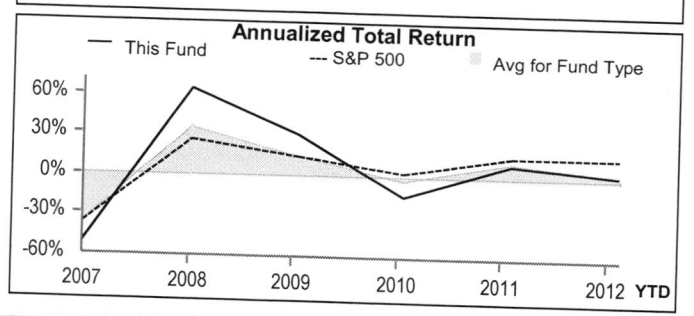

*iShares DJ US Broker-Dealers Idx (IAI)

D **Weak**

Fund Family: BlackRock Fund Advisors
Fund Type: Financial Services
Inception Date: May 1, 2006

Major Rating Factors:
Disappointing performance is the major factor driving the D (Weak) TheStreet.com Investment Rating for *iShares DJ US Broker-Dealers Idx. The fund currently has a performance rating of D (Weak) based on an annualized return of -2.15% over the last three years and a total return of 5.54% year to date 2012. Factored into the performance evaluation is an expense ratio of 0.47% (very low).

The fund's risk rating is currently C+ (Fair). It carries a beta of 1.13, meaning it is expected to move 11.3% for every 10% move in the market. Volatility, as measured by both the semi-deviation and a drawdown factor, is considered low. As of December 31, 2012, *iShares DJ US Broker-Dealers Idx traded at a discount of 5.21% below its net asset value, which is better than its one-year historical average discount of .04%.

Diane Hsiung has been running the fund for 5 years and currently receives a manager quality ranking of 11 (0=worst, 99=best). This fund offers only a moderate level of risk but investors looking for strong performance are still waiting.

Data Date	Investment Rating	Net Assets ($Mil)	Price	Performance Rating/Pts	Total Return Y-T-D	Risk Rating/Pts
12-12	D	44.90	23.63	D / 2.0	5.54%	C+ / 6.7
2011	D	52.20	20.92	D / 1.9	2.20%	C+ / 6.9
2010	D-	100.10	29.02	E+ / 0.8	4.89%	C / 4.7
2009	D-	138.16	28.13	E+ / 0.7	39.55%	C / 4.9

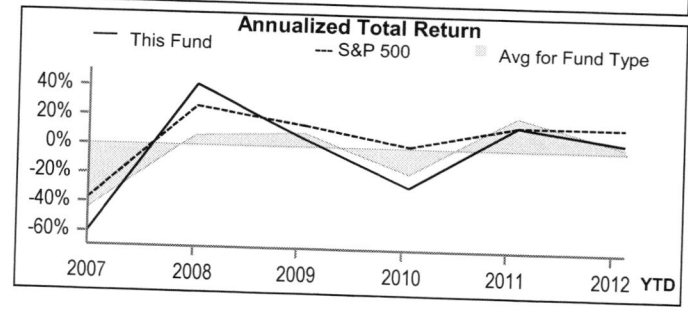

* Denotes ETF Fund

*iShares DJ US Consumer Goods (IYK)

B-   **Good**

Fund Family: BlackRock Fund Advisors
Fund Type: Income
Inception Date: June 12, 2000

Major Rating Factors: *iShares DJ US Consumer Goods receives a TheStreet.com Investment Rating of B- (Good). The fund currently has a performance rating of C+ (Fair) based on an annualized return of 13.67% over the last three years and a total return of 3.67% year to date 2012. Factored into the performance evaluation is an expense ratio of 0.47% (very low).

The fund's risk rating is currently B (Good). It carries a beta of 0.67, meaning as fund's expected move will be 6.7% for every 10% move in the market. Volatility, as measured by both the semi-deviation and a drawdown factor, is considered low. As of December 31, 2012, *iShares DJ US Consumer Goods traded at a discount of 3.61% below its net asset value.

Diane Hsiung has been running the fund for 5 years and currently receives a manager quality ranking of 80 (0=worst, 99=best). If you desire an average level of risk, then this fund may be an option.

Data Date	Investment Rating	Net Assets ($Mil)	Price	Performance Rating/Pts	Total Return Y-T-D	Risk Rating/Pts
12-12	B-	394.30	74.99	C+ / 6.0	3.67%	B / 8.8
2011	B-	359.20	68.48	C+ / 6.1	0.26%	B / 8.5
2010	C+	306.70	64.55	C+ / 6.4	18.99%	C+ / 6.8
2009	C	308.32	55.53	C- / 3.4	20.43%	C+ / 6.8

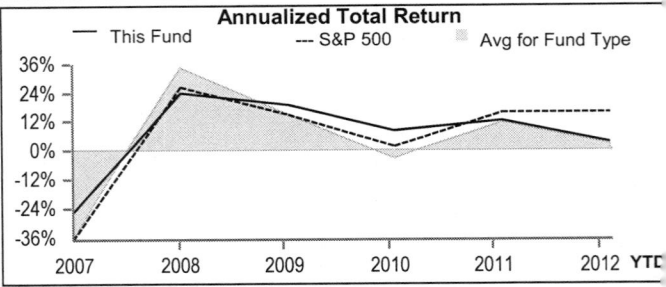

*iShares DJ US Consumer Services (IYC)

B+   **Good**

Fund Family: BlackRock Fund Advisors
Fund Type: Income
Inception Date: June 12, 2000

Major Rating Factors: Strong performance is the major factor driving the B+ (Good) TheStreet.com Investment Rating for *iShares DJ US Consumer Services. The fund currently has a performance rating of B (Good) based on an annualized return of 18.50% over the last three years and a total return of 3.06% year to date 2012. Factored into the performance evaluation is an expense ratio of 0.47% (very low).

The fund's risk rating is currently B (Good). It carries a beta of 0.96, meaning that its performance tracks fairly well with that of the overall stock market. Volatility, as measured by both the semi-deviation and a drawdown factor, is considered low. As of December 31, 2012, *iShares DJ US Consumer Services traded at a discount of 3.04% below its net asset value.

Diane Hsiung has been running the fund for 5 years and currently receives a manager quality ranking of 83 (0=worst, 99=best). If you desire only a moderate level of risk and strong performance, then this fund is an excellent option.

Data Date	Investment Rating	Net Assets ($Mil)	Price	Performance Rating/Pts	Total Return Y-T-D	Risk Rating/Pts
12-12	B+	334.30	86.80	B / 8.1	3.06%	B / 8.1
2011	B-	260.40	71.41	B- / 7.1	1.46%	B / 8.1
2010	B+	209.60	67.66	B- / 7.4	23.26%	C+ / 6.1
2009	C-	178.16	55.49	D+ / 2.6	28.24%	C+ / 6.2

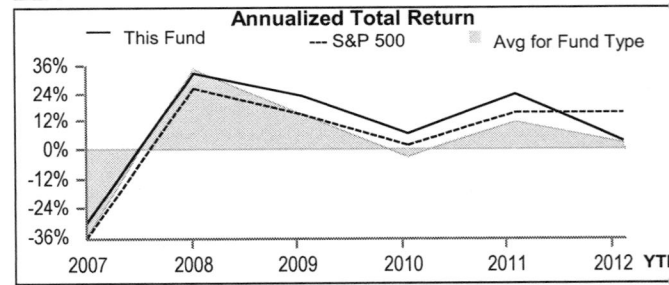

*iShares DJ US Energy (IYE)

C-   **Fair**

Fund Family: BlackRock Fund Advisors
Fund Type: Energy/Natural Resources
Inception Date: June 12, 2000

Major Rating Factors: Middle of the road best describes *iShares DJ US Energy whose TheStreet.com Investment Rating is currently a C- (Fair). The fund currently has a performance rating of C- (Fair) based on an annualized return of 8.85% over the last three years and a total return of 3.77% year to date 2012. Factored into the performance evaluation is an expense ratio of 0.47% (very low).

The fund's risk rating is currently B- (Good). It carries a beta of 1.00, meaning that its performance tracks fairly well with that of the overall stock market. Volatility, as measured by both the semi-deviation and a drawdown factor, is considered low. As of December 31, 2012, *iShares DJ US Energy traded at a discount of 3.54% below its net asset value, which is better than its one-year historical average premium of .01%.

Diane Hsiung has been running the fund for 5 years and currently receives a manager quality ranking of 47 (0=worst, 99=best). If you desire an average level of risk, then this fund may be an option.

Data Date	Investment Rating	Net Assets ($Mil)	Price	Performance Rating/Pts	Total Return Y-T-D	Risk Rating/Pts
12-12	C-	817.00	40.84	C- / 3.6	3.77%	B- / 7.4
2011	C	945.90	39.83	C / 5.0	1.78%	B- / 7.2
2010	D	806.00	38.96	C / 4.3	19.00%	D+ / 2.8
2009	D	597.62	33.24	C- / 3.9	13.74%	C- / 3.0

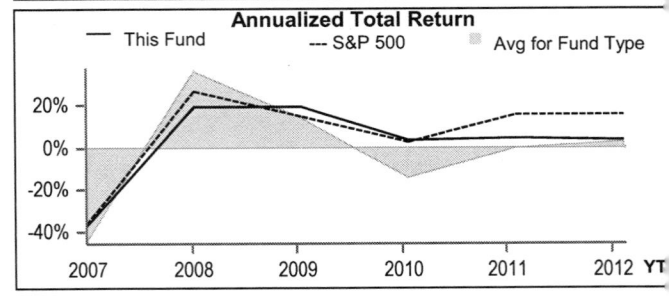

*iShares DJ US Financial Sector (IYF)

C   **Fair**

Fund Family: BlackRock Fund Advisors
Fund Type: Financial Services
Inception Date: May 22, 2000

Major Rating Factors: Middle of the road best describes *iShares DJ US Financial Sector whose TheStreet.com Investment Rating is currently a C (Fair). The fund currently has a performance rating of C (Fair) based on an annualized return of 7.56% over the last three years and a total return of 4.68% year to date 2012. Factored into the performance evaluation is an expense ratio of 0.47% (very low).

The fund's risk rating is currently B- (Good). It carries a beta of 1.00, meaning that its performance tracks fairly well with that of the overall stock market. Volatility, as measured by both the semi-deviation and a drawdown factor, is considered low. As of December 31, 2012, *iShares DJ US Financial Sector traded at a discount of 4.44% below its net asset value, which is better than its one-year historical average discount of .01%.

Diane Hsiung has been running the fund for 5 years and currently receives a manager quality ranking of 46 (0=worst, 99=best). If you desire an average level of risk, then this fund may be an option.

Data Date	Investment Rating	Net Assets ($Mil)	Price	Performance Rating/Pts	Total Return Y-T-D	Risk Rating/Pts
12-12	C	614.90	60.70	C / 5.3	4.68%	B- / 7.4
2011	D+	380.20	49.05	C- / 3.1	2.55%	C+ / 6.9
2010	D-	476.70	57.48	D- / 1.0	12.23%	C / 4.5
2009	E+	504.16	51.78	E+ / 0.6	16.17%	C / 4.5

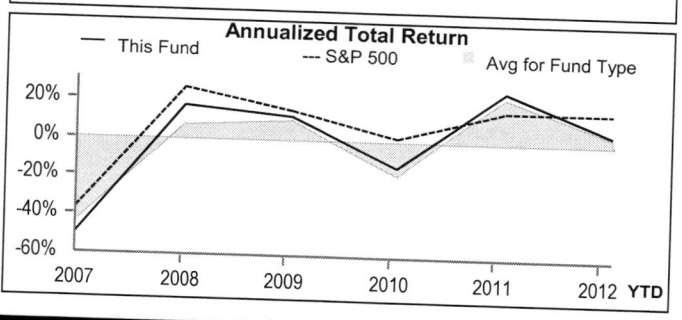

*iShares DJ US Financial Services (IYG)

C   **Fair**

Fund Family: BlackRock Fund Advisors
Fund Type: Financial Services
Inception Date: June 12, 2000

Major Rating Factors: Middle of the road best describes *iShares DJ US Financial Services whose TheStreet.com Investment Rating is currently a C (Fair). The fund currently has a performance rating of C (Fair) based on an annualized return of 4.67% over the last three years and a total return of 4.92% year to date 2012. Factored into the performance evaluation is an expense ratio of 0.47% (very low).

The fund's risk rating is currently B- (Good). It carries a beta of 1.15, meaning it is expected to move 11.5% for every 10% move in the market. Volatility, as measured by both the semi-deviation and a drawdown factor, is considered low. As of December 31, 2012, *iShares DJ US Financial Services traded at a discount of 4.66% below its net asset value, which is better than its one-year historical average discount of .01%.

Diane Hsiung has been running the fund for 5 years and currently receives a manager quality ranking of 25 (0=worst, 99=best). If you desire an average level of risk, then this fund may be an option.

Data Date	Investment Rating	Net Assets ($Mil)	Price	Performance Rating/Pts	Total Return Y-T-D	Risk Rating/Pts
12-12	C	353.00	59.31	C / 5.1	4.92%	B- / 7.0
2011	D	172.10	45.27	D / 2.2	4.02%	C+ / 6.8
2010	D-	221.50	57.57	E+ / 0.8	7.71%	C / 4.3
2009	E+	317.11	53.71	E / 0.5	14.53%	C / 4.3

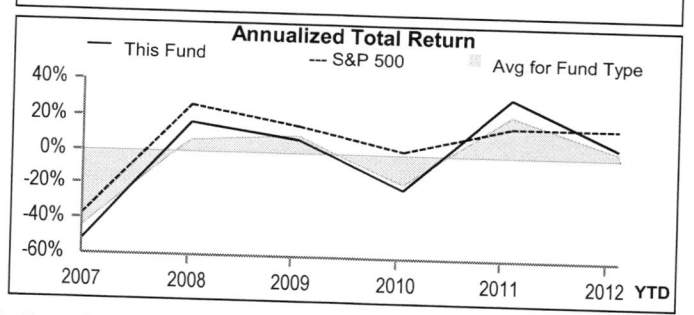

*iShares DJ US Healthcare (IYH)

C+   **Fair**

Fund Family: BlackRock Fund Advisors
Fund Type: Health
Inception Date: June 12, 2000

Major Rating Factors: Middle of the road best describes *iShares DJ US Healthcare whose TheStreet.com Investment Rating is currently a C+ (Fair). The fund currently has a performance rating of C+ (Fair) based on an annualized return of 11.62% over the last three years and a total return of 4.67% year to date 2012. Factored into the performance evaluation is an expense ratio of 0.47% (very low).

The fund's risk rating is currently B (Good). It carries a beta of 0.65, meaning the fund's expected move will be 6.5% for every 10% move in the market. Volatility, as measured by both the semi-deviation and a drawdown factor, is considered low. As of December 31, 2012, *iShares DJ US Healthcare traded at a discount of 4.44% below its net asset value.

Diane Hsiung has been running the fund for 5 years and currently receives a manager quality ranking of 76 (0=worst, 99=best). If you desire an average level of risk, then this fund may be an option.

Data Date	Investment Rating	Net Assets ($Mil)	Price	Performance Rating/Pts	Total Return Y-T-D	Risk Rating/Pts
12-12	C+	705.70	83.51	C+ / 5.7	4.67%	B / 8.3
2011	C+	575.90	71.57	C / 5.0	1.17%	B / 8.2
2010	C-	552.10	65.37	D+ / 2.9	4.13%	B- / 7.0
2009	C	658.79	63.82	C- / 3.5	18.77%	C+ / 6.9

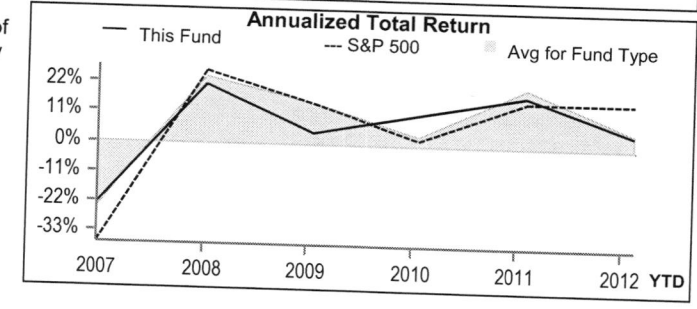

* Denotes ETF Fund

*iShares DJ US HealthCare Provide (IHF)

C   **Fair**

Fund Family: BlackRock Fund Advisors
Fund Type: Health
Inception Date: May 1, 2006

Major Rating Factors: Middle of the road best describes *iShares DJ US HealthCare Provide whose TheStreet.com Investment Rating is currently a C (Fair). The fund currently has a performance rating of C (Fair) based on an annualized return of 11.35% over the last three years and a total return of 2.00% year to date 2012. Factored into the performance evaluation is an expense ratio of 0.47% (very low).

The fund's risk rating is currently B- (Good). It carries a beta of 0.92, meaning that its performance tracks fairly well with that of the overall stock market. Volatility, as measured by both the semi-deviation and a drawdown factor, is considered low. As of December 31, 2012, *iShares DJ US HealthCare Provide traded at a discount of 2.02% below its net asset value, which is better than its one-year historical average premium of .01%.

Diane Hsiung has been running the fund for 5 years and currently receives a manager quality ranking of 69 (0=worst, 99=best). If you desire an average level of risk, then this fund may be an option.

Data Date	Investment Rating	Net Assets ($Mil)	Price	Performance Rating/Pts	Total Return Y-T-D	Risk Rating/Pts
12-12	C	225.60	68.45	C / 4.8	2.00%	B- / 7.9
2011	B-	217.70	58.85	C+ / 6.9	3.64%	B- / 7.8
2010	D	110.40	53.87	D / 2.2	11.47%	C+ / 5.7
2009	C-	74.88	48.42	C- / 3.8	33.10%	C / 5.5

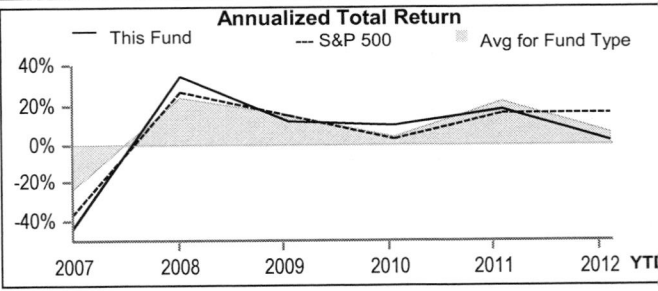

Annualized Total Return

---

*iShares DJ US Home Cons Idx (ITB)

B+   **Good**

Fund Family: BlackRock Fund Advisors
Fund Type: Income
Inception Date: May 1, 2006

Major Rating Factors:
Exceptional performance is the major factor driving the B+ (Good) TheStreet.com Investment Rating for *iShares DJ US Home Cons Idx. The fund currently has a performance rating of A+ (Excellent) based on an annualized return of 21.15% over the last three years and a total return of 4.96% year to date 2012. Factored into the performance evaluation is an expense ratio of 0.47% (very low).

The fund's risk rating is currently C+ (Fair). It carries a beta of 1.43, meaning it is expected to move 14.3% for every 10% move in the market. Volatility, as measured by both the semi-deviation and a drawdown factor, is considered low. As of December 31, 2012, *iShares DJ US Home Cons Idx traded at a discount of 4.68% below its net asset value.

Diane Hsiung has been running the fund for 5 years and currently receives a manager quality ranking of 80 (0=worst, 99=best). If you desire only a moderate level of risk and strong performance, then this fund is an excellent option.

Data Date	Investment Rating	Net Assets ($Mil)	Price	Performance Rating/Pts	Total Return Y-T-D	Risk Rating/Pts
12-12	B+	1,627.60	21.16	A+ / 9.7	4.96%	C+ / 6.4
2011	D+	374.60	11.88	C- / 3.6	4.88%	C+ / 6.4
2010	D	505.20	13.18	D+ / 2.4	10.43%	C / 4.5
2009	E	198.46	12.01	E / 0.5	20.18%	C- / 3.8

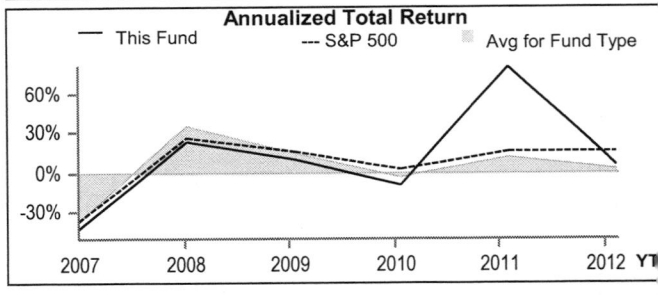

Annualized Total Return

---

*iShares DJ US Index (IYY)

C   **Fair**

Fund Family: BlackRock Fund Advisors
Fund Type: Income
Inception Date: June 12, 2000

Major Rating Factors: Middle of the road best describes *iShares DJ US Index whose TheStreet.com Investment Rating is currently a C (Fair). The fund currently has a performance rating of C (Fair) based on an annualized return of 11.49% over the last three years and a total return of 3.38% year to date 2012. Factored into the performance evaluation is an expense ratio of 0.20% (very low).

The fund's risk rating is currently B- (Good). It carries a beta of 1.03, meaning that its performance tracks fairly well with that of the overall stock market. Volatility, as measured by both the semi-deviation and a drawdown factor, is considered low. As of December 31, 2012, *iShares DJ US Index traded at a discount of 3.27% below its net asset value, which is better than its one-year historical average discount of .02%.

Diane Hsiung has been running the fund for 5 years and currently receives a manager quality ranking of 50 (0=worst, 99=best). If you desire an average level of risk, then this fund may be an option.

Data Date	Investment Rating	Net Assets ($Mil)	Price	Performance Rating/Pts	Total Return Y-T-D	Risk Rating/Pts
12-12	C	608.90	71.64	C / 5.3	3.38%	B- / 7.9
2011	C+	582.20	62.95	C / 5.4	1.64%	B- / 7.9
2010	C	621.20	63.40	C / 4.4	16.50%	C+ / 5.9
2009	D+	487.85	55.39	D+ / 2.5	25.07%	C+ / 6.1

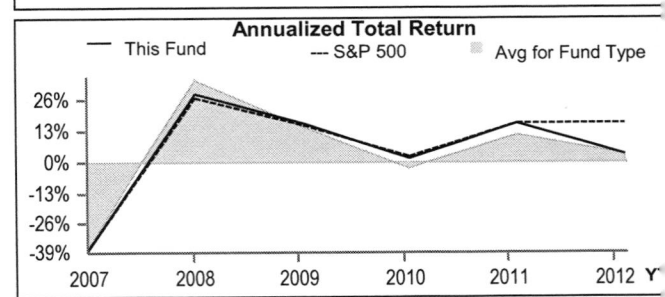

Annualized Total Return

*iShares DJ US Industrial (IYJ)

Fund Family: BlackRock Fund Advisors
Fund Type: Income
Inception Date: June 12, 2000

C+   **Fair**

Major Rating Factors: Middle of the road best describes *iShares DJ US Industrial whose TheStreet.com Investment Rating is currently a C+ (Fair). The fund currently has a performance rating of C+ (Fair) based on an annualized return of 13.10% over the last three years and a total return of 3.18% year to date 2012. Factored into the performance evaluation is an expense ratio of 0.47% (very low).

The fund's risk rating is currently B- (Good). It carries a beta of 1.24, meaning it is expected to move 12.4% for every 10% move in the market. Volatility, as measured by both the semi-deviation and a drawdown factor, is considered low. As of December 31, 2012, *iShares DJ US Industrial traded at a discount of 3.13% below its net asset value, which is better than its one-year historical average discount of .02%.

Diane Hsiung has been running the fund for 5 years and currently receives a manager quality ranking of 49 (0=worst, 99=best). If you desire an average level of risk, then this fund may be an option.

Data Date	Investment Rating	Net Assets ($Mil)	Price	Performance Rating/Pts	Total Return Y-T-D	Risk Rating/Pts
12-12	C+	689.30	73.33	C+ / 6.4	3.18%	B- / 7.6
2011	C	343.20	63.62	C+ / 5.6	2.14%	B- / 7.5
2010	C	369.30	65.40	C+ / 5.7	25.49%	C / 5.4
2009	D+	213.85	53.03	D+ / 2.5	21.44%	C+ / 5.7

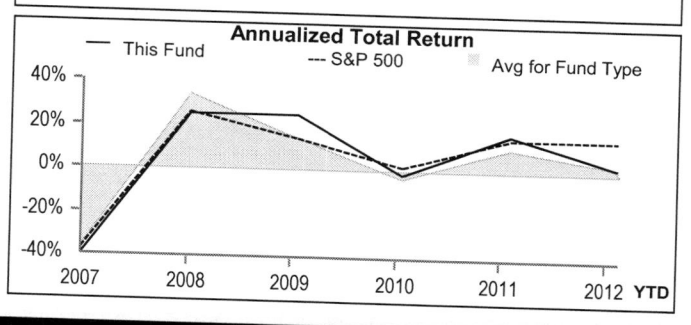

*iShares DJ US Insurance Idx (IAK)

Fund Family: BlackRock Fund Advisors
Fund Type: Income
Inception Date: May 1, 2006

C   **Fair**

Major Rating Factors: Middle of the road best describes *iShares DJ US Insurance Idx whose TheStreet.com Investment Rating is currently a C (Fair). The fund currently has a performance rating of C (Fair) based on an annualized return of 9.77% over the last three years and a total return of 4.59% year to date 2012. Factored into the performance evaluation is an expense ratio of 0.47% (very low).

The fund's risk rating is currently B- (Good). It carries a beta of 1.12, meaning it is expected to move 11.2% for every 10% move in the market. Volatility, as measured by both the semi-deviation and a drawdown factor, is considered low. As of December 31, 2012, *iShares DJ US Insurance Idx traded at a discount of 4.35% below its net asset value, which is better than its one-year historical average discount of .04%.

Diane Hsiung has been running the fund for 5 years and currently receives a manager quality ranking of 31 (0=worst, 99=best). If you desire an average level of risk, then this fund may be an option.

Data Date	Investment Rating	Net Assets ($Mil)	Price	Performance Rating/Pts	Total Return Y-T-D	Risk Rating/Pts
12-12	C	79.20	32.99	C / 5.4	4.59%	B- / 7.8
2011	C-	59.80	28.57	C- / 3.7	1.48%	B- / 7.0
2010	D-	81.50	31.34	D- / 1.1	20.03%	C / 4.5
2009	E+	28.35	26.67	E+ / 0.7	12.63%	C / 4.6

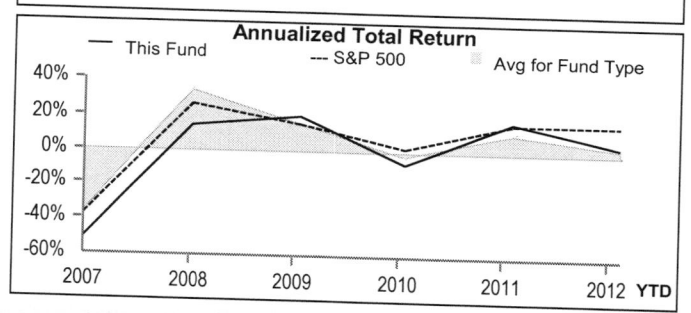

*iShares DJ US Medical Devices Id (IHI)

Fund Family: BlackRock Fund Advisors
Fund Type: Health
Inception Date: May 1, 2006

C-   **Fair**

Major Rating Factors: Middle of the road best describes *iShares DJ US Medical Devices Id whose TheStreet.com Investment Rating is currently a C- (Fair). The fund currently has a performance rating of C (Fair) based on an annualized return of 9.32% over the last three years and a total return of 4.87% year to date 2012. Factored into the performance evaluation is an expense ratio of 0.47% (very low).

The fund's risk rating is currently B- (Good). It carries a beta of 0.96, meaning that its performance tracks fairly well with that of the overall stock market. Volatility, as measured by both the semi-deviation and a drawdown factor, is considered low. As of December 31, 2012, *iShares DJ US Medical Devices Id traded at a discount of 4.69% below its net asset value, which is better than its one-year historical average discount of .03%.

Diane Hsiung has been running the fund for 5 years and currently receives a manager quality ranking of 40 (0=worst, 99=best). If you desire an average level of risk, then this fund may be an option.

Data Date	Investment Rating	Net Assets ($Mil)	Price	Performance Rating/Pts	Total Return Y-T-D	Risk Rating/Pts
12-12	C-	274.00	67.60	C / 4.9	4.87%	B- / 7.0
2011	C	331.90	58.76	C / 5.3	1.14%	C+ / 6.9
2010	C-	338.80	58.91	C- / 3.7	11.35%	C+ / 5.6
2009	C	214.90	52.98	C / 5.1	35.04%	C+ / 5.7

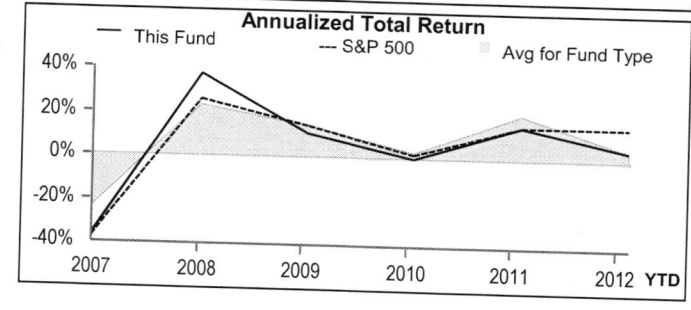

*iShares DJ US Oil & Gas Exp & Pr (IEO)   D+   Weak

Fund Family: BlackRock Fund Advisors
Fund Type: Energy/Natural Resources
Inception Date: May 1, 2006

Major Rating Factors: *iShares DJ US Oil & Gas Exp & Pr receives a TheStreet.com Investment Rating of D+ (Weak). The fund currently has a performance rating of C- (Fair) based on an annualized return of 6.20% over the last three years and a total return of 3.02% year to date 2012. Factored into the performance evaluation is an expense ratio of 0.47% (very low).

The fund's risk rating is currently C+ (Fair). It carries a beta of 1.18, meaning it is expected to move 11.8% for every 10% move in the market. Volatility, as measured by both the semi-deviation and a drawdown factor, is considered low. As of December 31, 2012, *iShares DJ US Oil & Gas Exp & Pr traded at a discount of 2.95% below its net asset value, which is better than its one-year historical average discount of .01%.

Diane Hsiung has been running the fund for 5 years and currently receives a manager quality ranking of 24 (0=worst, 99=best). If you desire an average level of risk, then this fund may be an option.

Data Date	Investment Rating	Net Assets ($Mil)	Price	Performance Rating/Pts	Total Return Y-T-D	Risk Rating/Pts
12-12	D+	314.70	63.54	C- / 3.0	3.02%	C+ / 6.8
2011	C	343.80	61.42	C+ / 6.0	3.79%	C+ / 6.9
2010	C	427.70	63.85	C / 5.5	18.64%	C / 4.9
2009	C	335.06	53.99	C / 5.5	33.25%	C / 4.9

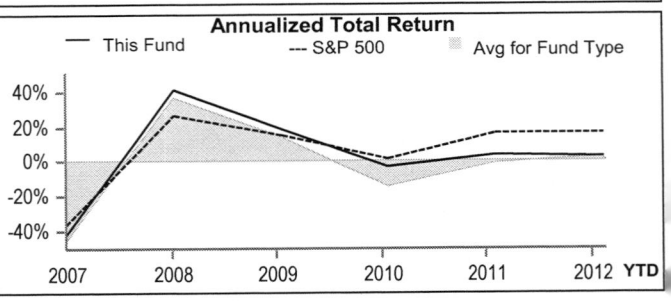

*iShares DJ US Oil Equip & Svcs (IEZ)   D   Weak

Fund Family: BlackRock Fund Advisors
Fund Type: Energy/Natural Resources
Inception Date: May 1, 2006

Major Rating Factors:
Disappointing performance is the major factor driving the D (Weak) TheStreet.com Investment Rating for *iShares DJ US Oil Equip & Svcs. The fund currently has a performance rating of D+ (Weak) based on an annualized return of 5.42% over the last three years and a total return of 5.39% year to date 2012. Factored into the performance evaluation is an expense ratio of 0.47% (very low).

The fund's risk rating is currently C+ (Fair). It carries a beta of 1.40, meaning it is expected to move 14.0% for every 10% move in the market. Volatility, as measured by both the semi-deviation and a drawdown factor, is considered low. As of December 31, 2012, *iShares DJ US Oil Equip & Svcs traded at a discount of 5.22% below its net asset value, which is better than its one-year historical average discount of .02%.

Diane Hsiung has been running the fund for 5 years and currently receives a manager quality ranking of 19 (0=worst, 99=best). This fund offers only a moderate level of risk but investors looking for strong performance are still waiting.

Data Date	Investment Rating	Net Assets ($Mil)	Price	Performance Rating/Pts	Total Return Y-T-D	Risk Rating/Pts
12-12	D	324.10	51.01	D+ / 2.8	5.39%	C+ / 6.2
2011	C+	417.80	51.92	B- / 7.1	2.25%	C+ / 6.3
2010	C-	495.60	56.35	C+ / 5.9	31.77%	C- / 4.2
2009	C	194.24	43.02	C+ / 6.3	52.96%	C / 4.6

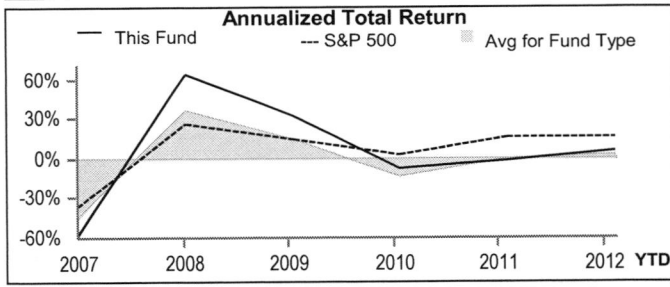

*iShares DJ US Pharmaceuticals (IHE)   B-   Good

Fund Family: BlackRock Fund Advisors
Fund Type: Health
Inception Date: May 1, 2006

Major Rating Factors: *iShares DJ US Pharmaceuticals receives a TheStreet.com Investment Rating of B- (Good). The fund currently has a performance rating of C+ (Fair) based on an annualized return of 16.92% over the last three years and a total return of 6.03% year to date 2012. Factored into the performance evaluation is an expense ratio of 0.47% (very low).

The fund's risk rating is currently B (Good). It carries a beta of 0.62, meaning the fund's expected move will be 6.2% for every 10% move in the market. Volatility, as measured by both the semi-deviation and a drawdown factor, is considered low. As of December 31, 2012, *iShares DJ US Pharmaceuticals traded at a discount of 5.70% below its net asset value.

Diane Hsiung has been running the fund for 5 years and currently receives a manager quality ranking of 87 (0=worst, 99=best). If you desire an average level of risk, then this fund may be an option.

Data Date	Investment Rating	Net Assets ($Mil)	Price	Performance Rating/Pts	Total Return Y-T-D	Risk Rating/Pts
12-12	B-	348.70	85.02	C+ / 6.7	6.03%	B / 8.0
2011	B-	344.10	76.45	B / 7.6	-0.16%	B- / 7.3
2010	B+	159.80	64.04	B- / 7.1	12.72%	C+ / 6.7
2009	C+	98.68	57.66	C / 5.5	28.19%	B- / 7.0

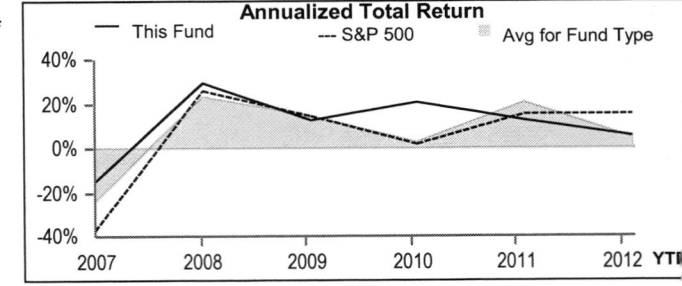

*iShares DJ US Real Estate (IYR)

Fund Family: BlackRock Fund Advisors
Fund Type: Income
Inception Date: June 12, 2000

B-   **Good**

Major Rating Factors: Strong performance is the major factor driving the B- (Good) TheStreet.com Investment Rating for *iShares DJ US Real Estate. The fund currently has a performance rating of B- (Good) based on an annualized return of 17.69% over the last three years and a total return of 2.81% year to date 2012. Factored into the performance evaluation is an expense ratio of 0.47% (very low).

The fund's risk rating is currently B- (Good). It carries a beta of 0.98, meaning that its performance tracks fairly well with that of the overall stock market. Volatility, as measured by both the semi-deviation and a drawdown factor, is considered low. As of December 31, 2012, *iShares DJ US Real Estate traded at a discount of 2.81% below its net asset value, which is better than its one-year historical average premium of .01%.

Diane Hsiung has been running the fund for 5 years and currently receives a manager quality ranking of 80 (0=worst, 99=best). If you desire only a moderate level of risk and strong performance, then this fund is an excellent option.

Data Date	Investment Rating	Net Assets ($Mil)	Price	Perfor-mance Rating/Pts	Total Return Y-T-D	Risk Rating/Pts
12-12	B-	4,590.90	64.67	B- / 7.4	2.81%	B- / 7.7
2011	C+	3,294.80	56.81	B- / 7.4	0.04%	C+ / 6.6
2010	C+	3,080.10	55.96	B- / 7.1	26.59%	C / 4.3
2009	D-	1,721.08	45.92	D- / 1.5	34.13%	C- / 3.9

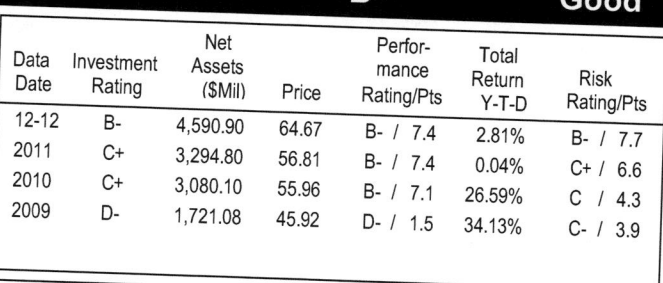

*iShares DJ US Regional Banks (IAT)

Fund Family: BlackRock Fund Advisors
Fund Type: Financial Services
Inception Date: May 1, 2006

D+   **Weak**

Major Rating Factors: *iShares DJ US Regional Banks receives a TheStreet.com Investment Rating of D+ (Weak). The fund currently has a performance rating of C- (Fair) based on an annualized return of 5.78% over the last three years and a total return of 3.64% year to date 2012. Factored into the performance evaluation is an expense ratio of 0.47% (very low).

The fund's risk rating is currently B- (Good). It carries a beta of 0.96, meaning that its performance tracks fairly well with that of the overall stock market. Volatility, as measured by both the semi-deviation and a drawdown factor, is considered low. As of December 31, 2012, *iShares DJ US Regional Banks traded at a discount of 3.63% below its net asset value, which is better than its one-year historical average discount of .01%.

Diane Hsiung has been running the fund for 5 years and currently receives a manager quality ranking of 52 (0=worst, 99=best). If you desire an average level of risk, then this fund may be an option.

Data Date	Investment Rating	Net Assets ($Mil)	Price	Perfor-mance Rating/Pts	Total Return Y-T-D	Risk Rating/Pts
12-12	D+	173.60	24.43	C- / 3.0	3.64%	B- / 7.3
2011	D+	95.10	21.16	D+ / 2.4	4.25%	C+ / 6.9
2010	D	135.90	24.74	D / 1.6	20.25%	C / 4.7
2009	E	121.02	20.82	E / 0.5	-11.00%	C- / 3.8

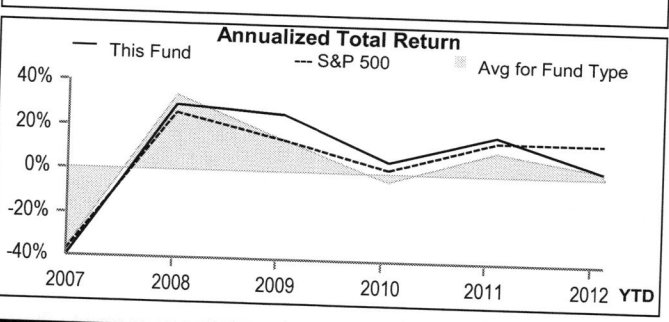

*iShares DJ US Technology (IYW)

Fund Family: BlackRock Fund Advisors
Fund Type: Growth
Inception Date: May 15, 2000

D+   **Weak**

Major Rating Factors: *iShares DJ US Technology receives a TheStreet.com Investment Rating of D+ (Weak). The fund currently has a performance rating of C- (Fair) based on an annualized return of 8.73% over the last three years and a total return of 2.28% year to date 2012. Factored into the performance evaluation is an expense ratio of 0.47% (very low).

The fund's risk rating is currently C+ (Fair). It carries a beta of 1.17, meaning it is expected to move 11.7% for every 10% move in the market. Volatility, as measured by both the semi-deviation and a drawdown factor, is considered low. As of December 31, 2012, *iShares DJ US Technology traded at a discount of 2.21% below its net asset value, which is better than its one-year historical average discount of .01%.

Diane Hsiung has been running the fund for 5 years and currently receives a manager quality ranking of 24 (0=worst, 99=best). If you desire an average level of risk, then this fund may be an option.

Data Date	Investment Rating	Net Assets ($Mil)	Price	Perfor-mance Rating/Pts	Total Return Y-T-D	Risk Rating/Pts
12-12	D+	1,514.40	70.72	C- / 3.4	2.28%	C+ / 6.9
2011	C+	1,300.00	63.90	B- / 7.1	2.77%	B- / 7.3
2010	C+	1,451.40	64.38	C+ / 6.3	12.42%	C+ / 5.6
2009	C+	826.01	57.54	C+ / 6.6	57.55%	C+ / 5.6

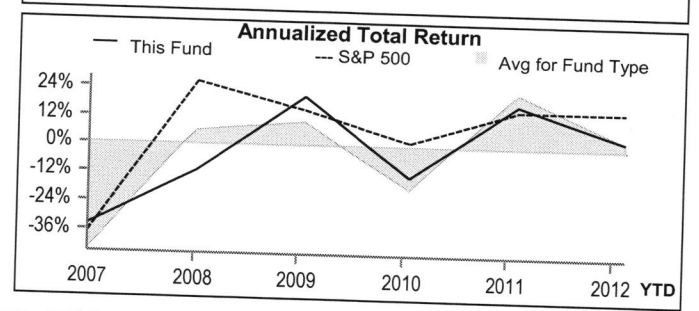

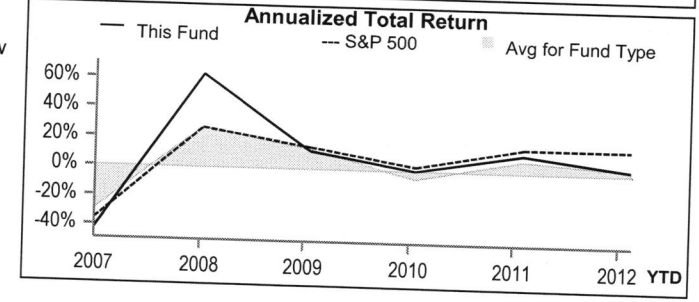

* Denotes ETF Fund

II. Analysis of ETFs and Other Closed-End Funds

| | | C+ | | Fair |

*iShares DJ US Telecommunications (IYZ)

Fund Family: BlackRock Fund Advisors
Fund Type: Income
Inception Date: May 22, 2000

Major Rating Factors: Middle of the road best describes *iShares DJ US Telecommunications whose TheStreet.com Investment Rating is currently a C+ (Fair). The fund currently has a performance rating of C (Fair) based on an annualized return of 11.70% over the last three years and a total return of 2.07% year to date 2012. Factored into the performance evaluation is an expense ratio of 0.47% (very low).

The fund's risk rating is currently B (Good). It carries a beta of 0.85, meaning the fund's expected move will be 8.5% for every 10% move in the market. Volatility, as measured by both the semi-deviation and a drawdown factor, is considered low. As of December 31, 2012, *iShares DJ US Telecommunications traded at a discount of 2.06% below its net asset value, which is better than its one-year historical average discount of .03%.

Diane Hsiung has been running the fund for 5 years and currently receives a manager quality ranking of 58 (0=worst, 99=best). If you desire an average level of risk, then this fund may be an option.

Data Date	Investment Rating	Net Assets ($Mil)	Price	Performance Rating/Pts	Total Return Y-T-D	Risk Rating/Pts
12-12	C+	479.30	24.26	C / 5.2	2.07%	B / 8.2
2011	C-	512.30	21.00	C- / 3.5	-0.57%	B / 8.1
2010	C-	761.10	23.37	C- / 3.8	20.72%	C+ / 6.1
2009	D-	531.48	20.02	D- / 1.4	22.35%	C / 5.4

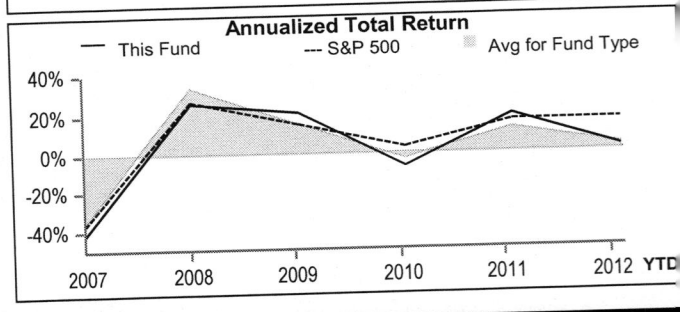

*iShares DJ US Utilities (IDU)

| | | C | | Fair |

Fund Family: BlackRock Fund Advisors
Fund Type: Utilities
Inception Date: June 12, 2000

Major Rating Factors: Middle of the road best describes *iShares DJ US Utilities whose TheStreet.com Investment Rating is currently a C (Fair). The fund currently has a performance rating of C- (Fair) based on an annualized return of 9.28% over the last three years and a total return of 1.51% year to date 2012. Factored into the performance evaluation is an expense ratio of 0.47% (very low).

The fund's risk rating is currently B+ (Good). It carries a beta of 0.92, meaning that its performance tracks fairly well with that of the overall stock market. Volatility, as measured by both the semi-deviation and a drawdown factor, is considered very low. As of December 31, 2012, *iShares DJ US Utilities traded at a discount of 1.51% below its net asset value, which is better than its one-year historical average discount of .01%.

Diane Hsiung has been running the fund for 5 years and currently receives a manager quality ranking of 56 (0=worst, 99=best). If you desire an average level of risk, then this fund may be an option.

Data Date	Investment Rating	Net Assets ($Mil)	Price	Performance Rating/Pts	Total Return Y-T-D	Risk Rating/Pts
12-12	C	838.40	86.36	C- / 3.2	1.51%	B+ / 9.2
2011	C+	772.40	88.32	C / 4.9	-2.59%	B / 8.6
2010	D+	497.30	77.10	D / 1.6	7.21%	C+ / 6.6
2009	C-	405.86	74.79	D / 2.2	10.08%	C+ / 6.7

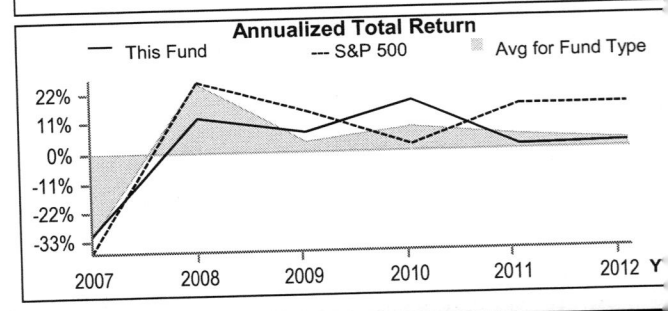

*iShares Emerging Mkts Lcl Cur Bo (LEMB)

| | | B- | | Good |

Fund Family: BlackRock Fund Advisors
Fund Type: Global
Inception Date: October 18, 2011

Major Rating Factors: *iShares Emerging Mkts Lcl Cur Bo receives a TheStreet.com Investment Rating of B- (Good). The fund currently has a performance rating of C (Fair) based on an annualized return of 0.00% over the last three years and a total return of 0.11% year to date 2012. Factored into the performance evaluation is an expense ratio of 0.60% (very low).

The fund's risk rating is currently B+ (Good). It carries a beta of 0.00, meaning the fund's expected move will be 0.0% for every 10% move in the market. Volatility, as measured by both the semi-deviation and a drawdown factor, is considered very low. As of December 31, 2012, *iShares Emerging Mkts Lcl Cur Bo traded at a premium of 1.18% above its net asset value, which is better than its one-year historical average premium of 1.45%.

James J. Mauro has been running the fund for 2 years and currently receives a manager quality ranking of 90 (0=worst, 99=best). If you desire an average level of risk, then this fund may be an option.

Data Date	Investment Rating	Net Assets ($Mil)	Price	Performance Rating/Pts	Total Return Y-T-D	Risk Rating/P
12-12	B-	381.00	53.86	C / 5.5	0.11%	B+ / 9

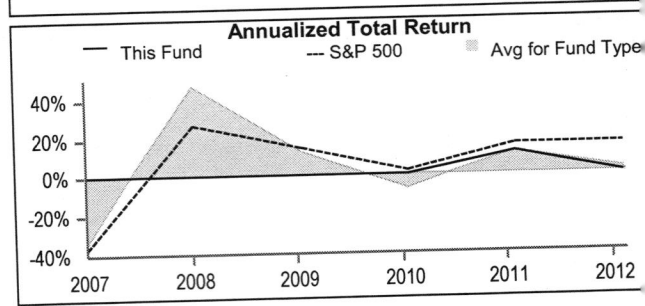

*iShares Floating Rate Note (FLOT)

C-   **Fair**

Fund Family: BlackRock Fund Advisors
Fund Type: Corporate - Investment Grade
Inception Date: June 14, 2011

Major Rating Factors:
Disappointing performance is the major factor driving the C- (Fair) TheStreet.com Investment Rating for *iShares Floating Rate Note. The fund currently has a performance rating of D (Weak) based on an annualized return of 0.00% over the last three years and a total return of 0.04% year to date 2012. Factored into the performance evaluation is an expense ratio of 0.20% (very low).

The fund's risk rating is currently B+ (Good). It carries a beta of 0.00, meaning the fund's expected move will be 0.0% for every 10% move in the market. Volatility, as measured by both the semi-deviation and a drawdown factor, is considered very low. As of December 31, 2012, *iShares Floating Rate Note traded at a premium of .34% above its net asset value, which is better than its one-year historical average premium of .36%.

James J. Mauro has been running the fund for 2 years and currently receives a manager quality ranking of 72 (0=worst, 99=best). This fund offers only a moderate level of risk but investors looking for strong performance are still waiting.

Data Date	Investment Rating	Net Assets ($Mil)	Price	Performance Rating/Pts	Total Return Y-T-D	Risk Rating/Pts
12-12	C-	402.70	50.59	D / 2.2	0.04%	B+ / 9.9

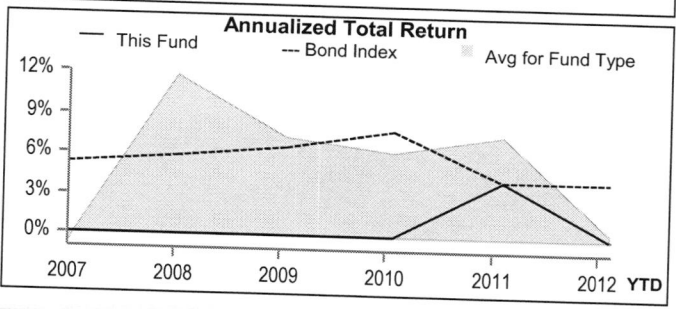

*iShares FTSE China 25 (FXI)

D   **Weak**

Fund Family: BlackRock Fund Advisors
Fund Type: Foreign
Inception Date: October 5, 2004

Major Rating Factors:
Disappointing performance is the major factor driving the D (Weak) TheStreet.com Investment Rating for *iShares FTSE China 25. The fund currently has a performance rating of D+ (Weak) based on an annualized return of 1.77% over the last three years and a total return of 1.58% year to date 2012. Factored into the performance evaluation is an expense ratio of 0.74% (very low).

The fund's risk rating is currently C+ (Fair). It carries a beta of 0.92, meaning that its performance tracks fairly well with that of the overall stock market. Volatility, as measured by both the semi-deviation and a drawdown factor, is considered low. As of December 31, 2012, *iShares FTSE China 25 traded at a discount of .93% below its net asset value, which is better than its one-year historical average premium of .04%.

Diane Hsiung has been running the fund for 5 years and currently receives a manager quality ranking of 29 (0=worst, 99=best). This fund offers only a moderate level of risk but investors looking for strong performance are still waiting.

Data Date	Investment Rating	Net Assets ($Mil)	Price	Performance Rating/Pts	Total Return Y-T-D	Risk Rating/Pts
12-12	D	8,478.30	40.45	D+ / 2.8	1.58%	C+ / 6.5
2011	D+	5,838.20	34.87	C- / 3.2	0.86%	C+ / 6.8
2010	E	8,139.90	43.09	D- / 1.3	3.51%	D- / 1.5
2009	D	11,300.67	42.26	C+ / 6.0	37.72%	D / 1.7

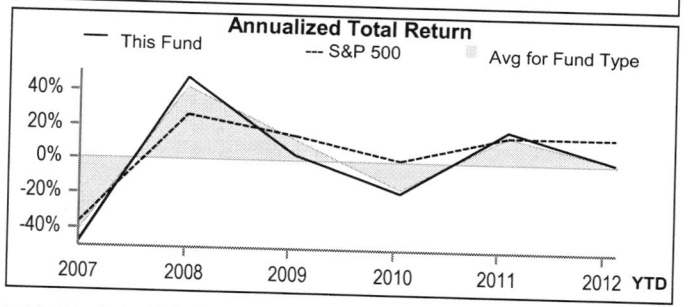

*iShares FTSE China Index (FCHI)

D+   **Weak**

Fund Family: BlackRock Fund Advisors
Fund Type: Foreign
Inception Date: June 24, 2008

Major Rating Factors: *iShares FTSE China Index receives a TheStreet.com Investment Rating of D+ (Weak). The fund currently has a performance rating of C- (Fair) based on an annualized return of 3.72% over the last three years and a total return of 2.13% year to date 2012. Factored into the performance evaluation is an expense ratio of 0.74% (very low).

The fund's risk rating is currently C+ (Fair). It carries a beta of 0.87, meaning the fund's expected move will be 8.7% for every 10% move in the market. Volatility, as measured by both the semi-deviation and a drawdown factor, is considered low. As of December 31, 2012, *iShares FTSE China Index traded at a discount of 1.64% below its net asset value, which is better than its one-year historical average discount of .19%.

Diane Hsiung has been running the fund for 5 years and currently receives a manager quality ranking of 44 (0=worst, 99=best). If you desire an average level of risk, then this fund may be an option.

Data Date	Investment Rating	Net Assets ($Mil)	Price	Performance Rating/Pts	Total Return Y-T-D	Risk Rating/Pts
12-12	D+	34.30	49.65	C- / 3.4	2.13%	C+ / 6.6
2011	C-	37.30	41.39	C- / 3.4	0.90%	B- / 7.0
2010	B	56.60	51.20	B / 7.6	6.88%	C / 5.2
2009	B+	42.71	48.81	B+ / 8.6	39.80%	C / 5.2

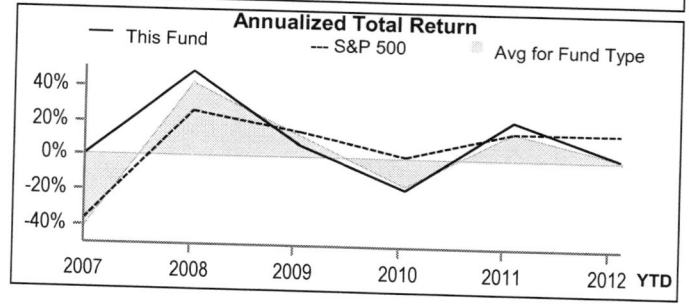

*iShares FTSE Dev Sm Cap ex-North (IFSM)

C **Fair**

Fund Family: BlackRock Fund Advisors
Fund Type: Foreign
Inception Date: November 12, 2007

Major Rating Factors: Middle of the road best describes *iShares FTSE Dev Sm Cap ex-North whose TheStreet.com Investment Rating is currently a C (Fair). The fund currently has a performance rating of C (Fair) based on an annualized return of 5.88% over the last three years and a total return of 2.92% year to date 2012. Factored into the performance evaluation is an expense ratio of 0.50% (very low).

The fund's risk rating is currently B- (Good). It carries a beta of 1.06, meaning that its performance tracks fairly well with that of the overall stock market. Volatility, as measured by both the semi-deviation and a drawdown factor, is considered low. As of December 31, 2012, *iShares FTSE Dev Sm Cap ex-North traded at a discount of 2.58% below its net asset value, which is better than its one-year historical average premium of .34%.

Diane Hsiung has been running the fund for 5 years and currently receives a manager quality ranking of 68 (0=worst, 99=best). If you desire an average level of risk, then this fund may be an option.

Data Date	Investment Rating	Net Assets ($Mil)	Price	Performance Rating/Pts	Total Return Y-T-D	Risk Rating/Pts
12-12	C	28.60	36.26	C / 5.1	2.92%	B- / 7.5
2011	C-	30.70	30.52	C- / 3.4	0.43%	B- / 7.7
2010	C-	38.70	38.69	C- / 4.1	20.80%	C / 5.4
2009	A-	23.33	32.89	B+ / 8.8	40.76%	C / 5.4

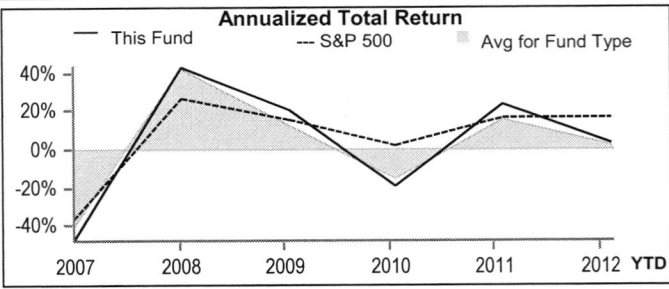

Annualized Total Return

*iShares FTSE EPRA/NAREIT Asia In (IFAS)

B **Good**

Fund Family: BlackRock Fund Advisors
Fund Type: Growth and Income
Inception Date: November 12, 2007

Major Rating Factors: Strong performance is the major factor driving the B (Good) TheStreet.com Investment Rating for *iShares FTSE EPRA/NAREIT Asia In. The fund currently has a performance rating of B+ (Good) based on an annualized return of 11.60% over the last three years and a total return of 1.01% year to date 2012. Factored into the performance evaluation is an expense ratio of 0.48% (very low).

The fund's risk rating is currently B- (Good). It carries a beta of 1.16, meaning it is expected to move 11.6% for every 10% move in the market. Volatility, as measured by both the semi-deviation and a drawdown factor, is considered low. As of December 31, 2012, *iShares FTSE EPRA/NAREIT Asia In traded at a discount of .27% below its net asset value, which is better than its one-year historical average premium of .18%.

Diane Hsiung has been running the fund for 5 years and currently receives a manager quality ranking of 39 (0=worst, 99=best). If you desire only a moderate level of risk and strong performance, then this fund is an excellent option.

Data Date	Investment Rating	Net Assets ($Mil)	Price	Performance Rating/Pts	Total Return Y-T-D	Risk Rating/Pts
12-12	B	36.30	33.67	B+ / 8.4	1.01%	B- / 7.1
2011	D+	19.60	24.15	D+ / 2.8	2.19%	B- / 7.1
2010	D-	25.40	31.86	D / 2.0	16.32%	C- / 4.2
2009	C+	10.31	28.92	B+ / 8.4	37.63%	C- / 4.2

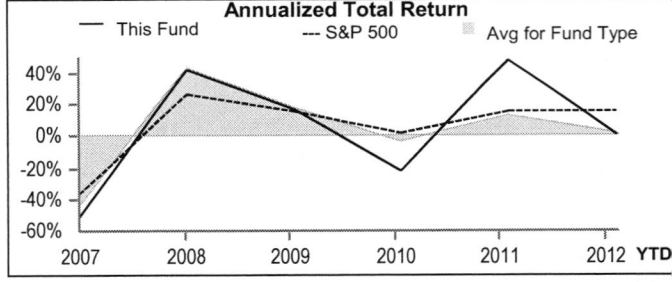

Annualized Total Return

*iShares FTSE EPRA/NAREIT Dev RE (IFGL)

C **Fair**

Fund Family: BlackRock Fund Advisors
Fund Type: Growth and Income
Inception Date: November 12, 2007

Major Rating Factors: Strong performance is the major factor driving the C (Fair) TheStreet.com Investment Rating for *iShares FTSE EPRA/NAREIT Dev RE. The fund currently has a performance rating of B- (Good) based on an annualized return of 10.54% over the last three years and a total return of 0.51% year to date 2012. Factored into the performance evaluation is an expense ratio of 0.48% (very low).

The fund's risk rating is currently C+ (Fair). It carries a beta of 1.14, meaning it is expected to move 11.4% for every 10% move in the market. Volatility, as measured by both the semi-deviation and a drawdown factor, is considered low. As of December 31, 2012, *iShares FTSE EPRA/NAREIT Dev RE traded at a price exactly equal to its net asset value, which is better than its one-year historical average premium of .30%.

Diane Hsiung has been running the fund for 5 years and currently receives a manager quality ranking of 37 (0=worst, 99=best). If you desire only a moderate level of risk and strong performance, then this fund is an excellent option.

Data Date	Investment Rating	Net Assets ($Mil)	Price	Performance Rating/Pts	Total Return Y-T-D	Risk Rating/Pts
12-12	C	1,546.20	33.13	B- / 7.5	0.51%	C+ / 5.6
2011	D	336.00	25.25	C- / 3.1	0.40%	C+ / 5.6
2010	E+	380.50	31.01	D / 1.6	14.55%	C- / 3.1
2009	C+	194.74	28.92	B+ / 8.6	36.54%	C- / 3.2

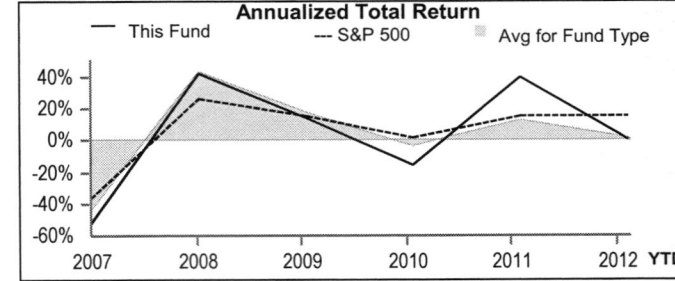

Annualized Total Return

*iShares FTSE EPRA/NAREIT Europe (IFEU)

C **Fair**

Fund Family: BlackRock Fund Advisors
Fund Type: Growth and Income
Inception Date: November 12, 2007

Major Rating Factors: Middle of the road best describes *iShares FTSE EPRA/NAREIT Europe whose TheStreet.com Investment Rating is currently a C (Fair). The fund currently has a performance rating of C+ (Fair) based on an annualized return of 6.63% over the last three years and a total return of 0.98% year to date 2012. Factored into the performance evaluation is an expense ratio of 0.48% (very low).

The fund's risk rating is currently C+ (Fair). It carries a beta of 1.30, meaning it is expected to move 13.0% for every 10% move in the market. Volatility, as measured by both the semi-deviation and a drawdown factor, is considered low. As of December 31, 2012, *iShares FTSE EPRA/NAREIT Europe traded at a discount of .52% below its net asset value, which is better than its one-year historical average premium of .47%.

Diane Hsiung has been running the fund for 5 years and currently receives a manager quality ranking of 19 (0=worst, 99=best). If you desire an average level of risk, then this fund may be an option.

Data Date	Investment Rating	Net Assets ($Mil)	Price	Performance Rating/Pts	Total Return Y-T-D	Risk Rating/Pts
12-12	C	13.90	30.75	C+ / 6.0	0.98%	C+ / 6.6
2011	D	11.20	24.69	D / 1.8	-3.51%	C+ / 6.7
2010	E+	9.00	29.97	D- / 1.2	9.46%	C- / 3.6
2009	C+	3.16	29.30	B+ / 8.6	29.85%	C- / 3.9

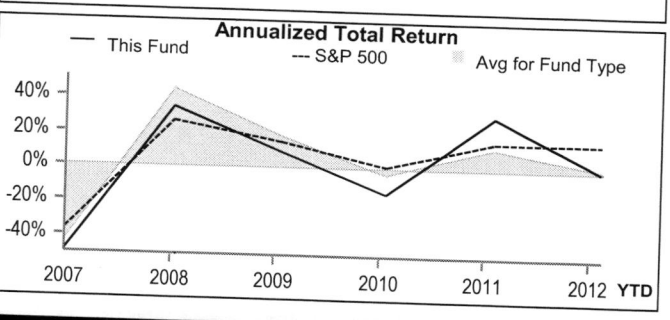

*iShares FTSE EPRA/NAREIT NA Idx (IFNA)

C+ **Fair**

Fund Family: BlackRock Fund Advisors
Fund Type: Growth and Income
Inception Date: November 12, 2007

Major Rating Factors: Strong performance is the major factor driving the C+ (Fair) TheStreet.com Investment Rating for *iShares FTSE EPRA/NAREIT NA Idx. The fund currently has a performance rating of B- (Good) based on an annualized return of 17.88% over the last three years and a total return of 2.96% year to date 2012. Factored into the performance evaluation is an expense ratio of 0.48% (very low).

The fund's risk rating is currently B- (Good). It carries a beta of 0.93, meaning that its performance tracks fairly well with that of the overall stock market. Volatility, as measured by both the semi-deviation and a drawdown factor, is considered low. As of December 31, 2012, *iShares FTSE EPRA/NAREIT NA Idx traded at a discount of 3.30% below its net asset value, which is better than its one-year historical average premium of .13%.

Diane Hsiung has been running the fund for 5 years and currently receives a manager quality ranking of 80 (0=worst, 99=best). If you desire only a moderate level of risk and strong performance, then this fund is an excellent option.

Data Date	Investment Rating	Net Assets ($Mil)	Price	Performance Rating/Pts	Total Return Y-T-D	Risk Rating/Pts
12-12	C+	21.50	47.17	B- / 7.2	2.96%	B- / 7.3
2011	C+	12.60	42.14	B- / 7.5	0.12%	C+ / 6.0
2010	C	10.10	40.00	C+ / 6.9	24.46%	C- / 4.0
2009	B	2.28	33.20	A- / 9.2	33.80%	C- / 4.0

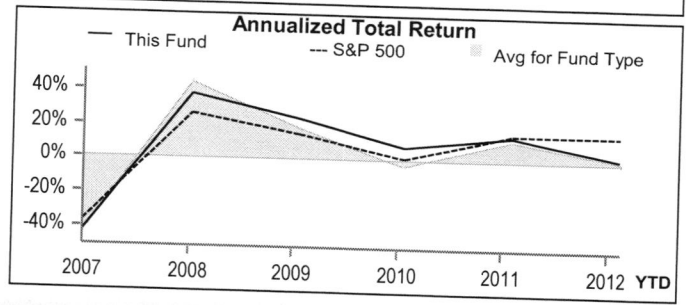

*iShares FTSE NAREIT Indl/Off Idx (FNIO)

C **Fair**

Fund Family: BlackRock Fund Advisors
Fund Type: Income
Inception Date: May 1, 2007

Major Rating Factors: Middle of the road best describes *iShares FTSE NAREIT Indl/Off Idx whose TheStreet.com Investment Rating is currently a C (Fair). The fund currently has a performance rating of C (Fair) based on an annualized return of 11.13% over the last three years and a total return of 2.96% year to date 2012. Factored into the performance evaluation is an expense ratio of 0.48% (very low).

The fund's risk rating is currently B- (Good). It carries a beta of 1.14, meaning it is expected to move 11.4% for every 10% move in the market. Volatility, as measured by both the semi-deviation and a drawdown factor, is considered low. As of December 31, 2012, *iShares FTSE NAREIT Indl/Off Idx traded at a discount of 2.97% below its net asset value, which is better than its one-year historical average discount of .08%.

Diane Hsiung has been running the fund for 5 years and currently receives a manager quality ranking of 34 (0=worst, 99=best). If you desire an average level of risk, then this fund may be an option.

Data Date	Investment Rating	Net Assets ($Mil)	Price	Performance Rating/Pts	Total Return Y-T-D	Risk Rating/Pts
12-12	C	10.10	28.73	C / 5.0	2.96%	B- / 7.3
2011	C-	10.00	25.08	C / 5.1	0.28%	C+ / 6.6
2010	D-	9.30	26.65	D / 2.1	16.27%	C- / 3.8
2009	B-	2.52	23.72	A- / 9.2	28.62%	C- / 3.8

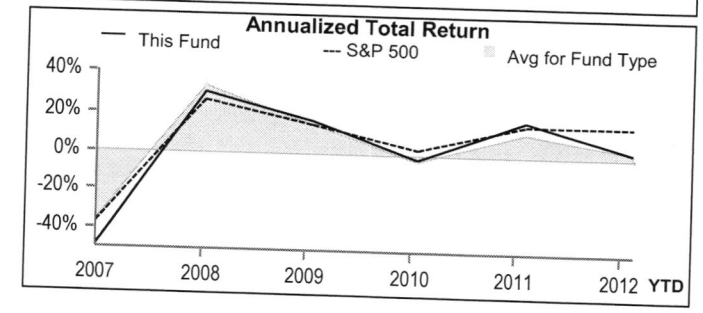

* Denotes ETF Fund

*iShares FTSE NAREIT Mtge+Capped (REM)

C+   **Fair**

Fund Family: BlackRock Fund Advisors
Fund Type: Income
Inception Date: May 1, 2007

Major Rating Factors: Middle of the road best describes *iShares FTSE NAREIT Mtge+Capped whose TheStreet.com Investment Rating is currently a C+ (Fair). The fund currently has a performance rating of C+ (Fair) based on an annualized return of 11.10% over the last three years and a total return of 6.88% year to date 2012. Factored into the performance evaluation is an expense ratio of 0.48% (very low).

The fund's risk rating is currently B (Good). It carries a beta of 0.60, meaning the fund's expected move will be 6.0% for every 10% move in the market. Volatility, as measured by both the semi-deviation and a drawdown factor, is considered low. As of December 31, 2012, *iShares FTSE NAREIT Mtge+Capped traded at a discount of 6.37% below its net asset value, which is better than its one-year historical average premium of .06%.

Diane Hsiung has been running the fund for 5 years and currently receives a manager quality ranking of 68 (0=worst, 99=best). If you desire an average level of risk, then this fund may be an option.

Data Date	Investment Rating	Net Assets ($Mil)	Price	Performance Rating/Pts	Total Return Y-T-D	Risk Rating/Pts
12-12	C+	862.10	13.67	C+ / 5.8	6.88%	B / 8.1
2011	C-	215.00	12.66	D+ / 2.6	1.26%	B / 8.0
2010	D-	102.10	15.59	D- / 1.5	16.49%	C- / 4.2
2009	C	30.51	14.71	C+ / 6.9	13.12%	C / 4.4

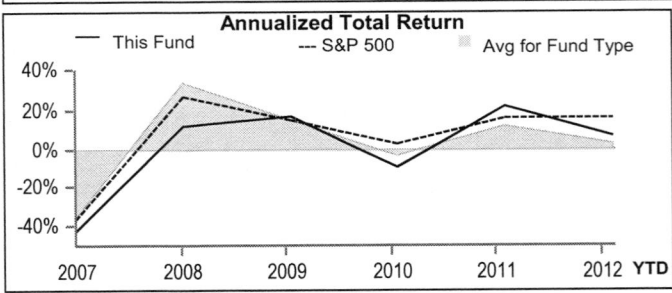

*iShares FTSE NAREIT Real Estate (FTY)

B   **Good**

Fund Family: BlackRock Fund Advisors
Fund Type: Income
Inception Date: May 1, 2007

Major Rating Factors: Strong performance is the major factor driving the B (Good) TheStreet.com Investment Rating for *iShares FTSE NAREIT Real Estate. The fund currently has a performance rating of B- (Good) based on an annualized return of 18.58% over the last three years and a total return of 2.66% year to date 2012. Factored into the performance evaluation is an expense ratio of 0.48% (very low).

The fund's risk rating is currently B- (Good). It carries a beta of 0.94, meaning that its performance tracks fairly well with that of the overall stock market. Volatility, as measured by both the semi-deviation and a drawdown factor, is considered low. As of December 31, 2012, *iShares FTSE NAREIT Real Estate traded at a discount of 2.59% below its net asset value, which is better than its one-year historical average premium of .01%.

Diane Hsiung has been running the fund for 5 years and currently receives a manager quality ranking of 83 (0=worst, 99=best). If you desire only a moderate level of risk and strong performance, then this fund is an excellent option.

Data Date	Investment Rating	Net Assets ($Mil)	Price	Performance Rating/Pts	Total Return Y-T-D	Risk Rating/Pts
12-12	B	69.80	39.82	B- / 7.5	2.66%	B- / 7.9
2011	C+	42.20	35.35	B- / 7.5	-0.83%	C+ / 6.7
2010	C+	50.40	33.72	B- / 7.2	26.21%	C / 4.3
2009	B	14.04	27.77	A- / 9.1	30.12%	C / 4.4

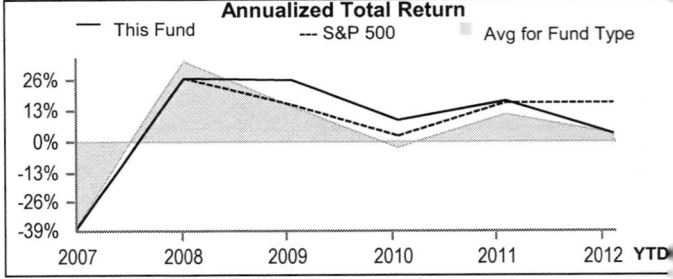

*iShares FTSE NAREIT Residential (REZ)

B+   **Good**

Fund Family: BlackRock Fund Advisors
Fund Type: Income
Inception Date: May 1, 2007

Major Rating Factors: Strong performance is the major factor driving the B+ (Good) TheStreet.com Investment Rating for *iShares FTSE NAREIT Residential. The fund currently has a performance rating of B (Good) based on an annualized return of 21.25% over the last three years and a total return of 2.03% year to date 2012. Factored into the performance evaluation is an expense ratio of 0.48% (very low).

The fund's risk rating is currently B- (Good). It carries a beta of 0.77, meaning the fund's expected move will be 7.7% for every 10% move in the market. Volatility, as measured by both the semi-deviation and a drawdown factor, is considered low. As of December 31, 2012, *iShares FTSE NAREIT Residential traded at a discount of 1.98% below its net asset value, which is better than its one-year historical average premium of .02%.

Diane Hsiung has been running the fund for 5 years and currently receives a manager quality ranking of 91 (0=worst, 99=best). If you desire only a moderate level of risk and strong performance, then this fund is an excellent option.

Data Date	Investment Rating	Net Assets ($Mil)	Price	Performance Rating/Pts	Total Return Y-T-D	Risk Rating/Pts
12-12	B+	257.20	48.47	B / 8.2	2.03%	B- / 7.9
2011	C+	143.50	44.22	B / 8.2	-1.31%	C+ / 6.2
2010	B	70.90	39.39	B+ / 8.3	31.61%	C / 4.5
2009	B	14.23	30.94	A- / 9.0	25.84%	C / 4.4

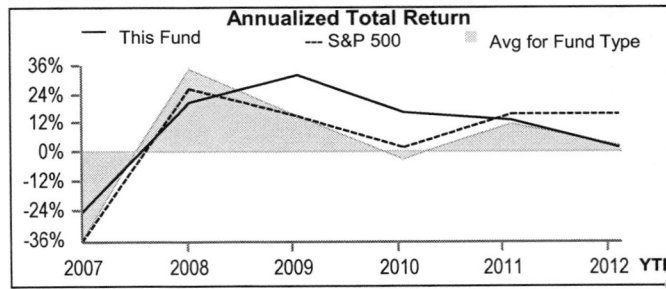

*iShares FTSE NAREIT Retail Idx (RTL)

B+ **Good**

Fund Family: BlackRock Fund Advisors
Fund Type: Income
Inception Date: May 1, 2007

Major Rating Factors: Strong performance is the major factor driving the B+ (Good) TheStreet.com Investment Rating for *iShares FTSE NAREIT Retail Idx. The fund currently has a performance rating of B+ (Good) based on an annualized return of 22.92% over the last three years and a total return of 1.65% year to date 2012. Factored into the performance evaluation is an expense ratio of 0.48% (very low).

The fund's risk rating is currently B- (Good). It carries a beta of 1.01, meaning that its performance tracks fairly well with that of the overall stock market. Volatility, as measured by both the semi-deviation and a drawdown factor, is considered low. As of December 31, 2012, *iShares FTSE NAREIT Retail Idx traded at a discount of 1.71% below its net asset value.

Diane Hsiung has been running the fund for 5 years and currently receives a manager quality ranking of 90 (0=worst, 99=best). If you desire only a moderate level of risk and strong performance, then this fund is an excellent option.

Data Date	Investment Rating	Net Assets ($Mil)	Price	Perfor-mance Rating/Pts	Total Return Y-T-D	Risk Rating/Pts
12-12	B+	22.80	35.08	B+ / 8.7	1.65%	B- / 7.7
2011	C+	8.60	28.94	B / 7.7	-0.21%	C+ / 6.2
2010	C-	14.00	28.13	C+ / 6.1	36.08%	C- / 3.7
2009	C+	1.63	21.36	B+ / 8.9	25.55%	D+ / 2.9

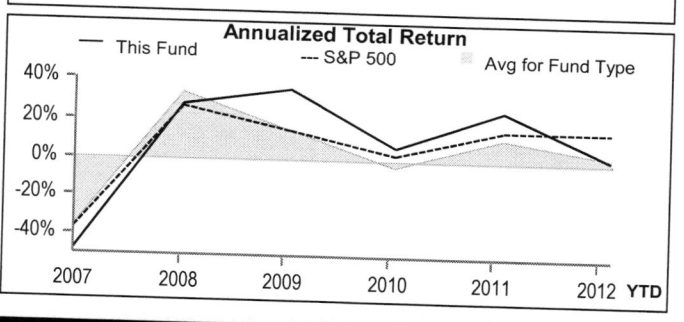

*iShares Global Inflation-Linked (GTIP)

B **Good**

Fund Family: BlackRock Fund Advisors
Fund Type: Global
Inception Date: May 18, 2011

Major Rating Factors: *iShares Global Inflation-Linked receives a TheStreet.com Investment Rating of B (Good). The fund currently has a performance rating of C+ (Fair) based on an annualized return of 0.00% over the last three years and a total return of 0.64% year to date 2012. Factored into the performance evaluation is an expense ratio of 0.40% (very low).

The fund's risk rating is currently B+ (Good). It carries a beta of 0.00, meaning the fund's expected move will be 0.0% for every 10% move in the market. Volatility, as measured by both the semi-deviation and a drawdown factor, is considered very low. As of December 31, 2012, *iShares Global Inflation-Linked traded at a premium of .80% above its net asset value, which is worse than its one-year historical average discount of 1.07%.

James J. Mauro has been running the fund for 2 years and currently receives a manager quality ranking of 90 (0=worst, 99=best). If you desire an average level of risk, then this fund may be an option.

Data Date	Investment Rating	Net Assets ($Mil)	Price	Perfor-mance Rating/Pts	Total Return Y-T-D	Risk Rating/Pts
12-12	B	16.00	54.08	C+ / 6.0	0.64%	B+ / 9.2

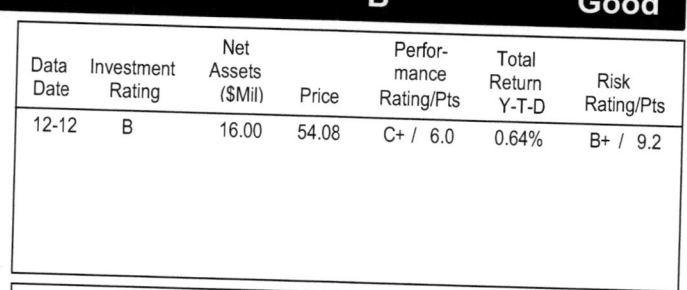

*iShares Gold Trust (IAU)

D- **Weak**

Fund Family: BlackRock Fund Advisors
Fund Type: Precious Metals
Inception Date: January 21, 2005

Major Rating Factors: *iShares Gold Trust has adopted a very risky asset allocation strategy and currently receives an overall TheStreet.com Investment Rating of D- (Weak). The fund has a high level of volatility, as measured by both semi-deviation and drawdown factors. It carries a beta of 0.92, meaning that its performance tracks fairly well with that of the overall stock market. As of December 31, 2012, *iShares Gold Trust traded at a premium of .99% above its net asset value, which is worse than its one-year historical average premium of .15%. Unfortunately, the high level of risk (D, Weak) has only provided investors with average performance.

The fund's performance rating is currently C (Fair). It has registered an annualized return of 13.37% over the last three years but is down -0.67% year to date 2012. Factored into the performance evaluation is an expense ratio of 0.25% (very low).

Index Strategies Group has been running the fund for 8 years and currently receives a manager quality ranking of 60 (0=worst, 99=best). If you are comfortable owning a very high risk investment, then this fund may be an option.

Data Date	Investment Rating	Net Assets ($Mil)	Price	Perfor-mance Rating/Pts	Total Return Y-T-D	Risk Rating/Pts
12-12	D-	11,645.30	16.28	C / 4.3	-0.67%	D / 1.9
2011	D+	8,416.90	15.23	B / 7.6	3.48%	D / 1.9
2010	C-	5,316.70	13.90	B+ / 8.9	29.46%	D- / 1.0
2009	A+	2,667.82	107.37	B- / 7.5	24.34%	B- / 7.2

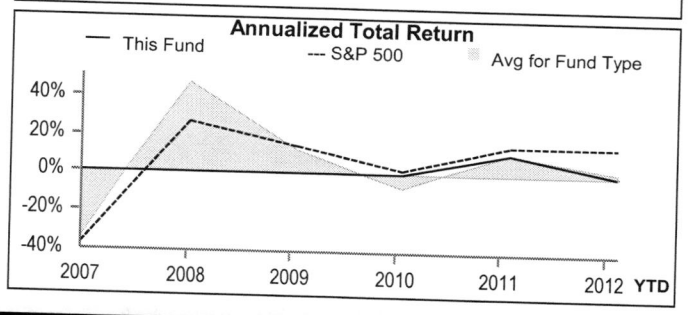

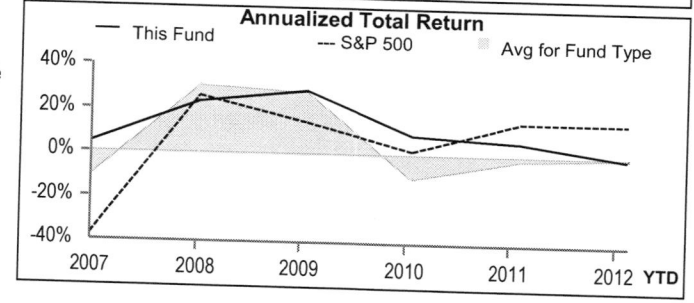

*iShares High Dividend Equity (HDV)

C+ **Fair**

Fund Family: BlackRock Fund Advisors
Fund Type: Global
Inception Date: March 29, 2011

Data Date	Investment Rating	Net Assets ($Mil)	Price	Performance Rating/Pts	Total Return Y-T-D	Risk Rating/Pts
12-12	C+	2,135.80	58.79	C / 4.5	3.21%	B+ / 9.4

Major Rating Factors: Middle of the road best describes *iShares High Dividend Equity whose TheStreet.com Investment Rating is currently a C+ (Fair). The fund currently has a performance rating of C (Fair) based on an annualized return of 0.00% over the last three years and a total return of 3.21% year to date 2012. Factored into the performance evaluation is an expense ratio of 0.40% (very low).

The fund's risk rating is currently B+ (Good). It carries a beta of 0.00, meaning the fund's expected move will be 0.0% for every 10% move in the market. Volatility, as measured by both the semi-deviation and a drawdown factor, is considered very low. As of December 31, 2012, *iShares High Dividend Equity traded at a discount of 3.11% below its net asset value, which is better than its one-year historical average premium of .02%.

Greg Savage has been running the fund for 2 years and currently receives a manager quality ranking of 89 (0=worst, 99=best). If you desire an average level of risk, then this fund may be an option.

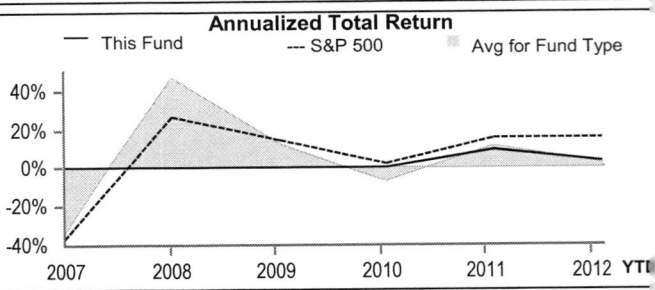

Annualized Total Return
— This Fund   --- S&P 500   Avg for Fund Type

*iShares iBoxx $ High Yld Corp Bo (HYG)

C- **Fair**

Fund Family: BlackRock Fund Advisors
Fund Type: Corporate - High Yield
Inception Date: April 4, 2007

Data Date	Investment Rating	Net Assets ($Mil)	Price	Performance Rating/Pts	Total Return Y-T-D	Risk Rating/Pts
12-12	C-	15,972.30	93.35	C / 4.4	1.25%	B- / 7.7
2011	C	10,636.60	89.43	C / 5.0	-0.59%	B- / 7.0
2010	C+	7,273.10	90.29	C+ / 6.7	11.98%	C / 5.2
2009	B	3,765.79	87.84	B / 8.2	29.16%	C / 5.2

Major Rating Factors: Middle of the road best describes *iShares iBoxx $ High Yld Corp Bo whose TheStreet.com Investment Rating is currently a C- (Fair). The fund currently has a performance rating of C (Fair) based on an annualized return of 10.08% over the last three years and a total return of 1.25% year to date 2012. Factored into the performance evaluation is an expense ratio of 0.50% (very low).

The fund's risk rating is currently B- (Good). It carries a beta of 1.19, meaning it is expected to move 11.9% for every 10% move in the market. Volatility, as measured by both the semi-deviation and a drawdown factor, is considered low. As of December 31, 2012, *iShares iBoxx $ High Yld Corp Bo traded at a discount of .78% below its net asset value, which is better than its one-year historical average premium of .45%.

Scott F. Radell has been running the fund for 3 years and currently receives a manager quality ranking of 29 (0=worst, 99=best). If you desire an average level of risk, then this fund may be an option.

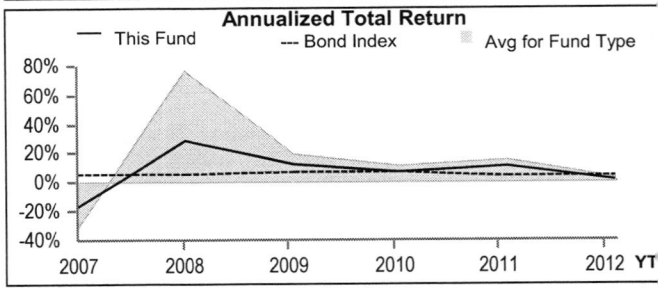

Annualized Total Return
— This Fund   --- Bond Index   Avg for Fund Type

*iShares iBoxx $ Inves Grade Corp (LQD)

C **Fair**

Fund Family: BlackRock Fund Advisors
Fund Type: Corporate - Investment Grade
Inception Date: July 22, 2002

Data Date	Investment Rating	Net Assets ($Mil)	Price	Performance Rating/Pts	Total Return Y-T-D	Risk Rating/Pts
12-12	C	25,350.40	120.99	C- / 3.5	0.09%	B+ / 9.4
2011	C+	16,990.80	113.76	C- / 4.0	-0.04%	B+ / 9.2
2010	B	13,098.30	108.44	C / 5.5	9.35%	B / 8.5
2009	B-	12,969.09	104.15	C- / 4.0	9.68%	B / 8.7

Major Rating Factors: Middle of the road best describes *iShares iBoxx $ Inves Grade Corp whose TheStreet.com Investment Rating is currently a C (Fair). The fund currently has a performance rating of C- (Fair) based on an annualized return of 9.47% over the last three years and a total return of 0.09% year to date 2012. Factored into the performance evaluation is an expense ratio of 0.15% (very low).

The fund's risk rating is currently B+ (Good). It carries a beta of 1.38, meaning it is expected to move 13.8% for every 10% move in the market. Volatility, as measured by both the semi-deviation and a drawdown factor, is considered very low. As of December 31, 2012, *iShares iBoxx $ Inves Grade Corp traded at a premium of .20% above its net asset value, which is better than its one-year historical average premium of .43%.

Scott F. Radell has been running the fund for 3 years and currently receives a manager quality ranking of 35 (0=worst, 99=best). If you desire an average level of risk, then this fund may be an option.

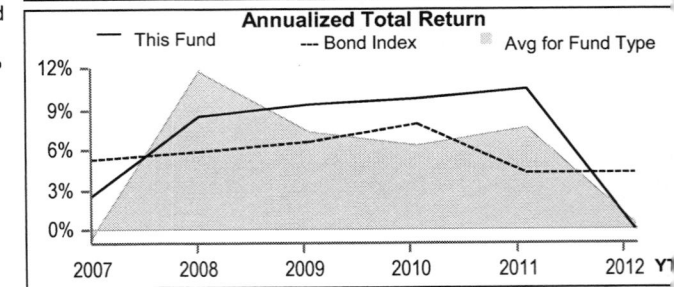

Annualized Total Return
— This Fund   --- Bond Index   Avg for Fund Type

*iShares Internat Inflation-Link (ITIP)

B **Good**

Fund Family: BlackRock Fund Advisors
Fund Type: Global
Inception Date: May 18, 2011

Major Rating Factors: Strong performance is the major factor driving the B (Good) TheStreet.com Investment Rating for *iShares Internat Inflation-Link. The fund currently has a performance rating of B- (Good) based on an annualized return of 0.00% over the last three years and a total return of 0.47% year to date 2012. Factored into the performance evaluation is an expense ratio of 0.40% (very low).

The fund's risk rating is currently B (Good). It carries a beta of 0.00, meaning the fund's expected move will be 0.0% for every 10% move in the market. Volatility, as measured by both the semi-deviation and a drawdown factor, is considered low. As of December 31, 2012, *iShares Internat Inflation-Link traded at a premium of 1.08% above its net asset value, which is worse than its one-year historical average premium of .85%.

James J. Mauro has been running the fund for 2 years and currently receives a manager quality ranking of 93 (0=worst, 99=best). If you desire only a moderate level of risk and strong performance, then this fund is an excellent option.

Data Date	Investment Rating	Net Assets ($Mil)	Price	Performance Rating/Pts	Total Return Y-T-D	Risk Rating/Pts
12-12	B	65.60	51.29	B- / 7.1	0.47%	B / 8.7

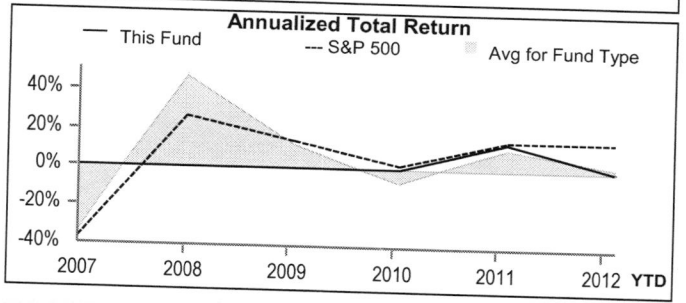

*iShares JPMorgan USD Emg Mkts Bo (EMB)

C+ **Fair**

Fund Family: BlackRock Fund Advisors
Fund Type: Emerging Market
Inception Date: December 17, 2007

Major Rating Factors: Middle of the road best describes *iShares JPMorgan USD Emg Mkts Bo whose TheStreet.com Investment Rating is currently a C+ (Fair). The fund currently has a performance rating of C (Fair) based on an annualized return of 11.17% over the last three years and a total return of -1.10% year to date 2012. Factored into the performance evaluation is an expense ratio of 0.60% (very low).

The fund's risk rating is currently B (Good). It carries a beta of 0.66, meaning the fund's expected move will be 6.6% for every 10% move in the market. Volatility, as measured by both the semi-deviation and a drawdown factor, is considered low. As of December 31, 2012, *iShares JPMorgan USD Emg Mkts Bo traded at a premium of 1.34% above its net asset value, which is worse than its one-year historical average premium of .55%.

Scott F. Radell has been running the fund for 3 years and currently receives a manager quality ranking of 88 (0=worst, 99=best). If you desire an average level of risk, then this fund may be an option.

Data Date	Investment Rating	Net Assets ($Mil)	Price	Performance Rating/Pts	Total Return Y-T-D	Risk Rating/Pts
12-12	C+	6,902.90	122.79	C / 4.6	-1.10%	B / 8.9
2011	C+	3,554.20	109.75	C / 4.7	-1.23%	B / 8.6
2010	C+	2,187.50	107.08	C+ / 6.4	10.89%	C+ / 6.8
2009	B-	405.50	101.78	C+ / 5.9	13.50%	B- / 7.0

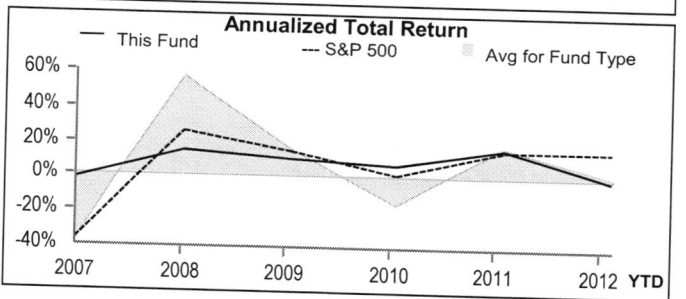

*iShares Morningstar Large Core (JKD)

C+ **Fair**

Fund Family: BlackRock Fund Advisors
Fund Type: Growth
Inception Date: June 28, 2004

Major Rating Factors: Middle of the road best describes *iShares Morningstar Large Core whose TheStreet.com Investment Rating is currently a C+ (Fair). The fund currently has a performance rating of C (Fair) based on an annualized return of 11.51% over the last three years and a total return of 3.19% year to date 2012. Factored into the performance evaluation is an expense ratio of 0.20% (very low).

The fund's risk rating is currently B (Good). It carries a beta of 0.92, meaning that its performance tracks fairly well with that of the overall stock market. Volatility, as measured by both the semi-deviation and a drawdown factor, is considered low. As of December 31, 2012, *iShares Morningstar Large Core traded at a discount of 3.11% below its net asset value, which is better than its one-year historical average discount of .03%.

Diane Hsiung has been running the fund for 5 years and currently receives a manager quality ranking of 60 (0=worst, 99=best). If you desire an average level of risk, then this fund may be an option.

Data Date	Investment Rating	Net Assets ($Mil)	Price	Performance Rating/Pts	Total Return Y-T-D	Risk Rating/Pts
12-12	C+	287.00	82.04	C / 5.5	3.19%	B / 8.4
2011	C	285.80	71.50	C / 4.9	1.66%	B / 8.0
2010	C-	275.90	70.70	C- / 3.8	12.68%	C+ / 6.2
2009	C-	195.88	63.97	D+ / 2.5	18.04%	C+ / 6.3

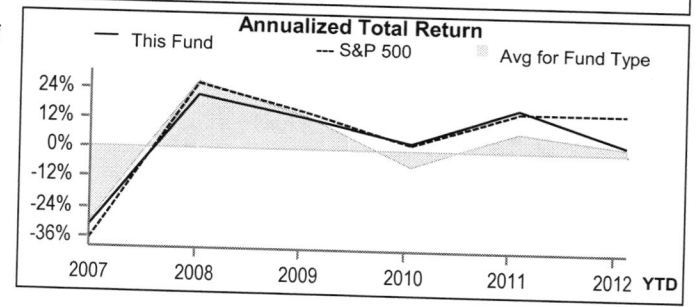

*iShares Morningstar Large Growth (JKE)

C   **Fair**

Fund Family: BlackRock Fund Advisors
Fund Type: Growth
Inception Date: June 28, 2004

Major Rating Factors: Middle of the road best describes *iShares Morningstar Large Growth whose TheStreet.com Investment Rating is currently a C (Fair). The fund currently has a performance rating of C (Fair) based on an annualized return of 11.12% over the last three years and a total return of 3.16% year to date 2012. Factored into the performance evaluation is an expense ratio of 0.25% (very low).

The fund's risk rating is currently B- (Good). It carries a beta of 1.10, meaning it is expected to move 11.0% for every 10% move in the market. Volatility, as measured by both the semi-deviation and a drawdown factor, is considered low. As of December 31, 2012, *iShares Morningstar Large Growth traded at a discount of 3.09% below its net asset value, which is better than its one-year historical average discount of .03%.

Diane Hsiung has been running the fund for 5 years and currently receives a manager quality ranking of 39 (0=worst, 99=best). If you desire an average level of risk, then this fund may be an option.

Data Date	Investment Rating	Net Assets ($Mil)	Price	Perfor-mance Rating/Pts	Total Return Y-T-D	Risk Rating/Pts
12-12	C	447.50	76.50	C / 5.0	3.16%	B- / 7.1
2011	C+	355.30	65.95	C+ / 6.2	1.88%	B- / 7.4
2010	C-	370.40	65.53	C / 4.3	12.57%	C+ / 5.7
2009	C-	331.59	58.69	C- / 3.9	39.27%	C+ / 5.8

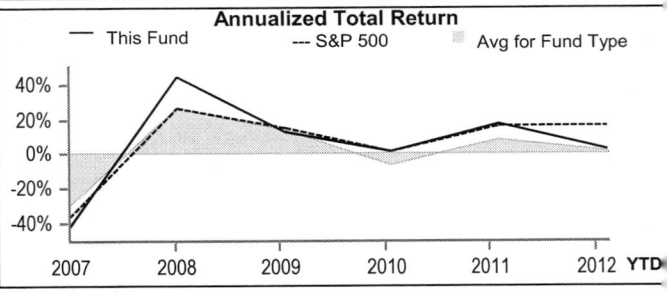

*iShares Morningstar Large Value (JKF)

C   **Fair**

Fund Family: BlackRock Fund Advisors
Fund Type: Income
Inception Date: June 28, 2004

Major Rating Factors: Middle of the road best describes *iShares Morningstar Large Value whose TheStreet.com Investment Rating is currently a C (Fair). The fund currently has a performance rating of C (Fair) based on an annualized return of 9.60% over the last three years and a total return of 3.43% year to date 2012. Factored into the performance evaluation is an expense ratio of 0.25% (very low).

The fund's risk rating is currently B (Good). It carries a beta of 0.93, meaning that its performance tracks fairly well with that of the overall stock market. Volatility, as measured by both the semi-deviation and a drawdown factor, is considered low. As of December 31, 2012, *iShares Morningstar Large Value traded at a discount of 3.31% below its net asset value, which is better than its one-year historical average discount of .01%.

Diane Hsiung has been running the fund for 5 years and currently receives a manager quality ranking of 47 (0=worst, 99=best). If you desire an average level of risk, then this fund may be an option.

Data Date	Investment Rating	Net Assets ($Mil)	Price	Perfor-mance Rating/Pts	Total Return Y-T-D	Risk Rating/Pts
12-12	C	244.70	64.47	C / 4.4	3.43%	B / 8.2
2011	C	244.40	58.90	C- / 4.1	1.21%	B / 8.0
2010	D+	208.20	59.53	D / 2.1	14.57%	C+ / 6.1
2009	D	159.31	53.41	D- / 1.1	8.17%	C+ / 5.7

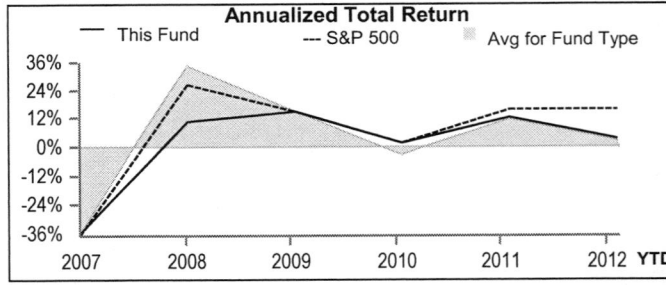

*iShares Morningstar Mid Core (JKG)

B   **Good**

Fund Family: BlackRock Fund Advisors
Fund Type: Growth
Inception Date: June 28, 2004

Major Rating Factors: Strong performance is the major factor driving the B (Good) TheStreet.com Investment Rating for *iShares Morningstar Mid Core. The fund currently has a performance rating of B- (Good) based on an annualized return of 15.27% over the last three years and a total return of 3.85% year to date 2012. Factored into the performance evaluation is an expense ratio of 0.25% (very low).

The fund's risk rating is currently B- (Good). It carries a beta of 1.13, meaning it is expected to move 11.3% for every 10% move in the market. Volatility, as measured by both the semi-deviation and a drawdown factor, is considered low. As of December 31, 2012, *iShares Morningstar Mid Core traded at a discount of 3.74% below its net asset value, which is better than its one-year historical average discount of .03%.

Diane Hsiung has been running the fund for 5 years and currently receives a manager quality ranking of 67 (0=worst, 99=best). If you desire only a moderate level of risk and strong performance, then this fund is an excellent option.

Data Date	Investment Rating	Net Assets ($Mil)	Price	Perfor-mance Rating/Pts	Total Return Y-T-D	Risk Rating/Pts
12-12	B	158.30	98.60	B- / 7.3	3.85%	B- / 7.8
2011	B-	140.60	85.15	B- / 7.0	1.59%	B- / 7.8
2010	B-	143.90	84.94	B- / 7.1	26.50%	C+ / 5.6
2009	C-	77.66	68.17	C- / 3.2	34.75%	C+ / 5.7

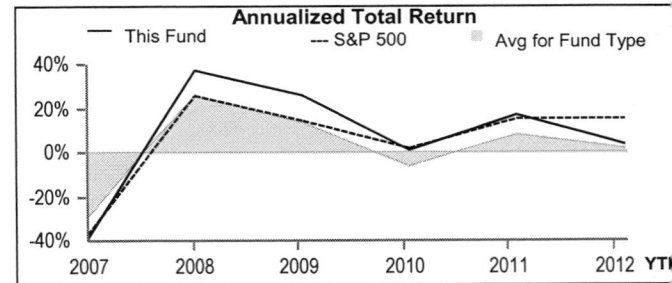

*iShares Morningstar Mid Growth (JKH)

C+   **Fair**

Fund Family: BlackRock Fund Advisors
Fund Type: Growth
Inception Date: June 28, 2004

Major Rating Factors: Middle of the road best describes *iShares Morningstar Mid Growth whose TheStreet.com Investment Rating is currently a C+ (Fair). The fund currently has a performance rating of C+ (Fair) based on an annualized return of 13.52% over the last three years and a total return of 3.27% year to date 2012. Factored into the performance evaluation is an expense ratio of 0.30% (very low).

The fund's risk rating is currently B- (Good). It carries a beta of 1.09, meaning that its performance tracks fairly well with that of the overall stock market. Volatility, as measured by both the semi-deviation and a drawdown factor, is considered low. As of December 31, 2012, *iShares Morningstar Mid Growth traded at a discount of 3.20% below its net asset value, which is better than its one-year historical average discount of .03%.

Diane Hsiung has been running the fund for 5 years and currently receives a manager quality ranking of 59 (0=worst, 99=best). If you desire an average level of risk, then this fund may be an option.

Data Date	Investment Rating	Net Assets ($Mil)	Price	Performance Rating/Pts	Total Return Y-T-D	Risk Rating/Pts
12-12	C+	160.50	106.95	C+ / 6.2	3.27%	B- / 7.8
2011	C+	158.70	93.33	C+ / 6.5	1.95%	B- / 7.5
2010	C	192.00	96.31	C+ / 6.1	27.84%	C / 4.9
2009	C-	195.61	75.60	C- / 3.5	36.46%	C / 5.5

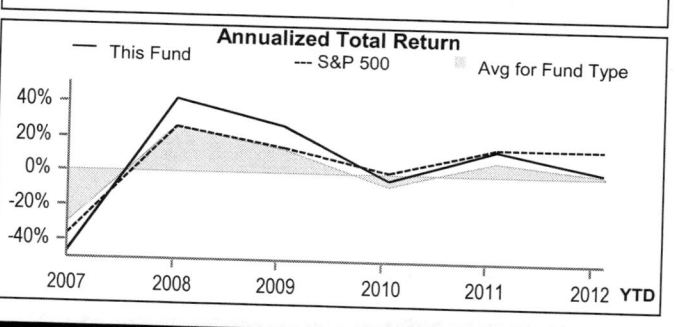

*iShares Morningstar Mid Value (JKI)

C+   **Fair**

Fund Family: BlackRock Fund Advisors
Fund Type: Growth
Inception Date: June 28, 2004

Major Rating Factors: Middle of the road best describes *iShares Morningstar Mid Value whose TheStreet.com Investment Rating is currently a C+ (Fair). The fund currently has a performance rating of C+ (Fair) based on an annualized return of 11.50% over the last three years and a total return of 3.80% year to date 2012. Factored into the performance evaluation is an expense ratio of 0.30% (very low).

The fund's risk rating is currently B- (Good). It carries a beta of 1.08, meaning that its performance tracks fairly well with that of the overall stock market. Volatility, as measured by both the semi-deviation and a drawdown factor, is considered low. As of December 31, 2012, *iShares Morningstar Mid Value traded at a discount of 3.67% below its net asset value, which is better than its one-year historical average discount of .02%.

Diane Hsiung has been running the fund for 5 years and currently receives a manager quality ranking of 46 (0=worst, 99=best). If you desire an average level of risk, then this fund may be an option.

Data Date	Investment Rating	Net Assets ($Mil)	Price	Performance Rating/Pts	Total Return Y-T-D	Risk Rating/Pts
12-12	C+	98.90	82.35	C+ / 6.1	3.80%	B- / 7.9
2011	C+	93.50	72.09	C+ / 5.7	1.42%	B- / 7.7
2010	C+	109.70	75.75	C+ / 6.5	20.46%	C+ / 5.6
2009	D+	69.65	64.71	D+ / 2.6	31.64%	C+ / 5.6

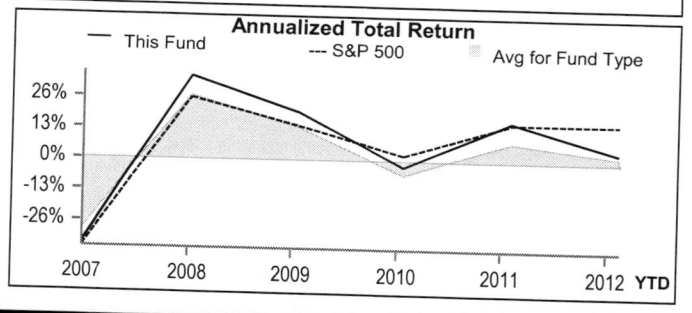

*iShares Morningstar Small Core (JKJ)

C   **Fair**

Fund Family: BlackRock Fund Advisors
Fund Type: Growth
Inception Date: June 28, 2004

Major Rating Factors: Middle of the road best describes *iShares Morningstar Small Core whose TheStreet.com Investment Rating is currently a C (Fair). The fund currently has a performance rating of C+ (Fair) based on an annualized return of 12.33% over the last three years and a total return of 3.74% year to date 2012. Factored into the performance evaluation is an expense ratio of 0.25% (very low).

The fund's risk rating is currently B- (Good). It carries a beta of 1.30, meaning it is expected to move 13.0% for every 10% move in the market. Volatility, as measured by both the semi-deviation and a drawdown factor, is considered low. As of December 31, 2012, *iShares Morningstar Small Core traded at a discount of 3.61% below its net asset value, which is better than its one-year historical average discount of .06%.

Diane Hsiung has been running the fund for 5 years and currently receives a manager quality ranking of 35 (0=worst, 99=best). If you desire an average level of risk, then this fund may be an option.

Data Date	Investment Rating	Net Assets ($Mil)	Price	Performance Rating/Pts	Total Return Y-T-D	Risk Rating/Pts
12-12	C	134.10	95.27	C+ / 6.0	3.74%	B- / 7.2
2011	C+	138.30	83.78	C+ / 6.4	1.73%	B- / 7.3
2010	B	173.60	89.11	B / 7.8	27.70%	C / 5.5
2009	D+	80.55	70.57	C- / 3.0	36.83%	C+ / 5.6

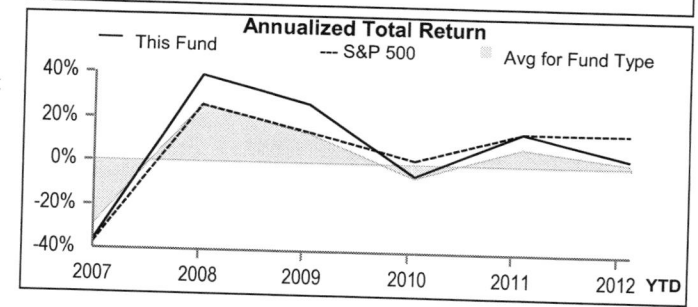

* Denotes ETF Fund

*iShares Morningstar Small Growth (JKK)

C+ | **Fair**

Fund Family: BlackRock Fund Advisors
Fund Type: Growth
Inception Date: June 28, 2004

Major Rating Factors: Middle of the road best describes *iShares Morningstar Small Growth whose TheStreet.com Investment Rating is currently a C+ (Fair). The fund currently has a performance rating of C+ (Fair) based on an annualized return of 14.98% over the last three years and a total return of 3.67% year to date 2012. Factored into the performance evaluation is an expense ratio of 0.30% (very low).

The fund's risk rating is currently B- (Good). It carries a beta of 1.26, meaning it is expected to move 12.6% for every 10% move in the market. Volatility, as measured by both the semi-deviation and a drawdown factor, is considered low. As of December 31, 2012, *iShares Morningstar Small Growth traded at a discount of 3.70% below its net asset value, which is better than its one-year historical average discount of .01%.

Diane Hsiung has been running the fund for 5 years and currently receives a manager quality ranking of 54 (0=worst, 99=best). If you desire an average level of risk, then this fund may be an option.

Data Date	Investment Rating	Net Assets ($Mil)	Price	Performance Rating/Pts	Total Return Y-T-D	Risk Rating/Pts
12-12	C+	89.20	93.85	C+ / 6.6	3.67%	B- / 7.1
2011	C+	83.20	83.29	C+ / 6.4	0.62%	C+ / 6.8
2010	B-	109.80	84.51	B- / 7.2	31.19%	C / 5.3
2009	D+	66.16	64.58	D+ / 2.8	29.95%	C / 5.3

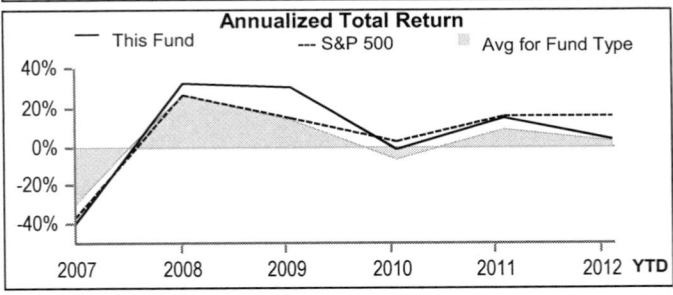

*iShares Morningstar Small Value (JKL)

C+ | **Fair**

Fund Family: BlackRock Fund Advisors
Fund Type: Growth
Inception Date: June 28, 2004

Major Rating Factors: Middle of the road best describes *iShares Morningstar Small Value whose TheStreet.com Investment Rating is currently a C+ (Fair). The fund currently has a performance rating of C+ (Fair) based on an annualized return of 13.47% over the last three years and a total return of 3.36% year to date 2012. Factored into the performance evaluation is an expense ratio of 0.30% (very low).

The fund's risk rating is currently B- (Good). It carries a beta of 1.19, meaning it is expected to move 11.9% for every 10% move in the market. Volatility, as measured by both the semi-deviation and a drawdown factor, is considered low. As of December 31, 2012, *iShares Morningstar Small Value traded at a discount of 3.27% below its net asset value, which is better than its one-year historical average discount of .01%.

Diane Hsiung has been running the fund for 5 years and currently receives a manager quality ranking of 54 (0=worst, 99=best). If you desire an average level of risk, then this fund may be an option.

Data Date	Investment Rating	Net Assets ($Mil)	Price	Performance Rating/Pts	Total Return Y-T-D	Risk Rating/Pts
12-12	C+	208.50	90.76	C+ / 6.7	3.36%	B- / 7.7
2011	C+	153.80	78.90	C+ / 6.7	1.66%	B- / 7.5
2010	B+	185.90	82.67	B / 8.0	25.80%	C+ / 5.6
2009	C-	65.09	67.02	C- / 3.6	36.72%	C / 5.5

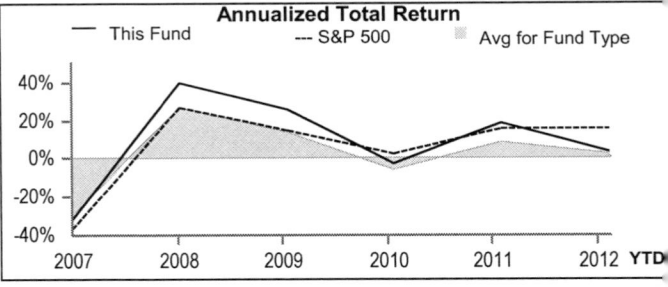

*iShares MSCI ACW Minimum Vol Ind (ACWV)

C+ | **Fair**

Fund Family: BlackRock Fund Advisors
Fund Type: Global
Inception Date: October 18, 2011

Major Rating Factors: Middle of the road best describes *iShares MSCI ACW Minimum Vol Ind whose TheStreet.com Investment Rating is currently a C+ (Fair). The fund currently has a performance rating of C (Fair) based on an annualized return of 0.00% over the last three years and a total return of 2.34% year to date 2012. Factored into the performance evaluation is an expense ratio of 0.23% (very low).

The fund's risk rating is currently B+ (Good). It carries a beta of 0.00, meaning the fund's expected move will be 0.0% for every 10% move in the market. Volatility, as measured by both the semi-deviation and a drawdown factor, is considered very low. As of December 31, 2012, *iShares MSCI ACW Minimum Vol Ind traded at a discount of 1.82% below its net asset value, which is better than its one-year historical average premium of .55%.

Greg Savage has been running the fund for 2 years and currently receives a manager quality ranking of 80 (0=worst, 99=best). If you desire an average level of risk, then this fund may be an option.

Data Date	Investment Rating	Net Assets ($Mil)	Price	Performance Rating/Pts	Total Return Y-T-D	Risk Rating/Pts
12-12	C+	648.00	55.63	C / 4.6	2.34%	B+ / 9.5

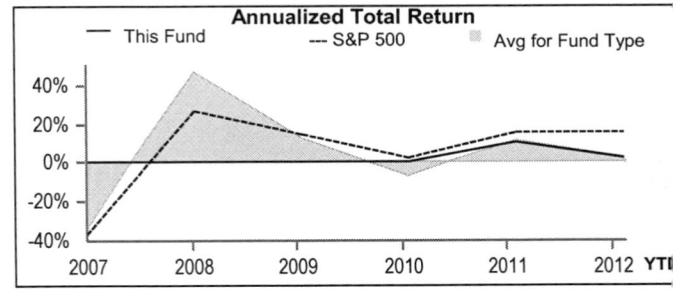

*iShares MSCI ACWI ex US Enrgy Id (AXEN)

D+ **Weak**

Fund Family: BlackRock Fund Advisors
Fund Type: Energy/Natural Resources
Inception Date: July 13, 2010

Data Date	Investment Rating	Net Assets ($Mil)	Price	Performance Rating/Pts	Total Return Y-T-D	Risk Rating/Pts
12-12	D+	5.40	53.92	C- / 3.1	2.58%	C+ / 6.6
2011	D	5.50	54.74	D / 1.7	3.05%	C+ / 6.9

Major Rating Factors: *iShares MSCI ACWI ex US Enrgy Id receives a TheStreet.com Investment Rating of D+ (Weak). The fund currently has a performance rating of C- (Fair) based on an annualized return of 0.00% over the last three years and a total return of 2.58% year to date 2012. Factored into the performance evaluation is an expense ratio of 0.48% (very low).

The fund's risk rating is currently C+ (Fair). It carries a beta of 0.00, meaning the fund's expected move will be 0.0% for every 10% move in the market. Volatility, as measured by both the semi-deviation and a drawdown factor, is considered low. As of December 31, 2012, *iShares MSCI ACWI ex US Enrgy Id traded at a discount of 2.92% below its net asset value, which is better than its one-year historical average discount of .11%.

Rene Casis has been running the fund for 3 years and currently receives a manager quality ranking of 26 (0=worst, 99=best). If you desire an average level of risk, then this fund may be an option.

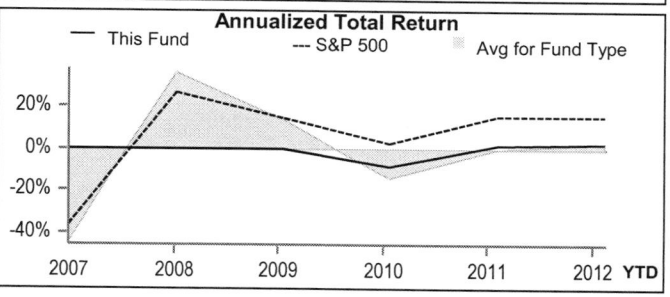

*iShares MSCI ACWI ex US Fn Sctr (AXFN)

B+ **Good**

Fund Family: BlackRock Fund Advisors
Fund Type: Financial Services
Inception Date: January 20, 2010

Data Date	Investment Rating	Net Assets ($Mil)	Price	Performance Rating/Pts	Total Return Y-T-D	Risk Rating/Pts
12-12	B+	1.20	23.40	A+ / 9.7	3.80%	C+ / 6.6
2011	D-	1.90	18.24	E+ / 0.7	0.05%	C+ / 6.7

Major Rating Factors:
Exceptional performance is the major factor driving the B+ (Good) TheStreet.com Investment Rating for *iShares MSCI ACWI ex US Fn Sctr. The fund currently has a performance rating of A+ (Excellent) based on an annualized return of 0.00% over the last three years and a total return of 3.80% year to date 2012. Factored into the performance evaluation is an expense ratio of 0.48% (very low).

The fund's risk rating is currently C+ (Fair). It carries a beta of 0.00, meaning the fund's expected move will be 0.0% for every 10% move in the market. Volatility, as measured by both the semi-deviation and a drawdown factor, is considered low. As of December 31, 2012, *iShares MSCI ACWI ex US Fn Sctr traded at a discount of 2.42% below its net asset value, which is better than its one-year historical average premium of .13%.

Rene Casis has been running the fund for 3 years and currently receives a manager quality ranking of 65 (0=worst, 99=best). If you desire only a moderate level of risk and strong performance, then this fund is an excellent option.

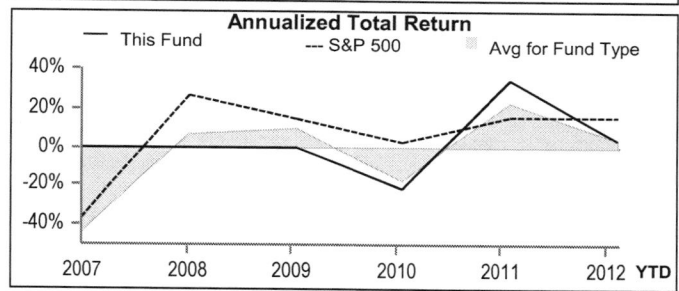

*iShares MSCI ACWI ex US HlthCre (AXHE)

A+ **Excellent**

Fund Family: BlackRock Fund Advisors
Fund Type: Health
Inception Date: July 13, 2010

Data Date	Investment Rating	Net Assets ($Mil)	Price	Performance Rating/Pts	Total Return Y-T-D	Risk Rating/Pts
12-12	A+	9.70	65.41	A / 9.3	4.45%	B / 8.4
2011	C-	8.50	56.07	D+ / 2.4	0.87%	B / 8.4

Major Rating Factors:
Exceptional performance is the major factor driving the A+ (Excellent) TheStreet.com Investment Rating for *iShares MSCI ACWI ex US HlthCre. The fund currently has a performance rating of A (Excellent) based on an annualized return of 0.00% over the last three years and a total return of 4.45% year to date 2012. Factored into the performance evaluation is an expense ratio of 0.48% (very low).

The fund's risk rating is currently B (Good). It carries a beta of 0.00, meaning the fund's expected move will be 0.0% for every 10% move in the market. Volatility, as measured by both the semi-deviation and a drawdown factor, is considered low. As of December 31, 2012, *iShares MSCI ACWI ex US HlthCre traded at a discount of 2.69% below its net asset value, which is better than its one-year historical average premium of .48%.

Rene Casis has been running the fund for 3 years and currently receives a manager quality ranking of 78 (0=worst, 99=best). If you desire only a moderate level of risk and strong performance, then this fund is an excellent option.

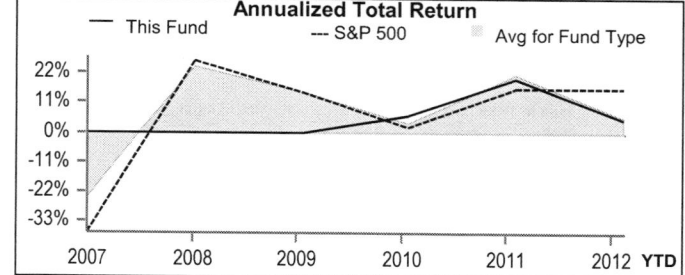

*iShares MSCI ACWI ex US Index (ACWX)   C-   Fair

Fund Family: BlackRock Fund Advisors
Fund Type: Foreign
Inception Date: March 26, 2008

Major Rating Factors: Middle of the road best describes *iShares MSCI ACWI ex US Index whose TheStreet.com Investment Rating is currently a C- (Fair). The fund currently has a performance rating of C- (Fair) based on an annualized return of 3.32% over the last three years and a total return of 1.96% year to date 2012. Factored into the performance evaluation is an expense ratio of 0.34% (very low).

The fund's risk rating is currently B- (Good). It carries a beta of 1.02, meaning that its performance tracks fairly well with that of the overall stock market. Volatility, as measured by both the semi-deviation and a drawdown factor, is considered low. As of December 31, 2012, *iShares MSCI ACWI ex US Index traded at a discount of 1.71% below its net asset value, which is better than its one-year historical average premium of .19%.

Diane Hsiung has been running the fund for 5 years and currently receives a manager quality ranking of 47 (0=worst, 99=best). If you desire an average level of risk, then this fund may be an option.

Data Date	Investment Rating	Net Assets ($Mil)	Price	Performance Rating/Pts	Total Return Y-T-D	Risk Rating/Pts
12-12	C-	1,276.00	41.88	C- / 3.7	1.96%	B- / 7.4
2011	D+	835.90	36.81	C- / 3.0	-0.65%	B- / 7.3
2010	B+	771.80	44.04	B+ / 8.9	10.44%	C / 5.0
2009	B+	270.64	40.91	B+ / 8.6	34.14%	C / 5.3

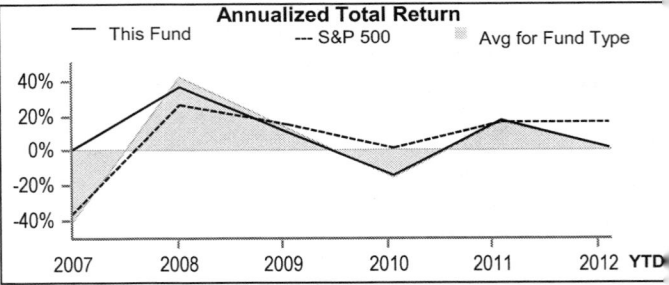

Annualized Total Return — This Fund — S&P 500 — Avg for Fund Type

*iShares MSCI ACWI ex US Indsl In (AXID)   B-   Good

Fund Family: BlackRock Fund Advisors
Fund Type: Foreign
Inception Date: July 13, 2010

Major Rating Factors: Strong performance is the major factor driving the B- (Good) TheStreet.com Investment Rating for *iShares MSCI ACWI ex US Indsl In. The fund currently has a performance rating of B (Good) based on an annualized return of 0.00% over the last three years and a total return of 3.68% year to date 2012. Factored into the performance evaluation is an expense ratio of 0.48% (very low).

The fund's risk rating is currently B- (Good). It carries a beta of 0.00, meaning the fund's expected move will be 0.0% for every 10% move in the market. Volatility, as measured by both the semi-deviation and a drawdown factor, is considered low. As of December 31, 2012, *iShares MSCI ACWI ex US Indsl In traded at a discount of 3.94% below its net asset value, which is better than its one-year historical average discount of .44%.

Rene Casis has been running the fund for 3 years and currently receives a manager quality ranking of 94 (0=worst, 99=best). If you desire only a moderate level of risk and strong performance, then this fund is an excellent option.

Data Date	Investment Rating	Net Assets ($Mil)	Price	Performance Rating/Pts	Total Return Y-T-D	Risk Rating/Pts
12-12	B-	2.80	55.86	B / 7.7	3.68%	B- / 7.0

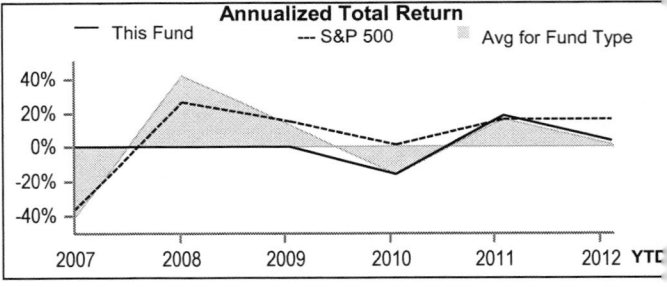

Annualized Total Return — This Fund — S&P 500 — Avg for Fund Type

*iShares MSCI ACWI ex US Mtls Ind (AXMT)   C   Fair

Fund Family: BlackRock Fund Advisors
Fund Type: Precious Metals
Inception Date: July 13, 2010

Major Rating Factors: Strong performance is the major factor driving the C (Fair) TheStreet.com Investment Rating for *iShares MSCI ACWI ex US Mtls Ind. The fund currently has a performance rating of B- (Good) based on an annualized return of 0.00% over the last three years and a total return of 1.31% year to date 2012. Factored into the performance evaluation is an expense ratio of 0.48% (very low).

The fund's risk rating is currently C+ (Fair). It carries a beta of 0.00, meaning the fund's expected move will be 0.0% for every 10% move in the market. Volatility, as measured by both the semi-deviation and a drawdown factor, is considered low. As of December 31, 2012, *iShares MSCI ACWI ex US Mtls Ind traded at a discount of 1.51% below its net asset value, which is better than its one-year historical average discount of .69%.

Rene Casis has been running the fund for 3 years and currently receives a manager quality ranking of 74 (0=worst, 99=best). If you desire only a moderate level of risk and strong performance, then this fund is an excellent option.

Data Date	Investment Rating	Net Assets ($Mil)	Price	Performance Rating/Pts	Total Return Y-T-D	Risk Rating/Pts
12-12	C	2.80	54.92	B- / 7.4	1.31%	C+ / 5.9
2011	D-	2.50	50.51	E+ / 0.8	3.88%	C+ / 6.5

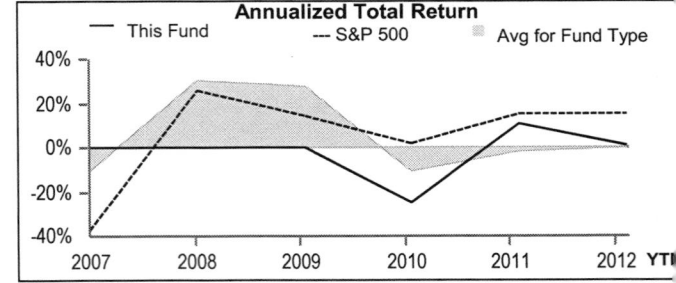

Annualized Total Return — This Fund — S&P 500 — Avg for Fund Type

*iShares MSCI ACWI ex US TS Index (AXTE)

D+   **Weak**

Fund Family: BlackRock Fund Advisors
Fund Type: Emerging Market
Inception Date: July 13, 2010

Major Rating Factors:
Disappointing performance is the major factor driving the D+ (Weak) TheStreet.com Investment Rating for *iShares MSCI ACWI ex US TS Index. The fund currently has a performance rating of D+ (Weak) based on an annualized return of 0.00% over the last three years and a total return of 3.00% year to date 2012. Factored into the performance evaluation is an expense ratio of 0.48% (very low).

The fund's risk rating is currently B- (Good). It carries a beta of 0.00, meaning the fund's expected move will be 0.0% for every 10% move in the market. Volatility, as measured by both the semi-deviation and a drawdown factor, is considered low. As of December 31, 2012, *iShares MSCI ACWI ex US TS Index traded at a discount of 2.10% below its net asset value, which is better than its one-year historical average premium of .03%.

Rene Casis has been running the fund for 3 years and currently receives a manager quality ranking of 29 (0=worst, 99=best). This fund offers only a moderate level of risk but investors looking for strong performance are still waiting.

Data Date	Investment Rating	Net Assets ($Mil)	Price	Perfor-mance Rating/Pts	Total Return Y-T-D	Risk Rating/Pts
12-12	D+	2.60	51.37	D+ / 2.4	3.00%	B- / 7.9

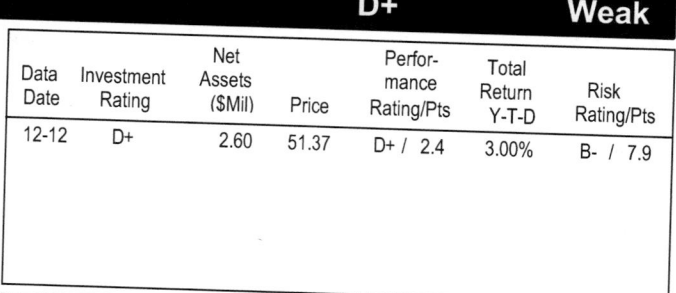

*iShares MSCI ACWI ex US Utl Sct (AXUT)

D+   **Weak**

Fund Family: BlackRock Fund Advisors
Fund Type: Utilities
Inception Date: July 13, 2010

Major Rating Factors:
Disappointing performance is the major factor driving the D+ (Weak) TheStreet.com Investment Rating for *iShares MSCI ACWI ex US Utl Sct. The fund currently has a performance rating of D+ (Weak) based on an annualized return of 0.00% over the last three years and a total return of 0.95% year to date 2012. Factored into the performance evaluation is an expense ratio of 0.48% (very low).

The fund's risk rating is currently B- (Good). It carries a beta of 0.00, meaning the fund's expected move will be 0.0% for every 10% move in the market. Volatility, as measured by both the semi-deviation and a drawdown factor, is considered low. As of December 31, 2012, *iShares MSCI ACWI ex US Utl Sct traded at a discount of 2.50% below its net asset value, which is better than its one-year historical average premium of .13%.

Rene Casis has been running the fund for 3 years and currently receives a manager quality ranking of 76 (0=worst, 99=best). This fund offers only a moderate level of risk but investors looking for strong performance are still waiting.

Data Date	Investment Rating	Net Assets ($Mil)	Price	Perfor-mance Rating/Pts	Total Return Y-T-D	Risk Rating/Pts
12-12	D+	6.30	41.26	D+ / 2.8	0.95%	B- / 7.0
2011	D	2.10	41.26	E+ / 0.8	1.14%	B- / 7.4

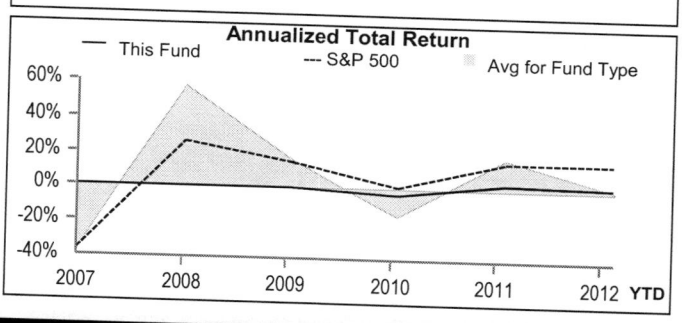

*iShares MSCI ACWI Index Fund (ACWI)

C-   **Fair**

Fund Family: BlackRock Fund Advisors
Fund Type: Global
Inception Date: March 26, 2008

Major Rating Factors: Middle of the road best describes *iShares MSCI ACWI Index Fund whose TheStreet.com Investment Rating is currently a C- (Fair). The fund currently has a performance rating of C- (Fair) based on an annualized return of 6.70% over the last three years and a total return of 2.48% year to date 2012. Factored into the performance evaluation is an expense ratio of 0.34% (very low).

The fund's risk rating is currently B- (Good). It carries a beta of 0.90, meaning that its performance tracks fairly well with that of the overall stock market. Volatility, as measured by both the semi-deviation and a drawdown factor, is considered low. As of December 31, 2012, *iShares MSCI ACWI Index Fund traded at a discount of 2.18% below its net asset value, which is better than its one-year historical average premium of .07%.

Diane Hsiung has been running the fund for 5 years and currently receives a manager quality ranking of 72 (0=worst, 99=best). If you desire an average level of risk, then this fund may be an option.

Data Date	Investment Rating	Net Assets ($Mil)	Price	Perfor-mance Rating/Pts	Total Return Y-T-D	Risk Rating/Pts
12-12	C-	3,262.00	48.08	C- / 4.2	2.48%	B- / 7.5
2011	C-	2,189.90	42.17	C- / 4.0	0.71%	B- / 7.6
2010	A-	1,501.30	46.81	A- / 9.0	12.82%	C+ / 5.6
2009	A-	492.82	42.29	B+ / 8.4	29.48%	C+ / 5.7

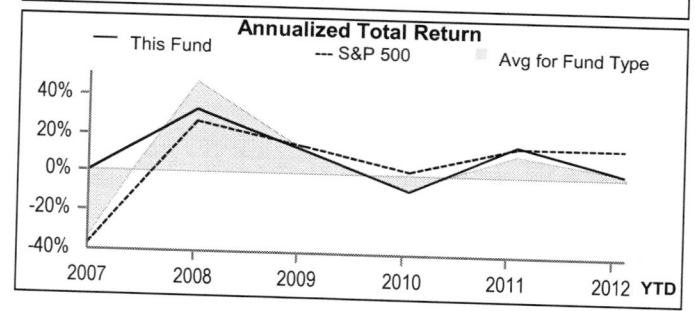

* Denotes ETF Fund

*iShares MSCI ACWI xUS Cnsmr Dis (AXDI)

B+ **Good**

Fund Family: BlackRock Fund Advisors
Fund Type: Foreign
Inception Date: July 13, 2010

Data Date	Investment Rating	Net Assets ($Mil)	Price	Performance Rating/Pts	Total Return Y-T-D	Risk Rating/Pts
12-12	B+	3.30	66.77	A- / 9.1	0.31%	B- / 7.1
2011	D	5.40	53.89	D- / 1.0	1.52%	B- / 7.1

Major Rating Factors:
Exceptional performance is the major factor driving the B+ (Good) TheStreet.com Investment Rating for *iShares MSCI ACWI xUS Cnsmr Dis. The fund currently has a performance rating of A- (Excellent) based on an annualized return of 0.00% over the last three years and a total return of 0.31% year to date 2012. Factored into the performance evaluation is an expense ratio of 0.48% (very low).

The fund's risk rating is currently B- (Good). It carries a beta of 0.00, meaning the fund's expected move will be 0.0% for every 10% move in the market. Volatility, as measured by both the semi-deviation and a drawdown factor, is considered low. As of December 31, 2012, *iShares MSCI ACWI xUS Cnsmr Dis traded at a discount of .89% below its net asset value, which is better than its one-year historical average discount of .31%.

Rene Casis has been running the fund for 3 years and currently receives a manager quality ranking of 91 (0=worst, 99=best). If you desire only a moderate level of risk and strong performance, then this fund is an excellent option.

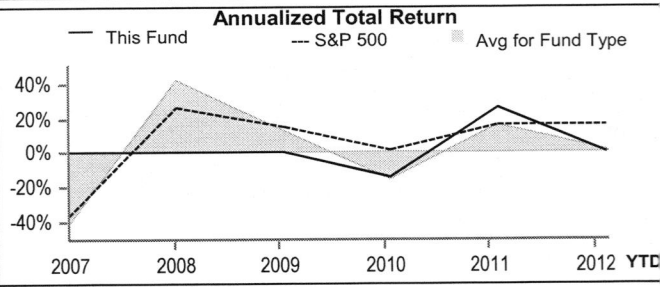

Annualized Total Return
— This Fund   --- S&P 500   Avg for Fund Type

*iShares MSCI ACWI xUS Cnsmr Stp (AXSL)

A- **Excellent**

Fund Family: BlackRock Fund Advisors
Fund Type: Foreign
Inception Date: July 13, 2010

Data Date	Investment Rating	Net Assets ($Mil)	Price	Performance Rating/Pts	Total Return Y-T-D	Risk Rating/Pts
12-12	A-	3.50	71.04	B / 8.2	2.20%	B / 8.6
2011	C-	3.10	62.17	C- / 3.3	-0.77%	B / 8.7

Major Rating Factors:
Strong performance is the major factor driving the A- (Excellent) TheStreet.com Investment Rating for *iShares MSCI ACWI xUS Cnsmr Stp. The fund currently has a performance rating of B (Good) based on an annualized return of 0.00% over the last three years and a total return of 2.20% year to date 2012. Factored into the performance evaluation is an expense ratio of 0.48% (very low).

The fund's risk rating is currently B (Good). It carries a beta of 0.00, meaning the fund's expected move will be 0.0% for every 10% move in the market. Volatility, as measured by both the semi-deviation and a drawdown factor, is considered low. As of December 31, 2012, *iShares MSCI ACWI xUS Cnsmr Stp traded at a discount of 1.36% below its net asset value, which is better than its one-year historical average premium of .18%.

Rene Casis has been running the fund for 3 years and currently receives a manager quality ranking of 88 (0=worst, 99=best). If you desire only a moderate level of risk and strong performance, then this fund is an excellent option.

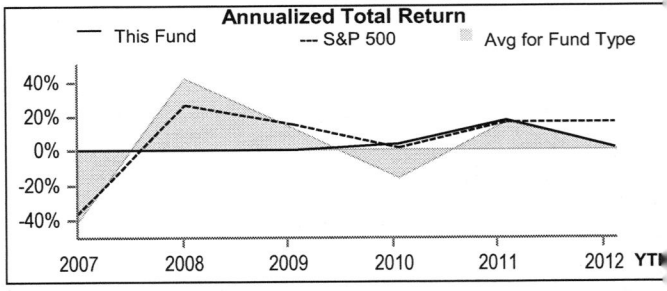

Annualized Total Return
— This Fund   --- S&P 500   Avg for Fund Type

*iShares MSCI All Cntry Asia ex J (AAXJ)

C- **Fair**

Fund Family: BlackRock Fund Advisors
Fund Type: Foreign
Inception Date: August 13, 2008

Data Date	Investment Rating	Net Assets ($Mil)	Price	Performance Rating/Pts	Total Return Y-T-D	Risk Rating/Pts
12-12	C-	2,128.30	60.52	C- / 3.9	0.48%	C+ / 6.9
2011	C-	2,006.60	49.90	C / 4.5	1.04%	B- / 7.1
2010	A-	2,657.90	63.70	A- / 9.0	16.22%	C+ / 6.0
2009	A+	1,045.35	55.71	A / 9.4	60.65%	C+ / 6.0

Major Rating Factors: Middle of the road best describes *iShares MSCI All Cntry Asia ex J whose TheStreet.com Investment Rating is currently a C- (Fair). The fund currently has a performance rating of C- (Fair) based on an annualized return of 4.13% over the last three years and a total return of 0.48% year to date 2012. Factored into the performance evaluation is an expense ratio of 0.69% (very low).

The fund's risk rating is currently C+ (Fair). It carries a beta of 0.99, meaning that its performance tracks fairly well with that of the overall stock market. Volatility, as measured by both the semi-deviation and a drawdown factor, is considered low. As of December 31, 2012, *iShares MSCI All Cntry Asia ex J traded at a discount of .03% below its net asset value, which is better than its one-year historical average premium of .10%.

Diane Hsiung has been running the fund for 5 years and currently receives a manager quality ranking of 58 (0=worst, 99=best). If you desire an average level of risk, then this fund may be an option.

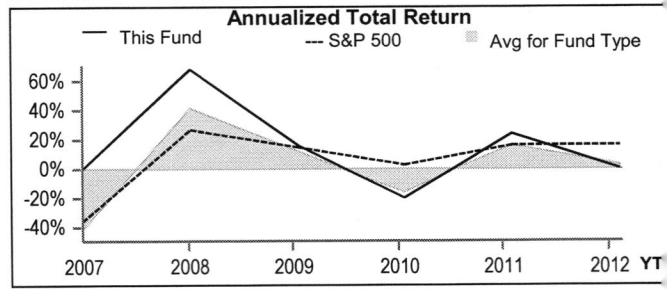

Annualized Total Return
— This Fund   --- S&P 500   Avg for Fund Type

*iShares MSCI All Peru Capped Idx (EPU)

C+   **Fair**

Fund Family: BlackRock Fund Advisors
Fund Type: Foreign
Inception Date: June 19, 2009

Major Rating Factors: Strong performance is the major factor driving the C+ (Fair) TheStreet.com Investment Rating for *iShares MSCI All Peru Capped Idx. The fund currently has a performance rating of B (Good) based on an annualized return of 15.53% over the last three years and a total return of 3.55% year to date 2012. Factored into the performance evaluation is an expense ratio of 0.51% (very low).

The fund's risk rating is currently C+ (Fair). It carries a beta of 0.69, meaning the fund's expected move will be 6.9% for every 10% move in the market. Volatility, as measured by both the semi-deviation and a drawdown factor, is considered low. As of December 31, 2012, *iShares MSCI All Peru Capped Idx traded at a discount of 3.10% below its net asset value, which is better than its one-year historical average discount of .11%.

Diane Hsiung has been running the fund for 4 years and currently receives a manager quality ranking of 92 (0=worst, 99=best). If you desire only a moderate level of risk and strong performance, then this fund is an excellent option.

Data Date	Investment Rating	Net Assets ($Mil)	Price	Performance Rating/Pts	Total Return Y-T-D	Risk Rating/Pts
12-12	C+	509.60	45.88	B / 7.7	3.55%	C+ / 6.7
2011	D	429.60	38.37	D- / 1.4	2.35%	B- / 7.4
2010	A+	556.20	50.36	A+ / 9.8	57.46%	B / 8.3

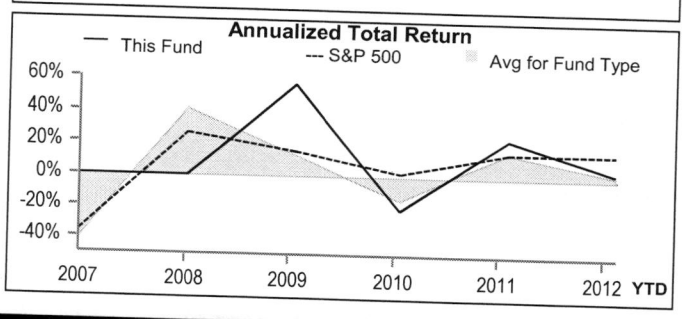

*iShares MSCI Australia (EWA)

C-   **Fair**

Fund Family: BlackRock Fund Advisors
Fund Type: Foreign
Inception Date: March 12, 1996

Major Rating Factors: Middle of the road best describes *iShares MSCI Australia whose TheStreet.com Investment Rating is currently a C- (Fair). The fund currently has a performance rating of C (Fair) based on an annualized return of 7.39% over the last three years and a total return of 1.27% year to date 2012. Factored into the performance evaluation is an expense ratio of 0.53% (very low).

The fund's risk rating is currently C+ (Fair). It carries a beta of 1.21, meaning it is expected to move 12.1% for every 10% move in the market. Volatility, as measured by both the semi-deviation and a drawdown factor, is considered low. As of December 31, 2012, *iShares MSCI Australia traded at a discount of 1.06% below its net asset value, which is better than its one-year historical average premium of .07%.

Diane Hsiung has been running the fund for 5 years and currently receives a manager quality ranking of 73 (0=worst, 99=best). If you desire an average level of risk, then this fund may be an option.

Data Date	Investment Rating	Net Assets ($Mil)	Price	Performance Rating/Pts	Total Return Y-T-D	Risk Rating/Pts
12-12	C-	2,387.70	25.14	C / 4.3	1.27%	C+ / 6.6
2011	C+	2,637.80	21.44	C+ / 6.3	1.49%	C+ / 6.9
2010	C-	2,958.40	25.44	C+ / 5.6	15.35%	C- / 4.1
2009	C+	1,593.68	22.84	B- / 7.4	66.12%	C / 4.3

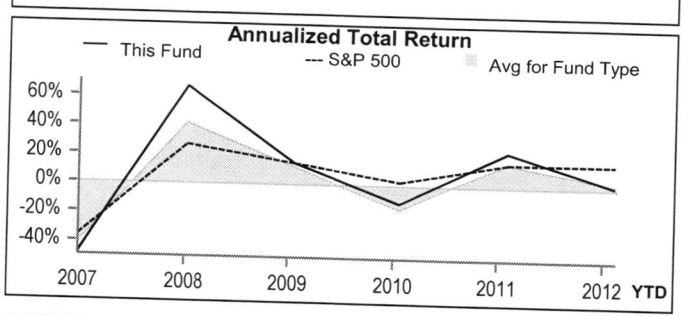

*iShares MSCI Austria Inv Mkt (EWO)

D   **Weak**

Fund Family: BlackRock Fund Advisors
Fund Type: Foreign
Inception Date: March 12, 1996

Major Rating Factors:
Disappointing performance is the major factor driving the D (Weak) TheStreet.com Investment Rating for *iShares MSCI Austria Inv Mkt. The fund currently has a performance rating of D+ (Weak) based on an annualized return of -2.18% over the last three years and a total return of 1.92% year to date 2012. Factored into the performance evaluation is an expense ratio of 0.52% (very low).

The fund's risk rating is currently C (Fair). It carries a beta of 1.42, meaning it is expected to move 14.2% for every 10% move in the market. Volatility, as measured by both the semi-deviation and a drawdown factor, is considered average. As of December 31, 2012, *iShares MSCI Austria Inv Mkt traded at a discount of 1.62% below its net asset value, which is better than its one-year historical average premium of .07%.

Diane Hsiung has been running the fund for 5 years and currently receives a manager quality ranking of 20 (0=worst, 99=best). This fund offers an average level of risk but investors looking for strong performance will be frustrated.

Data Date	Investment Rating	Net Assets ($Mil)	Price	Performance Rating/Pts	Total Return Y-T-D	Risk Rating/Pts
12-12	D	121.30	18.19	D+ / 2.9	1.92%	C / 5.4
2011	D-	53.90	14.22	D / 1.6	-3.31%	C+ / 5.7
2010	E+	119.50	22.33	D- / 1.3	15.81%	D+ / 2.8
2009	E+	159.67	19.56	D- / 1.2	52.05%	C- / 3.3

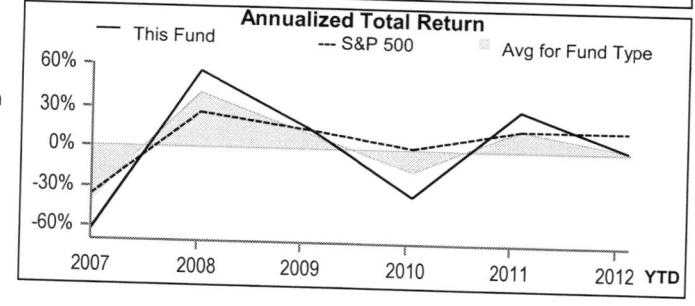

*iShares MSCI Belgium Cp Inv Mkt (EWK)

C   **Fair**

Fund Family: BlackRock Fund Advisors
Fund Type: Foreign
Inception Date: March 12, 1996

Major Rating Factors: Middle of the road best describes *iShares MSCI Belgium Cp Inv Mkt whose TheStreet.com Investment Rating is currently a C (Fair). The fund currently has a performance rating of C+ (Fair) based on an annualized return of 5.28% over the last three years and a total return of 1.37% year to date 2012. Factored into the performance evaluation is an expense ratio of 0.53% (very low).

The fund's risk rating is currently C+ (Fair). It carries a beta of 1.03, meaning that its performance tracks fairly well with that of the overall stock market. Volatility, as measured by both the semi-deviation and a drawdown factor, is considered low. As of December 31, 2012, *iShares MSCI Belgium Cp Inv Mkt traded at a discount of 1.07% below its net asset value, which is better than its one-year historical average premium of .13%.

Diane Hsiung has been running the fund for 5 years and currently receives a manager quality ranking of 67 (0=worst, 99=best). If you desire an average level of risk, then this fund may be an option.

Data Date	Investment Rating	Net Assets ($Mil)	Price	Performance Rating/Pts	Total Return Y-T-D	Risk Rating/Pts
12-12	C	57.20	13.85	C+ / 6.4	1.37%	C+ / 6.6
2011	D+	23.40	10.59	D+ / 2.6	-1.79%	C+ / 6.8
2010	E+	50.40	13.13	E+ / 0.7	5.07%	C- / 3.3
2009	E+	53.04	12.76	D- / 1.0	44.41%	C- / 4.0

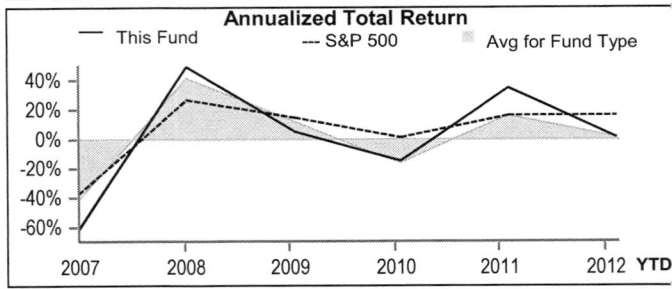

Annualized Total Return

*iShares MSCI Brazil (EWZ)

D-   **Weak**

Fund Family: BlackRock Fund Advisors
Fund Type: Foreign
Inception Date: July 10, 2000

Major Rating Factors:
Disappointing performance is the major factor driving the D- (Weak) TheStreet.com Investment Rating for *iShares MSCI Brazil. The fund currently has a performance rating of D- (Weak) based on an annualized return of -5.74% over the last three years and a total return of 0.84% year to date 2012. Factored into the performance evaluation is an expense ratio of 0.53% (very low).

The fund's risk rating is currently C+ (Fair). It carries a beta of 1.25, meaning it is expected to move 12.5% for every 10% move in the market. Volatility, as measured by both the semi-deviation and a drawdown factor, is considered low. As of December 31, 2012, *iShares MSCI Brazil traded at a discount of .85% below its net asset value, which is better than its one-year historical average discount of .04%.

Diane Hsiung has been running the fund for 5 years and currently receives a manager quality ranking of 12 (0=worst, 99=best). This fund offers only a moderate level of risk but investors looking for strong performance are still waiting.

Data Date	Investment Rating	Net Assets ($Mil)	Price	Performance Rating/Pts	Total Return Y-T-D	Risk Rating/Pts
12-12	D-	9,303.80	55.94	D- / 1.0	0.84%	C+ / 6.2
2011	C-	9,346.00	57.39	C / 4.9	1.97%	C+ / 6.5
2010	C-	11,699.30	77.40	C+ / 5.6	7.42%	C- / 3.6
2009	B-	8,777.37	74.61	B+ / 8.9	111.28%	C- / 4.2

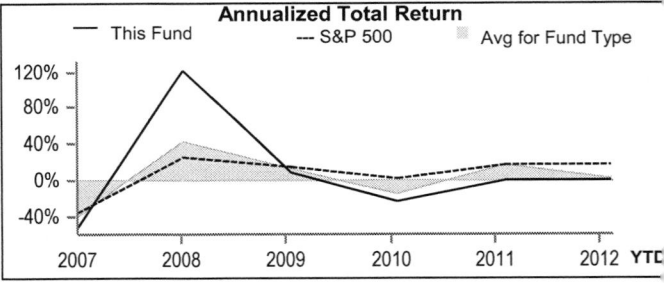

Annualized Total Return

*iShares MSCI Brazil Small Cap In (EWZS)

B   **Good**

Fund Family: BlackRock Fund Advisors
Fund Type: Foreign
Inception Date: September 28, 2010

Major Rating Factors:
Exceptional performance is the major factor driving the B (Good) TheStreet.com Investment Rating for *iShares MSCI Brazil Small Cap In. The fund currently has a performance rating of A (Excellent) based on an annualized return of 0.00% over the last three years and a total return of -0.25% year to date 2012. Factored into the performance evaluation is an expense ratio of 0.61% (very low).

The fund's risk rating is currently C+ (Fair). It carries a beta of 0.00, meaning the fund's expected move will be 0.0% for every 10% move in the market. Volatility, as measured by both the semi-deviation and a drawdown factor, is considered low. As of December 31, 2012, *iShares MSCI Brazil Small Cap In traded at a discount of .14% below its net asset value, which is worse than its one-year historical average discount of .16%.

Diane Hsiung has been running the fund for 3 years and currently receives a manager quality ranking of 76 (0=worst, 99=best). If you desire only a moderate level of risk and strong performance, then this fund is an excellent option.

Data Date	Investment Rating	Net Assets ($Mil)	Price	Performance Rating/Pts	Total Return Y-T-D	Risk Rating/Pts
12-12	B	55.00	27.80	A / 9.5	-0.25%	C+ / 6.1
2011	D-	45.30	22.41	E+ / 0.7	1.07%	C+ / 6.1

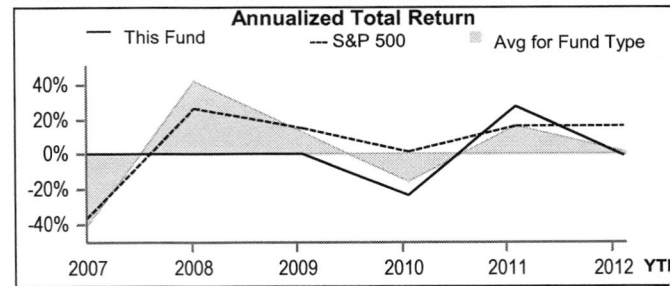

Annualized Total Return

*iShares MSCI BRIC (BKF)

D **Weak**

Fund Family: BlackRock Fund Advisors
Fund Type: Foreign
Inception Date: November 12, 2007

Major Rating Factors:

Disappointing performance is the major factor driving the D (Weak) TheStreet.com Investment Rating for *iShares MSCI BRIC. The fund currently has a performance rating of D (Weak) based on an annualized return of -1.72% over the last three years and a total return of 1.18% year to date 2012. Factored into the performance evaluation is an expense ratio of 0.69% (very low).

The fund's risk rating is currently C+ (Fair). It carries a beta of 1.14, meaning it is expected to move 11.4% for every 10% move in the market. Volatility, as measured by both the semi-deviation and a drawdown factor, is considered low. As of December 31, 2012, *iShares MSCI BRIC traded at a discount of .85% below its net asset value, which is better than its one-year historical average discount of .11%.

Diane Hsiung has been running the fund for 5 years and currently receives a manager quality ranking of 19 (0=worst, 99=best). This fund offers only a moderate level of risk but investors looking for strong performance are still waiting.

Data Date	Investment Rating	Net Assets ($Mil)	Price	Performance Rating/Pts	Total Return Y-T-D	Risk Rating/Pts
12-12	D	772.60	40.84	D / 1.8	1.18%	C+ / 6.4
2011	C-	683.90	36.27	C- / 4.0	1.96%	C+ / 6.7
2010	D-	1,188.10	49.13	D / 2.2	9.13%	C- / 4.0
2009	B+	497.84	45.85	A+ / 9.6	74.91%	C- / 4.0

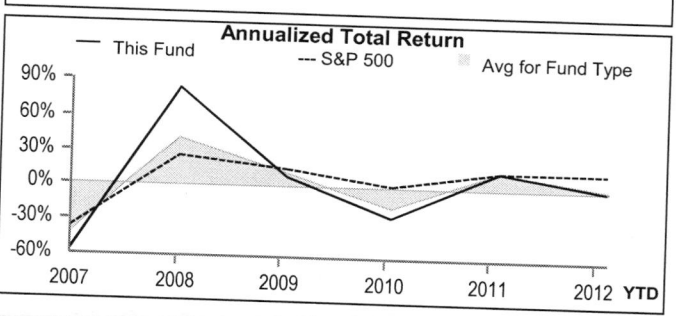

*iShares MSCI Canada (EWC)

D+ **Weak**

Fund Family: BlackRock Fund Advisors
Fund Type: Foreign
Inception Date: March 12, 1996

Major Rating Factors:

Disappointing performance is the major factor driving the D+ (Weak) TheStreet.com Investment Rating for *iShares MSCI Canada. The fund currently has a performance rating of D+ (Weak) based on an annualized return of 4.88% over the last three years and a total return of 2.29% year to date 2012. Factored into the performance evaluation is an expense ratio of 0.53% (very low).

The fund's risk rating is currently B- (Good). It carries a beta of 0.82, meaning the fund's expected move will be 8.2% for every 10% move in the market. Volatility, as measured by both the semi-deviation and a drawdown factor, is considered low. As of December 31, 2012, *iShares MSCI Canada traded at a discount of 2.41% below its net asset value, which is better than its one-year historical average discount of .10%.

Diane Hsiung has been running the fund for 5 years and currently receives a manager quality ranking of 62 (0=worst, 99=best). This fund offers only a moderate level of risk but investors looking for strong performance are still waiting.

Data Date	Investment Rating	Net Assets ($Mil)	Price	Performance Rating/Pts	Total Return Y-T-D	Risk Rating/Pts
12-12	D+	4,733.20	28.40	D+ / 2.9	2.29%	B- / 7.5
2011	C	4,471.00	26.60	C / 4.6	1.13%	B- / 7.4
2010	C	4,647.50	31.00	C+ / 5.6	19.80%	C / 5.0
2009	C+	2,393.64	26.33	C+ / 6.3	49.22%	C / 5.4

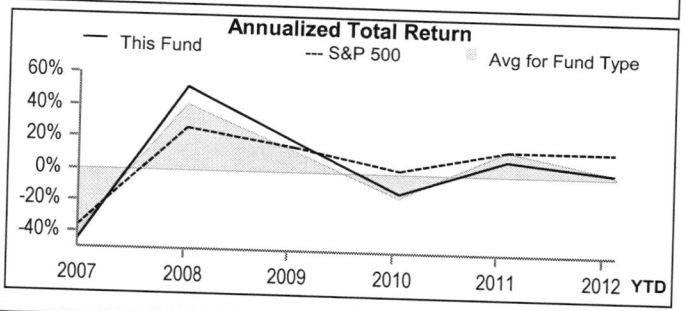

*iShares MSCI Chile Inv Market (ECH)

D **Weak**

Fund Family: BlackRock Fund Advisors
Fund Type: Foreign
Inception Date: November 12, 2007

Major Rating Factors:

Disappointing performance is the major factor driving the D (Weak) TheStreet.com Investment Rating for *iShares MSCI Chile Inv Market. The fund currently has a performance rating of D+ (Weak) based on an annualized return of 4.19% over the last three years and a total return of 3.26% year to date 2012. Factored into the performance evaluation is an expense ratio of 0.61% (very low).

The fund's risk rating is currently C+ (Fair). It carries a beta of 0.82, meaning the fund's expected move will be 8.2% for every 10% move in the market. Volatility, as measured by both the semi-deviation and a drawdown factor, is considered low. As of December 31, 2012, *iShares MSCI Chile Inv Market traded at a discount of 2.95% below its net asset value, which is better than its one-year historical average discount of .18%.

Diane Hsiung has been running the fund for 5 years and currently receives a manager quality ranking of 71 (0=worst, 99=best). This fund offers only a moderate level of risk but investors looking for strong performance are still waiting.

Data Date	Investment Rating	Net Assets ($Mil)	Price	Performance Rating/Pts	Total Return Y-T-D	Risk Rating/Pts
12-12	D	548.40	63.24	D+ / 2.7	3.26%	C+ / 6.4
2011	C+	505.80	57.71	C+ / 6.5	2.55%	C+ / 6.7
2010	A-	1,006.80	79.60	A / 9.3	46.59%	C+ / 5.6
2009	A+	263.21	54.79	A+ / 9.7	82.77%	C+ / 5.8

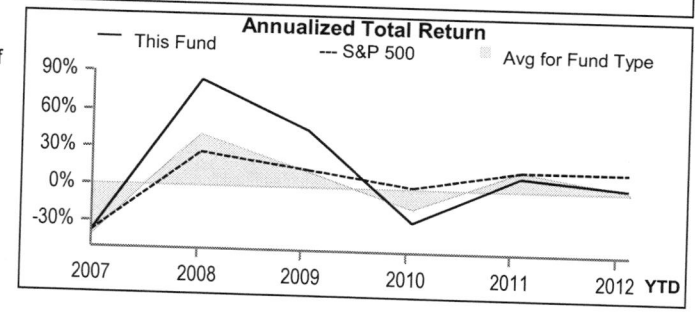

* Denotes ETF Fund

*iShares MSCI China Index (MCHI)   B   Good

Fund Family: BlackRock Fund Advisors
Fund Type: Foreign
Inception Date: March 29, 2011

Data Date	Investment Rating	Net Assets ($Mil)	Price	Performance Rating/Pts	Total Return Y-T-D	Risk Rating/Pts
12-12	B	831.30	48.54	A+ / 9.6	1.46%	C+ / 6.3

Major Rating Factors:
Exceptional performance is the major factor driving the B (Good) TheStreet.com Investment Rating for *iShares MSCI China Index. The fund currently has a performance rating of A+ (Excellent) based on an annualized return of 0.00% over the last three years and a total return of 1.46% year to date 2012. Factored into the performance evaluation is an expense ratio of 0.61% (very low).

The fund's risk rating is currently C+ (Fair). It carries a beta of 0.00, meaning the fund's expected move will be 0.0% for every 10% move in the market. Volatility, as measured by both the semi-deviation and a drawdown factor, is considered low. As of December 31, 2012, *iShares MSCI China Index traded at a discount of .65% below its net asset value, which is better than its one-year historical average premium of .25%.

Christopher Bliss has been running the fund for 2 years and currently receives a manager quality ranking of 84 (0=worst, 99=best). If you desire only a moderate level of risk and strong performance, then this fund is an excellent option.

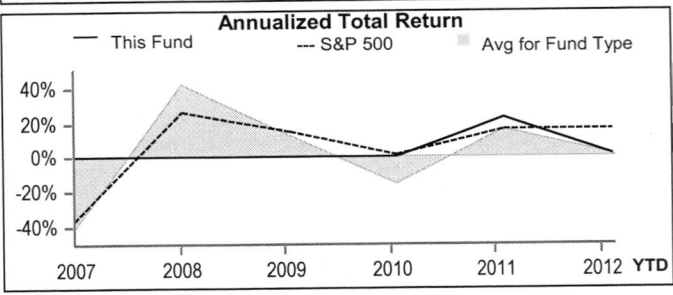

Annualized Total Return
— This Fund   --- S&P 500   Avg for Fund Type

*iShares MSCI China Small Cap Ind (ECNS)   B-   Good

Fund Family: BlackRock Fund Advisors
Fund Type: Foreign
Inception Date: September 28, 2010

Data Date	Investment Rating	Net Assets ($Mil)	Price	Performance Rating/Pts	Total Return Y-T-D	Risk Rating/Pts
12-12	B-	22.00	41.09	A+ / 9.8	5.82%	C / 5.2
2011	E+	15.10	33.19	E / 0.3	-1.02%	C / 5.2

Major Rating Factors:
Exceptional performance is the major factor driving the B- (Good) TheStreet.com Investment Rating for *iShares MSCI China Small Cap Ind. The fund currently has a performance rating of A+ (Excellent) based on an annualized return of 0.00% over the last three years and a total return of 5.82% year to date 2012. Factored into the performance evaluation is an expense ratio of 0.61% (very low).

The fund's risk rating is currently C (Fair). It carries a beta of 0.00, meaning the fund's expected move will be 0.0% for every 10% move in the market. Volatility, as measured by both the semi-deviation and a drawdown factor, is considered average. As of December 31, 2012, *iShares MSCI China Small Cap Ind traded at a discount of 3.93% below its net asset value, which is better than its one-year historical average discount of .26%.

Diane Hsiung has been running the fund for 3 years and currently receives a manager quality ranking of 91 (0=worst, 99=best). If you desire an average level of risk and strong performance, then this fund is a good option.

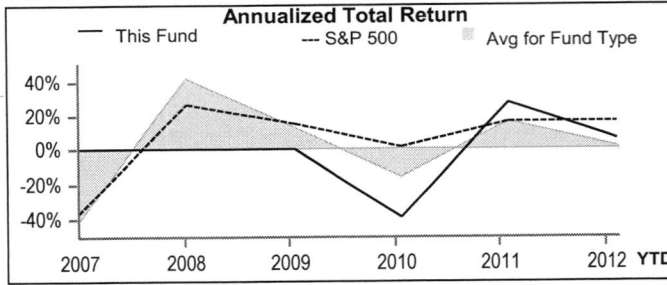

Annualized Total Return
— This Fund   --- S&P 500   Avg for Fund Type

*iShares MSCI EAFE (EFA)   C-   Fair

Fund Family: BlackRock Fund Advisors
Fund Type: Foreign
Inception Date: August 14, 2001

Data Date	Investment Rating	Net Assets ($Mil)	Price	Performance Rating/Pts	Total Return Y-T-D	Risk Rating/Pts
12-12	C-	38,814.70	56.86	C- / 4.1	2.08%	B- / 7.3
2011	D+	36,543.40	49.53	D+ / 2.6	-0.77%	B- / 7.4
2010	D	36,829.10	58.22	D / 1.7	8.25%	C / 5.2
2009	D	32,048.10	55.28	D / 2.0	25.26%	C / 5.0

Major Rating Factors: Middle of the road best describes *iShares MSCI EAFE whose TheStreet.com Investment Rating is currently a C- (Fair). The fund currently has a performance rating of C- (Fair) based on an annualized return of 3.74% over the last three years and a total return of 2.08% year to date 2012. Factored into the performance evaluation is an expense ratio of 0.34% (very low).

The fund's risk rating is currently B- (Good). It carries a beta of 1.02, meaning that its performance tracks fairly well with that of the overall stock market. Volatility, as measured by both the semi-deviation and a drawdown factor, is considered low. As of December 31, 2012, *iShares MSCI EAFE traded at a discount of 1.66% below its net asset value, which is better than its one-year historical average premium of .15%.

Diane Hsiung has been running the fund for 5 years and currently receives a manager quality ranking of 52 (0=worst, 99=best). If you desire an average level of risk, then this fund may be an option.

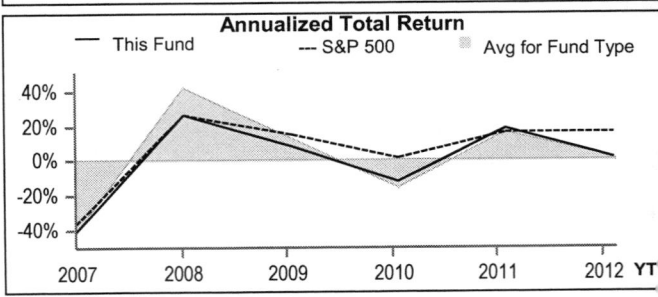

Annualized Total Return
— This Fund   --- S&P 500   Avg for Fund Type

*iShares MSCI EAFE Growth (EFG)

C-   **Fair**

Fund Family: BlackRock Fund Advisors
Fund Type: Foreign
Inception Date: August 1, 2005

Major Rating Factors: Middle of the road best describes *iShares MSCI EAFE Growth whose TheStreet.com Investment Rating is currently a C- (Fair). The fund currently has a performance rating of C- (Fair) based on an annualized return of 4.62% over the last three years and a total return of 1.43% year to date 2012. Factored into the performance evaluation is an expense ratio of 0.40% (very low).

The fund's risk rating is currently B- (Good). It carries a beta of 1.00, meaning that its performance tracks fairly well with that of the overall stock market. Volatility, as measured by both the semi-deviation and a drawdown factor, is considered low. As of December 31, 2012, *iShares MSCI EAFE Growth traded at a discount of 1.17% below its net asset value, which is better than its one-year historical average premium of .14%.

Diane Hsiung has been running the fund for 5 years and currently receives a manager quality ranking of 62 (0=worst, 99=best). If you desire an average level of risk, then this fund may be an option.

Data Date	Investment Rating	Net Assets ($Mil)	Price	Performance Rating/Pts	Total Return Y-T-D	Risk Rating/Pts
12-12	C-	1,375.90	60.04	C- / 3.9	1.43%	B- / 7.3
2011	D+	1,106.10	52.01	D+ / 2.8	0.00%	B- / 7.4
2010	D	1,338.40	61.08	D+ / 2.3	13.12%	C / 5.3
2009	D	1,198.70	55.12	D / 2.2	22.80%	C / 5.2

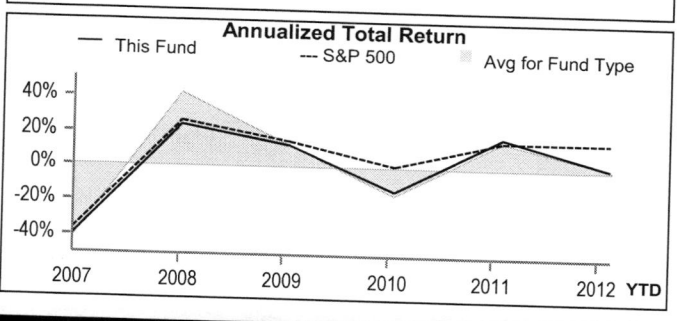

*iShares MSCI EAFE Minimum Vol Id (EFAV)

B-   **Good**

Fund Family: BlackRock Fund Advisors
Fund Type: Foreign
Inception Date: October 18, 2011

Major Rating Factors: *iShares MSCI EAFE Minimum Vol Id receives a TheStreet.com Investment Rating of B- (Good). The fund currently has a performance rating of C+ (Fair) based on an annualized return of 0.00% over the last three years and a total return of 0.42% year to date 2012. Factored into the performance evaluation is an expense ratio of 0.20% (very low).

The fund's risk rating is currently B+ (Good). It carries a beta of 0.00, meaning the fund's expected move will be 0.0% for every 10% move in the market. Volatility, as measured by both the semi-deviation and a drawdown factor, is considered very low. As of December 31, 2012, *iShares MSCI EAFE Minimum Vol Id traded at a discount of .46% below its net asset value, which is better than its one-year historical average premium of .55%.

Greg Savage has been running the fund for 2 years and currently receives a manager quality ranking of 54 (0=worst, 99=best). If you desire an average level of risk, then this fund may be an option.

Data Date	Investment Rating	Net Assets ($Mil)	Price	Performance Rating/Pts	Total Return Y-T-D	Risk Rating/Pts
12-12	B-	210.60	54.68	C+ / 5.7	0.42%	B+ / 9.0

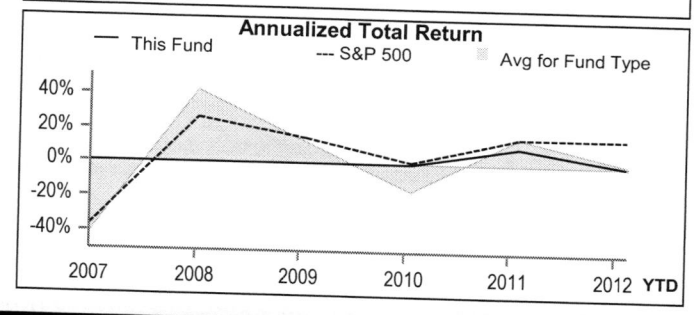

*iShares MSCI EAFE Small Cap Idx (SCZ)

C   **Fair**

Fund Family: BlackRock Fund Advisors
Fund Type: Foreign
Inception Date: December 10, 2007

Major Rating Factors: Middle of the road best describes *iShares MSCI EAFE Small Cap Idx whose TheStreet.com Investment Rating is currently a C (Fair). The fund currently has a performance rating of C (Fair) based on an annualized return of 7.12% over the last three years and a total return of 3.24% year to date 2012. Factored into the performance evaluation is an expense ratio of 0.40% (very low).

The fund's risk rating is currently B- (Good). It carries a beta of 1.02, meaning that its performance tracks fairly well with that of the overall stock market. Volatility, as measured by both the semi-deviation and a drawdown factor, is considered low. As of December 31, 2012, *iShares MSCI EAFE Small Cap Idx traded at a discount of 2.44% below its net asset value, which is better than its one-year historical average premium of .16%.

Diane Hsiung has been running the fund for 5 years and currently receives a manager quality ranking of 74 (0=worst, 99=best). If you desire an average level of risk, then this fund may be an option.

Data Date	Investment Rating	Net Assets ($Mil)	Price	Performance Rating/Pts	Total Return Y-T-D	Risk Rating/Pts
12-12	C	1,619.00	40.71	C / 5.5	3.24%	B- / 7.7
2011	C-	1,231.60	34.76	C- / 3.9	-0.03%	B- / 7.9
2010	C-	1,373.40	42.21	C / 4.4	21.51%	C / 5.3
2009	A-	378.00	35.81	B+ / 8.7	41.30%	C / 5.5

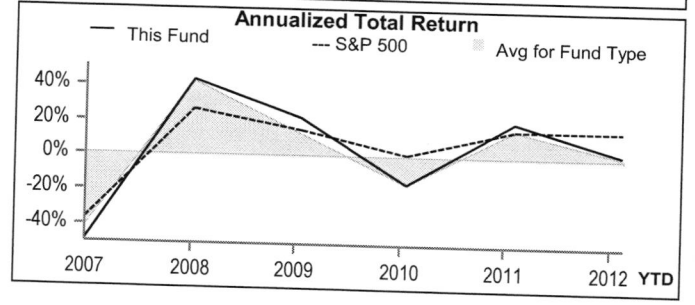

*iShares MSCI EAFE Value (EFV)

C-   **Fair**

Fund Family: BlackRock Fund Advisors
Fund Type: Foreign
Inception Date: August 1, 2005

Major Rating Factors: Middle of the road best describes *iShares MSCI EAFE Value whose TheStreet.com Investment Rating is currently a C- (Fair). The fund currently has a performance rating of C- (Fair) based on an annualized return of 2.70% over the last three years and a total return of 3.29% year to date 2012. Factored into the performance evaluation is an expense ratio of 0.40% (very low).

The fund's risk rating is currently C+ (Fair). It carries a beta of 1.06, meaning that its performance tracks fairly well with that of the overall stock market. Volatility, as measured by both the semi-deviation and a drawdown factor, is considered low. As of December 31, 2012, *iShares MSCI EAFE Value traded at a discount of 2.66% below its net asset value, which is better than its one-year historical average premium of .25%.

Diane Hsiung has been running the fund for 5 years and currently receives a manager quality ranking of 40 (0=worst, 99=best). If you desire an average level of risk, then this fund may be an option.

Data Date	Investment Rating	Net Assets ($Mil)	Price	Performance Rating/Pts	Total Return Y-T-D	Risk Rating/Pts
12-12	C-	1,613.90	48.64	C- / 4.2	3.29%	C+ / 6.9
2011	D+	1,210.30	42.70	D+ / 2.3	-1.10%	B- / 7.2
2010	D-	1,355.20	50.77	D- / 1.4	4.59%	C / 4.7
2009	D-	1,142.40	50.34	D / 1.7	26.53%	C / 4.8

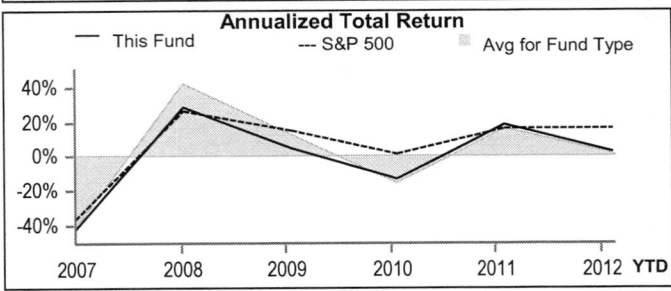

Annualized Total Return — This Fund — S&P 500 — Avg for Fund Type

*IShares MSCI EM Eastern Europe (ESR)

D-   **Weak**

Fund Family: BlackRock Fund Advisors
Fund Type: Emerging Market
Inception Date: September 30, 2009

Major Rating Factors:
Disappointing performance is the major factor driving the D- (Weak) TheStreet.com Investment Rating for *IShares MSCI EM Eastern Europe. The fund currently has a performance rating of D+ (Weak) based on an annualized return of 0.42% over the last three years and a total return of -0.11% year to date 2012. Factored into the performance evaluation is an expense ratio of 0.69% (very low).

The fund's risk rating is currently C (Fair). It carries a beta of 1.35, meaning it is expected to move 13.5% for every 10% move in the market. Volatility, as measured by both the semi-deviation and a drawdown factor, is considered average. As of December 31, 2012, *IShares MSCI EM Eastern Europe traded at a premium of .45% above its net asset value, which is worse than its one-year historical average premium of .07%.

Diane Hsiung has been running the fund for 4 years and currently receives a manager quality ranking of 25 (0=worst, 99=best). This fund offers an average level of risk but investors looking for strong performance will be frustrated.

Data Date	Investment Rating	Net Assets ($Mil)	Price	Performance Rating/Pts	Total Return Y-T-D	Risk Rating/Pts
12-12	D-	17.10	27.06	D+ / 2.3	-0.11%	C / 5.3
2011	D-	22.30	23.52	E+ / 0.7	1.07%	C+ / 5.7
2010	A+	18.80	31.66	A / 9.4	17.16%	B- / 7.2

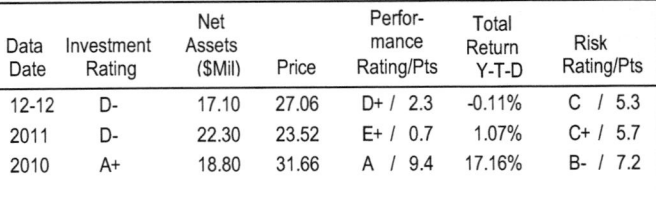

Annualized Total Return — This Fund — S&P 500 — Avg for Fund Type

*iShares MSCI Emerging Markets (EEM)

D+   **Weak**

Fund Family: BlackRock Fund Advisors
Fund Type: Emerging Market
Inception Date: April 7, 2003

Major Rating Factors:
Disappointing performance is the major factor driving the D+ (Weak) TheStreet.com Investment Rating for *iShares MSCI Emerging Markets. The fund currently has a performance rating of D+ (Weak) based on an annualized return of 3.76% over the last three years and a total return of 0.27% year to date 2012. Factored into the performance evaluation is an expense ratio of 0.68% (very low).

The fund's risk rating is currently C+ (Fair). It carries a beta of 1.07, meaning that its performance tracks fairly well with that of the overall stock market. Volatility, as measured by both the semi-deviation and a drawdown factor, is considered low. As of December 31, 2012, *iShares MSCI Emerging Markets traded at a premium of .05% above its net asset value, which is better than its one-year historical average premium of .18%.

Diane Hsiung has been running the fund for 5 years and currently receives a manager quality ranking of 41 (0=worst, 99=best). This fund offers only a moderate level of risk but investors looking for strong performance are still waiting.

Data Date	Investment Rating	Net Assets ($Mil)	Price	Performance Rating/Pts	Total Return Y-T-D	Risk Rating/Pts
12-12	D+	48,189.60	44.35	D+ / 2.9	0.27%	C+ / 6.8
2011	C-	32,493.30	37.94	C / 4.5	0.75%	B- / 7.5
2010	D+	47,459.00	47.64	C / 5.3	16.47%	D+ / 2.7
2009	C	30,268.12	41.50	B- / 7.2	61.14%	C- / 3.1

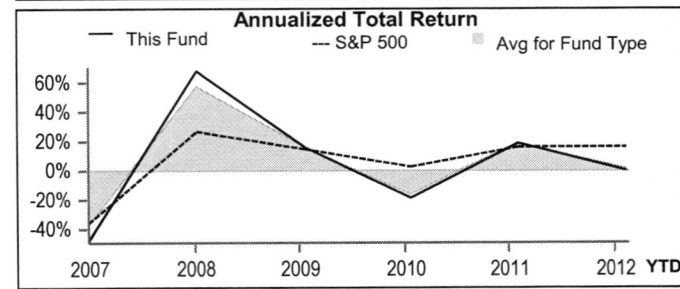

Annualized Total Return — This Fund — S&P 500 — Avg for Fund Type

*iShares MSCI Emg Mkts Finls Sctr (EMFN)

B+   **Good**

Fund Family: BlackRock Fund Advisors
Fund Type: Emerging Market
Inception Date: January 20, 2010

Major Rating Factors:
Exceptional performance is the major factor driving the B+ (Good) TheStreet.com Investment Rating for *iShares MSCI Emg Mkts Finls Sctr. The fund currently has a performance rating of A+ (Excellent) based on an annualized return of 0.00% over the last three years and a total return of 0.00% year to date 2012. Factored into the performance evaluation is an expense ratio of 0.69% (very low).

The fund's risk rating is currently C+ (Fair). It carries a beta of 0.00, meaning the fund's expected move will be 0.0% for every 10% move in the market. Volatility, as measured by both the semi-deviation and a drawdown factor, is considered low. As of December 31, 2012, *iShares MSCI Emg Mkts Finls Sctr traded at a premium of .58% above its net asset value, which is worse than its one-year historical average premium of .44%.

Rene Casis has been running the fund for 3 years and currently receives a manager quality ranking of 94 (0=worst, 99=best). If you desire only a moderate level of risk and strong performance, then this fund is an excellent option.

Data Date	Investment Rating	Net Assets ($Mil)	Price	Performance Rating/Pts	Total Return Y-T-D	Risk Rating/Pts
12-12	B+	4.00	27.65	A+ / 9.7	0.00%	C+ / 6.6
2011	D-	3.10	20.87	D- / 1.0	5.03%	C+ / 6.6

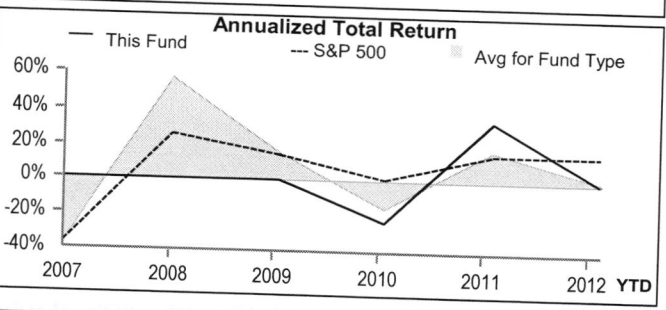

*iShares MSCI Emg Mkts Matl Sctr (EMMT)

C+   **Fair**

Fund Family: BlackRock Fund Advisors
Fund Type: Emerging Market
Inception Date: January 20, 2010

Major Rating Factors: Strong performance is the major factor driving the C+ (Fair) TheStreet.com Investment Rating for *iShares MSCI Emg Mkts Matl Sctr. The fund currently has a performance rating of B+ (Good) based on an annualized return of 0.00% over the last three years and a total return of 2.46% year to date 2012. Factored into the performance evaluation is an expense ratio of 0.69% (very low).

The fund's risk rating is currently C+ (Fair). It carries a beta of 0.00, meaning the fund's expected move will be 0.0% for every 10% move in the market. Volatility, as measured by both the semi-deviation and a drawdown factor, is considered low. As of December 31, 2012, *iShares MSCI Emg Mkts Matl Sctr traded at a discount of 2.04% below its net asset value, which is better than its one-year historical average discount of .59%.

Rene Casis has been running the fund for 3 years and currently receives a manager quality ranking of 14 (0=worst, 99=best). If you desire only a moderate level of risk and strong performance, then this fund is an excellent option.

Data Date	Investment Rating	Net Assets ($Mil)	Price	Performance Rating/Pts	Total Return Y-T-D	Risk Rating/Pts
12-12	C+	5.30	21.18	B+ / 8.3	2.46%	C+ / 5.9
2011	D-	7.80	19.29	E+ / 0.6	2.18%	C+ / 6.2

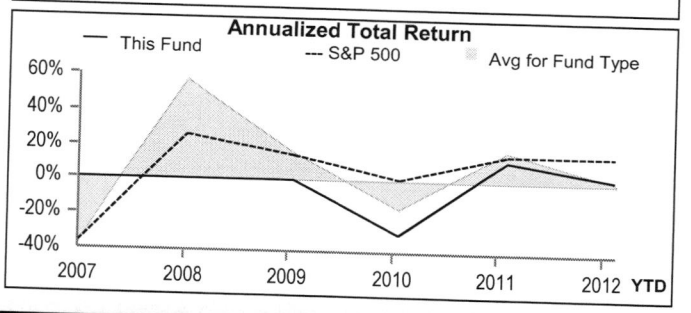

*iShares MSCI Emg Mkts Min Vol In (EEMV)

A   **Excellent**

Fund Family: BlackRock Fund Advisors
Fund Type: Emerging Market
Inception Date: October 18, 2011

Major Rating Factors:
Strong performance is the major factor driving the A (Excellent) TheStreet.com Investment Rating for *iShares MSCI Emg Mkts Min Vol In. The fund currently has a performance rating of B+ (Good) based on an annualized return of 0.00% over the last three years and a total return of 0.23% year to date 2012. Factored into the performance evaluation is an expense ratio of 0.25% (very low).

The fund's risk rating is currently B (Good). It carries a beta of 0.00, meaning the fund's expected move will be 0.0% for every 10% move in the market. Volatility, as measured by both the semi-deviation and a drawdown factor, is considered low. As of December 31, 2012, *iShares MSCI Emg Mkts Min Vol In traded at a premium of .25% above its net asset value, which is better than its one-year historical average premium of .43%.

Christopher Bliss has been running the fund for 2 years and currently receives a manager quality ranking of 88 (0=worst, 99=best). If you desire only a moderate level of risk and strong performance, then this fund is an excellent option.

Data Date	Investment Rating	Net Assets ($Mil)	Price	Performance Rating/Pts	Total Return Y-T-D	Risk Rating/Pts
12-12	A	846.60	60.56	B+ / 8.7	0.23%	B / 8.7

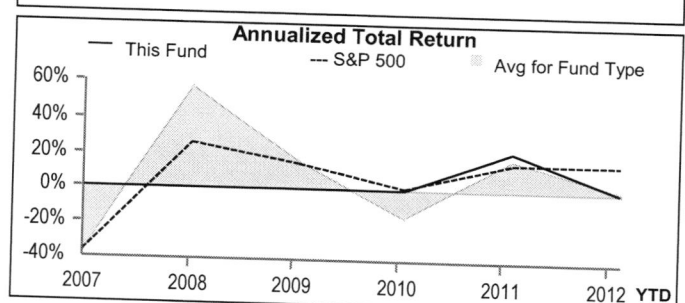

* Denotes ETF Fund

*iShares MSCI Emg Mkts Sm Cap Ind (EEMS)   B+   Good

Fund Family: BlackRock Fund Advisors
Fund Type: Emerging Market
Inception Date: August 16, 2011

Data Date	Investment Rating	Net Assets ($Mil)	Price	Performance Rating/Pts	Total Return Y-T-D	Risk Rating/Pts
12-12	B+	9.40	47.30	A / 9.3	3.34%	B- / 7.3

Major Rating Factors:
Exceptional performance is the major factor driving the B+ (Good) TheStreet.com Investment Rating for *iShares MSCI Emg Mkts Sm Cap Ind. The fund currently has a performance rating of A (Excellent) based on an annualized return of 0.00% over the last three years and a total return of 3.34% year to date 2012. Factored into the performance evaluation is an expense ratio of 0.69% (very low).

The fund's risk rating is currently B- (Good). It carries a beta of 0.00, meaning the fund's expected move will be 0.0% for every 10% move in the market. Volatility, as measured by both the semi-deviation and a drawdown factor, is considered low. As of December 31, 2012, *iShares MSCI Emg Mkts Sm Cap Ind traded at a discount of 3.11% below its net asset value.

Christopher Bliss has been running the fund for 2 years and currently receives a manager quality ranking of 69 (0=worst, 99=best). If you desire only a moderate level of risk and strong performance, then this fund is an excellent option.

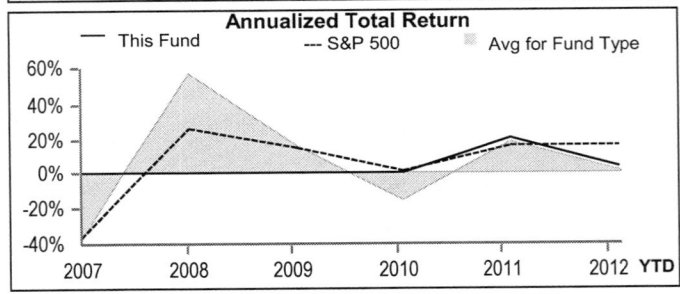

---

*iShares MSCI EMU (EZU)   D   Weak

Fund Family: BlackRock Fund Advisors
Fund Type: Foreign
Inception Date: July 25, 2000

Data Date	Investment Rating	Net Assets ($Mil)	Price	Performance Rating/Pts	Total Return Y-T-D	Risk Rating/Pts
12-12	D	2,195.00	33.46	D+ / 2.9	2.36%	C+ / 6.1
2011	D	624.10	27.90	D- / 1.5	-2.15%	C+ / 6.4
2010	E	741.50	35.27	E+ / 0.8	-3.00%	D+ / 2.8
2009	E+	741.27	37.47	D / 1.9	24.42%	D+ / 2.9

Major Rating Factors:
Disappointing performance is the major factor driving the D (Weak) TheStreet.com Investment Rating for *iShares MSCI EMU. The fund currently has a performance rating of D+ (Weak) based on an annualized return of -0.15% over the last three years and a total return of 2.36% year to date 2012. Factored into the performance evaluation is an expense ratio of 0.53% (very low).

The fund's risk rating is currently C+ (Fair). It carries a beta of 1.34, meaning it is expected to move 13.4% for every 10% move in the market. Volatility, as measured by both the semi-deviation and a drawdown factor, is considered low. As of December 31, 2012, *iShares MSCI EMU traded at a discount of 1.96% below its net asset value, which is better than its one-year historical average premium of .11%.

Diane Hsiung has been running the fund for 5 years and currently receives a manager quality ranking of 20 (0=worst, 99=best). This fund offers only a moderate level of risk but investors looking for strong performance are still waiting.

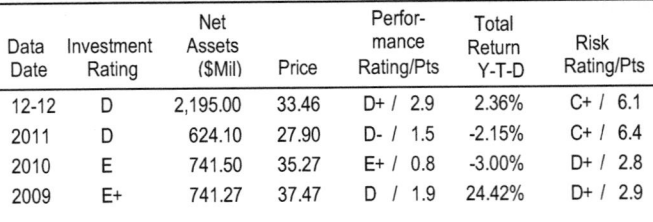

---

*iShares MSCI Europ Finls Sctr Id (EUFN)   B-   Good

Fund Family: BlackRock Fund Advisors
Fund Type: Financial Services
Inception Date: January 20, 2010

Data Date	Investment Rating	Net Assets ($Mil)	Price	Performance Rating/Pts	Total Return Y-T-D	Risk Rating/Pts
12-12	B-	33.00	19.80	A+ / 9.9	6.01%	C / 5.2
2011	E+	20.40	15.15	E / 0.4	-4.57%	C+ / 5.6

Major Rating Factors:
Exceptional performance is the major factor driving the B- (Good) TheStreet.com Investment Rating for *iShares MSCI Europ Finls Sctr Id. The fund currently has a performance rating of A+ (Excellent) based on an annualized return of 0.00% over the last three years and a total return of 6.01% year to date 2012. Factored into the performance evaluation is an expense ratio of 0.48% (very low).

The fund's risk rating is currently C (Fair). It carries a beta of 0.00, meaning the fund's expected move will be 0.0% for every 10% move in the market. Volatility, as measured by both the semi-deviation and a drawdown factor, is considered average. As of December 31, 2012, *iShares MSCI Europ Finls Sctr Id traded at a discount of 5.17% below its net asset value, which is better than its one-year historical average premium of .14%.

Rene Casis has been running the fund for 3 years and currently receives a manager quality ranking of 18 (0=worst, 99=best). If you desire an average level of risk and strong performance, then this fund is a good option.

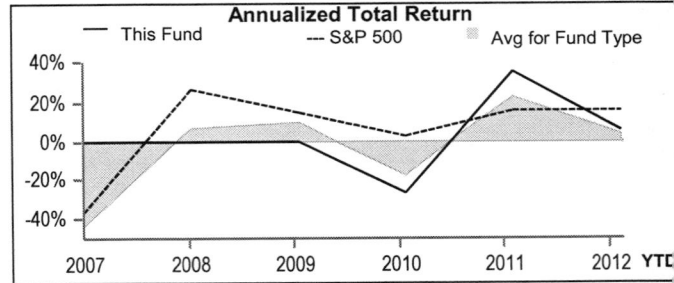

---

*iShares MSCI France (EWQ)

D　　　**Weak**

Fund Family: BlackRock Fund Advisors
Fund Type: Foreign
Inception Date: March 12, 1996

Major Rating Factors:

Disappointing performance is the major factor driving the D (Weak) TheStreet.com Investment Rating for *iShares MSCI France. The fund currently has a performance rating of D+ (Weak) based on an annualized return of -0.54% over the last three years and a total return of 0.93% year to date 2012. Factored into the performance evaluation is an expense ratio of 0.53% (very low).

The fund's risk rating is currently C+ (Fair). It carries a beta of 1.31, meaning it is expected to move 13.1% for every 10% move in the market. Volatility, as measured by both the semi-deviation and a drawdown factor, is considered low. As of December 31, 2012, *iShares MSCI France traded at a discount of .84% below its net asset value, which is better than its one-year historical average premium of .09%.

Diane Hsiung has been running the fund for 5 years and currently receives a manager quality ranking of 22 (0=worst, 99=best). This fund offers only a moderate level of risk but investors looking for strong performance are still waiting.

Data Date	Investment Rating	Net Assets ($Mil)	Price	Performance Rating/Pts	Total Return Y-T-D	Risk Rating/Pts
12-12	D	448.20	23.59	D+ / 2.6	0.93%	C+ / 6.0
2011	D	251.40	19.58	D- / 1.5	-2.71%	C+ / 6.3
2010	D-	286.50	24.45	D- / 1.0	-2.38%	C / 4.3
2009	D	184.51	25.85	D / 2.2	24.15%	C / 4.7

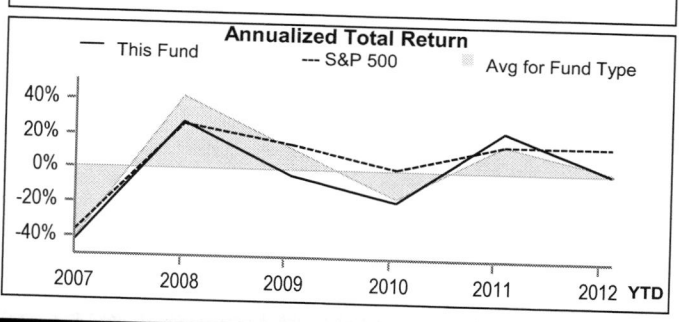

*iShares MSCI Germany (EWG)

C　　　**Fair**

Fund Family: BlackRock Fund Advisors
Fund Type: Foreign
Inception Date: March 12, 1996

Major Rating Factors: Middle of the road best describes *iShares MSCI Germany whose TheStreet.com Investment Rating is currently a C (Fair). The fund currently has a performance rating of C+ (Fair) based on an annualized return of 6.29% over the last three years and a total return of 1.54% year to date 2012. Factored into the performance evaluation is an expense ratio of 0.53% (very low).

The fund's risk rating is currently C+ (Fair). It carries a beta of 1.35, meaning it is expected to move 13.5% for every 10% move in the market. Volatility, as measured by both the semi-deviation and a drawdown factor, is considered low. As of December 31, 2012, *iShares MSCI Germany traded at a discount of 1.44% below its net asset value, which is better than its one-year historical average premium of .06%.

Diane Hsiung has been running the fund for 5 years and currently receives a manager quality ranking of 55 (0=worst, 99=best). If you desire an average level of risk, then this fund may be an option.

Data Date	Investment Rating	Net Assets ($Mil)	Price	Performance Rating/Pts	Total Return Y-T-D	Risk Rating/Pts
12-12	C	3,991.80	24.70	C+ / 6.4	1.54%	C+ / 6.2
2011	D	2,313.50	19.22	D / 2.0	0.36%	C+ / 6.3
2010	D-	1,892.70	23.94	D- / 1.3	8.31%	C / 4.7
2009	D	619.64	22.44	D+ / 2.8	19.62%	C- / 4.2

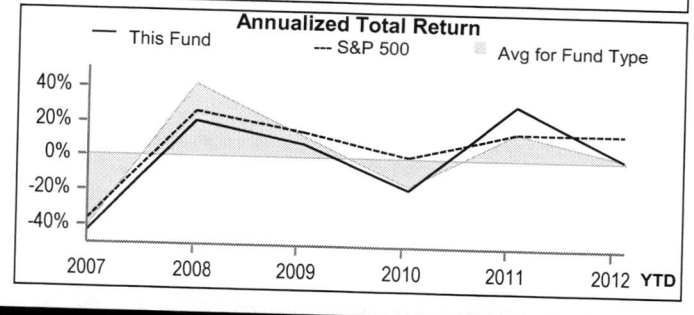

*iShares MSCI Hong Kong (EWH)

B-　　　**Good**

Fund Family: BlackRock Fund Advisors
Fund Type: Foreign
Inception Date: March 12, 1996

Major Rating Factors: Strong performance is the major factor driving the B- (Good) TheStreet.com Investment Rating for *iShares MSCI Hong Kong. The fund currently has a performance rating of B- (Good) based on an annualized return of 11.23% over the last three years and a total return of 2.63% year to date 2012. Factored into the performance evaluation is an expense ratio of 0.53% (very low).

The fund's risk rating is currently B- (Good). It carries a beta of 0.89, meaning the fund's expected move will be 8.9% for every 10% move in the market. Volatility, as measured by both the semi-deviation and a drawdown factor, is considered low. As of December 31, 2012, *iShares MSCI Hong Kong traded at a discount of 2.07% below its net asset value, which is better than its one-year historical average premium of .08%.

Diane Hsiung has been running the fund for 5 years and currently receives a manager quality ranking of 84 (0=worst, 99=best). If you desire only a moderate level of risk and strong performance, then this fund is an excellent option.

Data Date	Investment Rating	Net Assets ($Mil)	Price	Performance Rating/Pts	Total Return Y-T-D	Risk Rating/Pts
12-12	B-	3,001.60	19.42	B- / 7.5	2.63%	B- / 7.1
2011	C-	1,814.00	15.47	C / 4.5	0.52%	B- / 7.3
2010	C-	2,059.00	18.92	C / 4.7	24.16%	C / 5.0
2009	C	1,951.78	15.66	C+ / 5.6	48.91%	C / 5.0

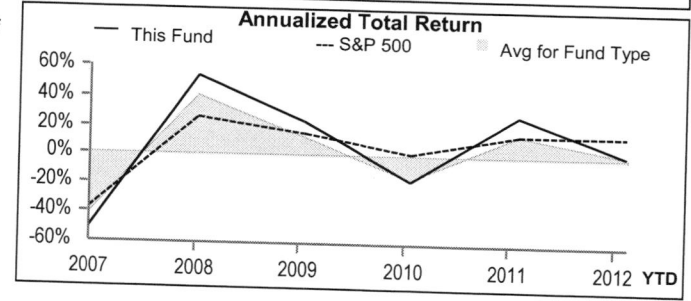

* Denotes ETF Fund

*iShares MSCI Indonesia Inv Mkt I (EIDO)

D   **Weak**

Fund Family: BlackRock Fund Advisors
Fund Type: Foreign
Inception Date: May 5, 2010

Data Date	Investment Rating	Net Assets ($Mil)	Price	Performance Rating/Pts	Total Return Y-T-D	Risk Rating/Pts
12-12	D	387.10	30.26	D- / 1.5	-2.28%	C+ / 6.8
2011	D+	295.60	29.31	C- / 3.0	0.96%	C+ / 6.9

Major Rating Factors:
Disappointing performance is the major factor driving the D (Weak) TheStreet.com Investment Rating for *iShares MSCI Indonesia Inv Mkt I. The fund currently has a performance rating of D- (Weak) based on an annualized return of 0.00% over the last three years and a total return of -2.28% year to date 2012. Factored into the performance evaluation is an expense ratio of 0.61% (very low).

    The fund's risk rating is currently C+ (Fair). It carries a beta of 0.00, meaning the fund's expected move will be 0.0% for every 10% move in the market. Volatility, as measured by both the semi-deviation and a drawdown factor, is considered low. As of December 31, 2012, *iShares MSCI Indonesia Inv Mkt I traded at a premium of .43% above its net asset value, which is worse than its one-year historical average discount of .50%.

    Diane Hsiung has been running the fund for 3 years and currently receives a manager quality ranking of 13 (0=worst, 99=best). This fund offers only a moderate level of risk but investors looking for strong performance are still waiting.

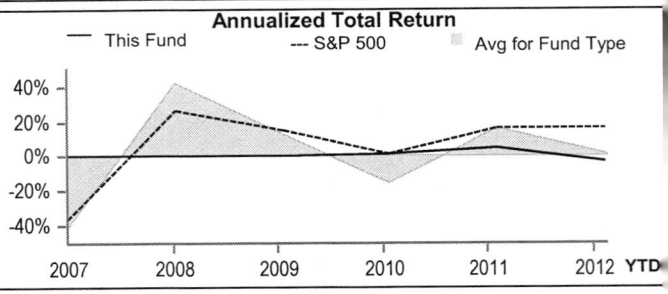

Annualized Total Return

*iShares MSCI Irlnd Capd Inv Mkt (EIRL)

A   **Excellent**

Fund Family: BlackRock Fund Advisors
Fund Type: Foreign
Inception Date: May 5, 2010

Data Date	Investment Rating	Net Assets ($Mil)	Price	Performance Rating/Pts	Total Return Y-T-D	Risk Rating/Pts
12-12	A	35.40	25.09	A+ / 9.8	1.67%	B- / 7.3
2011	D	7.60	18.99	D- / 1.3	-1.95%	B- / 7.3

Major Rating Factors:
Exceptional performance is the major factor driving the A (Excellent) TheStreet.com Investment Rating for *iShares MSCI Irlnd Capd Inv Mkt. The fund currently has a performance rating of A+ (Excellent) based on an annualized return of 0.00% over the last three years and a total return of 1.67% year to date 2012. Factored into the performance evaluation is an expense ratio of 0.53% (very low).

    The fund's risk rating is currently B- (Good). It carries a beta of 0.00, meaning the fund's expected move will be 0.0% for every 10% move in the market. Volatility, as measured by both the semi-deviation and a drawdown factor, is considered low. As of December 31, 2012, *iShares MSCI Irlnd Capd Inv Mkt traded at a discount of .28% below its net asset value, which is better than its one-year historical average premium of .57%.

    Diane Hsiung has been running the fund for 3 years and currently receives a manager quality ranking of 93 (0=worst, 99=best). If you desire only a moderate level of risk and strong performance, then this fund is an excellent option.

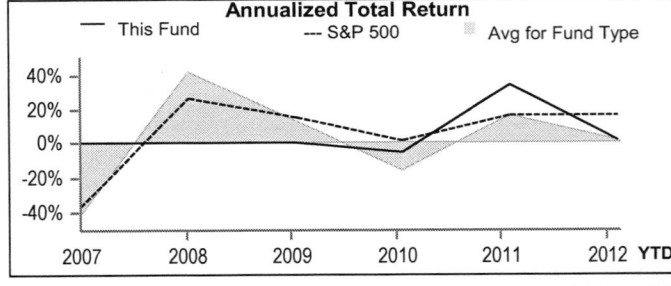

Annualized Total Return

*iShares MSCI Israel Capped Inv M (EIS)

D-   **Weak**

Fund Family: BlackRock Fund Advisors
Fund Type: Foreign
Inception Date: March 26, 2008

Data Date	Investment Rating	Net Assets ($Mil)	Price	Performance Rating/Pts	Total Return Y-T-D	Risk Rating/Pts
12-12	D-	79.50	41.90	D- / 1.1	1.89%	C+ / 5.9
2011	D+	75.20	39.56	D+ / 2.8	3.44%	C+ / 6.6
2010	A-	141.30	60.52	A / 9.3	15.39%	C+ / 5.6
2009	A+	107.79	54.40	A+ / 9.6	71.67%	C+ / 5.9

Major Rating Factors:
Disappointing performance is the major factor driving the D- (Weak) TheStreet.com Investment Rating for *iShares MSCI Israel Capped Inv M. The fund currently has a performance rating of D- (Weak) based on an annualized return of -6.06% over the last three years and a total return of 1.89% year to date 2012. Factored into the performance evaluation is an expense ratio of 0.61% (very low).

    The fund's risk rating is currently C+ (Fair). It carries a beta of 0.91, meaning that its performance tracks fairly well with that of the overall stock market. Volatility, as measured by both the semi-deviation and a drawdown factor, is considered low. As of December 31, 2012, *iShares MSCI Israel Capped Inv M traded at a discount of 3.05% below its net asset value, which is better than its one-year historical average discount of .19%.

    Diane Hsiung has been running the fund for 5 years and currently receives a manager quality ranking of 14 (0=worst, 99=best). This fund offers only a moderate level of risk but investors looking for strong performance are still waiting.

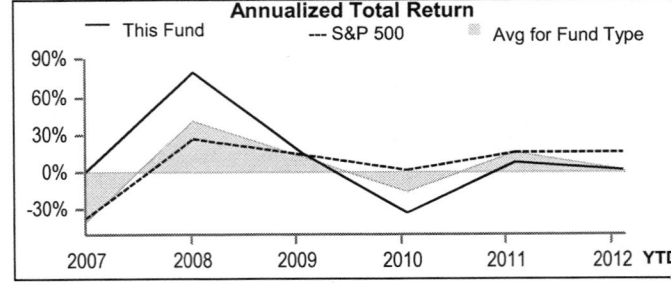

Annualized Total Return

*iShares MSCI Italy (EWI)

Fund Family: BlackRock Fund Advisors
Fund Type: Foreign
Inception Date: March 12, 1996

D-   Weak

Major Rating Factors:
Disappointing performance is the major factor driving the D- (Weak) TheStreet.com Investment Rating for *iShares MSCI Italy. The fund currently has a performance rating of D (Weak) based on an annualized return of -7.79% over the last three years and a total return of 6.32% year to date 2012. Factored into the performance evaluation is an expense ratio of 0.53% (very low).

The fund's risk rating is currently C (Fair). It carries a beta of 1.55, meaning it is expected to move 15.5% for every 10% move in the market. Volatility, as measured by both the semi-deviation and a drawdown factor, is considered average. As of December 31, 2012, *iShares MSCI Italy traded at a discount of 5.61% below its net asset value, which is better than its one-year historical average premium of .16%.

Diane Hsiung has been running the fund for 5 years and currently receives a manager quality ranking of 8 (0=worst, 99=best). This fund offers an average level of risk but investors looking for strong performance will be frustrated.

Data Date	Investment Rating	Net Assets ($Mil)	Price	Performance Rating/Pts	Total Return Y-T-D	Risk Rating/Pts
12-12	D-	384.40	13.45	D / 1.6	6.32%	C / 4.6
2011	D-	100.80	11.99	D- / 1.1	-5.25%	C / 5.5
2010	E+	95.80	16.38	E+ / 0.6	-14.12%	C- / 3.8
2009	D-	125.72	19.51	D- / 1.1	20.86%	C / 4.3

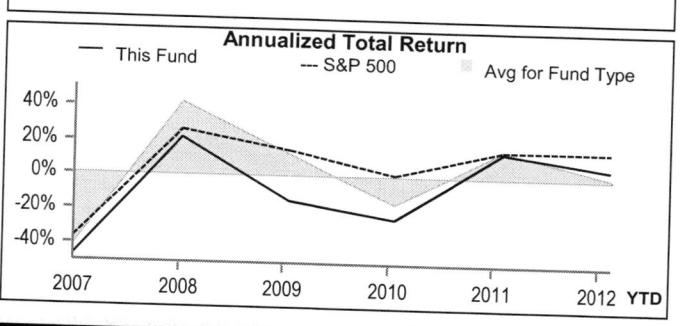

*iShares MSCI Japan (EWJ)

Fund Family: BlackRock Fund Advisors
Fund Type: Foreign
Inception Date: March 12, 1996

D   Weak

Major Rating Factors:
Disappointing performance is the major factor driving the D (Weak) TheStreet.com Investment Rating for *iShares MSCI Japan. The fund currently has a performance rating of D (Weak) based on an annualized return of -0.12% over the last three years and a total return of 1.33% year to date 2012. Factored into the performance evaluation is an expense ratio of 0.53% (very low).

The fund's risk rating is currently B- (Good). It carries a beta of 0.60, meaning the fund's expected move will be 6.0% for every 10% move in the market. Volatility, as measured by both the semi-deviation and a drawdown factor, is considered low. As of December 31, 2012, *iShares MSCI Japan traded at a discount of .41% below its net asset value, which is better than its one-year historical average premium of .12%.

Diane Hsiung has been running the fund for 5 years and currently receives a manager quality ranking of 46 (0=worst, 99=best). This fund offers only a moderate level of risk but investors looking for strong performance are still waiting.

Data Date	Investment Rating	Net Assets ($Mil)	Price	Performance Rating/Pts	Total Return Y-T-D	Risk Rating/Pts
12-12	D	5,156.00	9.75	D / 2.0	1.33%	B- / 7.5
2011	D+	5,345.00	9.11	D / 1.7	-0.49%	B- / 7.6
2010	D+	4,904.70	10.91	D+ / 2.4	13.61%	C+ / 5.6
2009	D-	6,164.17	9.74	E+ / 0.9	2.60%	C+ / 5.8

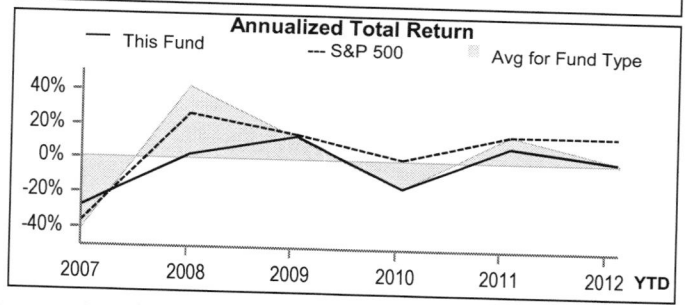

*iShares MSCI Japan Small Cap (SCJ)

Fund Family: BlackRock Fund Advisors
Fund Type: Foreign
Inception Date: December 20, 2007

C-   Fair

Major Rating Factors:
Disappointing performance is the major factor driving the C- (Fair) TheStreet.com Investment Rating for *iShares MSCI Japan Small Cap. The fund currently has a performance rating of D+ (Weak) based on an annualized return of 4.52% over the last three years and a total return of 1.05% year to date 2012. Factored into the performance evaluation is an expense ratio of 0.53% (very low).

The fund's risk rating is currently B (Good). It carries a beta of 0.41, meaning the fund's expected move will be 4.1% for every 10% move in the market. Volatility, as measured by both the semi-deviation and a drawdown factor, is considered low. As of December 31, 2012, *iShares MSCI Japan Small Cap traded at a premium of .11% above its net asset value, which is worse than its one-year historical average discount of .15%.

Diane Hsiung has been running the fund for 5 years and currently receives a manager quality ranking of 78 (0=worst, 99=best). This fund offers only a moderate level of risk but investors looking for strong performance are still waiting.

Data Date	Investment Rating	Net Assets ($Mil)	Price	Performance Rating/Pts	Total Return Y-T-D	Risk Rating/Pts
12-12	C-	39.50	44.39	D+ / 2.6	1.05%	B / 8.3
2011	C-	52.20	43.33	C- / 3.0	0.08%	B- / 7.8
2010	C	42.00	46.66	C / 4.3	19.07%	C+ / 6.1
2009	D+	35.56	39.99	D / 2.1	3.32%	C+ / 6.3

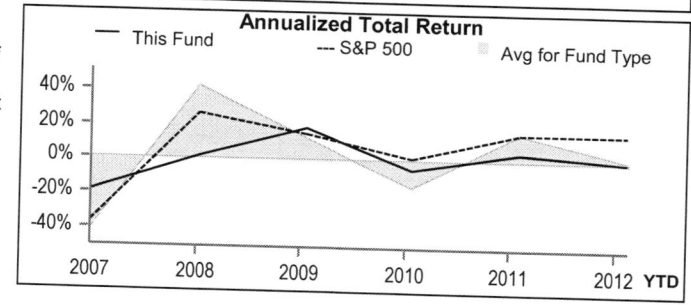

*iShares MSCI KLD 400 Social Idx (DSI)   C   Fair

Fund Family: BlackRock Fund Advisors
Fund Type: Income
Inception Date: November 14, 2006

Major Rating Factors: Middle of the road best describes *iShares MSCI KLD 400 Social Idx whose TheStreet.com Investment Rating is currently a C (Fair). The fund currently has a performance rating of C- (Fair) based on an annualized return of 8.84% over the last three years and a total return of 3.30% year to date 2012. Factored into the performance evaluation is an expense ratio of 0.50% (very low).

The fund's risk rating is currently B (Good). It carries a beta of 0.96, meaning that its performance tracks fairly well with that of the overall stock market. Volatility, as measured by both the semi-deviation and a drawdown factor, is considered low. As of December 31, 2012, *iShares MSCI KLD 400 Social Idx traded at a discount of 3.22% below its net asset value, which is better than its one-year historical average discount of .02%.

Diane Hsiung has been running the fund for 5 years and currently receives a manager quality ranking of 35 (0=worst, 99=best). If you desire an average level of risk, then this fund may be an option.

Data Date	Investment Rating	Net Assets ($Mil)	Price	Performance Rating/Pts	Total Return Y-T-D	Risk Rating/Pts
12-12	C	165.50	51.74	C- / 4.2	3.30%	B / 8.2
2011	C	161.20	46.89	C / 5.1	1.30%	B / 8.0
2010	C-	140.70	46.91	C- / 4.0	11.42%	C+ / 6.0
2009	C-	65.81	42.71	D+ / 2.8	27.31%	C+ / 6.1

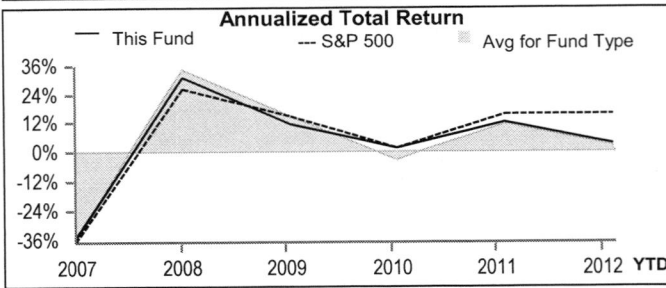

*iShares MSCI Kokusai Index (TOK)   C-   Fair

Fund Family: BlackRock Fund Advisors
Fund Type: Global
Inception Date: December 10, 2007

Major Rating Factors: Middle of the road best describes *iShares MSCI Kokusai Index whose TheStreet.com Investment Rating is currently a C- (Fair). The fund currently has a performance rating of C- (Fair) based on an annualized return of 7.66% over the last three years and a total return of 1.71% year to date 2012. Factored into the performance evaluation is an expense ratio of 0.25% (very low).

The fund's risk rating is currently B- (Good). It carries a beta of 0.82, meaning the fund's expected move will be 8.2% for every 10% move in the market. Volatility, as measured by both the semi-deviation and a drawdown factor, is considered low. As of December 31, 2012, *iShares MSCI Kokusai Index traded at a discount of 2.69% below its net asset value, which is better than its one-year historical average premium of .31%.

Diane Hsiung has been running the fund for 5 years and currently receives a manager quality ranking of 77 (0=worst, 99=best). If you desire an average level of risk, then this fund may be an option.

Data Date	Investment Rating	Net Assets ($Mil)	Price	Performance Rating/Pts	Total Return Y-T-D	Risk Rating/Pts
12-12	C-	636.20	42.69	C- / 4.2	1.71%	B- / 7.7
2011	C	611.30	37.81	C / 4.3	0.50%	B- / 7.7
2010	D+	287.30	40.24	D+ / 2.9	11.45%	C+ / 5.7
2009	A	83.82	36.95	B+ / 8.6	31.91%	C+ / 5.8

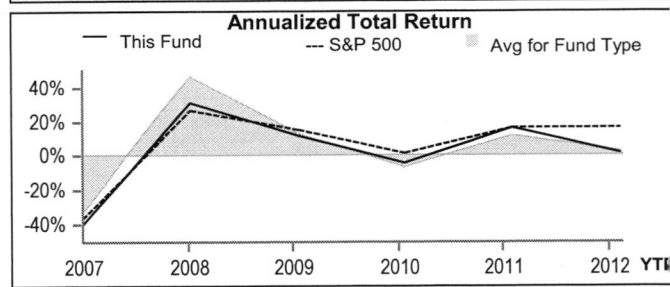

*iShares MSCI Malaysia (EWM)   C+   Fair

Fund Family: BlackRock Fund Advisors
Fund Type: Foreign
Inception Date: March 12, 1996

Major Rating Factors: Middle of the road best describes *iShares MSCI Malaysia whose TheStreet.com Investment Rating is currently a C+ (Fair). The fund currently has a performance rating of C+ (Fair) based on an annualized return of 14.36% over the last three years and a total return of 0.73% year to date 2012. Factored into the performance evaluation is an expense ratio of 0.53% (very low).

The fund's risk rating is currently B- (Good). It carries a beta of 0.68, meaning the fund's expected move will be 6.8% for every 10% move in the market. Volatility, as measured by both the semi-deviation and a drawdown factor, is considered low. As of December 31, 2012, *iShares MSCI Malaysia traded at a discount of .72% below its net asset value, which is better than its one-year historical average premium of .07%.

Diane Hsiung has been running the fund for 5 years and currently receives a manager quality ranking of 93 (0=worst, 99=best). If you desire an average level of risk, then this fund may be an option.

Data Date	Investment Rating	Net Assets ($Mil)	Price	Performance Rating/Pts	Total Return Y-T-D	Risk Rating/Pts
12-12	C+	971.30	15.13	C+ / 5.9	0.73%	B- / 7.8
2011	B	855.70	13.40	B- / 7.4	0.90%	B / 8.0
2010	B+	973.10	14.38	B+ / 8.4	38.97%	C+ / 5.7
2009	C+	513.00	10.62	C+ / 6.5	44.77%	C+ / 5.7

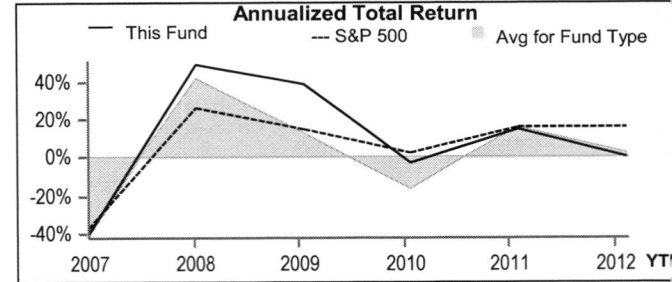

*iShares MSCI Mexico Inv Market (EWW)

B   **Good**

Fund Family: BlackRock Fund Advisors
Fund Type: Foreign
Inception Date: March 12, 1996

Major Rating Factors: Strong performance is the major factor driving the B (Good) TheStreet.com Investment Rating for *iShares MSCI Mexico Inv Market. The fund currently has a performance rating of B+ (Good) based on an annualized return of 14.89% over the last three years and a total return of 4.00% year to date 2012. Factored into the performance evaluation is an expense ratio of 0.53% (very low).

The fund's risk rating is currently B- (Good). It carries a beta of 0.95, meaning that its performance tracks fairly well with that of the overall stock market. Volatility, as measured by both the semi-deviation and a drawdown factor, is considered low. As of December 31, 2012, *iShares MSCI Mexico Inv Market traded at a discount of 3.87% below its net asset value, which is better than its one-year historical average premium of .08%.

Diane Hsiung has been running the fund for 5 years and currently receives a manager quality ranking of 90 (0=worst, 99=best). If you desire only a moderate level of risk and strong performance, then this fund is an excellent option.

Data Date	Investment Rating	Net Assets ($Mil)	Price	Performance Rating/Pts	Total Return Y-T-D	Risk Rating/Pts
12-12	B	1,928.70	70.53	B+ / 8.4	4.00%	B- / 7.3
2011	C+	1,133.30	53.76	C+ / 6.1	1.00%	B- / 7.3
2010	B-	1,720.10	61.92	B / 7.8	27.91%	C / 4.6
2009	C	694.28	48.87	C+ / 6.3	47.42%	C / 4.6

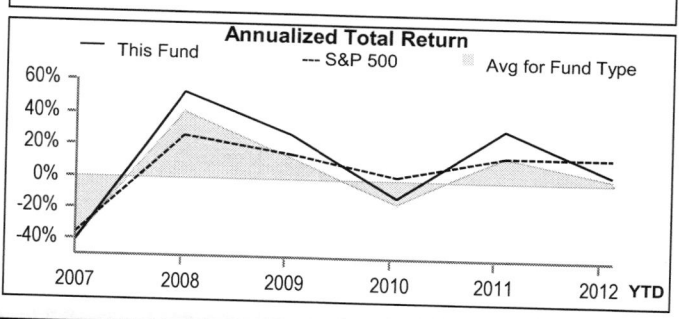

---

*iShares MSCI Netherlands Inv Mar (EWN)

C-   **Fair**

Fund Family: BlackRock Fund Advisors
Fund Type: Foreign
Inception Date: March 12, 1996

Major Rating Factors: Middle of the road best describes *iShares MSCI Netherlands Inv Mar whose TheStreet.com Investment Rating is currently a C- (Fair). The fund currently has a performance rating of C (Fair) based on an annualized return of 2.42% over the last three years and a total return of 2.68% year to date 2012. Factored into the performance evaluation is an expense ratio of 0.53% (very low).

The fund's risk rating is currently C+ (Fair). It carries a beta of 1.17, meaning it is expected to move 11.7% for every 10% move in the market. Volatility, as measured by both the semi-deviation and a drawdown factor, is considered low. As of December 31, 2012, *iShares MSCI Netherlands Inv Mar traded at a discount of 2.38% below its net asset value, which is better than its one-year historical average premium of .08%.

Diane Hsiung has been running the fund for 5 years and currently receives a manager quality ranking of 34 (0=worst, 99=best). If you desire an average level of risk, then this fund may be an option.

Data Date	Investment Rating	Net Assets ($Mil)	Price	Performance Rating/Pts	Total Return Y-T-D	Risk Rating/Pts
12-12	C-	148.40	20.51	C / 4.7	2.68%	C+ / 6.5
2011	D	73.50	17.23	D / 2.2	-3.02%	C+ / 6.7
2010	D-	172.20	21.09	D- / 1.3	4.95%	C- / 4.1
2009	D+	83.35	20.46	C- / 3.4	36.55%	C / 4.9

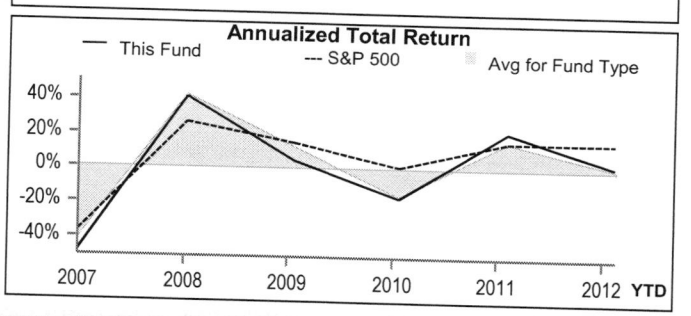

---

*iShares MSCI New Zealand Inv Mk (ENZL)

A+   **Excellent**

Fund Family: BlackRock Fund Advisors
Fund Type: Foreign
Inception Date: September 1, 2010

Major Rating Factors:
Exceptional performance is the major factor driving the A+ (Excellent) TheStreet.com Investment Rating for *iShares MSCI New Zealand Inv Mk. The fund currently has a performance rating of A+ (Excellent) based on an annualized return of 0.00% over the last three years and a total return of 2.28% year to date 2012. Factored into the performance evaluation is an expense ratio of 0.53% (very low).

The fund's risk rating is currently B- (Good). It carries a beta of 0.00, meaning the fund's expected move will be 0.0% for every 10% move in the market. Volatility, as measured by the semi-deviation and a drawdown factor, is considered low. As of December 31, 2012, *iShares MSCI New Zealand Inv Mk traded at a discount of 2.21% below its net asset value, which is better than its one-year historical average premium of .10%.

Diane Hsiung has been running the fund for 3 years and currently receives a manager quality ranking of 96 (0=worst, 99=best). If you desire only a moderate level of risk and strong performance, then this fund is an excellent option.

Data Date	Investment Rating	Net Assets ($Mil)	Price	Performance Rating/Pts	Total Return Y-T-D	Risk Rating/Pts
12-12	A+	157.20	34.58	A+ / 9.7	2.28%	B- / 7.8
2011	D	95.80	27.56	D- / 1.4	-0.51%	B- / 7.9

*iShares MSCI Pacific ex-Japan (EPP) — C — Fair

Fund Family: BlackRock Fund Advisors
Fund Type: Foreign
Inception Date: October 25, 2001

Major Rating Factors: Middle of the road best describes *iShares MSCI Pacific ex-Japan whose TheStreet.com Investment Rating is currently a C (Fair). The fund currently has a performance rating of C+ (Fair) based on an annualized return of 8.34% over the last three years and a total return of 1.29% year to date 2012. Factored into the performance evaluation is an expense ratio of 0.50% (very low).

The fund's risk rating is currently C+ (Fair). It carries a beta of 1.11, meaning it is expected to move 11.1% for every 10% move in the market. Volatility, as measured by both the semi-deviation and a drawdown factor, is considered low. As of December 31, 2012, *iShares MSCI Pacific ex-Japan traded at a discount of 1.11% below its net asset value, which is better than its one-year historical average premium of .09%.

Diane Hsiung has been running the fund for 5 years and currently receives a manager quality ranking of 77 (0=worst, 99=best). If you desire an average level of risk, then this fund may be an option.

Data Date	Investment Rating	Net Assets ($Mil)	Price	Perfor-mance Rating/Pts	Total Return Y-T-D	Risk Rating/Pts
12-12	C	3,798.50	47.14	C+ / 5.8	1.29%	C+ / 6.9
2011	C	3,099.70	38.93	C+ / 6.0	1.59%	B- / 7.1
2010	D	4,319.90	46.98	C+ / 5.7	17.77%	D- / 1.4
2009	C-	3,382.55	41.37	B- / 7.1	61.99%	D / 1.8

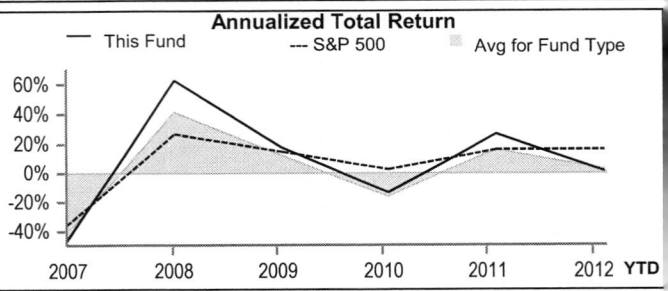

Annualized Total Return

*iShares MSCI Philipps Invst Mkt (EPHE) — A — Excellent

Fund Family: BlackRock Fund Advisors
Fund Type: Foreign
Inception Date: September 28, 2010

Major Rating Factors:
Exceptional performance is the major factor driving the A (Excellent) TheStreet.com Investment Rating for *iShares MSCI Philipps Invst Mkt. The fund currently has a performance rating of A+ (Excellent) based on an annualized return of 0.00% over the last three years and a total return of 4.34% year to date 2012. Factored into the performance evaluation is an expense ratio of 0.61% (very low).

The fund's risk rating is currently B- (Good). It carries a beta of 0.00, meaning the fund's expected move will be 0.0% for every 10% move in the market. Volatility, as measured by both the semi-deviation and a drawdown factor, is considered low. As of December 31, 2012, *iShares MSCI Philipps Invst Mkt traded at a discount of 3.57% below its net asset value, which is better than its one-year historical average premium of .14%.

Diane Hsiung has been running the fund for 3 years and currently receives a manager quality ranking of 98 (0=worst, 99=best). If you desire only a moderate level of risk and strong performance, then this fund is an excellent option.

Data Date	Investment Rating	Net Assets ($Mil)	Price	Perfor-mance Rating/Pts	Total Return Y-T-D	Risk Rating/Pts
12-12	A	218.40	34.55	A+ / 9.8	4.34%	B- / 7.5
2011	D+	69.80	23.57	D / 2.2	2.21%	B- / 7.3

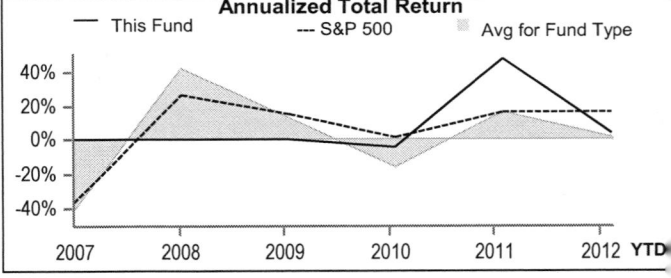

Annualized Total Return

*iShares MSCI Poland Invstbl Mkt (EPOL) — B- — Good

Fund Family: BlackRock Fund Advisors
Fund Type: Foreign
Inception Date: May 25, 2010

Major Rating Factors:
Exceptional performance is the major factor driving the B- (Good) TheStreet.com Investment Rating for *iShares MSCI Poland Invstbl Mkt. The fund currently has a performance rating of A+ (Excellent) based on an annualized return of 0.00% over the last three years and a total return of -1.45% year to date 2012. Factored into the performance evaluation is an expense ratio of 0.61% (very low).

The fund's risk rating is currently C (Fair). It carries a beta of 0.00, meaning the fund's expected move will be 0.0% for every 10% move in the market. Volatility, as measured by both the semi-deviation and a drawdown factor, is considered average. As of December 31, 2012, *iShares MSCI Poland Invstbl Mkt traded at a premium of 2.00% above its net asset value, which is worse than its one-year historical average premium of .21%.

Diane Hsiung has been running the fund for 3 years and currently receives a manager quality ranking of 84 (0=worst, 99=best). If you desire an average level of risk and strong performance, then this fund is a good option.

Data Date	Investment Rating	Net Assets ($Mil)	Price	Perfor-mance Rating/Pts	Total Return Y-T-D	Risk Rating/Pts
12-12	B-	184.50	29.62	A+ / 9.8	-1.45%	C / 4.8
2011	E+	109.80	21.64	E- / 0.2	-3.19%	C / 4.9

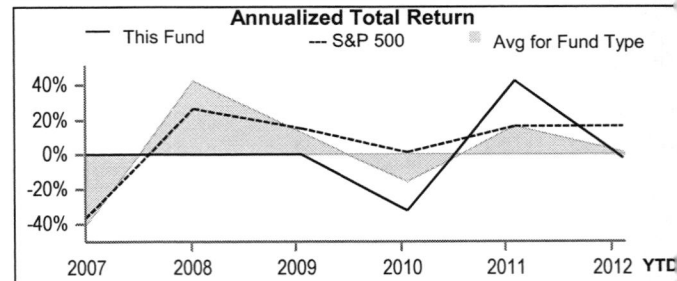

Annualized Total Return

*iShares MSCI Russia Capped Index (ERUS)

C-   **Fair**

Fund Family: BlackRock Fund Advisors
Fund Type: Foreign
Inception Date: November 9, 2010

Major Rating Factors: Middle of the road best describes *iShares MSCI Russia Capped Index whose TheStreet.com Investment Rating is currently a C- (Fair). The fund currently has a performance rating of C+ (Fair) based on an annualized return of 0.00% over the last three years and a total return of -0.04% year to date 2012. Factored into the performance evaluation is an expense ratio of 0.61% (very low).

The fund's risk rating is currently C (Fair). It carries a beta of 0.00, meaning the fund's expected move will be 0.0% for every 10% move in the market. Volatility, as measured by both the semi-deviation and a drawdown factor, is considered average. As of December 31, 2012, *iShares MSCI Russia Capped Index traded at a premium of .17% above its net asset value, which is better than its one-year historical average premium of .36%.

Diane Hsiung has been running the fund for 3 years and currently receives a manager quality ranking of 9 (0=worst, 99=best). If you desire an average level of risk, then this fund may be an option.

Data Date	Investment Rating	Net Assets ($Mil)	Price	Performance Rating/Pts	Total Return Y-T-D	Risk Rating/Pts
12-12	C-	205.50	23.65	C+ / 6.8	-0.04%	C / 5.1

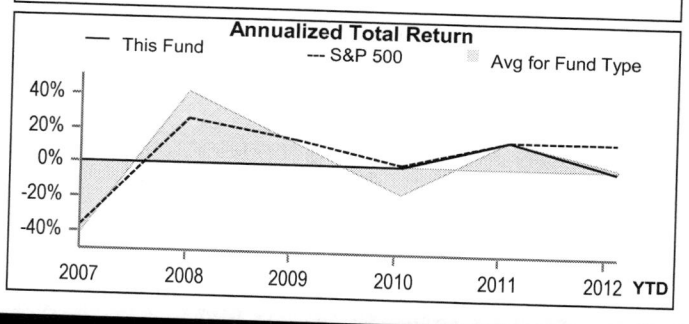

*iShares MSCI Singapore (EWS)

C   **Fair**

Fund Family: BlackRock Fund Advisors
Fund Type: Foreign
Inception Date: March 12, 1996

Major Rating Factors: Middle of the road best describes *iShares MSCI Singapore whose TheStreet.com Investment Rating is currently a C (Fair). The fund currently has a performance rating of C (Fair) based on an annualized return of 9.79% over the last three years and a total return of 0.15% year to date 2012. Factored into the performance evaluation is an expense ratio of 0.53% (very low).

The fund's risk rating is currently B- (Good). It carries a beta of 0.93, meaning that its performance tracks fairly well with that of the overall stock market. Volatility, as measured by both the semi-deviation and a drawdown factor, is considered low. As of December 31, 2012, *iShares MSCI Singapore traded at a discount of .15% below its net asset value, which is better than its one-year historical average premium of .11%.

Diane Hsiung has been running the fund for 5 years and currently receives a manager quality ranking of 82 (0=worst, 99=best). If you desire an average level of risk, then this fund may be an option.

Data Date	Investment Rating	Net Assets ($Mil)	Price	Performance Rating/Pts	Total Return Y-T-D	Risk Rating/Pts
12-12	C	1,520.80	13.69	C / 5.5	0.15%	B- / 7.1
2011	C	1,282.60	10.83	C+ / 5.6	2.40%	B- / 7.3
2010	C+	2,205.60	13.85	B / 7.7	24.51%	C / 4.5
2009	C+	1,294.04	11.49	B- / 7.2	63.20%	C / 4.6

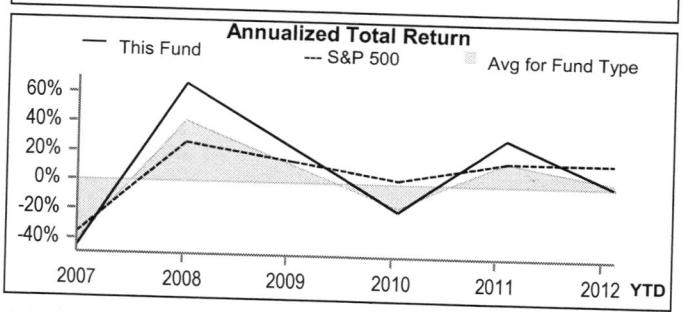

*iShares MSCI South Africa (EZA)

C-   **Fair**

Fund Family: BlackRock Fund Advisors
Fund Type: Foreign
Inception Date: February 3, 2003

Major Rating Factors: Middle of the road best describes *iShares MSCI South Africa whose TheStreet.com Investment Rating is currently a C- (Fair). The fund currently has a performance rating of C (Fair) based on an annualized return of 10.03% over the last three years and a total return of -4.08% year to date 2012. Factored into the performance evaluation is an expense ratio of 0.61% (very low).

The fund's risk rating is currently C+ (Fair). It carries a beta of 1.02, meaning that its performance tracks fairly well with that of the overall stock market. Volatility, as measured by both the semi-deviation and a drawdown factor, is considered low. As of December 31, 2012, *iShares MSCI South Africa traded at a premium of 4.65% above its net asset value, which is worse than its one-year historical average premium of .10%.

Diane Hsiung has been running the fund for 5 years and currently receives a manager quality ranking of 86 (0=worst, 99=best). If you desire an average level of risk, then this fund may be an option.

Data Date	Investment Rating	Net Assets ($Mil)	Price	Performance Rating/Pts	Total Return Y-T-D	Risk Rating/Pts
12-12	C-	533.50	71.58	C / 5.1	-4.08%	C+ / 6.9
2011	C+	504.20	61.07	C+ / 6.2	0.34%	B- / 7.1
2010	C	684.40	74.68	B+ / 8.5	36.91%	D+ / 2.3
2009	C-	488.73	55.97	C+ / 6.2	47.55%	D+ / 2.6

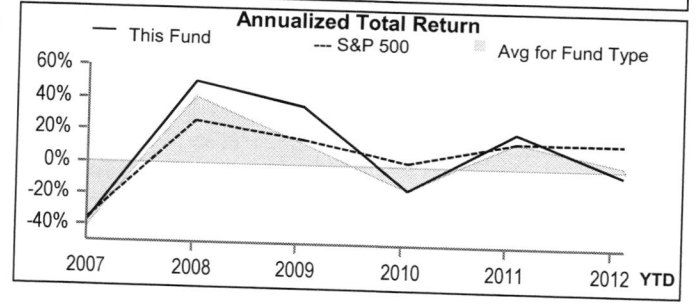

* Denotes ETF Fund

*iShares MSCI South Korea (EWY)   C-   Fair

Fund Family: BlackRock Fund Advisors
Fund Type: Foreign
Inception Date: May 9, 2000

Major Rating Factors: Middle of the road best describes *iShares MSCI South Korea whose TheStreet.com Investment Rating is currently a C- (Fair). The fund currently has a performance rating of C (Fair) based on an annualized return of 9.46% over the last three years and a total return of -0.46% year to date 2012. Factored into the performance evaluation is an expense ratio of 0.61% (very low).

The fund's risk rating is currently C+ (Fair). It carries a beta of 1.20, meaning it is expected to move 12.0% for every 10% move in the market. Volatility, as measured by both the semi-deviation and a drawdown factor, is considered low. As of December 31, 2012, *iShares MSCI South Korea traded at a premium of .68% above its net asset value, which is worse than its one-year historical average discount of .02%.

Diane Hsiung has been running the fund for 5 years and currently receives a manager quality ranking of 82 (0=worst, 99=best). If you desire an average level of risk, then this fund may be an option.

Data Date	Investment Rating	Net Assets ($Mil)	Price	Perfor-mance Rating/Pts	Total Return Y-T-D	Risk Rating/Pts
12-12	C-	3,344.80	63.35	C / 5.1	-0.46%	C+ / 6.3
2011	C	3,038.60	52.26	C+ / 6.5	-0.13%	C+ / 6.3
2010	C	4,170.10	61.19	C+ / 6.7	29.58%	C- / 3.8
2009	C	2,398.55	47.64	C+ / 6.7	65.51%	C- / 3.8

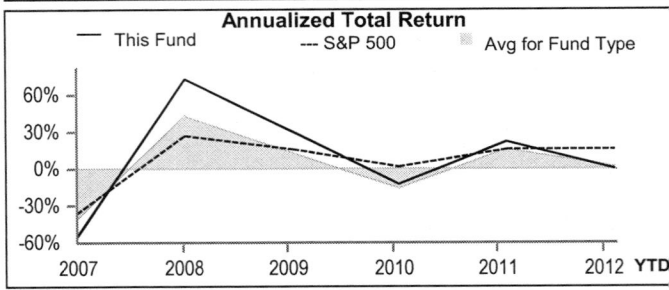

*iShares MSCI Spain (EWP)   E+   Very Weak

Fund Family: BlackRock Fund Advisors
Fund Type: Foreign
Inception Date: March 12, 1996

Major Rating Factors:
Disappointing performance is the major factor driving the E+ (Very Weak) TheStreet.com Investment Rating for *iShares MSCI Spain. The fund currently has a performance rating of D (Weak) based on an annualized return of -6.66% over the last three years and a total return of 6.44% year to date 2012. Factored into the performance evaluation is an expense ratio of 0.53% (very low).

The fund's risk rating is currently C (Fair). It carries a beta of 1.48, meaning it is expected to move 14.8% for every 10% move in the market. Volatility, as measured by both the semi-deviation and a drawdown factor, is considered average. As of December 31, 2012, *iShares MSCI Spain traded at a discount of 5.70% below its net asset value, which is better than its one-year historical average premium of .03%.

Diane Hsiung has been running the fund for 5 years and currently receives a manager quality ranking of 9 (0=worst, 99=best). This fund offers an average level of risk but investors looking for strong performance will be frustrated.

Data Date	Investment Rating	Net Assets ($Mil)	Price	Perfor-mance Rating/Pts	Total Return Y-T-D	Risk Rating/Pts
12-12	E+	241.50	30.26	D / 1.7	6.44%	C / 4.4
2011	D-	99.70	30.27	D- / 1.5	-5.45%	C+ / 5.7
2010	E+	137.40	36.74	E+ / 0.7	-18.61%	C- / 4.2
2009	C-	278.73	48.04	C / 4.7	31.23%	C / 5.2

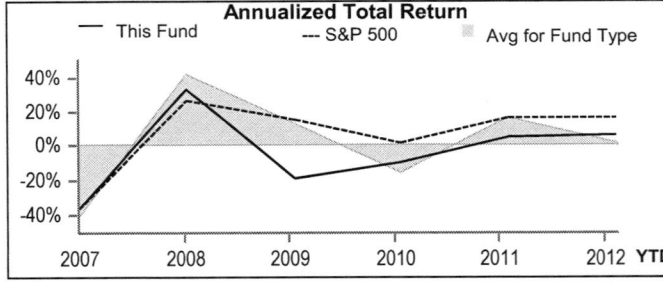

*iShares MSCI Sweden (EWD)   C   Fair

Fund Family: BlackRock Fund Advisors
Fund Type: Foreign
Inception Date: March 12, 1996

Major Rating Factors: Strong performance is the major factor driving the C (Fair) TheStreet.com Investment Rating for *iShares MSCI Sweden. The fund currently has a performance rating of B- (Good) based on an annualized return of 10.96% over the last three years and a total return of 1.46% year to date 2012. Factored into the performance evaluation is an expense ratio of 0.53% (very low).

The fund's risk rating is currently C+ (Fair). It carries a beta of 1.29, meaning it is expected to move 12.9% for every 10% move in the market. Volatility, as measured by both the semi-deviation and a drawdown factor, is considered low. As of December 31, 2012, *iShares MSCI Sweden traded at a discount of 1.27% below its net asset value, which is better than its one-year historical average premium of .05%.

Diane Hsiung has been running the fund for 5 years and currently receives a manager quality ranking of 84 (0=worst, 99=best). If you desire only a moderate level of risk and strong performance, then this fund is an excellent option.

Data Date	Investment Rating	Net Assets ($Mil)	Price	Perfor-mance Rating/Pts	Total Return Y-T-D	Risk Rating/Pts
12-12	C	366.00	30.20	B- / 7.0	1.46%	C+ / 6.2
2011	C	267.20	25.14	C+ / 5.8	0.08%	C+ / 6.5
2010	B-	421.90	31.23	B+ / 8.4	36.11%	C- / 4.1
2009	D+	190.33	23.50	C- / 3.2	48.14%	C / 4.7

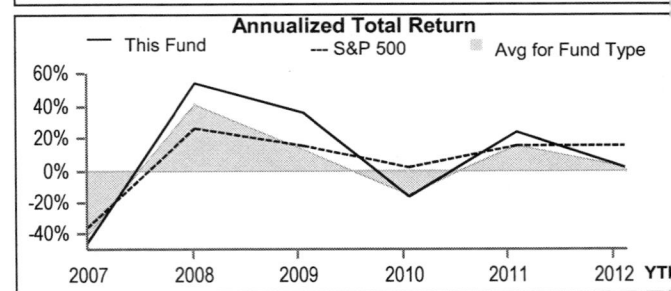

*iShares MSCI Switzerland (EWL)

| | C+ | Fair |

Fund Family: BlackRock Fund Advisors
Fund Type: Foreign
Inception Date: March 12, 1996

Major Rating Factors: Middle of the road best describes *iShares MSCI Switzerland whose TheStreet.com Investment Rating is currently a C+ (Fair). The fund currently has a performance rating of C+ (Fair) based on an annualized return of 9.37% over the last three years and a total return of 4.25% year to date 2012. Factored into the performance evaluation is an expense ratio of 0.53% (very low).

The fund's risk rating is currently B- (Good). It carries a beta of 0.88, meaning the fund's expected move will be 8.8% for every 10% move in the market. Volatility, as measured by both the semi-deviation and a drawdown factor, is considered low. As of December 31, 2012, *iShares MSCI Switzerland traded at a discount of 4.11% below its net asset value, which is better than its one-year historical average premium of .08%.

Diane Hsiung has been running the fund for 5 years and currently receives a manager quality ranking of 79 (0=worst, 99=best). If you desire an average level of risk, then this fund may be an option.

Data Date	Investment Rating	Net Assets ($Mil)	Price	Performance Rating/Pts	Total Return Y-T-D	Risk Rating/Pts
12-12	C+	698.90	26.80	C+ / 6.9	4.25%	B- / 7.4
2011	C-	475.80	22.62	C- / 3.4	-1.06%	B- / 7.5
2010	C	464.90	25.08	C / 5.2	14.48%	C / 5.5
2009	C-	271.86	22.26	C- / 3.1	22.38%	C+ / 5.8

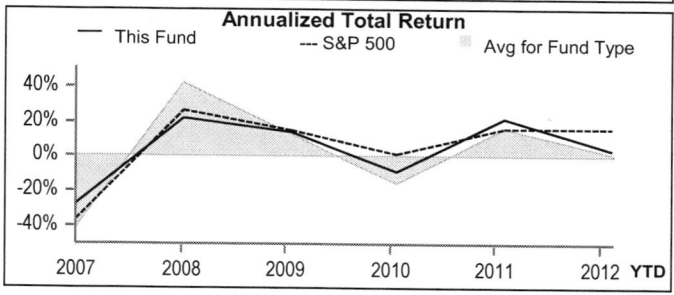

*iShares MSCI Taiwan (EWT)

| | D+ | Weak |

Fund Family: BlackRock Fund Advisors
Fund Type: Foreign
Inception Date: June 20, 2000

Major Rating Factors:
Disappointing performance is the major factor driving the D+ (Weak) TheStreet.com Investment Rating for *iShares MSCI Taiwan. The fund currently has a performance rating of D+ (Weak) based on an annualized return of 3.64% over the last three years and a total return of -0.07% year to date 2012. Factored into the performance evaluation is an expense ratio of 0.61% (very low).

The fund's risk rating is currently B- (Good). It carries a beta of 0.98, meaning that its performance tracks fairly well with that of the overall stock market. Volatility, as measured by both the semi-deviation and a drawdown factor, is considered low. As of December 31, 2012, *iShares MSCI Taiwan traded at a price exactly equal to its net asset value, which is better than its one-year historical average premium of .21%.

Diane Hsiung has been running the fund for 5 years and currently receives a manager quality ranking of 55 (0=worst, 99=best). This fund offers only a moderate level of risk but investors looking for strong performance are still waiting.

Data Date	Investment Rating	Net Assets ($Mil)	Price	Performance Rating/Pts	Total Return Y-T-D	Risk Rating/Pts
12-12	D+	2,693.80	13.62	D+ / 2.9	-0.07%	B- / 7.0
2011	C	2,193.10	11.71	C / 5.4	0.98%	B- / 7.1
2010	B-	3,435.30	15.62	B / 8.0	22.70%	C / 4.5
2009	C	3,035.33	12.97	C+ / 6.5	68.95%	C / 4.6

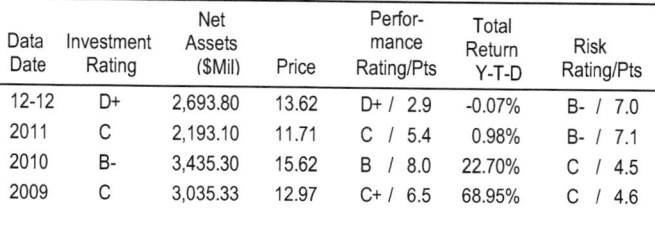

*iShares MSCI Thailand Inv Market (THD)

| | B+ | Good |

Fund Family: BlackRock Fund Advisors
Fund Type: Foreign
Inception Date: March 26, 2008

Major Rating Factors:
Exceptional performance is the major factor driving the B+ (Good) TheStreet.com Investment Rating for *iShares MSCI Thailand Inv Market. The fund currently has a performance rating of A+ (Excellent) based on an annualized return of 26.94% over the last three years and a total return of 0.25% year to date 2012. Factored into the performance evaluation is an expense ratio of 0.61% (very low).

The fund's risk rating is currently C+ (Fair). It carries a beta of 0.93, meaning that its performance tracks fairly well with that of the overall stock market. Volatility, as measured by both the semi-deviation and a drawdown factor, is considered low. As of December 31, 2012, *iShares MSCI Thailand Inv Market traded at a premium of .01% above its net asset value, which is better than its one-year historical average premium of .25%.

Diane Hsiung has been running the fund for 5 years and currently receives a manager quality ranking of 97 (0=worst, 99=best). If you desire only a moderate level of risk and strong performance, then this fund is an excellent option.

Data Date	Investment Rating	Net Assets ($Mil)	Price	Performance Rating/Pts	Total Return Y-T-D	Risk Rating/Pts
12-12	B+	788.90	82.49	A+ / 9.6	0.25%	C+ / 6.9
2011	B+	459.40	60.11	A / 9.3	-0.07%	B- / 7.2
2010	B+	694.00	64.61	A+ / 9.8	56.76%	C- / 4.2
2009	B+	94.02	42.49	A / 9.5	74.19%	C- / 4.1

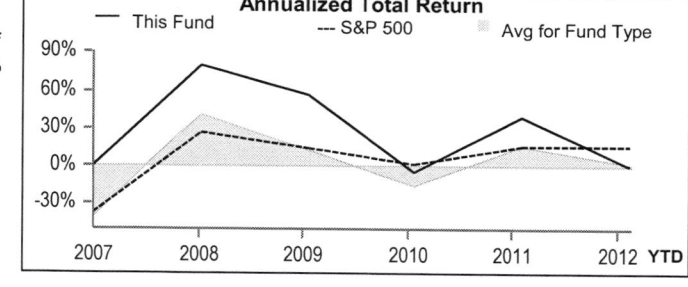

*iShares MSCI Turkey Inv Market (TUR)   B-   Good

Fund Family: BlackRock Fund Advisors
Fund Type: Foreign
Inception Date: March 26, 2008

Data Date	Investment Rating	Net Assets ($Mil)	Price	Performance Rating/Pts	Total Return Y-T-D	Risk Rating/Pts
12-12	B-	767.60	66.78	A- / 9.1	3.86%	C / 5.4
2011	D	352.10	41.14	C- / 3.3	-2.14%	C+ / 5.8
2010	B	787.90	66.21	A- / 9.1	25.64%	C- / 3.8
2009	B+	242.44	53.90	A+ / 9.8	98.29%	C- / 3.9

Major Rating Factors:
Exceptional performance is the major factor driving the B- (Good) TheStreet.com Investment Rating for *iShares MSCI Turkey Inv Market. The fund currently has a performance rating of A- (Excellent) based on an annualized return of 8.64% over the last three years and a total return of 3.86% year to date 2012. Factored into the performance evaluation is an expense ratio of 0.61% (very low).

The fund's risk rating is currently C (Fair). It carries a beta of 1.08, meaning that its performance tracks fairly well with that of the overall stock market. Volatility, as measured by both the semi-deviation and a drawdown factor, is considered average. As of December 31, 2012, *iShares MSCI Turkey Inv Market traded at a discount of 2.94% below its net asset value, which is better than its one-year historical average premium of .17%.

Diane Hsiung has been running the fund for 5 years and currently receives a manager quality ranking of 80 (0=worst, 99=best). If you desire an average level of risk and strong performance, then this fund is a good option.

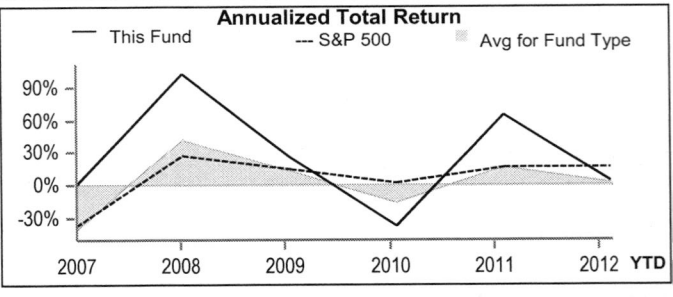

*iShares MSCI United Kingdom (EWU)   C-   Fair

Fund Family: BlackRock Fund Advisors
Fund Type: Foreign
Inception Date: March 12, 1996

Data Date	Investment Rating	Net Assets ($Mil)	Price	Performance Rating/Pts	Total Return Y-T-D	Risk Rating/Pts
12-12	C-	1,423.50	17.94	C- / 4.1	1.84%	B- / 7.4
2011	C-	1,296.50	16.16	C- / 4.2	0.62%	B- / 7.6
2010	D	1,143.80	17.37	D / 1.8	10.28%	C / 4.8
2009	D	739.12	16.20	D / 2.1	35.56%	C / 4.9

Major Rating Factors: Middle of the road best describes *iShares MSCI United Kingdom whose TheStreet.com Investment Rating is currently a C- (Fair). The fund currently has a performance rating of C- (Fair) based on an annualized return of 6.50% over the last three years and a total return of 1.84% year to date 2012. Factored into the performance evaluation is an expense ratio of 0.53% (very low).

The fund's risk rating is currently B- (Good). It carries a beta of 1.02, meaning that its performance tracks fairly well with that of the overall stock market. Volatility, as measured by both the semi-deviation and a drawdown factor, is considered low. As of December 31, 2012, *iShares MSCI United Kingdom traded at a discount of 1.86% below its net asset value, which is better than its one-year historical average premium of .27%.

Diane Hsiung has been running the fund for 5 years and currently receives a manager quality ranking of 70 (0=worst, 99=best). If you desire an average level of risk, then this fund may be an option.

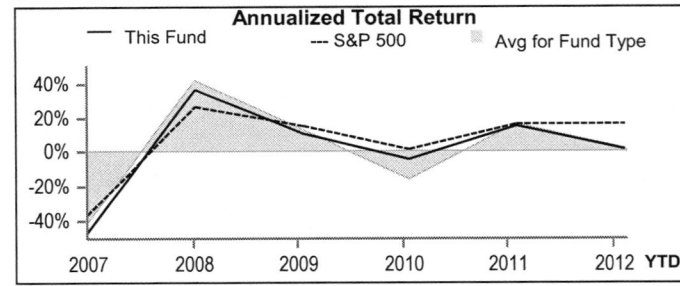

*iShares MSCI USA (EUSA)   B   Good

Fund Family: BlackRock Fund Advisors
Fund Type: Income
Inception Date: May 5, 2010

Data Date	Investment Rating	Net Assets ($Mil)	Price	Performance Rating/Pts	Total Return Y-T-D	Risk Rating/Pts
12-12	B	150.10	30.68	B / 7.7	3.26%	B / 8.1
2011	C-	122.80	27.20	D+ / 2.9	1.03%	B / 8.1

Major Rating Factors: Strong performance is the major factor driving the B (Good) TheStreet.com Investment Rating for *iShares MSCI USA. The fund currently has a performance rating of B (Good) based on an annualized return of 0.00% over the last three years and a total return of 3.26% year to date 2012. Factored into the performance evaluation is an expense ratio of 0.15% (very low).

The fund's risk rating is currently B (Good). It carries a beta of 0.00, meaning the fund's expected move will be 0.0% for every 10% move in the market. Volatility, as measured by both the semi-deviation and a drawdown factor, is considered low. As of December 31, 2012, *iShares MSCI USA traded at a discount of 3.10% below its net asset value, which is better than its one-year historical average discount of .05%.

Diane Hsiung has been running the fund for 3 years and currently receives a manager quality ranking of 50 (0=worst, 99=best). If you desire only a moderate level of risk and strong performance, then this fund is an excellent option.

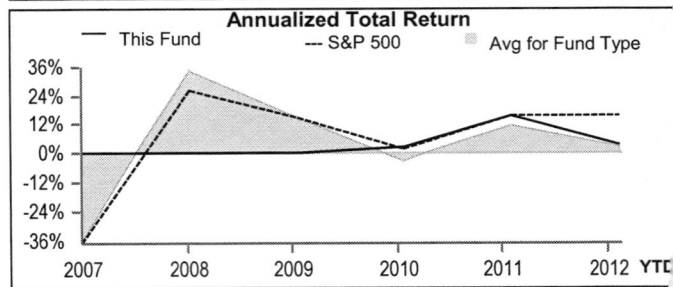

*iShares MSCI USA ESG Select Soc (KLD)

C   **Fair**

Fund Family: BlackRock Fund Advisors
Fund Type: Growth
Inception Date: January 24, 2005

Major Rating Factors: Middle of the road best describes *iShares MSCI USA ESG Select Soc whose TheStreet.com Investment Rating is currently a C (Fair). The fund currently has a performance rating of C- (Fair) based on an annualized return of 9.03% over the last three years and a total return of 3.71% year to date 2012. Factored into the performance evaluation is an expense ratio of 0.50% (very low).

The fund's risk rating is currently B (Good). It carries a beta of 0.99, meaning that its performance tracks fairly well with that of the overall stock market. Volatility, as measured by both the semi-deviation and a drawdown factor, is considered low. As of December 31, 2012, *iShares MSCI USA ESG Select Soc traded at a discount of 3.58% below its net asset value, which is better than its one-year historical average discount of .03%.

Diane Hsiung has been running the fund for 5 years and currently receives a manager quality ranking of 34 (0=worst, 99=best). If you desire an average level of risk, then this fund may be an option.

Data Date	Investment Rating	Net Assets ($Mil)	Price	Performance Rating/Pts	Total Return Y-T-D	Risk Rating/Pts
12-12	C	172.60	59.33	C- / 4.1	3.71%	B / 8.1
2011	C+	164.80	55.03	C / 5.4	1.60%	B / 8.1
2010	C	145.50	54.91	C / 4.5	13.88%	C+ / 6.1
2009	C-	94.91	49.00	D+ / 2.8	26.93%	C+ / 6.1

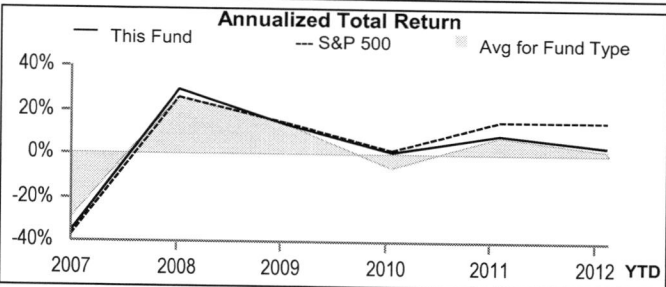

*iShares MSCI USA Minimum Vol Idx (USMV)

B-   **Good**

Fund Family: BlackRock Fund Advisors
Fund Type: Income
Inception Date: October 18, 2011

Major Rating Factors: *iShares MSCI USA Minimum Vol Idx receives a TheStreet.com Investment Rating of B- (Good). The fund currently has a performance rating of C (Fair) based on an annualized return of 0.00% over the last three years and a total return of 3.24% year to date 2012. Factored into the performance evaluation is an expense ratio of 0.15% (very low).

The fund's risk rating is currently B+ (Good). It carries a beta of 0.00, meaning the fund's expected move will be 0.0% for every 10% move in the market. Volatility, as measured by both the semi-deviation and a drawdown factor, is considered very low. As of December 31, 2012, *iShares MSCI USA Minimum Vol Idx traded at a discount of 3.07% below its net asset value, which is better than its one-year historical average premium of .09%.

Greg Savage has been running the fund for 2 years and currently receives a manager quality ranking of 76 (0=worst, 99=best). If you desire an average level of risk, then this fund may be an option.

Data Date	Investment Rating	Net Assets ($Mil)	Price	Performance Rating/Pts	Total Return Y-T-D	Risk Rating/Pts
12-12	B-	751.60	29.04	C / 4.8	3.24%	B+ / 9.8

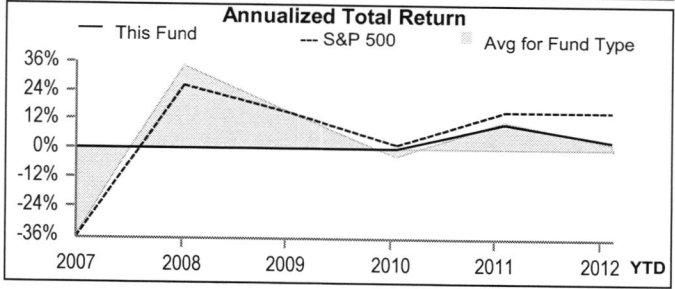

*iShares Nasdaq Biotechnology (IBB)

B-   **Good**

Fund Family: BlackRock Fund Advisors
Fund Type: Health
Inception Date: February 5, 2001

Major Rating Factors: Strong performance is the major factor driving the B- (Good) TheStreet.com Investment Rating for *iShares Nasdaq Biotechnology. The fund currently has a performance rating of B+ (Good) based on an annualized return of 20.43% over the last three years and a total return of 6.02% year to date 2012. Factored into the performance evaluation is an expense ratio of 0.48% (very low).

The fund's risk rating is currently C+ (Fair). It carries a beta of 0.87, meaning the fund's expected move will be 8.7% for every 10% move in the market. Volatility, as measured by both the semi-deviation and a drawdown factor, is considered low. As of December 31, 2012, *iShares Nasdaq Biotechnology traded at a discount of 5.66% below its net asset value, which is better than its one-year historical average premium of .02%.

Diane Hsiung has been running the fund for 5 years and currently receives a manager quality ranking of 88 (0=worst, 99=best). If you desire only a moderate level of risk and strong performance, then this fund is an excellent option.

Data Date	Investment Rating	Net Assets ($Mil)	Price	Performance Rating/Pts	Total Return Y-T-D	Risk Rating/Pts
12-12	B-	2,145.90	137.22	B+ / 8.6	6.02%	C+ / 6.4
2011	C	1,393.90	104.35	C+ / 6.1	2.74%	C+ / 6.2
2010	C+	1,446.90	93.42	C+ / 6.8	14.84%	C+ / 5.9
2009	C-	1,627.16	81.83	C- / 3.3	13.54%	C+ / 5.9

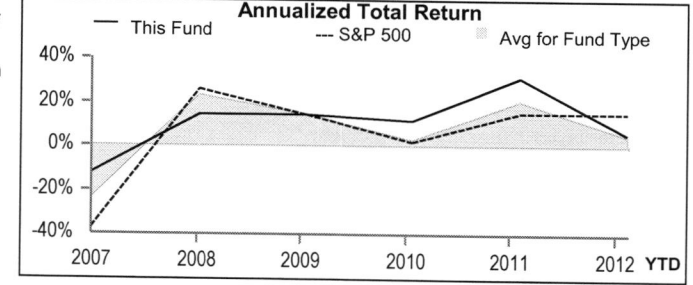

*iShares NYSE 100 (NY)

C   **Fair**

Fund Family: BlackRock Fund Advisors
Fund Type: Income
Inception Date: March 29, 2004

Major Rating Factors: Middle of the road best describes *iShares NYSE 100 whose TheStreet.com Investment Rating is currently a C (Fair). The fund currently has a performance rating of C (Fair) based on an annualized return of 9.84% over the last three years and a total return of 4.33% year to date 2012. Factored into the performance evaluation is an expense ratio of 0.20% (very low).

The fund's risk rating is currently B (Good). It carries a beta of 0.92, meaning that its performance tracks fairly well with that of the overall stock market. Volatility, as measured by both the semi-deviation and a drawdown factor, is considered low. As of December 31, 2012, *iShares NYSE 100 traded at a discount of 4.28% below its net asset value, which is better than its one-year historical average premium of .01%.

Diane Hsiung has been running the fund for 5 years and currently receives a manager quality ranking of 44 (0=worst, 99=best). If you desire an average level of risk, then this fund may be an option.

Data Date	Investment Rating	Net Assets ($Mil)	Price	Performance Rating/Pts	Total Return Y-T-D	Risk Rating/Pts
12-12	C	53.40	66.21	C / 4.6	4.33%	B / 8.3
2011	C	54.00	60.10	C / 4.3	1.01%	B / 8.1
2010	D+	63.20	60.14	D+ / 2.5	12.35%	C+ / 6.2
2009	D	64.58	54.75	D- / 1.4	13.34%	C+ / 6.3

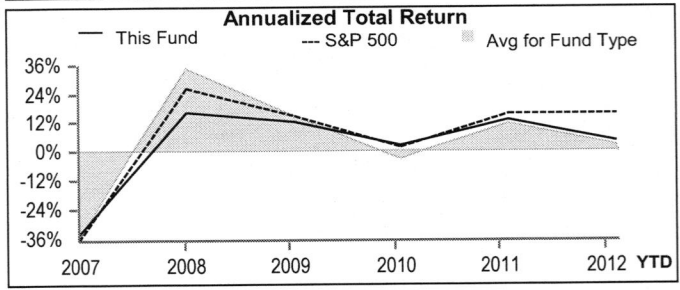

*iShares NYSE Composite (NYC)

C   **Fair**

Fund Family: BlackRock Fund Advisors
Fund Type: Income
Inception Date: March 30, 2004

Major Rating Factors: Middle of the road best describes *iShares NYSE Composite whose TheStreet.com Investment Rating is currently a C (Fair). The fund currently has a performance rating of C (Fair) based on an annualized return of 8.28% over the last three years and a total return of 3.60% year to date 2012. Factored into the performance evaluation is an expense ratio of 0.25% (very low).

The fund's risk rating is currently B (Good). It carries a beta of 1.07, meaning that its performance tracks fairly well with that of the overall stock market. Volatility, as measured by both the semi-deviation and a drawdown factor, is considered low. As of December 31, 2012, *iShares NYSE Composite traded at a discount of 3.50% below its net asset value, which is better than its one-year historical average discount of .03%.

Diane Hsiung has been running the fund for 5 years and currently receives a manager quality ranking of 28 (0=worst, 99=best). If you desire an average level of risk, then this fund may be an option.

Data Date	Investment Rating	Net Assets ($Mil)	Price	Performance Rating/Pts	Total Return Y-T-D	Risk Rating/Pts
12-12	C	61.60	76.69	C / 4.7	3.60%	B / 8.0
2011	C	71.70	68.45	C- / 4.2	0.91%	B- / 7.9
2010	D+	98.30	72.76	C- / 3.1	13.12%	C+ / 5.8
2009	D+	100.24	65.83	D+ / 2.4	25.08%	C+ / 5.9

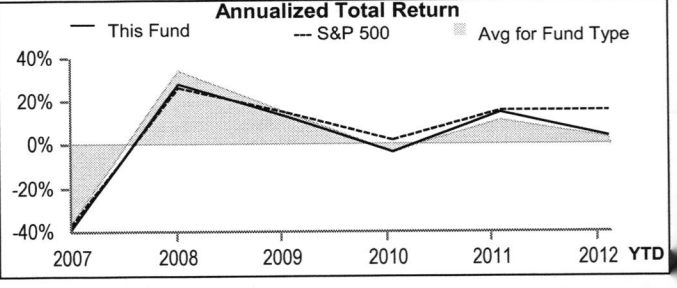

*iShares PHLX SOX Semicon Sector (SOXX)

D+   **Weak**

Fund Family: BlackRock Fund Advisors
Fund Type: Income
Inception Date: July 10, 2001

Major Rating Factors: *iShares PHLX SOX Semicon Sector receives a TheStreet.com Investment Rating of D+ (Weak). The fund currently has a performance rating of C- (Fair) based on an annualized return of 6.29% over the last three years and a total return of 5.02% year to date 2012. Factored into the performance evaluation is an expense ratio of 0.48% (very low).

The fund's risk rating is currently B- (Good). It carries a beta of 1.36, meaning it is expected to move 13.6% for every 10% move in the market. Volatility, as measured by both the semi-deviation and a drawdown factor, is considered low. As of December 31, 2012, *iShares PHLX SOX Semicon Sector traded at a discount of 4.79% below its net asset value, which is better than its one-year historical average discount of .02%.

Diane Hsiung has been running the fund for 5 years and currently receives a manager quality ranking of 12 (0=worst, 99=best). If you desire an average level of risk, then this fund may be an option.

Data Date	Investment Rating	Net Assets ($Mil)	Price	Performance Rating/Pts	Total Return Y-T-D	Risk Rating/Pts
12-12	D+	216.30	52.04	C- / 3.2	5.02%	B- / 7.4
2011	C+	177.90	49.40	C+ / 6.3	2.89%	B- / 7.4
2010	C	230.90	55.70	C+ / 6.0	14.35%	C / 5.2
2009	C-	226.25	49.23	C / 4.3	67.14%	C / 4.9

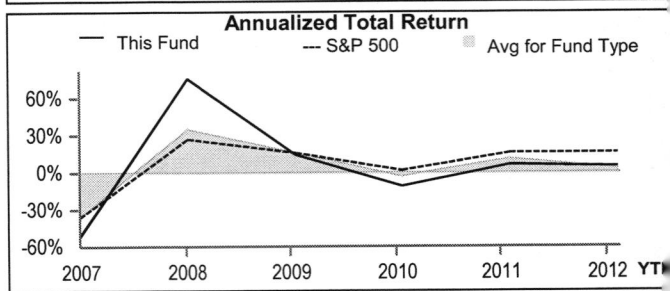

*iShares Russell 1000 (IWB)

C+   **Fair**

Fund Family: BlackRock Fund Advisors
Fund Type: Growth
Inception Date: May 15, 2000

Major Rating Factors: Middle of the road best describes *iShares Russell 1000 whose TheStreet.com Investment Rating is currently a C+ (Fair). The fund currently has a performance rating of C (Fair) based on an annualized return of 11.47% over the last three years and a total return of 3.28% year to date 2012. Factored into the performance evaluation is an expense ratio of 0.15% (very low).

The fund's risk rating is currently B (Good). It carries a beta of 1.02, meaning that its performance tracks fairly well with that of the overall stock market. Volatility, as measured by both the semi-deviation and a drawdown factor, is considered low. As of December 31, 2012, *iShares Russell 1000 traded at a discount of 3.17% below its net asset value, which is better than its one-year historical average discount of .02%.

Diane Hsiung has been running the fund for 5 years and currently receives a manager quality ranking of 51 (0=worst, 99=best). If you desire an average level of risk, then this fund may be an option.

Data Date	Investment Rating	Net Assets ($Mil)	Price	Performance Rating/Pts	Total Return Y-T-D	Risk Rating/Pts
12-12	C+	6,546.30	79.15	C / 5.4	3.28%	B / 8.0
2011	C+	6,300.80	69.37	C / 5.3	1.82%	B- / 7.9
2010	C-	6,452.00	69.86	C- / 4.2	16.02%	C+ / 5.9
2009	D+	4,885.21	61.31	D+ / 2.4	24.71%	C+ / 6.1

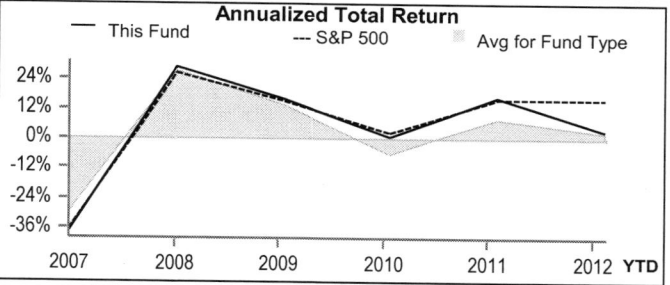

*iShares Russell 1000 Growth (IWF)

C   **Fair**

Fund Family: BlackRock Fund Advisors
Fund Type: Growth
Inception Date: May 22, 2000

Major Rating Factors: Middle of the road best describes *iShares Russell 1000 Growth whose TheStreet.com Investment Rating is currently a C (Fair). The fund currently has a performance rating of C (Fair) based on an annualized return of 11.89% over the last three years and a total return of 3.22% year to date 2012. Factored into the performance evaluation is an expense ratio of 0.20% (very low).

The fund's risk rating is currently B- (Good). It carries a beta of 1.02, meaning that its performance tracks fairly well with that of the overall stock market. Volatility, as measured by both the semi-deviation and a drawdown factor, is considered low. As of December 31, 2012, *iShares Russell 1000 Growth traded at a discount of 3.06% below its net asset value.

Diane Hsiung has been running the fund for 5 years and currently receives a manager quality ranking of 53 (0=worst, 99=best). If you desire an average level of risk, then this fund may be an option.

Data Date	Investment Rating	Net Assets ($Mil)	Price	Performance Rating/Pts	Total Return Y-T-D	Risk Rating/Pts
12-12	C	16,907.00	65.49	C / 5.2	3.22%	B- / 7.6
2011	C+	14,210.50	57.79	C+ / 6.2	1.77%	B- / 7.7
2010	C	12,576.60	57.26	C / 5.3	16.48%	C+ / 5.9
2009	C-	10,436.97	49.85	C- / 3.6	32.68%	C+ / 6.1

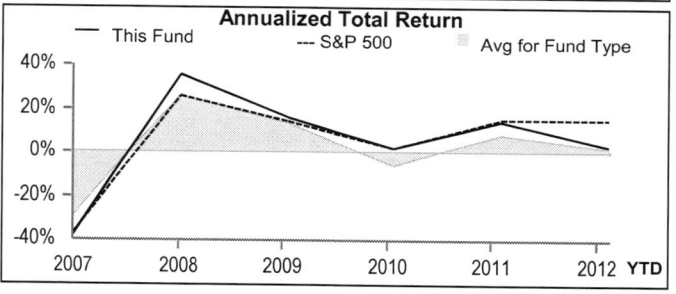

*iShares Russell 1000 Value (IWD)

C+   **Fair**

Fund Family: BlackRock Fund Advisors
Fund Type: Income
Inception Date: May 22, 2000

Major Rating Factors: Middle of the road best describes *iShares Russell 1000 Value whose TheStreet.com Investment Rating is currently a C+ (Fair). The fund currently has a performance rating of C (Fair) based on an annualized return of 10.94% over the last three years and a total return of 3.43% year to date 2012. Factored into the performance evaluation is an expense ratio of 0.20% (very low).

The fund's risk rating is currently B (Good). It carries a beta of 1.02, meaning that its performance tracks fairly well with that of the overall stock market. Volatility, as measured by both the semi-deviation and a drawdown factor, is considered low. As of December 31, 2012, *iShares Russell 1000 Value traded at a discount of 3.32% below its net asset value, which is better than its one-year historical average discount of .01%.

Diane Hsiung has been running the fund for 5 years and currently receives a manager quality ranking of 48 (0=worst, 99=best). If you desire an average level of risk, then this fund may be an option.

Data Date	Investment Rating	Net Assets ($Mil)	Price	Performance Rating/Pts	Total Return Y-T-D	Risk Rating/Pts
12-12	C+	14,536.20	72.82	C / 5.5	3.43%	B / 8.2
2011	C	11,359.00	63.48	C / 4.6	1.78%	B- / 7.8
2010	C-	10,698.20	64.87	C- / 3.1	15.44%	C+ / 5.9
2009	D	8,355.94	57.40	D- / 1.4	16.66%	C+ / 5.9

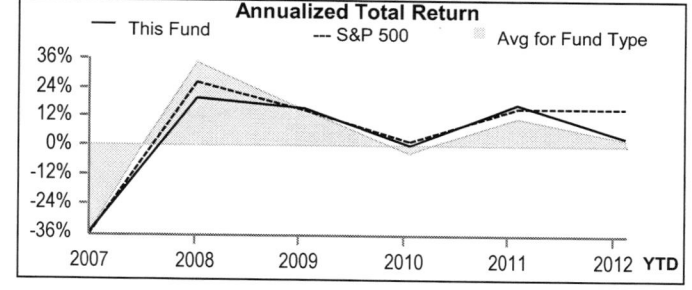

*iShares Russell 2000 (IWM)

C+   **Fair**

Fund Family: BlackRock Fund Advisors
Fund Type: Growth
Inception Date: May 22, 2000

Major Rating Factors: Middle of the road best describes *iShares Russell 2000 whose TheStreet.com Investment Rating is currently a C+ (Fair). The fund currently has a performance rating of C+ (Fair) based on an annualized return of 12.85% over the last three years and a total return of 3.58% year to date 2012. Factored into the performance evaluation is an expense ratio of 0.20% (very low).

The fund's risk rating is currently B- (Good). It carries a beta of 1.28, meaning it is expected to move 12.8% for every 10% move in the market. Volatility, as measured by both the semi-deviation and a drawdown factor, is considered low. As of December 31, 2012, *iShares Russell 2000 traded at a discount of 3.54% below its net asset value, which is better than its one-year historical average discount of .02%.

Diane Hsiung has been running the fund for 5 years and currently receives a manager quality ranking of 38 (0=worst, 99=best). If you desire an average level of risk, then this fund may be an option.

Data Date	Investment Rating	Net Assets ($Mil)	Price	Performance Rating/Pts	Total Return Y-T-D	Risk Rating/Pts
12-12	C+	15,997.10	84.32	C+ / 6.1	3.58%	B- / 7.3
2011	C	14,101.20	73.75	C+ / 5.6	1.42%	B- / 7.2
2010	B	17,565.80	78.24	B- / 7.2	26.90%	C+ / 6.1
2009	D+	12,883.49	62.44	D+ / 2.3	26.02%	C+ / 5.6

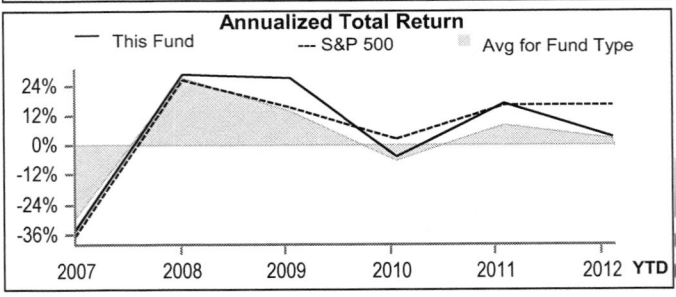

*iShares Russell 2000 Growth (IWO)

C   **Fair**

Fund Family: BlackRock Fund Advisors
Fund Type: Growth
Inception Date: July 24, 2000

Major Rating Factors: Middle of the road best describes *iShares Russell 2000 Growth whose TheStreet.com Investment Rating is currently a C (Fair). The fund currently has a performance rating of C+ (Fair) based on an annualized return of 13.78% over the last three years and a total return of 4.10% year to date 2012. Factored into the performance evaluation is an expense ratio of 0.25% (very low).

The fund's risk rating is currently B- (Good). It carries a beta of 1.30, meaning it is expected to move 13.0% for every 10% move in the market. Volatility, as measured by both the semi-deviation and a drawdown factor, is considered low. As of December 31, 2012, *iShares Russell 2000 Growth traded at a discount of 4.04% below its net asset value, which is better than its one-year historical average discount of .02%.

Diane Hsiung has been running the fund for 5 years and currently receives a manager quality ranking of 42 (0=worst, 99=best). If you desire an average level of risk, then this fund may be an option.

Data Date	Investment Rating	Net Assets ($Mil)	Price	Performance Rating/Pts	Total Return Y-T-D	Risk Rating/Pts
12-12	C	3,915.00	95.31	C+ / 6.2	4.10%	B- / 7.0
2011	C+	3,492.10	84.23	C+ / 6.3	1.14%	C+ / 6.9
2010	B-	4,134.90	87.42	B- / 7.4	29.35%	C / 5.4
2009	D+	3,313.21	68.07	C- / 3.0	31.86%	C / 5.0

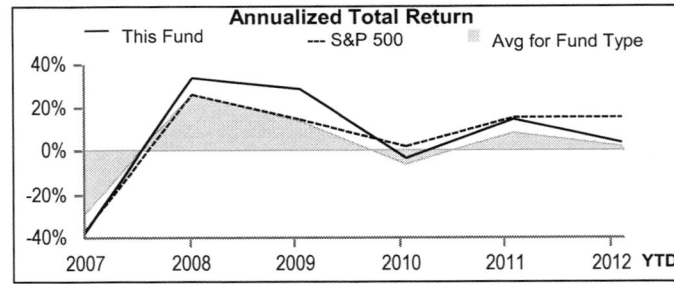

*iShares Russell 2000 Value (IWN)

C+   **Fair**

Fund Family: BlackRock Fund Advisors
Fund Type: Growth
Inception Date: July 24, 2000

Major Rating Factors: Middle of the road best describes *iShares Russell 2000 Value whose TheStreet.com Investment Rating is currently a C+ (Fair). The fund currently has a performance rating of C+ (Fair) based on an annualized return of 11.74% over the last three years and a total return of 3.31% year to date 2012. Factored into the performance evaluation is an expense ratio of 0.25% (very low).

The fund's risk rating is currently B- (Good). It carries a beta of 1.26, meaning it is expected to move 12.6% for every 10% move in the market. Volatility, as measured by both the semi-deviation and a drawdown factor, is considered low. As of December 31, 2012, *iShares Russell 2000 Value traded at a discount of 3.23% below its net asset value, which is better than its one-year historical average discount of .01%.

Diane Hsiung has been running the fund for 5 years and currently receives a manager quality ranking of 34 (0=worst, 99=best). If you desire an average level of risk, then this fund may be an option.

Data Date	Investment Rating	Net Assets ($Mil)	Price	Performance Rating/Pts	Total Return Y-T-D	Risk Rating/Pts
12-12	C+	4,260.00	75.51	C+ / 5.9	3.31%	B- / 7.5
2011	C	3,887.90	65.64	C / 4.8	1.63%	B- / 7.4
2010	B-	4,728.40	71.09	B- / 7.1	24.68%	C+ / 5.7
2009	D	3,864.02	58.04	D / 1.6	20.27%	C+ / 5.6

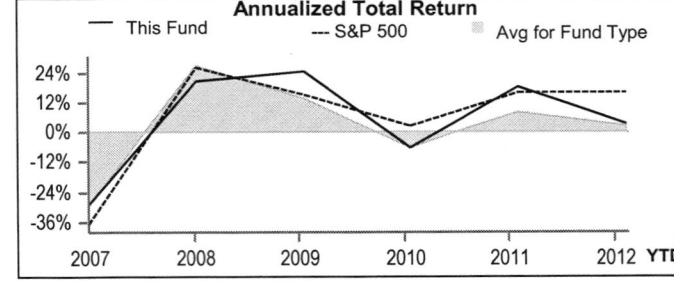

*iShares Russell 3000 (IWV)

C+   **Fair**

Fund Family: BlackRock Fund Advisors
Fund Type: Income
Inception Date: May 22, 2000

Major Rating Factors: Middle of the road best describes *iShares Russell 3000 whose TheStreet.com Investment Rating is currently a C+ (Fair). The fund currently has a performance rating of C (Fair) based on an annualized return of 11.59% over the last three years and a total return of 3.27% year to date 2012. Factored into the performance evaluation is an expense ratio of 0.20% (very low).

The fund's risk rating is currently B- (Good). It carries a beta of 1.03, meaning that its performance tracks fairly well with that of the overall stock market. Volatility, as measured by both the semi-deviation and a drawdown factor, is considered low. As of December 31, 2012, *iShares Russell 3000 traded at a discount of 3.15% below its net asset value, which is better than its one-year historical average discount of .01%.

Diane Hsiung has been running the fund for 5 years and currently receives a manager quality ranking of 50 (0=worst, 99=best). If you desire an average level of risk, then this fund may be an option.

Data Date	Investment Rating	Net Assets ($Mil)	Price	Performance Rating/Pts	Total Return Y-T-D	Risk Rating/Pts
12-12	C+	3,660.90	84.68	C / 5.4	3.27%	B- / 7.9
2011	C+	3,209.30	74.18	C / 5.3	1.70%	B- / 7.9
2010	C	3,250.80	74.95	C / 4.5	16.82%	C+ / 5.9
2009	D+	2,958.22	65.28	D+ / 2.3	24.83%	C+ / 6.0

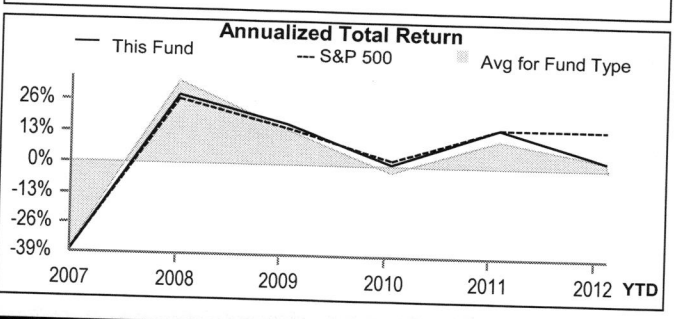

*iShares Russell 3000 Growth (IWZ)

C   **Fair**

Fund Family: BlackRock Fund Advisors
Fund Type: Growth
Inception Date: July 24, 2000

Major Rating Factors: Middle of the road best describes *iShares Russell 3000 Growth whose TheStreet.com Investment Rating is currently a C (Fair). The fund currently has a performance rating of C (Fair) based on an annualized return of 11.92% over the last three years and a total return of 3.30% year to date 2012. Factored into the performance evaluation is an expense ratio of 0.25% (very low).

The fund's risk rating is currently B- (Good). It carries a beta of 1.04, meaning that its performance tracks fairly well with that of the overall stock market. Volatility, as measured by both the semi-deviation and a drawdown factor, is considered low. As of December 31, 2012, *iShares Russell 3000 Growth traded at a discount of 3.17% below its net asset value, which is better than its one-year historical average discount of .01%.

Diane Hsiung has been running the fund for 5 years and currently receives a manager quality ranking of 51 (0=worst, 99=best). If you desire an average level of risk, then this fund may be an option.

Data Date	Investment Rating	Net Assets ($Mil)	Price	Performance Rating/Pts	Total Return Y-T-D	Risk Rating/Pts
12-12	C	363.20	53.41	C / 5.2	3.30%	B- / 7.6
2011	C+	346.90	47.19	C+ / 6.2	1.57%	B- / 7.7
2010	C+	333.00	46.93	C / 5.5	17.42%	C+ / 5.9
2009	C-	343.73	40.49	C- / 3.5	32.47%	C+ / 6.0

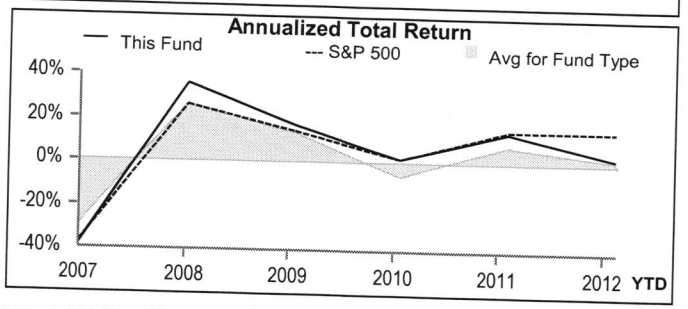

*iShares Russell 3000 Value (IWW)

C+   **Fair**

Fund Family: BlackRock Fund Advisors
Fund Type: Income
Inception Date: July 24, 2000

Major Rating Factors: Middle of the road best describes *iShares Russell 3000 Value whose TheStreet.com Investment Rating is currently a C+ (Fair). The fund currently has a performance rating of C (Fair) based on an annualized return of 10.95% over the last three years and a total return of 3.50% year to date 2012. Factored into the performance evaluation is an expense ratio of 0.25% (very low).

The fund's risk rating is currently B (Good). It carries a beta of 1.03, meaning that its performance tracks fairly well with that of the overall stock market. Volatility, as measured by both the semi-deviation and a drawdown factor, is considered low. As of December 31, 2012, *iShares Russell 3000 Value traded at a discount of 3.35% below its net asset value, which is better than its one-year historical average discount of .02%.

Diane Hsiung has been running the fund for 5 years and currently receives a manager quality ranking of 47 (0=worst, 99=best). If you desire an average level of risk, then this fund may be an option.

Data Date	Investment Rating	Net Assets ($Mil)	Price	Performance Rating/Pts	Total Return Y-T-D	Risk Rating/Pts
12-12	C+	366.80	95.35	C / 5.5	3.50%	B / 8.1
2011	C	307.60	83.14	C / 4.6	1.64%	B- / 7.8
2010	C-	324.00	85.25	C- / 3.4	15.76%	C+ / 5.9
2009	D	392.18	75.23	D- / 1.4	17.15%	C+ / 5.9

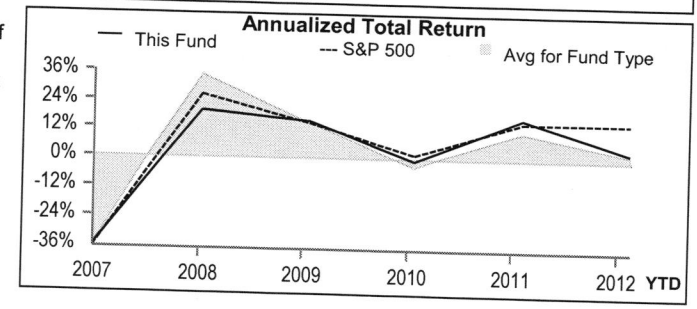

* Denotes ETF Fund

*iShares Russell Micro Cap (IWC)

			C			Fair

Fund Family: BlackRock Fund Advisors
Fund Type: Growth
Inception Date: August 12, 2005

Major Rating Factors: Middle of the road best describes *iShares Russell Micro Cap whose TheStreet.com Investment Rating is currently a C (Fair). The fund currently has a performance rating of C+ (Fair) based on an annualized return of 12.08% over the last three years and a total return of 3.94% year to date 2012. Factored into the performance evaluation is an expense ratio of 0.60% (very low).

The fund's risk rating is currently B- (Good). It carries a beta of 1.34, meaning it is expected to move 13.4% for every 10% move in the market. Volatility, as measured by both the semi-deviation and a drawdown factor, is considered low. As of December 31, 2012, *iShares Russell Micro Cap traded at a discount of 3.68% below its net asset value, which is better than its one-year historical average discount of .05%.

Diane Hsiung has been running the fund for 5 years and currently receives a manager quality ranking of 31 (0=worst, 99=best). If you desire an average level of risk, then this fund may be an option.

Data Date	Investment Rating	Net Assets ($Mil)	Price	Performance Rating/Pts	Total Return Y-T-D	Risk Rating/Pts
12-12	C	460.60	52.32	C+ / 5.8	3.94%	B- / 7.3
2011	C-	388.90	44.65	C / 4.4	1.41%	B- / 7.1
2010	C+	529.90	50.11	C+ / 6.6	29.55%	C / 5.5
2009	D-	353.54	39.03	D- / 1.2	23.06%	C / 5.4

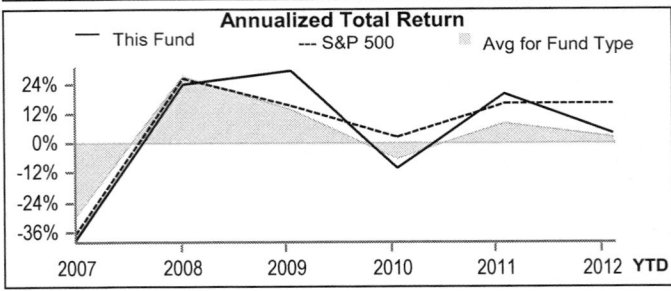

*iShares Russell Mid Cap (IWR)

			C+			Fair

Fund Family: BlackRock Fund Advisors
Fund Type: Growth
Inception Date: July 17, 2001

Major Rating Factors: Middle of the road best describes *iShares Russell Mid Cap whose TheStreet.com Investment Rating is currently a C+ (Fair). The fund currently has a performance rating of C+ (Fair) based on an annualized return of 13.38% over the last three years and a total return of 3.30% year to date 2012. Factored into the performance evaluation is an expense ratio of 0.20% (very low).

The fund's risk rating is currently B- (Good). It carries a beta of 1.11, meaning it is expected to move 11.1% for every 10% move in the market. Volatility, as measured by both the semi-deviation and a drawdown factor, is considered low. As of December 31, 2012, *iShares Russell Mid Cap traded at a discount of 3.24% below its net asset value, which is better than its one-year historical average discount of .01%.

Diane Hsiung has been running the fund for 5 years and currently receives a manager quality ranking of 59 (0=worst, 99=best). If you desire an average level of risk, then this fund may be an option.

Data Date	Investment Rating	Net Assets ($Mil)	Price	Performance Rating/Pts	Total Return Y-T-D	Risk Rating/Pts
12-12	C+	6,523.60	113.10	C+ / 6.5	3.30%	B- / 7.9
2011	C+	6,009.40	98.42	C+ / 6.5	1.47%	B- / 7.8
2010	C+	6,018.40	101.75	C+ / 6.6	25.31%	C / 5.5
2009	C-	4,561.94	82.51	C- / 3.2	36.03%	C+ / 6.1

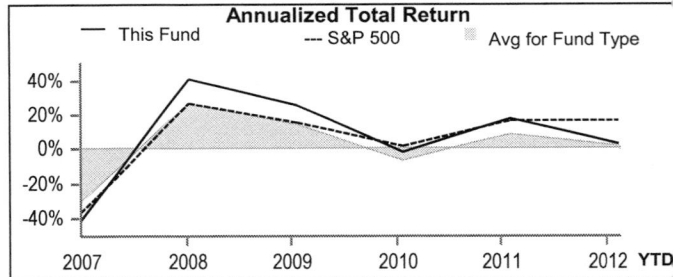

*iShares Russell Mid Cap Growth (IWP)

			C+			Fair

Fund Family: BlackRock Fund Advisors
Fund Type: Growth
Inception Date: July 17, 2001

Major Rating Factors: Middle of the road best describes *iShares Russell Mid Cap Growth whose TheStreet.com Investment Rating is currently a C+ (Fair). The fund currently has a performance rating of C+ (Fair) based on an annualized return of 13.35% over the last three years and a total return of 3.31% year to date 2012. Factored into the performance evaluation is an expense ratio of 0.25% (very low).

The fund's risk rating is currently B- (Good). It carries a beta of 1.14, meaning it is expected to move 11.4% for every 10% move in the market. Volatility, as measured by both the semi-deviation and a drawdown factor, is considered low. As of December 31, 2012, *iShares Russell Mid Cap Growth traded at a discount of 3.24% below its net asset value, which is better than its one-year historical average discount of .01%.

Diane Hsiung has been running the fund for 5 years and currently receives a manager quality ranking of 54 (0=worst, 99=best). If you desire an average level of risk, then this fund may be an option.

Data Date	Investment Rating	Net Assets ($Mil)	Price	Performance Rating/Pts	Total Return Y-T-D	Risk Rating/Pts
12-12	C+	3,289.00	62.80	C+ / 6.2	3.31%	B- / 7.7
2011	C+	2,896.90	55.05	C+ / 6.7	1.80%	B- / 7.6
2010	C-	3,161.20	56.61	C+ / 6.7	26.03%	C- / 3.2
2009	D	2,542.46	45.34	C- / 3.7	40.24%	C- / 3.6

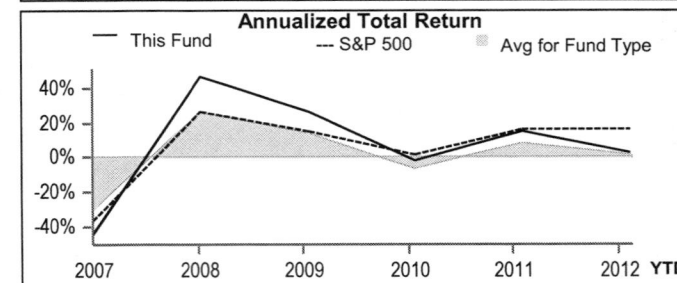

*iShares Russell Mid Cap Value (IWS)

B-   **Good**

Fund Family: BlackRock Fund Advisors
Fund Type: Growth
Inception Date: July 17, 2001

Major Rating Factors: *iShares Russell Mid Cap Value receives a TheStreet.com Investment Rating of B- (Good). The fund currently has a performance rating of C+ (Fair) based on an annualized return of 13.31% over the last three years and a total return of 3.24% year to date 2012. Factored into the performance evaluation is an expense ratio of 0.25% (very low).

The fund's risk rating is currently B- (Good). It carries a beta of 1.09, meaning that its performance tracks fairly well with that of the overall stock market. Volatility, as measured by both the semi-deviation and a drawdown factor, is considered low. As of December 31, 2012, *iShares Russell Mid Cap Value traded at a discount of 3.22% below its net asset value.

Diane Hsiung has been running the fund for 5 years and currently receives a manager quality ranking of 62 (0=worst, 99=best). If you desire an average level of risk, then this fund may be an option.

Data Date	Investment Rating	Net Assets ($Mil)	Price	Performance Rating/Pts	Total Return Y-T-D	Risk Rating/Pts
12-12	B-	3,907.30	50.24	C+ / 6.6	3.24%	B- / 7.9
2011	C+	2,744.40	43.40	C+ / 6.1	1.29%	B- / 7.9
2010	C-	3,100.30	45.01	C+ / 6.5	24.43%	D+ / 2.8
2009	D-	2,890.41	36.95	D+ / 2.5	30.87%	C- / 3.0

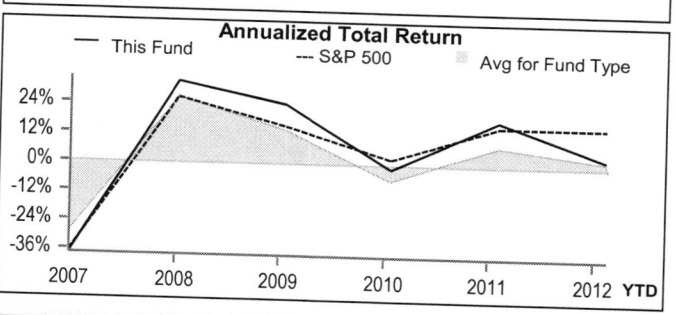

*iShares Russell Top 200 Growth (IWY)

C+   **Fair**

Fund Family: BlackRock Fund Advisors
Fund Type: Growth
Inception Date: September 22, 2009

Major Rating Factors: Middle of the road best describes *iShares Russell Top 200 Growth whose TheStreet.com Investment Rating is currently a C+ (Fair). The fund currently has a performance rating of C (Fair) based on an annualized return of 11.32% over the last three years and a total return of 3.17% year to date 2012. Factored into the performance evaluation is an expense ratio of 0.20% (very low).

The fund's risk rating is currently B (Good). It carries a beta of 0.97, meaning that its performance tracks fairly well with that of the overall stock market. Volatility, as measured by both the semi-deviation and a drawdown factor, is considered low. As of December 31, 2012, *iShares Russell Top 200 Growth traded at a discount of 3.07% below its net asset value.

Diane Hsiung has been running the fund for 4 years and currently receives a manager quality ranking of 50 (0=worst, 99=best). If you desire an average level of risk, then this fund may be an option.

Data Date	Investment Rating	Net Assets ($Mil)	Price	Performance Rating/Pts	Total Return Y-T-D	Risk Rating/Pts
12-12	C+	352.30	34.71	C / 4.8	3.17%	B / 8.5
2011	C-	401.70	30.82	C- / 3.3	1.62%	B / 8.6
2010	A+	331.00	29.93	A- / 9.0	11.98%	B- / 7.8

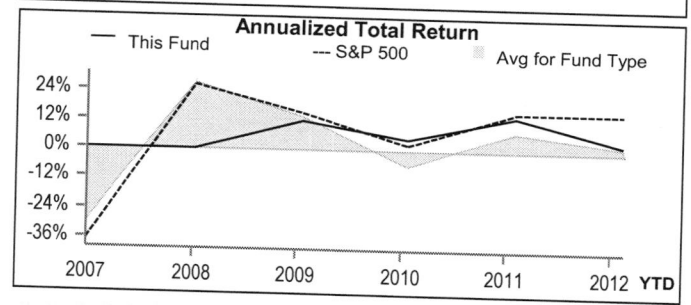

*iShares Russell Top 200 Idx (IWL)

C   **Fair**

Fund Family: BlackRock Fund Advisors
Fund Type: Income
Inception Date: September 22, 2009

Major Rating Factors: Middle of the road best describes *iShares Russell Top 200 Idx whose TheStreet.com Investment Rating is currently a C (Fair). The fund currently has a performance rating of C (Fair) based on an annualized return of 10.61% over the last three years and a total return of 3.38% year to date 2012. Factored into the performance evaluation is an expense ratio of 0.15% (very low).

The fund's risk rating is currently B (Good). It carries a beta of 0.91, meaning that its performance tracks fairly well with that of the overall stock market. Volatility, as measured by both the semi-deviation and a drawdown factor, is considered low. As of December 31, 2012, *iShares Russell Top 200 Idx traded at a discount of 3.27% below its net asset value, which is better than its one-year historical average discount of .01%.

Diane Hsiung has been running the fund for 4 years and currently receives a manager quality ranking of 51 (0=worst, 99=best). If you desire an average level of risk, then this fund may be an option.

Data Date	Investment Rating	Net Assets ($Mil)	Price	Performance Rating/Pts	Total Return Y-T-D	Risk Rating/Pts
12-12	C	52.00	32.50	C / 4.9	3.38%	B / 8.4
2011	C-	109.10	29.17	C- / 3.2	1.65%	B / 8.5
2010	A+	11.60	28.87	B+ / 8.9	11.26%	B- / 7.9

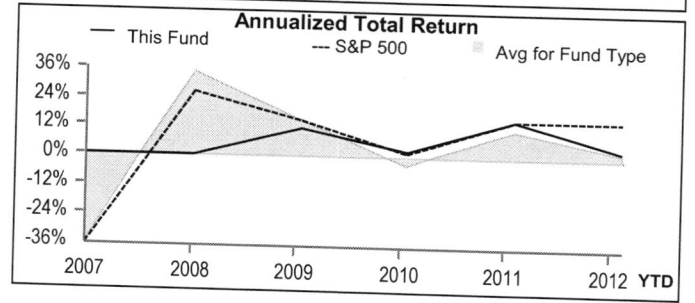

*iShares Russell Top 200 Value Id (IWX)   C   Fair

Fund Family: BlackRock Fund Advisors
Fund Type: Income
Inception Date: September 22, 2009

Major Rating Factors: Middle of the road best describes *iShares Russell Top 200 Value Id whose TheStreet.com Investment Rating is currently a C (Fair). The fund currently has a performance rating of C (Fair) based on an annualized return of 9.58% over the last three years and a total return of 3.66% year to date 2012. Factored into the performance evaluation is an expense ratio of 0.20% (very low).

The fund's risk rating is currently B (Good). It carries a beta of 0.98, meaning that its performance tracks fairly well with that of the overall stock market. Volatility, as measured by both the semi-deviation and a drawdown factor, is considered low. As of December 31, 2012, *iShares Russell Top 200 Value Id traded at a discount of 3.53% below its net asset value, which is better than its one-year historical average discount of .03%.

Diane Hsiung has been running the fund for 4 years and currently receives a manager quality ranking of 40 (0=worst, 99=best). If you desire an average level of risk, then this fund may be an option.

Data Date	Investment Rating	Net Assets ($Mil)	Price	Performance Rating/Pts	Total Return Y-T-D	Risk Rating/Pts
12-12	C	79.50	31.17	C / 4.8	3.66%	B / 8.0
2011	C-	137.30	27.54	D+ / 2.9	1.56%	B / 8.1
2010	A+	212.20	27.94	B+ / 8.8	10.59%	B- / 7.8

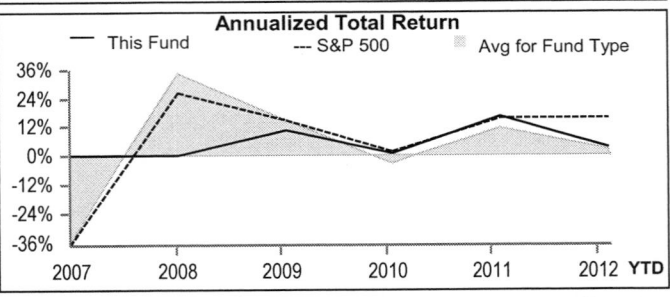

*iShares S&P 100 (OEF)   C   Fair

Fund Family: BlackRock Fund Advisors
Fund Type: Growth
Inception Date: October 23, 2000

Major Rating Factors: Middle of the road best describes *iShares S&P 100 whose TheStreet.com Investment Rating is currently a C (Fair). The fund currently has a performance rating of C (Fair) based on an annualized return of 10.72% over the last three years and a total return of 3.37% year to date 2012. Factored into the performance evaluation is an expense ratio of 0.20% (very low).

The fund's risk rating is currently B (Good). It carries a beta of 0.97, meaning that its performance tracks fairly well with that of the overall stock market. Volatility, as measured by both the semi-deviation and a drawdown factor, is considered low. As of December 31, 2012, *iShares S&P 100 traded at a discount of 3.27% below its net asset value, which is better than its one-year historical average discount of .01%.

Diane Hsiung has been running the fund for 5 years and currently receives a manager quality ranking of 50 (0=worst, 99=best). If you desire an average level of risk, then this fund may be an option.

Data Date	Investment Rating	Net Assets ($Mil)	Price	Performance Rating/Pts	Total Return Y-T-D	Risk Rating/Pts
12-12	C	3,940.10	64.69	C / 4.8	3.37%	B / 8.0
2011	C	2,878.00	57.03	C / 4.9	1.93%	B- / 7.9
2010	C-	2,415.40	56.67	C- / 3.2	12.48%	C+ / 6.1
2009	D+	2,163.95	51.45	D / 1.9	18.80%	C+ / 6.1

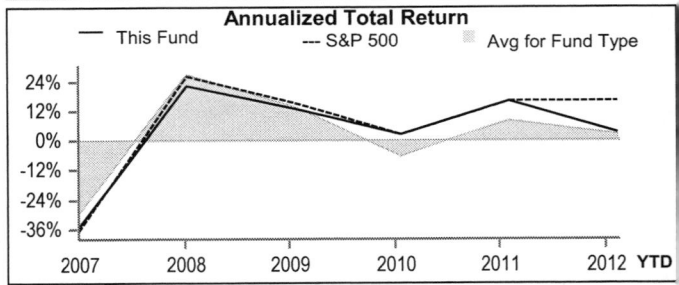

*iShares S&P 500 Growth (IVW)   C   Fair

Fund Family: BlackRock Fund Advisors
Fund Type: Growth
Inception Date: May 22, 2000

Major Rating Factors: Middle of the road best describes *iShares S&P 500 Growth whose TheStreet.com Investment Rating is currently a C (Fair). The fund currently has a performance rating of C (Fair) based on an annualized return of 11.90% over the last three years and a total return of 3.22% year to date 2012. Factored into the performance evaluation is an expense ratio of 0.18% (very low).

The fund's risk rating is currently B- (Good). It carries a beta of 0.97, meaning that its performance tracks fairly well with that of the overall stock market. Volatility, as measured by both the semi-deviation and a drawdown factor, is considered low. As of December 31, 2012, *iShares S&P 500 Growth traded at a discount of 3.12% below its net asset value, which is better than its one-year historical average discount of .01%.

Diane Hsiung has been running the fund for 5 years and currently receives a manager quality ranking of 57 (0=worst, 99=best). If you desire an average level of risk, then this fund may be an option.

Data Date	Investment Rating	Net Assets ($Mil)	Price	Performance Rating/Pts	Total Return Y-T-D	Risk Rating/Pts
12-12	C	6,644.40	75.74	C / 5.1	3.22%	B- / 7.8
2011	C+	6,403.90	67.43	C+ / 6.0	1.29%	B- / 7.8
2010	C	5,806.90	65.65	C / 5.0	14.91%	C+ / 6.1
2009	C-	5,513.11	57.99	C- / 3.3	27.19%	C+ / 6.3

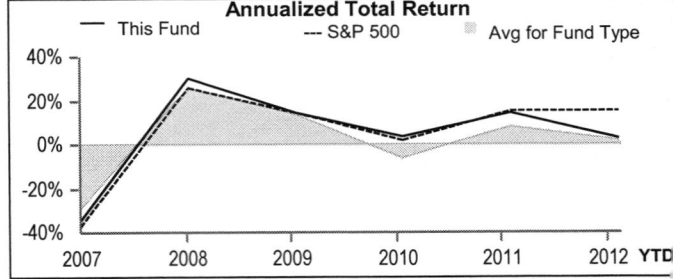

*iShares S&P 500 Value (IVE)

C+   **Fair**

Fund Family: BlackRock Fund Advisors
Fund Type: Income
Inception Date: May 22, 2000

Major Rating Factors: Middle of the road best describes *iShares S&P 500 Value whose TheStreet.com Investment Rating is currently a C+ (Fair). The fund currently has a performance rating of C (Fair) based on an annualized return of 10.54% over the last three years and a total return of 3.31% year to date 2012. Factored into the performance evaluation is an expense ratio of 0.18% (very low).

The fund's risk rating is currently B (Good). It carries a beta of 1.03, meaning that its performance tracks fairly well with that of the overall stock market. Volatility, as measured by both the semi-deviation and a drawdown factor, is considered low. As of December 31, 2012, *iShares S&P 500 Value traded at a discount of 3.21% below its net asset value, which is better than its one-year historical average discount of .02%.

Diane Hsiung has been running the fund for 5 years and currently receives a manager quality ranking of 44 (0=worst, 99=best). If you desire an average level of risk, then this fund may be an option.

Data Date	Investment Rating	Net Assets ($Mil)	Price	Performance Rating/Pts	Total Return Y-T-D	Risk Rating/Pts
12-12	C+	4,830.60	66.39	C / 5.3	3.31%	B / 8.1
2011	C	3,901.70	57.83	C / 4.7	2.21%	B- / 7.8
2010	D+	4,115.90	59.59	D+ / 2.7	14.97%	C+ / 5.7
2009	D	3,503.61	53.01	D- / 1.3	18.12%	C+ / 5.8

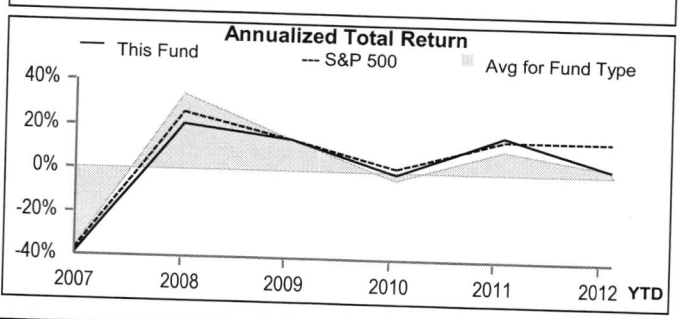

*iShares S&P Aggressive Allocatio (AOA)

C   **Fair**

Fund Family: BlackRock Fund Advisors
Fund Type: Growth and Income
Inception Date: November 4, 2008

Major Rating Factors: Middle of the road best describes *iShares S&P Aggressive Allocatio whose TheStreet.com Investment Rating is currently a C (Fair). The fund currently has a performance rating of C (Fair) based on an annualized return of 9.82% over the last three years and a total return of 2.50% year to date 2012. Factored into the performance evaluation is an expense ratio of 0.11% (very low).

The fund's risk rating is currently B (Good). It carries a beta of 0.99, meaning that its performance tracks fairly well with that of the overall stock market. Volatility, as measured by both the semi-deviation and a drawdown factor, is considered low. As of December 31, 2012, *iShares S&P Aggressive Allocatio traded at a discount of 2.39% below its net asset value, which is better than its one-year historical average premium of .03%.

Diane Hsiung has been running the fund for 5 years and currently receives a manager quality ranking of 43 (0=worst, 99=best). If you desire an average level of risk, then this fund may be an option.

Data Date	Investment Rating	Net Assets ($Mil)	Price	Performance Rating/Pts	Total Return Y-T-D	Risk Rating/Pts
12-12	C	105.90	37.17	C / 4.8	2.50%	B / 8.1
2011	C	82.50	33.05	C / 4.7	1.05%	B / 8.1
2010	A+	56.70	34.37	A- / 9.2	16.77%	B- / 7.5
2009	A+	18.88	29.97	B / 8.1	23.89%	B- / 7.8

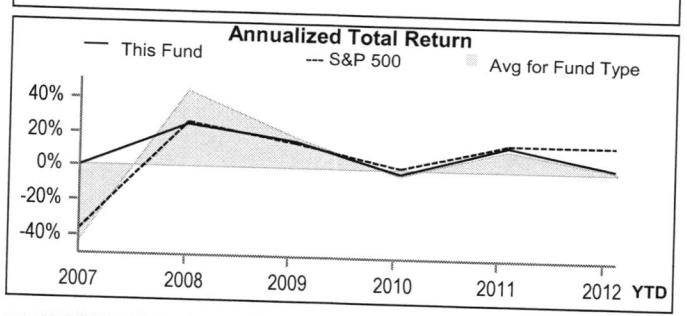

*iShares S&P Asia 50 Index (AIA)

C   **Fair**

Fund Family: BlackRock Fund Advisors
Fund Type: Foreign
Inception Date: November 13, 2007

Major Rating Factors: Middle of the road best describes *iShares S&P Asia 50 Index whose TheStreet.com Investment Rating is currently a C (Fair). The fund currently has a performance rating of C+ (Fair) based on an annualized return of 8.45% over the last three years and a total return of 0.23% year to date 2012. Factored into the performance evaluation is an expense ratio of 0.50% (very low).

The fund's risk rating is currently B- (Good). It carries a beta of 0.94, meaning that its performance tracks fairly well with that of the overall stock market. Volatility, as measured by both the semi-deviation and a drawdown factor, is considered low. As of December 31, 2012, *iShares S&P Asia 50 Index traded at a premium of .27% above its net asset value, which is worse than its one-year historical average premium of .04%.

Diane Hsiung has been running the fund for 5 years and currently receives a manager quality ranking of 79 (0=worst, 99=best). If you desire an average level of risk, then this fund may be an option.

Data Date	Investment Rating	Net Assets ($Mil)	Price	Performance Rating/Pts	Total Return Y-T-D	Risk Rating/Pts
12-12	C	227.10	48.15	C+ / 5.8	0.23%	B- / 7.1
2011	C	177.10	39.15	C / 5.2	1.10%	B- / 7.3
2010	C	209.60	46.95	C+ / 6.3	19.62%	C / 4.9
2009	A-	111.28	39.95	A- / 9.1	51.24%	C / 5.1

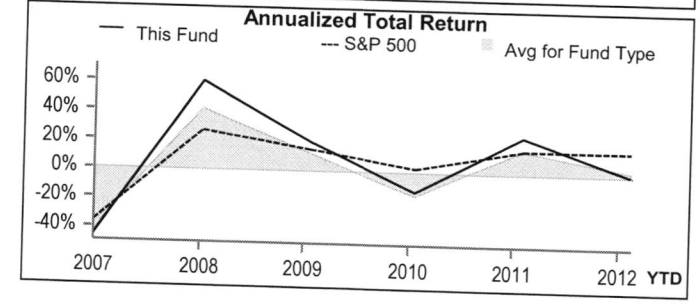

*iShares S&P CA AMT-Free Muni Bon (CMF)   C   Fair

Fund Family: BlackRock Fund Advisors
Fund Type: Municipal - Single State
Inception Date: October 4, 2007

Major Rating Factors: Middle of the road best describes *iShares S&P CA AMT-Free Muni Bon whose TheStreet.com Investment Rating is currently a C (Fair). The fund currently has a performance rating of C- (Fair) based on an annualized return of 6.82% over the last three years and a total return of 0.75% year to date 2012. Factored into the performance evaluation is an expense ratio of 0.25% (very low).

The fund's risk rating is currently B+ (Good). It carries a beta of 1.51, meaning it is expected to move 15.1% for every 10% move in the market. Volatility, as measured by both the semi-deviation and a drawdown factor, is considered very low. As of December 31, 2012, *iShares S&P CA AMT-Free Muni Bon traded at a discount of .44% below its net asset value, which is better than its one-year historical average premium of .55%.

James J. Mauro currently receives a manager quality ranking of 30 (0=worst, 99=best). If you desire an average level of risk, then this fund may be an option.

Data Date	Investment Rating	Net Assets ($Mil)	Price	Performance Rating/Pts	Total Return Y-T-D	Risk Rating/Pts
12-12	C	282.10	115.30	C- / 3.9	0.75%	B+ / 9.1
2011	B-	193.00	110.79	C / 5.5	0.59%	B+ / 9.2
2010	C	225.30	98.85	D / 2.2	-2.64%	B / 8.5
2009	B	167.56	105.55	C / 5.3	8.17%	B / 8.9

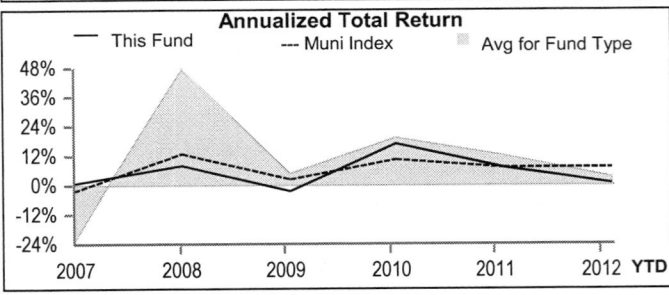

*iShares S&P Conservative Allocat (AOK)   C   Fair

Fund Family: BlackRock Fund Advisors
Fund Type: Growth and Income
Inception Date: November 4, 2008

Major Rating Factors:
Disappointing performance is the major factor driving the C (Fair) TheStreet.com Investment Rating for *iShares S&P Conservative Allocat. The fund currently has a performance rating of D+ (Weak) based on an annualized return of 5.70% over the last three years and a total return of 0.62% year to date 2012. Factored into the performance evaluation is an expense ratio of 0.11% (very low).

The fund's risk rating is currently B+ (Good). It carries a beta of 0.23, meaning the fund's expected move will be 2.3% for every 10% move in the market. Volatility, as measured by both the semi-deviation and a drawdown factor, is considered very low. As of December 31, 2012, *iShares S&P Conservative Allocat traded at a discount of .71% below its net asset value, which is better than its one-year historical average premium of .01%.

Diane Hsiung has been running the fund for 5 years and currently receives a manager quality ranking of 74 (0=worst, 99=best). This fund offers only a moderate level of risk but investors looking for strong performance are still waiting.

Data Date	Investment Rating	Net Assets ($Mil)	Price	Performance Rating/Pts	Total Return Y-T-D	Risk Rating/Pts
12-12	C	116.20	30.58	D+ / 2.7	0.62%	B+ / 9.8
2011	C	95.30	29.35	C- / 3.4	0.20%	B+ / 9.6
2010	B	44.60	28.79	C+ / 6.6	7.08%	B / 8.7
2009	B+	10.51	27.30	C / 4.8	8.46%	B / 8.9

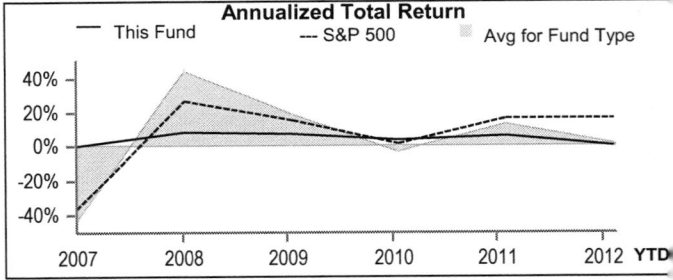

*iShares S&P Dev ex-US Property (WPS)   C+   Fair

Fund Family: BlackRock Fund Advisors
Fund Type: Foreign
Inception Date: July 30, 2007

Major Rating Factors: Strong performance is the major factor driving the C+ (Fair) TheStreet.com Investment Rating for *iShares S&P Dev ex-US Property. The fund currently has a performance rating of B (Good) based on an annualized return of 11.11% over the last three years and a total return of 0.91% year to date 2012. Factored into the performance evaluation is an expense ratio of 0.48% (very low).

The fund's risk rating is currently C+ (Fair). It carries a beta of 0.96, meaning that its performance tracks fairly well with that of the overall stock market. Volatility, as measured by both the semi-deviation and a drawdown factor, is considered low. As of December 31, 2012, *iShares S&P Dev ex-US Property traded at a discount of .38% below its net asset value, which is better than its one-year historical average premium of .14%.

Diane Hsiung has been running the fund for 5 years and currently receives a manager quality ranking of 85 (0=worst, 99=best). If you desire only a moderate level of risk and strong performance, then this fund is an excellent option.

Data Date	Investment Rating	Net Assets ($Mil)	Price	Performance Rating/Pts	Total Return Y-T-D	Risk Rating/Pts
12-12	C+	233.20	36.31	B / 7.8	0.91%	C+ / 5.6
2011	D	116.30	27.53	C- / 3.2	0.41%	C / 5.5
2010	D-	143.30	34.25	D+ / 2.4	18.13%	C- / 3.1
2009	C	90.88	30.69	B+ / 8.4	33.92%	C- / 3.1

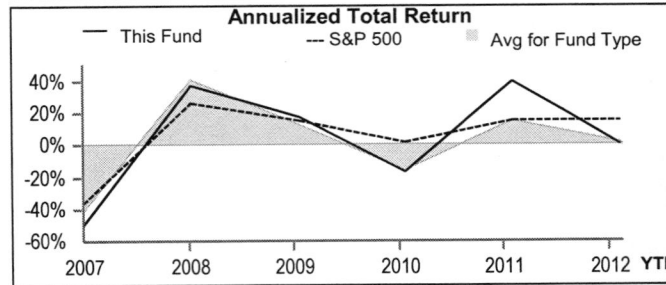

*iShares S&P Emerging Mkts Infr (EMIF)

C-   **Fair**

Fund Family: BlackRock Fund Advisors
Fund Type: Global
Inception Date: June 16, 2009

Major Rating Factors: Middle of the road best describes *iShares S&P Emerging Mkts Infr whose TheStreet.com Investment Rating is currently a C- (Fair). The fund currently has a performance rating of C (Fair) based on an annualized return of 6.84% over the last three years and a total return of 2.48% year to date 2012. Factored into the performance evaluation is an expense ratio of 0.72% (very low).

The fund's risk rating is currently C+ (Fair). It carries a beta of 0.91, meaning that its performance tracks fairly well with that of the overall stock market. Volatility, as measured by both the semi-deviation and a drawdown factor, is considered low. As of December 31, 2012, *iShares S&P Emerging Mkts Infr traded at a discount of 2.06% below its net asset value, which is better than its one-year historical average premium of .09%.

Diane Hsiung has been running the fund for 4 years and currently receives a manager quality ranking of 77 (0=worst, 99=best). If you desire an average level of risk, then this fund may be an option.

Data Date	Investment Rating	Net Assets ($Mil)	Price	Performance Rating/Pts	Total Return Y-T-D	Risk Rating/Pts
12-12	C-	130.80	34.24	C / 4.3	2.48%	C+ / 6.9
2011	D	102.60	28.84	D- / 1.3	2.01%	B- / 7.1
2010	A+	109.40	34.32	A- / 9.0	18.30%	B / 8.2

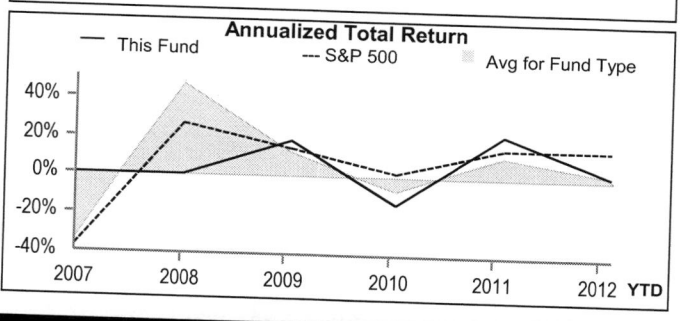

Annualized Total Return

*iShares S&P Europe 350 (IEV)

C-   **Fair**

Fund Family: BlackRock Fund Advisors
Fund Type: Foreign
Inception Date: July 25, 2000

Major Rating Factors: Middle of the road best describes *iShares S&P Europe 350 whose TheStreet.com Investment Rating is currently a C- (Fair). The fund currently has a performance rating of C (Fair) based on an annualized return of 3.78% over the last three years and a total return of 2.80% year to date 2012. Factored into the performance evaluation is an expense ratio of 0.60% (very low).

The fund's risk rating is currently C+ (Fair). It carries a beta of 1.17, meaning it is expected to move 11.7% for every 10% move in the market. Volatility, as measured by both the semi-deviation and a drawdown factor, is considered low. As of December 31, 2012, *iShares S&P Europe 350 traded at a discount of 2.34% below its net asset value, which is better than its one-year historical average premium of .12%.

Diane Hsiung has been running the fund for 5 years and currently receives a manager quality ranking of 42 (0=worst, 99=best). If you desire an average level of risk, then this fund may be an option.

Data Date	Investment Rating	Net Assets ($Mil)	Price	Performance Rating/Pts	Total Return Y-T-D	Risk Rating/Pts
12-12	C-	1,200.90	39.30	C / 4.5	2.80%	C+ / 6.9
2011	D	915.60	33.74	D+ / 2.4	-1.04%	B- / 7.0
2010	E+	1,156.80	39.28	D- / 1.2	3.83%	C- / 3.0
2009	E+	1,509.85	38.96	D / 2.2	27.55%	C- / 3.1

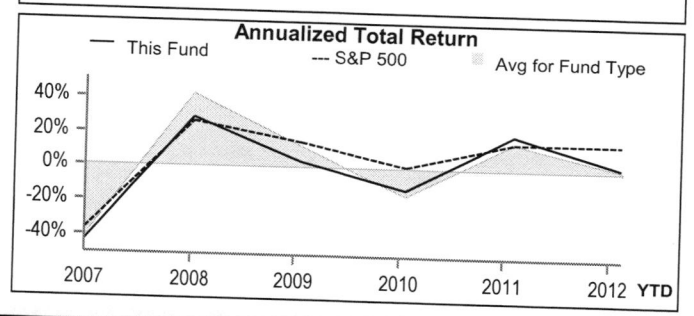

Annualized Total Return

*iShares S&P Gl Cons Staples Sect (KXI)

C+   **Fair**

Fund Family: BlackRock Fund Advisors
Fund Type: Global
Inception Date: September 12, 2006

Major Rating Factors: Middle of the road best describes *iShares S&P Gl Cons Staples Sect whose TheStreet.com Investment Rating is currently a C+ (Fair). The fund currently has a performance rating of C+ (Fair) based on an annualized return of 12.46% over the last three years and a total return of 2.21% year to date 2012. Factored into the performance evaluation is an expense ratio of 0.48% (very low).

The fund's risk rating is currently B (Good). It carries a beta of 0.49, meaning the fund's expected move will be 4.9% for every 10% move in the market. Volatility, as measured by both the semi-deviation and a drawdown factor, is considered low. As of December 31, 2012, *iShares S&P Gl Cons Staples Sect traded at a discount of 1.94% below its net asset value, which is better than its one-year historical average premium of .02%.

Diane Hsiung has been running the fund for 5 years and currently receives a manager quality ranking of 90 (0=worst, 99=best). If you desire an average level of risk, then this fund may be an option.

Data Date	Investment Rating	Net Assets ($Mil)	Price	Performance Rating/Pts	Total Return Y-T-D	Risk Rating/Pts
12-12	C+	440.20	73.63	C+ / 5.6	2.21%	B / 8.9
2011	C+	465.70	66.56	C+ / 5.7	-1.10%	B / 8.5
2010	C+	327.50	62.47	C / 5.4	13.19%	C+ / 6.9
2009	C	251.25	56.61	C / 4.5	20.16%	B- / 7.0

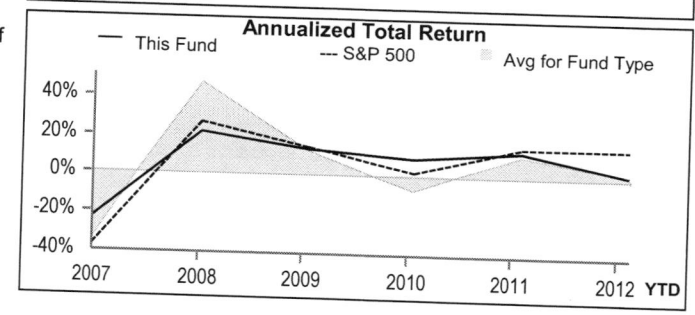

Annualized Total Return

* Denotes ETF Fund

*iShares S&P Glb Infrastructure (IGF)

C-   **Fair**

Fund Family: BlackRock Fund Advisors
Fund Type: Global
Inception Date: December 10, 2007

Major Rating Factors: Middle of the road best describes *iShares S&P Glb Infrastructure whose TheStreet.com Investment Rating is currently a C- (Fair). The fund currently has a performance rating of C- (Fair) based on an annualized return of 5.05% over the last three years and a total return of 1.09% year to date 2012. Factored into the performance evaluation is an expense ratio of 0.48% (very low).

The fund's risk rating is currently B (Good). It carries a beta of 0.77, meaning the fund's expected move will be 7.7% for every 10% move in the market. Volatility, as measured by both the semi-deviation and a drawdown factor, is considered low. As of December 31, 2012, *iShares S&P Glb Infrastructure traded at a discount of .81% below its net asset value.

Diane Hsiung has been running the fund for 5 years and currently receives a manager quality ranking of 70 (0=worst, 99=best). If you desire an average level of risk, then this fund may be an option.

Data Date	Investment Rating	Net Assets ($Mil)	Price	Performance Rating/Pts	Total Return Y-T-D	Risk Rating/Pts
12-12	C-	357.10	35.71	C- / 3.1	1.09%	B / 8.2
2011	C-	415.10	33.20	C- / 3.3	-1.33%	B- / 7.8
2010	D	468.90	35.06	D- / 1.3	7.05%	C+ / 5.7
2009	B	409.90	34.08	B / 7.6	16.96%	C+ / 5.8

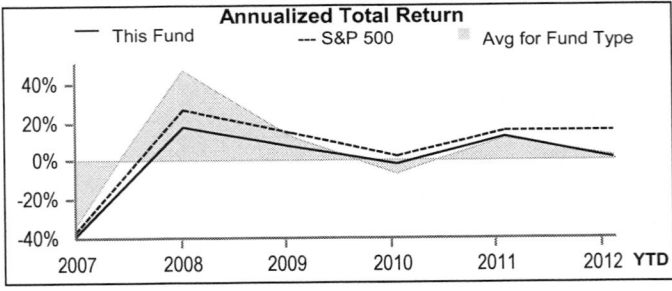

*iShares S&P Glb Timber & Forestr (WOOD)

C-   **Fair**

Fund Family: BlackRock Fund Advisors
Fund Type: Global
Inception Date: June 24, 2008

Major Rating Factors: Middle of the road best describes *iShares S&P Glb Timber & Forestr whose TheStreet.com Investment Rating is currently a C- (Fair). The fund currently has a performance rating of C (Fair) based on an annualized return of 6.83% over the last three years and a total return of 3.31% year to date 2012. Factored into the performance evaluation is an expense ratio of 0.48% (very low).

The fund's risk rating is currently B- (Good). It carries a beta of 0.89, meaning the fund's expected move will be 8.9% for every 10% move in the market. Volatility, as measured by both the semi-deviation and a drawdown factor, is considered low. As of December 31, 2012, *iShares S&P Glb Timber & Forestr traded at a discount of 2.80% below its net asset value, which is better than its one-year historical average premium of .13%.

Diane Hsiung has been running the fund for 5 years and currently receives a manager quality ranking of 72 (0=worst, 99=best). If you desire an average level of risk, then this fund may be an option.

Data Date	Investment Rating	Net Assets ($Mil)	Price	Performance Rating/Pts	Total Return Y-T-D	Risk Rating/Pts
12-12	C-	226.90	45.10	C / 4.5	3.31%	B- / 7.1
2011	C-	142.00	37.19	C- / 3.8	1.50%	B- / 7.0
2010	B+	166.70	44.95	A- / 9.1	16.19%	C / 5.0
2009	A-	35.72	39.68	A- / 9.2	38.44%	C / 4.9

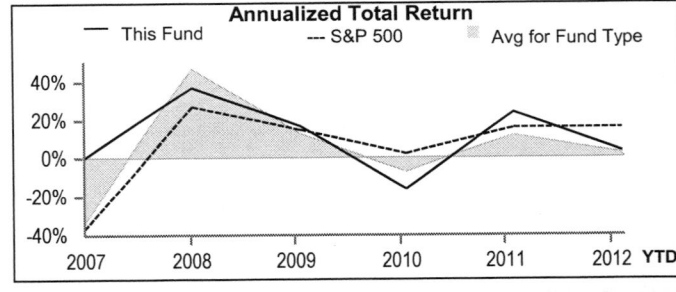

*iShares S&P Global 100 (IOO)

C-   **Fair**

Fund Family: BlackRock Fund Advisors
Fund Type: Growth
Inception Date: December 5, 2000

Major Rating Factors: Middle of the road best describes *iShares S&P Global 100 whose TheStreet.com Investment Rating is currently a C- (Fair). The fund currently has a performance rating of C- (Fair) based on an annualized return of 5.71% over the last three years and a total return of 3.30% year to date 2012. Factored into the performance evaluation is an expense ratio of 0.40% (very low).

The fund's risk rating is currently B- (Good). It carries a beta of 1.13, meaning it is expected to move 11.3% for every 10% move in the market. Volatility, as measured by both the semi-deviation and a drawdown factor, is considered low. As of December 31, 2012, *iShares S&P Global 100 traded at a discount of 2.96% below its net asset value, which is better than its one-year historical average premium of .01%.

Diane Hsiung has been running the fund for 5 years and currently receives a manager quality ranking of 18 (0=worst, 99=best). If you desire an average level of risk, then this fund may be an option.

Data Date	Investment Rating	Net Assets ($Mil)	Price	Performance Rating/Pts	Total Return Y-T-D	Risk Rating/Pts
12-12	C-	1,054.00	63.96	C- / 4.2	3.30%	B- / 7.9
2011	C-	975.50	57.94	C- / 3.5	0.57%	B- / 7.8
2010	D+	953.10	62.27	D / 1.9	5.96%	C+ / 6.0
2009	C-	707.27	60.25	D+ / 2.6	21.62%	C+ / 6.4

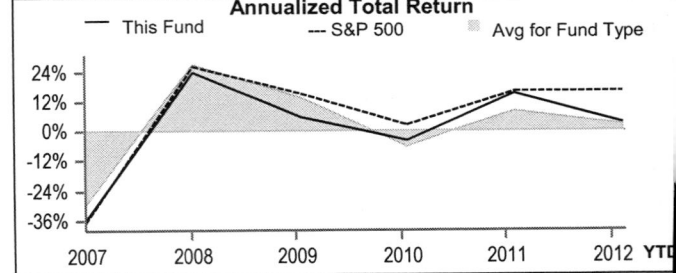

*iShares S&P Global Clean Energy (ICLN)

Fund Family: BlackRock Fund Advisors
Fund Type: Energy/Natural Resources
Inception Date: June 24, 2008

E+   Very Weak

Major Rating Factors:
Very poor performance is the major factor driving the E+ (Very Weak) TheStreet.com Investment Rating for *iShares S&P Global Clean Energy. The fund currently has a performance rating of E (Very Weak) based on an annualized return of -27.66% over the last three years and a total return of 6.89% year to date 2012. Factored into the performance evaluation is an expense ratio of 0.48% (very low).

The fund's risk rating is currently C (Fair). It carries a beta of 1.12, meaning it is expected to move 11.2% for every 10% move in the market. Volatility, as measured by both the semi-deviation and a drawdown factor, is considered average. As of December 31, 2012, *iShares S&P Global Clean Energy traded at a discount of 6.03% below its net asset value, which is better than its one-year historical average discount of .01%.

Diane Hsiung has been running the fund for 5 years and currently receives a manager quality ranking of 1 (0=worst, 99=best). This fund offers an average level of risk but investors looking for strong performance will be frustrated.

Data Date	Investment Rating	Net Assets ($Mil)	Price	Performance Rating/Pts	Total Return Y-T-D	Risk Rating/Pts
12-12	E+	26.40	7.17	E / 0.4	6.89%	C / 4.4
2011	E+	32.00	8.54	E+ / 0.6	0.00%	C / 4.3
2010	E+	50.60	15.84	E / 0.5	-27.64%	C- / 3.5
2009	E+	90.43	22.26	D / 2.0	-0.14%	C- / 3.3

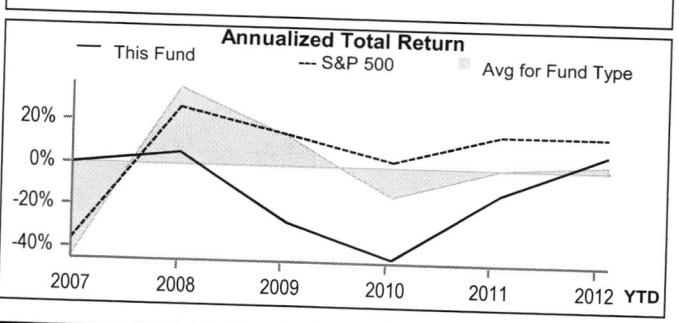

*iShares S&P Global Cons Disc (RXI)

Fund Family: BlackRock Fund Advisors
Fund Type: Global
Inception Date: September 12, 2006

B   Good

Major Rating Factors: Strong performance is the major factor driving the B (Good) TheStreet.com Investment Rating for *iShares S&P Global Cons Disc. The fund currently has a performance rating of B (Good) based on an annualized return of 13.64% over the last three years and a total return of 2.80% year to date 2012. Factored into the performance evaluation is an expense ratio of 0.48% (very low).

The fund's risk rating is currently B- (Good). It carries a beta of 0.83, meaning the fund's expected move will be 8.3% for every 10% move in the market. Volatility, as measured by both the semi-deviation and a drawdown factor, is considered low. As of December 31, 2012, *iShares S&P Global Cons Disc traded at a discount of 2.48% below its net asset value, which is better than its one-year historical average premium of .10%.

Diane Hsiung has been running the fund for 5 years and currently receives a manager quality ranking of 90 (0=worst, 99=best). If you desire only a moderate level of risk and strong performance, then this fund is an excellent option.

Data Date	Investment Rating	Net Assets ($Mil)	Price	Performance Rating/Pts	Total Return Y-T-D	Risk Rating/Pts
12-12	B	162.80	61.71	B / 7.6	2.80%	B- / 7.8
2011	C	112.60	49.95	C / 5.3	1.88%	B- / 7.8
2010	C+	130.60	53.41	C+ / 6.6	23.32%	C+ / 5.8
2009	D+	78.77	43.84	D+ / 2.4	33.34%	C+ / 5.7

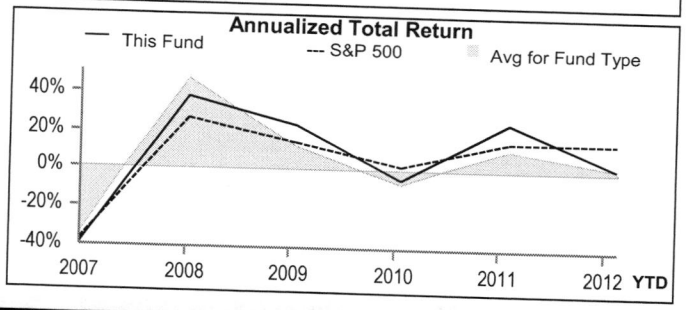

*iShares S&P Global Energy (IXC)

Fund Family: BlackRock Fund Advisors
Fund Type: Energy/Natural Resources
Inception Date: November 12, 2001

D+   Weak

Major Rating Factors:
Disappointing performance is the major factor driving the D+ (Weak) TheStreet.com Investment Rating for *iShares S&P Global Energy. The fund currently has a performance rating of D+ (Weak) based on an annualized return of 4.63% over the last three years and a total return of 2.64% year to date 2012. Factored into the performance evaluation is an expense ratio of 0.48% (very low).

The fund's risk rating is currently B- (Good). It carries a beta of 0.99, meaning that its performance tracks fairly well with that of the overall stock market. Volatility, as measured by both the semi-deviation and a drawdown factor, is considered low. As of December 31, 2012, *iShares S&P Global Energy traded at a discount of 2.82% below its net asset value, which is better than its one-year historical average discount of .03%.

Diane Hsiung has been running the fund for 5 years and currently receives a manager quality ranking of 26 (0=worst, 99=best). This fund offers only a moderate level of risk but investors looking for strong performance are still waiting.

Data Date	Investment Rating	Net Assets ($Mil)	Price	Performance Rating/Pts	Total Return Y-T-D	Risk Rating/Pts
12-12	D+	990.70	38.25	D+ / 2.5	2.64%	B- / 7.4
2011	C-	1,123.40	38.19	C / 4.3	1.44%	B- / 7.5
2010	D-	1,313.20	39.06	C- / 3.3	11.85%	D+ / 2.8
2009	D	930.27	35.68	C- / 4.2	18.86%	C- / 3.1

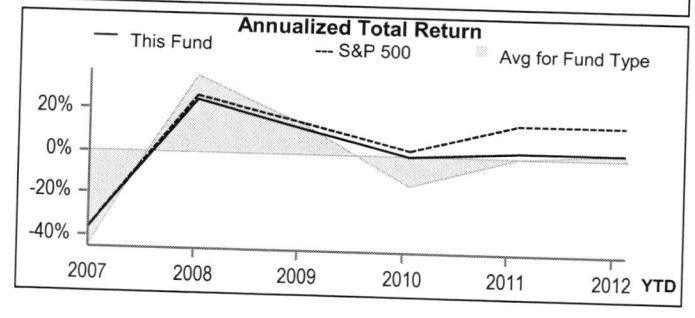

* Denotes ETF Fund

*iShares S&P Global Financials (IXG)

C   **Fair**

Fund Family: BlackRock Fund Advisors
Fund Type: Financial Services
Inception Date: November 12, 2001

Data Date	Investment Rating	Net Assets ($Mil)	Price	Performance Rating/Pts	Total Return Y-T-D	Risk Rating/Pts
12-12	C	219.50	45.66	C / 5.4	4.25%	B- / 7.0
2011	D	147.40	35.78	D / 2.0	0.70%	C+ / 6.8
2010	D-	287.80	46.13	E+ / 0.8	3.97%	C / 4.4
2009	E+	330.25	45.41	E+ / 0.8	30.85%	C / 4.5

Major Rating Factors: Middle of the road best describes *iShares S&P Global Financials whose TheStreet.com Investment Rating is currently a C (Fair). The fund currently has a performance rating of C (Fair) based on an annualized return of 3.30% over the last three years and a total return of 4.25% year to date 2012. Factored into the performance evaluation is an expense ratio of 0.48% (very low).

The fund's risk rating is currently B- (Good). It carries a beta of 1.11, meaning it is expected to move 11.1% for every 10% move in the market. Volatility, as measured by both the semi-deviation and a drawdown factor, is considered low. As of December 31, 2012, *iShares S&P Global Financials traded at a discount of 3.63% below its net asset value, which is better than its one-year historical average premium of .01%.

Diane Hsiung has been running the fund for 5 years and currently receives a manager quality ranking of 22 (0=worst, 99=best). If you desire an average level of risk, then this fund may be an option.

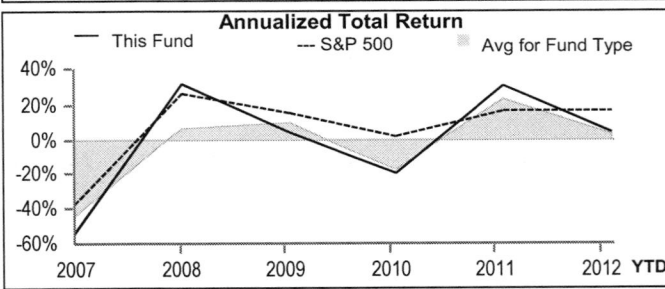

Annualized Total Return — This Fund --- S&P 500 — Avg for Fund Type

*iShares S&P Global Healthcare (IXJ)

C+   **Fair**

Fund Family: BlackRock Fund Advisors
Fund Type: Health
Inception Date: November 13, 2001

Data Date	Investment Rating	Net Assets ($Mil)	Price	Performance Rating/Pts	Total Return Y-T-D	Risk Rating/Pts
12-12	C+	572.70	64.50	C+ / 5.7	4.16%	B / 8.3
2011	C	530.40	56.12	C / 4.4	0.55%	B- / 7.9
2010	C-	477.00	51.76	D+ / 2.4	1.91%	C+ / 6.8
2009	C-	445.26	52.01	C- / 3.0	16.26%	C+ / 6.7

Major Rating Factors: Middle of the road best describes *iShares S&P Global Healthcare whose TheStreet.com Investment Rating is currently a C+ (Fair). The fund currently has a performance rating of C+ (Fair) based on an annualized return of 10.59% over the last three years and a total return of 4.16% year to date 2012. Factored into the performance evaluation is an expense ratio of 0.48% (very low).

The fund's risk rating is currently B (Good). It carries a beta of 0.63, meaning the fund's expected move will be 6.3% for every 10% move in the market. Volatility, as measured by both the semi-deviation and a drawdown factor, is considered low. As of December 31, 2012, *iShares S&P Global Healthcare traded at a discount of 3.92% below its net asset value, which is better than its one-year historical average discount of .01%.

Diane Hsiung has been running the fund for 5 years and currently receives a manager quality ranking of 72 (0=worst, 99=best). If you desire an average level of risk, then this fund may be an option.

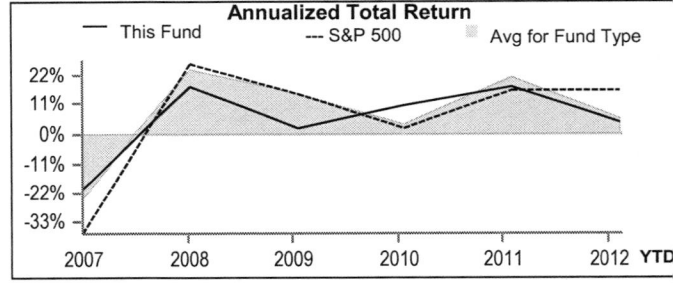

Annualized Total Return — This Fund --- S&P 500 — Avg for Fund Type

*iShares S&P Global Industrials (EXI)

C-   **Fair**

Fund Family: BlackRock Fund Advisors
Fund Type: Global
Inception Date: September 12, 2006

Data Date	Investment Rating	Net Assets ($Mil)	Price	Performance Rating/Pts	Total Return Y-T-D	Risk Rating/Pts
12-12	C-	153.20	54.89	C / 4.5	3.04%	B- / 7.5
2011	C-	167.10	48.23	C- / 4.1	1.24%	B- / 7.4
2010	C-	199.00	53.85	C / 4.6	23.33%	C / 5.3
2009	D+	124.62	44.41	D+ / 2.3	22.53%	C / 5.5

Major Rating Factors: Middle of the road best describes *iShares S&P Global Industrials whose TheStreet.com Investment Rating is currently a C- (Fair). The fund currently has a performance rating of C (Fair) based on an annualized return of 8.93% over the last three years and a total return of 3.04% year to date 2012. Factored into the performance evaluation is an expense ratio of 0.48% (very low).

The fund's risk rating is currently B- (Good). It carries a beta of 0.94, meaning that its performance tracks fairly well with that of the overall stock market. Volatility, as measured by both the semi-deviation and a drawdown factor, is considered low. As of December 31, 2012, *iShares S&P Global Industrials traded at a discount of 2.59% below its net asset value, which is better than its one-year historical average discount of .04%.

Diane Hsiung has been running the fund for 5 years and currently receives a manager quality ranking of 81 (0=worst, 99=best). If you desire an average level of risk, then this fund may be an option.

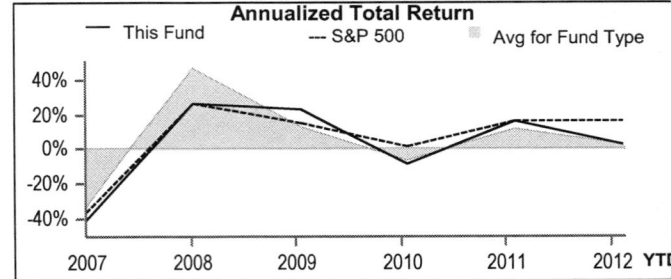

Annualized Total Return — This Fund --- S&P 500 — Avg for Fund Type

*iShares S&P Global Materials (MXI)

| | D | Weak |

Fund Family: BlackRock Fund Advisors
Fund Type: Global
Inception Date: September 12, 2006

Data Date	Investment Rating	Net Assets ($Mil)	Price	Performance Rating/Pts	Total Return Y-T-D	Risk Rating/Pts
12-12	D	486.00	62.45	D+ / 2.3	1.17%	C+ / 6.6
2011	C-	476.20	57.20	C- / 4.2	2.40%	C+ / 6.5
2010	C	777.40	73.25	C+ / 6.0	19.99%	C / 4.6
2009	C+	757.32	62.22	B- / 7.3	56.43%	C / 5.2

Major Rating Factors:
Disappointing performance is the major factor driving the D (Weak) TheStreet.com Investment Rating for *iShares S&P Global Materials. The fund currently has a performance rating of D+ (Weak) based on an annualized return of 1.64% over the last three years and a total return of 1.17% year to date 2012. Factored into the performance evaluation is an expense ratio of 0.48% (very low).

The fund's risk rating is currently C+ (Fair). It carries a beta of 1.19, meaning it is expected to move 11.9% for every 10% move in the market. Volatility, as measured by both the semi-deviation and a drawdown factor, is considered low. As of December 31, 2012, *iShares S&P Global Materials traded at a discount of .94% below its net asset value, which is better than its one-year historical average premium of .12%.

Diane Hsiung has been running the fund for 5 years and currently receives a manager quality ranking of 32 (0=worst, 99=best). This fund offers only a moderate level of risk but investors looking for strong performance are still waiting.

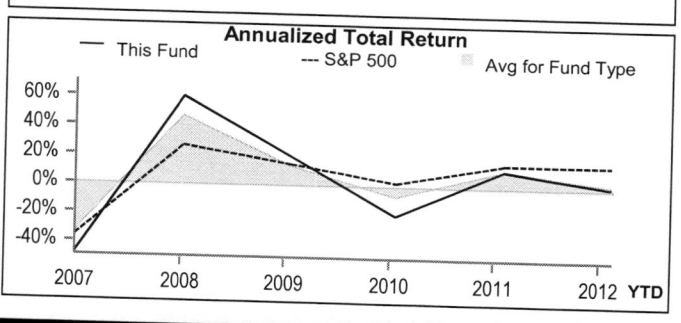

*iShares S&P Global Nuclear (NUCL)

| | D | Weak |

Fund Family: BlackRock Fund Advisors
Fund Type: Energy/Natural Resources
Inception Date: June 24, 2008

Data Date	Investment Rating	Net Assets ($Mil)	Price	Performance Rating/Pts	Total Return Y-T-D	Risk Rating/Pts
12-12	D	8.90	31.93	D- / 1.1	3.01%	C+ / 6.8
2011	D	11.10	32.34	D / 1.8	-0.46%	B- / 7.2
2010	A-	17.30	43.38	B+ / 8.9	7.11%	C+ / 5.9
2009	B+	16.19	41.90	B / 8.2	35.10%	C+ / 5.8

Major Rating Factors:
Disappointing performance is the major factor driving the D (Weak) TheStreet.com Investment Rating for *iShares S&P Global Nuclear. The fund currently has a performance rating of D- (Weak) based on an annualized return of -4.92% over the last three years and a total return of 3.01% year to date 2012. Factored into the performance evaluation is an expense ratio of 0.48% (very low).

The fund's risk rating is currently C+ (Fair). It carries a beta of 0.67, meaning the fund's expected move will be 6.7% for every 10% move in the market. Volatility, as measured by both the semi-deviation and a drawdown factor, is considered low. As of December 31, 2012, *iShares S&P Global Nuclear traded at a discount of 2.65% below its net asset value, which is better than its one-year historical average discount of .44%.

Diane Hsiung has been running the fund for 5 years and currently receives a manager quality ranking of 11 (0=worst, 99=best). This fund offers only a moderate level of risk but investors looking for strong performance are still waiting.

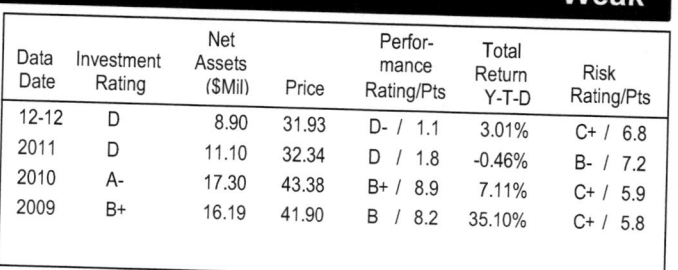

*iShares S&P Global Technology (IXN)

| | D+ | Weak |

Fund Family: BlackRock Fund Advisors
Fund Type: Global
Inception Date: November 12, 2001

Data Date	Investment Rating	Net Assets ($Mil)	Price	Performance Rating/Pts	Total Return Y-T-D	Risk Rating/Pts
12-12	D+	484.00	67.31	C- / 3.9	2.20%	C+ / 6.7
2011	C	475.80	58.71	C+ / 5.7	1.87%	B- / 7.1
2010	C-	601.00	61.42	C / 4.7	10.48%	C / 5.4
2009	C-	373.23	56.01	C / 4.5	48.00%	C / 5.5

Major Rating Factors: *iShares S&P Global Technology receives a TheStreet.com Investment Rating of D+ (Weak). The fund currently has a performance rating of C- (Fair) based on an annualized return of 7.64% over the last three years and a total return of 2.20% year to date 2012. Factored into the performance evaluation is an expense ratio of 0.48% (very low).

The fund's risk rating is currently C+ (Fair). It carries a beta of 0.84, meaning the fund's expected move will be 8.4% for every 10% move in the market. Volatility, as measured by both the semi-deviation and a drawdown factor, is considered low. As of December 31, 2012, *iShares S&P Global Technology traded at a discount of 2.21% below its net asset value, which is better than its one-year historical average discount of .03%.

Diane Hsiung has been running the fund for 5 years and currently receives a manager quality ranking of 76 (0=worst, 99=best). If you desire an average level of risk, then this fund may be an option.

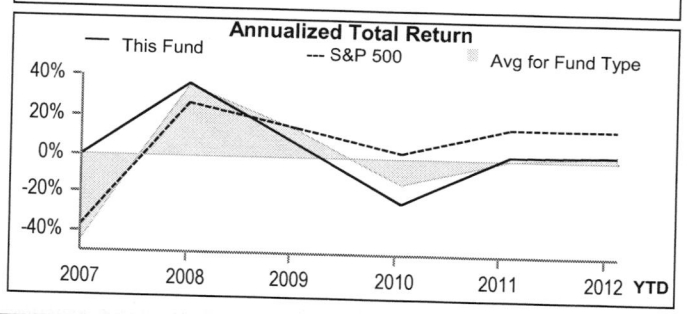

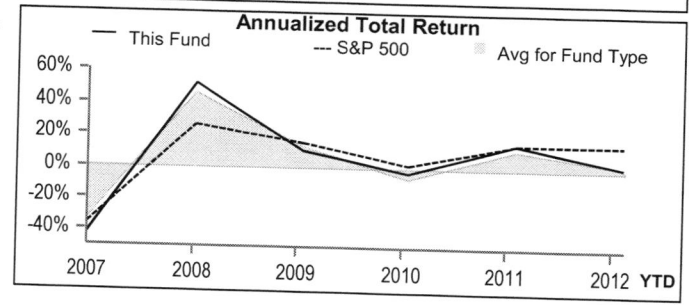

*iShares S&P Global Telecom (IXP)   C-   Fair

Fund Family: BlackRock Fund Advisors
Fund Type: Global
Inception Date: November 12, 2001

Major Rating Factors: Middle of the road best describes *iShares S&P Global Telecom whose TheStreet.com Investment Rating is currently a C- (Fair). The fund currently has a performance rating of C- (Fair) based on an annualized return of 8.22% over the last three years and a total return of 2.83% year to date 2012. Factored into the performance evaluation is an expense ratio of 0.48% (very low).

The fund's risk rating is currently B (Good). It carries a beta of 0.59, meaning the fund's expected move will be 5.9% for every 10% move in the market. Volatility, as measured by both the semi-deviation and a drawdown factor, is considered low. As of December 31, 2012, *iShares S&P Global Telecom traded at a discount of 2.71% below its net asset value, which is better than its one-year historical average premium of .15%.

Diane Hsiung has been running the fund for 5 years and currently receives a manager quality ranking of 77 (0=worst, 99=best). If you desire an average level of risk, then this fund may be an option.

Data Date	Investment Rating	Net Assets ($Mil)	Price	Performance Rating/Pts	Total Return Y-T-D	Risk Rating/Pts
12-12	C-	475.30	57.17	C- / 3.4	2.83%	B / 8.6
2011	C-	440.60	55.79	C- / 3.5	-1.57%	B / 8.5
2010	D+	409.50	58.27	D+ / 2.3	11.74%	C+ / 6.4
2009	C-	243.98	54.68	D+ / 2.6	9.97%	C+ / 6.4

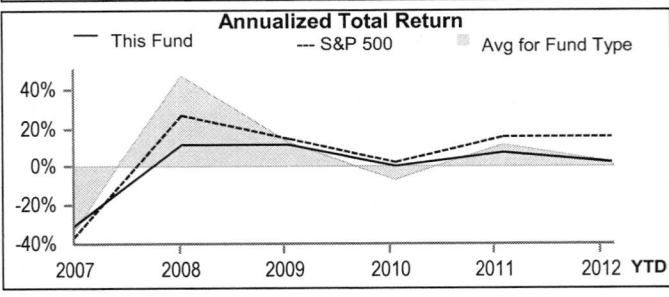

Annualized Total Return

*iShares S&P Global Utilities (JXI)   D+   Weak

Fund Family: BlackRock Fund Advisors
Fund Type: Utilities
Inception Date: September 12, 2006

Major Rating Factors:
Disappointing performance is the major factor driving the D+ (Weak) TheStreet.com Investment Rating for *iShares S&P Global Utilities. The fund currently has a performance rating of D- (Weak) based on an annualized return of -0.62% over the last three years and a total return of 0.34% year to date 2012. Factored into the performance evaluation is an expense ratio of 0.48% (very low).

The fund's risk rating is currently B (Good). It carries a beta of 0.91, meaning that its performance tracks fairly well with that of the overall stock market. Volatility, as measured by both the semi-deviation and a drawdown factor, is considered low. As of December 31, 2012, *iShares S&P Global Utilities traded at a discount of .22% below its net asset value, which is better than its one-year historical average premium of .16%.

Diane Hsiung has been running the fund for 5 years and currently receives a manager quality ranking of 15 (0=worst, 99=best). This fund offers only a moderate level of risk but investors looking for strong performance are still waiting.

Data Date	Investment Rating	Net Assets ($Mil)	Price	Performance Rating/Pts	Total Return Y-T-D	Risk Rating/Pts
12-12	D+	235.00	41.23	D- / 1.4	0.34%	B / 8.4
2011	D+	238.40	41.90	D / 1.9	-1.91%	B / 8.0
2010	D	252.70	45.08	E+ / 0.9	-1.70%	C+ / 6.3
2009	C-	157.41	47.99	D / 2.2	6.09%	C+ / 6.5

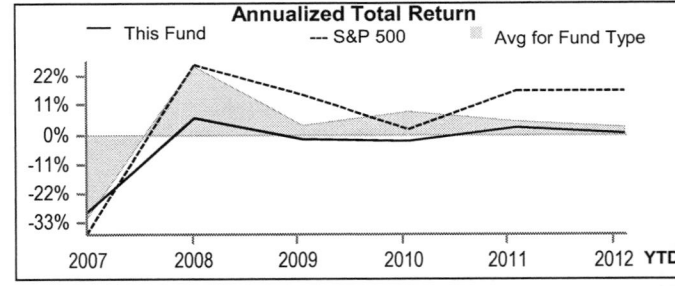

Annualized Total Return

*iShares S&P Growth Allocation (AOR)   C   Fair

Fund Family: BlackRock Fund Advisors
Fund Type: Growth and Income
Inception Date: November 4, 2008

Major Rating Factors: Middle of the road best describes *iShares S&P Growth Allocation whose TheStreet.com Investment Rating is currently a C (Fair). The fund currently has a performance rating of C- (Fair) based on an annualized return of 7.71% over the last three years and a total return of 1.61% year to date 2012. Factored into the performance evaluation is an expense ratio of 0.11% (very low).

The fund's risk rating is currently B (Good). It carries a beta of 0.63, meaning the fund's expected move will be 6.3% for every 10% move in the market. Volatility, as measured by both the semi-deviation and a drawdown factor, is considered low. As of December 31, 2012, *iShares S&P Growth Allocation traded at a discount of 1.59% below its net asset value, which is better than its one-year historical average premium of .04%.

Diane Hsiung has been running the fund for 5 years and currently receives a manager quality ranking of 61 (0=worst, 99=best). If you desire an average level of risk, then this fund may be an option.

Data Date	Investment Rating	Net Assets ($Mil)	Price	Performance Rating/Pts	Total Return Y-T-D	Risk Rating/Pts
12-12	C	152.50	33.97	C- / 3.6	1.61%	B / 8.8
2011	C	118.20	31.14	C- / 4.0	0.64%	B / 8.8
2010	A+	81.90	31.54	B+ / 8.5	11.14%	B- / 7.8
2009	A+	26.80	28.94	B- / 7.3	17.44%	B- / 7.9

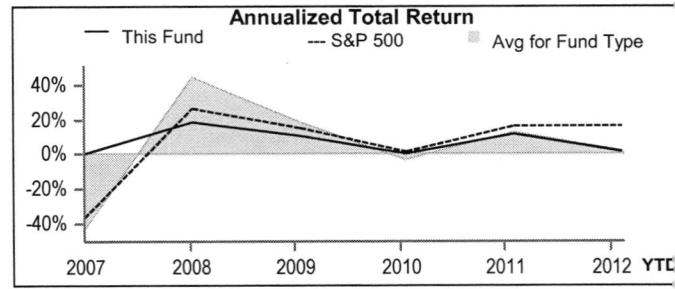

Annualized Total Return

*iShares S&P GSCI Commodity-Index (GSG)

Fund Family: BlackRock Fund Advisors
Fund Type: Income
Inception Date: July 21, 2006

D　　**Weak**

Major Rating Factors:
Disappointing performance is the major factor driving the D (Weak) TheStreet.com Investment Rating for *iShares S&P GSCI Commodity-Index. The fund currently has a performance rating of D- (Weak) based on an annualized return of 1.15% over the last three years and a total return of 0.27% year to date 2012. Factored into the performance evaluation is an expense ratio of 0.80% (very low).

　　The fund's risk rating is currently B- (Good). It carries a beta of 1.13, meaning it is expected to move 11.3% for every 10% move in the market. Volatility, as measured by both the semi-deviation and a drawdown factor, is considered low. As of December 31, 2012, *iShares S&P GSCI Commodity-Index traded at a discount of .64% below its net asset value, which is better than its one-year historical average discount of .32%.

　　This fund has been team managed for 7 years and currently receives a manager quality ranking of 13 (0=worst, 99=best). This fund offers only a moderate level of risk but investors looking for strong performance are still waiting.

Data Date	Investment Rating	Net Assets ($Mil)	Price	Performance Rating/Pts	Total Return Y-T-D	Risk Rating/Pts
12-12	D	1,167.60	32.79	D- / 1.5	0.27%	B- / 7.3
2011	C-	1,313.30	32.98	C- / 3.2	2.94%	B- / 7.6
2010	E+	1,799.90	34.10	E+ / 0.8	7.17%	C- / 3.7
2009	D-	1,092.84	31.82	D- / 1.4	7.46%	C / 4.3

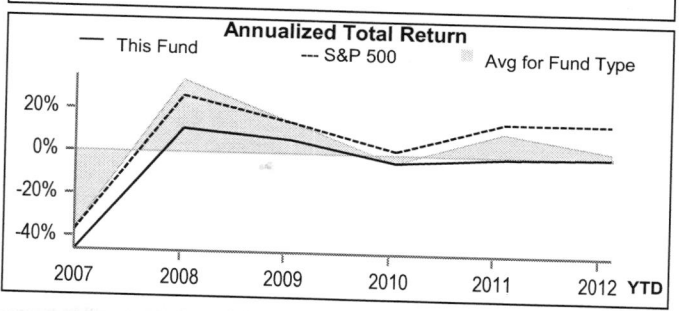

*iShares S&P India Nifty 50 (INDY)

Fund Family: BlackRock Fund Advisors
Fund Type: Emerging Market
Inception Date: November 18, 2009

D　　**Weak**

Major Rating Factors:
Disappointing performance is the major factor driving the D (Weak) TheStreet.com Investment Rating for *iShares S&P India Nifty 50. The fund currently has a performance rating of D (Weak) based on an annualized return of -0.94% over the last three years and a total return of 0.08% year to date 2012. Factored into the performance evaluation is an expense ratio of 0.92% (low).

　　The fund's risk rating is currently C+ (Fair). It carries a beta of 1.13, meaning it is expected to move 11.3% for every 10% move in the market. Volatility, as measured by both the semi-deviation and a drawdown factor, is considered low. As of December 31, 2012, *iShares S&P India Nifty 50 traded at a premium of .24% above its net asset value, which is better than its one-year historical average premium of .34%.

　　Diane Hsiung has been running the fund for 4 years and currently receives a manager quality ranking of 21 (0=worst, 99=best). This fund offers only a moderate level of risk but investors looking for strong performance are still waiting.

Data Date	Investment Rating	Net Assets ($Mil)	Price	Performance Rating/Pts	Total Return Y-T-D	Risk Rating/Pts
12-12	D	358.40	24.97	D / 1.9	0.08%	C+ / 6.0
2011	D-	214.40	19.75	E / 0.4	3.85%	C+ / 6.1
2010	A+	174.70	31.35	A- / 9.2	24.42%	B / 8.0

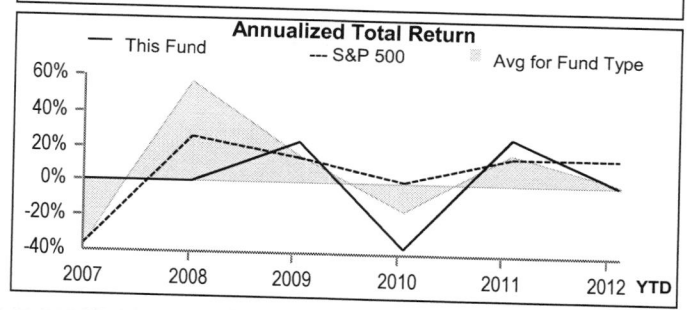

*iShares S&P Intl Preferred Stock (IPFF)

Fund Family: BlackRock Fund Advisors
Fund Type: Corporate - Investment Grade
Inception Date: November 15, 2011

B　　**Good**

Major Rating Factors: *iShares S&P Intl Preferred Stock receives a TheStreet.com Investment Rating of B (Good). The fund currently has a performance rating of C+ (Fair) based on an annualized return of 0.00% over the last three years and a total return of 0.77% year to date 2012.

　　The fund's risk rating is currently B+ (Good). It carries a beta of 0.00, meaning the fund's expected move will be 0.0% for every 10% move in the market. Volatility, as measured by both the semi-deviation and a drawdown factor, is considered very low. As of December 31, 2012, *iShares S&P Intl Preferred Stock traded at a discount of .04% below its net asset value, which is better than its one-year historical average premium of .31%.

　　Greg Savage has been running the fund for 2 years and currently receives a manager quality ranking of 72 (0=worst, 99=best). If you desire an average level of risk, then this fund may be an option.

Data Date	Investment Rating	Net Assets ($Mil)	Price	Performance Rating/Pts	Total Return Y-T-D	Risk Rating/Pts
12-12	B	123.20	27.10	C+ / 6.1	0.77%	B+ / 9.1

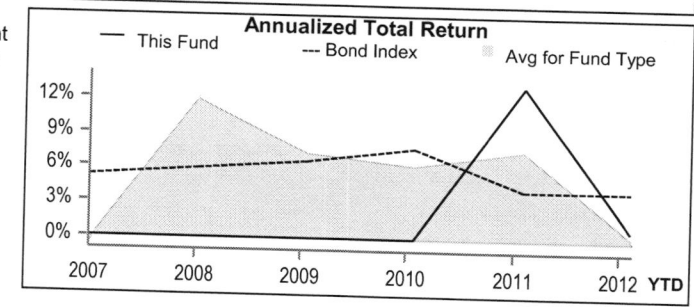

*iShares S&P Latin American 40 (ILF)   D   Weak

Fund Family: BlackRock Fund Advisors
Fund Type: Foreign
Inception Date: October 25, 2001

Major Rating Factors:
Disappointing performance is the major factor driving the D (Weak) TheStreet.com Investment Rating for *iShares S&P Latin American 40. The fund currently has a performance rating of D (Weak) based on an annualized return of 1.10% over the last three years and a total return of 3.01% year to date 2012. Factored into the performance evaluation is an expense ratio of 0.50% (very low).

The fund's risk rating is currently C+ (Fair). It carries a beta of 1.08, meaning that its performance tracks fairly well with that of the overall stock market. Volatility, as measured by both the semi-deviation and a drawdown factor, is considered low. As of December 31, 2012, *iShares S&P Latin American 40 traded at a discount of 2.84% below its net asset value, which is better than its one-year historical average discount of .02%.

Diane Hsiung has been running the fund for 5 years and currently receives a manager quality ranking of 25 (0=worst, 99=best). This fund offers only a moderate level of risk but investors looking for strong performance are still waiting.

Data Date	Investment Rating	Net Assets ($Mil)	Price	Performance Rating/Pts	Total Return Y-T-D	Risk Rating/Pts
12-12	D	1,603.20	43.84	D / 2.0	3.01%	C+ / 6.9
2011	C	1,733.60	42.57	C / 5.5	1.25%	B- / 7.5
2010	C-	3,334.70	53.86	B- / 7.1	15.58%	D / 2.1
2009	C	2,557.89	47.79	B+ / 8.4	81.50%	D+ / 2.4

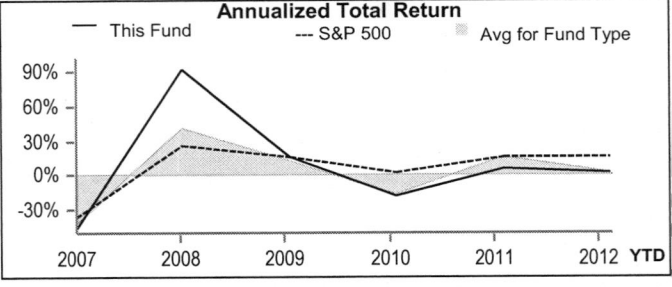

*iShares S&P Mid Cap 400 Growth (IJK)   B-   Good

Fund Family: BlackRock Fund Advisors
Fund Type: Growth
Inception Date: July 24, 2000

Major Rating Factors: Strong performance is the major factor driving the B- (Good) TheStreet.com Investment Rating for *iShares S&P Mid Cap 400 Growth. The fund currently has a performance rating of B- (Good) based on an annualized return of 15.38% over the last three years and a total return of 3.90% year to date 2012. Factored into the performance evaluation is an expense ratio of 0.25% (very low).

The fund's risk rating is currently B- (Good). It carries a beta of 1.12, meaning it is expected to move 11.2% for every 10% move in the market. Volatility, as measured by both the semi-deviation and a drawdown factor, is considered low. As of December 31, 2012, *iShares S&P Mid Cap 400 Growth traded at a discount of 3.77% below its net asset value, which is better than its one-year historical average discount of .01%.

Diane Hsiung has been running the fund for 5 years and currently receives a manager quality ranking of 67 (0=worst, 99=best). If you desire only a moderate level of risk and strong performance, then this fund is an excellent option.

Data Date	Investment Rating	Net Assets ($Mil)	Price	Performance Rating/Pts	Total Return Y-T-D	Risk Rating/Pts
12-12	B-	3,117.10	114.41	B- / 7.3	3.90%	B- / 7.7
2011	B-	2,632.90	98.73	C+ / 6.9	1.13%	B- / 7.7
2010	B	2,962.90	100.72	B / 7.7	30.44%	C / 5.5
2009	C	1,941.63	77.71	C / 4.3	37.15%	C+ / 6.1

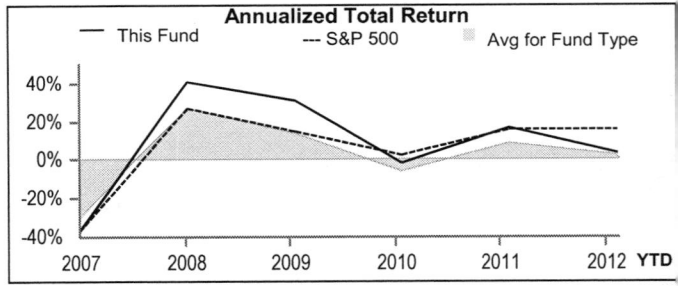

*iShares S&P Mid Cap 400 Value (IJJ)   C+   Fair

Fund Family: BlackRock Fund Advisors
Fund Type: Growth
Inception Date: July 24, 2000

Major Rating Factors: Middle of the road best describes *iShares S&P Mid Cap 400 Value whose TheStreet.com Investment Rating is currently a C+ (Fair). The fund currently has a performance rating of C+ (Fair) based on an annualized return of 12.49% over the last three years and a total return of 3.64% year to date 2012. Factored into the performance evaluation is an expense ratio of 0.25% (very low).

The fund's risk rating is currently B- (Good). It carries a beta of 1.16, meaning it is expected to move 11.6% for every 10% move in the market. Volatility, as measured by both the semi-deviation and a drawdown factor, is considered low. As of December 31, 2012, *iShares S&P Mid Cap 400 Value traded at a discount of 3.50% below its net asset value, which is better than its one-year historical average discount of .01%.

Diane Hsiung has been running the fund for 5 years and currently receives a manager quality ranking of 47 (0=worst, 99=best). If you desire an average level of risk, then this fund may be an option.

Data Date	Investment Rating	Net Assets ($Mil)	Price	Performance Rating/Pts	Total Return Y-T-D	Risk Rating/Pts
12-12	C+	2,253.60	88.14	C+ / 6.4	3.64%	B- / 7.6
2011	C+	1,988.30	75.98	C+ / 6.0	1.84%	B- / 7.6
2010	C+	2,082.10	79.46	C+ / 6.8	22.58%	C+ / 5.8
2009	C-	1,701.89	65.94	C- / 3.3	31.50%	C+ / 5.9

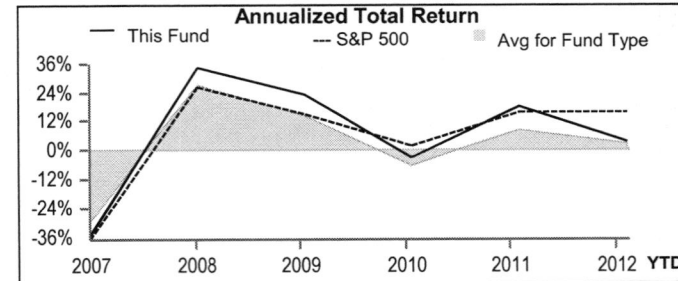

*iShares S&P Moderate Allocation (AOM)

C   **Fair**

Fund Family: BlackRock Fund Advisors
Fund Type: Growth and Income
Inception Date: November 4, 2008

Major Rating Factors: Middle of the road best describes *iShares S&P Moderate Allocation whose TheStreet.com Investment Rating is currently a C (Fair). The fund currently has a performance rating of C- (Fair) based on an annualized return of 6.08% over the last three years and a total return of 1.01% year to date 2012. Factored into the performance evaluation is an expense ratio of 0.11% (very low).

The fund's risk rating is currently B+ (Good). It carries a beta of 0.40, meaning the fund's expected move will be 4.0% for every 10% move in the market. Volatility, as measured by both the semi-deviation and a drawdown factor, is considered very low. As of December 31, 2012, *iShares S&P Moderate Allocation traded at a discount of 1.09% below its net asset value, which is better than its one-year historical average premium of .02%.

Diane Hsiung has been running the fund for 5 years and currently receives a manager quality ranking of 66 (0=worst, 99=best). If you desire an average level of risk, then this fund may be an option.

Data Date	Investment Rating	Net Assets ($Mil)	Price	Performance Rating/Pts	Total Return Y-T-D	Risk Rating/Pts
12-12	C	145.80	31.73	C- / 3.0	1.01%	B+ / 9.3
2011	C	125.40	29.90	C- / 3.6	0.30%	B+ / 9.2
2010	A	74.80	29.92	B- / 7.5	7.90%	B / 8.4
2009	B	18.59	28.23	C+ / 6.2	12.74%	B / 8.6

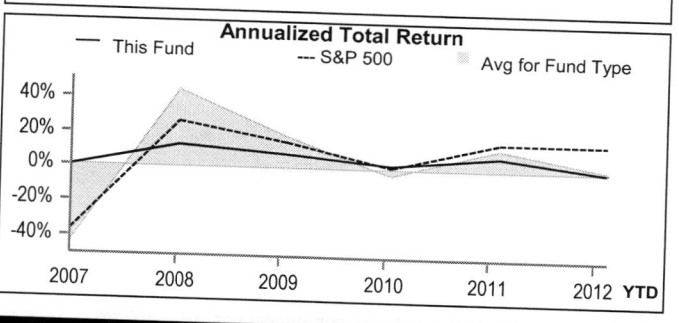

*iShares S&P NA Natural Resource (IGE)

D+   **Weak**

Fund Family: BlackRock Fund Advisors
Fund Type: Energy/Natural Resources
Inception Date: October 22, 2001

Major Rating Factors:
Disappointing performance is the major factor driving the D+ (Weak) TheStreet.com Investment Rating for *iShares S&P NA Natural Resource. The fund currently has a performance rating of D+ (Weak) based on an annualized return of 4.92% over the last three years and a total return of 2.65% year to date 2012. Factored into the performance evaluation is an expense ratio of 0.48% (very low).

The fund's risk rating is currently B- (Good). It carries a beta of 1.02, meaning that its performance tracks fairly well with that of the overall stock market. Volatility, as measured by both the semi-deviation and a drawdown factor, is considered low. As of December 31, 2012, *iShares S&P NA Natural Resource traded at a discount of 2.53% below its net asset value.

Diane Hsiung has been running the fund for 5 years and currently receives a manager quality ranking of 26 (0=worst, 99=best). This fund offers only a moderate level of risk but investors looking for strong performance are still waiting.

Data Date	Investment Rating	Net Assets ($Mil)	Price	Performance Rating/Pts	Total Return Y-T-D	Risk Rating/Pts
12-12	D+	1,744.70	38.16	D+ / 2.5	2.65%	B- / 7.1
2011	C	1,816.50	38.00	C / 5.1	2.47%	B- / 7.0
2010	D+	2,097.00	41.69	C+ / 5.8	23.35%	D+ / 2.6
2009	D+	1,427.86	34.31	C / 5.5	30.65%	D+ / 2.8

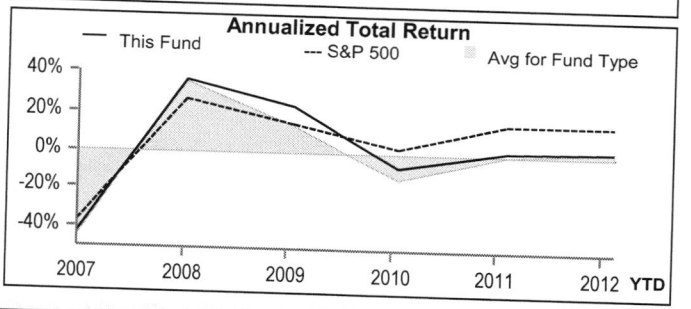

*iShares S&P NA Tech-Multimedia N (IGN)

D   **Weak**

Fund Family: BlackRock Fund Advisors
Fund Type: Growth
Inception Date: July 10, 2001

Major Rating Factors:
Disappointing performance is the major factor driving the D (Weak) TheStreet.com Investment Rating for *iShares S&P NA Tech-Multimedia N. The fund currently has a performance rating of D+ (Weak) based on an annualized return of 2.68% over the last three years and a total return of 3.06% year to date 2012. Factored into the performance evaluation is an expense ratio of 0.48% (very low).

The fund's risk rating is currently C+ (Fair). It carries a beta of 1.50, meaning it is expected to move 15.0% for every 10% move in the market. Volatility, as measured by both the semi-deviation and a drawdown factor, is considered low. As of December 31, 2012, *iShares S&P NA Tech-Multimedia N traded at a discount of 3.00% below its net asset value, which is better than its one-year historical average discount of .01%.

Diane Hsiung has been running the fund for 5 years and currently receives a manager quality ranking of 10 (0=worst, 99=best). This fund offers only a moderate level of risk but investors looking for strong performance are still waiting.

Data Date	Investment Rating	Net Assets ($Mil)	Price	Performance Rating/Pts	Total Return Y-T-D	Risk Rating/Pts
12-12	D	253.60	28.14	D+ / 2.7	3.06%	C+ / 6.6
2011	C-	203.80	27.35	C / 4.3	1.68%	C+ / 6.8
2010	C+	217.60	33.51	C+ / 6.8	24.30%	C / 5.2
2009	D+	161.78	26.98	C- / 3.1	55.41%	C / 5.3

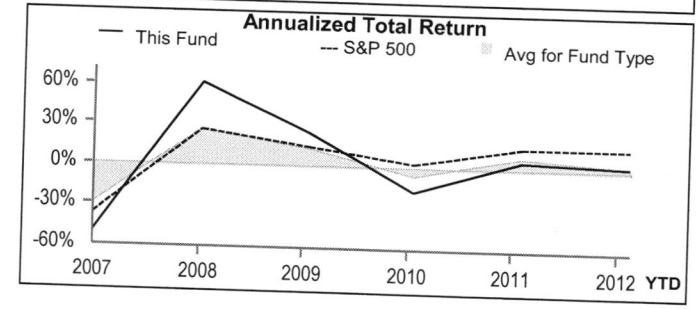

* Denotes ETF Fund

*iShares S&P NA Technology Sector (IGM)

C-　　**Fair**

Fund Family: BlackRock Fund Advisors
Fund Type: Growth
Inception Date: March 13, 2001

Major Rating Factors: Middle of the road best describes *iShares S&P NA Technology Sector whose TheStreet.com Investment Rating is currently a C- (Fair). The fund currently has a performance rating of C (Fair) based on an annualized return of 9.65% over the last three years and a total return of 3.42% year to date 2012. Factored into the performance evaluation is an expense ratio of 0.48% (very low).

The fund's risk rating is currently B- (Good). It carries a beta of 1.18, meaning it is expected to move 11.8% for every 10% move in the market. Volatility, as measured by both the semi-deviation and a drawdown factor, is considered low. As of December 31, 2012, *iShares S&P NA Technology Sector traded at a discount of 3.31% below its net asset value, which is better than its one-year historical average discount of .01%.

Diane Hsiung has been running the fund for 5 years and currently receives a manager quality ranking of 25 (0=worst, 99=best). If you desire an average level of risk, then this fund may be an option.

Data Date	Investment Rating	Net Assets ($Mil)	Price	Performance Rating/Pts	Total Return Y-T-D	Risk Rating/Pts
12-12	C-	493.80	67.46	C / 4.5	3.42%	B- / 7.3
2011	C+	365.20	59.41	C+ / 6.7	2.41%	B- / 7.3
2010	C+	450.90	60.45	C+ / 6.0	11.98%	C / 5.5
2009	C+	332.97	54.22	C+ / 6.5	56.00%	C / 5.3

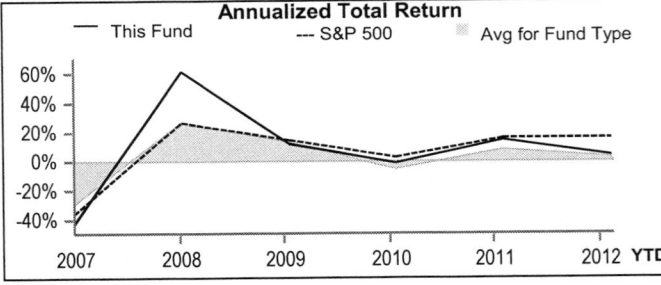

*iShares S&P NA Technology-Softwa (IGV)

C-　　**Fair**

Fund Family: BlackRock Fund Advisors
Fund Type: Income
Inception Date: July 10, 2001

Major Rating Factors: Middle of the road best describes *iShares S&P NA Technology-Softwa whose TheStreet.com Investment Rating is currently a C- (Fair). The fund currently has a performance rating of C+ (Fair) based on an annualized return of 11.65% over the last three years and a total return of 3.93% year to date 2012. Factored into the performance evaluation is an expense ratio of 0.48% (very low).

The fund's risk rating is currently C+ (Fair). It carries a beta of 1.16, meaning it is expected to move 11.6% for every 10% move in the market. Volatility, as measured by both the semi-deviation and a drawdown factor, is considered low. As of December 31, 2012, *iShares S&P NA Technology-Softwa traded at a discount of 3.77% below its net asset value, which is better than its one-year historical premium of .01%.

Diane Hsiung has been running the fund for 5 years and currently receives a manager quality ranking of 35 (0=worst, 99=best). If you desire an average level of risk, then this fund may be an option.

Data Date	Investment Rating	Net Assets ($Mil)	Price	Performance Rating/Pts	Total Return Y-T-D	Risk Rating/Pts
12-12	C-	640.60	63.03	C+ / 5.7	3.93%	C+ / 5.9
2011	C-	492.40	54.12	C+ / 5.6	1.39%	C+ / 6.2
2010	C+	385.10	58.42	B- / 7.5	24.64%	C / 4.6
2009	C	301.15	46.87	C / 5.4	41.64%	C+ / 5.7

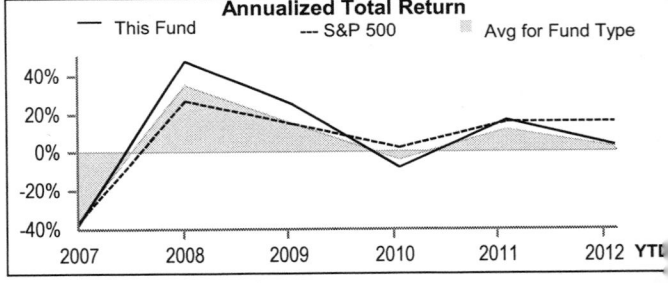

*iShares S&P Natl AMT-Free Muni B (MUB)

C　　**Fair**

Fund Family: BlackRock Fund Advisors
Fund Type: Municipal - National
Inception Date: September 7, 2007

Major Rating Factors: Middle of the road best describes *iShares S&P Natl AMT-Free Muni B whose TheStreet.com Investment Rating is currently a C (Fair). The fund currently has a performance rating of C- (Fair) based on an annualized return of 6.23% over the last three years and a total return of 1.61% year to date 2012. Factored into the performance evaluation is an expense ratio of 0.25% (very low).

The fund's risk rating is currently B+ (Good). It carries a beta of 1.38, meaning it is expected to move 13.8% for every 10% move in the market. Volatility, as measured by both the semi-deviation and a drawdown factor, is considered very low. As of December 31, 2012, *iShares S&P Natl AMT-Free Muni B traded at a discount of .65% below its net asset value, which is better than its one-year historical premium of .65%.

Scott F. Radell has been running the fund for 3 years and currently receives a manager quality ranking of 29 (0=worst, 99=best). If you desire an average level of risk, then this fund may be an option.

Data Date	Investment Rating	Net Assets ($Mil)	Price	Performance Rating/Pts	Total Return Y-T-D	Risk Rating/Pts
12-12	C	3,476.20	110.64	C- / 3.6	1.61%	B+ / 9.4
2011	B	2,512.30	108.25	C+ / 5.8	2.13%	B+ / 9.5
2010	C+	1,975.60	99.18	C- / 3.2	-0.22%	B / 8.7
2009	B+	1,409.80	102.75	C / 4.9	7.12%	B+ / 9.0

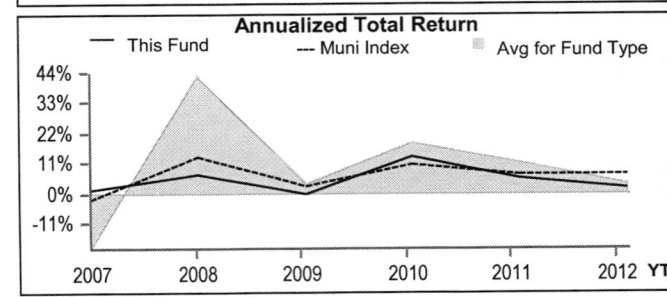

*iShares S&P NY AMT-Free Muni Bon (NYF)

C   **Fair**

Fund Family: BlackRock Fund Advisors
Fund Type: Municipal - Single State
Inception Date: October 4, 2007

Major Rating Factors: Middle of the road best describes *iShares S&P NY AMT-Free Muni Bon whose TheStreet.com Investment Rating is currently a C (Fair). The fund currently has a performance rating of C- (Fair) based on an annualized return of 6.14% over the last three years and a total return of 1.13% year to date 2012. Factored into the performance evaluation is an expense ratio of 0.25% (very low).

The fund's risk rating is currently B+ (Good). It carries a beta of 1.14, meaning it is expected to move 11.4% for every 10% move in the market. Volatility, as measured by both the semi-deviation and a drawdown factor, is considered very low. As of December 31, 2012, *iShares S&P NY AMT-Free Muni Bon traded at a discount of .40% below its net asset value, which is better than its one-year historical average premium of .61%.

Scott F. Radell has been running the fund for 3 years and currently receives a manager quality ranking of 39 (0=worst, 99=best). If you desire an average level of risk, then this fund may be an option.

Data Date	Investment Rating	Net Assets ($Mil)	Price	Performance Rating/Pts	Total Return Y-T-D	Risk Rating/Pts
12-12	C	128.00	111.52	C- / 3.6	1.13%	B+ / 9.4
2011	C+	97.10	108.23	C / 4.5	-0.13%	B+ / 9.4
2010	C+	70.90	99.98	C- / 3.4	-0.26%	B / 8.6
2009	B	56.54	103.87	C / 5.3	10.75%	B / 8.8

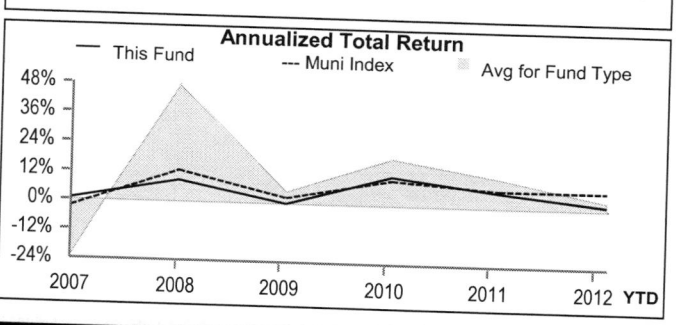

*iShares S&P Sh Tm Ntl AMT-Fr Mun (SUB)

C-   **Fair**

Fund Family: BlackRock Fund Advisors
Fund Type: Municipal - National
Inception Date: November 5, 2008

Major Rating Factors:
Disappointing performance is the major factor driving the C- (Fair) TheStreet.com Investment Rating for *iShares S&P Sh Tm Ntl AMT-Fr Mun. The fund currently has a performance rating of D (Weak) based on an annualized return of 1.64% over the last three years and a total return of 0.49% year to date 2012. Factored into the performance evaluation is an expense ratio of 0.25% (very low).

The fund's risk rating is currently B+ (Good). It carries a beta of 0.24, meaning the fund's expected move will be 2.4% for every 10% move in the market. Volatility, as measured by both the semi-deviation and a drawdown factor, is considered very low. As of December 31, 2012, *iShares S&P Sh Tm Ntl AMT-Fr Mun traded at a discount of .09% below its net asset value, which is better than its one-year historical average premium of .26%.

Scott F. Radell has been running the fund for 3 years and currently receives a manager quality ranking of 52 (0=worst, 99=best). This fund offers only a moderate level of risk but investors looking for strong performance are still waiting.

Data Date	Investment Rating	Net Assets ($Mil)	Price	Performance Rating/Pts	Total Return Y-T-D	Risk Rating/Pts
12-12	C-	621.00	106.23	D / 1.8	0.49%	B+ / 9.9
2011	C	472.60	106.73	D+ / 2.9	0.23%	B+ / 9.9
2010	C	449.90	104.10	D / 2.0	0.36%	B / 8.9
2009	C+	156.17	105.05	C- / 3.0	4.31%	B+ / 9.1

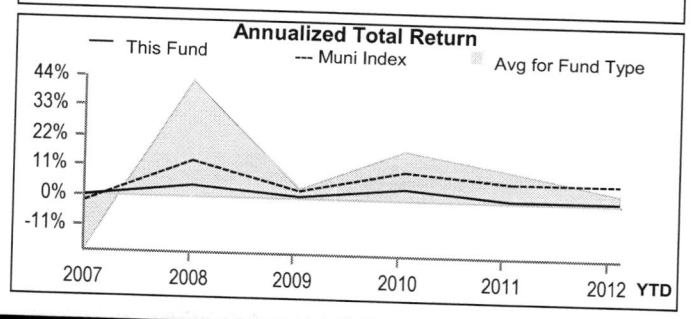

*iShares S&P Small Cap 600 Growth (IJT)

C+   **Fair**

Fund Family: BlackRock Fund Advisors
Fund Type: Growth
Inception Date: July 24, 2000

Major Rating Factors: Strong performance is the major factor driving the C+ (Fair) TheStreet.com Investment Rating for *iShares S&P Small Cap 600 Growth. The fund currently has a performance rating of B- (Good) based on an annualized return of 15.69% over the last three years and a total return of 3.68% year to date 2012. Factored into the performance evaluation is an expense ratio of 0.25% (very low).

The fund's risk rating is currently B- (Good). It carries a beta of 1.13, meaning it is expected to move 11.3% for every 10% move in the market. Volatility, as measured by both the semi-deviation and a drawdown factor, is considered low. As of December 31, 2012, *iShares S&P Small Cap 600 Growth traded at a discount of 3.62% below its net asset value, which is better than its one-year historical average discount of .01%.

Diane Hsiung has been running the fund for 5 years and currently receives a manager quality ranking of 68 (0=worst, 99=best). If you desire only a moderate level of risk and strong performance, then this fund is an excellent option.

Data Date	Investment Rating	Net Assets ($Mil)	Price	Performance Rating/Pts	Total Return Y-T-D	Risk Rating/Pts
12-12	C+	1,606.40	84.04	B- / 7.0	3.68%	B- / 7.4
2011	C+	1,561.20	74.47	C+ / 6.8	0.60%	B- / 7.2
2010	C	1,885.30	72.59	B- / 7.4	28.24%	C- / 3.4
2009	D	1,469.61	57.14	C- / 3.1	26.12%	C- / 3.8

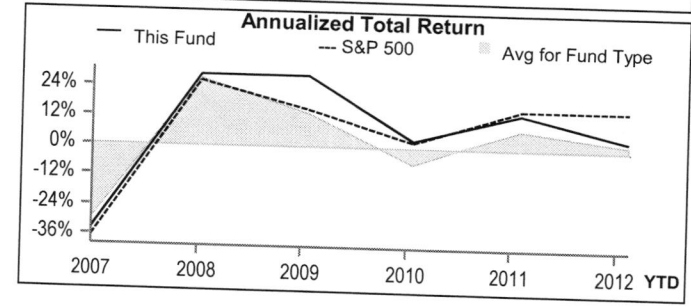

* Denotes ETF Fund

*iShares S&P Small Cap 600 Value (IJS)

C+ **Fair**

Fund Family: BlackRock Fund Advisors
Fund Type: Growth
Inception Date: July 24, 2000

Data Date	Investment Rating	Net Assets ($Mil)	Price	Performance Rating/Pts	Total Return Y-T-D	Risk Rating/Pts
12-12	C+	1,904.10	80.91	C+ / 6.4	2.76%	B- / 7.6
2011	C+	1,591.40	69.76	C+ / 6.1	2.05%	B- / 7.4
2010	B	1,792.50	71.89	B- / 7.2	24.70%	C+ / 5.7
2009	D	1,542.08	58.38	D / 2.0	21.43%	C+ / 5.6

Major Rating Factors: Middle of the road best describes *iShares S&P Small Cap 600 Value whose TheStreet.com Investment Rating is currently a C+ (Fair). The fund currently has a performance rating of C+ (Fair) based on an annualized return of 13.40% over the last three years and a total return of 2.76% year to date 2012. Factored into the performance evaluation is an expense ratio of 0.25% (very low).

The fund's risk rating is currently B- (Good). It carries a beta of 1.26, meaning it is expected to move 12.6% for every 10% move in the market. Volatility, as measured by both the semi-deviation and a drawdown factor, is considered low. As of December 31, 2012, *iShares S&P Small Cap 600 Value traded at a discount of 2.71% below its net asset value.

Diane Hsiung has been running the fund for 5 years and currently receives a manager quality ranking of 46 (0=worst, 99=best). If you desire an average level of risk, then this fund may be an option.

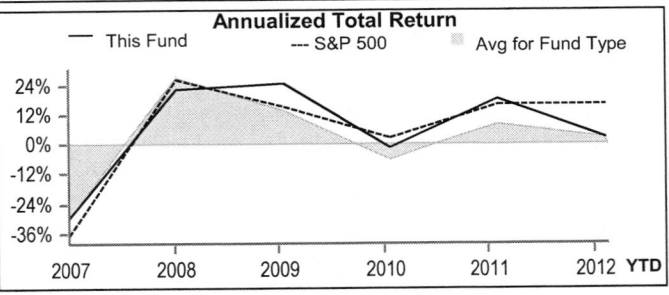
Annualized Total Return

*iShares S&P Target Date 2010 Ind (TZD)

C **Fair**

Fund Family: BlackRock Fund Advisors
Fund Type: Growth and Income
Inception Date: November 4, 2008

Data Date	Investment Rating	Net Assets ($Mil)	Price	Performance Rating/Pts	Total Return Y-T-D	Risk Rating/Pts
12-12	C	4.90	32.96	C- / 3.2	1.07%	B+ / 9.3
2011	C+	6.20	30.86	C- / 3.9	0.84%	B+ / 9.4
2010	A+	6.20	30.93	B / 8.1	10.22%	B / 8.8
2009	A+	2.71	28.62	B- / 7.1	17.54%	B+ / 9.0

Major Rating Factors: Middle of the road best describes *iShares S&P Target Date 2010 Ind whose TheStreet.com Investment Rating is currently a C (Fair). The fund currently has a performance rating of C- (Fair) based on an annualized return of 7.04% over the last three years and a total return of 1.07% year to date 2012. Factored into the performance evaluation is an expense ratio of 0.11% (very low).

The fund's risk rating is currently B+ (Good). It carries a beta of 0.41, meaning the fund's expected move will be 4.1% for every 10% move in the market. Volatility, as measured by both the semi-deviation and a drawdown factor, is considered very low. As of December 31, 2012, *iShares S&P Target Date 2010 Ind traded at a discount of .78% below its net asset value, which is better than its one-year historical average discount of .05%.

Diane Hsiung has been running the fund for 5 years and currently receives a manager quality ranking of 70 (0=worst, 99=best). If you desire an average level of risk, then this fund may be an option.

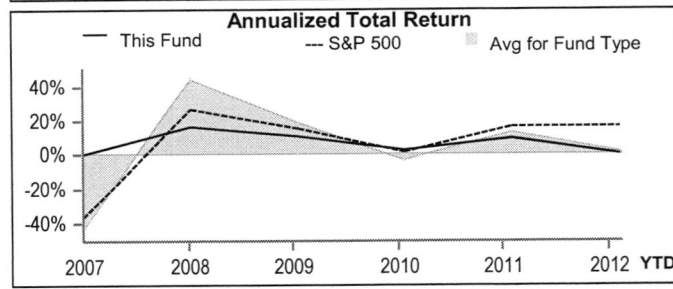
Annualized Total Return

*iShares S&P Target Date 2015 Ind (TZE)

C **Fair**

Fund Family: BlackRock Fund Advisors
Fund Type: Growth and Income
Inception Date: November 4, 2008

Data Date	Investment Rating	Net Assets ($Mil)	Price	Performance Rating/Pts	Total Return Y-T-D	Risk Rating/Pts
12-12	C	15.40	34.13	C- / 3.5	1.85%	B / 8.9
2011	C	9.50	31.63	C- / 3.7	1.01%	B+ / 9.0
2010	A+	9.60	32.04	B+ / 8.5	11.35%	B / 8.5
2009	A+	2.72	29.24	B- / 7.3	19.00%	B / 8.8

Major Rating Factors: Middle of the road best describes *iShares S&P Target Date 2015 Ind whose TheStreet.com Investment Rating is currently a C (Fair). The fund currently has a performance rating of C- (Fair) based on an annualized return of 7.75% over the last three years and a total return of 1.85% year to date 2012. Factored into the performance evaluation is an expense ratio of 0.11% (very low).

The fund's risk rating is currently B (Good). It carries a beta of 0.59, meaning the fund's expected move will be 5.9% for every 10% move in the market. Volatility, as measured by both the semi-deviation and a drawdown factor, is considered low. As of December 31, 2012, *iShares S&P Target Date 2015 Ind traded at a discount of 1.67% below its net asset value, which is better than its one-year historical average discount of .02%.

Diane Hsiung has been running the fund for 5 years and currently receives a manager quality ranking of 61 (0=worst, 99=best). If you desire an average level of risk, then this fund may be an option.

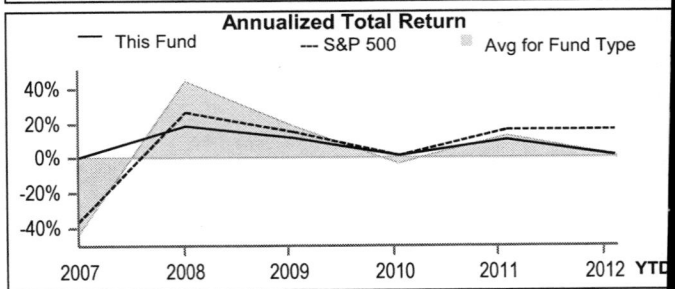
Annualized Total Return

*iShares S&P Target Date 2020 Ind (TZG)

Fund Family: BlackRock Fund Advisors
Fund Type: Growth and Income
Inception Date: November 4, 2008

C **Fair**

Major Rating Factors: Middle of the road best describes *iShares S&P Target Date 2020 Ind whose TheStreet.com Investment Rating is currently a C (Fair). The fund currently has a performance rating of C- (Fair) based on an annualized return of 7.89% over the last three years and a total return of 1.69% year to date 2012. Factored into the performance evaluation is an expense ratio of 0.11% (very low).

The fund's risk rating is currently B (Good). It carries a beta of 0.66, meaning the fund's expected move will be 6.6% for every 10% move in the market. Volatility, as measured by both the semi-deviation and a drawdown factor, is considered low. As of December 31, 2012, *iShares S&P Target Date 2020 Ind traded at a discount of 1.58% below its net asset value, which is better than its one-year historical average premium of .08%.

Diane Hsiung has been running the fund for 5 years and currently receives a manager quality ranking of 60 (0=worst, 99=best). If you desire an average level of risk, then this fund may be an option.

Data Date	Investment Rating	Net Assets ($Mil)	Price	Performance Rating/Pts	Total Return Y-T-D	Risk Rating/Pts
12-12	C	26.20	34.99	C- / 3.7	1.69%	B / 8.8
2011	C	17.60	32.26	C- / 4.1	-0.06%	B / 8.9
2010	A+	11.40	32.73	B+ / 8.7	12.58%	B / 8.4
2009	A+	2.72	29.67	B / 8.0	27.96%	B / 8.8

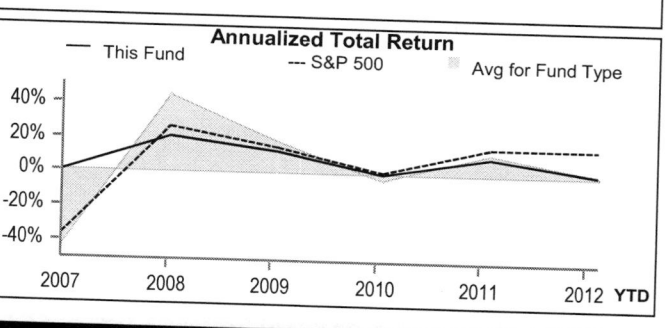

*iShares S&P Target Date 2025 Ind (TZI)

Fund Family: BlackRock Fund Advisors
Fund Type: Growth and Income
Inception Date: November 4, 2008

C **Fair**

Major Rating Factors: Middle of the road best describes *iShares S&P Target Date 2025 Ind whose TheStreet.com Investment Rating is currently a C (Fair). The fund currently has a performance rating of C- (Fair) based on an annualized return of 8.39% over the last three years and a total return of 2.32% year to date 2012. Factored into the performance evaluation is an expense ratio of 0.11% (very low).

The fund's risk rating is currently B (Good). It carries a beta of 0.78, meaning the fund's expected move will be 7.8% for every 10% move in the market. Volatility, as measured by both the semi-deviation and a drawdown factor, is considered low. As of December 31, 2012, *iShares S&P Target Date 2025 Ind traded at a discount of 2.27% below its net asset value, which is better than its one-year historical average premium of .03%.

Diane Hsiung has been running the fund for 5 years and currently receives a manager quality ranking of 48 (0=worst, 99=best). If you desire an average level of risk, then this fund may be an option.

Data Date	Investment Rating	Net Assets ($Mil)	Price	Performance Rating/Pts	Total Return Y-T-D	Risk Rating/Pts
12-12	C	19.50	35.33	C- / 3.9	2.32%	B / 8.6
2011	C	27.40	32.24	C- / 4.1	0.81%	B / 8.6
2010	A+	13.30	33.24	B+ / 8.8	13.02%	B / 8.1
2009	A+	4.08	29.90	B / 8.0	22.36%	B / 8.3

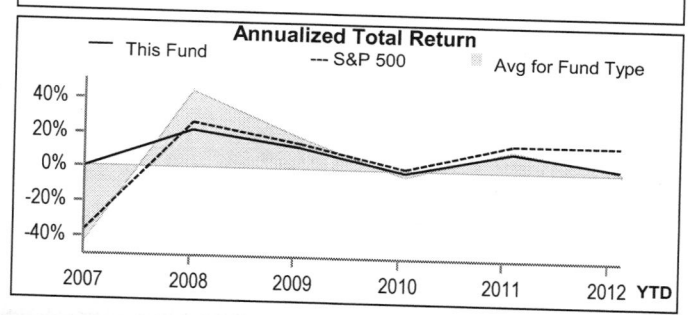

*iShares S&P Target Date 2030 Ind (TZL)

Fund Family: BlackRock Fund Advisors
Fund Type: Growth and Income
Inception Date: November 4, 2008

C **Fair**

Major Rating Factors: Middle of the road best describes *iShares S&P Target Date 2030 Ind whose TheStreet.com Investment Rating is currently a C (Fair). The fund currently has a performance rating of C- (Fair) based on an annualized return of 8.61% over the last three years and a total return of 2.42% year to date 2012. Factored into the performance evaluation is an expense ratio of 0.11% (very low).

The fund's risk rating is currently B (Good). It carries a beta of 0.77, meaning the fund's expected move will be 7.7% for every 10% move in the market. Volatility, as measured by both the semi-deviation and a drawdown factor, is considered low. As of December 31, 2012, *iShares S&P Target Date 2030 Ind traded at a discount of 2.21% below its net asset value, which is better than its one-year historical average premium of .04%.

Diane Hsiung has been running the fund for 5 years and currently receives a manager quality ranking of 42 (0=worst, 99=best). If you desire an average level of risk, then this fund may be an option.

Data Date	Investment Rating	Net Assets ($Mil)	Price	Performance Rating/Pts	Total Return Y-T-D	Risk Rating/Pts
12-12	C	17.90	35.78	C- / 4.2	2.42%	B / 8.5
2011	C+	12.90	32.41	C / 4.6	0.56%	B / 8.6
2010	A+	10.00	33.57	B+ / 8.9	13.90%	B / 8.1
2009	A+	4.07	30.00	B+ / 8.3	28.66%	B / 8.4

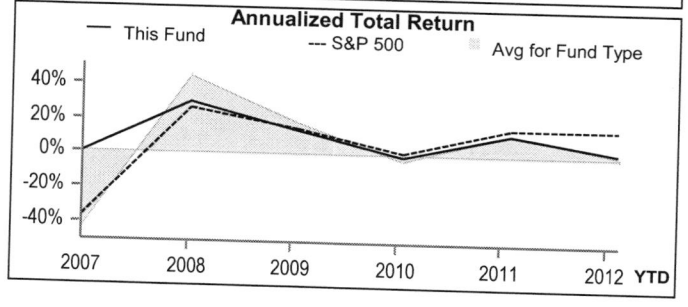

*iShares S&P Target Date 2035 Ind (TZO)

C   **Fair**

Fund Family: BlackRock Fund Advisors
Fund Type: Growth and Income
Inception Date: November 4, 2008

Major Rating Factors: Middle of the road best describes *iShares S&P Target Date 2035 Ind whose TheStreet.com Investment Rating is currently a C (Fair). The fund currently has a performance rating of C (Fair) based on an annualized return of 8.95% over the last three years and a total return of 2.77% year to date 2012. Factored into the performance evaluation is an expense ratio of 0.11% (very low).

The fund's risk rating is currently B (Good). It carries a beta of 0.91, meaning that its performance tracks fairly well with that of the overall stock market. Volatility, as measured by both the semi-deviation and a drawdown factor, is considered low. As of December 31, 2012, *iShares S&P Target Date 2035 Ind traded at a discount of 2.59% below its net asset value, which is better than its one-year historical average premium of .12%.

Diane Hsiung has been running the fund for 5 years and currently receives a manager quality ranking of 41 (0=worst, 99=best). If you desire an average level of risk, then this fund may be an option.

Data Date	Investment Rating	Net Assets ($Mil)	Price	Performance Rating/Pts	Total Return Y-T-D	Risk Rating/Pts
12-12	C	12.60	35.80	C / 4.4	2.77%	B / 8.2
2011	C	8.00	32.31	C- / 4.2	0.65%	B / 8.3
2010	A+	6.70	33.51	B+ / 8.9	14.19%	B- / 7.6
2009	A+	2.71	29.90	B / 8.1	25.09%	B- / 7.8

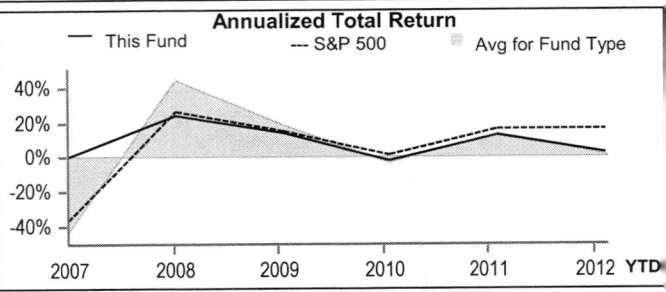

*iShares S&P Target Date 2040 Ind (TZV)

C   **Fair**

Fund Family: BlackRock Fund Advisors
Fund Type: Growth and Income
Inception Date: November 4, 2008

Major Rating Factors: Middle of the road best describes *iShares S&P Target Date 2040 Ind whose TheStreet.com Investment Rating is currently a C (Fair). The fund currently has a performance rating of C (Fair) based on an annualized return of 9.02% over the last three years and a total return of 2.37% year to date 2012. Factored into the performance evaluation is an expense ratio of 0.11% (very low).

The fund's risk rating is currently B (Good). It carries a beta of 0.98, meaning that its performance tracks fairly well with that of the overall stock market. Volatility, as measured by both the semi-deviation and a drawdown factor, is considered low. As of December 31, 2012, *iShares S&P Target Date 2040 Ind traded at a discount of 2.31% below its net asset value, which is better than its one-year historical average premium of .03%.

Daine Hsiung has been running the fund for 5 years and currently receives a manager quality ranking of 36 (0=worst, 99=best). If you desire an average level of risk, then this fund may be an option.

Data Date	Investment Rating	Net Assets ($Mil)	Price	Performance Rating/Pts	Total Return Y-T-D	Risk Rating/Pts
12-12	C	21.80	36.30	C / 4.5	2.37%	B / 8.0
2011	C	16.20	32.45	C- / 4.1	0.86%	B / 8.1
2010	A+	11.90	33.94	A- / 9.0	14.56%	B / 8.0
2009	A+	2.71	30.20	B / 8.1	23.48%	B / 8.4

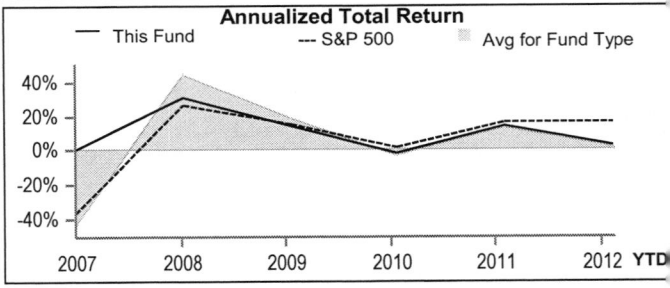

*iShares S&P Target Date 2045 Ind (TZW)

B+   **Good**

Fund Family: BlackRock Fund Advisors
Fund Type: Global
Inception Date: August 16, 2011

Major Rating Factors: Strong performance is the major factor driving the B+ (Good) TheStreet.com Investment Rating for *iShares S&P Target Date 2045 Ind. The fund currently has a performance rating of B (Good) based on an annualized return of 0.00% over the last three years and a total return of 2.85% year to date 2012. Factored into the performance evaluation is an expense ratio of 0.11% (very low).

The fund's risk rating is currently B (Good). It carries a beta of 0.00, meaning the fund's expected move will be 0.0% for every 10% move in the market. Volatility, as measured by both the semi-deviation and a drawdown factor, is considered low. As of December 31, 2012, *iShares S&P Target Date 2045 Ind traded at a discount of 2.60% below its net asset value, which is better than its one-year historical average premium of .02%.

Diane Hsiung has been running the fund for 2 years and currently receives a manager quality ranking of 65 (0=worst, 99=best). If you desire only a moderate level of risk and strong performance, then this fund is an excellent option.

Data Date	Investment Rating	Net Assets ($Mil)	Price	Performance Rating/Pts	Total Return Y-T-D	Risk Rating/Pts
12-12	B+	4.20	28.05	B / 7.9	2.85%	B / 8.6

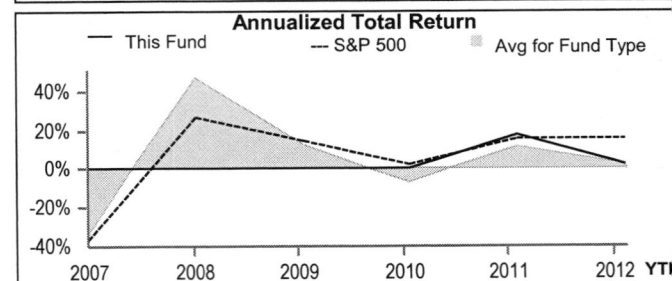

*iShares S&P Target Date 2050 Ind (TZY)

B+ **Good**

Fund Family: BlackRock Fund Advisors
Fund Type: Global
Inception Date: August 16, 2011

Major Rating Factors: Strong performance is the major factor driving the B+ (Good) TheStreet.com Investment Rating for *iShares S&P Target Date 2050 Ind. The fund currently has a performance rating of B (Good) based on an annualized return of 0.00% over the last three years and a total return of 3.54% year to date 2012. Factored into the performance evaluation is an expense ratio of 0.11% (very low).

The fund's risk rating is currently B (Good). It carries a beta of 0.00, meaning the fund's expected move will be 0.0% for every 10% move in the market. Volatility, as measured by both the semi-deviation and a drawdown factor, is considered low. As of December 31, 2012, *iShares S&P Target Date 2050 Ind traded at a discount of 3.29% below its net asset value, which is better than its one-year historical average premium of .02%.

Diane Hsiung has been running the fund for 2 years and currently receives a manager quality ranking of 55 (0=worst, 99=best). If you desire only a moderate level of risk and strong performance, then this fund is an excellent option.

Data Date	Investment Rating	Net Assets ($Mil)	Price	Performance Rating/Pts	Total Return Y-T-D	Risk Rating/Pts
12-12	B+	5.60	27.95	B / 8.0	3.54%	B / 8.5

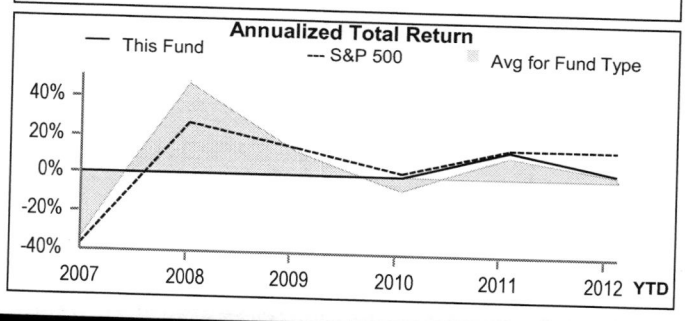

*iShares S&P Target Date Ret Inco (TGR)

C **Fair**

Fund Family: BlackRock Fund Advisors
Fund Type: Growth and Income
Inception Date: November 4, 2008

Major Rating Factors:
Disappointing performance is the major factor driving the C (Fair) TheStreet.com Investment Rating for *iShares S&P Target Date Ret Inco. The fund currently has a performance rating of D+ (Weak) based on an annualized return of 6.50% over the last three years and a total return of 1.50% year to date 2012. Factored into the performance evaluation is an expense ratio of 0.11% (very low).

The fund's risk rating is currently B+ (Good). It carries a beta of 0.28, meaning the fund's expected move will be 2.8% for every 10% move in the market. Volatility, as measured by both the semi-deviation and a drawdown factor, is considered very low. As of December 31, 2012, *iShares S&P Target Date Ret Inco traded at a discount of 1.41% below its net asset value, which is better than its one-year historical average premium of .07%.

Diane Hsiung has been running the fund for 5 years and currently receives a manager quality ranking of 73 (0=worst, 99=best). This fund offers only a moderate level of risk but investors looking for strong performance are still waiting.

Data Date	Investment Rating	Net Assets ($Mil)	Price	Performance Rating/Pts	Total Return Y-T-D	Risk Rating/Pts
12-12	C	7.90	31.45	D+ / 2.9	1.50%	B+ / 9.6
2011	C	9.00	30.00	C- / 3.6	0.54%	B+ / 9.4
2010	A	4.50	29.70	B- / 7.2	8.31%	B / 8.5
2009	B	2.66	28.00	C+ / 5.6	11.05%	B / 8.7

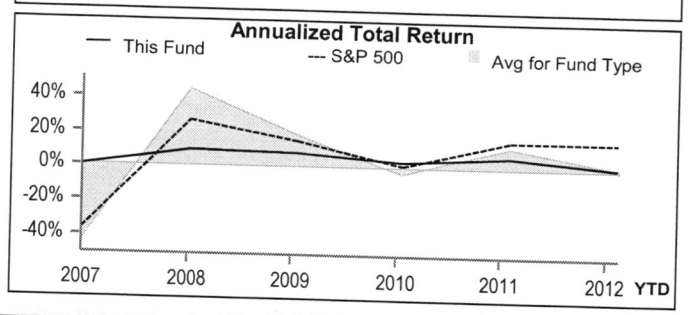

*iShares S&P USPreferred Stock (PFF)

C **Fair**

Fund Family: BlackRock Fund Advisors
Fund Type: Income
Inception Date: March 26, 2007

Major Rating Factors: Middle of the road best describes *iShares S&P USPreferred Stock whose TheStreet.com Investment Rating is currently a C (Fair). The fund currently has a performance rating of C- (Fair) based on an annualized return of 9.10% over the last three years and a total return of 1.49% year to date 2012. Factored into the performance evaluation is an expense ratio of 0.48% (very low).

The fund's risk rating is currently B (Good). It carries a beta of 0.37, meaning the fund's expected move will be 3.7% for every 10% move in the market. Volatility, as measured by both the semi-deviation and a drawdown factor, is considered low. As of December 31, 2012, *iShares S&P USPreferred Stock traded at a discount of 1.39% below its net asset value, which is better than its one-year historical average premium of .07%.

Diane Hsiung has been running the fund for 5 years and currently receives a manager quality ranking of 81 (0=worst, 99=best). If you desire an average level of risk, then this fund may be an option.

Data Date	Investment Rating	Net Assets ($Mil)	Price	Performance Rating/Pts	Total Return Y-T-D	Risk Rating/Pts
12-12	C	10,747.30	39.62	C- / 4.0	1.49%	B / 8.9
2011	C-	6,979.90	35.62	C / 4.7	3.34%	C+ / 6.6
2010	C	6,127.40	38.80	C+ / 6.2	13.87%	C / 4.4
2009	B-	2,763.48	36.70	B+ / 8.4	33.66%	C / 4.5

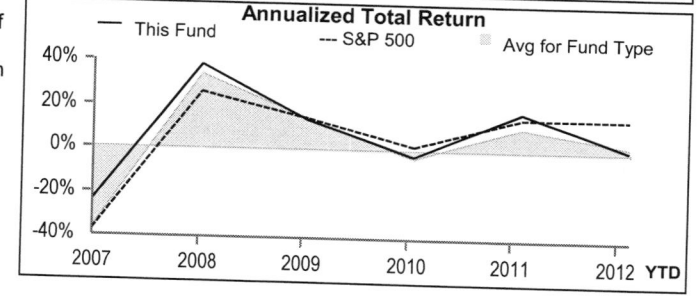

* Denotes ETF Fund

*iShares S&P/Citigroup 1-3 Year I (ISHG)   D+   Weak

Fund Family: BlackRock Fund Advisors
Fund Type: Global
Inception Date: January 21, 2009

Major Rating Factors:
Disappointing performance is the major factor driving the D+ (Weak) TheStreet.com Investment Rating for *iShares S&P/Citigroup 1-3 Year I. The fund currently has a performance rating of D- (Weak) based on an annualized return of -0.29% over the last three years and a total return of 0.46% year to date 2012. Factored into the performance evaluation is an expense ratio of 0.35% (very low).

The fund's risk rating is currently B (Good). It carries a beta of 1.07, meaning that its performance tracks fairly well with that of the overall stock market. Volatility, as measured by both the semi-deviation and a drawdown factor, is considered low. As of December 31, 2012, *iShares S&P/Citigroup 1-3 Year I traded at a discount of .19% below its net asset value, which is better than its one-year historical average premium of .48%.

Scott F. Radell has been running the fund for 3 years and currently receives a manager quality ranking of 25 (0=worst, 99=best). This fund offers only a moderate level of risk but investors looking for strong performance are still waiting.

Data Date	Investment Rating	Net Assets ($Mil)	Price	Perfor-mance Rating/Pts	Total Return Y-T-D	Risk Rating/Pts
12-12	D+	203.60	97.02	D- / 1.4	0.46%	B / 8.5
2011	D+	154.80	96.99	D- / 1.5	-0.56%	B / 8.7
2010	C+	114.70	104.21	C- / 4.1	0.99%	B / 8.1

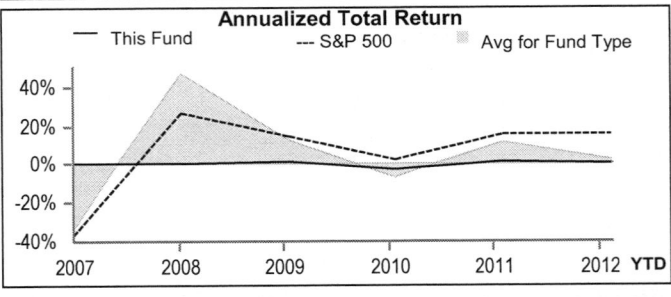
Annualized Total Return
— This Fund   --- S&P 500   Avg for Fund Type

*iShares S&P/Citigroup Intl Treas (IGOV)   C-   Fair

Fund Family: BlackRock Fund Advisors
Fund Type: Global
Inception Date: January 21, 2009

Major Rating Factors:
Disappointing performance is the major factor driving the C- (Fair) TheStreet.com Investment Rating for *iShares S&P/Citigroup Intl Treas. The fund currently has a performance rating of D (Weak) based on an annualized return of 2.33% over the last three years and a total return of -0.08% year to date 2012. Factored into the performance evaluation is an expense ratio of 0.35% (very low).

The fund's risk rating is currently B (Good). It carries a beta of 1.05, meaning that its performance tracks fairly well with that of the overall stock market. Volatility, as measured by both the semi-deviation and a drawdown factor, is considered low. As of December 31, 2012, *iShares S&P/Citigroup Intl Treas traded at a premium of .30% above its net asset value, which is worse than its one-year historical average premium of .17%.

Scott F. Radell has been running the fund for 3 years and currently receives a manager quality ranking of 41 (0=worst, 99=best). This fund offers only a moderate level of risk but investors looking for strong performance are still waiting.

Data Date	Investment Rating	Net Assets ($Mil)	Price	Perfor-mance Rating/Pts	Total Return Y-T-D	Risk Rating/Pts
12-12	C-	365.00	102.93	D / 2.2	-0.08%	B / 8.8
2011	C-	273.90	99.90	D / 1.8	-2.15%	B / 8.8
2010	C+	163.30	102.27	C- / 3.3	1.40%	B / 8.1

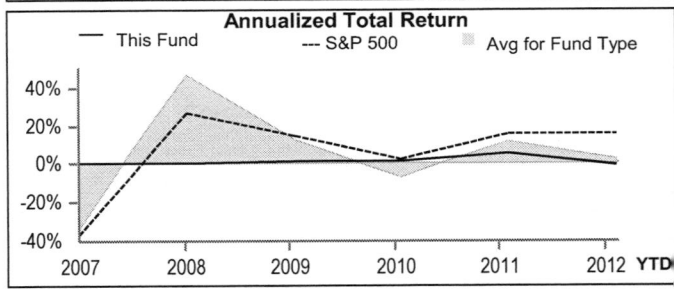
Annualized Total Return
— This Fund   --- S&P 500   Avg for Fund Type

*iShares S&P/Topix 150 (ITF)   D+   Weak

Fund Family: BlackRock Fund Advisors
Fund Type: Foreign
Inception Date: October 23, 2001

Major Rating Factors:
Disappointing performance is the major factor driving the D+ (Weak) TheStreet.com Investment Rating for *iShares S&P/Topix 150. The fund currently has a performance rating of D (Weak) based on an annualized return of 0.13% over the last three years and a total return of 1.73% year to date 2012. Factored into the performance evaluation is an expense ratio of 0.50% (very low).

The fund's risk rating is currently B- (Good). It carries a beta of 0.63, meaning the fund's expected move will be 6.3% for every 10% move in the market. Volatility, as measured by both the semi-deviation and a drawdown factor, is considered low. As of December 31, 2012, *iShares S&P/Topix 150 traded at a discount of .09% below its net asset value, which is worse than its one-year historical average discount of .44%.

Diane Hsiung has been running the fund for 5 years and currently receives a manager quality ranking of 48 (0=worst, 99=best). This fund offers only a moderate level of risk but investors looking for strong performance are still waiting.

Data Date	Investment Rating	Net Assets ($Mil)	Price	Perfor-mance Rating/Pts	Total Return Y-T-D	Risk Rating/Pts
12-12	D+	72.10	42.45	D / 2.2	1.73%	B- / 7.4
2011	D	70.50	38.68	D / 1.7	0.34%	B- / 7.6
2010	D-	100.20	47.53	D+ / 2.4	14.07%	D+ / 2.7
2009	E	116.70	42.34	E+ / 0.9	2.74%	C- / 3.1

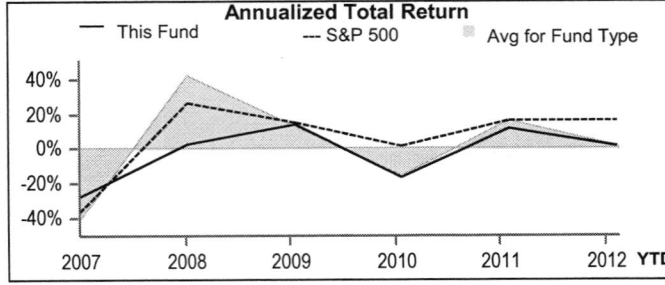
Annualized Total Return
— This Fund   --- S&P 500   Avg for Fund Type

*iShares Silver Trust (SLV)

C-   **Fair**

Fund Family: BlackRock Fund Advisors
Fund Type: Precious Metals
Inception Date: April 28, 2006

Major Rating Factors: Middle of the road best describes *iShares Silver Trust whose TheStreet.com Investment Rating is currently a C- (Fair). The fund currently has a performance rating of C+ (Fair) based on an annualized return of 17.77% over the last three years and a total return of 0.37% year to date 2012. Factored into the performance evaluation is an expense ratio of 0.50% (very low).

The fund's risk rating is currently C (Fair). It carries a beta of 1.72, meaning it is expected to move 17.2% for every 10% move in the market. Volatility, as measured by both the semi-deviation and a drawdown factor, is considered average. As of December 31, 2012, *iShares Silver Trust traded at a discount of 1.01% below its net asset value, which is better than its one-year historical average premium of .51%.

This fund has been team managed for 7 years and currently receives a manager quality ranking of 22 (0=worst, 99=best). If you desire an average level of risk, then this fund may be an option.

Data Date	Investment Rating	Net Assets ($Mil)	Price	Performance Rating/Pts	Total Return Y-T-D	Risk Rating/Pts
12-12	C-	9,706.70	29.37	C+ / 6.3	0.37%	C / 4.9
2011	C+	8,699.00	26.94	B+ / 8.5	3.60%	C / 5.2
2010	C	10,750.90	30.18	A+ / 9.7	82.47%	D- / 1.0
2009	D+	4,292.92	16.54	B- / 7.0	44.96%	D- / 1.5

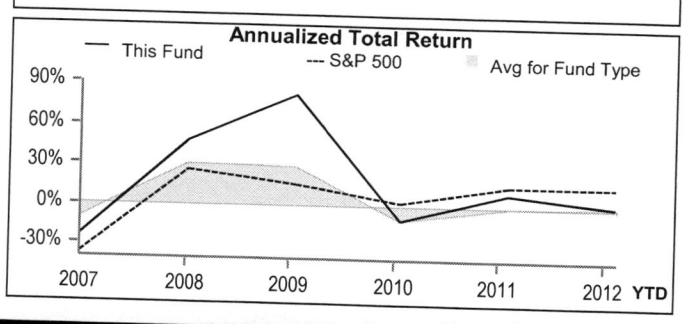

*JPMorgan Alerian MLP Idx ETN (AMJ)

C   **Fair**

Fund Family: JP Morgan Investment Management Inc
Fund Type: Energy/Natural Resources
Inception Date: April 2, 2009

Major Rating Factors: Strong performance is the major factor driving the C (Fair) TheStreet.com Investment Rating for *JPMorgan Alerian MLP Idx ETN. The fund currently has a performance rating of B- (Good) based on an annualized return of 17.74% over the last three years and a total return of 7.33% year to date 2012.

The fund's risk rating is currently C (Fair). It carries a beta of 0.45, meaning the fund's expected move will be 4.5% for every 10% move in the market. Volatility, as measured by both the semi-deviation and a drawdown factor, is considered average. As of December 31, 2012, *JPMorgan Alerian MLP Idx ETN traded at a discount of 6.92% below its net asset value, which is better than its one-year historical average premium of .13%.

This fund has been team managed for 4 years and currently receives a manager quality ranking of 91 (0=worst, 99=best). If you desire an average level of risk and strong performance, then this fund is a good option.

Data Date	Investment Rating	Net Assets ($Mil)	Price	Performance Rating/Pts	Total Return Y-T-D	Risk Rating/Pts
12-12	C	4,869.00	38.46	B- / 7.0	7.33%	C / 5.1
2011	C	3,639.00	38.97	B- / 7.2	1.03%	C / 5.2
2010	A-	2,271.30	36.35	A / 9.5	34.55%	C / 4.7

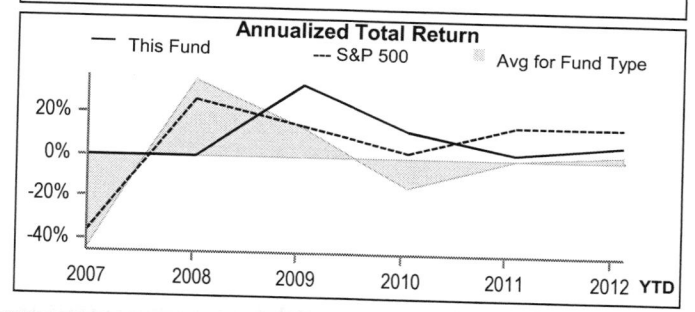

*JPMorgan Dbl Short 10 Year Trs E (DSXJ)

E-   **Very Weak**

Fund Family: JP Morgan Investment Management Inc
Fund Type: Growth
Inception Date: October 4, 2010

Major Rating Factors: *JPMorgan Dbl Short 10 Year Trs E has adopted a risky asset allocation strategy and currently receives an overall TheStreet.com Investment Rating of E- (Very Weak). The fund has an above average level of volatility, as measured by both semi-deviation and drawdown factors. It carries a beta of 0.00, meaning the fund's expected move will be 0.0% for every 10% move in the market. As of December 31, 2012, *JPMorgan Dbl Short 10 Year Trs E traded at a discount of 28.21% below its net asset value, which is better than its one-year historical average discount of 3.51%. Unfortunately, the high level of risk (D+, Weak) failed to pay off as investors endured very poor performance.

The fund's performance rating is currently E- (Very Weak). It has registered an annualized return of 0.00% over the last three years but is down -3.21% year to date 2012.

This is team managed and currently receives a manager quality ranking of 1 (0=worst, 99=best). If you can tolerate high levels of risk in the hope of improved future returns, holding this fund may be an option.

Data Date	Investment Rating	Net Assets ($Mil)	Price	Performance Rating/Pts	Total Return Y-T-D	Risk Rating/Pts
12-12	E-	0.10	28.00	E- / 0.2	-3.21%	D+ / 2.7
2011	E+	0.00	41.59	E+ / 0.7	0.75%	C / 4.5

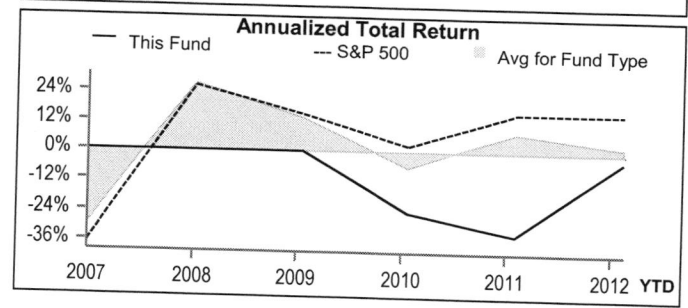

* Denotes ETF Fund

*Madrona Domestic ETF (FWDD)

B+   Good

Fund Family: AdvisorShares Investments LLC
Fund Type: Growth
Inception Date: June 20, 2011

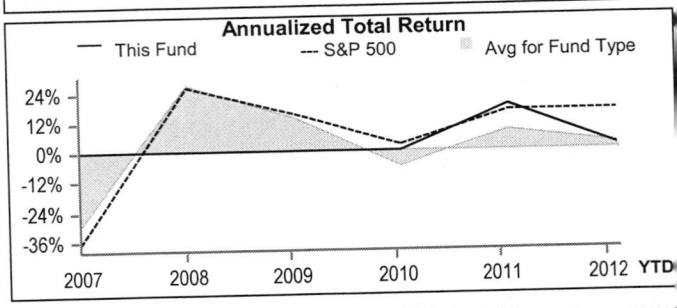

Data Date	Investment Rating	Net Assets ($Mil)	Price	Performance Rating/Pts	Total Return Y-T-D	Risk Rating/Pts
12-12	B+	15.20	27.80	B+ / 8.5	1.87%	B- / 7.9

Major Rating Factors: Strong performance is the major factor driving the B+ (Good) TheStreet.com Investment Rating for *Madrona Domestic ETF. The fund currently has a performance rating of B+ (Good) based on an annualized return of 0.00% over the last three years and a total return of 1.87% year to date 2012. Factored into the performance evaluation is an expense ratio of 1.25% (average).

The fund's risk rating is currently B- (Good). It carries a beta of 0.00, meaning the fund's expected move will be 0.0% for every 10% move in the market. Volatility, as measured by both the semi-deviation and a drawdown factor, is considered low. As of December 31, 2012, *Madrona Domestic ETF traded at a discount of 1.56% below its net asset value, which is better than its one-year historical average discount of .19%.

Brian K. Evans has been running the fund for 2 years and currently receives a manager quality ranking of 48 (0=worst, 99=best). If you desire only a moderate level of risk and strong performance, then this fund is an excellent option.

Annualized Total Return

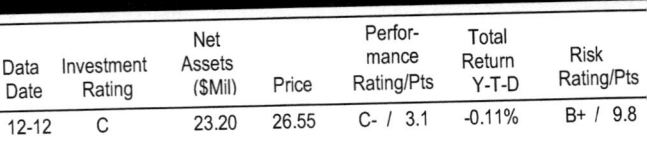

*Madrona Global Bond ETF (FWDB)

C   Fair

Fund Family: AdvisorShares Investments LLC
Fund Type: Global
Inception Date: June 20, 2011

Data Date	Investment Rating	Net Assets ($Mil)	Price	Performance Rating/Pts	Total Return Y-T-D	Risk Rating/Pts
12-12	C	23.20	26.55	C- / 3.1	-0.11%	B+ / 9.8

Major Rating Factors: Middle of the road best describes *Madrona Global Bond ETF whose TheStreet.com Investment Rating is currently a C (Fair). The fund currently has a performance rating of C- (Fair) based on an annualized return of 0.00% over the last three years and a total return of -0.11% year to date 2012. Factored into the performance evaluation is an expense ratio of 0.95% (low).

The fund's risk rating is currently B+ (Good). It carries a beta of 0.00, meaning the fund's expected move will be 0.0% for every 10% move in the market. Volatility, as measured by both the semi-deviation and a drawdown factor, is considered very low. As of December 31, 2012, *Madrona Global Bond ETF traded at a premium of .04% above its net asset value, which is better than its one-year historical average premium of .07%.

Robert W. Bauer has been running the fund for 2 years and currently receives a manager quality ranking of 86 (0=worst, 99=best). If you desire an average level of risk, then this fund may be an option.

Annualized Total Return

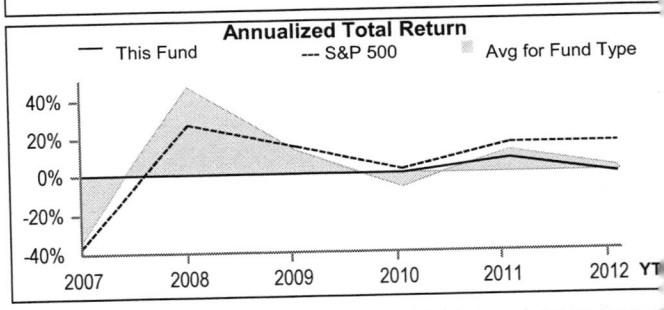

*Madrona International ETF (FWDI)

B+   Good

Fund Family: AdvisorShares Investments LLC
Fund Type: Foreign
Inception Date: June 20, 2011

Data Date	Investment Rating	Net Assets ($Mil)	Price	Performance Rating/Pts	Total Return Y-T-D	Risk Rating/Pts
12-12	B+	15.00	24.03	A / 9.5	2.37%	C+ / 6.7

Major Rating Factors:
Exceptional performance is the major factor driving the B+ (Good) TheStreet.com Investment Rating for *Madrona International ETF. The fund currently has a performance rating of A (Excellent) based on an annualized return of 0.00% over the last three years and a total return of 2.37% year to date 2012. Factored into the performance evaluation is an expense ratio of 1.25% (average).

The fund's risk rating is currently C+ (Fair). It carries a beta of 0.00, meaning the fund's expected move will be 0.0% for every 10% move in the market. Volatility, as measured by both the semi-deviation and a drawdown factor, is considered low. As of December 31, 2012, *Madrona International ETF traded at a discount of 2.32% below its net asset value, which is better than its one-year historical average discount of .23%.

Brian K. Evans has been running the fund for 2 years and currently receives a manager quality ranking of 38 (0=worst, 99=best). If you desire only a moderate level of risk and strong performance, then this fund is an excellent option.

Annualized Total Return

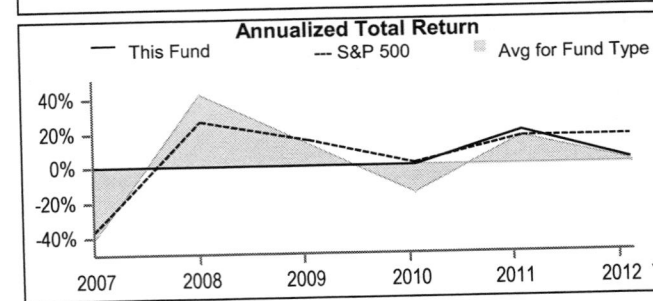

*Market Vector RVE Hard Asst Prd (HAP)

D+   **Weak**

Fund Family: Van Eck Associates Corporation
Fund Type: Global
Inception Date: August 29, 2008

Major Rating Factors:
Disappointing performance is the major factor driving the D+ (Weak) TheStreet.com Investment Rating for *Market Vector RVE Hard Asst Prd. The fund currently has a performance rating of D+ (Weak) based on an annualized return of 3.66% over the last three years and a total return of 2.76% year to date 2012. Factored into the performance evaluation is an expense ratio of 0.52% (very low).

The fund's risk rating is currently B- (Good). It carries a beta of 1.06, meaning that its performance tracks fairly well with that of the overall stock market. Volatility, as measured by both the semi-deviation and a drawdown factor, is considered low. As of December 31, 2012, *Market Vector RVE Hard Asst Prd traded at a discount of 2.92% below its net asset value, which is better than its one-year historical average discount of .12%.

George Cao has been running the fund for 5 years and currently receives a manager quality ranking of 47 (0=worst, 99=best). This fund offers only a moderate level of risk but investors looking for strong performance are still waiting.

Data Date	Investment Rating	Net Assets ($Mil)	Price	Performance Rating/Pts	Total Return Y-T-D	Risk Rating/Pts
12-12	D+	122.20	35.85	D+ / 2.5	2.76%	B- / 7.0
2011	C-	158.70	33.73	C- / 4.2	2.55%	B- / 7.1
2010	A+	209.70	38.95	A / 9.5	16.52%	C+ / 6.9
2009	A+	47.89	33.70	B+ / 8.9	38.05%	B- / 7.0

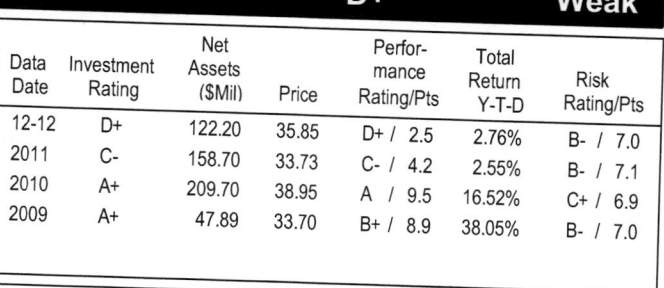

*Market Vectors Africa Index ETF (AFK)

C-   **Fair**

Fund Family: Van Eck Associates Corporation
Fund Type: Foreign
Inception Date: July 10, 2008

Major Rating Factors: Middle of the road best describes *Market Vectors Africa Index ETF whose TheStreet.com Investment Rating is currently a C- (Fair). The fund currently has a performance rating of C- (Fair) based on an annualized return of 4.71% over the last three years and a total return of -0.48% year to date 2012. Factored into the performance evaluation is an expense ratio of 0.78% (very low).

The fund's risk rating is currently B- (Good). It carries a beta of 0.87, meaning the fund's expected move will be 8.7% for every 10% move in the market. Volatility, as measured by both the semi-deviation and a drawdown factor, is considered low. As of December 31, 2012, *Market Vectors Africa Index ETF traded at a premium of .84% above its net asset value, which is worse than its one-year historical average premium of .12%.

George Cao has been running the fund for 5 years and currently receives a manager quality ranking of 70 (0=worst, 99=best). If you desire an average level of risk, then this fund may be an option.

Data Date	Investment Rating	Net Assets ($Mil)	Price	Performance Rating/Pts	Total Return Y-T-D	Risk Rating/Pts
12-12	C-	84.60	31.35	C- / 3.8	-0.48%	B- / 7.6
2011	C-	63.80	25.75	D+ / 2.9	0.89%	B- / 7.7
2010	B	107.50	35.18	A / 9.4	25.26%	C- / 3.4
2009	C	18.60	28.40	B- / 7.5	29.79%	C- / 3.4

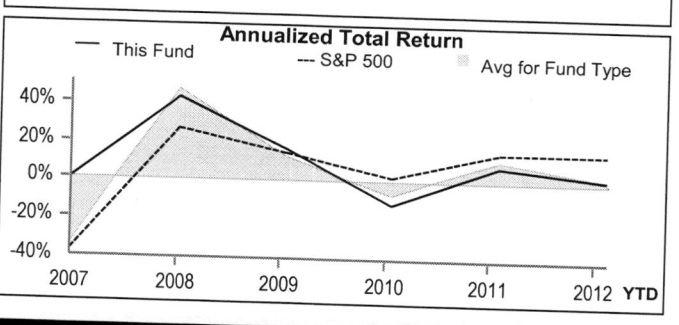

*Market Vectors Agribusiness ETF (MOO)

C-   **Fair**

Fund Family: Van Eck Associates Corporation
Fund Type: Global
Inception Date: August 31, 2007

Major Rating Factors: Middle of the road best describes *Market Vectors Agribusiness ETF whose TheStreet.com Investment Rating is currently a C- (Fair). The fund currently has a performance rating of C- (Fair) based on an annualized return of 7.43% over the last three years and a total return of 4.00% year to date 2012. Factored into the performance evaluation is an expense ratio of 0.54% (very low).

The fund's risk rating is currently B- (Good). It carries a beta of 1.01, meaning that its performance tracks fairly well with that of the overall stock market. Volatility, as measured by both the semi-deviation and a drawdown factor, is considered low. As of December 31, 2012, *Market Vectors Agribusiness ETF traded at a discount of 3.76% below its net asset value, which is better than its one-year historical average discount of .07%.

Hao-Hung Liao has been running the fund for 6 years and currently receives a manager quality ranking of 74 (0=worst, 99=best). If you desire an average level of risk, then this fund may be an option.

Data Date	Investment Rating	Net Assets ($Mil)	Price	Performance Rating/Pts	Total Return Y-T-D	Risk Rating/Pts
12-12	C-	5,667.20	52.76	C- / 3.6	4.00%	B- / 7.2
2011	C	5,530.60	47.15	C+ / 5.6	3.46%	B- / 7.3
2010	C	2,624.20	53.54	C+ / 5.8	23.02%	C / 4.7
2009	B+	1,389.32	43.79	A / 9.3	50.12%	C / 4.6

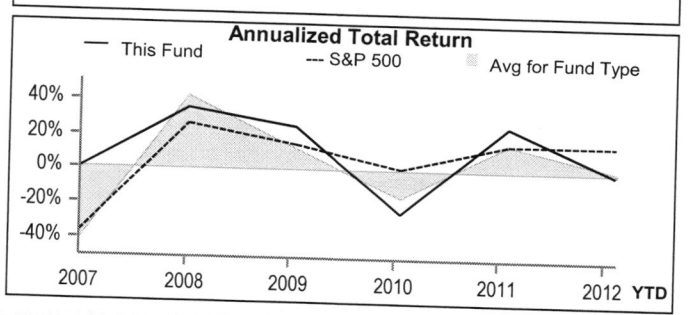

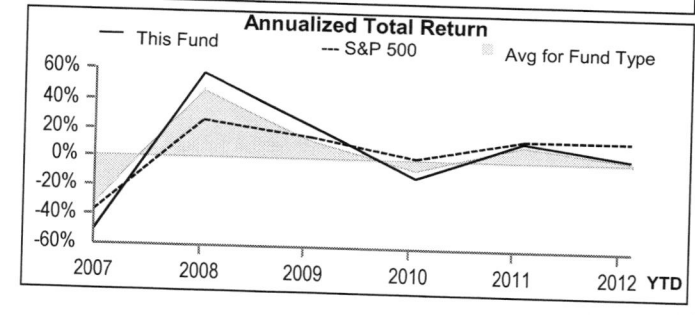

* Denotes ETF Fund

*Market Vectors Bank and Brokerag (RKH)

B   **Good**

Fund Family: Van Eck Associates Corporation
Fund Type: Income
Inception Date: December 20, 2011

Data Date	Investment Rating	Net Assets ($Mil)	Price	Performance Rating/Pts	Total Return Y-T-D	Risk Rating/Pts
12-12	B	33.40	45.73	A+ / 9.8	4.85%	C+ / 6.0

Major Rating Factors:
Exceptional performance is the major factor driving the B (Good) TheStreet.com Investment Rating for *Market Vectors Bank and Brokerag. The fund currently has a performance rating of A+ (Excellent) based on an annualized return of 0.00% over the last three years and a total return of 4.85% year to date 2012. Factored into the performance evaluation is an expense ratio of 0.35% (very low).

The fund's risk rating is currently C+ (Fair). It carries a beta of 0.00, meaning the fund's expected move will be 0.0% for every 10% move in the market. Volatility, as measured by both the semi-deviation and a drawdown factor, is considered low. As of December 31, 2012, *Market Vectors Bank and Brokerag traded at a discount of 4.65% below its net asset value, which is better than its one-year historical average premium of .01%.

George Cao has been running the fund for 2 years and currently receives a manager quality ranking of 62 (0=worst, 99=best). If you desire only a moderate level of risk and strong performance, then this fund is an excellent option.

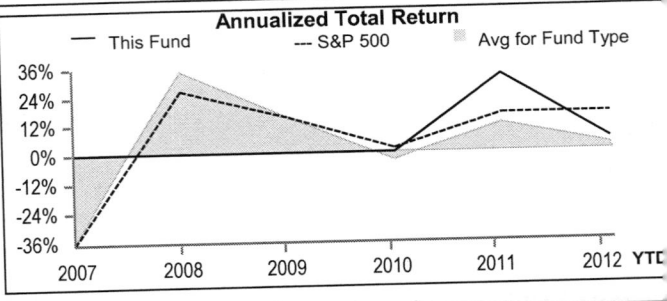

Annualized Total Return — This Fund --- S&P 500 ■ Avg for Fund Type

*Market Vectors Biotech ETF (BBH)

B   **Good**

Fund Family: Van Eck Associates Corporation
Fund Type: Income
Inception Date: December 20, 2011

Data Date	Investment Rating	Net Assets ($Mil)	Price	Performance Rating/Pts	Total Return Y-T-D	Risk Rating/Pts
12-12	B	146.90	53.50	A+ / 9.8	6.15%	C+ / 6.1

Major Rating Factors:
Exceptional performance is the major factor driving the B (Good) TheStreet.com Investment Rating for *Market Vectors Biotech ETF. The fund currently has a performance rating of A+ (Excellent) based on an annualized return of 0.00% over the last three years and a total return of 6.15% year to date 2012. Factored into the performance evaluation is an expense ratio of 0.35% (very low).

The fund's risk rating is currently C+ (Fair). It carries a beta of 0.00, meaning the fund's expected move will be 0.0% for every 10% move in the market. Volatility, as measured by both the semi-deviation and a drawdown factor, is considered low. As of December 31, 2012, *Market Vectors Biotech ETF traded at a discount of 5.73% below its net asset value, which is better than its one-year historical average premium of .05%.

George Cao has been running the fund for 2 years and currently receives a manager quality ranking of 98 (0=worst, 99=best). If you desire only a moderate level of risk and strong performance, then this fund is an excellent option.

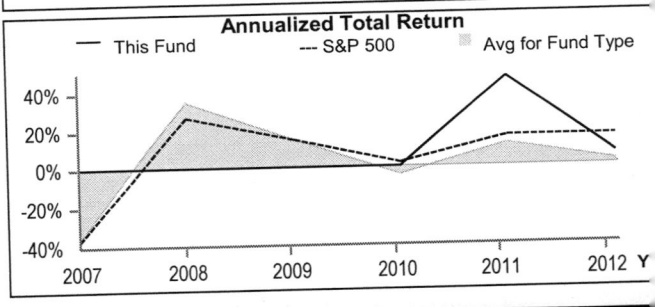

Annualized Total Return — This Fund --- S&P 500 ■ Avg for Fund Type

*Market Vectors Brazil Small-Cap (BRF)

D   **Weak**

Fund Family: Van Eck Associates Corporation
Fund Type: Foreign
Inception Date: May 12, 2009

Data Date	Investment Rating	Net Assets ($Mil)	Price	Performance Rating/Pts	Total Return Y-T-D	Risk Rating/Pts
12-12	D	552.80	42.62	D+ / 2.5	-0.75%	C / 5
2011	D-	512.60	36.44	E+ / 0.6	1.21%	C+ / 5
2010	A+	1,078.10	57.68	A / 9.5	24.05%	C+ / 6

Major Rating Factors:
Disappointing performance is the major factor driving the D (Weak) TheStreet.com Investment Rating for *Market Vectors Brazil Small-Cap. The fund currently has a performance rating of D+ (Weak) based on an annualized return of 2.17% over the last three years and a total return of -0.75% year to date 2012. Factored into the performance evaluation is an expense ratio of 0.59% (very low).

The fund's risk rating is currently C (Fair). It carries a beta of 1.15, meaning it is expected to move 11.5% for every 10% move in the market. Volatility, as measured by both the semi-deviation and a drawdown factor, is considered average. As of December 31, 2012, *Market Vectors Brazil Small-Cap traded at a premium of .78% above its net asset value, which is worse than its one-year historical average discount of .11%.

George Cao has been running the fund for 4 years and currently receives a manager quality ranking of 32 (0=worst, 99=best). This fund offers an average level of risk but investors looking for strong performance will be frustrated.

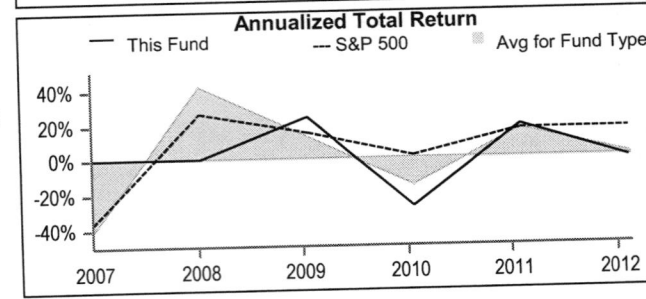

Annualized Total Return — This Fund --- S&P 500 ■ Avg for Fund Type

*Market Vectors CEF Muni Inc ETF (XMPT)

A+   **Excellent**

Fund Family: Van Eck Associates Corporation
Fund Type: Municipal - National
Inception Date: July 12, 2011

Major Rating Factors:
Strong performance is the major factor driving the A+ (Excellent) TheStreet.com Investment Rating for *Market Vectors CEF Muni Inc ETF. The fund currently has a performance rating of B+ (Good) based on an annualized return of 0.00% over the last three years and a total return of 4.88% year to date 2012. Factored into the performance evaluation is an expense ratio of 0.40% (very low).

The fund's risk rating is currently B+ (Good). It carries a beta of 0.00, meaning the fund's expected move will be 0.0% for every 10% move in the market. Volatility, as measured by both the semi-deviation and a drawdown factor, is considered very low. As of December 31, 2012, *Market Vectors CEF Muni Inc ETF traded at a discount of 4.59% below its net asset value, which is better than its one-year historical average premium of .11%.

Hao-Hung Liao has been running the fund for 2 years and currently receives a manager quality ranking of 27 (0=worst, 99=best). If you desire only a moderate level of risk and strong performance, then this fund is an excellent option.

Data Date	Investment Rating	Net Assets ($Mil)	Price	Performance Rating/Pts	Total Return Y-T-D	Risk Rating/Pts
12-12	A+	15.60	28.30	B+ / 8.6	4.88%	B+ / 9.2

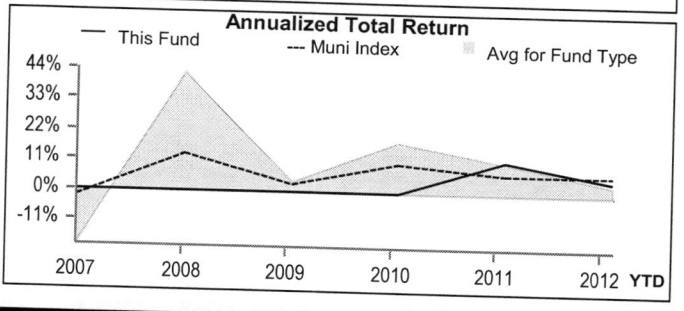

*Market Vectors China ETF (PEK)

C   **Fair**

Fund Family: Van Eck Associates Corporation
Fund Type: Foreign
Inception Date: October 13, 2010

Major Rating Factors: Middle of the road best describes *Market Vectors China ETF whose TheStreet.com Investment Rating is currently a C (Fair). The fund currently has a performance rating of C+ (Fair) based on an annualized return of 0.00% over the last three years and a total return of -1.45% year to date 2012. Factored into the performance evaluation is an expense ratio of 0.72% (very low).

The fund's risk rating is currently C+ (Fair). It carries a beta of 0.00, meaning the fund's expected move will be 0.0% for every 10% move in the market. Volatility, as measured by both the semi-deviation and a drawdown factor, is considered low. As of December 31, 2012, *Market Vectors China ETF traded at a premium of 12.14% above its net asset value, which is worse than its one-year historical average premium of 5.64%.

George Cao has been running the fund for 3 years and currently receives a manager quality ranking of 86 (0=worst, 99=best). If you desire an average level of risk, then this fund may be an option.

Data Date	Investment Rating	Net Assets ($Mil)	Price	Performance Rating/Pts	Total Return Y-T-D	Risk Rating/Pts
12-12	C	33.20	36.50	C+ / 6.8	-1.45%	C+ / 6.2
2011	D-	15.10	31.64	E / 0.4	-1.49%	C+ / 6.4

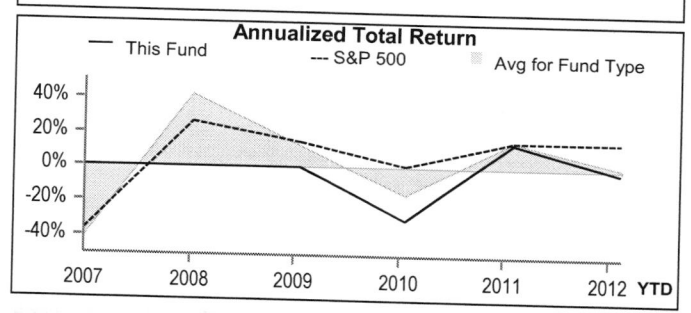

*Market Vectors Chinese RMB USD E (CNY)

C-   **Fair**

Fund Family: Morgan Stanley Investment Managemen
Fund Type: Foreign
Inception Date: March 14, 2008

Major Rating Factors:
Disappointing performance is the major factor driving the C- (Fair) TheStreet.com Investment Rating for *Market Vectors Chinese RMB USD E. The fund currently has a performance rating of D (Weak) based on an annualized return of 1.03% over the last three years and a total return of -0.06% year to date 2012. Factored into the performance evaluation is an expense ratio of 0.55% (very low).

The fund's risk rating is currently B+ (Good). It carries a beta of 0.07, meaning the fund's expected move will be 0.7% for every 10% move in the market. Volatility, as measured by both the semi-deviation and a drawdown factor, is considered very low. As of December 31, 2012, *Market Vectors Chinese RMB USD E traded at a premium of .34% above its net asset value, which is worse than its one-year historical average discount of .07%.

This fund has been team managed for 5 years and currently receives a manager quality ranking of 59 (0=worst, 99=best). This fund offers only a moderate level of risk but investors looking for strong performance are still waiting.

Data Date	Investment Rating	Net Assets ($Mil)	Price	Performance Rating/Pts	Total Return Y-T-D	Risk Rating/Pts
12-12	C-	27.05	41.62	D / 1.7	-0.06%	B+ / 9.9
2011	C	27.05	40.95	D / 2.2	0.15%	B+ / 9.8
2010	C+	27.05	40.57	D+ / 2.9	0.87%	B / 8.8
2009	C	27.05	40.22	D / 2.1	1.69%	B+ / 9.0

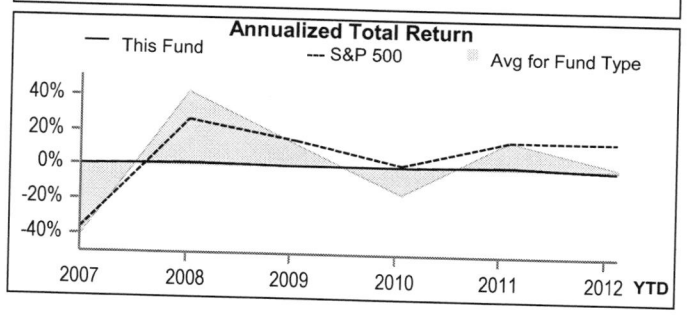

*Market Vectors Coal ETF (KOL)

E+   Very Weak

Fund Family: Van Eck Associates Corporation
Fund Type: Energy/Natural Resources
Inception Date: January 10, 2008

Major Rating Factors:

Very poor performance is the major factor driving the E+ (Very Weak) TheStreet.com Investment Rating for *Market Vectors Coal ETF. The fund currently has a performance rating of E+ (Very Weak) based on an annualized return of -12.07% over the last three years and a total return of 1.31% year to date 2012. Factored into the performance evaluation is an expense ratio of 0.59% (very low).

The fund's risk rating is currently C (Fair). It carries a beta of 1.40, meaning it is expected to move 14.0% for every 10% move in the market. Volatility, as measured by both the semi-deviation and a drawdown factor, is considered average. As of December 31, 2012, *Market Vectors Coal ETF traded at a discount of 1.02% below its net asset value, which is better than its one-year historical average discount of .05%.

George Cao has been running the fund for 5 years and currently receives a manager quality ranking of 5 (0=worst, 99=best). This fund offers an average level of risk but investors looking for strong performance will be frustrated.

Data Date	Investment Rating	Net Assets ($Mil)	Price	Performance Rating/Pts	Total Return Y-T-D	Risk Rating/Pts
12-12	E+	235.40	25.14	E+ / 0.7	1.31%	C / 4.9
2011	C	314.40	32.25	B- / 7.1	3.01%	C+ / 5.9
2010	B	529.60	47.24	A+ / 9.8	31.33%	C- / 3.1
2009	B-	268.98	36.12	A+ / 9.9	123.90%	C- / 3.2

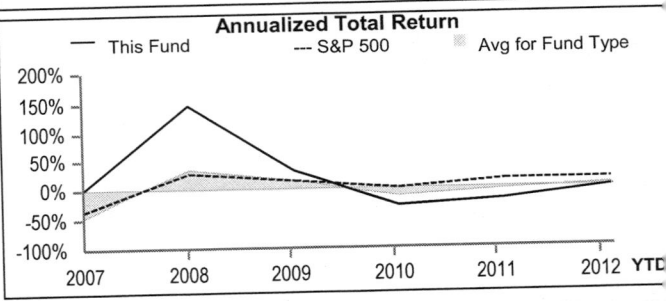

---

*Market Vectors Colombia ETF (COLX)

B+   Good

Fund Family: Van Eck Associates Corporation
Fund Type: Global
Inception Date: March 14, 2011

Major Rating Factors: Strong performance is the major factor driving the B+ (Good) TheStreet.com Investment Rating for *Market Vectors Colombia ETF. The fund currently has a performance rating of B+ (Good) based on an annualized return of 0.00% over the last three years and a total return of 2.52% year to date 2012. Factored into the performance evaluation is an expense ratio of 0.75% (very low).

The fund's risk rating is currently B- (Good). It carries a beta of 0.00, meaning the fund's expected move will be 0.0% for every 10% move in the market. Volatility, as measured by both the semi-deviation and a drawdown factor, is considered low. As of December 31, 2012, *Market Vectors Colombia ETF traded at a discount of 1.44% below its net asset value, which is better than its one-year historical average premium of .80%.

George Cao has been running the fund for 2 years and currently receives a manager quality ranking of 92 (0=worst, 99=best). If you desire only a moderate level of risk and strong performance, then this fund is an excellent option.

Data Date	Investment Rating	Net Assets ($Mil)	Price	Performance Rating/Pts	Total Return Y-T-D	Risk Rating/Pts
12-12	B+	3.00	19.81	B+ / 8.9	2.52%	B- / 7.3

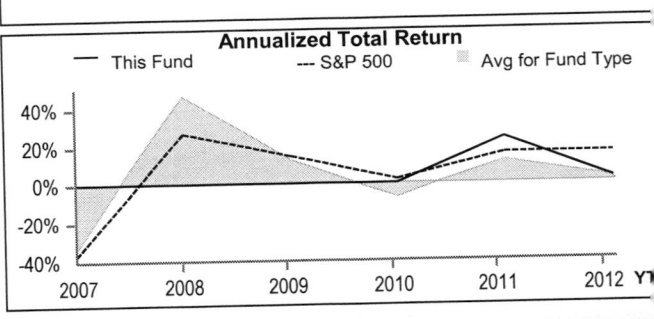

---

*Market Vectors Double Long Euro (URR)

D-   Weak

Fund Family: Morgan Stanley Investment Managemen
Fund Type: Foreign
Inception Date: May 7, 2008

Major Rating Factors:

Very poor performance is the major factor driving the D- (Weak) TheStreet.com Investment Rating for *Market Vectors Double Long Euro. The fund currently has a performance rating of E+ (Very Weak) based on an annualized return of -9.01% over the last three years and a total return of -3.14% year to date 2012. Factored into the performance evaluation is an expense ratio of 0.65% (very low).

The fund's risk rating is currently C+ (Fair). It carries a beta of 1.02, meaning that its performance tracks fairly well with that of the overall stock market. Volatility, as measured by both the semi-deviation and a drawdown factor, is considered low. As of December 31, 2012, *Market Vectors Double Long Euro traded at a discount of 1.75% below its net asset value, which is better than its one-year historical average discount of .93%.

This fund has been team managed for 5 years and currently receives a manager quality ranking of 11 (0=worst, 99=best). This fund offers only a moderate level of risk but investors looking for strong performance are still waiting.

Data Date	Investment Rating	Net Assets ($Mil)	Price	Performance Rating/Pts	Total Return Y-T-D	Risk Rating/Pt
12-12	D-	4.84	27.00	E+ / 0.8	-3.14%	C+ / 6.
2011	D-	4.84	26.24	D- / 1.3	-1.87%	C+ / 6.
2010	D	4.84	29.10	D- / 1.1	-14.24%	C / 5.
2009	C-	4.84	33.93	C- / 3.2	5.97%	C+ / 5.

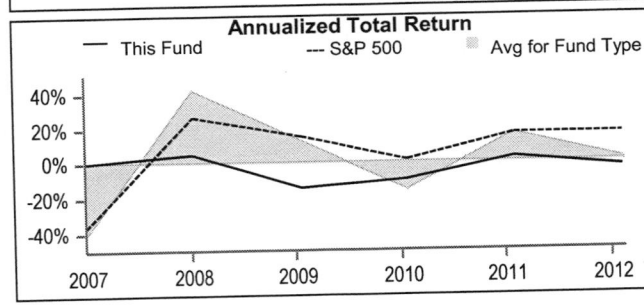

www.thestreetratings.c

*Market Vectors Double Shrt Euro (DRR)

D-   **Weak**

Fund Family: Morgan Stanley Investment Managemen
Fund Type: Foreign
Inception Date: May 7, 2008

Major Rating Factors:
Disappointing performance is the major factor driving the D- (Weak) TheStreet.com Investment Rating for *Market Vectors Double Shrt Euro. The fund currently has a performance rating of D- (Weak) based on an annualized return of 0.51% over the last three years and a total return of -2.62% year to date 2012. Factored into the performance evaluation is an expense ratio of 0.65% (very low).

The fund's risk rating is currently C+ (Fair). It carries a beta of -1.06, meaning the fund's expected move will be -10.6% for every 10% move in the market. Volatility, as measured by both the semi-deviation and a drawdown factor, is considered low. As of December 31, 2012, *Market Vectors Double Shrt Euro traded at a premium of 2.74% above its net asset value, which is worse than its one-year historical average discount of .02%.

This fund has been team managed for 5 years and currently receives a manager quality ranking of 80 (0=worst, 99=best). This fund offers only a moderate level of risk but investors looking for strong performance are still waiting.

Data Date	Investment Rating	Net Assets ($Mil)	Price	Performance Rating/Pts	Total Return Y-T-D	Risk Rating/Pts
12-12	D-	28.43	43.15	D- / 1.1	-2.62%	C+ / 6.3
2011	D	28.43	45.66	D / 2.0	3.57%	C+ / 6.4
2010	C-	28.43	45.64	C- / 3.2	9.24%	C+ / 5.9
2009	D	28.43	41.78	E+ / 0.8	-11.91%	C+ / 6.3

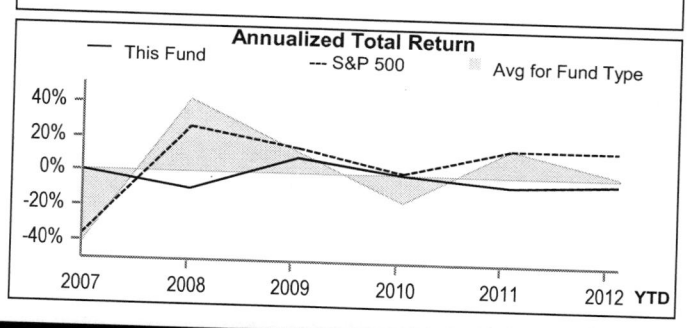

*Market Vectors Egypt Index ETF (EGPT)

C+   **Fair**

Fund Family: Van Eck Associates Corporation
Fund Type: Emerging Market
Inception Date: February 16, 2010

Major Rating Factors:
Exceptional performance is the major factor driving the C+ (Fair) TheStreet.com Investment Rating for *Market Vectors Egypt Index ETF. The fund currently has a performance rating of A+ (Excellent) based on an annualized return of 0.00% over the last three years and a total return of 0.54% year to date 2012. Factored into the performance evaluation is an expense ratio of 0.94% (low).

The fund's risk rating is currently C- (Fair). It carries a beta of 0.00, meaning the fund's expected move will be 0.0% for every 10% move in the market. Volatility, as measured by both the semi-deviation and a drawdown factor, is considered average. As of December 31, 2012, *Market Vectors Egypt Index ETF traded at a discount of .23% below its net asset value, which is worse than its one-year historical average discount of .56%.

George Cao has been running the fund for 3 years and currently receives a manager quality ranking of 95 (0=worst, 99=best). If you desire an average level of risk and strong performance, then this fund is a good option.

Data Date	Investment Rating	Net Assets ($Mil)	Price	Performance Rating/Pts	Total Return Y-T-D	Risk Rating/Pts
12-12	C+	36.30	13.08	A+ / 9.6	0.54%	C- / 4.2
2011	E+	36.20	9.46	E- / 0	0.42%	C / 4.4

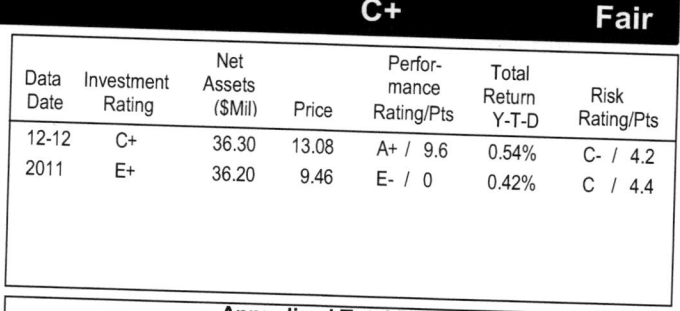

*Market Vectors EM Lcl Curr Bnd E (EMLC)

B   **Good**

Fund Family: Van Eck Associates Corporation
Fund Type: Global
Inception Date: July 22, 2010

Major Rating Factors: Strong performance is the major factor driving the B (Good) TheStreet.com Investment Rating for *Market Vectors EM Lcl Curr Bnd E. The fund currently has a performance rating of B- (Good) based on an annualized return of 0.00% over the last three years and a total return of -0.04% year to date 2012. Factored into the performance evaluation is an expense ratio of 0.47% (very low).

The fund's risk rating is currently B (Good). It carries a beta of 0.00, meaning the fund's expected move will be 0.0% for every 10% move in the market. Volatility, as measured by both the semi-deviation and a drawdown factor, is considered low. As of December 31, 2012, *Market Vectors EM Lcl Curr Bnd E traded at a premium of .59% above its net asset value, which is worse than its one-year historical average premium of .53%.

Michael F. Mazier has been running the fund for 3 years and currently receives a manager quality ranking of 95 (0=worst, 99=best). If you desire only a moderate level of risk and strong performance, then this fund is an excellent option.

Data Date	Investment Rating	Net Assets ($Mil)	Price	Performance Rating/Pts	Total Return Y-T-D	Risk Rating/Pts
12-12	B	927.00	27.45	B- / 7.1	-0.04%	B / 8.4
2011	D+	491.80	24.51	D- / 1.3	-0.16%	B / 8.5

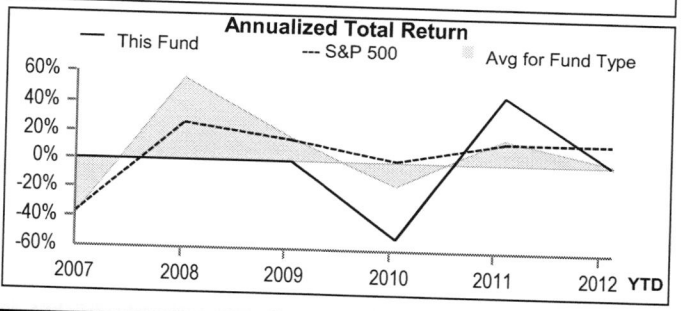

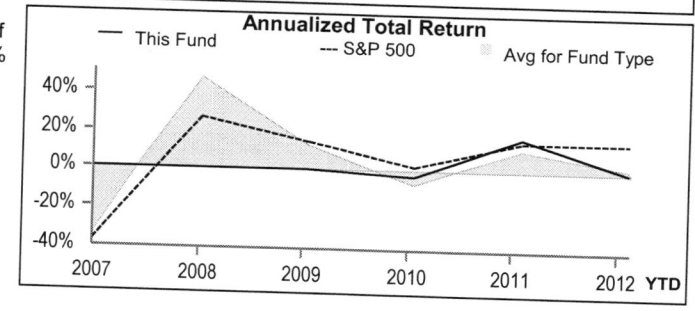

* Denotes ETF Fund

II. Analysis of ETFs and Other Closed-End Funds

*Market Vectors Environment Svc E (EVX)

	C-	Fair

Fund Family: Van Eck Associates Corporation
Fund Type: Income
Inception Date: October 10, 2006

Major Rating Factors: Middle of the road best describes *Market Vectors Environment Svc E whose TheStreet.com Investment Rating is currently a C- (Fair). The fund currently has a performance rating of C- (Fair) based on an annualized return of 7.55% over the last three years and a total return of 3.00% year to date 2012. Factored into the performance evaluation is an expense ratio of 0.55% (very low).

The fund's risk rating is currently B- (Good). It carries a beta of 0.91, meaning that its performance tracks fairly well with that of the overall stock market. Volatility, as measured by both the semi-deviation and a drawdown factor, is considered low. As of December 31, 2012, *Market Vectors Environment Svc E traded at a discount of 3.19% below its net asset value, which is better than its one-year historical average discount of .16%.

Hao-Hung Liao has been running the fund for 7 years and currently receives a manager quality ranking of 34 (0=worst, 99=best). If you desire an average level of risk, then this fund may be an option.

Data Date	Investment Rating	Net Assets ($Mil)	Price	Performance Rating/Pts	Total Return Y-T-D	Risk Rating/Pts
12-12	C-	20.50	50.97	C- / 3.6	3.00%	B- / 7.8
2011	C-	23.30	46.59	C- / 3.4	0.04%	B- / 7.1
2010	C+	30.90	51.60	C+ / 6.2	22.10%	C / 5.3
2009	C-	19.56	42.67	C- / 3.7	19.57%	C / 5.5

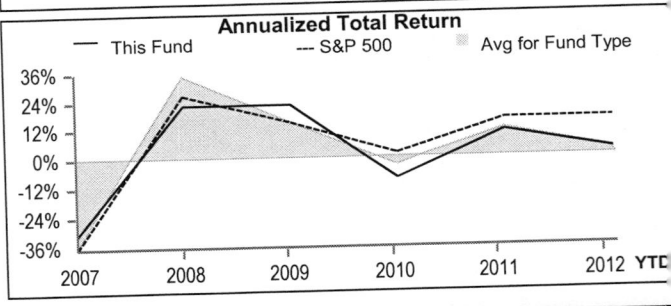

*Market Vectors Gaming ETF (BJK)

	B	Good

Fund Family: Van Eck Associates Corporation
Fund Type: Global
Inception Date: January 22, 2008

Major Rating Factors: Strong performance is the major factor driving the B (Good) TheStreet.com Investment Rating for *Market Vectors Gaming ETF. The fund currently has a performance rating of B+ (Good) based on an annualized return of 17.62% over the last three years and a total return of 6.43% year to date 2012. Factored into the performance evaluation is an expense ratio of 0.65% (very low).

The fund's risk rating is currently B- (Good). It carries a beta of 1.08, meaning that its performance tracks fairly well with that of the overall stock market. Volatility, as measured by both the semi-deviation and a drawdown factor, is considered low. As of December 31, 2012, *Market Vectors Gaming ETF traded at a discount of 6.27% below its net asset value, which is better than its one-year historical average discount of .33%.

George Cao has been running the fund for 5 years and currently receives a manager quality ranking of 93 (0=worst, 99=best). If you desire only a moderate level of risk and strong performance, then this fund is an excellent option.

Data Date	Investment Rating	Net Assets ($Mil)	Price	Performance Rating/Pts	Total Return Y-T-D	Risk Rating/Pts
12-12	B	60.80	35.45	B+ / 8.5	6.43%	B- / 7.2
2011	C-	96.70	30.07	C+ / 6.1	-0.19%	C / 5.5
2010	B+	129.10	31.49	A+ / 9.7	37.89%	C / 4.4
2009	C+	104.09	23.45	B / 8.0	30.79%	C / 4.7

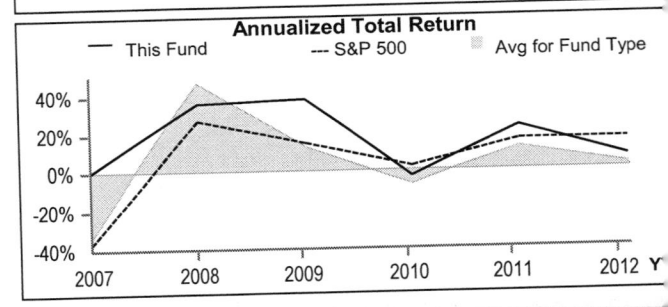

*Market Vectors Germany SmallCap (GERJ)

	B	Good

Fund Family: Van Eck Associates Corporation
Fund Type: Foreign
Inception Date: April 4, 2011

Major Rating Factors:
Exceptional performance is the major factor driving the B (Good) TheStreet.com Investment Rating for *Market Vectors Germany SmallCap. The fund currently has a performance rating of A+ (Excellent) based on an annualized return of 0.00% over the last three years and a total return of 1.96% year to date 2012. Factored into the performance evaluation is an expense ratio of 0.55% (very low).

The fund's risk rating is currently C+ (Fair). It carries a beta of 0.00, meaning the fund's expected move will be 0.0% for every 10% move in the market. Volatility, as measured by both the semi-deviation and a drawdown factor, is considered low. As of December 31, 2012, *Market Vectors Germany SmallCap traded at a discount of 2.26% below its net asset value, which is better than its one-year historical average premium of .01%.

George Cao has been running the fund for 2 years and currently receives a manager quality ranking of 95 (0=worst, 99=best). If you desire only a moderate level of risk and strong performance, then this fund is an excellent option.

Data Date	Investment Rating	Net Assets ($Mil)	Price	Performance Rating/Pts	Total Return Y-T-D	Risk Rating/P..
12-12	B	4.50	22.91	A+ / 9.7	1.96%	C+ / 6.

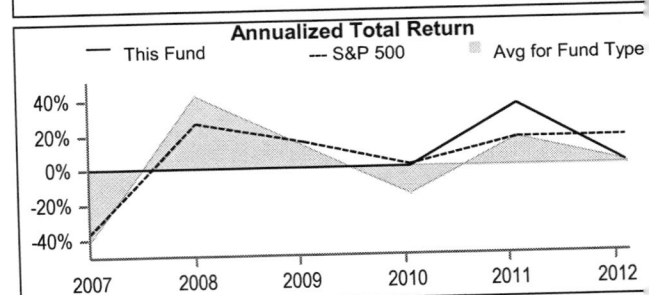

www.thestreetratings.

* Denotes ETF Fund

*Market Vectors Global Alt Enrgy (GEX)

E+   Very Weak

Fund Family: Van Eck Associates Corporation
Fund Type: Energy/Natural Resources
Inception Date: May 3, 2007

Data Date	Investment Rating	Net Assets ($Mil)	Price	Performance Rating/Pts	Total Return Y-T-D	Risk Rating/Pts
12-12	E+	46.00	11.04	E+ / 0.6	5.07%	C / 4.7
2011	E+	58.60	10.91	E+ / 0.6	0.46%	C / 4.8
2010	E+	134.50	20.01	E / 0.4	-19.20%	C- / 3.5
2009	D	231.99	25.00	C- / 3.4	1.88%	C- / 3.6

Major Rating Factors:

Very poor performance is the major factor driving the E+ (Very Weak) TheStreet.com Investment Rating for *Market Vectors Global Alt Enrgy. The fund currently has a performance rating of E+ (Very Weak) based on an annualized return of -21.16% over the last three years and a total return of 5.07% year to date 2012. Factored into the performance evaluation is an expense ratio of 0.62% (very low).

The fund's risk rating is currently C (Fair). It carries a beta of 0.95, meaning that its performance tracks fairly well with that of the overall stock market. Volatility, as measured by both the semi-deviation and a drawdown factor, is considered average. As of December 31, 2012, *Market Vectors Global Alt Enrgy traded at a discount of 5.24% below its net asset value, which is better than its one-year historical average discount of .46%.

Hao-Hung Liao has been running the fund for 6 years and currently receives a manager quality ranking of 3 (0=worst, 99=best). This fund offers an average level of risk but investors looking for strong performance will be frustrated.

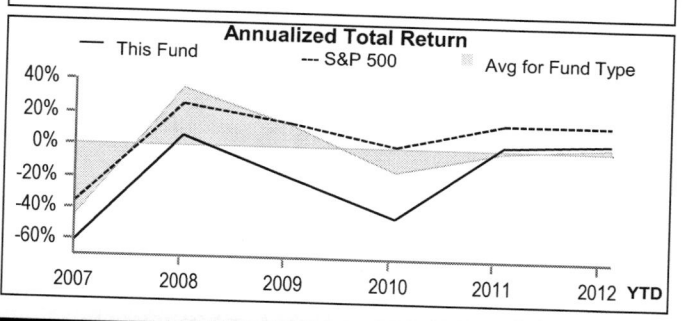

*Market Vectors Gold Miners ETF (GDX)

D-   Weak

Fund Family: Van Eck Associates Corporation
Fund Type: Precious Metals
Inception Date: May 16, 2006

Data Date	Investment Rating	Net Assets ($Mil)	Price	Performance Rating/Pts	Total Return Y-T-D	Risk Rating/Pts
12-12	D-	9,406.10	46.39	D- / 1.1	-2.13%	C / 5.1
2011	C	8,772.70	51.43	C+ / 6.0	3.73%	B- / 7.1
2010	C+	7,677.40	61.47	B+ / 8.4	33.90%	C- / 3.3
2009	C-	4,322.09	46.21	C+ / 6.4	39.02%	C- / 3.2

Major Rating Factors:

Disappointing performance is the major factor driving the D- (Weak) TheStreet.com Investment Rating for *Market Vectors Gold Miners ETF. The fund currently has a performance rating of D- (Weak) based on an annualized return of -0.80% over the last three years and a total return of -2.13% year to date 2012. Factored into the performance evaluation is an expense ratio of 0.52% (very low).

The fund's risk rating is currently C (Fair). It carries a beta of 1.18, meaning it is expected to move 11.8% for every 10% move in the market. Volatility, as measured by both the semi-deviation and a drawdown factor, is considered average. As of December 31, 2012, *Market Vectors Gold Miners ETF traded at a premium of 2.27% above its net asset value, which is worse than its one-year historical average discount of .03%.

Hao-Hung Liao has been running the fund for 7 years and currently receives a manager quality ranking of 8 (0=worst, 99=best). This fund offers an average level of risk but investors looking for strong performance will be frustrated.

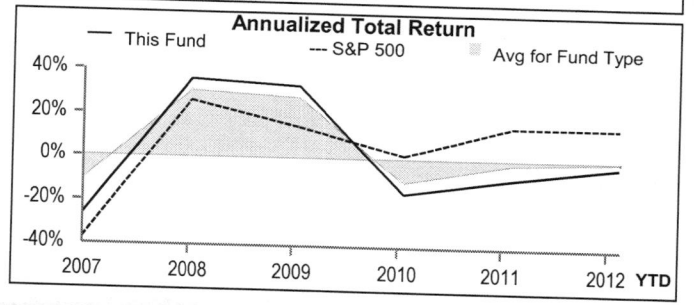

*Market Vectors Gulf States Idx E (MES)

C-   Fair

Fund Family: Van Eck Associates Corporation
Fund Type: Foreign
Inception Date: July 22, 2008

Data Date	Investment Rating	Net Assets ($Mil)	Price	Performance Rating/Pts	Total Return Y-T-D	Risk Rating/Pts
12-12	C-	10.30	20.25	C- / 3.6	5.28%	B- / 7.9
2011	D+	14.10	19.56	D+ / 2.4	-0.26%	B- / 7.3
2010	B	22.10	23.81	A / 9.4	23.81%	C- / 3.8
2009	E+	8.06	19.42	D- / 1.0	1.62%	C- / 3.7

Major Rating Factors: Middle of the road best describes *Market Vectors Gulf States Idx E whose TheStreet.com Investment Rating is currently a C- (Fair). The fund currently has a performance rating of C- (Fair) based on an annualized return of 6.36% over the last three years and a total return of 5.28% year to date 2012. Factored into the performance evaluation is an expense ratio of 0.98% (low).

The fund's risk rating is currently B- (Good). It carries a beta of 0.52, meaning the fund's expected move will be 5.2% for every 10% move in the market. Volatility, as measured by both the semi-deviation and a drawdown factor, is considered low. As of December 31, 2012, *Market Vectors Gulf States Idx E traded at a discount of 5.64% below its net asset value, which is better than its one-year historical average discount of 1.81%.

George Cao has been running the fund for 5 years and currently receives a manager quality ranking of 66 (0=worst, 99=best). If you desire an average level of risk, then this fund may be an option.

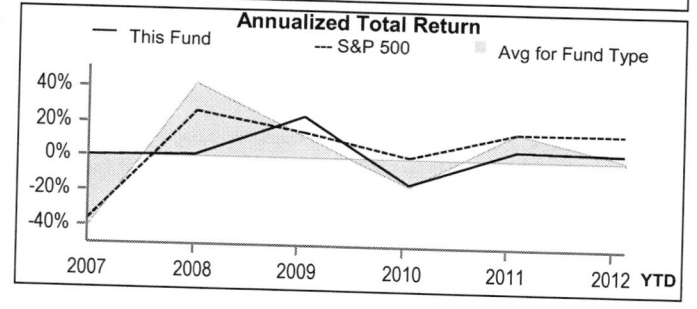

*Market Vectors Hi-Yld Mun Idx ET (HYD)   B   Good

Fund Family: Van Eck Associates Corporation
Fund Type: Municipal - High Yield
Inception Date: February 4, 2009

Major Rating Factors: *Market Vectors Hi-Yld Mun Idx ET receives a TheStreet.com Investment Rating of B (Good). The fund currently has a performance rating of C+ (Fair) based on an annualized return of 8.70% over the last three years and a total return of 0.79% year to date 2012. Factored into the performance evaluation is an expense ratio of 0.35% (very low).

The fund's risk rating is currently B+ (Good). It carries a beta of 1.16, meaning it is expected to move 11.6% for every 10% move in the market. Volatility, as measured by both the semi-deviation and a drawdown factor, is considered very low. As of December 31, 2012, *Market Vectors Hi-Yld Mun Idx ET traded at a discount of .67% below its net asset value, which is better than its one-year historical average premium of .21%.

Jeffrey A. Herrmann has been running the fund for 5 years and currently receives a manager quality ranking of 61 (0=worst, 99=best). If you desire an average level of risk, then this fund may be an option.

Data Date	Investment Rating	Net Assets ($Mil)	Price	Performance Rating/Pts	Total Return Y-T-D	Risk Rating/Pts
12-12	B	1,044.10	32.84	C+ / 6.1	0.79%	B+ / 9.1
2011	B	340.80	29.80	C+ / 6.8	0.64%	B+ / 9.1
2010	C-	175.50	28.51	D- / 1.0	-0.40%	B / 8.4

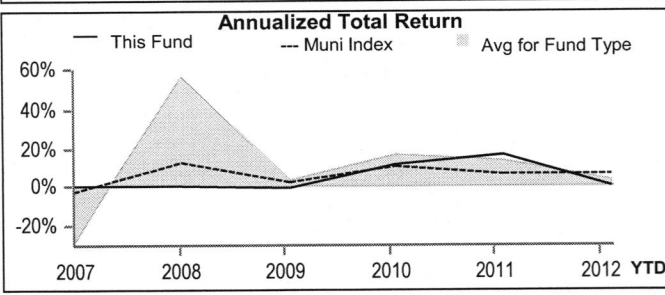

*Market Vectors India Small-Cap E (SCIF)   D   Weak

Fund Family: Van Eck Associates Corporation
Fund Type: Foreign
Inception Date: August 24, 2010

Major Rating Factors: *Market Vectors India Small-Cap E receives a TheStreet.com Investment Rating of D (Weak). The fund currently has a performance rating of C (Fair) based on an annualized return of 0.00% over the last three years and a total return of 1.80% year to date 2012. Factored into the performance evaluation is an expense ratio of 0.85% (very low).

The fund's risk rating is currently C- (Fair). It carries a beta of 0.00, meaning the fund's expected move will be 0.0% for every 10% move in the market. Volatility, as measured by both the semi-deviation and a drawdown factor, is considered average. As of December 31, 2012, *Market Vectors India Small-Cap E traded at a discount of .80% below its net asset value, which is better than its one-year historical average premium of .37%.

George Cao has been running the fund for 3 years and currently receives a manager quality ranking of 16 (0=worst, 99=best). If you desire an average level of risk, then this fund may be an option.

Data Date	Investment Rating	Net Assets ($Mil)	Price	Performance Rating/Pts	Total Return Y-T-D	Risk Rating/Pts
12-12	D	81.10	11.12	C / 4.9	1.80%	C- / 3.3
2011	E	30.90	8.73	E- / 0	5.38%	C- / 3.3

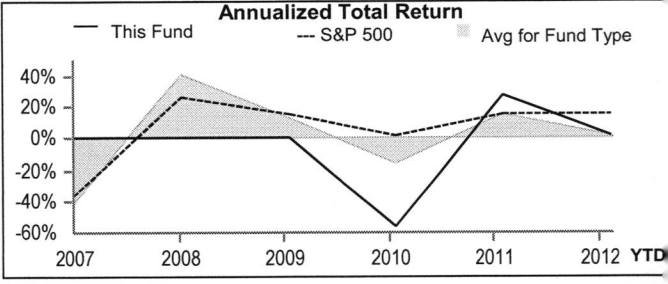

*Market Vectors Indian Rupee USD (INR)   D   Weak

Fund Family: Morgan Stanley Investment Managemen
Fund Type: Foreign
Inception Date: March 14, 2008

Major Rating Factors:
Disappointing performance is the major factor driving the D (Weak) TheStreet.com Investment Rating for *Market Vectors Indian Rupee USD. The fund currently has a performance rating of D- (Weak) based on an annualized return of -1.73% over the last three years and a total return of -0.14% year to date 2012. Factored into the performance evaluation is an expense ratio of 0.55% (very low).

The fund's risk rating is currently B (Good). It carries a beta of 0.41, meaning the fund's expected move will be 4.1% for every 10% move in the market. Volatility, as measured by both the semi-deviation and a drawdown factor, is considered low. As of December 31, 2012, *Market Vectors Indian Rupee USD traded at a discount of 1.53% below its net asset value, which is better than its one-year historical average discount of .77%.

This fund has been team managed for 5 years and currently receives a manager quality ranking of 31 (0=worst, 99=best). This fund offers only a moderate level of risk but investors looking for strong performance are still waiting.

Data Date	Investment Rating	Net Assets ($Mil)	Price	Performance Rating/Pts	Total Return Y-T-D	Risk Rating/Pts
12-12	D	6.60	36.75	D- / 1.2	-0.14%	B / 8.2
2011	D+	6.60	35.70	D / 1.6	-0.90%	B / 8.5
2010	A-	6.60	40.85	B- / 7.0	7.78%	B- / 7.8
2009	C+	6.60	37.90	C / 4.4	8.13%	B / 8.0

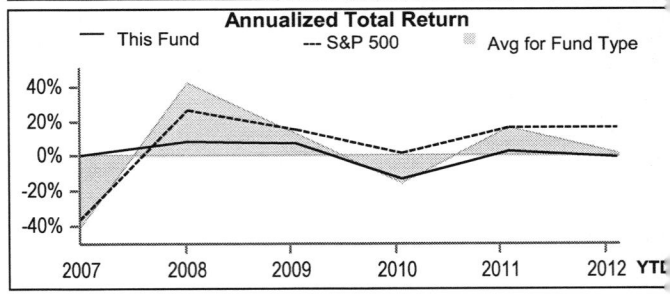

*Market Vectors Indonesia Idx ETF (IDX)

D-　**Weak**

Fund Family: Van Eck Associates Corporation
Fund Type: Foreign
Inception Date: January 15, 2009

Major Rating Factors: *Market Vectors Indonesia Idx ETF receives a TheStreet.com Investment Rating of D- (Weak). The fund currently has a performance rating of C- (Fair) based on an annualized return of 9.41% over the last three years and a total return of -2.03% year to date 2012. Factored into the performance evaluation is an expense ratio of 0.59% (very low).

The fund's risk rating is currently C (Fair). It carries a beta of 0.98, meaning that its performance tracks fairly well with that of the overall stock market. Volatility, as measured by both the semi-deviation and a drawdown factor, is considered average. As of December 31, 2012, *Market Vectors Indonesia Idx ETF traded at a premium of .74% above its net asset value, which is worse than its one-year historical average discount of .42%.

George Cao has been running the fund for 4 years and currently receives a manager quality ranking of 88 (0=worst, 99=best). If you desire an average level of risk, then this fund may be an option.

Data Date	Investment Rating	Net Assets ($Mil)	Price	Performance Rating/Pts	Total Return Y-T-D	Risk Rating/Pts
12-12	D-	405.10	28.64	C- / 3.1	-2.03%	C / 4.5
2011	D-	471.30	28.47	D+ / 2.5	1.40%	C / 4.9
2010	A+	623.50	87.31	A / 9.5	41.77%	B- / 7.9

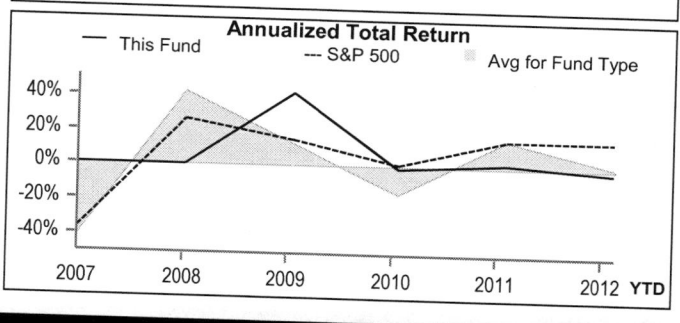
Annualized Total Return

---

*Market Vectors Interm Muni Idx E (ITM)

C+　**Fair**

Fund Family: Van Eck Associates Corporation
Fund Type: Municipal - National
Inception Date: December 4, 2007

Major Rating Factors: Middle of the road best describes *Market Vectors Interm Muni Idx E whose TheStreet.com Investment Rating is currently a C+ (Fair). The fund currently has a performance rating of C- (Fair) based on an annualized return of 7.01% over the last three years and a total return of 0.55% year to date 2012. Factored into the performance evaluation is an expense ratio of 0.24% (very low).

The fund's risk rating is currently B+ (Good). It carries a beta of 1.38, meaning it is expected to move 13.8% for every 10% move in the market. Volatility, as measured by both the semi-deviation and a drawdown factor, is considered very low. As of December 31, 2012, *Market Vectors Interm Muni Idx E traded at a discount of .42% below its net asset value, which is better than its one-year historical average premium of .17%.

James T. Colby, III has been running the fund for 6 years and currently receives a manager quality ranking of 35 (0=worst, 99=best). If you desire an average level of risk, then this fund may be an option.

Data Date	Investment Rating	Net Assets ($Mil)	Price	Performance Rating/Pts	Total Return Y-T-D	Risk Rating/Pts
12-12	C+	690.00	23.64	C- / 4.0	0.55%	B+ / 9.4
2011	B-	351.40	22.86	C+ / 5.8	0.52%	B+ / 9.4
2010	D	209.70	20.89	C- / 4.1	1.47%	D+ / 2.7
2009	D+	51.92	21.29	C+ / 5.8	10.41%	D+ / 2.6

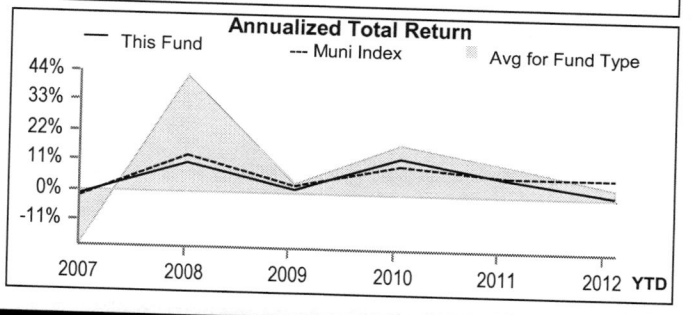
Annualized Total Return

---

*Market Vectors Invest Grade FR E (FLTR)

C　**Fair**

Fund Family: Van Eck Associates Corporation
Fund Type: Corporate - Investment Grade
Inception Date: April 25, 2011

Major Rating Factors: Middle of the road best describes *Market Vectors Invest Grade FR E whose TheStreet.com Investment Rating is currently a C (Fair). The fund currently has a performance rating of C- (Fair) based on an annualized return of 0.00% over the last three years and a total return of 0.36% year to date 2012. Factored into the performance evaluation is an expense ratio of 0.19% (very low).

The fund's risk rating is currently B+ (Good). It carries a beta of 0.00, meaning the fund's expected move will be 0.0% for every 10% move in the market. Volatility, as measured by both the semi-deviation and a drawdown factor, is considered very low. As of December 31, 2012, *Market Vectors Invest Grade FR E traded at a discount of .20% below its net asset value, which is worse than its one-year historical average discount of 1.04%.

Michael F. Mazier has been running the fund for 2 years and currently receives a manager quality ranking of 71 (0=worst, 99=best). If you desire an average level of risk, then this fund may be an option.

Data Date	Investment Rating	Net Assets ($Mil)	Price	Performance Rating/Pts	Total Return Y-T-D	Risk Rating/Pts
12-12	C	7.30	24.72	C- / 3.1	0.36%	B+ / 9.4

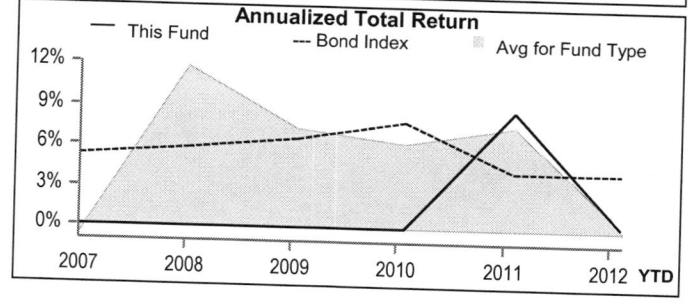
Annualized Total Return

* Denotes ETF Fund

*Market Vectors Junior Gold Mnrs (GDXJ)

E+ **Very Weak**

Fund Family: Van Eck Associates Corporation
Fund Type: Precious Metals
Inception Date: November 10, 2009

Data Date	Investment Rating	Net Assets ($Mil)	Price	Performance Rating/Pts	Total Return Y-T-D	Risk Rating/Pts
12-12	E+	2,537.20	19.80	E+ / 0.9	2.02%	C- / 4.1
2011	E+	1,922.70	24.70	E+ / 0.6	3.72%	C / 5.2
2010	A+	2,123.90	39.89	A+ / 9.9	66.53%	B- / 7.6

Major Rating Factors:

Very poor performance is the major factor driving the E+ (Very Weak) TheStreet.com Investment Rating for *Market Vectors Junior Gold Mnrs. The fund currently has a performance rating of E+ (Very Weak) based on an annualized return of -4.17% over the last three years and a total return of 2.02% year to date 2012. Factored into the performance evaluation is an expense ratio of 0.55% (very low).

The fund's risk rating is currently C- (Fair). It carries a beta of 1.54, meaning it is expected to move 15.4% for every 10% move in the market. Volatility, as measured by both the semi-deviation and a drawdown factor, is considered average. As of December 31, 2012, *Market Vectors Junior Gold Mnrs traded at a discount of 1.93% below its net asset value, which is better than its one-year historical average premium of .17%.

George Cao has been running the fund for 4 years and currently receives a manager quality ranking of 4 (0=worst, 99=best). This fund offers an average level of risk but investors looking for strong performance will be frustrated.

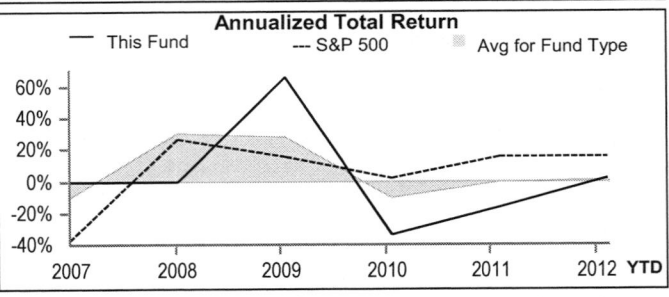

*Market Vectors Lat Am SC Index E (LATM)

B- **Good**

Fund Family: Van Eck Associates Corporation
Fund Type: Foreign
Inception Date: April 6, 2010

Data Date	Investment Rating	Net Assets ($Mil)	Price	Performance Rating/Pts	Total Return Y-T-D	Risk Rating/Pts
12-12	B-	13.60	24.41	B+ / 8.9	3.97%	C+ / 5.9
2011	D-	14.20	21.94	E+ / 0.6	3.01%	C+ / 6.2

Major Rating Factors: Strong performance is the major factor driving the B- (Good) TheStreet.com Investment Rating for *Market Vectors Lat Am SC Index E. The fund currently has a performance rating of B+ (Good) based on an annualized return of 0.00% over the last three years and a total return of 3.97% year to date 2012. Factored into the performance evaluation is an expense ratio of 0.63% (very low).

The fund's risk rating is currently C+ (Fair). It carries a beta of 0.00, meaning the fund's expected move will be 0.0% for every 10% move in the market. Volatility, as measured by both the semi-deviation and a drawdown factor, is considered low. As of December 31, 2012, *Market Vectors Lat Am SC Index E traded at a discount of 3.75% below its net asset value, which is better than its one-year historical average discount of .30%.

George Cao has been running the fund for 3 years and currently receives a manager quality ranking of 21 (0=worst, 99=best). If you desire only a moderate level of risk and strong performance, then this fund is an excellent option.

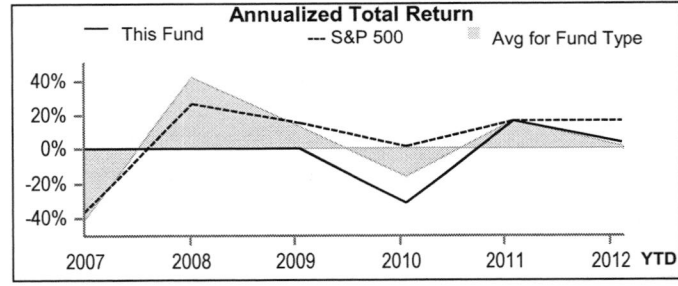

*Market Vectors LatAm Aggrgte Bd (BONO)

B **Good**

Fund Family: Van Eck Associates Corporation
Fund Type: General - Investment Grade
Inception Date: May 11, 2011

Data Date	Investment Rating	Net Assets ($Mil)	Price	Performance Rating/Pts	Total Return Y-T-D	Risk Rating/Pts
12-12	B	7.50	26.15	C+ / 6.5	0.61%	B / 8.9

Major Rating Factors: *Market Vectors LatAm Aggrgte Bd receives a TheStreet.com Investment Rating of B (Good). The fund currently has a performance rating of C+ (Fair) based on an annualized return of 0.00% over the last three years and a total return of 0.61% year to date 2012. Factored into the performance evaluation is an expense ratio of 0.49% (very low).

The fund's risk rating is currently B (Good). It carries a beta of 0.00, meaning the fund's expected move will be 0.0% for every 10% move in the market. Volatility, as measured by both the semi-deviation and a drawdown factor, is considered low. As of December 31, 2012, *Market Vectors LatAm Aggrgte Bd traded at a premium of 1.04% above its net asset value, which is worse than its one-year historical average premium of .49%.

Michael F. Mazier has been running the fund for 2 years and currently receives a manager quality ranking of 97 (0=worst, 99=best). If you desire an average level of risk, then this fund may be an option.

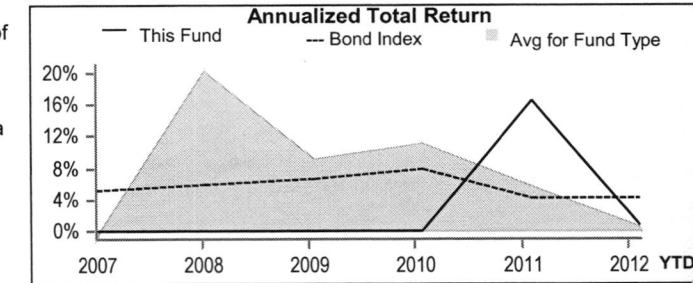

*Market Vectors Long Muni Index E (MLN)

Fund Family: Van Eck Associates Corporation
Fund Type: Municipal - National
Inception Date: January 2, 2008

C+   **Fair**

Major Rating Factors: Middle of the road best describes *Market Vectors Long Muni Index E whose TheStreet.com Investment Rating is currently a C+ (Fair). The fund currently has a performance rating of C (Fair) based on an annualized return of 8.14% over the last three years and a total return of 0.94% year to date 2012. Factored into the performance evaluation is an expense ratio of 0.24% (very low).

The fund's risk rating is currently B+ (Good). It carries a beta of 1.76, meaning it is expected to move 17.6% for every 10% move in the market. Volatility, as measured by both the semi-deviation and a drawdown factor, is considered very low. As of December 31, 2012, *Market Vectors Long Muni Index E traded at a discount of 1.08% below its net asset value, which is better than its one-year historical average premium of .11%.

James T. Colby, III has been running the fund for 5 years and currently receives a manager quality ranking of 29 (0=worst, 99=best). If you desire an average level of risk, then this fund may be an option.

Data Date	Investment Rating	Net Assets ($Mil)	Price	Performance Rating/Pts	Total Return Y-T-D	Risk Rating/Pts
12-12	C+	119.60	20.12	C / 4.9	0.94%	B+ / 9.0
2011	B	67.30	19.03	C+ / 6.9	0.60%	B+ / 9.1
2010	E	56.00	17.17	E+ / 0.9	-1.26%	D+ / 2.7
2009	C-	30.25	18.18	B- / 7.4	17.84%	D+ / 2.5

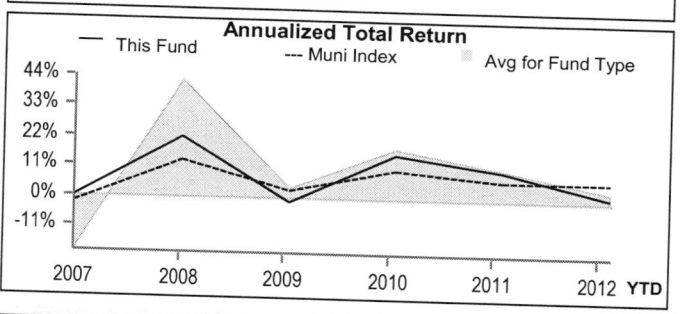

*Market Vectors Mtge REIT Income (MORT)

Fund Family: Van Eck Associates Corporation
Fund Type: Mortgage
Inception Date: August 16, 2011

A+   **Excellent**

Major Rating Factors:
Exceptional performance is the major factor driving the A+ (Excellent) TheStreet.com Investment Rating for *Market Vectors Mtge REIT Income. The fund currently has a performance rating of A- (Excellent) based on an annualized return of 0.00% over the last three years and a total return of 7.19% year to date 2012. Factored into the performance evaluation is an expense ratio of 0.40% (very low).

The fund's risk rating is currently B (Good). It carries a beta of 0.00, meaning the fund's expected move will be 0.0% for every 10% move in the market. Volatility, as measured by both the semi-deviation and a drawdown factor, is considered low. As of December 31, 2012, *Market Vectors Mtge REIT Income traded at a discount of 6.78% below its net asset value, which is better than its one-year historical average premium of .12%.

George Cao has been running the fund for 2 years and currently receives a manager quality ranking of 80 (0=worst, 99=best). If you desire only a moderate level of risk and strong performance, then this fund is an excellent option.

Data Date	Investment Rating	Net Assets ($Mil)	Price	Performance Rating/Pts	Total Return Y-T-D	Risk Rating/Pts
12-12	A+	79.30	25.18	A- / 9.1	7.19%	B / 8.8

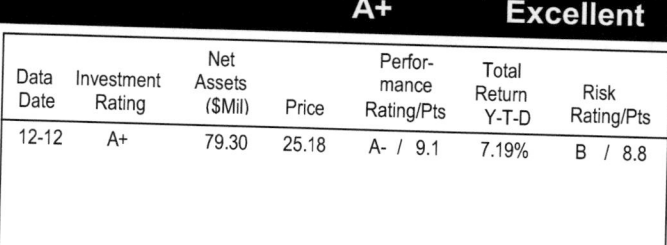

*Market Vectors Oil Services ETF (OIH)

Fund Family: Van Eck Associates Corporation
Fund Type: Income
Inception Date: December 20, 2011

D-   **Weak**

Major Rating Factors: *Market Vectors Oil Services ETF has adopted a very risky asset allocation strategy and currently receives an overall TheStreet.com Investment Rating of D- (Weak). The fund has a high level of volatility, as measured by both semi-deviation and drawdown factors. It carries a beta of 0.00, meaning the fund's expected move will be 0.0% for every 10% move in the market. As of December 31, 2012, *Market Vectors Oil Services ETF traded at a discount of 5.02% below its net asset value, which is better than its one-year historical average discount of .02%. Unfortunately, the high level of risk (D, Weak) has only provided investors with average performance.

The fund's performance rating is currently C (Fair). It has registered an annualized return of 0.00% over the last three years and is up 5.33% year to date 2012. Factored into the performance evaluation is an expense ratio of 0.35% (very low).

George Cao has been running the fund for 2 years and currently receives a manager quality ranking of 6 (0=worst, 99=best). If you are comfortable owning a very high risk investment, then this fund may be an option.

Data Date	Investment Rating	Net Assets ($Mil)	Price	Performance Rating/Pts	Total Return Y-T-D	Risk Rating/Pts
12-12	D-	1,283.30	38.63	C / 4.5	5.33%	D / 1.9

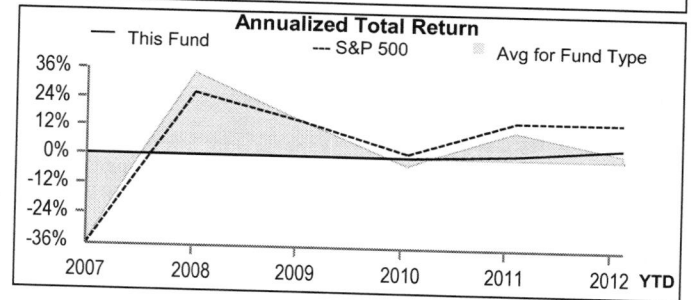

* Denotes ETF Fund

*Market Vectors Pharmaceutical ET (PPH) — B- — Good

Fund Family: Van Eck Associates Corporation
Fund Type: Income
Inception Date: December 20, 2011

Data Date	Investment Rating	Net Assets ($Mil)	Price	Performance Rating/Pts	Total Return Y-T-D	Risk Rating/Pts
12-12	B-	164.40	39.73	B / 7.9	4.86%	B- / 7.1

Major Rating Factors: Strong performance is the major factor driving the B- (Good) TheStreet.com Investment Rating for *Market Vectors Pharmaceutical ET. The fund currently has a performance rating of B (Good) based on an annualized return of 0.00% over the last three years and a total return of 4.86% year to date 2012. Factored into the performance evaluation is an expense ratio of 0.35% (very low).

The fund's risk rating is currently B- (Good). It carries a beta of 0.00, meaning the fund's expected move will be 0.0% for every 10% move in the market. Volatility, as measured by both the semi-deviation and a drawdown factor, is considered low. As of December 31, 2012, *Market Vectors Pharmaceutical ET traded at a discount of 4.59% below its net asset value.

George Cao has been running the fund for 2 years and currently receives a manager quality ranking of 65 (0=worst, 99=best). If you desire only a moderate level of risk and strong performance, then this fund is an excellent option.

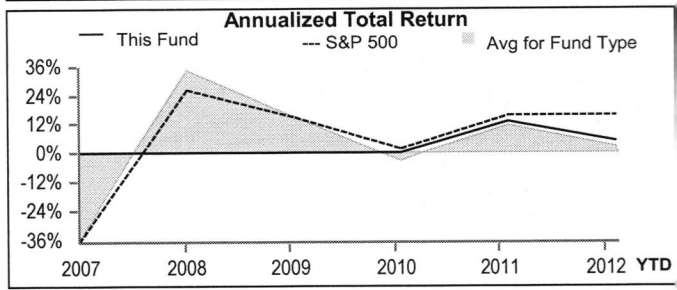

*Market Vectors Poland ETF (PLND) — D- — Weak

Fund Family: Van Eck Associates Corporation
Fund Type: Emerging Market
Inception Date: November 24, 2009

Data Date	Investment Rating	Net Assets ($Mil)	Price	Performance Rating/Pts	Total Return Y-T-D	Risk Rating/Pts
12-12	D-	32.30	22.47	D+ / 2.9	-0.22%	C / 4.8
2011	E+	31.00	17.18	E- / 0.2	-3.14%	C / 5.1
2010	A	52.80	27.02	A- / 9.1	12.50%	C+ / 6.5

Major Rating Factors:
Disappointing performance is the major factor driving the D- (Weak) TheStreet.com Investment Rating for *Market Vectors Poland ETF. The fund currently has a performance rating of D+ (Weak) based on an annualized return of -1.04% over the last three years and a total return of -0.22% year to date 2012. Factored into the performance evaluation is an expense ratio of 0.60% (very low).

The fund's risk rating is currently C (Fair). It carries a beta of 1.45, meaning it is expected to move 14.5% for every 10% move in the market. Volatility, as measured by both the semi-deviation and a drawdown factor, is considered average. As of December 31, 2012, *Market Vectors Poland ETF traded at a premium of .36% above its net asset value, which is worse than its one-year historical average premium of .16%.

George Cao has been running the fund for 4 years and currently receives a manager quality ranking of 18 (0=worst, 99=best). This fund offers an average level of risk but investors looking for strong performance will be frustrated.

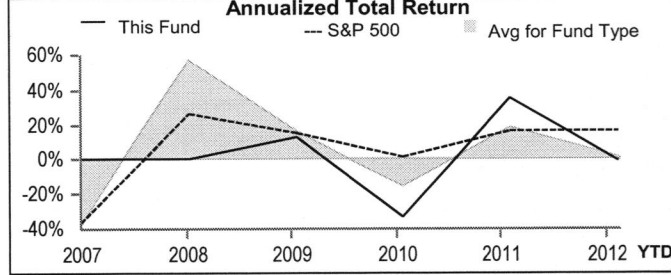

*Market Vectors Pre-Refnded Muni (PRB) — C- — Fair

Fund Family: Van Eck Associates Corporation
Fund Type: Municipal - National
Inception Date: February 2, 2009

Data Date	Investment Rating	Net Assets ($Mil)	Price	Performance Rating/Pts	Total Return Y-T-D	Risk Rating/Pts
12-12	C-	36.00	25.36	D / 1.9	0.01%	B+ / 9.7
2011	C	35.40	25.20	C- / 3.1	0.09%	B+ / 9.8
2010	D	37.20	24.76	D / 2.0	0.49%	C / 4.9

Major Rating Factors:
Disappointing performance is the major factor driving the C- (Fair) TheStreet.com Investment Rating for *Market Vectors Pre-Refnded Muni. The fund currently has a performance rating of D (Weak) based on an annualized return of 1.81% over the last three years and a total return of 0.01% year to date 2012. Factored into the performance evaluation is an expense ratio of 0.24% (very low).

The fund's risk rating is currently B+ (Good). It carries a beta of 0.56, meaning the fund's expected move will be 5.6% for every 10% move in the market. Volatility, as measured by both the semi-deviation and a drawdown factor, is considered very low. As of December 31, 2012, *Market Vectors Pre-Refnded Muni traded at a discount of .43% below its net asset value, which is better than its one-year historical average discount of .11%.

Jack W. Bauer has been running the fund for 5 years and currently receives a manager quality ranking of 38 (0=worst, 99=best). This fund offers only a moderate level of risk but investors looking for strong performance are still waiting.

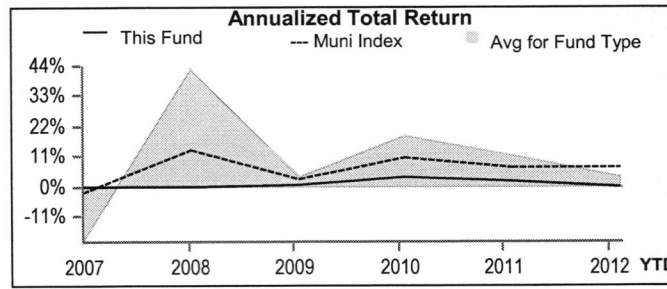

*Market Vectors Renminbi Bond ETF (CHLC)

C-   **Fair**

Fund Family: Van Eck Associates Corporation
Fund Type: Emerging Market
Inception Date: October 11, 2011

Major Rating Factors:
Disappointing performance is the major factor driving the C- (Fair) TheStreet.com Investment Rating for *Market Vectors Renminbi Bond ETF. The fund currently has a performance rating of D- (Weak) based on an annualized return of 0.00% over the last three years and a total return of -0.04% year to date 2012. Factored into the performance evaluation is an expense ratio of 0.39% (very low).

The fund's risk rating is currently B+ (Good). It carries a beta of 0.00, meaning the fund's expected move will be 0.0% for every 10% move in the market. Volatility, as measured by both the semi-deviation and a drawdown factor, is considered very low. As of December 31, 2012, *Market Vectors Renminbi Bond ETF traded at a discount of 2.30% below its net asset value, which is better than its one-year historical average premium of .15%.

Michael F. Mazier has been running the fund for 2 years and currently receives a manager quality ranking of 63 (0=worst, 99=best). This fund offers only a moderate level of risk but investors looking for strong performance are still waiting.

Data Date	Investment Rating	Net Assets ($Mil)	Price	Performance Rating/Pts	Total Return Y-T-D	Risk Rating/Pts
12-12	C-	5.10	25.53	D- / 1.5	-0.04%	B+ / 9.7

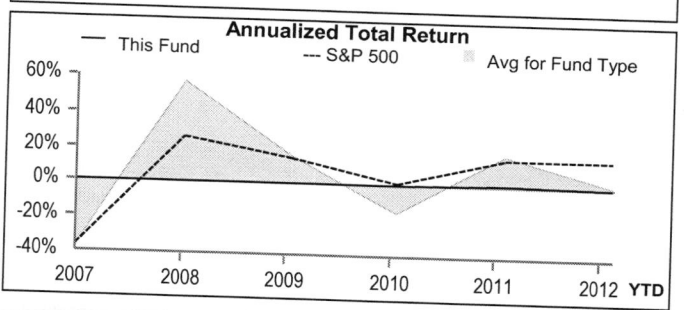

*Market Vectors Retail ETF (RTH)

C+   **Fair**

Fund Family: Van Eck Associates Corporation
Fund Type: Income
Inception Date: December 20, 2011

Major Rating Factors: Strong performance is the major factor driving the C+ (Fair) TheStreet.com Investment Rating for *Market Vectors Retail ETF. The fund currently has a performance rating of B- (Good) based on an annualized return of 0.00% over the last three years and a total return of 1.73% year to date 2012. Factored into the performance evaluation is an expense ratio of 0.35% (very low).

The fund's risk rating is currently C+ (Fair). It carries a beta of 0.00, meaning the fund's expected move will be 0.0% for every 10% move in the market. Volatility, as measured by both the semi-deviation and a drawdown factor, is considered low. As of December 31, 2012, *Market Vectors Retail ETF traded at a discount of 1.62% below its net asset value, which is better than its one-year historical average premium of .02%.

George Cao has been running the fund for 2 years and currently receives a manager quality ranking of 88 (0=worst, 99=best). If you desire only a moderate level of risk and strong performance, then this fund is an excellent option.

Data Date	Investment Rating	Net Assets ($Mil)	Price	Performance Rating/Pts	Total Return Y-T-D	Risk Rating/Pts
12-12	C+	33.80	43.83	B- / 7.4	1.73%	C+ / 6.3

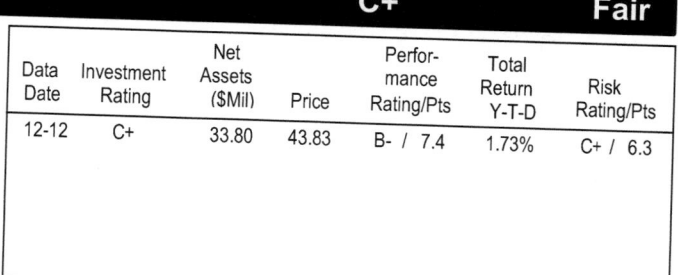

*Market Vectors Russia ETF (RSX)

D-   **Weak**

Fund Family: Van Eck Associates Corporation
Fund Type: Foreign
Inception Date: April 24, 2007

Major Rating Factors:
Disappointing performance is the major factor driving the D- (Weak) TheStreet.com Investment Rating for *Market Vectors Russia ETF. The fund currently has a performance rating of D (Weak) based on an annualized return of -2.52% over the last three years and a total return of -0.47% year to date 2012. Factored into the performance evaluation is an expense ratio of 0.62% (very low).

The fund's risk rating is currently C (Fair). It carries a beta of 1.47, meaning it is expected to move 14.7% for every 10% move in the market. Volatility, as measured by both the semi-deviation and a drawdown factor, is considered average. As of December 31, 2012, *Market Vectors Russia ETF traded at a premium of .03% above its net asset value, which is better than its one-year historical average premium of .14%.

Hao-Hung Liao has been running the fund for 6 years and currently receives a manager quality ranking of 21 (0=worst, 99=best). This fund offers an average level of risk but investors looking for strong performance will be frustrated.

Data Date	Investment Rating	Net Assets ($Mil)	Price	Performance Rating/Pts	Total Return Y-T-D	Risk Rating/Pts
12-12	D-	1,634.20	29.90	D / 1.6	-0.47%	C / 5.0
2011	C-	1,557.00	26.65	C+ / 6.2	1.61%	C+ / 5.8
2010	E+	2,609.60	37.91	D / 2.0	22.14%	D+ / 2.3
2009	C+	726.96	31.19	A+ / 9.9	120.06%	D+ / 2.6

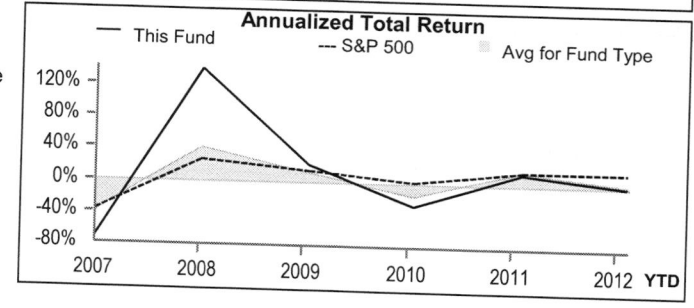

* Denotes ETF Fund

*Market Vectors Russia SmallCap E (RSXJ)

E+   **Very Weak**

Fund Family: Van Eck Associates Corporation
Fund Type: Foreign
Inception Date: April 13, 2011

Data Date	Investment Rating	Net Assets ($Mil)	Price	Performance Rating/Pts	Total Return Y-T-D	Risk Rating/Pts
12-12	E+	8.30	15.24	D- / 1.3	-0.79%	C / 4.8

Major Rating Factors:
Disappointing performance is the major factor driving the E+ (Very Weak) TheStreet.com Investment Rating for *Market Vectors Russia SmallCap E. The fund currently has a performance rating of D- (Weak) based on an annualized return of 0.00% over the last three years and a total return of -0.79% year to date 2012. Factored into the performance evaluation is an expense ratio of 0.67% (very low).

The fund's risk rating is currently C (Fair). It carries a beta of 0.00, meaning the fund's expected move will be 0.0% for every 10% move in the market. Volatility, as measured by both the semi-deviation and a drawdown factor, is considered average. As of December 31, 2012, *Market Vectors Russia SmallCap E traded at a premium of .79% above its net asset value, which is worse than its one-year historical average premium of .35%.

George Cao has been running the fund for 2 years and currently receives a manager quality ranking of 3 (0=worst, 99=best). This fund offers an average level of risk but investors looking for strong performance will be frustrated.

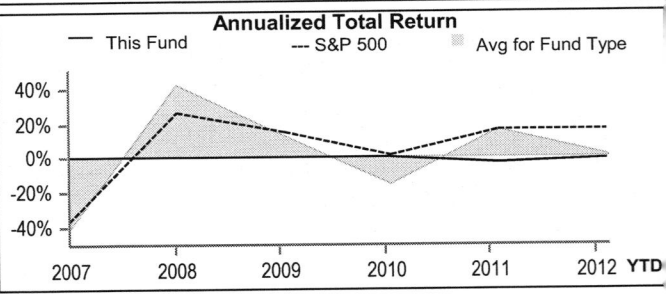
Annualized Total Return

---

*Market Vectors Short Muni Index (SMB)

C-   **Fair**

Fund Family: Van Eck Associates Corporation
Fund Type: Municipal - National
Inception Date: February 22, 2008

Data Date	Investment Rating	Net Assets ($Mil)	Price	Performance Rating/Pts	Total Return Y-T-D	Risk Rating/Pts
12-12	C-	177.40	17.68	D / 2.2	0.68%	B+ / 9.7
2011	C+	113.80	17.71	C- / 3.6	0.17%	B+ / 9.7
2010	D-	102.40	17.12	D / 2.0	0.86%	C- / 3.8
2009	D+	24.54	17.32	C / 5.0	7.88%	C- / 3.5

Major Rating Factors:
Disappointing performance is the major factor driving the C- (Fair) TheStreet.com Investment Rating for *Market Vectors Short Muni Index. The fund currently has a performance rating of D (Weak) based on an annualized return of 2.79% over the last three years and a total return of 0.68% year to date 2012. Factored into the performance evaluation is an expense ratio of 0.20% (very low).

The fund's risk rating is currently B+ (Good). It carries a beta of 0.55, meaning the fund's expected move will be 5.5% for every 10% move in the market. Volatility, as measured by both the semi-deviation and a drawdown factor, is considered very low. As of December 31, 2012, *Market Vectors Short Muni Index traded at a discount of .34% below its net asset value, which is better than its one-year historical average premium of .19%.

James T. Colby, III has been running the fund for 5 years and currently receives a manager quality ranking of 43 (0=worst, 99=best). This fund offers only a moderate level of risk but investors looking for strong performance are still waiting.

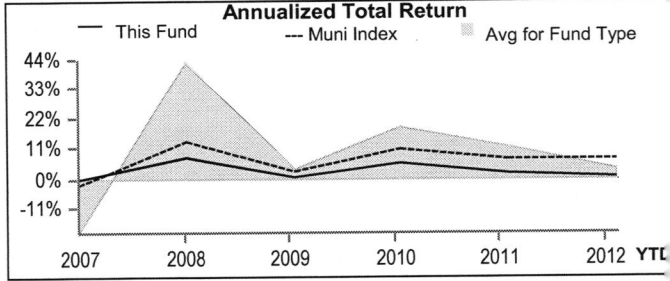
Annualized Total Return

---

*Market Vectors Solar Energy ETF (KWT)

E   **Very Weak**

Fund Family: Van Eck Associates Corporation
Fund Type: Energy/Natural Resources
Inception Date: April 21, 2008

Data Date	Investment Rating	Net Assets ($Mil)	Price	Performance Rating/Pts	Total Return Y-T-D	Risk Rating/Pts
12-12	E	10.90	35.83	E / 0.3	23.95%	C- / 3.6
2011	E	9.90	3.69	E / 0.3	2.98%	C- / 3.8
2010	E	24.90	10.99	E / 0.5	-28.71%	C- / 3.0
2009	D	29.87	15.51	C / 4.4	2.47%	C- / 3.0

Major Rating Factors: Very poor performance is the major factor driving the E (Very Weak) TheStreet.com Investment Rating for *Market Vectors Solar Energy ETF. The fund currently has a performance rating of E (Very Weak) based on an annualized return of -39.94% over the last three years and a total return of 23.95% year to date 2012. Factored into the performance evaluation is an expense ratio of 0.65% (very low).

The fund's risk rating is currently C- (Fair). It carries a beta of 1.59, meaning it is expected to move 15.9% for every 10% move in the market. Volatility, as measured by both the semi-deviation and a drawdown factor, is considered average. As of December 31, 2012, *Market Vectors Solar Energy ETF traded at a discount of 19.16% below its net asset value, which is better than its one-year historical average premium of .32%.

George Cao has been running the fund for 5 years and currently receives a manager quality ranking of 0 (0=worst, 99=best). This fund offers an average level of risk but investors looking for strong performance will be frustrated.

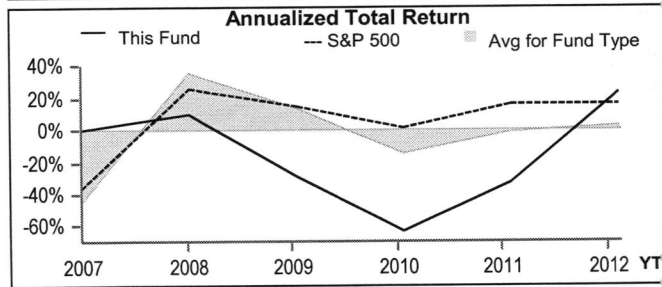
Annualized Total Return

*Market Vectors Steel Index ETF (SLX)

D-   **Weak**

Fund Family: Van Eck Associates Corporation
Fund Type: Income
Inception Date: October 10, 2006

Major Rating Factors:

Disappointing performance is the major factor driving the D- (Weak) TheStreet.com Investment Rating for *Market Vectors Steel Index ETF. The fund currently has a performance rating of D- (Weak) based on an annualized return of -7.12% over the last three years and a total return of 0.76% year to date 2012. Factored into the performance evaluation is an expense ratio of 0.55% (very low).

The fund's risk rating is currently C+ (Fair). It carries a beta of 1.92, meaning it is expected to move 19.2% for every 10% move in the market. Volatility, as measured by both the semi-deviation and a drawdown factor, is considered low. As of December 31, 2012, *Market Vectors Steel Index ETF traded at a discount of .86% below its net asset value, which is better than its one-year historical average discount of .05%.

Hao-Hung Liao has been running the fund for 7 years and currently receives a manager quality ranking of 4 (0=worst, 99=best). This fund offers only a moderate level of risk but investors looking for strong performance are still waiting.

Data Date	Investment Rating	Net Assets ($Mil)	Price	Performance Rating/Pts	Total Return Y-T-D	Risk Rating/Pts
12-12	D-	153.90	48.69	D- / 1.0	0.76%	C+ / 5.9
2011	C-	181.00	47.55	C- / 4.2	4.65%	C+ / 6.3
2010	C-	279.10	72.58	C / 5.4	19.65%	C- / 3.7
2009	B-	227.48	61.52	B+ / 8.6	97.08%	C- / 4.1

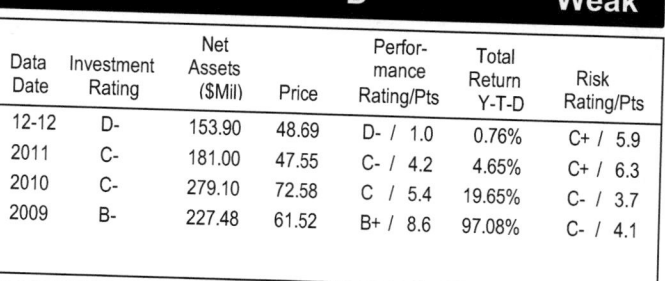

*Market Vectors Uranium+Nuc Engy (NLR)

D-   **Weak**

Fund Family: Van Eck Associates Corporation
Fund Type: Global
Inception Date: August 13, 2007

Major Rating Factors:

Very poor performance is the major factor driving the D- (Weak) TheStreet.com Investment Rating for *Market Vectors Uranium+Nuc Engy. The fund currently has a performance rating of E+ (Very Weak) based on an annualized return of -9.64% over the last three years and a total return of 3.20% year to date 2012. Factored into the performance evaluation is an expense ratio of 0.60% (very low).

The fund's risk rating is currently C+ (Fair). It carries a beta of 1.06, meaning that its performance tracks fairly well with that of the overall stock market. Volatility, as measured by both the semi-deviation and a drawdown factor, is considered low. As of December 31, 2012, *Market Vectors Uranium+Nuc Engy traded at a discount of 3.51% below its net asset value, which is better than its one-year historical average discount of .01%.

Hao-Hung Liao has been running the fund for 6 years and currently receives a manager quality ranking of 10 (0=worst, 99=best). This fund offers only a moderate level of risk but investors looking for strong performance are still waiting.

Data Date	Investment Rating	Net Assets ($Mil)	Price	Performance Rating/Pts	Total Return Y-T-D	Risk Rating/Pts
12-12	D-	78.60	13.76	E+ / 0.8	3.20%	C+ / 5.7
2011	D-	86.70	14.84	D- / 1.3	-0.27%	C+ / 5.8
2010	D	260.40	25.35	D+ / 2.3	16.59%	C / 5.1
2009	C-	164.63	22.66	C / 5.1	12.63%	C / 4.8

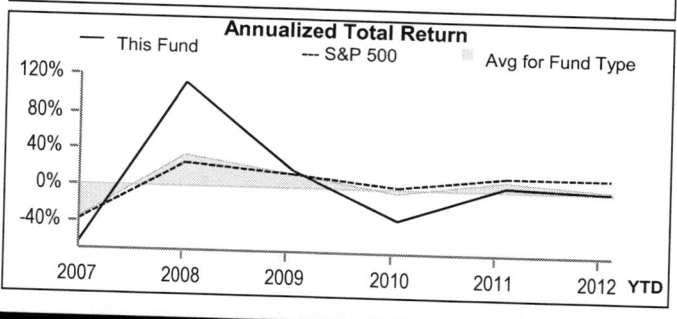

*Market Vectors Vietnam ETF (VNM)

D-   **Weak**

Fund Family: Van Eck Associates Corporation
Fund Type: Foreign
Inception Date: August 11, 2009

Major Rating Factors:

Disappointing performance is the major factor driving the D- (Weak) TheStreet.com Investment Rating for *Market Vectors Vietnam ETF. The fund currently has a performance rating of D- (Weak) based on an annualized return of -7.93% over the last three years and a total return of 10.00% year to date 2012. Factored into the performance evaluation is an expense ratio of 0.73% (very low).

The fund's risk rating is currently C (Fair). It carries a beta of 0.72, meaning the fund's expected move will be 7.2% for every 10% move in the market. Volatility, as measured by both the semi-deviation and a drawdown factor, is considered average. As of December 31, 2012, *Market Vectors Vietnam ETF traded at a discount of 6.40% below its net asset value, which is better than its one-year historical average premium of .89%.

George Cao has been running the fund for 4 years and currently receives a manager quality ranking of 10 (0=worst, 99=best). This fund offers an average level of risk but investors looking for strong performance will be frustrated.

Data Date	Investment Rating	Net Assets ($Mil)	Price	Performance Rating/Pts	Total Return Y-T-D	Risk Rating/Pts
12-12	D-	286.70	18.00	D- / 1.4	10.00%	C / 4.9
2011	E+	198.50	14.55	E- / 0.1	-1.03%	C / 5.1
2010	B-	243.30	26.18	C+ / 6.8	4.10%	B- / 7.3

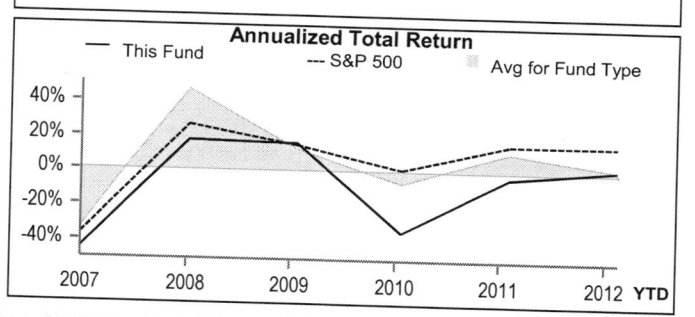

* Denotes ETF Fund

*Materials Select Sector SPDR (XLB)

| C- | Fair |

Fund Family: SSgA Funds Management Inc
Fund Type: Growth
Inception Date: December 16, 1998

Data Date	Investment Rating	Net Assets ($Mil)	Price	Performance Rating/Pts	Total Return Y-T-D	Risk Rating/Pts
12-12	C-	2,445.50	37.54	C- / 3.6	3.92%	B- / 7.1
2011	C	1,635.40	33.50	C / 5.3	3.79%	B- / 7.1
2010	C+	2,594.70	38.41	C+ / 6.4	20.56%	C / 5.3
2009	C	1,725.05	32.99	C+ / 5.8	42.89%	C / 5.5

Major Rating Factors: Middle of the road best describes *Materials Select Sector SPDR whose TheStreet.com Investment Rating is currently a C- (Fair). The fund currently has a performance rating of C- (Fair) based on an annualized return of 7.71% over the last three years and a total return of 3.92% year to date 2012. Factored into the performance evaluation is an expense ratio of 0.18% (very low).

The fund's risk rating is currently B- (Good). It carries a beta of 1.39, meaning it is expected to move 13.9% for every 10% move in the market. Volatility, as measured by both the semi-deviation and a drawdown factor, is considered low. As of December 31, 2012, *Materials Select Sector SPDR traded at a discount of 3.74% below its net asset value.

John A. Tucker has been running the fund for 15 years and currently receives a manager quality ranking of 17 (0=worst, 99=best). If you desire an average level of risk, then this fund may be an option.

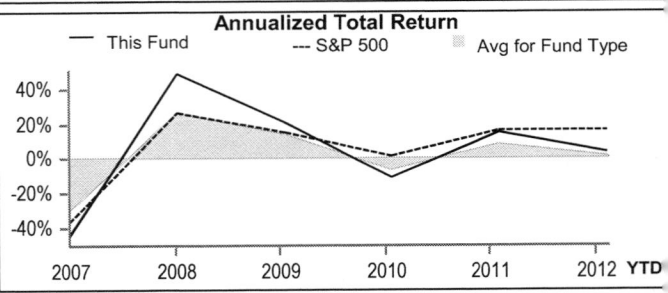

*Meidell Tactical Advantage ETF (MATH)

| C+ | Fair |

Fund Family: AdvisorShares Investments LLC
Fund Type: Growth and Income
Inception Date: June 23, 2011

Data Date	Investment Rating	Net Assets ($Mil)	Price	Performance Rating/Pts	Total Return Y-T-D	Risk Rating/Pts
12-12	C+	7.10	25.93	C- / 4.0	2.78%	B+ / 9.3

Major Rating Factors: Middle of the road best describes *Meidell Tactical Advantage ETF whose TheStreet.com Investment Rating is currently a C+ (Fair). The fund currently has a performance rating of C- (Fair) based on an annualized return of 0.00% over the last three years and a total return of 2.78% year to date 2012. Factored into the performance evaluation is an expense ratio of 1.35% (average).

The fund's risk rating is currently B+ (Good). It carries a beta of 0.00, meaning the fund's expected move will be 0.0% for every 10% move in the market. Volatility, as measured by both the semi-deviation and a drawdown factor, is considered very low. As of December 31, 2012, *Meidell Tactical Advantage ETF traded at a discount of 2.26% below its net asset value, which is better than its one-year historical average premium of .48%.

Laif Meidell has been running the fund for 2 years and currently receives a manager quality ranking of 28 (0=worst, 99=best). If you desire an average level of risk, then this fund may be an option.

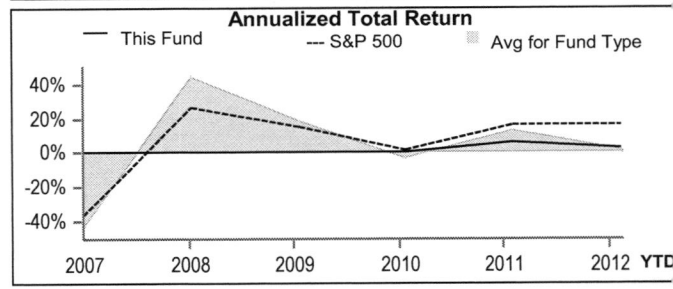

*Morgan Stanley Technology ETF (MTK)

| C- | Fair |

Fund Family: SSgA Funds Management Inc
Fund Type: Growth
Inception Date: September 25, 2000

Data Date	Investment Rating	Net Assets ($Mil)	Price	Performance Rating/Pts	Total Return Y-T-D	Risk Rating/Pts
12-12	C-	163.80	68.37	C / 5.0	3.85%	C+ / 6.5
2011	C	155.30	58.66	C+ / 5.7	1.99%	B- / 7.0
2010	C+	218.00	66.08	C+ / 6.9	15.31%	C / 4.7
2009	C+	197.82	57.61	C+ / 6.5	63.10%	C / 5.2

Major Rating Factors: Middle of the road best describes *Morgan Stanley Technology ETF whose TheStreet.com Investment Rating is currently a C- (Fair). The fund currently has a performance rating of C (Fair) based on an annualized return of 8.16% over the last three years and a total return of 3.85% year to date 2012. Factored into the performance evaluation is an expense ratio of 0.50% (very low).

The fund's risk rating is currently C+ (Fair). It carries a beta of 1.29, meaning it is expected to move 12.9% for every 10% move in the market. Volatility, as measured by both the semi-deviation and a drawdown factor, is considered low. As of December 31, 2012, *Morgan Stanley Technology ETF traded at a discount of 3.73% below its net asset value, which is better than its one-year historical average discount of .05%.

John A. Tucker has been running the fund for 13 years and currently receives a manager quality ranking of 18 (0=worst, 99=best). If you desire an average level of risk, then this fund may be an option.

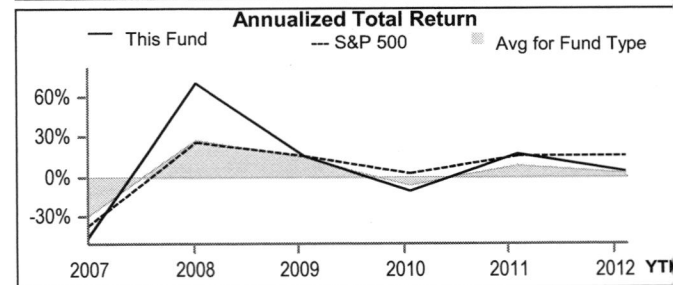

*Mrkt Vectors Rare Earth/Str Met (REMX)

Fund Family: Van Eck Associates Corporation
Fund Type: Growth
Inception Date: October 27, 2010

| | E+ | Very Weak |

Major Rating Factors:

Very poor performance is the major factor driving the E+ (Very Weak) TheStreet.com Investment Rating for *Mrkt Vectors Rare Earth/Str Met. The fund currently has a performance rating of E+ (Very Weak) based on an annualized return of 0.00% over the last three years and a total return of 1.44% year to date 2012. Factored into the performance evaluation is an expense ratio of 0.57% (very low).

The fund's risk rating is currently C- (Fair). It carries a beta of 0.00, meaning the fund's expected move will be 0.0% for every 10% move in the market. Volatility, as measured by both the semi-deviation and a drawdown factor, is considered average. As of December 31, 2012, *Mrkt Vectors Rare Earth/Str Met traded at a discount of 1.72% below its net asset value, which is better than its one-year historical average discount of .13%.

George Cao has been running the fund for 3 years and currently receives a manager quality ranking of 2 (0=worst, 99=best). This fund offers an average level of risk but investors looking for strong performance will be frustrated.

Data Date	Investment Rating	Net Assets ($Mil)	Price	Performance Rating/Pts	Total Return Y-T-D	Risk Rating/Pts
12-12	E+	174.60	13.16	E+ / 0.9	1.44%	C- / 3.8
2011	E+	198.50	14.92	E / 0.5	3.95%	C / 4.3

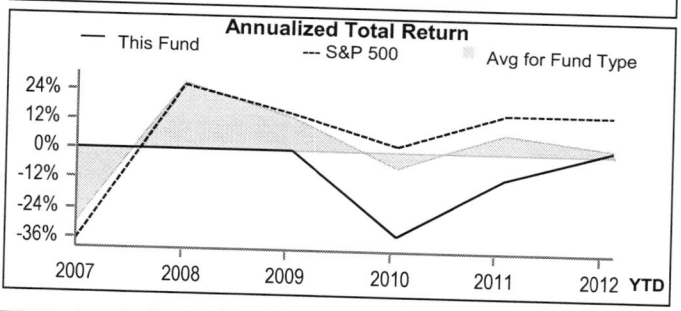

*Nuveen Diversified Commodity (CFD)

Fund Family: Nuveen Commodities Asset Management
Fund Type: Growth
Inception Date: September 28, 2010

| | D | Weak |

Major Rating Factors:

Disappointing performance is the major factor driving the D (Weak) TheStreet.com Investment Rating for *Nuveen Diversified Commodity. The fund currently has a performance rating of D (Weak) based on an annualized return of 0.00% over the last three years and a total return of 3.22% year to date 2012. Factored into the performance evaluation is an expense ratio of 1.63% (above average).

The fund's risk rating is currently C+ (Fair). It carries a beta of 0.00, meaning the fund's expected move will be 0.0% for every 10% move in the market. Volatility, as measured by both the semi-deviation and a drawdown factor, is considered low. As of December 31, 2012, *Nuveen Diversified Commodity traded at a discount of 6.55% below its net asset value, which is better than its one-year historical average discount of 4.51%.

This fund has been team managed for 3 years and currently receives a manager quality ranking of 8 (0=worst, 99=best). This fund offers only a moderate level of risk but investors looking for strong performance are still waiting.

Data Date	Investment Rating	Net Assets ($Mil)	Price	Performance Rating/Pts	Total Return Y-T-D	Risk Rating/Pts
12-12	D	197.10	19.97	D / 1.7	3.22%	C+ / 6.3
2011	D-	214.30	20.30	D- / 1.0	2.61%	C+ / 6.6

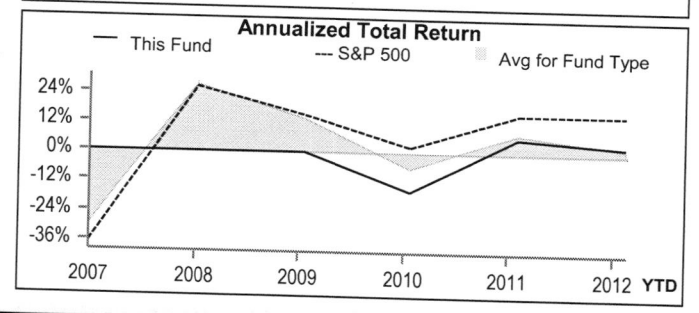

*Pax MSCI EAFE ESG Index ETF (EAPS)

Fund Family: Pax World Management LLC
Fund Type: Foreign
Inception Date: January 28, 2011

| | B+ | Good |

Major Rating Factors:

Exceptional performance is the major factor driving the B+ (Good) TheStreet.com Investment Rating for *Pax MSCI EAFE ESG Index ETF. The fund currently has a performance rating of A- (Excellent) based on an annualized return of 0.00% over the last three years and a total return of 1.39% year to date 2012. Factored into the performance evaluation is an expense ratio of 0.55% (very low).

The fund's risk rating is currently B- (Good). It carries a beta of 0.00, meaning the fund's expected move will be 0.0% for every 10% move in the market. Volatility, as measured by both the semi-deviation and a drawdown factor, is considered low. As of December 31, 2012, *Pax MSCI EAFE ESG Index ETF traded at a discount of .49% below its net asset value, which is better than its one-year historical average premium of .76%.

Christopher H. Brown has been running the fund for 2 years and currently receives a manager quality ranking of 67 (0=worst, 99=best). If you desire only a moderate level of risk and strong performance, then this fund is an excellent option.

Data Date	Investment Rating	Net Assets ($Mil)	Price	Performance Rating/Pts	Total Return Y-T-D	Risk Rating/Pts
12-12	B+	13.20	24.51	A- / 9.1	1.39%	B- / 7.4

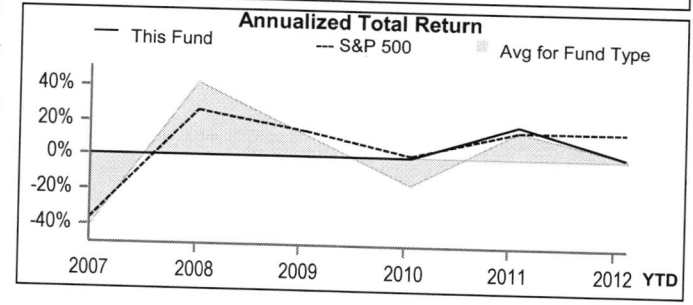

* Denotes ETF Fund

*Pax MSCI North America ESG Idx E (NASI)

| | C+ | Fair |

Fund Family: Pax World Management LLC
Fund Type: Growth
Inception Date: May 18, 2010

Major Rating Factors: Middle of the road best describes *Pax MSCI North America ESG Idx E whose TheStreet.com Investment Rating is currently a C+ (Fair). The fund currently has a performance rating of C+ (Fair) based on an annualized return of 0.00% over the last three years and a total return of 4.19% year to date 2012. Factored into the performance evaluation is an expense ratio of 0.50% (very low).

The fund's risk rating is currently B (Good). It carries a beta of 0.00, meaning the fund's expected move will be 0.0% for every 10% move in the market. Volatility, as measured by both the semi-deviation and a drawdown factor, is considered low. As of December 31, 2012, *Pax MSCI North America ESG Idx E traded at a discount of 4.27% below its net asset value, which is better than its one-year historical average premium of .37%.

Christopher H. Brown has been running the fund for 3 years and currently receives a manager quality ranking of 48 (0=worst, 99=best). If you desire an average level of risk, then this fund may be an option.

Data Date	Investment Rating	Net Assets ($Mil)	Price	Performance Rating/Pts	Total Return Y-T-D	Risk Rating/Pts
12-12	C+	12.00	29.62	C+ / 6.1	4.19%	B / 8.3
2011	C-	5.40	27.09	D+ / 2.3	1.77%	B / 8.4

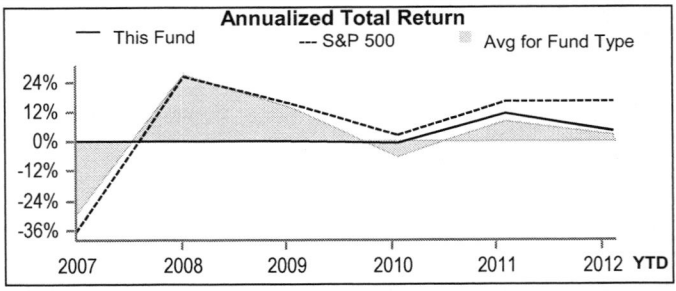

*Peritus High Yield ETF (HYLD)

| | B | Good |

Fund Family: AdvisorShares Investments LLC
Fund Type: Corporate - High Yield
Inception Date: December 1, 2010

Major Rating Factors: *Peritus High Yield ETF receives a TheStreet.com Investment Rating of B (Good). The fund currently has a performance rating of C+ (Fair) based on an annualized return of 0.00% over the last three years and a total return of 1.34% year to date 2012. Factored into the performance evaluation is an expense ratio of 1.35% (average).

The fund's risk rating is currently B+ (Good). It carries a beta of 0.00, meaning the fund's expected move will be 0.0% for every 10% move in the market. Volatility, as measured by both the semi-deviation and a drawdown factor, is considered very low. As of December 31, 2012, *Peritus High Yield ETF traded at a discount of 1.38% below its net asset value, which is better than its one-year historical average premium of .15%.

Ronald J. Heller currently receives a manager quality ranking of 69 (0=worst, 99=best). If you desire an average level of risk, then this fund may be an option.

Data Date	Investment Rating	Net Assets ($Mil)	Price	Performance Rating/Pts	Total Return Y-T-D	Risk Rating/Pts
12-12	B	177.20	50.07	C+ / 6.3	1.34%	B+ / 9.0
2011	C-	61.40	47.52	D / 1.9	0.23%	B+ / 9.0

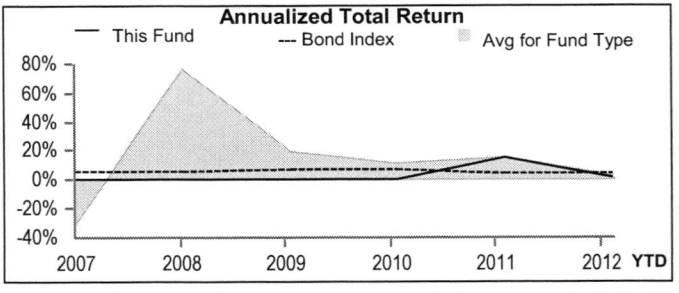

*PIMCO 0-5 Year Hi Yield Corp Bd (HYS)

| | B- | Good |

Fund Family: PIMCO
Fund Type: Corporate - Investment Grade
Inception Date: June 16, 2011

Major Rating Factors: *PIMCO 0-5 Year Hi Yield Corp Bd receives a TheStreet.com Investment Rating of B- (Good). The fund currently has a performance rating of C (Fair) based on an annualized return of 0.00% over the last three years and a total return of 0.86% year to date 2012. Factored into the performance evaluation is an expense ratio of 0.55% (very low).

The fund's risk rating is currently B+ (Good). It carries a beta of 0.00, meaning the fund's expected move will be 0.0% for every 10% move in the market. Volatility, as measured by both the semi-deviation and a drawdown factor, is considered very low. As of December 31, 2012, *PIMCO 0-5 Year Hi Yield Corp Bd traded at a discount of .49% below its net asset value, which is better than its one-year historical average premium of .20%.

Vineer Bhansali has been running the fund for 2 years and currently receives a manager quality ranking of 91 (0=worst, 99=best). If you desire an average level of risk, then this fund may be an option.

Data Date	Investment Rating	Net Assets ($Mil)	Price	Performance Rating/Pts	Total Return Y-T-D	Risk Rating/Pts
12-12	B-	791.70	103.43	C / 5.0	0.86%	B+ / 9.6

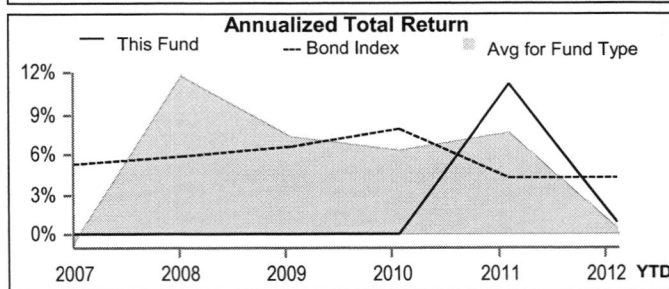

*PIMCO 1-3 Year US Treasury Idx E (TUZ)

C- **Fair**

Fund Family: PIMCO
Fund Type: US Government/Agency
Inception Date: June 1, 2009

Data Date	Investment Rating	Net Assets ($Mil)	Price	Perfor-mance Rating/Pts	Total Return Y-T-D	Risk Rating/Pts
12-12	C-	122.20	50.85	D / 1.6	0.12%	B+ / 9.9
2011	C	143.10	51.12	D / 2.2	-0.11%	B+ / 9.9
2010	C+	106.80	50.92	C- / 3.1	2.37%	B+ / 9.0

Major Rating Factors:
Disappointing performance is the major factor driving the C- (Fair) TheStreet.com Investment Rating for *PIMCO 1-3 Year US Treasury Idx E. The fund currently has a performance rating of D (Weak) based on an annualized return of 1.20% over the last three years and a total return of 0.12% year to date 2012. Factored into the performance evaluation is an expense ratio of 0.09% (very low).

The fund's risk rating is currently B+ (Good). It carries a beta of 0.03, meaning the fund's expected move will be 0.3% for every 10% move in the market. Volatility, as measured by both the semi-deviation and a drawdown factor, is considered very low. As of December 31, 2012, *PIMCO 1-3 Year US Treasury Idx E traded at a discount of .10% below its net asset value, which is better than its one-year historical average discount of .02%.

Vineer Bhansali has been running the fund for 4 years and currently receives a manager quality ranking of 59 (0=worst, 99=best). This fund offers only a moderate level of risk but investors looking for strong performance are still waiting.

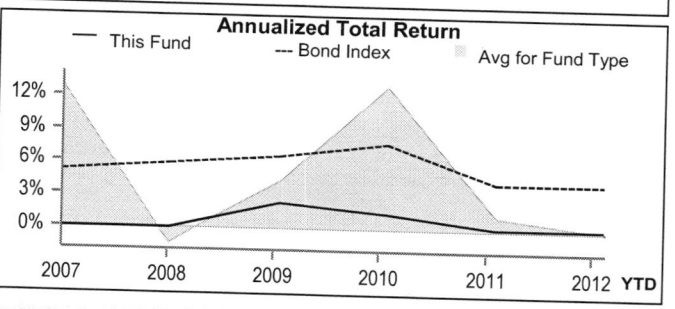

*PIMCO 1-5 Year US TIPS Index ETF (STPZ)

C- **Fair**

Fund Family: PIMCO
Fund Type: US Government/Agency
Inception Date: August 20, 2009

Data Date	Investment Rating	Net Assets ($Mil)	Price	Perfor-mance Rating/Pts	Total Return Y-T-D	Risk Rating/Pts
12-12	C-	992.70	54.06	D / 2.1	0.04%	B+ / 9.9
2011	C	933.90	53.34	D+ / 2.8	0.41%	B+ / 9.9
2010	B	672.80	52.58	C- / 4.0	3.40%	B+ / 9.0

Major Rating Factors:
Disappointing performance is the major factor driving the C- (Fair) TheStreet.com Investment Rating for *PIMCO 1-5 Year US TIPS Index ETF. The fund currently has a performance rating of D (Weak) based on an annualized return of 3.32% over the last three years and a total return of 0.04% year to date 2012. Factored into the performance evaluation is an expense ratio of 0.20% (very low).

The fund's risk rating is currently B+ (Good). It carries a beta of -0.06, meaning the fund's expected move will be -0.6% for every 10% move in the market. Volatility, as measured by both the semi-deviation and a drawdown factor, is considered very low. As of December 31, 2012, *PIMCO 1-5 Year US TIPS Index ETF traded at a premium of .02% above its net asset value, which is worse than its one-year historical average discount of .01%.

Vineer Bhansali has been running the fund for 4 years and currently receives a manager quality ranking of 77 (0=worst, 99=best). This fund offers only a moderate level of risk but investors looking for strong performance are still waiting.

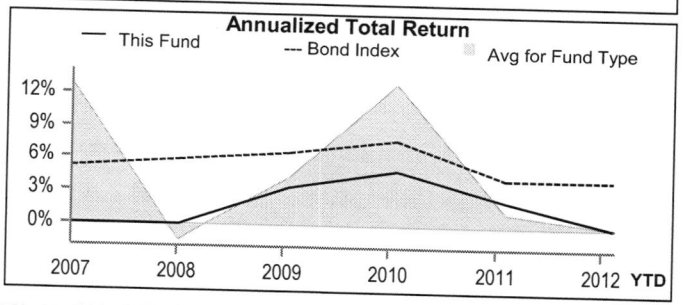

*PIMCO 15 Plus Year US TIPS Idx E (LTPZ)

C+ **Fair**

Fund Family: PIMCO
Fund Type: US Government/Agency
Inception Date: September 3, 2009

Data Date	Investment Rating	Net Assets ($Mil)	Price	Perfor-mance Rating/Pts	Total Return Y-T-D	Risk Rating/Pts
12-12	C+	155.90	71.65	C / 5.3	-0.48%	B+ / 9.1
2011	A	360.50	65.25	B+ / 8.7	0.92%	B+ / 9.1
2010	B	250.80	54.35	C / 5.2	8.49%	B / 8.4

Major Rating Factors: Middle of the road best describes *PIMCO 15 Plus Year US TIPS Idx E whose TheStreet.com Investment Rating is currently a C+ (Fair). The fund currently has a performance rating of C (Fair) based on an annualized return of 14.46% over the last three years and a total return of -0.48% year to date 2012. Factored into the performance evaluation is an expense ratio of 0.20% (very low).

The fund's risk rating is currently B+ (Good). It carries a beta of 0.44, meaning the fund's expected move will be 4.4% for every 10% move in the market. Volatility, as measured by both the semi-deviation and a drawdown factor, is considered very low. As of December 31, 2012, *PIMCO 15 Plus Year US TIPS Idx E traded at a premium of .58% above its net asset value, which is worse than its one-year historical average premium of .01%.

Vineer Bhansali has been running the fund for 4 years and currently receives a manager quality ranking of 88 (0=worst, 99=best). If you desire an average level of risk, then this fund may be an option.

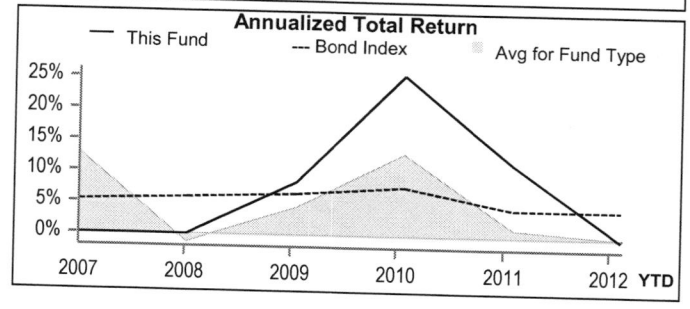

* Denotes ETF Fund

*PIMCO 25+ Year Zero Coupon US Tr (ZROZ)

C+ **Fair**

Fund Family: PIMCO
Fund Type: US Government/Agency
Inception Date: October 30, 2009

Major Rating Factors: Middle of the road best describes *PIMCO 25+ Year Zero Coupon US Tr whose TheStreet.com Investment Rating is currently a C+ (Fair). The fund currently has a performance rating of C+ (Fair) based on an annualized return of 20.20% over the last three years and a total return of -1.60% year to date 2012. Factored into the performance evaluation is an expense ratio of 0.15% (very low).

The fund's risk rating is currently B- (Good). It carries a beta of 2.15, meaning it is expected to move 21.5% for every 10% move in the market. Volatility, as measured by both the semi-deviation and a drawdown factor, is considered low. As of December 31, 2012, *PIMCO 25+ Year Zero Coupon US Tr traded at a premium of 1.92% above its net asset value, which is worse than its one-year historical average discount of .20%.

Vineer Bhansali has been running the fund for 4 years and currently receives a manager quality ranking of 16 (0=worst, 99=best). If you desire an average level of risk, then this fund may be an option.

Data Date	Investment Rating	Net Assets ($Mil)	Price	Performance Rating/Pts	Total Return Y-T-D	Risk Rating/Pts
12-12	C+	100.90	109.12	C+ / 6.5	-1.60%	B- / 7.1
2011	B+	64.50	111.50	A+ / 9.9	-3.82%	B- / 7.2
2010	D	53.50	72.30	D- / 1.0	8.61%	C+ / 6.8

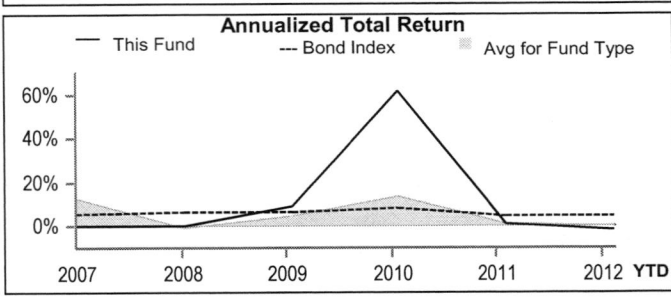

*PIMCO 3-7 Year US Treasury Idx E (FIVZ)

C- **Fair**

Fund Family: PIMCO
Fund Type: US Government/Agency
Inception Date: October 30, 2009

Major Rating Factors:
Disappointing performance is the major factor driving the C- (Fair) TheStreet.com Investment Rating for *PIMCO 3-7 Year US Treasury Idx E. The fund currently has a performance rating of D+ (Weak) based on an annualized return of 4.99% over the last three years and a total return of -0.36% year to date 2012. Factored into the performance evaluation is an expense ratio of 0.15% (very low).

The fund's risk rating is currently B+ (Good). It carries a beta of 0.18, meaning the fund's expected move will be 1.8% for every 10% move in the market. Volatility, as measured by both the semi-deviation and a drawdown factor, is considered very low. As of December 31, 2012, *PIMCO 3-7 Year US Treasury Idx E traded at a premium of .17% above its net asset value, which is worse than its one-year historical average discount of .03%.

Vineer Bhansali has been running the fund for 4 years and currently receives a manager quality ranking of 72 (0=worst, 99=best). This fund offers only a moderate level of risk but investors looking for strong performance are still waiting.

Data Date	Investment Rating	Net Assets ($Mil)	Price	Performance Rating/Pts	Total Return Y-T-D	Risk Rating/Pts
12-12	C-	21.70	81.36	D+ / 2.3	-0.36%	B+ / 9.7
2011	C+	21.70	81.26	C- / 3.7	0.14%	B+ / 9.7
2010	B-	51.30	76.95	C- / 4.0	6.22%	B / 8.8

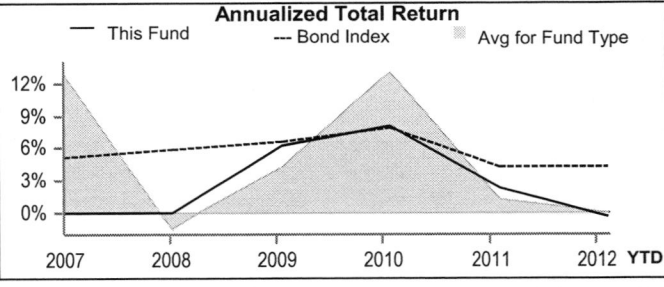

*PIMCO 7-15 Year US Treasury Idx (TENZ)

C **Fair**

Fund Family: PIMCO
Fund Type: US Government/Agency
Inception Date: September 10, 2009

Major Rating Factors: Middle of the road best describes *PIMCO 7-15 Year US Treasury Idx whose TheStreet.com Investment Rating is currently a C (Fair). The fund currently has a performance rating of C- (Fair) based on an annualized return of 8.64% over the last three years and a total return of -0.84% year to date 2012. Factored into the performance evaluation is an expense ratio of 0.15% (very low).

The fund's risk rating is currently B+ (Good). It carries a beta of 0.45, meaning the fund's expected move will be 4.5% for every 10% move in the market. Volatility, as measured by both the semi-deviation and a drawdown factor, is considered very low. As of December 31, 2012, *PIMCO 7-15 Year US Treasury Idx traded at a premium of .92% above its net asset value, which is worse than its one-year historical average discount of .02%.

Vineer Bhansali has been running the fund for 4 years and currently receives a manager quality ranking of 73 (0=worst, 99=best). If you desire an average level of risk, then this fund may be an option.

Data Date	Investment Rating	Net Assets ($Mil)	Price	Performance Rating/Pts	Total Return Y-T-D	Risk Rating/Pts
12-12	C	16.20	86.82	C- / 3.0	-0.84%	B+ / 9.3
2011	B	16.00	85.79	C+ / 6.0	-0.49%	B+ / 9.3
2010	C+	14.30	76.37	C- / 3.7	8.28%	B / 8.4

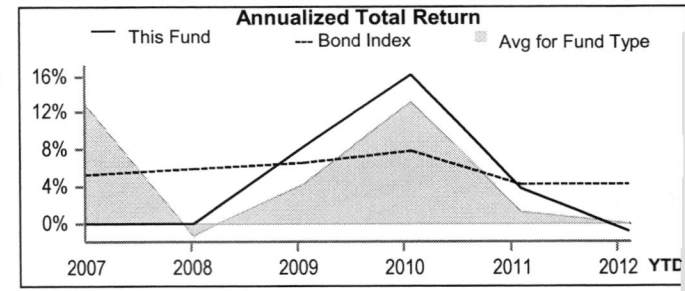

*PIMCO Australia Bond Index ETF (AUD)

C **Fair**

Fund Family: PIMCO
Fund Type: Global
Inception Date: October 31, 2011

Major Rating Factors: Middle of the road best describes *PIMCO Australia Bond Index ETF whose TheStreet.com Investment Rating is currently a C (Fair). The fund currently has a performance rating of C- (Fair) based on an annualized return of 0.00% over the last three years and a total return of 0.51% year to date 2012. Factored into the performance evaluation is an expense ratio of 0.45% (very low).

The fund's risk rating is currently B+ (Good). It carries a beta of 0.00, meaning the fund's expected move will be 0.0% for every 10% move in the market. Volatility, as measured by both the semi-deviation and a drawdown factor, is considered very low. As of December 31, 2012, *PIMCO Australia Bond Index ETF traded at a discount of .62% below its net asset value, which is better than its one-year historical average premium of .16%.

Robert Mead has been running the fund for 2 years and currently receives a manager quality ranking of 85 (0=worst, 99=best). If you desire an average level of risk, then this fund may be an option.

Data Date	Investment Rating	Net Assets ($Mil)	Price	Performance Rating/Pts	Total Return Y-T-D	Risk Rating/Pts
12-12	C	39.60	104.36	C- / 3.5	0.51%	B+ / 9.3

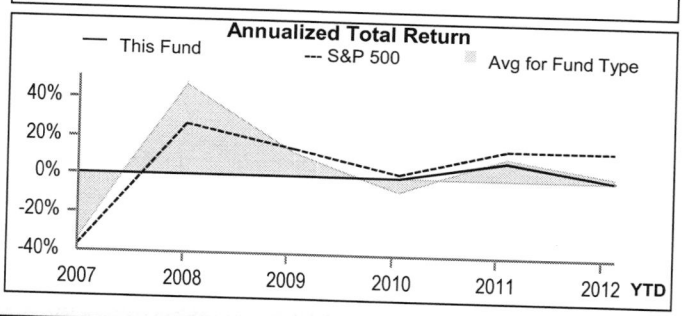

*PIMCO Broad US TIPS Index ETF (TIPZ)

C **Fair**

Fund Family: PIMCO
Fund Type: US Government/Agency
Inception Date: September 3, 2009

Major Rating Factors: Middle of the road best describes *PIMCO Broad US TIPS Index ETF whose TheStreet.com Investment Rating is currently a C (Fair). The fund currently has a performance rating of C- (Fair) based on an annualized return of 8.52% over the last three years and a total return of -0.29% year to date 2012. Factored into the performance evaluation is an expense ratio of 0.20% (very low).

The fund's risk rating is currently B+ (Good). It carries a beta of 0.16, meaning the fund's expected move will be 1.6% for every 10% move in the market. Volatility, as measured by both the semi-deviation and a drawdown factor, is considered very low. As of December 31, 2012, *PIMCO Broad US TIPS Index ETF traded at a premium of .33% above its net asset value.

Vineer Bhansali has been running the fund for 4 years and currently receives a manager quality ranking of 84 (0=worst, 99=best). If you desire an average level of risk, then this fund may be an option.

Data Date	Investment Rating	Net Assets ($Mil)	Price	Performance Rating/Pts	Total Return Y-T-D	Risk Rating/Pts
12-12	C	136.50	61.20	C- / 3.1	-0.29%	B+ / 9.7
2011	B	95.00	58.29	C+ / 5.7	0.63%	B+ / 9.7
2010	B	38.80	53.13	C / 4.5	5.94%	B / 8.8

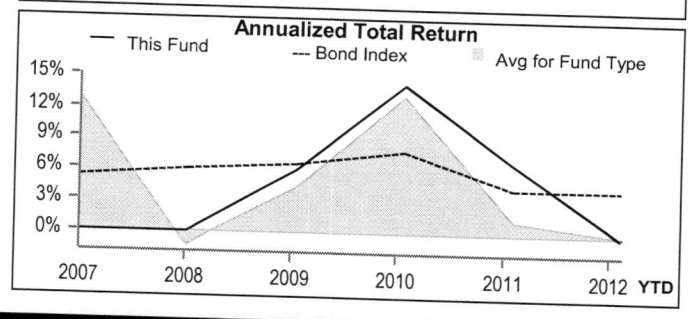

*PIMCO Broad US Treasury Index ET (TRSY)

C- **Fair**

Fund Family: PIMCO
Fund Type: US Government/Agency
Inception Date: October 29, 2010

Major Rating Factors:
Disappointing performance is the major factor driving the C- (Fair) TheStreet.com Investment Rating for *PIMCO Broad US Treasury Index ET. The fund currently has a performance rating of D- (Weak) based on an annualized return of 0.00% over the last three years and a total return of -2.48% year to date 2012. Factored into the performance evaluation is an expense ratio of 0.15% (very low).

The fund's risk rating is currently B+ (Good). It carries a beta of 0.00, meaning the fund's expected move will be 0.0% for every 10% move in the market. Volatility, as measured by both the semi-deviation and a drawdown factor, is considered very low. As of December 31, 2012, *PIMCO Broad US Treasury Index ET traded at a premium of 2.17% above its net asset value, which is worse than its one-year historical average premium of .21%.

Vineer Bhansali has been running the fund for 3 years and currently receives a manager quality ranking of 67 (0=worst, 99=best). This fund offers only a moderate level of risk but investors looking for strong performance are still waiting.

Data Date	Investment Rating	Net Assets ($Mil)	Price	Performance Rating/Pts	Total Return Y-T-D	Risk Rating/Pts
12-12	C-	18.90	106.66	D- / 1.4	-2.48%	B+ / 9.6

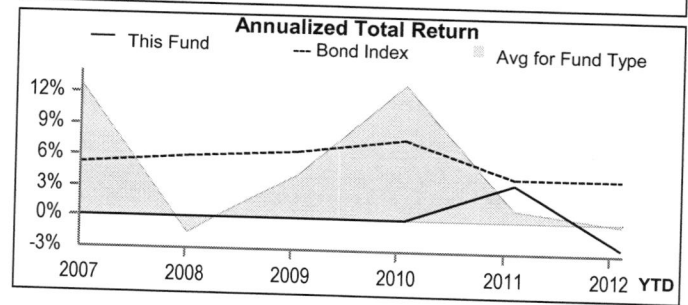

*PIMCO Build America Bond ETF (BABZ)   C-   Fair

Fund Family: PIMCO
Fund Type: US Government/Agency
Inception Date: September 20, 2010

Data Date	Investment Rating	Net Assets ($Mil)	Price	Performance Rating/Pts	Total Return Y-T-D	Risk Rating/Pts
12-12	C-	42.00	55.00	D+ / 2.8	-0.33%	B+ / 9.3
2011	B+	24.60	53.47	B- / 7.2	-0.97%	B+ / 9.5

Major Rating Factors:
Disappointing performance is the major factor driving the C- (Fair) TheStreet.com Investment Rating for *PIMCO Build America Bond ETF. The fund currently has a performance rating of D+ (Weak) based on an annualized return of 0.00% over the last three years and a total return of -0.33% year to date 2012. Factored into the performance evaluation is an expense ratio of 0.45% (very low).

The fund's risk rating is currently B+ (Good). It carries a beta of 0.00, meaning the fund's expected move will be 0.0% for every 10% move in the market. Volatility, as measured by both the semi-deviation and a drawdown factor, is considered very low. As of December 31, 2012, *PIMCO Build America Bond ETF traded at a premium of .60% above its net asset value, which is worse than its one-year historical average discount of .01%.

Joseph P. Deane has been running the fund for 2 years and currently receives a manager quality ranking of 87 (0=worst, 99=best). This fund offers only a moderate level of risk but investors looking for strong performance are still waiting.

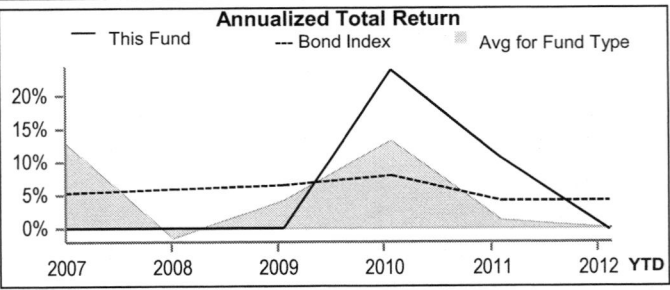

*PIMCO Canada Bond Index ETF (CAD)   C-   Fair

Fund Family: PIMCO
Fund Type: Global
Inception Date: November 9, 2011

Data Date	Investment Rating	Net Assets ($Mil)	Price	Performance Rating/Pts	Total Return Y-T-D	Risk Rating/Pts
12-12	C-	29.50	105.58	D+ / 2.4	0.12%	B+ / 9.6

Major Rating Factors:
Disappointing performance is the major factor driving the C- (Fair) TheStreet.com Investment Rating for *PIMCO Canada Bond Index ETF. The fund currently has a performance rating of D+ (Weak) based on an annualized return of 0.00% over the last three years and a total return of 0.12% year to date 2012. Factored into the performance evaluation is an expense ratio of 0.45% (very low).

The fund's risk rating is currently B+ (Good). It carries a beta of 0.00, meaning the fund's expected move will be 0.0% for every 10% move in the market. Volatility, as measured by both the semi-deviation and a drawdown factor, is considered very low. As of December 31, 2012, *PIMCO Canada Bond Index ETF traded at a price exactly equal to its net asset value, which is better than its one-year historical average premium of .20%.

Edward Devlin has been running the fund for 2 years and currently receives a manager quality ranking of 75 (0=worst, 99=best). This fund offers only a moderate level of risk but investors looking for strong performance are still waiting.

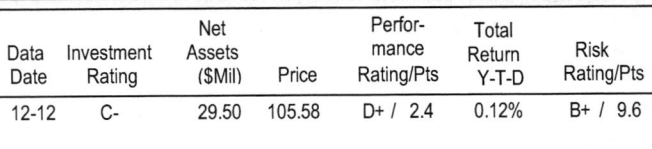
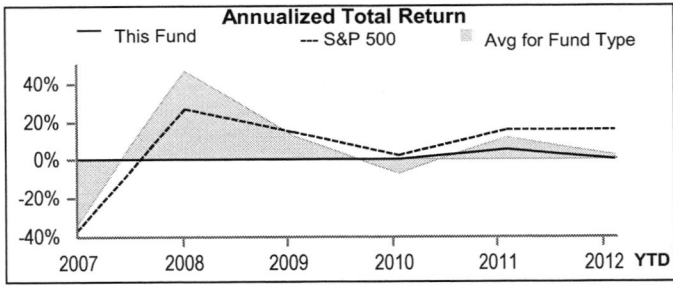

*PIMCO Enhanced Short Maturity ET (MINT)   C-   Fair

Fund Family: PIMCO
Fund Type: Corporate - Investment Grade
Inception Date: November 16, 2009

Data Date	Investment Rating	Net Assets ($Mil)	Price	Performance Rating/Pts	Total Return Y-T-D	Risk Rating/Pts
12-12	C-	2,169.30	101.48	D / 1.7	0.07%	B+ / 9.9
2011	C-	1,803.30	100.16	D / 2.0	-0.03%	B+ / 9.9
2010	C+	785.20	100.71	C- / 3.0	1.61%	B+ / 9.0

Major Rating Factors:
Disappointing performance is the major factor driving the C- (Fair) TheStreet.com Investment Rating for *PIMCO Enhanced Short Maturity ET. The fund currently has a performance rating of D (Weak) based on an annualized return of 1.49% over the last three years and a total return of 0.07% year to date 2012. Factored into the performance evaluation is an expense ratio of 0.35% (very low).

The fund's risk rating is currently B+ (Good). It carries a beta of 0.06, meaning the fund's expected move will be 0.6% for every 10% move in the market. Volatility, as measured by both the semi-deviation and a drawdown factor, is considered very low. As of December 31, 2012, *PIMCO Enhanced Short Maturity ET traded at a discount of .04% below its net asset value, which is better than its one-year historical average premium of .01%.

Jerome M. Schneider has been running the fund for 4 years and currently receives a manager quality ranking of 60 (0=worst, 99=best). This fund offers only a moderate level of risk but investors looking for strong performance are still waiting.

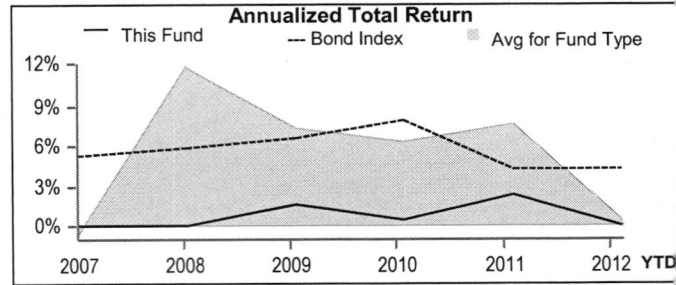

*PIMCO Germany Bond Index ETF (BUND)

C | **Fair**

Fund Family: PIMCO
Fund Type: Global
Inception Date: November 9, 2011

Major Rating Factors: Middle of the road best describes *PIMCO Germany Bond Index ETF whose TheStreet.com Investment Rating is currently a C (Fair). The fund currently has a performance rating of C- (Fair) based on an annualized return of 0.00% over the last three years and a total return of -0.14% year to date 2012. Factored into the performance evaluation is an expense ratio of 0.45% (very low).

The fund's risk rating is currently B+ (Good). It carries a beta of 0.00, meaning the fund's expected move will be 0.0% for every 10% move in the market. Volatility, as measured by both the semi-deviation and a drawdown factor, is considered very low. As of December 31, 2012, *PIMCO Germany Bond Index ETF traded at a premium of .41% above its net asset value, which is worse than its one-year historical average discount of .16%.

Lorenzo P. Pagani has been running the fund for 2 years and currently receives a manager quality ranking of 84 (0=worst, 99=best). If you desire an average level of risk, then this fund may be an option.

Data Date	Investment Rating	Net Assets ($Mil)	Price	Performance Rating/Pts	Total Return Y-T-D	Risk Rating/Pts
12-12	C	3.10	102.50	C- / 3.0	-0.14%	B+ / 9.2

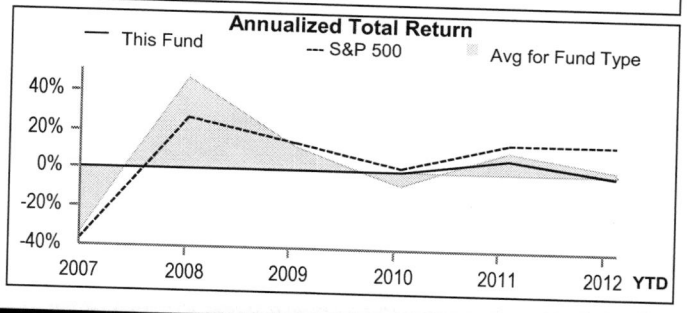

*PIMCO Intermediate Municipal Bd (MUNI)

C | **Fair**

Fund Family: PIMCO
Fund Type: Municipal - National
Inception Date: November 30, 2009

Major Rating Factors: Middle of the road best describes *PIMCO Intermediate Municipal Bd whose TheStreet.com Investment Rating is currently a C (Fair). The fund currently has a performance rating of C- (Fair) based on an annualized return of 5.52% over the last three years and a total return of 0.51% year to date 2012. Factored into the performance evaluation is an expense ratio of 0.35% (very low).

The fund's risk rating is currently B+ (Good). It carries a beta of 0.82, meaning the fund's expected move will be 8.2% for every 10% move in the market. Volatility, as measured by both the semi-deviation and a drawdown factor, is considered very low. As of December 31, 2012, *PIMCO Intermediate Municipal Bd traded at a discount of .44% below its net asset value, which is better than its one-year historical average premium of .05%.

Joseph P. Deane has been running the fund for 2 years and currently receives a manager quality ranking of 53 (0=worst, 99=best). If you desire an average level of risk, then this fund may be an option.

Data Date	Investment Rating	Net Assets ($Mil)	Price	Performance Rating/Pts	Total Return Y-T-D	Risk Rating/Pts
12-12	C	204.20	54.37	C- / 3.3	0.51%	B+ / 9.7
2011	B	98.60	53.12	C+ / 5.6	0.17%	B+ / 9.8
2010	C+	63.40	50.37	C- / 3.4	3.50%	B / 8.9

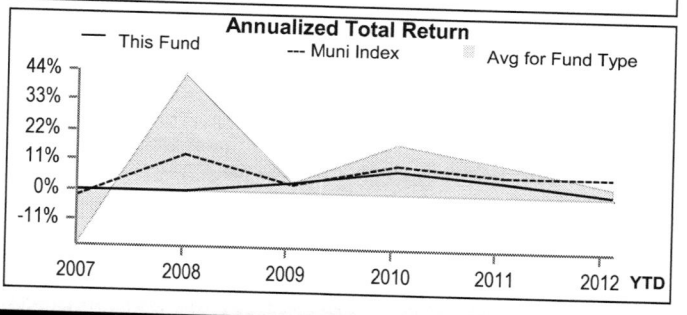

*PIMCO Short Term Muncipal Bond E (SMMU)

C- | **Fair**

Fund Family: PIMCO
Fund Type: Municipal - National
Inception Date: February 1, 2010

Major Rating Factors:
Disappointing performance is the major factor driving the C- (Fair) TheStreet.com Investment Rating for *PIMCO Short Term Municipal Bond E. The fund currently has a performance rating of D- (Weak) based on an annualized return of 0.00% over the last three years and a total return of -0.04% year to date 2012. Factored into the performance evaluation is an expense ratio of 0.35% (very low).

The fund's risk rating is currently B+ (Good). It carries a beta of 0.00, meaning the fund's expected move will be 0.0% for every 10% move in the market. Volatility, as measured by both the semi-deviation and a drawdown factor, is considered very low. As of December 31, 2012, *PIMCO Short Term Municipal Bond E traded at a discount of .04% below its net asset value, which is better than its one-year historical average premium of .02%.

Joseph P. Deane has been running the fund for 2 years and currently receives a manager quality ranking of 56 (0=worst, 99=best). This fund offers only a moderate level of risk but investors looking for strong performance are still waiting.

Data Date	Investment Rating	Net Assets ($Mil)	Price	Performance Rating/Pts	Total Return Y-T-D	Risk Rating/Pts
12-12	C-	58.40	50.42	D- / 1.5	-0.04%	B+ / 9.9
2011	C	38.30	50.44	D+ / 2.4	-0.10%	B+ / 9.9

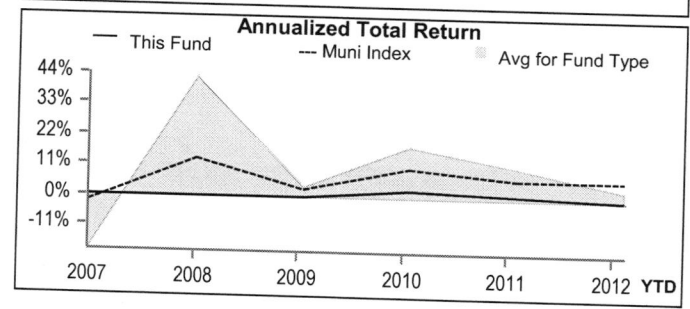

*PowerShares 1-30 Laddered Treasu (PLW)

C **Fair**

Fund Family: Invesco Powershares Capital Mgmt LL
Fund Type: US Government/Agency
Inception Date: October 11, 2007

Major Rating Factors: Middle of the road best describes *PowerShares 1-30 Laddered Treasu whose TheStreet.com Investment Rating is currently a C (Fair). The fund currently has a performance rating of C- (Fair) based on an annualized return of 9.61% over the last three years and a total return of -0.58% year to date 2012. Factored into the performance evaluation is an expense ratio of 0.25% (very low).

The fund's risk rating is currently B+ (Good). It carries a beta of 0.71, meaning the fund's expected move will be 7.1% for every 10% move in the market. Volatility, as measured by both the semi-deviation and a drawdown factor, is considered very low. As of December 31, 2012, *PowerShares 1-30 Laddered Treasu traded at a premium of .77% above its net asset value, which is worse than its one-year historical average premium of .06%.

Peter Hubbard has been running the fund for 6 years and currently receives a manager quality ranking of 60 (0=worst, 99=best). If you desire an average level of risk, then this fund may be an option.

Data Date	Investment Rating	Net Assets ($Mil)	Price	Performance Rating/Pts	Total Return Y-T-D	Risk Rating/Pts
12-12	C	167.00	32.60	C- / 3.2	-0.58%	B+ / 9.2
2011	C	0.00	32.47	C- / 4.2	-0.80%	B / 8.8
2010	B-	280.30	27.95	C / 4.4	9.11%	B / 8.3
2009	C-	89.22	26.57	E+ / 0.8	-9.60%	B / 8.5

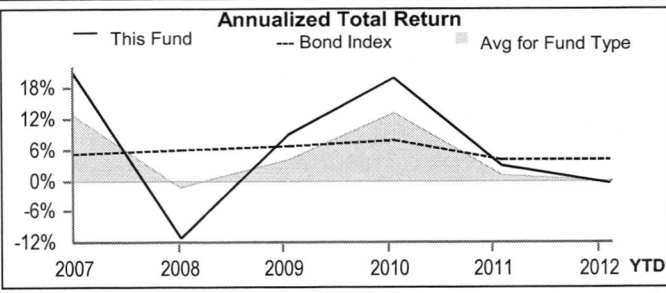

Annualized Total Return

*PowerShares Act US Real Estate (PSR)

B **Good**

Fund Family: Invesco Powershares Capital Mgmt LL
Fund Type: Growth and Income
Inception Date: November 19, 2008

Major Rating Factors: Strong performance is the major factor driving the B (Good) TheStreet.com Investment Rating for *PowerShares Act US Real Estate. The fund currently has a performance rating of B (Good) based on an annualized return of 19.25% over the last three years and a total return of 2.76% year to date 2012. Factored into the performance evaluation is an expense ratio of 0.80% (very low).

The fund's risk rating is currently B- (Good). It carries a beta of 0.98, meaning that its performance tracks fairly well with that of the overall stock market. Volatility, as measured by both the semi-deviation and a drawdown factor, is considered low. As of December 31, 2012, *PowerShares Act US Real Estate traded at a discount of 2.89% below its net asset value, which is better than its one-year historical average premium of .02%.

Joseph V. Rodriguez, Jr. has been running the fund for 5 years and currently receives a manager quality ranking of 82 (0=worst, 99=best). If you desire only a moderate level of risk and strong performance, then this fund is an excellent option.

Data Date	Investment Rating	Net Assets ($Mil)	Price	Performance Rating/Pts	Total Return Y-T-D	Risk Rating/Pts
12-12	B	17.20	56.83	B / 7.7	2.76%	B- / 7.8
2011	C+	20.10	50.42	B / 7.6	-0.09%	C+ / 6.8
2010	A	16.00	45.81	A / 9.4	26.87%	C+ / 6.6
2009	A+	2.62	37.42	A- / 9.1	29.23%	C+ / 6.5

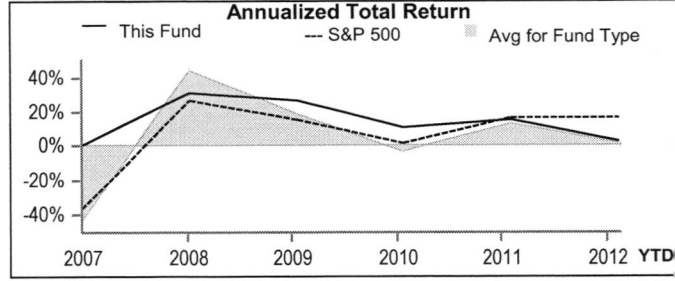

Annualized Total Return

*PowerShares Active Low Dur Fd (PLK)

C- **Fair**

Fund Family: Invesco Powershares Capital Mgmt LL
Fund Type: Growth and Income
Inception Date: April 8, 2008

Major Rating Factors:
Disappointing performance is the major factor driving the C- (Fair) TheStreet.com Investment Rating for *PowerShares Active Low Dur Fd. The fund currently has a performance rating of D (Weak) based on an annualized return of 1.03% over the last three years and a total return of 0.04% year to date 2012. Factored into the performance evaluation is an expense ratio of 0.29% (very low).

The fund's risk rating is currently B+ (Good). It carries a beta of -0.03, meaning the fund's expected move will be -0.3% for every 10% move in the market. Volatility, as measured by both the semi-deviation and a drawdown factor, is considered very low. As of December 31, 2012, *PowerShares Active Low Dur Fd traded at a discount of .55% below its net asset value, which is better than its one-year historical average discount of .24%.

Brian Schneider has been running the fund for 4 years and currently receives a manager quality ranking of 63 (0=worst, 99=best). This fund offers only a moderate level of risk but investors looking for strong performance are still waiting.

Data Date	Investment Rating	Net Assets ($Mil)	Price	Performance Rating/Pts	Total Return Y-T-D	Risk Rating/Pts
12-12	C-	7.60	25.25	D / 1.6	0.04%	B+ / 9.9
2011	C	7.60	25.43	D / 2.1	-0.51%	B+ / 9.9
2010	C+	10.10	25.33	D+ / 2.6	1.68%	B+ / 9.1
2009	C	6.32	25.32	D / 2.1	1.52%	B+ / 9.2

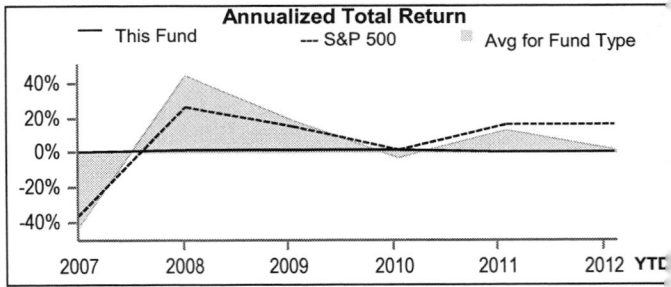

Annualized Total Return

*PowerShares Active Mega-Cap Fd (PMA)

Fund Family: Invesco Powershares Capital Mgmt LL
Fund Type: Growth
Inception Date: April 8, 2008

C **Fair**

Major Rating Factors: Middle of the road best describes *PowerShares Active Mega-Cap Fd whose TheStreet.com Investment Rating is currently a C (Fair). The fund currently has a performance rating of C (Fair) based on an annualized return of 10.96% over the last three years and a total return of 4.47% year to date 2012. Factored into the performance evaluation is an expense ratio of 0.75% (very low).

The fund's risk rating is currently B (Good). It carries a beta of 0.96, meaning that its performance tracks fairly well with that of the overall stock market. Volatility, as measured by both the semi-deviation and a drawdown factor, is considered low. As of December 31, 2012, *PowerShares Active Mega-Cap Fd traded at a discount of 4.25% below its net asset value, which is better than its one-year historical average premium of .04%.

Glen E. Murphy has been running the fund for 5 years and currently receives a manager quality ranking of 49 (0=worst, 99=best). If you desire an average level of risk, then this fund may be an option.

Data Date	Investment Rating	Net Assets ($Mil)	Price	Perfor- mance Rating/Pts	Total Return Y-T-D	Risk Rating/Pts
12-12	C	5.90	28.84	C / 4.7	4.47%	B / 8.2
2011	C+	5.30	26.36	C+ / 5.8	1.63%	B / 8.2
2010	A	3.70	24.90	A- / 9.0	11.55%	C+ / 6.4
2009	A	1.82	22.83	B / 8.0	22.63%	C+ / 6.4

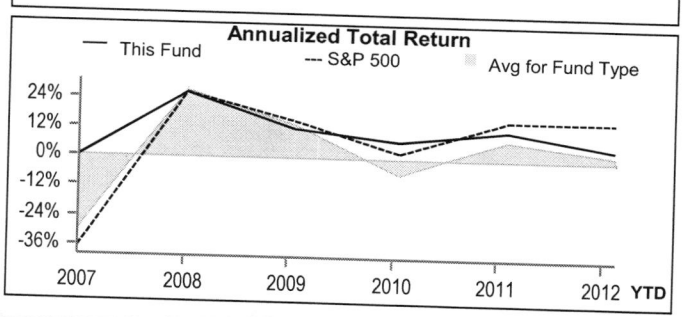

*PowerShares Aerospace & Defense (PPA)

Fund Family: Invesco Powershares Capital Mgmt LL
Fund Type: Income
Inception Date: October 26, 2005

C **Fair**

Major Rating Factors: Middle of the road best describes *PowerShares Aerospace & Defense whose TheStreet.com Investment Rating is currently a C (Fair). The fund currently has a performance rating of C (Fair) based on an annualized return of 8.17% over the last three years and a total return of 2.49% year to date 2012. Factored into the performance evaluation is an expense ratio of 0.66% (very low).

The fund's risk rating is currently B- (Good). It carries a beta of 1.06, meaning that its performance tracks fairly well with that of the overall stock market. Volatility, as measured by both the semi-deviation and a drawdown factor, is considered low. As of December 31, 2012, *PowerShares Aerospace & Defense traded at a discount of 2.56% below its net asset value, which is better than its one-year historical average discount of .09%.

Peter Hubbard has been running the fund for 6 years and currently receives a manager quality ranking of 31 (0=worst, 99=best). If you desire an average level of risk, then this fund may be an option.

Data Date	Investment Rating	Net Assets ($Mil)	Price	Perfor- mance Rating/Pts	Total Return Y-T-D	Risk Rating/Pts
12-12	C	46.20	20.94	C / 5.0	2.49%	B- / 7.9
2011	C-	53.70	18.20	C- / 3.7	1.21%	B- / 7.7
2010	D+	110.40	18.71	D+ / 2.3	10.93%	C+ / 5.8
2009	C-	116.43	17.07	C- / 3.0	18.16%	C+ / 5.9

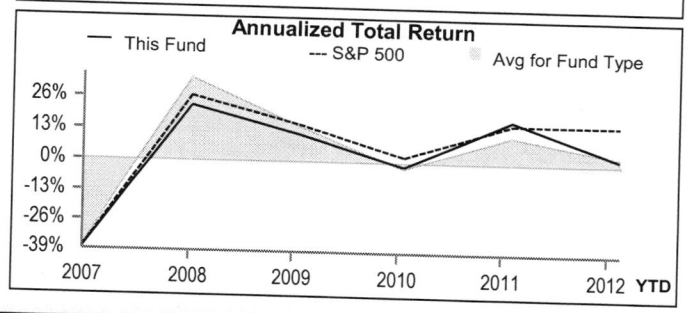

*PowerShares Build America Bond (BAB)

Fund Family: Invesco Powershares Capital Mgmt LL
Fund Type: US Government/Agency
Inception Date: November 17, 2009

C+ **Fair**

Major Rating Factors: Middle of the road best describes *PowerShares Build America Bond whose TheStreet.com Investment Rating is currently a C+ (Fair). The fund currently has a performance rating of C (Fair) based on an annualized return of 12.68% over the last three years and a total return of -0.40% year to date 2012. Factored into the performance evaluation is an expense ratio of 0.28% (very low).

The fund's risk rating is currently B+ (Good). It carries a beta of 0.47, meaning the fund's expected move will be 4.7% for every 10% move in the market. Volatility, as measured by both the semi-deviation and a drawdown factor, is considered very low. As of December 31, 2012, *PowerShares Build America Bond traded at a premium of .47% above its net asset value, which is worse than its one-year historical average premium of .10%.

Peter Hubbard has been running the fund for 4 years and currently receives a manager quality ranking of 84 (0=worst, 99=best). If you desire an average level of risk, then this fund may be an option.

Data Date	Investment Rating	Net Assets ($Mil)	Price	Perfor- mance Rating/Pts	Total Return Y-T-D	Risk Rating/Pts
12-12	C+	1,124.00	30.24	C / 4.6	-0.40%	B+ / 9.3
2011	B+	777.10	28.70	B- / 7.2	-0.42%	B+ / 9.4
2010	B-	606.70	25.08	C- / 4.0	8.81%	B / 8.6

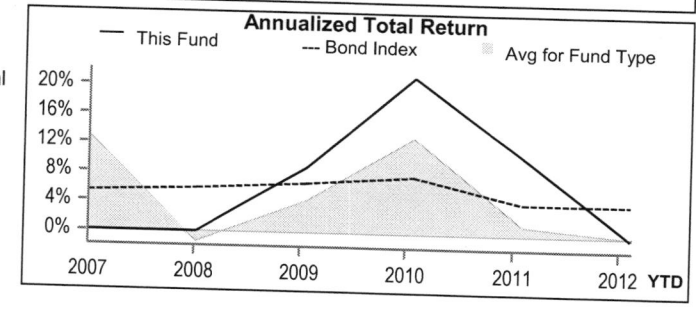

* Denotes ETF Fund

*PowerShares Buyback Achievers (PKW)

B-   **Good**

Fund Family: Invesco Powershares Capital Mgmt LL
Fund Type: Income
Inception Date: December 20, 2006

Major Rating Factors: *PowerShares Buyback Achievers receives a TheStreet.com Investment Rating of B- (Good). The fund currently has a performance rating of C+ (Fair) based on an annualized return of 14.44% over the last three years and a total return of 3.42% year to date 2012. Factored into the performance evaluation is an expense ratio of 0.71% (very low).

The fund's risk rating is currently B (Good). It carries a beta of 0.89, meaning the fund's expected move will be 8.9% for every 10% move in the market. Volatility, as measured by both the semi-deviation and a drawdown factor, is considered low. As of December 31, 2012, *PowerShares Buyback Achievers traded at a discount of 3.25% below its net asset value, which is better than its one-year historical average premium of .07%.

Peter Hubbard has been running the fund for 6 years and currently receives a manager quality ranking of 76 (0=worst, 99=best). If you desire an average level of risk, then this fund may be an option.

Data Date	Investment Rating	Net Assets ($Mil)	Price	Performance Rating/Pts	Total Return Y-T-D	Risk Rating/Pts
12-12	B-	214.30	29.80	C+ / 6.3	3.42%	B / 8.5
2011	B-	74.20	26.53	C+ / 6.9	1.06%	B / 8.1
2010	C+	35.20	24.32	C+ / 6.1	18.11%	C / 5.2
2009	C-	27.46	20.70	D+ / 2.7	29.72%	C+ / 6.2

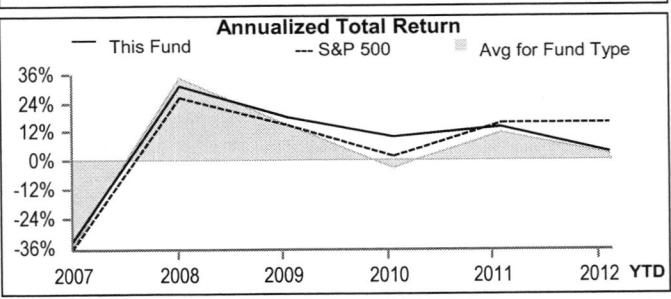

*PowerShares CEF Inc Composite Po (PCEF)

B   **Good**

Fund Family: Invesco Powershares Capital Mgmt LL
Fund Type: Income
Inception Date: February 18, 2010

Major Rating Factors: *PowerShares CEF Inc Composite Po receives a TheStreet.com Investment Rating of B (Good). The fund currently has a performance rating of C+ (Fair) based on an annualized return of 0.00% over the last three years and a total return of 3.48% year to date 2012. Factored into the performance evaluation is an expense ratio of 0.50% (very low).

The fund's risk rating is currently B (Good). It carries a beta of 0.00, meaning the fund's expected move will be 0.0% for every 10% move in the market. Volatility, as measured by both the semi-deviation and a drawdown factor, is considered low. As of December 31, 2012, *PowerShares CEF Inc Composite Po traded at a discount of 3.38% below its net asset value, which is better than its one-year historical average premium of .09%.

This fund has been team managed for 3 years and currently receives a manager quality ranking of 79 (0=worst, 99=best). If you desire an average level of risk, then this fund may be an option.

Data Date	Investment Rating	Net Assets ($Mil)	Price	Performance Rating/Pts	Total Return Y-T-D	Risk Rating/Pts
12-12	B	394.30	25.14	C+ / 6.7	3.48%	B / 8.6
2011	C-	233.40	23.51	D+ / 2.6	1.61%	B / 8.6

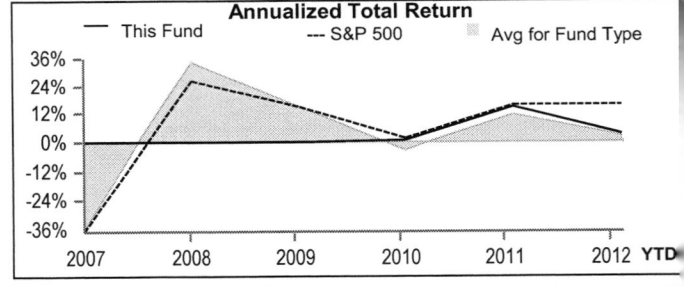

*PowerShares Chinese YDS Bd (DSUM)

C+   **Fair**

Fund Family: Invesco Powershares Capital Mgmt LL
Fund Type: Global
Inception Date: September 23, 2011

Major Rating Factors: Middle of the road best describes *PowerShares Chinese YDS Bd whose TheStreet.com Investment Rating is currently a C+ (Fair). The fund currently has a performance rating of C- (Fair) based on an annualized return of 0.00% over the last three years and a total return of 1.23% year to date 2012.

The fund's risk rating is currently B+ (Good). It carries a beta of 0.00, meaning the fund's expected move will be 0.0% for every 10% move in the market. Volatility, as measured by both the semi-deviation and a drawdown factor, is considered very low. As of December 31, 2012, *PowerShares Chinese YDS Bd traded at a discount of .44% below its net asset value, which is better than its one-year historical average premium of .63%.

Peter Hubbard has been running the fund for 2 years and currently receives a manager quality ranking of 87 (0=worst, 99=best). If you desire an average level of risk, then this fund may be an option.

Data Date	Investment Rating	Net Assets ($Mil)	Price	Performance Rating/Pts	Total Return Y-T-D	Risk Rating/Pts
12-12	C+	35.70	24.79	C- / 3.8	1.23%	B+ / 9.8

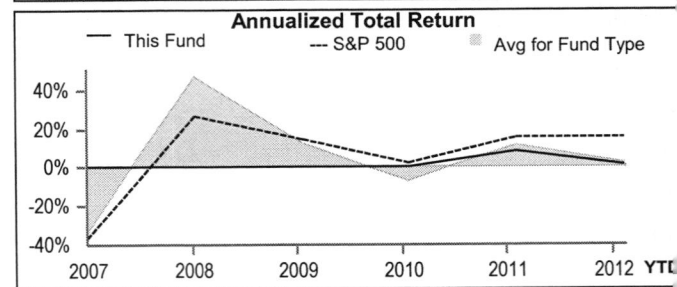

*PowerShares Cleantech Portfolio (PZD)   D   Weak

Fund Family: Invesco Powershares Capital Mgmt LL
Fund Type: Income
Inception Date: October 24, 2006

Major Rating Factors:
Disappointing performance is the major factor driving the D (Weak) TheStreet.com Investment Rating for *PowerShares Cleantech Portfolio. The fund currently has a performance rating of D (Weak) based on an annualized return of -0.36% over the last three years and a total return of 3.94% year to date 2012. Factored into the performance evaluation is an expense ratio of 0.67% (very low).

The fund's risk rating is currently C+ (Fair). It carries a beta of 1.37, meaning it is expected to move 13.7% for every 10% move in the market. Volatility, as measured by both the semi-deviation and a drawdown factor, is considered low. As of December 31, 2012, *PowerShares Cleantech Portfolio traded at a discount of 4.23% below its net asset value, which is better than its one-year historical average discount of .41%.

Peter Hubbard has been running the fund for 6 years and currently receives a manager quality ranking of 8 (0=worst, 99=best). This fund offers only a moderate level of risk but investors looking for strong performance are still waiting.

Data Date	Investment Rating	Net Assets ($Mil)	Price	Perfor-mance Rating/Pts	Total Return Y-T-D	Risk Rating/Pts
12-12	D	66.10	23.12	D / 2.1	3.94%	C+ / 6.8
2011	D	97.30	21.51	D / 2.2	0.69%	C+ / 6.5
2010	D-	147.10	26.40	D- / 1.5	7.61%	C / 4.4
2009	D+	111.67	24.54	C- / 3.9	30.82%	C / 4.6

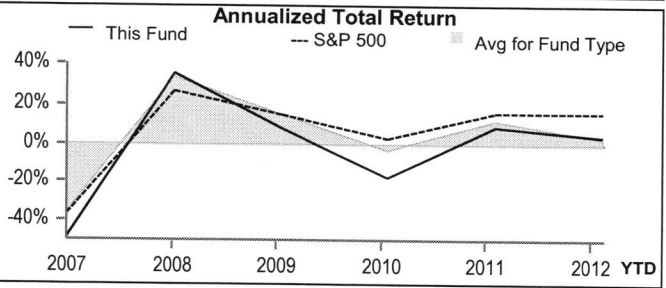

*PowerShares Convertible Secs Por (CVRT)   C   Fair

Fund Family: Invesco Powershares Capital Mgmt LL
Fund Type: Growth and Income
Inception Date: May 26, 2011

Major Rating Factors: Middle of the road best describes *PowerShares Convertible Secs Por whose TheStreet.com Investment Rating is currently a C (Fair). The fund currently has a performance rating of C (Fair) based on an annualized return of 0.00% over the last three years and a total return of 1.64% year to date 2012. Factored into the performance evaluation is an expense ratio of 0.35% (very low).

The fund's risk rating is currently B (Good). It carries a beta of 0.00, meaning the fund's expected move will be 0.0% for every 10% move in the market. Volatility, as measured by both the semi-deviation and a drawdown factor, is considered low. As of December 31, 2012, *PowerShares Convertible Secs Por traded at a discount of 3.01% below its net asset value, which is better than its one-year historical average discount of .65%.

Peter Hubbard has been running the fund for 2 years and currently receives a manager quality ranking of 20 (0=worst, 99=best). If you desire an average level of risk, then this fund may be an option.

Data Date	Investment Rating	Net Assets ($Mil)	Price	Perfor-mance Rating/Pts	Total Return Y-T-D	Risk Rating/Pts
12-12	C	9.60	23.84	C / 4.4	1.64%	B / 8.6

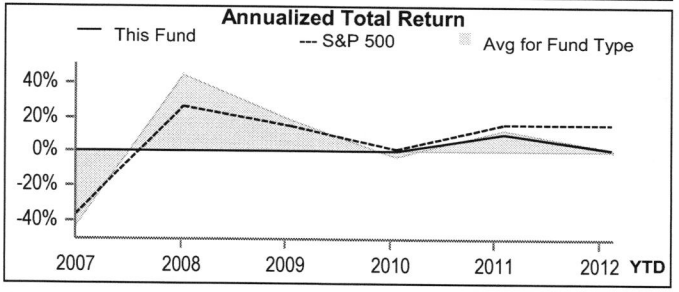

*PowerShares DB 3x German Bd Fut (BUNT)   D-   Weak

Fund Family: DB Commodity Services LLC
Fund Type: Global
Inception Date: March 22, 2011

Major Rating Factors:
Disappointing performance is the major factor driving the D- (Weak) TheStreet.com Investment Rating for *PowerShares DB 3x German Bd Fut. The fund currently has a performance rating of D (Weak) based on an annualized return of 0.00% over the last three years and a total return of -6.19% year to date 2012.

The fund's risk rating is currently C (Fair). It carries a beta of 0.00, meaning the fund's expected move will be 0.0% for every 10% move in the market. Volatility, as measured by both the semi-deviation and a drawdown factor, is considered average. As of December 31, 2012, *PowerShares DB 3x German Bd Fut traded at a premium of 6.36% above its net asset value.

This fund has been team managed for 2 years and currently receives a manager quality ranking of 96 (0=worst, 99=best). This fund offers an average level of risk but investors looking for strong performance will be frustrated.

Data Date	Investment Rating	Net Assets ($Mil)	Price	Perfor-mance Rating/Pts	Total Return Y-T-D	Risk Rating/Pts
12-12	D-	0.00	34.64	D / 1.6	-6.19%	C / 5.4

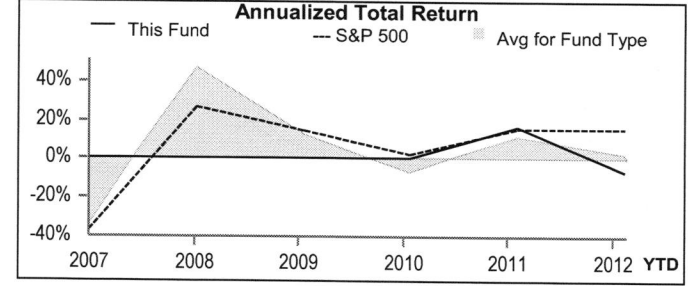

*PowerShares DB 3x Inv Jpnese Gvt (JGBD)   D-   Weak

Fund Family: DB Commodity Services LLC
Fund Type: Global
Inception Date: November 8, 2011

Major Rating Factors:
Disappointing performance is the major factor driving the D- (Weak) TheStreet.com Investment Rating for *PowerShares DB 3x Inv Jpnese Gvt. The fund currently has a performance rating of D- (Weak) based on an annualized return of 0.00% over the last three years and a total return of 0.42% year to date 2012.

The fund's risk rating is currently C (Fair). It carries a beta of 0.00, meaning the fund's expected move will be 0.0% for every 10% move in the market. Volatility, as measured by both the semi-deviation and a drawdown factor, is considered average. As of December 31, 2012, *PowerShares DB 3x Inv Jpnese Gvt traded at a discount of 4.41% below its net asset value, which is better than its one-year historical average discount of 2.89%.

This fund has been team managed for 2 years and currently receives a manager quality ranking of 19 (0=worst, 99=best). This fund offers an average level of risk but investors looking for strong performance will be frustrated.

Data Date	Investment Rating	Net Assets ($Mil)	Price	Performance Rating/Pts	Total Return Y-T-D	Risk Rating/Pts
12-12	D-	0.00	18.63	D- / 1.0	0.42%	C / 5.5

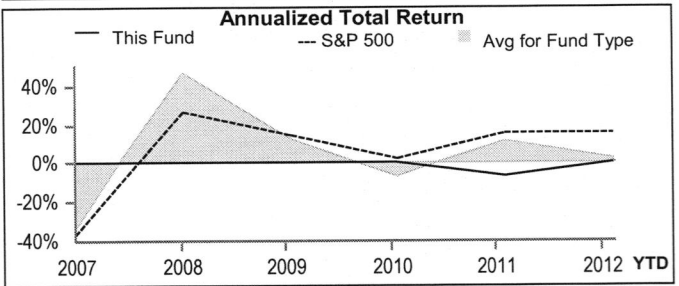

Annualized Total Return

---

*PowerShares DB 3x Itn Trs B Fut (ITLT)   C+   Fair

Fund Family: DB Commodity Services LLC
Fund Type: Global
Inception Date: March 22, 2011

Major Rating Factors:
Exceptional performance is the major factor driving the C+ (Fair) TheStreet.com Investment Rating for *PowerShares DB 3x Itn Trs B Fut. The fund currently has a performance rating of A+ (Excellent) based on an annualized return of 0.00% over the last three years and a total return of 8.34% year to date 2012.

The fund's risk rating is currently C- (Fair). It carries a beta of 0.00, meaning the fund's expected move will be 0.0% for every 10% move in the market. Volatility, as measured by both the semi-deviation and a drawdown factor, is considered average. As of December 31, 2012, *PowerShares DB 3x Itn Trs B Fut traded at a premium of 23.51% above its net asset value, which is worse than its one-year historical average premium of 6.18%.

This fund has been team managed for 2 years and currently receives a manager quality ranking of 99 (0=worst, 99=best). If you desire an average level of risk and strong performance, then this fund is a good option.

Data Date	Investment Rating	Net Assets ($Mil)	Price	Performance Rating/Pts	Total Return Y-T-D	Risk Rating/Pts
12-12	C+	0.00	30.05	A+ / 9.9	8.34%	C- / 3.8

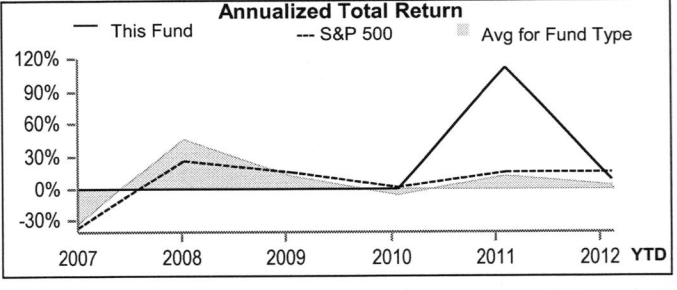

Annualized Total Return

---

*PowerShares DB 3x Lg 25+ Yr Tr E (LBND)   E+   Very Weak

Fund Family: DB Commodity Services LLC
Fund Type: US Government/Agency
Inception Date: June 28, 2010

Major Rating Factors:
Very poor performance is the major factor driving the E+ (Very Weak) TheStreet.com Investment Rating for *PowerShares DB 3x Lg 25+ Yr Tr E. The fund currently has a performance rating of E+ (Very Weak) based on an annualized return of 0.00% over the last three years and a total return of -3.23% year to date 2012.

The fund's risk rating is currently C (Fair). It carries a beta of 0.00, meaning the fund's expected move will be 0.0% for every 10% move in the market. Volatility, as measured by both the semi-deviation and a drawdown factor, is considered average. As of December 31, 2012, *PowerShares DB 3x Lg 25+ Yr Tr E traded at a premium of 4.22% above its net asset value, which is worse than its one-year historical average premium of .01%.

This fund has been team managed for 3 years and currently receives a manager quality ranking of 14 (0=worst, 99=best). This fund offers an average level of risk but investors looking for strong performance will be frustrated.

Data Date	Investment Rating	Net Assets ($Mil)	Price	Performance Rating/Pts	Total Return Y-T-D	Risk Rating/Pts
12-12	E+	0.00	47.22	E+ / 0.7	-3.23%	C / 4.8
2011	B	0.00	45.77	A+ / 9.9	-7.78%	C / 5.4

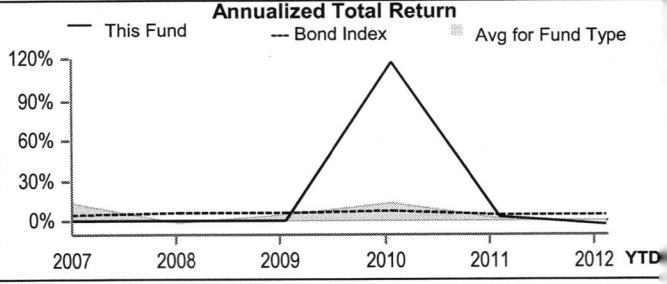

Annualized Total Return

---

*PowerShares DB 3x Lng USD I Fut (UUPT)

Fund Family: DB Commodity Services LLC
Fund Type: Growth and Income
Inception Date: May 23, 2011

E+   Very Weak

Major Rating Factors:
Very poor performance is the major factor driving the E+ (Very Weak) TheStreet.com Investment Rating for *PowerShares DB 3x Lng USD I Fut. The fund currently has a performance rating of E (Very Weak) based on an annualized return of 0.00% over the last three years and a total return of -1.38% year to date 2012.

The fund's risk rating is currently C (Fair). It carries a beta of 0.00, meaning the fund's expected move will be 0.0% for every 10% move in the market. Volatility, as measured by both the semi-deviation and a drawdown factor, is considered average. As of December 31, 2012, *PowerShares DB 3x Lng USD I Fut traded at a premium of 1.21% above its net asset value, which is worse than its one-year historical average discount of .16%.

This fund has been team managed for 2 years and currently receives a manager quality ranking of 96 (0=worst, 99=best). This fund offers an average level of risk but investors looking for strong performance will be frustrated.

Data Date	Investment Rating	Net Assets ($Mil)	Price	Performance Rating/Pts	Total Return Y-T-D	Risk Rating/Pts
12-12	E+	0.00	20.00	E / 0.5	-1.38%	C / 5.1

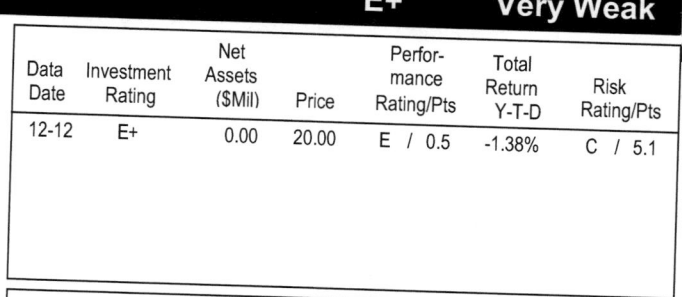

Annualized Total Return

*PowerShares DB 3x Sh 25+ Yr Tr E (SBND)

Fund Family: DB Commodity Services LLC
Fund Type: US Government/Agency
Inception Date: June 28, 2010

E   Very Weak

Major Rating Factors: *PowerShares DB 3x Sh 25+ Yr Tr E has adopted a very risky asset allocation strategy and currently receives an overall TheStreet.com Investment Rating of E (Very Weak). The fund has a high level of volatility, as measured by both semi-deviation and drawdown factors. It carries a beta of 0.00, meaning the fund's expected move will be 0.0% for every 10% move in the market. As of December 31, 2012, *PowerShares DB 3x Sh 25+ Yr Tr E traded at a discount of 3.86% below its net asset value, which is better than its one-year historical average discount of .15%. Unfortunately, the high level of risk (D, Weak) failed to pay off as investors endured poor performance.

The fund's performance rating is currently D (Weak). It has registered an annualized return of 0.00% over the last three years and is up 3.21% year to date 2012.

This fund has been team managed for 3 years and currently receives a manager quality ranking of 23 (0=worst, 99=best). If you can tolerate very high levels of risk in the hope of improved future returns, holding this fund may be an option.

Data Date	Investment Rating	Net Assets ($Mil)	Price	Performance Rating/Pts	Total Return Y-T-D	Risk Rating/Pts
12-12	E	0.10	7.47	D / 1.7	3.21%	D / 1.9
2011	E-	0.00	8.97	E- / 0	7.80%	D / 1.9

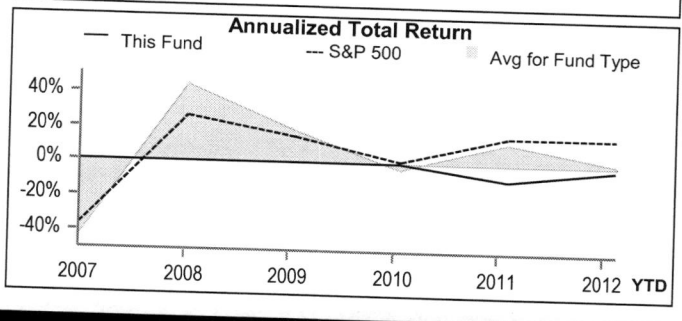

Annualized Total Return

*PowerShares DB 3x Sht USD I Fut (UDNT)

Fund Family: DB Commodity Services LLC
Fund Type: Growth and Income
Inception Date: May 23, 2011

D   Weak

Major Rating Factors: *PowerShares DB 3x Sht USD I Fut receives a TheStreet.com Investment Rating of D (Weak). The fund currently has a performance rating of C (Fair) based on an annualized return of 0.00% over the last three years and a total return of 0.41% year to date 2012.

The fund's risk rating is currently C- (Fair). It carries a beta of 0.00, meaning the fund's expected move will be 0.0% for every 10% move in the market. Volatility, as measured by both the semi-deviation and a drawdown factor, is considered average. As of December 31, 2012, *PowerShares DB 3x Sht USD I Fut traded at a discount of .62% below its net asset value, which is better than its one-year historical average discount of .04%.

This fund has been team managed for 2 years and currently receives a manager quality ranking of 5 (0=worst, 99=best). If you desire an average level of risk, then this fund may be an option.

Data Date	Investment Rating	Net Assets ($Mil)	Price	Performance Rating/Pts	Total Return Y-T-D	Risk Rating/Pts
12-12	D	0.00	17.71	C / 5.1	0.41%	C- / 4.0

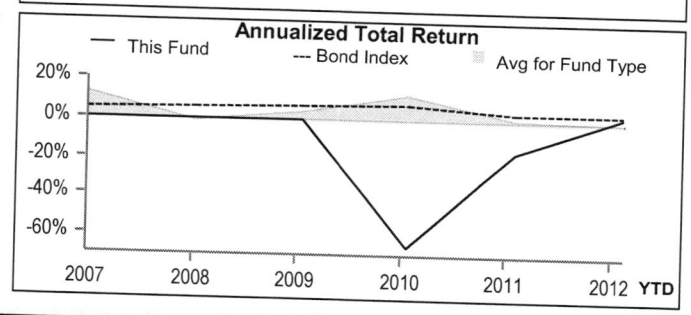

Annualized Total Return

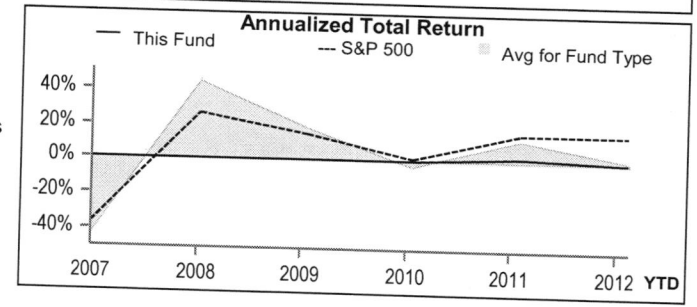

* Denotes ETF Fund

*PowerShares DB Agri Double Long (DAG)

E   **Very Weak**

Fund Family: Deutsche Bank AG (London)
Fund Type: Growth
Inception Date: April 15, 2008

Major Rating Factors:
Disappointing performance is the major factor driving the E (Very Weak) TheStreet.com Investment Rating for *PowerShares DB Agri Double Long. The fund currently has a performance rating of D- (Weak) based on an annualized return of 4.25% over the last three years and a total return of -4.66% year to date 2012. Factored into the performance evaluation is an expense ratio of 0.75% (very low).

The fund's risk rating is currently C- (Fair). It carries a beta of 1.43, meaning it is expected to move 14.3% for every 10% move in the market. Volatility, as measured by both the semi-deviation and a drawdown factor, is considered average. As of December 31, 2012, *PowerShares DB Agri Double Long traded at a premium of 4.80% above its net asset value, which is worse than its one-year historical average premium of .75%.

This fund has been team managed for 5 years and currently receives a manager quality ranking of 12 (0=worst, 99=best). This fund offers an average level of risk but investors looking for strong performance will be frustrated.

Data Date	Investment Rating	Net Assets ($Mil)	Price	Performance Rating/Pts	Total Return Y-T-D	Risk Rating/Pts
12-12	E	87.09	11.79	D- / 1.5	-4.66%	C- / 3.0
2011	E+	87.09	10.79	D- / 1.5	-0.83%	C- / 3.1
2010	C	87.09	14.07	A+ / 9.9	30.88%	D- / 1.2
2009	C-	87.09	10.75	B- / 7.4	5.29%	D / 1.8

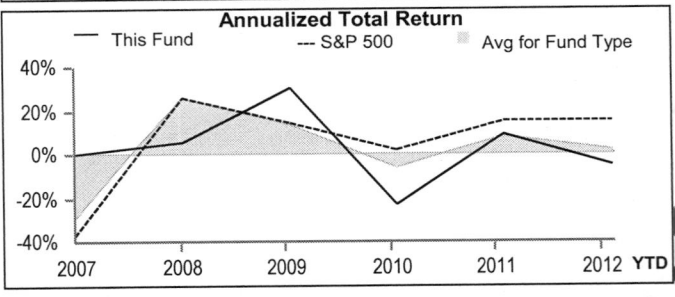

*PowerShares DB Agri Double Sht (AGA)

E-   **Very Weak**

Fund Family: Deutsche Bank AG (London)
Fund Type: Growth
Inception Date: April 15, 2008

Major Rating Factors: *PowerShares DB Agri Double Sht has adopted a very risky asset allocation strategy and currently receives an overall TheStreet.com Investment Rating of E- (Very Weak). The fund has a high level of volatility, as measured by both semi-deviation and drawdown factors. It carries a beta of -1.46, meaning the fund's expected move will be -14.6% for every 10% move in the market. As of December 31, 2012, *PowerShares DB Agri Double Sht traded at a discount of 5.44% below its net asset value, which is better than its one-year historical average premium of 8.21%. Unfortunately, the high level of risk (D, Weak) failed to pay off as investors endured very poor performance.

The fund's performance rating is currently E (Very Weak). It has registered an annualized return of -25.49% over the last three years and is up 7.37% year to date 2012. Factored into the performance evaluation is an expense ratio of 0.75% (very low).

This fund has been team managed for 5 years and currently receives a manager quality ranking of 7 (0=worst, 99=best). If you can tolerate very high levels of risk in the hope of improved future returns, holding this fund may be an option.

Data Date	Investment Rating	Net Assets ($Mil)	Price	Performance Rating/Pts	Total Return Y-T-D	Risk Rating/Pts
12-12	E-	3.98	13.03	E / 0.4	7.37%	D / 1.9
2011	E-	3.98	17.79	E+ / 0.9	3.42%	D / 1.9
2010	E-	3.98	18.00	E- / 0	-47.14%	D / 1.7
2009	E	3.98	34.05	E / 0.4	-19.90%	C- / 3.5

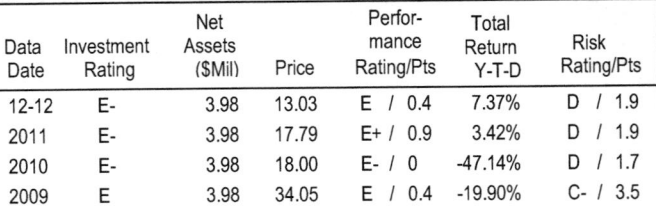

*PowerShares DB Agriculture Fund (DBA)

D   **Weak**

Fund Family: DB Commodity Services LLC
Fund Type: Income
Inception Date: January 3, 2007

Major Rating Factors:
Disappointing performance is the major factor driving the D (Weak) TheStreet.com Investment Rating for *PowerShares DB Agriculture Fund. The fund currently has a performance rating of D- (Weak) based on an annualized return of 2.09% over the last three years and a total return of -0.64% year to date 2012. Factored into the performance evaluation is an expense ratio of 0.92% (low).

The fund's risk rating is currently B- (Good). It carries a beta of 0.60, meaning the fund's expected move will be 6.0% for every 10% move in the market. Volatility, as measured by both the semi-deviation and a drawdown factor, is considered low. As of December 31, 2012, *PowerShares DB Agriculture Fund traded at a premium of .83% above its net asset value, which is worse than its one-year historical average discount of .04%.

Benjamin A. Pace, III currently receives a manager quality ranking of 25 (0=worst, 99=best). This fund offers only a moderate level of risk but investors looking for strong performance are still waiting.

Data Date	Investment Rating	Net Assets ($Mil)	Price	Performance Rating/Pts	Total Return Y-T-D	Risk Rating/Pts
12-12	D	1,661.30	27.95	D- / 1.5	-0.64%	B- / 7.5
2011	D+	2,034.30	28.88	D / 1.8	-1.84%	B / 8.1
2010	C	2,712.70	32.35	C / 5.3	22.35%	C+ / 5.6
2009	C-	2,327.02	26.44	C- / 4.1	1.15%	C+ / 6.0

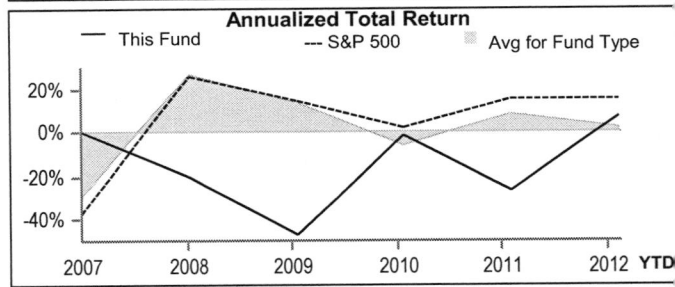

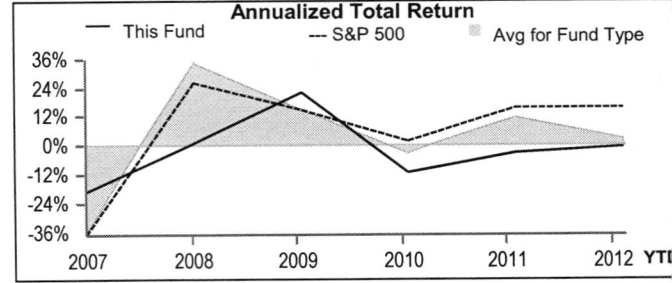

*PowerShares DB Agriculture Long (AGF)

D-   **Weak**

Fund Family: Deutsche Bank AG (London)
Fund Type: Growth
Inception Date: April 15, 2008

Major Rating Factors:
Disappointing performance is the major factor driving the D- (Weak) TheStreet.com Investment Rating for *PowerShares DB Agriculture Long. The fund currently has a performance rating of D (Weak) based on an annualized return of 5.05% over the last three years and a total return of -1.45% year to date 2012. Factored into the performance evaluation is an expense ratio of 0.75% (very low).

The fund's risk rating is currently C (Fair). It carries a beta of 0.80, meaning the fund's expected move will be 8.0% for every 10% move in the market. Volatility, as measured by both the semi-deviation and a drawdown factor, is considered average. As of December 31, 2012, *PowerShares DB Agriculture Long traded at a premium of 1.52% above its net asset value, which is worse than its one-year historical average premium of .43%.

This fund has been team managed for 5 years and currently receives a manager quality ranking of 27 (0=worst, 99=best). This fund offers an average level of risk but investors looking for strong performance will be frustrated.

Data Date	Investment Rating	Net Assets ($Mil)	Price	Performance Rating/Pts	Total Return Y-T-D	Risk Rating/Pts
12-12	D-	4.96	20.00	D / 2.1	-1.45%	C / 4.6
2011	E+	4.96	18.71	D / 1.9	-1.92%	C- / 4.1
2010	C+	4.96	20.96	A+ / 9.6	19.57%	D+ / 2.5
2009	D	4.96	17.53	C / 4.5	1.15%	C- / 3.2

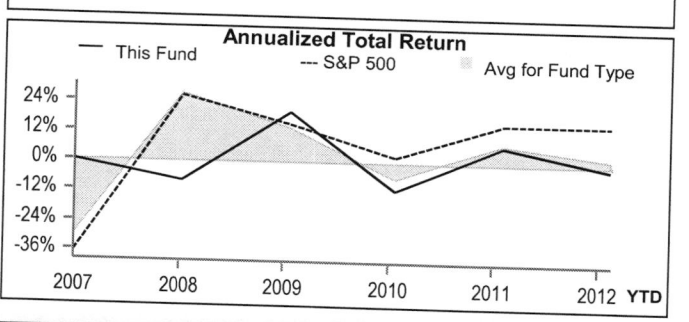

*PowerShares DB Agriculture Sht E (ADZ)

E   **Very Weak**

Fund Family: Deutsche Bank AG (London)
Fund Type: Growth
Inception Date: April 15, 2008

Major Rating Factors: *PowerShares DB Agriculture Sht E has adopted a risky asset allocation strategy and currently receives an overall TheStreet.com Investment Rating of E (Very Weak). The fund has an above average level of volatility, as measured by both semi-deviation and drawdown factors. It carries a beta of -0.78, meaning the fund's expected move will be -7.8% for every 10% move in the market. As of December 31, 2012, *PowerShares DB Agriculture Sht E traded at a discount of 1.89% below its net asset value, which is better than its one-year historical average premium of .69%. Unfortunately, the high level of risk (D+, Weak) failed to pay off as investors endured very poor performance.

The fund's performance rating is currently E+ (Very Weak). It has registered an annualized return of -12.68% over the last three years and is up 0.52% year to date 2012. Factored into the performance evaluation is an expense ratio of 0.75% (very low).

This fund has been team managed for 5 years and currently receives a manager quality ranking of 24 (0=worst, 99=best). If you can tolerate high levels of risk in the hope of improved future returns, holding this fund may be an option.

Data Date	Investment Rating	Net Assets ($Mil)	Price	Performance Rating/Pts	Total Return Y-T-D	Risk Rating/Pts
12-12	E	3.34	21.34	E+ / 0.7	0.52%	D+ / 2.7
2011	E+	3.34	24.38	D- / 1.4	1.61%	C- / 3.1
2010	E	3.34	23.93	E- / 0.2	-23.05%	C- / 3.1
2009	E+	3.34	31.10	E+ / 0.6	-8.02%	C / 4.4

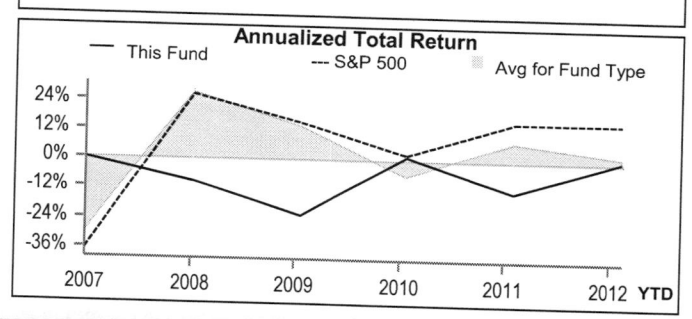

*PowerShares DB Base Metals Fund (DBB)

D-   **Weak**

Fund Family: DB Commodity Services LLC
Fund Type: Income
Inception Date: January 3, 2007

Major Rating Factors:
Disappointing performance is the major factor driving the D- (Weak) TheStreet.com Investment Rating for *PowerShares DB Base Metals Fund. The fund currently has a performance rating of D- (Weak) based on an annualized return of -5.41% over the last three years and a total return of -1.19% year to date 2012. Factored into the performance evaluation is an expense ratio of 0.77% (very low).

The fund's risk rating is currently C+ (Fair). It carries a beta of 1.37, meaning it is expected to move 13.7% for every 10% move in the market. Volatility, as measured by both the semi-deviation and a drawdown factor, is considered low. As of December 31, 2012, *PowerShares DB Base Metals Fund traded at a premium of 1.47% above its net asset value, which is worse than its one-year historical average discount of .03%.

Benjamin A. Pace, III currently receives a manager quality ranking of 6 (0=worst, 99=best). This fund offers only a moderate level of risk but investors looking for strong performance are still waiting.

Data Date	Investment Rating	Net Assets ($Mil)	Price	Performance Rating/Pts	Total Return Y-T-D	Risk Rating/Pts
12-12	D-	310.00	19.28	D- / 1.0	-1.19%	C+ / 6.5
2011	C-	366.90	18.65	C- / 3.4	0.70%	B- / 7.0
2010	C	511.70	24.43	C+ / 6.1	8.58%	C / 4.4
2009	A	441.46	22.50	A+ / 9.8	81.01%	C / 4.9

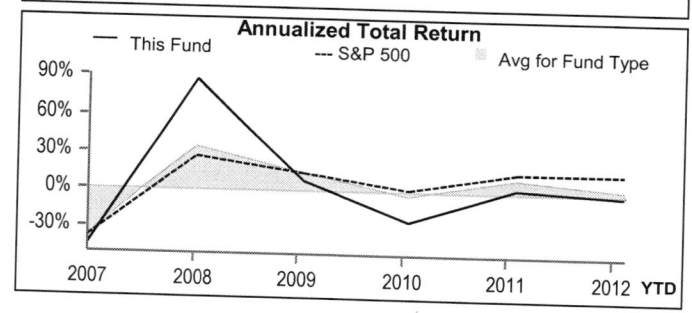

*PowerShares DB Base Metals Sht E (BOS)

E+   Very Weak

Fund Family: Deutsche Bank AG (London)
Fund Type: Precious Metals
Inception Date: June 16, 2008

Major Rating Factors:
Disappointing performance is the major factor driving the E+ (Very Weak) TheStreet.com Investment Rating for *PowerShares DB Base Metals Sht E. The fund currently has a performance rating of D- (Weak) based on an annualized return of -2.79% over the last three years and a total return of -1.33% year to date 2012. Factored into the performance evaluation is an expense ratio of 0.75% (very low).

The fund's risk rating is currently C- (Fair). It carries a beta of -0.55, meaning the fund's expected move will be -5.5% for every 10% move in the market. Volatility, as measured by both the semi-deviation and a drawdown factor, is considered average. As of December 31, 2012, *PowerShares DB Base Metals Sht E traded at a premium of .05% above its net asset value, which is worse than its one-year historical average discount of .27%.

This fund has been team managed for 5 years and currently receives a manager quality ranking of 82 (0=worst, 99=best). This fund offers an average level of risk but investors looking for strong performance will be frustrated.

Data Date	Investment Rating	Net Assets ($Mil)	Price	Performance Rating/Pts	Total Return Y-T-D	Risk Rating/Pts
12-12	E+	2.52	20.34	D- / 1.0	-1.33%	C- / 3.9
2011	E	2.52	22.14	D- / 1.2	0.29%	D / 2.0
2010	E-	2.52	18.49	E / 0.4	-13.44%	D / 2.0
2009	E-	2.52	21.36	E- / 0.2	-49.29%	D+ / 2.5

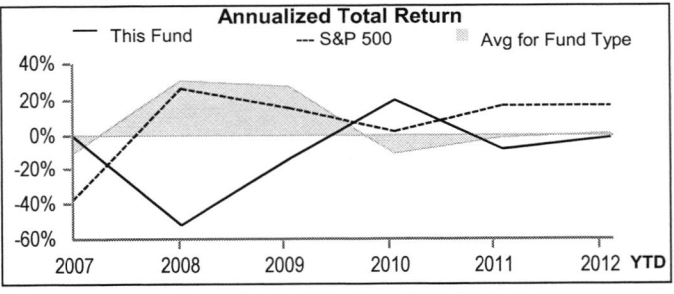

Annualized Total Return

---

*PowerShares DB Base Mtls Dbl Lg (BDD)

E-   Very Weak

Fund Family: Deutsche Bank AG (London)
Fund Type: Precious Metals
Inception Date: June 16, 2008

Major Rating Factors: *PowerShares DB Base Mtls Dbl Lg has adopted a risky asset allocation strategy and currently receives an overall TheStreet.com Investment Rating of E- (Very Weak). The fund has an above average level of volatility, as measured by both semi-deviation and drawdown factors. It carries a beta of 1.24, meaning it is expected to move 12.4% for every 10% move in the market. As of December 31, 2012, *PowerShares DB Base Mtls Dbl Lg traded at a premium of 2.08% above its net asset value, which is worse than its one-year historical average discount of .07%. Unfortunately, the high level of risk (D+, Weak) failed to pay off as investors endured very poor performance.

The fund's performance rating is currently E+ (Very Weak). It has registered an annualized return of -15.22% over the last three years and is down -1.57% year to date 2012. Factored into the performance evaluation is an expense ratio of 0.75% (very low).

This fund has been team managed for 5 years and currently receives a manager quality ranking of 3 (0=worst, 99=best). If you can tolerate high levels of risk in the hope of improved future returns, holding this fund may be an option.

Data Date	Investment Rating	Net Assets ($Mil)	Price	Performance Rating/Pts	Total Return Y-T-D	Risk Rating/Pts
12-12	E-	22.78	10.82	E+ / 0.7	-1.57%	D+ / 2.4
2011	E+	22.78	10.47	C- / 3.1	1.05%	D+ / 2.9
2010	C	22.78	19.27	A+ / 9.7	9.12%	D- / 1.0
2009	C	22.78	17.66	A+ / 9.9	202.40%	D- / 1.2

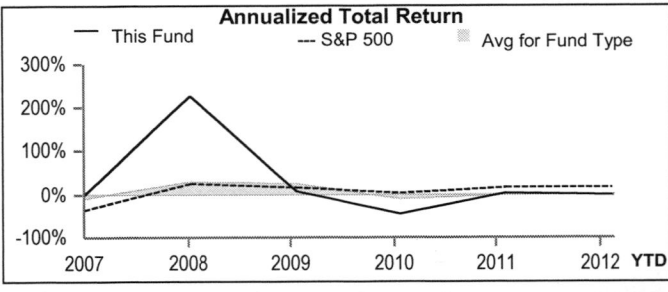

Annualized Total Return

---

*PowerShares DB Base Mtls Dbl Sh (BOM)

E-   Very Weak

Fund Family: Deutsche Bank AG (London)
Fund Type: Precious Metals
Inception Date: June 16, 2008

Major Rating Factors: *PowerShares DB Base Mtls Dbl Sh has adopted a very risky asset allocation strategy and currently receives an overall TheStreet.com Investment Rating of E- (Very Weak). The fund has a high level of volatility, as measured by both semi-deviation and drawdown factors. It carries a beta of -1.09, meaning the fund's expected move will be -10.9% for every 10% move in the market. As of December 31, 2012, *PowerShares DB Base Mtls Dbl Sh traded at a discount of 3.02% below its net asset value, which is better than its one-year historical average discount of .19%. Unfortunately, the high level of risk (D, Weak) failed to pay off as investors endured very poor performance.

The fund's performance rating is currently E+ (Very Weak). It has registered an annualized return of -8.93% over the last three years and is up 2.09% year to date 2012. Factored into the performance evaluation is an expense ratio of 0.75% (very low).

This fund has been team managed for 5 years and currently receives a manager quality ranking of 81 (0=worst, 99=best). If you can tolerate very high levels of risk in the hope of improved future returns, holding this fund may be an option.

Data Date	Investment Rating	Net Assets ($Mil)	Price	Performance Rating/Pts	Total Return Y-T-D	Risk Rating/Pts
12-12	E-	2.20	11.87	E+ / 0.7	2.09%	D / 2.2
2011	E-	2.20	14.95	E+ / 0.8	-0.33%	D / 1.9
2010	E-	2.20	10.54	E- / 0.1	-33.71%	D- / 1.0
2009	E-	2.20	15.90	E- / 0	-75.52%	D- / 1.2

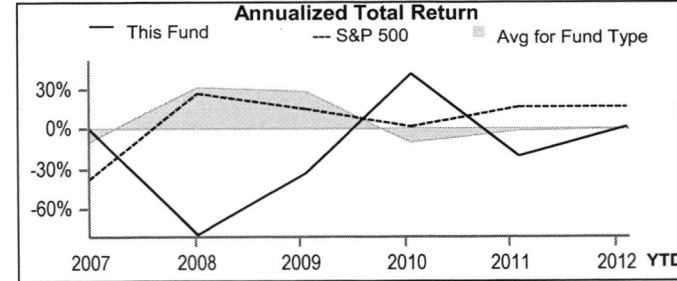

Annualized Total Return

*PowerShares DB Commodity Double (DEE)

E- **Very Weak**

Fund Family: Deutsche Bank AG (London)
Fund Type: Growth
Inception Date: April 28, 2008

Major Rating Factors: *PowerShares DB Commodity Double has adopted a very risky asset allocation strategy and currently receives an overall TheStreet.com Investment Rating of E- (Very Weak). The fund has a high level of volatility, as measured by both semi-deviation and drawdown factors. It carries a beta of -1.92, meaning the fund's expected move will be -19.2% for every 10% move in the market. As of December 31, 2012, *PowerShares DB Commodity Double traded at a discount of 4.64% below its net asset value, which is better than its one-year historical average premium of .23%. Unfortunately, the high level of risk (D, Weak) failed to pay off as investors endured very poor performance.

The fund's performance rating is currently E (Very Weak). It has registered an annualized return of -19.48% over the last three years and is up 5.13% year to date 2012. Factored into the performance evaluation is an expense ratio of 0.75% (very low).

This fund has been team managed for 5 years and currently receives a manager quality ranking of 35 (0=worst, 99=best). If you can tolerate very high levels of risk in the hope of improved future returns, holding this fund may be an option.

Data Date	Investment Rating	Net Assets ($Mil)	Price	Perfor- mance Rating/Pts	Total Return Y-T-D	Risk Rating/Pts
12-12	E-	5.65	26.50	E / 0.5	5.13%	D / 2.1
2011	E-	5.65	30.65	E+ / 0.6	-6.30%	D / 1.9
2010	E-	5.65	35.00	E- / 0.1	-30.83%	D / 1.9
2009	E	5.65	50.60	E / 0.3	-27.24%	C- / 3.0

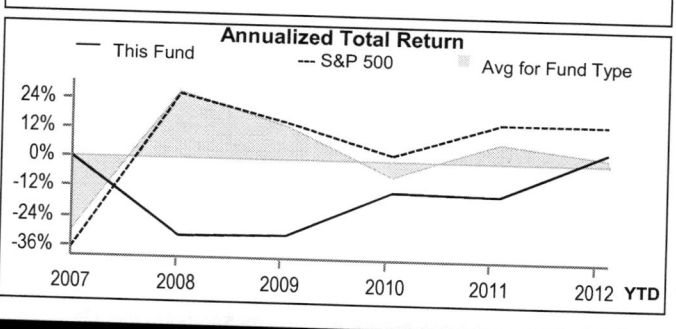

*PowerShares DB Commodity Double (DYY)

E+ **Very Weak**

Fund Family: Deutsche Bank AG (London)
Fund Type: Growth
Inception Date: April 28, 2008

Major Rating Factors:
Disappointing performance is the major factor driving the E+ (Very Weak) TheStreet.com Investment Rating for *PowerShares DB Commodity Double. The fund currently has a performance rating of D (Weak) based on an annualized return of 4.00% over the last three years and a total return of -1.30% year to date 2012. Factored into the performance evaluation is an expense ratio of 0.75% (very low).

The fund's risk rating is currently C- (Fair). It carries a beta of 2.26, meaning it is expected to move 22.6% for every 10% move in the market. Volatility, as measured by both the semi-deviation and a drawdown factor, is considered average. As of December 31, 2012, *PowerShares DB Commodity Double traded at a premium of 1.54% above its net asset value, which is worse than its one-year historical average premium of .81%.

This fund has been team managed for 5 years and currently receives a manager quality ranking of 6 (0=worst, 99=best). This fund offers an average level of risk but investors looking for strong performance will be frustrated.

Data Date	Investment Rating	Net Assets ($Mil)	Price	Perfor- mance Rating/Pts	Total Return Y-T-D	Risk Rating/Pts
12-12	E+	43.11	9.21	D / 2.1	-1.30%	C- / 3.1
2011	D	43.11	9.18	C / 4.6	4.03%	C- / 3.7
2010	C	43.11	10.00	A+ / 9.7	19.62%	D- / 1.0
2009	C-	43.11	8.36	B+ / 8.8	24.59%	D- / 1.1

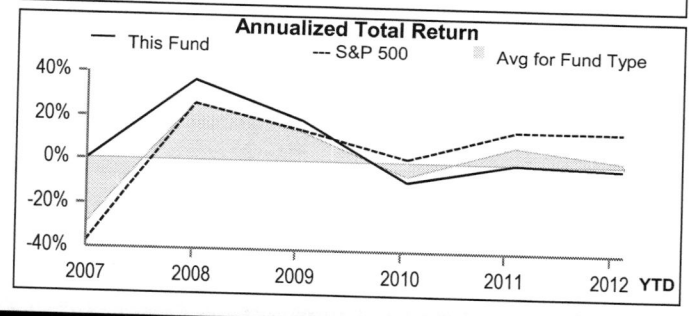

*PowerShares DB Commodity Idx Tra (DBC)

D+ **Weak**

Fund Family: DB Commodity Services LLC
Fund Type: Growth
Inception Date: February 3, 2006

Major Rating Factors:
Disappointing performance is the major factor driving the D+ (Weak) TheStreet.com Investment Rating for *PowerShares DB Commodity Idx Tra. The fund currently has a performance rating of D (Weak) based on an annualized return of 4.22% over the last three years and a total return of -0.68% year to date 2012. Factored into the performance evaluation is an expense ratio of 0.87% (low).

The fund's risk rating is currently B- (Good). It carries a beta of 1.05, meaning that its performance tracks fairly well with that of the overall stock market. Volatility, as measured by both the semi-deviation and a drawdown factor, is considered low. As of December 31, 2012, *PowerShares DB Commodity Idx Tra traded at a premium of .83% above its net asset value, which is worse than its one-year historical average premium of .03%.

Benjamin A. Pace, III currently receives a manager quality ranking of 18 (0=worst, 99=best). This fund offers only a moderate level of risk but investors looking for strong performance are still waiting.

Data Date	Investment Rating	Net Assets ($Mil)	Price	Perfor- mance Rating/Pts	Total Return Y-T-D	Risk Rating/Pts
12-12	D+	6,607.50	27.78	D / 2.2	-0.68%	B- / 7.5
2011	C-	5,456.80	26.84	C- / 3.6	2.79%	B- / 7.8
2010	D	5,106.80	27.55	D+ / 2.7	11.90%	C / 4.7
2009	C-	3,731.03	24.62	C- / 4.0	12.27%	C / 5.2

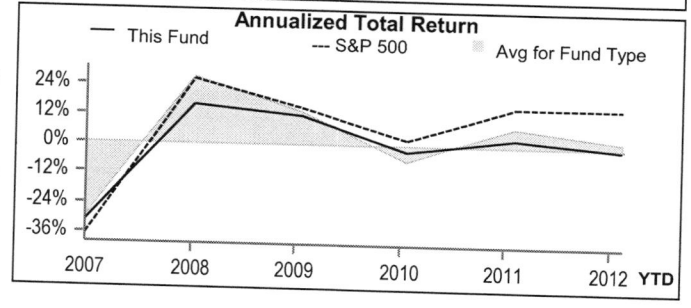

* Denotes ETF Fund

*PowerShares DB Commodity Short E (DDP) — E+ Very Weak

Fund Family: Deutsche Bank AG (London)
Fund Type: Growth
Inception Date: April 28, 2008

Major Rating Factors:
Very poor performance is the major factor driving the E+ (Very Weak) TheStreet.com Investment Rating for *PowerShares DB Commodity Short E. The fund currently has a performance rating of E+ (Very Weak) based on an annualized return of -7.92% over the last three years and a total return of -0.02% year to date 2012. Factored into the performance evaluation is an expense ratio of 0.75% (very low).

The fund's risk rating is currently C- (Fair). It carries a beta of -1.18, meaning the fund's expected move will be -11.8% for every 10% move in the market. Volatility, as measured by both the semi-deviation and a drawdown factor, is considered average. As of December 31, 2012, *PowerShares DB Commodity Short E traded at a premium of 2.71% above its net asset value, which is better than its one-year historical average premium of 10.83%.

This fund has been team managed for 5 years and currently receives a manager quality ranking of 80 (0=worst, 99=best). This fund offers an average level of risk but investors looking for strong performance will be frustrated.

Data Date	Investment Rating	Net Assets ($Mil)	Price	Performance Rating/Pts	Total Return Y-T-D	Risk Rating/Pts
12-12	E+	10.11	30.70	E+ / 0.8	-0.02%	C- / 3.7
2011	E	10.11	31.38	D- / 1.2	-1.24%	C- / 3.1
2010	E+	10.11	32.50	E / 0.4	-14.16%	C- / 3.2
2009	E+	10.11	37.86	E / 0.5	-13.46%	C- / 4.0

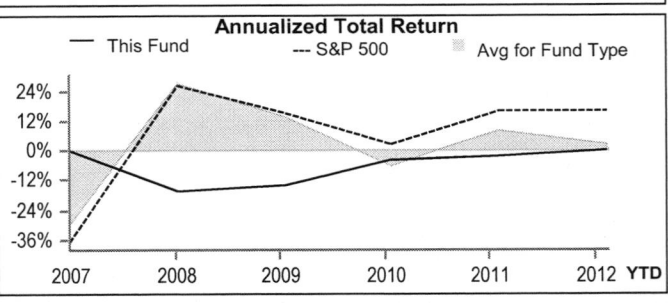

*PowerShares DB Crude Oil Dbl Sh (DTO) — E- Very Weak

Fund Family: Deutsche Bank AG (London)
Fund Type: Growth
Inception Date: June 16, 2008

Major Rating Factors: *PowerShares DB Crude Oil Dbl Sh has adopted a very risky asset allocation strategy and currently receives an overall TheStreet.com Investment Rating of E- (Very Weak). The fund has a high level of volatility, as measured by both semi-deviation and drawdown factors. It carries a beta of -2.76, meaning the fund's expected move will be -27.6% for every 10% move in the market. As of December 31, 2012, *PowerShares DB Crude Oil Dbl Sh traded at a premium of 4.17% above its net asset value, which is worse than its one-year historical average discount of .02%. Unfortunately, the high level of risk (D, Weak) failed to pay off as investors endured very poor performance.

The fund's performance rating is currently E+ (Very Weak). It has registered an annualized return of -15.01% over the last three years and is down -4.24% year to date 2012. Factored into the performance evaluation is an expense ratio of 0.75% (very low).

This fund has been team managed for 5 years and currently receives a manager quality ranking of 95 (0=worst, 99=best). If you can tolerate very high levels of risk in the hope of improved future returns, holding this fund may be an option.

Data Date	Investment Rating	Net Assets ($Mil)	Price	Performance Rating/Pts	Total Return Y-T-D	Risk Rating/Pts
12-12	E-	97.05	44.69	E+ / 0.6	-4.24%	D / 2.1
2011	E-	97.05	41.42	E / 0.4	-5.55%	D / 1.9
2010	E-	97.05	53.35	E / 0.3	-20.25%	D- / 1.3
2009	E-	97.05	66.90	E / 0.3	-46.99%	D / 1.9

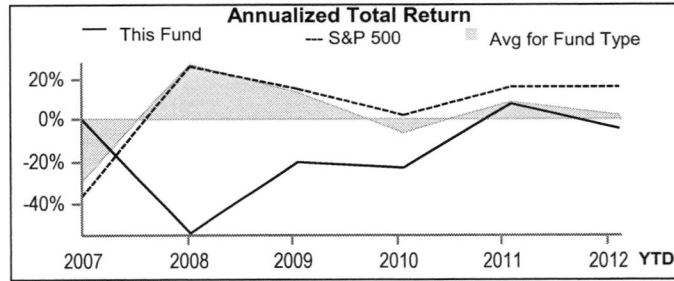

*PowerShares DB Crude Oil Long ET (OLO) — E+ Very Weak

Fund Family: Deutsche Bank AG (London)
Fund Type: Growth
Inception Date: June 16, 2008

Major Rating Factors:
Disappointing performance is the major factor driving the E+ (Very Weak) TheStreet.com Investment Rating for *PowerShares DB Crude Oil Long ET. The fund currently has a performance rating of D- (Weak) based on an annualized return of -0.93% over the last three years and a total return of 2.00% year to date 2012. Factored into the performance evaluation is an expense ratio of 0.75% (very low).

The fund's risk rating is currently C- (Fair). It carries a beta of 1.35, meaning it is expected to move 13.5% for every 10% move in the market. Volatility, as measured by both the semi-deviation and a drawdown factor, is considered average. As of December 31, 2012, *PowerShares DB Crude Oil Long ET traded at a discount of 2.00% below its net asset value, which is better than its one-year historical average discount of .09%.

This fund has been team managed for 5 years and currently receives a manager quality ranking of 8 (0=worst, 99=best). This fund offers an average level of risk but investors looking for strong performance will be frustrated.

Data Date	Investment Rating	Net Assets ($Mil)	Price	Performance Rating/Pts	Total Return Y-T-D	Risk Rating/Pts
12-12	E+	14.59	12.72	D- / 1.2	2.00%	C- / 3.9
2011	D+	14.59	14.02	C / 5.4	3.08%	C- / 4.0
2010	C	14.59	14.00	B+ / 8.5	3.09%	D / 2.0
2009	C	14.59	13.58	B+ / 8.4	32.62%	D / 2.2

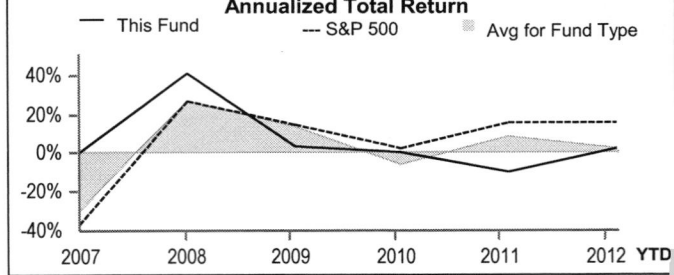

*PowerShares DB Crude Oil Short E (SZO)

E+ **Very Weak**

Fund Family: Deutsche Bank AG (London)
Fund Type: Growth
Inception Date: June 16, 2008

Major Rating Factors:
Disappointing performance is the major factor driving the E+ (Very Weak) TheStreet.com Investment Rating for *PowerShares DB Crude Oil Short E. The fund currently has a performance rating of D- (Weak) based on an annualized return of -4.62% over the last three years and a total return of -1.96% year to date 2012. Factored into the performance evaluation is an expense ratio of 0.75% (very low).

The fund's risk rating is currently C- (Fair). It carries a beta of -1.34, meaning the fund's expected move will be -13.4% for every 10% move in the market. Volatility, as measured by both the semi-deviation and a drawdown factor, is considered average. As of December 31, 2012, *PowerShares DB Crude Oil Short E traded at a premium of 2.24% above its net asset value, which is worse than its one-year historical average discount of .09%.

This fund has been team managed for 5 years and currently receives a manager quality ranking of 91 (0=worst, 99=best). This fund offers an average level of risk but investors looking for strong performance will be frustrated.

Data Date	Investment Rating	Net Assets ($Mil)	Price	Performance Rating/Pts	Total Return Y-T-D	Risk Rating/Pts
12-12	E+	14.43	43.41	D- / 1.0	-1.96%	C- / 3.9
2011	E	14.43	40.74	D- / 1.0	-2.80%	D+ / 2.7
2010	E	14.43	44.31	E+ / 0.6	-7.69%	D+ / 2.9
2009	E	14.43	48.00	E / 0.5	-20.83%	C- / 3.3

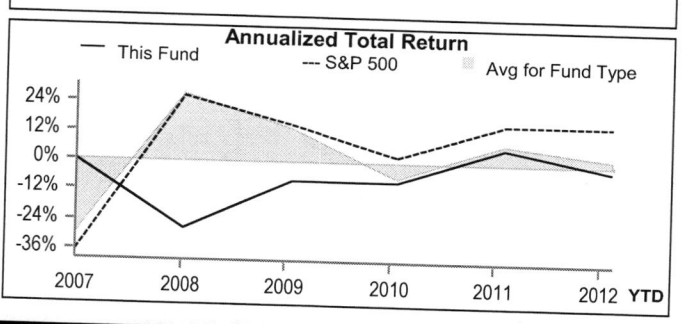

*PowerShares DB Energy Fund (DBE)

D **Weak**

Fund Family: DB Commodity Services LLC
Fund Type: Energy/Natural Resources
Inception Date: January 3, 2007

Major Rating Factors:
Disappointing performance is the major factor driving the D (Weak) TheStreet.com Investment Rating for *PowerShares DB Energy Fund. The fund currently has a performance rating of D (Weak) based on an annualized return of 2.97% over the last three years and a total return of 0.39% year to date 2012. Factored into the performance evaluation is an expense ratio of 0.77% (very low).

The fund's risk rating is currently B- (Good). It carries a beta of 0.87, meaning the fund's expected move will be 8.7% for every 10% move in the market. Volatility, as measured by both the semi-deviation and a drawdown factor, is considered low. As of December 31, 2012, *PowerShares DB Energy Fund traded at a discount of .39% below its net asset value, which is better than its one-year historical average premium of .02%.

Benjamin A. Pace, III currently receives a manager quality ranking of 21 (0=worst, 99=best). This fund offers only a moderate level of risk but investors looking for strong performance are still waiting.

Data Date	Investment Rating	Net Assets ($Mil)	Price	Performance Rating/Pts	Total Return Y-T-D	Risk Rating/Pts
12-12	D	139.90	27.94	D / 2.0	0.39%	B- / 7.1
2011	C	149.10	27.62	C / 4.6	5.32%	B- / 7.5
2010	E+	161.40	26.88	D- / 1.2	2.63%	C- / 3.8
2009	C+	364.70	26.19	B / 7.7	21.70%	C / 4.4

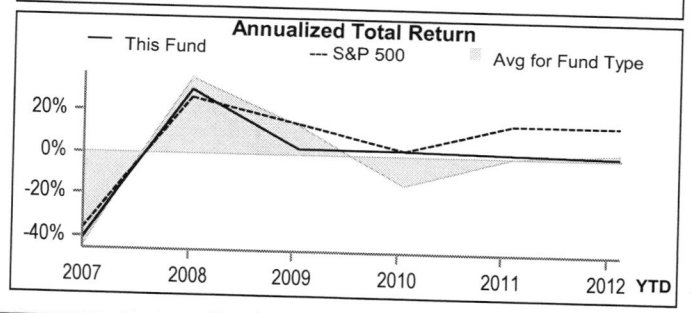

*PowerShares DB G10 Currency Harv (DBV)

C- **Fair**

Fund Family: DB Commodity Services LLC
Fund Type: Income
Inception Date: September 18, 2006

Major Rating Factors:
Disappointing performance is the major factor driving the C- (Fair) TheStreet.com Investment Rating for *PowerShares DB G10 Currency Harv. The fund currently has a performance rating of D+ (Weak) based on an annualized return of 3.77% over the last three years and a total return of 1.61% year to date 2012. Factored into the performance evaluation is an expense ratio of 0.79% (very low).

The fund's risk rating is currently B (Good). It carries a beta of 0.65, meaning the fund's expected move will be 6.5% for every 10% move in the market. Volatility, as measured by both the semi-deviation and a drawdown factor, is considered low. As of December 31, 2012, *PowerShares DB G10 Currency Harv traded at a discount of 1.62% below its net asset value, which is better than its one-year historical average discount of .03%.

Benjamin A. Pace, III currently receives a manager quality ranking of 29 (0=worst, 99=best). This fund offers only a moderate level of risk but investors looking for strong performance are still waiting.

Data Date	Investment Rating	Net Assets ($Mil)	Price	Performance Rating/Pts	Total Return Y-T-D	Risk Rating/Pts
12-12	C-	345.10	26.15	D+ / 2.8	1.61%	B / 8.9
2011	C	286.00	23.76	C- / 3.2	0.76%	B+ / 9.0
2010	D+	356.10	23.74	D / 1.6	0.85%	C+ / 6.7
2009	C-	411.67	23.54	D+ / 2.6	19.80%	C+ / 6.8

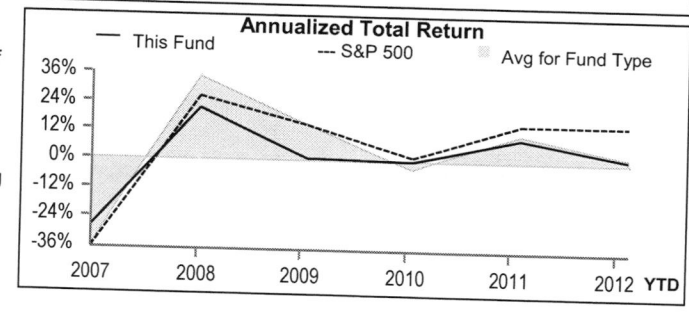

* Denotes ETF Fund

*PowerShares DB German Bond Fut E (BUNL)

D-   Weak

Fund Family: DB Commodity Services LLC
Fund Type: Global
Inception Date: March 22, 2011

Data Date	Investment Rating	Net Assets ($Mil)	Price	Performance Rating/Pts	Total Return Y-T-D	Risk Rating/Pts
12-12	D-	0.00	23.93	D / 1.9	-0.17%	C+ / 5.8

Major Rating Factors:
Disappointing performance is the major factor driving the D- (Weak) TheStreet.com Investment Rating for *PowerShares DB German Bond Fut E. The fund currently has a performance rating of D (Weak) based on an annualized return of 0.00% over the last three years and a total return of -0.17% year to date 2012.

The fund's risk rating is currently C+ (Fair). It carries a beta of 0.00, meaning the fund's expected move will be 0.0% for every 10% move in the market. Volatility, as measured by both the semi-deviation and a drawdown factor, is considered low. As of December 31, 2012, *PowerShares DB German Bond Fut E traded at a premium of .17% above its net asset value, which is worse than its one-year historical average discount of .15%.

This fund has been team managed for 2 years and currently receives a manager quality ranking of 78 (0=worst, 99=best). This fund offers only a moderate level of risk but investors looking for strong performance are still waiting.

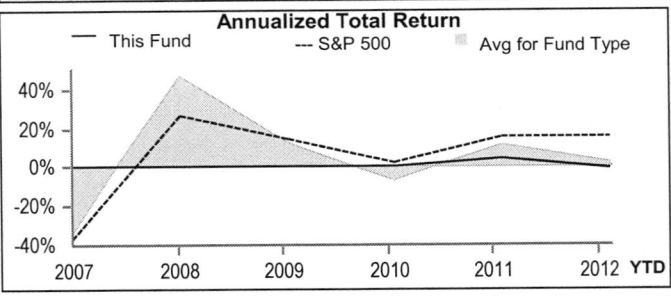

*PowerShares DB Gold Double Lg ET (DGP)

C-   Fair

Fund Family: Deutsche Bank AG (London)
Fund Type: Precious Metals
Inception Date: February 28, 2008

Data Date	Investment Rating	Net Assets ($Mil)	Price	Performance Rating/Pts	Total Return Y-T-D	Risk Rating/Pts
12-12	C-	0.10	52.03	B- / 7.5	-1.27%	C- / 3.9
2011	C+	0.00	47.61	A+ / 9.8	7.50%	C- / 4.2
2010	B-	0.10	42.93	A+ / 9.8	62.37%	D+ / 2.8
2009	C+	0.00	26.44	A- / 9.2	46.48%	C- / 3.0

Major Rating Factors: Strong performance is the major factor driving the C- (Fair) TheStreet.com Investment Rating for *PowerShares DB Gold Double Lg ET. The fund currently has a performance rating of B- (Good) based on an annualized return of 22.20% over the last three years and a total return of -1.27% to date 2012.

The fund's risk rating is currently C- (Fair). It carries a beta of 1.85, meaning it is expected to move 18.5% for every 10% move in the market. Volatility, as measured by both the semi-deviation and a drawdown factor, is considered average. As of December 31, 2012, *PowerShares DB Gold Double Lg ET traded at a premium of 1.62% above its net asset value, which is worse than its one-year historical average premium of .02%.

This fund has been team managed for 5 years and currently receives a manager quality ranking of 29 (0=worst, 99=best). If you desire an average level of risk and strong performance, then this fund is a good option.

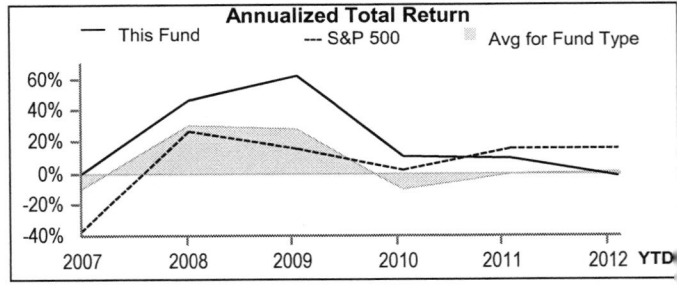

*PowerShares DB Gold Double Sht E (DZZ)

E-   Very Weak

Fund Family: Deutsche Bank AG (London)
Fund Type: Precious Metals
Inception Date: February 28, 2008

Data Date	Investment Rating	Net Assets ($Mil)	Price	Performance Rating/Pts	Total Return Y-T-D	Risk Rating/Pts
12-12	E-	0.10	4.47	E / 0.4	1.34%	D / 1.9
2011	E-	0.00	5.45	E / 0.3	-7.62%	D / 1.9
2010	E-	0.10	7.98	E- / 0.2	-43.08%	D- / 1.0
2009	E-	0.00	14.02	E- / 0.2	-44.08%	D / 1.8

Major Rating Factors: *PowerShares DB Gold Double Sht E has adopted a very risky asset allocation strategy and currently receives an overall TheStreet.com Investment Rating of E- (Very Weak). The fund has a high level of volatility, as measured by both semi-deviation and drawdown factors. It carries a beta of -1.87, meaning the fund's expected move will be -18.7% for every 10% move in the market. As of December 31, 2012, *PowerShares DB Gold Double Sht E traded at a discount of 1.76% below its net asset value, which is better than its one-year historical average discount of .07%. Unfortunately, the high level of risk (D, Weak) failed to pay off as investors endured very poor performance.

The fund's performance rating is currently E (Very Weak). It has registered an annualized return of -29.85% over the last three years and is up 1.34% year to date 2012.

This fund has been team managed for 5 years and currently receives a manager quality ranking of 11 (0=worst, 99=best). If you can tolerate very high levels of risk in the hope of improved future returns, holding this fund may be an option.

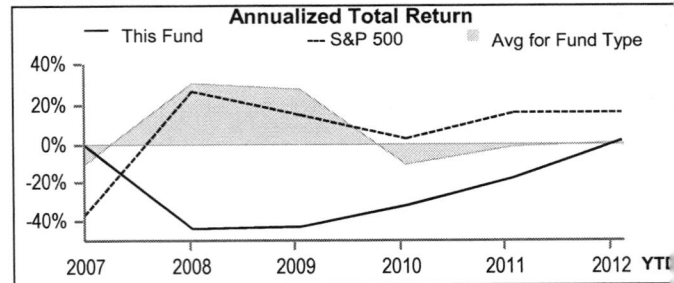

*PowerShares DB Gold Fund (DGL)

C-   **Fair**

Fund Family: DB Commodity Services LLC
Fund Type: Precious Metals
Inception Date: January 3, 2007

Major Rating Factors: Middle of the road best describes *PowerShares DB Gold Fund whose TheStreet.com Investment Rating is currently a C- (Fair). The fund currently has a performance rating of C- (Fair) based on an annualized return of 12.06% over the last three years and a total return of -0.66% year to date 2012. Factored into the performance evaluation is an expense ratio of 0.76% (very low).

The fund's risk rating is currently B (Good). It carries a beta of 0.92, meaning that its performance tracks fairly well with that of the overall stock market. Volatility, as measured by both the semi-deviation and a drawdown factor, is considered low. As of December 31, 2012, *PowerShares DB Gold Fund traded at a premium of .81% above its net asset value, which is worse than its one-year historical average premium of .01%.

Benjamin A. Pace, III currently receives a manager quality ranking of 49 (0=worst, 99=best). If you desire an average level of risk, then this fund may be an option.

Data Date	Investment Rating	Net Assets ($Mil)	Price	Performance Rating/Pts	Total Return Y-T-D	Risk Rating/Pts
12-12	C-	516.90	57.35	C- / 3.8	-0.66%	B / 8.1
2011	B	458.10	54.45	B- / 7.3	3.40%	B / 8.2
2010	A	331.30	50.16	B+ / 8.7	27.89%	C+ / 6.9
2009	A+	149.38	39.22	B / 7.9	22.99%	B- / 7.2

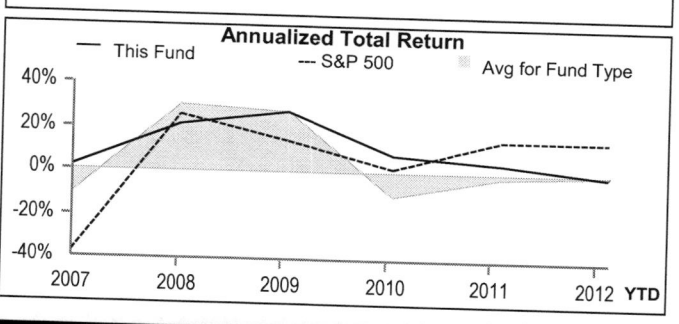

*PowerShares DB Gold Short ETN (DGZ)

E   **Very Weak**

Fund Family: Deutsche Bank AG (London)
Fund Type: Precious Metals
Inception Date: February 29, 2008

Major Rating Factors: Very poor performance is the major factor driving the E (Very Weak) TheStreet.com Investment Rating for *PowerShares DB Gold Short ETN. The fund currently has a performance rating of E+ (Very Weak) based on an annualized return of -14.98% over the last three years and a total return of 0.59% year to date 2012.

The fund's risk rating is currently C- (Fair). It carries a beta of -0.92, meaning the fund's expected move will be -9.2% for every 10% move in the market. Volatility, as measured by both the semi-deviation and a drawdown factor, is considered average. As of December 31, 2012, *PowerShares DB Gold Short ETN traded at a discount of .76% below its net asset value, which is better than its one-year historical average discount of .04%.

This fund has been team managed for 5 years and currently receives a manager quality ranking of 23 (0=worst, 99=best). This fund offers an average level of risk but investors looking for strong performance will be frustrated.

Data Date	Investment Rating	Net Assets ($Mil)	Price	Performance Rating/Pts	Total Return Y-T-D	Risk Rating/Pts
12-12	E	0.10	11.81	E+ / 0.6	0.59%	C- / 3.0
2011	E	0.00	12.89	E+ / 0.8	-3.72%	D+ / 2.5
2010	E	0.10	15.16	E / 0.4	-24.05%	D+ / 2.4
2009	E	0.00	19.96	E / 0.4	-23.52%	C- / 3.1

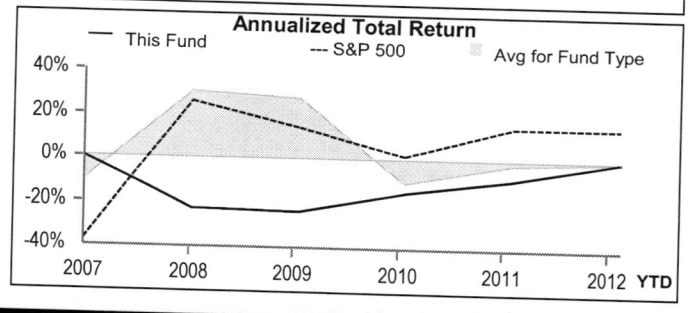

*PowerShares DB Inv Jpnese Gvt Bd (JGBS)

D-   **Weak**

Fund Family: DB Commodity Services LLC
Fund Type: Global
Inception Date: November 8, 2011

Major Rating Factors:
Disappointing performance is the major factor driving the D- (Weak) TheStreet.com Investment Rating for *PowerShares DB Inv Jpnese Gvt Bd. The fund currently has a performance rating of D- (Weak) based on an annualized return of 0.00% over the last three years and a total return of 0.20% year to date 2012.

The fund's risk rating is currently C+ (Fair). It carries a beta of 0.00, meaning the fund's expected move will be 0.0% for every 10% move in the market. Volatility, as measured by both the semi-deviation and a drawdown factor, is considered low. As of December 31, 2012, *PowerShares DB Inv Jpnese Gvt Bd traded at a premium of 4.60% above its net asset value, which is worse than its one-year historical average premium of 3.21%.

This fund has been team managed for 2 years and currently receives a manager quality ranking of 34 (0=worst, 99=best). This fund offers only a moderate level of risk but investors looking for strong performance are still waiting.

Data Date	Investment Rating	Net Assets ($Mil)	Price	Performance Rating/Pts	Total Return Y-T-D	Risk Rating/Pts
12-12	D-	0.00	19.54	D- / 1.2	0.20%	C+ / 5.8

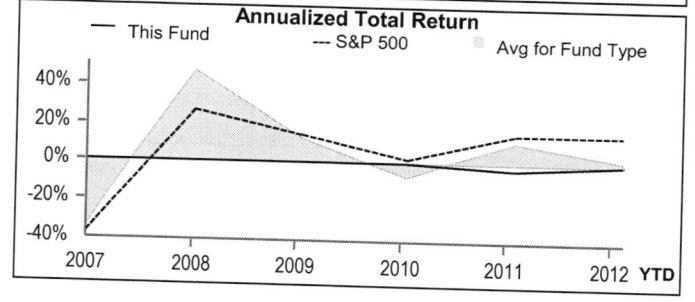

* Denotes ETF Fund

*PowerShares DB Itn Trs B Fut ETN (ITLY)

B-   **Good**

Fund Family: DB Commodity Services LLC
Fund Type: Global
Inception Date: March 22, 2011

Major Rating Factors:
Exceptional performance is the major factor driving the B- (Good) TheStreet.com Investment Rating for *PowerShares DB Itn Trs B Fut ETN. The fund currently has a performance rating of A+ (Excellent) based on an annualized return of 0.00% over the last three years and a total return of 1.77% year to date 2012.

The fund's risk rating is currently C (Fair). It carries a beta of 0.00, meaning the fund's expected move will be 0.0% for every 10% move in the market. Volatility, as measured by both the semi-deviation and a drawdown factor, is considered average. As of December 31, 2012, *PowerShares DB Itn Trs B Fut ETN traded at a discount of 26.67% below its net asset value, which is better than its one-year historical average discount of 4.23%.

This fund has been team managed for 2 years and currently receives a manager quality ranking of 98 (0=worst, 99=best). If you desire an average level of risk and strong performance, then this fund is a good option.

Data Date	Investment Rating	Net Assets ($Mil)	Price	Performance Rating/Pts	Total Return Y-T-D	Risk Rating/Pts
12-12	B-	0.00	23.84	A+ / 9.6	1.77%	C / 5.3

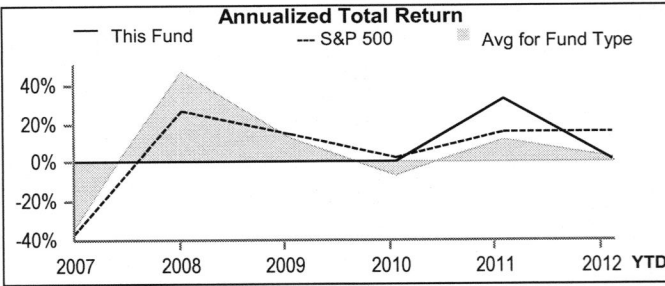

*PowerShares DB Japanese GvBd Fut (JGBL)

D-   **Weak**

Fund Family: DB Commodity Services LLC
Fund Type: Global
Inception Date: March 22, 2011

Major Rating Factors:
Disappointing performance is the major factor driving the D- (Weak) TheStreet.com Investment Rating for *PowerShares DB Japanese GvBd Fut. The fund currently has a performance rating of D- (Weak) based on an annualized return of 0.00% over the last three years and a total return of 0.10% year to date 2012.

The fund's risk rating is currently C+ (Fair). It carries a beta of 0.00, meaning the fund's expected move will be 0.0% for every 10% move in the market. Volatility, as measured by both the semi-deviation and a drawdown factor, is considered low. As of December 31, 2012, *PowerShares DB Japanese GvBd Fut traded at a premium of .43% above its net asset value, which is worse than its one-year historical average premium of .11%.

This fund has been team managed for 2 years and currently receives a manager quality ranking of 66 (0=worst, 99=best). This fund offers only a moderate level of risk but investors looking for strong performance are still waiting.

Data Date	Investment Rating	Net Assets ($Mil)	Price	Performance Rating/Pts	Total Return Y-T-D	Risk Rating/Pts
12-12	D-	0.00	20.81	D- / 1.5	0.10%	C+ / 5.9

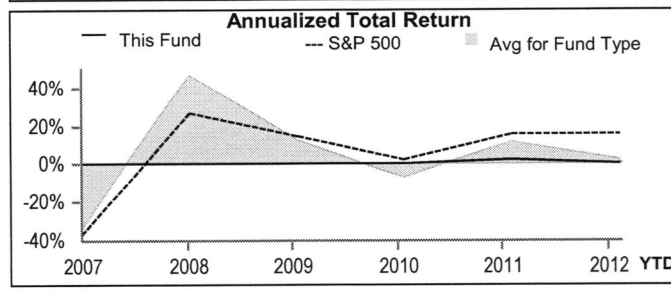

*PowerShares DB Oil Fund (DBO)

D-   **Weak**

Fund Family: DB Commodity Services LLC
Fund Type: Energy/Natural Resources
Inception Date: January 3, 2007

Major Rating Factors:
Disappointing performance is the major factor driving the D- (Weak) TheStreet.com Investment Rating for *PowerShares DB Oil Fund. The fund currently has a performance rating of D- (Weak) based on an annualized return of -0.97% over the last three years and a total return of 1.54% year to date 2012. Factored into the performance evaluation is an expense ratio of 0.77% (very low).

The fund's risk rating is currently C+ (Fair). It carries a beta of 1.02, meaning that its performance tracks fairly well with that of the overall stock market. Volatility, as measured by both the semi-deviation and a drawdown factor, is considered low. As of December 31, 2012, *PowerShares DB Oil Fund traded at a discount of 1.56% below its net asset value, which is better than its one-year historical average discount of .02%.

Benjamin A. Pace, III currently receives a manager quality ranking of 12 (0=worst, 99=best). This fund offers only a moderate level of risk but investors looking for strong performance are still waiting.

Data Date	Investment Rating	Net Assets ($Mil)	Price	Performance Rating/Pts	Total Return Y-T-D	Risk Rating/Pts
12-12	D-	774.50	25.94	D- / 1.2	1.54%	C+ / 6.2
2011	C	508.40	28.57	C / 5.4	3.36%	C+ / 6.7
2010	D-	597.80	28.22	D- / 1.4	2.36%	C- / 3.7
2009	B-	302.15	27.57	B+ / 8.4	32.61%	C / 4.4

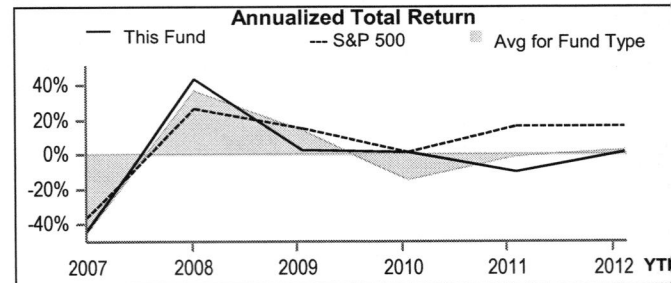

*PowerShares DB Precious Metals F (DBP)

C-   **Fair**

Fund Family: DB Commodity Services LLC
Fund Type: Precious Metals
Inception Date: January 3, 2007

Major Rating Factors: Middle of the road best describes *PowerShares DB Precious Metals F whose TheStreet.com Investment Rating is currently a C- (Fair). The fund currently has a performance rating of C- (Fair) based on an annualized return of 13.05% over the last three years and a total return of -0.51% year to date 2012. Factored into the performance evaluation is an expense ratio of 0.77% (very low).

The fund's risk rating is currently B- (Good). It carries a beta of 1.10, meaning it is expected to move 11.0% for every 10% move in the market. Volatility, as measured by both the semi-deviation and a drawdown factor, is considered low. As of December 31, 2012, *PowerShares DB Precious Metals F traded at a premium of .63% above its net asset value.

Benjamin A. Pace, III currently receives a manager quality ranking of 38 (0=worst, 99=best). If you desire an average level of risk, then this fund may be an option.

Data Date	Investment Rating	Net Assets ($Mil)	Price	Performance Rating/Pts	Total Return Y-T-D	Risk Rating/Pts
12-12	C-	354.00	57.09	C- / 4.2	-0.51%	B- / 7.5
2011	B-	454.10	53.88	B- / 7.5	3.36%	B- / 7.7
2010	A	404.20	51.82	A- / 9.1	37.56%	C+ / 6.5
2009	A+	201.07	37.67	B / 8.2	27.05%	C+ / 6.8

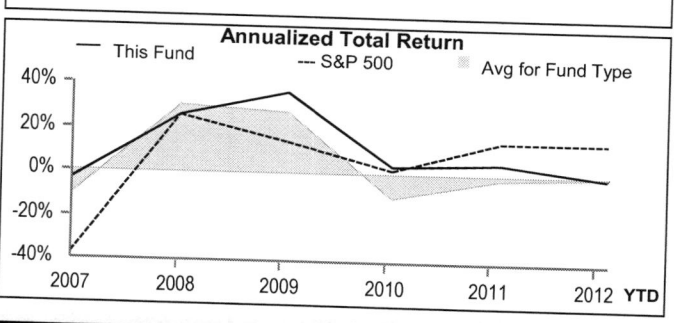

*PowerShares DB Silver Fund (DBS)

D+   **Weak**

Fund Family: DB Commodity Services LLC
Fund Type: Precious Metals
Inception Date: January 3, 2007

Major Rating Factors: *PowerShares DB Silver Fund receives a TheStreet.com Investment Rating of D+ (Weak). The fund currently has a performance rating of C+ (Fair) based on an annualized return of 16.82% over the last three years and a total return of -0.08% year to date 2012. Factored into the performance evaluation is an expense ratio of 0.76% (very low).

The fund's risk rating is currently C (Fair). It carries a beta of 1.76, meaning it is expected to move 17.6% for every 10% move in the market. Volatility, as measured by both the semi-deviation and a drawdown factor, is considered average. As of December 31, 2012, *PowerShares DB Silver Fund traded at a premium of .13% above its net asset value, which is worse than its one-year historical average premium of .04%.

Benjamin A. Pace, III currently receives a manager quality ranking of 19 (0=worst, 99=best). If you desire an average level of risk, then this fund may be an option.

Data Date	Investment Rating	Net Assets ($Mil)	Price	Performance Rating/Pts	Total Return Y-T-D	Risk Rating/Pts
12-12	D+	62.30	52.35	C+ / 5.8	-0.08%	C / 4.8
2011	C+	77.70	47.99	B+ / 8.4	3.83%	C / 5.1
2010	A-	207.60	54.51	A+ / 9.7	81.16%	C / 4.8
2009	B+	81.26	30.09	B+ / 8.9	45.93%	C / 5.1

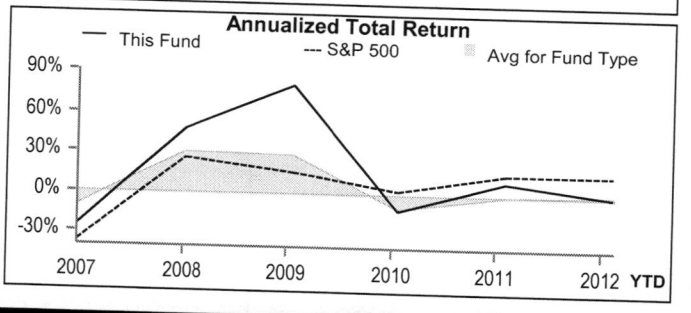

*PowerShares DB US Deflation ETN (DEFL)

D-   **Weak**

Fund Family: Deutsche Bank AG (London)
Fund Type: US Government/Agency
Inception Date: December 5, 2011

Major Rating Factors:
Very poor performance is the major factor driving the D- (Weak) TheStreet.com Investment Rating for *PowerShares DB US Deflation ETN. The fund currently has a performance rating of E+ (Very Weak) based on an annualized return of 0.00% over the last three years and a total return of 0.81% year to date 2012.

The fund's risk rating is currently C+ (Fair). It carries a beta of 0.00, meaning the fund's expected move will be 0.0% for every 10% move in the market. Volatility, as measured by both the semi-deviation and a drawdown factor, is considered low. As of December 31, 2012, *PowerShares DB US Deflation ETN traded at a premium of .32% above its net asset value, which is worse than its one-year historical average premium of .01%.

LUKE OLIVER has been running the fund for 2 years and currently receives a manager quality ranking of 10 (0=worst, 99=best). This fund offers only a moderate level of risk but investors looking for strong performance are still waiting.

Data Date	Investment Rating	Net Assets ($Mil)	Price	Performance Rating/Pts	Total Return Y-T-D	Risk Rating/Pts
12-12	D-	0.10	46.77	E+ / 0.9	0.81%	C+ / 5.6

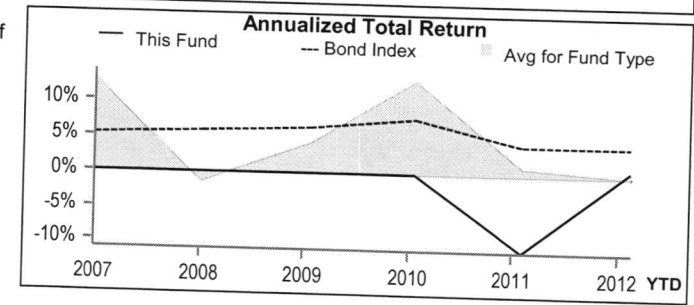

*PowerShares DB US Dollar Bearish (UDN)   D+   Weak

Fund Family: DB Commodity Services LLC
Fund Type: Growth
Inception Date: February 15, 2007

Major Rating Factors:
Disappointing performance is the major factor driving the D+ (Weak) TheStreet.com Investment Rating for *PowerShares DB US Dollar Bearish. The fund currently has a performance rating of D- (Weak) based on an annualized return of -0.71% over the last three years and a total return of 0.26% year to date 2012. Factored into the performance evaluation is an expense ratio of 0.80% (very low).

The fund's risk rating is currently B (Good). It carries a beta of 0.47, meaning the fund's expected move will be 4.7% for every 10% move in the market. Volatility, as measured by both the semi-deviation and a drawdown factor, is considered low. As of December 31, 2012, *PowerShares DB US Dollar Bearish traded at a discount of .29% below its net asset value.

Benjamin A. Pace, III currently receives a manager quality ranking of 22 (0=worst, 99=best). This fund offers only a moderate level of risk but investors looking for strong performance are still waiting.

Data Date	Investment Rating	Net Assets ($Mil)	Price	Performance Rating/Pts	Total Return Y-T-D	Risk Rating/Pts
12-12	D+	92.50	27.21	D- / 1.4	0.26%	B / 8.8
2011	C-	102.20	26.85	D / 2.0	-1.27%	B / 8.7
2010	C-	151.50	27.10	D / 2.1	-1.60%	B- / 7.8
2009	C+	382.19	27.54	C- / 3.5	6.00%	B / 8.2

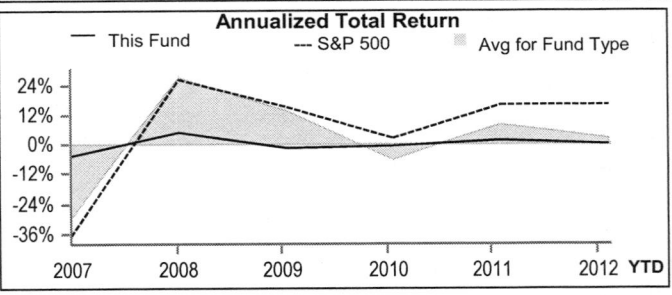
Annualized Total Return

*PowerShares DB US Dollar Bullish (UUP)   D+   Weak

Fund Family: DB Commodity Services LLC
Fund Type: Growth
Inception Date: February 15, 2007

Major Rating Factors:
Disappointing performance is the major factor driving the D+ (Weak) TheStreet.com Investment Rating for *PowerShares DB US Dollar Bullish. The fund currently has a performance rating of D- (Weak) based on an annualized return of -1.53% over the last three years and a total return of -0.32% year to date 2012. Factored into the performance evaluation is an expense ratio of 0.81% (very low).

The fund's risk rating is currently B (Good). It carries a beta of -0.46, meaning the fund's expected move will be -4.6% for every 10% move in the market. Volatility, as measured by both the semi-deviation and a drawdown factor, is considered low. As of December 31, 2012, *PowerShares DB US Dollar Bullish traded at a premium of .37% above its net asset value, which is worse than its one-year historical average discount of .03%.

Benjamin A. Pace, III currently receives a manager quality ranking of 71 (0=worst, 99=best). This fund offers only a moderate level of risk but investors looking for strong performance are still waiting.

Data Date	Investment Rating	Net Assets ($Mil)	Price	Performance Rating/Pts	Total Return Y-T-D	Risk Rating/Pts
12-12	D+	689.10	21.81	D- / 1.1	-0.32%	B / 8.4
2011	D+	0.00	22.47	D / 1.7	1.11%	B / 8.2
2010	C-	997.50	22.71	D / 1.8	-1.60%	B- / 7.8
2009	C-	770.21	23.08	D- / 1.0	-7.38%	B / 8.2

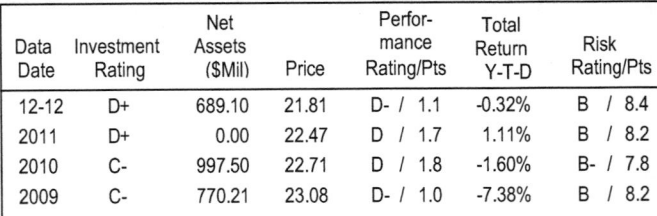
Annualized Total Return

*PowerShares DB US Inflation ETN (INFL)   D   Weak

Fund Family: Deutsche Bank AG (London)
Fund Type: US Government/Agency
Inception Date: December 5, 2011

Major Rating Factors:
Disappointing performance is the major factor driving the D (Weak) TheStreet.com Investment Rating for *PowerShares DB US Inflation ETN. The fund currently has a performance rating of D+ (Weak) based on an annualized return of 0.00% over the last three years and a total return of -0.32% year to date 2012.

The fund's risk rating is currently C+ (Fair). It carries a beta of 0.00, meaning the fund's expected move will be 0.0% for every 10% move in the market. Volatility, as measured by both the semi-deviation and a drawdown factor, is considered low. As of December 31, 2012, *PowerShares DB US Inflation ETN traded at a premium of .14% above its net asset value, which is better than its one-year historical average premium of .19%.

This fund has been team managed for 2 years and currently receives a manager quality ranking of 85 (0=worst, 99=best). This fund offers only a moderate level of risk but investors looking for strong performance are still waiting.

Data Date	Investment Rating	Net Assets ($Mil)	Price	Performance Rating/Pts	Total Return Y-T-D	Risk Rating/Pts
12-12	D	0.10	51.33	D+ / 2.4	-0.32%	C+ / 5.7

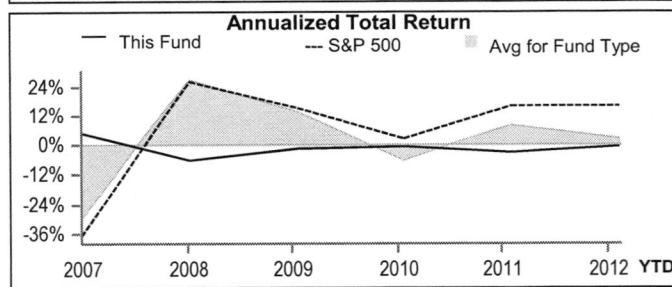

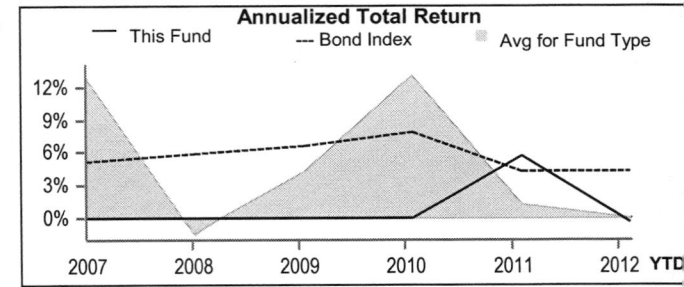
Annualized Total Return

*PowerShares Div Achievers (PFM)

Fund Family: Invesco Powershares Capital Mgmt LL
Fund Type: Income
Inception Date: September 15, 2005

C+   **Fair**

Major Rating Factors: Middle of the road best describes *PowerShares Div Achievers whose TheStreet.com Investment Rating is currently a C+ (Fair). The fund currently has a performance rating of C (Fair) based on an annualized return of 12.28% over the last three years and a total return of 3.16% year to date 2012. Factored into the performance evaluation is an expense ratio of 0.60% (very low).

The fund's risk rating is currently B (Good). It carries a beta of 0.71, meaning the fund's expected move will be 7.1% for every 10% move in the market. Volatility, as measured by both the semi-deviation and a drawdown factor, is considered low. As of December 31, 2012, *PowerShares Div Achievers traded at a discount of 3.12% below its net asset value, which is better than its one-year historical average discount of .02%.

Peter Hubbard has been running the fund for 6 years and currently receives a manager quality ranking of 76 (0=worst, 99=best). If you desire an average level of risk, then this fund may be an option.

Data Date	Investment Rating	Net Assets ($Mil)	Price	Performance Rating/Pts	Total Return Y-T-D	Risk Rating/Pts
12-12	C+	254.70	16.16	C / 5.1	3.16%	B / 8.8
2011	C	256.30	14.96	C / 5.0	0.00%	B / 8.0
2010	C-	193.50	14.02	C- / 3.5	15.87%	C+ / 6.1
2009	D+	85.45	12.47	D- / 1.3	8.45%	C+ / 6.5

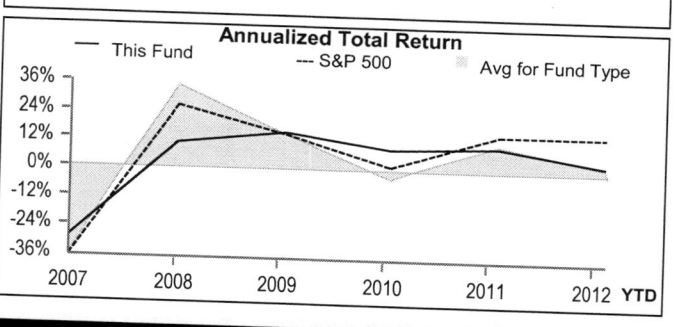

*PowerShares DWA Dev Mkt Tech Lea (PIZ)

Fund Family: Invesco Powershares Capital Mgmt LL
Fund Type: Foreign
Inception Date: December 27, 2007

D+   **Weak**

Major Rating Factors: *PowerShares DWA Dev Mkt Tech Lea receives a TheStreet.com Investment Rating of D+ (Weak). The fund currently has a performance rating of C- (Fair) based on an annualized return of 4.19% over the last three years and a total return of 2.04% year to date 2012. Factored into the performance evaluation is an expense ratio of 0.80% (very low).

The fund's risk rating is currently C+ (Fair). It carries a beta of 1.14, meaning it is expected to move 11.4% for every 10% move in the market. Volatility, as measured by both the semi-deviation and a drawdown factor, is considered low. As of December 31, 2012, *PowerShares DWA Dev Mkt Tech Lea traded at a discount of 1.42% below its net asset value, which is better than its one-year historical average premium of .15%.

Peter Hubbard has been running the fund for 6 years and currently receives a manager quality ranking of 57 (0=worst, 99=best). If you desire an average level of risk, then this fund may be an option.

Data Date	Investment Rating	Net Assets ($Mil)	Price	Performance Rating/Pts	Total Return Y-T-D	Risk Rating/Pts
12-12	D+	101.40	20.14	C- / 3.9	2.04%	C+ / 6.8
2011	D+	54.30	17.47	C- / 3.3	-0.11%	C+ / 6.9
2010	C-	120.70	22.15	C / 4.4	21.32%	C / 5.3
2009	B+	16.83	18.39	B+ / 8.9	36.06%	C / 5.2

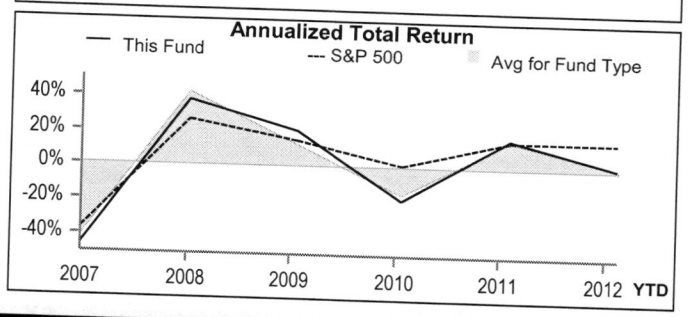

*PowerShares DWA Emg Mkts Tech Le (PIE)

Fund Family: Invesco Powershares Capital Mgmt LL
Fund Type: Emerging Market
Inception Date: December 27, 2007

C-   **Fair**

Major Rating Factors: Middle of the road best describes *PowerShares DWA Emg Mkts Tech Le whose TheStreet.com Investment Rating is currently a C- (Fair). The fund currently has a performance rating of C (Fair) based on an annualized return of 8.30% over the last three years and a total return of 0.91% year to date 2012. Factored into the performance evaluation is an expense ratio of 0.90% (low).

The fund's risk rating is currently C+ (Fair). It carries a beta of 1.03, meaning that its performance tracks fairly well with that of the overall stock market. Volatility, as measured by both the semi-deviation and a drawdown factor, is considered low. As of December 31, 2012, *PowerShares DWA Emg Mkts Tech Le traded at a discount of .64% below its net asset value, which is better than its one-year historical average premium of .15%.

Peter Hubbard has been running the fund for 6 years and currently receives a manager quality ranking of 75 (0=worst, 99=best). If you desire an average level of risk, then this fund may be an option.

Data Date	Investment Rating	Net Assets ($Mil)	Price	Performance Rating/Pts	Total Return Y-T-D	Risk Rating/Pts
12-12	C-	239.40	18.59	C / 4.6	0.91%	C+ / 6.9
2011	C	147.90	15.94	C+ / 6.0	0.56%	B- / 7.0
2010	D-	392.00	18.37	D / 1.7	25.56%	C- / 3.8
2009	B	14.94	14.73	A / 9.4	53.10%	C- / 4.2

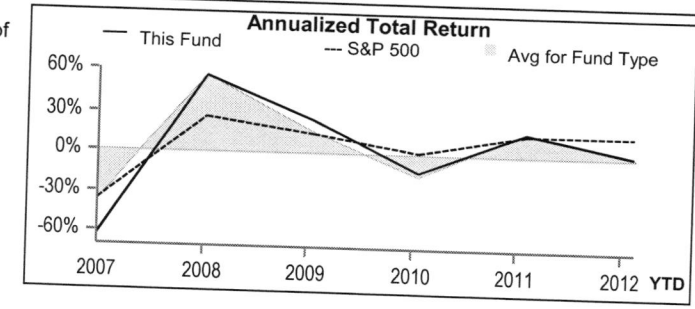

* Denotes ETF Fund

*PowerShares DWA Technical Leader (PDP)

B- **Good**

Fund Family: Invesco Powershares Capital Mgmt LL
Fund Type: Income
Inception Date: March 1, 2007

Major Rating Factors: *PowerShares DWA Technical Leader receives a
TheStreet.com Investment Rating of B- (Good). The fund currently has a performance
rating of C+ (Fair) based on an annualized return of 15.44% over the last three years
and a total return of 2.97% year to date 2012. Factored into the performance
evaluation is an expense ratio of 0.65% (very low).

The fund's risk rating is currently B- (Good). It carries a beta of 1.04, meaning
that its performance tracks fairly well with that of the overall stock market. Volatility,
as measured by both the semi-deviation and a drawdown factor, is considered low.
As of December 31, 2012, *PowerShares DWA Technical Leader traded at a discount
of 2.85% below its net asset value, which is better than its one-year historical average
premium of .03%.

Peter Hubbard has been running the fund for 6 years and currently receives a
manager quality ranking of 74 (0=worst, 99=best). If you desire an average level of
risk, then this fund may be an option.

Data Date	Investment Rating	Net Assets ($Mil)	Price	Performance Rating/Pts	Total Return Y-T-D	Risk Rating/Pts
12-12	B-	721.00	27.92	C+ / 6.9	2.97%	B- / 7.8
2011	C+	441.40	23.83	C+ / 6.2	1.26%	B- / 7.3
2010	D+	323.90	23.51	C- / 4.2	26.79%	C / 4.6
2009	B+	138.55	18.62	B+ / 8.5	24.87%	C / 5.4

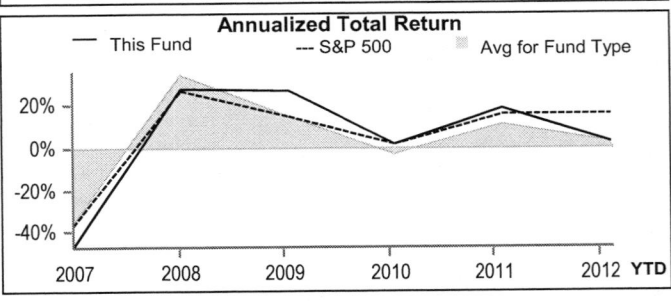

Annualized Total Return

---

*PowerShares Dynamic Banking Port (PJB)

D+ **Weak**

Fund Family: Invesco Powershares Capital Mgmt LL
Fund Type: Financial Services
Inception Date: October 12, 2006

Major Rating Factors:
Disappointing performance is the major factor driving the D+ (Weak) TheStreet.com
Investment Rating for *PowerShares Dynamic Banking Port. The fund currently has a
performance rating of D+ (Weak) based on an annualized return of 5.27% over the
last three years and a total return of 3.68% year to date 2012. Factored into the
performance evaluation is an expense ratio of 0.65% (very low).

The fund's risk rating is currently B- (Good). It carries a beta of 0.92, meaning
that its performance tracks fairly well with that of the overall stock market. Volatility,
as measured by both the semi-deviation and a drawdown factor, is considered low.
As of December 31, 2012, *PowerShares Dynamic Banking Port traded at a discount
of 3.97% below its net asset value, which is better than its one-year historical average
discount of .17%.

Peter Hubbard has been running the fund for 6 years and currently receives a
manager quality ranking of 38 (0=worst, 99=best). This fund offers only a moderate
level of risk but investors looking for strong performance are still waiting.

Data Date	Investment Rating	Net Assets ($Mil)	Price	Performance Rating/Pts	Total Return Y-T-D	Risk Rating/Pts
12-12	D+	10.10	13.31	D+ / 2.8	3.68%	B- / 7.3
2011	D	11.80	11.79	D / 1.8	3.39%	C+ / 6.8
2010	D	24.50	13.27	D / 1.6	12.42%	C+ / 5.9
2009	D-	74.77	12.00	E / 0.5	-21.61%	C+ / 5.8

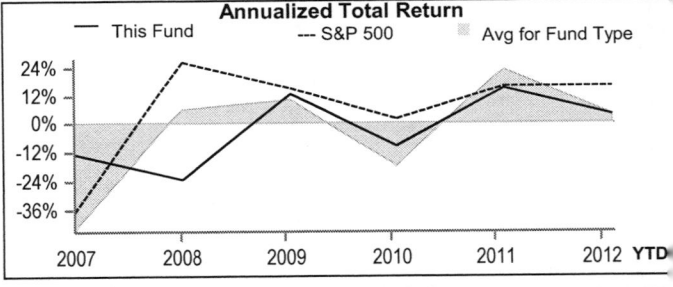

Annualized Total Return

---

*PowerShares Dynamic Basic Materi (PYZ)

B **Good**

Fund Family: Invesco Powershares Capital Mgmt LL
Fund Type: Income
Inception Date: October 12, 2006

Major Rating Factors: Strong performance is the major factor driving the B (Good)
TheStreet.com Investment Rating for *PowerShares Dynamic Basic Materi. The fund
currently has a performance rating of B+ (Good) based on an annualized return of
16.67% over the last three years and a total return of 5.05% year to date 2012.
Factored into the performance evaluation is an expense ratio of 0.65% (very low).

The fund's risk rating is currently C+ (Fair). It carries a beta of 1.55, meaning it is
expected to move 15.5% for every 10% move in the market. Volatility, as measured
by both the semi-deviation and a drawdown factor, is considered low. As of
December 31, 2012, *PowerShares Dynamic Basic Materi traded at a discount of
4.67% below its net asset value.

Peter Hubbard has been running the fund for 6 years and currently receives a
manager quality ranking of 37 (0=worst, 99=best). If you desire only a moderate level
of risk and strong performance, then this fund is an excellent option.

Data Date	Investment Rating	Net Assets ($Mil)	Price	Performance Rating/Pts	Total Return Y-T-D	Risk Rating/Pts
12-12	B	70.60	40.45	B+ / 8.5	5.05%	C+ / 6.8
2011	C+	54.40	32.03	C+ / 6.7	4.28%	B- / 7.0
2010	B-	76.20	35.44	B / 7.7	30.88%	C / 4.9
2009	C	18.13	28.30	C+ / 6.3	42.86%	C / 5.2

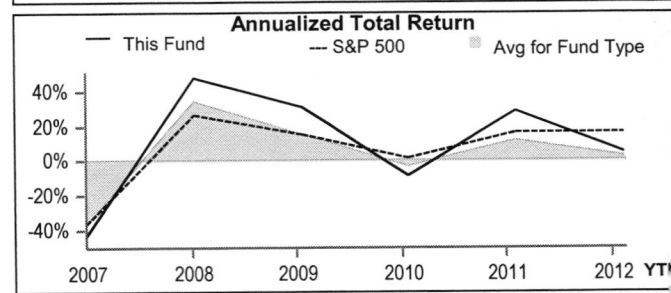

Annualized Total Return

---

*PowerShares Dynamic Biotech&Geno (PBE)

D+   **Weak**

Fund Family: Invesco Powershares Capital Mgmt LL
Fund Type: Health
Inception Date: June 23, 2005

Major Rating Factors: *PowerShares Dynamic Biotech&Geno receives a TheStreet.com Investment Rating of D+ (Weak). The fund currently has a performance rating of C (Fair) based on an annualized return of 12.18% over the last three years and a total return of 6.32% year to date 2012. Factored into the performance evaluation is an expense ratio of 0.63% (very low).

The fund's risk rating is currently C+ (Fair). It carries a beta of 1.06, meaning that its performance tracks fairly well with that of the overall stock market. Volatility, as measured by both the semi-deviation and a drawdown factor, is considered low. As of December 31, 2012, *PowerShares Dynamic Biotech&Geno traded at a discount of 6.09% below its net asset value, which is better than its one-year historical average discount of .16%.

Peter Hubbard has been running the fund for 6 years and currently receives a manager quality ranking of 48 (0=worst, 99=best). If you desire an average level of risk, then this fund may be an option.

Data Date	Investment Rating	Net Assets ($Mil)	Price	Performance Rating/Pts	Total Return Y-T-D	Risk Rating/Pts
12-12	D+	126.90	22.84	C / 4.7	6.32%	C+ / 5.8
2011	C-	135.40	20.06	C / 4.8	2.59%	C+ / 5.8
2010	B	205.30	21.89	B+ / 8.4	31.47%	C / 4.5
2009	D	139.30	16.65	D+ / 2.8	19.13%	C / 4.8

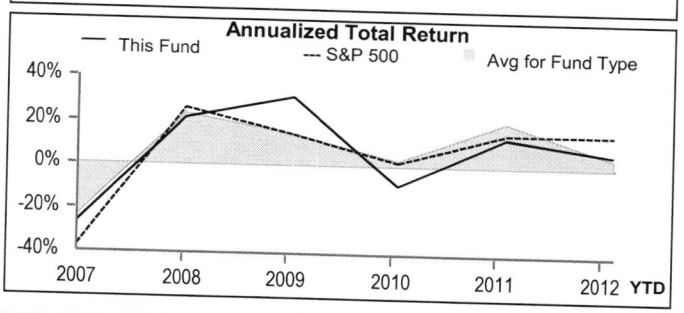

Annualized Total Return

*PowerShares Dynamic Bldg & Cons (PKB)

B+   **Good**

Fund Family: Invesco Powershares Capital Mgmt LL
Fund Type: Income
Inception Date: October 26, 2005

Major Rating Factors:
Exceptional performance is the major factor driving the B+ (Good) TheStreet.com Investment Rating for *PowerShares Dynamic Bldg & Cons. The fund currently has a performance rating of A (Excellent) based on an annualized return of 18.58% over the last three years and a total return of 3.32% year to date 2012. Factored into the performance evaluation is an expense ratio of 0.63% (very low).

The fund's risk rating is currently B- (Good). It carries a beta of 1.48, meaning it is expected to move 14.8% for every 10% move in the market. Volatility, as measured by both the semi-deviation and a drawdown factor, is considered low. As of December 31, 2012, *PowerShares Dynamic Bldg & Cons traded at a discount of 3.06% below its net asset value, which is better than its one-year historical average discount of .03%.

Peter Hubbard has been running the fund for 6 years and currently receives a manager quality ranking of 63 (0=worst, 99=best). If you desire only a moderate level of risk and strong performance, then this fund is an excellent option.

Data Date	Investment Rating	Net Assets ($Mil)	Price	Performance Rating/Pts	Total Return Y-T-D	Risk Rating/Pts
12-12	B+	65.90	17.41	A / 9.4	3.32%	B- / 7.1
2011	D+	25.80	11.98	D+ / 2.9	1.84%	C+ / 6.9
2010	D+	42.50	13.00	C- / 3.5	22.05%	C / 5.1
2009	D-	49.14	11.94	D- / 1.0	-1.11%	C / 5.2

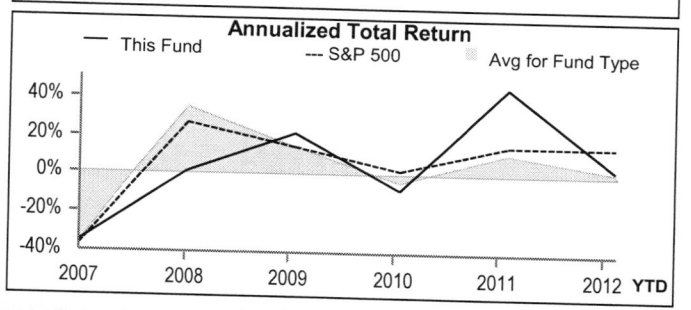

Annualized Total Return

*PowerShares Dynamic Consumer Dis (PEZ)

C+   **Fair**

Fund Family: Invesco Powershares Capital Mgmt LL
Fund Type: Income
Inception Date: October 12, 2006

Major Rating Factors: Middle of the road best describes *PowerShares Dynamic Consumer Dis whose TheStreet.com Investment Rating is currently a C+ (Fair). The fund currently has a performance rating of C+ (Fair) based on an annualized return of 15.41% over the last three years and a total return of 2.15% year to date 2012. Factored into the performance evaluation is an expense ratio of 0.65% (very low).

The fund's risk rating is currently B- (Good). It carries a beta of 1.14, meaning it is expected to move 11.4% for every 10% move in the market. Volatility, as measured by both the semi-deviation and a drawdown factor, is considered low. As of December 31, 2012, *PowerShares Dynamic Consumer Dis traded at a discount of 1.88% below its net asset value, which is better than its one-year historical average premium of .03%.

Peter Hubbard has been running the fund for 6 years and currently receives a manager quality ranking of 71 (0=worst, 99=best). If you desire an average level of risk, then this fund may be an option.

Data Date	Investment Rating	Net Assets ($Mil)	Price	Performance Rating/Pts	Total Return Y-T-D	Risk Rating/Pts
12-12	C+	31.20	29.74	C+ / 6.4	2.15%	B- / 7.9
2011	C+	17.70	25.52	C+ / 6.2	1.02%	B- / 7.8
2010	B+	22.80	25.42	B / 7.6	29.87%	C+ / 6.2
2009	D	13.66	19.81	D- / 1.3	22.42%	C+ / 5.8

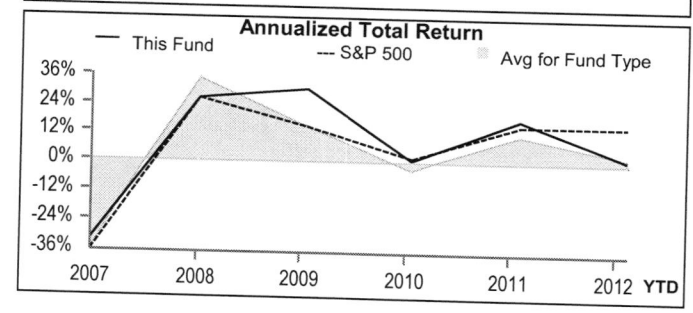

Annualized Total Return

* Denotes ETF Fund

*PowerShares Dynamic Consumer Sta (PSL)

C+   **Fair**

Fund Family: Invesco Powershares Capital Mgmt LL
Fund Type: Income
Inception Date: October 12, 2006

Major Rating Factors: Middle of the road best describes *PowerShares Dynamic Consumer Sta whose TheStreet.com Investment Rating is currently a C+ (Fair). The fund currently has a performance rating of C (Fair) based on an annualized return of 13.46% over the last three years and a total return of 2.74% year to date 2012. Factored into the performance evaluation is an expense ratio of 0.65% (very low).

The fund's risk rating is currently B (Good). It carries a beta of 0.66, meaning the fund's expected move will be 6.6% for every 10% move in the market. Volatility, as measured by both the semi-deviation and a drawdown factor, is considered low. As of December 31, 2012, *PowerShares Dynamic Consumer Sta traded at a discount of 2.84% below its net asset value, which is better than its one-year historical average discount of .05%.

Peter Hubbard has been running the fund for 6 years and currently receives a manager quality ranking of 80 (0=worst, 99=best). If you desire an average level of risk, then this fund may be an option.

Data Date	Investment Rating	Net Assets ($Mil)	Price	Performance Rating/Pts	Total Return Y-T-D	Risk Rating/Pts
12-12	C+	33.30	33.22	C / 5.4	2.74%	B / 8.7
2011	B-	38.80	31.12	C+ / 6.0	-1.09%	B / 8.4
2010	C+	40.40	28.98	C+ / 6.8	20.56%	C+ / 6.9
2009	C-	37.45	24.67	C- / 3.1	18.05%	B- / 7.0

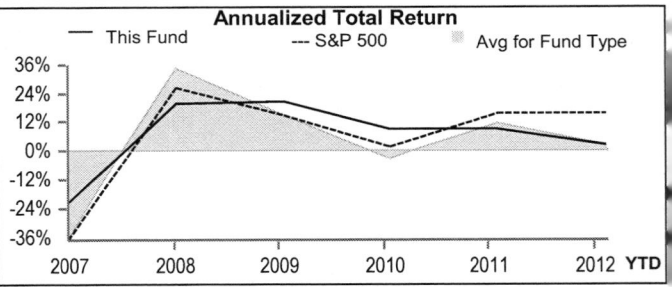

*PowerShares Dynamic Energy (PXI)

B-   **Good**

Fund Family: Invesco Powershares Capital Mgmt LL
Fund Type: Energy/Natural Resources
Inception Date: October 12, 2006

Major Rating Factors: Strong performance is the major factor driving the B- (Good) TheStreet.com Investment Rating for *PowerShares Dynamic Energy. The fund currently has a performance rating of B (Good) based on an annualized return of 18.10% over the last three years and a total return of 3.52% year to date 2012. Factored into the performance evaluation is an expense ratio of 0.65% (very low).

The fund's risk rating is currently B- (Good). It carries a beta of 1.07, meaning that its performance tracks fairly well with that of the overall stock market. Volatility, as measured by both the semi-deviation and a drawdown factor, is considered low. As of December 31, 2012, *PowerShares Dynamic Energy traded at a discount of 3.51% below its net asset value, which is better than its one-year historical average discount of .05%.

Peter Hubbard has been running the fund for 6 years and currently receives a manager quality ranking of 85 (0=worst, 99=best). If you desire only a moderate level of risk and strong performance, then this fund is an excellent option.

Data Date	Investment Rating	Net Assets ($Mil)	Price	Performance Rating/Pts	Total Return Y-T-D	Risk Rating/Pts
12-12	B-	113.70	42.89	B / 7.8	3.52%	B- / 7.1
2011	B-	135.50	38.15	B / 7.9	3.07%	B- / 7.1
2010	B-	106.50	37.41	B / 7.6	40.04%	C / 4.9
2009	C	25.88	26.98	C / 5.2	33.80%	C / 5.1

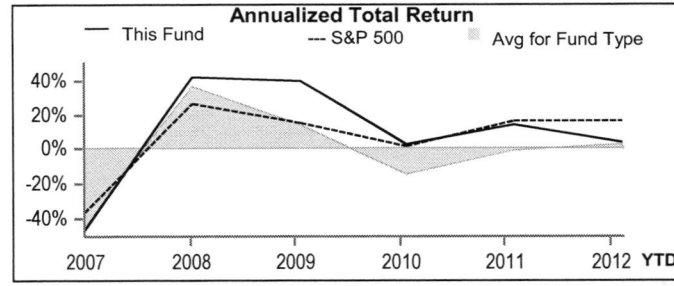

*PowerShares Dynamic Enrg Exp & P (PXE)

B   **Good**

Fund Family: Invesco Powershares Capital Mgmt LL
Fund Type: Energy/Natural Resources
Inception Date: October 26, 2005

Major Rating Factors: Strong performance is the major factor driving the B (Good) TheStreet.com Investment Rating for *PowerShares Dynamic Enrg Exp & P. The fund currently has a performance rating of B+ (Good) based on an annualized return of 19.40% over the last three years and a total return of 3.15% year to date 2012. Factored into the performance evaluation is an expense ratio of 0.65% (very low).

The fund's risk rating is currently B- (Good). It carries a beta of 1.11, meaning it is expected to move 11.1% for every 10% move in the market. Volatility, as measured by both the semi-deviation and a drawdown factor, is considered low. As of December 31, 2012, *PowerShares Dynamic Enrg Exp & P traded at a discount of 3.30% below its net asset value, which is better than its one-year historical average discount of .03%.

Peter Hubbard has been running the fund for 6 years and currently receives a manager quality ranking of 87 (0=worst, 99=best). If you desire only a moderate level of risk and strong performance, then this fund is an excellent option.

Data Date	Investment Rating	Net Assets ($Mil)	Price	Performance Rating/Pts	Total Return Y-T-D	Risk Rating/Pts
12-12	B	65.10	26.97	B+ / 8.7	3.15%	B- / 7.1
2011	C+	67.30	22.43	C+ / 6.2	3.21%	B- / 7.0
2010	C+	76.10	23.07	C+ / 6.8	40.36%	C / 4.9
2009	D+	51.34	16.58	D+ / 2.7	13.13%	C / 5.2

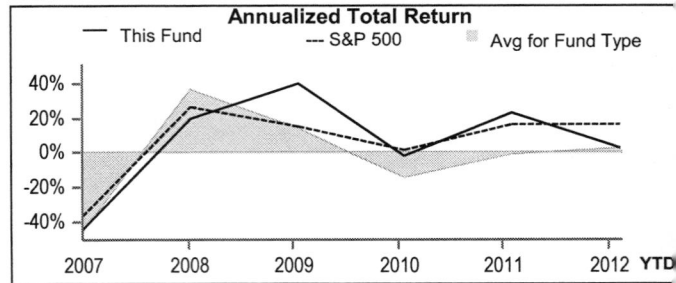

*PowerShares Dynamic Financial (PFI)

C+ **Fair**

Fund Family: Invesco Powershares Capital Mgmt LL
Fund Type: Financial Services
Inception Date: October 12, 2006

Major Rating Factors: Middle of the road best describes *PowerShares Dynamic Financial whose TheStreet.com Investment Rating is currently a C+ (Fair). The fund currently has a performance rating of C+ (Fair) based on an annualized return of 10.76% over the last three years and a total return of 4.02% year to date 2012. Factored into the performance evaluation is an expense ratio of 0.65% (very low).

The fund's risk rating is currently B- (Good). It carries a beta of 0.86, meaning the fund's expected move will be 8.6% for every 10% move in the market. Volatility, as measured by both the semi-deviation and a drawdown factor, is considered low. As of December 31, 2012, *PowerShares Dynamic Financial traded at a discount of 3.99% below its net asset value, which is better than its one-year historical average discount of .05%.

Peter Hubbard has been running the fund for 6 years and currently receives a manager quality ranking of 72 (0=worst, 99=best). If you desire an average level of risk, then this fund may be an option.

Data Date	Investment Rating	Net Assets ($Mil)	Price	Performance Rating/Pts	Total Return Y-T-D	Risk Rating/Pts
12-12	C+	19.10	21.15	C+ / 5.8	4.02%	B- / 7.9
2011	D+	17.00	17.93	D+ / 2.7	1.76%	B- / 7.5
2010	D+	19.00	19.01	D / 2.2	15.84%	C+ / 6.0
2009	D-	14.63	16.87	E+ / 0.8	-5.95%	C+ / 5.9

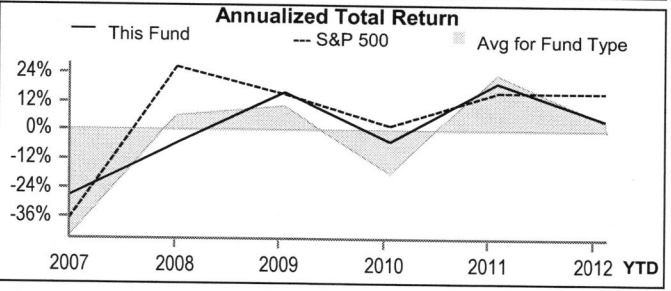

*PowerShares Dynamic Food & Bever (PBJ)

C+ **Fair**

Fund Family: Invesco Powershares Capital Mgmt LL
Fund Type: Income
Inception Date: June 23, 2005

Major Rating Factors: Middle of the road best describes *PowerShares Dynamic Food & Bever whose TheStreet.com Investment Rating is currently a C+ (Fair). The fund currently has a performance rating of C+ (Fair) based on an annualized return of 14.54% over the last three years and a total return of 3.01% year to date 2012. Factored into the performance evaluation is an expense ratio of 0.63% (very low).

The fund's risk rating is currently B (Good). It carries a beta of 0.55, meaning the fund's expected move will be 5.5% for every 10% move in the market. Volatility, as measured by both the semi-deviation and a drawdown factor, is considered low. As of December 31, 2012, *PowerShares Dynamic Food & Bever traded at a discount of 2.88% below its net asset value, which is better than its one-year historical average discount of .06%.

Peter Hubbard has been running the fund for 6 years and currently receives a manager quality ranking of 85 (0=worst, 99=best). If you desire an average level of risk, then this fund may be an option.

Data Date	Investment Rating	Net Assets ($Mil)	Price	Performance Rating/Pts	Total Return Y-T-D	Risk Rating/Pts
12-12	C+	102.70	19.91	C+ / 5.6	3.01%	B / 8.8
2011	C+	190.90	19.17	C / 5.5	-0.94%	B / 8.5
2010	A	126.70	18.23	B / 8.2	30.78%	B- / 7.0
2009	C-	86.59	14.20	D / 1.9	8.78%	B- / 7.0

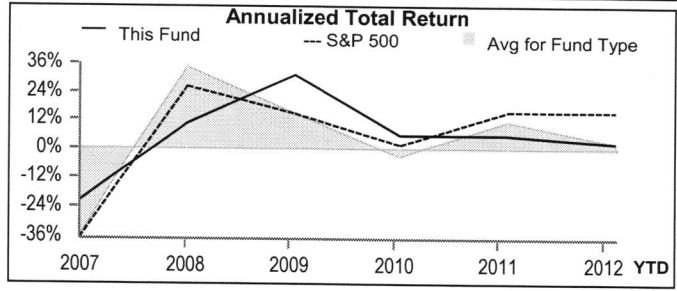

*PowerShares Dynamic Hlthcare (PTH)

C **Fair**

Fund Family: Invesco Powershares Capital Mgmt LL
Fund Type: Health
Inception Date: October 12, 2006

Major Rating Factors: Middle of the road best describes *PowerShares Dynamic Hlthcare whose TheStreet.com Investment Rating is currently a C (Fair). The fund currently has a performance rating of C (Fair) based on an annualized return of 12.62% over the last three years and a total return of 4.72% year to date 2012. Factored into the performance evaluation is an expense ratio of 0.65% (very low).

The fund's risk rating is currently B- (Good). It carries a beta of 0.89, meaning the fund's expected move will be 8.9% for every 10% move in the market. Volatility, as measured by both the semi-deviation and a drawdown factor, is considered low. As of December 31, 2012, *PowerShares Dynamic Hlthcare traded at a discount of 4.51% below its net asset value, which is better than its one-year historical average discount of .02%.

Peter Hubbard has been running the fund for 6 years and currently receives a manager quality ranking of 67 (0=worst, 99=best). If you desire an average level of risk, then this fund may be an option.

Data Date	Investment Rating	Net Assets ($Mil)	Price	Performance Rating/Pts	Total Return Y-T-D	Risk Rating/Pts
12-12	C	49.50	32.82	C / 5.5	4.72%	B- / 7.1
2011	C+	45.90	28.69	C+ / 5.6	1.92%	B- / 7.8
2010	D+	49.70	26.85	D+ / 2.7	13.58%	C+ / 5.9
2009	C-	71.58	23.64	D+ / 2.9	19.54%	C+ / 6.0

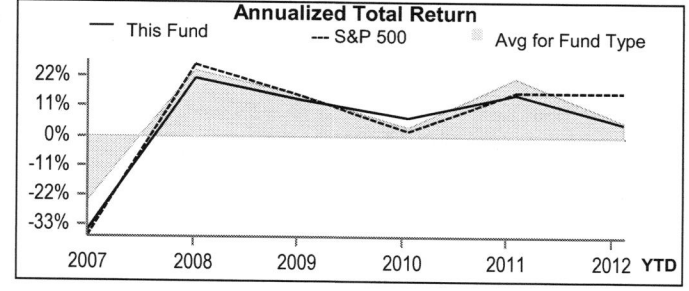

*PowerShares Dynamic Industrials (PRN)   B   Good

Fund Family: Invesco Powershares Capital Mgmt LL
Fund Type: Income
Inception Date: October 12, 2006

Major Rating Factors: Strong performance is the major factor driving the B (Good) TheStreet.com Investment Rating for *PowerShares Dynamic Industrials. The fund currently has a performance rating of B (Good) based on an annualized return of 15.30% over the last three years and a total return of 4.58% year to date 2012. Factored into the performance evaluation is an expense ratio of 0.65% (very low).

The fund's risk rating is currently B- (Good). It carries a beta of 1.28, meaning it is expected to move 12.8% for every 10% move in the market. Volatility, as measured by both the semi-deviation and a drawdown factor, is considered low. As of December 31, 2012, *PowerShares Dynamic Industrials traded at a discount of 4.39% below its net asset value, which is better than its one-year historical average discount of .13%.

Peter Hubbard has been running the fund for 6 years and currently receives a manager quality ranking of 54 (0=worst, 99=best). If you desire only a moderate level of risk and strong performance, then this fund is an excellent option.

Data Date	Investment Rating	Net Assets ($Mil)	Price	Performance Rating/Pts	Total Return Y-T-D	Risk Rating/Pts
12-12	B	29.00	31.82	B / 7.8	4.58%	B- / 7.4
2011	C-	46.30	27.31	C / 4.4	2.00%	B- / 7.2
2010	B-	55.60	29.35	B- / 7.0	33.38%	C / 5.5
2009	D	60.32	22.25	D / 1.8	12.95%	C+ / 5.6

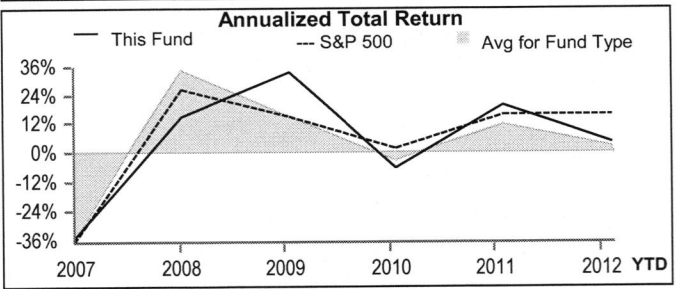

*PowerShares Dynamic Insurance (PIC)   B-   Good

Fund Family: Invesco Powershares Capital Mgmt LL
Fund Type: Income
Inception Date: October 26, 2005

Major Rating Factors: Strong performance is the major factor driving the B- (Good) TheStreet.com Investment Rating for *PowerShares Dynamic Insurance. The fund currently has a performance rating of B- (Good) based on an annualized return of 12.86% over the last three years and a total return of 5.09% year to date 2012. Factored into the performance evaluation is an expense ratio of 0.63% (very low).

The fund's risk rating is currently B- (Good). It carries a beta of 1.01, meaning that its performance tracks fairly well with that of the overall stock market. Volatility, as measured by both the semi-deviation and a drawdown factor, is considered low. As of December 31, 2012, *PowerShares Dynamic Insurance traded at a discount of 4.56% below its net asset value, which is better than its one-year historical average discount of .08%.

Peter Hubbard has been running the fund for 6 years and currently receives a manager quality ranking of 54 (0=worst, 99=best). If you desire only a moderate level of risk and strong performance, then this fund is an excellent option.

Data Date	Investment Rating	Net Assets ($Mil)	Price	Performance Rating/Pts	Total Return Y-T-D	Risk Rating/Pts
12-12	B-	8.00	17.60	B- / 7.1	5.09%	B- / 7.9
2011	C-	6.70	14.99	C- / 3.0	0.93%	B- / 7.6
2010	C+	18.80	16.36	C+ / 6.9	23.35%	C+ / 6.5
2009	D	26.81	13.68	D- / 1.1	-3.54%	C+ / 6.2

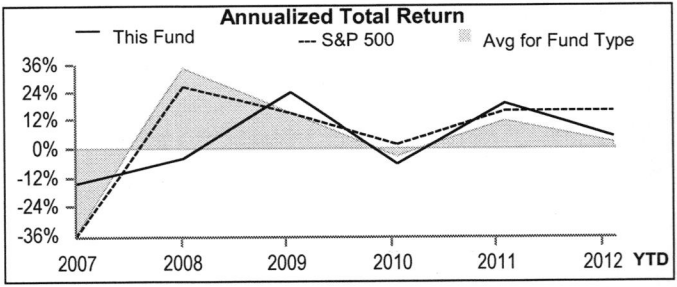

*PowerShares Dynamic Large Cap Gr (PWB)   C+   Fair

Fund Family: Invesco Powershares Capital Mgmt LL
Fund Type: Growth
Inception Date: March 3, 2005

Major Rating Factors: Middle of the road best describes *PowerShares Dynamic Large Cap Gr whose TheStreet.com Investment Rating is currently a C+ (Fair). The fund currently has a performance rating of C+ (Fair) based on an annualized return of 11.42% over the last three years and a total return of 3.33% year to date 2012. Factored into the performance evaluation is an expense ratio of 0.61% (very low).

The fund's risk rating is currently B- (Good). It carries a beta of 1.07, meaning that its performance tracks fairly well with that of the overall stock market. Volatility, as measured by both the semi-deviation and a drawdown factor, is considered low. As of December 31, 2012, *PowerShares Dynamic Large Cap Gr traded at a discount of 3.17% below its net asset value, which is better than its one-year historical average discount of .04%.

Peter Hubbard has been running the fund for 6 years and currently receives a manager quality ranking of 43 (0=worst, 99=best). If you desire an average level of risk, then this fund may be an option.

Data Date	Investment Rating	Net Assets ($Mil)	Price	Performance Rating/Pts	Total Return Y-T-D	Risk Rating/Pts
12-12	C+	188.20	18.93	C+ / 5.7	3.33%	B- / 7.6
2011	C	163.70	16.12	C / 5.1	0.87%	B- / 7.5
2010	C-	215.50	16.25	C- / 3.6	14.11%	C+ / 5.9
2009	C-	281.17	14.39	C- / 3.0	30.17%	C+ / 5.9

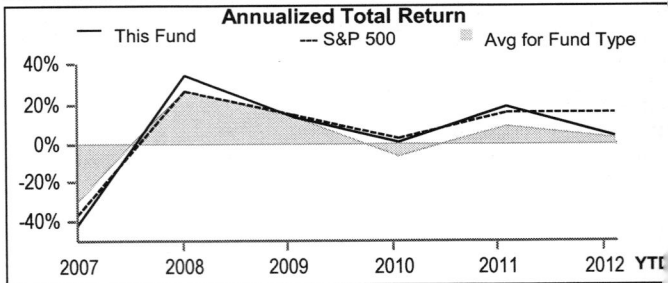

*PowerShares Dynamic Large Cap Va (PWV)

C+   **Fair**

Fund Family: Invesco Powershares Capital Mgmt LL
Fund Type: Income
Inception Date: March 3, 2005

Major Rating Factors: Middle of the road best describes *PowerShares Dynamic Large Cap Va whose TheStreet.com Investment Rating is currently a C+ (Fair). The fund currently has a performance rating of C+ (Fair) based on an annualized return of 12.90% over the last three years and a total return of 3.30% year to date 2012. Factored into the performance evaluation is an expense ratio of 0.59% (very low).

The fund's risk rating is currently B (Good). It carries a beta of 0.91, meaning that its performance tracks fairly well with that of the overall stock market. Volatility, as measured by both the semi-deviation and a drawdown factor, is considered low. As of December 31, 2012, *PowerShares Dynamic Large Cap Va traded at a discount of 3.15% below its net asset value, which is better than its one-year historical average discount of .01%.

Peter Hubbard has been running the fund for 6 years and currently receives a manager quality ranking of 67 (0=worst, 99=best). If you desire an average level of risk, then this fund may be an option.

Data Date	Investment Rating	Net Assets ($Mil)	Price	Performance Rating/Pts	Total Return Y-T-D	Risk Rating/Pts
12-12	C+	459.60	21.85	C+ / 6.0	3.30%	B / 8.5
2011	C+	393.90	19.28	C / 5.1	1.02%	B / 8.1
2010	C	374.50	18.53	C / 4.6	14.34%	C+ / 6.6
2009	C-	262.70	16.75	D+ / 2.6	15.25%	C+ / 6.6

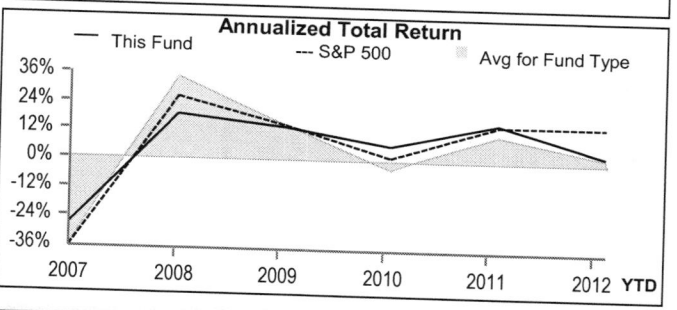

*PowerShares Dynamic Leisure&Ente (PEJ)

A-   **Excellent**

Fund Family: Invesco Powershares Capital Mgmt LL
Fund Type: Income
Inception Date: June 23, 2005

Major Rating Factors:
Strong performance is the major factor driving the A- (Excellent) TheStreet.com Investment Rating for *PowerShares Dynamic Leisure&Ente. The fund currently has a performance rating of B+ (Good) based on an annualized return of 21.77% over the last three years and a total return of 4.84% year to date 2012. Factored into the performance evaluation is an expense ratio of 0.63% (very low).

The fund's risk rating is currently B (Good). It carries a beta of 1.14, meaning it is expected to move 11.4% for every 10% move in the market. Volatility, as measured by both the semi-deviation and a drawdown factor, is considered low. As of December 31, 2012, *PowerShares Dynamic Leisure&Ente traded at a discount of 4.49% below its net asset value.

Peter Hubbard has been running the fund for 6 years and currently receives a manager quality ranking of 86 (0=worst, 99=best). If you desire only a moderate level of risk and strong performance, then this fund is an excellent option.

Data Date	Investment Rating	Net Assets ($Mil)	Price	Performance Rating/Pts	Total Return Y-T-D	Risk Rating/Pts
12-12	A-	58.50	22.95	B+ / 8.8	4.84%	B / 8.0
2011	B	35.50	18.69	B / 7.7	0.64%	B- / 7.6
2010	A-	66.30	18.47	B+ / 8.8	39.93%	C+ / 5.6
2009	D	12.78	13.39	D / 2.1	37.52%	C / 5.4

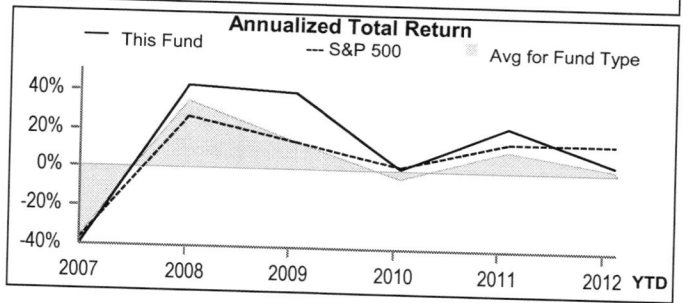

*PowerShares Dynamic MagniQuant (PIQ)

C+   **Fair**

Fund Family: Invesco Powershares Capital Mgmt LL
Fund Type: Income
Inception Date: October 12, 2006

Major Rating Factors: Middle of the road best describes *PowerShares Dynamic MagniQuant whose TheStreet.com Investment Rating is currently a C+ (Fair). The fund currently has a performance rating of C+ (Fair) based on an annualized return of 12.29% over the last three years and a total return of 4.70% year to date 2012. Factored into the performance evaluation is an expense ratio of 0.65% (very low).

The fund's risk rating is currently B- (Good). It carries a beta of 1.27, meaning it is expected to move 12.7% for every 10% move in the market. Volatility, as measured by both the semi-deviation and a drawdown factor, is considered low. As of December 31, 2012, *PowerShares Dynamic MagniQuant traded at a discount of 4.55% below its net asset value, which is better than its one-year historical average discount of .09%.

Peter Hubbard has been running the fund for 6 years and currently receives a manager quality ranking of 31 (0=worst, 99=best). If you desire an average level of risk, then this fund may be an option.

Data Date	Investment Rating	Net Assets ($Mil)	Price	Performance Rating/Pts	Total Return Y-T-D	Risk Rating/Pts
12-12	C+	16.40	27.05	C+ / 6.1	4.70%	B- / 7.6
2011	C-	16.50	23.70	C / 4.4	0.42%	B- / 7.5
2010	C	25.60	24.54	C / 5.2	20.68%	C+ / 6.0
2009	D	28.65	20.59	D / 1.6	16.89%	C+ / 6.0

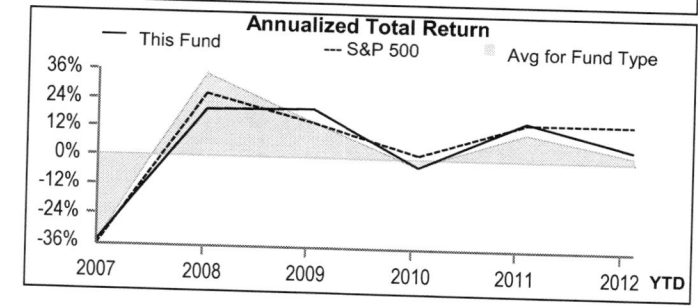

*PowerShares Dynamic Market (PWC)   C+   Fair

Fund Family: Invesco Powershares Capital Mgmt LL
Fund Type: Growth
Inception Date: May 1, 2003

Major Rating Factors: Middle of the road best describes *PowerShares Dynamic Market whose TheStreet.com Investment Rating is currently a C+ (Fair). The fund currently has a performance rating of C+ (Fair) based on an annualized return of 11.31% over the last three years and a total return of 3.85% year to date 2012. Factored into the performance evaluation is an expense ratio of 0.60% (very low).

The fund's risk rating is currently B- (Good). It carries a beta of 1.13, meaning it is expected to move 11.3% for every 10% move in the market. Volatility, as measured by both the semi-deviation and a drawdown factor, is considered low. As of December 31, 2012, *PowerShares Dynamic Market traded at a discount of 3.73% below its net asset value, which is better than its one-year historical average discount of .04%.

Peter Hubbard has been running the fund for 6 years and currently receives a manager quality ranking of 37 (0=worst, 99=best). If you desire an average level of risk, then this fund may be an option.

Data Date	Investment Rating	Net Assets ($Mil)	Price	Perfor-mance Rating/Pts	Total Return Y-T-D	Risk Rating/Pts
12-12	C+	132.10	48.78	C+ / 6.0	3.85%	B- / 7.6
2011	C-	131.10	41.02	C- / 3.7	1.27%	B- / 7.7
2010	C-	195.80	44.01	C- / 3.8	18.15%	C+ / 6.3
2009	D	260.78	38.05	D- / 1.4	15.86%	C+ / 6.2

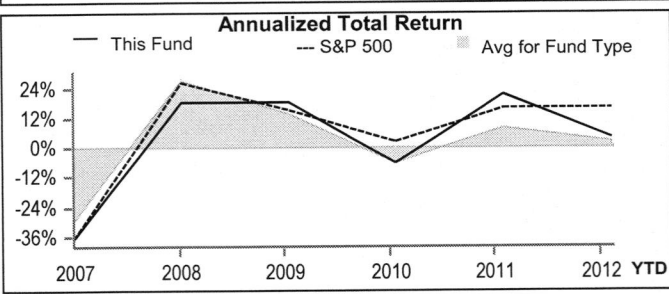

*PowerShares Dynamic Media (PBS)   B-   Good

Fund Family: Invesco Powershares Capital Mgmt LL
Fund Type: Income
Inception Date: June 23, 2005

Major Rating Factors: Strong performance is the major factor driving the B- (Good) TheStreet.com Investment Rating for *PowerShares Dynamic Media. The fund currently has a performance rating of B- (Good) based on an annualized return of 14.43% over the last three years and a total return of 3.12% year to date 2012. Factored into the performance evaluation is an expense ratio of 0.63% (very low).

The fund's risk rating is currently B- (Good). It carries a beta of 1.32, meaning it is expected to move 13.2% for every 10% move in the market. Volatility, as measured by both the semi-deviation and a drawdown factor, is considered low. As of December 31, 2012, *PowerShares Dynamic Media traded at a discount of 3.08% below its net asset value, which is better than its one-year historical average premium of .01%.

Peter Hubbard has been running the fund for 6 years and currently receives a manager quality ranking of 44 (0=worst, 99=best). If you desire only a moderate level of risk and strong performance, then this fund is an excellent option.

Data Date	Investment Rating	Net Assets ($Mil)	Price	Perfor-mance Rating/Pts	Total Return Y-T-D	Risk Rating/Pts
12-12	B-	84.50	16.69	B- / 7.5	3.12%	B- / 7.4
2011	B-	124.00	13.25	B- / 7.0	2.03%	B- / 7.5
2010	C+	84.10	13.92	C+ / 6.1	20.54%	C / 5.4
2009	D+	8.25	11.64	D+ / 2.7	55.05%	C / 5.1

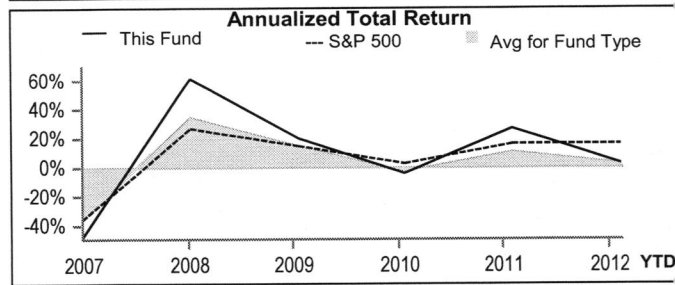

*PowerShares Dynamic Networking (PXQ)   C-   Fair

Fund Family: Invesco Powershares Capital Mgmt LL
Fund Type: Growth
Inception Date: June 23, 2005

Major Rating Factors: Middle of the road best describes *PowerShares Dynamic Networking whose TheStreet.com Investment Rating is currently a C- (Fair). The fund currently has a performance rating of C (Fair) based on an annualized return of 12.41% over the last three years and a total return of 2.61% year to date 2012. Factored into the performance evaluation is an expense ratio of 0.63% (very low).

The fund's risk rating is currently C+ (Fair). It carries a beta of 1.49, meaning it is expected to move 14.9% for every 10% move in the market. Volatility, as measured by both the semi-deviation and a drawdown factor, is considered low. As of December 31, 2012, *PowerShares Dynamic Networking traded at a discount of 2.69% below its net asset value, which is better than its one-year historical average discount of .10%.

Peter Hubbard has been running the fund for 6 years and currently receives a manager quality ranking of 27 (0=worst, 99=best). If you desire an average level of risk, then this fund may be an option.

Data Date	Investment Rating	Net Assets ($Mil)	Price	Perfor-mance Rating/Pts	Total Return Y-T-D	Risk Rating/Pts
12-12	C-	39.40	25.33	C / 5.0	2.61%	C+ / 6.9
2011	B-	81.40	24.29	B / 7.6	0.95%	B- / 7.0
2010	A	116.10	26.46	A- / 9.2	47.05%	C+ / 5.8
2009	C	16.28	18.14	C+ / 6.1	63.13%	C / 5.5

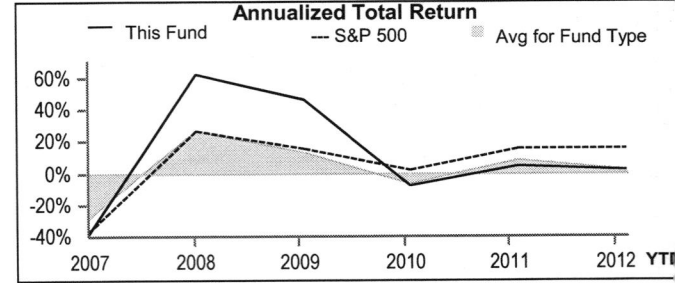

*PowerShares Dynamic Oil & Gas Sv (PXJ)

D　**Weak**

Fund Family: Invesco Powershares Capital Mgmt LL
Fund Type: Energy/Natural Resources
Inception Date: October 26, 2005

Major Rating Factors: *PowerShares Dynamic Oil & Gas Sv receives a TheStreet.com Investment Rating of D (Weak). The fund currently has a performance rating of C- (Fair) based on an annualized return of 6.46% over the last three years and a total return of 5.16% year to date 2012. Factored into the performance evaluation is an expense ratio of 0.63% (very low).

The fund's risk rating is currently C+ (Fair). It carries a beta of 1.44, meaning it is expected to move 14.4% for every 10% move in the market. Volatility, as measured by both the semi-deviation and a drawdown factor, is considered low. As of December 31, 2012, *PowerShares Dynamic Oil & Gas Sv traded at a discount of 5.00% below its net asset value, which is better than its one-year historical average discount of .08%.

Peter Hubbard has been running the fund for 6 years and currently receives a manager quality ranking of 19 (0=worst, 99=best). If you desire an average level of risk, then this fund may be an option.

Data Date	Investment Rating	Net Assets ($Mil)	Price	Performance Rating/Pts	Total Return Y-T-D	Risk Rating/Pts
12-12	D	113.00	20.34	C- / 3.3	5.16%	C+ / 6.0
2011	C	169.50	20.16	C+ / 6.6	2.93%	C+ / 6.0
2010	D+	199.50	21.83	C- / 4.0	29.63%	C- / 4.1
2009	D+	155.72	16.96	C- / 3.9	43.35%	C / 4.4

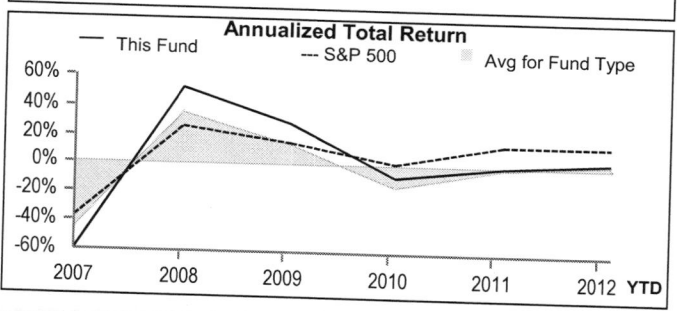

*PowerShares Dynamic OTC Portfoli (PWO)

D+　**Weak**

Fund Family: Invesco Powershares Capital Mgmt LL
Fund Type: Growth
Inception Date: May 1, 2003

Major Rating Factors: *PowerShares Dynamic OTC Portfoli receives a TheStreet.com Investment Rating of D+ (Weak). The fund currently has a performance rating of C- (Fair) based on an annualized return of 7.72% over the last three years and a total return of 3.35% year to date 2012. Factored into the performance evaluation is an expense ratio of 0.60% (very low).

The fund's risk rating is currently B- (Good). It carries a beta of 1.17, meaning it is expected to move 11.7% for every 10% move in the market. Volatility, as measured by both the semi-deviation and a drawdown factor, is considered low. As of December 31, 2012, *PowerShares Dynamic OTC Portfoli traded at a discount of 3.57% below its net asset value, which is better than its one-year historical average discount of .06%.

Peter Hubbard has been running the fund for 6 years and currently receives a manager quality ranking of 21 (0=worst, 99=best). If you desire an average level of risk, then this fund may be an option.

Data Date	Investment Rating	Net Assets ($Mil)	Price	Performance Rating/Pts	Total Return Y-T-D	Risk Rating/Pts
12-12	D+	21.80	48.10	C- / 3.3	3.35%	B- / 7.1
2011	C-	27.20	45.44	C- / 3.9	1.47%	B- / 7.4
2010	C+	37.20	49.80	C / 5.5	23.64%	C+ / 6.0
2009	D	39.39	40.45	D- / 1.4	17.93%	C+ / 5.6

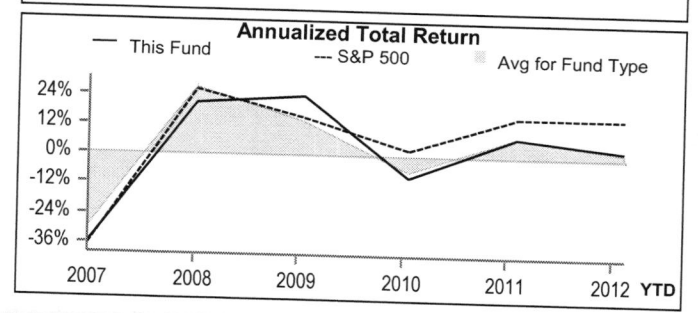

*PowerShares Dynamic Pharmaceutic (PJP)

B+　**Good**

Fund Family: Invesco Powershares Capital Mgmt LL
Fund Type: Health
Inception Date: June 23, 2005

Major Rating Factors:
Exceptional performance is the major factor driving the B+ (Good) TheStreet.com Investment Rating for *PowerShares Dynamic Pharmaceutic. The fund currently has a performance rating of A (Excellent) based on an annualized return of 25.51% over the last three years and a total return of 5.85% year to date 2012. Factored into the performance evaluation is an expense ratio of 0.63% (very low).

The fund's risk rating is currently B- (Good). It carries a beta of 0.70, meaning the fund's expected move will be 7.0% for every 10% move in the market. Volatility, as measured by both the semi-deviation and a drawdown factor, is considered low. As of December 31, 2012, *PowerShares Dynamic Pharmaceutic traded at a discount of 5.47% below its net asset value, which is better than its one-year historical average premium of .03%.

Peter Hubbard has been running the fund for 6 years and currently receives a manager quality ranking of 95 (0=worst, 99=best). If you desire only a moderate level of risk and strong performance, then this fund is an excellent option.

Data Date	Investment Rating	Net Assets ($Mil)	Price	Performance Rating/Pts	Total Return Y-T-D	Risk Rating/Pts
12-12	B+	316.00	34.53	A / 9.3	5.85%	B- / 7.1
2011	B	182.80	28.18	B / 7.9	0.50%	B- / 7.5
2010	A-	94.60	23.64	B+ / 8.3	27.81%	C+ / 5.9
2009	C-	104.35	18.65	C- / 3.8	15.07%	C / 5.2

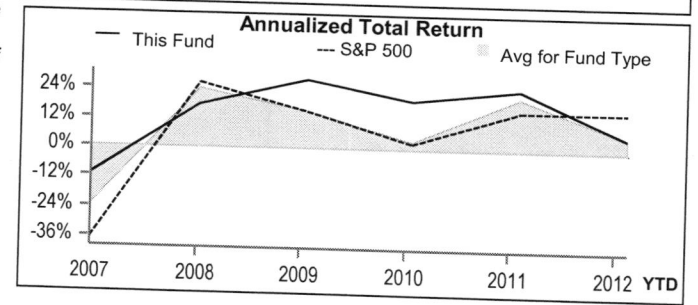

*PowerShares Dynamic Retail (PMR)   B   Good

Fund Family: Invesco Powershares Capital Mgmt LL
Fund Type: Income
Inception Date: October 26, 2005

Major Rating Factors: Strong performance is the major factor driving the B (Good) TheStreet.com Investment Rating for *PowerShares Dynamic Retail. The fund currently has a performance rating of B- (Good) based on an annualized return of 18.09% over the last three years and a total return of -0.32% year to date 2012. Factored into the performance evaluation is an expense ratio of 0.63% (very low).

The fund's risk rating is currently B (Good). It carries a beta of 0.99, meaning that its performance tracks fairly well with that of the overall stock market. Volatility, as measured by both the semi-deviation and a drawdown factor, is considered low. As of December 31, 2012, *PowerShares Dynamic Retail traded at a premium of .20% above its net asset value, which is worse than its one-year historical average discount of .04%.

Peter Hubbard has been running the fund for 6 years and currently receives a manager quality ranking of 85 (0=worst, 99=best). If you desire only a moderate level of risk and strong performance, then this fund is an excellent option.

Data Date	Investment Rating	Net Assets ($Mil)	Price	Performance Rating/Pts	Total Return Y-T-D	Risk Rating/Pts
12-12	B	53.00	25.22	B- / 7.2	-0.32%	B / 8.2
2011	B	29.70	21.96	B / 8.0	1.46%	B / 8.0
2010	A-	13.60	19.45	B+ / 8.3	24.90%	C+ / 6.7
2009	D+	77.61	15.82	D / 1.9	27.20%	C+ / 6.2

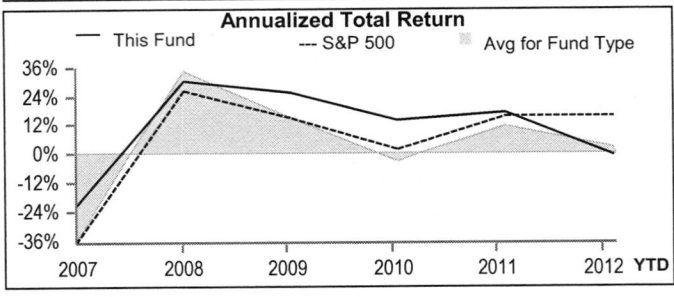

*PowerShares Dynamic Semiconducto (PSI)   D   Weak

Fund Family: Invesco Powershares Capital Mgmt LL
Fund Type: Income
Inception Date: June 23, 2005

Major Rating Factors:
Disappointing performance is the major factor driving the D (Weak) TheStreet.com Investment Rating for *PowerShares Dynamic Semiconducto. The fund currently has a performance rating of D+ (Weak) based on an annualized return of 5.02% over the last three years and a total return of 2.76% year to date 2012. Factored into the performance evaluation is an expense ratio of 0.63% (very low).

The fund's risk rating is currently C+ (Fair). It carries a beta of 1.58, meaning it is expected to move 15.8% for every 10% move in the market. Volatility, as measured by both the semi-deviation and a drawdown factor, is considered low. As of December 31, 2012, *PowerShares Dynamic Semiconducto traded at a discount of 2.96% below its net asset value, which is better than its one-year historical average discount of .03%.

Peter Hubbard has been running the fund for 6 years and currently receives a manager quality ranking of 10 (0=worst, 99=best). This fund offers only a moderate level of risk but investors looking for strong performance are still waiting.

Data Date	Investment Rating	Net Assets ($Mil)	Price	Performance Rating/Pts	Total Return Y-T-D	Risk Rating/Pts
12-12	D	15.90	14.40	D+ / 2.7	2.76%	C+ / 6.7
2011	C-	22.30	13.89	C / 4.4	1.73%	C+ / 6.7
2010	C+	37.40	16.28	C+ / 6.6	20.74%	C / 5.3
2009	D+	36.37	13.53	D+ / 2.6	41.71%	C / 5.2

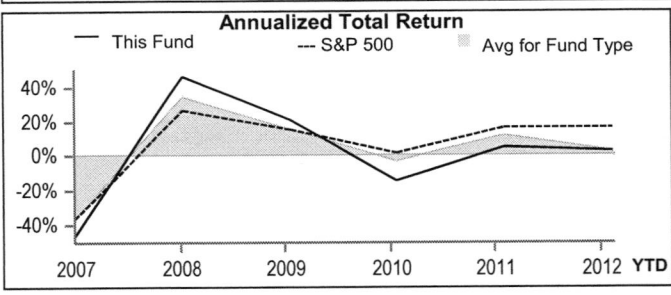

*PowerShares Dynamic Software (PSJ)   C-   Fair

Fund Family: Invesco Powershares Capital Mgmt LL
Fund Type: Growth
Inception Date: June 23, 2005

Major Rating Factors: Middle of the road best describes *PowerShares Dynamic Software whose TheStreet.com Investment Rating is currently a C- (Fair). The fund currently has a performance rating of C (Fair) based on an annualized return of 10.07% over the last three years and a total return of 3.57% year to date 2012. Factored into the performance evaluation is an expense ratio of 0.63% (very low).

The fund's risk rating is currently C+ (Fair). It carries a beta of 1.05, meaning that its performance tracks fairly well with that of the overall stock market. Volatility, as measured by both the semi-deviation and a drawdown factor, is considered low. As of December 31, 2012, *PowerShares Dynamic Software traded at a discount of 3.52% below its net asset value, which is better than its one-year historical average discount of .04%.

Peter Hubbard has been running the fund for 6 years and currently receives a manager quality ranking of 35 (0=worst, 99=best). If you desire an average level of risk, then this fund may be an option.

Data Date	Investment Rating	Net Assets ($Mil)	Price	Performance Rating/Pts	Total Return Y-T-D	Risk Rating/Pts
12-12	C-	44.80	27.14	C / 4.9	3.57%	C+ / 6.8
2011	C+	50.20	23.45	C+ / 5.9	-0.99%	B- / 7.4
2010	A-	66.00	24.96	B / 7.9	20.06%	C+ / 6.4
2009	C+	36.90	20.79	C+ / 6.2	51.42%	C+ / 5.9

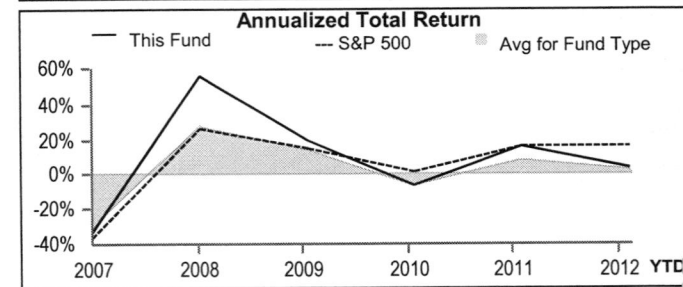

*PowerShares Dynamic Technology (PTF)

D+   **Weak**

Fund Family: Invesco Powershares Capital Mgmt LL
Fund Type: Growth
Inception Date: October 12, 2006

Major Rating Factors: *PowerShares Dynamic Technology receives a TheStreet.com Investment Rating of D+ (Weak). The fund currently has a performance rating of C- (Fair) based on an annualized return of 6.78% over the last three years and a total return of 4.64% year to date 2012. Factored into the performance evaluation is an expense ratio of 0.65% (very low).

    The fund's risk rating is currently C+ (Fair). It carries a beta of 1.36, meaning it is expected to move 13.6% for every 10% move in the market. Volatility, as measured by both the semi-deviation and a drawdown factor, is considered low. As of December 31, 2012, *PowerShares Dynamic Technology traded at a discount of 4.63% below its net asset value, which is better than its one-year historical average discount of .10%.

    Peter Hubbard has been running the fund for 6 years and currently receives a manager quality ranking of 14 (0=worst, 99=best). If you desire an average level of risk, then this fund may be an option.

Data Date	Investment Rating	Net Assets ($Mil)	Price	Performance Rating/Pts	Total Return Y-T-D	Risk Rating/Pts
12-12	D+	29.00	26.17	C- / 3.9	4.64%	C+ / 6.8
2011	C-	27.70	23.28	C- / 4.0	0.83%	B- / 7.1
2010	C	42.30	25.63	C / 4.9	11.21%	C+ / 5.7
2009	C-	25.93	23.07	C- / 3.5	38.89%	C+ / 5.6

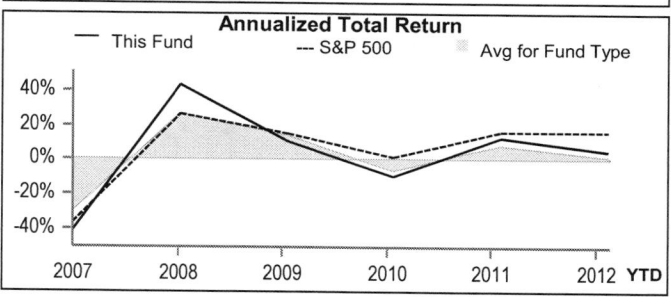

*PowerShares Dynamic Utilities (PUI)

C   **Fair**

Fund Family: Invesco Powershares Capital Mgmt LL
Fund Type: Utilities
Inception Date: October 26, 2005

Major Rating Factors: Middle of the road best describes *PowerShares Dynamic Utilities whose TheStreet.com Investment Rating is currently a C (Fair). The fund currently has a performance rating of C- (Fair) based on an annualized return of 9.34% over the last three years and a total return of 2.25% year to date 2012. Factored into the performance evaluation is an expense ratio of 0.63% (very low).

    The fund's risk rating is currently B (Good). It carries a beta of 0.85, meaning the fund's expected move will be 8.5% for every 10% move in the market. Volatility, as measured by both the semi-deviation and a drawdown factor, is considered low. As of December 31, 2012, *PowerShares Dynamic Utilities traded at a discount of 2.42% below its net asset value, which is better than its one-year historical average discount of .16%.

    Peter Hubbard has been running the fund for 6 years and currently receives a manager quality ranking of 59 (0=worst, 99=best). If you desire an average level of risk, then this fund may be an option.

Data Date	Investment Rating	Net Assets ($Mil)	Price	Performance Rating/Pts	Total Return Y-T-D	Risk Rating/Pts
12-12	C	38.20	17.31	C- / 3.7	2.25%	B / 8.8
2011	C-	47.10	16.25	C- / 3.2	-1.48%	B / 8.3
2010	C-	41.30	15.59	D+ / 2.3	8.56%	C+ / 6.8
2009	D+	42.07	15.04	D / 1.6	1.82%	C+ / 6.9

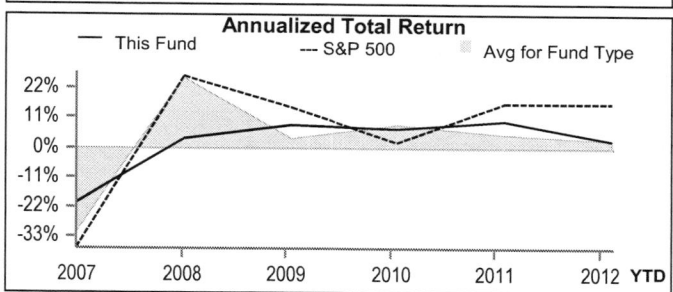

*PowerShares Emg Mkts Infrastruct (PXR)

D   **Weak**

Fund Family: Invesco Powershares Capital Mgmt LL
Fund Type: Emerging Market
Inception Date: October 15, 2008

Major Rating Factors:
Disappointing performance is the major factor driving the D (Weak) TheStreet.com Investment Rating for *PowerShares Emg Mkts Infrastruct. The fund currently has a performance rating of D+ (Weak) based on an annualized return of 1.15% over the last three years and a total return of 2.23% year to date 2012. Factored into the performance evaluation is an expense ratio of 0.75% (very low).

    The fund's risk rating is currently C+ (Fair). It carries a beta of 1.30, meaning it is expected to move 13.0% for every 10% move in the market. Volatility, as measured by both the semi-deviation and a drawdown factor, is considered low. As of December 31, 2012, *PowerShares Emg Mkts Infrastruct traded at a discount of 2.08% below its net asset value, which is better than its one-year historical average discount of .20%.

    Brian McGreal has been running the fund for 5 years and currently receives a manager quality ranking of 25 (0=worst, 99=best). This fund offers only a moderate level of risk but investors looking for strong performance are still waiting.

Data Date	Investment Rating	Net Assets ($Mil)	Price	Performance Rating/Pts	Total Return Y-T-D	Risk Rating/Pts
12-12	D	101.10	43.21	D+ / 2.5	2.23%	C+ / 6.2
2011	C-	112.20	37.13	C- / 4.1	0.57%	C+ / 6.4
2010	A+	192.00	53.62	A+ / 9.6	27.00%	B- / 7.6
2009	A+	21.23	42.84	A+ / 9.7	77.81%	B / 8.0

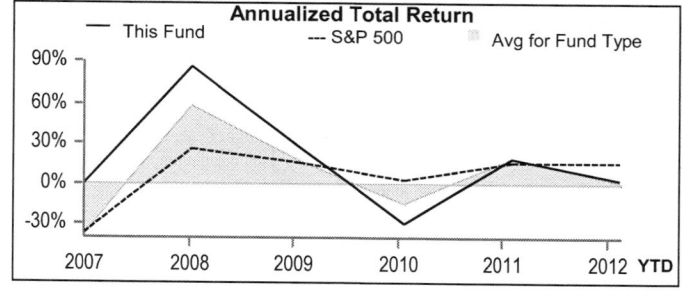

* Denotes ETF Fund

*PowerShares Emrg Mkt Sovereign D (PCY)

B-   **Good**

Fund Family: Invesco Powershares Capital Mgmt LL
Fund Type: Emerging Market
Inception Date: October 11, 2007

Major Rating Factors: *PowerShares Emrg Mkt Sovereign D receives a TheStreet.com Investment Rating of B- (Good). The fund currently has a performance rating of C+ (Fair) based on an annualized return of 13.01% over the last three years and a total return of -0.75% year to date 2012. Factored into the performance evaluation is an expense ratio of 0.50% (very low).

The fund's risk rating is currently B (Good). It carries a beta of 0.65, meaning the fund's expected move will be 6.5% for every 10% move in the market. Volatility, as measured by both the semi-deviation and a drawdown factor, is considered low. As of December 31, 2012, *PowerShares Emrg Mkt Sovereign D traded at a premium of .87% above its net asset value, which is worse than its one-year historical average premium of .05%.

Peter Hubbard has been running the fund for 6 years and currently receives a manager quality ranking of 90 (0=worst, 99=best). If you desire an average level of risk, then this fund may be an option.

Data Date	Investment Rating	Net Assets ($Mil)	Price	Perfor-mance Rating/Pts	Total Return Y-T-D	Risk Rating/Pts
12-12	B-	3,032.70	31.45	C+ / 5.8	-0.75%	B / 8.9
2011	C+	1,405.50	27.36	C / 5.2	-0.88%	B / 8.8
2010	C+	893.80	26.67	C+ / 6.4	11.40%	C+ / 6.2
2009	B+	133.19	25.53	B / 7.7	29.03%	C+ / 6.1

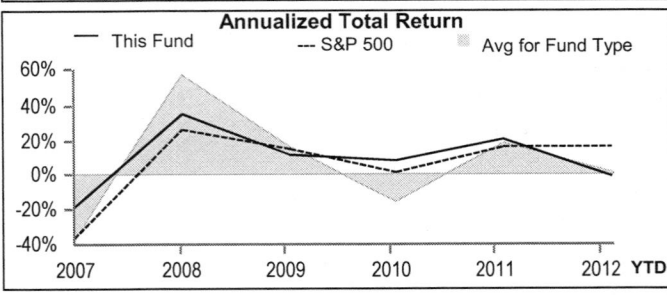

*PowerShares Financial Preferred (PGF)

C   **Fair**

Fund Family: Invesco Powershares Capital Mgmt LL
Fund Type: Financial Services
Inception Date: December 1, 2006

Major Rating Factors: Middle of the road best describes *PowerShares Financial Preferred whose TheStreet.com Investment Rating is currently a C (Fair). The fund currently has a performance rating of C (Fair) based on an annualized return of 10.33% over the last three years and a total return of 1.81% year to date 2012. Factored into the performance evaluation is an expense ratio of 0.66% (very low).

The fund's risk rating is currently B (Good). It carries a beta of 0.32, meaning the fund's expected move will be 3.2% for every 10% move in the market. Volatility, as measured by both the semi-deviation and a drawdown factor, is considered low. As of December 31, 2012, *PowerShares Financial Preferred traded at a discount of 1.67% below its net asset value, which is better than its one-year historical average premium of .08%.

Peter Hubbard has been running the fund for 6 years and currently receives a manager quality ranking of 88 (0=worst, 99=best). If you desire an average level of risk, then this fund may be an option.

Data Date	Investment Rating	Net Assets ($Mil)	Price	Perfor-mance Rating/Pts	Total Return Y-T-D	Risk Rating/Pts
12-12	C	1,720.40	18.28	C / 4.4	1.81%	B / 8.8
2011	D+	1,423.20	16.12	C / 4.6	4.09%	C+ / 5.6
2010	C-	1,735.70	17.61	C+ / 5.6	16.71%	C- / 3.4
2009	D-	773.64	16.32	D+ / 2.3	30.76%	C- / 3.7

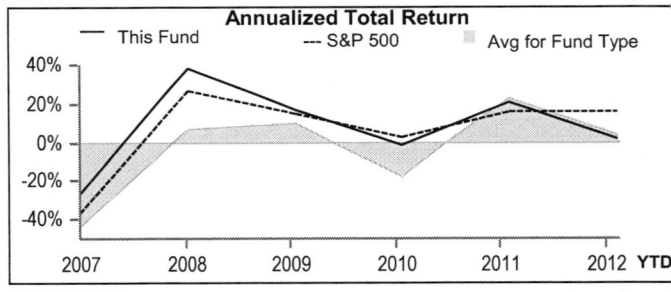

*PowerShares FTSE RAFI Asia Pac E (PAF)

C+   **Fair**

Fund Family: Invesco Powershares Capital Mgmt LL
Fund Type: Foreign
Inception Date: June 25, 2007

Major Rating Factors: Middle of the road best describes *PowerShares FTSE RAFI Asia Pac E whose TheStreet.com Investment Rating is currently a C+ (Fair). The fund currently has a performance rating of C+ (Fair) based on an annualized return of 9.68% over the last three years and a total return of 1.31% year to date 2012. Factored into the performance evaluation is an expense ratio of 0.80% (very low).

The fund's risk rating is currently C+ (Fair). It carries a beta of 1.13, meaning it is expected to move 11.3% for every 10% move in the market. Volatility, as measured by both the semi-deviation and a drawdown factor, is considered low. As of December 31, 2012, *PowerShares FTSE RAFI Asia Pac E traded at a discount of .78% below its net asset value, which is better than its one-year historical average discount of .01%.

Peter Hubbard currently receives a manager quality ranking of 81 (0=worst, 99=best). If you desire an average level of risk, then this fund may be an option.

Data Date	Investment Rating	Net Assets ($Mil)	Price	Perfor-mance Rating/Pts	Total Return Y-T-D	Risk Rating/Pts
12-12	C+	65.10	57.17	C+ / 6.7	1.31%	C+ / 6.7
2011	C+	53.70	46.53	C+ / 6.2	1.31%	B- / 7.0
2010	C+	49.50	55.67	B- / 7.2	23.18%	C / 4.6
2009	A-	15.59	46.81	A+ / 9.7	71.61%	C / 4.6

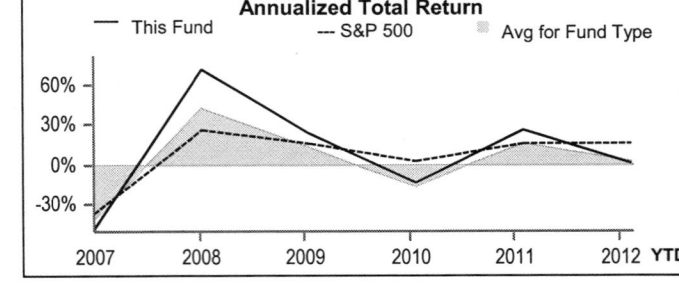

*PowerShares FTSE RAFI DM exUS Sm (PDN)

D+ **Weak**

Fund Family: Invesco Powershares Capital Mgmt LL
Fund Type: Foreign
Inception Date: September 27, 2007

Major Rating Factors: *PowerShares FTSE RAFI DM exUS Sm receives a TheStreet.com Investment Rating of D+ (Weak). The fund currently has a performance rating of C- (Fair) based on an annualized return of 5.98% over the last three years and a total return of 3.28% year to date 2012. Factored into the performance evaluation is an expense ratio of 0.75% (very low).

The fund's risk rating is currently C+ (Fair). It carries a beta of 0.94, meaning that its performance tracks fairly well with that of the overall stock market. Volatility, as measured by both the semi-deviation and a drawdown factor, is considered low. As of December 31, 2012, *PowerShares FTSE RAFI DM exUS Sm traded at a discount of 1.55% below its net asset value, which is better than its one-year historical average discount of .29%.

Peter Hubbard has been running the fund for 6 years and currently receives a manager quality ranking of 70 (0=worst, 99=best). If you desire an average level of risk, then this fund may be an option.

Data Date	Investment Rating	Net Assets ($Mil)	Price	Performance Rating/Pts	Total Return Y-T-D	Risk Rating/Pts
12-12	D+	62.70	23.50	C- / 3.8	3.28%	C+ / 6.6
2011	C-	60.30	20.56	C / 4.6	0.19%	C+ / 6.6
2010	C+	70.20	24.49	C+ / 6.9	20.35%	C / 5.3
2009	B+	14.70	21.04	A- / 9.0	51.55%	C / 5.0

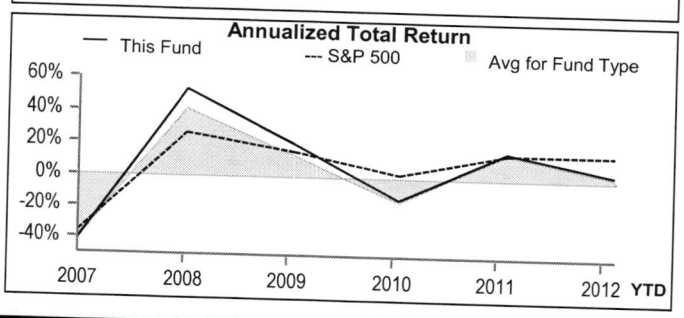

*PowerShares FTSE RAFI Dvlp Mkt e (PXF)

D+ **Weak**

Fund Family: Invesco Powershares Capital Mgmt LL
Fund Type: Foreign
Inception Date: June 25, 2007

Major Rating Factors:
Disappointing performance is the major factor driving the D+ (Weak) TheStreet.com Investment Rating for *PowerShares FTSE RAFI Dvlp Mkt e. The fund currently has a performance rating of D+ (Weak) based on an annualized return of 1.81% over the last three years and a total return of 3.00% year to date 2012. Factored into the performance evaluation is an expense ratio of 0.75% (very low).

The fund's risk rating is currently B- (Good). It carries a beta of 1.14, meaning it is expected to move 11.4% for every 10% move in the market. Volatility, as measured by both the semi-deviation and a drawdown factor, is considered low. As of December 31, 2012, *PowerShares FTSE RAFI Dvlp Mkt e traded at a discount of 2.72% below its net asset value, which is better than its one-year historical average premium of .18%.

Peter Hubbard has been running the fund for 6 years and currently receives a manager quality ranking of 32 (0=worst, 99=best). This fund offers only a moderate level of risk but investors looking for strong performance are still waiting.

Data Date	Investment Rating	Net Assets ($Mil)	Price	Performance Rating/Pts	Total Return Y-T-D	Risk Rating/Pts
12-12	D+	301.20	36.45	D+ / 2.8	3.00%	B- / 7.0
2011	D+	229.70	32.15	D+ / 2.5	-0.56%	B- / 7.2
2010	D	214.60	39.41	D+ / 2.5	8.95%	C / 5.4
2009	A-	93.57	37.86	B+ / 8.7	37.76%	C / 5.5

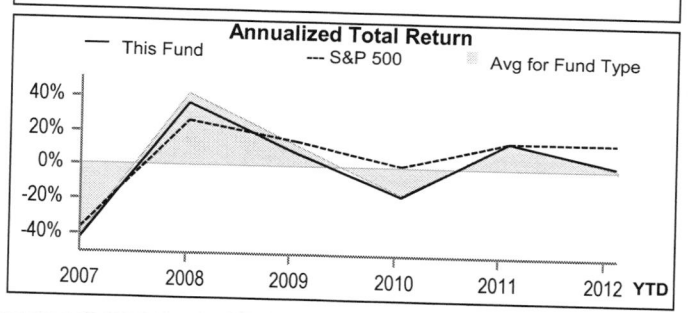

*PowerShares FTSE RAFI Emg Mkts (PXH)

D **Weak**

Fund Family: Invesco Powershares Capital Mgmt LL
Fund Type: Emerging Market
Inception Date: September 27, 2007

Major Rating Factors:
Disappointing performance is the major factor driving the D (Weak) TheStreet.com Investment Rating for *PowerShares FTSE RAFI Emg Mkts. The fund currently has a performance rating of D+ (Weak) based on an annualized return of 1.51% over the last three years and a total return of 0.31% year to date 2012. Factored into the performance evaluation is an expense ratio of 0.85% (very low).

The fund's risk rating is currently C+ (Fair). It carries a beta of 1.02, meaning that its performance tracks fairly well with that of the overall stock market. Volatility, as measured by both the semi-deviation and a drawdown factor, is considered low. As of December 31, 2012, *PowerShares FTSE RAFI Emg Mkts traded at a discount of .35% below its net asset value, which is better than its one-year historical average premium of .16%.

Peter Hubbard has been running the fund for 6 years and currently receives a manager quality ranking of 29 (0=worst, 99=best). This fund offers only a moderate level of risk but investors looking for strong performance are still waiting.

Data Date	Investment Rating	Net Assets ($Mil)	Price	Performance Rating/Pts	Total Return Y-T-D	Risk Rating/Pts
12-12	D	384.30	22.82	D+ / 2.3	0.31%	C+ / 6.7
2011	C-	327.50	20.23	C / 4.4	1.29%	B- / 7.0
2010	C	533.90	25.78	C+ / 5.9	14.23%	C / 4.6
2009	B+	102.87	23.01	A / 9.5	60.22%	C / 4.6

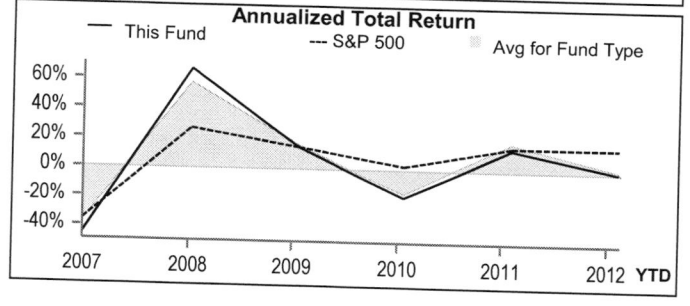

* Denotes ETF Fund

*PowerShares FTSE RAFI US 1000 (PRF)

C+ **Fair**

Fund Family: Invesco Powershares Capital Mgmt LL
Fund Type: Income
Inception Date: December 19, 2005

Major Rating Factors: Middle of the road best describes *PowerShares FTSE RAFI US 1000 whose TheStreet.com Investment Rating is currently a C+ (Fair). The fund currently has a performance rating of C+ (Fair) based on an annualized return of 11.92% over the last three years and a total return of 3.43% year to date 2012. Factored into the performance evaluation is an expense ratio of 0.39% (very low).

The fund's risk rating is currently B (Good). It carries a beta of 1.06, meaning that its performance tracks fairly well with that of the overall stock market. Volatility, as measured by both the semi-deviation and a drawdown factor, is considered low. As of December 31, 2012, *PowerShares FTSE RAFI US 1000 traded at a discount of 3.27% below its net asset value, which is better than its one-year historical average premium of .02%.

Peter Hubbard has been running the fund for 6 years and currently receives a manager quality ranking of 55 (0=worst, 99=best). If you desire an average level of risk, then this fund may be an option.

Data Date	Investment Rating	Net Assets ($Mil)	Price	Perfor-mance Rating/Pts	Total Return Y-T-D	Risk Rating/Pts
12-12	C+	1,479.00	62.43	C+ / 5.8	3.43%	B / 8.1
2011	B-	1,164.80	54.58	C+ / 6.5	1.48%	B- / 7.9
2010	C+	927.40	55.95	C+ / 6.1	20.41%	C+ / 5.8
2009	C-	396.44	47.47	C- / 3.2	37.47%	C+ / 6.3

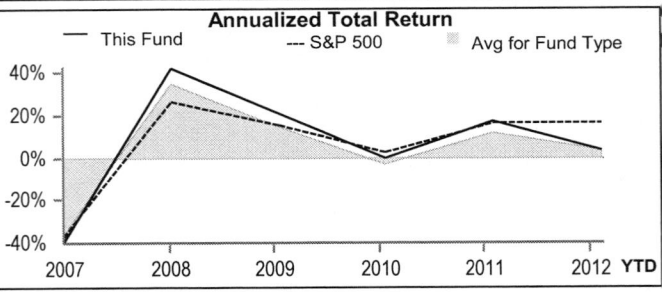

*PowerShares FTSE RAFI US 1500 Sm (PRFZ)

C+ **Fair**

Fund Family: Invesco Powershares Capital Mgmt LL
Fund Type: Income
Inception Date: September 20, 2006

Major Rating Factors: Middle of the road best describes *PowerShares FTSE RAFI US 1500 Sm whose TheStreet.com Investment Rating is currently a C+ (Fair). The fund currently has a performance rating of C+ (Fair) based on an annualized return of 12.88% over the last three years and a total return of 3.65% year to date 2012. Factored into the performance evaluation is an expense ratio of 0.39% (very low).

The fund's risk rating is currently B- (Good). It carries a beta of 1.33, meaning it is expected to move 13.3% for every 10% move in the market. Volatility, as measured by both the semi-deviation and a drawdown factor, is considered low. As of December 31, 2012, *PowerShares FTSE RAFI US 1500 Sm traded at a discount of 3.46% below its net asset value, which is better than its one-year historical average discount of .02%.

Peter Hubbard has been running the fund for 6 years and currently receives a manager quality ranking of 36 (0=worst, 99=best). If you desire an average level of risk, then this fund may be an option.

Data Date	Investment Rating	Net Assets ($Mil)	Price	Perfor-mance Rating/Pts	Total Return Y-T-D	Risk Rating/Pts
12-12	C+	487.20	69.54	C+ / 6.5	3.65%	B- / 7.3
2011	B-	344.40	60.00	B- / 7.4	1.35%	B- / 7.2
2010	B+	389.60	64.47	B+ / 8.3	28.81%	C / 5.4
2009	C	94.40	50.64	C / 4.7	55.35%	C+ / 5.6

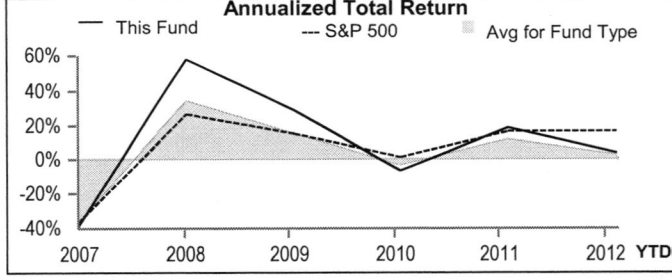

*PowerShares Fundamental High Yie (PHB)

C- **Fair**

Fund Family: Invesco Powershares Capital Mgmt LL
Fund Type: Corporate - High Yield
Inception Date: November 13, 2007

Major Rating Factors: Middle of the road best describes *PowerShares Fundamental High Yie whose TheStreet.com Investment Rating is currently a C- (Fair). The fund currently has a performance rating of C- (Fair) based on an annualized return of 8.89% over the last three years and a total return of 1.09% year to date 2012. Factored into the performance evaluation is an expense ratio of 0.50% (very low).

The fund's risk rating is currently B (Good). It carries a beta of 0.83, meaning the fund's expected move will be 8.3% for every 10% move in the market. Volatility, as measured by both the semi-deviation and a drawdown factor, is considered low. As of December 31, 2012, *PowerShares Fundamental High Yie traded at a discount of 1.08% below its net asset value, which is better than its one-year historical average discount of .01%.

Peter Hubbard has been running the fund for 6 years and currently receives a manager quality ranking of 48 (0=worst, 99=best). If you desire an average level of risk, then this fund may be an option.

Data Date	Investment Rating	Net Assets ($Mil)	Price	Perfor-mance Rating/Pts	Total Return Y-T-D	Risk Rating/Pts
12-12	C-	845.30	19.25	C- / 3.7	1.09%	B / 8.1
2011	C	637.10	18.47	C / 4.7	-1.14%	B- / 7.7
2010	D	407.30	18.19	D+ / 2.5	9.83%	C / 5.2
2009	C+	95.70	18.01	B / 7.7	21.99%	C / 4.8

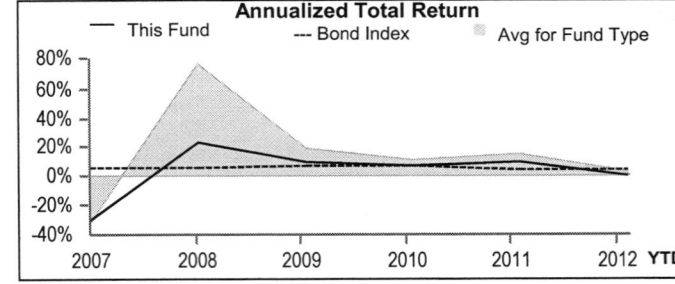

*PowerShares Fundamental Pure Lg (PXLC)

C+ **Fair**

Fund Family: Invesco Powershares Capital Mgmt LL
Fund Type: Growth
Inception Date: December 1, 2006

Major Rating Factors: Middle of the road best describes *PowerShares Fundamental Pure Lg whose TheStreet.com Investment Rating is currently a C+ (Fair). The fund currently has a performance rating of C (Fair) based on an annualized return of 10.94% over the last three years and a total return of 4.69% year to date 2012. Factored into the performance evaluation is an expense ratio of 0.43% (very low).

The fund's risk rating is currently B (Good). It carries a beta of 0.88, meaning the fund's expected move will be 8.8% for every 10% move in the market. Volatility, as measured by both the semi-deviation and a drawdown factor, is considered low. As of December 31, 2012, *PowerShares Fundamental Pure Lg traded at a discount of 4.62% below its net asset value, which is better than its one-year historical average discount of .06%.

Peter Hubbard has been running the fund for 6 years and currently receives a manager quality ranking of 54 (0=worst, 99=best). If you desire an average level of risk, then this fund may be an option.

Data Date	Investment Rating	Net Assets ($Mil)	Price	Performance Rating/Pts	Total Return Y-T-D	Risk Rating/Pts
12-12	C+	25.40	26.64	C / 5.0	4.69%	B / 8.5
2011	C+	23.20	24.44	C / 4.8	1.29%	B / 8.3
2010	C-	32.80	24.27	C- / 3.8	14.84%	C+ / 6.3
2009	D+	33.36	21.67	D / 2.2	16.53%	C+ / 6.4

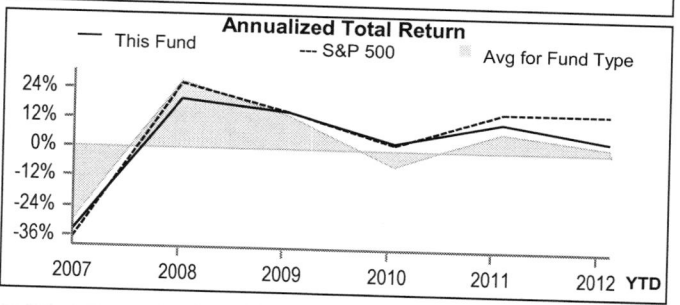

*PowerShares Fundamental Pure Lg (PXLG)

B **Good**

Fund Family: Invesco Powershares Capital Mgmt LL
Fund Type: Growth
Inception Date: June 16, 2011

Major Rating Factors: *PowerShares Fundamental Pure Lg receives a TheStreet.com Investment Rating of B (Good). The fund currently has a performance rating of C+ (Fair) based on an annualized return of 0.00% over the last three years and a total return of 4.01% year to date 2012. Factored into the performance evaluation is an expense ratio of 0.39% (very low).

The fund's risk rating is currently B (Good). It carries a beta of 0.00, meaning the fund's expected move will be 0.0% for every 10% move in the market. Volatility, as measured by both the semi-deviation and a drawdown factor, is considered low. As of December 31, 2012, *PowerShares Fundamental Pure Lg traded at a discount of 3.77% below its net asset value, which is better than its one-year historical average premium of .05%.

Joshua Betts has been running the fund for 2 years and currently receives a manager quality ranking of 65 (0=worst, 99=best). If you desire an average level of risk, then this fund may be an option.

Data Date	Investment Rating	Net Assets ($Mil)	Price	Performance Rating/Pts	Total Return Y-T-D	Risk Rating/Pts
12-12	B	5.60	22.47	C+ / 6.6	4.01%	B / 8.5

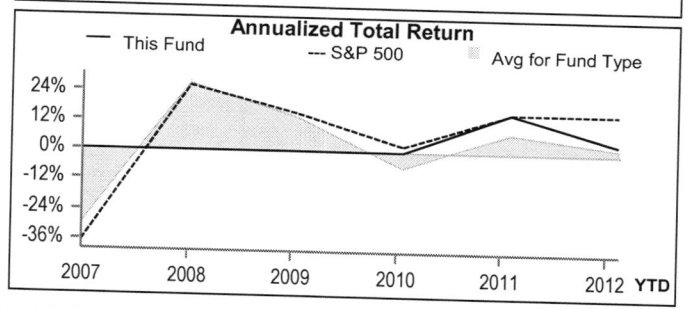

*PowerShares Fundamental Pure Lg (PXLV)

A **Excellent**

Fund Family: Invesco Powershares Capital Mgmt LL
Fund Type: Growth
Inception Date: June 16, 2011

Major Rating Factors:
Strong performance is the major factor driving the A (Excellent) TheStreet.com Investment Rating for *PowerShares Fundamental Pure Lg. The fund currently has a performance rating of B+ (Good) based on an annualized return of 0.00% over the last three years and a total return of 3.72% year to date 2012. Factored into the performance evaluation is an expense ratio of 0.39% (very low).

The fund's risk rating is currently B (Good). It carries a beta of 0.00, meaning the fund's expected move will be 0.0% for every 10% move in the market. Volatility, as measured by both the semi-deviation and a drawdown factor, is considered low. As of December 31, 2012, *PowerShares Fundamental Pure Lg traded at a discount of 3.45% below its net asset value, which is better than its one-year historical average discount of .01%.

Joshua Betts has been running the fund for 2 years and currently receives a manager quality ranking of 58 (0=worst, 99=best). If you desire only a moderate level of risk and strong performance, then this fund is an excellent option.

Data Date	Investment Rating	Net Assets ($Mil)	Price	Performance Rating/Pts	Total Return Y-T-D	Risk Rating/Pts
12-12	A	5.50	21.86	B+ / 8.9	3.72%	B / 8.1

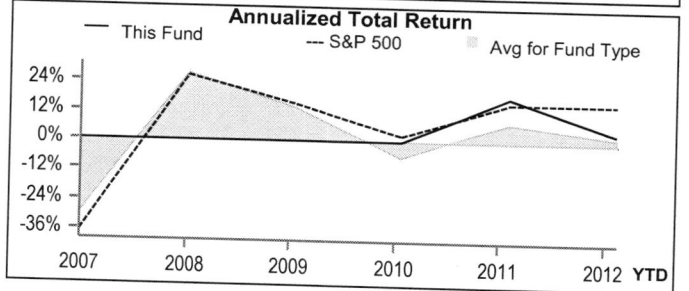

*PowerShares Fundamental Pure Md (PXMC)   C+   Fair

Fund Family: Invesco Powershares Capital Mgmt LL
Fund Type: Growth
Inception Date: December 1, 2006

Major Rating Factors: Middle of the road best describes *PowerShares Fundamental Pure Md whose TheStreet.com Investment Rating is currently a C+ (Fair). The fund currently has a performance rating of C (Fair) based on an annualized return of 11.33% over the last three years and a total return of 3.16% year to date 2012. Factored into the performance evaluation is an expense ratio of 0.43% (very low).

The fund's risk rating is currently B (Good). It carries a beta of 1.07, meaning that its performance tracks fairly well with that of the overall stock market. Volatility, as measured by both the semi-deviation and a drawdown factor, is considered low. As of December 31, 2012, *PowerShares Fundamental Pure Md traded at a discount of 3.03% below its net asset value, which is better than its one-year historical average discount of .02%.

Peter Hubbard has been running the fund for 6 years and currently receives a manager quality ranking of 45 (0=worst, 99=best). If you desire an average level of risk, then this fund may be an option.

Data Date	Investment Rating	Net Assets ($Mil)	Price	Performance Rating/Pts	Total Return Y-T-D	Risk Rating/Pts
12-12	C+	17.30	26.92	C / 5.5	3.16%	B / 8.0
2011	C+	20.50	24.16	C / 5.5	1.59%	B- / 7.8
2010	C	22.20	24.76	C / 4.7	21.78%	C+ / 5.8
2009	D+	17.93	20.62	D / 2.1	27.00%	C+ / 5.7

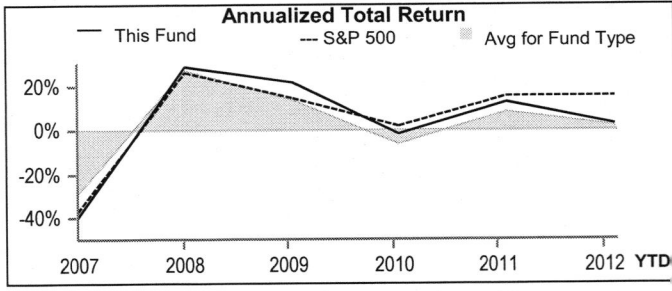

*PowerShares Fundamental Pure Md (PXMG)   C+   Fair

Fund Family: Invesco Powershares Capital Mgmt LL
Fund Type: Growth
Inception Date: March 3, 2005

Major Rating Factors: Middle of the road best describes *PowerShares Fundamental Pure Md whose TheStreet.com Investment Rating is currently a C+ (Fair). The fund currently has a performance rating of C+ (Fair) based on an annualized return of 12.76% over the last three years and a total return of 3.38% year to date 2012. Factored into the performance evaluation is an expense ratio of 0.43% (very low).

The fund's risk rating is currently B- (Good). It carries a beta of 1.21, meaning it is expected to move 12.1% for every 10% move in the market. Volatility, as measured by both the semi-deviation and a drawdown factor, is considered low. As of December 31, 2012, *PowerShares Fundamental Pure Md traded at a discount of 3.39% below its net asset value, which is better than its one-year historical average discount of .07%.

Peter Hubbard has been running the fund for 6 years and currently receives a manager quality ranking of 42 (0=worst, 99=best). If you desire an average level of risk, then this fund may be an option.

Data Date	Investment Rating	Net Assets ($Mil)	Price	Performance Rating/Pts	Total Return Y-T-D	Risk Rating/Pts
12-12	C+	75.40	23.09	C+ / 6.2	3.38%	B- / 7.4
2011	C	86.40	20.35	C / 4.9	2.01%	B- / 7.5
2010	C-	131.10	21.66	C / 5.1	29.95%	C / 4.6
2009	D+	140.04	16.76	D+ / 2.4	19.98%	C+ / 5.6

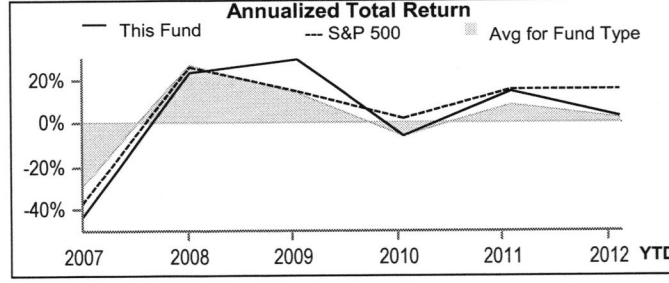

*PowerShares Fundamental Pure Md (PXMV)   C+   Fair

Fund Family: Invesco Powershares Capital Mgmt LL
Fund Type: Growth
Inception Date: March 3, 2005

Major Rating Factors: Middle of the road best describes *PowerShares Fundamental Pure Md whose TheStreet.com Investment Rating is currently a C+ (Fair). The fund currently has a performance rating of C+ (Fair) based on an annualized return of 11.23% over the last three years and a total return of 3.97% year to date 2012. Factored into the performance evaluation is an expense ratio of 0.43% (very low).

The fund's risk rating is currently B (Good). It carries a beta of 1.04, meaning that its performance tracks fairly well with that of the overall stock market. Volatility, as measured by both the semi-deviation and a drawdown factor, is considered low. As of December 31, 2012, *PowerShares Fundamental Pure Md traded at a discount of 4.04% below its net asset value, which is better than its one-year historical average discount of .13%.

Peter Hubbard has been running the fund for 6 years and currently receives a manager quality ranking of 44 (0=worst, 99=best). If you desire an average level of risk, then this fund may be an option.

Data Date	Investment Rating	Net Assets ($Mil)	Price	Performance Rating/Pts	Total Return Y-T-D	Risk Rating/Pts
12-12	C+	27.40	17.82	C+ / 6.2	3.97%	B / 8.0
2011	C	32.30	15.42	C / 4.7	0.91%	B- / 7.8
2010	C-	39.40	15.79	C- / 3.6	15.31%	C+ / 5.7
2009	D	39.06	13.90	D / 1.7	21.68%	C / 5.5

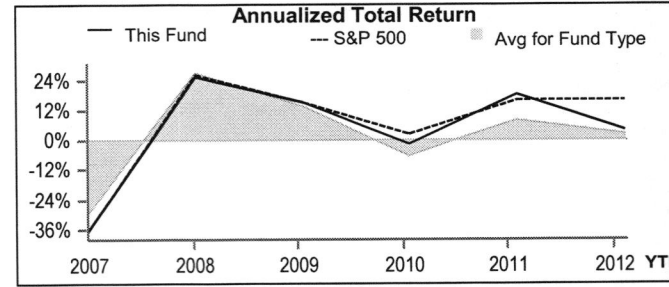

*PowerShares Fundamental Pure Sm (PXSG)

C   **Fair**

Fund Family: Invesco Powershares Capital Mgmt LL
Fund Type: Growth
Inception Date: March 3, 2005

Major Rating Factors: Middle of the road best describes *PowerShares Fundamental Pure Sm whose TheStreet.com Investment Rating is currently a C (Fair). The fund currently has a performance rating of C+ (Fair) based on an annualized return of 13.33% over the last three years and a total return of 4.02% year to date 2012. Factored into the performance evaluation is an expense ratio of 0.48% (very low).

The fund's risk rating is currently C+ (Fair). It carries a beta of 1.20, meaning it is expected to move 12.0% for every 10% move in the market. Volatility, as measured by both the semi-deviation and a drawdown factor, is considered low. As of December 31, 2012, *PowerShares Fundamental Pure Sm traded at a discount of 3.81% below its net asset value, which is better than its one-year historical average discount of .12%.

Peter Hubbard has been running the fund for 6 years and currently receives a manager quality ranking of 47 (0=worst, 99=best). If you desire an average level of risk, then this fund may be an option.

Data Date	Investment Rating	Net Assets ($Mil)	Price	Performance Rating/Pts	Total Return Y-T-D	Risk Rating/Pts
12-12	C	27.20	17.93	C+ / 6.1	4.02%	C+ / 6.9
2011	C-	33.30	15.91	C / 5.0	1.45%	C+ / 6.8
2010	C+	38.70	16.13	C+ / 5.7	27.31%	C+ / 5.8
2009	D-	31.48	12.67	D- / 1.2	16.22%	C / 5.5

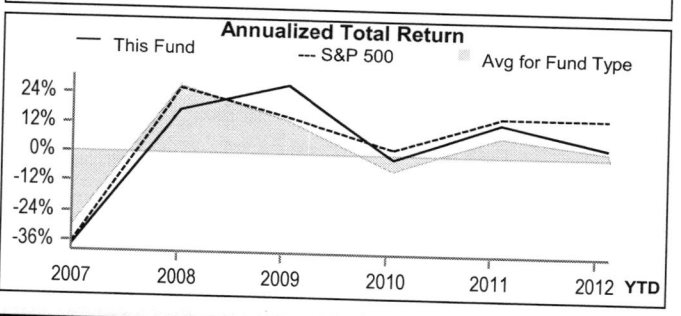

Annualized Total Return

---

*PowerShares Fundamental Pure Sm (PXSV)

C+   **Fair**

Fund Family: Invesco Powershares Capital Mgmt LL
Fund Type: Growth
Inception Date: March 3, 2005

Major Rating Factors: Strong performance is the major factor driving the C+ (Fair) TheStreet.com Investment Rating for *PowerShares Fundamental Pure Sm. The fund currently has a performance rating of B- (Good) based on an annualized return of 13.37% over the last three years and a total return of 3.40% year to date 2012. Factored into the performance evaluation is an expense ratio of 0.43% (very low).

The fund's risk rating is currently B- (Good). It carries a beta of 1.29, meaning it is expected to move 12.9% for every 10% move in the market. Volatility, as measured by both the semi-deviation and a drawdown factor, is considered low. As of December 31, 2012, *PowerShares Fundamental Pure Sm traded at a discount of 3.21% below its net asset value, which is better than its one-year historical average discount of .13%.

Peter Hubbard has been running the fund for 6 years and currently receives a manager quality ranking of 40 (0=worst, 99=best). If you desire only a moderate level of risk and strong performance, then this fund is an excellent option.

Data Date	Investment Rating	Net Assets ($Mil)	Price	Performance Rating/Pts	Total Return Y-T-D	Risk Rating/Pts
12-12	C+	44.80	17.47	B- / 7.0	3.40%	B- / 7.5
2011	C	52.30	14.74	C / 4.6	1.42%	B- / 7.4
2010	C+	65.60	15.08	C+ / 5.8	19.92%	C+ / 5.7
2009	D	62.25	12.84	D- / 1.3	16.77%	C+ / 5.7

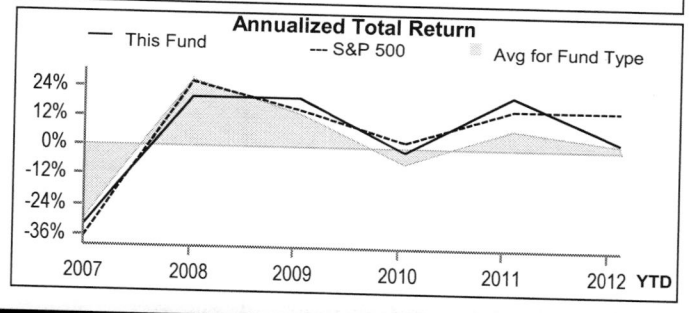

Annualized Total Return

---

*PowerShares Fundamental Pure Sm (PXSC)

C   **Fair**

Fund Family: Invesco Powershares Capital Mgmt LL
Fund Type: Growth
Inception Date: December 1, 2006

Major Rating Factors: Middle of the road best describes *PowerShares Fundamental Pure Sm whose TheStreet.com Investment Rating is currently a C (Fair). The fund currently has a performance rating of C+ (Fair) based on an annualized return of 12.18% over the last three years and a total return of 4.82% year to date 2012. Factored into the performance evaluation is an expense ratio of 0.43% (very low).

The fund's risk rating is currently B- (Good). It carries a beta of 1.22, meaning it is expected to move 12.2% for every 10% move in the market. Volatility, as measured by both the semi-deviation and a drawdown factor, is considered low. As of December 31, 2012, *PowerShares Fundamental Pure Sm traded at a discount of 4.86% below its net asset value, which is better than its one-year historical average discount of .21%.

Peter Hubbard has been running the fund for 6 years and currently receives a manager quality ranking of 34 (0=worst, 99=best). If you desire an average level of risk, then this fund may be an option.

Data Date	Investment Rating	Net Assets ($Mil)	Price	Performance Rating/Pts	Total Return Y-T-D	Risk Rating/Pts
12-12	C	13.40	24.26	C+ / 5.8	4.82%	B- / 7.5
2011	C-	14.20	21.98	C / 4.5	0.79%	B- / 7.4
2010	C	17.80	22.45	C+ / 5.6	23.30%	C+ / 5.6
2009	D	13.53	18.35	D- / 1.2	15.57%	C+ / 5.6

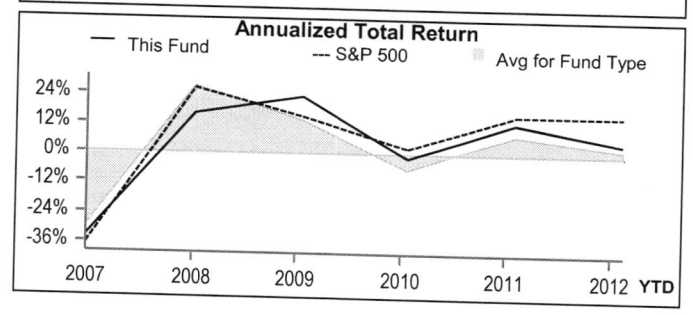

Annualized Total Return

* Denotes ETF Fund

*PowerShares Fundmntl Inv Gr Corp (PFIG)   C   Fair

Fund Family: Invesco Powershares Capital Mgmt LL
Fund Type: Corporate - Investment Grade
Inception Date: September 15, 2011

Major Rating Factors:
Disappointing performance is the major factor driving the C (Fair) TheStreet.com Investment Rating for *PowerShares Fundmntl Inv Gr Corp. The fund currently has a performance rating of D (Weak) based on an annualized return of 0.00% over the last three years and a total return of -0.12% year to date 2012. Factored into the performance evaluation is an expense ratio of 0.22% (very low).

The fund's risk rating is currently B+ (Good). It carries a beta of 0.00, meaning the fund's expected move will be 0.0% for every 10% move in the market. Volatility, as measured by both the semi-deviation and a drawdown factor, is considered very low. As of December 31, 2012, *PowerShares Fundmntl Inv Gr Corp traded at a premium of .04% above its net asset value, which is better than its one-year historical average premium of .38%.

Peter Hubbard has been running the fund for 2 years and currently receives a manager quality ranking of 56 (0=worst, 99=best). This fund offers only a moderate level of risk but investors looking for strong performance are still waiting.

Data Date	Investment Rating	Net Assets ($Mil)	Price	Performance Rating/Pts	Total Return Y-T-D	Risk Rating/Pts
12-12	C	33.40	25.69	D / 2.2	-0.12%	B+ / 9.9

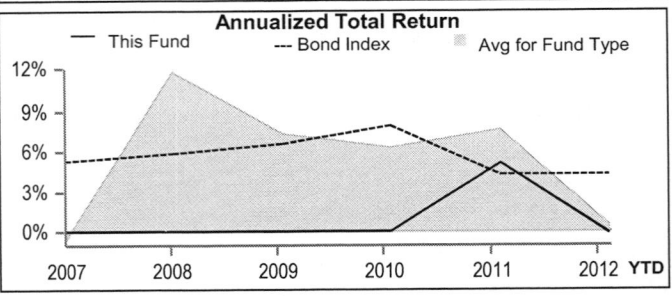

Annualized Total Return

---

*PowerShares Gb Nuclear Energy Po (PKN)   D   Weak

Fund Family: Invesco Powershares Capital Mgmt LL
Fund Type: Energy/Natural Resources
Inception Date: April 1, 2008

Major Rating Factors:
Disappointing performance is the major factor driving the D (Weak) TheStreet.com Investment Rating for *PowerShares Gb Nuclear Energy Po. The fund currently has a performance rating of D- (Weak) based on an annualized return of -2.52% over the last three years and a total return of 2.97% year to date 2012. Factored into the performance evaluation is an expense ratio of 0.75% (very low).

The fund's risk rating is currently C+ (Fair). It carries a beta of 0.84, meaning the fund's expected move will be 8.4% for every 10% move in the market. Volatility, as measured by both the semi-deviation and a drawdown factor, is considered low. As of December 31, 2012, *PowerShares Gb Nuclear Energy Po traded at a discount of 3.60% below its net asset value, which is better than its one-year historical average discount of .48%.

Peter Hubbard has been running the fund for 5 years and currently receives a manager quality ranking of 13 (0=worst, 99=best). This fund offers only a moderate level of risk but investors looking for strong performance are still waiting.

Data Date	Investment Rating	Net Assets ($Mil)	Price	Performance Rating/Pts	Total Return Y-T-D	Risk Rating/Pts
12-12	D	10.40	15.80	D- / 1.3	2.97%	C+ / 6.8
2011	D	14.90	15.58	D / 1.8	0.26%	B- / 7.0
2010	A-	36.80	21.15	A / 9.5	20.01%	C / 5.1
2009	C+	28.57	18.70	B- / 7.3	21.35%	C / 5.0

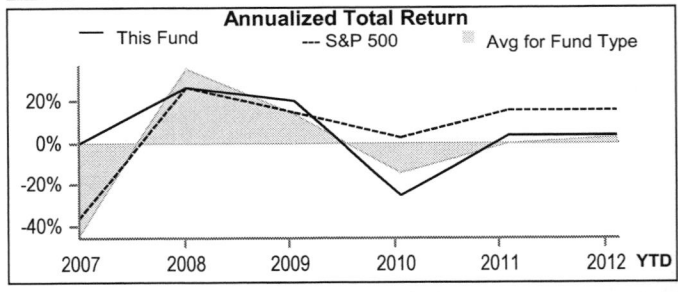

Annualized Total Return

---

*PowerShares Glb Gold & Precious (PSAU)   E+   Very Weak

Fund Family: Invesco Powershares Capital Mgmt LL
Fund Type: Precious Metals
Inception Date: September 16, 2008

Major Rating Factors:
Disappointing performance is the major factor driving the E+ (Very Weak) TheStreet.com Investment Rating for *PowerShares Glb Gold & Precious. The fund currently has a performance rating of D- (Weak) based on an annualized return of -1.00% over the last three years and a total return of -2.67% year to date 2012. Factored into the performance evaluation is an expense ratio of 0.75% (very low).

The fund's risk rating is currently C (Fair). It carries a beta of 1.14, meaning it is expected to move 11.4% for every 10% move in the market. Volatility, as measured by both the semi-deviation and a drawdown factor, is considered average. As of December 31, 2012, *PowerShares Glb Gold & Precious traded at a premium of 2.66% above its net asset value, which is worse than its one-year historical average discount of .17%.

Brian McGreal has been running the fund for 5 years and currently receives a manager quality ranking of 9 (0=worst, 99=best). This fund offers an average level of risk but investors looking for strong performance will be frustrated.

Data Date	Investment Rating	Net Assets ($Mil)	Price	Performance Rating/Pts	Total Return Y-T-D	Risk Rating/Pts
12-12	E+	36.70	37.08	D- / 1.1	-2.67%	C / 4.7
2011	C-	47.80	39.81	C+ / 5.7	2.66%	C / 5.4
2010	A-	67.50	50.01	A+ / 9.6	37.48%	C / 5.3
2009	B+	7.73	38.21	A- / 9.0	45.33%	C / 4.6

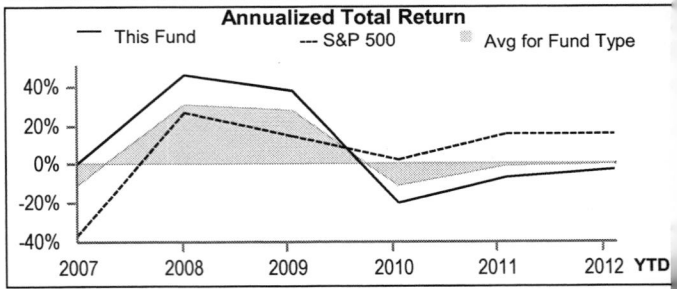

Annualized Total Return

*PowerShares Global Agriculture P (PAGG)

D+   **Weak**

Fund Family: Invesco Powershares Capital Mgmt LL
Fund Type: Global
Inception Date: September 16, 2008

Major Rating Factors: *PowerShares Global Agriculture P receives a TheStreet.com Investment Rating of D+ (Weak). The fund currently has a performance rating of C- (Fair) based on an annualized return of 5.21% over the last three years and a total return of 3.48% year to date 2012. Factored into the performance evaluation is an expense ratio of 0.75% (very low).

The fund's risk rating is currently B- (Good). It carries a beta of 1.05, meaning that its performance tracks fairly well with that of the overall stock market. Volatility, as measured by both the semi-deviation and a drawdown factor, is considered low. As of December 31, 2012, *PowerShares Global Agriculture P traded at a discount of 3.49% below its net asset value, which is better than its one-year historical average discount of .28%.

Brian McGreal has been running the fund for 5 years and currently receives a manager quality ranking of 65 (0=worst, 99=best). If you desire an average level of risk, then this fund may be an option.

Data Date	Investment Rating	Net Assets ($Mil)	Price	Perfor-mance Rating/Pts	Total Return Y-T-D	Risk Rating/Pts
12-12	D+	109.40	30.73	C- / 3.5	3.48%	B- / 7.0
2011	C-	106.40	26.88	C / 4.4	2.55%	C+ / 6.9
2010	A	68.50	32.03	A+ / 9.7	21.91%	C+ / 6.2
2009	A+	9.56	26.74	A / 9.3	51.75%	C+ / 6.6

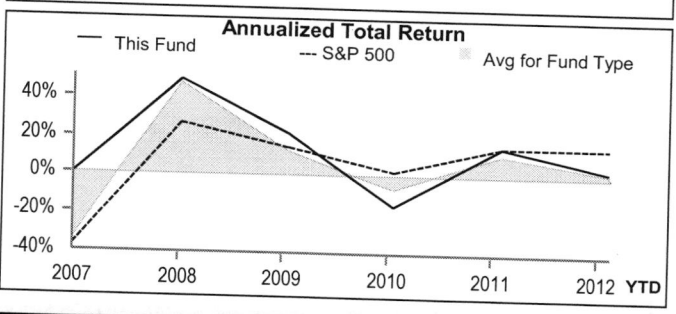

*PowerShares Global Clean Energy (PBD)

E+   **Very Weak**

Fund Family: Invesco Powershares Capital Mgmt LL
Fund Type: Energy/Natural Resources
Inception Date: June 13, 2007

Major Rating Factors:
Very poor performance is the major factor driving the E+ (Very Weak) TheStreet.com Investment Rating for *PowerShares Global Clean Energy. The fund currently has a performance rating of E+ (Very Weak) based on an annualized return of -19.16% over the last three years and a total return of 7.60% year to date 2012. Factored into the performance evaluation is an expense ratio of 0.75% (very low).

The fund's risk rating is currently C (Fair). It carries a beta of 1.04, meaning that its performance tracks fairly well with that of the overall stock market. Volatility, as measured by both the semi-deviation and a drawdown factor, is considered average. As of December 31, 2012, *PowerShares Global Clean Energy traded at a discount of 7.39% below its net asset value, which is better than its one-year historical average discount of .58%.

Peter Hubbard has been running the fund for 6 years and currently receives a manager quality ranking of 3 (0=worst, 99=best). This fund offers an average level of risk but investors looking for strong performance will be frustrated.

Data Date	Investment Rating	Net Assets ($Mil)	Price	Perfor-mance Rating/Pts	Total Return Y-T-D	Risk Rating/Pts
12-12	E+	57.30	7.89	E+ / 0.6	7.60%	C / 4.9
2011	D-	97.00	8.23	E+ / 0.9	0.49%	C / 5.4
2010	E+	147.40	13.96	E / 0.5	-15.98%	C- / 4.0
2009	C+	140.69	16.66	B / 7.9	28.38%	C- / 3.9

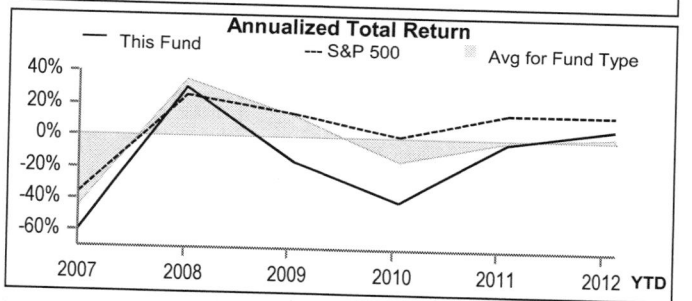

*PowerShares Global Coal Portfoli (PKOL)

D-   **Weak**

Fund Family: Invesco Powershares Capital Mgmt LL
Fund Type: Energy/Natural Resources
Inception Date: September 16, 2008

Major Rating Factors:
Very poor performance is the major factor driving the D- (Weak) TheStreet.com Investment Rating for *PowerShares Global Coal Portfoli. The fund currently has a performance rating of E+ (Very Weak) based on an annualized return of -11.57% over the last three years and a total return of 0.81% year to date 2012. Factored into the performance evaluation is an expense ratio of 0.75% (very low).

The fund's risk rating is currently C (Fair). It carries a beta of 1.27, meaning it is expected to move 12.7% for every 10% move in the market. Volatility, as measured by both the semi-deviation and a drawdown factor, is considered average. As of December 31, 2012, *PowerShares Global Coal Portfoli traded at a discount of 1.89% below its net asset value, which is better than its one-year historical average premium of .11%.

Brian McGreal has been running the fund for 5 years and currently receives a manager quality ranking of 5 (0=worst, 99=best). This fund offers an average level of risk but investors looking for strong performance will be frustrated.

Data Date	Investment Rating	Net Assets ($Mil)	Price	Perfor-mance Rating/Pts	Total Return Y-T-D	Risk Rating/Pts
12-12	D-	9.00	19.76	E+ / 0.7	0.81%	C / 5.4
2011	C	14.90	24.52	C+ / 6.1	3.47%	C+ / 6.5
2010	A	27.80	37.40	A+ / 9.7	31.63%	C+ / 6.3
2009	A+	4.78	28.92	A+ / 9.9	119.44%	C+ / 6.1

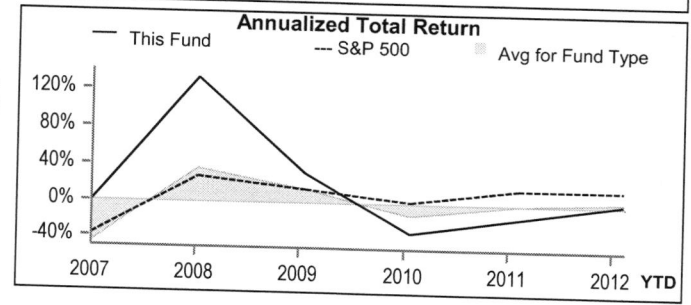

*PowerShares Global Listed Priv E (PSP)

C+   **Fair**

Fund Family: Invesco Powershares Capital Mgmt LL
Fund Type: Income
Inception Date: October 24, 2006

Major Rating Factors: Strong performance is the major factor driving the C+ (Fair) TheStreet.com Investment Rating for *PowerShares Global Listed Priv E. The fund currently has a performance rating of B- (Good) based on an annualized return of 9.74% over the last three years and a total return of 4.84% year to date 2012. Factored into the performance evaluation is an expense ratio of 0.71% (very low).

    The fund's risk rating is currently C+ (Fair). It carries a beta of 1.55, meaning it is expected to move 15.5% for every 10% move in the market. Volatility, as measured by both the semi-deviation and a drawdown factor, is considered low. As of December 31, 2012, *PowerShares Global Listed Priv E traded at a discount of 4.08% below its net asset value, which is better than its one-year historical average premium of .03%.

    Peter Hubbard has been running the fund for 6 years and currently receives a manager quality ranking of 20 (0=worst, 99=best). If you desire only a moderate level of risk and strong performance, then this fund is an excellent option.

Data Date	Investment Rating	Net Assets ($Mil)	Price	Performance Rating/Pts	Total Return Y-T-D	Risk Rating/Pts
12-12	C+	300.60	10.12	B- / 7.5	4.84%	C+ / 6.0
2011	D	240.60	7.99	D / 2.0	1.00%	C+ / 6.4
2010	E+	309.90	10.75	D- / 1.3	30.23%	C- / 3.5
2009	E	60.48	9.01	E+ / 0.6	25.84%	C- / 3.6

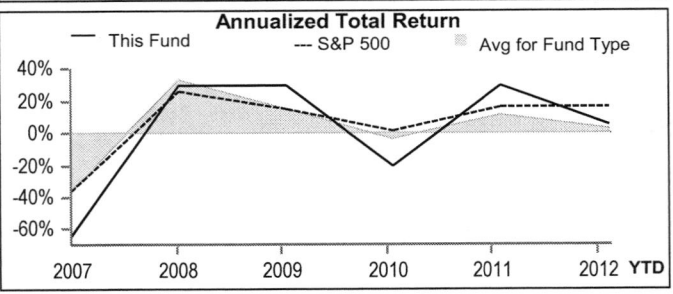

Annualized Total Return

*PowerShares Global Steel Portfol (PSTL)

D-   **Weak**

Fund Family: Invesco Powershares Capital Mgmt LL
Fund Type: Global
Inception Date: September 16, 2008

Major Rating Factors:
Very poor performance is the major factor driving the D- (Weak) TheStreet.com Investment Rating for *PowerShares Global Steel Portfol. The fund currently has a performance rating of E+ (Very Weak) based on an annualized return of -11.99% over the last three years and a total return of 1.59% year to date 2012. Factored into the performance evaluation is an expense ratio of 0.75% (very low).

    The fund's risk rating is currently C+ (Fair). It carries a beta of 1.40, meaning it is expected to move 14.0% for every 10% move in the market. Volatility, as measured by both the semi-deviation and a drawdown factor, is considered low. As of December 31, 2012, *PowerShares Global Steel Portfol traded at a discount of 2.21% below its net asset value, which is better than its one-year historical average discount of .53%.

    Brian McGreal has been running the fund for 5 years and currently receives a manager quality ranking of 7 (0=worst, 99=best). This fund offers only a moderate level of risk but investors looking for strong performance are still waiting.

Data Date	Investment Rating	Net Assets ($Mil)	Price	Performance Rating/Pts	Total Return Y-T-D	Risk Rating/Pts
12-12	D-	2.20	14.57	E+ / 0.8	1.59%	C+ / 5.8
2011	D	3.80	14.88	D / 1.8	2.96%	C+ / 6.5
2010	A	5.90	23.82	A- / 9.2	8.29%	C+ / 6.3
2009	A+	1.38	22.38	A+ / 9.6	66.07%	C+ / 6.3

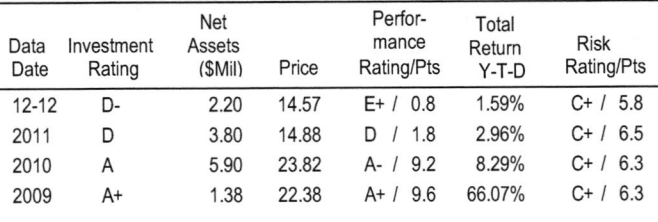

Annualized Total Return

*PowerShares Global Water Portfol (PIO)

D   **Weak**

Fund Family: Invesco Powershares Capital Mgmt LL
Fund Type: Energy/Natural Resources
Inception Date: June 13, 2007

Major Rating Factors:
Disappointing performance is the major factor driving the D (Weak) TheStreet.com Investment Rating for *PowerShares Global Water Portfol. The fund currently has a performance rating of D+ (Weak) based on an annualized return of 1.02% over the last three years and a total return of 2.00% year to date 2012. Factored into the performance evaluation is an expense ratio of 0.75% (very low).

    The fund's risk rating is currently C+ (Fair). It carries a beta of 0.72, meaning the fund's expected move will be 7.2% for every 10% move in the market. Volatility, as measured by both the semi-deviation and a drawdown factor, is considered low. As of December 31, 2012, *PowerShares Global Water Portfol traded at a discount of 1.96% below its net asset value, which is better than its one-year historical average discount of .38%.

    Peter Hubbard has been running the fund for 6 years and currently receives a manager quality ranking of 22 (0=worst, 99=best). This fund offers only a moderate level of risk but investors looking for strong performance are still waiting.

Data Date	Investment Rating	Net Assets ($Mil)	Price	Performance Rating/Pts	Total Return Y-T-D	Risk Rating/Pts
12-12	D	196.90	18.01	D+ / 2.9	2.00%	C+ / 6.6
2011	D	234.10	15.59	D+ / 2.4	0.77%	C / 5.5
2010	D	352.70	20.01	D+ / 2.5	11.80%	C / 4.3
2009	C+	179.20	18.16	B+ / 8.7	36.57%	C- / 3.8

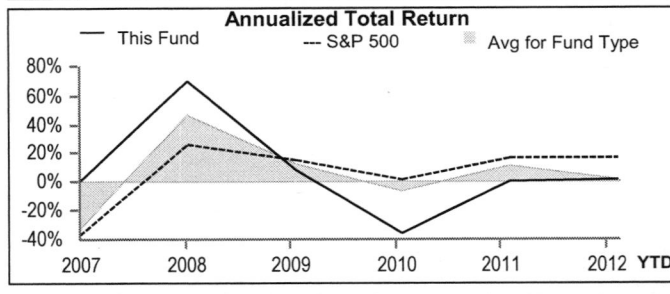

Annualized Total Return

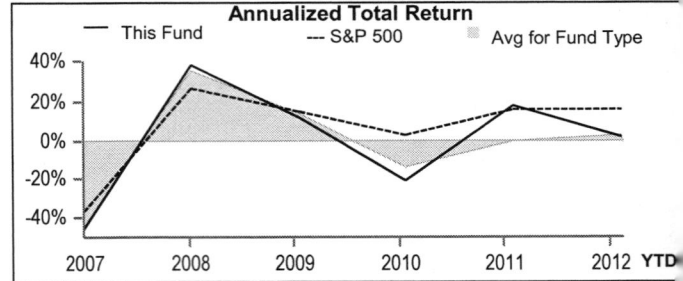

*PowerShares Global Wind Energy P (PWND)

E+   **Very Weak**

Fund Family: Invesco Powershares Capital Mgmt LL
Fund Type: Energy/Natural Resources
Inception Date: June 27, 2008

Data Date	Investment Rating	Net Assets ($Mil)	Price	Performance Rating/Pts	Total Return Y-T-D	Risk Rating/Pts
12-12	E+	9.10	5.63	E / 0.5	12.73%	C / 4.9
2011	D-	14.90	6.85	E+ / 0.8	-0.47%	C / 5.3
2010	E+	25.90	9.87	E / 0.4	-35.81%	C / 4.5
2009	C	27.53	15.43	C+ / 6.9	26.49%	C / 4.6

Major Rating Factors:
Very poor performance is the major factor driving the E+ (Very Weak) TheStreet.com Investment Rating for *PowerShares Global Wind Energy P. The fund currently has a performance rating of E (Very Weak) based on an annualized return of -25.32% over the last three years and a total return of 12.73% year to date 2012. Factored into the performance evaluation is an expense ratio of 0.75% (very low).

The fund's risk rating is currently C (Fair). It carries a beta of 0.94, meaning that its performance tracks fairly well with that of the overall stock market. Volatility, as measured by both the semi-deviation and a drawdown factor, is considered average. As of December 31, 2012, *PowerShares Global Wind Energy P traded at a discount of 11.89% below its net asset value, which is better than its one-year historical average discount of .72%.

Peter Hubbard has been running the fund for 5 years and currently receives a manager quality ranking of 2 (0=worst, 99=best). This fund offers an average level of risk but investors looking for strong performance will be frustrated.

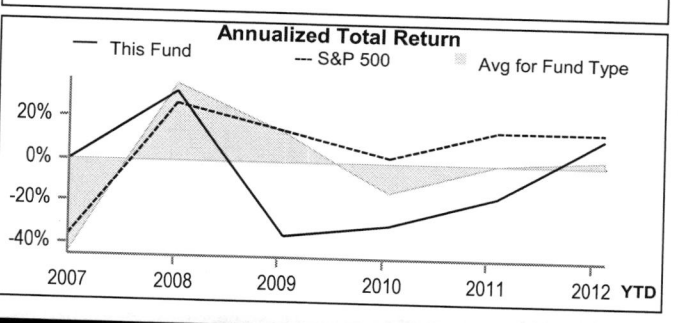

*PowerShares Golden Dragon China (PGJ)

D-   **Weak**

Fund Family: Invesco Powershares Capital Mgmt LL
Fund Type: Global
Inception Date: December 9, 2004

Data Date	Investment Rating	Net Assets ($Mil)	Price	Performance Rating/Pts	Total Return Y-T-D	Risk Rating/Pts
12-12	D-	196.90	19.16	D- / 1.1	5.17%	C+ / 5.9
2011	D+	228.90	19.61	C- / 3.1	1.53%	C+ / 6.3
2010	D-	450.30	26.64	D / 1.7	11.77%	C / 4.4
2009	C-	279.49	24.10	C+ / 6.4	54.14%	C- / 3.3

Major Rating Factors:
Disappointing performance is the major factor driving the D- (Weak) TheStreet.com Investment Rating for *PowerShares Golden Dragon China. The fund currently has a performance rating of D- (Weak) based on an annualized return of -5.19% over the last three years and a total return of 5.17% year to date 2012. Factored into the performance evaluation is an expense ratio of 0.69% (very low).

The fund's risk rating is currently C+ (Fair). It carries a beta of 1.00, meaning that its performance tracks fairly well with that of the overall stock market. Volatility, as measured by both the semi-deviation and a drawdown factor, is considered low. As of December 31, 2012, *PowerShares Golden Dragon China traded at a discount of 4.91% below its net asset value, which is better than its one-year historical average discount of .13%.

Peter Hubbard has been running the fund for 6 years and currently receives a manager quality ranking of 13 (0=worst, 99=best). This fund offers only a moderate level of risk but investors looking for strong performance are still waiting.

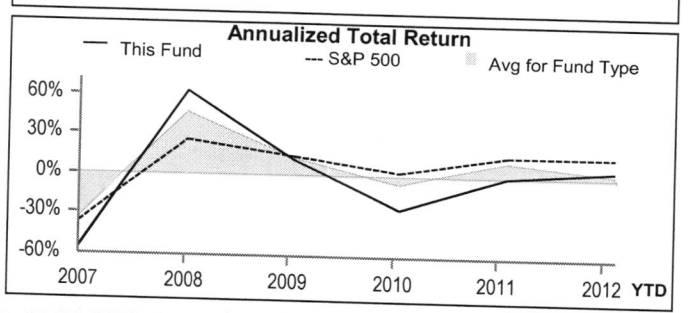

*PowerShares High Yld Eq Div Ach (PEY)

C+   **Fair**

Fund Family: Invesco Powershares Capital Mgmt LL
Fund Type: Income
Inception Date: December 9, 2004

Data Date	Investment Rating	Net Assets ($Mil)	Price	Performance Rating/Pts	Total Return Y-T-D	Risk Rating/Pts
12-12	C+	276.40	9.41	C / 4.6	2.98%	B+ / 9.1
2011	C	357.50	9.25	C / 5.3	-0.11%	C+ / 6.9
2010	D	182.60	8.86	D / 1.9	21.32%	C / 4.7
2009	D-	86.85	7.65	E+ / 0.7	3.21%	C / 4.8

Major Rating Factors: Middle of the road best describes *PowerShares High Yld Eq Div Ach whose TheStreet.com Investment Rating is currently a C+ (Fair). The fund currently has a performance rating of C (Fair) based on an annualized return of 12.11% over the last three years and a total return of 2.98% year to date 2012. Factored into the performance evaluation is an expense ratio of 0.60% (very low).

The fund's risk rating is currently B+ (Good). It carries a beta of 0.64, meaning the fund's expected move will be 6.4% for every 10% move in the market. Volatility, as measured by both the semi-deviation and a drawdown factor, is considered very low. As of December 31, 2012, *PowerShares High Yld Eq Div Ach traded at a discount of 2.79% below its net asset value, which is better than its one-year historical average discount of .02%.

Peter Hubbard has been running the fund for 6 years and currently receives a manager quality ranking of 79 (0=worst, 99=best). If you desire an average level of risk, then this fund may be an option.

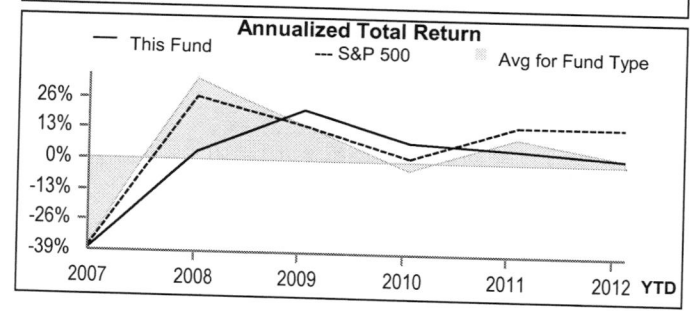

*PowerShares Ibbotson Altv Comp (PTO)

C-   **Fair**

Fund Family: Invesco Powershares Capital Mgmt LL
Fund Type: Global
Inception Date: May 16, 2008

Major Rating Factors:
Disappointing performance is the major factor driving the C- (Fair) TheStreet.com Investment Rating for *PowerShares Ibbotson Altv Comp. The fund currently has a performance rating of D+ (Weak) based on an annualized return of 4.14% over the last three years and a total return of 0.77% year to date 2012. Factored into the performance evaluation is an expense ratio of 0.25% (very low).

The fund's risk rating is currently B (Good). It carries a beta of 0.63, meaning the fund's expected move will be 6.3% for every 10% move in the market. Volatility, as measured by both the semi-deviation and a drawdown factor, is considered low. As of December 31, 2012, *PowerShares Ibbotson Altv Comp traded at a discount of 1.36% below its net asset value, which is better than its one-year historical average discount of .34%.

Peter Hubbard has been running the fund for 5 years and currently receives a manager quality ranking of 71 (0=worst, 99=best). This fund offers only a moderate level of risk but investors looking for strong performance are still waiting.

Data Date	Investment Rating	Net Assets ($Mil)	Price	Performance Rating/Pts	Total Return Y-T-D	Risk Rating/Pts
12-12	C-	8.20	11.62	D+ / 2.6	0.77%	B / 8.4
2011	C-	8.20	10.75	C- / 3.8	2.79%	B / 8.1
2010	B+	9.40	11.70	B+ / 8.9	13.32%	C / 5.1
2009	B-	7.70	10.72	B / 7.8	21.67%	C / 5.1

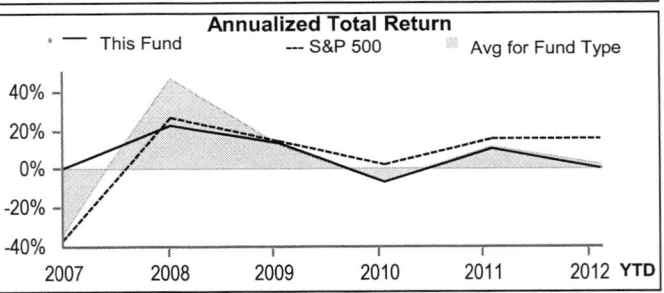

*PowerShares India Portfolio (PIN)

D-   **Weak**

Fund Family: Invesco Powershares Capital Mgmt LL
Fund Type: Foreign
Inception Date: March 4, 2008

Major Rating Factors:
Disappointing performance is the major factor driving the D- (Weak) TheStreet.com Investment Rating for *PowerShares India Portfolio. The fund currently has a performance rating of D- (Weak) based on an annualized return of -6.03% over the last three years and a total return of 1.14% year to date 2012. Factored into the performance evaluation is an expense ratio of 0.80% (very low).

The fund's risk rating is currently C+ (Fair). It carries a beta of 0.95, meaning that its performance tracks fairly well with that of the overall stock market. Volatility, as measured by both the semi-deviation and a drawdown factor, is considered low. As of December 31, 2012, *PowerShares India Portfolio traded at a discount of 1.45% below its net asset value, which is better than its one-year historical average premium of .08%.

Peter Hubbard has been running the fund for 5 years and currently receives a manager quality ranking of 14 (0=worst, 99=best). This fund offers only a moderate level of risk but investors looking for strong performance are still waiting.

Data Date	Investment Rating	Net Assets ($Mil)	Price	Performance Rating/Pts	Total Return Y-T-D	Risk Rating/Pts
12-12	D-	406.80	18.36	D- / 1.1	1.14%	C+ / 6.0
2011	D	286.00	16.30	D+ / 2.9	3.68%	C+ / 6.4
2010	B-	566.00	25.42	B+ / 8.5	16.25%	C- / 4.2
2009	B+	97.45	22.07	A / 9.5	70.44%	C- / 4.1

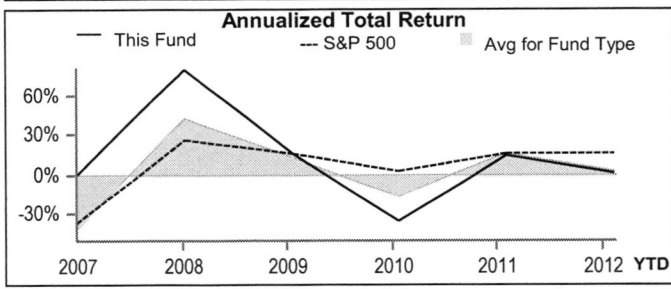

*PowerShares Insured CA Mun Bond (PWZ)

C+   **Fair**

Fund Family: Invesco Powershares Capital Mgmt LL
Fund Type: Municipal - National
Inception Date: October 11, 2007

Major Rating Factors: Middle of the road best describes *PowerShares Insured CA Mun Bond whose TheStreet.com Investment Rating is currently a C+ (Fair). The fund currently has a performance rating of C- (Fair) based on an annualized return of 7.08% over the last three years and a total return of 0.74% year to date 2012. Factored into the performance evaluation is an expense ratio of 0.28% (very low).

The fund's risk rating is currently B+ (Good). It carries a beta of 1.38, meaning it is expected to move 13.8% for every 10% move in the market. Volatility, as measured by both the semi-deviation and a drawdown factor, is considered very low. As of December 31, 2012, *PowerShares Insured CA Mun Bond traded at a discount of .63% below its net asset value, which is better than its one-year historical average premium of .08%.

Peter Hubbard has been running the fund for 6 years and currently receives a manager quality ranking of 36 (0=worst, 99=best). If you desire an average level of risk, then this fund may be an option.

Data Date	Investment Rating	Net Assets ($Mil)	Price	Performance Rating/Pts	Total Return Y-T-D	Risk Rating/Pts
12-12	C+	72.10	25.26	C- / 4.2	0.74%	B+ / 9.3
2011	B-	39.90	24.21	C+ / 5.9	0.52%	B+ / 9.3
2010	C	38.30	22.57	D+ / 2.4	1.06%	B / 8.1
2009	B	27.02	23.45	C+ / 6.8	14.62%	B / 8.3

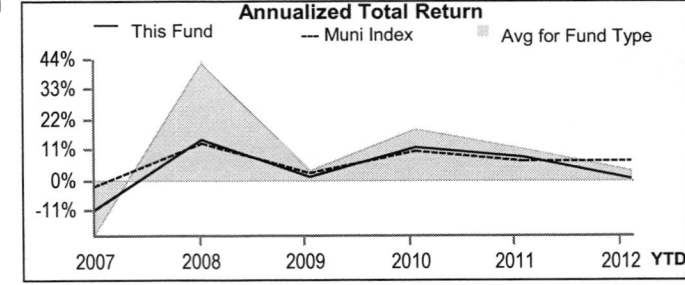

*PowerShares Insured National Mun (PZA)

C+   **Fair**

Fund Family: Invesco Powershares Capital Mgmt LL
Fund Type: Municipal - National
Inception Date: October 11, 2007

Major Rating Factors: Middle of the road best describes *PowerShares Insured National Mun whose TheStreet.com Investment Rating is currently a C+ (Fair). The fund currently has a performance rating of C (Fair) based on an annualized return of 7.70% over the last three years and a total return of 0.70% year to date 2012. Factored into the performance evaluation is an expense ratio of 0.28% (very low).

The fund's risk rating is currently B+ (Good). It carries a beta of 1.46, meaning it is expected to move 14.6% for every 10% move in the market. Volatility, as measured by both the semi-deviation and a drawdown factor, is considered very low. As of December 31, 2012, *PowerShares Insured National Mun traded at a discount of .50% below its net asset value, which is better than its one-year historical average premium of .07%.

Peter Hubbard has been running the fund for 6 years and currently receives a manager quality ranking of 36 (0=worst, 99=best). If you desire an average level of risk, then this fund may be an option.

Data Date	Investment Rating	Net Assets ($Mil)	Price	Performance Rating/Pts	Total Return Y-T-D	Risk Rating/Pts
12-12	C+	982.20	25.75	C / 4.6	0.70%	B+ / 9.3
2011	B	588.30	24.45	C+ / 6.4	0.41%	B+ / 9.3
2010	C	507.10	22.54	D / 2.2	-0.09%	B / 8.2
2009	A+	303.83	23.72	B / 7.6	17.92%	B / 8.3

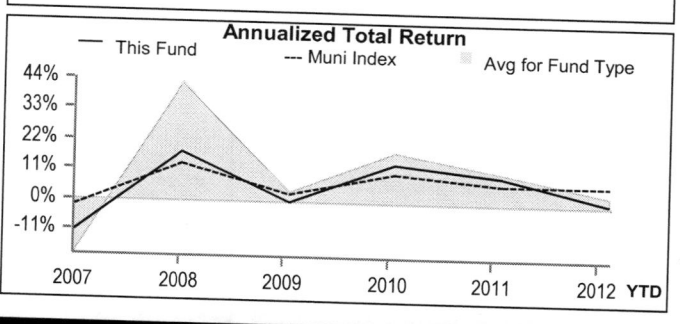

*PowerShares Insured NY Mun Bond (PZT)

C   **Fair**

Fund Family: Invesco Powershares Capital Mgmt LL
Fund Type: Municipal - National
Inception Date: October 11, 2007

Major Rating Factors: Middle of the road best describes *PowerShares Insured NY Mun Bond whose TheStreet.com Investment Rating is currently a C (Fair). The fund currently has a performance rating of C- (Fair) based on an annualized return of 6.65% over the last three years and a total return of 0.94% year to date 2012. Factored into the performance evaluation is an expense ratio of 0.28% (very low).

The fund's risk rating is currently B+ (Good). It carries a beta of 1.36, meaning it is expected to move 13.6% for every 10% move in the market. Volatility, as measured by both the semi-deviation and a drawdown factor, is considered very low. As of December 31, 2012, *PowerShares Insured NY Mun Bond traded at a discount of .85% below its net asset value, which is better than its one-year historical average premium of .06%.

Peter Hubbard has been running the fund for 6 years and currently receives a manager quality ranking of 33 (0=worst, 99=best). If you desire an average level of risk, then this fund may be an option.

Data Date	Investment Rating	Net Assets ($Mil)	Price	Performance Rating/Pts	Total Return Y-T-D	Risk Rating/Pts
12-12	C	68.80	24.57	C- / 3.8	0.94%	B+ / 9.3
2011	B	40.60	23.90	C+ / 6.1	0.54%	B+ / 9.4
2010	C-	37.80	22.15	D / 2.1	0.22%	B / 8.1
2009	A+	28.72	23.22	B- / 7.4	16.89%	B / 8.3

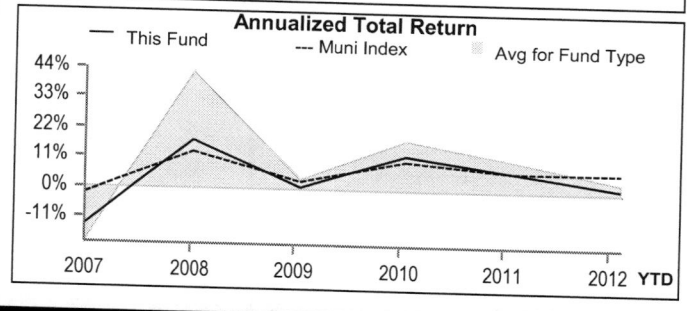

*PowerShares International Corp B (PICB)

B+   **Good**

Fund Family: Invesco Powershares Capital Mgmt LL
Fund Type: Global
Inception Date: June 2, 2010

Major Rating Factors: Strong performance is the major factor driving the B+ (Good) TheStreet.com Investment Rating for *PowerShares International Corp B. The fund currently has a performance rating of B (Good) based on an annualized return of 0.00% over the last three years and a total return of 0.47% year to date 2012. Factored into the performance evaluation is an expense ratio of 0.50% (very low).

The fund's risk rating is currently B (Good). It carries a beta of 0.00, meaning the fund's expected move will be 0.0% for every 10% move in the market. Volatility, as measured by both the semi-deviation and a drawdown factor, is considered low. As of December 31, 2012, *PowerShares International Corp B traded at a discount of .07% below its net asset value, which is better than its one-year historical average premium of .17%.

Peter Hubbard has been running the fund for 3 years and currently receives a manager quality ranking of 94 (0=worst, 99=best). If you desire only a moderate level of risk and strong performance, then this fund is an excellent option.

Data Date	Investment Rating	Net Assets ($Mil)	Price	Performance Rating/Pts	Total Return Y-T-D	Risk Rating/Pts
12-12	B+	133.10	29.61	B / 7.8	0.47%	B / 8.7
2011	C-	77.50	26.46	D / 1.9	-1.32%	B / 8.7

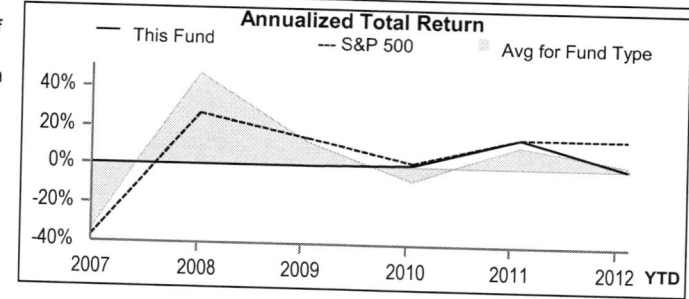

*PowerShares Intl Dividend Ach (PID)

C   **Fair**

Fund Family: Invesco Powershares Capital Mgmt LL
Fund Type: Foreign
Inception Date: September 15, 2005

Data Date	Investment Rating	Net Assets ($Mil)	Price	Performance Rating/Pts	Total Return Y-T-D	Risk Rating/Pts
12-12	C	738.10	15.83	C / 4.3	2.91%	B / 8.0
2011	C	585.20	14.57	C / 4.8	0.27%	B / 8.0
2010	D	468.80	15.40	D+ / 2.4	15.04%	C / 5.1
2009	D	256.58	13.97	D+ / 2.6	34.13%	C / 5.0

Major Rating Factors: Middle of the road best describes *PowerShares Intl Dividend Ach whose TheStreet.com Investment Rating is currently a C (Fair). The fund currently has a performance rating of C (Fair) based on an annualized return of 7.66% over the last three years and a total return of 2.91% year to date 2012. Factored into the performance evaluation is an expense ratio of 0.55% (very low).

The fund's risk rating is currently B (Good). It carries a beta of 0.81, meaning the fund's expected move will be 8.1% for every 10% move in the market. Volatility, as measured by both the semi-deviation and a drawdown factor, is considered low. As of December 31, 2012, *PowerShares Intl Dividend Ach traded at a discount of 2.82% below its net asset value, which is better than its one-year historical average premium of .09%.

Peter Hubbard has been running the fund for 6 years and currently receives a manager quality ranking of 78 (0=worst, 99=best). If you desire an average level of risk, then this fund may be an option.

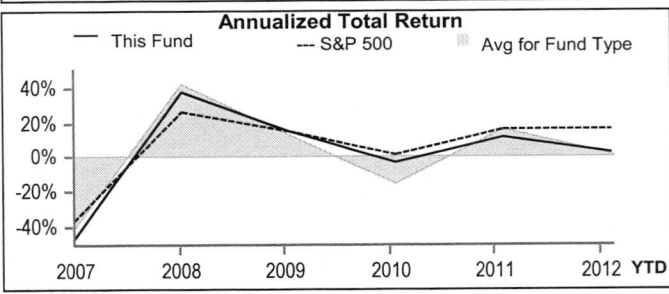

*PowerShares KBW Bank (KBWB)

A+   **Excellent**

Fund Family: Invesco Powershares Capital Mgmt LL
Fund Type: Income
Inception Date: November 1, 2011

Data Date	Investment Rating	Net Assets ($Mil)	Price	Performance Rating/Pts	Total Return Y-T-D	Risk Rating/Pts
12-12	A+	38.70	26.27	A / 9.4	3.77%	B / 8.6

Major Rating Factors:
Exceptional performance is the major factor driving the A+ (Excellent) TheStreet.com Investment Rating for *PowerShares KBW Bank. The fund currently has a performance rating of A (Excellent) based on an annualized return of 0.00% over the last three years and a total return of 3.77% year to date 2012. Factored into the performance evaluation is an expense ratio of 0.15% (very low).

The fund's risk rating is currently B (Good). It carries a beta of 0.00, meaning the fund's expected move will be 0.0% for every 10% move in the market. Volatility, as measured by both the semi-deviation and a drawdown factor, is considered low. As of December 31, 2012, *PowerShares KBW Bank traded at a discount of 3.70% below its net asset value, which is better than its one-year historical average discount of .03%.

Michael C. Jeanette has been running the fund for 2 years and currently receives a manager quality ranking of 82 (0=worst, 99=best). If you desire only a moderate level of risk and strong performance, then this fund is an excellent option.

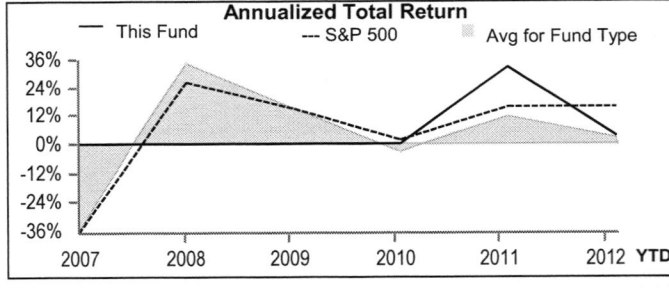

*PowerShares KBW Capital Markets (KBWC)

A   **Excellent**

Fund Family: Invesco Powershares Capital Mgmt LL
Fund Type: Income
Inception Date: November 1, 2011

Data Date	Investment Rating	Net Assets ($Mil)	Price	Performance Rating/Pts	Total Return Y-T-D	Risk Rating/Pts
12-12	A	1.70	32.72	A / 9.3	7.67%	B- / 7.8

Major Rating Factors:
Exceptional performance is the major factor driving the A (Excellent) TheStreet.com Investment Rating for *PowerShares KBW Capital Markets. The fund currently has a performance rating of A (Excellent) based on an annualized return of 0.00% over the last three years and a total return of 7.67% year to date 2012. Factored into the performance evaluation is an expense ratio of 0.12% (very low).

The fund's risk rating is currently B- (Good). It carries a beta of 0.00, meaning the fund's expected move will be 0.0% for every 10% move in the market. Volatility, as measured by both the semi-deviation and a drawdown factor, is considered low. As of December 31, 2012, *PowerShares KBW Capital Markets traded at a discount of 7.36% below its net asset value, which is better than its one-year historical average discount of .07%.

Michael C. Jeanette has been running the fund for 2 years and currently receives a manager quality ranking of 11 (0=worst, 99=best). If you desire only a moderate level of risk and strong performance, then this fund is an excellent option.

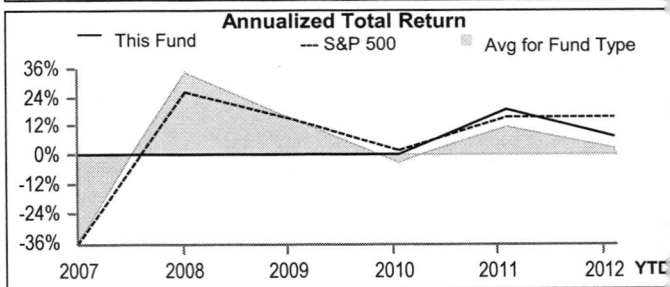

*PowerShares KBW High Div Yield F (KBWD)

C+ **Fair**

Fund Family: Invesco Powershares Capital Mgmt LL
Fund Type: Growth and Income
Inception Date: December 1, 2010

Major Rating Factors: Middle of the road best describes *PowerShares KBW High Div Yield F whose TheStreet.com Investment Rating is currently a C+ (Fair). The fund currently has a performance rating of C+ (Fair) based on an annualized return of 0.00% over the last three years and a total return of 4.75% year to date 2012. Factored into the performance evaluation is an expense ratio of 0.35% (very low).

The fund's risk rating is currently B (Good). It carries a beta of 0.00, meaning the fund's expected move will be 0.0% for every 10% move in the market. Volatility, as measured by both the semi-deviation and a drawdown factor, is considered low. As of December 31, 2012, *PowerShares KBW High Div Yield F traded at a discount of 4.61% below its net asset value, which is better than its one-year historical average premium of .11%.

Michael C. Jeanette has been running the fund for 3 years and currently receives a manager quality ranking of 74 (0=worst, 99=best). If you desire an average level of risk, then this fund may be an option.

Data Date	Investment Rating	Net Assets ($Mil)	Price	Performance Rating/Pts	Total Return Y-T-D	Risk Rating/Pts
12-12	C+	169.10	23.15	C+ / 5.6	4.75%	B / 8.4
2011	C-	33.60	21.76	C- / 3.1	2.21%	B / 8.3

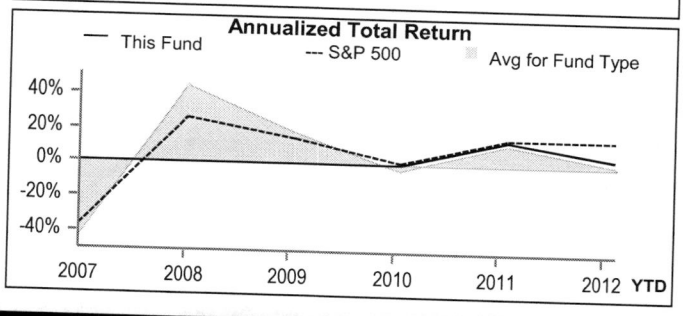

*PowerShares KBW Premium Yld Eq R (KBWY)

A **Excellent**

Fund Family: Invesco Powershares Capital Mgmt LL
Fund Type: Income
Inception Date: December 1, 2010

Major Rating Factors:
Exceptional performance is the major factor driving the A (Excellent) TheStreet.com Investment Rating for *PowerShares KBW Premium Yld Eq R. The fund currently has a performance rating of A (Excellent) based on an annualized return of 0.00% over the last three years and a total return of 3.27% year to date 2012. Factored into the performance evaluation is an expense ratio of 0.35% (very low).

The fund's risk rating is currently B- (Good). It carries a beta of 0.00, meaning the fund's expected move will be 0.0% for every 10% move in the market. Volatility, as measured by both the semi-deviation and a drawdown factor, is considered low. As of December 31, 2012, *PowerShares KBW Premium Yld Eq R traded at a discount of 2.97% below its net asset value, which is better than its one-year historical average premium of .16%.

Michael C. Jeanette has been running the fund for 3 years and currently receives a manager quality ranking of 92 (0=worst, 99=best). If you desire only a moderate level of risk and strong performance, then this fund is an excellent option.

Data Date	Investment Rating	Net Assets ($Mil)	Price	Performance Rating/Pts	Total Return Y-T-D	Risk Rating/Pts
12-12	A	29.60	28.10	A / 9.4	3.27%	B- / 7.7
2011	D+	6.90	23.04	D / 2.1	2.34%	B- / 7.6

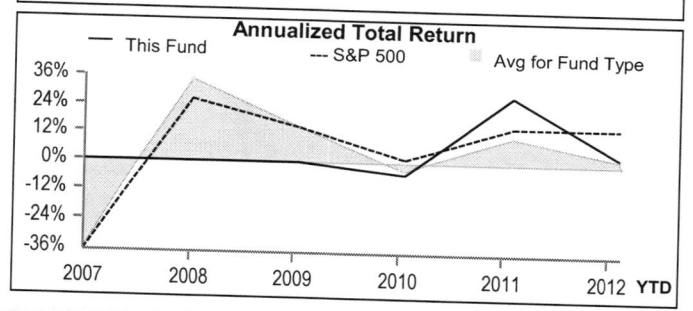

*PowerShares KBW Regional Banking (KBWR)

C **Fair**

Fund Family: Invesco Powershares Capital Mgmt LL
Fund Type: Income
Inception Date: November 1, 2011

Major Rating Factors: Middle of the road best describes *PowerShares KBW Regional Banking whose TheStreet.com Investment Rating is currently a C (Fair). The fund currently has a performance rating of C- (Fair) based on an annualized return of 0.00% over the last three years and a total return of 3.95% year to date 2012. Factored into the performance evaluation is an expense ratio of 0.05% (very low).

The fund's risk rating is currently B+ (Good). It carries a beta of 0.00, meaning the fund's expected move will be 0.0% for every 10% move in the market. Volatility, as measured by both the semi-deviation and a drawdown factor, is considered very low. As of December 31, 2012, *PowerShares KBW Regional Banking traded at a discount of 3.93% below its net asset value, which is better than its one-year historical average discount of .09%.

Michael C. Jeanette has been running the fund for 2 years and currently receives a manager quality ranking of 28 (0=worst, 99=best). If you desire an average level of risk, then this fund may be an option.

Data Date	Investment Rating	Net Assets ($Mil)	Price	Performance Rating/Pts	Total Return Y-T-D	Risk Rating/Pts
12-12	C	20.70	27.35	C- / 3.4	3.95%	B+ / 9.2

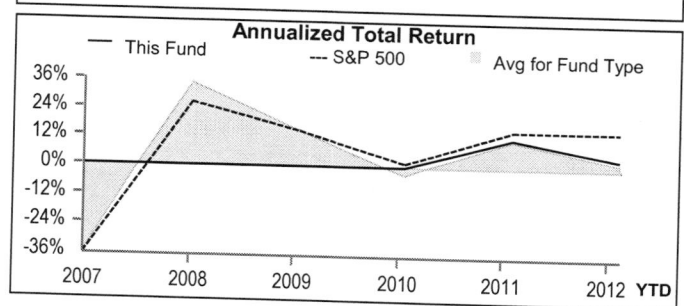

* Denotes ETF Fund

*PowerShares Lux Nanotech (PXN)

D- **Weak**

Fund Family: Invesco Powershares Capital Mgmt LL
Fund Type: Growth
Inception Date: October 26, 2005

Data Date	Investment Rating	Net Assets ($Mil)	Price	Perfor-mance Rating/Pts	Total Return Y-T-D	Risk Rating/Pts
12-12	D-	19.80	5.96	E+ / 0.7	6.54%	C+ / 5.9
2011	D-	22.10	6.05	D- / 1.1	1.49%	C+ / 5.8
2010	D-	46.10	9.80	E+ / 0.8	-6.58%	C / 4.9
2009	D-	39.48	10.49	E+ / 0.9	32.41%	C / 5.1

Major Rating Factors:
Very poor performance is the major factor driving the D- (Weak) TheStreet.com Investment Rating for *PowerShares Lux Nanotech. The fund currently has a performance rating of E+ (Very Weak) based on an annualized return of -14.95% over the last three years and a total return of 6.54% year to date 2012. Factored into the performance evaluation is an expense ratio of 0.70% (very low).

The fund's risk rating is currently C+ (Fair). It carries a beta of 1.40, meaning it is expected to move 14.0% for every 10% move in the market. Volatility, as measured by both the semi-deviation and a drawdown factor, is considered low. As of December 31, 2012, *PowerShares Lux Nanotech traded at a discount of 6.58% below its net asset value, which is better than its one-year historical average discount of .24%.

Peter Hubbard has been running the fund for 6 years and currently receives a manager quality ranking of 3 (0=worst, 99=best). This fund offers only a moderate level of risk but investors looking for strong performance are still waiting.

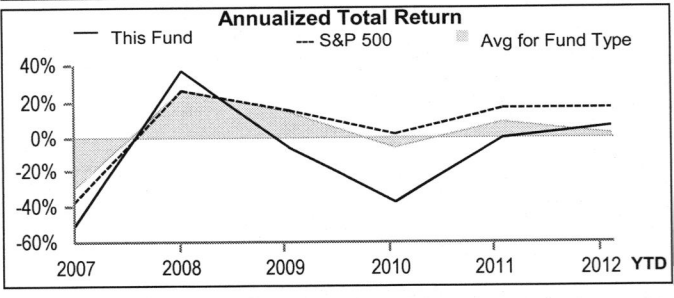

*PowerShares MENA Frontier Countr (PMNA)

D **Weak**

Fund Family: Invesco Powershares Capital Mgmt LL
Fund Type: Foreign
Inception Date: July 7, 2008

Data Date	Investment Rating	Net Assets ($Mil)	Price	Perfor-mance Rating/Pts	Total Return Y-T-D	Risk Rating/Pts
12-12	D	15.90	10.83	D- / 1.3	1.11%	B- / 7.6
2011	D	18.70	10.45	D- / 1.4	-2.30%	B- / 7.3
2010	B-	21.80	13.71	B+ / 8.5	9.76%	C / 4.3
2009	D-	10.34	12.90	D / 1.6	4.07%	C- / 4.1

Major Rating Factors:
Disappointing performance is the major factor driving the D (Weak) TheStreet.com Investment Rating for *PowerShares MENA Frontier Countr. The fund currently has a performance rating of D- (Weak) based on an annualized return of -2.43% over the last three years and a total return of 1.11% year to date 2012. Factored into the performance evaluation is an expense ratio of 0.70% (very low).

The fund's risk rating is currently B- (Good). It carries a beta of 0.57, meaning the fund's expected move will be 5.7% for every 10% move in the market. Volatility, as measured by both the semi-deviation and a drawdown factor, is considered low. As of December 31, 2012, *PowerShares MENA Frontier Countr traded at a discount of 2.43% below its net asset value, which is better than its one-year historical average discount of .75%.

Peter Hubbard has been running the fund for 5 years and currently receives a manager quality ranking of 23 (0=worst, 99=best). This fund offers only a moderate level of risk but investors looking for strong performance are still waiting.

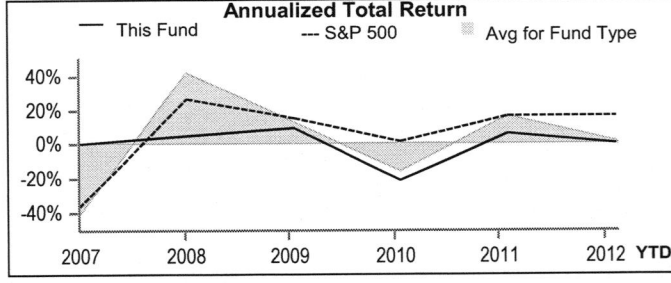

*PowerShares Mrnngstr StockInv Co (PYH)

C+ **Fair**

Fund Family: Invesco Powershares Capital Mgmt LL
Fund Type: Income
Inception Date: December 1, 2006

Data Date	Investment Rating	Net Assets ($Mil)	Price	Perfor-mance Rating/Pts	Total Return Y-T-D	Risk Rating/Pts
12-12	C+	14.00	23.25	C / 5.3	4.18%	B / 8.2
2011	C-	16.30	20.37	C- / 3.8	0.54%	B / 8.1
2010	D	18.00	20.04	D- / 1.0	10.63%	C+ / 5.7
2009	D-	26.51	18.33	D- / 1.1	8.44%	C / 5.5

Major Rating Factors: Middle of the road best describes *PowerShares Mrnngstr StockInv Co whose TheStreet.com Investment Rating is currently a C+ (Fair). The fund currently has a performance rating of C (Fair) based on an annualized return of 10.13% over the last three years and a total return of 4.18% year to date 2012. Factored into the performance evaluation is an expense ratio of 0.50% (very low).

The fund's risk rating is currently B (Good). It carries a beta of 0.94, meaning that its performance tracks fairly well with that of the overall stock market. Volatility, as measured by both the semi-deviation and a drawdown factor, is considered low. As of December 31, 2012, *PowerShares Mrnngstr StockInv Co traded at a discount of 4.20% below its net asset value, which is better than its one-year historical average discount of .16%.

Peter Hubbard has been running the fund for 6 years and currently receives a manager quality ranking of 47 (0=worst, 99=best). If you desire an average level of risk, then this fund may be an option.

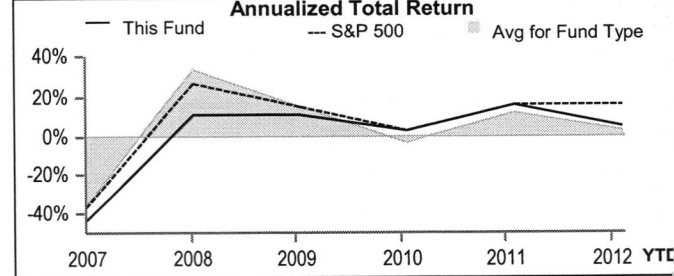

*PowerShares NASDAQ Internet Port (PNQI)

B-   **Good**

Fund Family: Invesco Powershares Capital Mgmt LL
Fund Type: Income
Inception Date: June 10, 2008

Major Rating Factors: Strong performance is the major factor driving the B- (Good) TheStreet.com Investment Rating for *PowerShares NASDAQ Internet Port. The fund currently has a performance rating of B+ (Good) based on an annualized return of 19.47% over the last three years and a total return of 4.61% year to date 2012. Factored into the performance evaluation is an expense ratio of 0.60% (very low).

The fund's risk rating is currently C+ (Fair). It carries a beta of 1.20, meaning it is expected to move 12.0% for every 10% move in the market. Volatility, as measured by both the semi-deviation and a drawdown factor, is considered low. As of December 31, 2012, *PowerShares NASDAQ Internet Port traded at a discount of 4.47% below its net asset value, which is better than its one-year historical average discount of .05%.

Peter Hubbard has been running the fund for 5 years and currently receives a manager quality ranking of 74 (0=worst, 99=best). If you desire only a moderate level of risk and strong performance, then this fund is an excellent option.

Data Date	Investment Rating	Net Assets ($Mil)	Price	Performance Rating/Pts	Total Return Y-T-D	Risk Rating/Pts
12-12	B-	48.20	41.46	B+ / 8.4	4.61%	C+ / 6.3
2011	B	53.50	34.54	B+ / 8.8	1.69%	C+ / 6.5
2010	B+	31.10	34.69	A+ / 9.6	34.20%	C- / 3.9
2009	A-	1.79	25.85	A+ / 9.8	88.03%	C / 4.3

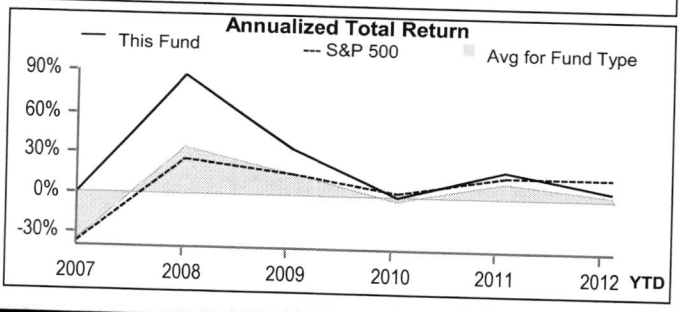

*PowerShares Preferred Port (PGX)

C+   **Fair**

Fund Family: Invesco Powershares Capital Mgmt LL
Fund Type: General - Investment Grade
Inception Date: January 28, 2008

Major Rating Factors: Middle of the road best describes *PowerShares Preferred Port whose TheStreet.com Investment Rating is currently a C+ (Fair). The fund currently has a performance rating of C- (Fair) based on an annualized return of 9.96% over the last three years and a total return of 1.57% year to date 2012. Factored into the performance evaluation is an expense ratio of 0.50% (very low).

The fund's risk rating is currently B+ (Good). It carries a beta of 0.24, meaning the fund's expected move will be 2.4% for every 10% move in the market. Volatility, as measured by both the semi-deviation and a drawdown factor, is considered very low. As of December 31, 2012, *PowerShares Preferred Port traded at a discount of 1.41% below its net asset value, which is better than its one-year historical average premium of .15%.

Peter Hubbard has been running the fund for 5 years and currently receives a manager quality ranking of 87 (0=worst, 99=best). If you desire an average level of risk, then this fund may be an option.

Data Date	Investment Rating	Net Assets ($Mil)	Price	Performance Rating/Pts	Total Return Y-T-D	Risk Rating/Pts
12-12	C+	2,149.00	14.68	C- / 4.0	1.57%	B+ / 9.4
2011	C-	1,359.70	13.69	C- / 3.8	2.34%	C+ / 6.8
2010	C+	1,353.90	14.12	B- / 7.3	12.18%	C / 4.4
2009	C	387.66	13.55	C+ / 6.6	14.01%	C / 4.3

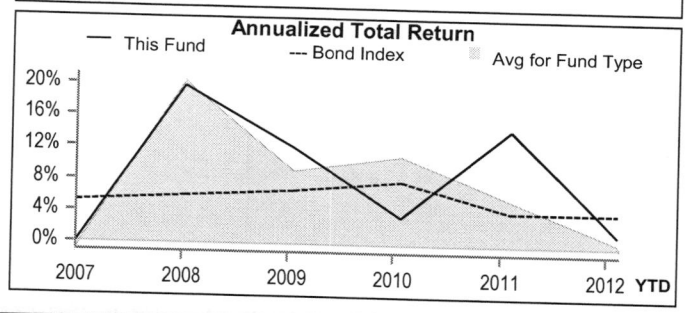

*PowerShares QQQ (QQQ)

C   **Fair**

Fund Family: Bank of New York Mellon
Fund Type: Growth
Inception Date: March 10, 1999

Major Rating Factors: Middle of the road best describes *PowerShares QQQ whose TheStreet.com Investment Rating is currently a C (Fair). The fund currently has a performance rating of C+ (Fair) based on an annualized return of 14.59% over the last three years and a total return of 3.27% year to date 2012. Factored into the performance evaluation is an expense ratio of 0.20% (very low).

The fund's risk rating is currently B- (Good). It carries a beta of 1.09, meaning that its performance tracks fairly well with that of the overall stock market. Volatility, as measured by both the semi-deviation and a drawdown factor, is considered low. As of December 31, 2012, *PowerShares QQQ traded at a discount of 3.17% below its net asset value.

Steven M. Hill currently receives a manager quality ranking of 63 (0=worst, 99=best). If you desire an average level of risk, then this fund may be an option.

Data Date	Investment Rating	Net Assets ($Mil)	Price	Performance Rating/Pts	Total Return Y-T-D	Risk Rating/Pts
12-12	C	30,416.90	65.13	C+ / 6.0	3.27%	B- / 7.1
2011	B	25,574.40	55.83	B- / 7.5	3.55%	B / 8.6
2010	C+	22,061.00	54.46	C+ / 6.9	20.16%	C+ / 5.6
2009	C	13,357.13	45.75	C+ / 6.0	48.21%	C / 5.5

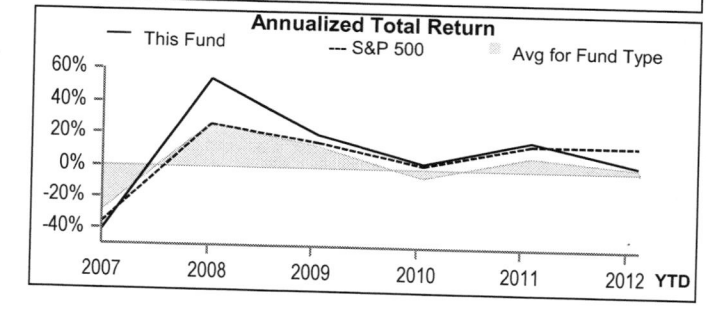

* Denotes ETF Fund

*PowerShares RiverFront Tact Bal (PAO)

C-   **Fair**

Fund Family: Invesco Powershares Capital Mgmt LL
Fund Type: Growth and Income
Inception Date: May 16, 2008

Major Rating Factors: Middle of the road best describes *PowerShares RiverFront Tact Bal whose TheStreet.com Investment Rating is currently a C- (Fair). The fund currently has a performance rating of C- (Fair) based on an annualized return of 5.57% over the last three years and a total return of 2.15% year to date 2012. Factored into the performance evaluation is an expense ratio of 0.25% (very low).

The fund's risk rating is currently B- (Good). It carries a beta of 0.88, meaning the fund's expected move will be 8.8% for every 10% move in the market. Volatility, as measured by both the semi-deviation and a drawdown factor, is considered low. As of December 31, 2012, *PowerShares RiverFront Tact Bal traded at a discount of 2.86% below its net asset value, which is better than its one-year historical average discount of .33%.

Peter Hubbard has been running the fund for 5 years and currently receives a manager quality ranking of 27 (0=worst, 99=best). If you desire an average level of risk, then this fund may be an option.

Data Date	Investment Rating	Net Assets ($Mil)	Price	Performance Rating/Pts	Total Return Y-T-D	Risk Rating/Pts
12-12	C-	15.80	12.58	C- / 3.3	2.15%	B- / 7.9
2011	C-	20.60	11.43	C- / 3.4	0.91%	B- / 7.9
2010	A-	18.20	12.63	B+ / 8.9	13.24%	C / 5.5
2009	B	8.32	11.44	B / 7.8	20.46%	C+ / 5.6

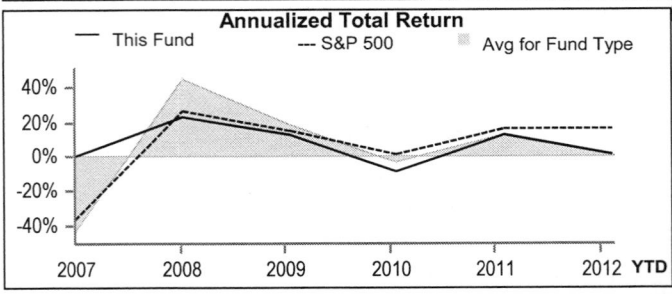

*PowerShares RiverFront Tact Gr & (PCA)

C   **Fair**

Fund Family: Invesco Powershares Capital Mgmt LL
Fund Type: Growth and Income
Inception Date: May 16, 2008

Major Rating Factors: Middle of the road best describes *PowerShares RiverFront Tact Gr & whose TheStreet.com Investment Rating is currently a C (Fair). The fund currently has a performance rating of C- (Fair) based on an annualized return of 6.76% over the last three years and a total return of 1.99% year to date 2012. Factored into the performance evaluation is an expense ratio of 0.25% (very low).

The fund's risk rating is currently B (Good). It carries a beta of 0.60, meaning the fund's expected move will be 6.0% for every 10% move in the market. Volatility, as measured by both the semi-deviation and a drawdown factor, is considered low. As of December 31, 2012, *PowerShares RiverFront Tact Gr & traded at a discount of 1.93% below its net asset value, which is better than its one-year historical average discount of .25%.

Peter Hubbard has been running the fund for 5 years and currently receives a manager quality ranking of 55 (0=worst, 99=best). If you desire an average level of risk, then this fund may be an option.

Data Date	Investment Rating	Net Assets ($Mil)	Price	Performance Rating/Pts	Total Return Y-T-D	Risk Rating/Pts
12-12	C	15.20	13.24	C- / 3.5	1.99%	B / 8.7
2011	C	29.10	12.44	C- / 3.7	-0.16%	B / 8.4
2010	A-	17.90	12.81	B+ / 8.6	11.98%	C+ / 6.3
2009	B	10.05	11.84	B- / 7.3	15.43%	C+ / 6.1

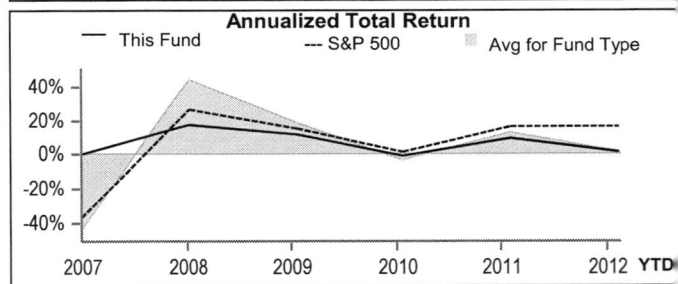

*PowerShares S&P 500 BuyWrite Por (PBP)

C-   **Fair**

Fund Family: Invesco Powershares Capital Mgmt LL
Fund Type: Income
Inception Date: December 20, 2007

Major Rating Factors:
Disappointing performance is the major factor driving the C- (Fair) TheStreet.com Investment Rating for *PowerShares S&P 500 BuyWrite Por. The fund currently has a performance rating of D+ (Weak) based on an annualized return of 7.29% over the last three years and a total return of 1.78% year to date 2012. Factored into the performance evaluation is an expense ratio of 0.75% (very low).

The fund's risk rating is currently B (Good). It carries a beta of 0.65, meaning the fund's expected move will be 6.5% for every 10% move in the market. Volatility, as measured by both the semi-deviation and a drawdown factor, is considered low. As of December 31, 2012, *PowerShares S&P 500 BuyWrite Por traded at a discount of 1.60% below its net asset value, which is better than its one-year historical average premium of .17%.

Jeffrey W. Kernagis has been running the fund for 6 years and currently receives a manager quality ranking of 48 (0=worst, 99=best). This fund offers only a moderate level of risk but investors looking for strong performance are still waiting.

Data Date	Investment Rating	Net Assets ($Mil)	Price	Performance Rating/Pts	Total Return Y-T-D	Risk Rating/Pts
12-12	C-	274.90	19.65	D+ / 2.9	1.78%	B / 8.2
2011	C+	89.50	19.62	C+ / 5.8	1.38%	B / 8.2
2010	C-	140.70	20.89	D+ / 2.8	5.51%	C+ / 6.4
2009	A	84.21	21.51	B / 7.9	21.32%	C+ / 6.5

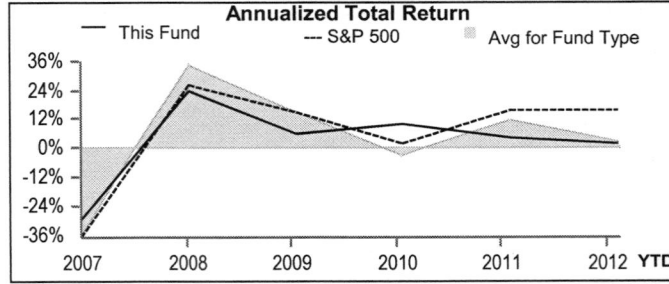

*Powershares S&P 500 High Beta Po (SPHB)

Fund Family: Invesco Powershares Capital Mgmt LL
Fund Type: Income
Inception Date: May 5, 2011

B+   Good

Data Date	Investment Rating	Net Assets ($Mil)	Price	Performance Rating/Pts	Total Return Y-T-D	Risk Rating/Pts
12-12	B+	119.30	21.92	A- / 9.1	3.97%	B- / 7.2

Major Rating Factors:
Exceptional performance is the major factor driving the B+ (Good) TheStreet.com Investment Rating for *Powershares S&P 500 High Beta Po. The fund currently has a performance rating of A- (Excellent) based on an annualized return of 0.00% over the last three years and a total return of 3.97% year to date 2012. Factored into the performance evaluation is an expense ratio of 0.25% (very low).

The fund's risk rating is currently B- (Good). It carries a beta of 0.00, meaning the fund's expected move will be 0.0% for every 10% move in the market. Volatility, as measured by both the semi-deviation and a drawdown factor, is considered low. As of December 31, 2012, *Powershares S&P 500 High Beta Po traded at a discount of 3.78% below its net asset value, which is better than its one-year historical average premium of .01%.

Michael C. Jeanette has been running the fund for 2 years and currently receives a manager quality ranking of 14 (0=worst, 99=best). If you desire only a moderate level of risk and strong performance, then this fund is an excellent option.

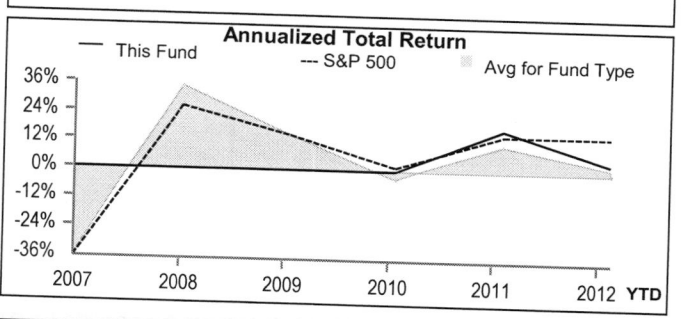

*PowerShares S&P 500 High Quality (SPHQ)

Fund Family: Invesco Powershares Capital Mgmt LL
Fund Type: Income
Inception Date: December 6, 2005

B-   Good

Data Date	Investment Rating	Net Assets ($Mil)	Price	Performance Rating/Pts	Total Return Y-T-D	Risk Rating/Pts
12-12	B-	175.70	15.72	C+ / 6.5	3.12%	B / 8.6
2011	C+	134.50	14.03	C / 5.1	0.86%	B / 8.4
2010	D	108.80	13.44	D / 1.7	21.20%	C+ / 6.0
2009	D-	71.05	11.22	D- / 1.0	10.06%	C / 5.1

Major Rating Factors: *PowerShares S&P 500 High Quality receives a TheStreet.com Investment Rating of B- (Good). The fund currently has a performance rating of C+ (Fair) based on an annualized return of 14.94% over the last three years and a total return of 3.12% year to date 2012. Factored into the performance evaluation is an expense ratio of 0.50% (very low).

The fund's risk rating is currently B (Good). It carries a beta of 0.86, meaning the fund's expected move will be 8.6% for every 10% move in the market. Volatility, as measured by both the semi-deviation and a drawdown factor, is considered low. As of December 31, 2012, *PowerShares S&P 500 High Quality traded at a discount of 2.96% below its net asset value, which is better than its one-year historical average discount of .01%.

Peter Hubbard has been running the fund for 6 years and currently receives a manager quality ranking of 77 (0=worst, 99=best). If you desire an average level of risk, then this fund may be an option.

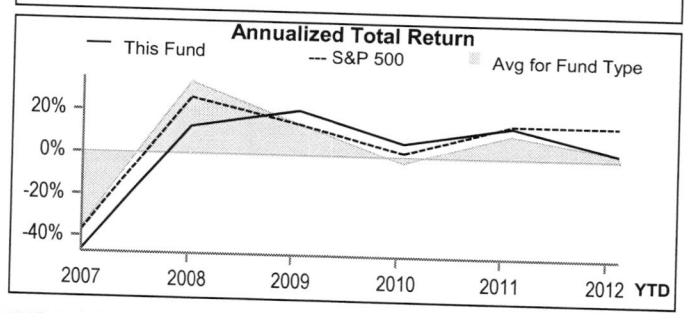

*Powershares S&P 500 Low Vol Port (SPLV)

Fund Family: Invesco Powershares Capital Mgmt LL
Fund Type: Growth
Inception Date: May 5, 2011

C+   Fair

Data Date	Investment Rating	Net Assets ($Mil)	Price	Performance Rating/Pts	Total Return Y-T-D	Risk Rating/Pts
12-12	C+	3,092.20	27.68	C / 4.5	2.53%	B+ / 9.7

Major Rating Factors: Middle of the road best describes *Powershares S&P 500 Low Vol Port whose TheStreet.com Investment Rating is currently a C+ (Fair). The fund currently has a performance rating of C (Fair) based on an annualized return of 0.00% over the last three years and a total return of 2.53% year to date 2012. Factored into the performance evaluation is an expense ratio of 0.25% (very low).

The fund's risk rating is currently B+ (Good). It carries a beta of 0.00, meaning the fund's expected move will be 0.0% for every 10% move in the market. Volatility, as measured by both the semi-deviation and a drawdown factor, is considered very low. As of December 31, 2012, *Powershares S&P 500 Low Vol Port traded at a discount of 2.47% below its net asset value, which is better than its one-year historical average premium of .03%.

Michael C. Jeanette has been running the fund for 2 years and currently receives a manager quality ranking of 79 (0=worst, 99=best). If you desire an average level of risk, then this fund may be an option.

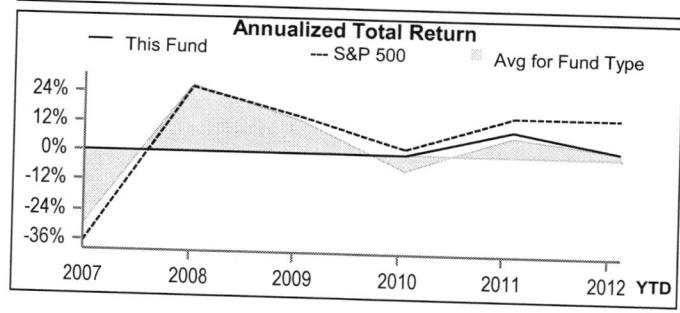

*PowerShares S&P Intl Dev High Qu (IDHQ)

C-   **Fair**

Fund Family: Invesco Powershares Capital Mgmt LL
Fund Type: Foreign
Inception Date: June 13, 2007

Major Rating Factors: Middle of the road best describes *PowerShares S&P Intl Dev High Qu whose TheStreet.com Investment Rating is currently a C- (Fair). The fund currently has a performance rating of C (Fair) based on an annualized return of 5.23% over the last three years and a total return of 2.42% year to date 2012. Factored into the performance evaluation is an expense ratio of 0.75% (very low).

The fund's risk rating is currently B- (Good). It carries a beta of 1.07, meaning that its performance tracks fairly well with that of the overall stock market. Volatility, as measured by both the semi-deviation and a drawdown factor, is considered low. As of December 31, 2012, *PowerShares S&P Intl Dev High Qu traded at a discount of 1.31% below its net asset value, which is better than its one-year historical average discount of .28%.

Peter Hubbard has been running the fund for 6 years and currently receives a manager quality ranking of 64 (0=worst, 99=best). If you desire an average level of risk, then this fund may be an option.

Data Date	Investment Rating	Net Assets ($Mil)	Price	Performance Rating/Pts	Total Return Y-T-D	Risk Rating/Pts
12-12	C-	18.90	17.33	C / 4.3	2.42%	B- / 7.5
2011	C-	17.70	14.57	C- / 3.3	-0.36%	B- / 7.5
2010	D	31.70	17.48	D+ / 2.5	16.28%	C / 4.7
2009	B+	44.15	15.96	B+ / 8.8	40.21%	C / 4.7

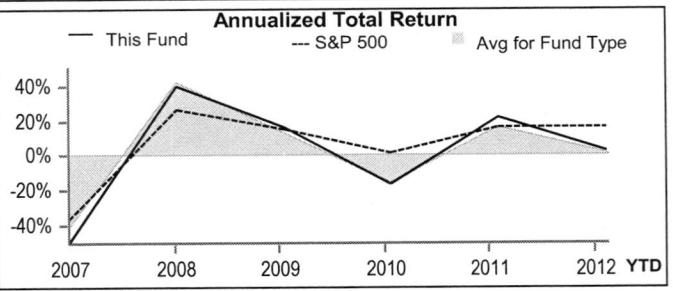

Annualized Total Return
— This Fund   --- S&P 500   Avg for Fund Type

*PowerShares S&P SC Cnsmr Discr (PSCD)

B+   **Good**

Fund Family: Invesco Powershares Capital Mgmt LL
Fund Type: Growth
Inception Date: April 6, 2010

Major Rating Factors:
Exceptional performance is the major factor driving the B+ (Good) TheStreet.com Investment Rating for *PowerShares S&P SC Cnsmr Discr. The fund currently has a performance rating of A- (Excellent) based on an annualized return of 0.00% over the last three years and a total return of 3.18% year to date 2012. Factored into the performance evaluation is an expense ratio of 0.29% (very low).

The fund's risk rating is currently B- (Good). It carries a beta of 0.00, meaning the fund's expected move will be 0.0% for every 10% move in the market. Volatility, as measured by both the semi-deviation and a drawdown factor, is considered low. As of December 31, 2012, *PowerShares S&P SC Cnsmr Discr traded at a discount of 3.11% below its net asset value, which is better than its one-year historical average discount of .04%.

Michael C. Jeanette has been running the fund for 3 years and currently receives a manager quality ranking of 82 (0=worst, 99=best). If you desire only a moderate level of risk and strong performance, then this fund is an excellent option.

Data Date	Investment Rating	Net Assets ($Mil)	Price	Performance Rating/Pts	Total Return Y-T-D	Risk Rating/Pts
12-12	B+	63.00	32.98	A- / 9.1	3.18%	B- / 7.4
2011	D	43.30	27.10	D / 1.8	0.92%	B- / 7.3

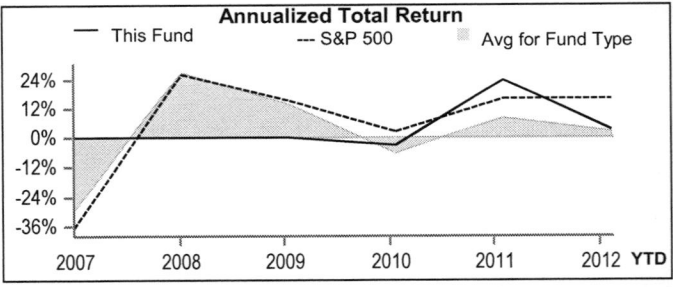

Annualized Total Return
— This Fund   --- S&P 500   Avg for Fund Type

*PowerShares S&P SC Cnsmr Staples (PSCC)

C+   **Fair**

Fund Family: Invesco Powershares Capital Mgmt LL
Fund Type: Growth
Inception Date: April 6, 2010

Major Rating Factors: Middle of the road best describes *PowerShares S&P SC Cnsmr Staples whose TheStreet.com Investment Rating is currently a C+ (Fair). The fund currently has a performance rating of C (Fair) based on an annualized return of 0.00% over the last three years and a total return of 2.47% year to date 2012. Factored into the performance evaluation is an expense ratio of 0.29% (very low).

The fund's risk rating is currently B (Good). It carries a beta of 0.00, meaning the fund's expected move will be 0.0% for every 10% move in the market. Volatility, as measured by both the semi-deviation and a drawdown factor, is considered low. As of December 31, 2012, *PowerShares S&P SC Cnsmr Staples traded at a discount of 2.27% below its net asset value, which is better than its one-year historical average premium of .02%.

Michael C. Jeanette has been running the fund for 3 years and currently receives a manager quality ranking of 56 (0=worst, 99=best). If you desire an average level of risk, then this fund may be an option.

Data Date	Investment Rating	Net Assets ($Mil)	Price	Performance Rating/Pts	Total Return Y-T-D	Risk Rating/Pts
12-12	C+	27.70	34.44	C / 4.9	2.47%	B / 8.7
2011	C	20.30	31.45	C- / 3.3	-1.24%	B / 8.7

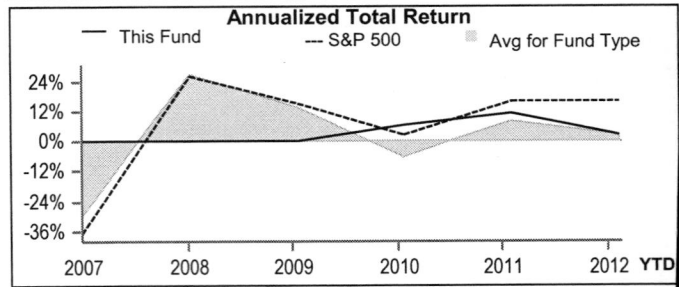

Annualized Total Return
— This Fund   --- S&P 500   Avg for Fund Type

*PowerShares S&P SC Energy (PSCE)

D   **Weak**

Fund Family: Invesco Powershares Capital Mgmt LL
Fund Type: Growth
Inception Date: April 6, 2010

Major Rating Factors: *PowerShares S&P SC Energy receives a TheStreet.com Investment Rating of D (Weak). The fund currently has a performance rating of C- (Fair) based on an annualized return of 0.00% over the last three years and a total return of 3.24% year to date 2012. Factored into the performance evaluation is an expense ratio of 0.29% (very low).

The fund's risk rating is currently C+ (Fair). It carries a beta of 0.00, meaning the fund's expected move will be 0.0% for every 10% move in the market. Volatility, as measured by both the semi-deviation and a drawdown factor, is considered low. As of December 31, 2012, *PowerShares S&P SC Energy traded at a discount of 3.19% below its net asset value, which is better than its one-year historical average discount of .10%.

Michael C. Jeanette has been running the fund for 3 years and currently receives a manager quality ranking of 3 (0=worst, 99=best). If you desire an average level of risk, then this fund may be an option.

Data Date	Investment Rating	Net Assets ($Mil)	Price	Perfor-mance Rating/Pts	Total Return Y-T-D	Risk Rating/Pts
12-12	D	30.30	33.64	C- / 3.1	3.24%	C+ / 5.7
2011	D+	54.80	34.30	C- / 4.0	2.33%	C+ / 5.8

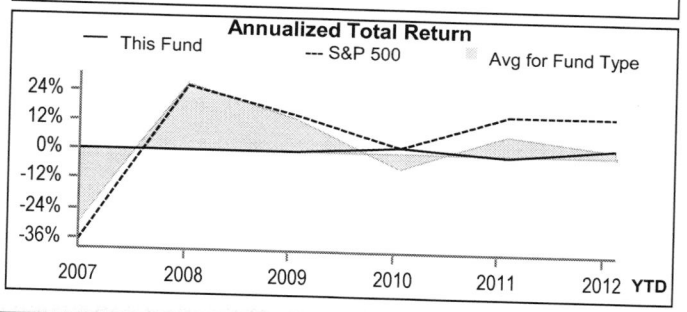

*PowerShares S&P SC Financials (PSCF)

B-   **Good**

Fund Family: Invesco Powershares Capital Mgmt LL
Fund Type: Growth
Inception Date: April 6, 2010

Major Rating Factors: Strong performance is the major factor driving the B- (Good) TheStreet.com Investment Rating for *PowerShares S&P SC Financials. The fund currently has a performance rating of B- (Good) based on an annualized return of 0.00% over the last three years and a total return of 2.75% year to date 2012. Factored into the performance evaluation is an expense ratio of 0.29% (very low).

The fund's risk rating is currently B- (Good). It carries a beta of 0.00, meaning the fund's expected move will be 0.0% for every 10% move in the market. Volatility, as measured by both the semi-deviation and a drawdown factor, is considered low. As of December 31, 2012, *PowerShares S&P SC Financials traded at a discount of 2.71% below its net asset value, which is better than its one-year historical average discount of .11%.

Michael C. Jeanette has been running the fund for 3 years and currently receives a manager quality ranking of 73 (0=worst, 99=best). If you desire only a moderate level of risk and strong performance, then this fund is an excellent option.

Data Date	Investment Rating	Net Assets ($Mil)	Price	Perfor-mance Rating/Pts	Total Return Y-T-D	Risk Rating/Pts
12-12	B-	74.10	30.89	B- / 7.1	2.75%	B- / 7.8
2011	C	62.00	27.04	C / 4.3	1.47%	B- / 7.8

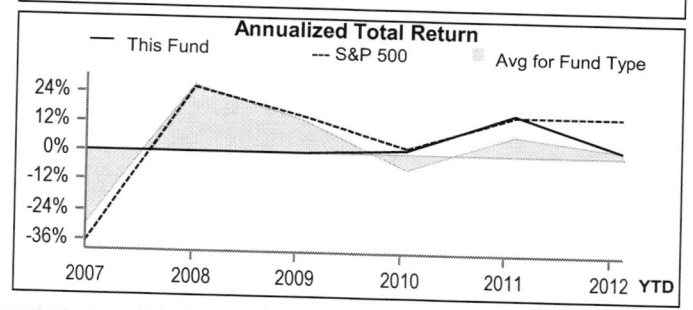

*PowerShares S&P SC Health Care (PSCH)

C+   **Fair**

Fund Family: Invesco Powershares Capital Mgmt LL
Fund Type: Growth
Inception Date: April 6, 2010

Major Rating Factors: Middle of the road best describes *PowerShares S&P SC Health Care whose TheStreet.com Investment Rating is currently a C+ (Fair). The fund currently has a performance rating of C+ (Fair) based on an annualized return of 0.00% over the last three years and a total return of 4.55% year to date 2012. Factored into the performance evaluation is an expense ratio of 0.29% (very low).

The fund's risk rating is currently B- (Good). It carries a beta of 0.00, meaning the fund's expected move will be 0.0% for every 10% move in the market. Volatility, as measured by both the semi-deviation and a drawdown factor, is considered low. As of December 31, 2012, *PowerShares S&P SC Health Care traded at a discount of 4.36% below its net asset value, which is better than its one-year historical average discount of .08%.

Michael C. Jeanette has been running the fund for 3 years and currently receives a manager quality ranking of 24 (0=worst, 99=best). If you desire an average level of risk, then this fund may be an option.

Data Date	Investment Rating	Net Assets ($Mil)	Price	Perfor-mance Rating/Pts	Total Return Y-T-D	Risk Rating/Pts
12-12	C+	109.80	35.35	C+ / 6.2	4.55%	B- / 7.9
2011	C	103.80	31.53	C- / 4.1	0.33%	B / 8.0

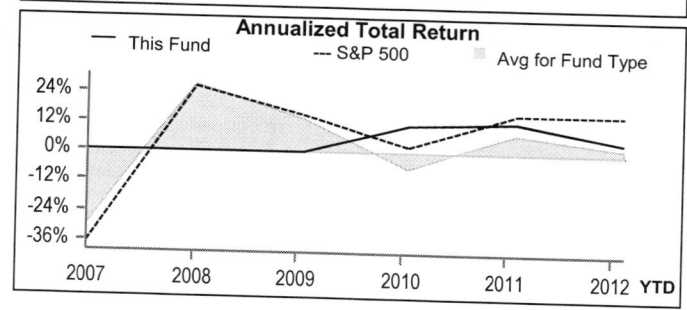

* Denotes ETF Fund

*PowerShares S&P SC Industrials (PSCI)

	B+	Good

Fund Family: Invesco Powershares Capital Mgmt LL
Fund Type: Growth
Inception Date: April 6, 2010

Data Date	Investment Rating	Net Assets ($Mil)	Price	Performance Rating/Pts	Total Return Y-T-D	Risk Rating/Pts
12-12	B+	24.30	32.03	A / 9.5	4.62%	B- / 7.2
2011	D	25.90	27.38	D / 1.9	1.61%	B- / 7.2

Major Rating Factors:
Exceptional performance is the major factor driving the B+ (Good) TheStreet.com Investment Rating for *PowerShares S&P SC Industrials. The fund currently has a performance rating of A (Excellent) based on an annualized return of 0.00% over the last three years and a total return of 4.62% year to date 2012. Factored into the performance evaluation is an expense ratio of 0.29% (very low).

The fund's risk rating is currently B- (Good). It carries a beta of 0.00, meaning the fund's expected move will be 0.0% for every 10% move in the market. Volatility, as measured by both the semi-deviation and a drawdown factor, is considered low. As of December 31, 2012, *PowerShares S&P SC Industrials traded at a discount of 4.33% below its net asset value, which is better than its one-year historical average discount of .05%.

Michael C. Jeanette has been running the fund for 3 years and currently receives a manager quality ranking of 70 (0=worst, 99=best). If you desire only a moderate level of risk and strong performance, then this fund is an excellent option.

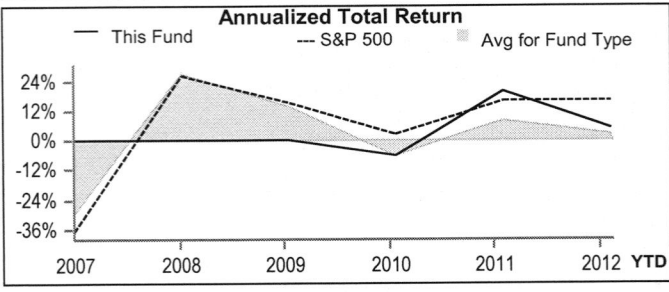

*PowerShares S&P SC Information T (PSCT)

	B	Good

Fund Family: Invesco Powershares Capital Mgmt LL
Fund Type: Growth
Inception Date: April 6, 2010

Data Date	Investment Rating	Net Assets ($Mil)	Price	Performance Rating/Pts	Total Return Y-T-D	Risk Rating/Pts
12-12	B	84.90	30.69	B / 8.2	4.04%	B- / 7.0
2011	D	78.10	28.03	D / 1.7	0.88%	B- / 7.0

Major Rating Factors: Strong performance is the major factor driving the B (Good) TheStreet.com Investment Rating for *PowerShares S&P SC Information T. The fund currently has a performance rating of B (Good) based on an annualized return of 0.00% over the last three years and a total return of 4.04% year to date 2012. Factored into the performance evaluation is an expense ratio of 0.29% (very low).

The fund's risk rating is currently B- (Good). It carries a beta of 0.00, meaning the fund's expected move will be 0.0% for every 10% move in the market. Volatility, as measured by both the semi-deviation and a drawdown factor, is considered low. As of December 31, 2012, *PowerShares S&P SC Information T traded at a discount of 3.76% below its net asset value, which is better than its one-year historical average discount of .08%.

Michael C. Jeanette has been running the fund for 3 years and currently receives a manager quality ranking of 18 (0=worst, 99=best). If you desire only a moderate level of risk and strong performance, then this fund is an excellent option.

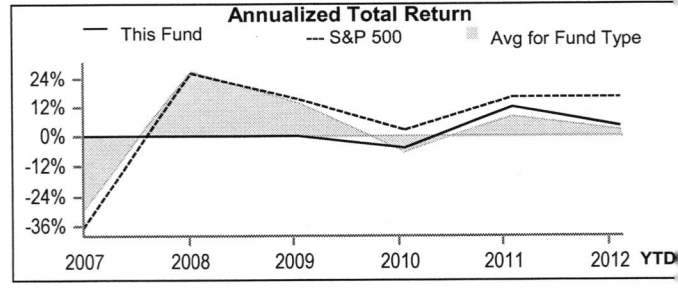

*PowerShares S&P SC Materials (PSCM)

	B+	Good

Fund Family: Invesco Powershares Capital Mgmt LL
Fund Type: Growth
Inception Date: April 6, 2010

Data Date	Investment Rating	Net Assets ($Mil)	Price	Performance Rating/Pts	Total Return Y-T-D	Risk Rating/Pts
12-12	B+	6.40	31.49	B+ / 8.8	6.73%	B- / 7.2
2011	D	3.90	25.84	D- / 1.4	1.47%	B- / 7.2

Major Rating Factors: Strong performance is the major factor driving the B+ (Good) TheStreet.com Investment Rating for *PowerShares S&P SC Materials. The fund currently has a performance rating of B+ (Good) based on an annualized return of 0.00% over the last three years and a total return of 6.73% year to date 2012. Factored into the performance evaluation is an expense ratio of 0.29% (very low).

The fund's risk rating is currently B- (Good). It carries a beta of 0.00, meaning the fund's expected move will be 0.0% for every 10% move in the market. Volatility, as measured by both the semi-deviation and a drawdown factor, is considered low. As of December 31, 2012, *PowerShares S&P SC Materials traded at a discount of 6.81% below its net asset value, which is better than its one-year historical average discount of .09%.

Michael C. Jeanette has been running the fund for 3 years and currently receives a manager quality ranking of 63 (0=worst, 99=best). If you desire only a moderate level of risk and strong performance, then this fund is an excellent option.

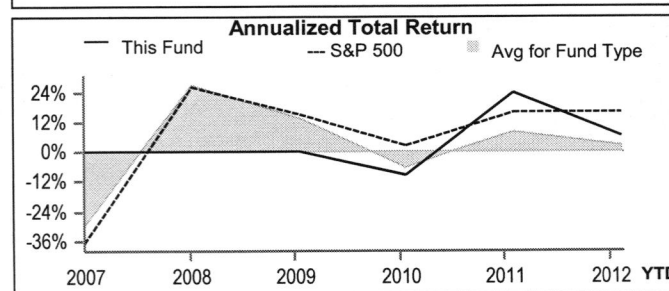

*PowerShares S&P SC Utilities (PSCU)

D+   **Weak**

Fund Family: Invesco Powershares Capital Mgmt LL
Fund Type: Growth
Inception Date: April 6, 2010

Major Rating Factors:
Disappointing performance is the major factor driving the D+ (Weak) TheStreet.com Investment Rating for *PowerShares S&P SC Utilities. The fund currently has a performance rating of D- (Weak) based on an annualized return of 0.00% over the last three years and a total return of 1.77% year to date 2012. Factored into the performance evaluation is an expense ratio of 0.29% (very low).

The fund's risk rating is currently B (Good). It carries a beta of 0.00, meaning the fund's expected move will be 0.0% for every 10% move in the market. Volatility, as measured by both the semi-deviation and a drawdown factor, is considered low. As of December 31, 2012, *PowerShares S&P SC Utilities traded at a discount of 2.35% below its net asset value, which is better than its one-year historical average discount of .08%.

Michael C. Jeanette has been running the fund for 3 years and currently receives a manager quality ranking of 20 (0=worst, 99=best). This fund offers only a moderate level of risk but investors looking for strong performance are still waiting.

Data Date	Investment Rating	Net Assets ($Mil)	Price	Performance Rating/Pts	Total Return Y-T-D	Risk Rating/Pts
12-12	D+	28.40	29.56	D- / 1.5	1.77%	B / 8.9
2011	C+	46.10	30.75	C / 4.8	-1.17%	B+ / 9.0

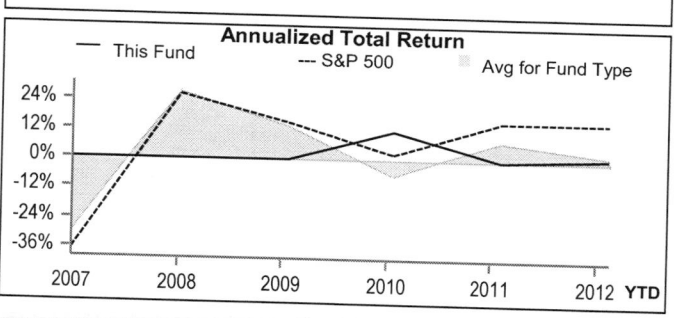

*PowerShares Senior Loan (BKLN)

C   **Fair**

Fund Family: Invesco Powershares Capital Mgmt LL
Fund Type: Loan Participation
Inception Date: March 1, 2011

Major Rating Factors: Middle of the road best describes *PowerShares Senior Loan whose TheStreet.com Investment Rating is currently a C (Fair). The fund currently has a performance rating of C- (Fair) based on an annualized return of 0.00% over the last three years and a total return of 0.88% year to date 2012. Factored into the performance evaluation is an expense ratio of 0.65% (very low).

The fund's risk rating is currently B+ (Good). It carries a beta of 0.00, meaning the fund's expected move will be 0.0% for every 10% move in the market. Volatility, as measured by both the semi-deviation and a drawdown factor, is considered very low. As of December 31, 2012, *PowerShares Senior Loan traded at a discount of .64% below its net asset value, which is better than its one-year historical average premium of .40%.

Peter Hubbard has been running the fund for 2 years and currently receives a manager quality ranking of 87 (0=worst, 99=best). If you desire an average level of risk, then this fund may be an option.

Data Date	Investment Rating	Net Assets ($Mil)	Price	Performance Rating/Pts	Total Return Y-T-D	Risk Rating/Pts
12-12	C	1,499.40	24.98	C- / 3.7	0.88%	B+ / 9.6

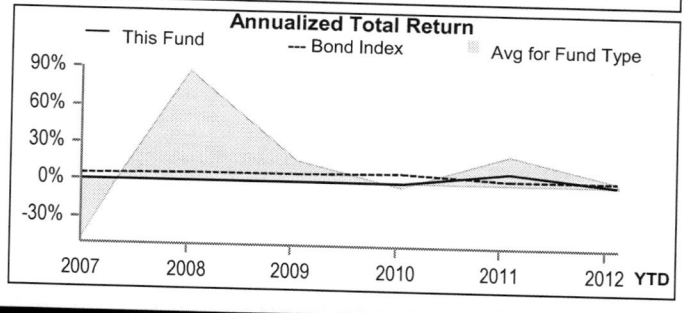

*PowerShares VRDO Tax-Free Weekly (PVI)

C-   **Fair**

Fund Family: Invesco Powershares Capital Mgmt LL
Fund Type: Municipal - High Yield
Inception Date: November 14, 2007

Major Rating Factors:
Disappointing performance is the major factor driving the C- (Fair) TheStreet.com Investment Rating for *PowerShares VRDO Tax-Free Weekly. The fund currently has a performance rating of D- (Weak) based on an annualized return of 0.33% over the last three years and a total return of -0.04% year to date 2012. Factored into the performance evaluation is an expense ratio of 0.25% (very low).

The fund's risk rating is currently B+ (Good). It carries a beta of 0.00, meaning the fund's expected move will be 0.0% for every 10% move in the market. Volatility, as measured by both the semi-deviation and a drawdown factor, is considered very low. As of December 31, 2012, *PowerShares VRDO Tax-Free Weekly traded at a discount of .04% below its net asset value, which is better than its one-year historical average discount of .03%.

Peter Hubbard has been running the fund for 6 years and currently receives a manager quality ranking of 55 (0=worst, 99=best). This fund offers only a moderate level of risk but investors looking for strong performance are still waiting.

Data Date	Investment Rating	Net Assets ($Mil)	Price	Performance Rating/Pts	Total Return Y-T-D	Risk Rating/Pts
12-12	C-	274.90	24.99	D- / 1.4	-0.04%	B+ / 9.9
2011	C	436.20	25.02	D / 2.1	-0.12%	B+ / 9.9
2010	B-	566.30	24.99	C- / 3.3	0.32%	B+ / 9.1
2009	C	380.13	25.00	D+ / 2.3	0.96%	B+ / 9.2

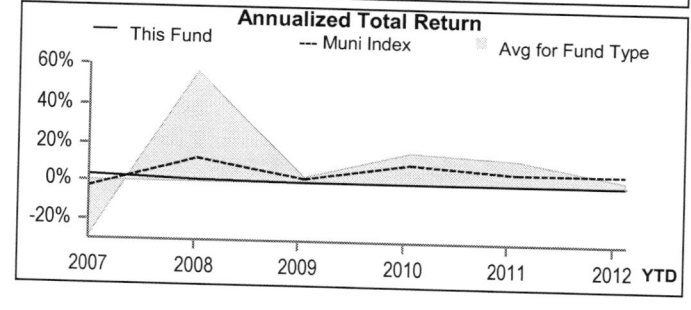

*PowerShares Water Resources (PHO)   C   Fair

Fund Family: Invesco Powershares Capital Mgmt LL
Fund Type: Income
Inception Date: December 6, 2005

Major Rating Factors: Middle of the road best describes *PowerShares Water Resources whose TheStreet.com Investment Rating is currently a C (Fair). The fund currently has a performance rating of C+ (Fair) based on an annualized return of 8.55% over the last three years and a total return of 3.86% year to date 2012. Factored into the performance evaluation is an expense ratio of 0.62% (very low).

The fund's risk rating is currently C+ (Fair). It carries a beta of 1.29, meaning it is expected to move 12.9% for every 10% move in the market. Volatility, as measured by both the semi-deviation and a drawdown factor, is considered low. As of December 31, 2012, *PowerShares Water Resources traded at a discount of 3.76% below its net asset value, which is better than its one-year historical average discount of .09%.

Peter Hubbard has been running the fund for 6 years and currently receives a manager quality ranking of 21 (0=worst, 99=best). If you desire an average level of risk, then this fund may be an option.

Data Date	Investment Rating	Net Assets ($Mil)	Price	Performance Rating/Pts	Total Return Y-T-D	Risk Rating/Pts
12-12	C	823.70	20.75	C+ / 5.9	3.86%	C+ / 6.8
2011	D+	808.80	16.85	C- / 3.1	2.14%	C+ / 6.4
2010	D+	1,162.50	18.99	C- / 3.9	13.73%	C / 5.0
2009	D	1,220.03	16.86	D+ / 2.7	13.90%	C / 4.9

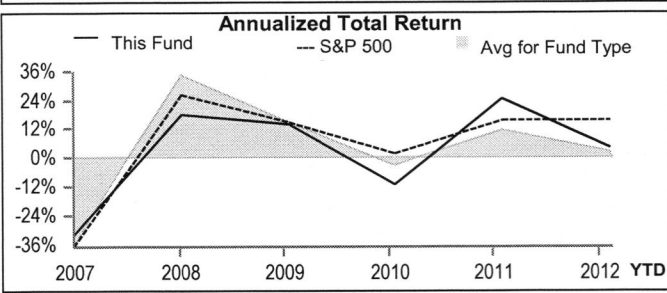

*PowerShares Wilder Clean Energy (PBW)   E+   Very Weak

Fund Family: Invesco Powershares Capital Mgmt LL
Fund Type: Energy/Natural Resources
Inception Date: March 3, 2005

Major Rating Factors:
Very poor performance is the major factor driving the E+ (Very Weak) TheStreet.com Investment Rating for *PowerShares Wilder Clean Energy. The fund currently has a performance rating of E (Very Weak) based on an annualized return of -24.84% over the last three years and a total return of 7.11% year to date 2012. Factored into the performance evaluation is an expense ratio of 0.70% (very low).

The fund's risk rating is currently C (Fair). It carries a beta of 1.13, meaning it is expected to move 11.3% for every 10% move in the market. Volatility, as measured by both the semi-deviation and a drawdown factor, is considered average. As of December 31, 2012, *PowerShares Wilder Clean Energy traded at a discount of 6.85% below its net asset value, which is better than its one-year historical average discount of .19%.

Peter Hubbard has been running the fund for 6 years and currently receives a manager quality ranking of 2 (0=worst, 99=best). This fund offers an average level of risk but investors looking for strong performance will be frustrated.

Data Date	Investment Rating	Net Assets ($Mil)	Price	Performance Rating/Pts	Total Return Y-T-D	Risk Rating/Pts
12-12	E+	123.10	4.08	E / 0.4	7.11%	C / 4.5
2011	E+	194.50	5.07	E+ / 0.8	2.96%	C / 4.8
2010	E+	547.20	10.39	E / 0.5	-5.55%	C- / 3.7
2009	E+	658.40	11.00	E+ / 0.9	21.28%	C- / 3.7

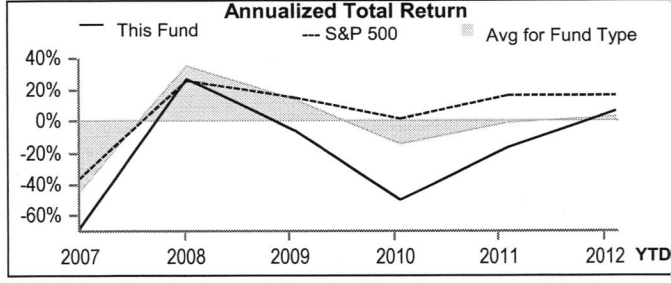

*PowerShares WilderHill Progr Ene (PUW)   D   Weak

Fund Family: Invesco Powershares Capital Mgmt LL
Fund Type: Energy/Natural Resources
Inception Date: October 24, 2006

Major Rating Factors:
Disappointing performance is the major factor driving the D (Weak) TheStreet.com Investment Rating for *PowerShares WilderHill Progr Ene. The fund currently has a performance rating of D+ (Weak) based on an annualized return of 3.16% over the last three years and a total return of 3.13% year to date 2012. Factored into the performance evaluation is an expense ratio of 0.71% (very low).

The fund's risk rating is currently C+ (Fair). It carries a beta of 1.03, meaning that its performance tracks fairly well with that of the overall stock market. Volatility, as measured by both the semi-deviation and a drawdown factor, is considered low. As of December 31, 2012, *PowerShares WilderHill Progr Ene traded at a discount of 3.65% below its net asset value, which is better than its one-year historical average discount of .12%.

Peter Hubbard has been running the fund for 6 years and currently receives a manager quality ranking of 21 (0=worst, 99=best). This fund offers only a moderate level of risk but investors looking for strong performance are still waiting.

Data Date	Investment Rating	Net Assets ($Mil)	Price	Performance Rating/Pts	Total Return Y-T-D	Risk Rating/Pts
12-12	D	37.20	25.58	D+ / 2.6	3.13%	C+ / 6.7
2011	C-	43.90	22.53	C / 4.3	3.32%	C+ / 6.8
2010	C	61.70	28.13	C+ / 5.8	20.44%	C / 5.1
2009	C-	39.97	23.54	C / 4.5	51.77%	C / 5.3

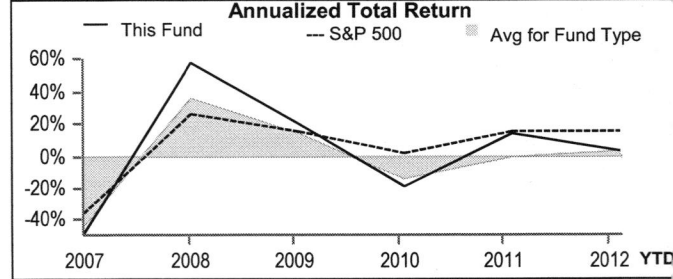

*PowerShares Zacks Micro Cap (PZI)

C | **Fair**

Fund Family: Invesco Powershares Capital Mgmt LL
Fund Type: Growth
Inception Date: August 18, 2005

Major Rating Factors: Middle of the road best describes *PowerShares Zacks Micro Cap whose TheStreet.com Investment Rating is currently a C (Fair). The fund currently has a performance rating of C (Fair) based on an annualized return of 8.57% over the last three years and a total return of 4.33% year to date 2012. Factored into the performance evaluation is an expense ratio of 0.70% (very low).

The fund's risk rating is currently B- (Good). It carries a beta of 1.51, meaning it is expected to move 15.1% for every 10% move in the market. Volatility, as measured by both the semi-deviation and a drawdown factor, is considered low. As of December 31, 2012, *PowerShares Zacks Micro Cap traded at a discount of 4.21% below its net asset value, which is better than its one-year historical average discount of .24%.

Peter Hubbard has been running the fund for 6 years and currently receives a manager quality ranking of 16 (0=worst, 99=best). If you desire an average level of risk, then this fund may be an option.

Data Date	Investment Rating	Net Assets ($Mil)	Price	Performance Rating/Pts	Total Return Y-T-D	Risk Rating/Pts
12-12	C	29.20	11.83	C / 5.0	4.33%	B- / 7.1
2011	D+	31.60	10.19	D+ / 2.9	0.98%	C+ / 6.8
2010	C-	110.70	12.01	C- / 4.0	23.70%	C / 5.3
2009	D-	46.96	9.80	E+ / 0.7	9.89%	C / 5.1

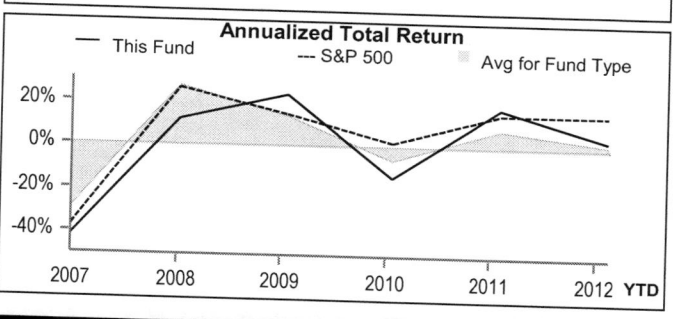

Annualized Total Return

---

*Precidian Maxis Nikkei 225 Index (NKY)

B+ | **Good**

Fund Family: Precidian Funds LLC
Fund Type: Global
Inception Date: July 8, 2011

Major Rating Factors: Strong performance is the major factor driving the B+ (Good) TheStreet.com Investment Rating for *Precidian Maxis Nikkei 225 Index. The fund currently has a performance rating of B (Good) based on an annualized return of 0.00% over the last three years and a total return of 1.04% year to date 2012. Factored into the performance evaluation is an expense ratio of 0.50% (very low).

The fund's risk rating is currently B (Good). It carries a beta of 0.00, meaning the fund's expected move will be 0.0% for every 10% move in the market. Volatility, as measured by both the semi-deviation and a drawdown factor, is considered low. As of December 31, 2012, *Precidian Maxis Nikkei 225 Index traded at a price exactly equal to its net asset value, which is better than its one-year historical average premium of .10%.

This fund has been team managed for 2 years and currently receives a manager quality ranking of 92 (0=worst, 99=best). If you desire only a moderate level of risk and strong performance, then this fund is an excellent option.

Data Date	Investment Rating	Net Assets ($Mil)	Price	Performance Rating/Pts	Total Return Y-T-D	Risk Rating/Pts
12-12	B+	192.90	14.45	B / 7.9	1.04%	B / 8.3

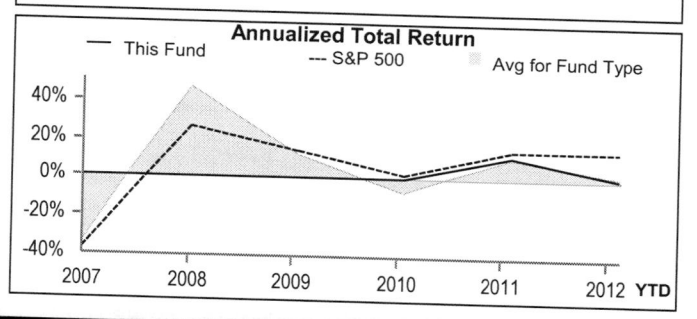

Annualized Total Return

---

*ProShares Credit Suisse 130/30 (CSM)

C | **Fair**

Fund Family: ProShare Advisors LLC
Fund Type: Income
Inception Date: July 13, 2009

Major Rating Factors: Middle of the road best describes *ProShares Credit Suisse 130/30 whose TheStreet.com Investment Rating is currently a C (Fair). The fund currently has a performance rating of C (Fair) based on an annualized return of 10.64% over the last three years and a total return of 3.13% year to date 2012. Factored into the performance evaluation is an expense ratio of 0.95% (low).

The fund's risk rating is currently B (Good). It carries a beta of 1.04, meaning that its performance tracks fairly well with that of the overall stock market. Volatility, as measured by both the semi-deviation and a drawdown factor, is considered low. As of December 31, 2012, *ProShares Credit Suisse 130/30 traded at a discount of 3.11% below its net asset value, which is better than its one-year historical average discount of .05%.

Ryan Dofflemeyer has been running the fund for 3 years and currently receives a manager quality ranking of 43 (0=worst, 99=best). If you desire an average level of risk, then this fund may be an option.

Data Date	Investment Rating	Net Assets ($Mil)	Price	Performance Rating/Pts	Total Return Y-T-D	Risk Rating/Pts
12-12	C	75.60	65.83	C / 5.1	3.13%	B / 8.1
2011	D+	91.00	56.77	D / 2.1	1.41%	B / 8.2
2010	A+	62.70	57.03	A- / 9.0	14.17%	B- / 7.9

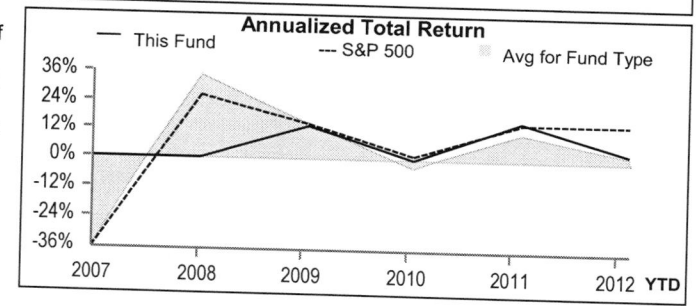

Annualized Total Return

*ProShares Hedge Replication ETF (HDG)

C-   Fair

Fund Family: ProShare Advisors LLC
Fund Type: Global
Inception Date: July 12, 2011

Major Rating Factors:
Disappointing performance is the major factor driving the C- (Fair) TheStreet.com Investment Rating for *ProShares Hedge Replication ETF. The fund currently has a performance rating of D+ (Weak) based on an annualized return of 0.00% over the last three years and a total return of 1.14% year to date 2012. Factored into the performance evaluation is an expense ratio of 0.95% (low).

The fund's risk rating is currently B+ (Good). It carries a beta of 0.00, meaning the fund's expected move will be 0.0% for every 10% move in the market. Volatility, as measured by both the semi-deviation and a drawdown factor, is considered very low. As of December 31, 2012, *ProShares Hedge Replication ETF traded at a discount of 1.12% below its net asset value, which is better than its one-year historical average premium of .09%.

Ryan Dofflemeyer has been running the fund for 1 year and currently receives a manager quality ranking of 34 (0=worst, 99=best). This fund offers only a moderate level of risk but investors looking for strong performance are still waiting.

Data Date	Investment Rating	Net Assets ($Mil)	Price	Performance Rating/Pts	Total Return Y-T-D	Risk Rating/Pts
12-12	C-	22.00	39.89	D+ / 2.5	1.14%	B+ / 9.4

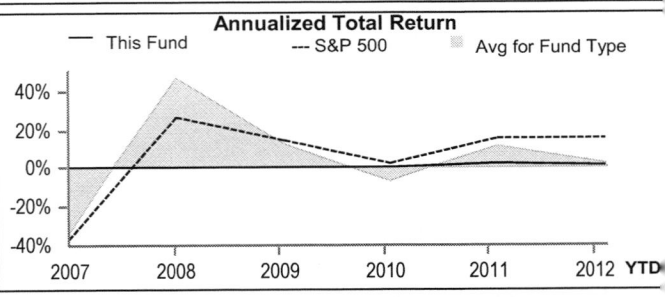

*ProShares RAFI Long/Short (RALS)

C-   Fair

Fund Family: ProShare Advisors LLC
Fund Type: Income
Inception Date: December 2, 2010

Major Rating Factors:
Disappointing performance is the major factor driving the C- (Fair) TheStreet.com Investment Rating for *ProShares RAFI Long/Short. The fund currently has a performance rating of D+ (Weak) based on an annualized return of 0.00% over the last three years and a total return of -1.44% year to date 2012. Factored into the performance evaluation is an expense ratio of 0.95% (low).

The fund's risk rating is currently B (Good). It carries a beta of 0.00, meaning the fund's expected move will be 0.0% for every 10% move in the market. Volatility, as measured by both the semi-deviation and a drawdown factor, is considered low. As of December 31, 2012, *ProShares RAFI Long/Short traded at a discount of .23% below its net asset value, which is better than its one-year historical average discount of .18%.

Ryan Dofflemeyer currently receives a manager quality ranking of 64 (0=worst, 99=best). This fund offers only a moderate level of risk but investors looking for strong performance are still waiting.

Data Date	Investment Rating	Net Assets ($Mil)	Price	Performance Rating/Pts	Total Return Y-T-D	Risk Rating/Pts
12-12	C-	11.70	38.82	D+ / 2.4	-1.44%	B / 8.7
2011	C-	15.40	38.37	D- / 1.4	0.21%	B+ / 9.1

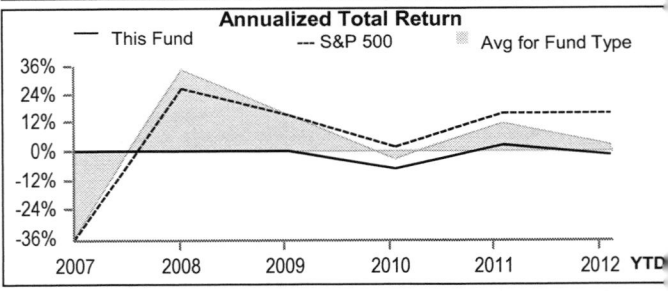

*ProShares Short 20+ Year Treas (TBF)

D-   Weak

Fund Family: ProShare Advisors LLC
Fund Type: US Government/Agency
Inception Date: August 18, 2009

Major Rating Factors:
Very poor performance is the major factor driving the D- (Weak) TheStreet.com Investment Rating for *ProShares Short 20+ Year Treas. The fund currently has a performance rating of E+ (Very Weak) based on an annualized return of -15.89% over the last three years and a total return of 0.92% year to date 2012. Factored into the performance evaluation is an expense ratio of 0.95% (low).

The fund's risk rating is currently C+ (Fair). It carries a beta of -1.25, meaning the fund's expected move will be -12.5% for every 10% move in the market. Volatility, as measured by both the semi-deviation and a drawdown factor, is considered low. As of December 31, 2012, *ProShares Short 20+ Year Treas traded at a discount of 1.28% below its net asset value, which is better than its one-year historical average discount of .11%.

Michelle Lui has been running the fund for 3 years and currently receives a manager quality ranking of 33 (0=worst, 99=best). This fund offers only a moderate level of risk but investors looking for strong performance are still waiting.

Data Date	Investment Rating	Net Assets ($Mil)	Price	Performance Rating/Pts	Total Return Y-T-D	Risk Rating/Pts
12-12	D-	780.60	29.38	E+ / 0.6	0.92%	C+ / 5.9
2011	D-	712.30	31.17	E / 0.5	2.09%	C+ / 6.5
2010	D+	812.00	44.25	D- / 1.4	-12.39%	B- / 7.3

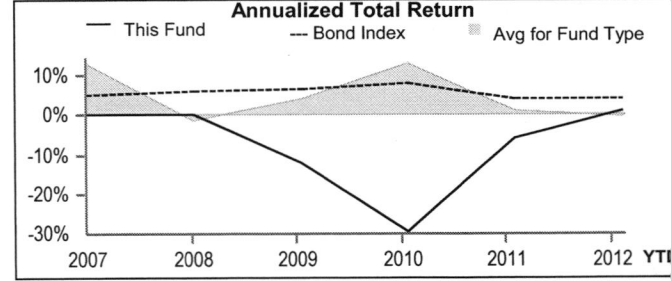

*ProShares Short 7-10 Year Treasu (TBX)

D **Weak**

Fund Family: ProShare Advisors LLC
Fund Type: General - Investment Grade
Inception Date: April 4, 2011

Major Rating Factors:

Disappointing performance is the major factor driving the D (Weak) TheStreet.com Investment Rating for *ProShares Short 7-10 Year Treasu. The fund currently has a performance rating of D- (Weak) based on an annualized return of 0.00% over the last three years and a total return of 0.34% year to date 2012. Factored into the performance evaluation is an expense ratio of 0.95% (low).

The fund's risk rating is currently B (Good). It carries a beta of 0.00, meaning the fund's expected move will be 0.0% for every 10% move in the market. Volatility, as measured by both the semi-deviation and a drawdown factor, is considered low. As of December 31, 2012, *ProShares Short 7-10 Year Treasu traded at a discount of .37% below its net asset value, which is better than its one-year historical average discount of .03%.

Michelle Lui has been running the fund for 2 years and currently receives a manager quality ranking of 69 (0=worst, 99=best). This fund offers only a moderate level of risk but investors looking for strong performance are still waiting.

Data Date	Investment Rating	Net Assets ($Mil)	Price	Performance Rating/Pts	Total Return Y-T-D	Risk Rating/Pts
12-12	D	15.30	32.42	D- / 1.1	0.34%	B / 8.4

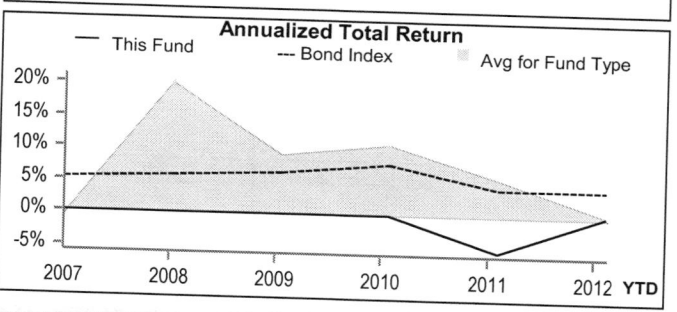

*ProShares Short Basic Materials (SBM)

D- **Weak**

Fund Family: ProShare Advisors LLC
Fund Type: Growth
Inception Date: March 16, 2010

Major Rating Factors:

Very poor performance is the major factor driving the D- (Weak) TheStreet.com Investment Rating for *ProShares Short Basic Materials. The fund currently has a performance rating of E (Very Weak) based on an annualized return of 0.00% over the last three years and a total return of -3.11% year to date 2012. Factored into the performance evaluation is an expense ratio of 0.95% (low).

The fund's risk rating is currently C+ (Fair). It carries a beta of 0.00, meaning the fund's expected move will be 0.0% for every 10% move in the market. Volatility, as measured by both the semi-deviation and a drawdown factor, is considered low. As of December 31, 2012, *ProShares Short Basic Materials traded at a premium of 3.18% above its net asset value, which is worse than its one-year historical average discount of .03%.

Hratch Najarian has been running the fund for 2 years and currently receives a manager quality ranking of 74 (0=worst, 99=best). This fund offers only a moderate level of risk but investors looking for strong performance are still waiting.

Data Date	Investment Rating	Net Assets ($Mil)	Price	Performance Rating/Pts	Total Return Y-T-D	Risk Rating/Pts
12-12	D-	6.80	33.75	E / 0.5	-3.11%	C+ / 5.7
2011	D-	7.80	39.21	D / 1.6	-3.55%	C+ / 5.9

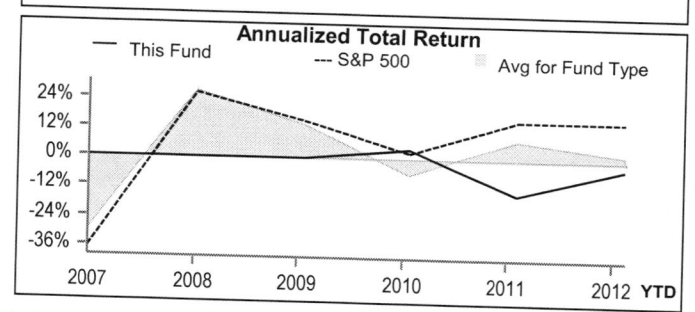

*ProShares Short Dow30 (DOG)

D- **Weak**

Fund Family: ProShare Advisors LLC
Fund Type: Growth
Inception Date: June 19, 2006

Major Rating Factors:

Very poor performance is the major factor driving the D- (Weak) TheStreet.com Investment Rating for *ProShares Short Dow30. The fund currently has a performance rating of E+ (Very Weak) based on an annualized return of -13.35% over the last three years and a total return of -2.91% year to date 2012. Factored into the performance evaluation is an expense ratio of 0.95% (low).

The fund's risk rating is currently C+ (Fair). It carries a beta of -0.86, meaning the fund's expected move will be -8.6% for every 10% move in the market. Volatility, as measured by both the semi-deviation and a drawdown factor, is considered low. As of December 31, 2012, *ProShares Short Dow30 traded at a premium of 3.02% above its net asset value, which is worse than its one-year historical average discount of .02%.

Hratch Najarian has been running the fund for 4 years and currently receives a manager quality ranking of 22 (0=worst, 99=best). This fund offers only a moderate level of risk but investors looking for strong performance are still waiting.

Data Date	Investment Rating	Net Assets ($Mil)	Price	Performance Rating/Pts	Total Return Y-T-D	Risk Rating/Pts
12-12	D-	260.80	34.40	E+ / 0.6	-2.91%	C+ / 6.6
2011	D-	293.90	38.80	D- / 1.0	-1.39%	C / 5.5
2010	D	246.20	44.33	E+ / 0.8	-15.29%	C+ / 5.7
2009	D	234.48	52.33	D- / 1.0	-21.40%	C+ / 6.7

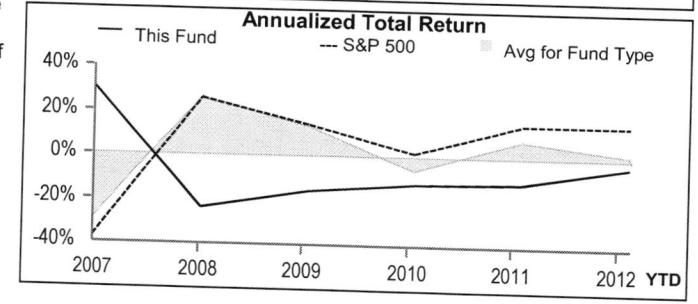

*ProShares Short Financials (SEF)

D-   **Weak**

Fund Family: ProShare Advisors LLC
Fund Type: Financial Services
Inception Date: June 10, 2008

Major Rating Factors:

Very poor performance is the major factor driving the D- (Weak) TheStreet.com Investment Rating for *ProShares Short Financials. The fund currently has a performance rating of E (Very Weak) based on an annualized return of -14.10% over the last three years and a total return of -4.12% year to date 2012. Factored into the performance evaluation is an expense ratio of 0.95% (low).

The fund's risk rating is currently C+ (Fair). It carries a beta of -0.96, meaning the fund's expected move will be -9.6% for every 10% move in the market. Volatility, as measured by both the semi-deviation and a drawdown factor, is considered low. As of December 31, 2012, *ProShares Short Financials traded at a premium of 4.30% above its net asset value.

Hratch Najarian has been running the fund for 2 years and currently receives a manager quality ranking of 16 (0=worst, 99=best). This fund offers only a moderate level of risk but investors looking for strong performance are still waiting.

Data Date	Investment Rating	Net Assets ($Mil)	Price	Performance Rating/Pts	Total Return Y-T-D	Risk Rating/Pts
12-12	D-	70.40	28.39	E / 0.5	-4.12%	C+ / 6.3
2011	E+	131.90	37.38	E+ / 0.8	-2.49%	C- / 3.9
2010	E+	96.30	36.66	E / 0.4	-17.43%	C- / 3.7
2009	E+	157.37	44.40	E / 0.3	-40.93%	C- / 4.1

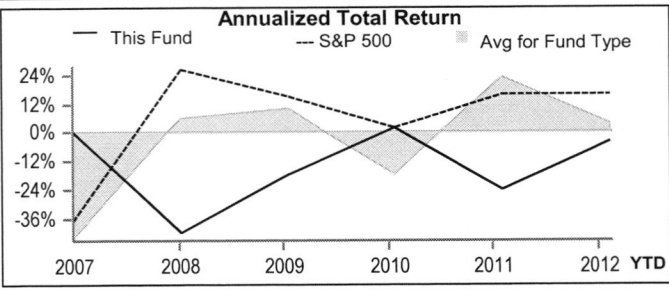
Annualized Total Return

*ProShares Short FTSE China 25 (YXI)

D-   **Weak**

Fund Family: ProShare Advisors LLC
Fund Type: Foreign
Inception Date: March 16, 2010

Major Rating Factors:

Very poor performance is the major factor driving the D- (Weak) TheStreet.com Investment Rating for *ProShares Short FTSE China 25. The fund currently has a performance rating of E (Very Weak) based on an annualized return of 0.00% over the last three years and a total return of -2.51% year to date 2012. Factored into the performance evaluation is an expense ratio of 0.95% (low).

The fund's risk rating is currently C+ (Fair). It carries a beta of 0.00, meaning the fund's expected move will be 0.0% for every 10% move in the market. Volatility, as measured by both the semi-deviation and a drawdown factor, is considered low. As of December 31, 2012, *ProShares Short FTSE China 25 traded at a premium of 2.51% above its net asset value, which is worse than its one-year historical average premium of .01%.

Alexander V. Ilyasov has been running the fund for 3 years and currently receives a manager quality ranking of 14 (0=worst, 99=best). This fund offers only a moderate level of risk but investors looking for strong performance are still waiting.

Data Date	Investment Rating	Net Assets ($Mil)	Price	Performance Rating/Pts	Total Return Y-T-D	Risk Rating/Pts
12-12	D-	8.80	35.50	E / 0.3	-2.51%	C+ / 6.3
2011	D+	11.30	45.31	D / 2.1	-0.88%	B- / 7.4

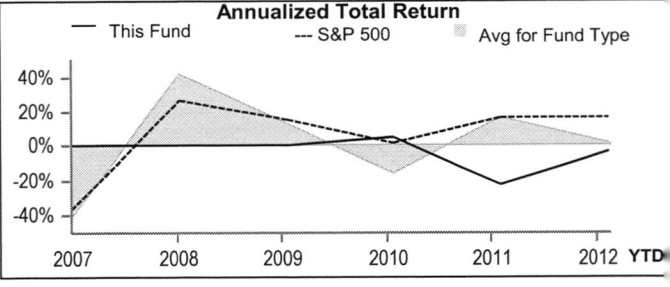
Annualized Total Return

*ProShares Short High Yield (SJB)

D   **Weak**

Fund Family: ProShare Advisors LLC
Fund Type: General - Investment Grade
Inception Date: March 21, 2011

Major Rating Factors:

Very poor performance is the major factor driving the D (Weak) TheStreet.com Investment Rating for *ProShares Short High Yield. The fund currently has a performance rating of E (Very Weak) based on an annualized return of 0.00% over the last three years and a total return of -1.21% year to date 2012. Factored into the performance evaluation is an expense ratio of 0.95% (low).

The fund's risk rating is currently B- (Good). It carries a beta of 0.00, meaning the fund's expected move will be 0.0% for every 10% move in the market. Volatility, as measured by both the semi-deviation and a drawdown factor, is considered low. As of December 31, 2012, *ProShares Short High Yield traded at a premium of 1.26% above its net asset value, which is worse than its one-year historical average discount of .02%.

Jeff Ploshnick has been running the fund for 2 years and currently receives a manager quality ranking of 8 (0=worst, 99=best). This fund offers only a moderate level of risk but investors looking for strong performance are still waiting.

Data Date	Investment Rating	Net Assets ($Mil)	Price	Performance Rating/Pts	Total Return Y-T-D	Risk Rating/Pts
12-12	D	40.20	32.15	E / 0.5	-1.21%	B- / 7.8

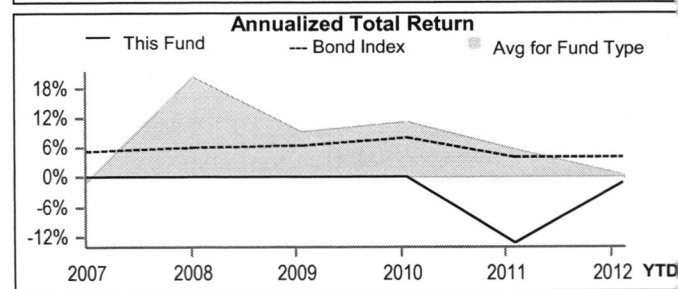
Annualized Total Return

*ProShares Short Inv Grade Corp (IGS)

Fund Family: ProShare Advisors LLC
Fund Type: Corporate - Investment Grade
Inception Date: March 28, 2011

D — Weak

Data Date	Investment Rating	Net Assets ($Mil)	Price	Performance Rating/Pts	Total Return Y-T-D	Risk Rating/Pts
12-12	D	4.80	31.90	E+ / 0.7	0.31%	B / 8.3

Major Rating Factors:

Very poor performance is the major factor driving the D (Weak) TheStreet.com Investment Rating for *ProShares Short Inv Grade Corp. The fund currently has a performance rating of E+ (Very Weak) based on an annualized return of 0.00% over the last three years and a total return of 0.31% year to date 2012. Factored into the performance evaluation is an expense ratio of 0.95% (low).

The fund's risk rating is currently B (Good). It carries a beta of 0.00, meaning the fund's expected move will be 0.0% for every 10% move in the market. Volatility, as measured by both the semi-deviation and a drawdown factor, is considered low. As of December 31, 2012, *ProShares Short Inv Grade Corp traded at a premium of .03% above its net asset value, which is better than its one-year historical average premium of .26%.

Jeff Ploshnick has been running the fund for 2 years and currently receives a manager quality ranking of 65 (0=worst, 99=best). This fund offers only a moderate level of risk but investors looking for strong performance are still waiting.

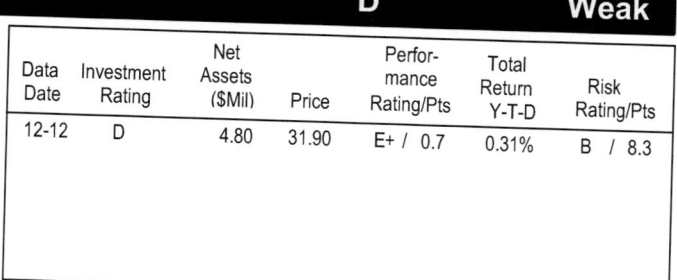

*ProShares Short KBW Regional Ban (KRS)

Fund Family: ProShare Advisors LLC
Fund Type: Financial Services
Inception Date: April 20, 2010

D- — Weak

Data Date	Investment Rating	Net Assets ($Mil)	Price	Performance Rating/Pts	Total Return Y-T-D	Risk Rating/Pts
12-12	D-	4.40	43.91	E+ / 0.7	-3.01%	C / 5.5
2011	D-	10.50	51.74	E+ / 0.6	-3.34%	C+ / 6.3

Major Rating Factors:

Very poor performance is the major factor driving the D- (Weak) TheStreet.com Investment Rating for *ProShares Short KBW Regional Ban. The fund currently has a performance rating of E+ (Very Weak) based on an annualized return of 0.00% over the last three years and a total return of -3.01% year to date 2012. Factored into the performance evaluation is an expense ratio of 0.95% (low).

The fund's risk rating is currently C (Fair). It carries a beta of 0.00, meaning the fund's expected move will be 0.0% for every 10% move in the market. Volatility, as measured by both the semi-deviation and a drawdown factor, is considered average. As of December 31, 2012, *ProShares Short KBW Regional Ban traded at a premium of 3.51% above its net asset value, which is worse than its one-year historical average discount of .18%.

Hratch Najarian has been running the fund for 2 years and currently receives a manager quality ranking of 81 (0=worst, 99=best). This fund offers an average level of risk but investors looking for strong performance will be frustrated.

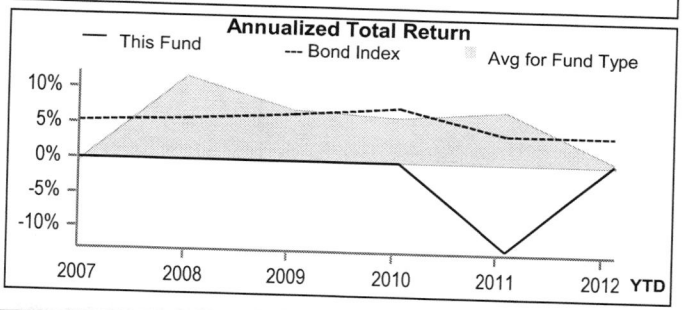

*ProShares Short Midcap 400 (MYY)

Fund Family: ProShare Advisors LLC
Fund Type: Growth
Inception Date: June 19, 2006

D- — Weak

Data Date	Investment Rating	Net Assets ($Mil)	Price	Performance Rating/Pts	Total Return Y-T-D	Risk Rating/Pts
12-12	D-	19.00	25.35	E / 0.5	-3.75%	C+ / 5.8
2011	E+	32.40	30.85	E+ / 0.8	-1.46%	C / 4.5
2010	D-	32.40	33.15	E / 0.5	-25.40%	C / 4.5
2009	D-	30.63	44.44	E+ / 0.7	-33.39%	C+ / 5.7

Major Rating Factors:

Very poor performance is the major factor driving the D- (Weak) TheStreet.com Investment Rating for *ProShares Short Midcap 400. The fund currently has a performance rating of E (Very Weak) based on an annualized return of -17.36% over the last three years and a total return of -3.75% year to date 2012. Factored into the performance evaluation is an expense ratio of 0.95% (low).

The fund's risk rating is currently C+ (Fair). It carries a beta of -1.11, meaning the fund's expected move will be -11.1% for every 10% move in the market. Volatility, as measured by both the semi-deviation and a drawdown factor, is considered low. As of December 31, 2012, *ProShares Short Midcap 400 traded at a premium of 3.89% above its net asset value, which is worse than its one-year historical average discount of .04%.

Hratch Najarian has been running the fund for 3 years and currently receives a manager quality ranking of 17 (0=worst, 99=best). This fund offers only a moderate level of risk but investors looking for strong performance are still waiting.

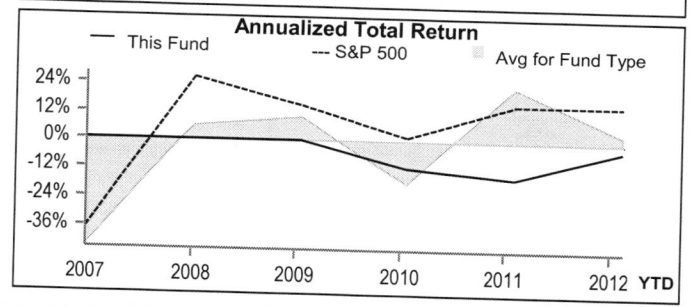

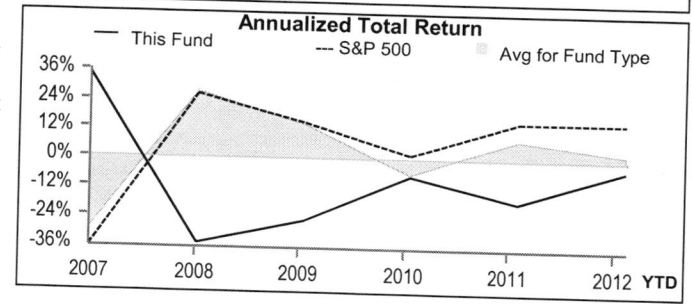

*ProShares Short MSCI EAFE (EFZ)

D-   **Weak**

Fund Family: ProShare Advisors LLC
Fund Type: Foreign
Inception Date: October 23, 2007

Major Rating Factors:
Very poor performance is the major factor driving the D- (Weak) TheStreet.com Investment Rating for *ProShares Short MSCI EAFE. The fund currently has a performance rating of E+ (Very Weak) based on an annualized return of -10.34% over the last three years and a total return of -2.00% year to date 2012. Factored into the performance evaluation is an expense ratio of 0.95% (low).

The fund's risk rating is currently C+ (Fair). It carries a beta of -0.98, meaning the fund's expected move will be -9.8% for every 10% move in the market. Volatility, as measured by both the semi-deviation and a drawdown factor, is considered low. As of December 31, 2012, *ProShares Short MSCI EAFE traded at a premium of 1.99% above its net asset value, which is worse than its one-year historical average discount of .01%.

Alexander V. Ilyasov has been running the fund for 4 years and currently receives a manager quality ranking of 16 (0=worst, 99=best). This fund offers only a moderate level of risk but investors looking for strong performance are still waiting.

Data Date	Investment Rating	Net Assets ($Mil)	Price	Performance Rating/Pts	Total Return Y-T-D	Risk Rating/Pts
12-12	D-	134.20	41.51	E+ / 0.6	-2.00%	C+ / 6.4
2011	D-	251.10	51.50	D- / 1.2	0.61%	C / 4.9
2010	D-	105.20	50.06	E+ / 0.8	-14.24%	C / 4.6
2009	D-	60.46	58.37	E / 0.3	-29.66%	C / 5.4

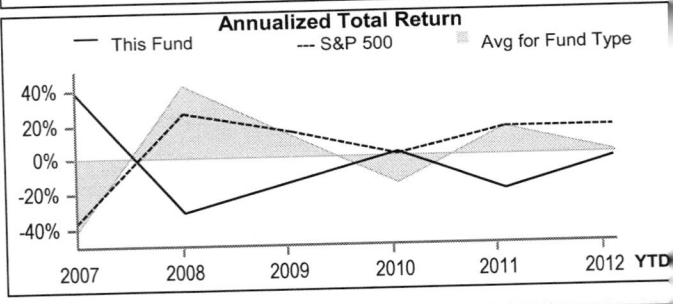

*ProShares Short MSCI Emg Mkts (EUM)

D-   **Weak**

Fund Family: ProShare Advisors LLC
Fund Type: Emerging Market
Inception Date: October 30, 2007

Major Rating Factors:
Very poor performance is the major factor driving the D- (Weak) TheStreet.com Investment Rating for *ProShares Short MSCI Emg Mkts. The fund currently has a performance rating of E+ (Very Weak) based on an annualized return of -11.45% over the last three years and a total return of -0.38% year to date 2012. Factored into the performance evaluation is an expense ratio of 0.95% (low).

The fund's risk rating is currently C+ (Fair). It carries a beta of -1.03, meaning the fund's expected move will be -10.3% for every 10% move in the market. Volatility, as measured by both the semi-deviation and a drawdown factor, is considered low. As of December 31, 2012, *ProShares Short MSCI Emg Mkts traded at a premium of .38% above its net asset value.

Alexander V. Ilyasov has been running the fund for 4 years and currently receives a manager quality ranking of 17 (0=worst, 99=best). This fund offers only a moderate level of risk but investors looking for strong performance are still waiting.

Data Date	Investment Rating	Net Assets ($Mil)	Price	Performance Rating/Pts	Total Return Y-T-D	Risk Rating/Pts
12-12	D-	214.10	26.68	E+ / 0.6	-0.38%	C+ / 6.1
2011	E+	280.80	33.39	E+ / 0.9	-0.93%	C- / 4.0
2010	E+	200.20	30.66	E / 0.4	-20.92%	C- / 3.7
2009	E+	54.70	38.77	E- / 0.2	-48.04%	C / 4.4

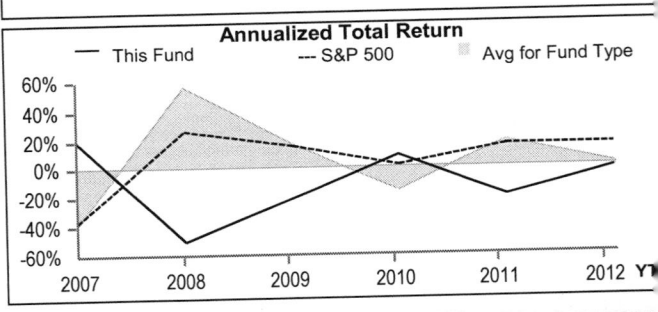

*ProShares Short Oil and Gas (DDG)

D-   **Weak**

Fund Family: ProShare Advisors LLC
Fund Type: Income
Inception Date: June 10, 2008

Major Rating Factors:
Very poor performance is the major factor driving the D- (Weak) TheStreet.com Investment Rating for *ProShares Short Oil and Gas. The fund currently has a performance rating of E+ (Very Weak) based on an annualized return of -14.72% over the last three years and a total return of -4.18% year to date 2012. Factored into the performance evaluation is an expense ratio of 0.95% (low).

The fund's risk rating is currently C+ (Fair). It carries a beta of -1.23, meaning the fund's expected move will be -12.3% for every 10% move in the market. Volatility, as measured by both the semi-deviation and a drawdown factor, is considered low. As of December 31, 2012, *ProShares Short Oil and Gas traded at a premium of 3.95% above its net asset value, which is worse than its one-year historical average discount of .11%.

Hratch Najarian has been running the fund for 2 years and currently receives a manager quality ranking of 30 (0=worst, 99=best). This fund offers only a moderate level of risk but investors looking for strong performance are still waiting.

Data Date	Investment Rating	Net Assets ($Mil)	Price	Performance Rating/Pts	Total Return Y-T-D	Risk Rating/Pt
12-12	D-	4.80	32.08	E+ / 0.6	-4.18%	C+ / 5.
2011	D-	7.90	34.85	E+ / 0.9	-1.81%	C / 5.
2010	E+	12.10	40.38	E / 0.3	-21.02%	C / 4.
2009	D-	4.44	51.13	E / 0.4	-20.86%	C / 5.

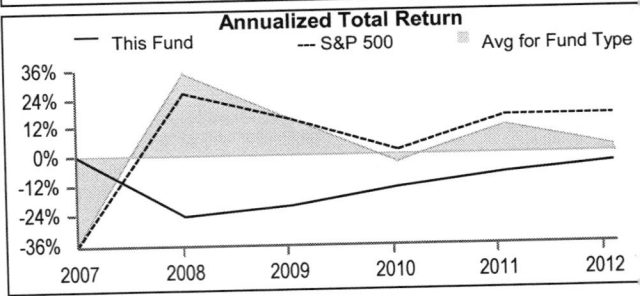

*ProShares Short QQQ (PSQ)

D-   **Weak**

Fund Family: ProShare Advisors LLC
Fund Type: Growth
Inception Date: June 19, 2006

Major Rating Factors:

Very poor performance is the major factor driving the D- (Weak) TheStreet.com Investment Rating for *ProShares Short QQQ. The fund currently has a performance rating of E (Very Weak) based on an annualized return of -17.17% over the last three years and a total return of -3.29% year to date 2012. Factored into the performance evaluation is an expense ratio of 0.95% (low).

The fund's risk rating is currently C+ (Fair). It carries a beta of -1.06, meaning the fund's expected move will be -10.6% for every 10% move in the market. Volatility, as measured by both the semi-deviation and a drawdown factor, is considered low. As of December 31, 2012, *ProShares Short QQQ traded at a premium of 3.44% above its net asset value, which is worse than its one-year historical average discount of .01%.

Hratch Najarian has been running the fund for 4 years and currently receives a manager quality ranking of 17 (0=worst, 99=best). This fund offers only a moderate level of risk but investors looking for strong performance are still waiting.

Data Date	Investment Rating	Net Assets ($Mil)	Price	Performance Rating/Pts	Total Return Y-T-D	Risk Rating/Pts
12-12	D-	184.10	25.57	E / 0.5	-3.29%	C+ / 5.6
2011	E+	293.30	31.29	E+ / 0.8	-3.39%	C / 4.8
2010	D-	200.30	34.67	E+ / 0.6	-20.61%	C / 4.9
2009	D-	174.68	43.67	E+ / 0.6	-37.79%	C+ / 6.0

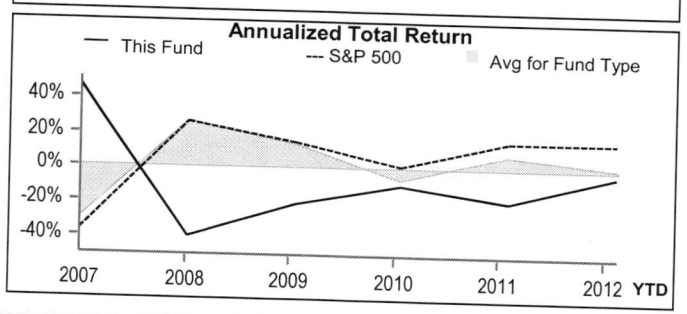

Annualized Total Return

*ProShares Short Real Estate (REK)

D-   **Weak**

Fund Family: ProShare Advisors LLC
Fund Type: Growth and Income
Inception Date: March 16, 2010

Major Rating Factors:

Very poor performance is the major factor driving the D- (Weak) TheStreet.com Investment Rating for *ProShares Short Real Estate. The fund currently has a performance rating of E (Very Weak) based on an annualized return of 0.00% over the last three years and a total return of -2.76% year to date 2012. Factored into the performance evaluation is an expense ratio of 0.95% (low).

The fund's risk rating is currently C+ (Fair). It carries a beta of 0.00, meaning the fund's expected move will be 0.0% for every 10% move in the market. Volatility, as measured by both the semi-deviation and a drawdown factor, is considered low. As of December 31, 2012, *ProShares Short Real Estate traded at a premium of 2.94% above its net asset value, which is worse than its one-year historical average discount of .07%.

Hratch Najarian has been running the fund for 2 years and currently receives a manager quality ranking of 13 (0=worst, 99=best). This fund offers only a moderate level of risk but investors looking for strong performance are still waiting.

Data Date	Investment Rating	Net Assets ($Mil)	Price	Performance Rating/Pts	Total Return Y-T-D	Risk Rating/Pts
12-12	D-	28.00	28.00	E / 0.5	-2.76%	C+ / 5.9
2011	D-	42.90	34.29	D- / 1.0	-0.09%	C+ / 6.8

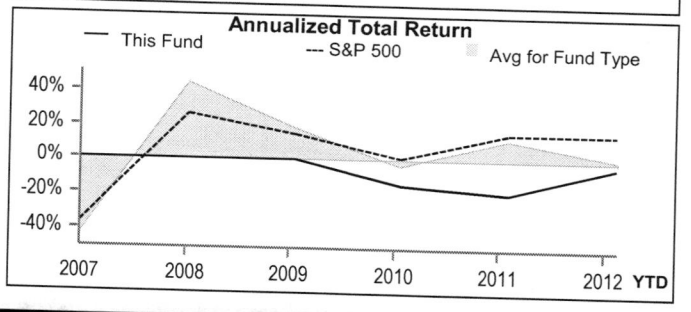

Annualized Total Return

*ProShares Short Russell 2000 (RWM)

E+   **Very Weak**

Fund Family: ProShare Advisors LLC
Fund Type: Growth
Inception Date: January 23, 2007

Major Rating Factors:

Very poor performance is the major factor driving the E+ (Very Weak) TheStreet.com Investment Rating for *ProShares Short Russell 2000. The fund currently has a performance rating of E (Very Weak) based on an annualized return of -18.50% over the last three years and a total return of -3.70% year to date 2012. Factored into the performance evaluation is an expense ratio of 0.95% (low).

The fund's risk rating is currently C (Fair). It carries a beta of -1.24, meaning the fund's expected move will be -12.4% for every 10% move in the market. Volatility, as measured by both the semi-deviation and a drawdown factor, is considered average. As of December 31, 2012, *ProShares Short Russell 2000 traded at a premium of 3.98% above its net asset value, which is worse than its one-year historical average premium of .02%.

Hratch Najarian has been running the fund for 4 years and currently receives a manager quality ranking of 17 (0=worst, 99=best). This fund offers an average level of risk but investors looking for strong performance will be frustrated.

Data Date	Investment Rating	Net Assets ($Mil)	Price	Performance Rating/Pts	Total Return Y-T-D	Risk Rating/Pts
12-12	E+	437.30	24.32	E / 0.5	-3.70%	C / 5.5
2011	E+	475.30	29.68	E+ / 0.8	-1.45%	C / 4.3
2010	E+	224.60	32.18	E / 0.5	-27.39%	C- / 3.7
2009	E+	78.49	44.32	E / 0.3	-31.44%	C / 4.9

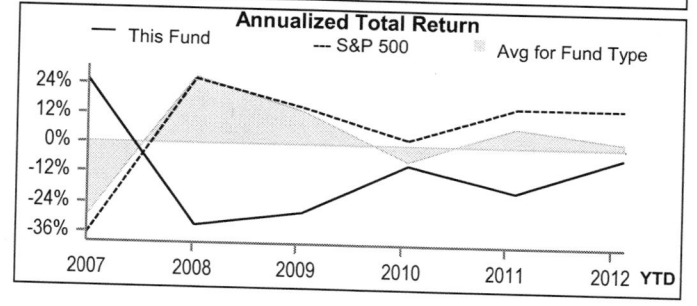

Annualized Total Return

* Denotes ETF Fund

*ProShares Short S&P500 (SH)   D-   Weak

Fund Family: ProShare Advisors LLC
Fund Type: Growth
Inception Date: June 19, 2006

Major Rating Factors:
Very poor performance is the major factor driving the D- (Weak) TheStreet.com Investment Rating for *ProShares Short S&P500. The fund currently has a performance rating of E+ (Very Weak) based on an annualized return of -13.89% over the last three years and a total return of -3.35% year to date 2012. Factored into the performance evaluation is an expense ratio of 0.89% (low).

The fund's risk rating is currently C+ (Fair). It carries a beta of -0.98, meaning the fund's expected move will be -9.8% for every 10% move in the market. Volatility, as measured by both the semi-deviation and a drawdown factor, is considered low. As of December 31, 2012, *ProShares Short S&P500 traded at a premium of 3.40% above its net asset value.

Hratch Najarian has been running the fund for 3 years and currently receives a manager quality ranking of 24 (0=worst, 99=best). This fund offers only a moderate level of risk but investors looking for strong performance are still waiting.

Data Date	Investment Rating	Net Assets ($Mil)	Price	Performance Rating/Pts	Total Return Y-T-D	Risk Rating/Pts
12-12	D-	1,849.60	34.03	E+ / 0.6	-3.35%	C+ / 6.4
2011	D-	2,366.70	40.41	D- / 1.0	-1.76%	C / 5.4
2010	D-	1,553.90	43.84	E+ / 0.7	-16.59%	C / 5.4
2009	D	1,282.50	52.56	D- / 1.1	-24.87%	C+ / 6.4

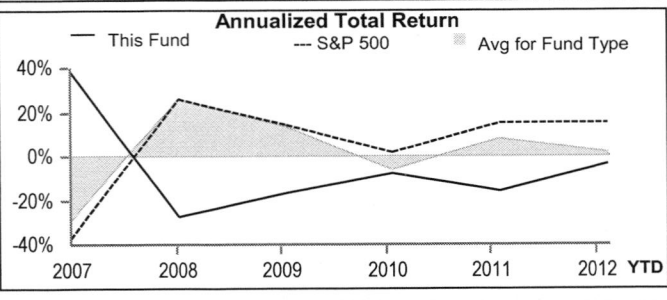

*ProShares Short Small Cap 600 (SBB)   E+   Very Weak

Fund Family: ProShare Advisors LLC
Fund Type: Growth
Inception Date: January 23, 2007

Major Rating Factors:
Very poor performance is the major factor driving the E+ (Very Weak) TheStreet.com Investment Rating for *ProShares Short Small Cap 600. The fund currently has a performance rating of E (Very Weak) based on an annualized return of -19.06% over the last three years and a total return of -3.24% year to date 2012. Factored into the performance evaluation is an expense ratio of 0.95% (low).

The fund's risk rating is currently C (Fair). It carries a beta of -1.17, meaning the fund's expected move will be -11.7% for every 10% move in the market. Volatility, as measured by both the semi-deviation and a drawdown factor, is considered average. As of December 31, 2012, *ProShares Short Small Cap 600 traded at a premium of 3.00% above its net asset value, which is worse than its one-year historical average discount of .09%.

Hratch Najarian has been running the fund for 3 years and currently receives a manager quality ranking of 15 (0=worst, 99=best). This fund offers an average level of risk but investors looking for strong performance will be frustrated.

Data Date	Investment Rating	Net Assets ($Mil)	Price	Performance Rating/Pts	Total Return Y-T-D	Risk Rating/Pts
12-12	E+	15.80	20.97	E / 0.4	-3.24%	C / 5.4
2011	E+	28.60	25.37	E+ / 0.7	-1.19%	C / 4.3
2010	E+	23.80	28.76	E / 0.5	-26.33%	C- / 3.3
2009	E+	23.16	39.04	E / 0.3	-29.68%	C / 4.4

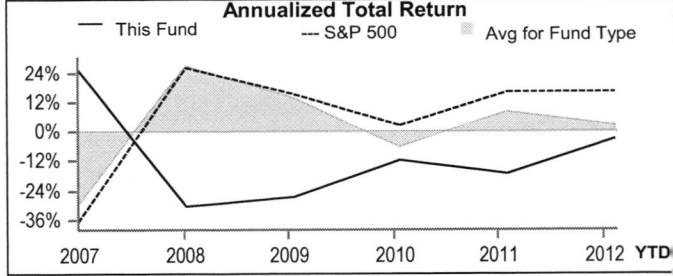

*ProShares Short VIX Sh-Tm Fut ET (SVXY)   C   Fair

Fund Family: ProShare Advisors LLC
Fund Type: Growth and Income
Inception Date: October 3, 2011

Major Rating Factors: *ProShares Short VIX Sh-Tm Fut ET has adopted a risky asset allocation strategy and currently receives an overall TheStreet.com Investment Rating of C (Fair). The fund has shown an above average level of volatility, as measured by both semi-deviation and drawdown factors. It carries a beta of 0.00, meaning the fund's expected move will be 0.0% for every 10% move in the market. As of December 31, 2012, *ProShares Short VIX Sh-Tm Fut ET traded at a discount of 15.95% below its net asset value, which is better than its one-year historical average premium of .19%. The high level of risk (D+, Weak) did however, reward investors with excellent performance.

The fund's performance rating is currently A+ (Excellent). It has registered an annualized return of 0.00% over the last three years and is up 17.86% year to date 2012.

HOWARD S RUBIN has been running the fund for 2 years and currently receives a manager quality ranking of 97 (0=worst, 99=best). If you are comfortable owning a high risk investment, this fund may be an option.

Data Date	Investment Rating	Net Assets ($Mil)	Price	Performance Rating/Pts	Total Return Y-T-D	Risk Rating/Pts
12-12	C	79.40	65.45	A+ / 9.9	17.86%	D+ / 2.5

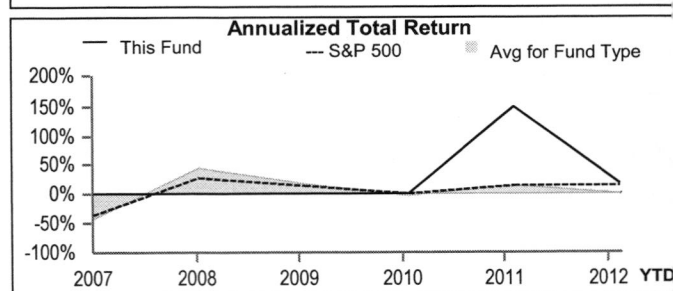

*ProShares Ult Telecommunications (LTL)

B   **Good**

Fund Family: ProShare Advisors LLC
Fund Type: Income
Inception Date: March 25, 2008

Major Rating Factors: Strong performance is the major factor driving the B (Good) TheStreet.com Investment Rating for *ProShares Ult Telecommunications. The fund currently has a performance rating of B+ (Good) based on an annualized return of 19.59% over the last three years and a total return of 5.16% year to date 2012. Factored into the performance evaluation is an expense ratio of 0.95% (low).

The fund's risk rating is currently C+ (Fair). It carries a beta of 1.64, meaning it is expected to move 16.4% for every 10% move in the market. Volatility, as measured by both the semi-deviation and a drawdown factor, is considered low. As of December 31, 2012, *ProShares Ult Telecommunications traded at a discount of 5.23% below its net asset value, which is better than its one-year historical average premium of .16%.

Hratch Najarian has been running the fund for 2 years and currently receives a manager quality ranking of 30 (0=worst, 99=best). If you desire only a moderate level of risk and strong performance, then this fund is an excellent option.

Data Date	Investment Rating	Net Assets ($Mil)	Price	Performance Rating/Pts	Total Return Y-T-D	Risk Rating/Pts
12-12	B	4.50	58.58	B+ / 8.8	5.16%	C+ / 6.9
2011	C-	3.30	43.59	C- / 3.7	-1.06%	C+ / 6.7
2010	B+	8.20	54.58	A+ / 9.8	40.39%	C- / 3.6
2009	B-	11.65	39.55	A- / 9.2	38.86%	C- / 3.5

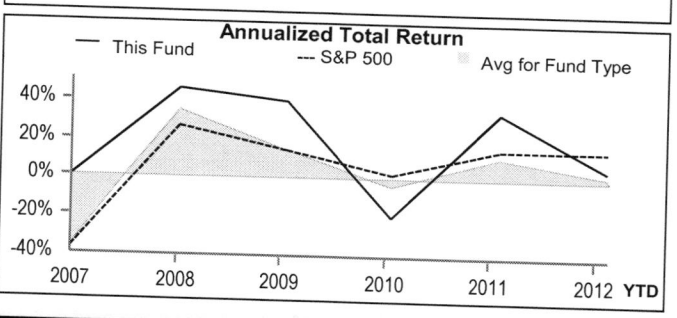

*ProShares Ultra 20+ Year Treasur (UBT)

E+   **Very Weak**

Fund Family: ProShare Advisors LLC
Fund Type: US Government/Agency
Inception Date: January 19, 2010

Major Rating Factors:
Very poor performance is the major factor driving the E+ (Very Weak) TheStreet.com Investment Rating for *ProShares Ultra 20+ Year Treasur. The fund currently has a performance rating of E+ (Very Weak) based on an annualized return of 0.00% over the last three years and a total return of -2.93% year to date 2012. Factored into the performance evaluation is an expense ratio of 0.95% (low).

The fund's risk rating is currently C (Fair). It carries a beta of 0.00, meaning the fund's expected move will be 0.0% for every 10% move in the market. Volatility, as measured by both the semi-deviation and a drawdown factor, is considered average. As of December 31, 2012, *ProShares Ultra 20+ Year Treasur traded at a premium of 3.30% above its net asset value, which is worse than its one-year historical average premium of .19%.

Michelle Lui has been running the fund for 3 years and currently receives a manager quality ranking of 19 (0=worst, 99=best). This fund offers an average level of risk but investors looking for strong performance will be frustrated.

Data Date	Investment Rating	Net Assets ($Mil)	Price	Performance Rating/Pts	Total Return Y-T-D	Risk Rating/Pts
12-12	E+	14.10	69.53	E+ / 0.8	-2.93%	C / 4.4
2011	B+	33.90	135.46	A+ / 9.9	-4.22%	B- / 7.2

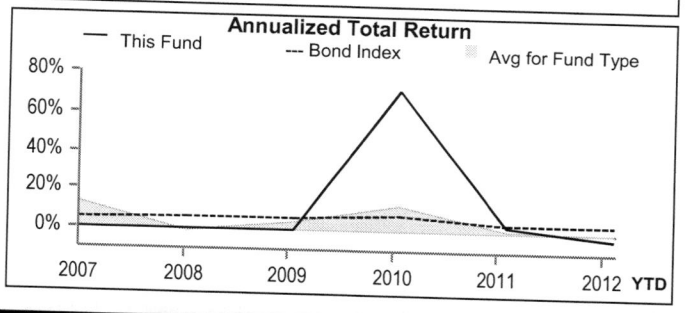

*ProShares Ultra 7-10 Year Treasu (UST)

E+   **Very Weak**

Fund Family: ProShare Advisors LLC
Fund Type: US Government/Agency
Inception Date: January 19, 2010

Major Rating Factors:
Disappointing performance is the major factor driving the E+ (Very Weak) TheStreet.com Investment Rating for *ProShares Ultra 7-10 Year Treasu. The fund currently has a performance rating of D (Weak) based on an annualized return of 0.00% over the last three years and a total return of -1.13% year to date 2012. Factored into the performance evaluation is an expense ratio of 0.95% (low).

The fund's risk rating is currently C (Fair). It carries a beta of 0.00, meaning the fund's expected move will be 0.0% for every 10% move in the market. Volatility, as measured by both the semi-deviation and a drawdown factor, is considered average. As of December 31, 2012, *ProShares Ultra 7-10 Year Treasu traded at a premium of 1.30% above its net asset value, which is worse than its one-year historical average premium of .09%.

Michelle Lui has been running the fund for 3 years and currently receives a manager quality ranking of 73 (0=worst, 99=best). This fund offers an average level of risk but investors looking for strong performance will be frustrated.

Data Date	Investment Rating	Net Assets ($Mil)	Price	Performance Rating/Pts	Total Return Y-T-D	Risk Rating/Pts
12-12	E+	741.30	56.75	D / 1.6	-1.13%	C / 4.3
2011	A+	181.10	106.40	A- / 9.1	-0.70%	B+ / 9.1

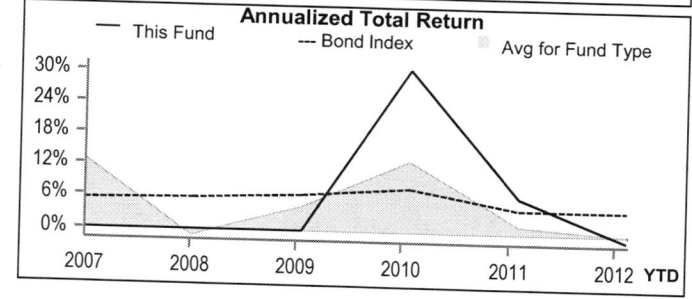

*ProShares Ultra Basic Materials (UYM)
D-   **Weak**

Fund Family: ProShare Advisors LLC
Fund Type: Income
Inception Date: January 30, 2007

Major Rating Factors: *ProShares Ultra Basic Materials receives a TheStreet.com Investment Rating of D- (Weak). The fund currently has a performance rating of C- (Fair) based on an annualized return of 4.40% over the last three years and a total return of 6.82% year to date 2012. Factored into the performance evaluation is an expense ratio of 0.95% (low).

The fund's risk rating is currently C (Fair). It carries a beta of 3.09, meaning it is expected to move 30.9% for every 10% move in the market. Volatility, as measured by both the semi-deviation and a drawdown factor, is considered average. As of December 31, 2012, *ProShares Ultra Basic Materials traded at a discount of 6.40% below its net asset value, which is better than its one-year historical average discount of .04%.

Hratch Najarian has been running the fund for 2 years and currently receives a manager quality ranking of 4 (0=worst, 99=best). If you desire an average level of risk, then this fund may be an option.

Data Date	Investment Rating	Net Assets ($Mil)	Price	Performance Rating/Pts	Total Return Y-T-D	Risk Rating/Pts
12-12	D-	157.40	36.68	C- / 3.2	6.82%	C / 4.4
2011	C	224.00	32.12	B / 7.6	6.82%	C / 4.5
2010	D+	368.30	50.65	C+ / 5.8	57.39%	D+ / 2.3
2009	C+	466.53	32.23	A+ / 9.9	106.64%	D+ / 2.6

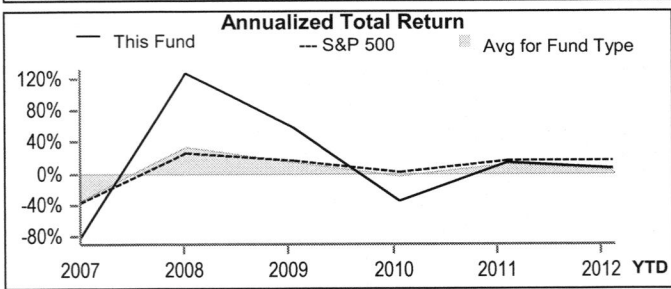

*ProShares Ultra Consumer Goods (UGE)
A   **Excellent**

Fund Family: ProShare Advisors LLC
Fund Type: Income
Inception Date: January 30, 2007

Major Rating Factors:
Exceptional performance is the major factor driving the A (Excellent) TheStreet.com Investment Rating for *ProShares Ultra Consumer Goods. The fund currently has a performance rating of A (Excellent) based on an annualized return of 25.65% over the last three years and a total return of 9.40% year to date 2012. Factored into the performance evaluation is an expense ratio of 0.95% (low).

The fund's risk rating is currently B- (Good). It carries a beta of 1.40, meaning it is expected to move 14.0% for every 10% move in the market. Volatility, as measured by both the semi-deviation and a drawdown factor, is considered low. As of December 31, 2012, *ProShares Ultra Consumer Goods traded at a discount of 9.16% below its net asset value, which is better than its one-year historical average discount of .16%.

Hratch Najarian has been running the fund for 2 years and currently receives a manager quality ranking of 83 (0=worst, 99=best). If you desire only a moderate level of risk and strong performance, then this fund is an excellent option.

Data Date	Investment Rating	Net Assets ($Mil)	Price	Performance Rating/Pts	Total Return Y-T-D	Risk Rating/Pts
12-12	A	14.50	94.10	A / 9.4	9.40%	B- / 7.9
2011	B+	11.80	78.34	B+ / 8.9	0.80%	B- / 7.4
2010	C+	20.80	69.61	B- / 7.4	36.67%	C / 4.8
2009	B+	15.92	51.46	A / 9.3	41.11%	C / 4.8

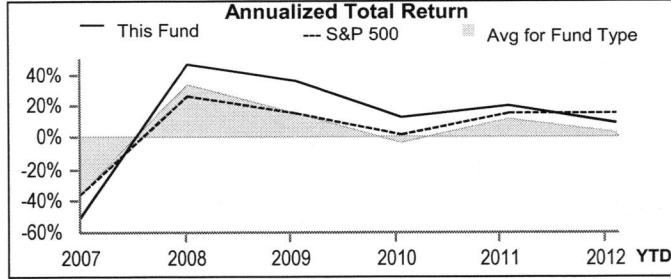

*ProShares Ultra Consumer Service (UCC)
A-   **Excellent**

Fund Family: ProShare Advisors LLC
Fund Type: Income
Inception Date: January 30, 2007

Major Rating Factors:
Exceptional performance is the major factor driving the A- (Excellent) TheStreet.com Investment Rating for *ProShares Ultra Consumer Service. The fund currently has a performance rating of A+ (Excellent) based on an annualized return of 35.36% over the last three years and a total return of 6.62% year to date 2012. Factored into the performance evaluation is an expense ratio of 0.95% (low).

The fund's risk rating is currently B- (Good). It carries a beta of 1.90, meaning it is expected to move 19.0% for every 10% move in the market. Volatility, as measured by both the semi-deviation and a drawdown factor, is considered low. As of December 31, 2012, *ProShares Ultra Consumer Service traded at a discount of 6.35% below its net asset value, which is better than its one-year historical average premium of .08%.

Hratch Najarian has been running the fund for 2 years and currently receives a manager quality ranking of 89 (0=worst, 99=best). If you desire only a moderate level of risk and strong performance, then this fund is an excellent option.

Data Date	Investment Rating	Net Assets ($Mil)	Price	Performance Rating/Pts	Total Return Y-T-D	Risk Rating/Pts
12-12	A-	11.80	78.44	A+ / 9.8	6.62%	B- / 7.1
2011	B+	7.90	52.93	A / 9.5	2.57%	B- / 7.1
2010	C+	11.00	49.20	B / 8.1	46.07%	C- / 3.8
2009	B	11.44	33.73	A+ / 9.7	54.04%	C- / 3.9

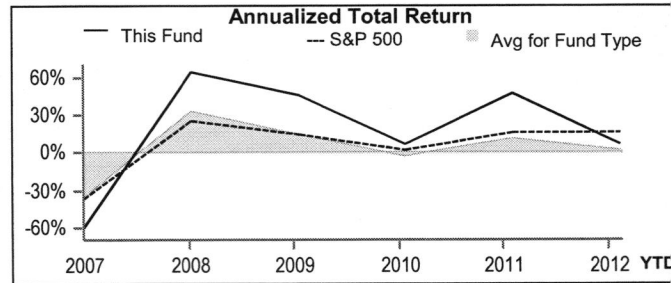

*ProShares Ultra DJ-UBS Commodity (UCD)

E+   Very Weak

Fund Family: ProShare Advisors LLC
Fund Type: Income
Inception Date: November 25, 2008

Major Rating Factors:
Very poor performance is the major factor driving the E+ (Very Weak) TheStreet.com Investment Rating for *ProShares Ultra DJ-UBS Commodity. The fund currently has a performance rating of E+ (Very Weak) based on an annualized return of -4.82% over the last three years and a total return of -0.54% year to date 2012. Factored into the performance evaluation is an expense ratio of 0.95% (low).

The fund's risk rating is currently C (Fair). It carries a beta of 1.83, meaning it is expected to move 18.3% for every 10% move in the market. Volatility, as measured by both the semi-deviation and a drawdown factor, is considered average. As of December 31, 2012, *ProShares Ultra DJ-UBS Commodity traded at a discount of 1.07% below its net asset value, which is better than its one-year historical average discount of .85%.

Michael Neches currently receives a manager quality ranking of 4 (0=worst, 99=best). This fund offers an average level of risk but investors looking for strong performance will be frustrated.

Data Date	Investment Rating	Net Assets ($Mil)	Price	Performance Rating/Pts	Total Return Y-T-D	Risk Rating/Pts
12-12	E+	6.10	23.93	E+ / 0.8	-0.54%	C / 4.5
2011	D-	9.10	25.64	D / 2.0	3.74%	C+ / 5.6
2010	A+	18.20	36.27	A+ / 9.8	27.58%	C+ / 6.6
2009	A+	3.33	28.43	B+ / 8.6	21.08%	B- / 7.2

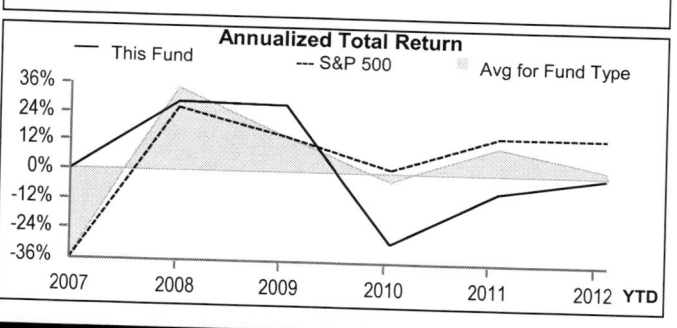

*ProShares Ultra DJ-UBS Crude Oil (UCO)

E   Very Weak

Fund Family: ProShare Advisors LLC
Fund Type: Energy/Natural Resources
Inception Date: November 25, 2008

Major Rating Factors: *ProShares Ultra DJ-UBS Crude Oil has adopted a risky asset allocation strategy and currently receives an overall TheStreet.com Investment Rating of E (Very Weak). The fund has an above average level of volatility, as measured by both semi-deviation and drawdown factors. It carries a beta of 2.01, meaning it is expected to move 20.1% for every 10% move in the market. As of December 31, 2012, *ProShares Ultra DJ-UBS Crude Oil traded at a discount of 3.81% below its net asset value. Unfortunately, the high level of risk (D+, Weak) failed to pay off as investors endured very poor performance.

The fund's performance rating is currently E+ (Very Weak). It has registered an annualized return of -14.21% over the last three years and is up 4.06% year to date 2012. Factored into the performance evaluation is an expense ratio of 0.98% (low).

Michael Neches currently receives a manager quality ranking of 2 (0=worst, 99=best). If you can tolerate high levels of risk in the hope of improved future returns, holding this fund may be an option.

Data Date	Investment Rating	Net Assets ($Mil)	Price	Performance Rating/Pts	Total Return Y-T-D	Risk Rating/Pts
12-12	E	495.20	29.32	E+ / 0.6	4.06%	D+ / 2.8
2011	E+	251.40	40.94	D / 1.7	5.94%	C- / 3.4
2010	B-	228.10	12.50	A- / 9.2	-1.42%	C- / 3.2
2009	E+	99.77	12.68	D- / 1.2	-19.03%	C- / 4.1

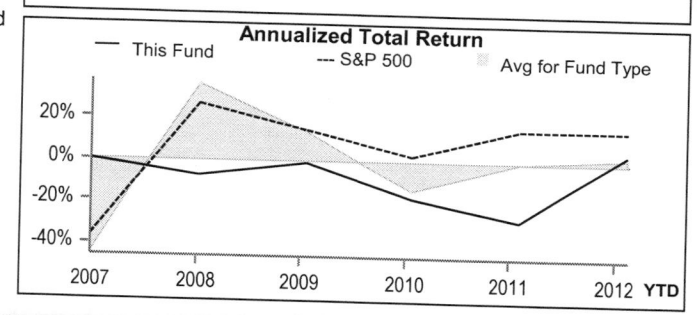

*ProShares Ultra DJ-UBS Natural G (BOIL)

E-   Very Weak

Fund Family: ProShare Advisors LLC
Fund Type: Energy/Natural Resources
Inception Date: October 6, 2011

Major Rating Factors: *ProShares Ultra DJ-UBS Natural G has adopted a very risky asset allocation strategy and currently receives an overall TheStreet.com Investment Rating of E- (Very Weak). The fund has a high level of volatility, as measured by both semi-deviation and drawdown factors. It carries a beta of 0.00, meaning the fund's expected move will be 0.0% for every 10% move in the market. As of December 31, 2012, *ProShares Ultra DJ-UBS Natural G traded at a premium of 2.83% above its net asset value, which is worse than its one-year historical average discount of .04%. Unfortunately, the high level of risk (D, Weak) failed to pay off as investors endured very poor performance.

The fund's performance rating is currently E- (Very Weak). It has registered an annualized return of 0.00% over the last three years but is down -2.80% year to date 2012.

Michael Neches currently receives a manager quality ranking of 0 (0=worst, 99=best). If you can tolerate very high levels of risk in the hope of improved future returns, holding this fund may be an option.

Data Date	Investment Rating	Net Assets ($Mil)	Price	Performance Rating/Pts	Total Return Y-T-D	Risk Rating/Pts
12-12	E-	73.00	39.24	E- / 0	-2.80%	D / 1.9

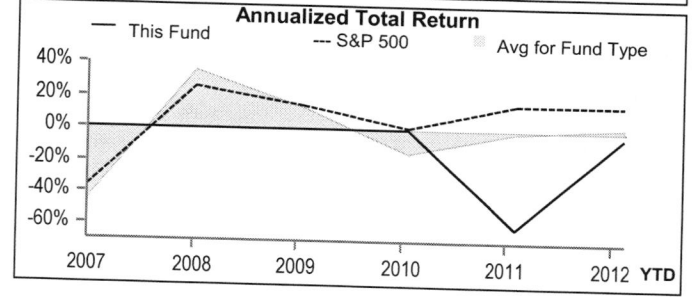

* Denotes ETF Fund

*ProShares Ultra Dow30 (DDM)

B-   **Good**

Fund Family: ProShare Advisors LLC
Fund Type: Growth
Inception Date: June 19, 2006

Major Rating Factors: Strong performance is the major factor driving the B- (Good) TheStreet.com Investment Rating for *ProShares Ultra Dow30. The fund currently has a performance rating of B (Good) based on an annualized return of 18.74% over the last three years and a total return of 6.61% year to date 2012. Factored into the performance evaluation is an expense ratio of 0.95% (low).

The fund's risk rating is currently C+ (Fair). It carries a beta of 1.78, meaning it is expected to move 17.8% for every 10% move in the market. Volatility, as measured by both the semi-deviation and a drawdown factor, is considered low. As of December 31, 2012, *ProShares Ultra Dow30 traded at a discount of 6.17% below its net asset value.

Howard Rubin has been running the fund for 6 years and currently receives a manager quality ranking of 34 (0=worst, 99=best). If you desire only a moderate level of risk and strong performance, then this fund is an excellent option.

Data Date	Investment Rating	Net Assets ($Mil)	Price	Performance Rating/Pts	Total Return Y-T-D	Risk Rating/Pts
12-12	B-	217.10	70.23	B / 8.1	6.61%	C+ / 6.8
2011	B-	269.80	59.89	B / 8.2	2.71%	C+ / 6.2
2010	E+	314.20	54.52	D / 1.9	25.37%	C- / 3.0
2009	E+	602.47	43.81	D- / 1.3	32.45%	C- / 3.2

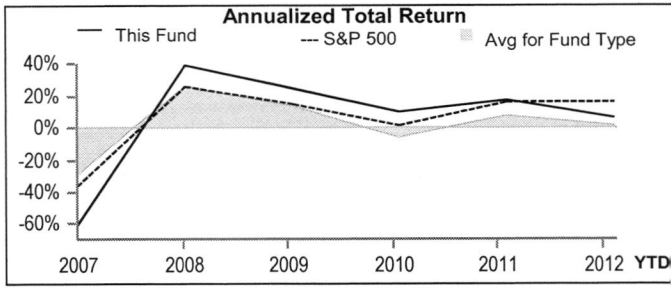

*ProShares Ultra Euro (ULE)

D-   **Weak**

Fund Family: ProShare Advisors LLC
Fund Type: Foreign
Inception Date: November 25, 2008

Major Rating Factors:
Disappointing performance is the major factor driving the D- (Weak) TheStreet.com Investment Rating for *ProShares Ultra Euro. The fund currently has a performance rating of D- (Weak) based on an annualized return of -6.72% over the last three years and a total return of 1.60% year to date 2012. Factored into the performance evaluation is an expense ratio of 0.95% (low).

The fund's risk rating is currently C+ (Fair). It carries a beta of 1.05, meaning that its performance tracks fairly well with that of the overall stock market. Volatility, as measured by both the semi-deviation and a drawdown factor, is considered low. As of December 31, 2012, *ProShares Ultra Euro traded at a discount of 2.17% below its net asset value, which is better than its one-year historical average discount of .14%.

Michael Neches currently receives a manager quality ranking of 12 (0=worst, 99=best). This fund offers only a moderate level of risk but investors looking for strong performance are still waiting.

Data Date	Investment Rating	Net Assets ($Mil)	Price	Performance Rating/Pts	Total Return Y-T-D	Risk Rating/Pts
12-12	D-	4.90	24.32	D- / 1.1	1.60%	C+ / 6.3
2011	D-	9.60	23.87	D- / 1.3	-3.27%	C+ / 6.5
2010	D	7.70	25.86	D- / 1.0	-14.29%	C+ / 5.9
2009	C-	4.39	30.17	D+ / 2.8	3.39%	B- / 7.2

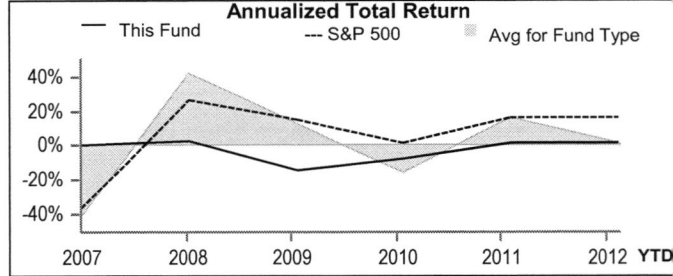

*ProShares Ultra Financials (UYG)

C+   **Fair**

Fund Family: ProShare Advisors LLC
Fund Type: Financial Services
Inception Date: January 30, 2007

Major Rating Factors: Strong performance is the major factor driving the C+ (Fair) TheStreet.com Investment Rating for *ProShares Ultra Financials. The fund currently has a performance rating of B+ (Good) based on an annualized return of 7.65% over the last three years and a total return of 8.73% year to date 2012. Factored into the performance evaluation is an expense ratio of 0.95% (low).

The fund's risk rating is currently C (Fair). It carries a beta of 2.04, meaning it is expected to move 20.4% for every 10% move in the market. Volatility, as measured by both the semi-deviation and a drawdown factor, is considered average. As of December 31, 2012, *ProShares Ultra Financials traded at a discount of 8.10% below its net asset value, which is better than its one-year historical average discount of .05%.

Hratch Najarian has been running the fund for 2 years and currently receives a manager quality ranking of 16 (0=worst, 99=best). If you desire an average level of risk and strong performance, then this fund is a good option.

Data Date	Investment Rating	Net Assets ($Mil)	Price	Performance Rating/Pts	Total Return Y-T-D	Risk Rating/Pts
12-12	C+	754.80	67.81	B+ / 8.4	8.73%	C / 5.1
2011	E+	770.40	44.37	D- / 1.4	4.82%	C- / 4.2
2010	E	1,372.70	66.38	E / 0.3	18.04%	D+ / 2.4
2009	C-	2,517.92	5.63	B- / 7.4	-6.27%	D+ / 2.4

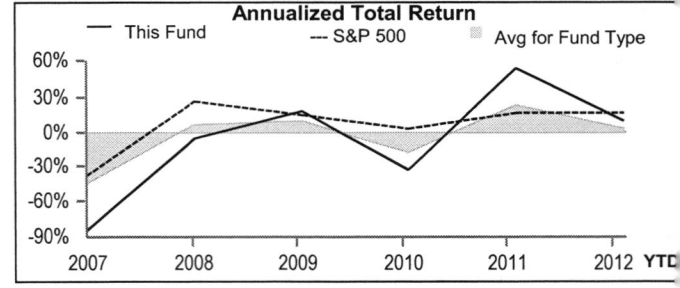

*ProShares Ultra FTSE China 25 (XPP)

D-   **Weak**

Fund Family: ProShare Advisors LLC
Fund Type: Foreign
Inception Date: June 2, 2009

Major Rating Factors: *ProShares Ultra FTSE China 25 receives a TheStreet.com Investment Rating of D- (Weak). The fund currently has a performance rating of C- (Fair) based on an annualized return of -2.15% over the last three years and a total return of 2.87% year to date 2012. Factored into the performance evaluation is an expense ratio of 0.95% (low).

The fund's risk rating is currently C- (Fair). It carries a beta of 1.86, meaning it is expected to move 18.6% for every 10% move in the market. Volatility, as measured by both the semi-deviation and a drawdown factor, is considered average. As of December 31, 2012, *ProShares Ultra FTSE China 25 traded at a discount of 2.82% below its net asset value, which is better than its one-year historical average discount of .01%.

Alexander V. Ilyasov has been running the fund for 4 years and currently receives a manager quality ranking of 11 (0=worst, 99=best). If you desire an average level of risk, then this fund may be an option.

Data Date	Investment Rating	Net Assets ($Mil)	Price	Performance Rating/Pts	Total Return Y-T-D	Risk Rating/Pts
12-12	D-	43.70	62.37	C- / 3.3	2.87%	C- / 3.6
2011	E+	24.90	45.40	E / 0.5	1.23%	C- / 4.0
2010	B+	47.50	73.12	B- / 7.5	2.74%	C+ / 6.3

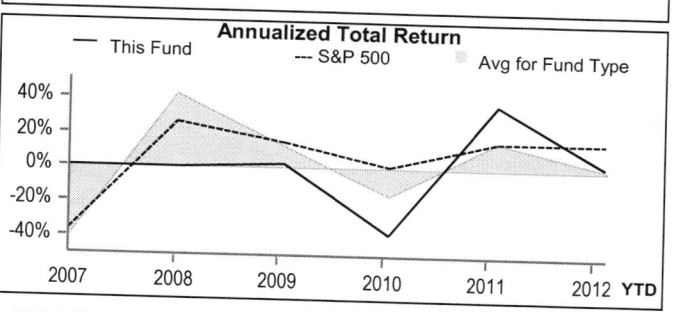

*ProShares Ultra Gold (UGL)

C   **Fair**

Fund Family: ProShare Advisors LLC
Fund Type: Precious Metals
Inception Date: December 2, 2008

Major Rating Factors: Strong performance is the major factor driving the C (Fair) TheStreet.com Investment Rating for *ProShares Ultra Gold. The fund currently has a performance rating of B- (Good) based on an annualized return of 20.99% over the last three years and a total return of -1.25% year to date 2012. Factored into the performance evaluation is an expense ratio of 0.95% (low).

The fund's risk rating is currently C+ (Fair). It carries a beta of 1.84, meaning it is expected to move 18.4% for every 10% move in the market. Volatility, as measured by both the semi-deviation and a drawdown factor, is considered low. As of December 31, 2012, *ProShares Ultra Gold traded at a premium of 2.00% above its net asset value, which is worse than its one-year historical average premium of .24%.

Michael Neches currently receives a manager quality ranking of 25 (0=worst, 99=best). If you desire only a moderate level of risk and strong performance, then this fund is an excellent option.

Data Date	Investment Rating	Net Assets ($Mil)	Price	Performance Rating/Pts	Total Return Y-T-D	Risk Rating/Pts
12-12	C	364.40	85.26	B- / 7.0	-1.25%	C+ / 5.9
2011	B	322.60	79.01	A+ / 9.8	6.73%	C+ / 6.3
2010	A+	252.80	70.72	A+ / 9.8	58.28%	B- / 7.1
2009	A+	27.74	44.68	A- / 9.2	42.29%	B- / 7.2

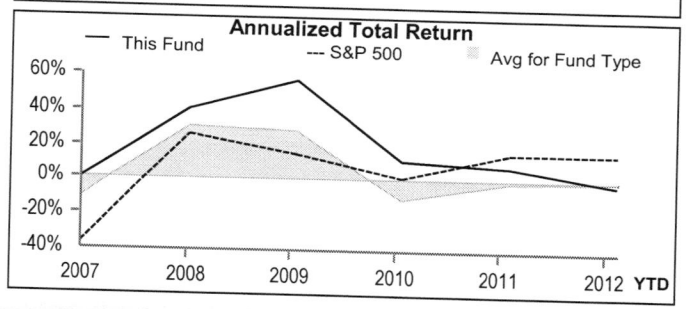

*ProShares Ultra Health Care (RXL)

B+   **Good**

Fund Family: ProShare Advisors LLC
Fund Type: Health
Inception Date: January 30, 2007

Major Rating Factors:
Exceptional performance is the major factor driving the B+ (Good) TheStreet.com Investment Rating for *ProShares Ultra Health Care. The fund currently has a performance rating of A (Excellent) based on an annualized return of 20.46% over the last three years and a total return of 9.08% year to date 2012. Factored into the performance evaluation is an expense ratio of 0.95% (low).

The fund's risk rating is currently B- (Good). It carries a beta of 1.30, meaning it is expected to move 13.0% for every 10% move in the market. Volatility, as measured by both the semi-deviation and a drawdown factor, is considered low. As of December 31, 2012, *ProShares Ultra Health Care traded at a discount of 8.62% below its net asset value, which is better than its one-year historical average discount of .06%.

Hratch Najarian has been running the fund for 2 years and currently receives a manager quality ranking of 79 (0=worst, 99=best). If you desire only a moderate level of risk and strong performance, then this fund is an excellent option.

Data Date	Investment Rating	Net Assets ($Mil)	Price	Performance Rating/Pts	Total Return Y-T-D	Risk Rating/Pts
12-12	B+	44.00	83.83	A / 9.3	9.08%	B- / 7.2
2011	B-	36.60	60.90	B- / 7.5	2.63%	B- / 7.1
2010	D	46.80	52.02	D- / 1.5	5.01%	C / 4.9
2009	B+	48.66	49.96	A / 9.3	35.65%	C / 4.8

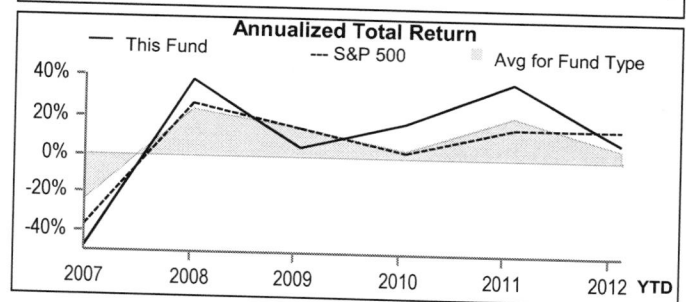

*ProShares Ultra High Yield (UJB)   A+   Excellent

Fund Family: ProShare Advisors LLC
Fund Type: Corporate - High Yield
Inception Date: April 13, 2011

Major Rating Factors:
Exceptional performance is the major factor driving the A+ (Excellent) TheStreet.com Investment Rating for *ProShares Ultra High Yield. The fund currently has a performance rating of A (Excellent) based on an annualized return of 0.00% over the last three years and a total return of 2.28% year to date 2012. Factored into the performance evaluation is an expense ratio of 0.95% (low).

The fund's risk rating is currently B (Good). It carries a beta of 0.00, meaning the fund's expected move will be 0.0% for every 10% move in the market. Volatility, as measured by both the semi-deviation and a drawdown factor, is considered low. As of December 31, 2012, *ProShares Ultra High Yield traded at a discount of 2.46% below its net asset value, which is better than its one-year historical average discount of .04%.

Jeff Ploshnick has been running the fund for 2 years and currently receives a manager quality ranking of 7 (0=worst, 99=best). If you desire only a moderate level of risk and strong performance, then this fund is an excellent option.

Data Date	Investment Rating	Net Assets ($Mil)	Price	Performance Rating/Pts	Total Return Y-T-D	Risk Rating/Pts
12-12	A+	5.10	50.37	A / 9.3	2.28%	B / 8.2

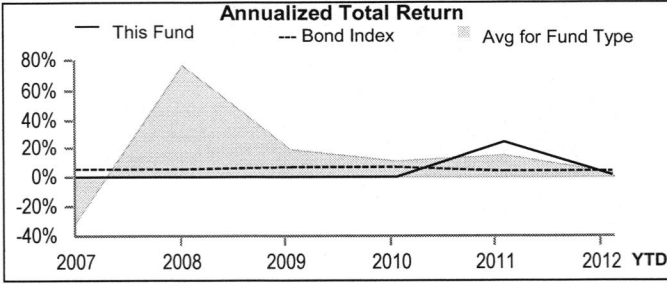

*ProShares Ultra Industrials (UXI)   C+   Fair

Fund Family: ProShare Advisors LLC
Fund Type: Income
Inception Date: January 30, 2007

Major Rating Factors:
Exceptional performance is the major factor driving the C+ (Fair) TheStreet.com Investment Rating for *ProShares Ultra Industrials. The fund currently has a performance rating of A- (Excellent) based on an annualized return of 20.77% over the last three years and a total return of 6.85% year to date 2012. Factored into the performance evaluation is an expense ratio of 0.95% (low).

The fund's risk rating is currently C (Fair). It carries a beta of 2.52, meaning it is expected to move 25.2% for every 10% move in the market. Volatility, as measured by both the semi-deviation and a drawdown factor, is considered average. As of December 31, 2012, *ProShares Ultra Industrials traded at a discount of 6.39% below its net asset value, which is better than its one-year historical average discount of .09%.

Hratch Najarian has been running the fund for 2 years and currently receives a manager quality ranking of 18 (0=worst, 99=best). If you desire an average level of risk and strong performance, then this fund is a good option.

Data Date	Investment Rating	Net Assets ($Mil)	Price	Performance Rating/Pts	Total Return Y-T-D	Risk Rating/Pts
12-12	C+	20.60	54.60	A- / 9.0	6.85%	C / 5.5
2011	C	24.80	41.42	B- / 7.3	4.42%	C / 5.4
2010	D	34.70	46.31	C- / 3.9	49.21%	D+ / 2.9
2009	B-	30.23	31.13	A / 9.5	30.86%	C- / 3.3

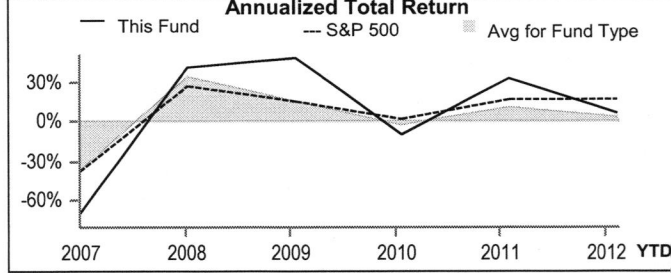

*ProShares Ultra Invest Grade Cor (IGU)   B   Good

Fund Family: ProShare Advisors LLC
Fund Type: Corporate - Investment Grade
Inception Date: April 13, 2011

Major Rating Factors: *ProShares Ultra Invest Grade Cor receives a TheStreet.com Investment Rating of B (Good). The fund currently has a performance rating of C+ (Fair) based on an annualized return of 0.00% over the last three years and a total return of -0.03% year to date 2012. Factored into the performance evaluation is an expense ratio of 0.95% (low).

The fund's risk rating is currently B+ (Good). It carries a beta of 0.00, meaning the fund's expected move will be 0.0% for every 10% move in the market. Volatility, as measured by both the semi-deviation and a drawdown factor, is considered very low. As of December 31, 2012, *ProShares Ultra Invest Grade Cor traded at a discount of .22% below its net asset value, which is better than its one-year historical average premium of .13%.

Jeff Ploshnick has been running the fund for 2 years and currently receives a manager quality ranking of 27 (0=worst, 99=best). If you desire an average level of risk, then this fund may be an option.

Data Date	Investment Rating	Net Assets ($Mil)	Price	Performance Rating/Pts	Total Return Y-T-D	Risk Rating/Pts
12-12	B	5.60	55.58	C+ / 6.0	-0.03%	B+ / 9.2

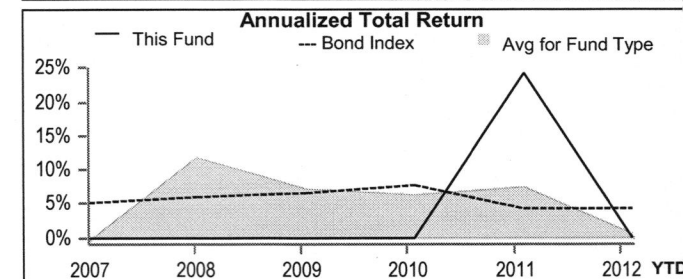

*ProShares Ultra KBW Regional Ban (KRU)

D   **Weak**

Fund Family: ProShare Advisors LLC
Fund Type: Financial Services
Inception Date: April 20, 2010

Major Rating Factors: *ProShares Ultra KBW Regional Ban receives a TheStreet.com Investment Rating of D (Weak). The fund currently has a performance rating of C (Fair) based on an annualized return of 0.00% over the last three years and a total return of 6.22% year to date 2012. Factored into the performance evaluation is an expense ratio of 0.95% (low).

The fund's risk rating is currently C- (Fair). It carries a beta of 0.00, meaning the fund's expected move will be 0.0% for every 10% move in the market. Volatility, as measured by both the semi-deviation and a drawdown factor, is considered average. As of December 31, 2012, *ProShares Ultra KBW Regional Ban traded at a discount of 6.16% below its net asset value, which is better than its one-year historical average premium of .04%.

Hratch Najarian has been running the fund for 2 years and currently receives a manager quality ranking of 7 (0=worst, 99=best). If you desire an average level of risk, then this fund may be an option.

Data Date	Investment Rating	Net Assets ($Mil)	Price	Performance Rating/Pts	Total Return Y-T-D	Risk Rating/Pts
12-12	D	2.30	45.21	C / 4.9	6.22%	C- / 3.8
2011	D-	3.80	38.20	C- / 3.9	7.41%	D+ / 2.8

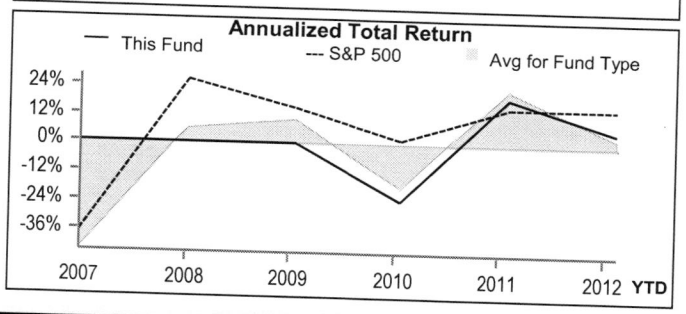

*ProShares Ultra MidCap 400 (MVV)

B   **Good**

Fund Family: ProShare Advisors LLC
Fund Type: Growth
Inception Date: June 19, 2006

Major Rating Factors:
Exceptional performance is the major factor driving the B (Good) TheStreet.com Investment Rating for *ProShares Ultra MidCap 400. The fund currently has a performance rating of A (Excellent) based on an annualized return of 21.99% over the last three years and a total return of 7.33% year to date 2012. Factored into the performance evaluation is an expense ratio of 0.95% (low).

The fund's risk rating is currently C+ (Fair). It carries a beta of 2.32, meaning it is expected to move 23.2% for every 10% move in the market. Volatility, as measured by both the semi-deviation and a drawdown factor, is considered low. As of December 31, 2012, *ProShares Ultra MidCap 400 traded at a discount of 6.83% below its net asset value, which is better than its one-year historical average discount of .02%.

Hratch Najarian has been running the fund for 3 years and currently receives a manager quality ranking of 24 (0=worst, 99=best). If you desire only a moderate level of risk and strong performance, then this fund is an excellent option.

Data Date	Investment Rating	Net Assets ($Mil)	Price	Performance Rating/Pts	Total Return Y-T-D	Risk Rating/Pts
12-12	B	644.40	74.05	A / 9.5	7.33%	C+ / 5.7
2011	C+	91.50	55.36	B / 8.2	3.03%	C+ / 5.9
2010	C	137.90	63.68	B- / 7.4	52.88%	C- / 3.1
2009	E+	158.90	41.69	D / 1.8	60.55%	C- / 3.5

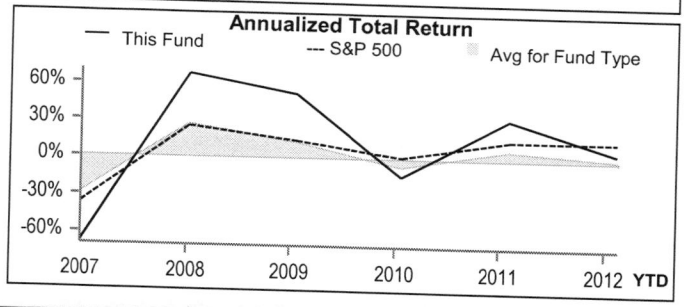

*ProShares Ultra MSCI Brazil (UBR)

E+   **Very Weak**

Fund Family: ProShare Advisors LLC
Fund Type: Foreign
Inception Date: April 27, 2010

Major Rating Factors: *ProShares Ultra MSCI Brazil has adopted a risky asset allocation strategy and currently receives an overall TheStreet.com Investment Rating of E+ (Very Weak). The fund has an above average level of volatility, as measured by both semi-deviation and drawdown factors. It carries a beta of 0.00, meaning the fund's expected move will be 0.0% for every 10% move in the market. As of December 31, 2012, *ProShares Ultra MSCI Brazil traded at a discount of 1.60% below its net asset value, which is better than its one-year historical average premium of .01%. Unfortunately, the high level of risk (D+, Weak) failed to pay off as investors endured poor performance.

The fund's performance rating is currently D (Weak). It has registered an annualized return of 0.00% over the last three years and is up 1.58% year to date 2012. Factored into the performance evaluation is an expense ratio of 0.95% (low).

Alexander V. Ilyasov has been running the fund for 3 years and currently receives a manager quality ranking of 1 (0=worst, 99=best). If you can tolerate high levels of risk in the hope of improved future returns, holding this fund may be an option.

Data Date	Investment Rating	Net Assets ($Mil)	Price	Performance Rating/Pts	Total Return Y-T-D	Risk Rating/Pts
12-12	E+	14.10	70.24	D / 1.8	1.58%	D+ / 2.6
2011	E	10.30	18.66	E- / 0.2	3.54%	C- / 3.0

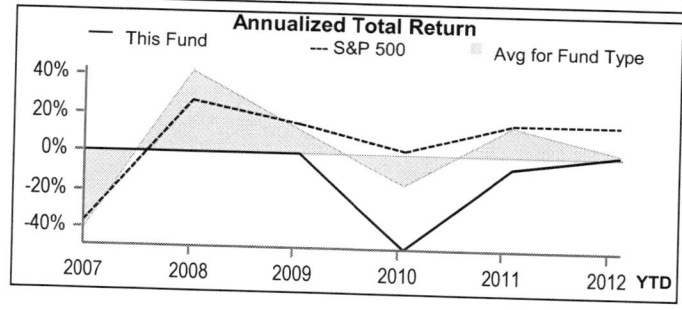

* Denotes ETF Fund

*ProShares Ultra MSCI EAFE (EFO)

| | **C+** | | **Fair** |

Fund Family: ProShare Advisors LLC
Fund Type: Income
Inception Date: June 2, 2009

Data Date	Investment Rating	Net Assets ($Mil)	Price	Performance Rating/Pts	Total Return Y-T-D	Risk Rating/Pts
12-12	C+	11.90	78.88	A+ / 9.9	4.49%	C / 4.4
2011	E+	5.90	58.18	E / 0.4	-0.62%	C / 5.0
2010	A	8.50	85.89	A / 9.5	9.53%	C+ / 5.9

Major Rating Factors:
Exceptional performance is the major factor driving the C+ (Fair) TheStreet.com Investment Rating for *ProShares Ultra MSCI EAFE. The fund currently has a performance rating of A+ (Excellent) based on an annualized return of 0.00% over the last three years and a total return of 4.49% year to date 2012. Factored into the performance evaluation is an expense ratio of 0.95% (low).

The fund's risk rating is currently C (Fair). It carries a beta of 2.49, meaning it is expected to move 24.9% for every 10% move in the market. Volatility, as measured by both the semi-deviation and a drawdown factor, is considered average. As of December 31, 2012, *ProShares Ultra MSCI EAFE traded at a discount of 4.33% below its net asset value, which is better than its one-year historical average discount of .11%.

Alexander V. Ilyasov has been running the fund for 4 years and currently receives a manager quality ranking of 4 (0=worst, 99=best). If you desire an average level of risk and strong performance, then this fund is a good option.

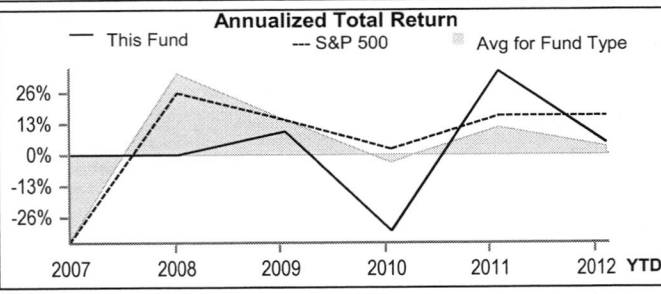

*ProShares Ultra MSCI Emerging Mk (EET)

| | **D-** | | **Weak** |

Fund Family: ProShare Advisors LLC
Fund Type: Emerging Market
Inception Date: June 2, 2009

Data Date	Investment Rating	Net Assets ($Mil)	Price	Performance Rating/Pts	Total Return Y-T-D	Risk Rating/Pts
12-12	D-	42.80	85.62	D+ / 2.7	0.54%	C- / 3.8
2011	E	22.20	63.92	E- / 0.2	0.91%	C- / 4.1
2010	A	43.80	109.55	A+ / 9.6	25.18%	C+ / 6.3

Major Rating Factors:
Disappointing performance is the major factor driving the D- (Weak) TheStreet.com Investment Rating for *ProShares Ultra MSCI Emerging Mk. The fund currently has a performance rating of D+ (Weak) based on an annualized return of -1.45% over the last three years and a total return of 0.54% year to date 2012. Factored into the performance evaluation is an expense ratio of 0.95% (low).

The fund's risk rating is currently C- (Fair). It carries a beta of 2.14, meaning it is expected to move 21.4% for every 10% move in the market. Volatility, as measured by both the semi-deviation and a drawdown factor, is considered average. As of December 31, 2012, *ProShares Ultra MSCI Emerging Mk traded at a discount of .42% below its net asset value, which is better than its one-year historical average discount of .02%.

Alexander V. Ilyasov has been running the fund for 4 years and currently receives a manager quality ranking of 12 (0=worst, 99=best). This fund offers an average level of risk but investors looking for strong performance will be frustrated.

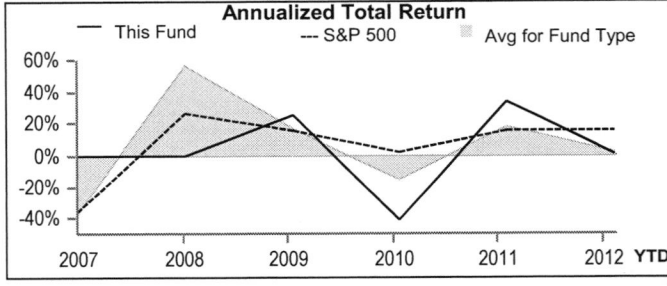

*ProShares Ultra MSCI Europe (UPV)

| | **C+** | | **Fair** |

Fund Family: ProShare Advisors LLC
Fund Type: Foreign
Inception Date: April 27, 2010

Data Date	Investment Rating	Net Assets ($Mil)	Price	Performance Rating/Pts	Total Return Y-T-D	Risk Rating/Pts
12-12	C+	8.40	33.44	A+ / 9.9	6.00%	C- / 3.7
2011	E	2.40	23.87	E / 0.4	-2.26%	C- / 3.8

Major Rating Factors:
Exceptional performance is the major factor driving the C+ (Fair) TheStreet.com Investment Rating for *ProShares Ultra MSCI Europe. The fund currently has a performance rating of A+ (Excellent) based on an annualized return of 0.00% over the last three years and a total return of 6.00% year to date 2012. Factored into the performance evaluation is an expense ratio of 0.95% (low).

The fund's risk rating is currently C- (Fair). It carries a beta of 0.00, meaning the fund's expected move will be 0.0% for every 10% move in the market. Volatility, as measured by both the semi-deviation and a drawdown factor, is considered average. As of December 31, 2012, *ProShares Ultra MSCI Europe traded at a discount of 5.70% below its net asset value, which is better than its one-year historical average discount of .04%.

Alexander V. Ilyasov has been running the fund for 4 years and currently receives a manager quality ranking of 41 (0=worst, 99=best). If you desire an average level of risk and strong performance, then this fund is a good option.

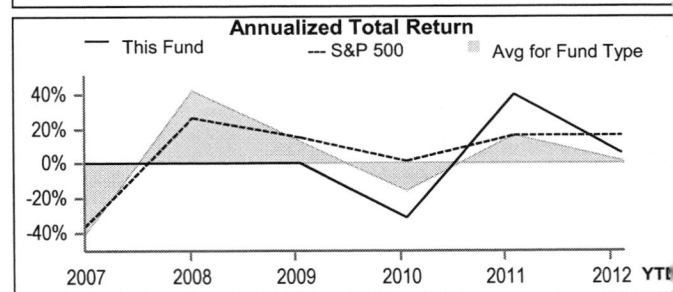

*ProShares Ultra MSCI Japan (EZJ)

D-   **Weak**

Fund Family: ProShare Advisors LLC
Fund Type: Foreign
Inception Date: June 2, 2009

Major Rating Factors:

Disappointing performance is the major factor driving the D- (Weak) TheStreet.com Investment Rating for *ProShares Ultra MSCI Japan. The fund currently has a performance rating of D (Weak) based on an annualized return of -4.80% over the last three years and a total return of 2.25% year to date 2012. Factored into the performance evaluation is an expense ratio of 0.95% (low).

The fund's risk rating is currently C (Fair). It carries a beta of 1.22, meaning it is expected to move 12.2% for every 10% move in the market. Volatility, as measured by both the semi-deviation and a drawdown factor, is considered average. As of December 31, 2012, *ProShares Ultra MSCI Japan traded at a discount of 2.23% below its net asset value, which is better than its one-year historical average discount of .11%.

Alexander V. Ilyasov has been running the fund for 4 years and currently receives a manager quality ranking of 20 (0=worst, 99=best). This fund offers an average level of risk but investors looking for strong performance will be frustrated.

Data Date	Investment Rating	Net Assets ($Mil)	Price	Performance Rating/Pts	Total Return Y-T-D	Risk Rating/Pts
12-12	D-	18.10	60.62	D / 1.7	2.25%	C / 5.1
2011	D-	23.60	52.38	E / 0.4	-1.16%	C+ / 5.7
2010	A+	11.70	78.49	A+ / 9.6	24.81%	C+ / 6.8

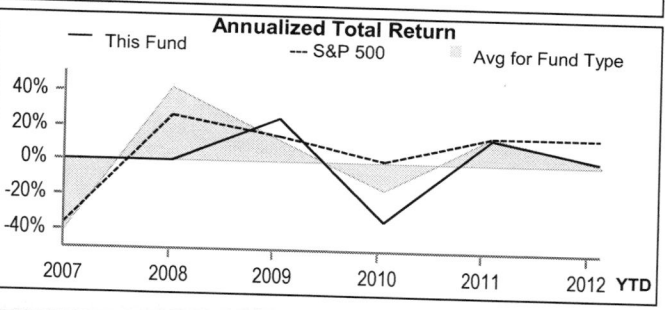

*ProShares Ultra MSCI Mex Invest (UMX)

C+   **Fair**

Fund Family: ProShare Advisors LLC
Fund Type: Foreign
Inception Date: April 27, 2010

Major Rating Factors:

Exceptional performance is the major factor driving the C+ (Fair) TheStreet.com Investment Rating for *ProShares Ultra MSCI Mex Invest. The fund currently has a performance rating of A+ (Excellent) based on an annualized return of 0.00% over the last three years and a total return of 8.49% year to date 2012. Factored into the performance evaluation is an expense ratio of 0.95% (low).

The fund's risk rating is currently C (Fair). It carries a beta of 0.00, meaning the fund's expected move will be 0.0% for every 10% move in the market. Volatility, as measured by both the semi-deviation and a drawdown factor, is considered average. As of December 31, 2012, *ProShares Ultra MSCI Mex Invest traded at a discount of 7.68% below its net asset value, which is better than its one-year historical average discount of .25%.

Alexander V. Ilyasov has been running the fund for 3 years and currently receives a manager quality ranking of 98 (0=worst, 99=best). If you desire an average level of risk and strong performance, then this fund is a good option.

Data Date	Investment Rating	Net Assets ($Mil)	Price	Performance Rating/Pts	Total Return Y-T-D	Risk Rating/Pts
12-12	C+	2.50	49.02	A+ / 9.9	8.49%	C / 4.6
2011	E+	1.50	29.11	E+ / 0.6	1.79%	C / 4.5

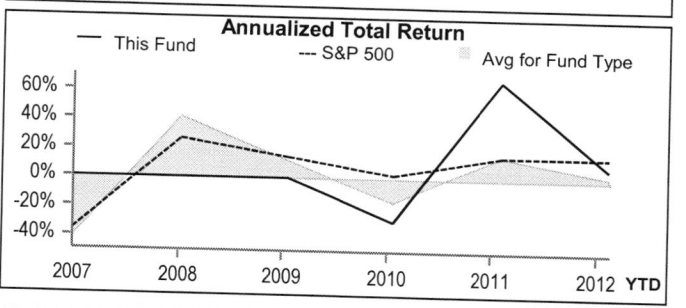

*ProShares Ultra MSCI Pacific ex- (UXJ)

C+   **Fair**

Fund Family: ProShare Advisors LLC
Fund Type: Foreign
Inception Date: April 27, 2010

Major Rating Factors:

Exceptional performance is the major factor driving the C+ (Fair) TheStreet.com Investment Rating for *ProShares Ultra MSCI Pacific ex-. The fund currently has a performance rating of A+ (Excellent) based on an annualized return of 0.00% over the last three years and a total return of 2.58% year to date 2012. Factored into the performance evaluation is an expense ratio of 0.95% (low).

The fund's risk rating is currently C- (Fair). It carries a beta of 0.00, meaning the fund's expected move will be 0.0% for every 10% move in the market. Volatility, as measured by both the semi-deviation and a drawdown factor, is considered average. As of December 31, 2012, *ProShares Ultra MSCI Pacific ex- traded at a discount of 2.69% below its net asset value, which is better than its one-year historical average discount of .10%.

Alexander V. Ilyasov has been running the fund for 3 years and currently receives a manager quality ranking of 75 (0=worst, 99=best). If you desire an average level of risk and strong performance, then this fund is a good option.

Data Date	Investment Rating	Net Assets ($Mil)	Price	Performance Rating/Pts	Total Return Y-T-D	Risk Rating/Pts
12-12	C+	3.80	37.92	A+ / 9.9	2.58%	C- / 4.0
2011	E+	2.50	24.98	E / 0.5	2.36%	C- / 4.0

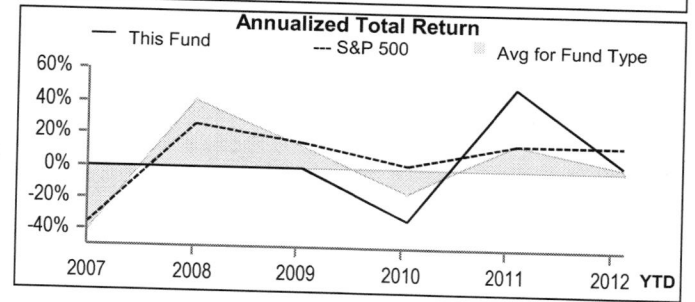

* Denotes ETF Fund

*ProShares Ultra Nasdaq Biotech (BIB)

C   **Fair**

Fund Family: ProShare Advisors LLC
Fund Type: Health
Inception Date: April 7, 2010

Major Rating Factors: *ProShares Ultra Nasdaq Biotech has adopted a risky asset allocation strategy and currently receives an overall TheStreet.com Investment Rating of C (Fair). The fund has shown an above average level of volatility, as measured by both semi-deviation and drawdown factors. It carries a beta of 0.00, meaning the fund's expected move will be 0.0% for every 10% move in the market. As of December 31, 2012, *ProShares Ultra Nasdaq Biotech traded at a discount of 10.86% below its net asset value, which is better than its one-year historical average discount of .03%. The high level of risk (D+, Weak) did however, reward investors with excellent performance.

The fund's performance rating is currently A+ (Excellent). It has registered an annualized return of 0.00% over the last three years and is up 11.99% year to date 2012. Factored into the performance evaluation is an expense ratio of 0.95% (low).

Hratch Najarian has been running the fund for 2 years and currently receives a manager quality ranking of 97 (0=worst, 99=best). If you are comfortable owning a high risk investment, this fund may be an option.

Data Date	Investment Rating	Net Assets ($Mil)	Price	Performance Rating/Pts	Total Return Y-T-D	Risk Rating/Pts
12-12	C	37.60	57.97	A+ / 9.9	11.99%	D+ / 2.6
2011	C+	13.90	69.52	B- / 7.1	5.16%	C+ / 6.2

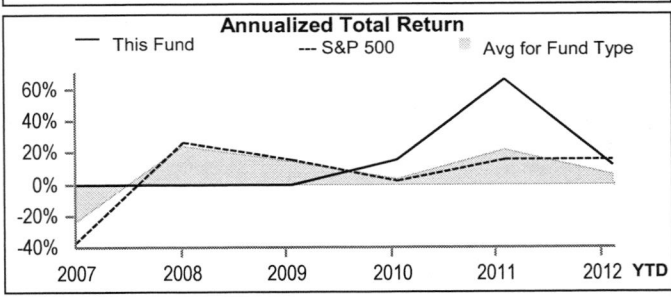

*ProShares Ultra Oil and Gas (DIG)

D   **Weak**

Fund Family: ProShare Advisors LLC
Fund Type: Energy/Natural Resources
Inception Date: January 30, 2007

Major Rating Factors: *ProShares Ultra Oil and Gas receives a TheStreet.com Investment Rating of D (Weak). The fund currently has a performance rating of C (Fair) based on an annualized return of 10.31% over the last three years and a total return of 7.33% year to date 2012. Factored into the performance evaluation is an expense ratio of 0.95% (low).

The fund's risk rating is currently C- (Fair). It carries a beta of 2.03, meaning it is expected to move 20.3% for every 10% move in the market. Volatility, as measured by both the semi-deviation and a drawdown factor, is considered average. As of December 31, 2012, *ProShares Ultra Oil and Gas traded at a discount of 6.83% below its net asset value, which is better than its one-year historical average discount of .01%.

Hratch Najarian has been running the fund for 2 years and currently receives a manager quality ranking of 16 (0=worst, 99=best). If you desire an average level of risk, then this fund may be an option.

Data Date	Investment Rating	Net Assets ($Mil)	Price	Performance Rating/Pts	Total Return Y-T-D	Risk Rating/Pts
12-12	D	192.00	45.73	C / 4.6	7.33%	C- / 4.2
2011	D+	254.00	43.91	C / 5.5	3.67%	C / 4.5
2010	E	366.70	45.81	D- / 1.1	33.69%	D / 1.7
2009	C+	818.55	34.53	B+ / 8.3	10.42%	C- / 3.4

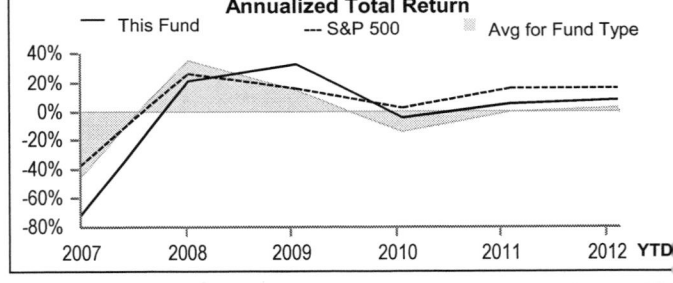

*ProShares Ultra QQQ (QLD)

C-   **Fair**

Fund Family: ProShare Advisors LLC
Fund Type: Growth
Inception Date: June 19, 2006

Major Rating Factors: *ProShares Ultra QQQ has adopted a risky asset allocation strategy and currently receives an overall TheStreet.com Investment Rating of C- (Fair). The fund has shown an above average level of volatility, as measured by both semi-deviation and drawdown factors. It carries a beta of 2.22, meaning it is expected to move 22.2% for every 10% move in the market. As of December 31, 2012, *ProShares Ultra QQQ traded at a discount of 6.28% below its net asset value, which is better than its one-year historical average discount of .01%. The high level of risk (D+, Weak) did however, reward investors with excellent performance.

The fund's performance rating is currently A (Excellent). It has registered an annualized return of 25.27% over the last three years and is up 6.73% year to date 2012. Factored into the performance evaluation is an expense ratio of 0.95% (low).

Hratch Najarian has been running the fund for 4 years and currently receives a manager quality ranking of 33 (0=worst, 99=best). If you are comfortable owning a high risk investment, this fund may be an option.

Data Date	Investment Rating	Net Assets ($Mil)	Price	Performance Rating/Pts	Total Return Y-T-D	Risk Rating/Pts
12-12	C-	671.10	54.81	A / 9.3	6.73%	D+ / 2.8
2011	B+	678.20	81.46	A+ / 9.8	7.00%	C+ / 6.8
2010	C-	842.00	81.43	C+ / 6.8	36.90%	C- / 3.1
2009	D+	1,080.61	59.48	C / 5.2	103.28%	C- / 3.1

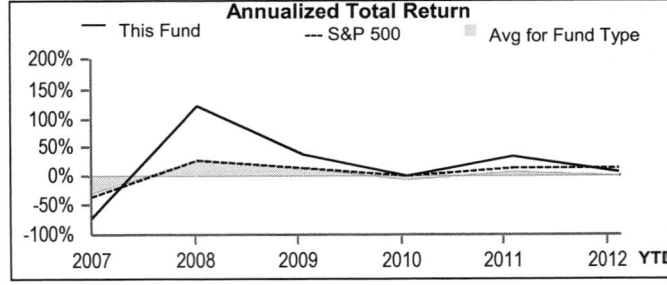

*ProShares Ultra Real Estate (URE)

B　　**Good**

Fund Family: ProShare Advisors LLC
Fund Type: Income
Inception Date: January 30, 2007

Major Rating Factors:

Exceptional performance is the major factor driving the B (Good) TheStreet.com Investment Rating for *ProShares Ultra Real Estate. The fund currently has a performance rating of A+ (Excellent) based on an annualized return of 30.24% over the last three years and a total return of 5.64% year to date 2012. Factored into the performance evaluation is an expense ratio of 0.95% (low).

The fund's risk rating is currently C+ (Fair). It carries a beta of 2.02, meaning it is expected to move 20.2% for every 10% move in the market. Volatility, as measured by both the semi-deviation and a drawdown factor, is considered low. As of December 31, 2012, *ProShares Ultra Real Estate traded at a discount of 5.37% below its net asset value, which is better than its one-year historical average discount of .02%.

Hratch Najarian has been running the fund for 2 years and currently receives a manager quality ranking of 75 (0=worst, 99=best). If you desire only a moderate level of risk and strong performance, then this fund is an excellent option.

Data Date	Investment Rating	Net Assets ($Mil)	Price	Performance Rating/Pts	Total Return Y-T-D	Risk Rating/Pts
12-12	B	349.60	69.09	A+ / 9.6	5.64%	C+ / 6.0
2011	C	353.40	51.00	B / 7.9	-0.22%	C- / 4.2
2010	E	535.30	50.62	E+ / 0.7	48.36%	D / 2.1
2009	C+	451.44	6.89	A+ / 9.7	19.77%	D / 2.1

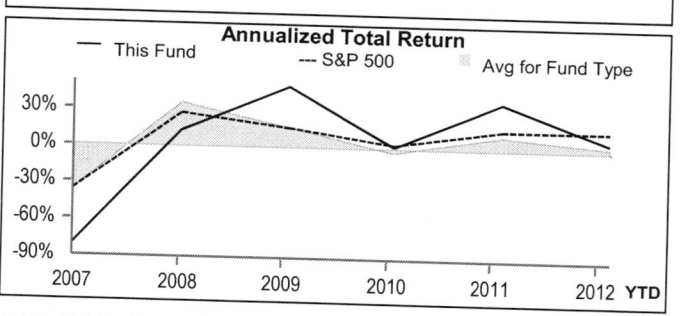

*ProShares Ultra Rus Mid Cap Grow (UKW)

B-　　**Good**

Fund Family: ProShare Advisors LLC
Fund Type: Growth
Inception Date: February 20, 2007

Major Rating Factors:

Exceptional performance is the major factor driving the B- (Good) TheStreet.com Investment Rating for *ProShares Ultra Rus Mid Cap Grow. The fund currently has a performance rating of A- (Excellent) based on an annualized return of 20.58% over the last three years and a total return of 7.44% year to date 2012. Factored into the performance evaluation is an expense ratio of 0.95% (low).

The fund's risk rating is currently C+ (Fair). It carries a beta of 2.32, meaning it is expected to move 23.2% for every 10% move in the market. Volatility, as measured by both the semi-deviation and a drawdown factor, is considered low. As of December 31, 2012, *ProShares Ultra Rus Mid Cap Grow traded at a discount of 8.18% below its net asset value, which is better than its one-year historical average discount of .04%.

Hratch Najarian has been running the fund for 4 years and currently receives a manager quality ranking of 18 (0=worst, 99=best). If you desire only a moderate level of risk and strong performance, then this fund is an excellent option.

Data Date	Investment Rating	Net Assets ($Mil)	Price	Performance Rating/Pts	Total Return Y-T-D	Risk Rating/Pts
12-12	B-	8.10	53.08	A- / 9.0	7.44%	C+ / 5.8
2011	B-	12.60	42.20	B+ / 8.8	3.08%	C+ / 6.1
2010	C-	14.30	48.03	C+ / 6.4	51.71%	D+ / 2.9
2009	B-	15.46	31.66	A+ / 9.8	78.84%	C- / 3.2

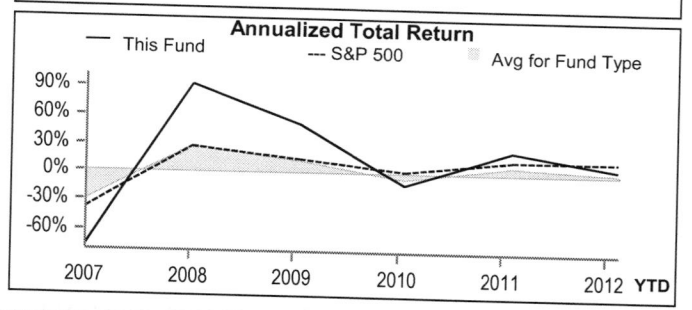

*ProShares Ultra Rus Mid Cap Valu (UVU)

B　　**Good**

Fund Family: ProShare Advisors LLC
Fund Type: Growth
Inception Date: February 20, 2007

Major Rating Factors:

Exceptional performance is the major factor driving the B (Good) TheStreet.com Investment Rating for *ProShares Ultra Rus Mid Cap Valu. The fund currently has a performance rating of A- (Excellent) based on an annualized return of 20.79% over the last three years and a total return of 6.68% year to date 2012. Factored into the performance evaluation is an expense ratio of 0.95% (low).

The fund's risk rating is currently C+ (Fair). It carries a beta of 2.20, meaning it is expected to move 22.0% for every 10% move in the market. Volatility, as measured by both the semi-deviation and a drawdown factor, is considered low. As of December 31, 2012, *ProShares Ultra Rus Mid Cap Valu traded at a discount of 7.26% below its net asset value, which is better than its one-year historical average discount of .33%.

Hratch Najarian has been running the fund for 4 years and currently receives a manager quality ranking of 26 (0=worst, 99=best). If you desire only a moderate level of risk and strong performance, then this fund is an excellent option.

Data Date	Investment Rating	Net Assets ($Mil)	Price	Performance Rating/Pts	Total Return Y-T-D	Risk Rating/Pts
12-12	B	6.50	42.95	A- / 9.2	6.68%	C+ / 6.1
2011	C+	7.20	32.17	B / 7.9	3.29%	C+ / 6.0
2010	D+	8.10	36.22	C / 4.9	46.79%	C- / 3.1
2009	B-	13.78	24.76	A+ / 9.7	50.94%	C- / 3.3

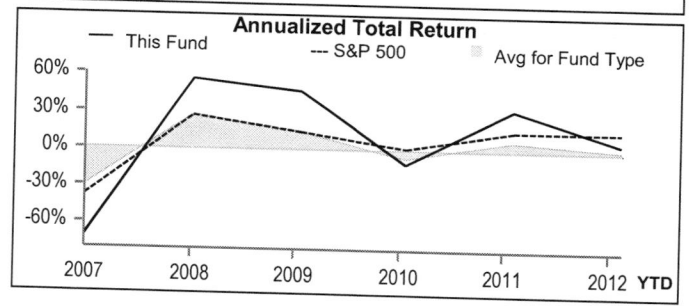

*ProShares Ultra Russell 3000 (UWC)

B-   **Good**

Fund Family: ProShare Advisors LLC
Fund Type: Income
Inception Date: June 30, 2009

Major Rating Factors: Strong performance is the major factor driving the B- (Good) TheStreet.com Investment Rating for *ProShares Ultra Russell 3000. The fund currently has a performance rating of B+ (Good) based on an annualized return of 17.85% over the last three years and a total return of 0.21% year to date 2012. Factored into the performance evaluation is an expense ratio of 0.95% (low).

The fund's risk rating is currently C+ (Fair). It carries a beta of 2.27, meaning it is expected to move 22.7% for every 10% move in the market. Volatility, as measured by both the semi-deviation and a drawdown factor, is considered low. As of December 31, 2012, *ProShares Ultra Russell 3000 traded at a discount of .34% below its net asset value, which is better than its one-year historical average discount of .08%.

Howard Rubin has been running the fund for 6 years and currently receives a manager quality ranking of 19 (0=worst, 99=best). If you desire only a moderate level of risk and strong performance, then this fund is an excellent option.

Data Date	Investment Rating	Net Assets ($Mil)	Price	Perfor- mance Rating/Pts	Total Return Y-T-D	Risk Rating/Pts
12-12	B-	4.80	100.12	B+ / 8.6	0.21%	C+ / 6.0
2011	D	7.30	73.00	D / 1.8	3.48%	C+ / 6.2
2010	A	7.70	76.69	A+ / 9.7	27.20%	C+ / 6.3

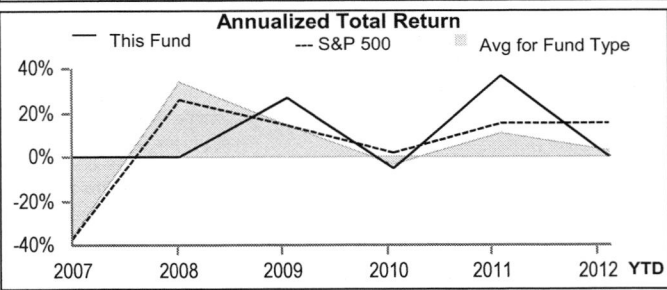

*ProShares Ultra Russell1000 Grow (UKF)

B-   **Good**

Fund Family: ProShare Advisors LLC
Fund Type: Growth
Inception Date: February 20, 2007

Major Rating Factors: Strong performance is the major factor driving the B- (Good) TheStreet.com Investment Rating for *ProShares Ultra Russell1000 Grow. The fund currently has a performance rating of B+ (Good) based on an annualized return of 19.06% over the last three years and a total return of 7.43% year to date 2012. Factored into the performance evaluation is an expense ratio of 0.95% (low).

The fund's risk rating is currently C+ (Fair). It carries a beta of 2.05, meaning it is expected to move 20.5% for every 10% move in the market. Volatility, as measured by both the semi-deviation and a drawdown factor, is considered low. As of December 31, 2012, *ProShares Ultra Russell1000 Grow traded at a discount of 7.81% below its net asset value, which is better than its one-year historical average discount of .25%.

Hratch Najarian has been running the fund for 4 years and currently receives a manager quality ranking of 22 (0=worst, 99=best). If you desire only a moderate level of risk and strong performance, then this fund is an excellent option.

Data Date	Investment Rating	Net Assets ($Mil)	Price	Perfor- mance Rating/Pts	Total Return Y-T-D	Risk Rating/Pts
12-12	B-	14.30	62.41	B+ / 8.5	7.43%	C+ / 6.2
2011	B-	14.90	50.00	B+ / 8.5	2.86%	C+ / 6.7
2010	D	15.20	50.68	C- / 4.0	30.70%	C- / 3.6
2009	B	29.07	38.90	A+ / 9.8	63.98%	C- / 3.7

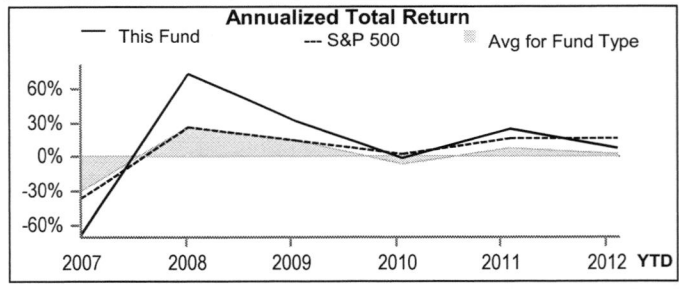

*ProShares Ultra Russell1000 Valu (UVG)

B   **Good**

Fund Family: ProShare Advisors LLC
Fund Type: Income
Inception Date: February 20, 2007

Major Rating Factors: Strong performance is the major factor driving the B (Good) TheStreet.com Investment Rating for *ProShares Ultra Russell1000 Valu. The fund currently has a performance rating of B+ (Good) based on an annualized return of 16.76% over the last three years and a total return of 8.03% year to date 2012. Factored into the performance evaluation is an expense ratio of 0.95% (low).

The fund's risk rating is currently C+ (Fair). It carries a beta of 2.11, meaning it is expected to move 21.1% for every 10% move in the market. Volatility, as measured by both the semi-deviation and a drawdown factor, is considered low. As of December 31, 2012, *ProShares Ultra Russell1000 Valu traded at a discount of 8.35% below its net asset value, which is better than its one-year historical average discount of .21%.

Hratch Najarian has been running the fund for 4 years and currently receives a manager quality ranking of 17 (0=worst, 99=best). If you desire only a moderate level of risk and strong performance, then this fund is an excellent option.

Data Date	Investment Rating	Net Assets ($Mil)	Price	Perfor- mance Rating/Pts	Total Return Y-T-D	Risk Rating/Pts
12-12	B	5.40	35.35	B+ / 8.8	8.03%	C+ / 6.5
2011	C	6.10	27.12	C+ / 6.1	3.25%	C+ / 5.9
2010	E+	13.10	29.14	E+ / 0.9	25.43%	C- / 3.4
2009	C+	20.48	23.42	A- / 9.1	23.90%	C- / 3.6

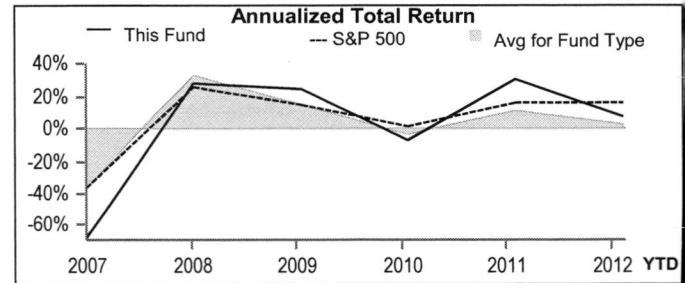

*ProShares Ultra Russell2000 (UWM)

Fund Family: ProShare Advisors LLC
Fund Type: Growth
Inception Date: January 23, 2007

C+　　　　**Fair**

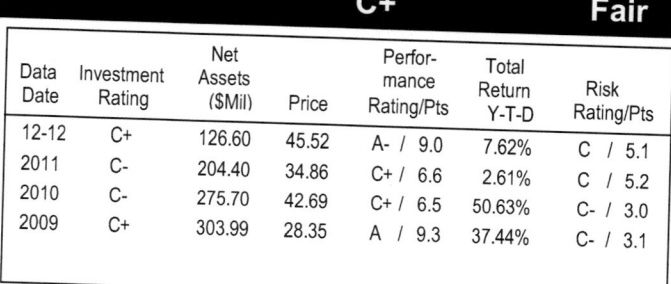

Data Date	Investment Rating	Net Assets ($Mil)	Price	Performance Rating/Pts	Total Return Y-T-D	Risk Rating/Pts
12-12	C+	126.60	45.52	A- / 9.0	7.62%	C / 5.1
2011	C-	204.40	34.86	C+ / 6.6	2.61%	C / 5.2
2010	C-	275.70	42.69	C+ / 6.5	50.63%	C- / 3.0
2009	C+	303.99	28.35	A / 9.3	37.44%	C- / 3.1

Major Rating Factors:
Exceptional performance is the major factor driving the C+ (Fair) TheStreet.com Investment Rating for *ProShares Ultra Russell2000. The fund currently has a performance rating of A- (Excellent) based on an annualized return of 18.47% over the last three years and a total return of 7.62% year to date 2012. Factored into the performance evaluation is an expense ratio of 0.95% (low).

The fund's risk rating is currently C (Fair). It carries a beta of 2.61, meaning it is expected to move 26.1% for every 10% move in the market. Volatility, as measured by both the semi-deviation and a drawdown factor, is considered average. As of December 31, 2012, *ProShares Ultra Russell2000 traded at a discount of 7.05% below its net asset value, which is better than its one-year historical average discount of .02%.

Hratch Najarian has been running the fund for 4 years and currently receives a manager quality ranking of 12 (0=worst, 99=best). If you desire an average level of risk and strong performance, then this fund is a good option.

---

*ProShares Ultra Russell2000 Grow (UKK)

Fund Family: ProShare Advisors LLC
Fund Type: Growth
Inception Date: February 20, 2007

C+　　　　**Fair**

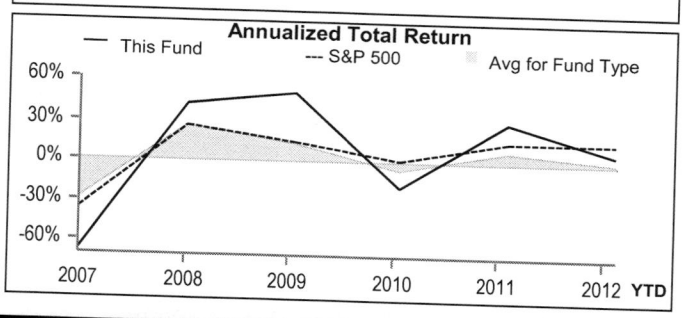

Data Date	Investment Rating	Net Assets ($Mil)	Price	Performance Rating/Pts	Total Return Y-T-D	Risk Rating/Pts
12-12	C+	11.20	50.13	B+ / 8.9	8.16%	C / 4.8
2011	C	17.90	40.18	B / 7.7	1.05%	C / 5.4
2010	C-	28.80	47.94	B- / 7.2	55.80%	D+ / 2.8
2009	C+	23.18	30.77	A / 9.5	54.42%	D+ / 2.8

Major Rating Factors: Strong performance is the major factor driving the C+ (Fair) TheStreet.com Investment Rating for *ProShares Ultra Russell2000 Grow. The fund currently has a performance rating of B+ (Good) based on an annualized return of 19.52% over the last three years and a total return of 8.16% year to date 2012. Factored into the performance evaluation is an expense ratio of 0.95% (low).

The fund's risk rating is currently C (Fair). It carries a beta of 2.65, meaning it is expected to move 26.5% for every 10% move in the market. Volatility, as measured by both the semi-deviation and a drawdown factor, is considered average. As of December 31, 2012, *ProShares Ultra Russell2000 Grow traded at a discount of 7.36% below its net asset value, which is better than its one-year historical average discount of .11%.

Hratch Najarian has been running the fund for 4 years and currently receives a manager quality ranking of 12 (0=worst, 99=best). If you desire an average level of risk and strong performance, then this fund is a good option.

---

*ProShares Ultra Russell2000 Valu (UVT)

Fund Family: ProShare Advisors LLC
Fund Type: Income
Inception Date: February 20, 2007

C+　　　　**Fair**

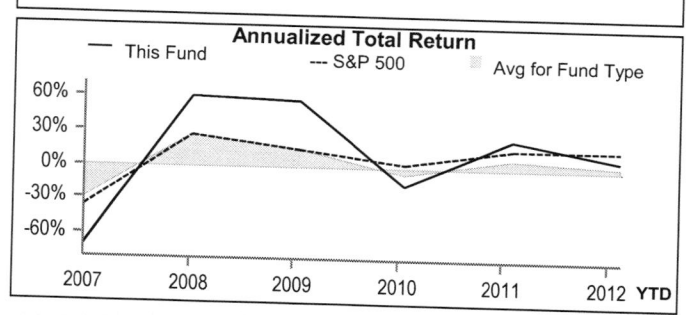

Data Date	Investment Rating	Net Assets ($Mil)	Price	Performance Rating/Pts	Total Return Y-T-D	Risk Rating/Pts
12-12	C+	10.00	33.21	B+ / 8.7	6.44%	C / 5.5
2011	D+	9.40	24.97	C / 4.8	3.36%	C / 5.1
2010	D+	23.70	31.80	C+ / 5.7	44.93%	D+ / 2.9
2009	C+	18.45	22.02	A- / 9.1	22.37%	C- / 3.1

Major Rating Factors: Strong performance is the major factor driving the C+ (Fair) TheStreet.com Investment Rating for *ProShares Ultra Russell2000 Valu. The fund currently has a performance rating of B+ (Good) based on an annualized return of 15.65% over the last three years and a total return of 6.44% year to date 2012. Factored into the performance evaluation is an expense ratio of 0.95% (low).

The fund's risk rating is currently C (Fair). It carries a beta of 2.55, meaning it is expected to move 25.5% for every 10% move in the market. Volatility, as measured by both the semi-deviation and a drawdown factor, is considered average. As of December 31, 2012, *ProShares Ultra Russell2000 Valu traded at a discount of 6.27% below its net asset value, which is better than its one-year historical average discount of .08%.

Hratch Najarian has been running the fund for 4 years and currently receives a manager quality ranking of 11 (0=worst, 99=best). If you desire an average level of risk and strong performance, then this fund is a good option.

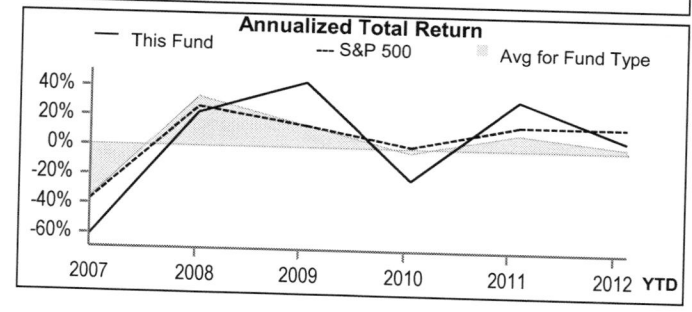

* Denotes ETF Fund

*ProShares Ultra S&P500 (SSO)   B-   Good

Fund Family: ProShare Advisors LLC
Fund Type: Growth
Inception Date: June 19, 2006

Major Rating Factors: Strong performance is the major factor driving the B- (Good) TheStreet.com Investment Rating for *ProShares Ultra S&P500. The fund currently has a performance rating of B+ (Good) based on an annualized return of 18.21% over the last three years and a total return of 6.35% year to date 2012. Factored into the performance evaluation is an expense ratio of 0.91% (low).

The fund's risk rating is currently C+ (Fair). It carries a beta of 2.03, meaning it is expected to move 20.3% for every 10% move in the market. Volatility, as measured by both the semi-deviation and a drawdown factor, is considered low. As of December 31, 2012, *ProShares Ultra S&P500 traded at a discount of 5.98% below its net asset value, which is better than its one-year historical average discount of .04%.

Hratch Najarian has been running the fund for 3 years and currently receives a manager quality ranking of 23 (0=worst, 99=best). If you desire only a moderate level of risk and strong performance, then this fund is an excellent option.

Data Date	Investment Rating	Net Assets ($Mil)	Price	Performance Rating/Pts	Total Return Y-T-D	Risk Rating/Pts
12-12	B-	1,279.30	60.35	B+ / 8.7	6.35%	C+ / 6.4
2011	C+	1,654.20	46.39	B- / 7.4	3.56%	C+ / 6.5
2010	D-	1,589.60	48.05	D / 1.6	26.86%	C- / 3.5
2009	E+	2,398.03	38.24	E+ / 0.9	38.72%	C- / 3.7

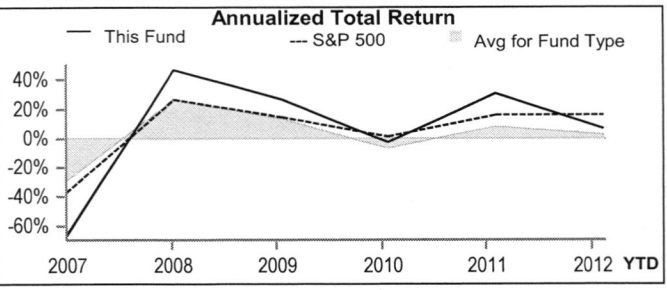

*ProShares Ultra Semiconductors (USD)   D-   Weak

Fund Family: ProShare Advisors LLC
Fund Type: Income
Inception Date: January 30, 2007

Major Rating Factors:
Disappointing performance is the major factor driving the D- (Weak) TheStreet.com Investment Rating for *ProShares Ultra Semiconductors. The fund currently has a performance rating of D (Weak) based on an annualized return of 2.04% over the last three years and a total return of 9.62% year to date 2012. Factored into the performance evaluation is an expense ratio of 0.95% (low).

The fund's risk rating is currently C (Fair). It carries a beta of 2.52, meaning it is expected to move 25.2% for every 10% move in the market. Volatility, as measured by both the semi-deviation and a drawdown factor, is considered average. As of December 31, 2012, *ProShares Ultra Semiconductors traded at a discount of 8.91% below its net asset value, which is better than its one-year historical average discount of .03%.

Hratch Najarian has been running the fund for 2 years and currently receives a manager quality ranking of 3 (0=worst, 99=best). This fund offers an average level of risk but investors looking for strong performance will be frustrated.

Data Date	Investment Rating	Net Assets ($Mil)	Price	Performance Rating/Pts	Total Return Y-T-D	Risk Rating/Pts
12-12	D-	38.70	30.25	D / 1.9	9.62%	C / 4.9
2011	C+	43.30	33.90	B+ / 8.8	6.52%	C / 5.3
2010	E+	74.60	39.82	D+ / 2.6	19.43%	D / 1.6
2009	C+	105.49	33.44	A+ / 9.9	124.24%	D / 1.9

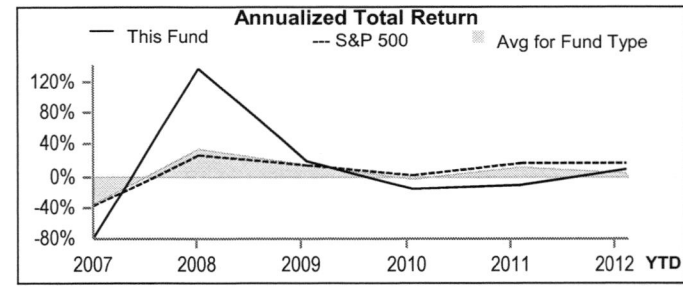

*ProShares Ultra Silver (AGQ)   E+   Very Weak

Fund Family: ProShare Advisors LLC
Fund Type: Energy/Natural Resources
Inception Date: December 2, 2008

Major Rating Factors: *ProShares Ultra Silver has adopted a very risky asset allocation strategy and currently receives an overall TheStreet.com Investment Rating of E+ (Very Weak). The fund has a high level of volatility, as measured by both semi-deviation and drawdown factors. It carries a beta of 2.15, meaning it is expected to move 21.5% for every 10% move in the market. As of December 31, 2012, *ProShares Ultra Silver traded at a discount of 1.56% below its net asset value, which is better than its one-year historical average premium of .96%. Unfortunately, the high level of risk (D, Weak) has only provided investors with average performance.

The fund's performance rating is currently C- (Fair). It has registered an annualized return of 9.91% over the last three years and is up 0.32% year to date 2012. Factored into the performance evaluation is an expense ratio of 0.95% (low).

Michael Neches currently receives a manager quality ranking of 26 (0=worst, 99=best). If you are comfortable owning a very high risk investment, then this fund may be an option.

Data Date	Investment Rating	Net Assets ($Mil)	Price	Performance Rating/Pts	Total Return Y-T-D	Risk Rating/Pts
12-12	E+	745.50	44.10	C- / 3.0	0.32%	D / 1.9
2011	D+	600.40	41.65	B / 8.2	7.20%	D / 1.9
2010	A	546.70	158.59	A+ / 9.9	182.44%	C+ / 5.8
2009	A+	10.01	56.15	A+ / 9.6	71.35%	C / 5.5

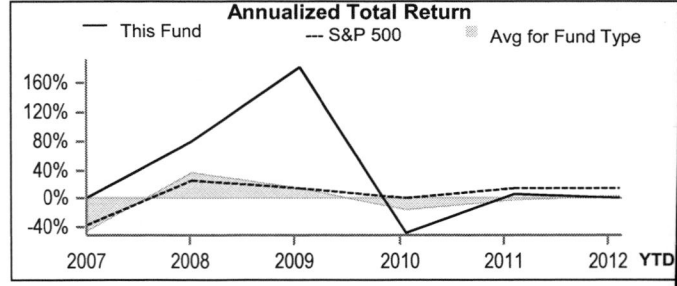

*ProShares Ultra SmallCap 600 (SAA)

B-   **Good**

Fund Family: ProShare Advisors LLC
Fund Type: Growth
Inception Date: January 23, 2007

Major Rating Factors:
Exceptional performance is the major factor driving the B- (Good) TheStreet.com Investment Rating for *ProShares Ultra SmallCap 600. The fund currently has a performance rating of A (Excellent) based on an annualized return of 22.10% over the last three years and a total return of 6.76% year to date 2012. Factored into the performance evaluation is an expense ratio of 0.95% (low).

The fund's risk rating is currently C (Fair). It carries a beta of 2.45, meaning it is expected to move 24.5% for every 10% move in the market. Volatility, as measured by both the semi-deviation and a drawdown factor, is considered average. As of December 31, 2012, *ProShares Ultra SmallCap 600 traded at a discount of 6.46% below its net asset value, which is better than its one-year historical average discount of .09%.

Hratch Najarian has been running the fund for 3 years and currently receives a manager quality ranking of 19 (0=worst, 99=best). If you desire an average level of risk and strong performance, then this fund is a good option.

Data Date	Investment Rating	Net Assets ($Mil)	Price	Perfor- mance Rating/Pts	Total Return Y-T-D	Risk Rating/Pts
12-12	B-	20.60	54.60	A / 9.3	6.76%	C / 5.5
2011	C+	37.90	41.99	B / 7.8	2.50%	C+ / 5.6
2010	C-	48.50	46.37	B- / 7.1	49.95%	C- / 3.0
2009	C+	54.57	30.93	A / 9.3	34.54%	C- / 3.2

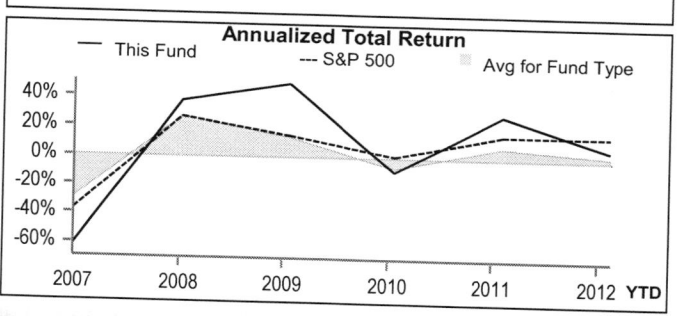

*ProShares Ultra Technology (ROM)

D+   **Weak**

Fund Family: ProShare Advisors LLC
Fund Type: Growth
Inception Date: January 30, 2007

Major Rating Factors: *ProShares Ultra Technology receives a TheStreet.com Investment Rating of D+ (Weak). The fund currently has a performance rating of C (Fair) based on an annualized return of 11.75% over the last three years and a total return of 4.91% year to date 2012. Factored into the performance evaluation is an expense ratio of 0.95% (low).

The fund's risk rating is currently C (Fair). It carries a beta of 2.38, meaning it is expected to move 23.8% for every 10% move in the market. Volatility, as measured by both the semi-deviation and a drawdown factor, is considered average. As of December 31, 2012, *ProShares Ultra Technology traded at a discount of 4.88% below its net asset value, which is better than its one-year historical average discount of .03%.

Hratch Najarian has been running the fund for 2 years and currently receives a manager quality ranking of 9 (0=worst, 99=best). If you desire an average level of risk, then this fund may be an option.

Data Date	Investment Rating	Net Assets ($Mil)	Price	Perfor- mance Rating/Pts	Total Return Y-T-D	Risk Rating/Pts
12-12	D+	74.10	70.01	C / 4.8	4.91%	C / 5.4
2011	B	88.10	58.71	A / 9.4	5.65%	C+ / 6.5
2010	D+	151.80	63.37	C / 5.4	19.91%	C- / 3.2
2009	B-	128.44	52.85	A+ / 9.9	127.15%	C- / 3.2

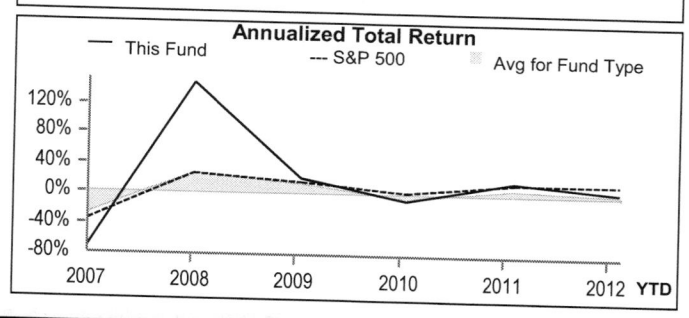

*ProShares Ultra Utilities (UPW)

C+   **Fair**

Fund Family: ProShare Advisors LLC
Fund Type: Utilities
Inception Date: January 30, 2007

Major Rating Factors: Middle of the road best describes *ProShares Ultra Utilities whose TheStreet.com Investment Rating is currently a C+ (Fair). The fund currently has a performance rating of C (Fair) based on an annualized return of 15.55% over the last three years and a total return of 3.63% year to date 2012. Factored into the performance evaluation is an expense ratio of 0.95% (low).

The fund's risk rating is currently B (Good). It carries a beta of 1.85, meaning it is expected to move 18.5% for every 10% move in the market. Volatility, as measured by both the semi-deviation and a drawdown factor, is considered low. As of December 31, 2012, *ProShares Ultra Utilities traded at a discount of 3.86% below its net asset value, which is better than its one-year historical average discount of .15%.

Hratch Najarian has been running the fund for 2 years and currently receives a manager quality ranking of 31 (0=worst, 99=best). If you desire an average level of risk, then this fund may be an option.

Data Date	Investment Rating	Net Assets ($Mil)	Price	Perfor- mance Rating/Pts	Total Return Y-T-D	Risk Rating/Pts
12-12	C+	16.40	54.01	C / 5.3	3.63%	B / 8.3
2011	B-	20.80	55.62	B- / 7.5	-5.17%	B- / 7.3
2010	D-	22.10	42.00	E+ / 0.7	11.49%	C / 4.4
2009	B-	25.18	38.77	B+ / 8.3	14.29%	C / 4.4

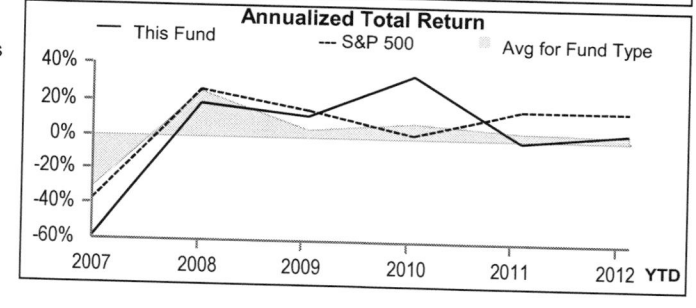

* Denotes ETF Fund

*ProShares Ultra VIX Sh-Tm Fut ET (UVXY)   E-   Very Weak

Fund Family: ProShare Advisors LLC
Fund Type: Growth and Income
Inception Date: October 3, 2011

Data Date	Investment Rating	Net Assets ($Mil)	Price	Performance Rating/Pts	Total Return Y-T-D	Risk Rating/Pts
12-12	E-	72.60	20.90	E- / 0	-32.25%	D / 1.9

Major Rating Factors: *ProShares Ultra VIX Sh-Tm Fut ET has adopted a very risky asset allocation strategy and currently receives an overall TheStreet.com Investment Rating of E- (Very Weak). The fund has a high level of volatility, as measured by both semi-deviation and drawdown factors. It carries a beta of 0.00, meaning the fund's expected move will be 0.0% for every 10% move in the market. As of December 31, 2012, *ProShares Ultra VIX Sh-Tm Fut ET traded at a premium of 50.14% above its net asset value, which is worse than its one-year historical average discount of .19%. Unfortunately, the high level of risk (D, Weak) failed to pay off as investors endured very poor performance.

The fund's performance rating is currently E- (Very Weak). It has registered an annualized return of 0.00% over the last three years but is down -32.25% year to date 2012.

HOWARD S RUBIN has been running the fund for 2 years and currently receives a manager quality ranking of 0 (0=worst, 99=best). If you can tolerate very high levels of risk in the hope of improved future returns, holding this fund may be an option.

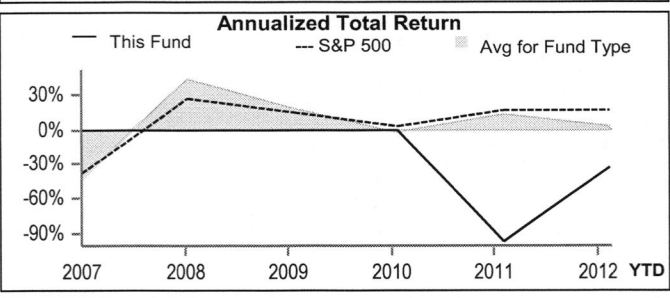

*ProShares Ultra Yen (YCL)   D   Weak

Fund Family: ProShare Advisors LLC
Fund Type: Foreign
Inception Date: November 25, 2008

Data Date	Investment Rating	Net Assets ($Mil)	Price	Performance Rating/Pts	Total Return Y-T-D	Risk Rating/Pts
12-12	D	4.20	28.28	E+ / 0.8	-5.80%	B- / 7.3
2011	C-	5.50	36.50	C- / 4.0	-0.11%	B- / 7.8
2010	A+	5.00	33.29	A- / 9.1	25.24%	B- / 7.0
2009	D+	2.85	26.58	D- / 1.4	-3.90%	B- / 7.1

Major Rating Factors:
Very poor performance is the major factor driving the D (Weak) TheStreet.com Investment Rating for *ProShares Ultra Yen. The fund currently has a performance rating of E+ (Very Weak) based on an annualized return of -0.93% over the last three years and a total return of -5.80% year to date 2012. Factored into the performance evaluation is an expense ratio of 0.95% (low).

The fund's risk rating is currently B- (Good). It carries a beta of -0.20, meaning the fund's expected move will be -2.0% for every 10% move in the market. Volatility, as measured by both the semi-deviation and a drawdown factor, is considered low. As of December 31, 2012, *ProShares Ultra Yen traded at a premium of 6.24% above its net asset value, which is worse than its one-year historical average discount of .11%.

Michael Neches currently receives a manager quality ranking of 71 (0=worst, 99=best). This fund offers only a moderate level of risk but investors looking for strong performance are still waiting.

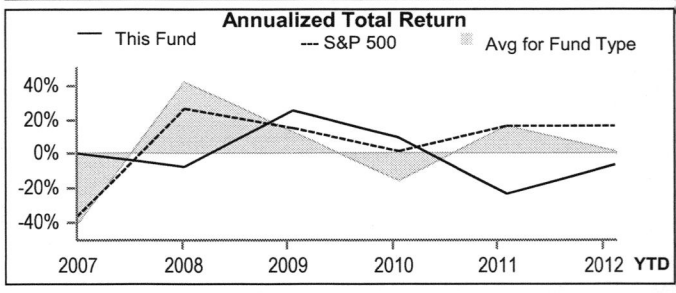

*ProShares UltraPro Dow30 (UDOW)   C   Fair

Fund Family: ProShare Advisors LLC
Fund Type: Growth
Inception Date: February 9, 2010

Data Date	Investment Rating	Net Assets ($Mil)	Price	Performance Rating/Pts	Total Return Y-T-D	Risk Rating/Pts
12-12	C	46.60	54.82	A+ / 9.6	8.81%	C- / 3.1
2011	C-	58.80	130.31	C+ / 5.7	4.01%	C+ / 5.7

Major Rating Factors:
Exceptional performance is the major factor driving the C (Fair) TheStreet.com Investment Rating for *ProShares UltraPro Dow30. The fund currently has a performance rating of A+ (Excellent) based on an annualized return of 0.00% over the last three years and a total return of 8.81% year to date 2012. Factored into the performance evaluation is an expense ratio of 0.95% (low).

The fund's risk rating is currently C- (Fair). It carries a beta of 0.00, meaning the fund's expected move will be 0.0% for every 10% move in the market. Volatility, as measured by both the semi-deviation and a drawdown factor, is considered average. As of December 31, 2012, *ProShares UltraPro Dow30 traded at a discount of 8.30% below its net asset value, which is better than its one-year historical average discount of .03%.

Hratch Najarian has been running the fund for 4 years and currently receives a manager quality ranking of 8 (0=worst, 99=best). If you desire an average level of risk and strong performance, then this fund is a good option.

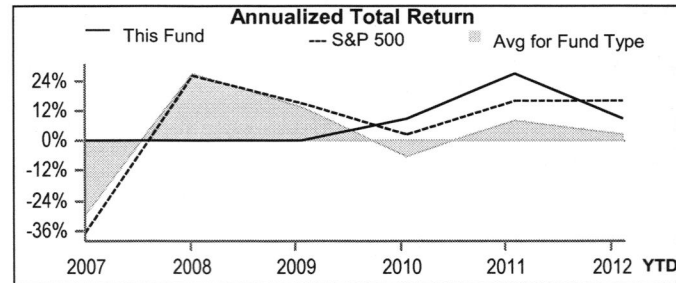

*ProShares UltraPro MidCap400 (UMDD)

		C-				Fair

Fund Family: ProShare Advisors LLC
Fund Type: Growth
Inception Date: February 9, 2010

Major Rating Factors: *ProShares UltraPro MidCap400 has adopted a very risky asset allocation strategy and currently receives an overall TheStreet.com Investment Rating of C- (Fair). The fund has shown a high level of volatility, as measured by both semi-deviation and drawdown factors. It carries a beta of 0.00, meaning the fund's expected move will be 0.0% for every 10% move in the market. As of December 31, 2012, *ProShares UltraPro MidCap400 traded at a discount of 9.91% below its net asset value, which is better than its one-year historical average discount of .07%. The high level of risk (D, Weak) did however, reward investors with excellent performance.

The fund's performance rating is currently A+ (Excellent). It has registered an annualized return of 0.00% over the last three years and is up 11.01% year to date 2012. Factored into the performance evaluation is an expense ratio of 0.95% (low).

Hratch Najarian has been running the fund for 3 years and currently receives a manager quality ranking of 33 (0=worst, 99=best). If you are comfortable owning a very high risk investment, this fund may be an option.

Data Date	Investment Rating	Net Assets ($Mil)	Price	Performance Rating/Pts	Total Return Y-T-D	Risk Rating/Pts
12-12	C-	25.50	84.85	A+ / 9.9	11.01%	D / 2.1
2011	E-	34.00	56.60	E+ / 0.7	4.47%	D / 1.9

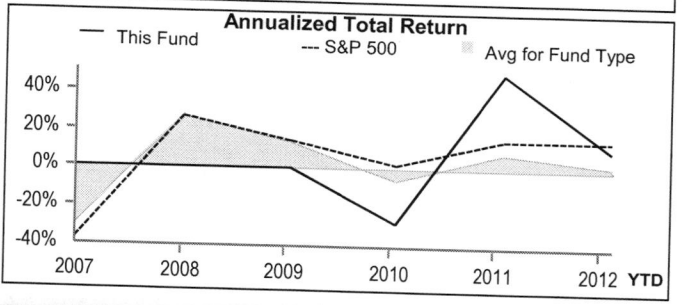

*ProShares UltraPro QQQ (TQQQ)

		C-				Fair

Fund Family: ProShare Advisors LLC
Fund Type: Growth
Inception Date: February 9, 2010

Major Rating Factors: *ProShares UltraPro QQQ has adopted a very risky asset allocation strategy and currently receives an overall TheStreet.com Investment Rating of C- (Fair). The fund has shown a high level of volatility, as measured by both semi-deviation and drawdown factors. It carries a beta of 0.00, meaning the fund's expected move will be 0.0% for every 10% move in the market. As of December 31, 2012, *ProShares UltraPro QQQ traded at a discount of 8.96% below its net asset value, which is better than its one-year historical average discount of .01%. The high level of risk (D, Weak) did however, reward investors with excellent performance.

The fund's performance rating is currently A+ (Excellent). It has registered an annualized return of 0.00% over the last three years and is up 9.81% year to date 2012. Factored into the performance evaluation is an expense ratio of 0.95% (low).

Hratch Najarian has been running the fund for 3 years and currently receives a manager quality ranking of 6 (0=worst, 99=best). If you are comfortable owning a very high risk investment, this fund may be an option.

Data Date	Investment Rating	Net Assets ($Mil)	Price	Performance Rating/Pts	Total Return Y-T-D	Risk Rating/Pts
12-12	C-	317.90	51.69	A+ / 9.8	9.81%	D / 1.9
2011	E	183.70	67.97	D- / 1.5	10.74%	D / 2.1

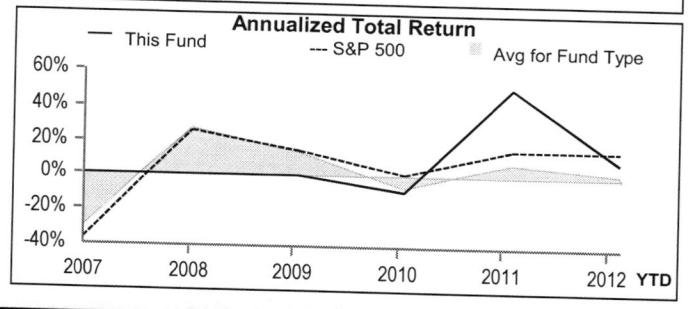

*ProShares UltraPro Russell2000 (URTY)

		C-				Fair

Fund Family: ProShare Advisors LLC
Fund Type: Growth
Inception Date: February 9, 2010

Major Rating Factors: *ProShares UltraPro Russell2000 has adopted a very risky asset allocation strategy and currently receives an overall TheStreet.com Investment Rating of C- (Fair). The fund has shown a high level of volatility, as measured by both semi-deviation and drawdown factors. It carries a beta of 0.00, meaning the fund's expected move will be 0.0% for every 10% move in the market. As of December 31, 2012, *ProShares UltraPro Russell2000 traded at a discount of 10.39% below its net asset value, which is better than its one-year historical average discount of .05%. The high level of risk (D, Weak) did however, reward investors with excellent performance.

The fund's performance rating is currently A+ (Excellent). It has registered an annualized return of 0.00% over the last three years and is up 11.57% year to date 2012. Factored into the performance evaluation is an expense ratio of 0.95% (low).

Hratch Najarian has been running the fund for 3 years and currently receives a manager quality ranking of 10 (0=worst, 99=best). If you are comfortable owning a very high risk investment, this fund may be an option.

Data Date	Investment Rating	Net Assets ($Mil)	Price	Performance Rating/Pts	Total Return Y-T-D	Risk Rating/Pts
12-12	C-	67.90	71.13	A+ / 9.9	11.57%	D / 1.9
2011	E-	99.40	49.48	E+ / 0.6	3.88%	D / 1.9

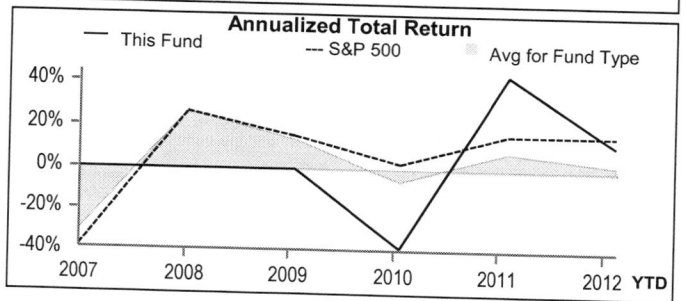

*ProShares UltraPro S&P500 (UPRO)

C-   **Fair**

Fund Family: ProShare Advisors LLC
Fund Type: Income
Inception Date: June 23, 2009

Data Date	Investment Rating	Net Assets ($Mil)	Price	Performance Rating/Pts	Total Return Y-T-D	Risk Rating/Pts
12-12	C-	365.80	87.86	A+ / 9.6	10.19%	D / 1.9
2011	E	343.60	60.15	D- / 1.4	5.29%	D / 1.9
2010	A-	204.50	204.91	A+ / 9.9	36.37%	C / 5.1

Major Rating Factors: *ProShares UltraPro S&P500 has adopted a very risky asset allocation strategy and currently receives an overall TheStreet.com Investment Rating of C- (Fair). The fund has shown a high level of volatility, as measured by both semi-deviation and drawdown factors. It carries a beta of 3.07, meaning it is expected to move 30.7% for every 10% move in the market. As of December 31, 2012, *ProShares UltraPro S&P500 traded at a discount of 9.16% below its net asset value, which is better than its one-year historical average discount of .05%. The high level of risk (D, Weak) did however, reward investors with excellent performance.

The fund's performance rating is currently A+ (Excellent). It has registered an annualized return of 22.26% over the last three years and is up 10.19% year to date 2012. Factored into the performance evaluation is an expense ratio of 0.95% (low).

Hratch Najarian has been running the fund for 3 years and currently receives a manager quality ranking of 10 (0=worst, 99=best). If you are comfortable owning a very high risk investment, this fund may be an option.

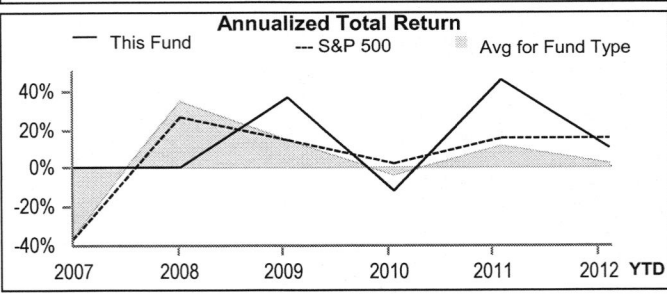

*ProShares UltraPro Short Dow30 (SDOW)

E   **Very Weak**

Fund Family: ProShare Advisors LLC
Fund Type: Growth
Inception Date: February 9, 2010

Data Date	Investment Rating	Net Assets ($Mil)	Price	Performance Rating/Pts	Total Return Y-T-D	Risk Rating/Pts
12-12	E	82.10	68.47	E- / 0.2	-8.68%	C- / 3.1
2011	E	68.00	25.21	E- / 0.1	-4.28%	D+ / 2.9

Major Rating Factors: Very poor performance is the major factor driving the E (Very Weak) TheStreet.com Investment Rating for *ProShares UltraPro Short Dow30. The fund currently has a performance rating of E- (Very Weak) based on an annualized return of 0.00% over the last three years and a total return of -8.68% year to date 2012. Factored into the performance evaluation is an expense ratio of 0.95% (low).

The fund's risk rating is currently C- (Fair). It carries a beta of 0.00, meaning the fund's expected move will be 0.0% for every 10% move in the market. Volatility, as measured by both the semi-deviation and a drawdown factor, is considered average. As of December 31, 2012, *ProShares UltraPro Short Dow30 traded at a premium of 9.73% above its net asset value, which is worse than its one-year historical average discount of .02%.

Hratch Najarian has been running the fund for 3 years and currently receives a manager quality ranking of 58 (0=worst, 99=best). This fund offers an average level of risk but investors looking for strong performance will be frustrated.

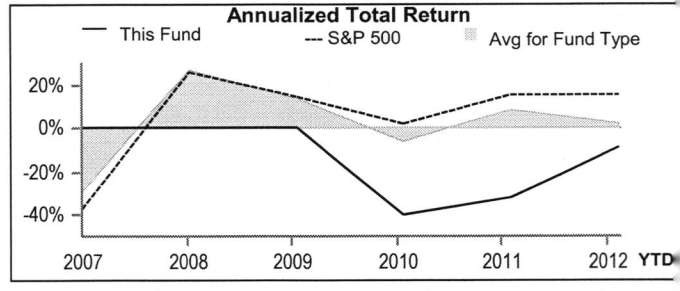

*ProShares UltraPro Short MidCap4 (SMDD)

E-   **Very Weak**

Fund Family: ProShare Advisors LLC
Fund Type: Growth
Inception Date: February 9, 2010

Data Date	Investment Rating	Net Assets ($Mil)	Price	Performance Rating/Pts	Total Return Y-T-D	Risk Rating/Pts
12-12	E-	6.40	36.87	E- / 0	-10.82%	D / 2.2
2011	E-	11.40	17.57	E- / 0.2	-4.38%	D / 1.9

Major Rating Factors: *ProShares UltraPro Short MidCap4 has adopted a very risky asset allocation strategy and currently receives an overall TheStreet.com Investment Rating of E- (Very Weak). The fund has a high level of volatility, as measured by both semi-deviation and drawdown factors. It carries a beta of 0.00, meaning the fund's expected move will be 0.0% for every 10% move in the market. As of December 31, 2012, *ProShares UltraPro Short MidCap4 traded at a premium of 12.03% above its net asset value, which is worse than its one-year historical average premium of .01%. Unfortunately, the high level of risk (D, Weak) failed to pay off as investors endured very poor performance.

The fund's performance rating is currently E- (Very Weak). It has registered an annualized return of 0.00% over the last three years but is down -10.82% year to date 2012. Factored into the performance evaluation is an expense ratio of 0.95% (low).

Hratch Najarian has been running the fund for 3 years and currently receives a manager quality ranking of 5 (0=worst, 99=best). If you can tolerate very high levels of risk in the hope of improved future returns, holding this fund may be an option.

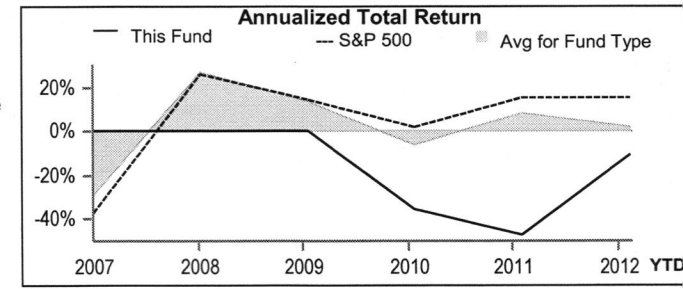

*ProShares UltraPro Short QQQ (SQQQ)

E-   Very Weak

Fund Family: ProShare Advisors LLC
Fund Type: Growth
Inception Date: February 9, 2010

Data Date	Investment Rating	Net Assets ($Mil)	Price	Perfor-mance Rating/Pts	Total Return Y-T-D	Risk Rating/Pts
12-12	E-	134.00	40.55	E- / 0.1	-9.78%	D / 2.2
2011	E-	94.50	19.69	E- / 0.1	-9.95%	D+ / 2.3

Major Rating Factors: *ProShares UltraPro Short QQQ has adopted a very risky asset allocation strategy and currently receives an overall TheStreet.com Investment Rating of E- (Very Weak). The fund has a high level of volatility, as measured by both semi-deviation and drawdown factors. It carries a beta of 0.00, meaning the fund's expected move will be 0.0% for every 10% move in the market. As of December 31, 2012, *ProShares UltraPro Short QQQ traded at a premium of 10.88% above its net asset value, which is worse than its one-year historical average premium of .07%. Unfortunately, the high level of risk (D, Weak) failed to pay off as investors endured very poor performance.

The fund's performance rating is currently E- (Very Weak). It has registered an annualized return of 0.00% over the last three years but is down -9.78% year to date 2012. Factored into the performance evaluation is an expense ratio of 0.95% (low).

Hratch Najarian has been running the fund for 4 years and currently receives a manager quality ranking of 23 (0=worst, 99=best). If you can tolerate very high levels of risk in the hope of improved future returns, holding this fund may be an option.

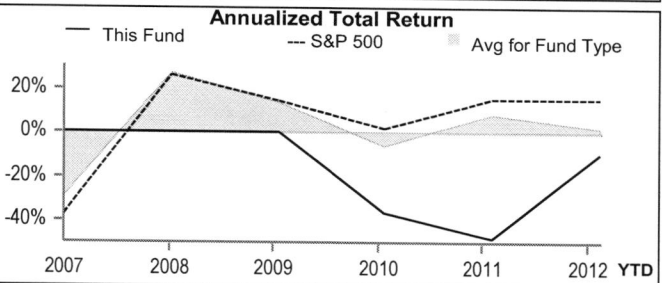

*ProShares UltraPro Short S&P500 (SPXU)

E-   Very Weak

Fund Family: ProShare Advisors LLC
Fund Type: Growth
Inception Date: June 23, 2009

Data Date	Investment Rating	Net Assets ($Mil)	Price	Perfor-mance Rating/Pts	Total Return Y-T-D	Risk Rating/Pts
12-12	E-	462.00	37.86	E- / 0.1	-9.83%	D+ / 2.8
2011	E-	596.80	13.13	E- / 0.2	-5.18%	D+ / 2.6
2010	E-	290.10	19.41	E- / 0	-46.51%	D+ / 2.3

Major Rating Factors: *ProShares UltraPro Short S&P500 has adopted a risky asset allocation strategy and currently receives an overall TheStreet.com Investment Rating of E- (Very Weak). The fund has an above average level of volatility, as measured by both semi-deviation and drawdown factors. It carries a beta of -2.82, meaning the fund's expected move will be -28.2% for every 10% move in the market. As of December 31, 2012, *ProShares UltraPro Short S&P500 traded at a premium of 10.77% above its net asset value, which is worse than its one-year historical average discount of .01%. Unfortunately, the high level of risk (D+, Weak) failed to pay off as investors endured very poor performance.

The fund's performance rating is currently E- (Very Weak). It has registered an annualized return of -41.50% over the last three years and is down -9.83% year to date 2012. Factored into the performance evaluation is an expense ratio of 0.93% (low).

Hratch Najarian has been running the fund for 3 years and currently receives a manager quality ranking of 5 (0=worst, 99=best). If you can tolerate high levels of risk in the hope of improved future returns, holding this fund may be an option.

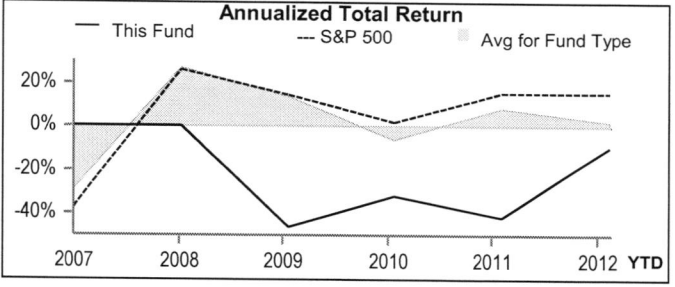

*ProShares UltraPro Shrt Russell2 (SRTY)

E-   Very Weak

Fund Family: ProShare Advisors LLC
Fund Type: Growth
Inception Date: February 9, 2010

Data Date	Investment Rating	Net Assets ($Mil)	Price	Perfor-mance Rating/Pts	Total Return Y-T-D	Risk Rating/Pts
12-12	E-	61.40	33.74	E- / 0	-10.82%	D / 1.9
2011	E-	66.90	13.12	E- / 0	-3.73%	D / 1.9

Major Rating Factors: *ProShares UltraPro Shrt Russell2 has adopted a very risky asset allocation strategy and currently receives an overall TheStreet.com Investment Rating of E- (Very Weak). The fund has a high level of volatility, as measured by both semi-deviation and drawdown factors. It carries a beta of 0.00, meaning the fund's expected move will be 0.0% for every 10% move in the market. As of December 31, 2012, *ProShares UltraPro Shrt Russell2 traded at a premium of 12.20% above its net asset value, which is worse than its one-year historical average premium of .01%. Unfortunately, the high level of risk (D, Weak) failed to pay off as investors endured very poor performance.

The fund's performance rating is currently E- (Very Weak). It has registered an annualized return of 0.00% over the last three years but is down -10.82% year to date 2012. Factored into the performance evaluation is an expense ratio of 0.95% (low).

Hratch Najarian has been running the fund for 3 years and currently receives a manager quality ranking of 8 (0=worst, 99=best). If you can tolerate very high levels of risk in the hope of improved future returns, holding this fund may be an option.

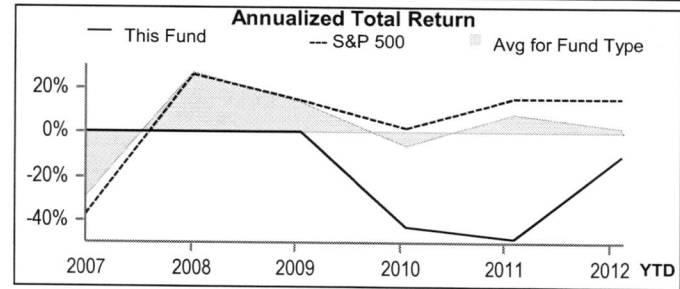

*ProShares UltraShort 20+ Year Tr (TBT)

E **Very Weak**

Fund Family: ProShare Advisors LLC
Fund Type: Income
Inception Date: April 29, 2008

Major Rating Factors: Very poor performance is the major factor driving the E (Very Weak) TheStreet.com Investment Rating for *ProShares UltraShort 20+ Year Tr. The fund currently has a performance rating of E (Very Weak) based on an annualized return of -30.70% over the last three years and a total return of 1.94% year to date 2012. Factored into the performance evaluation is an expense ratio of 0.92% (low).

The fund's risk rating is currently C- (Fair). It carries a beta of 1.54, meaning it is expected to move 15.4% for every 10% move in the market. Volatility, as measured by both the semi-deviation and a drawdown factor, is considered average. As of December 31, 2012, *ProShares UltraShort 20+ Year Tr traded at a discount of 2.62% below its net asset value, which is better than its one-year historical average discount of .21%.

Michelle Lui has been running the fund for 5 years and currently receives a manager quality ranking of 1 (0=worst, 99=best). This fund offers an average level of risk but investors looking for strong performance will be frustrated.

Data Date	Investment Rating	Net Assets ($Mil)	Price	Performance Rating/Pts	Total Return Y-T-D	Risk Rating/Pts
12-12	E	2,902.10	63.45	E / 0.4	1.94%	C- / 3.6
2011	E+	3,106.50	18.07	E+ / 0.6	4.15%	C- / 3.9
2010	E+	5,392.20	37.04	E+ / 0.8	-25.74%	C- / 4.2
2009	C+	4,058.21	49.88	B / 7.7	27.90%	C / 5.0

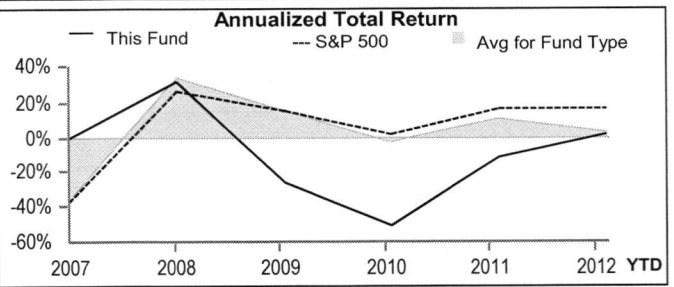

Annualized Total Return

*ProShares UltraShort 3-7 Yr Trea (TBZ)

D **Weak**

Fund Family: ProShare Advisors LLC
Fund Type: General - Investment Grade
Inception Date: April 4, 2011

Major Rating Factors:
Disappointing performance is the major factor driving the D (Weak) TheStreet.com Investment Rating for *ProShares UltraShort 3-7 Yr Trea. The fund currently has a performance rating of D- (Weak) based on an annualized return of 0.00% over the last three years and a total return of 0.63% year to date 2012. Factored into the performance evaluation is an expense ratio of 0.95% (low).

The fund's risk rating is currently B (Good). It carries a beta of 0.00, meaning the fund's expected move will be 0.0% for every 10% move in the market. Volatility, as measured by both the semi-deviation and a drawdown factor, is considered low. As of December 31, 2012, *ProShares UltraShort 3-7 Yr Trea traded at a discount of .71% below its net asset value, which is better than its one-year historical average discount of .21%.

Michelle Lui has been running the fund for 2 years and currently receives a manager quality ranking of 68 (0=worst, 99=best). This fund offers only a moderate level of risk but investors looking for strong performance are still waiting.

Data Date	Investment Rating	Net Assets ($Mil)	Price	Performance Rating/Pts	Total Return Y-T-D	Risk Rating/Pts
12-12	D	4.80	31.94	D- / 1.0	0.63%	B / 8.5

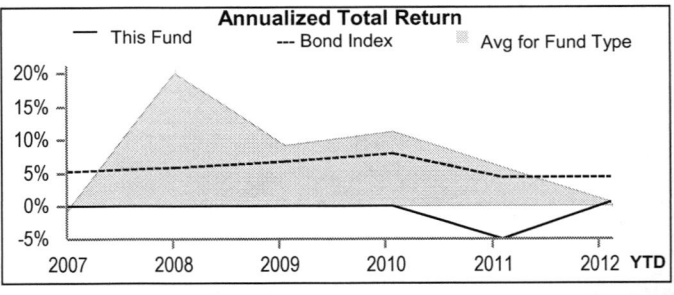

Annualized Total Return

*ProShares UltraShort 7-10 Year T (PST)

D- **Weak**

Fund Family: ProShare Advisors LLC
Fund Type: Income
Inception Date: April 29, 2008

Major Rating Factors:
Very poor performance is the major factor driving the D- (Weak) TheStreet.com Investment Rating for *ProShares UltraShort 7-10 Year T. The fund currently has a performance rating of E (Very Weak) based on an annualized return of -18.88% over the last three years and a total return of 0.94% year to date 2012. Factored into the performance evaluation is an expense ratio of 0.95% (low).

The fund's risk rating is currently C+ (Fair). It carries a beta of 0.56, meaning the fund's expected move will be 5.6% for every 10% move in the market. Volatility, as measured by both the semi-deviation and a drawdown factor, is considered low. As of December 31, 2012, *ProShares UltraShort 7-10 Year T traded at a discount of 1.22% below its net asset value, which is better than its one-year historical average discount of .09%.

Michelle Lui has been running the fund for 5 years and currently receives a manager quality ranking of 4 (0=worst, 99=best). This fund offers only a moderate level of risk but investors looking for strong performance are still waiting.

Data Date	Investment Rating	Net Assets ($Mil)	Price	Performance Rating/Pts	Total Return Y-T-D	Risk Rating/Pts
12-12	D-	292.50	27.60	E / 0.5	0.94%	C+ / 5.9
2011	D-	380.80	30.51	E+ / 0.9	1.11%	C+ / 6.2
2010	D	451.30	42.34	E+ / 0.6	-21.51%	C+ / 5.8
2009	C-	445.82	53.94	D / 1.9	0.04%	C+ / 6.8

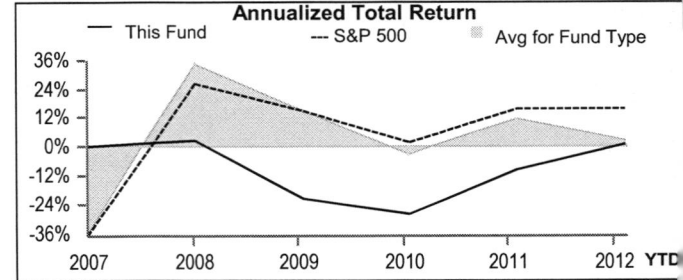

Annualized Total Return

*ProShares UltraShort Basic Mater (SMN)

E-   **Very Weak**

Fund Family: ProShare Advisors LLC
Fund Type: Income
Inception Date: January 30, 2007

Major Rating Factors: *ProShares UltraShort Basic Mater has adopted a risky asset allocation strategy and currently receives an overall TheStreet.com Investment Rating of E- (Very Weak). The fund has an above average level of volatility, as measured by both semi-deviation and drawdown factors. It carries a beta of -2.90, meaning the fund's expected move will be -29.0% for every 10% move in the market. As of December 31, 2012, *ProShares UltraShort Basic Mater traded at a premium of 7.13% above its net asset value, which is worse than its one-year historical average premium of .01%. Unfortunately, the high level of risk (D+, Weak) failed to pay off as investors endured very poor performance.

The fund's performance rating is currently E (Very Weak). It has registered an annualized return of -31.56% over the last three years and is down -6.62% year to date 2012. Factored into the performance evaluation is an expense ratio of 0.95% (low).

Hratch Najarian has been running the fund for 2 years and currently receives a manager quality ranking of 15 (0=worst, 99=best). If you can tolerate high levels of risk in the hope of improved future returns, holding this fund may be an option.

Data Date	Investment Rating	Net Assets ($Mil)	Price	Perfor-mance Rating/Pts	Total Return Y-T-D	Risk Rating/Pts
12-12	E-	30.40	53.77	E / 0.3	-6.62%	D+ / 2.7
2011	E-	64.50	18.63	E- / 0.1	-7.03%	D / 1.9
2010	E-	73.90	19.24	E- / 0.1	-54.68%	D- / 1.0
2009	E-	62.69	8.49	E- / 0	-75.87%	D / 1.4

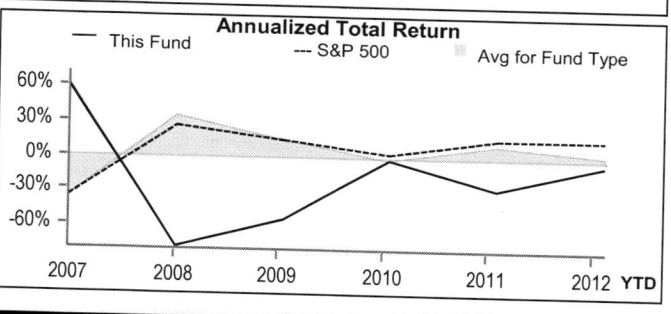

*ProShares UltraShort Consumer Go (SZK)

E+   **Very Weak**

Fund Family: ProShare Advisors LLC
Fund Type: Income
Inception Date: January 30, 2007

Major Rating Factors:
Very poor performance is the major factor driving the E+ (Very Weak) TheStreet.com Investment Rating for *ProShares UltraShort Consumer Go. The fund currently has a performance rating of E (Very Weak) based on an annualized return of -28.65% over the last three years and a total return of -5.26% year to date 2012. Factored into the performance evaluation is an expense ratio of 0.95% (low).

The fund's risk rating is currently C- (Fair). It carries a beta of -1.32, meaning the fund's expected move will be -13.2% for every 10% move in the market. Volatility, as measured by both the semi-deviation and a drawdown factor, is considered average. As of December 31, 2012, *ProShares UltraShort Consumer Go traded at a premium of 5.23% above its net asset value, which is worse than its one-year historical average premium of .01%.

Hratch Najarian has been running the fund for 2 years and currently receives a manager quality ranking of 6 (0=worst, 99=best). This fund offers an average level of risk but investors looking for strong performance will be frustrated.

Data Date	Investment Rating	Net Assets ($Mil)	Price	Perfor-mance Rating/Pts	Total Return Y-T-D	Risk Rating/Pts
12-12	E+	2.40	62.39	E / 0.3	-5.26%	C- / 4.2
2011	E	4.70	20.84	E / 0.5	-1.34%	C- / 3.8
2010	E+	8.30	27.52	E / 0.4	-34.86%	C- / 3.3
2009	E+	19.67	42.25	E / 0.3	-40.09%	C / 4.8

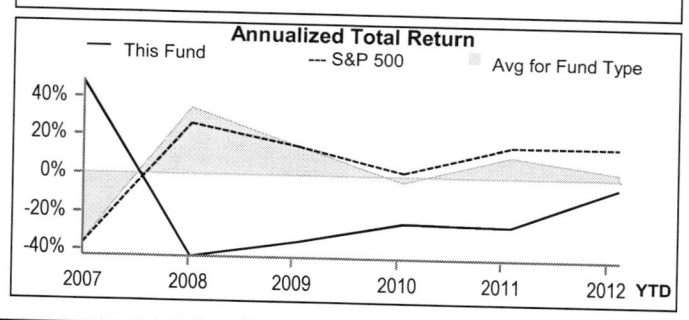

*ProShares UltraShort Consumer Se (SCC)

E   **Very Weak**

Fund Family: ProShare Advisors LLC
Fund Type: Income
Inception Date: January 30, 2007

Major Rating Factors: Very poor performance is the major factor driving the E (Very Weak) TheStreet.com Investment Rating for *ProShares UltraShort Consumer Se. The fund currently has a performance rating of E- (Very Weak) based on an annualized return of -37.41% over the last three years and a total return of -6.56% year to date 2012. Factored into the performance evaluation is an expense ratio of 0.95% (low).

The fund's risk rating is currently C- (Fair). It carries a beta of -1.82, meaning the fund's expected move will be -18.2% for every 10% move in the market. Volatility, as measured by both the semi-deviation and a drawdown factor, is considered average. As of December 31, 2012, *ProShares UltraShort Consumer Se traded at a premium of 6.97% above its net asset value, which is worse than its one-year historical average discount of .03%.

Hratch Najarian has been running the fund for 2 years and currently receives a manager quality ranking of 4 (0=worst, 99=best). This fund offers an average level of risk but investors looking for strong performance will be frustrated.

Data Date	Investment Rating	Net Assets ($Mil)	Price	Perfor-mance Rating/Pts	Total Return Y-T-D	Risk Rating/Pts
12-12	E	5.80	39.00	E- / 0.2	-6.56%	C- / 3.6
2011	E	12.00	15.94	E / 0.3	-3.33%	C- / 3.2
2010	E-	22.90	21.81	E / 0.3	-42.09%	D / 2.0
2009	E	72.41	37.66	E- / 0.1	-52.35%	C- / 3.3

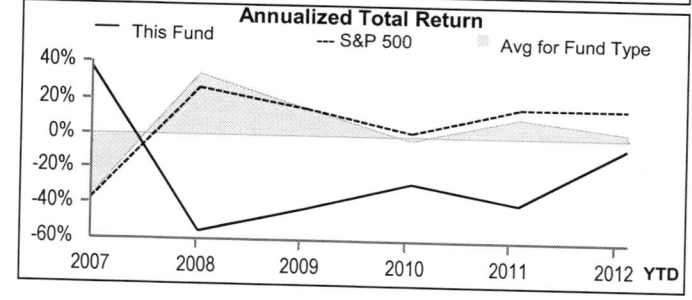

*ProShares UltraShort DJ-UBS Com (CMD)   E+   Very Weak

Fund Family: ProShare Advisors LLC
Fund Type: Income
Inception Date: November 25, 2008

Major Rating Factors:
Very poor performance is the major factor driving the E+ (Very Weak) TheStreet.com Investment Rating for *ProShares UltraShort DJ-UBS Com. The fund currently has a performance rating of E+ (Very Weak) based on an annualized return of -10.02% over the last three years and a total return of 5.52% year to date 2012. Factored into the performance evaluation is an expense ratio of 0.95% (low).

The fund's risk rating is currently C (Fair). It carries a beta of -1.73, meaning the fund's expected move will be -17.3% for every 10% move in the market. Volatility, as measured by both the semi-deviation and a drawdown factor, is considered average. As of December 31, 2012, *ProShares UltraShort DJ-UBS Com traded at a discount of 5.16% below its net asset value, which is better than its one-year historical average discount of .41%.

Michael Neches currently receives a manager quality ranking of 83 (0=worst, 99=best). This fund offers an average level of risk but investors looking for strong performance will be frustrated.

Data Date	Investment Rating	Net Assets ($Mil)	Price	Performance Rating/Pts	Total Return Y-T-D	Risk Rating/Pts
12-12	E+	3.20	51.64	E+ / 0.8	5.52%	C / 5.0
2011	E+	9.10	56.19	E+ / 0.9	-1.76%	C- / 3.8
2010	E	1.40	9.66	E- / 0.1	-34.06%	C- / 3.5
2009	E+	2.68	14.65	E- / 0.2	-42.64%	C / 5.0

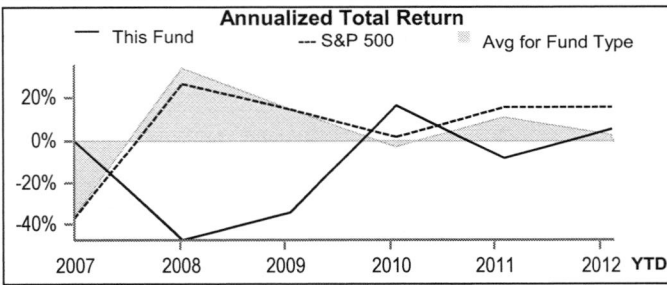

*ProShares UltraShort DJ-UBS Cr O (SCO)   E   Very Weak

Fund Family: ProShare Advisors LLC
Fund Type: Energy/Natural Resources
Inception Date: November 25, 2008

Major Rating Factors: Very poor performance is the major factor driving the E (Very Weak) TheStreet.com Investment Rating for *ProShares UltraShort DJ-UBS Cr O. The fund currently has a performance rating of E (Very Weak) based on an annualized return of -18.25% over the last three years and a total return of -4.28% year to date 2012. Factored into the performance evaluation is an expense ratio of 0.99% (low).

The fund's risk rating is currently C- (Fair). It carries a beta of -1.93, meaning the fund's expected move will be -19.3% for every 10% move in the market. Volatility, as measured by both the semi-deviation and a drawdown factor, is considered average. As of December 31, 2012, *ProShares UltraShort DJ-UBS Cr O traded at a premium of 4.23% above its net asset value, which is worse than its one-year historical average discount of .04%.

Michael Neches currently receives a manager quality ranking of 46 (0=worst, 99=best). This fund offers an average level of risk but investors looking for strong performance will be frustrated.

Data Date	Investment Rating	Net Assets ($Mil)	Price	Performance Rating/Pts	Total Return Y-T-D	Risk Rating/Pts
12-12	E	85.40	40.44	E / 0.5	-4.28%	C- / 3.7
2011	E-	144.40	38.69	E / 0.3	-6.25%	D+ / 2.4
2010	E-	132.20	10.17	E- / 0.2	-25.49%	D / 1.9
2009	E-	14.50	13.65	E- / 0.2	-49.82%	D+ / 2.3

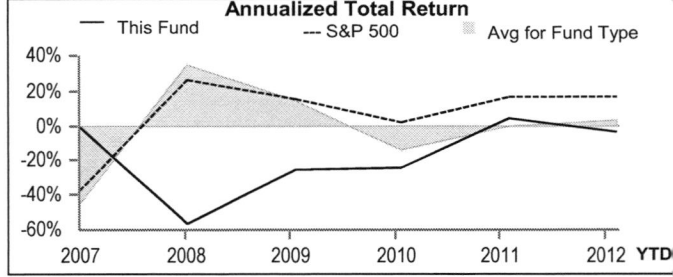

*ProShares UltraShort DJ-UBS Nat (KOLD)   E-   Very Weak

Fund Family: ProShare Advisors LLC
Fund Type: Income
Inception Date: October 6, 2011

Major Rating Factors: *ProShares UltraShort DJ-UBS Nat has adopted a very risky asset allocation strategy and currently receives an overall TheStreet.com Investment Rating of E- (Very Weak). The fund has a high level of volatility, as measured by both semi-deviation and drawdown factors. It carries a beta of 0.00, meaning the fund's expected move will be 0.0% for every 10% move in the market. As of December 31, 2012, *ProShares UltraShort DJ-UBS Nat traded at a discount of .55% below its net asset value, which is better than its one-year historical average premium of .01%. Unfortunately, the high level of risk (D, Weak) failed to pay off as investors endured poor performance.

The fund's performance rating is currently D- (Weak). It has registered an annualized return of 0.00% over the last three years and is up 0.48% year to date 2012.

Michael Neches currently receives a manager quality ranking of 8 (0=worst, 99=best). If you can tolerate very high levels of risk in the hope of improved future returns, holding this fund may be an option.

Data Date	Investment Rating	Net Assets ($Mil)	Price	Performance Rating/Pts	Total Return Y-T-D	Risk Rating/Pts
12-12	E-	12.80	25.41	D- / 1.1	0.48%	D / 1.9

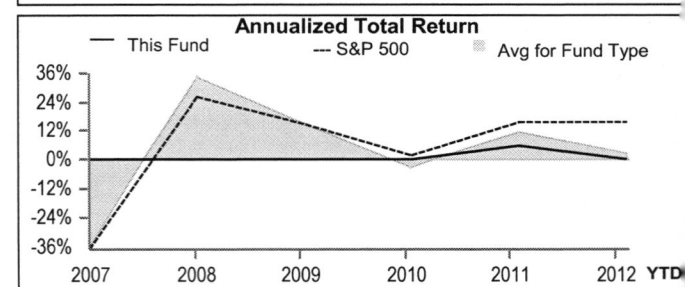

*ProShares UltraShort Dow 30 (DXD)

E+   Very Weak

Fund Family: ProShare Advisors LLC
Fund Type: Growth
Inception Date: July 11, 2006

Major Rating Factors:
Very poor performance is the major factor driving the E+ (Very Weak) TheStreet.com Investment Rating for *ProShares UltraShort Dow 30. The fund currently has a performance rating of E (Very Weak) based on an annualized return of -26.53% over the last three years and a total return of -5.88% year to date 2012. Factored into the performance evaluation is an expense ratio of 0.95% (low).

The fund's risk rating is currently C- (Fair). It carries a beta of -1.69, meaning the fund's expected move will be -16.9% for every 10% move in the market. Volatility, as measured by both the semi-deviation and a drawdown factor, is considered average. As of December 31, 2012, *ProShares UltraShort Dow 30 traded at a premium of 6.27% above its net asset value, which is worse than its one-year historical average discount of .01%.

Hratch Najarian has been running the fund for 4 years and currently receives a manager quality ranking of 10 (0=worst, 99=best). This fund offers an average level of risk but investors looking for strong performance will be frustrated.

Data Date	Investment Rating	Net Assets ($Mil)	Price	Performance Rating/Pts	Total Return Y-T-D	Risk Rating/Pts
12-12	E+	272.40	47.78	E / 0.4	-5.88%	C- / 4.1
2011	E	288.20	15.31	E / 0.5	-2.68%	C- / 3.6
2010	E	379.70	20.70	E / 0.4	-29.76%	C- / 3.1
2009	E+	639.20	29.47	E / 0.5	-41.74%	C / 4.3

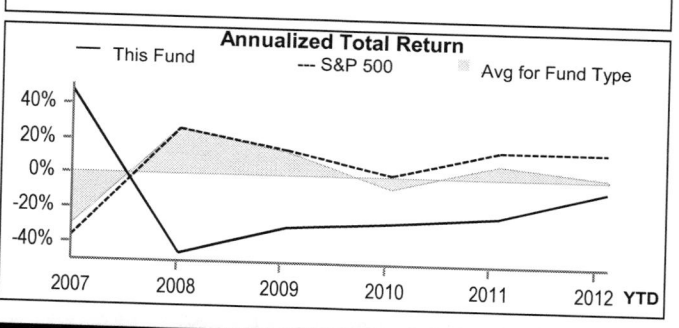

*ProShares UltraShort Euro (EUO)

D-   Weak

Fund Family: ProShare Advisors LLC
Fund Type: Foreign
Inception Date: November 25, 2008

Major Rating Factors:
Disappointing performance is the major factor driving the D- (Weak) TheStreet.com Investment Rating for *ProShares UltraShort Euro. The fund currently has a performance rating of D- (Weak) based on an annualized return of 0.16% over the last three years and a total return of -2.21% year to date 2012. Factored into the performance evaluation is an expense ratio of 0.95% (low).

The fund's risk rating is currently C+ (Fair). It carries a beta of -1.03, meaning the fund's expected move will be -10.3% for every 10% move in the market. Volatility, as measured by both the semi-deviation and a drawdown factor, is considered low. As of December 31, 2012, *ProShares UltraShort Euro traded at a premium of 2.26% above its net asset value, which is worse than its one-year historical average discount of .02%.

Michael Neches currently receives a manager quality ranking of 78 (0=worst, 99=best). This fund offers only a moderate level of risk but investors looking for strong performance are still waiting.

Data Date	Investment Rating	Net Assets ($Mil)	Price	Performance Rating/Pts	Total Return Y-T-D	Risk Rating/Pts
12-12	D-	530.60	19.01	D- / 1.1	-2.21%	C+ / 6.5
2011	D	1,095.10	20.35	D / 2.0	3.24%	C+ / 6.6
2010	D+	444.40	20.31	D+ / 2.8	8.61%	C+ / 5.9
2009	D	7.33	18.70	E+ / 0.7	-12.90%	C+ / 6.1

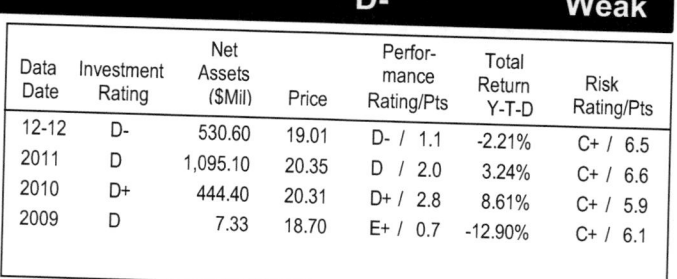

*ProShares UltraShort Financials (SKF)

E   Very Weak

Fund Family: ProShare Advisors LLC
Fund Type: Financial Services
Inception Date: January 30, 2007

Major Rating Factors: Very poor performance is the major factor driving the E (Very Weak) TheStreet.com Investment Rating for *ProShares UltraShort Financials. The fund currently has a performance rating of E- (Very Weak) based on an annualized return of -30.26% over the last three years and a total return of -8.29% year to date 2012. Factored into the performance evaluation is an expense ratio of 0.95% (low).

The fund's risk rating is currently C- (Fair). It carries a beta of -1.89, meaning the fund's expected move will be -18.9% for every 10% move in the market. Volatility, as measured by both the semi-deviation and a drawdown factor, is considered average. As of December 31, 2012, *ProShares UltraShort Financials traded at a premium of 9.11% above its net asset value, which is worse than its one-year historical average premium of .01%.

Hratch Najarian has been running the fund for 2 years and currently receives a manager quality ranking of 5 (0=worst, 99=best). This fund offers an average level of risk but investors looking for strong performance will be frustrated.

Data Date	Investment Rating	Net Assets ($Mil)	Price	Performance Rating/Pts	Total Return Y-T-D	Risk Rating/Pts
12-12	E	168.90	33.54	E- / 0.2	-8.29%	C- / 3.3
2011	E-	350.30	59.32	E- / 0.2	-5.09%	D / 1.9
2010	E-	389.10	15.67	E- / 0.2	-35.33%	D- / 1.0
2009	E-	1,204.27	24.23	E- / 0.1	-76.26%	D- / 1.5

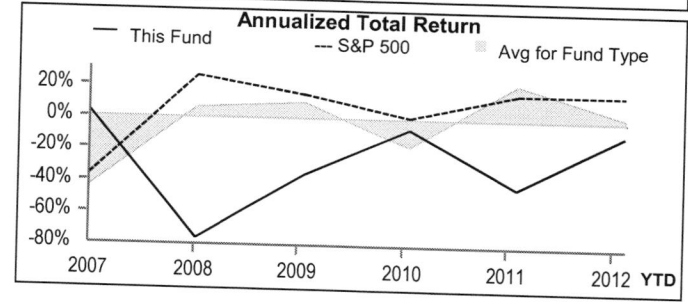

* Denotes ETF Fund

*ProShares UltraShort FTSE China (FXP)

			E	Very Weak

Fund Family: ProShare Advisors LLC
Fund Type: Foreign
Inception Date: November 6, 2007

Major Rating Factors: Very poor performance is the major factor driving the E (Very Weak) TheStreet.com Investment Rating for *ProShares UltraShort FTSE China. The fund currently has a performance rating of E (Very Weak) based on an annualized return of -26.75% over the last three years and a total return of -3.64% year to date 2012. Factored into the performance evaluation is an expense ratio of 0.95% (low).

The fund's risk rating is currently C- (Fair). It carries a beta of -1.73, meaning the fund's expected move will be -17.3% for every 10% move in the market. Volatility, as measured by both the semi-deviation and a drawdown factor, is considered average. As of December 31, 2012, *ProShares UltraShort FTSE China traded at a premium of 3.72% above its net asset value, which is worse than its one-year historical average discount of .05%.

Alexander V. Ilyasov has been running the fund for 4 years and currently receives a manager quality ranking of 5 (0=worst, 99=best). This fund offers an average level of risk but investors looking for strong performance will be frustrated.

Data Date	Investment Rating	Net Assets ($Mil)	Price	Perfor- mance Rating/Pts	Total Return Y-T-D	Risk Rating/Pts
12-12	E	111.50	17.58	E / 0.3	-3.64%	C- / 3.0
2011	E-	192.70	30.37	E / 0.4	-2.21%	D / 2.2
2010	E-	211.10	30.08	E- / 0.1	-28.29%	D- / 1.0
2009	E-	169.69	8.39	E- / 0.1	-72.69%	D- / 1.1

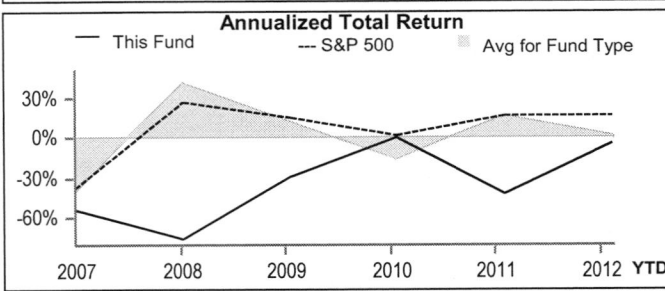

*ProShares UltraShort Gold (GLL)

			E	Very Weak

Fund Family: ProShare Advisors LLC
Fund Type: Energy/Natural Resources
Inception Date: December 2, 2008

Major Rating Factors: Very poor performance is the major factor driving the E (Very Weak) TheStreet.com Investment Rating for *ProShares UltraShort Gold. The fund currently has a performance rating of E (Very Weak) based on an annualized return of -31.04% over the last three years and a total return of 0.89% year to date 2012. Factored into the performance evaluation is an expense ratio of 0.95% (low).

The fund's risk rating is currently C- (Fair). It carries a beta of -0.35, meaning the fund's expected move will be -3.5% for every 10% move in the market. Volatility, as measured by both the semi-deviation and a drawdown factor, is considered average. As of December 31, 2012, *ProShares UltraShort Gold traded at a discount of 1.60% below its net asset value, which is better than its one-year historical average discount of .29%.

Michael Neches currently receives a manager quality ranking of 2 (0=worst, 99=best). This fund offers an average level of risk but investors looking for strong performance will be frustrated.

Data Date	Investment Rating	Net Assets ($Mil)	Price	Perfor- mance Rating/Pts	Total Return Y-T-D	Risk Rating/Pts
12-12	E	94.40	62.60	E / 0.4	0.89%	C- / 3.4
2011	E	194.20	19.81	E / 0.3	-7.12%	C- / 3.4
2010	E+	81.10	27.80	E- / 0.1	-46.28%	C / 4.5
2009	E+	3.88	10.35	E- / 0.2	-46.29%	C / 4.4

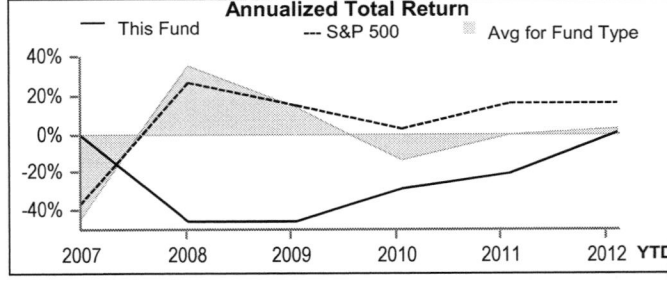

*ProShares UltraShort Health Care (RXD)

			E+	Very Weak

Fund Family: ProShare Advisors LLC
Fund Type: Health
Inception Date: January 30, 2007

Major Rating Factors:
Very poor performance is the major factor driving the E+ (Very Weak) TheStreet.com Investment Rating for *ProShares UltraShort Health Care. The fund currently has a performance rating of E (Very Weak) based on an annualized return of -27.07% over the last three years and a total return of -10.02% year to date 2012. Factored into the performance evaluation is an expense ratio of 0.95% (low).

The fund's risk rating is currently C- (Fair). It carries a beta of -1.21, meaning the fund's expected move will be -12.1% for every 10% move in the market. Volatility, as measured by both the semi-deviation and a drawdown factor, is considered average. As of December 31, 2012, *ProShares UltraShort Health Care traded at a premium of 11.27% above its net asset value, which is worse than its one-year historical average premium of .06%.

Hratch Najarian has been running the fund for 2 years and currently receives a manager quality ranking of 7 (0=worst, 99=best). This fund offers an average level of risk but investors looking for strong performance will be frustrated.

Data Date	Investment Rating	Net Assets ($Mil)	Price	Perfor- mance Rating/Pts	Total Return Y-T-D	Risk Rating/Pts
12-12	E+	5.20	56.06	E / 0.3	-10.02%	C- / 4.2
2011	E+	3.10	20.55	E / 0.5	-2.19%	C- / 4.0
2010	E	4.40	29.22	E+ / 0.6	-15.62%	D+ / 2.8
2009	E	12.34	34.63	E / 0.3	-37.01%	C- / 3.6

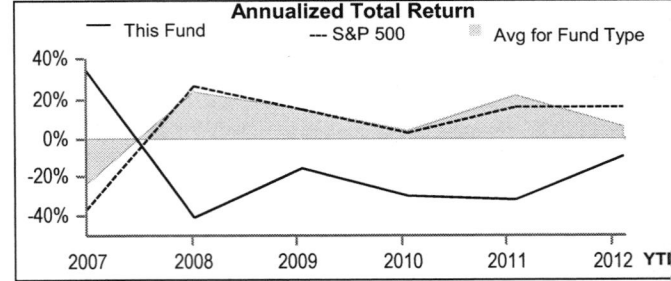

*ProShares UltraShort Industrials (SIJ)

E   **Very Weak**

Fund Family: ProShare Advisors LLC
Fund Type: Income
Inception Date: January 30, 2007

Major Rating Factors: Very poor performance is the major factor driving the E (Very Weak) TheStreet.com Investment Rating for *ProShares UltraShort Industrials. The fund currently has a performance rating of E- (Very Weak) based on an annualized return of -34.12% over the last three years and a total return of -6.44% year to date 2012. Factored into the performance evaluation is an expense ratio of 0.95% (low).

The fund's risk rating is currently C- (Fair). It carries a beta of -2.37, meaning the fund's expected move will be -23.7% for every 10% move in the market. Volatility, as measured by both the semi-deviation and a drawdown factor, is considered average. As of December 31, 2012, *ProShares UltraShort Industrials traded at a premium of 6.89% above its net asset value, which is worse than its one-year historical average premium of .04%.

Hratch Najarian has been running the fund for 2 years and currently receives a manager quality ranking of 7 (0=worst, 99=best). This fund offers an average level of risk but investors looking for strong performance will be frustrated.

Data Date	Investment Rating	Net Assets ($Mil)	Price	Performance Rating/Pts	Total Return Y-T-D	Risk Rating/Pts
12-12	E	6.70	27.63	E- / 0.2	-6.44%	C- / 3.6
2011	E-	7.00	41.56	E / 0.3	-4.33%	D+ / 2.6
2010	E-	8.90	13.07	E / 0.3	-46.26%	D- / 1.3
2009	E-	35.75	24.32	E- / 0.1	-52.04%	D+ / 2.3

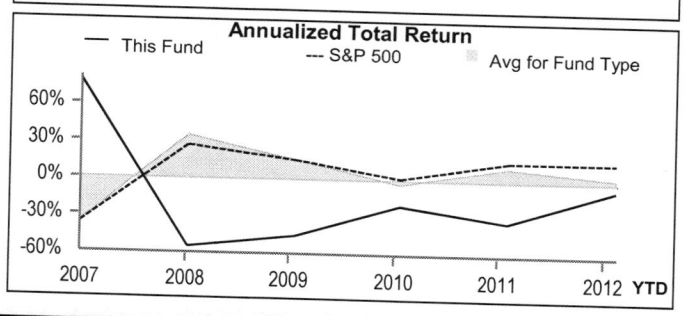

*ProShares UltraShort MidCap 400 (MZZ)

E   **Very Weak**

Fund Family: ProShare Advisors LLC
Fund Type: Growth
Inception Date: July 11, 2006

Major Rating Factors: Very poor performance is the major factor driving the E (Very Weak) TheStreet.com Investment Rating for *ProShares UltraShort MidCap 400. The fund currently has a performance rating of E- (Very Weak) based on an annualized return of -34.55% over the last three years and a total return of -6.99% year to date 2012. Factored into the performance evaluation is an expense ratio of 0.95% (low).

The fund's risk rating is currently C- (Fair). It carries a beta of -2.16, meaning the fund's expected move will be -21.6% for every 10% move in the market. Volatility, as measured by both the semi-deviation and a drawdown factor, is considered average. As of December 31, 2012, *ProShares UltraShort MidCap 400 traded at a premium of 7.56% above its net asset value, which is worse than its one-year historical average premium of .02%.

Howard Rubin has been running the fund for 6 years and currently receives a manager quality ranking of 6 (0=worst, 99=best). This fund offers an average level of risk but investors looking for strong performance will be frustrated.

Data Date	Investment Rating	Net Assets ($Mil)	Price	Performance Rating/Pts	Total Return Y-T-D	Risk Rating/Pts
12-12	E	25.20	25.31	E- / 0.2	-6.99%	C- / 4.0
2011	E	40.80	38.03	E / 0.3	-2.34%	D+ / 2.9
2010	E-	19.60	11.89	E- / 0.2	-46.22%	D / 1.8
2009	E	61.46	22.11	E / 0.4	-59.99%	D+ / 2.8

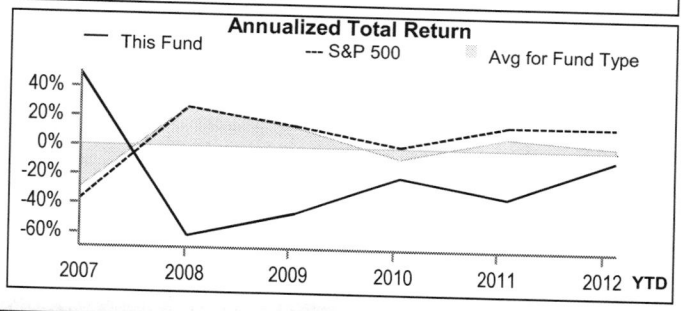

*ProShares UltraShort MSCI Brazil (BZQ)

E   **Very Weak**

Fund Family: ProShare Advisors LLC
Fund Type: Foreign
Inception Date: June 16, 2009

Major Rating Factors: *ProShares UltraShort MSCI Brazil has adopted a risky asset allocation strategy and currently receives an overall TheStreet.com Investment Rating of E (Very Weak). The fund has an above average level of volatility, as measured by both semi-deviation and drawdown factors. It carries a beta of -2.36, meaning the fund's expected move will be -23.6% for every 10% move in the market. As of December 31, 2012, *ProShares UltraShort MSCI Brazil traded at a premium of 2.19% above its net asset value, which is worse than its one-year historical average discount of .01%. Unfortunately, the high level of risk (D+, Weak) failed to pay off as investors endured very poor performance.

The fund's performance rating is currently E+ (Very Weak). It has registered an annualized return of -13.19% over the last three years and is down -2.23% year to date 2012. Factored into the performance evaluation is an expense ratio of 0.95% (low).

Alexander V. Ilyasov has been running the fund for 4 years and currently receives a manager quality ranking of 28 (0=worst, 99=best). If you can tolerate high levels of risk in the hope of improved future returns, holding this fund may be an option.

Data Date	Investment Rating	Net Assets ($Mil)	Price	Performance Rating/Pts	Total Return Y-T-D	Risk Rating/Pts
12-12	E	14.20	63.59	E+ / 0.6	-2.23%	D+ / 2.8
2011	D-	17.00	18.95	C- / 3.9	-4.64%	D+ / 2.4
2010	E-	18.80	15.06	E- / 0.2	-34.97%	D / 1.9

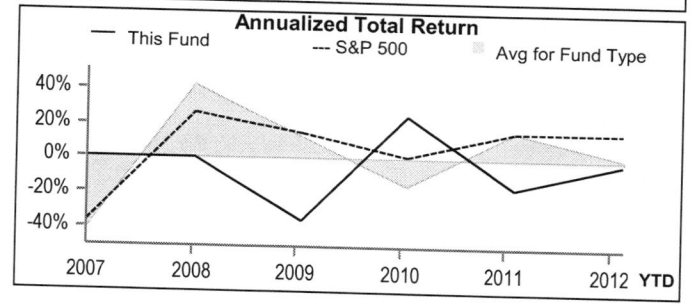

*ProShares UltraShort MSCI EAFE (EFU)

E **Very Weak**

Fund Family: ProShare Advisors LLC
Fund Type: Foreign
Inception Date: October 23, 2007

Major Rating Factors: Very poor performance is the major factor driving the E (Very Weak) TheStreet.com Investment Rating for *ProShares UltraShort MSCI EAFE. The fund currently has a performance rating of E (Very Weak) based on an annualized return of -23.93% over the last three years and a total return of -4.13% year to date 2012. Factored into the performance evaluation is an expense ratio of 0.95% (low).

The fund's risk rating is currently C- (Fair). It carries a beta of -1.91, meaning the fund's expected move will be -19.1% for every 10% move in the market. Volatility, as measured by both the semi-deviation and a drawdown factor, is considered average. As of December 31, 2012, *ProShares UltraShort MSCI EAFE traded at a premium of 4.11% above its net asset value, which is worse than its one-year historical average discount of .04%.

Alexander V. Ilyasov has been running the fund for 4 years and currently receives a manager quality ranking of 6 (0=worst, 99=best). This fund offers an average level of risk but investors looking for strong performance will be frustrated.

Data Date	Investment Rating	Net Assets ($Mil)	Price	Performance Rating/Pts	Total Return Y-T-D	Risk Rating/Pts
12-12	E	11.20	16.47	E / 0.4	-4.13%	C- / 3.4
2011	E	27.20	25.94	E+ / 0.6	1.12%	D+ / 2.9
2010	E-	18.00	26.70	E / 0.3	-30.72%	D / 1.9
2009	E	56.21	38.54	E- / 0.2	-55.40%	D+ / 2.7

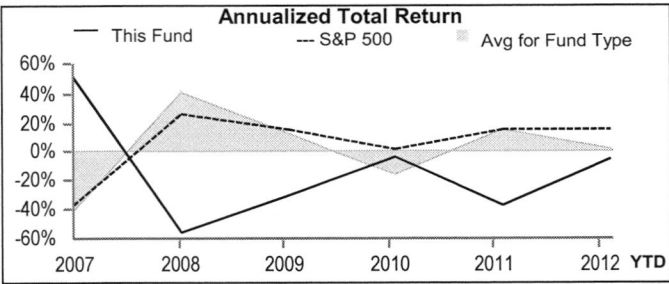

*ProShares UltraShort MSCI Emg Mk (EEV)

E **Very Weak**

Fund Family: ProShare Advisors LLC
Fund Type: Emerging Market
Inception Date: October 30, 2007

Major Rating Factors: *ProShares UltraShort MSCI Emg Mk has adopted a risky asset allocation strategy and currently receives an overall TheStreet.com Investment Rating of E (Very Weak). The fund has an above average level of volatility, as measured by both semi-deviation and drawdown factors. It carries a beta of -2.02, meaning the fund's expected move will be -20.2% for every 10% move in the market. As of December 31, 2012, *ProShares UltraShort MSCI Emg Mk traded at a premium of .67% above its net asset value, which is worse than its one-year historical average discount of .02%. Unfortunately, the high level of risk (D+, Weak) failed to pay off as investors endured very poor performance.

The fund's performance rating is currently E (Very Weak). It has registered an annualized return of -26.47% over the last three years and is down -0.71% year to date 2012. Factored into the performance evaluation is an expense ratio of 0.95% (low).

Alexander V. Ilyasov has been running the fund for 4 years and currently receives a manager quality ranking of 5 (0=worst, 99=best). If you can tolerate high levels of risk in the hope of improved future returns, holding this fund may be an option.

Data Date	Investment Rating	Net Assets ($Mil)	Price	Performance Rating/Pts	Total Return Y-T-D	Risk Rating/Pts
12-12	E	48.60	21.18	E / 0.3	-0.71%	D+ / 3.0
2011	E-	91.60	34.32	E / 0.3	-2.13%	D / 2.0
2010	E-	103.80	31.71	E- / 0.1	-41.82%	D- / 1.2
2009	E-	207.08	10.90	E- / 0	-76.97%	D- / 1.3

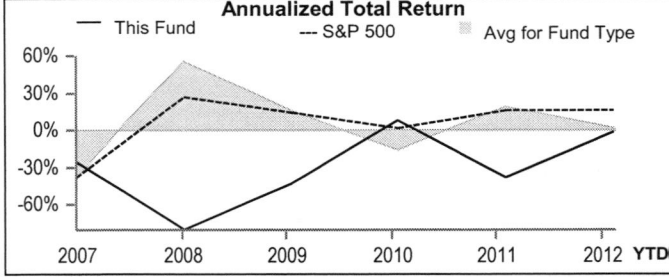

*ProShares UltraShort MSCI Europe (EPV)

E **Very Weak**

Fund Family: ProShare Advisors LLC
Fund Type: Foreign
Inception Date: June 16, 2009

Major Rating Factors: Very poor performance is the major factor driving the E (Very Weak) TheStreet.com Investment Rating for *ProShares UltraShort MSCI Europe. The fund currently has a performance rating of E- (Very Weak) based on an annualized return of -33.55% over the last three years and a total return of -4.87% year to date 2012. Factored into the performance evaluation is an expense ratio of 0.95% (low).

The fund's risk rating is currently C- (Fair). It carries a beta of -2.16, meaning the fund's expected move will be -21.6% for every 10% move in the market. Volatility, as measured by both the semi-deviation and a drawdown factor, is considered average. As of December 31, 2012, *ProShares UltraShort MSCI Europe traded at a premium of 5.33% above its net asset value, which is worse than its one-year historical average premium of .02%.

Howard Rubin has been running the fund for 4 years and currently receives a manager quality ranking of 3 (0=worst, 99=best). This fund offers an average level of risk but investors looking for strong performance will be frustrated.

Data Date	Investment Rating	Net Assets ($Mil)	Price	Performance Rating/Pts	Total Return Y-T-D	Risk Rating/Pts
12-12	E	84.80	26.10	E- / 0.2	-4.87%	C- / 3.1
2011	E	149.20	46.60	D- / 1.0	1.67%	C- / 3.3
2010	E	51.40	14.29	E- / 0.1	-34.66%	C- / 3.2

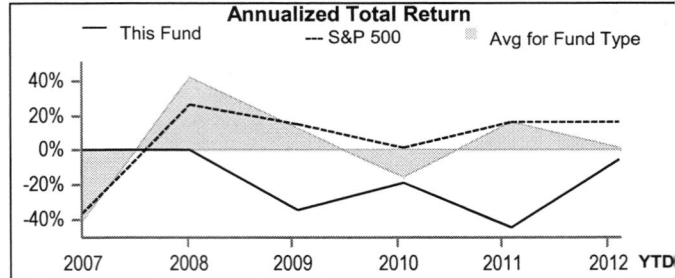

*ProShares UltraShort MSCI Japan (EWV)

Fund Family: ProShare Advisors LLC
Fund Type: Foreign
Inception Date: November 6, 2007

E+   Very Weak

Major Rating Factors:
Very poor performance is the major factor driving the E+ (Very Weak) TheStreet.com Investment Rating for *ProShares UltraShort MSCI Japan. The fund currently has a performance rating of E (Very Weak) based on an annualized return of -12.64% over the last three years and a total return of -2.65% year to date 2012. Factored into the performance evaluation is an expense ratio of 0.95% (low).

The fund's risk rating is currently C (Fair). It carries a beta of -1.15, meaning the fund's expected move will be -11.5% for every 10% move in the market. Volatility, as measured by both the semi-deviation and a drawdown factor, is considered average. As of December 31, 2012, *ProShares UltraShort MSCI Japan traded at a premium of 3.02% above its net asset value, which is worse than its one-year historical average premium of .02%.

Alexander V. Ilyasov has been running the fund for 4 years and currently receives a manager quality ranking of 10 (0=worst, 99=best). This fund offers an average level of risk but investors looking for strong performance will be frustrated.

Data Date	Investment Rating	Net Assets ($Mil)	Price	Perfor- mance Rating/Pts	Total Return Y-T-D	Risk Rating/Pts
12-12	E+	10.90	29.01	E / 0.5	-2.65%	C / 5.3
2011	E+	17.10	37.92	D- / 1.1	0.47%	C- / 3.9
2010	E	12.80	34.00	E / 0.4	-30.85%	C- / 3.2
2009	E+	13.23	49.17	E / 0.4	-26.12%	C- / 4.1

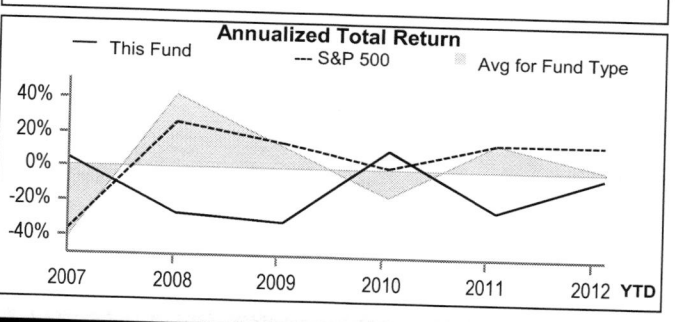

*ProShares UltraShort MSCI Mex In (SMK)

Fund Family: ProShare Advisors LLC
Fund Type: Foreign
Inception Date: June 16, 2009

E-   Very Weak

Major Rating Factors: Very poor performance is the major factor driving the E- (Very Weak) TheStreet.com Investment Rating for *ProShares UltraShort MSCI Mex In. The fund currently has a performance rating of E- (Very Weak) based on an annualized return of -39.05% over the last three years and a total return of -8.42% year to date 2012. Factored into the performance evaluation is an expense ratio of 0.95% (low).

The fund's risk rating is currently C- (Fair). It carries a beta of -1.70, meaning the fund's expected move will be -17.0% for every 10% move in the market. Volatility, as measured by both the semi-deviation and a drawdown factor, is considered average. As of December 31, 2012, *ProShares UltraShort MSCI Mex In traded at a premium of 9.34% above its net asset value, which is worse than its one-year historical average premium of .13%.

Alexander V. Ilyasov has been running the fund for 4 years and currently receives a manager quality ranking of 2 (0=worst, 99=best). This fund offers an average level of risk but investors looking for strong performance will be frustrated.

Data Date	Investment Rating	Net Assets ($Mil)	Price	Perfor- mance Rating/Pts	Total Return Y-T-D	Risk Rating/Pts
12-12	E-	1.20	24.81	E- / 0.1	-8.42%	C- / 3.0
2011	E	2.50	49.44	D- / 1.2	-1.13%	C- / 3.1
2010	E	2.60	13.26	E- / 0.1	-49.66%	D+ / 2.5

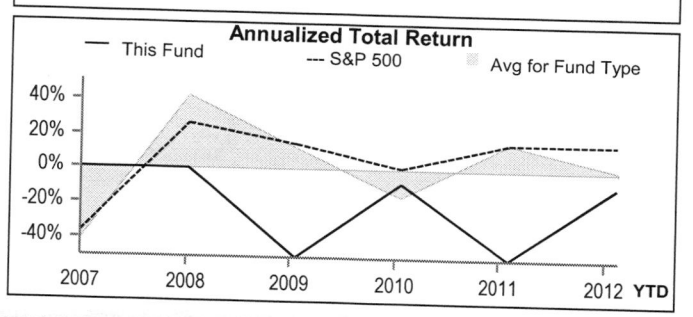

*ProShares UltraShort MSCI PXJ (JPX)

Fund Family: ProShare Advisors LLC
Fund Type: Foreign
Inception Date: June 16, 2009

E   Very Weak

Major Rating Factors: Very poor performance is the major factor driving the E (Very Weak) TheStreet.com Investment Rating for *ProShares UltraShort MSCI PXJ. The fund currently has a performance rating of E- (Very Weak) based on an annualized return of -31.91% over the last three years and a total return of -5.27% year to date 2012. Factored into the performance evaluation is an expense ratio of 0.95% (low).

The fund's risk rating is currently C- (Fair). It carries a beta of -2.01, meaning the fund's expected move will be -20.1% for every 10% move in the market. Volatility, as measured by both the semi-deviation and a drawdown factor, is considered average. As of December 31, 2012, *ProShares UltraShort MSCI PXJ traded at a premium of 5.71% above its net asset value, which is worse than its one-year historical average premium of .17%.

Alexander V. Ilyasov has been running the fund for 4 years and currently receives a manager quality ranking of 3 (0=worst, 99=best). This fund offers an average level of risk but investors looking for strong performance will be frustrated.

Data Date	Investment Rating	Net Assets ($Mil)	Price	Perfor- mance Rating/Pts	Total Return Y-T-D	Risk Rating/Pts
12-12	E	1.50	30.19	E- / 0.2	-5.27%	C- / 3.4
2011	E	2.60	52.11	D- / 1.1	-2.80%	D+ / 2.7
2010	E	2.70	10.88	E- / 0.1	-43.22%	D+ / 2.4

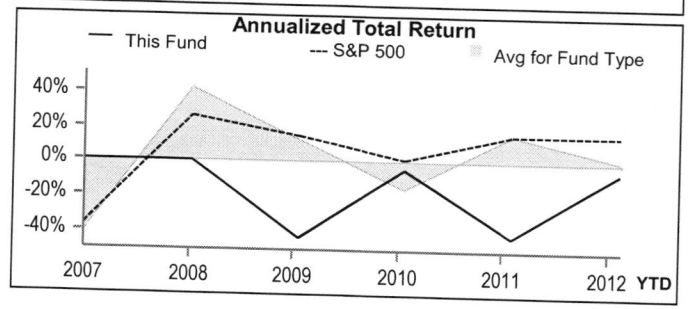

*ProShares UltraShort Nasdaq Biot (BIS) E Very Weak

Fund Family: ProShare Advisors LLC
Fund Type: Health
Inception Date: April 7, 2010

Major Rating Factors: Very poor performance is the major factor driving the E (Very Weak) TheStreet.com Investment Rating for *ProShares UltraShort Nasdaq Biot. The fund currently has a performance rating of E- (Very Weak) based on an annualized return of 0.00% over the last three years and a total return of -11.17% year to date 2012. Factored into the performance evaluation is an expense ratio of 0.95% (low).

The fund's risk rating is currently C- (Fair). It carries a beta of 0.00, meaning the fund's expected move will be 0.0% for every 10% move in the market. Volatility, as measured by both the semi-deviation and a drawdown factor, is considered average. As of December 31, 2012, *ProShares UltraShort Nasdaq Biot traded at a premium of 13.08% above its net asset value, which is worse than its one-year historical average premium of .06%.

Hratch Najarian has been running the fund for 2 years and currently receives a manager quality ranking of 2 (0=worst, 99=best). This fund offers an average level of risk but investors looking for strong performance will be frustrated.

Data Date	Investment Rating	Net Assets ($Mil)	Price	Performance Rating/Pts	Total Return Y-T-D	Risk Rating/Pts
12-12	E	5.00	66.33	E- / 0.1	-11.17%	C- / 3.4
2011	E	1.60	32.60	E / 0.3	-4.39%	C- / 4.0

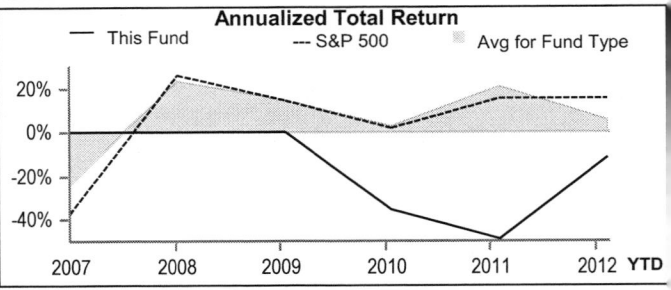

*ProShares UltraShort Oil & Gas (DUG) E Very Weak

Fund Family: ProShare Advisors LLC
Fund Type: Energy/Natural Resources
Inception Date: January 30, 2007

Major Rating Factors: Very poor performance is the major factor driving the E (Very Weak) TheStreet.com Investment Rating for *ProShares UltraShort Oil & Gas. The fund currently has a performance rating of E (Very Weak) based on an annualized return of -30.84% over the last three years and a total return of -7.18% year to date 2012. Factored into the performance evaluation is an expense ratio of 0.95% (low).

The fund's risk rating is currently C- (Fair). It carries a beta of -1.92, meaning the fund's expected move will be -19.2% for every 10% move in the market. Volatility, as measured by both the semi-deviation and a drawdown factor, is considered average. As of December 31, 2012, *ProShares UltraShort Oil & Gas traded at a premium of 8.01% above its net asset value, which is worse than its one-year historical average discount of .01%.

Hratch Najarian has been running the fund for 2 years and currently receives a manager quality ranking of 6 (0=worst, 99=best). This fund offers an average level of risk but investors looking for strong performance will be frustrated.

Data Date	Investment Rating	Net Assets ($Mil)	Price	Performance Rating/Pts	Total Return Y-T-D	Risk Rating/Pts
12-12	E	57.70	21.04	E / 0.3	-7.18%	C- / 3.1
2011	E	89.50	25.63	E / 0.3	-3.75%	C- / 3.0
2010	E	86.20	37.42	E- / 0.2	-41.26%	D+ / 2.6
2009	E	219.57	12.74	E- / 0.2	-43.88%	D+ / 2.7

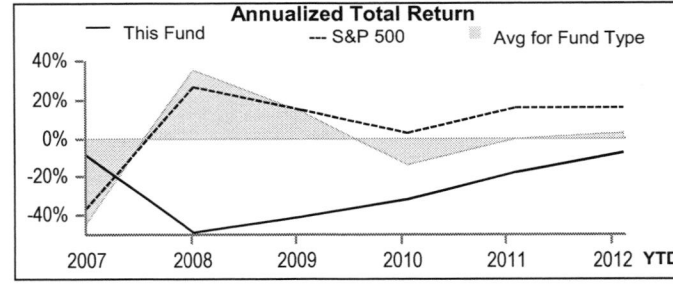

*ProShares UltraShort QQQ (QID) E Very Weak

Fund Family: ProShare Advisors LLC
Fund Type: Growth
Inception Date: July 11, 2006

Major Rating Factors: Very poor performance is the major factor driving the E (Very Weak) TheStreet.com Investment Rating for *ProShares UltraShort QQQ. The fund currently has a performance rating of E (Very Weak) based on an annualized return of -33.61% over the last three years and a total return of -6.68% year to date 2012. Factored into the performance evaluation is an expense ratio of 0.95% (low).

The fund's risk rating is currently C- (Fair). It carries a beta of -2.08, meaning the fund's expected move will be -20.8% for every 10% move in the market. Volatility, as measured by both the semi-deviation and a drawdown factor, is considered average. As of December 31, 2012, *ProShares UltraShort QQQ traded at a premium of 7.16% above its net asset value, which is worse than its one-year historical average discount of .02%.

Howard Rubin has been running the fund for 6 years and currently receives a manager quality ranking of 7 (0=worst, 99=best). This fund offers an average level of risk but investors looking for strong performance will be frustrated.

Data Date	Investment Rating	Net Assets ($Mil)	Price	Performance Rating/Pts	Total Return Y-T-D	Risk Rating/Pts
12-12	E	377.30	29.65	E / 0.3	-6.68%	C- / 4.2
2011	E	601.70	45.13	E- / 0.2	-6.82%	C- / 3.1
2010	E	629.70	11.63	E / 0.3	-38.92%	D / 2.2
2009	E	956.42	19.04	E / 0.4	-63.73%	C- / 3.3

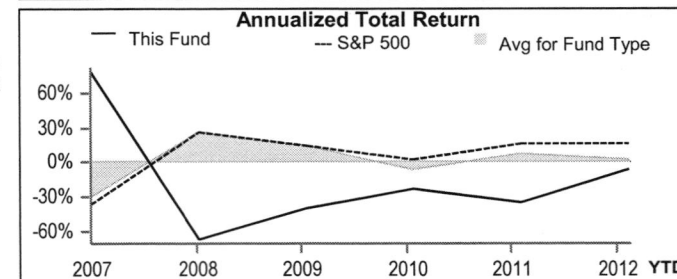

*ProShares UltraShort Real Estate (SRS)

E | **Very Weak**

Fund Family: ProShare Advisors LLC
Fund Type: Income
Inception Date: January 30, 2007

Major Rating Factors: Very poor performance is the major factor driving the E (Very Weak) TheStreet.com Investment Rating for *ProShares UltraShort Real Estate. The fund currently has a performance rating of E- (Very Weak) based on an annualized return of -41.30% over the last three years and a total return of -5.57% year to date 2012. Factored into the performance evaluation is an expense ratio of 0.95% (low).

The fund's risk rating is currently C- (Fair). It carries a beta of -1.84, meaning the fund's expected move will be -18.4% for every 10% move in the market. Volatility, as measured by both the semi-deviation and a drawdown factor, is considered average. As of December 31, 2012, *ProShares UltraShort Real Estate traded at a premium of 5.80% above its net asset value.

Hratch Najarian has been running the fund for 2 years and currently receives a manager quality ranking of 3 (0=worst, 99=best). This fund offers an average level of risk but investors looking for strong performance will be frustrated.

Data Date	Investment Rating	Net Assets ($Mil)	Price	Performance Rating/Pts	Total Return Y-T-D	Risk Rating/Pts
12-12	E	108.90	24.26	E- / 0.1	-5.57%	C- / 4.2
2011	E-	134.80	36.76	E- / 0	-0.16%	D / 1.9
2010	E-	242.40	18.14	E- / 0	-51.63%	D- / 1.0
2009	E-	1,239.19	7.50	E- / 0	-85.91%	D- / 1.1

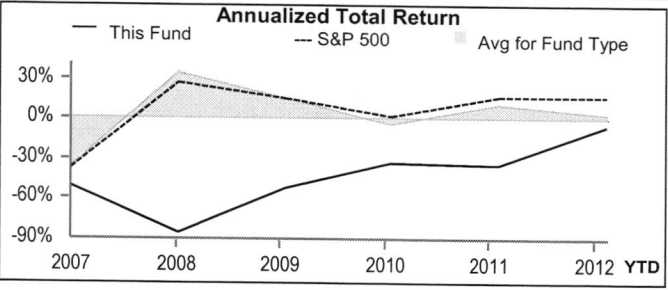

*ProShares UltraShort Russell 300 (TWQ)

E | **Very Weak**

Fund Family: ProShare Advisors LLC
Fund Type: Growth
Inception Date: June 30, 2009

Major Rating Factors: Very poor performance is the major factor driving the E (Very Weak) TheStreet.com Investment Rating for *ProShares UltraShort Russell 300. The fund currently has a performance rating of E (Very Weak) based on an annualized return of -29.13% over the last three years and a total return of -7.90% year to date 2012. Factored into the performance evaluation is an expense ratio of 0.95% (low).

The fund's risk rating is currently C- (Fair). It carries a beta of -2.00, meaning the fund's expected move will be -20.0% for every 10% move in the market. Volatility, as measured by both the semi-deviation and a drawdown factor, is considered average. As of December 31, 2012, *ProShares UltraShort Russell 300 traded at a premium of 8.68% above its net asset value, which is worse than its one-year historical average premium of .17%.

Hratch Najarian has been running the fund for 4 years and currently receives a manager quality ranking of 11 (0=worst, 99=best). This fund offers an average level of risk but investors looking for strong performance will be frustrated.

Data Date	Investment Rating	Net Assets ($Mil)	Price	Performance Rating/Pts	Total Return Y-T-D	Risk Rating/Pts
12-12	E	1.40	46.22	E / 0.3	-7.90%	C- / 3.7
2011	E+	2.00	13.25	E+ / 0.7	-4.53%	C- / 3.9
2010	E+	1.60	16.28	E- / 0.1	-33.82%	C- / 4.2

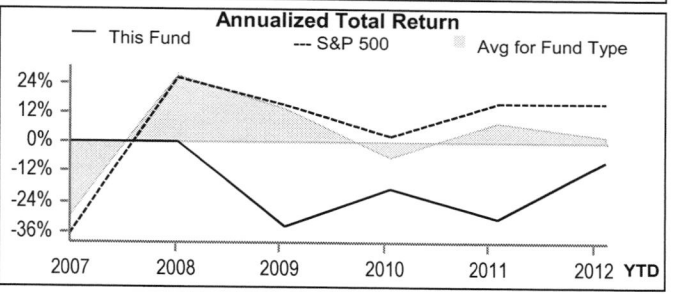

*ProShares UltraShort Russell MC (SJL)

E | **Very Weak**

Fund Family: ProShare Advisors LLC
Fund Type: Growth
Inception Date: February 20, 2007

Major Rating Factors: Very poor performance is the major factor driving the E (Very Weak) TheStreet.com Investment Rating for *ProShares UltraShort Russell MC. The fund currently has a performance rating of E (Very Weak) based on an annualized return of -32.94% over the last three years and a total return of -5.74% year to date 2012. Factored into the performance evaluation is an expense ratio of 0.95% (low).

The fund's risk rating is currently C- (Fair). It carries a beta of -2.10, meaning the fund's expected move will be -21.0% for every 10% move in the market. Volatility, as measured by both the semi-deviation and a drawdown factor, is considered average. As of December 31, 2012, *ProShares UltraShort Russell MC traded at a premium of 6.09% above its net asset value, which is worse than its one-year historical average premium of .59%.

Hratch Najarian has been running the fund for 4 years and currently receives a manager quality ranking of 7 (0=worst, 99=best). This fund offers an average level of risk but investors looking for strong performance will be frustrated.

Data Date	Investment Rating	Net Assets ($Mil)	Price	Performance Rating/Pts	Total Return Y-T-D	Risk Rating/Pts
12-12	E	1.20	32.04	E / 0.3	-5.74%	C- / 4.0
2011	E	1.80	47.63	E / 0.4	1.30%	D+ / 2.6
2010	E-	2.20	14.60	E- / 0.2	-45.07%	D- / 1.4
2009	E-	4.09	26.58	E- / 0.1	-59.92%	D / 2.0

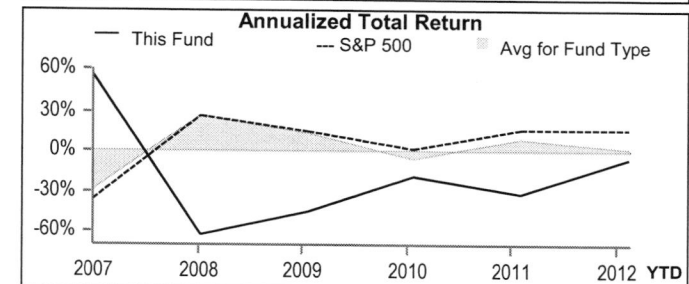

*ProShares UltraShort Russell1000 (SFK)   E   Very Weak

Fund Family: ProShare Advisors LLC
Fund Type: Growth
Inception Date: February 20, 2007

Major Rating Factors: Very poor performance is the major factor driving the E (Very Weak) TheStreet.com Investment Rating for *ProShares UltraShort Russell1000. The fund currently has a performance rating of E (Very Weak) based on an annualized return of -28.84% over the last three years and a total return of -8.62% year to date 2012. Factored into the performance evaluation is an expense ratio of 0.95% (low).

The fund's risk rating is currently C- (Fair). It carries a beta of -2.01, meaning the fund's expected move will be -20.1% for every 10% move in the market. Volatility, as measured by both the semi-deviation and a drawdown factor, is considered average. As of December 31, 2012, *ProShares UltraShort Russell1000 traded at a premium of 9.95% above its net asset value, which is worse than its one-year historical average premium of .03%.

Hratch Najarian has been running the fund for 4 years and currently receives a manager quality ranking of 12 (0=worst, 99=best). This fund offers an average level of risk but investors looking for strong performance will be frustrated.

Data Date	Investment Rating	Net Assets ($Mil)	Price	Performance Rating/Pts	Total Return Y-T-D	Risk Rating/Pts
12-12	E	2.00	54.05	E / 0.3	-8.62%	C- / 3.8
2011	E	5.60	18.47	E / 0.4	-3.18%	C- / 3.4
2010	E	5.20	23.21	E / 0.4	-33.91%	D+ / 2.4
2009	E	17.25	35.12	E- / 0.2	-53.28%	C- / 3.5

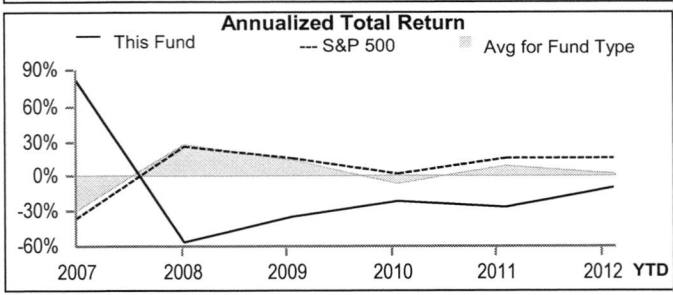

*ProShares UltraShort Russell2000 (SKK)   E   Very Weak

Fund Family: ProShare Advisors LLC
Fund Type: Growth
Inception Date: February 20, 2007

Major Rating Factors: Very poor performance is the major factor driving the E (Very Weak) TheStreet.com Investment Rating for *ProShares UltraShort Russell2000. The fund currently has a performance rating of E- (Very Weak) based on an annualized return of -38.60% over the last three years and a total return of -8.41% year to date 2012. Factored into the performance evaluation is an expense ratio of 0.95% (low).

The fund's risk rating is currently C- (Fair). It carries a beta of -2.49, meaning the fund's expected move will be -24.9% for every 10% move in the market. Volatility, as measured by both the semi-deviation and a drawdown factor, is considered average. As of December 31, 2012, *ProShares UltraShort Russell2000 traded at a premium of 9.59% above its net asset value, which is worse than its one-year historical average discount of .15%.

Hratch Najarian has been running the fund for 4 years and currently receives a manager quality ranking of 5 (0=worst, 99=best). This fund offers an average level of risk but investors looking for strong performance will be frustrated.

Data Date	Investment Rating	Net Assets ($Mil)	Price	Performance Rating/Pts	Total Return Y-T-D	Risk Rating/Pts
12-12	E	6.50	24.12	E- / 0.2	-8.41%	C- / 3.4
2011	E-	17.50	35.39	E- / 0.1	-2.75%	D+ / 2.3
2010	E-	8.00	9.64	E- / 0.2	-51.56%	D- / 1.2
2009	E-	11.43	19.90	E- / 0.1	-60.06%	D / 1.9

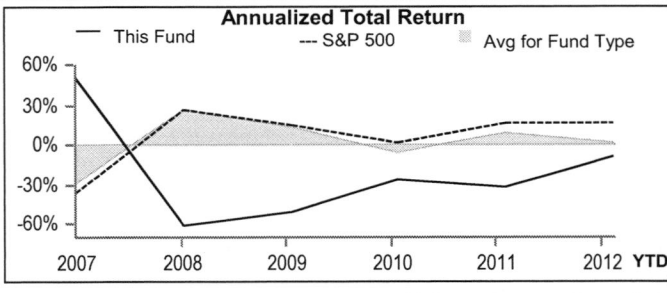

*ProShares UltraShort Russell2000 (TWM)   E   Very Weak

Fund Family: ProShare Advisors LLC
Fund Type: Growth
Inception Date: January 23, 2007

Major Rating Factors: Very poor performance is the major factor driving the E (Very Weak) TheStreet.com Investment Rating for *ProShares UltraShort Russell2000. The fund currently has a performance rating of E- (Very Weak) based on an annualized return of -37.55% over the last three years and a total return of -7.35% year to date 2012. Factored into the performance evaluation is an expense ratio of 0.95% (low).

The fund's risk rating is currently C- (Fair). It carries a beta of -2.44, meaning the fund's expected move will be -24.4% for every 10% move in the market. Volatility, as measured by both the semi-deviation and a drawdown factor, is considered average. As of December 31, 2012, *ProShares UltraShort Russell2000 traded at a premium of 8.10% above its net asset value, which is worse than its one-year historical average discount of .02%.

Hratch Najarian has been running the fund for 4 years and currently receives a manager quality ranking of 5 (0=worst, 99=best). This fund offers an average level of risk but investors looking for strong performance will be frustrated.

Data Date	Investment Rating	Net Assets ($Mil)	Price	Performance Rating/Pts	Total Return Y-T-D	Risk Rating/Pts
12-12	E	264.30	25.35	E- / 0.2	-7.35%	C- / 3.4
2011	E-	297.60	38.61	E- / 0.2	-2.95%	D+ / 2.6
2010	E-	299.00	12.56	E- / 0.2	-50.14%	D / 1.6
2009	E	578.47	25.19	E- / 0.1	-59.03%	D+ / 2.7

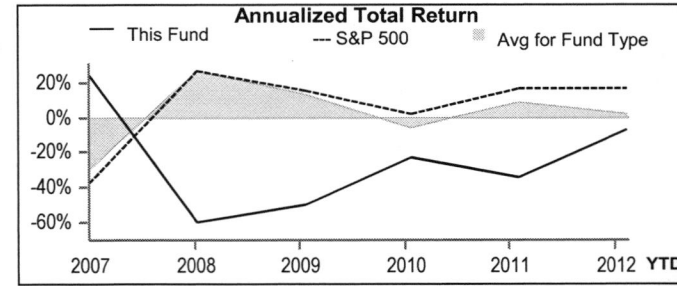

*ProShares UltraShort S&P500 (SDS)

E | **Very Weak**

Fund Family: ProShare Advisors LLC
Fund Type: Growth
Inception Date: July 11, 2006

Major Rating Factors: Very poor performance is the major factor driving the E (Very Weak) TheStreet.com Investment Rating for *ProShares UltraShort S&P500. The fund currently has a performance rating of E (Very Weak) based on an annualized return of -27.77% over the last three years and a total return of -6.28% year to date 2012. Factored into the performance evaluation is an expense ratio of 0.89% (low).

The fund's risk rating is currently C- (Fair). It carries a beta of -1.91, meaning the fund's expected move will be -19.1% for every 10% move in the market. Volatility, as measured by both the semi-deviation and a drawdown factor, is considered average. As of December 31, 2012, *ProShares UltraShort S&P500 traded at a premium of 6.79% above its net asset value.

Hratch Najarian has been running the fund for 3 years and currently receives a manager quality ranking of 11 (0=worst, 99=best). This fund offers an average level of risk but investors looking for strong performance will be frustrated.

Data Date	Investment Rating	Net Assets ($Mil)	Price	Performance Rating/Pts	Total Return Y-T-D	Risk Rating/Pts
12-12	E	1,561.00	54.11	E / 0.3	-6.28%	C- / 3.8
2011	E	2,013.10	19.29	E / 0.5	-3.57%	C- / 3.4
2010	E	2,052.80	23.76	E / 0.4	-32.21%	D+ / 2.9
2009	E+	3,872.85	35.05	E / 0.5	-47.35%	C- / 4.2

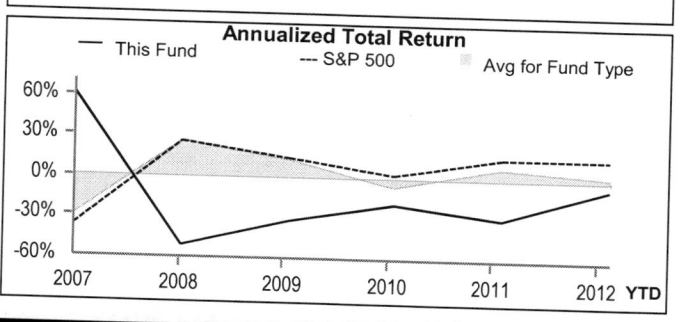

*ProShares UltraShort Semiconduct (SSG)

E | **Very Weak**

Fund Family: ProShare Advisors LLC
Fund Type: Income
Inception Date: January 30, 2007

Major Rating Factors: Very poor performance is the major factor driving the E (Very Weak) TheStreet.com Investment Rating for *ProShares UltraShort Semiconduct. The fund currently has a performance rating of E (Very Weak) based on an annualized return of -26.64% over the last three years and a total return of -9.22% year to date 2012. Factored into the performance evaluation is an expense ratio of 0.95% (low).

The fund's risk rating is currently C- (Fair). It carries a beta of -2.41, meaning the fund's expected move will be -24.1% for every 10% move in the market. Volatility, as measured by both the semi-deviation and a drawdown factor, is considered average. As of December 31, 2012, *ProShares UltraShort Semiconduct traded at a premium of 10.56% above its net asset value, which is worse than its one-year historical average discount of .01%.

Hratch Najarian has been running the fund for 2 years and currently receives a manager quality ranking of 38 (0=worst, 99=best). This fund offers an average level of risk but investors looking for strong performance will be frustrated.

Data Date	Investment Rating	Net Assets ($Mil)	Price	Performance Rating/Pts	Total Return Y-T-D	Risk Rating/Pts
12-12	E	10.60	41.56	E / 0.4	-9.22%	C- / 3.5
2011	E-	15.00	45.59	E- / 0.1	-6.01%	D+ / 2.3
2010	E-	20.10	11.17	E- / 0.2	-38.59%	D- / 1.1
2009	E-	34.53	18.19	E- / 0	-74.59%	D / 1.7

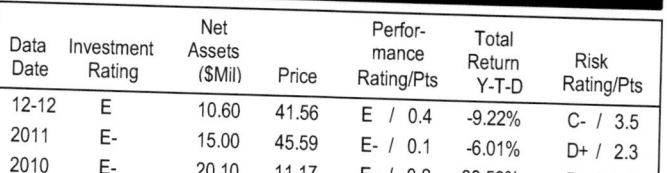
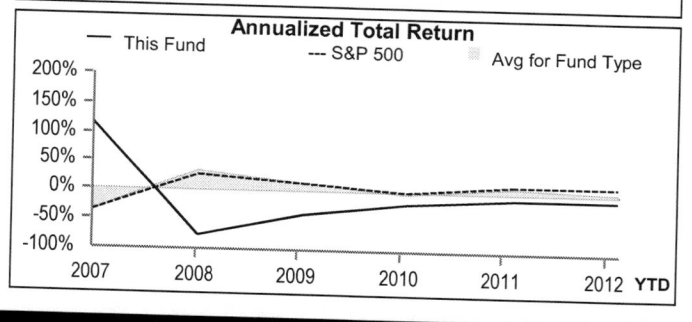

*ProShares UltraShort Silver (ZSL)

E- | **Very Weak**

Fund Family: ProShare Advisors LLC
Fund Type: Energy/Natural Resources
Inception Date: December 2, 2008

Major Rating Factors: *ProShares UltraShort Silver has adopted a very risky asset allocation strategy and currently receives an overall TheStreet.com Investment Rating of E- (Very Weak). The fund has a high level of volatility, as measured by both semi-deviation and drawdown factors. It carries a beta of -1.74, meaning the fund's expected move will be -17.4% for every 10% move in the market. As of December 31, 2012, *ProShares UltraShort Silver traded at a premium of 3.54% above its net asset value, which is worse than its one-year historical average discount of 1.08%. Unfortunately, the high level of risk (D, Weak) failed to pay off as investors endured very poor performance.

The fund's performance rating is currently E- (Very Weak). It has registered an annualized return of -60.50% over the last three years and is down -2.27% year to date 2012. Factored into the performance evaluation is an expense ratio of 0.95% (low).

Michael Neches currently receives a manager quality ranking of 0 (0=worst, 99=best). If you can tolerate very high levels of risk in the hope of improved future returns, holding this fund may be an option.

Data Date	Investment Rating	Net Assets ($Mil)	Price	Performance Rating/Pts	Total Return Y-T-D	Risk Rating/Pts
12-12	E-	105.80	50.07	E- / 0	-2.27%	D / 1.9
2011	E-	245.30	15.87	E- / 0	-7.56%	D / 1.9
2010	E-	99.10	9.82	E- / 0	-79.50%	D- / 1.4
2009	E-	1.96	4.79	E- / 0	-71.91%	D / 1.8

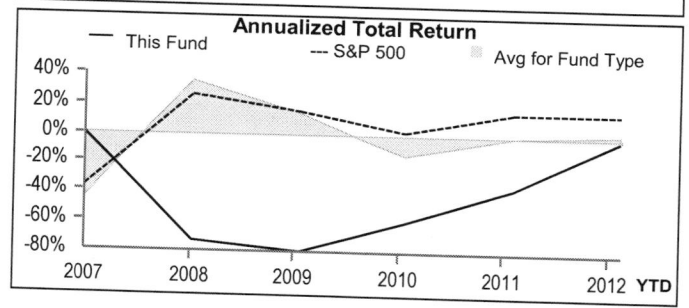

* Denotes ETF Fund

*ProShares UltraShort SmallCap 60 (SDD)

E **Very Weak**

Fund Family: ProShare Advisors LLC
Fund Type: Growth
Inception Date: January 23, 2007

Major Rating Factors: Very poor performance is the major factor driving the E (Very Weak) TheStreet.com Investment Rating for *ProShares UltraShort SmallCap 60. The fund currently has a performance rating of E- (Very Weak) based on an annualized return of -37.91% over the last three years and a total return of -5.97% year to date 2012. Factored into the performance evaluation is an expense ratio of 0.95% (low).

The fund's risk rating is currently C- (Fair). It carries a beta of -2.29, meaning the fund's expected move will be -22.9% for every 10% move in the market. Volatility, as measured by both the semi-deviation and a drawdown factor, is considered average. As of December 31, 2012, *ProShares UltraShort SmallCap 60 traded at a premium of 6.48% above its net asset value, which is worse than its one-year historical average discount of .09%.

Hratch Najarian has been running the fund for 3 years and currently receives a manager quality ranking of 5 (0=worst, 99=best). This fund offers an average level of risk but investors looking for strong performance will be frustrated.

Data Date	Investment Rating	Net Assets ($Mil)	Price	Performance Rating/Pts	Total Return Y-T-D	Risk Rating/Pts
12-12	E	8.30	25.80	E- / 0.2	-5.97%	C- / 3.4
2011	E-	18.10	38.51	E- / 0.1	-2.30%	D+ / 2.6
2010	E-	15.30	13.59	E- / 0.2	-48.39%	D- / 1.5
2009	E-	24.73	26.33	E- / 0.1	-56.67%	D+ / 2.7

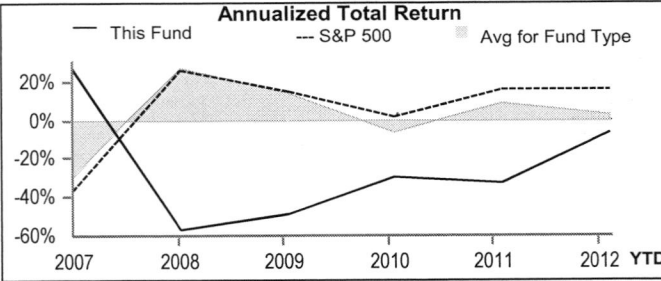

*ProShares UltraShort Technology (REW)

E+ **Very Weak**

Fund Family: ProShare Advisors LLC
Fund Type: Growth
Inception Date: January 30, 2007

Major Rating Factors:
Very poor performance is the major factor driving the E+ (Very Weak) TheStreet.com Investment Rating for *ProShares UltraShort Technology. The fund currently has a performance rating of E (Very Weak) based on an annualized return of -26.76% over the last three years and a total return of -4.95% year to date 2012. Factored into the performance evaluation is an expense ratio of 0.95% (low).

The fund's risk rating is currently C- (Fair). It carries a beta of -2.24, meaning the fund's expected move will be -22.4% for every 10% move in the market. Volatility, as measured by both the semi-deviation and a drawdown factor, is considered average. As of December 31, 2012, *ProShares UltraShort Technology traded at a premium of 5.11% above its net asset value, which is worse than its one-year historical average discount of .03%.

Hratch Najarian has been running the fund for 2 years and currently receives a manager quality ranking of 18 (0=worst, 99=best). This fund offers an average level of risk but investors looking for strong performance will be frustrated.

Data Date	Investment Rating	Net Assets ($Mil)	Price	Performance Rating/Pts	Total Return Y-T-D	Risk Rating/Pts
12-12	E+	12.50	37.00	E / 0.4	-4.95%	C- / 4.2
2011	E	13.40	51.06	E / 0.3	-5.56%	C- / 3.0
2010	E-	18.60	15.51	E / 0.3	-30.82%	D / 2.0
2009	E-	36.39	22.42	E- / 0	-68.81%	D+ / 2.7

*ProShares UltraShort Telecomncti (TLL)

E+ **Very Weak**

Fund Family: ProShare Advisors LLC
Fund Type: Income
Inception Date: March 25, 2008

Major Rating Factors:
Very poor performance is the major factor driving the E+ (Very Weak) TheStreet.com Investment Rating for *ProShares UltraShort Telecomncti. The fund currently has a performance rating of E (Very Weak) based on an annualized return of -29.39% over the last three years and a total return of -8.05% year to date 2012. Factored into the performance evaluation is an expense ratio of 0.95% (low).

The fund's risk rating is currently C (Fair). It carries a beta of -1.60, meaning the fund's expected move will be -16.0% for every 10% move in the market. Volatility, as measured by both the semi-deviation and a drawdown factor, is considered average. As of December 31, 2012, *ProShares UltraShort Telecomncti traded at a premium of 9.16% above its net asset value, which is worse than its one-year historical average premium of .22%.

Hratch Najarian has been running the fund for 2 years and currently receives a manager quality ranking of 10 (0=worst, 99=best). This fund offers an average level of risk but investors looking for strong performance will be frustrated.

Data Date	Investment Rating	Net Assets ($Mil)	Price	Performance Rating/Pts	Total Return Y-T-D	Risk Rating/Pts
12-12	E+	1.70	29.19	E / 0.3	-8.05%	C / 4.5
2011	E	2.60	42.74	E+ / 0.7	0.98%	D+ / 2.8
2010	E-	2.00	8.84	E- / 0.1	-37.96%	D- / 1.3
2009	E-	2.33	14.25	E- / 0.2	-50.15%	D- / 1.1

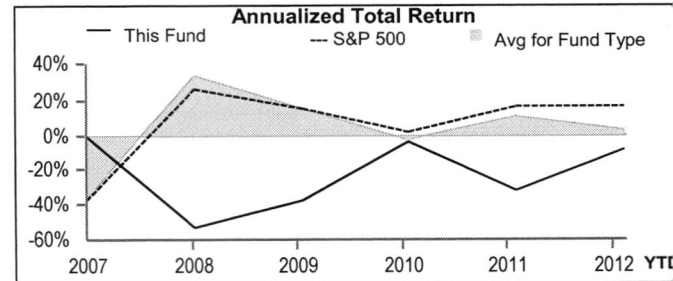

*ProShares UltraShort TIPS (TPS)

D | **Weak**

Fund Family: ProShare Advisors LLC
Fund Type: Growth
Inception Date: February 9, 2011

Major Rating Factors:

Very poor performance is the major factor driving the D (Weak) TheStreet.com Investment Rating for *ProShares UltraShort TIPS. The fund currently has a performance rating of E+ (Very Weak) based on an annualized return of 0.00% over the last three years and a total return of 1.09% year to date 2012. Factored into the performance evaluation is an expense ratio of 0.95% (low).

The fund's risk rating is currently B- (Good). It carries a beta of 0.00, meaning the fund's expected move will be 0.0% for every 10% move in the market. Volatility, as measured by both the semi-deviation and a drawdown factor, is considered low. As of December 31, 2012, *ProShares UltraShort TIPS traded at a discount of .97% below its net asset value.

Michelle Lui has been running the fund for 2 years and currently receives a manager quality ranking of 7 (0=worst, 99=best). This fund offers only a moderate level of risk but investors looking for strong performance are still waiting.

Data Date	Investment Rating	Net Assets ($Mil)	Price	Performance Rating/Pts	Total Return Y-T-D	Risk Rating/Pts
12-12	D	3.80	25.57	E+ / 0.7	1.09%	B- / 7.4

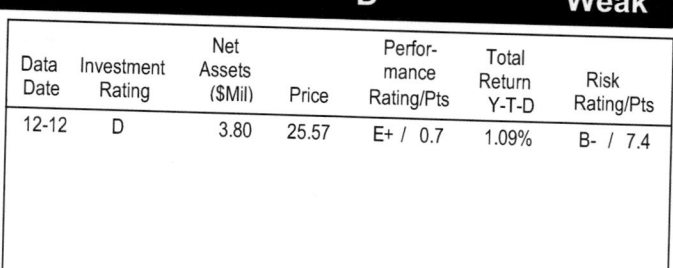

*ProShares UltraShort Utilities (SDP)

D- | **Weak**

Fund Family: ProShare Advisors LLC
Fund Type: Utilities
Inception Date: January 30, 2007

Major Rating Factors:

Very poor performance is the major factor driving the D- (Weak) TheStreet.com Investment Rating for *ProShares UltraShort Utilities. The fund currently has a performance rating of E (Very Weak) based on an annualized return of -22.97% over the last three years and a total return of -4.37% year to date 2012. Factored into the performance evaluation is an expense ratio of 0.95% (low).

The fund's risk rating is currently C+ (Fair). It carries a beta of -1.89, meaning the fund's expected move will be -18.9% for every 10% move in the market. Volatility, as measured by both the semi-deviation and a drawdown factor, is considered low. As of December 31, 2012, *ProShares UltraShort Utilities traded at a premium of 4.76% above its net asset value, which is worse than its one-year historical average premium of .02%.

Hratch Najarian has been running the fund for 2 years and currently receives a manager quality ranking of 16 (0=worst, 99=best). This fund offers only a moderate level of risk but investors looking for strong performance are still waiting.

Data Date	Investment Rating	Net Assets ($Mil)	Price	Performance Rating/Pts	Total Return Y-T-D	Risk Rating/Pts
12-12	D-	2.90	29.74	E / 0.4	-4.37%	C+ / 5.8
2011	E+	3.10	31.14	E+ / 0.6	5.94%	C- / 3.8
2010	E	6.20	16.44	E+ / 0.7	-19.80%	D+ / 2.4
2009	E	12.32	20.50	E / 0.3	-29.85%	C- / 3.1

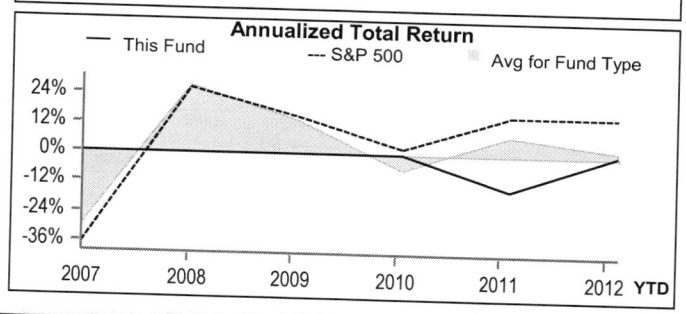

*ProShares UltraShort Yen (YCS)

D | **Weak**

Fund Family: ProShare Advisors LLC
Fund Type: Foreign
Inception Date: November 25, 2008

Major Rating Factors:

Disappointing performance is the major factor driving the D (Weak) TheStreet.com Investment Rating for *ProShares UltraShort Yen. The fund currently has a performance rating of D+ (Weak) based on an annualized return of -4.32% over the last three years and a total return of 5.57% year to date 2012. Factored into the performance evaluation is an expense ratio of 0.95% (low).

The fund's risk rating is currently C+ (Fair). It carries a beta of 0.21, meaning the fund's expected move will be 2.1% for every 10% move in the market. Volatility, as measured by both the semi-deviation and a drawdown factor, is considered low. As of December 31, 2012, *ProShares UltraShort Yen traded at a discount of 5.32% below its net asset value, which is better than its one-year historical average discount of .01%.

Michael Neches currently receives a manager quality ranking of 15 (0=worst, 99=best). This fund offers only a moderate level of risk but investors looking for strong performance are still waiting.

Data Date	Investment Rating	Net Assets ($Mil)	Price	Performance Rating/Pts	Total Return Y-T-D	Risk Rating/Pts
12-12	D	400.90	50.77	D+ / 2.4	5.57%	C+ / 6.5
2011	D-	221.20	40.95	D- / 1.1	0.02%	C+ / 6.0
2010	D	207.70	15.67	E / 0.3	-26.43%	C+ / 6.0
2009	D+	2.17	21.30	D- / 1.2	-3.97%	B- / 7.0

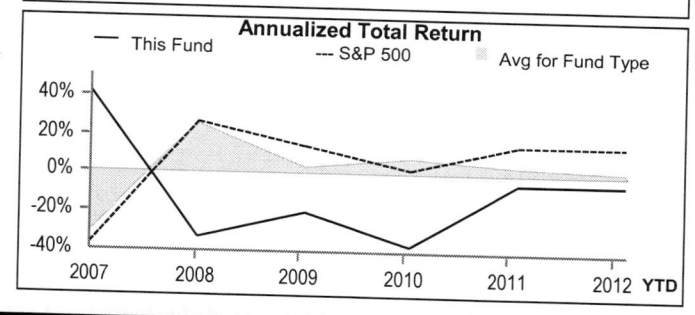

*ProShares VIX Mid-Term Futures E (VIXM)

E   **Very Weak**

Fund Family: ProShare Advisors LLC
Fund Type: General - Investment Grade
Inception Date: January 3, 2011

Major Rating Factors: Very poor performance is the major factor driving the E (Very Weak) TheStreet.com Investment Rating for *ProShares VIX Mid-Term Futures E. The fund currently has a performance rating of E- (Very Weak) based on an annualized return of 0.00% over the last three years and a total return of -8.68% year to date 2012. Factored into the performance evaluation is an expense ratio of 0.85% (very low).

The fund's risk rating is currently C- (Fair). It carries a beta of 0.00, meaning the fund's expected move will be 0.0% for every 10% move in the market. Volatility, as measured by both the semi-deviation and a drawdown factor, is considered average. As of December 31, 2012, *ProShares VIX Mid-Term Futures E traded at a premium of 9.40% above its net asset value, which is worse than its one-year historical average discount of .16%.

Michelle Liu has been running the fund for 2 years and currently receives a manager quality ranking of 0 (0=worst, 99=best). This fund offers an average level of risk but investors looking for strong performance will be frustrated.

Data Date	Investment Rating	Net Assets ($Mil)	Price	Performance Rating/Pts	Total Return Y-T-D	Risk Rating/Pts
12-12	E	37.30	34.22	E- / 0	-8.68%	C- / 3.6

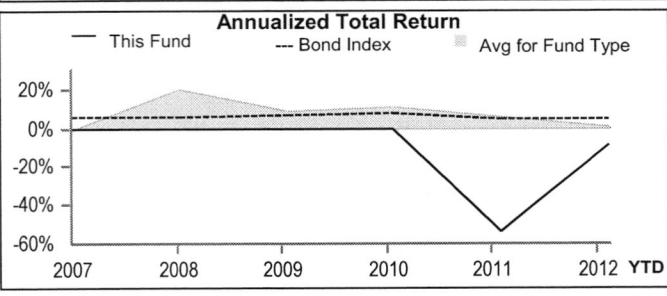

*ProShares VIX Short-Term Futures (VIXY)

E-   **Very Weak**

Fund Family: ProShare Advisors LLC
Fund Type: General - Investment Grade
Inception Date: January 3, 2011

Major Rating Factors: *ProShares VIX Short-Term Futures has adopted a very risky asset allocation strategy and currently receives an overall TheStreet.com Investment Rating of E- (Very Weak). The fund has a high level of volatility, as measured by both semi-deviation and drawdown factors. It carries a beta of 0.00, meaning the fund's expected move will be 0.0% for every 10% move in the market. As of December 31, 2012, *ProShares VIX Short-Term Futures traded at a premium of 20.90% above its net asset value, which is worse than its one-year historical average discount of .13%. Unfortunately, the high level of risk (D, Weak) failed to pay off as investors endured very poor performance.

The fund's performance rating is currently E- (Very Weak). It has registered an annualized return of 0.00% over the last three years but is down -16.64% year to date 2012. Factored into the performance evaluation is an expense ratio of 0.85% (very low).

Michelle Liu has been running the fund for 2 years and currently receives a manager quality ranking of 0 (0=worst, 99=best). If you can tolerate very high levels of risk in the hope of improved future returns, holding this fund may be an option.

Data Date	Investment Rating	Net Assets ($Mil)	Price	Performance Rating/Pts	Total Return Y-T-D	Risk Rating/Pts
12-12	E-	147.70	17.01	E- / 0	-16.64%	D / 1.9

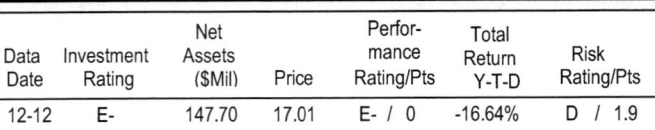
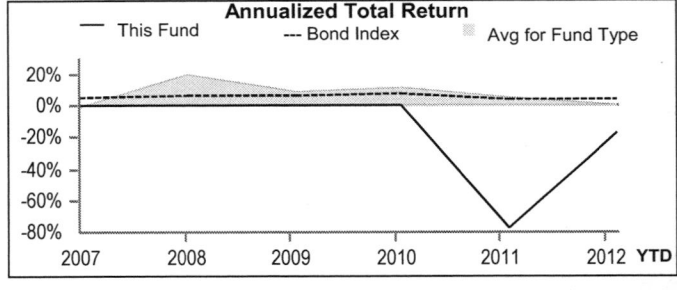

*QuantShares US Market Neutral Si (SIZ)

C-   **Fair**

Fund Family: FFCM LLC
Fund Type: Growth
Inception Date: September 7, 2011

Major Rating Factors:
Disappointing performance is the major factor driving the C- (Fair) TheStreet.com Investment Rating for *QuantShares US Market Neutral Si. The fund currently has a performance rating of D (Weak) based on an annualized return of 0.00% over the last three years and a total return of -0.14% year to date 2012. Factored into the performance evaluation is an expense ratio of 0.99% (low).

The fund's risk rating is currently B+ (Good). It carries a beta of 0.00, meaning the fund's expected move will be 0.0% for every 10% move in the market. Volatility, as measured by both the semi-deviation and a drawdown factor, is considered very low. As of December 31, 2012, *QuantShares US Market Neutral Si traded at a discount of .08% below its net asset value, which is worse than its one-year historical average discount of .24%.

Charles Martin has been running the fund for 2 years and currently receives a manager quality ranking of 36 (0=worst, 99=best). This fund offers only a moderate level of risk but investors looking for strong performance are still waiting.

Data Date	Investment Rating	Net Assets ($Mil)	Price	Performance Rating/Pts	Total Return Y-T-D	Risk Rating/Pts
12-12	C-	5.00	25.12	D / 1.6	-0.14%	B+ / 9.5

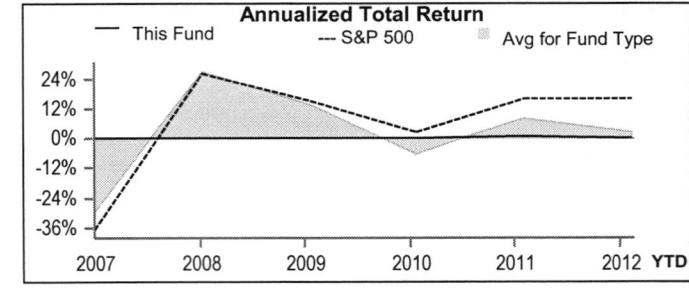

*QuantShares US Market Neutral Va (CHEP)

D+ **Weak**

Fund Family: FFCM LLC
Fund Type: Income
Inception Date: September 13, 2011

Major Rating Factors:

Disappointing performance is the major factor driving the D+ (Weak) TheStreet.com Investment Rating for *QuantShares US Market Neutral Va. The fund currently has a performance rating of D- (Weak) based on an annualized return of 0.00% over the last three years and a total return of 0.49% year to date 2012. Factored into the performance evaluation is an expense ratio of 0.99% (low).

The fund's risk rating is currently B+ (Good). It carries a beta of 0.00, meaning the fund's expected move will be 0.0% for every 10% move in the market. Volatility, as measured by both the semi-deviation and a drawdown factor, is considered very low. As of December 31, 2012, *QuantShares US Market Neutral Va traded at a discount of .69% below its net asset value, which is better than its one-year historical average discount of .09%.

Charles Martin has been running the fund for 2 years and currently receives a manager quality ranking of 27 (0=worst, 99=best). This fund offers only a moderate level of risk but investors looking for strong performance are still waiting.

Data Date	Investment Rating	Net Assets ($Mil)	Price	Performance Rating/Pts	Total Return Y-T-D	Risk Rating/Pts
12-12	D+	3.70	24.57	D- / 1.5	0.49%	B+ / 9.1

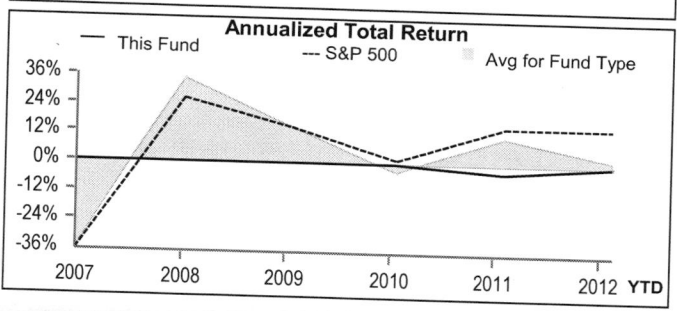

*QuantShares US Mkt Neut Anti-Bet (BTAL)

D **Weak**

Fund Family: FFCM LLC
Fund Type: Growth
Inception Date: September 13, 2011

Major Rating Factors:

Very poor performance is the major factor driving the D (Weak) TheStreet.com Investment Rating for *QuantShares US Mkt Neut Anti-Bet. The fund currently has a performance rating of E+ (Very Weak) based on an annualized return of 0.00% over the last three years and a total return of -3.17% year to date 2012. Factored into the performance evaluation is an expense ratio of 0.99% (low).

The fund's risk rating is currently B (Good). It carries a beta of 0.00, meaning the fund's expected move will be 0.0% for every 10% move in the market. Volatility, as measured by both the semi-deviation and a drawdown factor, is considered low. As of December 31, 2012, *QuantShares US Mkt Neut Anti-Bet traded at a premium of 2.94% above its net asset value, which is worse than its one-year historical average discount of .04%.

Charles Martin has been running the fund for 2 years and currently receives a manager quality ranking of 82 (0=worst, 99=best). This fund offers only a moderate level of risk but investors looking for strong performance are still waiting.

Data Date	Investment Rating	Net Assets ($Mil)	Price	Performance Rating/Pts	Total Return Y-T-D	Risk Rating/Pts
12-12	D	17.40	22.04	E+ / 0.7	-3.17%	B / 8.1

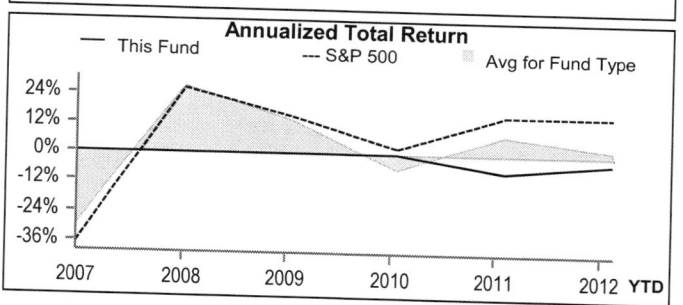

*QuantShares US Mkt Neutral Momen (MOM)

D **Weak**

Fund Family: FFCM LLC
Fund Type: Growth
Inception Date: September 7, 2011

Major Rating Factors:

Very poor performance is the major factor driving the D (Weak) TheStreet.com Investment Rating for *QuantShares US Mkt Neutral Momen. The fund currently has a performance rating of E+ (Very Weak) based on an annualized return of 0.00% over the last three years and a total return of -0.08% year to date 2012. Factored into the performance evaluation is an expense ratio of 0.99% (low).

The fund's risk rating is currently B (Good). It carries a beta of 0.00, meaning the fund's expected move will be 0.0% for every 10% move in the market. Volatility, as measured by both the semi-deviation and a drawdown factor, is considered low. As of December 31, 2012, *QuantShares US Mkt Neutral Momen traded at a discount of 1.45% below its net asset value, which is better than its one-year historical average discount of .31%.

Charles Martin has been running the fund for 2 years and currently receives a manager quality ranking of 94 (0=worst, 99=best). This fund offers only a moderate level of risk but investors looking for strong performance are still waiting.

Data Date	Investment Rating	Net Assets ($Mil)	Price	Performance Rating/Pts	Total Return Y-T-D	Risk Rating/Pts
12-12	D	1.20	24.42	E+ / 0.7	-0.08%	B / 8.6

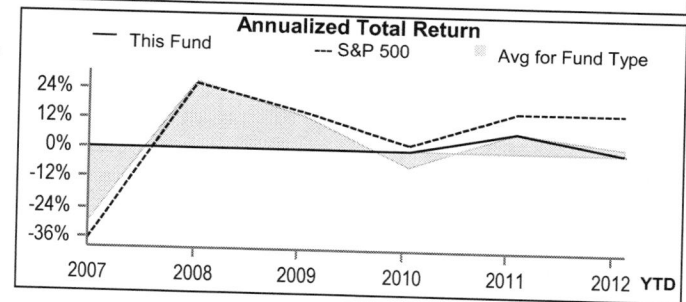

*Ranger Equity Bear ETF (HDGE)

D-   **Weak**

Fund Family: AdvisorShares Investments LLC
Fund Type: Growth
Inception Date: January 26, 2011

Data Date	Investment Rating	Net Assets ($Mil)	Price	Performance Rating/Pts	Total Return Y-T-D	Risk Rating/Pts
12-12	D-	218.90	18.28	E- / 0.2	-2.90%	C+ / 6.2

Major Rating Factors:
Very poor performance is the major factor driving the D- (Weak) TheStreet.com Investment Rating for *Ranger Equity Bear ETF. The fund currently has a performance rating of E- (Very Weak) based on an annualized return of 0.00% over the last three years and a total return of -2.90% year to date 2012. Factored into the performance evaluation is an expense ratio of 1.69% (above average).

The fund's risk rating is currently C+ (Fair). It carries a beta of 0.00, meaning the fund's expected move will be 0.0% for every 10% move in the market. Volatility, as measured by both the semi-deviation and a drawdown factor, is considered low. As of December 31, 2012, *Ranger Equity Bear ETF traded at a premium of 3.10% above its net asset value, which is worse than its one-year historical average premium of .05%.

Brad H. Lamensdorf currently receives a manager quality ranking of 19 (0=worst, 99=best). This fund offers only a moderate level of risk but investors looking for strong performance are still waiting.

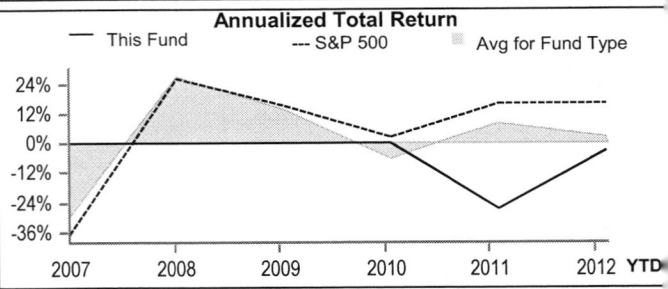

*RBS Global Big Pharma ETN (DRGS)

C+   **Fair**

Fund Family: Royal Bank of Scotland NV
Fund Type: Global
Inception Date: October 21, 2011

Data Date	Investment Rating	Net Assets ($Mil)	Price	Performance Rating/Pts	Total Return Y-T-D	Risk Rating/Pts
12-12	C+	4.00	29.57	B / 7.9	5.41%	C+ / 5.7

Major Rating Factors: Strong performance is the major factor driving the C+ (Fair) TheStreet.com Investment Rating for *RBS Global Big Pharma ETN. The fund currently has a performance rating of B (Good) based on an annualized return of 0.00% over the last three years and a total return of 5.41% year to date 2012.

The fund's risk rating is currently C+ (Fair). It carries a beta of 0.00, meaning the fund's expected move will be 0.0% for every 10% move in the market. Volatility, as measured by both the semi-deviation and a drawdown factor, is considered low. As of December 31, 2012, *RBS Global Big Pharma ETN traded at a discount of 4.15% below its net asset value, which is better than its one-year historical average premium of .02%.

This fund has been team managed for 2 years and currently receives a manager quality ranking of 76 (0=worst, 99=best). If you desire only a moderate level of risk and strong performance, then this fund is an excellent option.

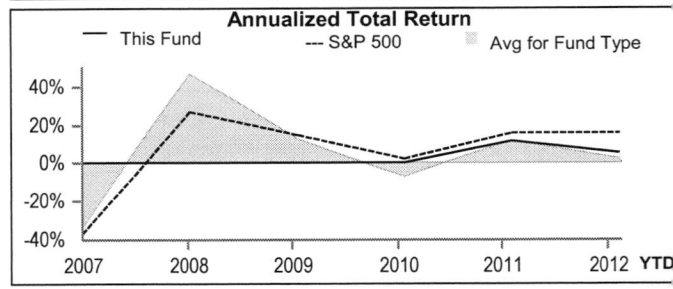

*RBS Gold Trendpilot ETN (TBAR)

D-   **Weak**

Fund Family: Royal Bank of Scotland NV
Fund Type: Energy/Natural Resources
Inception Date: February 17, 2011

Data Date	Investment Rating	Net Assets ($Mil)	Price	Performance Rating/Pts	Total Return Y-T-D	Risk Rating/Pts
12-12	D-	25.60	29.38	D- / 1.1	-1.19%	C / 5.0

Major Rating Factors:
Disappointing performance is the major factor driving the D- (Weak) TheStreet.com Investment Rating for *RBS Gold Trendpilot ETN. The fund currently has a performance rating of D- (Weak) based on an annualized return of 0.00% over the last three years and a total return of -1.19% year to date 2012.

The fund's risk rating is currently C (Fair). It carries a beta of 0.00, meaning the fund's expected move will be 0.0% for every 10% move in the market. Volatility, as measured by both the semi-deviation and a drawdown factor, is considered average. As of December 31, 2012, *RBS Gold Trendpilot ETN traded at a premium of 1.42% above its net asset value, which is worse than its one-year historical average premium of .14%.

This fund has been team managed for 2 years and currently receives a manager quality ranking of 75 (0=worst, 99=best). This fund offers an average level of risk but investors looking for strong performance will be frustrated.

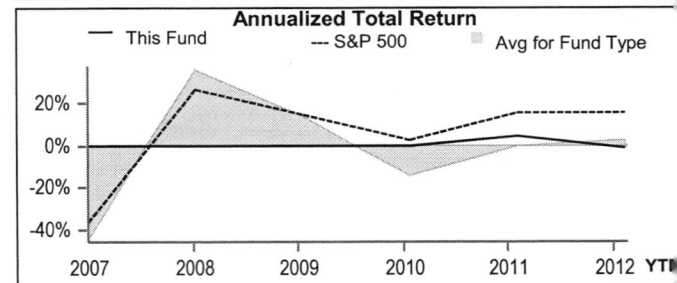

*RBS NASDAQ 100 Trendpilot ETN (TNDQ)

| | | | | | **D-** | | **Weak** |

Fund Family: Royal Bank of Scotland NV
Fund Type: Income
Inception Date: December 8, 2011

Data Date	Investment Rating	Net Assets ($Mil)	Price	Performance Rating/Pts	Total Return Y-T-D	Risk Rating/Pts
12-12	D-	0.00	27.51	D / 2.0	0.11%	C / 5.3

Major Rating Factors:

Disappointing performance is the major factor driving the D- (Weak) TheStreet.com Investment Rating for *RBS NASDAQ 100 Trendpilot ETN. The fund currently has a performance rating of D (Weak) based on an annualized return of 0.00% over the last three years and a total return of 0.11% year to date 2012.

The fund's risk rating is currently C (Fair). It carries a beta of 0.00, meaning the fund's expected move will be 0.0% for every 10% move in the market. Volatility, as measured by both the semi-deviation and a drawdown factor, is considered average. As of December 31, 2012, *RBS NASDAQ 100 Trendpilot ETN traded at a discount of .65% below its net asset value, which is better than its one-year historical average premium of .13%.

This fund has been team managed for 2 years and currently receives a manager quality ranking of 16 (0=worst, 99=best). This fund offers an average level of risk but investors looking for strong performance will be frustrated.

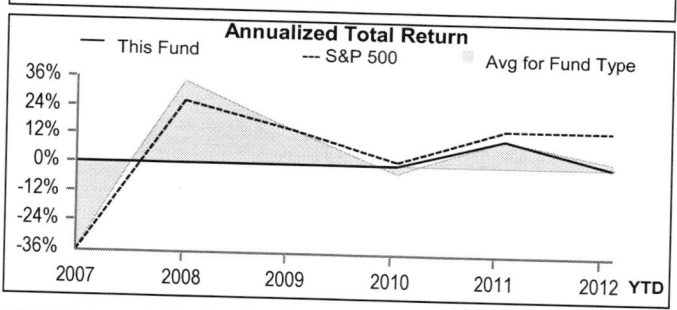

*RBS Oil Trendpilot ETN (TWTI)

| | | | | | **E+** | | **Very Weak** |

Fund Family: Royal Bank of Scotland NV
Fund Type: Global
Inception Date: September 15, 2011

Data Date	Investment Rating	Net Assets ($Mil)	Price	Performance Rating/Pts	Total Return Y-T-D	Risk Rating/Pts
12-12	E+	8.80	22.99	E+ / 0.6	0.26%	C / 4.8

Major Rating Factors:

Very poor performance is the major factor driving the E+ (Very Weak) TheStreet.com Investment Rating for *RBS Oil Trendpilot ETN. The fund currently has a performance rating of E+ (Very Weak) based on an annualized return of 0.00% over the last three years and a total return of 0.26% year to date 2012.

The fund's risk rating is currently C (Fair). It carries a beta of 0.00, meaning the fund's expected move will be 0.0% for every 10% move in the market. Volatility, as measured by both the semi-deviation and a drawdown factor, is considered average. As of December 31, 2012, *RBS Oil Trendpilot ETN traded at a discount of .13% below its net asset value, which is worse than its one-year historical average discount of .17%.

This fund has been team managed for 2 years and currently receives a manager quality ranking of 6 (0=worst, 99=best). This fund offers an average level of risk but investors looking for strong performance will be frustrated.

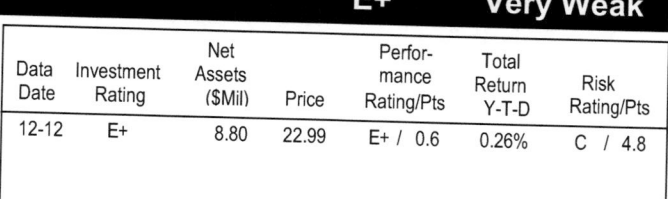

*RBS US Large Cap Trendpilot ETN (TRND)

| | | | | | **B** | | **Good** |

Fund Family: Royal Bank of Scotland NV
Fund Type: Growth
Inception Date: December 6, 2010

Data Date	Investment Rating	Net Assets ($Mil)	Price	Performance Rating/Pts	Total Return Y-T-D	Risk Rating/Pts
12-12	B	69.50	27.70	C+ / 6.9	3.18%	B / 8.5
2011	D+	0.00	24.06	D- / 1.3	1.89%	B / 8.5

Major Rating Factors: *RBS US Large Cap Trendpilot ETN receives a TheStreet.com Investment Rating of B (Good). The fund currently has a performance rating of C+ (Fair) based on an annualized return of 0.00% over the last three years and a total return of 3.18% year to date 2012.

The fund's risk rating is currently B (Good). It carries a beta of 0.00, meaning the fund's expected move will be 0.0% for every 10% move in the market. Volatility, as measured by both the semi-deviation and a drawdown factor, is considered low. As of December 31, 2012, *RBS US Large Cap Trendpilot ETN traded at a discount of 2.91% below its net asset value, which is better than its one-year historical average premium of .08%.

This fund has been team managed for 3 years and currently receives a manager quality ranking of 45 (0=worst, 99=best). If you desire an average level of risk, then this fund may be an option.

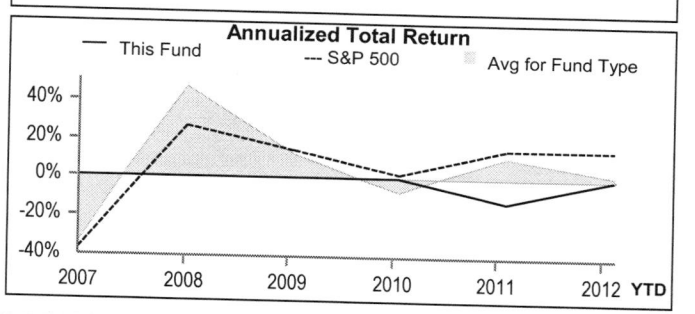

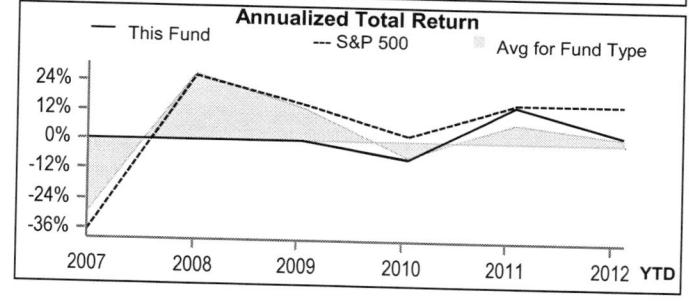

*RBS US Mid Cap Trendpilot ETN (TRNM)

		C		**Fair**

Fund Family: Royal Bank of Scotland NV
Fund Type: Growth
Inception Date: January 27, 2011

Data Date	Investment Rating	Net Assets ($Mil)	Price	Performance Rating/Pts	Total Return Y-T-D	Risk Rating/Pts
12-12	C	32.90	24.78	B / 8.0	3.60%	C / 4.7

Major Rating Factors: Strong performance is the major factor driving the C (Fair) TheStreet.com Investment Rating for *RBS US Mid Cap Trendpilot ETN. The fund currently has a performance rating of B (Good) based on an annualized return of 0.00% over the last three years and a total return of 3.60% year to date 2012.

The fund's risk rating is currently C (Fair). It carries a beta of 0.00, meaning the fund's expected move will be 0.0% for every 10% move in the market. Volatility, as measured by both the semi-deviation and a drawdown factor, is considered average. As of December 31, 2012, *RBS US Mid Cap Trendpilot ETN traded at a discount of 3.58% below its net asset value, which is better than its one-year historical average discount of .05%.

This fund has been team managed for 2 years and currently receives a manager quality ranking of 30 (0=worst, 99=best). If you desire an average level of risk and strong performance, then this fund is a good option.

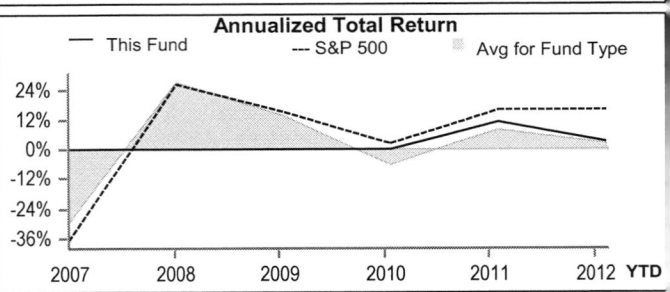

*RevenueShares ADR Fund (RTR)

		D+		**Weak**

Fund Family: VTL Associates LLC
Fund Type: Income
Inception Date: November 18, 2008

Data Date	Investment Rating	Net Assets ($Mil)	Price	Performance Rating/Pts	Total Return Y-T-D	Risk Rating/Pts
12-12	D+	26.50	35.29	D+ / 2.7	3.23%	C+ / 6.9
2011	C-	38.10	31.71	C- / 3.2	1.83%	B- / 7.4
2010	A	59.10	38.13	B+ / 8.6	6.85%	B- / 7.1
2009	A+	7.52	36.38	B+ / 8.7	38.63%	B- / 7.4

Major Rating Factors:
Disappointing performance is the major factor driving the D+ (Weak) TheStreet.com Investment Rating for *RevenueShares ADR Fund. The fund currently has a performance rating of D+ (Weak) based on an annualized return of 2.12% over the last three years and a total return of 3.23% year to date 2012. Factored into the performance evaluation is an expense ratio of 0.49% (very low).

The fund's risk rating is currently C+ (Fair). It carries a beta of 1.32, meaning it is expected to move 13.2% for every 10% move in the market. Volatility, as measured by both the semi-deviation and a drawdown factor, is considered low. As of December 31, 2012, *RevenueShares ADR Fund traded at a discount of 3.02% below its net asset value, which is better than its one-year historical average discount of .10%.

Michael Gompers currently receives a manager quality ranking of 12 (0=worst, 99=best). This fund offers only a moderate level of risk but investors looking for strong performance are still waiting.

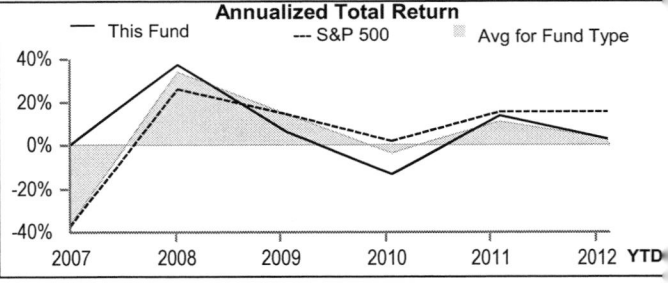

*RevenueShares Financials Sector (RWW)

		C		**Fair**

Fund Family: VTL Associates LLC
Fund Type: Financial Services
Inception Date: November 10, 2008

Data Date	Investment Rating	Net Assets ($Mil)	Price	Performance Rating/Pts	Total Return Y-T-D	Risk Rating/Pts
12-12	C	9.60	32.04	C+ / 5.9	4.53%	C+ / 6.6
2011	D	7.20	23.91	D / 2.1	2.80%	C+ / 6.1
2010	A-	20.70	31.84	A- / 9.0	15.52%	C / 5.3
2009	B	5.59	27.63	B / 8.2	27.10%	C / 5.2

Major Rating Factors: Middle of the road best describes *RevenueShares Financials Sector whose TheStreet.com Investment Rating is currently a C (Fair). The fund currently has a performance rating of C+ (Fair) based on an annualized return of 6.00% over the last three years and a total return of 4.53% year to date 2012. Factored into the performance evaluation is an expense ratio of 0.49% (very low).

The fund's risk rating is currently C+ (Fair). It carries a beta of 1.18, meaning it is expected to move 11.8% for every 10% move in the market. Volatility, as measured by both the semi-deviation and a drawdown factor, is considered low. As of December 31, 2012, *RevenueShares Financials Sector traded at a discount of 4.53% below its net asset value, which is better than its one-year historical average discount of .16%.

Vincent T. Lowry has been running the fund for 5 years and currently receives a manager quality ranking of 30 (0=worst, 99=best). If you desire an average level of risk, then this fund may be an option.

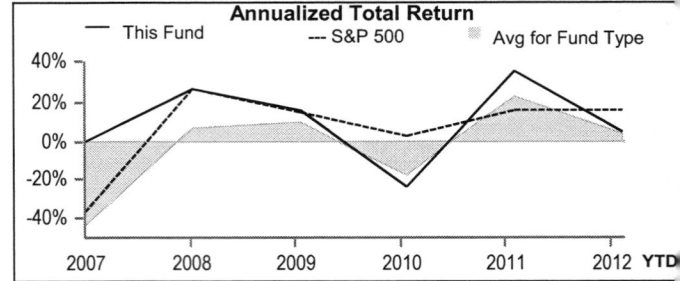

*RevenueShares Large Cap Fund (RWL)

Fund Family: VTL Associates LLC
Fund Type: Growth
Inception Date: February 22, 2008

Major Rating Factors: Middle of the road best describes *RevenueShares Large Cap Fund whose TheStreet.com Investment Rating is currently a C+ (Fair). The fund currently has a performance rating of C+ (Fair) based on an annualized return of 11.42% over the last three years and a total return of 3.34% year to date 2012. Factored into the performance evaluation is an expense ratio of 0.49% (very low).

The fund's risk rating is currently B (Good). It carries a beta of 1.03, meaning that its performance tracks fairly well with that of the overall stock market. Volatility, as measured by both the semi-deviation and a drawdown factor, is considered low. As of December 31, 2012, *RevenueShares Large Cap Fund traded at a discount of 3.17% below its net asset value, which is better than its one-year historical average discount of .04%.

Vincent T. Lowry has been running the fund for 5 years and currently receives a manager quality ranking of 52 (0=worst, 99=best). If you desire an average level of risk, then this fund may be an option.

C+ **Fair**

Data Date	Investment Rating	Net Assets ($Mil)	Price	Performance Rating/Pts	Total Return Y-T-D	Risk Rating/Pts
12-12	C+	151.00	26.92	C+ / 5.7	3.34%	B / 8.1
2011	C	162.90	23.27	C / 5.1	1.80%	B / 8.0
2010	B-	188.90	23.64	A- / 9.2	16.38%	C- / 3.6
2009	C+	53.23	20.53	B+ / 8.4	26.40%	C- / 3.4

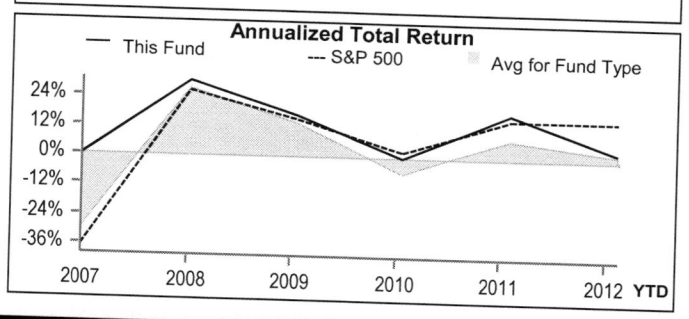

*RevenueShares Mid Cap Fund (RWK)

Fund Family: VTL Associates LLC
Fund Type: Growth
Inception Date: February 22, 2008

Major Rating Factors: Middle of the road best describes *RevenueShares Mid Cap Fund whose TheStreet.com Investment Rating is currently a C+ (Fair). The fund currently has a performance rating of C+ (Fair) based on an annualized return of 12.49% over the last three years and a total return of 4.64% year to date 2012. Factored into the performance evaluation is an expense ratio of 0.54% (very low).

The fund's risk rating is currently B- (Good). It carries a beta of 1.27, meaning it is expected to move 12.7% for every 10% move in the market. Volatility, as measured by both the semi-deviation and a drawdown factor, is considered low. As of December 31, 2012, *RevenueShares Mid Cap Fund traded at a discount of 4.47% below its net asset value, which is better than its one-year historical average discount of .06%.

Vincent T. Lowry has been running the fund for 5 years and currently receives a manager quality ranking of 36 (0=worst, 99=best). If you desire an average level of risk, then this fund may be an option.

C+ **Fair**

Data Date	Investment Rating	Net Assets ($Mil)	Price	Performance Rating/Pts	Total Return Y-T-D	Risk Rating/Pts
12-12	C+	104.60	32.08	C+ / 6.9	4.64%	B- / 7.6
2011	B-	126.70	28.16	C+ / 6.9	1.80%	B- / 7.6
2010	B-	138.60	29.51	A / 9.4	23.00%	C- / 3.3
2009	C+	30.17	24.10	A- / 9.1	47.01%	C- / 3.2

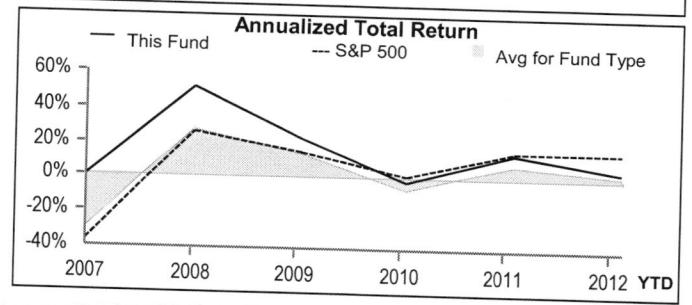

*RevenueShares Navellier OA A100 (RWV)

Fund Family: VTL Associates LLC
Fund Type: Income
Inception Date: January 21, 2009

Major Rating Factors: Middle of the road best describes *RevenueShares Navellier OA A100 whose TheStreet.com Investment Rating is currently a C (Fair). The fund currently has a performance rating of C (Fair) based on an annualized return of 10.34% over the last three years and a total return of 3.63% year to date 2012. Factored into the performance evaluation is an expense ratio of 0.60% (very low).

The fund's risk rating is currently B- (Good). It carries a beta of 1.08, meaning that its performance tracks fairly well with that of the overall stock market. Volatility, as measured by both the semi-deviation and a drawdown factor, is considered low. As of December 31, 2012, *RevenueShares Navellier OA A100 traded at a discount of 4.11% below its net asset value, which is better than its one-year historical average discount of .12%.

Michael Gompers currently receives a manager quality ranking of 31 (0=worst, 99=best). If you desire an average level of risk, then this fund may be an option.

C **Fair**

Data Date	Investment Rating	Net Assets ($Mil)	Price	Performance Rating/Pts	Total Return Y-T-D	Risk Rating/Pts
12-12	C	8.00	39.66	C / 4.4	3.63%	B- / 7.8
2011	D	9.00	35.93	D- / 1.4	1.00%	B- / 7.9
2010	A+	9.60	38.66	A / 9.5	21.99%	B- / 7.8

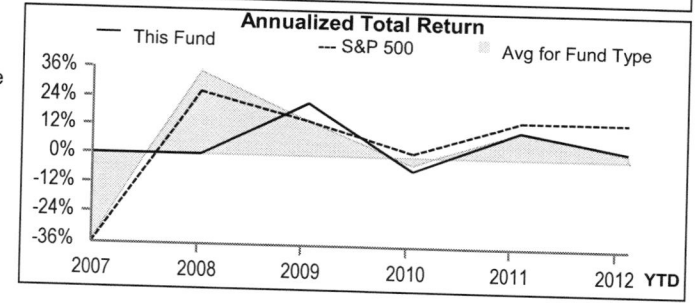

* Denotes ETF Fund

*RevenueShares Small Cap Fund (RWJ)

C+   **Fair**

Fund Family: VTL Associates LLC
Fund Type: Growth
Inception Date: February 22, 2008

Major Rating Factors: Strong performance is the major factor driving the C+ (Fair) TheStreet.com Investment Rating for *RevenueShares Small Cap Fund. The fund currently has a performance rating of B- (Good) based on an annualized return of 14.08% over the last three years and a total return of 3.12% year to date 2012. Factored into the performance evaluation is an expense ratio of 0.54% (very low).

The fund's risk rating is currently B- (Good). It carries a beta of 1.35, meaning it is expected to move 13.5% for every 10% move in the market. Volatility, as measured by both the semi-deviation and a drawdown factor, is considered low. As of December 31, 2012, *RevenueShares Small Cap Fund traded at a discount of 3.18% below its net asset value, which is better than its one-year historical average discount of .03%.

Vincent T. Lowry has been running the fund for 5 years and currently receives a manager quality ranking of 43 (0=worst, 99=best). If you desire only a moderate level of risk and strong performance, then this fund is an excellent option.

Data Date	Investment Rating	Net Assets ($Mil)	Price	Performance Rating/Pts	Total Return Y-T-D	Risk Rating/Pts
12-12	C+	122.00	37.44	B- / 7.0	3.12%	B- / 7.5
2011	B-	104.30	32.07	B- / 7.3	1.40%	B- / 7.4
2010	B	128.20	32.49	A / 9.5	25.66%	C- / 3.3
2009	C+	32.10	25.90	A- / 9.0	44.07%	C- / 3.2

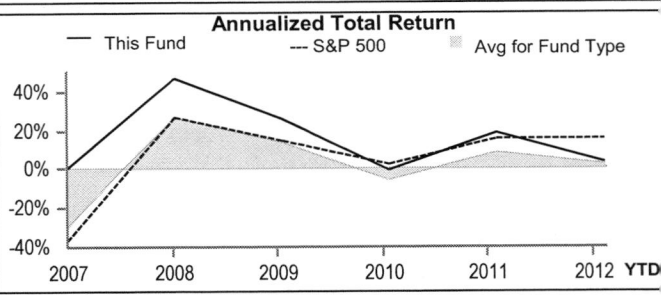

*Russell Equity ETF (ONEF)

B   **Good**

Fund Family: Russell Investment Management Compa
Fund Type: Global
Inception Date: May 11, 2010

Major Rating Factors: Strong performance is the major factor driving the B (Good) TheStreet.com Investment Rating for *Russell Equity ETF. The fund currently has a performance rating of B (Good) based on an annualized return of 0.00% over the last three years and a total return of 2.55% year to date 2012. Factored into the performance evaluation is an expense ratio of 0.35% (very low).

The fund's risk rating is currently B- (Good). It carries a beta of 0.00, meaning the fund's expected move will be 0.0% for every 10% move in the market. Volatility, as measured by both the semi-deviation and a drawdown factor, is considered low. As of December 31, 2012, *Russell Equity ETF traded at a discount of 2.35% below its net asset value, which is better than its one-year historical average discount of .06%.

Paul Hrabal has been running the fund for 3 years and currently receives a manager quality ranking of 82 (0=worst, 99=best). If you desire only a moderate level of risk and strong performance, then this fund is an excellent option.

Data Date	Investment Rating	Net Assets ($Mil)	Price	Performance Rating/Pts	Total Return Y-T-D	Risk Rating/Pts
12-12	B	2.90	29.14	B / 8.0	2.55%	B- / 7.8
2011	D	6.40	25.38	D- / 1.3	1.30%	B- / 7.9

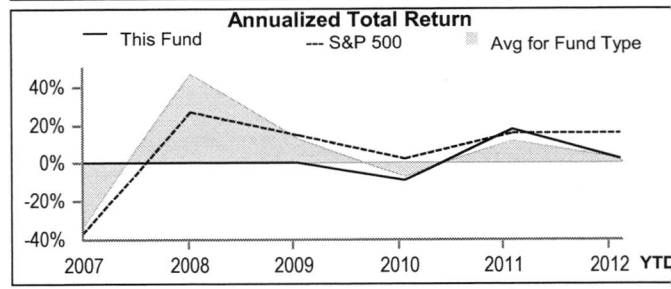

*Schwab Emerging Markets Equity E (SCHE)

B+   **Good**

Fund Family: Charles Schwab Investment Managemen
Fund Type: Foreign
Inception Date: January 13, 2010

Major Rating Factors:
Exceptional performance is the major factor driving the B+ (Good) TheStreet.com Investment Rating for *Schwab Emerging Markets Equity E. The fund currently has a performance rating of A- (Excellent) based on an annualized return of 0.00% over the last three years and a total return of 0.68% year to date 2012. Factored into the performance evaluation is an expense ratio of 0.25% (very low).

The fund's risk rating is currently C+ (Fair). It carries a beta of 0.00, meaning the fund's expected move will be 0.0% for every 10% move in the market. Volatility, as measured by both the semi-deviation and a drawdown factor, is considered low. As of December 31, 2012, *Schwab Emerging Markets Equity E traded at a premium of .11% above its net asset value, which is better than its one-year historical average premium of .38%.

Agnes Hong has been running the fund for 3 years and currently receives a manager quality ranking of 62 (0=worst, 99=best). If you desire only a moderate level of risk and strong performance, then this fund is an excellent option.

Data Date	Investment Rating	Net Assets ($Mil)	Price	Performance Rating/Pts	Total Return Y-T-D	Risk Rating/Pts
12-12	B+	694.10	26.39	A- / 9.0	0.68%	C+ / 6.9
2011	D	0.00	22.87	D- / 1.0	1.05%	B- / 7.0

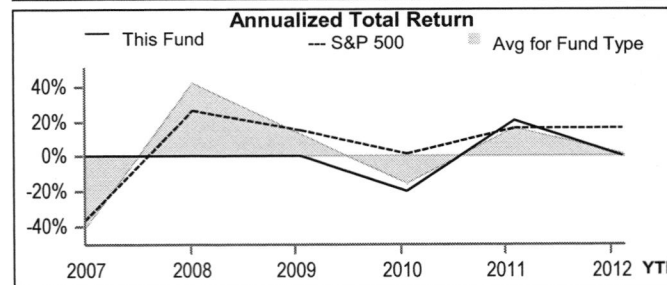

*Schwab International Equity ETF (SCHF)

C   **Fair**

Fund Family: Charles Schwab Investment Managemen
Fund Type: Foreign
Inception Date: October 30, 2009

Major Rating Factors: Middle of the road best describes *Schwab International Equity ETF whose TheStreet.com Investment Rating is currently a C (Fair). The fund currently has a performance rating of C (Fair) based on an annualized return of 4.85% over the last three years and a total return of 1.85% year to date 2012. Factored into the performance evaluation is an expense ratio of 0.13% (very low).

The fund's risk rating is currently B- (Good). It carries a beta of 1.03, meaning that its performance tracks fairly well with that of the overall stock market. Volatility, as measured by both the semi-deviation and a drawdown factor, is considered low. As of December 31, 2012, *Schwab International Equity ETF traded at a discount of 1.28% below its net asset value, which is better than its one-year historical average premium of .55%.

Agnes Hong has been running the fund for 4 years and currently receives a manager quality ranking of 61 (0=worst, 99=best). If you desire an average level of risk, then this fund may be an option.

Data Date	Investment Rating	Net Assets ($Mil)	Price	Perfor- mance Rating/Pts	Total Return Y-T-D	Risk Rating/Pts
12-12	C	979.30	27.10	C / 5.0	1.85%	B- / 7.5
2011	D	632.50	23.43	D- / 1.1	-0.17%	B- / 7.4
2010	A+	359.70	27.69	B+ / 8.7	9.26%	B- / 7.7

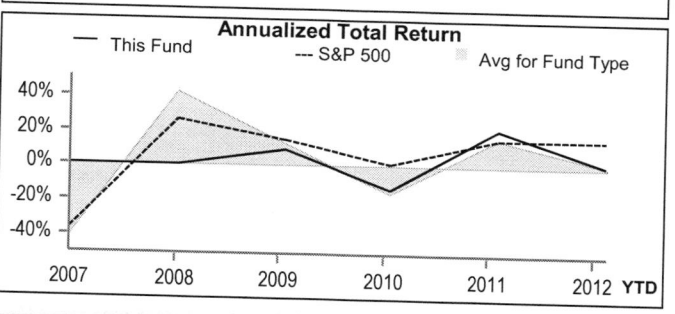

*Schwab Intl Small-Cap Equity ETF (SCHC)

B   **Good**

Fund Family: Charles Schwab Investment Managemen
Fund Type: Foreign
Inception Date: January 13, 2010

Major Rating Factors:
Exceptional performance is the major factor driving the B (Good) TheStreet.com Investment Rating for *Schwab Intl Small-Cap Equity ETF. The fund currently has a performance rating of A+ (Excellent) based on an annualized return of 0.00% over the last three years and a total return of 2.92% year to date 2012. Factored into the performance evaluation is an expense ratio of 0.35% (very low).

The fund's risk rating is currently C+ (Fair). It carries a beta of 0.00, meaning the fund's expected move will be 0.0% for every 10% move in the market. Volatility, as measured by both the semi-deviation and a drawdown factor, is considered low. As of December 31, 2012, *Schwab Intl Small-Cap Equity ETF traded at a discount of 1.74% below its net asset value, which is better than its one-year historical average premium of .48%.

Agnes Hong has been running the fund for 3 years and currently receives a manager quality ranking of 77 (0=worst, 99=best). If you desire only a moderate level of risk and strong performance, then this fund is an excellent option.

Data Date	Investment Rating	Net Assets ($Mil)	Price	Perfor- mance Rating/Pts	Total Return Y-T-D	Risk Rating/Pts
12-12	B	205.00	27.05	A+ / 9.7	2.92%	C+ / 6.0
2011	D-	137.80	23.38	E+ / 0.9	0.38%	C+ / 6.1

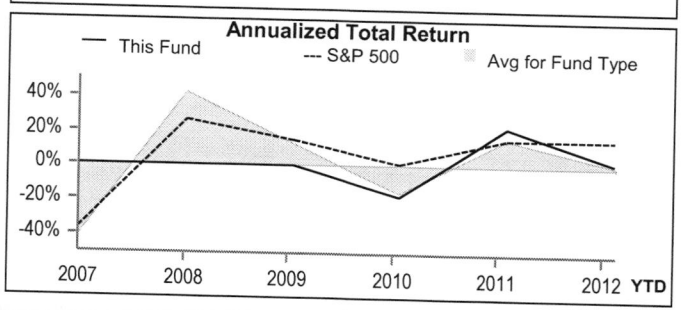

*Schwab Intmdt-Term US Treasury E (SCHR)

C-   **Fair**

Fund Family: Charles Schwab Investment Managemen
Fund Type: US Government/Agency
Inception Date: August 4, 2010

Major Rating Factors:
Disappointing performance is the major factor driving the C- (Fair) TheStreet.com Investment Rating for *Schwab Intmdt-Term US Treasury E. The fund currently has a performance rating of D (Weak) based on an annualized return of 0.00% over the last three years and a total return of -0.20% year to date 2012. Factored into the performance evaluation is an expense ratio of 0.12% (very low).

The fund's risk rating is currently B+ (Good). It carries a beta of 0.00, meaning the fund's expected move will be 0.0% for every 10% move in the market. Volatility, as measured by both the semi-deviation and a drawdown factor, is considered very low. As of December 31, 2012, *Schwab Intmdt-Term US Treasury E traded at a premium of .20% above its net asset value.

Matthew Hastings has been running the fund for 3 years and currently receives a manager quality ranking of 62 (0=worst, 99=best). This fund offers only a moderate level of risk but investors looking for strong performance are still waiting.

Data Date	Investment Rating	Net Assets ($Mil)	Price	Perfor- mance Rating/Pts	Total Return Y-T-D	Risk Rating/Pts
12-12	C-	216.70	54.08	D / 1.6	-0.20%	B+ / 9.7
2011	C+	117.50	53.52	C- / 4.1	-0.32%	B+ / 9.7

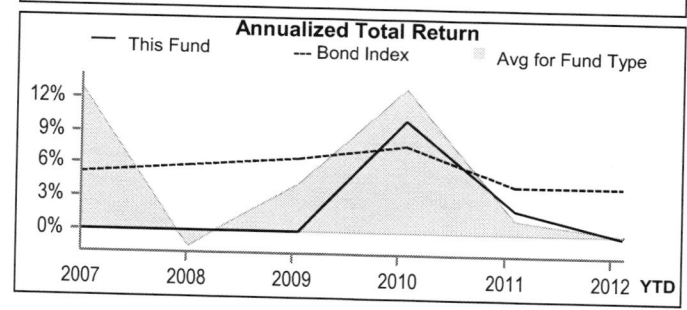

* Denotes ETF Fund

*Schwab Short-Term US Treas ETF (SCHO)   C-   Fair

Fund Family: Charles Schwab Investment Managemen
Fund Type: US Government/Agency
Inception Date: August 4, 2010

Major Rating Factors:
Disappointing performance is the major factor driving the C- (Fair) TheStreet.com Investment Rating for *Schwab Short-Term US Treas ETF. The fund currently has a performance rating of D- (Weak) based on an annualized return of 0.00% over the last three years and a total return of 0.06% year to date 2012. Factored into the performance evaluation is an expense ratio of 0.12% (very low).

The fund's risk rating is currently B+ (Good). It carries a beta of 0.00, meaning the fund's expected move will be 0.0% for every 10% move in the market. Volatility, as measured by both the semi-deviation and a drawdown factor, is considered very low. As of December 31, 2012, *Schwab Short-Term US Treas ETF traded at a discount of .08% below its net asset value.

Matthew Hastings has been running the fund for 3 years and currently receives a manager quality ranking of 52 (0=worst, 99=best). This fund offers only a moderate level of risk but investors looking for strong performance are still waiting.

Data Date	Investment Rating	Net Assets ($Mil)	Price	Performance Rating/Pts	Total Return Y-T-D	Risk Rating/Pts
12-12	C-	250.10	50.49	D- / 1.4	0.06%	B+ / 9.9
2011	C	197.00	50.54	D / 2.2	-0.06%	B+ / 9.9

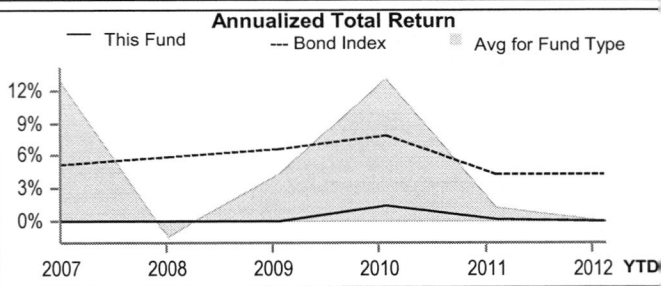

*Schwab US Aggregate Bond ETF (SCHZ)   C-   Fair

Fund Family: Charles Schwab Investment Managemen
Fund Type: General Bond
Inception Date: July 14, 2011

Major Rating Factors:
Disappointing performance is the major factor driving the C- (Fair) TheStreet.com Investment Rating for *Schwab US Aggregate Bond ETF. The fund currently has a performance rating of D (Weak) based on an annualized return of 0.00% over the last three years and a total return of -0.15% year to date 2012. Factored into the performance evaluation is an expense ratio of 0.10% (very low).

The fund's risk rating is currently B+ (Good). It carries a beta of 0.00, meaning the fund's expected move will be 0.0% for every 10% move in the market. Volatility, as measured by both the semi-deviation and a drawdown factor, is considered very low. As of December 31, 2012, *Schwab US Aggregate Bond ETF traded at a premium of .13% above its net asset value, which is better than its one-year historical average premium of .18%.

Matthew Hastings has been running the fund for 2 years and currently receives a manager quality ranking of 40 (0=worst, 99=best). This fund offers only a moderate level of risk but investors looking for strong performance are still waiting.

Data Date	Investment Rating	Net Assets ($Mil)	Price	Performance Rating/Pts	Total Return Y-T-D	Risk Rating/Pts
12-12	C-	388.00	52.34	D / 1.8	-0.15%	B+ / 9.9

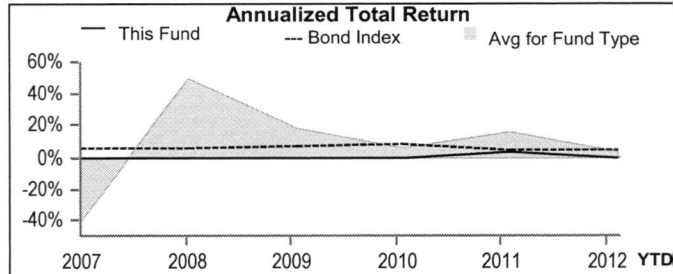

*Schwab US Broad Market ETF (SCHB)   C+   Fair

Fund Family: Charles Schwab Investment Managemen
Fund Type: Income
Inception Date: October 30, 2009

Major Rating Factors: Middle of the road best describes *Schwab US Broad Market ETF whose TheStreet.com Investment Rating is currently a C+ (Fair). The fund currently has a performance rating of C+ (Fair) based on an annualized return of 12.12% over the last three years and a total return of 3.28% year to date 2012. Factored into the performance evaluation is an expense ratio of 0.06% (very low).

The fund's risk rating is currently B (Good). It carries a beta of 1.03, meaning that its performance tracks fairly well with that of the overall stock market. Volatility, as measured by both the semi-deviation and a drawdown factor, is considered low. As of December 31, 2012, *Schwab US Broad Market ETF traded at a discount of 3.13% below its net asset value, which is better than its one-year historical average premium of .03%.

Agnes Hong has been running the fund for 4 years and currently receives a manager quality ranking of 56 (0=worst, 99=best). If you desire an average level of risk, then this fund may be an option.

Data Date	Investment Rating	Net Assets ($Mil)	Price	Performance Rating/Pts	Total Return Y-T-D	Risk Rating/Pts
12-12	C+	1,334.50	34.41	C+ / 5.8	3.28%	B / 8.1
2011	C-	815.30	30.22	D+ / 2.8	1.75%	B / 8.1
2010	A+	405.40	30.38	A- / 9.2	17.11%	B- / 7.8

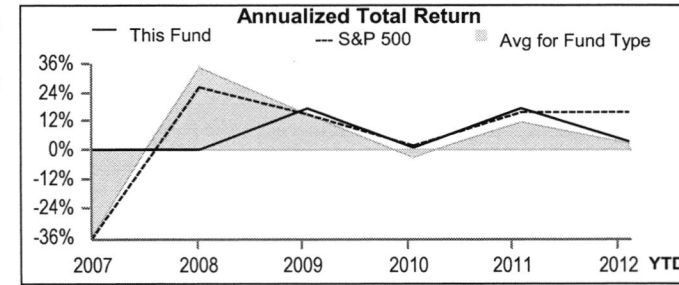

*Schwab US Dividend Equity ETF (SCHD)

B+   **Good**

Fund Family: Charles Schwab Investment Managemen
Fund Type: Growth and Income
Inception Date: October 18, 2011

Data Date	Investment Rating	Net Assets ($Mil)	Price	Performance Rating/Pts	Total Return Y-T-D	Risk Rating/Pts
12-12	B+	575.00	28.34	C+ / 6.4	3.07%	B+ / 9.6

Major Rating Factors: *Schwab US Dividend Equity ETF receives a TheStreet.com Investment Rating of B+ (Good). The fund currently has a performance rating of C+ (Fair) based on an annualized return of 0.00% over the last three years and a total return of 3.07% year to date 2012.

The fund's risk rating is currently B+ (Good). It carries a beta of 0.00, meaning the fund's expected move will be 0.0% for every 10% move in the market. Volatility, as measured by both the semi-deviation and a drawdown factor, is considered very low. As of December 31, 2012, *Schwab US Dividend Equity ETF traded at a discount of 2.95% below its net asset value, which is better than its one-year historical average premium of .04%.

Agnes Hong has been running the fund for 2 years and currently receives a manager quality ranking of 69 (0=worst, 99=best). If you desire an average level of risk, then this fund may be an option.

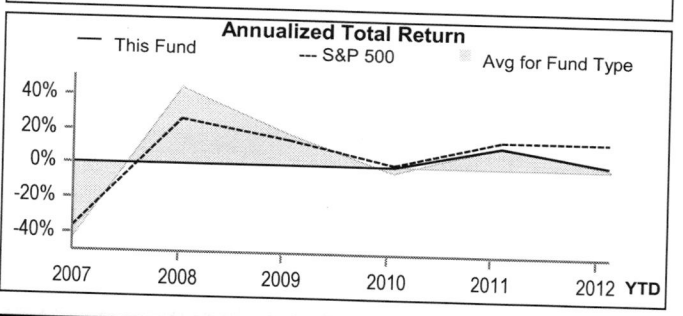

*Schwab US Large-Cap ETF (SCHX)

C+   **Fair**

Fund Family: Charles Schwab Investment Managemen
Fund Type: Income
Inception Date: October 30, 2009

Data Date	Investment Rating	Net Assets ($Mil)	Price	Performance Rating/Pts	Total Return Y-T-D	Risk Rating/Pts
12-12	C+	1,018.00	33.89	C+ / 5.7	3.45%	B / 8.1
2011	C-	704.30	29.85	D+ / 2.8	1.71%	B / 8.2
2010	A+	368.00	29.96	A- / 9.2	15.93%	B- / 7.8

Major Rating Factors: Middle of the road best describes *Schwab US Large-Cap ETF whose TheStreet.com Investment Rating is currently a C+ (Fair). The fund currently has a performance rating of C+ (Fair) based on an annualized return of 11.81% over the last three years and a total return of 3.45% year to date 2012. Factored into the performance evaluation is an expense ratio of 0.08% (very low).

The fund's risk rating is currently B (Good). It carries a beta of 1.01, meaning that its performance tracks fairly well with that of the overall stock market. Volatility, as measured by both the semi-deviation and a drawdown factor, is considered low. As of December 31, 2012, *Schwab US Large-Cap ETF traded at a discount of 3.25% below its net asset value, which is better than its one-year historical average premium of .01%.

Agnes Hong has been running the fund for 4 years and currently receives a manager quality ranking of 55 (0=worst, 99=best). If you desire an average level of risk, then this fund may be an option.

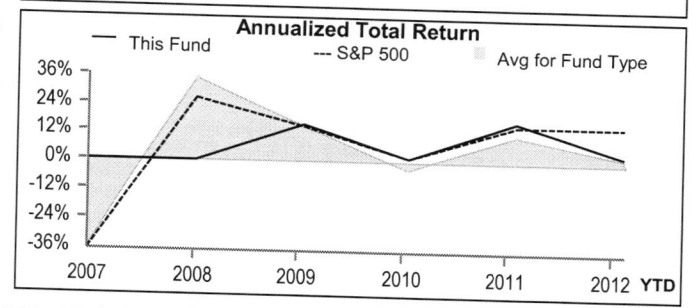

*Schwab US Large-Cap Growth ETF (SCHG)

C+   **Fair**

Fund Family: Charles Schwab Investment Managemen
Fund Type: Growth
Inception Date: December 9, 2009

Data Date	Investment Rating	Net Assets ($Mil)	Price	Performance Rating/Pts	Total Return Y-T-D	Risk Rating/Pts
12-12	C+	528.30	34.15	C / 5.5	3.60%	B / 8.0
2011	D+	324.40	29.63	D+ / 2.3	2.40%	B / 8.0
2010	A+	162.30	30.16	A- / 9.2	16.85%	B- / 7.6

Major Rating Factors: Middle of the road best describes *Schwab US Large-Cap Growth ETF whose TheStreet.com Investment Rating is currently a C+ (Fair). The fund currently has a performance rating of C (Fair) based on an annualized return of 11.62% over the last three years and a total return of 3.60% year to date 2012. Factored into the performance evaluation is an expense ratio of 0.13% (very low).

The fund's risk rating is currently B (Good). It carries a beta of 1.11, meaning it is expected to move 11.1% for every 10% move in the market. Volatility, as measured by both the semi-deviation and a drawdown factor, is considered low. As of December 31, 2012, *Schwab US Large-Cap Growth ETF traded at a discount of 3.42% below its net asset value, which is better than its one-year historical average premium of .03%.

Agnes Hong has been running the fund for 4 years and currently receives a manager quality ranking of 42 (0=worst, 99=best). If you desire an average level of risk, then this fund may be an option.

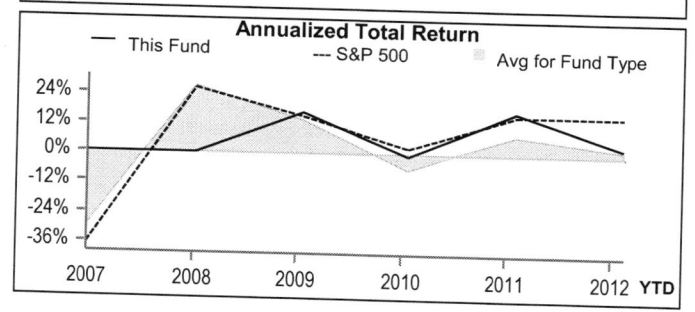

*Schwab US Large-Cap Value ETF (SCHV)

C+   **Fair**

Fund Family: Charles Schwab Investment Managemen
Fund Type: Income
Inception Date: December 9, 2009

Major Rating Factors: Middle of the road best describes *Schwab US Large-Cap Value ETF whose TheStreet.com Investment Rating is currently a C+ (Fair). The fund currently has a performance rating of C+ (Fair) based on an annualized return of 11.78% over the last three years and a total return of 3.42% year to date 2012. Factored into the performance evaluation is an expense ratio of 0.13% (very low).

The fund's risk rating is currently B (Good). It carries a beta of 0.91, meaning that its performance tracks fairly well with that of the overall stock market. Volatility, as measured by both the semi-deviation and a drawdown factor, is considered low. As of December 31, 2012, *Schwab US Large-Cap Value ETF traded at a discount of 3.25% below its net asset value, which is better than its one-year historical average premium of .04%.

Agnes Hong has been running the fund for 4 years and currently receives a manager quality ranking of 63 (0=worst, 99=best). If you desire an average level of risk, then this fund may be an option.

Data Date	Investment Rating	Net Assets ($Mil)	Price	Performance Rating/Pts	Total Return Y-T-D	Risk Rating/Pts
12-12	C+	420.00	31.83	C+ / 5.7	3.42%	B / 8.2
2011	C-	256.50	28.49	C- / 3.4	1.16%	B / 8.3
2010	A+	114.10	28.25	A- / 9.0	14.86%	B- / 7.8

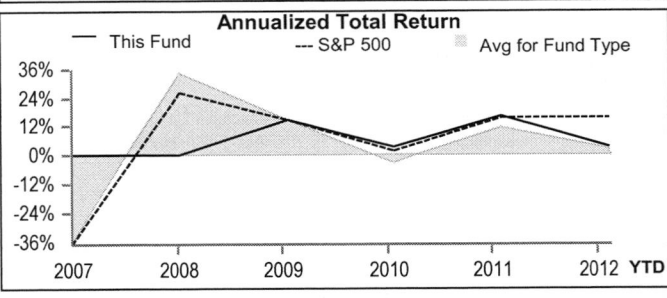

*Schwab US Mid-Cap ETF (SCHM)

B+   **Good**

Fund Family: Charles Schwab Investment Managemen
Fund Type: Growth
Inception Date: January 12, 2011

Major Rating Factors: Strong performance is the major factor driving the B+ (Good) TheStreet.com Investment Rating for *Schwab US Mid-Cap ETF. The fund currently has a performance rating of B+ (Good) based on an annualized return of 0.00% over the last three years and a total return of 3.62% year to date 2012. Factored into the performance evaluation is an expense ratio of 0.13% (very low).

The fund's risk rating is currently B- (Good). It carries a beta of 0.00, meaning the fund's expected move will be 0.0% for every 10% move in the market. Volatility, as measured by both the semi-deviation and a drawdown factor, is considered low. As of December 31, 2012, *Schwab US Mid-Cap ETF traded at a discount of 3.46% below its net asset value, which is better than its one-year historical average premium of .05%.

Agnes Hong has been running the fund for 2 years and currently receives a manager quality ranking of 64 (0=worst, 99=best). If you desire only a moderate level of risk and strong performance, then this fund is an excellent option.

Data Date	Investment Rating	Net Assets ($Mil)	Price	Performance Rating/Pts	Total Return Y-T-D	Risk Rating/Pts
12-12	B+	292.60	27.87	B+ / 8.8	3.62%	B- / 7.5

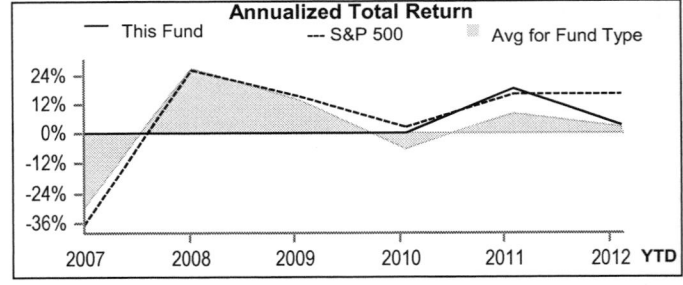

*Schwab US REIT ETF (SCHH)

B-   **Good**

Fund Family: Charles Schwab Investment Managemen
Fund Type: Growth and Income
Inception Date: January 12, 2011

Major Rating Factors: Strong performance is the major factor driving the B- (Good) TheStreet.com Investment Rating for *Schwab US REIT ETF. The fund currently has a performance rating of B- (Good) based on an annualized return of 0.00% over the last three years and a total return of 1.99% year to date 2012. Factored into the performance evaluation is an expense ratio of 0.13% (very low).

The fund's risk rating is currently B- (Good). It carries a beta of 0.00, meaning the fund's expected move will be 0.0% for every 10% move in the market. Volatility, as measured by both the semi-deviation and a drawdown factor, is considered low. As of December 31, 2012, *Schwab US REIT ETF traded at a discount of 1.98% below its net asset value, which is better than its one-year historical average premium of .03%.

Agnes Hong has been running the fund for 2 years and currently receives a manager quality ranking of 83 (0=worst, 99=best). If you desire only a moderate level of risk and strong performance, then this fund is an excellent option.

Data Date	Investment Rating	Net Assets ($Mil)	Price	Performance Rating/Pts	Total Return Y-T-D	Risk Rating/Pts
12-12	B-	372.50	30.64	B- / 7.0	1.99%	B- / 7.9

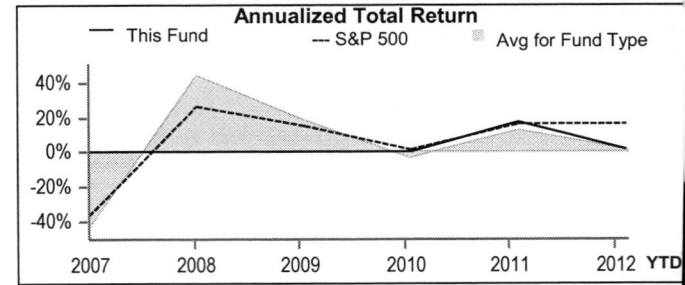

*Schwab US Small-Cap ETF (SCHA)

B-   **Good**

Fund Family: Charles Schwab Investment Managemen
Fund Type: Growth
Inception Date: October 30, 2009

Major Rating Factors: Strong performance is the major factor driving the B- (Good) TheStreet.com Investment Rating for *Schwab US Small-Cap ETF. The fund currently has a performance rating of B- (Good) based on an annualized return of 14.50% over the last three years and a total return of 3.54% year to date 2012. Factored into the performance evaluation is an expense ratio of 0.13% (very low).

The fund's risk rating is currently B- (Good). It carries a beta of 1.28, meaning it is expected to move 12.8% for every 10% move in the market. Volatility, as measured by both the semi-deviation and a drawdown factor, is considered low. As of December 31, 2012, *Schwab US Small-Cap ETF traded at a discount of 3.40% below its net asset value, which is better than its one-year historical average premium of .04%.

Agnes Hong has been running the fund for 4 years and currently receives a manager quality ranking of 54 (0=worst, 99=best). If you desire only a moderate level of risk and strong performance, then this fund is an excellent option.

Data Date	Investment Rating	Net Assets ($Mil)	Price	Performance Rating/Pts	Total Return Y-T-D	Risk Rating/Pts
12-12	B-	707.10	38.12	B- / 7.2	3.54%	B- / 7.4
2011	D	506.10	32.84	D / 1.9	1.64%	B- / 7.4
2010	A+	277.00	34.30	A+ / 9.6	28.64%	B- / 7.5

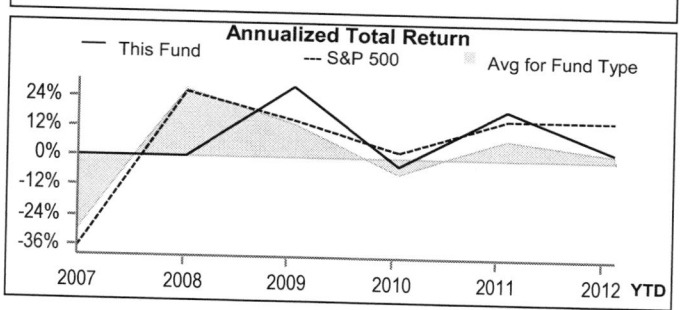

*Schwab US TIPS ETF (SCHP)

C-   **Fair**

Fund Family: Charles Schwab Investment Managemen
Fund Type: General - Investment Grade
Inception Date: August 4, 2010

Major Rating Factors:
Disappointing performance is the major factor driving the C- (Fair) TheStreet.com Investment Rating for *Schwab US TIPS ETF. The fund currently has a performance rating of D (Weak) based on an annualized return of 0.00% over the last three years and a total return of -0.22% year to date 2012. Factored into the performance evaluation is an expense ratio of 0.14% (very low).

The fund's risk rating is currently B+ (Good). It carries a beta of 0.00, meaning the fund's expected move will be 0.0% for every 10% move in the market. Volatility, as measured by both the semi-deviation and a drawdown factor, is considered very low. As of December 31, 2012, *Schwab US TIPS ETF traded at a premium of .34% above its net asset value, which is worse than its one-year historical average premium of .08%.

Matthew Hastings has been running the fund for 3 years and currently receives a manager quality ranking of 38 (0=worst, 99=best). This fund offers only a moderate level of risk but investors looking for strong performance are still waiting.

Data Date	Investment Rating	Net Assets ($Mil)	Price	Performance Rating/Pts	Total Return Y-T-D	Risk Rating/Pts
12-12	C-	571.40	58.30	D / 2.2	-0.22%	B+ / 9.7
2011	B-	288.40	55.62	C / 4.9	0.50%	B+ / 9.8

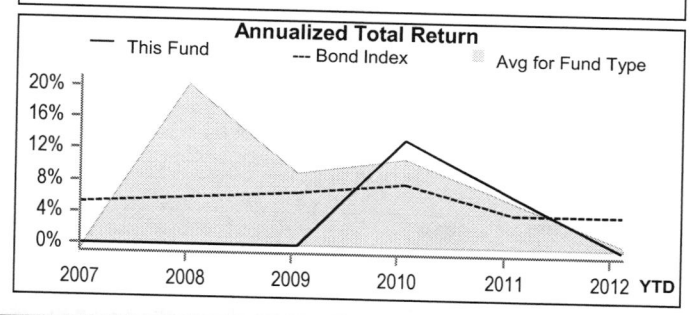

*SP Bank ETF (KBE)

D+   **Weak**

Fund Family: SSgA Funds Management Inc
Fund Type: Financial Services
Inception Date: November 8, 2005

Major Rating Factors: *SP Bank ETF receives a TheStreet.com Investment Rating of D+ (Weak). The fund currently has a performance rating of C- (Fair) based on an annualized return of 3.79% over the last three years and a total return of 3.90% year to date 2012. Factored into the performance evaluation is an expense ratio of 0.35% (very low).

The fund's risk rating is currently C+ (Fair). It carries a beta of 1.10, meaning it is expected to move 11.0% for every 10% move in the market. Volatility, as measured by both the semi-deviation and a drawdown factor, is considered low. As of December 31, 2012, *SP Bank ETF traded at a discount of 3.76% below its net asset value, which is better than its one-year historical average discount of .02%.

John A. Tucker has been running the fund for 8 years and currently receives a manager quality ranking of 32 (0=worst, 99=best). If you desire an average level of risk, then this fund may be an option.

Data Date	Investment Rating	Net Assets ($Mil)	Price	Performance Rating/Pts	Total Return Y-T-D	Risk Rating/Pts
12-12	D+	1,678.90	23.83	C- / 3.3	3.90%	C+ / 6.9
2011	D	1,140.60	19.83	D / 2.1	4.84%	C+ / 6.4
2010	D-	1,988.30	25.91	D- / 1.0	23.06%	C- / 4.0
2009	E+	821.69	21.17	E / 0.5	-3.26%	C- / 4.1

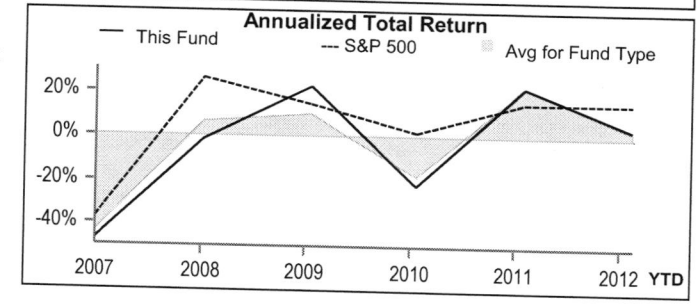

* Denotes ETF Fund

*SP Capital Markets ETF (KCE)

C-   **Fair**

Fund Family: SSgA Funds Management Inc
Fund Type: Financial Services
Inception Date: November 8, 2005

Major Rating Factors: Middle of the road best describes *SP Capital Markets ETF whose TheStreet.com Investment Rating is currently a C- (Fair). The fund currently has a performance rating of C (Fair) based on an annualized return of 1.96% over the last three years and a total return of 6.30% year to date 2012. Factored into the performance evaluation is an expense ratio of 0.36% (very low).

The fund's risk rating is currently C+ (Fair). It carries a beta of 1.16, meaning it is expected to move 11.6% for every 10% move in the market. Volatility, as measured by both the semi-deviation and a drawdown factor, is considered low. As of December 31, 2012, *SP Capital Markets ETF traded at a discount of 5.90% below its net asset value, which is better than its one-year historical average discount of .05%.

John A. Tucker has been running the fund for 8 years and currently receives a manager quality ranking of 15 (0=worst, 99=best). If you desire an average level of risk, then this fund may be an option.

Data Date	Investment Rating	Net Assets ($Mil)	Price	Performance Rating/Pts	Total Return Y-T-D	Risk Rating/Pts
12-12	C-	20.40	34.11	C / 4.3	6.30%	C+ / 6.7
2011	D	22.40	27.95	D / 2.2	3.61%	C+ / 6.9
2010	D-	76.80	38.39	E+ / 0.9	6.23%	C / 4.8
2009	D-	80.19	36.78	E+ / 0.8	37.48%	C / 4.9

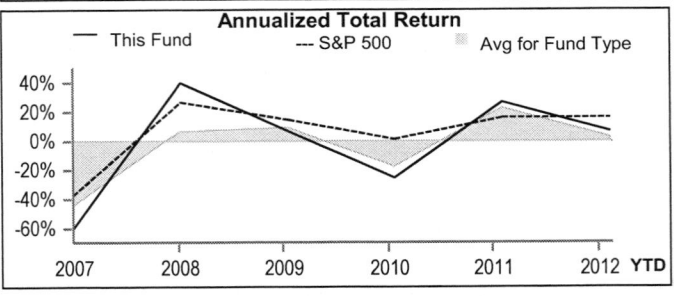

Annualized Total Return

*SP Insurance ETF (KIE)

C   **Fair**

Fund Family: SSgA Funds Management Inc
Fund Type: Income
Inception Date: November 8, 2005

Major Rating Factors: Middle of the road best describes *SP Insurance ETF whose TheStreet.com Investment Rating is currently a C (Fair). The fund currently has a performance rating of C+ (Fair) based on an annualized return of 10.08% over the last three years and a total return of 4.55% year to date 2012. Factored into the performance evaluation is an expense ratio of 0.35% (very low).

The fund's risk rating is currently B- (Good). It carries a beta of 1.22, meaning it is expected to move 12.2% for every 10% move in the market. Volatility, as measured by both the semi-deviation and a drawdown factor, is considered low. As of December 31, 2012, *SP Insurance ETF traded at a discount of 4.37% below its net asset value.

John A. Tucker has been running the fund for 8 years and currently receives a manager quality ranking of 30 (0=worst, 99=best). If you desire an average level of risk, then this fund may be an option.

Data Date	Investment Rating	Net Assets ($Mil)	Price	Performance Rating/Pts	Total Return Y-T-D	Risk Rating/Pts
12-12	C	143.10	44.00	C+ / 5.9	4.55%	B- / 7.3
2011	C-	120.90	37.21	C / 4.3	0.59%	C+ / 6.7
2010	D+	236.80	43.03	C- / 3.7	26.06%	C / 4.5
2009	D-	139.21	34.71	D- / 1.1	26.28%	C / 4.5

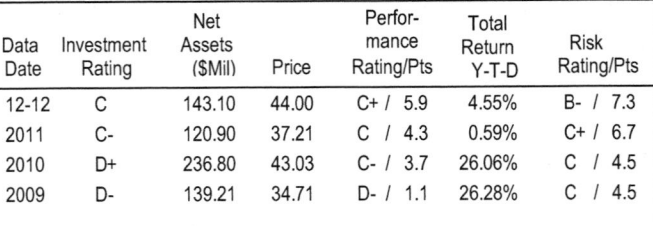

Annualized Total Return

*SP Regional Banking ETF (KRE)

C-   **Fair**

Fund Family: SSgA Funds Management Inc
Fund Type: Financial Services
Inception Date: June 19, 2006

Major Rating Factors: Middle of the road best describes *SP Regional Banking ETF whose TheStreet.com Investment Rating is currently a C- (Fair). The fund currently has a performance rating of C- (Fair) based on an annualized return of 8.84% over the last three years and a total return of 3.43% year to date 2012. Factored into the performance evaluation is an expense ratio of 0.35% (very low).

The fund's risk rating is currently B- (Good). It carries a beta of 1.09, meaning that its performance tracks fairly well with that of the overall stock market. Volatility, as measured by both the semi-deviation and a drawdown factor, is considered low. As of December 31, 2012, *SP Regional Banking ETF traded at a discount of 3.42% below its net asset value, which is better than its one-year historical average premium of .01%.

John A. Tucker currently receives a manager quality ranking of 63 (0=worst, 99=best). If you desire an average level of risk, then this fund may be an option.

Data Date	Investment Rating	Net Assets ($Mil)	Price	Performance Rating/Pts	Total Return Y-T-D	Risk Rating/Pts
12-12	C-	1,147.00	27.97	C- / 3.8	3.43%	B- / 7.3
2011	D+	721.40	24.41	D+ / 2.9	4.59%	C+ / 6.8
2010	D	793.50	26.45	D+ / 2.3	20.66%	C / 5.3
2009	D-	434.94	22.25	E / 0.5	-21.83%	C / 5.2

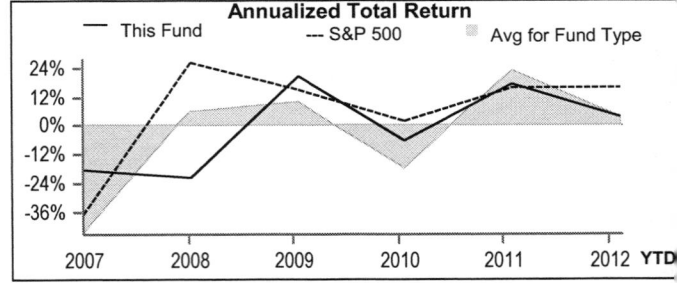

Annualized Total Return

*SPDR Barclays 1-3 Month T-Bill E (BIL)

C-   **Fair**

Fund Family: SSgA Funds Management Inc
Fund Type: US Government/Agency
Inception Date: May 25, 2007

Major Rating Factors:
Disappointing performance is the major factor driving the C- (Fair) TheStreet.com Investment Rating for *SPDR Barclays 1-3 Month T-Bill E. The fund currently has a performance rating of D- (Weak) based on an annualized return of -0.03% over the last three years and a total return of -0.02% year to date 2012. Factored into the performance evaluation is an expense ratio of 0.14% (very low).

The fund's risk rating is currently B+ (Good). It carries a beta of 0.00, meaning the fund's expected move will be 0.0% for every 10% move in the market. Volatility, as measured by both the semi-deviation and a drawdown factor, is considered very low. As of December 31, 2012, *SPDR Barclays 1-3 Month T-Bill E traded at a price exactly equal to its net asset value.

Jeffrey A. St. Peters currently receives a manager quality ranking of 50 (0=worst, 99=best). This fund offers only a moderate level of risk but investors looking for strong performance are still waiting.

Data Date	Investment Rating	Net Assets ($Mil)	Price	Performance Rating/Pts	Total Return Y-T-D	Risk Rating/Pts
12-12	C-	1,296.50	45.81	D- / 1.3	-0.02%	B+ / 9.9
2011	C-	1,654.50	45.83	D / 1.9	-0.02%	B+ / 9.9
2010	C	1,013.40	45.85	D+ / 2.3	-0.04%	B+ / 9.0
2009	C	985.94	45.87	D / 1.9	0.25%	B+ / 9.1

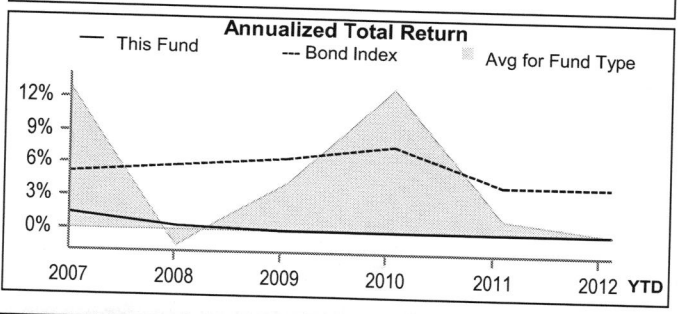

*SPDR Barclays Aggregate Bond ETF (LAG)

C   **Fair**

Fund Family: SSgA Funds Management Inc
Fund Type: General - Investment Grade
Inception Date: May 23, 2007

Major Rating Factors:
Disappointing performance is the major factor driving the C (Fair) TheStreet.com Investment Rating for *SPDR Barclays Aggregate Bond ETF. The fund currently has a performance rating of D+ (Weak) based on an annualized return of 5.19% over the last three years and a total return of -0.32% year to date 2012. Factored into the performance evaluation is an expense ratio of 0.13% (very low).

The fund's risk rating is currently B+ (Good). It carries a beta of 1.11, meaning it is expected to move 11.1% for every 10% move in the market. Volatility, as measured by both the semi-deviation and a drawdown factor, is considered very low. As of December 31, 2012, *SPDR Barclays Aggregate Bond ETF traded at a premium of .46% above its net asset value.

Max DeSantis currently receives a manager quality ranking of 41 (0=worst, 99=best). This fund offers only a moderate level of risk but investors looking for strong performance are still waiting.

Data Date	Investment Rating	Net Assets ($Mil)	Price	Performance Rating/Pts	Total Return Y-T-D	Risk Rating/Pts
12-12	C	621.70	58.77	D+ / 2.4	-0.32%	B+ / 9.7
2011	C	306.20	57.90	C- / 3.2	-0.32%	B+ / 9.6
2010	B	222.40	55.56	C / 4.5	4.48%	B / 8.8
2009	C+	196.09	54.69	C- / 3.3	3.97%	B+ / 9.1

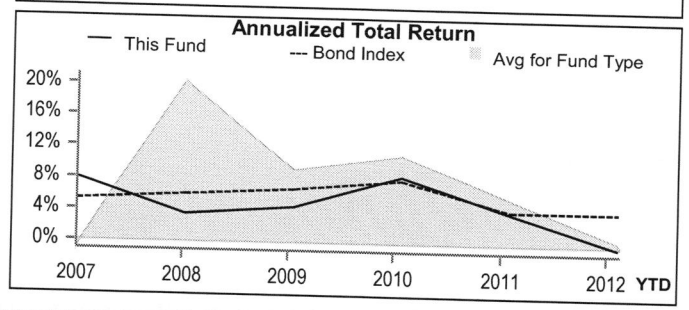

*SPDR Barclays Conv Sec ETF (CWB)

C   **Fair**

Fund Family: SSgA Funds Management Inc
Fund Type: Growth and Income
Inception Date: April 14, 2009

Major Rating Factors: Middle of the road best describes *SPDR Barclays Conv Sec ETF whose TheStreet.com Investment Rating is currently a C (Fair). The fund currently has a performance rating of C- (Fair) based on an annualized return of 6.78% over the last three years and a total return of 2.27% year to date 2012. Factored into the performance evaluation is an expense ratio of 0.40% (very low).

The fund's risk rating is currently B (Good). It carries a beta of 0.70, meaning the fund's expected move will be 7.0% for every 10% move in the market. Volatility, as measured by both the semi-deviation and a drawdown factor, is considered low. As of December 31, 2012, *SPDR Barclays Conv Sec ETF traded at a discount of 1.90% below its net asset value, which is better than its one-year historical average premium of .05%.

Michael J. Brunell currently receives a manager quality ranking of 45 (0=worst, 99=best). If you desire an average level of risk, then this fund may be an option.

Data Date	Investment Rating	Net Assets ($Mil)	Price	Performance Rating/Pts	Total Return Y-T-D	Risk Rating/Pts
12-12	C	918.40	40.30	C- / 3.9	2.27%	B / 8.3
2011	D+	680.90	36.17	D- / 1.5	2.35%	B / 8.5
2010	A+	532.30	41.05	B+ / 8.6	13.01%	B / 8.4

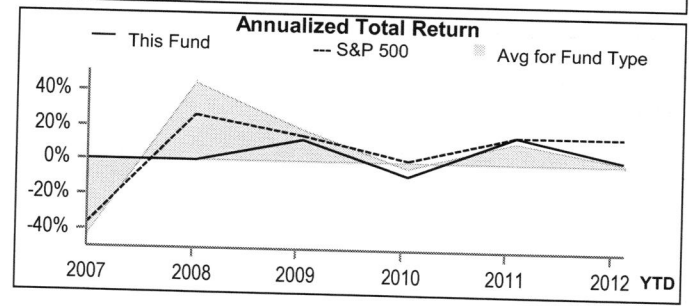

*SPDR Barclays Em Mkt Local Bond (EBND)   C+   Fair

Fund Family: SSgA Funds Management Inc
Fund Type: Growth and Income
Inception Date: February 23, 2011

Major Rating Factors: Middle of the road best describes *SPDR Barclays Em Mkt Local Bond whose TheStreet.com Investment Rating is currently a C+ (Fair). The fund currently has a performance rating of C+ (Fair) based on an annualized return of 0.00% over the last three years and a total return of 0.28% year to date 2012. Factored into the performance evaluation is an expense ratio of 0.50% (very low).

The fund's risk rating is currently B (Good). It carries a beta of 0.00, meaning the fund's expected move will be 0.0% for every 10% move in the market. Volatility, as measured by both the semi-deviation and a drawdown factor, is considered low. As of December 31, 2012, *SPDR Barclays Em Mkt Local Bond traded at a premium of .31% above its net asset value, which is better than its one-year historical average premium of .86%.

Abhishek Kumar currently receives a manager quality ranking of 68 (0=worst, 99=best). If you desire an average level of risk, then this fund may be an option.

Data Date	Investment Rating	Net Assets ($Mil)	Price	Performance Rating/Pts	Total Return Y-T-D	Risk Rating/Pts
12-12	C+	150.50	32.29	C+ / 5.8	0.28%	B / 8.7

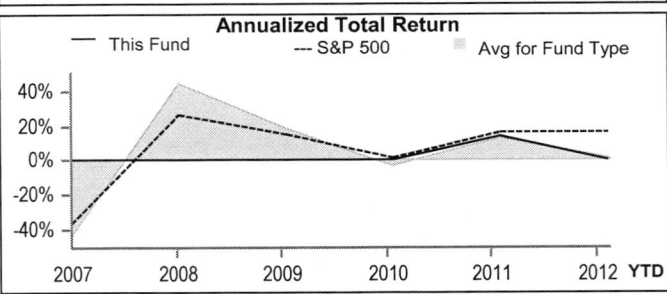

*SPDR Barclays High Yield Bond ET (JNK)   C-   Fair

Fund Family: SSgA Funds Management Inc
Fund Type: Corporate - High Yield
Inception Date: November 28, 2007

Major Rating Factors: Middle of the road best describes *SPDR Barclays High Yield Bond ET whose TheStreet.com Investment Rating is currently a C- (Fair). The fund currently has a performance rating of C (Fair) based on an annualized return of 10.05% over the last three years and a total return of 1.23% year to date 2012. Factored into the performance evaluation is an expense ratio of 0.40% (very low).

The fund's risk rating is currently B- (Good). It carries a beta of 1.28, meaning it is expected to move 12.8% for every 10% move in the market. Volatility, as measured by both the semi-deviation and a drawdown factor, is considered low. As of December 31, 2012, *SPDR Barclays High Yield Bond ET traded at a discount of .88% below its net asset value, which is better than its one-year historical average premium of .24%.

Michael J. Brunell currently receives a manager quality ranking of 26 (0=worst, 99=best). If you desire an average level of risk, then this fund may be an option.

Data Date	Investment Rating	Net Assets ($Mil)	Price	Performance Rating/Pts	Total Return Y-T-D	Risk Rating/Pts
12-12	C-	12,502.30	40.71	C / 4.5	1.23%	B- / 7.3
2011	B-	8,852.60	38.45	C+ / 6.1	0.05%	B / 8.6
2010	C+	6,315.30	39.71	C+ / 6.1	11.68%	C+ / 6.0
2009	B	1,900.71	38.81	B+ / 8.7	39.76%	C / 4.7

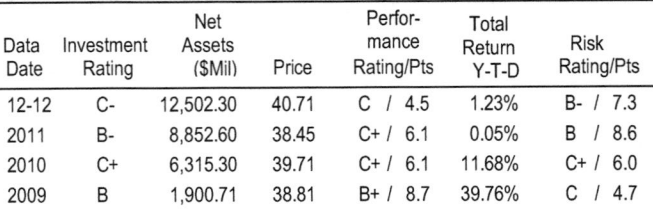
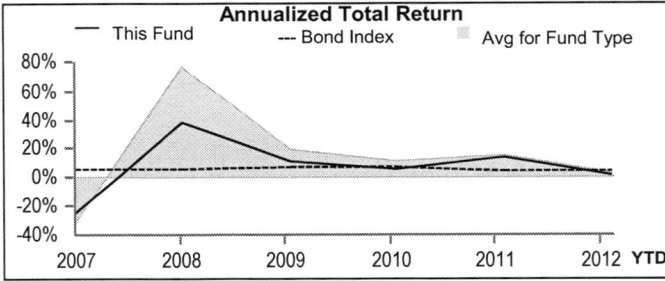

*SPDR Barclays Int Term Crp Bond (ITR)   C   Fair

Fund Family: SSgA Funds Management Inc
Fund Type: General - Investment Grade
Inception Date: February 10, 2009

Major Rating Factors:
Disappointing performance is the major factor driving the C (Fair) TheStreet.com Investment Rating for *SPDR Barclays Int Term Crp Bond. The fund currently has a performance rating of D+ (Weak) based on an annualized return of 6.53% over the last three years and a total return of -0.34% year to date 2012. Factored into the performance evaluation is an expense ratio of 0.15% (very low).

The fund's risk rating is currently B+ (Good). It carries a beta of 0.81, meaning the fund's expected move will be 8.1% for every 10% move in the market. Volatility, as measured by both the semi-deviation and a drawdown factor, is considered very low. As of December 31, 2012, *SPDR Barclays Int Term Crp Bond traded at a premium of .52% above its net asset value, which is better than its one-year historical average premium of .54%.

Max DeSantis currently receives a manager quality ranking of 66 (0=worst, 99=best). This fund offers only a moderate level of risk but investors looking for strong performance are still waiting.

Data Date	Investment Rating	Net Assets ($Mil)	Price	Performance Rating/Pts	Total Return Y-T-D	Risk Rating/Pts
12-12	C	349.80	34.82	D+ / 2.8	-0.34%	B+ / 9.7
2011	C	217.60	33.21	C- / 3.1	0.03%	B+ / 9.8
2010	B	143.10	32.56	C- / 4.2	6.35%	B / 8.9

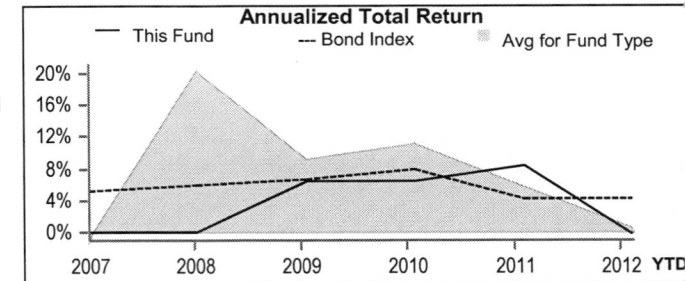

*SPDR Barclays Int Tr Treas ETF (ITE)

C-   **Fair**

Fund Family: SSgA Funds Management Inc
Fund Type: US Government/Agency
Inception Date: May 23, 2007

Major Rating Factors:
Disappointing performance is the major factor driving the C- (Fair) TheStreet.com Investment Rating for *SPDR Barclays Int Tr Treas ETF. The fund currently has a performance rating of D (Weak) based on an annualized return of 3.91% over the last three years and a total return of -0.03% year to date 2012. Factored into the performance evaluation is an expense ratio of 0.14% (very low).

The fund's risk rating is currently B+ (Good). It carries a beta of 0.16, meaning the fund's expected move will be 1.6% for every 10% move in the market. Volatility, as measured by both the semi-deviation and a drawdown factor, is considered very low. As of December 31, 2012, *SPDR Barclays Int Tr Treas ETF traded at a premium of .03% above its net asset value, which is worse than its one-year historical average discount of .06%.

Karen Tsang currently receives a manager quality ranking of 67 (0=worst, 99=best). This fund offers only a moderate level of risk but investors looking for strong performance are still waiting.

Data Date	Investment Rating	Net Assets ($Mil)	Price	Performance Rating/Pts	Total Return Y-T-D	Risk Rating/Pts
12-12	C-	170.30	60.72	D / 2.1	-0.03%	B+ / 9.8
2011	C	226.10	61.05	D+ / 2.8	-0.16%	B+ / 9.8
2010	B	205.30	58.57	C- / 3.9	4.53%	B+ / 9.1
2009	C	143.07	57.07	D / 1.7	-1.02%	B+ / 9.2

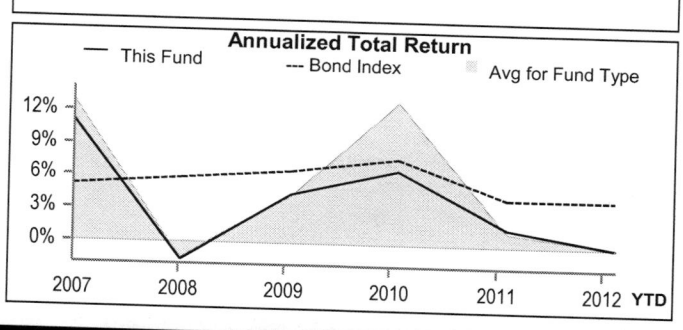

*SPDR Barclays Intl Corporate Bd (IBND)

B+   **Good**

Fund Family: SSgA Funds Management Inc
Fund Type: Corporate - Investment Grade
Inception Date: May 19, 2010

Major Rating Factors: Strong performance is the major factor driving the B+ (Good) TheStreet.com Investment Rating for *SPDR Barclays Intl Corporate Bd. The fund currently has a performance rating of B- (Good) based on an annualized return of 0.00% over the last three years and a total return of 0.34% year to date 2012. Factored into the performance evaluation is an expense ratio of 0.55% (very low).

The fund's risk rating is currently B (Good). It carries a beta of 0.00, meaning the fund's expected move will be 0.0% for every 10% move in the market. Volatility, as measured by both the semi-deviation and a drawdown factor, is considered low. As of December 31, 2012, *SPDR Barclays Intl Corporate Bd traded at a premium of .11% above its net asset value, which is better than its one-year historical average premium of .38%.

John P. Philpot currently receives a manager quality ranking of 95 (0=worst, 99=best). If you desire only a moderate level of risk and strong performance, then this fund is an excellent option.

Data Date	Investment Rating	Net Assets ($Mil)	Price	Performance Rating/Pts	Total Return Y-T-D	Risk Rating/Pts
12-12	B+	116.10	35.40	B- / 7.3	0.34%	B / 8.7
2011	D+	53.60	31.52	D- / 1.4	-1.52%	B / 8.7

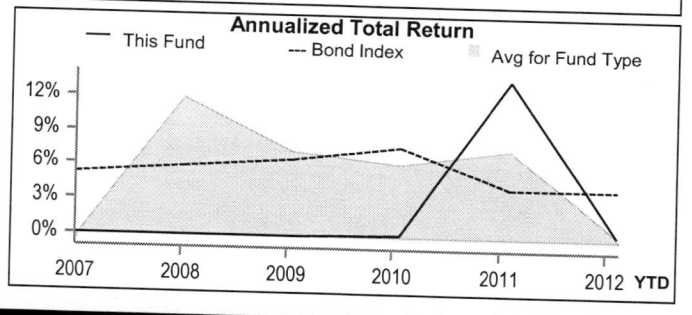

*SPDR Barclays Intl Treasury Bd E (BWX)

C-   **Fair**

Fund Family: SSgA Funds Management Inc
Fund Type: Global
Inception Date: October 2, 2007

Major Rating Factors:
Disappointing performance is the major factor driving the C- (Fair) TheStreet.com Investment Rating for *SPDR Barclays Intl Treasury Bd E. The fund currently has a performance rating of D (Weak) based on an annualized return of 3.57% over the last three years and a total return of -0.74% year to date 2012. Factored into the performance evaluation is an expense ratio of 0.50% (very low).

The fund's risk rating is currently B+ (Good). It carries a beta of 1.08, meaning that its performance tracks fairly well with that of the overall stock market. Volatility, as measured by both the semi-deviation and a drawdown factor, is considered very low. As of December 31, 2012, *SPDR Barclays Intl Treasury Bd E traded at a premium of .89% above its net asset value, which is worse than its one-year historical average premium of .23%.

Mahesh Jayakumar currently receives a manager quality ranking of 53 (0=worst, 99=best). This fund offers only a moderate level of risk but investors looking for strong performance are still waiting.

Data Date	Investment Rating	Net Assets ($Mil)	Price	Performance Rating/Pts	Total Return Y-T-D	Risk Rating/Pts
12-12	C-	1,975.10	61.01	D / 2.2	-0.74%	B+ / 9.3
2011	C-	1,616.60	58.83	D+ / 2.6	-1.58%	B / 8.8
2010	C+	1,342.40	58.46	C- / 4.1	3.17%	B- / 7.8
2009	C+	1,089.23	56.83	C- / 3.7	6.31%	B / 8.4

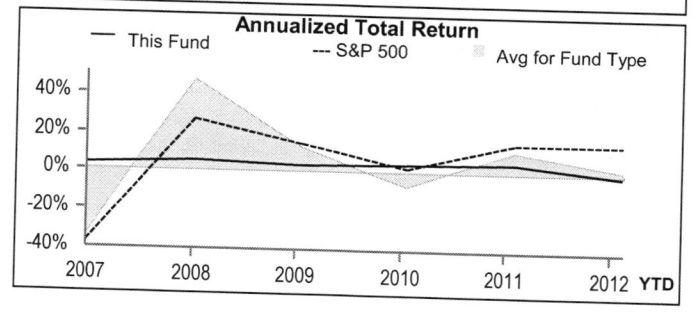

* Denotes ETF Fund

*SPDR Barclays Invest Grade FlRt (FLRN)   C-   Fair

Fund Family: SSgA Funds Management Inc
Fund Type: Corporate - Investment Grade
Inception Date: December 1, 2011

Data Date	Investment Rating	Net Assets ($Mil)	Price	Perfor-mance Rating/Pts	Total Return Y-T-D	Risk Rating/Pts
12-12	C-	15.20	30.66	D / 2.1	0.61%	B+ / 9.6

Major Rating Factors:
Disappointing performance is the major factor driving the C- (Fair) TheStreet.com Investment Rating for *SPDR Barclays Invest Grade FlRt. The fund currently has a performance rating of D (Weak) based on an annualized return of 0.00% over the last three years and a total return of 0.61% year to date 2012. Factored into the performance evaluation is an expense ratio of 0.15% (very low).

The fund's risk rating is currently B+ (Good). It carries a beta of 0.00, meaning the fund's expected move will be 0.0% for every 10% move in the market. Volatility, as measured by both the semi-deviation and a drawdown factor, is considered very low. As of December 31, 2012, *SPDR Barclays Invest Grade FlRt traded at a premium of .56% above its net asset value, which is better than its one-year historical average premium of .81%.

Peter R. Breault currently receives a manager quality ranking of 27 (0=worst, 99=best). This fund offers only a moderate level of risk but investors looking for strong performance are still waiting.

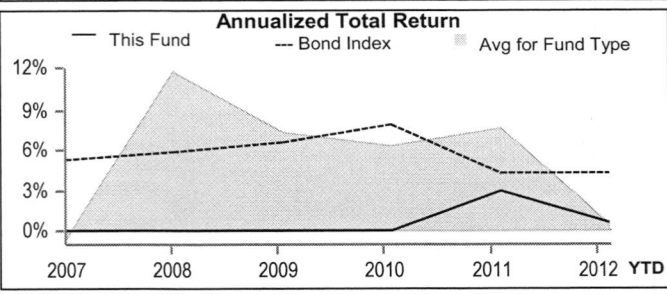

*SPDR Barclays Iss Sco Corp Bond (CBND)   C   Fair

Fund Family: SSgA Funds Management Inc
Fund Type: Corporate - Investment Grade
Inception Date: April 6, 2011

Data Date	Investment Rating	Net Assets ($Mil)	Price	Perfor-mance Rating/Pts	Total Return Y-T-D	Risk Rating/Pts
12-12	C	29.30	32.58	D+ / 2.8	0.52%	B+ / 9.9

Major Rating Factors:
Disappointing performance is the major factor driving the C (Fair) TheStreet.com Investment Rating for *SPDR Barclays Iss Sco Corp Bond. The fund currently has a performance rating of D+ (Weak) based on an annualized return of 0.00% over the last three years and a total return of 0.52% year to date 2012. Factored into the performance evaluation is an expense ratio of 0.16% (very low).

The fund's risk rating is currently B+ (Good). It carries a beta of 0.00, meaning the fund's expected move will be 0.0% for every 10% move in the market. Volatility, as measured by both the semi-deviation and a drawdown factor, is considered very low. As of December 31, 2012, *SPDR Barclays Iss Sco Corp Bond traded at a premium of .09% above its net asset value, which is better than its one-year historical average premium of .70%.

Max DeSantis currently receives a manager quality ranking of 50 (0=worst, 99=best). This fund offers only a moderate level of risk but investors looking for strong performance are still waiting.

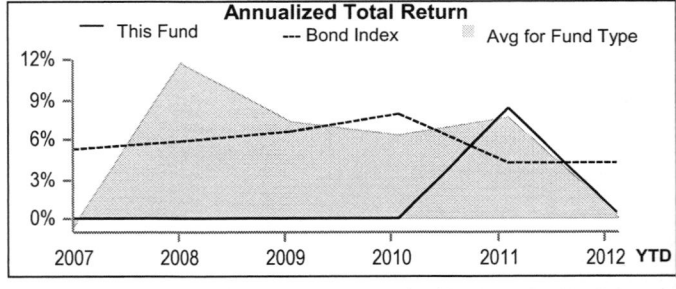

*SPDR Barclays LongTerm Treasury (TLO)   C   Fair

Fund Family: SSgA Funds Management Inc
Fund Type: US Government/Agency
Inception Date: May 23, 2007

Data Date	Investment Rating	Net Assets ($Mil)	Price	Perfor-mance Rating/Pts	Total Return Y-T-D	Risk Rating/Pts
12-12	C	42.40	70.11	C- / 3.9	-0.97%	B / 8.7
2011	C+	56.00	69.93	C / 5.5	-1.82%	B / 8.5
2010	C+	27.90	55.55	C- / 3.6	8.41%	B / 8.1
2009	C-	16.50	53.07	E+ / 0.7	-11.08%	B / 8.4

Major Rating Factors: Middle of the road best describes *SPDR Barclays LongTerm Treasury whose TheStreet.com Investment Rating is currently a C (Fair). The fund currently has a performance rating of C- (Fair) based on an annualized return of 12.50% over the last three years and a total return of -0.97% year to date 2012. Factored into the performance evaluation is an expense ratio of 0.14% (very low).

The fund's risk rating is currently B (Good). It carries a beta of 1.04, meaning that its performance tracks fairly well with that of the overall stock market. Volatility, as measured by both the semi-deviation and a drawdown factor, is considered low. As of December 31, 2012, *SPDR Barclays LongTerm Treasury traded at a premium of 1.17% above its net asset value, which is worse than its one-year historical average premium of .05%.

Karen Tsang currently receives a manager quality ranking of 46 (0=worst, 99=best). If you desire an average level of risk, then this fund may be an option.

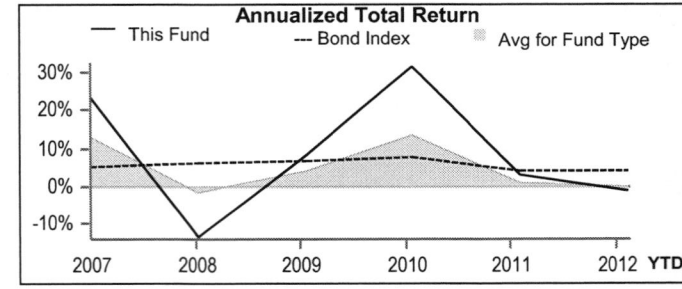

*SPDR Barclays LongTrm Corp Bond (LWC)

C **Fair**

Fund Family: SSgA Funds Management Inc
Fund Type: General - Investment Grade
Inception Date: March 10, 2009

Major Rating Factors: Middle of the road best describes *SPDR Barclays LongTrm Corp Bond whose TheStreet.com Investment Rating is currently a C (Fair). The fund currently has a performance rating of C- (Fair) based on an annualized return of 10.57% over the last three years and a total return of 0.19% year to date 2012. Factored into the performance evaluation is an expense ratio of 0.15% (very low).

The fund's risk rating is currently B+ (Good). It carries a beta of 2.43, meaning it is expected to move 24.3% for every 10% move in the market. Volatility, as measured by both the semi-deviation and a drawdown factor, is considered very low. As of December 31, 2012, *SPDR Barclays LongTrm Corp Bond traded at a premium of .15% above its net asset value, which is better than its one-year historical average premium of .59%.

John P. Kirby currently receives a manager quality ranking of 26 (0=worst, 99=best). If you desire an average level of risk, then this fund may be an option.

Data Date	Investment Rating	Net Assets ($Mil)	Price	Performance Rating/Pts	Total Return Y-T-D	Risk Rating/Pts
12-12	C	128.00	41.14	C- / 3.8	0.19%	B+ / 9.0
2011	B	65.90	39.49	C+ / 6.8	-1.27%	B+ / 9.1
2010	C+	28.40	35.65	D+ / 2.9	6.18%	B / 8.5

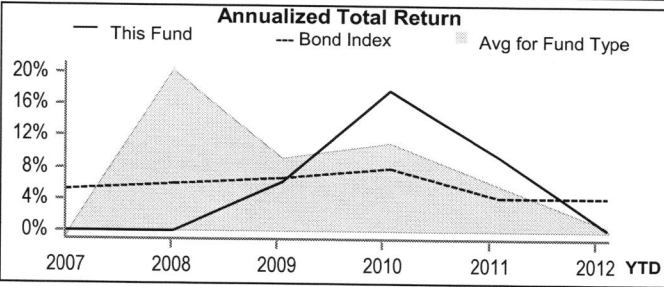
Annualized Total Return — This Fund / Bond Index / Avg for Fund Type

*SPDR Barclays Mortg Backed Bond (MBG)

C- **Fair**

Fund Family: SSgA Funds Management Inc
Fund Type: Mortgage
Inception Date: January 15, 2009

Major Rating Factors:
Disappointing performance is the major factor driving the C- (Fair) TheStreet.com Investment Rating for *SPDR Barclays Mortg Backed Bond. The fund currently has a performance rating of D (Weak) based on an annualized return of 3.71% over the last three years and a total return of -0.04% year to date 2012. Factored into the performance evaluation is an expense ratio of 0.20% (very low).

The fund's risk rating is currently B+ (Good). It carries a beta of 1.36, meaning it is expected to move 13.6% for every 10% move in the market. Volatility, as measured by both the semi-deviation and a drawdown factor, is considered very low. As of December 31, 2012, *SPDR Barclays Mortg Backed Bond traded at a premium of .22% above its net asset value.

Karen Tsang currently receives a manager quality ranking of 33 (0=worst, 99=best). This fund offers only a moderate level of risk but investors looking for strong performance are still waiting.

Data Date	Investment Rating	Net Assets ($Mil)	Price	Performance Rating/Pts	Total Return Y-T-D	Risk Rating/Pts
12-12	C-	35.50	27.31	D / 2.1	-0.04%	B+ / 9.6
2011	C	41.10	27.38	C- / 3.5	0.21%	B+ / 9.6
2010	C	32.20	26.44	D / 1.9	2.55%	B / 8.8

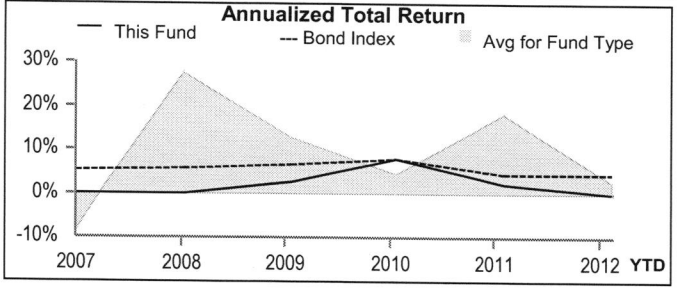
Annualized Total Return — This Fund / Bond Index / Avg for Fund Type

*SPDR Barclays Sht Trm Corp Bond (SCPB)

C- **Fair**

Fund Family: SSgA Funds Management Inc
Fund Type: Corporate - Investment Grade
Inception Date: December 16, 2009

Major Rating Factors:
Disappointing performance is the major factor driving the C- (Fair) TheStreet.com Investment Rating for *SPDR Barclays Sht Trm Corp Bond. The fund currently has a performance rating of D (Weak) based on an annualized return of 2.68% over the last three years and a total return of 0.26% year to date 2012. Factored into the performance evaluation is an expense ratio of 0.23% (very low).

The fund's risk rating is currently B+ (Good). It carries a beta of 0.24, meaning the fund's expected move will be 2.4% for every 10% move in the market. Volatility, as measured by both the semi-deviation and a drawdown factor, is considered very low. As of December 31, 2012, *SPDR Barclays Sht Trm Corp Bond traded at a premium of .07% above its net asset value, which is better than its one-year historical average premium of .32%.

Max DeSantis currently receives a manager quality ranking of 57 (0=worst, 99=best). This fund offers only a moderate level of risk but investors looking for strong performance are still waiting.

Data Date	Investment Rating	Net Assets ($Mil)	Price	Performance Rating/Pts	Total Return Y-T-D	Risk Rating/Pts
12-12	C-	1,723.10	30.72	D / 2.0	0.26%	B+ / 9.9
2011	C	390.60	30.11	D+ / 2.3	0.60%	B+ / 9.9
2010	B-	196.40	30.25	C- / 3.4	2.52%	B+ / 9.0

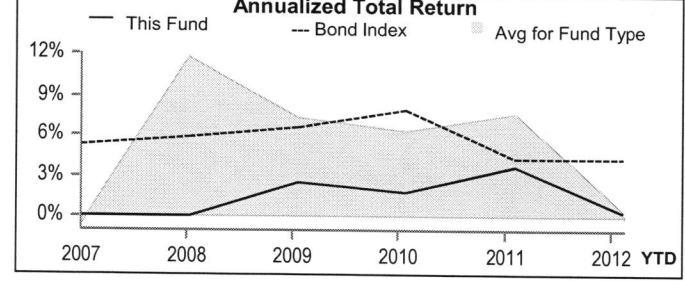
Annualized Total Return — This Fund / Bond Index / Avg for Fund Type

*SPDR Barclays Sht Trm Treasury E (SST)

C-   **Fair**

Fund Family: SSgA Funds Management Inc
Fund Type: US Government/Agency
Inception Date: December 1, 2011

Major Rating Factors:
Disappointing performance is the major factor driving the C- (Fair) TheStreet.com Investment Rating for *SPDR Barclays Sht Trm Treasury E. The fund currently has a performance rating of D- (Weak) based on an annualized return of 0.00% over the last three years and a total return of -0.03% year to date 2012. Factored into the performance evaluation is an expense ratio of 0.12% (very low).

The fund's risk rating is currently B+ (Good). It carries a beta of 0.00, meaning the fund's expected move will be 0.0% for every 10% move in the market. Volatility, as measured by both the semi-deviation and a drawdown factor, is considered very low. As of December 31, 2012, *SPDR Barclays Sht Trm Treasury E traded at a premium of .10% above its net asset value, which is worse than its one-year historical average premium of .02%.

Karen Tsang currently receives a manager quality ranking of 58 (0=worst, 99=best). This fund offers only a moderate level of risk but investors looking for strong performance are still waiting.

Data Date	Investment Rating	Net Assets ($Mil)	Price	Performance Rating/Pts	Total Return Y-T-D	Risk Rating/Pts
12-12	C-	3.00	30.17	D- / 1.5	-0.03%	B+ / 9.9

Annualized Total Return

— This Fund --- Bond Index ▨ Avg for Fund Type

*SPDR Barclays ST Intl Treas Bd E (BWZ)

D+   **Weak**

Fund Family: SSgA Funds Management Inc
Fund Type: Global
Inception Date: January 15, 2009

Major Rating Factors:
Disappointing performance is the major factor driving the D+ (Weak) TheStreet.com Investment Rating for *SPDR Barclays ST Intl Treas Bd E. The fund currently has a performance rating of D (Weak) based on an annualized return of 1.02% over the last three years and a total return of 0.07% year to date 2012. Factored into the performance evaluation is an expense ratio of 0.35% (very low).

The fund's risk rating is currently B (Good). It carries a beta of 0.82, meaning fund's expected move will be 8.2% for every 10% move in the market. Volatility, as measured by both the semi-deviation and a drawdown factor, is considered low. As of December 31, 2012, *SPDR Barclays ST Intl Treas Bd E traded at a discount of .11% below its net asset value, which is better than its one-year historical average premium of .12%.

Mahesh Jayakumar currently receives a manager quality ranking of 36 (0=worst, 99=best). This fund offers only a moderate level of risk but investors looking for strong performance are still waiting.

Data Date	Investment Rating	Net Assets ($Mil)	Price	Performance Rating/Pts	Total Return Y-T-D	Risk Rating/Pts
12-12	D+	256.50	36.65	D / 1.7	0.07%	B / 8.7
2011	C-	218.90	35.59	D / 1.6	-0.24%	B / 8.9
2010	B	166.60	37.00	C / 4.7	1.59%	B / 8.2

Annualized Total Return

— This Fund --- S&P 500 ▨ Avg for Fund Type

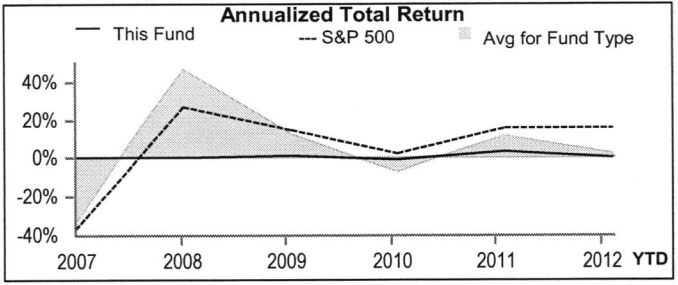

*SPDR Barclays TIPS ETF (IPE)

C   **Fair**

Fund Family: SSgA Funds Management Inc
Fund Type: US Government/Agency
Inception Date: May 25, 2007

Major Rating Factors: Middle of the road best describes *SPDR Barclays TIPS ETF whose TheStreet.com Investment Rating is currently a C (Fair). The fund currently has a performance rating of C- (Fair) based on an annualized return of 8.92% over the last three years and a total return of -0.36% year to date 2012. Factored into the performance evaluation is an expense ratio of 0.19% (very low).

The fund's risk rating is currently B+ (Good). It carries a beta of 0.15, meaning the fund's expected move will be 1.5% for every 10% move in the market. Volatility, as measured by both the semi-deviation and a drawdown factor, is considered very low. As of December 31, 2012, *SPDR Barclays TIPS ETF traded at a premium of .36% above its net asset value, which is worse than its one-year historical average premium of .01%.

Max DeSantis currently receives a manager quality ranking of 85 (0=worst, 99=best). If you desire an average level of risk, then this fund may be an option.

Data Date	Investment Rating	Net Assets ($Mil)	Price	Performance Rating/Pts	Total Return Y-T-D	Risk Rating/Pts
12-12	C	771.60	60.72	C- / 3.3	-0.36%	B+ / 9.7
2011	B-	613.60	58.02	C / 4.7	0.52%	B+ / 9.7
2010	B-	360.60	53.12	C / 4.3	6.03%	B / 8.3
2009	B	288.50	51.18	C / 5.0	11.53%	B / 8.5

Annualized Total Return

— This Fund --- Bond Index ▨ Avg for Fund Type

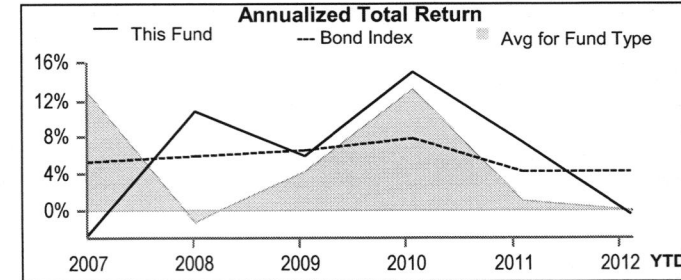

*SPDR DB Intl Gvt Inflation Pt Bo (WIP)

Fund Family: SSgA Funds Management Inc
Fund Type: Global
Inception Date: March 13, 2008

Major Rating Factors: Middle of the road best describes *SPDR DB Intl Gvt Inflation Pt Bo whose TheStreet.com Investment Rating is currently a C (Fair). The fund currently has a performance rating of C- (Fair) based on an annualized return of 6.70% over the last three years and a total return of 0.13% year to date 2012. Factored into the performance evaluation is an expense ratio of 0.50% (very low).

The fund's risk rating is currently B (Good). It carries a beta of 1.09, meaning that its performance tracks fairly well with that of the overall stock market. Volatility, as measured by both the semi-deviation and a drawdown factor, is considered low. As of December 31, 2012, *SPDR DB Intl Gvt Inflation Pt Bo traded at a premium of .32% above its net asset value, which is worse than its one-year historical average premium of .18%.

Max DeSantis currently receives a manager quality ranking of 72 (0=worst, 99=best). If you desire an average level of risk, then this fund may be an option.

						C			Fair
Data Date	Investment Rating	Net Assets ($Mil)	Price	Performance Rating/Pts		Total Return Y-T-D	Risk Rating/Pts	
12-12	C	1,426.90	63.54	C- / 3.6		0.13%	B / 8.8	
2011	C	1,171.50	56.75	C- / 3.4		-0.42%	B / 8.8	
2010	C+	893.40	58.11	C+ / 6.2		4.78%	C+ / 6.8	
2009	B-	394.48	55.86	C+ / 6.0		17.38%	B- / 7.5	

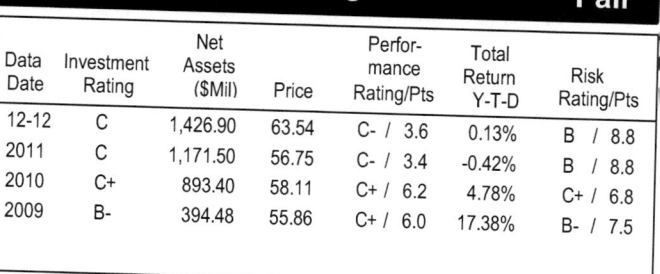

*SPDR DJ REIT ETF (RWR)

Fund Family: SSgA Funds Management Inc
Fund Type: Income
Inception Date: April 23, 2001

Major Rating Factors: Strong performance is the major factor driving the B (Good) TheStreet.com Investment Rating for *SPDR DJ REIT ETF. The fund currently has a performance rating of B (Good) based on an annualized return of 18.69% over the last three years and a total return of 1.90% year to date 2012. Factored into the performance evaluation is an expense ratio of 0.25% (very low).

The fund's risk rating is currently B- (Good). It carries a beta of 1.02, meaning that its performance tracks fairly well with that of the overall stock market. Volatility, as measured by both the semi-deviation and a drawdown factor, is considered low. As of December 31, 2012, *SPDR DJ REIT ETF traded at a discount of 1.91% below its net asset value.

Amos J. Rogers, III currently receives a manager quality ranking of 82 (0=worst, 99=best). If you desire only a moderate level of risk and strong performance, then this fund is an excellent option.

						B			Good
Data Date	Investment Rating	Net Assets ($Mil)	Price	Performance Rating/Pts		Total Return Y-T-D	Risk Rating/Pts	
12-12	B	1,892.20	72.97	B / 7.6		1.90%	B- / 7.6	
2011	C+	1,513.00	64.40	B / 7.9		-0.28%	C+ / 6.3	
2010	C+	1,367.30	61.02	B- / 7.4		28.03%	C- / 4.1	
2009	D-	908.89	49.21	D / 1.6		32.11%	C- / 4.0	

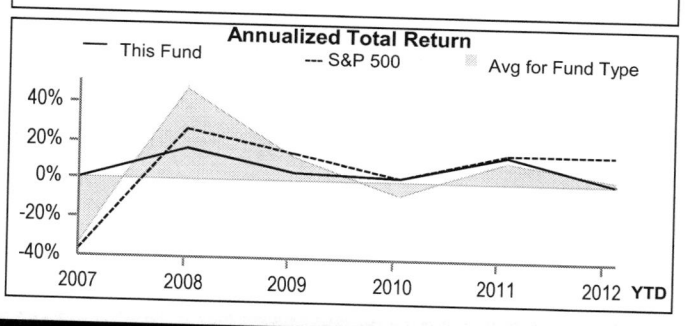

*SPDR DJ Total Market ETF (TMW)

Fund Family: SSgA Funds Management Inc
Fund Type: Growth
Inception Date: October 4, 2000

Major Rating Factors: Middle of the road best describes *SPDR DJ Total Market ETF whose TheStreet.com Investment Rating is currently a C+ (Fair). The fund currently has a performance rating of C (Fair) based on an annualized return of 11.52% over the last three years and a total return of 3.49% year to date 2012. Factored into the performance evaluation is an expense ratio of 0.20% (very low).

The fund's risk rating is currently B (Good). It carries a beta of 1.02, meaning that its performance tracks fairly well with that of the overall stock market. Volatility, as measured by both the semi-deviation and a drawdown factor, is considered low. As of December 31, 2012, *SPDR DJ Total Market ETF traded at a discount of 3.43% below its net asset value, which is better than its one-year historical average discount of .05%.

John A. Tucker has been running the fund for 13 years and currently receives a manager quality ranking of 51 (0=worst, 99=best). If you desire an average level of risk, then this fund may be an option.

						C+			Fair
Data Date	Investment Rating	Net Assets ($Mil)	Price	Performance Rating/Pts		Total Return Y-T-D	Risk Rating/Pts	
12-12	C+	431.10	106.26	C / 5.4		3.49%	B / 8.0	
2011	C+	163.90	93.54	C / 5.4		1.76%	B- / 7.9	
2010	C	202.90	94.54	C / 4.7		17.34%	C+ / 5.9	
2009	D+	158.24	81.95	D+ / 2.4		24.23%	C+ / 6.0	

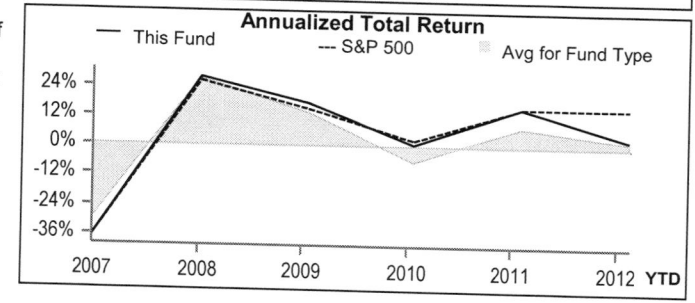

*SPDR DJ Wilshire Glb Real Est ET (RWO)   B   Good

Fund Family: SSgA Funds Management Inc
Fund Type: Growth and Income
Inception Date: May 7, 2008

Major Rating Factors: Strong performance is the major factor driving the B (Good) TheStreet.com Investment Rating for *SPDR DJ Wilshire Glb Real Est ET. The fund currently has a performance rating of B- (Good) based on an annualized return of 15.26% over the last three years and a total return of 1.09% year to date 2012. Factored into the performance evaluation is an expense ratio of 0.50% (very low).

The fund's risk rating is currently B- (Good). It carries a beta of 1.07, meaning that its performance tracks fairly well with that of the overall stock market. Volatility, as measured by both the semi-deviation and a drawdown factor, is considered low. As of December 31, 2012, *SPDR DJ Wilshire Glb Real Est ET traded at a discount of .73% below its net asset value, which is better than its one-year historical average premium of .29%.

Amos J. Rogers III has been running the fund for 5 years and currently receives a manager quality ranking of 71 (0=worst, 99=best). If you desire only a moderate level of risk and strong performance, then this fund is an excellent option.

Data Date	Investment Rating	Net Assets ($Mil)	Price	Performance Rating/Pts	Total Return Y-T-D	Risk Rating/Pts
12-12	B	685.10	42.12	B- / 7.4	1.09%	B- / 7.8
2011	C	323.70	34.89	C+ / 5.9	0.00%	B- / 7.0
2010	B	162.20	37.07	A / 9.3	24.01%	C- / 4.0
2009	B	81.08	32.13	B+ / 8.8	31.12%	C / 4.3

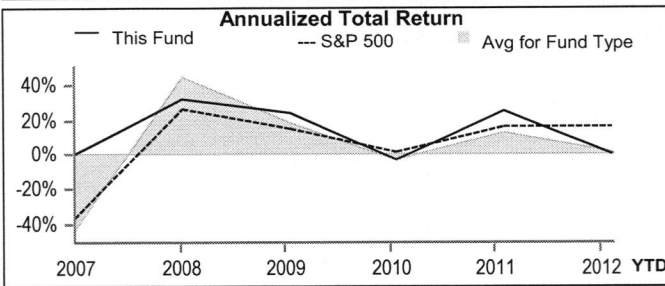

*SPDR DJ Wilshire Intl Real Estat (RWX)   C   Fair

Fund Family: SSgA Funds Management Inc
Fund Type: Foreign
Inception Date: December 15, 2006

Major Rating Factors: Strong performance is the major factor driving the C (Fair) TheStreet.com Investment Rating for *SPDR DJ Wilshire Intl Real Estat. The fund currently has a performance rating of B (Good) based on an annualized return of 12.37% over the last three years and a total return of -0.05% year to date 2012. Factored into the performance evaluation is an expense ratio of 0.59% (very low).

The fund's risk rating is currently C+ (Fair). It carries a beta of 0.96, meaning that its performance tracks fairly well with that of the overall stock market. Volatility, as measured by both the semi-deviation and a drawdown factor, is considered low. As of December 31, 2012, *SPDR DJ Wilshire Intl Real Estat traded at a premium of .34% above its net asset value, which is worse than its one-year historical average premium of .25%.

Amos J. Rogers, III currently receives a manager quality ranking of 88 (0=worst, 99=best). If you desire only a moderate level of risk and strong performance, then this fund is an excellent option.

Data Date	Investment Rating	Net Assets ($Mil)	Price	Performance Rating/Pts	Total Return Y-T-D	Risk Rating/Pts
12-12	C	3,452.60	41.35	B / 7.7	-0.05%	C+ / 5.6
2011	D	2,007.70	31.83	C- / 3.4	0.47%	C+ / 5.6
2010	D	1,430.50	38.93	D+ / 2.8	21.77%	C- / 3.9
2009	E+	939.27	34.89	D- / 1.1	31.75%	C- / 3.4

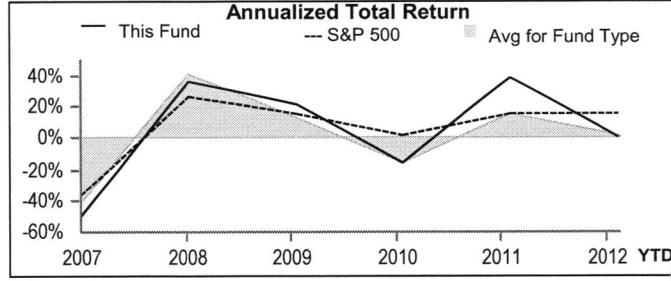

*SPDR DJ Wilshire Large Cap ETF (ELR)   C+   Fair

Fund Family: SSgA Funds Management Inc
Fund Type: Growth
Inception Date: November 8, 2005

Major Rating Factors: Middle of the road best describes *SPDR DJ Wilshire Large Cap ETF whose TheStreet.com Investment Rating is currently a C+ (Fair). The fund currently has a performance rating of C (Fair) based on an annualized return of 11.39% over the last three years and a total return of 3.84% year to date 2012. Factored into the performance evaluation is an expense ratio of 0.20% (very low).

The fund's risk rating is currently B (Good). It carries a beta of 0.92, meaning that its performance tracks fairly well with that of the overall stock market. Volatility, as measured by both the semi-deviation and a drawdown factor, is considered low. As of December 31, 2012, *SPDR DJ Wilshire Large Cap ETF traded at a discount of 3.84% below its net asset value, which is better than its one-year historical average discount of .04%.

John A. Tucker has been running the fund for 7 years and currently receives a manager quality ranking of 58 (0=worst, 99=best). If you desire an average level of risk, then this fund may be an option.

Data Date	Investment Rating	Net Assets ($Mil)	Price	Performance Rating/Pts	Total Return Y-T-D	Risk Rating/Pts
12-12	C+	43.40	66.40	C / 5.2	3.84%	B / 8.2
2011	C+	35.30	58.88	C / 5.2	1.70%	B / 8.0
2010	C-	41.30	59.00	C- / 4.0	15.91%	C+ / 6.0
2009	D+	38.42	51.83	D+ / 2.4	24.27%	C+ / 6.1

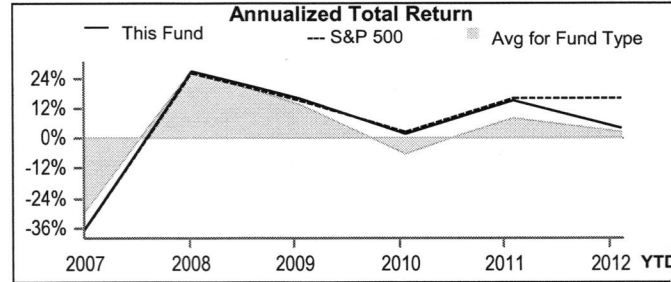

*SPDR DJ Wilshire Mid Cap ETF (EMM)

C+   **Fair**

Fund Family: SSgA Funds Management Inc
Fund Type: Growth
Inception Date: November 8, 2005

Major Rating Factors: Middle of the road best describes *SPDR DJ Wilshire Mid Cap ETF whose TheStreet.com Investment Rating is currently a C+ (Fair). The fund currently has a performance rating of C+ (Fair) based on an annualized return of 13.68% over the last three years and a total return of 3.62% year to date 2012. Factored into the performance evaluation is an expense ratio of 0.25% (very low).

The fund's risk rating is currently B- (Good). It carries a beta of 1.17, meaning it is expected to move 11.7% for every 10% move in the market. Volatility, as measured by both the semi-deviation and a drawdown factor, is considered low. As of December 31, 2012, *SPDR DJ Wilshire Mid Cap ETF traded at a discount of 3.66% below its net asset value, which is better than its one-year historical average discount of .03%.

John A. Tucker has been running the fund for 8 years and currently receives a manager quality ranking of 54 (0=worst, 99=best). If you desire an average level of risk, then this fund may be an option.

Data Date	Investment Rating	Net Assets ($Mil)	Price	Performance Rating/Pts	Total Return Y-T-D	Risk Rating/Pts
12-12	C+	76.10	66.09	C+ / 6.7	3.62%	B- / 7.6
2011	B-	66.60	57.95	C+ / 6.8	1.69%	B- / 7.6
2010	B	59.10	59.43	B- / 7.3	24.63%	C+ / 5.8
2009	C-	31.26	48.30	C / 4.4	43.69%	C+ / 5.8

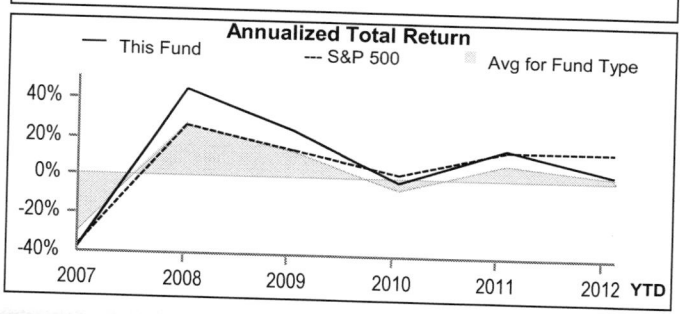

*SPDR Dow Jones Industrial Averag (DIA)

C   **Fair**

Fund Family: State Street Bank and Trust Company
Fund Type: Growth
Inception Date: January 14, 1998

Major Rating Factors: Middle of the road best describes *SPDR Dow Jones Industrial Averag whose TheStreet.com Investment Rating is currently a C (Fair). The fund currently has a performance rating of C (Fair) based on an annualized return of 11.18% over the last three years and a total return of 3.17% year to date 2012. Factored into the performance evaluation is an expense ratio of 0.17% (very low).

The fund's risk rating is currently B (Good). It carries a beta of 0.88, meaning the fund's expected move will be 8.8% for every 10% move in the market. Volatility, as measured by both the semi-deviation and a drawdown factor, is considered low. As of December 31, 2012, *SPDR Dow Jones Industrial Averag traded at a discount of 3.05% below its net asset value.

David K. Chin currently receives a manager quality ranking of 61 (0=worst, 99=best). If you desire an average level of risk, then this fund may be an option.

Data Date	Investment Rating	Net Assets ($Mil)	Price	Performance Rating/Pts	Total Return Y-T-D	Risk Rating/Pts
12-12	C	10,923.40	130.58	C / 4.4	3.17%	B / 8.5
2011	C+	10,842.40	121.85	C+ / 6.0	1.38%	B / 8.1
2010	C	8,721.10	115.63	C- / 4.1	14.26%	C+ / 6.3
2009	C-	7,500.73	104.07	D+ / 2.8	19.06%	C+ / 6.4

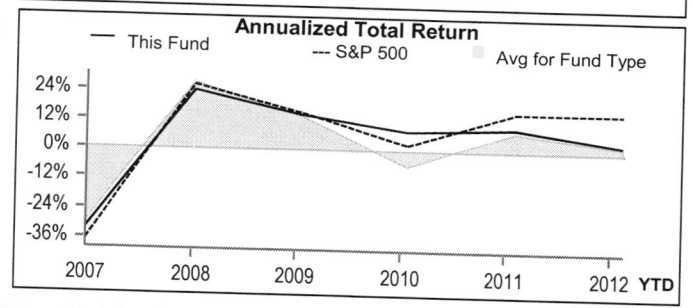

*SPDR Euro STOXX 50 ETF (FEZ)

D   **Weak**

Fund Family: SSgA Funds Management Inc
Fund Type: Foreign
Inception Date: October 15, 2002

Major Rating Factors:
Disappointing performance is the major factor driving the D (Weak) TheStreet.com Investment Rating for *SPDR Euro STOXX 50 ETF. The fund currently has a performance rating of D+ (Weak) based on an annualized return of -1.14% over the last three years and a total return of 2.68% year to date 2012. Factored into the performance evaluation is an expense ratio of 0.29% (very low).

The fund's risk rating is currently C+ (Fair). It carries a beta of 1.37, meaning it is expected to move 13.7% for every 10% move in the market. Volatility, as measured by both the semi-deviation and a drawdown factor, is considered low. As of December 31, 2012, *SPDR Euro STOXX 50 ETF traded at a discount of 2.31% below its net asset value, which is better than its one-year historical average premium of .16%.

John A. Tucker has been running the fund for 11 years and currently receives a manager quality ranking of 17 (0=worst, 99=best). This fund offers only a moderate level of risk but investors looking for strong performance are still waiting.

Data Date	Investment Rating	Net Assets ($Mil)	Price	Performance Rating/Pts	Total Return Y-T-D	Risk Rating/Pts
12-12	D	1,304.60	34.66	D+ / 2.7	2.68%	C+ / 5.7
2011	D-	138.40	29.51	D- / 1.5	-3.12%	C+ / 6.2
2010	E+	163.70	36.84	E+ / 0.8	-7.75%	C- / 4.2
2009	D-	181.92	41.48	D / 1.6	18.75%	C / 4.6

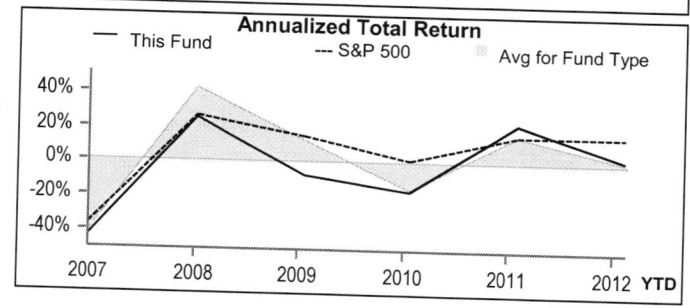

* Denotes ETF Fund

*SPDR FTSE/Macquarie Glob Infr 10 (GII)

C-   **Fair**

Fund Family: SSgA Funds Management Inc
Fund Type: Global
Inception Date: January 25, 2007

Major Rating Factors:
Disappointing performance is the major factor driving the C- (Fair) TheStreet.com Investment Rating for *SPDR FTSE/Macquarie Glob Infr 10. The fund currently has a performance rating of D (Weak) based on an annualized return of 2.31% over the last three years and a total return of 0.42% year to date 2012. Factored into the performance evaluation is an expense ratio of 0.59% (very low).

The fund's risk rating is currently B (Good). It carries a beta of 0.56, meaning the fund's expected move will be 5.6% for every 10% move in the market. Volatility, as measured by both the semi-deviation and a drawdown factor, is considered low. As of December 31, 2012, *SPDR FTSE/Macquarie Glob Infr 10 traded at a discount of .22% below its net asset value, which is better than its one-year historical average discount of .07%.

John A. Tucker currently receives a manager quality ranking of 50 (0=worst, 99=best). This fund offers only a moderate level of risk but investors looking for strong performance are still waiting.

Data Date	Investment Rating	Net Assets ($Mil)	Price	Perfor-mance Rating/Pts	Total Return Y-T-D	Risk Rating/Pts
12-12	C-	59.60	40.26	D / 2.2	0.42%	B / 8.6
2011	C-	35.70	39.51	D+ / 2.6	-0.40%	B / 8.1
2010	D	49.70	41.32	D- / 1.0	1.22%	C+ / 6.3
2009	C+	67.10	42.52	C+ / 6.1	7.09%	C+ / 6.5

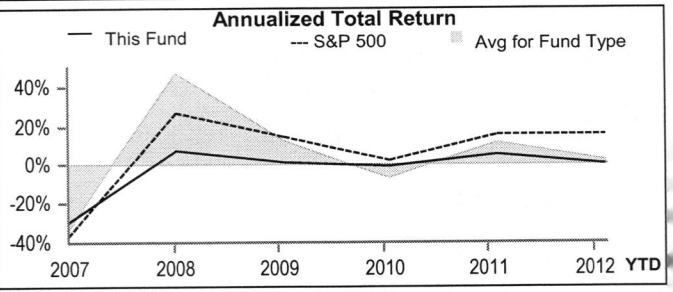

---

*SPDR Global Dow ETF (DGT)

D+   **Weak**

Fund Family: SSgA Funds Management Inc
Fund Type: Global
Inception Date: September 25, 2000

Major Rating Factors:
Disappointing performance is the major factor driving the D+ (Weak) TheStreet.com Investment Rating for *SPDR Global Dow ETF. The fund currently has a performance rating of D+ (Weak) based on an annualized return of 2.59% over the last three years and a total return of 3.53% year to date 2012. Factored into the performance evaluation is an expense ratio of 0.50% (very low).

The fund's risk rating is currently B- (Good). It carries a beta of 0.88, meaning the fund's expected move will be 8.8% for every 10% move in the market. Volatility, as measured by both the semi-deviation and a drawdown factor, is considered low. As of December 31, 2012, *SPDR Global Dow ETF traded at a discount of 3.19% below its net asset value, which is better than its one-year historical average discount of .14%.

John A. Tucker has been running the fund for 8 years and currently receives a manager quality ranking of 38 (0=worst, 99=best). This fund offers only a moderate level of risk but investors looking for strong performance are still waiting.

Data Date	Investment Rating	Net Assets ($Mil)	Price	Perfor-mance Rating/Pts	Total Return Y-T-D	Risk Rating/Pts
12-12	D+	89.30	56.18	D+ / 2.7	3.53%	B- / 7.5
2011	D+	98.20	50.18	D+ / 2.3	0.60%	B- / 7.6
2010	D	122.50	58.46	D / 1.6	4.99%	C+ / 5.9
2009	D+	70.92	57.02	D / 1.8	19.90%	C+ / 6.0

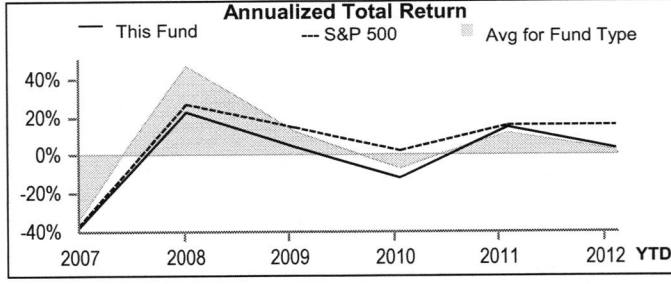

---

*SPDR Gold Shares (GLD)

C   **Fair**

Fund Family: SSgA Funds Management Inc
Fund Type: Precious Metals
Inception Date: November 18, 2004

Major Rating Factors: Middle of the road best describes *SPDR Gold Shares whose TheStreet.com Investment Rating is currently a C (Fair). The fund currently has a performance rating of C (Fair) based on an annualized return of 13.26% over the last three years and a total return of -0.59% year to date 2012. Factored into the performance evaluation is an expense ratio of 0.40% (very low).

The fund's risk rating is currently B (Good). It carries a beta of 0.92, meaning that its performance tracks fairly well with that of the overall stock market. Volatility, as measured by both the semi-deviation and a drawdown factor, is considered low. As of December 31, 2012, *SPDR Gold Shares traded at a premium of .95% above its net asset value, which is worse than its one-year historical average premium of .14%.

This fund has been team managed for 9 years and currently receives a manager quality ranking of 59 (0=worst, 99=best). If you desire an average level of risk, then this fund may be an option.

Data Date	Investment Rating	Net Assets ($Mil)	Price	Perfor-mance Rating/Pts	Total Return Y-T-D	Risk Rating/Pts
12-12	C	72,239.30	162.02	C / 4.3	-0.59%	B / 8.1
2011	B	63,484.30	151.99	B- / 7.5	3.43%	B / 8.3
2010	A	57,210.20	138.72	B+ / 8.8	29.27%	C+ / 6.9
2009	A+	36,885.82	107.31	B / 7.6	24.45%	B- / 7.2

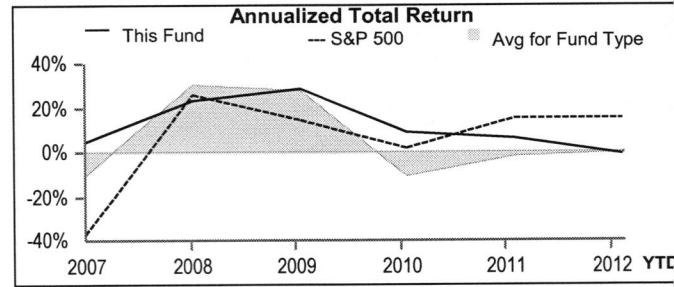

---

*SPDR MSCI ACWI ex-US ETF (CWI)

C- **Fair**

Fund Family: SSgA Funds Management Inc
Fund Type: Global
Inception Date: January 10, 2007

Major Rating Factors: Middle of the road best describes *SPDR MSCI ACWI ex-US ETF whose TheStreet.com Investment Rating is currently a C- (Fair). The fund currently has a performance rating of C- (Fair) based on an annualized return of 3.60% over the last three years and a total return of 1.58% year to date 2012. Factored into the performance evaluation is an expense ratio of 0.34% (very low).

The fund's risk rating is currently B- (Good). It carries a beta of 1.02, meaning that its performance tracks fairly well with that of the overall stock market. Volatility, as measured by both the semi-deviation and a drawdown factor, is considered low. As of December 31, 2012, *SPDR MSCI ACWI ex-US ETF traded at a discount of 1.44% below its net asset value, which is better than its one-year historical average discount of .11%.

John A. Tucker currently receives a manager quality ranking of 51 (0=worst, 99=best). If you desire an average level of risk, then this fund may be an option.

Data Date	Investment Rating	Net Assets ($Mil)	Price	Performance Rating/Pts	Total Return Y-T-D	Risk Rating/Pts
12-12	C-	368.30	32.19	C- / 3.7	1.58%	B- / 7.3
2011	C-	527.50	28.46	C- / 3.3	-0.25%	B- / 7.5
2010	D+	410.90	33.91	C- / 3.0	11.59%	C / 5.5
2009	A-	309.90	31.20	B+ / 8.6	35.34%	C+ / 5.6

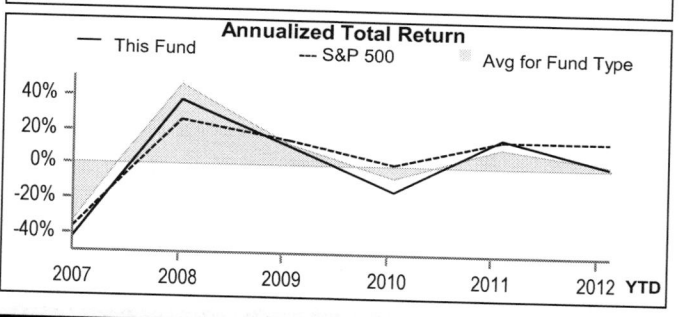

*SPDR Nuveen Barclays Bld Amr Bd (BABS)

B- **Good**

Fund Family: SSgA Funds Management Inc
Fund Type: Municipal - National
Inception Date: May 12, 2010

Major Rating Factors: *SPDR Nuveen Barclays Bld Amr Bd receives a TheStreet.com Investment Rating of B- (Good). The fund currently has a performance rating of C+ (Fair) based on an annualized return of 0.00% over the last three years and a total return of -0.84% year to date 2012. Factored into the performance evaluation is an expense ratio of 0.35% (very low).

The fund's risk rating is currently B+ (Good). It carries a beta of 0.00, meaning the fund's expected move will be 0.0% for every 10% move in the market. Volatility, as measured by both the semi-deviation and a drawdown factor, is considered very low. As of December 31, 2012, *SPDR Nuveen Barclays Bld Amr Bd traded at a premium of .97% above its net asset value, which is worse than its one-year historical average discount of .07%.

Daniel J. Close currently receives a manager quality ranking of 53 (0=worst, 99=best). If you desire an average level of risk, then this fund may be an option.

Data Date	Investment Rating	Net Assets ($Mil)	Price	Performance Rating/Pts	Total Return Y-T-D	Risk Rating/Pts
12-12	B-	104.90	61.55	C+ / 5.6	-0.84%	B+ / 9.0
2011	A	39.90	56.90	A- / 9.1	-2.69%	B+ / 9.0

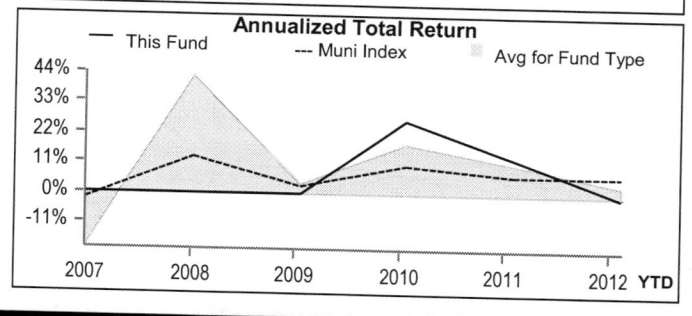

*SPDR Nuveen Barclays CA Muni Bd (CXA)

C+ **Fair**

Fund Family: SSgA Funds Management Inc
Fund Type: Municipal - National
Inception Date: October 10, 2007

Major Rating Factors: Middle of the road best describes *SPDR Nuveen Barclays CA Muni Bd whose TheStreet.com Investment Rating is currently a C+ (Fair). The fund currently has a performance rating of C (Fair) based on an annualized return of 7.93% over the last three years and a total return of 1.12% year to date 2012. Factored into the performance evaluation is an expense ratio of 0.20% (very low).

The fund's risk rating is currently B+ (Good). It carries a beta of 1.80, meaning it is expected to move 18.0% for every 10% move in the market. Volatility, as measured by both the semi-deviation and a drawdown factor, is considered very low. As of December 31, 2012, *SPDR Nuveen Barclays CA Muni Bd traded at a discount of 1.06% below its net asset value, which is better than its one-year historical average discount of .06%.

Steven M. Hlavin currently receives a manager quality ranking of 26 (0=worst, 99=best). If you desire an average level of risk, then this fund may be an option.

Data Date	Investment Rating	Net Assets ($Mil)	Price	Performance Rating/Pts	Total Return Y-T-D	Risk Rating/Pts
12-12	C+	99.60	24.18	C / 4.7	1.12%	B+ / 9.0
2011	B	75.10	23.44	C+ / 6.4	0.99%	B+ / 9.0
2010	C	65.60	20.76	D / 2.0	-2.80%	B / 8.5
2009	B	40.38	22.18	C / 4.4	4.28%	B / 8.8

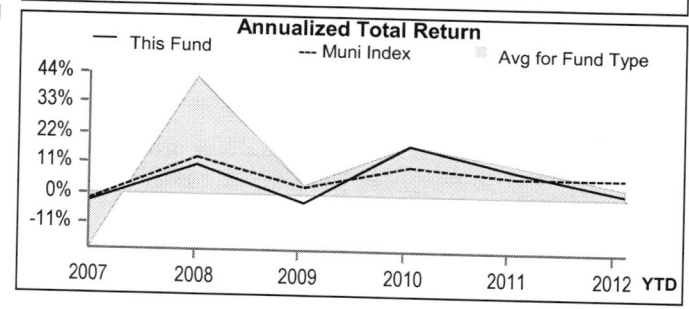

*SPDR Nuveen Barclays Muni Bond E (TFI)

C   **Fair**

Fund Family: SSgA Funds Management Inc
Fund Type: Municipal - National
Inception Date: September 11, 2007

Major Rating Factors: Middle of the road best describes *SPDR Nuveen Barclays Muni Bond E whose TheStreet.com Investment Rating is currently a C (Fair). The fund currently has a performance rating of C- (Fair) based on an annualized return of 6.35% over the last three years and a total return of 0.45% year to date 2012. Factored into the performance evaluation is an expense ratio of 0.23% (very low).

The fund's risk rating is currently B+ (Good). It carries a beta of 1.37, meaning it is expected to move 13.7% for every 10% move in the market. Volatility, as measured by both the semi-deviation and a drawdown factor, is considered very low. As of December 31, 2012, *SPDR Nuveen Barclays Muni Bond E traded at a discount of .53% below its net asset value, which is better than its one-year historical average discount of .16%.

Steven M. Hlavin currently receives a manager quality ranking of 32 (0=worst, 99=best). If you desire an average level of risk, then this fund may be an option.

Data Date	Investment Rating	Net Assets ($Mil)	Price	Perfor- mance Rating/Pts	Total Return Y-T-D	Risk Rating/Pts
12-12	C	1,216.70	24.24	C- / 3.7	0.45%	B+ / 9.3
2011	B-	982.20	23.74	C / 5.2	0.21%	B+ / 9.4
2010	C+	862.00	21.63	D+ / 2.8	-1.42%	B / 8.6
2009	B	583.86	22.68	C+ / 5.8	10.82%	B / 8.9

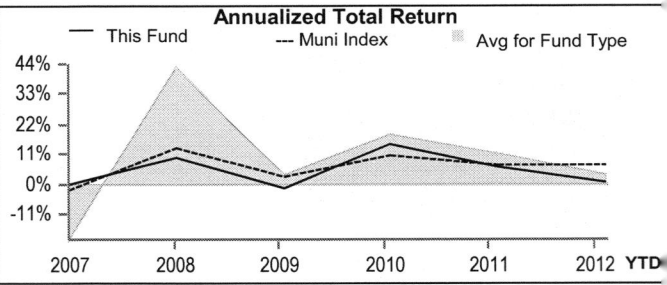

*SPDR Nuveen Barclays NY Muni Bd (INY)

C   **Fair**

Fund Family: SSgA Funds Management Inc
Fund Type: Municipal - National
Inception Date: October 11, 2007

Major Rating Factors: Middle of the road best describes *SPDR Nuveen Barclays NY Muni Bd whose TheStreet.com Investment Rating is currently a C (Fair). The fund currently has a performance rating of C- (Fair) based on an annualized return of 6.56% over the last three years and a total return of 1.46% year to date 2012. Factored into the performance evaluation is an expense ratio of 0.20% (very low).

The fund's risk rating is currently B+ (Good). It carries a beta of 1.51, meaning it is expected to move 15.1% for every 10% move in the market. Volatility, as measured by both the semi-deviation and a drawdown factor, is considered very low. As of December 31, 2012, *SPDR Nuveen Barclays NY Muni Bd traded at a discount of .79% below its net asset value, which is better than its one-year historical average premium of .03%.

Steven M. Hlavin currently receives a manager quality ranking of 28 (0=worst, 99=best). If you desire an average level of risk, then this fund may be an option.

Data Date	Investment Rating	Net Assets ($Mil)	Price	Perfor- mance Rating/Pts	Total Return Y-T-D	Risk Rating/Pts
12-12	C	31.20	23.95	C- / 3.9	1.46%	B+ / 9.2
2011	B-	25.70	23.34	C+ / 5.8	0.34%	B+ / 9.3
2010	C	26.00	21.42	D+ / 2.8	-0.91%	B / 8.3
2009	B	15.05	22.36	C+ / 6.6	14.34%	B / 8.5

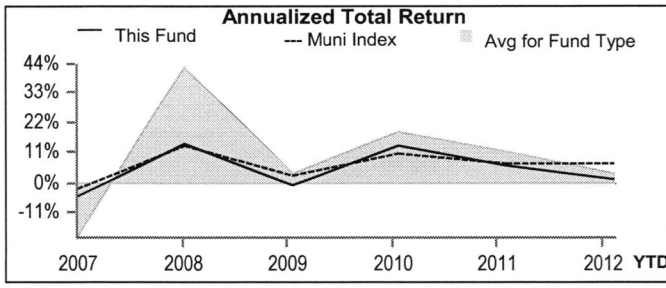

*SPDR Nuveen Barclays ST Muni Bd (SHM)

C-   **Fair**

Fund Family: SSgA Funds Management Inc
Fund Type: Municipal - National
Inception Date: October 10, 2007

Major Rating Factors:
Disappointing performance is the major factor driving the C- (Fair) TheStreet.com Investment Rating for *SPDR Nuveen Barclays ST Muni Bd. The fund currently has a performance rating of D (Weak) based on an annualized return of 1.93% over the last three years and a total return of 0.08% year to date 2012. Factored into the performance evaluation is an expense ratio of 0.20% (very low).

The fund's risk rating is currently B+ (Good). It carries a beta of 0.35, meaning the fund's expected move will be 3.5% for every 10% move in the market. Volatility, as measured by both the semi-deviation and a drawdown factor, is considered very low. As of December 31, 2012, *SPDR Nuveen Barclays ST Muni Bd traded at a discount of .04% below its net asset value, which is better than its one-year historical average discount of .01%.

Steven M. Hlavin currently receives a manager quality ranking of 49 (0=worst, 99=best). This fund offers only a moderate level of risk but investors looking for strong performance are still waiting.

Data Date	Investment Rating	Net Assets ($Mil)	Price	Perfor- mance Rating/Pts	Total Return Y-T-D	Risk Rating/Pts
12-12	C-	1,614.10	24.31	D / 1.9	0.08%	B+ / 9.8
2011	C	1,455.50	24.34	C- / 3.0	-0.12%	B+ / 9.9
2010	B+	1,300.60	23.81	C / 4.3	0.59%	B+ / 9.1
2009	B	501.79	24.02	C- / 4.1	4.28%	B+ / 9.2

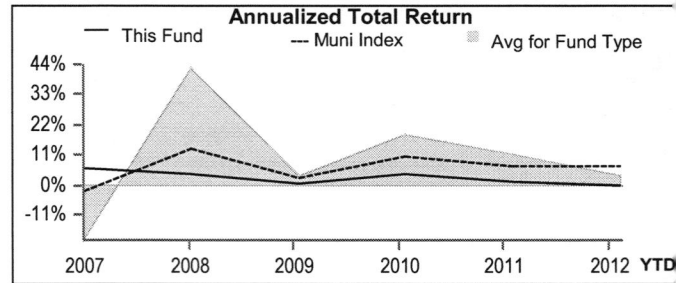

*SPDR Nuveen S&P Hi Yld Muni Bd E (HYMB)

Fund Family: SSgA Funds Management Inc
Fund Type: Corporate - High Yield
Inception Date: April 13, 2011

B+   **Good**

Major Rating Factors: *SPDR Nuveen S&P Hi Yld Muni Bd E receives a TheStreet.com Investment Rating of B+ (Good). The fund currently has a performance rating of C+ (Fair) based on an annualized return of 0.00% over the last three years and a total return of 1.45% year to date 2012. Factored into the performance evaluation is an expense ratio of 0.45% (very low).

The fund's risk rating is currently B+ (Good). It carries a beta of 0.00, meaning the fund's expected move will be 0.0% for every 10% move in the market. Volatility, as measured by both the semi-deviation and a drawdown factor, is considered very low. As of December 31, 2012, *SPDR Nuveen S&P Hi Yld Muni Bd E traded at a discount of 1.21% below its net asset value, which is better than its one-year historical average discount of .01%.

Steven M. Hlavin currently receives a manager quality ranking of 95 (0=worst, 99=best). If you desire an average level of risk, then this fund may be an option.

Data Date	Investment Rating	Net Assets ($Mil)	Price	Performance Rating/Pts	Total Return Y-T-D	Risk Rating/Pts
12-12	B+	192.50	58.00	C+ / 6.5	1.45%	B+ / 9.8

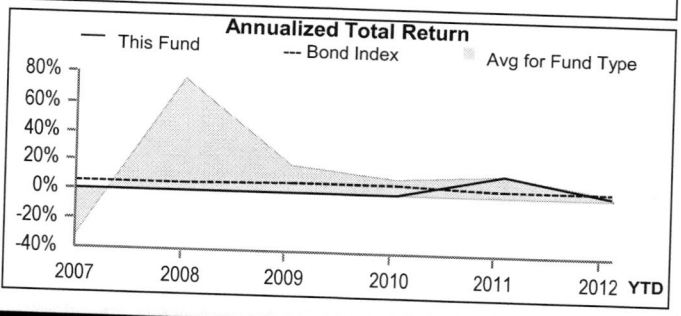

*SPDR Nuveen S&P VRDO Muni Bond E (VRD)

Fund Family: SSgA Funds Management Inc
Fund Type: General - Investment Grade
Inception Date: September 23, 2009

C-   **Fair**

Major Rating Factors:
Disappointing performance is the major factor driving the C- (Fair) TheStreet.com Investment Rating for *SPDR Nuveen S&P VRDO Muni Bond E. The fund currently has a performance rating of D- (Weak) based on an annualized return of 0.38% over the last three years and a total return of -0.07% year to date 2012. Factored into the performance evaluation is an expense ratio of 0.21% (very low).

The fund's risk rating is currently B+ (Good). It carries a beta of -0.03, meaning the fund's expected move will be -0.3% for every 10% move in the market. Volatility, as measured by both the semi-deviation and a drawdown factor, is considered low. As of December 31, 2012, *SPDR Nuveen S&P VRDO Muni Bond E traded at a discount of .43% below its net asset value, which is better than its one-year historical average discount of .24%.

Steven M. Hlavin currently receives a manager quality ranking of 57 (0=worst, 99=best). This fund offers only a moderate level of risk but investors looking for strong performance are still waiting.

Data Date	Investment Rating	Net Assets ($Mil)	Price	Performance Rating/Pts	Total Return Y-T-D	Risk Rating/Pts
12-12	C-	12.00	29.88	D- / 1.4	-0.07%	B+ / 9.9
2011	C	12.00	30.01	D / 2.1	-0.20%	B+ / 9.9
2010	C+	9.00	30.01	D+ / 2.4	0.42%	B+ / 9.0

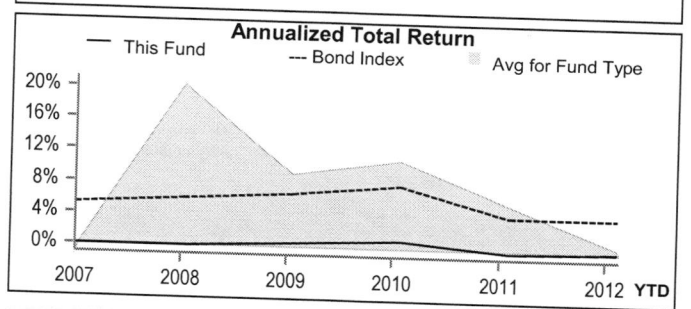

*SPDR Russell/Nomura PRIME Japan (JPP)

Fund Family: SSgA Funds Management Inc
Fund Type: Foreign
Inception Date: November 9, 2006

D+   **Weak**

Major Rating Factors:
Disappointing performance is the major factor driving the D+ (Weak) TheStreet.com Investment Rating for *SPDR Russell/Nomura PRIME Japan. The fund currently has a performance rating of D (Weak) based on an annualized return of 1.02% over the last three years and a total return of 2.86% year to date 2012. Factored into the performance evaluation is an expense ratio of 0.50% (very low).

The fund's risk rating is currently B- (Good). It carries a beta of 0.61, meaning the fund's expected move will be 6.1% for every 10% move in the market. Volatility, as measured by both the semi-deviation and a drawdown factor, is considered low. As of December 31, 2012, *SPDR Russell/Nomura PRIME Japan traded at a discount of .86% below its net asset value, which is better than its one-year historical average discount of .03%.

John A. Tucker currently receives a manager quality ranking of 45 (0=worst, 99=best). This fund offers only a moderate level of risk but investors looking for strong performance are still waiting.

Data Date	Investment Rating	Net Assets ($Mil)	Price	Performance Rating/Pts	Total Return Y-T-D	Risk Rating/Pts
12-12	D+	14.70	37.10	D / 2.2	2.86%	B- / 7.5
2011	D+	14.10	35.45	D / 1.9	-0.14%	B- / 7.6
2010	D+	8.30	41.07	D+ / 2.5	12.14%	C+ / 5.7
2009	D-	15.36	37.45	E+ / 0.9	4.59%	C+ / 5.7

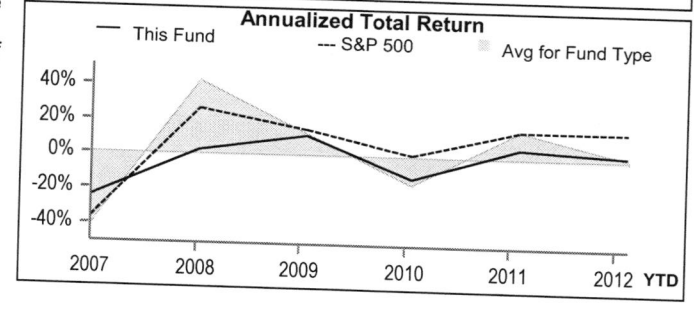

* Denotes ETF Fund

*SPDR Russell/Nomura Small Cap Ja (JSC)   C-   Fair

Fund Family: SSgA Funds Management Inc
Fund Type: Foreign
Inception Date: November 9, 2006

Major Rating Factors:
Disappointing performance is the major factor driving the C- (Fair) TheStreet.com Investment Rating for *SPDR Russell/Nomura Small Cap Ja. The fund currently has a performance rating of D+ (Weak) based on an annualized return of 4.93% over the last three years and a total return of 1.07% year to date 2012. Factored into the performance evaluation is an expense ratio of 0.55% (very low).

The fund's risk rating is currently B (Good). It carries a beta of 0.39, meaning the fund's expected move will be 3.9% for every 10% move in the market. Volatility, as measured by both the semi-deviation and a drawdown factor, is considered low. As of December 31, 2012, *SPDR Russell/Nomura Small Cap Ja traded at a premium of .05% above its net asset value, which is worse than its one-year historical average discount of .19%.

John A. Tucker currently receives a manager quality ranking of 78 (0=worst, 99=best). This fund offers only a moderate level of risk but investors looking for strong performance are still waiting.

Data Date	Investment Rating	Net Assets ($Mil)	Price	Performance Rating/Pts	Total Return Y-T-D	Risk Rating/Pts
12-12	C-	60.70	42.35	D+ / 2.6	1.07%	B / 8.4
2011	C-	88.90	41.09	C- / 3.2	0.38%	B- / 7.6
2010	C+	69.30	43.12	C+ / 6.4	17.94%	C+ / 6.1
2009	D	85.08	37.20	E+ / 0.9	3.01%	C+ / 6.0

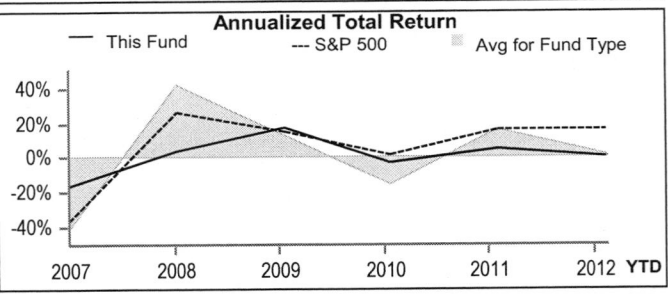

*SPDR S&P 400 Mid Cap Growth ETF (MDYG)   B-   Good

Fund Family: SSgA Funds Management Inc
Fund Type: Growth
Inception Date: November 8, 2005

Major Rating Factors: Strong performance is the major factor driving the B- (Good) TheStreet.com Investment Rating for *SPDR S&P 400 Mid Cap Growth ETF. The fund currently has a performance rating of B- (Good) based on an annualized return of 14.18% over the last three years and a total return of 3.56% year to date 2012. Factored into the performance evaluation is an expense ratio of 0.25% (very low).

The fund's risk rating is currently B- (Good). It carries a beta of 1.15, meaning it is expected to move 11.5% for every 10% move in the market. Volatility, as measured by both the semi-deviation and a drawdown factor, is considered low. As of December 31, 2012, *SPDR S&P 400 Mid Cap Growth ETF traded at a discount of 3.54% below its net asset value, which is better than its one-year historical average premium of .04%.

John A. Tucker currently receives a manager quality ranking of 61 (0=worst, 99=best). If you desire only a moderate level of risk and strong performance, then this fund is an excellent option.

Data Date	Investment Rating	Net Assets ($Mil)	Price	Performance Rating/Pts	Total Return Y-T-D	Risk Rating/Pts
12-12	B-	68.10	85.22	B- / 7.0	3.56%	B- / 7.7
2011	B-	58.80	73.69	B- / 7.2	0.88%	B- / 7.7
2010	B+	71.00	75.32	B / 7.9	27.62%	C / 5.5
2009	C+	42.94	59.22	C+ / 6.0	50.31%	C+ / 5.7

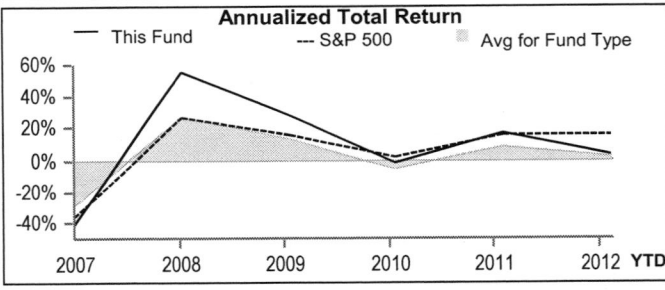

*SPDR S&P 400 Mid Cap Value ETF (MDYV)   C+   Fair

Fund Family: SSgA Funds Management Inc
Fund Type: Growth
Inception Date: November 8, 2005

Major Rating Factors: Middle of the road best describes *SPDR S&P 400 Mid Cap Value ETF whose TheStreet.com Investment Rating is currently a C+ (Fair). The fund currently has a performance rating of C+ (Fair) based on an annualized return of 12.29% over the last three years and a total return of 3.74% year to date 2012. Factored into the performance evaluation is an expense ratio of 0.25% (very low).

The fund's risk rating is currently B- (Good). It carries a beta of 1.12, meaning it is expected to move 11.2% for every 10% move in the market. Volatility, as measured by both the semi-deviation and a drawdown factor, is considered low. As of December 31, 2012, *SPDR S&P 400 Mid Cap Value ETF traded at a discount of 3.64% below its net asset value, which is better than its one-year historical average premium of .03%.

John A. Tucker has been running the fund for 8 years and currently receives a manager quality ranking of 45 (0=worst, 99=best). If you desire an average level of risk, then this fund may be an option.

Data Date	Investment Rating	Net Assets ($Mil)	Price	Performance Rating/Pts	Total Return Y-T-D	Risk Rating/Pts
12-12	C+	24.00	59.85	C+ / 6.3	3.74%	B- / 7.7
2011	C+	25.90	51.91	C+ / 5.7	1.73%	B- / 7.7
2010	C+	27.10	54.48	C+ / 6.2	21.37%	C+ / 5.7
2009	C-	8.82	46.00	C- / 3.0	31.68%	C+ / 5.7

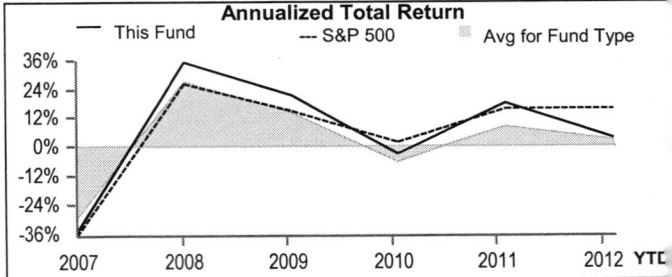

*SPDR S&P 500 ETF (SPY)

C   **Fair**

Fund Family: State Street Bank and Trust Company
Fund Type: Growth
Inception Date: January 22, 1993

Major Rating Factors: Middle of the road best describes *SPDR S&P 500 ETF whose TheStreet.com Investment Rating is currently a C (Fair). The fund currently has a performance rating of C (Fair) based on an annualized return of 11.26% over the last three years and a total return of 3.27% year to date 2012. Factored into the performance evaluation is an expense ratio of 0.09% (very low).

The fund's risk rating is currently B (Good). It carries a beta of 1.00, meaning that its performance tracks fairly well with that of the overall stock market. Volatility, as measured by both the semi-deviation and a drawdown factor, is considered low. As of December 31, 2012, *SPDR S&P 500 ETF traded at a discount of 3.17% below its net asset value, which is better than its one-year historical average discount of .01%.

David K. Chin currently receives a manager quality ranking of 52 (0=worst, 99=best). If you desire an average level of risk, then this fund may be an option.

Data Date	Investment Rating	Net Assets ($Mil)	Price	Performance Rating/Pts	Total Return Y-T-D	Risk Rating/Pts
12-12	C	123,000.90	142.41	C / 5.2	3.27%	B / 8.0
2011	C	95,397.40	125.50	C / 5.2	1.76%	B- / 7.9
2010	C-	89,875.00	125.75	C- / 3.8	15.08%	C+ / 6.0
2009	D+	63,691.96	111.44	D / 2.2	22.53%	C+ / 6.1

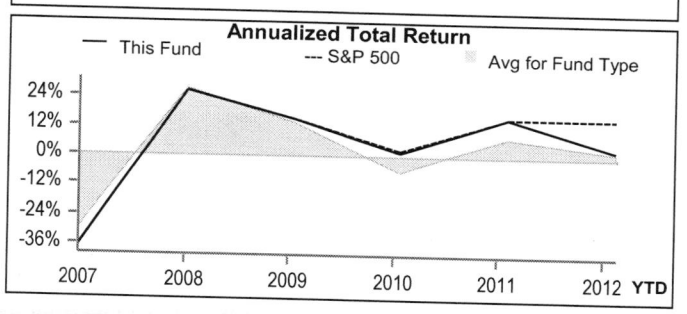

*SPDR S&P 500 Growth ETF (SPYG)

C   **Fair**

Fund Family: SSgA Funds Management Inc
Fund Type: Growth
Inception Date: September 25, 2000

Major Rating Factors: Middle of the road best describes *SPDR S&P 500 Growth ETF whose TheStreet.com Investment Rating is currently a C (Fair). The fund currently has a performance rating of C (Fair) based on an annualized return of 12.20% over the last three years and a total return of 3.16% year to date 2012. Factored into the performance evaluation is an expense ratio of 0.20% (very low).

The fund's risk rating is currently B- (Good). It carries a beta of 0.99, meaning that its performance tracks fairly well with that of the overall stock market. Volatility, as measured by both the semi-deviation and a drawdown factor, is considered low. As of December 31, 2012, *SPDR S&P 500 Growth ETF traded at a discount of 3.09% below its net asset value, which is better than its one-year historical average discount of .01%.

John A. Tucker has been running the fund for 13 years and currently receives a manager quality ranking of 59 (0=worst, 99=best). If you desire an average level of risk, then this fund may be an option.

Data Date	Investment Rating	Net Assets ($Mil)	Price	Performance Rating/Pts	Total Return Y-T-D	Risk Rating/Pts
12-12	C	216.40	65.56	C / 5.2	3.16%	B- / 7.8
2011	C+	207.30	58.47	C+ / 6.3	1.12%	B- / 7.8
2010	C+	190.40	56.94	C / 5.5	16.50%	C+ / 5.8
2009	C-	154.82	49.26	C- / 3.8	32.07%	C+ / 6.1

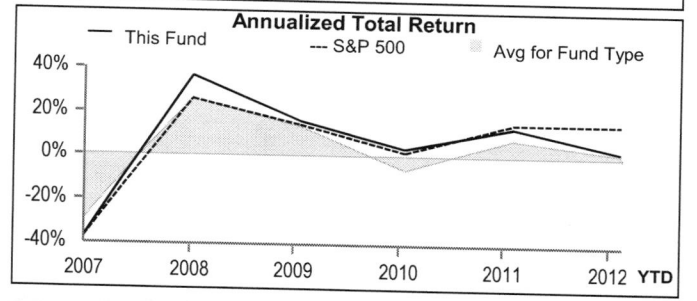

*SPDR S&P 500 Value ETF (SPYV)

C+   **Fair**

Fund Family: SSgA Funds Management Inc
Fund Type: Income
Inception Date: September 25, 2000

Major Rating Factors: Middle of the road best describes *SPDR S&P 500 Value ETF whose TheStreet.com Investment Rating is currently a C+ (Fair). The fund currently has a performance rating of C (Fair) based on an annualized return of 10.76% over the last three years and a total return of 3.57% year to date 2012. Factored into the performance evaluation is an expense ratio of 0.20% (very low).

The fund's risk rating is currently B (Good). It carries a beta of 1.00, meaning that its performance tracks fairly well with that of the overall stock market. Volatility, as measured by both the semi-deviation and a drawdown factor, is considered low. As of December 31, 2012, *SPDR S&P 500 Value ETF traded at a discount of 3.44% below its net asset value, which is better than its one-year historical average premium of .02%.

John A. Tucker has been running the fund for 8 years and currently receives a manager quality ranking of 47 (0=worst, 99=best). If you desire an average level of risk, then this fund may be an option.

Data Date	Investment Rating	Net Assets ($Mil)	Price	Performance Rating/Pts	Total Return Y-T-D	Risk Rating/Pts
12-12	C+	115.10	71.79	C / 5.4	3.57%	B / 8.1
2011	C	160.30	62.80	C / 4.4	2.17%	B / 8.0
2010	D+	168.20	64.69	D+ / 2.8	15.51%	C+ / 6.0
2009	D	99.22	57.50	D- / 1.3	14.66%	C+ / 6.0

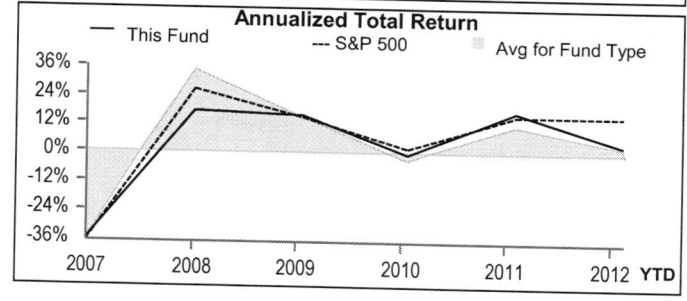

* Denotes ETF Fund

*SPDR S&P 600 Small Cap ETF (SLY)   C+   Fair

Fund Family: SSgA Funds Management Inc
Fund Type: Growth
Inception Date: November 8, 2005

Major Rating Factors: Middle of the road best describes *SPDR S&P 600 Small Cap ETF whose TheStreet.com Investment Rating is currently a C+ (Fair). The fund currently has a performance rating of C+ (Fair) based on an annualized return of 14.56% over the last three years and a total return of 3.37% year to date 2012. Factored into the performance evaluation is an expense ratio of 0.20% (very low).

The fund's risk rating is currently B- (Good). It carries a beta of 1.24, meaning it is expected to move 12.4% for every 10% move in the market. Volatility, as measured by both the semi-deviation and a drawdown factor, is considered low. As of December 31, 2012, *SPDR S&P 600 Small Cap ETF traded at a discount of 3.21% below its net asset value, which is better than its one-year historical average premium of .08%.

John A. Tucker has been running the fund for 8 years and currently receives a manager quality ranking of 57 (0=worst, 99=best). If you desire an average level of risk, then this fund may be an option.

Data Date	Investment Rating	Net Assets ($Mil)	Price	Perfor-mance Rating/Pts	Total Return Y-T-D	Risk Rating/Pts
12-12	C+	229.20	75.11	C+ / 6.7	3.37%	B- / 7.5
2011	B-	72.40	66.07	B- / 7.3	1.45%	B- / 7.5
2010	B	62.60	66.87	B / 7.8	28.92%	C / 5.4
2009	C-	22.65	52.54	C- / 3.6	38.80%	C+ / 5.6

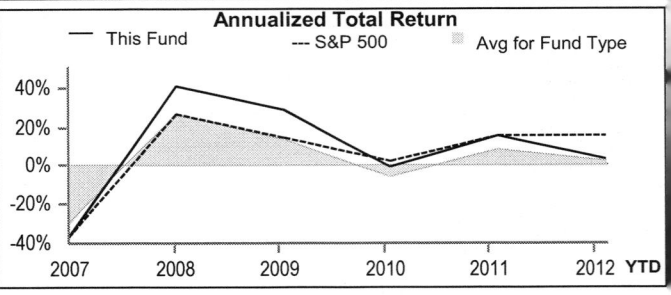

*SPDR S&P 600 Small Cap Growth ET (SLYG)   B-   Good

Fund Family: SSgA Funds Management Inc
Fund Type: Growth
Inception Date: September 25, 2000

Major Rating Factors: Strong performance is the major factor driving the B- (Good) TheStreet.com Investment Rating for *SPDR S&P 600 Small Cap Growth ET. The fund currently has a performance rating of B- (Good) based on an annualized return of 15.91% over the last three years and a total return of 3.71% year to date 2012. Factored into the performance evaluation is an expense ratio of 0.25% (very low).

The fund's risk rating is currently B- (Good). It carries a beta of 1.22, meaning it is expected to move 12.2% for every 10% move in the market. Volatility, as measured by both the semi-deviation and a drawdown factor, is considered low. As of December 31, 2012, *SPDR S&P 600 Small Cap Growth ET traded at a discount of 3.62% below its net asset value, which is better than its one-year historical average discount of .02%.

John A. Tucker has been running the fund for 13 years and currently receives a manager quality ranking of 66 (0=worst, 99=best). If you desire only a moderate level of risk and strong performance, then this fund is an excellent option.

Data Date	Investment Rating	Net Assets ($Mil)	Price	Perfor-mance Rating/Pts	Total Return Y-T-D	Risk Rating/Pts
12-12	B-	164.40	126.35	B- / 7.1	3.71%	B- / 7.4
2011	B-	145.80	112.28	B / 7.7	0.84%	B- / 7.2
2010	B	174.60	110.57	B / 8.0	32.09%	C / 5.2
2009	C-	94.08	83.96	C- / 4.2	43.53%	C / 5.3

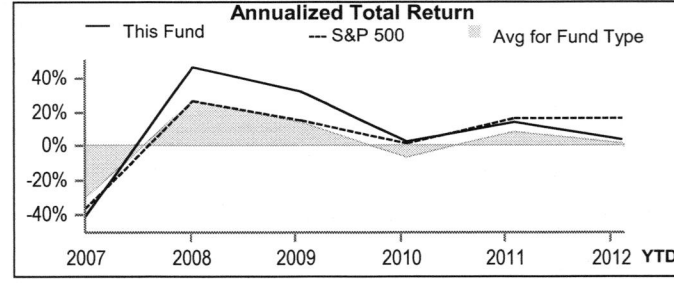

*SPDR S&P 600 Small Cap Value ETF (SLYV)   C+   Fair

Fund Family: SSgA Funds Management Inc
Fund Type: Growth
Inception Date: September 25, 2000

Major Rating Factors: Middle of the road best describes *SPDR S&P 600 Small Cap Value ETF whose TheStreet.com Investment Rating is currently a C+ (Fair). The fund currently has a performance rating of C+ (Fair) based on an annualized return of 13.08% over the last three years and a total return of 3.40% year to date 2012. Factored into the performance evaluation is an expense ratio of 0.25% (very low).

The fund's risk rating is currently B- (Good). It carries a beta of 1.26, meaning it is expected to move 12.6% for every 10% move in the market. Volatility, as measured by both the semi-deviation and a drawdown factor, is considered low. As of December 31, 2012, *SPDR S&P 600 Small Cap Value ETF traded at a discount of 3.38% below its net asset value, which is better than its one-year historical average discount of .01%.

John A. Tucker has been running the fund for 13 years and currently receives a manager quality ranking of 43 (0=worst, 99=best). If you desire an average level of risk, then this fund may be an option.

Data Date	Investment Rating	Net Assets ($Mil)	Price	Perfor-mance Rating/Pts	Total Return Y-T-D	Risk Rating/Pts
12-12	C+	131.80	77.01	C+ / 6.3	3.40%	B- / 7.6
2011	B-	114.00	66.98	C+ / 6.9	2.56%	B- / 7.5
2010	B	134.50	69.75	B / 7.6	25.97%	C+ / 5.6
2009	C-	69.89	56.60	C- / 3.2	34.22%	C+ / 5.7

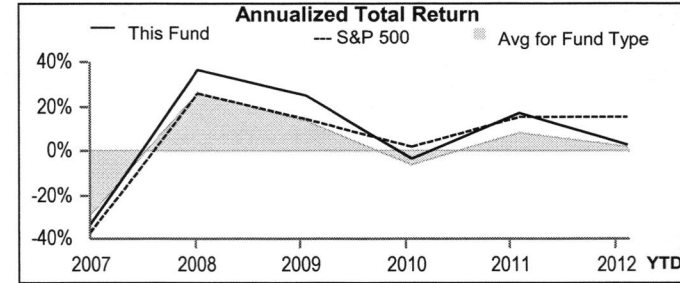

*SPDR S&P Aerospace & Defense ETF (XAR)

A+   Excellent

Fund Family: SSgA Funds Management Inc
Fund Type: Income
Inception Date: September 29, 2011

Major Rating Factors:
Strong performance is the major factor driving the A+ (Excellent) TheStreet.com Investment Rating for *SPDR S&P Aerospace & Defense ETF. The fund currently has a performance rating of B+ (Good) based on an annualized return of 0.00% over the last three years and a total return of 4.82% year to date 2012. Factored into the performance evaluation is an expense ratio of 0.35% (very low).

The fund's risk rating is currently B+ (Good). It carries a beta of 0.00, meaning the fund's expected move will be 0.0% for every 10% move in the market. Volatility, as measured by both the semi-deviation and a drawdown factor, is considered very low. As of December 31, 2012, *SPDR S&P Aerospace & Defense ETF traded at a discount of 4.57% below its net asset value, which is better than its one-year historical average discount of .01%.

John A. Tucker currently receives a manager quality ranking of 62 (0=worst, 99=best). If you desire only a moderate level of risk and strong performance, then this fund is an excellent option.

Data Date	Investment Rating	Net Assets ($Mil)	Price	Performance Rating/Pts	Total Return Y-T-D	Risk Rating/Pts
12-12	A+	12.80	62.80	B+ / 8.7	4.82%	B+ / 9.1

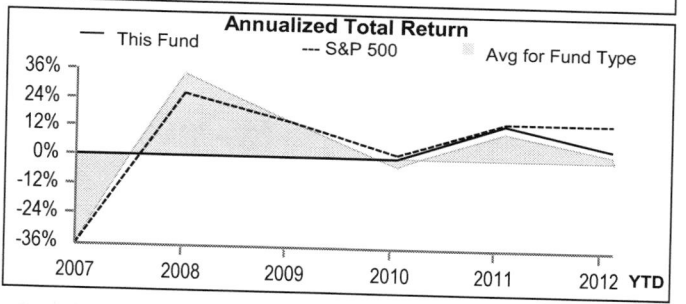

*SPDR S&P Biotech ETF (XBI)

B-   Good

Fund Family: SSgA Funds Management Inc
Fund Type: Health
Inception Date: January 31, 2006

Major Rating Factors: Strong performance is the major factor driving the B- (Good) TheStreet.com Investment Rating for *SPDR S&P Biotech ETF. The fund currently has a performance rating of B+ (Good) based on an annualized return of 20.18% over the last three years and a total return of 8.65% year to date 2012. Factored into the performance evaluation is an expense ratio of 0.35% (very low).

The fund's risk rating is currently C+ (Fair). It carries a beta of 1.08, meaning that its performance tracks fairly well with that of the overall stock market. Volatility, as measured by both the semi-deviation and a drawdown factor, is considered low. As of December 31, 2012, *SPDR S&P Biotech ETF traded at a discount of 7.92% below its net asset value, which is better than its one-year historical average premium of .03%.

John A. Tucker currently receives a manager quality ranking of 81 (0=worst, 99=best). If you desire only a moderate level of risk and strong performance, then this fund is an excellent option.

Data Date	Investment Rating	Net Assets ($Mil)	Price	Performance Rating/Pts	Total Return Y-T-D	Risk Rating/Pts
12-12	B-	629.20	87.91	B+ / 8.4	8.65%	C+ / 6.5
2011	D+	418.20	66.40	C- / 4.1	4.79%	C+ / 6.0
2010	C+	491.90	63.08	C+ / 5.9	17.60%	C+ / 6.0
2009	C-	428.51	53.64	C- / 3.7	-0.82%	C+ / 6.1

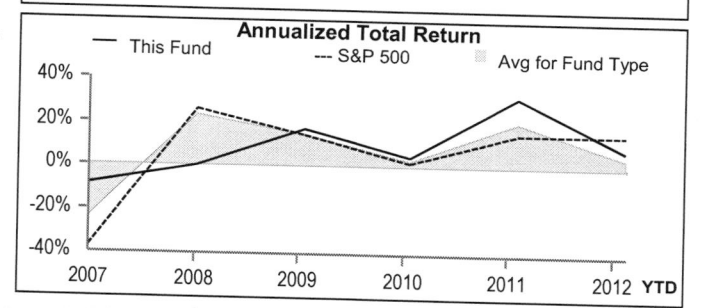

*SPDR S&P BRIC 40 ETF (BIK)

D   Weak

Fund Family: SSgA Funds Management Inc
Fund Type: Foreign
Inception Date: June 19, 2007

Major Rating Factors:
Disappointing performance is the major factor driving the D (Weak) TheStreet.com Investment Rating for *SPDR S&P BRIC 40 ETF. The fund currently has a performance rating of D+ (Weak) based on an annualized return of 2.07% over the last three years and a total return of 2.13% year to date 2012. Factored into the performance evaluation is an expense ratio of 0.50% (very low).

The fund's risk rating is currently C+ (Fair). It carries a beta of 1.07, meaning that its performance tracks fairly well with that of the overall stock market. Volatility, as measured by both the semi-deviation and a drawdown factor, is considered low. As of December 31, 2012, *SPDR S&P BRIC 40 ETF traded at a discount of 1.65% below its net asset value, which is better than its one-year historical average discount of .01%.

John A. Tucker currently receives a manager quality ranking of 30 (0=worst, 99=best). This fund offers only a moderate level of risk but investors looking for strong performance are still waiting.

Data Date	Investment Rating	Net Assets ($Mil)	Price	Performance Rating/Pts	Total Return Y-T-D	Risk Rating/Pts
12-12	D	320.30	24.40	D+ / 2.5	2.13%	C+ / 6.6
2011	C-	342.00	21.92	C / 4.9	2.33%	C+ / 6.9
2010	D	503.00	27.43	C- / 3.1	11.36%	C- / 4.2
2009	B+	340.81	25.07	A / 9.5	67.09%	C- / 4.2

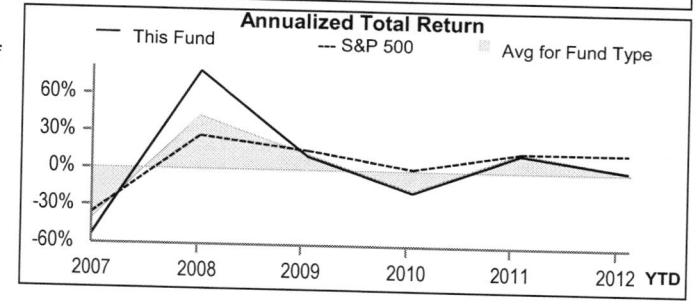

*SPDR S&P China ETF (GXC) D+ Weak

Fund Family: SSgA Funds Management Inc
Fund Type: Foreign
Inception Date: March 20, 2007

Major Rating Factors: *SPDR S&P China ETF receives a TheStreet.com Investment Rating of D+ (Weak). The fund currently has a performance rating of C- (Fair) based on an annualized return of 3.54% over the last three years and a total return of 2.46% year to date 2012. Factored into the performance evaluation is an expense ratio of 0.59% (very low).

The fund's risk rating is currently C+ (Fair). It carries a beta of 0.94, meaning that its performance tracks fairly well with that of the overall stock market. Volatility, as measured by both the semi-deviation and a drawdown factor, is considered low. As of December 31, 2012, *SPDR S&P China ETF traded at a discount of 1.62% below its net asset value, which is better than its one-year historical average premium of .11%.

John A. Tucker currently receives a manager quality ranking of 44 (0=worst, 99=best). If you desire an average level of risk, then this fund may be an option.

Data Date	Investment Rating	Net Assets ($Mil)	Price	Performance Rating/Pts	Total Return Y-T-D	Risk Rating/Pts
12-12	D+	1,067.30	74.09	C- / 3.2	2.46%	C+ / 6.4
2011	D+	584.70	62.30	C- / 4.0	0.88%	C+ / 6.1
2010	D	703.70	76.24	D / 2.1	7.57%	C / 4.6
2009	B	445.54	71.85	A- / 9.0	50.76%	C / 4.3

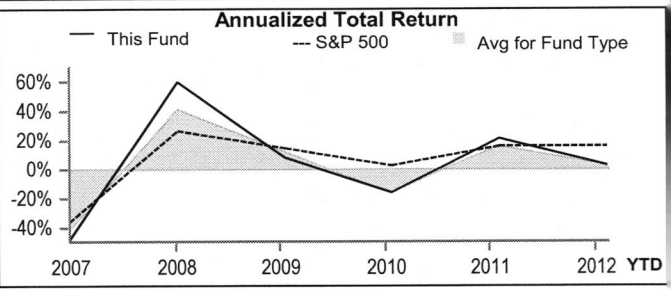

*SPDR S&P Dividend ETF (SDY) C+ Fair

Fund Family: SSgA Funds Management Inc
Fund Type: Income
Inception Date: November 8, 2005

Major Rating Factors: Middle of the road best describes *SPDR S&P Dividend ETF whose TheStreet.com Investment Rating is currently a C+ (Fair). The fund currently has a performance rating of C (Fair) based on an annualized return of 12.30% over the last three years and a total return of 3.13% year to date 2012. Factored into the performance evaluation is an expense ratio of 0.35% (very low).

The fund's risk rating is currently B (Good). It carries a beta of 0.76, meaning the fund's expected move will be 7.6% for every 10% move in the market. Volatility, as measured by both the semi-deviation and a drawdown factor, is considered low. As of December 31, 2012, *SPDR S&P Dividend ETF traded at a discount of 3.05% below its net asset value.

John A. Tucker has been running the fund for 8 years and currently receives a manager quality ranking of 73 (0=worst, 99=best). If you desire an average level of risk, then this fund may be an option.

Data Date	Investment Rating	Net Assets ($Mil)	Price	Performance Rating/Pts	Total Return Y-T-D	Risk Rating/Pts
12-12	C+	9,399.00	58.16	C / 5.5	3.13%	B / 8.7
2011	C+	8,252.90	53.87	C / 5.5	0.09%	B- / 7.8
2010	C+	5,031.90	51.98	C+ / 6.0	16.43%	C+ / 6.1
2009	D+	658.66	46.25	D / 2.1	16.49%	C+ / 6.1

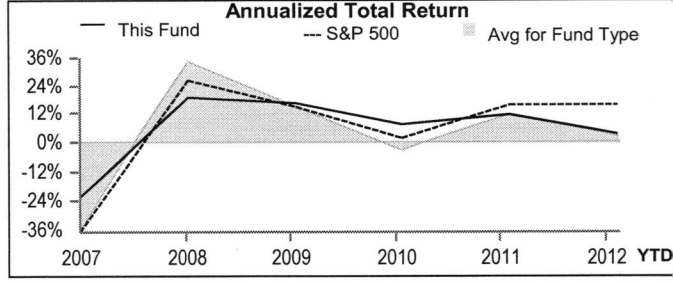

*SPDR S&P Emerg Middle East&Afric (GAF) C- Fair

Fund Family: SSgA Funds Management Inc
Fund Type: Emerging Market
Inception Date: March 20, 2007

Major Rating Factors: Middle of the road best describes *SPDR S&P Emerg Middle East&Afric whose TheStreet.com Investment Rating is currently a C- (Fair). The fund currently has a performance rating of C (Fair) based on an annualized return of 7.62% over the last three years and a total return of -2.73% year to date 2012. Factored into the performance evaluation is an expense ratio of 0.59% (very low).

The fund's risk rating is currently B- (Good). It carries a beta of 0.89, meaning the fund's expected move will be 8.9% for every 10% move in the market. Volatility, as measured by both the semi-deviation and a drawdown factor, is considered low. As of December 31, 2012, *SPDR S&P Emerg Middle East&Afric traded at a premium of 3.41% above its net asset value, which is worse than its one-year historical average discount of .09%.

John A. Tucker currently receives a manager quality ranking of 78 (0=worst, 99=best). If you desire an average level of risk, then this fund may be an option.

Data Date	Investment Rating	Net Assets ($Mil)	Price	Performance Rating/Pts	Total Return Y-T-D	Risk Rating/Pts
12-12	C-	94.90	73.91	C / 4.3	-2.73%	B- / 7.2
2011	C	94.70	62.75	C / 5.0	0.48%	B- / 7.4
2010	B+	181.70	79.59	B / 8.1	30.45%	C+ / 5.8
2009	A	129.23	62.39	A- / 9.0	46.98%	C+ / 5.8

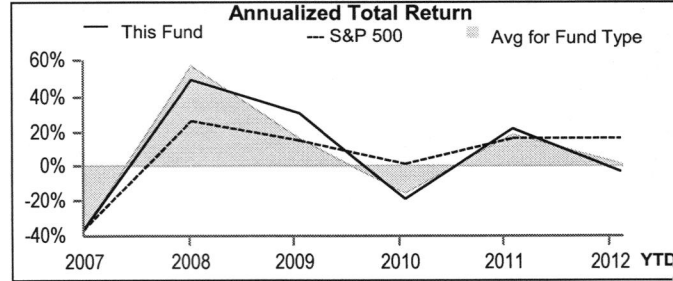

*SPDR S&P Emerging Asia Pacific E (GMF)

Fund Family: SSgA Funds Management Inc
Fund Type: Emerging Market
Inception Date: March 20, 2007

D+   **Weak**

Major Rating Factors: *SPDR S&P Emerging Asia Pacific E receives a TheStreet.com Investment Rating of D+ (Weak). The fund currently has a performance rating of C- (Fair) based on an annualized return of 4.80% over the last three years and a total return of 1.41% year to date 2012. Factored into the performance evaluation is an expense ratio of 0.60% (very low).

The fund's risk rating is currently B- (Good). It carries a beta of 0.97, meaning that its performance tracks fairly well with that of the overall stock market. Volatility, as measured by both the semi-deviation and a drawdown factor, is considered low. As of December 31, 2012, *SPDR S&P Emerging Asia Pacific E traded at a discount of 1.22% below its net asset value, which is better than its one-year historical average discount of .04%.

John A. Tucker currently receives a manager quality ranking of 53 (0=worst, 99=best). If you desire an average level of risk, then this fund may be an option.

Data Date	Investment Rating	Net Assets ($Mil)	Price	Performance Rating/Pts	Total Return Y-T-D	Risk Rating/Pts
12-12	D+	481.60	77.49	C- / 3.2	1.41%	B- / 7.0
2011	C-	450.30	65.99	C / 5.2	1.73%	C+ / 6.5
2010	C	770.30	84.75	C+ / 5.9	19.44%	C / 4.8
2009	A-	436.77	74.18	A / 9.4	63.77%	C / 4.7

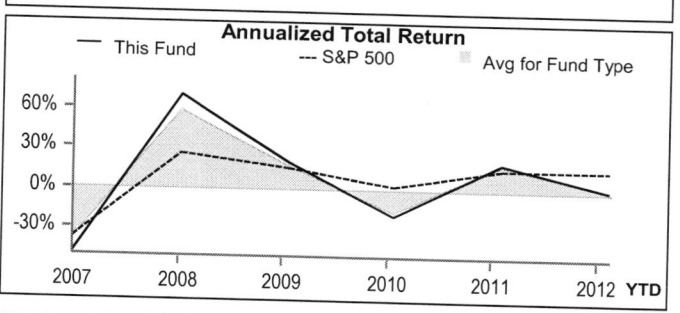

*SPDR S&P Emerging Europe ETF (GUR)

Fund Family: SSgA Funds Management Inc
Fund Type: Emerging Market
Inception Date: March 20, 2007

D   **Weak**

Major Rating Factors: *SPDR S&P Emerging Europe ETF receives a TheStreet.com Investment Rating of D (Weak). The fund currently has a performance rating of C- (Fair) based on an annualized return of 1.00% over the last three years and a total return of 0.77% year to date 2012. Factored into the performance evaluation is an expense ratio of 0.60% (very low).

The fund's risk rating is currently C (Fair). It carries a beta of 1.28, meaning it is expected to move 12.8% for every 10% move in the market. Volatility, as measured by both the semi-deviation and a drawdown factor, is considered average. As of December 31, 2012, *SPDR S&P Emerging Europe ETF traded at a discount of .54% below its net asset value, which is better than its one-year historical average premium of .02%.

John A. Tucker currently receives a manager quality ranking of 29 (0=worst, 99=best). If you desire an average level of risk, then this fund may be an option.

Data Date	Investment Rating	Net Assets ($Mil)	Price	Performance Rating/Pts	Total Return Y-T-D	Risk Rating/Pts
12-12	D	94.90	43.95	C- / 3.4	0.77%	C / 5.4
2011	D+	86.00	35.99	C- / 3.6	0.58%	C+ / 6.1
2010	E+	217.30	49.55	D- / 1.4	15.70%	C- / 3.2
2009	B	137.98	43.34	A+ / 9.6	67.53%	C- / 3.6

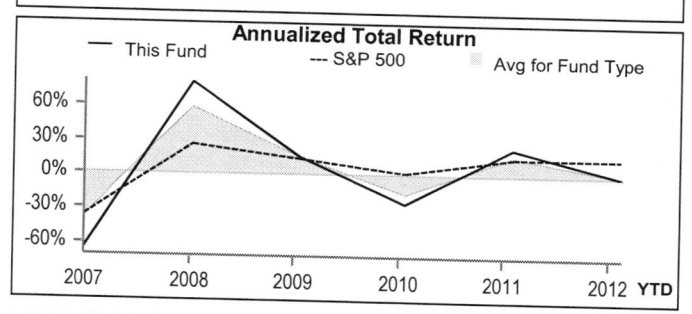

*SPDR S&P Emerging Latin America (GML)

Fund Family: SSgA Funds Management Inc
Fund Type: Emerging Market
Inception Date: March 20, 2007

D   **Weak**

Major Rating Factors:
Disappointing performance is the major factor driving the D (Weak) TheStreet.com Investment Rating for *SPDR S&P Emerging Latin America. The fund currently has a performance rating of D (Weak) based on an annualized return of 0.65% over the last three years and a total return of 1.99% year to date 2012. Factored into the performance evaluation is an expense ratio of 0.59% (very low).

The fund's risk rating is currently C+ (Fair). It carries a beta of 1.13, meaning it is expected to move 11.3% for every 10% move in the market. Volatility, as measured by both the semi-deviation and a drawdown factor, is considered low. As of December 31, 2012, *SPDR S&P Emerging Latin America traded at a discount of 2.00% below its net asset value, which is better than its one-year historical average discount of .08%.

John A. Tucker currently receives a manager quality ranking of 21 (0=worst, 99=best). This fund offers only a moderate level of risk but investors looking for strong performance are still waiting.

Data Date	Investment Rating	Net Assets ($Mil)	Price	Performance Rating/Pts	Total Return Y-T-D	Risk Rating/Pts
12-12	D	110.80	74.30	D / 2.0	1.99%	C+ / 6.7
2011	C	117.20	68.99	C+ / 5.7	2.01%	C+ / 6.9
2010	C+	276.80	89.74	B- / 7.2	15.38%	C / 4.5
2009	A+	132.84	80.06	A+ / 9.8	93.33%	C / 5.0

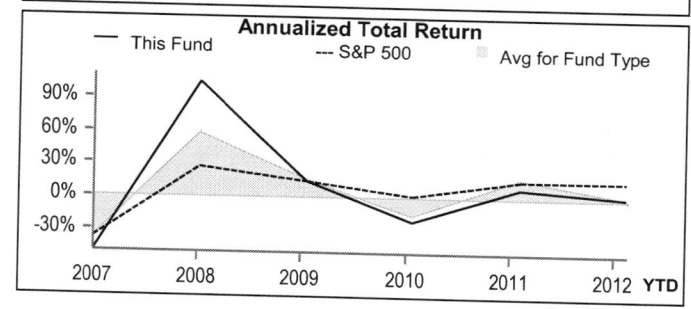

*SPDR S&P Emerging Markets ETF (GMM)

D+ **Weak**

Fund Family: SSgA Funds Management Inc
Fund Type: Emerging Market
Inception Date: March 20, 2007

Major Rating Factors: *SPDR S&P Emerging Markets ETF receives a TheStreet.com Investment Rating of D+ (Weak). The fund currently has a performance rating of C- (Fair) based on an annualized return of 4.06% over the last three years and a total return of 1.21% year to date 2012. Factored into the performance evaluation is an expense ratio of 0.59% (very low).

The fund's risk rating is currently B- (Good). It carries a beta of 1.00, meaning that its performance tracks fairly well with that of the overall stock market. Volatility, as measured by both the semi-deviation and a drawdown factor, is considered low. As of December 31, 2012, *SPDR S&P Emerging Markets ETF traded at a discount of .59% below its net asset value, which is better than its one-year historical average premium of .10%.

John A. Tucker currently receives a manager quality ranking of 46 (0=worst, 99=best). If you desire an average level of risk, then this fund may be an option.

Data Date	Investment Rating	Net Assets ($Mil)	Price	Performance Rating/Pts	Total Return Y-T-D	Risk Rating/Pts
12-12	D+	159.10	67.22	C- / 3.0	1.21%	B- / 7.0
2011	C	139.10	58.21	C / 5.1	1.58%	B- / 7.1
2010	C	237.10	74.37	C+ / 5.9	18.75%	C / 5.0
2009	A	94.40	64.21	A / 9.5	65.38%	C / 5.1

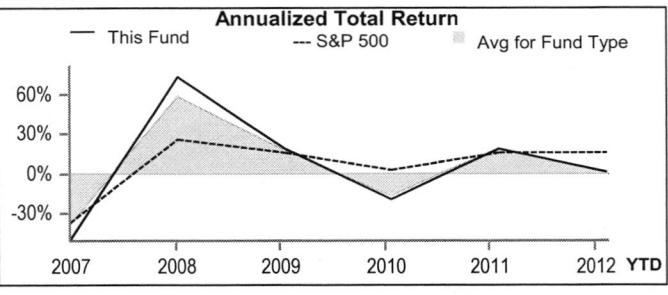

Annualized Total Return

*SPDR S&P Emg Markets Dividend ET (EDIV)

C- **Fair**

Fund Family: SSgA Funds Management Inc
Fund Type: Growth and Income
Inception Date: February 23, 2011

Major Rating Factors: Middle of the road best describes *SPDR S&P Emg Markets Dividend ET whose TheStreet.com Investment Rating is currently a C- (Fair). The fund currently has a performance rating of C (Fair) based on an annualized return of 0.00% over the last three years and a total return of 0.45% year to date 2012. Factored into the performance evaluation is an expense ratio of 0.61% (very low).

The fund's risk rating is currently B- (Good). It carries a beta of 0.00, meaning the fund's expected move will be 0.0% for every 10% move in the market. Volatility, as measured by both the semi-deviation and a drawdown factor, is considered low. As of December 31, 2012, *SPDR S&P Emg Markets Dividend ET traded at a premium of .28% above its net asset value, which is in line with its one-year historical average premium of .28%.

John A. Tucker currently receives a manager quality ranking of 9 (0=worst, 99=best). If you desire an average level of risk, then this fund may be an option.

Data Date	Investment Rating	Net Assets ($Mil)	Price	Performance Rating/Pts	Total Return Y-T-D	Risk Rating/Pts
12-12	C-	358.30	47.18	C / 4.8	0.45%	B- / 7.1

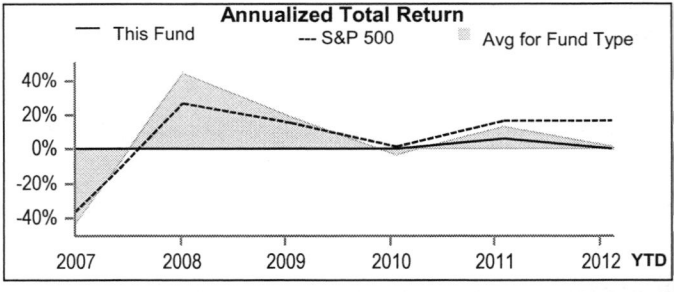

Annualized Total Return

*SPDR S&P Emg Markets Sm Cap ETF (EWX)

D+ **Weak**

Fund Family: SSgA Funds Management Inc
Fund Type: Global
Inception Date: May 12, 2008

Major Rating Factors: *SPDR S&P Emg Markets Sm Cap ETF receives a TheStreet.com Investment Rating of D+ (Weak). The fund currently has a performance rating of C- (Fair) based on an annualized return of 2.73% over the last three years and a total return of 2.57% year to date 2012. Factored into the performance evaluation is an expense ratio of 0.66% (very low).

The fund's risk rating is currently C+ (Fair). It carries a beta of 1.08, meaning that its performance tracks fairly well with that of the overall stock market. Volatility, as measured by both the semi-deviation and a drawdown factor, is considered low. As of December 31, 2012, *SPDR S&P Emg Markets Sm Cap ETF traded at a discount of 2.65% below its net asset value, which is better than its one-year historical average premium of .28%.

John A. Tucker currently receives a manager quality ranking of 40 (0=worst, 99=best). If you desire an average level of risk, then this fund may be an option.

Data Date	Investment Rating	Net Assets ($Mil)	Price	Performance Rating/Pts	Total Return Y-T-D	Risk Rating/Pts
12-12	D+	875.30	46.64	C- / 3.9	2.57%	C+ / 5.9
2011	D+	736.60	37.73	C / 4.7	1.33%	C / 5.0
2010	B+	1,245.10	57.01	A / 9.3	23.48%	C / 4.8
2009	A	65.67	47.60	A+ / 9.8	92.32%	C / 5.0

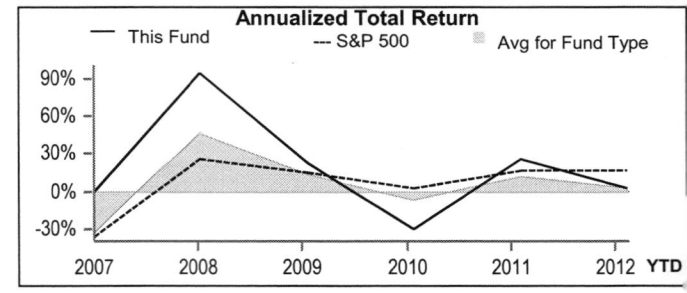

Annualized Total Return

*SPDR S&P Glbl Natural Resources (GNR)

C-   **Fair**

Fund Family: SSgA Funds Management Inc
Fund Type: Energy/Natural Resources
Inception Date: September 13, 2010

Major Rating Factors: Middle of the road best describes *SPDR S&P Glbl Natural Resources whose TheStreet.com Investment Rating is currently a C- (Fair). The fund currently has a performance rating of C (Fair) based on an annualized return of 0.00% over the last three years and a total return of 2.40% year to date 2012. Factored into the performance evaluation is an expense ratio of 0.40% (very low).

The fund's risk rating is currently C+ (Fair). It carries a beta of 0.00, meaning the fund's expected move will be 0.0% for every 10% move in the market. Volatility, as measured by both the semi-deviation and a drawdown factor, is considered low. As of December 31, 2012, *SPDR S&P Glbl Natural Resources traded at a discount of 2.09% below its net asset value, which is better than its one-year historical average premium of .22%.

John A. Tucker currently receives a manager quality ranking of 70 (0=worst, 99=best). If you desire an average level of risk, then this fund may be an option.

Data Date	Investment Rating	Net Assets ($Mil)	Price	Perfor-mance Rating/Pts	Total Return Y-T-D	Risk Rating/Pts
12-12	C-	490.30	51.56	C / 4.7	2.40%	C+ / 6.7
2011	D	171.40	49.02	D- / 1.1	2.75%	C+ / 6.8

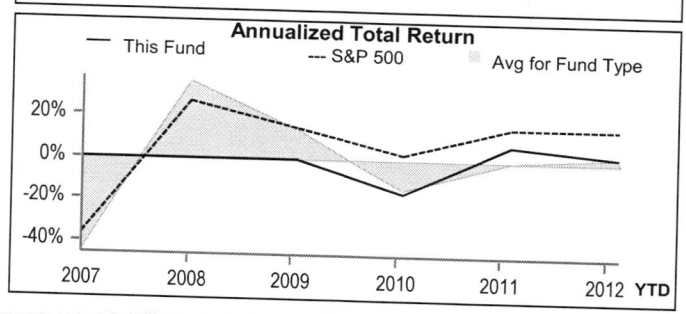

*SPDR S&P Health Care Equipment E (XHE)

B-   **Good**

Fund Family: SSgA Funds Management Inc
Fund Type: Health
Inception Date: January 26, 2011

Major Rating Factors: Strong performance is the major factor driving the B- (Good) TheStreet.com Investment Rating for *SPDR S&P Health Care Equipment E. The fund currently has a performance rating of B- (Good) based on an annualized return of 0.00% over the last three years and a total return of 6.32% year to date 2012. Factored into the performance evaluation is an expense ratio of 0.35% (very low).

The fund's risk rating is currently B (Good). It carries a beta of 0.00, meaning the fund's expected move will be 0.0% for every 10% move in the market. Volatility, as measured by both the semi-deviation and a drawdown factor, is considered low. As of December 31, 2012, *SPDR S&P Health Care Equipment E traded at a discount of 5.56% below its net asset value, which is better than its one-year historical average discount of .04%.

John A. Tucker currently receives a manager quality ranking of 20 (0=worst, 99=best). If you desire only a moderate level of risk and strong performance, then this fund is an excellent option.

Data Date	Investment Rating	Net Assets ($Mil)	Price	Perfor-mance Rating/Pts	Total Return Y-T-D	Risk Rating/Pts
12-12	B-	19.70	54.90	B- / 7.1	6.32%	B / 8.1

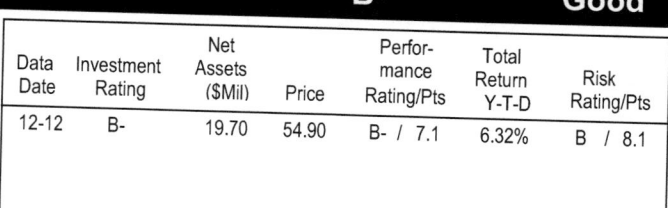

*SPDR S&P Health Care Services ET (XHS)

A+   **Excellent**

Fund Family: SSgA Funds Management Inc
Fund Type: Health
Inception Date: September 29, 2011

Major Rating Factors:
Exceptional performance is the major factor driving the A+ (Excellent) TheStreet.com Investment Rating for *SPDR S&P Health Care Services ET. The fund currently has a performance rating of A- (Excellent) based on an annualized return of 0.00% over the last three years and a total return of 3.54% year to date 2012. Factored into the performance evaluation is an expense ratio of 0.35% (very low).

The fund's risk rating is currently B (Good). It carries a beta of 0.00, meaning the fund's expected move will be 0.0% for every 10% move in the market. Volatility, as measured by both the semi-deviation and a drawdown factor, is considered low. As of December 31, 2012, *SPDR S&P Health Care Services ET traded at a discount of 3.40% below its net asset value, which is better than its one-year historical average discount of .02%.

John A. Tucker currently receives a manager quality ranking of 49 (0=worst, 99=best). If you desire only a moderate level of risk and strong performance, then this fund is an excellent option.

Data Date	Investment Rating	Net Assets ($Mil)	Price	Perfor-mance Rating/Pts	Total Return Y-T-D	Risk Rating/Pts
12-12	A+	13.30	66.30	A- / 9.2	3.54%	B / 8.9

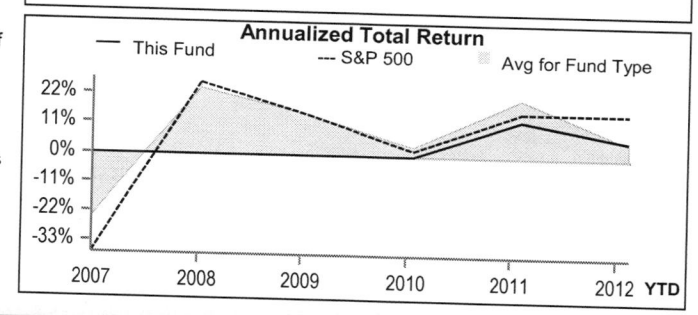

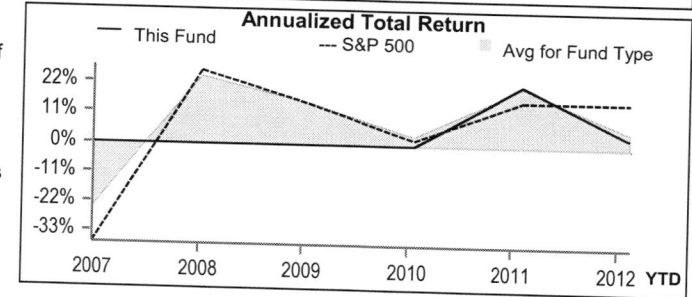

*SPDR S&P Homebuilders ETF (XHB)

A-   **Excellent**

Fund Family: SSgA Funds Management Inc
Fund Type: Income
Inception Date: January 31, 2006

Data Date	Investment Rating	Net Assets ($Mil)	Price	Performance Rating/Pts	Total Return Y-T-D	Risk Rating/Pts
12-12	A-	2,206.30	26.60	A+ / 9.6	4.40%	B- / 7.1
2011	C	876.90	17.10	C+ / 5.8	4.85%	B- / 7.0
2010	C	874.70	17.39	C+ / 6.1	17.40%	C / 4.9
2009	E+	556.11	15.11	E+ / 0.6	24.61%	C / 4.3

Major Rating Factors:
Exceptional performance is the major factor driving the A- (Excellent) TheStreet.com Investment Rating for *SPDR S&P Homebuilders ETF. The fund currently has a performance rating of A+ (Excellent) based on an annualized return of 22.76% over the last three years and a total return of 4.40% year to date 2012. Factored into the performance evaluation is an expense ratio of 0.35% (very low).

The fund's risk rating is currently B- (Good). It carries a beta of 1.46, meaning it is expected to move 14.6% for every 10% move in the market. Volatility, as measured by both the semi-deviation and a drawdown factor, is considered low. As of December 31, 2012, *SPDR S&P Homebuilders ETF traded at a discount of 4.25% below its net asset value, which is better than its one-year historical average discount of .01%.

John A. Tucker currently receives a manager quality ranking of 80 (0=worst, 99=best). If you desire only a moderate level of risk and strong performance, then this fund is an excellent option.

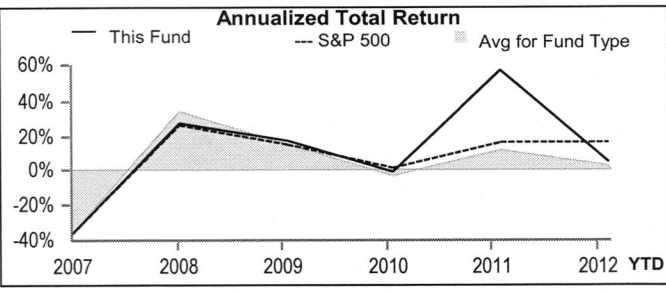

Annualized Total Return

---

*SPDR S&P International Div ETF (DWX)

D   **Weak**

Fund Family: SSgA Funds Management Inc
Fund Type: Emerging Market
Inception Date: February 12, 2008

Data Date	Investment Rating	Net Assets ($Mil)	Price	Performance Rating/Pts	Total Return Y-T-D	Risk Rating/Pts
12-12	D	1,146.80	48.11	D+ / 2.4	2.99%	C+ / 6.4
2011	C-	603.60	46.49	C- / 4.2	-0.17%	B- / 7.1
2010	B	351.30	56.00	B+ / 8.6	7.87%	C / 4.7
2009	A-	126.04	54.40	A / 9.3	56.71%	C / 4.9

Major Rating Factors:
Disappointing performance is the major factor driving the D (Weak) TheStreet.com Investment Rating for *SPDR S&P International Div ETF. The fund currently has a performance rating of D+ (Weak) based on an annualized return of 1.57% over the last three years and a total return of 2.99% year to date 2012. Factored into the performance evaluation is an expense ratio of 0.45% (very low).

The fund's risk rating is currently C+ (Fair). It carries a beta of 0.90, meaning that its performance tracks fairly well with that of the overall stock market. Volatility, as measured by both the semi-deviation and a drawdown factor, is considered low. As of December 31, 2012, *SPDR S&P International Div ETF traded at a discount of 2.51% below its net asset value, which is better than its one-year historical average premium of .23%.

John A. Tucker currently receives a manager quality ranking of 32 (0=worst, 99=best). This fund offers only a moderate level of risk but investors looking for strong performance are still waiting.

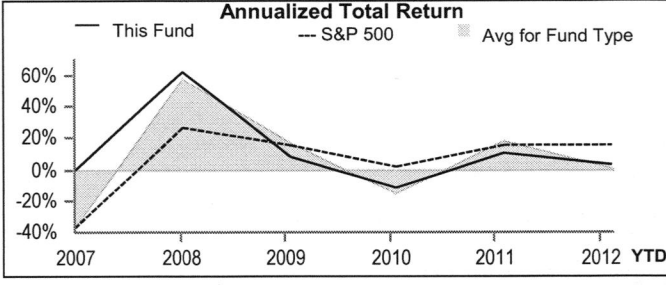

Annualized Total Return

---

*SPDR S&P International Mid Cap E (MDD)

C-   **Fair**

Fund Family: SSgA Funds Management Inc
Fund Type: Global
Inception Date: May 7, 2008

Data Date	Investment Rating	Net Assets ($Mil)	Price	Performance Rating/Pts	Total Return Y-T-D	Risk Rating/Pts
12-12	C-	34.30	28.69	C / 4.9	2.53%	B- / 7.1
2011	C-	35.10	24.88	C- / 3.5	0.92%	B- / 7.4
2010	B+	40.10	31.00	A / 9.4	23.05%	C / 4.3
2009	B	21.72	26.24	B / 8.1	30.50%	C / 5.1

Major Rating Factors: Middle of the road best describes *SPDR S&P International Mid Cap E whose TheStreet.com Investment Rating is currently a C- (Fair). The fund currently has a performance rating of C (Fair) based on an annualized return of 6.75% over the last three years and a total return of 2.53% year to date 2012. Factored into the performance evaluation is an expense ratio of 0.45% (very low).

The fund's risk rating is currently B- (Good). It carries a beta of 0.99, meaning that its performance tracks fairly well with that of the overall stock market. Volatility, as measured by both the semi-deviation and a drawdown factor, is considered low. As of December 31, 2012, *SPDR S&P International Mid Cap E traded at a discount of 2.35% below its net asset value, which is better than its one-year historical average discount of .19%.

John A. Tucker currently receives a manager quality ranking of 74 (0=worst, 99=best). If you desire an average level of risk, then this fund may be an option.

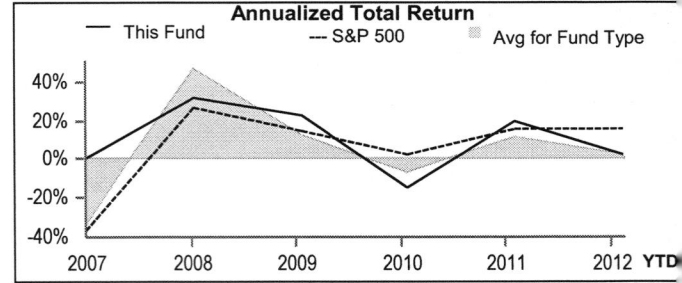

Annualized Total Return

---

*SPDR S&P International Small Cap (GWX)

C　　**Fair**

Fund Family: SSgA Funds Management Inc
Fund Type: Foreign
Inception Date: April 20, 2007

Major Rating Factors: Middle of the road best describes *SPDR S&P International Small Cap whose TheStreet.com Investment Rating is currently a C (Fair). The fund currently has a performance rating of C (Fair) based on an annualized return of 6.27% over the last three years and a total return of 3.27% year to date 2012. Factored into the performance evaluation is an expense ratio of 0.59% (very low).

The fund's risk rating is currently B- (Good). It carries a beta of 0.99, meaning that its performance tracks fairly well with that of the overall stock market. Volatility, as measured by both the semi-deviation and a drawdown factor, is considered low. As of December 31, 2012, *SPDR S&P International Small Cap traded at a discount of 2.50% below its net asset value, which is better than its one-year historical average premium of .14%.

John A. Tucker currently receives a manager quality ranking of 71 (0=worst, 99=best). If you desire an average level of risk, then this fund may be an option.

Data Date	Investment Rating	Net Assets ($Mil)	Price	Performance Rating/Pts	Total Return Y-T-D	Risk Rating/Pts
12-12	C	694.20	28.45	C / 4.6	3.27%	B- / 7.6
2011	C-	656.90	25.17	C- / 3.9	0.20%	B- / 7.7
2010	C	806.70	30.84	C / 5.4	24.94%	C / 5.4
2009	B+	509.03	25.33	B+ / 8.5	35.65%	C / 5.3

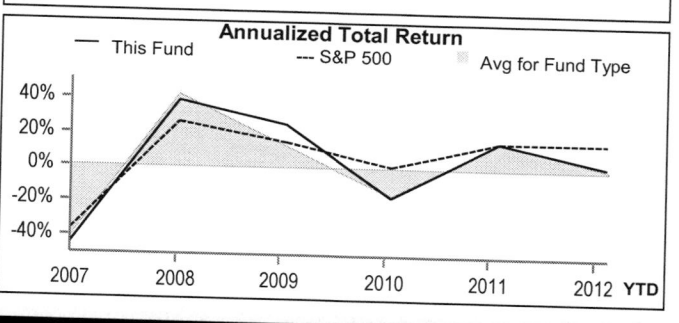

*SPDR S&P Metals & Mining ETF (XME)

D-　　**Weak**

Fund Family: SSgA Funds Management Inc
Fund Type: Income
Inception Date: June 19, 2006

Major Rating Factors:
Very poor performance is the major factor driving the D- (Weak) TheStreet.com Investment Rating for *SPDR S&P Metals & Mining ETF. The fund currently has a performance rating of E+ (Very Weak) based on an annualized return of -5.57% over the last three years and a total return of 0.38% year to date 2012. Factored into the performance evaluation is an expense ratio of 0.35% (very low).

The fund's risk rating is currently C+ (Fair). It carries a beta of 1.80, meaning it is expected to move 18.0% for every 10% move in the market. Volatility, as measured by both the semi-deviation and a drawdown factor, is considered low. As of December 31, 2012, *SPDR S&P Metals & Mining ETF traded at a discount of .46% below its net asset value, which is better than its one-year historical average discount of .02%.

John A. Tucker currently receives a manager quality ranking of 5 (0=worst, 99=best). This fund offers only a moderate level of risk but investors looking for strong performance are still waiting.

Data Date	Investment Rating	Net Assets ($Mil)	Price	Performance Rating/Pts	Total Return Y-T-D	Risk Rating/Pts
12-12	D-	1,004.30	45.13	E+ / 0.9	0.38%	C+ / 5.6
2011	C-	707.50	48.99	C / 5.1	4.74%	C+ / 6.2
2010	C+	1,220.90	68.78	B / 7.8	34.14%	C- / 3.7
2009	C+	602.42	51.61	B / 7.7	73.19%	C- / 4.1

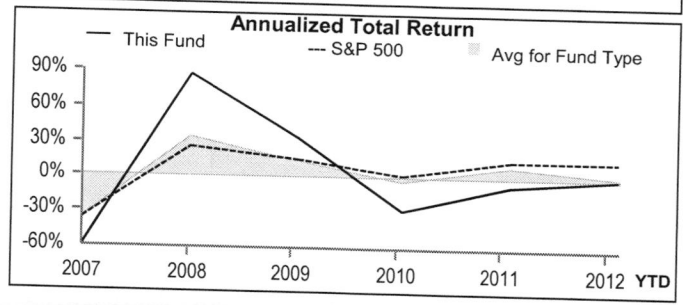

*SPDR S&P MidCap 400 ETF (MDY)

C+　　**Fair**

Fund Family: Bank of New York Mellon
Fund Type: Growth
Inception Date: April 28, 1995

Major Rating Factors: Middle of the road best describes *SPDR S&P MidCap 400 ETF whose TheStreet.com Investment Rating is currently a C+ (Fair). The fund currently has a performance rating of C+ (Fair) based on an annualized return of 13.77% over the last three years and a total return of 3.54% year to date 2012. Factored into the performance evaluation is an expense ratio of 0.25% (very low).

The fund's risk rating is currently B- (Good). It carries a beta of 1.17, meaning it is expected to move 11.7% for every 10% move in the market. Volatility, as measured by both the semi-deviation and a drawdown factor, is considered low. As of December 31, 2012, *SPDR S&P MidCap 400 ETF traded at a discount of 3.49% below its net asset value, which is better than its one-year historical average discount of .01%.

Alistair Lowe currently receives a manager quality ranking of 57 (0=worst, 99=best). If you desire an average level of risk, then this fund may be an option.

Data Date	Investment Rating	Net Assets ($Mil)	Price	Performance Rating/Pts	Total Return Y-T-D	Risk Rating/Pts
12-12	C+	10,616.80	185.71	C+ / 6.8	3.54%	B- / 7.7
2011	C+	0.00	159.49	C+ / 6.4	1.53%	B- / 7.7
2010	B-	10,875.80	164.68	B- / 7.2	25.93%	C / 5.5
2009	C-	7,581.13	131.74	C- / 3.8	33.85%	C+ / 6.0

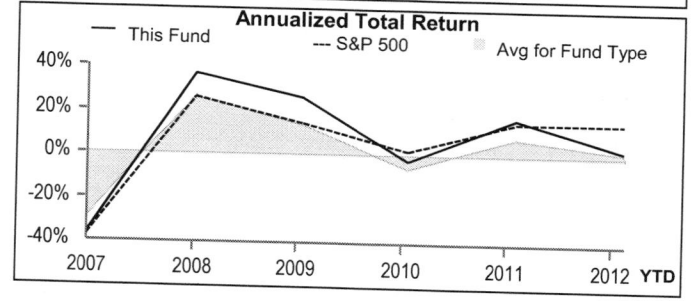

*SPDR S&P Oil & Gas Equip & Serv (XES)

D+   **Weak**

Fund Family: SSgA Funds Management Inc
Fund Type: Energy/Natural Resources
Inception Date: June 19, 2006

Major Rating Factors: *SPDR S&P Oil & Gas Equip & Serv receives a TheStreet.com Investment Rating of D+ (Weak). The fund currently has a performance rating of C- (Fair) based on an annualized return of 6.61% over the last three years and a total return of 4.85% year to date 2012. Factored into the performance evaluation is an expense ratio of 0.35% (very low).

The fund's risk rating is currently C+ (Fair). It carries a beta of 1.34, meaning it is expected to move 13.4% for every 10% move in the market. Volatility, as measured by both the semi-deviation and a drawdown factor, is considered low. As of December 31, 2012, *SPDR S&P Oil & Gas Equip & Serv traded at a discount of 4.63% below its net asset value.

John A. Tucker currently receives a manager quality ranking of 23 (0=worst, 99=best). If you desire an average level of risk, then this fund may be an option.

Data Date	Investment Rating	Net Assets ($Mil)	Price	Perfor-mance Rating/Pts	Total Return Y-T-D	Risk Rating/Pts
12-12	D+	277.10	34.62	C- / 3.3	4.85%	C+ / 6.3
2011	C+	341.50	34.66	B- / 7.5	2.71%	C+ / 6.3
2010	C-	451.20	36.71	C+ / 6.0	30.10%	C- / 4.2
2009	C	199.10	28.48	C+ / 6.5	57.09%	C / 4.6

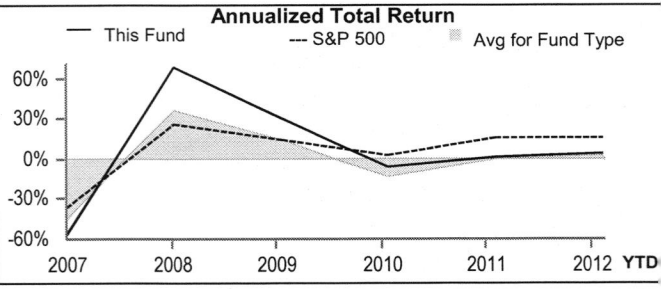

*SPDR S&P Oil & Gas Expl & Prod (XOP)

C-   **Fair**

Fund Family: SSgA Funds Management Inc
Fund Type: Income
Inception Date: June 19, 2006

Major Rating Factors: Middle of the road best describes *SPDR S&P Oil & Gas Expl & Prod whose TheStreet.com Investment Rating is currently a C- (Fair). The fund currently has a performance rating of C- (Fair) based on an annualized return of 10.27% over the last three years and a total return of 3.77% year to date 2012. Factored into the performance evaluation is an expense ratio of 0.35% (very low).

The fund's risk rating is currently C+ (Fair). It carries a beta of 1.54, meaning it is expected to move 15.4% for every 10% move in the market. Volatility, as measured by both the semi-deviation and a drawdown factor, is considered low. As of December 31, 2012, *SPDR S&P Oil & Gas Expl & Prod traded at a discount of 3.53% below its net asset value, which is better than its one-year historical average premium of .02%.

John A. Tucker currently receives a manager quality ranking of 20 (0=worst, 99=best). If you desire an average level of risk, then this fund may be an option.

Data Date	Investment Rating	Net Assets ($Mil)	Price	Perfor-mance Rating/Pts	Total Return Y-T-D	Risk Rating/Pts
12-12	C-	721.90	54.08	C- / 4.2	3.77%	C+ / 6.7
2011	C+	776.50	52.69	B- / 7.1	3.61%	C+ / 6.7
2010	C+	722.10	52.75	B- / 7.0	28.57%	C / 4.8
2009	C	280.28	41.21	C / 5.1	31.82%	C / 5.1

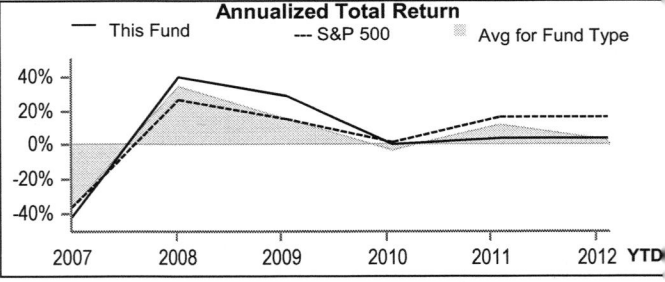

*SPDR S&P Pharmaceuticals ETF (XPH)

C+   **Fair**

Fund Family: SSgA Funds Management Inc
Fund Type: Health
Inception Date: June 19, 2006

Major Rating Factors: Middle of the road best describes *SPDR S&P Pharmaceuticals ETF whose TheStreet.com Investment Rating is currently a C+ (Fair). The fund currently has a performance rating of C+ (Fair) based on an annualized return of 16.15% over the last three years and a total return of 5.78% year to date 2012. Factored into the performance evaluation is an expense ratio of 0.35% (very low).

The fund's risk rating is currently B- (Good). It carries a beta of 0.71, meaning the fund's expected move will be 7.1% for every 10% move in the market. Volatility, as measured by both the semi-deviation and a drawdown factor, is considered low. As of December 31, 2012, *SPDR S&P Pharmaceuticals ETF traded at a discount of 5.41% below its net asset value.

John A. Tucker currently receives a manager quality ranking of 85 (0=worst, 99=best). If you desire an average level of risk, then this fund may be an option.

Data Date	Investment Rating	Net Assets ($Mil)	Price	Perfor-mance Rating/Pts	Total Return Y-T-D	Risk Rating/Pts
12-12	C+	307.70	55.91	C+ / 6.3	5.78%	B- / 7.3
2011	C+	289.90	51.33	B- / 7.3	0.66%	C+ / 6.3
2010	B+	209.50	46.09	B+ / 8.5	22.48%	C / 5.4
2009	C+	40.50	38.08	C / 4.8	25.17%	B- / 7.2

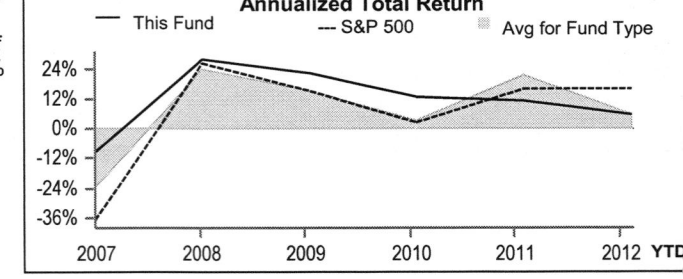

*SPDR S&P Retail ETF (XRT)

B+   **Good**

Fund Family: SSgA Funds Management Inc
Fund Type: Income
Inception Date: June 19, 2006

Major Rating Factors: Strong performance is the major factor driving the B+ (Good) TheStreet.com Investment Rating for *SPDR S&P Retail ETF. The fund currently has a performance rating of B+ (Good) based on an annualized return of 22.25% over the last three years and a total return of 1.06% year to date 2012. Factored into the performance evaluation is an expense ratio of 0.35% (very low).

The fund's risk rating is currently B (Good). It carries a beta of 1.14, meaning it is expected to move 11.4% for every 10% move in the market. Volatility, as measured by both the semi-deviation and a drawdown factor, is considered low. As of December 31, 2012, *SPDR S&P Retail ETF traded at a discount of 1.16% below its net asset value, which is better than its one-year historical average discount of .01%.

John A. Tucker currently receives a manager quality ranking of 88 (0=worst, 99=best). If you desire only a moderate level of risk and strong performance, then this fund is an excellent option.

Data Date	Investment Rating	Net Assets ($Mil)	Price	Performance Rating/Pts	Total Return Y-T-D	Risk Rating/Pts
12-12	B+	536.40	62.38	B+ / 8.6	1.06%	B / 8.0
2011	A-	614.50	52.55	A / 9.3	-0.91%	B / 8.1
2010	A-	976.70	48.36	A- / 9.2	37.38%	C / 5.3
2009	C-	1,018.01	35.60	C / 4.7	70.31%	C / 5.4

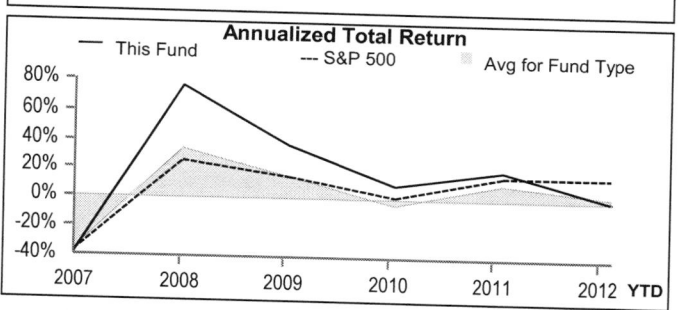

*SPDR S&P Russia (RBL)

C-   **Fair**

Fund Family: SSgA Funds Management Inc
Fund Type: Emerging Market
Inception Date: March 10, 2010

Major Rating Factors: Middle of the road best describes *SPDR S&P Russia whose TheStreet.com Investment Rating is currently a C- (Fair). The fund currently has a performance rating of C+ (Fair) based on an annualized return of 0.00% over the last three years and a total return of 0.14% year to date 2012. Factored into the performance evaluation is an expense ratio of 0.59% (very low).

The fund's risk rating is currently C (Fair). It carries a beta of 0.00, meaning the fund's expected move will be 0.0% for every 10% move in the market. Volatility, as measured by both the semi-deviation and a drawdown factor, is considered average. As of December 31, 2012, *SPDR S&P Russia traded at a discount of .34% below its net asset value, which is better than its one-year historical average premium of .12%.

John A. Tucker currently receives a manager quality ranking of 9 (0=worst, 99=best). If you desire an average level of risk, then this fund may be an option.

Data Date	Investment Rating	Net Assets ($Mil)	Price	Performance Rating/Pts	Total Return Y-T-D	Risk Rating/Pts
12-12	C-	37.20	29.11	C+ / 6.1	0.14%	C / 5.3
2011	D-	35.20	26.32	E+ / 0.7	1.52%	C+ / 5.6

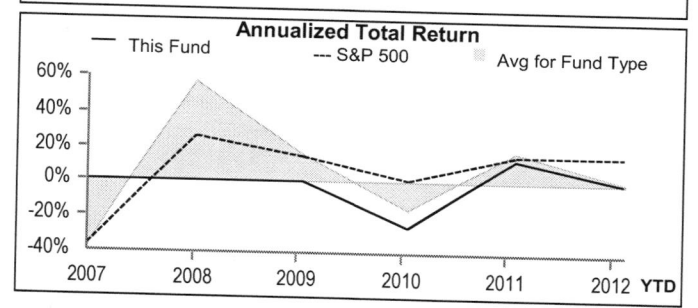

*SPDR S&P Semiconductor ETF (XSD)

D   **Weak**

Fund Family: SSgA Funds Management Inc
Fund Type: Income
Inception Date: January 31, 2006

Major Rating Factors:
Disappointing performance is the major factor driving the D (Weak) TheStreet.com Investment Rating for *SPDR S&P Semiconductor ETF. The fund currently has a performance rating of D+ (Weak) based on an annualized return of 2.01% over the last three years and a total return of 4.06% year to date 2012. Factored into the performance evaluation is an expense ratio of 0.35% (very low).

The fund's risk rating is currently C+ (Fair). It carries a beta of 1.45, meaning it is expected to move 14.5% for every 10% move in the market. Volatility, as measured by both the semi-deviation and a drawdown factor, is considered low. As of December 31, 2012, *SPDR S&P Semiconductor ETF traded at a discount of 3.90% below its net asset value, which is better than its one-year historical average discount of .02%.

John A. Tucker currently receives a manager quality ranking of 8 (0=worst, 99=best). This fund offers only a moderate level of risk but investors looking for strong performance are still waiting.

Data Date	Investment Rating	Net Assets ($Mil)	Price	Performance Rating/Pts	Total Return Y-T-D	Risk Rating/Pts
12-12	D	33.90	45.07	D+ / 2.3	4.06%	C+ / 6.8
2011	C	33.20	44.32	C+ / 6.2	2.30%	C+ / 6.7
2010	B	109.20	54.60	B / 8.1	15.71%	C / 5.0
2009	C	103.28	47.60	C+ / 6.2	91.09%	C / 4.9

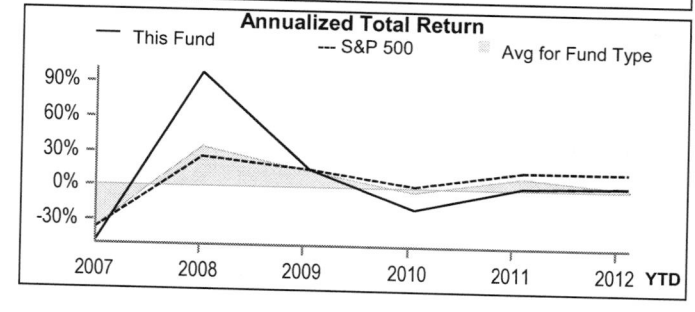

*SPDR S&P Software & Services ETF (XSW) A Excellent

Fund Family: SSgA Funds Management Inc
Fund Type: Growth
Inception Date: September 29, 2011

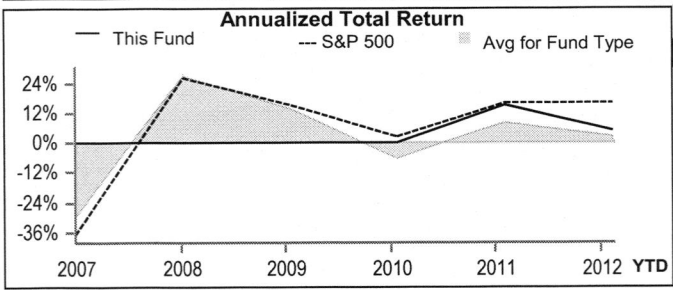

Data Date	Investment Rating	Net Assets ($Mil)	Price	Performance Rating/Pts	Total Return Y-T-D	Risk Rating/Pts
12-12	A	12.50	62.39	B+ / 8.3	4.44%	B / 8.9

Major Rating Factors:

Strong performance is the major factor driving the A (Excellent) TheStreet.com Investment Rating for *SPDR S&P Software & Services ETF. The fund currently has a performance rating of B+ (Good) based on an annualized return of 0.00% over the last three years and a total return of 4.44% year to date 2012. Factored into the performance evaluation is an expense ratio of 0.35% (very low).

The fund's risk rating is currently B (Good). It carries a beta of 0.00, meaning the fund's expected move will be 0.0% for every 10% move in the market. Volatility, as measured by both the semi-deviation and a drawdown factor, is considered low. As of December 31, 2012, *SPDR S&P Software & Services ETF traded at a discount of 4.38% below its net asset value, which is better than its one-year historical average discount of .02%.

John A. Tucker currently receives a manager quality ranking of 23 (0=worst, 99=best). If you desire only a moderate level of risk and strong performance, then this fund is an excellent option.

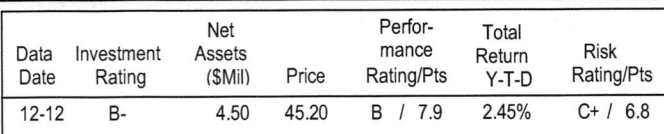

Annualized Total Return
— This Fund   --- S&P 500   Avg for Fund Type

*SPDR S&P Telecom ETF (XTL) B- Good

Fund Family: SSgA Funds Management Inc
Fund Type: Growth
Inception Date: January 26, 2011

Data Date	Investment Rating	Net Assets ($Mil)	Price	Performance Rating/Pts	Total Return Y-T-D	Risk Rating/Pts
12-12	B-	4.50	45.20	B / 7.9	2.45%	C+ / 6.8

Major Rating Factors: Strong performance is the major factor driving the B- (Good) TheStreet.com Investment Rating for *SPDR S&P Telecom ETF. The fund currently has a performance rating of B (Good) based on an annualized return of 0.00% over the last three years and a total return of 2.45% year to date 2012. Factored into the performance evaluation is an expense ratio of 0.35% (very low).

The fund's risk rating is currently C+ (Fair). It carries a beta of 0.00, meaning the fund's expected move will be 0.0% for every 10% move in the market. Volatility, as measured by both the semi-deviation and a drawdown factor, is considered low. As of December 31, 2012, *SPDR S&P Telecom ETF traded at a discount of 2.77% below its net asset value, which is better than its one-year historical average discount of .04%.

John A. Tucker currently receives a manager quality ranking of 10 (0=worst, 99=best). If you desire only a moderate level of risk and strong performance, then this fund is an excellent option.

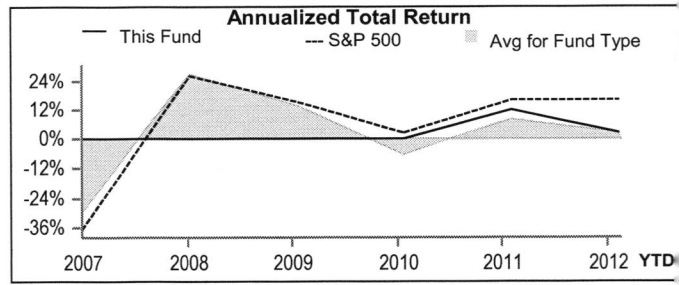

Annualized Total Return
— This Fund   --- S&P 500   Avg for Fund Type

*SPDR S&P Transportation ETF (XTN) B+ Good

Fund Family: SSgA Funds Management Inc
Fund Type: Utilities
Inception Date: January 26, 2011

Data Date	Investment Rating	Net Assets ($Mil)	Price	Performance Rating/Pts	Total Return Y-T-D	Risk Rating/Pts
12-12	B+	13.50	53.78	A / 9.4	5.62%	B- / 7.1

Major Rating Factors:

Exceptional performance is the major factor driving the B+ (Good) TheStreet.com Investment Rating for *SPDR S&P Transportation ETF. The fund currently has a performance rating of A (Excellent) based on an annualized return of 0.00% over the last three years and a total return of 5.62% year to date 2012. Factored into the performance evaluation is an expense ratio of 0.35% (very low).

The fund's risk rating is currently B- (Good). It carries a beta of 0.00, meaning the fund's expected move will be 0.0% for every 10% move in the market. Volatility, as measured by both the semi-deviation and a drawdown factor, is considered low. As of December 31, 2012, *SPDR S&P Transportation ETF traded at a discount of 5.30% below its net asset value, which is better than its one-year historical average discount of .08%.

John A. Tucker currently receives a manager quality ranking of 97 (0=worst, 99=best). If you desire only a moderate level of risk and strong performance, then this fund is an excellent option.

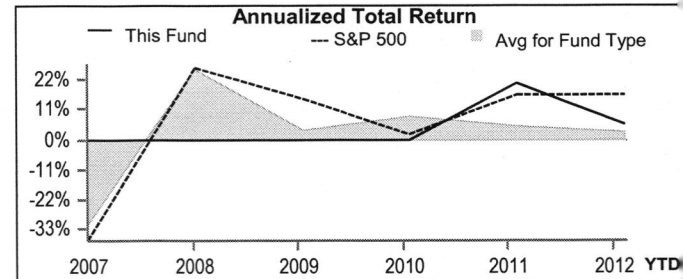

Annualized Total Return
— This Fund   --- S&P 500   Avg for Fund Type

*SPDR S&P WORLD EX-US ETF (GWL)

C- **Fair**

Fund Family: SSgA Funds Management Inc
Fund Type: Global
Inception Date: April 20, 2007

Major Rating Factors: Middle of the road best describes *SPDR S&P WORLD EX-US ETF whose TheStreet.com Investment Rating is currently a C- (Fair). The fund currently has a performance rating of C- (Fair) based on an annualized return of 4.36% over the last three years and a total return of 2.53% year to date 2012. Factored into the performance evaluation is an expense ratio of 0.34% (very low).

The fund's risk rating is currently B- (Good). It carries a beta of 1.02, meaning that its performance tracks fairly well with that of the overall stock market. Volatility, as measured by both the semi-deviation and a drawdown factor, is considered low. As of December 31, 2012, *SPDR S&P WORLD EX-US ETF traded at a discount of 1.86% below its net asset value, which is better than its one-year historical average premium of .27%.

John A. Tucker currently receives a manager quality ranking of 57 (0=worst, 99=best). If you desire an average level of risk, then this fund may be an option.

Data Date	Investment Rating	Net Assets ($Mil)	Price	Performance Rating/Pts	Total Return Y-T-D	Risk Rating/Pts
12-12	C-	460.00	25.33	C- / 4.2	2.53%	B- / 7.3
2011	D+	140.20	21.79	D+ / 2.7	-0.09%	B- / 7.2
2010	D	118.30	25.95	D+ / 2.3	11.26%	C / 5.4
2009	B+	84.89	23.93	B+ / 8.3	27.01%	C / 5.5

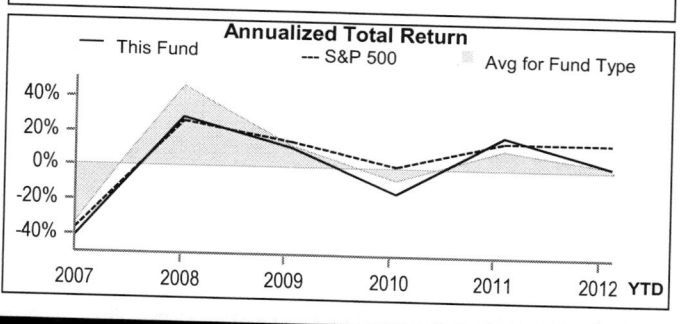

Annualized Total Return

---

*SPDR SP Intl Con Disc Sect ETF (IPD)

C+ **Fair**

Fund Family: SSgA Funds Management Inc
Fund Type: Global
Inception Date: July 16, 2008

Major Rating Factors: Middle of the road best describes *SPDR SP Intl Con Disc Sect ETF whose TheStreet.com Investment Rating is currently a C+ (Fair). The fund currently has a performance rating of C+ (Fair) based on an annualized return of 9.11% over the last three years and a total return of 1.52% year to date 2012. Factored into the performance evaluation is an expense ratio of 0.51% (very low).

The fund's risk rating is currently B- (Good). It carries a beta of 0.97, meaning that its performance tracks fairly well with that of the overall stock market. Volatility, as measured by both the semi-deviation and a drawdown factor, is considered low. As of December 31, 2012, *SPDR SP Intl Con Disc Sect ETF traded at a discount of 1.62% below its net asset value, which is better than its one-year historical average premium of .13%.

John A. Tucker currently receives a manager quality ranking of 81 (0=worst, 99=best). If you desire an average level of risk, then this fund may be an option.

Data Date	Investment Rating	Net Assets ($Mil)	Price	Performance Rating/Pts	Total Return Y-T-D	Risk Rating/Pts
12-12	C+	6.00	30.32	C+ / 6.7	1.52%	B- / 7.5
2011	C	4.90	24.37	C / 5.0	0.86%	B- / 7.9
2010	A	22.00	29.34	A / 9.3	19.59%	C+ / 6.2
2009	A+	4.82	24.87	A / 9.3	61.86%	C+ / 6.2

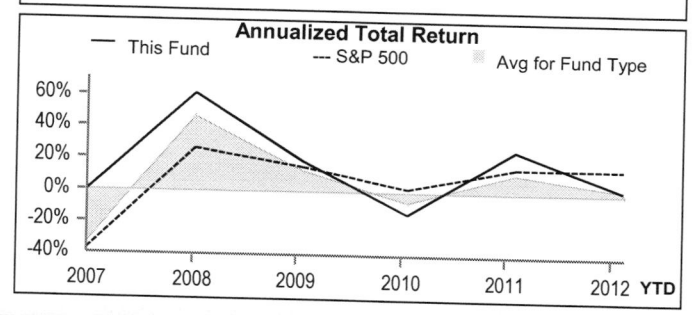

Annualized Total Return

---

*SPDR SP Intl Con Stap Sect ETF (IPS)

C+ **Fair**

Fund Family: SSgA Funds Management Inc
Fund Type: Global
Inception Date: July 16, 2008

Major Rating Factors: Middle of the road best describes *SPDR SP Intl Con Stap Sect ETF whose TheStreet.com Investment Rating is currently a C+ (Fair). The fund currently has a performance rating of C+ (Fair) based on an annualized return of 10.63% over the last three years and a total return of 1.21% year to date 2012. Factored into the performance evaluation is an expense ratio of 0.50% (very low).

The fund's risk rating is currently B (Good). It carries a beta of 0.66, meaning the fund's expected move will be 6.6% for every 10% move in the market. Volatility, as measured by both the semi-deviation and a drawdown factor, is considered low. As of December 31, 2012, *SPDR SP Intl Con Stap Sect ETF traded at a discount of .67% below its net asset value, which is better than its one-year historical average premium of .20%.

John A. Tucker currently receives a manager quality ranking of 86 (0=worst, 99=best). If you desire an average level of risk, then this fund may be an option.

Data Date	Investment Rating	Net Assets ($Mil)	Price	Performance Rating/Pts	Total Return Y-T-D	Risk Rating/Pts
12-12	C+	19.40	35.67	C+ / 5.6	1.21%	B / 8.6
2011	C+	17.20	31.31	C / 4.9	-1.09%	B / 8.3
2010	A	12.40	30.95	B+ / 8.6	11.72%	C+ / 6.8
2009	A+	5.26	28.32	B+ / 8.3	26.07%	B- / 7.0

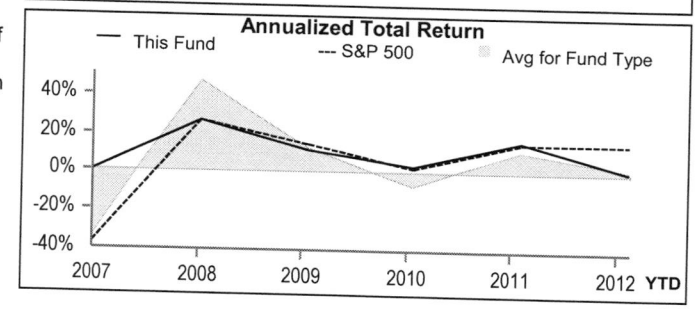

Annualized Total Return

*SPDR SP Intl Energy Sector ETF (IPW)   D   Weak

Fund Family: SSgA Funds Management Inc
Fund Type: Energy/Natural Resources
Inception Date: July 16, 2008

Data Date	Investment Rating	Net Assets ($Mil)	Price	Performance Rating/Pts	Total Return Y-T-D	Risk Rating/Pts
12-12	D	11.10	24.96	D / 2.0	3.01%	B- / 7.3
2011	C-	10.20	25.25	C- / 3.7	1.60%	B- / 7.4
2010	A-	15.00	27.44	B+ / 8.9	4.68%	C+ / 6.1
2009	A+	6.37	26.86	B+ / 8.6	34.41%	C+ / 6.2

Major Rating Factors:
Disappointing performance is the major factor driving the D (Weak) TheStreet.com Investment Rating for *SPDR SP Intl Energy Sector ETF. The fund currently has a performance rating of D (Weak) based on an annualized return of 0.99% over the last three years and a total return of 3.01% year to date 2012. Factored into the performance evaluation is an expense ratio of 0.50% (very low).

The fund's risk rating is currently B- (Good). It carries a beta of 0.99, meaning that its performance tracks fairly well with that of the overall stock market. Volatility, as measured by both the semi-deviation and a drawdown factor, is considered low. As of December 31, 2012, *SPDR SP Intl Energy Sector ETF traded at a discount of 1.96% below its net asset value, which is better than its one-year historical average discount of .41%.

John A. Tucker currently receives a manager quality ranking of 15 (0=worst, 99=best). This fund offers only a moderate level of risk but investors looking for strong performance are still waiting.

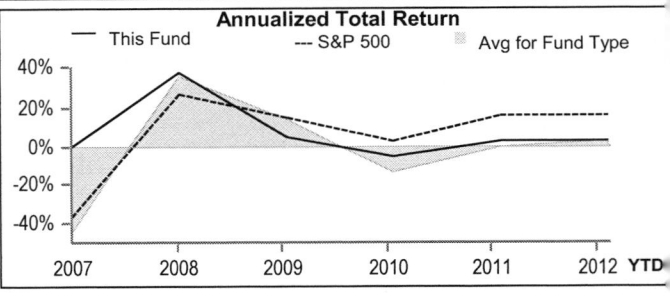

*SPDR SP Intl Finl Sector ETF (IPF)   D+   Weak

Fund Family: SSgA Funds Management Inc
Fund Type: Financial Services
Inception Date: July 16, 2008

Data Date	Investment Rating	Net Assets ($Mil)	Price	Performance Rating/Pts	Total Return Y-T-D	Risk Rating/Pts
12-12	D+	5.70	19.33	C- / 3.1	3.47%	B- / 7.0
2011	D	4.60	15.05	D / 1.7	-0.98%	B- / 7.1
2010	C+	6.00	19.81	B- / 7.0	0.56%	C / 5.1
2009	B	5.35	20.45	B+ / 8.5	36.11%	C / 5.0

Major Rating Factors: *SPDR SP Intl Finl Sector ETF receives a TheStreet.com Investment Rating of D+ (Weak). The fund currently has a performance rating of C- (Fair) based on an annualized return of 2.26% over the last three years and a total return of 3.47% year to date 2012. Factored into the performance evaluation is an expense ratio of 0.50% (very low).

The fund's risk rating is currently B- (Good). It carries a beta of 1.00, meaning that its performance tracks fairly well with that of the overall stock market. Volatility, as measured by both the semi-deviation and a drawdown factor, is considered low. As of December 31, 2012, *SPDR SP Intl Finl Sector ETF traded at a discount of 2.67% below its net asset value, which is better than its one-year historical average discount of .13%.

John A. Tucker currently receives a manager quality ranking of 22 (0=worst, 99=best). If you desire an average level of risk, then this fund may be an option.

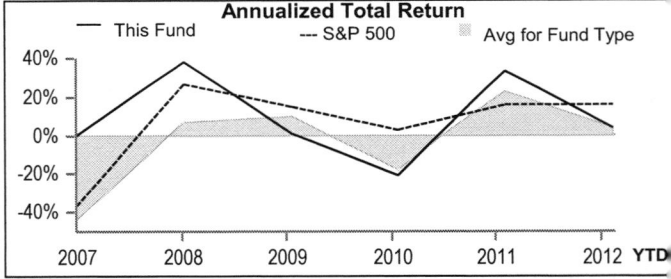

*SPDR SP Intl Health Care ETF (IRY)   C+   Fair

Fund Family: SSgA Funds Management Inc
Fund Type: Health
Inception Date: July 16, 2008

Data Date	Investment Rating	Net Assets ($Mil)	Price	Performance Rating/Pts	Total Return Y-T-D	Risk Rating/Pts
12-12	C+	30.20	35.81	C+ / 5.7	2.88%	B / 8.2
2011	C-	15.50	31.00	C- / 3.7	-0.65%	B / 8.1
2010	C+	12.10	30.12	C+ / 6.9	3.51%	C+ / 6.5
2009	B+	5.70	29.75	B / 7.7	16.78%	C+ / 6.2

Major Rating Factors: Middle of the road best describes *SPDR SP Intl Health Care ETF whose TheStreet.com Investment Rating is currently a C+ (Fair). The fund currently has a performance rating of C+ (Fair) based on an annualized return of 9.67% over the last three years and a total return of 2.88% year to date 2012. Factored into the performance evaluation is an expense ratio of 0.50% (very low).

The fund's risk rating is currently B (Good). It carries a beta of 0.70, meaning the fund's expected move will be 7.0% for every 10% move in the market. Volatility, as measured by both the semi-deviation and a drawdown factor, is considered low. As of December 31, 2012, *SPDR SP Intl Health Care ETF traded at a discount of 2.80% below its net asset value, which is better than its one-year historical average premium of .10%.

John A. Tucker currently receives a manager quality ranking of 63 (0=worst, 99=best). If you desire an average level of risk, then this fund may be an option.

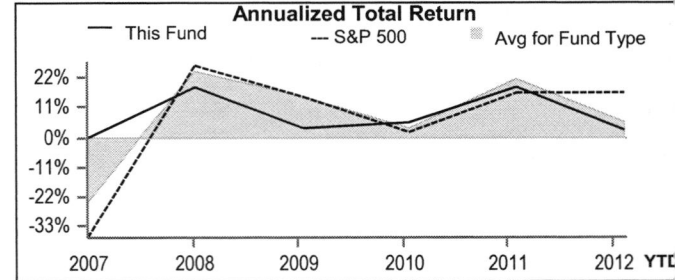

*SPDR SP Intl Industrial ETF (IPN)

C-   **Fair**

Fund Family: SSgA Funds Management Inc
Fund Type: Global
Inception Date: July 16, 2008

Major Rating Factors: Middle of the road best describes *SPDR SP Intl Industrial ETF whose TheStreet.com Investment Rating is currently a C- (Fair). The fund currently has a performance rating of C- (Fair) based on an annualized return of 5.18% over the last three years and a total return of 2.66% year to date 2012. Factored into the performance evaluation is an expense ratio of 0.50% (very low).

The fund's risk rating is currently B- (Good). It carries a beta of 0.97, meaning that its performance tracks fairly well with that of the overall stock market. Volatility, as measured by both the semi-deviation and a drawdown factor, is considered low. As of December 31, 2012, *SPDR SP Intl Industrial ETF traded at a discount of 2.08% below its net asset value, which is better than its one-year historical average discount of .06%.

John A. Tucker currently receives a manager quality ranking of 67 (0=worst, 99=best). If you desire an average level of risk, then this fund may be an option.

Data Date	Investment Rating	Net Assets ($Mil)	Price	Performance Rating/Pts	Total Return Y-T-D	Risk Rating/Pts
12-12	C-	6.50	26.35	C- / 3.6	2.66%	B- / 7.4
2011	C-	12.80	23.02	C- / 3.0	-0.17%	B- / 7.6
2010	A-	28.30	28.28	A / 9.3	20.35%	C+ / 5.7
2009	A	4.65	23.88	B+ / 8.8	40.88%	C+ / 5.6

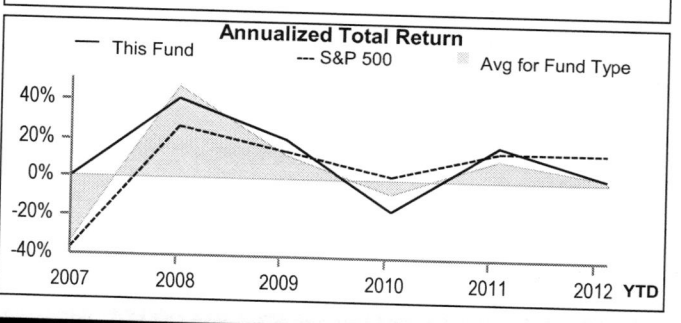

Annualized Total Return

*SPDR SP Intl Materials Sec ETF (IRV)

D   **Weak**

Fund Family: SSgA Funds Management Inc
Fund Type: Global
Inception Date: July 16, 2008

Major Rating Factors:
Disappointing performance is the major factor driving the D (Weak) TheStreet.com Investment Rating for *SPDR SP Intl Materials Sec ETF. The fund currently has a performance rating of D (Weak) based on an annualized return of -0.11% over the last three years and a total return of 1.27% year to date 2012. Factored into the performance evaluation is an expense ratio of 0.50% (very low).

The fund's risk rating is currently C+ (Fair). It carries a beta of 1.24, meaning it is expected to move 12.4% for every 10% move in the market. Volatility, as measured by both the semi-deviation and a drawdown factor, is considered low. As of December 31, 2012, *SPDR SP Intl Materials Sec ETF traded at a discount of 1.27% below its net asset value, which is better than its one-year historical average discount of .32%.

John A. Tucker currently receives a manager quality ranking of 25 (0=worst, 99=best). This fund offers only a moderate level of risk but investors looking for strong performance are still waiting.

Data Date	Investment Rating	Net Assets ($Mil)	Price	Performance Rating/Pts	Total Return Y-T-D	Risk Rating/Pts
12-12	D	9.90	24.87	D / 2.0	1.27%	C+ / 5.9
2011	D	12.80	23.06	C- / 3.5	1.97%	C+ / 5.8
2010	B	35.40	30.94	A+ / 9.6	21.94%	C- / 3.6
2009	B	9.22	25.69	A / 9.4	55.87%	C- / 4.1

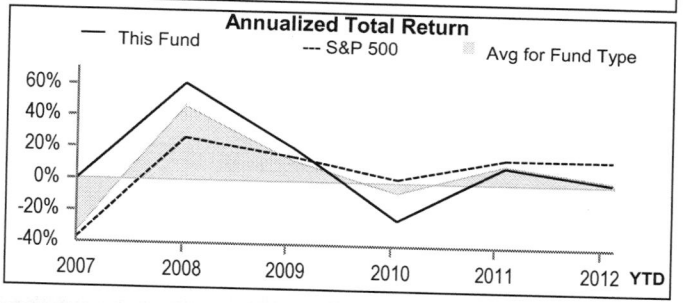

Annualized Total Return

*SPDR SP Intl Tech Sector ETF (IPK)

D+   **Weak**

Fund Family: SSgA Funds Management Inc
Fund Type: Global
Inception Date: July 16, 2008

Major Rating Factors: *SPDR SP Intl Tech Sector ETF receives a TheStreet.com Investment Rating of D+ (Weak). The fund currently has a performance rating of C- (Fair) based on an annualized return of 3.81% over the last three years and a total return of 1.91% year to date 2012. Factored into the performance evaluation is an expense ratio of 0.50% (very low).

The fund's risk rating is currently C+ (Fair). It carries a beta of 1.01, meaning that its performance tracks fairly well with that of the overall stock market. Volatility, as measured by both the semi-deviation and a drawdown factor, is considered low. As of December 31, 2012, *SPDR SP Intl Tech Sector ETF traded at a discount of .55% below its net asset value, which is better than its one-year historical average discount of .26%.

John A. Tucker currently receives a manager quality ranking of 61 (0=worst, 99=best). If you desire an average level of risk, then this fund may be an option.

Data Date	Investment Rating	Net Assets ($Mil)	Price	Performance Rating/Pts	Total Return Y-T-D	Risk Rating/Pts
12-12	D+	11.90	27.11	C- / 3.7	1.91%	C+ / 6.7
2011	D+	12.50	22.55	C- / 3.1	0.22%	C+ / 6.6
2010	A-	26.40	27.79	A- / 9.1	15.11%	C / 5.3
2009	B+	11.06	24.48	B+ / 8.6	40.34%	C / 5.4

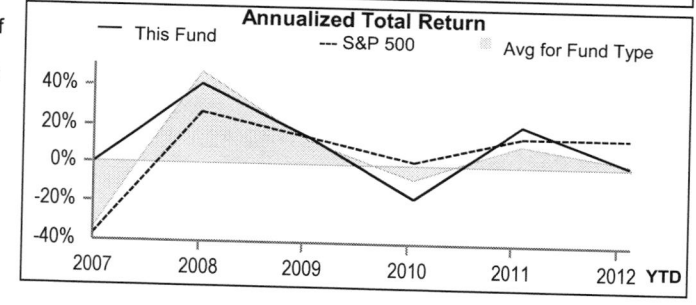

Annualized Total Return

* Denotes ETF Fund

*SPDR SP Intl Telecom Sect ETF (IST)   D+   Weak

Fund Family: SSgA Funds Management Inc
Fund Type: Global
Inception Date: July 16, 2008

Data Date	Investment Rating	Net Assets ($Mil)	Price	Performance Rating/Pts	Total Return Y-T-D	Risk Rating/Pts
12-12	D+	25.10	22.00	D+ / 2.6	3.73%	B- / 7.6
2011	C-	14.80	22.59	D+ / 2.9	-1.24%	B- / 7.9
2010	B	15.90	24.45	B+ / 8.3	9.02%	C / 4.7
2009	C	9.43	23.57	C+ / 6.5	11.21%	C / 4.8

Major Rating Factors:
Disappointing performance is the major factor driving the D+ (Weak) TheStreet.com Investment Rating for *SPDR SP Intl Telecom Sect ETF. The fund currently has a performance rating of D+ (Weak) based on an annualized return of 4.12% over the last three years and a total return of 3.73% year to date 2012. Factored into the performance evaluation is an expense ratio of 0.50% (very low).

The fund's risk rating is currently B- (Good). It carries a beta of 0.74, meaning the fund's expected move will be 7.4% for every 10% move in the market. Volatility, as measured by both the semi-deviation and a drawdown factor, is considered low. As of December 31, 2012, *SPDR SP Intl Telecom Sect ETF traded at a discount of 2.74% below its net asset value, which is better than its one-year historical average premium of .38%.

John A. Tucker currently receives a manager quality ranking of 54 (0=worst, 99=best). This fund offers only a moderate level of risk but investors looking for strong performance are still waiting.

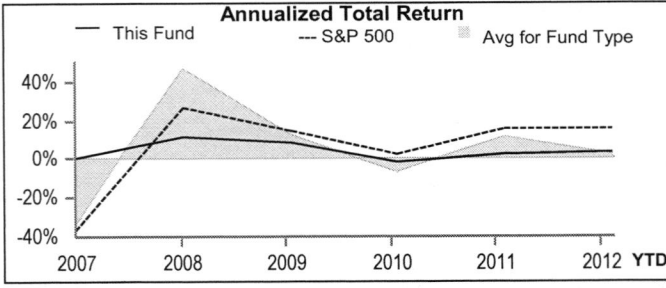

Annualized Total Return — This Fund --- S&P 500 Avg for Fund Type

*SPDR SP Intl Utils Sector ETF (IPU)   D   Weak

Fund Family: SSgA Funds Management Inc
Fund Type: Utilities
Inception Date: July 16, 2008

Data Date	Investment Rating	Net Assets ($Mil)	Price	Performance Rating/Pts	Total Return Y-T-D	Risk Rating/Pts
12-12	D	27.20	16.73	D- / 1.1	0.42%	B- / 7.2
2011	D	11.60	16.50	D- / 1.3	-0.59%	B- / 7.4
2010	C-	8.40	20.86	C- / 3.8	-5.61%	C+ / 6.2
2009	C	4.56	22.98	C / 5.1	3.92%	C+ / 6.3

Major Rating Factors:
Disappointing performance is the major factor driving the D (Weak) TheStreet.com Investment Rating for *SPDR SP Intl Utils Sector ETF. The fund currently has a performance rating of D- (Weak) based on an annualized return of -5.75% over the last three years and a total return of 0.42% year to date 2012. Factored into the performance evaluation is an expense ratio of 0.50% (very low).

The fund's risk rating is currently B- (Good). It carries a beta of 0.74, meaning the fund's expected move will be 7.4% for every 10% move in the market. Volatility, as measured by both the semi-deviation and a drawdown factor, is considered low. As of December 31, 2012, *SPDR SP Intl Utils Sector ETF traded at a premium of .36% above its net asset value, which is in line with its one-year historical average premium of .36%.

John A. Tucker currently receives a manager quality ranking of 11 (0=worst, 99=best). This fund offers only a moderate level of risk but investors looking for strong performance are still waiting.

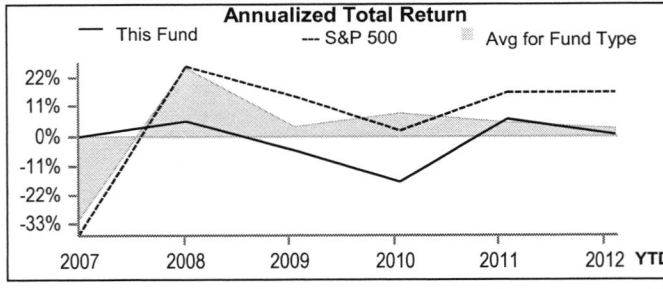

Annualized Total Return — This Fund --- S&P 500 Avg for Fund Type

*SPDR SP Mortgage Finance ETF (KME)   D+   Weak

Fund Family: SSgA Funds Management Inc
Fund Type: Financial Services
Inception Date: April 29, 2009

Data Date	Investment Rating	Net Assets ($Mil)	Price	Performance Rating/Pts	Total Return Y-T-D	Risk Rating/Pts
12-12	D+	4.30	42.70	C / 4.7	5.01%	C+ / 5.9
2011	D-	3.30	33.28	D- / 1.1	0.78%	C+ / 5.9
2010	B+	2.10	42.34	B- / 7.5	6.16%	C+ / 6.4

Major Rating Factors: *SPDR SP Mortgage Finance ETF receives a TheStreet.com Investment Rating of D+ (Weak). The fund currently has a performance rating of C (Fair) based on an annualized return of 3.37% over the last three years and a total return of 5.01% year to date 2012. Factored into the performance evaluation is an expense ratio of 0.35% (very low).

The fund's risk rating is currently C+ (Fair). It carries a beta of 0.94, meaning that its performance tracks fairly well with that of the overall stock market. Volatility, as measured by both the semi-deviation and a drawdown factor, is considered low. As of December 31, 2012, *SPDR SP Mortgage Finance ETF traded at a discount of 4.96% below its net asset value, which is better than its one-year historical average discount of .02%.

John A. Tucker currently receives a manager quality ranking of 29 (0=worst, 99=best). If you desire an average level of risk, then this fund may be an option.

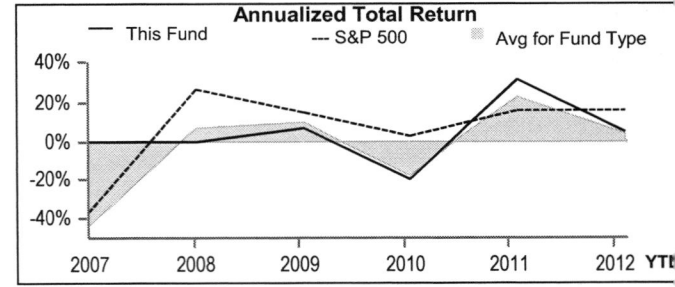

Annualized Total Return — This Fund --- S&P 500 Avg for Fund Type

*SPDR STOXX Europe 50 ETF (FEU)

D+   **Weak**

Fund Family: SSgA Funds Management Inc
Fund Type: Foreign
Inception Date: October 15, 2002

Major Rating Factors: *SPDR STOXX Europe 50 ETF receives a TheStreet.com Investment Rating of D+ (Weak). The fund currently has a performance rating of C- (Fair) based on an annualized return of 2.18% over the last three years and a total return of 2.65% year to date 2012. Factored into the performance evaluation is an expense ratio of 0.29% (very low).

The fund's risk rating is currently C+ (Fair). It carries a beta of 1.13, meaning it is expected to move 11.3% for every 10% move in the market. Volatility, as measured by both the semi-deviation and a drawdown factor, is considered low. As of December 31, 2012, *SPDR STOXX Europe 50 ETF traded at a discount of 2.01% below its net asset value, which is better than its one-year historical average premium of .47%.

John A. Tucker has been running the fund for 11 years and currently receives a manager quality ranking of 30 (0=worst, 99=best). If you desire an average level of risk, then this fund may be an option.

Data Date	Investment Rating	Net Assets ($Mil)	Price	Performance Rating/Pts	Total Return Y-T-D	Risk Rating/Pts
12-12	D+	44.60	33.62	C- / 3.5	2.65%	C+ / 6.9
2011	D+	28.40	29.79	D+ / 2.3	-0.72%	B- / 7.0
2010	D-	39.00	33.80	E+ / 0.9	-3.15%	C / 4.7
2009	D	56.51	35.85	D+ / 2.3	27.29%	C / 5.3

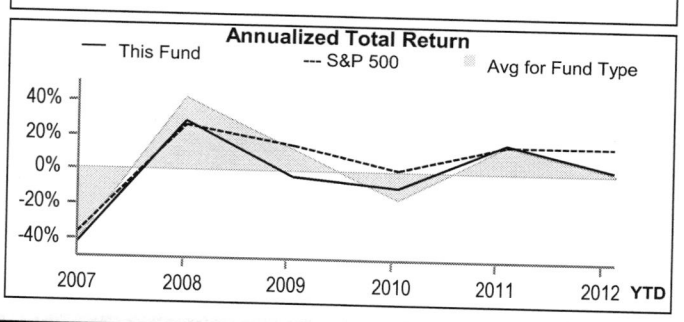

*SPDR Wells Fargo Preferred Stk E (PSK)

C   **Fair**

Fund Family: SSgA Funds Management Inc
Fund Type: Income
Inception Date: September 16, 2009

Major Rating Factors: Middle of the road best describes *SPDR Wells Fargo Preferred Stk E whose TheStreet.com Investment Rating is currently a C (Fair). The fund currently has a performance rating of C- (Fair) based on an annualized return of 8.90% over the last three years and a total return of 1.11% year to date 2012. Factored into the performance evaluation is an expense ratio of 0.45% (very low).

The fund's risk rating is currently B+ (Good). It carries a beta of 0.25, meaning the fund's expected move will be 2.5% for every 10% move in the market. Volatility, as measured by both the semi-deviation and a drawdown factor, is considered very low. As of December 31, 2012, *SPDR Wells Fargo Preferred Stk E traded at a discount of 1.08% below its net asset value, which is better than its one-year historical average premium of .13%.

John A. Tucker currently receives a manager quality ranking of 83 (0=worst, 99=best). If you desire an average level of risk, then this fund may be an option.

Data Date	Investment Rating	Net Assets ($Mil)	Price	Performance Rating/Pts	Total Return Y-T-D	Risk Rating/Pts
12-12	C	321.40	44.98	C- / 3.5	1.11%	B+ / 9.1
2011	C-	126.40	42.17	D+ / 2.6	2.59%	B+ / 9.2
2010	A+	102.80	44.59	B / 7.9	13.95%	B / 8.9

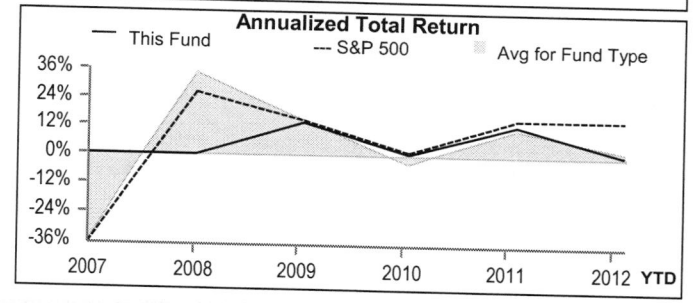

*Technology Select Sector SPDR (XLK)

C-   **Fair**

Fund Family: SSgA Funds Management Inc
Fund Type: Growth
Inception Date: December 16, 1998

Major Rating Factors: Middle of the road best describes *Technology Select Sector SPDR whose TheStreet.com Investment Rating is currently a C- (Fair). The fund currently has a performance rating of C (Fair) based on an annualized return of 11.01% over the last three years and a total return of 2.57% year to date 2012. Factored into the performance evaluation is an expense ratio of 0.18% (very low).

The fund's risk rating is currently B- (Good). It carries a beta of 1.06, meaning that its performance tracks fairly well with that of the overall stock market. Volatility, as measured by both the semi-deviation and a drawdown factor, is considered low. As of December 31, 2012, *Technology Select Sector SPDR traded at a discount of 2.57% below its net asset value, which is better than its one-year historical average discount of .01%.

John A. Tucker has been running the fund for 15 years and currently receives a manager quality ranking of 37 (0=worst, 99=best). If you desire an average level of risk, then this fund may be an option.

Data Date	Investment Rating	Net Assets ($Mil)	Price	Performance Rating/Pts	Total Return Y-T-D	Risk Rating/Pts
12-12	C-	8,283.80	28.85	C / 4.4	2.57%	B- / 7.2
2011	C+	8,195.60	25.45	C+ / 6.6	2.04%	B- / 7.5
2010	C	5,849.30	25.19	C / 5.1	11.41%	C+ / 5.7
2009	C	3,854.17	22.93	C+ / 5.7	45.76%	C+ / 5.8

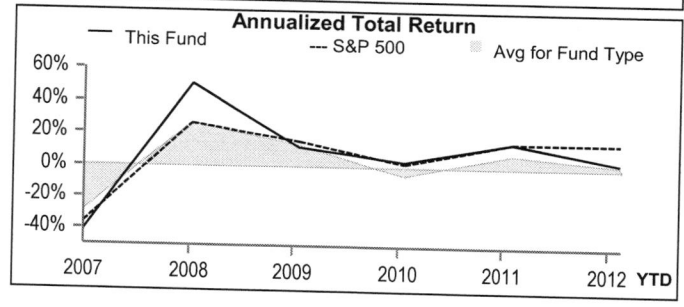

*Teucrium Corn (CORN)

D **Weak**

Fund Family: Teucrium Trading LLC
Fund Type: Growth
Inception Date: June 9, 2010

Major Rating Factors:
Disappointing performance is the major factor driving the D (Weak) TheStreet.com Investment Rating for *Teucrium Corn. The fund currently has a performance rating of D (Weak) based on an annualized return of 0.00% over the last three years and a total return of -0.74% year to date 2012. Factored into the performance evaluation is an expense ratio of 2.55% (high).

The fund's risk rating is currently C+ (Fair). It carries a beta of 0.00, meaning the fund's expected move will be 0.0% for every 10% move in the market. Volatility, as measured by both the semi-deviation and a drawdown factor, is considered low. As of December 31, 2012, *Teucrium Corn traded at a premium of 1.19% above its net asset value, which is worse than its one-year historical average discount of .01%.

Gilbertie/Teevan has been running the fund for 3 years and currently receives a manager quality ranking of 19 (0=worst, 99=best). This fund offers only a moderate level of risk but investors looking for strong performance are still waiting.

Data Date	Investment Rating	Net Assets ($Mil)	Price	Performance Rating/Pts	Total Return Y-T-D	Risk Rating/Pts
12-12	D	37.70	44.32	D / 1.6	-0.74%	C+ / 6.6
2011	D+	71.30	41.98	C- / 3.2	-1.50%	B- / 7.0

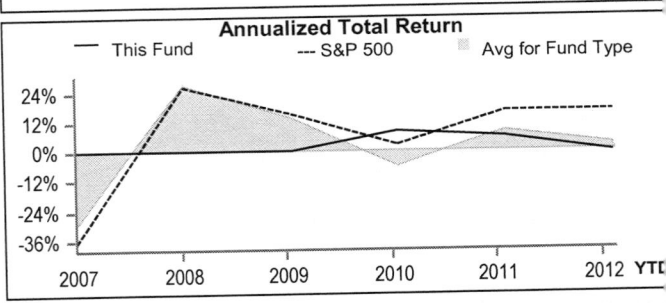

Annualized Total Return
— This Fund --- S&P 500 Avg for Fund Type

*Teucrium Natural Gas (NAGS)

E+ **Very Weak**

Fund Family: Teucrium Trading LLC
Fund Type: Growth
Inception Date: February 1, 2011

Major Rating Factors:
Very poor performance is the major factor driving the E+ (Very Weak) TheStreet.com Investment Rating for *Teucrium Natural Gas. The fund currently has a performance rating of E+ (Very Weak) based on an annualized return of 0.00% over the last three years and a total return of -1.55% year to date 2012. Factored into the performance evaluation is an expense ratio of 11.59% (high).

The fund's risk rating is currently C (Fair). It carries a beta of 0.00, meaning the fund's expected move will be 0.0% for every 10% move in the market. Volatility, as measured by both the semi-deviation and a drawdown factor, is considered average. As of December 31, 2012, *Teucrium Natural Gas traded at a premium of 1.05% above its net asset value, which is worse than its one-year historical average discount of .11%.

This fund has been team managed for 2 years and currently receives a manager quality ranking of 13 (0=worst, 99=best). This fund offers an average level of risk but investors looking for strong performance will be frustrated.

Data Date	Investment Rating	Net Assets ($Mil)	Price	Performance Rating/Pts	Total Return Y-T-D	Risk Rating/Pts
12-12	E+	4.60	11.58	E+ / 0.6	-1.55%	C / 4.6

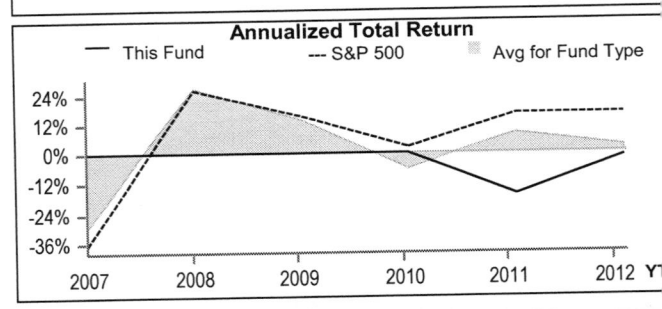

Annualized Total Return
— This Fund --- S&P 500 Avg for Fund Type

*Teucrium Soybean (SOYB)

D **Weak**

Fund Family: Teucrium Trading LLC
Fund Type: Global
Inception Date: September 19, 2011

Major Rating Factors:
Disappointing performance is the major factor driving the D (Weak) TheStreet.com Investment Rating for *Teucrium Soybean. The fund currently has a performance rating of D- (Weak) based on an annualized return of 0.00% over the last three years and a total return of -2.47% year to date 2012.

The fund's risk rating is currently B (Good). It carries a beta of 0.00, meaning the fund's expected move will be 0.0% for every 10% move in the market. Volatility, as measured by both the semi-deviation and a drawdown factor, is considered low. As of December 31, 2012, *Teucrium Soybean traded at a premium of 2.64% above its net asset value, which is worse than its one-year historical average discount of .05%.

SAL GILBERTIE has been running the fund for 2 years and currently receives a manager quality ranking of 65 (0=worst, 99=best). This fund offers only a moderate level of risk but investors looking for strong performance are still waiting.

Data Date	Investment Rating	Net Assets ($Mil)	Price	Performance Rating/Pts	Total Return Y-T-D	Risk Rating/Pts
12-12	D	6.60	24.07	D- / 1.2	-2.47%	B / 8.

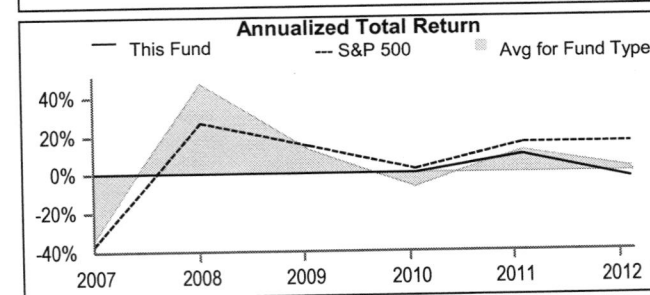

Annualized Total Return
— This Fund --- S&P 500 Avg for Fund Type

*Teucrium Sugar (CANE)

D-   **Weak**

Fund Family: Teucrium Trading LLC
Fund Type: Global
Inception Date: September 19, 2011

Major Rating Factors:

Very poor performance is the major factor driving the D- (Weak) TheStreet.com Investment Rating for *Teucrium Sugar. The fund currently has a performance rating of E (Very Weak) based on an annualized return of 0.00% over the last three years and a total return of -0.95% year to date 2012.

The fund's risk rating is currently C+ (Fair). It carries a beta of 0.00, meaning the fund's expected move will be 0.0% for every 10% move in the market. Volatility, as measured by both the semi-deviation and a drawdown factor, is considered low. As of December 31, 2012, *Teucrium Sugar traded at a premium of .79% above its net asset value, which is worse than its one-year historical average premium of .37%.

This fund has been team managed for 2 years and currently receives a manager quality ranking of 3 (0=worst, 99=best). This fund offers only a moderate level of risk but investors looking for strong performance are still waiting.

Data Date	Investment Rating	Net Assets ($Mil)	Price	Performance Rating/Pts	Total Return Y-T-D	Risk Rating/Pts
12-12	D-	2.20	17.84	E / 0.4	-0.95%	C+ / 6.6

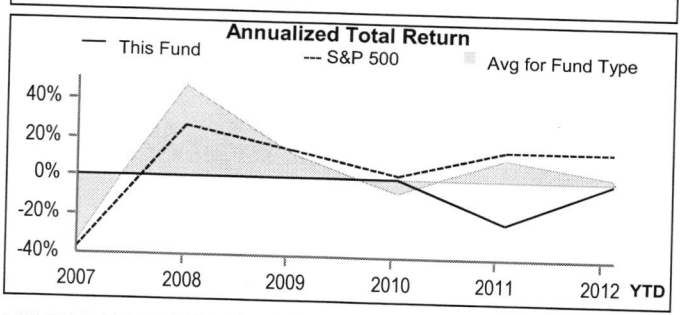

*Teucrium Wheat (WEAT)

D   **Weak**

Fund Family: Teucrium Trading LLC
Fund Type: Global
Inception Date: September 19, 2011

Major Rating Factors:

Very poor performance is the major factor driving the D (Weak) TheStreet.com Investment Rating for *Teucrium Wheat. The fund currently has a performance rating of E+ (Very Weak) based on an annualized return of 0.00% over the last three years and a total return of -3.44% year to date 2012.

The fund's risk rating is currently B (Good). It carries a beta of 0.00, meaning the fund's expected move will be 0.0% for every 10% move in the market. Volatility, as measured by both the semi-deviation and a drawdown factor, is considered low. As of December 31, 2012, *Teucrium Wheat traded at a premium of 4.10% above its net asset value, which is worse than its one-year historical average premium of .01%.

This fund has been team managed for 2 years and currently receives a manager quality ranking of 15 (0=worst, 99=best). This fund offers only a moderate level of risk but investors looking for strong performance are still waiting.

Data Date	Investment Rating	Net Assets ($Mil)	Price	Performance Rating/Pts	Total Return Y-T-D	Risk Rating/Pts
12-12	D	3.70	21.32	E+ / 0.6	-3.44%	B / 8.1

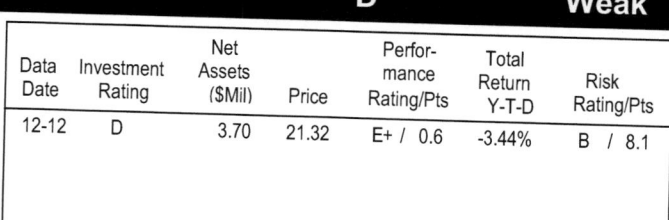

*Teucrium WTI Crude Oil (CRUD)

D-   **Weak**

Fund Family: Teucrium Trading LLC
Fund Type: Growth and Income
Inception Date: February 22, 2011

Major Rating Factors:

Very poor performance is the major factor driving the D- (Weak) TheStreet.com Investment Rating for *Teucrium WTI Crude Oil. The fund currently has a performance rating of E+ (Very Weak) based on an annualized return of 0.00% over the last three years and a total return of 1.05% year to date 2012. Factored into the performance evaluation is an expense ratio of 10.76% (high).

The fund's risk rating is currently C+ (Fair). It carries a beta of 0.00, meaning the fund's expected move will be 0.0% for every 10% move in the market. Volatility, as measured by both the semi-deviation and a drawdown factor, is considered low. As of December 31, 2012, *Teucrium WTI Crude Oil traded at a discount of 1.35% below its net asset value, which is better than its one-year historical average discount of .02%.

This fund has been team managed for 2 years and currently receives a manager quality ranking of 3 (0=worst, 99=best). This fund offers only a moderate level of risk but investors looking for strong performance are still waiting.

Data Date	Investment Rating	Net Assets ($Mil)	Price	Performance Rating/Pts	Total Return Y-T-D	Risk Rating/Pts
12-12	D-	2.00	39.53	E+ / 0.8	1.05%	C+ / 6.2

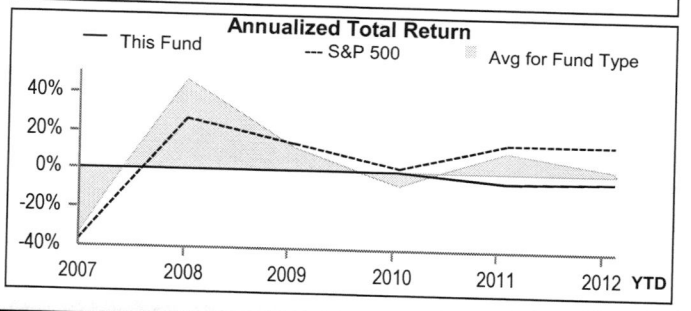
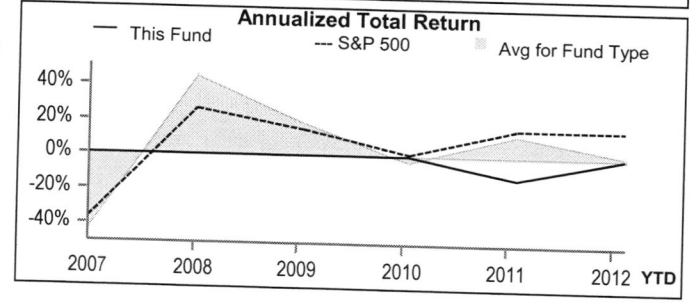

*TrimTabs Float Shrink ETF (TTFS)

B   **Good**

Fund Family: AdvisorShares Investments LLC
Fund Type: Income
Inception Date: October 4, 2011

Data Date	Investment Rating	Net Assets ($Mil)	Price	Performance Rating/Pts	Total Return Y-T-D	Risk Rating/Pts
12-12	B	11.10	33.89	C+ / 6.5	3.75%	B / 8.8

Major Rating Factors: *TrimTabs Float Shrink ETF receives a TheStreet.com Investment Rating of B (Good). The fund currently has a performance rating of C+ (Fair) based on an annualized return of 0.00% over the last three years and a total return of 3.75% year to date 2012. Factored into the performance evaluation is an expense ratio of 0.99% (low).

The fund's risk rating is currently B (Good). It carries a beta of 0.00, meaning the fund's expected move will be 0.0% for every 10% move in the market. Volatility, as measured by both the semi-deviation and a drawdown factor, is considered low. As of December 31, 2012, *TrimTabs Float Shrink ETF traded at a discount of 3.99% below its net asset value, which is better than its one-year historical average discount of .12%.

Charles Biderman has been running the fund for 2 years and currently receives a manager quality ranking of 38 (0=worst, 99=best). If you desire an average level of risk, then this fund may be an option.

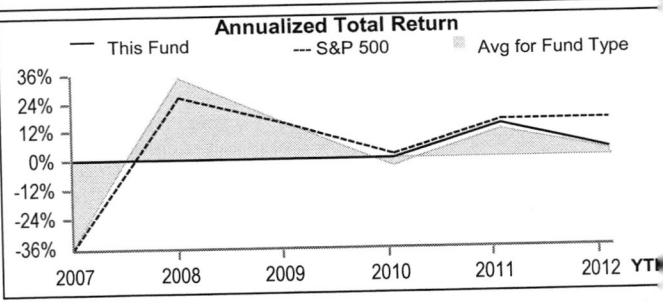

Annualized Total Return
— This Fund   --- S&P 500   ▨ Avg for Fund Type

*UBS E Tracs Alerian MLP Infrast (MLPI)

D   **Weak**

Fund Family: UBS Global Asset Mgmt (Americas) In
Fund Type: Income
Inception Date: April 1, 2010

Data Date	Investment Rating	Net Assets ($Mil)	Price	Performance Rating/Pts	Total Return Y-T-D	Risk Rating/Pts
12-12	D	499.10	32.54	C- / 3.9	5.90%	C / 5.3
2011	C	213.10	33.10	B- / 7.2	1.69%	C / 5.4

Major Rating Factors: *UBS E Tracs Alerian MLP Infrast receives a TheStreet.com Investment Rating of D (Weak). The fund currently has a performance rating of C- (Fair) based on an annualized return of 0.00% over the last three years and a total return of 5.90% year to date 2012.

The fund's risk rating is currently C (Fair). It carries a beta of 0.00, meaning the fund's expected move will be 0.0% for every 10% move in the market. Volatility, as measured by both the semi-deviation and a drawdown factor, is considered average. As of December 31, 2012, *UBS E Tracs Alerian MLP Infrast traded at a discount of 5.43% below its net asset value.

This fund has been team managed for 3 years and currently receives a manager quality ranking of 14 (0=worst, 99=best). If you desire an average level of risk, then this fund may be an option.

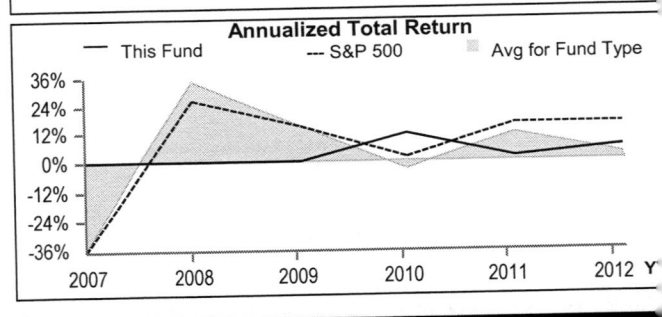

Annualized Total Return
— This Fund   --- S&P 500   ▨ Avg for Fund Type

*UBS E Tracs CMCI Agriculture TR (UAG)

D   **Weak**

Fund Family: UBS Global Asset Mgmt (Americas) In
Fund Type: Growth
Inception Date: April 1, 2008

Data Date	Investment Rating	Net Assets ($Mil)	Price	Performance Rating/Pts	Total Return Y-T-D	Risk Rating/P
12-12	D	3.43	28.82	C- / 3.2	-0.79%	C / 4.
2011	D	13.50	27.67	C- / 3.7	-1.16%	C / 4
2010	B	3.43	30.40	A+ / 9.8	35.17%	C- / 3
2009	C	3.43	22.49	B / 7.8	20.98%	C- / 3

Major Rating Factors: *UBS E Tracs CMCI Agriculture TR receives a TheStreet.com Investment Rating of D (Weak). The fund currently has a performance rating of C- (Fair) based on an annualized return of 10.33% over the last three years and a total return of -0.79% year to date 2012. Factored into the performance evaluation is an expense ratio of 0.65% (very low).

The fund's risk rating is currently C (Fair). It carries a beta of 0.86, meaning the fund's expected move will be 8.6% for every 10% move in the market. Volatility, as measured by both the semi-deviation and a drawdown factor, is considered average. As of December 31, 2012, *UBS E Tracs CMCI Agriculture TR traded at a premium of 1.09% above its net asset value, which is worse than its one-year historical average discount of .20%.

This fund has been team managed for 5 years and currently receives a manager quality ranking of 45 (0=worst, 99=best). If you desire an average level of risk, then this fund may be an option.

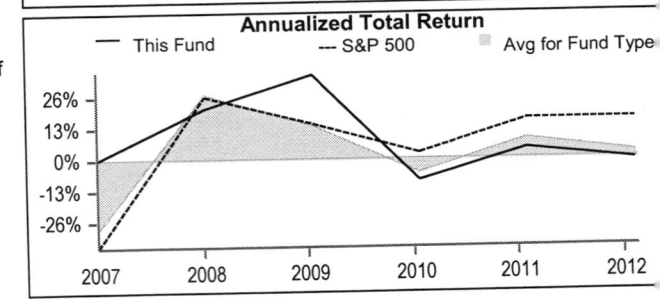

Annualized Total Return
— This Fund   --- S&P 500   ▨ Avg for Fund Type

*UBS E Tracs CMCI Food Tr (FUD)

D-   **Weak**

Fund Family: UBS Global Asset Mgmt (Americas) In
Fund Type: Growth
Inception Date: April 1, 2008

Major Rating Factors: *UBS E Tracs CMCI Food Tr receives a TheStreet.com Investment Rating of D- (Weak). The fund currently has a performance rating of C- (Fair) based on an annualized return of 9.25% over the last three years and a total return of -1.00% year to date 2012. Factored into the performance evaluation is an expense ratio of 0.65% (very low).

The fund's risk rating is currently C (Fair). It carries a beta of 0.81, meaning the fund's expected move will be 8.1% for every 10% move in the market. Volatility, as measured by both the semi-deviation and a drawdown factor, is considered average. As of December 31, 2012, *UBS E Tracs CMCI Food Tr traded at a premium of 1.45% above its net asset value, which is worse than its one-year historical average discount of .02%.

This fund has been team managed for 5 years and currently receives a manager quality ranking of 47 (0=worst, 99=best). If you desire an average level of risk, then this fund may be an option.

Data Date	Investment Rating	Net Assets ($Mil)	Price	Performance Rating/Pts	Total Return Y-T-D	Risk Rating/Pts
12-12	D-	6.32	28.03	C- / 3.1	-1.00%	C / 4.6
2011	D	41.60	26.73	C- / 3.5	-0.34%	C / 4.9
2010	B	6.32	29.23	A+ / 9.7	32.26%	C- / 3.1
2009	C	6.32	22.10	B- / 7.3	16.19%	C- / 3.3

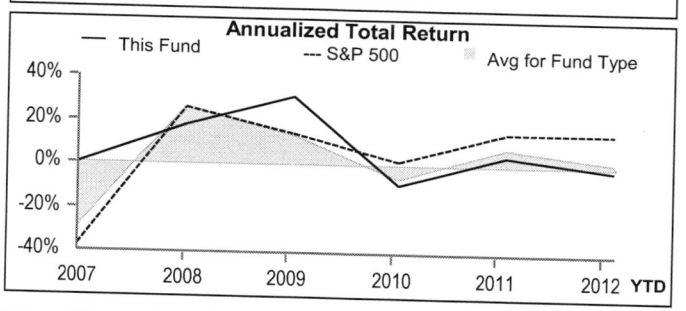

*UBS E Tracs CMCI Gold TR (UBG)

D   **Weak**

Fund Family: UBS Global Asset Mgmt (Americas) In
Fund Type: Growth
Inception Date: April 1, 2008

Major Rating Factors: *UBS E Tracs CMCI Gold TR receives a TheStreet.com Investment Rating of D (Weak). The fund currently has a performance rating of C- (Fair) based on an annualized return of 11.89% over the last three years and a total return of -1.17% year to date 2012. Factored into the performance evaluation is an expense ratio of 0.30% (very low).

The fund's risk rating is currently C (Fair). It carries a beta of 0.13, meaning the fund's expected move will be 1.3% for every 10% move in the market. Volatility, as measured by both the semi-deviation and a drawdown factor, is considered average. As of December 31, 2012, *UBS E Tracs CMCI Gold TR traded at a premium of .82% above its net asset value, which is worse than its one-year historical average discount of .10%.

This fund has been team managed for 5 years and currently receives a manager quality ranking of 93 (0=worst, 99=best). If you desire an average level of risk, then this fund may be an option.

Data Date	Investment Rating	Net Assets ($Mil)	Price	Performance Rating/Pts	Total Return Y-T-D	Risk Rating/Pts
12-12	D	4.56	44.34	C- / 3.7	-1.17%	C / 5.0
2011	C	8.00	41.78	B- / 7.5	4.00%	C / 5.1
2010	B	4.56	38.25	A / 9.3	28.05%	C- / 3.9
2009	C+	4.56	29.87	B / 8.1	27.54%	C- / 4.1

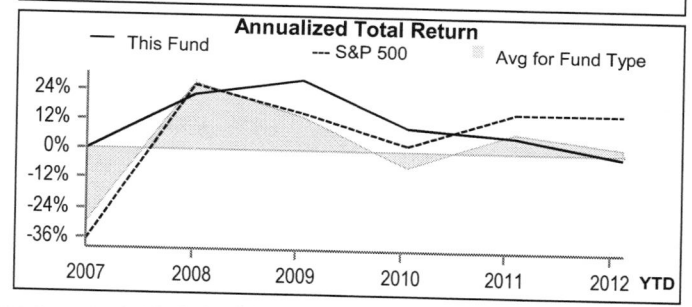

*UBS E Tracs CMCI Industrial Meta (UBM)

E+   **Very Weak**

Fund Family: UBS Global Asset Mgmt (Americas) In
Fund Type: Growth
Inception Date: April 1, 2008

Major Rating Factors:
Disappointing performance is the major factor driving the E+ (Very Weak) TheStreet.com Investment Rating for *UBS E Tracs CMCI Industrial Meta. The fund currently has a performance rating of D- (Weak) based on an annualized return of -2.48% over the last three years and a total return of 1.14% year to date 2012. Factored into the performance evaluation is an expense ratio of 0.65% (very low).

The fund's risk rating is currently C- (Fair). It carries a beta of 1.25, meaning it is expected to move 12.5% for every 10% move in the market. Volatility, as measured by both the semi-deviation and a drawdown factor, is considered average. As of December 31, 2012, *UBS E Tracs CMCI Industrial Meta traded at a discount of 1.10% below its net asset value, which is better than its one-year historical average discount of .12%.

This fund has been team managed for 5 years and currently receives a manager quality ranking of 9 (0=worst, 99=best). This fund offers an average level of risk but investors looking for strong performance will be frustrated.

Data Date	Investment Rating	Net Assets ($Mil)	Price	Performance Rating/Pts	Total Return Y-T-D	Risk Rating/Pts
12-12	E+	3.90	19.77	D- / 1.2	1.14%	C- / 4.1
2011	D	5.20	19.47	C- / 3.7	0.00%	C / 4.5
2010	C+	3.90	25.16	A+ / 9.6	18.46%	D+ / 2.4
2009	C+	3.90	21.24	A+ / 9.8	86.32%	D+ / 2.6

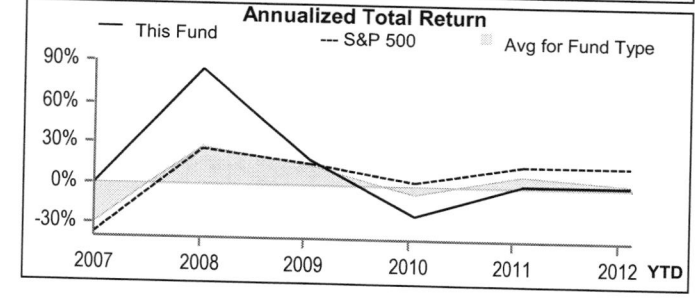

*UBS E Tracs CMCI Livestock Tr (UBC)

D-   **Weak**

Fund Family: UBS Global Asset Mgmt (Americas) In
Fund Type: Growth
Inception Date: April 1, 2008

Major Rating Factors:
Disappointing performance is the major factor driving the D- (Weak) TheStreet.com Investment Rating for *UBS E Tracs CMCI Livestock Tr. The fund currently has a performance rating of D- (Weak) based on an annualized return of 0.74% over the last three years and a total return of -1.58% year to date 2012. Factored into the performance evaluation is an expense ratio of 0.65% (very low).

    The fund's risk rating is currently C (Fair). It carries a beta of -0.02, meaning the fund's expected move will be -0.2% for every 10% move in the market. Volatility, as measured by both the semi-deviation and a drawdown factor, is considered average. As of December 31, 2012, *UBS E Tracs CMCI Livestock Tr traded at a premium of 1.60% above its net asset value, which is worse than its one-year historical average discount of .08%.

    This fund has been team managed for 5 years and currently receives a manager quality ranking of 71 (0=worst, 99=best). This fund offers an average level of risk but investors looking for strong performance will be frustrated.

Data Date	Investment Rating	Net Assets ($Mil)	Price	Performance Rating/Pts	Total Return Y-T-D	Risk Rating/Pts
12-12	D-	7.84	19.68	D- / 1.2	-1.58%	C / 4.8
2011	D-	5.00	21.09	D / 1.8	-0.76%	C / 4.6
2010	C+	7.84	21.14	B+ / 8.6	16.60%	C- / 3.1
2009	E	7.84	18.13	E+ / 0.8	-16.37%	C- / 3.3

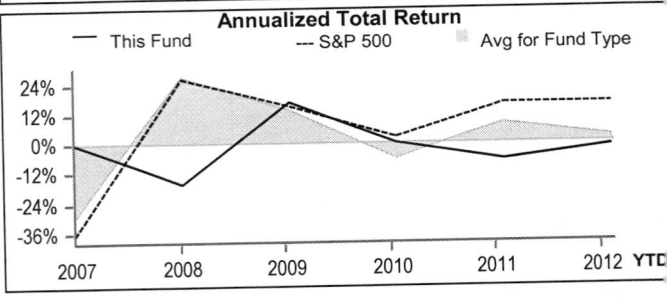
Annualized Total Return

*UBS E Tracs CMCI Silver TR (USV)

D   **Weak**

Fund Family: UBS Global Asset Mgmt (Americas) In
Fund Type: Growth
Inception Date: April 1, 2008

Major Rating Factors: *UBS E Tracs CMCI Silver TR receives a TheStreet.com Investment Rating of D (Weak). The fund currently has a performance rating of C (Fair) based on an annualized return of 16.59% over the last three years and a total return of 0.74% year to date 2012. Factored into the performance evaluation is an expense ratio of 0.40% (very low).

    The fund's risk rating is currently C- (Fair). It carries a beta of 1.23, meaning it is expected to move 12.3% for every 10% move in the market. Volatility, as measured by both the semi-deviation and a drawdown factor, is considered average. As of December 31, 2012, *UBS E Tracs CMCI Silver TR traded at a discount of 1.36% below its net asset value, which is better than its one-year historical average discount of .36%.

    This fund has been team managed for 5 years and currently receives a manager quality ranking of 81 (0=worst, 99=best). If you desire an average level of risk, then this fund may be an option.

Data Date	Investment Rating	Net Assets ($Mil)	Price	Performance Rating/Pts	Total Return Y-T-D	Risk Rating/Pts
12-12	D	3.74	41.96	C / 5.5	0.74%	C- / 3.0
2011	C	6.10	39.02	B+ / 8.7	5.89%	C- / 3.3
2010	B-	3.74	44.05	A+ / 9.9	80.74%	D+ / 2.7
2009	C	3.74	24.37	B+ / 8.7	43.69%	D+ / 2.9

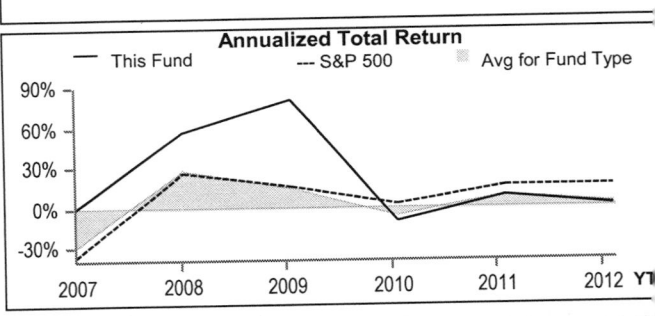
Annualized Total Return

*UBS E Tracs CMCI Total Return (UCI)

D-   **Weak**

Fund Family: UBS Global Asset Mgmt (Americas) In
Fund Type: Growth
Inception Date: April 1, 2008

Major Rating Factors:
Disappointing performance is the major factor driving the D- (Weak) TheStreet.com Investment Rating for *UBS E Tracs CMCI Total Return. The fund currently has a performance rating of D (Weak) based on an annualized return of 3.59% over the last three years and a total return of -0.14% year to date 2012. Factored into the performance evaluation is an expense ratio of 0.65% (very low).

    The fund's risk rating is currently C (Fair). It carries a beta of 1.06, meaning that its performance tracks fairly well with that of the overall stock market. Volatility, as measured by both the semi-deviation and a drawdown factor, is considered average. As of December 31, 2012, *UBS E Tracs CMCI Total Return traded at a premium of .27% above its net asset value, which is worse than its one-year historical average premium of .04%.

    This fund has been team managed for 5 years and currently receives a manager quality ranking of 17 (0=worst, 99=best). This fund offers an average level of risk but investors looking for strong performance will be frustrated.

Data Date	Investment Rating	Net Assets ($Mil)	Price	Performance Rating/Pts	Total Return Y-T-D	Risk Rating/Pt
12-12	D-	11.63	22.06	D / 2.0	-0.14%	C / 4.
2011	D	137.50	21.56	C- / 3.9	1.03%	C / 4.
2010	C+	11.63	23.61	A / 9.4	18.61%	D+ / 2.
2009	C	11.63	19.91	B+ / 8.7	40.61%	D+ / 2.

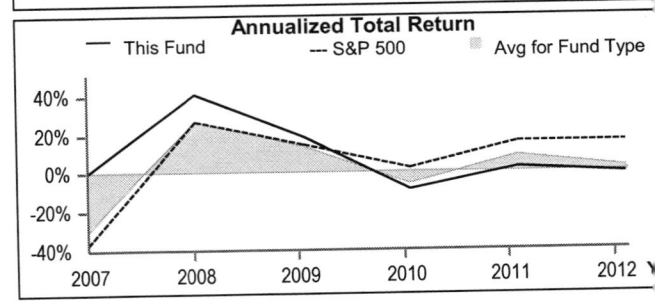
Annualized Total Return

*UBS E Tracs DJ-UBS Comm Idx Tot (DJCI)

E+ **Very Weak**

Fund Family: UBS Global Asset Mgmt (Americas) In
Fund Type: Income
Inception Date: October 29, 2009

Major Rating Factors:

Disappointing performance is the major factor driving the E+ (Very Weak) TheStreet.com Investment Rating for *UBS E Tracs DJ-UBS Comm Idx Tot. The fund currently has a performance rating of D- (Weak) based on an annualized return of -0.37% over the last three years and a total return of -0.35% year to date 2012.

The fund's risk rating is currently C- (Fair). It carries a beta of 0.93, meaning that its performance tracks fairly well with that of the overall stock market. Volatility, as measured by both the semi-deviation and a drawdown factor, is considered average. As of December 31, 2012, *UBS E Tracs DJ-UBS Comm Idx Tot traded at a premium of .35% above its net asset value, which is worse than its one-year historical average discount of .10%.

This fund has been team managed for 4 years and currently receives a manager quality ranking of 13 (0=worst, 99=best). This fund offers an average level of risk but investors looking for strong performance will be frustrated.

Data Date	Investment Rating	Net Assets ($Mil)	Price	Performance Rating/Pts	Total Return Y-T-D	Risk Rating/Pts
12-12	E+	70.30	26.03	D- / 1.2	-0.35%	C- / 4.2
2011	E+	22.00	26.45	D- / 1.2	1.01%	C / 4.7
2010	B+	13.80	30.60	A / 9.3	14.86%	C / 4.7

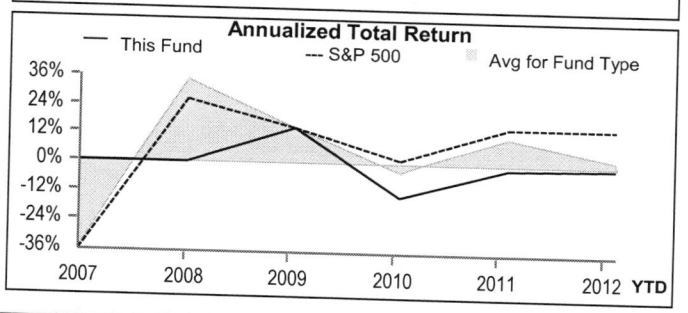

*UBS E Tracs Long Platinum ETN (PTM)

E+ **Very Weak**

Fund Family: UBS Global Asset Mgmt (Americas) In
Fund Type: Growth
Inception Date: May 8, 2008

Major Rating Factors:

Disappointing performance is the major factor driving the E+ (Very Weak) TheStreet.com Investment Rating for *UBS E Tracs Long Platinum ETN. The fund currently has a performance rating of D- (Weak) based on an annualized return of -1.24% over the last three years and a total return of 5.80% year to date 2012. Factored into the performance evaluation is an expense ratio of 0.65% (very low).

The fund's risk rating is currently C- (Fair). It carries a beta of 1.18, meaning it is expected to move 11.8% for every 10% move in the market. Volatility, as measured by both the semi-deviation and a drawdown factor, is considered average. As of December 31, 2012, *UBS E Tracs Long Platinum ETN traded at a discount of 5.53% below its net asset value, which is better than its one-year historical average premium of 3.28%.

This fund has been team managed for 5 years and currently receives a manager quality ranking of 10 (0=worst, 99=best). This fund offers an average level of risk but investors looking for strong performance will be frustrated.

Data Date	Investment Rating	Net Assets ($Mil)	Price	Performance Rating/Pts	Total Return Y-T-D	Risk Rating/Pts
12-12	E+	66.49	17.59	D- / 1.3	5.80%	C- / 4.0
2011	D-	32.20	16.12	D+ / 2.5	1.74%	C- / 4.1
2010	C	66.49	20.92	B+ / 8.7	13.70%	D+ / 2.5
2009	C+	66.49	18.40	A / 9.4	55.80%	D+ / 2.7

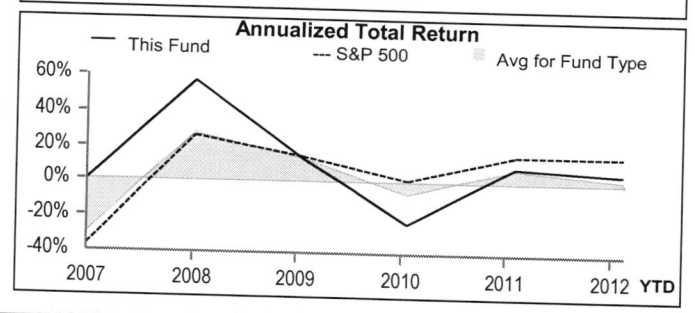

*UBS E-TRACS 2x Levd Lng Alerian (MLPL)

C+ **Fair**

Fund Family: UBS Global Asset Mgmt (Americas) In
Fund Type: Energy/Natural Resources
Inception Date: July 7, 2010

Major Rating Factors: Strong performance is the major factor driving the C+ (Fair) TheStreet.com Investment Rating for *UBS E-TRACS 2x Levd Lng Alerian. The fund currently has a performance rating of B+ (Good) based on an annualized return of 0.00% over the last three years and a total return of 14.14% year to date 2012.

The fund's risk rating is currently C (Fair). It carries a beta of 0.00, meaning the fund's expected move will be 0.0% for every 10% move in the market. Volatility, as measured by both the semi-deviation and a drawdown factor, is considered average. As of December 31, 2012, *UBS E-TRACS 2x Levd Lng Alerian traded at a discount of 10.08% below its net asset value, which is better than its one-year historical average discount of .07%.

This fund has been team managed for 3 years and currently receives a manager quality ranking of 26 (0=worst, 99=best). If you desire an average level of risk and strong performance, then this fund is a good option.

Data Date	Investment Rating	Net Assets ($Mil)	Price	Performance Rating/Pts	Total Return Y-T-D	Risk Rating/Pts
12-12	C+	127.50	38.55	B+ / 8.8	14.14%	C / 4.6
2011	B-	93.90	40.70	A+ / 9.8	2.97%	C / 4.8

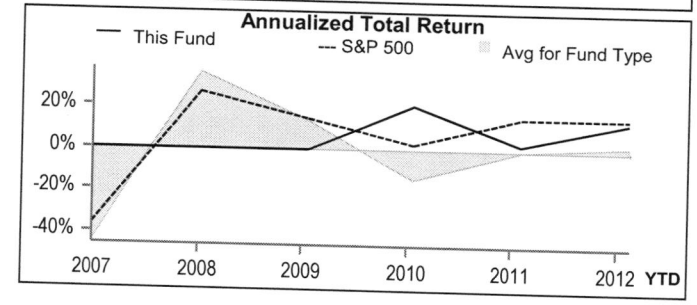

*UBS E-TRACS 2x Levd Long WF BDC (BDCL)

C+   Fair

Fund Family: UBS Global Asset Mgmt (Americas) In
Fund Type: Growth
Inception Date: May 25, 2011

Data Date	Investment Rating	Net Assets ($Mil)	Price	Performance Rating/Pts	Total Return Y-T-D	Risk Rating/Pts
12-12	C+	73.60	26.06	A+ / 9.9	4.77%	C- / 4.2

Major Rating Factors:

Exceptional performance is the major factor driving the C+ (Fair) TheStreet.com Investment Rating for *UBS E-TRACS 2x Levd Long WF BDC. The fund currently has a performance rating of A+ (Excellent) based on an annualized return of 0.00% over the last three years and a total return of 4.77% year to date 2012.

The fund's risk rating is currently C- (Fair). It carries a beta of 0.00, meaning the fund's expected move will be 0.0% for every 10% move in the market. Volatility, as measured by both the semi-deviation and a drawdown factor, is considered average. As of December 31, 2012, *UBS E-TRACS 2x Levd Long WF BDC traded at a discount of 4.65% below its net asset value, which is better than its one-year historical average discount of .03%.

This fund has been team managed for 2 years and currently receives a manager quality ranking of 98 (0=worst, 99=best). If you desire an average level of risk and strong performance, then this fund is a good option.

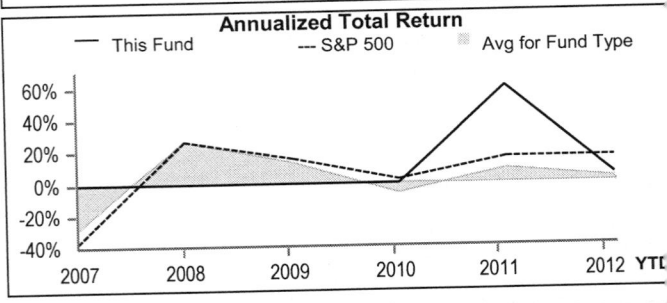

Annualized Total Return

---

*UBS E-TRACS Alerian Nat Gas MLP (MLPG)

D-   Weak

Fund Family: UBS Global Asset Mgmt (Americas) In
Fund Type: Energy/Natural Resources
Inception Date: July 14, 2010

Data Date	Investment Rating	Net Assets ($Mil)	Price	Performance Rating/Pts	Total Return Y-T-D	Risk Rating/Pts
12-12	D-	25.70	28.56	D+ / 2.6	5.86%	C / 5.1
2011	D+	14.90	29.71	C / 5.1	3.50%	C / 5.2

Major Rating Factors:

Disappointing performance is the major factor driving the D- (Weak) TheStreet.com Investment Rating for *UBS E-TRACS Alerian Nat Gas MLP. The fund currently has a performance rating of D+ (Weak) based on an annualized return of 0.00% over the last three years and a total return of 5.86% year to date 2012.

The fund's risk rating is currently C (Fair). It carries a beta of 0.00, meaning the fund's expected move will be 0.0% for every 10% move in the market. Volatility, as measured by both the semi-deviation and a drawdown factor, is considered average. As of December 31, 2012, *UBS E-TRACS Alerian Nat Gas MLP traded at a discount of 3.97% below its net asset value, which is better than its one-year historical average discount of .08%.

This fund has been team managed for 3 years and currently receives a manager quality ranking of 32 (0=worst, 99=best). This fund offers an average level of risk but investors looking for strong performance will be frustrated.

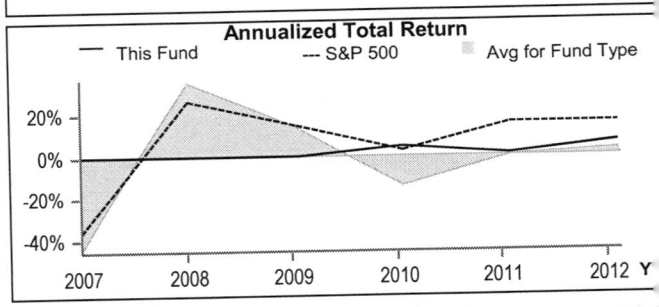

Annualized Total Return

---

*UBS E-TRACS Internet IPO ETN (EIPO)

E+   Very Weak

Fund Family: UBS Global Asset Mgmt (Americas) In
Fund Type: Growth
Inception Date: July 20, 2011

Data Date	Investment Rating	Net Assets ($Mil)	Price	Performance Rating/Pts	Total Return Y-T-D	Risk Rating/Pts
12-12	E+	5.60	13.90	D- / 1.1	5.68%	C- / 4.

Major Rating Factors:

Disappointing performance is the major factor driving the E+ (Very Weak) TheStreet.com Investment Rating for *UBS E-TRACS Internet IPO ETN. The fund currently has a performance rating of D- (Weak) based on an annualized return of 0.00% over the last three years and a total return of 5.68% year to date 2012.

The fund's risk rating is currently C- (Fair). It carries a beta of 0.00, meaning the fund's expected move will be 0.0% for every 10% move in the market. Volatility, as measured by both the semi-deviation and a drawdown factor, is considered average. As of December 31, 2012, *UBS E-TRACS Internet IPO ETN traded at a discount of 6.08% below its net asset value, which is better than its one-year historical average discount of .34%.

This fund has been team managed for 2 years and currently receives a manager quality ranking of 4 (0=worst, 99=best). This fund offers an average level of risk but investors looking for strong performance will be frustrated.

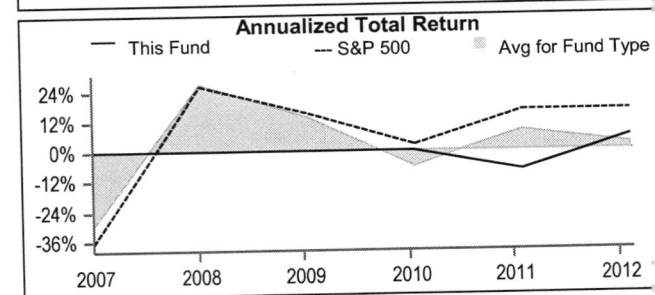

Annualized Total Return

*UBS E-TRACS Mnth 2xLevd ltr IPO (EIPL)

E-   **Very Weak**

Fund Family: UBS Global Asset Mgmt (Americas) In
Fund Type: Growth
Inception Date: July 20, 2011

Major Rating Factors: *UBS E-TRACS Mnth 2xLevd ltr IPO has adopted a very risky asset allocation strategy and currently receives an overall TheStreet.com Investment Rating of E- (Very Weak). The fund has a high level of volatility, as measured by both semi-deviation and drawdown factors. It carries a beta of 0.00, meaning the fund's expected move will be 0.0% for every 10% move in the market. As of December 31, 2012, *UBS E-TRACS Mnth 2xLevd ltr IPO traded at a discount of 9.53% below its net asset value, which is better than its one-year historical average discount of 1.34%. Unfortunately, the high level of risk (D, Weak) failed to pay off as investors endured very poor performance.

The fund's performance rating is currently E+ (Very Weak). It has registered an annualized return of 0.00% over the last three years and is up 9.31% year to date 2012.

This fund has been team managed for 2 years and currently receives a manager quality ranking of 0 (0=worst, 99=best). If you can tolerate very high levels of risk in the hope of improved future returns, holding this fund may be an option.

Data Date	Investment Rating	Net Assets ($Mil)	Price	Performance Rating/Pts	Total Return Y-T-D	Risk Rating/Pts
12-12	E-	2.30	25.36	E+ / 0.9	9.31%	D / 1.9

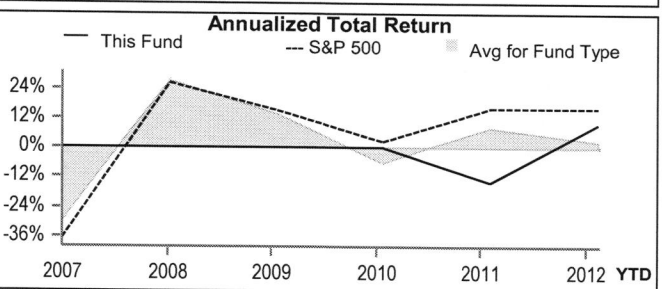

*UBS E-TRACS Monthly 2X LISE CCTR (LSKY)

C+   **Fair**

Fund Family: UBS Global Asset Mgmt (Americas) In
Fund Type: Global
Inception Date: October 4, 2011

Major Rating Factors:
Exceptional performance is the major factor driving the C+ (Fair) TheStreet.com Investment Rating for *UBS E-TRACS Monthly 2X LISE CCTR. The fund currently has a performance rating of A+ (Excellent) based on an annualized return of 0.00% over the last three years and a total return of 8.33% year to date 2012.

The fund's risk rating is currently C- (Fair). It carries a beta of 0.00, meaning the fund's expected move will be 0.0% for every 10% move in the market. Volatility, as measured by both the semi-deviation and a drawdown factor, is considered average. As of December 31, 2012, *UBS E-TRACS Monthly 2X LISE CCTR traded at a discount of 8.56% below its net asset value, which is better than its one-year historical average discount of .03%.

This fund has been team managed for 2 years and currently receives a manager quality ranking of 7 (0=worst, 99=best). If you desire an average level of risk and strong performance, then this fund is a good option.

Data Date	Investment Rating	Net Assets ($Mil)	Price	Performance Rating/Pts	Total Return Y-T-D	Risk Rating/Pts
12-12	C+	14.40	36.00	A+ / 9.7	8.33%	C- / 3.8

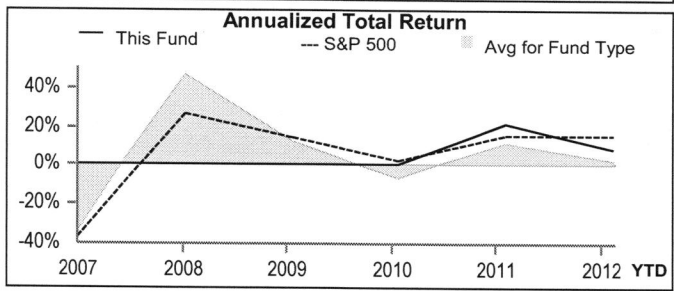

*UBS E-TRACS Nat Gas Ft Contango (GASZ)

D-   **Weak**

Fund Family: UBS Global Asset Mgmt (Americas) In
Fund Type: Growth
Inception Date: June 15, 2011

Major Rating Factors:
Disappointing performance is the major factor driving the D- (Weak) TheStreet.com Investment Rating for *UBS E-TRACS Nat Gas Ft Contango. The fund currently has a performance rating of D+ (Weak) based on an annualized return of 0.00% over the last three years and a total return of 0.17% year to date 2012.

The fund's risk rating is currently C (Fair). It carries a beta of 0.00, meaning the fund's expected move will be 0.0% for every 10% move in the market. Volatility, as measured by both the semi-deviation and a drawdown factor, is considered average. As of December 31, 2012, *UBS E-TRACS Nat Gas Ft Contango traded at a discount of .24% below its net asset value, which is better than its one-year historical average premium of .02%.

This fund has been team managed for 2 years and currently receives a manager quality ranking of 48 (0=worst, 99=best). This fund offers an average level of risk but investors looking for strong performance will be frustrated.

Data Date	Investment Rating	Net Assets ($Mil)	Price	Performance Rating/Pts	Total Return Y-T-D	Risk Rating/Pts
12-12	D-	11.60	28.87	D+ / 2.4	0.17%	C / 5.2

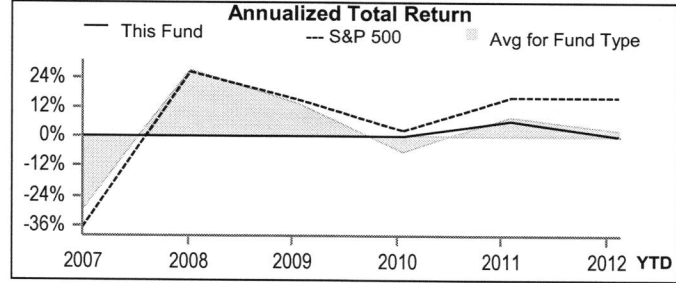

*UBS E-TRACS S&P 500 Gold Hedged (SPGH)

C   Fai

Fund Family: UBS Global Asset Mgmt (Americas) In
Fund Type: Precious Metals
Inception Date: January 28, 2010

Major Rating Factors: Strong performance is the major factor driving the C (Fair) TheStreet.com Investment Rating for *UBS E-TRACS S&P 500 Gold Hedged. The fund currently has a performance rating of B (Good) based on an annualized return of 0.00% over the last three years and a total return of 3.96% year to date 2012.

The fund's risk rating is currently C (Fair). It carries a beta of 0.00, meaning the fund's expected move will be 0.0% for every 10% move in the market. Volatility, as measured by both the semi-deviation and a drawdown factor, is considered average. As of December 31, 2012, *UBS E-TRACS S&P 500 Gold Hedged traded at a discount of 4.05% below its net asset value, which is better than its one-year historical average discount of .10%.

This fund has been team managed for 3 years and currently receives a manager quality ranking of 91 (0=worst, 99=best). If you desire an average level of risk and strong performance, then this fund is a good option.

Data Date	Investment Rating	Net Assets ($Mil)	Price	Performance Rating/Pts	Total Return Y-T-D	Risk Rating/P
12-12	C	18.90	50.99	B / 7.9	3.96%	C / 4
2011	C-	15.80	42.60	C+ / 6.4	3.71%	C / 4

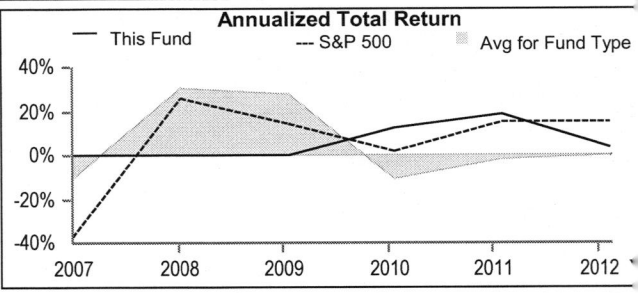

Annualized Total Return — This Fund --- S&P 500 — Avg for Fund Type

*UBS E-TRACS Wells Fargo BDC Inde (BDCS)

C+   Fai

Fund Family: UBS Global Asset Mgmt (Americas) In
Fund Type: Growth
Inception Date: April 27, 2011

Major Rating Factors:
Exceptional performance is the major factor driving the C+ (Fair) TheStreet.com Investment Rating for *UBS E-TRACS Wells Fargo BDC Inde. The fund currently has a performance rating of A (Excellent) based on an annualized return of 0.00% over the last three years and a total return of 2.43% year to date 2012.

The fund's risk rating is currently C (Fair). It carries a beta of 0.00, meaning the fund's expected move will be 0.0% for every 10% move in the market. Volatility, as measured by both the semi-deviation and a drawdown factor, is considered average. As of December 31, 2012, *UBS E-TRACS Wells Fargo BDC Inde traded at a discount of 2.26% below its net asset value, which is better than its one-year historical average discount of .02%.

This fund has been team managed for 2 years and currently receives a manager quality ranking of 94 (0=worst, 99=best). If you desire an average level of risk and strong performance, then this fund is a good option.

Data Date	Investment Rating	Net Assets ($Mil)	Price	Performance Rating/Pts	Total Return Y-T-D	Risk Rating/F
12-12	C+	21.10	25.12	A / 9.4	2.43%	C / 4

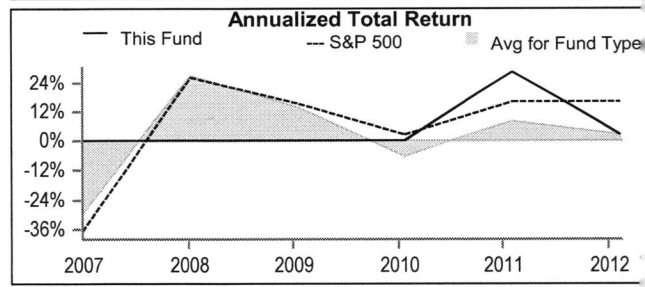

Annualized Total Return — This Fund --- S&P 500 — Avg for Fund Type

*UBS E-TRACS Wells Fargo MLP Inde (MLPW)

D+   Wea

Fund Family: UBS Global Asset Mgmt (Americas) In
Fund Type: Energy/Natural Resources
Inception Date: November 1, 2010

Major Rating Factors: *UBS E-TRACS Wells Fargo MLP Inde receives a TheStreet.com Investment Rating of D+ (Weak). The fund currently has a performance rating of C (Fair) based on an annualized return of 0.00% over the last three years and a total return of 2.68% year to date 2012.

The fund's risk rating is currently C (Fair). It carries a beta of 0.00, meaning the fund's expected move will be 0.0% for every 10% move in the market. Volatility, as measured by both the semi-deviation and a drawdown factor, is considered average. As of December 31, 2012, *UBS E-TRACS Wells Fargo MLP Inde traded at a discount of 2.74% below its net asset value, which is better than its one-year historical average discount of .13%.

This is team managed and currently receives a manager quality ranking of 84 (0=worst, 99=best). If you desire an average level of risk, then this fund may be an option.

Data Date	Investment Rating	Net Assets ($Mil)	Price	Performance Rating/Pts	Total Return Y-T-D	Risk Rating/I
12-12	D+	10.90	28.71	C / 4.6	2.68%	C / 5
2011	C-	19.00	27.21	C+ / 5.9	2.81%	C / 5

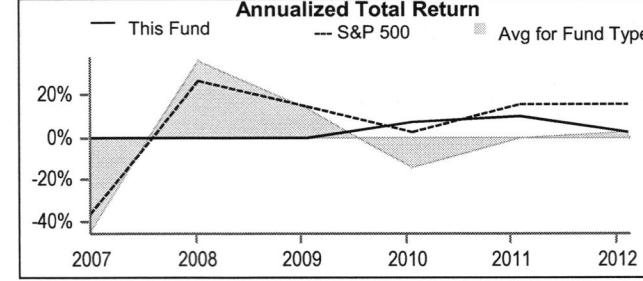

Annualized Total Return — This Fund --- S&P 500 — Avg for Fund Type

*UBS ETRACS FsherGartman Rsk Off (OFF)

E+   Very Weak

Fund Family: UBS Global Asset Mgmt (Americas) In
Fund Type: Income
Inception Date: November 30, 2011

Major Rating Factors:
Very poor performance is the major factor driving the E+ (Very Weak) TheStreet.com Investment Rating for *UBS ETRACS FsherGartman Rsk Off. The fund currently has a performance rating of E (Very Weak) based on an annualized return of 0.00% over the last three years and a total return of -2.80% year to date 2012.

The fund's risk rating is currently C (Fair). It carries a beta of 0.00, meaning the fund's expected move will be 0.0% for every 10% move in the market. Volatility, as measured by both the semi-deviation and a drawdown factor, is considered average. As of December 31, 2012, *UBS ETRACS FsherGartman Rsk Off traded at a premium of 2.89% above its net asset value, which is worse than its one-year historical average discount of .01%.

This fund has been team managed for 2 years and currently receives a manager quality ranking of 94 (0=worst, 99=best). This fund offers an average level of risk but investors looking for strong performance will be frustrated.

Data Date	Investment Rating	Net Assets ($Mil)	Price	Performance Rating/Pts	Total Return Y-T-D	Risk Rating/Pts
12-12	E+	12.40	20.65	E / 0.5	-2.80%	C / 4.7

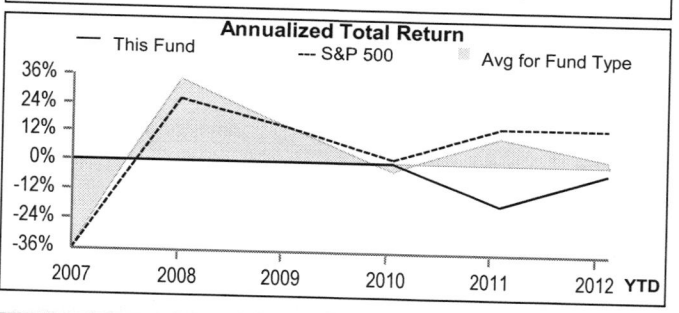

Annualized Total Return

*UBS ETRACS FsherGartman Rsk On E (ONN)

D+   Weak

Fund Family: UBS Global Asset Mgmt (Americas) In
Fund Type: Income
Inception Date: November 30, 2011

Major Rating Factors: *UBS ETRACS FsherGartman Rsk On E receives a TheStreet.com Investment Rating of D+ (Weak). The fund currently has a performance rating of C (Fair) based on an annualized return of 0.00% over the last three years and a total return of 2.03% year to date 2012.

The fund's risk rating is currently C (Fair). It carries a beta of 0.00, meaning the fund's expected move will be 0.0% for every 10% move in the market. Volatility, as measured by both the semi-deviation and a drawdown factor, is considered average. As of December 31, 2012, *UBS ETRACS FsherGartman Rsk On E traded at a discount of 2.78% below its net asset value, which is better than its one-year historical average discount of .01%.

This fund has been team managed for 2 years and currently receives a manager quality ranking of 6 (0=worst, 99=best). If you desire an average level of risk, then this fund may be an option.

Data Date	Investment Rating	Net Assets ($Mil)	Price	Performance Rating/Pts	Total Return Y-T-D	Risk Rating/Pts
12-12	D+	11.00	27.60	C / 5.0	2.03%	C / 4.8

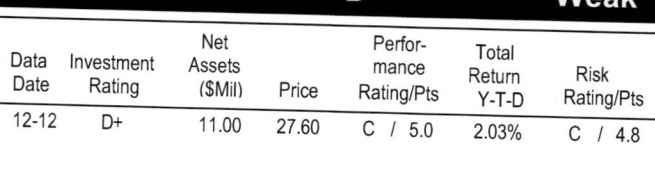

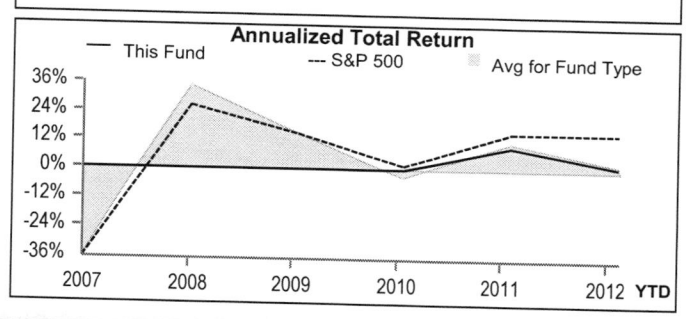

Annualized Total Return

*United States 12 Month Oil Fund (USL)

D-   Weak

Fund Family: United States Commodity Funds LLC
Fund Type: Energy/Natural Resources
Inception Date: December 6, 2007

Major Rating Factors:
Disappointing performance is the major factor driving the D- (Weak) TheStreet.com Investment Rating for *United States 12 Month Oil Fund. The fund currently has a performance rating of D- (Weak) based on an annualized return of 0.38% over the last three years and a total return of 1.54% year to date 2012. Factored into the performance evaluation is an expense ratio of 0.77% (very low).

The fund's risk rating is currently C+ (Fair). It carries a beta of 0.97, meaning that its performance tracks fairly well with that of the overall stock market. Volatility, as measured by both the semi-deviation and a drawdown factor, is considered low. As of December 31, 2012, *United States 12 Month Oil Fund traded at a discount of 1.54% below its net asset value, which is better than its one-year historical average discount of .06%.

This fund has been team managed for 6 years and currently receives a manager quality ranking of 14 (0=worst, 99=best). This fund offers only a moderate level of risk but investors looking for strong performance are still waiting.

Data Date	Investment Rating	Net Assets ($Mil)	Price	Performance Rating/Pts	Total Return Y-T-D	Risk Rating/Pts
12-12	D-	99.50	39.67	D- / 1.3	1.54%	C+ / 6.4
2011	C	169.50	43.48	C / 5.5	3.24%	C+ / 6.8
2010	D-	180.20	43.10	D- / 1.4	6.52%	C- / 3.6
2009	C+	181.22	40.46	B / 8.0	26.44%	C- / 3.8

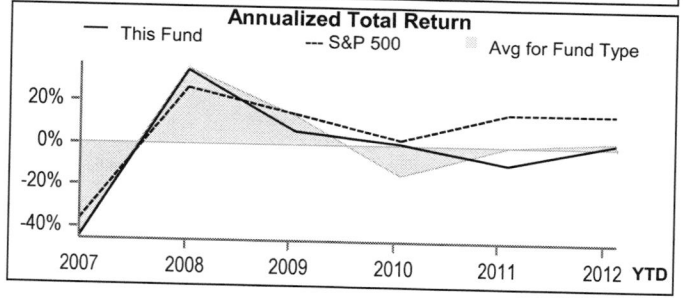

Annualized Total Return

*United States Brent Oil Fund (BNO)

C- **Fair**

Fund Family: United States Commodity Funds LLC
Fund Type: Energy/Natural Resources
Inception Date: June 1, 2010

Major Rating Factors: Middle of the road best describes *United States Brent Oil Fund whose TheStreet.com Investment Rating is currently a C- (Fair). The fund currently has a performance rating of C- (Fair) based on an annualized return of 0.00% over the last three years and a total return of -0.30% year to date 2012. Factored into the performance evaluation is an expense ratio of 0.94% (low).

The fund's risk rating is currently B- (Good). It carries a beta of 0.00, meaning the fund's expected move will be 0.0% for every 10% move in the market. Volatility, as measured by both the semi-deviation and a drawdown factor, is considered low. As of December 31, 2012, *United States Brent Oil Fund traded at a premium of .27% above its net asset value, which is worse than its one-year historical average premium of .03%.

Nicholas D. Gerber currently receives a manager quality ranking of 78 (0=worst, 99=best). If you desire an average level of risk, then this fund may be an option.

Data Date	Investment Rating	Net Assets ($Mil)	Price	Performance Rating/Pts	Total Return Y-T-D	Risk Rating/Pts
12-12	C-	45.10	82.07	C- / 3.7	-0.30%	B- / 7.6
2011	B	37.30	74.64	B / 7.7	5.64%	B- / 7.9

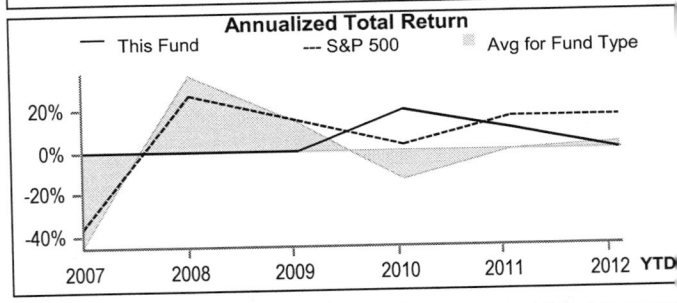

*United States Commodity Index (USCI)

D **Weak**

Fund Family: United States Commodity Funds LLC
Fund Type: Income
Inception Date: August 9, 2010

Major Rating Factors:
Disappointing performance is the major factor driving the D (Weak) TheStreet.com Investment Rating for *United States Commodity Index. The fund currently has a performance rating of D- (Weak) based on an annualized return of 0.00% over the last three years and a total return of -0.46% year to date 2012. Factored into the performance evaluation is an expense ratio of 1.15% (low).

The fund's risk rating is currently B- (Good). It carries a beta of 0.00, meaning the fund's expected move will be 0.0% for every 10% move in the market. Volatility, as measured by both the semi-deviation and a drawdown factor, is considered low. As of December 31, 2012, *United States Commodity Index traded at a premium of .72% above its net asset value, which is worse than its one-year historical average premium of .04%.

Nicholas D. Gerber currently receives a manager quality ranking of 10 (0=worst, 99=best). This fund offers only a moderate level of risk but investors looking for strong performance are still waiting.

Data Date	Investment Rating	Net Assets ($Mil)	Price	Performance Rating/Pts	Total Return Y-T-D	Risk Rating/Pts
12-12	D	485.20	58.63	D- / 1.0	-0.46%	B- / 7.7
2011	D	350.80	58.37	D- / 1.4	2.88%	B- / 7.9

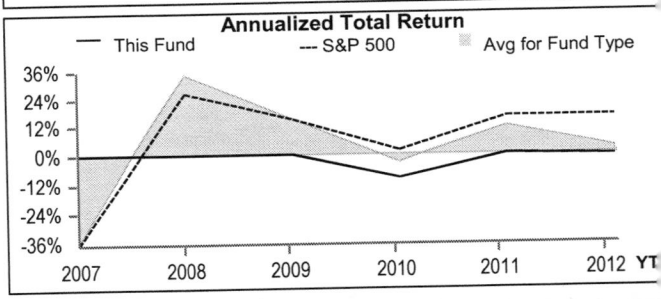

*United States Copper Index (CPER)

D+ **Weak**

Fund Family: United States Commodity Funds LLC
Fund Type: Income
Inception Date: November 14, 2011

Major Rating Factors:
Disappointing performance is the major factor driving the D+ (Weak) TheStreet.com Investment Rating for *United States Copper Index. The fund currently has a performance rating of D (Weak) based on an annualized return of 0.00% over the last three years and a total return of 1.95% year to date 2012.

The fund's risk rating is currently B (Good). It carries a beta of 0.00, meaning the fund's expected move will be 0.0% for every 10% move in the market. Volatility, as measured by both the semi-deviation and a drawdown factor, is considered low. As of December 31, 2012, *United States Copper Index traded at a discount of 1.81% below its net asset value, which is better than its one-year historical average discount of .12%.

This fund has been team managed for 2 years and currently receives a manager quality ranking of 6 (0=worst, 99=best). This fund offers only a moderate level of risk but investors looking for strong performance are still waiting.

Data Date	Investment Rating	Net Assets ($Mil)	Price	Performance Rating/Pts	Total Return Y-T-D	Risk Rating/Pt
12-12	D+	2.50	25.01	D / 1.7	1.95%	B / 8.1

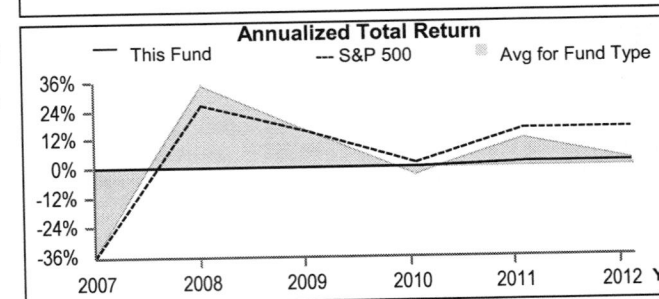

*United States Gasoline Fund LP (UGA)

	C+	Fair

Fund Family: United States Commodity Funds LLC
Fund Type: Energy/Natural Resources
Inception Date: February 26, 2008

Major Rating Factors: Middle of the road best describes *United States Gasoline Fund LP whose TheStreet.com Investment Rating is currently a C+ (Fair). The fund currently has a performance rating of C+ (Fair) based on an annualized return of 16.73% over the last three years and a total return of -1.16% year to date 2012. Factored into the performance evaluation is an expense ratio of 0.84% (very low).

The fund's risk rating is currently B- (Good). It carries a beta of 0.81, meaning the fund's expected move will be 8.1% for every 10% move in the market. Volatility, as measured by both the semi-deviation and a drawdown factor, is considered low. As of December 31, 2012, *United States Gasoline Fund LP traded at a premium of .93% above its net asset value, which is worse than its one-year historical average premium of .05%.

Nicholas D. Gerber currently receives a manager quality ranking of 88 (0=worst, 99=best). If you desire an average level of risk, then this fund may be an option.

Data Date	Investment Rating	Net Assets ($Mil)	Price	Performance Rating/Pts	Total Return Y-T-D	Risk Rating/Pts
12-12	C+	64.20	58.44	C+ / 6.8	-1.16%	B- / 7.3
2011	B+	77.40	48.32	A- / 9.0	4.12%	B- / 7.6
2010	C+	67.30	42.11	A / 9.3	15.12%	C- / 3.0
2009	C+	91.54	36.58	A / 9.5	73.20%	C- / 3.1

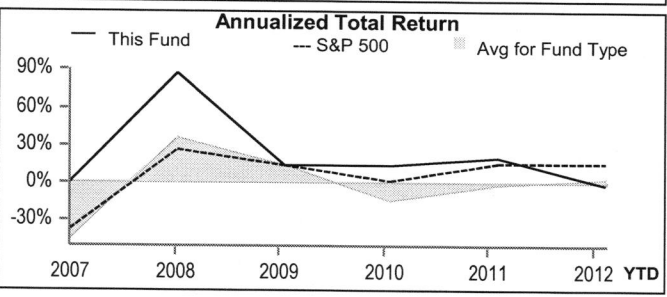

*United States Heating Oil Fund (UHN)

	D+	Weak

Fund Family: United States Commodity Funds LLC
Fund Type: Energy/Natural Resources
Inception Date: April 9, 2008

Major Rating Factors:
Disappointing performance is the major factor driving the D+ (Weak) TheStreet.com Investment Rating for *United States Heating Oil Fund. The fund currently has a performance rating of D+ (Weak) based on an annualized return of 7.88% over the last three years and a total return of -0.71% year to date 2012. Factored into the performance evaluation is an expense ratio of 0.90% (low).

The fund's risk rating is currently B- (Good). It carries a beta of 0.85, meaning the fund's expected move will be 8.5% for every 10% move in the market. Volatility, as measured by both the semi-deviation and a drawdown factor, is considered low. As of December 31, 2012, *United States Heating Oil Fund traded at a premium of .69% above its net asset value, which is worse than its one-year historical average premium of .03%.

Nicholas Gerber has been running the fund for 5 years and currently receives a manager quality ranking of 44 (0=worst, 99=best). This fund offers only a moderate level of risk but investors looking for strong performance are still waiting.

Data Date	Investment Rating	Net Assets ($Mil)	Price	Performance Rating/Pts	Total Return Y-T-D	Risk Rating/Pts
12-12	D+	6.80	33.73	D+ / 2.8	-0.71%	B- / 7.4
2011	C+	9.80	32.87	C+ / 5.7	4.96%	B- / 7.8
2010	C+	11.90	29.86	B+ / 8.8	8.15%	C- / 3.3
2009	C	7.71	27.61	B / 7.9	23.09%	C- / 3.4

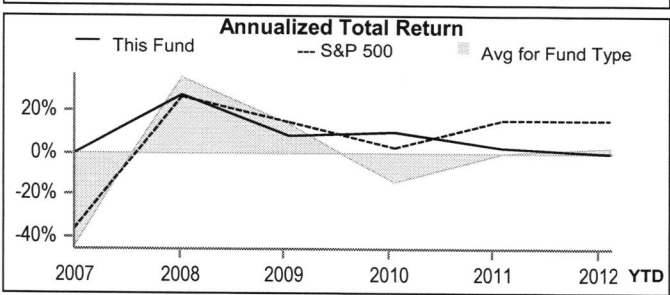

*United States Natural Gas Fund (UNG)

	E	Very Weak

Fund Family: United States Commodity Funds LLC
Fund Type: Energy/Natural Resources
Inception Date: April 18, 2007

Major Rating Factors: Very poor performance is the major factor driving the E (Very Weak) TheStreet.com Investment Rating for *United States Natural Gas Fund. The fund currently has a performance rating of E- (Very Weak) based on an annualized return of -38.86% over the last three years and a total return of -0.95% year to date 2012. Factored into the performance evaluation is an expense ratio of 0.96% (low).

The fund's risk rating is currently C- (Fair). It carries a beta of 0.24, meaning the fund's expected move will be 2.4% for every 10% move in the market. Volatility, as measured by both the semi-deviation and a drawdown factor, is considered average. As of December 31, 2012, *United States Natural Gas Fund traded at a premium of .91% above its net asset value, which is worse than its one-year historical average discount of .05%.

Nicholas D. Gerber currently receives a manager quality ranking of 1 (0=worst, 99=best). This fund offers an average level of risk but investors looking for strong performance will be frustrated.

Data Date	Investment Rating	Net Assets ($Mil)	Price	Performance Rating/Pts	Total Return Y-T-D	Risk Rating/Pts
12-12	E	1,175.00	18.90	E- / 0.2	-0.95%	C- / 3.4
2011	E	1,072.10	6.46	E- / 0.1	2.79%	C- / 3.4
2010	E-	2,724.40	5.99	E- / 0.2	-40.58%	D / 2.1
2009	E-	3,722.20	10.08	E- / 0.2	-59.37%	D+ / 2.4

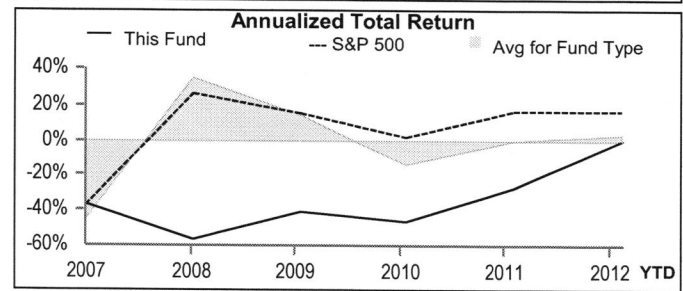

*United States Oil Fund (USO)   D-   Weak

Fund Family: United States Commodity Funds LLC
Fund Type: Energy/Natural Resources
Inception Date: April 10, 2006

Major Rating Factors:

Disappointing performance is the major factor driving the D- (Weak) TheStreet.com Investment Rating for *United States Oil Fund. The fund currently has a performance rating of D- (Weak) based on an annualized return of -3.92% over the last three years and a total return of 2.07% year to date 2012. Factored into the performance evaluation is an expense ratio of 0.65% (very low).

The fund's risk rating is currently C+ (Fair). It carries a beta of 1.02, meaning that its performance tracks fairly well with that of the overall stock market. Volatility, as measured by both the semi-deviation and a drawdown factor, is considered low. As of December 31, 2012, *United States Oil Fund traded at a discount of 1.97% below its net asset value, which is better than its one-year historical average premium of .01%.

Nicholas D.Gerber / John T. Hy has been running the fund for 7 years and currently receives a manager quality ranking of 9 (0=worst, 99=best). This fund offers only a moderate level of risk but investors looking for strong performance are still waiting.

Data Date	Investment Rating	Net Assets ($Mil)	Price	Performance Rating/Pts	Total Return Y-T-D	Risk Rating/P
12-12	D-	1,199.80	33.37	D- / 1.0	2.07%	C+ / 6
2011	D+	1,134.60	38.11	C- / 3.7	2.91%	C+ / 6
2010	E	1,819.80	39.00	E+ / 0.6	-0.71%	D+ / 2
2009	E+	2,303.34	39.28	D- / 1.3	10.24%	C- / 3

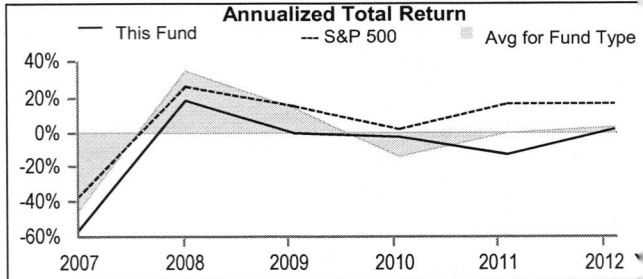

*United States Short Oil Fund (DNO)   D-   Wea

Fund Family: United States Commodity Funds LLC
Fund Type: Energy/Natural Resources
Inception Date: September 23, 2009

Major Rating Factors:

Disappointing performance is the major factor driving the D- (Weak) TheStreet.com Investment Rating for *United States Short Oil Fund. The fund currently has a performance rating of D- (Weak) based on an annualized return of -5.53% over the last three years and a total return of -0.53% year to date 2012. Factored into the performance evaluation is an expense ratio of 0.85% (very low).

The fund's risk rating is currently C+ (Fair). It carries a beta of -1.00, meaning the fund's expected move will be -10.0% for every 10% move in the market. Volatility, as measured by both the semi-deviation and a drawdown factor, is considered low. As of December 31, 2012, *United States Short Oil Fund traded at a premium of 1.88% above its net asset value, which is worse than its one-year historical average discount of .01%.

Nicholas Gerber has been running the fund for 4 years and currently receives a manager quality ranking of 76 (0=worst, 99=best). This fund offers only a moderate level of risk but investors looking for strong performance are still waiting.

Data Date	Investment Rating	Net Assets ($Mil)	Price	Performance Rating/Pts	Total Return Y-T-D	Risk Rating/
12-12	D-	13.30	37.88	D- / 1.0	-0.53%	C+ / 6
2011	D-	10.80	36.11	E+ / 0.7	-3.05%	C+ / 6
2010	D	8.10	40.42	E / 0.5	-7.93%	C+ / 6

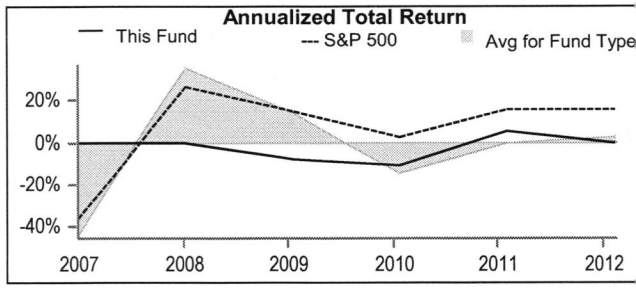

*US 12 Month Natural Gas Fund (UNL)   E   Very Wea

Fund Family: United States Commodity Funds LLC
Fund Type: Energy/Natural Resources
Inception Date: November 19, 2009

Major Rating Factors: Very poor performance is the major factor driving the E (Very Weak) TheStreet.com Investment Rating for *US 12 Month Natural Gas Fund. The fund currently has a performance rating of E (Very Weak) based on an annualized return of -32.38% over the last three years and a total return of -1.57% year to date 2012. Factored into the performance evaluation is an expense ratio of 0.92% (low).

The fund's risk rating is currently C- (Fair). It carries a beta of 0.15, meaning the fund's expected move will be 1.5% for every 10% move in the market. Volatility, as measured by both the semi-deviation and a drawdown factor, is considered average. As of December 31, 2012, *US 12 Month Natural Gas Fund traded at a premium of 3.79% above its net asset value, which is worse than its one-year historical average premium of .06%.

Nicholas D. Gerber currently receives a manager quality ranking of 2 (0=worst, 99=best). This fund offers an average level of risk but investors looking for strong performance will be frustrated.

Data Date	Investment Rating	Net Assets ($Mil)	Price	Performance Rating/Pts	Total Return Y-T-D	Risk Rating/
12-12	E	43.10	17.24	E / 0.3	-1.57%	C- / 4
2011	E+	21.20	21.12	E- / 0.1	2.69%	C / 4
2010	D-	35.00	34.97	E / 0.3	-35.48%	C+ /

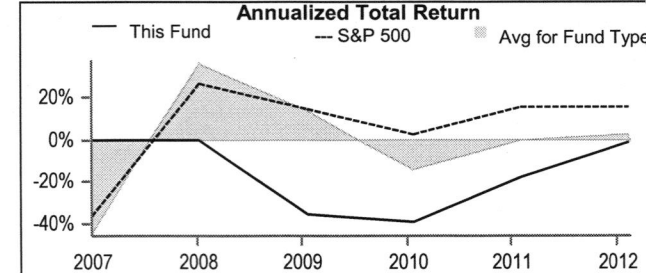

*Utilities Select Sector SPDR (XLU)

C   **Fair**

Fund Family: SSgA Funds Management Inc
Fund Type: Utilities
Inception Date: December 16, 1998

Major Rating Factors: Middle of the road best describes *Utilities Select Sector SPDR whose TheStreet.com Investment Rating is currently a C (Fair). The fund currently has a performance rating of C- (Fair) based on an annualized return of 8.99% over the last three years and a total return of 1.37% year to date 2012. Factored into the performance evaluation is an expense ratio of 0.18% (very low).

The fund's risk rating is currently B+ (Good). It carries a beta of 0.94, meaning that its performance tracks fairly well with that of the overall stock market. Volatility, as measured by both the semi-deviation and a drawdown factor, is considered very low. As of December 31, 2012, *Utilities Select Sector SPDR traded at a discount of 1.33% below its net asset value, which is better than its one-year historical average discount of .02%.

John A. Tucker has been running the fund for 15 years and currently receives a manager quality ranking of 51 (0=worst, 99=best). If you desire an average level of risk, then this fund may be an option.

Data Date	Investment Rating	Net Assets ($Mil)	Price	Performance Rating/Pts	Total Return Y-T-D	Risk Rating/Pts
12-12	C	5,457.90	34.92	C- / 3.1	1.37%	B+ / 9.1
2011	C+	7,662.30	35.98	C / 5.0	-2.67%	B / 8.6
2010	D+	3,756.60	31.34	D- / 1.5	5.35%	C+ / 6.7
2009	C-	2,462.73	31.02	D+ / 2.5	9.12%	C+ / 6.8

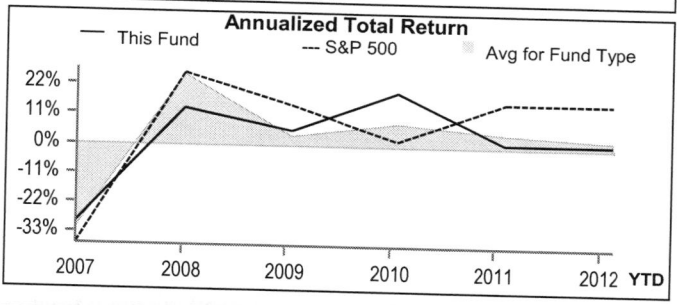

*Vanguard Consumer Discret ETF (VCR)

B+   **Good**

Fund Family: Vanguard Group Inc
Fund Type: Income
Inception Date: January 26, 2004

Major Rating Factors: Strong performance is the major factor driving the B+ (Good) TheStreet.com Investment Rating for *Vanguard Consumer Discret ETF. The fund currently has a performance rating of B+ (Good) based on an annualized return of 19.81% over the last three years and a total return of 3.27% year to date 2012. Factored into the performance evaluation is an expense ratio of 0.14% (very low).

The fund's risk rating is currently B- (Good). It carries a beta of 1.13, meaning it is expected to move 11.3% for every 10% move in the market. Volatility, as measured by both the semi-deviation and a drawdown factor, is considered low. As of December 31, 2012, *Vanguard Consumer Discret ETF traded at a discount of 3.17% below its net asset value, which is better than its one-year historical average premium of .03%.

Michael A. Johnson has been running the fund for 3 years and currently receives a manager quality ranking of 82 (0=worst, 99=best). If you desire only a moderate level of risk and strong performance, then this fund is an excellent option.

Data Date	Investment Rating	Net Assets ($Mil)	Price	Performance Rating/Pts	Total Return Y-T-D	Risk Rating/Pts
12-12	B+	572.80	75.87	B+ / 8.5	3.27%	B- / 7.9
2011	B	346.20	61.81	B / 7.9	2.44%	B- / 7.9
2010	B+	362.70	60.47	B / 8.2	30.57%	C+ / 5.6
2009	D+	140.76	46.77	D+ / 2.9	40.69%	C+ / 5.6

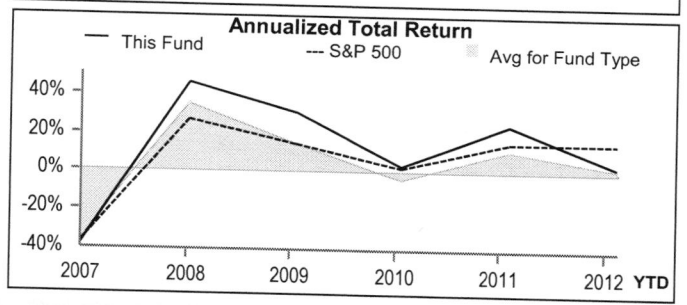

*Vanguard Consumer Staples ETF (VDC)

C+   **Fair**

Fund Family: Vanguard Group Inc
Fund Type: Income
Inception Date: January 26, 2004

Major Rating Factors: Middle of the road best describes *Vanguard Consumer Staples ETF whose TheStreet.com Investment Rating is currently a C+ (Fair). The fund currently has a performance rating of C (Fair) based on an annualized return of 13.65% over the last three years and a total return of 2.93% year to date 2012. Factored into the performance evaluation is an expense ratio of 0.14% (very low).

The fund's risk rating is currently B+ (Good). It carries a beta of 0.51, meaning the fund's expected move will be 5.1% for every 10% move in the market. Volatility, as measured by both the semi-deviation and a drawdown factor, is considered very low. As of December 31, 2012, *Vanguard Consumer Staples ETF traded at a discount of 2.87% below its net asset value, which is better than its one-year historical average premium of .01%.

Michael A. Johnson has been running the fund for 3 years and currently receives a manager quality ranking of 85 (0=worst, 99=best). If you desire an average level of risk, then this fund may be an option.

Data Date	Investment Rating	Net Assets ($Mil)	Price	Performance Rating/Pts	Total Return Y-T-D	Risk Rating/Pts
12-12	C+	1,202.60	87.91	C / 5.4	2.93%	B+ / 9.0
2011	B-	879.50	81.47	C+ / 6.0	-0.99%	B / 8.6
2010	B-	608.70	73.39	C+ / 6.2	14.62%	B- / 7.3
2009	C	552.45	65.69	C- / 4.0	15.05%	B- / 7.3

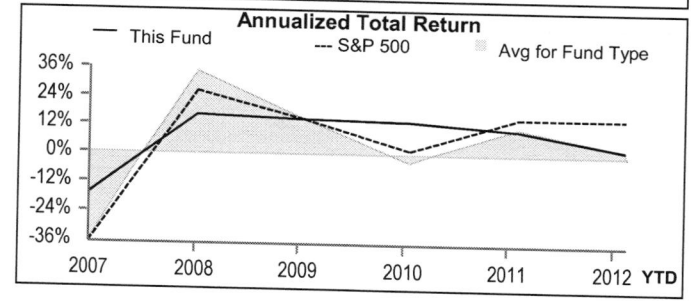

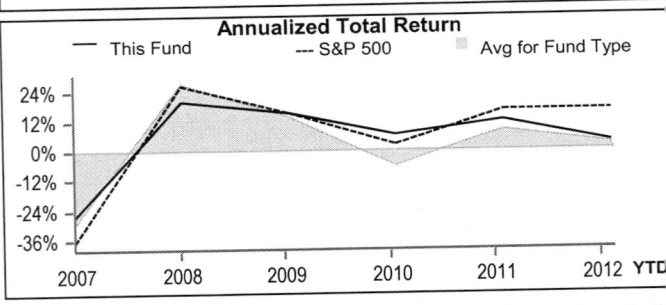
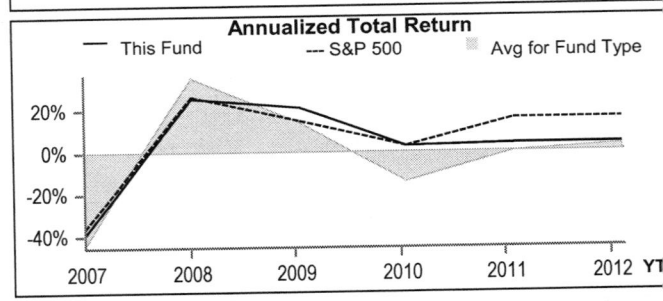
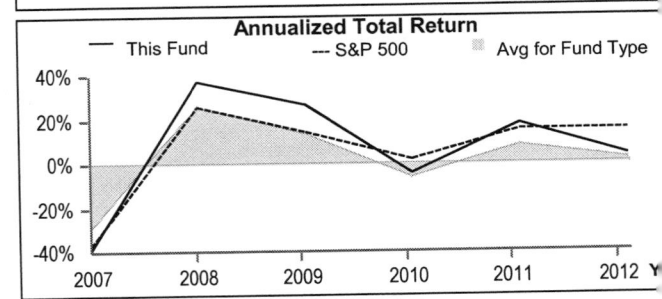

*Vanguard Div Appreciation ETF (VIG)

C+   Fair

Fund Family: Vanguard Group Inc
Fund Type: Growth
Inception Date: April 21, 2006

Data Date	Investment Rating	Net Assets ($Mil)	Price	Performance Rating/Pts	Total Return Y-T-D	Risk Rating/Pts
12-12	C+	12,040.10	59.57	C / 5.1	3.22%	B / 8.4
2011	C+	8,964.40	54.65	C / 5.3	0.75%	B / 8.2
2010	C+	4,606.30	52.63	C / 5.0	14.76%	C+ / 6.6
2009	C-	1,203.27	46.86	D+ / 2.7	16.54%	B- / 7.1

Major Rating Factors: Middle of the road best describes *Vanguard Div Appreciation ETF whose TheStreet.com Investment Rating is currently a C+ (Fair). The fund currently has a performance rating of C (Fair) based on an annualized return of 11.34% over the last three years and a total return of 3.22% year to date 2012. Factored into the performance evaluation is an expense ratio of 0.10% (very low).

The fund's risk rating is currently B (Good). It carries a beta of 0.82, meaning the fund's expected move will be 8.2% for every 10% move in the market. Volatility, as measured by both the semi-deviation and a drawdown factor, is considered low. As of December 31, 2012, *Vanguard Div Appreciation ETF traded at a discount of 3.09% below its net asset value, which is better than its one-year historical average premium of .01%.

Ryan E. Ludt has been running the fund for 7 years and currently receives a manager quality ranking of 66 (0=worst, 99=best). If you desire an average level of risk, then this fund may be an option.

*Vanguard Energy ETF (VDE)

C-   Fair

Fund Family: Vanguard Group Inc
Fund Type: Energy/Natural Resources
Inception Date: September 23, 2004

Data Date	Investment Rating	Net Assets ($Mil)	Price	Performance Rating/Pts	Total Return Y-T-D	Risk Rating/Pts
12-12	C-	1,880.60	102.26	C- / 3.5	3.47%	B- / 7.3
2011	C	1,728.20	100.81	C+ / 5.6	1.95%	B- / 7.1
2010	C-	1,548.60	99.67	C / 5.0	21.05%	C / 4.8
2009	C-	869.27	83.37	C / 4.3	18.95%	C+ / 5.9

Major Rating Factors: Middle of the road best describes *Vanguard Energy ETF whose TheStreet.com Investment Rating is currently a C- (Fair). The fund currently has a performance rating of C- (Fair) based on an annualized return of 8.54% over the last three years and a total return of 3.47% year to date 2012. Factored into the performance evaluation is an expense ratio of 0.14% (very low).

The fund's risk rating is currently B- (Good). It carries a beta of 1.03, meaning that its performance tracks fairly well with that of the overall stock market. Volatility, as measured by both the semi-deviation and a drawdown factor, is considered low. As of December 31, 2012, *Vanguard Energy ETF traded at a discount of 3.35% below its net asset value, which is better than its one-year historical average premium of .01%.

Jeffrey D. Miller has been running the fund for 3 years and currently receives a manager quality ranking of 45 (0=worst, 99=best). If you desire an average level of risk, then this fund may be an option.

*Vanguard Extended Market Index E (VXF)

C+   Fair

Fund Family: Vanguard Group Inc
Fund Type: Growth
Inception Date: December 27, 2001

Data Date	Investment Rating	Net Assets ($Mil)	Price	Performance Rating/Pts	Total Return Y-T-D	Risk Rating/Pts
12-12	C+	1,400.70	60.50	C+ / 6.9	3.88%	B- / 7.5
2011	C+	1,148.20	51.84	C+ / 6.1	1.64%	B- / 7.4
2010	C	1,112.90	54.41	B- / 7.3	27.62%	C- / 3.2
2009	D	633.03	43.06	C- / 3.2	34.79%	C- / 3.4

Major Rating Factors: Middle of the road best describes *Vanguard Extended Market Index E whose TheStreet.com Investment Rating is currently a C+ (Fair). The fund currently has a performance rating of C+ (Fair) based on an annualized return of 13.87% over the last three years and a total return of 3.88% year to date 2012. Factored into the performance evaluation is an expense ratio of 0.10% (very low).

The fund's risk rating is currently B- (Good). It carries a beta of 1.22, meaning it is expected to move 12.2% for every 10% move in the market. Volatility, as measured by both the semi-deviation and a drawdown factor, is considered low. As of December 31, 2012, *Vanguard Extended Market Index E traded at a discount of 3.72% below its net asset value, which is better than its one-year historical average premium of .01%.

Donald M. Butler has been running the fund for 16 years and currently receives a manager quality ranking of 59 (0=worst, 99=best). If you desire an average level of risk, then this fund may be an option.

*Vanguard Extnd Durtn Trea Idx ET (EDV)

C+ **Fair**

Fund Family: Vanguard Group Inc
Fund Type: US Government/Agency
Inception Date: December 6, 2007

Major Rating Factors: Middle of the road best describes *Vanguard Extnd Durtn Trea Idx ET whose TheStreet.com Investment Rating is currently a C+ (Fair). The fund currently has a performance rating of C+ (Fair) based on an annualized return of 19.69% over the last three years and a total return of -1.49% year to date 2012. Factored into the performance evaluation is an expense ratio of 0.12% (very low).

The fund's risk rating is currently B- (Good). It carries a beta of 1.97, meaning it is expected to move 19.7% for every 10% move in the market. Volatility, as measured by both the semi-deviation and a drawdown factor, is considered low. As of December 31, 2012, *Vanguard Extnd Durtn Trea Idx ET traded at a premium of 2.10% above its net asset value, which is worse than its one-year historical average premium of .27%.

Gregory Davis has been running the fund for 6 years and currently receives a manager quality ranking of 19 (0=worst, 99=best). If you desire an average level of risk, then this fund may be an option.

Data Date	Investment Rating	Net Assets ($Mil)	Price	Performance Rating/Pts	Total Return Y-T-D	Risk Rating/Pts
12-12	C+	176.60	116.00	C+ / 6.4	-1.49%	B- / 7.7
2011	C+	187.90	121.94	B- / 7.2	-3.21%	C+ / 6.3
2010	D+	132.00	82.80	D / 2.0	9.79%	C+ / 5.9
2009	D-	45.86	78.87	E / 0.4	-31.22%	C+ / 6.1

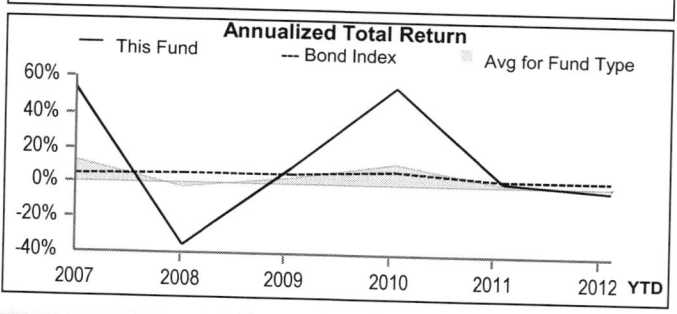
Annualized Total Return — This Fund — Bond Index — Avg for Fund Type

*Vanguard Financials ETF (VFH)

C **Fair**

Fund Family: Vanguard Group Inc
Fund Type: Financial Services
Inception Date: January 26, 2004

Major Rating Factors: Middle of the road best describes *Vanguard Financials ETF whose TheStreet.com Investment Rating is currently a C (Fair). The fund currently has a performance rating of C (Fair) based on an annualized return of 8.02% over the last three years and a total return of 4.16% year to date 2012. Factored into the performance evaluation is an expense ratio of 0.14% (very low).

The fund's risk rating is currently B- (Good). It carries a beta of 1.02, meaning that its performance tracks fairly well with that of the overall stock market. Volatility, as measured by both the semi-deviation and a drawdown factor, is considered low. As of December 31, 2012, *Vanguard Financials ETF traded at a discount of 3.89% below its net asset value, which is better than its one-year historical average premium of .02%.

Jeffrey D. Miller has been running the fund for 3 years and currently receives a manager quality ranking of 51 (0=worst, 99=best). If you desire an average level of risk, then this fund may be an option.

Data Date	Investment Rating	Net Assets ($Mil)	Price	Performance Rating/Pts	Total Return Y-T-D	Risk Rating/Pts
12-12	C	850.50	34.10	C / 5.5	4.16%	B- / 7.4
2011	D+	534.20	27.62	C- / 3.0	2.72%	C+ / 6.8
2010	D-	576.20	32.88	D- / 1.1	14.83%	C / 4.5
2009	E+	579.62	29.04	E+ / 0.6	13.97%	C / 4.5

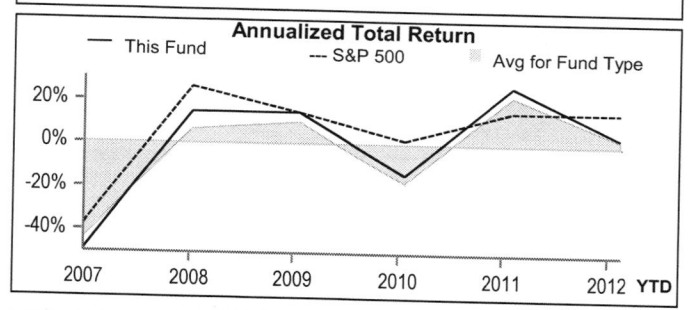
Annualized Total Return — This Fund — S&P 500 — Avg for Fund Type

*Vanguard FTSE All-Wld ex-US S/C (VSS)

C- **Fair**

Fund Family: Vanguard Group Inc
Fund Type: Foreign
Inception Date: April 2, 2009

Major Rating Factors: Middle of the road best describes *Vanguard FTSE All-Wld ex-US S/C whose TheStreet.com Investment Rating is currently a C- (Fair). The fund currently has a performance rating of C (Fair) based on an annualized return of 6.11% over the last three years and a total return of 2.73% year to date 2012. Factored into the performance evaluation is an expense ratio of 0.27% (very low).

The fund's risk rating is currently C+ (Fair). It carries a beta of 1.06, meaning that its performance tracks fairly well with that of the overall stock market. Volatility, as measured by both the semi-deviation and a drawdown factor, is considered low. As of December 31, 2012, *Vanguard FTSE All-Wld ex-US S/C traded at a discount of 1.77% below its net asset value, which is better than its one-year historical average premium of .51%.

Ryan E. Ludt has been running the fund for 4 years and currently receives a manager quality ranking of 69 (0=worst, 99=best). If you desire an average level of risk, then this fund may be an option.

Data Date	Investment Rating	Net Assets ($Mil)	Price	Performance Rating/Pts	Total Return Y-T-D	Risk Rating/Pts
12-12	C-	1,067.20	90.89	C / 4.9	2.73%	C+ / 6.1
2011	D-	814.40	77.57	E+ / 0.8	1.33%	C+ / 6.3
2010	A+	673.30	99.62	A / 9.5	25.62%	B- / 7.8

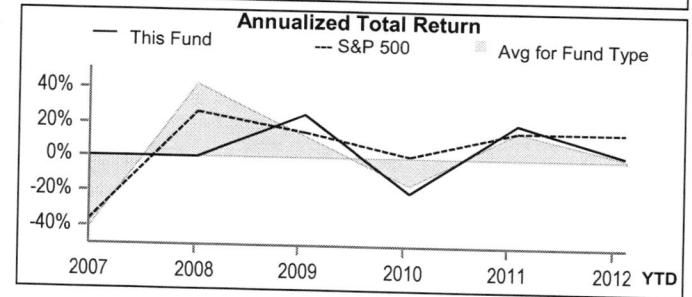
Annualized Total Return — This Fund — S&P 500 — Avg for Fund Type

*Vanguard FTSE All-World ex-US ET (VEU)

C-   **Fair**

Fund Family: Vanguard Group Inc
Fund Type: Foreign
Inception Date: March 2, 2007

Major Rating Factors: Middle of the road best describes *Vanguard FTSE All-World ex-US ET whose TheStreet.com Investment Rating is currently a C- (Fair). The fund currently has a performance rating of C- (Fair) based on an annualized return of 4.24% over the last three years and a total return of 1.77% year to date 2012. Factored into the performance evaluation is an expense ratio of 0.17% (very low).

The fund's risk rating is currently B- (Good). It carries a beta of 1.05, meaning that its performance tracks fairly well with that of the overall stock market. Volatility, as measured by both the semi-deviation and a drawdown factor, is considered low. As of December 31, 2012, *Vanguard FTSE All-World ex-US ET traded at a discount of 1.36% below its net asset value, which is better than its one-year historical average premium of .26%.

Ryan E. Ludt has been running the fund for 5 years and currently receives a manager quality ranking of 55 (0=worst, 99=best). If you desire an average level of risk, then this fund may be an option.

Data Date	Investment Rating	Net Assets ($Mil)	Price	Performance Rating/Pts	Total Return Y-T-D	Risk Rating/Pts
12-12	C-	7,829.50	45.75	C- / 4.1	1.77%	B- / 7.3
2011	C-	5,864.70	39.65	C- / 3.3	-0.10%	B- / 7.3
2010	D+	6,174.60	47.73	D+ / 2.7	11.80%	C / 5.3
2009	A-	2,600.53	43.61	B+ / 8.6	35.10%	C+ / 5.6

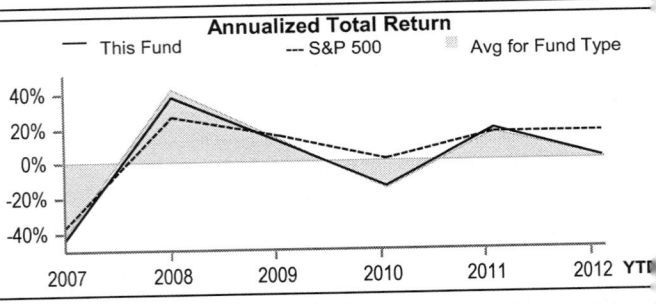

Annualized Total Return
— This Fund   --- S&P 500   Avg for Fund Type

*Vanguard FTSE Emerging Markets E (VWO)

D+   **Weak**

Fund Family: Vanguard Group Inc
Fund Type: Emerging Market
Inception Date: March 4, 2005

Major Rating Factors: *Vanguard FTSE Emerging Markets E receives a TheStreet.com Investment Rating of D+ (Weak). The fund currently has a performance rating of C- (Fair) based on an annualized return of 4.64% over the last three years and a total return of 0.70% year to date 2012. Factored into the performance evaluation is an expense ratio of 0.19% (very low).

The fund's risk rating is currently C+ (Fair). It carries a beta of 1.06, meaning that its performance tracks fairly well with that of the overall stock market. Volatility, as measured by both the semi-deviation and a drawdown factor, is considered low. As of December 31, 2012, *Vanguard FTSE Emerging Markets E traded at a discount of .49% below its net asset value, which is better than its one-year historical average premium of .10%.

Michael Perre has been running the fund for 5 years and currently receives a manager quality ranking of 49 (0=worst, 99=best). If you desire an average level of risk, then this fund may be an option.

Data Date	Investment Rating	Net Assets ($Mil)	Price	Performance Rating/Pts	Total Return Y-T-D	Risk Rating/Pts
12-12	D+	56,968.50	44.53	C- / 3.1	0.70%	C+ / 6.8
2011	C	42,454.50	38.21	C / 5.2	0.94%	B- / 7.0
2010	D+	44,730.40	48.15	C / 5.3	19.46%	C- / 3.0
2009	C	6,767.32	41.00	B- / 7.4	66.71%	C- / 3.4

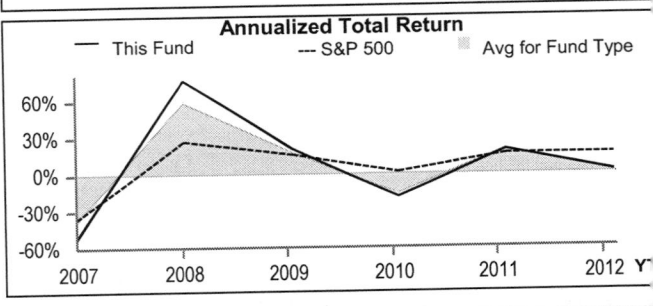

Annualized Total Return
— This Fund   --- S&P 500   Avg for Fund Type

*Vanguard Global ex-US RE I Fd ET (VNQI)

A   **Excellent**

Fund Family: Vanguard Group Inc
Fund Type: Global
Inception Date: November 1, 2010

Major Rating Factors:
Exceptional performance is the major factor driving the A (Excellent) TheStreet.com Investment Rating for *Vanguard Global ex-US RE I Fd ET. The fund currently has a performance rating of A+ (Excellent) based on an annualized return of 0.00% over the last three years and a total return of 0.80% year to date 2012. Factored into the performance evaluation is an expense ratio of 0.34% (very low).

The fund's risk rating is currently B- (Good). It carries a beta of 0.00, meaning the fund's expected move will be 0.0% for every 10% move in the market. Volatility, as measured by both the semi-deviation and a drawdown factor, is considered low. As of December 31, 2012, *Vanguard Global ex-US RE I Fd ET traded at a discount of .09% below its net asset value, which is better than its one-year historical average premium of .41%.

Gerard C. O'Reilly has been running the fund for 3 years and currently receives a manager quality ranking of 97 (0=worst, 99=best). If you desire only a moderate level of risk and strong performance, then this fund is an excellent option.

Data Date	Investment Rating	Net Assets ($Mil)	Price	Performance Rating/Pts	Total Return Y-T-D	Risk Rating/Pts
12-12	A	423.30	55.03	A+ / 9.8	0.80%	B- / 7.
2011	D	166.70	40.70	D- / 1.0	1.55%	B- / 7.

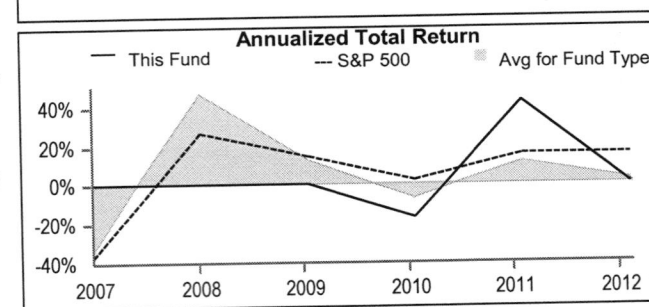

Annualized Total Return
— This Fund   --- S&P 500   Avg for Fund Type

*Vanguard Growth ETF (VUG)

C　　　**Fair**

Fund Family: Vanguard Group Inc
Fund Type: Growth
Inception Date: January 26, 2004

Major Rating Factors: Middle of the road best describes *Vanguard Growth ETF whose TheStreet.com Investment Rating is currently a C (Fair). The fund currently has a performance rating of C+ (Fair) based on an annualized return of 12.38% over the last three years and a total return of 3.32% year to date 2012. Factored into the performance evaluation is an expense ratio of 0.10% (very low).

The fund's risk rating is currently B- (Good). It carries a beta of 1.06, meaning that its performance tracks fairly well with that of the overall stock market. Volatility, as measured by both the semi-deviation and a drawdown factor, is considered low. As of December 31, 2012, *Vanguard Growth ETF traded at a discount of 3.18% below its net asset value.

Gerard C. O'Reilly has been running the fund for 19 years and currently receives a manager quality ranking of 55 (0=worst, 99=best). If you desire an average level of risk, then this fund may be an option.

Data Date	Investment Rating	Net Assets ($Mil)	Price	Performance Rating/Pts	Total Return Y-T-D	Risk Rating/Pts
12-12	C	8,446.50	71.18	C+ / 5.7	3.32%	B- / 7.6
2011	C+	6,045.60	61.76	C+ / 6.2	1.98%	B- / 7.7
2010	C+	5,099.50	61.42	C / 5.5	17.23%	C+ / 5.9
2009	C-	3,294.13	53.06	C- / 3.7	32.17%	C+ / 6.1

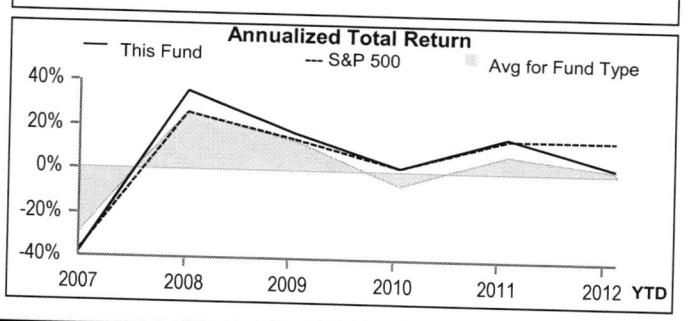

*Vanguard HealthCare Index ETF (VHT)

C+　　　**Fair**

Fund Family: Vanguard Group Inc
Fund Type: Health
Inception Date: January 26, 2004

Major Rating Factors: Middle of the road best describes *Vanguard HealthCare Index ETF whose TheStreet.com Investment Rating is currently a C+ (Fair). The fund currently has a performance rating of C+ (Fair) based on an annualized return of 12.12% over the last three years and a total return of 4.79% year to date 2012. Factored into the performance evaluation is an expense ratio of 0.14% (very low).

The fund's risk rating is currently B (Good). It carries a beta of 0.67, meaning the fund's expected move will be 6.7% for every 10% move in the market. Volatility, as measured by both the semi-deviation and a drawdown factor, is considered low. As of December 31, 2012, *Vanguard HealthCare Index ETF traded at a discount of 4.52% below its net asset value, which is better than its one-year historical average premium of .04%.

Ryan E. Ludt has been running the fund for 9 years and currently receives a manager quality ranking of 77 (0=worst, 99=best). If you desire an average level of risk, then this fund may be an option.

Data Date	Investment Rating	Net Assets ($Mil)	Price	Performance Rating/Pts	Total Return Y-T-D	Risk Rating/Pts
12-12	C+	1,014.30	71.67	C+ / 5.9	4.79%	B / 8.4
2011	C+	728.90	61.21	C / 5.2	1.27%	B / 8.2
2010	C	614.30	56.25	C- / 3.4	5.60%	C+ / 6.9
2009	C	554.25	54.19	C- / 3.6	19.98%	C+ / 6.9

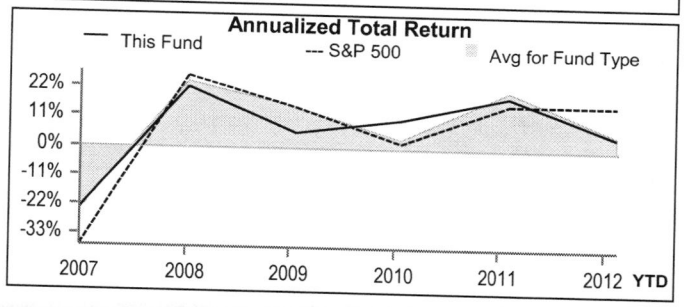

*Vanguard High Dividend Yield ETF (VYM)

C+　　　**Fair**

Fund Family: Vanguard Group Inc
Fund Type: Income
Inception Date: November 10, 2006

Major Rating Factors: Middle of the road best describes *Vanguard High Dividend Yield ETF whose TheStreet.com Investment Rating is currently a C+ (Fair). The fund currently has a performance rating of C (Fair) based on an annualized return of 12.87% over the last three years and a total return of 3.02% year to date 2012. Factored into the performance evaluation is an expense ratio of 0.11% (very low).

The fund's risk rating is currently B (Good). It carries a beta of 0.81, meaning the fund's expected move will be 8.1% for every 10% move in the market. Volatility, as measured by both the semi-deviation and a drawdown factor, is considered low. As of December 31, 2012, *Vanguard High Dividend Yield ETF traded at a discount of 2.93% below its net asset value, which is better than its one-year historical average premium of .03%.

Michael Perre has been running the fund for 7 years and currently receives a manager quality ranking of 74 (0=worst, 99=best). If you desire an average level of risk, then this fund may be an option.

Data Date	Investment Rating	Net Assets ($Mil)	Price	Performance Rating/Pts	Total Return Y-T-D	Risk Rating/Pts
12-12	C+	4,230.70	49.38	C / 5.3	3.02%	B / 8.7
2011	C+	2,407.50	45.26	C+ / 5.9	0.71%	B- / 7.8
2010	C-	931.40	42.22	C- / 3.5	14.25%	C+ / 6.0
2009	D	278.92	38.00	D / 1.6	14.68%	C+ / 6.1

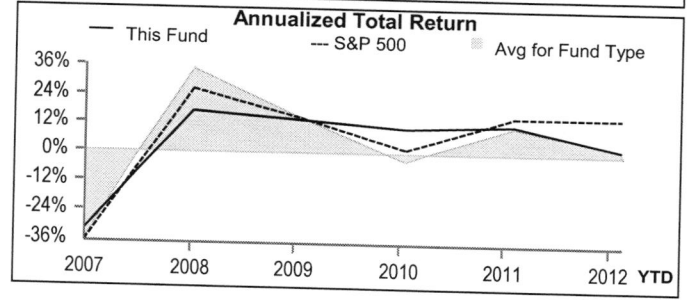

*Vanguard Industrials Index ETF (VIS)

C+   Fair

Fund Family: Vanguard Group Inc
Fund Type: Income
Inception Date: September 23, 2004

Major Rating Factors: Middle of the road best describes *Vanguard Industrials Index ETF whose TheStreet.com Investment Rating is currently a C+ (Fair). The fund currently has a performance rating of C+ (Fair) based on an annualized return of 12.92% over the last three years and a total return of 3.20% year to date 2012. Factored into the performance evaluation is an expense ratio of 0.14% (very low).

The fund's risk rating is currently B- (Good). It carries a beta of 1.25, meaning it is expected to move 12.5% for every 10% move in the market. Volatility, as measured by both the semi-deviation and a drawdown factor, is considered low. As of December 31, 2012, *Vanguard Industrials Index ETF traded at a discount of 3.06% below its net asset value, which is better than its one-year historical average discount of .01%.

Jeffrey D. Miller has been running the fund for 3 years and currently receives a manager quality ranking of 48 (0=worst, 99=best). If you desire an average level of risk, then this fund may be an option.

Data Date	Investment Rating	Net Assets ($Mil)	Price	Performance Rating/Pts	Total Return Y-T-D	Risk Rating/Pts
12-12	C+	515.50	71.25	C+ / 6.4	3.20%	B- / 7.6
2011	C	435.10	62.09	C / 5.3	2.37%	B- / 7.3
2010	C	440.40	64.82	C / 5.5	27.32%	C / 5.3
2009	D	185.86	51.58	D / 2.1	17.86%	C+ / 5.6

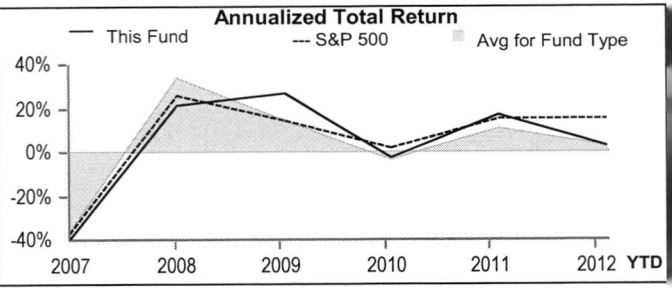

Annualized Total Return

*Vanguard Info Tech Ind ETF (VGT)

C-   Fair

Fund Family: Vanguard Group Inc
Fund Type: Growth
Inception Date: January 26, 2004

Major Rating Factors: Middle of the road best describes *Vanguard Info Tech Ind ETF whose TheStreet.com Investment Rating is currently a C- (Fair). The fund currently has a performance rating of C- (Fair) based on an annualized return of 9.94% over the last three years and a total return of 2.79% year to date 2012. Factored into the performance evaluation is an expense ratio of 0.14% (very low).

The fund's risk rating is currently B- (Good). It carries a beta of 1.19, meaning it is expected to move 11.9% for every 10% move in the market. Volatility, as measured by both the semi-deviation and a drawdown factor, is considered low. As of December 31, 2012, *Vanguard Info Tech Ind ETF traded at a discount of 2.69% below its net asset value, which is better than its one-year historical average premium of .04%.

Jeffrey D. Miller has been running the fund for 3 years and currently receives a manager quality ranking of 28 (0=worst, 99=best). If you desire an average level of risk, then this fund may be an option.

Data Date	Investment Rating	Net Assets ($Mil)	Price	Performance Rating/Pts	Total Return Y-T-D	Risk Rating/Pts
12-12	C-	2,484.10	69.11	C- / 4.2	2.79%	B- / 7.0
2011	C+	1,891.00	61.37	B- / 7.0	2.31%	B- / 7.3
2010	C+	1,501.60	61.52	C+ / 6.3	12.78%	C+ / 5.6
2009	C+	639.19	54.87	C+ / 6.5	55.70%	C+ / 5.6

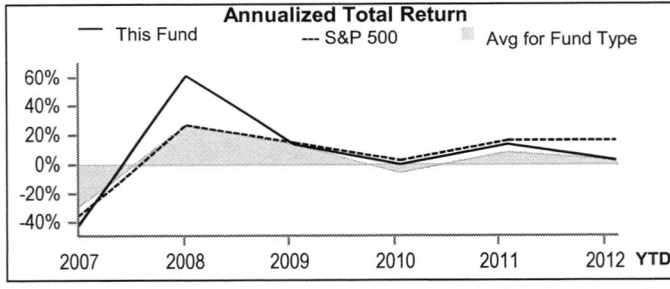

Annualized Total Return

*Vanguard Intermediate Term Bond (BIV)

C   Fair

Fund Family: Vanguard Group Inc
Fund Type: General - Investment Grade
Inception Date: April 3, 2007

Major Rating Factors: Middle of the road best describes *Vanguard Intermediate Term Bond whose TheStreet.com Investment Rating is currently a C (Fair). The fund currently has a performance rating of C- (Fair) based on an annualized return of 8.39% over the last three years and a total return of -0.22% year to date 2012. Factored into the performance evaluation is an expense ratio of 0.10% (very low).

The fund's risk rating is currently B+ (Good). It carries a beta of 1.64, meaning it is expected to move 16.4% for every 10% move in the market. Volatility, as measured by both the semi-deviation and a drawdown factor, is considered very low. As of December 31, 2012, *Vanguard Intermediate Term Bond traded at a premium of .46% above its net asset value, which is worse than its one-year historical average premium of .28%.

Joshua C. Barrickman has been running the fund for 5 years and currently receives a manager quality ranking of 41 (0=worst, 99=best). If you desire an average level of risk, then this fund may be an option.

Data Date	Investment Rating	Net Assets ($Mil)	Price	Performance Rating/Pts	Total Return Y-T-D	Risk Rating/Pts
12-12	C	4,368.20	88.25	C- / 3.1	-0.22%	B+ / 9.5
2011	C+	2,780.90	86.97	C- / 3.9	-0.01%	B+ / 9.6
2010	B	1,931.90	82.49	C / 5.4	9.13%	B / 8.6
2009	C+	852.24	79.07	C- / 3.6	5.14%	B / 8.8

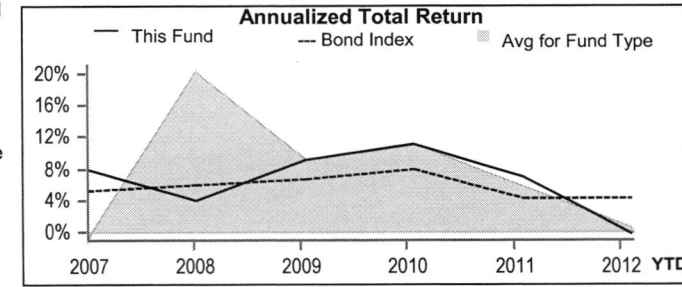

Annualized Total Return

*Vanguard Intm-Term Corp Bd Idx E (VCIT)

C   **Fair**

Fund Family: Vanguard Group Inc
Fund Type: Corporate - Investment Grade
Inception Date: November 19, 2009

Major Rating Factors: Middle of the road best describes *Vanguard Intm-Term Corp Bd Idx E whose TheStreet.com Investment Rating is currently a C (Fair). The fund currently has a performance rating of C- (Fair) based on an annualized return of 9.19% over the last three years and a total return of 0.01% year to date 2012. Factored into the performance evaluation is an expense ratio of 0.12% (very low).

The fund's risk rating is currently B+ (Good). It carries a beta of 1.12, meaning it is expected to move 11.2% for every 10% move in the market. Volatility, as measured by both the semi-deviation and a drawdown factor, is considered very low. As of December 31, 2012, *Vanguard Intm-Term Corp Bd Idx E traded at a premium of .26% above its net asset value, which is better than its one-year historical average premium of .58%.

Joshua C. Barrickman has been running the fund for 4 years and currently receives a manager quality ranking of 52 (0=worst, 99=best). If you desire an average level of risk, then this fund may be an option.

Data Date	Investment Rating	Net Assets ($Mil)	Price	Performance Rating/Pts	Total Return Y-T-D	Risk Rating/Pts
12-12	C	3,222.70	87.66	C- / 3.5	0.01%	B+ / 9.7
2011	C+	953.70	82.37	C- / 4.0	-0.11%	B+ / 9.7
2010	B	386.10	78.68	C+ / 6.2	9.96%	B / 8.9

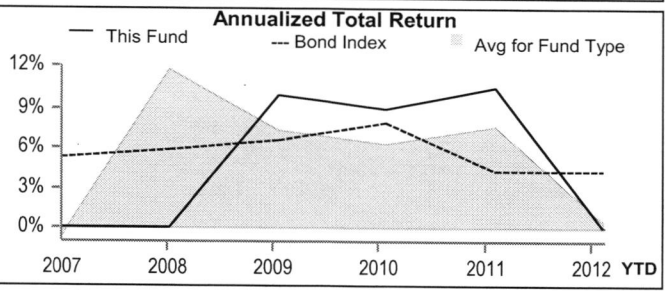

*Vanguard Intm-Term Govt Bd Idx E (VGIT)

C-   **Fair**

Fund Family: Vanguard Group Inc
Fund Type: US Government/Agency
Inception Date: November 19, 2009

Major Rating Factors:
Disappointing performance is the major factor driving the C- (Fair) TheStreet.com Investment Rating for *Vanguard Intm-Term Govt Bd Idx E. The fund currently has a performance rating of D+ (Weak) based on an annualized return of 5.80% over the last three years and a total return of -0.14% year to date 2012. Factored into the performance evaluation is an expense ratio of 0.12% (very low).

The fund's risk rating is currently B+ (Good). It carries a beta of 0.25, meaning the fund's expected move will be 2.5% for every 10% move in the market. Volatility, as measured by both the semi-deviation and a drawdown factor, is considered very low. As of December 31, 2012, *Vanguard Intm-Term Govt Bd Idx E traded at a premium of .17% above its net asset value, which is worse than its one-year historical average premium of .05%.

Gregory Davis has been running the fund for 4 years and currently receives a manager quality ranking of 72 (0=worst, 99=best). This fund offers only a moderate level of risk but investors looking for strong performance are still waiting.

Data Date	Investment Rating	Net Assets ($Mil)	Price	Performance Rating/Pts	Total Return Y-T-D	Risk Rating/Pts
12-12	C-	126.30	65.41	D+ / 2.4	-0.14%	B+ / 9.6
2011	C+	81.80	65.66	C- / 4.0	-0.32%	B+ / 9.6
2010	B	34.70	61.23	C / 4.5	7.51%	B / 8.8

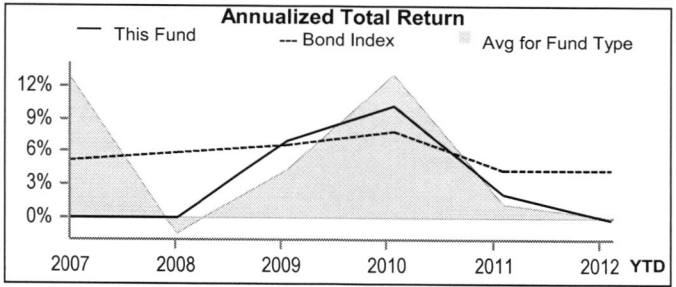

*Vanguard Large Cap ETF (VV)

C   **Fair**

Fund Family: Vanguard Group Inc
Fund Type: Growth
Inception Date: January 27, 2004

Major Rating Factors: Middle of the road best describes *Vanguard Large Cap ETF whose TheStreet.com Investment Rating is currently a C (Fair). The fund currently has a performance rating of C (Fair) based on an annualized return of 11.46% over the last three years and a total return of 3.41% year to date 2012. Factored into the performance evaluation is an expense ratio of 0.10% (very low).

The fund's risk rating is currently B (Good). It carries a beta of 1.02, meaning that its performance tracks fairly well with that of the overall stock market. Volatility, as measured by both the semi-deviation and a drawdown factor, is considered low. As of December 31, 2012, *Vanguard Large Cap ETF traded at a discount of 3.27% below its net asset value.

Ryan E. Ludt has been running the fund for 9 years and currently receives a manager quality ranking of 51 (0=worst, 99=best). If you desire an average level of risk, then this fund may be an option.

Data Date	Investment Rating	Net Assets ($Mil)	Price	Performance Rating/Pts	Total Return Y-T-D	Risk Rating/Pts
12-12	C	3,559.80	65.16	C / 5.3	3.41%	B / 8.0
2011	C+	3,020.90	57.30	C / 5.3	1.78%	B- / 7.9
2010	C-	2,857.80	57.61	C- / 4.2	15.93%	C+ / 6.0
2009	D+	2,173.77	50.67	D+ / 2.5	24.07%	C+ / 6.1

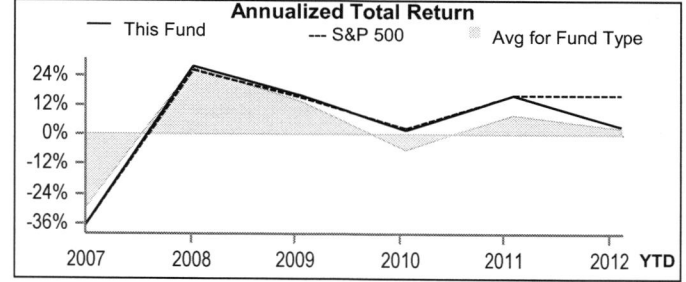

*Vanguard Long Term Bd Idx ETF (BLV)   C+   Fair

Fund Family: Vanguard Group Inc
Fund Type: General - Investment Grade
Inception Date: April 3, 2007

Major Rating Factors: Middle of the road best describes *Vanguard Long Term Bd Idx ETF whose TheStreet.com Investment Rating is currently a C+ (Fair). The fund currently has a performance rating of C (Fair) based on an annualized return of 12.84% over the last three years and a total return of -0.54% year to date 2012. Factored into the performance evaluation is an expense ratio of 0.10% (very low).

The fund's risk rating is currently B+ (Good). It carries a beta of 3.04, meaning it is expected to move 30.4% for every 10% move in the market. Volatility, as measured by both the semi-deviation and a drawdown factor, is considered very low. As of December 31, 2012, *Vanguard Long Term Bd Idx ETF traded at a premium of .74% above its net asset value, which is worse than its one-year historical average premium of .28%.

Gregory Davis has been running the fund for 5 years and currently receives a manager quality ranking of 21 (0=worst, 99=best). If you desire an average level of risk, then this fund may be an option.

Data Date	Investment Rating	Net Assets ($Mil)	Price	Performance Rating/Pts	Total Return Y-T-D	Risk Rating/Pts
12-12	C+	832.40	93.87	C / 4.4	-0.54%	B+ / 9.1
2011	B-	511.80	92.01	C / 5.5	-0.85%	B+ / 9.1
2010	B	324.20	79.09	C / 5.1	10.01%	B / 8.2
2009	C	140.92	76.16	D+ / 2.7	2.26%	B / 8.4

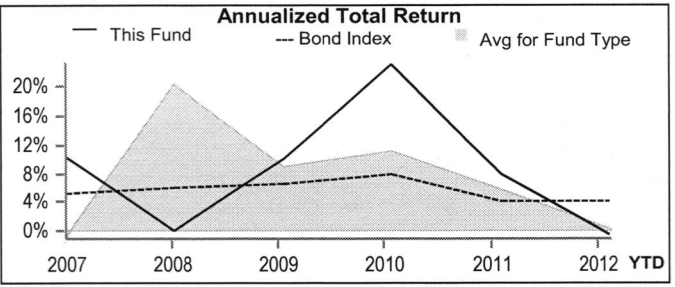

*Vanguard Long-Term Corp Bd Idx E (VCLT)   C+   Fair

Fund Family: Vanguard Group Inc
Fund Type: Corporate - Investment Grade
Inception Date: November 19, 2009

Major Rating Factors: Middle of the road best describes *Vanguard Long-Term Corp Bd Idx E whose TheStreet.com Investment Rating is currently a C+ (Fair). The fund currently has a performance rating of C (Fair) based on an annualized return of 12.48% over the last three years and a total return of 0.04% year to date 2012. Factored into the performance evaluation is an expense ratio of 0.12% (very low).

The fund's risk rating is currently B+ (Good). It carries a beta of 1.88, meaning it is expected to move 18.8% for every 10% move in the market. Volatility, as measured by both the semi-deviation and a drawdown factor, is considered very low. As of December 31, 2012, *Vanguard Long-Term Corp Bd Idx E traded at a premium of .21% above its net asset value, which is better than its one-year historical average premium of .74%.

Joshua C. Barrickman has been running the fund for 4 years and currently receives a manager quality ranking of 28 (0=worst, 99=best). If you desire an average level of risk, then this fund may be an option.

Data Date	Investment Rating	Net Assets ($Mil)	Price	Performance Rating/Pts	Total Return Y-T-D	Risk Rating/Pts
12-12	C+	1,164.00	91.70	C / 4.5	0.04%	B+ / 9.2
2011	B+	401.30	86.70	B- / 7.0	-0.36%	B+ / 9.3
2010	B	54.90	77.52	C+ / 6.2	10.62%	B / 8.6

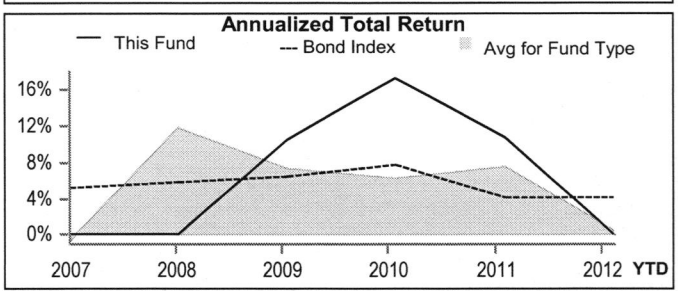

*Vanguard Long-Term Govt Bd Idx E (VGLT)   C   Fair

Fund Family: Vanguard Group Inc
Fund Type: US Government/Agency
Inception Date: November 19, 2009

Major Rating Factors: Middle of the road best describes *Vanguard Long-Term Govt Bd Idx E whose TheStreet.com Investment Rating is currently a C (Fair). The fund currently has a performance rating of C- (Fair) based on an annualized return of 12.28% over the last three years and a total return of -1.05% year to date 2012. Factored into the performance evaluation is an expense ratio of 0.12% (very low).

The fund's risk rating is currently B (Good). It carries a beta of 1.04, meaning that its performance tracks fairly well with that of the overall stock market. Volatility, as measured by both the semi-deviation and a drawdown factor, is considered low. As of December 31, 2012, *Vanguard Long-Term Govt Bd Idx E traded at a premium of 1.06% above its net asset value, which is worse than its one-year historical average premium of .09%.

Gregory Davis has been running the fund for 4 years and currently receives a manager quality ranking of 44 (0=worst, 99=best). If you desire an average level of risk, then this fund may be an option.

Data Date	Investment Rating	Net Assets ($Mil)	Price	Performance Rating/Pts	Total Return Y-T-D	Risk Rating/Pts
12-12	C	81.20	75.30	C- / 3.8	-1.05%	B / 8.7
2011	A	63.90	75.11	A- / 9.0	-1.36%	B / 8.8
2010	C	72.30	60.27	D+ / 2.9	8.98%	B / 8.1

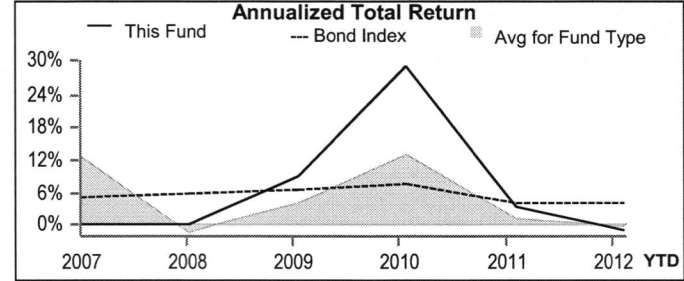

*Vanguard Materials ETF (VAW)

C-   **Fair**

Fund Family: Vanguard Group Inc
Fund Type: Income
Inception Date: January 26, 2004

Major Rating Factors: Middle of the road best describes *Vanguard Materials ETF whose TheStreet.com Investment Rating is currently a C- (Fair). The fund currently has a performance rating of C (Fair) based on an annualized return of 10.26% over the last three years and a total return of 3.91% year to date 2012. Factored into the performance evaluation is an expense ratio of 0.14% (very low).

The fund's risk rating is currently B- (Good). It carries a beta of 1.42, meaning it is expected to move 14.2% for every 10% move in the market. Volatility, as measured by both the semi-deviation and a drawdown factor, is considered low. As of December 31, 2012, *Vanguard Materials ETF traded at a discount of 3.75% below its net asset value, which is better than its one-year historical average premium of .01%.

Michael D. Eyre has been running the fund for 3 years and currently receives a manager quality ranking of 22 (0=worst, 99=best). If you desire an average level of risk, then this fund may be an option.

Data Date	Investment Rating	Net Assets ($Mil)	Price	Perfor-mance Rating/Pts	Total Return Y-T-D	Risk Rating/Pts
12-12	C-	700.40	84.21	C / 4.8	3.91%	B- / 7.1
2011	C+	530.10	73.13	C+ / 6.2	3.65%	B- / 7.0
2010	C+	614.30	82.60	C+ / 6.7	24.46%	C / 5.0
2009	C	375.30	67.82	C+ / 6.1	46.33%	C / 5.2

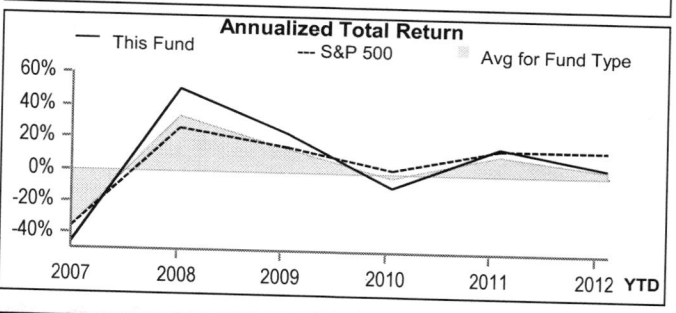

*Vanguard Mega Cap 300 ETF (MGC)

C   **Fair**

Fund Family: Vanguard Group Inc
Fund Type: Income
Inception Date: December 17, 2007

Major Rating Factors: Middle of the road best describes *Vanguard Mega Cap 300 ETF whose TheStreet.com Investment Rating is currently a C (Fair). The fund currently has a performance rating of C (Fair) based on an annualized return of 11.05% over the last three years and a total return of 3.26% year to date 2012. Factored into the performance evaluation is an expense ratio of 0.12% (very low).

The fund's risk rating is currently B (Good). It carries a beta of 0.99, meaning that its performance tracks fairly well with that of the overall stock market. Volatility, as measured by both the semi-deviation and a drawdown factor, is considered low. As of December 31, 2012, *Vanguard Mega Cap 300 ETF traded at a discount of 3.15% below its net asset value, which is better than its one-year historical average premium of .02%.

Ryan E. Ludt has been running the fund for 6 years and currently receives a manager quality ranking of 50 (0=worst, 99=best). If you desire an average level of risk, then this fund may be an option.

Data Date	Investment Rating	Net Assets ($Mil)	Price	Perfor-mance Rating/Pts	Total Return Y-T-D	Risk Rating/Pts
12-12	C	454.00	48.83	C / 5.1	3.26%	B / 8.0
2011	C	331.00	43.01	C / 5.1	1.68%	B- / 7.9
2010	C-	246.60	42.92	C- / 3.7	13.77%	C+ / 6.1
2009	A-	198.72	38.50	B / 8.2	21.99%	C+ / 6.2

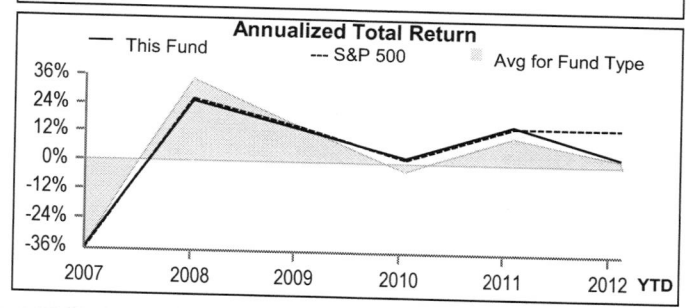

*Vanguard Mega Cap 300 Growth ETF (MGK)

C   **Fair**

Fund Family: Vanguard Group Inc
Fund Type: Growth
Inception Date: December 17, 2007

Major Rating Factors: Middle of the road best describes *Vanguard Mega Cap 300 Growth ETF whose TheStreet.com Investment Rating is currently a C (Fair). The fund currently has a performance rating of C (Fair) based on an annualized return of 12.03% over the last three years and a total return of 3.23% year to date 2012. Factored into the performance evaluation is an expense ratio of 0.12% (very low).

The fund's risk rating is currently B- (Good). It carries a beta of 1.04, meaning that its performance tracks fairly well with that of the overall stock market. Volatility, as measured by both the semi-deviation and a drawdown factor, is considered low. As of December 31, 2012, *Vanguard Mega Cap 300 Growth ETF traded at a discount of 3.13% below its net asset value, which is better than its one-year historical average premium of .02%.

Michael D. Eyre has been running the fund for 3 years and currently receives a manager quality ranking of 53 (0=worst, 99=best). If you desire an average level of risk, then this fund may be an option.

Data Date	Investment Rating	Net Assets ($Mil)	Price	Perfor-mance Rating/Pts	Total Return Y-T-D	Risk Rating/Pts
12-12	C	779.70	55.46	C / 5.4	3.23%	B- / 7.6
2011	C+	533.90	48.10	C+ / 6.1	1.85%	B- / 7.7
2010	C	346.90	47.31	C / 5.1	14.53%	C+ / 6.1
2009	A	36.25	41.87	B+ / 8.6	31.09%	C+ / 6.1

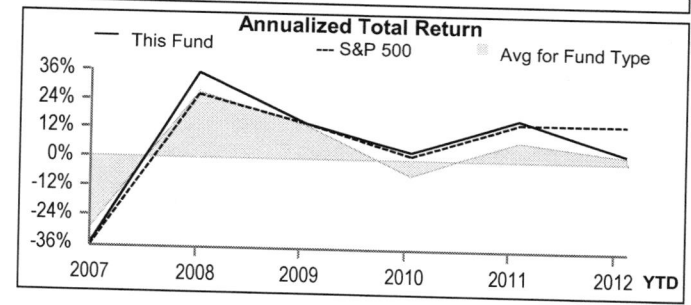

*Vanguard Mega Cap 300 Value ETF (MGV)

C **Fair**

Fund Family: Vanguard Group Inc
Fund Type: Income
Inception Date: December 17, 2007

Major Rating Factors: Middle of the road best describes *Vanguard Mega Cap 300 Value ETF whose TheStreet.com Investment Rating is currently a C (Fair). The fund currently has a performance rating of C (Fair) based on an annualized return of 10.08% over the last three years and a total return of 3.49% year to date 2012. Factored into the performance evaluation is an expense ratio of 0.12% (very low).

The fund's risk rating is currently B (Good). It carries a beta of 0.96, meaning that its performance tracks fairly well with that of the overall stock market. Volatility, as measured by both the semi-deviation and a drawdown factor, is considered low. As of December 31, 2012, *Vanguard Mega Cap 300 Value ETF traded at a discount of 3.35% below its net asset value, which is better than its one-year historical average premium of .03%.

Michael D. Eyre has been running the fund for 3 years and currently receives a manager quality ranking of 45 (0=worst, 99=best). If you desire an average level of risk, then this fund may be an option.

Data Date	Investment Rating	Net Assets ($Mil)	Price	Performance Rating/Pts	Total Return Y-T-D	Risk Rating/Pts
12-12	C	430.70	42.67	C / 4.8	3.49%	B / 8.2
2011	C	347.40	38.17	C / 4.3	1.55%	B- / 7.8
2010	D+	259.50	38.72	D+ / 2.4	13.16%	C+ / 6.0
2009	B	163.14	35.10	B- / 7.5	13.22%	C+ / 6.1

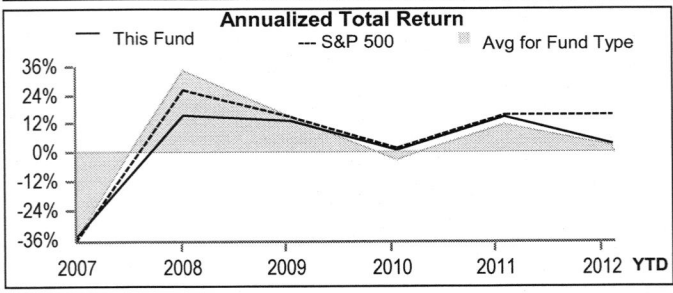

Annualized Total Return

*Vanguard Mid Cap ETF (VO)

C+ **Fair**

Fund Family: Vanguard Group Inc
Fund Type: Growth
Inception Date: January 26, 2004

Major Rating Factors: Middle of the road best describes *Vanguard Mid Cap ETF whose TheStreet.com Investment Rating is currently a C+ (Fair). The fund currently has a performance rating of C+ (Fair) based on an annualized return of 12.95% over the last three years and a total return of 3.37% year to date 2012. Factored into the performance evaluation is an expense ratio of 0.10% (very low).

The fund's risk rating is currently B- (Good). It carries a beta of 1.13, meaning it is expected to move 11.3% for every 10% move in the market. Volatility, as measured by both the semi-deviation and a drawdown factor, is considered low. As of December 31, 2012, *Vanguard Mid Cap ETF traded at a discount of 3.25% below its net asset value.

Donald M. Butler has been running the fund for 15 years and currently receives a manager quality ranking of 55 (0=worst, 99=best). If you desire an average level of risk, then this fund may be an option.

Data Date	Investment Rating	Net Assets ($Mil)	Price	Performance Rating/Pts	Total Return Y-T-D	Risk Rating/Pts
12-12	C+	3,828.60	82.44	C+ / 6.3	3.37%	B- / 7.8
2011	C+	3,241.00	71.94	C+ / 6.5	1.83%	B- / 7.7
2010	C+	3,356.30	74.46	C+ / 6.7	25.68%	C / 5.4
2009	C-	1,482.72	59.95	C- / 3.3	36.24%	C+ / 5.7

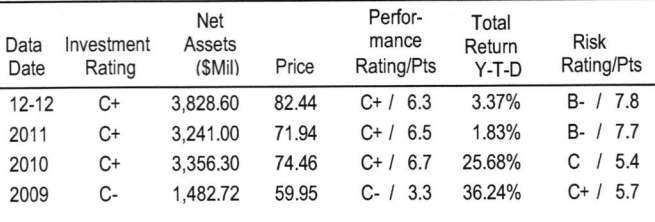

Annualized Total Return

*Vanguard Mid Cap Growth ETF (VOT)

C+ **Fair**

Fund Family: Vanguard Group Inc
Fund Type: Growth
Inception Date: August 17, 2006

Major Rating Factors: Middle of the road best describes *Vanguard Mid Cap Growth ETF whose TheStreet.com Investment Rating is currently a C+ (Fair). The fund currently has a performance rating of C+ (Fair) based on an annualized return of 13.53% over the last three years and a total return of 3.65% year to date 2012. Factored into the performance evaluation is an expense ratio of 0.10% (very low).

The fund's risk rating is currently B- (Good). It carries a beta of 1.18, meaning it is expected to move 11.8% for every 10% move in the market. Volatility, as measured by both the semi-deviation and a drawdown factor, is considered low. As of December 31, 2012, *Vanguard Mid Cap Growth ETF traded at a discount of 3.49% below its net asset value, which is better than its one-year historical average discount of .01%.

Gerard C. O'Reilly has been running the fund for 7 years and currently receives a manager quality ranking of 51 (0=worst, 99=best). If you desire an average level of risk, then this fund may be an option.

Data Date	Investment Rating	Net Assets ($Mil)	Price	Performance Rating/Pts	Total Return Y-T-D	Risk Rating/Pts
12-12	C+	1,165.30	68.58	C+ / 6.4	3.65%	B- / 7.7
2011	C+	1,095.50	59.54	C+ / 6.6	2.27%	B- / 7.5
2010	C+	913.50	62.30	C+ / 6.5	29.14%	C / 5.1
2009	C-	523.74	48.49	C- / 3.5	37.89%	C / 5.5

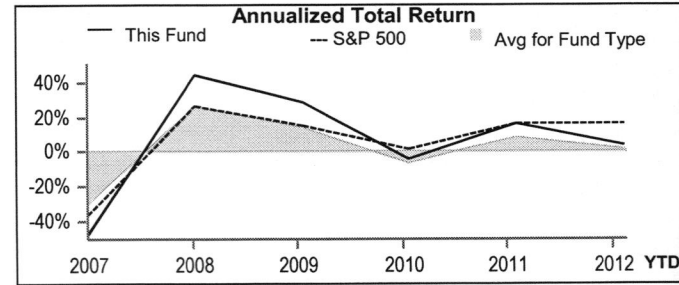

Annualized Total Return

*Vanguard Mid Cap Value Index ETF (VOE)

C+ **Fair**

Fund Family: Vanguard Group Inc
Fund Type: Growth
Inception Date: August 17, 2006

Major Rating Factors: Middle of the road best describes *Vanguard Mid Cap Value Index ETF whose TheStreet.com Investment Rating is currently a C+ (Fair). The fund currently has a performance rating of C+ (Fair) based on an annualized return of 12.24% over the last three years and a total return of 3.50% year to date 2012. Factored into the performance evaluation is an expense ratio of 0.10% (very low).

The fund's risk rating is currently B (Good). It carries a beta of 1.07, meaning that its performance tracks fairly well with that of the overall stock market. Volatility, as measured by both the semi-deviation and a drawdown factor, is considered low. As of December 31, 2012, *Vanguard Mid Cap Value Index ETF traded at a discount of 3.37% below its net asset value, which is better than its one-year historical average premium of .02%.

Donald M. Butler has been running the fund for 7 years and currently receives a manager quality ranking of 55 (0=worst, 99=best). If you desire an average level of risk, then this fund may be an option.

Data Date	Investment Rating	Net Assets ($Mil)	Price	Performance Rating/Pts	Total Return Y-T-D	Risk Rating/Pts
12-12	C+	1,123.40	58.81	C+ / 6.0	3.50%	B / 8.0
2011	C+	784.60	51.67	C+ / 6.3	1.41%	B- / 7.9
2010	C+	688.10	53.01	C+ / 6.7	21.76%	C+ / 5.7
2009	C-	492.35	44.37	C- / 3.0	34.58%	C+ / 5.7

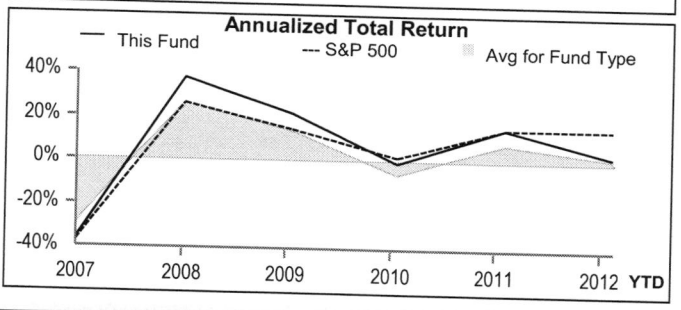

*Vanguard Mort-Backed Secs Idx ET (VMBS)

C- **Fair**

Fund Family: Vanguard Group Inc
Fund Type: Mortgage
Inception Date: November 19, 2009

Major Rating Factors:
Disappointing performance is the major factor driving the C- (Fair) TheStreet.com Investment Rating for *Vanguard Mort-Backed Secs Idx ET. The fund currently has a performance rating of D (Weak) based on an annualized return of 4.10% over the last three years and a total return of -0.10% year to date 2012. Factored into the performance evaluation is an expense ratio of 0.12% (very low).

The fund's risk rating is currently B+ (Good). It carries a beta of 1.04, meaning that its performance tracks fairly well with that of the overall stock market. Volatility, as measured by both the semi-deviation and a drawdown factor, is considered very low. As of December 31, 2012, *Vanguard Mort-Backed Secs Idx ET traded at a premium of .13% above its net asset value, which is better than its one-year historical average premium of .20%.

Gregory Davis has been running the fund for 4 years and currently receives a manager quality ranking of 48 (0=worst, 99=best). This fund offers only a moderate level of risk but investors looking for strong performance are still waiting.

Data Date	Investment Rating	Net Assets ($Mil)	Price	Performance Rating/Pts	Total Return Y-T-D	Risk Rating/Pts
12-12	C-	288.60	52.20	D / 2.1	-0.10%	B+ / 9.8
2011	C+	129.50	51.88	C- / 3.3	0.13%	B+ / 9.9
2010	B	36.00	50.28	C / 4.4	5.44%	B / 8.9

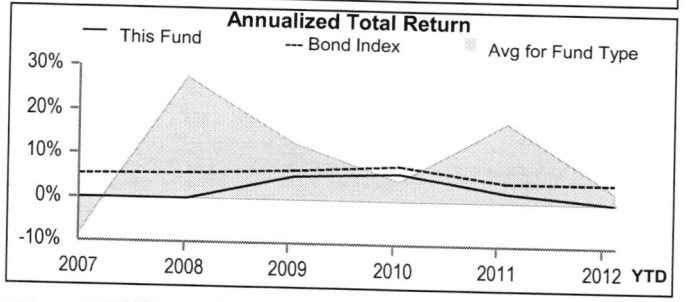

*Vanguard MSCI EAFE ETF (VEA)

D **Weak**

Fund Family: Vanguard Group Inc
Fund Type: Foreign
Inception Date: July 20, 2007

Major Rating Factors: *Vanguard MSCI EAFE ETF receives a TheStreet.com Investment Rating of D (Weak). The fund currently has a performance rating of C- (Fair) based on an annualized return of 3.81% over the last three years and a total return of 2.19% year to date 2012. Factored into the performance evaluation is an expense ratio of 0.11% (very low).

The fund's risk rating is currently C (Fair). It carries a beta of 1.03, meaning that its performance tracks fairly well with that of the overall stock market. Volatility, as measured by both the semi-deviation and a drawdown factor, is considered average. As of December 31, 2012, *Vanguard MSCI EAFE ETF traded at a discount of 1.87% below its net asset value, which is better than its one-year historical average premium of .21%.

Donald M. Butler has been running the fund for 5 years and currently receives a manager quality ranking of 51 (0=worst, 99=best). If you desire an average level of risk, then this fund may be an option.

Data Date	Investment Rating	Net Assets ($Mil)	Price	Performance Rating/Pts	Total Return Y-T-D	Risk Rating/Pts
12-12	D	10,212.70	35.23	C- / 4.1	2.19%	C / 5.4
2011	D+	6,435.30	30.63	D+ / 2.6	-0.55%	B- / 7.4
2010	D-	4,829.40	36.15	D / 1.8	8.33%	C- / 3.6
2009	B	3,068.69	34.20	B / 8.2	26.41%	C / 4.9

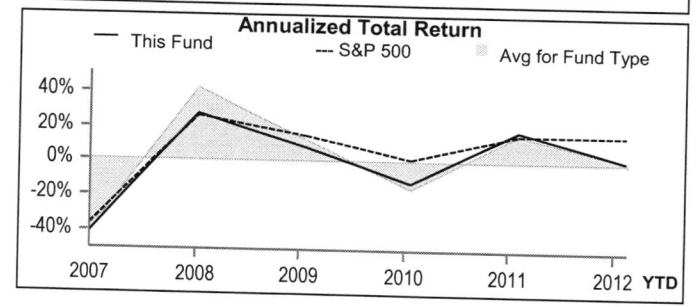

* Denotes ETF Fund

*Vanguard MSCI Europe ETF (VGK)

D+   **Weak**

Fund Family: Vanguard Group Inc
Fund Type: Foreign
Inception Date: March 4, 2005

Major Rating Factors: *Vanguard MSCI Europe ETF receives a TheStreet.com Investment Rating of D+ (Weak). The fund currently has a performance rating of C (Fair) based on an annualized return of 4.57% over the last three years and a total return of 2.48% year to date 2012. Factored into the performance evaluation is an expense ratio of 0.13% (very low).

The fund's risk rating is currently C (Fair). It carries a beta of 1.17, meaning it is expected to move 11.7% for every 10% move in the market. Volatility, as measured by both the semi-deviation and a drawdown factor, is considered average. As of December 31, 2012, *Vanguard MSCI Europe ETF traded at a discount of 2.12% below its net asset value, which is better than its one-year historical average premium of .15%.

Gerard C. O'Reilly has been running the fund for 5 years and currently receives a manager quality ranking of 49 (0=worst, 99=best). If you desire an average level of risk, then this fund may be an option.

Data Date	Investment Rating	Net Assets ($Mil)	Price	Performance Rating/Pts	Total Return Y-T-D	Risk Rating/Pts
12-12	D+	4,379.10	48.84	C / 4.9	2.48%	C / 5.1
2011	D+	2,220.40	41.43	D+ / 2.7	-1.16%	B- / 7.1
2010	E+	2,784.40	49.09	D- / 1.4	6.05%	C- / 3.4
2009	D	1,544.20	48.48	D / 2.2	29.11%	C / 4.8

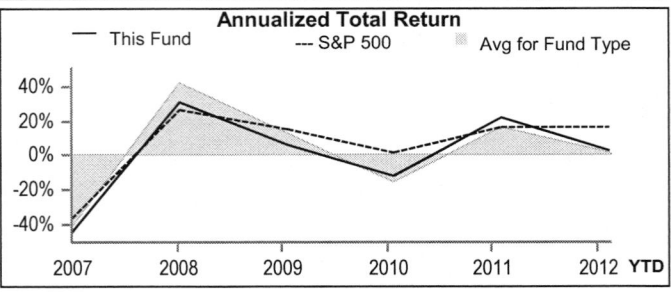

---

*Vanguard MSCI Pacific Fund ETF (VPL)

C-   **Fair**

Fund Family: Vanguard Group Inc
Fund Type: Foreign
Inception Date: March 4, 2005

Major Rating Factors: Middle of the road best describes *Vanguard MSCI Pacific Fund ETF whose TheStreet.com Investment Rating is currently a C- (Fair). The fund currently has a performance rating of C- (Fair) based on an annualized return of 3.45% over the last three years and a total return of 1.42% year to date 2012. Factored into the performance evaluation is an expense ratio of 0.14% (very low).

The fund's risk rating is currently B- (Good). It carries a beta of 0.78, meaning the fund's expected move will be 7.8% for every 10% move in the market. Volatility, as measured by both the semi-deviation and a drawdown factor, is considered low. As of December 31, 2012, *Vanguard MSCI Pacific Fund ETF traded at a discount of 1.09% below its net asset value, which is better than its one-year historical average premium of .02%.

Michael H. Buek has been running the fund for 16 years and currently receives a manager quality ranking of 65 (0=worst, 99=best). If you desire an average level of risk, then this fund may be an option.

Data Date	Investment Rating	Net Assets ($Mil)	Price	Performance Rating/Pts	Total Return Y-T-D	Risk Rating/Pts
12-12	C-	1,599.30	53.39	C- / 3.4	1.42%	B- / 7.7
2011	C-	1,415.50	47.59	D+ / 2.7	0.25%	B- / 7.8
2010	C-	1,548.70	57.04	C- / 3.7	15.50%	C / 5.3
2009	D	1,130.26	51.32	D / 1.7	19.44%	C / 5.4

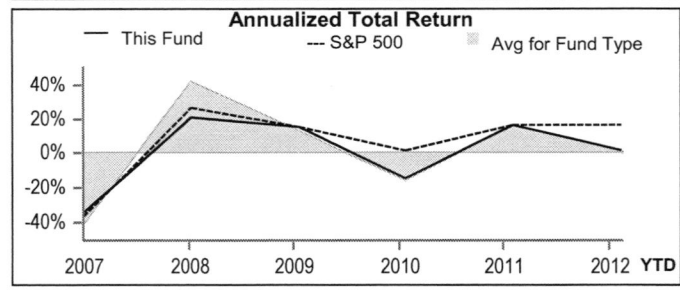

---

*Vanguard REIT ETF (VNQ)

B   **Good**

Fund Family: Vanguard Group Inc
Fund Type: Income
Inception Date: September 23, 2004

Major Rating Factors: Strong performance is the major factor driving the B (Good) TheStreet.com Investment Rating for *Vanguard REIT ETF. The fund currently has a performance rating of B (Good) based on an annualized return of 18.86% over the last three years and a total return of 2.07% year to date 2012. Factored into the performance evaluation is an expense ratio of 0.10% (very low).

The fund's risk rating is currently B- (Good). It carries a beta of 1.01, meaning that its performance tracks fairly well with that of the overall stock market. Volatility, as measured by both the semi-deviation and a drawdown factor, is considered low. As of December 31, 2012, *Vanguard REIT ETF traded at a discount of 2.05% below its net asset value.

Gerard C. O'Reilly has been running the fund for 17 years and currently receives a manager quality ranking of 83 (0=worst, 99=best). If you desire only a moderate level of risk and strong performance, then this fund is an excellent option.

Data Date	Investment Rating	Net Assets ($Mil)	Price	Performance Rating/Pts	Total Return Y-T-D	Risk Rating/Pts
12-12	B	14,609.30	65.80	B / 7.6	2.07%	B- / 7.6
2011	C+	9,307.90	58.00	B / 7.8	-0.28%	C+ / 6.4
2010	C+	7,532.70	55.37	B / 7.7	28.43%	C- / 4.2
2009	D-	2,491.89	44.74	D / 1.9	34.15%	C- / 4.1

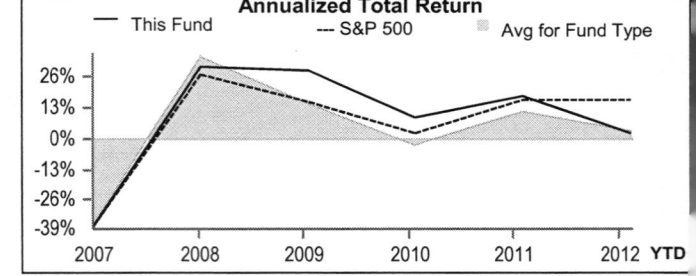

*Vanguard Russell 1000 Gro Idx ET (VONG)

B **Good**

Fund Family: Vanguard Group Inc
Fund Type: Growth
Inception Date: September 20, 2010

Major Rating Factors: *Vanguard Russell 1000 Gro Idx ET receives a TheStreet.com Investment Rating of B (Good). The fund currently has a performance rating of C+ (Fair) based on an annualized return of 0.00% over the last three years and a total return of 3.25% year to date 2012. Factored into the performance evaluation is an expense ratio of 0.15% (very low).

The fund's risk rating is currently B (Good). It carries a beta of 0.00, meaning the fund's expected move will be 0.0% for every 10% move in the market. Volatility, as measured by both the semi-deviation and a drawdown factor, is considered low. As of December 31, 2012, *Vanguard Russell 1000 Gro Idx ET traded at a discount of 3.08% below its net asset value, which is better than its one-year historical average discount of .04%.

Michael A. Johnson has been running the fund for 3 years and currently receives a manager quality ranking of 43 (0=worst, 99=best). If you desire an average level of risk, then this fund may be an option.

Data Date	Investment Rating	Net Assets ($Mil)	Price	Performance Rating/Pts	Total Return Y-T-D	Risk Rating/Pts
12-12	B	82.90	67.12	C+ / 6.8	3.25%	B / 8.4
2011	C-	53.40	59.26	D+ / 2.7	1.82%	B / 8.5

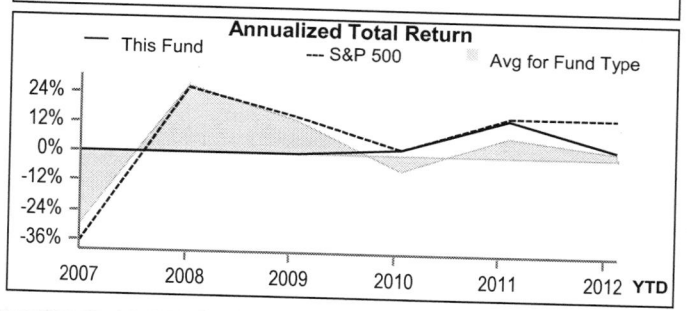

*Vanguard Russell 1000 Index ETF (VONE)

B **Good**

Fund Family: Vanguard Group Inc
Fund Type: Growth
Inception Date: September 20, 2010

Major Rating Factors: Strong performance is the major factor driving the B (Good) TheStreet.com Investment Rating for *Vanguard Russell 1000 Index ETF. The fund currently has a performance rating of B (Good) based on an annualized return of 0.00% over the last three years and a total return of 3.42% year to date 2012. Factored into the performance evaluation is an expense ratio of 0.12% (very low).

The fund's risk rating is currently B (Good). It carries a beta of 0.00, meaning the fund's expected move will be 0.0% for every 10% move in the market. Volatility, as measured by both the semi-deviation and a drawdown factor, is considered low. As of December 31, 2012, *Vanguard Russell 1000 Index ETF traded at a discount of 3.34% below its net asset value, which is better than its one-year historical average discount of .06%.

Jeffrey D. Miller has been running the fund for 3 years and currently receives a manager quality ranking of 51 (0=worst, 99=best). If you desire only a moderate level of risk and strong performance, then this fund is an excellent option.

Data Date	Investment Rating	Net Assets ($Mil)	Price	Performance Rating/Pts	Total Return Y-T-D	Risk Rating/Pts
12-12	B	175.60	65.21	B / 7.6	3.42%	B / 8.2
2011	C-	34.40	57.25	D+ / 2.8	1.99%	B / 8.3

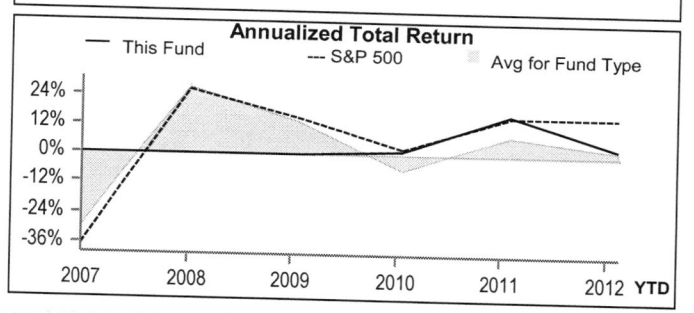

*Vanguard Russell 1000 Val Index (VONV)

B+ **Good**

Fund Family: Vanguard Group Inc
Fund Type: Growth
Inception Date: September 20, 2010

Major Rating Factors: Strong performance is the major factor driving the B+ (Good) TheStreet.com Investment Rating for *Vanguard Russell 1000 Val Index. The fund currently has a performance rating of B (Good) based on an annualized return of 0.00% over the last three years and a total return of 3.85% year to date 2012. Factored into the performance evaluation is an expense ratio of 0.15% (very low).

The fund's risk rating is currently B (Good). It carries a beta of 0.00, meaning the fund's expected move will be 0.0% for every 10% move in the market. Volatility, as measured by both the semi-deviation and a drawdown factor, is considered low. As of December 31, 2012, *Vanguard Russell 1000 Val Index traded at a discount of 3.65% below its net asset value.

Michael A. Johnson has been running the fund for 3 years and currently receives a manager quality ranking of 67 (0=worst, 99=best). If you desire only a moderate level of risk and strong performance, then this fund is an excellent option.

Data Date	Investment Rating	Net Assets ($Mil)	Price	Performance Rating/Pts	Total Return Y-T-D	Risk Rating/Pts
12-12	B+	47.00	63.35	B / 8.2	3.85%	B / 8.1
2011	C-	36.00	55.54	D+ / 2.8	1.66%	B / 8.1

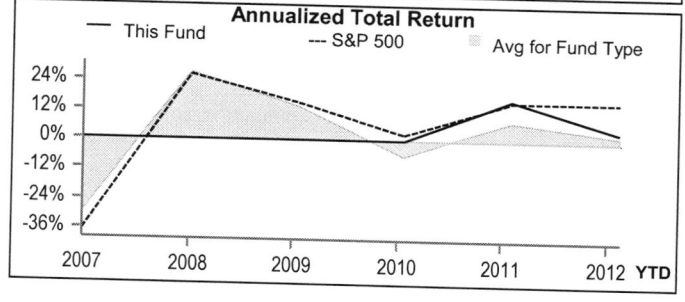

* Denotes ETF Fund

*Vanguard Russell 2000 Gro Idx ET (VTWG)   B   Good

Fund Family: Vanguard Group Inc
Fund Type: Growth
Inception Date: September 20, 2010

Major Rating Factors: Strong performance is the major factor driving the B (Good) TheStreet.com Investment Rating for *Vanguard Russell 2000 Gro Idx ET. The fund currently has a performance rating of B (Good) based on an annualized return of 0.00% over the last three years and a total return of 4.08% year to date 2012. Factored into the performance evaluation is an expense ratio of 0.20% (very low).

The fund's risk rating is currently B- (Good). It carries a beta of 0.00, meaning the fund's expected move will be 0.0% for every 10% move in the market. Volatility, as measured by both the semi-deviation and a drawdown factor, is considered low. As of December 31, 2012, *Vanguard Russell 2000 Gro Idx ET traded at a discount of 3.93% below its net asset value, which is better than its one-year historical average discount of .02%.

Andrew H. Maack has been running the fund for 3 years and currently receives a manager quality ranking of 25 (0=worst, 99=best). If you desire only a moderate level of risk and strong performance, then this fund is an excellent option.

Data Date	Investment Rating	Net Assets ($Mil)	Price	Performance Rating/Pts	Total Return Y-T-D	Risk Rating/Pts
12-12	B	47.40	69.11	B / 7.8	4.08%	B- / 7.4
2011	D	12.20	60.93	D / 1.8	1.10%	B- / 7.4

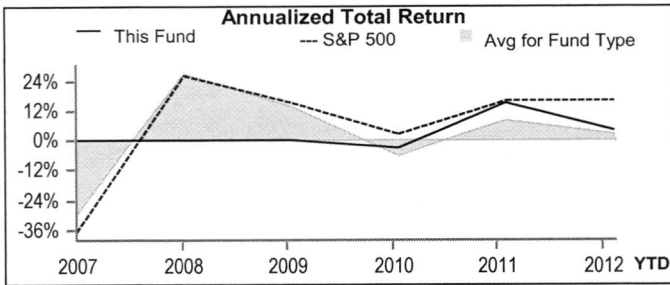

*Vanguard Russell 2000 Idx ETF (VTWO)   B   Good

Fund Family: Vanguard Group Inc
Fund Type: Growth
Inception Date: September 20, 2010

Major Rating Factors: Strong performance is the major factor driving the B (Good) TheStreet.com Investment Rating for *Vanguard Russell 2000 Idx ETF. The fund currently has a performance rating of B (Good) based on an annualized return of 0.00% over the last three years and a total return of 3.79% year to date 2012. Factored into the performance evaluation is an expense ratio of 0.15% (very low).

The fund's risk rating is currently B- (Good). It carries a beta of 0.00, meaning the fund's expected move will be 0.0% for every 10% move in the market. Volatility, as measured by both the semi-deviation and a drawdown factor, is considered low. As of December 31, 2012, *Vanguard Russell 2000 Idx ETF traded at a discount of 3.62% below its net asset value, which is better than its one-year historical average discount of .05%.

Andrew H. Maack has been running the fund for 3 years and currently receives a manager quality ranking of 38 (0=worst, 99=best). If you desire only a moderate level of risk and strong performance, then this fund is an excellent option.

Data Date	Investment Rating	Net Assets ($Mil)	Price	Performance Rating/Pts	Total Return Y-T-D	Risk Rating/Pts
12-12	B	164.40	67.00	B / 8.0	3.79%	B- / 7.5
2011	D	52.70	58.53	D / 1.7	1.54%	B- / 7.5

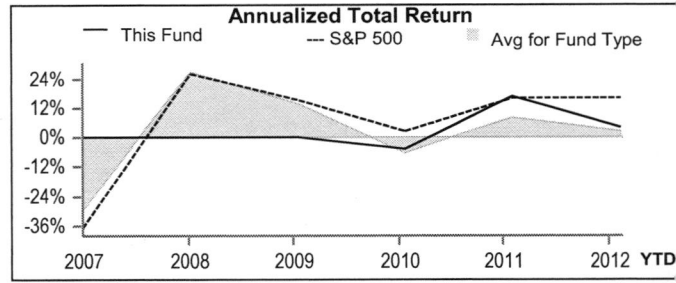

*Vanguard Russell 2000 Val Index (VTWV)   B   Good

Fund Family: Vanguard Group Inc
Fund Type: Growth
Inception Date: September 20, 2010

Major Rating Factors: Strong performance is the major factor driving the B (Good) TheStreet.com Investment Rating for *Vanguard Russell 2000 Val Index. The fund currently has a performance rating of B+ (Good) based on an annualized return of 0.00% over the last three years and a total return of 3.68% year to date 2012. Factored into the performance evaluation is an expense ratio of 0.20% (very low).

The fund's risk rating is currently B- (Good). It carries a beta of 0.00, meaning the fund's expected move will be 0.0% for every 10% move in the market. Volatility, as measured by both the semi-deviation and a drawdown factor, is considered low. As of December 31, 2012, *Vanguard Russell 2000 Val Index traded at a discount of 3.68% below its net asset value, which is better than its one-year historical average premium of .07%.

Andrew H. Maack has been running the fund for 3 years and currently receives a manager quality ranking of 37 (0=worst, 99=best). If you desire only a moderate level of risk and strong performance, then this fund is an excellent option.

Data Date	Investment Rating	Net Assets ($Mil)	Price	Performance Rating/Pts	Total Return Y-T-D	Risk Rating/Pts
12-12	B	19.10	64.62	B+ / 8.3	3.68%	B- / 7.5
2011	D+	11.20	56.67	D / 1.9	0.97%	B- / 7.5

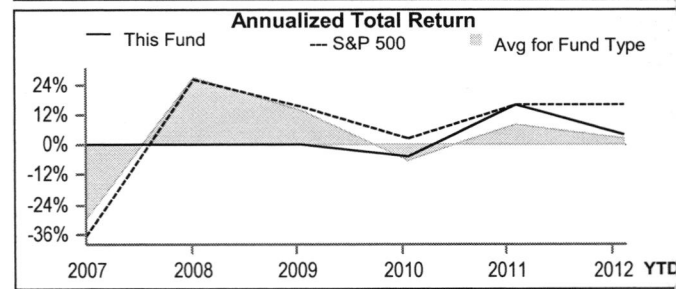

*Vanguard Russell 3000 Index ETF (VTHR)

B **Good**

Fund Family: Vanguard Group Inc
Fund Type: Growth
Inception Date: September 20, 2010

Major Rating Factors: Strong performance is the major factor driving the B (Good) TheStreet.com Investment Rating for *Vanguard Russell 3000 Index ETF. The fund currently has a performance rating of B (Good) based on an annualized return of 0.00% over the last three years and a total return of 3.62% year to date 2012. Factored into the performance evaluation is an expense ratio of 0.15% (very low).

The fund's risk rating is currently B (Good). It carries a beta of 0.00, meaning the fund's expected move will be 0.0% for every 10% move in the market. Volatility, as measured by both the semi-deviation and a drawdown factor, is considered low. As of December 31, 2012, *Vanguard Russell 3000 Index ETF traded at a discount of 3.58% below its net asset value, which is better than its one-year historical average discount of .05%.

Jeffrey D. Miller has been running the fund for 3 years and currently receives a manager quality ranking of 46 (0=worst, 99=best). If you desire only a moderate level of risk and strong performance, then this fund is an excellent option.

Data Date	Investment Rating	Net Assets ($Mil)	Price	Performance Rating/Pts	Total Return Y-T-D	Risk Rating/Pts
12-12	B	39.00	65.22	B / 7.7	3.62%	B / 8.2
2011	C-	22.90	57.42	D+ / 2.5	1.66%	B / 8.2

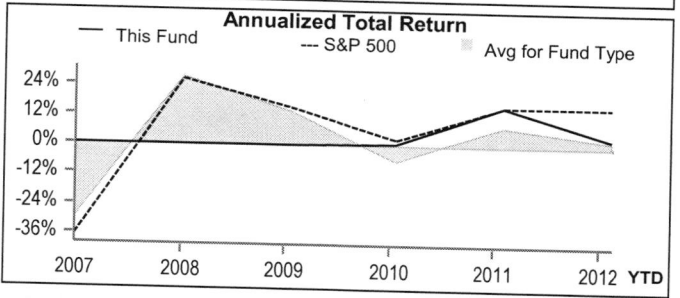

*Vanguard S&P 500 Val Indx ETF (VOOV)

B+ **Good**

Fund Family: Vanguard Group Inc
Fund Type: Growth
Inception Date: September 7, 2010

Major Rating Factors: Strong performance is the major factor driving the B+ (Good) TheStreet.com Investment Rating for *Vanguard S&P 500 Val Indx ETF. The fund currently has a performance rating of B (Good) based on an annualized return of 0.00% over the last three years and a total return of 3.40% year to date 2012. Factored into the performance evaluation is an expense ratio of 0.15% (very low).

The fund's risk rating is currently B (Good). It carries a beta of 0.00, meaning the fund's expected move will be 0.0% for every 10% move in the market. Volatility, as measured by both the semi-deviation and a drawdown factor, is considered low. As of December 31, 2012, *Vanguard S&P 500 Val Indx ETF traded at a discount of 3.24% below its net asset value, which is better than its one-year historical average premium of .02%.

Ryan E. Ludt has been running the fund for 3 years and currently receives a manager quality ranking of 64 (0=worst, 99=best). If you desire only a moderate level of risk and strong performance, then this fund is an excellent option.

Data Date	Investment Rating	Net Assets ($Mil)	Price	Performance Rating/Pts	Total Return Y-T-D	Risk Rating/Pts
12-12	B+	62.60	63.61	B / 8.2	3.40%	B / 8.0
2011	C-	33.20	55.53	D+ / 2.7	2.03%	B / 8.0

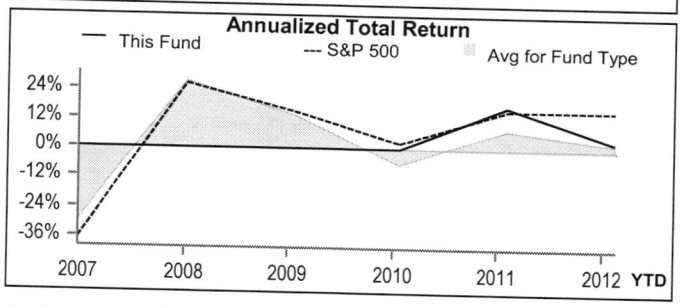

*Vanguard S&P Mid-Cap 400 Gro ETF (IVOG)

A- **Excellent**

Fund Family: Vanguard Group Inc
Fund Type: Growth
Inception Date: September 7, 2010

Major Rating Factors:
Strong performance is the major factor driving the A- (Excellent) TheStreet.com Investment Rating for *Vanguard S&P Mid-Cap 400 Gro ETF. The fund currently has a performance rating of B+ (Good) based on an annualized return of 0.00% over the last three years and a total return of 3.92% year to date 2012. Factored into the performance evaluation is an expense ratio of 0.20% (very low).

The fund's risk rating is currently B- (Good). It carries a beta of 0.00, meaning the fund's expected move will be 0.0% for every 10% move in the market. Volatility, as measured by both the semi-deviation and a drawdown factor, is considered low. As of December 31, 2012, *Vanguard S&P Mid-Cap 400 Gro ETF traded at a discount of 3.72% below its net asset value, which is better than its one-year historical average premium of .03%.

Donald M. Butler has been running the fund for 3 years and currently receives a manager quality ranking of 68 (0=worst, 99=best). If you desire only a moderate level of risk and strong performance, then this fund is an excellent option.

Data Date	Investment Rating	Net Assets ($Mil)	Price	Performance Rating/Pts	Total Return Y-T-D	Risk Rating/Pts
12-12	A-	97.40	69.97	B+ / 8.8	3.92%	B- / 7.9
2011	D+	30.10	60.35	D / 1.7	0.89%	B- / 7.9

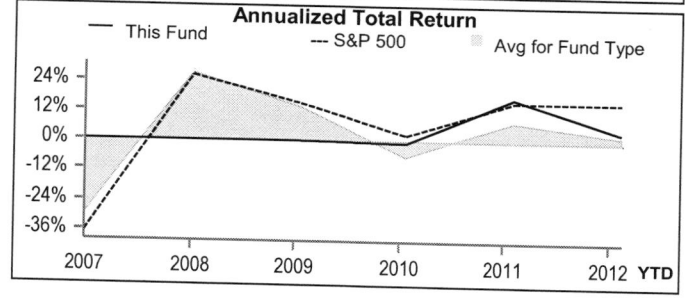

* Denotes ETF Fund

*Vanguard S&P Mid-Cap 400 Index E (IVOO)

B+   Good

Fund Family: Vanguard Group Inc
Fund Type: Growth
Inception Date: September 7, 2010

Major Rating Factors: Strong performance is the major factor driving the B+ (Good) TheStreet.com Investment Rating for *Vanguard S&P Mid-Cap 400 Index E. The fund currently has a performance rating of B+ (Good) based on an annualized return of 0.00% over the last three years and a total return of 3.76% year to date 2012. Factored into the performance evaluation is an expense ratio of 0.15% (very low).

The fund's risk rating is currently B- (Good). It carries a beta of 0.00, meaning the fund's expected move will be 0.0% for every 10% move in the market. Volatility, as measured by both the semi-deviation and a drawdown factor, is considered low. As of December 31, 2012, *Vanguard S&P Mid-Cap 400 Index E traded at a discount of 3.64% below its net asset value, which is better than its one-year historical average premium of .04%.

Donald M. Butler has been running the fund for 3 years and currently receives a manager quality ranking of 69 (0=worst, 99=best). If you desire only a moderate level of risk and strong performance, then this fund is an excellent option.

Data Date	Investment Rating	Net Assets ($Mil)	Price	Performance Rating/Pts	Total Return Y-T-D	Risk Rating/Pts
12-12	B+	101.10	68.07	B+ / 8.6	3.76%	B- / 7.8
2011	D+	26.30	58.66	D / 1.8	1.14%	B- / 7.8

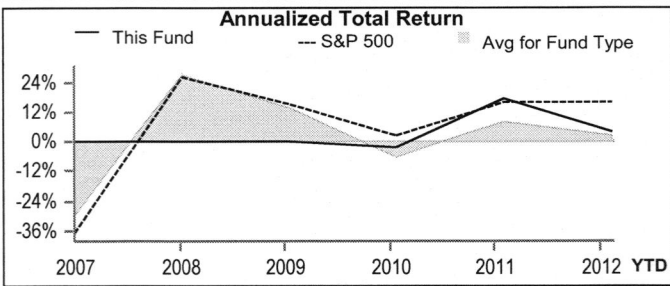

*Vanguard S&P Mid-Cap 400 Value E (IVOV)

B+   Good

Fund Family: Vanguard Group Inc
Fund Type: Growth
Inception Date: September 7, 2010

Major Rating Factors: Strong performance is the major factor driving the B+ (Good) TheStreet.com Investment Rating for *Vanguard S&P Mid-Cap 400 Value E. The fund currently has a performance rating of B+ (Good) based on an annualized return of 0.00% over the last three years and a total return of 3.98% year to date 2012. Factored into the performance evaluation is an expense ratio of 0.20% (very low).

The fund's risk rating is currently B- (Good). It carries a beta of 0.00, meaning the fund's expected move will be 0.0% for every 10% move in the market. Volatility, as measured by both the semi-deviation and a drawdown factor, is considered low. As of December 31, 2012, *Vanguard S&P Mid-Cap 400 Value E traded at a discount of 3.78% below its net asset value, which is better than its one-year historical average premium of .06%.

Donald M. Butler has been running the fund for 3 years and currently receives a manager quality ranking of 64 (0=worst, 99=best). If you desire only a moderate level of risk and strong performance, then this fund is an excellent option.

Data Date	Investment Rating	Net Assets ($Mil)	Price	Performance Rating/Pts	Total Return Y-T-D	Risk Rating/Pts
12-12	B+	9.70	65.63	B+ / 8.8	3.98%	B- / 7.6
2011	D	11.30	56.91	D / 1.7	-0.93%	B- / 7.6

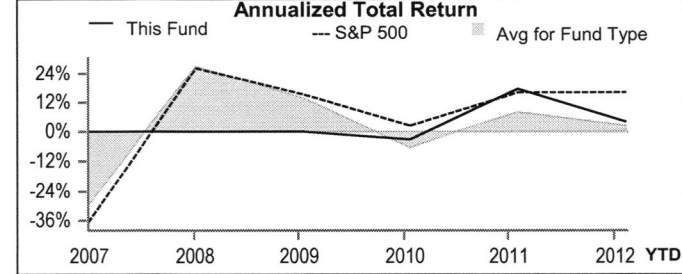

*Vanguard S&P SC 600 G Indx ETF (VIOG)

B   Good

Fund Family: Vanguard Group Inc
Fund Type: Growth
Inception Date: September 7, 2010

Major Rating Factors: Strong performance is the major factor driving the B (Good) TheStreet.com Investment Rating for *Vanguard S&P SC 600 G Indx ETF. The fund currently has a performance rating of B (Good) based on an annualized return of 0.00% over the last three years and a total return of 4.03% year to date 2012. Factored into the performance evaluation is an expense ratio of 0.20% (very low).

The fund's risk rating is currently B- (Good). It carries a beta of 0.00, meaning the fund's expected move will be 0.0% for every 10% move in the market. Volatility, as measured by both the semi-deviation and a drawdown factor, is considered low. As of December 31, 2012, *Vanguard S&P SC 600 G Indx ETF traded at a discount of 3.81% below its net asset value, which is better than its one-year historical average premium of .03%.

Michael Perre has been running the fund for 3 years and currently receives a manager quality ranking of 44 (0=worst, 99=best). If you desire only a moderate level of risk and strong performance, then this fund is an excellent option.

Data Date	Investment Rating	Net Assets ($Mil)	Price	Performance Rating/Pts	Total Return Y-T-D	Risk Rating/Pts
12-12	B	14.10	71.64	B / 7.7	4.03%	B- / 7.9
2011	C-	19.10	63.82	D+ / 2.7	-0.28%	B- / 7.9

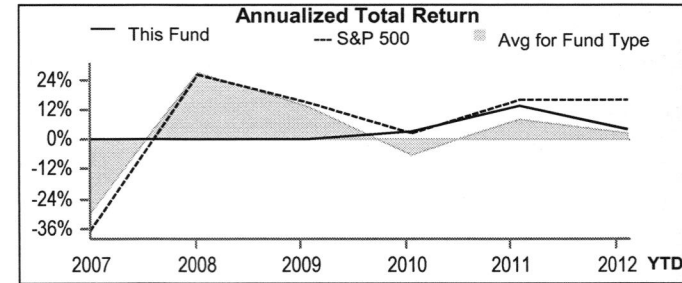

*Vanguard S&P SC 600 Indx ETF (VIOO)

B   **Good**

Fund Family: Vanguard Group Inc
Fund Type: Growth
Inception Date: September 7, 2010

Major Rating Factors: Strong performance is the major factor driving the B (Good) TheStreet.com Investment Rating for *Vanguard S&P SC 600 Indx ETF. The fund currently has a performance rating of B (Good) based on an annualized return of 0.00% over the last three years and a total return of 3.27% year to date 2012. Factored into the performance evaluation is an expense ratio of 0.15% (very low).

The fund's risk rating is currently B- (Good). It carries a beta of 0.00, meaning the fund's expected move will be 0.0% for every 10% move in the market. Volatility, as measured by both the semi-deviation and a drawdown factor, is considered low. As of December 31, 2012, *Vanguard S&P SC 600 Indx ETF traded at a discount of 3.13% below its net asset value, which is better than its one-year historical average premium of .03%.

Michael H. Buek has been running the fund for 3 years and currently receives a manager quality ranking of 44 (0=worst, 99=best). If you desire only a moderate level of risk and strong performance, then this fund is an excellent option.

Data Date	Investment Rating	Net Assets ($Mil)	Price	Performance Rating/Pts	Total Return Y-T-D	Risk Rating/Pts
12-12	B	48.30	70.25	B / 8.1	3.27%	B- / 7.8
2011	D+	12.30	61.80	D+ / 2.5	-0.23%	B- / 7.8

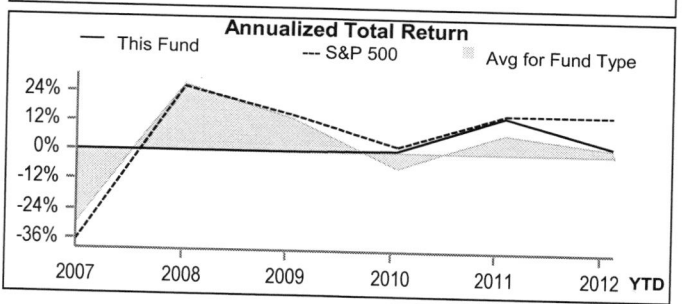

---

*Vanguard S&P SC 600 Val Indx ETF (VIOV)

B+   **Good**

Fund Family: Vanguard Group Inc
Fund Type: Growth
Inception Date: September 7, 2010

Major Rating Factors: Strong performance is the major factor driving the B+ (Good) TheStreet.com Investment Rating for *Vanguard S&P SC 600 Val Indx ETF. The fund currently has a performance rating of B+ (Good) based on an annualized return of 0.00% over the last three years and a total return of 2.72% year to date 2012. Factored into the performance evaluation is an expense ratio of 0.20% (very low).

The fund's risk rating is currently B- (Good). It carries a beta of 0.00, meaning the fund's expected move will be 0.0% for every 10% move in the market. Volatility, as measured by both the semi-deviation and a drawdown factor, is considered low. As of December 31, 2012, *Vanguard S&P SC 600 Val Indx ETF traded at a discount of 2.63% below its net asset value, which is better than its one-year historical average discount of .04%.

Michael H. Buek has been running the fund for 3 years and currently receives a manager quality ranking of 39 (0=worst, 99=best). If you desire only a moderate level of risk and strong performance, then this fund is an excellent option.

Data Date	Investment Rating	Net Assets ($Mil)	Price	Performance Rating/Pts	Total Return Y-T-D	Risk Rating/Pts
12-12	B+	16.90	69.17	B+ / 8.3	2.72%	B- / 7.7
2011	D+	14.80	59.59	D+ / 2.5	0.17%	B- / 7.7

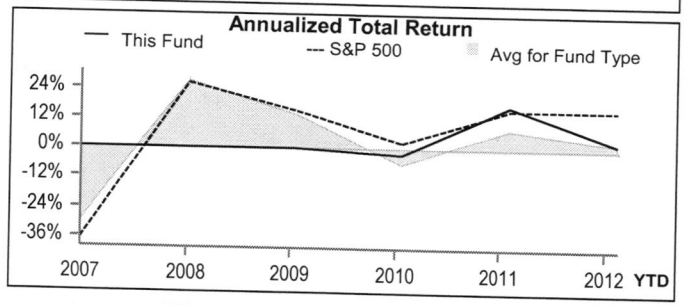

---

*Vanguard Short-Term Bd Idx ETF (BSV)

C-   **Fair**

Fund Family: Vanguard Group Inc
Fund Type: General - Investment Grade
Inception Date: April 3, 2007

Major Rating Factors:
Disappointing performance is the major factor driving the C- (Fair) TheStreet.com Investment Rating for *Vanguard Short-Term Bd Idx ETF. The fund currently has a performance rating of D (Weak) based on an annualized return of 2.69% over the last three years and a total return of 0.04% year to date 2012. Factored into the performance evaluation is an expense ratio of 0.10% (very low).

The fund's risk rating is currently B+ (Good). It carries a beta of 0.48, meaning the fund's expected move will be 4.8% for every 10% move in the market. Volatility, as measured by both the semi-deviation and a drawdown factor, is considered very low. As of December 31, 2012, *Vanguard Short-Term Bd Idx ETF traded at a premium of .06% above its net asset value, which is better than its one-year historical average premium of .08%.

Gregory Davis has been running the fund for 8 years and currently receives a manager quality ranking of 52 (0=worst, 99=best). This fund offers only a moderate level of risk but investors looking for strong performance are still waiting.

Data Date	Investment Rating	Net Assets ($Mil)	Price	Performance Rating/Pts	Total Return Y-T-D	Risk Rating/Pts
12-12	C-	9,274.40	80.99	D / 1.9	0.04%	B+ / 9.8
2011	C	7,481.70	80.84	D+ / 2.5	0.11%	B+ / 9.8
2010	B	5,640.40	80.46	C / 4.3	3.89%	B / 8.9
2009	C+	1,904.50	79.54	D+ / 2.8	2.93%	B+ / 9.1

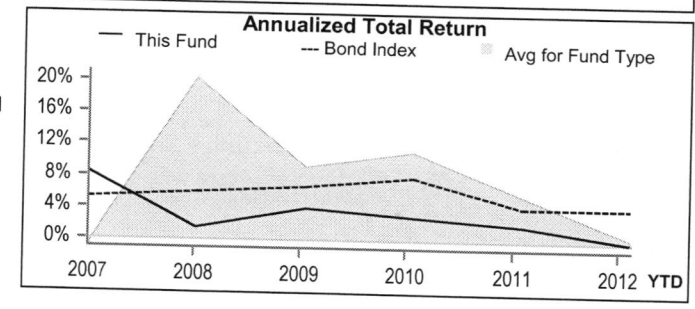

* Denotes ETF Fund

*Vanguard Short-Term Crp Bd Idx E (VCSH)   C   Fair

Fund Family: Vanguard Group Inc
Fund Type: Corporate - Investment Grade
Inception Date: November 19, 2009

Data Date	Investment Rating	Net Assets ($Mil)	Price	Perfor-mance Rating/Pts	Total Return Y-T-D	Risk Rating/Pts
12-12	C	4,648.50	80.33	D+ / 2.3	0.01%	B+ / 9.9
2011	C	2,230.20	77.83	D+ / 2.4	0.10%	B+ / 9.9
2010	B+	940.80	77.41	C / 4.5	5.27%	B+ / 9.0

Major Rating Factors:
Disappointing performance is the major factor driving the C (Fair) TheStreet.com Investment Rating for *Vanguard Short-Term Crp Bd Idx E. The fund currently has a performance rating of D+ (Weak) based on an annualized return of 4.22% over the last three years and a total return of 0.01% year to date 2012. Factored into the performance evaluation is an expense ratio of 0.12% (very low).

The fund's risk rating is currently B+ (Good). It carries a beta of 0.42, meaning the fund's expected move will be 4.2% for every 10% move in the market. Volatility, as measured by both the semi-deviation and a drawdown factor, is considered very low. As of December 31, 2012, *Vanguard Short-Term Crp Bd Idx E traded at a premium of .25% above its net asset value, which is better than its one-year historical average premium of .35%.

Joshua C. Barrickman has been running the fund for 4 years and currently receives a manager quality ranking of 60 (0=worst, 99=best). This fund offers only a moderate level of risk but investors looking for strong performance are still waiting.

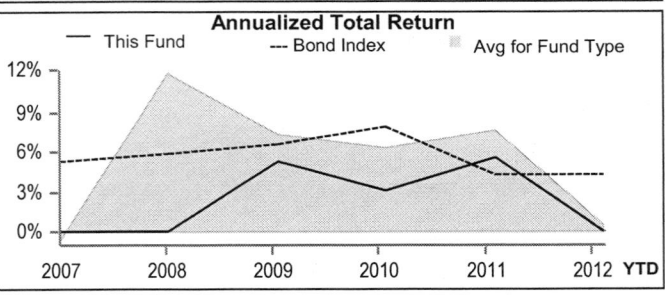

*Vanguard Short-Term Gvt Bd Idx E (VGSH)   C-   Fair

Fund Family: Vanguard Group Inc
Fund Type: US Government/Agency
Inception Date: November 19, 2009

Data Date	Investment Rating	Net Assets ($Mil)	Price	Perfor-mance Rating/Pts	Total Return Y-T-D	Risk Rating/Pts
12-12	C-	225.50	60.89	D / 1.6	0.00%	B+ / 9.9
2011	C	170.60	60.98	D / 2.2	-0.11%	B+ / 9.9
2010	C+	82.00	60.56	C- / 3.1	2.29%	B+ / 9.0

Major Rating Factors:
Disappointing performance is the major factor driving the C- (Fair) TheStreet.com Investment Rating for *Vanguard Short-Term Gvt Bd Idx E. The fund currently has a performance rating of D (Weak) based on an annualized return of 1.16% over the last three years and a total return of 0.00% year to date 2012. Factored into the performance evaluation is an expense ratio of 0.12% (very low).

The fund's risk rating is currently B+ (Good). It carries a beta of 0.03, meaning the fund's expected move will be 0.3% for every 10% move in the market. Volatility, as measured by both the semi-deviation and a drawdown factor, is considered very low. As of December 31, 2012, *Vanguard Short-Term Gvt Bd Idx E traded at a premium of .03% above its net asset value, which is in line with its one-year historical average premium of .03%.

Gregory Davis has been running the fund for 4 years and currently receives a manager quality ranking of 60 (0=worst, 99=best). This fund offers only a moderate level of risk but investors looking for strong performance are still waiting.

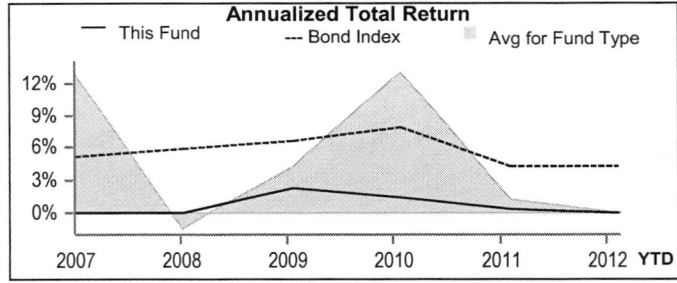

*Vanguard Small Cap ETF (VB)   C+   Fair

Fund Family: Vanguard Group Inc
Fund Type: Growth
Inception Date: January 26, 2004

Data Date	Investment Rating	Net Assets ($Mil)	Price	Perfor-mance Rating/Pts	Total Return Y-T-D	Risk Rating/Pts
12-12	C+	4,491.00	80.90	C+ / 6.9	3.55%	B- / 7.4
2011	C+	3,683.00	69.67	C+ / 6.5	1.42%	B- / 7.3
2010	B	4,843.10	72.63	B- / 7.5	28.12%	C / 5.5
2009	C-	1,621.53	57.35	C- / 3.3	34.18%	C+ / 5.6

Major Rating Factors: Middle of the road best describes *Vanguard Small Cap ETF whose TheStreet.com Investment Rating is currently a C+ (Fair). The fund currently has a performance rating of C+ (Fair) based on an annualized return of 14.23% over the last three years and a total return of 3.55% year to date 2012. Factored into the performance evaluation is an expense ratio of 0.10% (very low).

The fund's risk rating is currently B- (Good). It carries a beta of 1.27, meaning it is expected to move 12.7% for every 10% move in the market. Volatility, as measured by both the semi-deviation and a drawdown factor, is considered low. As of December 31, 2012, *Vanguard Small Cap ETF traded at a discount of 3.45% below its net asset value, which is better than its one-year historical average premium of .01%.

Michael H. Buek has been running the fund for 22 years and currently receives a manager quality ranking of 50 (0=worst, 99=best). If you desire an average level of risk, then this fund may be an option.

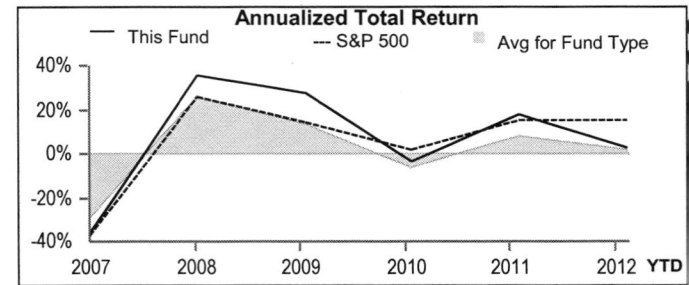

*Vanguard Small Cap Growth ETF (VBK)

C+   **Fair**

Fund Family: Vanguard Group Inc
Fund Type: Growth
Inception Date: January 26, 2004

Major Rating Factors: Strong performance is the major factor driving the C+ (Fair) TheStreet.com Investment Rating for *Vanguard Small Cap Growth ETF. The fund currently has a performance rating of B- (Good) based on an annualized return of 15.49% over the last three years and a total return of 3.64% year to date 2012. Factored into the performance evaluation is an expense ratio of 0.10% (very low).

The fund's risk rating is currently B- (Good). It carries a beta of 1.31, meaning it is expected to move 13.1% for every 10% move in the market. Volatility, as measured by both the semi-deviation and a drawdown factor, is considered low. As of December 31, 2012, *Vanguard Small Cap Growth ETF traded at a discount of 3.55% below its net asset value.

Gerard C. O'Reilly has been running the fund for 9 years and currently receives a manager quality ranking of 56 (0=worst, 99=best). If you desire only a moderate level of risk and strong performance, then this fund is an excellent option.

Data Date	Investment Rating	Net Assets ($Mil)	Price	Performance Rating/Pts	Total Return Y-T-D	Risk Rating/Pts
12-12	C+	2,101.10	89.03	B- / 7.2	3.64%	B- / 7.0
2011	C+	1,857.30	76.36	B- / 7.0	1.13%	C+ / 6.9
2010	B	1,841.90	78.04	B / 7.8	30.95%	C / 5.3
2009	C-	993.12	59.87	C- / 4.0	39.29%	C / 5.4

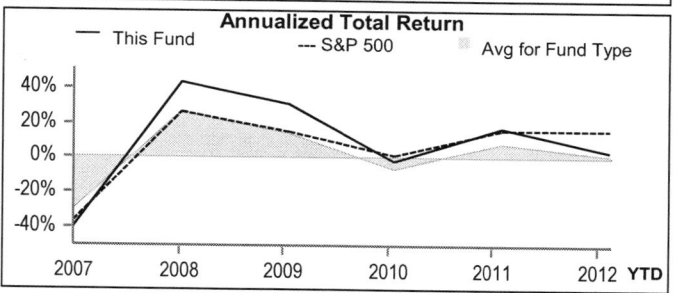

*Vanguard Small Cap Value ETF (VBR)

C+   **Fair**

Fund Family: Vanguard Group Inc
Fund Type: Growth
Inception Date: January 26, 2004

Major Rating Factors: Middle of the road best describes *Vanguard Small Cap Value ETF whose TheStreet.com Investment Rating is currently a C+ (Fair). The fund currently has a performance rating of C+ (Fair) based on an annualized return of 12.95% over the last three years and a total return of 3.36% year to date 2012. Factored into the performance evaluation is an expense ratio of 0.10% (very low).

The fund's risk rating is currently B- (Good). It carries a beta of 1.22, meaning it is expected to move 12.2% for every 10% move in the market. Volatility, as measured by both the semi-deviation and a drawdown factor, is considered low. As of December 31, 2012, *Vanguard Small Cap Value ETF traded at a discount of 3.28% below its net asset value, which is better than its one-year historical average premium of .03%.

Michael H. Buek has been running the fund for 15 years and currently receives a manager quality ranking of 45 (0=worst, 99=best). If you desire an average level of risk, then this fund may be an option.

Data Date	Investment Rating	Net Assets ($Mil)	Price	Performance Rating/Pts	Total Return Y-T-D	Risk Rating/Pts
12-12	C+	2,169.90	72.65	C+ / 6.4	3.36%	B- / 7.6
2011	C	1,755.20	62.67	C / 5.4	1.88%	B- / 7.5
2010	B	1,851.20	66.86	B- / 7.4	25.12%	C / 5.5
2009	D+	1,023.31	54.48	D+ / 2.5	29.32%	C+ / 5.6

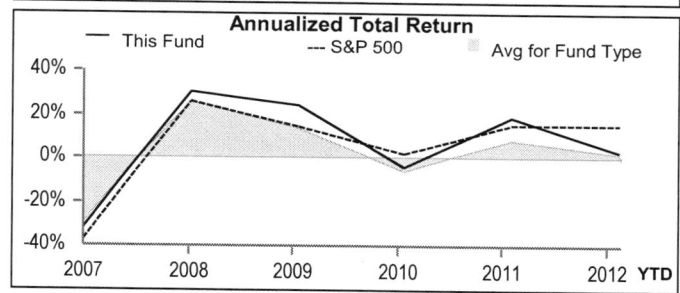

*Vanguard Telecom Serv ETF (VOX)

C+   **Fair**

Fund Family: Vanguard Group Inc
Fund Type: Income
Inception Date: September 23, 2004

Major Rating Factors: Middle of the road best describes *Vanguard Telecom Serv ETF whose TheStreet.com Investment Rating is currently a C+ (Fair). The fund currently has a performance rating of C (Fair) based on an annualized return of 12.58% over the last three years and a total return of 2.14% year to date 2012. Factored into the performance evaluation is an expense ratio of 0.14% (very low).

The fund's risk rating is currently B (Good). It carries a beta of 0.73, meaning the fund's expected move will be 7.3% for every 10% move in the market. Volatility, as measured by both the semi-deviation and a drawdown factor, is considered low. As of December 31, 2012, *Vanguard Telecom Serv ETF traded at a discount of 2.08% below its net asset value, which is better than its one-year historical average premium of .01%.

Ryan E. Ludt has been running the fund for 9 years and currently receives a manager quality ranking of 71 (0=worst, 99=best). If you desire an average level of risk, then this fund may be an option.

Data Date	Investment Rating	Net Assets ($Mil)	Price	Performance Rating/Pts	Total Return Y-T-D	Risk Rating/Pts
12-12	C+	484.90	70.01	C / 5.3	2.14%	B / 8.6
2011	C	373.10	62.17	C / 4.3	-1.34%	B / 8.4
2010	C	315.30	65.63	C / 4.7	19.52%	C+ / 6.4
2009	D+	146.79	56.51	D+ / 2.3	27.26%	C+ / 6.2

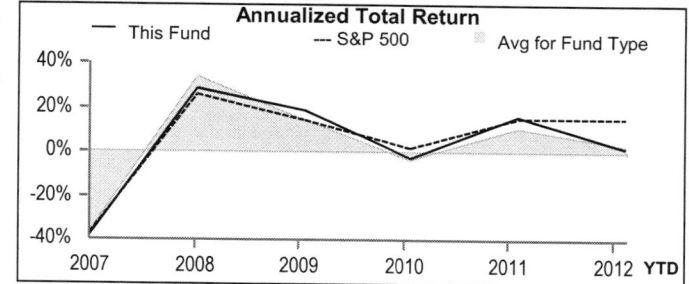

*Vanguard Total Bond Market ETF (BND)

C **Fair**

Fund Family: Vanguard Group Inc
Fund Type: General - Investment Grade
Inception Date: April 3, 2007

Data Date	Investment Rating	Net Assets ($Mil)	Price	Perfor-mance Rating/Pts	Total Return Y-T-D	Risk Rating/Pts
12-12	C	17,720.50	84.03	D+ / 2.4	-0.24%	B+ / 9.8
2011	C	14,595.70	83.54	C- / 3.3	-0.24%	B+ / 9.7
2010	B+	9,047.80	80.27	C / 4.8	6.20%	B / 8.9
2009	C+	4,435.15	78.59	C- / 3.3	4.15%	B+ / 9.0

Major Rating Factors:
Disappointing performance is the major factor driving the C (Fair) TheStreet.com Investment Rating for *Vanguard Total Bond Market ETF. The fund currently has a performance rating of D+ (Weak) based on an annualized return of 5.59% over the last three years and a total return of -0.24% year to date 2012. Factored into the performance evaluation is an expense ratio of 0.10% (very low).

The fund's risk rating is currently B+ (Good). It carries a beta of 1.01, meaning that its performance tracks fairly well with that of the overall stock market. Volatility, as measured by both the semi-deviation and a drawdown factor, is considered very low. As of December 31, 2012, *Vanguard Total Bond Market ETF traded at a premium of .30% above its net asset value, which is worse than its one-year historical average premium of .13%.

Kenneth E. Volpert has been running the fund for 21 years and currently receives a manager quality ranking of 49 (0=worst, 99=best). This fund offers only a moderate level of risk but investors looking for strong performance are still waiting.

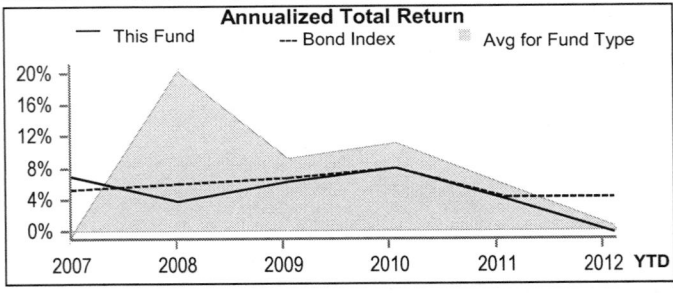

*Vanguard Total Intl Stock Index (VXUS)

B+ **Good**

Fund Family: Vanguard Group Inc
Fund Type: Global
Inception Date: January 26, 2011

Data Date	Investment Rating	Net Assets ($Mil)	Price	Perfor-mance Rating/Pts	Total Return Y-T-D	Risk Rating/Pts
12-12	B+	1,065.70	46.96	A- / 9.2	2.02%	B- / 7.2

Major Rating Factors:
Exceptional performance is the major factor driving the B+ (Good) TheStreet.com Investment Rating for *Vanguard Total Intl Stock Index. The fund currently has a performance rating of A- (Excellent) based on an annualized return of 0.00% over the last three years and a total return of 2.02% year to date 2012. Factored into the performance evaluation is an expense ratio of 0.17% (very low).

The fund's risk rating is currently B- (Good). It carries a beta of 0.00, meaning the fund's expected move will be 0.0% for every 10% move in the market. Volatility, as measured by both the semi-deviation and a drawdown factor, is considered low. As of December 31, 2012, *Vanguard Total Intl Stock Index traded at a discount of 1.47% below its net asset value, which is better than its one-year historical average premium of .29%.

Michael Perre has been running the fund for 5 years and currently receives a manager quality ranking of 58 (0=worst, 99=best). If you desire only a moderate level of risk and strong performance, then this fund is an excellent option.

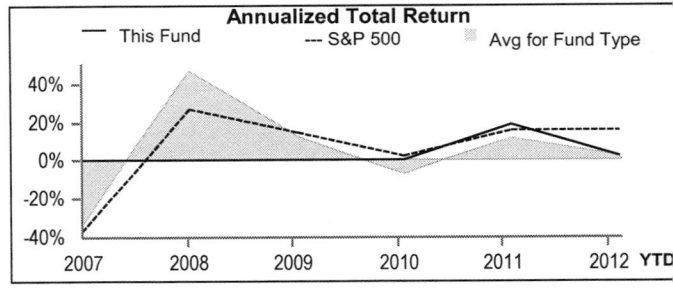

*Vanguard Total Stock Market ETF (VTI)

C+ **Fair**

Fund Family: Vanguard Group Inc
Fund Type: Growth and Income
Inception Date: May 24, 2001

Data Date	Investment Rating	Net Assets ($Mil)	Price	Perfor-mance Rating/Pts	Total Return Y-T-D	Risk Rating/Pts
12-12	C+	23,383.20	73.28	C / 5.5	3.40%	B- / 7.9
2011	C+	19,521.40	64.30	C / 5.5	1.68%	B- / 7.9
2010	D+	17,930.40	64.93	C / 4.8	17.45%	C- / 3.5
2009	D-	92,494.32	56.37	D+ / 2.5	25.19%	C- / 3.8

Major Rating Factors: Middle of the road best describes *Vanguard Total Stock Market ETF whose TheStreet.com Investment Rating is currently a C+ (Fair). The fund currently has a performance rating of C (Fair) based on an annualized return of 11.85% over the last three years and a total return of 3.40% year to date 2012. Factored into the performance evaluation is an expense ratio of 0.05% (very low).

The fund's risk rating is currently B- (Good). It carries a beta of 1.04, meaning that its performance tracks fairly well with that of the overall stock market. Volatility, as measured by both the semi-deviation and a drawdown factor, is considered low. As of December 31, 2012, *Vanguard Total Stock Market ETF traded at a discount of 3.26% below its net asset value, which is better than its one-year historical average premium of .01%.

Gerard C. O'Reilly has been running the fund for 19 years and currently receives a manager quality ranking of 52 (0=worst, 99=best). If you desire an average level of risk, then this fund may be an option.

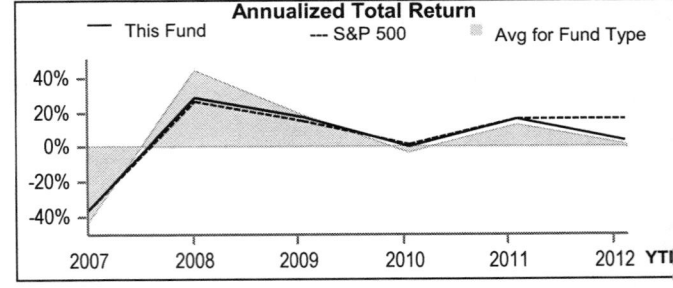

*Vanguard Total World Stock ETF (VT)

C- **Fair**

Fund Family: Vanguard Group Inc
Fund Type: Emerging Market
Inception Date: June 24, 2008

Major Rating Factors: Middle of the road best describes *Vanguard Total World Stock ETF whose TheStreet.com Investment Rating is currently a C- (Fair). The fund currently has a performance rating of C (Fair) based on an annualized return of 7.05% over the last three years and a total return of 2.65% year to date 2012. Factored into the performance evaluation is an expense ratio of 0.21% (very low).

The fund's risk rating is currently B- (Good). It carries a beta of 0.76, meaning the fund's expected move will be 7.6% for every 10% move in the market. Volatility, as measured by both the semi-deviation and a drawdown factor, is considered low. As of December 31, 2012, *Vanguard Total World Stock ETF traded at a discount of 2.27% below its net asset value, which is better than its one-year historical average premium of .17%.

Ryan E. Ludt has been running the fund for 5 years and currently receives a manager quality ranking of 73 (0=worst, 99=best). If you desire an average level of risk, then this fund may be an option.

Data Date	Investment Rating	Net Assets ($Mil)	Price	Performance Rating/Pts	Total Return Y-T-D	Risk Rating/Pts
12-12	C-	1,559.60	49.42	C / 4.4	2.65%	B- / 7.4
2011	C-	1,050.20	43.18	C- / 4.1	1.34%	B- / 7.7
2010	A-	742.10	47.80	A- / 9.0	13.09%	C+ / 5.9
2009	A-	114.19	43.09	B+ / 8.4	29.37%	C+ / 5.9

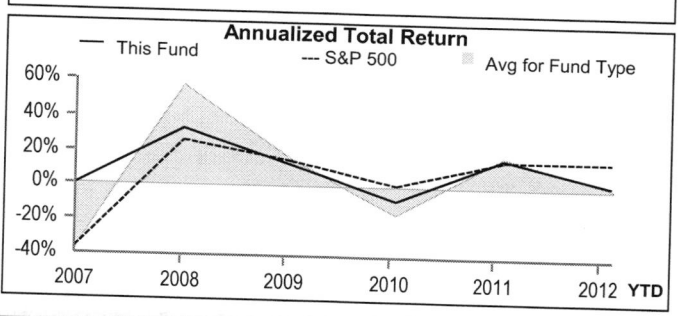

*Vanguard Utilities Index ETF (VPU)

C **Fair**

Fund Family: Vanguard Group Inc
Fund Type: Utilities
Inception Date: January 26, 2004

Major Rating Factors: Middle of the road best describes *Vanguard Utilities Index ETF whose TheStreet.com Investment Rating is currently a C (Fair). The fund currently has a performance rating of C- (Fair) based on an annualized return of 9.62% over the last three years and a total return of 1.51% year to date 2012. Factored into the performance evaluation is an expense ratio of 0.14% (very low).

The fund's risk rating is currently B+ (Good). It carries a beta of 0.92, meaning that its performance tracks fairly well with that of the overall stock market. Volatility, as measured by both the semi-deviation and a drawdown factor, is considered very low. As of December 31, 2012, *Vanguard Utilities Index ETF traded at a discount of 1.49% below its net asset value, which is better than its one-year historical average premium of .02%.

Michael D. Eyre has been running the fund for 3 years and currently receives a manager quality ranking of 59 (0=worst, 99=best). If you desire an average level of risk, then this fund may be an option.

Data Date	Investment Rating	Net Assets ($Mil)	Price	Performance Rating/Pts	Total Return Y-T-D	Risk Rating/Pts
12-12	C	1,129.80	75.30	C- / 3.4	1.51%	B+ / 9.2
2011	C+	1,048.80	76.89	C / 4.9	-2.74%	B / 8.5
2010	D+	647.00	67.08	D / 1.7	7.05%	C+ / 6.7
2009	C-	363.65	65.18	D+ / 2.5	9.30%	C+ / 6.8

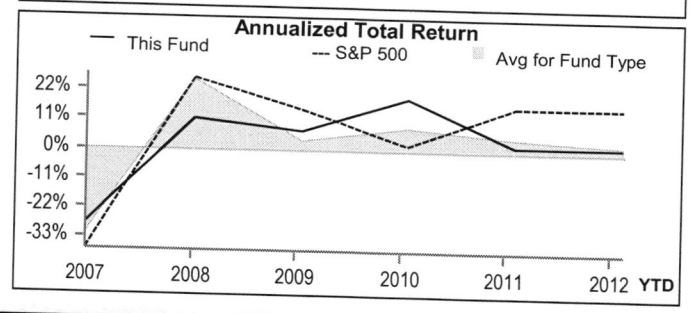

*Vanguard Value ETF (VTV)

C **Fair**

Fund Family: Vanguard Group Inc
Fund Type: Income
Inception Date: January 26, 2004

Major Rating Factors: Middle of the road best describes *Vanguard Value ETF whose TheStreet.com Investment Rating is currently a C (Fair). The fund currently has a performance rating of C (Fair) based on an annualized return of 10.48% over the last three years and a total return of 3.50% year to date 2012. Factored into the performance evaluation is an expense ratio of 0.10% (very low).

The fund's risk rating is currently B (Good). It carries a beta of 0.97, meaning that its performance tracks fairly well with that of the overall stock market. Volatility, as measured by both the semi-deviation and a drawdown factor, is considered low. As of December 31, 2012, *Vanguard Value ETF traded at a discount of 3.35% below its net asset value, which is better than its one-year historical average premium of .01%.

Gerard C. O'Reilly has been running the fund for 19 years and currently receives a manager quality ranking of 48 (0=worst, 99=best). If you desire an average level of risk, then this fund may be an option.

Data Date	Investment Rating	Net Assets ($Mil)	Price	Performance Rating/Pts	Total Return Y-T-D	Risk Rating/Pts
12-12	C	6,758.20	58.80	C / 5.0	3.50%	B / 8.2
2011	C	5,049.00	52.49	C / 4.6	1.58%	B- / 7.9
2010	C-	4,330.00	53.33	C- / 3.1	14.57%	C+ / 6.0
2009	D	2,357.82	47.75	D- / 1.5	16.53%	C+ / 6.0

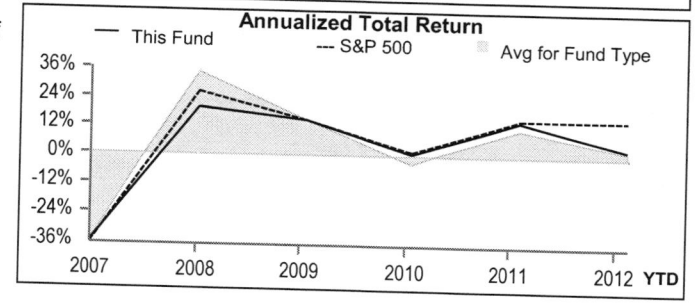

* Denotes ETF Fund

*VelocityShares 2x Long Platinum (LPLT)   E+   Very Weak

Fund Family: Credit Suisse AG
Fund Type: Global
Inception Date: October 14, 2011

Data Date	Investment Rating	Net Assets ($Mil)	Price	Performance Rating/Pts	Total Return Y-T-D	Risk Rating/Pts
12-12	E+	3.10	44.43	D / 1.8	1.64%	C- / 3.7

Major Rating Factors:
Disappointing performance is the major factor driving the E+ (Very Weak) TheStreet.com Investment Rating for *VelocityShares 2x Long Platinum. The fund currently has a performance rating of D (Weak) based on an annualized return of 0.00% over the last three years and a total return of 1.64% year to date 2012.

The fund's risk rating is currently C- (Fair). It carries a beta of 0.00, meaning the fund's expected move will be 0.0% for every 10% move in the market. Volatility, as measured by both the semi-deviation and a drawdown factor, is considered average. As of December 31, 2012, *VelocityShares 2x Long Platinum traded at a discount of 1.79% below its net asset value, which is better than its one-year historical average discount of .35%.

This fund has been team managed for 2 years and currently receives a manager quality ranking of 5 (0=worst, 99=best). This fund offers an average level of risk but investors looking for strong performance will be frustrated.

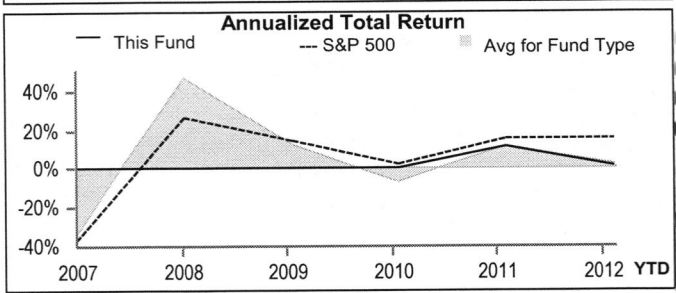

*VelocityShares 3x Inverse Gold E (DGLD)   E   Very Weak

Fund Family: Credit Suisse AG
Fund Type: Global
Inception Date: October 14, 2011

Data Date	Investment Rating	Net Assets ($Mil)	Price	Performance Rating/Pts	Total Return Y-T-D	Risk Rating/Pts
12-12	E	5.60	41.24	E+ / 0.6	1.65%	C- / 3.5

Major Rating Factors: Very poor performance is the major factor driving the E (Very Weak) TheStreet.com Investment Rating for *VelocityShares 3x Inverse Gold E. The fund currently has a performance rating of E+ (Very Weak) based on an annualized return of 0.00% over the last three years and a total return of 1.65% year to date 2012.

The fund's risk rating is currently C- (Fair). It carries a beta of 0.00, meaning the fund's expected move will be 0.0% for every 10% move in the market. Volatility, as measured by both the semi-deviation and a drawdown factor, is considered average. As of December 31, 2012, *VelocityShares 3x Inverse Gold E traded at a discount of 1.90% below its net asset value, which is better than its one-year historical average discount of .02%.

This fund has been team managed for 2 years and currently receives a manager quality ranking of 21 (0=worst, 99=best). This fund offers an average level of risk but investors looking for strong performance will be frustrated.

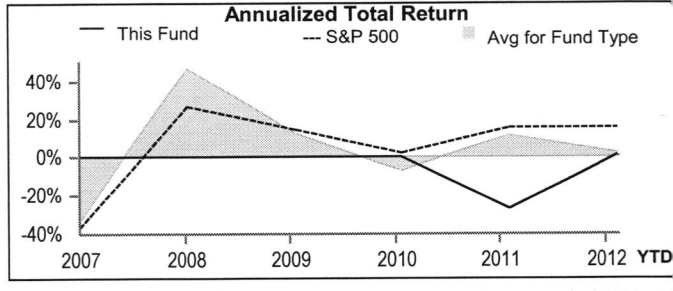

*VelocityShares 3x Inverse Silver (DSLV)   E-   Very Weak

Fund Family: Credit Suisse AG
Fund Type: Global
Inception Date: October 14, 2011

Data Date	Investment Rating	Net Assets ($Mil)	Price	Performance Rating/Pts	Total Return Y-T-D	Risk Rating/Pts
12-12	E-	16.90	26.91	E- / 0.1	-2.45%	D / 1.9

Major Rating Factors: *VelocityShares 3x Inverse Silver has adopted a very risky asset allocation strategy and currently receives an overall TheStreet.com Investment Rating of E- (Very Weak). The fund has a high level of volatility, as measured by both semi-deviation and drawdown factors. It carries a beta of 0.00, meaning the fund's expected move will be 0.0% for every 10% move in the market. As of December 31, 2012, *VelocityShares 3x Inverse Silver traded at a premium of 1.70% above its net asset value, which is worse than its one-year historical average discount of .17%. Unfortunately, the high level of risk (D, Weak) failed to pay off as investors endured very poor performance.

The fund's performance rating is currently E- (Very Weak). It has registered an annualized return of 0.00% over the last three years but is down -2.45% year to date 2012.

This fund has been team managed for 2 years and currently receives a manager quality ranking of 4 (0=worst, 99=best). If you can tolerate very high levels of risk in the hope of improved future returns, holding this fund may be an option.

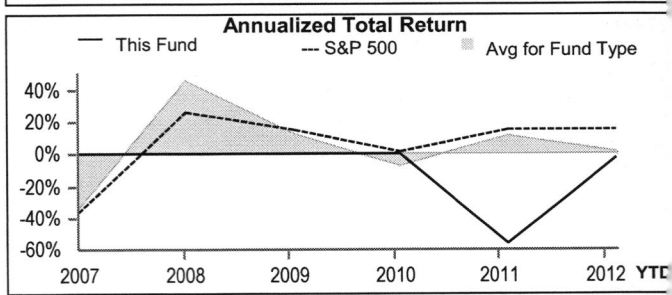

*VelocityShares 3x Long Gold ETN (UGLD)

E+   Very Weak

Fund Family: Credit Suisse AG
Fund Type: Global
Inception Date: October 14, 2011

Major Rating Factors:
Very poor performance is the major factor driving the E+ (Very Weak) TheStreet.com Investment Rating for *VelocityShares 3x Long Gold ETN. The fund currently has a performance rating of E+ (Very Weak) based on an annualized return of 0.00% over the last three years and a total return of -2.29% year to date 2012.

The fund's risk rating is currently C- (Fair). It carries a beta of 0.00, meaning the fund's expected move will be 0.0% for every 10% move in the market. Volatility, as measured by both the semi-deviation and a drawdown factor, is considered average. As of December 31, 2012, *VelocityShares 3x Long Gold ETN traded at a premium of 2.70% above its net asset value, which is worse than its one-year historical average premium of .07%.

This fund has been team managed for 2 years and currently receives a manager quality ranking of 7 (0=worst, 99=best). This fund offers an average level of risk but investors looking for strong performance will be frustrated.

Data Date	Investment Rating	Net Assets ($Mil)	Price	Performance Rating/Pts	Total Return Y-T-D	Risk Rating/Pts
12-12	E+	42.40	41.86	E+ / 0.8	-2.29%	C- / 3.7

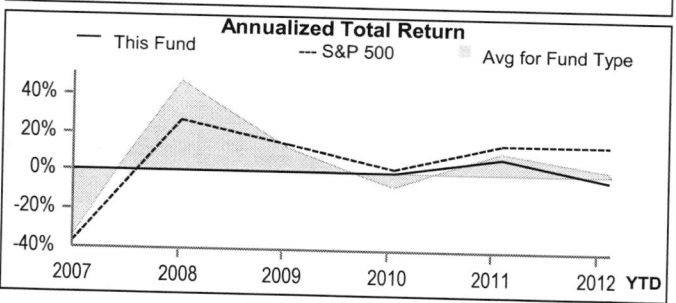

*VelocityShares 3x Long Silver ET (USLV)

E-   Very Weak

Fund Family: Credit Suisse AG
Fund Type: Global
Inception Date: October 14, 2011

Major Rating Factors: *VelocityShares 3x Long Silver ET has adopted a very risky asset allocation strategy and currently receives an overall TheStreet.com Investment Rating of E- (Very Weak). The fund has a high level of volatility, as measured by both semi-deviation and drawdown factors. It carries a beta of 0.00, meaning the fund's expected move will be 0.0% for every 10% move in the market. As of December 31, 2012, *VelocityShares 3x Long Silver ET traded at a premium of .50% above its net asset value, which is worse than its one-year historical average premium of .15%. Unfortunately, the high level of risk (D, Weak) failed to pay off as investors endured very poor performance.

The fund's performance rating is currently E (Very Weak). It has registered an annualized return of 0.00% over the last three years and is up 0.23% year to date 2012.

This fund has been team managed for 2 years and currently receives a manager quality ranking of 1 (0=worst, 99=best). If you can tolerate very high levels of risk in the hope of improved future returns, holding this fund may be an option.

Data Date	Investment Rating	Net Assets ($Mil)	Price	Performance Rating/Pts	Total Return Y-T-D	Risk Rating/Pts
12-12	E-	121.20	26.11	E / 0.5	0.23%	D / 2.2

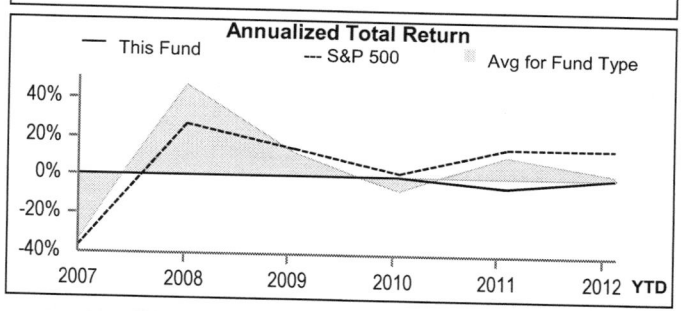

*VelocityShares Daily 2x VIX S-T (TVIX)

E-   Very Weak

Fund Family: Credit Suisse AG
Fund Type: Income
Inception Date: November 29, 2010

Major Rating Factors: *VelocityShares Daily 2x VIX S-T has adopted a very risky asset allocation strategy and currently receives an overall TheStreet.com Investment Rating of E- (Very Weak). The fund has a high level of volatility, as measured by both semi-deviation and drawdown factors. It carries a beta of 0.00, meaning the fund's expected move will be 0.0% for every 10% move in the market. As of December 31, 2012, *VelocityShares Daily 2x VIX S-T traded at a premium of 54.38% above its net asset value, which is worse than its one-year historical average premium of 8.42%. Unfortunately, the high level of risk (D, Weak) failed to pay off as investors endured very poor performance.

The fund's performance rating is currently E- (Very Weak). It has registered an annualized return of 0.00% over the last three years but is down -29.82% year to date 2012.

This fund has been team managed for 3 years and currently receives a manager quality ranking of 0 (0=worst, 99=best). If you can tolerate very high levels of risk in the hope of improved future returns, holding this fund may be an option.

Data Date	Investment Rating	Net Assets ($Mil)	Price	Performance Rating/Pts	Total Return Y-T-D	Risk Rating/Pts
12-12	E-	117.80	9.34	E- / 0	-29.82%	D / 1.9

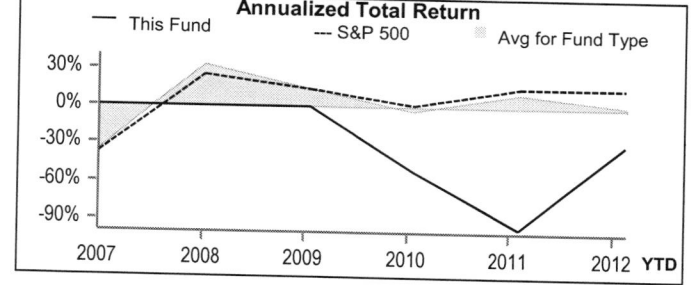

* Denotes ETF Fund

*VelocityShares Dly 2x VIX Med-T (TVIZ)

E-   **Very Weak**

Fund Family: Credit Suisse AG
Fund Type: Income
Inception Date: November 29, 2010

Major Rating Factors: *VelocityShares Dly 2x VIX Med-T has adopted a very risky asset allocation strategy and currently receives an overall TheStreet.com Investment Rating of E- (Very Weak). The fund has a high level of volatility, as measured by both semi-deviation and drawdown factors. It carries a beta of 0.00, meaning the fund's expected move will be 0.0% for every 10% move in the market. As of December 31, 2012, *VelocityShares Dly 2x VIX Med-T traded at a premium of 19.46% above its net asset value, which is worse than its one-year historical average discount of .31%. Unfortunately, the high level of risk (D, Weak) failed to pay off as investors endured very poor performance.

The fund's performance rating is currently E- (Very Weak). It has registered an annualized return of 0.00% over the last three years but is down -17.33% year to date 2012.

This fund has been team managed for 3 years and currently receives a manager quality ranking of 0 (0=worst, 99=best). If you can tolerate very high levels of risk in the hope of improved future returns, holding this fund may be an option.

Data Date	Investment Rating	Net Assets ($Mil)	Price	Performance Rating/Pts	Total Return Y-T-D	Risk Rating/Pts
12-12	E-	2.10	11.48	E- / 0	-17.33%	D / 1.9

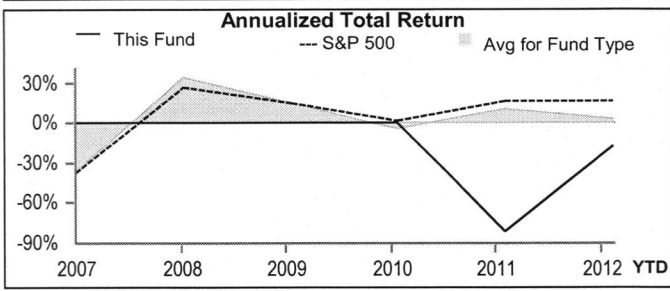

*VelocityShares Dly Invs VIX M-T (ZIV)

B   **Good**

Fund Family: Credit Suisse AG
Fund Type: General - Investment Grade
Inception Date: November 29, 2010

Major Rating Factors:
Exceptional performance is the major factor driving the B (Good) TheStreet.com Investment Rating for *VelocityShares Dly Invs VIX M-T. The fund currently has a performance rating of A+ (Excellent) based on an annualized return of 0.00% over the last three years and a total return of 9.30% year to date 2012.

The fund's risk rating is currently C (Fair). It carries a beta of 0.00, meaning the fund's expected move will be 0.0% for every 10% move in the market. Volatility, as measured by both the semi-deviation and a drawdown factor, is considered average. As of December 31, 2012, *VelocityShares Dly Invs VIX M-T traded at a discount of 8.05% below its net asset value, which is better than its one-year historical average premium of .27%.

This fund has been team managed for 3 years and currently receives a manager quality ranking of 99 (0=worst, 99=best). If you desire an average level of risk and strong performance, then this fund is a good option.

Data Date	Investment Rating	Net Assets ($Mil)	Price	Performance Rating/Pts	Total Return Y-T-D	Risk Rating/Pts
12-12	B	15.70	23.77	A+ / 9.9	9.30%	C / 5.3
2011	D-	7.10	12.46	D- / 1.3	5.77%	C / 5.4

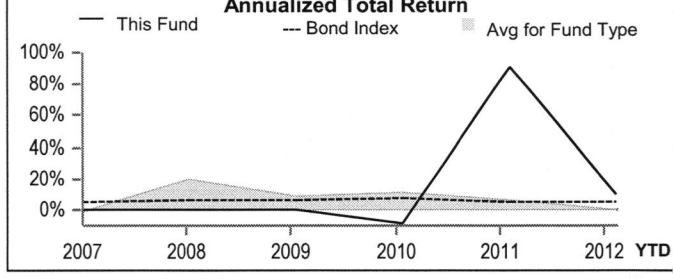

*VelocityShares Dly Invs VIX ST E (XIV)

C-   **Fair**

Fund Family: Credit Suisse AG
Fund Type: Growth and Income
Inception Date: November 29, 2010

Major Rating Factors: *VelocityShares Dly Invs VIX ST E has adopted a very risky asset allocation strategy and currently receives an overall TheStreet.com Investment Rating of C- (Fair). The fund has shown a high level of volatility, as measured by both semi-deviation and drawdown factors. It carries a beta of 0.00, meaning the fund's expected move will be 0.0% for every 10% move in the market. As of December 31, 2012, *VelocityShares Dly Invs VIX ST E traded at a discount of 16.06% below its net asset value, which is better than its one-year historical average discount of .03%. The high level of risk (D, Weak) did however, reward investors with excellent performance.

The fund's performance rating is currently A+ (Excellent). It has registered an annualized return of 0.00% over the last three years and is up 18.17% year to date 2012.

This fund has been team managed for 3 years and currently receives a manager quality ranking of 97 (0=worst, 99=best). If you are comfortable owning a very high risk investment, this fund may be an option.

Data Date	Investment Rating	Net Assets ($Mil)	Price	Performance Rating/Pts	Total Return Y-T-D	Risk Rating/Pts
12-12	C-	346.60	16.57	A+ / 9.9	18.17%	D / 1.9
2011	E-	387.60	6.51	E- / 0.2	11.37%	D / 1.9

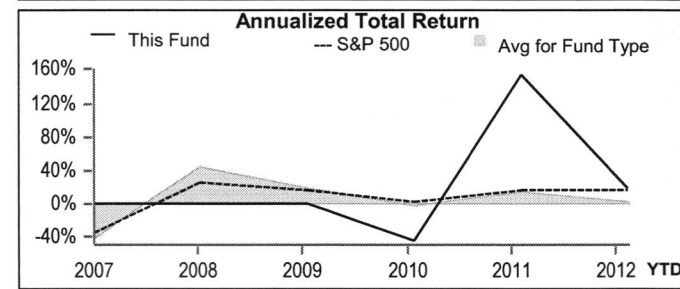

*VelocityShares VIX Medium-Term E (VIIZ)

E-   Very Weak

Fund Family: Credit Suisse AG
Fund Type: Growth and Income
Inception Date: November 29, 2010

Data Date	Investment Rating	Net Assets ($Mil)	Price	Performance Rating/Pts	Total Return Y-T-D	Risk Rating/Pts
12-12	E-	4.90	38.65	E- / 0	-8.64%	D / 1.9
2011	D-	8.30	83.32	D- / 1.3	-5.38%	C / 4.7

Major Rating Factors: *VelocityShares VIX Medium-Term E has adopted a very risky asset allocation strategy and currently receives an overall TheStreet.com Investment Rating of E- (Very Weak). The fund has a high level of volatility, as measured by both semi-deviation and drawdown factors. It carries a beta of 0.00, meaning the fund's expected move will be 0.0% for every 10% move in the market. As of December 31, 2012, *VelocityShares VIX Medium-Term E traded at a premium of 9.24% above its net asset value, which is worse than its one-year historical average discount of .39%. Unfortunately, the high level of risk (D, Weak) failed to pay off as investors endured very poor performance.

The fund's performance rating is currently E- (Very Weak). It has registered an annualized return of 0.00% over the last three years but is down -8.64% year to date 2012.

This fund has been team managed for 3 years and currently receives a manager quality ranking of 1 (0=worst, 99=best). If you can tolerate very high levels of risk in the hope of improved future returns, holding this fund may be an option.

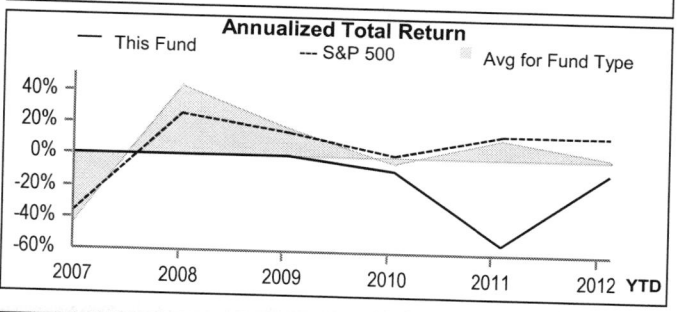

*VelocityShares VIX Short-Term ET (VIIX)

E-   Very Weak

Fund Family: Credit Suisse AG
Fund Type: Growth and Income
Inception Date: November 29, 2010

Data Date	Investment Rating	Net Assets ($Mil)	Price	Performance Rating/Pts	Total Return Y-T-D	Risk Rating/Pts
12-12	E-	13.60	17.19	E- / 0	-16.75%	D / 1.9
2011	D-	32.20	76.68	D+ / 2.5	-10.37%	C- / 3.9

Major Rating Factors: *VelocityShares VIX Short-Term ET has adopted a very risky asset allocation strategy and currently receives an overall TheStreet.com Investment Rating of E- (Very Weak). The fund has a high level of volatility, as measured by both semi-deviation and drawdown factors. It carries a beta of 0.00, meaning the fund's expected move will be 0.0% for every 10% move in the market. As of December 31, 2012, *VelocityShares VIX Short-Term ET traded at a premium of 21.06% above its net asset value, which is worse than its one-year historical average premium of .03%. Unfortunately, the high level of risk (D, Weak) failed to pay off as investors endured very poor performance.

The fund's performance rating is currently E- (Very Weak). It has registered an annualized return of 0.00% over the last three years but is down -16.75% year to date 2012.

This fund has been team managed for 3 years and currently receives a manager quality ranking of 0 (0=worst, 99=best). If you can tolerate very high levels of risk in the hope of improved future returns, holding this fund may be an option.

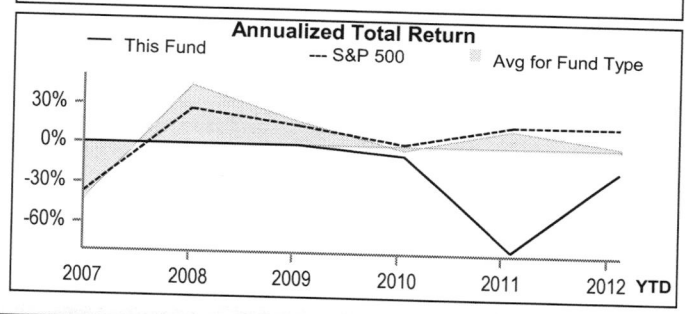

*WCM/BNY Mellon Focused Gro ADR E (AADR)

B+   Good

Fund Family: AdvisorShares Investments LLC
Fund Type: Global
Inception Date: July 20, 2010

Data Date	Investment Rating	Net Assets ($Mil)	Price	Performance Rating/Pts	Total Return Y-T-D	Risk Rating/Pts
12-12	B+	7.00	30.74	B+ / 8.5	5.06%	B- / 7.8
2011	D	6.30	28.11	D- / 1.4	-0.56%	B- / 7.8

Major Rating Factors: Strong performance is the major factor driving the B+ (Good) TheStreet.com Investment Rating for *WCM/BNY Mellon Focused Gro ADR E. The fund currently has a performance rating of B+ (Good) based on an annualized return of 0.00% over the last three years and a total return of 5.06% year to date 2012. Factored into the performance evaluation is an expense ratio of 1.25% (average).

The fund's risk rating is currently B- (Good). It carries a beta of 0.00, meaning the fund's expected move will be 0.0% for every 10% move in the market. Volatility, as measured by both the semi-deviation and a drawdown factor, is considered low. As of December 31, 2012, *WCM/BNY Mellon Focused Gro ADR E traded at a discount of 4.62% below its net asset value, which is better than its one-year historical average discount of .02%.

Kurt R. Winrich currently receives a manager quality ranking of 45 (0=worst, 99=best). If you desire only a moderate level of risk and strong performance, then this fund is an excellent option.

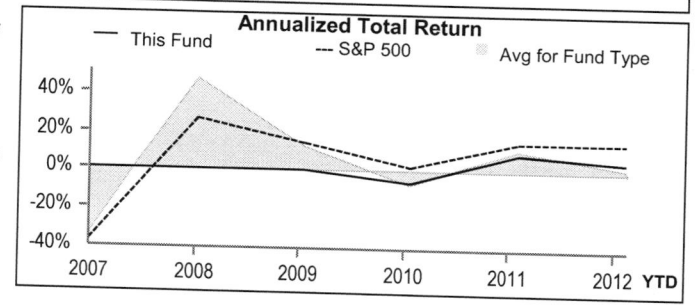

* Denotes ETF Fund

*WisdomTree Asia Local Debt (ALD)   C   Fair

Fund Family: WisdomTree Asset Management Inc
Fund Type: Global
Inception Date: March 17, 2011

Major Rating Factors: Middle of the road best describes *WisdomTree Asia Local Debt whose TheStreet.com Investment Rating is currently a C (Fair). The fund currently has a performance rating of C- (Fair) based on an annualized return of 0.00% over the last three years and a total return of 0.53% year to date 2012. Factored into the performance evaluation is an expense ratio of 0.55% (very low).

The fund's risk rating is currently B+ (Good). It carries a beta of 0.00, meaning the fund's expected move will be 0.0% for every 10% move in the market. Volatility, as measured by both the semi-deviation and a drawdown factor, is considered very low. As of December 31, 2012, *WisdomTree Asia Local Debt traded at a discount of .66% below its net asset value, which is better than its one-year historical average premium of .09%.

David C. Kwan has been running the fund for 2 years and currently receives a manager quality ranking of 81 (0=worst, 99=best). If you desire an average level of risk, then this fund may be an option.

Data Date	Investment Rating	Net Assets ($Mil)	Price	Perfor-mance Rating/Pts	Total Return Y-T-D	Risk Rating/Pts
12-12	C	456.60	52.55	C- / 3.1	0.53%	B+ / 9.1

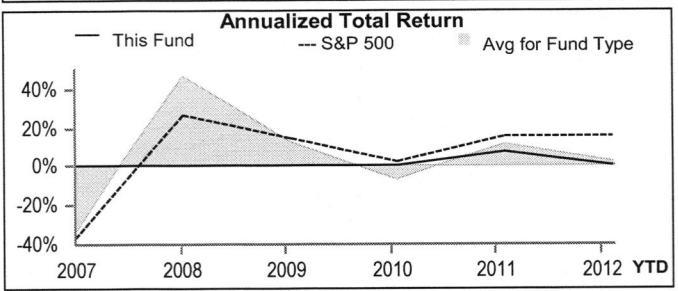

*WisdomTree Asia Pacific ex-Japan (AXJL)   C   Fair

Fund Family: WisdomTree Asset Management Inc
Fund Type: Foreign
Inception Date: June 16, 2006

Major Rating Factors: Middle of the road best describes *WisdomTree Asia Pacific ex-Japan whose TheStreet.com Investment Rating is currently a C (Fair). The fund currently has a performance rating of C (Fair) based on an annualized return of 8.40% over the last three years and a total return of 0.51% year to date 2012. Factored into the performance evaluation is an expense ratio of 0.48% (very low).

The fund's risk rating is currently B- (Good). It carries a beta of 0.96, meaning that its performance tracks fairly well with that of the overall stock market. Volatility, as measured by both the semi-deviation and a drawdown factor, is considered low. As of December 31, 2012, *WisdomTree Asia Pacific ex-Japan traded at a discount of .25% below its net asset value, which is better than its one-year historical average premium of .17%.

Karen Q. Wong has been running the fund for 5 years and currently receives a manager quality ranking of 80 (0=worst, 99=best). If you desire an average level of risk, then this fund may be an option.

Data Date	Investment Rating	Net Assets ($Mil)	Price	Perfor-mance Rating/Pts	Total Return Y-T-D	Risk Rating/Pts
12-12	C	91.80	69.06	C / 5.2	0.51%	B- / 7.2
2011	C+	72.50	58.05	C+ / 5.7	0.63%	B- / 7.5
2010	C-	89.80	66.42	C / 4.6	15.09%	C / 4.5
2009	C	151.37	60.00	C+ / 6.7	51.53%	C / 4.6

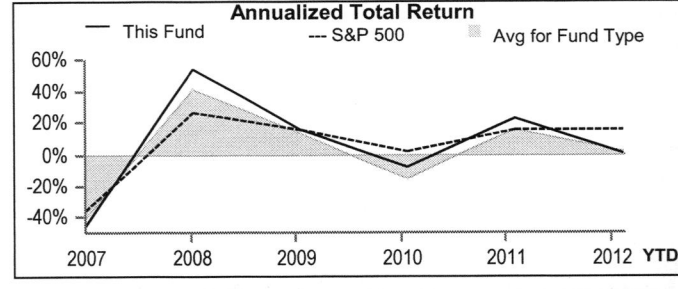

*WisdomTree Australia and NZ Debt (AUNZ)   D+   Weak

Fund Family: WisdomTree Asset Management Inc
Fund Type: Foreign
Inception Date: June 25, 2008

Major Rating Factors:
Disappointing performance is the major factor driving the D+ (Weak) TheStreet.com Investment Rating for *WisdomTree Australia and NZ Debt. The fund currently has a performance rating of D+ (Weak) based on an annualized return of 3.03% over the last three years and a total return of 0.88% year to date 2012. Factored into the performance evaluation is an expense ratio of 0.45% (very low).

The fund's risk rating is currently B- (Good). It carries a beta of 0.43, meaning the fund's expected move will be 4.3% for every 10% move in the market. Volatility, as measured by both the semi-deviation and a drawdown factor, is considered low. As of December 31, 2012, *WisdomTree Australia and NZ Debt traded at a discount of .74% below its net asset value, which is better than its one-year historical average premium of .27%.

David C. Kwan has been running the fund for 5 years and currently receives a manager quality ranking of 64 (0=worst, 99=best). This fund offers only a moderate level of risk but investors looking for strong performance are still waiting.

Data Date	Investment Rating	Net Assets ($Mil)	Price	Perfor-mance Rating/Pts	Total Return Y-T-D	Risk Rating/Pts
12-12	D+	63.40	22.74	D+ / 2.4	0.88%	B- / 7.8
2011	C-	25.90	21.50	D+ / 2.9	0.88%	B / 8.0
2010	A-	28.40	23.66	B+ / 8.3	9.97%	C+ / 6.5
2009	A-	9.47	22.65	B / 7.8	27.81%	C+ / 6.5

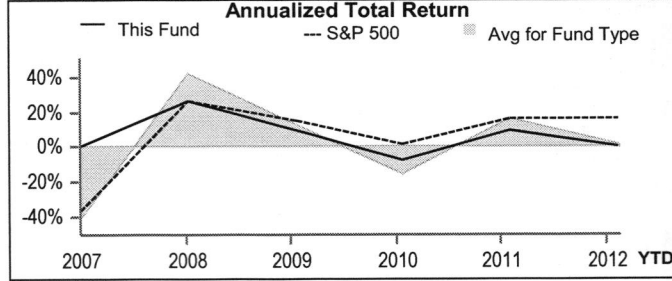

*WisdomTree Australia Divide (AUSE)

C-   Fair

Fund Family: WisdomTree Asset Management Inc
Fund Type: Foreign
Inception Date: June 16, 2006

Major Rating Factors: Middle of the road best describes *WisdomTree Australia Divide whose TheStreet.com Investment Rating is currently a C- (Fair). The fund currently has a performance rating of C (Fair) based on an annualized return of 7.35% over the last three years and a total return of 3.87% year to date 2012. Factored into the performance evaluation is an expense ratio of 0.58% (very low).

The fund's risk rating is currently C+ (Fair). It carries a beta of 1.15, meaning it is expected to move 11.5% for every 10% move in the market. Volatility, as measured by both the semi-deviation and a drawdown factor, is considered low. As of December 31, 2012, *WisdomTree Australia Divide traded at a discount of 3.53% below its net asset value, which is better than its one-year historical average premium of .20%.

Karen Q. Wong has been running the fund for 5 years and currently receives a manager quality ranking of 67 (0=worst, 99=best). If you desire an average level of risk, then this fund may be an option.

Data Date	Investment Rating	Net Assets ($Mil)	Price	Performance Rating/Pts	Total Return Y-T-D	Risk Rating/Pts
12-12	C-	69.00	58.17	C / 4.5	3.87%	C+ / 6.7
2011	C+	50.70	50.74	C+ / 6.6	0.61%	B- / 7.0
2010	C-	78.50	60.41	C+ / 6.2	12.82%	C- / 4.0
2009	C+	103.32	56.34	B / 7.7	75.23%	C- / 4.2

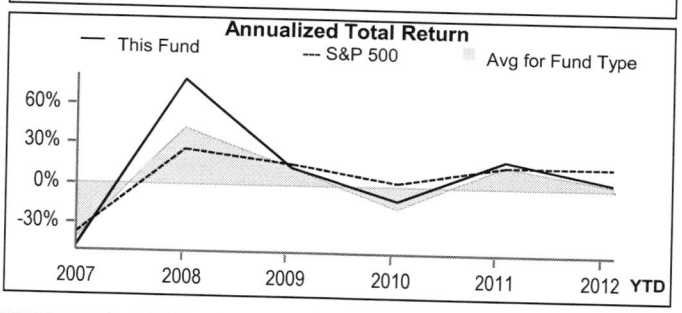

*WisdomTree Commodity Country Equ (CCXE)

C-   Fair

Fund Family: WisdomTree Asset Management Inc
Fund Type: Foreign
Inception Date: October 13, 2006

Major Rating Factors: Middle of the road best describes *WisdomTree Commodity Country Equ whose TheStreet.com Investment Rating is currently a C- (Fair). The fund currently has a performance rating of C (Fair) based on an annualized return of 7.33% over the last three years and a total return of 1.60% year to date 2012. Factored into the performance evaluation is an expense ratio of 0.58% (very low).

The fund's risk rating is currently B- (Good). It carries a beta of 1.21, meaning it is expected to move 12.1% for every 10% move in the market. Volatility, as measured by both the semi-deviation and a drawdown factor, is considered low. As of December 31, 2012, *WisdomTree Commodity Country Equ traded at a discount of 1.97% below its net asset value, which is better than its one-year historical average discount of .28%.

Karen Q. Wong has been running the fund for 5 years and currently receives a manager quality ranking of 70 (0=worst, 99=best). If you desire an average level of risk, then this fund may be an option.

Data Date	Investment Rating	Net Assets ($Mil)	Price	Performance Rating/Pts	Total Return Y-T-D	Risk Rating/Pts
12-12	C-	26.90	31.83	C / 4.6	1.60%	B- / 7.2
2011	C	30.80	28.00	C / 5.2	0.36%	B- / 7.3
2010	C-	41.90	32.15	C / 5.1	16.76%	C- / 3.9
2009	C	41.79	28.12	B- / 7.0	51.62%	C / 4.4

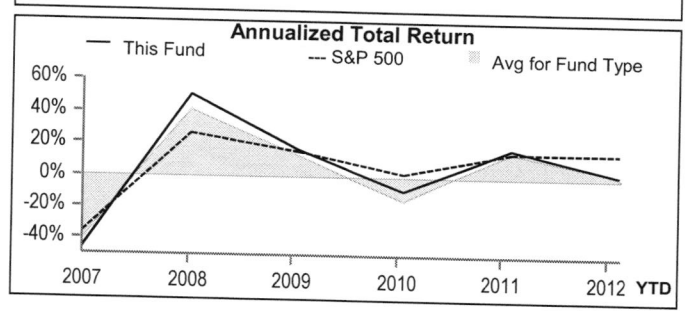

*WisdomTree DEFA (DWM)

C-   Fair

Fund Family: WisdomTree Asset Management Inc
Fund Type: Foreign
Inception Date: June 16, 2006

Major Rating Factors: Middle of the road best describes *WisdomTree DEFA whose TheStreet.com Investment Rating is currently a C- (Fair). The fund currently has a performance rating of C- (Fair) based on an annualized return of 3.78% over the last three years and a total return of 2.41% year to date 2012. Factored into the performance evaluation is an expense ratio of 0.48% (very low).

The fund's risk rating is currently B- (Good). It carries a beta of 1.03, meaning that its performance tracks fairly well with that of the overall stock market. Volatility, as measured by both the semi-deviation and a drawdown factor, is considered low. As of December 31, 2012, *WisdomTree DEFA traded at a discount of 1.98% below its net asset value, which is better than its one-year historical average premium of .36%.

Denise Krisko currently receives a manager quality ranking of 51 (0=worst, 99=best). If you desire an average level of risk, then this fund may be an option.

Data Date	Investment Rating	Net Assets ($Mil)	Price	Performance Rating/Pts	Total Return Y-T-D	Risk Rating/Pts
12-12	C-	418.20	46.47	C- / 4.0	2.41%	B- / 7.1
2011	D+	326.30	40.92	D+ / 2.7	-0.83%	B- / 7.4
2010	D-	426.80	47.37	D- / 1.4	5.19%	C / 4.8
2009	D	422.40	46.69	D+ / 2.3	24.55%	C / 5.0

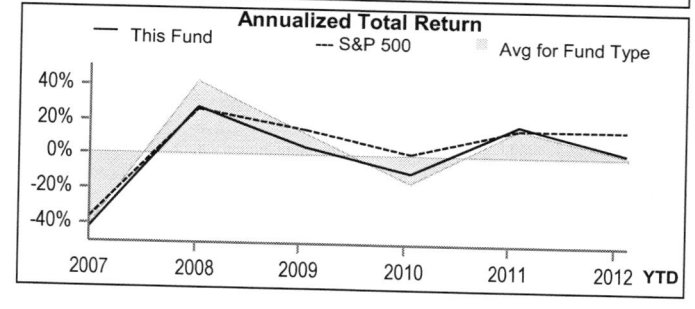

*WisdomTree DEFA Equity Income (DTH)   D+   Weak

Fund Family: WisdomTree Asset Management Inc
Fund Type: Foreign
Inception Date: June 16, 2006

Major Rating Factors: *WisdomTree DEFA Equity Income receives a TheStreet.com Investment Rating of D+ (Weak). The fund currently has a performance rating of C- (Fair) based on an annualized return of 3.23% over the last three years and a total return of 2.89% year to date 2012. Factored into the performance evaluation is an expense ratio of 0.58% (very low).

The fund's risk rating is currently C+ (Fair). It carries a beta of 1.07, meaning that its performance tracks fairly well with that of the overall stock market. Volatility, as measured by both the semi-deviation and a drawdown factor, is considered low. As of December 31, 2012, *WisdomTree DEFA Equity Income traded at a discount of 2.13% below its net asset value, which is better than its one-year historical average premium of .31%.

Karen Q. Wong has been running the fund for 5 years and currently receives a manager quality ranking of 37 (0=worst, 99=best). If you desire an average level of risk, then this fund may be an option.

Data Date	Investment Rating	Net Assets ($Mil)	Price	Performance Rating/Pts	Total Return Y-T-D	Risk Rating/Pts
12-12	D+	183.50	40.43	C- / 3.8	2.89%	C+ / 6.9
2011	D+	145.60	36.56	D+ / 2.8	-1.23%	B- / 7.3
2010	D-	120.50	41.10	D- / 1.0	-0.99%	C / 4.5
2009	D	155.16	43.50	D+ / 2.4	30.43%	C / 4.7

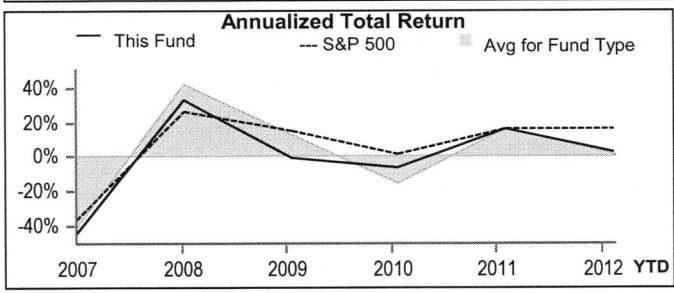

*WisdomTree Dividend Ex-Financial (DTN)   B   Good

Fund Family: WisdomTree Asset Management Inc
Fund Type: Income
Inception Date: June 16, 2006

Major Rating Factors: *WisdomTree Dividend Ex-Financial receives a TheStreet.com Investment Rating of B (Good). The fund currently has a performance rating of C+ (Fair) based on an annualized return of 15.88% over the last three years and a total return of 2.79% year to date 2012. Factored into the performance evaluation is an expense ratio of 0.38% (very low).

The fund's risk rating is currently B (Good). It carries a beta of 0.75, meaning the fund's expected move will be 7.5% for every 10% move in the market. Volatility, as measured by both the semi-deviation and a drawdown factor, is considered low. As of December 31, 2012, *WisdomTree Dividend Ex-Financial traded at a discount of 2.71% below its net asset value, which is better than its one-year historical average premium of .07%.

Karen Q. Wong has been running the fund for 5 years and currently receives a manager quality ranking of 84 (0=worst, 99=best). If you desire an average level of risk, then this fund may be an option.

Data Date	Investment Rating	Net Assets ($Mil)	Price	Performance Rating/Pts	Total Return Y-T-D	Risk Rating/Pts
12-12	B	1,080.80	55.58	C+ / 6.6	2.79%	B / 8.9
2011	B-	1,010.40	52.00	B- / 7.2	0.00%	B- / 7.7
2010	C	343.00	48.02	C / 5.4	21.44%	C+ / 5.6
2009	D	145.81	41.02	D / 2.0	22.73%	C+ / 5.7

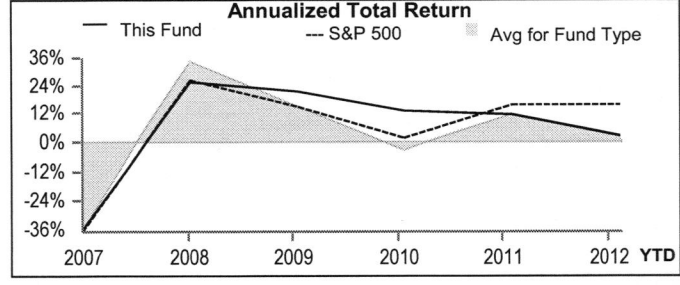

*WisdomTree Dr Brazilian Real Fun (BZF)   D   Weak

Fund Family: WisdomTree Asset Management Inc
Fund Type: Foreign
Inception Date: May 13, 2008

Major Rating Factors:
Disappointing performance is the major factor driving the D (Weak) TheStreet.com Investment Rating for *WisdomTree Dr Brazilian Real Fun. The fund currently has a performance rating of D (Weak) based on an annualized return of 5.29% over the last three years and a total return of 0.32% year to date 2012. Factored into the performance evaluation is an expense ratio of 0.45% (very low).

The fund's risk rating is currently C+ (Fair). It carries a beta of 0.62, meaning the fund's expected move will be 6.2% for every 10% move in the market. Volatility, as measured by both the semi-deviation and a drawdown factor, is considered low. As of December 31, 2012, *WisdomTree Dr Brazilian Real Fun traded at a discount of .79% below its net asset value, which is better than its one-year historical average discount of .15%.

David C. Kwan has been running the fund for 5 years and currently receives a manager quality ranking of 67 (0=worst, 99=best). This fund offers only a moderate level of risk but investors looking for strong performance are still waiting.

Data Date	Investment Rating	Net Assets ($Mil)	Price	Performance Rating/Pts	Total Return Y-T-D	Risk Rating/Pts
12-12	D	60.60	18.91	D / 2.2	0.32%	C+ / 5.8
2011	C-	81.90	19.47	C / 5.4	0.57%	C+ / 6.4
2010	A	132.80	26.55	A / 9.4	24.53%	C+ / 6.4
2009	A+	112.57	26.53	B+ / 8.6	44.17%	C+ / 6.5

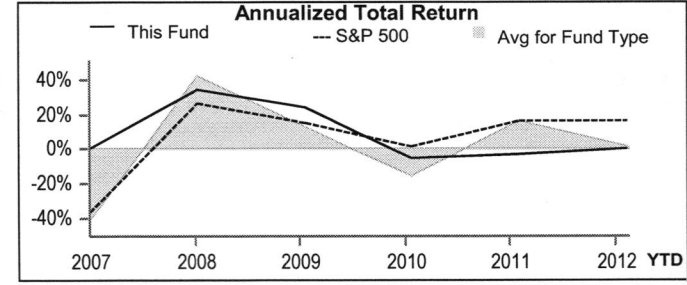

*WisdomTree Dr Chinese Yuan Fund (CYB)

C-   **Fair**

Fund Family: WisdomTree Asset Management Inc
Fund Type: Foreign
Inception Date: May 13, 2008

Major Rating Factors:

Disappointing performance is the major factor driving the C- (Fair) TheStreet.com Investment Rating for *WisdomTree Dr Chinese Yuan Fund. The fund currently has a performance rating of D (Weak) based on an annualized return of 2.64% over the last three years and a total return of 0.74% year to date 2012. Factored into the performance evaluation is an expense ratio of 0.45% (very low).

The fund's risk rating is currently B+ (Good). It carries a beta of 0.10, meaning the fund's expected move will be 1.0% for every 10% move in the market. Volatility, as measured by both the semi-deviation and a drawdown factor, is considered very low. As of December 31, 2012, *WisdomTree Dr Chinese Yuan Fund traded at a discount of .82% below its net asset value, which is better than its one-year historical average discount of .11%.

David C. Kwan has been running the fund for 5 years and currently receives a manager quality ranking of 67 (0=worst, 99=best). This fund offers only a moderate level of risk but investors looking for strong performance are still waiting.

Data Date	Investment Rating	Net Assets ($Mil)	Price	Performance Rating/Pts	Total Return Y-T-D	Risk Rating/Pts
12-12	C-	240.30	25.53	D / 2.0	0.74%	B+ / 9.8
2011	C	448.50	25.19	C- / 3.0	0.60%	B+ / 9.8
2010	B-	639.60	25.37	C- / 3.6	1.79%	B / 8.9
2009	C	136.66	25.21	D / 2.0	1.16%	B+ / 9.1

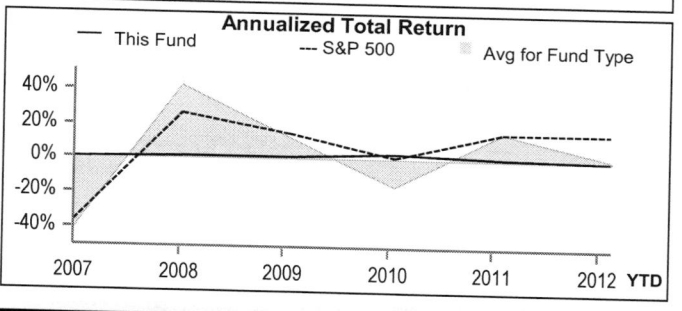

Annualized Total Return

*WisdomTree Dr Commodity Curr Fun (CCX)

D   **Weak**

Fund Family: WisdomTree Asset Management Inc
Fund Type: Global
Inception Date: September 24, 2010

Major Rating Factors:

Disappointing performance is the major factor driving the D (Weak) TheStreet.com Investment Rating for *WisdomTree Dr Commodity Curr Fun. The fund currently has a performance rating of D+ (Weak) based on an annualized return of 0.00% over the last three years and a total return of 0.37% year to date 2012. Factored into the performance evaluation is an expense ratio of 0.55% (very low).

The fund's risk rating is currently C+ (Fair). It carries a beta of 0.00, meaning the fund's expected move will be 0.0% for every 10% move in the market. Volatility, as measured by both the semi-deviation and a drawdown factor, is considered low. As of December 31, 2012, *WisdomTree Dr Commodity Curr Fun traded at a discount of .51% below its net asset value, which is better than its one-year historical average discount of .18%.

David C. Kwan has been running the fund for 3 years and currently receives a manager quality ranking of 27 (0=worst, 99=best). This fund offers only a moderate level of risk but investors looking for strong performance are still waiting.

Data Date	Investment Rating	Net Assets ($Mil)	Price	Performance Rating/Pts	Total Return Y-T-D	Risk Rating/Pts
12-12	D	23.60	21.48	D+ / 2.9	0.37%	C+ / 6.6
2011	D-	38.60	20.31	D- / 1.0	-0.24%	C+ / 6.5

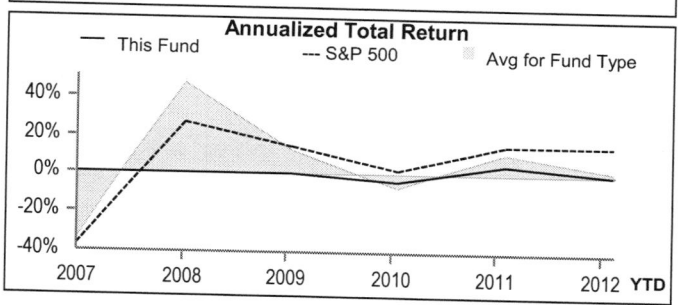

Annualized Total Return

*WisdomTree Dr Emerg Curr Fd (CEW)

D+   **Weak**

Fund Family: WisdomTree Asset Management Inc
Fund Type: Foreign
Inception Date: May 6, 2009

Major Rating Factors:

Disappointing performance is the major factor driving the D+ (Weak) TheStreet.com Investment Rating for *WisdomTree Dr Emerg Curr Fd. The fund currently has a performance rating of D+ (Weak) based on an annualized return of 2.98% over the last three years and a total return of 0.48% year to date 2012. Factored into the performance evaluation is an expense ratio of 0.55% (very low).

The fund's risk rating is currently B (Good). It carries a beta of 0.47, meaning the fund's expected move will be 4.7% for every 10% move in the market. Volatility, as measured by both the semi-deviation and a drawdown factor, is considered low. As of December 31, 2012, *WisdomTree Dr Emerg Curr Fd traded at a discount of .47% below its net asset value, which is better than its one-year historical average discount of .11%.

David C. Kwan has been running the fund for 4 years and currently receives a manager quality ranking of 63 (0=worst, 99=best). This fund offers only a moderate level of risk but investors looking for strong performance are still waiting.

Data Date	Investment Rating	Net Assets ($Mil)	Price	Performance Rating/Pts	Total Return Y-T-D	Risk Rating/Pts
12-12	D+	271.60	21.09	D+ / 2.3	0.48%	B / 8.2
2011	D+	344.00	19.70	D / 1.8	0.41%	B / 8.4
2010	B	296.90	22.56	C+ / 6.9	6.40%	B / 8.8

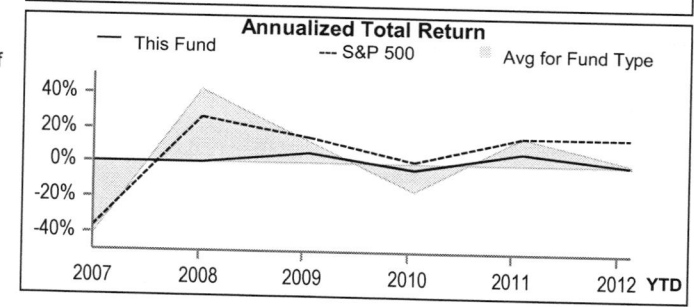

Annualized Total Return

* Denotes ETF Fund

*WisdomTree Dr Indian Rupee Fund (ICN)   D   Weak

Fund Family: WisdomTree Asset Management Inc
Fund Type: Foreign
Inception Date: May 13, 2008

Major Rating Factors:
Disappointing performance is the major factor driving the D (Weak) TheStreet.com Investment Rating for *WisdomTree Dr Indian Rupee Fund. The fund currently has a performance rating of D- (Weak) based on an annualized return of -0.70% over the last three years and a total return of -0.31% year to date 2012. Factored into the performance evaluation is an expense ratio of 0.45% (very low).

The fund's risk rating is currently B- (Good). It carries a beta of 0.45, meaning the fund's expected move will be 4.5% for every 10% move in the market. Volatility, as measured by both the semi-deviation and a drawdown factor, is considered low. As of December 31, 2012, *WisdomTree Dr Indian Rupee Fund traded at a discount of .57% below its net asset value, which is better than its one-year historical average premium of .06%.

David C. Kwan has been running the fund for 5 years and currently receives a manager quality ranking of 35 (0=worst, 99=best). This fund offers only a moderate level of risk but investors looking for strong performance are still waiting.

Data Date	Investment Rating	Net Assets ($Mil)	Price	Performance Rating/Pts	Total Return Y-T-D	Risk Rating/Pts
12-12	D	14.70	21.09	D- / 1.3	-0.31%	B- / 7.0
2011	D	16.10	20.12	D / 1.8	1.04%	B- / 7.4
2010	A-	21.20	26.58	B- / 7.0	7.89%	B / 8.0
2009	C+	11.89	25.17	C / 4.4	7.98%	B / 8.2

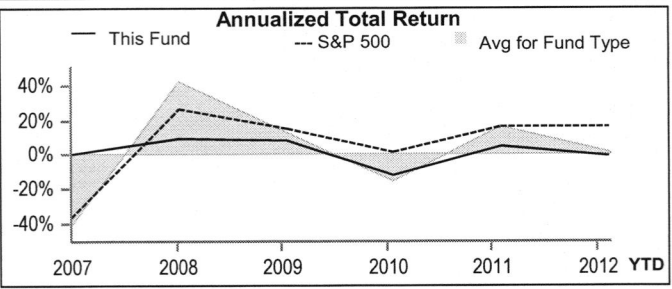

*WisdomTree Earnings 500 Fund (EPS)   C+   Fair

Fund Family: WisdomTree Asset Management Inc
Fund Type: Income
Inception Date: February 23, 2007

Major Rating Factors: Middle of the road best describes *WisdomTree Earnings 500 Fund whose TheStreet.com Investment Rating is currently a C+ (Fair). The fund currently has a performance rating of C (Fair) based on an annualized return of 11.37% over the last three years and a total return of 3.71% year to date 2012. Factored into the performance evaluation is an expense ratio of 0.28% (very low).

The fund's risk rating is currently B (Good). It carries a beta of 0.93, meaning that its performance tracks fairly well with that of the overall stock market. Volatility, as measured by both the semi-deviation and a drawdown factor, is considered low. As of December 31, 2012, *WisdomTree Earnings 500 Fund traded at a discount of 3.52% below its net asset value, which is better than its one-year historical average premium of .01%.

Karen Q. Wong has been running the fund for 5 years and currently receives a manager quality ranking of 57 (0=worst, 99=best). If you desire an average level of risk, then this fund may be an option.

Data Date	Investment Rating	Net Assets ($Mil)	Price	Performance Rating/Pts	Total Return Y-T-D	Risk Rating/Pts
12-12	C+	56.90	49.36	C / 5.2	3.71%	B / 8.2
2011	C+	61.50	44.03	C / 5.5	1.89%	B / 8.1
2010	C-	69.30	43.34	C- / 3.5	13.28%	C+ / 6.1
2009	A	55.24	38.97	B / 8.2	23.42%	C+ / 6.2

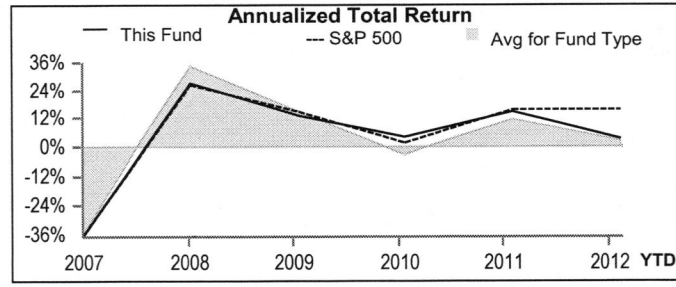

*WisdomTree Emg Mkts Eqty Inc Fd (DEM)   C-   Fair

Fund Family: WisdomTree Asset Management Inc
Fund Type: Emerging Market
Inception Date: July 13, 2007

Major Rating Factors: Middle of the road best describes *WisdomTree Emg Mkts Eqty Inc Fd whose TheStreet.com Investment Rating is currently a C- (Fair). The fund currently has a performance rating of C- (Fair) based on an annualized return of 7.99% over the last three years and a total return of -0.03% year to date 2012. Factored into the performance evaluation is an expense ratio of 0.63% (very low).

The fund's risk rating is currently B- (Good). It carries a beta of 0.90, meaning that its performance tracks fairly well with that of the overall stock market. Volatility, as measured by both the semi-deviation and a drawdown factor, is considered low. As of December 31, 2012, *WisdomTree Emg Mkts Eqty Inc Fd traded at a premium of .67% above its net asset value, which is worse than its one-year historical average premium of .52%.

Karen Q. Wong has been running the fund for 5 years and currently receives a manager quality ranking of 79 (0=worst, 99=best). If you desire an average level of risk, then this fund may be an option.

Data Date	Investment Rating	Net Assets ($Mil)	Price	Performance Rating/Pts	Total Return Y-T-D	Risk Rating/Pts
12-12	C-	4,866.00	57.19	C- / 3.8	-0.03%	B- / 7.1
2011	C+	2,144.70	51.27	C+ / 6.4	0.35%	B- / 7.3
2010	B+	1,166.90	59.69	B+ / 8.3	25.43%	C / 5.2
2009	A	356.50	49.71	A- / 9.2	53.72%	C / 5.4

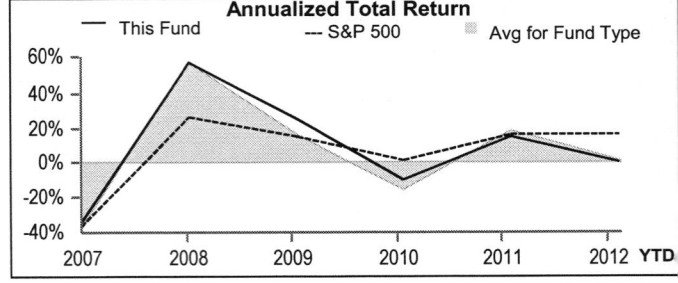

*WisdomTree Emg Mkts Local Debt F (ELD)

C+   **Fair**

Fund Family: WisdomTree Asset Management Inc
Fund Type: Emerging Market
Inception Date: August 9, 2010

Major Rating Factors: Middle of the road best describes *WisdomTree Emg Mkts Local Debt F whose TheStreet.com Investment Rating is currently a C+ (Fair). The fund currently has a performance rating of C+ (Fair) based on an annualized return of 0.00% over the last three years and a total return of 0.17% year to date 2012. Factored into the performance evaluation is an expense ratio of 0.55% (very low).

The fund's risk rating is currently B (Good). It carries a beta of 0.00, meaning the fund's expected move will be 0.0% for every 10% move in the market. Volatility, as measured by both the semi-deviation and a drawdown factor, is considered low. As of December 31, 2012, *WisdomTree Emg Mkts Local Debt F traded at a premium of .04% above its net asset value, which is better than its one-year historical average premium of .19%.

David C. Kwan has been running the fund for 3 years and currently receives a manager quality ranking of 92 (0=worst, 99=best). If you desire an average level of risk, then this fund may be an option.

Data Date	Investment Rating	Net Assets ($Mil)	Price	Performance Rating/Pts	Total Return Y-T-D	Risk Rating/Pts
12-12	C+	1,497.50	53.46	C+ / 5.6	0.17%	B / 8.6
2011	D+	1,078.10	48.64	D- / 1.5	0.12%	B / 8.6

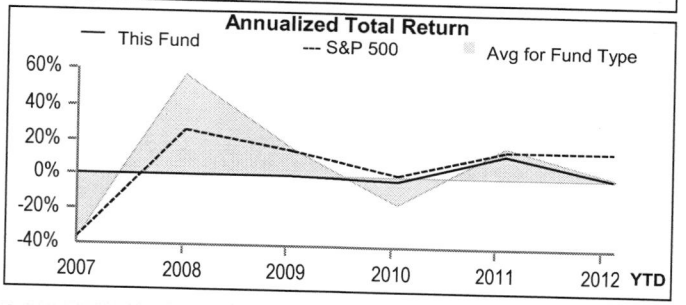

*WisdomTree Emg Mkts SmCap Div Fd (DGS)

C   **Fair**

Fund Family: WisdomTree Asset Management Inc
Fund Type: Emerging Market
Inception Date: October 30, 2007

Major Rating Factors: Middle of the road best describes *WisdomTree Emg Mkts SmCap Div Fd whose TheStreet.com Investment Rating is currently a C (Fair). The fund currently has a performance rating of C (Fair) based on an annualized return of 8.20% over the last three years and a total return of 1.31% year to date 2012. Factored into the performance evaluation is an expense ratio of 0.63% (very low).

The fund's risk rating is currently C+ (Fair). It carries a beta of 0.99, meaning that its performance tracks fairly well with that of the overall stock market. Volatility, as measured by both the semi-deviation and a drawdown factor, is considered low. As of December 31, 2012, *WisdomTree Emg Mkts SmCap Div Fd traded at a discount of .84% below its net asset value, which is better than its one-year historical average premium of .55%.

Karen Q. Wong has been running the fund for 5 years and currently receives a manager quality ranking of 74 (0=worst, 99=best). If you desire an average level of risk, then this fund may be an option.

Data Date	Investment Rating	Net Assets ($Mil)	Price	Performance Rating/Pts	Total Return Y-T-D	Risk Rating/Pts
12-12	C	1,191.60	49.44	C / 5.5	1.31%	C+ / 6.6
2011	C+	739.40	41.34	C+ / 6.5	1.21%	C+ / 6.9
2010	B	929.70	54.50	B+ / 8.4	30.88%	C / 4.9
2009	A	203.24	43.05	A+ / 9.7	78.53%	C / 4.9

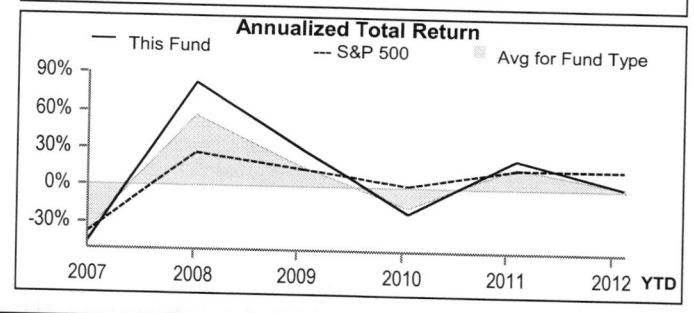

*WisdomTree Equity Income Fund (DHS)

B   **Good**

Fund Family: WisdomTree Asset Management Inc
Fund Type: Growth and Income
Inception Date: June 16, 2006

Major Rating Factors: *WisdomTree Equity Income Fund receives a TheStreet.com Investment Rating of B (Good). The fund currently has a performance rating of C+ (Fair) based on an annualized return of 15.60% over the last three years and a total return of 3.30% year to date 2012. Factored into the performance evaluation is an expense ratio of 0.38% (very low).

The fund's risk rating is currently B+ (Good). It carries a beta of 0.62, meaning the fund's expected move will be 6.2% for every 10% move in the market. Volatility, as measured by both the semi-deviation and a drawdown factor, is considered very low. As of December 31, 2012, *WisdomTree Equity Income Fund traded at a discount of 3.13% below its net asset value, which is better than its one-year historical average premium of .13%.

Karen Q. Wong has been running the fund for 5 years and currently receives a manager quality ranking of 86 (0=worst, 99=best). If you desire an average level of risk, then this fund may be an option.

Data Date	Investment Rating	Net Assets ($Mil)	Price	Performance Rating/Pts	Total Return Y-T-D	Risk Rating/Pts
12-12	B	535.90	45.80	C+ / 6.2	3.30%	B+ / 9.0
2011	C+	366.20	42.92	C+ / 6.8	-0.28%	B- / 7.4
2010	D	169.40	38.91	D+ / 2.6	17.63%	C / 5.1
2009	D-	141.20	34.57	D- / 1.1	14.64%	C / 5.2

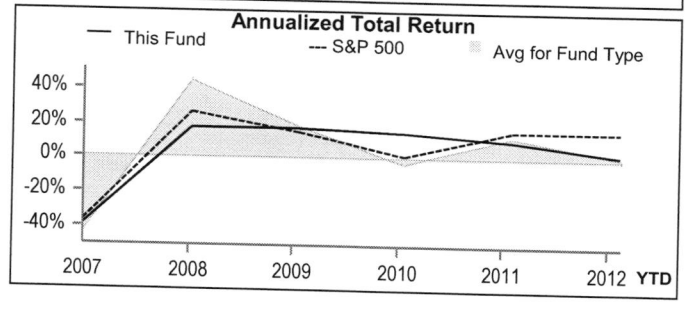

* Denotes ETF Fund

*WisdomTree Euro Debt (EU)

D+   **Weak**

Fund Family: WisdomTree Asset Management Inc
Fund Type: Foreign
Inception Date: May 13, 2008

Data Date	Investment Rating	Net Assets ($Mil)	Price	Performance Rating/Pts	Total Return Y-T-D	Risk Rating/Pts
12-12	D+	4.50	22.27	D / 2.1	0.96%	B- / 7.5
2011	D+	4.70	19.80	D / 1.6	1.87%	B / 8.2
2010	D+	9.20	21.55	D- / 1.5	-6.59%	B- / 7.2
2009	C	9.86	23.07	D+ / 2.6	3.73%	B- / 7.6

Major Rating Factors:
Disappointing performance is the major factor driving the D+ (Weak) TheStreet.com Investment Rating for *WisdomTree Euro Debt. The fund currently has a performance rating of D (Weak) based on an annualized return of 0.07% over the last three years and a total return of 0.96% year to date 2012. Factored into the performance evaluation is an expense ratio of 0.35% (very low).

The fund's risk rating is currently B- (Good). It carries a beta of 0.62, meaning the fund's expected move will be 6.2% for every 10% move in the market. Volatility, as measured by both the semi-deviation and a drawdown factor, is considered low. As of December 31, 2012, *WisdomTree Euro Debt traded at a discount of 1.63% below its net asset value, which is worse than its one-year historical average discount of 3.43%.

David C. Kwan has been running the fund for 5 years and currently receives a manager quality ranking of 32 (0=worst, 99=best). This fund offers only a moderate level of risk but investors looking for strong performance are still waiting.

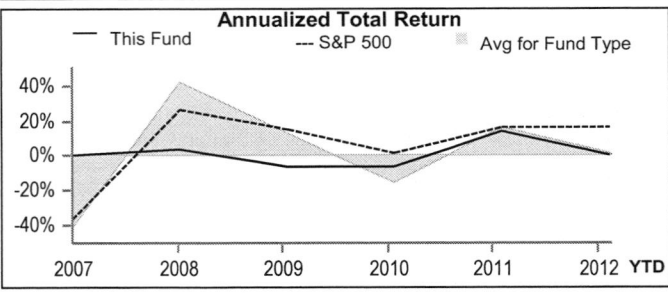

*WisdomTree Europe Hedged Equity (HEDJ)

C   **Fair**

Fund Family: WisdomTree Asset Management Inc
Fund Type: Foreign
Inception Date: December 31, 2009

Data Date	Investment Rating	Net Assets ($Mil)	Price	Performance Rating/Pts	Total Return Y-T-D	Risk Rating/Pts
12-12	C	35.10	47.67	C- / 4.0	1.96%	B / 8.2
2011	D+	18.40	41.20	D- / 1.3	0.46%	B / 8.2
2010	A-	21.00	46.85	B- / 7.1	3.53%	B- / 7.8

Major Rating Factors: Middle of the road best describes *WisdomTree Europe Hedged Equity whose TheStreet.com Investment Rating is currently a C (Fair). The fund currently has a performance rating of C- (Fair) based on an annualized return of 4.28% over the last three years and a total return of 1.96% year to date 2012. Factored into the performance evaluation is an expense ratio of 0.58% (very low).

The fund's risk rating is currently B (Good). It carries a beta of 0.57, meaning the fund's expected move will be 5.7% for every 10% move in the market. Volatility, as measured by both the semi-deviation and a drawdown factor, is considered low. As of December 31, 2012, *WisdomTree Europe Hedged Equity traded at a discount of 1.06% below its net asset value, which is better than its one-year historical average premium of .89%.

Karen Q. Wong has been running the fund for 4 years and currently receives a manager quality ranking of 64 (0=worst, 99=best). If you desire an average level of risk, then this fund may be an option.

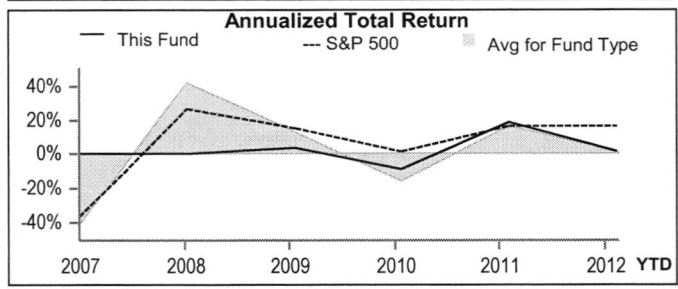

*WisdomTree Europe Small Cap Div (DFE)

C+   **Fair**

Fund Family: WisdomTree Asset Management Inc
Fund Type: Foreign
Inception Date: June 16, 2006

Data Date	Investment Rating	Net Assets ($Mil)	Price	Performance Rating/Pts	Total Return Y-T-D	Risk Rating/Pts
12-12	C+	34.10	41.08	B / 7.7	3.94%	C+ / 6.5
2011	D+	21.20	32.65	C- / 3.4	-0.56%	C+ / 6.8
2010	D	29.80	42.55	C- / 3.4	19.92%	C- / 4.1
2009	D-	25.71	36.50	D / 1.7	47.87%	C- / 4.1

Major Rating Factors: Strong performance is the major factor driving the C+ (Fair) TheStreet.com Investment Rating for *WisdomTree Europe Small Cap Div. The fund currently has a performance rating of B (Good) based on an annualized return of 7.93% over the last three years and a total return of 3.94% year to date 2012. Factored into the performance evaluation is an expense ratio of 0.58% (very low).

The fund's risk rating is currently C+ (Fair). It carries a beta of 1.18, meaning it is expected to move 11.8% for every 10% move in the market. Volatility, as measured by both the semi-deviation and a drawdown factor, is considered low. As of December 31, 2012, *WisdomTree Europe Small Cap Div traded at a discount of 2.84% below its net asset value, which is better than its one-year historical average premium of .68%.

Karen Q. Wong has been running the fund for 5 years and currently receives a manager quality ranking of 75 (0=worst, 99=best). If you desire only a moderate level of risk and strong performance, then this fund is an excellent option.

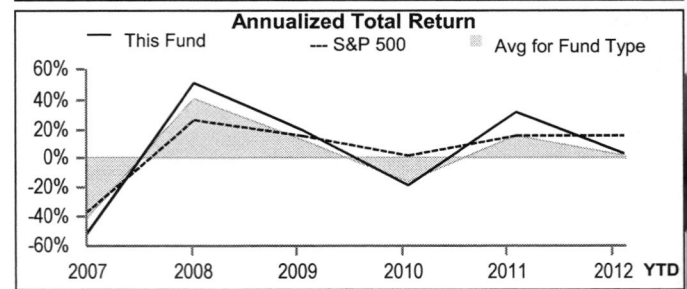

*WisdomTree Global Equity Income (DEW)

C-   **Fair**

Fund Family: WisdomTree Asset Management Inc
Fund Type: Global
Inception Date: June 16, 2006

Major Rating Factors: Middle of the road best describes *WisdomTree Global Equity Income whose TheStreet.com Investment Rating is currently a C- (Fair). The fund currently has a performance rating of C- (Fair) based on an annualized return of 6.46% over the last three years and a total return of 1.68% year to date 2012. Factored into the performance evaluation is an expense ratio of 0.58% (very low).

The fund's risk rating is currently B- (Good). It carries a beta of 0.88, meaning the fund's expected move will be 8.8% for every 10% move in the market. Volatility, as measured by both the semi-deviation and a drawdown factor, is considered low. As of December 31, 2012, *WisdomTree Global Equity Income traded at a discount of 1.88% below its net asset value, which is better than its one-year historical average premium of .49%.

Karen Q. Wong has been running the fund for 5 years and currently receives a manager quality ranking of 69 (0=worst, 99=best). If you desire an average level of risk, then this fund may be an option.

Data Date	Investment Rating	Net Assets ($Mil)	Price	Performance Rating/Pts	Total Return Y-T-D	Risk Rating/Pts
12-12	C-	98.60	43.27	C- / 4.1	1.68%	B- / 7.8
2011	C-	70.20	39.31	C- / 3.9	-1.14%	B- / 7.7
2010	D	69.30	42.15	D- / 1.3	5.82%	C / 5.3
2009	D-	38.13	41.36	D / 1.9	29.97%	C / 4.7

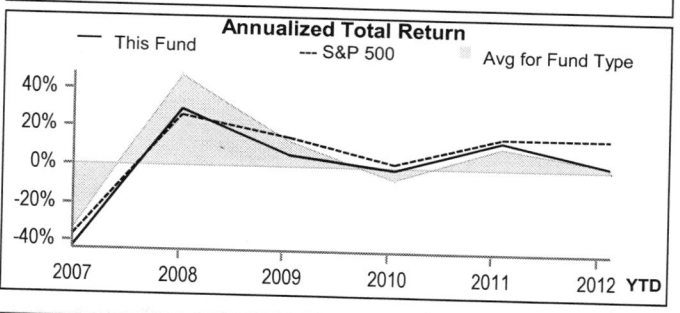

*WisdomTree Global ex-US Growth (DNL)

D+   **Weak**

Fund Family: WisdomTree Asset Management Inc
Fund Type: Global
Inception Date: June 16, 2006

Major Rating Factors: *WisdomTree Global ex-US Growth receives a TheStreet.com Investment Rating of D+ (Weak). The fund currently has a performance rating of C- (Fair) based on an annualized return of 5.32% over the last three years and a total return of 0.09% year to date 2012. Factored into the performance evaluation is an expense ratio of 0.58% (very low).

The fund's risk rating is currently C+ (Fair). It carries a beta of 1.06, meaning that its performance tracks fairly well with that of the overall stock market. Volatility, as measured by both the semi-deviation and a drawdown factor, is considered low. As of December 31, 2012, *WisdomTree Global ex-US Growth traded at a premium of .57% above its net asset value, which is worse than its one-year historical average premium of .06%.

Karen Q. Wong has been running the fund for 5 years and currently receives a manager quality ranking of 64 (0=worst, 99=best). If you desire an average level of risk, then this fund may be an option.

Data Date	Investment Rating	Net Assets ($Mil)	Price	Performance Rating/Pts	Total Return Y-T-D	Risk Rating/Pts
12-12	D+	67.60	52.94	C- / 3.3	0.09%	C+ / 6.7
2011	D+	55.50	46.37	D+ / 2.8	1.06%	B- / 7.4
2010	C+	37.80	54.19	C+ / 6.5	14.05%	C+ / 6.6
2009	C-	18.04	48.89	D+ / 2.5	11.74%	B- / 7.0

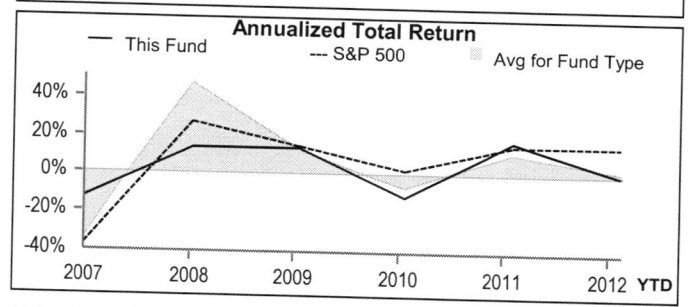

*WisdomTree Global ex-US Real Est (DRW)

C+   **Fair**

Fund Family: WisdomTree Asset Management Inc
Fund Type: Foreign
Inception Date: June 5, 2007

Major Rating Factors: Strong performance is the major factor driving the C+ (Fair) TheStreet.com Investment Rating for *WisdomTree Global ex-US Real Est. The fund currently has a performance rating of B+ (Good) based on an annualized return of 14.45% over the last three years and a total return of 1.57% year to date 2012. Factored into the performance evaluation is an expense ratio of 0.58% (very low).

The fund's risk rating is currently C (Fair). It carries a beta of 1.03, meaning that its performance tracks fairly well with that of the overall stock market. Volatility, as measured by both the semi-deviation and a drawdown factor, is considered average. As of December 31, 2012, *WisdomTree Global ex-US Real Est traded at a discount of 1.19% below its net asset value, which is better than its one-year historical average premium of .07%.

Karen Q. Wong has been running the fund for 5 years and currently receives a manager quality ranking of 89 (0=worst, 99=best). If you desire an average level of risk and strong performance, then this fund is a good option.

Data Date	Investment Rating	Net Assets ($Mil)	Price	Performance Rating/Pts	Total Return Y-T-D	Risk Rating/Pts
12-12	C+	108.00	29.97	B+ / 8.4	1.57%	C / 5.3
2011	D	102.80	23.21	C- / 3.9	0.39%	C / 5.3
2010	D	118.60	28.63	D+ / 2.8	24.49%	C- / 3.9
2009	C+	82.82	26.77	B+ / 8.7	38.41%	C- / 3.9

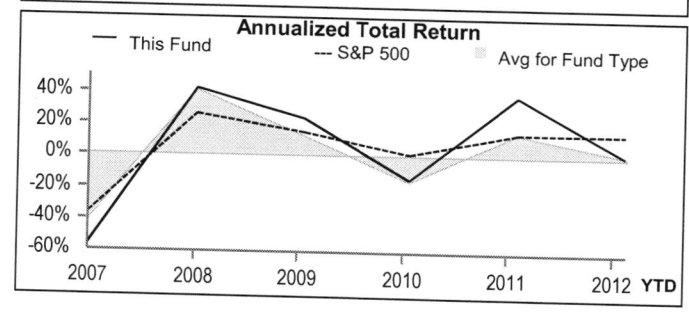

*WisdomTree Global ex-US Utilitie (DBU)   D   Weak

Fund Family: WisdomTree Asset Management Inc
Fund Type: Utilities
Inception Date: October 13, 2006

Data Date	Investment Rating	Net Assets ($Mil)	Price	Perfor-mance Rating/Pts	Total Return Y-T-D	Risk Rating/Pts
12-12	D	37.10	18.40	D- / 1.5	0.65%	B- / 7.5
2011	D	30.30	17.78	D / 1.7	-0.50%	B- / 7.4
2010	D-	36.30	20.14	E+ / 0.8	-4.91%	C / 5.1
2009	D	38.57	22.50	D / 1.7	0.96%	C+ / 5.6

Major Rating Factors:
Disappointing performance is the major factor driving the D (Weak) TheStreet.com Investment Rating for *WisdomTree Global ex-US Utilitie. The fund currently has a performance rating of D- (Weak) based on an annualized return of -1.76% over the last three years and a total return of 0.65% year to date 2012. Factored into the performance evaluation is an expense ratio of 0.58% (very low).

The fund's risk rating is currently B- (Good). It carries a beta of 1.00, meaning that its performance tracks fairly well with that of the overall stock market. Volatility, as measured by both the semi-deviation and a drawdown factor, is considered low. As of December 31, 2012, *WisdomTree Global ex-US Utilitie traded at a discount of .43% below its net asset value, which is better than its one-year historical average premium of .05%.

Karen Q. Wong has been running the fund for 5 years and currently receives a manager quality ranking of 13 (0=worst, 99=best). This fund offers only a moderate level of risk but investors looking for strong performance are still waiting.

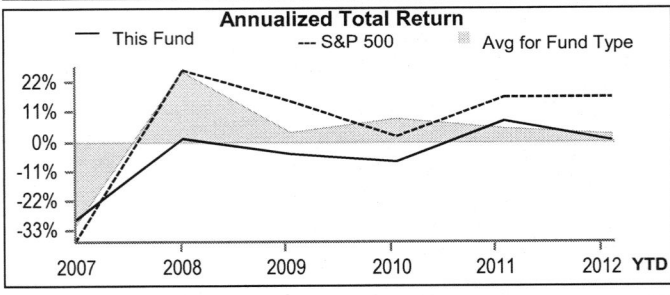

Annualized Total Return

*WisdomTree Global Natural Resour (GNAT)   D   Weak

Fund Family: WisdomTree Asset Management Inc
Fund Type: Energy/Natural Resources
Inception Date: October 13, 2006

Data Date	Investment Rating	Net Assets ($Mil)	Price	Perfor-mance Rating/Pts	Total Return Y-T-D	Risk Rating/Pts
12-12	D	27.90	24.54	D / 2.1	0.59%	C+ / 6.8
2011	C-	30.60	23.50	C- / 3.6	1.96%	C+ / 6.9
2010	D	52.20	26.65	C- / 3.0	7.25%	C / 4.7
2009	C-	38.97	25.60	C / 4.9	29.86%	C / 5.2

Major Rating Factors:
Disappointing performance is the major factor driving the D (Weak) TheStreet.com Investment Rating for *WisdomTree Global Natural Resour. The fund currently has a performance rating of D (Weak) based on an annualized return of 1.17% over the last three years and a total return of 0.59% year to date 2012. Factored into the performance evaluation is an expense ratio of 0.58% (very low).

The fund's risk rating is currently C+ (Fair). It carries a beta of 1.07, meaning that its performance tracks fairly well with that of the overall stock market. Volatility, as measured by both the semi-deviation and a drawdown factor, is considered low. As of December 31, 2012, *WisdomTree Global Natural Resour traded at a discount of .77% below its net asset value, which is better than its one-year historical average discount of .04%.

Karen Q. Wong has been running the fund for 5 years and currently receives a manager quality ranking of 17 (0=worst, 99=best). This fund offers only a moderate level of risk but investors looking for strong performance are still waiting.

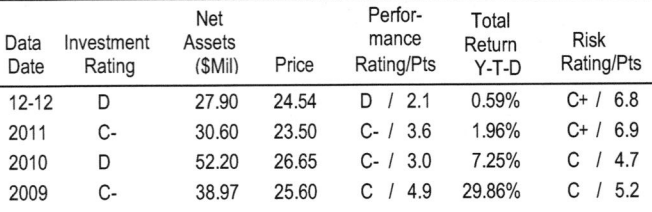

Annualized Total Return

*WisdomTree Global Real Return Fu (RRF)   D+   Weak

Fund Family: WisdomTree Asset Management Inc
Fund Type: Growth and Income
Inception Date: July 14, 2011

Data Date	Investment Rating	Net Assets ($Mil)	Price	Perfor-mance Rating/Pts	Total Return Y-T-D	Risk Rating/Pts
12-12	D+	4.90	47.79	D / 1.8	-2.06%	B / 8.8

Major Rating Factors:
Disappointing performance is the major factor driving the D+ (Weak) TheStreet.com Investment Rating for *WisdomTree Global Real Return Fu. The fund currently has a performance rating of D (Weak) based on an annualized return of 0.00% over the last three years and a total return of -2.06% year to date 2012. Factored into the performance evaluation is an expense ratio of 0.60% (very low).

The fund's risk rating is currently B (Good). It carries a beta of 0.00, meaning the fund's expected move will be 0.0% for every 10% move in the market. Volatility, as measured by both the semi-deviation and a drawdown factor, is considered low. As of December 31, 2012, *WisdomTree Global Real Return Fu traded at a discount of 1.63% below its net asset value, which is worse than its one-year historical average discount of 2.27%.

David C. Kwan has been running the fund for 2 years and currently receives a manager quality ranking of 62 (0=worst, 99=best). This fund offers only a moderate level of risk but investors looking for strong performance are still waiting.

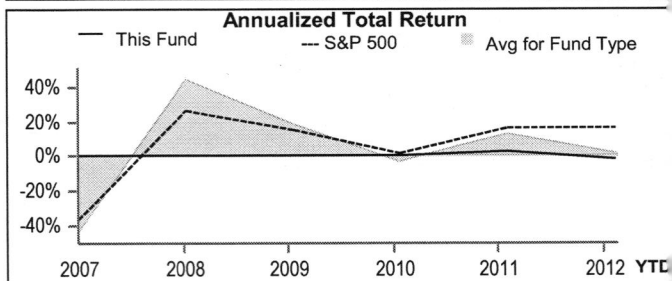

Annualized Total Return

*WisdomTree India Earnings Fund (EPI)

D-   **Weak**

Fund Family: WisdomTree Asset Management Inc
Fund Type: Foreign
Inception Date: February 22, 2008

Major Rating Factors:
Disappointing performance is the major factor driving the D- (Weak) TheStreet.com Investment Rating for *WisdomTree India Earnings Fund. The fund currently has a performance rating of D- (Weak) based on an annualized return of -4.31% over the last three years and a total return of 1.45% year to date 2012. Factored into the performance evaluation is an expense ratio of 0.76% (very low).

The fund's risk rating is currently C (Fair). It carries a beta of 1.08, meaning that its performance tracks fairly well with that of the overall stock market. Volatility, as measured by both the semi-deviation and a drawdown factor, is considered average. As of December 31, 2012, *WisdomTree India Earnings Fund traded at a discount of 1.07% below its net asset value, which is better than its one-year historical average premium of .37%.

Karen Q. Wong has been running the fund for 5 years and currently receives a manager quality ranking of 16 (0=worst, 99=best). This fund offers an average level of risk but investors looking for strong performance will be frustrated.

Data Date	Investment Rating	Net Assets ($Mil)	Price	Performance Rating/Pts	Total Return Y-T-D	Risk Rating/Pts
12-12	D-	1,232.30	19.37	D- / 1.3	1.45%	C / 5.5
2011	D	714.70	15.60	C- / 3.0	4.10%	C+ / 5.8
2010	B-	1,662.90	26.39	B+ / 8.7	20.34%	C- / 3.9
2009	B	553.94	22.07	A+ / 9.7	84.82%	C- / 3.9

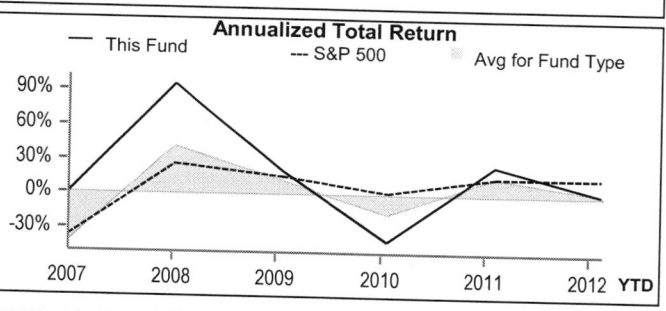

Annualized Total Return

*WisdomTree Intl Div Ex-Financial (DOO)

D+   **Weak**

Fund Family: WisdomTree Asset Management Inc
Fund Type: Foreign
Inception Date: June 16, 2006

Major Rating Factors:
Disappointing performance is the major factor driving the D+ (Weak) TheStreet.com Investment Rating for *WisdomTree Intl Div Ex-Financial. The fund currently has a performance rating of D+ (Weak) based on an annualized return of 3.86% over the last three years and a total return of 2.03% year to date 2012. Factored into the performance evaluation is an expense ratio of 0.58% (very low).

The fund's risk rating is currently B- (Good). It carries a beta of 0.98, meaning that its performance tracks fairly well with that of the overall stock market. Volatility, as measured by both the semi-deviation and a drawdown factor, is considered low. As of December 31, 2012, *WisdomTree Intl Div Ex-Financial traded at a discount of 1.83% below its net asset value, which is better than its one-year historical average premium of .28%.

Karen Q. Wong has been running the fund for 5 years and currently receives a manager quality ranking of 47 (0=worst, 99=best). This fund offers only a moderate level of risk but investors looking for strong performance are still waiting.

Data Date	Investment Rating	Net Assets ($Mil)	Price	Performance Rating/Pts	Total Return Y-T-D	Risk Rating/Pts
12-12	D+	347.00	41.90	D+ / 2.9	2.03%	B- / 7.1
2011	C-	264.50	39.58	C- / 3.5	-1.47%	B- / 7.5
2010	D-	171.80	44.16	D- / 1.3	5.70%	C- / 4.2
2009	D	149.40	43.59	D+ / 2.4	31.21%	C / 4.5

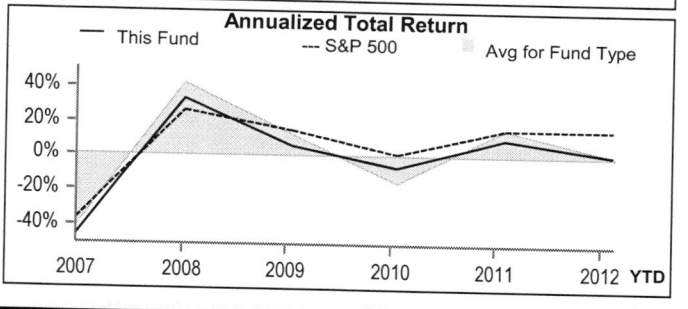

Annualized Total Return

*WisdomTree Intl LargeCap Dividen (DOL)

C-   **Fair**

Fund Family: WisdomTree Asset Management Inc
Fund Type: Foreign
Inception Date: June 16, 2006

Major Rating Factors: Middle of the road best describes *WisdomTree Intl LargeCap Dividen whose TheStreet.com Investment Rating is currently a C- (Fair). The fund currently has a performance rating of C- (Fair) based on an annualized return of 3.17% over the last three years and a total return of 2.07% year to date 2012. Factored into the performance evaluation is an expense ratio of 0.48% (very low).

The fund's risk rating is currently B- (Good). It carries a beta of 1.04, meaning that its performance tracks fairly well with that of the overall stock market. Volatility, as measured by both the semi-deviation and a drawdown factor, is considered low. As of December 31, 2012, *WisdomTree Intl LargeCap Dividen traded at a discount of 1.60% below its net asset value, which is better than its one-year historical average premium of .37%.

Karen Q. Wong has been running the fund for 5 years and currently receives a manager quality ranking of 43 (0=worst, 99=best). If you desire an average level of risk, then this fund may be an option.

Data Date	Investment Rating	Net Assets ($Mil)	Price	Performance Rating/Pts	Total Return Y-T-D	Risk Rating/Pts
12-12	C-	199.20	44.93	C- / 3.6	2.07%	B- / 7.1
2011	D+	127.70	40.00	D+ / 2.6	-0.65%	B- / 7.3
2010	D-	149.30	45.49	D- / 1.2	1.87%	C / 4.8
2009	D	117.33	46.41	D+ / 2.3	22.43%	C / 5.0

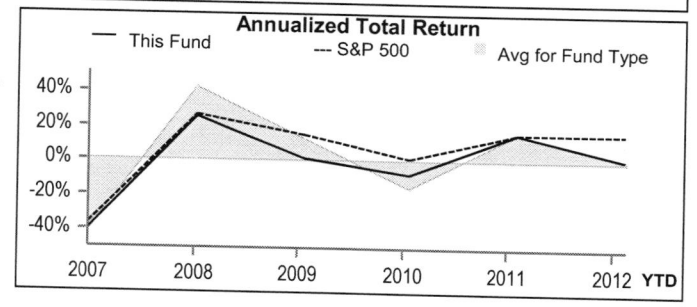

Annualized Total Return

* Denotes ETF Fund

*WisdomTree Intl MidCap Dividend (DIM)

C   **Fair**

Fund Family: WisdomTree Asset Management Inc
Fund Type: Foreign
Inception Date: June 16, 2006

Major Rating Factors: Middle of the road best describes *WisdomTree Intl MidCap Dividend whose TheStreet.com Investment Rating is currently a C (Fair). The fund currently has a performance rating of C (Fair) based on an annualized return of 5.34% over the last three years and a total return of 2.72% year to date 2012. Factored into the performance evaluation is an expense ratio of 0.38% (very low).

The fund's risk rating is currently B- (Good). It carries a beta of 1.03, meaning that its performance tracks fairly well with that of the overall stock market. Volatility, as measured by both the semi-deviation and a drawdown factor, is considered low. As of December 31, 2012, *WisdomTree Intl MidCap Dividend traded at a discount of 2.29% below its net asset value, which is better than its one-year historical average discount of .07%.

Karen Q. Wong has been running the fund for 5 years and currently receives a manager quality ranking of 61 (0=worst, 99=best). If you desire an average level of risk, then this fund may be an option.

Data Date	Investment Rating	Net Assets ($Mil)	Price	Performance Rating/Pts	Total Return Y-T-D	Risk Rating/Pts
12-12	C	104.60	50.29	C / 5.0	2.72%	B- / 7.1
2011	C-	112.60	43.05	C- / 3.0	-0.33%	B- / 7.4
2010	D	153.40	51.85	D+ / 2.7	11.31%	C / 4.7
2009	D	128.53	48.12	D+ / 2.7	32.42%	C / 4.9

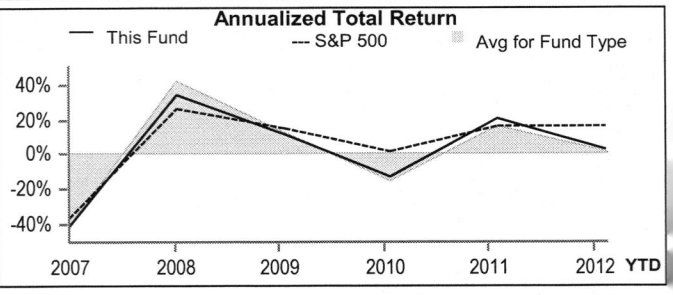

*WisdomTree Intl Small Cap Divide (DLS)

C+   **Fair**

Fund Family: WisdomTree Asset Management Inc
Fund Type: Foreign
Inception Date: June 16, 2006

Major Rating Factors: Middle of the road best describes *WisdomTree Intl Small Cap Divide whose TheStreet.com Investment Rating is currently a C+ (Fair). The fund currently has a performance rating of C+ (Fair) based on an annualized return of 8.45% over the last three years and a total return of 2.90% year to date 2012. Factored into the performance evaluation is an expense ratio of 0.38% (very low).

The fund's risk rating is currently B- (Good). It carries a beta of 0.91, meaning that its performance tracks fairly well with that of the overall stock market. Volatility, as measured by both the semi-deviation and a drawdown factor, is considered low. As of December 31, 2012, *WisdomTree Intl Small Cap Divide traded at a discount of 2.10% below its net asset value, which is better than its one-year historical average premium of .32%.

Karen Q. Wong has been running the fund for 5 years and currently receives a manager quality ranking of 81 (0=worst, 99=best). If you desire an average level of risk, then this fund may be an option.

Data Date	Investment Rating	Net Assets ($Mil)	Price	Performance Rating/Pts	Total Return Y-T-D	Risk Rating/Pts
12-12	C+	483.50	52.13	C+ / 6.8	2.90%	B- / 7.5
2011	C-	363.80	43.73	C- / 3.9	0.16%	B- / 7.7
2010	D+	471.20	51.77	C- / 3.9	19.41%	C / 4.6
2009	D-	389.97	44.78	D / 2.1	34.92%	C / 4.7

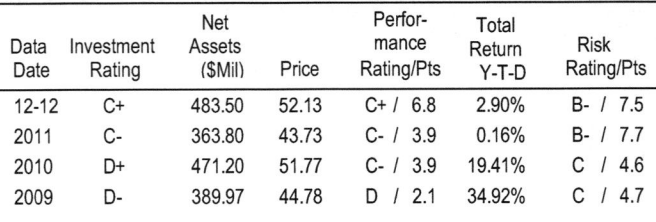

*WisdomTree Japan Hedged Equity (DXJ)

D+   **Weak**

Fund Family: WisdomTree Asset Management Inc
Fund Type: Foreign
Inception Date: June 16, 2006

Major Rating Factors:
Disappointing performance is the major factor driving the D+ (Weak) TheStreet.com Investment Rating for *WisdomTree Japan Hedged Equity. The fund currently has a performance rating of D+ (Weak) based on an annualized return of -1.10% over the last three years and a total return of 4.47% year to date 2012. Factored into the performance evaluation is an expense ratio of 0.48% (very low).

The fund's risk rating is currently B- (Good). It carries a beta of 0.56, meaning the fund's expected move will be 5.6% for every 10% move in the market. Volatility, as measured by both the semi-deviation and a drawdown factor, is considered low. As of December 31, 2012, *WisdomTree Japan Hedged Equity traded at a discount of 3.18% below its net asset value, which is better than its one-year historical average premium of .24%.

Karen Q. Wong has been running the fund for 5 years and currently receives a manager quality ranking of 32 (0=worst, 99=best). This fund offers only a moderate level of risk but investors looking for strong performance are still waiting.

Data Date	Investment Rating	Net Assets ($Mil)	Price	Performance Rating/Pts	Total Return Y-T-D	Risk Rating/Pts
12-12	D+	1,222.70	36.88	D+ / 2.6	4.47%	B- / 7.2
2011	D	399.20	31.34	D- / 1.4	0.26%	B- / 7.4
2010	D	121.80	38.17	D- / 1.2	-1.78%	C+ / 5.8
2009	D	87.80	39.33	E+ / 0.9	0.22%	C+ / 6.0

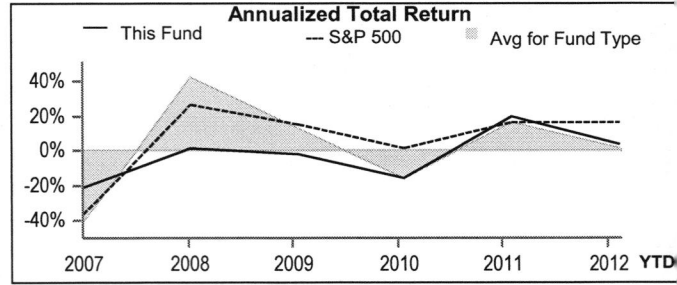

*WisdomTree Japan SmallCap Div Fd (DFJ)

C-   **Fair**

Fund Family: WisdomTree Asset Management Inc
Fund Type: Foreign
Inception Date: June 16, 2006

Major Rating Factors: Middle of the road best describes *WisdomTree Japan SmallCap Div Fd whose TheStreet.com Investment Rating is currently a C- (Fair). The fund currently has a performance rating of C- (Fair) based on an annualized return of 5.33% over the last three years and a total return of 0.34% year to date 2012. Factored into the performance evaluation is an expense ratio of 0.58% (very low).

The fund's risk rating is currently B (Good). It carries a beta of 0.36, meaning the fund's expected move will be 3.6% for every 10% move in the market. Volatility, as measured by both the semi-deviation and a drawdown factor, is considered low. As of December 31, 2012, *WisdomTree Japan SmallCap Div Fd traded at a premium of .25% above its net asset value, which is worse than its one-year historical average premium of .15%.

Karen Q. Wong has been running the fund for 5 years and currently receives a manager quality ranking of 81 (0=worst, 99=best). If you desire an average level of risk, then this fund may be an option.

Data Date	Investment Rating	Net Assets ($Mil)	Price	Performance Rating/Pts	Total Return Y-T-D	Risk Rating/Pts
12-12	C-	176.80	43.70	C- / 3.0	0.34%	B / 8.6
2011	C-	184.10	41.65	C- / 3.1	-0.31%	B- / 7.8
2010	C+	121.60	44.20	C+ / 6.3	17.37%	C+ / 6.3
2009	D	119.06	38.34	D- / 1.0	-0.93%	C+ / 6.3

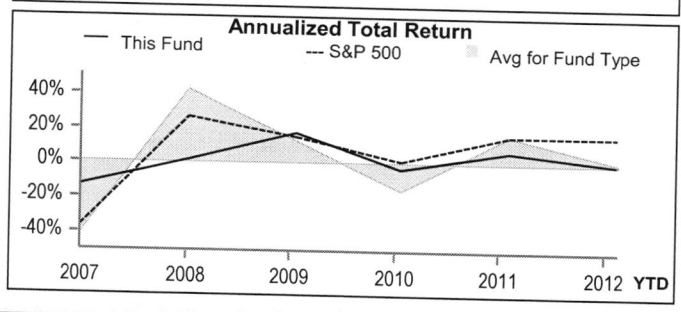

Annualized Total Return

---

*WisdomTree LargeCap Dividend Fun (DLN)

C+   **Fair**

Fund Family: WisdomTree Asset Management Inc
Fund Type: Growth and Income
Inception Date: June 16, 2006

Major Rating Factors: Middle of the road best describes *WisdomTree LargeCap Dividend Fun whose TheStreet.com Investment Rating is currently a C+ (Fair). The fund currently has a performance rating of C (Fair) based on an annualized return of 13.32% over the last three years and a total return of 3.08% year to date 2012. Factored into the performance evaluation is an expense ratio of 0.28% (very low).

The fund's risk rating is currently B (Good). It carries a beta of 0.79, meaning the fund's expected move will be 7.9% for every 10% move in the market. Volatility, as measured by both the semi-deviation and a drawdown factor, is considered low. As of December 31, 2012, *WisdomTree LargeCap Dividend Fun traded at a discount of 3.00% below its net asset value, which is better than its one-year historical average premium of .07%.

Karen Q. Wong has been running the fund for 5 years and currently receives a manager quality ranking of 75 (0=worst, 99=best). If you desire an average level of risk, then this fund may be an option.

Data Date	Investment Rating	Net Assets ($Mil)	Price	Performance Rating/Pts	Total Return Y-T-D	Risk Rating/Pts
12-12	C+	1,239.60	53.64	C / 5.5	3.08%	B / 8.7
2011	C+	930.90	49.03	C+ / 6.1	0.94%	B- / 7.9
2010	C-	554.90	46.10	C- / 3.0	14.98%	C+ / 5.9
2009	D	410.36	41.28	D- / 1.5	14.64%	C+ / 6.0

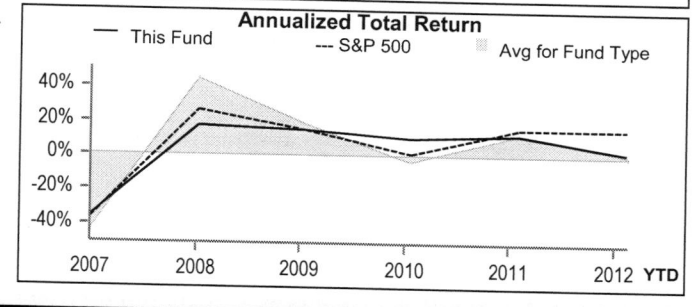

Annualized Total Return

---

*WisdomTree LargeCap Value Fund (EZY)

C-   **Fair**

Fund Family: WisdomTree Asset Management Inc
Fund Type: Income
Inception Date: February 23, 2007

Major Rating Factors: Middle of the road best describes *WisdomTree LargeCap Value Fund whose TheStreet.com Investment Rating is currently a C- (Fair). The fund currently has a performance rating of C- (Fair) based on an annualized return of 10.52% over the last three years and a total return of 1.90% year to date 2012. Factored into the performance evaluation is an expense ratio of 0.38% (very low).

The fund's risk rating is currently B- (Good). It carries a beta of 1.08, meaning that its performance tracks fairly well with that of the overall stock market. Volatility, as measured by both the semi-deviation and a drawdown factor, is considered low. As of December 31, 2012, *WisdomTree LargeCap Value Fund traded at a discount of 1.91% below its net asset value, which is better than its one-year historical average discount of .05%.

Karen Q. Wong has been running the fund for 5 years and currently receives a manager quality ranking of 41 (0=worst, 99=best). If you desire an average level of risk, then this fund may be an option.

Data Date	Investment Rating	Net Assets ($Mil)	Price	Performance Rating/Pts	Total Return Y-T-D	Risk Rating/Pts
12-12	C-	29.10	44.65	C- / 4.1	1.90%	B- / 7.8
2011	C+	30.70	41.06	C+ / 5.7	1.02%	B- / 7.9
2010	C-	23.80	39.68	C- / 3.4	14.24%	C+ / 5.7
2009	B+	28.00	35.26	B / 8.2	23.37%	C+ / 5.8

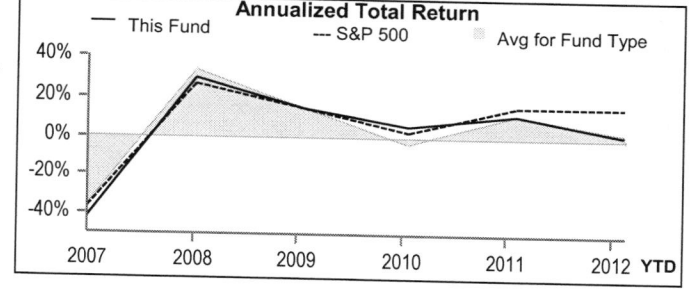

Annualized Total Return

*WisdomTree Mgd Futures Strategy (WDTI)

D   **Weak**

Fund Family: WisdomTree Asset Management Inc
Fund Type: Growth
Inception Date: January 5, 2011

Data Date	Investment Rating	Net Assets ($Mil)	Price	Perfor-mance Rating/Pts	Total Return Y-T-D	Risk Rating/Pts
12-12	D	117.00	40.30	E+ / 0.8	0.81%	B- / 7.8

Major Rating Factors:
Very poor performance is the major factor driving the D (Weak) TheStreet.com Investment Rating for *WisdomTree Mgd Futures Strategy. The fund currently has a performance rating of E+ (Very Weak) based on an annualized return of 0.00% over the last three years and a total return of 0.81% year to date 2012. Factored into the performance evaluation is an expense ratio of 0.95% (low).

The fund's risk rating is currently B- (Good). It carries a beta of 0.00, meaning the fund's expected move will be 0.0% for every 10% move in the market. Volatility, as measured by both the semi-deviation and a drawdown factor, is considered low. As of December 31, 2012, *WisdomTree Mgd Futures Strategy traded at a discount of .84% below its net asset value, which is better than its one-year historical average discount of .06%.

James H. Stavena has been running the fund for 2 years and currently receives a manager quality ranking of 12 (0=worst, 99=best). This fund offers only a moderate level of risk but investors looking for strong performance are still waiting.

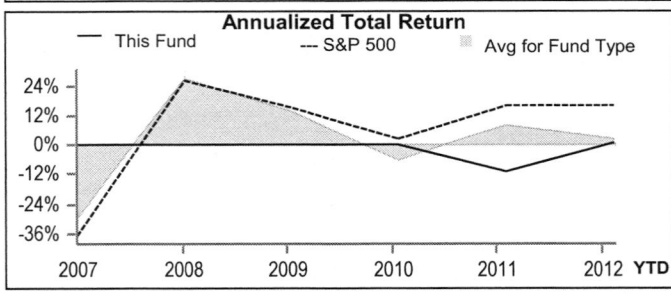

*WisdomTree MidCap Dividend Fund (DON)

B-   **Good**

Fund Family: WisdomTree Asset Management Inc
Fund Type: Growth
Inception Date: June 16, 2006

Data Date	Investment Rating	Net Assets ($Mil)	Price	Perfor-mance Rating/Pts	Total Return Y-T-D	Risk Rating/Pts
12-12	B-	390.90	57.41	C+ / 6.6	3.77%	B / 8.2
2011	B-	288.30	52.07	C+ / 6.9	0.71%	B- / 7.6
2010	C+	233.00	50.70	C+ / 6.8	21.65%	C+ / 5.6
2009	D+	102.89	42.97	C- / 3.0	30.02%	C+ / 5.6

Major Rating Factors: *WisdomTree MidCap Dividend Fund receives a TheStreet.com Investment Rating of B- (Good). The fund currently has a performance rating of C+ (Fair) based on an annualized return of 14.67% over the last three years and a total return of 3.77% year to date 2012. Factored into the performance evaluation is an expense ratio of 0.38% (very low).

The fund's risk rating is currently B (Good). It carries a beta of 0.96, meaning that its performance tracks fairly well with that of the overall stock market. Volatility, as measured by both the semi-deviation and a drawdown factor, is considered low. As of December 31, 2012, *WisdomTree MidCap Dividend Fund traded at a discount of 3.53% below its net asset value, which is better than its one-year historical average premium of .12%.

Karen Q. Wong has been running the fund for 5 years and currently receives a manager quality ranking of 72 (0=worst, 99=best). If you desire an average level of risk, then this fund may be an option.

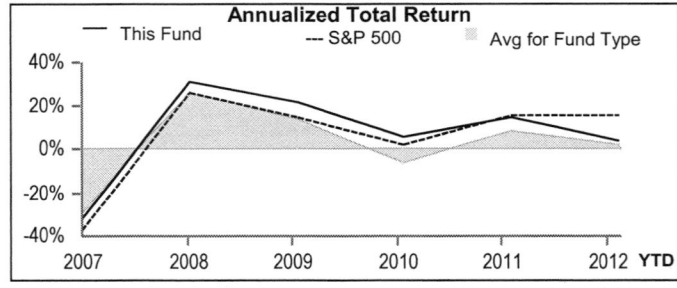

*WisdomTree MidCap Earnings Fund (EZM)

B   **Good**

Fund Family: WisdomTree Asset Management Inc
Fund Type: Growth
Inception Date: February 23, 2007

Data Date	Investment Rating	Net Assets ($Mil)	Price	Perfor-mance Rating/Pts	Total Return Y-T-D	Risk Rating/Pts
12-12	B	165.10	62.38	B- / 7.5	3.53%	B- / 7.7
2011	B-	121.20	53.95	B- / 7.4	1.93%	B- / 7.5
2010	B+	93.90	53.99	B / 8.0	25.60%	C+ / 5.8
2009	A+	22.35	43.65	A- / 9.2	46.05%	C+ / 5.8

Major Rating Factors: Strong performance is the major factor driving the B (Good) TheStreet.com Investment Rating for *WisdomTree MidCap Earnings Fund. The fund currently has a performance rating of B- (Good) based on an annualized return of 15.06% over the last three years and a total return of 3.53% year to date 2012. Factored into the performance evaluation is an expense ratio of 0.38% (very low).

The fund's risk rating is currently B- (Good). It carries a beta of 1.16, meaning it is expected to move 11.6% for every 10% move in the market. Volatility, as measured by both the semi-deviation and a drawdown factor, is considered low. As of December 31, 2012, *WisdomTree MidCap Earnings Fund traded at a discount of 3.23% below its net asset value, which is better than its one-year historical average premium of .08%.

Karen Q. Wong has been running the fund for 5 years and currently receives a manager quality ranking of 64 (0=worst, 99=best). If you desire only a moderate level of risk and strong performance, then this fund is an excellent option.

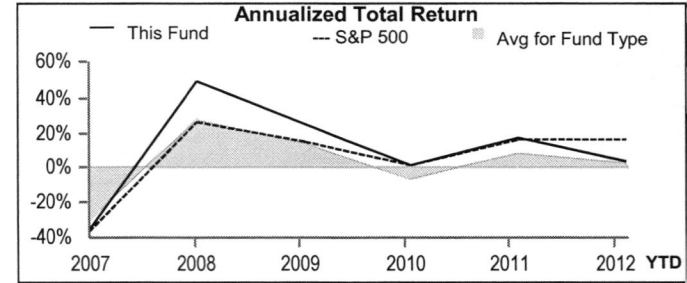

*WisdomTree Middle East Dividend (GULF)

C-   **Fair**

Fund Family: WisdomTree Asset Management Inc
Fund Type: Foreign
Inception Date: July 16, 2008

Major Rating Factors: Middle of the road best describes *WisdomTree Middle East Dividend whose TheStreet.com Investment Rating is currently a C- (Fair). The fund currently has a performance rating of C- (Fair) based on an annualized return of 7.19% over the last three years and a total return of 4.03% year to date 2012. Factored into the performance evaluation is an expense ratio of 0.88% (low).

The fund's risk rating is currently B (Good). It carries a beta of 0.50, meaning the fund's expected move will be 5.0% for every 10% move in the market. Volatility, as measured by both the semi-deviation and a drawdown factor, is considered low. As of December 31, 2012, *WisdomTree Middle East Dividend traded at a discount of 3.85% below its net asset value, which is better than its one-year historical average discount of .55%.

Michael C. Ho currently receives a manager quality ranking of 75 (0=worst, 99=best). If you desire an average level of risk, then this fund may be an option.

Data Date	Investment Rating	Net Assets ($Mil)	Price	Performance Rating/Pts	Total Return Y-T-D	Risk Rating/Pts
12-12	C-	11.90	14.99	C- / 4.1	4.03%	B / 8.0
2011	C-	14.70	14.63	D+ / 2.8	-0.48%	B / 8.0
2010	A-	20.30	17.04	A- / 9.2	22.43%	C / 5.0
2009	D-	10.94	14.40	D- / 1.4	0.64%	C / 4.9

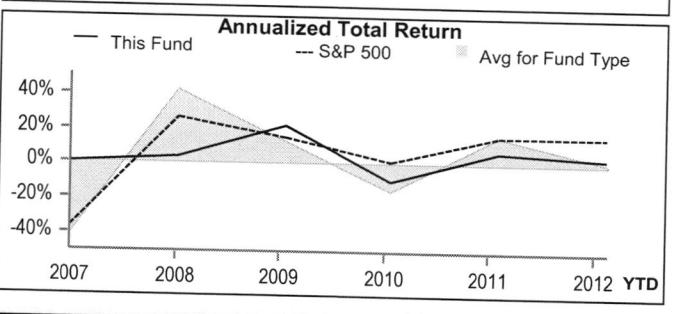

*WisdomTree SmallCap Dividend Fd (DES)

B-   **Good**

Fund Family: WisdomTree Asset Management Inc
Fund Type: Growth
Inception Date: June 16, 2006

Major Rating Factors: *WisdomTree SmallCap Dividend Fd receives a TheStreet.com Investment Rating of B- (Good). The fund currently has a performance rating of C+ (Fair) based on an annualized return of 14.49% over the last three years and a total return of 3.04% year to date 2012. Factored into the performance evaluation is an expense ratio of 0.38% (very low).

The fund's risk rating is currently B (Good). It carries a beta of 1.05, meaning that its performance tracks fairly well with that of the overall stock market. Volatility, as measured by both the semi-deviation and a drawdown factor, is considered low. As of December 31, 2012, *WisdomTree SmallCap Dividend Fd traded at a discount of 2.90% below its net asset value, which is better than its one-year historical average premium of .18%.

Karen Q. Wong has been running the fund for 5 years and currently receives a manager quality ranking of 68 (0=worst, 99=best). If you desire an average level of risk, then this fund may be an option.

Data Date	Investment Rating	Net Assets ($Mil)	Price	Performance Rating/Pts	Total Return Y-T-D	Risk Rating/Pts
12-12	B-	402.10	50.95	C+ / 6.6	3.04%	B / 8.0
2011	C	242.00	44.89	C / 5.2	1.69%	B- / 7.1
2010	B+	224.20	47.41	B / 8.2	27.05%	C / 5.4
2009	D	133.61	38.80	D / 1.7	20.06%	C / 5.4

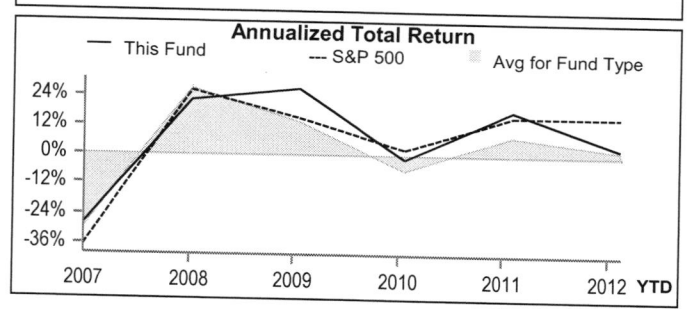

*WisdomTree SmallCap Earnings Fun (EES)

C+   **Fair**

Fund Family: WisdomTree Asset Management Inc
Fund Type: Growth
Inception Date: February 23, 2007

Major Rating Factors: Middle of the road best describes *WisdomTree SmallCap Earnings Fun whose TheStreet.com Investment Rating is currently a C+ (Fair). The fund currently has a performance rating of C+ (Fair) based on an annualized return of 13.08% over the last three years and a total return of 3.24% year to date 2012. Factored into the performance evaluation is an expense ratio of 0.38% (very low).

The fund's risk rating is currently B- (Good). It carries a beta of 1.20, meaning it is expected to move 12.0% for every 10% move in the market. Volatility, as measured by both the semi-deviation and a drawdown factor, is considered low. As of December 31, 2012, *WisdomTree SmallCap Earnings Fun traded at a discount of 3.26% below its net asset value, which is better than its one-year historical average premium of .11%.

Karen Q. Wong has been running the fund for 5 years and currently receives a manager quality ranking of 49 (0=worst, 99=best). If you desire an average level of risk, then this fund may be an option.

Data Date	Investment Rating	Net Assets ($Mil)	Price	Performance Rating/Pts	Total Return Y-T-D	Risk Rating/Pts
12-12	C+	155.80	56.71	C+ / 5.9	3.24%	B- / 7.6
2011	B-	120.30	50.31	B- / 7.2	1.88%	B- / 7.4
2010	B+	116.40	51.95	B+ / 8.4	26.97%	C+ / 5.7
2009	A	62.23	41.41	A- / 9.0	44.03%	C / 5.5

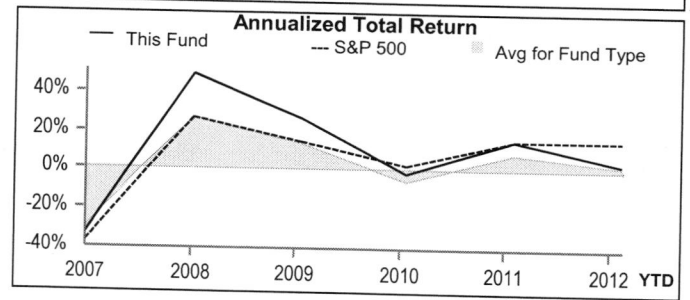

*WisdomTree Total Dividend (DTD)
C+   Fair

Fund Family: WisdomTree Asset Management Inc
Fund Type: Income
Inception Date: June 16, 2006

Major Rating Factors: Middle of the road best describes *WisdomTree Total Dividend whose TheStreet.com Investment Rating is currently a C+ (Fair). The fund currently has a performance rating of C+ (Fair) based on an annualized return of 13.52% over the last three years and a total return of 3.09% year to date 2012. Factored into the performance evaluation is an expense ratio of 0.28% (very low).

The fund's risk rating is currently B (Good). It carries a beta of 0.82, meaning the fund's expected move will be 8.2% for every 10% move in the market. Volatility, as measured by both the semi-deviation and a drawdown factor, is considered low. As of December 31, 2012, *WisdomTree Total Dividend traded at a discount of 3.05% below its net asset value, which is better than its one-year historical average premium of .07%.

Karen Q. Wong has been running the fund for 5 years and currently receives a manager quality ranking of 75 (0=worst, 99=best). If you desire an average level of risk, then this fund may be an option.

Data Date	Investment Rating	Net Assets ($Mil)	Price	Perfor-mance Rating/Pts	Total Return Y-T-D	Risk Rating/Pts
12-12	C+	266.30	53.79	C+ / 5.6	3.09%	B / 8.6
2011	C+	206.00	49.05	C+ / 6.1	0.92%	B- / 7.9
2010	C-	155.80	46.59	C- / 3.7	16.32%	C+ / 5.9
2009	D	124.25	41.32	D / 1.6	16.64%	C+ / 5.9

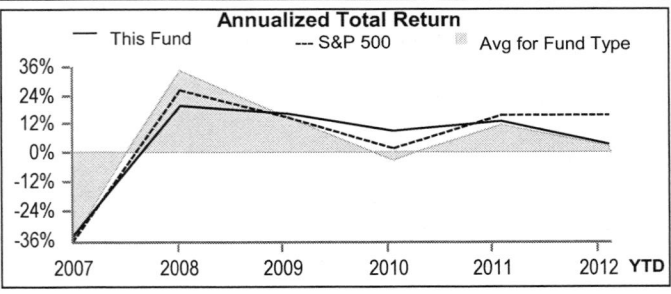

*WisdomTree Total Earnings Fund (EXT)
C+   Fair

Fund Family: WisdomTree Asset Management Inc
Fund Type: Income
Inception Date: February 23, 2007

Major Rating Factors: Middle of the road best describes *WisdomTree Total Earnings Fund whose TheStreet.com Investment Rating is currently a C+ (Fair). The fund currently has a performance rating of C (Fair) based on an annualized return of 11.66% over the last three years and a total return of 4.20% year to date 2012. Factored into the performance evaluation is an expense ratio of 0.28% (very low).

The fund's risk rating is currently B (Good). It carries a beta of 0.96, meaning that its performance tracks fairly well with that of the overall stock market. Volatility, as measured by both the semi-deviation and a drawdown factor, is considered low. As of December 31, 2012, *WisdomTree Total Earnings Fund traded at a discount of 4.13% below its net asset value, which is better than its one-year historical average premium of .03%.

Karen Q. Wong has been running the fund for 5 years and currently receives a manager quality ranking of 53 (0=worst, 99=best). If you desire an average level of risk, then this fund may be an option.

Data Date	Investment Rating	Net Assets ($Mil)	Price	Perfor-mance Rating/Pts	Total Return Y-T-D	Risk Rating/Pts
12-12	C+	48.30	50.39	C / 5.4	4.20%	B / 8.1
2011	C+	33.70	45.01	C+ / 6.0	1.98%	B / 8.0
2010	C-	51.20	44.62	C- / 4.1	13.78%	C+ / 5.9
2009	A	24.34	39.97	B+ / 8.5	29.03%	C+ / 6.0

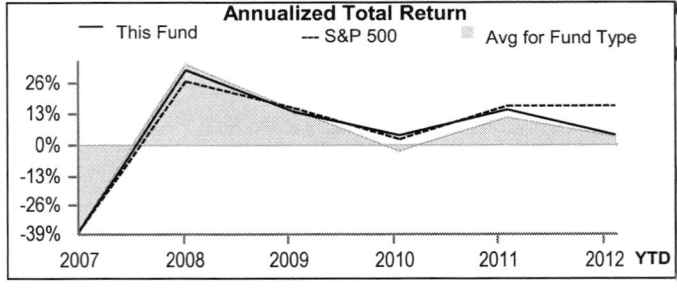

Aberdeen Asia-Pacific Income Fund (FAX)
C+   Fair

Fund Family: Aberdeen Asset Management Asia Ltd
Fund Type: Global
Inception Date: April 17, 1986

Major Rating Factors: Middle of the road best describes Aberdeen Asia-Pacific Income Fund whose TheStreet.com Investment Rating is currently a C+ (Fair). The fund currently has a performance rating of C (Fair) based on an annualized return of 13.38% over the last three years and a total return of 2.58% year to date 2012. Factored into the performance evaluation is an expense ratio of 1.49% (average).

The fund's risk rating is currently B (Good). It carries a beta of 0.93, meaning that its performance tracks fairly well with that of the overall stock market. Volatility, as measured by both the semi-deviation and a drawdown factor, is considered low. As of December 31, 2012, Aberdeen Asia-Pacific Income Fund traded at a discount of .77% below its net asset value, which is better than its one-year historical average premium of .94%.

Anthony Michael currently receives a manager quality ranking of 90 (0=worst, 99=best). If you desire an average level of risk, then this fund may be an option.

Data Date	Investment Rating	Net Assets ($Mil)	Price	Perfor-mance Rating/Pts	Total Return Y-T-D	Risk Rating/Pts
12-12	C+	1,951.74	7.74	C / 5.3	2.58%	B / 8.6
2011	B+	1,917.40	7.33	B / 8.0	1.50%	B / 8.6
2010	B+	1,777.77	6.75	B / 8.1	15.66%	C+ / 6.0
2009	C+	1,421.03	6.22	C+ / 6.4	49.04%	C+ / 6.3

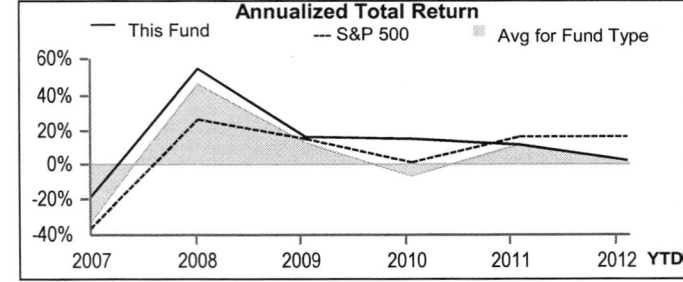

Aberdeen Australia Equity Fund (IAF)   D+   Weak

Fund Family: Aberdeen Asset Management Asia Ltd
Fund Type: Foreign
Inception Date: December 12, 1985

Major Rating Factors: Aberdeen Australia Equity Fund receives a TheStreet.com Investment Rating of D+ (Weak). The fund currently has a performance rating of C- (Fair) based on an annualized return of 5.15% over the last three years and a total return of 2.87% year to date 2012. Factored into the performance evaluation is an expense ratio of 1.34% (average).

The fund's risk rating is currently C+ (Fair). It carries a beta of 1.20, meaning it is expected to move 12.0% for every 10% move in the market. Volatility, as measured by both the semi-deviation and a drawdown factor, is considered low. As of December 31, 2012, Aberdeen Australia Equity Fund traded at a premium of 2.25% above its net asset value, which is better than its one-year historical average premium of 5.97%.

Mark Daniels currently receives a manager quality ranking of 56 (0=worst, 99=best). If you desire an average level of risk, then this fund may be an option.

Data Date	Investment Rating	Net Assets ($Mil)	Price	Perfor-mance Rating/Pts	Total Return Y-T-D	Risk Rating/Pts
12-12	D+	229.62	10.44	C- / 3.9	2.87%	C+ / 6.6
2011	C-	207.70	9.05	C / 5.0	3.76%	C+ / 6.6
2010	C-	219.93	11.98	C / 4.8	8.15%	C / 4.4
2009	C+	155.02	12.17	B / 7.8	73.27%	C- / 4.0

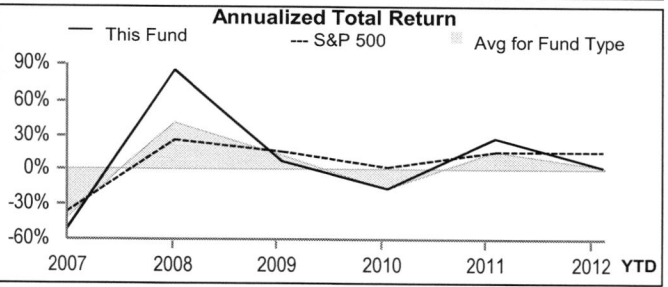

Aberdeen Chile Fund (CH)   D   Weak

Fund Family: Aberdeen Asset Management Inc
Fund Type: Foreign
Inception Date: September 27, 1989

Major Rating Factors: Aberdeen Chile Fund receives a TheStreet.com Investment Rating of D (Weak). The fund currently has a performance rating of C- (Fair) based on an annualized return of 10.13% over the last three years and a total return of 2.65% year to date 2012. Factored into the performance evaluation is an expense ratio of 1.90% (above average).

The fund's risk rating is currently C (Fair). It carries a beta of 1.10, meaning it is expected to move 11.0% for every 10% move in the market. Volatility, as measured by both the semi-deviation and a drawdown factor, is considered average. As of December 31, 2012, Aberdeen Chile Fund traded at a discount of 3.33% below its net asset value, which is better than its one-year historical average premium of 2.54%.

Devan Kaloo has been running the fund for 4 years and currently receives a manager quality ranking of 85 (0=worst, 99=best). If you desire an average level of risk, then this fund may be an option.

Data Date	Investment Rating	Net Assets ($Mil)	Price	Perfor-mance Rating/Pts	Total Return Y-T-D	Risk Rating/Pts
12-12	D	142.16	15.09	C- / 3.7	2.65%	C / 5.4
2011	C+	134.50	15.04	B / 8.2	1.60%	C+ / 5.9
2010	B+	190.85	22.67	A- / 9.1	48.63%	C / 4.7
2009	B	170.07	17.90	B / 8.2	93.26%	C / 5.1

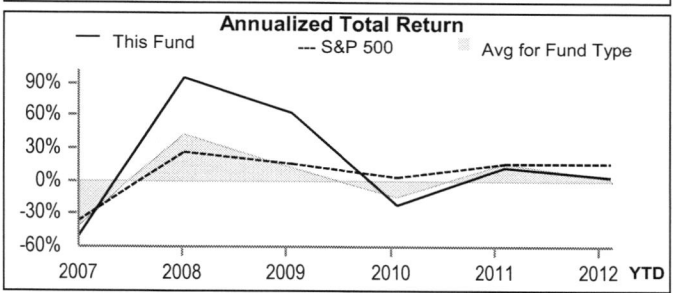

Aberdeen Emerging Mkt Tele & Infr (ETF)   B-   Good

Fund Family: Aberdeen Asset Managers Ltd
Fund Type: Emerging Market
Inception Date: June 17, 1992

Major Rating Factors: Aberdeen Emerging Mkt Tele & Infr receives a TheStreet.com Investment Rating of B- (Good). The fund currently has a performance rating of C+ (Fair) based on an annualized return of 11.55% over the last three years and a total return of 1.40% year to date 2012. Factored into the performance evaluation is an expense ratio of 1.50% (average).

The fund's risk rating is currently B (Good). It carries a beta of 0.73, meaning the fund's expected move will be 7.3% for every 10% move in the market. Volatility, as measured by both the semi-deviation and a drawdown factor, is considered low. As of December 31, 2012, Aberdeen Emerging Mkt Tele & Infr traded at a discount of 11.05% below its net asset value, which is worse than its one-year historical average discount of 11.42%.

Andrew P. S. Brown currently receives a manager quality ranking of 86 (0=worst, 99=best). If you desire an average level of risk, then this fund may be an option.

Data Date	Investment Rating	Net Assets ($Mil)	Price	Perfor-mance Rating/Pts	Total Return Y-T-D	Risk Rating/Pts
12-12	B-	165.08	21.50	C+ / 6.7	1.40%	B / 8.3
2011	C	161.40	17.53	C- / 4.2	1.60%	B / 8.0
2010	D-	157.63	19.36	D / 2.2	20.26%	C- / 3.3
2009	D-	125.36	16.58	D+ / 2.4	19.32%	C- / 4.1

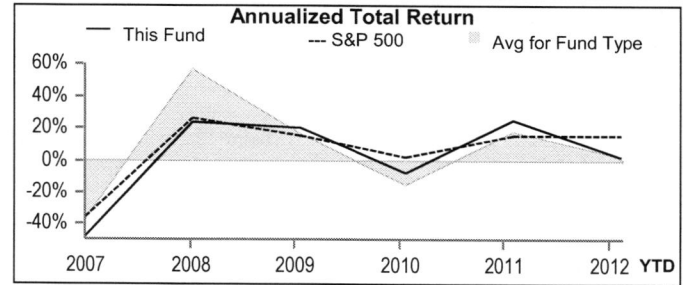

Aberdeen Global Income Fund (FCO)

C+   **Fair**

Fund Family: Aberdeen Asset Management Asia Ltd
Fund Type: Global
Inception Date: February 20, 1992

Major Rating Factors: Middle of the road best describes Aberdeen Global Income Fund whose TheStreet.com Investment Rating is currently a C+ (Fair). The fund currently has a performance rating of C (Fair) based on an annualized return of 13.66% over the last three years and a total return of 0.01% year to date 2012. Factored into the performance evaluation is an expense ratio of 2.13% (high).

    The fund's risk rating is currently B (Good). It carries a beta of 0.75, meaning the fund's expected move will be 7.5% for every 10% move in the market. Volatility, as measured by both the semi-deviation and a drawdown factor, is considered low. As of December 31, 2012, Aberdeen Global Income Fund traded at a premium of 1.79% above its net asset value, which is better than its one-year historical average premium of 1.90%.

    John A. Murphy currently receives a manager quality ranking of 90 (0=worst, 99=best). If you desire an average level of risk, then this fund may be an option.

Data Date	Investment Rating	Net Assets ($Mil)	Price	Performance Rating/Pts	Total Return Y-T-D	Risk Rating/Pts
12-12	C+	121.65	14.22	C / 5.2	0.01%	B / 8.5
2011	B+	119.80	13.90	B+ / 8.6	0.07%	B / 8.3
2010	B	108.85	12.31	B- / 7.5	5.93%	C+ / 5.6
2009	B-	87.89	12.46	B- / 7.2	54.30%	C+ / 5.6

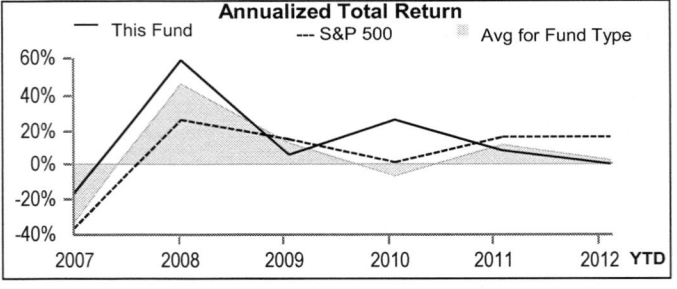

Aberdeen Indonesia Fund (IF)

B   **Good**

Fund Family: Aberdeen Asset Management Asia Ltd
Fund Type: Emerging Market
Inception Date: March 9, 1990

Major Rating Factors: Strong performance is the major factor driving the B (Good) TheStreet.com Investment Rating for Aberdeen Indonesia Fund. The fund currently has a performance rating of B (Good) based on an annualized return of 19.05% over the last three years and a total return of 2.74% year to date 2012. Factored into the performance evaluation is an expense ratio of 1.44% (average).

    The fund's risk rating is currently B- (Good). It carries a beta of 0.82, meaning the fund's expected move will be 8.2% for every 10% move in the market. Volatility, as measured by both the semi-deviation and a drawdown factor, is considered low. As of December 31, 2012, Aberdeen Indonesia Fund traded at a discount of 9.95% below its net asset value, which is better than its one-year historical average discount of 9.48%.

    Andrew Gillan currently receives a manager quality ranking of 95 (0=worst, 99=best). If you desire only a moderate level of risk and strong performance, then this fund is an excellent option.

Data Date	Investment Rating	Net Assets ($Mil)	Price	Performance Rating/Pts	Total Return Y-T-D	Risk Rating/Pts
12-12	B	116.42	11.67	B / 8.0	2.74%	B- / 7.3
2011	B+	106.50	11.78	A+ / 9.7	1.44%	B- / 7.5
2010	C+	84.14	13.31	B+ / 8.8	51.47%	D+ / 2.6
2009	C-	68.29	9.50	C+ / 6.2	102.19%	C- / 3.7

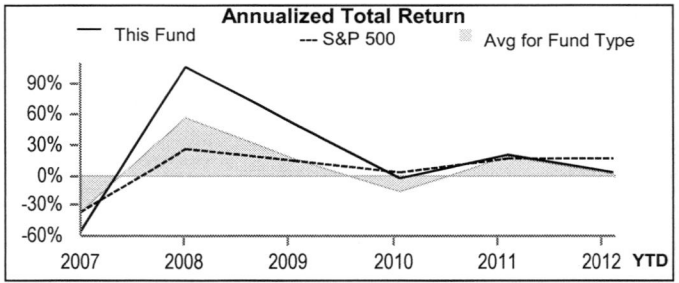

Aberdeen Israel Fund (ISL)

D   **Weak**

Fund Family: Aberdeen Asset Management Inc
Fund Type: Foreign
Inception Date: October 22, 1992

Major Rating Factors:
Disappointing performance is the major factor driving the D (Weak) TheStreet.com Investment Rating for Aberdeen Israel Fund. The fund currently has a performance rating of D (Weak) based on an annualized return of -0.60% over the last three years and a total return of 5.34% year to date 2012. Factored into the performance evaluation is an expense ratio of 1.68% (above average).

    The fund's risk rating is currently C+ (Fair). It carries a beta of 0.87, meaning the fund's expected move will be 8.7% for every 10% move in the market. Volatility, as measured by both the semi-deviation and a drawdown factor, is considered low. As of December 31, 2012, Aberdeen Israel Fund traded at a discount of 17.61% below its net asset value, which is better than its one-year historical average discount of 13.34%.

    Andrew P. S. Brown currently receives a manager quality ranking of 26 (0=worst, 99=best). This fund offers only a moderate level of risk but investors looking for strong performance are still waiting.

Data Date	Investment Rating	Net Assets ($Mil)	Price	Performance Rating/Pts	Total Return Y-T-D	Risk Rating/Pts
12-12	D	60.30	13.10	D / 2.0	5.34%	C+ / 6.7
2011	C-	62.40	12.75	C / 4.7	-0.24%	B- / 7.1
2010	C-	70.25	17.40	C- / 4.2	16.96%	C / 5.4
2009	B-	53.59	15.14	B / 7.6	81.32%	C / 5.3

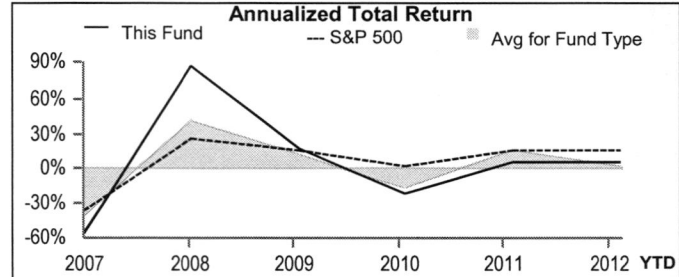

Aberdeen Latin America Equity Fund (LAQ)

C   **Fair**

Fund Family: Aberdeen Asset Management Inc
Fund Type: Foreign
Inception Date: October 30, 1991

Major Rating Factors: Middle of the road best describes Aberdeen Latin America Equity Fund whose TheStreet.com Investment Rating is currently a C (Fair). The fund currently has a performance rating of C+ (Fair) based on an annualized return of 10.96% over the last three years and a total return of 4.30% year to date 2012. Factored into the performance evaluation is an expense ratio of 1.20% (average).

The fund's risk rating is currently C+ (Fair). It carries a beta of 1.10, meaning it is expected to move 11.0% for every 10% move in the market. Volatility, as measured by both the semi-deviation and a drawdown factor, is considered low. As of December 31, 2012, Aberdeen Latin America Equity Fund traded at a discount of 11.46% below its net asset value, which is better than its one-year historical average discount of 9.30%.

Devan Kaloo has been running the fund for 4 years and currently receives a manager quality ranking of 79 (0=worst, 99=best). If you desire an average level of risk, then this fund may be an option.

Data Date	Investment Rating	Net Assets ($Mil)	Price	Performance Rating/Pts	Total Return Y-T-D	Risk Rating/Pts
12-12	C	264.11	36.24	C+ / 6.0	4.30%	C+ / 6.6
2011	B-	247.50	30.10	B / 7.6	2.66%	C+ / 6.8
2010	C	265.10	38.72	B / 8.1	26.93%	D+ / 2.7
2009	C+	190.98	39.42	B+ / 8.5	107.90%	C- / 4.0

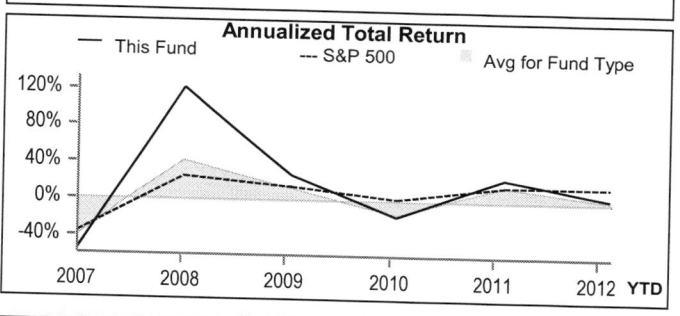

Adams Express Company (ADX)

C   **Fair**

Fund Family: Adams Express Company
Fund Type: Income
Inception Date: N/A

Major Rating Factors: Middle of the road best describes Adams Express Company whose TheStreet.com Investment Rating is currently a C (Fair). The fund currently has a performance rating of C (Fair) based on an annualized return of 8.85% over the last three years and a total return of 4.72% year to date 2012. Factored into the performance evaluation is an expense ratio of 0.68% (very low).

The fund's risk rating is currently B- (Good). It carries a beta of 1.09, meaning that its performance tracks fairly well with that of the overall stock market. Volatility, as measured by both the semi-deviation and a drawdown factor, is considered low. As of December 31, 2012, Adams Express Company traded at a discount of 17.59% below its net asset value, which is better than its one-year historical average discount of 14.12%.

Douglas G. Ober has been running the fund for 27 years and currently receives a manager quality ranking of 27 (0=worst, 99=best). If you desire an average level of risk, then this fund may be an option.

Data Date	Investment Rating	Net Assets ($Mil)	Price	Performance Rating/Pts	Total Return Y-T-D	Risk Rating/Pts
12-12	C	1,125.29	10.59	C / 4.3	4.72%	B- / 7.7
2011	C	1,050.70	9.64	C / 4.4	3.22%	B- / 7.7
2010	C	939.67	10.74	C- / 3.9	11.85%	C+ / 6.7
2009	C-	870.83	10.10	C- / 3.0	27.19%	C+ / 6.6

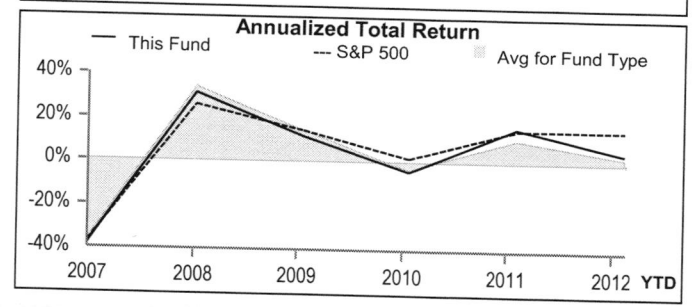

Advent Claymore Cnv Sec & Inc (AVK)

C-   **Fair**

Fund Family: Advent Capital Management LLC
Fund Type: Growth and Income
Inception Date: April 30, 2003

Major Rating Factors: Middle of the road best describes Advent Claymore Cnv Sec & Inc whose TheStreet.com Investment Rating is currently a C- (Fair). The fund currently has a performance rating of C (Fair) based on an annualized return of 9.68% over the last three years and a total return of 4.22% year to date 2012. Factored into the performance evaluation is an expense ratio of 1.58% (above average).

The fund's risk rating is currently C+ (Fair). It carries a beta of 0.92, meaning that its performance tracks fairly well with that of the overall stock market. Volatility, as measured by both the semi-deviation and a drawdown factor, is considered low. As of December 31, 2012, Advent Claymore Cnv Sec & Inc traded at a discount of 11.48% below its net asset value, which is better than its one-year historical average discount of 7.19%.

F. Barry Nelson has been running the fund for 10 years and currently receives a manager quality ranking of 49 (0=worst, 99=best). If you desire an average level of risk, then this fund may be an option.

Data Date	Investment Rating	Net Assets ($Mil)	Price	Performance Rating/Pts	Total Return Y-T-D	Risk Rating/Pts
12-12	C-	413.04	16.12	C / 4.3	4.22%	C+ / 6.7
2011	C	390.20	14.73	C+ / 6.2	6.59%	C+ / 6.6
2010	C	456.14	18.09	C+ / 6.9	27.15%	C- / 3.6
2009	D	304.08	15.59	D+ / 2.4	45.63%	C / 4.7

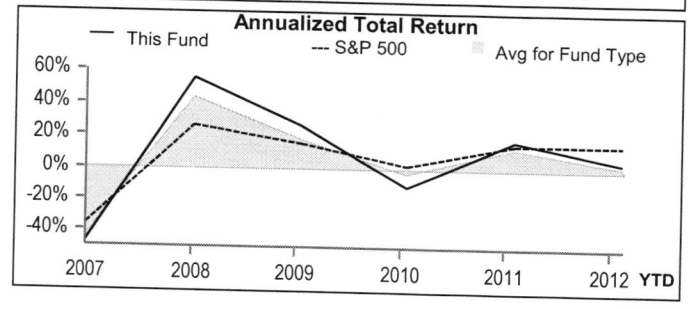

Advent Claymore Enhanced Gr & Inc (LCM)   D+   Weak

Fund Family: Guggenheim Funds Investment Advisor
Fund Type: Global
Inception Date: January 26, 2005

Data Date	Investment Rating	Net Assets ($Mil)	Price	Performance Rating/Pts	Total Return Y-T-D	Risk Rating/Pts
12-12	D+	144.53	9.10	D+ / 2.9	6.48%	C+ / 6.7
2011	C-	138.80	8.98	C- / 3.8	2.67%	B- / 7.3
2010	C-	171.50	11.80	C / 5.0	15.91%	C / 4.3
2009	D+	142.01	11.20	C- / 3.1	48.58%	C / 4.7

Major Rating Factors:
Disappointing performance is the major factor driving the D+ (Weak) TheStreet.com Investment Rating for Advent Claymore Enhanced Gr & Inc. The fund currently has a performance rating of D+ (Weak) based on an annualized return of 3.66% over the last three years and a total return of 6.48% year to date 2012. Factored into the performance evaluation is an expense ratio of 2.11% (high).

The fund's risk rating is currently C+ (Fair). It carries a beta of 0.63, meaning the fund's expected move will be 6.3% for every 10% move in the market. Volatility, as measured by both the semi-deviation and a drawdown factor, is considered low. As of December 31, 2012, Advent Claymore Enhanced Gr & Inc traded at a discount of 17.05% below its net asset value, which is better than its one-year historical average discount of 10.35%.

Paul L. Latronica has been running the fund for 6 years and currently receives a manager quality ranking of 51 (0=worst, 99=best). This fund offers only a moderate level of risk but investors looking for strong performance are still waiting.

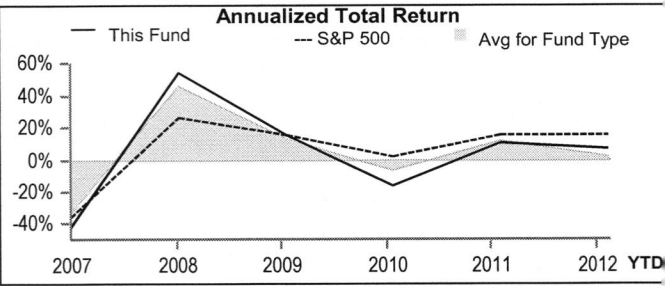

Advent/Claymore Gbl Con Sec & Inc (AGC)   D   Weak

Fund Family: Guggenheim Funds Investment Advisor
Fund Type: Growth and Income
Inception Date: May 25, 2007

Data Date	Investment Rating	Net Assets ($Mil)	Price	Performance Rating/Pts	Total Return Y-T-D	Risk Rating/Pts
12-12	D	238.69	6.48	D+ / 2.4	5.40%	C+ / 6.0
2011	D+	224.90	6.30	C- / 3.6	2.70%	C+ / 6.1
2010	E+	300.46	9.17	D / 1.9	22.95%	C- / 3.0
2009	C+	211.61	8.17	A- / 9.1	47.85%	C- / 3.3

Major Rating Factors:
Disappointing performance is the major factor driving the D (Weak) TheStreet.com Investment Rating for Advent/Claymore Gbl Con Sec & Inc. The fund currently has a performance rating of D+ (Weak) based on an annualized return of 0.82% over the last three years and a total return of 5.40% year to date 2012. Factored into the performance evaluation is an expense ratio of 1.99% (high).

The fund's risk rating is currently C+ (Fair). It carries a beta of 0.92, meaning its performance tracks fairly well with that of the overall stock market. Volatility, as measured by both the semi-deviation and a drawdown factor, is considered low. As of December 31, 2012, Advent/Claymore Gbl Con Sec & Inc traded at a discount of 14.85% below its net asset value, which is better than its one-year historical average discount of 8.99%.

Paul L. Latronica has been running the fund for 6 years and currently receives a manager quality ranking of 16 (0=worst, 99=best). This fund offers only a moderate level of risk but investors looking for strong performance are still waiting.

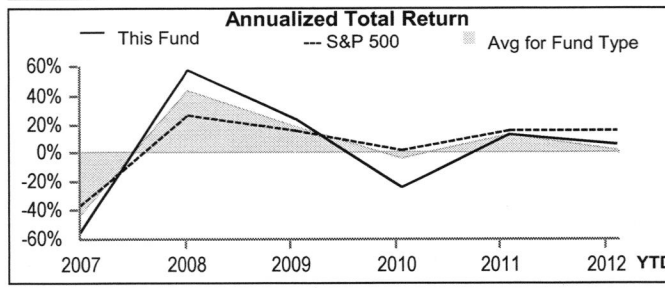

AGIC Convertible & Income Fund (NCV)   C-   Fair

Fund Family: Allianz Global Investors Fund Mgmt
Fund Type: Growth and Income
Inception Date: March 26, 2003

Data Date	Investment Rating	Net Assets ($Mil)	Price	Performance Rating/Pts	Total Return Y-T-D	Risk Rating/Pts
12-12	C-	627.09	8.69	C / 4.5	4.99%	B- / 7.2
2011	B	595.10	8.45	B+ / 8.8	4.02%	C+ / 6.5
2010	C-	644.41	10.24	B / 7.9	24.09%	D / 1.7
2009	D+	573.98	9.27	C+ / 5.9	119.23%	D+ / 2.6

Major Rating Factors: Middle of the road best describes AGIC Convertible & Income Fund whose TheStreet.com Investment Rating is currently a C- (Fair). The fund currently has a performance rating of C (Fair) based on an annualized return of 11.03% over the last three years and a total return of 4.99% year to date 2012. Factored into the performance evaluation is an expense ratio of 1.30% (average).

The fund's risk rating is currently B- (Good). It carries a beta of 1.07, meaning that its performance tracks fairly well with that of the overall stock market. Volatility, as measured by both the semi-deviation and a drawdown factor, is considered low. As of December 31, 2012, AGIC Convertible & Income Fund traded at a premium of .23% above its net asset value, which is better than its one-year historical average premium of 9.11%.

Douglas G. Forsyth has been running the fund for 10 years and currently receives a manager quality ranking of 42 (0=worst, 99=best). If you desire an average level of risk, then this fund may be an option.

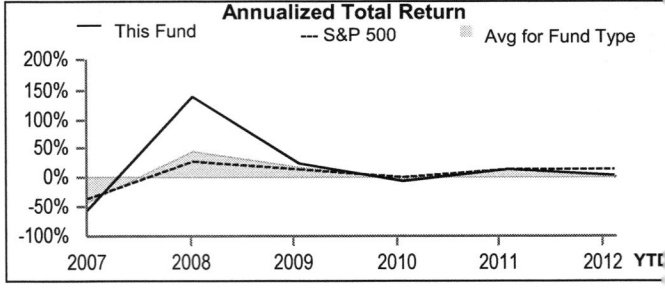

AGIC Convertible & Income Fund II (NCZ)

C-   **Fair**

Fund Family: Allianz Global Investors Fund Mgmt
Fund Type: Growth and Income
Inception Date: July 28, 2003

Major Rating Factors: Middle of the road best describes AGIC Convertible & Income Fund II whose TheStreet.com Investment Rating is currently a C- (Fair). The fund currently has a performance rating of C- (Fair) based on an annualized return of 10.36% over the last three years and a total return of 5.42% year to date 2012. Factored into the performance evaluation is an expense ratio of 1.33% (average).

The fund's risk rating is currently B- (Good). It carries a beta of 0.96, meaning that its performance tracks fairly well with that of the overall stock market. Volatility, as measured by both the semi-deviation and a drawdown factor, is considered low. As of December 31, 2012, AGIC Convertible & Income Fund II traded at a premium of .89% above its net asset value, which is better than its one-year historical average premium of 10.49%.

Douglas G. Forsyth has been running the fund for 10 years and currently receives a manager quality ranking of 52 (0=worst, 99=best). If you desire an average level of risk, then this fund may be an option.

Data Date	Investment Rating	Net Assets ($Mil)	Price	Perfor-mance Rating/Pts	Total Return Y-T-D	Risk Rating/Pts
12-12	C-	472.61	7.93	C- / 4.2	5.42%	B- / 7.4
2011	B	449.50	7.87	A- / 9.0	3.81%	B- / 7.0
2010	C-	487.13	9.37	B- / 7.2	24.41%	D / 1.8
2009	D+	438.12	8.48	C / 5.4	114.55%	D+ / 2.4

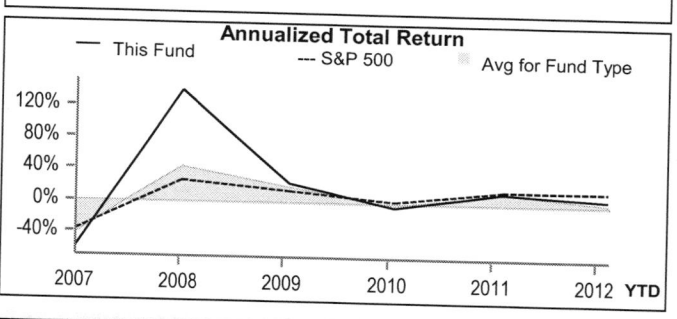

AGIC Equity & Convertible Income F (NIE)

C-   **Fair**

Fund Family: Allianz Global Investors Fund Mgmt
Fund Type: Income
Inception Date: February 27, 2007

Major Rating Factors: Middle of the road best describes AGIC Equity & Convertible Income F whose TheStreet.com Investment Rating is currently a C- (Fair). The fund currently has a performance rating of C- (Fair) based on an annualized return of 7.34% over the last three years and a total return of 4.15% year to date 2012. Factored into the performance evaluation is an expense ratio of 1.09% (low).

The fund's risk rating is currently B- (Good). It carries a beta of 0.96, meaning that its performance tracks fairly well with that of the overall stock market. Volatility, as measured by both the semi-deviation and a drawdown factor, is considered low. As of December 31, 2012, AGIC Equity & Convertible Income F traded at a discount of 15.49% below its net asset value, which is better than its one-year historical average discount of 10.60%.

Douglas G. Forsyth currently receives a manager quality ranking of 27 (0=worst, 99=best). If you desire an average level of risk, then this fund may be an option.

Data Date	Investment Rating	Net Assets ($Mil)	Price	Perfor-mance Rating/Pts	Total Return Y-T-D	Risk Rating/Pts
12-12	C-	416.87	16.64	C- / 3.4	4.15%	B- / 7.5
2011	C-	403.70	15.60	C- / 4.1	3.78%	B- / 7.4
2010	C	392.09	18.21	C+ / 5.6	15.68%	C / 5.1
2009	A-	361.94	16.56	B+ / 8.8	39.21%	C / 5.5

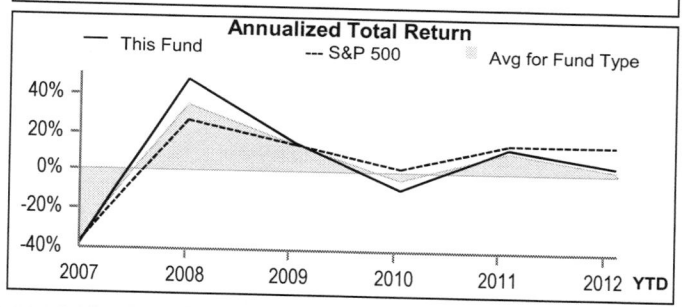

AGIC Global Equity & Conv Inc Fund (NGZ)

D+   **Weak**

Fund Family: Allianz Global Investors Fund Mgmt
Fund Type: Global
Inception Date: September 26, 2007

Major Rating Factors: AGIC Global Equity & Conv Inc Fund receives a TheStreet.com Investment Rating of D+ (Weak). The fund currently has a performance rating of C- (Fair) based on an annualized return of 4.20% over the last three years and a total return of 3.04% year to date 2012. Factored into the performance evaluation is an expense ratio of 1.29% (average).

The fund's risk rating is currently B- (Good). It carries a beta of 0.82, meaning the fund's expected move will be 8.2% for every 10% move in the market. Volatility, as measured by both the semi-deviation and a drawdown factor, is considered low. As of December 31, 2012, AGIC Global Equity & Conv Inc Fund traded at a discount of 12.52% below its net asset value, which is better than its one-year historical average discount of 10.45%.

Douglas G. Forsyth currently receives a manager quality ranking of 54 (0=worst, 99=best). If you desire an average level of risk, then this fund may be an option.

Data Date	Investment Rating	Net Assets ($Mil)	Price	Perfor-mance Rating/Pts	Total Return Y-T-D	Risk Rating/Pts
12-12	D+	104.35	13.49	C- / 3.3	3.04%	B- / 7.2
2011	C-	101.50	12.86	C / 4.6	2.57%	B- / 7.2
2010	C-	101.85	15.82	C- / 4.2	9.78%	C / 5.4
2009	B+	103.05	15.31	A / 9.5	58.23%	C / 4.5

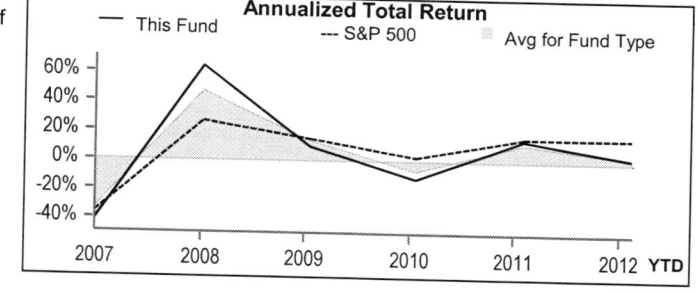

AGIC Intl & Premium Strategy Fund (NAI)

D-   **Weak**

Fund Family: Allianz Global Investors Fund Mgmt
Fund Type: Foreign
Inception Date: April 27, 2005

Major Rating Factors:
Disappointing performance is the major factor driving the D- (Weak) TheStreet.com Investment Rating for AGIC Intl & Premium Strategy Fund. The fund currently has a performance rating of D (Weak) based on an annualized return of -1.79% over the last three years and a total return of 6.29% year to date 2012. Factored into the performance evaluation is an expense ratio of 1.34% (average).

The fund's risk rating is currently C+ (Fair). It carries a beta of 0.90, meaning that its performance tracks fairly well with that of the overall stock market. Volatility, as measured by both the semi-deviation and a drawdown factor, is considered low. As of December 31, 2012, AGIC Intl & Premium Strategy Fund traded at a discount of 10.43% below its net asset value, which is better than its one-year historical average discount of 1.57%.

Kunal Ghosh currently receives a manager quality ranking of 17 (0=worst, 99=best). This fund offers only a moderate level of risk but investors looking for strong performance are still waiting.

Data Date	Investment Rating	Net Assets ($Mil)	Price	Performance Rating/Pts	Total Return Y-T-D	Risk Rating/Pts
12-12	D-	102.93	9.70	D / 1.6	6.29%	C+ / 5.9
2011	D	106.50	9.89	D+ / 2.6	1.72%	C+ / 6.0
2010	D-	140.36	14.12	D / 1.9	0.23%	C- / 3.4
2009	C-	145.11	15.48	C- / 4.1	54.35%	C / 4.6

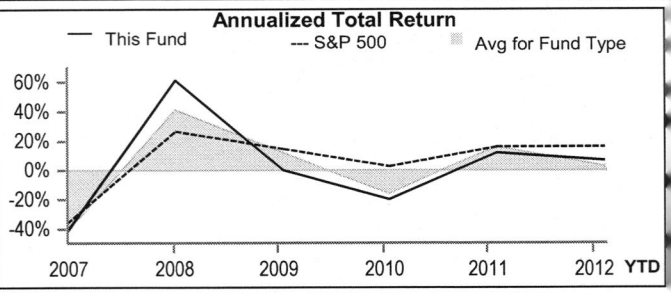

Alliance CA Municipal Income Fund (AKP)

B+   **Good**

Fund Family: AllianceBernstein LP
Fund Type: Municipal - Single State
Inception Date: January 28, 2002

Major Rating Factors: Strong performance is the major factor driving the B+ (Good) TheStreet.com Investment Rating for Alliance CA Municipal Income Fund. The fund currently has a performance rating of B- (Good) based on an annualized return of 13.02% over the last three years and a total return of 4.19% year to date 2012. Factored into the performance evaluation is an expense ratio of 1.30% (average).

The fund's risk rating is currently B (Good). It carries a beta of 1.92, meaning it is expected to move 19.2% for every 10% move in the market. Volatility, as measured by both the semi-deviation and a drawdown factor, is considered low. As of December 31, 2012, Alliance CA Municipal Income Fund traded at a discount of 3.24% below its net asset value, which is better than its one-year historical average premium of 3.72%.

Michael G. Brooks currently receives a manager quality ranking of 42 (0=worst, 99=best). If you desire only a moderate level of risk and strong performance, then this fund is an excellent option.

Data Date	Investment Rating	Net Assets ($Mil)	Price	Performance Rating/Pts	Total Return Y-T-D	Risk Rating/Pts
12-12	B+	119.97	14.65	B- / 7.1	4.19%	B / 8.8
2011	A	115.27	14.51	B+ / 8.9	-0.34%	B+ / 9.0
2010	C+	121.80	13.18	C / 4.8	10.12%	C+ / 6.5
2009	C+	112.32	12.80	C / 4.6	38.82%	B- / 7.6

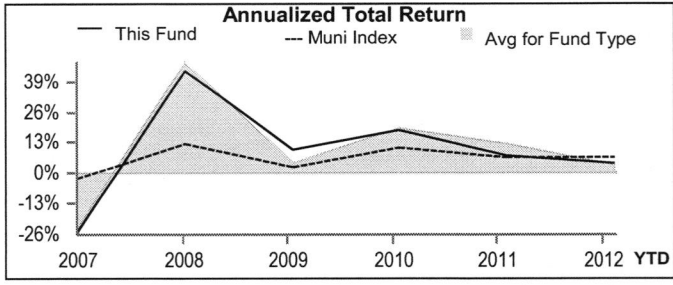

Alliance NY Municipal Income Fund (AYN)

C   **Fair**

Fund Family: AllianceBernstein LP
Fund Type: Municipal - Single State
Inception Date: January 28, 2002

Major Rating Factors: Middle of the road best describes Alliance NY Municipal Income Fund whose TheStreet.com Investment Rating is currently a C (Fair). The fund currently has a performance rating of C- (Fair) based on an annualized return of 8.90% over the last three years and a total return of 3.01% year to date 2012. Factored into the performance evaluation is an expense ratio of 1.44% (average).

The fund's risk rating is currently B+ (Good). It carries a beta of 1.86, meaning it is expected to move 18.6% for every 10% move in the market. Volatility, as measured by both the semi-deviation and a drawdown factor, is considered very low. As of December 31, 2012, Alliance NY Municipal Income Fund traded at a discount of 3.69% below its net asset value, which is better than its one-year historical average premium of 3.02%.

Michael G. Brooks currently receives a manager quality ranking of 30 (0=worst, 99=best). If you desire an average level of risk, then this fund may be an option.

Data Date	Investment Rating	Net Assets ($Mil)	Price	Performance Rating/Pts	Total Return Y-T-D	Risk Rating/Pts
12-12	C	69.61	14.37	C- / 4.1	3.01%	B+ / 9.0
2011	A	68.05	15.27	B+ / 8.8	-0.65%	B+ / 9.3
2010	B+	70.65	14.27	B / 7.8	15.62%	C+ / 6.2
2009	B-	66.38	13.11	C+ / 6.0	41.46%	B- / 7.7

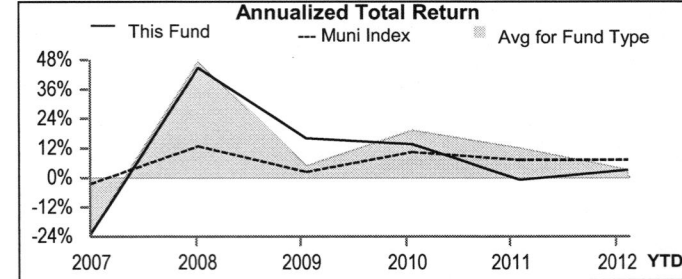

AllianceBernstein Global High Inc (AWF)

B **Good**

Fund Family: AllianceBernstein LP
Fund Type: Global
Inception Date: July 23, 1993

Major Rating Factors: Strong performance is the major factor driving the B (Good) TheStreet.com Investment Rating for AllianceBernstein Global High Inc. The fund currently has a performance rating of B (Good) based on an annualized return of 15.90% over the last three years and a total return of 3.96% year to date 2012. Factored into the performance evaluation is an expense ratio of 0.98% (low).

The fund's risk rating is currently B- (Good). It carries a beta of 0.77, meaning the fund's expected move will be 7.7% for every 10% move in the market. Volatility, as measured by both the semi-deviation and a drawdown factor, is considered low. As of December 31, 2012, AllianceBernstein Global High Inc traded at a premium of .13% above its net asset value, which is better than its one-year historical average premium of 2.60%.

Paul J. DeNoon has been running the fund for 21 years and currently receives a manager quality ranking of 93 (0=worst, 99=best). If you desire only a moderate level of risk and strong performance, then this fund is an excellent option.

Data Date	Investment Rating	Net Assets ($Mil)	Price	Performance Rating/Pts	Total Return Y-T-D	Risk Rating/Pts
12-12	B	1,267.20	15.65	B / 7.9	3.96%	B- / 7.7
2011	B+	1,186.30	14.17	B+ / 8.9	1.48%	B / 8.1
2010	B	1,232.80	14.30	B+ / 8.3	16.34%	C / 5.0
2009	B-	1,144.75	13.29	B / 8.1	86.73%	C / 4.9

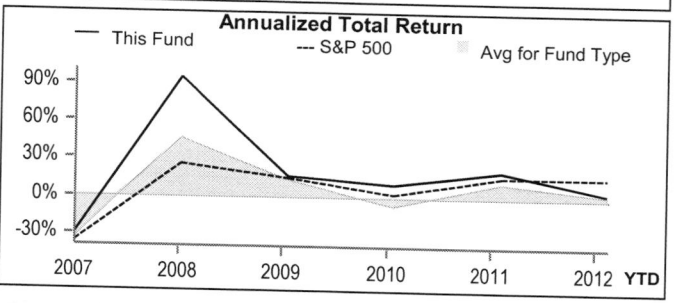

AllianceBernstein Income Fund (ACG)

C **Fair**

Fund Family: AllianceBernstein LP
Fund Type: Global
Inception Date: August 21, 1987

Major Rating Factors: Middle of the road best describes AllianceBernstein Income Fund whose TheStreet.com Investment Rating is currently a C (Fair). The fund currently has a performance rating of C- (Fair) based on an annualized return of 9.66% over the last three years and a total return of 1.23% year to date 2012. Factored into the performance evaluation is an expense ratio of 0.65% (very low).

The fund's risk rating is currently B+ (Good). It carries a beta of 0.16, meaning the fund's expected move will be 1.6% for every 10% move in the market. Volatility, as measured by both the semi-deviation and a drawdown factor, is considered very low. As of December 31, 2012, AllianceBernstein Income Fund traded at a discount of 9.09% below its net asset value, which is worse than its one-year historical average discount of 9.12%.

Douglas J. Peebles has been running the fund for 26 years and currently receives a manager quality ranking of 86 (0=worst, 99=best). If you desire an average level of risk, then this fund may be an option.

Data Date	Investment Rating	Net Assets ($Mil)	Price	Performance Rating/Pts	Total Return Y-T-D	Risk Rating/Pts
12-12	C	2.24	8.10	C- / 4.1	1.23%	B+ / 9.1
2011	C+	2,168.20	8.07	C / 4.5	0.74%	B+ / 9.2
2010	B	2,099.85	7.93	C / 4.7	2.11%	B / 8.3
2009	C+	1,909.28	8.25	C / 5.2	24.26%	B- / 7.4

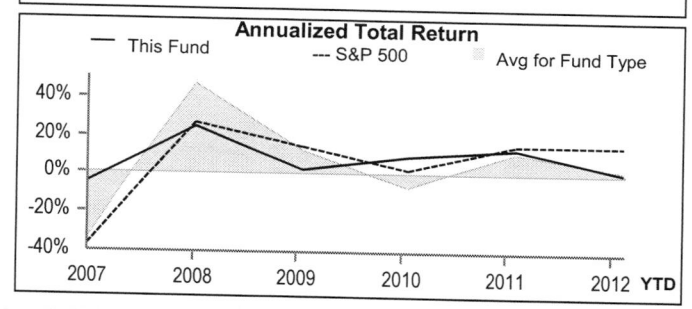

AllianceBernstein Nat Muni Inc Fun (AFB)

A+ **Excellent**

Fund Family: AllianceBernstein LP
Fund Type: Municipal - National
Inception Date: January 28, 2002

Major Rating Factors:
Exceptional performance is the major factor driving the A+ (Excellent) TheStreet.com Investment Rating for AllianceBernstein Nat Muni Inc Fun. The fund currently has a performance rating of A- (Excellent) based on an annualized return of 14.21% over the last three years and a total return of 7.30% year to date 2012. Factored into the performance evaluation is an expense ratio of 1.13% (low).

The fund's risk rating is currently B (Good). It carries a beta of 1.72, meaning it is expected to move 17.2% for every 10% move in the market. Volatility, as measured by both the semi-deviation and a drawdown factor, is considered low. As of December 31, 2012, AllianceBernstein Nat Muni Inc Fun traded at a premium of 2.30% above its net asset value, which is better than its one-year historical average premium of 3.24%.

Michael G. Brooks currently receives a manager quality ranking of 59 (0=worst, 99=best). If you desire only a moderate level of risk and strong performance, then this fund is an excellent option.

Data Date	Investment Rating	Net Assets ($Mil)	Price	Performance Rating/Pts	Total Return Y-T-D	Risk Rating/Pts
12-12	A+	409.20	15.55	A- / 9.1	7.30%	B / 8.8
2011	A+	386.44	14.78	A / 9.5	0.81%	B / 8.9
2010	C	403.45	12.94	C / 4.5	3.32%	C+ / 6.1
2009	C+	356.77	13.39	C+ / 6.5	46.57%	C+ / 6.9

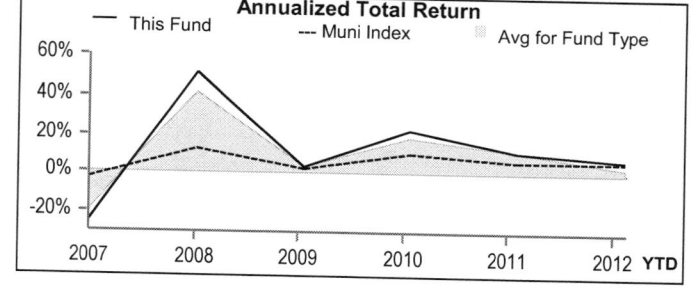

Alpine Global Dynamic Div Fd (AGD)

E+   **Very Weak**

Fund Family: Alpine Woods Capital Investors LLC
Fund Type: Global
Inception Date: July 26, 2006

Major Rating Factors:
Very poor performance is the major factor driving the E+ (Very Weak) TheStreet.com Investment Rating for Alpine Global Dynamic Div Fd. The fund currently has a performance rating of E+ (Very Weak) based on an annualized return of -7.67% over the last three years and a total return of 4.40% year to date 2012. Factored into the performance evaluation is an expense ratio of 1.39% (average).

The fund's risk rating is currently C (Fair). It carries a beta of 1.31, meaning it is expected to move 13.1% for every 10% move in the market. Volatility, as measured by both the semi-deviation and a drawdown factor, is considered average. As of December 31, 2012, Alpine Global Dynamic Div Fd traded at a premium of 2.35% above its net asset value, which is better than its one-year historical average premium of 7.59%.

Jill K. Evans has been running the fund for 7 years and currently receives a manager quality ranking of 9 (0=worst, 99=best). This fund offers an average level of risk but investors looking for strong performance will be frustrated.

Data Date	Investment Rating	Net Assets ($Mil)	Price	Performance Rating/Pts	Total Return Y-T-D	Risk Rating/Pts
12-12	E+	142.83	5.23	E+ / 0.9	4.40%	C / 4.6
2011	D-	192.55	5.17	D / 1.6	2.90%	C / 4.8
2010	D-	177.05	7.29	E+ / 0.6	-17.71%	C / 4.6
2009	D	147.78	10.13	C- / 3.7	58.82%	C- / 3.3

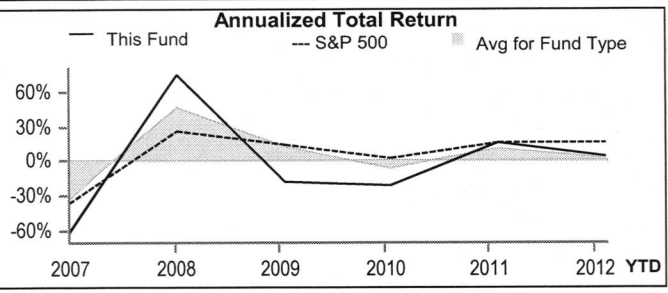

Alpine Global Premier Properties F (AWP)

B   **Good**

Fund Family: Alpine Woods Capital Investors LLC
Fund Type: Growth and Income
Inception Date: April 25, 2007

Major Rating Factors: Strong performance is the major factor driving the B (Good) TheStreet.com Investment Rating for Alpine Global Premier Properties F. The fund currently has a performance rating of B+ (Good) based on an annualized return of 13.65% over the last three years and a total return of 5.08% year to date 2012. Factored into the performance evaluation is an expense ratio of 1.29% (average).

The fund's risk rating is currently C+ (Fair). It carries a beta of 1.38, meaning it is expected to move 13.8% for every 10% move in the market. Volatility, as measured by both the semi-deviation and a drawdown factor, is considered low. As of December 31, 2012, Alpine Global Premier Properties F traded at a discount of 11.00% below its net asset value, which is better than its one-year historical average discount of 9.18%.

Samuel A. Lieber has been running the fund for 6 years and currently receives a manager quality ranking of 39 (0=worst, 99=best). If you desire only a moderate level of risk and strong performance, then this fund is an excellent option.

Data Date	Investment Rating	Net Assets ($Mil)	Price	Performance Rating/Pts	Total Return Y-T-D	Risk Rating/Pts
12-12	B	758.72	7.28	B+ / 8.8	5.08%	C+ / 6.8
2011	C	956.40	5.30	C / 5.5	3.02%	C+ / 6.7
2010	D-	794.94	7.09	D / 1.9	21.04%	C / 4.3
2009	B+	528.19	6.23	A+ / 9.7	73.64%	C- / 4.1

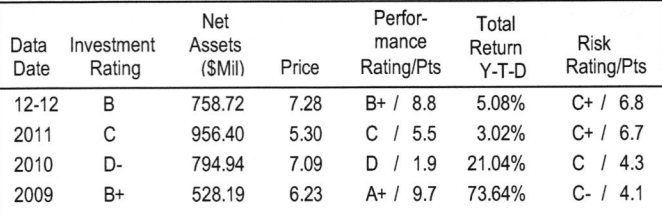

Alpine Total Dynamic Dividend Fund (AOD)

E+   **Very Weak**

Fund Family: Alpine Woods Capital Investors LLC
Fund Type: Global
Inception Date: January 26, 2007

Major Rating Factors:
Very poor performance is the major factor driving the E+ (Very Weak) TheStreet.com Investment Rating for Alpine Total Dynamic Dividend Fund. The fund currently has a performance rating of E+ (Very Weak) based on an annualized return of -11.03% over the last three years and a total return of 4.22% year to date 2012. Factored into the performance evaluation is an expense ratio of 1.35% (average).

The fund's risk rating is currently C (Fair). It carries a beta of 1.08, meaning that its performance tracks fairly well with that of the overall stock market. Volatility, as measured by both the semi-deviation and a drawdown factor, is considered average. As of December 31, 2012, Alpine Total Dynamic Dividend Fund traded at a discount of 12.77% below its net asset value, which is better than its one-year historical average discount of 7.82%.

Jill K. Evans has been running the fund for 6 years and currently receives a manager quality ranking of 8 (0=worst, 99=best). This fund offers an average level of risk but investors looking for strong performance will be frustrated.

Data Date	Investment Rating	Net Assets ($Mil)	Price	Performance Rating/Pts	Total Return Y-T-D	Risk Rating/Pts
12-12	E+	1,134.04	4.03	E+ / 0.8	4.22%	C / 4.7
2011	D-	1,504.33	4.38	D / 1.6	1.83%	C / 5.0
2010	D-	1,424.57	5.92	E+ / 0.7	-22.17%	C / 4.6
2009	B-	1,321.60	8.92	A / 9.4	61.13%	C- / 3.5

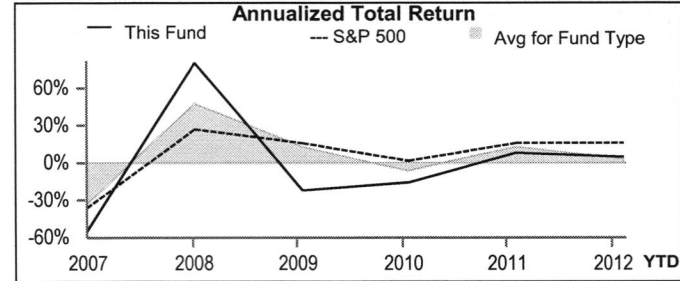

American Income Fund (MRF)

Fund Family: US Bancorp Asset Management Inc
Fund Type: Mortgage
Inception Date: December 23, 1988

C+   **Fair**

Data Date	Investment Rating	Net Assets ($Mil)	Price	Perfor-mance Rating/Pts	Total Return Y-T-D	Risk Rating/Pts
12-12	C+	80.00	8.37	C+ / 6.6	3.94%	B- / 7.1
2011	C	77.80	7.69	C+ / 5.9	-1.30%	B- / 7.0
2010	B+	79.00	8.38	B / 7.8	22.25%	C+ / 5.7
2009	C	70.89	7.44	C+ / 5.6	41.22%	C+ / 5.7

Major Rating Factors: Middle of the road best describes American Income Fund whose TheStreet.com Investment Rating is currently a C+ (Fair). The fund currently has a performance rating of C+ (Fair) based on an annualized return of 13.67% over the last three years and a total return of 3.94% year to date 2012. Factored into the performance evaluation is an expense ratio of 1.25% (average).

The fund's risk rating is currently B- (Good). It carries a beta of 0.45, meaning the fund's expected move will be 4.5% for every 10% move in the market. Volatility, as measured by both the semi-deviation and a drawdown factor, is considered low. As of December 31, 2012, American Income Fund traded at a discount of 3.46% below its net asset value, which is worse than its one-year historical average discount of 4.40%.

Chris J. Neuharth currently receives a manager quality ranking of 90 (0=worst, 99=best). If you desire an average level of risk, then this fund may be an option.

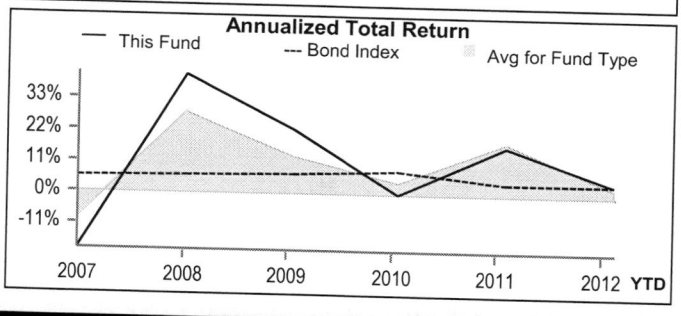

American Municipal Income Portfoli (XAA)

Fund Family: US Bancorp Asset Management Inc
Fund Type: Municipal - National
Inception Date: June 18, 1993

A   **Excellent**

Data Date	Investment Rating	Net Assets ($Mil)	Price	Perfor-mance Rating/Pts	Total Return Y-T-D	Risk Rating/Pts
12-12	A	91.00	15.77	B+ / 8.9	6.47%	B / 8.5
2011	A+	84.30	14.55	A+ / 9.6	0.70%	B / 8.9
2010	C+	85.00	12.94	C / 5.4	-1.06%	C+ / 6.1
2009	A-	75.12	13.95	B / 7.8	71.92%	C+ / 6.3

Major Rating Factors:
Strong performance is the major factor driving the A (Excellent) TheStreet.com Investment Rating for American Municipal Income Portfoli. The fund currently has a performance rating of B+ (Good) based on an annualized return of 13.00% over the last three years and a total return of 6.47% year to date 2012. Factored into the performance evaluation is an expense ratio of 1.32% (average).

The fund's risk rating is currently B (Good). It carries a beta of 1.97, meaning it is expected to move 19.7% for every 10% move in the market. Volatility, as measured by both the semi-deviation and a drawdown factor, is considered low. As of December 31, 2012, American Municipal Income Portfoli traded at a discount of .57% below its net asset value, which is better than its one-year historical average premium of 1.79%.

Christopher L. Drahn currently receives a manager quality ranking of 37 (0=worst, 99=best). If you desire only a moderate level of risk and strong performance, then this fund is an excellent option.

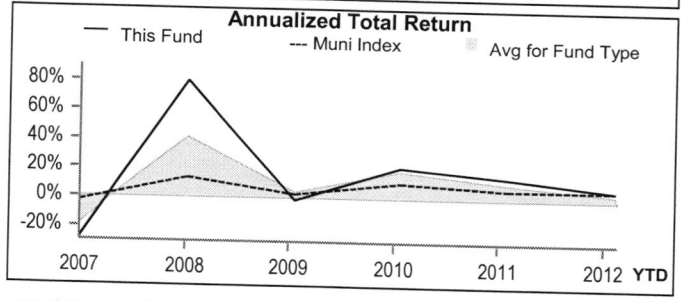

American Select Portfolio (SLA)

Fund Family: US Bancorp Asset Management Inc
Fund Type: Mortgage
Inception Date: September 14, 1993

C   **Fair**

Data Date	Investment Rating	Net Assets ($Mil)	Price	Perfor-mance Rating/Pts	Total Return Y-T-D	Risk Rating/Pts
12-12	C	128.00	10.93	C / 4.4	1.01%	B / 8.2
2011	C	121.80	10.00	C / 4.8	-0.30%	B- / 7.9
2010	C+	129.00	10.46	C / 4.9	3.75%	B- / 7.2
2009	C	131.42	11.37	C / 5.1	28.48%	C+ / 6.5

Major Rating Factors: Middle of the road best describes American Select Portfolio whose TheStreet.com Investment Rating is currently a C (Fair). The fund currently has a performance rating of C (Fair) based on an annualized return of 9.72% over the last three years and a total return of 1.01% year to date 2012. Factored into the performance evaluation is an expense ratio of 1.95% (above average).

The fund's risk rating is currently B (Good). It carries a beta of 0.95, meaning that its performance tracks fairly well with that of the overall stock market. Volatility, as measured by both the semi-deviation and a drawdown factor, is considered low. As of December 31, 2012, American Select Portfolio traded at a discount of 10.12% below its net asset value, which is worse than its one-year historical average discount of 10.34%.

Jason J. O'Brien currently receives a manager quality ranking of 78 (0=worst, 99=best). If you desire an average level of risk, then this fund may be an option.

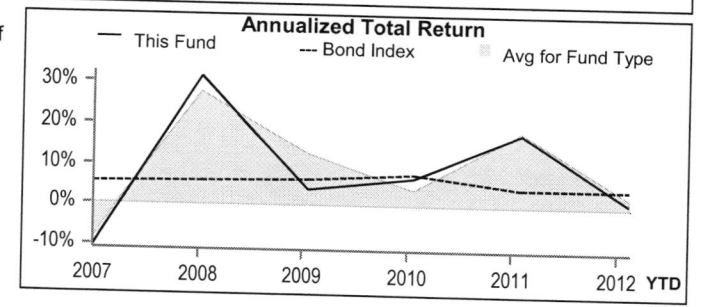

American Strat Inc Portfolio (ASP)

C   Fair

Fund Family: US Bancorp Asset Management Inc
Fund Type: Mortgage
Inception Date: December 19, 1991

Major Rating Factors: Middle of the road best describes American Strat Inc Portfolio whose TheStreet.com Investment Rating is a C (Fair). The fund currently has a performance rating of C- (Fair) based on an annualized return of 10.64% over the last three years and a total return of 0.44% year to date 2012. Factored into the performance evaluation is an expense ratio of 1.93% (above average).

The fund's risk rating is currently B (Good). It carries a beta of 1.19, meaning it is expected to move 11.9% for every 10% move in the market. Volatility, as measured by both the semi-deviation and a drawdown factor, is considered low. As of December 31, 2012, American Strat Inc Portfolio traded at a discount of 9.13% below its net asset value, which is better than its one-year historical average discount of 8.53%.

Jason J. O'Brien currently receives a manager quality ranking of 80 (0=worst, 99=best). If you desire an average level of risk, then this fund may be an option.

Data Date	Investment Rating	Net Assets ($Mil)	Price	Performance Rating/Pts	Total Return Y-T-D	Risk Rating/Pts
12-12	C	55.00	11.45	C- / 4.1	0.44%	B / 8.1
2011	C+	52.70	10.67	C+ / 5.6	0.37%	B- / 7.9
2010	B+	56.00	12.06	B / 7.6	16.86%	C+ / 5.8
2009	B-	52.66	11.31	C+ / 6.1	37.38%	B- / 7.1

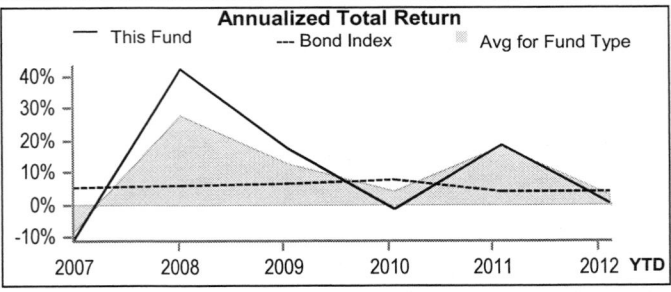

American Strat Inc Portfolio II (BSP)

C-   Fair

Fund Family: US Bancorp Asset Management Inc
Fund Type: Mortgage
Inception Date: July 23, 1992

Major Rating Factors: Middle of the road best describes American Strat Inc Portfolio II whose TheStreet.com Investment Rating is currently a C- (Fair). The fund currently has a performance rating of C- (Fair) based on an annualized return of 6.59% over the last three years and a total return of 2.61% year to date 2012. Factored into the performance evaluation is an expense ratio of 2.00% (high).

The fund's risk rating is currently B- (Good). It carries a beta of 0.09, meaning the fund's expected move will be 0.9% for every 10% move in the market. Volatility, as measured by both the semi-deviation and a drawdown factor, is considered low. As of December 31, 2012, American Strat Inc Portfolio II traded at a discount of 14.12% below its net asset value, which is worse than its one-year historical average discount of 14.31%.

Jason J. O'Brien currently receives a manager quality ranking of 80 (0=worst, 99=best). If you desire an average level of risk, then this fund may be an option.

Data Date	Investment Rating	Net Assets ($Mil)	Price	Performance Rating/Pts	Total Return Y-T-D	Risk Rating/Pts
12-12	C-	163.00	8.82	C- / 3.7	2.61%	B- / 7.9
2011	C-	155.30	8.06	C- / 3.5	-0.74%	B- / 7.9
2010	C+	173.00	9.32	C / 4.6	4.13%	B- / 7.4
2009	C+	181.53	10.16	C / 5.0	29.23%	B- / 7.0

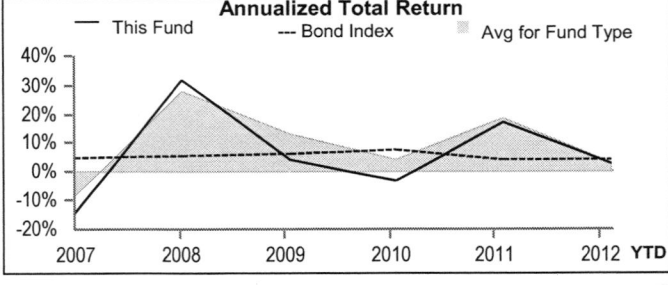

American Strat Inc Portfolio III (CSP)

C-   Fair

Fund Family: US Bancorp Asset Management Inc
Fund Type: Mortgage
Inception Date: March 18, 1993

Major Rating Factors: Middle of the road best describes American Strat Inc Portfolio III whose TheStreet.com Investment Rating is currently a C- (Fair). The fund currently has a performance rating of C- (Fair) based on an annualized return of 5.13% over the last three years and a total return of 0.00% year to date 2012. Factored into the performance evaluation is an expense ratio of 2.11% (high).

The fund's risk rating is currently B- (Good). It carries a beta of 0.05, meaning the fund's expected move will be 0.5% for every 10% move in the market. Volatility, as measured by both the semi-deviation and a drawdown factor, is considered low. As of December 31, 2012, American Strat Inc Portfolio III traded at a discount of 7.99% below its net asset value, which is worse than its one-year historical average discount of 11.93%.

Jason J. O'Brien currently receives a manager quality ranking of 80 (0=worst, 99=best). If you desire an average level of risk, then this fund may be an option.

Data Date	Investment Rating	Net Assets ($Mil)	Price	Performance Rating/Pts	Total Return Y-T-D	Risk Rating/Pts
12-12	C-	175.00	7.49	C- / 3.4	0.00%	B- / 7.5
2011	D	172.80	6.52	D / 1.9	0.61%	B- / 7.3
2010	C-	196.00	7.65	D / 1.8	0.02%	B- / 7.2
2009	C-	227.89	8.79	D / 1.9	9.46%	C+ / 6.9

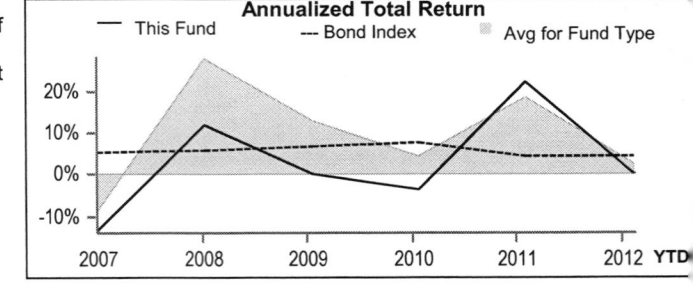

Apollo Senior Floating Rate Fd Inc (AFT)

B+   **Good**

Fund Family: Apollo Investment Management LP
Fund Type: Loan Participation
Inception Date: February 24, 2011

Major Rating Factors: Strong performance is the major factor driving the B+ (Good) TheStreet.com Investment Rating for Apollo Senior Floating Rate Fd Inc. The fund currently has a performance rating of B (Good) based on an annualized return of 0.00% over the last three years and a total return of 2.56% year to date 2012. Factored into the performance evaluation is an expense ratio of 3.24% (high).

The fund's risk rating is currently B- (Good). It carries a beta of 0.00, meaning the fund's expected move will be 0.0% for every 10% move in the market. Volatility, as measured by both the semi-deviation and a drawdown factor, is considered low. As of December 31, 2012, Apollo Senior Floating Rate Fd Inc traded at a discount of 1.16% below its net asset value, which is better than its one-year historical average discount of .04%.

Joseph A. Moroney currently receives a manager quality ranking of 99 (0=worst, 99=best). If you desire only a moderate level of risk and strong performance, then this fund is an excellent option.

Data Date	Investment Rating	Net Assets ($Mil)	Price	Performance Rating/Pts	Total Return Y-T-D	Risk Rating/Pts
12-12	B+	283.96	18.77	B / 8.2	2.56%	B- / 7.8

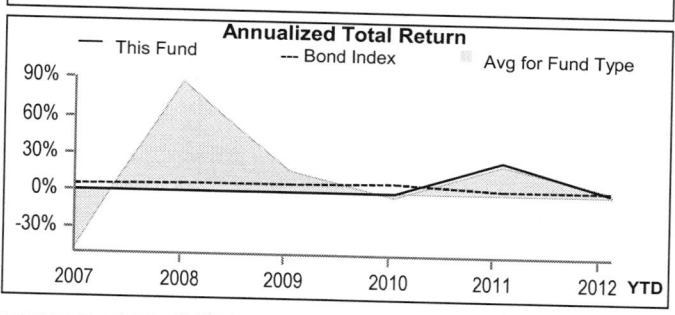

ASA Gold & Precious Metals Ltd (ASA)

E   **Very Weak**

Fund Family: ASA Limited
Fund Type: Precious Metals
Inception Date: N/A

Major Rating Factors: ASA Gold & Precious Metals Ltd has adopted a risky asset allocation strategy and currently receives an overall TheStreet.com Investment Rating of E (Very Weak). The fund has an above average level of volatility, as measured by both semi-deviation and drawdown factors. It carries a beta of 1.01, meaning that its performance tracks fairly well with that of the overall stock market. As of December 31, 2012, ASA Gold & Precious Metals Ltd traded at a discount of 8.89% below its net asset value, which is better than its one-year historical average discount of 7.98%. Unfortunately, the high level of risk (D+, Weak) failed to pay off as investors endured very poor performance.

The fund's performance rating is currently E+ (Very Weak). It has registered an annualized return of -3.98% over the last three years and is up 1.53% year to date 2012. Factored into the performance evaluation is an expense ratio of 0.76% (very low).

David J. Christensen currently receives a manager quality ranking of 7 (0=worst, 99=best). If you can tolerate high levels of risk in the hope of improved future returns, holding this fund may be an option.

Data Date	Investment Rating	Net Assets ($Mil)	Price	Performance Rating/Pts	Total Return Y-T-D	Risk Rating/Pts
12-12	E	455.24	21.53	E+ / 0.9	1.53%	D+ / 2.8
2011	D	549.40	26.19	C+ / 6.3	2.90%	D+ / 2.5
2010	C	580.36	34.71	B+ / 8.9	35.98%	D / 1.6
2009	C	552.52	77.45	B / 7.6	57.73%	C- / 4.0

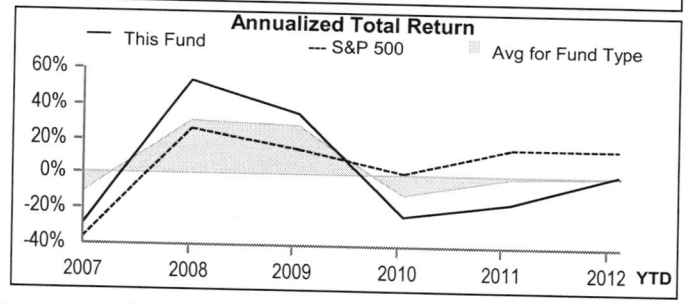

Asia Pacific Fund (APB)

D+   **Weak**

Fund Family: Baring Asset Management (Asia) Limi
Fund Type: Foreign
Inception Date: April 24, 1987

Major Rating Factors:
Disappointing performance is the major factor driving the D+ (Weak) TheStreet.com Investment Rating for Asia Pacific Fund. The fund currently has a performance rating of D+ (Weak) based on an annualized return of 1.92% over the last three years and a total return of 1.85% year to date 2012. Factored into the performance evaluation is an expense ratio of 2.15% (high).

The fund's risk rating is currently B- (Good). It carries a beta of 1.01, meaning that its performance tracks fairly well with that of the overall stock market. Volatility, as measured by both the semi-deviation and a drawdown factor, is considered low. As of December 31, 2012, Asia Pacific Fund traded at a discount of 12.10% below its net asset value, which is better than its one-year historical average discount of 10.15%.

Khiem T. Do has been running the fund for 9 years and currently receives a manager quality ranking of 31 (0=worst, 99=best). This fund offers only a moderate level of risk but investors looking for strong performance are still waiting.

Data Date	Investment Rating	Net Assets ($Mil)	Price	Performance Rating/Pts	Total Return Y-T-D	Risk Rating/Pts
12-12	D+	120.72	10.82	D+ / 2.5	1.85%	B- / 7.1
2011	C-	107.30	9.40	C- / 3.6	1.06%	B- / 7.2
2010	D	113.44	11.95	C / 4.6	14.90%	C- / 3.3
2009	C-	105.97	10.40	C+ / 6.7	54.07%	D+ / 2.4

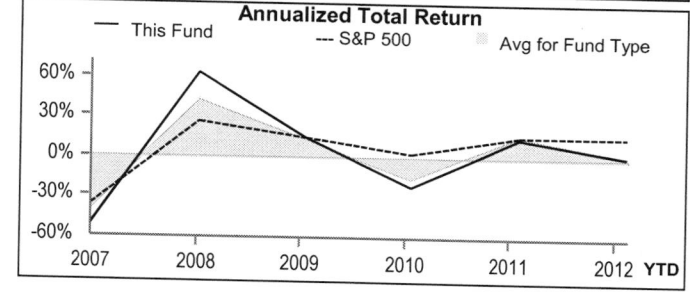

Asia Tigers Fund (GRR)

D-　　　**Weak**

Fund Family: Aberdeen Asset Management Asia Ltd
Fund Type: Foreign
Inception Date: November 29, 1993

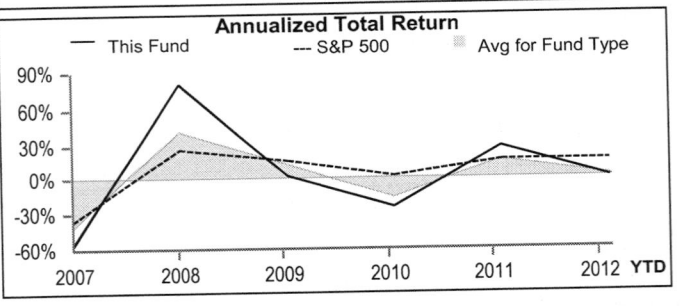

Data Date	Investment Rating	Net Assets ($Mil)	Price	Performance Rating/Pts	Total Return Y-T-D	Risk Rating/Pts
12-12	D-	57.14	12.59	D / 2.2	1.03%	C / 5.2
2011	D	79.92	12.01	C- / 3.3	2.25%	C / 5.5
2010	D-	77.15	19.68	D- / 1.3	2.50%	C- / 3.7
2009	C	54.83	19.20	B- / 7.2	70.92%	C / 4.3

Major Rating Factors:
Disappointing performance is the major factor driving the D- (Weak) TheStreet.com Investment Rating for Asia Tigers Fund. The fund currently has a performance rating of D (Weak) based on an annualized return of -1.55% over the last three years and a total return of 1.03% year to date 2012. Factored into the performance evaluation is an expense ratio of 2.36% (high).

The fund's risk rating is currently C (Fair). It carries a beta of 0.81, meaning the fund's expected move will be 8.1% for every 10% move in the market. Volatility, as measured by both the semi-deviation and a drawdown factor, is considered average. As of December 31, 2012, Asia Tigers Fund traded at a discount of 7.83% below its net asset value, which is worse than its one-year historical average discount of 8.49%.

Gregory S. Geiling currently receives a manager quality ranking of 27 (0=worst, 99=best). This fund offers an average level of risk but investors looking for strong performance will be frustrated.

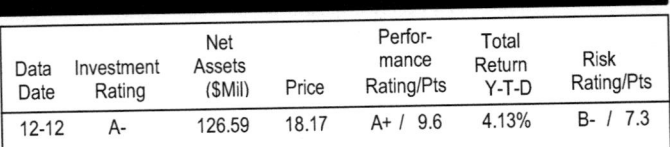

Avenue Income Credit Strategies (ACP)

A-　　　**Excellent**

Fund Family: Avenue Capital Management II LP
Fund Type: Loan Participation
Inception Date: January 27, 2011

Data Date	Investment Rating	Net Assets ($Mil)	Price	Performance Rating/Pts	Total Return Y-T-D	Risk Rating/Pts
12-12	A-	126.59	18.17	A+ / 9.6	4.13%	B- / 7.3

Major Rating Factors:
Exceptional performance is the major factor driving the A- (Excellent) TheStreet.com Investment Rating for Avenue Income Credit Strategies. The fund currently has a performance rating of A+ (Excellent) based on an annualized return of 0.00% over the last three years and a total return of 4.13% year to date 2012. Factored into the performance evaluation is an expense ratio of 2.50% (high).

The fund's risk rating is currently B- (Good). It carries a beta of 0.00, meaning the fund's expected move will be 0.0% for every 10% move in the market. Volatility, as measured by both the semi-deviation and a drawdown factor, is considered low. As of December 31, 2012, Avenue Income Credit Strategies traded at a discount of 4.72% below its net asset value, which is better than its one-year historical average discount of 3.24%.

Robert T. Symington currently receives a manager quality ranking of 97 (0=worst, 99=best). If you desire only a moderate level of risk and strong performance, then this fund is an excellent option.

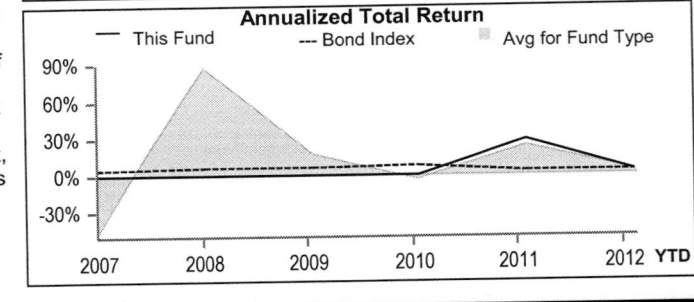

Bancroft Fund Ltd. (BCV)

C-　　　**Fair**

Fund Family: Dinsmore Capital Management Co
Fund Type: Growth and Income
Inception Date: April 20, 1971

Data Date	Investment Rating	Net Assets ($Mil)	Price	Performance Rating/Pts	Total Return Y-T-D	Risk Rating/Pts
12-12	C-	98.21	16.40	C- / 3.5	3.48%	B / 8.2
2011	C	95.00	15.12	C- / 4.2	2.31%	B / 8.3
2010	C	97.60	16.92	C / 4.9	17.38%	C+ / 5.7
2009	C	72.89	15.03	C- / 4.2	41.99%	C+ / 6.0

Major Rating Factors: Middle of the road best describes Bancroft Fund Ltd. whose TheStreet.com Investment Rating is currently a C- (Fair). The fund currently has a performance rating of C- (Fair) based on an annualized return of 7.18% over the last three years and a total return of 3.48% year to date 2012. Factored into the performance evaluation is an expense ratio of 1.10% (low).

The fund's risk rating is currently B (Good). It carries a beta of 0.70, meaning the fund's expected move will be 7.0% for every 10% move in the market. Volatility, as measured by both the semi-deviation and a drawdown factor, is considered low. As of December 31, 2012, Bancroft Fund Ltd. traded at a discount of 17.13% below its net asset value, which is better than its one-year historical average discount of 13.83%.

Thomas H. Dinsmore has been running the fund for 17 years and currently receives a manager quality ranking of 46 (0=worst, 99=best). If you desire an average level of risk, then this fund may be an option.

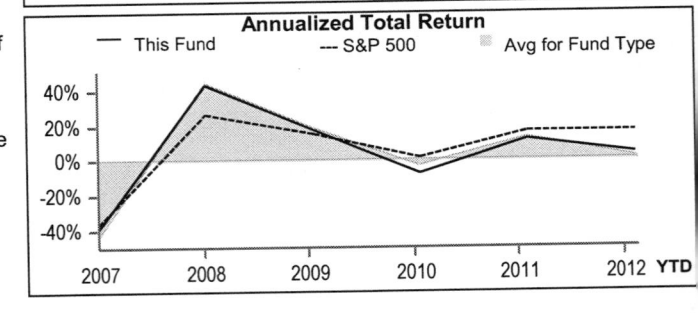

BlackRock Build America Bond (BBN)

B   **Good**

Fund Family: BlackRock Inc
Fund Type: Municipal - National
Inception Date: August 27, 2010

Major Rating Factors: BlackRock Build America Bond receives a TheStreet.com Investment Rating of B (Good). The fund currently has a performance rating of C+ (Fair) based on an annualized return of 0.00% over the last three years and a total return of 0.48% year to date 2012. Factored into the performance evaluation is an expense ratio of 1.09% (low).

The fund's risk rating is currently B (Good). It carries a beta of 0.00, meaning the fund's expected move will be 0.0% for every 10% move in the market. Volatility, as measured by both the semi-deviation and a drawdown factor, is considered low. As of December 31, 2012, BlackRock Build America Bond traded at a discount of 2.31% below its net asset value, which is worse than its one-year historical average discount of 3.08%.

Jonathan A. Clark currently receives a manager quality ranking of 66 (0=worst, 99=best). If you desire an average level of risk, then this fund may be an option.

Data Date	Investment Rating	Net Assets ($Mil)	Price	Performance Rating/Pts	Total Return Y-T-D	Risk Rating/Pts
12-12	B	1,367.83	22.87	C+ / 6.9	0.48%	B / 8.5
2011	A+	1,260.90	21.35	A+ / 9.9	0.23%	B / 8.5

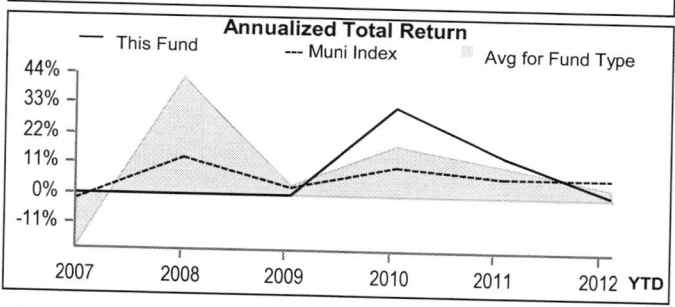

BlackRock CA Muni 2018 Income Trus (BJZ)

C+   **Fair**

Fund Family: BlackRock Inc
Fund Type: Municipal - Single State
Inception Date: October 25, 2001

Major Rating Factors: Middle of the road best describes BlackRock CA Muni 2018 Income Trus whose TheStreet.com Investment Rating is currently a C+ (Fair). The fund currently has a performance rating of C (Fair) based on an annualized return of 8.43% over the last three years and a total return of 0.06% year to date 2012. Factored into the performance evaluation is an expense ratio of 0.95% (low).

The fund's risk rating is currently B+ (Good). It carries a beta of 0.59, meaning the fund's expected move will be 5.9% for every 10% move in the market. Volatility, as measured by both the semi-deviation and a drawdown factor, is considered very low. As of December 31, 2012, BlackRock CA Muni 2018 Income Trus traded at a premium of 2.34% above its net asset value, which is better than its one-year historical average premium of 3.39%.

Theodore R. Jaeckel, Jr. has been running the fund for 7 years and currently receives a manager quality ranking of 77 (0=worst, 99=best). If you desire an average level of risk, then this fund may be an option.

Data Date	Investment Rating	Net Assets ($Mil)	Price	Performance Rating/Pts	Total Return Y-T-D	Risk Rating/Pts
12-12	C+	100.60	16.21	C / 4.7	0.06%	B+ / 9.4
2011	B	100.30	16.34	C+ / 6.7	-0.18%	B+ / 9.4
2010	C+	94.69	15.38	C+ / 6.9	8.02%	C+ / 6.8
2009	B-	85.16	15.09	C+ / 6.4	39.10%	B- / 7.4

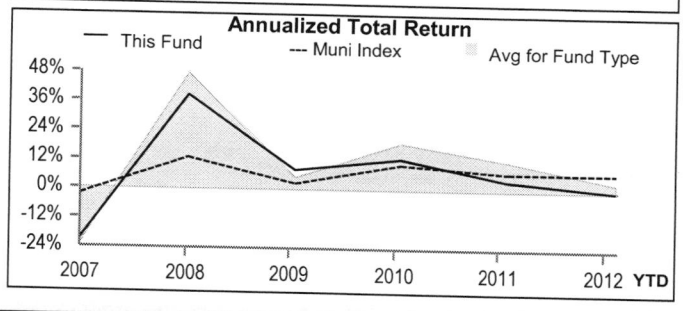

BlackRock CA Municipal Income Trus (BFZ)

A+   **Excellent**

Fund Family: BlackRock Inc
Fund Type: Municipal - Single State
Inception Date: July 26, 2001

Major Rating Factors:
Exceptional performance is the major factor driving the A+ (Excellent) TheStreet.com Investment Rating for BlackRock CA Municipal Income Trus. The fund currently has a performance rating of A (Excellent) based on an annualized return of 16.94% over the last three years and a total return of 6.98% year to date 2012. Factored into the performance evaluation is an expense ratio of 1.46% (average).

The fund's risk rating is currently B (Good). It carries a beta of 2.35, meaning it is expected to move 23.5% for every 10% move in the market. Volatility, as measured by both the semi-deviation and a drawdown factor, is considered low. As of December 31, 2012, BlackRock CA Municipal Income Trus traded at a discount of 1.15% below its net asset value, which is better than its one-year historical average discount of .21%.

Theodore R. Jaeckel, Jr. has been running the fund for 7 years and currently receives a manager quality ranking of 41 (0=worst, 99=best). If you desire only a moderate level of risk and strong performance, then this fund is an excellent option.

Data Date	Investment Rating	Net Assets ($Mil)	Price	Performance Rating/Pts	Total Return Y-T-D	Risk Rating/Pts
12-12	A+	519.58	16.34	A / 9.5	6.98%	B / 8.4
2011	A	472.90	14.71	A / 9.3	1.32%	B / 8.4
2010	D+	454.30	12.80	D / 1.7	3.76%	C+ / 6.7
2009	C	192.55	13.18	C / 4.3	47.74%	C+ / 6.7

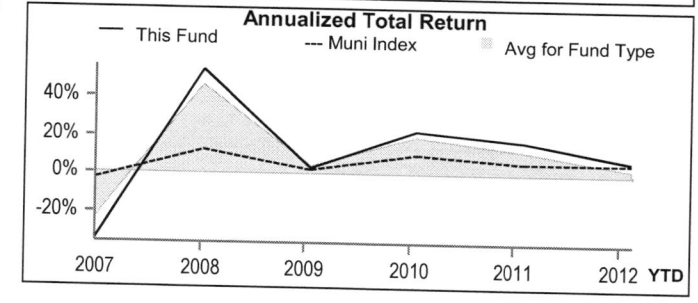

BlackRock Core Bond Trust (BHK)   B-   Good

Fund Family: BlackRock Inc
Fund Type: General - Investment Grade
Inception Date: November 27, 2001

Data Date	Investment Rating	Net Assets ($Mil)	Price	Performance Rating/Pts	Total Return Y-T-D	Risk Rating/Pts
12-12	B-	411.14	14.90	C+ / 6.1	2.21%	B / 8.8
2011	B-	382.30	13.52	C+ / 6.3	-0.22%	B / 8.8
2010	C+	383.54	12.52	C+ / 6.1	12.69%	C+ / 6.6
2009	C	339.52	11.89	C / 4.4	14.41%	C+ / 6.8

Major Rating Factors: BlackRock Core Bond Trust receives a TheStreet.com Investment Rating of B- (Good). The fund currently has a performance rating of C+ (Fair) based on an annualized return of 15.58% over the last three years and a total return of 2.21% year to date 2012. Factored into the performance evaluation is an expense ratio of 0.94% (low).

The fund's risk rating is currently B (Good). It carries a beta of 2.17, meaning it is expected to move 21.7% for every 10% move in the market. Volatility, as measured by both the semi-deviation and a drawdown factor, is considered low. As of December 31, 2012, BlackRock Core Bond Trust traded at a discount of 2.68% below its net asset value, which is better than its one-year historical average discount of 1.48%.

James E. Keenan currently receives a manager quality ranking of 61 (0=worst, 99=best). If you desire an average level of risk, then this fund may be an option.

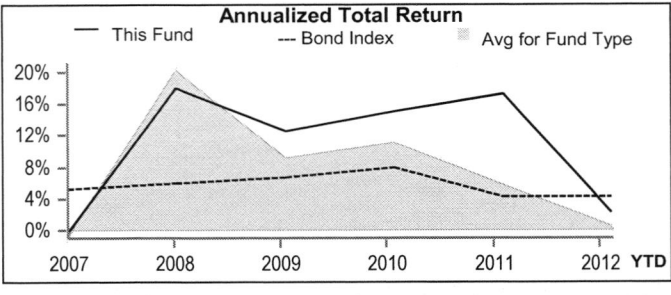

BlackRock Corporate High Yield Fun (COY)   C   Fair

Fund Family: BlackRock Inc
Fund Type: Corporate - High Yield
Inception Date: June 18, 1993

Data Date	Investment Rating	Net Assets ($Mil)	Price	Performance Rating/Pts	Total Return Y-T-D	Risk Rating/Pts
12-12	C	258.49	7.74	C+ / 5.9	2.33%	B- / 7.1
2011	B	237.10	7.21	B+ / 8.8	0.42%	B- / 7.0
2010	C	237.85	6.79	B- / 7.1	7.13%	C- / 3.3
2009	C+	202.65	6.89	B / 7.9	93.36%	C- / 3.8

Major Rating Factors: Middle of the road best describes BlackRock Corporate High Yield Fun whose TheStreet.com Investment Rating is currently a C (Fair). The fund currently has a performance rating of C+ (Fair) based on an annualized return of 13.31% over the last three years and a total return of 2.33% year to date 2012. Factored into the performance evaluation is an expense ratio of 1.26% (average).

The fund's risk rating is currently B- (Good). It carries a beta of 0.59, meaning the fund's expected move will be 5.9% for every 10% move in the market. Volatility, as measured by both the semi-deviation and a drawdown factor, is considered low. As of December 31, 2012, BlackRock Corporate High Yield Fun traded at a discount of .13% below its net asset value, which is better than its one-year historical average premium of 4.19%.

James E. Keenan has been running the fund for 7 years and currently receives a manager quality ranking of 82 (0=worst, 99=best). If you desire an average level of risk, then this fund may be an option.

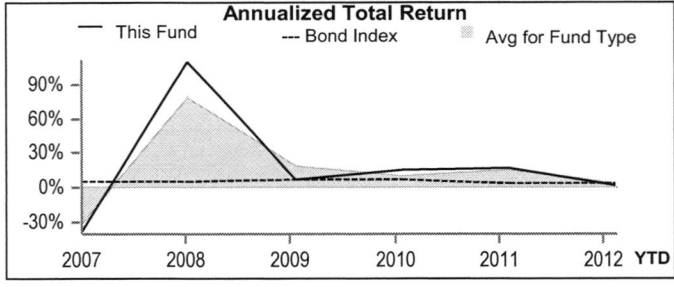

BlackRock Corporate High Yield III (CYE)   C+   Fair

Fund Family: BlackRock Inc
Fund Type: Corporate - High Yield
Inception Date: January 27, 1998

Data Date	Investment Rating	Net Assets ($Mil)	Price	Performance Rating/Pts	Total Return Y-T-D	Risk Rating/Pts
12-12	C+	282.43	7.57	C+ / 6.5	3.30%	B- / 7.1
2011	B	257.80	7.08	B+ / 8.9	-0.56%	C+ / 6.8
2010	C	257.76	6.77	B / 7.7	16.70%	C- / 3.6
2009	C	215.35	6.35	B / 7.6	86.99%	C- / 3.4

Major Rating Factors: Middle of the road best describes BlackRock Corporate High Yield III whose TheStreet.com Investment Rating is currently a C+ (Fair). The fund currently has a performance rating of C+ (Fair) based on an annualized return of 15.07% over the last three years and a total return of 3.30% year to date 2012. Factored into the performance evaluation is an expense ratio of 1.44% (average).

The fund's risk rating is currently B- (Good). It carries a beta of 1.12, meaning it is expected to move 11.2% for every 10% move in the market. Volatility, as measured by both the semi-deviation and a drawdown factor, is considered low. As of December 31, 2012, BlackRock Corporate High Yield III traded at a discount of 3.81% below its net asset value, which is better than its one-year historical average premium of 3.04%.

James E. Keenan has been running the fund for 7 years and currently receives a manager quality ranking of 70 (0=worst, 99=best). If you desire an average level of risk, then this fund may be an option.

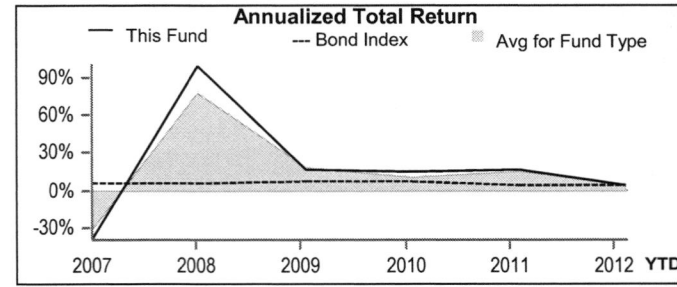

BlackRock Corporate High Yield V (HYV)

C+   **Fair**

Fund Family: BlackRock Inc
Fund Type: Corporate - High Yield
Inception Date: November 27, 2001

Major Rating Factors: Strong performance is the major factor driving the C+ (Fair) TheStreet.com Investment Rating for BlackRock Corporate High Yield V. The fund currently has a performance rating of B- (Good) based on an annualized return of 16.43% over the last three years and a total return of 3.34% year to date 2012. Factored into the performance evaluation is an expense ratio of 1.42% (average).

The fund's risk rating is currently B- (Good). It carries a beta of 1.09, meaning that its performance tracks fairly well with that of the overall stock market. Volatility, as measured by both the semi-deviation and a drawdown factor, is considered low. As of December 31, 2012, BlackRock Corporate High Yield V traded at a discount of 4.56% below its net asset value, which is better than its one-year historical average premium of 2.37%.

Gary Giamo currently receives a manager quality ranking of 73 (0=worst, 99=best). If you desire only a moderate level of risk and strong performance, then this fund is an excellent option.

Data Date	Investment Rating	Net Assets ($Mil)	Price	Performance Rating/Pts	Total Return Y-T-D	Risk Rating/Pts
12-12	C+	416.70	12.56	B- / 7.0	3.34%	B- / 7.1
2011	B	380.60	11.69	A- / 9.0	1.37%	C+ / 6.9
2010	C+	382.60	11.54	B / 8.2	20.80%	C- / 3.7
2009	C	320.05	10.48	B / 7.6	84.43%	C- / 3.6

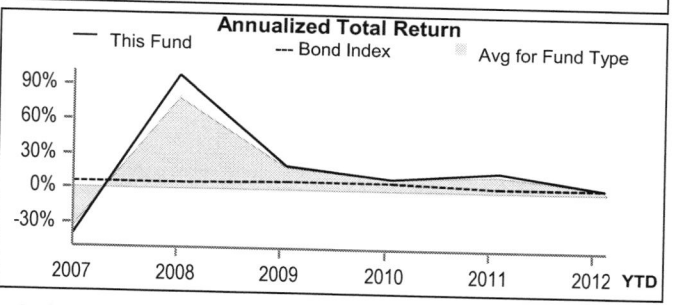

BlackRock Corporate High Yield VI (HYT)

C+   **Fair**

Fund Family: BlackRock Inc
Fund Type: Corporate - High Yield
Inception Date: May 28, 2003

Major Rating Factors: Middle of the road best describes BlackRock Corporate High Yield VI whose TheStreet.com Investment Rating is currently a C+ (Fair). The fund currently has a performance rating of C+ (Fair) based on an annualized return of 15.45% over the last three years and a total return of 4.12% year to date 2012. Factored into the performance evaluation is an expense ratio of 1.51% (average).

The fund's risk rating is currently B- (Good). It carries a beta of 1.08, meaning that its performance tracks fairly well with that of the overall stock market. Volatility, as measured by both the semi-deviation and a drawdown factor, is considered low. As of December 31, 2012, BlackRock Corporate High Yield VI traded at a discount of 3.50% below its net asset value, which is better than its one-year historical average premium of 2.75%.

James E. Keenan has been running the fund for 7 years and currently receives a manager quality ranking of 68 (0=worst, 99=best). If you desire an average level of risk, then this fund may be an option.

Data Date	Investment Rating	Net Assets ($Mil)	Price	Performance Rating/Pts	Total Return Y-T-D	Risk Rating/Pts
12-12	C+	435.96	12.39	C+ / 6.8	4.12%	B- / 7.2
2011	B	399.40	11.38	B+ / 8.7	1.67%	B- / 7.1
2010	C+	401.76	11.63	B+ / 8.3	19.98%	C- / 3.7
2009	C	341.42	10.60	B / 7.7	84.31%	C- / 3.8

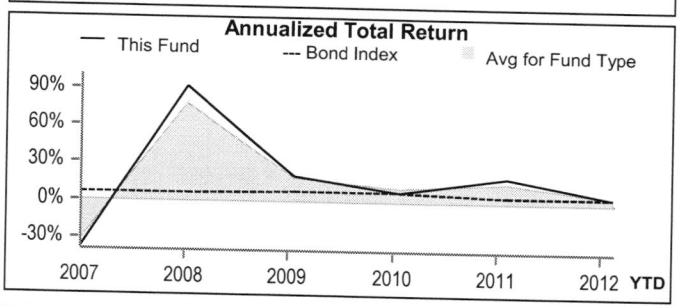

BlackRock Credit Alloc Inc Tr IV (BTZ)

B   **Good**

Fund Family: BlackRock Inc
Fund Type: Income
Inception Date: December 27, 2006

Major Rating Factors: BlackRock Credit Alloc Inc Tr IV receives a TheStreet.com Investment Rating of B (Good). The fund currently has a performance rating of C+ (Fair) based on an annualized return of 14.60% over the last three years and a total return of 2.99% year to date 2012. Factored into the performance evaluation is an expense ratio of 1.09% (low).

The fund's risk rating is currently B (Good). It carries a beta of 0.26, meaning the fund's expected move will be 2.6% for every 10% move in the market. Volatility, as measured by both the semi-deviation and a drawdown factor, is considered low. As of December 31, 2012, BlackRock Credit Alloc Inc Tr IV traded at a discount of 10.90% below its net asset value, which is better than its one-year historical average discount of 8.03%.

Jeffrey Cucunato has been running the fund for 2 years and currently receives a manager quality ranking of 91 (0=worst, 99=best). If you desire an average level of risk, then this fund may be an option.

Data Date	Investment Rating	Net Assets ($Mil)	Price	Performance Rating/Pts	Total Return Y-T-D	Risk Rating/Pts
12-12	B	722.34	13.73	C+ / 6.6	2.99%	B / 8.8
2011	C+	708.60	12.15	B- / 7.5	0.58%	C+ / 6.8
2010	D	723.87	12.10	D+ / 2.8	14.66%	C / 4.4
2009	D-	449.72	11.38	D- / 1.5	52.37%	C- / 3.9

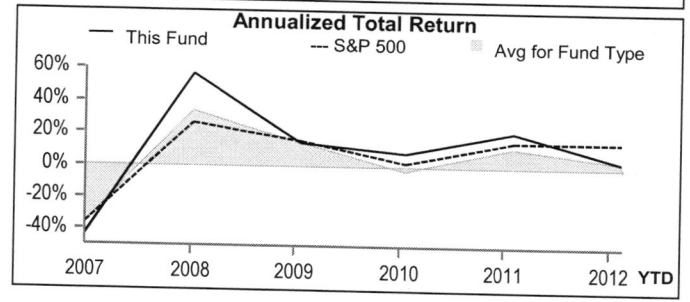

BlackRock Debt Strategies Fund Inc (DSU)

B+　　**Good**

Fund Family: BlackRock Inc
Fund Type: Corporate - High Yield
Inception Date: March 24, 1998

Major Rating Factors: Strong performance is the major factor driving the B+ (Good) TheStreet.com Investment Rating for BlackRock Debt Strategies Fund Inc. The fund currently has a performance rating of B- (Good) based on an annualized return of 15.43% over the last three years and a total return of 3.95% year to date 2012. Factored into the performance evaluation is an expense ratio of 1.39% (average).

The fund's risk rating is currently B (Good). It carries a beta of 1.01, meaning that its performance tracks fairly well with that of the overall stock market. Volatility, as measured by both the semi-deviation and a drawdown factor, is considered low. As of December 31, 2012, BlackRock Debt Strategies Fund Inc traded at a discount of 1.15% below its net asset value, which is better than its one-year historical average premium of 1.14%.

Leland T. Hart has been running the fund for 4 years and currently receives a manager quality ranking of 72 (0=worst, 99=best). If you desire only a moderate level of risk and strong performance, then this fund is an excellent option.

Data Date	Investment Rating	Net Assets ($Mil)	Price	Performance Rating/Pts	Total Return Y-T-D	Risk Rating/Pts
12-12	B+	453.44	4.30	B- / 7.4	3.95%	B / 8.6
2011	C	428.20	3.88	B- / 7.2	2.58%	C / 5.0
2010	D	431.56	3.81	D+ / 2.6	14.79%	C- / 3.7
2009	E+	355.59	3.60	D / 2.0	49.66%	C- / 3.0

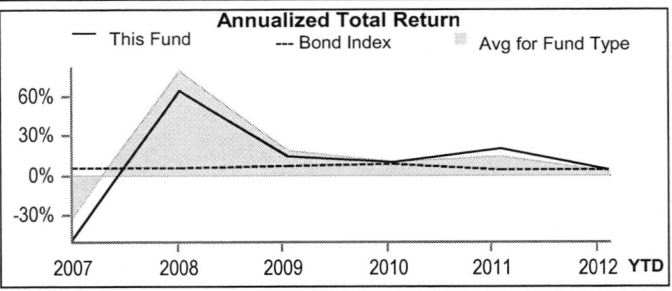

BlackRock Defined Opp Credit Trust (BHL)

C+　　**Fair**

Fund Family: BlackRock Inc
Fund Type: Loan Participation
Inception Date: January 31, 2008

Major Rating Factors: Middle of the road best describes BlackRock Defined Opp Credit Trust whose TheStreet.com Investment Rating is currently a C+ (Fair). The fund currently has a performance rating of C (Fair) based on an annualized return of 11.28% over the last three years and a total return of 1.13% year to date 2012. Factored into the performance evaluation is an expense ratio of 1.91% (above average).

The fund's risk rating is currently B (Good). It carries a beta of -165.10, meaning the fund's expected move will be -1651.0% for every 10% move in the market. Volatility, as measured by both the semi-deviation and a drawdown factor, is considered low. As of December 31, 2012, BlackRock Defined Opp Credit Trust traded at a discount of 1.46% below its net asset value, which is worse than its one-year historical average discount of 2.88%.

James E. Keenan currently receives a manager quality ranking of 98 (0=worst, 99=best). If you desire an average level of risk, then this fund may be an option.

Data Date	Investment Rating	Net Assets ($Mil)	Price	Performance Rating/Pts	Total Return Y-T-D	Risk Rating/Pts
12-12	C+	127.46	14.18	C / 5.3	1.13%	B / 8.2
2011	C	121.10	12.45	C / 4.8	2.65%	B / 8.2
2010	A	122.06	13.51	B+ / 8.7	19.14%	C+ / 6.8
2009	A+	112.86	11.94	B+ / 8.5	34.51%	C+ / 6.7

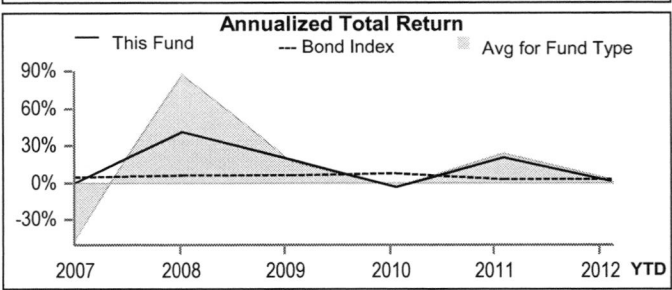

BlackRock EcoSolutions Investment (BQR)

D　　**Weak**

Fund Family: BlackRock Inc
Fund Type: Energy/Natural Resources
Inception Date: September 28, 2007

Major Rating Factors:
Disappointing performance is the major factor driving the D (Weak) TheStreet.com Investment Rating for BlackRock EcoSolutions Investment. The fund currently has a performance rating of D+ (Weak) based on an annualized return of 1.64% over the last three years and a total return of 5.24% year to date 2012. Factored into the performance evaluation is an expense ratio of 1.40% (average).

The fund's risk rating is currently C+ (Fair). It carries a beta of 0.67, meaning the fund's expected move will be 6.7% for every 10% move in the market. Volatility, as measured by both the semi-deviation and a drawdown factor, is considered low. As of December 31, 2012, BlackRock EcoSolutions Investment traded at a discount of 11.68% below its net asset value, which is better than its one-year historical average discount of 3.20%.

Robert M. Shearer has been running the fund for 6 years and currently receives a manager quality ranking of 25 (0=worst, 99=best). This fund offers only a moderate level of risk but investors looking for strong performance are still waiting.

Data Date	Investment Rating	Net Assets ($Mil)	Price	Performance Rating/Pts	Total Return Y-T-D	Risk Rating/Pts
12-12	D	117.50	8.39	D+ / 2.5	5.24%	C+ / 6.3
2011	D	110.10	7.82	D+ / 2.5	6.14%	C+ / 6.1
2010	D-	128.66	10.95	D / 1.9	12.25%	C- / 3.6
2009	C+	115.51	10.95	B+ / 8.3	42.30%	C- / 4.1

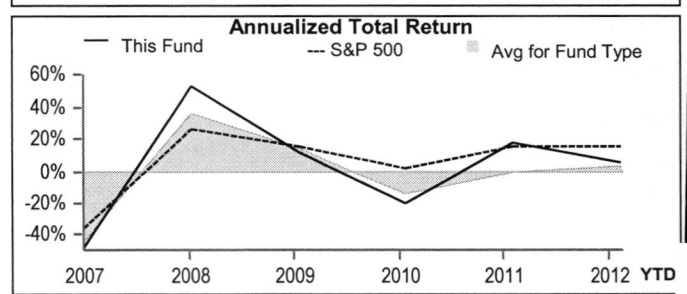

BlackRock Energy & Resources (BGR)

D+ **Weak**

Fund Family: BlackRock Inc
Fund Type: Energy/Natural Resources
Inception Date: December 23, 2004

Major Rating Factors:

Disappointing performance is the major factor driving the D+ (Weak) TheStreet.com Investment Rating for BlackRock Energy & Resources. The fund currently has a performance rating of D+ (Weak) based on an annualized return of 5.00% over the last three years and a total return of 5.14% year to date 2012. Factored into the performance evaluation is an expense ratio of 1.15% (low).

The fund's risk rating is currently B- (Good). It carries a beta of 0.96, meaning that its performance tracks fairly well with that of the overall stock market. Volatility, as measured by both the semi-deviation and a drawdown factor, is considered low. As of December 31, 2012, BlackRock Energy & Resources traded at a discount of 11.53% below its net asset value, which is better than its one-year historical average discount of 5.49%.

Daniel J. Neumann currently receives a manager quality ranking of 23 (0=worst, 99=best). This fund offers only a moderate level of risk but investors looking for strong performance are still waiting.

Data Date	Investment Rating	Net Assets ($Mil)	Price	Performance Rating/Pts	Total Return Y-T-D	Risk Rating/Pts
12-12	D+	843.33	23.55	D+ / 2.5	5.14%	B- / 7.1
2011	C+	794.70	24.45	B- / 7.0	4.83%	B- / 7.1
2010	C	795.72	28.74	B- / 7.2	19.58%	C- / 3.9
2009	C+	554.46	25.63	B / 7.8	67.69%	C- / 4.1

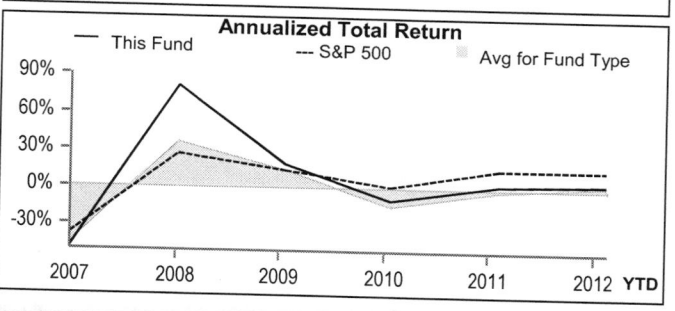

BlackRock Enhanced Capital and Inc (CII)

D+ **Weak**

Fund Family: BlackRock Inc
Fund Type: Growth and Income
Inception Date: April 30, 2004

Major Rating Factors:

Disappointing performance is the major factor driving the D+ (Weak) TheStreet.com Investment Rating for BlackRock Enhanced Capital and Inc. The fund currently has a performance rating of D+ (Weak) based on an annualized return of 5.72% over the last three years and a total return of 3.78% year to date 2012. Factored into the performance evaluation is an expense ratio of 0.93% (low).

The fund's risk rating is currently B- (Good). It carries a beta of 0.74, meaning the fund's expected move will be 7.4% for every 10% move in the market. Volatility, as measured by both the semi-deviation and a drawdown factor, is considered low. As of December 31, 2012, BlackRock Enhanced Capital and Inc traded at a discount of 12.54% below its net asset value, which is better than its one-year historical average discount of 7.95%.

Christopher M. Accettella has been running the fund for 1 year and currently receives a manager quality ranking of 28 (0=worst, 99=best). This fund offers only a moderate level of risk but investors looking for strong performance are still waiting.

Data Date	Investment Rating	Net Assets ($Mil)	Price	Performance Rating/Pts	Total Return Y-T-D	Risk Rating/Pts
12-12	D+	612.15	12.42	D+ / 2.9	3.78%	B- / 7.8
2011	C	614.10	12.30	C / 5.1	3.01%	B- / 7.6
2010	C	659.60	14.85	C+ / 5.7	8.97%	C / 4.9
2009	C	552.92	15.57	C+ / 6.8	54.92%	C / 4.7

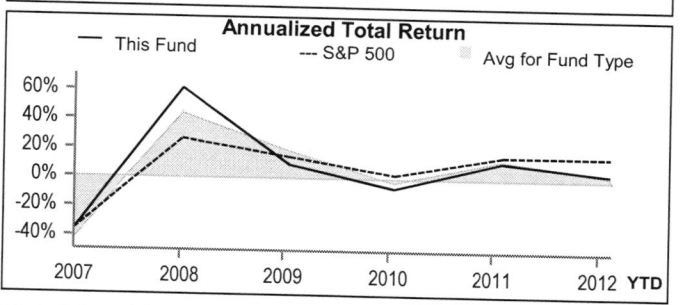

BlackRock Enhanced Equity Div (BDJ)

D+ **Weak**

Fund Family: BlackRock Inc
Fund Type: Income
Inception Date: August 25, 2005

Major Rating Factors:

Disappointing performance is the major factor driving the D+ (Weak) TheStreet.com Investment Rating for BlackRock Enhanced Equity Div. The fund currently has a performance rating of D+ (Weak) based on an annualized return of 3.98% over the last three years and a total return of 3.34% year to date 2012. Factored into the performance evaluation is an expense ratio of 1.14% (low).

The fund's risk rating is currently B- (Good). It carries a beta of 0.68, meaning the fund's expected move will be 6.8% for every 10% move in the market. Volatility, as measured by both the semi-deviation and a drawdown factor, is considered low. As of December 31, 2012, BlackRock Enhanced Equity Div traded at a discount of 14.73% below its net asset value, which is better than its one-year historical average discount of 11.13%.

Kathleen M. Anderson has been running the fund for 3 years and currently receives a manager quality ranking of 27 (0=worst, 99=best). This fund offers only a moderate level of risk but investors looking for strong performance are still waiting.

Data Date	Investment Rating	Net Assets ($Mil)	Price	Performance Rating/Pts	Total Return Y-T-D	Risk Rating/Pts
12-12	D+	575.71	7.18	D+ / 2.6	3.34%	B- / 7.9
2011	D+	578.80	7.07	D+ / 2.7	1.70%	B- / 7.2
2010	C	603.70	8.70	C+ / 5.8	11.31%	C / 4.9
2009	D-	526.67	8.80	D / 1.7	15.23%	C / 4.9

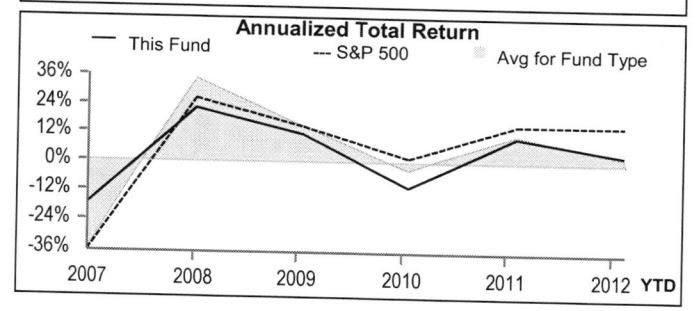

BlackRock Enhanced Government (EGF)

C-   **Fair**

Fund Family: BlackRock Inc
Fund Type: US Government/Agency
Inception Date: October 27, 2005

Major Rating Factors:
Disappointing performance is the major factor driving the C- (Fair) TheStreet.com Investment Rating for BlackRock Enhanced Government. The fund currently has a performance rating of D+ (Weak) based on an annualized return of 3.33% over the last three years and a total return of -0.06% year to date 2012. Factored into the performance evaluation is an expense ratio of 1.46% (average).

The fund's risk rating is currently B+ (Good). It carries a beta of 0.11, meaning the fund's expected move will be 1.1% for every 10% move in the market. Volatility, as measured by both the semi-deviation and a drawdown factor, is considered very low. As of December 31, 2012, BlackRock Enhanced Government traded at a discount of 2.50% below its net asset value, which is worse than its one-year historical average discount of 4.97%.

Stuart Spodek currently receives a manager quality ranking of 63 (0=worst, 99=best). This fund offers only a moderate level of risk but investors looking for strong performance are still waiting.

Data Date	Investment Rating	Net Assets ($Mil)	Price	Performance Rating/Pts	Total Return Y-T-D	Risk Rating/Pts
12-12	C-	177.92	15.63	D+ / 2.3	-0.06%	B+ / 9.1
2011	C-	187.90	15.25	D+ / 2.9	0.59%	B / 8.8
2010	C+	196.51	15.51	C- / 3.8	-4.02%	B / 8.2
2009	C	192.56	17.07	C- / 3.8	9.93%	B- / 7.5

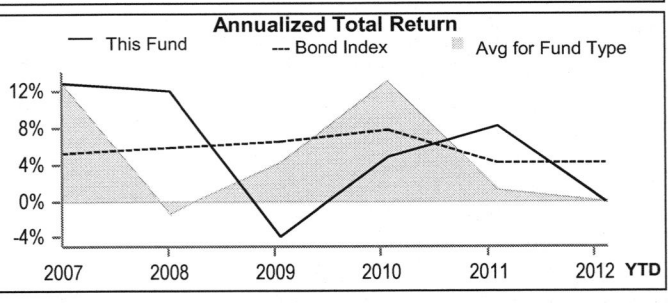

BlackRock FL Muni 2020 Term Tr (BFO)

B+   **Good**

Fund Family: BlackRock Inc
Fund Type: Municipal - Single State
Inception Date: September 26, 2003

Major Rating Factors: Strong performance is the major factor driving the B+ (Good) TheStreet.com Investment Rating for BlackRock FL Muni 2020 Term Tr. The fund currently has a performance rating of B- (Good) based on an annualized return of 11.40% over the last three years and a total return of 2.17% year to date 2012. Factored into the performance evaluation is an expense ratio of 1.06% (low).

The fund's risk rating is currently B+ (Good). It carries a beta of 1.18, meaning it is expected to move 11.8% for every 10% move in the market. Volatility, as measured by both the semi-deviation and a drawdown factor, is considered very low. As of December 31, 2012, BlackRock FL Muni 2020 Term Tr traded at a discount of 3.04% below its net asset value, which is better than its one-year historical average discount of 1.83%.

Theodore R. Jaeckel, Jr. has been running the fund for 7 years and currently receives a manager quality ranking of 69 (0=worst, 99=best). If you desire only a moderate level of risk and strong performance, then this fund is an excellent option.

Data Date	Investment Rating	Net Assets ($Mil)	Price	Performance Rating/Pts	Total Return Y-T-D	Risk Rating/Pts
12-12	B+	89.25	15.64	B- / 7.1	2.17%	B+ / 9.3
2011	B+	86.30	15.20	B / 7.9	-1.05%	B+ / 9.4
2010	C+	82.93	13.62	C+ / 6.0	7.01%	C+ / 6.6
2009	C+	74.26	13.35	C+ / 6.6	36.10%	C+ / 6.9

BlackRock Floating Rate Inc Strat (FRA)

C   **Fair**

Fund Family: BlackRock Inc
Fund Type: Loan Participation
Inception Date: October 28, 2003

Major Rating Factors: Middle of the road best describes BlackRock Floating Rate Inc Strat whose TheStreet.com Investment Rating is currently a C (Fair). The fund currently has a performance rating of C (Fair) based on an annualized return of 9.41% over the last three years and a total return of 2.05% year to date 2012. Factored into the performance evaluation is an expense ratio of 1.67% (above average).

The fund's risk rating is currently B- (Good). It carries a beta of -284.49, meaning the fund's expected move will be -2844.9% for every 10% move in the market. Volatility, as measured by both the semi-deviation and a drawdown factor, is considered low. As of December 31, 2012, BlackRock Floating Rate Inc Strat traded at a discount of .66% below its net asset value, which is worse than its one-year historical average discount of .79%.

C. Adrian Marshall has been running the fund for 4 years and currently receives a manager quality ranking of 99 (0=worst, 99=best). If you desire an average level of risk, then this fund may be an option.

Data Date	Investment Rating	Net Assets ($Mil)	Price	Performance Rating/Pts	Total Return Y-T-D	Risk Rating/Pts
12-12	C	276.99	15.15	C / 5.1	2.05%	B- / 7.5
2011	C+	263.10	13.36	C+ / 6.7	3.29%	B- / 7.6
2010	C-	264.38	14.88	C+ / 5.9	10.94%	C- / 4.2
2009	C	237.16	14.23	B- / 7.0	66.45%	C / 4.5

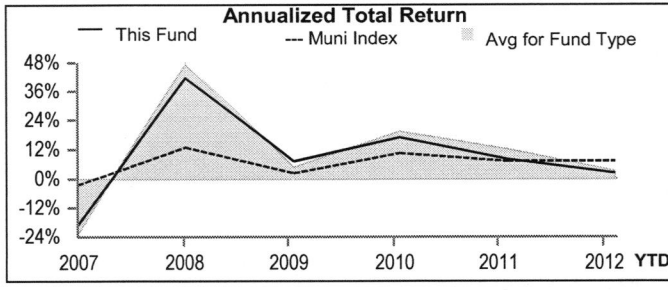

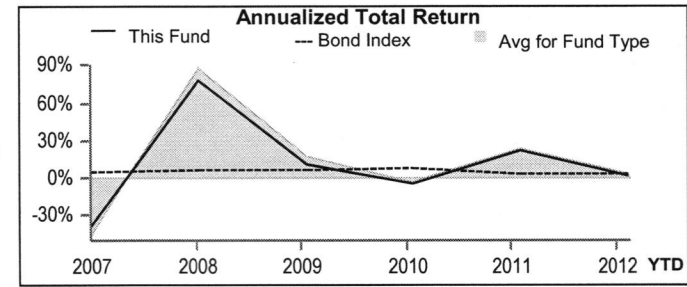

BlackRock Floating Rt Income (BGT)

C **Fair**

Fund Family: BlackRock Inc
Fund Type: Loan Participation
Inception Date: August 30, 2004

Major Rating Factors: Middle of the road best describes BlackRock Floating Rt Income whose TheStreet.com Investment Rating is currently a C (Fair). The fund currently has a performance rating of C+ (Fair) based on an annualized return of 11.23% over the last three years and a total return of 1.40% year to date 2012. Factored into the performance evaluation is an expense ratio of 1.60% (above average).

The fund's risk rating is currently B- (Good). It carries a beta of -172.54, meaning the fund's expected move will be -1725.4% for every 10% move in the market. Volatility, as measured by both the semi-deviation and a drawdown factor, is considered low. As of December 31, 2012, BlackRock Floating Rt Income traded at a premium of 2.94% above its net asset value, which is worse than its one-year historical average premium of 1.94%.

C. Adrian Marshall has been running the fund for 4 years and currently receives a manager quality ranking of 98 (0=worst, 99=best). If you desire an average level of risk, then this fund may be an option.

Data Date	Investment Rating	Net Assets ($Mil)	Price	Performance Rating/Pts	Total Return Y-T-D	Risk Rating/Pts
12-12	C	329.83	15.05	C+ / 5.6	1.40%	B- / 7.6
2011	B-	320.00	13.47	B- / 7.1	0.52%	B- / 7.7
2010	B	337.34	16.55	B+ / 8.6	27.16%	C- / 4.2
2009	C	245.13	13.95	B- / 7.1	80.57%	C / 4.5

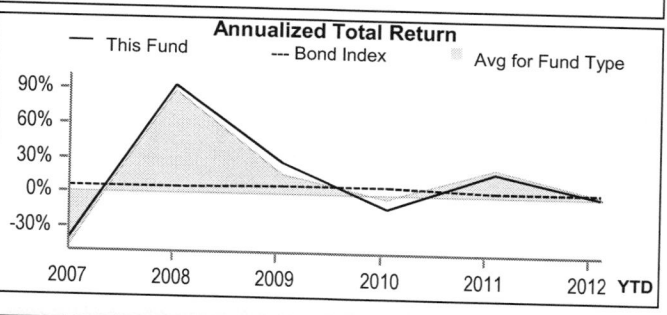

BlackRock Global Opportunities Eq (BOE)

D **Weak**

Fund Family: BlackRock Inc
Fund Type: Global
Inception Date: May 26, 2005

Major Rating Factors:
Disappointing performance is the major factor driving the D (Weak) TheStreet.com Investment Rating for BlackRock Global Opportunities Eq. The fund currently has a performance rating of D+ (Weak) based on an annualized return of 1.81% over the last three years and a total return of 5.23% year to date 2012. Factored into the performance evaluation is an expense ratio of 1.09% (low).

The fund's risk rating is currently C+ (Fair). It carries a beta of 0.88, meaning the fund's expected move will be 8.8% for every 10% move in the market. Volatility, as measured by both the semi-deviation and a drawdown factor, is considered low. As of December 31, 2012, BlackRock Global Opportunities Eq traded at a discount of 14.73% below its net asset value, which is better than its one-year historical average discount of 8.48%.

Kyle McClements has been running the fund for 4 years and currently receives a manager quality ranking of 41 (0=worst, 99=best). This fund offers only a moderate level of risk but investors looking for strong performance are still waiting.

Data Date	Investment Rating	Net Assets ($Mil)	Price	Performance Rating/Pts	Total Return Y-T-D	Risk Rating/Pts
12-12	D	1,113.92	13.20	D+ / 2.6	5.23%	C+ / 6.2
2011	D+	1,056.00	13.21	D+ / 2.8	3.63%	C+ / 6.7
2010	D+	1,316.01	18.35	C- / 3.5	10.46%	C / 5.1
2009	D+	209.23	18.89	C- / 3.3	30.43%	C / 5.3

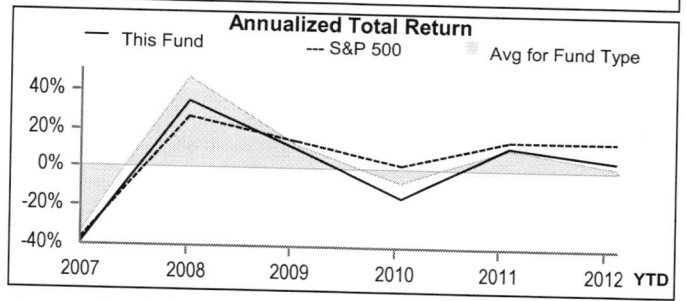

BlackRock Health Sciences Trust (BME)

C+ **Fair**

Fund Family: BlackRock Inc
Fund Type: Health
Inception Date: March 31, 2005

Major Rating Factors: Strong performance is the major factor driving the C+ (Fair) TheStreet.com Investment Rating for BlackRock Health Sciences Trust. The fund currently has a performance rating of B- (Good) based on an annualized return of 14.24% over the last three years and a total return of 6.89% year to date 2012. Factored into the performance evaluation is an expense ratio of 1.13% (low).

The fund's risk rating is currently B- (Good). It carries a beta of 0.88, meaning the fund's expected move will be 8.8% for every 10% move in the market. Volatility, as measured by both the semi-deviation and a drawdown factor, is considered low. As of December 31, 2012, BlackRock Health Sciences Trust traded at a discount of 3.25% below its net asset value, which is better than its one-year historical average discount of .21%.

Erin Z. Xie has been running the fund for 8 years and currently receives a manager quality ranking of 66 (0=worst, 99=best). If you desire only a moderate level of risk and strong performance, then this fund is an excellent option.

Data Date	Investment Rating	Net Assets ($Mil)	Price	Performance Rating/Pts	Total Return Y-T-D	Risk Rating/Pts
12-12	C+	202.68	28.02	B- / 7.4	6.89%	B- / 7.1
2011	C+	196.00	25.13	C+ / 5.9	2.79%	B- / 7.6
2010	C+	213.38	26.22	C+ / 6.6	8.94%	C+ / 5.7
2009	C+	166.97	26.23	C+ / 6.7	38.58%	C+ / 6.5

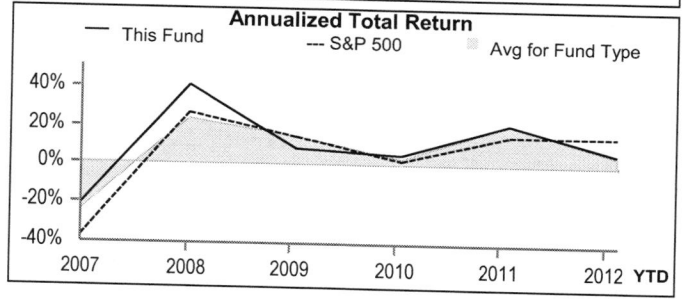

BlackRock High Income Shares (HIS)

B+   **Good**

Fund Family: BlackRock Inc
Fund Type: Corporate - High Yield
Inception Date: August 10, 1988

Data Date	Investment Rating	Net Assets ($Mil)	Price	Performance Rating/Pts	Total Return Y-T-D	Risk Rating/Pts
12-12	B+	123.75	2.36	B- / 7.4	0.97%	B / 8.6
2011	A-	116.20	2.18	A- / 9.1	0.00%	B / 8.4
2010	C+	119.64	2.06	B / 7.8	20.50%	C- / 3.6
2009	C+	100.92	1.89	B- / 7.1	75.75%	C / 5.1

Major Rating Factors: Strong performance is the major factor driving the B+ (Good) TheStreet.com Investment Rating for BlackRock High Income Shares. The fund currently has a performance rating of B- (Good) based on an annualized return of 17.94% over the last three years and a total return of 0.97% year to date 2012. Factored into the performance evaluation is an expense ratio of 1.54% (average).

The fund's risk rating is currently B (Good). It carries a beta of 1.15, meaning it is expected to move 11.5% for every 10% move in the market. Volatility, as measured by both the semi-deviation and a drawdown factor, is considered low. As of December 31, 2012, BlackRock High Income Shares traded at a premium of 1.72% above its net asset value, which is better than its one-year historical average premium of 3.34%.

Robert S. Kapito currently receives a manager quality ranking of 77 (0=worst, 99=best). If you desire only a moderate level of risk and strong performance, then this fund is an excellent option.

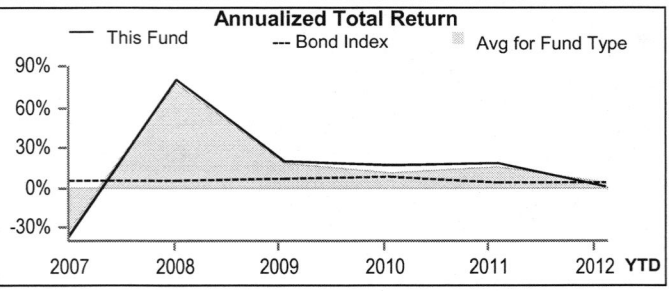

BlackRock High Yield Trust (BHY)

C   **Fair**

Fund Family: BlackRock Inc
Fund Type: Corporate - High Yield
Inception Date: December 17, 1998

Data Date	Investment Rating	Net Assets ($Mil)	Price	Performance Rating/Pts	Total Return Y-T-D	Risk Rating/Pts
12-12	C	46.88	7.37	C+ / 5.9	3.53%	B- / 7.2
2011	B	43.50	6.74	C+ / 6.6	1.78%	B / 8.8
2010	B-	42.98	6.60	B- / 7.3	17.23%	C / 5.3
2009	C	37.14	6.06	C / 5.3	42.96%	C+ / 5.8

Major Rating Factors: Middle of the road best describes BlackRock High Yield Trust whose TheStreet.com Investment Rating is currently a C (Fair). The fund currently has a performance rating of C+ (Fair) based on an annualized return of 15.56% over the last three years and a total return of 3.53% year to date 2012. Factored into the performance evaluation is an expense ratio of 2.01% (high).

The fund's risk rating is currently B- (Good). It carries a beta of 1.23, meaning it is expected to move 12.3% for every 10% move in the market. Volatility, as measured by both the semi-deviation and a drawdown factor, is considered low. As of December 31, 2012, BlackRock High Yield Trust traded at a discount of 2.90% below its net asset value, which is better than its one-year historical average premium of 3.98%.

Robert S. Kapito currently receives a manager quality ranking of 56 (0=worst, 99=best). If you desire an average level of risk, then this fund may be an option.

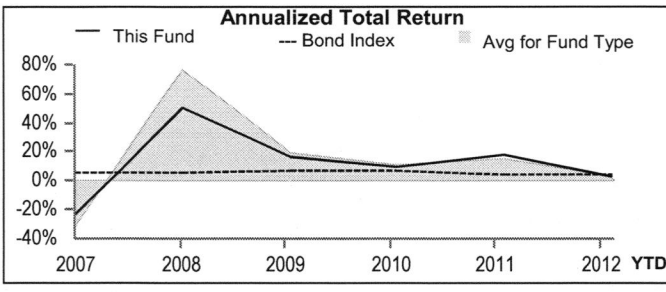

BlackRock Income Opportunity Trust (BNA)

C+   **Fair**

Fund Family: BlackRock Inc
Fund Type: General - Investment Grade
Inception Date: December 20, 1991

Data Date	Investment Rating	Net Assets ($Mil)	Price	Performance Rating/Pts	Total Return Y-T-D	Risk Rating/Pts
12-12	C+	408.07	11.34	C / 5.3	0.44%	B / 8.7
2011	B-	381.20	10.22	C+ / 5.8	-0.29%	B+ / 9.0
2010	C+	381.38	9.69	C+ / 5.6	11.60%	C+ / 6.5
2009	C	345.10	9.27	C- / 3.9	14.47%	B- / 7.1

Major Rating Factors: Middle of the road best describes BlackRock Income Opportunity Trust whose TheStreet.com Investment Rating is currently a C+ (Fair). The fund currently has a performance rating of C (Fair) based on an annualized return of 13.66% over the last three years and a total return of 0.44% year to date 2012. Factored into the performance evaluation is an expense ratio of 0.90% (low).

The fund's risk rating is currently B (Good). It carries a beta of 1.80, meaning it is expected to move 18.0% for every 10% move in the market. Volatility, as measured by both the semi-deviation and a drawdown factor, is considered low. As of December 31, 2012, BlackRock Income Opportunity Trust traded at a discount of 5.18% below its net asset value, which is better than its one-year historical average discount of 4.27%.

Robert S. Kapito currently receives a manager quality ranking of 68 (0=worst, 99=best). If you desire an average level of risk, then this fund may be an option.

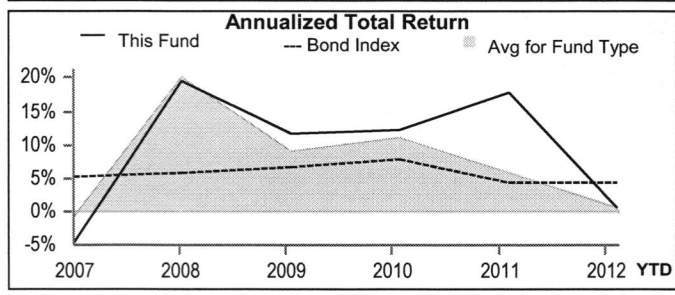

BlackRock Income Trust (BKT)

C **Fair**

Fund Family: BlackRock Inc
Fund Type: Mortgage
Inception Date: July 22, 1988

Major Rating Factors: Middle of the road best describes BlackRock Income Trust whose TheStreet.com Investment Rating is currently a C (Fair). The fund currently has a performance rating of C- (Fair) based on an annualized return of 10.46% over the last three years and a total return of -0.82% year to date 2012. Factored into the performance evaluation is an expense ratio of 0.97% (low).

The fund's risk rating is currently B+ (Good). It carries a beta of 1.40, meaning it is expected to move 14.0% for every 10% move in the market. Volatility, as measured by both the semi-deviation and a drawdown factor, is considered very low. As of December 31, 2012, BlackRock Income Trust traded at a discount of 4.17% below its net asset value, which is worse than its one-year historical average discount of 4.76%.

Robert S. Kapito has been running the fund for 25 years and currently receives a manager quality ranking of 75 (0=worst, 99=best). If you desire an average level of risk, then this fund may be an option.

Data Date	Investment Rating	Net Assets ($Mil)	Price	Performance Rating/Pts	Total Return Y-T-D	Risk Rating/Pts
12-12	C	507.85	7.35	C- / 3.5	-0.82%	B+ / 9.6
2011	C+	509.30	7.33	C / 4.8	0.27%	B+ / 9.6
2010	A	496.26	6.84	B- / 7.2	11.86%	B / 8.1
2009	B-	455.53	6.36	C / 4.3	11.72%	B / 8.7

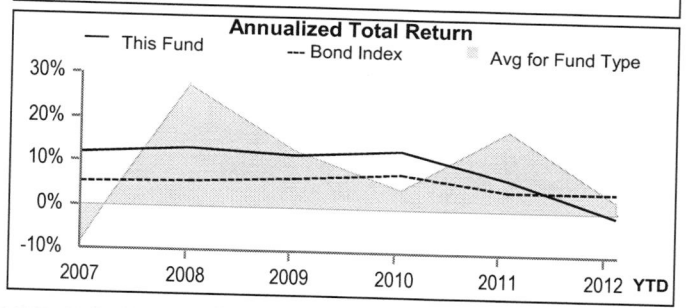

BlackRock Intl Grth and Inc Tr (BGY)

D- **Weak**

Fund Family: BlackRock Inc
Fund Type: Foreign
Inception Date: May 30, 2007

Major Rating Factors:
Disappointing performance is the major factor driving the D- (Weak) TheStreet.com Investment Rating for BlackRock Intl Grth and Inc Tr. The fund currently has a performance rating of D (Weak) based on an annualized return of -0.53% over the last three years and a total return of 4.63% year to date 2012. Factored into the performance evaluation is an expense ratio of 1.10% (low).

The fund's risk rating is currently C (Fair). It carries a beta of 0.82, meaning the fund's expected move will be 8.2% for every 10% move in the market. Volatility, as measured by both the semi-deviation and a drawdown factor, is considered average. As of December 31, 2012, BlackRock Intl Grth and Inc Tr traded at a discount of 14.53% below its net asset value, which is better than its one-year historical average discount of 9.73%.

Robert S. Kapito currently receives a manager quality ranking of 23 (0=worst, 99=best). This fund offers an average level of risk but investors looking for strong performance will be frustrated.

Data Date	Investment Rating	Net Assets ($Mil)	Price	Performance Rating/Pts	Total Return Y-T-D	Risk Rating/Pts
12-12	D-	959.15	7.35	D / 2.1	4.63%	C / 4.6
2011	D	890.80	7.16	D+ / 2.5	1.40%	C+ / 6.5
2010	D	1,158.58	10.17	D+ / 2.4	1.66%	C / 4.6
2009	B+	1,025.51	11.56	A- / 9.1	55.63%	C / 4.7

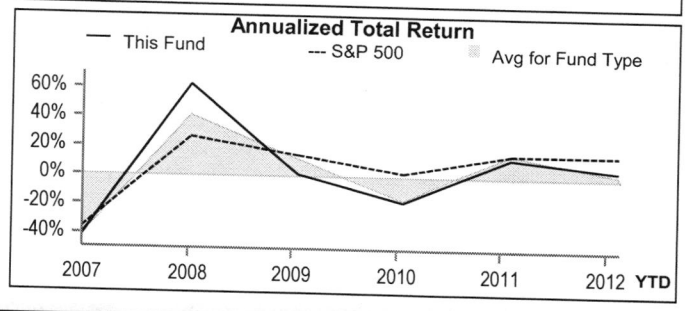

BlackRock Investment Qual Muni Tr (BKN)

A **Excellent**

Fund Family: BlackRock Inc
Fund Type: Municipal - National
Inception Date: February 19, 1993

Major Rating Factors:
Strong performance is the major factor driving the A (Excellent) TheStreet.com Investment Rating for BlackRock Investment Qual Muni Tr. The fund currently has a performance rating of B+ (Good) based on an annualized return of 14.89% over the last three years and a total return of 3.00% year to date 2012. Factored into the performance evaluation is an expense ratio of 1.26% (average).

The fund's risk rating is currently B (Good). It carries a beta of 2.13, meaning it is expected to move 21.3% for every 10% move in the market. Volatility, as measured by both the semi-deviation and a drawdown factor, is considered low. As of December 31, 2012, BlackRock Investment Qual Muni Tr traded at a premium of .31% above its net asset value, which is better than its one-year historical average premium of 3.89%.

Theodore R. Jaeckel, Jr. has been running the fund for 7 years and currently receives a manager quality ranking of 54 (0=worst, 99=best). If you desire only a moderate level of risk and strong performance, then this fund is an excellent option.

Data Date	Investment Rating	Net Assets ($Mil)	Price	Performance Rating/Pts	Total Return Y-T-D	Risk Rating/Pts
12-12	A	263.38	16.34	B+ / 8.7	3.00%	B / 8.4
2011	A+	247.10	15.02	A+ / 9.8	3.73%	B / 8.6
2010	C-	232.47	13.14	D+ / 2.5	5.52%	C+ / 6.9
2009	C	196.81	13.40	C / 4.3	60.82%	C+ / 6.6

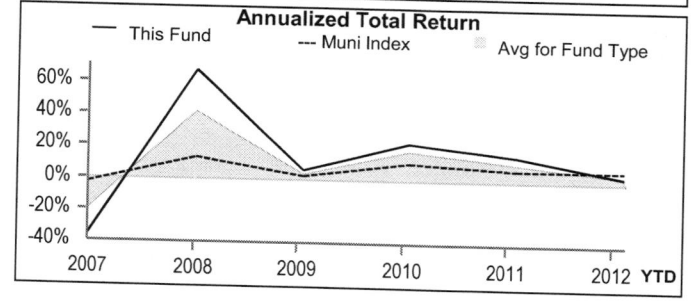

BlackRock Limited Duration Income (BLW)   B-   Good

Fund Family: BlackRock Inc
Fund Type: General Bond
Inception Date: July 30, 2003

Major Rating Factors: Strong performance is the major factor driving the B- (Good) TheStreet.com Investment Rating for BlackRock Limited Duration Income. The fund currently has a performance rating of B- (Good) based on an annualized return of 15.21% over the last three years and a total return of 2.09% year to date 2012. Factored into the performance evaluation is an expense ratio of 1.05% (low).

The fund's risk rating is currently B- (Good). It carries a beta of -0.09, meaning the fund's expected move will be -0.9% for every 10% move in the market. Volatility, as measured by both the semi-deviation and a drawdown factor, is considered low. As of December 31, 2012, BlackRock Limited Duration Income traded at a premium of 2.14% above its net asset value, which is better than its one-year historical average premium of 2.90%.

James E. Keenan has been running the fund for 6 years and currently receives a manager quality ranking of 95 (0=worst, 99=best). If you desire only a moderate level of risk and strong performance, then this fund is an excellent option.

Data Date	Investment Rating	Net Assets ($Mil)	Price	Perfor- mance Rating/Pts	Total Return Y-T-D	Risk Rating/Pts
12-12	B-	642.39	18.17	B- / 7.2	2.09%	B- / 7.4
2011	B	603.70	15.97	B- / 7.1	2.94%	B / 8.7
2010	C+	619.38	16.30	C+ / 6.7	17.46%	C+ / 5.8
2009	C	551.51	14.66	C- / 4.0	40.87%	C+ / 6.5

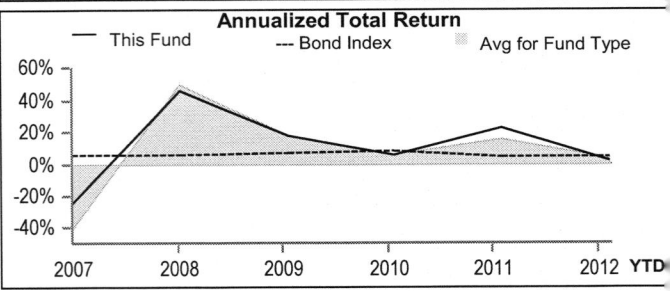

BlackRock Long Term Muni Adv (BTA)   A   Excellent

Fund Family: BlackRock Inc
Fund Type: Municipal - National
Inception Date: February 27, 2006

Major Rating Factors:
Exceptional performance is the major factor driving the A (Excellent) TheStreet.com Investment Rating for BlackRock Long Term Muni Adv. The fund currently has a performance rating of A- (Excellent) based on an annualized return of 15.62% over the last three years and a total return of 4.61% year to date 2012. Factored into the performance evaluation is an expense ratio of 1.42% (average).

The fund's risk rating is currently B (Good). It carries a beta of 2.38, meaning it is expected to move 23.8% for every 10% move in the market. Volatility, as measured by both the semi-deviation and a drawdown factor, is considered low. As of December 31, 2012, BlackRock Long Term Muni Adv traded at a discount of 1.95% below its net asset value, which is better than its one-year historical average premium of 1.67%.

Theodore R. Jaeckel, Jr. currently receives a manager quality ranking of 40 (0=worst, 99=best). If you desire only a moderate level of risk and strong performance, then this fund is an excellent option.

Data Date	Investment Rating	Net Assets ($Mil)	Price	Perfor- mance Rating/Pts	Total Return Y-T-D	Risk Rating/Pts
12-12	A	163.22	12.59	A- / 9.0	4.61%	B / 8.3
2011	A+	154.80	11.67	A+ / 9.7	0.69%	B / 8.4
2010	D	150.36	10.08	D / 1.8	5.39%	C+ / 5.9
2009	C-	127.08	10.22	C- / 3.4	53.14%	C+ / 5.9

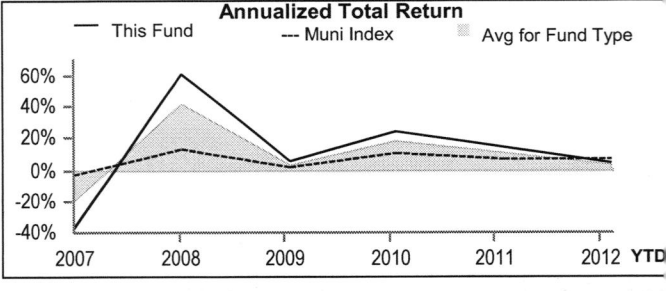

BlackRock MD Muni Bond Trust (BZM)   C+   Fair

Fund Family: BlackRock Inc
Fund Type: Municipal - Single State
Inception Date: April 26, 2002

Major Rating Factors: Middle of the road best describes BlackRock MD Muni Bond Trust whose TheStreet.com Investment Rating is currently a C+ (Fair). The fund currently has a performance rating of C+ (Fair) based on an annualized return of 12.09% over the last three years and a total return of 3.83% year to date 2012. Factored into the performance evaluation is an expense ratio of 1.60% (above average).

The fund's risk rating is currently B- (Good). It carries a beta of 1.75, meaning it is expected to move 17.5% for every 10% move in the market. Volatility, as measured by both the semi-deviation and a drawdown factor, is considered low. As of December 31, 2012, BlackRock MD Muni Bond Trust traded at a premium of 2.80% above its net asset value, which is better than its one-year historical average premium of 13.82%.

Theodore R. Jaeckel, Jr. has been running the fund for 7 years and currently receives a manager quality ranking of 40 (0=worst, 99=best). If you desire an average level of risk, then this fund may be an option.

Data Date	Investment Rating	Net Assets ($Mil)	Price	Perfor- mance Rating/Pts	Total Return Y-T-D	Risk Rating/Pts
12-12	C+	32.32	16.17	C+ / 6.4	3.83%	B- / 7.9
2011	B+	30.80	16.61	B+ / 8.4	1.26%	B / 8.5
2010	C	31.35	14.67	C- / 3.0	8.04%	B- / 7.7
2009	C	28.31	14.44	C- / 3.1	35.37%	B- / 7.5

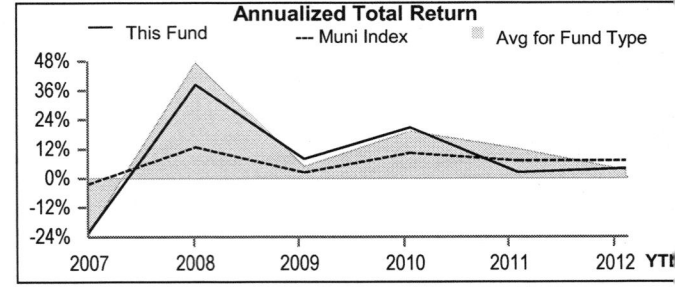

BlackRock Muni 2020 Term Trust (BKK)

B+   **Good**

Fund Family: BlackRock Inc
Fund Type: Municipal - National
Inception Date: September 26, 2003

Major Rating Factors: Strong performance is the major factor driving the B+ (Good) TheStreet.com Investment Rating for BlackRock Muni 2020 Term Trust. The fund currently has a performance rating of B- (Good) based on an annualized return of 9.99% over the last three years and a total return of 2.93% year to date 2012. Factored into the performance evaluation is an expense ratio of 0.99% (low).

The fund's risk rating is currently B+ (Good). It carries a beta of 0.96, meaning that its performance tracks fairly well with that of the overall stock market. Volatility, as measured by both the semi-deviation and a drawdown factor, is considered very low. As of December 31, 2012, BlackRock Muni 2020 Term Trust traded at a discount of .36% below its net asset value, which is better than its one-year historical average discount of .23%.

Theodore R. Jaeckel, Jr. has been running the fund for 7 years and currently receives a manager quality ranking of 73 (0=worst, 99=best). If you desire only a moderate level of risk and strong performance, then this fund is an excellent option.

Data Date	Investment Rating	Net Assets ($Mil)	Price	Performance Rating/Pts	Total Return Y-T-D	Risk Rating/Pts
12-12	B+	331.06	16.70	B- / 7.1	2.93%	B+ / 9.4
2011	B+	320.80	15.77	B / 8.0	1.14%	B+ / 9.3
2010	B-	293.55	14.67	C+ / 6.6	5.70%	B- / 7.1
2009	C+	243.57	14.60	C+ / 6.6	42.74%	C+ / 6.6

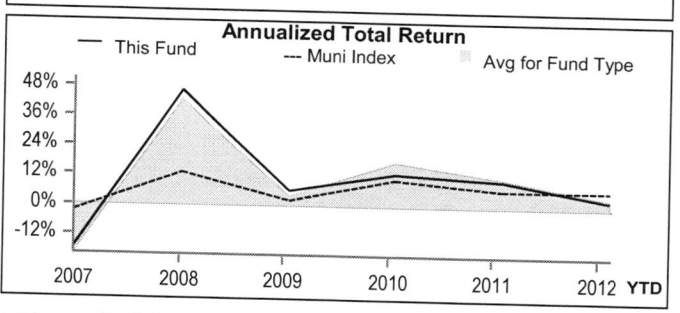

BlackRock Muni Bond Invt Trust (BIE)

A+   **Excellent**

Fund Family: BlackRock Inc
Fund Type: Municipal - Single State
Inception Date: April 26, 2002

Major Rating Factors:
Exceptional performance is the major factor driving the A+ (Excellent) TheStreet.com Investment Rating for BlackRock Muni Bond Invt Trust. The fund currently has a performance rating of A- (Excellent) based on an annualized return of 15.80% over the last three years and a total return of 1.46% year to date 2012. Factored into the performance evaluation is an expense ratio of 2.12% (high).

The fund's risk rating is currently B (Good). It carries a beta of 2.27, meaning it is expected to move 22.7% for every 10% move in the market. Volatility, as measured by both the semi-deviation and a drawdown factor, is considered low. As of December 31, 2012, BlackRock Muni Bond Invt Trust traded at a premium of .53% above its net asset value, which is worse than its one-year historical average discount of .12%.

Robert S. Kapito currently receives a manager quality ranking of 57 (0=worst, 99=best). If you desire only a moderate level of risk and strong performance, then this fund is an excellent option.

Data Date	Investment Rating	Net Assets ($Mil)	Price	Performance Rating/Pts	Total Return Y-T-D	Risk Rating/Pts
12-12	A+	56.33	17.18	A- / 9.0	1.46%	B / 8.6
2011	A	51.10	15.17	A- / 9.1	1.85%	B / 8.6
2010	C-	51.71	13.28	D / 2.0	6.26%	B- / 7.2
2009	C	47.20	13.33	C- / 4.1	42.09%	B- / 7.3

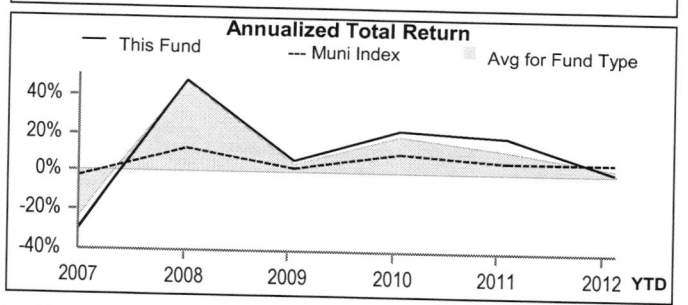

BlackRock Muni Interm Duration (MUI)

A+   **Excellent**

Fund Family: BlackRock Inc
Fund Type: Municipal - National
Inception Date: July 29, 2003

Major Rating Factors:
Exceptional performance is the major factor driving the A+ (Excellent) TheStreet.com Investment Rating for BlackRock Muni Interm Duration. The fund currently has a performance rating of A- (Excellent) based on an annualized return of 15.93% over the last three years and a total return of 4.63% year to date 2012. Factored into the performance evaluation is an expense ratio of 1.88% (above average).

The fund's risk rating is currently B (Good). It carries a beta of 2.09, meaning it is expected to move 20.9% for every 10% move in the market. Volatility, as measured by both the semi-deviation and a drawdown factor, is considered low. As of December 31, 2012, BlackRock Muni Interm Duration traded at a premium of .24% above its net asset value, which is better than its one-year historical average premium of 1.64%.

Theodore R. Jaeckel, Jr. has been running the fund for 7 years and currently receives a manager quality ranking of 57 (0=worst, 99=best). If you desire only a moderate level of risk and strong performance, then this fund is an excellent option.

Data Date	Investment Rating	Net Assets ($Mil)	Price	Performance Rating/Pts	Total Return Y-T-D	Risk Rating/Pts
12-12	A+	617.44	16.63	A- / 9.1	4.63%	B / 8.8
2011	A	596.00	15.32	A- / 9.1	2.61%	B+ / 9.0
2010	C+	561.14	13.79	C+ / 5.7	10.91%	C+ / 6.4
2009	C+	496.25	13.16	C / 4.9	30.77%	B- / 7.6

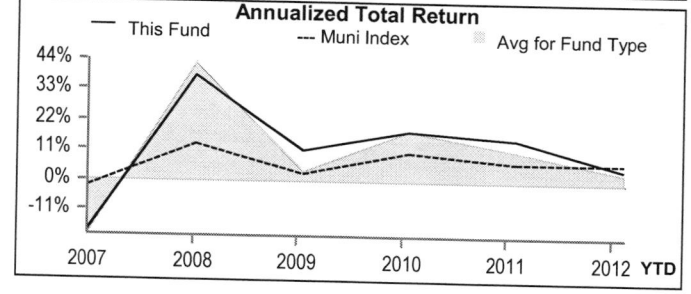

* Denotes ETF Fund

BlackRock Muni NY Interm Duration (MNE)

A+ Excellent

Fund Family: BlackRock Inc
Fund Type: Municipal - Single State
Inception Date: July 29, 2003

Data Date	Investment Rating	Net Assets ($Mil)	Price	Performance Rating/Pts	Total Return Y-T-D	Risk Rating/Pts
12-12	A+	67.16	15.44	B+ / 8.8	3.76%	B+ / 9.1
2011	A+	63.40	14.38	A / 9.3	1.39%	B+ / 9.1
2010	C+	61.01	12.85	C+ / 5.8	11.07%	C+ / 6.1
2009	B-	54.64	12.25	C+ / 5.9	43.61%	B- / 7.6

Major Rating Factors:
Strong performance is the major factor driving the A+ (Excellent) TheStreet.com Investment Rating for BlackRock Muni NY Interm Duration. The fund currently has a performance rating of B+ (Good) based on an annualized return of 14.72% over the last three years and a total return of 3.76% year to date 2012. Factored into the performance evaluation is an expense ratio of 1.81% (above average).

The fund's risk rating is currently B+ (Good). It carries a beta of 1.94, meaning it is expected to move 19.4% for every 10% move in the market. Volatility, as measured by both the semi-deviation and a drawdown factor, is considered very low. As of December 31, 2012, BlackRock Muni NY Interm Duration traded at a discount of 3.38% below its net asset value, which is better than its one-year historical average discount of 2.24%.

Timothy T. Browse has been running the fund for 10 years and currently receives a manager quality ranking of 58 (0=worst, 99=best). If you desire only a moderate level of risk and strong performance, then this fund is an excellent option.

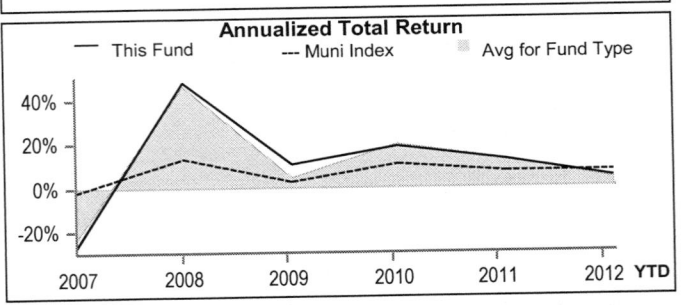

BlackRock MuniAssets Fund (MUA)

A- Excellent

Fund Family: BlackRock Inc
Fund Type: Municipal - National
Inception Date: June 18, 1993

Data Date	Investment Rating	Net Assets ($Mil)	Price	Performance Rating/Pts	Total Return Y-T-D	Risk Rating/Pts
12-12	A-	481.60	13.92	B / 8.1	3.74%	B / 8.6
2011	B+	456.80	12.53	B+ / 8.3	1.36%	B / 8.5
2010	C-	266.83	11.64	D+ / 2.9	1.63%	B- / 7.3
2009	C	221.90	12.18	C / 4.5	43.12%	C+ / 6.8

Major Rating Factors:
Strong performance is the major factor driving the A- (Excellent) TheStreet.com Investment Rating for BlackRock MuniAssets Fund. The fund currently has a performance rating of B (Good) based on an annualized return of 10.97% over the last three years and a total return of 3.74% year to date 2012. Factored into the performance evaluation is an expense ratio of 0.77% (very low).

The fund's risk rating is currently B (Good). It carries a beta of 1.72, meaning it is expected to move 17.2% for every 10% move in the market. Volatility, as measured by both the semi-deviation and a drawdown factor, is considered low. As of December 31, 2012, BlackRock MuniAssets Fund traded at a discount of 1.90% below its net asset value, which is better than its one-year historical average discount of 1.34%.

Gary Giamo currently receives a manager quality ranking of 48 (0=worst, 99=best). If you desire only a moderate level of risk and strong performance, then this fund is an excellent option.

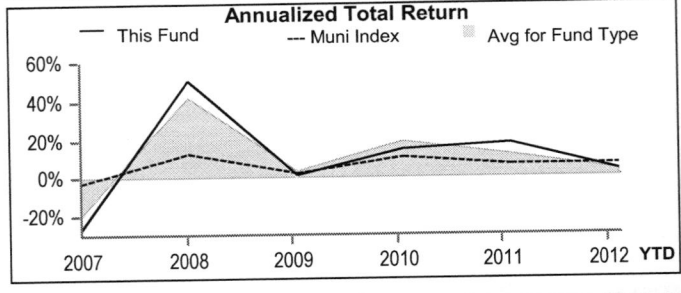

BlackRock Municipal 2018 Income Tr (BPK)

B- Good

Fund Family: BlackRock Inc
Fund Type: Municipal - National
Inception Date: October 25, 2001

Data Date	Investment Rating	Net Assets ($Mil)	Price	Performance Rating/Pts	Total Return Y-T-D	Risk Rating/Pts
12-12	B-	254.59	16.56	C+ / 5.6	2.66%	B+ / 9.3
2011	B	249.10	16.59	C+ / 6.7	0.24%	B+ / 9.4
2010	A-	235.85	15.72	B- / 7.1	10.28%	B- / 7.4
2009	C+	208.01	15.16	C / 4.7	20.30%	B- / 7.5

Major Rating Factors: BlackRock Municipal 2018 Income Tr receives a TheStreet.com Investment Rating of B- (Good). The fund currently has a performance rating of C+ (Fair) based on an annualized return of 9.37% over the last three years and a total return of 2.66% year to date 2012. Factored into the performance evaluation is an expense ratio of 0.82% (very low).

The fund's risk rating is currently B+ (Good). It carries a beta of 0.79, meaning the fund's expected move will be 7.9% for every 10% move in the market. Volatility, as measured by both the semi-deviation and a drawdown factor, is considered very low. As of December 31, 2012, BlackRock Municipal 2018 Income Tr traded at a premium of 2.99% above its net asset value, which is better than its one-year historical average premium of 5.11%.

Theodore R. Jaeckel, Jr. has been running the fund for 7 years and currently receives a manager quality ranking of 76 (0=worst, 99=best). If you desire an average level of risk, then this fund may be an option.

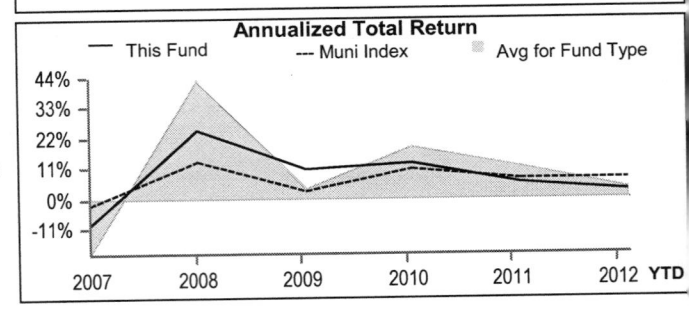

BlackRock Municipal Bond Trust (BBK)

A+   **Excellent**

Fund Family: BlackRock Inc
Fund Type: Municipal - National
Inception Date: April 26, 2002

Major Rating Factors:
Exceptional performance is the major factor driving the A+ (Excellent) TheStreet.com Investment Rating for BlackRock Municipal Bond Trust. The fund currently has a performance rating of A- (Excellent) based on an annualized return of 15.95% over the last three years and a total return of 5.24% year to date 2012. Factored into the performance evaluation is an expense ratio of 1.64% (above average).

The fund's risk rating is currently B (Good). It carries a beta of 2.24, meaning it is expected to move 22.4% for every 10% move in the market. Volatility, as measured by both the semi-deviation and a drawdown factor, is considered low. As of December 31, 2012, BlackRock Municipal Bond Trust traded at a premium of .29% above its net asset value, which is better than its one-year historical average premium of 3.74%.

Theodore R. Jaeckel, Jr. has been running the fund for 7 years and currently receives a manager quality ranking of 50 (0=worst, 99=best). If you desire only a moderate level of risk and strong performance, then this fund is an excellent option.

Data Date	Investment Rating	Net Assets ($Mil)	Price	Performance Rating/Pts	Total Return Y-T-D	Risk Rating/Pts
12-12	A+	176.22	17.00	A- / 9.1	5.24%	B / 8.4
2011	A+	159.40	15.72	A / 9.5	1.59%	B / 8.6
2010	C-	159.22	13.73	D+ / 2.9	6.18%	B- / 7.1
2009	C	137.03	13.88	C- / 4.2	50.74%	C+ / 6.5

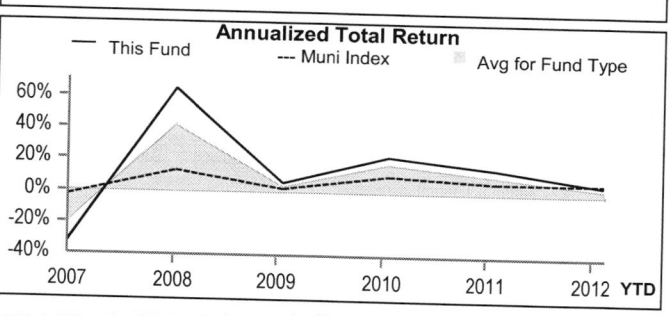

BlackRock Municipal Income Inv Qly (BAF)

A-   **Excellent**

Fund Family: BlackRock Inc
Fund Type: Municipal - Single State
Inception Date: October 28, 2002

Major Rating Factors:
Strong performance is the major factor driving the A- (Excellent) TheStreet.com Investment Rating for BlackRock Municipal Income Inv Qly. The fund currently has a performance rating of B+ (Good) based on an annualized return of 14.38% over the last three years and a total return of 3.72% year to date 2012. Factored into the performance evaluation is an expense ratio of 1.49% (average).

The fund's risk rating is currently B (Good). It carries a beta of 2.64, meaning it is expected to move 26.4% for every 10% move in the market. Volatility, as measured by both the semi-deviation and a drawdown factor, is considered low. As of December 31, 2012, BlackRock Municipal Income Inv Qly traded at a discount of 2.26% below its net asset value, which is better than its one-year historical average discount of .99%.

Robert S. Kapito currently receives a manager quality ranking of 26 (0=worst, 99=best). If you desire only a moderate level of risk and strong performance, then this fund is an excellent option.

Data Date	Investment Rating	Net Assets ($Mil)	Price	Performance Rating/Pts	Total Return Y-T-D	Risk Rating/Pts
12-12	A-	144.59	16.40	B+ / 8.6	3.72%	B / 8.2
2011	A-	132.60	15.24	A- / 9.2	1.25%	B / 8.4
2010	C	131.77	13.07	C / 4.5	3.44%	C+ / 6.4
2009	C+	122.83	13.43	C+ / 6.8	39.37%	C+ / 6.9

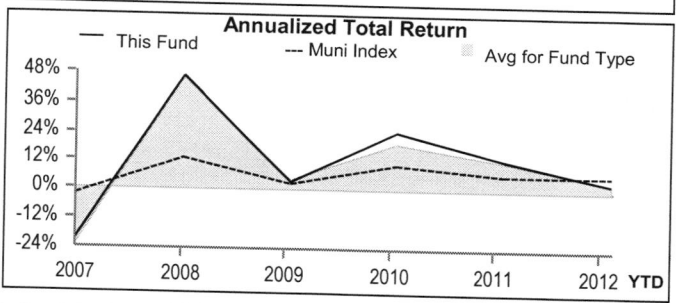

BlackRock Municipal Income Invt Tr (BBF)

A   **Excellent**

Fund Family: BlackRock Inc
Fund Type: Municipal - Single State
Inception Date: July 26, 2001

Major Rating Factors:
Exceptional performance is the major factor driving the A (Excellent) TheStreet.com Investment Rating for BlackRock Municipal Income Invt Tr. The fund currently has a performance rating of A- (Excellent) based on an annualized return of 15.43% over the last three years and a total return of 4.22% year to date 2012. Factored into the performance evaluation is an expense ratio of 1.99% (high).

The fund's risk rating is currently B (Good). It carries a beta of 2.32, meaning it is expected to move 23.2% for every 10% move in the market. Volatility, as measured by both the semi-deviation and a drawdown factor, is considered low. As of December 31, 2012, BlackRock Municipal Income Invt Tr traded at a discount of 1.55% below its net asset value, which is better than its one-year historical average premium of .04%.

Robert D. Sneeden has been running the fund for 7 years and currently receives a manager quality ranking of 42 (0=worst, 99=best). If you desire only a moderate level of risk and strong performance, then this fund is an excellent option.

Data Date	Investment Rating	Net Assets ($Mil)	Price	Performance Rating/Pts	Total Return Y-T-D	Risk Rating/Pts
12-12	A	106.63	15.87	A- / 9.1	4.22%	B / 8.2
2011	B+	96.10	14.30	B+ / 8.6	0.49%	B / 8.2
2010	C-	93.07	12.34	D / 1.8	3.01%	B- / 7.5
2009	C	85.05	12.80	C- / 3.2	37.79%	B- / 7.3

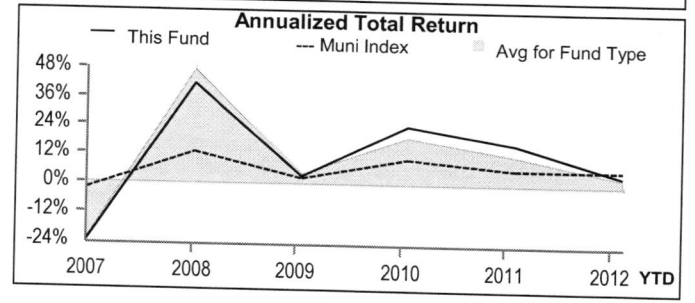

BlackRock Municipal Income Quality (BYM)

A+   **Excellent**

Fund Family: BlackRock Inc
Fund Type: Municipal - National
Inception Date: October 28, 2002

Data Date	Investment Rating	Net Assets ($Mil)	Price	Performance Rating/Pts	Total Return Y-T-D	Risk Rating/Pts
12-12	A+	424.79	16.20	A / 9.4	7.72%	B / 8.2
2011	B+	388.20	14.84	B+ / 8.5	-0.54%	B / 8.5
2010	D+	384.56	12.95	D / 1.6	1.32%	C+ / 6.9
2009	C+	355.33	13.61	C / 5.4	32.69%	C+ / 6.9

Major Rating Factors:
Exceptional performance is the major factor driving the A+ (Excellent) TheStreet.com Investment Rating for BlackRock Municipal Income Quality. The fund currently has a performance rating of A (Excellent) based on an annualized return of 15.38% over the last three years and a total return of 7.72% year to date 2012. Factored into the performance evaluation is an expense ratio of 1.46% (average).

The fund's risk rating is currently B (Good). It carries a beta of 2.30, meaning it is expected to move 23.0% for every 10% move in the market. Volatility, as measured by both the semi-deviation and a drawdown factor, is considered low. As of December 31, 2012, BlackRock Municipal Income Quality traded at a premium of .25% above its net asset value, which is better than its one-year historical average premium of 1.44%.

Robert S. Kapito currently receives a manager quality ranking of 33 (0=worst, 99=best). If you desire only a moderate level of risk and strong performance, then this fund is an excellent option.

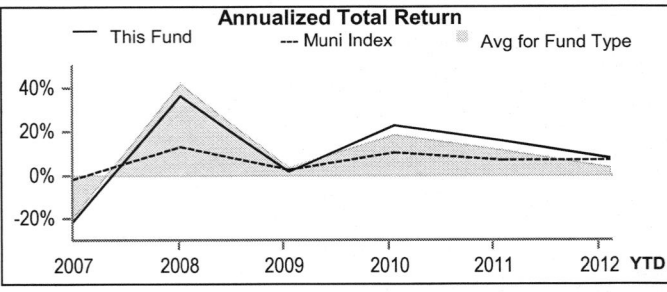

BlackRock Municipal Income Trust (BFK)

A   **Excellent**

Fund Family: BlackRock Inc
Fund Type: Municipal - National
Inception Date: July 27, 2001

Data Date	Investment Rating	Net Assets ($Mil)	Price	Performance Rating/Pts	Total Return Y-T-D	Risk Rating/Pts
12-12	A	648.50	15.52	B+ / 8.6	4.32%	B / 8.4
2011	A+	609.10	13.95	A+ / 9.7	3.44%	B / 8.5
2010	C	587.25	12.69	C- / 3.5	6.50%	C+ / 6.8
2009	C	474.81	12.80	C / 4.4	61.74%	C+ / 6.2

Major Rating Factors:
Strong performance is the major factor driving the A (Excellent) TheStreet.com Investment Rating for BlackRock Municipal Income Trust. The fund currently has a performance rating of B+ (Good) based on an annualized return of 14.71% over the last three years and a total return of 4.32% year to date 2012. Factored into the performance evaluation is an expense ratio of 1.45% (average).

The fund's risk rating is currently B (Good). It carries a beta of 2.28, meaning it is expected to move 22.8% for every 10% move in the market. Volatility, as measured by both the semi-deviation and a drawdown factor, is considered low. As of December 31, 2012, BlackRock Municipal Income Trust traded at a premium of 1.04% above its net asset value, which is better than its one-year historical average premium of 3.88%.

Theodore R. Jaeckel, Jr. has been running the fund for 7 years and currently receives a manager quality ranking of 43 (0=worst, 99=best). If you desire only a moderate level of risk and strong performance, then this fund is an excellent option.

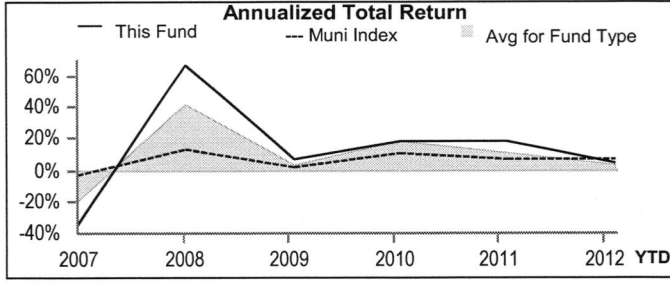

BlackRock Municipal Income Trust I (BLE)

A+   **Excellent**

Fund Family: BlackRock Inc
Fund Type: Municipal - National
Inception Date: July 25, 2002

Data Date	Investment Rating	Net Assets ($Mil)	Price	Performance Rating/Pts	Total Return Y-T-D	Risk Rating/Pts
12-12	A+	376.77	16.21	A- / 9.0	5.98%	B / 8.4
2011	A+	340.50	15.21	A+ / 9.8	0.72%	B / 8.7
2010	C	340.27	13.10	C- / 3.2	2.63%	B- / 7.1
2009	C	296.07	13.69	C / 5.2	53.95%	C+ / 6.3

Major Rating Factors:
Exceptional performance is the major factor driving the A+ (Excellent) TheStreet.com Investment Rating for BlackRock Municipal Income Trust I. The fund currently has a performance rating of A- (Excellent) based on an annualized return of 15.19% over the last three years and a total return of 5.98% year to date 2012. Factored into the performance evaluation is an expense ratio of 1.48% (average).

The fund's risk rating is currently B (Good). It carries a beta of 2.30, meaning it is expected to move 23.0% for every 10% move in the market. Volatility, as measured by both the semi-deviation and a drawdown factor, is considered low. As of December 31, 2012, BlackRock Municipal Income Trust I traded at a discount of .18% below its net asset value, which is better than its one-year historical average premium of 3.15%.

Theodore R. Jaeckel, Jr. has been running the fund for 7 years and currently receives a manager quality ranking of 36 (0=worst, 99=best). If you desire only a moderate level of risk and strong performance, then this fund is an excellent option.

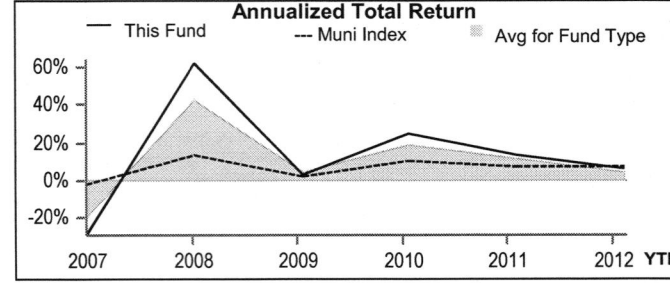

BlackRock MuniEnhanced Fund (MEN)

A- **Excellent**

Fund Family: BlackRock Inc
Fund Type: Municipal - National
Inception Date: February 23, 1989

Major Rating Factors:

Strong performance is the major factor driving the A- (Excellent) TheStreet.com Investment Rating for BlackRock MuniEnhanced Fund. The fund currently has a performance rating of B+ (Good) based on an annualized return of 13.68% over the last three years and a total return of 3.58% year to date 2012. Factored into the performance evaluation is an expense ratio of 1.70% (above average).

The fund's risk rating is currently B (Good). It carries a beta of 2.44, meaning it is expected to move 24.4% for every 10% move in the market. Volatility, as measured by both the semi-deviation and a drawdown factor, is considered low. As of December 31, 2012, BlackRock MuniEnhanced Fund traded at a discount of 2.61% below its net asset value, which is better than its one-year historical average discount of 1.21%.

Michael A. Kalinoski has been running the fund for 24 years and currently receives a manager quality ranking of 28 (0=worst, 99=best). If you desire only a moderate level of risk and strong performance, then this fund is an excellent option.

Data Date	Investment Rating	Net Assets ($Mil)	Price	Performance Rating/Pts	Total Return Y-T-D	Risk Rating/Pts
12-12	A-	357.02	12.29	B+ / 8.4	3.58%	B / 8.6
2011	A	339.70	11.64	A- / 9.1	-1.20%	B / 8.8
2010	C+	320.08	10.45	C / 5.4	7.20%	C+ / 6.3
2009	B+	287.08	10.38	B- / 7.1	42.52%	C+ / 6.8

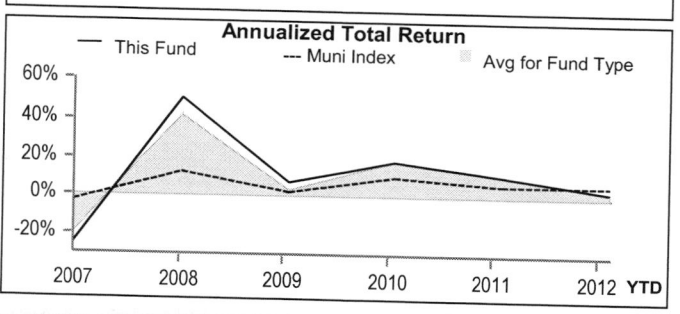

BlackRock MuniHoldings CA Qly (MUC)

A+ **Excellent**

Fund Family: BlackRock Inc
Fund Type: Municipal - Single State
Inception Date: February 27, 1998

Major Rating Factors:

Exceptional performance is the major factor driving the A+ (Excellent) TheStreet.com Investment Rating for BlackRock MuniHoldings CA Qly. The fund currently has a performance rating of A (Excellent) based on an annualized return of 17.93% over the last three years and a total return of 4.16% year to date 2012. Factored into the performance evaluation is an expense ratio of 1.39% (average).

The fund's risk rating is currently B (Good). It carries a beta of 2.08, meaning it is expected to move 20.8% for every 10% move in the market. Volatility, as measured by both the semi-deviation and a drawdown factor, is considered low. As of December 31, 2012, BlackRock MuniHoldings CA Qly traded at a discount of .91% below its net asset value, which is better than its one-year historical average discount of .64%.

Walter O'Connor has been running the fund for 15 years and currently receives a manager quality ranking of 66 (0=worst, 99=best). If you desire only a moderate level of risk and strong performance, then this fund is an excellent option.

Data Date	Investment Rating	Net Assets ($Mil)	Price	Performance Rating/Pts	Total Return Y-T-D	Risk Rating/Pts
12-12	A+	671.08	16.34	A / 9.5	4.16%	B / 8.6
2011	A	618.00	14.88	A / 9.3	0.81%	B / 8.7
2010	C+	254.00	13.05	C+ / 5.7	10.47%	C+ / 6.4
2009	B-	540.14	12.57	C+ / 5.6	39.83%	B- / 7.5

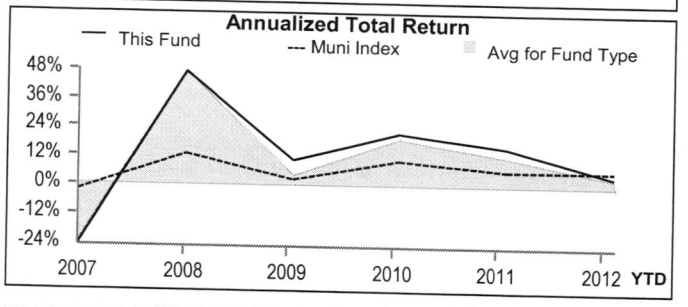

BlackRock MuniHoldings Fund (MHD)

A+ **Excellent**

Fund Family: BlackRock Inc
Fund Type: Municipal - National
Inception Date: April 29, 1997

Major Rating Factors:

Exceptional performance is the major factor driving the A+ (Excellent) TheStreet.com Investment Rating for BlackRock MuniHoldings Fund. The fund currently has a performance rating of A+ (Excellent) based on an annualized return of 17.52% over the last three years and a total return of 6.59% year to date 2012. Factored into the performance evaluation is an expense ratio of 1.41% (average).

The fund's risk rating is currently B (Good). It carries a beta of 1.98, meaning it is expected to move 19.8% for every 10% move in the market. Volatility, as measured by both the semi-deviation and a drawdown factor, is considered low. As of December 31, 2012, BlackRock MuniHoldings Fund traded at a premium of 1.60% above its net asset value, which is better than its one-year historical average premium of 3.24%.

Robert M. Shearer currently receives a manager quality ranking of 70 (0=worst, 99=best). If you desire only a moderate level of risk and strong performance, then this fund is an excellent option.

Data Date	Investment Rating	Net Assets ($Mil)	Price	Performance Rating/Pts	Total Return Y-T-D	Risk Rating/Pts
12-12	A+	243.99	18.36	A+ / 9.6	6.59%	B / 8.7
2011	A+	229.90	16.58	A / 9.5	1.03%	B / 8.9
2010	C+	219.13	15.03	C+ / 6.7	11.71%	C+ / 5.9
2009	C+	184.69	14.49	C+ / 6.9	50.85%	C+ / 6.9

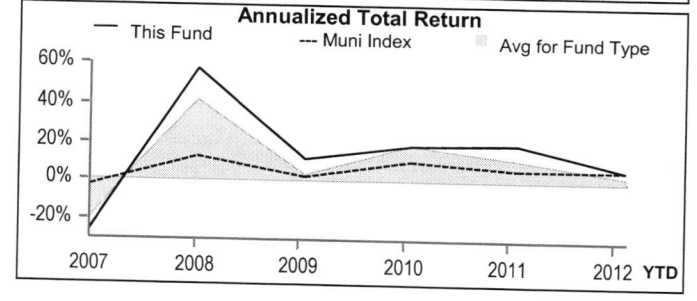

BlackRock MuniHoldings Fund II (MUH)

A+   **Excellent**

Fund Family: BlackRock Inc
Fund Type: Municipal - National
Inception Date: February 24, 1998

Major Rating Factors:
Exceptional performance is the major factor driving the A+ (Excellent) TheStreet.com Investment Rating for BlackRock MuniHoldings Fund II. The fund currently has a performance rating of A- (Excellent) based on an annualized return of 16.54% over the last three years and a total return of 5.11% year to date 2012. Factored into the performance evaluation is an expense ratio of 1.37% (average).

    The fund's risk rating is currently B (Good). It carries a beta of 2.41, meaning it is expected to move 24.1% for every 10% move in the market. Volatility, as measured by both the semi-deviation and a drawdown factor, is considered low. As of December 31, 2012, BlackRock MuniHoldings Fund II traded at a discount of 1.42% below its net asset value, which is better than its one-year historical average premium of 1.38%.

    Robert M. Shearer currently receives a manager quality ranking of 40 (0=worst, 99=best). If you desire only a moderate level of risk and strong performance, then this fund is an excellent option.

Data Date	Investment Rating	Net Assets ($Mil)	Price	Performance Rating/Pts	Total Return Y-T-D	Risk Rating/Pts
12-12	A+	182.62	16.64	A- / 9.2	5.11%	B / 8.5
2011	A+	172.60	15.49	A+ / 9.6	1.25%	B / 8.7
2010	C+	163.72	13.66	C+ / 5.6	8.03%	C+ / 6.0
2009	B+	139.38	13.58	B- / 7.1	48.72%	C+ / 6.9

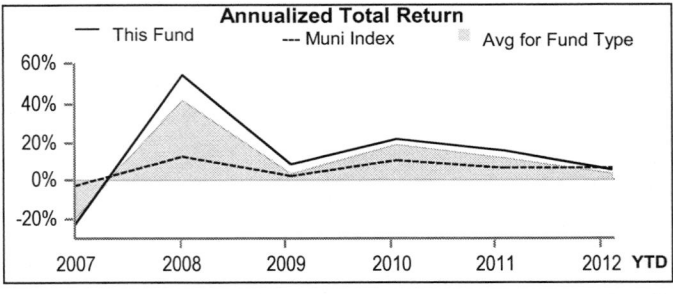

BlackRock MuniHoldings Inv Quality (MFL)

A+   **Excellent**

Fund Family: BlackRock Inc
Fund Type: Municipal - Single State
Inception Date: September 23, 1997

Major Rating Factors:
Exceptional performance is the major factor driving the A+ (Excellent) TheStreet.com Investment Rating for BlackRock MuniHoldings Inv Quality. The fund currently has a performance rating of A- (Excellent) based on an annualized return of 15.59% over the last three years and a total return of 4.35% year to date 2012. Factored into the performance evaluation is an expense ratio of 1.80% (above average).

    The fund's risk rating is currently B (Good). It carries a beta of 1.99, meaning it is expected to move 19.9% for every 10% move in the market. Volatility, as measured by both the semi-deviation and a drawdown factor, is considered low. As of December 31, 2012, BlackRock MuniHoldings Inv Quality traded at a discount of .43% below its net asset value, which is better than its one-year historical average discount of .23%.

    Robert M. Shearer currently receives a manager quality ranking of 61 (0=worst, 99=best). If you desire only a moderate level of risk and strong performance, then this fund is an excellent option.

Data Date	Investment Rating	Net Assets ($Mil)	Price	Performance Rating/Pts	Total Return Y-T-D	Risk Rating/Pts
12-12	A+	602.78	16.10	A- / 9.2	4.35%	B / 8.5
2011	A	550.70	14.61	A- / 9.2	-0.14%	B / 8.7
2010	C+	553.37	12.78	C+ / 5.8	4.98%	C+ / 6.3
2009	A-	511.01	12.97	B- / 7.0	46.26%	B- / 7.0

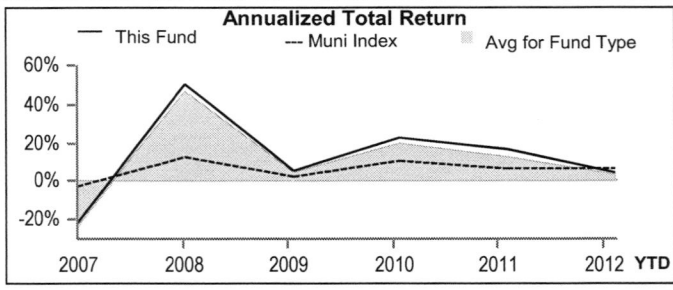

BlackRock MuniHoldings New York QI (MHN)

A   **Excellent**

Fund Family: BlackRock Inc
Fund Type: Municipal - Single State
Inception Date: September 16, 1997

Major Rating Factors:
Strong performance is the major factor driving the A (Excellent) TheStreet.com Investment Rating for BlackRock MuniHoldings New York QI. The fund currently has a performance rating of B+ (Good) based on an annualized return of 13.80% over the last three years and a total return of 2.41% year to date 2012. Factored into the performance evaluation is an expense ratio of 1.87% (above average).

    The fund's risk rating is currently B (Good). It carries a beta of 2.18, meaning it is expected to move 21.8% for every 10% move in the market. Volatility, as measured by both the semi-deviation and a drawdown factor, is considered low. As of December 31, 2012, BlackRock MuniHoldings New York QI traded at a premium of 3.46% above its net asset value, which is worse than its one-year historical average premium of 2.00%.

    Robert M. Shearer currently receives a manager quality ranking of 44 (0=worst, 99=best). If you desire only a moderate level of risk and strong performance, then this fund is an excellent option.

Data Date	Investment Rating	Net Assets ($Mil)	Price	Performance Rating/Pts	Total Return Y-T-D	Risk Rating/Pts
12-12	A	485.45	16.15	B+ / 8.7	2.41%	B / 8.4
2011	A+	459.90	15.16	A / 9.5	0.20%	B / 8.7
2010	C+	464.85	13.46	C+ / 5.7	8.10%	C+ / 6.1
2009	A-	422.98	13.28	B- / 7.3	55.22%	C+ / 6.9

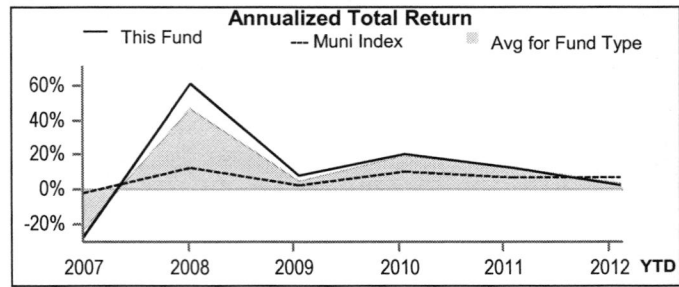

BlackRock MuniHoldings NJ Qly (MUJ)

A+ **Excellent**

Fund Family: BlackRock Inc
Fund Type: Municipal - Single State
Inception Date: March 6, 1998

Major Rating Factors:

Strong performance is the major factor driving the A+ (Excellent) TheStreet.com Investment Rating for BlackRock MuniHoldings NJ Qly. The fund currently has a performance rating of B+ (Good) based on an annualized return of 13.38% over the last three years and a total return of 3.18% year to date 2012. Factored into the performance evaluation is an expense ratio of 1.78% (above average).

The fund's risk rating is currently B (Good). It carries a beta of 1.73, meaning it is expected to move 17.3% for every 10% move in the market. Volatility, as measured by both the semi-deviation and a drawdown factor, is considered low. As of December 31, 2012, BlackRock MuniHoldings NJ Qly traded at a premium of .60% above its net asset value, which is worse than its one-year historical average discount of 1.72%.

Robert M. Shearer currently receives a manager quality ranking of 66 (0=worst, 99=best). If you desire only a moderate level of risk and strong performance, then this fund is an excellent option.

Data Date	Investment Rating	Net Assets ($Mil)	Price	Performance Rating/Pts	Total Return Y-T-D	Risk Rating/Pts
12-12	A+	351.84	16.67	B+ / 8.7	3.18%	B / 8.7
2011	A	330.80	15.74	A / 9.3	-0.19%	B / 8.8
2010	C+	322.68	13.49	C / 5.3	5.19%	C+ / 6.5
2009	B	305.86	13.61	C / 5.4	37.36%	B- / 7.7

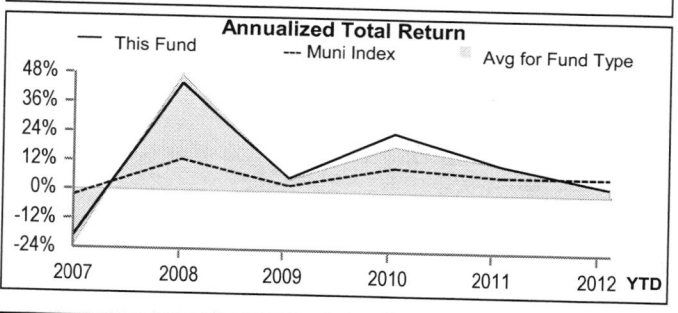

BlackRock MuniHoldings Quality (MUS)

A- **Excellent**

Fund Family: BlackRock Inc
Fund Type: Municipal - National
Inception Date: April 28, 1998

Major Rating Factors:

Strong performance is the major factor driving the A- (Excellent) TheStreet.com Investment Rating for BlackRock MuniHoldings Quality. The fund currently has a performance rating of B+ (Good) based on an annualized return of 14.33% over the last three years and a total return of 4.57% year to date 2012. Factored into the performance evaluation is an expense ratio of 1.41% (average).

The fund's risk rating is currently B (Good). It carries a beta of 2.57, meaning it is expected to move 25.7% for every 10% move in the market. Volatility, as measured by both the semi-deviation and a drawdown factor, is considered low. As of December 31, 2012, BlackRock MuniHoldings Quality traded at a discount of 2.01% below its net asset value, which is better than its one-year historical average premium of 1.13%.

Robert M. Shearer currently receives a manager quality ranking of 26 (0=worst, 99=best). If you desire only a moderate level of risk and strong performance, then this fund is an excellent option.

Data Date	Investment Rating	Net Assets ($Mil)	Price	Performance Rating/Pts	Total Return Y-T-D	Risk Rating/Pts
12-12	A-	189.57	15.10	B+ / 8.6	4.57%	B / 8.3
2011	A	181.00	14.12	A / 9.4	0.42%	B / 8.5
2010	C	171.98	12.10	C / 4.5	1.24%	C+ / 6.5
2009	B+	158.06	12.77	B- / 7.2	42.01%	C+ / 6.8

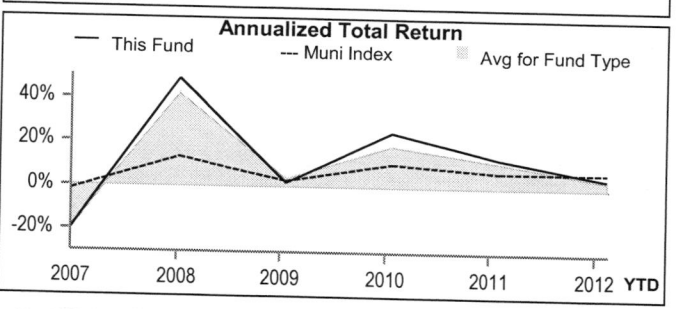

BlackRock MuniHoldings Quality II (MUE)

A **Excellent**

Fund Family: BlackRock Inc
Fund Type: Municipal - National
Inception Date: February 23, 1999

Major Rating Factors:

Exceptional performance is the major factor driving the A (Excellent) TheStreet.com Investment Rating for BlackRock MuniHoldings Quality II. The fund currently has a performance rating of A- (Excellent) based on an annualized return of 14.55% over the last three years and a total return of 5.90% year to date 2012. Factored into the performance evaluation is an expense ratio of 1.46% (average).

The fund's risk rating is currently B (Good). It carries a beta of 2.49, meaning it is expected to move 24.9% for every 10% move in the market. Volatility, as measured by both the semi-deviation and a drawdown factor, is considered low. As of December 31, 2012, BlackRock MuniHoldings Quality II traded at a discount of 2.01% below its net asset value, which is better than its one-year historical average discount of .21%.

Robert M. Shearer currently receives a manager quality ranking of 25 (0=worst, 99=best). If you desire only a moderate level of risk and strong performance, then this fund is an excellent option.

Data Date	Investment Rating	Net Assets ($Mil)	Price	Performance Rating/Pts	Total Return Y-T-D	Risk Rating/Pts
12-12	A	341.14	15.08	A- / 9.0	5.90%	B / 8.3
2011	A	313.70	14.30	A+ / 9.6	1.61%	B / 8.5
2010	C	303.67	11.96	C- / 4.0	-1.83%	C+ / 6.4
2009	B+	274.34	13.01	B- / 7.5	44.33%	C+ / 6.5

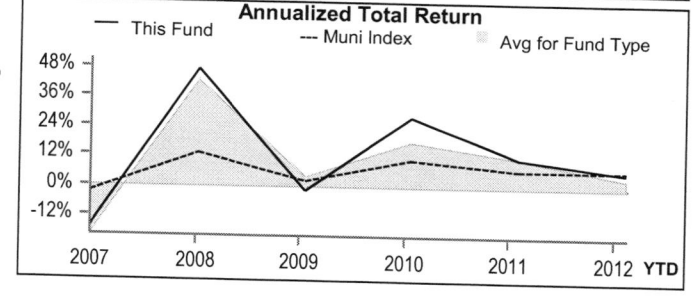

BlackRock MuniVest Fund (MVF)

A+   **Excellent**

Fund Family: BlackRock Inc
Fund Type: Municipal - National
Inception Date: September 22, 1988

Major Rating Factors:
Exceptional performance is the major factor driving the A+ (Excellent) TheStreet.com Investment Rating for BlackRock MuniVest Fund. The fund currently has a performance rating of A- (Excellent) based on an annualized return of 15.19% over the last three years and a total return of 5.97% year to date 2012. Factored into the performance evaluation is an expense ratio of 1.51% (average).

The fund's risk rating is currently B (Good). It carries a beta of 2.23, meaning it is expected to move 22.3% for every 10% move in the market. Volatility, as measured by both the semi-deviation and a drawdown factor, is considered low. As of December 31, 2012, BlackRock MuniVest Fund traded at a premium of 2.80% above its net asset value, which is better than its one-year historical average premium of 4.59%.

Fred K. Stuebe has been running the fund for 25 years and currently receives a manager quality ranking of 43 (0=worst, 99=best). If you desire only a moderate level of risk and strong performance, then this fund is an excellent option.

Data Date	Investment Rating	Net Assets ($Mil)	Price	Performance Rating/Pts	Total Return Y-T-D	Risk Rating/Pts
12-12	A+	679.21	11.03	A- / 9.2	5.97%	B / 8.8
2011	A+	626.10	10.44	A- / 9.2	0.38%	B / 8.9
2010	C+	625.20	9.46	C+ / 6.7	9.27%	C+ / 6.3
2009	B-	555.89	9.22	C+ / 6.6	39.12%	B- / 7.2

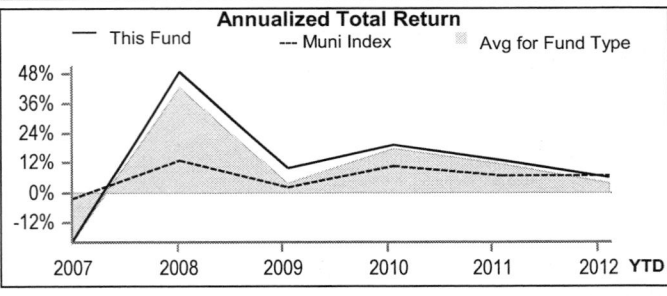

Annualized Total Return

BlackRock MuniVest Fund II (MVT)

A+   **Excellent**

Fund Family: BlackRock Inc
Fund Type: Municipal - National
Inception Date: March 19, 1993

Major Rating Factors:
Exceptional performance is the major factor driving the A+ (Excellent) TheStreet.com Investment Rating for BlackRock MuniVest Fund II. The fund currently has a performance rating of A- (Excellent) based on an annualized return of 16.07% over the last three years and a total return of 4.45% year to date 2012. Factored into the performance evaluation is an expense ratio of 1.41% (average).

The fund's risk rating is currently B (Good). It carries a beta of 1.88, meaning it is expected to move 18.8% for every 10% move in the market. Volatility, as measured by both the semi-deviation and a drawdown factor, is considered low. As of December 31, 2012, BlackRock MuniVest Fund II traded at a premium of 5.10% above its net asset value, which is better than its one-year historical average premium of 5.84%.

Fred K. Stuebe has been running the fund for 14 years and currently receives a manager quality ranking of 71 (0=worst, 99=best). If you desire only a moderate level of risk and strong performance, then this fund is an excellent option.

Data Date	Investment Rating	Net Assets ($Mil)	Price	Performance Rating/Pts	Total Return Y-T-D	Risk Rating/Pts
12-12	A+	330.94	17.51	A- / 9.2	4.45%	B / 8.6
2011	A+	312.40	15.88	A+ / 9.8	3.02%	B / 8.6
2010	C+	295.47	14.00	C+ / 5.6	7.54%	C+ / 6.7
2009	B+	243.58	13.99	B- / 7.4	57.70%	C+ / 6.7

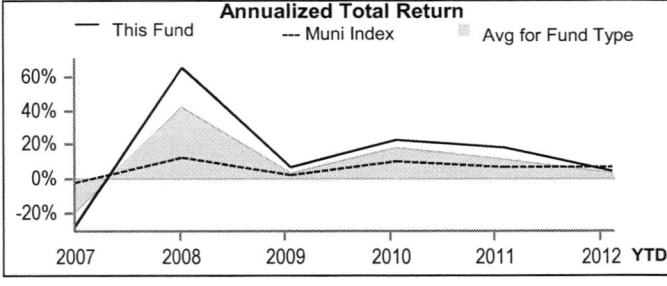

Annualized Total Return

BlackRock MuniYield AZ Fund (MZA)

A   **Excellent**

Fund Family: BlackRock Inc
Fund Type: Municipal - Single State
Inception Date: October 22, 1993

Major Rating Factors:
Strong performance is the major factor driving the A (Excellent) TheStreet.com Investment Rating for BlackRock MuniYield AZ Fund. The fund currently has a performance rating of B+ (Good) based on an annualized return of 14.29% over the last three years and a total return of 3.91% year to date 2012. Factored into the performance evaluation is an expense ratio of 1.96% (above average).

The fund's risk rating is currently B (Good). It carries a beta of 1.65, meaning it is expected to move 16.5% for every 10% move in the market. Volatility, as measured by both the semi-deviation and a drawdown factor, is considered low. As of December 31, 2012, BlackRock MuniYield AZ Fund traded at a premium of .66% above its net asset value, which is better than its one-year historical average premium of 1.30%.

Michael A. Kalinoski has been running the fund for 20 years and currently receives a manager quality ranking of 72 (0=worst, 99=best). If you desire only a moderate level of risk and strong performance, then this fund is an excellent option.

Data Date	Investment Rating	Net Assets ($Mil)	Price	Performance Rating/Pts	Total Return Y-T-D	Risk Rating/Pts
12-12	A	69.07	15.34	B+ / 8.6	3.91%	B / 8.7
2011	A+	64.90	14.12	A / 9.4	1.27%	B / 8.8
2010	C	62.62	12.62	C- / 3.9	8.80%	B- / 7.4
2009	C+	56.45	12.34	C / 5.0	48.15%	B- / 7.2

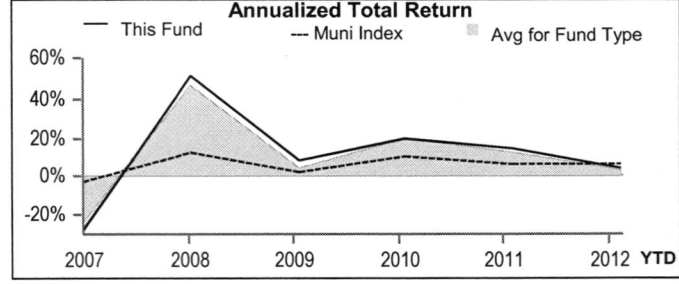

Annualized Total Return

BlackRock MuniYield CA Fund (MYC)

A+   Excellent

Fund Family: BlackRock Inc
Fund Type: Municipal - Single State
Inception Date: February 21, 1992

Major Rating Factors:

Exceptional performance is the major factor driving the A+ (Excellent) TheStreet.com Investment Rating for BlackRock MuniYield CA Fund. The fund currently has a performance rating of A (Excellent) based on an annualized return of 17.83% over the last three years and a total return of 3.37% year to date 2012. Factored into the performance evaluation is an expense ratio of 1.64% (above average).

The fund's risk rating is currently B (Good). It carries a beta of 2.35, meaning it is expected to move 23.5% for every 10% move in the market. Volatility, as measured by both the semi-deviation and a drawdown factor, is considered low. As of December 31, 2012, BlackRock MuniYield CA Fund traded at a discount of 1.23% below its net asset value, which is better than its one-year historical average discount of .95%.

Walter O'Connor has been running the fund for 21 years and currently receives a manager quality ranking of 58 (0=worst, 99=best). If you desire only a moderate level of risk and strong performance, then this fund is an excellent option.

Data Date	Investment Rating	Net Assets ($Mil)	Price	Performance Rating/Pts	Total Return Y-T-D	Risk Rating/Pts
12-12	A+	361.34	16.93	A / 9.4	3.37%	B / 8.7
2011	A+	327.80	15.08	A / 9.3	1.33%	B / 8.8
2010	C+	314.33	13.28	C / 5.4	9.82%	C+ / 6.2
2009	B-	286.81	12.88	C+ / 6.3	42.95%	B- / 7.5

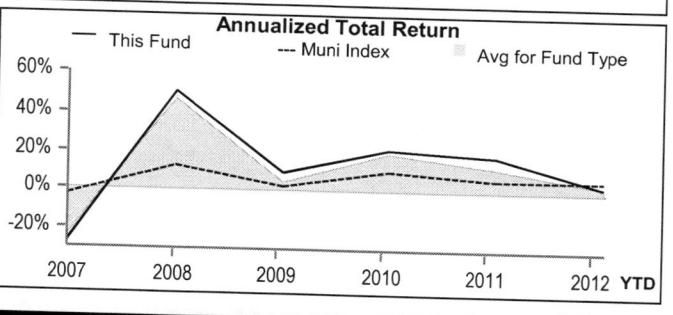

BlackRock MuniYield California Qly (MCA)

A+   Excellent

Fund Family: BlackRock Inc
Fund Type: Municipal - Single State
Inception Date: October 23, 1992

Major Rating Factors:

Exceptional performance is the major factor driving the A+ (Excellent) TheStreet.com Investment Rating for BlackRock MuniYield California Qly. The fund currently has a performance rating of A (Excellent) based on an annualized return of 17.78% over the last three years and a total return of 3.83% year to date 2012. Factored into the performance evaluation is an expense ratio of 1.61% (above average).

The fund's risk rating is currently B (Good). It carries a beta of 2.31, meaning it is expected to move 23.1% for every 10% move in the market. Volatility, as measured by both the semi-deviation and a drawdown factor, is considered low. As of December 31, 2012, BlackRock MuniYield California Qly traded at a discount of 1.73% below its net asset value, which is worse than its one-year historical average discount of 2.52%.

Walter O'Connor has been running the fund for 21 years and currently receives a manager quality ranking of 57 (0=worst, 99=best). If you desire only a moderate level of risk and strong performance, then this fund is an excellent option.

Data Date	Investment Rating	Net Assets ($Mil)	Price	Performance Rating/Pts	Total Return Y-T-D	Risk Rating/Pts
12-12	A+	570.56	16.43	A / 9.5	3.83%	B / 8.6
2011	A-	523.90	14.34	B+ / 8.9	2.02%	B / 8.7
2010	C	503.87	12.79	C / 4.6	8.05%	C+ / 6.1
2009	B	461.51	12.57	C / 5.5	36.21%	B- / 7.7

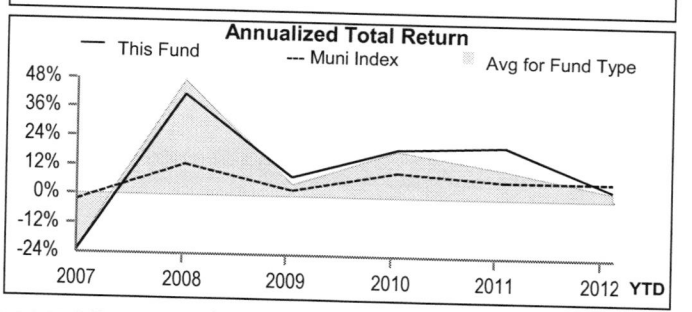

BlackRock MuniYield Fund (MYD)

A+   Excellent

Fund Family: BlackRock Inc
Fund Type: Municipal - National
Inception Date: November 21, 1991

Major Rating Factors:

Exceptional performance is the major factor driving the A+ (Excellent) TheStreet.com Investment Rating for BlackRock MuniYield Fund. The fund currently has a performance rating of A (Excellent) based on an annualized return of 16.92% over the last three years and a total return of 4.52% year to date 2012. Factored into the performance evaluation is an expense ratio of 1.53% (average).

The fund's risk rating is currently B (Good). It carries a beta of 2.06, meaning it is expected to move 20.6% for every 10% move in the market. Volatility, as measured by both the semi-deviation and a drawdown factor, is considered low. As of December 31, 2012, BlackRock MuniYield Fund traded at a premium of 2.44% above its net asset value, which is better than its one-year historical average premium of 3.64%.

Robert M. Shearer currently receives a manager quality ranking of 66 (0=worst, 99=best). If you desire only a moderate level of risk and strong performance, then this fund is an excellent option.

Data Date	Investment Rating	Net Assets ($Mil)	Price	Performance Rating/Pts	Total Return Y-T-D	Risk Rating/Pts
12-12	A+	703.29	16.37	A / 9.4	4.52%	B / 8.5
2011	A-	660.60	14.79	B+ / 8.7	0.20%	B / 8.6
2010	C+	630.61	13.41	C / 4.7	11.94%	C+ / 6.8
2009	C+	523.59	12.82	C / 4.4	32.31%	B- / 7.3

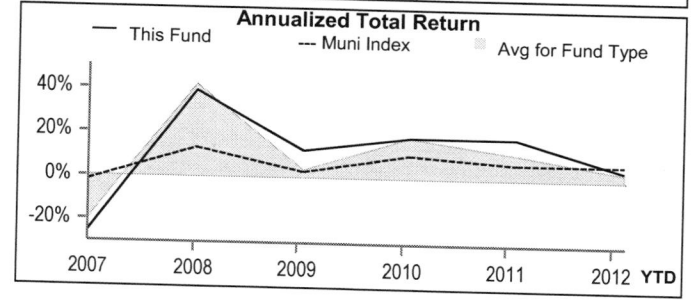

BlackRock MuniYield Inv Quality (MFT)

A+   Excellent

Fund Family: BlackRock Inc
Fund Type: Municipal - Single State
Inception Date: October 23, 1992

Data Date	Investment Rating	Net Assets ($Mil)	Price	Performance Rating/Pts	Total Return Y-T-D	Risk Rating/Pts
12-12	A+	133.16	15.70	A- / 9.1	4.46%	B / 8.7
2011	A+	121.40	14.41	A / 9.4	0.35%	B / 8.8
2010	C-	117.34	12.31	C- / 4.1	2.49%	C / 5.4
2009	C+	108.43	12.78	C+ / 6.9	44.89%	C+ / 6.7

Major Rating Factors:
Exceptional performance is the major factor driving the A+ (Excellent) TheStreet.com Investment Rating for BlackRock MuniYield Inv Quality. The fund currently has a performance rating of A- (Excellent) based on an annualized return of 15.41% over the last three years and a total return of 4.46% year to date 2012. Factored into the performance evaluation is an expense ratio of 1.58% (above average).

The fund's risk rating is currently B (Good). It carries a beta of 1.93, meaning it is expected to move 19.3% for every 10% move in the market. Volatility, as measured by both the semi-deviation and a drawdown factor, is considered low. As of December 31, 2012, BlackRock MuniYield Inv Quality traded at a discount of 1.81% below its net asset value, which is better than its one-year historical average discount of 1.02%.

Robert M. Shearer currently receives a manager quality ranking of 60 (0=worst, 99=best). If you desire only a moderate level of risk and strong performance, then this fund is an excellent option.

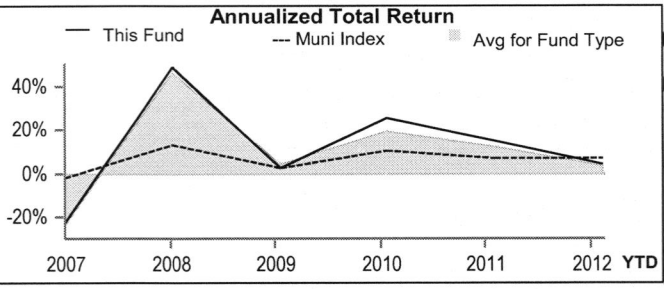

BlackRock MuniYield Invt Fund (MYF)

A+   Excellent

Fund Family: BlackRock Inc
Fund Type: Municipal - Single State
Inception Date: February 21, 1992

Data Date	Investment Rating	Net Assets ($Mil)	Price	Performance Rating/Pts	Total Return Y-T-D	Risk Rating/Pts
12-12	A+	221.78	16.87	A+ / 9.6	3.92%	B / 8.8
2011	A+	198.90	14.69	A+ / 9.7	2.45%	B / 8.8
2010	C+	193.27	12.98	C / 5.3	9.07%	C+ / 6.2
2009	B-	175.61	12.68	C+ / 6.8	45.37%	B- / 7.0

Major Rating Factors:
Exceptional performance is the major factor driving the A+ (Excellent) TheStreet.com Investment Rating for BlackRock MuniYield Invt Fund. The fund currently has a performance rating of A+ (Excellent) based on an annualized return of 17.94% over the last three years and a total return of 3.92% year to date 2012. Factored into the performance evaluation is an expense ratio of 1.66% (above average).

The fund's risk rating is currently B (Good). It carries a beta of 2.00, meaning it is expected to move 20.0% for every 10% move in the market. Volatility, as measured by both the semi-deviation and a drawdown factor, is considered low. As of December 31, 2012, BlackRock MuniYield Invt Fund traded at a premium of 2.12% above its net asset value, which is worse than its one-year historical average premium of 1.78%.

Robert M. Shearer currently receives a manager quality ranking of 74 (0=worst, 99=best). If you desire only a moderate level of risk and strong performance, then this fund is an excellent option.

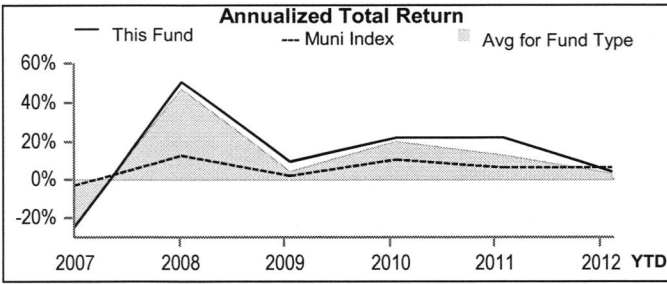

BlackRock MuniYield Michigan Qly (MIY)

A+   Excellent

Fund Family: BlackRock Inc
Fund Type: Municipal - Single State
Inception Date: October 23, 1992

Data Date	Investment Rating	Net Assets ($Mil)	Price	Performance Rating/Pts	Total Return Y-T-D	Risk Rating/Pts
12-12	A+	294.80	15.65	B+ / 8.9	6.65%	B / 8.6
2011	A+	279.40	15.50	A / 9.3	-2.00%	B / 8.9
2010	C+	271.61	13.35	C / 5.3	9.67%	C+ / 6.2
2009	B-	253.63	12.98	C+ / 6.4	40.50%	B- / 7.6

Major Rating Factors:
Strong performance is the major factor driving the A+ (Excellent) TheStreet.com Investment Rating for BlackRock MuniYield Michigan Qly. The fund currently has a performance rating of B+ (Good) based on an annualized return of 15.07% over the last three years and a total return of 6.65% year to date 2012. Factored into the performance evaluation is an expense ratio of 1.72% (above average).

The fund's risk rating is currently B (Good). It carries a beta of 2.34, meaning it is expected to move 23.4% for every 10% move in the market. Volatility, as measured by both the semi-deviation and a drawdown factor, is considered low. As of December 31, 2012, BlackRock MuniYield Michigan Qly traded at a discount of 3.69% below its net asset value, which is better than its one-year historical average discount of 1.60%.

Fred K. Stuebe has been running the fund for 21 years and currently receives a manager quality ranking of 34 (0=worst, 99=best). If you desire only a moderate level of risk and strong performance, then this fund is an excellent option.

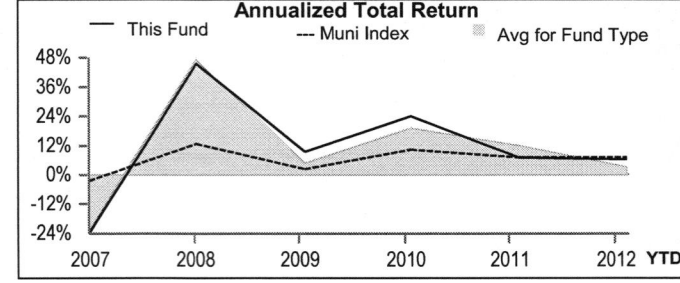

BlackRock MuniYield Michigan Qly I (MYM)

A- **Excellent**

Fund Family: BlackRock Inc
Fund Type: Municipal - Single State
Inception Date: February 21, 1992

Major Rating Factors:

Strong performance is the major factor driving the A- (Excellent) TheStreet.com Investment Rating for BlackRock MuniYield Michigan Qly I. The fund currently has a performance rating of B+ (Good) based on an annualized return of 14.48% over the last three years and a total return of 3.69% year to date 2012. Factored into the performance evaluation is an expense ratio of 1.71% (above average).

The fund's risk rating is currently B (Good). It carries a beta of 2.21, meaning it is expected to move 22.1% for every 10% move in the market. Volatility, as measured by both the semi-deviation and a drawdown factor, is considered low. As of December 31, 2012, BlackRock MuniYield Michigan Qly I traded at a discount of 5.59% below its net asset value, which is better than its one-year historical average discount of 2.34%.

Fred K. Stuebe has been running the fund for 21 years and currently receives a manager quality ranking of 41 (0=worst, 99=best). If you desire only a moderate level of risk and strong performance, then this fund is an excellent option.

Data Date	Investment Rating	Net Assets ($Mil)	Price	Performance Rating/Pts	Total Return Y-T-D	Risk Rating/Pts
12-12	A-	183.08	14.35	B+ / 8.3	3.69%	B / 8.6
2011	A+	172.10	14.83	A+ / 9.7	-2.29%	B / 8.9
2010	C	166.77	12.11	C / 4.5	8.82%	C+ / 6.2
2009	B-	155.36	11.88	C+ / 5.7	40.26%	B- / 7.7

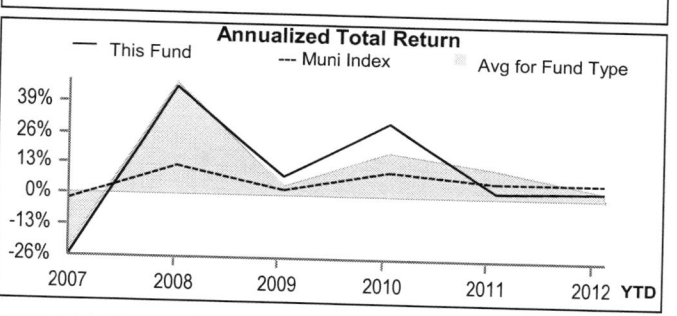

BlackRock MuniYield New Jersey Qly (MJI)

A- **Excellent**

Fund Family: BlackRock Inc
Fund Type: Municipal - Single State
Inception Date: October 23, 1992

Major Rating Factors:

Strong performance is the major factor driving the A- (Excellent) TheStreet.com Investment Rating for BlackRock MuniYield New Jersey Qly. The fund currently has a performance rating of B+ (Good) based on an annualized return of 14.00% over the last three years and a total return of 4.93% year to date 2012. Factored into the performance evaluation is an expense ratio of 1.70% (above average).

The fund's risk rating is currently B (Good). It carries a beta of 1.94, meaning it is expected to move 19.4% for every 10% move in the market. Volatility, as measured by both the semi-deviation and a drawdown factor, is considered low. As of December 31, 2012, BlackRock MuniYield New Jersey Qly traded at a discount of .92% below its net asset value, which is better than its one-year historical average premium of .93%.

Robert M. Shearer currently receives a manager quality ranking of 54 (0=worst, 99=best). If you desire only a moderate level of risk and strong performance, then this fund is an excellent option.

Data Date	Investment Rating	Net Assets ($Mil)	Price	Performance Rating/Pts	Total Return Y-T-D	Risk Rating/Pts
12-12	A-	144.94	16.23	B+ / 8.3	4.93%	B / 8.6
2011	A+	135.20	15.56	A+ / 9.6	1.03%	B / 8.7
2010	C-	132.28	13.34	C- / 3.6	5.58%	C+ / 6.6
2009	B-	123.81	13.40	C+ / 6.0	41.85%	B- / 7.6

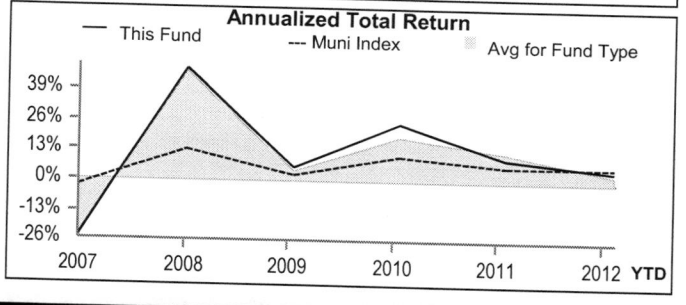

BlackRock MuniYield New York Qly (MYN)

A **Excellent**

Fund Family: BlackRock Inc
Fund Type: Municipal - Single State
Inception Date: February 21, 1992

Major Rating Factors:

Strong performance is the major factor driving the A (Excellent) TheStreet.com Investment Rating for BlackRock MuniYield New York Qly. The fund currently has a performance rating of B+ (Good) based on an annualized return of 15.35% over the last three years and a total return of 1.79% year to date 2012. Factored into the performance evaluation is an expense ratio of 1.65% (above average).

The fund's risk rating is currently B (Good). It carries a beta of 2.30, meaning it is expected to move 23.0% for every 10% move in the market. Volatility, as measured by both the semi-deviation and a drawdown factor, is considered low. As of December 31, 2012, BlackRock MuniYield New York Qly traded at a premium of .53% above its net asset value, which is worse than its one-year historical average discount of .85%.

Timothy T. Browse has been running the fund for 21 years and currently receives a manager quality ranking of 50 (0=worst, 99=best). If you desire only a moderate level of risk and strong performance, then this fund is an excellent option.

Data Date	Investment Rating	Net Assets ($Mil)	Price	Performance Rating/Pts	Total Return Y-T-D	Risk Rating/Pts
12-12	A	594.81	15.10	B+ / 8.9	1.79%	B / 8.4
2011	A	559.70	14.08	A / 9.4	0.00%	B / 8.6
2010	C	547.81	12.45	C / 5.5	12.09%	C / 5.4
2009	B-	499.09	11.80	C / 5.3	38.08%	B- / 7.7

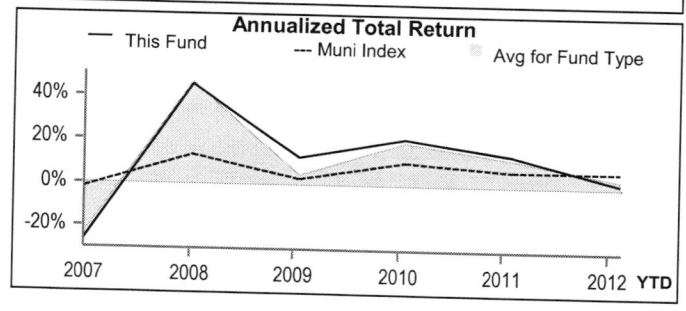

* Denotes ETF Fund

BlackRock MuniYield NJ Fund (MYJ)   A   Excellent

Fund Family: BlackRock Inc
Fund Type: Municipal - Single State
Inception Date: April 23, 1992

Data Date	Investment Rating	Net Assets ($Mil)	Price	Perfor-mance Rating/Pts	Total Return Y-T-D	Risk Rating/Pts
12-12	A	240.76	16.60	B+ / 8.5	4.16%	B / 8.7
2011	A-	224.80	15.60	B+ / 8.6	-1.60%	B / 8.8
2010	C	216.43	13.78	C- / 4.1	5.74%	C+ / 6.7
2009	B-	200.74	13.81	C+ / 5.7	38.87%	B- / 7.5

Major Rating Factors:
Strong performance is the major factor driving the A (Excellent) TheStreet.com Investment Rating for BlackRock MuniYield NJ Fund. The fund currently has a performance rating of B+ (Good) based on an annualized return of 13.90% over the last three years and a total return of 4.16% year to date 2012. Factored into the performance evaluation is an expense ratio of 1.60% (above average).

The fund's risk rating is currently B (Good). It carries a beta of 2.11, meaning it is expected to move 21.1% for every 10% move in the market. Volatility, as measured by both the semi-deviation and a drawdown factor, is considered low. As of December 31, 2012, BlackRock MuniYield NJ Fund traded at a discount of 2.18% below its net asset value, which is better than its one-year historical average discount of .43%.

Robert M. Shearer currently receives a manager quality ranking of 41 (0=worst, 99=best). If you desire only a moderate level of risk and strong performance, then this fund is an excellent option.

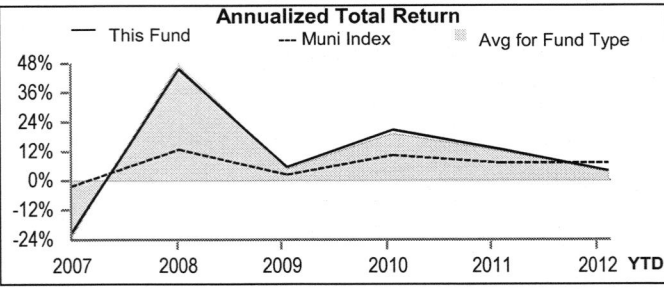

BlackRock MuniYield PA Qly (MPA)   A   Excellent

Fund Family: BlackRock Inc
Fund Type: Municipal - Single State
Inception Date: October 23, 1992

Data Date	Investment Rating	Net Assets ($Mil)	Price	Perfor-mance Rating/Pts	Total Return Y-T-D	Risk Rating/Pts
12-12	A	190.56	16.35	B+ / 8.4	2.26%	B / 8.7
2011	A+	180.10	15.79	A- / 9.2	0.06%	B / 8.9
2010	C	176.53	13.45	C- / 4.0	7.26%	C+ / 6.3
2009	B-	163.92	13.32	C+ / 6.0	43.71%	B- / 7.4

Major Rating Factors:
Strong performance is the major factor driving the A (Excellent) TheStreet.com Investment Rating for BlackRock MuniYield PA Qly. The fund currently has a performance rating of B+ (Good) based on an annualized return of 14.12% over the last three years and a total return of 2.26% year to date 2012. Factored into the performance evaluation is an expense ratio of 1.65% (above average).

The fund's risk rating is currently B (Good). It carries a beta of 1.52, meaning it is expected to move 15.2% for every 10% move in the market. Volatility, as measured by both the semi-deviation and a drawdown factor, is considered low. As of December 31, 2012, BlackRock MuniYield PA Qly traded at a discount of 2.10% below its net asset value, which is better than its one-year historical average discount of 2.04%.

William R. Bock has been running the fund for 21 years and currently receives a manager quality ranking of 73 (0=worst, 99=best). If you desire only a moderate level of risk and strong performance, then this fund is an excellent option.

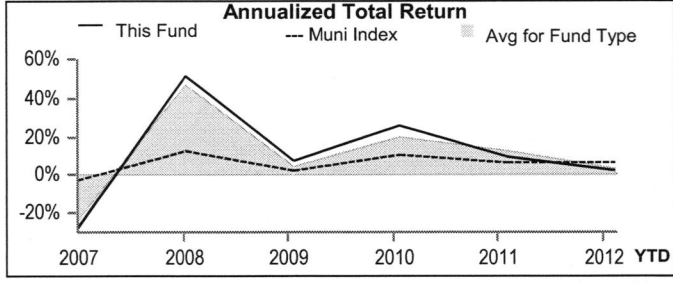

BlackRock MuniYield Quality Fund (MQY)   A+   Excellent

Fund Family: BlackRock Inc
Fund Type: Municipal - National
Inception Date: June 19, 1992

Data Date	Investment Rating	Net Assets ($Mil)	Price	Perfor-mance Rating/Pts	Total Return Y-T-D	Risk Rating/Pts
12-12	A+	495.26	17.64	A / 9.4	2.38%	B / 8.4
2011	A-	470.20	15.82	A- / 9.1	-1.07%	B / 8.5
2010	C+	445.16	13.72	C+ / 6.0	5.54%	C+ / 5.9
2009	B-	403.80	13.84	C+ / 6.7	37.31%	B- / 7.1

Major Rating Factors:
Exceptional performance is the major factor driving the A+ (Excellent) TheStreet.com Investment Rating for BlackRock MuniYield Quality Fund. The fund currently has a performance rating of A (Excellent) based on an annualized return of 15.80% over the last three years and a total return of 2.38% year to date 2012. Factored into the performance evaluation is an expense ratio of 1.46% (average).

The fund's risk rating is currently B (Good). It carries a beta of 2.47, meaning it is expected to move 24.7% for every 10% move in the market. Volatility, as measured by both the semi-deviation and a drawdown factor, is considered low. As of December 31, 2012, BlackRock MuniYield Quality Fund traded at a premium of 4.69% above its net asset value, which is worse than its one-year historical average premium of 1.98%.

Michael A. Kalinoski has been running the fund for 21 years and currently receives a manager quality ranking of 41 (0=worst, 99=best). If you desire only a moderate level of risk and strong performance, then this fund is an excellent option.

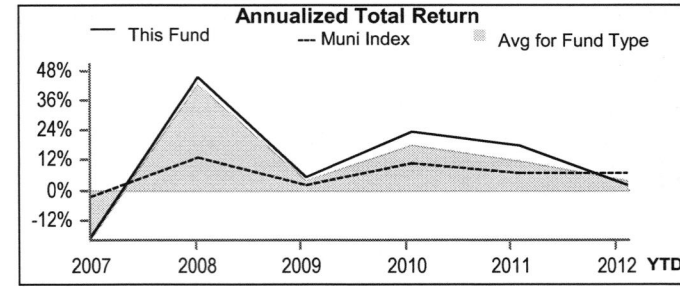

BlackRock MuniYield Quality Fund I (MQT)

A   **Excellent**

Fund Family: BlackRock Inc
Fund Type: Municipal - National
Inception Date: August 21, 1992

Major Rating Factors:

Strong performance is the major factor driving the A (Excellent) TheStreet.com Investment Rating for BlackRock MuniYield Quality Fund I. The fund currently has a performance rating of B+ (Good) based on an annualized return of 15.29% over the last three years and a total return of 3.88% year to date 2012. Factored into the performance evaluation is an expense ratio of 1.31% (average).

The fund's risk rating is currently B (Good). It carries a beta of 2.80, meaning it is expected to move 28.0% for every 10% move in the market. Volatility, as measured by both the semi-deviation and a drawdown factor, is considered low. As of December 31, 2012, BlackRock MuniYield Quality Fund I traded at a discount of 1.57% below its net asset value, which is better than its one-year historical average premium of .13%.

Michael A. Kalinoski currently receives a manager quality ranking of 24 (0=worst, 99=best). If you desire only a moderate level of risk and strong performance, then this fund is an excellent option.

Data Date	Investment Rating	Net Assets ($Mil)	Price	Performance Rating/Pts	Total Return Y-T-D	Risk Rating/Pts
12-12	A	317.28	14.44	B+ / 8.9	3.88%	B / 8.4
2011	A+	300.70	13.70	A+ / 9.7	-0.44%	B / 8.6
2010	C	284.40	11.35	C- / 4.2	2.87%	C+ / 6.3
2009	C+	258.26	11.76	C+ / 6.5	40.16%	C+ / 6.8

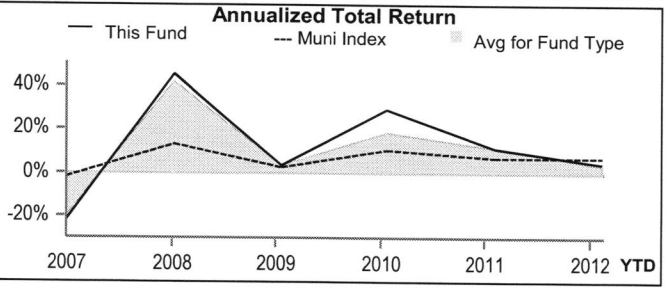

BlackRock MuniYield Quality III (MYI)

A   **Excellent**

Fund Family: BlackRock Inc
Fund Type: Municipal - National
Inception Date: March 20, 1992

Major Rating Factors:

Exceptional performance is the major factor driving the A (Excellent) TheStreet.com Investment Rating for BlackRock MuniYield Quality III. The fund currently has a performance rating of A- (Excellent) based on an annualized return of 15.23% over the last three years and a total return of 4.51% year to date 2012. Factored into the performance evaluation is an expense ratio of 1.56% (average).

The fund's risk rating is currently B (Good). It carries a beta of 2.26, meaning it is expected to move 22.6% for every 10% move in the market. Volatility, as measured by both the semi-deviation and a drawdown factor, is considered low. As of December 31, 2012, BlackRock MuniYield Quality III traded at a discount of .97% below its net asset value, which is better than its one-year historical average premium of .38%.

William R. Bock has been running the fund for 21 years and currently receives a manager quality ranking of 46 (0=worst, 99=best). If you desire only a moderate level of risk and strong performance, then this fund is an excellent option.

Data Date	Investment Rating	Net Assets ($Mil)	Price	Performance Rating/Pts	Total Return Y-T-D	Risk Rating/Pts
12-12	A	1,036.02	15.30	A- / 9.0	4.51%	B / 8.4
2011	A	955.20	14.14	A / 9.5	1.27%	B / 8.6
2010	D+	920.23	12.47	C- / 3.4	8.16%	C / 5.5
2009	C+	825.62	12.26	C / 5.1	37.13%	B- / 7.0

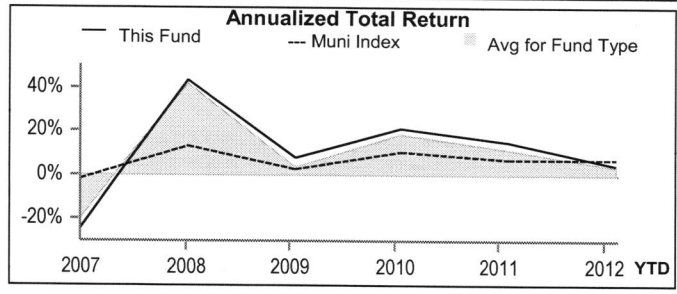

BlackRock New York Muni Inc Qly (BSE)

A   **Excellent**

Fund Family: BlackRock Inc
Fund Type: Municipal - Single State
Inception Date: October 28, 2002

Major Rating Factors:

Strong performance is the major factor driving the A (Excellent) TheStreet.com Investment Rating for BlackRock New York Muni Inc Qly. The fund currently has a performance rating of B+ (Good) based on an annualized return of 14.22% over the last three years and a total return of 3.10% year to date 2012. Factored into the performance evaluation is an expense ratio of 1.82% (above average).

The fund's risk rating is currently B (Good). It carries a beta of 2.35, meaning it is expected to move 23.5% for every 10% move in the market. Volatility, as measured by both the semi-deviation and a drawdown factor, is considered low. As of December 31, 2012, BlackRock New York Muni Inc Qly traded at a premium of 3.53% above its net asset value, which is worse than its one-year historical average premium of 2.94%.

Timothy T. Browse has been running the fund for 7 years and currently receives a manager quality ranking of 31 (0=worst, 99=best). If you desire only a moderate level of risk and strong performance, then this fund is an excellent option.

Data Date	Investment Rating	Net Assets ($Mil)	Price	Performance Rating/Pts	Total Return Y-T-D	Risk Rating/Pts
12-12	A	100.87	16.11	B+ / 8.5	3.10%	B / 8.5
2011	B+	95.80	14.91	B+ / 8.4	0.03%	B / 8.7
2010	C-	96.62	13.05	D / 2.1	3.27%	B- / 7.1
2009	B-	88.14	13.41	C+ / 6.2	47.95%	B- / 7.2

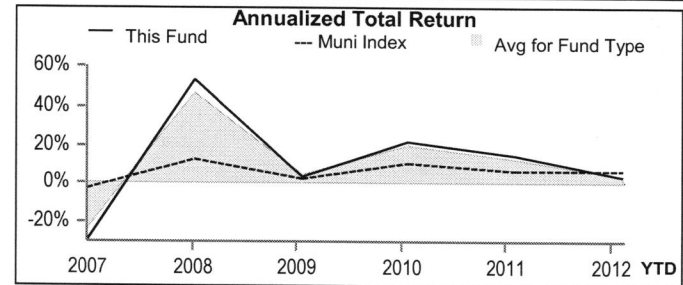

BlackRock NJ Muni Bond Trust (BLJ)

B+ **Good**

Fund Family: BlackRock Inc
Fund Type: Municipal - Single State
Inception Date: April 26, 2002

Major Rating Factors: Strong performance is the major factor driving the B+ (Good) TheStreet.com Investment Rating for BlackRock NJ Muni Bond Trust. The fund currently has a performance rating of B+ (Good) based on an annualized return of 15.03% over the last three years and a total return of 4.88% year to date 2012. Factored into the performance evaluation is an expense ratio of 1.59% (above average).

The fund's risk rating is currently B- (Good). It carries a beta of 2.63, meaning it is expected to move 26.3% for every 10% move in the market. Volatility, as measured by both the semi-deviation and a drawdown factor, is considered low. As of December 31, 2012, BlackRock NJ Muni Bond Trust traded at a premium of 1.19% above its net asset value, which is better than its one-year historical average premium of 4.64%.

Theodore R. Jaeckel, Jr. has been running the fund for 7 years and currently receives a manager quality ranking of 23 (0=worst, 99=best). If you desire only a moderate level of risk and strong performance, then this fund is an excellent option.

Data Date	Investment Rating	Net Assets ($Mil)	Price	Performance Rating/Pts	Total Return Y-T-D	Risk Rating/Pts
12-12	B+	38.73	17.00	B+ / 8.6	4.88%	B- / 7.7
2011	A-	35.50	15.33	A / 9.3	1.37%	B / 8.0
2010	D+	35.28	13.38	D- / 1.3	-1.22%	C+ / 6.9
2009	C	31.24	14.47	C- / 3.6	33.40%	C+ / 6.8

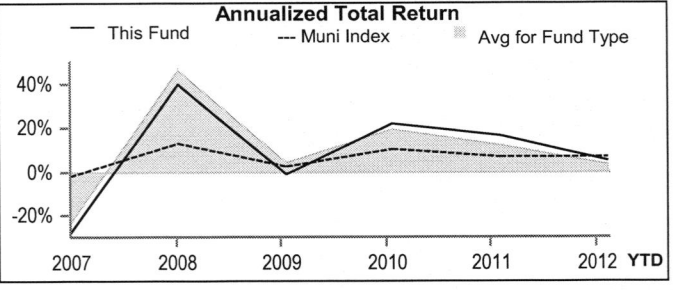

BlackRock NJ Municipal Income Trus (BNJ)

A **Excellent**

Fund Family: BlackRock Inc
Fund Type: Municipal - Single State
Inception Date: July 26, 2001

Major Rating Factors:
Exceptional performance is the major factor driving the A (Excellent) TheStreet.com Investment Rating for BlackRock NJ Municipal Income Trus. The fund currently has a performance rating of A- (Excellent) based on an annualized return of 15.55% over the last three years and a total return of 5.98% year to date 2012. Factored into the performance evaluation is an expense ratio of 1.46% (average).

The fund's risk rating is currently B (Good). It carries a beta of 2.42, meaning it is expected to move 24.2% for every 10% move in the market. Volatility, as measured by both the semi-deviation and a drawdown factor, is considered low. As of December 31, 2012, BlackRock NJ Municipal Income Trus traded at a premium of 4.92% above its net asset value, which is better than its one-year historical average premium of 7.48%.

Theodore R. Jaeckel, Jr. has been running the fund for 7 years and currently receives a manager quality ranking of 42 (0=worst, 99=best). If you desire only a moderate level of risk and strong performance, then this fund is an excellent option.

Data Date	Investment Rating	Net Assets ($Mil)	Price	Performance Rating/Pts	Total Return Y-T-D	Risk Rating/Pts
12-12	A	123.50	17.05	A- / 9.0	5.98%	B / 8.3
2011	B+	114.10	15.69	B+ / 8.8	1.02%	B / 8.4
2010	D+	109.26	13.43	D / 1.6	5.96%	C+ / 6.9
2009	C-	96.70	13.53	D / 1.8	25.91%	B- / 7.0

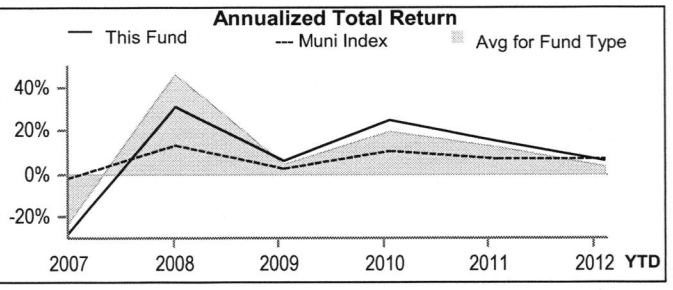

BlackRock NY Muni 2018 Income Trus (BLH)

C **Fair**

Fund Family: BlackRock Inc
Fund Type: Municipal - Single State
Inception Date: October 25, 2001

Major Rating Factors: Middle of the road best describes BlackRock NY Muni 2018 Income Trus whose TheStreet.com Investment Rating is currently a C (Fair). The fund currently has a performance rating of C- (Fair) based on an annualized return of 5.76% over the last three years and a total return of 2.55% year to date 2012. Factored into the performance evaluation is an expense ratio of 0.95% (low).

The fund's risk rating is currently B+ (Good). It carries a beta of 1.01, meaning that its performance tracks fairly well with that of the overall stock market. Volatility, as measured by both the semi-deviation and a drawdown factor, is considered very low. As of December 31, 2012, BlackRock NY Muni 2018 Income Trus traded at a premium of 1.97% above its net asset value, which is better than its one-year historical average premium of 4.42%.

F. Howard Downs has been running the fund for 7 years and currently receives a manager quality ranking of 35 (0=worst, 99=best). If you desire an average level of risk, then this fund may be an option.

Data Date	Investment Rating	Net Assets ($Mil)	Price	Performance Rating/Pts	Total Return Y-T-D	Risk Rating/Pts
12-12	C	57.06	16.05	C- / 3.3	2.55%	B+ / 9.2
2011	B	56.80	16.71	C+ / 6.2	1.56%	B+ / 9.5
2010	B-	56.98	16.10	C+ / 6.3	1.84%	B- / 7.3
2009	A	53.50	16.90	B- / 7.0	26.06%	B- / 7.5

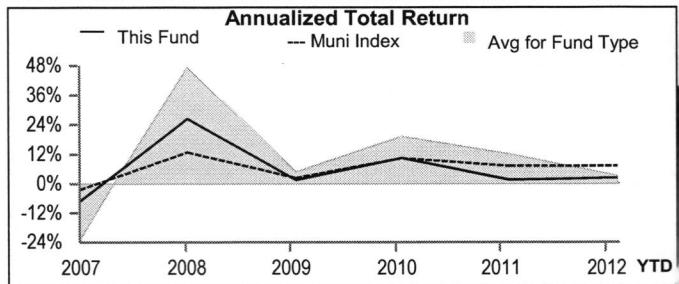

BlackRock NY Muni Bond Trust (BQH)

B+ **Good**

Fund Family: BlackRock Inc
Fund Type: Municipal - Single State
Inception Date: April 26, 2002

Major Rating Factors: Strong performance is the major factor driving the B+ (Good) TheStreet.com Investment Rating for BlackRock NY Muni Bond Trust. The fund currently has a performance rating of B (Good) based on an annualized return of 10.82% over the last three years and a total return of 2.29% year to date 2012. Factored into the performance evaluation is an expense ratio of 2.20% (high).

The fund's risk rating is currently B (Good). It carries a beta of 1.70, meaning it is expected to move 17.0% for every 10% move in the market. Volatility, as measured by both the semi-deviation and a drawdown factor, is considered low. As of December 31, 2012, BlackRock NY Muni Bond Trust traded at a discount of .24% below its net asset value, which is better than its one-year historical average premium of 1.34%.

Robert S. Kapito currently receives a manager quality ranking of 39 (0=worst, 99=best). If you desire only a moderate level of risk and strong performance, then this fund is an excellent option.

Data Date	Investment Rating	Net Assets ($Mil)	Price	Perfor-mance Rating/Pts	Total Return Y-T-D	Risk Rating/Pts
12-12	B+	46.16	16.57	B / 7.7	2.29%	B / 8.7
2011	B+	42.40	15.71	B+ / 8.4	-1.74%	B / 8.7
2010	C-	43.41	14.01	D / 1.9	-2.55%	B- / 7.1
2009	B-	40.20	15.33	C+ / 6.8	56.78%	B- / 7.1

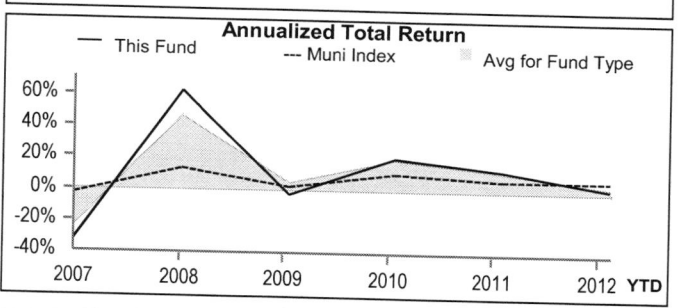

BlackRock NY Municipal Income Tr I (BFY)

B+ **Good**

Fund Family: BlackRock Inc
Fund Type: Municipal - Single State
Inception Date: July 25, 2002

Major Rating Factors: Strong performance is the major factor driving the B+ (Good) TheStreet.com Investment Rating for BlackRock NY Municipal Income Tr I. The fund currently has a performance rating of B- (Good) based on an annualized return of 12.48% over the last three years and a total return of 4.38% year to date 2012. Factored into the performance evaluation is an expense ratio of 1.95% (above average).

The fund's risk rating is currently B (Good). It carries a beta of 1.75, meaning it is expected to move 17.5% for every 10% move in the market. Volatility, as measured by both the semi-deviation and a drawdown factor, is considered low. As of December 31, 2012, BlackRock NY Municipal Income Tr I traded at a discount of 1.23% below its net asset value, which is better than its one-year historical average premium of 4.18%.

Timothy T. Browse has been running the fund for 7 years and currently receives a manager quality ranking of 46 (0=worst, 99=best). If you desire only a moderate level of risk and strong performance, then this fund is an excellent option.

Data Date	Investment Rating	Net Assets ($Mil)	Price	Perfor-mance Rating/Pts	Total Return Y-T-D	Risk Rating/Pts
12-12	B+	80.23	16.00	B- / 7.4	4.38%	B / 8.7
2011	A+	74.70	15.75	A+ / 9.6	1.17%	B+ / 9.1
2010	C	75.87	14.09	C / 4.9	5.74%	C+ / 5.8
2009	B+	69.32	14.24	B- / 7.3	57.11%	C+ / 6.5

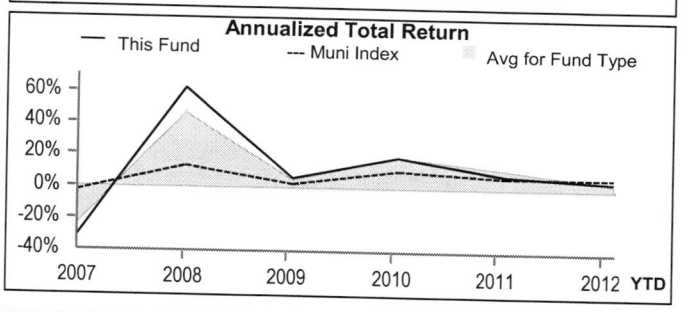

BlackRock NY Municipal Income Trus (BNY)

A- **Excellent**

Fund Family: BlackRock Inc
Fund Type: Municipal - Single State
Inception Date: July 26, 2001

Major Rating Factors:
Strong performance is the major factor driving the A- (Excellent) TheStreet.com Investment Rating for BlackRock NY Municipal Income Trus. The fund currently has a performance rating of B (Good) based on an annualized return of 12.17% over the last three years and a total return of 2.18% year to date 2012. Factored into the performance evaluation is an expense ratio of 1.49% (average).

The fund's risk rating is currently B (Good). It carries a beta of 1.76, meaning it is expected to move 17.6% for every 10% move in the market. Volatility, as measured by both the semi-deviation and a drawdown factor, is considered low. As of December 31, 2012, BlackRock NY Municipal Income Trus traded at a premium of 5.63% above its net asset value, which is better than its one-year historical average premium of 6.69%.

Timothy T. Browse has been running the fund for 7 years and currently receives a manager quality ranking of 51 (0=worst, 99=best). If you desire only a moderate level of risk and strong performance, then this fund is an excellent option.

Data Date	Investment Rating	Net Assets ($Mil)	Price	Perfor-mance Rating/Pts	Total Return Y-T-D	Risk Rating/Pts
12-12	A-	200.02	16.51	B / 8.0	2.18%	B / 8.8
2011	B+	185.20	15.32	B+ / 8.3	0.00%	B / 8.9
2010	C-	182.37	13.63	D / 2.1	0.74%	B- / 7.1
2009	C	161.73	14.50	C / 4.7	47.20%	C+ / 6.8

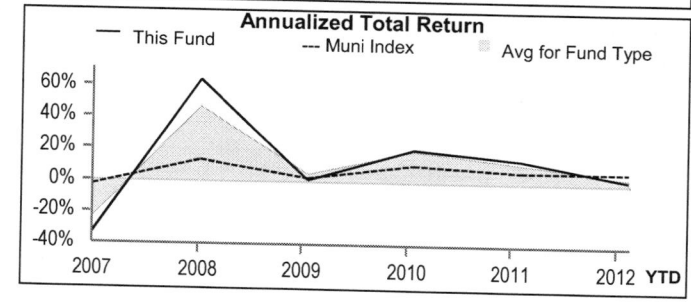

* Denotes ETF Fund

BlackRock PA Strategic Muni Tr (BPS)

A   **Excellent**

Fund Family: BlackRock Inc
Fund Type: Municipal - Single State
Inception Date: August 24, 1999

Data Date	Investment Rating	Net Assets ($Mil)	Price	Performance Rating/Pts	Total Return Y-T-D	Risk Rating/Pts
12-12	A	30.58	15.21	A- / 9.1	7.00%	B / 8.2
2011	A+	29.40	14.69	A+ / 9.7	0.00%	B / 8.4
2010	D+	28.04	12.44	D / 1.9	4.49%	C+ / 6.8
2009	C	24.02	12.68	C / 4.8	56.70%	C+ / 6.8

Major Rating Factors:
Exceptional performance is the major factor driving the A (Excellent) TheStreet.com Investment Rating for BlackRock PA Strategic Muni Tr. The fund currently has a performance rating of A- (Excellent) based on an annualized return of 15.45% over the last three years and a total return of 7.00% year to date 2012. Factored into the performance evaluation is an expense ratio of 1.71% (above average).

The fund's risk rating is currently B (Good). It carries a beta of 2.64, meaning it is expected to move 26.4% for every 10% move in the market. Volatility, as measured by both the semi-deviation and a drawdown factor, is considered low. As of December 31, 2012, BlackRock PA Strategic Muni Tr traded at a discount of 2.00% below its net asset value, which is better than its one-year historical average premium of .29%.

Theodore R. Jaeckel, Jr. has been running the fund for 7 years and currently receives a manager quality ranking of 25 (0=worst, 99=best). If you desire only a moderate level of risk and strong performance, then this fund is an excellent option.

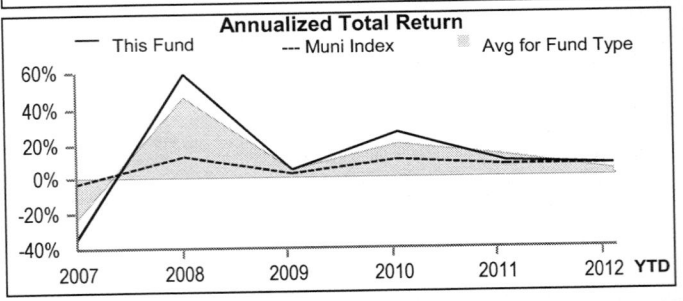

BlackRock Real Asset Equity Trust (BCF)

D   **Weak**

Fund Family: BlackRock Inc
Fund Type: Income
Inception Date: September 29, 2006

Data Date	Investment Rating	Net Assets ($Mil)	Price	Performance Rating/Pts	Total Return Y-T-D	Risk Rating/Pts
12-12	D	711.92	10.26	D / 1.8	2.73%	C+ / 6.6
2011	C+	664.50	10.67	C+ / 6.8	5.06%	C+ / 6.8
2010	C	664.93	14.62	B- / 7.5	25.56%	C- / 3.6
2009	C+	526.63	12.67	B / 8.1	90.33%	C- / 4.0

Major Rating Factors:
Disappointing performance is the major factor driving the D (Weak) TheStreet.com Investment Rating for BlackRock Real Asset Equity Trust. The fund currently has a performance rating of D (Weak) based on an annualized return of 1.72% over the last three years and a total return of 2.73% year to date 2012. Factored into the performance evaluation is an expense ratio of 1.09% (low).

The fund's risk rating is currently C+ (Fair). It carries a beta of 1.37, meaning it is expected to move 13.7% for every 10% move in the market. Volatility, as measured by both the semi-deviation and a drawdown factor, is considered low. As of December 31, 2012, BlackRock Real Asset Equity Trust traded at a discount of 8.80% below its net asset value, which is better than its one-year historical average discount of 3.17%.

Denis J. Walsh, III has been running the fund for 7 years and currently receives a manager quality ranking of 11 (0=worst, 99=best). This fund offers only a moderate level of risk but investors looking for strong performance are still waiting.

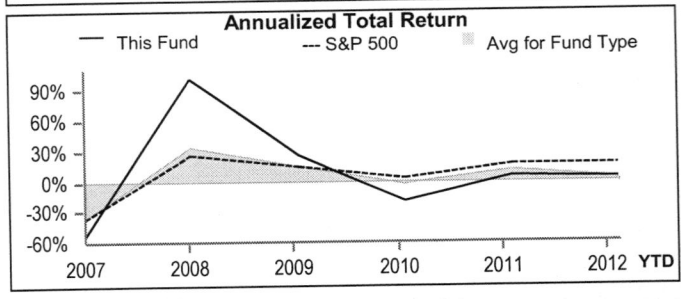

BlackRock Res & Commdty Strat Trus (BCX)

D   **Weak**

Fund Family: BlackRock Inc
Fund Type: Income
Inception Date: March 30, 2011

Data Date	Investment Rating	Net Assets ($Mil)	Price	Performance Rating/Pts	Total Return Y-T-D	Risk Rating/Pts
12-12	D	783.79	12.82	D / 2.2	5.46%	C+ / 5.8

Major Rating Factors:
Disappointing performance is the major factor driving the D (Weak) TheStreet.com Investment Rating for BlackRock Res & Commdty Strat Trus. The fund currently has a performance rating of D (Weak) based on an annualized return of 0.00% over the last three years and a total return of 5.46% year to date 2012. Factored into the performance evaluation is an expense ratio of 1.13% (low).

The fund's risk rating is currently C+ (Fair). It carries a beta of 0.00, meaning the fund's expected move will be 0.0% for every 10% move in the market. Volatility, as measured by both the semi-deviation and a drawdown factor, is considered low. As of December 31, 2012, BlackRock Res & Commdty Strat Trus traded at a discount of 14.59% below its net asset value, which is better than its one-year historical average discount of 8.01%.

This fund has been team managed for 2 years and currently receives a manager quality ranking of 7 (0=worst, 99=best). This fund offers only a moderate level of risk but investors looking for strong performance are still waiting.

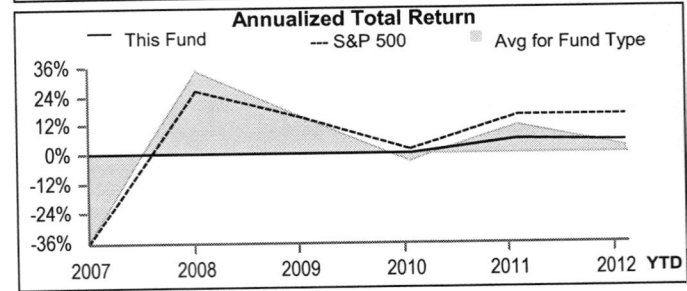

BlackRock S&P Qual Rkg Glob Eq Mgd (BQY)

C-   **Fair**

Fund Family: BlackRock Inc
Fund Type: Global
Inception Date: May 26, 2004

Major Rating Factors: Middle of the road best describes BlackRock S&P Qual Rkg Glob Eq Mgd whose TheStreet.com Investment Rating is currently a C- (Fair). The fund currently has a performance rating of C- (Fair) based on an annualized return of 9.26% over the last three years and a total return of 1.47% year to date 2012. Factored into the performance evaluation is an expense ratio of 1.19% (average).

The fund's risk rating is currently B (Good). It carries a beta of 0.68, meaning the fund's expected move will be 6.8% for every 10% move in the market. Volatility, as measured by both the semi-deviation and a drawdown factor, is considered low. As of December 31, 2012, BlackRock S&P Qual Rkg Glob Eq Mgd traded at a discount of 10.53% below its net asset value, which is better than its one-year historical average discount of 7.31%.

Kathleen M. Anderson has been running the fund for 3 years and currently receives a manager quality ranking of 81 (0=worst, 99=best). If you desire an average level of risk, then this fund may be an option.

Data Date	Investment Rating	Net Assets ($Mil)	Price	Perfor-mance Rating/Pts	Total Return Y-T-D	Risk Rating/Pts
12-12	C-	82.10	12.24	C- / 3.7	1.47%	B / 8.1
2011	C+	79.10	12.03	C+ / 5.7	1.58%	B- / 7.9
2010	C-	80.72	13.26	C / 4.3	13.87%	C / 4.9
2009	D+	67.40	12.52	D+ / 2.8	32.50%	C+ / 5.7

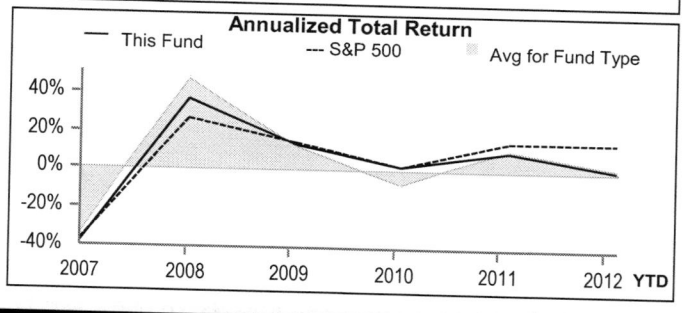

BlackRock Senior High Income Fund (ARK)

B   **Good**

Fund Family: BlackRock Inc
Fund Type: Corporate - High Yield
Inception Date: April 30, 1993

Major Rating Factors: Strong performance is the major factor driving the B (Good) TheStreet.com Investment Rating for BlackRock Senior High Income Fund. The fund currently has a performance rating of B- (Good) based on an annualized return of 16.18% over the last three years and a total return of 5.48% year to date 2012. Factored into the performance evaluation is an expense ratio of 1.26% (average).

The fund's risk rating is currently B (Good). It carries a beta of 0.85, meaning the fund's expected move will be 8.5% for every 10% move in the market. Volatility, as measured by both the semi-deviation and a drawdown factor, is considered low. As of December 31, 2012, BlackRock Senior High Income Fund traded at a discount of 3.23% below its net asset value, which is better than its one-year historical average premium of .41%.

Leland T. Hart has been running the fund for 4 years and currently receives a manager quality ranking of 79 (0=worst, 99=best). If you desire only a moderate level of risk and strong performance, then this fund is an excellent option.

Data Date	Investment Rating	Net Assets ($Mil)	Price	Perfor-mance Rating/Pts	Total Return Y-T-D	Risk Rating/Pts
12-12	B	239.45	4.20	B- / 7.3	5.48%	B / 8.6
2011	B-	226.90	3.85	C+ / 6.8	0.26%	B- / 7.6
2010	D+	225.89	3.89	C- / 3.3	19.17%	C / 4.8
2009	D-	196.31	3.50	D / 2.0	47.80%	C- / 3.9

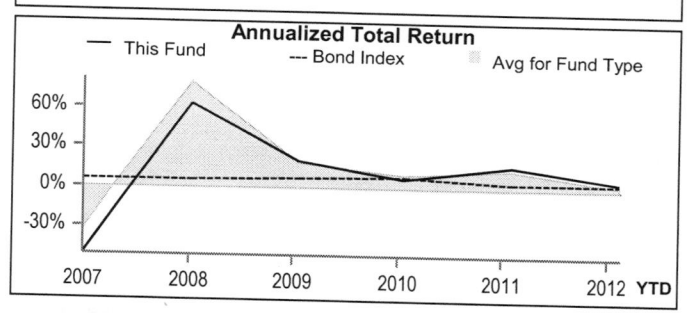

BlackRock Strategic Bond Trust (BHD)

B+   **Good**

Fund Family: BlackRock Inc
Fund Type: Corporate - High Yield
Inception Date: February 26, 2002

Major Rating Factors: Strong performance is the major factor driving the B+ (Good) TheStreet.com Investment Rating for BlackRock Strategic Bond Trust. The fund currently has a performance rating of B (Good) based on an annualized return of 15.88% over the last three years and a total return of 6.24% year to date 2012. Factored into the performance evaluation is an expense ratio of 1.45% (average).

The fund's risk rating is currently B (Good). It carries a beta of 0.67, meaning the fund's expected move will be 6.7% for every 10% move in the market. Volatility, as measured by both the semi-deviation and a drawdown factor, is considered low. As of December 31, 2012, BlackRock Strategic Bond Trust traded at a discount of 1.62% below its net asset value, which is better than its one-year historical average premium of 1.14%.

James E. Keenan has been running the fund for 6 years and currently receives a manager quality ranking of 83 (0=worst, 99=best). If you desire only a moderate level of risk and strong performance, then this fund is an excellent option.

Data Date	Investment Rating	Net Assets ($Mil)	Price	Perfor-mance Rating/Pts	Total Return Y-T-D	Risk Rating/Pts
12-12	B+	4.39	14.59	B / 7.8	6.24%	B / 8.4
2011	B+	94.90	12.99	B- / 7.3	1.08%	B+ / 9.1
2010	C+	95.79	12.70	C+ / 6.9	12.20%	C+ / 5.8
2009	C+	85.58	12.08	C+ / 5.6	42.64%	C+ / 6.2

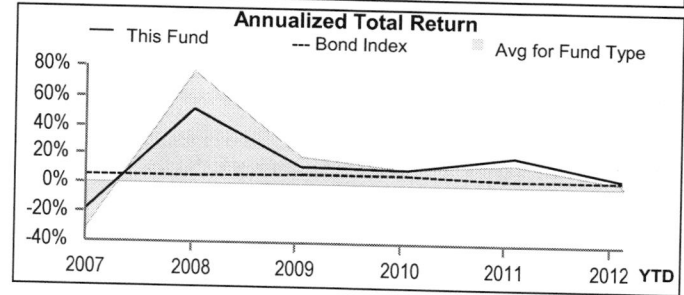

BlackRock Strategic Municipal Tr (BSD)

A+ **Excellent**

Fund Family: BlackRock Inc
Fund Type: Municipal - National
Inception Date: August 24, 1999

Major Rating Factors:
Exceptional performance is the major factor driving the A+ (Excellent) TheStreet.com Investment Rating for BlackRock Strategic Municipal Tr. The fund currently has a performance rating of A- (Excellent) based on an annualized return of 16.32% over the last three years and a total return of 4.65% year to date 2012. Factored into the performance evaluation is an expense ratio of 1.55% (average).

The fund's risk rating is currently B (Good). It carries a beta of 1.99, meaning it is expected to move 19.9% for every 10% move in the market. Volatility, as measured by both the semi-deviation and a drawdown factor, is considered low. As of December 31, 2012, BlackRock Strategic Municipal Tr traded at a discount of 2.69% below its net asset value, which is better than its one-year historical average premium of .66%.

Theodore R. Jaeckel, Jr. has been running the fund for 7 years and currently receives a manager quality ranking of 63 (0=worst, 99=best). If you desire only a moderate level of risk and strong performance, then this fund is an excellent option.

Data Date	Investment Rating	Net Assets ($Mil)	Price	Performance Rating/Pts	Total Return Y-T-D	Risk Rating/Pts
12-12	A+	105.31	14.84	A- / 9.2	4.65%	B / 8.5
2011	A+	99.10	13.68	A / 9.5	0.95%	B / 8.8
2010	C-	94.74	12.32	C- / 3.0	10.86%	B- / 7.0
2009	D+	79.82	11.89	D / 2.0	48.29%	C+ / 6.4

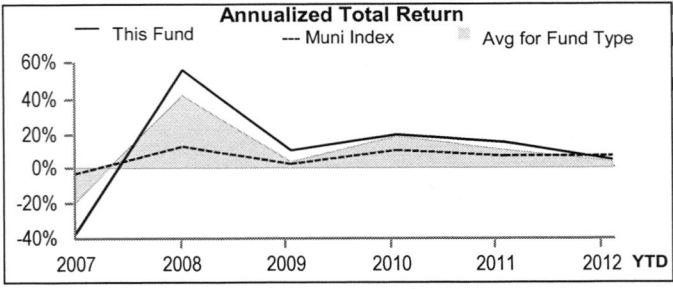

BlackRock Utility & Infrastructure (BUI)

D+ **Weak**

Fund Family: BlackRock Fund Advisors
Fund Type: Global
Inception Date: November 23, 2011

Major Rating Factors:
Disappointing performance is the major factor driving the D+ (Weak) TheStreet.com Investment Rating for BlackRock Utility & Infrastructure. The fund currently has a performance rating of D- (Weak) based on an annualized return of 0.00% over the last three years and a total return of 4.08% year to date 2012.

The fund's risk rating is currently B (Good). It carries a beta of 0.00, meaning the fund's expected move will be 0.0% for every 10% move in the market. Volatility, as measured by both the semi-deviation and a drawdown factor, is considered low. As of December 31, 2012, BlackRock Utility & Infrastructure traded at a discount of 11.00% below its net asset value, which is better than its one-year historical average discount of 4.90%.

Daniel J. Neumann has been running the fund for 2 years and currently receives a manager quality ranking of 28 (0=worst, 99=best). This fund offers only a moderate level of risk but investors looking for strong performance are still waiting.

Data Date	Investment Rating	Net Assets ($Mil)	Price	Performance Rating/Pts	Total Return Y-T-D	Risk Rating/Pts
12-12	D+	330.60	17.89	D- / 1.4	4.08%	B / 8.7

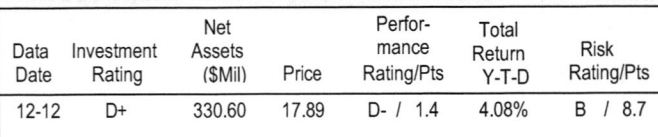

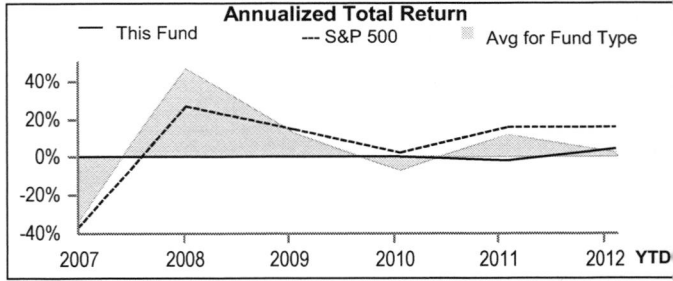

BlackRock VA Muni Bond Trust (BHV)

C+ **Fair**

Fund Family: BlackRock Inc
Fund Type: Municipal - Single State
Inception Date: April 26, 2002

Major Rating Factors: Middle of the road best describes BlackRock VA Muni Bond Trust whose TheStreet.com Investment Rating is currently a C+ (Fair). The fund currently has a performance rating of C+ (Fair) based on an annualized return of 10.01% over the last three years and a total return of 7.98% year to date 2012. Factored into the performance evaluation is an expense ratio of 1.64% (above average).

The fund's risk rating is currently B- (Good). It carries a beta of 1.98, meaning it is expected to move 19.8% for every 10% move in the market. Volatility, as measured by both the semi-deviation and a drawdown factor, is considered low. As of December 31, 2012, BlackRock VA Muni Bond Trust traded at a premium of 15.08% above its net asset value, which is better than its one-year historical average premium of 22.11%.

Theodore R. Jaeckel, Jr. has been running the fund for 7 years and currently receives a manager quality ranking of 24 (0=worst, 99=best). If you desire an average level of risk, then this fund may be an option.

Data Date	Investment Rating	Net Assets ($Mil)	Price	Performance Rating/Pts	Total Return Y-T-D	Risk Rating/Pts
12-12	C+	26.47	19.31	C+ / 6.4	7.98%	B- / 7.8
2011	B+	24.70	20.11	B+ / 8.3	2.78%	B / 8.2
2010	B-	25.14	17.66	C / 5.5	3.71%	B- / 7.3
2009	C+	23.48	18.07	C / 4.9	12.81%	B- / 7.7

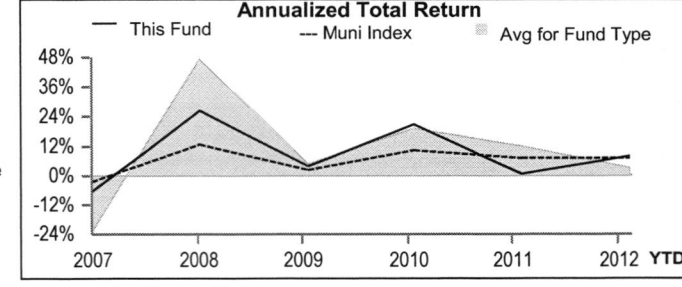

Blackstone / GSO Lng-Sht Credit In (BGX)

B-   **Good**

Fund Family: GSO/Blackstone Debt Funds Managemen
Fund Type: Loan Participation
Inception Date: January 26, 2011

Major Rating Factors: Blackstone / GSO Lng-Sht Credit In receives a TheStreet.com Investment Rating of B- (Good). The fund currently has a performance rating of C+ (Fair) based on an annualized return of 0.00% over the last three years and a total return of 2.13% year to date 2012. Factored into the performance evaluation is an expense ratio of 1.78% (above average).

The fund's risk rating is currently B (Good). It carries a beta of 0.00, meaning the fund's expected move will be 0.0% for every 10% move in the market. Volatility, as measured by both the semi-deviation and a drawdown factor, is considered low. As of December 31, 2012, Blackstone / GSO Lng-Sht Credit In traded at a discount of 2.14% below its net asset value, which is better than its one-year historical average discount of .78%.

James M. Didden, Jr. has been running the fund for 2 years and currently receives a manager quality ranking of 98 (0=worst, 99=best). If you desire an average level of risk, then this fund may be an option.

Data Date	Investment Rating	Net Assets ($Mil)	Price	Performance Rating/Pts	Total Return Y-T-D	Risk Rating/Pts
12-12	B-	229.73	18.75	C+ / 6.5	2.13%	B / 8.3

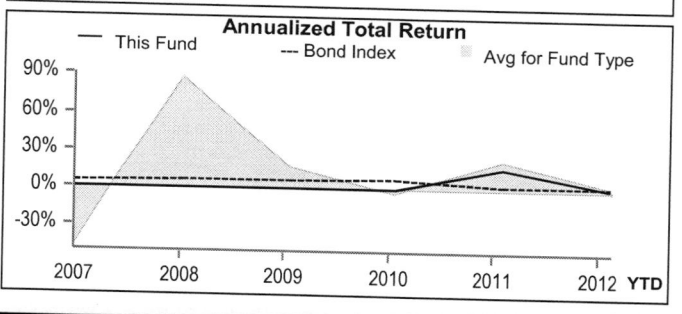

Blackstone/GSO Sr Floating Rate Tr (BSL)

B+   **Good**

Fund Family: GSO/Blackstone Debt Funds Managemen
Fund Type: Loan Participation
Inception Date: May 26, 2010

Major Rating Factors: Strong performance is the major factor driving the B+ (Good) TheStreet.com Investment Rating for Blackstone/GSO Sr Floating Rate Tr. The fund currently has a performance rating of B (Good) based on an annualized return of 0.00% over the last three years and a total return of 1.67% year to date 2012. Factored into the performance evaluation is an expense ratio of 2.79% (high).

The fund's risk rating is currently B (Good). It carries a beta of 0.00, meaning the fund's expected move will be 0.0% for every 10% move in the market. Volatility, as measured by both the semi-deviation and a drawdown factor, is considered low. As of December 31, 2012, Blackstone/GSO Sr Floating Rate Tr traded at a premium of 4.58% above its net asset value, which is worse than its one-year historical average premium of 1.81%.

Debra Anderson currently receives a manager quality ranking of 97 (0=worst, 99=best). If you desire only a moderate level of risk and strong performance, then this fund is an excellent option.

Data Date	Investment Rating	Net Assets ($Mil)	Price	Performance Rating/Pts	Total Return Y-T-D	Risk Rating/Pts
12-12	B+	285.30	20.33	B / 7.8	1.67%	B / 8.3
2011	C-	285.10	18.36	D+ / 2.4	3.43%	B / 8.2

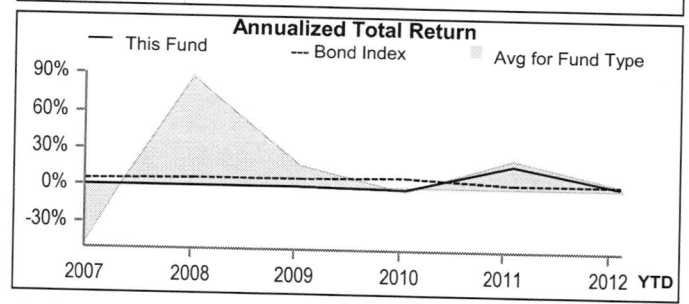

Boulder Growth&Income Fund (BIF)

C   **Fair**

Fund Family: Boulder Investment Advisors LLC
Fund Type: Growth and Income
Inception Date: December 7, 1972

Major Rating Factors: Middle of the road best describes Boulder Growth&Income Fund whose TheStreet.com Investment Rating is currently a C (Fair). The fund currently has a performance rating of C (Fair) based on an annualized return of 7.57% over the last three years and a total return of 5.69% year to date 2012. Factored into the performance evaluation is an expense ratio of 2.84% (high).

The fund's risk rating is currently B (Good). It carries a beta of 0.74, meaning the fund's expected move will be 7.4% for every 10% move in the market. Volatility, as measured by both the semi-deviation and a drawdown factor, is considered low. As of December 31, 2012, Boulder Growth&Income Fund traded at a discount of 26.99% below its net asset value, which is better than its one-year historical average discount of 21.67%.

Stewart R. Horejsi has been running the fund for 41 years and currently receives a manager quality ranking of 36 (0=worst, 99=best). If you desire an average level of risk, then this fund may be an option.

Data Date	Investment Rating	Net Assets ($Mil)	Price	Performance Rating/Pts	Total Return Y-T-D	Risk Rating/Pts
12-12	C	186.67	6.33	C / 4.7	5.69%	B / 8.0
2011	C-	185.00	5.74	D+ / 2.7	1.05%	B / 8.0
2010	D	169.15	6.23	D- / 1.1	8.35%	C / 5.3
2009	D	148.23	5.75	D / 1.8	18.80%	C+ / 5.6

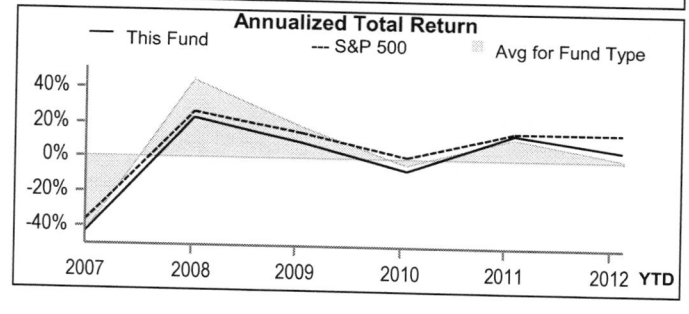

Boulder Total Return Fund (BTF)   B-   Good

Fund Family: Boulder Investment Advisors LLC
Fund Type: Income
Inception Date: February 19, 1993

Major Rating Factors: Strong performance is the major factor driving the B- (Good) TheStreet.com Investment Rating for Boulder Total Return Fund. The fund currently has a performance rating of B- (Good) based on an annualized return of 14.28% over the last three years and a total return of 5.82% year to date 2012. Factored into the performance evaluation is an expense ratio of 2.12% (high).

The fund's risk rating is currently B- (Good). It carries a beta of 0.90, meaning that its performance tracks fairly well with that of the overall stock market. Volatility, as measured by both the semi-deviation and a drawdown factor, is considered low. As of December 31, 2012, Boulder Total Return Fund traded at a discount of 24.96% below its net asset value, which is better than its one-year historical average discount of 20.95%.

Stewart R. Horejsi has been running the fund for 20 years and currently receives a manager quality ranking of 68 (0=worst, 99=best). If you desire only a moderate level of risk and strong performance, then this fund is an excellent option.

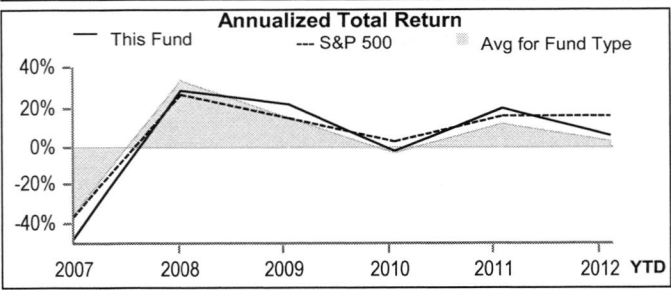

Data Date	Investment Rating	Net Assets ($Mil)	Price	Performance Rating/Pts	Total Return Y-T-D	Risk Rating/Pts
12-12	B-	234.10	18.04	B- / 7.3	5.82%	B- / 7.7
2011	C-	235.10	15.10	C / 4.3	1.59%	B- / 7.6
2010	D	194.19	15.52	D / 1.9	22.01%	C / 4.9
2009	D-	155.03	12.72	D- / 1.3	24.11%	C / 5.2

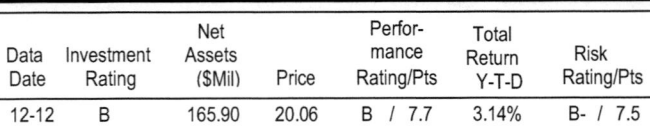

Brookfield Gl Lstd Infr Inc Fd (INF)   B   Good

Fund Family: Brookfield Investment Management In
Fund Type: Global
Inception Date: August 26, 2011

Major Rating Factors: Strong performance is the major factor driving the B (Good) TheStreet.com Investment Rating for Brookfield Gl Lstd Infr Inc Fd. The fund currently has a performance rating of B (Good) based on an annualized return of 0.00% over the last three years and a total return of 3.14% year to date 2012.

The fund's risk rating is currently B- (Good). It carries a beta of 0.00, meaning the fund's expected move will be 0.0% for every 10% move in the market. Volatility, as measured by both the semi-deviation and a drawdown factor, is considered low. As of December 31, 2012, Brookfield Gl Lstd Infr Inc Fd traded at a discount of 10.37% below its net asset value, which is better than its one-year historical average discount of 7.48%.

This fund has been team managed for 2 years and currently receives a manager quality ranking of 87 (0=worst, 99=best). If you desire only a moderate level of risk and strong performance, then this fund is an excellent option.

Data Date	Investment Rating	Net Assets ($Mil)	Price	Performance Rating/Pts	Total Return Y-T-D	Risk Rating/Pts
12-12	B	165.90	20.06	B / 7.7	3.14%	B- / 7.5

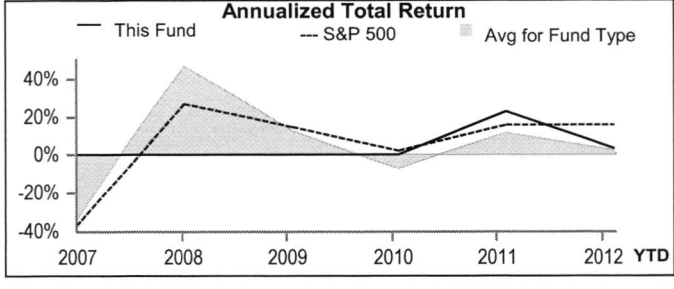

Calamos Convertible Opport&Income (CHI)   C   Fair

Fund Family: Calamos Advisors LLC
Fund Type: Growth and Income
Inception Date: June 25, 2002

Major Rating Factors: Middle of the road best describes Calamos Convertible Opport&Income whose TheStreet.com Investment Rating is currently a C (Fair). The fund currently has a performance rating of C- (Fair) based on an annualized return of 8.98% over the last three years and a total return of 4.52% year to date 2012. Factored into the performance evaluation is an expense ratio of 1.55% (average).

The fund's risk rating is currently B (Good). It carries a beta of 0.67, meaning the fund's expected move will be 6.7% for every 10% move in the market. Volatility, as measured by both the semi-deviation and a drawdown factor, is considered low. As of December 31, 2012, Calamos Convertible Opport&Income traded at a discount of 5.91% below its net asset value, which is better than its one-year historical average discount of .26%.

John P. Calamos, Sr. has been running the fund for 11 years and currently receives a manager quality ranking of 62 (0=worst, 99=best). If you desire an average level of risk, then this fund may be an option.

Data Date	Investment Rating	Net Assets ($Mil)	Price	Performance Rating/Pts	Total Return Y-T-D	Risk Rating/Pts
12-12	C	827.34	11.94	C- / 4.0	4.52%	B / 8.2
2011	C+	860.64	11.26	C / 5.5	3.73%	B / 8.2
2010	B-	733.71	13.18	B- / 7.4	17.29%	C / 5.0
2009	C-	492.27	12.32	C- / 3.9	54.54%	C / 5.0

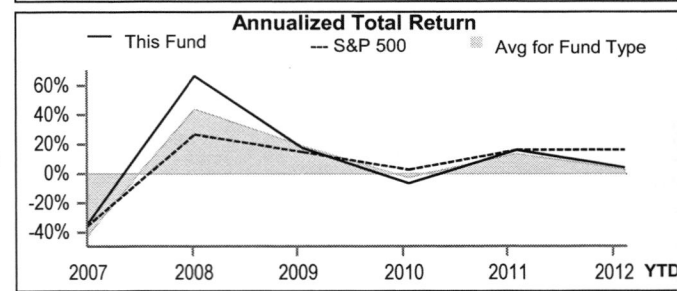

Calamos Convertible&High Income (CHY)

C   **Fair**

Fund Family: Calamos Advisors LLC
Fund Type: Growth and Income
Inception Date: May 28, 2003

Major Rating Factors: Middle of the road best describes Calamos Convertible&High Income whose TheStreet.com Investment Rating is currently a C (Fair). The fund currently has a performance rating of C (Fair) based on an annualized return of 10.34% over the last three years and a total return of 4.53% year to date 2012. Factored into the performance evaluation is an expense ratio of 1.61% (above average).

The fund's risk rating is currently B (Good). It carries a beta of 0.69, meaning the fund's expected move will be 6.9% for every 10% move in the market. Volatility, as measured by both the semi-deviation and a drawdown factor, is considered low. As of December 31, 2012, Calamos Convertible&High Income traded at a discount of 8.78% below its net asset value, which is better than its one-year historical average discount of 3.78%.

John P. Calamos, Sr. has been running the fund for 10 years and currently receives a manager quality ranking of 72 (0=worst, 99=best). If you desire an average level of risk, then this fund may be an option.

Data Date	Investment Rating	Net Assets ($Mil)	Price	Performance Rating/Pts	Total Return Y-T-D	Risk Rating/Pts
12-12	C	917.54	12.15	C / 4.3	4.53%	B / 8.0
2011	B-	973.05	11.56	C+ / 6.6	4.76%	B / 8.0
2010	C+	896.19	12.66	B- / 7.3	19.18%	C / 5.0
2009	C-	658.52	11.54	C- / 4.0	45.58%	C / 5.1

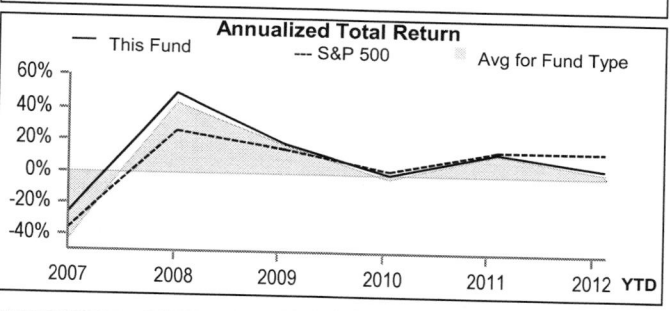

Calamos Global Dynamic Income Fd (CHW)

C+   **Fair**

Fund Family: Calamos Advisors LLC
Fund Type: Global
Inception Date: June 26, 2007

Major Rating Factors: Middle of the road best describes Calamos Global Dynamic Income Fd whose TheStreet.com Investment Rating is currently a C+ (Fair). The fund currently has a performance rating of C+ (Fair) based on an annualized return of 11.38% over the last three years and a total return of 4.91% year to date 2012. Factored into the performance evaluation is an expense ratio of 1.93% (above average).

The fund's risk rating is currently B- (Good). It carries a beta of 0.93, meaning that its performance tracks fairly well with that of the overall stock market. Volatility, as measured by both the semi-deviation and a drawdown factor, is considered low. As of December 31, 2012, Calamos Global Dynamic Income Fd traded at a discount of 13.11% below its net asset value, which is better than its one-year historical average discount of 9.21%.

John P. Calamos, Sr. has been running the fund for 6 years and currently receives a manager quality ranking of 84 (0=worst, 99=best). If you desire an average level of risk, then this fund may be an option.

Data Date	Investment Rating	Net Assets ($Mil)	Price	Performance Rating/Pts	Total Return Y-T-D	Risk Rating/Pts
12-12	C+	534.74	8.35	C+ / 6.0	4.91%	B- / 7.5
2011	C	620.56	7.30	C / 4.9	2.88%	B- / 7.2
2010	D+	534.65	8.37	C- / 3.5	15.01%	C / 4.5
2009	B+	428.98	7.86	B+ / 8.9	45.02%	C / 4.8

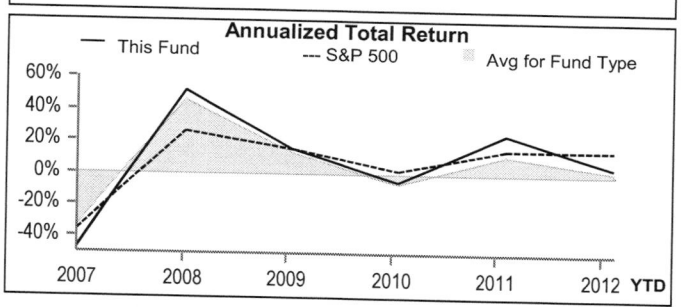

Calamos Global Total Return Fund (CGO)

C-   **Fair**

Fund Family: Calamos Advisors LLC
Fund Type: Growth and Income
Inception Date: October 27, 2005

Major Rating Factors: Middle of the road best describes Calamos Global Total Return Fund whose TheStreet.com Investment Rating is currently a C- (Fair). The fund currently has a performance rating of C- (Fair) based on an annualized return of 6.84% over the last three years and a total return of 3.28% year to date 2012. Factored into the performance evaluation is an expense ratio of 1.90% (above average).

The fund's risk rating is currently B- (Good). It carries a beta of 0.82, meaning the fund's expected move will be 8.2% for every 10% move in the market. Volatility, as measured by both the semi-deviation and a drawdown factor, is considered low. As of December 31, 2012, Calamos Global Total Return Fund traded at a discount of 4.65% below its net asset value, which is better than its one-year historical average discount of .84%.

John P. Calamos, Sr. has been running the fund for 8 years and currently receives a manager quality ranking of 40 (0=worst, 99=best). If you desire an average level of risk, then this fund may be an option.

Data Date	Investment Rating	Net Assets ($Mil)	Price	Performance Rating/Pts	Total Return Y-T-D	Risk Rating/Pts
12-12	C-	119.60	13.74	C- / 3.3	3.28%	B- / 7.6
2011	B-	131.71	13.64	C+ / 6.7	1.10%	B- / 7.8
2010	C-	117.48	14.60	C / 4.3	10.83%	C / 5.3
2009	C+	92.94	14.35	C+ / 6.6	56.52%	C / 5.1

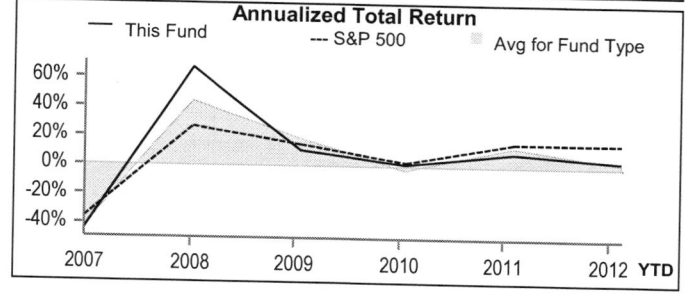

Calamos Strategic Total Return Fun (CSQ)

C+ **Fair**

Fund Family: Calamos Advisors LLC
Fund Type: Growth and Income
Inception Date: March 26, 2004

Data Date	Investment Rating	Net Assets ($Mil)	Price	Performance Rating/Pts	Total Return Y-T-D	Risk Rating/Pts
12-12	C+	1,567.88	9.81	C+ / 6.9	4.89%	B- / 7.7
2011	C+	1,776.33	8.35	C+ / 5.8	3.59%	B- / 7.5
2010	D	1,596.21	9.26	C- / 3.1	13.63%	C / 4.6
2009	D	1,177.69	8.76	D+ / 2.5	47.54%	C / 5.0

Major Rating Factors: Middle of the road best describes Calamos Strategic Total Return Fun whose TheStreet.com Investment Rating is currently a C+ (Fair). The fund currently has a performance rating of C+ (Fair) based on an annualized return of 13.07% over the last three years and a total return of 4.89% year to date 2012. Factored into the performance evaluation is an expense ratio of 1.93% (above average).

The fund's risk rating is currently B- (Good). It carries a beta of 1.07, meaning that its performance tracks fairly well with that of the overall stock market. Volatility, as measured by both the semi-deviation and a drawdown factor, is considered low. As of December 31, 2012, Calamos Strategic Total Return Fun traded at a discount of 9.67% below its net asset value, which is better than its one-year historical average discount of 6.86%.

John P. Calamos, Sr. has been running the fund for 9 years and currently receives a manager quality ranking of 55 (0=worst, 99=best). If you desire an average level of risk, then this fund may be an option.

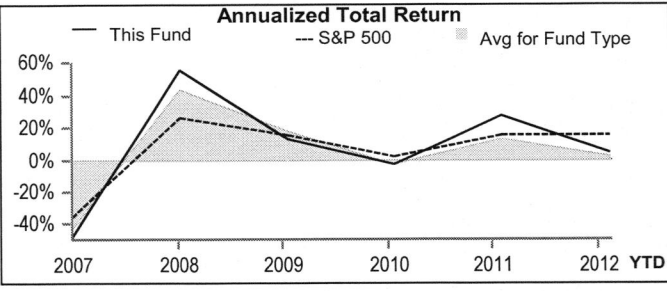

Canadian General Investments Ltd (T.CGI)

D **Weak**

Fund Family: Morgan Meighen & Associates Limited
Fund Type: Foreign
Inception Date: N/A

Data Date	Investment Rating	Net Assets ($Mil)	Price	Performance Rating/Pts	Total Return Y-T-D	Risk Rating/Pts
12-12	D	288.01	15.75	D+ / 2.8	1.27%	C / 4.9
2011	C	425.80	16.00	C+ / 6.8	0.63%	C / 5.2
2010	D-	288.01	19.18	C- / 3.2	27.89%	D+ / 2.9
2009	D-	288.01	15.83	D+ / 2.7	67.47%	D+ / 2.9

Major Rating Factors:
Disappointing performance is the major factor driving the D (Weak) TheStreet.com Investment Rating for Canadian General Investments Ltd. The fund currently has a performance rating of D+ (Weak) based on an annualized return of 5.63% over the last three years and a total return of 1.27% year to date 2012. Factored into the performance evaluation is an expense ratio of 3.57% (high).

The fund's risk rating is currently C (Fair). It carries a beta of 0.58, meaning the fund's expected move will be 5.8% for every 10% move in the market. Volatility, as measured by both the semi-deviation and a drawdown factor, is considered average. As of December 31, 2012, Canadian General Investments Ltd traded at a discount of 29.44% below its net asset value, which is better than its one-year historical average discount of 27.61%.

Michael A. Smedley has been running the fund for 25 years and currently receives a manager quality ranking of 70 (0=worst, 99=best). This fund offers an average level of risk but investors looking for strong performance will be frustrated.

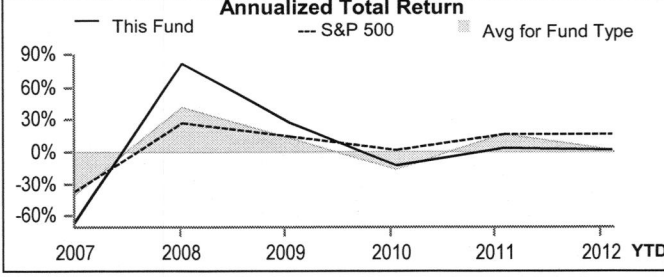

Canadian World Fund Limited (T.CWF)

D- **Weak**

Fund Family: Morgan Meighen & Associates Limited
Fund Type: Global
Inception Date: February 25, 1994

Data Date	Investment Rating	Net Assets ($Mil)	Price	Performance Rating/Pts	Total Return Y-T-D	Risk Rating/Pts
12-12	D-	20.47	3.45	D / 1.9	1.45%	C / 4.4
2011	D+	35.50	3.56	C / 5.2	0.84%	C / 4.9
2010	E	20.47	4.14	D- / 1.4	20.70%	D / 1.8
2009	E	20.47	3.43	D- / 1.0	43.51%	D+ / 2.5

Major Rating Factors:
Disappointing performance is the major factor driving the D- (Weak) TheStreet.com Investment Rating for Canadian World Fund Limited. The fund currently has a performance rating of D (Weak) based on an annualized return of 1.47% over the last three years and a total return of 1.45% year to date 2012. Factored into the performance evaluation is an expense ratio of 3.04% (high).

The fund's risk rating is currently C (Fair). It carries a beta of 0.51, meaning the fund's expected move will be 5.1% for every 10% move in the market. Volatility, as measured by both the semi-deviation and a drawdown factor, is considered average. As of December 31, 2012, Canadian World Fund Limited traded at a discount of 36.11% below its net asset value, which is better than its one-year historical average discount of 33.14%.

Alex Sulzer currently receives a manager quality ranking of 36 (0=worst, 99=best). This fund offers an average level of risk but investors looking for strong performance will be frustrated.

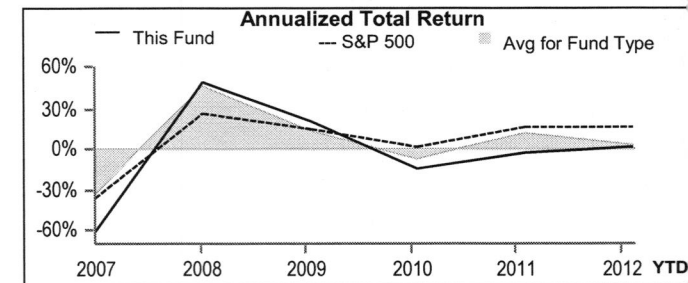

CBRE Clarion Global Real Estate In (IGR)

B+   **Good**

Fund Family: CBRE Clarion Securities LLC
Fund Type: Growth and Income
Inception Date: February 25, 2004

Major Rating Factors: Strong performance is the major factor driving the B+ (Good) TheStreet.com Investment Rating for CBRE Clarion Global Real Estate In. The fund currently has a performance rating of B+ (Good) based on an annualized return of 17.61% over the last three years and a total return of 2.71% year to date 2012. Factored into the performance evaluation is an expense ratio of 1.03% (low).

The fund's risk rating is currently B- (Good). It carries a beta of 1.11, meaning it is expected to move 11.1% for every 10% move in the market. Volatility, as measured by both the semi-deviation and a drawdown factor, is considered low. As of December 31, 2012, CBRE Clarion Global Real Estate In traded at a discount of 7.90% below its net asset value, which is worse than its one-year historical average discount of 8.40%.

T. Ritson Ferguson has been running the fund for 7 years and currently receives a manager quality ranking of 85 (0=worst, 99=best). If you desire only a moderate level of risk and strong performance, then this fund is an excellent option.

Data Date	Investment Rating	Net Assets ($Mil)	Price	Performance Rating/Pts	Total Return Y-T-D	Risk Rating/Pts
12-12	B+	949.58	8.86	B+ / 8.6	2.71%	B- / 7.5
2011	C+	949.60	6.84	B / 7.6	3.36%	C+ / 6.7
2010	D-	839.24	7.75	D / 1.7	31.18%	C- / 3.6
2009	E+	570.07	6.37	E+ / 0.8	68.37%	C- / 3.6

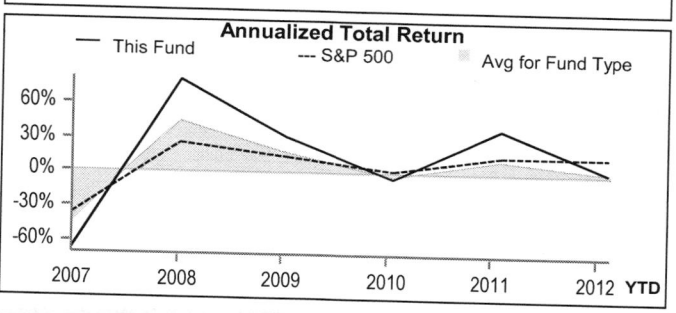

Central Europe & Russia Fund (CEE)

D+   **Weak**

Fund Family: Deutsche Asset Mgmt International G
Fund Type: Foreign
Inception Date: March 6, 1990

Major Rating Factors: Central Europe & Russia Fund receives a TheStreet.com Investment Rating of D+ (Weak). The fund currently has a performance rating of C (Fair) based on an annualized return of 5.68% over the last three years and a total return of 1.65% year to date 2012. Factored into the performance evaluation is an expense ratio of 1.11% (low).

The fund's risk rating is currently C (Fair). It carries a beta of 1.36, meaning it is expected to move 13.6% for every 10% move in the market. Volatility, as measured by both the semi-deviation and a drawdown factor, is considered average. As of December 31, 2012, Central Europe & Russia Fund traded at a discount of 11.76% below its net asset value, which is better than its one-year historical average discount of 9.59%.

Rainer Vermehren currently receives a manager quality ranking of 70 (0=worst, 99=best). If you desire an average level of risk, then this fund may be an option.

Data Date	Investment Rating	Net Assets ($Mil)	Price	Performance Rating/Pts	Total Return Y-T-D	Risk Rating/Pts
12-12	D+	505.93	33.92	C / 4.8	1.65%	C / 5.4
2011	C	416.00	28.55	B- / 7.0	1.93%	C+ / 5.8
2010	D-	575.79	41.84	D / 2.1	27.56%	C- / 3.2
2009	D+	353.02	32.99	C / 4.9	91.61%	C- / 3.1

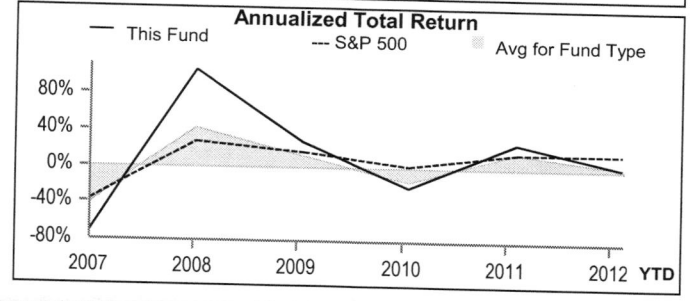

Central Fund of Canada (CEF)

C-   **Fair**

Fund Family: Central Group Alberta Ltd
Fund Type: Precious Metals
Inception Date: September 14, 1983

Major Rating Factors: Middle of the road best describes Central Fund of Canada whose TheStreet.com Investment Rating is currently a C- (Fair). The fund currently has a performance rating of C (Fair) based on an annualized return of 14.14% over the last three years and a total return of 1.66% year to date 2012. Factored into the performance evaluation is an expense ratio of 0.30% (very low).

The fund's risk rating is currently B- (Good). It carries a beta of 1.26, meaning it is expected to move 12.6% for every 10% move in the market. Volatility, as measured by both the semi-deviation and a drawdown factor, is considered low. As of December 31, 2012, Central Fund of Canada traded at a premium of 2.59% above its net asset value, which is better than its one-year historical average premium of 4.19%.

Philip M. Spicer has been running the fund for 7 years and currently receives a manager quality ranking of 28 (0=worst, 99=best). If you desire an average level of risk, then this fund may be an option.

Data Date	Investment Rating	Net Assets ($Mil)	Price	Performance Rating/Pts	Total Return Y-T-D	Risk Rating/Pts
12-12	C-	5,620.88	21.03	C / 4.8	1.66%	B- / 7.0
2011	B-	4,902.00	19.61	B- / 7.2	1.84%	B- / 7.5
2010	A	2,382.34	20.73	A / 9.4	50.52%	C+ / 5.8
2009	B	1,204.00	13.78	B- / 7.1	26.29%	C+ / 6.3

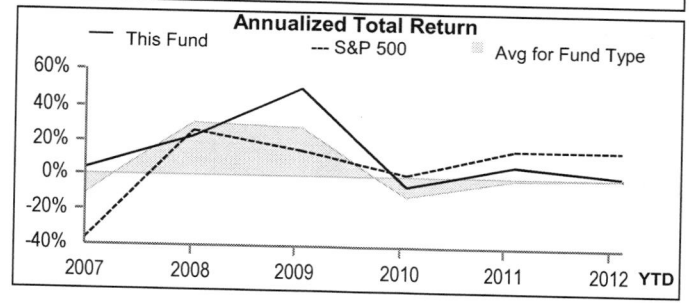

Central Gold-Trust (GTU)   C-   Fair

Fund Family: Central Gold Trust
Fund Type: Precious Metals
Inception Date: September 22, 2006

Major Rating Factors: Middle of the road best describes Central Gold-Trust whose TheStreet.com Investment Rating is currently a C- (Fair). The fund currently has a performance rating of C- (Fair) based on an annualized return of 11.87% over the last three years and a total return of 0.33% year to date 2012. Factored into the performance evaluation is an expense ratio of 0.35% (very low).

The fund's risk rating is currently B- (Good). It carries a beta of 1.00, meaning that its performance tracks fairly well with that of the overall stock market. Volatility, as measured by both the semi-deviation and a drawdown factor, is considered low. As of December 31, 2012, Central Gold-Trust traded at a premium of 2.25% above its net asset value, which is better than its one-year historical average premium of 3.23%.

This fund has been team managed for 10 years and currently receives a manager quality ranking of 32 (0=worst, 99=best). If you desire an average level of risk, then this fund may be an option.

Data Date	Investment Rating	Net Assets ($Mil)	Price	Performance Rating/Pts	Total Return Y-T-D	Risk Rating/Pts
12-12	C-	1,130.49	62.78	C- / 3.7	0.33%	B- / 7.7
2011	B	1,130.50	59.17	B- / 7.3	4.17%	B / 8.0
2010	A+	451.92	54.35	B+ / 8.8	22.44%	B- / 7.5
2009	A+	138.60	44.39	B- / 7.4	12.32%	B- / 7.8

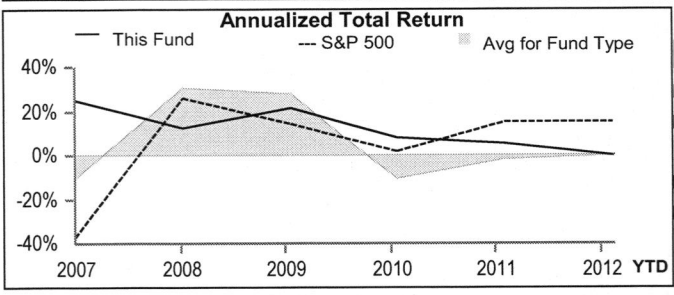

Central Securities (CET)   C-   Fair

Fund Family: Central Securities Corporation
Fund Type: Growth
Inception Date: N/A

Major Rating Factors: Middle of the road best describes Central Securities whose TheStreet.com Investment Rating is currently a C- (Fair). The fund currently has a performance rating of C- (Fair) based on an annualized return of 7.90% over the last three years and a total return of 1.00% year to date 2012. Factored into the performance evaluation is an expense ratio of 0.66% (very low).

The fund's risk rating is currently B- (Good). It carries a beta of 0.94, meaning that its performance tracks fairly well with that of the overall stock market. Volatility, as measured by both the semi-deviation and a drawdown factor, is considered low. As of December 31, 2012, Central Securities traded at a discount of 20.56% below its net asset value, which is better than its one-year historical average discount of 17.65%.

Wilmot H. Kidd, III has been running the fund for 40 years and currently receives a manager quality ranking of 35 (0=worst, 99=best). If you desire an average level of risk, then this fund may be an option.

Data Date	Investment Rating	Net Assets ($Mil)	Price	Performance Rating/Pts	Total Return Y-T-D	Risk Rating/Pts
12-12	C-	556.49	19.98	C- / 3.0	1.00%	B- / 7.8
2011	C	574.20	20.46	C / 5.2	0.98%	B- / 7.8
2010	B+	499.95	21.97	B / 7.7	27.63%	C+ / 6.1
2009	C-	429.43	17.98	C- / 3.1	29.57%	C+ / 6.4

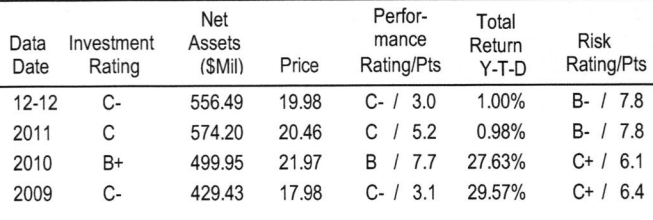

China Fund (CHN)   D   Weak

Fund Family: Martin Currie Inc
Fund Type: Foreign
Inception Date: July 10, 1992

Major Rating Factors:
China Fund receives a TheStreet.com Investment Rating of D (Weak). The fund currently has a performance rating of C- (Fair) based on an annualized return of 2.28% over the last three years and a total return of 2.52% year to date 2012. Factored into the performance evaluation is an expense ratio of 1.01% (low).

The fund's risk rating is currently C+ (Fair). It carries a beta of 0.85, meaning the fund's expected move will be 8.5% for every 10% move in the market. Volatility, as measured by both the semi-deviation and a drawdown factor, is considered low. As of December 31, 2012, China Fund traded at a discount of 6.99% below its net asset value, which is worse than its one-year historical average discount of 8.92%.

Christina Chung has been running the fund for 1 year and currently receives a manager quality ranking of 45 (0=worst, 99=best). If you desire an average level of risk, then this fund may be an option.

Data Date	Investment Rating	Net Assets ($Mil)	Price	Performance Rating/Pts	Total Return Y-T-D	Risk Rating/Pts
12-12	D	660.44	21.41	C- / 3.6	2.52%	C+ / 5.9
2011	D	529.60	20.51	D / 2.1	0.73%	C+ / 6.2
2010	C+	620.47	32.50	B / 8.2	23.60%	C- / 3.5
2009	C+	437.13	28.22	B+ / 8.3	65.10%	C- / 3.8

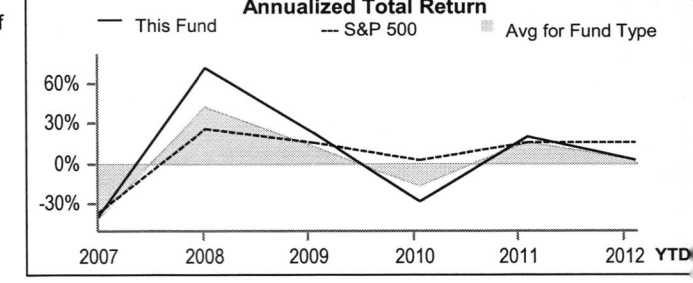

ClearBridge Energy MLP Fund Inc (CEM)

B-   **Good**

Fund Family: Legg Mason Partners Fund Advisor LL
Fund Type: Energy/Natural Resources
Inception Date: June 25, 2010

Major Rating Factors: ClearBridge Energy MLP Fund Inc receives a TheStreet.com Investment Rating of B- (Good). The fund currently has a performance rating of C+ (Fair) based on an annualized return of 0.00% over the last three years and a total return of 8.12% year to date 2012. Factored into the performance evaluation is an expense ratio of 1.71% (above average).

The fund's risk rating is currently B (Good). It carries a beta of 0.00, meaning the fund's expected move will be 0.0% for every 10% move in the market. Volatility, as measured by both the semi-deviation and a drawdown factor, is considered low. As of December 31, 2012, ClearBridge Energy MLP Fund Inc traded at a discount of 2.66% below its net asset value, which is better than its one-year historical average premium of 3.20%.

Christopher Eades currently receives a manager quality ranking of 83 (0=worst, 99=best). If you desire an average level of risk, then this fund may be an option.

Data Date	Investment Rating	Net Assets ($Mil)	Price	Performance Rating/Pts	Total Return Y-T-D	Risk Rating/Pts
12-12	B-	1,363.00	23.03	C+ / 6.8	8.12%	B / 8.1
2011	C	1,441.10	22.44	C+ / 6.9	2.23%	C / 5.2

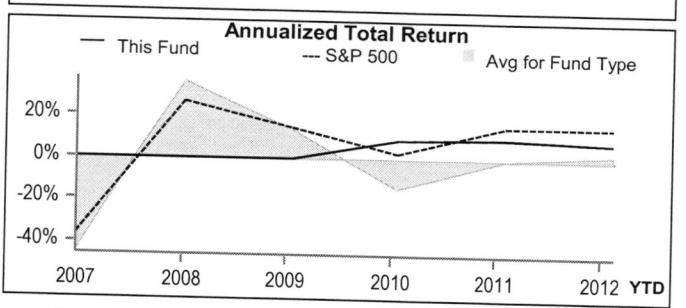

ClearBridge Energy MLP Oppty Fd In (EMO)

B-   **Good**

Fund Family: Legg Mason Partners Fund Advisor LL
Fund Type: Energy/Natural Resources
Inception Date: June 10, 2011

Major Rating Factors: Strong performance is the major factor driving the B- (Good) TheStreet.com Investment Rating for ClearBridge Energy MLP Oppty Fd In. The fund currently has a performance rating of B- (Good) based on an annualized return of 0.00% over the last three years and a total return of 3.82% year to date 2012. Factored into the performance evaluation is an expense ratio of 1.66% (above average).

The fund's risk rating is currently B (Good). It carries a beta of 0.00, meaning the fund's expected move will be 0.0% for every 10% move in the market. Volatility, as measured by both the semi-deviation and a drawdown factor, is considered low. As of December 31, 2012, ClearBridge Energy MLP Oppty Fd In traded at a discount of .29% below its net asset value, which is better than its one-year historical average premium of 1.06%.

Christopher Eades currently receives a manager quality ranking of 93 (0=worst, 99=best). If you desire only a moderate level of risk and strong performance, then this fund is an excellent option.

Data Date	Investment Rating	Net Assets ($Mil)	Price	Performance Rating/Pts	Total Return Y-T-D	Risk Rating/Pts
12-12	B-	568.00	20.70	B- / 7.1	3.82%	B / 8.0

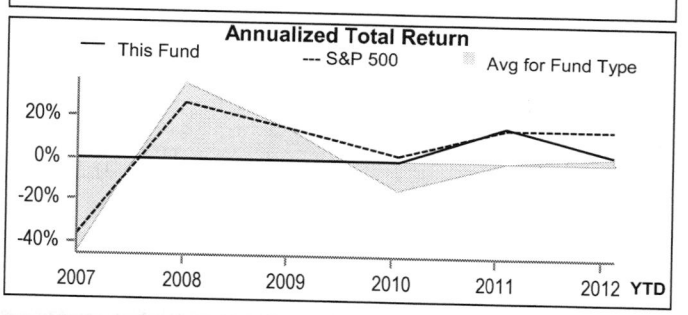

Clough Global Allocation Fund (GLV)

C-   **Fair**

Fund Family: Clough Capital Partners LP
Fund Type: Growth and Income
Inception Date: July 28, 2004

Major Rating Factors: Middle of the road best describes Clough Global Allocation Fund whose TheStreet.com Investment Rating is currently a C- (Fair). The fund currently has a performance rating of C- (Fair) based on an annualized return of 4.97% over the last three years and a total return of 4.09% year to date 2012. Factored into the performance evaluation is an expense ratio of 3.05% (high).

The fund's risk rating is currently B- (Good). It carries a beta of 1.00, meaning that its performance tracks fairly well with that of the overall stock market. Volatility, as measured by both the semi-deviation and a drawdown factor, is considered low. As of December 31, 2012, Clough Global Allocation Fund traded at a discount of 16.36% below its net asset value, which is better than its one-year historical average discount of 13.81%.

Charles I. Clough, Jr. has been running the fund for 9 years and currently receives a manager quality ranking of 21 (0=worst, 99=best). If you desire an average level of risk, then this fund may be an option.

Data Date	Investment Rating	Net Assets ($Mil)	Price	Performance Rating/Pts	Total Return Y-T-D	Risk Rating/Pts
12-12	C-	170.12	13.70	C- / 3.8	4.09%	B- / 7.3
2011	C-	156.20	12.75	C- / 4.2	1.25%	B- / 7.4
2010	D+	176.32	15.76	D+ / 2.9	10.41%	C / 5.5
2009	C-	177.64	15.17	C- / 4.0	49.89%	C+ / 5.6

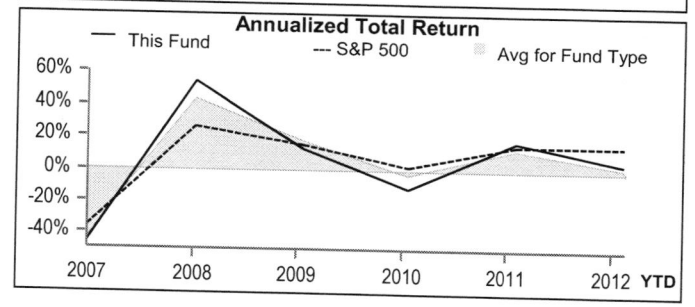

* Denotes ETF Fund

Clough Global Equity Fund (GLQ)   C   Fair

Fund Family: Clough Capital Partners LP
Fund Type: Global
Inception Date: April 26, 2005

Data Date	Investment Rating	Net Assets ($Mil)	Price	Performance Rating/Pts	Total Return Y-T-D	Risk Rating/Pts
12-12	C	277.06	13.00	C / 4.8	5.54%	B- / 7.3
2011	C-	254.70	12.04	C / 4.4	1.25%	B- / 7.4
2010	C-	409.63	15.12	C- / 4.1	15.67%	C / 5.0
2009	C-	290.82	14.19	C- / 4.1	53.37%	C+ / 5.7

Major Rating Factors: Middle of the road best describes Clough Global Equity Fund whose TheStreet.com Investment Rating is currently a C (Fair). The fund currently has a performance rating of C (Fair) based on an annualized return of 6.18% over the last three years and a total return of 5.54% year to date 2012. Factored into the performance evaluation is an expense ratio of 3.43% (high).

The fund's risk rating is currently B- (Good). It carries a beta of 0.84, meaning the fund's expected move will be 8.4% for every 10% move in the market. Volatility, as measured by both the semi-deviation and a drawdown factor, is considered low. As of December 31, 2012, Clough Global Equity Fund traded at a discount of 16.34% below its net asset value, which is better than its one-year historical average discount of 14.36%.

Charles I. Clough, Jr. has been running the fund for 8 years and currently receives a manager quality ranking of 68 (0=worst, 99=best). If you desire an average level of risk, then this fund may be an option.

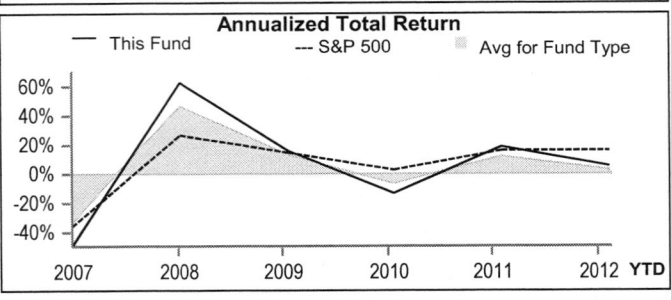

Clough Global Opportunities Fund (GLO)   C   Fair

Fund Family: Clough Capital Partners LP
Fund Type: Global
Inception Date: April 25, 2006

Data Date	Investment Rating	Net Assets ($Mil)	Price	Performance Rating/Pts	Total Return Y-T-D	Risk Rating/Pts
12-12	C	716.21	11.74	C / 4.9	5.28%	B- / 7.3
2011	C-	657.70	10.57	C- / 3.8	1.80%	B- / 7.3
2010	D+	759.60	13.45	C- / 3.7	13.63%	C / 5.2
2009	C-	769.65	12.88	C- / 4.2	48.12%	C+ / 5.7

Major Rating Factors: Middle of the road best describes Clough Global Opportunities Fund whose TheStreet.com Investment Rating is currently a C (Fair). The fund currently has a performance rating of C (Fair) based on an annualized return of 5.88% over the last three years and a total return of 5.28% year to date 2012. Factored into the performance evaluation is an expense ratio of 3.61% (high).

The fund's risk rating is currently B- (Good). It carries a beta of 0.80, meaning the fund's expected move will be 8.0% for every 10% move in the market. Volatility, as measured by both the semi-deviation and a drawdown factor, is considered low. As of December 31, 2012, Clough Global Opportunities Fund traded at a discount of 14.87% below its net asset value, which is better than its one-year historical average discount of 13.99%.

Charles I. Clough, Jr. has been running the fund for 7 years and currently receives a manager quality ranking of 70 (0=worst, 99=best). If you desire an average level of risk, then this fund may be an option.

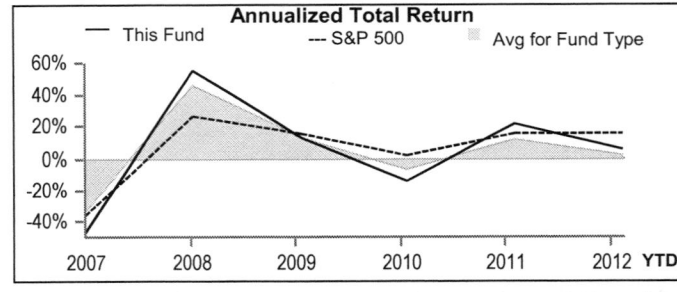

Cohen & Steers Closed-End Opp Fd (FOF)   C   Fair

Fund Family: Cohen & Steers Capital Management I
Fund Type: Global
Inception Date: November 24, 2006

Data Date	Investment Rating	Net Assets ($Mil)	Price	Performance Rating/Pts	Total Return Y-T-D	Risk Rating/Pts
12-12	C	354.40	12.42	C / 4.6	5.07%	B / 8.4
2011	C+	389.10	11.97	C+ / 5.7	2.34%	B / 8.3
2010	C	344.90	13.03	C / 5.0	16.13%	C+ / 6.0
2009	D+	294.25	12.13	D+ / 2.6	38.37%	C / 5.4

Major Rating Factors: Middle of the road best describes Cohen & Steers Closed-End Opp Fd whose TheStreet.com Investment Rating is currently a C (Fair). The fund currently has a performance rating of C (Fair) based on an annualized return of 10.19% over the last three years and a total return of 5.07% year to date 2012. Factored into the performance evaluation is an expense ratio of 0.95% (low).

The fund's risk rating is currently B (Good). It carries a beta of 0.48, meaning the fund's expected move will be 4.8% for every 10% move in the market. Volatility, as measured by both the semi-deviation and a drawdown factor, is considered low. As of December 31, 2012, Cohen & Steers Closed-End Opp Fd traded at a discount of 13.03% below its net asset value, which is better than its one-year historical average discount of 8.28%.

Douglas R. Bond currently receives a manager quality ranking of 85 (0=worst, 99=best). If you desire an average level of risk, then this fund may be an option.

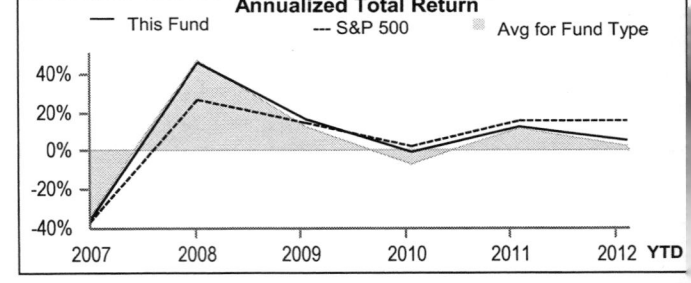

Cohen & Steers Global Inc Builder (INB)

C-   **Fair**

Fund Family: Cohen & Steers Capital Management I
Fund Type: Global
Inception Date: July 27, 2007

Major Rating Factors: Middle of the road best describes Cohen & Steers Global Inc Builder whose TheStreet.com Investment Rating is currently a C- (Fair). The fund currently has a performance rating of C (Fair) based on an annualized return of 8.37% over the last three years and a total return of 2.71% year to date 2012. Factored into the performance evaluation is an expense ratio of 2.01% (high).

The fund's risk rating is currently B- (Good). It carries a beta of 0.89, meaning the fund's expected move will be 8.9% for every 10% move in the market. Volatility, as measured by both the semi-deviation and a drawdown factor, is considered low. As of December 31, 2012, Cohen & Steers Global Inc Builder traded at a discount of 10.88% below its net asset value, which is better than its one-year historical average discount of 7.67%.

Joseph M. Harvey currently receives a manager quality ranking of 77 (0=worst, 99=best). If you desire an average level of risk, then this fund may be an option.

Data Date	Investment Rating	Net Assets ($Mil)	Price	Performance Rating/Pts	Total Return Y-T-D	Risk Rating/Pts
12-12	C-	245.70	10.32	C / 4.5	2.71%	B- / 7.2
2011	C	276.10	9.30	C / 5.4	2.47%	B- / 7.1
2010	D	224.60	11.21	C- / 3.1	10.13%	C / 4.4
2009	B+	227.62	11.29	A / 9.3	53.12%	C / 4.5

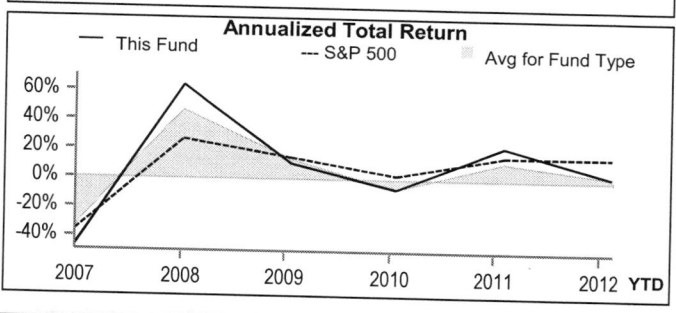

Cohen&Steers Dividend Majors (DVM)

B-   **Good**

Fund Family: Cohen & Steers Capital Management I
Fund Type: Income
Inception Date: January 28, 2005

Major Rating Factors: Strong performance is the major factor driving the B- (Good) TheStreet.com Investment Rating for Cohen&Steers Dividend Majors. The fund currently has a performance rating of B- (Good) based on an annualized return of 18.69% over the last three years and a total return of 3.47% year to date 2012. Factored into the performance evaluation is an expense ratio of 0.96% (low).

The fund's risk rating is currently B- (Good). It carries a beta of 1.16, meaning it is expected to move 11.6% for every 10% move in the market. Volatility, as measured by both the semi-deviation and a drawdown factor, is considered low. As of December 31, 2012, Cohen&Steers Dividend Majors traded at a discount of 9.07% below its net asset value, which is better than its one-year historical average discount of 5.91%.

Joseph M. Harvey has been running the fund for 8 years and currently receives a manager quality ranking of 76 (0=worst, 99=best). If you desire only a moderate level of risk and strong performance, then this fund is an excellent option.

Data Date	Investment Rating	Net Assets ($Mil)	Price	Performance Rating/Pts	Total Return Y-T-D	Risk Rating/Pts
12-12	B-	186.90	13.84	B- / 7.3	3.47%	B- / 7.6
2011	C	175.50	12.09	C+ / 5.7	3.89%	C+ / 6.7
2010	C	150.70	12.96	C+ / 6.5	31.87%	C- / 4.0
2009	D-	129.23	10.45	D- / 1.0	10.95%	C / 5.4

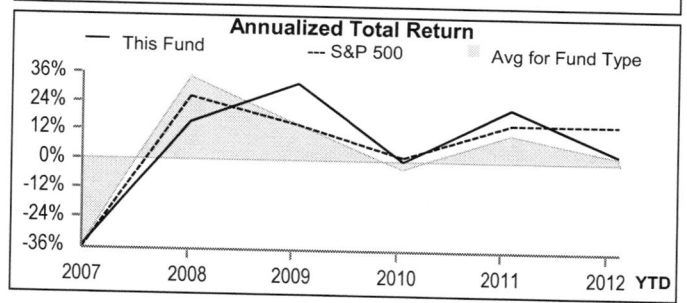

Cohen&Steers Infrastructure Fund (UTF)

B+   **Good**

Fund Family: Cohen & Steers Capital Management I
Fund Type: Utilities
Inception Date: March 26, 2004

Major Rating Factors: Strong performance is the major factor driving the B+ (Good) TheStreet.com Investment Rating for Cohen&Steers Infrastructure Fund. The fund currently has a performance rating of B (Good) based on an annualized return of 15.68% over the last three years and a total return of 3.04% year to date 2012. Factored into the performance evaluation is an expense ratio of 2.09% (high).

The fund's risk rating is currently B (Good). It carries a beta of 1.18, meaning it is expected to move 11.8% for every 10% move in the market. Volatility, as measured by both the semi-deviation and a drawdown factor, is considered low. As of December 31, 2012, Cohen&Steers Infrastructure Fund traded at a discount of 10.84% below its net asset value, which is better than its one-year historical average discount of 8.85%.

Robert S. Becker has been running the fund for 9 years and currently receives a manager quality ranking of 74 (0=worst, 99=best). If you desire only a moderate level of risk and strong performance, then this fund is an excellent option.

Data Date	Investment Rating	Net Assets ($Mil)	Price	Performance Rating/Pts	Total Return Y-T-D	Risk Rating/Pts
12-12	B+	1,609.10	18.75	B / 8.0	3.04%	B / 8.3
2011	B-	1,593.10	15.80	B- / 7.0	3.10%	B- / 7.7
2010	D	1,314.10	16.42	D / 1.7	11.40%	C / 5.4
2009	C-	592.33	15.95	C / 4.6	54.65%	C / 4.6

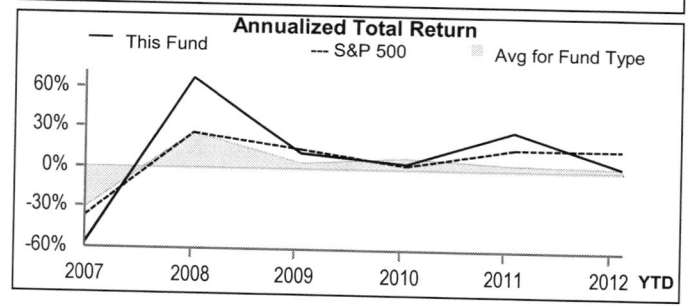

Cohen&Steers Quality Income Realty (RQI)

B+   **Good**

Fund Family: Cohen & Steers Capital Management I
Fund Type: Growth and Income
Inception Date: February 25, 2002

Major Rating Factors:
Exceptional performance is the major factor driving the B+ (Good) TheStreet.com Investment Rating for Cohen&Steers Quality Income Realty. The fund currently has a performance rating of A (Excellent) based on an annualized return of 28.55% over the last three years and a total return of 3.64% year to date 2012. Factored into the performance evaluation is an expense ratio of 1.84% (above average).

The fund's risk rating is currently B- (Good). It carries a beta of 1.36, meaning it is expected to move 13.6% for every 10% move in the market. Volatility, as measured by both the semi-deviation and a drawdown factor, is considered low. As of December 31, 2012, Cohen&Steers Quality Income Realty traded at a discount of 9.12% below its net asset value, which is better than its one-year historical average discount of 4.66%.

Joseph M. Harvey currently receives a manager quality ranking of 91 (0=worst, 99=best). If you desire only a moderate level of risk and strong performance, then this fund is an excellent option.

Data Date	Investment Rating	Net Assets ($Mil)	Price	Performance Rating/Pts	Total Return Y-T-D	Risk Rating/Pts
12-12	B+	1,191.30	10.16	A / 9.4	3.64%	B- / 7.0
2011	B-	1,051.80	8.47	A+ / 9.7	1.06%	C / 5.0
2010	D+	852.60	8.65	C / 5.4	53.21%	C- / 3.0
2009	E	167.73	6.07	E+ / 0.8	67.00%	C- / 3.1

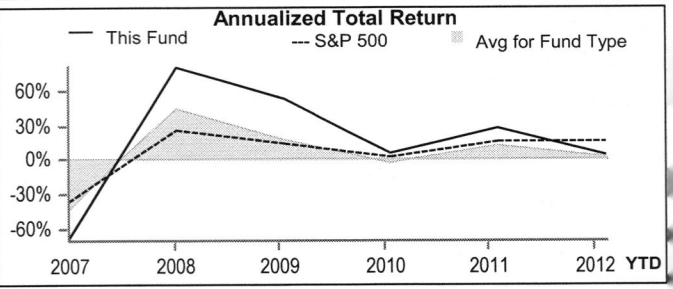

Cohen&Steers REIT& Preferred Incom (RNP)

A-   **Excellent**

Fund Family: Cohen & Steers Capital Management I
Fund Type: Income
Inception Date: June 25, 2003

Major Rating Factors:
Exceptional performance is the major factor driving the A- (Excellent) TheStreet.com Investment Rating for Cohen&Steers REIT& Preferred Incom. The fund currently has a performance rating of A (Excellent) based on an annualized return of 27.64% over the last three years and a total return of 4.18% year to date 2012. Factored into the performance evaluation is an expense ratio of 1.72% (above average).

The fund's risk rating is currently B- (Good). It carries a beta of 1.09, meaning that its performance tracks fairly well with that of the overall stock market. Volatility, as measured by both the semi-deviation and a drawdown factor, is considered low. As of December 31, 2012, Cohen&Steers REIT& Preferred Incom traded at a discount of 9.72% below its net asset value, which is better than its one-year historical average discount of 5.81%.

Joseph M. Harvey has been running the fund for 10 years and currently receives a manager quality ranking of 94 (0=worst, 99=best). If you desire only a moderate level of risk and strong performance, then this fund is an excellent option.

Data Date	Investment Rating	Net Assets ($Mil)	Price	Performance Rating/Pts	Total Return Y-T-D	Risk Rating/Pts
12-12	A-	737.70	16.99	A / 9.4	4.18%	B- / 7.5
2011	B	750.90	14.15	A+ / 9.9	5.02%	C+ / 6.2
2010	C+	632.80	14.29	B+ / 8.6	49.38%	C- / 3.6
2009	D-	395.61	10.35	D- / 1.5	81.08%	C- / 3.9

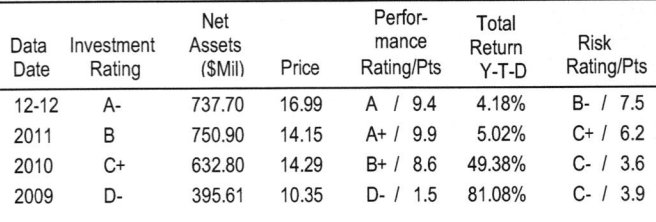

Cohen&Steers Sel Preferred & Incom (PSF)

A+   **Excellent**

Fund Family: Cohen & Steers Capital Management I
Fund Type: Income
Inception Date: November 24, 2010

Major Rating Factors:
Exceptional performance is the major factor driving the A+ (Excellent) TheStreet.com Investment Rating for Cohen&Steers Sel Preferred & Incom. The fund currently has a performance rating of A+ (Excellent) based on an annualized return of 0.00% over the last three years and a total return of 6.88% year to date 2012. Factored into the performance evaluation is an expense ratio of 1.78% (above average).

The fund's risk rating is currently B (Good). It carries a beta of 0.00, meaning the fund's expected move will be 0.0% for every 10% move in the market. Volatility, as measured by both the semi-deviation and a drawdown factor, is considered low. As of December 31, 2012, Cohen&Steers Sel Preferred & Incom traded at a discount of 3.46% below its net asset value, which is better than its one-year historical average premium of .72%.

Joseph M. Harvey currently receives a manager quality ranking of 97 (0=worst, 99=best). If you desire only a moderate level of risk and strong performance, then this fund is an excellent option.

Data Date	Investment Rating	Net Assets ($Mil)	Price	Performance Rating/Pts	Total Return Y-T-D	Risk Rating/Pts
12-12	A+	271.40	26.76	A+ / 9.7	6.88%	B / 8.7
2011	D+	0.00	21.68	D / 1.6	4.38%	B / 8.7

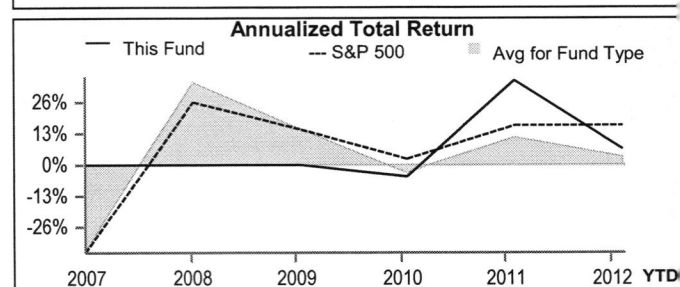

Cohen&Steers Total Return Realty (RFI)

A-　　**Excellent**

Fund Family: Cohen & Steers Capital Management I
Fund Type: Growth and Income
Inception Date: September 17, 1993

Major Rating Factors:

Exceptional performance is the major factor driving the A- (Excellent) TheStreet.com Investment Rating for Cohen&Steers Total Return Realty. The fund currently has a performance rating of A (Excellent) based on an annualized return of 25.32% over the last three years and a total return of 0.41% year to date 2012. Factored into the performance evaluation is an expense ratio of 0.95% (low).

The fund's risk rating is currently B- (Good). It carries a beta of 1.12, meaning it is expected to move 11.2% for every 10% move in the market. Volatility, as measured by both the semi-deviation and a drawdown factor, is considered low. As of December 31, 2012, Cohen&Steers Total Return Realty traded at a premium of 11.35% above its net asset value, which is worse than its one-year historical average premium of 2.89%.

Joseph M. Harvey currently receives a manager quality ranking of 92 (0=worst, 99=best). If you desire only a moderate level of risk and strong performance, then this fund is an excellent option.

Data Date	Investment Rating	Net Assets ($Mil)	Price	Performance Rating/Pts	Total Return Y-T-D	Risk Rating/Pts
12-12	A-	128.80	14.72	A / 9.5	0.41%	B- / 7.4
2011	C+	117.90	11.91	B / 7.6	3.27%	C+ / 6.7
2010	B	107.40	14.88	A / 9.5	71.18%	C- / 3.4
2009	D-	73.26	9.68	D- / 1.5	36.20%	C / 4.8

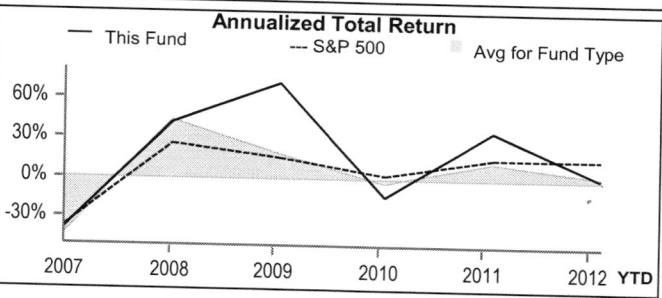

Columbia Seligman Prem Tech Gro (STK)

D　　**Weak**

Fund Family: Columbia Management Inv Advisers LL
Fund Type: Growth
Inception Date: November 30, 2009

Major Rating Factors:

Disappointing performance is the major factor driving the D (Weak) TheStreet.com Investment Rating for Columbia Seligman Prem Tech Gro. The fund currently has a performance rating of D (Weak) based on an annualized return of 0.13% over the last three years and a total return of 5.03% year to date 2012. Factored into the performance evaluation is an expense ratio of 1.10% (low).

The fund's risk rating is currently B- (Good). It carries a beta of 0.77, meaning the fund's expected move will be 7.7% for every 10% move in the market. Volatility, as measured by both the semi-deviation and a drawdown factor, is considered low. As of December 31, 2012, Columbia Seligman Prem Tech Gro traded at a discount of 7.34% below its net asset value, which is better than its one-year historical average discount of 3.00%.

Ajay Diwan currently receives a manager quality ranking of 16 (0=worst, 99=best). This fund offers only a moderate level of risk but investors looking for strong performance are still waiting.

Data Date	Investment Rating	Net Assets ($Mil)	Price	Performance Rating/Pts	Total Return Y-T-D	Risk Rating/Pts
12-12	D	260.82	14.51	D / 1.6	5.03%	B- / 7.0
2011	D	260.80	15.66	D- / 1.4	3.51%	B- / 7.7
2010	A	0.00	19.17	B / 7.9	6.01%	B / 8.0

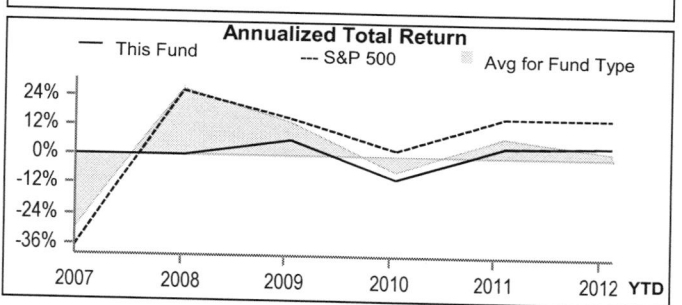

Cornerstone Progressive Return Fun (CFP)

D　　**Weak**

Fund Family: Cornerstone Advisors Inc
Fund Type: Income
Inception Date: September 10, 2007

Major Rating Factors:

Disappointing performance is the major factor driving the D (Weak) TheStreet.com Investment Rating for Cornerstone Progressive Return Fun. The fund currently has a performance rating of D+ (Weak) based on an annualized return of 4.76% over the last three years and a total return of 9.98% year to date 2012. Factored into the performance evaluation is an expense ratio of 1.45% (average).

The fund's risk rating is currently C (Fair). It carries a beta of 0.78, meaning the fund's expected move will be 7.8% for every 10% move in the market. Volatility, as measured by both the semi-deviation and a drawdown factor, is considered average. As of December 31, 2012, Cornerstone Progressive Return Fun traded at a premium of 3.73% above its net asset value, which is better than its one-year historical average premium of 16.53%.

Ralph W. Bradshaw has been running the fund for 6 years and currently receives a manager quality ranking of 19 (0=worst, 99=best). This fund offers an average level of risk but investors looking for strong performance will be frustrated.

Data Date	Investment Rating	Net Assets ($Mil)	Price	Performance Rating/Pts	Total Return Y-T-D	Risk Rating/Pts
12-12	D	78.44	5.01	D+ / 2.7	9.98%	C / 5.5
2011	D	55.28	6.05	C- / 3.3	3.14%	C+ / 6.0
2010	D	48.87	7.50	D+ / 2.4	5.28%	C / 4.7
2009	C+	57.27	8.90	B+ / 8.7	55.21%	C- / 4.0

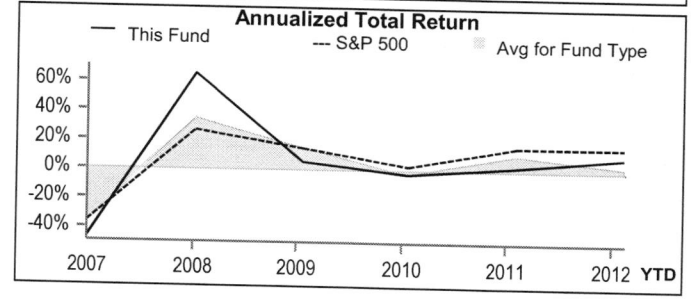

Cornerstone Strategic Value Fund (CLM)   D-   Weak

Fund Family: Cornerstone Advisors Inc
Fund Type: Income
Inception Date: June 30, 1987

Major Rating Factors:
Disappointing performance is the major factor driving the D- (Weak) TheStreet.com Investment Rating for Cornerstone Strategic Value Fund. The fund currently has a performance rating of D- (Weak) based on an annualized return of -1.87% over the last three years and a total return of 12.17% year to date 2012. Factored into the performance evaluation is an expense ratio of 1.40% (average).

The fund's risk rating is currently C (Fair). It carries a beta of 0.76, meaning the fund's expected move will be 7.6% for every 10% move in the market. Volatility, as measured by both the semi-deviation and a drawdown factor, is considered average. As of December 31, 2012, Cornerstone Strategic Value Fund traded at a premium of 4.17% above its net asset value, which is better than its one-year historical average premium of 19.23%.

Ralph W. Bradshaw has been running the fund for 12 years and currently receives a manager quality ranking of 11 (0=worst, 99=best). This fund offers an average level of risk but investors looking for strong performance will be frustrated.

Data Date	Investment Rating	Net Assets ($Mil)	Price	Performance Rating/Pts	Total Return Y-T-D	Risk Rating/Pts
12-12	D-	87.14	6.00	D- / 1.3	12.17%	C / 4.9
2011	D-	64.27	6.60	D+ / 2.4	1.67%	C / 5.5
2010	D-	57.45	8.84	E+ / 0.8	-10.20%	C / 4.3
2009	D-	53.18	11.61	D / 2.0	78.06%	C- / 3.7

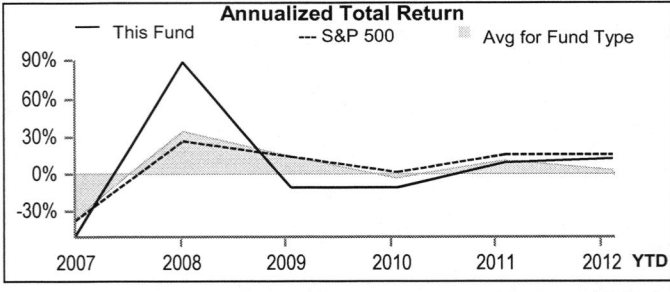

Annualized Total Return

Cornerstone Total Return Fund (CRF)   D-   Weak

Fund Family: Cornerstone Advisors Inc
Fund Type: Income
Inception Date: May 3, 1973

Major Rating Factors:
Disappointing performance is the major factor driving the D- (Weak) TheStreet.com Investment Rating for Cornerstone Total Return Fund. The fund currently has a performance rating of D- (Weak) based on an annualized return of -3.51% over the last three years and a total return of 8.77% year to date 2012. Factored into the performance evaluation is an expense ratio of 1.76% (above average).

The fund's risk rating is currently C (Fair). It carries a beta of 0.67, meaning the fund's expected move will be 6.7% for every 10% move in the market. Volatility, as measured by both the semi-deviation and a drawdown factor, is considered average. As of December 31, 2012, Cornerstone Total Return Fund traded at a premium of 4.28% above its net asset value, which is better than its one-year historical average premium of 18.70%.

Ralph W. Bradshaw currently receives a manager quality ranking of 12 (0=worst, 99=best). This fund offers an average level of risk but investors looking for strong performance will be frustrated.

Data Date	Investment Rating	Net Assets ($Mil)	Price	Performance Rating/Pts	Total Return Y-T-D	Risk Rating/Pts
12-12	D-	35.92	5.36	D- / 1.1	8.77%	C / 5.0
2011	D-	25.91	5.97	D / 1.7	1.68%	C / 5.0
2010	E+	17.08	7.88	E+ / 0.7	-9.94%	C- / 4.1
2009	E	19.08	10.25	E+ / 0.7	57.12%	C- / 3.4

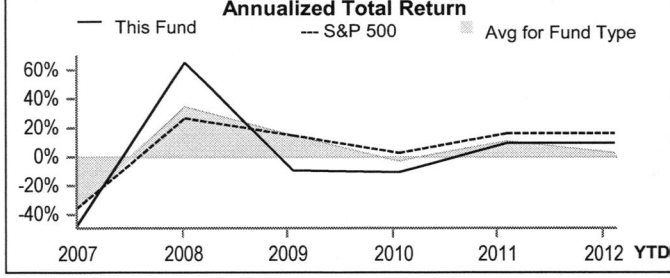

Annualized Total Return

Credit Suisse Asset Mgmt Income (CIK)   B+   Good

Fund Family: Credit Suisse Asset Management LLC
Fund Type: Corporate - High Yield
Inception Date: April 8, 1987

Major Rating Factors: Strong performance is the major factor driving the B+ (Good) TheStreet.com Investment Rating for Credit Suisse Asset Mgmt Income. The fund currently has a performance rating of B- (Good) based on an annualized return of 16.02% over the last three years and a total return of 2.44% year to date 2012. Factored into the performance evaluation is an expense ratio of 0.73% (very low).

The fund's risk rating is currently B (Good). It carries a beta of 1.02, meaning that its performance tracks fairly well with that of the overall stock market. Volatility, as measured by both the semi-deviation and a drawdown factor, is considered low. As of December 31, 2012, Credit Suisse Asset Mgmt Income traded at a premium of 5.50% above its net asset value, which is worse than its one-year historical average premium of 4.51%.

Thomas J. Flannery currently receives a manager quality ranking of 74 (0=worst, 99=best). If you desire only a moderate level of risk and strong performance, then this fund is an excellent option.

Data Date	Investment Rating	Net Assets ($Mil)	Price	Performance Rating/Pts	Total Return Y-T-D	Risk Rating/Pts
12-12	B+	184.89	4.03	B- / 7.4	2.44%	B / 8.5
2011	B+	180.00	3.65	B / 7.8	0.82%	B / 8.4
2010	C+	176.38	3.56	B / 7.6	16.04%	C / 4.7
2009	C	152.99	3.36	C+ / 6.1	58.04%	C / 5.4

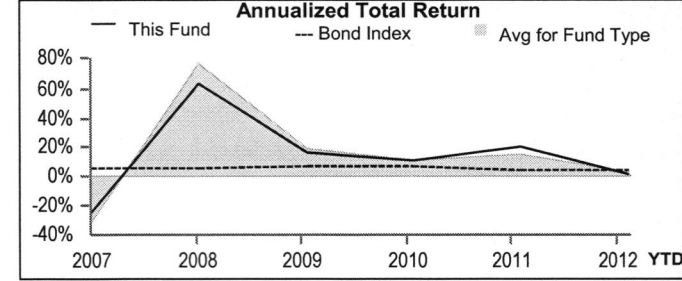

Annualized Total Return

Credit Suisse High Yield Bond Fund (DHY)

B-   **Good**

Fund Family: Credit Suisse Asset Management LLC
Fund Type: Corporate - High Yield
Inception Date: July 28, 1998

Major Rating Factors: Credit Suisse High Yield Bond Fund receives a TheStreet.com Investment Rating of B- (Good). The fund currently has a performance rating of C+ (Fair) based on an annualized return of 13.32% over the last three years and a total return of 1.88% year to date 2012. Factored into the performance evaluation is an expense ratio of 2.00% (high).

The fund's risk rating is currently B (Good). It carries a beta of 0.54, meaning the fund's expected move will be 5.4% for every 10% move in the market. Volatility, as measured by both the semi-deviation and a drawdown factor, is considered low. As of December 31, 2012, Credit Suisse High Yield Bond Fund traded at a premium of 2.89% above its net asset value, which is better than its one-year historical average premium of 6.77%.

Thomas J. Flannery currently receives a manager quality ranking of 87 (0=worst, 99=best). If you desire an average level of risk, then this fund may be an option.

Data Date	Investment Rating	Net Assets ($Mil)	Price	Performance Rating/Pts	Total Return Y-T-D	Risk Rating/Pts
12-12	B-	212.12	3.20	C+ / 6.1	1.88%	B / 8.6
2011	B+	210.60	2.88	B+ / 8.8	1.04%	B / 8.0
2010	C-	165.31	2.89	C+ / 6.6	10.19%	C- / 3.1
2009	C	112.77	2.93	B / 7.7	102.64%	D+ / 2.6

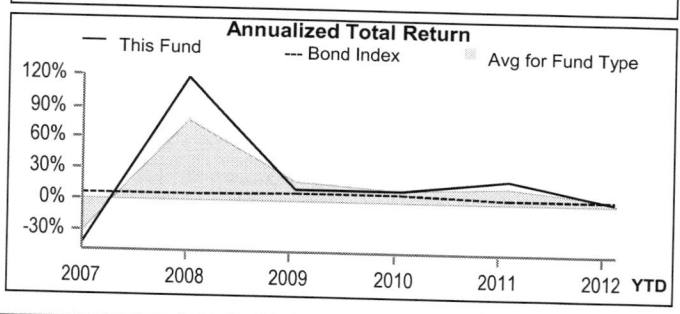

Cutwater Select Income (CSI)

B-   **Good**

Fund Family: Cutwater Asset Management Corp
Fund Type: Corporate - Investment Grade
Inception Date: September 29, 1971

Major Rating Factors: Cutwater Select Income receives a TheStreet.com Investment Rating of B- (Good). The fund currently has a performance rating of C (Fair) based on an annualized return of 13.10% over the last three years and a total return of 2.54% year to date 2012. Factored into the performance evaluation is an expense ratio of 0.74% (very low).

The fund's risk rating is currently B+ (Good). It carries a beta of 0.55, meaning the fund's expected move will be 5.5% for every 10% move in the market. Volatility, as measured by both the semi-deviation and a drawdown factor, is considered very low. As of December 31, 2012, Cutwater Select Income traded at a discount of 8.26% below its net asset value, which is better than its one-year historical average discount of 4.93%.

Gautam Khanna has been running the fund for 8 years and currently receives a manager quality ranking of 86 (0=worst, 99=best). If you desire an average level of risk, then this fund may be an option.

Data Date	Investment Rating	Net Assets ($Mil)	Price	Performance Rating/Pts	Total Return Y-T-D	Risk Rating/Pts
12-12	B-	218.32	19.65	C / 5.1	2.54%	B+ / 9.6
2010	B-	125.25	17.70	C+ / 6.6	15.48%	B- / 7.5
2009	C+	118.87	16.34	C- / 4.2	19.06%	B- / 7.6

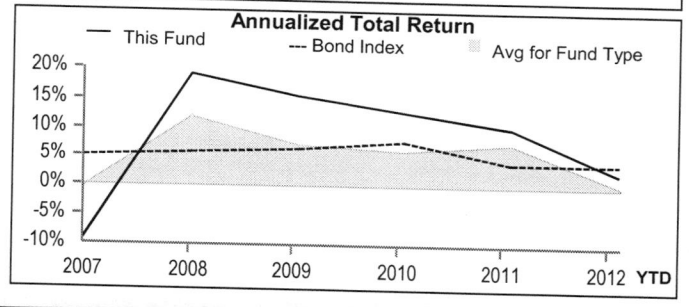

Delaware Enhanced Glb Div & Inc Fd (DEX)

C-   **Fair**

Fund Family: Delaware Management Company
Fund Type: Global
Inception Date: June 29, 2007

Major Rating Factors: Middle of the road best describes Delaware Enhanced Glb Div & Inc Fd whose TheStreet.com Investment Rating is currently a C- (Fair). The fund currently has a performance rating of C (Fair) based on an annualized return of 10.20% over the last three years and a total return of 3.50% year to date 2012. Factored into the performance evaluation is an expense ratio of 2.09% (high).

The fund's risk rating is currently C+ (Fair). It carries a beta of 0.70, meaning the fund's expected move will be 7.0% for every 10% move in the market. Volatility, as measured by both the semi-deviation and a drawdown factor, is considered low. As of December 31, 2012, Delaware Enhanced Glb Div & Inc Fd traded at a discount of 6.90% below its net asset value, which is better than its one-year historical average discount of .95%.

Babak Zenouzi has been running the fund for 6 years and currently receives a manager quality ranking of 84 (0=worst, 99=best). If you desire an average level of risk, then this fund may be an option.

Data Date	Investment Rating	Net Assets ($Mil)	Price	Performance Rating/Pts	Total Return Y-T-D	Risk Rating/Pts
12-12	C-	176.47	11.60	C / 4.5	3.50%	C+ / 6.9
2011	B	180.90	10.77	B / 7.9	3.71%	B- / 7.5
2010	C-	149.94	12.40	C+ / 6.8	16.55%	C- / 3.2
2009	B	133.47	11.79	A+ / 9.7	78.76%	C- / 3.6

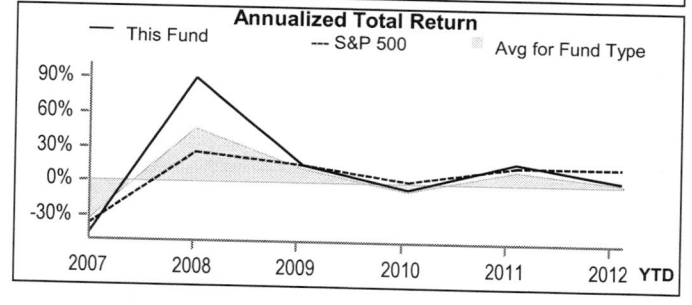

Delaware Inv CO Muni Inc (VCF)

B+   **Good**

Fund Family: Delaware Management Company
Fund Type: Municipal - Single State
Inception Date: July 22, 1993

Major Rating Factors: Strong performance is the major factor driving the B+ (Good) TheStreet.com Investment Rating for Delaware Inv CO Muni Inc. The fund currently has a performance rating of B- (Good) based on an annualized return of 9.94% over the last three years and a total return of 4.51% year to date 2012. Factored into the performance evaluation is an expense ratio of 0.73% (very low).

The fund's risk rating is currently B+ (Good). It carries a beta of 1.29, meaning it is expected to move 12.9% for every 10% move in the market. Volatility, as measured by both the semi-deviation and a drawdown factor, is considered very low. As of December 31, 2012, Delaware Inv CO Muni Inc traded at a discount of 3.26% below its net asset value, which is better than its one-year historical average discount of 1.19%.

Denise A. Franchetti has been running the fund for 9 years and currently receives a manager quality ranking of 60 (0=worst, 99=best). If you desire only a moderate level of risk and strong performance, then this fund is an excellent option.

Data Date	Investment Rating	Net Assets ($Mil)	Price	Performance Rating/Pts	Total Return Y-T-D	Risk Rating/Pts
12-12	B+	72.61	15.12	B- / 7.4	4.51%	B+ / 9.0
2011	C+	70.80	13.61	C+ / 5.6	1.44%	B / 8.7
2010	C-	67.65	12.86	D / 2.0	1.76%	B / 8.2
2009	C-	68.76	13.18	D- / 1.4	7.19%	B / 8.1

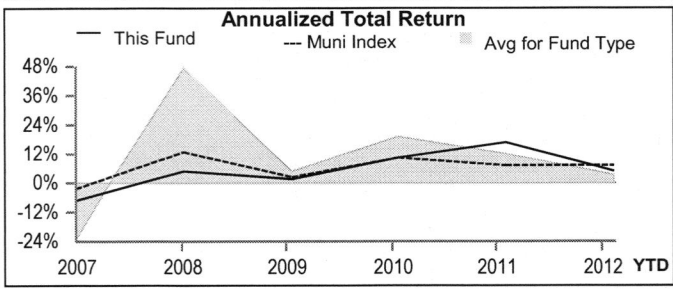

Delaware Inv Div & Inc (DDF)

B-   **Good**

Fund Family: Delaware Management Company
Fund Type: Growth and Income
Inception Date: March 18, 1993

Major Rating Factors: Strong performance is the major factor driving the B- (Good) TheStreet.com Investment Rating for Delaware Inv Div & Inc. The fund currently has a performance rating of B- (Good) based on an annualized return of 15.33% over the last three years and a total return of 6.73% year to date 2012. Factored into the performance evaluation is an expense ratio of 1.57% (above average).

The fund's risk rating is currently B- (Good). It carries a beta of 0.79, meaning the fund's expected move will be 7.9% for every 10% move in the market. Volatility, as measured by both the semi-deviation and a drawdown factor, is considered low. As of December 31, 2012, Delaware Inv Div & Inc traded at a discount of 12.39% below its net asset value, which is better than its one-year historical average discount of 6.33%.

Babak Zenouzi has been running the fund for 7 years and currently receives a manager quality ranking of 73 (0=worst, 99=best). If you desire only a moderate level of risk and strong performance, then this fund is an excellent option.

Data Date	Investment Rating	Net Assets ($Mil)	Price	Performance Rating/Pts	Total Return Y-T-D	Risk Rating/Pts
12-12	B-	76.09	7.92	B- / 7.3	6.73%	B- / 7.8
2011	B	74.50	7.07	B / 7.8	4.34%	B- / 7.8
2010	D+	67.11	7.79	C / 5.3	16.18%	C- / 3.4
2009	D	58.09	7.36	C- / 3.9	54.31%	C- / 3.4

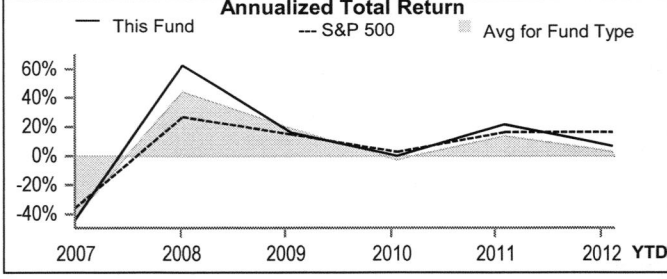

Delaware Inv MN Muni Inc Fund II (VMM)

A+   **Excellent**

Fund Family: Delaware Management Company
Fund Type: Municipal - Single State
Inception Date: February 19, 1993

Major Rating Factors:
Strong performance is the major factor driving the A+ (Excellent) TheStreet.com Investment Rating for Delaware Inv MN Muni Inc Fund II. The fund currently has a performance rating of B+ (Good) based on an annualized return of 12.84% over the last three years and a total return of 2.88% year to date 2012. Factored into the performance evaluation is an expense ratio of 0.70% (very low).

The fund's risk rating is currently B+ (Good). It carries a beta of 1.15, meaning it is expected to move 11.5% for every 10% move in the market. Volatility, as measured by both the semi-deviation and a drawdown factor, is considered very low. As of December 31, 2012, Delaware Inv MN Muni Inc Fund II traded at a discount of 1.55% below its net asset value, which is worse than its one-year historical average discount of 2.68%.

Denise A. Franchetti has been running the fund for 10 years and currently receives a manager quality ranking of 78 (0=worst, 99=best). If you desire only a moderate level of risk and strong performance, then this fund is an excellent option.

Data Date	Investment Rating	Net Assets ($Mil)	Price	Performance Rating/Pts	Total Return Y-T-D	Risk Rating/Pts
12-12	A+	171.84	15.22	B+ / 8.5	2.88%	B+ / 9.4
2011	B	170.00	13.51	C+ / 6.7	1.14%	B+ / 9.3
2010	C+	161.72	12.62	C- / 3.9	7.83%	B / 8.3
2009	C	163.21	12.23	D+ / 2.4	19.72%	B / 8.2

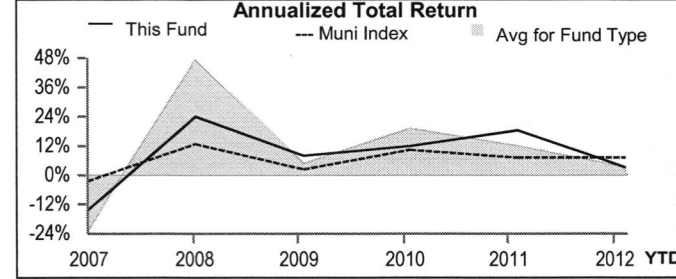

Delaware Inv Nat Muni Inc (VFL)

A-   **Excellent**

Fund Family: Delaware Management Company
Fund Type: Municipal - National
Inception Date: February 19, 1993

Major Rating Factors:
Strong performance is the major factor driving the A- (Excellent) TheStreet.com Investment Rating for Delaware Inv Nat Muni Inc. The fund currently has a performance rating of B (Good) based on an annualized return of 10.79% over the last three years and a total return of 4.56% year to date 2012. Factored into the performance evaluation is an expense ratio of 0.99% (low).

The fund's risk rating is currently B+ (Good). It carries a beta of 1.64, meaning it is expected to move 16.4% for every 10% move in the market. Volatility, as measured by both the semi-deviation and a drawdown factor, is considered very low. As of December 31, 2012, Delaware Inv Nat Muni Inc traded at a discount of 7.76% below its net asset value, which is better than its one-year historical average discount of 5.44%.

Denise A. Franchetti has been running the fund for 10 years and currently receives a manager quality ranking of 37 (0=worst, 99=best). If you desire only a moderate level of risk and strong performance, then this fund is an excellent option.

Data Date	Investment Rating	Net Assets ($Mil)	Price	Performance Rating/Pts	Total Return Y-T-D	Risk Rating/Pts
12-12	A-	63.49	14.03	B / 7.9	4.56%	B+ / 9.0
2011	B	61.90	12.91	B- / 7.2	0.31%	B / 8.9
2010	C-	31.65	12.09	C- / 3.7	2.62%	C+ / 6.1
2009	C	32.15	12.28	C- / 3.9	34.80%	C+ / 6.7

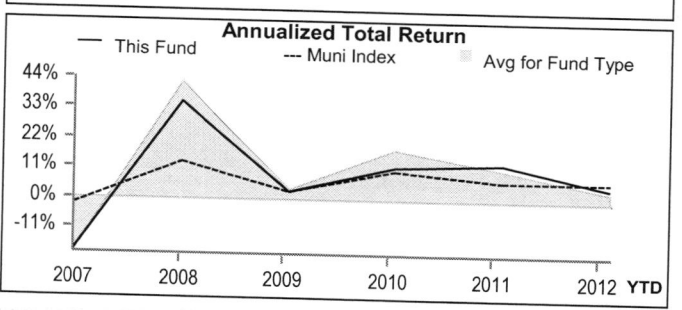

Dividend and Income Fund Inc (DNI)

D+   **Weak**

Fund Family: Bexil Advisers LLC
Fund Type: Growth and Income
Inception Date: June 23, 1998

Major Rating Factors: Dividend and Income Fund Inc receives a TheStreet.com Investment Rating of D+ (Weak). The fund currently has a performance rating of C- (Fair) based on an annualized return of 6.71% over the last three years and a total return of 4.07% year to date 2012. Factored into the performance evaluation is an expense ratio of 2.57% (high).

The fund's risk rating is currently B- (Good). It carries a beta of 0.85, meaning the fund's expected move will be 8.5% for every 10% move in the market. Volatility, as measured by both the semi-deviation and a drawdown factor, is considered low. As of December 31, 2012, Dividend and Income Fund Inc traded at a discount of 15.78% below its net asset value, which is better than its one-year historical average discount of 11.95%.

John F. Ramirez has been running the fund for 2 years and currently receives a manager quality ranking of 31 (0=worst, 99=best). If you desire an average level of risk, then this fund may be an option.

Data Date	Investment Rating	Net Assets ($Mil)	Price	Performance Rating/Pts	Total Return Y-T-D	Risk Rating/Pts
12-12	D+	93.38	13.50	C- / 3.2	4.07%	B- / 7.2
2011	C-	73.32	3.41	C- / 3.8	-2.05%	B- / 7.0
2010	D	70.85	4.27	D+ / 2.7	25.35%	C- / 4.1
2009	D-	63.00	3.77	E+ / 0.9	35.29%	C / 4.6

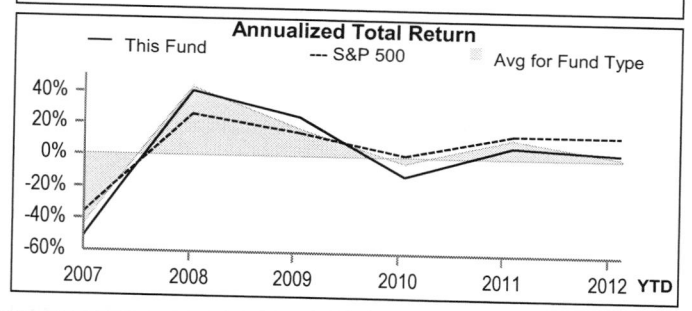

DNP Select Income Fund Inc (DNP)

C-   **Fair**

Fund Family: Duff & Phelps Investment Mgmt Co
Fund Type: Utilities
Inception Date: January 28, 1987

Major Rating Factors: Middle of the road best describes DNP Select Income Fund Inc whose TheStreet.com Investment Rating is currently a C- (Fair). The fund currently has a performance rating of C- (Fair) based on an annualized return of 12.13% over the last three years and a total return of 5.39% year to date 2012. Factored into the performance evaluation is an expense ratio of 1.84% (above average).

The fund's risk rating is currently B (Good). It carries a beta of 0.41, meaning the fund's expected move will be 4.1% for every 10% move in the market. Volatility, as measured by both the semi-deviation and a drawdown factor, is considered low. As of December 31, 2012, DNP Select Income Fund Inc traded at a premium of 12.07% above its net asset value, which is better than its one-year historical average premium of 26.18%.

Geoffrey P. Dybas has been running the fund for 17 years and currently receives a manager quality ranking of 84 (0=worst, 99=best). If you desire an average level of risk, then this fund may be an option.

Data Date	Investment Rating	Net Assets ($Mil)	Price	Performance Rating/Pts	Total Return Y-T-D	Risk Rating/Pts
12-12	C-	2,052.35	9.47	C- / 3.6	5.39%	B / 8.1
2011	B+	2,014.00	10.92	B+ / 8.3	0.37%	B / 8.2
2010	C	1,703.40	9.14	C / 5.1	11.31%	C / 5.5
2009	C	1,467.93	8.95	C / 5.4	48.07%	C+ / 5.6

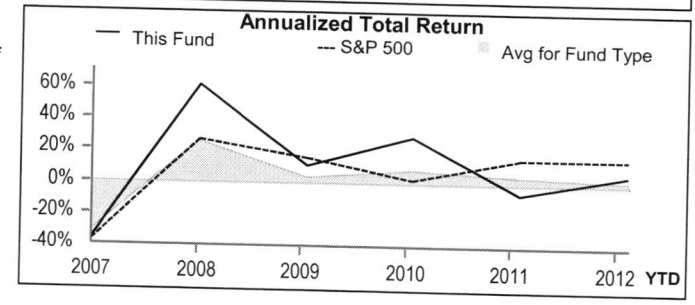

Dow 30 Enhanced Premium & Income F (DPO)

C **Fair**

Fund Family: Nuveen Fund Advisors Inc
Fund Type: Income
Inception Date: May 30, 2007

Major Rating Factors: Middle of the road best describes Dow 30 Enhanced Premium & Income F whose TheStreet.com Investment Rating is currently a C (Fair). The fund currently has a performance rating of C (Fair) based on an annualized return of 10.48% over the last three years and a total return of 2.89% year to date 2012. Factored into the performance evaluation is an expense ratio of 1.01% (low).

The fund's risk rating is currently B- (Good). It carries a beta of 0.89, meaning the fund's expected move will be 8.9% for every 10% move in the market. Volatility, as measured by both the semi-deviation and a drawdown factor, is considered low. As of December 31, 2012, Dow 30 Enhanced Premium & Income F traded at a discount of 8.13% below its net asset value, which is better than its one-year historical average discount of 5.64%.

James A. Colon has been running the fund for 2 years and currently receives a manager quality ranking of 44 (0=worst, 99=best). If you desire an average level of risk, then this fund may be an option.

Data Date	Investment Rating	Net Assets ($Mil)	Price	Performance Rating/Pts	Total Return Y-T-D	Risk Rating/Pts
12-12	C	306.13	10.73	C / 4.3	2.89%	B- / 7.9
2011	C+	306.10	10.16	C+ / 6.3	1.57%	B- / 7.3
2010	C-	285.17	10.38	C- / 3.6	5.19%	C+ / 6.1
2009	B	244.94	10.94	B+ / 8.3	43.79%	C / 5.0

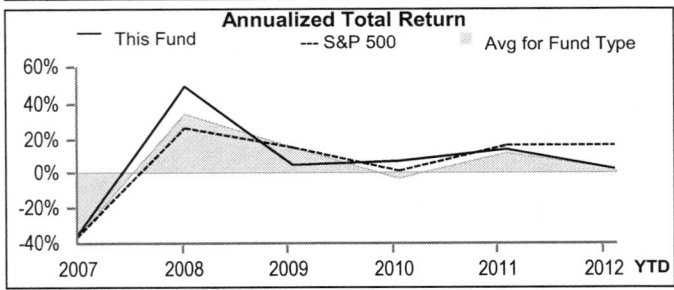

Dow 30 Premium & Dividend Income (DPD)

C- **Fair**

Fund Family: Nuveen Fund Advisors Inc
Fund Type: Income
Inception Date: May 6, 2005

Major Rating Factors: Middle of the road best describes Dow 30 Premium & Dividend Income whose TheStreet.com Investment Rating is currently a C- (Fair). The fund currently has a performance rating of C- (Fair) based on an annualized return of 5.53% over the last three years and a total return of 3.62% year to date 2012. Factored into the performance evaluation is an expense ratio of 1.00% (low).

The fund's risk rating is currently B (Good). It carries a beta of 0.84, meaning the fund's expected move will be 8.4% for every 10% move in the market. Volatility, as measured by both the semi-deviation and a drawdown factor, is considered low. As of December 31, 2012, Dow 30 Premium & Dividend Income traded at a discount of 9.93% below its net asset value, which is better than its one-year historical average discount of 6.69%.

James A. Colon has been running the fund for 2 years and currently receives a manager quality ranking of 27 (0=worst, 99=best). If you desire an average level of risk, then this fund may be an option.

Data Date	Investment Rating	Net Assets ($Mil)	Price	Performance Rating/Pts	Total Return Y-T-D	Risk Rating/Pts
12-12	C-	173.87	13.25	C- / 3.0	3.62%	B / 8.2
2011	C-	171.00	13.12	C- / 3.6	1.30%	B- / 7.5
2010	C	165.40	14.53	C+ / 5.6	7.76%	C / 5.3
2009	C-	144.47	14.74	D+ / 2.9	20.31%	C+ / 5.8

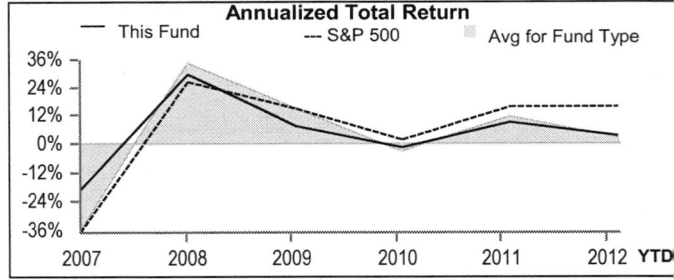

Dreyfus High Yield Strategies Fund (DHF)

C- **Fair**

Fund Family: Dreyfus Corporation
Fund Type: Corporate - High Yield
Inception Date: April 23, 1998

Major Rating Factors: Middle of the road best describes Dreyfus High Yield Strategies Fund whose TheStreet.com Investment Rating is currently a C- (Fair). The fund currently has a performance rating of C+ (Fair) based on an annualized return of 15.64% over the last three years and a total return of 3.64% year to date 2012. Factored into the performance evaluation is an expense ratio of 1.90% (above average).

The fund's risk rating is currently C+ (Fair). It carries a beta of 1.20, meaning it is expected to move 12.0% for every 10% move in the market. Volatility, as measured by both the semi-deviation and a drawdown factor, is considered low. As of December 31, 2012, Dreyfus High Yield Strategies Fund traded at a premium of 1.23% above its net asset value, which is better than its one-year historical average premium of 13.08%.

Chris E. Barris currently receives a manager quality ranking of 61 (0=worst, 99=best). If you desire an average level of risk, then this fund may be an option.

Data Date	Investment Rating	Net Assets ($Mil)	Price	Performance Rating/Pts	Total Return Y-T-D	Risk Rating/Pts
12-12	C-	281.90	4.12	C+ / 5.6	3.64%	C+ / 6.2
2011	B	384.10	4.43	A- / 9.1	1.13%	C+ / 6.3
2010	C+	291.96	4.43	B+ / 8.9	33.00%	C- / 3.0
2009	C	273.02	3.76	B / 7.6	77.12%	C- / 3.8

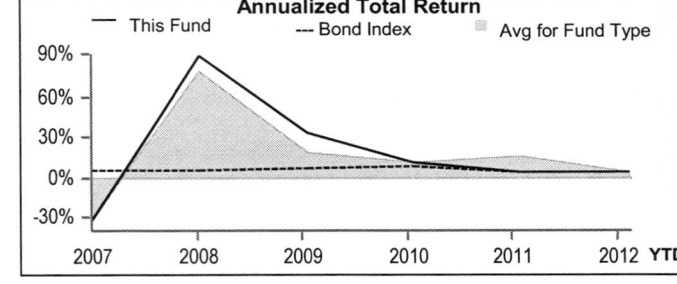

Dreyfus Municipal Income (DMF)   A-   Excellent

Fund Family: Dreyfus Corporation
Fund Type: Municipal - National
Inception Date: October 21, 1988

Data Date	Investment Rating	Net Assets ($Mil)	Price	Perfor-mance Rating/Pts	Total Return Y-T-D	Risk Rating/Pts
12-12	A-	204.08	10.43	B+ / 8.4	5.13%	B / 8.6
2011	A+	273.80	9.88	A+ / 9.6	2.63%	B / 8.8
2010	C+	199.20	8.93	C+ / 6.9	12.10%	C+ / 6.4
2009	B-	193.03	8.48	C / 5.5	28.94%	B- / 7.5

Major Rating Factors:
Strong performance is the major factor driving the A- (Excellent) TheStreet.com Investment Rating for Dreyfus Municipal Income. The fund currently has a performance rating of B+ (Good) based on an annualized return of 14.53% over the last three years and a total return of 5.13% year to date 2012. Factored into the performance evaluation is an expense ratio of 1.27% (average).

The fund's risk rating is currently B (Good). It carries a beta of 1.81, meaning it is expected to move 18.1% for every 10% move in the market. Volatility, as measured by both the semi-deviation and a drawdown factor, is considered low. As of December 31, 2012, Dreyfus Municipal Income traded at a premium of .10% above its net asset value, which is better than its one-year historical average premium of 4.18%.

James S. Welch has been running the fund for 4 years and currently receives a manager quality ranking of 66 (0=worst, 99=best). If you desire only a moderate level of risk and strong performance, then this fund is an excellent option.

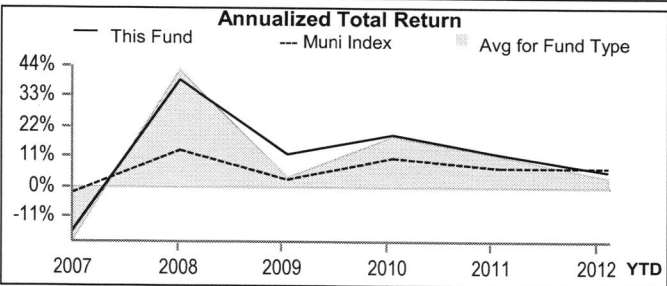

Dreyfus Strategic Muni Bond Fund (DSM)   A+   Excellent

Fund Family: Dreyfus Corporation
Fund Type: Municipal - National
Inception Date: November 22, 1989

Data Date	Investment Rating	Net Assets ($Mil)	Price	Perfor-mance Rating/Pts	Total Return Y-T-D	Risk Rating/Pts
12-12	A+	430.99	9.36	A- / 9.0	4.38%	B / 8.7
2011	A+	545.10	8.69	A / 9.4	-0.01%	B / 8.7
2010	C-	384.46	7.58	C- / 3.2	5.39%	C+ / 6.2
2009	C+	363.86	7.69	C / 4.8	45.02%	C+ / 6.9

Major Rating Factors:
Exceptional performance is the major factor driving the A+ (Excellent) TheStreet.com Investment Rating for Dreyfus Strategic Muni Bond Fund. The fund currently has a performance rating of A- (Excellent) based on an annualized return of 14.99% over the last three years and a total return of 4.38% year to date 2012. Factored into the performance evaluation is an expense ratio of 1.09% (low).

The fund's risk rating is currently B (Good). It carries a beta of 1.55, meaning it is expected to move 15.5% for every 10% move in the market. Volatility, as measured by both the semi-deviation and a drawdown factor, is considered low. As of December 31, 2012, Dreyfus Strategic Muni Bond Fund traded at a premium of 3.20% above its net asset value, which is better than its one-year historical average premium of 3.98%.

James S. Welch has been running the fund for 12 years and currently receives a manager quality ranking of 75 (0=worst, 99=best). If you desire only a moderate level of risk and strong performance, then this fund is an excellent option.

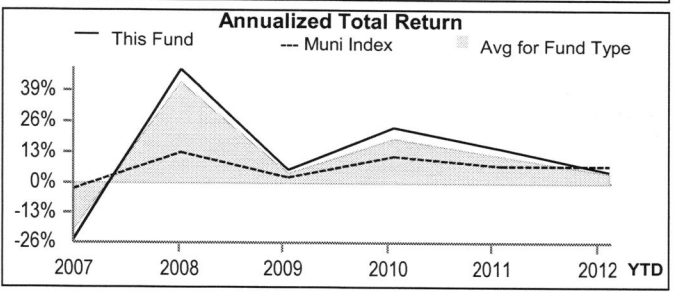

Dreyfus Strategic Municipals (LEO)   A   Excellent

Fund Family: Dreyfus Corporation
Fund Type: Municipal - National
Inception Date: September 23, 1987

Data Date	Investment Rating	Net Assets ($Mil)	Price	Perfor-mance Rating/Pts	Total Return Y-T-D	Risk Rating/Pts
12-12	A	541.93	9.55	B+ / 8.8	4.89%	B / 8.4
2011	A	738.90	8.89	A / 9.4	0.22%	B / 8.6
2010	C-	528.61	7.80	C- / 3.8	3.55%	C+ / 6.0
2009	C+	514.79	8.08	C+ / 6.8	46.73%	C+ / 6.8

Major Rating Factors:
Strong performance is the major factor driving the A (Excellent) TheStreet.com Investment Rating for Dreyfus Strategic Municipals. The fund currently has a performance rating of B+ (Good) based on an annualized return of 14.00% over the last three years and a total return of 4.89% year to date 2012. Factored into the performance evaluation is an expense ratio of 1.19% (average).

The fund's risk rating is currently B (Good). It carries a beta of 1.88, meaning it is expected to move 18.8% for every 10% move in the market. Volatility, as measured by both the semi-deviation and a drawdown factor, is considered low. As of December 31, 2012, Dreyfus Strategic Municipals traded at a premium of 2.36% above its net asset value, which is better than its one-year historical average premium of 4.29%.

James S. Welch has been running the fund for 4 years and currently receives a manager quality ranking of 58 (0=worst, 99=best). If you desire only a moderate level of risk and strong performance, then this fund is an excellent option.

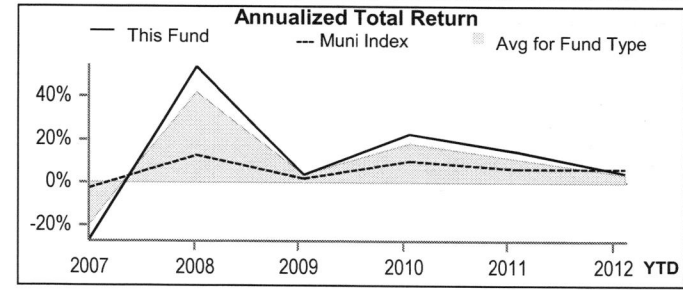

DTF Tax Free Income (DTF)   B+   Good

Fund Family: Duff & Phelps Investment Mgmt Co
Fund Type: Municipal - National
Inception Date: November 29, 1991

Major Rating Factors: Strong performance is the major factor driving the B+ (Good) TheStreet.com Investment Rating for DTF Tax Free Income. The fund currently has a performance rating of B (Good) based on an annualized return of 12.19% over the last three years and a total return of 4.34% year to date 2012. Factored into the performance evaluation is an expense ratio of 1.23% (average).

The fund's risk rating is currently B (Good). It carries a beta of 2.07, meaning it is expected to move 20.7% for every 10% move in the market. Volatility, as measured by both the semi-deviation and a drawdown factor, is considered low. As of December 31, 2012, DTF Tax Free Income traded at a discount of 3.05% below its net asset value, which is better than its one-year historical average premium of .60%.

Amy L. Robinson currently receives a manager quality ranking of 31 (0=worst, 99=best). If you desire only a moderate level of risk and strong performance, then this fund is an excellent option.

Data Date	Investment Rating	Net Assets ($Mil)	Price	Perfor-mance Rating/Pts	Total Return Y-T-D	Risk Rating/Pts
12-12	B+	138.11	16.82	B / 7.6	4.34%	B / 8.7
2011	B+	131.89	16.06	B / 8.2	1.00%	B / 8.9
2010	C+	136.53	14.82	C+ / 6.3	7.59%	C+ / 6.8
2009	B	128.43	14.56	C / 5.5	27.07%	B- / 7.6

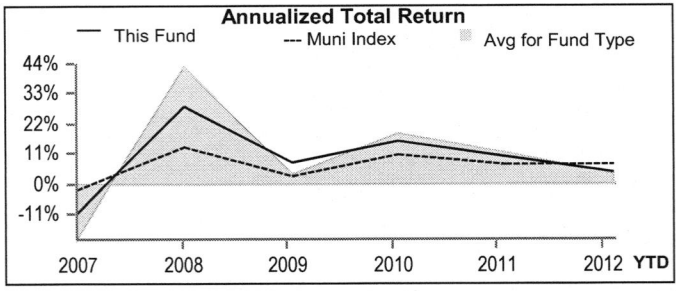

Duff & Phelps Global Utility Incom (DPG)   D+   Weak

Fund Family: Duff & Phelps Investment Mgmt Co
Fund Type: Utilities
Inception Date: July 29, 2011

Major Rating Factors:
Disappointing performance is the major factor driving the D+ (Weak) TheStreet.com Investment Rating for Duff & Phelps Global Utility Incom. The fund currently has a performance rating of D (Weak) based on an annualized return of 0.00% over the last three years and a total return of 7.05% year to date 2012.

The fund's risk rating is currently B- (Good). It carries a beta of 0.00, meaning the fund's expected move will be 0.0% for every 10% move in the market. Volatility, as measured by both the semi-deviation and a drawdown factor, is considered low. As of December 31, 2012, Duff & Phelps Global Utility Incom traded at a discount of 13.13% below its net asset value, which is better than its one-year historical average discount of 4.55%.

This fund has been team managed for 2 years and currently receives a manager quality ranking of 53 (0=worst, 99=best). This fund offers only a moderate level of risk but investors looking for strong performance are still waiting.

Data Date	Investment Rating	Net Assets ($Mil)	Price	Perfor-mance Rating/Pts	Total Return Y-T-D	Risk Rating/Pts
12-12	D+	704.20	16.87	D / 1.9	7.05%	B- / 7.9

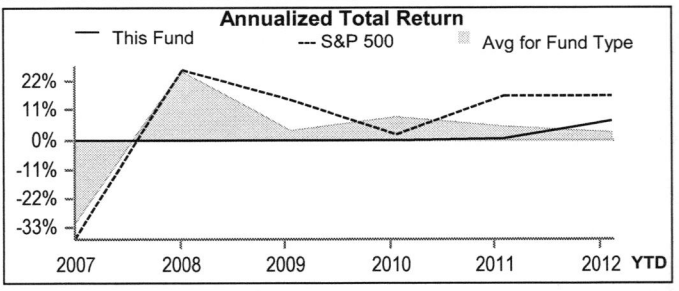

Duff & Phelps Utilities & Crp Bd T (DUC)   C-   Fair

Fund Family: Duff & Phelps Investment Mgmt Co
Fund Type: General - Investment Grade
Inception Date: January 22, 1993

Major Rating Factors: Middle of the road best describes Duff & Phelps Utilities & Crp Bd T whose TheStreet.com Investment Rating is currently a C- (Fair). The fund currently has a performance rating of C- (Fair) based on an annualized return of 8.52% over the last three years and a total return of 2.20% year to date 2012. Factored into the performance evaluation is an expense ratio of 1.78% (above average).

The fund's risk rating is currently B (Good). It carries a beta of 2.05, meaning it is expected to move 20.5% for every 10% move in the market. Volatility, as measured by both the semi-deviation and a drawdown factor, is considered low. As of December 31, 2012, Duff & Phelps Utilities & Crp Bd T traded at a premium of 3.37% above its net asset value, which is better than its one-year historical average premium of 4.06%.

Daniel J. Petrisko has been running the fund for 17 years and currently receives a manager quality ranking of 23 (0=worst, 99=best). If you desire an average level of risk, then this fund may be an option.

Data Date	Investment Rating	Net Assets ($Mil)	Price	Perfor-mance Rating/Pts	Total Return Y-T-D	Risk Rating/Pts
12-12	C-	324.21	12.26	C- / 3.3	2.20%	B / 8.7
2011	C+	319.92	12.04	C / 5.5	1.16%	B / 8.8
2010	B-	318.39	11.39	C+ / 5.9	-0.60%	B- / 7.3
2009	B-	306.51	12.29	C / 5.3	27.90%	B- / 7.4

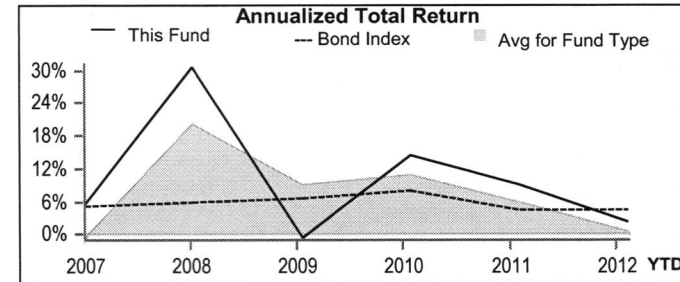

DWS Global High Income Fund (LBF)

B **Good**

Fund Family: DWS Investments
Fund Type: Global
Inception Date: July 24, 1992

Major Rating Factors: Strong performance is the major factor driving the B (Good) TheStreet.com Investment Rating for DWS Global High Income Fund. The fund currently has a performance rating of B- (Good) based on an annualized return of 14.82% over the last three years and a total return of 5.01% year to date 2012. Factored into the performance evaluation is an expense ratio of 2.22% (high).

The fund's risk rating is currently B- (Good). It carries a beta of 0.91, meaning that its performance tracks fairly well with that of the overall stock market. Volatility, as measured by both the semi-deviation and a drawdown factor, is considered low. As of December 31, 2012, DWS Global High Income Fund traded at a discount of 11.58% below its net asset value, which is better than its one-year historical average discount of 9.80%.

Gary A. Russell currently receives a manager quality ranking of 89 (0=worst, 99=best). If you desire only a moderate level of risk and strong performance, then this fund is an excellent option.

Data Date	Investment Rating	Net Assets ($Mil)	Price	Performance Rating/Pts	Total Return Y-T-D	Risk Rating/Pts
12-12	B	63.00	8.78	B- / 7.5	5.01%	B- / 7.8
2011	C+	61.70	7.57	C+ / 6.6	2.11%	B- / 7.4
2010	C	84.00	7.80	C+ / 6.5	13.94%	C / 4.3
2009	C	68.95	7.29	C / 5.2	46.23%	C / 5.1

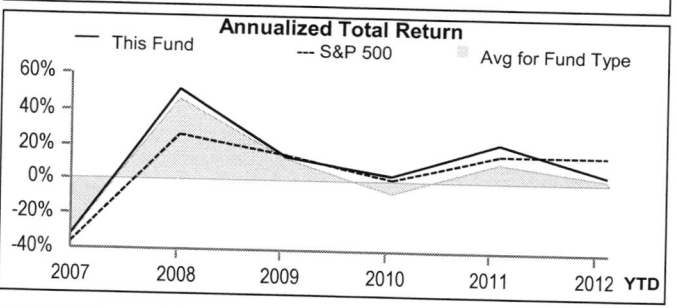

DWS High Income Opportunities Fund (DHG)

C+ **Fair**

Fund Family: DWS Investments
Fund Type: Global
Inception Date: November 22, 2006

Major Rating Factors: Middle of the road best describes DWS High Income Opportunities Fund whose TheStreet.com Investment Rating is currently a C+ (Fair). The fund currently has a performance rating of C+ (Fair) based on an annualized return of 16.37% over the last three years and a total return of 4.16% year to date 2012. Factored into the performance evaluation is an expense ratio of 2.08% (high).

The fund's risk rating is currently B- (Good). It carries a beta of 0.41, meaning the fund's expected move will be 4.1% for every 10% move in the market. Volatility, as measured by both the semi-deviation and a drawdown factor, is considered low. As of December 31, 2012, DWS High Income Opportunities Fund traded at a discount of 8.07% below its net asset value, which is better than its one-year historical average discount of .88%.

Gary A. Russell has been running the fund for 3 years and currently receives a manager quality ranking of 95 (0=worst, 99=best). If you desire an average level of risk, then this fund may be an option.

Data Date	Investment Rating	Net Assets ($Mil)	Price	Performance Rating/Pts	Total Return Y-T-D	Risk Rating/Pts
12-12	C+	270.00	15.16	C+ / 6.8	4.16%	B- / 7.0
2011	B+	252.50	13.86	B / 8.1	1.95%	B / 8.3
2010	E	365.00	14.08	D- / 1.2	25.15%	D / 2.0
2009	E	350.43	12.07	E+ / 0.8	57.98%	C- / 3.1

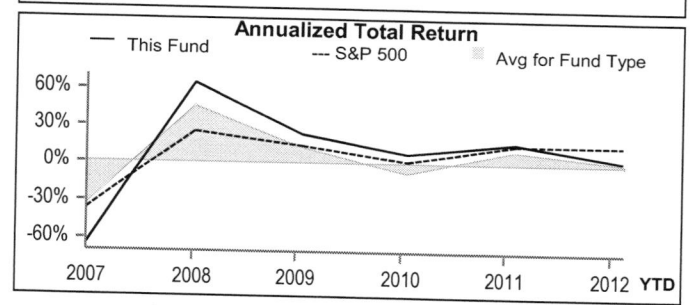

DWS High Income Trust (KHI)

B- **Good**

Fund Family: DWS Investments
Fund Type: Corporate - High Yield
Inception Date: April 21, 1988

Major Rating Factors: DWS High Income Trust receives a TheStreet.com Investment Rating of B- (Good). The fund currently has a performance rating of C+ (Fair) based on an annualized return of 16.66% over the last three years and a total return of 3.82% year to date 2012. Factored into the performance evaluation is an expense ratio of 1.73% (above average).

The fund's risk rating is currently B (Good). It carries a beta of 1.27, meaning it is expected to move 12.7% for every 10% move in the market. Volatility, as measured by both the semi-deviation and a drawdown factor, is considered low. As of December 31, 2012, DWS High Income Trust traded at a price exactly equal to its net asset value, which is better than its one-year historical average premium of 5.59%.

Gary A. Russell has been running the fund for 15 years and currently receives a manager quality ranking of 62 (0=worst, 99=best). If you desire an average level of risk, then this fund may be an option.

Data Date	Investment Rating	Net Assets ($Mil)	Price	Performance Rating/Pts	Total Return Y-T-D	Risk Rating/Pts
12-12	B-	154.00	10.20	C+ / 6.7	3.82%	B / 8.0
2011	B-	151.60	10.23	B+ / 8.6	-0.10%	C+ / 6.5
2010	C+	146.00	9.39	B- / 7.5	21.08%	C- / 4.1
2009	C	120.46	8.47	C+ / 5.9	60.93%	C / 4.5

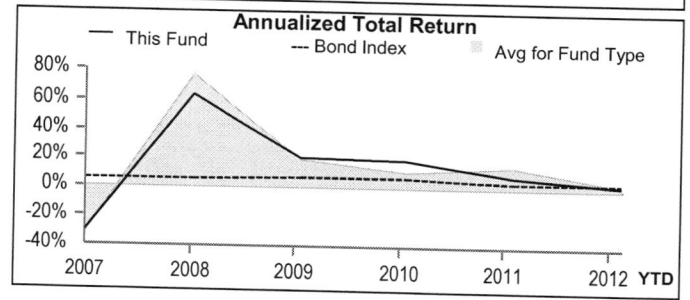

* Denotes ETF Fund

DWS Multi-Market Income Trust (KMM)   C+   Fair

Fund Family: DWS Investments
Fund Type: Global
Inception Date: January 23, 1989

Major Rating Factors: Strong performance is the major factor driving the C+ (Fair) TheStreet.com Investment Rating for DWS Multi-Market Income Trust. The fund currently has a performance rating of B- (Good) based on an annualized return of 17.17% over the last three years and a total return of 4.69% year to date 2012. Factored into the performance evaluation is an expense ratio of 1.63% (above average).

The fund's risk rating is currently B- (Good). It carries a beta of 0.72, meaning the fund's expected move will be 7.2% for every 10% move in the market. Volatility, as measured by both the semi-deviation and a drawdown factor, is considered low. As of December 31, 2012, DWS Multi-Market Income Trust traded at a discount of .57% below its net asset value, which is better than its one-year historical average premium of 5.87%.

Gary A. Russell currently receives a manager quality ranking of 94 (0=worst, 99=best). If you desire only a moderate level of risk and strong performance, then this fund is an excellent option.

Data Date	Investment Rating	Net Assets ($Mil)	Price	Performance Rating/Pts	Total Return Y-T-D	Risk Rating/Pts
12-12	C+	238.00	10.44	B- / 7.0	4.69%	B- / 7.2
2011	B	234.40	10.10	B+ / 8.6	1.68%	B- / 7.0
2010	B	218.10	9.91	B+ / 8.6	26.07%	C / 4.3
2009	C+	190.98	8.61	C+ / 6.7	62.81%	C / 5.1

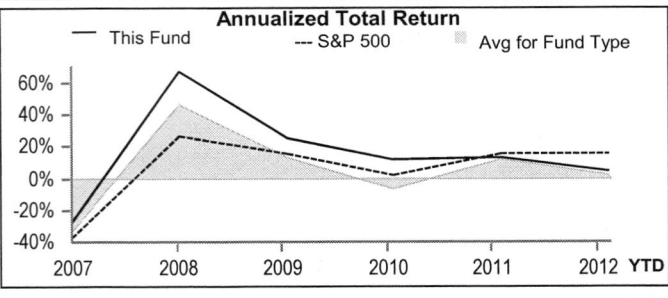

DWS Municipal Income Trust (KTF)   A+   Excellent

Fund Family: DWS Investments
Fund Type: Municipal - National
Inception Date: October 20, 1988

Major Rating Factors:
Exceptional performance is the major factor driving the A+ (Excellent) TheStreet.com Investment Rating for DWS Municipal Income Trust. The fund currently has a performance rating of A (Excellent) based on an annualized return of 16.63% over the last three years and a total return of 6.67% year to date 2012. Factored into the performance evaluation is an expense ratio of 1.14% (low).

The fund's risk rating is currently B (Good). It carries a beta of 2.25, meaning it is expected to move 22.5% for every 10% move in the market. Volatility, as measured by both the semi-deviation and a drawdown factor, is considered low. As of December 31, 2012, DWS Municipal Income Trust traded at a premium of .14% above its net asset value, which is better than its one-year historical average premium of 4.36%.

Philip G. Condon currently receives a manager quality ranking of 44 (0=worst, 99=best). If you desire only a moderate level of risk and strong performance, then this fund is an excellent option.

Data Date	Investment Rating	Net Assets ($Mil)	Price	Performance Rating/Pts	Total Return Y-T-D	Risk Rating/Pts
12-12	A+	536.00	14.39	A / 9.3	6.67%	B / 8.6
2011	A+	505.20	13.80	A+ / 9.8	-1.45%	B / 8.8
2010	B+	465.33	11.42	B- / 7.0	3.85%	C+ / 6.5
2009	A+	440.43	11.78	B / 7.9	49.68%	C+ / 6.9

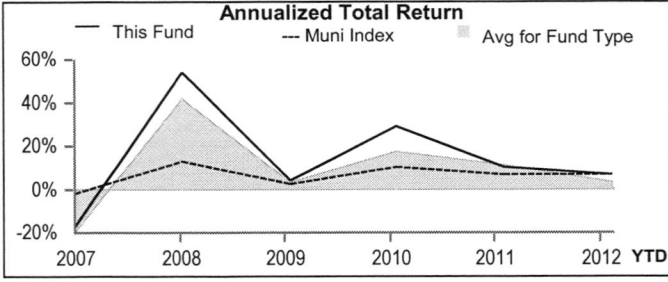

DWS Strategic Income Fund (KST)   B-   Good

Fund Family: DWS Investments
Fund Type: Global
Inception Date: April 29, 1994

Major Rating Factors: Strong performance is the major factor driving the B- (Good) TheStreet.com Investment Rating for DWS Strategic Income Fund. The fund currently has a performance rating of B- (Good) based on an annualized return of 17.46% over the last three years and a total return of 4.13% year to date 2012. Factored into the performance evaluation is an expense ratio of 2.03% (high).

The fund's risk rating is currently B- (Good). It carries a beta of 0.44, meaning the fund's expected move will be 4.4% for every 10% move in the market. Volatility, as measured by both the semi-deviation and a drawdown factor, is considered low. As of December 31, 2012, DWS Strategic Income Fund traded at a discount of 2.46% below its net asset value, which is better than its one-year historical average premium of 2.07%.

Gary A. Russell currently receives a manager quality ranking of 95 (0=worst, 99=best). If you desire only a moderate level of risk and strong performance, then this fund is an excellent option.

Data Date	Investment Rating	Net Assets ($Mil)	Price	Performance Rating/Pts	Total Return Y-T-D	Risk Rating/Pts
12-12	B-	63.00	14.26	B- / 7.0	4.13%	B- / 7.6
2011	B	62.40	13.35	B+ / 8.4	0.15%	B- / 7.4
2010	B-	60.13	12.68	B / 8.0	19.44%	C / 4.8
2009	C-	51.68	11.57	C / 4.6	55.85%	C / 5.2

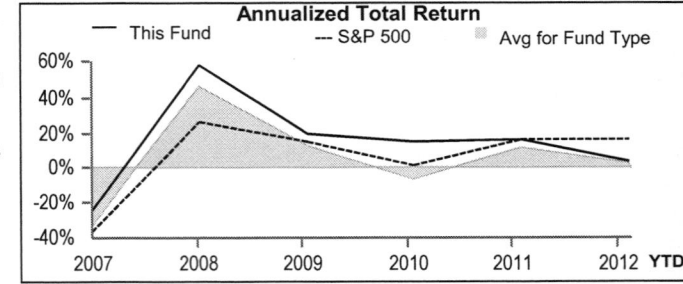

DWS Strategic Municipal Inc Tr (KSM)

A-   **Excellent**

Fund Family: DWS Investments
Fund Type: Municipal - National
Inception Date: March 22, 1989

Major Rating Factors:
Strong performance is the major factor driving the A- (Excellent) TheStreet.com Investment Rating for DWS Strategic Municipal Inc Tr. The fund currently has a performance rating of B (Good) based on an annualized return of 13.95% over the last three years and a total return of 5.57% year to date 2012. Factored into the performance evaluation is an expense ratio of 1.26% (average).

The fund's risk rating is currently B (Good). It carries a beta of 1.73, meaning it is expected to move 17.3% for every 10% move in the market. Volatility, as measured by both the semi-deviation and a drawdown factor, is considered low. As of December 31, 2012, DWS Strategic Municipal Inc Tr traded at a premium of 2.18% above its net asset value, which is better than its one-year historical average premium of 8.40%.

Philip G. Condon has been running the fund for 15 years and currently receives a manager quality ranking of 62 (0=worst, 99=best). If you desire only a moderate level of risk and strong performance, then this fund is an excellent option.

Data Date	Investment Rating	Net Assets ($Mil)	Price	Perfor-mance Rating/Pts	Total Return Y-T-D	Risk Rating/Pts
12-12	A-	150.00	14.55	B / 8.2	5.57%	B / 8.6
2011	A+	141.20	13.90	A+ / 9.9	2.81%	B / 8.9
2010	B+	138.00	12.28	B / 8.0	5.37%	C+ / 6.0
2009	A	121.32	12.60	B / 8.2	69.48%	C+ / 6.4

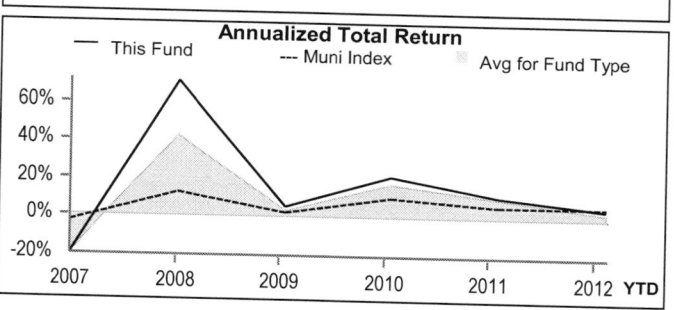

Eagle Capital Growth Fund (GRF)

C+   **Fair**

Fund Family: Sims Capital Management LLC
Fund Type: Growth
Inception Date: July 2, 1990

Major Rating Factors: Middle of the road best describes Eagle Capital Growth Fund whose TheStreet.com Investment Rating is currently a C+ (Fair). The fund currently has a performance rating of C+ (Fair) based on an annualized return of 12.64% over the last three years and a total return of -2.68% year to date 2012. Factored into the performance evaluation is an expense ratio of 1.31% (average).

The fund's risk rating is currently B (Good). It carries a beta of 0.69, meaning the fund's expected move will be 6.9% for every 10% move in the market. Volatility, as measured by both the semi-deviation and a drawdown factor, is considered low. As of December 31, 2012, Eagle Capital Growth Fund traded at a discount of 9.67% below its net asset value, which is worse than its one-year historical average discount of 12.43%.

David C. Sims currently receives a manager quality ranking of 77 (0=worst, 99=best). If you desire an average level of risk, then this fund may be an option.

Data Date	Investment Rating	Net Assets ($Mil)	Price	Perfor-mance Rating/Pts	Total Return Y-T-D	Risk Rating/Pts
12-12	C+	23.68	7.10	C+ / 5.8	-2.68%	B / 8.3
2011	B	22.20	7.00	B / 7.8	8.17%	B- / 7.7
2010	C-	21.00	6.62	C- / 3.3	9.34%	C+ / 6.3
2009	C-	16.80	6.39	C- / 3.3	28.82%	C / 5.5

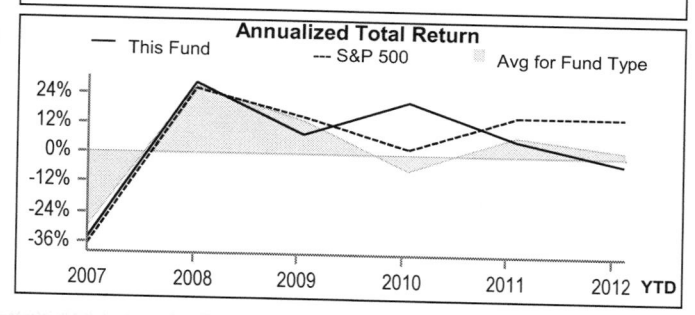

Eaton Vance CA Muni Bond (EVM)

C+   **Fair**

Fund Family: Eaton Vance Management
Fund Type: Municipal - Single State
Inception Date: August 27, 2002

Major Rating Factors: Middle of the road best describes Eaton Vance CA Muni Bond whose TheStreet.com Investment Rating is currently a C+ (Fair). The fund currently has a performance rating of C (Fair) based on an annualized return of 9.33% over the last three years and a total return of 3.95% year to date 2012. Factored into the performance evaluation is an expense ratio of 1.73% (above average).

The fund's risk rating is currently B (Good). It carries a beta of 2.89, meaning it is expected to move 28.9% for every 10% move in the market. Volatility, as measured by both the semi-deviation and a drawdown factor, is considered low. As of December 31, 2012, Eaton Vance CA Muni Bond traded at a discount of 7.75% below its net asset value, which is better than its one-year historical average discount of 2.23%.

Cynthia J. Clemson has been running the fund for 11 years and currently receives a manager quality ranking of 14 (0=worst, 99=best). If you desire an average level of risk, then this fund may be an option.

Data Date	Investment Rating	Net Assets ($Mil)	Price	Perfor-mance Rating/Pts	Total Return Y-T-D	Risk Rating/Pts
12-12	C+	282.35	12.14	C / 5.5	3.95%	B / 8.1
2011	B+	257.20	12.82	B+ / 8.8	-1.09%	B / 8.0
2010	D	273.91	11.25	D- / 1.5	5.61%	C+ / 6.2
2009	C-	280.74	11.43	C- / 3.4	43.32%	C+ / 6.5

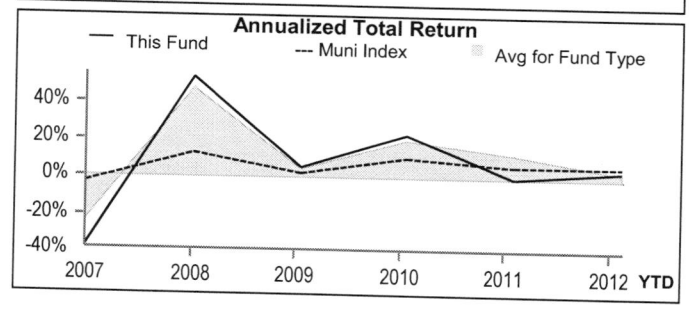

Eaton Vance CA Muni Bond II (EIA)

A+   **Excellent**

Fund Family: Eaton Vance Management
Fund Type: Municipal - Single State
Inception Date: November 25, 2002

Major Rating Factors:

Exceptional performance is the major factor driving the A+ (Excellent) TheStreet.com Investment Rating for Eaton Vance CA Muni Bond II. The fund currently has a performance rating of A+ (Excellent) based on an annualized return of 16.50% over the last three years and a total return of 7.52% year to date 2012. Factored into the performance evaluation is an expense ratio of 1.50% (average).

The fund's risk rating is currently B (Good). It carries a beta of 2.78, meaning it is expected to move 27.8% for every 10% move in the market. Volatility, as measured by both the semi-deviation and a drawdown factor, is considered low. As of December 31, 2012, Eaton Vance CA Muni Bond II traded at a premium of 3.91% above its net asset value, which is worse than its one-year historical average premium of 1.85%.

Cynthia J. Clemson has been running the fund for 11 years and currently receives a manager quality ranking of 28 (0=worst, 99=best). If you desire only a moderate level of risk and strong performance, then this fund is an excellent option.

Data Date	Investment Rating	Net Assets ($Mil)	Price	Performance Rating/Pts	Total Return Y-T-D	Risk Rating/Pts
12-12	A+	52.06	14.10	A+ / 9.6	7.52%	B / 8.2
2011	B+	46.50	12.77	B+ / 8.9	-0.82%	B / 8.2
2010	D	48.53	11.00	D / 1.6	3.14%	C+ / 6.1
2009	C-	50.08	11.46	C- / 3.3	39.64%	C+ / 6.3

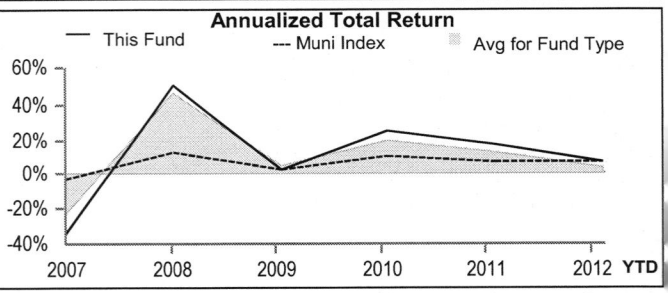

Eaton Vance CA Muni Inc Tr (CEV)

A-   **Excellent**

Fund Family: Eaton Vance Management
Fund Type: Municipal - Single State
Inception Date: January 26, 1999

Major Rating Factors:

Strong performance is the major factor driving the A- (Excellent) TheStreet.com Investment Rating for Eaton Vance CA Muni Inc Tr. The fund currently has a performance rating of B+ (Good) based on an annualized return of 12.75% over the last three years and a total return of 2.73% year to date 2012. Factored into the performance evaluation is an expense ratio of 1.80% (above average).

The fund's risk rating is currently B (Good). It carries a beta of 2.21, meaning it is expected to move 22.1% for every 10% move in the market. Volatility, as measured by both the semi-deviation and a drawdown factor, is considered low. As of December 31, 2012, Eaton Vance CA Muni Inc Tr traded at a discount of .07% below its net asset value, which is better than its one-year historical average premium of 1.14%.

Cynthia J. Clemson has been running the fund for 14 years and currently receives a manager quality ranking of 42 (0=worst, 99=best). If you desire only a moderate level of risk and strong performance, then this fund is an excellent option.

Data Date	Investment Rating	Net Assets ($Mil)	Price	Performance Rating/Pts	Total Return Y-T-D	Risk Rating/Pts
12-12	A-	100.33	14.27	B+ / 8.3	2.73%	B / 8.5
2011	A	93.00	13.06	A / 9.3	-0.77%	B / 8.5
2010	D	93.25	11.67	D / 1.9	5.21%	C+ / 5.7
2009	C	84.48	11.90	C / 4.9	60.17%	C+ / 6.1

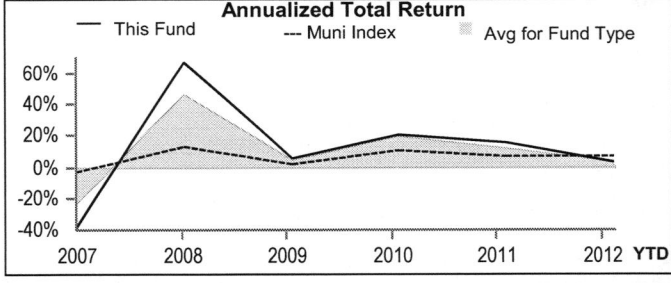

Eaton Vance Enhanced Eqty Inc (EOI)

D+   **Weak**

Fund Family: Eaton Vance Management
Fund Type: Income
Inception Date: October 29, 2004

Major Rating Factors:

Disappointing performance is the major factor driving the D+ (Weak) TheStreet.com Investment Rating for Eaton Vance Enhanced Eqty Inc. The fund currently has a performance rating of D+ (Weak) based on an annualized return of 2.37% over the last three years and a total return of 4.78% year to date 2012. Factored into the performance evaluation is an expense ratio of 1.15% (low).

The fund's risk rating is currently B- (Good). It carries a beta of 0.84, meaning the fund's expected move will be 8.4% for every 10% move in the market. Volatility, as measured by both the semi-deviation and a drawdown factor, is considered low. As of December 31, 2012, Eaton Vance Enhanced Eqty Inc traded at a discount of 15.93% below its net asset value, which is better than its one-year historical average discount of 13.04%.

Walter A. Row, III has been running the fund for 9 years and currently receives a manager quality ranking of 16 (0=worst, 99=best). This fund offers only a moderate level of risk but investors looking for strong performance are still waiting.

Data Date	Investment Rating	Net Assets ($Mil)	Price	Performance Rating/Pts	Total Return Y-T-D	Risk Rating/Pts
12-12	D+	503.83	10.66	D+ / 2.8	4.78%	B- / 7.1
2011	D	476.70	10.18	D+ / 2.4	1.57%	C+ / 6.8
2010	D	513.95	12.64	D / 2.1	-1.01%	C+ / 5.6
2009	C-	534.95	14.19	C- / 3.7	30.32%	C / 5.3

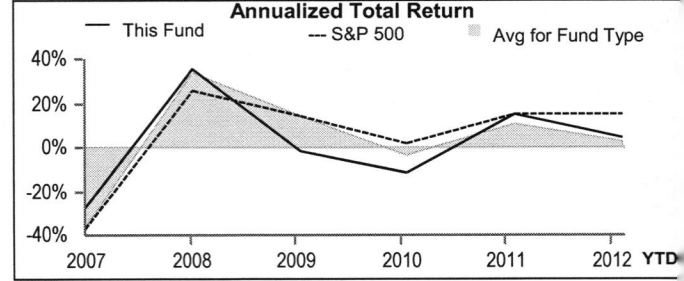

Eaton Vance Enhanced Eqty Inc II (EOS)

D   **Weak**

Fund Family: Eaton Vance Management
Fund Type: Income
Inception Date: January 26, 2005

Major Rating Factors:
Disappointing performance is the major factor driving the D (Weak) TheStreet.com Investment Rating for Eaton Vance Enhanced Eqty Inc II. The fund currently has a performance rating of D+ (Weak) based on an annualized return of 3.24% over the last three years and a total return of 4.21% year to date 2012. Factored into the performance evaluation is an expense ratio of 1.11% (low).

The fund's risk rating is currently C+ (Fair). It carries a beta of 0.81, meaning the fund's expected move will be 8.1% for every 10% move in the market. Volatility, as measured by both the semi-deviation and a drawdown factor, is considered low. As of December 31, 2012, Eaton Vance Enhanced Eqty Inc II traded at a discount of 14.78% below its net asset value, which is better than its one-year historical average discount of 12.12%.

Walter A. Row, III has been running the fund for 8 years and currently receives a manager quality ranking of 15 (0=worst, 99=best). This fund offers only a moderate level of risk but investors looking for strong performance are still waiting.

Data Date	Investment Rating	Net Assets ($Mil)	Price	Perfor-mance Rating/Pts	Total Return Y-T-D	Risk Rating/Pts
12-12	D	588.56	10.44	D+ / 2.7	4.21%	C+ / 6.8
2011	C-	569.60	10.21	C / 4.3	1.76%	C+ / 6.4
2010	D+	563.82	12.21	D / 2.2	-4.47%	C+ / 5.9
2009	C	566.26	14.32	C+ / 5.6	45.56%	C / 4.7

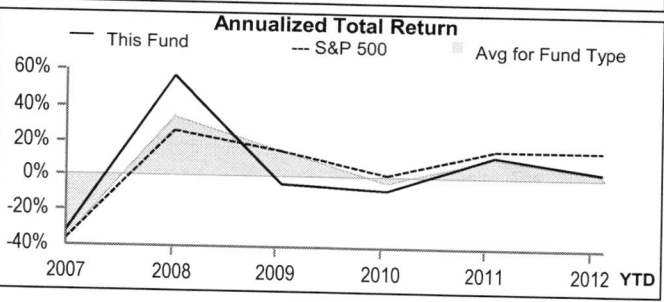

Eaton Vance Floating Rate Income T (EFT)

B   **Good**

Fund Family: Eaton Vance Management
Fund Type: Loan Participation
Inception Date: June 29, 2004

Major Rating Factors: Strong performance is the major factor driving the B (Good) TheStreet.com Investment Rating for Eaton Vance Floating Rate Income T. The fund currently has a performance rating of B (Good) based on an annualized return of 13.38% over the last three years and a total return of 3.64% year to date 2012. Factored into the performance evaluation is an expense ratio of 1.86% (above average).

The fund's risk rating is currently B (Good). It carries a beta of -247.42, meaning the fund's expected move will be -2474.2% for every 10% move in the market. Volatility, as measured by both the semi-deviation and a drawdown factor, is considered low. As of December 31, 2012, Eaton Vance Floating Rate Income T traded at a premium of 5.77% above its net asset value, which is worse than its one-year historical average premium of 2.68%.

Scott H. Page has been running the fund for 9 years and currently receives a manager quality ranking of 99 (0=worst, 99=best). If you desire only a moderate level of risk and strong performance, then this fund is an excellent option.

Data Date	Investment Rating	Net Assets ($Mil)	Price	Perfor-mance Rating/Pts	Total Return Y-T-D	Risk Rating/Pts
12-12	B	582.01	17.04	B / 7.8	3.64%	B / 8.1
2011	B	564.10	14.23	B / 7.7	3.72%	B / 8.2
2010	C+	556.61	16.00	B / 7.6	20.23%	C / 4.3
2009	C	425.90	14.16	C+ / 5.8	83.29%	C / 4.9

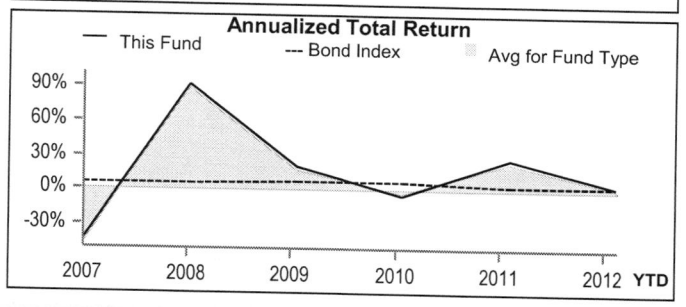

Eaton Vance Limited Duration Incom (EVV)

C   **Fair**

Fund Family: Eaton Vance Management
Fund Type: General Bond
Inception Date: May 30, 2003

Major Rating Factors: Middle of the road best describes Eaton Vance Limited Duration Incom whose TheStreet.com Investment Rating is currently a C (Fair). The fund currently has a performance rating of C+ (Fair) based on an annualized return of 12.09% over the last three years and a total return of 3.32% year to date 2012. Factored into the performance evaluation is an expense ratio of 1.71% (above average).

The fund's risk rating is currently B- (Good). It carries a beta of 0.47, meaning the fund's expected move will be 4.7% for every 10% move in the market. Volatility, as measured by both the semi-deviation and a drawdown factor, is considered low. As of December 31, 2012, Eaton Vance Limited Duration Incom traded at a discount of .95% below its net asset value, which is better than its one-year historical average discount of .92%.

Payson F. Swaffield has been running the fund for 10 years and currently receives a manager quality ranking of 88 (0=worst, 99=best). If you desire an average level of risk, then this fund may be an option.

Data Date	Investment Rating	Net Assets ($Mil)	Price	Perfor-mance Rating/Pts	Total Return Y-T-D	Risk Rating/Pts
12-12	C	1,941.50	16.66	C+ / 5.6	3.32%	B- / 7.7
2011	B-	1,899.70	15.23	B- / 7.1	1.58%	B- / 7.7
2010	C+	1,950.18	16.05	B / 7.6	16.59%	C / 4.4
2009	C	1,456.96	14.90	C+ / 6.4	60.33%	C / 5.1

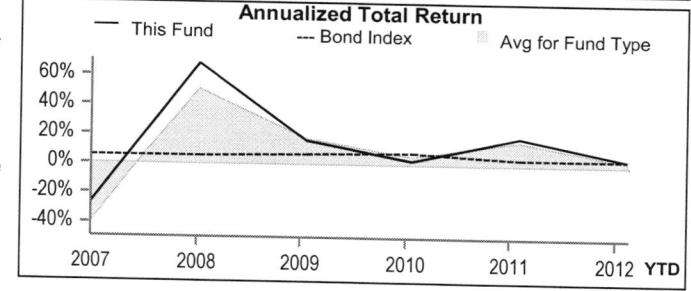

Eaton Vance MA Muni Bond (MAB)

B   **Good**

Fund Family: Eaton Vance Management
Fund Type: Municipal - Single State
Inception Date: November 25, 2002

Major Rating Factors: Strong performance is the major factor driving the B (Good) TheStreet.com Investment Rating for Eaton Vance MA Muni Bond. The fund currently has a performance rating of B- (Good) based on an annualized return of 10.29% over the last three years and a total return of 3.65% year to date 2012. Factored into the performance evaluation is an expense ratio of 1.55% (average).

The fund's risk rating is currently B (Good). It carries a beta of 2.53, meaning it is expected to move 25.3% for every 10% move in the market. Volatility, as measured by both the semi-deviation and a drawdown factor, is considered low. As of December 31, 2012, Eaton Vance MA Muni Bond traded at a discount of .31% below its net asset value, which is better than its one-year historical average premium of 3.31%.

Craig R. Brandon has been running the fund for 3 years and currently receives a manager quality ranking of 15 (0=worst, 99=best). If you desire only a moderate level of risk and strong performance, then this fund is an excellent option.

Data Date	Investment Rating	Net Assets ($Mil)	Price	Perfor-mance Rating/Pts	Total Return Y-T-D	Risk Rating/Pts
12-12	B	28.14	15.90	B- / 7.3	3.65%	B / 8.4
2011	B-	25.60	14.36	C+ / 6.9	1.18%	B / 8.2
2010	C-	25.92	12.91	D / 1.8	-9.86%	B- / 7.3
2009	B+	25.77	15.20	B- / 7.5	53.12%	C+ / 6.3

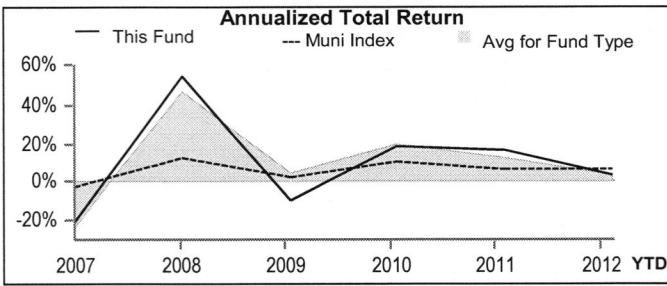

Eaton Vance MA Muni Inc Tr (MMV)

B-   **Good**

Fund Family: Eaton Vance Management
Fund Type: Municipal - Single State
Inception Date: January 26, 1999

Major Rating Factors: Eaton Vance MA Muni Inc Tr receives a TheStreet.com Investment Rating of B- (Good). The fund currently has a performance rating of C+ (Fair) based on an annualized return of 10.59% over the last three years and a total return of 2.28% year to date 2012. Factored into the performance evaluation is an expense ratio of 1.85% (above average).

The fund's risk rating is currently B (Good). It carries a beta of 1.72, meaning it is expected to move 17.2% for every 10% move in the market. Volatility, as measured by both the semi-deviation and a drawdown factor, is considered low. As of December 31, 2012, Eaton Vance MA Muni Inc Tr traded at a discount of 3.11% below its net asset value, which is better than its one-year historical average premium of .22%.

Craig R. Brandon has been running the fund for 3 years and currently receives a manager quality ranking of 39 (0=worst, 99=best). If you desire an average level of risk, then this fund may be an option.

Data Date	Investment Rating	Net Assets ($Mil)	Price	Perfor-mance Rating/Pts	Total Return Y-T-D	Risk Rating/Pts
12-12	B-	42.00	15.26	C+ / 6.4	2.28%	B / 8.6
2011	A-	39.70	14.46	B+ / 8.7	3.53%	B / 8.7
2010	C+	39.13	13.50	C+ / 6.0	4.02%	C+ / 6.1
2009	B	34.26	13.84	B- / 7.0	54.15%	C+ / 6.2

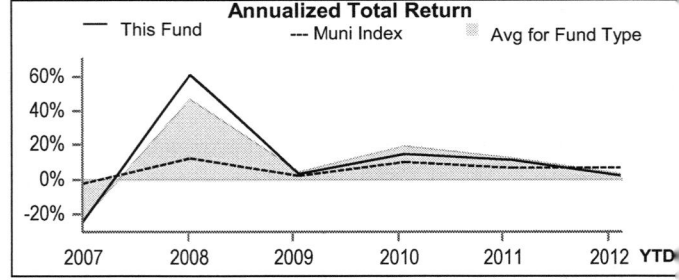

Eaton Vance MI Muni Bond (MIW)

C+   **Fair**

Fund Family: Eaton Vance Management
Fund Type: Municipal - Single State
Inception Date: November 25, 2002

Major Rating Factors: Middle of the road best describes Eaton Vance MI Muni Bond whose TheStreet.com Investment Rating is currently a C+ (Fair). The fund currently has a performance rating of C (Fair) based on an annualized return of 9.90% over the last three years and a total return of 3.75% year to date 2012. Factored into the performance evaluation is an expense ratio of 1.54% (average).

The fund's risk rating is currently B (Good). It carries a beta of 1.52, meaning it is expected to move 15.2% for every 10% move in the market. Volatility, as measured by both the semi-deviation and a drawdown factor, is considered low. As of December 31, 2012, Eaton Vance MI Muni Bond traded at a discount of 4.70% below its net asset value, which is better than its one-year historical average premium of 3.90%.

William H. Ahern, Jr. has been running the fund for 11 years and currently receives a manager quality ranking of 45 (0=worst, 99=best). If you desire an average level of risk, then this fund may be an option.

Data Date	Investment Rating	Net Assets ($Mil)	Price	Perfor-mance Rating/Pts	Total Return Y-T-D	Risk Rating/Pts
12-12	C+	22.76	14.40	C / 5.4	3.75%	B / 8.4
2011	A+	21.60	14.76	A+ / 9.7	0.05%	B / 8.6
2010	D+	21.99	12.32	D+ / 2.3	-1.32%	C+ / 6.6
2009	B+	22.28	13.31	B- / 7.1	55.88%	C+ / 6.7

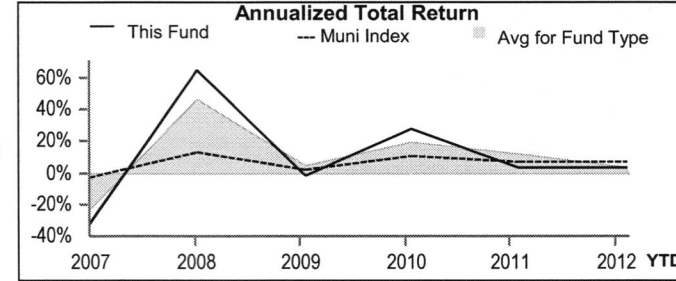

Eaton Vance MI Muni Inc Tr (EMI)

A   **Excellent**

Fund Family: Eaton Vance Management
Fund Type: Municipal - Single State
Inception Date: January 26, 1999

Major Rating Factors:
Strong performance is the major factor driving the A (Excellent) TheStreet.com Investment Rating for Eaton Vance MI Muni Inc Tr. The fund currently has a performance rating of B+ (Good) based on an annualized return of 13.32% over the last three years and a total return of 4.38% year to date 2012. Factored into the performance evaluation is an expense ratio of 1.91% (above average).

The fund's risk rating is currently B (Good). It carries a beta of 2.06, meaning it is expected to move 20.6% for every 10% move in the market. Volatility, as measured by both the semi-deviation and a drawdown factor, is considered low. As of December 31, 2012, Eaton Vance MI Muni Inc Tr traded at a discount of 7.44% below its net asset value, which is better than its one-year historical average discount of 5.69%.

William H. Ahern, Jr. has been running the fund for 14 years and currently receives a manager quality ranking of 39 (0=worst, 99=best). If you desire only a moderate level of risk and strong performance, then this fund is an excellent option.

Data Date	Investment Rating	Net Assets ($Mil)	Price	Performance Rating/Pts	Total Return Y-T-D	Risk Rating/Pts
12-12	A	30.72	13.80	B+ / 8.5	4.38%	B / 8.7
2011	A-	29.20	12.90	B+ / 8.8	-0.08%	B / 8.7
2010	D+	28.49	11.43	D / 2.2	3.24%	C+ / 5.9
2009	C+	26.11	11.86	C / 5.1	54.86%	C+ / 6.7

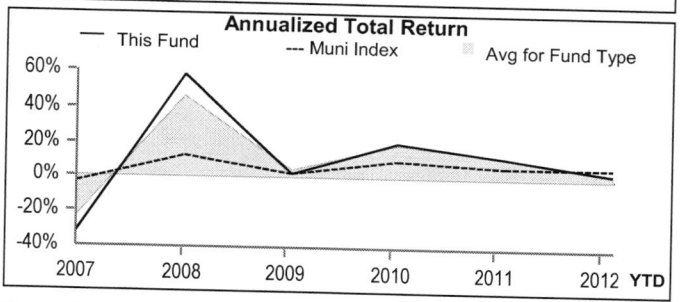

Eaton Vance Muni Bond Fund (EIM)

B+   **Good**

Fund Family: Eaton Vance Management
Fund Type: Municipal - National
Inception Date: August 27, 2002

Major Rating Factors: Strong performance is the major factor driving the B+ (Good) TheStreet.com Investment Rating for Eaton Vance Muni Bond Fund. The fund currently has a performance rating of B (Good) based on an annualized return of 10.94% over the last three years and a total return of 2.86% year to date 2012. Factored into the performance evaluation is an expense ratio of 1.78% (above average).

The fund's risk rating is currently B (Good). It carries a beta of 2.60, meaning it is expected to move 26.0% for every 10% move in the market. Volatility, as measured by both the semi-deviation and a drawdown factor, is considered low. As of December 31, 2012, Eaton Vance Muni Bond Fund traded at a discount of 2.10% below its net asset value, which is better than its one-year historical average discount of .57%.

William H. Ahern, Jr. has been running the fund for 3 years and currently receives a manager quality ranking of 21 (0=worst, 99=best). If you desire only a moderate level of risk and strong performance, then this fund is an excellent option.

Data Date	Investment Rating	Net Assets ($Mil)	Price	Performance Rating/Pts	Total Return Y-T-D	Risk Rating/Pts
12-12	B+	960.53	13.99	B / 7.9	2.86%	B / 8.3
2011	B+	866.50	12.68	B / 8.1	-0.32%	B / 8.4
2010	D+	889.54	11.48	D- / 1.3	-0.42%	C+ / 6.8
2009	C-	893.39	12.40	C- / 4.2	42.42%	C+ / 5.8

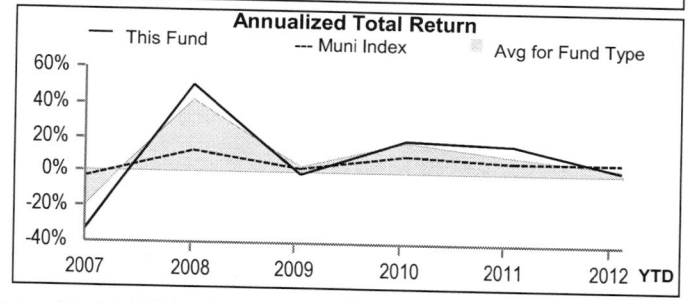

Eaton Vance Muni Bond II (EIV)

C+   **Fair**

Fund Family: Eaton Vance Management
Fund Type: Municipal - National
Inception Date: November 25, 2002

Major Rating Factors: Middle of the road best describes Eaton Vance Muni Bond II whose TheStreet.com Investment Rating is currently a C+ (Fair). The fund currently has a performance rating of C (Fair) based on an annualized return of 9.26% over the last three years and a total return of 5.78% year to date 2012. Factored into the performance evaluation is an expense ratio of 1.65% (above average).

The fund's risk rating is currently B (Good). It carries a beta of 2.37, meaning it is expected to move 23.7% for every 10% move in the market. Volatility, as measured by both the semi-deviation and a drawdown factor, is considered low. As of December 31, 2012, Eaton Vance Muni Bond II traded at a discount of 1.48% below its net asset value, which is better than its one-year historical average premium of 6.86%.

William H. Ahern, Jr. has been running the fund for 9 years and currently receives a manager quality ranking of 18 (0=worst, 99=best). If you desire an average level of risk, then this fund may be an option.

Data Date	Investment Rating	Net Assets ($Mil)	Price	Performance Rating/Pts	Total Return Y-T-D	Risk Rating/Pts
12-12	C+	133.77	13.32	C / 5.4	5.78%	B / 8.6
2011	A+	121.50	13.87	A / 9.4	0.94%	B / 8.8
2010	D	126.81	12.00	D / 2.0	0.15%	C+ / 5.8
2009	C+	128.15	12.90	C+ / 6.0	46.32%	C+ / 5.9

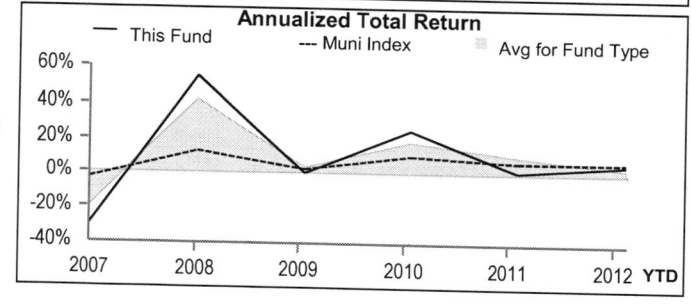

* Denotes ETF Fund

Eaton Vance Municipal Inc Tr (EVN)

A+   **Excellent**

Fund Family: Eaton Vance Management
Fund Type: Municipal - National
Inception Date: January 26, 1999

Major Rating Factors:
Exceptional performance is the major factor driving the A+ (Excellent) TheStreet.com Investment Rating for Eaton Vance Municipal Inc Tr. The fund currently has a performance rating of A- (Excellent) based on an annualized return of 15.65% over the last three years and a total return of 5.54% year to date 2012. Factored into the performance evaluation is an expense ratio of 2.09% (high).

The fund's risk rating is currently B (Good). It carries a beta of 2.07, meaning it is expected to move 20.7% for every 10% move in the market. Volatility, as measured by both the semi-deviation and a drawdown factor, is considered low. As of December 31, 2012, Eaton Vance Municipal Inc Tr traded at a premium of 6.09% above its net asset value, which is better than its one-year historical average premium of 12.52%.

Thomas M. Metzold has been running the fund for 14 years and currently receives a manager quality ranking of 60 (0=worst, 99=best). If you desire only a moderate level of risk and strong performance, then this fund is an excellent option.

Data Date	Investment Rating	Net Assets ($Mil)	Price	Perfor-mance Rating/Pts	Total Return Y-T-D	Risk Rating/Pts
12-12	A+	276.76	13.77	A- / 9.1	5.54%	B / 8.5
2011	A-	252.60	12.75	A- / 9.2	0.31%	B / 8.5
2010	D	260.25	11.13	D / 1.6	4.67%	C / 5.2
2009	C	214.07	11.53	C / 4.5	57.48%	C+ / 5.7

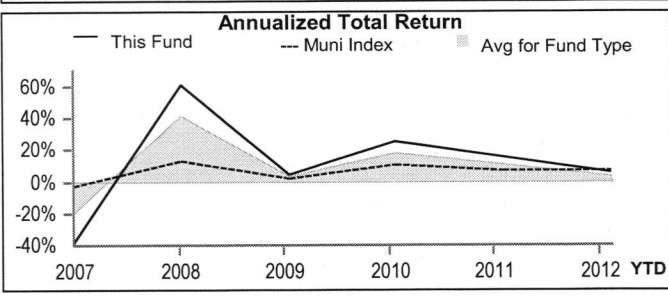

Eaton Vance National Municipal Opp (EOT)

B-   **Good**

Fund Family: Eaton Vance Management
Fund Type: Municipal - National
Inception Date: May 29, 2009

Major Rating Factors: Eaton Vance National Municipal Opp receives a TheStreet.com Investment Rating of B- (Good). The fund currently has a performance rating of C+ (Fair) based on an annualized return of 10.97% over the last three years and a total return of 2.98% year to date 2012. Factored into the performance evaluation is an expense ratio of 0.91% (low).

The fund's risk rating is currently B (Good). It carries a beta of 2.08, meaning it is expected to move 20.8% for every 10% move in the market. Volatility, as measured by both the semi-deviation and a drawdown factor, is considered low. As of December 31, 2012, Eaton Vance National Municipal Opp traded at a discount of 3.45% below its net asset value, which is better than its one-year historical average premium of .14%.

Dan Wasiolek has been running the fund for 4 years and currently receives a manager quality ranking of 33 (0=worst, 99=best). If you desire an average level of risk, then this fund may be an option.

Data Date	Investment Rating	Net Assets ($Mil)	Price	Perfor-mance Rating/Pts	Total Return Y-T-D	Risk Rating/Pts
12-12	B-	331.23	22.14	C+ / 6.8	2.98%	B / 8.3
2011	A-	318.80	20.90	A- / 9.1	-0.43%	B / 8.4
2010	C-	324.33	19.09	D / 1.7	5.76%	B- / 7.9

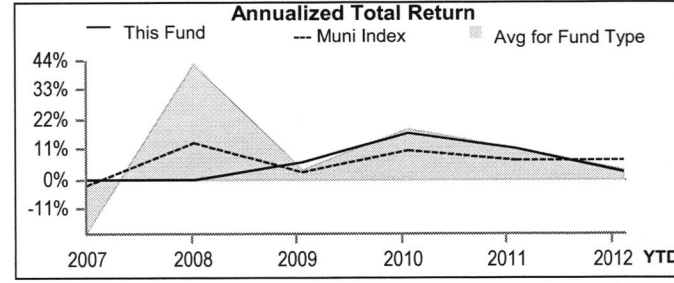

Eaton Vance NJ Muni Bond (EMJ)

B+   **Good**

Fund Family: Eaton Vance Management
Fund Type: Municipal - Single State
Inception Date: November 25, 2002

Major Rating Factors: Strong performance is the major factor driving the B+ (Good) TheStreet.com Investment Rating for Eaton Vance NJ Muni Bond. The fund currently has a performance rating of B (Good) based on an annualized return of 9.98% over the last three years and a total return of -1.22% year to date 2012. Factored into the performance evaluation is an expense ratio of 1.51% (average).

The fund's risk rating is currently B (Good). It carries a beta of 1.53, meaning it is expected to move 15.3% for every 10% move in the market. Volatility, as measured by both the semi-deviation and a drawdown factor, is considered low. As of December 31, 2012, Eaton Vance NJ Muni Bond traded at a premium of 9.43% above its net asset value, which is worse than its one-year historical average premium of 4.45%.

Adam Weigold has been running the fund for 3 years and currently receives a manager quality ranking of 59 (0=worst, 99=best). If you desire only a moderate level of risk and strong performance, then this fund is an excellent option.

Data Date	Investment Rating	Net Assets ($Mil)	Price	Perfor-mance Rating/Pts	Total Return Y-T-D	Risk Rating/Pts
12-12	B+	38.14	16.24	B / 8.1	-1.22%	B / 8.3
2011	B	34.90	14.16	B / 7.7	-1.84%	B / 8.3
2010	D+	37.22	12.61	D- / 1.5	-6.04%	C+ / 6.7
2009	C+	37.63	14.33	C+ / 6.7	51.54%	C+ / 6.4

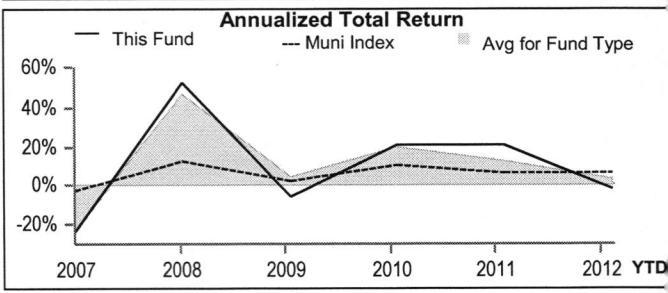

Eaton Vance NJ Muni Inc Tr (EVJ)

B+ **Good**

Fund Family: Eaton Vance Management
Fund Type: Municipal - Single State
Inception Date: January 26, 1999

Major Rating Factors: Strong performance is the major factor driving the B+ (Good) TheStreet.com Investment Rating for Eaton Vance NJ Muni Inc Tr. The fund currently has a performance rating of B (Good) based on an annualized return of 10.49% over the last three years and a total return of 4.12% year to date 2012. Factored into the performance evaluation is an expense ratio of 1.84% (above average).

The fund's risk rating is currently B (Good). It carries a beta of 2.38, meaning it is expected to move 23.8% for every 10% move in the market. Volatility, as measured by both the semi-deviation and a drawdown factor, is considered low. As of December 31, 2012, Eaton Vance NJ Muni Inc Tr traded at a premium of 3.92% above its net asset value, which is better than its one-year historical average premium of 3.97%.

Adam Weigold has been running the fund for 3 years and currently receives a manager quality ranking of 21 (0=worst, 99=best). If you desire only a moderate level of risk and strong performance, then this fund is an excellent option.

Data Date	Investment Rating	Net Assets ($Mil)	Price	Perfor- mance Rating/Pts	Total Return Y-T-D	Risk Rating/Pts
12-12	B+	65.46	15.10	B / 7.6	4.12%	B / 8.4
2011	B+	62.10	13.95	B+ / 8.8	-1.43%	B / 8.5
2010	C-	65.22	12.48	C- / 3.3	-2.98%	C+ / 5.8
2009	B+	57.62	13.78	B / 8.0	79.67%	C+ / 5.8

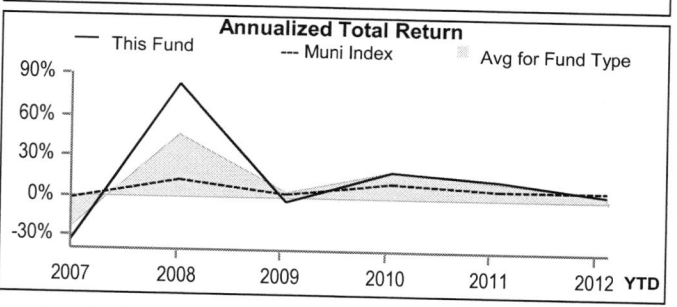

Eaton Vance NY Muni Bond (ENX)

C+ **Fair**

Fund Family: Eaton Vance Management
Fund Type: Municipal - Single State
Inception Date: August 27, 2002

Major Rating Factors: Middle of the road best describes Eaton Vance NY Muni Bond whose TheStreet.com Investment Rating is currently a C+ (Fair). The fund currently has a performance rating of C (Fair) based on an annualized return of 8.01% over the last three years and a total return of 3.88% year to date 2012. Factored into the performance evaluation is an expense ratio of 1.65% (above average).

The fund's risk rating is currently B (Good). It carries a beta of 2.36, meaning it is expected to move 23.6% for every 10% move in the market. Volatility, as measured by both the semi-deviation and a drawdown factor, is considered low. As of December 31, 2012, Eaton Vance NY Muni Bond traded at a discount of 4.33% below its net asset value, which is better than its one-year historical average premium of .79%.

Craig R. Brandon has been running the fund for 8 years and currently receives a manager quality ranking of 15 (0=worst, 99=best). If you desire an average level of risk, then this fund may be an option.

Data Date	Investment Rating	Net Assets ($Mil)	Price	Perfor- mance Rating/Pts	Total Return Y-T-D	Risk Rating/Pts
12-12	C+	229.79	13.93	C / 5.2	3.88%	B / 8.3
2011	B+	212.70	13.97	B / 7.9	-2.86%	B / 8.6
2010	D+	215.45	12.18	D- / 1.5	-5.41%	B- / 7.0
2009	C+	215.30	13.71	C+ / 6.6	45.33%	C+ / 6.2

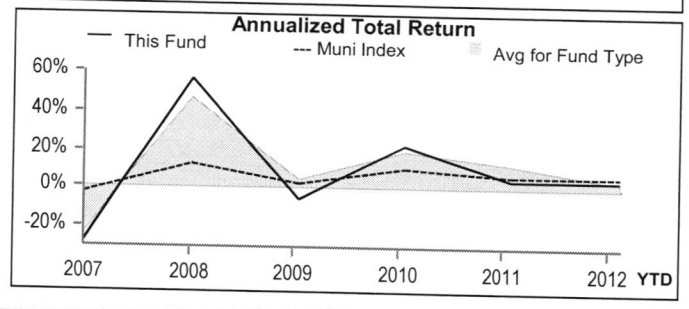

Eaton Vance NY Muni Bond II (NYH)

B- **Good**

Fund Family: Eaton Vance Management
Fund Type: Municipal - Single State
Inception Date: November 25, 2002

Major Rating Factors: Eaton Vance NY Muni Bond II receives a TheStreet.com Investment Rating of B- (Good). The fund currently has a performance rating of C+ (Fair) based on an annualized return of 9.86% over the last three years and a total return of 6.73% year to date 2012. Factored into the performance evaluation is an expense ratio of 1.64% (above average).

The fund's risk rating is currently B (Good). It carries a beta of 2.35, meaning it is expected to move 23.5% for every 10% move in the market. Volatility, as measured by both the semi-deviation and a drawdown factor, is considered low. As of December 31, 2012, Eaton Vance NY Muni Bond II traded at a discount of 4.64% below its net asset value, which is better than its one-year historical average premium of 2.28%.

Craig R. Brandon has been running the fund for 8 years and currently receives a manager quality ranking of 17 (0=worst, 99=best). If you desire an average level of risk, then this fund may be an option.

Data Date	Investment Rating	Net Assets ($Mil)	Price	Perfor- mance Rating/Pts	Total Return Y-T-D	Risk Rating/Pts
12-12	B-	35.67	13.37	C+ / 6.3	6.73%	B / 8.4
2011	B+	33.50	13.69	B+ / 8.6	0.73%	B / 8.5
2010	D+	34.33	12.03	D / 1.9	-0.31%	C+ / 6.6
2009	C+	34.85	12.91	C+ / 5.7	46.59%	C+ / 6.2

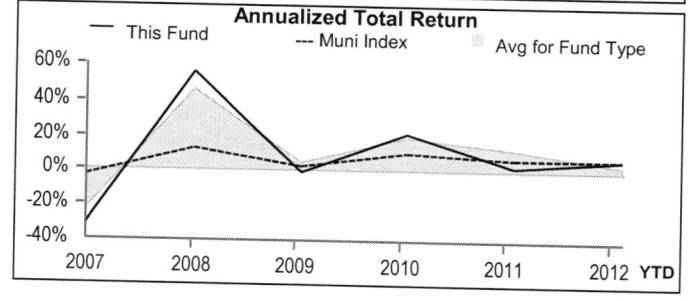

Eaton Vance NY Muni Inc Tr (EVY)

A+　　**Excellent**

Fund Family: Eaton Vance Management
Fund Type: Municipal - Single State
Inception Date: January 26, 1999

Data Date	Investment Rating	Net Assets ($Mil)	Price	Perfor-mance Rating/Pts	Total Return Y-T-D	Risk Rating/Pts
12-12	A+	79.95	15.64	A- / 9.1	3.77%	B / 8.6
2011	A+	74.80	13.99	A+ / 9.6	1.93%	B / 8.6
2010	D+	74.31	12.46	D+ / 2.7	-0.23%	C / 5.2
2009	B-	64.18	13.36	B / 7.6	83.39%	C / 5.2

Major Rating Factors:

Exceptional performance is the major factor driving the A+ (Excellent) TheStreet.com Investment Rating for Eaton Vance NY Muni Inc Tr. The fund currently has a performance rating of A- (Excellent) based on an annualized return of 14.38% over the last three years and a total return of 3.77% year to date 2012. Factored into the performance evaluation is an expense ratio of 1.87% (above average).

The fund's risk rating is currently B (Good). It carries a beta of 2.29, meaning it is expected to move 22.9% for every 10% move in the market. Volatility, as measured by both the semi-deviation and a drawdown factor, is considered low. As of December 31, 2012, Eaton Vance NY Muni Inc Tr traded at a premium of 3.64% above its net asset value, which is worse than its one-year historical average premium of 3.14%.

Craig R. Brandon has been running the fund for 14 years and currently receives a manager quality ranking of 33 (0=worst, 99=best). If you desire only a moderate level of risk and strong performance, then this fund is an excellent option.

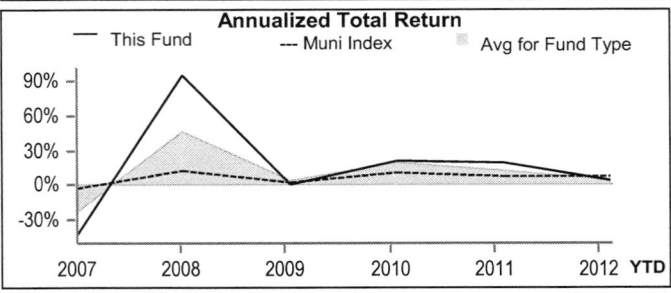

Eaton Vance OH Muni Bond (EIO)

B-　　**Good**

Fund Family: Eaton Vance Management
Fund Type: Municipal - Single State
Inception Date: November 25, 2002

Data Date	Investment Rating	Net Assets ($Mil)	Price	Perfor-mance Rating/Pts	Total Return Y-T-D	Risk Rating/Pts
12-12	B-	34.99	14.08	C+ / 6.7	5.54%	B / 8.2
2011	B+	31.70	13.10	B / 8.1	2.44%	B / 8.3
2010	D+	32.73	11.51	D / 1.7	-0.56%	C+ / 6.4
2009	C	32.71	12.30	C / 4.3	42.19%	C+ / 6.8

Major Rating Factors: Eaton Vance OH Muni Bond receives a TheStreet.com Investment Rating of B- (Good). The fund currently has a performance rating of C+ (Fair) based on an annualized return of 11.01% over the last three years and a total return of 5.54% year to date 2012. Factored into the performance evaluation is an expense ratio of 1.36% (average).

The fund's risk rating is currently B (Good). It carries a beta of 2.15, meaning it is expected to move 21.5% for every 10% move in the market. Volatility, as measured by both the semi-deviation and a drawdown factor, is considered low. As of December 31, 2012, Eaton Vance OH Muni Bond traded at a premium of .28% above its net asset value, which is better than its one-year historical average premium of 8.53%.

William H. Ahern, Jr. has been running the fund for 8 years and currently receives a manager quality ranking of 29 (0=worst, 99=best). If you desire an average level of risk, then this fund may be an option.

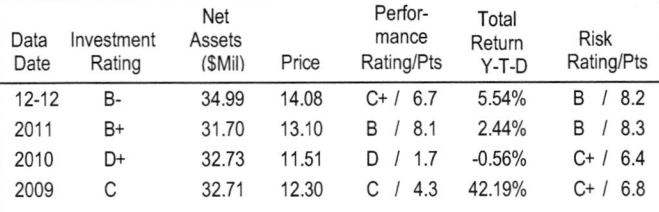

Eaton Vance OH Muni Inc Tr (EVO)

A　　**Excellent**

Fund Family: Eaton Vance Management
Fund Type: Municipal - Single State
Inception Date: January 26, 1999

Data Date	Investment Rating	Net Assets ($Mil)	Price	Perfor-mance Rating/Pts	Total Return Y-T-D	Risk Rating/Pts
12-12	A	42.42	16.45	A- / 9.0	-0.11%	B / 8.2
2011	A-	39.70	13.85	A- / 9.2	1.52%	B / 8.3
2010	C-	39.19	12.50	C- / 4.0	-0.23%	C+ / 5.9
2009	B	35.50	13.38	B- / 7.0	55.89%	C+ / 6.4

Major Rating Factors:

Exceptional performance is the major factor driving the A (Excellent) TheStreet.com Investment Rating for Eaton Vance OH Muni Inc Tr. The fund currently has a performance rating of A- (Excellent) based on an annualized return of 14.20% over the last three years and a total return of -0.11% year to date 2012. Factored into the performance evaluation is an expense ratio of 1.79% (above average).

The fund's risk rating is currently B (Good). It carries a beta of 1.73, meaning it is expected to move 17.3% for every 10% move in the market. Volatility, as measured by both the semi-deviation and a drawdown factor, is considered low. As of December 31, 2012, Eaton Vance OH Muni Inc Tr traded at a premium of 6.89% above its net asset value, which is worse than its one-year historical average premium of 3.34%.

William H. Ahern, Jr. has been running the fund for 8 years and currently receives a manager quality ranking of 68 (0=worst, 99=best). If you desire only a moderate level of risk and strong performance, then this fund is an excellent option.

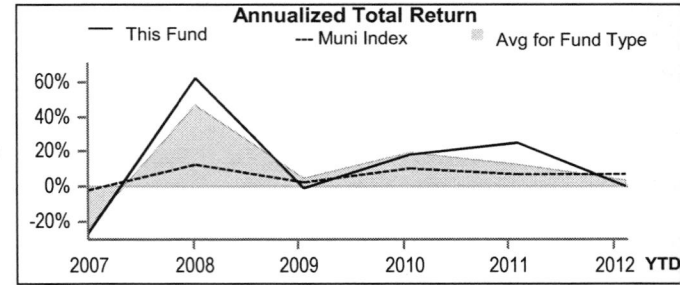

Eaton Vance PA Muni Bond (EIP)   B   Good

Fund Family: Eaton Vance Management
Fund Type: Municipal - Single State
Inception Date: November 25, 2002

Major Rating Factors: Strong performance is the major factor driving the B (Good) TheStreet.com Investment Rating for Eaton Vance PA Muni Bond. The fund currently has a performance rating of B (Good) based on an annualized return of 10.52% over the last three years and a total return of 2.88% year to date 2012. Factored into the performance evaluation is an expense ratio of 1.37% (average).

The fund's risk rating is currently B (Good). It carries a beta of 2.45, meaning it is expected to move 24.5% for every 10% move in the market. Volatility, as measured by both the semi-deviation and a drawdown factor, is considered low. As of December 31, 2012, Eaton Vance PA Muni Bond traded at a premium of 5.62% above its net asset value, which is better than its one-year historical average premium of 5.95%.

Adam Weigold has been running the fund for 6 years and currently receives a manager quality ranking of 20 (0=worst, 99=best). If you desire only a moderate level of risk and strong performance, then this fund is an excellent option.

Data Date	Investment Rating	Net Assets ($Mil)	Price	Performance Rating/Pts	Total Return Y-T-D	Risk Rating/Pts
12-12	B	42.79	15.40	B / 7.6	2.88%	B / 8.3
2011	B+	39.50	13.42	B+ / 8.7	2.09%	B / 8.1
2010	D+	40.26	11.73	D- / 1.5	-10.91%	C+ / 6.8
2009	B	40.96	14.04	B / 7.9	71.36%	C+ / 5.6

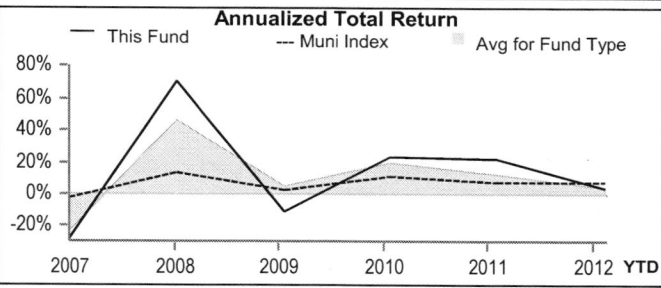

Eaton Vance PA Muni Inc Tr (EVP)   A-   Excellent

Fund Family: Eaton Vance Management
Fund Type: Municipal - Single State
Inception Date: January 26, 1999

Major Rating Factors:
Strong performance is the major factor driving the A- (Excellent) TheStreet.com Investment Rating for Eaton Vance PA Muni Inc Tr. The fund currently has a performance rating of B (Good) based on an annualized return of 11.60% over the last three years and a total return of 4.22% year to date 2012. Factored into the performance evaluation is an expense ratio of 1.90% (above average).

The fund's risk rating is currently B (Good). It carries a beta of 1.80, meaning it is expected to move 18.0% for every 10% move in the market. Volatility, as measured by both the semi-deviation and a drawdown factor, is considered low. As of December 31, 2012, Eaton Vance PA Muni Inc Tr traded at a premium of .42% above its net asset value, which is better than its one-year historical average premium of 1.07%.

Adam Weigold has been running the fund for 6 years and currently receives a manager quality ranking of 36 (0=worst, 99=best). If you desire only a moderate level of risk and strong performance, then this fund is an excellent option.

Data Date	Investment Rating	Net Assets ($Mil)	Price	Performance Rating/Pts	Total Return Y-T-D	Risk Rating/Pts
12-12	A-	38.40	14.46	B / 8.1	4.22%	B / 8.7
2011	A	36.80	13.46	A- / 9.2	0.13%	B / 8.6
2010	D+	37.74	12.30	C- / 3.1	-0.20%	C / 5.5
2009	B+	34.18	13.14	B / 7.7	69.56%	C+ / 6.1

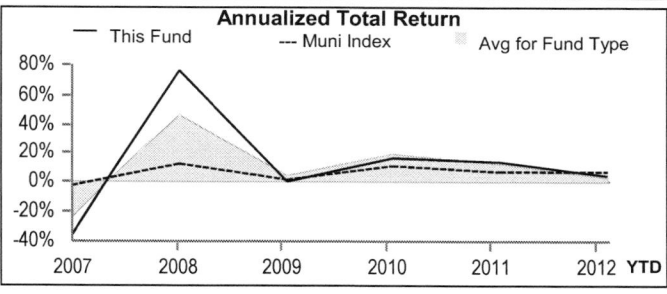

Eaton Vance Risk Mgd Div Eq Inc (ETJ)   D   Weak

Fund Family: Eaton Vance Management
Fund Type: Income
Inception Date: July 31, 2007

Major Rating Factors:
Disappointing performance is the major factor driving the D (Weak) TheStreet.com Investment Rating for Eaton Vance Risk Mgd Div Eq Inc. The fund currently has a performance rating of D- (Weak) based on an annualized return of -3.91% over the last three years and a total return of 3.84% year to date 2012. Factored into the performance evaluation is an expense ratio of 1.09% (low).

The fund's risk rating is currently C+ (Fair). It carries a beta of 0.23, meaning the fund's expected move will be 2.3% for every 10% move in the market. Volatility, as measured by both the semi-deviation and a drawdown factor, is considered low. As of December 31, 2012, Eaton Vance Risk Mgd Div Eq Inc traded at a discount of 14.72% below its net asset value, which is better than its one-year historical average discount of 14.15%.

Michael A. Allison has been running the fund for 6 years and currently receives a manager quality ranking of 18 (0=worst, 99=best). This fund offers only a moderate level of risk but investors looking for strong performance are still waiting.

Data Date	Investment Rating	Net Assets ($Mil)	Price	Performance Rating/Pts	Total Return Y-T-D	Risk Rating/Pts
12-12	D	922.23	10.43	D- / 1.3	3.84%	C+ / 6.6
2011	D	922.20	10.45	D- / 1.5	1.72%	C+ / 6.6
2010	C-	1,064.93	13.28	D / 2.1	-9.99%	B- / 7.9
2009	C	1,153.88	16.66	C- / 3.3	4.05%	B- / 7.3

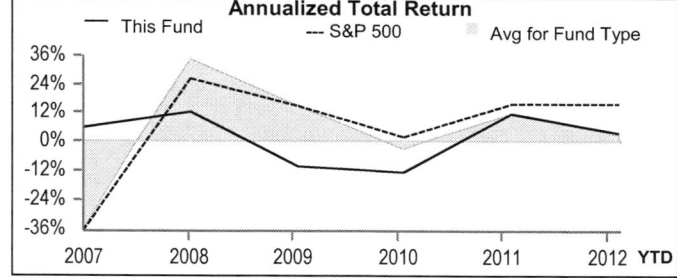

Eaton Vance Senior Floating Rate (EFR) C Fair

Fund Family: Eaton Vance Management
Fund Type: Loan Participation
Inception Date: November 28, 2003

Major Rating Factors: Middle of the road best describes Eaton Vance Senior Floating Rate whose TheStreet.com Investment Rating is currently a C (Fair). The fund currently has a performance rating of C+ (Fair) based on an annualized return of 10.35% over the last three years and a total return of 4.26% year to date 2012. Factored into the performance evaluation is an expense ratio of 1.73% (above average).

The fund's risk rating is currently B- (Good). It carries a beta of -196.88, meaning the fund's expected move will be -1968.8% for every 10% move in the market. Volatility, as measured by both the semi-deviation and a drawdown factor, is considered low. As of December 31, 2012, Eaton Vance Senior Floating Rate traded at a premium of 1.40% above its net asset value, which is better than its one-year historical average premium of 2.43%.

Craig P. Russ has been running the fund for 10 years and currently receives a manager quality ranking of 99 (0=worst, 99=best). If you desire an average level of risk, then this fund may be an option.

Data Date	Investment Rating	Net Assets ($Mil)	Price	Performance Rating/Pts	Total Return Y-T-D	Risk Rating/Pts
12-12	C	503.38	15.97	C+ / 5.7	4.26%	B- / 7.5
2011	B	496.40	14.38	B / 7.8	2.50%	B- / 7.6
2010	C+	505.67	16.22	B / 7.9	19.54%	C- / 4.1
2009	C+	340.98	14.58	B / 7.7	91.29%	C / 4.4

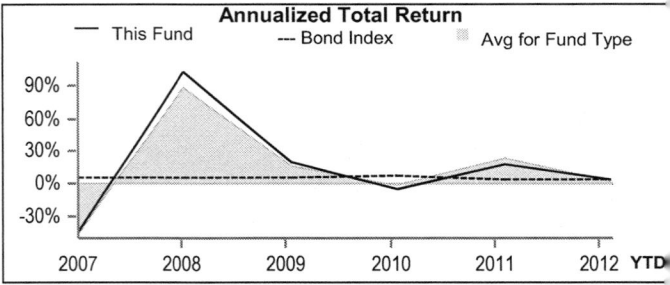

Eaton Vance Senior Income Trust (EVF) B- Good

Fund Family: Eaton Vance Management
Fund Type: Loan Participation
Inception Date: October 27, 1998

Major Rating Factors: Eaton Vance Senior Income Trust receives a TheStreet.com Investment Rating of B- (Good). The fund currently has a performance rating of C+ (Fair) based on an annualized return of 12.43% over the last three years and a total return of 1.59% year to date 2012. Factored into the performance evaluation is an expense ratio of 2.24% (high).

The fund's risk rating is currently B (Good). It carries a beta of -189.93, meaning the fund's expected move will be -1899.3% for every 10% move in the market. Volatility, as measured by both the semi-deviation and a drawdown factor, is considered low. As of December 31, 2012, Eaton Vance Senior Income Trust traded at a premium of 1.89% above its net asset value, which is worse than its one-year historical average discount of .16%.

Scott H. Page has been running the fund for 15 years and currently receives a manager quality ranking of 99 (0=worst, 99=best). If you desire an average level of risk, then this fund may be an option.

Data Date	Investment Rating	Net Assets ($Mil)	Price	Performance Rating/Pts	Total Return Y-T-D	Risk Rating/Pts
12-12	B-	263.17	7.54	C+ / 6.6	1.59%	B / 8.4
2011	B	254.50	6.53	B / 7.8	1.07%	B / 8.4
2010	C+	245.74	7.16	B- / 7.5	20.90%	C- / 4.1
2009	C	200.18	6.26	C+ / 5.6	84.34%	C / 4.9

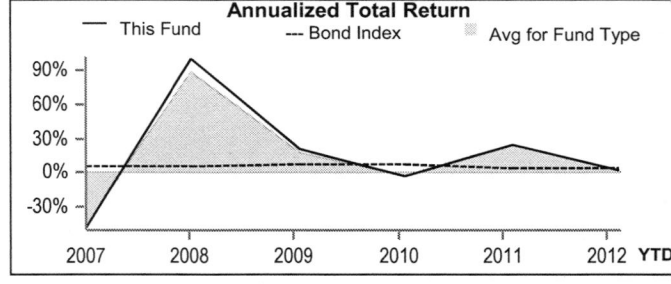

Eaton Vance Sh Dur Diversified Inc (EVG) C Fair

Fund Family: Eaton Vance Management
Fund Type: Global
Inception Date: February 23, 2005

Major Rating Factors: Middle of the road best describes Eaton Vance Sh Dur Diversified Inc whose TheStreet.com Investment Rating is currently a C (Fair). The fund currently has a performance rating of C- (Fair) based on an annualized return of 8.93% over the last three years and a total return of 0.92% year to date 2012. Factored into the performance evaluation is an expense ratio of 1.89% (above average).

The fund's risk rating is currently B (Good). It carries a beta of 0.07, meaning the fund's expected move will be 0.7% for every 10% move in the market. Volatility, as measured by both the semi-deviation and a drawdown factor, is considered low. As of December 31, 2012, Eaton Vance Sh Dur Diversified Inc traded at a discount of 3.30% below its net asset value, which is worse than its one-year historical average discount of 4.07%.

Payson F. Swaffield has been running the fund for 8 years and currently receives a manager quality ranking of 88 (0=worst, 99=best). If you desire an average level of risk, then this fund may be an option.

Data Date	Investment Rating	Net Assets ($Mil)	Price	Performance Rating/Pts	Total Return Y-T-D	Risk Rating/Pts
12-12	C	336.17	17.31	C- / 3.8	0.92%	B / 8.6
2011	C	330.80	16.20	C+ / 5.6	1.79%	B- / 7.6
2010	C+	347.81	16.88	C+ / 6.6	11.53%	C+ / 6.1
2009	C+	293.17	16.12	C / 5.5	41.66%	C+ / 6.9

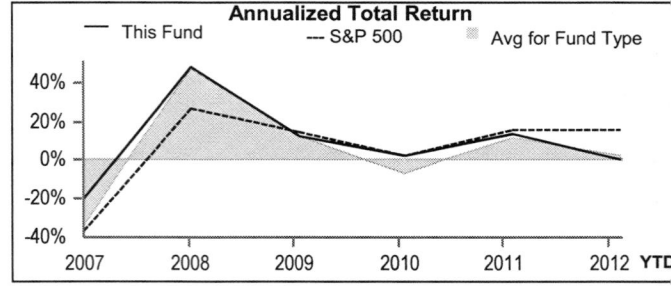

Eaton Vance Tax Adv Glob Div Inc (ETG)

C+   **Fair**

Fund Family: Eaton Vance Management
Fund Type: Global
Inception Date: January 30, 2004

Major Rating Factors: Middle of the road best describes Eaton Vance Tax Adv Glob Div Inc whose TheStreet.com Investment Rating is currently a C+ (Fair). The fund currently has a performance rating of C+ (Fair) based on an annualized return of 10.64% over the last three years and a total return of 9.28% year to date 2012. Factored into the performance evaluation is an expense ratio of 1.55% (average).

The fund's risk rating is currently B- (Good). It carries a beta of 0.95, meaning that its performance tracks fairly well with that of the overall stock market. Volatility, as measured by both the semi-deviation and a drawdown factor, is considered low. As of December 31, 2012, Eaton Vance Tax Adv Glob Div Inc traded at a discount of 12.72% below its net asset value, which is better than its one-year historical average discount of 5.82%.

Judith A. Saryan has been running the fund for 9 years and currently receives a manager quality ranking of 79 (0=worst, 99=best). If you desire an average level of risk, then this fund may be an option.

Data Date	Investment Rating	Net Assets ($Mil)	Price	Performance Rating/Pts	Total Return Y-T-D	Risk Rating/Pts
12-12	C+	1,097.14	13.58	C+ / 6.8	9.28%	B- / 7.5
2011	C-	1,064.30	12.22	C / 5.0	4.09%	C+ / 6.7
2010	E+	1,117.10	14.11	D- / 1.2	11.75%	C- / 3.7
2009	D-	837.49	13.73	D / 1.8	37.72%	C- / 4.2

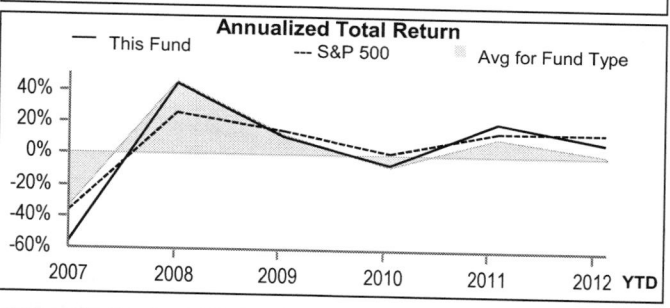

Eaton Vance Tax Adv Global Div Opp (ETO)

C+   **Fair**

Fund Family: Eaton Vance Management
Fund Type: Global
Inception Date: April 30, 2004

Major Rating Factors: Middle of the road best describes Eaton Vance Tax Adv Global Div Opp whose TheStreet.com Investment Rating is currently a C+ (Fair). The fund currently has a performance rating of C+ (Fair) based on an annualized return of 9.02% over the last three years and a total return of 4.78% year to date 2012. Factored into the performance evaluation is an expense ratio of 1.57% (above average).

The fund's risk rating is currently B- (Good). It carries a beta of 0.99, meaning that its performance tracks fairly well with that of the overall stock market. Volatility, as measured by both the semi-deviation and a drawdown factor, is considered low. As of December 31, 2012, Eaton Vance Tax Adv Global Div Opp traded at a discount of 14.58% below its net asset value, which is better than its one-year historical average discount of 12.33%.

Judith A. Saryan has been running the fund for 9 years and currently receives a manager quality ranking of 78 (0=worst, 99=best). If you desire an average level of risk, then this fund may be an option.

Data Date	Investment Rating	Net Assets ($Mil)	Price	Performance Rating/Pts	Total Return Y-T-D	Risk Rating/Pts
12-12	C+	303.82	20.09	C+ / 6.4	4.78%	B- / 7.2
2011	C-	291.70	17.00	C / 4.4	2.97%	C+ / 6.8
2010	D-	319.53	20.52	D / 1.7	13.17%	C / 4.3
2009	D+	220.47	19.38	C- / 3.7	41.37%	C / 4.9

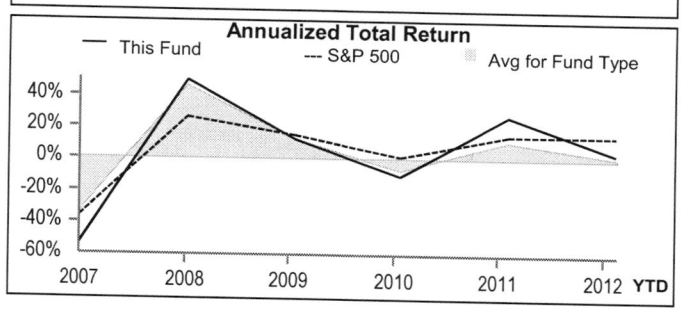

Eaton Vance Tax Advantage Div Inc (EVT)

C+   **Fair**

Fund Family: Eaton Vance Management
Fund Type: Income
Inception Date: September 30, 2003

Major Rating Factors: Middle of the road best describes Eaton Vance Tax Advantage Div Inc whose TheStreet.com Investment Rating is currently a C+ (Fair). The fund currently has a performance rating of C+ (Fair) based on an annualized return of 11.06% over the last three years and a total return of 6.91% year to date 2012. Factored into the performance evaluation is an expense ratio of 1.68% (above average).

The fund's risk rating is currently B- (Good). It carries a beta of 1.11, meaning it is expected to move 11.1% for every 10% move in the market. Volatility, as measured by both the semi-deviation and a drawdown factor, is considered low. As of December 31, 2012, Eaton Vance Tax Advantage Div Inc traded at a discount of 14.02% below its net asset value, which is better than its one-year historical average discount of 8.98%.

Judith A. Saryan has been running the fund for 10 years and currently receives a manager quality ranking of 33 (0=worst, 99=best). If you desire an average level of risk, then this fund may be an option.

Data Date	Investment Rating	Net Assets ($Mil)	Price	Performance Rating/Pts	Total Return Y-T-D	Risk Rating/Pts
12-12	C+	1,332.63	16.50	C+ / 6.0	6.91%	B- / 7.7
2011	C	1,223.00	14.60	C+ / 5.9	3.77%	C+ / 6.7
2010	E+	1,161.72	16.55	D / 1.8	13.21%	D+ / 2.9
2009	D	1,116.18	15.78	D+ / 2.7	44.47%	C / 4.3

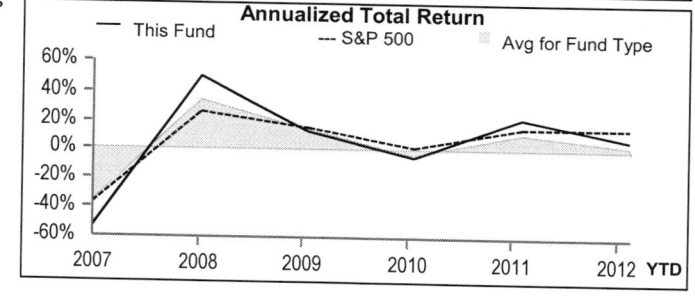

Eaton Vance Tax Mgd Buy Write Opp (ETV)   C-   Fair

Fund Family: Eaton Vance Management
Fund Type: Income
Inception Date: June 27, 2005

Data Date	Investment Rating	Net Assets ($Mil)	Price	Performance Rating/Pts	Total Return Y-T-D	Risk Rating/Pts
12-12	C-	896.71	12.50	C- / 4.1	3.44%	B- / 7.2
2011	C	871.20	11.72	C+ / 5.6	2.56%	C+ / 6.9
2010	C	805.34	13.08	C / 4.4	-2.70%	C+ / 6.1
2009	C+	821.69	15.05	C+ / 6.8	57.78%	C / 5.4

Major Rating Factors: Middle of the road best describes Eaton Vance Tax Mgd Buy Write Opp whose TheStreet.com Investment Rating is currently a C- (Fair). The fund currently has a performance rating of C- (Fair) based on an annualized return of 8.02% over the last three years and a total return of 3.44% year to date 2012. Factored into the performance evaluation is an expense ratio of 1.09% (low).

The fund's risk rating is currently B- (Good). It carries a beta of 0.66, meaning the fund's expected move will be 6.6% for every 10% move in the market. Volatility, as measured by both the semi-deviation and a drawdown factor, is considered low. As of December 31, 2012, Eaton Vance Tax Mgd Buy Write Opp traded at a discount of 11.28% below its net asset value, which is better than its one-year historical average discount of 10.77%.

David M. Stein has been running the fund for 8 years and currently receives a manager quality ranking of 34 (0=worst, 99=best). If you desire an average level of risk, then this fund may be an option.

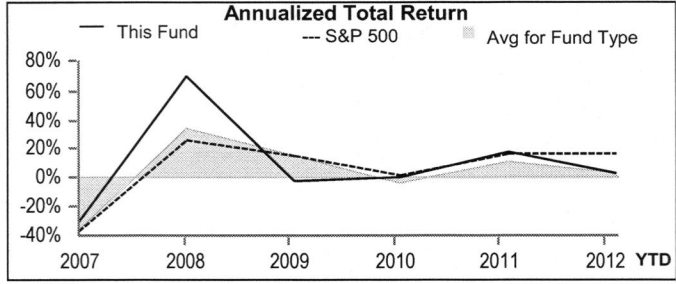

Eaton Vance Tax Mgd Div Eqty Inc (ETY)   D+   Weak

Fund Family: Eaton Vance Management
Fund Type: Income
Inception Date: November 30, 2006

Data Date	Investment Rating	Net Assets ($Mil)	Price	Performance Rating/Pts	Total Return Y-T-D	Risk Rating/Pts
12-12	D+	1,651.55	9.37	C- / 3.2	5.44%	C+ / 6.5
2011	D	1,612.60	8.87	D+ / 2.8	2.59%	C+ / 6.5
2010	D+	1,969.59	11.31	C- / 3.1	-1.22%	C+ / 5.8
2009	C-	1,742.10	13.13	C- / 3.9	37.09%	C+ / 5.6

Major Rating Factors: Eaton Vance Tax Mgd Div Eqty Inc receives a TheStreet.com Investment Rating of D+ (Weak). The fund currently has a performance rating of C- (Fair) based on an annualized return of 2.29% over the last three years and a total return of 5.44% year to date 2012. Factored into the performance evaluation is an expense ratio of 1.07% (low).

The fund's risk rating is currently C+ (Fair). It carries a beta of 0.88, meaning the fund's expected move will be 8.8% for every 10% move in the market. Volatility, as measured by both the semi-deviation and a drawdown factor, is considered low. As of December 31, 2012, Eaton Vance Tax Mgd Div Eqty Inc traded at a discount of 16.86% below its net asset value, which is better than its one-year historical average discount of 13.94%.

Michael A. Allison has been running the fund for 7 years and currently receives a manager quality ranking of 15 (0=worst, 99=best). If you desire an average level of risk, then this fund may be an option.

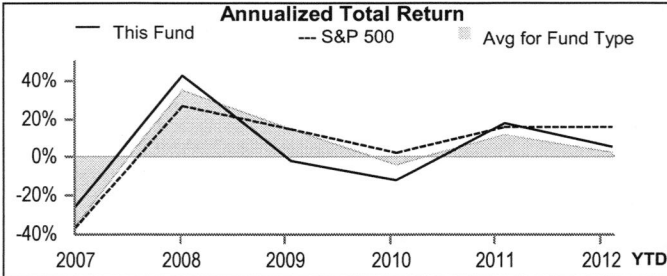

Eaton Vance Tax-Managed Buy-Write (ETB)   C-   Fair

Fund Family: Eaton Vance Management
Fund Type: Income
Inception Date: April 27, 2005

Data Date	Investment Rating	Net Assets ($Mil)	Price	Performance Rating/Pts	Total Return Y-T-D	Risk Rating/Pts
12-12	C-	371.29	14.03	C- / 3.9	6.06%	B- / 7.3
2011	C-	362.20	12.84	C / 5.0	2.80%	C+ / 6.8
2010	C-	335.31	14.41	C / 4.5	-3.39%	C / 5.4
2009	C+	343.03	16.85	C+ / 6.5	46.65%	C / 5.4

Major Rating Factors: Middle of the road best describes Eaton Vance Tax-Managed Buy-Write whose TheStreet.com Investment Rating is currently a C- (Fair). The fund currently has a performance rating of C- (Fair) based on an annualized return of 6.27% over the last three years and a total return of 6.06% year to date 2012. Factored into the performance evaluation is an expense ratio of 1.14% (low).

The fund's risk rating is currently B- (Good). It carries a beta of 0.69, meaning the fund's expected move will be 6.9% for every 10% move in the market. Volatility, as measured by both the semi-deviation and a drawdown factor, is considered low. As of December 31, 2012, Eaton Vance Tax-Managed Buy-Write traded at a discount of 8.06% below its net asset value, which is worse than its one-year historical average discount of 8.34%.

David M. Stein has been running the fund for 8 years and currently receives a manager quality ranking of 30 (0=worst, 99=best). If you desire an average level of risk, then this fund may be an option.

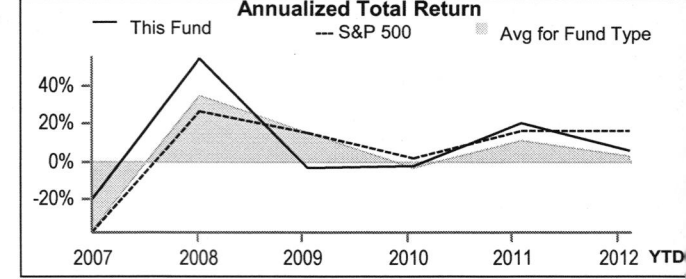

Eaton Vance Tax-Mgd Gbl Div Eq Inc (EXG)

D+   **Weak**

Fund Family: Eaton Vance Management
Fund Type: Global
Inception Date: February 27, 2007

Major Rating Factors: Eaton Vance Tax-Mgd Gbl Div Eq Inc receives a TheStreet.com Investment Rating of D+ (Weak). The fund currently has a performance rating of C- (Fair) based on an annualized return of 2.87% over the last three years and a total return of 5.45% year to date 2012. Factored into the performance evaluation is an expense ratio of 1.05% (low).

The fund's risk rating is currently C+ (Fair). It carries a beta of 0.81, meaning the fund's expected move will be 8.1% for every 10% move in the market. Volatility, as measured by both the semi-deviation and a drawdown factor, is considered low. As of December 31, 2012, Eaton Vance Tax-Mgd Gbl Div Eq Inc traded at a discount of 16.65% below its net asset value, which is better than its one-year historical average discount of 13.86%.

Michael A. Allison has been running the fund for 6 years and currently receives a manager quality ranking of 36 (0=worst, 99=best). If you desire an average level of risk, then this fund may be an option.

Data Date	Investment Rating	Net Assets ($Mil)	Price	Performance Rating/Pts	Total Return Y-T-D	Risk Rating/Pts
12-12	D+	3,122.46	8.81	C- / 3.6	5.45%	C+ / 6.5
2011	D+	3,023.50	8.25	C- / 3.3	2.67%	C+ / 6.4
2010	D+	3,638.43	10.53	D+ / 2.5	-1.72%	C / 5.5
2009	A-	3,281.57	12.33	B+ / 8.9	42.90%	C / 5.3

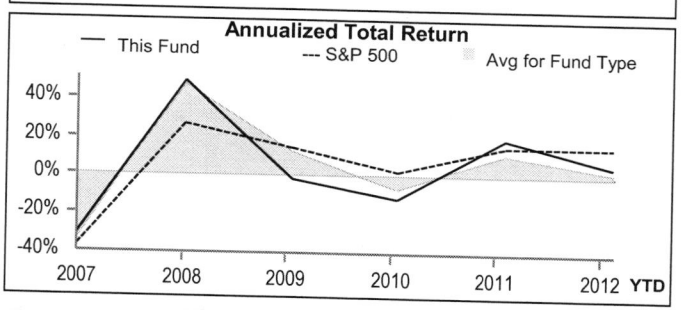

Eaton Vance Tx Adv Bd&Option Str (EXD)

A   **Excellent**

Fund Family: Eaton Vance Management
Fund Type: Municipal - National
Inception Date: June 29, 2010

Major Rating Factors:
Exceptional performance is the major factor driving the A (Excellent) TheStreet.com Investment Rating for Eaton Vance Tx Adv Bd&Option Str. The fund currently has a performance rating of A- (Excellent) based on an annualized return of 0.00% over the last three years and a total return of 1.47% year to date 2012. Factored into the performance evaluation is an expense ratio of 1.43% (average).

The fund's risk rating is currently B (Good). It carries a beta of 0.00, meaning the fund's expected move will be 0.0% for every 10% move in the market. Volatility, as measured by both the semi-deviation and a drawdown factor, is considered low. As of December 31, 2012, Eaton Vance Tx Adv Bd&Option Str traded at a discount of 3.07% below its net asset value, which is worse than its one-year historical average discount of 4.11%.

James H. Evans has been running the fund for 3 years and currently receives a manager quality ranking of 92 (0=worst, 99=best). If you desire only a moderate level of risk and strong performance, then this fund is an excellent option.

Data Date	Investment Rating	Net Assets ($Mil)	Price	Performance Rating/Pts	Total Return Y-T-D	Risk Rating/Pts
12-12	A	194.51	17.67	A- / 9.2	1.47%	B / 8.0
2011	C+	194.50	16.55	C / 5.3	2.42%	B / 8.0

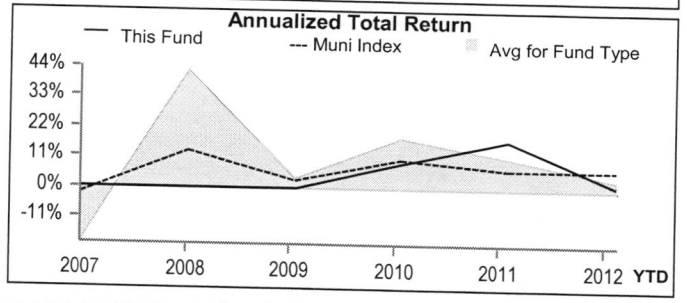

Eaton Vance Tx Mgd Glb Buy Wrt Opp (ETW)

D+   **Weak**

Fund Family: Eaton Vance Management
Fund Type: Global
Inception Date: September 27, 2005

Major Rating Factors: Eaton Vance Tx Mgd Glb Buy Wrt Opp receives a TheStreet.com Investment Rating of D+ (Weak). The fund currently has a performance rating of C- (Fair) based on an annualized return of 5.13% over the last three years and a total return of 4.77% year to date 2012. Factored into the performance evaluation is an expense ratio of 1.08% (low).

The fund's risk rating is currently C+ (Fair). It carries a beta of 0.68, meaning the fund's expected move will be 6.8% for every 10% move in the market. Volatility, as measured by both the semi-deviation and a drawdown factor, is considered low. As of December 31, 2012, Eaton Vance Tx Mgd Glb Buy Wrt Opp traded at a discount of 15.09% below its net asset value, which is better than its one-year historical average discount of 13.35%.

David M. Stein has been running the fund for 8 years and currently receives a manager quality ranking of 48 (0=worst, 99=best). If you desire an average level of risk, then this fund may be an option.

Data Date	Investment Rating	Net Assets ($Mil)	Price	Performance Rating/Pts	Total Return Y-T-D	Risk Rating/Pts
12-12	D+	1,318.02	10.69	C- / 3.6	4.77%	C+ / 6.9
2011	C-	1,310.00	10.28	C / 4.4	2.14%	C+ / 6.6
2010	D+	1,236.31	12.25	C- / 3.6	-0.83%	C / 5.3
2009	C	1,338.73	13.89	C+ / 5.7	51.30%	C / 5.2

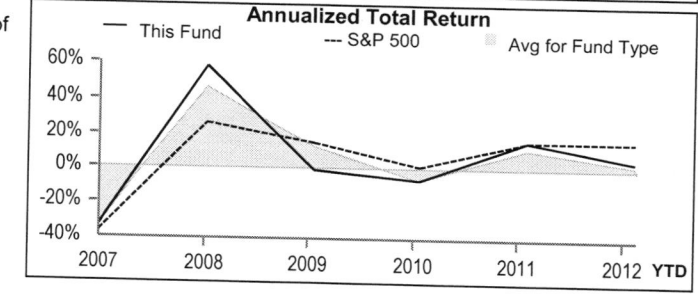

Ellsworth Fund Ltd (ECF)

C-   **Fair**

Fund Family: Dinsmore Capital Management Co
Fund Type: Growth and Income
Inception Date: June 20, 1986

Major Rating Factors: Middle of the road best describes Ellsworth Fund Ltd whose TheStreet.com Investment Rating is currently a C- (Fair). The fund currently has a performance rating of C- (Fair) based on an annualized return of 7.98% over the last three years and a total return of 3.92% year to date 2012. Factored into the performance evaluation is an expense ratio of 1.10% (low).

The fund's risk rating is currently B- (Good). It carries a beta of 0.71, meaning the fund's expected move will be 7.1% for every 10% move in the market. Volatility, as measured by both the semi-deviation and a drawdown factor, is considered low. As of December 31, 2012, Ellsworth Fund Ltd traded at a discount of 17.46% below its net asset value, which is better than its one-year historical average discount of 13.74%.

Thomas H. Dinsmore has been running the fund for 27 years and currently receives a manager quality ranking of 45 (0=worst, 99=best). If you desire an average level of risk, then this fund may be an option.

Data Date	Investment Rating	Net Assets ($Mil)	Price	Performance Rating/Pts	Total Return Y-T-D	Risk Rating/Pts
12-12	C-	114.15	7.14	C- / 3.5	3.92%	B- / 7.6
2011	C	104.60	6.60	C / 4.5	3.62%	B / 8.3
2010	C	106.23	7.35	C / 5.1	16.86%	C+ / 6.1
2009	C	94.97	6.55	C / 4.3	38.58%	C+ / 6.1

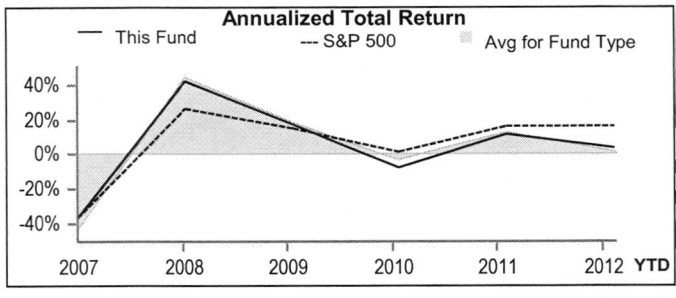

Engex (EGX)

E+   **Very Weak**

Fund Family: American Investors Advisors Inc
Fund Type: Health
Inception Date: November 20, 1968

Major Rating Factors: Engex has adopted a risky asset allocation strategy and currently receives an overall TheStreet.com Investment Rating of E+ (Very Weak). The fund has an above average level of volatility, as measured by both semi-deviation and drawdown factors. It carries a beta of 1.14, meaning it is expected to move 11.4% for every 10% move in the market. As of December 31, 2012, Engex traded at a discount of 48.76% below its net asset value, which is better than its one-year historical average discount of 24.42%. Unfortunately, the high level of risk (D+, Weak) failed to pay off as investors endured poor performance.

The fund's performance rating is currently D (Weak). It has registered an annualized return of -5.19% over the last three years and is up 20.39% year to date 2012. Factored into the performance evaluation is an expense ratio of 4.69% (high).

Joseph M. Davis currently receives a manager quality ranking of 6 (0=worst, 99=best). If you can tolerate high levels of risk in the hope of improved future returns, holding this fund may be an option.

Data Date	Investment Rating	Net Assets ($Mil)	Price	Performance Rating/Pts	Total Return Y-T-D	Risk Rating/Pts
12-12	E+	5.07	2.06	D / 2.1	20.39%	D+ / 2.7
2011	E	3.70	1.81	E+ / 0.9	3.87%	D+ / 2.5
2010	E	5.38	4.25	D / 1.6	57.41%	D / 1.9
2009	E-	6.26	2.70	E / 0.5	42.86%	D / 1.7

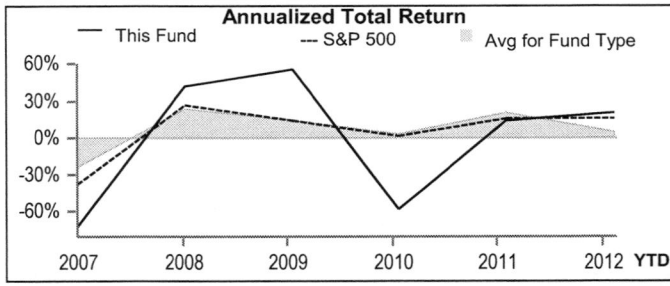

Equus Total Return (EQS)

D-   **Weak**

Fund Family: Equus Total Return Inc
Fund Type: Income
Inception Date: October 23, 1987

Major Rating Factors:
Very poor performance is the major factor driving the D- (Weak) TheStreet.com Investment Rating for Equus Total Return. The fund currently has a performance rating of E+ (Very Weak) based on an annualized return of -12.00% over the last three years and a total return of -2.97% year to date 2012. Factored into the performance evaluation is an expense ratio of 10.60% (high).

The fund's risk rating is currently C (Fair). It carries a beta of 0.95, meaning that its performance tracks fairly well with that of the overall stock market. Volatility, as measured by both the semi-deviation and a drawdown factor, is considered average. As of December 31, 2012, Equus Total Return traded at a discount of 29.13% below its net asset value, which is worse than its one-year historical average discount of 34.50%.

This fund has been team managed for 21 years and currently receives a manager quality ranking of 6 (0=worst, 99=best). This fund offers an average level of risk but investors looking for strong performance will be frustrated.

Data Date	Investment Rating	Net Assets ($Mil)	Price	Performance Rating/Pts	Total Return Y-T-D	Risk Rating/Pts
12-12	D-	38.15	2.36	E+ / 0.8	-2.97%	C / 5.4
2011	E+	38.05	2.24	E+ / 0.9	-2.23%	C- / 4.0
2010	E	50.90	2.50	E / 0.5	-21.87%	D / 2.0
2009	E+	73.00	3.20	E / 0.4	-31.94%	C / 4.3

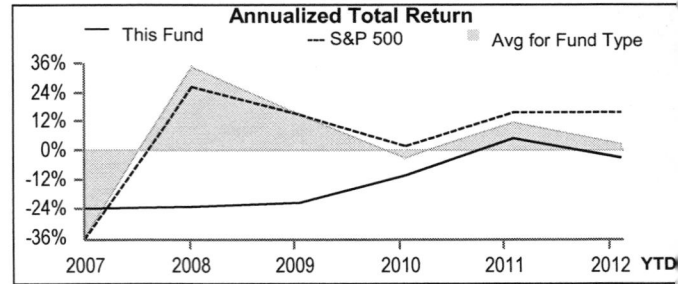

F&C/Claymore Preferred Sec Inc Fun (FFC)

A+ **Excellent**

Fund Family: Flaherty & Crumrine Inc
Fund Type: Income
Inception Date: January 28, 2003

Major Rating Factors:
Strong performance is the major factor driving the A+ (Excellent) TheStreet.com Investment Rating for F&C/Claymore Preferred Sec Inc Fun. The fund currently has a performance rating of B+ (Good) based on an annualized return of 23.07% over the last three years and a total return of 3.99% year to date 2012. Factored into the performance evaluation is an expense ratio of 1.68% (above average).

   The fund's risk rating is currently B (Good). It carries a beta of 0.38, meaning the fund's expected move will be 3.8% for every 10% move in the market. Volatility, as measured by both the semi-deviation and a drawdown factor, is considered low. As of December 31, 2012, F&C/Claymore Preferred Sec Inc Fun traded at a premium of 1.14% above its net asset value, which is better than its one-year historical average premium of 5.56%.

   Robert E. Chadwick has been running the fund for 10 years and currently receives a manager quality ranking of 96 (0=worst, 99=best). If you desire only a moderate level of risk and strong performance, then this fund is an excellent option.

Data Date	Investment Rating	Net Assets ($Mil)	Price	Performance Rating/Pts	Total Return Y-T-D	Risk Rating/Pts
12-12	A+	746.99	19.55	B+ / 8.9	3.99%	B / 8.9
2011	A-	699.40	17.46	A+ / 9.8	0.06%	B- / 7.6
2010	C	571.14	16.21	B+ / 8.3	27.69%	D+ / 2.5
2009	D+	419.99	13.97	C / 5.4	91.22%	D+ / 2.7

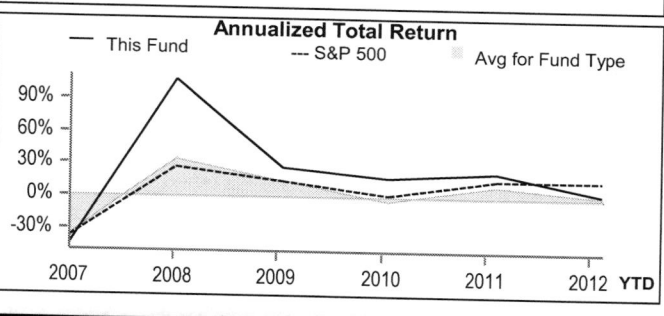

F&C/Claymore Total Return Fund (FLC)

A+ **Excellent**

Fund Family: Flaherty & Crumrine Inc
Fund Type: Income
Inception Date: August 29, 2003

Major Rating Factors:
Strong performance is the major factor driving the A+ (Excellent) TheStreet.com Investment Rating for F&C/Claymore Total Return Fund. The fund currently has a performance rating of B+ (Good) based on an annualized return of 23.05% over the last three years and a total return of 4.97% year to date 2012. Factored into the performance evaluation is an expense ratio of 2.02% (high).

   The fund's risk rating is currently B (Good). It carries a beta of 0.27, meaning the fund's expected move will be 2.7% for every 10% move in the market. Volatility, as measured by both the semi-deviation and a drawdown factor, is considered low. As of December 31, 2012, F&C/Claymore Total Return Fund traded at a discount of 2.00% below its net asset value, which is better than its one-year historical average premium of 3.78%.

   Robert M. Ettinger has been running the fund for 10 years and currently receives a manager quality ranking of 96 (0=worst, 99=best). If you desire only a moderate level of risk and strong performance, then this fund is an excellent option.

Data Date	Investment Rating	Net Assets ($Mil)	Price	Performance Rating/Pts	Total Return Y-T-D	Risk Rating/Pts
12-12	A+	182.40	20.14	B+ / 8.9	4.97%	B / 8.9
2011	A-	170.50	18.70	A+ / 9.8	-0.16%	B- / 7.9
2010	C	140.59	17.26	B+ / 8.4	30.49%	D+ / 2.6
2009	C-	101.59	14.52	C+ / 5.8	92.26%	D+ / 2.9

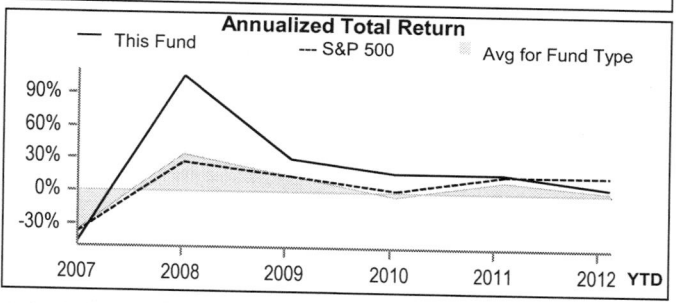

Federated Enhanced Treasury Income (FTT)

D **Weak**

Fund Family: Federated Investors
Fund Type: US Government/Agency
Inception Date: January 28, 2010

Major Rating Factors:
Disappointing performance is the major factor driving the D (Weak) TheStreet.com Investment Rating for Federated Enhanced Treasury Income. The fund currently has a performance rating of D (Weak) based on an annualized return of 0.00% over the last three years and a total return of 0.21% year to date 2012. Factored into the performance evaluation is an expense ratio of 1.02% (low).

   The fund's risk rating is currently B- (Good). It carries a beta of 0.00, meaning the fund's expected move will be 0.0% for every 10% move in the market. Volatility, as measured by both the semi-deviation and a drawdown factor, is considered low. As of December 31, 2012, Federated Enhanced Treasury Income traded at a discount of 10.31% below its net asset value, which is better than its one-year historical average discount of 9.76%.

   Donald T. Ellenberger currently receives a manager quality ranking of 81 (0=worst, 99=best). This fund offers only a moderate level of risk but investors looking for strong performance are still waiting.

Data Date	Investment Rating	Net Assets ($Mil)	Price	Performance Rating/Pts	Total Return Y-T-D	Risk Rating/Pts
12-12	D	151.30	14.18	D / 2.1	0.21%	B- / 7.5
2011	D	157.30	14.35	D- / 1.3	1.11%	B- / 7.5

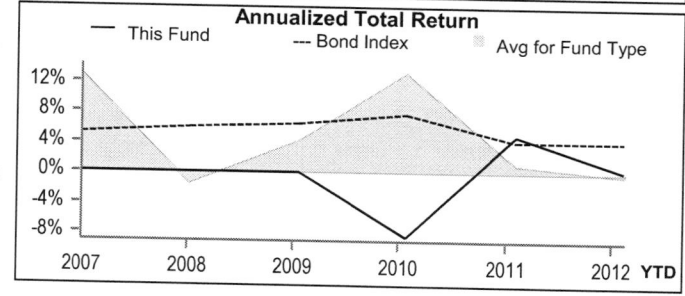

Federated Prem Intermediate Muni (FPT)

B-   **Good**

Fund Family: Federated Investors
Fund Type: Municipal - National
Inception Date: December 19, 2002

Major Rating Factors: Federated Prem Intermediate Muni receives a TheStreet.com Investment Rating of B- (Good). The fund currently has a performance rating of C+ (Fair) based on an annualized return of 9.79% over the last three years and a total return of 3.49% year to date 2012. Factored into the performance evaluation is an expense ratio of 1.15% (low).

The fund's risk rating is currently B (Good). It carries a beta of 2.43, meaning it is expected to move 24.3% for every 10% move in the market. Volatility, as measured by both the semi-deviation and a drawdown factor, is considered low. As of December 31, 2012, Federated Prem Intermediate Muni traded at a discount of 2.34% below its net asset value, which is better than its one-year historical average premium of 3.08%.

Lee R. Cunningham, II has been running the fund for 11 years and currently receives a manager quality ranking of 17 (0=worst, 99=best). If you desire an average level of risk, then this fund may be an option.

Data Date	Investment Rating	Net Assets ($Mil)	Price	Performance Rating/Pts	Total Return Y-T-D	Risk Rating/Pts
12-12	B-	102.67	14.61	C+ / 6.1	3.49%	B / 8.6
2011	A-	100.30	13.78	B+ / 8.6	1.89%	B / 8.9
2010	C+	93.60	12.59	C / 5.1	-2.48%	C+ / 6.4
2009	B+	88.99	13.75	B- / 7.5	49.23%	C+ / 6.5

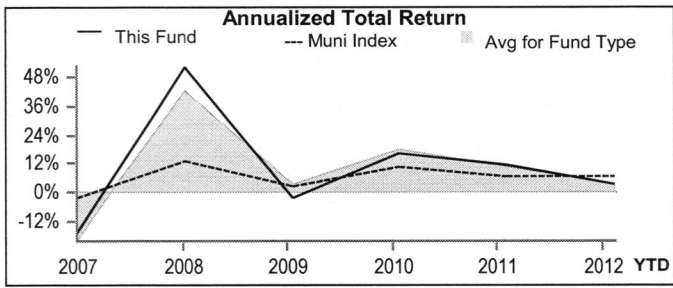

Federated Premier Muni Income (FMN)

B   **Good**

Fund Family: Federated Investors
Fund Type: Municipal - National
Inception Date: December 19, 2002

Major Rating Factors: Federated Premier Muni Income receives a TheStreet.com Investment Rating of B (Good). The fund currently has a performance rating of C+ (Fair) based on an annualized return of 11.51% over the last three years and a total return of 2.56% year to date 2012. Factored into the performance evaluation is an expense ratio of 1.14% (low).

The fund's risk rating is currently B (Good). It carries a beta of 1.77, meaning it is expected to move 17.7% for every 10% move in the market. Volatility, as measured by both the semi-deviation and a drawdown factor, is considered low. As of December 31, 2012, Federated Premier Muni Income traded at a premium of 1.65% above its net asset value, which is better than its one-year historical average premium of 6.16%.

Lee R. Cunningham, II has been running the fund for 11 years and currently receives a manager quality ranking of 37 (0=worst, 99=best). If you desire an average level of risk, then this fund may be an option.

Data Date	Investment Rating	Net Assets ($Mil)	Price	Performance Rating/Pts	Total Return Y-T-D	Risk Rating/Pts
12-12	B	94.19	15.99	C+ / 6.9	2.56%	B / 8.5
2011	A	88.50	15.14	A / 9.5	-0.59%	B / 8.4
2010	C	81.44	13.36	C / 5.2	-3.27%	C+ / 5.8
2009	B+	76.04	14.88	B / 8.0	72.04%	C+ / 5.7

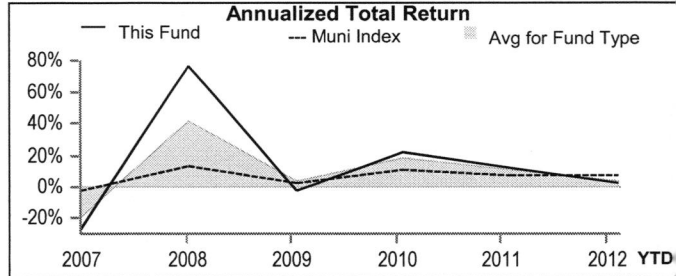

Fiduciary/Claymore MLP Opp (FMO)

C+   **Fair**

Fund Family: Guggenheim Funds Investment Advisor
Fund Type: Energy/Natural Resources
Inception Date: December 22, 2004

Major Rating Factors: Middle of the road best describes Fiduciary/Claymore MLP Opp whose TheStreet.com Investment Rating is currently a C+ (Fair). The fund currently has a performance rating of C+ (Fair) based on an annualized return of 15.40% over the last three years and a total return of 6.02% year to date 2012. Factored into the performance evaluation is an expense ratio of 2.04% (high).

The fund's risk rating is currently B- (Good). It carries a beta of 0.51, meaning the fund's expected move will be 5.1% for every 10% move in the market. Volatility, as measured by both the semi-deviation and a drawdown factor, is considered low. As of December 31, 2012, Fiduciary/Claymore MLP Opp traded at a discount of .59% below its net asset value, which is better than its one-year historical average premium of 7.23%.

James J. Cunnane, Jr. has been running the fund for 9 years and currently receives a manager quality ranking of 89 (0=worst, 99=best). If you desire an average level of risk, then this fund may be an option.

Data Date	Investment Rating	Net Assets ($Mil)	Price	Performance Rating/Pts	Total Return Y-T-D	Risk Rating/Pts
12-12	C+	499.30	21.77	C+ / 6.2	6.02%	B- / 7.9
2011	B	523.10	21.47	B / 7.8	2.61%	B- / 7.8
2010	B-	282.09	21.59	B / 8.2	29.19%	C / 4.5
2009	C	242.16	17.94	C+ / 6.4	59.78%	C / 4.5

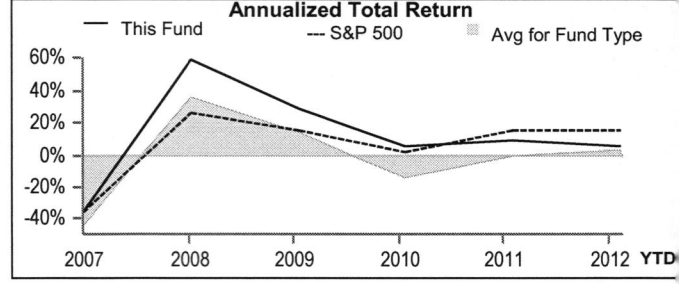

Financial Trends Fund (DHFT)

B+　　**Good**

Fund Family: Diamond Hill Capital Management Inc
Fund Type: Financial Services
Inception Date: August 23, 1989

Major Rating Factors: Strong performance is the major factor driving the B+ (Good) TheStreet.com Investment Rating for Financial Trends Fund. The fund currently has a performance rating of B+ (Good) based on an annualized return of 16.59% over the last three years and a total return of 5.24% year to date 2012. Factored into the performance evaluation is an expense ratio of 1.61% (above average).

The fund's risk rating is currently B- (Good). It carries a beta of 1.08, meaning that its performance tracks fairly well with that of the overall stock market. Volatility, as measured by both the semi-deviation and a drawdown factor, is considered low. As of December 31, 2012, Financial Trends Fund traded at a discount of 7.07% below its net asset value, which is worse than its one-year historical average discount of 7.60%.

Austin Hawley currently receives a manager quality ranking of 86 (0=worst, 99=best). If you desire only a moderate level of risk and strong performance, then this fund is an excellent option.

Data Date	Investment Rating	Net Assets ($Mil)	Price	Performance Rating/Pts	Total Return Y-T-D	Risk Rating/Pts
12-12	B+	45.00	11.44	B+ / 8.9	5.24%	B- / 7.7
2011	C-	39.60	8.27	C- / 4.0	6.17%	C+ / 6.9
2010	D	39.21	9.81	D+ / 2.5	25.68%	C / 5.2
2009	D-	32.67	7.88	E+ / 0.6	20.49%	C / 5.1

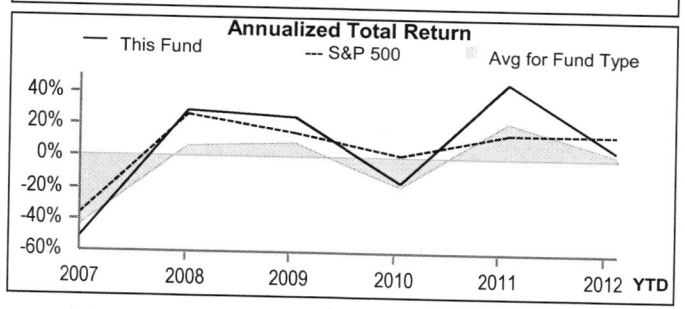

First Opportunity Fund (FOFI)

C-　　**Fair**

Fund Family: Rocky Mountain Advisers LLC
Fund Type: Financial Services
Inception Date: May 1, 1986

Major Rating Factors: Middle of the road best describes First Opportunity Fund whose TheStreet.com Investment Rating is currently a C- (Fair). The fund currently has a performance rating of C- (Fair) based on an annualized return of 7.32% over the last three years and a total return of 1.43% year to date 2012. Factored into the performance evaluation is an expense ratio of 1.05% (low).

The fund's risk rating is currently B (Good). It carries a beta of 0.61, meaning the fund's expected move will be 6.1% for every 10% move in the market. Volatility, as measured by both the semi-deviation and a drawdown factor, is considered low. As of December 31, 2012, First Opportunity Fund traded at a discount of 24.83% below its net asset value, which is better than its one-year historical average discount of 23.28%.

Stewart R. Horejsi has been running the fund for 3 years and currently receives a manager quality ranking of 75 (0=worst, 99=best). If you desire an average level of risk, then this fund may be an option.

Data Date	Investment Rating	Net Assets ($Mil)	Price	Performance Rating/Pts	Total Return Y-T-D	Risk Rating/Pts
12-12	C-	267.37	7.69	C- / 4.0	1.43%	B / 8.0
2011	C-	245.20	6.22	C- / 3.0	1.29%	B / 8.3
2010	D	234.57	7.43	D- / 1.5	23.42%	C / 5.1
2009	D-	219.74	6.02	E+ / 0.6	12.87%	C+ / 5.6

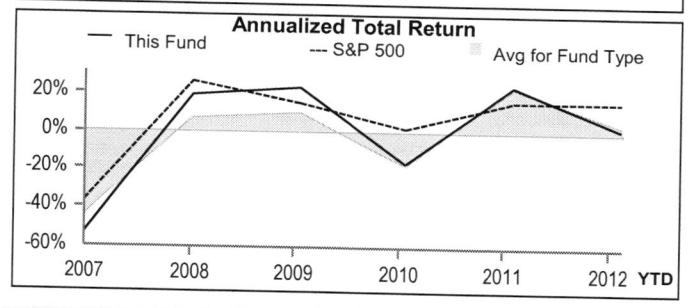

First Tr Senior Floating Rte Inc I (FCT)

B　　**Good**

Fund Family: First Trust Advisors LP
Fund Type: Loan Participation
Inception Date: May 25, 2004

Major Rating Factors: Strong performance is the major factor driving the B (Good) TheStreet.com Investment Rating for First Tr Senior Floating Rte Inc I. The fund currently has a performance rating of B- (Good) based on an annualized return of 15.41% over the last three years and a total return of 3.73% year to date 2012. Factored into the performance evaluation is an expense ratio of 1.88% (above average).

The fund's risk rating is currently B (Good). It carries a beta of -166.01, meaning the fund's expected move will be -1660.1% for every 10% move in the market. Volatility, as measured by both the semi-deviation and a drawdown factor, is considered low. As of December 31, 2012, First Tr Senior Floating Rte Inc I traded at a premium of .86% above its net asset value, which is better than its one-year historical average premium of 1.31%.

Scott D. Fries currently receives a manager quality ranking of 99 (0=worst, 99=best). If you desire only a moderate level of risk and strong performance, then this fund is an excellent option.

Data Date	Investment Rating	Net Assets ($Mil)	Price	Performance Rating/Pts	Total Return Y-T-D	Risk Rating/Pts
12-12	B	367.17	15.17	B- / 7.1	3.73%	B / 8.3
2011	B	357.00	13.19	B / 7.9	5.76%	B / 8.3
2010	C	353.11	13.97	C+ / 6.7	22.37%	C- / 3.9
2009	C-	298.10	11.90	C- / 3.6	63.80%	C / 5.2

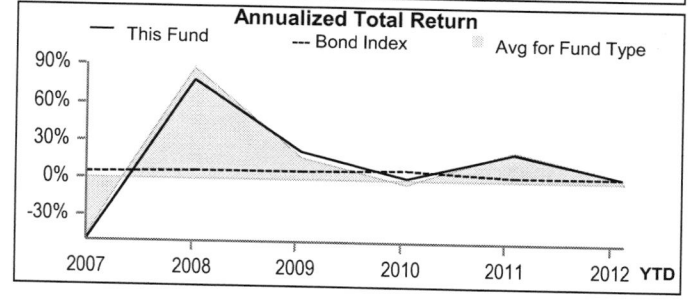

First Tr Specialty Finance &Fin Op (FGB)

B+   **Good**

Fund Family: First Trust Advisors LP
Fund Type: Financial Services
Inception Date: May 24, 2007

Data Date	Investment Rating	Net Assets ($Mil)	Price	Performance Rating/Pts	Total Return Y-T-D	Risk Rating/Pts
12-12	B+	101.81	7.80	A- / 9.1	8.33%	B- / 7.4
2010	C-	85.07	7.62	C+ / 5.7	39.34%	C- / 3.5
2009	B-	62.88	5.98	A+ / 9.6	58.86%	C- / 3.3

Major Rating Factors:
Exceptional performance is the major factor driving the B+ (Good) TheStreet.com Investment Rating for First Tr Specialty Finance &Fin Op. The fund currently has a performance rating of A- (Excellent) based on an annualized return of 19.96% over the last three years and a total return of 8.33% year to date 2012. Factored into the performance evaluation is an expense ratio of 1.84% (above average).

The fund's risk rating is currently B- (Good). It carries a beta of 0.75, meaning the fund's expected move will be 7.5% for every 10% move in the market. Volatility, as measured by both the semi-deviation and a drawdown factor, is considered low. As of December 31, 2012, First Tr Specialty Finance &Fin Op traded at a discount of 6.92% below its net asset value, which is better than its one-year historical average discount of 2.49%.

David B. Miyazaki currently receives a manager quality ranking of 93 (0=worst, 99=best). If you desire only a moderate level of risk and strong performance, then this fund is an excellent option.

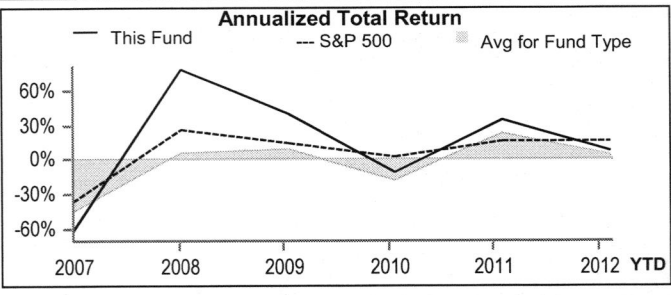
Annualized Total Return — This Fund / S&P 500 / Avg for Fund Type

First Trust Active Dividend Inc Fd (FAV)

D-   **Weak**

Fund Family: First Trust Advisors LP
Fund Type: Global
Inception Date: September 20, 2007

Data Date	Investment Rating	Net Assets ($Mil)	Price	Performance Rating/Pts	Total Return Y-T-D	Risk Rating/Pts
12-12	D-	70.36	7.55	E+ / 0.9	5.70%	C+ / 5.9
2011	D	77.40	8.38	D / 2.0	1.19%	C+ / 6.0
2010	D	76.20	11.02	C- / 3.6	-0.73%	C- / 4.0
2009	B-	71.15	12.63	B+ / 8.9	42.88%	C- / 4.1

Major Rating Factors:
Very poor performance is the major factor driving the D- (Weak) TheStreet.com Investment Rating for First Trust Active Dividend Inc Fd. The fund currently has a performance rating of E+ (Very Weak) based on an annualized return of -6.41% over the last three years and a total return of 5.70% year to date 2012. Factored into the performance evaluation is an expense ratio of 1.50% (average).

The fund's risk rating is currently C+ (Fair). It carries a beta of 0.72, meaning the fund's expected move will be 7.2% for every 10% move in the market. Volatility, as measured by both the semi-deviation and a drawdown factor, is considered low. As of December 31, 2012, First Trust Active Dividend Inc Fd traded at a discount of 14.50% below its net asset value, which is better than its one-year historical average discount of 10.12%.

Christian C. Bertelsen currently receives a manager quality ranking of 14 (0=worst, 99=best). This fund offers only a moderate level of risk but investors looking for strong performance are still waiting.

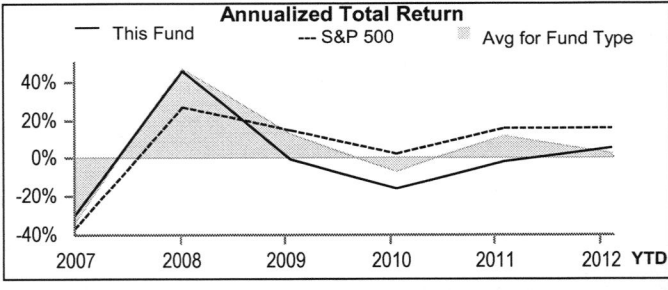
Annualized Total Return — This Fund / S&P 500 / Avg for Fund Type

First Trust Energy Income and Gro (FEN)

B+   **Good**

Fund Family: First Trust Advisors LP
Fund Type: Energy/Natural Resources
Inception Date: June 24, 2004

Data Date	Investment Rating	Net Assets ($Mil)	Price	Performance Rating/Pts	Total Return Y-T-D	Risk Rating/Pts
12-12	B+	385.33	30.65	B / 8.0	6.56%	B / 8.5
2011	B+	409.30	28.25	B+ / 8.8	3.01%	B / 8.3
2010	B+	136.52	26.88	B+ / 8.4	24.14%	C / 5.1
2009	C+	114.29	23.37	B- / 7.2	75.68%	C / 4.9

Major Rating Factors: Strong performance is the major factor driving the B+ (Good) TheStreet.com Investment Rating for First Trust Energy Income and Gro. The fund currently has a performance rating of B (Good) based on an annualized return of 19.11% over the last three years and a total return of 6.56% year to date 2012. Factored into the performance evaluation is an expense ratio of 2.26% (high).

The fund's risk rating is currently B (Good). It carries a beta of 0.40, meaning the fund's expected move will be 4.0% for every 10% move in the market. Volatility, as measured by both the semi-deviation and a drawdown factor, is considered low. As of December 31, 2012, First Trust Energy Income and Gro traded at a premium of .03% above its net asset value, which is better than its one-year historical average premium of 5.23%.

James J. Murchie currently receives a manager quality ranking of 93 (0=worst, 99=best). If you desire only a moderate level of risk and strong performance, then this fund is an excellent option.

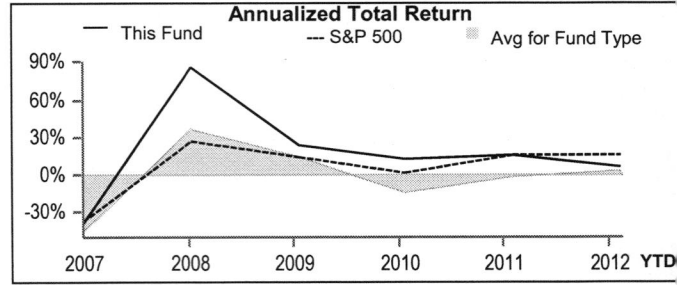
Annualized Total Return — This Fund / S&P 500 / Avg for Fund Type

First Trust Energy Infrastructure (FIF)

A+   **Excellent**

Fund Family: First Trust Advisors LP
Fund Type: Energy/Natural Resources
Inception Date: September 27, 2011

Major Rating Factors:
Strong performance is the major factor driving the A+ (Excellent) TheStreet.com Investment Rating for First Trust Energy Infrastructure. The fund currently has a performance rating of B+ (Good) based on an annualized return of 0.00% over the last three years and a total return of 4.30% year to date 2012.

The fund's risk rating is currently B+ (Good). It carries a beta of 0.00, meaning the fund's expected move will be 0.0% for every 10% move in the market. Volatility, as measured by both the semi-deviation and a drawdown factor, is considered very low. As of December 31, 2012, First Trust Energy Infrastructure traded at a discount of 6.13% below its net asset value, which is better than its one-year historical average discount of 5.78%.

This fund has been team managed for 2 years and currently receives a manager quality ranking of 94 (0=worst, 99=best). If you desire only a moderate level of risk and strong performance, then this fund is an excellent option.

Data Date	Investment Rating	Net Assets ($Mil)	Price	Performance Rating/Pts	Total Return Y-T-D	Risk Rating/Pts
12-12	A+	375.30	21.15	B+ / 8.5	4.30%	B+ / 9.2

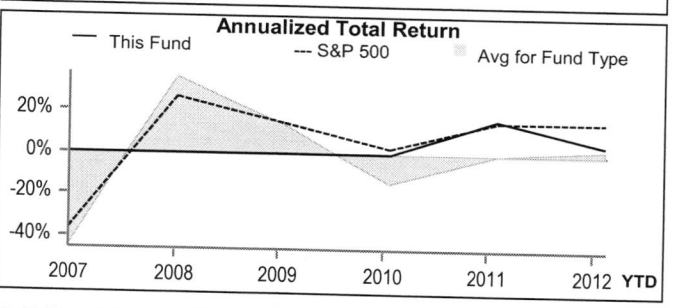

First Trust Enhanced Equity Income (FFA)

C   **Fair**

Fund Family: First Trust Advisors LP
Fund Type: Income
Inception Date: August 27, 2004

Major Rating Factors: Middle of the road best describes First Trust Enhanced Equity Income whose TheStreet.com Investment Rating is currently a C (Fair). The fund currently has a performance rating of C (Fair) based on an annualized return of 9.50% over the last three years and a total return of 4.39% year to date 2012. Factored into the performance evaluation is an expense ratio of 1.21% (average).

The fund's risk rating is currently B- (Good). It carries a beta of 1.00, meaning that its performance tracks fairly well with that of the overall stock market. Volatility, as measured by both the semi-deviation and a drawdown factor, is considered low. As of December 31, 2012, First Trust Enhanced Equity Income traded at a discount of 13.83% below its net asset value, which is better than its one-year historical average discount of 11.02%.

Douglas W. Kugler currently receives a manager quality ranking of 37 (0=worst, 99=best). If you desire an average level of risk, then this fund may be an option.

Data Date	Investment Rating	Net Assets ($Mil)	Price	Performance Rating/Pts	Total Return Y-T-D	Risk Rating/Pts
12-12	C	262.11	11.84	C / 4.6	4.39%	B- / 7.8
2011	C	249.80	10.83	C / 5.2	2.03%	B- / 7.8
2010	C+	225.65	12.64	C+ / 6.4	16.50%	C / 5.0
2009	C-	213.19	11.70	C- / 4.1	39.18%	C+ / 5.6

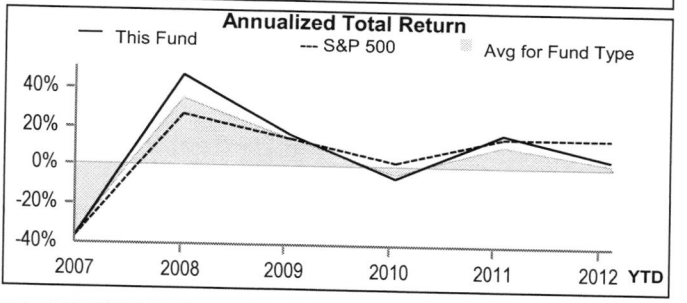

First Trust High Income Long/Short (FSD)

B+   **Good**

Fund Family: First Trust Advisors LP
Fund Type: Global
Inception Date: September 27, 2010

Major Rating Factors: Strong performance is the major factor driving the B+ (Good) TheStreet.com Investment Rating for First Trust High Income Long/Short. The fund currently has a performance rating of B+ (Good) based on an annualized return of 0.00% over the last three years and a total return of 3.15% year to date 2012. Factored into the performance evaluation is an expense ratio of 2.09% (high).

The fund's risk rating is currently B- (Good). It carries a beta of 0.00, meaning the fund's expected move will be 0.0% for every 10% move in the market. Volatility, as measured by both the semi-deviation and a drawdown factor, is considered low. As of December 31, 2012, First Trust High Income Long/Short traded at a discount of 8.39% below its net asset value, which is better than its one-year historical average discount of 2.80%.

Dan C. Roberts currently receives a manager quality ranking of 97 (0=worst, 99=best). If you desire only a moderate level of risk and strong performance, then this fund is an excellent option.

Data Date	Investment Rating	Net Assets ($Mil)	Price	Performance Rating/Pts	Total Return Y-T-D	Risk Rating/Pts
12-12	B+	642.41	18.12	B+ / 8.7	3.15%	B- / 7.7
2011	D	613.70	15.27	D- / 1.4	2.82%	B- / 7.7

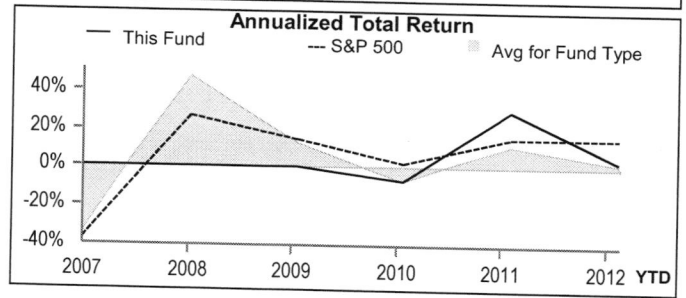

* Denotes ETF Fund

First Trust Mortgage Income Fund (FMY)

C-   **Fair**

Fund Family: First Trust Advisors LP
Fund Type: Mortgage
Inception Date: May 25, 2005

Major Rating Factors: Middle of the road best describes First Trust Mortgage Income Fund whose TheStreet.com Investment Rating is currently a C- (Fair). The fund currently has a performance rating of C- (Fair) based on an annualized return of 10.89% over the last three years and a total return of 4.87% year to date 2012. Factored into the performance evaluation is an expense ratio of 2.23% (high).

The fund's risk rating is currently B- (Good). It carries a beta of 0.21, meaning the fund's expected move will be 2.1% for every 10% move in the market. Volatility, as measured by both the semi-deviation and a drawdown factor, is considered low. As of December 31, 2012, First Trust Mortgage Income Fund traded at a discount of 1.51% below its net asset value, which is better than its one-year historical average premium of 9.41%.

Anthony Breaks currently receives a manager quality ranking of 87 (0=worst, 99=best). If you desire an average level of risk, then this fund may be an option.

Data Date	Investment Rating	Net Assets ($Mil)	Price	Performance Rating/Pts	Total Return Y-T-D	Risk Rating/Pts
12-12	C-	75.01	17.66	C- / 3.6	4.87%	B- / 7.2
2011	C	71.40	19.04	C+ / 5.9	0.16%	B- / 7.0
2010	B	82.10	19.40	B / 8.1	16.83%	C / 5.1
2009	B-	68.08	18.24	C+ / 5.8	20.93%	B- / 7.8

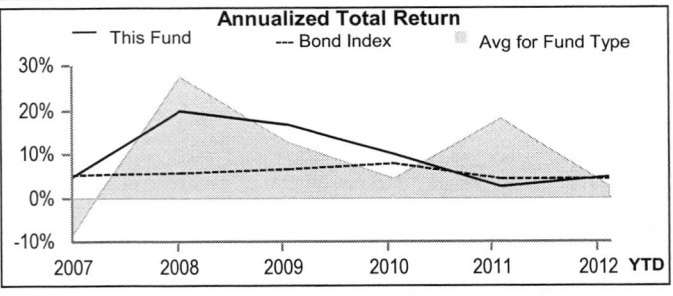

First Trust Strategic High Inc II (FHY)

B   **Good**

Fund Family: First Trust Advisors LP
Fund Type: General Bond
Inception Date: March 28, 2006

Major Rating Factors: Strong performance is the major factor driving the B (Good) TheStreet.com Investment Rating for First Trust Strategic High Inc II. The fund currently has a performance rating of B- (Good) based on an annualized return of 17.98% over the last three years and a total return of 3.25% year to date 2012. Factored into the performance evaluation is an expense ratio of 2.35% (high).

The fund's risk rating is currently B (Good). It carries a beta of 0.76, meaning the fund's expected move will be 7.6% for every 10% move in the market. Volatility, as measured by both the semi-deviation and a drawdown factor, is considered low. As of December 31, 2012, First Trust Strategic High Inc II traded at a discount of 5.25% below its net asset value, which is better than its one-year historical average premium of 2.18%.

Anthony Breaks currently receives a manager quality ranking of 92 (0=worst, 99=best). If you desire only a moderate level of risk and strong performance, then this fund is an excellent option.

Data Date	Investment Rating	Net Assets ($Mil)	Price	Performance Rating/Pts	Total Return Y-T-D	Risk Rating/Pts
12-12	B	131.11	16.60	B- / 7.3	3.25%	B / 8.6
2011	C-	129.70	15.28	C / 4.7	-0.46%	C+ / 5.9
2010	E+	48.16	4.68	E+ / 0.7	11.78%	C- / 4.1
2009	E	53.64	4.61	E / 0.5	-9.29%	C- / 3.2

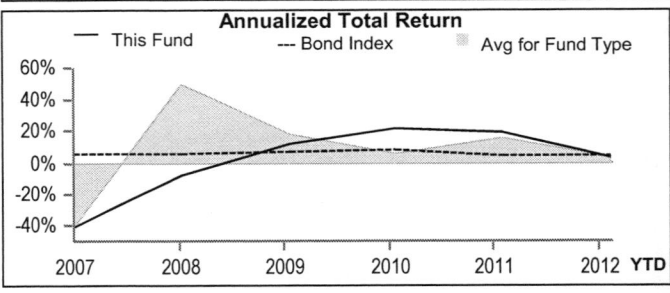

First Trust/Aberdeen Emerg Opp Fd (FEO)

B+   **Good**

Fund Family: First Trust Advisors LP
Fund Type: Global
Inception Date: August 28, 2006

Major Rating Factors: Strong performance is the major factor driving the B+ (Good) TheStreet.com Investment Rating for First Trust/Aberdeen Emerg Opp Fd. The fund currently has a performance rating of B+ (Good) based on an annualized return of 16.35% over the last three years and a total return of 6.08% year to date 2012. Factored into the performance evaluation is an expense ratio of 1.68% (above average).

The fund's risk rating is currently B- (Good). It carries a beta of 0.76, meaning the fund's expected move will be 7.6% for every 10% move in the market. Volatility, as measured by both the semi-deviation and a drawdown factor, is considered low. As of December 31, 2012, First Trust/Aberdeen Emerg Opp Fd traded at a discount of 7.66% below its net asset value, which is better than its one-year historical average discount of 6.91%.

Andrew P. S. Brown currently receives a manager quality ranking of 91 (0=worst, 99=best). If you desire only a moderate level of risk and strong performance, then this fund is an excellent option.

Data Date	Investment Rating	Net Assets ($Mil)	Price	Performance Rating/Pts	Total Return Y-T-D	Risk Rating/Pts
12-12	B+	108.17	22.05	B+ / 8.6	6.08%	B- / 7.6
2011	B	108.20	17.82	B / 7.6	2.49%	B- / 7.8
2010	B-	106.39	21.31	B+ / 8.4	26.55%	C- / 4.0
2009	B-	94.44	18.04	B / 7.7	78.12%	C / 5.0

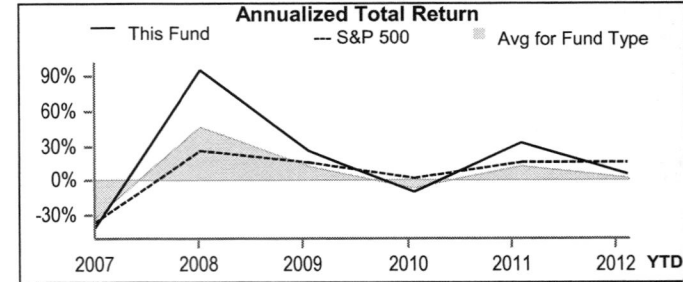

First Trust/Aberdeen Glob Opp Inc (FAM)

B-   **Good**

Fund Family: First Trust Advisors LP
Fund Type: Global
Inception Date: November 23, 2004

Major Rating Factors: First Trust/Aberdeen Glob Opp Inc receives a TheStreet.com Investment Rating of B- (Good). The fund currently has a performance rating of C+ (Fair) based on an annualized return of 13.56% over the last three years and a total return of 2.19% year to date 2012. Factored into the performance evaluation is an expense ratio of 2.09% (high).

The fund's risk rating is currently B (Good). It carries a beta of 1.09, meaning that its performance tracks fairly well with that of the overall stock market. Volatility, as measured by both the semi-deviation and a drawdown factor, is considered low. As of December 31, 2012, First Trust/Aberdeen Glob Opp Inc traded at a discount of 2.67% below its net asset value, which is better than its one-year historical average discount of 1.11%.

Esther S. E. Chan currently receives a manager quality ranking of 89 (0=worst, 99=best). If you desire an average level of risk, then this fund may be an option.

Data Date	Investment Rating	Net Assets ($Mil)	Price	Performance Rating/Pts	Total Return Y-T-D	Risk Rating/Pts
12-12	B-	303.29	17.85	C+ / 6.4	2.19%	B / 8.2
2011	B+	294.50	15.76	B / 7.8	1.59%	B / 8.6
2010	B	290.78	17.36	B / 8.2	18.95%	C / 4.9
2009	C+	259.99	16.03	B- / 7.1	69.35%	C / 5.5

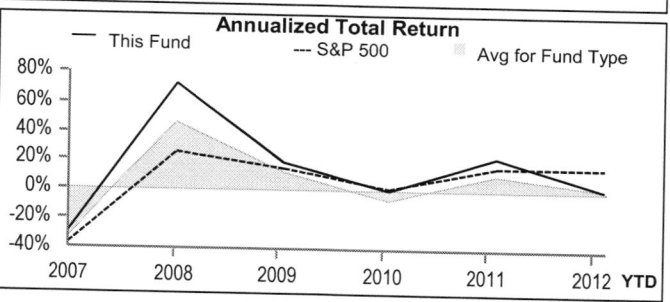

Flaherty&Crumrine Preferred Inc Op (PFO)

A-   **Excellent**

Fund Family: Flaherty & Crumrine Inc
Fund Type: Income
Inception Date: February 13, 1992

Major Rating Factors:
Strong performance is the major factor driving the A- (Excellent) TheStreet.com Investment Rating for Flaherty&Crumrine Preferred Inc Op. The fund currently has a performance rating of B+ (Good) based on an annualized return of 21.92% over the last three years and a total return of 5.70% year to date 2012. Factored into the performance evaluation is an expense ratio of 2.14% (high).

The fund's risk rating is currently B (Good). It carries a beta of 0.37, meaning the fund's expected move will be 3.7% for every 10% move in the market. Volatility, as measured by both the semi-deviation and a drawdown factor, is considered low. As of December 31, 2012, Flaherty&Crumrine Preferred Inc Op traded at a discount of .97% below its net asset value, which is better than its one-year historical average premium of 9.57%.

Robert E. Chadwick currently receives a manager quality ranking of 96 (0=worst, 99=best). If you desire only a moderate level of risk and strong performance, then this fund is an excellent option.

Data Date	Investment Rating	Net Assets ($Mil)	Price	Performance Rating/Pts	Total Return Y-T-D	Risk Rating/Pts
12-12	A-	124.39	11.22	B+ / 8.3	5.70%	B / 8.6
2011	A+	114.70	11.20	A+ / 9.8	0.98%	B / 8.9
2010	C+	95.02	9.48	B- / 7.0	25.08%	C / 4.3
2009	C-	67.90	8.27	C / 5.0	83.81%	C- / 4.1

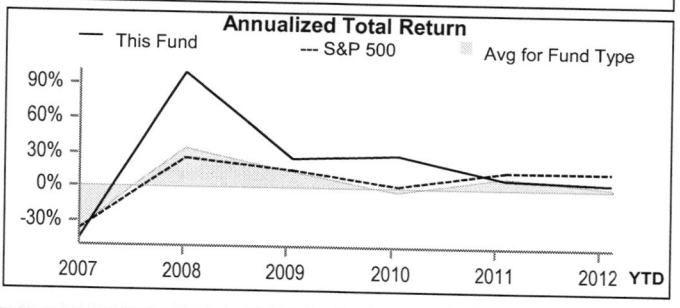

Flaherty&Crumrine Preferred Income (PFD)

B+   **Good**

Fund Family: Flaherty & Crumrine Inc
Fund Type: Income
Inception Date: January 31, 1991

Major Rating Factors: Strong performance is the major factor driving the B+ (Good) TheStreet.com Investment Rating for Flaherty&Crumrine Preferred Income. The fund currently has a performance rating of B (Good) based on an annualized return of 21.07% over the last three years and a total return of 8.07% year to date 2012. Factored into the performance evaluation is an expense ratio of 2.10% (high).

The fund's risk rating is currently B (Good). It carries a beta of 0.28, meaning the fund's expected move will be 2.8% for every 10% move in the market. Volatility, as measured by both the semi-deviation and a drawdown factor, is considered low. As of December 31, 2012, Flaherty&Crumrine Preferred Income traded at a discount of .37% below its net asset value, which is better than its one-year historical average premium of 14.48%.

Robert E. Chadwick currently receives a manager quality ranking of 96 (0=worst, 99=best). If you desire only a moderate level of risk and strong performance, then this fund is an excellent option.

Data Date	Investment Rating	Net Assets ($Mil)	Price	Performance Rating/Pts	Total Return Y-T-D	Risk Rating/Pts
12-12	B+	135.17	13.63	B / 7.9	8.07%	B / 8.3
2011	B+	125.40	14.14	A / 9.5	1.56%	B- / 7.4
2010	C-	104.76	11.62	C+ / 6.8	21.26%	C- / 3.4
2009	D+	76.36	10.47	C / 4.5	78.67%	C- / 3.8

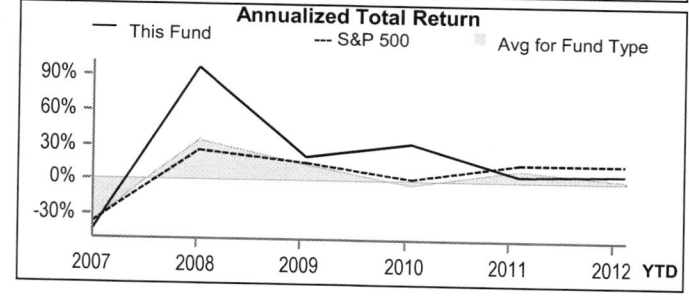

Fort Dearborn Inc. Secs. (FDI)

B+   Good

Fund Family: UBS Global Asset Mgmt (Americas) In
Fund Type: General - Investment Grade
Inception Date: December 15, 1972

Major Rating Factors: Strong performance is the major factor driving the B+ (Good) TheStreet.com Investment Rating for Fort Dearborn Inc. Secs.. The fund currently has a performance rating of B- (Good) based on an annualized return of 18.11% over the last three years and a total return of -0.60% year to date 2012. Factored into the performance evaluation is an expense ratio of 0.67% (very low).

The fund's risk rating is currently B (Good). It carries a beta of 1.36, meaning it is expected to move 13.6% for every 10% move in the market. Volatility, as measured by both the semi-deviation and a drawdown factor, is considered low. As of December 31, 2012, Fort Dearborn Inc. Secs. traded at a discount of 3.33% below its net asset value, which is worse than its one-year historical average discount of 5.09%.

Michael G. Dow currently receives a manager quality ranking of 89 (0=worst, 99=best). If you desire only a moderate level of risk and strong performance, then this fund is an excellent option.

Data Date	Investment Rating	Net Assets ($Mil)	Price	Performance Rating/Pts	Total Return Y-T-D	Risk Rating/Pts
12-12	B+	156.80	16.54	B- / 7.3	-0.60%	B / 8.9
2011	B+	151.70	15.96	B- / 7.4	-0.13%	B+ / 9.0
2010	B+	152.20	15.46	B / 7.6	17.35%	C+ / 6.4
2009	C+	144.77	14.48	C / 4.6	11.63%	B- / 7.9

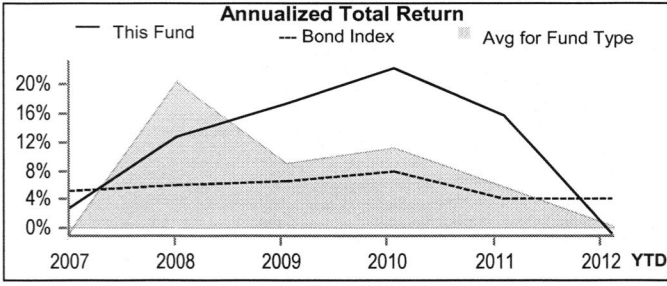

Foxby Corp (FXBY)

D+   Weak

Fund Family: CEF Advisers Inc
Fund Type: Income
Inception Date: October 26, 1999

Major Rating Factors:
Disappointing performance is the major factor driving the D+ (Weak) TheStreet.com Investment Rating for Foxby Corp. The fund currently has a performance rating of D+ (Weak) based on an annualized return of 7.48% over the last three years and a total return of 2.07% year to date 2012. Factored into the performance evaluation is an expense ratio of 2.63% (high).

The fund's risk rating is currently B- (Good). It carries a beta of 0.61, meaning the fund's expected move will be 6.1% for every 10% move in the market. Volatility, as measured by both the semi-deviation and a drawdown factor, is considered low. As of December 31, 2012, Foxby Corp traded at a discount of 33.49% below its net asset value, which is better than its one-year historical average discount of 27.05%.

Thomas B. Winmill has been running the fund for 8 years and currently receives a manager quality ranking of 82 (0=worst, 99=best). This fund offers only a moderate level of risk but investors looking for strong performance are still waiting.

Data Date	Investment Rating	Net Assets ($Mil)	Price	Performance Rating/Pts	Total Return Y-T-D	Risk Rating/Pts
12-12	D+	5.31	1.45	D+ / 2.8	2.07%	B- / 7.4
2011	C+	4.70	1.24	B- / 7.1	0.81%	B- / 7.0
2010	E	3.71	1.10	E / 0.5	7.84%	D+ / 2.3
2009	E	3.59	1.02	E+ / 0.8	82.14%	D+ / 2.6

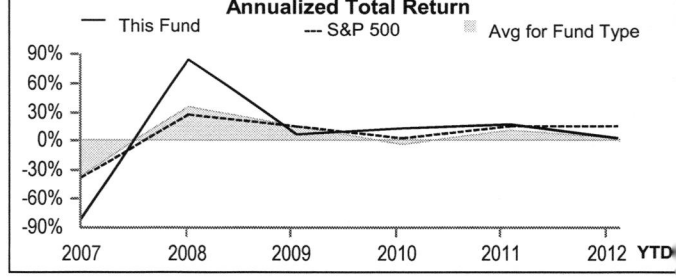

Franklin Templeton Ltd Duration In (FTF)

B-   Good

Fund Family: Franklin Advisers Inc
Fund Type: General Bond
Inception Date: August 27, 2003

Major Rating Factors: Franklin Templeton Ltd Duration In receives a TheStreet.com Investment Rating of B- (Good). The fund currently has a performance rating of C+ (Fair) based on an annualized return of 14.36% over the last three years and a total return of 1.81% year to date 2012. Factored into the performance evaluation is an expense ratio of 1.15% (low).

The fund's risk rating is currently B (Good). It carries a beta of -0.44, meaning the fund's expected move will be -4.4% for every 10% move in the market. Volatility, as measured by both the semi-deviation and a drawdown factor, is considered low. As of December 31, 2012, Franklin Templeton Ltd Duration In traded at a premium of .35% above its net asset value, which is better than its one-year historical average premium of 1.31%.

Christopher J. Molumphy currently receives a manager quality ranking of 96 (0=worst, 99=best). If you desire an average level of risk, then this fund may be an option.

Data Date	Investment Rating	Net Assets ($Mil)	Price	Performance Rating/Pts	Total Return Y-T-D	Risk Rating/Pts
12-12	B-	370.10	14.37	C+ / 6.6	1.81%	B / 8.5
2011	B	357.50	13.14	B- / 7.2	-1.07%	B / 8.6
2010	B-	360.80	13.10	B / 7.9	16.73%	C / 4.7
2009	C+	341.73	12.00	C+ / 6.2	52.91%	C+ / 6.0

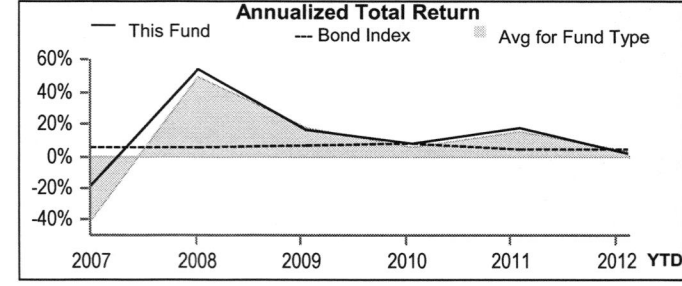

Franklin Universal Trust (FT)

C+ **Fair**

Fund Family: Franklin Advisers Inc
Fund Type: Growth and Income
Inception Date: September 23, 1988

Major Rating Factors: Middle of the road best describes Franklin Universal Trust whose TheStreet.com Investment Rating is currently a C+ (Fair). The fund currently has a performance rating of C+ (Fair) based on an annualized return of 15.77% over the last three years and a total return of 3.54% year to date 2012. Factored into the performance evaluation is an expense ratio of 2.46% (high).

The fund's risk rating is currently B- (Good). It carries a beta of 0.42, meaning the fund's expected move will be 4.2% for every 10% move in the market. Volatility, as measured by both the semi-deviation and a drawdown factor, is considered low. As of December 31, 2012, Franklin Universal Trust traded at a discount of 7.71% below its net asset value, which is better than its one-year historical average discount of 3.94%.

Christopher J. Molumphy has been running the fund for 22 years and currently receives a manager quality ranking of 90 (0=worst, 99=best). If you desire an average level of risk, then this fund may be an option.

Data Date	Investment Rating	Net Assets ($Mil)	Price	Performance Rating/Pts	Total Return Y-T-D	Risk Rating/Pts
12-12	C+	187.73	7.06	C+ / 6.3	3.54%	B- / 7.8
2011	B	179.20	6.69	B / 8.0	-1.05%	B- / 7.3
2010	C	165.08	6.33	C+ / 6.7	17.60%	C- / 4.2
2009	C	147.07	5.80	C+ / 6.6	59.54%	C / 4.9

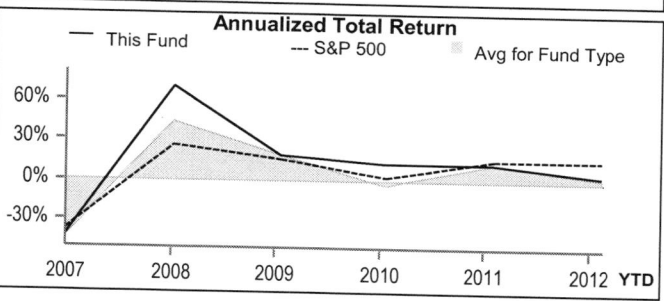

Gabelli Convertible&Income Sec Fun (GCV)

C- **Fair**

Fund Family: Gabelli Funds LLC
Fund Type: Growth and Income
Inception Date: July 3, 1989

Major Rating Factors: Middle of the road best describes Gabelli Convertible&Income Sec Fun whose TheStreet.com Investment Rating is currently a C- (Fair). The fund currently has a performance rating of C+ (Fair) based on an annualized return of 6.68% over the last three years and a total return of 3.75% year to date 2012. Factored into the performance evaluation is an expense ratio of 1.99% (high).

The fund's risk rating is currently B- (Good). It carries a beta of 0.83, meaning the fund's expected move will be 8.3% for every 10% move in the market. Volatility, as measured by both the semi-deviation and a drawdown factor, is considered low. As of December 31, 2012, Gabelli Convertible&Income Sec Fun traded at a discount of 7.94% below its net asset value, which is better than its one-year historical average discount of 2.56%.

Mario J. Gabelli has been running the fund for 24 years and currently receives a manager quality ranking of 32 (0=worst, 99=best). If you desire an average level of risk, then this fund may be an option.

Data Date	Investment Rating	Net Assets ($Mil)	Price	Performance Rating/Pts	Total Return Y-T-D	Risk Rating/Pts
12-12	C-	100.12	5.33	C- / 3.3	3.75%	B- / 7.5
2011	D+	98.20	5.11	D / 2.0	2.54%	B- / 7.6
2010	C+	74.08	6.12	C / 5.2	15.79%	C+ / 6.3
2009	D+	67.67	5.83	D / 1.8	8.95%	C+ / 6.8

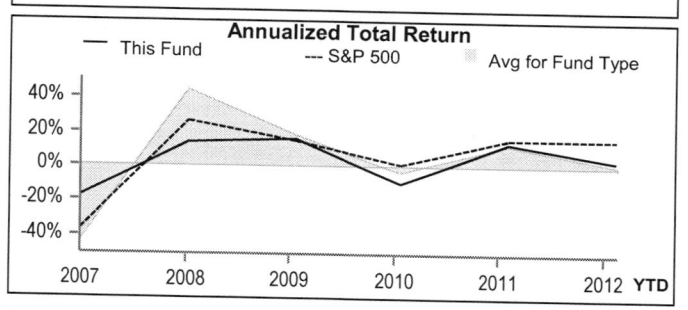

Gabelli Dividend & Income Trust (GDV)

C+ **Fair**

Fund Family: Gabelli Funds LLC
Fund Type: Income
Inception Date: November 24, 2003

Major Rating Factors: Middle of the road best describes Gabelli Dividend & Income Trust whose TheStreet.com Investment Rating is currently a C+ (Fair). The fund currently has a performance rating of C+ (Fair) based on an annualized return of 14.90% over the last three years and a total return of 5.87% year to date 2012. Factored into the performance evaluation is an expense ratio of 1.34% (average).

The fund's risk rating is currently B (Good). It carries a beta of 1.14, meaning it is expected to move 11.4% for every 10% move in the market. Volatility, as measured by both the semi-deviation and a drawdown factor, is considered low. As of December 31, 2012, Gabelli Dividend & Income Trust traded at a discount of 15.99% below its net asset value, which is better than its one-year historical average discount of 10.95%.

Barbara G. Marcin has been running the fund for 10 years and currently receives a manager quality ranking of 63 (0=worst, 99=best). If you desire an average level of risk, then this fund may be an option.

Data Date	Investment Rating	Net Assets ($Mil)	Price	Performance Rating/Pts	Total Return Y-T-D	Risk Rating/Pts
12-12	C+	1,923.33	16.18	C+ / 6.6	5.87%	B / 8.0
2011	C+	1,888.80	15.42	B- / 7.0	-0.32%	B- / 7.3
2010	C	1,168.13	15.36	C / 5.4	24.50%	C / 5.1
2009	D+	1,023.81	13.11	D+ / 2.6	32.13%	C+ / 5.7

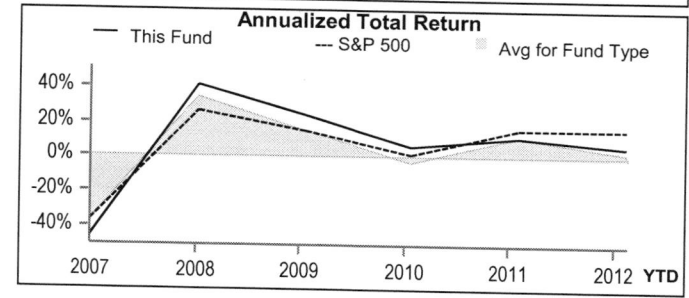

Gabelli Equity Trust (GAB)   B   Good

Fund Family: Gabelli Funds LLC
Fund Type: Income
Inception Date: August 14, 1986

Major Rating Factors: Strong performance is the major factor driving the B (Good) TheStreet.com Investment Rating for Gabelli Equity Trust. The fund currently has a performance rating of B (Good) based on an annualized return of 16.52% over the last three years and a total return of 5.73% year to date 2012. Factored into the performance evaluation is an expense ratio of 1.45% (average).

The fund's risk rating is currently B- (Good). It carries a beta of 1.10, meaning it is expected to move 11.0% for every 10% move in the market. Volatility, as measured by both the semi-deviation and a drawdown factor, is considered low. As of December 31, 2012, Gabelli Equity Trust traded at a discount of 4.29% below its net asset value, which is better than its one-year historical average premium of .55%.

Mario J. Gabelli has been running the fund for 27 years and currently receives a manager quality ranking of 72 (0=worst, 99=best). If you desire only a moderate level of risk and strong performance, then this fund is an excellent option.

Data Date	Investment Rating	Net Assets ($Mil)	Price	Performance Rating/Pts	Total Return Y-T-D	Risk Rating/Pts
12-12	B	1,293.17	5.58	B / 8.1	5.73%	B- / 7.6
2011	C+	1,265.50	4.99	B- / 7.2	2.61%	B- / 7.2
2010	C	822.41	5.67	C+ / 5.6	27.14%	C / 5.1
2009	D	711.52	5.04	D+ / 2.7	50.72%	C / 4.7

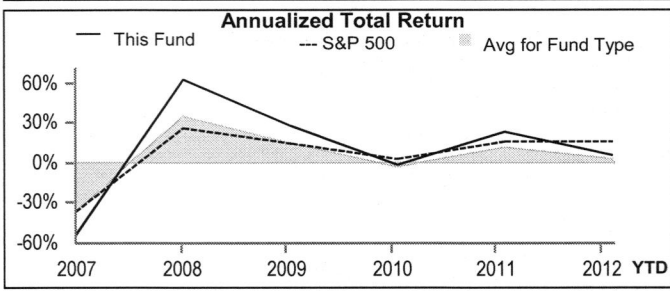

Gabelli Global Utility&Income Trus (GLU)   C   Fair

Fund Family: Gabelli Funds LLC
Fund Type: Utilities
Inception Date: May 26, 2004

Major Rating Factors: Middle of the road best describes Gabelli Global Utility&Income Trus whose TheStreet.com Investment Rating is currently a C (Fair). The fund currently has a performance rating of C- (Fair) based on an annualized return of 8.06% over the last three years and a total return of 1.53% year to date 2012. Factored into the performance evaluation is an expense ratio of 1.30% (average).

The fund's risk rating is currently B+ (Good). It carries a beta of 0.66, meaning the fund's expected move will be 6.6% for every 10% move in the market. Volatility, as measured by both the semi-deviation and a drawdown factor, is considered very low. As of December 31, 2012, Gabelli Global Utility&Income Trus traded at a premium of .24% above its net asset value, which is better than its one-year historical average premium of 2.12%.

Mario J. Gabelli has been running the fund for 9 years and currently receives a manager quality ranking of 72 (0=worst, 99=best). If you desire an average level of risk, then this fund may be an option.

Data Date	Investment Rating	Net Assets ($Mil)	Price	Performance Rating/Pts	Total Return Y-T-D	Risk Rating/Pts
12-12	C	63.11	20.88	C- / 3.3	1.53%	B+ / 9.0
2011	C+	63.30	21.04	C+ / 6.4	1.05%	B- / 7.9
2010	C	55.20	20.46	C / 5.3	12.68%	C / 5.2
2009	C	53.65	19.42	C / 5.1	28.04%	C / 5.2

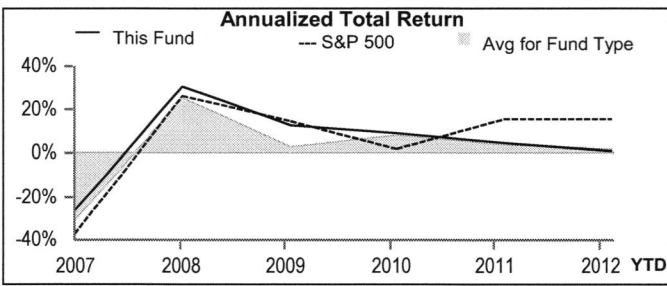

Gabelli Healthcare & WellnessRx Tr (GRX)   A   Excellent

Fund Family: Gabelli Funds LLC
Fund Type: Health
Inception Date: June 28, 2007

Major Rating Factors:
Strong performance is the major factor driving the A (Excellent) TheStreet.com Investment Rating for Gabelli Healthcare & WellnessRx Tr. The fund currently has a performance rating of B+ (Good) based on an annualized return of 16.98% over the last three years and a total return of 4.87% year to date 2012. Factored into the performance evaluation is an expense ratio of 2.22% (high).

The fund's risk rating is currently B (Good). It carries a beta of 0.83, meaning the fund's expected move will be 8.3% for every 10% move in the market. Volatility, as measured by both the semi-deviation and a drawdown factor, is considered low. As of December 31, 2012, Gabelli Healthcare & WellnessRx Tr traded at a discount of 12.13% below its net asset value, which is worse than its one-year historical average discount of 13.08%.

Kevin V. Dreyer currently receives a manager quality ranking of 83 (0=worst, 99=best). If you desire only a moderate level of risk and strong performance, then this fund is an excellent option.

Data Date	Investment Rating	Net Assets ($Mil)	Price	Performance Rating/Pts	Total Return Y-T-D	Risk Rating/Pts
12-12	A	95.58	8.62	B+ / 8.8	4.87%	B / 8.3
2011	C+	125.60	7.13	C / 5.4	1.54%	B / 8.3
2010	C+	63.00	7.10	C / 4.7	6.72%	B- / 7.3
2009	A+	55.89	6.70	B+ / 8.8	30.10%	C+ / 6.1

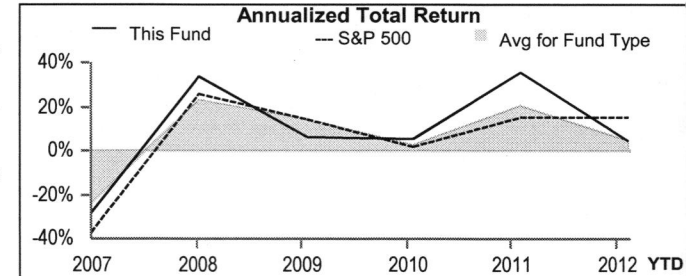

Gabelli Multimedia Trust (GGT)

B+   **Good**

Fund Family: Gabelli Funds LLC
Fund Type: Global
Inception Date: October 11, 1994

Major Rating Factors:
Exceptional performance is the major factor driving the B+ (Good) TheStreet.com Investment Rating for Gabelli Multimedia Trust. The fund currently has a performance rating of A (Excellent) based on an annualized return of 21.05% over the last three years and a total return of 7.01% year to date 2012. Factored into the performance evaluation is an expense ratio of 2.34% (high).

The fund's risk rating is currently C+ (Fair). It carries a beta of 0.91, meaning that its performance tracks fairly well with that of the overall stock market. Volatility, as measured by both the semi-deviation and a drawdown factor, is considered low. As of December 31, 2012, Gabelli Multimedia Trust traded at a discount of 8.61% below its net asset value, which is better than its one-year historical average discount of 7.90%.

Lawrence J. Haverty, Jr. has been running the fund for 19 years and currently receives a manager quality ranking of 95 (0=worst, 99=best). If you desire only a moderate level of risk and strong performance, then this fund is an excellent option.

Data Date	Investment Rating	Net Assets ($Mil)	Price	Performance Rating/Pts	Total Return Y-T-D	Risk Rating/Pts
12-12	B+	135.20	7.85	A / 9.5	7.01%	C+ / 6.9
2011	C	170.00	6.23	C+ / 6.6	5.14%	C+ / 6.6
2010	D-	106.39	8.21	C- / 3.0	34.34%	D+ / 2.7
2009	D-	80.51	6.61	D- / 1.3	39.45%	C- / 4.1

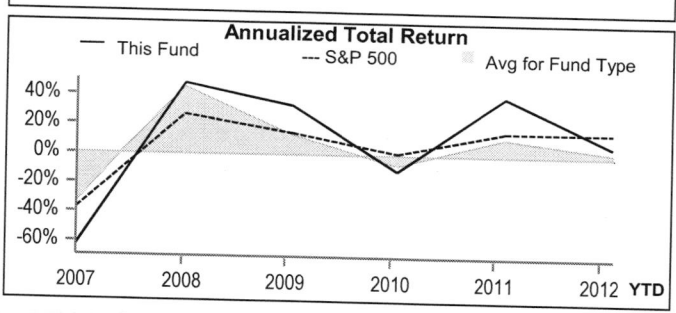

Gabelli Utility Trust (GUT)

D   **Weak**

Fund Family: Gabelli Funds LLC
Fund Type: Utilities
Inception Date: July 9, 1999

Major Rating Factors:
Disappointing performance is the major factor driving the D (Weak) TheStreet.com Investment Rating for Gabelli Utility Trust. The fund currently has a performance rating of D- (Weak) based on an annualized return of 1.11% over the last three years and a total return of 9.42% year to date 2012. Factored into the performance evaluation is an expense ratio of 1.61% (above average).

The fund's risk rating is currently C+ (Fair). It carries a beta of 0.55, meaning the fund's expected move will be 5.5% for every 10% move in the market. Volatility, as measured by both the semi-deviation and a drawdown factor, is considered low. As of December 31, 2012, Gabelli Utility Trust traded at a premium of 10.39% above its net asset value, which is better than its one-year historical average premium of 33.95%.

Mario J. Gabelli has been running the fund for 14 years and currently receives a manager quality ranking of 18 (0=worst, 99=best). This fund offers only a moderate level of risk but investors looking for strong performance are still waiting.

Data Date	Investment Rating	Net Assets ($Mil)	Price	Performance Rating/Pts	Total Return Y-T-D	Risk Rating/Pts
12-12	D	230.78	6.16	D- / 1.2	9.42%	C+ / 6.6
2011	C+	232.50	7.80	B / 8.1	1.67%	C+ / 6.2
2010	D	142.39	6.39	D- / 1.1	-20.15%	C+ / 6.1
2009	B-	138.32	8.95	B- / 7.5	60.52%	C / 5.2

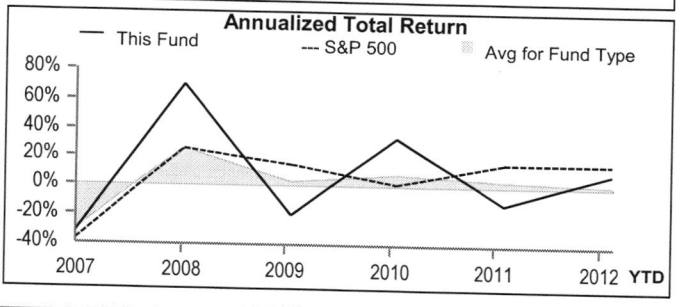

GAMCO Global Gold Nat ResandIncome (GGN)

D   **Weak**

Fund Family: Gabelli Funds LLC
Fund Type: Precious Metals
Inception Date: March 29, 2005

Major Rating Factors:
Disappointing performance is the major factor driving the D (Weak) TheStreet.com Investment Rating for GAMCO Global Gold Nat ResandIncome. The fund currently has a performance rating of D (Weak) based on an annualized return of 3.25% over the last three years and a total return of 6.80% year to date 2012. Factored into the performance evaluation is an expense ratio of 1.23% (average).

The fund's risk rating is currently C+ (Fair). It carries a beta of 0.79, meaning the fund's expected move will be 7.9% for every 10% move in the market. Volatility, as measured by both the semi-deviation and a drawdown factor, is considered low. As of December 31, 2012, GAMCO Global Gold Nat ResandIncome traded at a discount of 4.55% below its net asset value, which is better than its one-year historical average premium of 4.09%.

Caesar M. P. Bryan has been running the fund for 8 years and currently receives a manager quality ranking of 15 (0=worst, 99=best). This fund offers only a moderate level of risk but investors looking for strong performance are still waiting.

Data Date	Investment Rating	Net Assets ($Mil)	Price	Performance Rating/Pts	Total Return Y-T-D	Risk Rating/Pts
12-12	D	1,222.81	12.80	D / 2.1	6.80%	C+ / 6.2
2011	D+	1,206.10	14.11	C- / 3.7	6.31%	C+ / 5.9
2010	D	664.32	19.27	C / 4.9	32.00%	D / 2.2
2009	D	280.71	16.33	C- / 3.4	26.96%	C- / 3.5

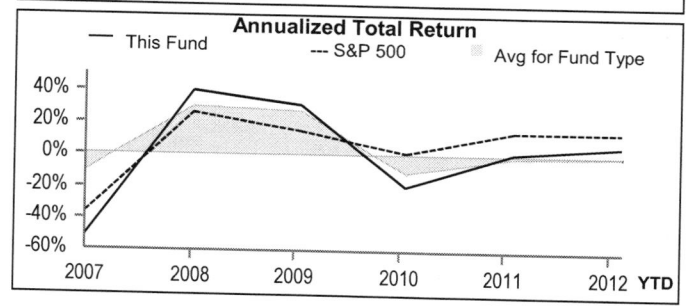

GAMCO Nat Res Gold & Income Trust (GNT)   D   Weak

Fund Family: Gabelli Funds LLC
Fund Type: Energy/Natural Resources
Inception Date: January 31, 2011

Major Rating Factors: GAMCO Nat Res Gold & Income Trust receives a
TheStreet.com Investment Rating of D (Weak). The fund currently has a performance
rating of C- (Fair) based on an annualized return of 0.00% over the last three years
and a total return of 6.08% year to date 2012. Factored into the performance
evaluation is an expense ratio of 1.17% (low).

The fund's risk rating is currently C+ (Fair). It carries a beta of 0.00, meaning the
fund's expected move will be 0.0% for every 10% move in the market. Volatility, as
measured by both the semi-deviation and a drawdown factor, is considered low. As of
December 31, 2012, GAMCO Nat Res Gold & Income Trust traded at a discount of
2.98% below its net asset value, which is better than its one-year historical average
premium of 4.62%.

CAESAR M.P. BRYAN has been running the fund for 2 years and currently
receives a manager quality ranking of 89 (0=worst, 99=best). If you desire an average
level of risk, then this fund may be an option.

Data Date	Investment Rating	Net Assets ($Mil)	Price	Performance Rating/Pts	Total Return Y-T-D	Risk Rating/Pts
12-12	D	310.78	13.66	C- / 3.0	6.08%	C+ / 6.1

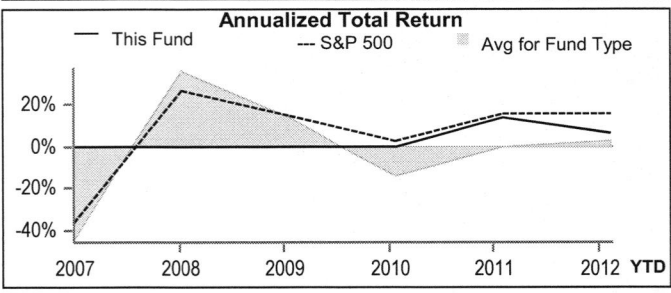

GDL Fund (GDL)   D+   Weak

Fund Family: Gabelli Funds LLC
Fund Type: Global
Inception Date: January 26, 2007

Major Rating Factors:
Disappointing performance is the major factor driving the D+ (Weak) TheStreet.com
Investment Rating for GDL Fund. The fund currently has a performance rating of D+
(Weak) based on an annualized return of 3.86% over the last three years and a total
return of 0.88% year to date 2012. Factored into the performance evaluation is an
expense ratio of 4.89% (high).

The fund's risk rating is currently B (Good). It carries a beta of 0.30, meaning the
fund's expected move will be 3.0% for every 10% move in the market. Volatility, as
measured by both the semi-deviation and a drawdown factor, is considered low. As of
December 31, 2012, GDL Fund traded at a discount of 14.39% below its net asset
value, which is better than its one-year historical average discount of 12.79%.

Mario J. Gabelli has been running the fund for 6 years and currently receives a
manager quality ranking of 66 (0=worst, 99=best). This fund offers only a moderate
level of risk but investors looking for strong performance are still waiting.

Data Date	Investment Rating	Net Assets ($Mil)	Price	Performance Rating/Pts	Total Return Y-T-D	Risk Rating/Pts
12-12	D+	293.77	11.42	D+ / 2.3	0.88%	B / 8.1
2011	C-	438.10	11.80	D+ / 2.9	0.68%	B / 8.1
2010	C+	315.08	13.37	C / 4.6	4.19%	C+ / 6.8
2009	C+	339.63	14.41	C+ / 6.4	17.32%	C+ / 6.8

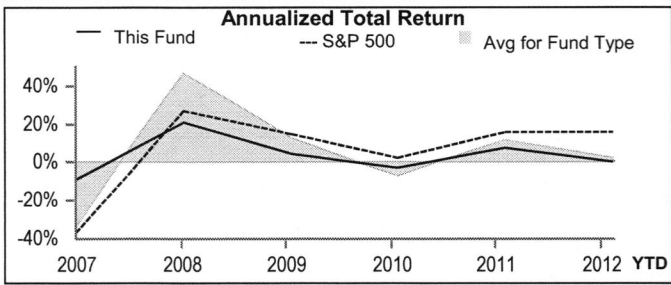

General American Investors (GAM)   C   Fair

Fund Family: General American Investors Company
Fund Type: Growth
Inception Date: N/A

Major Rating Factors: Middle of the road best describes General American
Investors whose TheStreet.com Investment Rating is currently a C (Fair). The fund
currently has a performance rating of C (Fair) based on an annualized return of
10.37% over the last three years and a total return of 4.06% year to date 2012.
Factored into the performance evaluation is an expense ratio of 1.51% (average).

The fund's risk rating is currently B- (Good). It carries a beta of 1.25, meaning it is
expected to move 12.5% for every 10% move in the market. Volatility, as measured
by both the semi-deviation and a drawdown factor, is considered low. As of
December 31, 2012, General American Investors traded at a discount of 17.64%
below its net asset value, which is better than its one-year historical average discount
of 14.63%.

Jeffrey W. Priest currently receives a manager quality ranking of 28 (0=worst,
99=best). If you desire an average level of risk, then this fund may be an option.

Data Date	Investment Rating	Net Assets ($Mil)	Price	Performance Rating/Pts	Total Return Y-T-D	Risk Rating/Pts
12-12	C	915.45	27.82	C / 5.3	4.06%	B- / 7.6
2011	C	1,076.70	24.91	C / 4.9	2.17%	B- / 7.6
2010	D+	864.32	26.82	D+ / 2.6	16.16%	C+ / 5.7
2009	D	732.06	23.46	D / 1.8	28.31%	C / 5.4

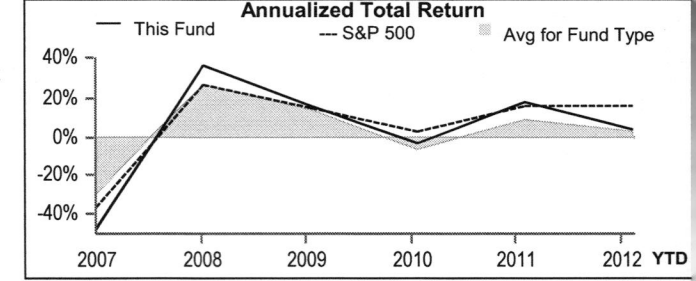

Global High Income Fund (GHI)

C   **Fair**

Fund Family: UBS Global Asset Mgmt (Americas) In
Fund Type: Emerging Market
Inception Date: September 30, 1993

Major Rating Factors: Middle of the road best describes Global High Income Fund whose TheStreet.com Investment Rating is currently a C (Fair). The fund currently has a performance rating of C+ (Fair) based on an annualized return of 13.08% over the last three years and a total return of 1.70% year to date 2012. Factored into the performance evaluation is an expense ratio of 1.44% (average).

The fund's risk rating is currently B- (Good). It carries a beta of 1.32, meaning it is expected to move 13.2% for every 10% move in the market. Volatility, as measured by both the semi-deviation and a drawdown factor, is considered low. As of December 31, 2012, Global High Income Fund traded at a discount of 6.24% below its net asset value, which is better than its one-year historical average discount of 3.18%.

John C. Leonard currently receives a manager quality ranking of 88 (0=worst, 99=best). If you desire an average level of risk, then this fund may be an option.

Data Date	Investment Rating	Net Assets ($Mil)	Price	Performance Rating/Pts	Total Return Y-T-D	Risk Rating/Pts
12-12	C	280.80	12.92	C+ / 5.7	1.70%	B- / 7.4
2011	B-	270.80	12.08	B / 7.7	1.24%	B- / 7.4
2010	B	291.28	13.05	B- / 7.5	23.01%	C / 5.4
2009	C	292.26	12.15	C / 5.4	57.81%	C+ / 5.7

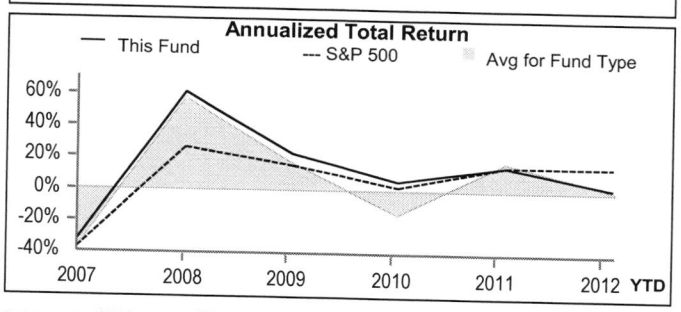

Global Income Fund (GIFD)

C   **Fair**

Fund Family: CEF Advisers Inc
Fund Type: Global
Inception Date: August 30, 1983

Major Rating Factors: Middle of the road best describes Global Income Fund whose TheStreet.com Investment Rating is currently a C (Fair). The fund currently has a performance rating of C (Fair) based on an annualized return of 10.53% over the last three years and a total return of 3.25% year to date 2012. Factored into the performance evaluation is an expense ratio of 1.96% (above average).

The fund's risk rating is currently B (Good). It carries a beta of 0.53, meaning the fund's expected move will be 5.3% for every 10% move in the market. Volatility, as measured by both the semi-deviation and a drawdown factor, is considered low. As of December 31, 2012, Global Income Fund traded at a discount of 23.44% below its net asset value, which is better than its one-year historical average discount of 19.61%.

Heidi Keating currently receives a manager quality ranking of 85 (0=worst, 99=best). If you desire an average level of risk, then this fund may be an option.

Data Date	Investment Rating	Net Assets ($Mil)	Price	Performance Rating/Pts	Total Return Y-T-D	Risk Rating/Pts
12-12	C	36.94	3.69	C / 4.5	3.25%	B / 8.0
2011	C	34.10	3.78	C / 4.8	-1.59%	B- / 7.8
2010	A-	31.19	4.17	B / 7.7	21.03%	B- / 7.0
2009	C+	28.99	3.65	C / 5.3	35.47%	C+ / 6.7

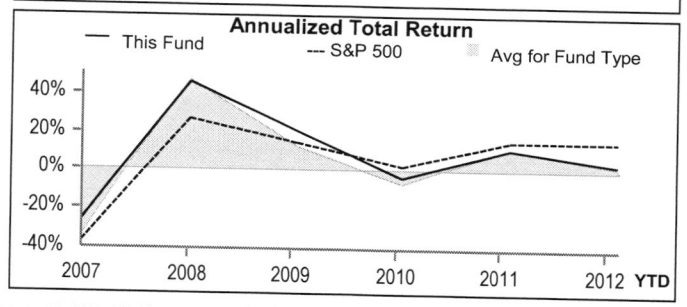

Greater China Fund (GCH)

D+   **Weak**

Fund Family: Aberdeen Asset Management Asia Ltd
Fund Type: Foreign
Inception Date: July 15, 1992

Major Rating Factors:
Disappointing performance is the major factor driving the D+ (Weak) TheStreet.com Investment Rating for Greater China Fund. The fund currently has a performance rating of D+ (Weak) based on an annualized return of -0.85% over the last three years and a total return of 2.56% year to date 2012. Factored into the performance evaluation is an expense ratio of 1.80% (above average).

The fund's risk rating is currently B- (Good). It carries a beta of 0.95, meaning that its performance tracks fairly well with that of the overall stock market. Volatility, as measured by both the semi-deviation and a drawdown factor, is considered low. As of December 31, 2012, Greater China Fund traded at a discount of 5.15% below its net asset value, which is worse than its one-year historical average discount of 8.08%.

Agnes Deng currently receives a manager quality ranking of 21 (0=worst, 99=best). This fund offers only a moderate level of risk but investors looking for strong performance are still waiting.

Data Date	Investment Rating	Net Assets ($Mil)	Price	Performance Rating/Pts	Total Return Y-T-D	Risk Rating/Pts
12-12	D+	282.12	12.88	D+ / 2.6	2.56%	B- / 7.1
2011	D	273.60	10.07	D+ / 2.5	1.79%	C+ / 6.4
2010	E+	368.48	13.15	D- / 1.4	-5.41%	C- / 3.1
2009	C-	273.67	13.92	B- / 7.2	58.49%	D / 2.0

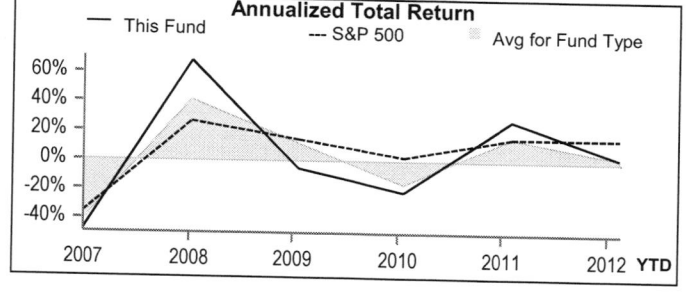

Guggenheim Build America Bd Mgd Du (GBAB)

C+   **Fair**

Fund Family: Guggenheim Funds Investment Advisor
Fund Type: General - Investment Grade
Inception Date: October 28, 2010

Major Rating Factors: Middle of the road best describes Guggenheim Build America Bd Mgd Du whose TheStreet.com Investment Rating is currently a C+ (Fair). The fund currently has a performance rating of C (Fair) based on an annualized return of 0.00% over the last three years and a total return of 1.70% year to date 2012. Factored into the performance evaluation is an expense ratio of 1.36% (average).

The fund's risk rating is currently B+ (Good). It carries a beta of 0.00, meaning the fund's expected move will be 0.0% for every 10% move in the market. Volatility, as measured by both the semi-deviation and a drawdown factor, is considered very low. As of December 31, 2012, Guggenheim Build America Bd Mgd Du traded at a discount of 2.63% below its net asset value, which is better than its one-year historical average discount of 2.36%.

Anne Walsh currently receives a manager quality ranking of 75 (0=worst, 99=best). If you desire an average level of risk, then this fund may be an option.

Data Date	Investment Rating	Net Assets ($Mil)	Price	Performance Rating/Pts	Total Return Y-T-D	Risk Rating/Pts
12-12	C+	408.96	22.95	C / 5.0	1.70%	B+ / 9.2
2011	A	359.44	21.41	B+ / 8.5	0.26%	B+ / 9.3

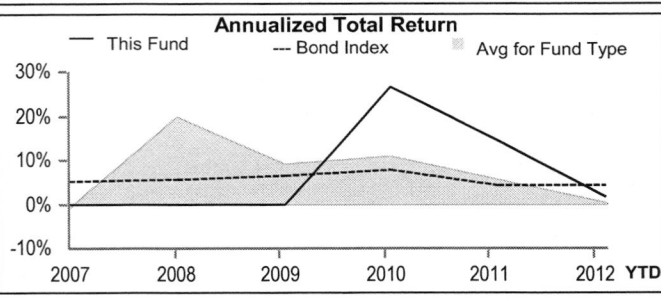

Guggenheim Enhanced Equity Income (GPM)

C-   **Fair**

Fund Family: Guggenheim Funds Investment Advisor
Fund Type: Income
Inception Date: August 25, 2005

Major Rating Factors: Middle of the road best describes Guggenheim Enhanced Equity Income whose TheStreet.com Investment Rating is currently a C- (Fair). The fund currently has a performance rating of C (Fair) based on an annualized return of 12.26% over the last three years and a total return of 6.71% year to date 2012. Factored into the performance evaluation is an expense ratio of 1.71% (above average).

The fund's risk rating is currently B- (Good). It carries a beta of 1.03, meaning that its performance tracks fairly well with that of the overall stock market. Volatility, as measured by both the semi-deviation and a drawdown factor, is considered low. As of December 31, 2012, Guggenheim Enhanced Equity Income traded at a discount of 10.77% below its net asset value, which is better than its one-year historical average discount of 4.43%.

Byron S. Minerd currently receives a manager quality ranking of 43 (0=worst, 99=best). If you desire an average level of risk, then this fund may be an option.

Data Date	Investment Rating	Net Assets ($Mil)	Price	Performance Rating/Pts	Total Return Y-T-D	Risk Rating/Pts
12-12	C-	177.84	8.20	C / 4.5	6.71%	B- / 7.4
2011	C-	176.70	8.16	C- / 4.1	2.21%	B- / 7.5
2010	D	154.55	9.33	C- / 3.8	22.63%	C- / 3.4
2009	D-	177.78	8.50	D- / 1.1	17.22%	C / 5.5

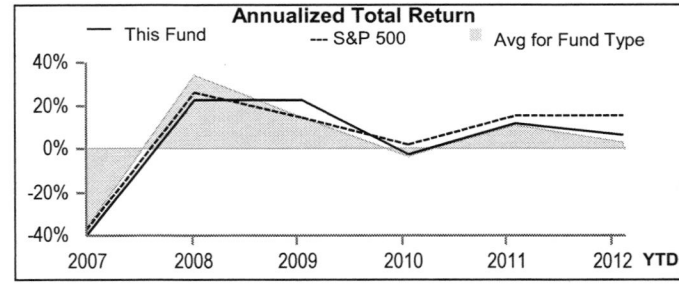

Guggenheim Enhanced Equity Strateg (GGE)

C+   **Fair**

Fund Family: Guggenheim Funds Investment Advisor
Fund Type: Income
Inception Date: January 28, 2004

Major Rating Factors: Middle of the road best describes Guggenheim Enhanced Equity Strateg whose TheStreet.com Investment Rating is currently a C+ (Fair). The fund currently has a performance rating of C+ (Fair) based on an annualized return of 13.92% over the last three years and a total return of 5.64% year to date 2012. Factored into the performance evaluation is an expense ratio of 2.23% (high).

The fund's risk rating is currently B- (Good). It carries a beta of 1.01, meaning that its performance tracks fairly well with that of the overall stock market. Volatility, as measured by both the semi-deviation and a drawdown factor, is considered low. As of December 31, 2012, Guggenheim Enhanced Equity Strateg traded at a discount of 13.41% below its net asset value, which is better than its one-year historical average discount of 11.04%.

Byron S. Minerd currently receives a manager quality ranking of 30 (0=worst, 99=best). If you desire an average level of risk, then this fund may be an option.

Data Date	Investment Rating	Net Assets ($Mil)	Price	Performance Rating/Pts	Total Return Y-T-D	Risk Rating/Pts
12-12	C+	90.33	16.66	C+ / 5.7	5.64%	B- / 7.7
2011	C+	93.70	16.03	B- / 7.3	2.15%	C+ / 6.1
2010	E	134.88	15.03	E / 0.3	-0.60%	C- / 3.0
2009	E-	104.28	15.65	E / 0.4	61.97%	D / 1.7

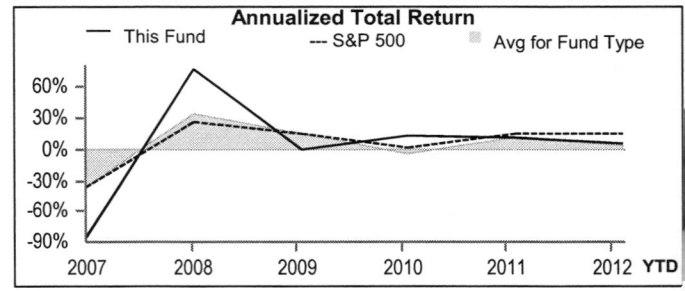

Guggenheim Equal Weight Enh Eq Inc (GEQ)

D+   **Weak**

Fund Family: Guggenheim Funds Investment Advisor
Fund Type: Income
Inception Date: October 27, 2011

Major Rating Factors:

Disappointing performance is the major factor driving the D+ (Weak) TheStreet.com Investment Rating for Guggenheim Equal Weight Enh Eq Inc. The fund currently has a performance rating of D (Weak) based on an annualized return of 0.00% over the last three years and a total return of 2.63% year to date 2012.

The fund's risk rating is currently B (Good). It carries a beta of 0.00, meaning the fund's expected move will be 0.0% for every 10% move in the market. Volatility, as measured by both the semi-deviation and a drawdown factor, is considered low. As of December 31, 2012, Guggenheim Equal Weight Enh Eq Inc traded at a discount of 6.98% below its net asset value, which is better than its one-year historical average discount of 2.89%.

Farhan Sharaff has been running the fund for 2 years and currently receives a manager quality ranking of 35 (0=worst, 99=best). This fund offers only a moderate level of risk but investors looking for strong performance are still waiting.

Data Date	Investment Rating	Net Assets ($Mil)	Price	Performance Rating/Pts	Total Return Y-T-D	Risk Rating/Pts
12-12	D+	168.00	17.73	D / 1.8	2.63%	B / 8.5

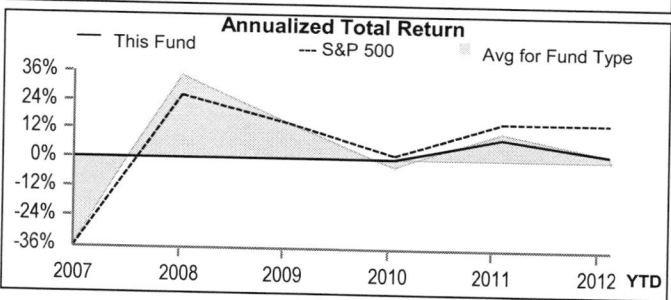

Guggenheim Strategic Opportunities (GOF)

A-   **Excellent**

Fund Family: Guggenheim Funds Investment Advisor
Fund Type: Growth and Income
Inception Date: July 27, 2007

Major Rating Factors:

Strong performance is the major factor driving the A- (Excellent) TheStreet.com Investment Rating for Guggenheim Strategic Opportunities. The fund currently has a performance rating of B+ (Good) based on an annualized return of 20.14% over the last three years and a total return of 4.51% year to date 2012. Factored into the performance evaluation is an expense ratio of 2.55% (high).

The fund's risk rating is currently B (Good). It carries a beta of 0.17, meaning the fund's expected move will be 1.7% for every 10% move in the market. Volatility, as measured by both the semi-deviation and a drawdown factor, is considered low. As of December 31, 2012, Guggenheim Strategic Opportunities traded at a premium of 5.03% above its net asset value, which is better than its one-year historical average premium of 7.95%.

Byron S. Minerd has been running the fund for 6 years and currently receives a manager quality ranking of 96 (0=worst, 99=best). If you desire only a moderate level of risk and strong performance, then this fund is an excellent option.

Data Date	Investment Rating	Net Assets ($Mil)	Price	Performance Rating/Pts	Total Return Y-T-D	Risk Rating/Pts
12-12	A-	207.35	21.50	B+ / 8.3	4.51%	B / 8.5
2011	A	174.10	20.59	A / 9.5	0.64%	B / 8.5
2010	B-	161.78	19.93	B+ / 8.8	31.55%	C- / 4.0
2009	A-	113.08	16.80	A+ / 9.7	78.82%	C / 4.3

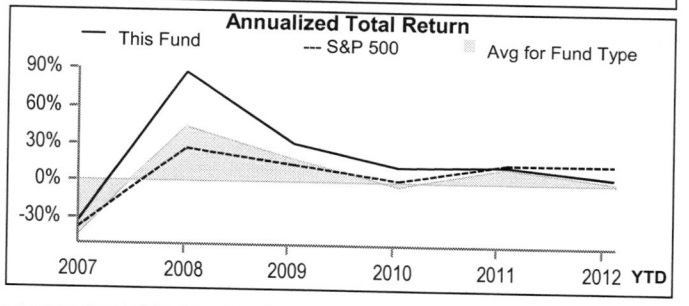

H&Q Healthcare Investors (HQH)

B   **Good**

Fund Family: Hambrecht & Quist Capital Mgmt LLC
Fund Type: Health
Inception Date: April 23, 1987

Major Rating Factors:

Exceptional performance is the major factor driving the B (Good) TheStreet.com Investment Rating for H&Q Healthcare Investors. The fund currently has a performance rating of A (Excellent) based on an annualized return of 24.16% over the last three years and a total return of 8.32% year to date 2012. Factored into the performance evaluation is an expense ratio of 1.43% (average).

The fund's risk rating is currently C+ (Fair). It carries a beta of 0.81, meaning the fund's expected move will be 8.1% for every 10% move in the market. Volatility, as measured by both the semi-deviation and a drawdown factor, is considered low. As of December 31, 2012, H&Q Healthcare Investors traded at a discount of 11.73% below its net asset value, which is better than its one-year historical average discount of 6.86%.

Daniel R. Omstead has been running the fund for 9 years and currently receives a manager quality ranking of 93 (0=worst, 99=best). If you desire only a moderate level of risk and strong performance, then this fund is an excellent option.

Data Date	Investment Rating	Net Assets ($Mil)	Price	Performance Rating/Pts	Total Return Y-T-D	Risk Rating/Pts
12-12	B	465.00	17.31	A / 9.3	8.32%	C+ / 6.3
2011	C+	404.80	14.11	C+ / 5.9	1.28%	B- / 7.4
2010	C+	365.00	13.37	C+ / 5.6	20.68%	C+ / 5.7
2009	D	356.28	11.85	D / 1.7	4.89%	C+ / 5.6

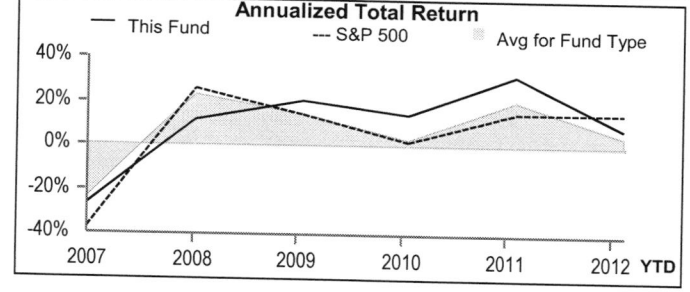

* Denotes ETF Fund

H&Q Life Sciences Investors (HQL)

B   **Good**

Fund Family: Hambrecht & Quist Capital Mgmt LLC
Fund Type: Health
Inception Date: May 8, 1992

Major Rating Factors:

Exceptional performance is the major factor driving the B (Good) TheStreet.com Investment Rating for H&Q Life Sciences Investors. The fund currently has a performance rating of A (Excellent) based on an annualized return of 27.58% over the last three years and a total return of 7.86% year to date 2012. Factored into the performance evaluation is an expense ratio of 1.75% (above average).

The fund's risk rating is currently C+ (Fair). It carries a beta of 0.80, meaning the fund's expected move will be 8.0% for every 10% move in the market. Volatility, as measured by both the semi-deviation and a drawdown factor, is considered low. As of December 31, 2012, H&Q Life Sciences Investors traded at a discount of 8.63% below its net asset value, which is better than its one-year historical average discount of 3.92%.

Daniel R. Omstead has been running the fund for 21 years and currently receives a manager quality ranking of 96 (0=worst, 99=best). If you desire only a moderate level of risk and strong performance, then this fund is an excellent option.

Data Date	Investment Rating	Net Assets ($Mil)	Price	Performance Rating/Pts	Total Return Y-T-D	Risk Rating/Pts
12-12	B	208.00	14.50	A / 9.5	7.86%	C+ / 6.2
2011	C+	178.80	11.47	B- / 7.3	2.70%	C+ / 6.1
2010	C	251.00	10.77	C+ / 5.9	21.84%	C / 4.5
2009	D-	248.58	9.44	D / 1.7	8.41%	C / 5.1

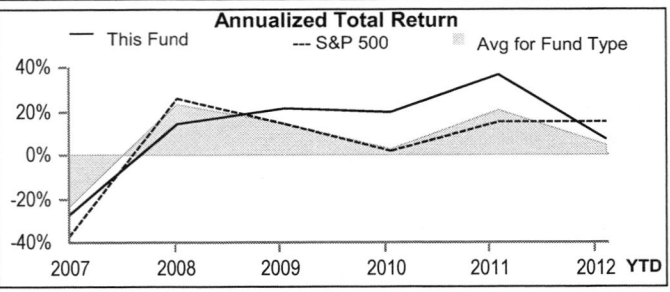

Helios Advantage Income Fund Inc (HAV)

A   **Excellent**

Fund Family: Brookfield Investment Management In
Fund Type: General Bond
Inception Date: November 8, 2004

Major Rating Factors:

Strong performance is the major factor driving the A (Excellent) TheStreet.com Investment Rating for Helios Advantage Income Fund Inc. The fund currently has a performance rating of B (Good) based on an annualized return of 21.10% over the last three years and a total return of 5.55% year to date 2012. Factored into the performance evaluation is an expense ratio of 2.48% (high).

The fund's risk rating is currently B+ (Good). It carries a beta of -1.06, meaning the fund's expected move will be -10.6% for every 10% move in the market. Volatility, as measured by both the semi-deviation and a drawdown factor, is considered very low. As of December 31, 2012, Helios Advantage Income Fund Inc traded at a discount of 8.47% below its net asset value, which is better than its one-year historical average discount of .85%.

Richard M. Cryan has been running the fund for 2 years and currently receives a manager quality ranking of 98 (0=worst, 99=best). If you desire only a moderate level of risk and strong performance, then this fund is an excellent option.

Data Date	Investment Rating	Net Assets ($Mil)	Price	Performance Rating/Pts	Total Return Y-T-D	Risk Rating/Pts
12-12	A	58.28	8.65	B / 8.2	5.55%	B+ / 9.0
2011	B	55.70	7.82	B+ / 8.6	2.81%	B- / 7.2
2010	E	49.02	7.65	E+ / 0.8	28.60%	D+ / 2.7
2009	E-	46.91	6.59	E / 0.4	58.89%	D+ / 2.3

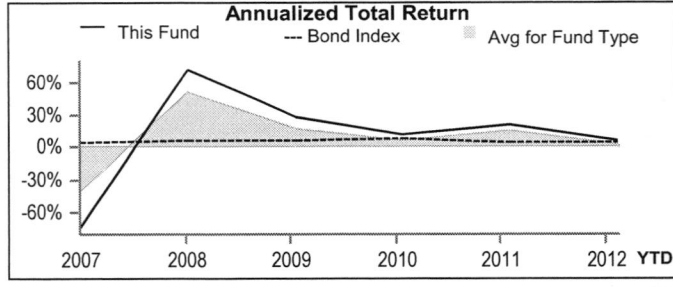

Helios High Income Fund Inc (HIH)

B+   **Good**

Fund Family: Brookfield Investment Management In
Fund Type: General Bond
Inception Date: June 26, 2003

Major Rating Factors: Strong performance is the major factor driving the B+ (Good) TheStreet.com Investment Rating for Helios High Income Fund Inc. The fund currently has a performance rating of B (Good) based on an annualized return of 18.71% over the last three years and a total return of 6.58% year to date 2012. Factored into the performance evaluation is an expense ratio of 2.70% (high).

The fund's risk rating is currently B (Good). It carries a beta of -0.80, meaning the fund's expected move will be -8.0% for every 10% move in the market. Volatility, as measured by both the semi-deviation and a drawdown factor, is considered low. As of December 31, 2012, Helios High Income Fund Inc traded at a discount of 6.90% below its net asset value, which is better than its one-year historical average premium of .89%.

Richard M. Cryan has been running the fund for 2 years and currently receives a manager quality ranking of 97 (0=worst, 99=best). If you desire only a moderate level of risk and strong performance, then this fund is an excellent option.

Data Date	Investment Rating	Net Assets ($Mil)	Price	Performance Rating/Pts	Total Return Y-T-D	Risk Rating/Pts
12-12	B+	41.07	8.36	B / 7.6	6.58%	B / 8.8
2011	B	39.30	7.71	B+ / 8.5	1.50%	B- / 7.1
2010	E	37.04	7.24	E+ / 0.6	18.85%	D+ / 2.5
2009	E-	35.08	6.74	E / 0.4	55.76%	D / 1.8

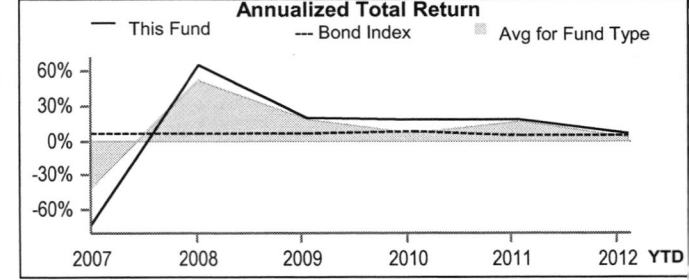

Helios High Yield Fund (HHY)

A-   **Excellent**

Fund Family: Brookfield Investment Management In
Fund Type: Corporate - High Yield
Inception Date: July 27, 1998

Major Rating Factors:
Strong performance is the major factor driving the A- (Excellent) TheStreet.com Investment Rating for Helios High Yield Fund. The fund currently has a performance rating of B (Good) based on an annualized return of 20.75% over the last three years and a total return of 5.14% year to date 2012. Factored into the performance evaluation is an expense ratio of 2.21% (high).

The fund's risk rating is currently B (Good). It carries a beta of 1.33, meaning it is expected to move 13.3% for every 10% move in the market. Volatility, as measured by both the semi-deviation and a drawdown factor, is considered low. As of December 31, 2012, Helios High Yield Fund traded at a discount of 4.26% below its net asset value, which is better than its one-year historical average premium of 2.75%.

Dana E. Erikson currently receives a manager quality ranking of 74 (0=worst, 99=best). If you desire only a moderate level of risk and strong performance, then this fund is an excellent option.

Data Date	Investment Rating	Net Assets ($Mil)	Price	Performance Rating/Pts	Total Return Y-T-D	Risk Rating/Pts
12-12	A-	67.49	10.12	B / 8.0	5.14%	B / 8.8
2011	B+	65.00	9.79	B / 8.1	1.93%	B / 8.8
2010	B-	63.26	8.94	B / 7.9	25.40%	C / 4.8
2009	C-	57.53	7.83	C / 4.7	31.73%	C / 5.0

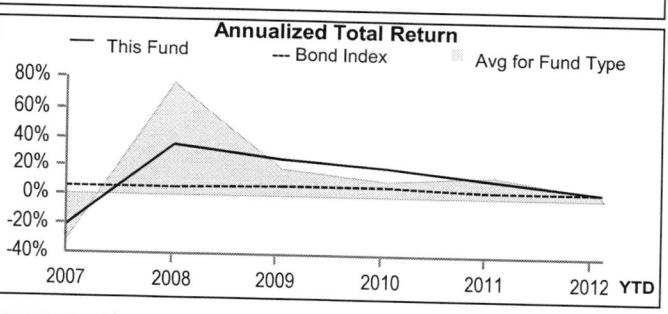

Annualized Total Return

Helios Multi Sector High Income (HMH)

A-   **Excellent**

Fund Family: Brookfield Investment Management In
Fund Type: General Bond
Inception Date: January 19, 2006

Major Rating Factors:
Strong performance is the major factor driving the A- (Excellent) TheStreet.com Investment Rating for Helios Multi Sector High Income. The fund currently has a performance rating of B (Good) based on an annualized return of 19.11% over the last three years and a total return of 2.98% year to date 2012. Factored into the performance evaluation is an expense ratio of 2.63% (high).

The fund's risk rating is currently B+ (Good). It carries a beta of -0.10, meaning the fund's expected move will be -1.0% for every 10% move in the market. Volatility, as measured by both the semi-deviation and a drawdown factor, is considered very low. As of December 31, 2012, Helios Multi Sector High Income traded at a discount of 7.22% below its net asset value, which is better than its one-year historical average discount of 2.10%.

Richard M. Cryan has been running the fund for 2 years and currently receives a manager quality ranking of 97 (0=worst, 99=best). If you desire only a moderate level of risk and strong performance, then this fund is an excellent option.

Data Date	Investment Rating	Net Assets ($Mil)	Price	Performance Rating/Pts	Total Return Y-T-D	Risk Rating/Pts
12-12	A-	46.48	6.04	B / 7.6	2.98%	B+ / 9.2
2011	B	44.40	5.50	B+ / 8.4	-0.55%	B- / 7.3
2010	E	37.04	5.03	E / 0.5	20.56%	D / 2.0
2009	E-	38.80	4.60	E / 0.3	49.04%	D / 2.0

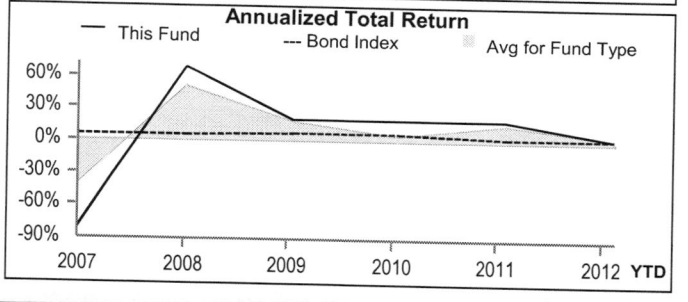

Annualized Total Return

Helios Strategic Income Fund Inc (HSA)

B   **Good**

Fund Family: Brookfield Investment Management In
Fund Type: General Bond
Inception Date: March 18, 2004

Major Rating Factors: Strong performance is the major factor driving the B (Good) TheStreet.com Investment Rating for Helios Strategic Income Fund Inc. The fund currently has a performance rating of B (Good) based on an annualized return of 16.53% over the last three years and a total return of 5.22% year to date 2012. Factored into the performance evaluation is an expense ratio of 2.69% (high).

The fund's risk rating is currently B- (Good). It carries a beta of 0.32, meaning the fund's expected move will be 3.2% for every 10% move in the market. Volatility, as measured by both the semi-deviation and a drawdown factor, is considered low. As of December 31, 2012, Helios Strategic Income Fund Inc traded at a discount of 10.86% below its net asset value, which is better than its one-year historical average discount of 8.73%.

Richard M. Cryan has been running the fund for 2 years and currently receives a manager quality ranking of 93 (0=worst, 99=best). If you desire only a moderate level of risk and strong performance, then this fund is an excellent option.

Data Date	Investment Rating	Net Assets ($Mil)	Price	Performance Rating/Pts	Total Return Y-T-D	Risk Rating/Pts
12-12	B	39.23	6.32	B / 7.8	5.22%	B- / 7.8
2011	B-	37.60	5.49	C+ / 6.7	1.09%	B- / 7.8
2010	E	34.97	5.33	E / 0.5	11.47%	D+ / 2.4
2009	E-	33.54	5.23	E / 0.3	44.16%	D+ / 2.3

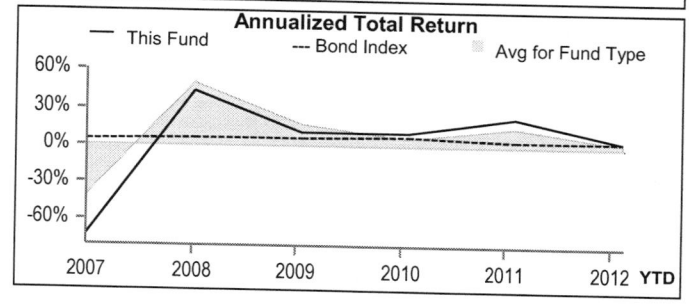

Annualized Total Return

Helios Total Return Fund Inc (HTR)   C   Fair

Fund Family: Brookfield Investment Management In
Fund Type: Mortgage
Inception Date: July 28, 1989

Major Rating Factors: Middle of the road best describes Helios Total Return Fund
Inc whose TheStreet.com Investment Rating is currently a C (Fair). The fund currently
has a performance rating of C+ (Fair) based on an annualized return of 15.06% over
the last three years and a total return of 3.56% year to date 2012. Factored into the
performance evaluation is an expense ratio of 1.88% (above average).

The fund's risk rating is currently B- (Good). It carries a beta of 1.96, meaning it is
expected to move 19.6% for every 10% move in the market. Volatility, as measured
by both the semi-deviation and a drawdown factor, is considered low. As of
December 31, 2012, Helios Total Return Fund Inc traded at a discount of 6.82%
below its net asset value, which is better than its one-year historical average premium
of .48%.

Michelle L. Russell-Dowe currently receives a manager quality ranking of 80
(0=worst, 99=best). If you desire an average level of risk, then this fund may be an
option.

Data Date	Investment Rating	Net Assets ($Mil)	Price	Performance Rating/Pts	Total Return Y-T-D	Risk Rating/Pts
12-12	C	245.30	23.62	C+ / 5.6	3.56%	B- / 7.0
2011	B-	178.20	5.72	C+ / 6.3	0.52%	B / 8.1
2010	C+	168.91	5.68	C+ / 6.2	21.84%	C+ / 6.8
2009	D	154.61	5.17	D- / 1.2	18.20%	C+ / 5.8

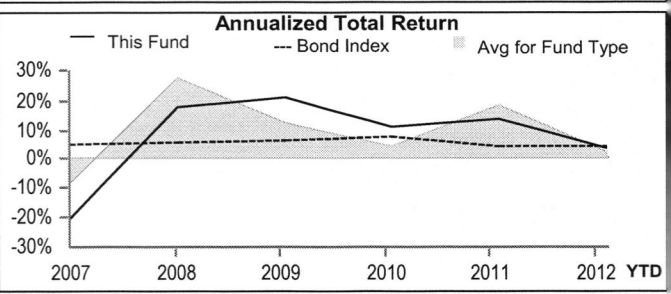

Herzfeld Caribbean Basin Fund (CUBA)   C+   Fair

Fund Family: Thomas J Herzfeld Advisors Inc
Fund Type: Foreign
Inception Date: September 10, 1993

Major Rating Factors: Middle of the road best describes Herzfeld Caribbean Basin
Fund whose TheStreet.com Investment Rating is currently a C+ (Fair). The fund
currently has a performance rating of C+ (Fair) based on an annualized return of
7.88% over the last three years and a total return of 6.06% year to date 2012.
Factored into the performance evaluation is an expense ratio of 2.68% (high).

The fund's risk rating is currently B (Good). It carries a beta of 0.71, meaning the
fund's expected move will be 7.1% for every 10% move in the market. Volatility, as
measured by both the semi-deviation and a drawdown factor, is considered low. As of
December 31, 2012, Herzfeld Caribbean Basin Fund traded at a discount of 14.83%
below its net asset value, which is better than its one-year historical average discount
of 10.14%.

Thomas J. Herzfeld has been running the fund for 19 years and currently
receives a manager quality ranking of 77 (0=worst, 99=best). If you desire an average
level of risk, then this fund may be an option.

Data Date	Investment Rating	Net Assets ($Mil)	Price	Performance Rating/Pts	Total Return Y-T-D	Risk Rating/Pts
12-12	C+	29.33	7.64	C+ / 5.9	6.06%	B / 8.2
2011	C-	26.60	6.42	C- / 3.5	2.06%	B / 8.0
2010	D+	22.71	7.17	C- / 3.4	11.68%	C / 5.4
2009	D-	19.88	6.42	E+ / 0.8	45.91%	C / 4.8

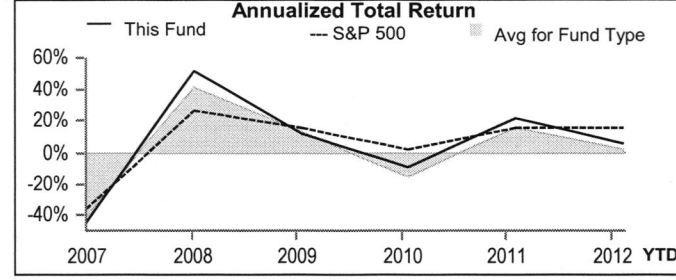

India Fund (IFN)   E+   Very Weak

Fund Family: Aberdeen Asset Management Asia Ltd
Fund Type: Foreign
Inception Date: February 14, 1994

Major Rating Factors:
Disappointing performance is the major factor driving the E+ (Very Weak)
TheStreet.com Investment Rating for India Fund. The fund currently has a
performance rating of D- (Weak) based on an annualized return of -8.09% over the
last three years and a total return of 0.72% year to date 2012. Factored into the
performance evaluation is an expense ratio of 1.26% (average).

The fund's risk rating is currently C (Fair). It carries a beta of 0.91, meaning that
its performance tracks fairly well with that of the overall stock market. Volatility, as
measured by both the semi-deviation and a drawdown factor, is considered average.
As of December 31, 2012, India Fund traded at a discount of 12.18% below its net
asset value, which is better than its one-year historical average discount of 11.28%.

Gregory S. Geiling currently receives a manager quality ranking of 12 (0=worst,
99=best). This fund offers an average level of risk but investors looking for strong
performance will be frustrated.

Data Date	Investment Rating	Net Assets ($Mil)	Price	Performance Rating/Pts	Total Return Y-T-D	Risk Rating/Pts
12-12	E+	899.34	20.91	D- / 1.0	0.72%	C / 4.8
2011	D-	1,581.37	19.04	D / 1.6	2.94%	C / 5.1
2010	E+	1,608.62	35.11	D / 1.8	14.63%	D+ / 2.7
2009	C-	1,003.13	30.70	C+ / 5.9	59.56%	C- / 3.6

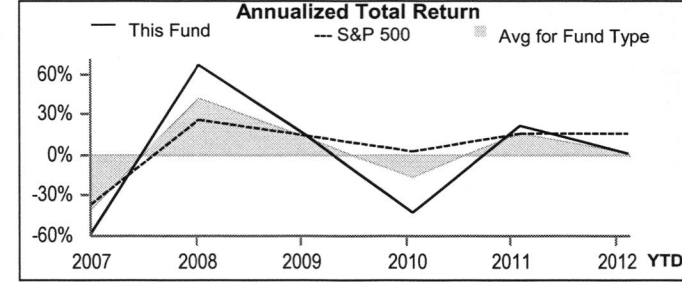

ING Asia Pacific High Div Eq Inc F (IAE)

C-   **Fair**

Fund Family: ING Investments LLC
Fund Type: Global
Inception Date: March 30, 2007

Major Rating Factors: Middle of the road best describes ING Asia Pacific High Div Eq Inc F whose TheStreet.com Investment Rating is currently a C- (Fair). The fund currently has a performance rating of C (Fair) based on an annualized return of 6.49% over the last three years and a total return of 4.01% year to date 2012. Factored into the performance evaluation is an expense ratio of 1.49% (average).

The fund's risk rating is currently C+ (Fair). It carries a beta of 1.05, meaning that its performance tracks fairly well with that of the overall stock market. Volatility, as measured by both the semi-deviation and a drawdown factor, is considered low. As of December 31, 2012, ING Asia Pacific High Div Eq Inc F traded at a discount of .63% below its net asset value, which is better than its one-year historical average premium of 2.13%.

Willem J.G. van Dommelen has been running the fund for 6 years and currently receives a manager quality ranking of 46 (0=worst, 99=best). If you desire an average level of risk, then this fund may be an option.

Data Date	Investment Rating	Net Assets ($Mil)	Price	Performance Rating/Pts	Total Return Y-T-D	Risk Rating/Pts
12-12	C-	207.42	15.72	C / 4.7	4.01%	C+ / 6.6
2011	C	179.00	14.19	C+ / 5.9	1.13%	C+ / 6.7
2010	C-	208.61	19.65	C+ / 6.2	11.12%	C- / 3.5
2009	B+	197.51	19.01	A+ / 9.8	85.35%	C- / 3.9

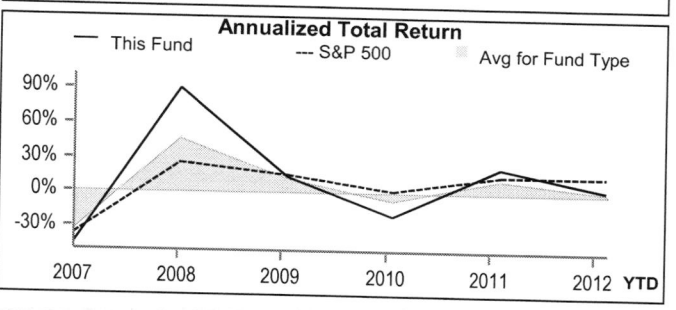

ING Emerging Markets High Div Eqty (IHD)

B   **Good**

Fund Family: ING Investments LLC
Fund Type: Emerging Market
Inception Date: April 26, 2011

Major Rating Factors:
Exceptional performance is the major factor driving the B (Good) TheStreet.com Investment Rating for ING Emerging Markets High Div Eqty. The fund currently has a performance rating of A+ (Excellent) based on an annualized return of 0.00% over the last three years and a total return of 6.36% year to date 2012. Factored into the performance evaluation is an expense ratio of 1.41% (average).

The fund's risk rating is currently C+ (Fair). It carries a beta of 0.00, meaning the fund's expected move will be 0.0% for every 10% move in the market. Volatility, as measured by both the semi-deviation and a drawdown factor, is considered low. As of December 31, 2012, ING Emerging Markets High Div Eqty traded at a discount of .61% below its net asset value, which is better than its one-year historical average discount of .60%.

Edwin Cuppen has been running the fund for 2 years and currently receives a manager quality ranking of 76 (0=worst, 99=best). If you desire only a moderate level of risk and strong performance, then this fund is an excellent option.

Data Date	Investment Rating	Net Assets ($Mil)	Price	Performance Rating/Pts	Total Return Y-T-D	Risk Rating/Pts
12-12	B	319.57	14.63	A+ / 9.6	6.36%	C+ / 6.1

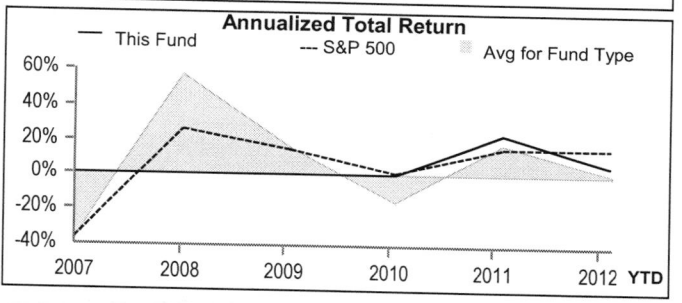

ING Global Advantage and Premium O (IGA)

C-   **Fair**

Fund Family: ING Investments LLC
Fund Type: Global
Inception Date: October 26, 2005

Major Rating Factors: Middle of the road best describes ING Global Advantage and Premium O whose TheStreet.com Investment Rating is currently a C- (Fair). The fund currently has a performance rating of C- (Fair) based on an annualized return of 6.03% over the last three years and a total return of 4.32% year to date 2012. Factored into the performance evaluation is an expense ratio of 1.00% (low).

The fund's risk rating is currently B- (Good). It carries a beta of 0.53, meaning the fund's expected move will be 5.3% for every 10% move in the market. Volatility, as measured by both the semi-deviation and a drawdown factor, is considered low. As of December 31, 2012, ING Global Advantage and Premium O traded at a discount of 10.77% below its net asset value, which is better than its one-year historical average discount of 7.66%.

Jody I. Hrazanek has been running the fund for 8 years and currently receives a manager quality ranking of 68 (0=worst, 99=best). If you desire an average level of risk, then this fund may be an option.

Data Date	Investment Rating	Net Assets ($Mil)	Price	Performance Rating/Pts	Total Return Y-T-D	Risk Rating/Pts
12-12	C-	232.16	11.35	C- / 4.2	4.32%	B- / 7.4
2011	C-	218.20	10.71	C- / 3.3	1.68%	B- / 7.2
2010	D+	242.43	13.55	C- / 3.5	7.04%	C / 5.1
2009	C-	238.91	13.69	C / 4.6	36.15%	C / 5.1

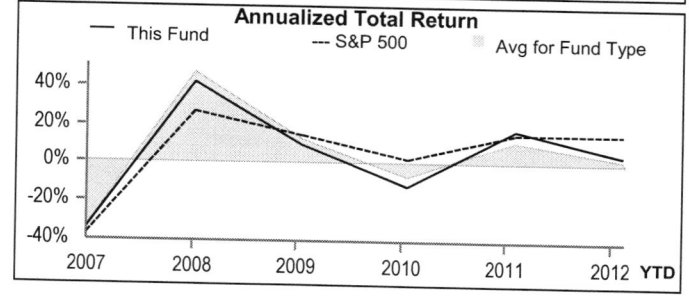

* Denotes ETF Fund

ING Gobal Equity Dividend Premium (IGD)　　　　D+　　Weak

Fund Family: ING Investments LLC
Fund Type: Global
Inception Date: March 29, 2005

Major Rating Factors:
Disappointing performance is the major factor driving the D+ (Weak) TheStreet.com Investment Rating for ING Gobal Equity Dividend Premium. The fund currently has a performance rating of D+ (Weak) based on an annualized return of 1.56% over the last three years and a total return of 4.84% year to date 2012. Factored into the performance evaluation is an expense ratio of 1.14% (low).

The fund's risk rating is currently B- (Good). It carries a beta of 0.65, meaning the fund's expected move will be 6.5% for every 10% move in the market. Volatility, as measured by both the semi-deviation and a drawdown factor, is considered low. As of December 31, 2012, ING Gobal Equity Dividend Premium traded at a discount of 11.80% below its net asset value, which is better than its one-year historical average discount of 5.88%.

Bas Peeters has been running the fund for 8 years and currently receives a manager quality ranking of 37 (0=worst, 99=best). This fund offers only a moderate level of risk but investors looking for strong performance are still waiting.

Data Date	Investment Rating	Net Assets ($Mil)	Price	Perfor-mance Rating/Pts	Total Return Y-T-D	Risk Rating/Pts
12-12	D+	976.69	8.67	D+ / 2.6	4.84%	B- / 7.0
2011	D+	947.30	8.64	D+ / 2.9	2.43%	C+ / 6.9
2010	D	1,117.91	10.85	D+ / 2.3	-0.57%	C / 5.5
2009	D+	1,130.16	12.17	D+ / 2.9	40.82%	C / 5.5

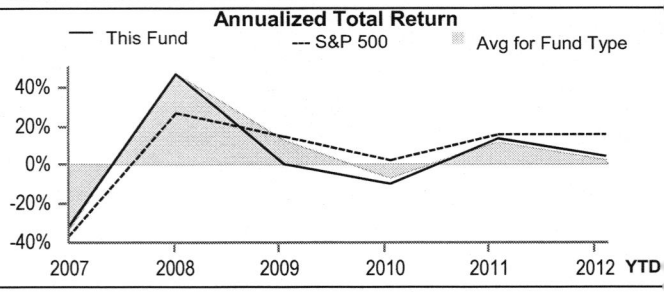

ING Infrastructure Indus & Mtrls (IDE)　　　　C+　　Fair

Fund Family: ING Investments LLC
Fund Type: Growth
Inception Date: January 26, 2010

Major Rating Factors: Strong performance is the major factor driving the C+ (Fair) TheStreet.com Investment Rating for ING Infrastructure Indus & Mtrls. The fund currently has a performance rating of B (Good) based on an annualized return of 0.00% over the last three years and a total return of 5.19% year to date 2012. Factored into the performance evaluation is an expense ratio of 1.21% (average).

The fund's risk rating is currently C+ (Fair). It carries a beta of 0.00, meaning the fund's expected move will be 0.0% for every 10% move in the market. Volatility, as measured by both the semi-deviation and a drawdown factor, is considered low. As of December 31, 2012, ING Infrastructure Indus & Mtrls traded at a discount of 10.29% below its net asset value, which is better than its one-year historical average discount of 5.29%.

Martin J. Jansen has been running the fund for 3 years and currently receives a manager quality ranking of 27 (0=worst, 99=best). If you desire only a moderate level of risk and strong performance, then this fund is an excellent option.

Data Date	Investment Rating	Net Assets ($Mil)	Price	Perfor-mance Rating/Pts	Total Return Y-T-D	Risk Rating/Pts
12-12	C+	394.27	16.39	B / 7.7	5.19%	C+ / 6.6
2011	D-	354.20	15.39	D- / 1.1	4.29%	C+ / 6.7

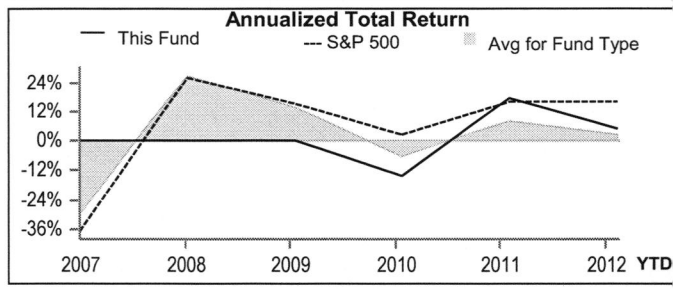

ING International High Div Eq Inc (IID)　　　　D+　　Weak

Fund Family: ING Investments LLC
Fund Type: Global
Inception Date: September 26, 2007

Major Rating Factors: ING International High Div Eq Inc receives a TheStreet.com Investment Rating of D+ (Weak). The fund currently has a performance rating of C- (Fair) based on an annualized return of 4.71% over the last three years and a total return of 3.32% year to date 2012. Factored into the performance evaluation is an expense ratio of 1.26% (average).

The fund's risk rating is currently C+ (Fair). It carries a beta of 0.97, meaning that its performance tracks fairly well with that of the overall stock market. Volatility, as measured by both the semi-deviation and a drawdown factor, is considered low. As of December 31, 2012, ING International High Div Eq Inc traded at a discount of .52% below its net asset value, which is better than its one-year historical average premium of 4.20%.

Martin J. Jansen has been running the fund for 6 years and currently receives a manager quality ranking of 56 (0=worst, 99=best). If you desire an average level of risk, then this fund may be an option.

Data Date	Investment Rating	Net Assets ($Mil)	Price	Perfor-mance Rating/Pts	Total Return Y-T-D	Risk Rating/Pts
12-12	D+	82.21	9.64	C- / 3.7	3.32%	C+ / 6.9
2011	D+	73.80	8.86	C- / 3.6	3.27%	C+ / 6.3
2010	D+	86.22	11.40	C / 4.4	6.43%	C / 4.4
2009	B-	86.65	11.87	B+ / 8.3	54.97%	C / 4.5

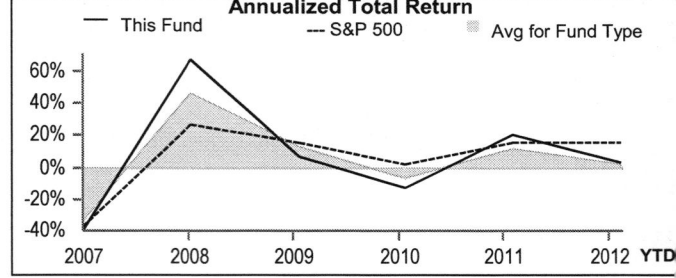

ING Prime Rate Trust (PPR)

C+ **Fair**

Fund Family: ING Investments LLC
Fund Type: Loan Participation
Inception Date: May 2, 1988

Major Rating Factors: Middle of the road best describes ING Prime Rate Trust whose TheStreet.com Investment Rating is currently a C+ (Fair). The fund currently has a performance rating of C+ (Fair) based on an annualized return of 10.54% over the last three years and a total return of 3.06% year to date 2012. Factored into the performance evaluation is an expense ratio of 2.20% (high).

The fund's risk rating is currently B- (Good). It carries a beta of -223.92, meaning the fund's expected move will be -2239.2% for every 10% move in the market. Volatility, as measured by both the semi-deviation and a drawdown factor, is considered low. As of December 31, 2012, ING Prime Rate Trust traded at a premium of 3.85% above its net asset value, which is worse than its one-year historical average discount of .02%.

Daniel A. Norman has been running the fund for 13 years and currently receives a manager quality ranking of 99 (0=worst, 99=best). If you desire an average level of risk, then this fund may be an option.

Data Date	Investment Rating	Net Assets ($Mil)	Price	Performance Rating/Pts	Total Return Y-T-D	Risk Rating/Pts
12-12	C+	851.28	6.21	C+ / 6.3	3.06%	B- / 8.0
2011	C+	822.30	5.10	C+ / 5.9	4.51%	B- / 7.9
2010	C-	830.79	5.69	C+ / 5.8	14.73%	C / 4.4
2009	C-	761.30	5.22	C / 4.3	55.82%	C / 5.4

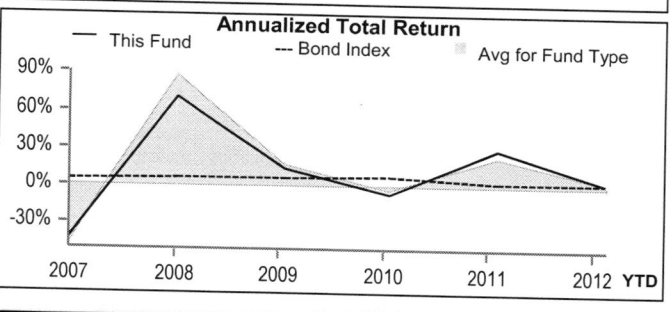

ING Risk Managed Nat Resources Fun (IRR)

D **Weak**

Fund Family: ING Investments LLC
Fund Type: Energy/Natural Resources
Inception Date: October 24, 2006

Major Rating Factors:
Very poor performance is the major factor driving the D (Weak) TheStreet.com Investment Rating for ING Risk Managed Nat Resources Fun. The fund currently has a performance rating of E+ (Very Weak) based on an annualized return of -5.82% over the last three years and a total return of 3.19% year to date 2012. Factored into the performance evaluation is an expense ratio of 1.22% (average).

The fund's risk rating is currently C+ (Fair). It carries a beta of 0.49, meaning the fund's expected move will be 4.9% for every 10% move in the market. Volatility, as measured by both the semi-deviation and a drawdown factor, is considered low. As of December 31, 2012, ING Risk Managed Nat Resources Fun traded at a discount of 10.94% below its net asset value, which is better than its one-year historical average discount of 6.05%.

Jody I. Hrazanek has been running the fund for 7 years and currently receives a manager quality ranking of 12 (0=worst, 99=best). This fund offers only a moderate level of risk but investors looking for strong performance are still waiting.

Data Date	Investment Rating	Net Assets ($Mil)	Price	Performance Rating/Pts	Total Return Y-T-D	Risk Rating/Pts
12-12	D	298.73	10.34	E+ / 0.9	3.19%	C+ / 6.8
2011	D+	289.10	11.40	D+ / 2.3	1.67%	B- / 7.1
2010	C+	357.35	15.33	C / 5.0	-3.43%	B- / 7.2
2009	C+	360.74	17.08	C+ / 5.6	36.95%	C+ / 6.5

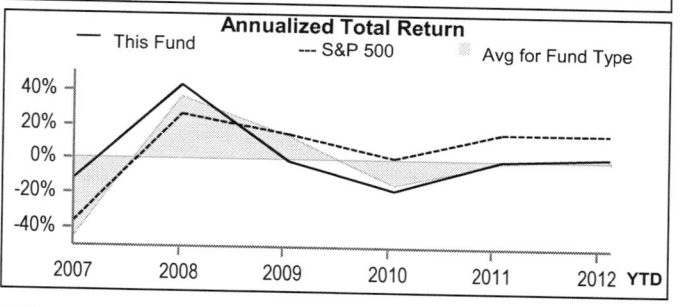

Invesco Municipal Income Opp Tr (OIA)

A **Excellent**

Fund Family: Invesco Advisers Inc
Fund Type: Municipal - National
Inception Date: August 12, 1988

Major Rating Factors:
Strong performance is the major factor driving the A (Excellent) TheStreet.com Investment Rating for Invesco Municipal Income Opp Tr. The fund currently has a performance rating of B+ (Good) based on an annualized return of 14.08% over the last three years and a total return of 5.54% year to date 2012. Factored into the performance evaluation is an expense ratio of 0.73% (very low).

The fund's risk rating is currently B (Good). It carries a beta of 1.98, meaning it is expected to move 19.8% for every 10% move in the market. Volatility, as measured by both the semi-deviation and a drawdown factor, is considered low. As of December 31, 2012, Invesco Municipal Income Opp Tr traded at a discount of 2.66% below its net asset value, which is better than its one-year historical average discount of 1.00%.

Mark Paris currently receives a manager quality ranking of 47 (0=worst, 99=best). If you desire only a moderate level of risk and strong performance, then this fund is an excellent option.

Data Date	Investment Rating	Net Assets ($Mil)	Price	Performance Rating/Pts	Total Return Y-T-D	Risk Rating/Pts
12-12	A	352.73	7.32	B+ / 8.9	5.54%	B / 8.5
2011	B+	135.00	6.66	B+ / 8.3	1.05%	B / 8.8
2010	C-	133.20	6.18	D / 2.2	6.65%	B- / 7.3
2009	D+	115.78	6.18	D / 1.6	37.04%	C+ / 6.6

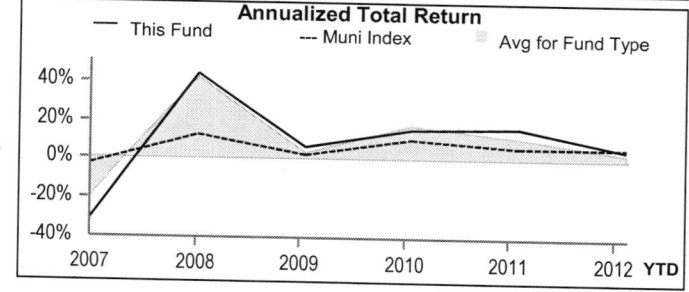

* Denotes ETF Fund

Invesco Quality Municipal Income T (IQI)   B   Good

Fund Family: Invesco Advisers Inc
Fund Type: Municipal - National
Inception Date: September 29, 1992

Major Rating Factors: Strong performance is the major factor driving the B (Good) TheStreet.com Investment Rating for Invesco Quality Municipal Income T. The fund currently has a performance rating of B- (Good) based on an annualized return of 11.99% over the last three years and a total return of 3.93% year to date 2012. Factored into the performance evaluation is an expense ratio of 1.14% (low).

The fund's risk rating is currently B (Good). It carries a beta of 1.81, meaning it is expected to move 18.1% for every 10% move in the market. Volatility, as measured by both the semi-deviation and a drawdown factor, is considered low. As of December 31, 2012, Invesco Quality Municipal Income T traded at a discount of 3.86% below its net asset value, which is better than its one-year historical average premium of 1.03%.

Robert J. Stryker currently receives a manager quality ranking of 46 (0=worst, 99=best). If you desire only a moderate level of risk and strong performance, then this fund is an excellent option.

Data Date	Investment Rating	Net Assets ($Mil)	Price	Performance Rating/Pts	Total Return Y-T-D	Risk Rating/Pts
12-12	B	333.57	13.70	B- / 7.0	3.93%	B / 8.7
2011	A+	314.70	13.44	A / 9.5	2.23%	B / 8.8
2010	C	296.50	12.30	C / 4.9	9.06%	C+ / 6.0
2009	C+	271.06	12.06	C / 5.1	32.90%	C+ / 6.6

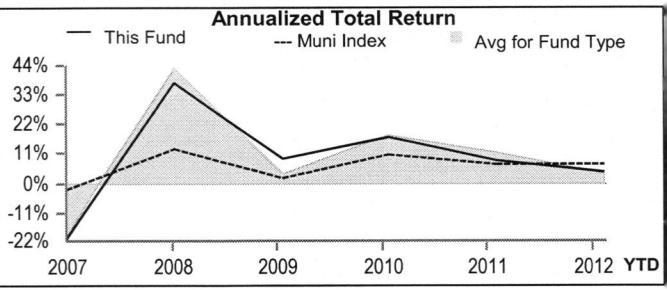

Invesco Value Municipal Income Tr (IIM)   B+   Good

Fund Family: Invesco Advisers Inc
Fund Type: Municipal - National
Inception Date: February 19, 1993

Major Rating Factors: Strong performance is the major factor driving the B+ (Good) TheStreet.com Investment Rating for Invesco Value Municipal Income Tr. The fund currently has a performance rating of B (Good) based on an annualized return of 12.98% over the last three years and a total return of 1.58% year to date 2012. Factored into the performance evaluation is an expense ratio of 1.09% (low).

The fund's risk rating is currently B (Good). It carries a beta of 2.29, meaning it is expected to move 22.9% for every 10% move in the market. Volatility, as measured by both the semi-deviation and a drawdown factor, is considered low. As of December 31, 2012, Invesco Value Municipal Income Tr traded at a premium of .36% above its net asset value, which is better than its one-year historical average premium of .37%.

Robert J. Stryker currently receives a manager quality ranking of 32 (0=worst, 99=best). If you desire only a moderate level of risk and strong performance, then this fund is an excellent option.

Data Date	Investment Rating	Net Assets ($Mil)	Price	Performance Rating/Pts	Total Return Y-T-D	Risk Rating/Pts
12-12	B+	344.32	16.81	B / 7.7	1.58%	B / 8.5
2011	A+	325.00	16.05	A+ / 9.7	4.36%	B / 8.7
2010	C+	303.16	13.50	C / 4.7	2.39%	C+ / 6.6
2009	B-	287.53	14.00	C+ / 6.6	34.89%	B- / 7.2

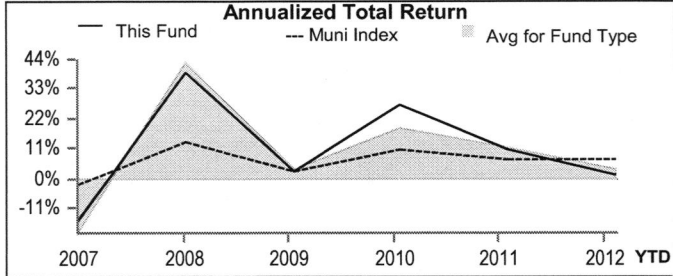

Invesco Van Kampen Adv Muni Inc II (VKI)   A-   Excellent

Fund Family: Invesco Advisers Inc
Fund Type: Municipal - National
Inception Date: August 27, 1993

Major Rating Factors:
Strong performance is the major factor driving the A- (Excellent) TheStreet.com Investment Rating for Invesco Van Kampen Adv Muni Inc II. The fund currently has a performance rating of B (Good) based on an annualized return of 13.30% over the last three years and a total return of 3.83% year to date 2012. Factored into the performance evaluation is an expense ratio of 1.58% (above average).

The fund's risk rating is currently B (Good). It carries a beta of 1.76, meaning it is expected to move 17.6% for every 10% move in the market. Volatility, as measured by both the semi-deviation and a drawdown factor, is considered low. As of December 31, 2012, Invesco Van Kampen Adv Muni Inc II traded at a premium of .61% above its net asset value, which is better than its one-year historical average premium of 3.44%.

Robert W. Wimmell has been running the fund for 11 years and currently receives a manager quality ranking of 58 (0=worst, 99=best). If you desire only a moderate level of risk and strong performance, then this fund is an excellent option.

Data Date	Investment Rating	Net Assets ($Mil)	Price	Performance Rating/Pts	Total Return Y-T-D	Risk Rating/Pts
12-12	A-	578.17	13.15	B / 8.2	3.83%	B / 8.7
2011	A+	544.80	12.46	A / 9.4	0.56%	B / 8.8
2010	C-	512.04	11.35	C- / 3.4	6.65%	C+ / 5.7
2009	C+	447.53	11.45	C+ / 6.8	55.30%	C+ / 6.1

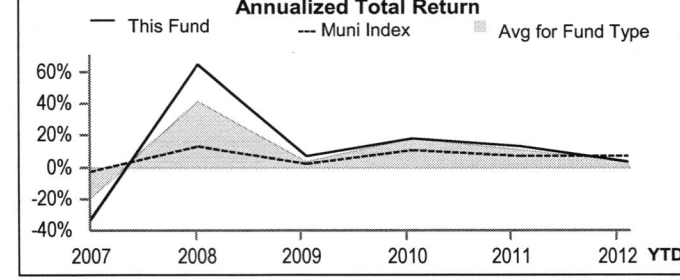

Invesco Van Kampen Bond (VBF)

C　　　**Fair**

Fund Family: Invesco Advisers Inc
Fund Type: General - Investment Grade
Inception Date: October 15, 1970

Major Rating Factors: Middle of the road best describes Invesco Van Kampen Bond whose TheStreet.com Investment Rating is currently a C (Fair). The fund currently has a performance rating of C- (Fair) based on an annualized return of 10.03% over the last three years and a total return of -1.09% year to date 2012. Factored into the performance evaluation is an expense ratio of 0.57% (very low).

The fund's risk rating is currently B (Good). It carries a beta of 1.15, meaning it is expected to move 11.5% for every 10% move in the market. Volatility, as measured by both the semi-deviation and a drawdown factor, is considered low. As of December 31, 2012, Invesco Van Kampen Bond traded at a premium of 1.96% above its net asset value, which is worse than its one-year historical average premium of 1.08%.

Chuck Burge has been running the fund for 3 years and currently receives a manager quality ranking of 75 (0=worst, 99=best). If you desire an average level of risk, then this fund may be an option.

Data Date	Investment Rating	Net Assets ($Mil)	Price	Performance Rating/Pts	Total Return Y-T-D	Risk Rating/Pts
12-12	C	241.51	21.34	C- / 4.0	-1.09%	B / 8.7
2011	C+	227.50	20.90	C / 5.0	-5.41%	B / 8.7
2010	B-	223.60	18.64	C+ / 5.8	3.81%	B- / 7.0
2009	C+	202.99	18.90	C / 5.1	18.86%	B- / 7.2

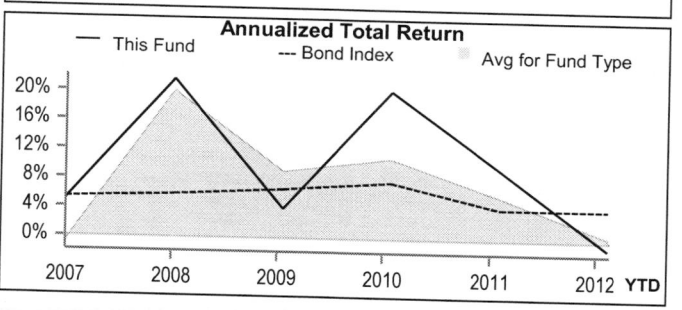

Invesco Van Kampen CA Val Muni Inc (VCV)

B+　　　**Good**

Fund Family: Invesco Advisers Inc
Fund Type: Municipal - Single State
Inception Date: April 30, 1993

Major Rating Factors: Strong performance is the major factor driving the B+ (Good) TheStreet.com Investment Rating for Invesco Van Kampen CA Val Muni Inc. The fund currently has a performance rating of B (Good) based on an annualized return of 13.13% over the last three years and a total return of 1.50% year to date 2012. Factored into the performance evaluation is an expense ratio of 1.70% (above average).

The fund's risk rating is currently B (Good). It carries a beta of 2.59, meaning it is expected to move 25.9% for every 10% move in the market. Volatility, as measured by both the semi-deviation and a drawdown factor, is considered low. As of December 31, 2012, Invesco Van Kampen CA Val Muni Inc traded at a discount of .36% below its net asset value, which is better than its one-year historical average premium of 3.09%.

Robert W. Wimmell has been running the fund for 11 years and currently receives a manager quality ranking of 24 (0=worst, 99=best). If you desire only a moderate level of risk and strong performance, then this fund is an excellent option.

Data Date	Investment Rating	Net Assets ($Mil)	Price	Performance Rating/Pts	Total Return Y-T-D	Risk Rating/Pts
12-12	B+	652.46	13.74	B / 8.0	1.50%	B / 8.4
2011	A	278.00	12.87	A / 9.5	1.79%	B / 8.5
2010	D	259.74	11.28	D- / 1.2	1.81%	C+ / 6.5
2009	C	225.69	11.94	C / 4.5	55.72%	C+ / 6.0

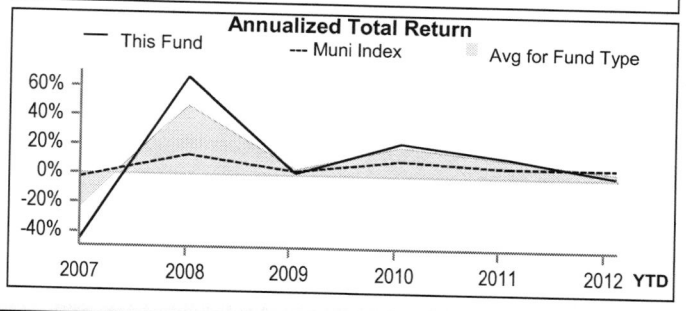

Invesco Van Kampen Dynamic Cred Op (VTA)

C+　　　**Fair**

Fund Family: Invesco Advisers Inc
Fund Type: Loan Participation
Inception Date: June 26, 2007

Major Rating Factors: Middle of the road best describes Invesco Van Kampen Dynamic Cred Op whose TheStreet.com Investment Rating is currently a C+ (Fair). The fund currently has a performance rating of C+ (Fair) based on an annualized return of 9.80% over the last three years and a total return of 4.13% year to date 2012. Factored into the performance evaluation is an expense ratio of 2.09% (high).

The fund's risk rating is currently B (Good). It carries a beta of -253.73, meaning the fund's expected move will be -2537.3% for every 10% move in the market. Volatility, as measured by both the semi-deviation and a drawdown factor, is considered low. As of December 31, 2012, Invesco Van Kampen Dynamic Cred Op traded at a discount of 4.59% below its net asset value, which is better than its one-year historical average discount of 3.91%.

Scott Baskind has been running the fund for 3 years and currently receives a manager quality ranking of 99 (0=worst, 99=best). If you desire an average level of risk, then this fund may be an option.

Data Date	Investment Rating	Net Assets ($Mil)	Price	Performance Rating/Pts	Total Return Y-T-D	Risk Rating/Pts
12-12	C+	938.27	12.48	C+ / 5.7	4.13%	B / 8.0
2011	B-	877.50	10.57	C+ / 6.8	2.74%	B- / 7.9
2010	C-	927.10	12.21	C / 5.4	12.20%	C / 4.5
2009	B+	814.40	11.84	A+ / 9.6	76.63%	C / 4.3

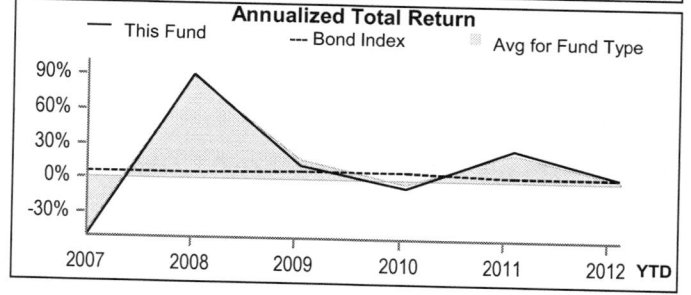

Invesco Van Kampen High Inc Tr II (VLT)

B   **Good**

Fund Family: Invesco Advisers Inc
Fund Type: Corporate - High Yield
Inception Date: April 28, 1989

Major Rating Factors: Strong performance is the major factor driving the B (Good) TheStreet.com Investment Rating for Invesco Van Kampen High Inc Tr II. The fund currently has a performance rating of B (Good) based on an annualized return of 17.34% over the last three years and a total return of 5.62% year to date 2012. Factored into the performance evaluation is an expense ratio of 1.93% (above average).

The fund's risk rating is currently B (Good). It carries a beta of 1.31, meaning it is expected to move 13.1% for every 10% move in the market. Volatility, as measured by both the semi-deviation and a drawdown factor, is considered low. As of December 31, 2012, Invesco Van Kampen High Inc Tr II traded at a discount of 1.77% below its net asset value, which is better than its one-year historical average premium of 3.78%.

Darren S. Hughes currently receives a manager quality ranking of 56 (0=worst, 99=best). If you desire only a moderate level of risk and strong performance, then this fund is an excellent option.

Data Date	Investment Rating	Net Assets ($Mil)	Price	Perfor-mance Rating/Pts	Total Return Y-T-D	Risk Rating/Pts
12-12	B	136.19	17.25	B / 7.6	5.62%	B / 8.1
2011	B	57.40	15.50	B+ / 8.5	2.58%	B- / 7.7
2010	C-	58.00	16.02	C+ / 6.3	22.05%	C- / 3.2
2009	C-	48.63	14.48	C / 5.0	70.00%	C- / 3.8

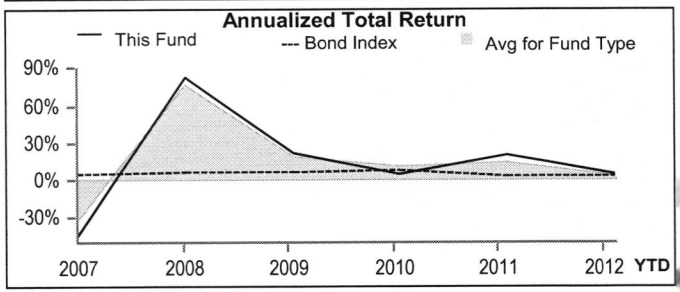

Invesco Van Kampen Muni Opp (VMO)

B+   **Good**

Fund Family: Invesco Advisers Inc
Fund Type: Municipal - National
Inception Date: April 24, 1992

Major Rating Factors: Strong performance is the major factor driving the B+ (Good) TheStreet.com Investment Rating for Invesco Van Kampen Muni Opp. The fund currently has a performance rating of B- (Good) based on an annualized return of 12.25% over the last three years and a total return of 4.55% year to date 2012. Factored into the performance evaluation is an expense ratio of 1.63% (above average).

The fund's risk rating is currently B (Good). It carries a beta of 1.55, meaning it is expected to move 15.5% for every 10% move in the market. Volatility, as measured by both the semi-deviation and a drawdown factor, is considered low. As of December 31, 2012, Invesco Van Kampen Muni Opp traded at a premium of .27% above its net asset value, which is better than its one-year historical average premium of 5.20%.

Robert W. Wimmell has been running the fund for 11 years and currently receives a manager quality ranking of 58 (0=worst, 99=best). If you desire only a moderate level of risk and strong performance, then this fund is an excellent option.

Data Date	Investment Rating	Net Assets ($Mil)	Price	Perfor-mance Rating/Pts	Total Return Y-T-D	Risk Rating/Pts
12-12	B+	492.56	14.59	B- / 7.4	4.55%	B / 8.7
2011	A+	462.60	14.48	A+ / 9.6	0.90%	B / 8.8
2010	C-	439.37	13.04	C- / 3.3	5.26%	C+ / 6.1
2009	C+	388.12	13.37	C+ / 6.3	44.98%	C+ / 6.3

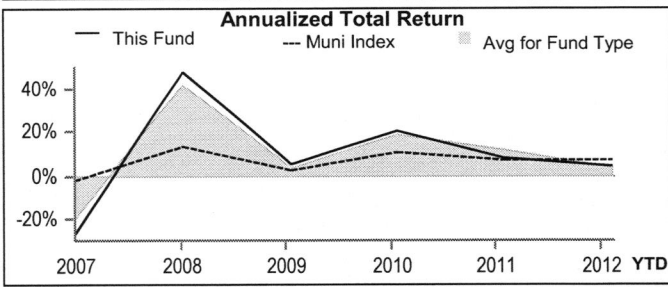

Invesco Van Kampen Muni Trust (VKQ)

B   **Good**

Fund Family: Invesco Advisers Inc
Fund Type: Municipal - National
Inception Date: September 20, 1991

Major Rating Factors: Strong performance is the major factor driving the B (Good) TheStreet.com Investment Rating for Invesco Van Kampen Muni Trust. The fund currently has a performance rating of B- (Good) based on an annualized return of 11.74% over the last three years and a total return of 4.71% year to date 2012. Factored into the performance evaluation is an expense ratio of 1.46% (average).

The fund's risk rating is currently B (Good). It carries a beta of 2.00, meaning it is expected to move 20.0% for every 10% move in the market. Volatility, as measured by both the semi-deviation and a drawdown factor, is considered low. As of December 31, 2012, Invesco Van Kampen Muni Trust traded at a discount of 1.23% below its net asset value, which is better than its one-year historical average premium of 3.17%.

This fund has been team managed for 22 years and currently receives a manager quality ranking of 33 (0=worst, 99=best). If you desire only a moderate level of risk and strong performance, then this fund is an excellent option.

Data Date	Investment Rating	Net Assets ($Mil)	Price	Perfor-mance Rating/Pts	Total Return Y-T-D	Risk Rating/Pts
12-12	B	569.97	14.40	B- / 7.3	4.71%	B / 8.4
2011	A	535.40	13.99	A- / 9.2	0.50%	B / 8.5
2010	D+	505.46	12.49	D / 1.7	2.88%	C+ / 6.9
2009	C	440.00	13.04	C+ / 6.0	49.25%	C+ / 5.6

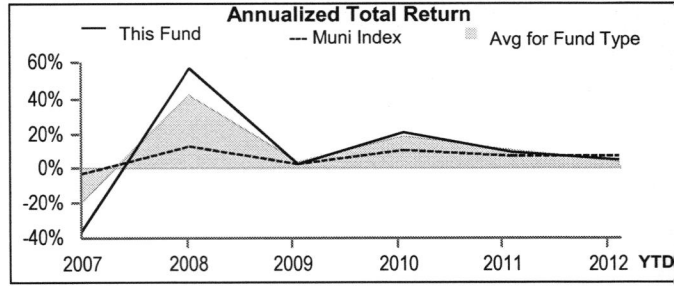

Invesco Van Kampen PA Val Muni Inc (VPV)

A+ **Excellent**

Fund Family: Invesco Advisers Inc
Fund Type: Municipal - Single State
Inception Date: April 23, 1993

Major Rating Factors:
Exceptional performance is the major factor driving the A+ (Excellent) TheStreet.com Investment Rating for Invesco Van Kampen PA Val Muni Inc. The fund currently has a performance rating of A- (Excellent) based on an annualized return of 14.54% over the last three years and a total return of 5.54% year to date 2012. Factored into the performance evaluation is an expense ratio of 1.49% (average).

The fund's risk rating is currently B (Good). It carries a beta of 2.24, meaning it is expected to move 22.4% for every 10% move in the market. Volatility, as measured by both the semi-deviation and a drawdown factor, is considered low. As of December 31, 2012, Invesco Van Kampen PA Val Muni Inc traded at a discount of 1.54% below its net asset value, which is better than its one-year historical average premium of .36%.

Robert W. Wimmell has been running the fund for 11 years and currently receives a manager quality ranking of 38 (0=worst, 99=best). If you desire only a moderate level of risk and strong performance, then this fund is an excellent option.

Data Date	Investment Rating	Net Assets ($Mil)	Price	Performance Rating/Pts	Total Return Y-T-D	Risk Rating/Pts
12-12	A+	367.39	15.30	A- / 9.0	5.54%	B / 8.5
2011	A+	343.00	14.22	A / 9.4	-0.39%	B / 8.7
2010	C-	321.18	12.65	C- / 3.6	6.03%	C+ / 6.2
2009	B+	294.63	12.74	B- / 7.1	52.07%	C+ / 6.6

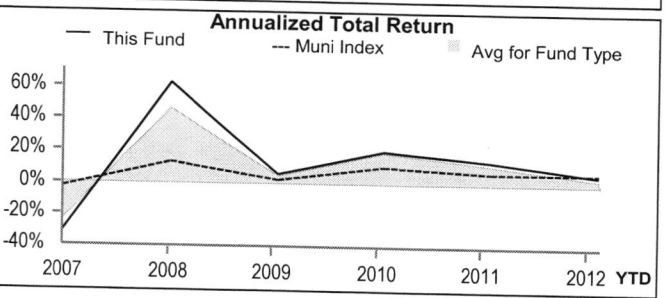

Invesco Van Kampen Senior Inc Tr (VVR)

B **Good**

Fund Family: Invesco Advisers Inc
Fund Type: Loan Participation
Inception Date: June 23, 1998

Major Rating Factors: Strong performance is the major factor driving the B (Good) TheStreet.com Investment Rating for Invesco Van Kampen Senior Inc Tr. The fund currently has a performance rating of B- (Good) based on an annualized return of 13.74% over the last three years and a total return of 4.28% year to date 2012. Factored into the performance evaluation is an expense ratio of 1.93% (above average).

The fund's risk rating is currently B (Good). It carries a beta of -188.48, meaning the fund's expected move will be -1884.8% for every 10% move in the market. Volatility, as measured by both the semi-deviation and a drawdown factor, is considered low. As of December 31, 2012, Invesco Van Kampen Senior Inc Tr traded at a premium of .97% above its net asset value, which is worse than its one-year historical average discount of 1.29%.

Philip Yarrow currently receives a manager quality ranking of 99 (0=worst, 99=best). If you desire only a moderate level of risk and strong performance, then this fund is an excellent option.

Data Date	Investment Rating	Net Assets ($Mil)	Price	Performance Rating/Pts	Total Return Y-T-D	Risk Rating/Pts
12-12	B	898.69	5.18	B- / 7.5	4.28%	B / 8.3
2011	B	849.20	4.28	B / 7.6	3.74%	B / 8.3
2010	D-	836.90	4.69	D / 2.2	18.70%	C- / 3.2
2009	D-	717.10	4.22	D / 2.1	66.80%	C / 4.3

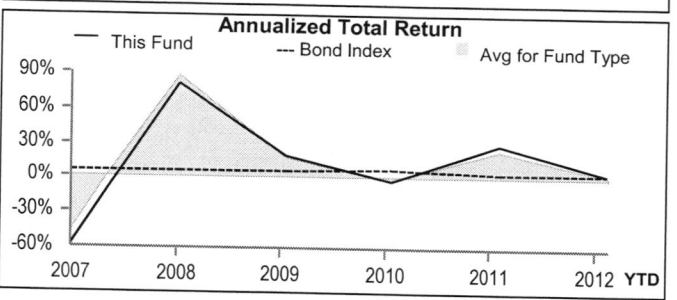

Invesco Van Kampen Tr Fr Inv Gr Mu (VGM)

B+ **Good**

Fund Family: Invesco Advisers Inc
Fund Type: Municipal - National
Inception Date: January 24, 1992

Major Rating Factors: Strong performance is the major factor driving the B+ (Good) TheStreet.com Investment Rating for Invesco Van Kampen Tr Fr Inv Gr Mu. The fund currently has a performance rating of B (Good) based on an annualized return of 12.61% over the last three years and a total return of 4.38% year to date 2012. Factored into the performance evaluation is an expense ratio of 1.52% (average).

The fund's risk rating is currently B (Good). It carries a beta of 1.50, meaning it is expected to move 15.0% for every 10% move in the market. Volatility, as measured by both the semi-deviation and a drawdown factor, is considered low. As of December 31, 2012, Invesco Van Kampen Tr Fr Inv Gr Mu traded at a premium of .13% above its net asset value, which is better than its one-year historical average premium of 3.14%.

Thomas M. Byron has been running the fund for 16 years and currently receives a manager quality ranking of 61 (0=worst, 99=best). If you desire only a moderate level of risk and strong performance, then this fund is an excellent option.

Data Date	Investment Rating	Net Assets ($Mil)	Price	Performance Rating/Pts	Total Return Y-T-D	Risk Rating/Pts
12-12	B+	823.16	15.22	B / 7.9	4.38%	B / 8.8
2011	A+	775.90	14.98	A / 9.4	-0.40%	B / 8.8
2010	C	733.60	13.35	C / 4.8	3.84%	C+ / 5.7
2009	B	646.45	13.86	B- / 7.4	55.46%	C+ / 6.0

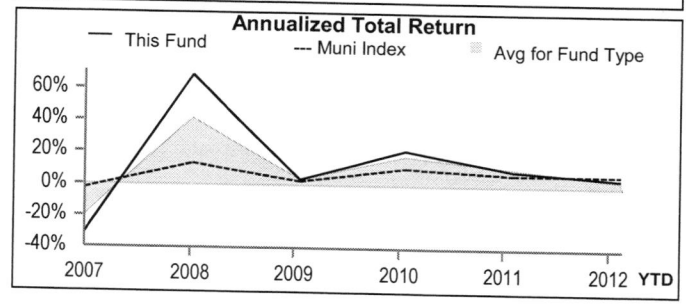

Invesco Van Kampen Tr Fr Inv NY Mu (VTN)   A   Excellent

Fund Family: Invesco Advisers Inc
Fund Type: Municipal - Single State
Inception Date: March 20, 1992

Data Date	Investment Rating	Net Assets ($Mil)	Price	Performance Rating/Pts	Total Return Y-T-D	Risk Rating/Pts
12-12	A	310.06	16.59	B+ / 8.7	3.55%	B / 8.8
2011	A+	228.00	15.25	A / 9.5	1.31%	B / 8.8
2010	C	212.05	13.63	C / 4.8	2.52%	C+ / 5.7
2009	B	190.53	14.25	B / 7.7	62.54%	C+ / 5.8

Major Rating Factors:
Strong performance is the major factor driving the A (Excellent) TheStreet.com Investment Rating for Invesco Van Kampen Tr Fr Inv NY Mu. The fund currently has a performance rating of B+ (Good) based on an annualized return of 13.31% over the last three years and a total return of 3.55% year to date 2012. Factored into the performance evaluation is an expense ratio of 1.63% (above average).

The fund's risk rating is currently B (Good). It carries a beta of 1.94, meaning it is expected to move 19.4% for every 10% move in the market. Volatility, as measured by both the semi-deviation and a drawdown factor, is considered low. As of December 31, 2012, Invesco Van Kampen Tr Fr Inv NY Mu traded at a premium of 4.14% above its net asset value, which is worse than its one-year historical average premium of 3.28%.

Robert J. Stryker has been running the fund for 6 years and currently receives a manager quality ranking of 48 (0=worst, 99=best). If you desire only a moderate level of risk and strong performance, then this fund is an excellent option.

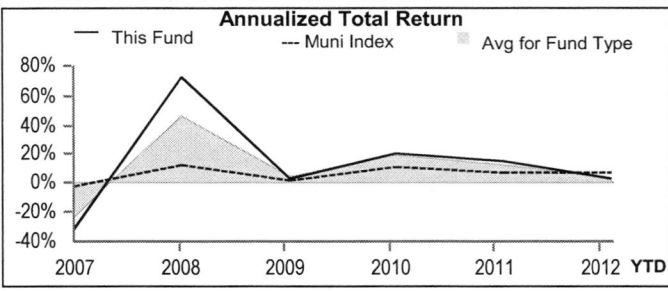

J Hancock Hedged Eqty & Inc Fd (HEQ)   C   Fair

Fund Family: John Hancock Advisers LLC
Fund Type: Growth and Income
Inception Date: May 25, 2011

Data Date	Investment Rating	Net Assets ($Mil)	Price	Performance Rating/Pts	Total Return Y-T-D	Risk Rating/Pts
12-12	C	241.10	15.26	C / 4.7	5.05%	B- / 7.4

Major Rating Factors: Middle of the road best describes J Hancock Hedged Eqty & Inc Fd whose TheStreet.com Investment Rating is currently a C (Fair). The fund currently has a performance rating of C (Fair) based on an annualized return of 0.00% over the last three years and a total return of 5.05% year to date 2012.

The fund's risk rating is currently B- (Good). It carries a beta of 0.00, meaning the fund's expected move will be 0.0% for every 10% move in the market. Volatility, as measured by both the semi-deviation and a drawdown factor, is considered low. As of December 31, 2012, J Hancock Hedged Eqty & Inc Fd traded at a discount of 15.27% below its net asset value, which is better than its one-year historical average discount of 10.73%.

Gregg R. Thomas has been running the fund for 2 years and currently receives a manager quality ranking of 28 (0=worst, 99=best). If you desire an average level of risk, then this fund may be an option.

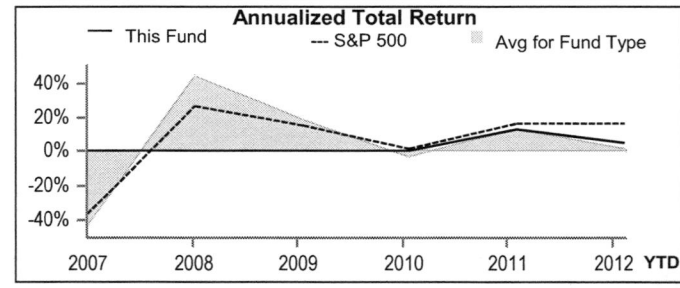

J Hancock Income Securities Tr (JHS)   B-   Good

Fund Family: John Hancock Advisers LLC
Fund Type: General - Investment Grade
Inception Date: February 14, 1973

Data Date	Investment Rating	Net Assets ($Mil)	Price	Performance Rating/Pts	Total Return Y-T-D	Risk Rating/Pts
12-12	B-	170.00	16.34	C+ / 6.3	2.14%	B / 8.7
2011	B+	253.60	14.60	B- / 7.4	1.23%	B+ / 9.0
2010	B+	164.00	15.10	B+ / 8.3	21.62%	C+ / 5.6
2009	C+	120.58	13.45	C+ / 6.4	49.48%	C+ / 5.8

Major Rating Factors: J Hancock Income Securities Tr receives a TheStreet.com Investment Rating of B- (Good). The fund currently has a performance rating of C+ (Fair) based on an annualized return of 14.33% over the last three years and a total return of 2.14% year to date 2012. Factored into the performance evaluation is an expense ratio of 1.56% (average).

The fund's risk rating is currently B (Good). It carries a beta of 0.86, meaning the fund's expected move will be 8.6% for every 10% move in the market. Volatility, as measured by both the semi-deviation and a drawdown factor, is considered low. As of December 31, 2012, J Hancock Income Securities Tr traded at a premium of 2.83% above its net asset value, which is better than its one-year historical average premium of 4.49%.

Howard C. Greene has been running the fund for 7 years and currently receives a manager quality ranking of 89 (0=worst, 99=best). If you desire an average level of risk, then this fund may be an option.

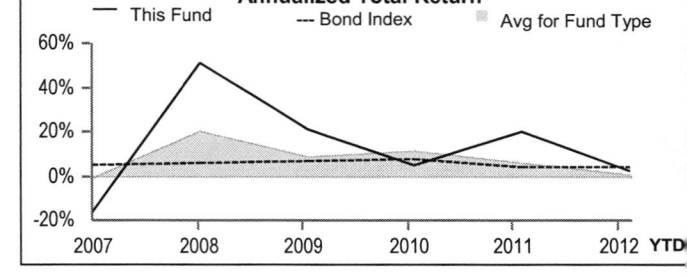

J Hancock Investors Trust (JHI)

B   **Good**

Fund Family: John Hancock Advisers LLC
Fund Type: General - Investment Grade
Inception Date: January 29, 1971

Major Rating Factors: J Hancock Investors Trust receives a TheStreet.com Investment Rating of B (Good). The fund currently has a performance rating of C+ (Fair) based on an annualized return of 17.55% over the last three years and a total return of 2.39% year to date 2012. Factored into the performance evaluation is an expense ratio of 1.62% (above average).

The fund's risk rating is currently B (Good). It carries a beta of 0.37, meaning the fund's expected move will be 3.7% for every 10% move in the market. Volatility, as measured by both the semi-deviation and a drawdown factor, is considered low. As of December 31, 2012, J Hancock Investors Trust traded at a premium of 9.30% above its net asset value, which is better than its one-year historical average premium of 17.59%.

John F. Iles has been running the fund for 7 years and currently receives a manager quality ranking of 95 (0=worst, 99=best). If you desire an average level of risk, then this fund may be an option.

Data Date	Investment Rating	Net Assets ($Mil)	Price	Performance Rating/Pts	Total Return Y-T-D	Risk Rating/Pts
12-12	B	164.00	22.57	C+ / 6.6	2.39%	B / 8.7
2011	B+	247.30	22.20	B+ / 8.9	0.32%	B- / 7.7
2010	B+	166.00	20.05	B / 8.1	21.55%	C+ / 5.9
2009	C+	119.03	18.27	C+ / 6.9	53.70%	C+ / 6.0

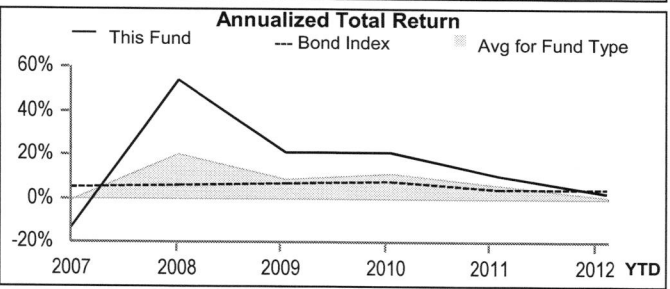

J Hancock Preferred Inc (HPI)

B+   **Good**

Fund Family: John Hancock Advisers LLC
Fund Type: Income
Inception Date: August 22, 2002

Major Rating Factors: Strong performance is the major factor driving the B+ (Good) TheStreet.com Investment Rating for J Hancock Preferred Inc. The fund currently has a performance rating of B- (Good) based on an annualized return of 18.69% over the last three years and a total return of 5.61% year to date 2012. Factored into the performance evaluation is an expense ratio of 1.74% (above average).

The fund's risk rating is currently B (Good). It carries a beta of 0.15, meaning the fund's expected move will be 1.5% for every 10% move in the market. Volatility, as measured by both the semi-deviation and a drawdown factor, is considered low. As of December 31, 2012, J Hancock Preferred Inc traded at a discount of 1.57% below its net asset value, which is better than its one-year historical average premium of 3.86%.

Gregory K. Phelps has been running the fund for 11 years and currently receives a manager quality ranking of 96 (0=worst, 99=best). If you desire only a moderate level of risk and strong performance, then this fund is an excellent option.

Data Date	Investment Rating	Net Assets ($Mil)	Price	Performance Rating/Pts	Total Return Y-T-D	Risk Rating/Pts
12-12	B+	572.00	21.91	B- / 7.4	5.61%	B / 8.9
2011	B-	786.50	21.48	B- / 7.5	0.42%	B- / 7.3
2010	B-	510.00	18.68	B- / 7.0	18.39%	C+ / 5.8
2009	D+	422.64	17.10	D+ / 2.9	28.20%	C+ / 5.6

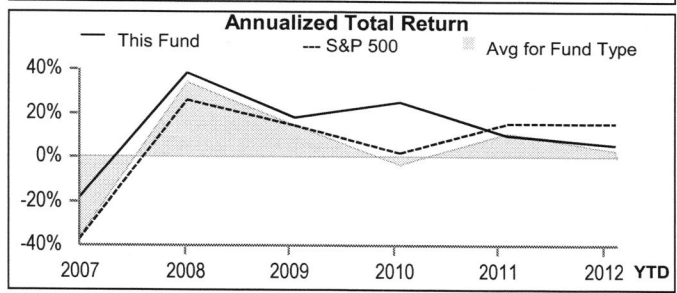

J Hancock Preferred Income II (HPF)

B+   **Good**

Fund Family: John Hancock Advisers LLC
Fund Type: Income
Inception Date: November 25, 2002

Major Rating Factors: Strong performance is the major factor driving the B+ (Good) TheStreet.com Investment Rating for J Hancock Preferred Income II. The fund currently has a performance rating of B- (Good) based on an annualized return of 18.26% over the last three years and a total return of 4.76% year to date 2012. Factored into the performance evaluation is an expense ratio of 1.75% (above average).

The fund's risk rating is currently B (Good). It carries a beta of 0.33, meaning the fund's expected move will be 3.3% for every 10% move in the market. Volatility, as measured by both the semi-deviation and a drawdown factor, is considered low. As of December 31, 2012, J Hancock Preferred Income II traded at a discount of 2.08% below its net asset value, which is better than its one-year historical average premium of 2.90%.

Gregory K. Phelps has been running the fund for 11 years and currently receives a manager quality ranking of 94 (0=worst, 99=best). If you desire only a moderate level of risk and strong performance, then this fund is an excellent option.

Data Date	Investment Rating	Net Assets ($Mil)	Price	Performance Rating/Pts	Total Return Y-T-D	Risk Rating/Pts
12-12	B+	466.00	21.66	B- / 7.4	4.76%	B / 8.8
2011	B	644.00	20.87	B / 7.8	0.34%	B- / 7.9
2010	B	414.00	18.59	B- / 7.1	19.23%	C+ / 5.9
2009	C-	343.55	17.03	C- / 3.1	33.74%	C+ / 5.7

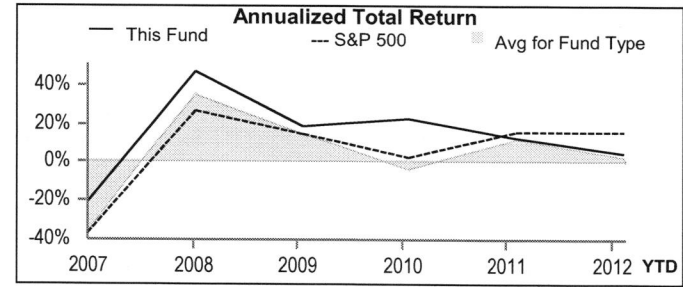

J Hancock Preferred Income III (HPS)

B   **Good**

Fund Family: John Hancock Advisers LLC
Fund Type: Income
Inception Date: June 19, 2003

Major Rating Factors: J Hancock Preferred Income III receives a TheStreet.com Investment Rating of B (Good). The fund currently has a performance rating of C+ (Fair) based on an annualized return of 17.27% over the last three years and a total return of 3.68% year to date 2012. Factored into the performance evaluation is an expense ratio of 1.73% (above average).

The fund's risk rating is currently B (Good). It carries a beta of 0.38, meaning the fund's expected move will be 3.8% for every 10% move in the market. Volatility, as measured by both the semi-deviation and a drawdown factor, is considered low. As of December 31, 2012, J Hancock Preferred Income III traded at a discount of 2.95% below its net asset value, which is better than its one-year historical average premium of 1.85%.

Gregory K. Phelps has been running the fund for 10 years and currently receives a manager quality ranking of 92 (0=worst, 99=best). If you desire an average level of risk, then this fund may be an option.

Data Date	Investment Rating	Net Assets ($Mil)	Price	Performance Rating/Pts	Total Return Y-T-D	Risk Rating/Pts
12-12	B	598.00	18.75	C+ / 6.8	3.68%	B / 8.8
2011	B-	819.80	17.07	B- / 7.4	1.52%	B- / 7.6
2010	C-	530.00	15.99	C / 4.8	15.17%	C- / 4.2
2009	D+	441.56	15.09	C- / 3.8	43.13%	C / 4.7

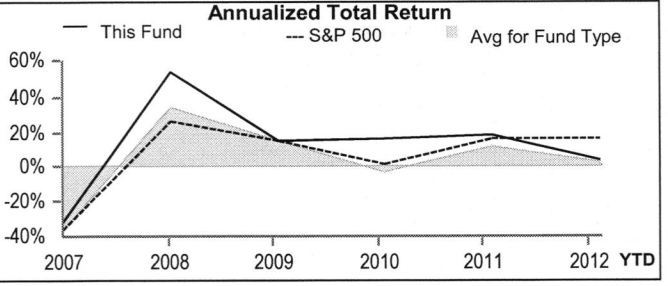

J Hancock Tax Adv Glb Shlr Yield (HTY)

C-   **Fair**

Fund Family: John Hancock Advisers LLC
Fund Type: Global
Inception Date: September 26, 2007

Major Rating Factors: Middle of the road best describes J Hancock Tax Adv Glb Shlr Yield whose TheStreet.com Investment Rating is currently a C- (Fair). The fund currently has a performance rating of C- (Fair) based on an annualized return of 10.64% over the last three years and a total return of 5.57% year to date 2012. Factored into the performance evaluation is an expense ratio of 1.28% (average).

The fund's risk rating is currently B- (Good). It carries a beta of 0.46, meaning the fund's expected move will be 4.6% for every 10% move in the market. Volatility, as measured by both the semi-deviation and a drawdown factor, is considered low. As of December 31, 2012, J Hancock Tax Adv Glb Shlr Yield traded at a premium of .34% above its net asset value, which is better than its one-year historical average premium of 5.41%.

Dennis M. Bein has been running the fund for 6 years and currently receives a manager quality ranking of 81 (0=worst, 99=best). If you desire an average level of risk, then this fund may be an option.

Data Date	Investment Rating	Net Assets ($Mil)	Price	Performance Rating/Pts	Total Return Y-T-D	Risk Rating/Pts
12-12	C-	115.00	11.84	C- / 4.1	5.57%	B- / 7.8
2011	B-	115.30	12.34	C+ / 6.7	2.27%	B / 8.0
2010	C+	115.00	12.73	C+ / 6.1	7.95%	C / 5.4
2009	A-	105.82	13.25	B+ / 8.8	33.81%	C / 5.5

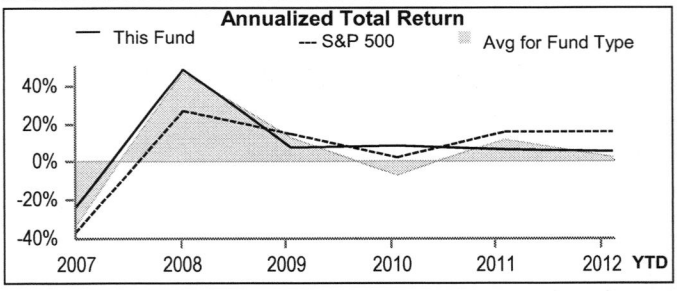

J Hancock Tax Advantage Div Income (HTD)

B+   **Good**

Fund Family: John Hancock Advisers LLC
Fund Type: Income
Inception Date: February 27, 2004

Major Rating Factors: Strong performance is the major factor driving the B+ (Good) TheStreet.com Investment Rating for J Hancock Tax Advantage Div Income. The fund currently has a performance rating of B (Good) based on an annualized return of 20.29% over the last three years and a total return of 3.43% year to date 2012. Factored into the performance evaluation is an expense ratio of 1.56% (average).

The fund's risk rating is currently B (Good). It carries a beta of 0.58, meaning the fund's expected move will be 5.8% for every 10% move in the market. Volatility, as measured by both the semi-deviation and a drawdown factor, is considered low. As of December 31, 2012, J Hancock Tax Advantage Div Income traded at a discount of 10.69% below its net asset value, which is better than its one-year historical average discount of 7.21%.

Dennis M. Bein currently receives a manager quality ranking of 93 (0=worst, 99=best). If you desire only a moderate level of risk and strong performance, then this fund is an excellent option.

Data Date	Investment Rating	Net Assets ($Mil)	Price	Performance Rating/Pts	Total Return Y-T-D	Risk Rating/Pts
12-12	B+	690.00	18.04	B / 7.6	3.43%	B / 8.8
2011	B	1,052.90	17.34	B+ / 8.8	1.27%	B- / 7.2
2010	B-	594.00	14.91	B- / 7.3	24.73%	C / 5.1
2009	C-	447.79	12.92	C- / 3.6	35.72%	C / 5.1

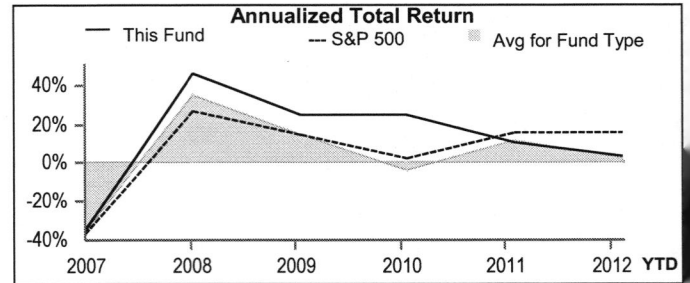

Japan Equity Fund (JEQ)

D+   **Weak**

Fund Family: Daiwa SB Investments
Fund Type: Foreign
Inception Date: July 24, 1992

Major Rating Factors:
Disappointing performance is the major factor driving the D+ (Weak) TheStreet.com Investment Rating for Japan Equity Fund. The fund currently has a performance rating of D+ (Weak) based on an annualized return of 2.34% over the last three years and a total return of 5.01% year to date 2012. Factored into the performance evaluation is an expense ratio of 1.38% (average).

The fund's risk rating is currently B- (Good). It carries a beta of 0.65, meaning the fund's expected move will be 6.5% for every 10% move in the market. Volatility, as measured by both the semi-deviation and a drawdown factor, is considered low. As of December 31, 2012, Japan Equity Fund traded at a discount of 11.87% below its net asset value, which is better than its one-year historical average discount of 10.76%.

Naoto Nagai has been running the fund for 7 years and currently receives a manager quality ranking of 56 (0=worst, 99=best). This fund offers only a moderate level of risk but investors looking for strong performance are still waiting.

Data Date	Investment Rating	Net Assets ($Mil)	Price	Performance Rating/Pts	Total Return Y-T-D	Risk Rating/Pts
12-12	D+	86.90	5.57	D+ / 2.9	5.01%	B- / 7.4
2011	D	82.40	5.00	D / 1.7	2.60%	B- / 7.4
2010	D+	94.00	6.12	D+ / 2.6	17.85%	C+ / 6.3
2009	D	74.32	5.24	E+ / 0.7	2.69%	C+ / 6.4

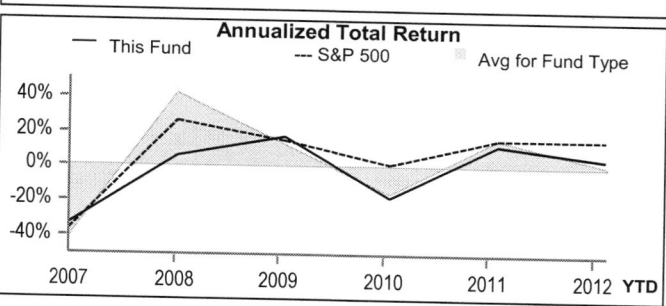

Japan Smaller Cap Fund Inc. (JOF)

D   **Weak**

Fund Family: Nomura Asset Management USA Inc
Fund Type: Foreign
Inception Date: March 14, 1990

Major Rating Factors:
Disappointing performance is the major factor driving the D (Weak) TheStreet.com Investment Rating for Japan Smaller Cap Fund Inc.. The fund currently has a performance rating of D- (Weak) based on an annualized return of -0.65% over the last three years and a total return of 4.31% year to date 2012. Factored into the performance evaluation is an expense ratio of 1.15% (low).

The fund's risk rating is currently B- (Good). It carries a beta of 0.46, meaning the fund's expected move will be 4.6% for every 10% move in the market. Volatility, as measured by both the semi-deviation and a drawdown factor, is considered low. As of December 31, 2012, Japan Smaller Cap Fund Inc. traded at a discount of 12.41% below its net asset value, which is worse than its one-year historical average discount of 12.83%.

Department Investment currently receives a manager quality ranking of 36 (0=worst, 99=best). This fund offers only a moderate level of risk but investors looking for strong performance are still waiting.

Data Date	Investment Rating	Net Assets ($Mil)	Price	Performance Rating/Pts	Total Return Y-T-D	Risk Rating/Pts
12-12	D	233.84	7.20	D- / 1.4	4.31%	B- / 7.3
2011	D	238.30	7.18	D / 1.7	1.95%	B- / 7.5
2010	C+	179.38	8.97	C+ / 6.2	23.86%	C+ / 6.1
2009	D-	190.28	7.32	E+ / 0.6	-2.22%	C+ / 5.8

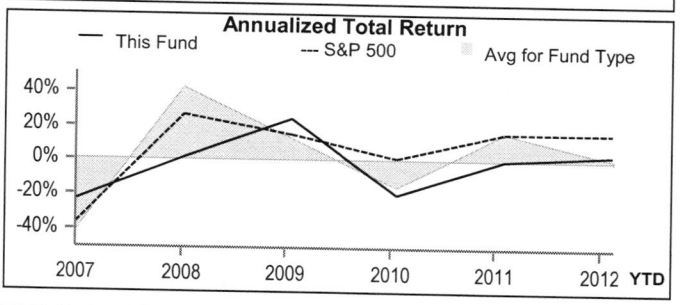

JF China Region Fund (JFC)

D+   **Weak**

Fund Family: JF International Management Inc
Fund Type: Foreign
Inception Date: July 16, 1992

Major Rating Factors: JF China Region Fund receives a TheStreet.com Investment Rating of D+ (Weak). The fund currently has a performance rating of C- (Fair) based on an annualized return of 1.91% over the last three years and a total return of 2.29% year to date 2012. Factored into the performance evaluation is an expense ratio of 1.89% (above average).

The fund's risk rating is currently C+ (Fair). It carries a beta of 1.03, meaning that its performance tracks fairly well with that of the overall stock market. Volatility, as measured by both the semi-deviation and a drawdown factor, is considered low. As of December 31, 2012, JF China Region Fund traded at a discount of 11.73% below its net asset value, which is worse than its one-year historical average discount of 11.95%.

Howard H. Wang has been running the fund for 8 years and currently receives a manager quality ranking of 30 (0=worst, 99=best). If you desire an average level of risk, then this fund may be an option.

Data Date	Investment Rating	Net Assets ($Mil)	Price	Performance Rating/Pts	Total Return Y-T-D	Risk Rating/Pts
12-12	D+	82.23	14.00	C- / 3.8	2.29%	C+ / 6.6
2011	D+	112.25	11.02	C- / 3.0	4.36%	C+ / 6.7
2010	D	89.71	15.79	C / 4.9	14.73%	D+ / 2.3
2009	C-	81.70	13.78	C+ / 6.6	49.97%	D+ / 2.6

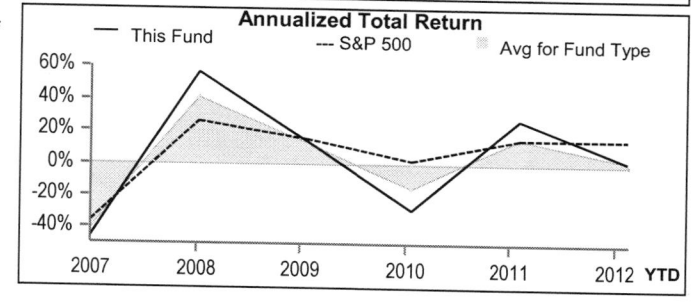

* Denotes ETF Fund

John Hancock Financial Opptys (BTO)

B- **Good**

Fund Family: John Hancock Advisers LLC
Fund Type: Financial Services
Inception Date: August 16, 1994

Major Rating Factors: Strong performance is the major factor driving the B- (Good) TheStreet.com Investment Rating for John Hancock Financial Opptys. The fund currently has a performance rating of B (Good) based on an annualized return of 15.20% over the last three years and a total return of 8.64% year to date 2012. Factored into the performance evaluation is an expense ratio of 1.37% (average).

The fund's risk rating is currently C+ (Fair). It carries a beta of 1.14, meaning it is expected to move 11.4% for every 10% move in the market. Volatility, as measured by both the semi-deviation and a drawdown factor, is considered low. As of December 31, 2012, John Hancock Financial Opptys traded at a discount of 9.28% below its net asset value, which is better than its one-year historical average discount of 8.12%.

Susan Curry has been running the fund for 7 years and currently receives a manager quality ranking of 79 (0=worst, 99=best). If you desire only a moderate level of risk and strong performance, then this fund is an excellent option.

Data Date	Investment Rating	Net Assets ($Mil)	Price	Performance Rating/Pts	Total Return Y-T-D	Risk Rating/Pts
12-12	B-	298.00	17.60	B / 8.2	8.64%	C+ / 6.9
2011	C-	300.00	13.70	C- / 3.8	7.45%	B- / 7.2
2010	C	418.00	17.22	C / 4.7	29.28%	C+ / 6.0
2009	D-	290.68	14.10	E+ / 0.6	4.44%	C+ / 6.0

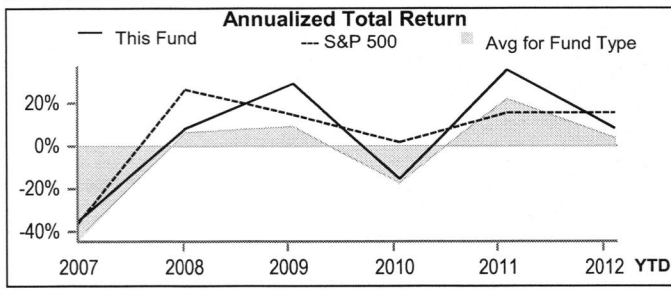

John Hancock Premium Dividend (PDT)

B+ **Good**

Fund Family: John Hancock Advisers LLC
Fund Type: Income
Inception Date: December 14, 1989

Major Rating Factors: Strong performance is the major factor driving the B+ (Good) TheStreet.com Investment Rating for John Hancock Premium Dividend. The fund currently has a performance rating of B- (Good) based on an annualized return of 19.76% over the last three years and a total return of 2.43% year to date 2012. Factored into the performance evaluation is an expense ratio of 1.87% (above average).

The fund's risk rating is currently B (Good). It carries a beta of 0.32, meaning the fund's expected move will be 3.2% for every 10% move in the market. Volatility, as measured by both the semi-deviation and a drawdown factor, is considered low. As of December 31, 2012, John Hancock Premium Dividend traded at a discount of 6.02% below its net asset value, which is better than its one-year historical average discount of .97%.

Gregory K. Phelps has been running the fund for 8 years and currently receives a manager quality ranking of 95 (0=worst, 99=best). If you desire only a moderate level of risk and strong performance, then this fund is an excellent option.

Data Date	Investment Rating	Net Assets ($Mil)	Price	Performance Rating/Pts	Total Return Y-T-D	Risk Rating/Pts
12-12	B+	660.00	13.57	B- / 7.2	2.43%	B / 8.9
2011	B+	991.20	13.44	A- / 9.1	-1.56%	B / 8.0
2010	B+	573.00	11.56	B+ / 8.5	25.73%	C / 5.3
2009	C+	385.52	9.96	C+ / 6.3	46.75%	C / 5.3

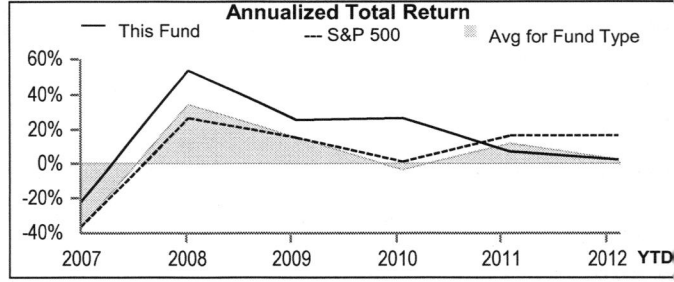

Kayne Anderson Energy Tot Ret (KYE)

C- **Fair**

Fund Family: KA Fund Advisors LLC
Fund Type: Energy/Natural Resources
Inception Date: June 28, 2005

Major Rating Factors: Middle of the road best describes Kayne Anderson Energy Tot Ret whose TheStreet.com Investment Rating is currently a C- (Fair). The fund currently has a performance rating of C (Fair) based on an annualized return of 12.93% over the last three years and a total return of 7.52% year to date 2012. Factored into the performance evaluation is an expense ratio of 4.30% (high).

The fund's risk rating is currently B- (Good). It carries a beta of 0.59, meaning the fund's expected move will be 5.9% for every 10% move in the market. Volatility, as measured by both the semi-deviation and a drawdown factor, is considered low. As of December 31, 2012, Kayne Anderson Energy Tot Ret traded at a discount of 7.07% below its net asset value, which is better than its one-year historical average premium of 1.86%.

John C. Frey has been running the fund for 8 years and currently receives a manager quality ranking of 79 (0=worst, 99=best). If you desire an average level of risk, then this fund may be an option.

Data Date	Investment Rating	Net Assets ($Mil)	Price	Performance Rating/Pts	Total Return Y-T-D	Risk Rating/Pts
12-12	C-	883.97	24.59	C / 4.3	7.52%	B- / 7.2
2011	B	915.06	25.31	B+ / 8.9	3.44%	B- / 7.3
2010	B-	677.68	29.11	B+ / 8.8	35.68%	C- / 3.6
2009	C+	547.78	23.10	B+ / 8.4	124.18%	C- / 3.9

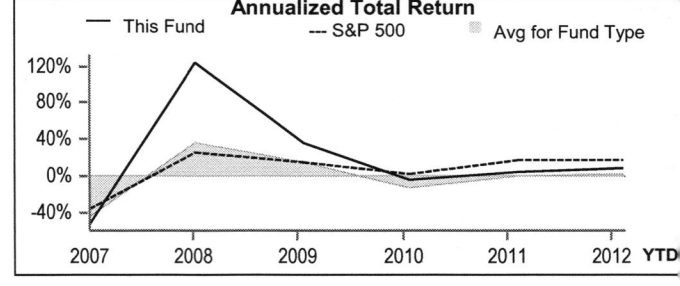

Kayne Anderson Engy Development Co (KED)

A   **Excellent**

Fund Family: KA Fund Advisors LLC
Fund Type: Energy/Natural Resources
Inception Date: September 21, 2006

Major Rating Factors:
Exceptional performance is the major factor driving the A (Excellent) TheStreet.com Investment Rating for Kayne Anderson Engy Development Co. The fund currently has a performance rating of A (Excellent) based on an annualized return of 27.89% over the last three years and a total return of 7.49% year to date 2012. Factored into the performance evaluation is an expense ratio of 3.90% (high).

The fund's risk rating is currently B (Good). It carries a beta of 0.20, meaning the fund's expected move will be 2.0% for every 10% move in the market. Volatility, as measured by both the semi-deviation and a drawdown factor, is considered low. As of December 31, 2012, Kayne Anderson Engy Development Co traded at a price exactly equal to its net asset value, which is better than its one-year historical average premium of 4.98%.

Robert V. Sinnott currently receives a manager quality ranking of 98 (0=worst, 99=best). If you desire only a moderate level of risk and strong performance, then this fund is an excellent option.

Data Date	Investment Rating	Net Assets ($Mil)	Price	Performance Rating/Pts	Total Return Y-T-D	Risk Rating/Pts
12-12	A	238.03	0.00	A / 9.3	7.49%	B / 8.0
2011	B	211.04	0.00	A- / 9.1	-0.75%	C+ / 6.2
2010	C-	168.54	18.01	B- / 7.4	33.91%	D+ / 2.8
2009	B-	158.60	14.55	A+ / 9.8	114.87%	C- / 3.3

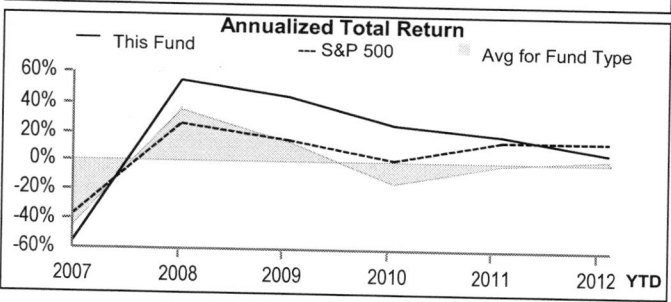

Kayne Anderson Midstream/Energy (KMF)

A+   **Excellent**

Fund Family: KA Fund Advisors LLC
Fund Type: Income
Inception Date: November 24, 2010

Major Rating Factors:
Exceptional performance is the major factor driving the A+ (Excellent) TheStreet.com Investment Rating for Kayne Anderson Midstream/Energy. The fund currently has a performance rating of A+ (Excellent) based on an annualized return of 0.00% over the last three years and a total return of 8.38% year to date 2012. Factored into the performance evaluation is an expense ratio of 2.90% (high).

The fund's risk rating is currently B (Good). It carries a beta of 0.00, meaning the fund's expected move will be 0.0% for every 10% move in the market. Volatility, as measured by both the semi-deviation and a drawdown factor, is considered low. As of December 31, 2012, Kayne Anderson Midstream/Energy traded at a discount of 4.86% below its net asset value, which is better than its one-year historical average discount of 3.70%.

Robert V. Sinnott currently receives a manager quality ranking of 89 (0=worst, 99=best). If you desire only a moderate level of risk and strong performance, then this fund is an excellent option.

Data Date	Investment Rating	Net Assets ($Mil)	Price	Performance Rating/Pts	Total Return Y-T-D	Risk Rating/Pts
12-12	A+	562.04	28.75	A+ / 9.6	8.38%	B / 8.5
2011	C-	0.00	24.60	C- / 3.1	1.71%	B / 8.5

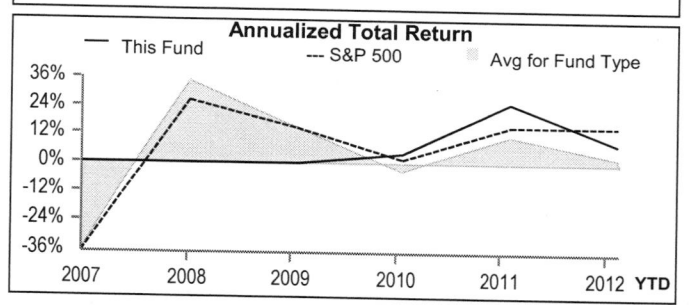

Kayne Anderson MLP Inv Co (KYN)

B   **Good**

Fund Family: KA Fund Advisors LLC
Fund Type: Energy/Natural Resources
Inception Date: September 27, 2004

Major Rating Factors: Strong performance is the major factor driving the B (Good) TheStreet.com Investment Rating for Kayne Anderson MLP Inv Co. The fund currently has a performance rating of B- (Good) based on an annualized return of 18.38% over the last three years and a total return of 7.63% year to date 2012. Factored into the performance evaluation is an expense ratio of 4.90% (high).

The fund's risk rating is currently B (Good). It carries a beta of 0.33, meaning the fund's expected move will be 3.3% for every 10% move in the market. Volatility, as measured by both the semi-deviation and a drawdown factor, is considered low. As of December 31, 2012, Kayne Anderson MLP Inv Co traded at a premium of .72% above its net asset value, which is better than its one-year historical average premium of 8.03%.

John C. Frey has been running the fund for 9 years and currently receives a manager quality ranking of 91 (0=worst, 99=best). If you desire only a moderate level of risk and strong performance, then this fund is an excellent option.

Data Date	Investment Rating	Net Assets ($Mil)	Price	Performance Rating/Pts	Total Return Y-T-D	Risk Rating/Pts
12-12	B	2,029.60	29.47	B- / 7.3	7.63%	B / 8.2
2011	B+	1,825.89	30.37	B+ / 8.6	1.02%	B / 8.1
2010	B-	1,038.28	0.00	B+ / 8.8	35.72%	C- / 4.0
2009	C+	763.65	25.04	B- / 7.0	65.38%	C / 4.8

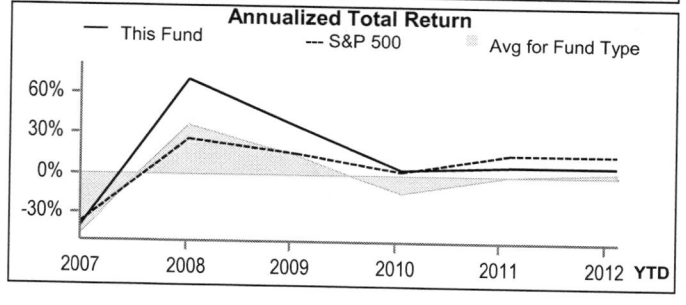

Korea Equity Fund (KEF)

C-   **Fair**

Fund Family: Nomura Asset Management USA Inc
Fund Type: Foreign
Inception Date: November 24, 1993

Data Date	Investment Rating	Net Assets ($Mil)	Price	Performance Rating/Pts	Total Return Y-T-D	Risk Rating/Pts
12-12	C-	121.20	9.22	C+ / 5.9	0.87%	C / 5.4
2011	C+	103.50	9.08	B / 8.0	0.77%	C+ / 5.8
2010	C-	109.46	12.23	C+ / 5.8	32.22%	C- / 4.0
2009	C-	84.14	9.25	C- / 4.1	55.59%	C / 4.5

Major Rating Factors: Middle of the road best describes Korea Equity Fund whose TheStreet.com Investment Rating is currently a C- (Fair). The fund currently has a performance rating of C+ (Fair) based on an annualized return of 13.10% over the last three years and a total return of 0.87% year to date 2012. Factored into the performance evaluation is an expense ratio of 1.90% (above average).

The fund's risk rating is currently C (Fair). It carries a beta of 0.98, meaning that its performance tracks fairly well with that of the overall stock market. Volatility, as measured by both the semi-deviation and a drawdown factor, is considered average. As of December 31, 2012, Korea Equity Fund traded at a discount of 8.26% below its net asset value, which is worse than its one-year historical average discount of 9.26%.

Shigeto Kasahara has been running the fund for 8 years and currently receives a manager quality ranking of 89 (0=worst, 99=best). If you desire an average level of risk, then this fund may be an option.

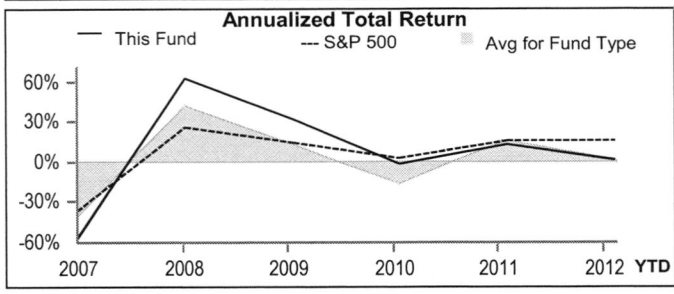

Korea Fund (KF)

C-   **Fair**

Fund Family: RCM Capital Management LLC
Fund Type: Foreign
Inception Date: August 22, 1984

Data Date	Investment Rating	Net Assets ($Mil)	Price	Performance Rating/Pts	Total Return Y-T-D	Risk Rating/Pts
12-12	C-	387.63	41.26	C / 4.3	1.33%	C+ / 6.4
2011	D	549.09	35.75	C- / 3.0	-0.06%	C / 5.2
2010	D	393.37	44.11	C- / 3.1	24.08%	C- / 3.7
2009	E	307.21	35.55	D- / 1.4	0.12%	D+ / 2.7

Major Rating Factors: Middle of the road best describes Korea Fund whose TheStreet.com Investment Rating is currently a C- (Fair). The fund currently has a performance rating of C (Fair) based on an annualized return of 8.80% over the last three years and a total return of 1.33% year to date 2012. Factored into the performance evaluation is an expense ratio of 1.12% (low).

The fund's risk rating is currently C+ (Fair). It carries a beta of 1.04, meaning that its performance tracks fairly well with that of the overall stock market. Volatility, as measured by both the semi-deviation and a drawdown factor, is considered low. As of December 31, 2012, Korea Fund traded at a discount of 8.96% below its net asset value, which is better than its one-year historical average discount of 8.77%.

Raymond Chan currently receives a manager quality ranking of 80 (0=worst, 99=best). If you desire an average level of risk, then this fund may be an option.

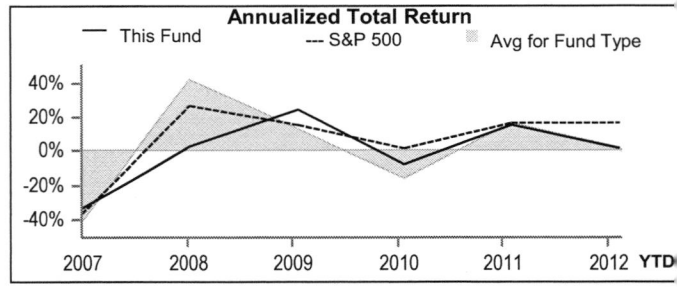

Latin American Discovery Fund (LDF)

D   **Weak**

Fund Family: Morgan Stanley Investment Managemen
Fund Type: Foreign
Inception Date: June 23, 1992

Data Date	Investment Rating	Net Assets ($Mil)	Price	Performance Rating/Pts	Total Return Y-T-D	Risk Rating/Pts
12-12	D	125.68	15.59	D+ / 2.5	4.36%	C+ / 6.3
2011	C	125.60	14.10	C / 5.5	3.19%	C+ / 6.9
2010	D+	130.76	19.17	C / 5.4	15.09%	C- / 3.5
2009	C	104.44	17.23	B / 8.1	86.30%	C- / 3.0

Major Rating Factors:
Disappointing performance is the major factor driving the D (Weak) TheStreet.com Investment Rating for Latin American Discovery Fund. The fund currently has a performance rating of D+ (Weak) based on an annualized return of 1.99% over the last three years and a total return of 4.36% year to date 2012. Factored into the performance evaluation is an expense ratio of 1.41% (average).

The fund's risk rating is currently C+ (Fair). It carries a beta of 1.13, meaning it is expected to move 11.3% for every 10% move in the market. Volatility, as measured by both the semi-deviation and a drawdown factor, is considered low. As of December 31, 2012, Latin American Discovery Fund traded at a discount of 11.72% below its net asset value, which is better than its one-year historical average discount of 8.94%.

Ana Cristina Piedrahita has been running the fund for 11 years and currently receives a manager quality ranking of 26 (0=worst, 99=best). This fund offers only a moderate level of risk but investors looking for strong performance are still waiting.

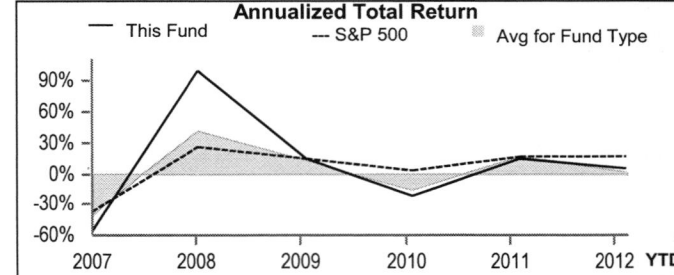

Lazard Global Total Return&Income (LGI)

C   **Fair**

Fund Family: Lazard Asset Management LLC
Fund Type: Global
Inception Date: April 27, 2004

Major Rating Factors: Middle of the road best describes Lazard Global Total Return&Income whose TheStreet.com Investment Rating is currently a C (Fair). The fund currently has a performance rating of C+ (Fair) based on an annualized return of 8.31% over the last three years and a total return of 4.09% year to date 2012. Factored into the performance evaluation is an expense ratio of 1.54% (average).

The fund's risk rating is currently B- (Good). It carries a beta of 0.90, meaning that its performance tracks fairly well with that of the overall stock market. Volatility, as measured by both the semi-deviation and a drawdown factor, is considered low. As of December 31, 2012, Lazard Global Total Return&Income traded at a discount of 15.27% below its net asset value, which is better than its one-year historical average discount of 11.97%.

Andrew D. Lacey currently receives a manager quality ranking of 78 (0=worst, 99=best). If you desire an average level of risk, then this fund may be an option.

Data Date	Investment Rating	Net Assets ($Mil)	Price	Performance Rating/Pts	Total Return Y-T-D	Risk Rating/Pts
12-12	C	148.82	15.09	C+ / 5.6	4.09%	B- / 7.6
2011	C-	148.80	13.39	C- / 3.8	0.90%	B- / 7.3
2010	D	139.30	15.06	D / 2.0	8.90%	C / 5.0
2009	D+	139.04	14.89	D+ / 2.7	29.89%	C+ / 5.8

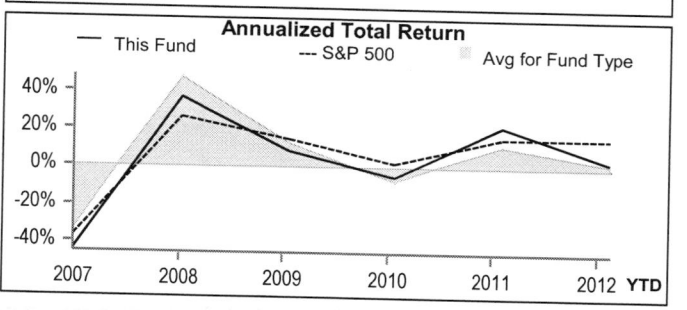

Lazard World Div&Inc Fd (LOR)

B   **Good**

Fund Family: Lazard Asset Management LLC
Fund Type: Global
Inception Date: June 27, 2005

Major Rating Factors: Strong performance is the major factor driving the B (Good) TheStreet.com Investment Rating for Lazard World Div&Inc Fd. The fund currently has a performance rating of B (Good) based on an annualized return of 13.01% over the last three years and a total return of 6.77% year to date 2012. Factored into the performance evaluation is an expense ratio of 1.97% (above average).

The fund's risk rating is currently B- (Good). It carries a beta of 0.95, meaning that its performance tracks fairly well with that of the overall stock market. Volatility, as measured by both the semi-deviation and a drawdown factor, is considered low. As of December 31, 2012, Lazard World Div&Inc Fd traded at a discount of 14.86% below its net asset value, which is better than its one-year historical average discount of 11.66%.

Andrew D. Lacey currently receives a manager quality ranking of 86 (0=worst, 99=best). If you desire only a moderate level of risk and strong performance, then this fund is an excellent option.

Data Date	Investment Rating	Net Assets ($Mil)	Price	Performance Rating/Pts	Total Return Y-T-D	Risk Rating/Pts
12-12	B	87.50	12.55	B / 8.1	6.77%	B- / 7.4
2011	C	84.30	10.86	C / 4.8	0.00%	B- / 7.6
2010	C-	78.78	12.85	C- / 4.1	23.81%	C / 4.9
2009	D+	72.22	11.17	D+ / 2.6	36.31%	C / 5.4

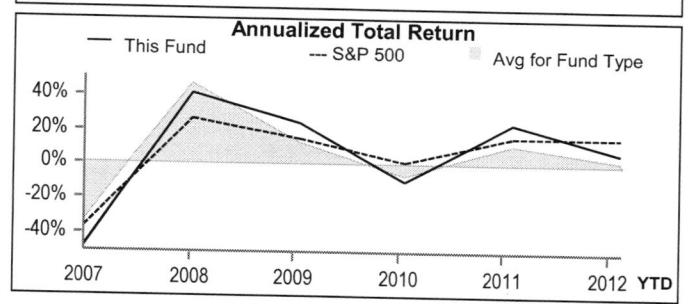

Liberty All-Star Equity Fund (USA)

C   **Fair**

Fund Family: ALPS Advisors Inc
Fund Type: Income
Inception Date: October 24, 1986

Major Rating Factors: Middle of the road best describes Liberty All-Star Equity Fund whose TheStreet.com Investment Rating is currently a C (Fair). The fund currently has a performance rating of C (Fair) based on an annualized return of 10.57% over the last three years and a total return of 3.14% year to date 2012. Factored into the performance evaluation is an expense ratio of 1.06% (low).

The fund's risk rating is currently B- (Good). It carries a beta of 1.29, meaning it is expected to move 12.9% for every 10% move in the market. Volatility, as measured by both the semi-deviation and a drawdown factor, is considered low. As of December 31, 2012, Liberty All-Star Equity Fund traded at a discount of 14.05% below its net asset value, which is better than its one-year historical average discount of 11.69%.

David A. Katz currently receives a manager quality ranking of 29 (0=worst, 99=best). If you desire an average level of risk, then this fund may be an option.

Data Date	Investment Rating	Net Assets ($Mil)	Price	Performance Rating/Pts	Total Return Y-T-D	Risk Rating/Pts
12-12	C	943.00	4.77	C / 5.2	3.14%	B- / 7.2
2011	C-	911.80	4.22	C / 4.9	4.27%	B- / 7.0
2010	C-	840.00	4.93	C / 4.6	21.80%	C / 5.4
2009	D	796.41	4.33	D- / 1.5	31.08%	C / 5.4

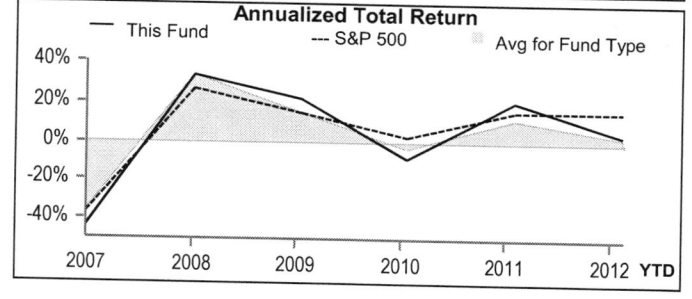

Liberty All-Star Growth Fund (ASG)   C   Fair

Fund Family: ALPS Advisors Inc
Fund Type: Income
Inception Date: March 6, 1986

Major Rating Factors: Middle of the road best describes Liberty All-Star Growth Fund whose TheStreet.com Investment Rating is currently a C (Fair). The fund currently has a performance rating of C+ (Fair) based on an annualized return of 14.18% over the last three years and a total return of 4.43% year to date 2012. Factored into the performance evaluation is an expense ratio of 1.45% (average).

The fund's risk rating is currently C+ (Fair). It carries a beta of 1.11, meaning it is expected to move 11.1% for every 10% move in the market. Volatility, as measured by both the semi-deviation and a drawdown factor, is considered low. As of December 31, 2012, Liberty All-Star Growth Fund traded at a discount of 13.43% below its net asset value, which is better than its one-year historical average discount of 9.17%.

Matthew A. Weatherbie has been running the fund for 27 years and currently receives a manager quality ranking of 63 (0=worst, 99=best). If you desire an average level of risk, then this fund may be an option.

Data Date	Investment Rating	Net Assets ($Mil)	Price	Performance Rating/Pts	Total Return Y-T-D	Risk Rating/Pts
12-12	C	130.00	4.06	C+ / 6.2	4.43%	C+ / 6.2
2011	C	127.60	3.81	C+ / 6.3	2.36%	C+ / 6.5
2010	C	113.00	4.25	C+ / 5.6	34.99%	C / 5.0
2009	D+	102.47	3.36	D+ / 2.9	30.11%	C+ / 5.7

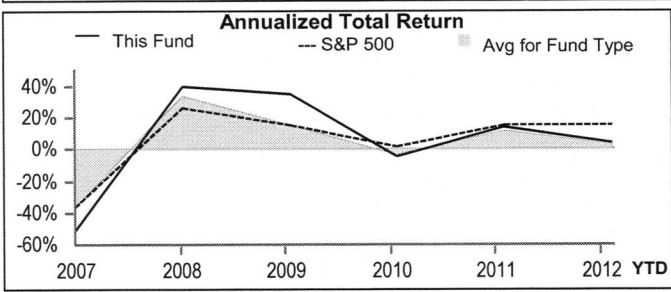

LMP Capital and Income Fund Inc (SCD)   B+   Good

Fund Family: Legg Mason Partners Fund Advisor LL
Fund Type: Growth and Income
Inception Date: February 24, 2004

Major Rating Factors: Strong performance is the major factor driving the B+ (Good) TheStreet.com Investment Rating for LMP Capital and Income Fund Inc. The fund currently has a performance rating of B+ (Good) based on an annualized return of 19.70% over the last three years and a total return of 7.28% year to date 2012. Factored into the performance evaluation is an expense ratio of 1.59% (above average).

The fund's risk rating is currently B (Good). It carries a beta of 0.89, meaning the fund's expected move will be 8.9% for every 10% move in the market. Volatility, as measured by both the semi-deviation and a drawdown factor, is considered low. As of December 31, 2012, LMP Capital and Income Fund Inc traded at a discount of 9.78% below its net asset value, which is better than its one-year historical average discount of 5.62%.

Mark J. McAllister currently receives a manager quality ranking of 83 (0=worst, 99=best). If you desire only a moderate level of risk and strong performance, then this fund is an excellent option.

Data Date	Investment Rating	Net Assets ($Mil)	Price	Performance Rating/Pts	Total Return Y-T-D	Risk Rating/Pts
12-12	B+	240.39	13.47	B+ / 8.4	7.28%	B / 8.0
2011	B-	268.30	12.36	C+ / 6.9	0.32%	B / 8.1
2010	C-	372.89	12.45	C- / 4.1	26.27%	C / 4.9
2009	D	325.30	10.35	D / 2.0	33.94%	C+ / 5.6

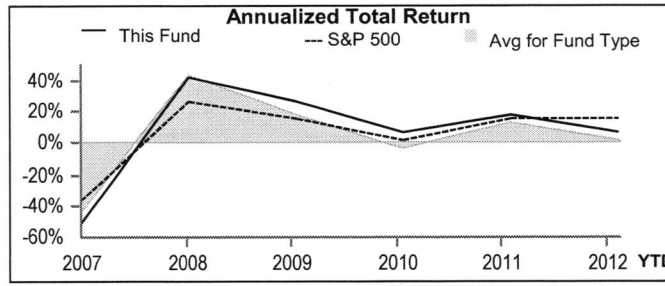

LMP Corporate Loan Fund Inc (TLI)   B-   Good

Fund Family: Legg Mason Partners Fund Advisor LL
Fund Type: Loan Participation
Inception Date: November 19, 1998

Major Rating Factors: LMP Corporate Loan Fund Inc receives a TheStreet.com Investment Rating of B- (Good). The fund currently has a performance rating of C+ (Fair) based on an annualized return of 14.26% over the last three years and a total return of 1.39% year to date 2012. Factored into the performance evaluation is an expense ratio of 1.94% (above average).

The fund's risk rating is currently B (Good). It carries a beta of -274.97, meaning the fund's expected move will be -2749.7% for every 10% move in the market. Volatility, as measured by both the semi-deviation and a drawdown factor, is considered low. As of December 31, 2012, LMP Corporate Loan Fund Inc traded at a discount of .62% below its net asset value, which is worse than its one-year historical average discount of 1.31%.

Jerry Pascucci currently receives a manager quality ranking of 99 (0=worst, 99=best). If you desire an average level of risk, then this fund may be an option.

Data Date	Investment Rating	Net Assets ($Mil)	Price	Performance Rating/Pts	Total Return Y-T-D	Risk Rating/Pts
12-12	B-	125.00	12.92	C+ / 6.4	1.39%	B / 8.4
2011	B+	120.00	11.11	B / 8.2	4.68%	B / 8.6
2010	C+	119.00	11.73	B- / 7.2	22.84%	C / 4.7
2009	C	111.29	10.04	C / 4.5	68.54%	C+ / 5.7

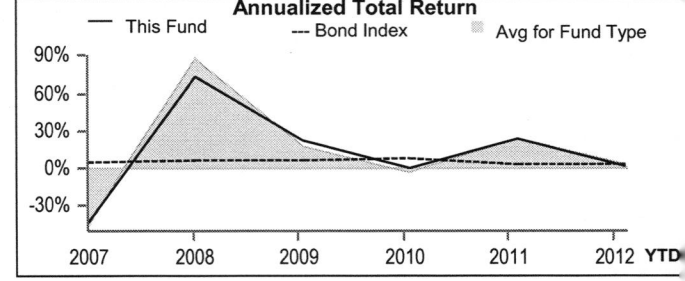

LMP Real Estate Income Fund Inc (RIT)

B+   **Good**

Fund Family: Legg Mason Partners Fund Advisor LL
Fund Type: Growth and Income
Inception Date: July 31, 2002

Major Rating Factors: Strong performance is the major factor driving the B+ (Good) TheStreet.com Investment Rating for LMP Real Estate Income Fund Inc. The fund currently has a performance rating of B+ (Good) based on an annualized return of 21.45% over the last three years and a total return of 5.76% year to date 2012. Factored into the performance evaluation is an expense ratio of 1.68% (above average).

The fund's risk rating is currently B- (Good). It carries a beta of 1.05, meaning that its performance tracks fairly well with that of the overall stock market. Volatility, as measured by both the semi-deviation and a drawdown factor, is considered low. As of December 31, 2012, LMP Real Estate Income Fund Inc traded at a discount of 12.10% below its net asset value, which is better than its one-year historical average discount of 8.87%.

John P. Baldi currently receives a manager quality ranking of 85 (0=worst, 99=best). If you desire only a moderate level of risk and strong performance, then this fund is an excellent option.

Data Date	Investment Rating	Net Assets ($Mil)	Price	Performance Rating/Pts	Total Return Y-T-D	Risk Rating/Pts
12-12	B+	37.00	10.97	B+ / 8.8	5.76%	B- / 7.8
2011	B	122.30	9.25	A- / 9.0	1.08%	C+ / 6.7
2010	C+	102.69	10.10	B / 8.1	35.86%	C- / 3.5
2009	E+	69.43	8.05	D / 2.1	89.96%	D+ / 2.5

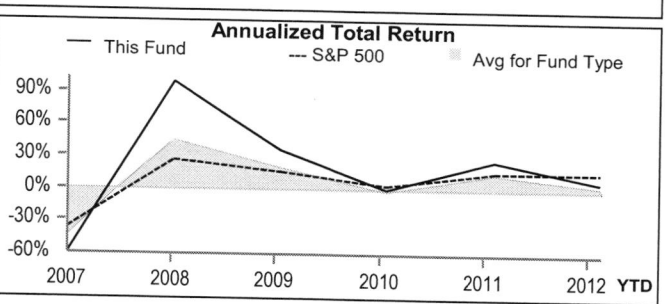

MA Health & Education Tax-Exempt T (MHE)

A-   **Excellent**

Fund Family: BlackRock Inc
Fund Type: Municipal - Single State
Inception Date: July 23, 1993

Major Rating Factors:
Strong performance is the major factor driving the A- (Excellent) TheStreet.com Investment Rating for MA Health & Education Tax-Exempt T. The fund currently has a performance rating of B (Good) based on an annualized return of 14.03% over the last three years and a total return of 3.37% year to date 2012. Factored into the performance evaluation is an expense ratio of 1.50% (average).

The fund's risk rating is currently B (Good). It carries a beta of 1.17, meaning it is expected to move 11.7% for every 10% move in the market. Volatility, as measured by both the semi-deviation and a drawdown factor, is considered low. As of December 31, 2012, MA Health & Education Tax-Exempt T traded at a premium of 2.56% above its net asset value, which is better than its one-year historical average premium of 6.84%.

Thomas M. Metzold currently receives a manager quality ranking of 83 (0=worst, 99=best). If you desire only a moderate level of risk and strong performance, then this fund is an excellent option.

Data Date	Investment Rating	Net Assets ($Mil)	Price	Performance Rating/Pts	Total Return Y-T-D	Risk Rating/Pts
12-12	A-	33.85	14.85	B / 8.0	3.37%	B / 8.8
2011	A+	32.00	14.60	A+ / 9.7	1.71%	B+ / 9.0
2010	A-	31.74	13.29	B+ / 8.5	18.59%	C+ / 6.3
2009	B-	28.58	12.00	C+ / 6.3	43.06%	B- / 7.0

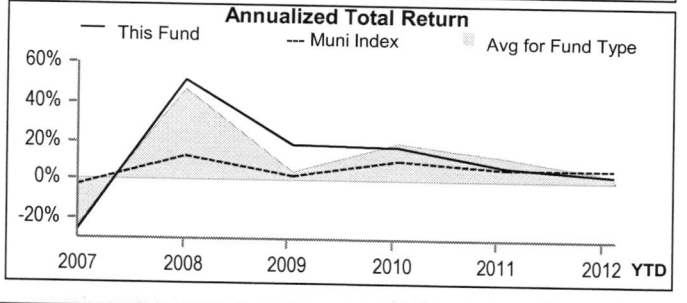

Macquarie Global Infr Total Return (MGU)

C+   **Fair**

Fund Family: Macquarie Capital Investment Mgmt L
Fund Type: Global
Inception Date: August 26, 2005

Major Rating Factors: Middle of the road best describes Macquarie Global Infr Total Return whose TheStreet.com Investment Rating is currently a C+ (Fair). The fund currently has a performance rating of C+ (Fair) based on an annualized return of 12.30% over the last three years and a total return of 5.03% year to date 2012. Factored into the performance evaluation is an expense ratio of 2.22% (high).

The fund's risk rating is currently B- (Good). It carries a beta of 0.96, meaning that its performance tracks fairly well with that of the overall stock market. Volatility, as measured by both the semi-deviation and a drawdown factor, is considered low. As of December 31, 2012, Macquarie Global Infr Total Return traded at a discount of 14.52% below its net asset value, which is better than its one-year historical average discount of 10.97%.

Brad L. Frishberg currently receives a manager quality ranking of 86 (0=worst, 99=best). If you desire an average level of risk, then this fund may be an option.

Data Date	Investment Rating	Net Assets ($Mil)	Price	Performance Rating/Pts	Total Return Y-T-D	Risk Rating/Pts
12-12	C+	325.95	19.07	C+ / 6.6	5.03%	B- / 7.8
2011	C	330.80	16.99	C+ / 5.6	0.82%	B- / 7.3
2010	D-	280.77	17.28	D- / 1.2	15.34%	C / 5.0
2009	D-	266.79	15.85	D / 1.6	31.62%	C / 5.1

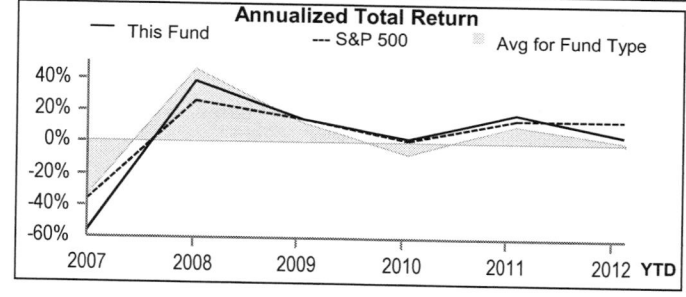

Macquarie/FTG Infr/ Util Div&Inc (MFD)

B- **Good**

Fund Family: First Trust Advisors LP
Fund Type: Global
Inception Date: March 25, 2004

Major Rating Factors: Macquarie/FTG Infr/ Util Div&Inc receives a TheStreet.com Investment Rating of B- (Good). The fund currently has a performance rating of C+ (Fair) based on an annualized return of 15.70% over the last three years and a total return of 3.34% year to date 2012. Factored into the performance evaluation is an expense ratio of 2.25% (high).

The fund's risk rating is currently B- (Good). It carries a beta of 0.89, meaning the fund's expected move will be 8.9% for every 10% move in the market. Volatility, as measured by both the semi-deviation and a drawdown factor, is considered low. As of December 31, 2012, Macquarie/FTG Infr/ Util Div&Inc traded at a discount of 7.58% below its net asset value, which is better than its one-year historical average discount of 2.61%.

Brad L. Frishberg currently receives a manager quality ranking of 92 (0=worst, 99=best). If you desire an average level of risk, then this fund may be an option.

Data Date	Investment Rating	Net Assets ($Mil)	Price	Performance Rating/Pts	Total Return Y-T-D	Risk Rating/Pts
12-12	B-	122.83	15.25	C+ / 6.7	3.34%	B- / 7.9
2011	C+	130.30	14.21	C+ / 6.7	3.45%	B- / 7.2
2010	D-	117.04	14.48	D / 1.8	23.62%	C- / 3.6
2009	E+	111.30	12.37	D- / 1.3	26.14%	C- / 4.0

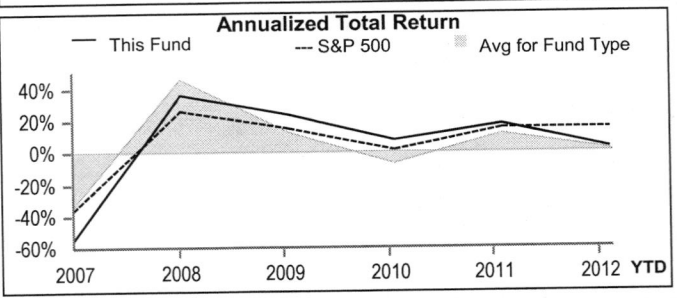

Madison Covered Call & Equity Stra (MCN)

D+ **Weak**

Fund Family: Guggenheim Funds Investment Advisor
Fund Type: Income
Inception Date: July 28, 2004

Major Rating Factors:
Disappointing performance is the major factor driving the D+ (Weak) TheStreet.com Investment Rating for Madison Covered Call & Equity Stra. The fund currently has a performance rating of D+ (Weak) based on an annualized return of 4.44% over the last three years and a total return of 3.41% year to date 2012. Factored into the performance evaluation is an expense ratio of 1.36% (average).

The fund's risk rating is currently B- (Good). It carries a beta of 0.95, meaning that its performance tracks fairly well with that of the overall stock market. Volatility, as measured by both the semi-deviation and a drawdown factor, is considered low. As of December 31, 2012, Madison Covered Call & Equity Stra traded at a discount of 13.80% below its net asset value, which is better than its one-year historical average discount of 11.02%.

Frank E. Burgess currently receives a manager quality ranking of 19 (0=worst, 99=best). This fund offers only a moderate level of risk but investors looking for strong performance are still waiting.

Data Date	Investment Rating	Net Assets ($Mil)	Price	Performance Rating/Pts	Total Return Y-T-D	Risk Rating/Pts
12-12	D+	166.38	7.62	D+ / 2.9	3.41%	B- / 7.5
2011	C	167.00	7.47	C / 4.7	1.34%	B- / 7.5
2010	C	185.39	9.05	C+ / 5.6	10.55%	C / 4.9
2009	C-	162.11	8.90	C- / 3.8	55.38%	C / 5.3

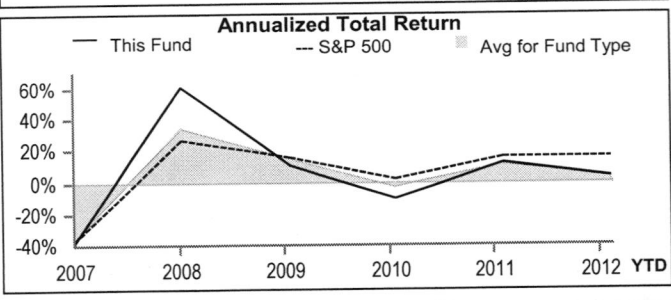

Madison Strategic Sector Premium (MSP)

C- **Fair**

Fund Family: Madison Asset Management LLC
Fund Type: Income
Inception Date: April 28, 2005

Major Rating Factors: Middle of the road best describes Madison Strategic Sector Premium whose TheStreet.com Investment Rating is currently a C- (Fair). The fund currently has a performance rating of C- (Fair) based on an annualized return of 6.76% over the last three years and a total return of 4.42% year to date 2012. Factored into the performance evaluation is an expense ratio of 0.97% (low).

The fund's risk rating is currently B- (Good). It carries a beta of 0.82, meaning the fund's expected move will be 8.2% for every 10% move in the market. Volatility, as measured by both the semi-deviation and a drawdown factor, is considered low. As of December 31, 2012, Madison Strategic Sector Premium traded at a discount of 15.47% below its net asset value, which is better than its one-year historical average discount of 12.74%.

Frank E. Burgess has been running the fund for 8 years and currently receives a manager quality ranking of 30 (0=worst, 99=best). If you desire an average level of risk, then this fund may be an option.

Data Date	Investment Rating	Net Assets ($Mil)	Price	Performance Rating/Pts	Total Return Y-T-D	Risk Rating/Pts
12-12	C-	74.20	11.09	C- / 3.4	4.42%	B- / 7.9
2011	C+	73.20	10.64	C / 5.2	4.04%	B- / 7.9
2010	C+	80.18	12.82	C+ / 6.3	14.04%	C / 5.4
2009	C-	69.89	12.23	C- / 3.2	49.47%	C+ / 5.8

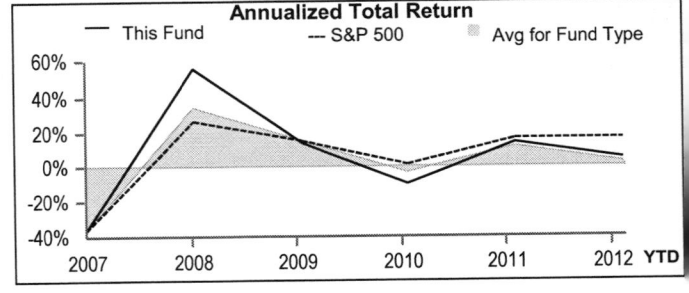

Managed Duration Investment Grd Mu (MZF)

B+   **Good**

Fund Family: Cutwater Asset Management Corp
Fund Type: Municipal - National
Inception Date: August 26, 2003

Major Rating Factors: Strong performance is the major factor driving the B+ (Good) TheStreet.com Investment Rating for Managed Duration Investment Grd Mu. The fund currently has a performance rating of B (Good) based on an annualized return of 13.55% over the last three years and a total return of 4.51% year to date 2012. Factored into the performance evaluation is an expense ratio of 1.36% (average).

The fund's risk rating is currently B (Good). It carries a beta of 2.15, meaning it is expected to move 21.5% for every 10% move in the market. Volatility, as measured by both the semi-deviation and a drawdown factor, is considered low. As of December 31, 2012, Managed Duration Investment Grd Mu traded at a discount of .58% below its net asset value, which is better than its one-year historical average premium of 3.19%.

Clifford D. Corso has been running the fund for 10 years and currently receives a manager quality ranking of 37 (0=worst, 99=best). If you desire only a moderate level of risk and strong performance, then this fund is an excellent option.

Data Date	Investment Rating	Net Assets ($Mil)	Price	Performance Rating/Pts	Total Return Y-T-D	Risk Rating/Pts
12-12	B+	104.62	15.30	B / 8.1	4.51%	B / 8.5
2011	A+	98.90	14.90	A+ / 9.8	0.00%	B / 8.6
2010	C+	97.19	13.11	C+ / 6.9	6.65%	C+ / 6.1
2009	A-	101.02	13.19	B / 8.0	61.84%	C+ / 6.2

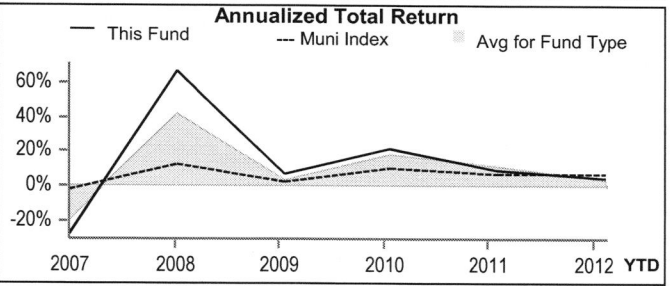

Managed High Yield Plus Fund (HYF)

C-   **Fair**

Fund Family: UBS Global Asset Mgmt (Americas) In
Fund Type: Global
Inception Date: June 24, 1998

Major Rating Factors: Middle of the road best describes Managed High Yield Plus Fund whose TheStreet.com Investment Rating is currently a C- (Fair). The fund currently has a performance rating of C- (Fair) based on an annualized return of 11.02% over the last three years and a total return of 2.34% year to date 2012. Factored into the performance evaluation is an expense ratio of 1.46% (average).

The fund's risk rating is currently B- (Good). It carries a beta of 0.86, meaning the fund's expected move will be 8.6% for every 10% move in the market. Volatility, as measured by both the semi-deviation and a drawdown factor, is considered low. As of December 31, 2012, Managed High Yield Plus Fund traded at a discount of 6.14% below its net asset value, which is better than its one-year historical average premium of 1.16%.

Matthew A. Iannucci has been running the fund for 4 years and currently receives a manager quality ranking of 90 (0=worst, 99=best). If you desire an average level of risk, then this fund may be an option.

Data Date	Investment Rating	Net Assets ($Mil)	Price	Performance Rating/Pts	Total Return Y-T-D	Risk Rating/Pts
12-12	C-	131.15	2.14	C- / 4.1	2.34%	B- / 7.3
2011	C+	126.90	2.13	B+ / 8.3	0.94%	C+ / 6.0
2010	D-	127.31	2.20	D+ / 2.7	23.34%	D+ / 2.3
2009	E+	103.92	1.99	D / 1.7	67.25%	C- / 3.3

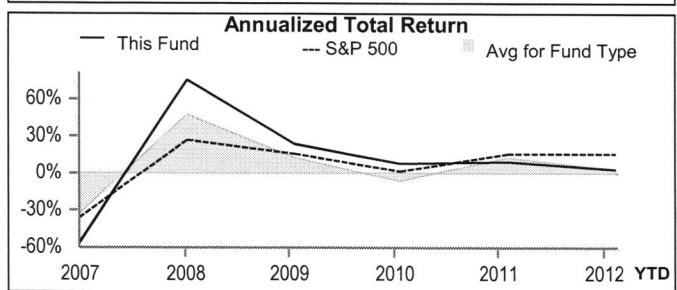

Mexico Equity & Income Fund (MXE)

A+   **Excellent**

Fund Family: Pichardo Asset Management SA de CV
Fund Type: Foreign
Inception Date: August 14, 1990

Major Rating Factors:
Exceptional performance is the major factor driving the A+ (Excellent) TheStreet.com Investment Rating for Mexico Equity & Income Fund. The fund currently has a performance rating of A+ (Excellent) based on an annualized return of 26.13% over the last three years and a total return of 9.26% year to date 2012. Factored into the performance evaluation is an expense ratio of 1.57% (above average).

The fund's risk rating is currently B (Good). It carries a beta of 0.80, meaning the fund's expected move will be 8.0% for every 10% move in the market. Volatility, as measured by both the semi-deviation and a drawdown factor, is considered low. As of December 31, 2012, Mexico Equity & Income Fund traded at a discount of 15.43% below its net asset value, which is better than its one-year historical average discount of 11.28%.

Maria-Eugenia Pichardo has been running the fund for 23 years and currently receives a manager quality ranking of 97 (0=worst, 99=best). If you desire only a moderate level of risk and strong performance, then this fund is an excellent option.

Data Date	Investment Rating	Net Assets ($Mil)	Price	Performance Rating/Pts	Total Return Y-T-D	Risk Rating/Pts
12-12	A+	86.97	14.25	A+ / 9.7	9.26%	B / 8.0
2011	D+	89.18	9.95	C / 4.7	0.20%	C+ / 5.7
2010	C-	74.61	11.33	B+ / 8.5	48.41%	D- / 1.5
2009	D-	61.43	7.65	C- / 3.4	15.91%	D+ / 2.5

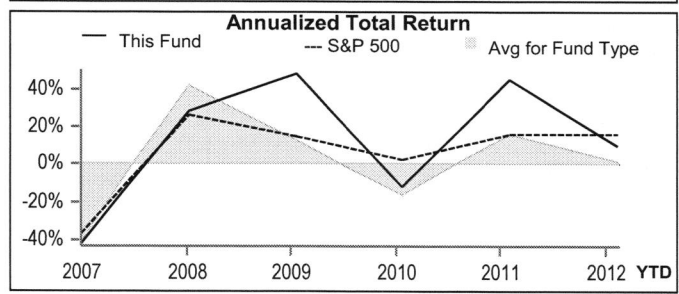

Mexico Fund (MXF)

A   **Excellent**

Fund Family: Impulsora Del Fondo Mexico SA De CV
Fund Type: Foreign
Inception Date: June 3, 1981

Major Rating Factors:
Exceptional performance is the major factor driving the A (Excellent) TheStreet.com Investment Rating for Mexico Fund. The fund currently has a performance rating of A+ (Excellent) based on an annualized return of 22.55% over the last three years and a total return of 7.31% year to date 2012. Factored into the performance evaluation is an expense ratio of 1.42% (average).

The fund's risk rating is currently B- (Good). It carries a beta of 0.96, meaning that its performance tracks fairly well with that of the overall stock market. Volatility, as measured by both the semi-deviation and a drawdown factor, is considered low. As of December 31, 2012, Mexico Fund traded at a discount of 9.88% below its net asset value, which is better than its one-year historical average discount of 7.81%.

José Luis Gómez Pimienta currently receives a manager quality ranking of 96 (0=worst, 99=best). If you desire only a moderate level of risk and strong performance, then this fund is an excellent option.

Data Date	Investment Rating	Net Assets ($Mil)	Price	Performance Rating/Pts	Total Return Y-T-D	Risk Rating/Pts
12-12	A	339.05	29.02	A+ / 9.7	7.31%	B- / 7.5
2011	C+	318.50	21.85	C+ / 6.9	1.83%	B- / 7.3
2010	B-	383.24	28.27	B+ / 8.7	42.37%	C- / 3.8
2009	D+	282.00	21.91	C / 4.3	52.65%	C / 4.3

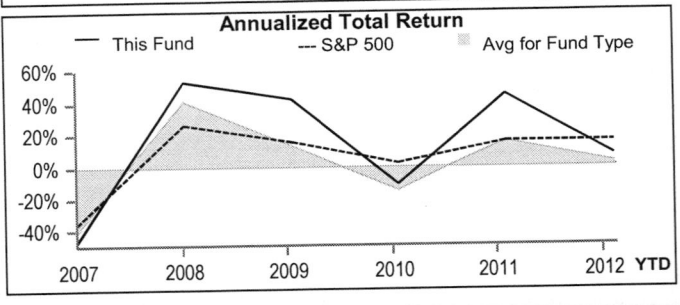

Annualized Total Return

MFS CA Muni (CCA)

B   **Good**

Fund Family: MFS Investment Management
Fund Type: Municipal - Single State
Inception Date: October 26, 1999

Major Rating Factors: Strong performance is the major factor driving the B (Good) TheStreet.com Investment Rating for MFS CA Muni. The fund currently has a performance rating of B- (Good) based on an annualized return of 10.89% over the last three years and a total return of 1.93% year to date 2012. Factored into the performance evaluation is an expense ratio of 1.41% (average).

The fund's risk rating is currently B (Good). It carries a beta of 2.31, meaning it is expected to move 23.1% for every 10% move in the market. Volatility, as measured by both the semi-deviation and a drawdown factor, is considered low. As of December 31, 2012, MFS CA Muni traded at a discount of 5.31% below its net asset value, which is better than its one-year historical average discount of 1.18%.

Geoffrey L. Schechter has been running the fund for 6 years and currently receives a manager quality ranking of 24 (0=worst, 99=best). If you desire only a moderate level of risk and strong performance, then this fund is an excellent option.

Data Date	Investment Rating	Net Assets ($Mil)	Price	Performance Rating/Pts	Total Return Y-T-D	Risk Rating/Pts
12-12	B	33.13	12.13	B- / 7.2	1.93%	B / 8.3
2011	B+	31.00	11.04	B+ / 8.7	1.90%	B / 8.3
2010	D	30.90	10.16	D / 1.6	-1.39%	C+ / 5.6
2009	C-	29.32	11.09	C / 4.6	53.70%	C / 5.5

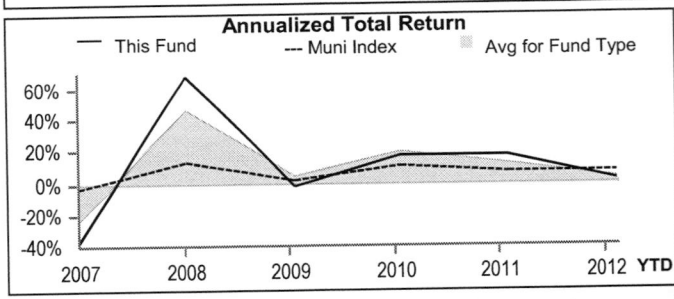

Annualized Total Return

MFS Charter Income Trust (MCR)

B-   **Good**

Fund Family: MFS Investment Management
Fund Type: General - Investment Grade
Inception Date: July 20, 1989

Major Rating Factors: MFS Charter Income Trust receives a TheStreet.com Investment Rating of B- (Good). The fund currently has a performance rating of C+ (Fair) based on an annualized return of 12.43% over the last three years and a total return of 4.05% year to date 2012. Factored into the performance evaluation is an expense ratio of 0.98% (low).

The fund's risk rating is currently B (Good). It carries a beta of 0.44, meaning the fund's expected move will be 4.4% for every 10% move in the market. Volatility, as measured by both the semi-deviation and a drawdown factor, is considered low. As of December 31, 2012, MFS Charter Income Trust traded at a discount of 3.89% below its net asset value, which is better than its one-year historical average discount of 3.50%.

Richard O. Hawkins has been running the fund for 9 years and currently receives a manager quality ranking of 87 (0=worst, 99=best). If you desire an average level of risk, then this fund may be an option.

Data Date	Investment Rating	Net Assets ($Mil)	Price	Performance Rating/Pts	Total Return Y-T-D	Risk Rating/Pts
12-12	B-	545.95	10.12	C+ / 5.9	4.05%	B / 8.8
2011	B-	535.80	9.15	C+ / 5.8	1.53%	B / 8.9
2010	A-	525.25	9.42	B / 7.6	11.32%	C+ / 6.6
2009	C+	473.08	9.18	C+ / 5.8	30.03%	C+ / 6.2

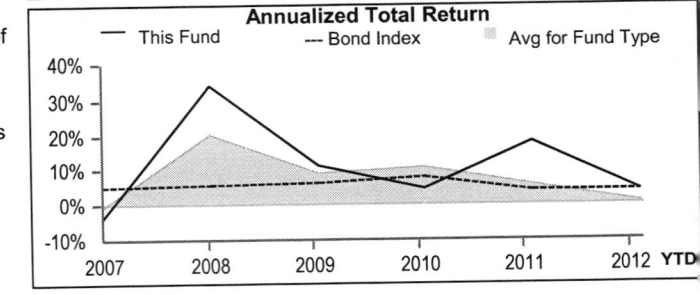

Annualized Total Return

MFS Government Markets Income Trus (MGF)

C-   **Fair**

Fund Family: MFS Investment Management
Fund Type: Global
Inception Date: May 20, 1987

Major Rating Factors:
Disappointing performance is the major factor driving the C- (Fair) TheStreet.com Investment Rating for MFS Government Markets Income Trus. The fund currently has a performance rating of D+ (Weak) based on an annualized return of 5.18% over the last three years and a total return of -0.73% year to date 2012. Factored into the performance evaluation is an expense ratio of 0.79% (very low).

    The fund's risk rating is currently B (Good). It carries a beta of 0.07, meaning the fund's expected move will be 0.7% for every 10% move in the market. Volatility, as measured by both the semi-deviation and a drawdown factor, is considered low. As of December 31, 2012, MFS Government Markets Income Trus traded at a premium of .88% above its net asset value, which is worse than its one-year historical average premium of .56%.

    Geoffrey L. Schechter currently receives a manager quality ranking of 78 (0=worst, 99=best). This fund offers only a moderate level of risk but investors looking for strong performance are still waiting.

Data Date	Investment Rating	Net Assets ($Mil)	Price	Perfor-mance Rating/Pts	Total Return Y-T-D	Risk Rating/Pts
12-12	C-	226.95	6.85	D+ / 2.3	-0.73%	B / 8.6
2011	C	228.00	6.96	C- / 3.8	0.43%	B / 8.4
2010	C+	232.78	6.80	C / 4.6	-1.88%	B- / 7.6
2009	C+	230.65	7.45	C / 4.9	0.84%	B- / 7.5

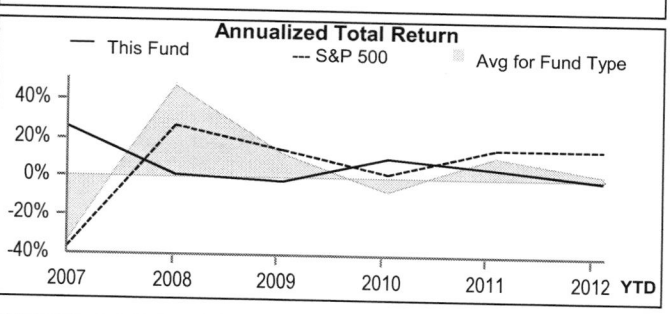

MFS High Inc Muni Tr (CXE)

B+   **Good**

Fund Family: MFS Investment Management
Fund Type: Municipal - High Yield
Inception Date: February 16, 1989

Major Rating Factors: Strong performance is the major factor driving the B+ (Good) TheStreet.com Investment Rating for MFS High Inc Muni Tr. The fund currently has a performance rating of B (Good) based on an annualized return of 13.30% over the last three years and a total return of 4.21% year to date 2012. Factored into the performance evaluation is an expense ratio of 1.45% (average).

    The fund's risk rating is currently B (Good). It carries a beta of 1.91, meaning it is expected to move 19.1% for every 10% move in the market. Volatility, as measured by both the semi-deviation and a drawdown factor, is considered low. As of December 31, 2012, MFS High Inc Muni Tr traded at a discount of 1.97% below its net asset value, which is better than its one-year historical average premium of 6.00%.

    Gary A. Lasman has been running the fund for 6 years and currently receives a manager quality ranking of 48 (0=worst, 99=best). If you desire only a moderate level of risk and strong performance, then this fund is an excellent option.

Data Date	Investment Rating	Net Assets ($Mil)	Price	Perfor-mance Rating/Pts	Total Return Y-T-D	Risk Rating/Pts
12-12	B+	163.71	5.46	B / 8.1	4.21%	B / 8.6
2011	A+	152.20	5.35	A+ / 9.9	-1.12%	B / 8.7
2010	D+	153.04	4.71	C- / 3.2	5.60%	C / 5.0
2009	C	134.11	4.83	C / 5.1	75.05%	C / 5.4

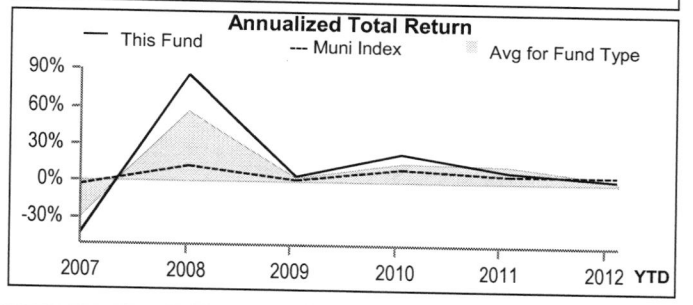

MFS High Yield Muni Trust (CMU)

B+   **Good**

Fund Family: MFS Investment Management
Fund Type: Municipal - High Yield
Inception Date: March 19, 1987

Major Rating Factors: Strong performance is the major factor driving the B+ (Good) TheStreet.com Investment Rating for MFS High Yield Muni Trust. The fund currently has a performance rating of B (Good) based on an annualized return of 12.54% over the last three years and a total return of 5.14% year to date 2012. Factored into the performance evaluation is an expense ratio of 1.33% (average).

    The fund's risk rating is currently B (Good). It carries a beta of 1.63, meaning it is expected to move 16.3% for every 10% move in the market. Volatility, as measured by both the semi-deviation and a drawdown factor, is considered low. As of December 31, 2012, MFS High Yield Muni Trust traded at a discount of 2.80% below its net asset value, which is better than its one-year historical average premium of 6.45%.

    Gary A. Lasman has been running the fund for 6 years and currently receives a manager quality ranking of 58 (0=worst, 99=best). If you desire only a moderate level of risk and strong performance, then this fund is an excellent option.

Data Date	Investment Rating	Net Assets ($Mil)	Price	Perfor-mance Rating/Pts	Total Return Y-T-D	Risk Rating/Pts
12-12	B+	132.05	4.86	B / 7.8	5.14%	B / 8.6
2011	A+	122.30	4.71	A+ / 9.8	1.06%	B / 8.8
2010	C-	122.46	4.32	C- / 3.7	5.92%	C+ / 5.7
2009	C	106.85	4.42	C / 5.2	65.78%	C+ / 5.7

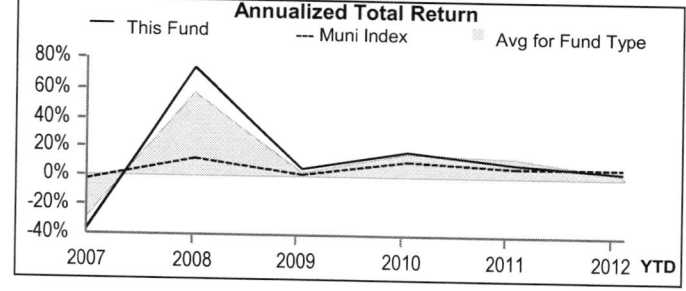

MFS Interm High Inc (CIF)

B   **Good**

Fund Family: MFS Investment Management
Fund Type: Corporate - High Yield
Inception Date: July 21, 1988

Major Rating Factors: Strong performance is the major factor driving the B (Good) TheStreet.com Investment Rating for MFS Interm High Inc. The fund currently has a performance rating of B- (Good) based on an annualized return of 17.51% over the last three years and a total return of 5.86% year to date 2012. Factored into the performance evaluation is an expense ratio of 1.74% (above average).

The fund's risk rating is currently B (Good). It carries a beta of 1.11, meaning it is expected to move 11.1% for every 10% move in the market. Volatility, as measured by both the semi-deviation and a drawdown factor, is considered low. As of December 31, 2012, MFS Interm High Inc traded at a discount of 3.76% below its net asset value, which is better than its one-year historical average premium of 2.80%.

David P. Cole has been running the fund for 6 years and currently receives a manager quality ranking of 49 (0=worst, 99=best). If you desire only a moderate level of risk and strong performance, then this fund is an excellent option.

Data Date	Investment Rating	Net Assets ($Mil)	Price	Performance Rating/Pts	Total Return Y-T-D	Risk Rating/Pts
12-12	B	61.96	3.07	B- / 7.2	5.86%	B / 8.7
2011	B+	60.50	2.94	B+ / 8.7	-0.34%	B- / 7.8
2010	C	58.49	2.95	B / 8.0	14.37%	C- / 3.0
2009	C	45.51	2.87	B / 7.9	82.47%	D+ / 2.8

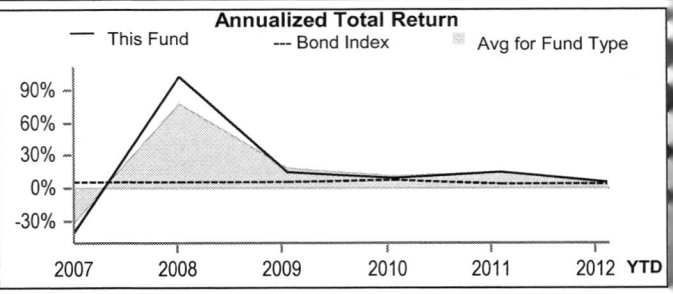

MFS Intermediate Income Trust (MIN)

C-   **Fair**

Fund Family: MFS Investment Management
Fund Type: Global
Inception Date: March 10, 1988

Major Rating Factors:
Disappointing performance is the major factor driving the C- (Fair) TheStreet.com Investment Rating for MFS Intermediate Income Trust. The fund currently has a performance rating of D+ (Weak) based on an annualized return of 6.88% over the last three years and a total return of -0.31% year to date 2012. Factored into the performance evaluation is an expense ratio of 0.71% (very low).

The fund's risk rating is currently B (Good). It carries a beta of 0.21, meaning the fund's expected move will be 2.1% for every 10% move in the market. Volatility, as measured by both the semi-deviation and a drawdown factor, is considered low. As of December 31, 2012, MFS Intermediate Income Trust traded at a premium of 4.04% above its net asset value, which is worse than its one-year historical average premium of 3.58%.

James J. Calmas has been running the fund for 11 years and currently receives a manager quality ranking of 84 (0=worst, 99=best). This fund offers only a moderate level of risk but investors looking for strong performance are still waiting.

Data Date	Investment Rating	Net Assets ($Mil)	Price	Performance Rating/Pts	Total Return Y-T-D	Risk Rating/Pts
12-12	C-	745.54	6.44	D+ / 2.9	-0.31%	B / 8.5
2011	C	735.30	6.30	C- / 4.1	0.00%	B / 8.7
2010	B-	792.81	6.31	C+ / 6.4	2.59%	B- / 7.6
2009	B-	774.71	6.70	C / 5.0	15.12%	B- / 7.9

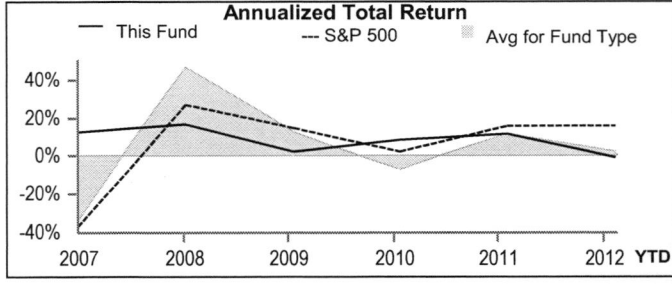

MFS InterMkt Inc Tr I (CMK)

C   **Fair**

Fund Family: MFS Investment Management
Fund Type: Global
Inception Date: September 22, 1989

Major Rating Factors: Middle of the road best describes MFS InterMkt Inc Tr I whose TheStreet.com Investment Rating is currently a C (Fair). The fund currently has a performance rating of C- (Fair) based on an annualized return of 8.93% over the last three years and a total return of 0.11% year to date 2012. Factored into the performance evaluation is an expense ratio of 1.12% (low).

The fund's risk rating is currently B (Good). It carries a beta of 0.41, meaning the fund's expected move will be 4.1% for every 10% move in the market. Volatility, as measured by both the semi-deviation and a drawdown factor, is considered low. As of December 31, 2012, MFS InterMkt Inc Tr I traded at a discount of 7.86% below its net asset value, which is worse than its one-year historical average discount of 8.02%.

James J. Calmas has been running the fund for 6 years and currently receives a manager quality ranking of 86 (0=worst, 99=best). If you desire an average level of risk, then this fund may be an option.

Data Date	Investment Rating	Net Assets ($Mil)	Price	Performance Rating/Pts	Total Return Y-T-D	Risk Rating/Pts
12-12	C	99.99	8.79	C- / 3.7	0.11%	B / 8.9
2011	C+	98.10	8.26	C / 4.6	-1.21%	B+ / 9.5
2010	B+	96.05	8.43	B- / 7.0	12.12%	C+ / 6.4
2009	C+	87.57	8.00	C / 4.7	18.49%	B- / 7.0

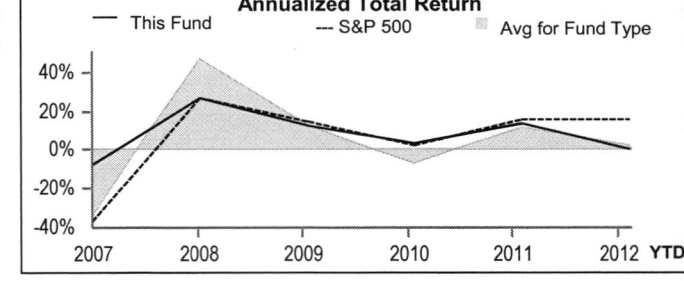

MFS Invst Gr Muni Tr (CXH)   B-   Good

Fund Family: MFS Investment Management
Fund Type: Municipal - National
Inception Date: May 19, 1989

Major Rating Factors: MFS Invst Gr Muni Tr receives a TheStreet.com Investment Rating of B- (Good). The fund currently has a performance rating of C+ (Fair) based on an annualized return of 11.55% over the last three years and a total return of 2.58% year to date 2012. Factored into the performance evaluation is an expense ratio of 1.21% (average).

The fund's risk rating is currently B (Good). It carries a beta of 2.13, meaning it is expected to move 21.3% for every 10% move in the market. Volatility, as measured by both the semi-deviation and a drawdown factor, is considered low. As of December 31, 2012, MFS Invst Gr Muni Tr traded at a discount of 3.33% below its net asset value, which is better than its one-year historical average premium of 3.07%.

Geoffrey L. Schechter has been running the fund for 6 years and currently receives a manager quality ranking of 31 (0=worst, 99=best). If you desire an average level of risk, then this fund may be an option.

Data Date	Investment Rating	Net Assets ($Mil)	Price	Performance Rating/Pts	Total Return Y-T-D	Risk Rating/Pts
12-12	B-	118.72	10.46	C+ / 6.2	2.58%	B / 8.6
2011	A	111.90	9.76	A- / 9.2	1.64%	B / 8.8
2010	C-	111.17	8.82	C- / 3.8	1.97%	C+ / 5.9
2009	C+	101.79	9.26	C+ / 6.9	56.01%	C+ / 6.3

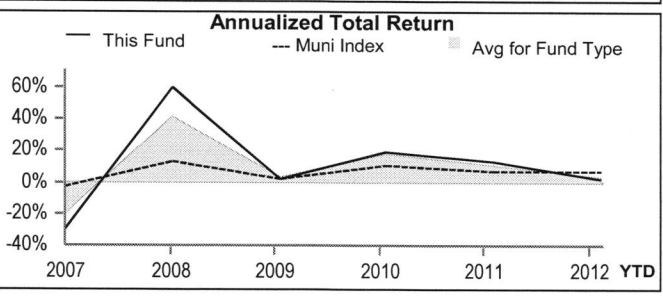

MFS Multimarket Income Trust (MMT)   C+   Fair

Fund Family: MFS Investment Management
Fund Type: General Bond
Inception Date: March 5, 1987

Major Rating Factors: Middle of the road best describes MFS Multimarket Income Trust whose TheStreet.com Investment Rating is currently a C+ (Fair). The fund currently has a performance rating of C (Fair) based on an annualized return of 11.91% over the last three years and a total return of 1.24% year to date 2012. Factored into the performance evaluation is an expense ratio of 1.12% (low).

The fund's risk rating is currently B (Good). It carries a beta of 0.31, meaning the fund's expected move will be 3.1% for every 10% move in the market. Volatility, as measured by both the semi-deviation and a drawdown factor, is considered low. As of December 31, 2012, MFS Multimarket Income Trust traded at a discount of 6.31% below its net asset value, which is better than its one-year historical average discount of 4.85%.

Richard O. Hawkins currently receives a manager quality ranking of 90 (0=worst, 99=best). If you desire an average level of risk, then this fund may be an option.

Data Date	Investment Rating	Net Assets ($Mil)	Price	Performance Rating/Pts	Total Return Y-T-D	Risk Rating/Pts
12-12	C+	564.45	7.28	C / 4.9	1.24%	B / 8.5
2011	B	558.30	6.72	C+ / 6.6	0.89%	B+ / 9.0
2010	B+	563.16	6.90	B / 8.2	15.16%	C+ / 5.8
2009	C+	466.51	6.50	C+ / 6.6	40.23%	C+ / 5.9

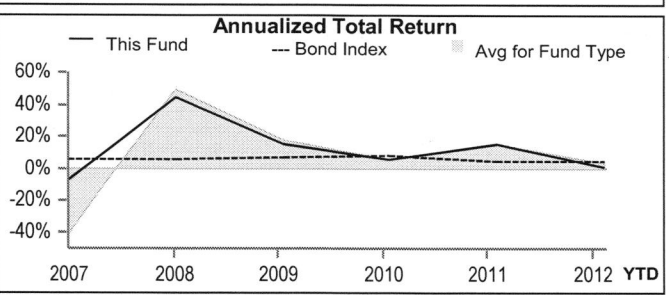

MFS Municipal Income Trust (MFM)   B+   Good

Fund Family: MFS Investment Management
Fund Type: Municipal - National
Inception Date: November 18, 1986

Major Rating Factors: Strong performance is the major factor driving the B+ (Good) TheStreet.com Investment Rating for MFS Municipal Income Trust. The fund currently has a performance rating of B- (Good) based on an annualized return of 11.65% over the last three years and a total return of 2.89% year to date 2012. Factored into the performance evaluation is an expense ratio of 1.42% (average).

The fund's risk rating is currently B (Good). It carries a beta of 1.57, meaning it is expected to move 15.7% for every 10% move in the market. Volatility, as measured by both the semi-deviation and a drawdown factor, is considered low. As of December 31, 2012, MFS Municipal Income Trust traded at a premium of .79% above its net asset value, which is better than its one-year historical average premium of 5.30%.

Geoffrey L. Schechter has been running the fund for 20 years and currently receives a manager quality ranking of 62 (0=worst, 99=best). If you desire only a moderate level of risk and strong performance, then this fund is an excellent option.

Data Date	Investment Rating	Net Assets ($Mil)	Price	Performance Rating/Pts	Total Return Y-T-D	Risk Rating/Pts
12-12	B+	271.03	7.62	B- / 7.5	2.89%	B / 8.6
2011	A+	274.80	7.11	A+ / 9.7	0.41%	B / 8.7
2010	C	273.60	6.41	C / 4.6	1.91%	C+ / 6.3
2009	B	221.67	6.78	B / 7.6	70.48%	C+ / 5.9

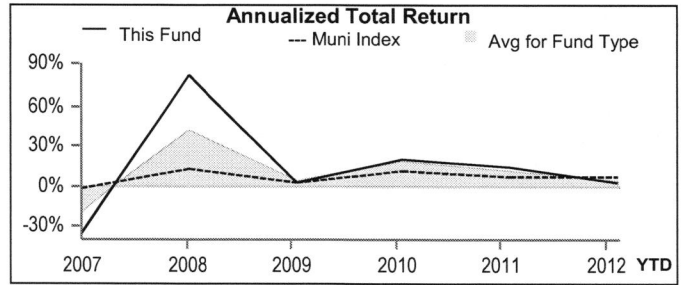

MFS Special Value Trust (MFV)

C   **Fair**

Fund Family: MFS Investment Management
Fund Type: Growth and Income
Inception Date: November 17, 1989

Data Date	Investment Rating	Net Assets ($Mil)	Price	Performance Rating/Pts	Total Return Y-T-D	Risk Rating/Pts
12-12	C	46.44	6.91	C / 5.2	6.93%	B- / 7.8
2011	B	45.70	6.43	B- / 7.5	3.11%	B- / 7.9
2010	C	49.44	7.38	C+ / 6.6	15.54%	C- / 3.8
2009	C-	36.38	7.03	C+ / 5.7	91.76%	C- / 4.0

Major Rating Factors: Middle of the road best describes MFS Special Value Trust whose TheStreet.com Investment Rating is currently a C (Fair). The fund currently has a performance rating of C (Fair) based on an annualized return of 12.54% over the last three years and a total return of 6.93% year to date 2012. Factored into the performance evaluation is an expense ratio of 1.39% (average).

The fund's risk rating is currently B- (Good). It carries a beta of 0.36, meaning the fund's expected move will be 3.6% for every 10% move in the market. Volatility, as measured by both the semi-deviation and a drawdown factor, is considered low. As of December 31, 2012, MFS Special Value Trust traded at a discount of 1.57% below its net asset value, which is better than its one-year historical average premium of 4.82%.

David P. Cole currently receives a manager quality ranking of 81 (0=worst, 99=best). If you desire an average level of risk, then this fund may be an option.

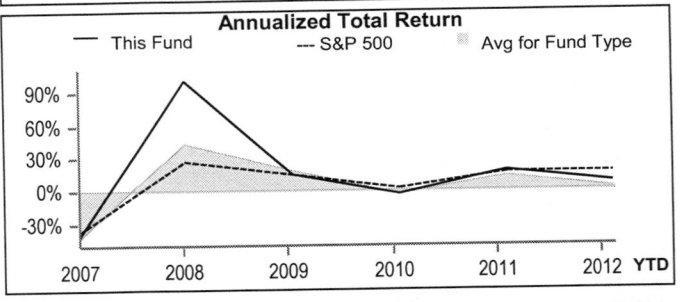

Annualized Total Return

Minnesota Municipal Inc Portfolio (MXA)

B   **Good**

Fund Family: US Bancorp Asset Management Inc
Fund Type: Municipal - Single State
Inception Date: June 18, 1993

Data Date	Investment Rating	Net Assets ($Mil)	Price	Performance Rating/Pts	Total Return Y-T-D	Risk Rating/Pts
12-12	B	67.00	17.17	C+ / 6.3	3.26%	B / 8.8
2011	A+	62.70	16.78	A+ / 9.7	0.70%	B+ / 9.0
2010	A-	63.00	14.36	B / 7.7	4.57%	C+ / 6.9
2009	A-	55.51	14.60	B- / 7.5	49.11%	C+ / 6.8

Major Rating Factors: Minnesota Municipal Inc Portfolio receives a TheStreet.com Investment Rating of B (Good). The fund currently has a performance rating of C+ (Fair) based on an annualized return of 10.72% over the last three years and a total return of 3.26% year to date 2012. Factored into the performance evaluation is an expense ratio of 1.42% (average).

The fund's risk rating is currently B (Good). It carries a beta of 1.76, meaning it is expected to move 17.6% for every 10% move in the market. Volatility, as measured by both the semi-deviation and a drawdown factor, is considered low. As of December 31, 2012, Minnesota Municipal Inc Portfolio traded at a premium of 5.66% above its net asset value, which is better than its one-year historical average premium of 8.48%.

James D. Palmer currently receives a manager quality ranking of 54 (0=worst, 99=best). If you desire an average level of risk, then this fund may be an option.

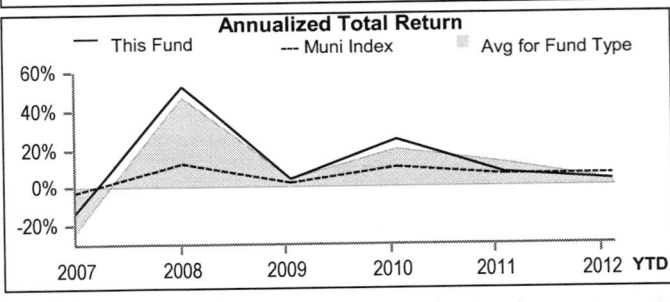

Annualized Total Return

Minnesota Municipal Income Fund II (MXN)

B+   **Good**

Fund Family: US Bancorp Asset Management Inc
Fund Type: Municipal - Single State
Inception Date: October 30, 2002

Data Date	Investment Rating	Net Assets ($Mil)	Price	Performance Rating/Pts	Total Return Y-T-D	Risk Rating/Pts
12-12	B+	23.00	16.15	B- / 7.1	5.94%	B+ / 9.0
2011	A+	22.10	16.68	A- / 9.0	-2.58%	B+ / 9.2
2010	A+	22.00	15.02	B+ / 8.4	6.58%	B- / 7.8
2009	A+	19.64	14.89	B / 7.9	53.71%	B- / 7.0

Major Rating Factors: Strong performance is the major factor driving the B+ (Good) TheStreet.com Investment Rating for Minnesota Municipal Income Fund II. The fund currently has a performance rating of B- (Good) based on an annualized return of 11.41% over the last three years and a total return of 5.94% year to date 2012. Factored into the performance evaluation is an expense ratio of 2.45% (high).

The fund's risk rating is currently B+ (Good). It carries a beta of 0.93, meaning that its performance tracks fairly well with that of the overall stock market. Volatility, as measured by both the semi-deviation and a drawdown factor, is considered very low. As of December 31, 2012, Minnesota Municipal Income Fund II traded at a premium of 2.02% above its net asset value, which is better than its one-year historical average premium of 7.42%.

James D. Palmer currently receives a manager quality ranking of 70 (0=worst, 99=best). If you desire only a moderate level of risk and strong performance, then this fund is an excellent option.

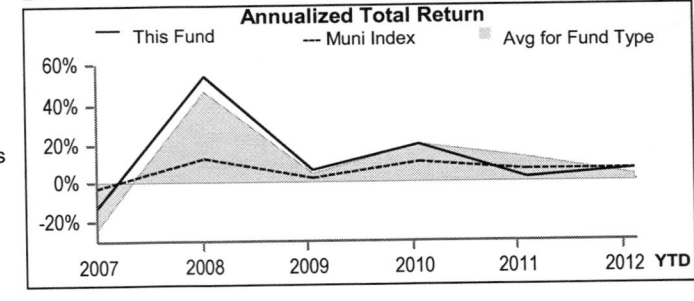

Annualized Total Return

Montgomery Street Inc. Sec. (MTS)

C+   **Fair**

Fund Family: PIMCO
Fund Type: General - Investment Grade
Inception Date: January 31, 1973

Major Rating Factors: Middle of the road best describes Montgomery Street Inc. Sec. whose TheStreet.com Investment Rating is currently a C+ (Fair). The fund currently has a performance rating of C (Fair) based on an annualized return of 10.05% over the last three years and a total return of 1.54% year to date 2012. Factored into the performance evaluation is an expense ratio of 0.71% (very low).

The fund's risk rating is currently B+ (Good). It carries a beta of 0.81, meaning the fund's expected move will be 8.1% for every 10% move in the market. Volatility, as measured by both the semi-deviation and a drawdown factor, is considered very low. As of December 31, 2012, Montgomery Street Inc. Sec. traded at a discount of 8.50% below its net asset value, which is worse than its one-year historical average discount of 9.16%.

Mark R. Kiesel currently receives a manager quality ranking of 78 (0=worst, 99=best). If you desire an average level of risk, then this fund may be an option.

Data Date	Investment Rating	Net Assets ($Mil)	Price	Performance Rating/Pts	Total Return Y-T-D	Risk Rating/Pts
12-12	C+	185.00	16.90	C / 4.7	1.54%	B+ / 9.5
2011	C	178.00	15.43	C- / 3.5	-0.13%	B+ / 9.4
2010	C+	170.34	15.78	C / 4.9	12.49%	B- / 7.1
2009	C	164.93	14.68	D+ / 2.9	9.05%	B / 8.0

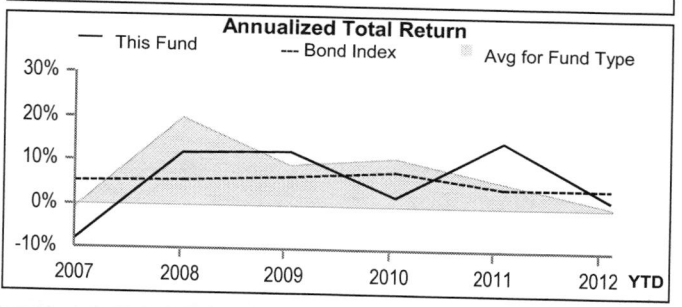

Annualized Total Return — This Fund, Bond Index, Avg for Fund Type

Morgan Stanley Asia Pacific Fund (APF)

D+   **Weak**

Fund Family: Morgan Stanley Investment Managemen
Fund Type: Foreign
Inception Date: July 25, 1994

Major Rating Factors: Morgan Stanley Asia Pacific Fund receives a TheStreet.com Investment Rating of D+ (Weak). The fund currently has a performance rating of C- (Fair) based on an annualized return of 4.35% over the last three years and a total return of 3.94% year to date 2012. Factored into the performance evaluation is an expense ratio of 1.22% (average).

The fund's risk rating is currently B- (Good). It carries a beta of 0.93, meaning that its performance tracks fairly well with that of the overall stock market. Volatility, as measured by both the semi-deviation and a drawdown factor, is considered low. As of December 31, 2012, Morgan Stanley Asia Pacific Fund traded at a discount of 14.11% below its net asset value, which is better than its one-year historical average discount of 10.90%.

John A. R. Pollock currently receives a manager quality ranking of 57 (0=worst, 99=best). If you desire an average level of risk, then this fund may be an option.

Data Date	Investment Rating	Net Assets ($Mil)	Price	Performance Rating/Pts	Total Return Y-T-D	Risk Rating/Pts
12-12	D+	301.88	14.98	C- / 3.1	3.94%	B- / 7.1
2011	C-	306.30	13.10	C- / 3.6	2.29%	C+ / 6.8
2010	C-	484.77	16.98	C / 5.5	17.90%	C- / 3.9
2009	C-	475.59	14.65	C / 4.8	32.84%	C / 4.3

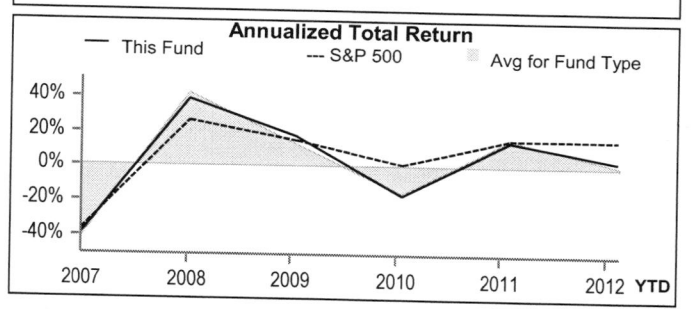

Annualized Total Return — This Fund, S&P 500, Avg for Fund Type

Morgan Stanley China A Share Fund (CAF)

D   **Weak**

Fund Family: Morgan Stanley Investment Managemen
Fund Type: Foreign
Inception Date: September 28, 2006

Major Rating Factors: Morgan Stanley China A Share Fund receives a TheStreet.com Investment Rating of D (Weak). The fund currently has a performance rating of C- (Fair) based on an annualized return of 1.07% over the last three years and a total return of -0.25% year to date 2012. Factored into the performance evaluation is an expense ratio of 2.13% (high).

The fund's risk rating is currently C+ (Fair). It carries a beta of 0.95, meaning that its performance tracks fairly well with that of the overall stock market. Volatility, as measured by both the semi-deviation and a drawdown factor, is considered low. As of December 31, 2012, Morgan Stanley China A Share Fund traded at a premium of 4.16% above its net asset value, which is worse than its one-year historical average discount of 7.37%.

Gary Cheung currently receives a manager quality ranking of 24 (0=worst, 99=best). If you desire an average level of risk, then this fund may be an option.

Data Date	Investment Rating	Net Assets ($Mil)	Price	Performance Rating/Pts	Total Return Y-T-D	Risk Rating/Pts
12-12	D	491.37	24.05	C- / 3.2	-0.25%	C+ / 5.8
2011	D	493.20	19.35	D+ / 2.5	2.02%	C / 5.3
2010	D	397.04	27.35	C- / 3.9	-0.73%	C- / 3.3
2009	C	531.73	31.37	B / 8.0	59.50%	C- / 3.3

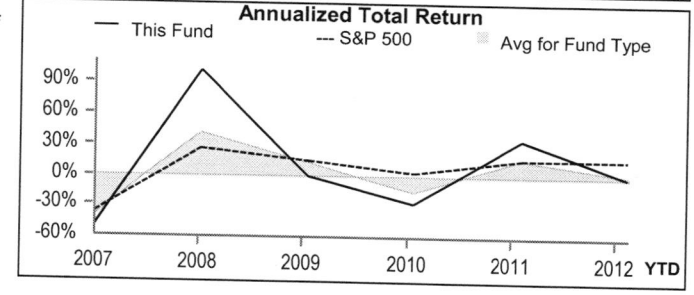

Annualized Total Return — This Fund, S&P 500, Avg for Fund Type

Morgan Stanley Eastern Europe (RNE)

D+   **Weak**

Fund Family: Morgan Stanley Investment Managemen
Fund Type: Foreign
Inception Date: September 24, 1996

Major Rating Factors: Morgan Stanley Eastern Europe receives a TheStreet.com Investment Rating of D+ (Weak). The fund currently has a performance rating of C- (Fair) based on an annualized return of 1.55% over the last three years and a total return of 1.83% year to date 2012. Factored into the performance evaluation is an expense ratio of 2.01% (high).

The fund's risk rating is currently C+ (Fair). It carries a beta of 1.34, meaning it is expected to move 13.4% for every 10% move in the market. Volatility, as measured by both the semi-deviation and a drawdown factor, is considered low. As of December 31, 2012, Morgan Stanley Eastern Europe traded at a discount of 12.02% below its net asset value, which is better than its one-year historical average discount of 10.86%.

Eric J. Carlson has been running the fund for 17 years and currently receives a manager quality ranking of 34 (0=worst, 99=best). If you desire an average level of risk, then this fund may be an option.

Data Date	Investment Rating	Net Assets ($Mil)	Price	Performance Rating/Pts	Total Return Y-T-D	Risk Rating/Pts
12-12	D+	67.52	17.13	C- / 3.4	1.83%	C+ / 6.3
2011	C-	63.60	13.46	C- / 3.6	1.82%	B- / 7.2
2010	E+	65.42	18.95	E+ / 0.9	21.09%	C- / 3.5
2009	E+	49.14	15.65	D+ / 2.7	77.65%	D+ / 2.6

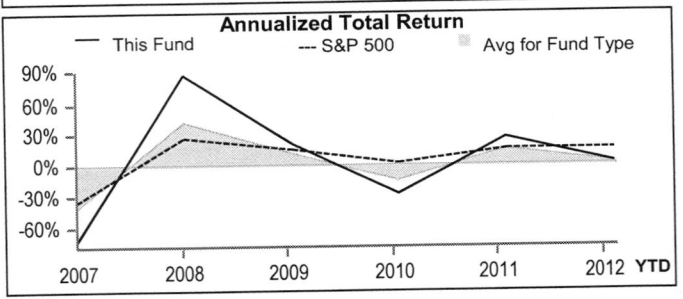
Annualized Total Return

Morgan Stanley Emerging Markets (MSF)

C-   **Fair**

Fund Family: Morgan Stanley Investment Managemen
Fund Type: Emerging Market
Inception Date: October 25, 1991

Major Rating Factors: Middle of the road best describes Morgan Stanley Emerging Markets whose TheStreet.com Investment Rating is currently a C- (Fair). The fund currently has a performance rating of C- (Fair) based on an annualized return of 4.51% over the last three years and a total return of 2.84% year to date 2012. Factored into the performance evaluation is an expense ratio of 1.50% (average).

The fund's risk rating is currently B- (Good). It carries a beta of 0.97, meaning that its performance tracks fairly well with that of the overall stock market. Volatility, as measured by both the semi-deviation and a drawdown factor, is considered low. As of December 31, 2012, Morgan Stanley Emerging Markets traded at a discount of 11.33% below its net asset value, which is better than its one-year historical average discount of 9.71%.

Ruchir Sharma has been running the fund for 22 years and currently receives a manager quality ranking of 44 (0=worst, 99=best). If you desire an average level of risk, then this fund may be an option.

Data Date	Investment Rating	Net Assets ($Mil)	Price	Performance Rating/Pts	Total Return Y-T-D	Risk Rating/Pts
12-12	C-	262.63	15.50	C- / 3.9	2.84%	B- / 7.3
2011	C-	248.00	12.92	C / 4.5	1.32%	B- / 7.5
2010	D	240.63	16.36	C / 4.5	17.74%	D+ / 2.7
2009	C	200.61	13.97	C+ / 6.9	62.20%	C- / 3.5

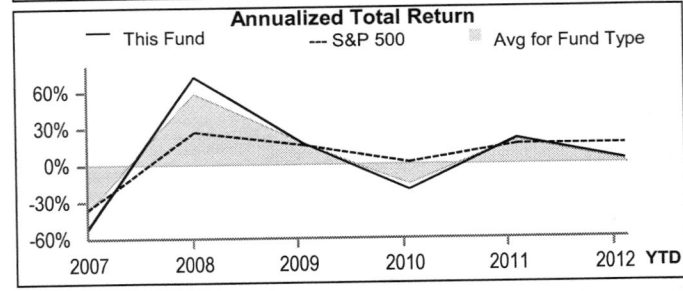
Annualized Total Return

Morgan Stanley Emerging Mkts Debt (MSD)

B-   **Good**

Fund Family: Morgan Stanley Investment Managemen
Fund Type: Emerging Market
Inception Date: July 16, 1993

Major Rating Factors: Morgan Stanley Emerging Mkts Debt receives a TheStreet.com Investment Rating of B- (Good). The fund currently has a performance rating of C+ (Fair) based on an annualized return of 13.70% over the last three years and a total return of 3.35% year to date 2012. Factored into the performance evaluation is an expense ratio of 1.12% (low).

The fund's risk rating is currently B (Good). It carries a beta of 0.98, meaning that its performance tracks fairly well with that of the overall stock market. Volatility, as measured by both the semi-deviation and a drawdown factor, is considered low. As of December 31, 2012, Morgan Stanley Emerging Mkts Debt traded at a discount of 8.29% below its net asset value, which is better than its one-year historical average discount of 8.16%.

Eric J. Baurmeister has been running the fund for 11 years and currently receives a manager quality ranking of 89 (0=worst, 99=best). If you desire an average level of risk, then this fund may be an option.

Data Date	Investment Rating	Net Assets ($Mil)	Price	Performance Rating/Pts	Total Return Y-T-D	Risk Rating/Pts
12-12	B-	286.47	11.95	C+ / 6.9	3.35%	B / 8.2
2011	B-	273.30	10.41	C+ / 6.8	0.00%	B / 8.1
2010	B-	267.21	10.48	B- / 7.5	13.75%	C / 5.1
2009	C+	210.80	10.08	C+ / 6.5	47.43%	C+ / 6.2

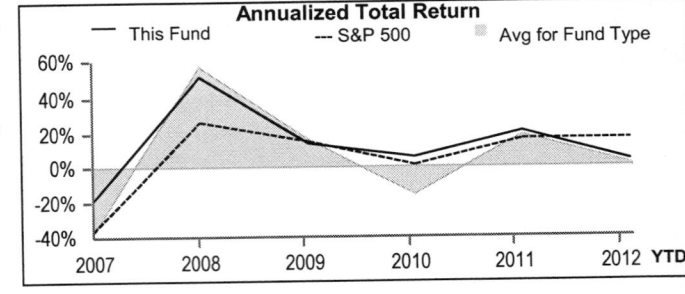
Annualized Total Return

Morgan Stanley Emg Mkts Dom Debt (EDD)

C+   Fair

Fund Family: Morgan Stanley Investment Managemen
Fund Type: Emerging Market
Inception Date: April 24, 2007

Major Rating Factors: Middle of the road best describes Morgan Stanley Emg Mkts Dom Debt whose TheStreet.com Investment Rating is currently a C+ (Fair). The fund currently has a performance rating of C+ (Fair) based on an annualized return of 13.71% over the last three years and a total return of 2.85% year to date 2012. Factored into the performance evaluation is an expense ratio of 2.16% (high).

The fund's risk rating is currently B- (Good). It carries a beta of 1.53, meaning it is expected to move 15.3% for every 10% move in the market. Volatility, as measured by both the semi-deviation and a drawdown factor, is considered low. As of December 31, 2012, Morgan Stanley Emg Mkts Dom Debt traded at a discount of 9.56% below its net asset value, which is better than its one-year historical average discount of 6.73%.

Eric J. Baurmeister has been running the fund for 6 years and currently receives a manager quality ranking of 87 (0=worst, 99=best). If you desire an average level of risk, then this fund may be an option.

Data Date	Investment Rating	Net Assets ($Mil)	Price	Performance Rating/Pts	Total Return Y-T-D	Risk Rating/Pts
12-12	C+	1,283.10	16.84	C+ / 6.6	2.85%	B- / 7.6
2011	C	1,153.50	14.15	C / 5.4	4.95%	B- / 7.6
2010	B+	1,264.52	16.15	B / 7.6	27.14%	C+ / 5.8
2009	B+	1,029.18	13.68	B / 8.2	36.17%	C+ / 5.6

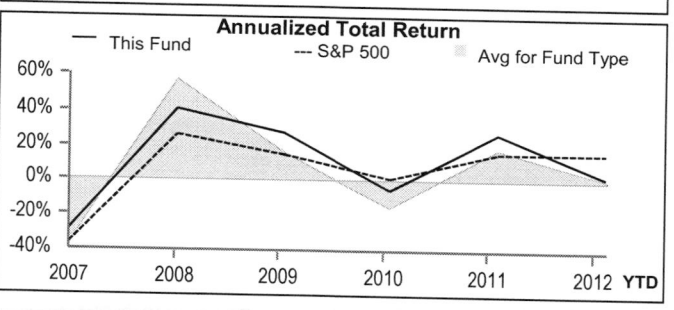

Morgan Stanley Income Sec (ICB)

C   Fair

Fund Family: Morgan Stanley Investment Advisors
Fund Type: General Bond
Inception Date: April 6, 1973

Major Rating Factors: Middle of the road best describes Morgan Stanley Income Sec whose TheStreet.com Investment Rating is currently a C (Fair). The fund currently has a performance rating of C- (Fair) based on an annualized return of 10.03% over the last three years and a total return of 0.60% year to date 2012. Factored into the performance evaluation is an expense ratio of 0.63% (very low).

The fund's risk rating is currently B+ (Good). It carries a beta of 0.87, meaning the fund's expected move will be 8.7% for every 10% move in the market. Volatility, as measured by both the semi-deviation and a drawdown factor, is considered very low. As of December 31, 2012, Morgan Stanley Income Sec traded at a discount of 6.77% below its net asset value, which is better than its one-year historical average discount of 4.56%.

Joseph M. Mehlman has been running the fund for 5 years and currently receives a manager quality ranking of 79 (0=worst, 99=best). If you desire an average level of risk, then this fund may be an option.

Data Date	Investment Rating	Net Assets ($Mil)	Price	Performance Rating/Pts	Total Return Y-T-D	Risk Rating/Pts
12-12	C	176.50	18.46	C- / 3.6	0.60%	B+ / 9.0
2011	B-	164.40	17.34	C / 5.4	1.04%	B+ / 9.1
2010	C+	165.95	16.83	C+ / 6.4	11.35%	C+ / 6.4
2009	C+	155.32	16.01	C / 4.7	18.94%	B- / 7.6

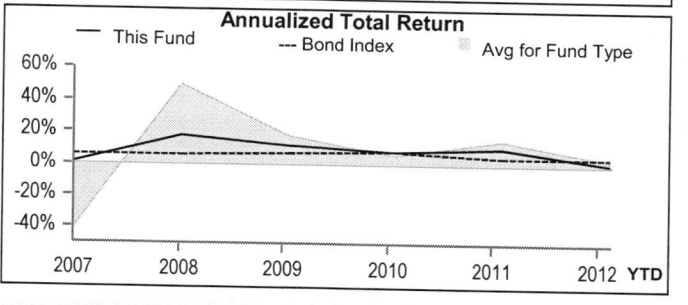

Morgan Stanley India Inv Fund (IIF)

D-   Weak

Fund Family: Morgan Stanley Investment Managemen
Fund Type: Foreign
Inception Date: February 17, 1994

Major Rating Factors:
Disappointing performance is the major factor driving the D- (Weak) TheStreet.com Investment Rating for Morgan Stanley India Inv Fund. The fund currently has a performance rating of D (Weak) based on an annualized return of -2.71% over the last three years and a total return of 0.27% year to date 2012. Factored into the performance evaluation is an expense ratio of 1.34% (average).

The fund's risk rating is currently C (Fair). It carries a beta of 1.03, meaning that its performance tracks fairly well with that of the overall stock market. Volatility, as measured by both the semi-deviation and a drawdown factor, is considered average. As of December 31, 2012, Morgan Stanley India Inv Fund traded at a discount of 10.44% below its net asset value, which is worse than its one-year historical average discount of 10.86%.

Ruchir Sharma has been running the fund for 19 years and currently receives a manager quality ranking of 20 (0=worst, 99=best). This fund offers an average level of risk but investors looking for strong performance will be frustrated.

Data Date	Investment Rating	Net Assets ($Mil)	Price	Performance Rating/Pts	Total Return Y-T-D	Risk Rating/Pts
12-12	D-	378.12	18.53	D / 1.9	0.27%	C / 5.2
2011	D-	350.00	14.01	D / 1.8	2.43%	C / 5.3
2010	D-	553.10	25.65	C- / 3.2	24.45%	D / 2.2
2009	D	372.04	22.61	C / 4.7	68.48%	D+ / 2.3

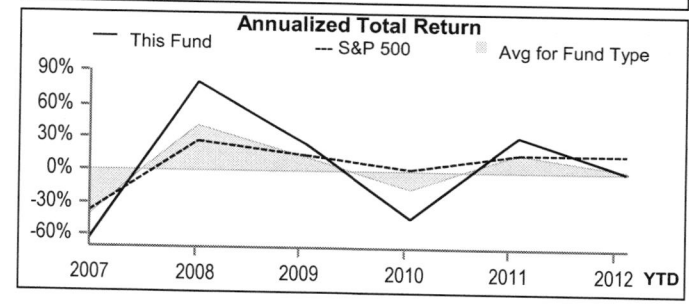

Nasdaq Premium Income & Growth Fun (QQQX)

C+   **Fair**

Fund Family: Nuveen Fund Advisors Inc
Fund Type: Income
Inception Date: January 30, 2007

Data Date	Investment Rating	Net Assets ($Mil)	Price	Performance Rating/Pts	Total Return Y-T-D	Risk Rating/Pts
12-12	C+	260.18	15.17	B- / 7.0	5.80%	B- / 7.0
2011	C+	260.20	12.97	B- / 7.3	4.93%	C+ / 6.9
2010	C-	259.73	14.10	C+ / 6.0	7.51%	C- / 4.0
2009	B+	229.87	14.41	A / 9.4	66.91%	C / 4.6

Major Rating Factors: Strong performance is the major factor driving the C+ (Fair) TheStreet.com Investment Rating for Nasdaq Premium Income & Growth Fun. The fund currently has a performance rating of B- (Good) based on an annualized return of 14.47% over the last three years and a total return of 5.80% year to date 2012. Factored into the performance evaluation is an expense ratio of 1.04% (low).

The fund's risk rating is currently B- (Good). It carries a beta of 1.00, meaning that its performance tracks fairly well with that of the overall stock market. Volatility, as measured by both the semi-deviation and a drawdown factor, is considered low. As of December 31, 2012, Nasdaq Premium Income & Growth Fun traded at a discount of 3.19% below its net asset value, which is better than its one-year historical average discount of 1.67%.

David A. Friar has been running the fund for 2 years and currently receives a manager quality ranking of 53 (0=worst, 99=best). If you desire only a moderate level of risk and strong performance, then this fund is an excellent option.

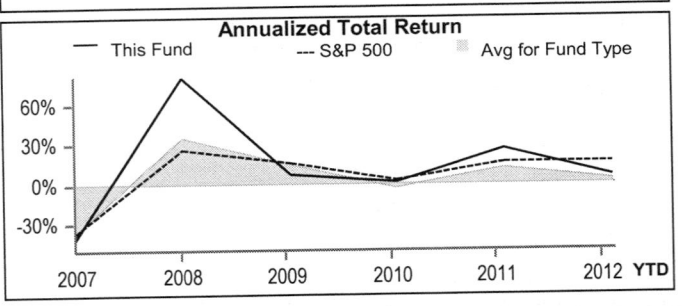

Neuberger Berman CA Inter Muni Fun (NBW)

B+   **Good**

Fund Family: Neuberger Berman Management LLC
Fund Type: Municipal - Single State
Inception Date: September 24, 2002

Data Date	Investment Rating	Net Assets ($Mil)	Price	Performance Rating/Pts	Total Return Y-T-D	Risk Rating/Pts
12-12	B+	83.10	15.50	B- / 7.2	2.90%	B+ / 9.1
2011	A-	84.70	15.27	B / 8.2	-0.24%	B+ / 9.2
2010	A-	59.54	14.34	B / 7.7	13.94%	C+ / 6.8
2009	B	92.34	13.27	C / 5.3	31.32%	B- / 7.9

Major Rating Factors: Strong performance is the major factor driving the B+ (Good) TheStreet.com Investment Rating for Neuberger Berman CA Inter Muni Fun. The fund currently has a performance rating of B- (Good) based on an annualized return of 12.38% over the last three years and a total return of 2.90% year to date 2012. Factored into the performance evaluation is an expense ratio of 1.29% (average).

The fund's risk rating is currently B+ (Good). It carries a beta of 1.32, meaning it is expected to move 13.2% for every 10% move in the market. Volatility, as measured by both the semi-deviation and a drawdown factor, is considered very low. As of December 31, 2012, Neuberger Berman CA Inter Muni Fun traded at a discount of 2.15% below its net asset value, which is better than its one-year historical average premium of 2.73%.

James L. Iselin currently receives a manager quality ranking of 68 (0=worst, 99=best). If you desire only a moderate level of risk and strong performance, then this fund is an excellent option.

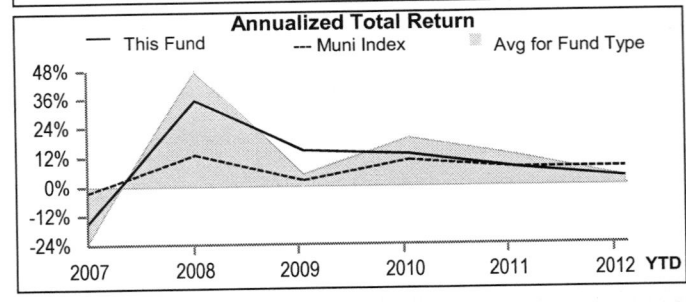

Neuberger Berman High Yield Strat (NHS)

C-   **Fair**

Fund Family: Neuberger Berman Management LLC
Fund Type: Corporate - High Yield
Inception Date: July 28, 2003

Data Date	Investment Rating	Net Assets ($Mil)	Price	Performance Rating/Pts	Total Return Y-T-D	Risk Rating/Pts
12-12	C-	253.17	13.90	C+ / 5.6	1.73%	C+ / 6.4
2011	B	249.40	13.65	A / 9.4	0.37%	C+ / 6.4
2010	B-	138.29	13.50	B+ / 8.6	24.86%	C- / 4.0
2009	C+	111.79	11.95	B / 8.0	103.10%	C- / 4.0

Major Rating Factors: Middle of the road best describes Neuberger Berman High Yield Strat whose TheStreet.com Investment Rating is currently a C- (Fair). The fund currently has a performance rating of C+ (Fair) based on an annualized return of 14.81% over the last three years and a total return of 1.73% year to date 2012. Factored into the performance evaluation is an expense ratio of 1.68% (above average).

The fund's risk rating is currently C+ (Fair). It carries a beta of 1.72, meaning it is expected to move 17.2% for every 10% move in the market. Volatility, as measured by both the semi-deviation and a drawdown factor, is considered low. As of December 31, 2012, Neuberger Berman High Yield Strat traded at a discount of 3.81% below its net asset value, which is better than its one-year historical average premium of 3.10%.

Ann H. Benjamin has been running the fund for 8 years and currently receives a manager quality ranking of 25 (0=worst, 99=best). If you desire an average level of risk, then this fund may be an option.

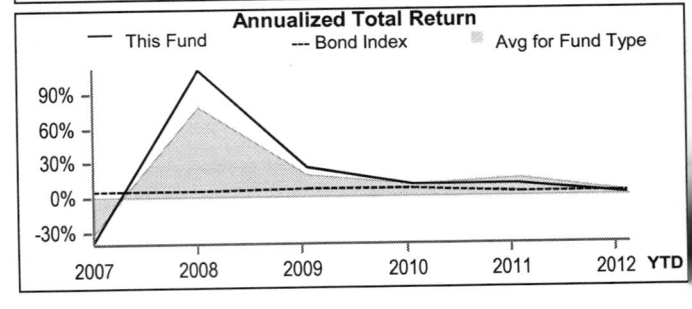

Neuberger Berman Intermediate Muni (NBH)   A+   Excellent

Fund Family: Neuberger Berman Management LLC
Fund Type: Municipal - National
Inception Date: September 24, 2002

Major Rating Factors:
Strong performance is the major factor driving the A+ (Excellent) TheStreet.com Investment Rating for Neuberger Berman Intermediate Muni. The fund currently has a performance rating of B+ (Good) based on an annualized return of 13.89% over the last three years and a total return of 5.32% year to date 2012. Factored into the performance evaluation is an expense ratio of 1.05% (low).

The fund's risk rating is currently B+ (Good). It carries a beta of 1.42, meaning it is expected to move 14.2% for every 10% move in the market. Volatility, as measured by both the semi-deviation and a drawdown factor, is considered very low. As of December 31, 2012, Neuberger Berman Intermediate Muni traded at a premium of .87% above its net asset value, which is better than its one-year historical average premium of 3.81%.

James L. Iselin currently receives a manager quality ranking of 71 (0=worst, 99=best). If you desire only a moderate level of risk and strong performance, then this fund is an excellent option.

Data Date	Investment Rating	Net Assets ($Mil)	Price	Perfor-mance Rating/Pts	Total Return Y-T-D	Risk Rating/Pts
12-12	A+	277.50	16.18	B+ / 8.4	5.32%	B+ / 9.1
2011	A	283.20	15.90	B+ / 8.8	-0.69%	B+ / 9.3
2010	B+	62.64	14.01	B- / 7.0	10.26%	B- / 7.1
2009	B	282.36	13.41	C / 5.3	22.50%	B- / 7.8

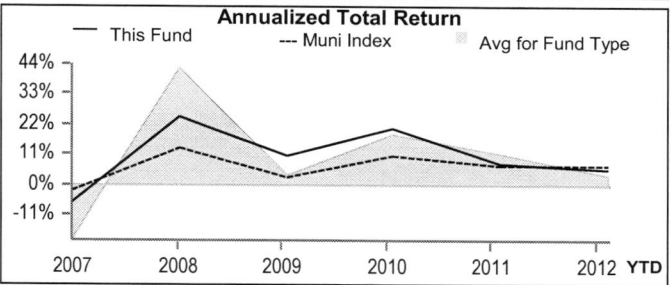

Neuberger Berman NY Int Muni (NBO)   B   Good

Fund Family: Neuberger Berman Management LLC
Fund Type: Municipal - Single State
Inception Date: September 24, 2002

Major Rating Factors: Strong performance is the major factor driving the B (Good) TheStreet.com Investment Rating for Neuberger Berman NY Int Muni. The fund currently has a performance rating of B- (Good) based on an annualized return of 11.98% over the last three years and a total return of 3.90% year to date 2012. Factored into the performance evaluation is an expense ratio of 1.29% (average).

The fund's risk rating is currently B (Good). It carries a beta of 1.84, meaning it is expected to move 18.4% for every 10% move in the market. Volatility, as measured by both the semi-deviation and a drawdown factor, is considered low. As of December 31, 2012, Neuberger Berman NY Int Muni traded at a premium of 1.33% above its net asset value, which is better than its one-year historical average premium of 4.00%.

James L. Iselin currently receives a manager quality ranking of 39 (0=worst, 99=best). If you desire only a moderate level of risk and strong performance, then this fund is an excellent option.

Data Date	Investment Rating	Net Assets ($Mil)	Price	Perfor-mance Rating/Pts	Total Return Y-T-D	Risk Rating/Pts
12-12	B	73.10	15.21	B- / 7.3	3.90%	B / 8.6
2011	A	74.40	15.47	A- / 9.0	-1.36%	B / 8.9
2010	C+	62.64	13.50	C+ / 5.7	8.09%	C+ / 6.7
2009	B-	74.46	13.13	C+ / 5.6	30.77%	B- / 7.6

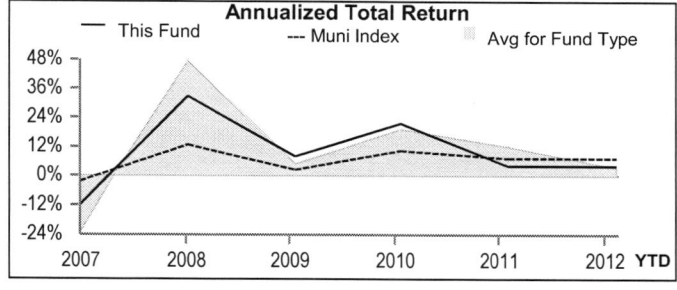

Neuberger Berman Real Est Secs Inc (NRO)   A-   Excellent

Fund Family: Neuberger Berman Management LLC
Fund Type: Growth and Income
Inception Date: October 28, 2003

Major Rating Factors:
Strong performance is the major factor driving the A- (Excellent) TheStreet.com Investment Rating for Neuberger Berman Real Est Secs Inc. The fund currently has a performance rating of B+ (Good) based on an annualized return of 22.92% over the last three years and a total return of 4.58% year to date 2012. Factored into the performance evaluation is an expense ratio of 2.21% (high).

The fund's risk rating is currently B- (Good). It carries a beta of 0.91, meaning that its performance tracks fairly well with that of the overall stock market. Volatility, as measured by both the semi-deviation and a drawdown factor, is considered low. As of December 31, 2012, Neuberger Berman Real Est Secs Inc traded at a discount of 15.00% below its net asset value, which is better than its one-year historical average discount of 12.27%.

Steve S. Shigekawa currently receives a manager quality ranking of 91 (0=worst, 99=best). If you desire only a moderate level of risk and strong performance, then this fund is an excellent option.

Data Date	Investment Rating	Net Assets ($Mil)	Price	Perfor-mance Rating/Pts	Total Return Y-T-D	Risk Rating/Pts
12-12	A-	257.20	4.59	B+ / 8.9	4.58%	B- / 7.9
2011	B-	245.60	3.75	B+ / 8.5	1.07%	C+ / 6.5
2010	E	260.60	3.99	D- / 1.5	40.04%	D / 2.1
2009	E	139.73	3.05	E+ / 0.8	78.23%	C- / 3.0

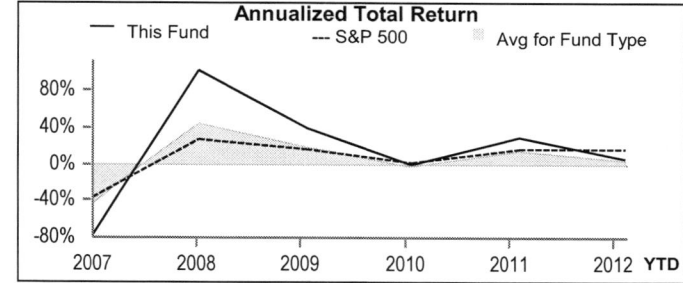

New America High Income Fund (HYB)   B   Good

Fund Family: T Rowe Price Associates Inc
Fund Type: Corporate - High Yield
Inception Date: February 26, 1988

Major Rating Factors: Strong performance is the major factor driving the B (Good) TheStreet.com Investment Rating for New America High Income Fund. The fund currently has a performance rating of B (Good) based on an annualized return of 17.82% over the last three years and a total return of 1.63% year to date 2012. Factored into the performance evaluation is an expense ratio of 1.10% (low).

The fund's risk rating is currently B (Good). It carries a beta of 1.19, meaning it is expected to move 11.9% for every 10% move in the market. Volatility, as measured by both the semi-deviation and a drawdown factor, is considered low. As of December 31, 2012, New America High Income Fund traded at a discount of 2.06% below its net asset value, which is better than its one-year historical average premium of 3.14%.

Brian C. Rogers currently receives a manager quality ranking of 70 (0=worst, 99=best). If you desire only a moderate level of risk and strong performance, then this fund is an excellent option.

Data Date	Investment Rating	Net Assets ($Mil)	Price	Performance Rating/Pts	Total Return Y-T-D	Risk Rating/Pts
12-12	B	321.16	10.45	B / 7.7	1.63%	B / 8.2
2011	B	221.50	10.21	A- / 9.1	-2.25%	C+ / 6.5
2010	B-	217.22	9.96	B+ / 8.6	22.09%	C- / 3.7
2009	C+	180.44	9.05	B+ / 8.4	110.83%	C- / 3.7

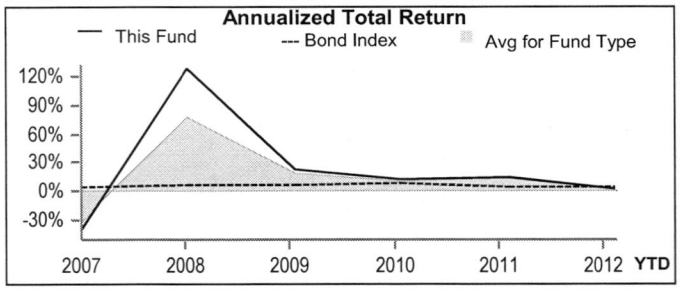

New Germany Fund (GF)   B   Good

Fund Family: Deutsche Asset Mgmt International G
Fund Type: Foreign
Inception Date: January 24, 1990

Major Rating Factors: Strong performance is the major factor driving the B (Good) TheStreet.com Investment Rating for New Germany Fund. The fund currently has a performance rating of B+ (Good) based on an annualized return of 14.21% over the last three years and a total return of 4.49% year to date 2012. Factored into the performance evaluation is an expense ratio of 1.17% (low).

The fund's risk rating is currently C+ (Fair). It carries a beta of 1.29, meaning it is expected to move 12.9% for every 10% move in the market. Volatility, as measured by both the semi-deviation and a drawdown factor, is considered low. As of December 31, 2012, New Germany Fund traded at a discount of 14.96% below its net asset value, which is better than its one-year historical average discount of 10.22%.

Rainer Vermehren currently receives a manager quality ranking of 89 (0=worst, 99=best). If you desire only a moderate level of risk and strong performance, then this fund is an excellent option.

Data Date	Investment Rating	Net Assets ($Mil)	Price	Performance Rating/Pts	Total Return Y-T-D	Risk Rating/Pts
12-12	B	262.51	15.58	B+ / 8.9	4.49%	C+ / 6.4
2011	C	241.50	12.24	C+ / 5.9	2.61%	C+ / 6.5
2010	C-	271.35	15.72	C+ / 5.9	32.19%	C- / 3.9
2009	C-	210.18	11.99	C- / 3.9	43.93%	C / 4.8

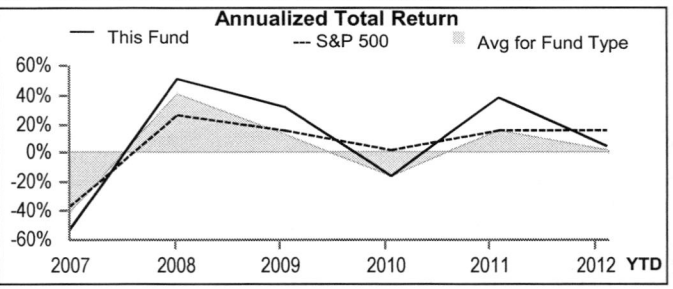

NexPoint Credit Strategies Fund (HCF)   C-   Fair

Fund Family: NexPoint Advisors LP
Fund Type: General Bond
Inception Date: June 26, 2006

Major Rating Factors: Middle of the road best describes NexPoint Credit Strategies Fund whose TheStreet.com Investment Rating is currently a C- (Fair). The fund currently has a performance rating of C (Fair) based on an annualized return of 8.57% over the last three years and a total return of 2.71% year to date 2012. Factored into the performance evaluation is an expense ratio of 3.15% (high).

The fund's risk rating is currently B- (Good). It carries a beta of -1.38, meaning the fund's expected move will be -13.8% for every 10% move in the market. Volatility, as measured by both the semi-deviation and a drawdown factor, is considered low. As of December 31, 2012, NexPoint Credit Strategies Fund traded at a discount of 12.86% below its net asset value, which is better than its one-year historical average discount of 10.40%.

Mark Okada currently receives a manager quality ranking of 96 (0=worst, 99=best). If you desire an average level of risk, then this fund may be an option.

Data Date	Investment Rating	Net Assets ($Mil)	Price	Performance Rating/Pts	Total Return Y-T-D	Risk Rating/Pts
12-12	C-	443.05	6.64	C / 4.3	2.71%	B- / 7.6
2011	C-	445.10	6.18	C- / 3.7	0.32%	B- / 7.5
2010	E+	458.76	7.58	D- / 1.3	30.86%	D+ / 2.8
2009	E+	400.79	6.31	E+ / 0.6	18.33%	C- / 4.0

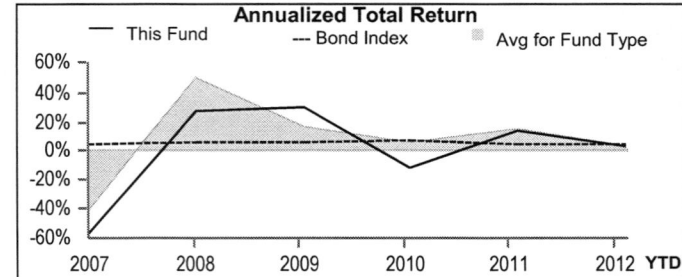

NFJ Dividend Interest & Premium St (NFJ)

C-   **Fair**

Fund Family: Allianz Global Investors Fund Mgmt
Fund Type: Growth and Income
Inception Date: February 23, 2005

Major Rating Factors: Middle of the road best describes NFJ Dividend Interest & Premium St whose TheStreet.com Investment Rating is currently a C- (Fair). The fund currently has a performance rating of C- (Fair) based on an annualized return of 10.65% over the last three years and a total return of 5.13% year to date 2012. Factored into the performance evaluation is an expense ratio of 0.97% (low).

The fund's risk rating is currently B- (Good). It carries a beta of 0.98, meaning that its performance tracks fairly well with that of the overall stock market. Volatility, as measured by both the semi-deviation and a drawdown factor, is considered low. As of December 31, 2012, NFJ Dividend Interest & Premium St traded at a discount of 11.11% below its net asset value, which is better than its one-year historical average discount of 4.90%.

Benno J. Fischer currently receives a manager quality ranking of 49 (0=worst, 99=best). If you desire an average level of risk, then this fund may be an option.

Data Date	Investment Rating	Net Assets ($Mil)	Price	Performance Rating/Pts	Total Return Y-T-D	Risk Rating/Pts
12-12	C-	1,644.18	15.60	C- / 3.8	5.13%	B- / 7.7
2011	C-	1,661.60	16.02	C / 4.4	3.68%	B- / 7.5
2010	C-	1,635.73	17.51	C- / 4.2	22.29%	C+ / 5.8
2009	D	1,481.95	14.75	D- / 1.4	13.27%	C+ / 6.1

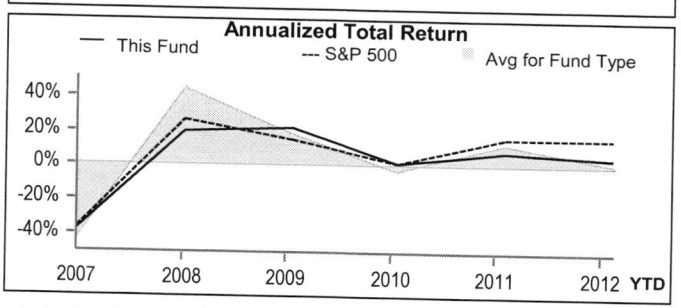

Nuveen AMT-Fr Muni Income (NEA)

C+   **Fair**

Fund Family: Nuveen Fund Advisors Inc
Fund Type: Municipal - National
Inception Date: November 21, 2002

Major Rating Factors: Middle of the road best describes Nuveen AMT-Fr Muni Income whose TheStreet.com Investment Rating is currently a C+ (Fair). The fund currently has a performance rating of C+ (Fair) based on an annualized return of 8.97% over the last three years and a total return of 4.65% year to date 2012. Factored into the performance evaluation is an expense ratio of 2.01% (high).

The fund's risk rating is currently B (Good). It carries a beta of 2.08, meaning it is expected to move 20.8% for every 10% move in the market. Volatility, as measured by both the semi-deviation and a drawdown factor, is considered low. As of December 31, 2012, Nuveen AMT-Fr Muni Income traded at a discount of 4.07% below its net asset value, which is better than its one-year historical average discount of 1.46%.

Paul L. Brennan has been running the fund for 7 years and currently receives a manager quality ranking of 22 (0=worst, 99=best). If you desire an average level of risk, then this fund may be an option.

Data Date	Investment Rating	Net Assets ($Mil)	Price	Performance Rating/Pts	Total Return Y-T-D	Risk Rating/Pts
12-12	C+	326.91	14.84	C+ / 5.8	4.65%	B / 8.6
2011	B+	332.40	14.61	B / 7.8	0.14%	B / 8.7
2010	C-	320.59	13.39	D+ / 2.6	1.90%	B- / 7.7
2009	B-	277.71	13.90	C+ / 6.2	34.27%	B- / 7.8

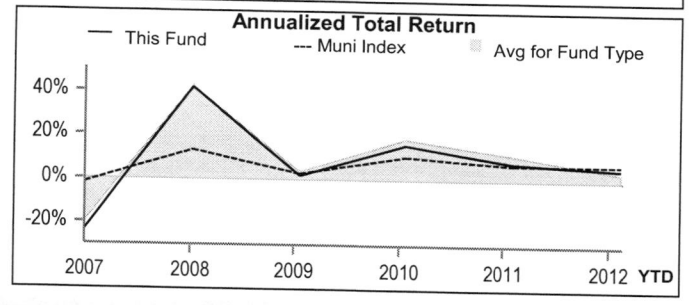

Nuveen AMT-Free Municipal Value (NUW)

C+   **Fair**

Fund Family: Nuveen Fund Advisors Inc
Fund Type: Municipal - National
Inception Date: February 25, 2009

Major Rating Factors: Middle of the road best describes Nuveen AMT-Free Municipal Value whose TheStreet.com Investment Rating is currently a C+ (Fair). The fund currently has a performance rating of C+ (Fair) based on an annualized return of 9.70% over the last three years and a total return of 3.63% year to date 2012. Factored into the performance evaluation is an expense ratio of 0.71% (very low).

The fund's risk rating is currently B (Good). It carries a beta of 2.46, meaning it is expected to move 24.6% for every 10% move in the market. Volatility, as measured by both the semi-deviation and a drawdown factor, is considered low. As of December 31, 2012, Nuveen AMT-Free Municipal Value traded at a discount of .90% below its net asset value, which is better than its one-year historical average premium of 1.91%.

Thomas C. Spalding has been running the fund for 4 years and currently receives a manager quality ranking of 18 (0=worst, 99=best). If you desire an average level of risk, then this fund may be an option.

Data Date	Investment Rating	Net Assets ($Mil)	Price	Performance Rating/Pts	Total Return Y-T-D	Risk Rating/Pts
12-12	C+	212.87	17.63	C+ / 6.2	3.63%	B / 8.3
2011	A-	215.20	17.32	A- / 9.0	0.40%	B / 8.7
2010	C-	205.71	15.38	D- / 1.0	2.98%	B / 8.1

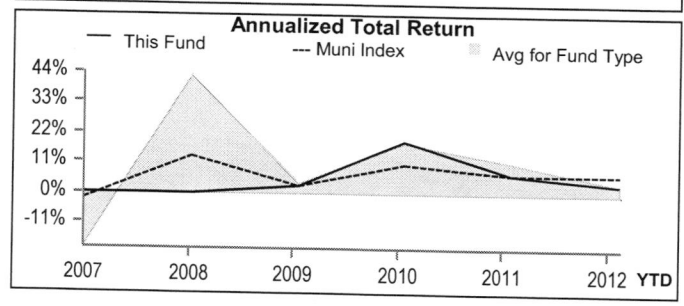

Nuveen AZ Div Adv Muni (NFZ)

B+   **Good**

Fund Family: Nuveen Fund Advisors Inc
Fund Type: Municipal - Single State
Inception Date: January 30, 2001

Data Date	Investment Rating	Net Assets ($Mil)	Price	Perfor-mance Rating/Pts	Total Return Y-T-D	Risk Rating/Pts
12-12	B+	23.95	14.98	B / 8.1	2.20%	B / 8.4
2011	B+	22.60	13.73	B+ / 8.3	-0.15%	B / 8.6
2010	C-	21.98	12.30	D / 2.0	5.01%	B- / 7.4
2009	C	21.52	12.39	C- / 3.8	38.67%	B- / 7.2

Major Rating Factors: Strong performance is the major factor driving the B+ (Good) TheStreet.com Investment Rating for Nuveen AZ Div Adv Muni. The fund currently has a performance rating of B (Good) based on an annualized return of 13.05% over the last three years and a total return of 2.20% year to date 2012. Factored into the performance evaluation is an expense ratio of 3.47% (high).

The fund's risk rating is currently B (Good). It carries a beta of 1.89, meaning it is expected to move 18.9% for every 10% move in the market. Volatility, as measured by both the semi-deviation and a drawdown factor, is considered low. As of December 31, 2012, Nuveen AZ Div Adv Muni traded at a discount of 3.17% below its net asset value, which is better than its one-year historical average discount of 3.09%.

Michael S. Hamilton has been running the fund for 2 years and currently receives a manager quality ranking of 51 (0=worst, 99=best). If you desire only a moderate level of risk and strong performance, then this fund is an excellent option.

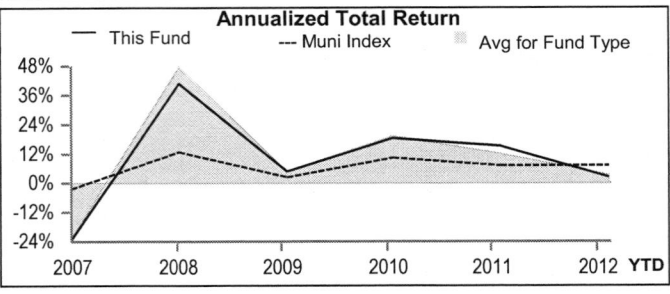

Nuveen AZ Div Adv Muni Fund 2 (NKR)

B+   **Good**

Fund Family: Nuveen Fund Advisors Inc
Fund Type: Municipal - Single State
Inception Date: March 25, 2002

Data Date	Investment Rating	Net Assets ($Mil)	Price	Perfor-mance Rating/Pts	Total Return Y-T-D	Risk Rating/Pts
12-12	B+	38.36	15.59	B / 7.7	1.99%	B+ / 9.0
2011	A-	36.30	14.17	B+ / 8.3	0.00%	B+ / 9.0
2010	C	35.73	12.88	D+ / 2.9	3.62%	B / 8.0
2009	B-	35.47	13.17	C / 5.5	39.56%	B- / 7.5

Major Rating Factors: Strong performance is the major factor driving the B+ (Good) TheStreet.com Investment Rating for Nuveen AZ Div Adv Muni Fund 2. The fund currently has a performance rating of B (Good) based on an annualized return of 11.84% over the last three years and a total return of 1.99% year to date 2012. Factored into the performance evaluation is an expense ratio of 2.94% (high).

The fund's risk rating is currently B+ (Good). It carries a beta of 1.64, meaning it is expected to move 16.4% for every 10% move in the market. Volatility, as measured by both the semi-deviation and a drawdown factor, is considered very low. As of December 31, 2012, Nuveen AZ Div Adv Muni Fund 2 traded at a discount of 1.45% below its net asset value, which is worse than its one-year historical average discount of 1.95%.

Michael S. Hamilton has been running the fund for 2 years and currently receives a manager quality ranking of 60 (0=worst, 99=best). If you desire only a moderate level of risk and strong performance, then this fund is an excellent option.

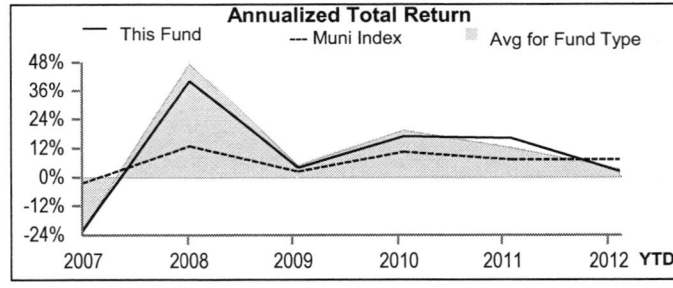

Nuveen AZ Div Adv Muni Fund 3 (NXE)

A-   **Excellent**

Fund Family: Nuveen Fund Advisors Inc
Fund Type: Municipal - Single State
Inception Date: September 25, 2002

Data Date	Investment Rating	Net Assets ($Mil)	Price	Perfor-mance Rating/Pts	Total Return Y-T-D	Risk Rating/Pts
12-12	A-	46.72	14.77	B / 8.0	2.26%	B+ / 9.0
2011	A-	44.40	13.36	B+ / 8.3	0.75%	B+ / 9.1
2010	C+	43.28	12.30	C- / 3.5	4.23%	B- / 7.9
2009	B-	42.94	12.50	C+ / 5.9	40.46%	B- / 7.8

Major Rating Factors:
Strong performance is the major factor driving the A- (Excellent) TheStreet.com Investment Rating for Nuveen AZ Div Adv Muni Fund 3. The fund currently has a performance rating of B (Good) based on an annualized return of 12.02% over the last three years and a total return of 2.26% year to date 2012. Factored into the performance evaluation is an expense ratio of 3.48% (high).

The fund's risk rating is currently B+ (Good). It carries a beta of 1.74, meaning it is expected to move 17.4% for every 10% move in the market. Volatility, as measured by both the semi-deviation and a drawdown factor, is considered very low. As of December 31, 2012, Nuveen AZ Div Adv Muni Fund 3 traded at a discount of 3.46% below its net asset value, which is worse than its one-year historical average discount of 3.82%.

Michael S. Hamilton has been running the fund for 2 years and currently receives a manager quality ranking of 54 (0=worst, 99=best). If you desire only a moderate level of risk and strong performance, then this fund is an excellent option.

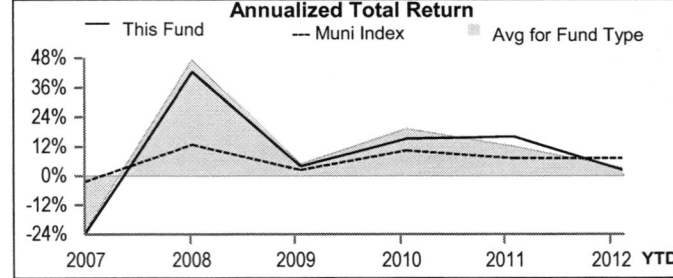

Nuveen AZ Prem Inc Muni (NAZ)

B-   **Good**

Fund Family: Nuveen Fund Advisors Inc
Fund Type: Municipal - Single State
Inception Date: November 19, 1992

Major Rating Factors: Nuveen AZ Prem Inc Muni receives a TheStreet.com Investment Rating of B- (Good). The fund currently has a performance rating of C+ (Fair) based on an annualized return of 9.98% over the last three years and a total return of 2.80% year to date 2012. Factored into the performance evaluation is an expense ratio of 1.82% (above average).

The fund's risk rating is currently B (Good). It carries a beta of 1.55, meaning it is expected to move 15.5% for every 10% move in the market. Volatility, as measured by both the semi-deviation and a drawdown factor, is considered low. As of December 31, 2012, Nuveen AZ Prem Inc Muni traded at a discount of .52% below its net asset value, which is better than its one-year historical average premium of .63%.

Michael S. Hamilton has been running the fund for 2 years and currently receives a manager quality ranking of 64 (0=worst, 99=best). If you desire an average level of risk, then this fund may be an option.

Data Date	Investment Rating	Net Assets ($Mil)	Price	Performance Rating/Pts	Total Return Y-T-D	Risk Rating/Pts
12-12	B-	68.02	15.33	C+ / 6.5	2.80%	B / 8.4
2011	B+	63.90	14.14	B+ / 8.5	0.14%	B / 8.5
2010	C+	62.55	12.72	C / 5.3	4.36%	C+ / 6.9
2009	B-	63.33	12.87	C+ / 6.0	40.82%	B- / 7.4

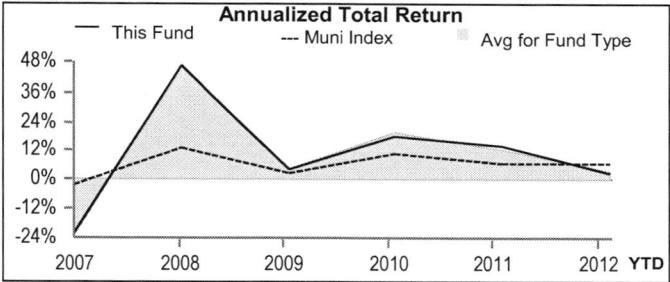

Nuveen Build America Bond Fund (NBB)

B-   **Good**

Fund Family: Nuveen Fund Advisors Inc
Fund Type: Municipal - National
Inception Date: April 27, 2010

Major Rating Factors: Nuveen Build America Bond Fund receives a TheStreet.com Investment Rating of B- (Good). The fund currently has a performance rating of C+ (Fair) based on an annualized return of 0.00% over the last three years and a total return of 1.27% year to date 2012. Factored into the performance evaluation is an expense ratio of 1.05% (low).

The fund's risk rating is currently B (Good). It carries a beta of 0.00, meaning the fund's expected move will be 0.0% for every 10% move in the market. Volatility, as measured by both the semi-deviation and a drawdown factor, is considered low. As of December 31, 2012, Nuveen Build America Bond Fund traded at a discount of 4.55% below its net asset value, which is worse than its one-year historical average discount of 4.91%.

Craig M. Chambers currently receives a manager quality ranking of 57 (0=worst, 99=best). If you desire an average level of risk, then this fund may be an option.

Data Date	Investment Rating	Net Assets ($Mil)	Price	Performance Rating/Pts	Total Return Y-T-D	Risk Rating/Pts
12-12	B-	565.95	21.18	C+ / 5.9	1.27%	B / 8.8
2011	A+	556.80	20.53	A / 9.4	0.58%	B / 8.9

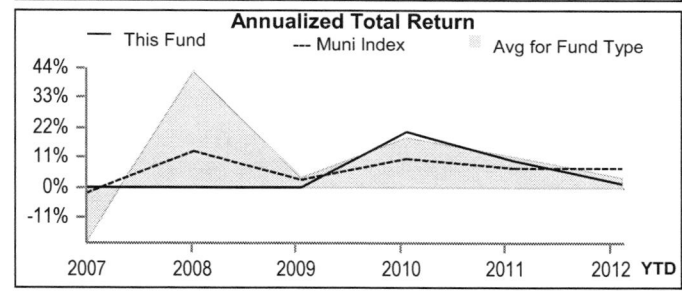

Nuveen Build America Bond Oppty Fd (NBD)

C-   **Fair**

Fund Family: Nuveen Fund Advisors Inc
Fund Type: General - Investment Grade
Inception Date: November 24, 2010

Major Rating Factors:
Disappointing performance is the major factor driving the C- (Fair) TheStreet.com Investment Rating for Nuveen Build America Bond Oppty Fd. The fund currently has a performance rating of D+ (Weak) based on an annualized return of 0.00% over the last three years and a total return of 1.20% year to date 2012. Factored into the performance evaluation is an expense ratio of 0.97% (low).

The fund's risk rating is currently B+ (Good). It carries a beta of 0.00, meaning the fund's expected move will be 0.0% for every 10% move in the market. Volatility, as measured by both the semi-deviation and a drawdown factor, is considered very low. As of December 31, 2012, Nuveen Build America Bond Oppty Fd traded at a discount of 7.24% below its net asset value, which is better than its one-year historical average discount of 6.74%.

Daniel J. Close currently receives a manager quality ranking of 20 (0=worst, 99=best). This fund offers only a moderate level of risk but investors looking for strong performance are still waiting.

Data Date	Investment Rating	Net Assets ($Mil)	Price	Performance Rating/Pts	Total Return Y-T-D	Risk Rating/Pts
12-12	C-	162.58	21.66	D+ / 2.8	1.20%	B+ / 9.3
2011	A-	158.80	21.62	B / 8.0	-0.14%	B+ / 9.3

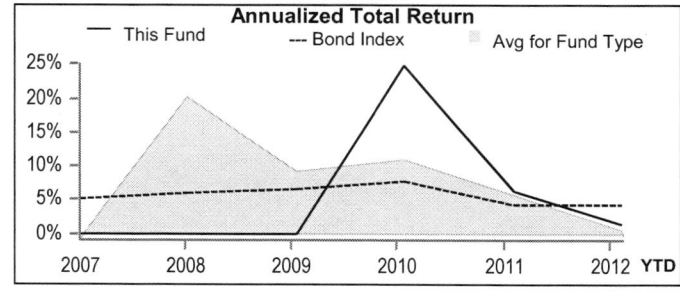

Nuveen CA AMT-Free Municipal Incom (NKX)　　　　　B+　　　Good

Fund Family: Nuveen Fund Advisors Inc
Fund Type:　Municipal - Single State
Inception Date:　November 21, 2002

Major Rating Factors: Strong performance is the major factor driving the B+ (Good) TheStreet.com Investment Rating for Nuveen CA AMT-Free Municipal Incom. The fund currently has a performance rating of B (Good) based on an annualized return of 12.99% over the last three years and a total return of 4.34% year to date 2012. Factored into the performance evaluation is an expense ratio of 1.65% (above average).

　　The fund's risk rating is currently B (Good). It carries a beta of 2.49, meaning it is expected to move 24.9% for every 10% move in the market. Volatility, as measured by both the semi-deviation and a drawdown factor, is considered low. As of December 31, 2012, Nuveen CA AMT-Free Municipal Incom traded at a discount of 5.15% below its net asset value, which is better than its one-year historical average discount of .47%.

　　Scott R. Romans has been running the fund for 11 years and currently receives a manager quality ranking of 24 (0=worst, 99=best). If you desire only a moderate level of risk and strong performance, then this fund is an excellent option.

Data Date	Investment Rating	Net Assets ($Mil)	Price	Performance Rating/Pts	Total Return Y-T-D	Risk Rating/Pts
12-12	B+	640.79	14.73	B / 7.9	4.34%	B / 8.4
2011	B+	84.50	14.60	B+ / 8.7	-0.36%	B / 8.5
2010	C-	39.30	12.18	D / 1.7	2.01%	B- / 7.8
2009	C+	85.77	12.68	C- / 3.7	26.23%	B / 8.0

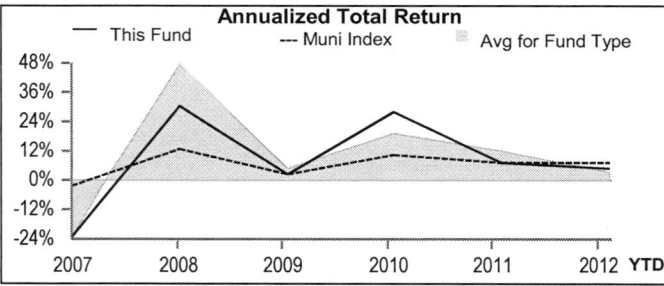

Nuveen CA Div Adv Muni (NAC)　　　　　A+　　　Excellent

Fund Family: Nuveen Fund Advisors Inc
Fund Type:　Municipal - Single State
Inception Date:　May 25, 1999

Major Rating Factors:
Exceptional performance is the major factor driving the A+ (Excellent) TheStreet.com Investment Rating for Nuveen CA Div Adv Muni. The fund currently has a performance rating of A (Excellent) based on an annualized return of 17.04% over the last three years and a total return of 1.74% year to date 2012. Factored into the performance evaluation is an expense ratio of 1.64% (above average).

　　The fund's risk rating is currently B (Good). It carries a beta of 2.08, meaning it is expected to move 20.8% for every 10% move in the market. Volatility, as measured by both the semi-deviation and a drawdown factor, is considered low. As of December 31, 2012, Nuveen CA Div Adv Muni traded at a premium of 1.51% above its net asset value, which is worse than its one-year historical average discount of .43%.

　　Scott R. Romans has been running the fund for 11 years and currently receives a manager quality ranking of 67 (0=worst, 99=best). If you desire only a moderate level of risk and strong performance, then this fund is an excellent option.

Data Date	Investment Rating	Net Assets ($Mil)	Price	Performance Rating/Pts	Total Return Y-T-D	Risk Rating/Pts
12-12	A+	364.25	16.10	A / 9.4	1.74%	B / 8.5
2011	A-	335.30	14.24	B+ / 8.8	-0.07%	B / 8.5
2010	C-	325.79	12.31	D+ / 2.5	6.08%	C+ / 6.5
2009	C	337.10	12.40	C- / 3.9	30.53%	B- / 7.2

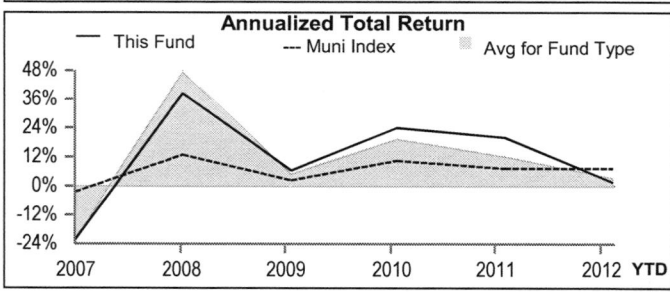

Nuveen CA Div Adv Muni 2 (NVX)　　　　　A-　　　Excellent

Fund Family: Nuveen Fund Advisors Inc
Fund Type:　Municipal - Single State
Inception Date:　March 27, 2001

Major Rating Factors:
Strong performance is the major factor driving the A- (Excellent) TheStreet.com Investment Rating for Nuveen CA Div Adv Muni 2. The fund currently has a performance rating of B (Good) based on an annualized return of 13.41% over the last three years and a total return of 3.20% year to date 2012. Factored into the performance evaluation is an expense ratio of 2.23% (high).

　　The fund's risk rating is currently B (Good). It carries a beta of 2.13, meaning it is expected to move 21.3% for every 10% move in the market. Volatility, as measured by both the semi-deviation and a drawdown factor, is considered low. As of December 31, 2012, Nuveen CA Div Adv Muni 2 traded at a discount of 4.53% below its net asset value, which is better than its one-year historical average discount of 1.04%.

　　Scott R. Romans has been running the fund for 11 years and currently receives a manager quality ranking of 36 (0=worst, 99=best). If you desire only a moderate level of risk and strong performance, then this fund is an excellent option.

Data Date	Investment Rating	Net Assets ($Mil)	Price	Performance Rating/Pts	Total Return Y-T-D	Risk Rating/Pts
12-12	A-	236.02	15.61	B / 8.2	3.20%	B / 8.7
2011	A	219.70	14.75	B+ / 8.9	0.34%	B / 8.9
2010	C	213.69	13.10	C / 4.9	4.11%	C+ / 6.3
2009	B-	219.78	13.47	C+ / 6.7	45.75%	B- / 7.1

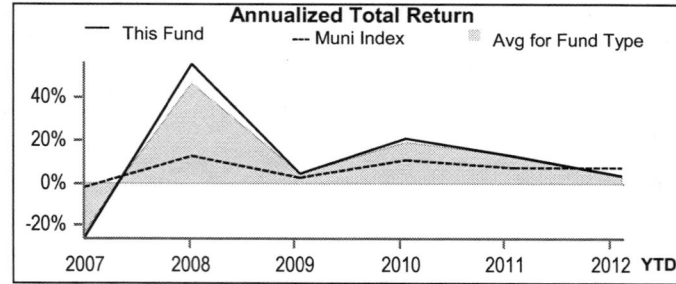

Nuveen CA Div Adv Muni 3 (NZH)

A-   **Excellent**

Fund Family: Nuveen Fund Advisors Inc
Fund Type: Municipal - Single State
Inception Date: September 25, 2001

Major Rating Factors:
Strong performance is the major factor driving the A- (Excellent) TheStreet.com Investment Rating for Nuveen CA Div Adv Muni 3. The fund currently has a performance rating of B (Good) based on an annualized return of 12.38% over the last three years and a total return of 1.53% year to date 2012. Factored into the performance evaluation is an expense ratio of 2.56% (high).

The fund's risk rating is currently B (Good). It carries a beta of 1.84, meaning it is expected to move 18.4% for every 10% move in the market. Volatility, as measured by both the semi-deviation and a drawdown factor, is considered low. As of December 31, 2012, Nuveen CA Div Adv Muni 3 traded at a discount of 2.38% below its net asset value, which is better than its one-year historical average discount of 1.00%.

Scott R. Romans has been running the fund for 11 years and currently receives a manager quality ranking of 52 (0=worst, 99=best). If you desire only a moderate level of risk and strong performance, then this fund is an excellent option.

Data Date	Investment Rating	Net Assets ($Mil)	Price	Performance Rating/Pts	Total Return Y-T-D	Risk Rating/Pts
12-12	A-	346.66	14.34	B / 8.0	1.53%	B / 8.7
2011	A-	322.20	13.51	B+ / 8.9	0.67%	B / 8.7
2010	D+	317.86	11.96	D / 2.2	3.36%	C+ / 6.1
2009	C	328.52	12.40	C / 4.6	41.00%	C+ / 6.9

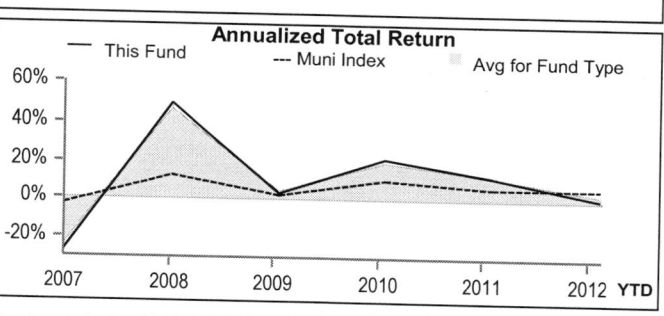

Nuveen CA Inv Quality Muni (NQC)

A   **Excellent**

Fund Family: Nuveen Fund Advisors Inc
Fund Type: Municipal - Single State
Inception Date: November 20, 1990

Major Rating Factors:
Strong performance is the major factor driving the A (Excellent) TheStreet.com Investment Rating for Nuveen CA Inv Quality Muni. The fund currently has a performance rating of B+ (Good) based on an annualized return of 15.90% over the last three years and a total return of 4.59% year to date 2012. Factored into the performance evaluation is an expense ratio of 1.63% (above average).

The fund's risk rating is currently B (Good). It carries a beta of 2.47, meaning it is expected to move 24.7% for every 10% move in the market. Volatility, as measured by both the semi-deviation and a drawdown factor, is considered low. As of December 31, 2012, Nuveen CA Inv Quality Muni traded at a discount of 2.91% below its net asset value, which is better than its one-year historical average premium of 1.87%.

Scott R. Romans has been running the fund for 11 years and currently receives a manager quality ranking of 34 (0=worst, 99=best). If you desire only a moderate level of risk and strong performance, then this fund is an excellent option.

Data Date	Investment Rating	Net Assets ($Mil)	Price	Performance Rating/Pts	Total Return Y-T-D	Risk Rating/Pts
12-12	A	216.25	15.68	B+ / 8.8	4.59%	B / 8.6
2011	A	200.00	14.68	A- / 9.2	0.82%	B / 8.7
2010	C-	190.88	12.59	C- / 3.2	4.89%	C+ / 6.0
2009	B-	197.13	12.83	C+ / 5.6	31.27%	B- / 7.1

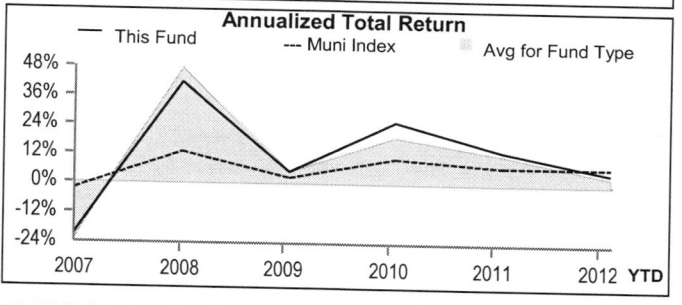

Nuveen CA Muni Market Opportunity (NCO)

A+   **Excellent**

Fund Family: Nuveen Fund Advisors Inc
Fund Type: Municipal - Single State
Inception Date: May 18, 1990

Major Rating Factors:
Exceptional performance is the major factor driving the A+ (Excellent) TheStreet.com Investment Rating for Nuveen CA Muni Market Opportunity. The fund currently has a performance rating of A (Excellent) based on an annualized return of 16.96% over the last three years and a total return of 5.02% year to date 2012. Factored into the performance evaluation is an expense ratio of 1.73% (above average).

The fund's risk rating is currently B (Good). It carries a beta of 2.05, meaning it is expected to move 20.5% for every 10% move in the market. Volatility, as measured by both the semi-deviation and a drawdown factor, is considered low. As of December 31, 2012, Nuveen CA Muni Market Opportunity traded at a discount of 1.09% below its net asset value, which is better than its one-year historical average premium of .53%.

Scott R. Romans has been running the fund for 11 years and currently receives a manager quality ranking of 59 (0=worst, 99=best). If you desire only a moderate level of risk and strong performance, then this fund is an excellent option.

Data Date	Investment Rating	Net Assets ($Mil)	Price	Performance Rating/Pts	Total Return Y-T-D	Risk Rating/Pts
12-12	A+	131.48	16.34	A / 9.5	5.02%	B / 8.7
2011	A-	120.60	14.64	B+ / 8.9	-0.68%	B / 8.8
2010	C-	115.07	12.73	C- / 3.9	3.08%	C+ / 6.2
2009	C+	119.38	13.16	C / 5.0	44.62%	B- / 7.1

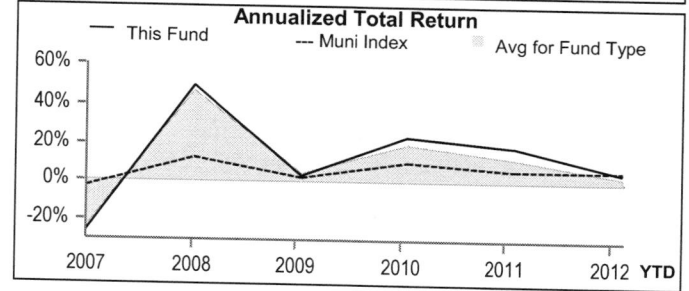

Nuveen CA Muni Value (NCA)   **B-**   **Good**

Fund Family: Nuveen Fund Advisors Inc
Fund Type: Municipal - Single State
Inception Date: October 7, 1987

Major Rating Factors: Nuveen CA Muni Value receives a TheStreet.com Investment Rating of B- (Good). The fund currently has a performance rating of C+ (Fair) based on an annualized return of 9.93% over the last three years and a total return of 4.09% year to date 2012. Factored into the performance evaluation is an expense ratio of 0.65% (very low).

The fund's risk rating is currently B (Good). It carries a beta of 1.31, meaning it is expected to move 13.1% for every 10% move in the market. Volatility, as measured by both the semi-deviation and a drawdown factor, is considered low. As of December 31, 2012, Nuveen CA Muni Value traded at a discount of 3.93% below its net asset value, which is better than its one-year historical average discount of .37%.

Scott R. Romans has been running the fund for 11 years and currently receives a manager quality ranking of 52 (0=worst, 99=best). If you desire an average level of risk, then this fund may be an option.

Data Date	Investment Rating	Net Assets ($Mil)	Price	Perfor-mance Rating/Pts	Total Return Y-T-D	Risk Rating/Pts
12-12	B-	261.05	10.03	C+ / 5.9	4.09%	B / 8.8
2011	B	248.50	9.51	C+ / 6.5	-0.11%	B / 8.9
2010	C	240.60	8.63	D+ / 2.6	-0.01%	B / 8.7
2009	C+	246.89	9.07	C- / 3.7	9.98%	B / 8.2

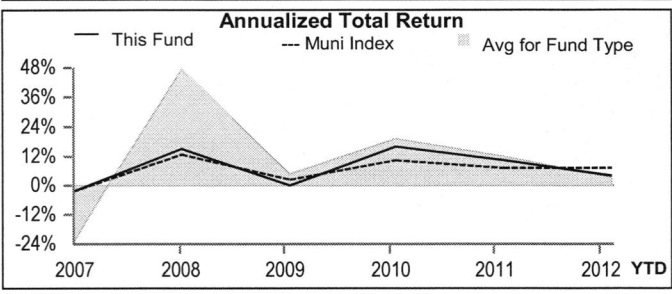

Nuveen CA Performance Plus Muni (NCP)   **A+**   **Excellent**

Fund Family: Nuveen Fund Advisors Inc
Fund Type: Municipal - Single State
Inception Date: November 16, 1989

Major Rating Factors:
Exceptional performance is the major factor driving the A+ (Excellent) TheStreet.com Investment Rating for Nuveen CA Performance Plus Muni. The fund currently has a performance rating of A (Excellent) based on an annualized return of 17.51% over the last three years and a total return of 2.34% year to date 2012. Factored into the performance evaluation is an expense ratio of 1.55% (average).

The fund's risk rating is currently B (Good). It carries a beta of 2.12, meaning it is expected to move 21.2% for every 10% move in the market. Volatility, as measured by both the semi-deviation and a drawdown factor, is considered low. As of December 31, 2012, Nuveen CA Performance Plus Muni traded at a premium of 1.37% above its net asset value, which is worse than its one-year historical average premium of 1.23%.

Scott R. Romans has been running the fund for 11 years and currently receives a manager quality ranking of 68 (0=worst, 99=best). If you desire only a moderate level of risk and strong performance, then this fund is an excellent option.

Data Date	Investment Rating	Net Assets ($Mil)	Price	Perfor-mance Rating/Pts	Total Return Y-T-D	Risk Rating/Pts
12-12	A+	204.79	16.26	A / 9.4	2.34%	B / 8.6
2011	A	191.30	14.87	A / 9.3	-0.81%	B / 8.7
2010	C-	182.06	12.42	D+ / 2.9	7.12%	C+ / 6.5
2009	B-	188.63	12.39	C / 5.4	40.37%	B- / 7.4

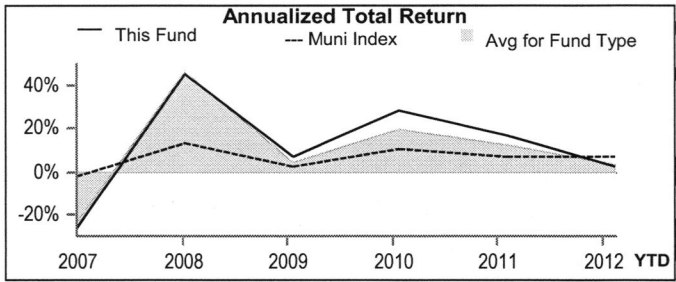

Nuveen CA Prem Inc Muni (NCU)   **A+**   **Excellent**

Fund Family: Nuveen Fund Advisors Inc
Fund Type: Municipal - Single State
Inception Date: June 18, 1993

Major Rating Factors:
Exceptional performance is the major factor driving the A+ (Excellent) TheStreet.com Investment Rating for Nuveen CA Prem Inc Muni. The fund currently has a performance rating of A- (Excellent) based on an annualized return of 16.97% over the last three years and a total return of 3.74% year to date 2012. Factored into the performance evaluation is an expense ratio of 2.16% (high).

The fund's risk rating is currently B (Good). It carries a beta of 2.17, meaning it is expected to move 21.7% for every 10% move in the market. Volatility, as measured by both the semi-deviation and a drawdown factor, is considered low. As of December 31, 2012, Nuveen CA Prem Inc Muni traded at a discount of 3.07% below its net asset value, which is better than its one-year historical average discount of 1.56%.

Scott R. Romans has been running the fund for 11 years and currently receives a manager quality ranking of 58 (0=worst, 99=best). If you desire only a moderate level of risk and strong performance, then this fund is an excellent option.

Data Date	Investment Rating	Net Assets ($Mil)	Price	Perfor-mance Rating/Pts	Total Return Y-T-D	Risk Rating/Pts
12-12	A+	90.44	15.46	A- / 9.2	3.74%	B / 8.7
2011	A	83.80	14.22	A / 9.3	1.05%	B / 8.8
2010	C	78.58	12.44	C / 4.6	9.46%	C+ / 6.1
2009	B-	81.65	12.13	C / 5.5	40.09%	B- / 7.4

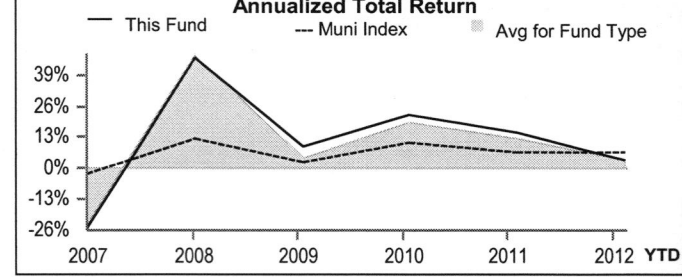

Nuveen CA Quality Inc Muni (NUC)

A+   **Excellent**

Fund Family: Nuveen Fund Advisors Inc
Fund Type: Municipal - Single State
Inception Date: November 20, 1991

Major Rating Factors:

Exceptional performance is the major factor driving the A+ (Excellent) TheStreet.com Investment Rating for Nuveen CA Quality Inc Muni. The fund currently has a performance rating of A+ (Excellent) based on an annualized return of 17.52% over the last three years and a total return of 3.34% year to date 2012. Factored into the performance evaluation is an expense ratio of 1.61% (above average).

The fund's risk rating is currently B (Good). It carries a beta of 2.43, meaning it is expected to move 24.3% for every 10% move in the market. Volatility, as measured by both the semi-deviation and a drawdown factor, is considered low. As of December 31, 2012, Nuveen CA Quality Inc Muni traded at a premium of 4.27% above its net asset value, which is worse than its one-year historical average premium of 3.28%.

Scott R. Romans has been running the fund for 11 years and currently receives a manager quality ranking of 49 (0=worst, 99=best). If you desire only a moderate level of risk and strong performance, then this fund is an excellent option.

Data Date	Investment Rating	Net Assets ($Mil)	Price	Performance Rating/Pts	Total Return Y-T-D	Risk Rating/Pts
12-12	A+	362.44	17.35	A+ / 9.6	3.34%	B / 8.4
2011	A	337.40	15.94	A / 9.5	-0.56%	B / 8.5
2010	C-	320.56	13.33	C- / 3.8	5.46%	C+ / 6.4
2009	B-	329.60	13.52	C+ / 5.9	38.93%	B- / 7.3

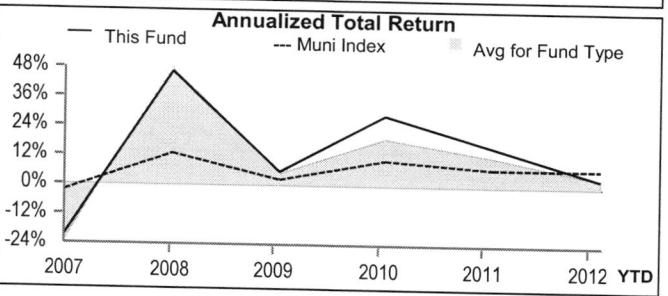

Nuveen CA Select Quality Muni (NVC)

A+   **Excellent**

Fund Family: Nuveen Fund Advisors Inc
Fund Type: Municipal - Single State
Inception Date: May 22, 1991

Major Rating Factors:

Exceptional performance is the major factor driving the A+ (Excellent) TheStreet.com Investment Rating for Nuveen CA Select Quality Muni. The fund currently has a performance rating of A (Excellent) based on an annualized return of 16.55% over the last three years and a total return of 5.11% year to date 2012. Factored into the performance evaluation is an expense ratio of 1.64% (above average).

The fund's risk rating is currently B (Good). It carries a beta of 2.31, meaning it is expected to move 23.1% for every 10% move in the market. Volatility, as measured by both the semi-deviation and a drawdown factor, is considered low. As of December 31, 2012, Nuveen CA Select Quality Muni traded at a premium of .12% above its net asset value, which is better than its one-year historical average premium of 2.43%.

Scott R. Romans has been running the fund for 11 years and currently receives a manager quality ranking of 49 (0=worst, 99=best). If you desire only a moderate level of risk and strong performance, then this fund is an excellent option.

Data Date	Investment Rating	Net Assets ($Mil)	Price	Performance Rating/Pts	Total Return Y-T-D	Risk Rating/Pts
12-12	A+	363.83	16.64	A / 9.4	5.11%	B / 8.4
2011	A	345.90	15.09	A / 9.3	0.40%	B / 8.6
2010	C+	329.54	13.04	C / 5.4	5.00%	C+ / 6.2
2009	B-	342.02	13.29	C+ / 5.8	39.57%	B- / 7.1

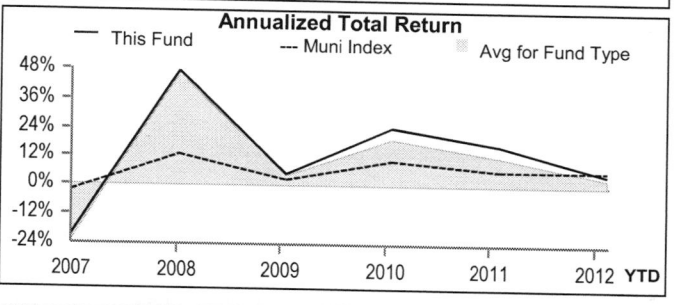

Nuveen CA Select Tax-Free Inc Port (NXC)

A-   **Excellent**

Fund Family: Nuveen Fund Advisors Inc
Fund Type: Municipal - Single State
Inception Date: June 26, 1992

Major Rating Factors:

Strong performance is the major factor driving the A- (Excellent) TheStreet.com Investment Rating for Nuveen CA Select Tax-Free Inc Port. The fund currently has a performance rating of B (Good) based on an annualized return of 12.27% over the last three years and a total return of 3.68% year to date 2012. Factored into the performance evaluation is an expense ratio of 0.42% (very low).

The fund's risk rating is currently B+ (Good). It carries a beta of 1.31, meaning it is expected to move 13.1% for every 10% move in the market. Volatility, as measured by both the semi-deviation and a drawdown factor, is considered very low. As of December 31, 2012, Nuveen CA Select Tax-Free Inc Port traded at a discount of 3.31% below its net asset value, which is better than its one-year historical average discount of 1.32%.

Scott R. Romans has been running the fund for 21 years and currently receives a manager quality ranking of 69 (0=worst, 99=best). If you desire only a moderate level of risk and strong performance, then this fund is an excellent option.

Data Date	Investment Rating	Net Assets ($Mil)	Price	Performance Rating/Pts	Total Return Y-T-D	Risk Rating/Pts
12-12	A-	94.45	15.21	B / 7.9	3.68%	B+ / 9.0
2011	B	91.40	14.08	C+ / 6.8	0.63%	B+ / 9.0
2010	C	87.55	12.75	D+ / 2.7	4.93%	B / 8.5
2009	C+	89.96	12.77	C- / 3.1	6.56%	B / 8.8

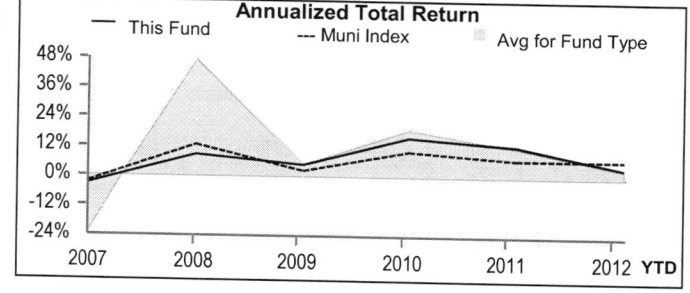

* Denotes ETF Fund

Nuveen California Municipal Value (NCB)

B   **Good**

Fund Family: Nuveen Fund Advisors Inc
Fund Type: Municipal - National
Inception Date: April 28, 2009

Major Rating Factors: Strong performance is the major factor driving the B (Good) TheStreet.com Investment Rating for Nuveen California Municipal Value. The fund currently has a performance rating of B- (Good) based on an annualized return of 10.81% over the last three years and a total return of 4.42% year to date 2012. Factored into the performance evaluation is an expense ratio of 0.76% (very low).

The fund's risk rating is currently B (Good). It carries a beta of 1.64, meaning it is expected to move 16.4% for every 10% move in the market. Volatility, as measured by both the semi-deviation and a drawdown factor, is considered low. As of December 31, 2012, Nuveen California Municipal Value traded at a discount of 6.91% below its net asset value, which is better than its one-year historical average discount of 3.79%.

Scott R. Romans currently receives a manager quality ranking of 39 (0=worst, 99=best). If you desire only a moderate level of risk and strong performance, then this fund is an excellent option.

Data Date	Investment Rating	Net Assets ($Mil)	Price	Performance Rating/Pts	Total Return Y-T-D	Risk Rating/Pts
12-12	B	56.44	16.29	B- / 7.3	4.42%	B / 8.6
2011	B+	52.60	15.06	B / 7.6	1.46%	B / 8.6
2010	C-	51.66	14.40	D / 2.0	3.81%	B / 8.1

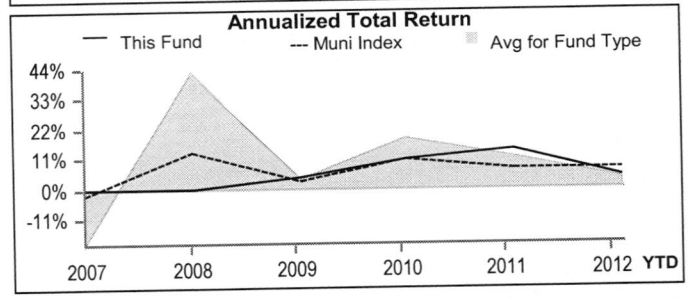

Nuveen Core Equity Alpha Fund (JCE)

C+   **Fair**

Fund Family: Nuveen Fund Advisors Inc
Fund Type: Income
Inception Date: March 28, 2007

Major Rating Factors: Middle of the road best describes Nuveen Core Equity Alpha Fund whose TheStreet.com Investment Rating is currently a C+ (Fair). The fund currently has a performance rating of C+ (Fair) based on an annualized return of 14.12% over the last three years and a total return of 4.34% year to date 2012. Factored into the performance evaluation is an expense ratio of 1.05% (low).

The fund's risk rating is currently B- (Good). It carries a beta of 0.92, meaning that its performance tracks fairly well with that of the overall stock market. Volatility, as measured by both the semi-deviation and a drawdown factor, is considered low. As of December 31, 2012, Nuveen Core Equity Alpha Fund traded at a discount of 11.71% below its net asset value, which is better than its one-year historical average discount of 7.35%.

Adrian D. Banner currently receives a manager quality ranking of 65 (0=worst, 99=best). If you desire an average level of risk, then this fund may be an option.

Data Date	Investment Rating	Net Assets ($Mil)	Price	Performance Rating/Pts	Total Return Y-T-D	Risk Rating/Pts
12-12	C+	222.46	13.35	C+ / 5.9	4.34%	B- / 7.8
2011	C+	222.50	12.47	C+ / 6.4	1.84%	B- / 7.6
2010	C	211.37	13.12	C / 5.5	17.29%	C / 5.2
2009	A	203.74	12.21	A- / 9.0	34.51%	C+ / 5.7

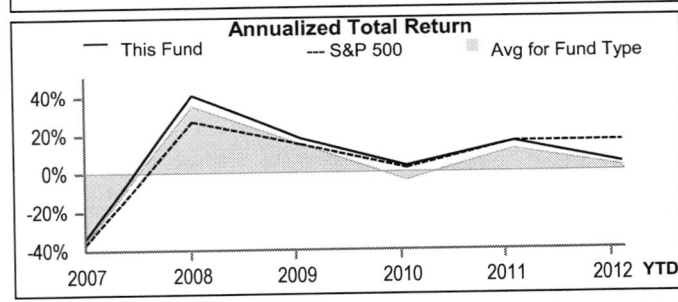

Nuveen Credit Strategies Income (JQC)

B+   **Good**

Fund Family: Nuveen Fund Advisors Inc
Fund Type: Growth and Income
Inception Date: June 25, 2003

Major Rating Factors: Strong performance is the major factor driving the B+ (Good) TheStreet.com Investment Rating for Nuveen Credit Strategies Income. The fund currently has a performance rating of B (Good) based on an annualized return of 17.80% over the last three years and a total return of 3.42% year to date 2012. Factored into the performance evaluation is an expense ratio of 1.86% (above average).

The fund's risk rating is currently B (Good). It carries a beta of 0.62, meaning the fund's expected move will be 6.2% for every 10% move in the market. Volatility, as measured by both the semi-deviation and a drawdown factor, is considered low. As of December 31, 2012, Nuveen Credit Strategies Income traded at a discount of 3.11% below its net asset value, which is worse than its one-year historical average discount of 4.24%.

Gunther M. Stein has been running the fund for 10 years and currently receives a manager quality ranking of 90 (0=worst, 99=best). If you desire only a moderate level of risk and strong performance, then this fund is an excellent option.

Data Date	Investment Rating	Net Assets ($Mil)	Price	Performance Rating/Pts	Total Return Y-T-D	Risk Rating/Pts
12-12	B+	1,388.24	9.65	B / 8.1	3.42%	B / 8.4
2011	B	1,250.00	8.05	B / 8.1	3.35%	B- / 7.7
2010	C+	839.85	8.80	C+ / 6.7	24.24%	C / 4.9
2009	D	1,194.98	7.69	C- / 3.4	65.23%	C- / 4.2

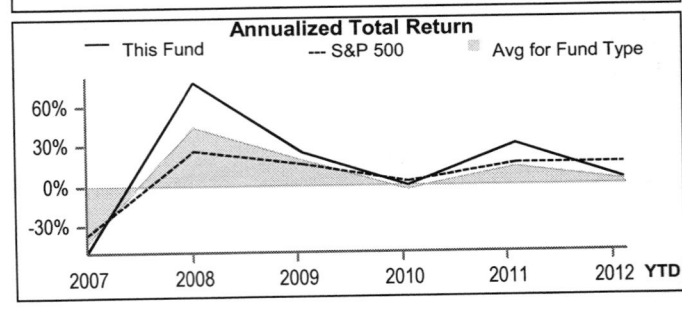

Nuveen CT Prem Inc Muni (NTC)

C+ **Fair**

Fund Family: Nuveen Fund Advisors Inc
Fund Type: Municipal - Single State
Inception Date: May 20, 1993

Major Rating Factors: Middle of the road best describes Nuveen CT Prem Inc Muni whose TheStreet.com Investment Rating is currently a C+ (Fair). The fund currently has a performance rating of C (Fair) based on an annualized return of 6.69% over the last three years and a total return of 2.03% year to date 2012. Factored into the performance evaluation is an expense ratio of 3.08% (high).

The fund's risk rating is currently B+ (Good). It carries a beta of 1.40, meaning it is expected to move 14.0% for every 10% move in the market. Volatility, as measured by both the semi-deviation and a drawdown factor, is considered very low. As of December 31, 2012, Nuveen CT Prem Inc Muni traded at a discount of 6.83% below its net asset value, which is better than its one-year historical average discount of 6.46%.

Michael S. Hamilton currently receives a manager quality ranking of 34 (0=worst, 99=best). If you desire an average level of risk, then this fund may be an option.

Data Date	Investment Rating	Net Assets ($Mil)	Price	Performance Rating/Pts		Total Return Y-T-D	Risk Rating/Pts	
12-12	C+	82.32	14.32	C	4.3	2.03%	B+	9.1
2011	B+	79.80	14.06	B	7.6	0.85%	B+	9.0
2010	C	78.11	13.05	C-	3.3	0.42%	B-	7.9
2009	B-	78.03	13.67	C+	5.7	33.94%	B-	7.6

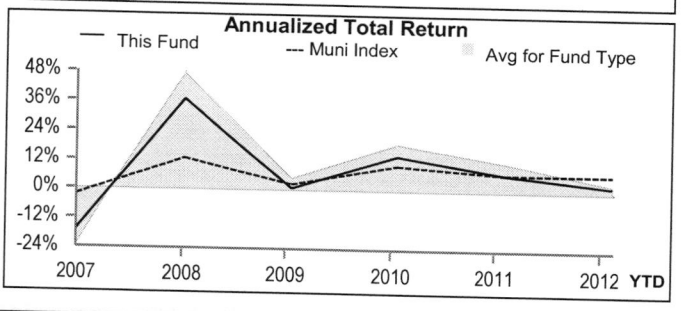

Nuveen Div Adv Muni (NAD)

A- **Excellent**

Fund Family: Nuveen Fund Advisors Inc
Fund Type: Municipal - National
Inception Date: May 25, 1999

Major Rating Factors:
Strong performance is the major factor driving the A- (Excellent) TheStreet.com Investment Rating for Nuveen Div Adv Muni. The fund currently has a performance rating of B+ (Good) based on an annualized return of 12.99% over the last three years and a total return of 3.88% year to date 2012. Factored into the performance evaluation is an expense ratio of 2.02% (high).

The fund's risk rating is currently B (Good). It carries a beta of 2.24, meaning it is expected to move 22.4% for every 10% move in the market. Volatility, as measured by both the semi-deviation and a drawdown factor, is considered low. As of December 31, 2012, Nuveen Div Adv Muni traded at a discount of 4.39% below its net asset value, which is better than its one-year historical average discount of 2.95%.

Thomas C. Spalding has been running the fund for 11 years and currently receives a manager quality ranking of 29 (0=worst, 99=best). If you desire only a moderate level of risk and strong performance, then this fund is an excellent option.

Data Date	Investment Rating	Net Assets ($Mil)	Price	Performance Rating/Pts		Total Return Y-T-D	Risk Rating/Pts	
12-12	A-	565.36	15.48	B+	8.4	3.88%	B	8.6
2011	A-	577.40	14.56	B+	8.7	-0.27%	B	8.7
2010	C-	561.83	12.90	C-	3.7	1.95%	C+	6.5
2009	C+	569.67	13.50	C+	5.6	38.15%	B-	7.1

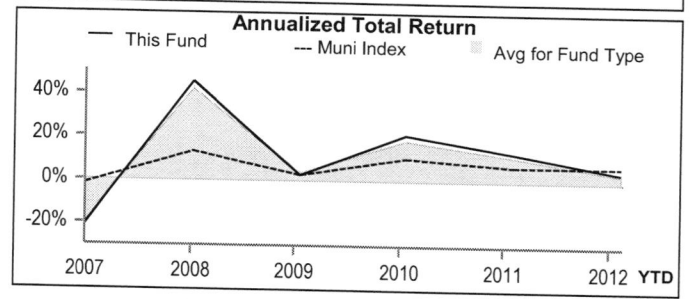

Nuveen Div Adv Muni 3 (NZF)

B **Good**

Fund Family: Nuveen Fund Advisors Inc
Fund Type: Municipal - National
Inception Date: September 25, 2001

Major Rating Factors: Strong performance is the major factor driving the B (Good) TheStreet.com Investment Rating for Nuveen Div Adv Muni 3. The fund currently has a performance rating of B- (Good) based on an annualized return of 11.47% over the last three years and a total return of 2.72% year to date 2012. Factored into the performance evaluation is an expense ratio of 1.46% (average).

The fund's risk rating is currently B (Good). It carries a beta of 1.89, meaning it is expected to move 18.9% for every 10% move in the market. Volatility, as measured by both the semi-deviation and a drawdown factor, is considered low. As of December 31, 2012, Nuveen Div Adv Muni 3 traded at a discount of 6.22% below its net asset value, which is better than its one-year historical average discount of 2.48%.

Paul L. Brennan has been running the fund for 7 years and currently receives a manager quality ranking of 40 (0=worst, 99=best). If you desire only a moderate level of risk and strong performance, then this fund is an excellent option.

Data Date	Investment Rating	Net Assets ($Mil)	Price	Performance Rating/Pts		Total Return Y-T-D	Risk Rating/Pts	
12-12	B	587.05	15.09	B-	7.2	2.72%	B	8.7
2011	B+	596.70	14.71	B+	8.3	-1.50%	B	8.8
2010	C	584.56	13.29	C-	3.9	5.81%	C+	6.8
2009	C+	592.68	13.45	C	5.0	36.58%	B-	7.4

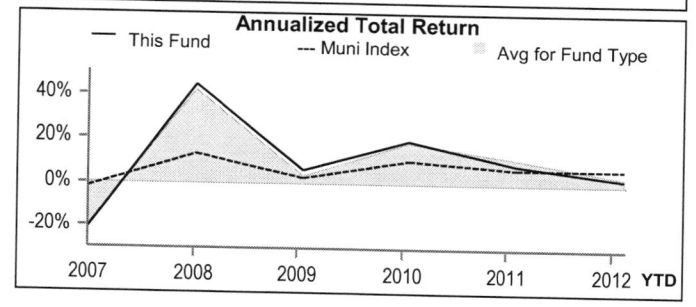

Nuveen Div Adv Muni Income (NVG)   B   Good

Fund Family: Nuveen Fund Advisors Inc
Fund Type: Municipal - National
Inception Date: March 25, 2002

Major Rating Factors: Nuveen Div Adv Muni Income receives a TheStreet.com Investment Rating of B (Good). The fund currently has a performance rating of C+ (Fair) based on an annualized return of 10.42% over the last three years and a total return of 3.32% year to date 2012. Factored into the performance evaluation is an expense ratio of 1.84% (above average).

The fund's risk rating is currently B+ (Good). It carries a beta of 1.68, meaning it is expected to move 16.8% for every 10% move in the market. Volatility, as measured by both the semi-deviation and a drawdown factor, is considered very low. As of December 31, 2012, Nuveen Div Adv Muni Income traded at a discount of 5.65% below its net asset value, which is better than its one-year historical average discount of 3.78%.

Paul L. Brennan has been running the fund for 7 years and currently receives a manager quality ranking of 35 (0=worst, 99=best). If you desire an average level of risk, then this fund may be an option.

Data Date	Investment Rating	Net Assets ($Mil)	Price	Performance Rating/Pts	Total Return Y-T-D	Risk Rating/Pts
12-12	B	448.07	15.35	C+ / 6.9	3.32%	B+ / 9.0
2011	B+	454.20	15.05	B / 7.8	-0.66%	B+ / 9.1
2010	C+	441.21	13.60	C / 4.9	0.77%	C+ / 6.9
2009	B-	457.06	14.30	C+ / 6.2	31.09%	B- / 7.5

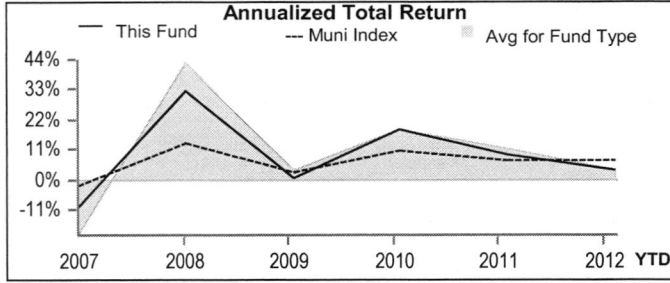

Nuveen Diversified Currency Opp (JGT)   D+   Weak

Fund Family: Nuveen Fund Advisors Inc
Fund Type: Global
Inception Date: April 25, 2007

Major Rating Factors:
Disappointing performance is the major factor driving the D+ (Weak) TheStreet.com Investment Rating for Nuveen Diversified Currency Opp. The fund currently has a performance rating of D+ (Weak) based on an annualized return of 2.89% over the last three years and a total return of 2.10% year to date 2012. Factored into the performance evaluation is an expense ratio of 1.06% (low).

The fund's risk rating is currently B- (Good). It carries a beta of 1.16, meaning it is expected to move 11.6% for every 10% move in the market. Volatility, as measured by both the semi-deviation and a drawdown factor, is considered low. As of December 31, 2012, Nuveen Diversified Currency Opp traded at a discount of 13.68% below its net asset value, which is better than its one-year historical average discount of 11.63%.

Steve S. Lee currently receives a manager quality ranking of 43 (0=worst, 99=best). This fund offers only a moderate level of risk but investors looking for strong performance are still waiting.

Data Date	Investment Rating	Net Assets ($Mil)	Price	Performance Rating/Pts	Total Return Y-T-D	Risk Rating/Pts
12-12	D+	605.96	12.87	D+ / 2.8	2.10%	B- / 7.8
2011	C-	606.00	12.11	D+ / 2.8	1.98%	B- / 7.7
2010	C-	748.96	13.77	C- / 3.0	-1.42%	B- / 7.0
2009	C+	762.97	15.41	C+ / 6.1	21.70%	C+ / 6.4

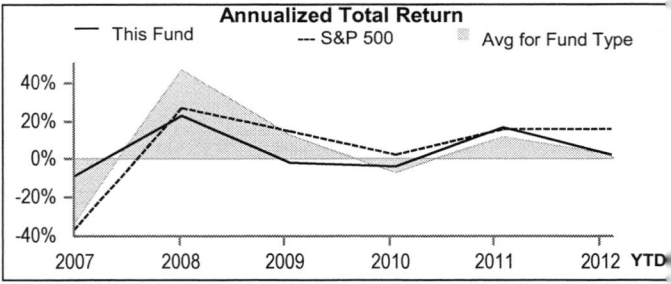

Nuveen Diversified Dividend&Income (JDD)   B   Good

Fund Family: Nuveen Fund Advisors Inc
Fund Type: Growth and Income
Inception Date: September 30, 2003

Major Rating Factors: Strong performance is the major factor driving the B (Good) TheStreet.com Investment Rating for Nuveen Diversified Dividend&Income. The fund currently has a performance rating of B- (Good) based on an annualized return of 16.78% over the last three years and a total return of 5.78% year to date 2012. Factored into the performance evaluation is an expense ratio of 1.92% (above average).

The fund's risk rating is currently B (Good). It carries a beta of 0.75, meaning the fund's expected move will be 7.5% for every 10% move in the market. Volatility, as measured by both the semi-deviation and a drawdown factor, is considered low. As of December 31, 2012, Nuveen Diversified Dividend&Income traded at a discount of 8.88% below its net asset value, which is better than its one-year historical average discount of 3.85%.

Gunther M. Stein has been running the fund for 10 years and currently receives a manager quality ranking of 85 (0=worst, 99=best). If you desire only a moderate level of risk and strong performance, then this fund is an excellent option.

Data Date	Investment Rating	Net Assets ($Mil)	Price	Performance Rating/Pts	Total Return Y-T-D	Risk Rating/Pts
12-12	B	239.89	11.60	B- / 7.4	5.78%	B / 8.0
2011	B	226.70	10.26	B+ / 8.4	3.61%	B- / 7.8
2010	C	222.57	10.89	C+ / 6.4	22.16%	C- / 4.0
2009	D	215.83	9.73	D+ / 2.4	63.04%	C / 4.6

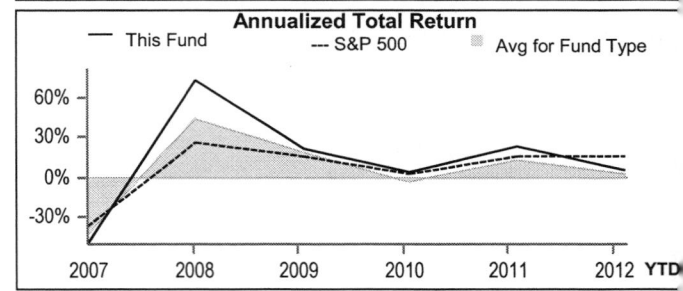

Nuveen Dividend Advantage Muni 2 (NXZ)   B   Good

Fund Family: Nuveen Fund Advisors Inc
Fund Type: Municipal - National
Inception Date: March 27, 2001

Data Date	Investment Rating	Net Assets ($Mil)	Price	Performance Rating/Pts	Total Return Y-T-D	Risk Rating/Pts
12-12	B	427.09	15.22	C+ / 6.5	3.09%	B / 8.7
2011	B+	431.20	14.76	B / 8.1	-0.54%	B / 8.7
2010	C-	436.38	13.30	D / 2.2	-1.17%	B- / 7.6
2009	C+	441.36	14.38	C / 5.3	29.54%	B- / 7.4

Major Rating Factors: Nuveen Dividend Advantage Muni 2 receives a TheStreet.com Investment Rating of B (Good). The fund currently has a performance rating of C+ (Fair) based on an annualized return of 10.10% over the last three years and a total return of 3.09% year to date 2012. Factored into the performance evaluation is an expense ratio of 1.75% (above average).

The fund's risk rating is currently B (Good). It carries a beta of 1.79, meaning it is expected to move 17.9% for every 10% move in the market. Volatility, as measured by both the semi-deviation and a drawdown factor, is considered low. As of December 31, 2012, Nuveen Dividend Advantage Muni 2 traded at a discount of 6.22% below its net asset value, which is better than its one-year historical average discount of 2.10%.

Thomas C. Spalding currently receives a manager quality ranking of 32 (0=worst, 99=best). If you desire an average level of risk, then this fund may be an option.

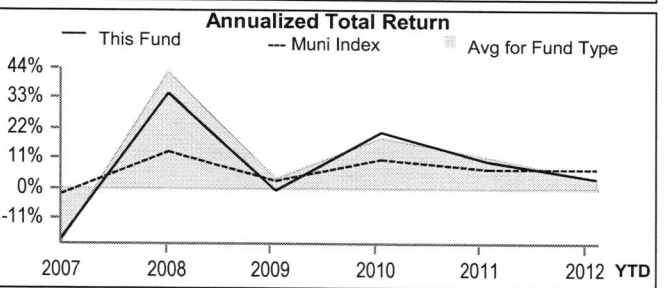

Nuveen Energy MLP Total Return Fun (JMF)   D+   Weak

Fund Family: Nuveen Fund Advisors Inc
Fund Type: Growth and Income
Inception Date: February 24, 2011

Data Date	Investment Rating	Net Assets ($Mil)	Price	Performance Rating/Pts	Total Return Y-T-D	Risk Rating/Pts
12-12	D+	409.91	17.70	C- / 3.4	5.48%	B- / 7.3

Major Rating Factors: Nuveen Energy MLP Total Return Fun receives a TheStreet.com Investment Rating of D+ (Weak). The fund currently has a performance rating of C- (Fair) based on an annualized return of 0.00% over the last three years and a total return of 5.48% year to date 2012. Factored into the performance evaluation is an expense ratio of 1.78% (above average).

The fund's risk rating is currently B- (Good). It carries a beta of 0.00, meaning the fund's expected move will be 0.0% for every 10% move in the market. Volatility, as measured by both the semi-deviation and a drawdown factor, is considered low. As of December 31, 2012, Nuveen Energy MLP Total Return Fun traded at a discount of 1.94% below its net asset value, which is better than its one-year historical average premium of 2.39%.

James J. Cunnane, Jr. currently receives a manager quality ranking of 15 (0=worst, 99=best). If you desire an average level of risk, then this fund may be an option.

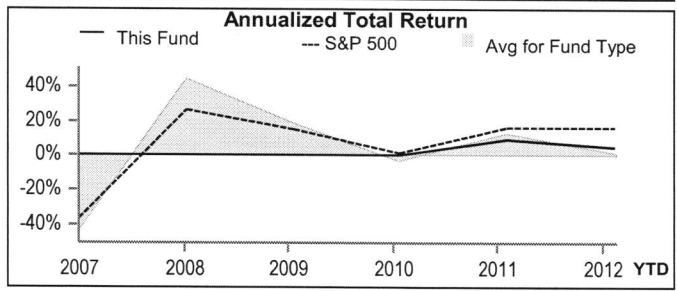

Nuveen EnhancedMunicipal Value (NEV)   B-   Good

Fund Family: Nuveen Fund Advisors Inc
Fund Type: General - Investment Grade
Inception Date: September 25, 2009

Data Date	Investment Rating	Net Assets ($Mil)	Price	Performance Rating/Pts	Total Return Y-T-D	Risk Rating/Pts
12-12	B-	269.05	16.10	C+ / 6.7	4.78%	B / 8.3
2011	B+	273.10	14.23	B+ / 8.3	3.23%	B / 8.2
2010	D+	240.98	12.71	E+ / 0.9	2.73%	B- / 7.6

Major Rating Factors: Nuveen EnhancedMunicipal Value receives a TheStreet.com Investment Rating of B- (Good). The fund currently has a performance rating of C+ (Fair) based on an annualized return of 14.06% over the last three years and a total return of 4.78% year to date 2012. Factored into the performance evaluation is an expense ratio of 1.17% (low).

The fund's risk rating is currently B (Good). It carries a beta of 2.17, meaning it is expected to move 21.7% for every 10% move in the market. Volatility, as measured by both the semi-deviation and a drawdown factor, is considered low. As of December 31, 2012, Nuveen EnhancedMunicipal Value traded at a premium of 1.07% above its net asset value, which is better than its one-year historical average premium of 2.12%.

Steven M. Hlavin has been running the fund for 3 years and currently receives a manager quality ranking of 55 (0=worst, 99=best). If you desire an average level of risk, then this fund may be an option.

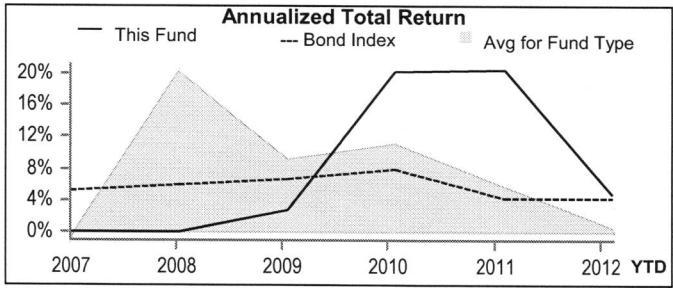

Nuveen Equity Premium & Growth Fun (JPG)   C   Fair

Fund Family: Nuveen Fund Advisors Inc
Fund Type: Income
Inception Date: November 22, 2005

Major Rating Factors: Middle of the road best describes Nuveen Equity Premium &
Growth Fun whose TheStreet.com Investment Rating is currently a C (Fair). The fund
currently has a performance rating of C (Fair) based on an annualized return of
10.30% over the last three years and a total return of 4.56% year to date 2012.
Factored into the performance evaluation is an expense ratio of 0.96% (low).

The fund's risk rating is currently B (Good). It carries a beta of 0.64, meaning the
fund's expected move will be 6.4% for every 10% move in the market. Volatility, as
measured by both the semi-deviation and a drawdown factor, is considered low. As of
December 31, 2012, Nuveen Equity Premium & Growth Fun traded at a discount of
11.62% below its net asset value, which is better than its one-year historical average
discount of 10.05%.

J. Patrick Rogers currently receives a manager quality ranking of 63 (0=worst,
99=best). If you desire an average level of risk, then this fund may be an option.

Data Date	Investment Rating	Net Assets ($Mil)	Price	Performance Rating/Pts	Total Return Y-T-D	Risk Rating/Pts
12-12	C	231.98	12.93	C / 5.0	4.56%	B / 8.1
2011	C	225.70	12.07	C / 4.5	1.08%	B / 8.0
2010	C	226.19	13.85	C+ / 6.0	14.90%	C / 5.3
2009	C-	217.79	13.09	D+ / 2.8	27.99%	C+ / 6.0

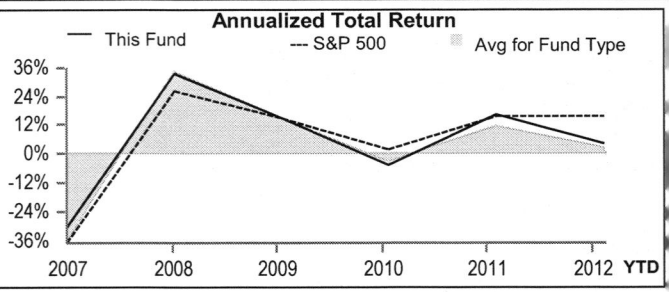

Nuveen Equity Premium Advantage (JLA)   C-   Fair

Fund Family: Nuveen Fund Advisors Inc
Fund Type: Income
Inception Date: May 26, 2005

Major Rating Factors: Middle of the road best describes Nuveen Equity Premium
Advantage whose TheStreet.com Investment Rating is currently a C- (Fair). The fund
currently has a performance rating of C- (Fair) based on an annualized return of
8.51% over the last three years and a total return of 4.12% year to date 2012.
Factored into the performance evaluation is an expense ratio of 0.99% (low).

The fund's risk rating is currently B- (Good). It carries a beta of 0.54, meaning the
fund's expected move will be 5.4% for every 10% move in the market. Volatility, as
measured by both the semi-deviation and a drawdown factor, is considered low. As of
December 31, 2012, Nuveen Equity Premium Advantage traded at a discount of
11.98% below its net asset value, which is better than its one-year historical average
discount of 10.59%.

J. Patrick Rogers currently receives a manager quality ranking of 61 (0=worst,
99=best). If you desire an average level of risk, then this fund may be an option.

Data Date	Investment Rating	Net Assets ($Mil)	Price	Performance Rating/Pts	Total Return Y-T-D	Risk Rating/Pts
12-12	C-	347.19	11.90	C- / 3.9	4.12%	B- / 7.5
2011	C	340.60	11.46	C / 5.0	1.66%	B- / 7.5
2010	C-	349.90	12.90	C / 4.4	8.94%	C / 5.3
2009	C-	339.64	13.07	C- / 3.6	34.61%	C+ / 5.8

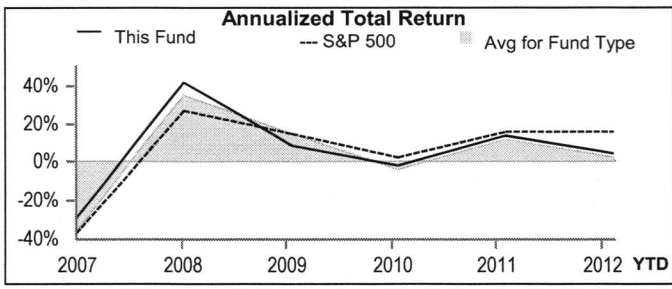

Nuveen Equity Premium Income Fund (JPZ)   C-   Fair

Fund Family: Nuveen Fund Advisors Inc
Fund Type: Income
Inception Date: October 26, 2004

Major Rating Factors: Middle of the road best describes Nuveen Equity Premium
Income Fund whose TheStreet.com Investment Rating is currently a C- (Fair). The
fund currently has a performance rating of C- (Fair) based on an annualized return of
8.43% over the last three years and a total return of 4.82% year to date 2012.
Factored into the performance evaluation is an expense ratio of 0.90% (low).

The fund's risk rating is currently B- (Good). It carries a beta of 0.61, meaning the
fund's expected move will be 6.1% for every 10% move in the market. Volatility, as
measured by both the semi-deviation and a drawdown factor, is considered low. As of
December 31, 2012, Nuveen Equity Premium Income Fund traded at a discount of
11.12% below its net asset value, which is better than its one-year historical average
discount of 9.07%.

J. Patrick Rogers currently receives a manager quality ranking of 82 (0=worst,
99=best). If you desire an average level of risk, then this fund may be an option.

Data Date	Investment Rating	Net Assets ($Mil)	Price	Performance Rating/Pts	Total Return Y-T-D	Risk Rating/Pts
12-12	C-	508.42	11.83	C- / 4.0	4.82%	B- / 7.9
2011	C	496.10	11.18	C- / 4.2	1.25%	B- / 7.8
2010	C-	502.49	12.76	C- / 4.2	8.13%	C / 5.4
2009	C-	487.49	13.00	C- / 3.5	28.97%	C+ / 5.8

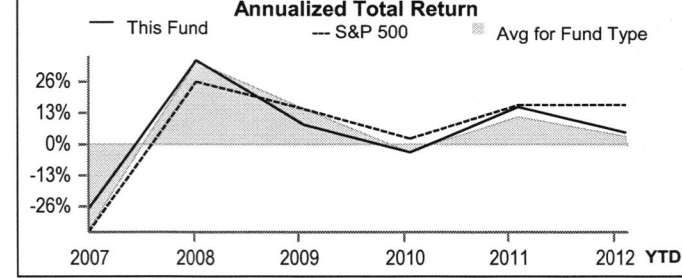

Nuveen Equity Premium Opportunity (JSN)

C-   Fair

Fund Family: Nuveen Fund Advisors Inc
Fund Type: Income
Inception Date: January 26, 2005

Major Rating Factors: Middle of the road best describes Nuveen Equity Premium Opportunity whose TheStreet.com Investment Rating is currently a C- (Fair). The fund currently has a performance rating of C- (Fair) based on an annualized return of 8.09% over the last three years and a total return of 2.32% year to date 2012. Factored into the performance evaluation is an expense ratio of 0.88% (low).

The fund's risk rating is currently B- (Good). It carries a beta of 0.57, meaning the fund's expected move will be 5.7% for every 10% move in the market. Volatility, as measured by both the semi-deviation and a drawdown factor, is considered low. As of December 31, 2012, Nuveen Equity Premium Opportunity traded at a discount of 8.70% below its net asset value, which is better than its one-year historical average discount of 8.45%.

J. Patrick Rogers currently receives a manager quality ranking of 59 (0=worst, 99=best). If you desire an average level of risk, then this fund may be an option.

Data Date	Investment Rating	Net Assets ($Mil)	Price	Perfor-mance Rating/Pts	Total Return Y-T-D	Risk Rating/Pts
12-12	C-	873.91	12.07	C- / 3.8	2.32%	B- / 7.8
2011	C	859.30	11.42	C / 4.5	0.79%	B- / 7.6
2010	C-	878.32	12.88	C / 4.4	7.85%	C / 5.3
2009	C-	858.14	13.20	C- / 4.0	32.50%	C+ / 5.7

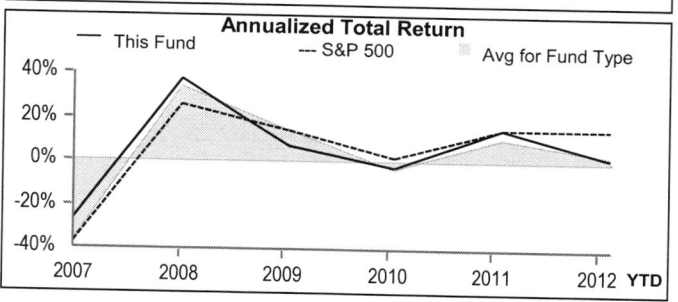

Annualized Total Return

Nuveen Floating Rate Income Fund (JFR)

C+   Fair

Fund Family: Nuveen Fund Advisors Inc
Fund Type: Loan Participation
Inception Date: March 26, 2004

Major Rating Factors: Middle of the road best describes Nuveen Floating Rate Income Fund whose TheStreet.com Investment Rating is currently a C+ (Fair). The fund currently has a performance rating of C+ (Fair) based on an annualized return of 13.40% over the last three years and a total return of 3.20% year to date 2012. Factored into the performance evaluation is an expense ratio of 1.72% (above average).

The fund's risk rating is currently B (Good). It carries a beta of -240.79, meaning the fund's expected move will be -2407.9% for every 10% move in the market. Volatility, as measured by both the semi-deviation and a drawdown factor, is considered low. As of December 31, 2012, Nuveen Floating Rate Income Fund traded at a discount of .49% below its net asset value, which is better than its one-year historical average discount of .17%.

Gunther M. Stein currently receives a manager quality ranking of 99 (0=worst, 99=best). If you desire an average level of risk, then this fund may be an option.

Data Date	Investment Rating	Net Assets ($Mil)	Price	Perfor-mance Rating/Pts	Total Return Y-T-D	Risk Rating/Pts
12-12	C+	572.12	12.19	C+ / 6.5	3.20%	B / 8.0
2011	B	543.20	10.86	B / 7.6	2.30%	B- / 7.9
2010	C+	542.46	11.81	B / 7.7	21.16%	C- / 3.7
2009	C-	500.80	10.35	C / 5.3	71.62%	C / 4.7

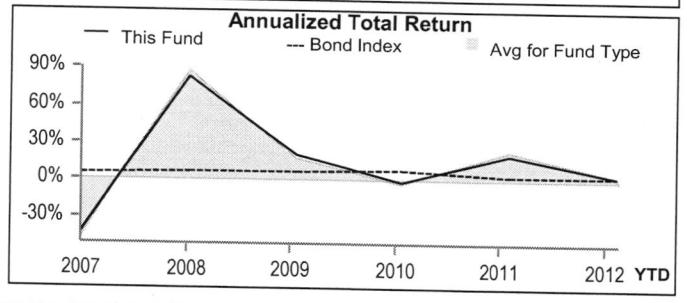

Annualized Total Return

Nuveen Floating Rate Income Opp (JRO)

C+   Fair

Fund Family: Nuveen Fund Advisors Inc
Fund Type: Loan Participation
Inception Date: July 30, 2004

Major Rating Factors: Middle of the road best describes Nuveen Floating Rate Income Opp whose TheStreet.com Investment Rating is currently a C+ (Fair). The fund currently has a performance rating of C+ (Fair) based on an annualized return of 12.32% over the last three years and a total return of 3.43% year to date 2012. Factored into the performance evaluation is an expense ratio of 1.65% (above average).

The fund's risk rating is currently B- (Good). It carries a beta of -235.78, meaning the fund's expected move will be -2357.8% for every 10% move in the market. Volatility, as measured by both the semi-deviation and a drawdown factor, is considered low. As of December 31, 2012, Nuveen Floating Rate Income Opp traded at a premium of .33% above its net asset value, which is better than its one-year historical average premium of 1.74%.

Gunther M. Stein has been running the fund for 6 years and currently receives a manager quality ranking of 99 (0=worst, 99=best). If you desire an average level of risk, then this fund may be an option.

Data Date	Investment Rating	Net Assets ($Mil)	Price	Perfor-mance Rating/Pts	Total Return Y-T-D	Risk Rating/Pts
12-12	C+	369.94	12.25	C+ / 5.9	3.43%	B- / 7.9
2011	B+	340.90	11.04	B+ / 8.6	2.45%	B- / 7.9
2010	C+	322.14	12.08	B / 7.9	19.90%	C- / 3.6
2009	C+	296.41	10.76	B / 7.9	106.49%	C / 4.3

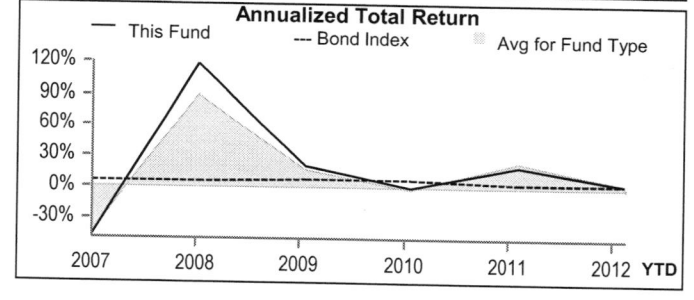

Annualized Total Return

Nuveen GA Div Adv Muni Fund 2 (NKG)

B-   **Good**

Fund Family: Nuveen Fund Advisors Inc
Fund Type: Municipal - Single State
Inception Date: September 25, 2002

Major Rating Factors: Nuveen GA Div Adv Muni Fund 2 receives a TheStreet.com Investment Rating of B- (Good). The fund currently has a performance rating of C+ (Fair) based on an annualized return of 9.95% over the last three years and a total return of 2.49% year to date 2012. Factored into the performance evaluation is an expense ratio of 2.95% (high).

The fund's risk rating is currently B (Good). It carries a beta of 1.42, meaning it is expected to move 14.2% for every 10% move in the market. Volatility, as measured by both the semi-deviation and a drawdown factor, is considered low. As of December 31, 2012, Nuveen GA Div Adv Muni Fund 2 traded at a discount of .34% below its net asset value, which is better than its one-year historical average premium of .08%.

Daniel J. Close has been running the fund for 6 years and currently receives a manager quality ranking of 57 (0=worst, 99=best). If you desire an average level of risk, then this fund may be an option.

Data Date	Investment Rating	Net Assets ($Mil)	Price	Performance Rating/Pts	Total Return Y-T-D	Risk Rating/Pts
12-12	B-	67.04	14.85	C+ / 6.3	2.49%	B / 8.7
2011	A-	65.10	14.63	B+ / 8.6	0.00%	B / 8.8
2010	C	64.72	12.58	C- / 3.1	2.09%	B- / 7.4
2009	B-	65.35	12.98	C+ / 6.3	44.26%	B- / 7.5

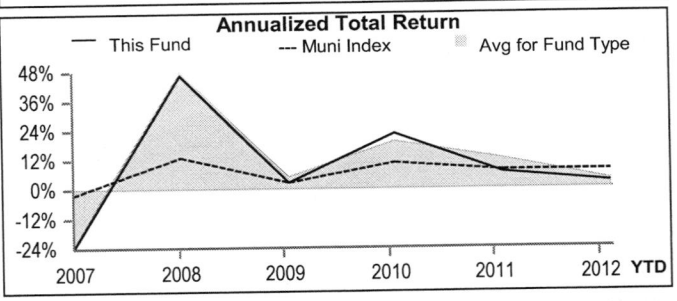

Annualized Total Return

Nuveen Global Income Oppportunitie (JGG)

C-   **Fair**

Fund Family: Nuveen Fund Advisors Inc
Fund Type: Global
Inception Date: June 30, 2006

Major Rating Factors:
Disappointing performance is the major factor driving the C- (Fair) TheStreet.com Investment Rating for Nuveen Global Income Oppportunitie. The fund currently has a performance rating of D+ (Weak) based on an annualized return of 3.68% over the last three years and a total return of 3.49% year to date 2012. Factored into the performance evaluation is an expense ratio of 1.06% (low).

The fund's risk rating is currently B (Good). It carries a beta of 0.36, meaning the fund's expected move will be 3.6% for every 10% move in the market. Volatility, as measured by both the semi-deviation and a drawdown factor, is considered low. As of December 31, 2012, Nuveen Global Income Oppportunitie traded at a discount of 10.53% below its net asset value, which is better than its one-year historical average discount of 6.72%.

Steve S. Lee currently receives a manager quality ranking of 57 (0=worst, 99=best). This fund offers only a moderate level of risk but investors looking for strong performance are still waiting.

Data Date	Investment Rating	Net Assets ($Mil)	Price	Performance Rating/Pts	Total Return Y-T-D	Risk Rating/Pts
12-12	C-	144.70	14.02	D+ / 2.5	3.49%	B / 8.3
2011	C-	144.70	14.16	D+ / 2.6	-0.57%	B / 8.1
2010	C+	156.25	15.65	C / 5.2	-0.21%	C+ / 6.9
2009	C	161.34	17.23	C- / 4.1	15.94%	C+ / 6.9

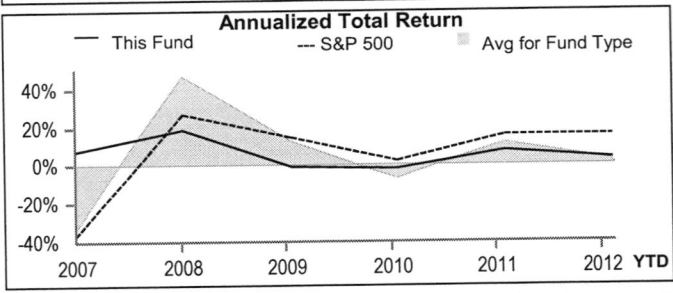

Annualized Total Return

Nuveen Global Value Opportunities (JGV)

D   **Weak**

Fund Family: Nuveen Fund Advisors Inc
Fund Type: Global
Inception Date: July 25, 2006

Major Rating Factors:
Disappointing performance is the major factor driving the D (Weak) TheStreet.com Investment Rating for Nuveen Global Value Opportunities. The fund currently has a performance rating of D (Weak) based on an annualized return of 1.74% over the last three years and a total return of 2.21% year to date 2012. Factored into the performance evaluation is an expense ratio of 1.16% (low).

The fund's risk rating is currently B- (Good). It carries a beta of 0.56, meaning the fund's expected move will be 5.6% for every 10% move in the market. Volatility, as measured by both the semi-deviation and a drawdown factor, is considered low. As of December 31, 2012, Nuveen Global Value Opportunities traded at a discount of 8.42% below its net asset value, which is better than its one-year historical average discount of 6.77%.

Michael A. Hart has been running the fund for 5 years and currently receives a manager quality ranking of 49 (0=worst, 99=best). This fund offers only a moderate level of risk but investors looking for strong performance are still waiting.

Data Date	Investment Rating	Net Assets ($Mil)	Price	Performance Rating/Pts	Total Return Y-T-D	Risk Rating/Pts
12-12	D	324.96	14.91	D / 2.0	2.21%	B- / 7.1
2011	C+	325.00	16.76	C+ / 5.8	-2.15%	B- / 7.7
2010	B+	351.82	20.30	B+ / 8.4	23.36%	C / 5.1
2009	C+	340.16	17.53	C+ / 6.9	52.59%	C+ / 5.6

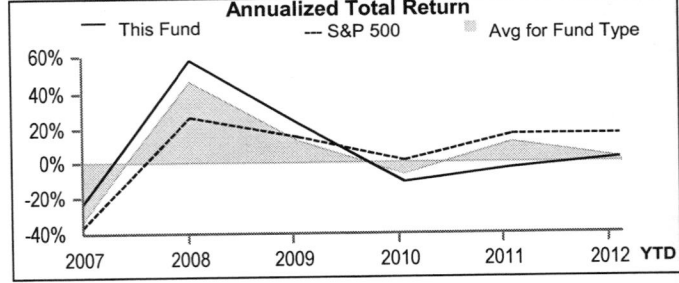

Annualized Total Return

Nuveen Investment Quality Muni Fun (NQM)

A   **Excellent**

Fund Family: Nuveen Fund Advisors Inc
Fund Type: Municipal - National
Inception Date: June 21, 1990

Major Rating Factors:
Strong performance is the major factor driving the A (Excellent) TheStreet.com Investment Rating for Nuveen Investment Quality Muni Fun. The fund currently has a performance rating of B+ (Good) based on an annualized return of 14.43% over the last three years and a total return of 4.99% year to date 2012. Factored into the performance evaluation is an expense ratio of 1.50% (average).

The fund's risk rating is currently B (Good). It carries a beta of 2.31, meaning it is expected to move 23.1% for every 10% move in the market. Volatility, as measured by both the semi-deviation and a drawdown factor, is considered low. As of December 31, 2012, Nuveen Investment Quality Muni Fun traded at a discount of 3.78% below its net asset value, which is better than its one-year historical average premium of .05%.

Christopher L. Drahn currently receives a manager quality ranking of 36 (0=worst, 99=best). If you desire only a moderate level of risk and strong performance, then this fund is an excellent option.

Data Date	Investment Rating	Net Assets ($Mil)	Price	Performance Rating/Pts	Total Return Y-T-D	Risk Rating/Pts
12-12	A	535.52	16.03	B+ / 8.6	4.99%	B / 8.6
2011	A	552.10	15.61	A- / 9.2	0.64%	B / 8.8
2010	C+	510.91	13.49	C / 4.3	7.98%	B- / 7.1
2009	C+	534.55	13.32	C / 4.8	29.90%	B- / 7.7

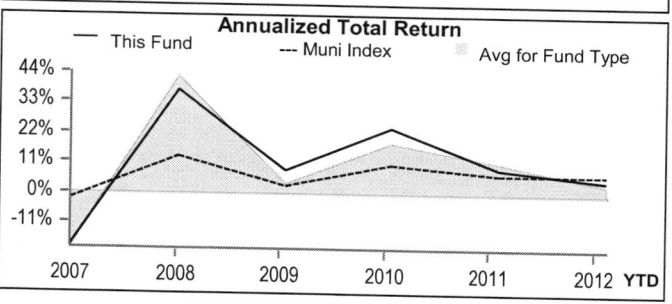

Nuveen MA AMT/F Muni Income (NGX)

D+   **Weak**

Fund Family: Nuveen Fund Advisors Inc
Fund Type: Municipal - Single State
Inception Date: November 21, 2002

Major Rating Factors:
Disappointing performance is the major factor driving the D+ (Weak) TheStreet.com Investment Rating for Nuveen MA AMT/F Muni Income. The fund currently has a performance rating of D+ (Weak) based on an annualized return of 3.40% over the last three years and a total return of 3.60% year to date 2012. Factored into the performance evaluation is an expense ratio of 3.16% (high).

The fund's risk rating is currently B (Good). It carries a beta of 1.89, meaning it is expected to move 18.9% for every 10% move in the market. Volatility, as measured by both the semi-deviation and a drawdown factor, is considered low. As of December 31, 2012, Nuveen MA AMT/F Muni Income traded at a discount of 7.56% below its net asset value, which is better than its one-year historical average discount of 1.79%.

Michael S. Hamilton currently receives a manager quality ranking of 15 (0=worst, 99=best). This fund offers only a moderate level of risk but investors looking for strong performance are still waiting.

Data Date	Investment Rating	Net Assets ($Mil)	Price	Performance Rating/Pts	Total Return Y-T-D	Risk Rating/Pts
12-12	D+	40.63	13.82	D+ / 2.4	3.60%	B / 8.3
2011	C+	40.20	13.84	C / 5.2	0.14%	B / 8.5
2010	C	40.10	13.68	D+ / 2.6	-1.26%	B- / 7.9
2009	B-	40.40	14.57	C+ / 6.8	34.25%	B- / 7.7

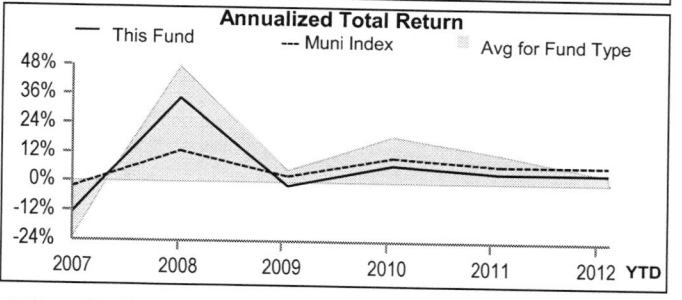

Nuveen MA Div Adv Muni (NMB)

C+   **Fair**

Fund Family: Nuveen Fund Advisors Inc
Fund Type: Municipal - Single State
Inception Date: January 30, 2001

Major Rating Factors: Middle of the road best describes Nuveen MA Div Adv Muni whose TheStreet.com Investment Rating is currently a C+ (Fair). The fund currently has a performance rating of C (Fair) based on an annualized return of 8.71% over the last three years and a total return of 2.81% year to date 2012. Factored into the performance evaluation is an expense ratio of 3.09% (high).

The fund's risk rating is currently B (Good). It carries a beta of 1.75, meaning it is expected to move 17.5% for every 10% move in the market. Volatility, as measured by both the semi-deviation and a drawdown factor, is considered low. As of December 31, 2012, Nuveen MA Div Adv Muni traded at a discount of 3.98% below its net asset value, which is better than its one-year historical average discount of 2.64%.

Michael S. Hamilton currently receives a manager quality ranking of 30 (0=worst, 99=best). If you desire an average level of risk, then this fund may be an option.

Data Date	Investment Rating	Net Assets ($Mil)	Price	Performance Rating/Pts	Total Return Y-T-D	Risk Rating/Pts
12-12	C+	30.12	14.96	C / 5.2	2.81%	B / 8.4
2011	B	28.90	13.90	B- / 7.1	1.44%	B / 8.3
2010	C	28.24	13.60	C / 4.6	4.30%	C+ / 6.7
2009	C+	28.60	13.80	C / 4.9	34.98%	B- / 7.5

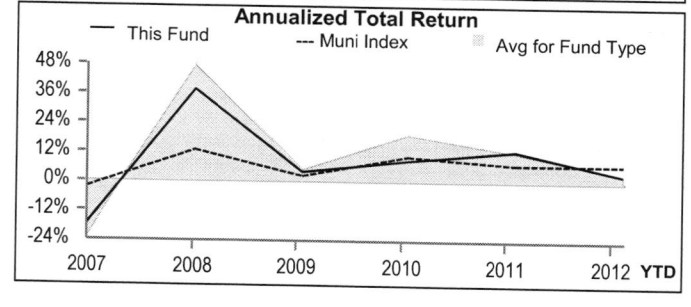

* Denotes ETF Fund

Nuveen MA Prem Inc Muni (NMT)

C+   **Fair**

Fund Family: Nuveen Fund Advisors Inc
Fund Type: Municipal - Single State
Inception Date: March 18, 1993

Major Rating Factors: Middle of the road best describes Nuveen MA Prem Inc Muni whose TheStreet.com Investment Rating is currently a C+ (Fair). The fund currently has a performance rating of C (Fair) based on an annualized return of 8.57% over the last three years and a total return of 3.52% year to date 2012. Factored into the performance evaluation is an expense ratio of 3.03% (high).

The fund's risk rating is currently B (Good). It carries a beta of 1.79, meaning it is expected to move 17.9% for every 10% move in the market. Volatility, as measured by both the semi-deviation and a drawdown factor, is considered low. As of December 31, 2012, Nuveen MA Prem Inc Muni traded at a discount of 4.57% below its net asset value, which is better than its one-year historical average discount of 1.48%.

Michael S. Hamilton currently receives a manager quality ranking of 31 (0=worst, 99=best). If you desire an average level of risk, then this fund may be an option.

Data Date	Investment Rating	Net Assets ($Mil)	Price	Performance Rating/Pts	Total Return Y-T-D	Risk Rating/Pts
12-12	C+	73.76	14.82	C / 4.9	3.52%	B / 8.7
2011	A-	71.10	14.61	B+ / 8.6	0.92%	B / 8.8
2010	C	69.03	13.35	C / 4.8	4.28%	C+ / 6.5
2009	B-	69.25	13.55	C+ / 6.0	42.87%	B- / 7.4

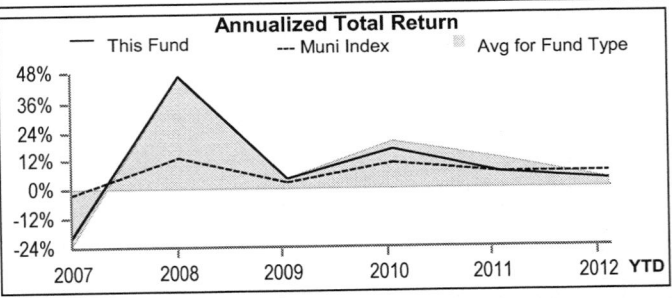

Nuveen MD Prem Inc Muni Fund (NMY)

C+   **Fair**

Fund Family: Nuveen Fund Advisors Inc
Fund Type: Municipal - Single State
Inception Date: March 18, 1993

Major Rating Factors: Middle of the road best describes Nuveen MD Prem Inc Muni Fund whose TheStreet.com Investment Rating is currently a C+ (Fair). The fund currently has a performance rating of C (Fair) based on an annualized return of 9.70% over the last three years and a total return of 2.23% year to date 2012. Factored into the performance evaluation is an expense ratio of 2.91% (high).

The fund's risk rating is currently B (Good). It carries a beta of 1.61, meaning it is expected to move 16.1% for every 10% move in the market. Volatility, as measured by both the semi-deviation and a drawdown factor, is considered low. As of December 31, 2012, Nuveen MD Prem Inc Muni Fund traded at a discount of 3.00% below its net asset value, which is better than its one-year historical average discount of .70%.

Thomas C. Spalding has been running the fund for 2 years and currently receives a manager quality ranking of 38 (0=worst, 99=best). If you desire an average level of risk, then this fund may be an option.

Data Date	Investment Rating	Net Assets ($Mil)	Price	Performance Rating/Pts	Total Return Y-T-D	Risk Rating/Pts
12-12	C+	167.21	15.20	C / 5.4	2.23%	B / 8.8
2011	A	160.60	14.93	A- / 9.0	3.25%	B / 8.9
2010	C+	157.24	13.45	C / 5.5	2.66%	C+ / 6.3
2009	B-	157.09	13.80	C+ / 6.1	45.56%	B- / 7.1

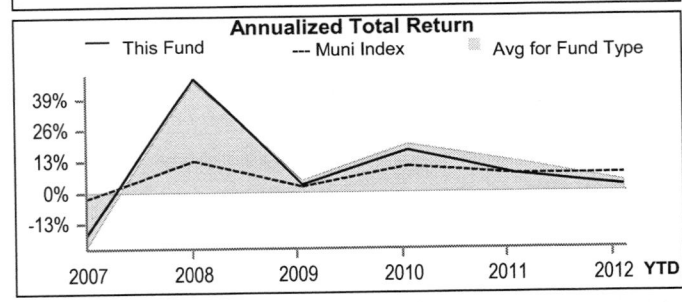

Nuveen MI Quality Inc Muni (NUM)

A-   **Excellent**

Fund Family: Nuveen Fund Advisors Inc
Fund Type: Municipal - Single State
Inception Date: October 24, 1991

Major Rating Factors:
Strong performance is the major factor driving the A- (Excellent) TheStreet.com Investment Rating for Nuveen MI Quality Inc Muni. The fund currently has a performance rating of B (Good) based on an annualized return of 13.65% over the last three years and a total return of 3.69% year to date 2012. Factored into the performance evaluation is an expense ratio of 1.75% (above average).

The fund's risk rating is currently B (Good). It carries a beta of 1.77, meaning it is expected to move 17.7% for every 10% move in the market. Volatility, as measured by both the semi-deviation and a drawdown factor, is considered low. As of December 31, 2012, Nuveen MI Quality Inc Muni traded at a discount of 6.42% below its net asset value, which is better than its one-year historical average discount of 3.19%.

Daniel J. Close has been running the fund for 6 years and currently receives a manager quality ranking of 60 (0=worst, 99=best). If you desire only a moderate level of risk and strong performance, then this fund is an excellent option.

Data Date	Investment Rating	Net Assets ($Mil)	Price	Performance Rating/Pts	Total Return Y-T-D	Risk Rating/Pts
12-12	A-	187.26	15.31	B / 8.1	3.69%	B / 8.9
2011	A-	178.30	14.62	B+ / 8.5	-0.41%	B+ / 9.1
2010	C	170.98	13.10	C / 4.8	9.07%	C+ / 6.5
2009	B	175.48	12.75	C / 5.4	34.07%	B- / 7.8

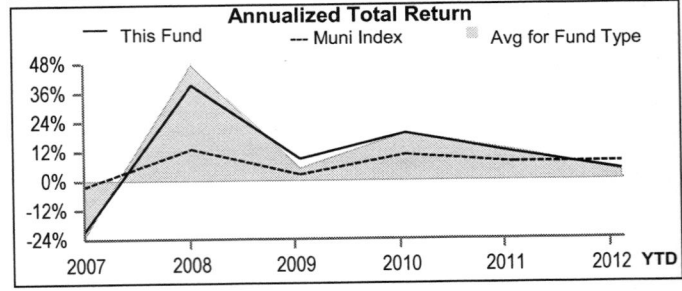

Nuveen MO Prem Inc Muni (NOM)

B   **Good**

Fund Family: Nuveen Fund Advisors Inc
Fund Type: Municipal - Single State
Inception Date: May 20, 1993

Major Rating Factors: Strong performance is the major factor driving the B (Good) TheStreet.com Investment Rating for Nuveen MO Prem Inc Muni. The fund currently has a performance rating of B- (Good) based on an annualized return of 11.19% over the last three years and a total return of 10.50% year to date 2012. Factored into the performance evaluation is an expense ratio of 2.95% (high).

The fund's risk rating is currently B (Good). It carries a beta of 1.42, meaning it is expected to move 14.2% for every 10% move in the market. Volatility, as measured by both the semi-deviation and a drawdown factor, is considered low. As of December 31, 2012, Nuveen MO Prem Inc Muni traded at a premium of 8.11% above its net asset value, which is better than its one-year historical average premium of 16.37%.

Christopher L. Drahn currently receives a manager quality ranking of 30 (0=worst, 99=best). If you desire only a moderate level of risk and strong performance, then this fund is an excellent option.

Data Date	Investment Rating	Net Assets ($Mil)	Price	Performance Rating/Pts	Total Return Y-T-D	Risk Rating/Pts
12-12	B	33.98	16.00	B- / 7.1	10.50%	B / 8.4
2011	A-	32.80	16.42	A- / 9.0	0.78%	B / 8.5
2010	C+	31.35	14.50	C / 5.0	-1.68%	C+ / 6.5
2009	B+	31.22	15.50	B- / 7.0	34.30%	C+ / 6.7

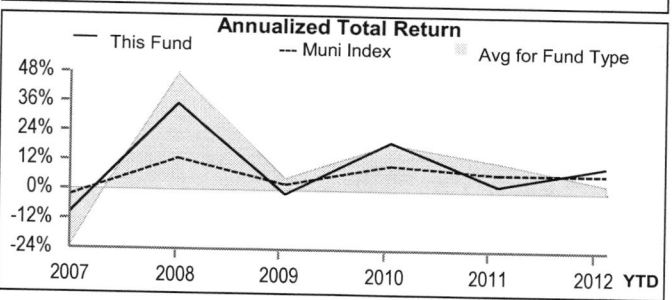

Nuveen Mortgage Opportunity Term (JLS)

B+   **Good**

Fund Family: Nuveen Fund Advisors Inc
Fund Type: Mortgage
Inception Date: November 25, 2009

Major Rating Factors: Strong performance is the major factor driving the B+ (Good) TheStreet.com Investment Rating for Nuveen Mortgage Opportunity Term. The fund currently has a performance rating of B+ (Good) based on an annualized return of 13.86% over the last three years and a total return of 5.18% year to date 2012. Factored into the performance evaluation is an expense ratio of 1.44% (average).

The fund's risk rating is currently B (Good). It carries a beta of -1.73, meaning the fund's expected move will be -17.3% for every 10% move in the market. Volatility, as measured by both the semi-deviation and a drawdown factor, is considered low. As of December 31, 2012, Nuveen Mortgage Opportunity Term traded at a discount of 1.45% below its net asset value, which is better than its one-year historical average premium of 2.77%.

John V. Miller currently receives a manager quality ranking of 97 (0=worst, 99=best). If you desire only a moderate level of risk and strong performance, then this fund is an excellent option.

Data Date	Investment Rating	Net Assets ($Mil)	Price	Performance Rating/Pts	Total Return Y-T-D	Risk Rating/Pts
12-12	B+	346.83	27.22	B+ / 8.3	5.18%	B / 8.2
2011	D+	346.80	20.35	D- / 1.4	4.67%	B / 8.3
2010	A+	0.00	25.50	B / 8.2	10.44%	B / 8.7

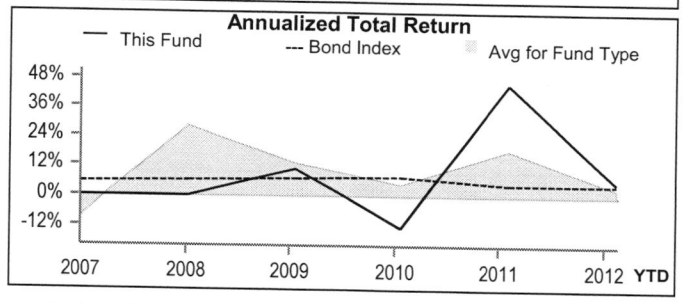

Nuveen Mortgage Opportunity Term 2 (JMT)

A+   **Excellent**

Fund Family: Nuveen Fund Advisors Inc
Fund Type: Mortgage
Inception Date: February 24, 2010

Major Rating Factors:
Exceptional performance is the major factor driving the A+ (Excellent) TheStreet.com Investment Rating for Nuveen Mortgage Opportunity Term 2. The fund currently has a performance rating of A+ (Excellent) based on an annualized return of 0.00% over the last three years and a total return of 4.67% year to date 2012. Factored into the performance evaluation is an expense ratio of 1.58% (above average).

The fund's risk rating is currently B (Good). It carries a beta of 0.00, meaning the fund's expected move will be 0.0% for every 10% move in the market. Volatility, as measured by both the semi-deviation and a drawdown factor, is considered low. As of December 31, 2012, Nuveen Mortgage Opportunity Term 2 traded at a discount of 2.65% below its net asset value, which is better than its one-year historical average premium of 1.68%.

John V. Miller currently receives a manager quality ranking of 98 (0=worst, 99=best). If you desire only a moderate level of risk and strong performance, then this fund is an excellent option.

Data Date	Investment Rating	Net Assets ($Mil)	Price	Performance Rating/Pts	Total Return Y-T-D	Risk Rating/Pts
12-12	A+	104.62	27.18	A+ / 9.8	4.67%	B / 8.3
2011	D+	104.60	20.40	D / 1.6	3.77%	B / 8.3

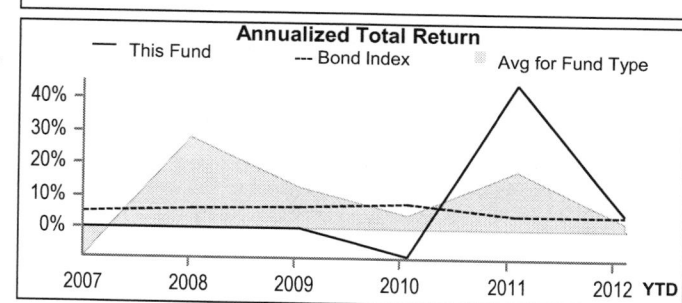

Nuveen Muni Advantage (NMA)

B   Good

Fund Family: Nuveen Fund Advisors Inc
Fund Type: Municipal - National
Inception Date: December 28, 1989

Major Rating Factors: Strong performance is the major factor driving the B (Good) TheStreet.com Investment Rating for Nuveen Muni Advantage. The fund currently has a performance rating of B- (Good) based on an annualized return of 10.80% over the last three years and a total return of 3.29% year to date 2012. Factored into the performance evaluation is an expense ratio of 2.01% (high).

The fund's risk rating is currently B (Good). It carries a beta of 2.10, meaning it is expected to move 21.0% for every 10% move in the market. Volatility, as measured by both the semi-deviation and a drawdown factor, is considered low. As of December 31, 2012, Nuveen Muni Advantage traded at a discount of 3.86% below its net asset value, which is better than its one-year historical average discount of 1.65%.

Thomas C. Spalding has been running the fund for 11 years and currently receives a manager quality ranking of 27 (0=worst, 99=best). If you desire only a moderate level of risk and strong performance, then this fund is an excellent option.

Data Date	Investment Rating	Net Assets ($Mil)	Price	Performance Rating/Pts	Total Return Y-T-D	Risk Rating/Pts
12-12	B	626.62	15.21	B- / 7.5	3.29%	B / 8.4
2011	B+	634.30	14.68	B / 8.0	-1.57%	B / 8.5
2010	C-	624.08	13.08	C- / 3.0	-1.70%	C+ / 6.5
2009	C+	634.51	14.25	C+ / 6.3	39.72%	C+ / 6.9

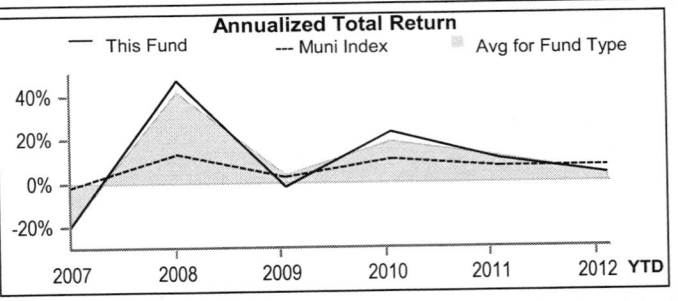

Annualized Total Return

Nuveen Muni High Income Opport (NMZ)

A-   Excellent

Fund Family: Nuveen Fund Advisors Inc
Fund Type: Municipal - High Yield
Inception Date: November 19, 2003

Major Rating Factors:
Strong performance is the major factor driving the A- (Excellent) TheStreet.com Investment Rating for Nuveen Muni High Income Opport. The fund currently has a performance rating of B+ (Good) based on an annualized return of 12.30% over the last three years and a total return of 1.56% year to date 2012. Factored into the performance evaluation is an expense ratio of 1.40% (average).

The fund's risk rating is currently B (Good). It carries a beta of 1.72, meaning it is expected to move 17.2% for every 10% move in the market. Volatility, as measured by both the semi-deviation and a drawdown factor, is considered low. As of December 31, 2012, Nuveen Muni High Income Opport traded at a premium of 3.75% above its net asset value, which is worse than its one-year historical average premium of 3.52%.

John V. Miller has been running the fund for 10 years and currently receives a manager quality ranking of 58 (0=worst, 99=best). If you desire only a moderate level of risk and strong performance, then this fund is an excellent option.

Data Date	Investment Rating	Net Assets ($Mil)	Price	Performance Rating/Pts	Total Return Y-T-D	Risk Rating/Pts
12-12	A-	323.09	14.10	B+ / 8.6	1.56%	B / 8.1
2011	B+	330.90	12.11	B+ / 8.3	1.49%	B / 8.3
2010	D+	288.96	11.45	D- / 1.5	-1.31%	C+ / 6.9
2009	C	300.97	12.60	C / 4.7	51.50%	C+ / 6.0

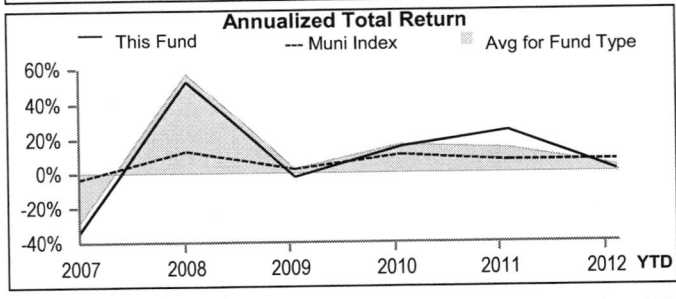

Annualized Total Return

Nuveen Muni High Income Opport 2 (NMD)

A   Excellent

Fund Family: Nuveen Fund Advisors Inc
Fund Type: Municipal - High Yield
Inception Date: November 16, 2007

Major Rating Factors:
Exceptional performance is the major factor driving the A (Excellent) TheStreet.com Investment Rating for Nuveen Muni High Income Opport 2. The fund currently has a performance rating of A- (Excellent) based on an annualized return of 12.94% over the last three years and a total return of 3.58% year to date 2012. Factored into the performance evaluation is an expense ratio of 1.61% (above average).

The fund's risk rating is currently B (Good). It carries a beta of 1.73, meaning it is expected to move 17.3% for every 10% move in the market. Volatility, as measured by both the semi-deviation and a drawdown factor, is considered low. As of December 31, 2012, Nuveen Muni High Income Opport 2 traded at a premium of 1.82% above its net asset value, which is worse than its one-year historical average premium of .86%.

John V. Miller currently receives a manager quality ranking of 66 (0=worst, 99=best). If you desire only a moderate level of risk and strong performance, then this fund is an excellent option.

Data Date	Investment Rating	Net Assets ($Mil)	Price	Performance Rating/Pts	Total Return Y-T-D	Risk Rating/Pts
12-12	A	199.43	13.42	A- / 9.1	3.58%	B / 8.2
2011	B	201.80	11.44	B / 7.8	0.52%	B / 8.4
2010	D	174.35	10.82	D- / 1.3	2.47%	C+ / 6.6
2009	A+	183.30	11.46	A+ / 9.6	57.72%	C+ / 6.4

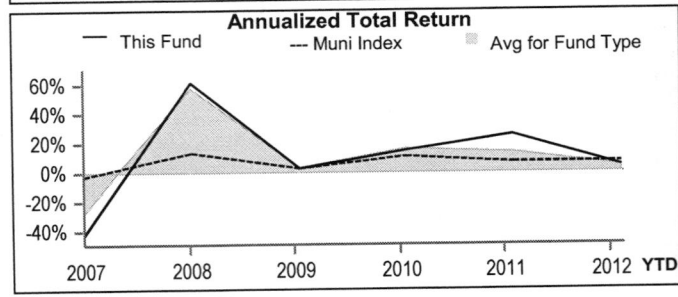

Annualized Total Return

Nuveen Muni Income (NMI)

B-   **Good**

Fund Family: Nuveen Fund Advisors Inc
Fund Type: Municipal - National
Inception Date: April 20, 1988

Major Rating Factors: Nuveen Muni Income receives a TheStreet.com Investment Rating of B- (Good). The fund currently has a performance rating of C+ (Fair) based on an annualized return of 9.82% over the last three years and a total return of 2.06% year to date 2012. Factored into the performance evaluation is an expense ratio of 0.77% (very low).

The fund's risk rating is currently B (Good). It carries a beta of 1.39, meaning it is expected to move 13.9% for every 10% move in the market. Volatility, as measured by both the semi-deviation and a drawdown factor, is considered low. As of December 31, 2012, Nuveen Muni Income traded at a premium of 3.67% above its net asset value, which is better than its one-year historical average premium of 5.40%.

Christopher L. Drahn currently receives a manager quality ranking of 50 (0=worst, 99=best). If you desire an average level of risk, then this fund may be an option.

Data Date	Investment Rating	Net Assets ($Mil)	Price	Perfor-mance Rating/Pts	Total Return Y-T-D	Risk Rating/Pts
12-12	B-	88.49	12.15	C+ / 6.2	2.06%	B / 8.7
2011	B+	90.20	11.53	B- / 7.4	0.35%	B / 8.9
2010	C+	84.88	10.30	C- / 3.9	-0.83%	B- / 7.9
2009	B-	87.01	10.95	C / 5.5	18.61%	B- / 7.3

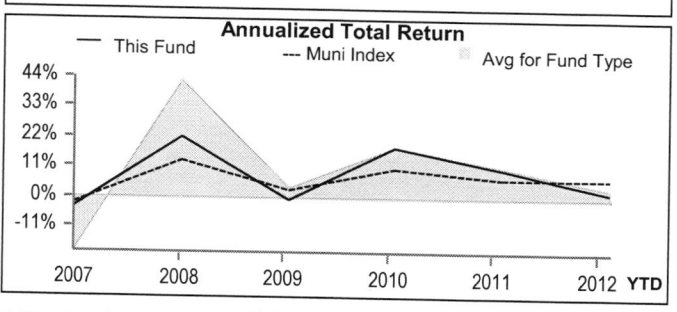

Nuveen Muni Market Opportunity (NMO)

B   **Good**

Fund Family: Nuveen Fund Advisors Inc
Fund Type: Municipal - National
Inception Date: March 22, 1990

Major Rating Factors: Strong performance is the major factor driving the B (Good) TheStreet.com Investment Rating for Nuveen Muni Market Opportunity. The fund currently has a performance rating of B- (Good) based on an annualized return of 10.51% over the last three years and a total return of 3.00% year to date 2012. Factored into the performance evaluation is an expense ratio of 2.10% (high).

The fund's risk rating is currently B (Good). It carries a beta of 2.17, meaning it is expected to move 21.7% for every 10% move in the market. Volatility, as measured by both the semi-deviation and a drawdown factor, is considered low. As of December 31, 2012, Nuveen Muni Market Opportunity traded at a discount of 4.68% below its net asset value, which is better than its one-year historical average discount of 2.67%.

Thomas C. Spalding has been running the fund for 11 years and currently receives a manager quality ranking of 27 (0=worst, 99=best). If you desire only a moderate level of risk and strong performance, then this fund is an excellent option.

Data Date	Investment Rating	Net Assets ($Mil)	Price	Perfor-mance Rating/Pts	Total Return Y-T-D	Risk Rating/Pts
12-12	B	622.82	14.66	B- / 7.3	3.00%	B / 8.5
2011	B+	636.00	13.84	B+ / 8.3	0.87%	B / 8.6
2010	C	636.76	12.87	C / 4.4	3.40%	C+ / 6.4
2009	C+	645.65	13.35	C / 5.5	31.35%	B- / 7.1

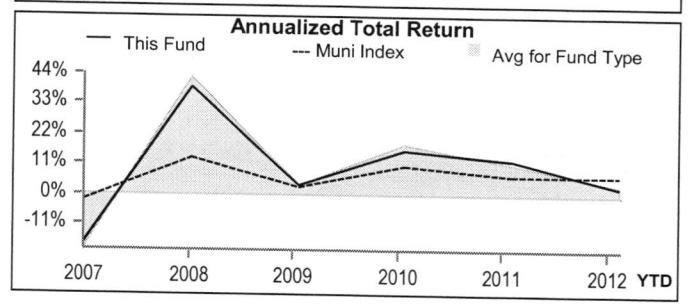

Nuveen Muni Opportunity (NIO)

B+   **Good**

Fund Family: Nuveen Fund Advisors Inc
Fund Type: Municipal - National
Inception Date: September 27, 1991

Major Rating Factors: Strong performance is the major factor driving the B+ (Good) TheStreet.com Investment Rating for Nuveen Muni Opportunity. The fund currently has a performance rating of B (Good) based on an annualized return of 11.79% over the last three years and a total return of 3.46% year to date 2012. Factored into the performance evaluation is an expense ratio of 1.63% (above average).

The fund's risk rating is currently B (Good). It carries a beta of 1.75, meaning it is expected to move 17.5% for every 10% move in the market. Volatility, as measured by both the semi-deviation and a drawdown factor, is considered low. As of December 31, 2012, Nuveen Muni Opportunity traded at a discount of 4.13% below its net asset value, which is better than its one-year historical average discount of 3.48%.

Paul L. Brennan has been running the fund for 7 years and currently receives a manager quality ranking of 45 (0=worst, 99=best). If you desire only a moderate level of risk and strong performance, then this fund is an excellent option.

Data Date	Investment Rating	Net Assets ($Mil)	Price	Perfor-mance Rating/Pts	Total Return Y-T-D	Risk Rating/Pts
12-12	B+	1,404.81	15.33	B / 7.8	3.46%	B / 8.8
2011	B+	1,435.40	14.92	B+ / 8.4	-0.80%	B / 8.9
2010	C	1,358.84	13.04	C- / 4.0	3.04%	B- / 7.0
2009	B-	1,205.12	13.44	C / 5.4	29.95%	B- / 7.6

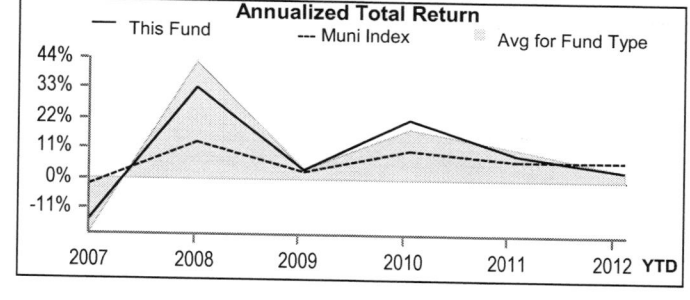

Nuveen Muni Value (NUV)   C+   Fair

Fund Family: Nuveen Fund Advisors Inc
Fund Type: Municipal - National
Inception Date: June 18, 1987

Major Rating Factors: Middle of the road best describes Nuveen Muni Value whose TheStreet.com Investment Rating is currently a C+ (Fair). The fund currently has a performance rating of C (Fair) based on an annualized return of 7.53% over the last three years and a total return of 2.24% year to date 2012. Factored into the performance evaluation is an expense ratio of 0.65% (very low).

The fund's risk rating is currently B+ (Good). It carries a beta of 1.34, meaning it is expected to move 13.4% for every 10% move in the market. Volatility, as measured by both the semi-deviation and a drawdown factor, is considered very low. As of December 31, 2012, Nuveen Muni Value traded at a discount of .97% below its net asset value, which is better than its one-year historical average premium of .68%.

Thomas C. Spalding has been running the fund for 26 years and currently receives a manager quality ranking of 39 (0=worst, 99=best). If you desire an average level of risk, then this fund may be an option.

Data Date	Investment Rating	Net Assets ($Mil)	Price	Performance Rating/Pts	Total Return Y-T-D	Risk Rating/Pts
12-12	C+	1,915.23	10.25	C / 4.8	2.24%	B+ / 9.0
2011	B-	1,939.10	9.80	C / 5.4	0.27%	B+ / 9.0
2010	C+	1,872.03	9.19	C- / 3.7	-0.22%	B / 8.1
2009	C+	1,931.30	9.69	C / 4.5	12.15%	B- / 7.8

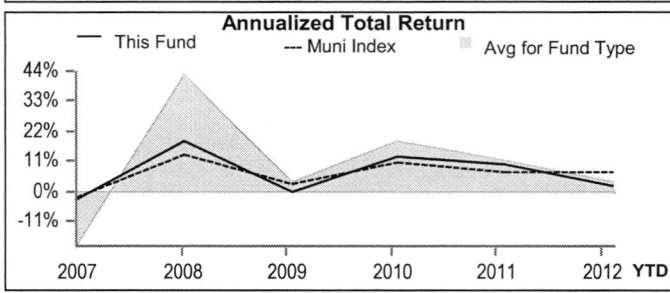

Nuveen NC Prem Inc Muni (NNC)   C   Fair

Fund Family: Nuveen Fund Advisors Inc
Fund Type: Municipal - Single State
Inception Date: May 20, 1993

Major Rating Factors: Middle of the road best describes Nuveen NC Prem Inc Muni whose TheStreet.com Investment Rating is currently a C (Fair). The fund currently has a performance rating of C (Fair) based on an annualized return of 7.49% over the last three years and a total return of 2.78% year to date 2012. Factored into the performance evaluation is an expense ratio of 3.28% (high).

The fund's risk rating is currently B (Good). It carries a beta of 1.39, meaning it is expected to move 13.9% for every 10% move in the market. Volatility, as measured by both the semi-deviation and a drawdown factor, is considered low. As of December 31, 2012, Nuveen NC Prem Inc Muni traded at a discount of 2.07% below its net asset value, which is better than its one-year historical average premium of .75%.

Daniel J. Close has been running the fund for 6 years and currently receives a manager quality ranking of 35 (0=worst, 99=best). If you desire an average level of risk, then this fund may be an option.

Data Date	Investment Rating	Net Assets ($Mil)	Price	Performance Rating/Pts	Total Return Y-T-D	Risk Rating/Pts
12-12	C	97.50	15.11	C / 4.4	2.78%	B / 8.8
2011	B+	95.10	15.25	B / 7.7	0.39%	B / 8.8
2010	C+	93.57	13.96	C+ / 6.3	2.69%	C+ / 6.9
2009	B-	93.88	14.30	C+ / 6.3	36.07%	B- / 7.4

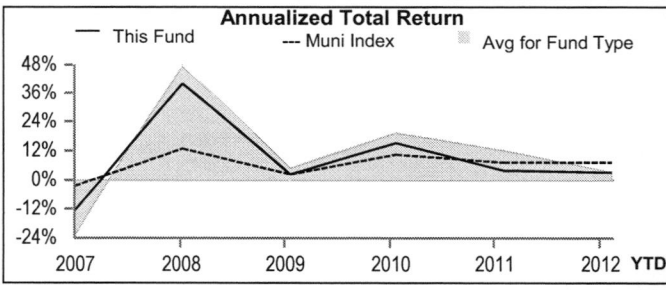

Nuveen New Jersey Municipal Value (NJV)   A   Excellent

Fund Family: Nuveen Fund Advisors Inc
Fund Type: Municipal - National
Inception Date: April 28, 2009

Major Rating Factors:
Strong performance is the major factor driving the A (Excellent) TheStreet.com Investment Rating for Nuveen New Jersey Municipal Value. The fund currently has a performance rating of B+ (Good) based on an annualized return of 11.68% over the last three years and a total return of 3.33% year to date 2012. Factored into the performance evaluation is an expense ratio of 0.85% (very low).

The fund's risk rating is currently B (Good). It carries a beta of 1.46, meaning it is expected to move 14.6% for every 10% move in the market. Volatility, as measured by both the semi-deviation and a drawdown factor, is considered low. As of December 31, 2012, Nuveen New Jersey Municipal Value traded at a premium of 1.30% above its net asset value, which is worse than its one-year historical average discount of .49%.

Paul L. Brennan currently receives a manager quality ranking of 61 (0=worst, 99=best). If you desire only a moderate level of risk and strong performance, then this fund is an excellent option.

Data Date	Investment Rating	Net Assets ($Mil)	Price	Performance Rating/Pts	Total Return Y-T-D	Risk Rating/Pts
12-12	A	25.96	17.14	B+ / 8.5	3.33%	B / 8.6
2011	B+	24.70	15.38	B+ / 8.3	0.13%	B / 8.7
2010	C+	24.72	14.87	C- / 3.7	5.49%	B / 8.5

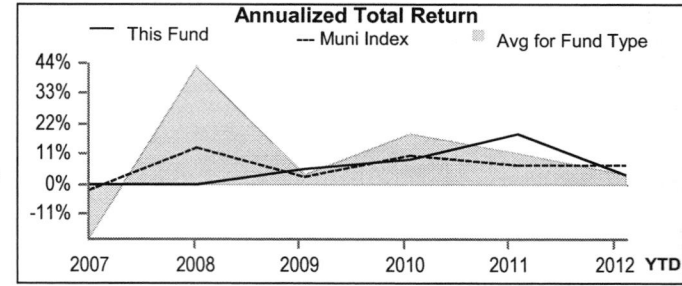

Nuveen New York Municipal Value 2 (NYV)

B-   **Good**

Fund Family: Nuveen Fund Advisors Inc
Fund Type: Municipal - National
Inception Date: April 28, 2009

Major Rating Factors: Nuveen New York Municipal Value 2 receives a TheStreet.com Investment Rating of B- (Good). The fund currently has a performance rating of C+ (Fair) based on an annualized return of 8.90% over the last three years and a total return of 3.77% year to date 2012. Factored into the performance evaluation is an expense ratio of 0.75% (very low).

The fund's risk rating is currently B (Good). It carries a beta of 1.48, meaning it is expected to move 14.8% for every 10% move in the market. Volatility, as measured by both the semi-deviation and a drawdown factor, is considered low. As of December 31, 2012, Nuveen New York Municipal Value 2 traded at a discount of 4.63% below its net asset value, which is better than its one-year historical average discount of 2.45%.

Scott R. Romans currently receives a manager quality ranking of 38 (0=worst, 99=best). If you desire an average level of risk, then this fund may be an option.

Data Date	Investment Rating	Net Assets ($Mil)	Price	Performance Rating/Pts	Total Return Y-T-D	Risk Rating/Pts
12-12	B-	38.43	15.66	C+ / 6.0	3.77%	B / 8.7
2011	B	36.10	14.56	B- / 7.3	0.62%	B / 8.7
2010	C-	37.80	13.98	D- / 1.3	2.54%	B / 8.0

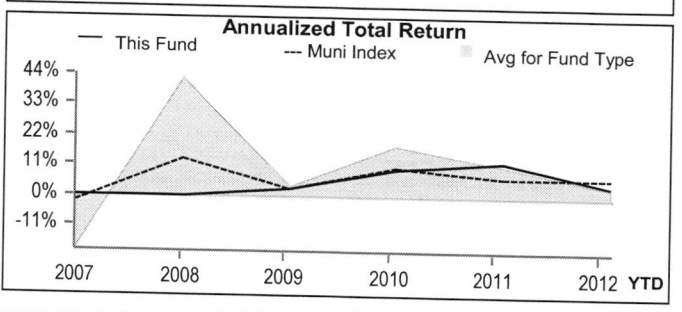

Nuveen NJ Div Adv Muni (NXJ)

A-   **Excellent**

Fund Family: Nuveen Fund Advisors Inc
Fund Type: Municipal - Single State
Inception Date: March 27, 2001

Major Rating Factors:
Strong performance is the major factor driving the A- (Excellent) TheStreet.com Investment Rating for Nuveen NJ Div Adv Muni. The fund currently has a performance rating of B (Good) based on an annualized return of 13.53% over the last three years and a total return of 4.56% year to date 2012. Factored into the performance evaluation is an expense ratio of 2.52% (high).

The fund's risk rating is currently B (Good). It carries a beta of 2.22, meaning it is expected to move 22.2% for every 10% move in the market. Volatility, as measured by both the semi-deviation and a drawdown factor, is considered low. As of December 31, 2012, Nuveen NJ Div Adv Muni traded at a discount of 5.02% below its net asset value, which is better than its one-year historical average discount of 1.92%.

Paul L. Brennan has been running the fund for 2 years and currently receives a manager quality ranking of 34 (0=worst, 99=best). If you desire only a moderate level of risk and strong performance, then this fund is an excellent option.

Data Date	Investment Rating	Net Assets ($Mil)	Price	Performance Rating/Pts	Total Return Y-T-D	Risk Rating/Pts
12-12	A-	100.58	15.34	B / 8.2	4.56%	B / 8.5
2011	B+	97.40	14.00	B+ / 8.6	1.07%	B / 8.7
2010	C	95.30	13.15	C / 5.0	9.08%	C+ / 6.3
2009	C	96.32	12.81	C / 4.4	42.00%	B- / 7.2

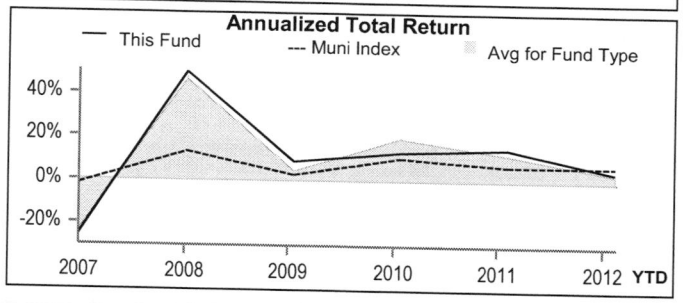

Nuveen NJ Div Adv Muni Fund 2 (NUJ)

A-   **Excellent**

Fund Family: Nuveen Fund Advisors Inc
Fund Type: Municipal - Single State
Inception Date: March 25, 2002

Major Rating Factors:
Strong performance is the major factor driving the A- (Excellent) TheStreet.com Investment Rating for Nuveen NJ Div Adv Muni Fund 2. The fund currently has a performance rating of B+ (Good) based on an annualized return of 13.81% over the last three years and a total return of 3.67% year to date 2012. Factored into the performance evaluation is an expense ratio of 2.52% (high).

The fund's risk rating is currently B (Good). It carries a beta of 1.87, meaning it is expected to move 18.7% for every 10% move in the market. Volatility, as measured by both the semi-deviation and a drawdown factor, is considered low. As of December 31, 2012, Nuveen NJ Div Adv Muni Fund 2 traded at a premium of 4.01% above its net asset value, which is worse than its one-year historical average premium of 3.43%.

Paul L. Brennan currently receives a manager quality ranking of 61 (0=worst, 99=best). If you desire only a moderate level of risk and strong performance, then this fund is an excellent option.

Data Date	Investment Rating	Net Assets ($Mil)	Price	Performance Rating/Pts	Total Return Y-T-D	Risk Rating/Pts
12-12	A-	68.91	16.34	B+ / 8.8	3.67%	B / 8.2
2011	A-	66.40	14.54	B+ / 8.9	0.76%	B / 8.5
2010	C-	65.41	13.08	D+ / 2.9	4.60%	C+ / 6.6
2009	C	65.93	13.30	C / 4.6	43.78%	B- / 7.0

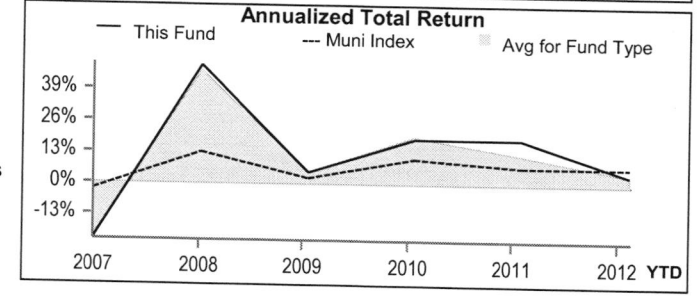

Nuveen NJ Investment Quality Muni (NQJ)

B+　　　**Good**

Fund Family: Nuveen Fund Advisors Inc
Fund Type:　Municipal - Single State
Inception Date:　February 21, 1991

Major Rating Factors: Strong performance is the major factor driving the B+ (Good) TheStreet.com Investment Rating for Nuveen NJ Investment Quality Muni. The fund currently has a performance rating of B (Good) based on an annualized return of 12.37% over the last three years and a total return of 3.59% year to date 2012. Factored into the performance evaluation is an expense ratio of 1.61% (above average).

The fund's risk rating is currently B (Good). It carries a beta of 1.91, meaning it is expected to move 19.1% for every 10% move in the market. Volatility, as measured by both the semi-deviation and a drawdown factor, is considered low. As of December 31, 2012, Nuveen NJ Investment Quality Muni traded at a discount of 3.41% below its net asset value, which is better than its one-year historical average discount of .83%.

Paul L. Brennan currently receives a manager quality ranking of 47 (0=worst, 99=best). If you desire only a moderate level of risk and strong performance, then this fund is an excellent option.

Data Date	Investment Rating	Net Assets ($Mil)	Price	Performance Rating/Pts	Total Return Y-T-D	Risk Rating/Pts
12-12	B+	313.08	15.30	B / 7.7	3.59%	B / 8.6
2011	B+	302.20	14.28	B / 8.2	0.01%	B / 8.8
2010	C+	295.38	13.12	C / 5.2	8.04%	C+ / 6.3
2009	B-	298.16	12.90	C+ / 5.8	37.89%	B- / 7.6

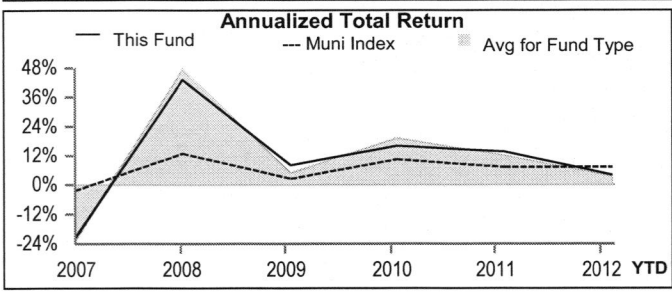

Nuveen NJ Prem Inc Muni (NNJ)

A+　　　**Excellent**

Fund Family: Nuveen Fund Advisors Inc
Fund Type:　Municipal - Single State
Inception Date:　December 17, 1992

Major Rating Factors:
Strong performance is the major factor driving the A+ (Excellent) TheStreet.com Investment Rating for Nuveen NJ Prem Inc Muni. The fund currently has a performance rating of B+ (Good) based on an annualized return of 14.32% over the last three years and a total return of 5.02% year to date 2012. Factored into the performance evaluation is an expense ratio of 1.64% (above average).

The fund's risk rating is currently B (Good). It carries a beta of 1.44, meaning it is expected to move 14.4% for every 10% move in the market. Volatility, as measured by both the semi-deviation and a drawdown factor, is considered low. As of December 31, 2012, Nuveen NJ Prem Inc Muni traded at a premium of 1.29% above its net asset value, which is better than its one-year historical average premium of 1.32%.

Paul L. Brennan currently receives a manager quality ranking of 74 (0=worst, 99=best). If you desire only a moderate level of risk and strong performance, then this fund is an excellent option.

Data Date	Investment Rating	Net Assets ($Mil)	Price	Performance Rating/Pts	Total Return Y-T-D	Risk Rating/Pts
12-12	A+	171.21	16.53	B+ / 8.8	5.02%	B / 8.6
2011	B+	184.90	15.49	B+ / 8.4	-2.00%	B / 8.8
2010	C	180.02	13.55	C / 4.4	6.43%	C+ / 6.7
2009	B-	182.23	13.47	C+ / 5.8	34.60%	B- / 7.6

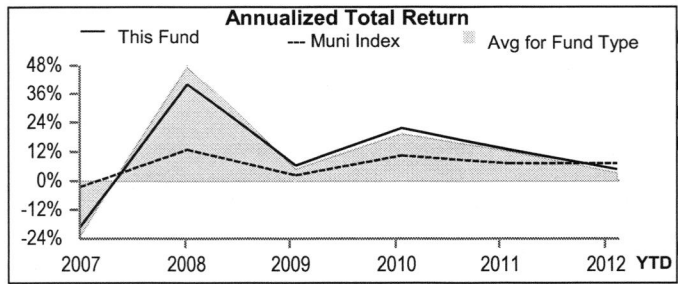

Nuveen NY AMT/Fr Muni Income (NRK)

B　　　**Good**

Fund Family: Nuveen Fund Advisors Inc
Fund Type:　Municipal - Single State
Inception Date:　November 21, 2002

Major Rating Factors: Nuveen NY AMT/Fr Muni Income receives a TheStreet.com Investment Rating of B (Good). The fund currently has a performance rating of C+ (Fair) based on an annualized return of 9.82% over the last three years and a total return of 2.78% year to date 2012. Factored into the performance evaluation is an expense ratio of 2.82% (high).

The fund's risk rating is currently B+ (Good). It carries a beta of 1.48, meaning it is expected to move 14.8% for every 10% move in the market. Volatility, as measured by both the semi-deviation and a drawdown factor, is considered very low. As of December 31, 2012, Nuveen NY AMT/Fr Muni Income traded at a discount of 1.24% below its net asset value, which is worse than its one-year historical average discount of 2.39%.

Scott R. Romans currently receives a manager quality ranking of 46 (0=worst, 99=best). If you desire an average level of risk, then this fund may be an option.

Data Date	Investment Rating	Net Assets ($Mil)	Price	Performance Rating/Pts	Total Return Y-T-D	Risk Rating/Pts
12-12	B	54.14	15.10	C+ / 6.8	2.78%	B+ / 9.0
2011	B+	52.90	14.13	B- / 7.3	1.70%	B+ / 9.0
2010	C+	53.87	13.17	C- / 3.6	2.25%	B / 8.0
2009	B-	53.22	13.57	C+ / 6.3	37.21%	B- / 7.9

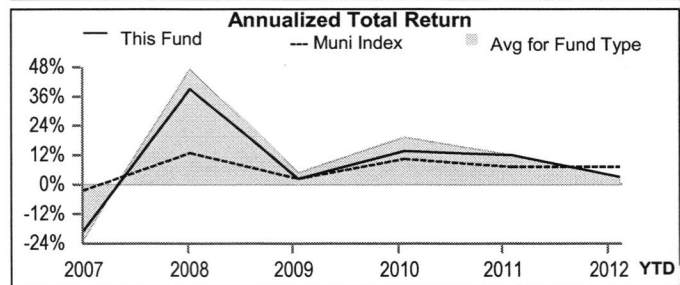

Nuveen NY Div Adv Muni (NAN)

A-   Excellent

Fund Family: Nuveen Fund Advisors Inc
Fund Type: Municipal - Single State
Inception Date: May 25, 1999

Major Rating Factors:
Strong performance is the major factor driving the A- (Excellent) TheStreet.com Investment Rating for Nuveen NY Div Adv Muni. The fund currently has a performance rating of B (Good) based on an annualized return of 12.43% over the last three years and a total return of 2.94% year to date 2012. Factored into the performance evaluation is an expense ratio of 2.37% (high).

The fund's risk rating is currently B (Good). It carries a beta of 1.82, meaning it is expected to move 18.2% for every 10% move in the market. Volatility, as measured by both the semi-deviation and a drawdown factor, is considered low. As of December 31, 2012, Nuveen NY Div Adv Muni traded at a discount of 4.56% below its net asset value, which is better than its one-year historical average discount of 3.92%.

Scott R. Romans currently receives a manager quality ranking of 50 (0=worst, 99=best). If you desire only a moderate level of risk and strong performance, then this fund is an excellent option.

Data Date	Investment Rating	Net Assets ($Mil)	Price	Performance Rating/Pts	Total Return Y-T-D	Risk Rating/Pts
12-12	A-	149.42	15.29	B / 7.8	2.94%	B / 8.9
2011	A	140.50	14.24	B+ / 8.7	1.83%	B+ / 9.0
2010	C	140.53	12.90	C- / 3.6	5.84%	B- / 7.8
2009	C+	137.27	12.94	C / 4.5	36.73%	B- / 7.6

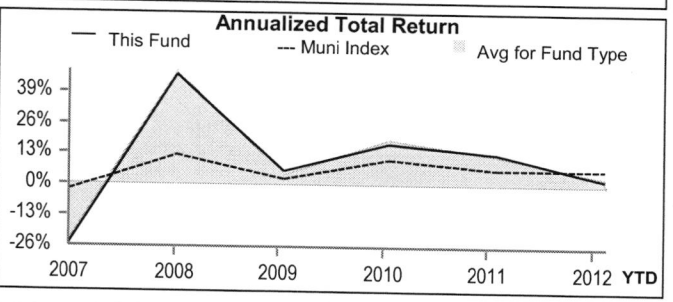

Nuveen NY Div Adv Muni 2 (NXK)

B+   Good

Fund Family: Nuveen Fund Advisors Inc
Fund Type: Municipal - Single State
Inception Date: March 27, 2001

Major Rating Factors: Strong performance is the major factor driving the B+ (Good) TheStreet.com Investment Rating for Nuveen NY Div Adv Muni 2. The fund currently has a performance rating of B (Good) based on an annualized return of 12.07% over the last three years and a total return of 3.33% year to date 2012. Factored into the performance evaluation is an expense ratio of 2.32% (high).

The fund's risk rating is currently B (Good). It carries a beta of 1.78, meaning it is expected to move 17.8% for every 10% move in the market. Volatility, as measured by both the semi-deviation and a drawdown factor, is considered low. As of December 31, 2012, Nuveen NY Div Adv Muni 2 traded at a discount of 5.30% below its net asset value, which is better than its one-year historical average discount of 4.17%.

Scott R. Romans currently receives a manager quality ranking of 47 (0=worst, 99=best). If you desire only a moderate level of risk and strong performance, then this fund is an excellent option.

Data Date	Investment Rating	Net Assets ($Mil)	Price	Performance Rating/Pts	Total Return Y-T-D	Risk Rating/Pts
12-12	B+	103.53	15.01	B / 7.6	3.33%	B / 8.9
2011	A-	98.00	14.26	B+ / 8.7	1.26%	B+ / 9.1
2010	C+	98.16	13.09	C / 4.8	7.35%	C+ / 6.6
2009	C+	95.75	12.92	C / 4.5	38.97%	B- / 7.3

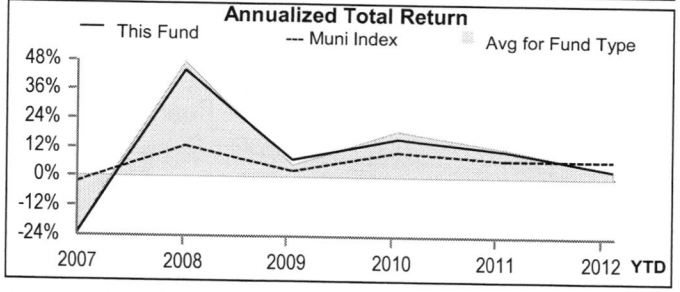

Nuveen NY Div Adv Muni Income (NKO)

B   Good

Fund Family: Nuveen Fund Advisors Inc
Fund Type: Municipal - Single State
Inception Date: March 25, 2002

Major Rating Factors: Nuveen NY Div Adv Muni Income receives a TheStreet.com Investment Rating of B (Good). The fund currently has a performance rating of C+ (Fair) based on an annualized return of 11.06% over the last three years and a total return of 4.44% year to date 2012. Factored into the performance evaluation is an expense ratio of 1.68% (above average).

The fund's risk rating is currently B+ (Good). It carries a beta of 1.58, meaning it is expected to move 15.8% for every 10% move in the market. Volatility, as measured by both the semi-deviation and a drawdown factor, is considered very low. As of December 31, 2012, Nuveen NY Div Adv Muni Income traded at a discount of 4.98% below its net asset value, which is better than its one-year historical average discount of 3.20%.

Scott R. Romans currently receives a manager quality ranking of 51 (0=worst, 99=best). If you desire an average level of risk, then this fund may be an option.

Data Date	Investment Rating	Net Assets ($Mil)	Price	Performance Rating/Pts	Total Return Y-T-D	Risk Rating/Pts
12-12	B	126.37	14.87	C+ / 6.7	4.44%	B+ / 9.0
2011	B+	122.60	14.94	B / 8.2	0.47%	B+ / 9.1
2010	C+	122.24	13.40	C / 4.7	8.08%	C+ / 6.8
2009	C+	120.41	13.10	C / 5.0	34.55%	B- / 7.5

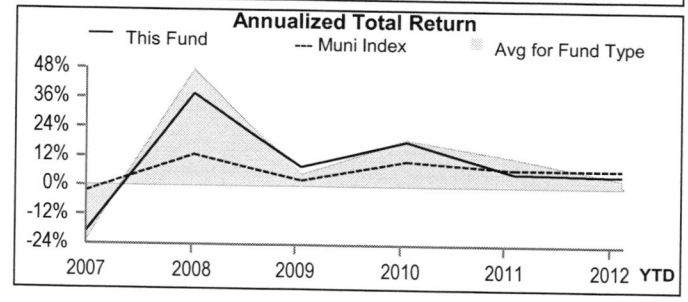

* Denotes ETF Fund

Nuveen NY Investment Quality Muni (NQN)   B   Good

Fund Family: Nuveen Fund Advisors Inc
Fund Type: Municipal - Single State
Inception Date: November 20, 1990

Major Rating Factors: Nuveen NY Investment Quality Muni receives a TheStreet.com Investment Rating of B (Good). The fund currently has a performance rating of C+ (Fair) based on an annualized return of 11.22% over the last three years and a total return of 1.10% year to date 2012. Factored into the performance evaluation is an expense ratio of 1.59% (above average).

    The fund's risk rating is currently B (Good). It carries a beta of 1.85, meaning it is expected to move 18.5% for every 10% move in the market. Volatility, as measured by both the semi-deviation and a drawdown factor, is considered low. As of December 31, 2012, Nuveen NY Investment Quality Muni traded at a discount of 2.03% below its net asset value, which is worse than its one-year historical average discount of 2.42%.

    Scott R. Romans currently receives a manager quality ranking of 43 (0=worst, 99=best). If you desire an average level of risk, then this fund may be an option.

Data Date	Investment Rating	Net Assets ($Mil)	Price	Performance Rating/Pts	Total Return Y-T-D	Risk Rating/Pts
12-12	B	278.96	15.46	C+ / 6.7	1.10%	B / 8.8
2011	A	270.20	15.41	A- / 9.0	0.39%	B / 8.9
2010	C+	272.03	13.48	C / 5.5	7.17%	C+ / 6.4
2009	B	264.17	13.34	C / 5.5	33.30%	B- / 7.7

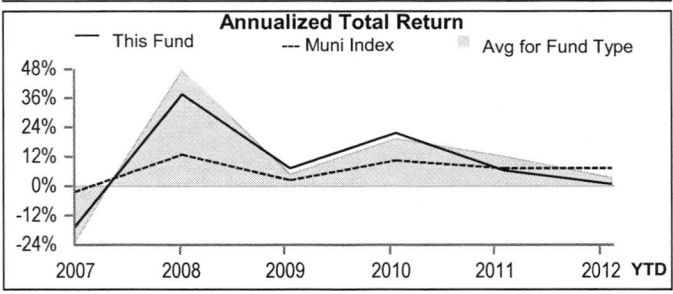

Nuveen NY Muni Value (NNY)   C+   Fair

Fund Family: Nuveen Fund Advisors Inc
Fund Type: Municipal - Single State
Inception Date: October 7, 1987

Major Rating Factors: Middle of the road best describes Nuveen NY Muni Value whose TheStreet.com Investment Rating is currently a C+ (Fair). The fund currently has a performance rating of C (Fair) based on an annualized return of 7.99% over the last three years and a total return of 1.67% year to date 2012. Factored into the performance evaluation is an expense ratio of 0.65% (very low).

    The fund's risk rating is currently B+ (Good). It carries a beta of 1.42, meaning it is expected to move 14.2% for every 10% move in the market. Volatility, as measured by both the semi-deviation and a drawdown factor, is considered very low. As of December 31, 2012, Nuveen NY Muni Value traded at a discount of .68% below its net asset value, which is better than its one-year historical average discount of .27%.

    Scott R. Romans currently receives a manager quality ranking of 37 (0=worst, 99=best). If you desire an average level of risk, then this fund may be an option.

Data Date	Investment Rating	Net Assets ($Mil)	Price	Performance Rating/Pts	Total Return Y-T-D	Risk Rating/Pts
12-12	C+	157.98	10.30	C / 4.6	1.67%	B+ / 9.1
2011	B	151.80	9.92	C+ / 6.5	1.11%	B+ / 9.2
2010	B	152.03	9.08	C- / 4.2	0.46%	B / 8.8
2009	B-	150.06	9.45	C / 4.6	11.40%	B / 8.3

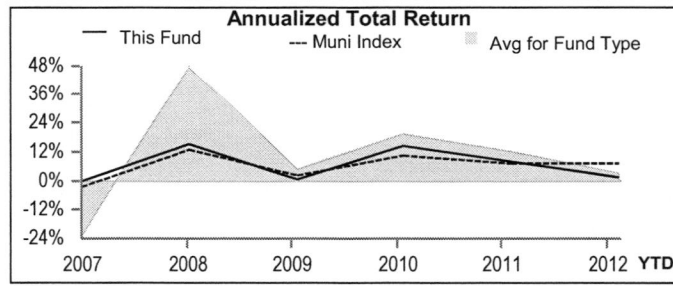

Nuveen NY Performance Plus Muni (NNP)   A   Excellent

Fund Family: Nuveen Fund Advisors Inc
Fund Type: Municipal - Single State
Inception Date: November 16, 1989

Major Rating Factors:
Strong performance is the major factor driving the A (Excellent) TheStreet.com Investment Rating for Nuveen NY Performance Plus Muni. The fund currently has a performance rating of B+ (Good) based on an annualized return of 13.34% over the last three years and a total return of 4.68% year to date 2012. Factored into the performance evaluation is an expense ratio of 1.64% (above average).

    The fund's risk rating is currently B+ (Good). It carries a beta of 1.64, meaning it is expected to move 16.4% for every 10% move in the market. Volatility, as measured by both the semi-deviation and a drawdown factor, is considered very low. As of December 31, 2012, Nuveen NY Performance Plus Muni traded at a discount of 1.50% below its net asset value, which is better than its one-year historical average discount of 1.20%.

    Scott R. Romans currently receives a manager quality ranking of 62 (0=worst, 99=best). If you desire only a moderate level of risk and strong performance, then this fund is an excellent option.

Data Date	Investment Rating	Net Assets ($Mil)	Price	Performance Rating/Pts	Total Return Y-T-D	Risk Rating/Pts
12-12	A	253.43	16.47	B+ / 8.5	4.68%	B+ / 9.0
2011	A-	240.50	15.44	B+ / 8.4	0.82%	B+ / 9.1
2010	C	241.45	13.98	C / 4.4	6.74%	C+ / 6.6
2009	C+	235.11	13.89	C / 5.1	38.65%	B- / 7.4

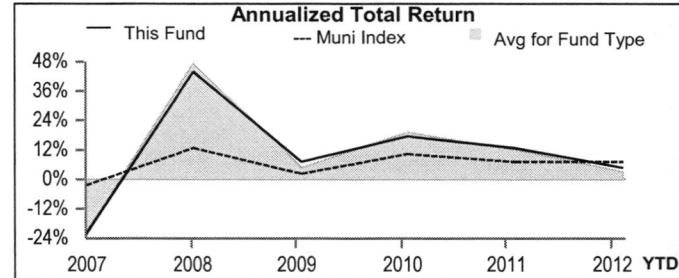

Nuveen NY Prem Inc Muni (NNF)

B　　**Good**

Fund Family: Nuveen Fund Advisors Inc
Fund Type: Municipal - Single State
Inception Date: December 17, 1992

Major Rating Factors: Strong performance is the major factor driving the B (Good) TheStreet.com Investment Rating for Nuveen NY Prem Inc Muni. The fund currently has a performance rating of B- (Good) based on an annualized return of 12.29% over the last three years and a total return of 2.34% year to date 2012. Factored into the performance evaluation is an expense ratio of 1.70% (above average).

The fund's risk rating is currently B (Good). It carries a beta of 1.92, meaning it is expected to move 19.2% for every 10% move in the market. Volatility, as measured by both the semi-deviation and a drawdown factor, is considered low. As of December 31, 2012, Nuveen NY Prem Inc Muni traded at a discount of 1.74% below its net asset value, which is better than its one-year historical average discount of .23%.

Scott R. Romans currently receives a manager quality ranking of 42 (0=worst, 99=best). If you desire only a moderate level of risk and strong performance, then this fund is an excellent option.

Data Date	Investment Rating	Net Assets ($Mil)	Price	Performance Rating/Pts	Total Return Y-T-D	Risk Rating/Pts
12-12	B	134.04	15.81	B- / 7.0	2.34%	B / 8.8
2011	A+	130.30	15.79	A- / 9.1	0.63%	B+ / 9.1
2010	C+	129.68	13.62	C / 5.0	7.23%	C+ / 6.8
2009	B-	126.26	13.39	C+ / 5.9	36.21%	B- / 7.8

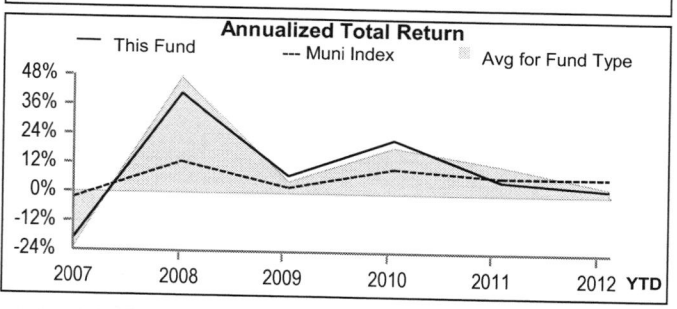

Nuveen NY Quality Inc Muni (NUN)

B+　　**Good**

Fund Family: Nuveen Fund Advisors Inc
Fund Type: Municipal - Single State
Inception Date: November 25, 1991

Major Rating Factors: Strong performance is the major factor driving the B+ (Good) TheStreet.com Investment Rating for Nuveen NY Quality Inc Muni. The fund currently has a performance rating of B- (Good) based on an annualized return of 11.79% over the last three years and a total return of 3.23% year to date 2012. Factored into the performance evaluation is an expense ratio of 1.58% (above average).

The fund's risk rating is currently B (Good). It carries a beta of 1.85, meaning it is expected to move 18.5% for every 10% move in the market. Volatility, as measured by both the semi-deviation and a drawdown factor, is considered low. As of December 31, 2012, Nuveen NY Quality Inc Muni traded at a discount of 3.68% below its net asset value, which is better than its one-year historical average discount of 2.62%.

Scott R. Romans currently receives a manager quality ranking of 40 (0=worst, 99=best). If you desire only a moderate level of risk and strong performance, then this fund is an excellent option.

Data Date	Investment Rating	Net Assets ($Mil)	Price	Performance Rating/Pts	Total Return Y-T-D	Risk Rating/Pts
12-12	B+	378.66	15.19	B- / 7.2	3.23%	B / 8.9
2011	A-	365.40	15.59	B+ / 8.6	-1.30%	B+ / 9.2
2010	C+	368.51	13.84	C+ / 6.5	10.17%	C+ / 6.4
2009	B-	359.83	13.30	C+ / 5.7	31.80%	B- / 7.6

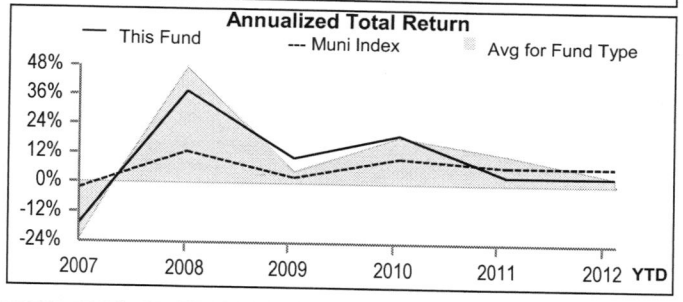

Nuveen NY Select Quality Muni (NVN)

B+　　**Good**

Fund Family: Nuveen Fund Advisors Inc
Fund Type: Municipal - Single State
Inception Date: May 22, 1991

Major Rating Factors: Strong performance is the major factor driving the B+ (Good) TheStreet.com Investment Rating for Nuveen NY Select Quality Muni. The fund currently has a performance rating of B (Good) based on an annualized return of 12.37% over the last three years and a total return of 4.02% year to date 2012. Factored into the performance evaluation is an expense ratio of 1.59% (above average).

The fund's risk rating is currently B (Good). It carries a beta of 1.96, meaning it is expected to move 19.6% for every 10% move in the market. Volatility, as measured by both the semi-deviation and a drawdown factor, is considered low. As of December 31, 2012, Nuveen NY Select Quality Muni traded at a discount of 3.09% below its net asset value, which is better than its one-year historical average discount of 2.65%.

Scott R. Romans currently receives a manager quality ranking of 38 (0=worst, 99=best). If you desire only a moderate level of risk and strong performance, then this fund is an excellent option.

Data Date	Investment Rating	Net Assets ($Mil)	Price	Performance Rating/Pts	Total Return Y-T-D	Risk Rating/Pts
12-12	B+	378.18	15.66	B / 7.9	4.02%	B / 8.7
2011	A-	363.40	15.65	B+ / 8.6	-1.15%	B+ / 9.0
2010	C+	366.20	13.70	C / 5.2	7.18%	C+ / 6.5
2009	B-	356.49	13.55	C+ / 6.0	35.70%	B- / 7.6

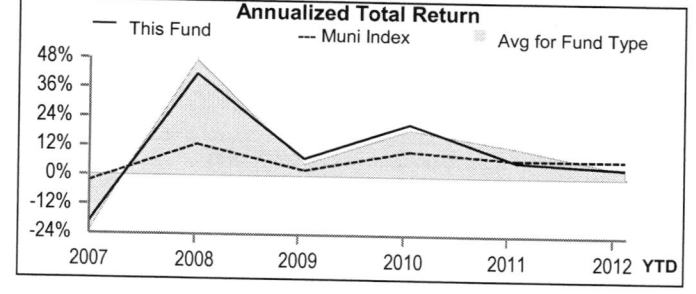

Nuveen NY Select Tax-Free Inc Port (NXN) B Good

Fund Family: Nuveen Fund Advisors Inc
Fund Type: Municipal - Single State
Inception Date: June 19, 1992

Major Rating Factors: Nuveen NY Select Tax-Free Inc Port receives a TheStreet.com Investment Rating of B (Good). The fund currently has a performance rating of C+ (Fair) based on an annualized return of 8.92% over the last three years and a total return of 0.98% year to date 2012. Factored into the performance evaluation is an expense ratio of 0.50% (very low).

The fund's risk rating is currently B+ (Good). It carries a beta of 1.53, meaning it is expected to move 15.3% for every 10% move in the market. Volatility, as measured by both the semi-deviation and a drawdown factor, is considered very low. As of December 31, 2012, Nuveen NY Select Tax-Free Inc Port traded at a premium of 2.97% above its net asset value, which is worse than its one-year historical average premium of .16%.

Scott R. Romans currently receives a manager quality ranking of 42 (0=worst, 99=best). If you desire an average level of risk, then this fund may be an option.

Data Date	Investment Rating	Net Assets ($Mil)	Price	Performance Rating/Pts	Total Return Y-T-D	Risk Rating/Pts
12-12	B	57.17	15.27	C+ / 6.1	0.98%	B+ / 9.1
2011	B+	56.70	14.22	B- / 7.1	3.45%	B+ / 9.2
2010	B	55.01	13.09	C- / 4.0	1.30%	B / 8.9
2009	C+	55.65	13.50	C- / 4.2	11.59%	B / 8.4

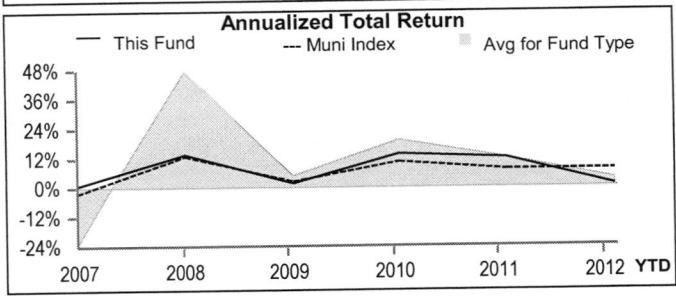

Nuveen OH Div Adv Muni (NXI) A Excellent

Fund Family: Nuveen Fund Advisors Inc
Fund Type: Municipal - Single State
Inception Date: March 27, 2001

Major Rating Factors:
Strong performance is the major factor driving the A (Excellent) TheStreet.com Investment Rating for Nuveen OH Div Adv Muni. The fund currently has a performance rating of B+ (Good) based on an annualized return of 12.45% over the last three years and a total return of 4.41% year to date 2012. Factored into the performance evaluation is an expense ratio of 3.07% (high).

The fund's risk rating is currently B (Good). It carries a beta of 2.10, meaning it is expected to move 21.0% for every 10% move in the market. Volatility, as measured by both the semi-deviation and a drawdown factor, is considered low. As of December 31, 2012, Nuveen OH Div Adv Muni traded at a premium of .25% above its net asset value, which is better than its one-year historical average premium of .36%.

Daniel J. Close has been running the fund for 6 years and currently receives a manager quality ranking of 32 (0=worst, 99=best). If you desire only a moderate level of risk and strong performance, then this fund is an excellent option.

Data Date	Investment Rating	Net Assets ($Mil)	Price	Performance Rating/Pts	Total Return Y-T-D	Risk Rating/Pts
12-12	A	68.35	16.31	B+ / 8.5	4.41%	B / 8.6
2011	B+	65.00	15.21	B+ / 8.4	1.17%	B / 8.9
2010	C+	64.29	13.56	C / 4.8	2.07%	B- / 7.2
2009	B-	65.57	14.08	C+ / 6.2	33.96%	B- / 7.8

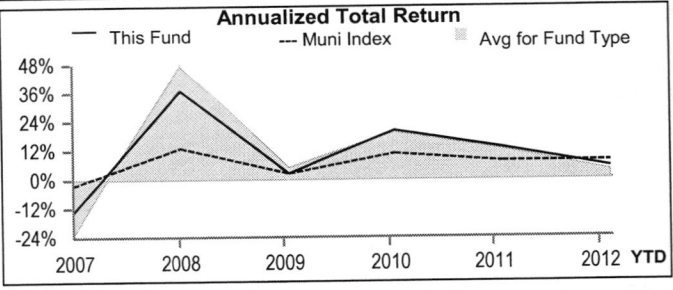

Nuveen OH Div Adv Muni 2 (NBJ) A- Excellent

Fund Family: Nuveen Fund Advisors Inc
Fund Type: Municipal - Single State
Inception Date: September 25, 2001

Major Rating Factors:
Strong performance is the major factor driving the A- (Excellent) TheStreet.com Investment Rating for Nuveen OH Div Adv Muni 2. The fund currently has a performance rating of B (Good) based on an annualized return of 11.48% over the last three years and a total return of 3.30% year to date 2012. Factored into the performance evaluation is an expense ratio of 3.22% (high).

The fund's risk rating is currently B (Good). It carries a beta of 1.95, meaning it is expected to move 19.5% for every 10% move in the market. Volatility, as measured by both the semi-deviation and a drawdown factor, is considered low. As of December 31, 2012, Nuveen OH Div Adv Muni 2 traded at a discount of .69% below its net asset value, which is better than its one-year historical average discount of .46%.

Daniel J. Close has been running the fund for 6 years and currently receives a manager quality ranking of 40 (0=worst, 99=best). If you desire only a moderate level of risk and strong performance, then this fund is an excellent option.

Data Date	Investment Rating	Net Assets ($Mil)	Price	Performance Rating/Pts	Total Return Y-T-D	Risk Rating/Pts
12-12	A-	49.24	15.89	B / 8.2	3.30%	B / 8.7
2011	B+	46.90	14.18	B / 8.1	0.63%	B / 8.8
2010	C+	46.00	13.20	C / 5.0	2.86%	B- / 7.0
2009	B-	46.46	13.60	C+ / 6.9	44.94%	B- / 7.4

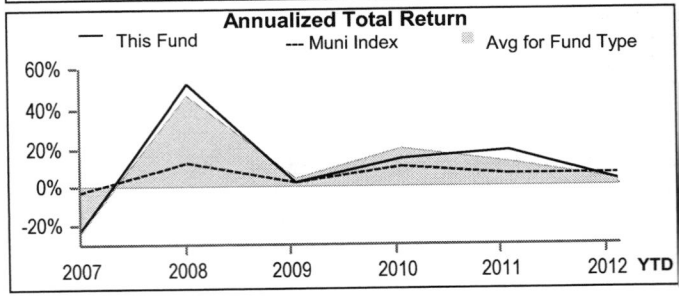

Nuveen OH Div Adv Muni Fund 3 (NVJ)

B+   **Good**

Fund Family: Nuveen Fund Advisors Inc
Fund Type: Municipal - Single State
Inception Date: March 26, 2002

Major Rating Factors: Strong performance is the major factor driving the B+ (Good) TheStreet.com Investment Rating for Nuveen OH Div Adv Muni Fund 3. The fund currently has a performance rating of B (Good) based on an annualized return of 10.34% over the last three years and a total return of 0.71% year to date 2012. Factored into the performance evaluation is an expense ratio of 3.42% (high).

The fund's risk rating is currently B (Good). It carries a beta of 2.25, meaning it is expected to move 22.5% for every 10% move in the market. Volatility, as measured by both the semi-deviation and a drawdown factor, is considered low. As of December 31, 2012, Nuveen OH Div Adv Muni Fund 3 traded at a premium of 3.31% above its net asset value, which is worse than its one-year historical average premium of 1.21%.

Daniel J. Close has been running the fund for 6 years and currently receives a manager quality ranking of 27 (0=worst, 99=best). If you desire only a moderate level of risk and strong performance, then this fund is an excellent option.

Data Date	Investment Rating	Net Assets ($Mil)	Price	Perfor-mance Rating/Pts	Total Return Y-T-D	Risk Rating/Pts
12-12	B+	34.62	16.84	B / 7.7	0.71%	B / 8.5
2011	B+	32.90	15.13	B / 8.1	0.86%	B / 8.7
2010	C+	33.06	13.95	C / 4.9	0.45%	C+ / 6.9
2009	A+	33.76	14.73	B- / 7.2	41.71%	B- / 7.6

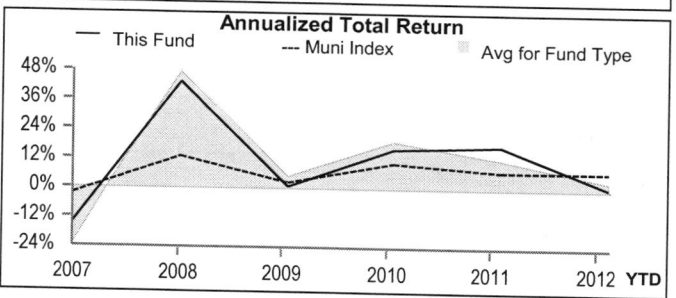

Nuveen OH Quality Inc Muni (NUO)

A+   **Excellent**

Fund Family: Nuveen Fund Advisors Inc
Fund Type: Municipal - Single State
Inception Date: October 11, 1991

Major Rating Factors:
Exceptional performance is the major factor driving the A+ (Excellent) TheStreet.com Investment Rating for Nuveen OH Quality Inc Muni. The fund currently has a performance rating of A (Excellent) based on an annualized return of 14.25% over the last three years and a total return of 4.67% year to date 2012. Factored into the performance evaluation is an expense ratio of 1.79% (above average).

The fund's risk rating is currently B (Good). It carries a beta of 1.39, meaning it is expected to move 13.9% for every 10% move in the market. Volatility, as measured by both the semi-deviation and a drawdown factor, is considered low. As of December 31, 2012, Nuveen OH Quality Inc Muni traded at a premium of 7.81% above its net asset value, which is worse than its one-year historical average premium of 4.66%.

Daniel J. Close currently receives a manager quality ranking of 71 (0=worst, 99=best). If you desire only a moderate level of risk and strong performance, then this fund is an excellent option.

Data Date	Investment Rating	Net Assets ($Mil)	Price	Perfor-mance Rating/Pts	Total Return Y-T-D	Risk Rating/Pts
12-12	A+	170.52	19.05	A / 9.3	4.67%	B / 8.8
2011	B+	162.30	16.70	B+ / 8.5	0.66%	B / 8.8
2010	C+	157.44	14.68	C / 5.1	-2.94%	C+ / 6.9
2009	A	160.55	16.00	B- / 7.3	34.98%	B- / 7.2

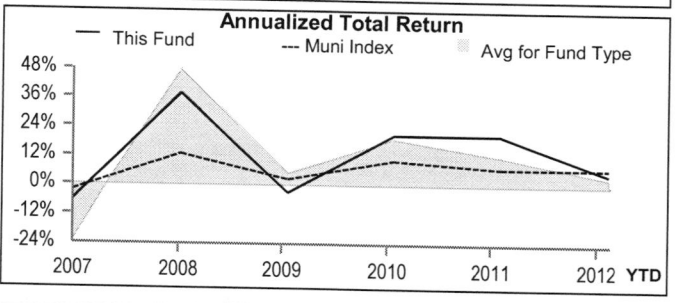

Nuveen PA Div Adv Muni (NXM)

B+   **Good**

Fund Family: Nuveen Fund Advisors Inc
Fund Type: Municipal - Single State
Inception Date: March 27, 2001

Major Rating Factors: Strong performance is the major factor driving the B+ (Good) TheStreet.com Investment Rating for Nuveen PA Div Adv Muni. The fund currently has a performance rating of B- (Good) based on an annualized return of 11.70% over the last three years and a total return of 2.13% year to date 2012. Factored into the performance evaluation is an expense ratio of 2.55% (high).

The fund's risk rating is currently B (Good). It carries a beta of 1.94, meaning it is expected to move 19.4% for every 10% move in the market. Volatility, as measured by both the semi-deviation and a drawdown factor, is considered low. As of December 31, 2012, Nuveen PA Div Adv Muni traded at a discount of 5.47% below its net asset value, which is better than its one-year historical average discount of 4.66%.

Paul L. Brennan currently receives a manager quality ranking of 39 (0=worst, 99=best). If you desire only a moderate level of risk and strong performance, then this fund is an excellent option.

Data Date	Investment Rating	Net Assets ($Mil)	Price	Perfor-mance Rating/Pts	Total Return Y-T-D	Risk Rating/Pts
12-12	B+	51.29	15.04	B- / 7.5	2.13%	B / 8.6
2011	B+	49.60	14.04	B / 8.1	1.14%	B / 8.7
2010	C-	48.93	12.97	D+ / 2.8	4.81%	B- / 7.3
2009	C+	49.17	13.20	C / 4.9	43.85%	B- / 7.3

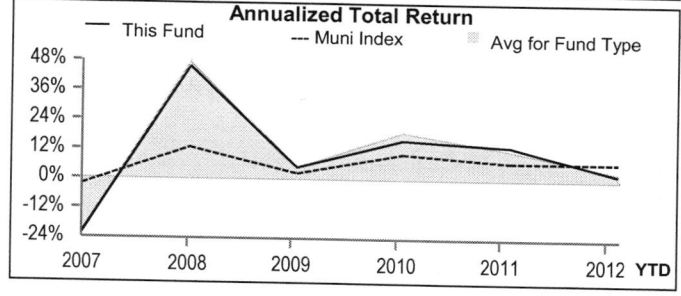

Nuveen PA Div Adv Muni Fund 2 (NVY)

B+   Good

Fund Family: Nuveen Fund Advisors Inc
Fund Type: Municipal - Single State
Inception Date: March 25, 2002

Major Rating Factors: Strong performance is the major factor driving the B+ (Good) TheStreet.com Investment Rating for Nuveen PA Div Adv Muni Fund 2. The fund currently has a performance rating of B- (Good) based on an annualized return of 11.53% over the last three years and a total return of 2.40% year to date 2012. Factored into the performance evaluation is an expense ratio of 2.47% (high).

The fund's risk rating is currently B (Good). It carries a beta of 1.70, meaning it is expected to move 17.0% for every 10% move in the market. Volatility, as measured by both the semi-deviation and a drawdown factor, is considered low. As of December 31, 2012, Nuveen PA Div Adv Muni Fund 2 traded at a discount of 3.59% below its net asset value, which is better than its one-year historical average discount of 2.03%.

Paul L. Brennan currently receives a manager quality ranking of 53 (0=worst, 99=best). If you desire only a moderate level of risk and strong performance, then this fund is an excellent option.

Data Date	Investment Rating	Net Assets ($Mil)	Price	Performance Rating/Pts	Total Return Y-T-D	Risk Rating/Pts
12-12	B+	56.58	15.02	B- / 7.4	2.40%	B / 8.7
2011	B+	54.80	14.03	B / 8.2	0.86%	B / 8.8
2010	C	54.92	13.18	C- / 3.2	6.40%	B- / 7.5
2009	B-	55.38	13.22	C+ / 6.8	57.14%	B- / 7.3

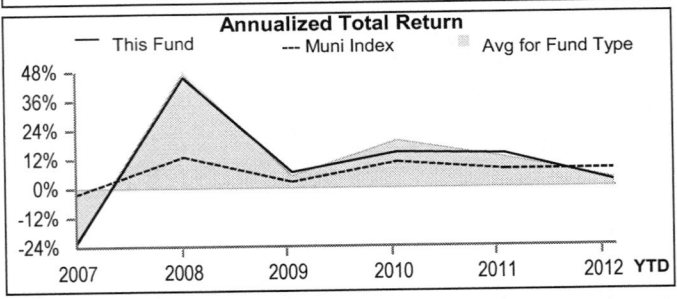

Nuveen PA Investment Quality Muni (NQP)

A   Excellent

Fund Family: Nuveen Fund Advisors Inc
Fund Type: Municipal - Single State
Inception Date: February 21, 1991

Major Rating Factors:
Strong performance is the major factor driving the A (Excellent) TheStreet.com Investment Rating for Nuveen PA Investment Quality Muni. The fund currently has a performance rating of B (Good) based on an annualized return of 13.66% over the last three years and a total return of 3.52% year to date 2012. Factored into the performance evaluation is an expense ratio of 1.63% (above average).

The fund's risk rating is currently B (Good). It carries a beta of 1.72, meaning it is expected to move 17.2% for every 10% move in the market. Volatility, as measured by both the semi-deviation and a drawdown factor, is considered low. As of December 31, 2012, Nuveen PA Investment Quality Muni traded at a discount of 3.69% below its net asset value, which is better than its one-year historical average discount of 1.01%.

Paul L. Brennan currently receives a manager quality ranking of 62 (0=worst, 99=best). If you desire only a moderate level of risk and strong performance, then this fund is an excellent option.

Data Date	Investment Rating	Net Assets ($Mil)	Price	Performance Rating/Pts	Total Return Y-T-D	Risk Rating/Pts
12-12	A	253.94	15.64	B / 8.2	3.52%	B / 8.9
2011	A	245.70	15.17	A- / 9.0	-0.07%	B+ / 9.0
2010	C+	238.37	13.33	C / 5.3	7.97%	C+ / 6.3
2009	A	241.54	13.15	B- / 7.0	44.57%	B- / 7.4

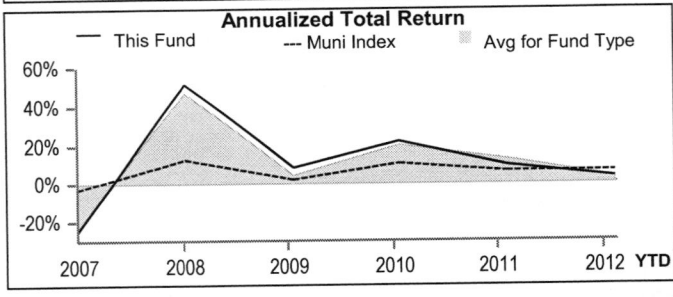

Nuveen PA Prem Inc Muni 2 (NPY)

A   Excellent

Fund Family: Nuveen Fund Advisors Inc
Fund Type: Municipal - Single State
Inception Date: March 18, 1993

Major Rating Factors:
Strong performance is the major factor driving the A (Excellent) TheStreet.com Investment Rating for Nuveen PA Prem Inc Muni 2. The fund currently has a performance rating of B+ (Good) based on an annualized return of 13.78% over the last three years and a total return of 2.32% year to date 2012. Factored into the performance evaluation is an expense ratio of 1.59% (above average).

The fund's risk rating is currently B (Good). It carries a beta of 1.84, meaning it is expected to move 18.4% for every 10% move in the market. Volatility, as measured by both the semi-deviation and a drawdown factor, is considered low. As of December 31, 2012, Nuveen PA Prem Inc Muni 2 traded at a discount of 2.65% below its net asset value, which is worse than its one-year historical average discount of 3.58%.

Paul L. Brennan currently receives a manager quality ranking of 59 (0=worst, 99=best). If you desire only a moderate level of risk and strong performance, then this fund is an excellent option.

Data Date	Investment Rating	Net Assets ($Mil)	Price	Performance Rating/Pts	Total Return Y-T-D	Risk Rating/Pts
12-12	A	236.04	15.08	B+ / 8.5	2.32%	B / 8.8
2011	A	228.60	13.97	A- / 9.0	0.00%	B / 8.9
2010	C	220.11	12.39	C- / 3.9	5.76%	C+ / 6.5
2009	B-	222.77	12.47	C+ / 6.8	46.95%	B- / 7.3

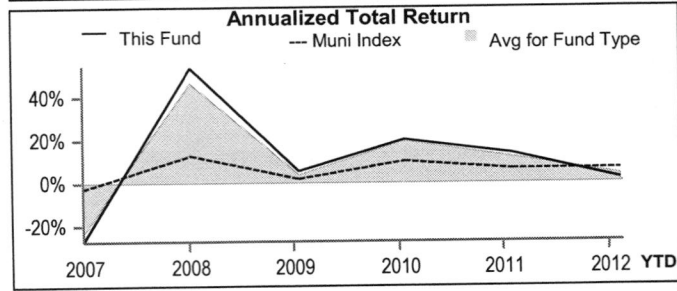

Nuveen Pennsylvania Municipal Valu (NPN)

C+   **Fair**

Fund Family: Nuveen Fund Advisors Inc
Fund Type: Municipal - National
Inception Date: April 28, 2009

Major Rating Factors: Middle of the road best describes Nuveen Pennsylvania Municipal Valu whose TheStreet.com Investment Rating is currently a C+ (Fair). The fund currently has a performance rating of C (Fair) based on an annualized return of 6.75% over the last three years and a total return of 3.62% year to date 2012. Factored into the performance evaluation is an expense ratio of 0.86% (very low).

The fund's risk rating is currently B (Good). It carries a beta of 1.53, meaning it is expected to move 15.3% for every 10% move in the market. Volatility, as measured by both the semi-deviation and a drawdown factor, is considered low. As of December 31, 2012, Nuveen Pennsylvania Municipal Valu traded at a discount of 4.31% below its net asset value, which is worse than its one-year historical average discount of 4.83%.

Paul L. Brennan currently receives a manager quality ranking of 28 (0=worst, 99=best). If you desire an average level of risk, then this fund may be an option.

Data Date	Investment Rating	Net Assets ($Mil)	Price	Performance Rating/Pts	Total Return Y-T-D	Risk Rating/Pts
12-12	C+	19.95	15.75	C / 5.2	3.62%	B / 8.6
2011	B+	19.40	15.26	B / 7.6	-0.07%	B / 8.8
2010	D+	18.81	14.20	E+ / 0.7	-3.16%	B / 8.2

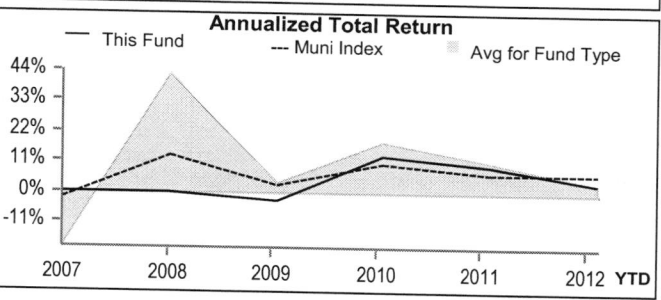

Nuveen Performance Plus Muni (NPP)

A   **Excellent**

Fund Family: Nuveen Fund Advisors Inc
Fund Type: Municipal - National
Inception Date: June 22, 1989

Major Rating Factors:
Strong performance is the major factor driving the A (Excellent) TheStreet.com Investment Rating for Nuveen Performance Plus Muni. The fund currently has a performance rating of B+ (Good) based on an annualized return of 13.20% over the last three years and a total return of 4.02% year to date 2012. Factored into the performance evaluation is an expense ratio of 1.62% (above average).

The fund's risk rating is currently B (Good). It carries a beta of 1.97, meaning it is expected to move 19.7% for every 10% move in the market. Volatility, as measured by both the semi-deviation and a drawdown factor, is considered low. As of December 31, 2012, Nuveen Performance Plus Muni traded at a discount of 3.75% below its net asset value, which is better than its one-year historical average discount of 1.72%.

Thomas C. Spalding has been running the fund for 11 years and currently receives a manager quality ranking of 41 (0=worst, 99=best). If you desire only a moderate level of risk and strong performance, then this fund is an excellent option.

Data Date	Investment Rating	Net Assets ($Mil)	Price	Performance Rating/Pts	Total Return Y-T-D	Risk Rating/Pts
12-12	A	892.60	16.17	B+ / 8.4	4.02%	B / 8.7
2011	A-	918.30	15.28	B+ / 8.7	0.72%	B / 8.8
2010	C+	893.85	13.55	C+ / 5.6	3.45%	C+ / 6.8
2009	B-	906.41	14.06	C+ / 5.8	29.74%	B- / 7.5

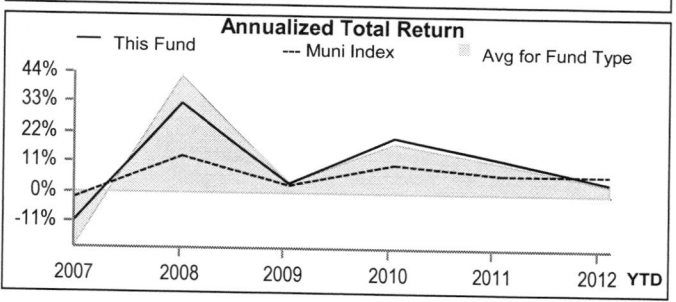

Nuveen Preferref Income Opps (JPC)

A-   **Excellent**

Fund Family: Nuveen Fund Advisors Inc
Fund Type: Growth and Income
Inception Date: March 26, 2003

Major Rating Factors:
Strong performance is the major factor driving the A- (Excellent) TheStreet.com Investment Rating for Nuveen Preferref Income Opps. The fund currently has a performance rating of B+ (Good) based on an annualized return of 18.80% over the last three years and a total return of 2.78% year to date 2012. Factored into the performance evaluation is an expense ratio of 1.86% (above average).

The fund's risk rating is currently B (Good). It carries a beta of 0.66, meaning the fund's expected move will be 6.6% for every 10% move in the market. Volatility, as measured by both the semi-deviation and a drawdown factor, is considered low. As of December 31, 2012, Nuveen Preferref Income Opps traded at a discount of 7.17% below its net asset value, which is better than its one-year historical average discount of 4.06%.

Kevin A. Hunter currently receives a manager quality ranking of 91 (0=worst, 99=best). If you desire only a moderate level of risk and strong performance, then this fund is an excellent option.

Data Date	Investment Rating	Net Assets ($Mil)	Price	Performance Rating/Pts	Total Return Y-T-D	Risk Rating/Pts
12-12	A-	914.51	9.71	B+ / 8.4	2.78%	B / 8.4
2011	B	840.50	8.01	B / 8.2	0.37%	B- / 7.7
2010	C	839.85	8.35	C+ / 6.2	21.28%	C / 4.6
2009	D+	809.16	7.49	C- / 3.5	73.30%	C / 4.6

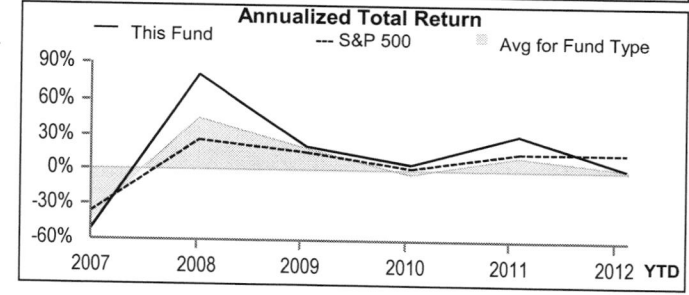

Nuveen Prem Inc Muni (NPI)   A-   Excellent

Fund Family: Nuveen Fund Advisors Inc
Fund Type: Municipal - National
Inception Date: July 21, 1988

Data Date	Investment Rating	Net Assets ($Mil)	Price	Performance Rating/Pts	Total Return Y-T-D	Risk Rating/Pts
12-12	A-	900.46	14.97	B / 8.1	3.94%	B / 8.8
2011	B+	922.10	14.47	B / 8.1	-1.31%	B / 8.9
2010	C	875.34	12.82	C- / 4.2	4.00%	C+ / 6.7
2009	C+	915.49	13.15	C / 5.4	27.21%	B- / 7.2

Major Rating Factors:
Strong performance is the major factor driving the A- (Excellent) TheStreet.com Investment Rating for Nuveen Prem Inc Muni. The fund currently has a performance rating of B (Good) based on an annualized return of 12.66% over the last three years and a total return of 3.94% year to date 2012. Factored into the performance evaluation is an expense ratio of 1.66% (above average).

The fund's risk rating is currently B (Good). It carries a beta of 1.58, meaning it is expected to move 15.8% for every 10% move in the market. Volatility, as measured by both the semi-deviation and a drawdown factor, is considered low. As of December 31, 2012, Nuveen Prem Inc Muni traded at a discount of 3.42% below its net asset value, which is better than its one-year historical average discount of 1.36%.

Paul L. Brennan has been running the fund for 7 years and currently receives a manager quality ranking of 59 (0=worst, 99=best). If you desire only a moderate level of risk and strong performance, then this fund is an excellent option.

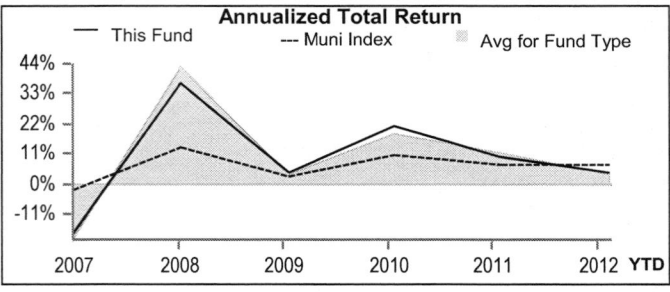

Nuveen Prem Inc Muni 4 (NPT)   A   Excellent

Fund Family: Nuveen Fund Advisors Inc
Fund Type: Municipal - National
Inception Date: February 19, 1993

Data Date	Investment Rating	Net Assets ($Mil)	Price	Performance Rating/Pts	Total Return Y-T-D	Risk Rating/Pts
12-12	A	565.53	14.11	B+ / 8.6	5.39%	B / 8.6
2011	A	579.30	13.44	A- / 9.2	0.60%	B / 8.7
2010	C+	543.81	11.97	C+ / 6.0	5.19%	C+ / 6.5
2009	B-	568.53	12.15	C+ / 6.2	32.99%	B- / 7.0

Major Rating Factors:
Strong performance is the major factor driving the A (Excellent) TheStreet.com Investment Rating for Nuveen Prem Inc Muni 4. The fund currently has a performance rating of B+ (Good) based on an annualized return of 13.56% over the last three years and a total return of 5.39% year to date 2012. Factored into the performance evaluation is an expense ratio of 1.99% (high).

The fund's risk rating is currently B (Good). It carries a beta of 1.79, meaning it is expected to move 17.9% for every 10% move in the market. Volatility, as measured by both the semi-deviation and a drawdown factor, is considered low. As of December 31, 2012, Nuveen Prem Inc Muni 4 traded at a discount of 3.16% below its net asset value, which is better than its one-year historical average discount of .95%.

Christopher L. Drahn currently receives a manager quality ranking of 54 (0=worst, 99=best). If you desire only a moderate level of risk and strong performance, then this fund is an excellent option.

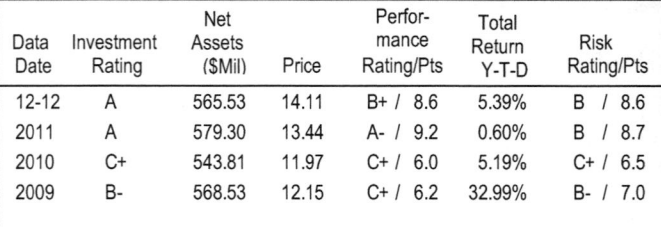

Nuveen Prem Inc Muni Oppty (NPX)   A-   Excellent

Fund Family: Nuveen Fund Advisors Inc
Fund Type: Municipal - National
Inception Date: July 22, 1993

Data Date	Investment Rating	Net Assets ($Mil)	Price	Performance Rating/Pts	Total Return Y-T-D	Risk Rating/Pts
12-12	A-	505.77	14.27	B / 8.0	4.77%	B / 8.7
2011	A-	518.10	13.78	B+ / 8.6	-1.89%	B / 8.9
2010	C	484.07	11.90	C- / 4.2	2.35%	C+ / 6.7
2009	B-	501.85	12.32	C+ / 6.2	35.39%	B- / 7.3

Major Rating Factors:
Strong performance is the major factor driving the A- (Excellent) TheStreet.com Investment Rating for Nuveen Prem Inc Muni Oppty. The fund currently has a performance rating of B (Good) based on an annualized return of 12.08% over the last three years and a total return of 4.77% year to date 2012. Factored into the performance evaluation is an expense ratio of 1.80% (above average).

The fund's risk rating is currently B (Good). It carries a beta of 2.07, meaning it is expected to move 20.7% for every 10% move in the market. Volatility, as measured by both the semi-deviation and a drawdown factor, is considered low. As of December 31, 2012, Nuveen Prem Inc Muni Oppty traded at a discount of 4.29% below its net asset value, which is better than its one-year historical average discount of 2.29%.

Douglas J. White currently receives a manager quality ranking of 32 (0=worst, 99=best). If you desire only a moderate level of risk and strong performance, then this fund is an excellent option.

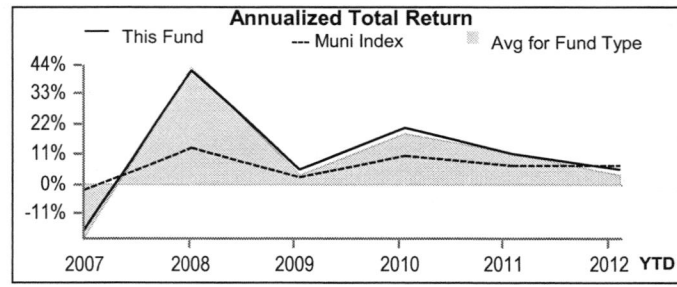

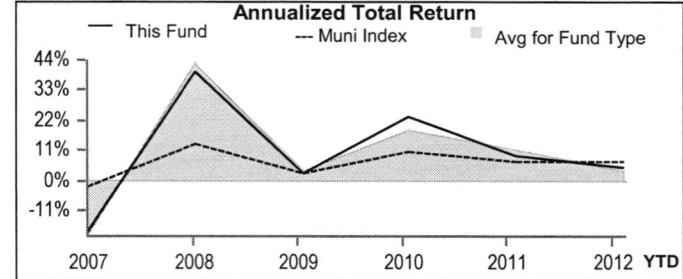

Nuveen Premier Muni Inc (NPF)

B+   **Good**

Fund Family: Nuveen Fund Advisors Inc
Fund Type: Municipal - National
Inception Date: December 18, 1991

Major Rating Factors: Strong performance is the major factor driving the B+ (Good) TheStreet.com Investment Rating for Nuveen Premier Muni Inc. The fund currently has a performance rating of B (Good) based on an annualized return of 12.70% over the last three years and a total return of 4.16% year to date 2012. Factored into the performance evaluation is an expense ratio of 1.55% (average).

The fund's risk rating is currently B (Good). It carries a beta of 2.08, meaning it is expected to move 20.8% for every 10% move in the market. Volatility, as measured by both the semi-deviation and a drawdown factor, is considered low. As of December 31, 2012, Nuveen Premier Muni Inc traded at a discount of 4.85% below its net asset value, which is better than its one-year historical average discount of 2.26%.

Daniel J. Close currently receives a manager quality ranking of 34 (0=worst, 99=best). If you desire only a moderate level of risk and strong performance, then this fund is an excellent option.

Data Date	Investment Rating	Net Assets ($Mil)	Price	Performance Rating/Pts	Total Return Y-T-D	Risk Rating/Pts
12-12	B+	287.47	14.92	B / 7.8	4.16%	B / 8.8
2011	A-	294.90	14.81	B+ / 8.9	-0.47%	B / 8.8
2010	C+	275.67	13.05	C / 5.1	7.17%	C+ / 6.4
2009	B-	290.67	12.96	C+ / 6.0	33.38%	B- / 7.2

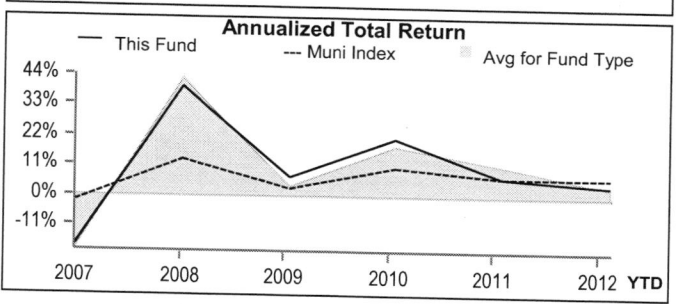

Nuveen Premier Muni Oppty (NIF)

B-   **Good**

Fund Family: Nuveen Fund Advisors Inc
Fund Type: Municipal - National
Inception Date: December 18, 1991

Major Rating Factors: Nuveen Premier Muni Oppty receives a TheStreet.com Investment Rating of B- (Good). The fund currently has a performance rating of C+ (Fair) based on an annualized return of 10.82% over the last three years and a total return of 3.98% year to date 2012. Factored into the performance evaluation is an expense ratio of 1.65% (above average).

The fund's risk rating is currently B (Good). It carries a beta of 2.46, meaning it is expected to move 24.6% for every 10% move in the market. Volatility, as measured by both the semi-deviation and a drawdown factor, is considered low. As of December 31, 2012, Nuveen Premier Muni Oppty traded at a discount of 4.78% below its net asset value, which is better than its one-year historical average discount of .57%.

Paul L. Brennan has been running the fund for 7 years and currently receives a manager quality ranking of 20 (0=worst, 99=best). If you desire an average level of risk, then this fund may be an option.

Data Date	Investment Rating	Net Assets ($Mil)	Price	Performance Rating/Pts	Total Return Y-T-D	Risk Rating/Pts
12-12	B-	287.07	15.34	C+ / 6.2	3.98%	B / 8.3
2011	A-	293.60	16.23	A- / 9.2	-2.09%	B / 8.6
2010	C+	279.31	13.50	C / 5.2	3.34%	C+ / 6.6
2009	B-	289.96	13.88	C+ / 6.1	32.10%	B- / 7.2

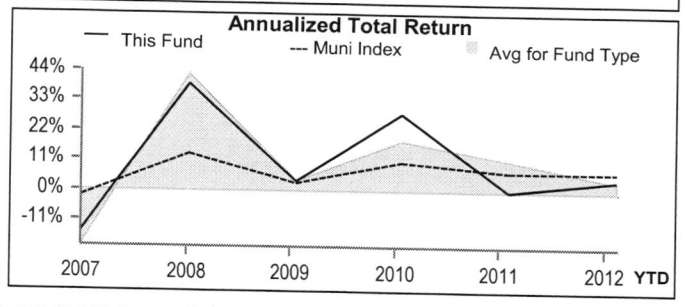

Nuveen Premium Income Muni 2 (NPM)

B+   **Good**

Fund Family: Nuveen Fund Advisors Inc
Fund Type: Municipal - National
Inception Date: July 23, 1992

Major Rating Factors: Strong performance is the major factor driving the B+ (Good) TheStreet.com Investment Rating for Nuveen Premium Income Muni 2. The fund currently has a performance rating of B (Good) based on an annualized return of 12.30% over the last three years and a total return of 3.88% year to date 2012. Factored into the performance evaluation is an expense ratio of 1.48% (average).

The fund's risk rating is currently B (Good). It carries a beta of 1.86, meaning it is expected to move 18.6% for every 10% move in the market. Volatility, as measured by both the semi-deviation and a drawdown factor, is considered low. As of December 31, 2012, Nuveen Premium Income Muni 2 traded at a discount of 5.06% below its net asset value, which is better than its one-year historical average discount of 2.55%.

Paul L. Brennan has been running the fund for 16 years and currently receives a manager quality ranking of 42 (0=worst, 99=best). If you desire only a moderate level of risk and strong performance, then this fund is an excellent option.

Data Date	Investment Rating	Net Assets ($Mil)	Price	Performance Rating/Pts	Total Return Y-T-D	Risk Rating/Pts
12-12	B+	1,039.72	15.20	B / 7.8	3.88%	B / 8.8
2011	A-	1,064.70	14.92	B+ / 8.5	-0.94%	B+ / 9.0
2010	C	1,003.37	13.24	C- / 3.9	5.79%	C+ / 6.5
2009	B-	603.44	13.33	C+ / 5.7	32.68%	B- / 7.3

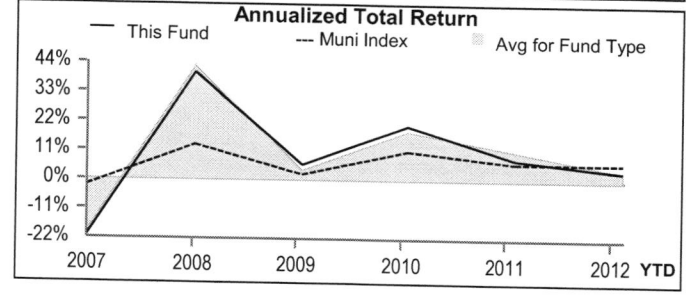

* Denotes ETF Fund

Nuveen Quality Inc Muni (NQU)

B+　　　**Good**

Fund Family: Nuveen Fund Advisors Inc
Fund Type: Municipal - National
Inception Date: June 19, 1991

Major Rating Factors: Strong performance is the major factor driving the B+ (Good) TheStreet.com Investment Rating for Nuveen Quality Inc Muni. The fund currently has a performance rating of B (Good) based on an annualized return of 11.71% over the last three years and a total return of 4.39% year to date 2012. Factored into the performance evaluation is an expense ratio of 1.92% (above average).

The fund's risk rating is currently B (Good). It carries a beta of 1.99, meaning it is expected to move 19.9% for every 10% move in the market. Volatility, as measured by both the semi-deviation and a drawdown factor, is considered low. As of December 31, 2012, Nuveen Quality Inc Muni traded at a discount of 5.92% below its net asset value, which is better than its one-year historical average discount of 1.91%.

Thomas C. Spalding has been running the fund for 11 years and currently receives a manager quality ranking of 33 (0=worst, 99=best). If you desire only a moderate level of risk and strong performance, then this fund is an excellent option.

Data Date	Investment Rating	Net Assets ($Mil)	Price	Performance Rating/Pts	Total Return Y-T-D	Risk Rating/Pts
12-12	B+	781.06	15.26	B / 7.7	4.39%	B / 8.7
2011	B+	800.60	14.60	B / 8.0	0.62%	B / 8.8
2010	C+	774.98	13.68	C / 4.8	7.08%	C+ / 6.6
2009	C+	808.36	13.63	C / 4.9	22.37%	B- / 7.5

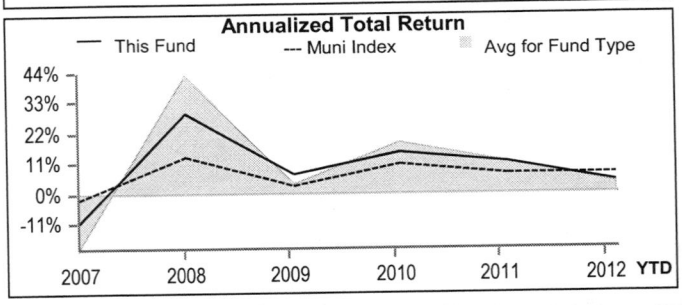

Nuveen Quality Municipal (NQI)

B　　　**Good**

Fund Family: Nuveen Fund Advisors Inc
Fund Type: Municipal - National
Inception Date: December 19, 1990

Major Rating Factors: Nuveen Quality Municipal receives a TheStreet.com Investment Rating of B (Good). The fund currently has a performance rating of C+ (Fair) based on an annualized return of 10.39% over the last three years and a total return of 3.67% year to date 2012. Factored into the performance evaluation is an expense ratio of 1.66% (above average).

The fund's risk rating is currently B (Good). It carries a beta of 2.09, meaning it is expected to move 20.9% for every 10% move in the market. Volatility, as measured by both the semi-deviation and a drawdown factor, is considered low. As of December 31, 2012, Nuveen Quality Municipal traded at a discount of 3.48% below its net asset value, which is better than its one-year historical average discount of 1.67%.

Douglas J. White currently receives a manager quality ranking of 27 (0=worst, 99=best). If you desire an average level of risk, then this fund may be an option.

Data Date	Investment Rating	Net Assets ($Mil)	Price	Performance Rating/Pts	Total Return Y-T-D	Risk Rating/Pts
12-12	B	544.50	14.97	C+ / 6.7	3.67%	B / 8.5
2011	B+	555.90	15.00	B+ / 8.5	-2.90%	B / 8.7
2010	C-	521.22	12.55	D / 2.1	-1.89%	B- / 7.5
2009	B-	542.09	13.60	C+ / 6.4	39.37%	B- / 7.0

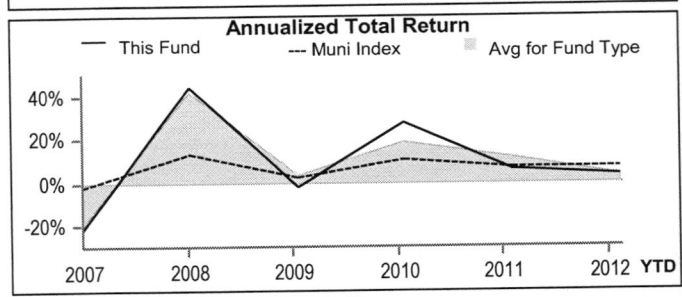

Nuveen Quality Preferred Income (JTP)

B+　　　**Good**

Fund Family: Nuveen Fund Advisors Inc
Fund Type: Income
Inception Date: June 25, 2002

Major Rating Factors: Strong performance is the major factor driving the B+ (Good) TheStreet.com Investment Rating for Nuveen Quality Preferred Income. The fund currently has a performance rating of B- (Good) based on an annualized return of 18.00% over the last three years and a total return of 1.38% year to date 2012. Factored into the performance evaluation is an expense ratio of 1.83% (above average).

The fund's risk rating is currently B (Good). It carries a beta of 0.28, meaning the fund's expected move will be 2.8% for every 10% move in the market. Volatility, as measured by both the semi-deviation and a drawdown factor, is considered low. As of December 31, 2012, Nuveen Quality Preferred Income traded at a discount of 5.04% below its net asset value, which is better than its one-year historical average discount of 1.10%.

Lewis P. Jacoby, IV currently receives a manager quality ranking of 95 (0=worst, 99=best). If you desire only a moderate level of risk and strong performance, then this fund is an excellent option.

Data Date	Investment Rating	Net Assets ($Mil)	Price	Performance Rating/Pts	Total Return Y-T-D	Risk Rating/Pts
12-12	B+	557.00	8.67	B- / 7.3	1.38%	B / 8.9
2011	C+	501.80	7.57	B- / 7.5	2.38%	C+ / 6.9
2010	D-	456.19	7.40	D+ / 2.3	21.90%	C- / 3.7
2009	E+	437.92	6.57	D- / 1.1	40.71%	C- / 3.8

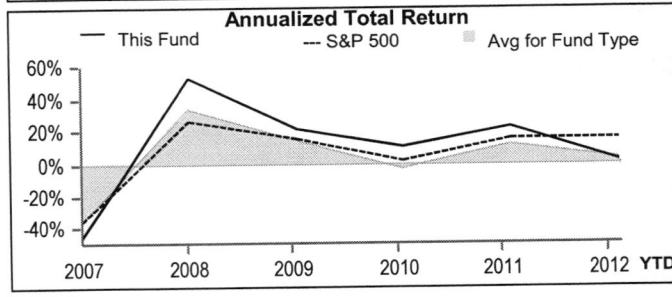

Nuveen Quality Preferred Income 2 (JPS)

B   Good

Fund Family: Nuveen Fund Advisors Inc
Fund Type: Income
Inception Date: September 23, 2002

Major Rating Factors: Strong performance is the major factor driving the B (Good) TheStreet.com Investment Rating for Nuveen Quality Preferred Income 2. The fund currently has a performance rating of B- (Good) based on an annualized return of 16.83% over the last three years and a total return of 0.21% year to date 2012. Factored into the performance evaluation is an expense ratio of 1.80% (above average).

The fund's risk rating is currently B (Good). It carries a beta of 0.42, meaning the fund's expected move will be 4.2% for every 10% move in the market. Volatility, as measured by both the semi-deviation and a drawdown factor, is considered low. As of December 31, 2012, Nuveen Quality Preferred Income 2 traded at a discount of 2.17% below its net asset value, which is better than its one-year historical average discount of .52%.

Lewis P. Jacoby, IV currently receives a manager quality ranking of 93 (0=worst, 99=best). If you desire only a moderate level of risk and strong performance, then this fund is an excellent option.

Data Date	Investment Rating	Net Assets ($Mil)	Price	Performance Rating/Pts	Total Return Y-T-D	Risk Rating/Pts
12-12	B	1,097.39	9.46	B- / 7.2	0.21%	B / 8.6
2011	C+	979.60	7.83	B- / 7.3	2.81%	C+ / 6.6
2010	D-	922.35	7.90	D+ / 2.5	18.30%	C- / 3.7
2009	E+	881.49	7.25	D- / 1.5	50.53%	C- / 3.6

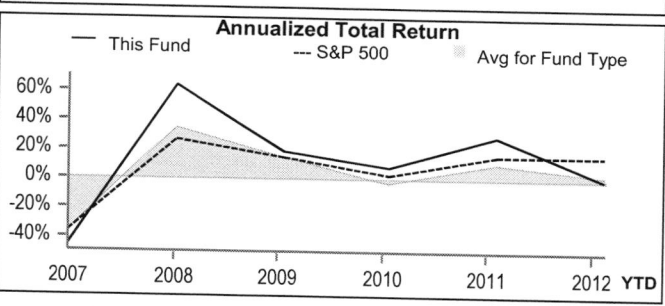

Annualized Total Return

Nuveen Quality Preferred Income 3 (JHP)

B   Good

Fund Family: Nuveen Fund Advisors Inc
Fund Type: Income
Inception Date: December 18, 2002

Major Rating Factors: Strong performance is the major factor driving the B (Good) TheStreet.com Investment Rating for Nuveen Quality Preferred Income 3. The fund currently has a performance rating of B- (Good) based on an annualized return of 17.36% over the last three years and a total return of 2.81% year to date 2012. Factored into the performance evaluation is an expense ratio of 1.84% (above average).

The fund's risk rating is currently B (Good). It carries a beta of 0.43, meaning the fund's expected move will be 4.3% for every 10% move in the market. Volatility, as measured by both the semi-deviation and a drawdown factor, is considered low. As of December 31, 2012, Nuveen Quality Preferred Income 3 traded at a discount of 5.43% below its net asset value, which is better than its one-year historical average discount of .53%.

Lewis P. Jacoby, IV currently receives a manager quality ranking of 92 (0=worst, 99=best). If you desire only a moderate level of risk and strong performance, then this fund is an excellent option.

Data Date	Investment Rating	Net Assets ($Mil)	Price	Performance Rating/Pts	Total Return Y-T-D	Risk Rating/Pts
12-12	B	208.73	8.89	B- / 7.2	2.81%	B / 8.5
2011	C+	186.50	7.84	B- / 7.4	1.53%	C+ / 6.8
2010	D	176.68	7.74	D+ / 2.8	20.63%	C- / 3.6
2009	E+	168.75	6.95	D- / 1.2	45.67%	C- / 3.8

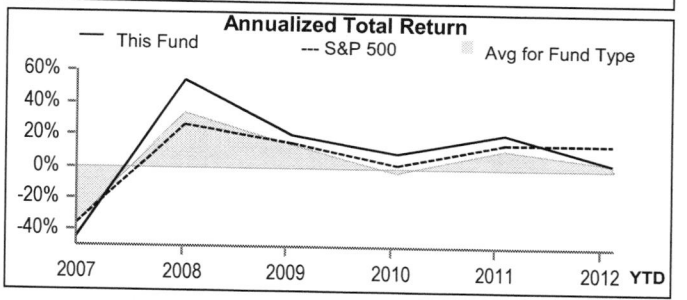

Annualized Total Return

Nuveen Real Estate Inc Fund (JRS)

B   Good

Fund Family: Nuveen Fund Advisors Inc
Fund Type: Growth and Income
Inception Date: November 15, 2001

Major Rating Factors: Strong performance is the major factor driving the B (Good) TheStreet.com Investment Rating for Nuveen Real Estate Inc Fund. The fund currently has a performance rating of B (Good) based on an annualized return of 20.72% over the last three years and a total return of 5.73% year to date 2012. Factored into the performance evaluation is an expense ratio of 1.93% (above average).

The fund's risk rating is currently B- (Good). It carries a beta of 0.93, meaning that its performance tracks fairly well with that of the overall stock market. Volatility, as measured by both the semi-deviation and a drawdown factor, is considered low. As of December 31, 2012, Nuveen Real Estate Inc Fund traded at a discount of 2.06% below its net asset value, which is better than its one-year historical average premium of 6.28%.

Anthony R. Manno, Jr. currently receives a manager quality ranking of 87 (0=worst, 99=best). If you desire only a moderate level of risk and strong performance, then this fund is an excellent option.

Data Date	Investment Rating	Net Assets ($Mil)	Price	Performance Rating/Pts	Total Return Y-T-D	Risk Rating/Pts
12-12	B	305.65	10.48	B / 7.9	5.73%	B- / 7.4
2011	B	275.80	10.44	A+ / 9.6	-0.19%	C+ / 6.4
2010	C-	230.33	10.11	B- / 7.3	37.66%	D+ / 2.3
2009	E	212.32	8.08	D- / 1.0	77.56%	C- / 3.1

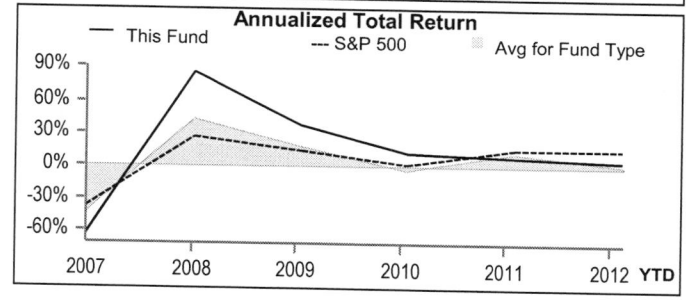

Annualized Total Return

Nuveen Select Maturities Muni (NIM)   C-   Fair

Fund Family: Nuveen Fund Advisors Inc
Fund Type: Municipal - National
Inception Date: September 18, 1992

Major Rating Factors:
Disappointing performance is the major factor driving the C- (Fair) TheStreet.com Investment Rating for Nuveen Select Maturities Muni. The fund currently has a performance rating of D+ (Weak) based on an annualized return of 4.57% over the last three years and a total return of 2.79% year to date 2012. Factored into the performance evaluation is an expense ratio of 0.62% (very low).

The fund's risk rating is currently B (Good). It carries a beta of 1.52, meaning it is expected to move 15.2% for every 10% move in the market. Volatility, as measured by both the semi-deviation and a drawdown factor, is considered low. As of December 31, 2012, Nuveen Select Maturities Muni traded at a discount of 2.53% below its net asset value, which is better than its one-year historical average premium of 2.17%.

Paul L. Brennan currently receives a manager quality ranking of 21 (0=worst, 99=best). This fund offers only a moderate level of risk but investors looking for strong performance are still waiting.

Data Date	Investment Rating	Net Assets ($Mil)	Price	Performance Rating/Pts	Total Return Y-T-D	Risk Rating/Pts
12-12	C-	129.87	10.39	D+ / 2.6	2.79%	B / 8.6
2011	C+	129.20	10.69	C / 5.4	-0.09%	B / 8.9
2010	B-	126.83	9.97	C / 5.3	0.24%	B- / 7.8
2009	B-	127.58	10.36	C / 5.2	13.82%	B / 8.0

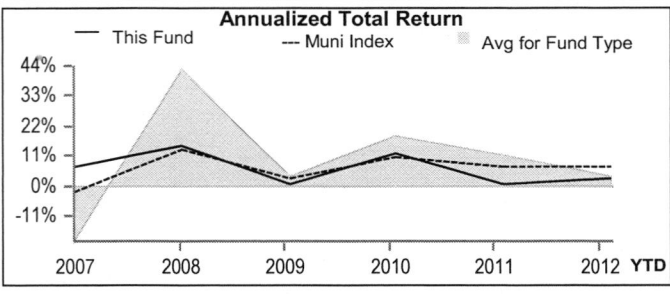

Nuveen Select Quality Muni (NQS)   B+   Good

Fund Family: Nuveen Fund Advisors Inc
Fund Type: Municipal - National
Inception Date: March 21, 1991

Major Rating Factors: Strong performance is the major factor driving the B+ (Good) TheStreet.com Investment Rating for Nuveen Select Quality Muni. The fund currently has a performance rating of B (Good) based on an annualized return of 12.20% over the last three years and a total return of 2.59% year to date 2012. Factored into the performance evaluation is an expense ratio of 1.53% (average).

The fund's risk rating is currently B (Good). It carries a beta of 2.07, meaning it is expected to move 20.7% for every 10% move in the market. Volatility, as measured by both the semi-deviation and a drawdown factor, is considered low. As of December 31, 2012, Nuveen Select Quality Muni traded at a discount of 1.12% below its net asset value, which is better than its one-year historical average premium of 1.18%.

Thomas C. Spalding has been running the fund for 11 years and currently receives a manager quality ranking of 37 (0=worst, 99=best). If you desire only a moderate level of risk and strong performance, then this fund is an excellent option.

Data Date	Investment Rating	Net Assets ($Mil)	Price	Performance Rating/Pts	Total Return Y-T-D	Risk Rating/Pts
12-12	B+	491.45	15.83	B / 7.8	2.59%	B / 8.5
2011	A	501.20	15.47	A / 9.4	0.13%	B / 8.6
2010	C+	481.23	13.64	C / 5.0	4.67%	C+ / 6.3
2009	B-	500.85	14.07	C+ / 5.8	40.53%	B- / 7.2

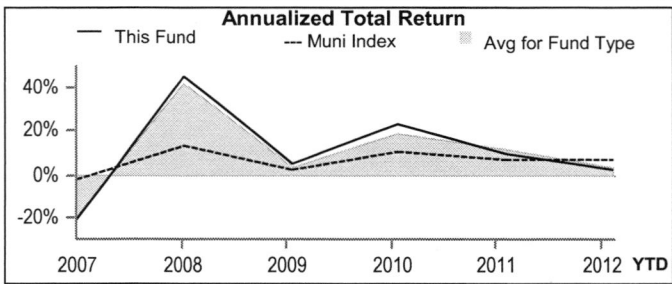

Nuveen Select T-F Inc Portf (NXP)   C   Fair

Fund Family: Nuveen Fund Advisors Inc
Fund Type: Municipal - National
Inception Date: March 19, 1992

Major Rating Factors: Middle of the road best describes Nuveen Select T-F Inc Portf whose TheStreet.com Investment Rating is currently a C (Fair). The fund currently has a performance rating of C- (Fair) based on an annualized return of 6.43% over the last three years and a total return of 3.62% year to date 2012. Factored into the performance evaluation is an expense ratio of 0.31% (very low).

The fund's risk rating is currently B (Good). It carries a beta of 1.65, meaning it is expected to move 16.5% for every 10% move in the market. Volatility, as measured by both the semi-deviation and a drawdown factor, is considered low. As of December 31, 2012, Nuveen Select T-F Inc Portf traded at a discount of 1.32% below its net asset value, which is better than its one-year historical average premium of 2.86%.

Thomas C. Spalding has been running the fund for 14 years and currently receives a manager quality ranking of 22 (0=worst, 99=best). If you desire an average level of risk, then this fund may be an option.

Data Date	Investment Rating	Net Assets ($Mil)	Price	Performance Rating/Pts	Total Return Y-T-D	Risk Rating/Pts
12-12	C	240.69	14.93	C- / 4.0	3.62%	B / 8.7
2011	B-	234.20	14.65	C+ / 5.8	0.15%	B / 8.9
2010	C	233.87	13.54	D+ / 2.5	-3.80%	B / 8.5
2009	B-	235.93	14.80	C / 5.2	12.38%	B- / 7.8

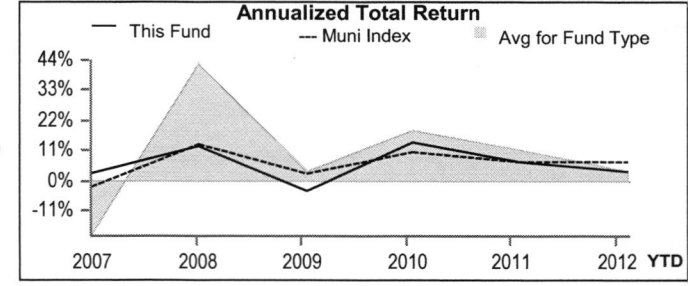

Nuveen Select T-F Inc Portf 2 (NXQ)

C　　　**Fair**

Fund Family: Nuveen Fund Advisors Inc
Fund Type: Municipal - National
Inception Date: May 21, 1992

Major Rating Factors: Middle of the road best describes Nuveen Select T-F Inc Portf 2 whose TheStreet.com Investment Rating is currently a C (Fair). The fund currently has a performance rating of C- (Fair) based on an annualized return of 5.53% over the last three years and a total return of 2.41% year to date 2012. Factored into the performance evaluation is an expense ratio of 0.35% (very low).

The fund's risk rating is currently B (Good). It carries a beta of 1.59, meaning it is expected to move 15.9% for every 10% move in the market. Volatility, as measured by both the semi-deviation and a drawdown factor, is considered low. As of December 31, 2012, Nuveen Select T-F Inc Portf 2 traded at a discount of 2.29% below its net asset value, which is better than its one-year historical average premium of .55%.

Thomas C. Spalding has been running the fund for 14 years and currently receives a manager quality ranking of 23 (0=worst, 99=best). If you desire an average level of risk, then this fund may be an option.

Data Date	Investment Rating	Net Assets ($Mil)	Price	Perfor-mance Rating/Pts	Total Return Y-T-D	Risk Rating/Pts
12-12	C	245.78	14.09	C- / 3.5	2.41%	B / 8.7
2011	C	239.50	13.56	C- / 4.2	-1.70%	B / 8.9
2010	C	239.10	12.73	C- / 3.0	-3.73%	B / 8.1
2009	C+	241.15	13.89	C / 4.6	9.06%	B- / 7.8

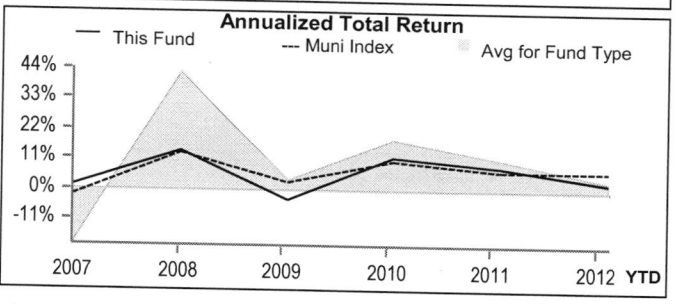

Nuveen Select Tax-Free Inc 3 (NXR)

C　　　**Fair**

Fund Family: Nuveen Fund Advisors Inc
Fund Type: Municipal - National
Inception Date: July 24, 1992

Major Rating Factors: Middle of the road best describes Nuveen Select Tax-Free Inc 3 whose TheStreet.com Investment Rating is currently a C (Fair). The fund currently has a performance rating of C- (Fair) based on an annualized return of 6.59% over the last three years and a total return of 4.45% year to date 2012. Factored into the performance evaluation is an expense ratio of 0.38% (very low).

The fund's risk rating is currently B (Good). It carries a beta of 1.51, meaning it is expected to move 15.1% for every 10% move in the market. Volatility, as measured by both the semi-deviation and a drawdown factor, is considered low. As of December 31, 2012, Nuveen Select Tax-Free Inc 3 traded at a discount of 2.66% below its net asset value, which is better than its one-year historical average premium of 1.54%.

Thomas C. Spalding has been running the fund for 14 years and currently receives a manager quality ranking of 23 (0=worst, 99=best). If you desire an average level of risk, then this fund may be an option.

Data Date	Investment Rating	Net Assets ($Mil)	Price	Perfor-mance Rating/Pts	Total Return Y-T-D	Risk Rating/Pts
12-12	C	188.01	14.62	C- / 4.0	4.45%	B / 8.7
2011	C+	183.10	14.31	C / 4.7	-1.40%	B / 8.9
2010	C+	182.78	13.10	C- / 3.0	-6.33%	B / 8.5
2009	B	184.84	14.64	C / 5.3	11.40%	B- / 7.9

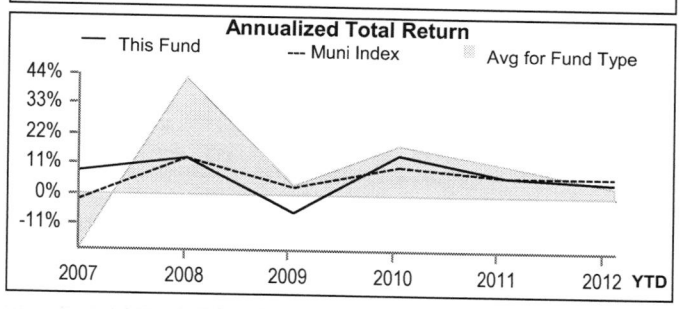

Nuveen Short Duration Credit Oppty (JSD)

A　　　**Excellent**

Fund Family: Nuveen Fund Advisors Inc
Fund Type: Growth and Income
Inception Date: May 25, 2011

Major Rating Factors:
Strong performance is the major factor driving the A (Excellent) TheStreet.com Investment Rating for Nuveen Short Duration Credit Oppty. The fund currently has a performance rating of B (Good) based on an annualized return of 0.00% over the last three years and a total return of 2.00% year to date 2012. Factored into the performance evaluation is an expense ratio of 1.75% (above average).

The fund's risk rating is currently B (Good). It carries a beta of 0.00, meaning the fund's expected move will be 0.0% for every 10% move in the market. Volatility, as measured by both the semi-deviation and a drawdown factor, is considered low. As of December 31, 2012, Nuveen Short Duration Credit Oppty traded at a premium of .91% above its net asset value, which is worse than its one-year historical average discount of .04%.

Gunther M. Stein has been running the fund for 2 years and currently receives a manager quality ranking of 92 (0=worst, 99=best). If you desire only a moderate level of risk and strong performance, then this fund is an excellent option.

Data Date	Investment Rating	Net Assets ($Mil)	Price	Perfor-mance Rating/Pts	Total Return Y-T-D	Risk Rating/Pts
12-12	A	195.17	19.95	B / 8.1	2.00%	B / 8.9

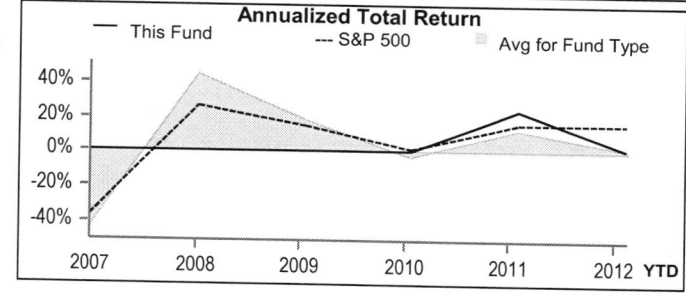

Nuveen Sr Inc (NSL)

| | C | Fair |

Fund Family: Nuveen Fund Advisors Inc
Fund Type: Loan Participation
Inception Date: October 26, 1999

Data Date	Investment Rating	Net Assets ($Mil)	Price	Performance Rating/Pts	Total Return Y-T-D	Risk Rating/Pts
12-12	C	231.87	7.31	C / 5.0	3.83%	B / 8.0
2011	B+	216.30	6.62	B+ / 8.5	2.42%	B / 8.1
2010	C	203.26	7.14	C+ / 6.8	7.64%	C- / 4.1
2009	C+	185.99	7.11	B+ / 8.5	127.45%	C- / 4.0

Major Rating Factors: Middle of the road best describes Nuveen Sr Inc whose TheStreet.com Investment Rating is currently a C (Fair). The fund currently has a performance rating of C (Fair) based on an annualized return of 9.68% over the last three years and a total return of 3.83% year to date 2012. Factored into the performance evaluation is an expense ratio of 1.82% (above average).

The fund's risk rating is currently B (Good). It carries a beta of -128.18, meaning the fund's expected move will be -1281.8% for every 10% move in the market. Volatility, as measured by both the semi-deviation and a drawdown factor, is considered low. As of December 31, 2012, Nuveen Sr Inc traded at a premium of .27% above its net asset value, which is better than its one-year historical average premium of 1.61%.

Gunther M. Stein has been running the fund for 14 years and currently receives a manager quality ranking of 98 (0=worst, 99=best). If you desire an average level of risk, then this fund may be an option.

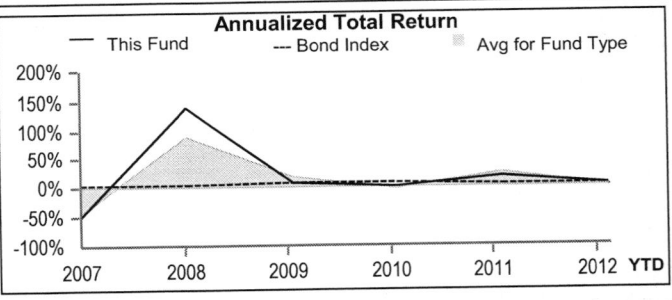

Nuveen Tax-Advant Tot Ret Strat Fd (JTA)

| | C | Fair |

Fund Family: Nuveen Fund Advisors Inc
Fund Type: Income
Inception Date: January 28, 2004

Data Date	Investment Rating	Net Assets ($Mil)	Price	Performance Rating/Pts	Total Return Y-T-D	Risk Rating/Pts
12-12	C	155.52	10.51	C / 4.9	5.99%	B / 8.0
2011	C+	151.90	9.56	C+ / 5.7	4.71%	B- / 7.6
2010	D-	161.40	11.24	D- / 1.1	14.72%	C / 4.3
2009	D-	157.14	10.66	D- / 1.1	46.20%	C / 4.4

Major Rating Factors: Middle of the road best describes Nuveen Tax-Advant Tot Ret Strat Fd whose TheStreet.com Investment Rating is currently a C (Fair). The fund currently has a performance rating of C (Fair) based on an annualized return of 9.06% over the last three years and a total return of 5.99% year to date 2012. Factored into the performance evaluation is an expense ratio of 2.03% (high).

The fund's risk rating is currently B (Good). It carries a beta of 0.90, meaning that its performance tracks fairly well with that of the overall stock market. Volatility, as measured by both the semi-deviation and a drawdown factor, is considered low. As of December 31, 2012, Nuveen Tax-Advant Tot Ret Strat Fd traded at a discount of 13.92% below its net asset value, which is better than its one-year historical average discount of 8.89%.

Gunther M. Stein has been running the fund for 9 years and currently receives a manager quality ranking of 40 (0=worst, 99=best). If you desire an average level of risk, then this fund may be an option.

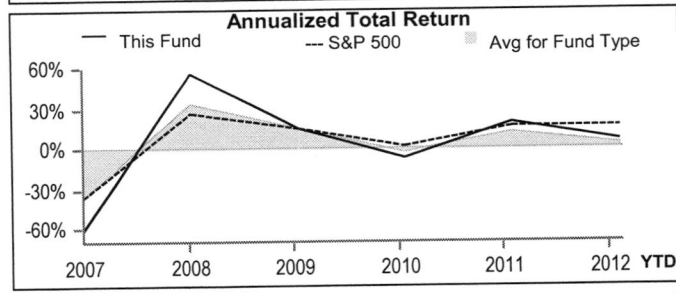

Nuveen Tax-Advantaged Dividend Grt (JTD)

| | A- | Excellent |

Fund Family: Nuveen Fund Advisors Inc
Fund Type: Growth and Income
Inception Date: June 27, 2007

Data Date	Investment Rating	Net Assets ($Mil)	Price	Performance Rating/Pts	Total Return Y-T-D	Risk Rating/Pts
12-12	A-	196.40	14.50	B+ / 8.7	4.34%	B / 8.3
2011	B-	196.40	12.29	B- / 7.2	2.44%	B- / 7.7
2010	C	189.01	13.01	C+ / 6.0	22.52%	C / 4.6
2009	A-	182.06	11.56	A- / 9.1	40.04%	C / 5.1

Major Rating Factors:
Strong performance is the major factor driving the A- (Excellent) TheStreet.com Investment Rating for Nuveen Tax-Advantaged Dividend Grt. The fund currently has a performance rating of B+ (Good) based on an annualized return of 18.68% over the last three years and a total return of 4.34% year to date 2012. Factored into the performance evaluation is an expense ratio of 1.87% (above average).

The fund's risk rating is currently B (Good). It carries a beta of 0.80, meaning the fund's expected move will be 8.0% for every 10% move in the market. Volatility, as measured by both the semi-deviation and a drawdown factor, is considered low. As of December 31, 2012, Nuveen Tax-Advantaged Dividend Grt traded at a discount of 7.17% below its net asset value, which is better than its one-year historical average discount of 6.36%.

James R. Boothe currently receives a manager quality ranking of 86 (0=worst, 99=best). If you desire only a moderate level of risk and strong performance, then this fund is an excellent option.

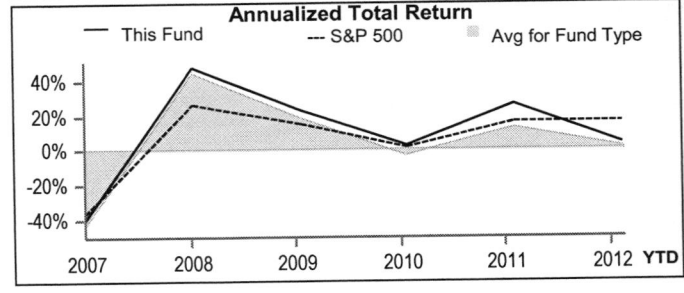

Nuveen TX Quality Inc Muni (NTX)

C   **Fair**

Fund Family: Nuveen Fund Advisors Inc
Fund Type: Municipal - Single State
Inception Date: October 17, 1991

Major Rating Factors: Middle of the road best describes Nuveen TX Quality Inc Muni whose TheStreet.com Investment Rating is currently a C (Fair). The fund currently has a performance rating of C- (Fair) based on an annualized return of 7.65% over the last three years and a total return of 2.97% year to date 2012. Factored into the performance evaluation is an expense ratio of 2.40% (high).

The fund's risk rating is currently B+ (Good). It carries a beta of 1.35, meaning it is expected to move 13.5% for every 10% move in the market. Volatility, as measured by both the semi-deviation and a drawdown factor, is considered very low. As of December 31, 2012, Nuveen TX Quality Inc Muni traded at a discount of .25% below its net asset value, which is better than its one-year historical average premium of 5.93%.

Daniel J. Close currently receives a manager quality ranking of 39 (0=worst, 99=best). If you desire an average level of risk, then this fund may be an option.

Data Date	Investment Rating	Net Assets ($Mil)	Price	Performance Rating/Pts	Total Return Y-T-D	Risk Rating/Pts
12-12	C	151.86	15.84	C- / 3.9	2.97%	B+ / 9.0
2011	B+	143.60	16.34	B / 8.2	0.69%	B+ / 9.1
2010	B+	143.08	14.92	B- / 7.4	4.43%	C+ / 6.6
2009	C+	141.86	15.10	C+ / 6.7	33.58%	C+ / 6.7

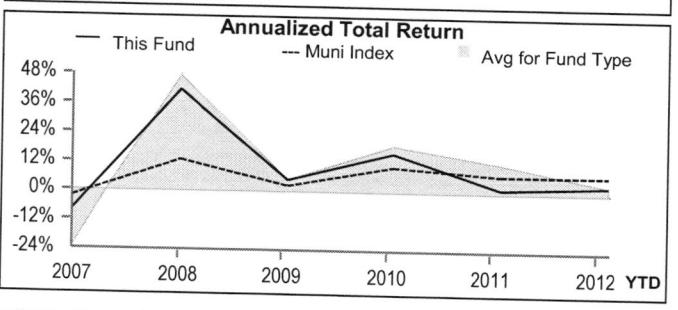

Nuveen VA Premium Income Municipal (NPV)

C   **Fair**

Fund Family: Nuveen Fund Advisors Inc
Fund Type: Municipal - Single State
Inception Date: March 18, 1993

Major Rating Factors: Middle of the road best describes Nuveen VA Premium Income Municipal whose TheStreet.com Investment Rating is currently a C (Fair). The fund currently has a performance rating of C- (Fair) based on an annualized return of 8.34% over the last three years and a total return of 3.15% year to date 2012. Factored into the performance evaluation is an expense ratio of 2.78% (high).

The fund's risk rating is currently B (Good). It carries a beta of 2.04, meaning it is expected to move 20.4% for every 10% move in the market. Volatility, as measured by both the semi-deviation and a drawdown factor, is considered low. As of December 31, 2012, Nuveen VA Premium Income Municipal traded at a discount of .64% below its net asset value, which is better than its one-year historical average premium of 5.26%.

Thomas C. Spalding currently receives a manager quality ranking of 19 (0=worst, 99=best). If you desire an average level of risk, then this fund may be an option.

Data Date	Investment Rating	Net Assets ($Mil)	Price	Performance Rating/Pts	Total Return Y-T-D	Risk Rating/Pts
12-12	C	141.10	15.55	C- / 4.2	3.15%	B / 8.5
2011	B	136.60	15.42	C+ / 6.7	-0.13%	B / 8.6
2010	C+	132.30	14.70	C+ / 6.7	3.78%	C+ / 6.8
2009	B-	133.23	14.94	C+ / 5.9	36.34%	B- / 7.3

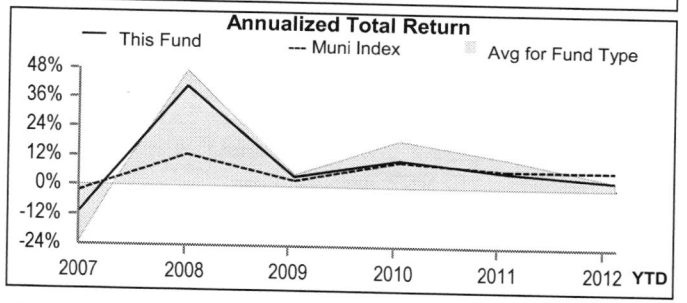

Pacholder High Yield Fund (PHF)

C+   **Fair**

Fund Family: JP Morgan Investment Management Inc
Fund Type: Corporate - High Yield
Inception Date: November 16, 1988

Major Rating Factors: Strong performance is the major factor driving the C+ (Fair) TheStreet.com Investment Rating for Pacholder High Yield Fund. The fund currently has a performance rating of B- (Good) based on an annualized return of 17.62% over the last three years and a total return of 4.40% year to date 2012. Factored into the performance evaluation is an expense ratio of 1.16% (low).

The fund's risk rating is currently B- (Good). It carries a beta of 0.86, meaning the fund's expected move will be 8.6% for every 10% move in the market. Volatility, as measured by both the semi-deviation and a drawdown factor, is considered low. As of December 31, 2012, Pacholder High Yield Fund traded at a premium of 1.60% above its net asset value, which is better than its one-year historical average premium of 10.15%.

James P. Shanahan, Jr. currently receives a manager quality ranking of 83 (0=worst, 99=best). If you desire only a moderate level of risk and strong performance, then this fund is an excellent option.

Data Date	Investment Rating	Net Assets ($Mil)	Price	Performance Rating/Pts	Total Return Y-T-D	Risk Rating/Pts
12-12	C+	106,346.02	8.87	B- / 7.0	4.40%	B- / 7.4
2011	A	101.90	8.95	A+ / 9.7	1.56%	B / 8.1
2010	C+	100.90	8.45	B / 8.2	21.63%	C- / 3.4
2009	C	77.08	7.38	B+ / 8.3	126.90%	C- / 3.0

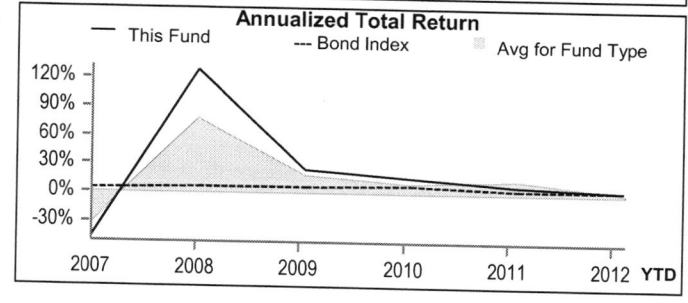

* Denotes ETF Fund

PCM Fund (PCM)

A+   Excellent

Fund Family: Allianz Global Investors Fund Mgmt
Fund Type: Mortgage
Inception Date: August 27, 1993

Major Rating Factors:
Exceptional performance is the major factor driving the A+ (Excellent) TheStreet.com Investment Rating for PCM Fund. The fund currently has a performance rating of A- (Excellent) based on an annualized return of 24.45% over the last three years and a total return of 1.86% year to date 2012. Factored into the performance evaluation is an expense ratio of 2.64% (high).

The fund's risk rating is currently B (Good). It carries a beta of -0.06, meaning the fund's expected move will be -0.6% for every 10% move in the market. Volatility, as measured by both the semi-deviation and a drawdown factor, is considered low. As of December 31, 2012, PCM Fund traded at a premium of 3.89% above its net asset value, which is better than its one-year historical average premium of 8.27%.

Daniel J. Ivascyn has been running the fund for 12 years and currently receives a manager quality ranking of 98 (0=worst, 99=best). If you desire only a moderate level of risk and strong performance, then this fund is an excellent option.

Data Date	Investment Rating	Net Assets ($Mil)	Price	Performance Rating/Pts	Total Return Y-T-D	Risk Rating/Pts
12-12	A+	117.80	12.02	A- / 9.0	1.86%	B / 8.8
2011	B+	113.02	10.77	B+ / 8.8	1.58%	B- / 7.8
2010	B-	88.29	10.80	B+ / 8.8	48.82%	C- / 4.0
2009	D+	68.87	7.97	C- / 3.1	45.58%	C / 4.8

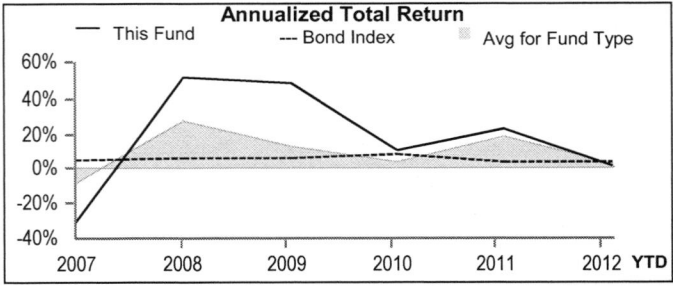

Petroleum and Resources Corp. (PEO)

D+   Weak

Fund Family: Adams Express Company
Fund Type: Energy/Natural Resources
Inception Date: January 21, 1969

Major Rating Factors: Petroleum and Resources Corp. receives a TheStreet.com Investment Rating of D+ (Weak). The fund currently has a performance rating of C- (Fair) based on an annualized return of 7.70% over the last three years and a total return of 4.77% year to date 2012. Factored into the performance evaluation is an expense ratio of 0.70% (very low).

The fund's risk rating is currently B- (Good). It carries a beta of 1.02, meaning that its performance tracks fairly well with that of the overall stock market. Volatility, as measured by both the semi-deviation and a drawdown factor, is considered low. As of December 31, 2012, Petroleum and Resources Corp. traded at a discount of 17.12% below its net asset value, which is better than its one-year historical average discount of 13.18%.

David D. Weaver has been running the fund for 3 years and currently receives a manager quality ranking of 33 (0=worst, 99=best). If you desire an average level of risk, then this fund may be an option.

Data Date	Investment Rating	Net Assets ($Mil)	Price	Performance Rating/Pts	Total Return Y-T-D	Risk Rating/Pts
12-12	D+	710.41	23.92	C- / 3.3	4.77%	B- / 7.3
2011	C	732.80	24.48	C / 4.7	1.96%	B- / 7.4
2010	C	650.72	27.02	C / 4.6	19.58%	C+ / 5.8
2009	C-	552.91	23.74	C- / 3.8	22.87%	C+ / 5.9

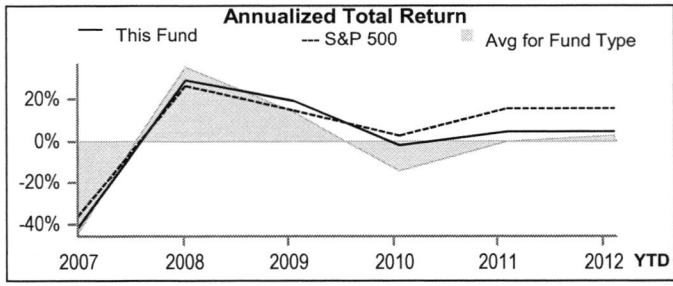

PIMCO CA Municipal Income Fund (PCQ)

A+   Excellent

Fund Family: Allianz Global Investors Fund Mgmt
Fund Type: Municipal - Single State
Inception Date: June 26, 2001

Major Rating Factors:
Exceptional performance is the major factor driving the A+ (Excellent) TheStreet.com Investment Rating for PIMCO CA Municipal Income Fund. The fund currently has a performance rating of A+ (Excellent) based on an annualized return of 17.46% over the last three years and a total return of 3.15% year to date 2012. Factored into the performance evaluation is an expense ratio of 1.36% (average).

The fund's risk rating is currently B (Good). It carries a beta of 2.28, meaning it is expected to move 22.8% for every 10% move in the market. Volatility, as measured by both the semi-deviation and a drawdown factor, is considered low. As of December 31, 2012, PIMCO CA Municipal Income Fund traded at a premium of 9.11% above its net asset value, which is worse than its one-year historical average premium of 8.32%.

Joseph P. Deane has been running the fund for 2 years and currently receives a manager quality ranking of 61 (0=worst, 99=best). If you desire only a moderate level of risk and strong performance, then this fund is an excellent option.

Data Date	Investment Rating	Net Assets ($Mil)	Price	Performance Rating/Pts	Total Return Y-T-D	Risk Rating/Pts
12-12	A+	253.87	15.93	A+ / 9.6	3.15%	B / 8.3
2011	A-	236.00	13.44	A- / 9.1	2.23%	B / 8.3
2010	D+	234.79	12.40	D / 1.7	7.56%	C+ / 6.6
2009	C	192.85	12.39	C- / 4.0	45.39%	C+ / 6.7

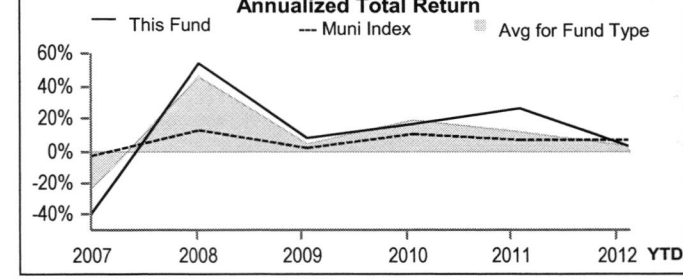

PIMCO CA Municipal Income Fund II (PCK)

A+   Excellent

Fund Family: Allianz Global Investors Fund Mgmt
Fund Type: Municipal - Single State
Inception Date: June 25, 2002

Major Rating Factors:

Exceptional performance is the major factor driving the A+ (Excellent) TheStreet.com Investment Rating for PIMCO CA Municipal Income Fund II. The fund currently has a performance rating of A (Excellent) based on an annualized return of 16.47% over the last three years and a total return of 3.36% year to date 2012. Factored into the performance evaluation is an expense ratio of 1.44% (average).

The fund's risk rating is currently B (Good). It carries a beta of 2.11, meaning it is expected to move 21.1% for every 10% move in the market. Volatility, as measured by both the semi-deviation and a drawdown factor, is considered low. As of December 31, 2012, PIMCO CA Municipal Income Fund II traded at a premium of 15.86% above its net asset value, which is better than its one-year historical average premium of 19.12%.

Joseph P. Deane has been running the fund for 2 years and currently receives a manager quality ranking of 64 (0=worst, 99=best). If you desire only a moderate level of risk and strong performance, then this fund is an excellent option.

Data Date	Investment Rating	Net Assets ($Mil)	Price	Performance Rating/Pts	Total Return Y-T-D	Risk Rating/Pts
12-12	A+	272.57	10.59	A / 9.3	3.36%	B / 8.7
2011	B+	247.80	9.40	B+ / 8.3	2.13%	B / 8.6
2010	D-	252.82	8.77	D- / 1.0	10.09%	C- / 4.3
2009	D-	231.42	8.68	D- / 1.2	47.00%	C / 4.8

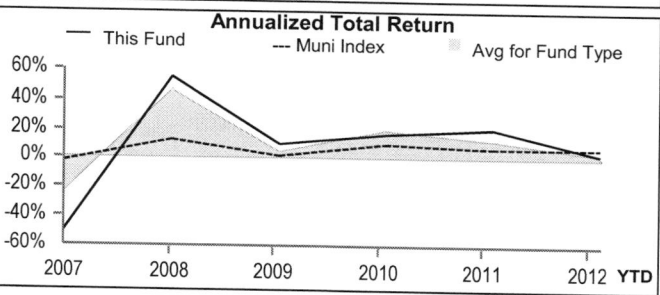

PIMCO CA Municipal Income Fund III (PZC)

A+   Excellent

Fund Family: Allianz Global Investors Fund Mgmt
Fund Type: Municipal - Single State
Inception Date: October 28, 2002

Major Rating Factors:

Exceptional performance is the major factor driving the A+ (Excellent) TheStreet.com Investment Rating for PIMCO CA Municipal Income Fund III. The fund currently has a performance rating of A- (Excellent) based on an annualized return of 16.10% over the last three years and a total return of 3.31% year to date 2012. Factored into the performance evaluation is an expense ratio of 1.34% (average).

The fund's risk rating is currently B (Good). It carries a beta of 2.07, meaning it is expected to move 20.7% for every 10% move in the market. Volatility, as measured by both the semi-deviation and a drawdown factor, is considered low. As of December 31, 2012, PIMCO CA Municipal Income Fund III traded at a premium of 8.88% above its net asset value, which is better than its one-year historical average premium of 9.33%.

Joseph P. Deane has been running the fund for 2 years and currently receives a manager quality ranking of 65 (0=worst, 99=best). If you desire only a moderate level of risk and strong performance, then this fund is an excellent option.

Data Date	Investment Rating	Net Assets ($Mil)	Price	Performance Rating/Pts	Total Return Y-T-D	Risk Rating/Pts
12-12	A+	224.60	11.28	A- / 9.2	3.31%	B / 8.6
2011	A-	202.10	9.76	A- / 9.1	2.36%	B / 8.6
2010	D-	210.32	9.01	E+ / 0.9	7.20%	C / 4.9
2009	D	207.17	9.08	D- / 1.3	56.52%	C / 5.5

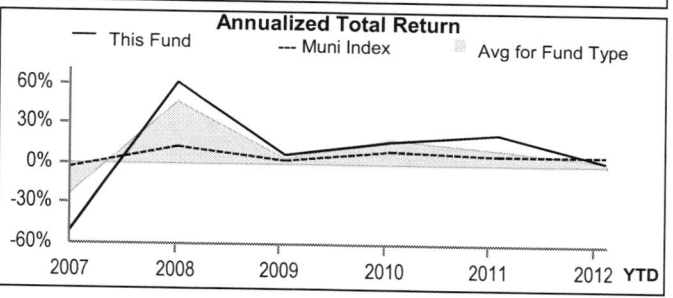

PIMCO Corporate and Income Oppty (PTY)

A   Excellent

Fund Family: Allianz Global Investors Fund Mgmt
Fund Type: Corporate - High Yield
Inception Date: December 23, 2002

Major Rating Factors:

Exceptional performance is the major factor driving the A (Excellent) TheStreet.com Investment Rating for PIMCO Corporate and Income Oppty. The fund currently has a performance rating of A- (Excellent) based on an annualized return of 24.05% over the last three years and a total return of 4.89% year to date 2012. Factored into the performance evaluation is an expense ratio of 1.12% (low).

The fund's risk rating is currently B- (Good). It carries a beta of 1.41, meaning it is expected to move 14.1% for every 10% move in the market. Volatility, as measured by both the semi-deviation and a drawdown factor, is considered low. As of December 31, 2012, PIMCO Corporate and Income Oppty traded at a premium of 14.78% above its net asset value, which is better than its one-year historical average premium of 19.68%.

William H. Gross currently receives a manager quality ranking of 83 (0=worst, 99=best). If you desire only a moderate level of risk and strong performance, then this fund is an excellent option.

Data Date	Investment Rating	Net Assets ($Mil)	Price	Performance Rating/Pts	Total Return Y-T-D	Risk Rating/Pts
12-12	A	1,046.09	19.41	A- / 9.2	4.89%	B- / 7.8
2011	C+	1,098.92	17.37	B / 7.9	2.19%	C+ / 6.4
2010	B	962.49	16.97	B+ / 8.7	28.50%	C / 4.3
2009	C+	669.92	14.40	B- / 7.3	54.08%	C / 4.9

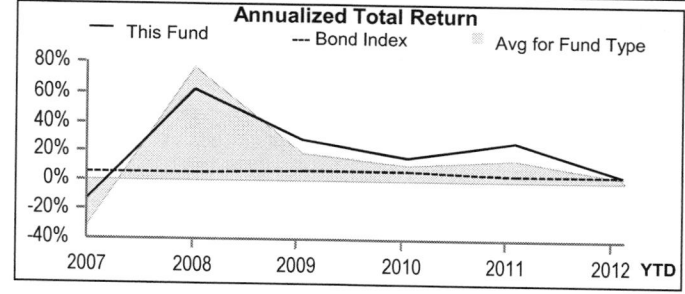

PIMCO Corporate and ncome Strategy (PCN)

B+ **Good**

Fund Family: Allianz Global Investors Fund Mgmt
Fund Type: Corporate - High Yield
Inception Date: December 19, 2001

Data Date	Investment Rating	Net Assets ($Mil)	Price	Perfor-mance Rating/Pts	Total Return Y-T-D	Risk Rating/Pts
12-12	B+	515.04	17.65	B+ / 8.7	5.50%	B- / 7.9
2011	C+	589.03	15.95	B- / 7.4	0.94%	C+ / 6.1
2010	B	529.37	15.49	B+ / 8.5	22.06%	C / 4.8
2009	C	286.56	13.85	C+ / 5.7	36.63%	C / 4.7

Major Rating Factors: Strong performance is the major factor driving the B+ (Good) TheStreet.com Investment Rating for PIMCO Corporate and ncome Strategy. The fund currently has a performance rating of B+ (Good) based on an annualized return of 20.62% over the last three years and a total return of 5.50% year to date 2012. Factored into the performance evaluation is an expense ratio of 1.30% (average).

The fund's risk rating is currently B- (Good). It carries a beta of 1.47, meaning it is expected to move 14.7% for every 10% move in the market. Volatility, as measured by both the semi-deviation and a drawdown factor, is considered low. As of December 31, 2012, PIMCO Corporate and ncome Strategy traded at a premium of 8.35% above its net asset value, which is better than its one-year historical average premium of 15.87%.

William H. Gross currently receives a manager quality ranking of 66 (0=worst, 99=best). If you desire only a moderate level of risk and strong performance, then this fund is an excellent option.

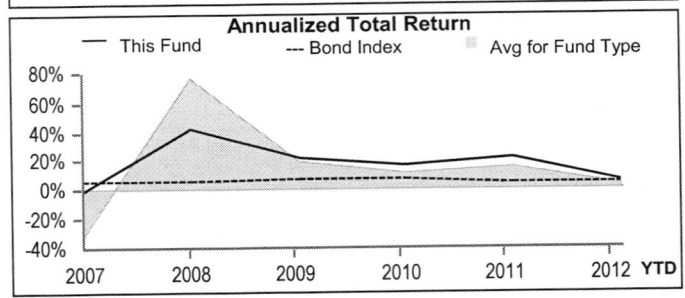

PIMCO Global StocksPLUS&Inc (PGP)

C+ **Fair**

Fund Family: Allianz Global Investors Fund Mgmt
Fund Type: Global
Inception Date: May 26, 2005

Data Date	Investment Rating	Net Assets ($Mil)	Price	Perfor-mance Rating/Pts	Total Return Y-T-D	Risk Rating/Pts
12-12	C+	128.95	17.83	C+ / 6.6	15.85%	C+ / 6.8
2011	B	150.88	18.75	A / 9.3	3.25%	C+ / 6.6
2010	C+	125.37	21.60	A- / 9.2	34.73%	D+ / 2.8
2009	C	103.34	18.02	B+ / 8.4	115.60%	D+ / 2.5

Major Rating Factors: Middle of the road best describes PIMCO Global StocksPLUS&Inc whose TheStreet.com Investment Rating is currently a C+ (Fair). The fund currently has a performance rating of C+ (Fair) based on an annualized return of 15.79% over the last three years and a total return of 15.85% year to date 2012. Factored into the performance evaluation is an expense ratio of 2.71% (high).

The fund's risk rating is currently C+ (Fair). It carries a beta of 0.75, meaning the fund's expected move will be 7.5% for every 10% move in the market. Volatility, as measured by both the semi-deviation and a drawdown factor, is considered low. As of December 31, 2012, PIMCO Global StocksPLUS&Inc traded at a premium of 27.08% above its net asset value, which is better than its one-year historical average premium of 67.14%.

Daniel J. Ivascyn has been running the fund for 8 years and currently receives a manager quality ranking of 87 (0=worst, 99=best). If you desire an average level of risk, then this fund may be an option.

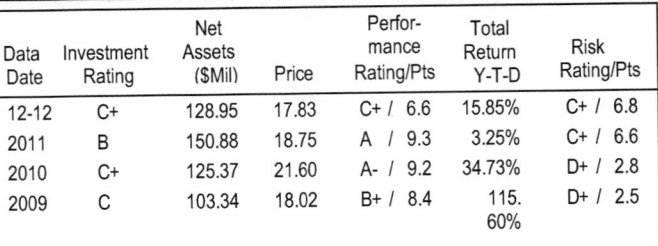

PIMCO High Income Fund (PHK)

C- **Fair**

Fund Family: Allianz Global Investors Fund Mgmt
Fund Type: Corporate - High Yield
Inception Date: April 24, 2003

Data Date	Investment Rating	Net Assets ($Mil)	Price	Perfor-mance Rating/Pts	Total Return Y-T-D	Risk Rating/Pts
12-12	C-	960.50	10.48	C / 5.1	15.21%	C+ / 6.8
2011	B	1,138.19	12.02	A+ / 9.6	3.58%	C+ / 6.3
2010	C	1,046.24	12.71	B+ / 8.7	32.67%	D / 2.1
2009	C	875.24	10.85	B / 7.9	111.17%	D+ / 2.3

Major Rating Factors: Middle of the road best describes PIMCO High Income Fund whose TheStreet.com Investment Rating is currently a C- (Fair). The fund currently has a performance rating of C (Fair) based on an annualized return of 14.96% over the last three years and a total return of 15.21% year to date 2012. Factored into the performance evaluation is an expense ratio of 1.16% (low).

The fund's risk rating is currently C+ (Fair). It carries a beta of 1.74, meaning it is expected to move 17.4% for every 10% move in the market. Volatility, as measured by both the semi-deviation and a drawdown factor, is considered low. As of December 31, 2012, PIMCO High Income Fund traded at a premium of 23.44% above its net asset value, which is better than its one-year historical average premium of 60.34%.

William H. Gross currently receives a manager quality ranking of 16 (0=worst, 99=best). If you desire an average level of risk, then this fund may be an option.

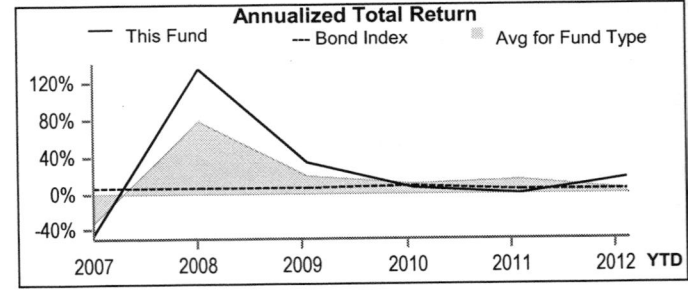

Pimco Income Opportunity Fund (PKO)

A   Excellent

Fund Family: Allianz Global Investors Fund Mgmt
Fund Type: Global
Inception Date: November 30, 2007

Major Rating Factors:
Strong performance is the major factor driving the A (Excellent) TheStreet.com Investment Rating for Pimco Income Opportunity Fund. The fund currently has a performance rating of B+ (Good) based on an annualized return of 21.87% over the last three years and a total return of 3.36% year to date 2012. Factored into the performance evaluation is an expense ratio of 2.44% (high).

The fund's risk rating is currently B (Good). It carries a beta of 0.61, meaning the fund's expected move will be 6.1% for every 10% move in the market. Volatility, as measured by both the semi-deviation and a drawdown factor, is considered low. As of December 31, 2012, Pimco Income Opportunity Fund traded at a premium of 1.43% above its net asset value, which is better than its one-year historical average premium of 7.21%.

Daniel J. Ivascyn has been running the fund for 6 years and currently receives a manager quality ranking of 96 (0=worst, 99=best). If you desire only a moderate level of risk and strong performance, then this fund is an excellent option.

Data Date	Investment Rating	Net Assets ($Mil)	Price	Performance Rating/Pts	Total Return Y-T-D	Risk Rating/Pts
12-12	A	359.91	29.12	B+ / 8.9	3.36%	B / 8.4
2011	B	391.73	25.18	B- / 7.4	3.53%	B / 8.2
2010	A-	307.68	25.59	B / 7.9	24.64%	C+ / 6.6
2009	A+	229.21	22.37	B+ / 8.8	39.16%	C+ / 6.1

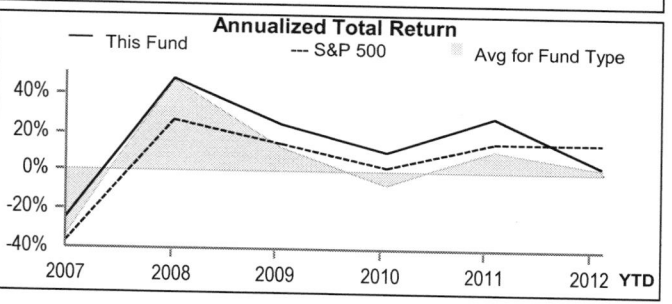

Annualized Total Return

PIMCO Income Strategy Fund (PFL)

B   Good

Fund Family: Allianz Global Investors Fund Mgmt
Fund Type: Loan Participation
Inception Date: August 26, 2003

Major Rating Factors: Strong performance is the major factor driving the B (Good) TheStreet.com Investment Rating for PIMCO Income Strategy Fund. The fund currently has a performance rating of B+ (Good) based on an annualized return of 15.40% over the last three years and a total return of 4.21% year to date 2012. Factored into the performance evaluation is an expense ratio of 1.85% (above average).

The fund's risk rating is currently B- (Good). It carries a beta of -227.70, meaning the fund's expected move will be -2277.0% for every 10% move in the market. Volatility, as measured by both the semi-deviation and a drawdown factor, is considered low. As of December 31, 2012, PIMCO Income Strategy Fund traded at a premium of 3.41% above its net asset value, which is better than its one-year historical average premium of 7.15%.

William H. Gross currently receives a manager quality ranking of 99 (0=worst, 99=best). If you desire only a moderate level of risk and strong performance, then this fund is an excellent option.

Data Date	Investment Rating	Net Assets ($Mil)	Price	Performance Rating/Pts	Total Return Y-T-D	Risk Rating/Pts
12-12	B	283.29	12.74	B+ / 8.3	4.21%	B- / 7.6
2011	C-	282.69	10.40	C+ / 5.6	2.50%	C+ / 5.7
2010	D	262.06	11.50	C- / 4.0	9.80%	D+ / 2.8
2009	D+	165.98	11.29	C / 4.9	71.37%	C- / 3.2

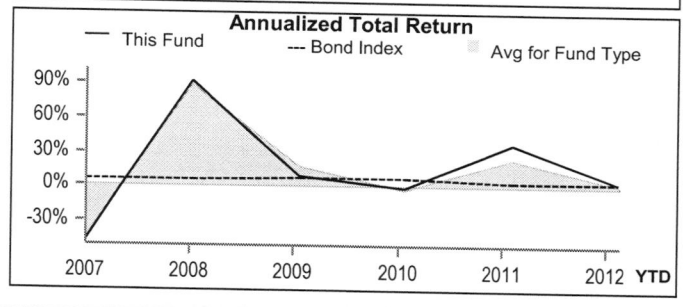

Annualized Total Return

PIMCO Income Strategy Fund II (PFN)

B+   Good

Fund Family: Allianz Global Investors Fund Mgmt
Fund Type: Loan Participation
Inception Date: October 29, 2004

Major Rating Factors: Strong performance is the major factor driving the B+ (Good) TheStreet.com Investment Rating for PIMCO Income Strategy Fund II. The fund currently has a performance rating of B+ (Good) based on an annualized return of 16.34% over the last three years and a total return of 3.85% year to date 2012. Factored into the performance evaluation is an expense ratio of 1.48% (average).

The fund's risk rating is currently B (Good). It carries a beta of -138.62, meaning the fund's expected move will be -1386.2% for every 10% move in the market. Volatility, as measured by both the semi-deviation and a drawdown factor, is considered low. As of December 31, 2012, PIMCO Income Strategy Fund II traded at a premium of 3.46% above its net asset value, which is better than its one-year historical average premium of 4.88%.

William H. Gross has been running the fund for 4 years and currently receives a manager quality ranking of 98 (0=worst, 99=best). If you desire only a moderate level of risk and strong performance, then this fund is an excellent option.

Data Date	Investment Rating	Net Assets ($Mil)	Price	Performance Rating/Pts	Total Return Y-T-D	Risk Rating/Pts
12-12	B+	597.68	11.05	B+ / 8.5	3.85%	B / 8.1
2011	C	584.35	9.15	C+ / 6.3	2.19%	C+ / 6.6
2010	D-	537.34	9.90	D / 2.1	8.28%	C- / 3.5
2009	D+	341.95	9.88	C / 4.7	78.67%	C- / 3.3

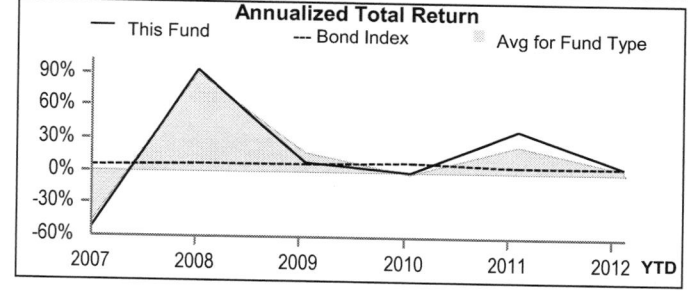

Annualized Total Return

PIMCO Municipal Income Fund (PMF)   A+   Excellent

Fund Family: Allianz Global Investors Fund Mgmt
Fund Type: Municipal - National
Inception Date: June 27, 2001

Major Rating Factors:
Exceptional performance is the major factor driving the A+ (Excellent) TheStreet.com Investment Rating for PIMCO Municipal Income Fund. The fund currently has a performance rating of A- (Excellent) based on an annualized return of 16.64% over the last three years and a total return of 3.41% year to date 2012. Factored into the performance evaluation is an expense ratio of 1.28% (average).

The fund's risk rating is currently B (Good). It carries a beta of 1.67, meaning it is expected to move 16.7% for every 10% move in the market. Volatility, as measured by both the semi-deviation and a drawdown factor, is considered low. As of December 31, 2012, PIMCO Municipal Income Fund traded at a premium of 13.60% above its net asset value, which is better than its one-year historical average premium of 17.21%.

Joseph P. Deane has been running the fund for 2 years and currently receives a manager quality ranking of 78 (0=worst, 99=best). If you desire only a moderate level of risk and strong performance, then this fund is an excellent option.

Data Date	Investment Rating	Net Assets ($Mil)	Price	Performance Rating/Pts	Total Return Y-T-D	Risk Rating/Pts
12-12	A+	326.74	15.70	A- / 9.1	3.41%	B / 8.5
2011	A-	305.90	14.22	A- / 9.1	1.62%	B / 8.4
2010	D+	294.46	12.61	D+ / 2.8	9.70%	C+ / 5.6
2009	C-	233.51	12.39	C- / 4.0	60.00%	C+ / 5.8

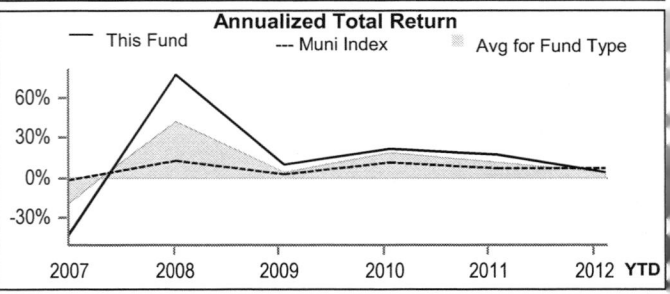

PIMCO Municipal Income Fund II (PML)   A+   Excellent

Fund Family: Allianz Global Investors Fund Mgmt
Fund Type: Municipal - National
Inception Date: June 25, 2002

Major Rating Factors:
Exceptional performance is the major factor driving the A+ (Excellent) TheStreet.com Investment Rating for PIMCO Municipal Income Fund II. The fund currently has a performance rating of A- (Excellent) based on an annualized return of 15.06% over the last three years and a total return of 3.24% year to date 2012. Factored into the performance evaluation is an expense ratio of 1.19% (average).

The fund's risk rating is currently B (Good). It carries a beta of 2.43, meaning it is expected to move 24.3% for every 10% move in the market. Volatility, as measured by both the semi-deviation and a drawdown factor, is considered low. As of December 31, 2012, PIMCO Municipal Income Fund II traded at a premium of 5.45% above its net asset value, which is better than its one-year historical average premium of 6.77%.

Joseph P. Deane has been running the fund for 2 years and currently receives a manager quality ranking of 44 (0=worst, 99=best). If you desire only a moderate level of risk and strong performance, then this fund is an excellent option.

Data Date	Investment Rating	Net Assets ($Mil)	Price	Performance Rating/Pts	Total Return Y-T-D	Risk Rating/Pts
12-12	A+	722.16	13.16	A- / 9.2	3.24%	B / 8.5
2011	A+	663.80	11.24	A+ / 9.7	3.02%	B / 8.6
2010	D	645.59	10.05	D- / 1.0	2.71%	C+ / 6.2
2009	C-	534.05	10.52	C- / 3.6	60.32%	C+ / 5.7

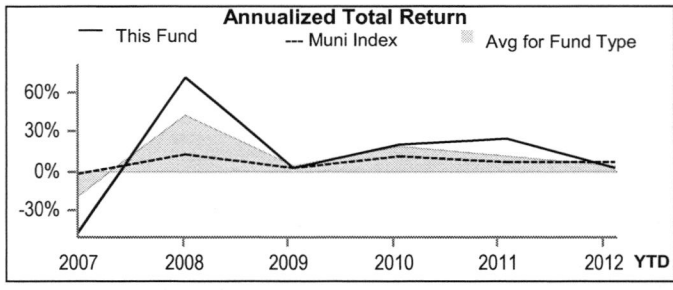

PIMCO Municipal Income Fund III (PMX)   A+   Excellent

Fund Family: Allianz Global Investors Fund Mgmt
Fund Type: Municipal - National
Inception Date: October 28, 2002

Major Rating Factors:
Strong performance is the major factor driving the A+ (Excellent) TheStreet.com Investment Rating for PIMCO Municipal Income Fund III. The fund currently has a performance rating of B+ (Good) based on an annualized return of 15.31% over the last three years and a total return of 4.98% year to date 2012. Factored into the performance evaluation is an expense ratio of 1.27% (average).

The fund's risk rating is currently B (Good). It carries a beta of 1.54, meaning it is expected to move 15.4% for every 10% move in the market. Volatility, as measured by both the semi-deviation and a drawdown factor, is considered low. As of December 31, 2012, PIMCO Municipal Income Fund III traded at a premium of 9.80% above its net asset value, which is better than its one-year historical average premium of 15.53%.

Joseph P. Deane has been running the fund for 2 years and currently receives a manager quality ranking of 77 (0=worst, 99=best). If you desire only a moderate level of risk and strong performance, then this fund is an excellent option.

Data Date	Investment Rating	Net Assets ($Mil)	Price	Performance Rating/Pts	Total Return Y-T-D	Risk Rating/Pts
12-12	A+	357.14	12.33	B+ / 8.9	4.98%	B / 8.8
2011	A+	321.10	11.05	A- / 9.2	3.17%	B / 8.9
2010	D-	330.84	10.44	D / 1.6	9.82%	C / 4.4
2009	C-	324.92	10.30	C- / 3.3	68.02%	C / 5.4

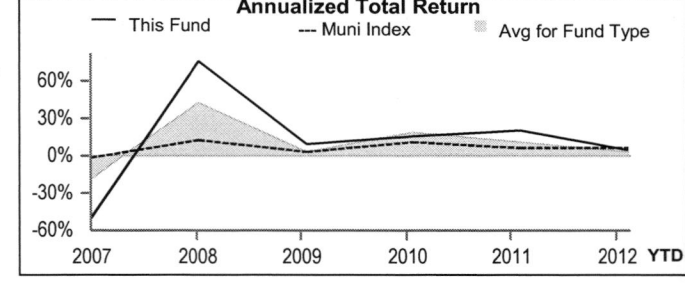

PIMCO NY Muni Income Fund (PNF)

A-   **Excellent**

Fund Family: Allianz Global Investors Fund Mgmt
Fund Type: Municipal - Single State
Inception Date: June 27, 2001

Major Rating Factors:

Strong performance is the major factor driving the A- (Excellent) TheStreet.com Investment Rating for PIMCO NY Muni Income Fund. The fund currently has a performance rating of B+ (Good) based on an annualized return of 13.36% over the last three years and a total return of 5.30% year to date 2012. Factored into the performance evaluation is an expense ratio of 1.37% (average).

The fund's risk rating is currently B (Good). It carries a beta of 2.17, meaning it is expected to move 21.7% for every 10% move in the market. Volatility, as measured by both the semi-deviation and a drawdown factor, is considered low. As of December 31, 2012, PIMCO NY Muni Income Fund traded at a premium of 1.74% above its net asset value, which is better than its one-year historical average premium of 4.85%.

Joseph P. Deane has been running the fund for 2 years and currently receives a manager quality ranking of 33 (0=worst, 99=best). If you desire only a moderate level of risk and strong performance, then this fund is an excellent option.

Data Date	Investment Rating	Net Assets ($Mil)	Price	Performance Rating/Pts	Total Return Y-T-D	Risk Rating/Pts
12-12	A-	87.13	12.28	B+ / 8.3	5.30%	B / 8.6
2011	A	82.70	11.29	A / 9.4	1.86%	B / 8.7
2010	D+	81.07	10.21	D / 1.8	3.36%	C+ / 6.3
2009	C-	69.48	10.53	C- / 3.7	58.92%	C+ / 5.9

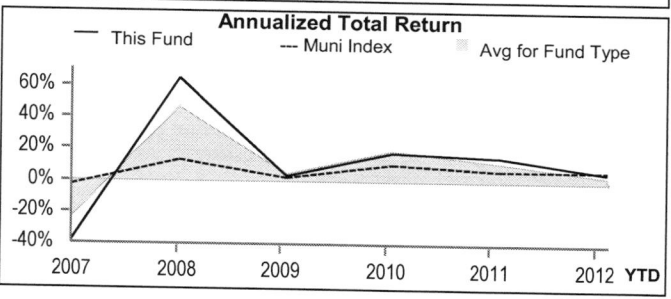

Annualized Total Return

PIMCO NY Municipal Income Fund II (PNI)

A+   **Excellent**

Fund Family: Allianz Global Investors Fund Mgmt
Fund Type: Municipal - Single State
Inception Date: June 25, 2002

Major Rating Factors:

Strong performance is the major factor driving the A+ (Excellent) TheStreet.com Investment Rating for PIMCO NY Municipal Income Fund II. The fund currently has a performance rating of B+ (Good) based on an annualized return of 14.50% over the last three years and a total return of 6.22% year to date 2012. Factored into the performance evaluation is an expense ratio of 1.45% (average).

The fund's risk rating is currently B (Good). It carries a beta of 2.06, meaning it is expected to move 20.6% for every 10% move in the market. Volatility, as measured by both the semi-deviation and a drawdown factor, is considered low. As of December 31, 2012, PIMCO NY Municipal Income Fund II traded at a premium of 8.67% above its net asset value, which is better than its one-year historical average premium of 11.24%.

Joseph P. Deane has been running the fund for 2 years and currently receives a manager quality ranking of 42 (0=worst, 99=best). If you desire only a moderate level of risk and strong performance, then this fund is an excellent option.

Data Date	Investment Rating	Net Assets ($Mil)	Price	Performance Rating/Pts	Total Return Y-T-D	Risk Rating/Pts
12-12	A+	123.67	12.78	B+ / 8.9	6.22%	B / 8.5
2011	B+	115.80	11.52	B+ / 8.7	2.08%	B / 8.6
2010	D	117.16	10.50	D- / 1.2	1.93%	C+ / 6.2
2009	C-	102.13	11.07	C / 4.3	62.39%	C / 5.4

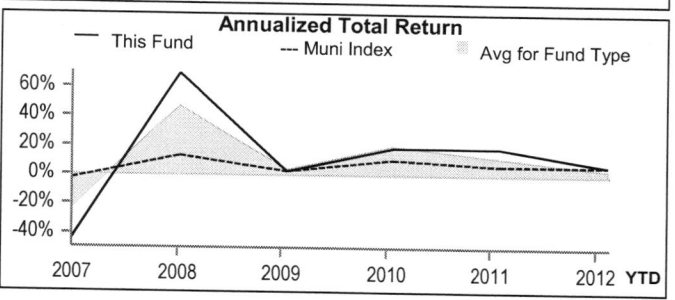

Annualized Total Return

PIMCO NY Municipal Income Fund III (PYN)

A   **Excellent**

Fund Family: Allianz Global Investors Fund Mgmt
Fund Type: Municipal - Single State
Inception Date: October 28, 2002

Major Rating Factors:

Strong performance is the major factor driving the A (Excellent) TheStreet.com Investment Rating for PIMCO NY Municipal Income Fund III. The fund currently has a performance rating of B+ (Good) based on an annualized return of 12.91% over the last three years and a total return of 1.25% year to date 2012. Factored into the performance evaluation is an expense ratio of 1.64% (above average).

The fund's risk rating is currently B (Good). It carries a beta of 2.01, meaning it is expected to move 20.1% for every 10% move in the market. Volatility, as measured by both the semi-deviation and a drawdown factor, is considered low. As of December 31, 2012, PIMCO NY Municipal Income Fund III traded at a premium of 9.47% above its net asset value, which is worse than its one-year historical average premium of 8.80%.

Joseph P. Deane has been running the fund for 2 years and currently receives a manager quality ranking of 53 (0=worst, 99=best). If you desire only a moderate level of risk and strong performance, then this fund is an excellent option.

Data Date	Investment Rating	Net Assets ($Mil)	Price	Performance Rating/Pts	Total Return Y-T-D	Risk Rating/Pts
12-12	A	54.33	10.63	B+ / 8.3	1.25%	B / 8.7
2011	A-	50.10	9.47	B+ / 8.7	1.58%	B / 8.8
2010	D-	65.94	8.79	E+ / 0.9	5.63%	C / 4.4
2009	D-	50.53	8.92	D- / 1.2	54.95%	C- / 4.2

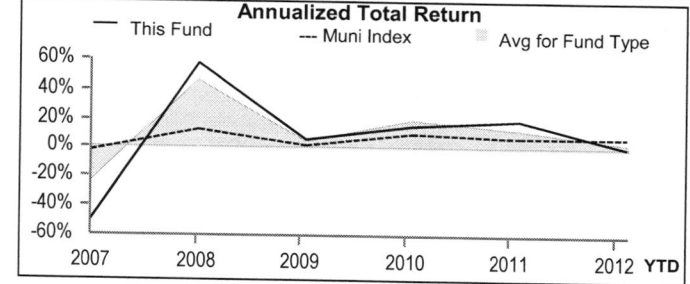

Annualized Total Return

PIMCO Strategic Glob Gov Fund (RCS)

C+   **Fair**

Fund Family: Allianz Global Investors Fund Mgmt
Fund Type: Mortgage
Inception Date: February 17, 1994

Major Rating Factors: Middle of the road best describes PIMCO Strategic Glob Gov Fund whose TheStreet.com Investment Rating is currently a C+ (Fair). The fund currently has a performance rating of C+ (Fair) based on an annualized return of 14.63% over the last three years and a total return of 1.98% year to date 2012. Factored into the performance evaluation is an expense ratio of 1.55% (average).

The fund's risk rating is currently B (Good). It carries a beta of 4.47, meaning it is expected to move 44.7% for every 10% move in the market. Volatility, as measured by both the semi-deviation and a drawdown factor, is considered low. As of December 31, 2012, PIMCO Strategic Glob Gov Fund traded at a premium of 18.35% above its net asset value, which is better than its one-year historical average premium of 23.53%.

Daniel J. Ivascyn has been running the fund for 8 years and currently receives a manager quality ranking of 19 (0=worst, 99=best). If you desire an average level of risk, then this fund may be an option.

Data Date	Investment Rating	Net Assets ($Mil)	Price	Perfor-mance Rating/Pts	Total Return Y-T-D	Risk Rating/Pts
12-12	C+	376.75	11.35	C+ / 5.9	1.98%	B / 8.4
2011	B-	394.70	11.15	C+ / 6.8	2.69%	B- / 7.7
2010	A-	254.12	10.19	B- / 7.5	7.69%	B- / 7.0
2009	C+	313.64	10.27	C+ / 6.8	28.06%	C+ / 6.1

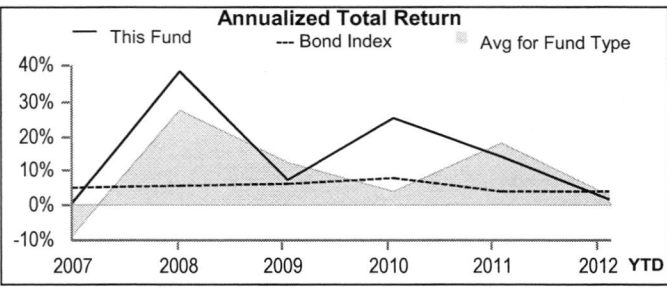

Pioneer Diversified High Income Tr (HNW)

C+   **Fair**

Fund Family: Pioneer Investment Management Inc
Fund Type: Global
Inception Date: May 24, 2007

Major Rating Factors: Middle of the road best describes Pioneer Diversified High Income Tr whose TheStreet.com Investment Rating is currently a C+ (Fair). The fund currently has a performance rating of C+ (Fair) based on an annualized return of 16.21% over the last three years and a total return of 4.03% year to date 2012. Factored into the performance evaluation is an expense ratio of 2.04% (high).

The fund's risk rating is currently B- (Good). It carries a beta of 0.28, meaning the fund's expected move will be 2.8% for every 10% move in the market. Volatility, as measured by both the semi-deviation and a drawdown factor, is considered low. As of December 31, 2012, Pioneer Diversified High Income Tr traded at a discount of 1.18% below its net asset value, which is better than its one-year historical average premium of 4.75%.

Andrew D. Feltus currently receives a manager quality ranking of 94 (0=worst, 99=best). If you desire an average level of risk, then this fund may be an option.

Data Date	Investment Rating	Net Assets ($Mil)	Price	Perfor-mance Rating/Pts	Total Return Y-T-D	Risk Rating/Pts
12-12	C+	161.15	20.08	C+ / 6.9	4.03%	B- / 7.2
2011	B	154.70	19.27	B / 7.9	0.21%	B / 8.2
2010	B-	165.28	20.20	B+ / 8.3	25.55%	C / 4.4
2009	B-	113.81	17.74	A / 9.3	68.14%	C- / 3.7

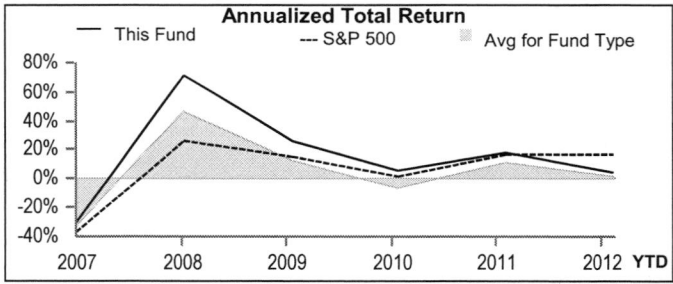

Pioneer Floating Rate Trust (PHD)

C+   **Fair**

Fund Family: Pioneer Investment Management Inc
Fund Type: Loan Participation
Inception Date: December 28, 2004

Major Rating Factors: Middle of the road best describes Pioneer Floating Rate Trust whose TheStreet.com Investment Rating is currently a C+ (Fair). The fund currently has a performance rating of C+ (Fair) based on an annualized return of 12.80% over the last three years and a total return of 2.41% year to date 2012. Factored into the performance evaluation is an expense ratio of 1.58% (above average).

The fund's risk rating is currently B (Good). It carries a beta of -218.30, meaning the fund's expected move will be -2183.0% for every 10% move in the market. Volatility, as measured by both the semi-deviation and a drawdown factor, is considered low. As of December 31, 2012, Pioneer Floating Rate Trust traded at a premium of .76% above its net asset value, which is better than its one-year historical average premium of 1.27%.

Jonathan D. Sharkey currently receives a manager quality ranking of 99 (0=worst, 99=best). If you desire an average level of risk, then this fund may be an option.

Data Date	Investment Rating	Net Assets ($Mil)	Price	Perfor-mance Rating/Pts	Total Return Y-T-D	Risk Rating/Pts
12-12	C+	314.68	13.27	C+ / 5.8	2.41%	B / 8.1
2011	B+	483.40	12.47	B / 8.1	0.56%	B / 8.3
2010	C-	278.57	12.89	C+ / 6.5	20.27%	C- / 3.6
2009	D+	230.91	11.52	C / 4.4	71.93%	C- / 4.2

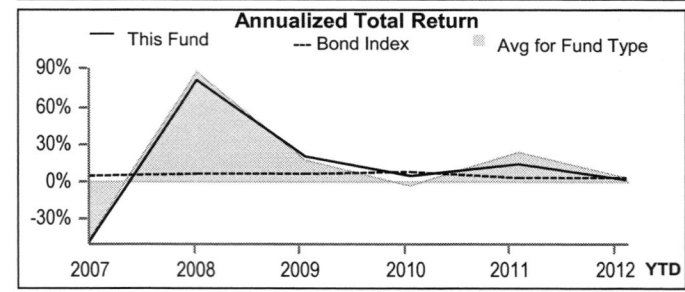

Pioneer High Income Trust (PHT)

C   **Fair**

Fund Family: Pioneer Investment Management Inc
Fund Type: Global
Inception Date: April 25, 2002

Major Rating Factors: Middle of the road best describes Pioneer High Income Trust whose TheStreet.com Investment Rating is currently a C (Fair). The fund currently has a performance rating of C+ (Fair) based on an annualized return of 15.91% over the last three years and a total return of 6.03% year to date 2012. Factored into the performance evaluation is an expense ratio of 1.05% (low).

The fund's risk rating is currently B- (Good). It carries a beta of 0.53, meaning the fund's expected move will be 5.3% for every 10% move in the market. Volatility, as measured by both the semi-deviation and a drawdown factor, is considered low. As of December 31, 2012, Pioneer High Income Trust traded at a premium of 13.96% above its net asset value, which is better than its one-year historical average premium of 29.07%.

Andrew D. Feltus currently receives a manager quality ranking of 93 (0=worst, 99=best). If you desire an average level of risk, then this fund may be an option.

Data Date	Investment Rating	Net Assets ($Mil)	Price	Performance Rating/Pts	Total Return Y-T-D	Risk Rating/Pts
12-12	C	379.52	15.92	C+ / 5.7	6.03%	B- / 7.4
2011	A	356.20	17.33	A+ / 9.9	2.71%	B- / 7.9
2010	B-	367.09	15.49	B+ / 8.5	21.64%	C- / 3.9
2009	C	326.42	14.11	B / 7.9	93.64%	C- / 3.0

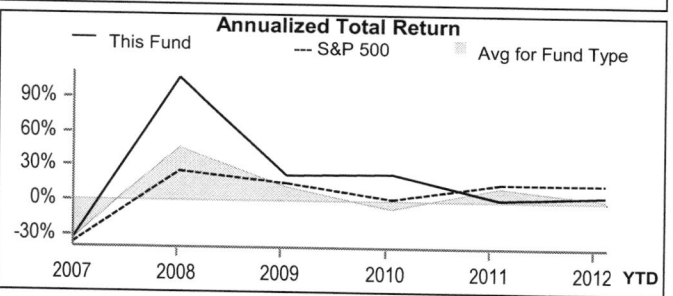

Pioneer Municipal High Income Adv (MAV)

A+   **Excellent**

Fund Family: Pioneer Investment Management Inc
Fund Type: Municipal - High Yield
Inception Date: October 20, 2003

Major Rating Factors:
Exceptional performance is the major factor driving the A+ (Excellent) TheStreet.com Investment Rating for Pioneer Municipal High Income Adv. The fund currently has a performance rating of A (Excellent) based on an annualized return of 16.94% over the last three years and a total return of 4.20% year to date 2012. Factored into the performance evaluation is an expense ratio of 1.36% (average).

The fund's risk rating is currently B (Good). It carries a beta of 1.87, meaning it is expected to move 18.7% for every 10% move in the market. Volatility, as measured by both the semi-deviation and a drawdown factor, is considered low. As of December 31, 2012, Pioneer Municipal High Income Adv traded at a premium of 12.10% above its net asset value, which is better than its one-year historical average premium of 15.38%.

David J. Eurkus currently receives a manager quality ranking of 76 (0=worst, 99=best). If you desire only a moderate level of risk and strong performance, then this fund is an excellent option.

Data Date	Investment Rating	Net Assets ($Mil)	Price	Performance Rating/Pts	Total Return Y-T-D	Risk Rating/Pts
12-12	A+	299.64	15.47	A / 9.3	4.20%	B / 8.4
2011	A+	288.40	14.40	A+ / 9.9	2.08%	B / 8.3
2010	D+	281.55	12.42	C- / 3.5	6.42%	C / 4.8
2009	B-	277.65	12.67	B / 7.9	72.76%	C / 5.0

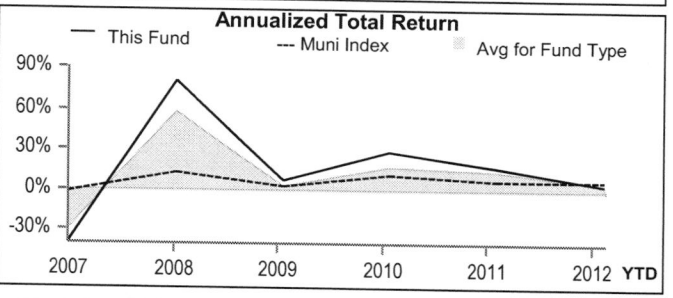

Pioneer Municipal High Income Trus (MHI)

A+   **Excellent**

Fund Family: Pioneer Investment Management Inc
Fund Type: Municipal - High Yield
Inception Date: July 17, 2003

Major Rating Factors:
Exceptional performance is the major factor driving the A+ (Excellent) TheStreet.com Investment Rating for Pioneer Municipal High Income Trus. The fund currently has a performance rating of A (Excellent) based on an annualized return of 15.03% over the last three years and a total return of 5.89% year to date 2012. Factored into the performance evaluation is an expense ratio of 1.08% (low).

The fund's risk rating is currently B (Good). It carries a beta of 1.58, meaning it is expected to move 15.8% for every 10% move in the market. Volatility, as measured by both the semi-deviation and a drawdown factor, is considered low. As of December 31, 2012, Pioneer Municipal High Income Trus traded at a premium of 6.33% above its net asset value, which is better than its one-year historical average premium of 8.47%.

David J. Eurkus currently receives a manager quality ranking of 71 (0=worst, 99=best). If you desire only a moderate level of risk and strong performance, then this fund is an excellent option.

Data Date	Investment Rating	Net Assets ($Mil)	Price	Performance Rating/Pts	Total Return Y-T-D	Risk Rating/Pts
12-12	A+	317.63	15.79	A / 9.3	5.89%	B / 8.4
2011	A+	304.60	14.87	A+ / 9.8	0.81%	B / 8.5
2010	C	308.46	13.42	C+ / 5.9	4.92%	C / 5.4
2009	B+	247.56	13.79	B / 8.2	70.35%	C+ / 5.7

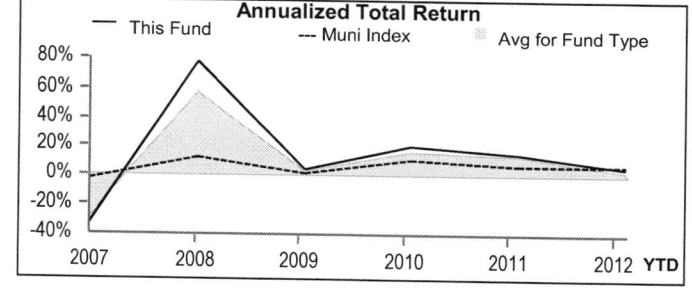

Putnam High Income Securities (PCF)   D+   Weak

Fund Family: Putnam Investment Management LLC
Fund Type: General Bond
Inception Date: July 9, 1987

Data Date	Investment Rating	Net Assets ($Mil)	Price	Performance Rating/Pts	Total Return Y-T-D	Risk Rating/Pts
12-12	D+	141.00	7.95	C- / 3.5	3.14%	B- / 7.0
2011	C+	133.80	7.68	C+ / 6.4	3.52%	C+ / 6.9
2010	B	135.78	8.38	B / 8.0	24.09%	C / 5.0
2009	C	123.26	7.21	C / 5.3	43.23%	C+ / 5.7

Major Rating Factors: Putnam High Income Securities receives a TheStreet.com Investment Rating of D+ (Weak). The fund currently has a performance rating of C- (Fair) based on an annualized return of 8.96% over the last three years and a total return of 3.14% year to date 2012. Factored into the performance evaluation is an expense ratio of 0.93% (low).

The fund's risk rating is currently B- (Good). It carries a beta of -0.50, meaning the fund's expected move will be -5.0% for every 10% move in the market. Volatility, as measured by both the semi-deviation and a drawdown factor, is considered low. As of December 31, 2012, Putnam High Income Securities traded at a discount of 8.52% below its net asset value, which is better than its one-year historical average discount of 1.06%.

Eric N. Harthun currently receives a manager quality ranking of 94 (0=worst, 99=best). If you desire an average level of risk, then this fund may be an option.

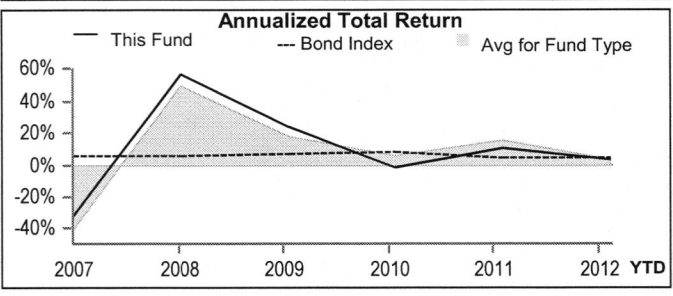

Annualized Total Return — This Fund --- Bond Index / Avg for Fund Type

Putnam Managed Muni Inc Tr (PMM)   A   Excellent

Fund Family: Putnam Investment Management LLC
Fund Type: Municipal - National
Inception Date: February 16, 1989

Data Date	Investment Rating	Net Assets ($Mil)	Price	Performance Rating/Pts	Total Return Y-T-D	Risk Rating/Pts
12-12	A	423.92	8.06	A- / 9.0	5.58%	B / 8.4
2011	A-	429.60	7.47	B+ / 8.9	0.13%	B / 8.6
2010	C+	422.05	6.91	C / 5.5	11.66%	C+ / 6.2
2009	B-	350.83	6.65	C+ / 6.0	38.99%	B- / 7.1

Major Rating Factors:
Exceptional performance is the major factor driving the A (Excellent) TheStreet.com Investment Rating for Putnam Managed Muni Inc Tr. The fund currently has a performance rating of A- (Excellent) based on an annualized return of 15.20% over the last three years and a total return of 5.58% year to date 2012. Factored into the performance evaluation is an expense ratio of 1.03% (low).

The fund's risk rating is currently B (Good). It carries a beta of 1.58, meaning it is expected to move 15.8% for every 10% move in the market. Volatility, as measured by both the semi-deviation and a drawdown factor, is considered low. As of December 31, 2012, Putnam Managed Muni Inc Tr traded at a discount of .98% below its net asset value, which is better than its one-year historical average premium of 1.23%.

Paul M. Drury has been running the fund for 24 years and currently receives a manager quality ranking of 73 (0=worst, 99=best). If you desire only a moderate level of risk and strong performance, then this fund is an excellent option.

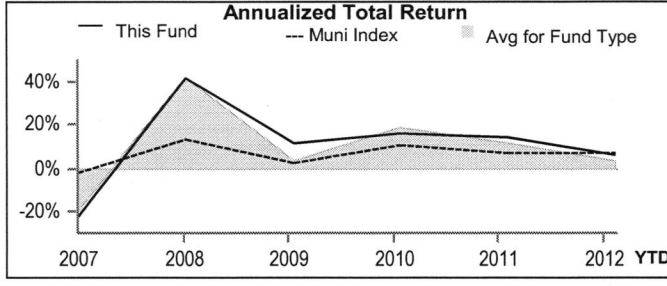

Annualized Total Return — This Fund --- Muni Index / Avg for Fund Type

Putnam Master Intermediate Inc Tr (PIM)   D   Weak

Fund Family: Putnam Investment Management LLC
Fund Type: General Bond
Inception Date: April 11, 1988

Data Date	Investment Rating	Net Assets ($Mil)	Price	Performance Rating/Pts	Total Return Y-T-D	Risk Rating/Pts
12-12	D	356.30	5.06	D / 2.2	2.47%	C+ / 6.2
2011	C-	345.80	5.08	C / 4.7	0.39%	C+ / 6.0
2010	C-	381.36	5.79	C / 5.3	6.52%	C / 4.5
2009	B-	383.39	6.03	B / 7.8	73.93%	C / 5.1

Major Rating Factors:
Disappointing performance is the major factor driving the D (Weak) TheStreet.com Investment Rating for Putnam Master Intermediate Inc Tr. The fund currently has a performance rating of D (Weak) based on an annualized return of 2.51% over the last three years and a total return of 2.47% year to date 2012. Factored into the performance evaluation is an expense ratio of 0.96% (low).

The fund's risk rating is currently C+ (Fair). It carries a beta of 0.79, meaning the fund's expected move will be 7.9% for every 10% move in the market. Volatility, as measured by both the semi-deviation and a drawdown factor, is considered low. As of December 31, 2012, Putnam Master Intermediate Inc Tr traded at a discount of 9.32% below its net asset value, which is better than its one-year historical average discount of 5.80%.

D. William Kohli has been running the fund for 19 years and currently receives a manager quality ranking of 32 (0=worst, 99=best). This fund offers only a moderate level of risk but investors looking for strong performance are still waiting.

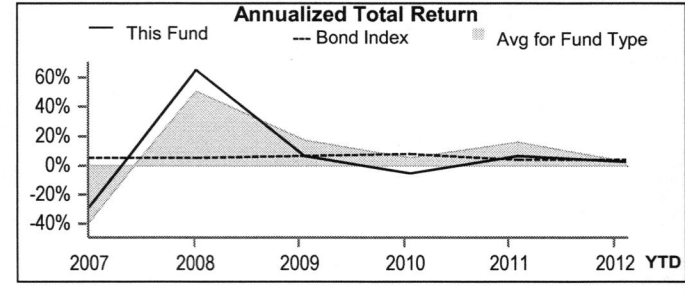

Annualized Total Return — This Fund --- Bond Index / Avg for Fund Type

Putnam Muni Opp Tr (PMO)

A- **Excellent**

Fund Family: Putnam Investment Management LLC
Fund Type: Municipal - National
Inception Date: May 21, 1993

Major Rating Factors:
Strong performance is the major factor driving the A- (Excellent) TheStreet.com Investment Rating for Putnam Muni Opp Tr. The fund currently has a performance rating of B (Good) based on an annualized return of 13.04% over the last three years and a total return of 3.47% year to date 2012. Factored into the performance evaluation is an expense ratio of 0.99% (low).

The fund's risk rating is currently B (Good). It carries a beta of 1.97, meaning it is expected to move 19.7% for every 10% move in the market. Volatility, as measured by both the semi-deviation and a drawdown factor, is considered low. As of December 31, 2012, Putnam Muni Opp Tr traded at a discount of 4.71% below its net asset value, which is better than its one-year historical average discount of 1.59%.

Paul M. Drury has been running the fund for 11 years and currently receives a manager quality ranking of 44 (0=worst, 99=best). If you desire only a moderate level of risk and strong performance, then this fund is an excellent option.

Data Date	Investment Rating	Net Assets ($Mil)	Price	Performance Rating/Pts	Total Return Y-T-D	Risk Rating/Pts
12-12	A-	556.12	12.95	B / 8.2	3.47%	B / 8.7
2011	A	532.10	12.27	B+ / 8.9	-0.24%	B / 8.8
2010	C+	514.09	10.87	C / 5.2	4.60%	C+ / 6.7
2009	B-	448.68	11.13	C+ / 6.4	34.79%	B- / 7.0

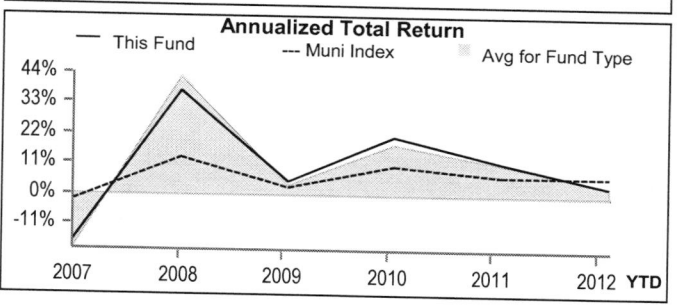

Putnam Premier Income Trust (PPT)

D **Weak**

Fund Family: Putnam Investment Management LLC
Fund Type: General Bond
Inception Date: February 29, 1988

Major Rating Factors:
Disappointing performance is the major factor driving the D (Weak) TheStreet.com Investment Rating for Putnam Premier Income Trust. The fund currently has a performance rating of D+ (Weak) based on an annualized return of 5.70% over the last three years and a total return of 0.92% year to date 2012. Factored into the performance evaluation is an expense ratio of 0.88% (low).

The fund's risk rating is currently C+ (Fair). It carries a beta of 0.87, meaning the fund's expected move will be 8.7% for every 10% move in the market. Volatility, as measured by both the semi-deviation and a drawdown factor, is considered low. As of December 31, 2012, Putnam Premier Income Trust traded at a discount of 8.39% below its net asset value, which is better than its one-year historical average discount of 4.55%.

Michael V. Salm has been running the fund for 21 years and currently receives a manager quality ranking of 50 (0=worst, 99=best). This fund offers only a moderate level of risk but investors looking for strong performance are still waiting.

Data Date	Investment Rating	Net Assets ($Mil)	Price	Performance Rating/Pts	Total Return Y-T-D	Risk Rating/Pts
12-12	D	818.08	5.46	D+ / 2.7	0.92%	C+ / 6.0
2011	C-	794.60	5.19	C / 5.5	1.35%	C+ / 5.9
2010	C+	887.22	6.28	B- / 7.1	14.15%	C / 4.7
2009	C+	803.32	6.13	B- / 7.5	70.88%	C / 5.0

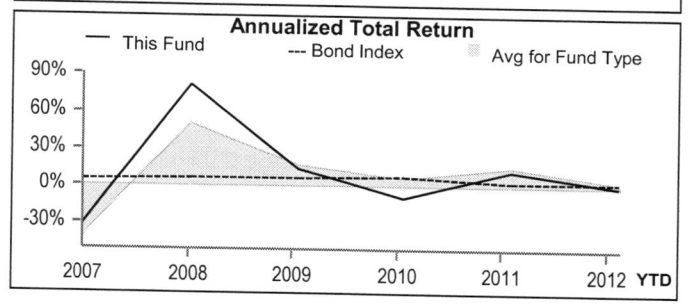

Reaves Utility Income Trust (UTG)

C+ **Fair**

Fund Family: W H Reaves & Company Inc
Fund Type: Utilities
Inception Date: February 24, 2004

Major Rating Factors: Middle of the road best describes Reaves Utility Income Trust whose TheStreet.com Investment Rating is currently a C+ (Fair). The fund currently has a performance rating of C+ (Fair) based on an annualized return of 17.13% over the last three years and a total return of 3.40% year to date 2012. Factored into the performance evaluation is an expense ratio of 1.93% (above average).

The fund's risk rating is currently B (Good). It carries a beta of 0.78, meaning the fund's expected move will be 7.8% for every 10% move in the market. Volatility, as measured by both the semi-deviation and a drawdown factor, is considered low. As of December 31, 2012, Reaves Utility Income Trust traded at a discount of 4.83% below its net asset value, which is better than its one-year historical average premium of 2.54%.

Ronald J. Sorenson has been running the fund for 9 years and currently receives a manager quality ranking of 88 (0=worst, 99=best). If you desire an average level of risk, then this fund may be an option.

Data Date	Investment Rating	Net Assets ($Mil)	Price	Performance Rating/Pts	Total Return Y-T-D	Risk Rating/Pts
12-12	C+	545.02	23.82	C+ / 5.8	3.40%	B / 8.7
2011	B+	557.60	26.01	A / 9.4	-3.19%	B- / 7.5
2010	B-	438.31	22.35	B / 8.1	29.08%	C / 4.3
2009	C	279.17	18.56	B- / 7.2	61.18%	C / 4.3

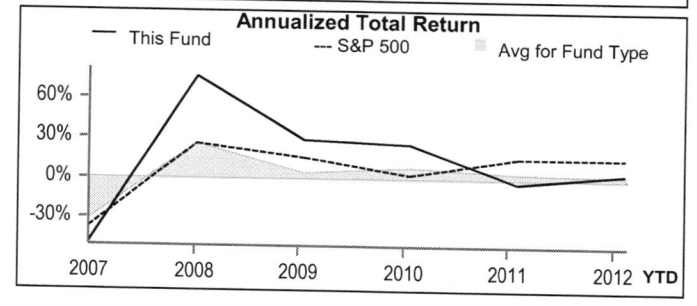

RENN Global Entrepreneurs Fund Inc (RCG)

E+   **Very Weak**

Fund Family: RENN Capital Group Inc
Fund Type: Growth and Income
Inception Date: May 25, 1994

Major Rating Factors:
Very poor performance is the major factor driving the E+ (Very Weak) TheStreet.com Investment Rating for RENN Global Entrepreneurs Fund Inc. The fund currently has a performance rating of E (Very Weak) based on an annualized return of -16.89% over the last three years and a total return of 6.34% year to date 2012. Factored into the performance evaluation is an expense ratio of 5.25% (high).

The fund's risk rating is currently C (Fair). It carries a beta of 0.60, meaning the fund's expected move will be 6.0% for every 10% move in the market. Volatility, as measured by both the semi-deviation and a drawdown factor, is considered average. As of December 31, 2012, RENN Global Entrepreneurs Fund Inc traded at a discount of 44.31% below its net asset value, which is better than its one-year historical average discount of 33.26%.

Russell G. Cleveland has been running the fund for 19 years and currently receives a manager quality ranking of 4 (0=worst, 99=best). This fund offers an average level of risk but investors looking for strong performance will be frustrated.

Data Date	Investment Rating	Net Assets ($Mil)	Price	Performance Rating/Pts	Total Return Y-T-D	Risk Rating/Pts
12-12	E+	9.50	1.42	E / 0.5	6.34%	C / 4.7
2011	D-	9.50	1.82	D- / 1.0	-3.85%	C / 5.1
2010	D-	18.17	1.96	E / 0.3	-24.62%	C / 4.7
2009	E+	17.41	2.60	E / 0.4	-19.75%	C / 4.9

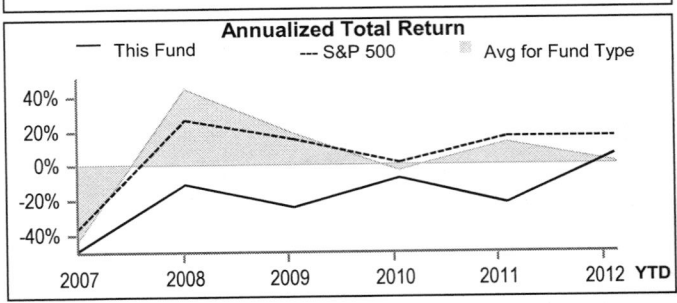

RMR Real Estate Income (RIF)

C+   **Fair**

Fund Family: RMR Advisors Inc
Fund Type: Growth and Income
Inception Date: May 26, 2006

Major Rating Factors: Strong performance is the major factor driving the C+ (Fair) TheStreet.com Investment Rating for RMR Real Estate Income. The fund currently has a performance rating of B (Good) based on an annualized return of 10.34% over the last three years and a total return of 5.08% year to date 2012. Factored into the performance evaluation is an expense ratio of 1.86% (above average).

The fund's risk rating is currently C+ (Fair). It carries a beta of 1.21, meaning it is expected to move 12.1% for every 10% move in the market. Volatility, as measured by both the semi-deviation and a drawdown factor, is considered low. As of December 31, 2012, RMR Real Estate Income traded at a discount of 15.07% below its net asset value, which is worse than its one-year historical average discount of 16.23%.

Craig Dunstan currently receives a manager quality ranking of 25 (0=worst, 99=best). If you desire only a moderate level of risk and strong performance, then this fund is an excellent option.

Data Date	Investment Rating	Net Assets ($Mil)	Price	Performance Rating/Pts	Total Return Y-T-D	Risk Rating/Pts
12-12	C+	153,778.87	18.21	B / 7.9	5.08%	C+ / 5.6
2011	D	54.80	14.02	D / 2.0	1.78%	C+ / 6.7
2011	D	54.80	14.02	D / 2.0	1.78%	C+ / 6.7
2010	D-	72.61	18.37	E+ / 0.9	15.99%	C / 4.4
2010	D-	72.61	18.37	E+ / 0.9	15.99%	C / 4.4
2009	E+	68.40	16.89	E+ / 0.7	30.41%	C- / 3.7
2009	E+	68.40	16.89	E+ / 0.7	30.41%	C- / 3.7

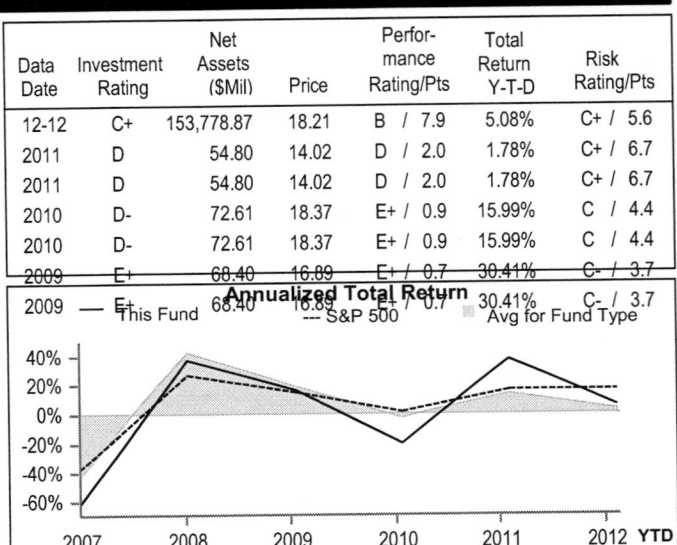

Royce Focus Trust (FUND)

D+   **Weak**

Fund Family: Royce & Associates LLC
Fund Type: Growth
Inception Date: March 2, 1988

Major Rating Factors: Royce Focus Trust receives a TheStreet.com Investment Rating of D+ (Weak). The fund currently has a performance rating of C- (Fair) based on an annualized return of 5.81% over the last three years and a total return of 5.30% year to date 2012. Factored into the performance evaluation is an expense ratio of 1.34% (average).

The fund's risk rating is currently B- (Good). It carries a beta of 1.29, meaning it is expected to move 12.9% for every 10% move in the market. Volatility, as measured by both the semi-deviation and a drawdown factor, is considered low. As of December 31, 2012, Royce Focus Trust traded at a discount of 15.49% below its net asset value, which is better than its one-year historical average discount of 12.57%.

Whitney W. George has been running the fund for 17 years and currently receives a manager quality ranking of 17 (0=worst, 99=best). If you desire an average level of risk, then this fund may be an option.

Data Date	Investment Rating	Net Assets ($Mil)	Price	Performance Rating/Pts	Total Return Y-T-D	Risk Rating/Pts
12-12	D+	148.84	6.60	C- / 3.2	5.30%	B- / 7.2
2011	C-	175.90	6.30	C / 4.3	3.97%	B- / 7.2
2010	C-	141.50	7.57	C / 4.7	19.59%	C+ / 5.6
2009	D	108.09	6.33	D / 2.2	33.33%	C / 5.4

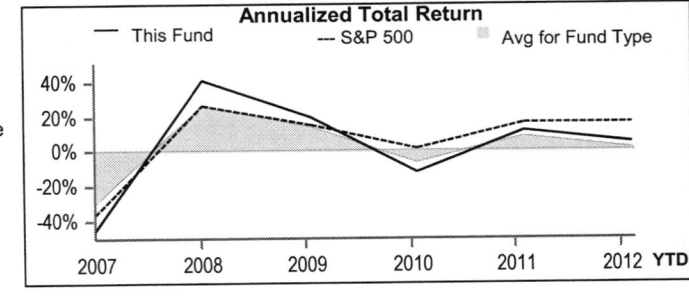

Royce Micro-Cap Trust (RMT)

C+ **Fair**

Fund Family: Royce & Associates LLC
Fund Type: Growth
Inception Date: December 14, 1993

Major Rating Factors: Middle of the road best describes Royce Micro-Cap Trust whose TheStreet.com Investment Rating is currently a C+ (Fair). The fund currently has a performance rating of C+ (Fair) based on an annualized return of 13.38% over the last three years and a total return of 5.08% year to date 2012. Factored into the performance evaluation is an expense ratio of 1.50% (average).

The fund's risk rating is currently B- (Good). It carries a beta of 1.35, meaning it is expected to move 13.5% for every 10% move in the market. Volatility, as measured by both the semi-deviation and a drawdown factor, is considered low. As of December 31, 2012, Royce Micro-Cap Trust traded at a discount of 16.45% below its net asset value, which is better than its one-year historical average discount of 12.76%.

Charles M. Royce has been running the fund for 20 years and currently receives a manager quality ranking of 38 (0=worst, 99=best). If you desire an average level of risk, then this fund may be an option.

Data Date	Investment Rating	Net Assets ($Mil)	Price	Performance Rating/Pts	Total Return Y-T-D	Risk Rating/Pts
12-12	C+	293.01	9.45	C+ / 6.7	5.08%	B- / 7.3
2011	C	339.30	8.77	C+ / 5.6	1.14%	B- / 7.0
2010	C+	243.16	9.80	C+ / 6.8	34.06%	C / 5.1
2009	D-	196.94	7.37	E+ / 0.9	29.62%	C / 4.8

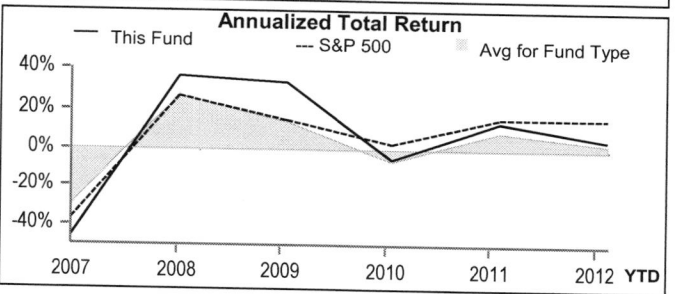

Royce Value Trust (RVT)

C+ **Fair**

Fund Family: Royce & Associates LLC
Fund Type: Growth
Inception Date: November 19, 1986

Major Rating Factors: Middle of the road best describes Royce Value Trust whose TheStreet.com Investment Rating is currently a C+ (Fair). The fund currently has a performance rating of C+ (Fair) based on an annualized return of 13.30% over the last three years and a total return of 5.07% year to date 2012. Factored into the performance evaluation is an expense ratio of 0.68% (very low).

The fund's risk rating is currently B- (Good). It carries a beta of 1.44, meaning it is expected to move 14.4% for every 10% move in the market. Volatility, as measured by both the semi-deviation and a drawdown factor, is considered low. As of December 31, 2012, Royce Value Trust traded at a discount of 16.13% below its net asset value, which is better than its one-year historical average discount of 12.62%.

Charles M. Royce has been running the fund for 27 years and currently receives a manager quality ranking of 29 (0=worst, 99=best). If you desire an average level of risk, then this fund may be an option.

Data Date	Investment Rating	Net Assets ($Mil)	Price	Performance Rating/Pts	Total Return Y-T-D	Risk Rating/Pts
12-12	C+	991.94	13.42	C+ / 6.9	5.07%	B- / 7.0
2011	C	1,186.90	12.27	C / 5.3	2.44%	C+ / 6.9
2010	C+	849.78	14.54	C+ / 6.6	35.03%	C / 5.2
2009	D-	656.68	10.79	D- / 1.2	28.12%	C / 5.0

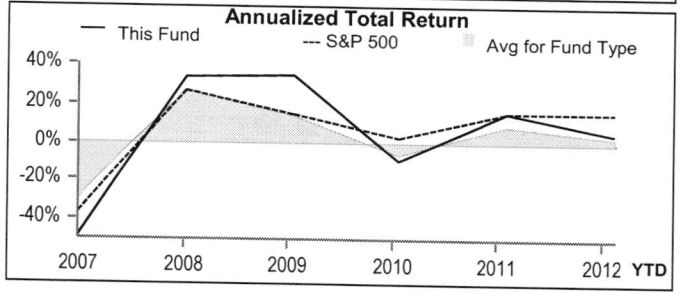

Salient MLP & Energy Infrastructur (SMF)

C **Fair**

Fund Family: Salient Capital Advisors LLC
Fund Type: Energy/Natural Resources
Inception Date: May 25, 2011

Major Rating Factors: Middle of the road best describes Salient MLP & Energy Infrastructur whose TheStreet.com Investment Rating is currently a C (Fair). The fund currently has a performance rating of C (Fair) based on an annualized return of 0.00% over the last three years and a total return of 2.15% year to date 2012.

The fund's risk rating is currently B (Good). It carries a beta of 0.00, meaning the fund's expected move will be 0.0% for every 10% move in the market. Volatility, as measured by both the semi-deviation and a drawdown factor, is considered low. As of December 31, 2012, Salient MLP & Energy Infrastructur traded at a price exactly equal to its net asset value, which is better than its one-year historical average premium of 2.75%.

Frank T. Gardner, III has been running the fund for 2 years and currently receives a manager quality ranking of 94 (0=worst, 99=best). If you desire an average level of risk, then this fund may be an option.

Data Date	Investment Rating	Net Assets ($Mil)	Price	Performance Rating/Pts	Total Return Y-T-D	Risk Rating/Pts
12-12	C	150.50	0.00	C / 4.3	2.15%	B / 8.3

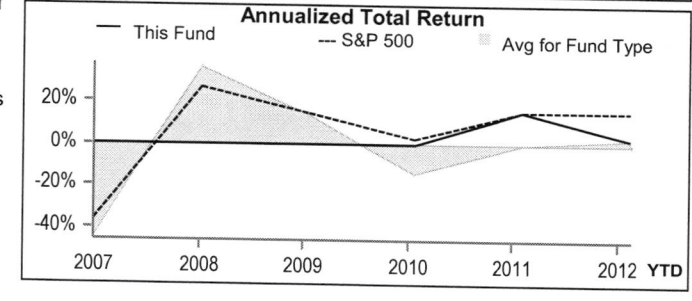

Singapore Fund (SGF)

C Fair

Fund Family: Aberdeen Asset Management Asia Ltd
Fund Type: Foreign
Inception Date: July 31, 1990

Data Date	Investment Rating	Net Assets ($Mil)	Price	Performance Rating/Pts	Total Return Y-T-D	Risk Rating/Pts
12-12	C	137.50	13.98	C+ / 6.0	1.86%	C+ / 6.5
2011	C-	119.40	10.91	C / 5.0	2.57%	C+ / 6.6
2010	C	146.90	15.19	B- / 7.3	28.33%	C- / 3.5
2009	C	85.06	13.30	B- / 7.0	69.74%	C- / 4.2

Major Rating Factors: Middle of the road best describes Singapore Fund whose TheStreet.com Investment Rating is currently a C (Fair). The fund currently has a performance rating of C+ (Fair) based on an annualized return of 9.22% over the last three years and a total return of 1.86% year to date 2012. Factored into the performance evaluation is an expense ratio of 1.83% (above average).

The fund's risk rating is currently C+ (Fair). It carries a beta of 0.93, meaning that its performance tracks fairly well with that of the overall stock market. Volatility, as measured by both the semi-deviation and a drawdown factor, is considered low. As of December 31, 2012, Singapore Fund traded at a discount of 10.38% below its net asset value, which is better than its one-year historical average discount of 9.94%.

Hugh Young has been running the fund for 2 years and currently receives a manager quality ranking of 78 (0=worst, 99=best). If you desire an average level of risk, then this fund may be an option.

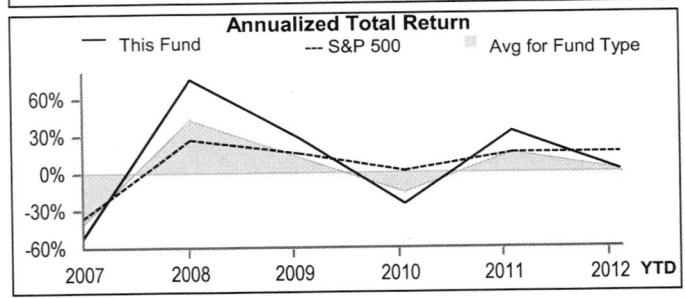

Source Capital (SOR)

C+ Fair

Fund Family: First Pacific Advisors LLC
Fund Type: Income
Inception Date: October 24, 1968

Data Date	Investment Rating	Net Assets ($Mil)	Price	Performance Rating/Pts	Total Return Y-T-D	Risk Rating/Pts
12-12	C+	472.48	52.22	B- / 7.2	4.71%	B- / 7.2
2011	C+	470.00	46.99	B- / 7.0	1.50%	B- / 7.2
2010	B+	490.04	53.13	B / 7.8	30.34%	C+ / 5.8
2009	C-	356.92	42.91	D+ / 2.8	51.58%	C+ / 5.8

Major Rating Factors: Strong performance is the major factor driving the C+ (Fair) TheStreet.com Investment Rating for Source Capital. The fund currently has a performance rating of B- (Good) based on an annualized return of 14.00% over the last three years and a total return of 4.71% year to date 2012. Factored into the performance evaluation is an expense ratio of 0.98% (low).

The fund's risk rating is currently B- (Good). It carries a beta of 1.24, meaning it is expected to move 12.4% for every 10% move in the market. Volatility, as measured by both the semi-deviation and a drawdown factor, is considered low. As of December 31, 2012, Source Capital traded at a discount of 14.24% below its net asset value, which is better than its one-year historical average discount of 11.15%.

Eric S. Ende has been running the fund for 17 years and currently receives a manager quality ranking of 49 (0=worst, 99=best). If you desire only a moderate level of risk and strong performance, then this fund is an excellent option.

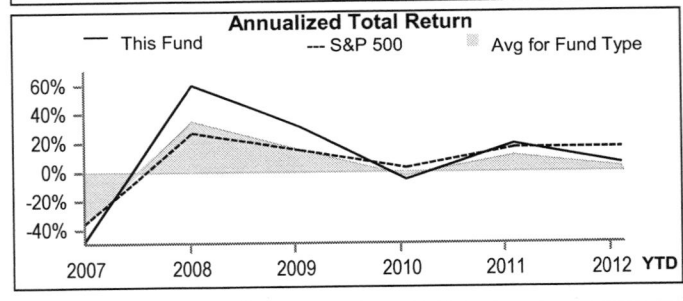

Special Opportunities Fund (SPE)

B Good

Fund Family: Brooklyn Capital Management LLC
Fund Type: Municipal - National
Inception Date: May 28, 1993

Data Date	Investment Rating	Net Assets ($Mil)	Price	Performance Rating/Pts	Total Return Y-T-D	Risk Rating/Pts
12-12	B	115.41	15.01	C+ / 6.3	4.66%	B+ / 9.1
2011	B	106.90	14.50	C+ / 6.9	2.04%	B+ / 9.1
2010	A	294.13	14.75	B / 8.1	4.90%	B- / 7.2
2009	A-	305.27	14.09	B- / 7.5	42.95%	C+ / 6.9

Major Rating Factors: Special Opportunities Fund receives a TheStreet.com Investment Rating of B (Good). The fund currently has a performance rating of C+ (Fair) based on an annualized return of 7.41% over the last three years and a total return of 4.66% year to date 2012. Factored into the performance evaluation is an expense ratio of 1.61% (above average).

The fund's risk rating is currently B+ (Good). It carries a beta of -0.62, meaning the fund's expected move will be -6.2% for every 10% move in the market. Volatility, as measured by both the semi-deviation and a drawdown factor, is considered very low. As of December 31, 2012, Special Opportunities Fund traded at a discount of 15.53% below its net asset value, which is better than its one-year historical average discount of 9.80%.

Andrew Dakos currently receives a manager quality ranking of 89 (0=worst, 99=best). If you desire an average level of risk, then this fund may be an option.

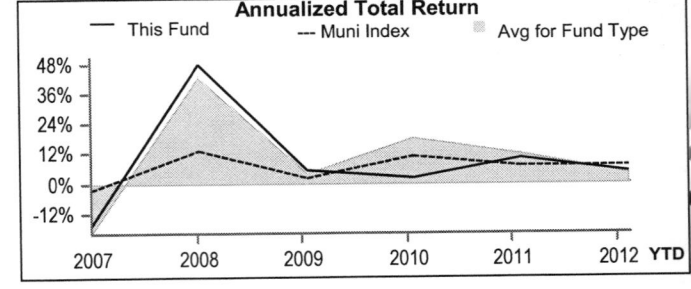

Stone Harbor Emg Markets Income (EDF)

A-   Excellent

Fund Family: Stone Harbor Investment Partners LP
Fund Type: Emerging Market
Inception Date: December 22, 2010

Major Rating Factors:
Strong performance is the major factor driving the A- (Excellent) TheStreet.com Investment Rating for Stone Harbor Emg Markets Income. The fund currently has a performance rating of B+ (Good) based on an annualized return of 0.00% over the last three years and a total return of 2.91% year to date 2012. Factored into the performance evaluation is an expense ratio of 1.76% (above average).

The fund's risk rating is currently B (Good). It carries a beta of 0.00, meaning the fund's expected move will be 0.0% for every 10% move in the market. Volatility, as measured by both the semi-deviation and a drawdown factor, is considered low. As of December 31, 2012, Stone Harbor Emg Markets Income traded at a premium of .45% above its net asset value, which is better than its one-year historical average premium of 3.57%.

Pablo Cisilino currently receives a manager quality ranking of 95 (0=worst, 99=best). If you desire only a moderate level of risk and strong performance, then this fund is an excellent option.

Data Date	Investment Rating	Net Assets ($Mil)	Price	Performance Rating/Pts	Total Return Y-T-D	Risk Rating/Pts
12-12	A-	335.27	24.76	B+ / 8.7	2.91%	B / 8.0
2011	D+	339.00	20.88	D / 1.6	6.42%	B / 8.0

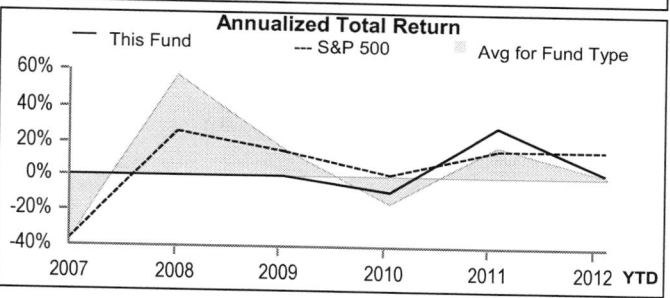

Strategic Global Income Fund (SGL)

B-   Good

Fund Family: UBS Global Asset Mgmt (Americas) In
Fund Type: Global
Inception Date: January 24, 1992

Major Rating Factors: Strong performance is the major factor driving the B- (Good) TheStreet.com Investment Rating for Strategic Global Income Fund. The fund currently has a performance rating of B- (Good) based on an annualized return of 16.91% over the last three years and a total return of 1.91% year to date 2012. Factored into the performance evaluation is an expense ratio of 1.16% (low).

The fund's risk rating is currently B- (Good). It carries a beta of 1.10, meaning it is expected to move 11.0% for every 10% move in the market. Volatility, as measured by both the semi-deviation and a drawdown factor, is considered low. As of December 31, 2012, Strategic Global Income Fund traded at a discount of 5.92% below its net asset value, which is better than its one-year historical average discount of 5.66%.

Uwe Schillhorn currently receives a manager quality ranking of 91 (0=worst, 99=best). If you desire only a moderate level of risk and strong performance, then this fund is an excellent option.

Data Date	Investment Rating	Net Assets ($Mil)	Price	Performance Rating/Pts	Total Return Y-T-D	Risk Rating/Pts
12-12	B-	203.46	10.97	B- / 7.1	1.91%	B- / 7.9
2011	B	204.10	10.17	B / 8.0	2.36%	B- / 7.9
2010	A-	209.28	11.00	A- / 9.0	28.41%	C+ / 6.0
2009	C+	183.83	10.99	C+ / 6.7	54.09%	C+ / 6.6

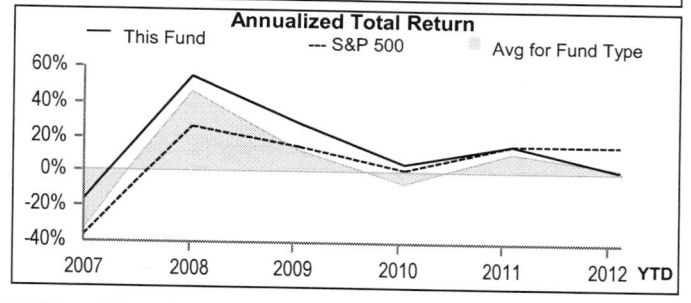

Swiss Helvetia Fund (SWZ)

C-   Fair

Fund Family: Hottinger Capital Corporation
Fund Type: Foreign
Inception Date: August 19, 1987

Major Rating Factors: Middle of the road best describes Swiss Helvetia Fund whose TheStreet.com Investment Rating is currently a C- (Fair). The fund currently has a performance rating of C (Fair) based on an annualized return of 8.41% over the last three years and a total return of 4.07% year to date 2012. Factored into the performance evaluation is an expense ratio of 1.46% (average).

The fund's risk rating is currently C+ (Fair). It carries a beta of 0.85, meaning the fund's expected move will be 8.5% for every 10% move in the market. Volatility, as measured by both the semi-deviation and a drawdown factor, is considered low. As of December 31, 2012, Swiss Helvetia Fund traded at a discount of 17.59% below its net asset value, which is better than its one-year historical average discount of 12.33%.

Rudolf S. Millisits has been running the fund for 17 years and currently receives a manager quality ranking of 73 (0=worst, 99=best). If you desire an average level of risk, then this fund may be an option.

Data Date	Investment Rating	Net Assets ($Mil)	Price	Performance Rating/Pts	Total Return Y-T-D	Risk Rating/Pts
12-12	C-	362.23	11.29	C / 5.0	4.07%	C+ / 6.5
2011	D	343.90	9.95	D / 2.1	1.71%	C+ / 6.5
2010	C-	433.93	13.54	C- / 4.1	20.89%	C / 4.9
2009	D-	374.26	11.62	D- / 1.0	-0.53%	C / 5.2

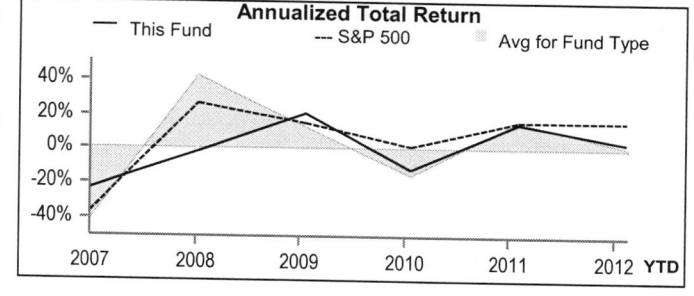

* Denotes ETF Fund

Taiwan Fund (TWN)

D+ **Weak**

Fund Family: Martin Currie Inc
Fund Type: Foreign
Inception Date: December 16, 1986

Major Rating Factors: Taiwan Fund receives a TheStreet.com Investment Rating of D+ (Weak). The fund currently has a performance rating of C- (Fair) based on an annualized return of 6.13% over the last three years and a total return of 2.33% year to date 2012. Factored into the performance evaluation is an expense ratio of 1.61% (above average).

The fund's risk rating is currently C+ (Fair). It carries a beta of 0.91, meaning that its performance tracks fairly well with that of the overall stock market. Volatility, as measured by both the semi-deviation and a drawdown factor, is considered low. As of December 31, 2012, Taiwan Fund traded at a discount of 11.39% below its net asset value, which is better than its one-year historical average discount of 8.22%.

James Liu currently receives a manager quality ranking of 69 (0=worst, 99=best). If you desire an average level of risk, then this fund may be an option.

Data Date	Investment Rating	Net Assets ($Mil)	Price	Performance Rating/Pts	Total Return Y-T-D	Risk Rating/Pts
12-12	D+	154.59	16.34	C- / 3.5	2.33%	C+ / 6.9
2011	C-	296.30	14.49	C / 4.8	0.14%	B- / 7.1
2010	B	303.41	19.24	B+ / 8.3	35.64%	C / 4.8
2009	C-	257.06	14.30	C- / 4.2	52.57%	C / 4.8

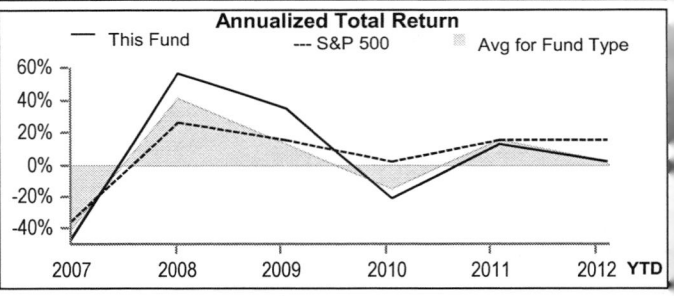

TCW Strategic Income Fund (TSI)

A **Excellent**

Fund Family: TCW Investment Management Company
Fund Type: Growth and Income
Inception Date: February 26, 1987

Major Rating Factors:
Exceptional performance is the major factor driving the A (Excellent) TheStreet.com Investment Rating for TCW Strategic Income Fund. The fund currently has a performance rating of A- (Excellent) based on an annualized return of 24.58% over the last three years and a total return of 6.16% year to date 2012. Factored into the performance evaluation is an expense ratio of 1.39% (average).

The fund's risk rating is currently B (Good). It carries a beta of 0.39, meaning the fund's expected move will be 3.9% for every 10% move in the market. Volatility, as measured by both the semi-deviation and a drawdown factor, is considered low. As of December 31, 2012, TCW Strategic Income Fund traded at a discount of 6.13% below its net asset value, which is better than its one-year historical average discount of 2.22%.

Mitchell A. Flack currently receives a manager quality ranking of 96 (0=worst, 99=best). If you desire only a moderate level of risk and strong performance, then this fund is an excellent option.

Data Date	Investment Rating	Net Assets ($Mil)	Price	Performance Rating/Pts	Total Return Y-T-D	Risk Rating/Pts
12-12	A	253.36	5.36	A- / 9.2	6.16%	B / 8.2
2011	B-	262.58	4.85	B- / 7.0	-2.27%	B- / 7.7
2010	B+	227.31	5.22	A- / 9.2	32.52%	C / 4.9
2009	C+	190.35	4.37	B- / 7.1	54.35%	C / 5.5

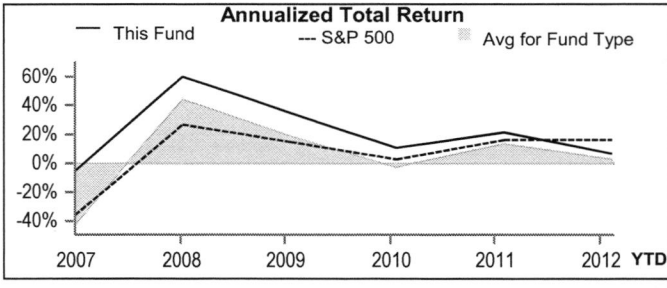

Templeton Dragon Fund (TDF)

C **Fair**

Fund Family: Templeton Asset Management Ltd
Fund Type: Foreign
Inception Date: September 21, 1994

Major Rating Factors: Middle of the road best describes Templeton Dragon Fund whose TheStreet.com Investment Rating is currently a C (Fair). The fund currently has a performance rating of C (Fair) based on an annualized return of 10.42% over the last three years and a total return of 3.16% year to date 2012. Factored into the performance evaluation is an expense ratio of 1.33% (average).

The fund's risk rating is currently B- (Good). It carries a beta of 0.72, meaning the fund's expected move will be 7.2% for every 10% move in the market. Volatility, as measured by both the semi-deviation and a drawdown factor, is considered low. As of December 31, 2012, Templeton Dragon Fund traded at a discount of 11.57% below its net asset value, which is better than its one-year historical average discount of 10.59%.

Mark J. Mobius has been running the fund for 19 years and currently receives a manager quality ranking of 81 (0=worst, 99=best). If you desire an average level of risk, then this fund may be an option.

Data Date	Investment Rating	Net Assets ($Mil)	Price	Performance Rating/Pts	Total Return Y-T-D	Risk Rating/Pts
12-12	C	1,089.56	28.44	C / 5.4	3.16%	B- / 7.3
2011	C+	1,054.50	25.45	C+ / 6.3	1.26%	C+ / 6.9
2010	C+	1,092.71	30.74	B / 7.7	19.81%	C- / 4.2
2009	C	968.58	27.25	B- / 7.4	56.75%	C- / 3.8

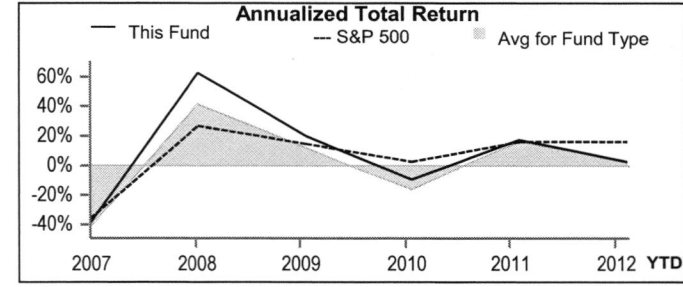

Templeton Emerging Markets Fd (EMF)

D   **Weak**

Fund Family: Templeton Asset Management Ltd
Fund Type: Emerging Market
Inception Date: March 5, 1987

Major Rating Factors:
Disappointing performance is the major factor driving the D (Weak) TheStreet.com Investment Rating for Templeton Emerging Markets Fd. The fund currently has a performance rating of D (Weak) based on an annualized return of -0.16% over the last three years and a total return of 3.55% year to date 2012. Factored into the performance evaluation is an expense ratio of 1.37% (average).

The fund's risk rating is currently C+ (Fair). It carries a beta of 1.19, meaning it is expected to move 11.9% for every 10% move in the market. Volatility, as measured by both the semi-deviation and a drawdown factor, is considered low. As of December 31, 2012, Templeton Emerging Markets Fd traded at a discount of 9.05% below its net asset value, which is better than its one-year historical average discount of 7.77%.

Mark J. Mobius has been running the fund for 22 years and currently receives a manager quality ranking of 25 (0=worst, 99=best). This fund offers only a moderate level of risk but investors looking for strong performance are still waiting.

Data Date	Investment Rating	Net Assets ($Mil)	Price	Performance Rating/Pts	Total Return Y-T-D	Risk Rating/Pts
12-12	D	348.00	20.00	D / 2.2	3.55%	C+ / 6.5
2011	C	343.20	17.86	C+ / 6.4	2.13%	C+ / 6.7
2010	C	355.29	23.57	B / 7.7	20.71%	D+ / 2.7
2009	C	283.40	19.65	B+ / 8.5	110.52%	D+ / 2.9

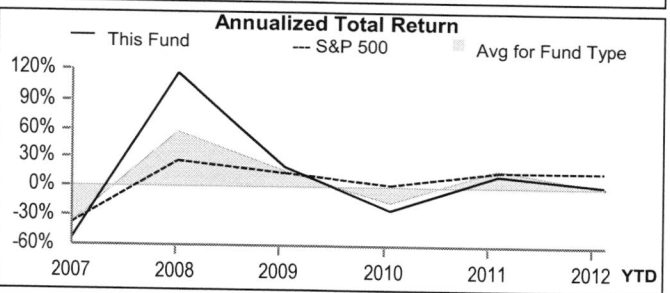

Templeton Emerging Markets Income (TEI)

B-   **Good**

Fund Family: Franklin Advisers Inc
Fund Type: Emerging Market
Inception Date: September 23, 1993

Major Rating Factors: Strong performance is the major factor driving the B- (Good) TheStreet.com Investment Rating for Templeton Emerging Markets Income. The fund currently has a performance rating of B- (Good) based on an annualized return of 15.55% over the last three years and a total return of -1.73% year to date 2012. Factored into the performance evaluation is an expense ratio of 1.15% (low).

The fund's risk rating is currently B- (Good). It carries a beta of 1.02, meaning that its performance tracks fairly well with that of the overall stock market. Volatility, as measured by both the semi-deviation and a drawdown factor, is considered low. As of December 31, 2012, Templeton Emerging Markets Income traded at a premium of 7.78% above its net asset value, which is worse than its one-year historical average premium of 3.74%.

Michael Hasenstab currently receives a manager quality ranking of 92 (0=worst, 99=best). If you desire only a moderate level of risk and strong performance, then this fund is an excellent option.

Data Date	Investment Rating	Net Assets ($Mil)	Price	Performance Rating/Pts	Total Return Y-T-D	Risk Rating/Pts
12-12	B-	759.02	17.31	B- / 7.4	-1.73%	B- / 7.4
2011	B	714.20	15.57	B / 7.8	0.39%	B- / 7.9
2010	B	769.97	16.39	B+ / 8.6	21.06%	C / 4.3
2009	B-	653.99	14.41	B / 7.7	59.87%	C / 5.1

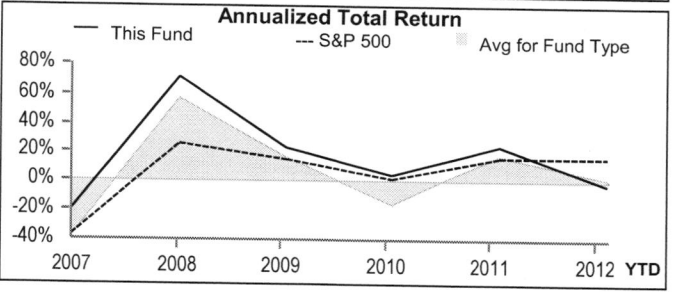

Templeton Global Income Fd (GIM)

C-   **Fair**

Fund Family: Franklin Advisers Inc
Fund Type: Global
Inception Date: March 17, 1988

Major Rating Factors: Middle of the road best describes Templeton Global Income Fd whose TheStreet.com Investment Rating is currently a C- (Fair). The fund currently has a performance rating of C- (Fair) based on an annualized return of 9.12% over the last three years and a total return of 2.33% year to date 2012. Factored into the performance evaluation is an expense ratio of 0.75% (very low).

The fund's risk rating is currently B- (Good). It carries a beta of 1.28, meaning it is expected to move 12.8% for every 10% move in the market. Volatility, as measured by both the semi-deviation and a drawdown factor, is considered low. As of December 31, 2012, Templeton Global Income Fd traded at a premium of 2.50% above its net asset value, which is better than its one-year historical average premium of 4.26%.

Michael Hasenstab has been running the fund for 25 years and currently receives a manager quality ranking of 75 (0=worst, 99=best). If you desire an average level of risk, then this fund may be an option.

Data Date	Investment Rating	Net Assets ($Mil)	Price	Performance Rating/Pts	Total Return Y-T-D	Risk Rating/Pts
12-12	C-	1,209.29	9.44	C- / 3.5	2.33%	B- / 7.7
2011	C	1,338.95	9.45	C / 5.1	-0.21%	B- / 7.9
2010	A-	1,307.68	10.70	B+ / 8.5	19.09%	C+ / 6.3
2009	B-	1,160.28	9.50	C+ / 6.2	28.31%	B- / 7.3

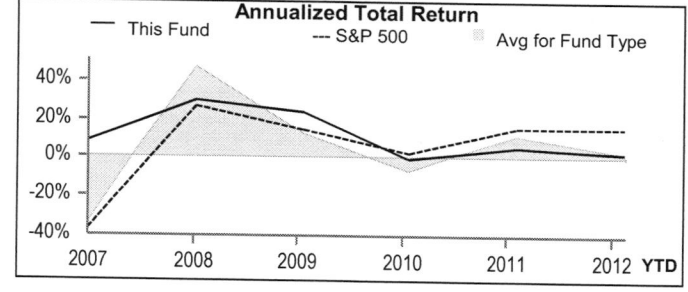

Templeton Russia&East European Fun (TRF)

E+   **Very Weak**

Fund Family: Templeton Asset Management Ltd
Fund Type: Foreign
Inception Date: June 15, 1995

Major Rating Factors:

Very poor performance is the major factor driving the E+ (Very Weak) TheStreet.com Investment Rating for Templeton Russia&East European Fun. The fund currently has a performance rating of E+ (Very Weak) based on an annualized return of -9.47% over the last three years and a total return of 1.30% year to date 2012. Factored into the performance evaluation is an expense ratio of 1.59% (above average).

The fund's risk rating is currently C (Fair). It carries a beta of 1.29, meaning it is expected to move 12.9% for every 10% move in the market. Volatility, as measured by both the semi-deviation and a drawdown factor, is considered average. As of December 31, 2012, Templeton Russia&East European Fun traded at a discount of 10.52% below its net asset value, which is better than its one-year historical average discount of 8.91%.

Mark J. Mobius has been running the fund for 18 years and currently receives a manager quality ranking of 11 (0=worst, 99=best). This fund offers an average level of risk but investors looking for strong performance will be frustrated.

Data Date	Investment Rating	Net Assets ($Mil)	Price	Perfor-mance Rating/Pts	Total Return Y-T-D	Risk Rating/Pts
12-12	E+	102.23	14.63	E+ / 0.8	1.30%	C / 5.1
2011	D-	86.30	13.61	D+ / 2.3	2.57%	C / 5.3
2010	E	119.22	22.90	D / 1.9	26.42%	D / 1.6
2009	E	90.37	18.20	D- / 1.5	79.31%	D- / 1.5

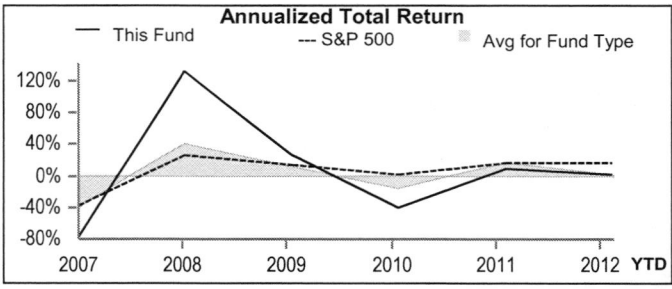

Thai Capital Fund (TF)

B-   **Good**

Fund Family: SCB Asset Management Co Ltd
Fund Type: Foreign
Inception Date: May 30, 1990

Major Rating Factors:

Exceptional performance is the major factor driving the B- (Good) TheStreet.com Investment Rating for Thai Capital Fund. The fund currently has a performance rating of A+ (Excellent) based on an annualized return of 28.26% over the last three years and a total return of 2.15% year to date 2012. Factored into the performance evaluation is an expense ratio of 2.32% (high).

The fund's risk rating is currently C (Fair). It carries a beta of 0.75, meaning the fund's expected move will be 7.5% for every 10% move in the market. Volatility, as measured by both the semi-deviation and a drawdown factor, is considered average. As of December 31, 2012, Thai Capital Fund traded at a discount of 5.39% below its net asset value, which is worse than its one-year historical average discount of 7.59%.

Tanavatt Bhanijkasem currently receives a manager quality ranking of 97 (0=worst, 99=best). If you desire an average level of risk and strong performance, then this fund is a good option.

Data Date	Investment Rating	Net Assets ($Mil)	Price	Perfor-mance Rating/Pts	Total Return Y-T-D	Risk Rating/Pts
12-12	B-	40.90	12.11	A+ / 9.7	2.15%	C / 5.1
2011	C+	35.80	8.59	B / 8.0	1.86%	C / 5.4
2010	B+	36.87	13.63	A / 9.3	71.62%	C / 4.6
2009	C-	31.05	9.83	C- / 4.1	51.36%	C / 5.3

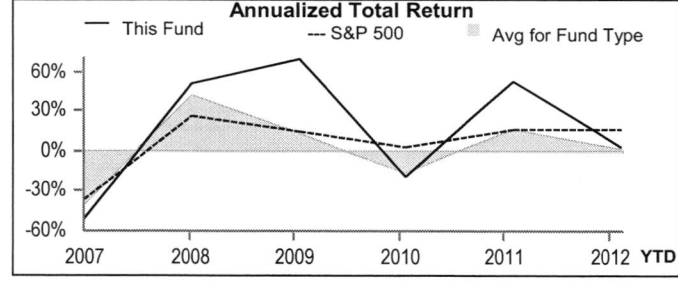

Thai Fund (TTF)

A+   **Excellent**

Fund Family: Morgan Stanley Investment Managemen
Fund Type: Foreign
Inception Date: February 17, 1988

Major Rating Factors:

Exceptional performance is the major factor driving the A+ (Excellent) TheStreet.com Investment Rating for Thai Fund. The fund currently has a performance rating of A+ (Excellent) based on an annualized return of 36.28% over the last three years and a total return of 3.86% year to date 2012. Factored into the performance evaluation is an expense ratio of 1.39% (average).

The fund's risk rating is currently B- (Good). It carries a beta of 0.80, meaning the fund's expected move will be 8.0% for every 10% move in the market. Volatility, as measured by both the semi-deviation and a drawdown factor, is considered low. As of December 31, 2012, Thai Fund traded at a discount of 14.52% below its net asset value, which is better than its one-year historical average discount of 12.77%.

Munib M. Madni has been running the fund for 5 years and currently receives a manager quality ranking of 98 (0=worst, 99=best). If you desire only a moderate level of risk and strong performance, then this fund is an excellent option.

Data Date	Investment Rating	Net Assets ($Mil)	Price	Perfor-mance Rating/Pts	Total Return Y-T-D	Risk Rating/Pts
12-12	A+	270.51	19.95	A+ / 9.8	3.86%	B- / 7.8
2011	B+	215.80	12.26	B+ / 8.4	0.00%	B- / 7.9
2010	B+	180.33	12.80	B+ / 8.7	49.50%	C / 5.0
2009	C	139.46	8.93	C / 5.2	48.85%	C / 5.1

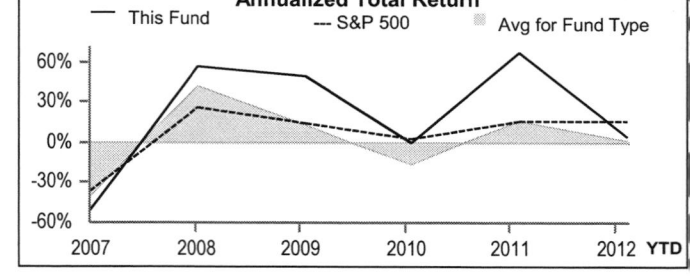

The Cushing MLP Total Return Fund (SRV)

D   Weak

Fund Family: Cushing MLP Asset Management LP
Fund Type: Growth and Income
Inception Date: August 27, 2007

Major Rating Factors:

Disappointing performance is the major factor driving the D (Weak) TheStreet.com Investment Rating for The Cushing MLP Total Return Fund. The fund currently has a performance rating of D- (Weak) based on an annualized return of 3.53% over the last three years and a total return of 7.11% year to date 2012. Factored into the performance evaluation is an expense ratio of 5.07% (high).

The fund's risk rating is currently C+ (Fair). It carries a beta of 0.71, meaning the fund's expected move will be 7.1% for every 10% move in the market. Volatility, as measured by both the semi-deviation and a drawdown factor, is considered low. As of December 31, 2012, The Cushing MLP Total Return Fund traded at a premium of 7.98% above its net asset value, which is better than its one-year historical average premium of 25.23%.

Jerry V. Swank currently receives a manager quality ranking of 31 (0=worst, 99=best). This fund offers only a moderate level of risk but investors looking for strong performance are still waiting.

Data Date	Investment Rating	Net Assets ($Mil)	Price	Perfor-mance Rating/Pts	Total Return Y-T-D	Risk Rating/Pts
12-12	D	216.30	7.17	D- / 1.4	7.11%	C+ / 6.7
2011	B	258.40	8.90	B+ / 8.5	1.57%	B- / 7.4
2010	D	64.51	10.52	C+ / 5.8	33.98%	D- / 1.2
2009	C+	50.46	8.51	A+ / 9.9	118.95%	D+ / 2.3

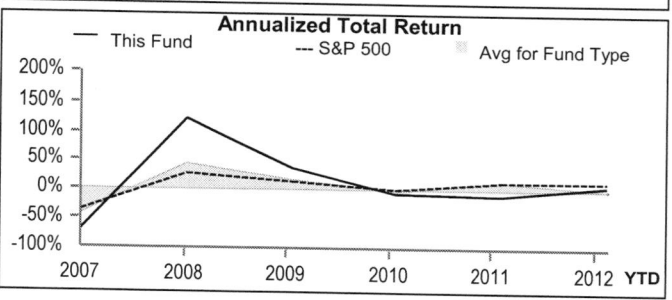

The Denali Fund Inc. (DNY)

C+   Fair

Fund Family: Boulder Investment Advisors LLC
Fund Type: Growth and Income
Inception Date: November 25, 2002

Major Rating Factors: Middle of the road best describes The Denali Fund Inc. whose TheStreet.com Investment Rating is currently a C+ (Fair). The fund currently has a performance rating of C+ (Fair) based on an annualized return of 10.54% over the last three years and a total return of 5.12% year to date 2012. Factored into the performance evaluation is an expense ratio of 2.64% (high).

The fund's risk rating is currently B- (Good). It carries a beta of 0.82, meaning the fund's expected move will be 8.2% for every 10% move in the market. Volatility, as measured by both the semi-deviation and a drawdown factor, is considered low. As of December 31, 2012, The Denali Fund Inc. traded at a discount of 24.10% below its net asset value, which is better than its one-year historical average discount of 19.58%.

Stewart R. Horejsi currently receives a manager quality ranking of 48 (0=worst, 99=best). If you desire an average level of risk, then this fund may be an option.

Data Date	Investment Rating	Net Assets ($Mil)	Price	Perfor-mance Rating/Pts	Total Return Y-T-D	Risk Rating/Pts
12-12	C+	74.92	16.22	C+ / 6.1	5.12%	B- / 7.8
2011	C-	70.50	13.23	C- / 3.8	4.01%	B- / 7.2
2010	C-	73.32	15.22	C- / 4.1	10.10%	C / 5.2
2009	D-	51.89	14.29	D / 1.6	33.76%	C / 4.9

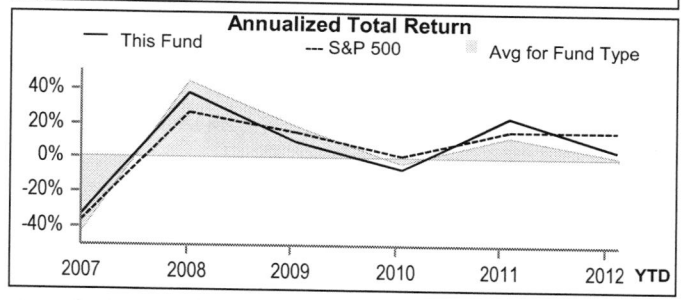

The European Equity Fund (EEA)

C   Fair

Fund Family: Deutsche Asset Mgmt International G
Fund Type: Foreign
Inception Date: July 18, 1986

Major Rating Factors: Middle of the road best describes The European Equity Fund whose TheStreet.com Investment Rating is currently a C (Fair). The fund currently has a performance rating of C+ (Fair) based on an annualized return of 4.51% over the last three years and a total return of 3.84% year to date 2012. Factored into the performance evaluation is an expense ratio of 1.75% (above average).

The fund's risk rating is currently C+ (Fair). It carries a beta of 1.19, meaning it is expected to move 11.9% for every 10% move in the market. Volatility, as measured by both the semi-deviation and a drawdown factor, is considered low. As of December 31, 2012, The European Equity Fund traded at a discount of 13.85% below its net asset value, which is better than its one-year historical average discount of 9.99%.

Gerd Kirsten has been running the fund for 4 years and currently receives a manager quality ranking of 39 (0=worst, 99=best). If you desire an average level of risk, then this fund may be an option.

Data Date	Investment Rating	Net Assets ($Mil)	Price	Perfor-mance Rating/Pts	Total Return Y-T-D	Risk Rating/Pts
12-12	C	73.09	7.03	C+ / 5.8	3.84%	C+ / 6.4
2011	D	72.00	5.94	D / 1.9	-0.17%	C+ / 6.5
2010	E+	97.38	7.58	D- / 1.2	8.61%	D+ / 2.9
2009	D-	77.28	7.03	D- / 1.4	30.74%	C / 4.6

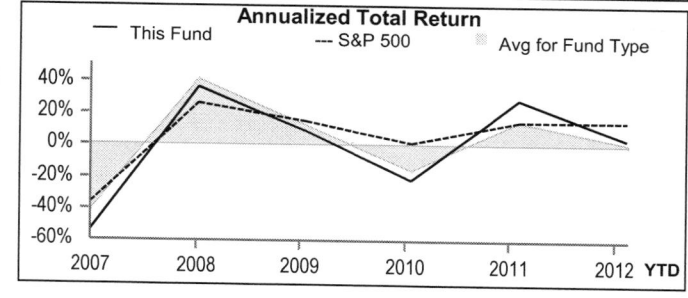

The New Ireland Fund (IRL)   B-   Good

Fund Family: Kleinwort Benson Investors Intl Ltd
Fund Type: Foreign
Inception Date: March 30, 1990

Data Date	Investment Rating	Net Assets ($Mil)	Price	Performance Rating/Pts	Total Return Y-T-D	Risk Rating/Pts
12-12	B-	54.07	9.10	B- / 7.5	3.63%	B- / 7.4
2011	D+	51.30	6.94	C- / 3.5	1.59%	C+ / 6.7
2010	E	58.57	6.86	E+ / 0.6	-2.52%	D+ / 2.5
2009	E	47.05	7.10	E+ / 0.6	42.03%	D+ / 2.6

Major Rating Factors: Strong performance is the major factor driving the B- (Good) TheStreet.com Investment Rating for The New Ireland Fund. The fund currently has a performance rating of B- (Good) based on an annualized return of 8.65% over the last three years and a total return of 3.63% year to date 2012. Factored into the performance evaluation is an expense ratio of 2.22% (high).

The fund's risk rating is currently B- (Good). It carries a beta of 0.91, meaning that its performance tracks fairly well with that of the overall stock market. Volatility, as measured by both the semi-deviation and a drawdown factor, is considered low. As of December 31, 2012, The New Ireland Fund traded at a discount of 15.51% below its net asset value, which is better than its one-year historical average discount of 12.29%.

Noel O'Halloran has been running the fund for 2 years and currently receives a manager quality ranking of 80 (0=worst, 99=best). If you desire only a moderate level of risk and strong performance, then this fund is an excellent option.

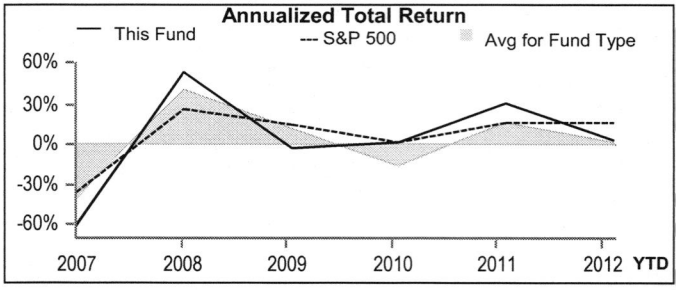

Tortoise Energy Capital (TYY)   C   Fair

Fund Family: Tortoise Capital Advisors LLC
Fund Type: Energy/Natural Resources
Inception Date: May 31, 2005

Data Date	Investment Rating	Net Assets ($Mil)	Price	Performance Rating/Pts	Total Return Y-T-D	Risk Rating/Pts
12-12	C	484.86	0.00	C+ / 6.9	3.93%	C+ / 6.3
2011	B+	532.30	26.83	A- / 9.0	1.90%	B- / 7.9
2010	B-	356.02	27.77	B+ / 8.6	29.80%	C- / 3.9
2009	C+	300.60	22.88	B / 7.8	90.71%	C- / 4.0

Major Rating Factors: Middle of the road best describes Tortoise Energy Capital whose TheStreet.com Investment Rating is currently a C (Fair). The fund currently has a performance rating of C+ (Fair) based on an annualized return of 15.21% over the last three years and a total return of 3.93% year to date 2012. Factored into the performance evaluation is an expense ratio of 4.01% (high).

The fund's risk rating is currently C+ (Fair). It carries a beta of 0.61, meaning the fund's expected move will be 6.1% for every 10% move in the market. Volatility, as measured by both the semi-deviation and a drawdown factor, is considered low. As of December 31, 2012, Tortoise Energy Capital traded at a price exactly equal to its net asset value, which is better than its one-year historical average premium of 2.91%.

H. Kevin Birzer has been running the fund for 8 years and currently receives a manager quality ranking of 87 (0=worst, 99=best). If you desire an average level of risk, then this fund may be an option.

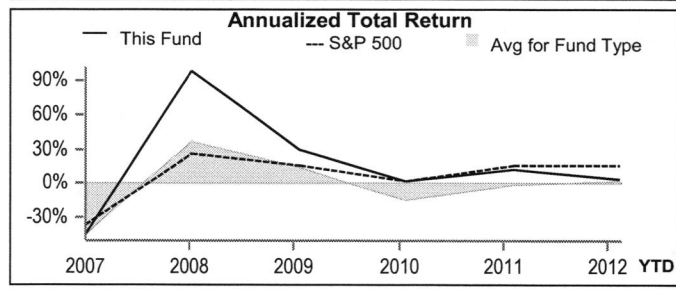

Tortoise Energy Infrastr Corp (TYG)   C   Fair

Fund Family: Tortoise Capital Advisors LLC
Fund Type: Energy/Natural Resources
Inception Date: February 27, 2004

Data Date	Investment Rating	Net Assets ($Mil)	Price	Performance Rating/Pts	Total Return Y-T-D	Risk Rating/Pts
12-12	C	907.10	0.00	C+ / 5.8	6.31%	C+ / 6.6
2011	A	990.20	39.99	A+ / 9.6	1.23%	B / 8.3
2010	B+	613.60	38.25	B+ / 8.8	32.04%	C / 5.0
2009	B	510.54	31.02	B / 8.0	95.84%	C / 5.4

Major Rating Factors: Middle of the road best describes Tortoise Energy Infrastr Corp whose TheStreet.com Investment Rating is currently a C (Fair). The fund currently has a performance rating of C+ (Fair) based on an annualized return of 15.88% over the last three years and a total return of 6.31% year to date 2012. Factored into the performance evaluation is an expense ratio of 3.40% (high).

The fund's risk rating is currently C+ (Fair). It carries a beta of 0.59, meaning the fund's expected move will be 5.9% for every 10% move in the market. Volatility, as measured by both the semi-deviation and a drawdown factor, is considered low. As of December 31, 2012, Tortoise Energy Infrastr Corp traded at a price exactly equal to its net asset value, which is better than its one-year historical average premium of 13.52%.

H. Kevin Birzer has been running the fund for 9 years and currently receives a manager quality ranking of 87 (0=worst, 99=best). If you desire an average level of risk, then this fund may be an option.

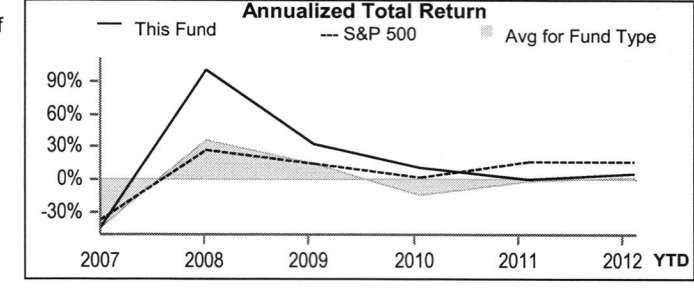

Tortoise MLP Fund Inc (NTG)　　　　C-　　　Fair

Fund Family: Tortoise Capital Advisors LLC
Fund Type: Growth
Inception Date: July 30, 2010

Major Rating Factors: Middle of the road best describes Tortoise MLP Fund Inc whose TheStreet.com Investment Rating is currently a C- (Fair). The fund currently has a performance rating of C- (Fair) based on an annualized return of 0.00% over the last three years and a total return of 5.10% year to date 2012. Factored into the performance evaluation is an expense ratio of 2.34% (high).

The fund's risk rating is currently B- (Good). It carries a beta of 0.00, meaning the fund's expected move will be 0.0% for every 10% move in the market. Volatility, as measured by both the semi-deviation and a drawdown factor, is considered low. As of December 31, 2012, Tortoise MLP Fund Inc traded at a price exactly equal to its net asset value, which is better than its one-year historical average premium of 2.79%.

This is team managed and currently receives a manager quality ranking of 21 (0=worst, 99=best). If you desire an average level of risk, then this fund may be an option.

Data Date	Investment Rating	Net Assets ($Mil)	Price	Performance Rating/Pts	Total Return Y-T-D	Risk Rating/Pts
12-12	C-	1,085.82	0.00	C- / 3.0	5.10%	B- / 7.8
2011	B-	1,178.50	25.77	C+ / 5.9	-0.31%	B / 8.5

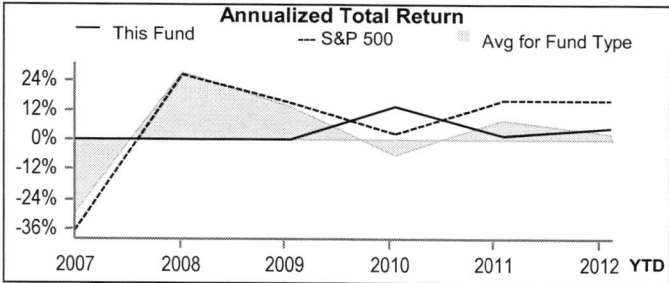

Tortoise North American Energy (TYN)　　　C　　　Fair

Fund Family: Tortoise Capital Advisors LLC
Fund Type: Energy/Natural Resources
Inception Date: October 31, 2005

Major Rating Factors: Middle of the road best describes Tortoise North American Energy whose TheStreet.com Investment Rating is currently a C (Fair). The fund currently has a performance rating of C (Fair) based on an annualized return of 11.62% over the last three years and a total return of 6.18% year to date 2012. Factored into the performance evaluation is an expense ratio of 1.90% (above average).

The fund's risk rating is currently C+ (Fair). It carries a beta of 0.33, meaning the fund's expected move will be 3.3% for every 10% move in the market. Volatility, as measured by both the semi-deviation and a drawdown factor, is considered low. As of December 31, 2012, Tortoise North American Energy traded at a price exactly equal to its net asset value, which is worse than its one-year historical average discount of .10%.

Zachary A. Hamel has been running the fund for 6 years and currently receives a manager quality ranking of 87 (0=worst, 99=best). If you desire an average level of risk, then this fund may be an option.

Data Date	Investment Rating	Net Assets ($Mil)	Price	Performance Rating/Pts	Total Return Y-T-D	Risk Rating/Pts
12-12	C	149.64	0.00	C / 5.5	6.18%	C+ / 6.9
2011	A-	162.20	24.46	B+ / 8.9	1.35%	B / 8.5
2010	C+	126.61	25.00	B / 7.8	21.51%	C- / 3.9
2009	C+	77.01	21.93	B+ / 8.4	103.63%	C- / 4.2

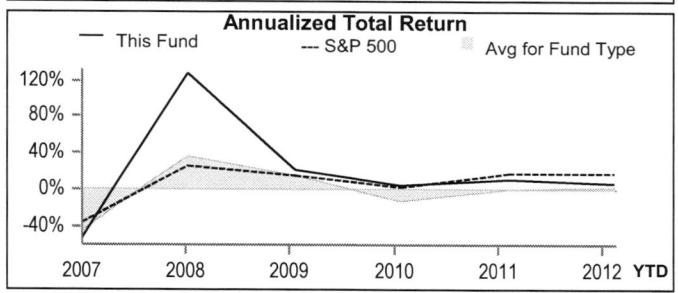

Tortoise Pipeline & Enrgy Fund Inc (TTP)　　　B　　　Good

Fund Family: Tortoise Capital Advisors LLC
Fund Type: Energy/Natural Resources
Inception Date: October 27, 2011

Major Rating Factors: Tortoise Pipeline & Enrgy Fund Inc receives a TheStreet.com Investment Rating of B (Good). The fund currently has a performance rating of C+ (Fair) based on an annualized return of 0.00% over the last three years and a total return of 6.93% year to date 2012. Factored into the performance evaluation is an expense ratio of 2.33% (high).

The fund's risk rating is currently B (Good). It carries a beta of 0.00, meaning the fund's expected move will be 0.0% for every 10% move in the market. Volatility, as measured by both the semi-deviation and a drawdown factor, is considered low. As of December 31, 2012, Tortoise Pipeline & Enrgy Fund Inc traded at a price exactly equal to its net asset value, which is worse than its one-year historical average discount of 3.33%.

H. Kevin Birzer has been running the fund for 2 years and currently receives a manager quality ranking of 87 (0=worst, 99=best). If you desire an average level of risk, then this fund may be an option.

Data Date	Investment Rating	Net Assets ($Mil)	Price	Performance Rating/Pts	Total Return Y-T-D	Risk Rating/Pts
12-12	B	237.75	0.00	C+ / 6.8	6.93%	B / 8.6

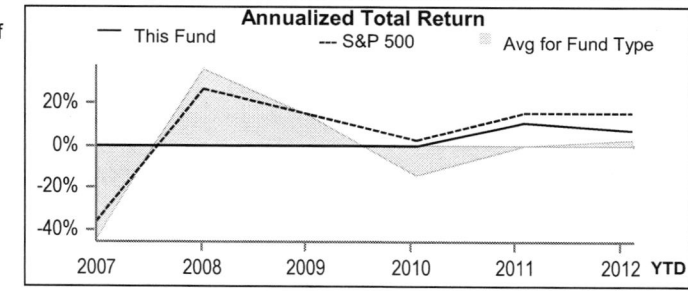

Tortoise Power and Energy Inf Fund (TPZ)   B   Good

Fund Family: Tortoise Capital Advisors LLC
Fund Type: Energy/Natural Resources
Inception Date: July 29, 2009

Major Rating Factors: Tortoise Power and Energy Inf Fund receives a TheStreet.com Investment Rating of B (Good). The fund currently has a performance rating of C+ (Fair) based on an annualized return of 17.06% over the last three years and a total return of 5.84% year to date 2012. Factored into the performance evaluation is an expense ratio of 1.73% (above average).

The fund's risk rating is currently B (Good). It carries a beta of 0.36, meaning the fund's expected move will be 3.6% for every 10% move in the market. Volatility, as measured by both the semi-deviation and a drawdown factor, is considered low. As of December 31, 2012, Tortoise Power and Energy Inf Fund traded at a price exactly equal to its net asset value, which is worse than its one-year historical average discount of 3.77%.

Zachary A. Hamel currently receives a manager quality ranking of 91 (0=worst, 99=best). If you desire an average level of risk, then this fund may be an option.

Data Date	Investment Rating	Net Assets ($Mil)	Price	Perfor-mance Rating/Pts	Total Return Y-T-D	Risk Rating/Pts
12-12	B	175.89	0.00	C+ / 6.8	5.84%	B / 8.3
2011	C+	182.50	24.99	C / 4.6	-0.36%	B / 8.6
2010	A+	0.00	24.49	A / 9.4	29.38%	B / 8.3

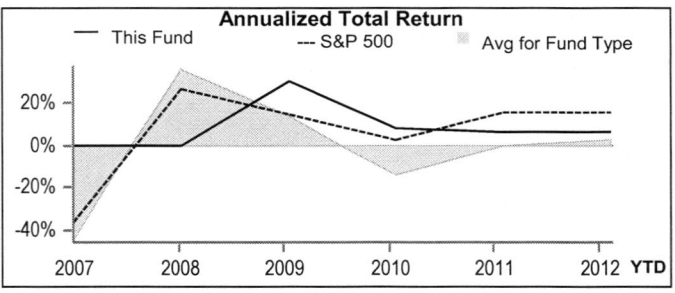

Transamerica Income Shares (TAI)   C   Fair

Fund Family: Transamerica Asset Management Inc
Fund Type: Global
Inception Date: November 9, 1972

Major Rating Factors: Middle of the road best describes Transamerica Income Shares whose TheStreet.com Investment Rating is currently a C (Fair). The fund currently has a performance rating of C- (Fair) based on an annualized return of 11.99% over the last three years and a total return of -0.65% year to date 2012. Factored into the performance evaluation is an expense ratio of 0.78% (very low).

The fund's risk rating is currently B (Good). It carries a beta of 0.25, meaning the fund's expected move will be 2.5% for every 10% move in the market. Volatility, as measured by both the semi-deviation and a drawdown factor, is considered low. As of December 31, 2012, Transamerica Income Shares traded at a premium of .26% above its net asset value, which is better than its one-year historical average premium of 3.03%.

Bradley J. Beman currently receives a manager quality ranking of 92 (0=worst, 99=best). If you desire an average level of risk, then this fund may be an option.

Data Date	Investment Rating	Net Assets ($Mil)	Price	Perfor-mance Rating/Pts	Total Return Y-T-D	Risk Rating/Pts
12-12	C	140.46	23.24	C- / 4.2	-0.65%	B / 8.6
2011	B	136.70	21.60	C+ / 6.7	0.49%	B+ / 9.0
2010	C+	139.24	20.70	C+ / 6.7	12.22%	C+ / 6.2
2009	C+	132.60	20.05	C / 5.5	33.33%	C+ / 6.8

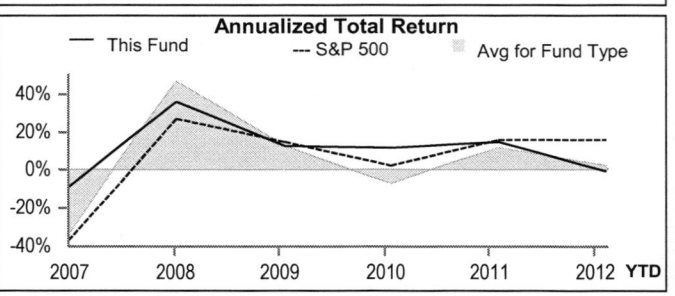

Tri-Continental Corporation (TY)   B-   Good

Fund Family: Columbia Management Inv Advisers LL
Fund Type: Income
Inception Date: N/A

Major Rating Factors: Strong performance is the major factor driving the B- (Good) TheStreet.com Investment Rating for Tri-Continental Corporation. The fund currently has a performance rating of B- (Good) based on an annualized return of 15.56% over the last three years and a total return of 4.24% year to date 2012. Factored into the performance evaluation is an expense ratio of 0.59% (very low).

The fund's risk rating is currently B (Good). It carries a beta of 1.10, meaning it is expected to move 11.0% for every 10% move in the market. Volatility, as measured by both the semi-deviation and a drawdown factor, is considered low. As of December 31, 2012, Tri-Continental Corporation traded at a discount of 16.75% below its net asset value, which is better than its one-year historical average discount of 14.38%.

Brian M. Condon has been running the fund for 3 years and currently receives a manager quality ranking of 69 (0=worst, 99=best). If you desire only a moderate level of risk and strong performance, then this fund is an excellent option.

Data Date	Investment Rating	Net Assets ($Mil)	Price	Perfor-mance Rating/Pts	Total Return Y-T-D	Risk Rating/Pts
12-12	B-	1,147.55	16.05	B- / 7.0	4.24%	B / 8.1
2011	C+	1,078.20	14.23	C+ / 6.0	1.97%	B / 8.0
2010	C-	946.34	13.76	D+ / 2.9	21.82%	C+ / 6.1
2009	D	778.22	11.52	D- / 1.0	14.61%	C+ / 5.8

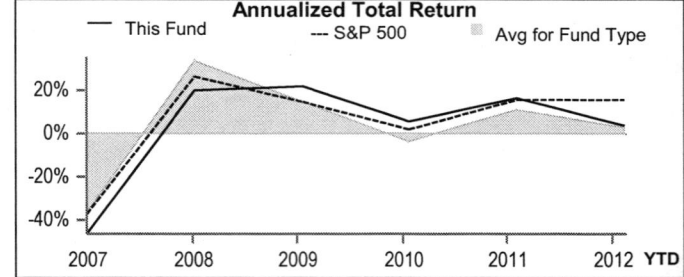

Turkish Investment Fund (TKF)   B-   Good

Fund Family: Morgan Stanley Investment Managemen
Fund Type: Foreign
Inception Date: December 5, 1989

Data Date	Investment Rating	Net Assets ($Mil)	Price	Performance Rating/Pts	Total Return Y-T-D	Risk Rating/Pts
12-12	B-	112.74	16.64	B+ / 8.7	6.63%	C+ / 5.9
2011	C-	93.40	11.06	C / 5.1	0.81%	C+ / 6.1
2010	D	97.73	16.50	C- / 3.0	24.92%	C- / 3.8
2009	C	60.26	13.37	C+ / 6.9	112.38%	C- / 3.7

Major Rating Factors: Strong performance is the major factor driving the B- (Good) TheStreet.com Investment Rating for Turkish Investment Fund. The fund currently has a performance rating of B+ (Good) based on an annualized return of 10.07% over the last three years and a total return of 6.63% year to date 2012. Factored into the performance evaluation is an expense ratio of 1.18% (low).

The fund's risk rating is currently C+ (Fair). It carries a beta of 1.05, meaning that its performance tracks fairly well with that of the overall stock market. Volatility, as measured by both the semi-deviation and a drawdown factor, is considered low. As of December 31, 2012, Turkish Investment Fund traded at a discount of 16.34% below its net asset value, which is better than its one-year historical average discount of 10.95%.

Paul C. Psaila has been running the fund for 16 years and currently receives a manager quality ranking of 79 (0=worst, 99=best). If you desire only a moderate level of risk and strong performance, then this fund is an excellent option.

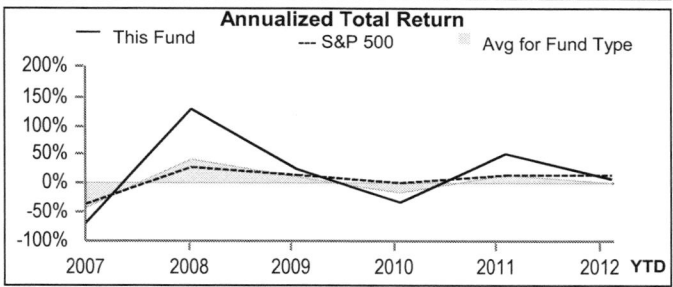

Virtus Total Return (DCA)   A+   Excellent

Fund Family: Virtus Investment Advisers Inc
Fund Type: Growth and Income
Inception Date: February 23, 2005

Data Date	Investment Rating	Net Assets ($Mil)	Price	Performance Rating/Pts	Total Return Y-T-D	Risk Rating/Pts
12-12	A+	115.01	3.87	A / 9.4	4.40%	B / 8.2
2011	C+	111.50	3.50	B+ / 8.4	-0.57%	C / 5.5
2010	D-	39.18	3.45	D / 2.1	53.64%	C- / 3.2
2009	E	30.47	2.39	E / 0.4	28.00%	C- / 3.4

Major Rating Factors:
Exceptional performance is the major factor driving the A+ (Excellent) TheStreet.com Investment Rating for Virtus Total Return. The fund currently has a performance rating of A (Excellent) based on an annualized return of 27.38% over the last three years and a total return of 4.40% year to date 2012. Factored into the performance evaluation is an expense ratio of 1.90% (above average).

The fund's risk rating is currently B (Good). It carries a beta of 1.13, meaning it is expected to move 11.3% for every 10% move in the market. Volatility, as measured by both the semi-deviation and a drawdown factor, is considered low. As of December 31, 2012, Virtus Total Return traded at a discount of 13.62% below its net asset value, which is better than its one-year historical average discount of 11.51%.

Connie M. Luecke currently receives a manager quality ranking of 91 (0=worst, 99=best). If you desire only a moderate level of risk and strong performance, then this fund is an excellent option.

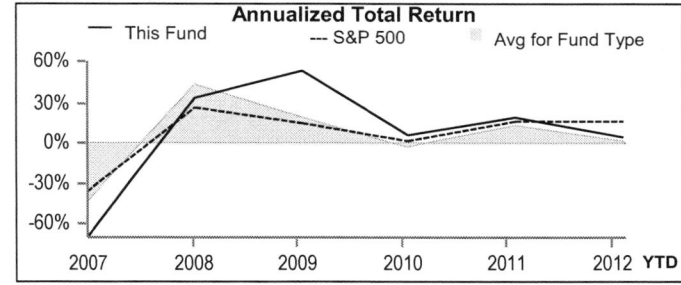

Wells Fargo Avtg Global Div Oppty (EOD)   D+   Weak

Fund Family: Wells Fargo Funds Management LLC
Fund Type: Global
Inception Date: March 28, 2007

Data Date	Investment Rating	Net Assets ($Mil)	Price	Performance Rating/Pts	Total Return Y-T-D	Risk Rating/Pts
12-12	D+	405.46	7.57	D+ / 2.3	3.43%	B- / 7.3
2011	D+	413.70	7.59	D+ / 2.4	3.56%	B- / 7.3
2010	D-	561.05	9.55	D- / 1.1	2.46%	C / 5.2
2009	C+	475.34	10.24	B- / 7.3	18.74%	C / 5.4

Major Rating Factors:
Disappointing performance is the major factor driving the D+ (Weak) TheStreet.com Investment Rating for Wells Fargo Avtg Global Div Oppty. The fund currently has a performance rating of D+ (Weak) based on an annualized return of 2.99% over the last three years and a total return of 3.43% year to date 2012. Factored into the performance evaluation is an expense ratio of 1.08% (low).

The fund's risk rating is currently B- (Good). It carries a beta of 0.68, meaning the fund's expected move will be 6.8% for every 10% move in the market. Volatility, as measured by both the semi-deviation and a drawdown factor, is considered low. As of December 31, 2012, Wells Fargo Avtg Global Div Oppty traded at a discount of 8.69% below its net asset value, which is better than its one-year historical average discount of 2.58%.

Jeffrey P. Mellas currently receives a manager quality ranking of 46 (0=worst, 99=best). This fund offers only a moderate level of risk but investors looking for strong performance are still waiting.

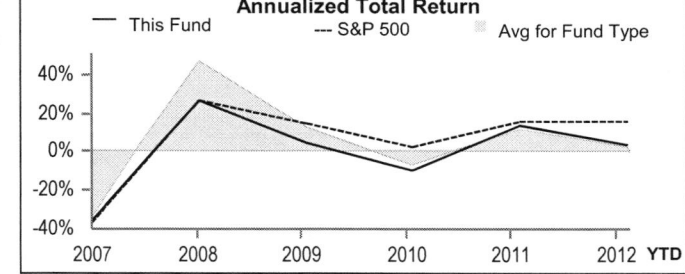

Wells Fargo Avtg Income Oppty (EAD)

C-   **Fair**

Fund Family: Wells Fargo Funds Management LLC
Fund Type: Corporate - High Yield
Inception Date: February 26, 2003

Major Rating Factors: Middle of the road best describes Wells Fargo Avtg Income Oppty whose TheStreet.com Investment Rating is currently a C- (Fair). The fund currently has a performance rating of C (Fair) based on an annualized return of 12.06% over the last three years and a total return of 2.28% year to date 2012. Factored into the performance evaluation is an expense ratio of 1.03% (low).

The fund's risk rating is currently B- (Good). It carries a beta of 1.17, meaning it is expected to move 11.7% for every 10% move in the market. Volatility, as measured by both the semi-deviation and a drawdown factor, is considered low. As of December 31, 2012, Wells Fargo Avtg Income Oppty traded at a discount of .10% below its net asset value, which is better than its one-year historical average premium of 5.32%.

Niklas Nordenfelt currently receives a manager quality ranking of 46 (0=worst, 99=best). If you desire an average level of risk, then this fund may be an option.

Data Date	Investment Rating	Net Assets ($Mil)	Price	Performance Rating/Pts	Total Return Y-T-D	Risk Rating/Pts
12-12	C-	683.81	10.07	C / 4.6	2.28%	B- / 7.3
2011	B	667.50	10.18	A- / 9.0	0.49%	B- / 7.1
2010	C-	676.14	9.63	C+ / 6.5	12.95%	C- / 3.4
2009	C-	508.60	9.51	C / 5.2	84.05%	C / 4.6

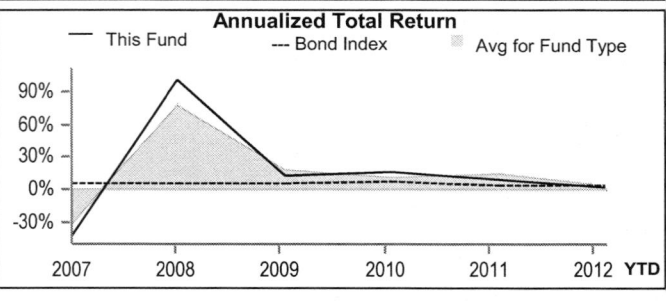

Wells Fargo Avtg Multi-Sector Inc (ERC)

C+   **Fair**

Fund Family: Wells Fargo Funds Management LLC
Fund Type: Global
Inception Date: June 25, 2003

Major Rating Factors: Middle of the road best describes Wells Fargo Avtg Multi-Sector Inc whose TheStreet.com Investment Rating is currently a C+ (Fair). The fund currently has a performance rating of C+ (Fair) based on an annualized return of 12.87% over the last three years and a total return of 1.24% year to date 2012. Factored into the performance evaluation is an expense ratio of 1.24% (average).

The fund's risk rating is currently B (Good). It carries a beta of 0.55, meaning the fund's expected move will be 5.5% for every 10% move in the market. Volatility, as measured by both the semi-deviation and a drawdown factor, is considered low. As of December 31, 2012, Wells Fargo Avtg Multi-Sector Inc traded at a discount of 6.53% below its net asset value, which is better than its one-year historical average discount of 5.54%.

Michael J. Bray currently receives a manager quality ranking of 91 (0=worst, 99=best). If you desire an average level of risk, then this fund may be an option.

Data Date	Investment Rating	Net Assets ($Mil)	Price	Performance Rating/Pts	Total Return Y-T-D	Risk Rating/Pts
12-12	C+	715.37	16.17	C+ / 5.7	1.24%	B / 8.7
2011	B	668.70	14.78	B- / 7.0	1.01%	B / 8.6
2010	B-	677.42	15.32	B / 7.7	17.47%	C / 4.9
2009	C+	546.30	14.18	C+ / 6.1	46.45%	C+ / 5.6

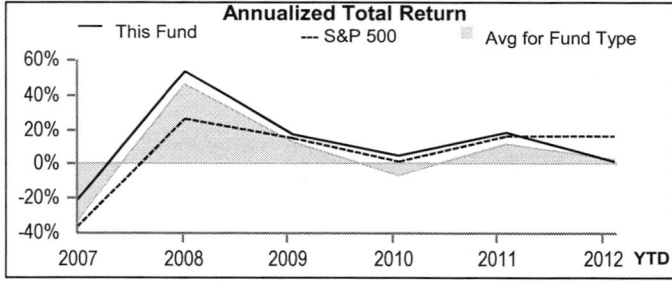

Wells Fargo Avtg Utilities&High In (ERH)

D   **Weak**

Fund Family: Wells Fargo Funds Management LLC
Fund Type: Utilities
Inception Date: April 28, 2004

Major Rating Factors:
Disappointing performance is the major factor driving the D (Weak) TheStreet.com Investment Rating for Wells Fargo Avtg Utilities&High In. The fund currently has a performance rating of D- (Weak) based on an annualized return of -1.60% over the last three years and a total return of 2.92% year to date 2012. Factored into the performance evaluation is an expense ratio of 1.20% (average).

The fund's risk rating is currently C+ (Fair). It carries a beta of 0.48, meaning the fund's expected move will be 4.8% for every 10% move in the market. Volatility, as measured by both the semi-deviation and a drawdown factor, is considered low. As of December 31, 2012, Wells Fargo Avtg Utilities&High In traded at a discount of 6.29% below its net asset value, which is better than its one-year historical average discount of .11%.

Timothy P. O'Brien has been running the fund for 9 years and currently receives a manager quality ranking of 22 (0=worst, 99=best). This fund offers only a moderate level of risk but investors looking for strong performance are still waiting.

Data Date	Investment Rating	Net Assets ($Mil)	Price	Performance Rating/Pts	Total Return Y-T-D	Risk Rating/Pts
12-12	D	108.33	11.18	D- / 1.3	2.92%	C+ / 6.5
2011	D+	107.60	11.15	C- / 3.5	1.08%	C+ / 6.2
2010	D-	103.25	11.59	E+ / 0.6	-14.38%	C / 4.9
2009	D	103.69	14.73	C- / 3.1	40.56%	C / 4.5

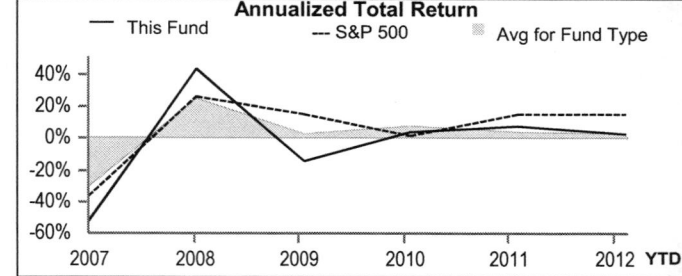

Western Asset Emerging Market Debt (ESD)   B+   Good

Fund Family: Legg Mason Partners Fund Advisor LL
Fund Type: Emerging Market
Inception Date: December 1, 2003

Data Date	Investment Rating	Net Assets ($Mil)	Price	Performance Rating/Pts	Total Return Y-T-D	Risk Rating/Pts
12-12	B+	653.87	21.80	B- / 7.5	2.57%	B / 8.6
2011	B	632.10	18.90	B / 7.9	0.74%	B- / 7.9
2010	B-	600.30	18.31	B- / 7.3	13.69%	C / 5.1
2009	C+	452.15	17.36	C+ / 6.8	51.88%	C / 5.3

Major Rating Factors: Strong performance is the major factor driving the B+ (Good) TheStreet.com Investment Rating for Western Asset Emerging Market Debt. The fund currently has a performance rating of B- (Good) based on an annualized return of 16.24% over the last three years and a total return of 2.57% year to date 2012. Factored into the performance evaluation is an expense ratio of 1.03% (low).

The fund's risk rating is currently B (Good). It carries a beta of 0.75, meaning the fund's expected move will be 7.5% for every 10% move in the market. Volatility, as measured by both the semi-deviation and a drawdown factor, is considered low. As of December 31, 2012, Western Asset Emerging Market Debt traded at a discount of 2.46% below its net asset value, which is worse than its one-year historical average discount of 4.19%.

S. Kenneth Leech currently receives a manager quality ranking of 93 (0=worst, 99=best). If you desire only a moderate level of risk and strong performance, then this fund is an excellent option.

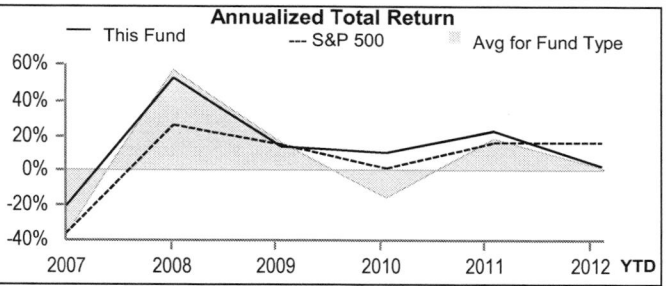

Western Asset Emerging Mkts Inc (EMD)   C+   Fair

Fund Family: Legg Mason Partners Fund Advisor LL
Fund Type: Emerging Market
Inception Date: June 18, 1993

Data Date	Investment Rating	Net Assets ($Mil)	Price	Performance Rating/Pts	Total Return Y-T-D	Risk Rating/Pts
12-12	C+	423.29	15.32	C+ / 6.1	0.65%	B / 8.1
2011	B	416.80	13.41	B / 7.9	0.75%	B / 8.0
2010	B	392.18	13.06	B- / 7.4	14.02%	C / 5.5
2009	B-	350.61	12.31	B- / 7.2	61.16%	C+ / 5.6

Major Rating Factors: Middle of the road best describes Western Asset Emerging Mkts Inc whose TheStreet.com Investment Rating is currently a C+ (Fair). The fund currently has a performance rating of C+ (Fair) based on an annualized return of 14.65% over the last three years and a total return of 0.65% year to date 2012. Factored into the performance evaluation is an expense ratio of 1.25% (average).

The fund's risk rating is currently B (Good). It carries a beta of 1.08, meaning that its performance tracks fairly well with that of the overall stock market. Volatility, as measured by both the semi-deviation and a drawdown factor, is considered low. As of December 31, 2012, Western Asset Emerging Mkts Inc traded at a discount of 2.92% below its net asset value, which is worse than its one-year historical average discount of 2.95%.

S. Kenneth Leech currently receives a manager quality ranking of 90 (0=worst, 99=best). If you desire an average level of risk, then this fund may be an option.

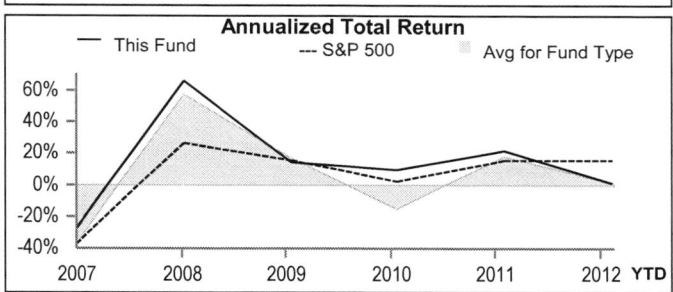

Western Asset Global Corp Def Oppt (GDO)   B-   Good

Fund Family: Legg Mason Partners Fund Advisor LL
Fund Type: Global
Inception Date: November 23, 2009

Data Date	Investment Rating	Net Assets ($Mil)	Price	Performance Rating/Pts	Total Return Y-T-D	Risk Rating/Pts
12-12	B-	291.50	20.75	C+ / 5.6	0.58%	B / 8.9
2011	C+	281.90	18.00	C / 4.8	2.06%	B / 8.5
2010	C-	0.00	17.93	D / 2.1	-2.44%	B- / 7.7

Major Rating Factors: Western Asset Global Corp Def Oppt receives a TheStreet.com Investment Rating of B- (Good). The fund currently has a performance rating of C+ (Fair) based on an annualized return of 10.90% over the last three years and a total return of 0.58% year to date 2012. Factored into the performance evaluation is an expense ratio of 1.40% (average).

The fund's risk rating is currently B (Good). It carries a beta of 0.69, meaning the fund's expected move will be 6.9% for every 10% move in the market. Volatility, as measured by both the semi-deviation and a drawdown factor, is considered low. As of December 31, 2012, Western Asset Global Corp Def Oppt traded at a discount of 1.43% below its net asset value, which is worse than its one-year historical average discount of 1.80%.

Michael C. Buchanan currently receives a manager quality ranking of 84 (0=worst, 99=best). If you desire an average level of risk, then this fund may be an option.

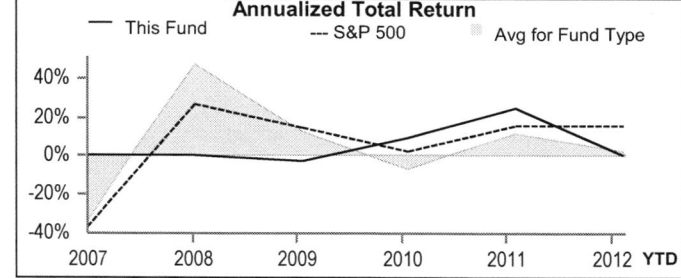

Western Asset Global High Income (EHI)

B-   **Good**

Fund Family: Legg Mason Partners Fund Advisor LL
Fund Type: Global
Inception Date: July 29, 2003

Major Rating Factors: Strong performance is the major factor driving the B- (Good) TheStreet.com Investment Rating for Western Asset Global High Income. The fund currently has a performance rating of B- (Good) based on an annualized return of 16.91% over the last three years and a total return of 1.60% year to date 2012. Factored into the performance evaluation is an expense ratio of 1.50% (average).

The fund's risk rating is currently B- (Good). It carries a beta of 0.73, meaning the fund's expected move will be 7.3% for every 10% move in the market. Volatility, as measured by both the semi-deviation and a drawdown factor, is considered low. As of December 31, 2012, Western Asset Global High Income traded at a discount of 1.99% below its net asset value, which is better than its one-year historical average premium of .22%.

S. Kenneth Leech currently receives a manager quality ranking of 94 (0=worst, 99=best). If you desire only a moderate level of risk and strong performance, then this fund is an excellent option.

Data Date	Investment Rating	Net Assets ($Mil)	Price	Performance Rating/Pts	Total Return Y-T-D	Risk Rating/Pts
12-12	B-	395.09	13.78	B- / 7.2	1.60%	B- / 7.7
2011	B-	380.80	12.60	B / 8.2	-0.87%	B- / 7.0
2010	B	369.75	12.88	B+ / 8.6	27.13%	C / 4.3
2009	C	313.21	11.08	C+ / 6.4	63.21%	C / 5.0

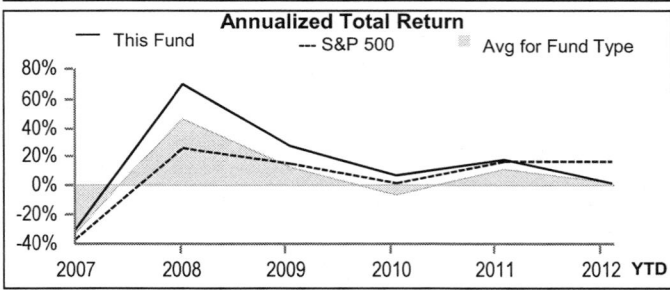

Western Asset Global Partners Inc (GDF)

C   **Fair**

Fund Family: Legg Mason Partners Fund Advisor LL
Fund Type: Global
Inception Date: October 21, 1993

Major Rating Factors: Middle of the road best describes Western Asset Global Partners Inc whose TheStreet.com Investment Rating is currently a C (Fair). The fund currently has a performance rating of C (Fair) based on an annualized return of 12.02% over the last three years and a total return of 2.21% year to date 2012. Factored into the performance evaluation is an expense ratio of 1.53% (average).

The fund's risk rating is currently B- (Good). It carries a beta of 0.75, meaning the fund's expected move will be 7.5% for every 10% move in the market. Volatility, as measured by both the semi-deviation and a drawdown factor, is considered low. As of December 31, 2012, Western Asset Global Partners Inc traded at a premium of .40% above its net asset value, which is better than its one-year historical average premium of 6.99%.

Stephen A. Walsh currently receives a manager quality ranking of 90 (0=worst, 99=best). If you desire an average level of risk, then this fund may be an option.

Data Date	Investment Rating	Net Assets ($Mil)	Price	Performance Rating/Pts	Total Return Y-T-D	Risk Rating/Pts
12-12	C	188.08	12.65	C / 4.7	2.21%	B- / 7.5
2011	B+	172.30	13.12	A+ / 9.6	0.69%	B- / 7.1
2010	C+	178.84	11.87	B / 8.2	13.69%	C- / 4.1
2009	C+	154.06	11.50	B / 8.0	98.86%	C- / 4.0

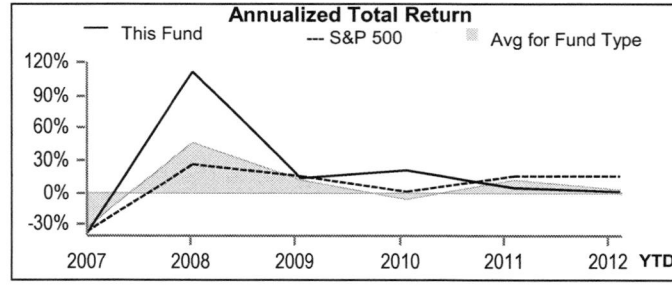

Western Asset High Inc Fd II (HIX)

C   **Fair**

Fund Family: Legg Mason Partners Fund Advisor LL
Fund Type: Global
Inception Date: May 22, 1998

Major Rating Factors: Middle of the road best describes Western Asset High Inc Fd II whose TheStreet.com Investment Rating is currently a C (Fair). The fund currently has a performance rating of C (Fair) based on an annualized return of 12.68% over the last three years and a total return of 4.55% year to date 2012. Factored into the performance evaluation is an expense ratio of 1.51% (average).

The fund's risk rating is currently B- (Good). It carries a beta of 0.57, meaning the fund's expected move will be 5.7% for every 10% move in the market. Volatility, as measured by both the semi-deviation and a drawdown factor, is considered low. As of December 31, 2012, Western Asset High Inc Fd II traded at a premium of 2.44% above its net asset value, which is better than its one-year historical average premium of 13.16%.

S. Kenneth Leech currently receives a manager quality ranking of 91 (0=worst, 99=best). If you desire an average level of risk, then this fund may be an option.

Data Date	Investment Rating	Net Assets ($Mil)	Price	Performance Rating/Pts	Total Return Y-T-D	Risk Rating/Pts
12-12	C	756.45	9.66	C / 4.8	4.55%	B- / 7.9
2011	B	709.60	9.64	A / 9.3	1.97%	C+ / 6.6
2010	C+	751.12	9.37	B / 7.8	15.24%	C- / 3.9
2009	C	504.96	9.16	B / 8.0	100.71%	D+ / 2.9

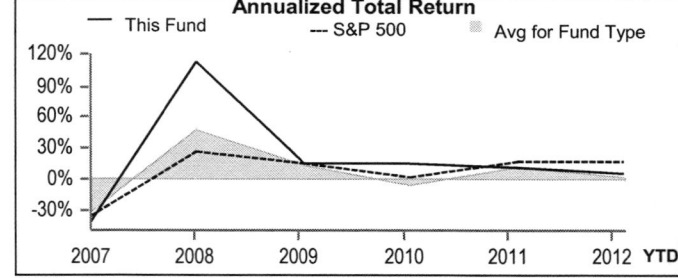

Western Asset High Income Fund (HIF)

C **Fair**

Fund Family: Legg Mason Partners Fund Advisor LL
Fund Type: Corporate - High Yield
Inception Date: January 22, 1993

Data Date	Investment Rating	Net Assets ($Mil)	Price	Performance Rating/Pts	Total Return Y-T-D	Risk Rating/Pts
12-12	C	48.19	9.41	C- / 4.0	2.58%	B / 8.5
2011	C+	46.40	8.93	C+ / 6.5	2.24%	B- / 7.2
2010	B-	46.79	10.05	B+ / 8.4	19.67%	C- / 4.2
2009	C+	40.02	9.24	B- / 7.3	63.57%	C / 5.1

Major Rating Factors: Middle of the road best describes Western Asset High Income Fund whose TheStreet.com Investment Rating is currently a C (Fair). The fund currently has a performance rating of C- (Fair) based on an annualized return of 9.17% over the last three years and a total return of 2.58% year to date 2012. Factored into the performance evaluation is an expense ratio of 1.18% (low).

The fund's risk rating is currently B (Good). It carries a beta of 0.76, meaning the fund's expected move will be 7.6% for every 10% move in the market. Volatility, as measured by both the semi-deviation and a drawdown factor, is considered low. As of December 31, 2012, Western Asset High Income Fund traded at a discount of 3.88% below its net asset value, which is better than its one-year historical average premium of 2.13%.

S. Kenneth Leech has been running the fund for 7 years and currently receives a manager quality ranking of 61 (0=worst, 99=best). If you desire an average level of risk, then this fund may be an option.

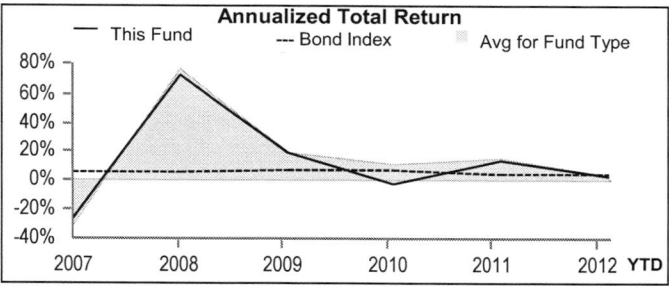

Western Asset High Income Opp Inc. (HIO)

C+ **Fair**

Fund Family: Legg Mason Partners Fund Advisor LL
Fund Type: Corporate - High Yield
Inception Date: October 21, 1993

Data Date	Investment Rating	Net Assets ($Mil)	Price	Performance Rating/Pts	Total Return Y-T-D	Risk Rating/Pts
12-12	C+	473.00	6.44	C+ / 5.7	5.59%	B- / 7.6
2011	B	443.00	6.17	B / 7.8	0.81%	B- / 7.4
2010	C	457.00	6.08	B / 7.6	12.07%	C- / 3.7
2009	C	423.86	5.98	B- / 7.1	61.55%	C- / 3.7

Major Rating Factors: Middle of the road best describes Western Asset High Income Opp Inc. whose TheStreet.com Investment Rating is currently a C+ (Fair). The fund currently has a performance rating of C+ (Fair) based on an annualized return of 12.71% over the last three years and a total return of 5.59% year to date 2012. Factored into the performance evaluation is an expense ratio of 0.88% (low).

The fund's risk rating is currently B- (Good). It carries a beta of 1.09, meaning that its performance tracks fairly well with that of the overall stock market. Volatility, as measured by both the semi-deviation and a drawdown factor, is considered low. As of December 31, 2012, Western Asset High Income Opp Inc. traded at a discount of .16% below its net asset value, which is better than its one-year historical average premium of 4.33%.

Michael C. Buchanan has been running the fund for 7 years and currently receives a manager quality ranking of 45 (0=worst, 99=best). If you desire an average level of risk, then this fund may be an option.

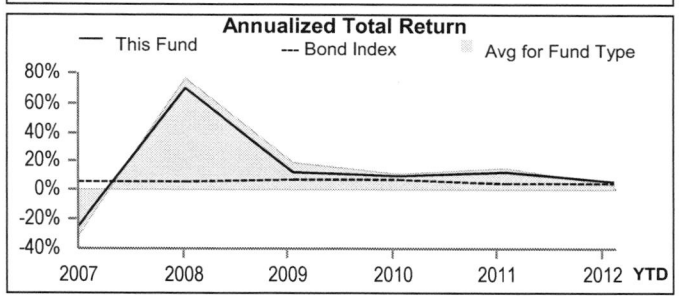

Western Asset High Yld Def Opp (HYI)

C **Fair**

Fund Family: Legg Mason Partners Fund Advisor LL
Fund Type: Corporate - High Yield
Inception Date: October 27, 2010

Data Date	Investment Rating	Net Assets ($Mil)	Price	Performance Rating/Pts	Total Return Y-T-D	Risk Rating/Pts
12-12	C	417.00	18.33	C / 4.8	4.15%	B- / 7.9
2011	D+	384.80	16.56	D+ / 2.3	5.13%	B- / 7.8

Major Rating Factors: Middle of the road best describes Western Asset High Yld Def Opp whose TheStreet.com Investment Rating is currently a C (Fair). The fund currently has a performance rating of C (Fair) based on an annualized return of 0.00% over the last three years and a total return of 4.15% year to date 2012. Factored into the performance evaluation is an expense ratio of 0.89% (low).

The fund's risk rating is currently B- (Good). It carries a beta of 0.00, meaning the fund's expected move will be 0.0% for every 10% move in the market. Volatility, as measured by both the semi-deviation and a drawdown factor, is considered low. As of December 31, 2012, Western Asset High Yld Def Opp traded at a discount of 5.66% below its net asset value, which is better than its one-year historical average premium of 3.17%.

Michael C. Buchanan currently receives a manager quality ranking of 16 (0=worst, 99=best). If you desire an average level of risk, then this fund may be an option.

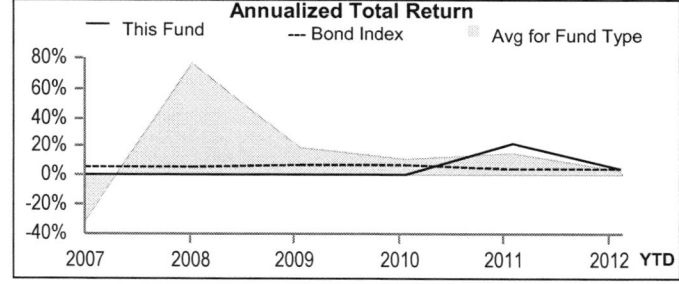

Western Asset Income Fund (PAI)   C+   Fair

Fund Family: Western Asset Management Company
Fund Type: General - Investment Grade
Inception Date: March 15, 1973

Major Rating Factors: Middle of the road best describes Western Asset Income Fund whose TheStreet.com Investment Rating is currently a C+ (Fair). The fund currently has a performance rating of C (Fair) based on an annualized return of 10.94% over the last three years and a total return of 1.28% year to date 2012. Factored into the performance evaluation is an expense ratio of 0.75% (very low).

The fund's risk rating is currently B+ (Good). It carries a beta of 0.31, meaning the fund's expected move will be 3.1% for every 10% move in the market. Volatility, as measured by both the semi-deviation and a drawdown factor, is considered very low. As of December 31, 2012, Western Asset Income Fund traded at a discount of 1.92% below its net asset value, which is better than its one-year historical average premium of 1.06%.

S. Kenneth Leech currently receives a manager quality ranking of 88 (0=worst, 99=best). If you desire an average level of risk, then this fund may be an option.

Data Date	Investment Rating	Net Assets ($Mil)	Price	Performance Rating/Pts	Total Return Y-T-D	Risk Rating/Pts
12-12	C+	135.15	14.82	C / 4.4	1.28%	B+ / 9.0
2011	B-	129.90	13.81	C+ / 6.1	-0.14%	B / 8.3
2010	C+	127.08	12.89	C+ / 6.3	12.19%	C+ / 6.4
2009	C	111.76	12.75	C- / 4.2	29.94%	C+ / 6.1

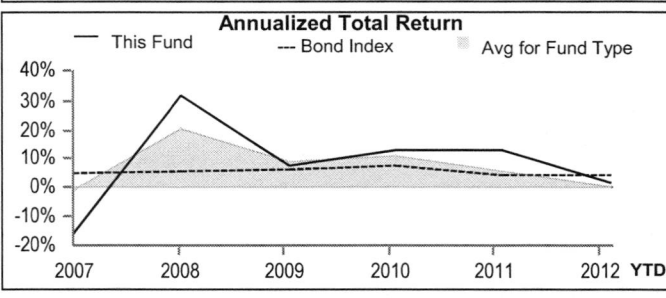

Annualized Total Return

Western Asset Inflation Mgmt (IMF)   C   Fair

Fund Family: Legg Mason Partners Fund Advisor LL
Fund Type: Global
Inception Date: May 25, 2004

Major Rating Factors: Middle of the road best describes Western Asset Inflation Mgmt whose TheStreet.com Investment Rating is currently a C (Fair). The fund currently has a performance rating of C- (Fair) based on an annualized return of 8.76% over the last three years and a total return of -0.85% year to date 2012. Factored into the performance evaluation is an expense ratio of 0.78% (very low).

The fund's risk rating is currently B+ (Good). It carries a beta of 0.10, meaning the fund's expected move will be 1.0% for every 10% move in the market. Volatility, as measured by both the semi-deviation and a drawdown factor, is considered very low. As of December 31, 2012, Western Asset Inflation Mgmt traded at a discount of 6.42% below its net asset value, which is worse than its one-year historical average discount of 8.29%.

S. Kenneth Leech has been running the fund for 7 years and currently receives a manager quality ranking of 89 (0=worst, 99=best). If you desire an average level of risk, then this fund may be an option.

Data Date	Investment Rating	Net Assets ($Mil)	Price	Performance Rating/Pts	Total Return Y-T-D	Risk Rating/Pts
12-12	C	140.72	18.79	C- / 3.3	-0.85%	B+ / 9.5
2011	C+	137.00	17.49	C- / 4.2	0.69%	B+ / 9.6
2010	B-	127.98	17.65	C+ / 6.8	13.46%	B- / 7.0
2009	C+	115.46	16.13	C- / 4.2	13.03%	B- / 7.6

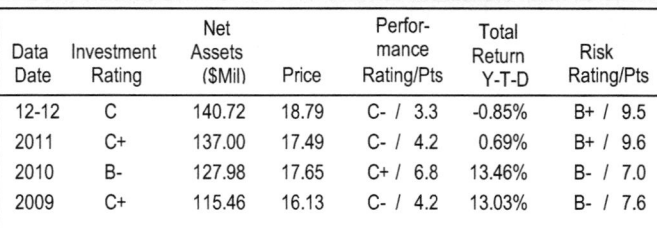

Annualized Total Return

Western Asset Intermediate Muni (SBI)   B+   Good

Fund Family: Legg Mason Partners Fund Advisor LL
Fund Type: Municipal - National
Inception Date: February 27, 1992

Major Rating Factors: Strong performance is the major factor driving the B+ (Good) TheStreet.com Investment Rating for Western Asset Intermediate Muni. The fund currently has a performance rating of B- (Good) based on an annualized return of 11.27% over the last three years and a total return of 1.80% year to date 2012. Factored into the performance evaluation is an expense ratio of 0.92% (low).

The fund's risk rating is currently B+ (Good). It carries a beta of 1.15, meaning it is expected to move 11.5% for every 10% move in the market. Volatility, as measured by both the semi-deviation and a drawdown factor, is considered very low. As of December 31, 2012, Western Asset Intermediate Muni traded at a premium of .47% above its net asset value, which is better than its one-year historical average premium of .57%.

Dennis J. McNamara currently receives a manager quality ranking of 73 (0=worst, 99=best). If you desire only a moderate level of risk and strong performance, then this fund is an excellent option.

Data Date	Investment Rating	Net Assets ($Mil)	Price	Performance Rating/Pts	Total Return Y-T-D	Risk Rating/Pts
12-12	B+	145.00	10.58	B- / 7.5	1.80%	B+ / 9.1
2011	B	141.60	9.80	C+ / 6.8	-0.15%	B+ / 9.2
2010	B-	137.00	9.43	C+ / 6.9	10.70%	B- / 7.2
2009	B	127.61	8.95	C+ / 5.6	25.03%	B / 8.1

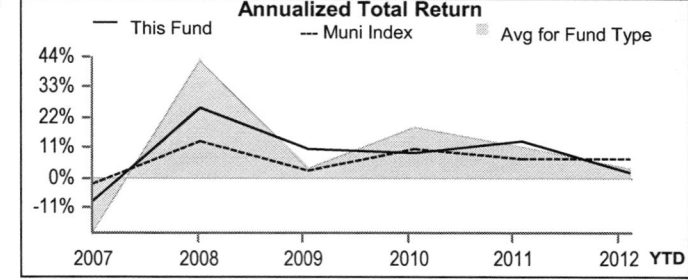

Annualized Total Return

Western Asset Managed High Income (MHY)   C   Fair

Fund Family: Legg Mason Partners Fund Advisor LL
Fund Type: Corporate - High Yield
Inception Date: March 18, 1993

Major Rating Factors: Middle of the road best describes Western Asset Managed High Income whose TheStreet.com Investment Rating is currently a C (Fair). The fund currently has a performance rating of C (Fair) based on an annualized return of 11.52% over the last three years and a total return of 2.92% year to date 2012. Factored into the performance evaluation is an expense ratio of 0.92% (low).

The fund's risk rating is currently B- (Good). It carries a beta of 0.97, meaning that its performance tracks fairly well with that of the overall stock market. Volatility, as measured by both the semi-deviation and a drawdown factor, is considered low. As of December 31, 2012, Western Asset Managed High Income traded at a discount of 1.12% below its net asset value, which is better than its one-year historical average premium of 5.27%.

Stephen A. Walsh currently receives a manager quality ranking of 57 (0=worst, 99=best). If you desire an average level of risk, then this fund may be an option.

Data Date	Investment Rating	Net Assets ($Mil)	Price	Performance Rating/Pts	Total Return Y-T-D	Risk Rating/Pts
12-12	C	283.00	6.17	C / 4.7	2.92%	B- / 7.6
2011	B-	267.50	6.04	B- / 7.2	0.66%	B / 8.0
2010	B	267.47	6.12	B / 7.9	16.81%	C / 5.1
2009	C-	244.39	5.79	C+ / 5.9	45.34%	C- / 4.1

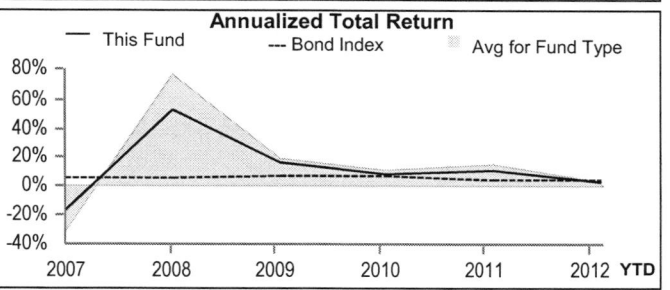

Western Asset Managed Municipals (MMU)   A+   Excellent

Fund Family: Legg Mason Partners Fund Advisor LL
Fund Type: Municipal - National
Inception Date: June 18, 1992

Major Rating Factors:
Strong performance is the major factor driving the A+ (Excellent) TheStreet.com Investment Rating for Western Asset Managed Municipals. The fund currently has a performance rating of B+ (Good) based on an annualized return of 14.08% over the last three years and a total return of 7.52% year to date 2012. Factored into the performance evaluation is an expense ratio of 0.90% (low).

The fund's risk rating is currently B (Good). It carries a beta of 1.68, meaning it is expected to move 16.8% for every 10% move in the market. Volatility, as measured by both the semi-deviation and a drawdown factor, is considered low. As of December 31, 2012, Western Asset Managed Municipals traded at a discount of .62% below its net asset value, which is better than its one-year historical average premium of 3.21%.

Joseph P. Deane has been running the fund for 21 years and currently receives a manager quality ranking of 59 (0=worst, 99=best). If you desire only a moderate level of risk and strong performance, then this fund is an excellent option.

Data Date	Investment Rating	Net Assets ($Mil)	Price	Performance Rating/Pts	Total Return Y-T-D	Risk Rating/Pts
12-12	A+	594.96	14.37	B+ / 8.9	7.52%	B / 8.7
2011	A+	559.40	13.41	A- / 9.2	0.22%	B+ / 9.0
2010	B+	539.18	12.07	B- / 7.3	5.24%	C+ / 6.3
2009	A	494.58	12.19	B- / 7.4	37.29%	B- / 7.2

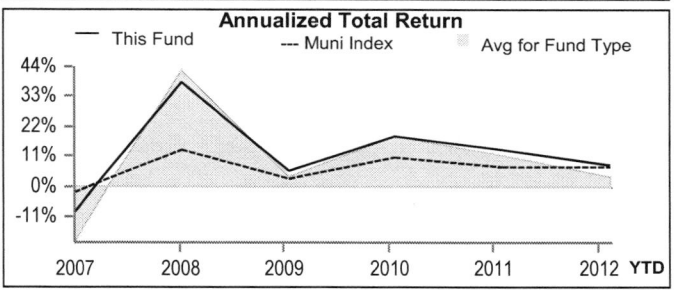

Western Asset Mtge Defined Oppty (DMO)   A+   Excellent

Fund Family: Legg Mason Partners Fund Advisor LL
Fund Type: Mortgage
Inception Date: February 24, 2010

Major Rating Factors:
Exceptional performance is the major factor driving the A+ (Excellent) TheStreet.com Investment Rating for Western Asset Mtge Defined Oppty. The fund currently has a performance rating of A+ (Excellent) based on an annualized return of 0.00% over the last three years and a total return of 6.65% year to date 2012. Factored into the performance evaluation is an expense ratio of 2.24% (high).

The fund's risk rating is currently B (Good). It carries a beta of 0.00, meaning fund's expected move will be 0.0% for every 10% move in the market. Volatility, as measured by both the semi-deviation and a drawdown factor, is considered low. As of December 31, 2012, Western Asset Mtge Defined Oppty traded at a discount of 1.98% below its net asset value, which is better than its one-year historical average premium of 3.69%.

S. Kenneth Leech currently receives a manager quality ranking of 98 (0=worst, 99=best). If you desire only a moderate level of risk and strong performance, then this fund is an excellent option.

Data Date	Investment Rating	Net Assets ($Mil)	Price	Performance Rating/Pts	Total Return Y-T-D	Risk Rating/Pts
12-12	A+	197.29	24.21	A+ / 9.8	6.65%	B / 8.5
2011	C-	197.30	19.61	D / 2.1	0.76%	B / 8.7

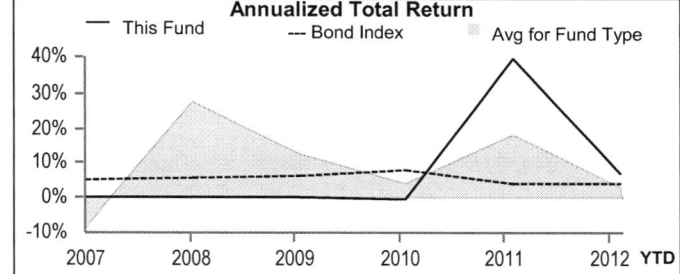

Western Asset Municipal Defined Op (MTT)   B   Good

Fund Family: Legg Mason Partners Fund Advisor LL
Fund Type: Municipal - National
Inception Date: March 27, 2009

Data Date	Investment Rating	Net Assets ($Mil)	Price	Performance Rating/Pts	Total Return Y-T-D	Risk Rating/Pts
12-12	B	272.25	23.06	B- / 7.0	5.59%	B / 8.7
2011	A-	260.30	22.06	B+ / 8.5	-0.27%	B+ / 9.0
2010	C-	256.21	19.89	D- / 1.1	0.51%	B / 8.4

Major Rating Factors: Strong performance is the major factor driving the B (Good) TheStreet.com Investment Rating for Western Asset Municipal Defined Op. The fund currently has a performance rating of B- (Good) based on an annualized return of 10.03% over the last three years and a total return of 5.59% year to date 2012. Factored into the performance evaluation is an expense ratio of 0.68% (very low).

The fund's risk rating is currently B (Good). It carries a beta of 1.56, meaning it is expected to move 15.6% for every 10% move in the market. Volatility, as measured by both the semi-deviation and a drawdown factor, is considered low. As of December 31, 2012, Western Asset Municipal Defined Op traded at a discount of .99% below its net asset value, which is better than its one-year historical average premium of 3.05%.

Robert E. Amodeo currently receives a manager quality ranking of 37 (0=worst, 99=best). If you desire only a moderate level of risk and strong performance, then this fund is an excellent option.

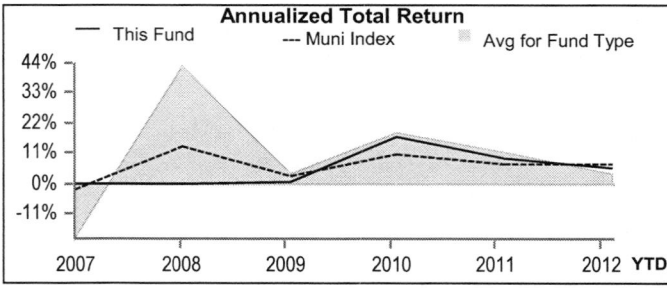

Western Asset Municipal High Inc (MHF)   C+   Fair

Fund Family: Legg Mason Partners Fund Advisor LL
Fund Type: Municipal - High Yield
Inception Date: November 17, 1988

Data Date	Investment Rating	Net Assets ($Mil)	Price	Performance Rating/Pts	Total Return Y-T-D	Risk Rating/Pts
12-12	C+	164.00	7.92	C / 5.4	4.67%	B / 8.7
2011	B+	166.00	7.83	B- / 7.5	-0.13%	B / 8.9
2010	C+	162.00	7.23	C / 4.9	3.19%	B- / 7.3
2009	C+	145.41	7.43	C / 5.1	18.79%	B- / 7.3

Major Rating Factors: Middle of the road best describes Western Asset Municipal High Inc whose TheStreet.com Investment Rating is currently a C+ (Fair). The fund currently has a performance rating of C (Fair) based on an annualized return of 9.21% over the last three years and a total return of 4.67% year to date 2012. Factored into the performance evaluation is an expense ratio of 0.68% (very low).

The fund's risk rating is currently B (Good). It carries a beta of 1.87, meaning it is expected to move 18.7% for every 10% move in the market. Volatility, as measured by both the semi-deviation and a drawdown factor, is considered low. As of December 31, 2012, Western Asset Municipal High Inc traded at a discount of 3.53% below its net asset value, which is better than its one-year historical average premium of 2.68%.

Ellen S. Cammer currently receives a manager quality ranking of 26 (0=worst, 99=best). If you desire an average level of risk, then this fund may be an option.

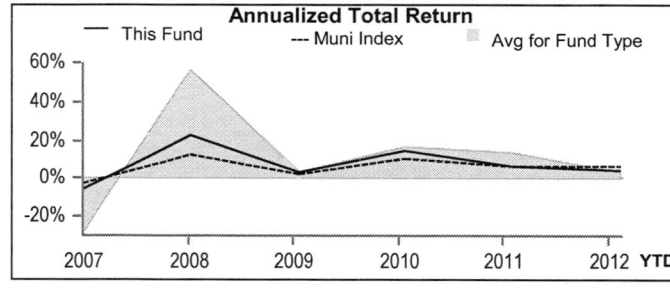

Western Asset Municipal Partners (MNP)   A+   Excellent

Fund Family: Legg Mason Partners Fund Advisor LL
Fund Type: Municipal - National
Inception Date: January 22, 1993

Data Date	Investment Rating	Net Assets ($Mil)	Price	Performance Rating/Pts	Total Return Y-T-D	Risk Rating/Pts
12-12	A+	159.77	17.22	A- / 9.2	2.96%	B / 8.7
2011	A+	152.10	15.36	A / 9.4	0.20%	B / 8.9
2010	C+	143.85	13.26	C+ / 5.7	5.45%	C+ / 6.6
2009	B-	131.23	13.32	C+ / 6.5	42.02%	B- / 7.5

Major Rating Factors:
Exceptional performance is the major factor driving the A+ (Excellent) TheStreet.com Investment Rating for Western Asset Municipal Partners. The fund currently has a performance rating of A- (Excellent) based on an annualized return of 16.43% over the last three years and a total return of 2.96% year to date 2012. Factored into the performance evaluation is an expense ratio of 1.16% (low).

The fund's risk rating is currently B (Good). It carries a beta of 2.08, meaning it is expected to move 20.8% for every 10% move in the market. Volatility, as measured by both the semi-deviation and a drawdown factor, is considered low. As of December 31, 2012, Western Asset Municipal Partners traded at a premium of 2.07% above its net asset value, which is worse than its one-year historical average premium of 1.92%.

Robert E. Amodeo currently receives a manager quality ranking of 62 (0=worst, 99=best). If you desire only a moderate level of risk and strong performance, then this fund is an excellent option.

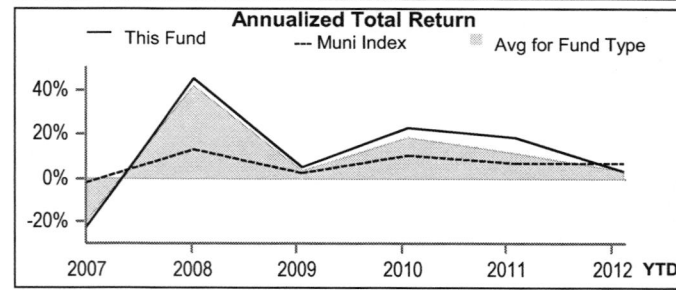

Western Asset Premier Bond Fund (WEA)   B-   Good

Fund Family: Western Asset Management Company
Fund Type: General - Investment Grade
Inception Date: March 25, 2002

Major Rating Factors: Western Asset Premier Bond Fund receives a TheStreet.com Investment Rating of B- (Good). The fund currently has a performance rating of C+ (Fair) based on an annualized return of 17.58% over the last three years and a total return of 5.73% year to date 2012. Factored into the performance evaluation is an expense ratio of 1.10% (low).

The fund's risk rating is currently B (Good). It carries a beta of 0.31, meaning the fund's expected move will be 3.1% for every 10% move in the market. Volatility, as measured by both the semi-deviation and a drawdown factor, is considered low. As of December 31, 2012, Western Asset Premier Bond Fund traded at a premium of 3.19% above its net asset value, which is better than its one-year historical average premium of 14.05%.

S. Kenneth Leech currently receives a manager quality ranking of 94 (0=worst, 99=best). If you desire an average level of risk, then this fund may be an option.

Data Date	Investment Rating	Net Assets ($Mil)	Price	Performance Rating/Pts	Total Return Y-T-D	Risk Rating/Pts
12-12	B-	163.49	15.54	C+ / 6.8	5.73%	B / 8.3
2011	B+	154.20	15.95	B+ / 8.8	0.31%	B- / 7.8
2010	B-	154.24	14.13	B / 7.7	17.57%	C / 4.9
2009	C	117.14	13.36	C+ / 6.6	60.72%	C / 4.5

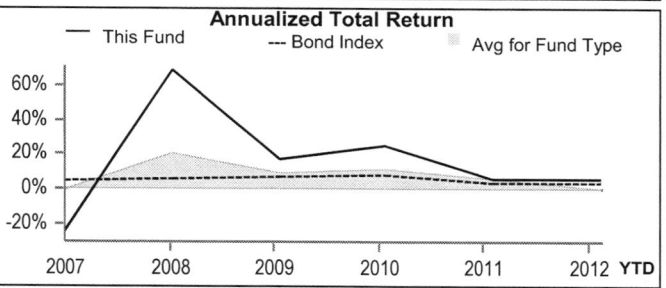

Western Asset Var Rt Strat Fd (GFY)   B-   Good

Fund Family: Legg Mason Partners Fund Advisor LL
Fund Type: Global
Inception Date: October 26, 2004

Major Rating Factors: Strong performance is the major factor driving the B- (Good) TheStreet.com Investment Rating for Western Asset Var Rt Strat Fd. The fund currently has a performance rating of B- (Good) based on an annualized return of 13.93% over the last three years and a total return of 5.16% year to date 2012. Factored into the performance evaluation is an expense ratio of 1.20% (average).

The fund's risk rating is currently B- (Good). It carries a beta of 0.15, meaning the fund's expected move will be 1.5% for every 10% move in the market. Volatility, as measured by both the semi-deviation and a drawdown factor, is considered low. As of December 31, 2012, Western Asset Var Rt Strat Fd traded at a discount of 5.98% below its net asset value, which is better than its one-year historical average discount of 4.98%.

Michael B. Zelouf currently receives a manager quality ranking of 92 (0=worst, 99=best). If you desire only a moderate level of risk and strong performance, then this fund is an excellent option.

Data Date	Investment Rating	Net Assets ($Mil)	Price	Performance Rating/Pts	Total Return Y-T-D	Risk Rating/Pts
12-12	B-	122.94	17.76	B- / 7.5	5.16%	B- / 7.5
2011	C	111.90	14.85	C- / 4.0	0.81%	B / 8.3
2010	B+	113.54	16.99	B / 7.9	25.48%	C / 5.5
2009	C-	126.39	14.14	C- / 3.4	26.80%	C+ / 6.2

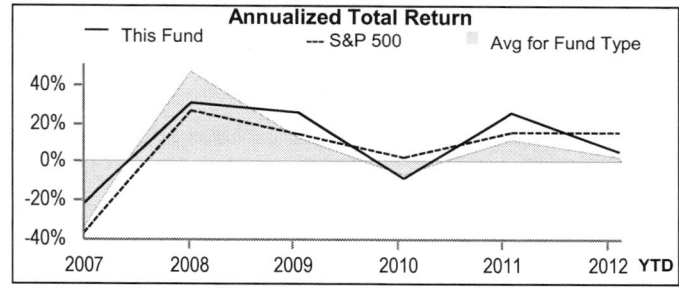

Western Asset Worldwide Inc Fd (SBW)   C+   Fair

Fund Family: Legg Mason Partners Fund Advisor LL
Fund Type: Emerging Market
Inception Date: December 31, 1993

Major Rating Factors: Middle of the road best describes Western Asset Worldwide Inc Fd whose TheStreet.com Investment Rating is currently a C+ (Fair). The fund currently has a performance rating of C+ (Fair) based on an annualized return of 13.68% over the last three years and a total return of 2.84% year to date 2012. Factored into the performance evaluation is an expense ratio of 1.29% (average).

The fund's risk rating is currently B (Good). It carries a beta of 1.00, meaning that its performance tracks fairly well with that of the overall stock market. Volatility, as measured by both the semi-deviation and a drawdown factor, is considered low. As of December 31, 2012, Western Asset Worldwide Inc Fd traded at a discount of 6.32% below its net asset value, which is better than its one-year historical average discount of 5.41%.

S. Kenneth Leech currently receives a manager quality ranking of 88 (0=worst, 99=best). If you desire an average level of risk, then this fund may be an option.

Data Date	Investment Rating	Net Assets ($Mil)	Price	Performance Rating/Pts	Total Return Y-T-D	Risk Rating/Pts
12-12	C+	200.54	15.12	C+ / 5.8	2.84%	B / 8.2
2011	B	194.10	13.78	B / 7.7	-0.29%	B / 8.2
2010	B	184.25	13.30	B- / 7.2	11.85%	C+ / 5.7
2009	B-	152.02	12.75	B- / 7.0	54.15%	C+ / 5.9

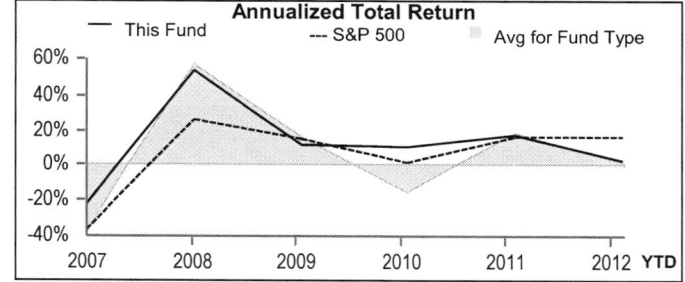

Western Asset/Claymore Inf-Link O& (WIW)
C   Fair

Fund Family: Guggenheim Funds Investment Advisor
Fund Type: US Government/Agency
Inception Date: February 25, 2004

Data Date	Investment Rating	Net Assets ($Mil)	Price	Performance Rating/Pts	Total Return Y-T-D	Risk Rating/Pts
12-12	C	896.97	13.20	D+ / 2.9	0.61%	B+ / 9.6
2011	C+	872.60	12.61	C / 4.5	0.87%	B+ / 9.6
2010	B-	813.12	12.51	C+ / 5.7	7.99%	B- / 7.0
2009	C+	749.85	12.04	C / 4.8	16.70%	B- / 7.3

Major Rating Factors:
Disappointing performance is the major factor driving the C (Fair) TheStreet.com Investment Rating for Western Asset/Claymore Inf-Link O&. The fund currently has a performance rating of D+ (Weak) based on an annualized return of 7.16% over the last three years and a total return of 0.61% year to date 2012. Factored into the performance evaluation is an expense ratio of 0.70% (very low).

The fund's risk rating is currently B+ (Good). It carries a beta of 0.05, meaning the fund's expected move will be 0.5% for every 10% move in the market. Volatility, as measured by both the semi-deviation and a drawdown factor, is considered very low. As of December 31, 2012, Western Asset/Claymore Inf-Link O& traded at a discount of 11.41% below its net asset value, which is better than its one-year historical average discount of 10.83%.

S. Kenneth Leech currently receives a manager quality ranking of 82 (0=worst, 99=best). This fund offers only a moderate level of risk but investors looking for strong performance are still waiting.

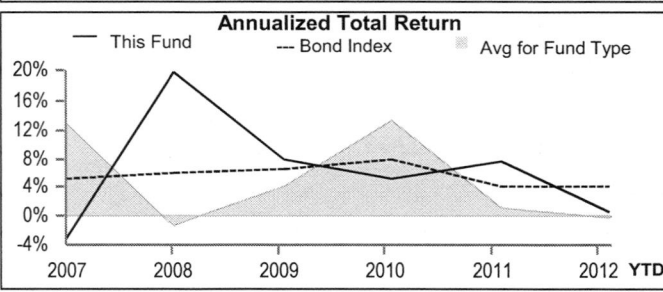

Western Asset/Claymore Inf-Link S& (WIA)
C-   Fair

Fund Family: Western Asset Management Company
Fund Type: US Government/Agency
Inception Date: September 26, 2003

Data Date	Investment Rating	Net Assets ($Mil)	Price	Performance Rating/Pts	Total Return Y-T-D	Risk Rating/Pts
12-12	C-	423.07	13.11	D+ / 2.5	-0.15%	B+ / 9.5
2011	C+	412.20	12.64	C- / 3.8	0.08%	B+ / 9.6
2010	B-	384.76	12.83	C+ / 6.1	8.11%	B- / 7.1
2009	C	356.52	12.30	C / 4.8	15.64%	C+ / 6.8

Major Rating Factors:
Disappointing performance is the major factor driving the C- (Fair) TheStreet.com Investment Rating for Western Asset/Claymore Inf-Link S&. The fund currently has a performance rating of D+ (Weak) based on an annualized return of 5.33% over the last three years and a total return of -0.15% year to date 2012. Factored into the performance evaluation is an expense ratio of 0.72% (very low).

The fund's risk rating is currently B+ (Good). It carries a beta of 0.07, meaning the fund's expected move will be 0.7% for every 10% move in the market. Volatility, as measured by both the semi-deviation and a drawdown factor, is considered very low. As of December 31, 2012, Western Asset/Claymore Inf-Link S& traded at a discount of 10.82% below its net asset value, which is better than its one-year historical average discount of 10.58%.

S. Kenneth Leech has been running the fund for 9 years and currently receives a manager quality ranking of 79 (0=worst, 99=best). This fund offers only a moderate level of risk but investors looking for strong performance are still waiting.

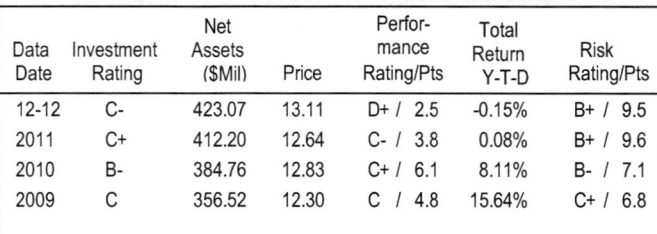

Western Asst Invst Grade Define Op (IGI)
C+   Fair

Fund Family: Legg Mason Partners Fund Advisor LL
Fund Type: Corporate - Investment Grade
Inception Date: June 26, 2009

Data Date	Investment Rating	Net Assets ($Mil)	Price	Performance Rating/Pts	Total Return Y-T-D	Risk Rating/Pts
12-12	C+	230.29	23.05	C / 5.5	3.30%	B / 8.9
2011	B	224.30	21.93	C+ / 6.5	0.05%	B+ / 9.1
2010	C	217.59	20.04	D+ / 2.6	8.40%	B / 8.4

Major Rating Factors: Middle of the road best describes Western Asst Invst Grade Define Op whose TheStreet.com Investment Rating is currently a C+ (Fair). The fund currently has a performance rating of C (Fair) based on an annualized return of 13.04% over the last three years and a total return of 3.30% year to date 2012. Factored into the performance evaluation is an expense ratio of 0.80% (very low).

The fund's risk rating is currently B (Good). It carries a beta of 1.10, meaning it is expected to move 11.0% for every 10% move in the market. Volatility, as measured by both the semi-deviation and a drawdown factor, is considered low. As of December 31, 2012, Western Asst Invst Grade Define Op traded at a premium of 1.72% above its net asset value, which is better than its one-year historical average premium of 3.47%.

Michael C. Buchanan currently receives a manager quality ranking of 67 (0=worst, 99=best). If you desire an average level of risk, then this fund may be an option.

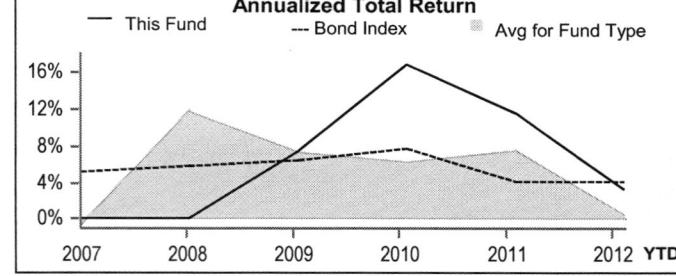

Zweig Fund (ZF)

| | **C-** | | | **Fair** |

Fund Family: Zweig Advisors LLC
Fund Type: Income
Inception Date: September 25, 1986

Major Rating Factors: Middle of the road best describes Zweig Fund whose TheStreet.com Investment Rating is currently a C- (Fair). The fund currently has a performance rating of C- (Fair) based on an annualized return of 7.72% over the last three years and a total return of 4.19% year to date 2012. Factored into the performance evaluation is an expense ratio of 1.13% (low).

The fund's risk rating is currently B- (Good). It carries a beta of 0.91, meaning that its performance tracks fairly well with that of the overall stock market. Volatility, as measured by both the semi-deviation and a drawdown factor, is considered low. As of December 31, 2012, Zweig Fund traded at a discount of 13.94% below its net asset value, which is better than its one-year historical average discount of 11.53%.

Carlton B. Neel has been running the fund for 10 years and currently receives a manager quality ranking of 35 (0=worst, 99=best). If you desire an average level of risk, then this fund may be an option.

Data Date	Investment Rating	Net Assets ($Mil)	Price	Performance Rating/Pts	Total Return Y-T-D	Risk Rating/Pts
12-12	C-	314.20	12.16	C- / 3.4	4.19%	B- / 7.6
2011	C-	310.00	2.90	C- / 4.0	1.38%	B- / 7.6
2010	C-	353.05	3.35	C- / 3.5	13.02%	C+ / 6.5
2009	D	317.86	3.31	D / 1.8	25.34%	C+ / 6.0

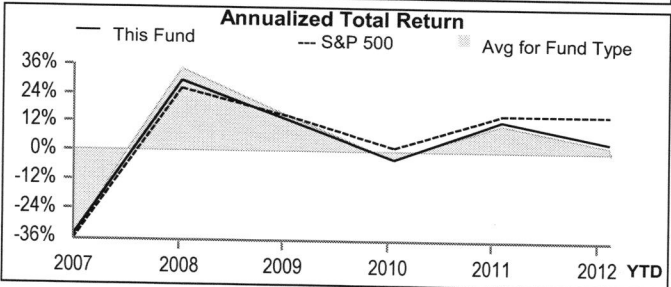

Annualized Total Return

Zweig Total Return Fund (ZTR)

| | **D+** | | | **Weak** |

Fund Family: Zweig Advisors LLC
Fund Type: Growth and Income
Inception Date: September 22, 1988

Major Rating Factors:
Disappointing performance is the major factor driving the D+ (Weak) TheStreet.com Investment Rating for Zweig Total Return Fund. The fund currently has a performance rating of D+ (Weak) based on an annualized return of 3.25% over the last three years and a total return of 3.67% year to date 2012. Factored into the performance evaluation is an expense ratio of 0.92% (low).

The fund's risk rating is currently B (Good). It carries a beta of 0.40, meaning the fund's expected move will be 4.0% for every 10% move in the market. Volatility, as measured by both the semi-deviation and a drawdown factor, is considered low. As of December 31, 2012, Zweig Total Return Fund traded at a discount of 13.80% below its net asset value, which is better than its one-year historical average discount of 12.26%.

Carlton B. Neel has been running the fund for 10 years and currently receives a manager quality ranking of 36 (0=worst, 99=best). This fund offers only a moderate level of risk but investors looking for strong performance are still waiting.

Data Date	Investment Rating	Net Assets ($Mil)	Price	Performance Rating/Pts	Total Return Y-T-D	Risk Rating/Pts
12-12	D+	507.70	12.31	D+ / 2.6	3.67%	B / 8.1
2011	C-	513.80	3.03	C- / 3.1	0.66%	B / 8.1
2010	C	473.22	3.56	C- / 3.5	1.07%	B- / 7.6
2009	C	451.62	3.91	C- / 3.7	27.12%	C+ / 6.9

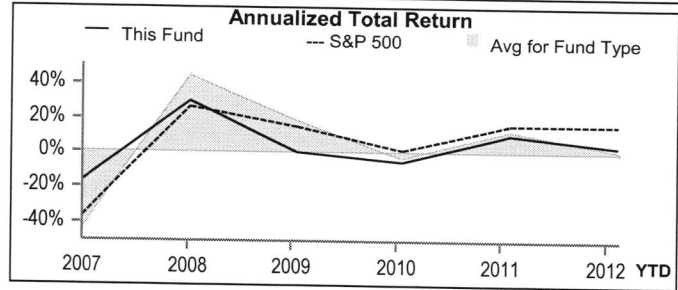

Annualized Total Return

* Denotes ETF Fund

Section III

Top ETFs and
Other Closed-End Funds

A compilation of those

Exchange-Traded Funds and Other

Closed-End Mutual Funds

receiving the highest TheStreet Investment Ratings.

Funds are listed in order by Overall Investment Rating.

Section III Contents

This section contains a summary analysis of each of the top ETFs and other closed-end mutual funds as determined by their overall TheStreet Investment Rating. You can use this section to identify those mutual funds that have achieved the best possible combination of total return on investment and reduced volatility over the past three years. Consult each fund's individual Performance Rating and Risk Rating to find the fund that best matches your investing style.

1. Fund Type

The mutual fund's peer category based on an analysis of its investment portfolio.

COH	Corporate – High Yield	HL	Health
COI	Corporate – Inv. Grade	IN	Income
EM	Emerging Market	LP	Loan Participation
EN	Energy/Natural Resources	MTG	Mortgage
FS	Financial Services	MUH	Municipal – High Yield
FO	Foreign	MUN	Municipal – National
GEI	General – Inv. Grade	MUS	Municipal – Single State
GEN	General Bond	PM	Precious Metals
GL	Global	USA	U.S. Gov. – Agency
GR	Growth	UT	Utilities
GI	Growth and Income		

A blank fund type means that the mutual fund has not yet been categorized.

2. Fund Name

The name of the mutual fund as stated in its prospectus, which can sometimes differ slightly from the name that the company uses for advertising. If you cannot find the particular mutual fund you are interested in, or if you have any doubts regarding the precise name, verify the information with your broker or on your account statement. Also, use the fund's ticker symbol for confirmation. (See column 3.)

3. Ticker Symbol

The unique alphabetic symbol used for identifying and trading a specific mutual fund. No two funds can have the same ticker symbol.

4. Overall Investment Rating

Our overall rating is measured on a scale from A to E based on each fund's risk-adjusted performance. Please see page 10 for specific descriptions of each letter grade. Also, refer to page 7 for information on how our ratings are derived. Most important, when using this rating, please be sure to consider the warnings beginning on page 11 regarding the ratings' limitations and the underlying assumptions.

5. Price

Closing price of the fund on the date shown.

6.	**Performance Rating/Points**	A letter grade rating based solely on the mutual fund's financial performance over the trailing three years, without any consideration for the amount of risk the fund poses. Like the overall Investment Rating, the Performance Rating is measured on a scale from A to E for ease of interpretation. The points score indicates where the Performance Rating falls on a scale of 0 to 10.
7.	**1-Year Total Return**	The total return the fund has provided investors over the preceeding 52 weeks. This total return figure is computed based on the fund's dividend distributions and share price appreciation/depreciation during the period, net of the expenses and fees it imposes on its shareholders.
8.	**1-Year Total Return Percentile**	The fund's percentile rank based on its one-year performance compared to that of all other closed-end funds in existence for at least one year. A score of 99 is the best possible, indicating that the fund outperformed 99% of the closed-end mutual funds. Zero is the worst possible percentile score.
9.	**3-Year Total Return**	The total annual return the fund has provided investors over the preceeding 156 weeks.
10.	**3-Year Total Return Percentile**	The fund's percentile rank based on its three-year performance compared to that of all other closed-end funds in existence for at least three years. A score of 99 is the best possible, indicating that the fund outperformed 99% of the closed-end mutual funds. Zero is the worst possible percentile score.
11.	**5-Year Total Return**	The total annual return the fund has provided investors over the preceeding 260 weeks.
12.	**5-Year Total Return Percentile**	The fund's percentile rank based on its five-year performance compared to that of all other closed-end funds in existence for at least five years. A score of 99 is the best possible, indicating that the fund outperformed 99% of the closed-end mutual funds. Zero is the worst possible percentile score.
13.	**Dividend Yield**	Most recent quarterly dividend to fund investors annualized, expressed as a percent of the fund's current share price. The dividend yield of a fund can have little correlation to the amount of dividends the fund has received from its underlying investments. Rather, dividend distributions are based on a fund's need to pass earnings from both dividends and gains on the sale of investments along to shareholders. Thus, these dividend distributions are included as a part of the fund's total return. Keep in mind that dividend income may be taxed at a different rate than capital gains depending on your income tax bracket.

14. Risk Rating/Points

A letter grade rating based solely on the mutual fund's risk as determined by its monthly performance volatility over the trailing three years. The risk rating does not take into consideration the overall financial performance the fund has achieved or the total return it has provided to its shareholders. Like the overall Investment Rating, the Risk Rating is measured on a scale from A to E for ease of interpretation. The points score indicates where the Risk Rating falls on a scale of 0 to 10.

15. Premium/ Discount

A comparison of the fund's price to its NAV as of the date indicated. The premium (+) or discount (-) indicates the percentage the shares are trading above or below the fund's NAV per share.

If the price is above the fund's NAV, the fund is said to be trading at a premium. If the price is lower than the fund's NAV, the fund is trading at a discount.

16. 1-Year Average Premium/ Discount

The average of the fund's premium/discount over the preceeding year.

It can be useful to compare the fund's current premium/discount to its one-year average. If the fund is currently trading at a premium/discount that is lower/higher than its one-year average, then there has been less demand for the fund in more recent times than over the past year. Conversely, if the fund is currently trading at a premium/discount that is higher/lower than its one-year average, this indicates that there has been greater demand for the fund in more recent times than over the past year.

Fund Type	Fund Name	Ticker Symbol	Overall Investment Rating	Price As of 12/31/12	Performance Rating/Pts	Annualized Total Return Through 12/31/12 1Yr/Pct	3Yr/Pct	5Yr/Pct	Dividend Yield %	Risk Rating/ Pts	Premium/Discount As of 12/31/12	1 Year Average
GR	*Direxion Daily Retail Bull 3X	RETL	A+	99.26	A+ / 9.9	84.71 / 99	--	--	0.00	B- / 7.9	-5.57	0.13
FO	*iShares MSCI New Zealand Inv Mk	ENZL	A+	34.58	A+ / 9.7	34.74 / 95	--	--	5.47	B- / 7.8	-2.21	0.10
FO	*DBX MSCI EAFE Currency-Hedged Eq	DBEF	A+	22.06	A / 9.5	19.21 / 68	--	--	2.71	B / 8.0	-2.43	-0.02
IN	*PowerShares KBW Bank	KBWB	A+	26.27	A / 9.4	24.09 / 82	--	--	1.33	B / 8.6	-3.70	-0.03
HL	*iShares MSCI ACWI ex US HlthCre	AXHE	A+	65.41	A / 9.3	24.29 / 82	--	--	1.18	B / 8.4	-2.69	0.48
COH	*ProShares Ultra High Yield	UJB	A+	50.37	A / 9.3	25.48 / 85	--	--	0.00	B / 8.2	-2.46	-0.04
HL	*SPDR S&P Health Care Services ET	XHS	A+	66.30	A- / 9.2	24.71 / 83	--	--	3.05	B / 8.9	-3.40	-0.02
MTG	*Market Vectors Mtge REIT Income	MORT	A+	25.18	A- / 9.1	26.96 / 87	--	--	12.39	B / 8.8	-6.78	0.12
IN	*SPDR S&P Aerospace & Defense ETF	XAR	A+	62.80	B+ / 8.7	17.14 / 59	--	--	3.59	B+ / 9.1	-4.57	-0.01
MUN	*Market Vectors CEF Muni Inc ETF	XMPT	A+	28.30	B+ / 8.6	15.31 / 81	--	--	6.11	B+ / 9.2	-4.59	0.11
FO	*iShares MSCI Irlnd Capd Inv Mkt	EIRL	A	25.09	A+ / 9.8	37.24 / 96	--	--	0.74	B- / 7.3	-0.28	0.57
FO	*iShares MSCI Philipps Invst Mkt	EPHE	A	34.55	A+ / 9.8	45.19 / 98	--	--	0.24	B- / 7.5	-3.57	0.14
GL	*Vanguard Global ex-US RE I Fd ET	VNQI	A	55.03	A+ / 9.8	40.47 / 97	--	--	8.49	B- / 7.3	-0.09	0.41
GI	*IQ US Real Estate SmCp ETF	ROOF	A	22.48	A+ / 9.7	36.39 / 96	--	--	3.62	B- / 7.5	-4.26	0.10
IN	*PowerShares KBW Premium Yld Eq R	KBWY	A	28.10	A / 9.4	27.82 / 88	--	--	5.53	B- / 7.7	-2.97	0.16
IN	*ProShares Ultra Consumer Goods	UGE	A	94.10	A / 9.4	29.99 / 91	25.65 / 98	11.17 / 74	0.85	B- / 7.9	-9.16	-0.16
IN	*PowerShares KBW Capital Markets	KBWC	A	32.72	A / 9.3	22.28 / 77	--	--	5.41	B- / 7.8	-7.36	-0.07
GR	*PowerShares Fundamental Pure Lg	PXLV	A	21.86	B+ / 8.9	19.60 / 69	--	--	3.07	B / 8.1	-3.45	-0.01
EM	*iShares MSCI Emg Mkts Min Vol In	EEMV	A	60.56	B+ / 8.7	20.57 / 72	--	--	1.27	B / 8.7	0.25	0.43
GR	*Guggenheim S&P Mid Cap 400 Eq Wg	EWMD	A	32.56	B+ / 8.6	17.80 / 61	--	--	2.17	B / 8.8	-3.58	0.01
GR	*Guggenheim S&P Sm Cap 600 Eq Wgh	EWSM	A	32.92	B+ / 8.5	19.87 / 70	--	--	2.56	B / 8.8	-3.46	-0.09
GR	*SPDR S&P Software & Services ETF	XSW	A	62.39	B+ / 8.3	18.88 / 67	--	--	2.63	B / 8.9	-4.38	-0.02
HL	*Direxion Daily Healthcare Bull 3	CURE	A-	52.92	A+ / 9.9	66.44 / 99	--	--	0.03	C+ / 6.9	-12.93	0.01
IN	*ProShares Ultra Consumer Service	UCC	A-	78.44	A+ / 9.8	52.14 / 99	35.36 / 99	14.45 / 88	0.22	B- / 7.1	-6.35	0.08
FO	*First Trust Europe AlphaDEX	FEP	A-	26.20	A+ / 9.7	24.40 / 83	--	--	0.29	B- / 7.2	-1.06	0.77
IN	*SPDR S&P Homebuilders ETF	XHB	A-	26.60	A+ / 9.6	52.39 / 99	22.76 / 94	11.72 / 76	1.18	B- / 7.1	-4.25	-0.01
HL	*EGShares Health Care GEMS ETF	HGEM	A-	22.32	A / 9.5	28.15 / 89	--	--	0.17	B- / 7.3	0.90	-0.06
GR	*First Trust US IPO Index Fund	FPX	A-	30.90	B+ / 8.8	31.61 / 93	17.71 / 82	9.57 / 68	1.28	B / 8.0	-4.04	-0.02
IN	*PowerShares Dynamic Leisure&Ente	PEJ	A-	22.95	B+ / 8.8	25.82 / 85	21.77 / 92	13.01 / 81	0.77	B / 8.0	-4.49	N/A
GR	*Vanguard S&P Mid-Cap 400 Gro ETF	IVOG	A-	69.97	B+ / 8.8	18.78 / 66	--	--	1.39	B- / 7.9	-3.72	0.03
GR	*First Trust Mid Cap Val AlphaDEX	FNK	A-	21.58	B+ / 8.5	17.45 / 60	--	--	1.35	B / 8.4	-3.23	0.21
GR	*First Trust Small Cap Val AlphaD	FYT	A-	22.38	B+ / 8.4	15.26 / 49	--	--	1.37	B / 8.3	-2.82	0.08
IN	*Guggenheim Spin-Off ETF	CSD	A-	29.64	B / 8.2	26.96 / 87	16.82 / 79	6.83 / 54	0.26	B / 8.5	-2.11	0.17
FO	*iShares MSCI ACWI xUS Cnsmr Stp	AXSL	A-	71.04	B / 8.2	20.43 / 72	--	--	1.36	B / 8.6	-1.36	0.18
IN	*FlexShs Morningstar US Mkt Fac T	TILT	A-	59.72	B / 7.9	16.96 / 58	--	--	1.11	B+ / 9.1	-3.33	0.11
IN	*iShares DJ US Home Cons Idx	ITB	B+	21.16	A+ / 9.7	69.50 / 99	21.15 / 91	9.55 / 67	0.48	C+ / 6.4	-4.68	N/A
FO	*iShares MSCI Thailand Inv Market	THD	B+	82.49	A+ / 9.6	39.82 / 97	26.94 / 99	--	1.01	C+ / 6.9	0.01	0.25
IN	*PowerShares Dynamic Bldg & Cons	PKB	B+	17.41	A / 9.4	41.98 / 97	18.58 / 84	5.46 / 47	0.93	B- / 7.1	-3.06	-0.03
GL	*EGShares COnsumer Services GEMS	VGEM	B+	22.14	A / 9.3	20.89 / 73	--	--	0.31	B- / 7.1	-0.09	-0.15
EM	*iShares MSCI Emg Mkts Sm Cap Ind	EEMS	B+	47.30	A / 9.3	20.19 / 71	--	--	6.63	B- / 7.3	-3.11	N/A
HL	*PowerShares Dynamic Pharmaceutic	PJP	B+	34.53	A / 9.3	28.77 / 90	25.51 / 98	16.42 / 94	4.32	B- / 7.1	-5.47	0.03
HL	*ProShares Ultra Health Care	RXL	B+	83.83	A / 9.3	44.11 / 98	20.46 / 89	7.21 / 56	0.71	B- / 7.2	-8.62	-0.06
USA	*Direxion Daily 7-10 Yr Trs Bull	TYD	B+	85.82	B+ / 8.7	6.67 / 27	27.23 / 99	--	0.00	B- / 7.8	1.68	-0.02
IN	*iShares FTSE NAREIT Retail Idx	RTL	B+	35.08	B+ / 8.7	27.54 / 88	22.92 / 94	6.92 / 54	4.79	B- / 7.7	-1.71	N/A
IN	*SPDR S&P Retail ETF	XRT	B+	62.38	B+ / 8.6	21.55 / 75	22.25 / 94	18.04 / 97	3.71	B / 8.0	-1.16	-0.01
IN	*Vanguard Consumer Discret ETF	VCR	B+	75.87	B+ / 8.5	23.94 / 82	19.81 / 88	12.24 / 78	1.52	B- / 7.9	-3.17	0.03
GR	*Consumer Discretionary Sel Sec S	XLY	B+	47.44	B+ / 8.4	23.04 / 80	19.54 / 87	12.42 / 78	2.58	B- / 7.9	-2.99	N/A
IN	*iShares FTSE NAREIT Residential	REZ	B+	48.47	B / 8.2	16.69 / 56	21.25 / 92	11.45 / 75	3.12	B- / 7.9	-1.98	0.02
IN	*iShares DJ US Consumer Services	IYC	B+	86.80	B / 8.1	24.62 / 83	18.50 / 84	11.05 / 73	3.11	B / 8.1	-3.04	N/A
IN	*Guggenheim S&P 500 Pure Value	RPV	B+	34.20	B / 8.0	23.82 / 81	14.15 / 69	7.52 / 57	1.71	B / 8.0	-3.01	-0.01

99 Pct = Best
0 Pct = Worst

Fund Type	Fund Name	Ticker Symbol	Overall Investment Rating	Price As of 12/31/12	Performance Rating/Pts	Annualized Total Return Through 12/31/12			Dividend Yield %	Risk Rating/Pts	Premium/Discount	
						1Yr/Pct	3Yr/Pct	5Yr/Pct			As of 12/31/12	1 Year Average
FO	Thai Fund	TTF	A+	19.95	A+ / 9.8	69.21 / 99	36.28 / 99	19.11 / 99	1.66	B- / 7.8	-14.52	-12.77
FO	Mexico Equity & Income Fund	MXE	A+	14.25	A+ / 9.7	54.56 / 99	26.13 / 98	11.30 / 74	0.00	B / 8.0	-15.43	-11.28
MUN	BlackRock MuniHoldings Fund	MHD	A+	18.36	A+ / 9.6	23.49 / 96	17.52 / 99	13.13 / 99	7.52	B / 8.7	1.60	3.24
MUS	BlackRock MuniYield Invt Fund	MYF	A+	16.87	A+ / 9.6	22.37 / 95	17.94 / 99	12.79 / 99	5.62	B / 8.8	2.12	1.78
MUS	Eaton Vance CA Muni Bond II	EIA	A+	14.10	A+ / 9.6	27.57 / 97	16.50 / 97	9.23 / 87	5.46	B / 8.2	3.91	1.85
MUS	Nuveen CA Quality Inc Muni	NUC	A+	17.35	A+ / 9.6	20.94 / 93	17.52 / 99	12.56 / 99	5.88	B / 8.4	4.27	3.28
MUS	PIMCO CA Municipal Income Fund	PCQ	A+	15.93	A+ / 9.6	24.29 / 96	17.46 / 98	8.79 / 84	5.80	B / 8.3	9.11	8.32
MUS	BlackRock CA Municipal Income Trus	BFZ	A+	16.34	A / 9.5	22.89 / 95	16.94 / 98	9.14 / 86	5.71	B / 8.4	-1.15	-0.21
MUS	BlackRock MuniHoldings CA Qly	MUC	A+	16.34	A / 9.5	18.55 / 89	17.93 / 99	11.85 / 98	5.80	B / 8.6	-0.91	-0.64
MUS	BlackRock MuniYield California Qly	MCA	A+	16.43	A / 9.5	21.56 / 94	17.78 / 99	11.33 / 97	5.55	B / 8.6	-1.73	-2.52
MUS	Nuveen CA Muni Market Opportunity	NCO	A+	16.34	A / 9.5	23.30 / 96	16.96 / 98	11.26 / 97	5.88	B / 8.7	-1.09	0.53
MUN	BlackRock Municipal Income Quality	BYM	A+	16.20	A / 9.4	22.96 / 95	15.38 / 96	10.27 / 92	5.78	B / 8.2	0.25	1.44
MUS	BlackRock MuniYield CA Fund	MYC	A+	16.93	A / 9.4	18.07 / 88	17.83 / 99	11.78 / 98	5.60	B / 8.7	-1.23	-0.95
MUN	BlackRock MuniYield Fund	MYD	A+	16.37	A / 9.4	21.19 / 94	16.92 / 98	11.05 / 96	7.21	B / 8.5	2.44	3.64
MUN	BlackRock MuniYield Quality Fund	MQY	A+	17.64	A / 9.4	20.98 / 93	15.80 / 96	12.39 / 99	5.47	B / 8.4	4.69	1.98
MUS	Nuveen CA Div Adv Muni	NAC	A+	16.10	A / 9.4	19.95 / 92	17.04 / 98	10.81 / 95	5.52	B / 8.5	1.51	-0.43
MUS	Nuveen CA Performance Plus Muni	NCP	A+	16.26	A / 9.4	16.94 / 85	17.51 / 98	11.06 / 96	5.83	B / 8.6	1.37	1.23
MUS	Nuveen CA Select Quality Muni	NVC	A+	16.64	A / 9.4	20.28 / 92	16.55 / 98	12.54 / 99	5.99	B / 8.4	0.12	2.43
MUN	DWS Municipal Income Trust	KTF	A+	14.39	A / 9.3	18.72 / 90	16.63 / 98	14.72 / 99	5.84	B / 8.6	0.14	4.36
MUS	Nuveen OH Quality Inc Muni	NUO	A+	19.05	A / 9.3	23.39 / 96	14.25 / 93	12.75 / 99	5.04	B / 8.8	7.81	4.66
MUS	PIMCO CA Municipal Income Fund II	PCK	A+	10.59	A / 9.3	21.87 / 94	16.47 / 97	3.12 / 43	7.08	B / 8.7	15.86	19.12
MUN	BlackRock MuniHoldings Fund II	MUH	A+	16.64	A- / 9.2	18.29 / 89	16.54 / 97	12.35 / 99	9.27	B / 8.5	-1.42	1.38
MUS	BlackRock MuniHoldings Inv Quality	MFL	A+	16.10	A- / 9.2	20.17 / 92	15.59 / 96	12.22 / 98	5.70	B / 8.5	-0.43	-0.23
MUN	BlackRock MuniVest Fund	MVF	A+	11.03	A- / 9.2	19.23 / 90	15.19 / 95	11.68 / 97	6.42	B / 8.8	2.80	4.59
MUN	BlackRock MuniVest Fund II	MVT	A+	17.51	A- / 9.2	20.33 / 92	16.07 / 97	12.83 / 99	6.60	B / 8.6	5.10	5.84
MUN	BlackRock Strategic Municipal Tr	BSD	A+	14.84	A- / 9.2	18.55 / 89	16.32 / 97	8.17 / 79	5.98	B / 8.5	-2.69	0.66
MUS	Nuveen CA Prem Inc Muni	NCU	A+	15.46	A- / 9.2	16.22 / 84	16.97 / 98	10.72 / 95	5.43	B / 8.7	-3.07	-1.56
MUS	PIMCO CA Municipal Income Fund III	PZC	A+	11.28	A- / 9.2	22.38 / 95	16.10 / 97	3.45 / 46	6.38	B / 8.6	8.88	9.33
MUN	PIMCO Municipal Income Fund II	PML	A+	13.16	A- / 9.2	21.57 / 94	15.06 / 95	5.40 / 61	5.93	B / 8.5	5.45	6.77
MUN	Western Asset Municipal Partners	MNP	A+	17.22	A- / 9.2	19.70 / 91	16.43 / 97	11.89 / 98	4.88	B / 8.7	2.07	1.92
MUN	AllianceBernstein Nat Muni Inc Fun	AFB	A+	15.55	A- / 9.1	19.71 / 91	14.21 / 93	10.59 / 94	5.98	B / 8.8	2.30	3.24
MUN	BlackRock Municipal Bond Trust	BBK	A+	17.00	A- / 9.1	18.70 / 90	15.95 / 97	10.67 / 94	6.05	B / 8.4	0.29	3.74
MUS	BlackRock MuniYield Inv Quality	MFT	A+	15.70	A- / 9.1	19.34 / 91	15.41 / 96	11.74 / 98	5.43	B / 8.7	-1.81	-1.02
MUN	Eaton Vance Municipal Inc Tr	EVN	A+	13.77	A- / 9.1	20.45 / 93	15.65 / 96	9.22 / 86	6.82	B / 8.5	6.09	12.52
MUS	Eaton Vance NY Muni Inc Tr	EVY	A+	15.64	A- / 9.1	18.28 / 88	14.38 / 93	9.26 / 87	5.82	B / 8.6	3.64	3.14
MUN	PIMCO Municipal Income Fund	PMF	A+	15.70	A- / 9.1	17.24 / 86	16.64 / 98	8.87 / 84	6.21	B / 8.5	13.60	17.21
MUS	BlackRock Muni Bond Invt Trust	BIE	A+	17.18	A- / 9.0	17.68 / 88	15.80 / 96	9.07 / 85	5.45	B / 8.6	0.53	-0.12
MUN	BlackRock Municipal Income Trust I	BLE	A+	16.21	A- / 9.0	18.50 / 89	15.19 / 95	10.06 / 91	6.93	B / 8.4	-0.18	3.15
MUN	Dreyfus Strategic Muni Bond Fund	DSM	A+	9.36	A- / 9.0	18.76 / 90	14.99 / 94	10.67 / 94	6.09	B / 8.7	3.20	3.98
MUS	Invesco Van Kampen PA Val Muni Inc	VPV	A+	15.30	A- / 9.0	18.95 / 90	14.54 / 94	10.50 / 93	5.88	B / 8.5	-1.54	0.36
MTG	PCM Fund	PCM	A+	12.02	A- / 9.0	24.67 / 83	24.45 / 96	16.99 / 96	16.76	B / 8.8	3.89	8.27
MUS	BlackRock MuniYield Michigan Qly	MIY	A+	15.65	B+ / 8.9	16.13 / 83	15.07 / 95	10.68 / 95	5.87	B / 8.6	-3.69	-1.60
IN	F&C/Claymore Preferred Sec Inc Fun	FFC	A+	19.55	B+ / 8.9	25.83 / 85	23.07 / 95	15.56 / 91	15.53	B / 8.9	1.14	5.56
MUN	PIMCO Municipal Income Fund III	PMX	A+	12.33	B+ / 8.9	18.28 / 88	15.31 / 95	5.17 / 59	6.81	B / 8.8	9.80	15.53
MUS	PIMCO NY Municipal Income Fund II	PNI	A+	12.78	B+ / 8.9	21.17 / 94	14.50 / 94	5.72 / 64	6.23	B / 8.5	8.67	11.24
MUN	Western Asset Managed Municipals	MMU	A+	14.37	B+ / 8.9	18.73 / 90	14.08 / 92	13.66 / 99	5.43	B / 8.7	-0.62	3.21
MUS	Nuveen NJ Prem Inc Muni	NNJ	A+	16.53	B+ / 8.8	18.59 / 89	14.32 / 93	10.92 / 96	5.15	B / 8.6	1.29	1.32
MUS	BlackRock MuniHoldings NJ Qly	MUJ	A+	16.67	B+ / 8.7	15.67 / 82	13.38 / 90	10.71 / 95	5.33	B / 8.7	0.60	-1.72
MUS	Delaware Inv MN Muni Inc Fund II	VMM	A+	15.22	B+ / 8.5	18.67 / 90	12.84 / 88	8.25 / 79	4.53	B+ / 9.4	-1.55	-2.68
MUN	Neuberger Berman Intermediate Muni	NBH	A+	16.18	B+ / 8.4	13.07 / 71	13.89 / 92	11.10 / 96	5.19	B+ / 9.1	0.87	3.81

* Denotes ETF Fund, N/A denotes number is not available

Section IV

Bottom ETFs and Other Closed-End Funds

A compilation of those

Exchange-Traded Funds and Other

Closed-End Mutual Funds

receiving the lowest TheStreet.com Investment Ratings.

Funds are listed in order by Overall Investment Rating.

Section IV Contents

This section contains a summary analysis of each of the bottom closed-end mutual funds as determined by their overall TheStreet.com Investment Rating. Typically, these funds have invested in securities that are currently out of favor, presenting a risky investment proposition. As such, these are the funds that you should generally avoid since they have historically underperformed most other mutual funds given the level of risk in their underlying investments.

1. **Fund Type**   The mutual fund's peer category based on an analysis of its investment portfolio.

COH	Corporate – High Yield	HL	Health
COI	Corporate – Inv. Grade	IN	Income
EM	Emerging Market	LP	Loan Participation
EN	Energy/Natural Resources	MTG	Mortgage
FS	Financial Services	MUH	Municipal – High Yield
FO	Foreign	MUN	Municipal – National
GEI	General – Inv. Grade	MUS	Municipal – Single State
GEN	General Bond	PM	Precious Metals
GL	Global	USA	U.S. Gov. – Agency
GR	Growth	UT	Utilities
GI	Growth and Income		

A blank fund type means that the mutual fund has not yet been categorized.

2. **Fund Name**   The name of the mutual fund as stated in its prospectus, which can sometimes differ slightly from the name that the company uses for advertising. If you cannot find the particular mutual fund you are interested in, or if you have any doubts regarding the precise name, verify the information with your broker or on your account statement. Also, use the fund's ticker symbol for confirmation. (See column 3.)

3. **Ticker Symbol**   The unique alphabetic symbol used for identifying and trading a specific mutual fund. No two funds can have the same ticker symbol.

4. **Overall Investment Rating**   Our overall rating is measured on a scale from A to E based on each fund's risk-adjusted performance. Please see page 10 for specific descriptions of each letter grade. Also, refer to page 7 for information on how our ratings are derived. Most important, when using this rating, please be sure to consider the warnings beginning on page 11 regarding the ratings' limitations and the underlying assumptions.

5.	**Price**	Closing price of the fund on the date shown.

6. **Performance Rating/Points**

A letter grade rating based solely on the mutual fund's financial performance over the trailing three years, without any consideration for the amount of risk the fund poses. Like the overall Investment Rating, the Performance Rating is measured on a scale from A to E for ease of interpretation. The points score indicates where the Performance Rating falls on a scale of 0 to 10.

7. **1-Year Total Return**

The total return the fund has provided investors over the preceeding 52 weeks. This total return figure is computed based on the fund's dividend distributions and share price appreciation/depreciation during the period, net of the expenses and fees it imposes on its shareholders.

8. **1-Year Total Return Percentile**

The fund's percentile rank based on its one-year performance compared to that of all other closed-end funds in existence for at least one year. A score of 99 is the best possible, indicating that the fund outperformed 99% of the closed-end mutual funds. Zero is the worst possible percentile score.

9. **3-Year Total Return**

The total annual return the fund has provided investors over the preceeding 156 weeks.

10. **3-Year Total Return Percentile**

The fund's percentile rank based on its three-year performance compared to that of all other closed-end funds in existence for at least three years. A score of 99 is the best possible, indicating that the fund outperformed 99% of the closed-end mutual funds. Zero is the worst possible percentile score.

11. **5-Year Total Return**

The total annual return the fund has provided investors over the preceeding 260 weeks.

12. **5-Year Total Return Percentile**

The fund's percentile rank based on its five-year performance compared to that of all other closed-end funds in existence for at least five years. A score of 99 is the best possible, indicating that the fund outperformed 99% of the closed-end mutual funds. Zero is the worst possible percentile score.

13. **Dividend Yield**

Most recent quarterly dividend to fund investors annualized, expressed as a percent of the fund's current share price. The dividend yield of a fund can have little correlation to the amount of dividends the fund has received from its underlying investments. Rather, dividend distributions are based on a fund's need to pass earnings from both dividends and gains on the sale of investments along to shareholders. Thus, these dividend distributions are included as a part of the fund's total return.

Keep in mind that dividend income may be taxed at a different rate than capital gains depending on your income tax bracket.

14. **Risk Rating/Points**   A letter grade rating based solely on the mutual fund's risk as determined by its monthly performance volatility over the trailing three years. The risk rating does not take into consideration the overall financial performance the fund has achieved or the total return it has provided to its shareholders. Like the overall Investment Rating, the Risk Rating is measured on a scale from A to E for ease of interpretation. The points score indicates where the Risk Rating falls on a scale of 0 to 10.

15. **Premium/Discount**   A comparison of the fund's price to its NAV as of the date indicated. The premium (+) or discount (-) indicates the percentage the shares are trading above or below the fund's NAV per share.

    If the price is above the fund's NAV, the fund is said to be trading at a premium. If the price is lower than the fund's NAV, the fund is trading at a discount.

16. **1-Year Average Premium/Discount**   The average of the fund's premium/discount over the preceeding year.

    It can be useful to compare the fund's current premium/discount to its one-year average. If the fund is currently trading at a premium/discount that is lower/higher than its one-year average, then there has been less demand for the fund in more recent times than over the past year. Conversely, if the fund is currently trading at a premium/discount that is higher/lower than its one-year average, this indicates that there has been greater demand for the fund in more recent times than over the past year.

Fund Type	Fund Name	Ticker Symbol	Overall Investment Rating	Price As of 12/31/12	Performance Rating/Pts	Annualized Total Return Through 12/31/12 1Yr/Pct	3Yr/Pct	5Yr/Pct	Dividend Yield %	Risk Rating/ Pts	Premium/Discount As of 12/31/12	1 Year Average
IN	*C-Tracks ETN Citi Volatility Idx	CVOL	E-	29.70	E- / 0.0	-90.16 / 0	--	--	0.00	D / 1.9	25.90	0.16
GR	*Direxion Daily Mid Cap Bear 3X	MIDZ	E-	16.41	E- / 0.0	-48.52 / 1	-49.62 / 0	--	0.00	D+ / 2.4	11.94	-0.01
GR	*Direxion Daily Real Estate Bear	DRV	E-	20.70	E- / 0.0	-48.85 / 1	-60.74 / 0	--	0.00	D / 1.9	6.76	N/A
GI	*Direxion Daily Russia Bear 3x	RUSS	E-	14.85	E- / 0.0	-54.83 / 1	--	--	0.00	D / 1.9	-0.60	-0.19
IN	*Direxion Daily Semiconductor Bea	SOXS	E-	32.84	E- / 0.0	-41.32 / 2	--	--	0.00	D / 1.9	16.45	-0.05
GR	*Direxion Daily Small Cap Bear 3x	TZA	E-	13.50	E- / 0.0	-49.42 / 1	-55.56 / 0	--	0.00	D / 1.9	12.31	-0.01
IN	*IPath S&P 500 VIX Sm-Trm Futr ET	VXX	E-	31.81	E- / 0.0	-78.99 / 0	-61.73 / 0	--	0.00	D / 1.9	21.13	-0.14
GI	*ProShares Ultra VIX Sh-Tm Fut ET	UVXY	E-	20.90	E- / 0.0	-97.51 / 0	--	--	0.00	D / 1.9	50.14	-0.19
GR	*ProShares UltraPro Short MidCap4	SMDD	E-	36.87	E- / 0.0	-48.24 / 1	--	--	0.00	D / 2.2	12.03	0.01
GR	*ProShares UltraPro Shrt Russell2	SRTY	E-	33.74	E- / 0.0	-49.17 / 1	--	--	0.00	D / 1.9	12.20	0.01
EN	*ProShares UltraShort Silver	ZSL	E-	50.07	E- / 0.0	-28.31 / 4	-60.50 / 0	--	0.00	D / 1.9	3.54	-1.08
GEI	*ProShares VIX Short-Term Futures	VIXY	E-	17.01	E- / 0.0	-78.89 / 0	--	--	0.00	D / 1.9	20.90	-0.13
IN	*VelocityShares Daily 2x VIX S-T	TVIX	E-	9.34	E- / 0.0	-97.36 / 0	--	--	0.00	D / 1.9	54.38	8.42
IN	*VelocityShares Dly 2x VIX Med-T	TVIZ	E-	11.48	E- / 0.0	-82.86 / 0	--	--	0.00	D / 1.9	19.46	-0.31
GI	*VelocityShares VIX Medium-Term E	VIIZ	E-	38.65	E- / 0.0	-54.85 / 1	--	--	0.00	D / 1.9	9.24	-0.39
GI	*VelocityShares VIX Short-Term ET	VIIX	E-	17.19	E- / 0.0	-79.00 / 0	--	--	0.00	D / 1.9	21.06	0.03
FO	*Direxion Daily China Bear 3x ETF	YANG	E-	10.45	E- / 0.1	-40.43 / 2	-37.71 / 2	--	0.00	D / 1.9	14.46	-0.18
PM	*Direxion Daily Gold Miners Bull	NUGT	E-	11.00	E- / 0.1	-54.60 / 1	--	--	0.00	D / 1.9	7.63	-0.03
GR	*Direxion Daily Nat Gas Rel Bull	GASL	E-	19.98	E- / 0.1	-36.84 / 2	--	--	0.00	D / 1.9	-6.50	N/A
GR	*Direxion Daily Technology Bear 3	TECS	E-	9.36	E- / 0.1	-41.82 / 2	-41.74 / 1	--	0.00	D+ / 2.3	8.46	N/A
GL	*Direxion Developed Markets Bear	DPK	E-	16.82	E- / 0.1	-53.99 / 1	-38.79 / 1	--	0.00	D / 2.2	6.79	0.02
GL	*Direxion Emerging Markets Bear 3	EDZ	E-	9.02	E- / 0.1	-49.14 / 1	-42.88 / 1	--	0.00	D / 1.9	1.35	-0.04
EN	*Direxion Energy Bear 3x Shares	ERY	E-	7.82	E- / 0.1	-36.27 / 2	-48.07 / 0	--	0.00	D / 1.9	10.45	-0.04
FS	*Direxion Financial Bear 3x Share	FAZ	E-	15.11	E- / 0.1	-58.56 / 1	-46.78 / 0	--	0.00	D / 2.0	14.64	-0.02
GR	*Direxion S&P 500 Bear 3X Shares	SPXS	E-	16.91	E- / 0.1	-43.62 / 2	-42.51 / 1	--	0.00	D+ / 2.7	10.74	N/A
GI	*FactorShares Oil Bull S&P 500 Be	FOL	E-	9.69	E- / 0.1	-53.93 / 1	--	--	0.00	D+ / 2.9	4.64	0.10
EN	*iPath DJ UBS Ntrl Gas Tot Ret Su	GAZ	E-	2.69	E- / 0.1	-21.07 / 5	-42.93 / 1	-44.34 / 0	0.00	D / 1.9	14.47	37.98
GR	*ProShares UltraPro Short QQQ	SQQQ	E-	40.55	E- / 0.1	-47.23 / 1	--	--	0.00	D / 2.2	10.88	0.07
GR	*ProShares UltraPro Short S&P500	SPXU	E-	37.86	E- / 0.1	-43.52 / 2	-41.50 / 1	--	0.00	D+ / 2.8	10.77	-0.01
FO	*ProShares UltraShort MSCI Mex In	SMK	E-	24.81	E- / 0.1	-53.40 / 1	-39.05 / 1	--	0.00	C- / 3.0	9.34	0.13
USA	*Direxion Daily 20+ Yr Treas Bear	TMV	E-	54.24	E- / 0.2	-18.14 / 5	-44.44 / 1	--	0.00	D+ / 2.4	-2.90	0.02
EN	*iPath Cptl Glbl Carbon Tot Ret E	GRN	E-	7.82	E- / 0.2	-29.17 / 4	-33.88 / 2	--	0.00	D / 1.9	3.30	-7.58
IN	*iPath Pure Beta Coffee ETN	CAFE	E-	21.23	E- / 0.2	-37.51 / 2	--	--	0.00	D+ / 2.3	-6.15	-0.06
IN	*IPath S&P 500 VIX Mid-Trm Futr E	VXZ	E-	27.95	E- / 0.2	-55.82 / 0	-28.99 / 3	--	0.00	D / 1.9	9.56	-0.15
GR	*JPMorgan Dbl Short 10 Year Trs E	DSXJ	E-	28.00	E- / 0.2	-34.50 / 3	--	--	0.00	D+ / 2.7	-28.21	-3.51
IN	*ProShares UltraShort Basic Mater	SMN	E-	53.77	E / 0.3	-21.94 / 5	-31.56 / 2	-39.30 / 1	0.00	D+ / 2.7	7.13	0.01
GR	*PowerShares DB Agri Double Sht	AGA	E-	13.03	E / 0.4	-26.22 / 4	-25.49 / 4	--	0.00	D / 1.9	-5.44	8.21
PM	*PowerShares DB Gold Double Sht E	DZZ	E-	4.47	E / 0.4	-8.11 / 9	-29.85 / 3	--	0.00	D / 1.9	-1.76	-0.07
GR	*Direxion Daily Nat Gas Rel Bear	GASX	E-	17.30	E / 0.5	-25.86 / 4	--	--	0.00	D / 2.1	7.99	-0.05
GL	*Global X Uranium ETF	URA	E-	6.51	E / 0.5	-22.62 / 5	--	--	1.90	D+ / 2.6	-4.41	0.25
GR	*PowerShares DB Commodity Double	DEE	E-	26.50	E / 0.5	-2.42 / 12	-19.48 / 4	--	0.00	D / 2.1	-4.64	0.23
GR	*PowerShares DB Crude Oil Dbl Sh	DTO	E-	44.69	E+ / 0.6	3.62 / 22	-15.01 / 5	--	0.00	D / 2.1	4.17	-0.02
FO	*Direxion Daily Latin Amer Bull 3	LBJ	E-	74.14	E+ / 0.7	1.19 / 16	-18.23 / 5	--	0.10	D / 1.9	-8.72	-0.10
EN	*iPath DJ UBS Coffee Tot Ret Sub	JO	E-	32.37	E+ / 0.7	-38.91 / 2	-4.97 / 9	--	0.00	D / 2.1	-6.15	0.05
PM	*PowerShares DB Base Mtls Dbl Lg	BDD	E-	10.82	E+ / 0.7	-10.92 / 8	-15.22 / 5	--	0.00	D+ / 2.4	2.08	-0.07
PM	*PowerShares DB Base Mtls Dbl Sh	BOM	E-	11.87	E+ / 0.7	-7.88 / 9	-8.93 / 7	--	0.00	D / 2.2	-3.02	-0.19
FO	*Direxion Daily China Bull 3x ETF	YINN	E-	18.70	E+ / 0.8	7.58 / 29	-17.61 / 5	--	0.00	D / 1.9	-10.78	0.16
EM	*EGShares Em Mkts Metals&Mining E	EMT	E-	14.50	E+ / 0.9	-2.59 / 12	-8.66 / 7	--	2.95	D / 2.2	-1.76	0.01
GR	*UBS E-TRACS Mnth 2xLevd Itr IPO	EIPL	E-	25.36	E+ / 0.9	-11.04 / 8	--	--	0.00	D / 1.9	-9.53	-1.34
GL	*Direxion Emerging Markets Bull 3	EDC	E-	109.28	D- / 1.2	33.47 / 94	-13.62 / 6	--	0.00	D / 1.9	-0.65	-0.03

99 Pct = Best
0 Pct = Worst

* Denotes ETF Fund, N/A denotes number is not available

99 Pct = Best
0 Pct = Worst

Fund Type	Fund Name	Ticker Symbol	Overall Investment Rating	Price As of 12/31/12	PERFORMANCE Perform-ance Rating/Pts	Annualized Total Return Through 12/31/12 1Yr/Pct	3Yr/Pct	5Yr/Pct	Dividend Yield %	RISK Risk Rating/Pts	VALUATION Premium/Discount As of 12/31/12	1 Year Average
PM	ASA Gold & Precious Metals Ltd	ASA	E	21.53	E+ / 0.9	-17.80 / 5	-3.98 / 10	-0.22 / 18	6.50	D+ / 2.8	-8.89	-7.98
GI	RENN Global Entrepreneurs Fund Inc	RCG	E+	1.42	E / 0.5	-10.12 / 8	-16.89 / 5	-23.48 / 2	0.00	C / 4.7	-44.31	-33.26
GL	Alpine Total Dynamic Dividend Fund	AOD	E+	4.03	E+ / 0.8	7.99 / 30	-11.03 / 7	-9.51 / 5	16.38	C / 4.7	-12.77	-7.82
FO	Templeton Russia&East European Fun	TRF	E+	14.63	E+ / 0.8	5.16 / 24	-9.47 / 7	-10.85 / 4	1.08	C / 5.1	-10.52	-8.91
GL	Alpine Global Dynamic Div Fd	AGD	E+	5.23	E+ / 0.9	13.20 / 42	-7.67 / 8	-9.18 / 5	7.66	C / 4.6	2.35	7.59
FO	India Fund	IFN	E+	20.91	D- / 1.0	14.13 / 45	-8.09 / 8	-8.34 / 6	0.72	C / 4.8	-12.18	-11.28
HL	Engex	EGX	E+	2.06	D / 2.1	31.91 / 93	-5.19 / 9	-18.20 / 3	0.00	D+ / 2.7	-48.76	-24.42
IN	Equus Total Return	EQS	D-	2.36	E+ / 0.8	12.09 / 39	-12.00 / 7	-15.61 / 4	0.00	C / 5.4	-29.13	-34.50
GL	First Trust Active Dividend Inc Fd	FAV	D-	7.55	E+ / 0.9	3.39 / 21	-6.41 / 8	-0.18 / 19	9.54	C+ / 5.9	-14.50	-10.12
IN	Cornerstone Total Return Fund	CRF	D-	5.36	D- / 1.1	13.65 / 43	-3.51 / 10	-4.06 / 10	21.85	C / 5.0	4.28	18.70
IN	Cornerstone Strategic Value Fund	CLM	D-	6.00	D- / 1.3	18.31 / 64	-1.87 / 12	-0.35 / 18	22.18	C / 4.9	4.17	19.23
FO	AGIC Intl & Premium Strategy Fund	NAI	D-	9.70	D / 1.6	16.26 / 54	-1.79 / 12	-0.69 / 17	11.34	C+ / 5.9	-10.43	-1.57
GL	Canadian World Fund Limited	T.CWF	D-	3.45	D / 1.9	-0.85 / 13	1.47 / 18	-8.00 / 6	0.00	C / 4.4	-36.11	-33.14
FO	Morgan Stanley India Inv Fund	IIF	D-	18.53	D / 1.9	22.96 / 79	-2.71 / 11	-5.44 / 8	0.00	C / 5.2	-10.44	-10.86
FO	BlackRock Intl Grth and Inc Tr	BGY	D-	7.35	D / 2.1	16.50 / 55	-0.53 / 14	-0.23 / 18	9.14	C / 4.6	-14.53	-9.73
FO	Asia Tigers Fund	GRR	D-	12.59	D / 2.2	22.72 / 79	-1.55 / 12	-1.73 / 14	0.16	C / 5.2	-7.83	-8.49
EN	ING Risk Managed Nat Resources Fun	IRR	D	10.34	E+ / 0.9	2.58 / 19	-5.82 / 8	1.95 / 27	10.83	C+ / 6.8	-10.94	-6.05
UT	Gabelli Utility Trust	GUT	D	6.16	D- / 1.2	-4.99 / 10	1.11 / 17	4.90 / 43	9.95	C+ / 6.6	10.39	33.95
IN	Eaton Vance Risk Mgd Div Eq Inc	ETJ	D	10.43	D- / 1.3	13.70 / 44	-3.91 / 10	1.89 / 26	10.70	C+ / 6.6	-14.72	-14.15
UT	Wells Fargo Avtg Utilities&High In	ERH	D	11.18	D- / 1.3	5.97 / 26	-1.60 / 12	-6.74 / 7	8.05	C+ / 6.5	-6.29	-0.11
FO	Japan Smaller Cap Fund Inc.	JOF	D	7.20	D- / 1.4	0.81 / 15	-0.65 / 14	-1.39 / 15	0.00	B- / 7.3	-12.41	-12.83
GI	The Cushing MLP Total Return Fund	SRV	D	7.17	D- / 1.4	-9.87 / 8	3.53 / 24	-3.44 / 10	12.55	C+ / 6.7	7.98	25.23
GR	Columbia Seligman Prem Tech Gro	STK	D	14.51	D / 1.6	3.36 / 21	0.13 / 15	--	12.75	B- / 7.0	-7.34	-3.00
IN	BlackRock Real Asset Equity Trust	BCF	D	10.26	D / 1.8	1.20 / 16	1.72 / 19	1.94 / 26	8.64	C+ / 6.6	-8.80	-3.17
FO	Aberdeen Israel Fund	ISL	D	13.10	D / 2.0	8.85 / 32	-0.60 / 14	-2.72 / 12	1.33	C+ / 6.7	-17.61	-13.34
GL	Nuveen Global Value Opportunities	JGV	D	14.91	D / 2.0	0.36 / 14	1.74 / 19	5.78 / 47	7.78	B- / 7.1	-8.42	-6.77
USA	Federated Enhanced Treasury Income	FTT	D	14.18	D / 2.1	2.73 / 19	--	--	6.18	B- / 7.5	-10.31	-9.76
PM	GAMCO Global Gold Nat ResandIncome	GGN	D	12.80	D / 2.1	-0.15 / 14	3.25 / 23	-3.39 / 10	11.25	C+ / 6.2	-4.55	4.09
IN	BlackRock Res & Commdty Strat Trus	BCX	D	12.82	D / 2.2	4.08 / 23	--	--	9.05	C+ / 5.8	-14.59	-8.01
GEN	Putnam Master Intermediate Inc Tr	PIM	D	5.06	D / 2.2	9.48 / 34	2.51 / 21	5.09 / 44	6.17	C+ / 6.2	-9.32	-5.80
EM	Templeton Emerging Markets Fd	EMF	D	20.00	D / 2.2	10.51 / 36	-0.16 / 14	4.31 / 39	1.44	C+ / 6.5	-9.05	-7.77
GI	Advent/Claymore Gbl Con Sec & Inc	AGC	D	6.48	D+ / 2.4	12.71 / 40	0.82 / 17	-4.28 / 9	8.70	C+ / 6.0	-14.85	-8.99
EN	BlackRock EcoSolutions Investment	BQR	D	8.39	D+ / 2.5	13.17 / 42	1.64 / 19	-2.08 / 13	8.55	C+ / 6.3	-11.68	-3.20
FO	Latin American Discovery Fund	LDF	D	15.59	D+ / 2.5	11.78 / 38	1.99 / 20	1.88 / 26	1.56	C+ / 6.3	-11.72	-8.94
GL	BlackRock Global Opportunities Eq	BOE	D	13.20	D+ / 2.6	13.65 / 43	1.81 / 19	2.21 / 28	9.45	C+ / 6.2	-14.73	-8.48
IN	Cornerstone Progressive Return Fun	CFP	D	5.01	D+ / 2.7	9.30 / 33	4.76 / 29	-0.34 / 18	21.89	C / 5.5	3.73	16.53
IN	Eaton Vance Enhanced Eqty Inc II	EOS	D	10.44	D+ / 2.7	14.39 / 46	3.24 / 23	2.55 / 29	10.06	C+ / 6.8	-14.78	-12.12
GEN	Putnam Premier Income Trust	PPT	D	5.46	D+ / 2.7	12.10 / 39	5.70 / 31	7.45 / 57	5.71	C+ / 6.0	-8.39	-4.55
FO	Canadian General Investments Ltd	T.CGI	D	15.75	D+ / 2.8	4.07 / 22	5.63 / 31	-3.67 / 10	1.52	C / 4.9	-29.44	-27.61
EN	GAMCO Nat Res Gold & Income Trust	GNT	D	13.66	C- / 3.0	10.33 / 35	--	--	12.30	C+ / 6.1	-2.98	4.62
FO	Morgan Stanley China A Share Fund	CAF	D	24.05	C- / 3.2	23.62 / 81	1.07 / 17	1.22 / 23	0.00	C+ / 5.8	4.16	-7.37
FO	China Fund	CHN	D	21.41	C- / 3.6	19.44 / 69	2.28 / 21	4.67 / 41	1.72	C+ / 5.9	-6.99	-8.92
FO	Aberdeen Chile Fund	CH	D	15.09	C- / 3.7	5.23 / 24	10.13 / 48	12.13 / 77	3.73	C / 5.4	-3.33	2.54
EN	BlackRock Energy & Resources	BGR	D+	23.55	D+ / 2.5	2.75 / 19	5.00 / 29	4.33 / 39	6.88	B- / 7.1	-11.53	-5.49
IN	BlackRock Enhanced Equity Div	BDJ	D+	7.18	D+ / 2.6	12.61 / 40	3.98 / 26	3.12 / 32	7.80	B- / 7.9	-14.73	-11.13
GL	ING Gobal Equity Dividend Premium	IGD	D+	8.67	D+ / 2.6	16.04 / 53	1.56 / 19	1.13 / 23	11.63	B- / 7.0	-11.80	-5.88
IN	Eaton Vance Enhanced Eqty Inc	EOI	D+	10.66	D+ / 2.8	18.28 / 64	2.37 / 21	2.21 / 28	9.73	B- / 7.1	-15.93	-13.04
GL	Advent Claymore Enhanced Gr & Inc	LCM	D+	9.10	D+ / 2.9	13.30 / 42	3.66 / 25	2.06 / 27	9.23	C+ / 6.7	-17.05	-10.35
IN	Madison Covered Call & Equity Stra	MCN	D+	7.62	D+ / 2.9	12.61 / 40	4.44 / 28	4.21 / 38	9.45	B- / 7.5	-13.80	-11.02
GL	Eaton Vance Tx Mgd Glb Buy Wrt Opp	ETW	D+	10.69	C- / 3.6	18.77 / 66	5.13 / 30	4.81 / 43	10.93	C+ / 6.9	-15.09	-13.35

* Denotes ETF Fund, N/A denotes number is not available

Section V

Performance:
Best and Worst
ETFs and Other
Closed-End Funds

A compilation of those

Exchange-Traded Funds and Other

Closed-End Mutual Funds

receiving the highest and lowest Performance Ratings.

Funds are listed in order by Performance Rating.

Section V Contents

This section contains a summary analysis of each of the top and bottom ETFs and other closed-end mutual funds as determined by their respective TheStreet Performance Ratings. Since the Performance Rating does not take into consideration the amount of risk a fund poses, the selection of funds presented here is based solely on each fund's financial performance over the past three years.

You can use this section to identify those funds that have historically given shareholders the highest returns on their investments. A word of caution though: past performance is not necessarily indicative of future results. While these funds have provided the highest returns, some of them may be currently overvalued and due for a correction.

1.	**Fund Type**	The mutual fund's peer category based on an analysis of its investment portfolio.	

COH	Corporate – High Yield
COI	Corporate – Inv. Grade
EM	Emerging Market
EN	Energy/Natural Resources
FS	Financial Services
FO	Foreign
GEI	General – Inv. Grade
GEN	General Bond
GL	Global
GR	Growth
GI	Growth and Income
HL	Health
IN	Income
LP	Loan Participation
MTG	Mortgage
MUH	Municipal – High Yield
MUN	Municipal – National
MUS	Municipal – Single State
PM	Precious Metals
USA	U.S. Gov. – Agency
UT	Utilities

A blank fund type means that the mutual fund has not yet been categorized.

2. Fund Name   The name of the mutual fund as stated in its prospectus, which can sometimes differ slightly from the name that the company uses for advertising. If you cannot find the particular mutual fund you are interested in, or if you have any doubts regarding the precise name, verify the information with your broker or on your account statement. Also, use the fund's ticker symbol for confirmation. (See column 3.)

3. Ticker Symbol   The unique alphabetic symbol used for identifying and trading a specific mutual fund. No two funds can have the same ticker symbol.

4. Overall Investment Rating   Our overall rating is measured on a scale from A to E based on each fund's risk-adjusted performance. Please see page 10 for specific descriptions of each letter grade. Also, refer to page 7 for information on how our ratings are derived. Most important, when using this rating, please be sure to consider the warnings beginning on page 11 regarding the ratings' limitations and the underlying assumptions.

5. Price   Closing price of the fund on the date shown.

6.	**Performance Rating/Points**	A letter grade rating based solely on the mutual fund's financial performance over the trailing three years, without any consideration for the amount of risk the fund poses. Like the overall Investment Rating, the Performance Rating is measured on a scale from A to E for ease of interpretation. The points score indicates where the Performance Rating falls on a scale of 0 to 10.
7.	**1-Year Total Return**	The total return the fund has provided investors over the preceeding 52 weeks. This total return figure is computed based on the fund's dividend distributions and share price appreciation/depreciation during the period, net of the expenses and fees it imposes on its shareholders.
8.	**1-Year Total Return Percentile**	The fund's percentile rank based on its one-year performance compared to that of all other closed-end funds in existence for at least one year. A score of 99 is the best possible, indicating that the fund outperformed 99% of the closed-end mutual funds. Zero is the worst possible percentile score.
9.	**3-Year Total Return**	The total annual return the fund has provided investors over the preceeding 156 weeks.
10.	**3-Year Total Return Percentile**	The fund's percentile rank based on its three-year performance compared to that of all other closed-end funds in existence for at least three years. A score of 99 is the best possible, indicating that the fund outperformed 99% of the closed-end mutual funds. Zero is the worst possible percentile score.
11.	**5-Year Total Return**	The total annual return the fund has provided investors over the preceeding 260 weeks.
12.	**5-Year Total Return Percentile**	The fund's percentile rank based on its five-year performance compared to that of all other closed-end funds in existence for at least five years. A score of 99 is the best possible, indicating that the fund outperformed 99% of the closed-end mutual funds. Zero is the worst possible percentile score.
13.	**Dividend Yield**	Most recent quarterly dividend to fund investors annualized, expressed as a percent of the fund's current share price. The dividend yield of a fund can have little correlation to the amount of dividends the fund has received from its underlying investments. Rather, dividend distributions are based on a fund's need to pass earnings from both dividends and gains on the sale of investments along to shareholders. Thus, these dividend distributions are included as a part of the fund's total return.
		Keep in mind that dividend income may be taxed at a different rate than capital gains depending on your income tax bracket.

14. Risk Rating/Points

A letter grade rating based solely on the mutual fund's risk as determined by its monthly performance volatility over the trailing three years. The risk rating does not take into consideration the overall financial performance the fund has achieved or the total return it has provided to its shareholders. Like the overall Investment Rating, the Risk Rating is measured on a scale from A to E for ease of interpretation. The points score indicates where the Risk Rating falls on a scale of 0 to 10.

15. Premium/ Discount

A comparison of the fund's price to its NAV as of the date indicated. The premium (+) or discount (-) indicates the percentage the shares are trading above or below the fund's NAV per share.

If the price is above the fund's NAV, the fund is said to be trading at a premium. If the price is lower than the fund's NAV, the fund is trading at a discount.

16. 1-Year Average Premium/ Discount

The average of the fund's premium/discount over the preceeding year.

It can be useful to compare the fund's current premium/discount to its one-year average. If the fund is currently trading at a premium/discount that is lower/higher than its one-year average, then there has been less demand for the fund in more recent times than over the past year. Conversely, if the fund is currently trading at a premium/discount that is higher/lower than its one-year average, this indicates that there has been greater demand for the fund in more recent times than over the past year.

Fund Type	Fund Name	Ticker Symbol	Overall Investment Rating	Price As of 12/31/12	Performance Rating/Pts	Annualized Total Return Through 12/31/12 1Yr/Pct	3Yr/Pct	5Yr/Pct	Dividend Yield %	Risk Rating/Pts	Premium/Discount As of 12/31/12	1 Year Average
GR	*Direxion Daily Retail Bull 3X	RETL	A+	99.26	A+ / 9.9	84.71 / 99	--	--	0.00	B- / 7.9	-5.57	0.13
HL	*Direxion Daily Healthcare Bull 3	CURE	A-	52.92	A+ / 9.9	66.44 / 99	--	--	0.03	C+ / 6.9	-12.93	0.01
GI	*EGShares India Consumer ETF	INCO	B+	24.32	A+ / 9.9	44.13 / 98	--	--	0.00	C+ / 6.7	2.83	0.48
GEI	*VelocityShares Dly Invs VIX M-T	ZIV	B	23.77	A+ / 9.9	99.69 / 99	--	--	0.00	C / 5.3	-8.05	0.27
FS	*iShares MSCI Europ Finls Sctr Id	EUFN	B-	19.80	A+ / 9.9	44.74 / 98	--	--	1.70	C / 5.2	-5.17	0.14
IN	*ProShares Ultra MSCI EAFE	EFO	C+	78.88	A+ / 9.9	40.38 / 97	--	--	0.00	C / 4.4	-4.33	-0.11
FO	*ProShares Ultra MSCI Pacific ex-	UXJ	C+	37.92	A+ / 9.9	44.88 / 98	--	--	0.00	C- / 4.0	-2.69	-0.10
FO	*ProShares Ultra MSCI Europe	UPV	C+	33.44	A+ / 9.9	50.40 / 99	--	--	0.00	C- / 3.7	-5.70	-0.04
FO	*ProShares Ultra MSCI Mex Invest	UMX	C+	49.02	A+ / 9.9	74.42 / 99	--	--	0.00	C / 4.6	-7.68	-0.25
GL	*PowerShares DB 3x Itn Trs B Fut	ITLT	C+	30.05	A+ / 9.9	119.41 / 99	--	--	0.00	C- / 3.8	23.51	6.18
GR	*UBS E-TRACS 2x Levd Long WF BDC	BDCL	C+	26.06	A+ / 9.9	60.83 / 99	--	--	7.04	C- / 4.2	-4.65	-0.03
FO	*Global X FTSE Greece 20 ETF	GREK	C+	18.06	A+ / 9.9	48.10 / 98	--	--	0.13	C / 4.4	-4.75	1.00
HL	*ProShares Ultra Nasdaq Biotech	BIB	C	57.97	A+ / 9.9	62.43 / 99	--	--	0.00	D+ / 2.6	-10.86	-0.03
GI	*ProShares Short VIX Sh-Tm Fut ET	SVXY	C	65.45	A+ / 9.9	164.27 / 99	--	--	0.00	D+ / 2.5	-15.95	0.19
GR	*ProShares UltraPro MidCap400	UMDD	C-	84.85	A+ / 9.9	51.19 / 99	--	--	0.00	D / 2.1	-9.91	-0.07
GR	*ProShares UltraPro Russell2000	URTY	C-	71.13	A+ / 9.9	45.22 / 98	--	--	0.03	D / 1.9	-10.39	-0.05
GI	*VelocityShares Dly Invs VIX ST E	XIV	C-	16.57	A+ / 9.9	168.59 / 99	--	--	0.00	D / 1.9	-16.06	-0.03
FO	*iShares MSCI Philipps Invst Mkt	EPHE	A	34.55	A+ / 9.8	45.19 / 98	--	--	0.24	B- / 7.5	-3.57	0.14
FO	*iShares MSCI Irlnd Capd Inv Mkt	EIRL	A	25.09	A+ / 9.8	37.24 / 96	--	--	0.74	B- / 7.3	-0.28	0.57
GL	*Vanguard Global ex-US RE I Fd ET	VNQI	A	55.03	A+ / 9.8	40.47 / 97	--	--	8.49	B- / 7.3	-0.09	0.41
IN	*ProShares Ultra Consumer Service	UCC	A-	78.44	A+ / 9.8	52.14 / 99	35.36 / 99	14.45 / 88	0.22	B- / 7.1	-6.35	0.08
GL	*First Trust NASDAQ Global Auto	CARZ	B+	29.12	A+ / 9.8	26.04 / 85	--	--	0.69	C+ / 6.6	-2.90	0.17
FO	*EGShares China Infrastructure ET	CHXX	B	19.63	A+ / 9.8	30.62 / 92	--	--	1.21	C / 5.4	-1.41	-0.13
FO	*First Trust China AlphaDEX	FCA	B	25.13	A+ / 9.8	29.58 / 90	--	--	1.06	C+ / 5.8	-2.10	0.23
IN	*Market Vectors Biotech ETF	BBH	B	53.50	A+ / 9.8	42.75 / 98	--	--	0.03	C+ / 6.1	-5.73	0.05
IN	*Market Vectors Bank and Brokerag	RKH	B	45.73	A+ / 9.8	31.01 / 92	--	--	1.88	C+ / 6.0	-4.65	0.01
FO	*iShares MSCI Poland Invstbl Mkt	EPOL	B-	29.62	A+ / 9.8	39.88 / 97	--	--	4.25	C / 4.8	2.00	0.21
FO	*iShares MSCI China Small Cap Ind	ECNS	B-	41.09	A+ / 9.8	31.87 / 93	--	--	2.18	C / 5.2	-3.93	-0.26
GR	*Direxion Daily Real Estate Bull	DRN	C-	77.50	A+ / 9.8	57.28 / 99	39.96 / 99	--	0.00	D / 1.9	-6.08	-0.02
GR	*ProShares UltraPro QQQ	TQQQ	C-	51.69	A+ / 9.8	47.95 / 98	--	--	0.00	D / 1.9	-8.96	-0.01
IN	*iPath Long Ext Rus 2000 TR Idx E	RTLA	C-	75.46	A+ / 9.8	43.34 / 98	--	--	0.00	D / 2.1	-9.37	-0.03
IN	*Direxion Daily Basic Mat Bull 3x	MATL	C-	29.33	A+ / 9.8	20.43 / 72	--	--	0.00	D / 2.0	-11.42	-0.06
FO	*iShares MSCI New Zealand Inv Mk	ENZL	A+	34.58	A+ / 9.7	34.74 / 95	--	--	5.47	B- / 7.8	-2.21	0.10
GI	*IQ US Real Estate SmCp ETF	ROOF	A	22.48	A+ / 9.7	36.39 / 96	--	--	3.62	B- / 7.5	-4.26	0.10
FO	*First Trust Europe AlphaDEX	FEP	A-	26.20	A+ / 9.7	24.40 / 83	--	--	0.29	B- / 7.2	-1.06	0.77
IN	*iShares DJ US Home Cons Idx	ITB	B+	21.16	A+ / 9.7	69.50 / 99	21.15 / 91	9.55 / 67	0.48	C+ / 6.4	-4.68	N/A
GL	*EGShares Industrials GEMS ETF	IGEM	B+	20.67	A+ / 9.7	29.56 / 90	--	--	0.94	C+ / 6.8	-0.34	-0.09
FS	*iShares MSCI ACWI ex US Fn Sctr	AXFN	B+	23.40	A+ / 9.7	33.40 / 94	--	--	4.76	C+ / 6.6	-2.42	0.13
EM	*iShares MSCI Emg Mkts Finls Sctr	EMFN	B+	27.65	A+ / 9.7	28.09 / 88	--	--	0.40	C+ / 6.6	0.58	0.44
FO	*Schwab Intl Small-Cap Equity ETF	SCHC	B	27.05	A+ / 9.7	24.30 / 82	--	--	5.99	C+ / 6.0	-1.74	0.48
FO	*Global X Brazil Consumer ETF	BRAQ	B	20.27	A+ / 9.7	26.72 / 87	--	--	1.21	C+ / 6.1	0.40	-0.13
FO	*Market Vectors Germany SmallCap	GERJ	B	22.91	A+ / 9.7	30.79 / 92	--	--	2.68	C+ / 6.0	-2.26	0.01
IN	*Brclys ETN+InvS&P500 VIX STF ETN	IVOP	B	35.44	A+ / 9.7	47.46 / 98	--	--	0.00	C / 5.5	-2.53	-0.14
GL	*UBS E-TRACS Monthly 2X LISE CCTR	LSKY	C+	36.00	A+ / 9.7	31.94 / 93	--	--	0.00	C- / 3.8	-8.56	-0.03
IN	*iPath Long Ext S&P 500 TR Idx ET	SFLA	C	85.71	A+ / 9.7	41.26 / 97	--	--	0.00	C- / 3.4	-6.79	-0.38
GR	*Direxion Daily Mid Cap Bull 3X	MIDU	C-	37.66	A+ / 9.7	54.09 / 99	27.74 / 99	--	0.00	D / 1.9	-10.63	-0.08
IN	*SPDR S&P Homebuilders ETF	XHB	A-	26.60	A+ / 9.6	52.39 / 99	22.76 / 94	11.72 / 76	1.18	B- / 7.1	-4.25	-0.01
FO	*iShares MSCI Thailand Inv Market	THD	B+	82.49	A+ / 9.6	39.82 / 97	26.94 / 99	--	1.01	C+ / 6.9	0.01	0.25
IN	*ProShares Ultra Real Estate	URE	B	69.09	A+ / 9.6	40.33 / 97	30.24 / 99	-9.85 / 5	0.50	C+ / 6.0	-5.37	-0.02
FO	*Global X FTSE Norway 30 ETF	NORW	B	15.25	A+ / 9.6	26.06 / 86	--	--	2.81	C+ / 6.2	-2.24	-0.03

* Denotes ETF Fund, N/A denotes number is not available

99 Pct = Best
0 Pct = Worst

Fund Type	Fund Name	Ticker Symbol	Overall Investment Rating	Price As of 12/31/12	Perform-ance Rating/Pts		Annualized Total Return Through 12/31/12			Dividend Yield %	Risk Rating/Pts		Premium/Discount As of 12/31/12	1 Year Average
							1Yr/Pct	3Yr/Pct	5Yr/Pct					
GR	*Direxion Daily Small Cap Bear 3x	TZA	E-	13.50	E-	0.0	-49.42 / 1	-55.56 / 0	--	0.00	D / 1.9	12.31	-0.01
EN	*ProShares UltraShort Silver	ZSL	E-	50.07	E-	0.0	-28.31 / 4	-60.50 / 0	--	0.00	D / 1.9	3.54	-1.08
GR	*Direxion Daily Mid Cap Bear 3X	MIDZ	E-	16.41	E-	0.0	-48.52 / 1	-49.62 / 0	--	0.00	D+ / 2.4	11.94	-0.01
IN	*IPath S&P 500 VIX Sm-Trm Futr ET	VXX	E-	31.81	E-	0.0	-78.99 / 0	-61.73 / 0	--	0.00	D / 1.9	21.13	-0.14
GR	*Direxion Daily Real Estate Bear	DRV	E-	20.70	E-	0.0	-48.85 / 1	-60.74 / 0	--	0.00	D / 1.9	6.76	N/A
GR	*ProShares UltraPro Short MidCap4	SMDD	E-	36.87	E-	0.0	-48.24 / 1	--	--	0.00	D / 2.2	12.03	0.01
GR	*ProShares UltraPro Shrt Russell2	SRTY	E-	33.74	E-	0.0	-49.17 / 1	--	--	0.00	D / 1.9	12.20	0.01
IN	*Direxion Daily Semiconductor Bea	SOXS	E-	32.84	E-	0.0	-41.32 / 2	--	--	0.00	D / 1.9	16.45	-0.05
IN	*C-Tracks ETN Citi Volatility Idx	CVOL	E-	29.70	E-	0.0	-90.16 / 0	--	--	0.00	D / 1.9	25.90	0.16
GI	*VelocityShares VIX Short-Term ET	VIIX	E-	17.19	E-	0.0	-79.00 / 0	--	--	0.00	D / 1.9	21.06	0.03
GI	*VelocityShares VIX Medium-Term E	VIIZ	E-	38.65	E-	0.0	-54.85 / 1	--	--	0.00	D / 1.9	9.24	-0.39
IN	*VelocityShares Daily 2x VIX S-T	TVIX	E-	9.34	E-	0.0	-97.36 / 0	--	--	0.00	D / 1.9	54.38	8.42
IN	*VelocityShares Dly 2x VIX Med-T	TVIZ	E-	11.48	E-	0.0	-82.86 / 0	--	--	0.00	D / 1.9	19.46	-0.31
GEI	*ProShares VIX Short-Term Futures	VIXY	E-	17.01	E-	0.0	-78.89 / 0	--	--	0.00	D / 1.9	20.90	-0.13
GI	*Direxion Daily Russia Bear 3x	RUSS	E-	14.85	E-	0.0	-54.83 / 1	--	--	0.00	D / 1.9	-0.60	-0.19
GI	*ProShares Ultra VIX Sh-Tm Fut ET	UVXY	E-	20.90	E-	0.0	-97.51 / 0	--	--	0.00	D / 1.9	50.14	-0.19
EN	*ProShares Ultra DJ-UBS Natural G	BOIL	E-	39.24	E-	0.0	-51.80 / 1	--	--	0.00	D / 1.9	2.83	-0.04
GEI	*ProShares VIX Mid-Term Futures E	VIXM	E	34.22	E-	0.0	-55.69 / 1	--	--	0.00	C- / 3.6	9.40	-0.16
EN	*iPath DJ UBS Ntrl Gas Tot Ret Su	GAZ	E-	2.69	E-	0.1	-21.07 / 5	-42.93 / 1	-44.34 / 0	0.00	D / 1.9	14.47	37.98
GR	*Direxion S&P 500 Bear 3X Shares	SPXS	E-	16.91	E-	0.1	-43.62 / 2	-42.51 / 1	--	0.00	D+ / 2.7	10.74	N/A
EN	*Direxion Energy Bear 3x Shares	ERY	E-	7.82	E-	0.1	-36.27 / 2	-48.07 / 0	--	0.00	D / 1.9	10.45	-0.04
FS	*Direxion Financial Bear 3x Share	FAZ	E-	15.11	E-	0.1	-58.56 / 0	-46.78 / 0	--	0.00	D / 2.0	14.64	-0.02
GL	*Direxion Developed Markets Bear	DPK	E-	16.82	E-	0.1	-53.99 / 1	-38.79 / 1	--	0.00	D / 2.2	6.79	0.02
GL	*Direxion Emerging Markets Bear 3	EDZ	E-	9.02	E-	0.1	-49.14 / 1	-42.88 / 1	--	0.00	D / 1.9	1.35	-0.04
GR	*Direxion Daily Technology Bear 3	TECS	E-	9.36	E-	0.1	-41.82 / 2	-41.74 / 1	--	0.00	D+ / 2.3	8.46	N/A
FO	*ProShares UltraShort MSCI Mex In	SMK	E-	24.81	E-	0.1	-53.40 / 1	-39.05 / 1	--	0.00	C- / 3.0	9.34	0.13
GR	*ProShares UltraPro Short S&P500	SPXU	E-	37.86	E-	0.1	-43.52 / 2	-41.50 / 1	--	0.00	D+ / 2.8	10.77	-0.01
FO	*Direxion Daily China Bear 3x ETF	YANG	E-	10.45	E-	0.1	-40.43 / 2	-37.71 / 2	--	0.00	D / 1.9	14.46	-0.18
GR	*ProShares UltraPro Short QQQ	SQQQ	E-	40.55	E-	0.1	-47.23 / 1	--	--	0.00	D / 2.2	10.88	0.07
GR	*Direxion Daily Nat Gas Rel Bull	GASL	E-	19.98	E-	0.1	-36.84 / 2	--	--	0.00	D / 1.9	-6.50	N/A
PM	*Direxion Daily Gold Miners Bull	NUGT	E-	11.00	E-	0.1	-54.60 / 1	--	--	0.00	D / 1.9	7.63	-0.03
GI	*FactorShares Oil Bull S&P 500 Be	FOL	E-	9.69	E-	0.1	-53.93 / 1	--	--	0.00	D+ / 2.9	4.64	0.10
GL	*VelocityShares 3x Inverse Silver	DSLV	E-	26.91	E-	0.1	-44.91 / 1	--	--	0.00	D / 1.9	1.70	-0.17
IN	*ProShares UltraShort Real Estate	SRS	E	24.26	E-	0.1	-35.57 / 2	-41.30 / 1	-58.70 / 0	0.00	C- / 4.2	5.80	N/A
HL	*ProShares UltraShort Nasdaq Biot	BIS	E	66.33	E-	0.1	-47.85 / 1	--	--	0.00	C- / 3.4	13.08	0.06
GR	*FactorShares Tbd Bull S&P 500 Be	FSA	E	19.40	E-	0.1	-40.23 / 2	--	--	0.00	C- / 3.9	10.73	-0.11
EN	*iPath Cptl Glbl Carbon Tot Ret E	GRN	E-	7.82	E-	0.2	-29.17 / 4	-33.88 / 2	--	0.00	D / 1.9	3.30	-7.58
IN	*IPath S&P 500 VIX Mid-Trm Futr E	VXZ	E-	27.95	E-	0.2	-55.82 / 0	-28.99 / 3	--	0.00	D / 1.9	9.56	-0.15
USA	*Direxion Daily 20+ Yr Treas Bear	TMV	E-	54.24	E-	0.2	-18.14 / 5	-44.44 / 1	--	0.00	D+ / 2.4	-2.90	0.02
GR	*JPMorgan Dbl Short 10 Year Trs E	DSXJ	E-	28.00	E-	0.2	-34.50 / 3	--	--	0.00	D+ / 2.7	-28.21	-3.51
IN	*iPath Pure Beta Coffee ETN	CAFE	E-	21.23	E-	0.2	-37.51 / 2	--	--	0.00	D+ / 2.3	-6.15	-0.06
GR	*ProShares UltraShort Russell2000	TWM	E	25.35	E-	0.2	-34.57 / 2	-37.55 / 2	-38.19 / 1	0.00	C- / 3.4	8.10	-0.02
GR	*ProShares UltraShort MidCap 400	MZZ	E	25.31	E-	0.2	-34.17 / 3	-34.55 / 2	-34.82 / 1	0.00	C- / 4.0	7.56	0.02
GR	*ProShares UltraShort SmallCap 60	SDD	E	25.80	E-	0.2	-33.79 / 3	-37.91 / 1	-36.96 / 1	0.00	C- / 3.4	6.48	-0.09
IN	*ProShares UltraShort Consumer Se	SCC	E	39.00	E-	0.2	-40.22 / 2	-37.41 / 2	-34.13 / 1	0.00	C- / 3.6	6.97	-0.03
FS	*ProShares UltraShort Financials	SKF	E	33.54	E-	0.2	-42.43 / 2	-30.26 / 3	-43.11 / 0	0.00	C- / 3.3	9.11	0.01
IN	*ProShares UltraShort Industrials	SIJ	E	27.63	E-	0.2	-31.41 / 3	-34.12 / 2	-30.06 / 1	0.00	C- / 3.6	6.89	0.04
GR	*ProShares UltraShort Russell2000	SKK	E	24.12	E-	0.2	-33.36 / 3	-38.60 / 1	-36.70 / 1	0.00	C- / 3.4	9.59	-0.15
EN	*United States Natural Gas Fund	UNG	E	18.90	E-	0.2	-17.46 / 6	-38.86 / 1	-42.85 / 0	0.00	C- / 3.4	0.91	-0.05
FO	*ProShares UltraShort MSCI Europe	EPV	E	26.10	E-	0.2	-46.89 / 1	-33.55 / 2	--	0.00	C- / 3.1	5.33	0.02

* Denotes ETF Fund, N/A denotes number is not available

99 Pct = Best
0 Pct = Worst

Fund Type	Fund Name	Ticker Symbol	Overall Investment Rating	Price As of 12/31/12	Performance Rating/Pts	1Yr/Pct	3Yr/Pct	5Yr/Pct	Dividend Yield %	Risk Rating/Pts	Premium/Discount As of 12/31/12	1 Year Average
FO	Thai Fund	TTF	A+	19.95	A+ / 9.8	69.21 / 99	36.28 / 99	19.11 / 99	1.66	B- / 7.8	-14.52	-12.77
MTG	Western Asset Mtge Defined Oppty	DMO	A+	24.21	A+ / 9.8	46.13 / 98	--	--	7.43	B / 8.5	-1.98	3.69
MTG	Nuveen Mortgage Opportunity Term 2	JMT	A+	27.18	A+ / 9.8	41.29 / 97	--	--	7.62	B / 8.3	-2.65	1.68
FO	Mexico Equity & Income Fund	MXE	A+	14.25	A+ / 9.7	54.56 / 99	26.13 / 98	11.30 / 74	0.00	B / 8.0	-15.43	-11.28
IN	Cohen&Steers Sel Preferred & Incom	PSF	A+	26.76	A+ / 9.7	35.33 / 95	--	--	6.51	B / 8.7	-3.46	0.72
FO	Mexico Fund	MXF	A	29.02	A+ / 9.7	52.02 / 99	22.55 / 94	12.25 / 78	1.08	B- / 7.5	-9.88	-7.81
FO	Thai Capital Fund	TF	B-	12.11	A+ / 9.7	49.86 / 98	28.26 / 99	15.14 / 90	0.00	C / 5.1	-5.39	-7.59
MUS	Nuveen CA Quality Inc Muni	NUC	A+	17.35	A+ / 9.6	20.94 / 93	17.52 / 99	12.56 / 99	5.88	B / 8.4	4.27	3.28
MUS	BlackRock MuniYield Invt Fund	MYF	A+	16.87	A+ / 9.6	22.37 / 95	17.94 / 99	12.79 / 99	5.62	B / 8.8	2.12	1.78
MUN	BlackRock MuniHoldings Fund	MHD	A+	18.36	A+ / 9.6	23.49 / 96	17.52 / 99	13.13 / 99	7.52	B / 8.7	1.60	3.24
MUS	PIMCO CA Municipal Income Fund	PCQ	A+	15.93	A+ / 9.6	24.29 / 96	17.46 / 98	8.79 / 84	5.80	B / 8.3	9.11	8.32
MUS	Eaton Vance CA Muni Bond II	EIA	A+	14.10	A+ / 9.6	27.57 / 97	16.50 / 97	9.23 / 87	5.46	B / 8.2	3.91	1.85
IN	Kayne Anderson Midstream/Energy	KMF	A+	28.75	A+ / 9.6	30.41 / 91	--	--	6.16	B / 8.5	-4.86	-3.70
LP	Avenue Income Credit Strategies	ACP	A-	18.17	A+ / 9.6	25.54 / 85	--	--	7.93	B- / 7.3	-4.72	-3.24
EM	ING Emerging Markets High Div Eqty	IHD	B	14.63	A+ / 9.6	23.70 / 81	--	--	9.84	C+ / 6.1	-0.61	-0.60
MUS	Nuveen CA Muni Market Opportunity	NCO	A+	16.34	A / 9.5	23.30 / 96	16.96 / 98	11.26 / 97	5.88	B / 8.7	-1.09	0.53
MUS	BlackRock MuniYield California Qly	MCA	A+	16.43	A / 9.5	21.56 / 94	17.78 / 99	11.33 / 97	5.55	B / 8.6	-1.73	-2.52
MUS	BlackRock MuniHoldings CA Qly	MUC	A+	16.34	A / 9.5	18.55 / 89	17.93 / 99	11.85 / 98	5.80	B / 8.6	-0.91	-0.64
MUS	BlackRock CA Municipal Income Trus	BFZ	A+	16.34	A / 9.5	22.89 / 95	16.94 / 98	9.14 / 86	5.71	B / 8.4	-1.15	-0.21
GI	Cohen&Steers Total Return Realty	RFI	A-	14.72	A / 9.5	30.01 / 91	25.32 / 97	13.44 / 83	5.98	B- / 7.4	11.35	2.89
GL	Gabelli Multimedia Trust	GGT	B+	7.85	A / 9.5	41.73 / 97	21.05 / 91	3.81 / 37	10.19	C+ / 6.9	-8.61	-7.90
HL	H&Q Life Sciences Investors	HQL	B	14.50	A / 9.5	37.86 / 96	27.58 / 99	12.77 / 80	6.21	C+ / 6.2	-8.63	-3.92
MUS	Nuveen CA Performance Plus Muni	NCP	A+	16.26	A / 9.4	16.94 / 85	17.51 / 99	11.06 / 96	5.83	B / 8.6	1.37	1.23
MUS	Nuveen CA Select Quality Muni	NVC	A+	16.64	A / 9.4	20.28 / 92	16.55 / 98	12.54 / 99	5.99	B / 8.4	0.12	2.43
MUN	BlackRock MuniYield Quality Fund	MQY	A+	17.64	A / 9.4	20.98 / 93	15.80 / 96	12.39 / 99	5.47	B / 8.4	4.69	1.98
MUS	BlackRock MuniYield CA Fund	MYC	A+	16.93	A / 9.4	18.07 / 88	17.83 / 99	11.78 / 98	5.60	B / 8.7	-1.23	-0.95
MUN	BlackRock MuniYield Fund	MYD	A+	16.37	A / 9.4	21.19 / 94	16.92 / 98	11.05 / 96	7.21	B / 8.5	2.44	3.64
MUS	Nuveen CA Div Adv Muni	NAC	A+	16.10	A / 9.4	19.95 / 92	17.04 / 98	10.81 / 95	5.52	B / 8.5	1.51	-0.43
MUN	BlackRock Municipal Income Quality	BYM	A+	16.20	A / 9.4	22.96 / 95	15.38 / 96	10.27 / 92	5.78	B / 8.2	0.25	1.44
GI	Virtus Total Return	DCA	A+	3.87	A / 9.4	26.28 / 86	27.38 / 99	-3.14 / 11	6.46	B / 8.2	-13.62	-11.51
IN	Cohen&Steers REIT& Preferred Incom	RNP	A-	16.99	A / 9.4	29.34 / 90	27.64 / 99	9.88 / 69	7.06	B- / 7.5	-9.72	-5.81
GI	Cohen&Steers Quality Income Realty	RQI	B+	10.16	A / 9.4	27.83 / 88	28.55 / 99	3.95 / 37	7.09	B- / 7.0	-9.12	-4.66
MUN	DWS Municipal Income Trust	KTF	A+	14.39	A / 9.3	18.72 / 90	16.63 / 98	14.72 / 99	5.84	B / 8.6	0.14	4.36
MUS	Nuveen OH Quality Inc Muni	NUO	A+	19.05	A / 9.3	23.39 / 96	14.25 / 93	12.75 / 99	5.04	B / 8.8	7.81	4.66
MUS	PIMCO CA Municipal Income Fund II	PCK	A+	10.59	A / 9.3	21.87 / 94	16.47 / 97	3.12 / 43	7.08	B / 8.7	15.86	19.12
MUH	Pioneer Municipal High Income Trus	MHI	A+	15.79	A / 9.3	20.52 / 93	15.03 / 95	11.53 / 97	7.85	B / 8.4	6.33	8.47
MUH	Pioneer Municipal High Income Adv	MAV	A+	15.47	A / 9.3	18.62 / 90	16.94 / 97	11.36 / 97	7.37	B / 8.4	12.10	15.38
EN	Kayne Anderson Engy Development Co	KED	A	0.00	A / 9.3	30.56 / 91	27.89 / 99	10.80 / 72	5.03	B / 8.0		4.98
HL	H&Q Healthcare Investors	HQH	B	17.31	A / 9.3	36.56 / 96	24.16 / 96	10.96 / 73	6.24	C+ / 6.3	-11.73	-6.86
MUN	BlackRock MuniHoldings Fund II	MUH	A+	16.64	A- / 9.2	18.29 / 89	16.54 / 97	12.35 / 99	9.27	B / 8.5	-1.42	1.38
MUN	BlackRock MuniVest Fund	MVF	A+	11.03	A- / 9.2	19.23 / 90	15.19 / 95	11.68 / 97	6.42	B / 8.8	2.80	4.59
MUN	Western Asset Municipal Partners	MNP	A+	17.22	A- / 9.2	19.70 / 91	16.43 / 97	11.89 / 98	4.88	B / 8.7	2.07	1.92
MUN	BlackRock MuniVest Fund II	MVT	A+	17.51	A- / 9.2	20.33 / 92	16.07 / 97	12.83 / 99	6.60	B / 8.6	5.10	5.84
MUS	Nuveen CA Prem Inc Muni	NCU	A+	15.46	A- / 9.2	16.22 / 84	16.97 / 98	10.72 / 95	5.43	B / 8.7	-3.07	-1.56
MUS	BlackRock MuniHoldings Inv Quality	MFL	A+	16.10	A- / 9.2	20.17 / 92	15.59 / 96	12.22 / 98	5.70	B / 8.5	-0.43	-0.23
MUN	BlackRock Strategic Municipal Tr	BSD	A+	14.84	A- / 9.2	18.55 / 89	16.32 / 97	8.17 / 79	5.98	B / 8.5	-2.69	0.66
MUN	PIMCO Municipal Income Fund II	PML	A+	13.16	A- / 9.2	21.57 / 94	15.06 / 95	5.40 / 61	5.93	B / 8.5	5.45	6.77
MUS	PIMCO CA Municipal Income Fund III	PZC	A+	11.28	A- / 9.2	22.38 / 95	16.10 / 97	3.45 / 46	6.38	B / 8.6	8.88	9.33
GI	TCW Strategic Income Fund	TSI	A	5.36	A- / 9.2	28.58 / 89	24.58 / 97	23.35 / 99	21.38	B / 8.2	-6.13	-2.22
COH	PIMCO Corporate and Income Oppty	PTY	A	19.41	A- / 9.2	30.62 / 92	24.05 / 96	20.98 / 99	26.46	B- / 7.8	14.78	19.68

* Denotes ETF Fund, N/A denotes number is not available

99 Pct = Best
0 Pct = Worst

Fund Type	Fund Name	Ticker Symbol	Overall Investment Rating	Price As of 12/31/12	PERFORMANCE Performance Rating/Pts	Annualized Total Return Through 12/31/12 1Yr/Pct	3Yr/Pct	5Yr/Pct	Dividend Yield %	RISK Risk Rating/Pts	VALUATION Premium/Discount As of 12/31/12	1 Year Average
GI	RENN Global Entrepreneurs Fund Inc	RCG	E+	1.42	E / 0.5	-10.12 / 8	-16.89 / 5	-23.48 / 2	0.00	C / 4.7	-44.31	-33.26
FO	Templeton Russia&East European Fun	TRF	E+	14.63	E+ / 0.8	5.16 / 24	-9.47 / 7	-10.85 / 4	1.08	C / 5.1	-10.52	-8.91
GL	Alpine Total Dynamic Dividend Fund	AOD	E+	4.03	E+ / 0.8	7.99 / 30	-11.03 / 7	-9.51 / 5	16.38	C / 4.7	-12.77	-7.82
IN	Equus Total Return	EQS	D-	2.36	E+ / 0.8	12.09 / 39	-12.00 / 7	-15.61 / 4	0.00	C / 5.4	-29.13	-34.50
PM	ASA Gold & Precious Metals Ltd	ASA	E	21.53	E+ / 0.9	-17.80 / 5	-3.98 / 10	-0.22 / 18	6.50	D+ / 2.8	-8.89	-7.98
GL	Alpine Global Dynamic Div Fd	AGD	E+	5.23	E+ / 0.9	13.20 / 42	-7.67 / 8	-9.18 / 5	7.66	C / 4.6	2.35	7.59
GL	First Trust Active Dividend Inc Fd	FAV	D-	7.55	E+ / 0.9	3.39 / 21	-6.41 / 8	-0.18 / 19	9.54	C+ / 5.9	-14.50	-10.12
EN	ING Risk Managed Nat Resources Fun	IRR	D	10.34	E+ / 0.9	2.58 / 19	-5.82 / 8	1.95 / 27	10.83	C+ / 6.8	-10.94	-6.05
FO	India Fund	IFN	E+	20.91	D- / 1.0	14.13 / 45	-8.09 / 8	-8.34 / 6	0.72	C / 4.8	-12.18	-11.28
IN	Cornerstone Total Return Fund	CRF	D-	5.36	D- / 1.1	13.65 / 43	-3.51 / 10	-4.06 / 10	21.85	C / 5.0	4.28	18.70
UT	Gabelli Utility Trust	GUT	D	6.16	D- / 1.2	-4.99 / 10	1.11 / 17	4.90 / 43	9.95	C+ / 6.6	10.39	33.95
IN	Cornerstone Strategic Value Fund	CLM	D-	6.00	D- / 1.3	18.31 / 64	-1.87 / 12	-0.35 / 18	22.18	C / 4.9	4.17	19.23
UT	Wells Fargo Avtg Utilities&High In	ERH	D	11.18	D- / 1.3	5.97 / 26	-1.60 / 12	-6.74 / 7	8.05	C+ / 6.5	-6.29	-0.11
IN	Eaton Vance Risk Mgd Div Eq Inc	ETJ	D	10.43	D- / 1.3	13.70 / 44	-3.91 / 9	1.89 / 26	10.70	C+ / 6.6	-14.72	-14.15
FO	Japan Smaller Cap Fund Inc.	JOF	D	7.20	D- / 1.4	0.81 / 15	-0.65 / 14	-1.39 / 15	0.00	B- / 7.3	-12.41	-12.83
GI	The Cushing MLP Total Return Fund	SRV	D	7.17	D- / 1.4	-9.87 / 8	3.53 / 24	-3.44 / 10	12.55	C+ / 6.7	7.98	25.23
GL	BlackRock Utility & Infrastructure	BUI	D+	17.89	D- / 1.4	2.36 / 19	--	--	8.11	B / 8.7	-11.00	-4.90
FO	AGIC Intl & Premium Strategy Fund	NAI	D-	9.70	D / 1.6	16.26 / 54	-1.79 / 12	-0.69 / 17	11.34	C+ / 5.9	-10.43	-1.57
GR	Columbia Seligman Prem Tech Gro	STK	D	14.51	D / 1.6	3.36 / 21	0.13 / 15	--	12.75	B- / 7.0	-7.34	-3.00
IN	BlackRock Real Asset Equity Trust	BCF	D	10.26	D / 1.8	1.20 / 16	1.72 / 19	1.94 / 26	8.64	C+ / 6.6	-8.80	-3.17
IN	Guggenheim Equal Weight Enh Eq Inc	GEQ	D+	17.73	D / 1.8	7.80 / 30	--	--	9.87	B / 8.5	-6.98	-2.89
FO	Morgan Stanley India Inv Fund	IIF	D-	18.53	D / 1.9	22.96 / 79	-2.71 / 11	-5.44 / 8	0.00	C / 5.2	-10.44	-10.86
GL	Canadian World Fund Limited	T.CWF	D-	3.45	D / 1.9	-0.85 / 13	1.47 / 18	-8.00 / 6	0.00	C / 4.4	-36.11	-33.14
UT	Duff & Phelps Global Utility Incom	DPG	D+	16.87	D / 1.9	4.66 / 23	--	--	8.30	B- / 7.9	-13.13	-4.55
FO	Aberdeen Israel Fund	ISL	D	13.10	D / 2.0	8.85 / 32	-0.60 / 14	-2.72 / 12	1.33	C+ / 6.7	-17.61	-13.34
GL	Nuveen Global Value Opportunities	JGV	D	14.91	D / 2.0	0.36 / 14	1.74 / 19	5.78 / 47	7.78	B- / 7.1	-8.42	-6.77
HL	Engex	EGX	E+	2.06	D / 2.1	31.91 / 93	-5.19 / 9	-18.20 / 3	0.00	D+ / 2.7	-48.76	-24.42
FO	BlackRock Intl Grth and Inc Tr	BGY	D-	7.35	D / 2.1	16.50 / 55	-0.53 / 14	-0.23 / 18	9.14	C / 4.6	-14.53	-9.73
PM	GAMCO Global Gold Nat ResandIncome	GGN	D	12.80	D / 2.1	-0.15 / 14	3.25 / 23	-3.39 / 10	11.25	C+ / 6.2	-4.55	4.09
USA	Federated Enhanced Treasury Income	FTT	D	14.18	D / 2.1	2.73 / 19	--	--	6.18	B- / 7.5	-10.31	-9.76
FO	Asia Tigers Fund	GRR	D-	12.59	D / 2.2	22.72 / 79	-1.55 / 12	-1.73 / 14	0.16	C / 5.2	-7.83	-8.49
EM	Templeton Emerging Markets Fd	EMF	D	20.00	D / 2.2	10.51 / 36	-0.16 / 14	4.31 / 39	1.44	C+ / 6.5	-9.05	-7.77
GEN	Putnam Master Intermediate Inc Tr	PIM	D	5.06	D / 2.2	9.48 / 34	2.51 / 21	5.09 / 44	6.17	C+ / 6.2	-9.32	-5.80
IN	BlackRock Res & Commdty Strat Trus	BCX	D	12.82	D / 2.2	4.08 / 23	--	--	9.05	C+ / 5.8	-14.59	-8.01
GL	GDL Fund	GDL	D+	11.42	D+ / 2.3	7.24 / 29	3.86 / 26	4.30 / 39	11.21	B / 8.1	-14.39	-12.79
GL	Wells Fargo Avtg Global Div Oppty	EOD	D+	7.57	D+ / 2.3	13.62 / 43	2.99 / 23	-1.41 / 15	11.10	B- / 7.3	-8.69	-2.58
GL	MFS Government Markets Income Trus	MGF	C-	6.85	D+ / 2.3	3.16 / 21	5.18 / 30	7.08 / 55	7.29	B / 8.6	0.88	0.56
USA	BlackRock Enhanced Government	EGF	C-	15.63	D+ / 2.3	7.24 / 29	3.33 / 24	5.72 / 47	4.99	B+ / 9.1	-2.50	-4.97
GI	Advent/Claymore Gbl Con Sec & Inc	AGC	D	6.48	D+ / 2.4	12.71 / 40	0.82 / 17	-4.28 / 9	8.70	C+ / 6.0	-14.85	-8.99
MUS	Nuveen MA AMT/F Muni Income	NGX	D+	13.82	D+ / 2.4	6.77 / 35	3.40 / 30	4.36 / 53	4.17	B / 8.3	-7.56	-1.79
FO	Latin American Discovery Fund	LDF	D	15.59	D+ / 2.5	11.78 / 38	1.99 / 20	1.88 / 26	1.56	C+ / 6.3	-11.72	-8.94
EN	BlackRock EcoSolutions Investment	BQR	D	8.39	D+ / 2.5	13.17 / 42	1.64 / 19	-2.08 / 13	8.55	C+ / 6.3	-11.68	-3.20
FO	Asia Pacific Fund	APB	D+	10.82	D+ / 2.5	13.03 / 41	1.92 / 20	-0.98 / 17	0.00	B- / 7.1	-12.10	-10.15
EN	BlackRock Energy & Resources	BGR	D+	23.55	D+ / 2.5	2.75 / 20	5.00 / 29	4.33 / 39	6.88	B- / 7.1	-11.53	-5.49
USA	Western Asset/Claymore Inf-Link S&	WIA	C-	13.11	D+ / 2.5	6.30 / 27	5.33 / 31	5.81 / 48	2.68	B+ / 9.5	-10.82	-10.58
GL	Nuveen Global Income Oppportunitie	JGG	C-	14.02	D+ / 2.5	10.39 / 35	3.68 / 25	5.84 / 48	8.42	B / 8.3	-10.53	-6.72
GL	BlackRock Global Opportunities Eq	BOE	D	13.20	D+ / 2.6	13.65 / 43	1.81 / 19	2.21 / 28	9.45	C+ / 6.2	-14.73	-8.48
GI	Zweig Total Return Fund	ZTR	D+	12.31	D+ / 2.6	11.71 / 38	3.25 / 23	3.83 / 37	7.99	B / 8.1	-13.80	-12.26
FO	Greater China Fund	GCH	D+	12.88	D+ / 2.6	25.37 / 84	-0.85 / 13	-1.05 / 16	0.79	B- / 7.1	-5.15	-8.08
GL	ING Gobal Equity Dividend Premium	IGD	D+	8.67	D+ / 2.6	16.04 / 53	1.56 / 19	1.13 / 23	11.63	B- / 7.0	-11.80	-5.88

* Denotes ETF Fund, N/A denotes number is not available

Section VI

Top-Rated
ETFs and Other
Closed-End Funds
by Fund Type

A compilation of those

Exchange-Traded Funds and Other

Closed-End Funds

receiving the highest TheStreet Investment Rating

within each type of fund.

Funds are listed in order by Overall Investment Rating.

Section VI Contents

This section contains a summary analysis of the top rated ETFs and other closed-end mutual funds within each fund type. If you are looking for a particular type of mutual fund, these pages show those funds that have achieved the best combination of risk and financial performance over the past three years.

1. Fund Type

The mutual fund's peer category based on an analysis of its investment portfolio.

COH	Corporate – High Yield	HL	Health
COI	Corporate – Inv. Grade	IN	Income
EM	Emerging Market	LP	Loan Participation
EN	Energy/Natural Resources	MTG	Mortgage
FS	Financial Services	MUH	Municipal – High Yield
FO	Foreign	MUN	Municipal – National
GEI	General – Inv. Grade	MUS	Municipal – Single State
GEN	General Bond	PM	Precious Metals
GL	Global	USA	U.S. Gov. – Agency
GR	Growth	UT	Utilities
GI	Growth and Income		

A blank fund type means that the mutual fund has not yet been categorized.

2. Fund Name

The name of the mutual fund as stated in its prospectus, which can sometimes differ slightly from the name that the company uses for advertising. If you cannot find the particular mutual fund you are interested in, or if you have any doubts regarding the precise name, verify the information with your broker or on your account statement. Also, use the fund's ticker symbol for confirmation. (See column 3.)

3. Ticker Symbol

The unique alphabetic symbol used for identifying and trading a specific mutual fund. No two funds can have the same ticker symbol.

4. Overall Investment Rating

Our overall rating is measured on a scale from A to E based on each fund's risk-adjusted performance. Please see page 10 for specific descriptions of each letter grade. Also, refer to page 7 for information on how our ratings are derived. Most important, when using this rating, please be sure to consider the warnings beginning on page 11 regarding the ratings' limitations and the underlying assumptions.

5. Price

Closing price of the fund on the date shown.

6.	Performance Rating/Points	A letter grade rating based solely on the mutual fund's financial performance over the trailing three years, without any consideration for the amount of risk the fund poses. Like the overall Investment Rating, the Performance Rating is measured on a scale from A to E for ease of interpretation. The points score indicates where the Performance Rating falls on a scale of 0 to 10.
7.	1-Year Total Return	The total return the fund has provided investors over the preceeding 52 weeks. This total return figure is computed based on the fund's dividend distributions and share price appreciation/depreciation during the period, net of the expenses and fees it imposes on its shareholders.
8.	1-Year Total Return Percentile	The fund's percentile rank based on its one-year performance compared to that of all other closed-end funds in existence for at least one year. A score of 99 is the best possible, indicating that the fund outperformed 99% of the closed-end mutual funds. Zero is the worst possible percentile score.
9.	3-Year Total Return	The total annual return the fund has provided investors over the preceeding 156 weeks.
10.	3-Year Total Return Percentile	The fund's percentile rank based on its three-year performance compared to that of all other closed-end funds in existence for at least three years. A score of 99 is the best possible, indicating that the fund outperformed 99% of the closed-end mutual funds. Zero is the worst possible percentile score.
11.	5-Year Total Return	The total annual return the fund has provided investors over the preceeding 260 weeks.
12.	5-Year Total Return Percentile	The fund's percentile rank based on its five-year performance compared to that of all other closed-end funds in existence for at least five years. A score of 99 is the best possible, indicating that the fund outperformed 99% of the closed-end mutual funds. Zero is the worst possible percentile score.
13.	Dividend Yield	Most recent quarterly dividend to fund investors annualized, expressed as a percent of the fund's current share price. The dividend yield of a fund can have little correlation to the amount of dividends the fund has received from its underlying investments. Rather, dividend distributions are based on a fund's need to pass earnings from both dividends and gains on the sale of investments along to shareholders. Thus, these dividend distributions are included as a part of the fund's total return.

Keep in mind that dividend income may be taxed at a different rate than capital gains depending on your income tax bracket. |

14. Risk Rating/Points

A letter grade rating based solely on the mutual fund's risk as determined by its monthly performance volatility over the trailing three years. The risk rating does not take into consideration the overall financial performance the fund has achieved or the total return it has provided to its shareholders. Like the overall Investment Rating, the Risk Rating is measured on a scale from A to E for ease of interpretation. The points score indicates where the Risk Rating falls on a scale of 0 to 10.

15. Premium/ Discount

A comparison of the fund's price to its NAV as of the date indicated. The premium (+) or discount (-) indicates the percentage the shares are trading above or below the fund's NAV per share.

If the price is above the fund's NAV, the fund is said to be trading at a premium. If the price is lower than the fund's NAV, the fund is trading at a discount.

16. 1-Year Average Premium/ Discount

The average of the fund's premium/discount over the preceeding year.

It can be useful to compare the fund's current premium/discount to its one-year average. If the fund is currently trading at a premium/discount that is lower/higher than its one-year average, then there has been less demand for the fund in more recent times than over the past year. Conversely, if the fund is currently trading at a premium/discount that is higher/lower than its one-year average, this indicates that there has been greater demand for the fund in more recent times than over the past year.

Fund Type	Fund Name	Ticker Symbol	Overall Investment Rating	Price As of 12/31/12	Performance Rating/Pts	Annualized Total Return Through 12/31/12			Dividend Yield %	Risk Rating/Pts	Premium/Discount	
						1Yr/Pct	3Yr/Pct	5Yr/Pct			As of 12/31/12	1 Year Average
COH	*ProShares Ultra High Yield	UJB	A+	50.37	A / 9.3	25.48 / 85	--	--	0.00	B / 8.2	-2.46	-0.04
COH	PIMCO Corporate and Income Oppty	PTY	A	19.41	A- / 9.2	30.62 / 92	24.05 / 96	20.98 / 99	26.46	B- / 7.8	14.78	19.68
COH	Helios High Yield Fund	HHY	A-	10.12	B / 8.0	13.30 / 42	20.75 / 90	14.03 / 86	10.08	B / 8.8	-4.26	2.75
COH	PIMCO Corporate and ncome Strategy	PCN	B+	17.65	B+ / 8.7	27.45 / 87	20.62 / 90	17.26 / 96	15.84	B- / 7.9	8.35	15.87
COH	BlackRock Strategic Bond Trust	BHD	B+	14.59	B / 7.8	28.00 / 88	15.88 / 76	14.34 / 88	7.53	B / 8.4	-1.62	1.14
COH	BlackRock Debt Strategies Fund Inc	DSU	B+	4.30	B- / 7.4	22.22 / 77	15.43 / 74	6.06 / 49	10.33	B / 8.6	-1.15	1.14
COH	BlackRock High Income Shares	HIS	B+	2.36	B- / 7.4	21.72 / 76	17.94 / 83	14.54 / 88	14.34	B / 8.6	1.72	3.34
COH	Credit Suisse Asset Mgmt Income	CIK	B+	4.03	B- / 7.4	21.64 / 75	16.02 / 77	14.27 / 87	7.89	B / 8.5	5.50	4.51
COH	*SPDR Nuveen S&P Hi Yld Muni Bd E	HYMB	B+	58.00	C+ / 6.5	16.79 / 57	--	--	4.58	B+ / 9.8	-1.21	-0.01
COH	New America High Income Fund	HYB	B	10.45	B / 7.7	22.82 / 79	17.82 / 82	17.51 / 97	57.42	B / 8.2	-2.06	3.14
COH	Invesco Van Kampen High Inc Tr II	VLT	B	17.25	B / 7.6	21.82 / 76	17.34 / 81	10.10 / 70	8.07	B / 8.1	-1.77	3.78
COH	BlackRock Senior High Income Fund	ARK	B	4.20	B- / 7.3	22.94 / 79	16.18 / 77	5.95 / 49	13.43	B / 8.6	-3.23	0.41
COH	MFS Interm High Inc	CIF	B	3.07	B- / 7.2	18.70 / 66	17.51 / 81	13.06 / 81	12.12	B / 8.7	-3.76	2.80
COH	*Peritus High Yield ETF	HYLD	B	50.07	C+ / 6.3	15.04 / 48	--	--	10.28	B+ / 9.0	-1.38	0.15
COH	DWS High Income Trust	KHI	B-	10.20	C+ / 6.7	12.73 / 40	16.66 / 79	12.05 / 77	7.47	B / 8.0	0.00	5.59
COH	Credit Suisse High Yield Bond Fund	DHY	B-	3.20	C+ / 6.1	23.25 / 80	13.32 / 65	13.39 / 83	9.94	B / 8.6	2.89	6.77
COH	BlackRock Corporate High Yield V	HYV	C+	12.56	B- / 7.0	20.08 / 71	16.43 / 78	14.71 / 89	17.87	B- / 7.1	-4.56	2.37
COH	Pacholder High Yield Fund	PHF	C+	8.87	B- / 7.0	13.51 / 43	17.62 / 81	15.21 / 91	9.47	B- / 7.4	1.60	10.15
COH	BlackRock Corporate High Yield VI	HYT	C+	12.39	C+ / 6.8	21.72 / 76	15.45 / 75	14.23 / 87	15.35	B- / 7.2	-3.50	2.75
COH	BlackRock Corporate High Yield III	CYE	C+	7.57	C+ / 6.5	20.51 / 72	15.07 / 73	14.78 / 89	15.61	B- / 7.1	-3.81	3.04
COH	Western Asset High Income Opp Inc.	HIO	C+	6.44	C+ / 5.7	17.36 / 60	12.71 / 62	14.18 / 86	7.73	B- / 7.6	-0.16	4.33
COH	*Guggenhm BltShs 2015 HY Corp Bd	BSJF	C+	26.60	C / 4.5	11.15 / 37	--	--	5.91	B+ / 9.4	-0.23	0.37
COH	*Guggenhm BltShs 2014 HY Corp Bd	BSJE	C+	26.48	C- / 3.8	10.11 / 35	--	--	4.98	B+ / 9.6	-0.15	0.38
COH	BlackRock Corporate High Yield Fun	COY	C	7.74	C+ / 5.9	19.92 / 70	13.31 / 65	14.57 / 89	7.91	B- / 7.1	-0.13	4.19
COH	BlackRock High Yield Trust	BHY	C	7.37	C+ / 5.9	19.15 / 68	15.56 / 75	13.01 / 81	7.25	B- / 7.2	-2.90	3.98
COH	Western Asset High Yld Def Opp	HYI	C	18.33	C / 4.8	16.05 / 53	--	--	9.17	B- / 7.9	-5.66	3.17
COH	Western Asset Managed High Income	MHY	C	6.17	C / 4.7	13.71 / 44	11.52 / 56	13.27 / 82	7.78	B- / 7.6	-1.12	5.27
COH	Western Asset High Income Fund	HIF	C	9.41	C- / 4.0	14.98 / 48	9.17 / 44	11.87 / 76	7.59	B / 8.5	-3.88	2.13
COH	*Guggenhm BltShs 2013 HY Corp Bd	BSJD	C	25.80	D+ / 2.7	6.78 / 28	--	--	4.42	B+ / 9.6	0.00	0.37
COH	Neuberger Berman High Yield Strat	NHS	C-	13.90	C+ / 5.6	13.14 / 42	14.81 / 72	15.85 / 93	7.77	C+ / 6.4	-3.81	3.10
COH	Dreyfus High Yield Strategies Fund	DHF	C-	4.12	C+ / 5.6	5.62 / 25	15.64 / 75	15.54 / 91	10.19	C+ / 6.2	1.23	13.08
COH	PIMCO High Income Fund	PHK	C-	10.48	C / 5.1	7.74 / 30	14.96 / 72	14.83 / 90	13.96	C+ / 6.8	23.44	60.34
COH	Wells Fargo Avtg Income Oppty	EAD	C-	10.07	C / 4.6	11.48 / 37	12.06 / 58	11.30 / 74	9.18	B- / 7.3	-0.10	5.32
COH	*SPDR Barclays High Yield Bond ET	JNK	C-	40.71	C / 4.5	14.40 / 46	10.05 / 47	7.98 / 60	6.33	B- / 7.3	-0.88	0.24
COH	*iShares iBoxx $ High Yld Corp Bo	HYG	C-	93.35	C / 4.4	13.60 / 43	10.08 / 48	8.19 / 60	6.49	B- / 7.7	-0.78	0.45
COH	*PowerShares Fundamental High Yie	PHB	C-	19.25	C- / 3.7	11.36 / 37	8.89 / 42	3.66 / 36	4.89	B / 8.1	-1.08	-0.01

99 Pct = Best
0 Pct = Worst

* Denotes ETF Fund, N/A denotes number is not available

www.thestreetratings.com

Fund Type	Fund Name	Ticker Symbol	Overall Investment Rating	Price As of 12/31/12	Performance Rating/Pts	Annualized Total Return Through 12/31/12 1Yr/Pct	3Yr/Pct	5Yr/Pct	Dividend Yield %	Risk Rating/ Pts	Premium/Discount As of 12/31/12	Premium/Discount 1 Year Average
COI	*SPDR Barclays Intl Corporate Bd	IBND	B+	35.40	B- / 7.3	15.22 / 49	--	--	1.64	B / 8.7	0.11	0.38
COI	*iShares S&P Intl Preferred Stock	IPFF	B	27.10	C+ / 6.1	12.72 / 40	--	--	3.53	B+/ 9.1	-0.04	0.31
COI	*ProShares Ultra Invest Grade Cor	IGU	B	55.58	C+ / 6.0	19.16 / 68	--	--	0.00	B+/ 9.2	-0.22	0.13
COI	Cutwater Select Income	CSI	B-	19.65	C / 5.1	12.22 / 39	13.10 / 64	9.44 / 67	5.39	B+/ 9.6	-8.26	-4.93
COI	*PIMCO 0-5 Year Hi Yield Corp Bd	HYS	B-	103.43	C / 5.0	11.95 / 38	--	--	5.57	B+/ 9.6	-0.49	0.20
COI	Western Asst Invst Grade Define Op	IGI	C+	23.05	C / 5.5	16.57 / 55	13.04 / 63	--	4.99	B / 8.9	1.72	3.47
COI	*Vanguard Long-Term Corp Bd Idx E	VCLT	C+	91.70	C / 4.5	10.39 / 35	12.48 / 61	--	4.42	B+/ 9.2	0.21	0.74
COI	*Vanguard Intm-Term Corp Bd Idx E	VCIT	C	87.66	C- / 3.5	10.02 / 34	9.19 / 44	--	3.15	B+/ 9.7	0.26	0.58
COI	*iShares iBoxx $ Inves Grade Corp	LQD	C	120.99	C- / 3.5	9.98 / 34	9.47 / 45	7.72 / 58	3.59	B+/ 9.4	0.20	0.43
COI	*Guggenheim BltShs 2017 Corp Bd E	BSCH	C	22.82	C- / 3.2	9.03 / 33	--	--	2.31	B+/ 9.7	0.09	0.43
COI	*Market Vectors Invest Grade FR E	FLTR	C	24.72	C- / 3.1	8.14 / 31	--	--	0.83	B+/ 9.4	-0.20	-1.04
COI	*iShares Barclays Credit Bond Fd	CFT	C	113.16	C- / 3.1	7.42 / 29	7.91 / 38	6.82 / 54	3.82	B+/ 9.5	0.06	0.41
COI	*SPDR Barclays Iss Sco Corp Bond	CBND	C	32.58	D+ / 2.8	7.08 / 28	--	--	3.15	B+/ 9.9	0.09	0.70
COI	*Guggenheim BltShs 2016 Corp Bd E	BSCG	C	22.22	D+ / 2.7	7.03 / 28	--	--	2.11	B+/ 9.7	0.05	0.37
COI	*iShares Barclays Intrm Credit Bd	CIU	C	111.29	D+ / 2.7	7.00 / 28	6.18 / 33	5.93 / 49	3.08	B+/ 9.7	0.24	0.26
COI	*Guggenheim BltShs 2015 Corp Bd E	BSCF	C	21.80	D+ / 2.4	5.30 / 24	--	--	1.93	B+/ 9.8	0.00	0.37
COI	*Vanguard Short-Term Crp Bd Idx E	VCSH	C	80.33	D+ / 2.3	5.34 / 24	4.22 / 27	--	1.97	B+/ 9.9	0.25	0.35
COI	*PowerShares Fundmntl Inv Gr Corp	PFIG	C	25.69	D / 2.2	5.04 / 24	--	--	3.48	B+/ 9.9	0.04	0.38
COI	*iShares Floating Rate Note	FLOT	C-	50.59	D / 2.2	4.00 / 22	--	--	0.93	B+/ 9.9	0.34	0.36
COI	*SPDR Barclays Invest Grade FlRt	FLRN	C-	30.66	D / 2.1	3.04 / 21	--	--	1.21	B+/ 9.6	0.56	0.81
COI	*Guggenheim BltShs 2014 Corp Bd E	BSCE	C-	21.27	D / 2.0	3.29 / 21	--	--	1.58	B+/ 9.9	0.14	0.35
COI	*SPDR Barclays Sht Trm Corp Bond	SCPB	C-	30.72	D / 2.0	2.97 / 20	2.68 / 22	--	1.25	B+/ 9.9	0.07	0.32
COI	*iShares Barclays 1-3 Year Credit	CSJ	C-	105.48	D / 1.9	2.94 / 20	2.39 / 21	3.41 / 34	1.56	B+/ 9.8	0.06	0.14
COI	*PIMCO Enhanced Short Maturity ET	MINT	C-	101.48	D / 1.7	2.31 / 19	1.49 / 18	--	1.19	B+/ 9.9	-0.04	0.01
COI	*Guggenheim BltShs 2013 Corp Bd E	BSCD	C-	20.80	D- / 1.5	1.10 / 16	--	--	1.27	B+/ 9.9	-0.19	0.20
COI	*ProShares Short Inv Grade Corp	IGS	D	31.90	E+ / 0.7	-10.86 / 8	--	--	0.00	B / 8.3	0.03	0.26

99 Pct = Best
0 Pct = Worst

* Denotes ETF Fund, N/A denotes number is not available

Fund Type	Fund Name	Ticker Symbol	Overall Investment Rating	Price As of 12/31/12	Performance Rating/Pts	Annualized Total Return Through 12/31/12			Dividend Yield %	Risk Rating/ Pts	Premium/Discount	
	99 Pct = Best *0 Pct = Worst*					1Yr/Pct	3Yr/Pct	5Yr/Pct			As of 12/31/12	1 Year Average
EM	*iShares MSCI Emg Mkts Min Vol In	EEMV	A	60.56	B+ / 8.7	20.57 / 72	--	--	1.27	B / 8.7	0.25	0.43
EM	Stone Harbor Emg Markets Income	EDF	A-	24.76	B+ / 8.7	21.77 / 76	--	--	8.00	B / 8.0	0.45	3.57
EM	*iShares MSCI Emg Mkts Finls Sctr	EMFN	B+	27.65	A+ / 9.7	28.09 / 88	--	--	0.40	C+ / 6.6	0.58	0.44
EM	*First Trust Emerg Mkt AlphaDEX	FEM	B+	26.39	A / 9.4	19.13 / 68	--	--	0.36	B- / 7.1	-1.49	0.43
EM	*Guggenheim MSCI EAFE Eq Weight E	EWEF	B+	38.56	A / 9.3	20.61 / 72	--	--	2.70	B- / 7.0	-3.62	-0.54
EM	*iShares MSCI Emg Mkts Sm Cap Ind	EEMS	B+	47.30	A / 9.3	20.19 / 71	--	--	6.63	B- / 7.3	-3.11	N/A
EM	*EGShares Emerging Markets Cons E	ECON	B+	26.64	A- / 9.0	19.39 / 69	--	--	0.40	B- / 7.6	0.57	0.23
EM	Western Asset Emerging Market Debt	ESD	B+	21.80	B- / 7.5	24.80 / 83	16.24 / 77	13.89 / 85	6.61	B / 8.6	-2.46	-4.19
EM	ING Emerging Markets High Div Eqty	IHD	B	14.63	A+ / 9.6	23.70 / 81	--	--	9.84	C+ / 6.1	-0.61	-0.60
EM	Aberdeen Indonesia Fund	IF	B	11.67	B / 8.0	18.78 / 66	19.05 / 86	12.91 / 80	1.86	B- / 7.3	-9.95	-9.48
EM	Templeton Emerging Markets Income	TEI	B-	17.31	B- / 7.4	22.22 / 77	15.55 / 75	16.23 / 94	16.04	B- / 7.4	7.78	3.74
EM	Morgan Stanley Emerging Mkts Debt	MSD	B-	11.95	C+ / 6.9	25.75 / 85	13.70 / 67	13.10 / 81	6.03	B / 8.2	-8.29	-8.16
EM	Aberdeen Emerging Mkt Tele & Infr	ETF	B-	21.50	C+ / 6.7	24.99 / 84	11.55 / 56	1.95 / 27	1.14	B / 8.3	-11.05	-11.42
EM	*PowerShares Emrg Mkt Sovereign D	PCY	B-	31.45	C+ / 5.8	21.90 / 76	13.01 / 63	10.09 / 70	4.44	B / 8.9	0.87	0.05
EM	*Market Vectors Egypt Index ETF	EGPT	C+	13.08	A+ / 9.6	39.59 / 97	--	--	7.13	C- / 4.2	-0.23	-0.56
EM	*iShares MSCI Emg Mkts Matl Sctr	EMMT	C+	21.18	B+ / 8.3	10.46 / 35	--	--	2.74	C+ / 5.9	-2.04	-0.59
EM	*Guggenheim MSCI Em Mkt Eq Weight	EWEM	C+	35.73	B / 8.1	13.69 / 44	--	--	1.06	C+ / 6.0	-1.65	-0.18
EM	*DBX MSCI Emg Mkt Currency-Hedged	DBEM	C+	22.84	B / 7.9	13.10 / 42	--	--	3.04	C / 5.5	-0.95	0.94
EM	Morgan Stanley Emg Mkts Dom Debt	EDD	C+	16.84	C+ / 6.6	19.69 / 70	13.71 / 68	9.39 / 67	5.94	B- / 7.6	-9.56	-6.73
EM	Western Asset Emerging Mkts Inc	EMD	C+	15.32	C+ / 6.1	22.25 / 77	14.65 / 71	13.11 / 82	6.66	B / 8.1	-2.92	-2.95
EM	Western Asset Worldwide Inc Fd	SBW	C+	15.12	C+ / 5.8	20.75 / 73	13.68 / 67	12.05 / 77	6.67	B / 8.2	-6.32	-5.41
EM	*WisdomTree Emg Mkts Local Debt F	ELD	C+	53.46	C+ / 5.6	12.93 / 41	--	--	10.44	B / 8.6	0.04	0.19
EM	*iShares JPMorgan USD Emg Mkts Bo	EMB	C+	122.79	C / 4.6	17.25 / 59	11.17 / 53	9.07 / 66	3.82	B / 8.9	1.34	0.55
EM	Global High Income Fund	GHI	C	12.92	C+ / 5.7	16.98 / 58	13.08 / 64	8.98 / 65	7.40	B- / 7.4	-6.24	-3.18
EM	*WisdomTree Emg Mkts SmCap Div Fd	DGS	C	49.44	C / 5.5	21.30 / 74	8.20 / 39	6.97 / 55	1.54	C+ / 6.6	-0.84	0.55
EM	*iPath Long Enh MSCI Em Mkt Idx E	EMLB	C-	108.98	A / 9.5	25.63 / 85	--	--	0.00	D+ / 2.5	3.91	-1.99
EM	*SPDR S&P Russia	RBL	C-	29.11	C+ / 6.1	9.23 / 33	--	--	4.68	C / 5.3	-0.34	0.12
EM	*PowerShares DWA Emg Mkts Tech Le	PIE	C-	18.59	C / 4.6	16.22 / 54	8.30 / 39	-3.30 / 11	0.33	C+ / 6.9	-0.64	0.15
EM	*Vanguard Total World Stock ETF	VT	C-	49.42	C / 4.4	18.18 / 63	7.05 / 36	--	2.25	B- / 7.4	-2.27	0.17
EM	*SPDR S&P Emerg Middle East&Afric	GAF	C-	73.91	C / 4.3	16.43 / 54	7.62 / 37	5.10 / 44	3.15	B- / 7.2	3.41	-0.09
EM	Morgan Stanley Emerging Markets	MSF	C-	15.50	C- / 3.9	19.93 / 71	4.51 / 28	1.04 / 22	0.53	B- / 7.3	-11.33	-9.71
EM	*WisdomTree Emg Mkts Eqty Inc Fd	DEM	C-	57.19	C- / 3.8	12.48 / 40	7.99 / 38	7.46 / 57	1.41	B- / 7.1	0.67	0.52
EM	*Market Vectors Renminbi Bond ETF	CHLC	C-	25.53	D- / 1.5	1.27 / 17	--	--	3.29	B+ / 9.7	-2.30	0.15
EM	*SPDR S&P Emerging Asia Pacific E	GMF	D+	77.49	C- / 3.2	15.56 / 50	4.80 / 29	2.43 / 29	2.24	B- / 7.0	-1.22	-0.04
EM	*Vanguard FTSE Emerging Markets E	VWO	D+	44.53	C- / 3.1	15.78 / 51	4.64 / 28	1.29 / 24	2.02	C+ / 6.8	-0.49	0.10
EM	*SPDR S&P Emerging Markets ETF	GMM	D+	67.22	C- / 3.0	14.50 / 47	4.06 / 26	2.04 / 27	2.31	B- / 7.0	-0.59	0.10
EM	*iShares MSCI Emerging Markets	EEM	D+	44.35	D+ / 2.9	15.33 / 49	3.76 / 25	1.58 / 25	0.10	C+ / 6.8	0.05	0.18
EM	*iShares MSCI ACWI ex US TS Index	AXTE	D+	51.37	D+ / 2.4	6.53 / 27	--	--	2.95	B- / 7.9	-2.10	0.03
EM	*Direxion Daily India Bull 3X	INDL	D	20.14	C+ / 6.0	2.97 / 20	--	--	0.00	D / 2.1	-2.99	0.08
EM	*SPDR S&P Emerging Europe ETF	GUR	D	43.95	C- / 3.4	21.40 / 75	1.00 / 17	-5.16 / 8	3.52	C / 5.4	-0.54	0.02
EM	*PowerShares Emg Mkts Infrastruct	PXR	D	43.21	D+ / 2.5	15.10 / 48	1.15 / 18	--	1.40	C+ / 6.2	-2.08	-0.20
EM	*SPDR S&P International Div ETF	DWX	D	48.11	D+ / 2.4	13.40 / 43	1.57 / 19	--	3.59	C+ / 6.4	-2.51	0.23
EM	*PowerShares FTSE RAFI Emg Mkts	PXH	D	22.82	D+ / 2.3	10.98 / 36	1.51 / 18	1.80 / 26	1.39	C+ / 6.7	-0.35	0.16
EM	Templeton Emerging Markets Fd	EMF	D	20.00	D / 2.2	10.51 / 36	-0.16 / 14	4.31 / 39	1.44	C+ / 6.5	-9.05	-7.77
EM	*SPDR S&P Emerging Latin America	GML	D	74.30	D / 2.0	6.48 / 27	0.65 / 16	3.39 / 34	1.71	C+ / 6.7	-2.00	-0.08
EM	*iShares S&P India Nifty 50	INDY	D	24.97	D / 1.9	17.19 / 59	-0.94 / 13	--	0.37	C+ / 6.0	0.24	0.34
EM	*BLDRS Emerging Market 50 ADR Ind	ADRE	D	40.22	D / 1.8	4.38 / 23	0.11 / 15	-1.17 / 16	2.81	B- / 7.1	-2.24	-0.09
EM	*Market Vectors Poland ETF	PLND	D-	22.47	D+ / 2.9	35.16 / 95	-1.04 / 13	--	3.65	C / 4.8	0.36	0.16
EM	*ProShares Ultra MSCI Emerging Mk	EET	D-	85.62	D+ / 2.7	26.98 / 87	-1.45 / 12	--	0.00	C- / 3.8	-0.42	-0.02
EM	*IShares MSCI EM Eastern Europe	ESR	D-	27.06	D+ / 2.3	16.28 / 54	0.42 / 16	--	1.27	C / 5.3	0.45	0.07
EM	*iPath MSCI India Index ETN	INP	D-	59.33	D / 1.7	18.28 / 64	-2.89 / 10	-7.27 / 7	0.00	C+ / 5.7	-0.65	0.30
EM	*ProShares Short MSCI Emg Mkts	EUM	D-	26.68	E+ / 0.6	-17.45 / 6	-11.45 / 7	-18.18 / 3	0.00	C+ / 6.1	0.38	N/A

* Denotes ETF Fund, N/A denotes number is not available

					PERFORMANCE					RISK	VALUATION	
99 Pct = Best 0 Pct = Worst					Perform-ance	Annualized Total Return Through 12/31/12				Risk	Premium/Discount	
Fund Type	Fund Name	Ticker Symbol	Overall Investment Rating	Price As of 12/31/12	Rating/Pts	1Yr/Pct	3Yr/Pct	5Yr/Pct	Dividend Yield %	Rating/ Pts	As of 12/31/12	1 Year Average
EN	First Trust Energy Infrastructure	FIF	A+	21.15	B+ / 8.5	18.49 / 65	--	--	6.24	B+ / 9.2	-6.13	-5.78
EN	Kayne Anderson Engy Development Co	KED	A	0.00	A / 9.3	30.56 / 91	27.89 / 99	10.80 / 72	5.03	B / 8.0		4.98
EN	First Trust Energy Income and Gro	FEN	B+	30.65	B / 8.0	20.42 / 72	19.11 / 86	16.16 / 93	6.39	B / 8.5	0.03	5.23
EN	*PowerShares Dynamic Enrg Exp & P	PXE	B	26.97	B+ / 8.7	24.36 / 82	19.40 / 87	5.95 / 49	5.49	B- / 7.1	-3.30	-0.03
EN	Kayne Anderson MLP Inv Co	KYN	B	29.47	B- / 7.3	12.10 / 39	18.38 / 84	9.85 / 69	9.33	B / 8.2	0.72	8.03
EN	Tortoise Pipeline & Enrgy Fund Inc	TTP	B	0.00	C+ / 6.8	13.89 / 44	--	--	6.69	B / 8.6		-3.33
EN	Tortoise Power and Energy Inf Fund	TPZ	B	0.00	C+ / 6.8	9.55 / 34	17.06 / 80	--	5.96	B / 8.3		-3.77
EN	*PowerShares Dynamic Energy	PXI	B-	42.89	B / 7.8	16.26 / 54	18.10 / 83	7.81 / 59	2.90	B- / 7.1	-3.51	-0.05
EN	ClearBridge Energy MLP Oppty Fd In	EMO	B-	20.70	B- / 7.1	15.96 / 52	--	--	6.47	B / 8.0	-0.29	1.06
EN	ClearBridge Energy MLP Fund Inc	CEM	B-	23.03	C+ / 6.8	14.80 / 47	--	--	6.43	B / 8.1	-2.66	3.20
EN	*UBS E-TRACS 2x Levd Lng Alerian	MLPL	C+	38.55	B+ / 8.8	19.74 / 70	--	--	8.42	C / 4.6	-10.08	-0.07
EN	*United States Gasoline Fund LP	UGA	C+	58.44	C+ / 6.8	15.34 / 49	16.73 / 79	--	0.00	B- / 7.3	0.93	0.05
EN	Fiduciary/Claymore MLP Opp	FMO	C+	21.77	C+ / 6.2	13.92 / 45	15.40 / 74	9.47 / 67	7.11	B- / 7.9	-0.59	7.23
EN	*JPMorgan Alerian MLP Idx ETN	AMJ	C	38.46	B- / 7.0	10.78 / 36	17.74 / 82	--	3.97	C / 5.1	-6.92	0.13
EN	Tortoise Energy Capital	TYY	C	0.00	C+ / 6.9	16.30 / 54	15.21 / 73	10.47 / 71	5.87	C+ / 6.3		2.91
EN	Tortoise Energy Infrastr Corp	TYG	C	0.00	C+ / 5.8	5.90 / 26	15.88 / 76	12.84 / 80	5.96	C+ / 6.6		13.52
EN	Tortoise North American Energy	TYN	C	0.00	C / 5.5	16.38 / 54	11.62 / 56	10.71 / 72	6.17	C+ / 6.9		-0.10
EN	*Guggenheim S&P Global Water Idx	CGW	C	22.24	C / 5.2	21.16 / 74	8.74 / 42	2.82 / 31	2.03	B / 8.0	-1.90	-0.16
EN	*FlexShs Morningstar Gl Upstream	GUNR	C	35.62	C / 4.9	7.60 / 29	--	--	1.03	B / 8.1	-1.71	0.34
EN	Salient MLP & Energy Infrastructur	SMF	C	0.00	C / 4.3	13.79 / 44	--	--	7.13	B / 8.3		2.75
EN	*Alps Alerian MLP ETF	AMLP	C	15.95	C- / 3.3	7.44 / 29	--	--	6.42	B+ / 9.0	-4.55	0.06
EN	*SPDR S&P Glbl Natural Resources	GNR	C-	51.56	C / 4.7	5.16 / 24	--	--	1.83	C+ / 6.7	-2.09	0.22
EN	Kayne Anderson Energy Tot Ret	KYE	C-	24.59	C / 4.3	3.21 / 21	12.93 / 63	9.72 / 68	7.81	B- / 7.2	-7.07	1.86
EN	*Energy Select Sector SPDR	XLE	C-	71.42	C- / 3.8	7.99 / 30	9.34 / 44	3.07 / 32	2.08	B- / 7.3	-3.01	N/A
EN	*United States Brent Oil Fund	BNO	C-	82.07	C- / 3.7	5.90 / 26	--	--	0.00	B- / 7.6	0.27	0.03
EN	*iShares DJ US Energy	IYE	C-	40.84	C- / 3.6	7.75 / 30	8.85 / 42	2.60 / 30	1.81	B- / 7.4	-3.54	0.01
EN	*Vanguard Energy ETF	VDE	C-	102.26	C- / 3.5	6.58 / 27	8.54 / 41	2.89 / 31	1.95	B- / 7.3	-3.35	0.01
EN	*IQ Global Resources ETF	GRES	C-	30.42	C- / 3.0	6.66 / 27	5.81 / 32	--	1.20	B- / 7.8	0.83	0.06
EN	*UBS E-TRACS Wells Fargo MLP Inde	MLPW	D+	28.71	C / 4.6	10.98 / 36	--	--	3.80	C / 5.2	-2.74	-0.13
EN	*Guggenheim S&P 500 Eq Wght Engy	RYE	D+	63.85	C- / 3.6	8.20 / 31	8.60 / 41	3.19 / 33	1.52	C+ / 6.9	-3.11	-0.07
EN	Petroleum and Resources Corp.	PEO	D+	23.92	C- / 3.3	7.74 / 29	7.70 / 37	1.43 / 24	3.01	B- / 7.3	-17.12	-13.18
EN	*SPDR S&P Oil & Gas Equip & Serv	XES	D+	34.62	C- / 3.3	5.58 / 25	6.61 / 34	1.14 / 23	1.21	C+ / 6.3	-4.63	N/A
EN	*iShares MSCI ACWI ex US Enrgy Id	AXEN	D+	53.92	C- / 3.1	1.84 / 18	--	--	2.59	C+ / 6.6	-2.92	-0.11
EN	*First Trust Energy AlphaDEX	FXN	D+	19.85	C- / 3.0	6.89 / 28	5.85 / 32	0.65 / 21	1.45	C+ / 6.7	-2.70	-0.01
EN	*iShares DJ US Oil & Gas Exp & Pr	IEO	D+	63.54	C- / 3.0	6.29 / 27	6.20 / 33	2.42 / 29	0.93	C+ / 6.8	-2.95	-0.01
EN	*United States Heating Oil Fund	UHN	D+	33.73	D+ / 2.8	-2.32 / 12	7.88 / 38	--	0.00	B- / 7.4	0.69	0.03
EN	*iShares S&P Global Energy	IXC	D+	38.25	D+ / 2.5	5.33 / 24	4.63 / 28	1.03 / 22	2.45	B- / 7.4	-2.82	-0.03
EN	*iShares S&P NA Natural Resource	IGE	D+	38.16	D+ / 2.5	2.92 / 20	4.92 / 29	1.15 / 23	2.34	B- / 7.1	-2.53	N/A
EN	BlackRock Energy & Resources	BGR	D+	23.55	D+ / 2.5	2.75 / 20	5.00 / 29	4.33 / 39	6.88	B- / 7.1	-11.53	-5.49
EN	*iPath DJ UBS Tin Tot Ret Sub	JJT	D	53.86	C+ / 6.1	18.00 / 62	10.26 / 49	--	0.00	D+ / 2.9	-5.94	-0.13
EN	*iPath DJ UBS Precious Mtls Tot R	JJP	D	89.23	C / 4.4	0.10 / 14	13.83 / 68	--	0.00	C / 4.7	0.45	-0.10
EN	*Credit Suisse Cushing 30 MLP ETN	MLPN	D	24.10	C- / 4.1	8.36 / 31	--	--	4.07	C / 5.0	-6.34	0.09
EN	*PowerShares Dynamic Oil & Gas Sv	PXJ	D	20.34	C- / 3.3	6.34 / 27	6.46 / 34	-2.07 / 13	0.13	C+ / 6.0	-5.00	-0.08
EN	GAMCO Nat Res Gold & Income Trust	GNT	D	13.66	C- / 3.0	10.33 / 35	--	--	12.30	C+ / 6.1	-2.98	4.62
EN	*PowerShares Global Water Portfol	PIO	D	18.01	D+ / 2.9	16.46 / 55	1.02 / 17	-1.22 / 16	1.05	C+ / 6.6	-1.96	-0.38
EN	*iShares DJ US Oil Equip & Svcs	IEZ	D	51.01	D+ / 2.8	3.36 / 21	5.42 / 31	-0.24 / 18	0.84	C+ / 6.2	-5.22	-0.02
EN	*Global X China Energy ETF	CHIE	D	14.50	D+ / 2.7	11.42 / 37	1.55 / 18	--	1.75	C+ / 6.4	-4.35	-0.24
EN	*PowerShares WilderHill Progr Ene	PUW	D	25.58	D+ / 2.6	12.24 / 39	3.16 / 23	1.57 / 25	1.19	C+ / 6.7	-3.65	-0.12
EN	BlackRock EcoSolutions Investment	BQR	D	8.39	D+ / 2.5	13.17 / 42	1.64 / 19	-2.08 / 13	8.55	C+ / 6.3	-11.68	-3.20
EN	*WisdomTree Global Natural Resour	GNAT	D	24.54	D / 2.1	5.89 / 26	1.17 / 18	-0.11 / 19	2.18	C+ / 6.8	-0.77	-0.04
EN	*SPDR SP Intl Energy Sector ETF	IPW	D	24.96	D / 2.0	6.14 / 26	0.99 / 17	--	4.54	B- / 7.3	-1.96	-0.41
EN	*PowerShares DB Energy Fund	DBE	D	27.94	D / 2.0	-0.99 / 13	2.97 / 23	-3.23 / 11	0.00	B- / 7.1	-0.39	0.02

* Denotes ETF Fund, N/A denotes number is not available

Fund Type	Fund Name	Ticker Symbol	Overall Investment Rating	Price As of 12/31/12	Perform-ance Rating/Pts	Annualized Total Return Through 12/31/12			Dividend Yield %	Risk Rating/ Pts	Premium/Discount	
	99 Pct = Best 0 Pct = Worst					1Yr/Pct	3Yr/Pct	5Yr/Pct			As of 12/31/12	1 Year Average
FS	*iShares MSCI ACWI ex US Fn Sctr	AXFN	B+	23.40	A+ / 9.7	33.40 / 94	--	--	4.76	C+ / 6.6	-2.42	0.13
FS	First Tr Specialty Finance &Fin Op	FGB	B+	7.80	A- / 9.1	36.89 / 96	19.96 / 88	6.26 / 50	8.46	B- / 7.4	-6.92	-2.49
FS	Financial Trends Fund	DHFT	B+	11.44	B+ / 8.9	38.91 / 97	16.59 / 78	3.08 / 32	0.10	B- / 7.7	-7.07	-7.60
FS	*iShares MSCI Europ Finls Sctr Id	EUFN	B-	19.80	A+ / 9.9	44.74 / 98	--	--	1.70	C / 5.2	-5.17	0.14
FS	John Hancock Financial Opptys	BTO	B-	17.60	B / 8.2	32.66 / 94	15.20 / 73	4.00 / 37	6.73	C+ / 6.9	-9.28	-8.12
FS	*ProShares Ultra Financials	UYG	C+	67.81	B+ / 8.4	51.91 / 99	7.65 / 37	-24.31 / 2	1.39	C / 5.1	-8.10	-0.05
FS	*Guggenheim S&P 500 Eq Wght Finl	RYF	C+	29.16	C+ / 6.6	25.08 / 84	10.73 / 51	-0.56 / 18	2.98	B- / 7.5	-4.55	-0.07
FS	*First Trust Financial AlphaDEX	FXO	C+	15.67	C+ / 6.0	21.27 / 74	10.99 / 53	5.18 / 45	2.71	B- / 7.7	-4.57	0.01
FS	*PowerShares Dynamic Financial	PFI	C+	21.15	C+ / 5.8	20.09 / 71	10.76 / 52	1.15 / 23	2.25	B- / 7.9	-3.99	-0.05
FS	*RevenueShares Financials Sector	RWW	C	32.04	C+ / 5.9	31.49 / 93	6.00 / 33	--	1.98	C+ / 6.6	-4.53	-0.16
FS	*Vanguard Financials ETF	VFH	C	34.10	C / 5.5	25.33 / 84	8.02 / 38	-2.71 / 12	3.46	B- / 7.4	-3.89	0.02
FS	*iShares S&P Global Financials	IXG	C	45.66	C / 5.4	32.05 / 93	3.30 / 24	-5.08 / 8	1.83	B- / 7.0	-3.63	0.01
FS	*iShares DJ US Financial Sector	IYF	C	60.70	C / 5.3	25.29 / 84	7.56 / 37	-3.17 / 11	2.33	B- / 7.4	-4.44	-0.01
FS	*iShares DJ US Financial Services	IYG	C	59.31	C / 5.1	29.73 / 91	4.67 / 28	-5.23 / 8	0.18	B- / 7.0	-4.66	-0.01
FS	*Financial Select Sector SPDR	XLF	C	16.39	C / 5.1	26.16 / 86	6.21 / 33	-5.65 / 7	2.54	B- / 7.2	-4.21	-0.01
FS	*PowerShares Financial Preferred	PGF	C	18.28	C / 4.4	16.96 / 58	10.33 / 49	4.99 / 44	7.60	B / 8.8	-1.67	0.08
FS	*Direxion Financial Bull 3x Share	FAS	C-	119.92	A- / 9.0	80.74 / 99	0.30 / 16	--	0.00	D / 1.9	-11.89	-0.06
FS	*SP Capital Markets ETF	KCE	C-	34.11	C / 4.3	26.88 / 87	1.96 / 20	-6.45 / 7	7.76	C+ / 6.7	-5.90	-0.05
FS	First Opportunity Fund	FOFI	C-	7.69	C- / 4.0	23.22 / 80	7.32 / 36	-3.28 / 11	0.00	B / 8.0	-24.83	-23.28
FS	*SP Regional Banking ETF	KRE	C-	27.97	C- / 3.8	12.58 / 40	8.84 / 42	0.33 / 21	3.27	B- / 7.3	-3.42	0.01
FS	*SPDR SP Mortgage Finance ETF	KME	D+	42.70	C / 4.7	35.02 / 95	3.37 / 24	--	4.80	C+ / 5.9	-4.96	-0.02
FS	*SP Bank ETF	KBE	D+	23.83	C- / 3.3	17.30 / 60	3.79 / 25	-6.30 / 7	3.47	C+ / 6.9	-3.76	-0.02
FS	*SPDR SP Intl Finl Sector ETF	IPF	D+	19.33	C- / 3.1	35.80 / 96	2.26 / 21	--	10.48	B- / 7.0	-2.67	-0.13
FS	*iShares DJ US Regional Banks	IAT	D+	24.43	C- / 3.0	12.77 / 41	5.78 / 32	-3.33 / 11	0.25	B- / 7.3	-3.63	-0.01
FS	*PowerShares Dynamic Banking Port	PJB	D+	13.31	D+ / 2.8	12.67 / 40	5.27 / 30	-1.79 / 14	2.27	B- / 7.3	-3.97	-0.17
FS	*ProShares Ultra KBW Regional Ban	KRU	D	45.21	C / 4.9	13.34 / 43	--	--	2.82	C- / 3.8	-6.16	0.04
FS	*Global X China Financials ETF	CHIX	D	13.66	C- / 4.1	32.91 / 94	2.33 / 21	--	2.73	C / 5.2	-2.15	-0.36
FS	*iShares DJ US Broker-Dealers Idx	IAI	D	23.63	D / 2.0	17.23 / 59	-2.15 / 11	-9.05 / 6	0.54	C+ / 6.7	-5.21	-0.04
FS	*EGShares Financials GEMS ETF	FGEM	D-	21.75	C- / 3.2	21.18 / 74	2.63 / 22	--	1.91	C- / 3.2	-2.51	-0.41
FS	*ProShares Short KBW Regional Ban	KRS	D-	43.91	E+ / 0.7	-13.08 / 7	--	--	0.00	C / 5.5	3.51	-0.18
FS	*ProShares Short Financials	SEF	D-	28.39	E / 0.5	-23.32 / 4	-14.10 / 6	--	0.00	C+ / 6.3	4.30	N/A
FS	*ProShares UltraShort Financials	SKF	E	33.54	E- / 0.2	-42.43 / 2	-30.26 / 3	-43.11 / 0	0.00	C- / 3.3	9.11	0.01
FS	*Direxion Financial Bear 3x Share	FAZ	E-	15.11	E- / 0.1	-58.56 / 0	-46.78 / 0	--	0.00	D / 2.0	14.64	-0.02

					PERFORMANCE					RISK	VALUATION	
					Perform-ance Rating/Pts	Annualized Total Return Through 12/31/12				Risk Rating/ Pts	Premium/Discount	
Fund Type	Fund Name	Ticker Symbol	Overall Investment Rating	Price As of 12/31/12		1Yr/Pct	3Yr/Pct	5Yr/Pct	Dividend Yield %		As of 12/31/12	1 Year Average
FO	Thai Fund	TTF	A+	19.95	A+ / 9.8	69.21 / 99	36.28 / 99	19.11 / 99	1.66	B- / 7.8	-14.52	-12.77
FO	Mexico Equity & Income Fund	MXE	A+	14.25	A+ / 9.7	54.56 / 99	26.13 / 98	11.30 / 74	0.00	B / 8.0	-15.43	-11.28
FO	*iShares MSCI New Zealand Inv Mk	ENZL	A+	34.58	A+ / 9.7	34.74 / 95	--	--	5.47	B- / 7.8	-2.21	0.10
FO	*DBX MSCI EAFE Currency-Hedged Eq	DBEF	A+	22.06	A / 9.5	19.21 / 68	--	--	2.71	B / 8.0	-2.43	-0.02
FO	*iShares MSCI Philipps Invst Mkt	EPHE	A	34.55	A+ / 9.8	45.19 / 98	--	--	0.24	B- / 7.5	-3.57	0.14
FO	*iShares MSCI Irlnd Capd Inv Mkt	EIRL	A	25.09	A+ / 9.8	37.24 / 96	--	--	0.74	B- / 7.3	-0.28	0.57
FO	Mexico Fund	MXF	A	29.02	A+ / 9.7	52.02 / 99	22.55 / 94	12.25 / 78	1.08	B- / 7.5	-9.88	-7.81
FO	*First Trust Europe AlphaDEX	FEP	A-	26.20	A+ / 9.7	24.40 / 83	--	--	0.29	B- / 7.2	-1.06	0.77
FO	*iShares MSCI ACWI xUS Cnsmr Stp	AXSL	A-	71.04	B / 8.2	20.43 / 72	--	--	1.36	B / 8.6	-1.36	0.18
FO	*iShares MSCI Thailand Inv Market	THD	B+	82.49	A+ / 9.6	39.82 / 97	26.94 / 99		1.01	C+ / 6.9	0.01	0.25
FO	*First Trust AsiaPac Ex-Jpn Alpha	FPA	B+	27.94	A / 9.5	22.14 / 77	--	--	0.62	C+ / 6.8	-0.46	0.35
FO	*Madrona International ETF	FWDI	B+	24.03	A / 9.5	19.96 / 71	--	--	1.23	C+ / 6.7	-2.32	-0.23
FO	*First Trust South Korea AlphaDEX	FKO	B+	26.83	A- / 9.2	18.28 / 64	--	--	0.92	C+ / 6.8	1.05	-0.01
FO	*iShares MSCI ACWI xUS Cnsmr Dis	AXDI	B+	66.77	A- / 9.1	22.69 / 78	--	--	1.62	B- / 7.1	-0.89	-0.31
FO	*Pax MSCI EAFE ESG Index ETF	EAPS	B+	24.51	A- / 9.1	18.41 / 65	--	--	1.79	B- / 7.4	-0.49	0.76
FO	*First Trust Dev Mkt Ex-US AlphaD	FDT	B+	44.27	A- / 9.0	16.75 / 57	--	--	1.91	B- / 7.5	-1.14	0.42
FO	*Schwab Emerging Markets Equity E	SCHE	B+	26.39	A- / 9.0	16.40 / 54	--	--	4.22	C+ / 6.9	0.11	0.38
FO	*EGShares China Infrastructure ET	CHXX	B	19.63	A+ / 9.8	30.62 / 92	--	--	1.21	C / 5.4	-1.41	-0.13
FO	*First Trust China AlphaDEX	FCA	B	25.13	A+ / 9.8	29.58 / 90	--	--	1.06	C+ / 5.8	-2.10	0.23
FO	*Market Vectors Germany SmallCap	GERJ	B	22.91	A+ / 9.7	30.79 / 92	--	--	2.68	C+ / 6.0	-2.26	0.01
FO	*Global X Brazil Consumer ETF	BRAQ	B	20.27	A+ / 9.7	26.72 / 87	--	--	1.21	C+ / 6.1	0.40	-0.13
FO	*Schwab Intl Small-Cap Equity ETF	SCHC	B	27.05	A+ / 9.7	24.30 / 82	--	--	5.99	C+ / 6.0	-1.74	0.48
FO	*Global X FTSE Norway 30 ETF	NORW	B	15.25	A+ / 9.6	26.06 / 86	--	--	2.81	C+ / 6.2	-2.24	-0.03
FO	*iShares MSCI China Index	MCHI	B	48.54	A+ / 9.6	20.53 / 72	--	--	0.38	C+ / 6.3	-0.65	0.25
FO	*iShares MSCI Brazil Small Cap In	EWZS	B	27.80	A / 9.5	21.15 / 74	--	--	2.36	C+ / 6.1	-0.14	-0.16
FO	New Germany Fund	GF	B	15.58	B+ / 8.9	38.58 / 97	14.21 / 69	6.29 / 50	8.13	C+ / 6.4	-14.96	-10.22
FO	*iShares MSCI Mexico Inv Market	EWW	B	70.53	B+ / 8.4	36.35 / 96	14.89 / 72	9.27 / 67	0.49	B- / 7.3	-3.87	0.08
FO	*iShares MSCI Poland Investbl Mkt	EPOL	B-	29.62	A+ / 9.8	39.88 / 97	--	--	4.25	C / 4.8	2.00	0.21
FO	*iShares MSCI China Small Cap Ind	ECNS	B-	41.09	A+ / 9.8	31.87 / 93	--	--	2.18	C / 5.2	-3.93	-0.26
FO	Thai Capital Fund	TF	B-	12.11	A+ / 9.7	49.86 / 98	28.26 / 99	15.14 / 90	0.00	C / 5.1	-5.39	-7.59
FO	*iShares MSCI Turkey Inv Market	TUR	B-	66.78	A- / 9.1	68.00 / 99	8.64 / 41	--	1.52	C / 5.4	-2.94	0.17
FO	*Market Vectors Lat Am SC Index E	LATM	B-	24.41	B+ / 8.9	15.21 / 49	--	--	4.47	C+ / 5.9	-3.75	-0.30
FO	Turkish Investment Fund	TKF	B-	16.64	B+ / 8.7	53.41 / 99	10.07 / 47	1.93 / 26	1.37	C+ / 5.9	-16.34	-10.95
FO	*iShares MSCI ACWI ex US Indsl In	AXID	B-	55.86	B / 7.7	19.19 / 68	--	--	1.28	B- / 7.0	-3.94	-0.44
FO	The New Ireland Fund	IRL	B-	9.10	B- / 7.5	35.49 / 95	8.65 / 41	-2.48 / 12	0.00	B- / 7.4	-15.51	-12.29
FO	*iShares MSCI Hong Kong	EWH	B-	19.42	B- / 7.5	30.54 / 91	11.23 / 54	3.17 / 33	1.36	B- / 7.1	-2.07	0.08
FO	*DBX MSCI Brazil Currency-Hedged	DBBR	B-	20.12	B- / 7.2	4.78 / 23	--	--	4.28	B- / 7.8	-1.90	0.10
FO	*iShares MSCI EAFE Minimum Vol Id	EFAV	B-	54.68	C+ / 5.7	13.87 / 44	--	--	1.83	B+ / 9.0	-0.46	0.55
FO	*ProShares Ultra MSCI Mex Invest	UMX	C+	49.02	A+ / 9.9	74.42 / 99	--	--	0.00	C / 4.6	-7.68	-0.25
FO	*ProShares Ultra MSCI Europe	UPV	C+	33.44	A+ / 9.9	50.40 / 99	--	--	0.00	C- / 3.7	-5.70	-0.04
FO	*Global X FTSE Greece 20 ETF	GREK	C+	18.06	A+ / 9.9	48.10 / 98	--	--	0.13	C / 4.4	-4.75	1.00
FO	*ProShares Ultra MSCI Pacific ex-	UXJ	C+	37.92	A+ / 9.9	44.88 / 98	--	--	0.00	C- / 4.0	-2.69	-0.10
FO	*Global X China Materials ETF	CHIM	C+	8.77	A / 9.5	8.46 / 31	--	--	1.53	C / 4.5	-7.39	0.18
FO	*WisdomTree Global ex-US Real Est	DRW	C+	29.97	B+ / 8.4	36.67 / 96	14.45 / 71	1.24 / 24	16.32	C / 5.3	-1.19	0.07
FO	*WisdomTree Europe Small Cap Div	DFE	C+	41.08	B / 7.7	34.63 / 95	7.93 / 38	1.31 / 24	2.58	C+ / 6.5	-2.84	0.68
FO	*iShares MSCI All Peru Capped Idx	EPU	C+	45.88	B / 7.7	21.53 / 75	15.53 / 75	--	2.34	C+ / 6.7	-3.10	-0.11
FO	*First Trust Latin America AlphaD	FLN	C+	27.16	B / 7.6	11.18 / 37	--	--	0.63	C+ / 6.8	-0.07	0.52
FO	*Global X FTSE Andean 40 ETF	AND	C+	14.58	B- / 7.4	15.73 / 51	--	--	1.78	B- / 7.1	-2.80	-0.26
FO	*iShares MSCI Switzerland	EWL	C+	26.80	C+ / 6.9	27.51 / 88	9.37 / 44	4.84 / 43	2.36	B- / 7.4	-4.11	0.08
FO	*WisdomTree Intl Small Cap Divide	DLS	C+	52.13	C+ / 6.8	26.39 / 86	8.45 / 40	2.36 / 28	2.42	B- / 7.5	-2.10	0.32
FO	Herzfeld Caribbean Basin Fund	CUBA	C+	7.64	C+ / 5.9	25.99 / 85	7.88 / 38	3.41 / 34	0.00	B / 8.2	-14.83	-10.14
FO	*iShares MSCI Malaysia	EWM	C+	15.13	C+ / 5.9	13.75 / 44	14.36 / 70	6.42 / 51	1.93	B- / 7.8	-0.72	0.07

* Denotes ETF Fund, N/A denotes number is not available

99 Pct = Best
0 Pct = Worst

Fund Type	Fund Name	Ticker Symbol	Overall Investment Rating	Price As of 12/31/12	Performance Rating/Pts	Annualized Total Return Through 12/31/12			Dividend Yield %	Risk Rating/ Pts	Premium/Discount	
						1Yr/Pct	3Yr/Pct	5Yr/Pct			As of 12/31/12	1 Year Average
GEI	Fort Dearborn Inc. Secs.	FDI	B+	16.54	B- / 7.3	15.56 / 50	18.11 / 83	13.39 / 83	4.23	B / 8.9	-3.33	-5.09
GEI	*VelocityShares Dly Invs VIX M-T	ZIV	B	23.77	A+ / 9.9	99.69 / 99	--	--	0.00	C / 5.3	-8.05	0.27
GEI	J Hancock Investors Trust	JHI	B	22.57	C+ / 6.6	13.20 / 42	17.55 / 81	17.15 / 96	8.84	B / 8.7	9.30	17.59
GEI	*Market Vectors LatAm Aggrgte Bd	BONO	B	26.15	C+ / 6.5	15.41 / 50	--	--	4.13	B / 8.9	1.04	0.49
GEI	Western Asset Premier Bond Fund	WEA	B-	15.54	C+ / 6.8	9.83 / 34	17.58 / 81	15.23 / 91	8.11	B / 8.3	3.19	14.05
GEI	Nuveen EnhancedMunicipal Value	NEV	B-	16.10	C+ / 6.7	23.56 / 81	14.06 / 69	--	6.19	B / 8.3	1.07	2.12
GEI	J Hancock Income Securities Tr	JHS	B-	16.34	C+ / 6.3	21.32 / 75	14.33 / 70	13.80 / 85	7.55	B / 8.7	2.83	4.49
GEI	BlackRock Core Bond Trust	BHK	B-	14.90	C+ / 6.1	17.36 / 60	15.58 / 75	11.88 / 76	10.63	B / 8.8	-2.68	-1.48
GEI	MFS Charter Income Trust	MCR	B-	10.12	C+ / 5.9	20.27 / 71	12.43 / 60	12.53 / 79	6.34	B / 8.8	-3.89	-3.50
GEI	BlackRock Income Opportunity Trust	BNA	C+	11.34	C / 5.3	16.45 / 55	13.66 / 67	10.06 / 70	6.03	B / 8.7	-5.18	-4.27
GEI	Guggenheim Build America Bd Mgd Du	GBAB	C+	22.95	C / 5.0	15.44 / 50	--	--	7.05	B+ / 9.2	-2.63	-2.36
GEI	Montgomery Street Inc. Sec.	MTS	C+	16.90	C / 4.7	16.75 / 57	10.05 / 47	5.95 / 49	6.86	B+ / 9.5	-8.50	-9.16
GEI	Western Asset Income Fund	PAI	C+	14.82	C / 4.4	17.35 / 60	10.94 / 52	8.15 / 60	4.66	B+ / 9.0	-1.92	1.06
GEI	*Vanguard Long Term Bd Idx ETF	BLV	C+	93.87	C / 4.4	7.10 / 28	12.84 / 62	9.61 / 68	4.15	B+ / 9.1	0.74	0.28
GEI	*PowerShares Preferred Port	PGX	C+	14.68	C- / 4.0	13.12 / 42	9.96 / 47	--	6.38	B+ / 9.4	-1.41	0.15
GEI	Invesco Van Kampen Bond	VBF	C	21.34	C- / 4.0	16.57 / 55	10.03 / 47	10.54 / 72	4.36	B / 8.7	1.96	1.08
GEI	*SPDR Barclays LongTrm Corp Bond	LWC	C	41.14	C- / 3.8	9.21 / 33	10.57 / 51	--	4.38	B+ / 9.0	0.15	0.59
GEI	*Vanguard Intermediate Term Bond	BIV	C	88.25	C- / 3.1	6.13 / 26	8.39 / 40	7.15 / 55	3.00	B+ / 9.5	0.46	0.28
GEI	*SPDR Barclays Int Term Crp Bond	ITR	C	34.82	D+ / 2.8	7.25 / 29	6.53 / 34	--	2.84	B+ / 9.7	0.52	0.54
GEI	*SPDR Barclays Aggregate Bond ETF	LAG	C	58.77	D+ / 2.4	3.48 / 21	5.19 / 30	5.16 / 45	1.57	B+ / 9.7	0.46	N/A
GEI	*Vanguard Total Bond Market ETF	BND	C	84.03	D+ / 2.4	3.45 / 21	5.59 / 31	5.40 / 46	2.39	B+ / 9.8	0.30	0.13
GEI	*iShares Core Total US Bond Mkt E	AGG	C	111.08	D+ / 2.4	3.26 / 21	5.49 / 31	5.26 / 45	2.49	B+ / 9.8	0.25	0.10
GEI	*iShares Barclays Intrm Govt/Crdt	GVI	C	112.41	D / 2.2	3.15 / 21	4.47 / 28	4.57 / 41	1.94	B+ / 9.8	0.20	0.21
GEI	Duff & Phelps Utilities & Crp Bd T	DUC	C-	12.26	C- / 3.3	9.35 / 33	8.52 / 41	10.89 / 73	6.85	B / 8.7	3.37	4.06
GEI	Nuveen Build America Bond Oppty Fd	NBD	C-	21.66	D+ / 2.8	6.45 / 27	--	--	6.01	B+ / 9.3	-7.24	-6.74
GEI	*Guggenheim Enhanced Core Bond ET	GIY	C-	51.75	D+ / 2.6	3.13 / 21	6.64 / 34	--	2.32	B+ / 9.4	-0.02	-0.09
GEI	*Schwab US TIPS ETF	SCHP	C-	58.30	D / 2.2	5.44 / 25	--	--	1.31	B+ / 9.7	0.34	0.08
GEI	*Vanguard Short-Term Bd Idx ETF	BSV	C-	80.99	D / 1.9	1.94 / 18	2.69 / 22	3.42 / 34	1.40	B+ / 9.8	0.06	0.08
GEI	*Columbia Core Bond Strategy	GMTB	C-	52.90	D / 1.8	4.41 / 23	--	--	2.55	B+ / 9.6	0.27	0.83
GEI	*iShares 2017 S&P AMT-Free Muni S	MUAF	C-	55.29	D / 1.7	1.85 / 18	--	--	1.35	B+ / 9.4	-0.07	0.45
GEI	*iShares 2016 S&P AMT-Free Muni S	MUAE	C-	53.56	D / 1.6	1.43 / 17	--	--	1.18	B+ / 9.7	0.11	0.49
GEI	*iShares 2015 S&P AMT-Free Muni S	MUAD	C-	53.23	D / 1.6	1.18 / 16	--	--	0.96	B+ / 9.8	0.21	0.47
GEI	*iShares 2014 S&P AMT-Free Muni S	MUAC	C-	51.68	D- / 1.5	0.51 / 15	--	--	0.64	B+ / 9.7	0.21	0.33
GEI	*SPDR Nuveen S&P VRDO Muni Bond E	VRD	C-	29.88	D- / 1.4	-0.26 / 13	0.38 / 16	--	0.05	B+ / 9.9	-0.43	-0.24
GEI	*iShares 2013 S&P AMT-Free Muni S	MUAB	C-	50.72	D- / 1.3	-0.16 / 14	--	--	0.67	B+ / 9.9	0.04	0.03
GEI	*ProShares Short 7-10 Year Treasu	TBX	D	32.42	D- / 1.1	-4.37 / 11	--	--	0.00	B / 8.4	-0.37	-0.03
GEI	*ProShares UltraShort 3-7 Yr Trea	TBZ	D	31.94	D- / 1.0	-4.91 / 10	--	--	0.00	B / 8.5	-0.71	-0.21
GEI	*ProShares Short High Yield	SJB	D	32.15	E / 0.5	-14.63 / 6	--	--	0.00	B- / 7.8	1.26	-0.02
GEI	*ProShares VIX Mid-Term Futures E	VIXM	E	34.22	E- / 0.0	-55.69 / 1	--	--	0.00	C- / 3.6	9.40	-0.16
GEI	*ProShares VIX Short-Term Futures	VIXY	E-	17.01	E- / 0.0	-78.89 / 0	--	--	0.00	D / 1.9	20.90	-0.13

* Denotes ETF Fund, N/A denotes number is not available

Fund Type	Fund Name	Ticker Symbol	Overall Investment Rating	Price As of 12/31/12	PERFORMANCE					Dividend Yield %	RISK	VALUATION	
					Perform-ance Rating/Pts	Annualized Total Return Through 12/31/12					Risk Rating/ Pts	Premium/Discount	
							1Yr/Pct	3Yr/Pct	5Yr/Pct			As of 12/31/12	1 Year Average
GEN	Helios Advantage Income Fund Inc	HAV	A	8.65	B / 8.2	22.30 / 78	21.10 / 91	-1.04 / 16	8.67	B+/ 9.0	-8.47	-0.85
GEN	Helios Multi Sector High Income	HMH	A-	6.04	B / 7.6	21.81 / 76	19.11 / 87	-7.41 / 6	8.44	B+/ 9.2	-7.22	-2.10
GEN	Helios High Income Fund Inc	HIH	B+	8.36	B / 7.6	20.30 / 71	18.71 / 85	-1.96 / 14	8.61	B / 8.8	-6.90	0.89
GEN	Helios Strategic Income Fund Inc	HSA	B	6.32	B / 7.8	26.56 / 86	16.53 / 78	-5.60 / 7	7.59	B- / 7.8	-10.86	-8.73
GEN	First Trust Strategic High Inc II	FHY	B	16.60	B- / 7.3	23.33 / 80	17.98 / 83	-1.71 / 15	8.67	B / 8.6	-5.25	2.18
GEN	BlackRock Limited Duration Income	BLW	B-	18.17	B- / 7.2	21.54 / 75	15.21 / 73	11.38 / 75	12.98	B- / 7.4	2.14	2.90
GEN	Franklin Templeton Ltd Duration In	FTF	B-	14.37	C+ / 6.6	21.69 / 76	14.36 / 70	13.33 / 82	6.93	B / 8.5	0.35	1.31
GEN	MFS Multimarket Income Trust	MMT	C+	7.28	C / 4.9	16.09 / 53	11.91 / 57	13.22 / 82	6.59	B / 8.5	-6.31	-4.85
GEN	Eaton Vance Limited Duration Incom	EVV	C	16.66	C+ / 5.6	19.59 / 69	12.09 / 58	11.90 / 77	7.51	B- / 7.7	-0.95	-0.92
GEN	Morgan Stanley Income Sec	ICB	C	18.46	C- / 3.6	10.77 / 36	10.03 / 47	8.85 / 64	3.74	B+/ 9.0	-6.77	-4.56
GEN	NexPoint Credit Strategies Fund	HCF	C-	6.64	C / 4.3	16.40 / 54	8.57 / 41	-3.48 / 10	6.33	B- / 7.6	-12.86	-10.40
GEN	*Schwab US Aggregate Bond ETF	SCHZ	C-	52.34	D / 1.8	2.77 / 20	--	--	1.98	B+/ 9.9	0.13	0.18
GEN	Putnam High Income Securities	PCF	D+	7.95	C- / 3.5	11.05 / 36	8.96 / 43	8.72 / 63	5.89	B- / 7.0	-8.52	-1.06
GEN	Putnam Premier Income Trust	PPT	D	5.46	D+ / 2.7	12.10 / 39	5.70 / 31	7.45 / 57	5.71	C+/ 6.0	-8.39	-4.55
GEN	Putnam Master Intermediate Inc Tr	PIM	D	5.06	D / 2.2	9.48 / 34	2.51 / 21	5.09 / 44	6.17	C+/ 6.2	-9.32	-5.80

99 Pct = Best
0 Pct = Worst

* Denotes ETF Fund, N/A denotes number is not available

www.thestreetratings.com
739
Data as of December 31, 2012

Fund Type	Fund Name	Ticker Symbol	Overall Investment Rating	Price As of 12/31/12	Performance Rating/Pts	Annualized Total Return Through 12/31/12			Dividend Yield %	Risk Rating/Pts	Premium/Discount As of 12/31/12	Premium/Discount 1 Year Average
	99 Pct = Best, 0 Pct = Worst					1Yr/Pct	3Yr/Pct	5Yr/Pct				
GL	*Vanguard Global ex-US RE I Fd ET	VNQI	A	55.03	A+ / 9.8	40.47 / 97	--	--	8.49	B- / 7.3	-0.09	0.41
GL	Pimco Income Opportunity Fund	PKO	A	29.12	B+ / 8.9	28.12 / 89	21.87 / 93	16.15 / 93	24.55	B / 8.4	1.43	7.21
GL	*First Trust NASDAQ Global Auto	CARZ	B+	29.12	A+ / 9.8	26.04 / 85	--	--	0.69	C+ / 6.6	-2.90	0.17
GL	*EGShares Industrials GEMS ETF	IGEM	B+	20.67	A+ / 9.7	29.56 / 90	--	--	0.94	C+ / 6.8	-0.34	-0.09
GL	Gabelli Multimedia Trust	GGT	B+	7.85	A / 9.5	41.73 / 97	21.05 / 91	3.81 / 37	10.19	C+ / 6.9	-8.61	-7.90
GL	*EGShares COnsumer Services GEMS	VGEM	B+	22.14	A / 9.3	20.89 / 73	--	--	0.31	B- / 7.1	-0.09	-0.15
GL	*Vanguard Total Intl Stock Index	VXUS	B+	46.96	A- / 9.2	19.12 / 68	--	--	2.71	B- / 7.2	-1.47	0.29
GL	*First Trust ISE Cloud Computing	SKYY	B+	19.87	A- / 9.1	18.50 / 65	--	--	0.00	B- / 7.6	-4.52	0.02
GL	*Market Vectors Colombia ETF	COLX	B+	19.81	B+ / 8.9	18.42 / 65	--	--	1.68	B- / 7.3	-1.44	0.80
GL	First Trust High Income Long/Short	FSD	B+	18.12	B+ / 8.7	26.83 / 87	--	--	7.65	B- / 7.7	-8.39	-2.80
GL	First Trust/Aberdeen Emerg Opp Fd	FEO	B+	22.05	B+ / 8.6	34.77 / 95	16.35 / 78	14.38 / 88	2.42	B- / 7.6	-7.66	-6.91
GL	*WCM/BNY Mellon Focused Gro ADR E	AADR	B+	30.74	B+ / 8.5	15.42 / 50	--	--	0.55	B- / 7.8	-4.62	-0.02
GL	*iShares S&P Target Date 2050 Ind	TZY	B+	27.95	B / 8.0	16.60 / 55	--	--	2.90	B / 8.5	-3.29	0.02
GL	*iShares S&P Target Date 2045 Ind	TZW	B+	28.05	B / 7.9	15.80 / 51	--	--	3.00	B / 8.6	-2.60	0.02
GL	*Precidian Maxis Nikkei 225 Index	NKY	B+	14.45	B / 7.9	13.48 / 43	--	--	1.59	B / 8.3	0.00	0.10
GL	*PowerShares International Corp B	PICB	B+	29.61	B / 7.8	17.65 / 61	--	--	2.98	B / 8.7	-0.07	0.17
GL	*First Trust NASDAQ CEA Smartphon	FONE	B	25.10	B+ / 8.7	7.56 / 29	--	--	1.33	B- / 7.2	-3.98	-0.37
GL	*Market Vectors Gaming ETF	BJK	B	35.45	B+ / 8.5	26.54 / 86	17.62 / 81	--	3.90	B- / 7.2	-6.27	-0.33
GL	*Global X SuperDividend ETF	SDIV	B	22.10	B / 8.2	17.79 / 61	--	--	16.47	B- / 7.6	-2.51	0.50
GL	Lazard World Div&Inc Fd	LOR	B	12.55	B / 8.1	30.82 / 92	13.01 / 63	4.36 / 39	6.35	B- / 7.4	-14.86	-11.66
GL	*EGShares Consumer Goods GEMS ETF	GGEM	B	23.82	B / 8.1	19.24 / 68	--	--	0.99	B- / 7.7	-0.58	-0.31
GL	*Russell Equity ETF	ONEF	B	29.14	B / 8.0	18.94 / 67	--	--	6.90	B- / 7.8	-2.35	-0.06
GL	*IQ Global Agribusiness SmCp ETF	CROP	B	25.58	B / 8.0	15.65 / 51	--	--	1.40	B- / 7.8	-1.69	-0.06
GL	AllianceBernstein Global High Inc	AWF	B	15.65	B / 7.9	24.71 / 83	15.90 / 76	16.74 / 95	20.82	B- / 7.7	0.13	2.60
GL	Brookfield Gl Lstd Infr Inc Fd	INF	B	20.06	B / 7.7	19.21 / 68	--	--	6.98	B- / 7.5	-10.37	-7.48
GL	*iShares S&P Global Cons Disc	RXI	B	61.71	B / 7.6	24.68 / 83	13.64 / 67	7.39 / 57	1.43	B- / 7.8	-2.48	0.10
GL	DWS Global High Income Fund	LBF	B	8.78	B- / 7.5	26.80 / 87	14.82 / 72	10.19 / 70	5.64	B- / 7.8	-11.58	-9.80
GL	*Market Vectors EM Lcl Curr Bnd E	EMLC	B	27.45	B- / 7.1	16.43 / 54	--	--	3.98	B / 8.4	0.59	0.53
GL	*iShares Internat Inflation-Link	ITIP	B	51.29	B- / 7.1	13.28 / 42	--	--	5.24	B / 8.7	1.08	0.85
GL	*iShares Global Inflation-Linked	GTIP	B	54.08	C+ / 6.0	11.11 / 36	--	--	3.92	B+ / 9.2	0.80	-1.07
GL	*PowerShares DB Itn Trs B Fut ETN	ITLY	B-	23.84	A+ / 9.6	31.28 / 92	--	--	0.00	C / 5.3	-26.67	-4.23
GL	*Global X Fertilizers/Potash ETF	SOIL	B-	14.04	B+ / 8.3	15.92 / 52	--	--	1.15	C+ / 6.5	-5.20	-0.03
GL	Western Asset Var Rt Strat Fd	GFY	B-	17.76	B- / 7.5	30.70 / 92	13.93 / 69	8.63 / 63	4.90	B- / 7.5	-5.98	-4.98
GL	Western Asset Global High Income	EHI	B-	13.78	B- / 7.2	19.75 / 70	16.91 / 80	14.07 / 86	8.39	B- / 7.7	-1.99	0.22
GL	Strategic Global Income Fund	SGL	B-	10.97	B- / 7.1	17.39 / 60	16.91 / 79	14.25 / 87	4.83	B- / 7.9	-5.92	-5.66
GL	DWS Strategic Income Fund	KST	B-	14.26	B- / 7.0	19.74 / 70	17.46 / 81	14.36 / 88	7.99	B- / 7.6	-2.46	2.07
GL	Macquarie/FTG Infr/ Util Div&Inc	MFD	B-	15.25	C+ / 6.7	19.15 / 68	15.70 / 76	-1.24 / 16	9.18	B- / 7.9	-7.58	-2.61
GL	First Trust/Aberdeen Glob Opp Inc	FAM	B-	17.85	C+ / 6.4	23.80 / 81	13.56 / 66	12.45 / 78	8.74	B / 8.2	-2.67	-1.11
GL	Western Asset Global Corp Def Oppt	GDO	B-	20.75	C+ / 5.6	22.16 / 77	10.90 / 52	--	2.44	B / 8.9	-1.43	-1.80
GL	*iShares Emerging Mkts Lcl Cur Bo	LEMB	B-	53.86	C / 5.5	11.82 / 38	--	--	4.16	B+ / 9.1	1.18	1.45
GL	*Global X FTSE ASEAN 40 ETF	ASEA	C+	17.04	B- / 7.1	16.74 / 57	--	--	2.20	B- / 7.3	1.19	0.37
GL	DWS Multi-Market Income Trust	KMM	C+	10.44	B- / 7.0	16.06 / 53	17.17 / 80	15.92 / 93	8.85	B- / 7.2	-0.57	5.87
GL	Pioneer Diversified High Income Tr	HNW	C+	20.08	C+ / 6.9	18.33 / 64	16.21 / 77	13.90 / 85	11.16	B- / 7.2	-1.18	4.75
GL	Eaton Vance Tax Adv Glob Div Inc	ETG	C+	13.58	C+ / 6.8	26.59 / 86	10.64 / 51	0.88 / 22	9.06	B- / 7.5	-12.72	-5.82
GL	*SPDR SP Intl Con Disc Sect ETF	IPD	C+	30.32	C+ / 6.7	25.38 / 84	9.11 / 43	--	4.92	B- / 7.5	-1.62	0.13
GL	Macquarie Global Infr Total Return	MGU	C+	19.07	C+ / 6.6	22.67 / 78	12.30 / 60	-0.09 / 19	6.71	B- / 7.8	-14.52	-10.97
GL	*EGShares Telecom GEMS ETF	TGEM	C+	20.22	C+ / 6.0	13.20 / 42	--	--	3.06	B- / 7.9	-1.27	0.13
GL	Wells Fargo Avtg Multi-Sector Inc	ERC	C+	16.17	C+ / 5.7	19.18 / 68	12.87 / 62	12.13 / 77	7.42	B / 8.7	-6.53	-5.54
GL	*SPDR SP Intl Con Stap Sect ETF	IPS	C+	35.67	C+ / 5.6	22.46 / 78	10.63 / 51	--	1.03	B / 8.6	-0.67	0.20
GL	*iShares S&P Gl Cons Staples Sect	KXI	C+	73.63	C+ / 5.6	19.05 / 67	12.46 / 61	7.75 / 58	2.84	B / 8.9	-1.94	0.02
GL	Aberdeen Asia-Pacific Income Fund	FAX	C+	7.74	C / 5.3	12.62 / 40	13.38 / 65	13.61 / 84	5.43	B / 8.6	-0.77	0.94
GL	*iShares MSCI ACW Minimum Vol Ind	ACWV	C+	55.63	C / 4.6	12.41 / 40	--	--	2.92	B+ / 9.5	-1.82	0.55

* Denotes ETF Fund, N/A denotes number is not available

Fund Type	Fund Name	Ticker Symbol	Overall Investment Rating	Price As of 12/31/12	PERFORMANCE Performance Rating/Pts	Annualized Total Return Through 12/31/12 1Yr/Pct	3Yr/Pct	5Yr/Pct	Dividend Yield %	RISK Risk Rating/ Pts	VALUATION Premium/Discount As of 12/31/12	1 Year Average
GR	*Direxion Daily Retail Bull 3X	RETL	A+	99.26	A+ / 9.9	84.71 / 99	--	--	0.00	B- / 7.9	-5.57	0.13
GR	*PowerShares Fundamental Pure Lg	PXLV	A	21.86	B+ / 8.9	19.60 / 69	--	--	3.07	B / 8.1	-3.45	-0.01
GR	*Guggenheim S&P Mid Cap 400 Eq Wg	EWMD	A	32.56	B+ / 8.6	17.80 / 61	--	--	2.17	B / 8.8	-3.58	0.01
GR	*Guggenheim S&P Sm Cap 600 Eq Wgh	EWSM	A	32.92	B+ / 8.5	19.87 / 70	--	--	2.56	B / 8.8	-3.46	-0.09
GR	*SPDR S&P Software & Services ETF	XSW	A	62.39	B+ / 8.3	18.88 / 67	--	--	2.63	B / 8.9	-4.38	-0.02
GR	*First Trust US IPO Index Fund	FPX	A-	30.90	B+ / 8.8	31.61 / 93	17.71 / 82	9.57 / 68	1.28	B / 8.0	-4.04	-0.02
GR	*Vanguard S&P Mid-Cap 400 Gro ETF	IVOG	A-	69.97	B+ / 8.8	18.78 / 66	--	--	1.39	B- / 7.9	-3.72	0.03
GR	*First Trust Mid Cap Val AlphaDEX	FNK	A-	21.58	B+ / 8.5	17.45 / 60	--	--	1.35	B / 8.4	-3.23	0.21
GR	*First Trust Small Cap Val AlphaD	FYT	A-	22.38	B+ / 8.4	15.26 / 49	--	--	1.37	B / 8.3	-2.82	0.08
GR	*PowerShares S&P SC Industrials	PSCI	B+	32.03	A / 9.5	20.37 / 72	--	--	6.26	B- / 7.2	-4.33	-0.05
GR	*PowerShares S&P SC Cnsmr Discr	PSCD	B+	32.98	A- / 9.1	23.09 / 80	--	--	6.72	B- / 7.4	-3.11	-0.04
GR	*PowerShares S&P SC Materials	PSCM	B+	31.49	B+ / 8.8	25.18 / 84	--	--	3.12	B- / 7.2	-6.81	-0.09
GR	*Vanguard S&P Mid-Cap 400 Value E	IVOV	B+	65.63	B+ / 8.8	18.81 / 66	--	--	1.64	B- / 7.6	-3.78	0.06
GR	*Schwab US Mid-Cap ETF	SCHM	B+	27.87	B+ / 8.8	18.38 / 64	--	--	5.36	B- / 7.5	-3.46	0.05
GR	*Vanguard S&P Mid-Cap 400 Index E	IVOO	B+	68.07	B+ / 8.6	18.42 / 65	--	--	1.07	B- / 7.8	-3.64	0.04
GR	*Madrona Domestic ETF	FWDD	B+	27.80	B+ / 8.5	17.09 / 59	--	--	0.46	B- / 7.9	-1.56	-0.19
GR	*Consumer Discretionary Sel Sec S	XLY	B+	47.44	B+ / 8.4	23.04 / 80	19.54 / 87	12.42 / 78	2.58	B- / 7.9	-2.99	N/A
GR	*Vanguard S&P SC 600 Val Indx ETF	VIOV	B+	69.17	B+ / 8.3	17.30 / 60	--	--	1.31	B- / 7.7	-2.63	-0.04
GR	*Guggenheim Russell MC Eq Wght ET	EWRM	B+	35.19	B+ / 8.3	16.88 / 57	--	--	2.46	B- / 7.8	-3.32	0.01
GR	*Guggenheim Russell 1000 Eq Wght	EWRI	B+	34.52	B+ / 8.3	16.66 / 56	--	--	2.72	B- / 7.8	-4.61	-0.04
GR	*Vanguard Russell 1000 Val Index	VONV	B+	63.35	B / 8.2	18.23 / 64	--	--	3.19	B / 8.1	-3.65	N/A
GR	*Vanguard S&P 500 Val Indx ETF	VOOV	B+	63.61	B / 8.2	17.89 / 62	--	--	2.58	B / 8.0	-3.24	0.02
GR	*Guggenheim Wilshire5000 Tot Mkt	WFVK	B+	31.45	B / 8.0	18.19 / 63	--	--	2.07	B / 8.1	-3.56	0.25
GR	*ProShares Ultra MidCap 400	MVV	B	74.05	A / 9.5	34.56 / 95	21.99 / 93	5.77 / 47	0.06	C+ / 5.7	-6.83	-0.02
GR	*ProShares Ultra Rus Mid Cap Valu	UVU	B	42.95	A- / 9.2	35.71 / 95	20.79 / 90	2.50 / 29	0.21	C+ / 6.1	-7.26	-0.33
GR	*Vanguard Russell 2000 Val Index	VTWV	B	64.62	B+ / 8.3	18.18 / 63	--	--	1.92	B- / 7.5	-3.68	0.07
GR	*PowerShares S&P SC Information T	PSCT	B	30.69	B / 8.2	12.31 / 39	--	--	1.88	B- / 7.0	-3.76	-0.08
GR	*Vanguard S&P SC 600 Indx ETF	VIOO	B	70.25	B / 8.1	16.69 / 56	--	--	1.45	B- / 7.8	-3.13	0.03
GR	*Vanguard Russell 2000 Idx ETF	VTWO	B	67.00	B / 8.0	16.75 / 57	--	--	1.56	B- / 7.5	-3.62	-0.05
GR	*Guggenheim S&P 500 Eq WgCon Dsc	RCD	B	56.42	B / 7.8	20.84 / 73	17.13 / 80	12.65 / 79	2.55	B- / 7.9	-2.91	-0.04
GR	*Guggenheim Wilshire 4500 Comp ET	WXSP	B	32.57	B / 7.8	17.92 / 62	--	--	1.75	B- / 7.5	-4.63	-0.03
GR	*Vanguard Russell 2000 Gro Idx ET	VTWG	B	69.11	B / 7.8	16.25 / 54	--	--	1.63	B- / 7.4	-3.93	-0.03
GR	*Vanguard Russell 3000 Index ETF	VTHR	B	65.22	B / 7.7	16.91 / 57	--	--	2.44	B / 8.2	-3.58	-0.05
GR	*Vanguard S&P SC 600 G Indx ETF	VIOG	B	71.64	B / 7.7	16.50 / 55	--	--	1.14	B- / 7.9	-3.81	0.03
GR	*Vanguard Russell 1000 Index ETF	VONE	B	65.21	B / 7.6	17.38 / 60	--	--	2.90	B / 8.2	-3.34	-0.06
GR	*WisdomTree MidCap Earnings Fund	EZM	B	62.38	B- / 7.5	17.84 / 61	15.06 / 73	11.19 / 74	3.04	B- / 7.7	-3.23	0.08
GR	*Guggenheim S&P Mid Cap 400 Pure	RFG	B	91.26	B- / 7.5	15.86 / 52	17.18 / 80	13.96 / 85	1.93	B- / 7.8	-3.08	-0.01
GR	*iShares Morningstar Mid Core	JKG	B	98.60	B- / 7.3	18.12 / 63	15.27 / 73	8.41 / 62	1.77	B- / 7.8	-3.74	-0.03
GR	*First Trust Small Cap Gro AlphaD	FYC	B	21.30	B- / 7.1	15.12 / 48	--	--	0.70	B / 8.5	-3.53	0.10
GR	*RBS US Large Cap Trendpilot ETN	TRND	B	27.70	C+ / 6.9	15.90 / 52	--	--	0.00	B / 8.5	-2.91	0.08
GR	*Vanguard Russell 1000 Gro Idx ET	VONG	B	67.12	C+ / 6.8	16.06 / 53	--	--	2.65	B / 8.4	-3.08	-0.04
GR	*PowerShares Fundamental Pure Lg	PXLG	B	22.47	C+ / 6.6	17.52 / 60	--	--	2.22	B / 8.5	-3.77	0.05
GR	*ProShares Ultra SmallCap 600	SAA	B-	54.60	A / 9.3	31.00 / 92	22.10 / 93	4.62 / 41	0.03	C / 5.5	-6.46	-0.09
GR	*ProShares Ultra Rus Mid Cap Grow	UKW	B-	53.08	A- / 9.0	26.71 / 86	20.58 / 90	2.03 / 27	0.00	C+ / 5.8	-8.18	-0.04
GR	*ProShares Ultra S&P500	SSO	B-	60.35	B+ / 8.7	32.03 / 93	18.21 / 84	0.01 / 20	0.74	C+ / 6.4	-5.98	-0.04
GR	*ProShares Ultra Dow30	DDM	B-	70.23	B / 8.1	21.02 / 74	18.74 / 85	2.22 / 28	0.50	C+ / 6.8	-6.17	N/A
GR	*iShares S&P Mid Cap 400 Growth	IJK	B-	114.41	B- / 7.3	17.85 / 62	15.38 / 74	9.27 / 67	1.76	B- / 7.7	-3.77	-0.01
GR	*PowerShares S&P SC Financials	PSCF	B-	30.89	B- / 7.1	17.63 / 61	--	--	6.68	B- / 7.8	-2.71	-0.11
GR	*Guggenheim Mid-Cap Core ETF	CZA	B-	33.75	C+ / 6.8	16.92 / 58	14.75 / 72	9.55 / 67	1.23	B / 8.1	-3.57	0.10
GR	*Guggenheim S&P 500 Eq Wght HC ET	RYH	B-	78.39	C+ / 6.6	22.02 / 76	12.90 / 63	8.77 / 64	1.06	B / 8.2	-4.67	N/A
GR	*WisdomTree MidCap Dividend Fund	DON	B-	57.41	C+ / 6.6	16.25 / 54	14.67 / 72	9.07 / 66	3.33	B / 8.2	-3.53	0.12
GR	*Guggenheim S&P 500 Eq WgCon St E	RHS	B-	69.18	C+ / 6.1	16.18 / 54	14.59 / 71	10.07 / 70	3.97	B / 8.9	-2.54	0.03

* Denotes ETF Fund, N/A denotes number is not available

Fund Type	Fund Name	Ticker Symbol	Overall Investment Rating	Price As of 12/31/12	Performance Rating/Pts	Annualized Total Return Through 12/31/12			Dividend Yield %	Risk Rating/ Pts	Premium/Discount	
						1Yr/Pct	3Yr/Pct	5Yr/Pct			As of 12/31/12	1 Year Average
GI	Virtus Total Return	DCA	A+	3.87	A / 9.4	26.28 / 86	27.38 / 99	-3.14 / 11	6.46	B / 8.2	-13.62	-11.51
GI	*IQ US Real Estate SmCp ETF	ROOF	A	22.48	A+ / 9.7	36.39 / 96	--	--	3.62	B- / 7.5	-4.26	0.10
GI	TCW Strategic Income Fund	TSI	A	5.36	A- / 9.2	28.58 / 89	24.58 / 97	23.35 / 99	21.38	B / 8.2	-6.13	-2.22
GI	Nuveen Short Duration Credit Oppty	JSD	A	19.95	B / 8.1	21.15 / 74	--	--	3.90	B / 8.9	0.91	-0.04
GI	Cohen&Steers Total Return Realty	RFI	A-	14.72	A / 9.5	30.01 / 91	25.32 / 97	13.44 / 83	5.98	B- / 7.4	11.35	2.89
GI	Neuberger Berman Real Est Secs Inc	NRO	A-	4.59	B+ / 8.9	31.62 / 93	22.92 / 94	-1.07 / 16	5.23	B- / 7.9	-15.00	-12.27
GI	Nuveen Tax-Advantaged Dividend Grt	JTD	A-	14.50	B+ / 8.7	28.18 / 89	18.68 / 85	8.93 / 65	7.17	B / 8.3	-7.17	-6.36
GI	Nuveen Preferref Income Opps	JPC	A-	9.71	B+ / 8.4	34.75 / 95	18.80 / 85	8.31 / 61	6.52	B / 8.4	-7.17	-4.06
GI	Guggenheim Strategic Opportunities	GOF	A-	21.50	B+ / 8.3	21.67 / 75	20.14 / 89	17.46 / 97	9.45	B / 8.5	5.03	7.95
GI	*EGShares India Consumer ETF	INCO	B+	24.32	A+ / 9.9	44.13 / 98	--	--	0.00	C+ / 6.7	2.83	0.48
GI	Cohen&Steers Quality Income Realty	RQI	B+	10.16	A / 9.4	27.83 / 88	28.55 / 99	3.95 / 37	7.09	B- / 7.0	-9.12	-4.66
GI	LMP Real Estate Income Fund Inc	RIT	B+	10.97	B+ / 8.8	30.01 / 91	21.45 / 92	9.03 / 65	6.56	B- / 7.8	-12.10	-8.87
GI	CBRE Clarion Global Real Estate In	IGR	B+	8.86	B+ / 8.6	36.06 / 96	17.61 / 81	1.29 / 24	11.78	B- / 7.5	-7.90	-8.40
GI	LMP Capital and Income Fund Inc	SCD	B+	13.47	B+ / 8.4	24.25 / 82	19.70 / 88	5.07 / 44	8.31	B / 8.0	-9.78	-5.62
GI	*EGShares Low Vol Em Mkts Div ETF	HILO	B+	20.29	B / 8.2	13.68 / 44	--	--	9.06	B- / 7.8	0.45	0.25
GI	Nuveen Credit Strategies Income	JQC	B+	9.65	B / 8.1	30.00 / 91	17.80 / 82	8.54 / 62	7.17	B / 8.4	-3.11	-4.24
GI	*Direxion All Cap Insider Sentime	KNOW	B+	43.64	B / 8.0	13.71 / 44	--	--	0.61	B / 8.0	-3.43	-0.12
GI	*Schwab US Dividend Equity ETF	SCHD	B+	28.34	C+ / 6.4	15.37 / 49	--	--	7.29	B+ / 9.6	-2.95	0.04
GI	*Guggenheim China Real Estate ETF	TAO	B	22.85	A / 9.3	57.22 / 99	12.72 / 62	3.14 / 33	1.70	C+ / 6.0	-2.85	0.02
GI	Alpine Global Premier Properties F	AWP	B	7.28	B+ / 8.8	51.27 / 99	13.65 / 67	1.21 / 23	8.24	C+ / 6.8	-11.00	-9.18
GI	*iShares FTSE EPRA/NAREIT Asia In	IFAS	B	33.67	B+ / 8.4	42.71 / 98	11.60 / 56	1.02 / 22	15.84	B- / 7.1	-0.27	0.18
GI	Nuveen Real Estate Inc Fund	JRS	B	10.48	B / 7.9	15.95 / 52	20.72 / 90	7.35 / 57	8.78	B- / 7.4	-2.06	6.28
GI	*PowerShares Act US Real Estate	PSR	B	56.83	B / 7.7	17.47 / 60	19.25 / 87	--	3.49	B- / 7.8	-2.89	0.02
GI	*SPDR DJ Wilshire Glb Real Est ET	RWO	B	42.12	B- / 7.4	25.71 / 85	15.26 / 73	--	6.70	B- / 7.8	-0.73	0.29
GI	Nuveen Diversified Dividend&Income	JDD	B	11.60	B- / 7.4	24.13 / 82	16.78 / 79	8.52 / 62	8.62	B / 8.0	-8.88	-3.85
GI	*WisdomTree Equity Income Fund	DHS	B	45.80	C+ / 6.2	14.10 / 45	15.60 / 75	4.32 / 39	3.34	B+ / 9.0	-3.13	0.13
GI	*Cohen & Steers Global Realty Maj	GRI	B-	39.25	B / 7.6	29.99 / 91	14.11 / 69	--	22.77	C+ / 6.9	-1.11	0.19
GI	Delaware Inv Div & Inc	DDF	B-	7.92	B- / 7.3	23.98 / 82	15.33 / 74	7.73 / 58	7.95	B- / 7.8	-12.39	-6.33
GI	*Schwab US REIT ETF	SCHH	B-	30.64	B- / 7.0	19.50 / 69	--	--	6.85	B- / 7.9	-1.98	0.03
GI	*Guggenheim Wilshire US REIT ETF	WREI	B-	36.10	C+ / 6.6	19.83 / 70	--	--	3.29	B / 8.0	-2.51	N/A
GI	RMR Real Estate Income	RIF	C+	18.21	B / 7.9	47.66 / 98	10.34 / 49	-5.54 / 7	6.81	C+ / 5.6	-15.07	-16.23
GI	*First Trust FTSE EPRA/NAREIT Glb	FFR	C+	39.37	B- / 7.2	28.61 / 89	13.21 / 64	2.84 / 31	10.62	B- / 7.0	-0.71	0.20
GI	*iShares FTSE EPRA/NAREIT NA Idx	IFNA	C+	47.17	B- / 7.2	18.22 / 63	17.88 / 82	7.82 / 59	3.54	B- / 7.3	-3.30	0.13
GI	Calamos Strategic Total Return Fun	CSQ	C+	9.81	C+ / 6.9	28.40 / 89	13.07 / 63	4.17 / 38	8.56	B- / 7.7	-9.67	-6.86
GI	Franklin Universal Trust	FT	C+	7.06	C+ / 6.3	18.11 / 63	15.77 / 76	10.45 / 71	6.46	B- / 7.8	-7.71	-3.94
GI	The Denali Fund Inc.	DNY	C+	16.22	C+ / 6.1	23.62 / 81	10.54 / 51	5.91 / 49	0.00	B- / 7.8	-24.10	-19.58
GI	*SPDR Barclays Em Mkt Local Bond	EBND	C+	32.29	C+ / 5.8	13.19 / 42	--	--	15.52	B / 8.7	0.31	0.86
GI	*PowerShares KBW High Div Yield F	KBWD	C+	23.15	C+ / 5.6	15.91 / 52	--	--	8.82	B / 8.4	-4.61	0.11
GI	*First Trust Lrg Cap Core AlphaDE	FEX	C+	30.65	C+ / 5.6	14.61 / 47	11.67 / 56	5.87 / 48	1.86	B / 8.0	-2.91	0.02
GI	*Vanguard Total Stock Market ETF	VTI	C+	73.28	C / 5.5	17.04 / 58	11.85 / 57	5.21 / 45	2.97	B- / 7.9	-3.26	0.01
GI	*WisdomTree LargeCap Dividend Fun	DLN	C+	53.64	C / 5.5	14.25 / 46	13.32 / 65	4.28 / 38	1.87	B / 8.7	-3.00	0.07
GI	*db-X 2030 Target Date Fund	TDN	C+	21.47	C / 5.2	19.79 / 70	8.73 / 42	2.60 / 30	4.80	B / 8.3	-9.18	-6.43
GI	*First Trust Value Line Dividend	FVD	C+	17.30	C / 5.2	13.66 / 43	12.58 / 61	7.40 / 57	3.46	B / 8.8	-2.43	0.07
GI	*Meidell Tactical Advantage ETF	MATH	C+	25.93	C- / 4.0	7.08 / 28	--	--	0.90	B+ / 9.3	-2.26	0.48
GI	*iShares FTSE EPRA/NAREIT Dev RE	IFGL	C	33.13	B- / 7.5	36.15 / 96	10.54 / 51	0.67 / 21	13.14	C+ / 5.6	0.00	0.30
GI	MFS Special Value Trust	MFV	C	6.91	C / 5.2	19.18 / 68	12.54 / 61	11.42 / 75	9.83	B- / 7.8	-1.57	4.82
GI	*iShares S&P Aggressive Allocatio	AOA	C	37.17	C / 4.8	15.48 / 50	9.82 / 46	--	2.98	B / 8.1	-2.39	0.03
GI	Boulder Growth&Income Fund	BIF	C	6.33	C / 4.7	20.65 / 72	7.57 / 37	-2.65 / 12	2.21	B / 8.0	-26.99	-21.67
GI	*iShares S&P Target Date 2035 Ind	TZO	C	35.80	C / 4.4	15.14 / 48	8.95 / 43	--	3.11	B / 8.2	-2.59	0.12
GI	*PowerShares Convertible Secs Por	CVRT	C	23.84	C / 4.4	10.02 / 34	--	--	2.85	B / 8.6	-3.01	-0.65
GI	*iShares S&P Target Date 2030 Ind	TZL	C	35.78	C- / 4.2	14.18 / 45	8.61 / 41	--	3.12	B / 8.5	-2.21	0.04
GI	*Cambria Global Tactical ETF Fund	GTAA	C	24.31	C- / 4.0	8.40 / 31	--	--	2.30	B / 8.7	-2.13	-0.20

* Denotes ETF Fund, N/A denotes number is not available

99 Pct = Best
0 Pct = Worst

Fund Type	Fund Name	Ticker Symbol	Overall Investment Rating	Price As of 12/31/12	PERFORMANCE Perform-ance Rating/Pts	Annualized Total Return Through 12/31/12 1Yr/Pct	3Yr/Pct	5Yr/Pct	Dividend Yield %	RISK Risk Rating/Pts	VALUATION Premium/Discount As of 12/31/12	Premium/Discount 1 Year Average
HL	*iShares MSCI ACWI ex US HlthCre	AXHE	A+	65.41	A / 9.3	24.29 / 82	--	--	1.18	B / 8.4	-2.69	0.48
HL	*SPDR S&P Health Care Services ET	XHS	A+	66.30	A- / 9.2	24.71 / 83	--	--	3.05	B / 8.9	-3.40	-0.02
HL	Gabelli Healthcare & WellnessRx Tr	GRX	A	8.62	B+ / 8.8	39.31 / 97	16.98 / 80	11.00 / 73	31.67	B / 8.3	-12.13	-13.08
HL	*Direxion Daily Healthcare Bull 3	CURE	A-	52.92	A+ / 9.9	66.44 / 99	--	--	0.03	C+ / 6.9	-12.93	0.01
HL	*EGShares Health Care GEMS ETF	HGEM	A-	22.32	A / 9.5	28.15 / 89	--	--	0.17	B- / 7.3	0.90	-0.06
HL	*ProShares Ultra Health Care	RXL	B+	83.83	A / 9.3	44.11 / 98	20.46 / 89	7.21 / 56	0.71	B- / 7.2	-8.62	-0.06
HL	*PowerShares Dynamic Pharmaceutic	PJP	B+	34.53	A / 9.3	28.77 / 90	25.51 / 98	16.42 / 94	4.32	B- / 7.1	-5.47	0.03
HL	H&Q Life Sciences Investors	HQL	B	14.50	A / 9.5	37.86 / 96	27.58 / 99	12.77 / 80	6.21	C+ / 6.2	-8.63	-3.92
HL	H&Q Healthcare Investors	HQH	B	17.31	A / 9.3	36.56 / 96	24.16 / 96	10.96 / 73	6.24	C+ / 6.3	-11.73	-6.86
HL	*First Trust Health Care AlphaDEX	FXH	B	32.57	B- / 7.2	22.85 / 79	15.26 / 73	11.27 / 74	0.76	B / 8.3	-4.46	0.01
HL	*iShares Nasdaq Biotechnology	IBB	B-	137.22	B+ / 8.6	30.12 / 91	20.43 / 89	12.68 / 79	0.30	C+ / 6.4	-5.66	0.02
HL	*SPDR S&P Biotech ETF	XBI	B-	87.91	B+ / 8.4	29.71 / 91	20.18 / 89	10.40 / 71	0.22	C+ / 6.5	-7.92	0.03
HL	*First Trust AMEX Biotechnology	FBT	B-	45.95	B+ / 8.3	31.41 / 92	17.93 / 83	15.17 / 90	0.00	C+ / 6.3	-5.74	0.02
HL	*SPDR S&P Health Care Equipment E	XHE	B-	54.90	B- / 7.1	19.17 / 68	--	--	1.01	B / 8.1	-5.56	-0.04
HL	*iShares DJ US Pharmaceuticals	IHE	B-	85.02	C+ / 6.7	18.29 / 64	16.92 / 80	12.90 / 80	1.90	B / 8.0	-5.70	N/A
HL	BlackRock Health Sciences Trust	BME	C+	28.02	B- / 7.4	22.56 / 78	14.24 / 70	10.51 / 72	17.62	B- / 7.1	-3.25	-0.21
HL	*SPDR S&P Pharmaceuticals ETF	XPH	C+	55.91	C+ / 6.3	14.43 / 46	16.15 / 77	13.63 / 84	1.74	B- / 7.3	-5.41	N/A
HL	*Vanguard HealthCare Index ETF	VHT	C+	71.67	C+ / 5.9	21.78 / 76	12.12 / 59	6.77 / 53	1.67	B / 8.4	-4.52	0.04
HL	*SPDR SP Intl Health Care ETF	IRY	C+	35.81	C+ / 5.7	22.07 / 77	9.67 / 46	--	1.77	B / 8.2	-2.80	0.10
HL	*iShares S&P Global Healthcare	IXJ	C+	64.50	C+ / 5.7	21.92 / 76	10.59 / 51	5.41 / 46	1.62	B / 8.3	-3.92	-0.01
HL	*iShares DJ US Healthcare	IYH	C+	83.51	C+ / 5.7	21.45 / 75	11.62 / 56	6.45 / 52	1.85	B / 8.3	-4.44	N/A
HL	*Health Care Select Sector SPDR	XLV	C+	39.88	C+ / 5.6	20.36 / 72	11.23 / 54	5.90 / 49	2.20	B / 8.4	-4.43	-0.01
HL	*ProShares Ultra Nasdaq Biotech	BIB	C	57.97	A+ / 9.9	62.43 / 99	--	--	0.00	D+ / 2.6	-10.86	-0.03
HL	*PowerShares Dynamic Hlthcare	PTH	C	32.82	C / 5.5	18.86 / 67	12.62 / 61	3.28 / 34	1.99	B- / 7.1	-4.51	-0.02
HL	*iShares DJ US HealthCare Provide	IHF	C	68.45	C / 4.8	15.86 / 52	11.35 / 54	2.59 / 30	2.44	B- / 7.9	-2.02	0.01
HL	*iShares DJ US Medical Devices Id	IHI	C-	67.60	C / 4.9	18.76 / 66	9.32 / 44	4.48 / 40	1.39	B- / 7.0	-4.69	-0.03
HL	*PowerShares Dynamic Biotech&Geno	PBE	D+	22.84	C / 4.7	14.24 / 46	12.18 / 59	6.01 / 49	0.00	C+ / 5.8	-6.09	-0.16
HL	Engex	EGX	E+	2.06	D / 2.1	31.91 / 93	-5.19 / 9	-18.20 / 3	0.00	D+ / 2.7	-48.76	-24.42
HL	*ProShares UltraShort Health Care	RXD	E+	56.06	E / 0.3	-36.15 / 2	-27.07 / 3	-22.54 / 3	0.00	C- / 4.2	11.27	0.06
HL	*ProShares UltraShort Nasdaq Biot	BIS	E	66.33	E- / 0.1	-47.85 / 1	--	--	0.00	C- / 3.4	13.08	0.06

* Denotes ETF Fund, N/A denotes number is not available

www.thestreetratings.com
743
Data as of December 31, 2012

VI. Top-Rated ETFs and Other Closed-End Funds: Income

					PERFORMANCE					RISK	VALUATION	
						Annualized Total Return Through 12/31/12					Premium/Discount	
Fund Type	Fund Name	Ticker Symbol	Overall Investment Rating	Price As of 12/31/12	Perform-ance Rating/Pts	1Yr/Pct	3Yr/Pct	5Yr/Pct	Dividend Yield %	Risk Rating/Pts	As of 12/31/12	1 Year Average
IN	Cohen&Steers Sel Preferred & Incom	PSF	A+	26.76	A+ / 9.7	35.33 / 95	--	--	6.51	B / 8.7	-3.46	0.72
IN	Kayne Anderson Midstream/Energy	KMF	A+	28.75	A+ / 9.6	30.41 / 91	--	--	6.16	B / 8.5	-4.86	-3.70
IN	*PowerShares KBW Bank	KBWB	A+	26.27	A / 9.4	24.09 / 82	--	--	1.33	B / 8.6	-3.70	-0.03
IN	F&C/Claymore Preferred Sec Inc Fun	FFC	A+	19.55	B+ / 8.9	25.83 / 85	23.07 / 95	15.56 / 91	15.53	B / 8.9	1.14	5.56
IN	F&C/Claymore Total Return Fund	FLC	A+	20.14	B+ / 8.9	25.26 / 84	23.05 / 95	15.84 / 93	13.17	B / 8.9	-2.00	3.78
IN	*SPDR S&P Aerospace & Defense ETF	XAR	A+	62.80	B+ / 8.7	17.14 / 59	--	--	3.59	B+ / 9.1	-4.57	-0.01
IN	*ProShares Ultra Consumer Goods	UGE	A	94.10	A / 9.4	29.99 / 91	25.65 / 98	11.17 / 74	0.85	B- / 7.9	-9.16	-0.16
IN	*PowerShares KBW Premium Yld Eq R	KBWY	A	28.10	A / 9.4	27.82 / 88	--	--	5.53	B- / 7.7	-2.97	0.16
IN	*PowerShares KBW Capital Markets	KBWC	A	32.72	A / 9.3	22.28 / 77	--	--	5.41	B- / 7.8	-7.36	-0.07
IN	*ProShares Ultra Consumer Service	UCC	A-	78.44	A+ / 9.8	52.14 / 99	35.36 / 99	14.45 / 88	0.22	B- / 7.1	-6.35	0.08
IN	*SPDR S&P Homebuilders ETF	XHB	A-	26.60	A+ / 9.6	52.39 / 99	22.76 / 94	11.72 / 76	1.18	B- / 7.1	-4.25	-0.01
IN	Cohen&Steers REIT& Preferred Incom	RNP	A-	16.99	A / 9.4	29.34 / 90	27.64 / 99	9.88 / 69	7.06	B- / 7.5	-9.72	-5.81
IN	*PowerShares Dynamic Leisure&Ente	PEJ	A-	22.95	B+ / 8.8	25.82 / 85	21.77 / 92	13.01 / 81	0.77	B / 8.0	-4.49	N/A
IN	Flaherty&Crumrine Preferred Inc Op	PFO	A-	11.22	B+ / 8.3	13.33 / 42	21.92 / 93	12.62 / 79	20.27	B / 8.6	-0.97	9.57
IN	*Guggenheim Spin-Off ETF	CSD	A-	29.64	B / 8.2	26.96 / 87	16.82 / 79	6.83 / 54	0.26	B / 8.5	-2.11	0.17
IN	*FlexShs Morningstar US Mkt Fac T	TILT	A-	59.72	B / 7.9	16.96 / 58	--	--	1.11	B+ / 9.1	-3.33	0.11
IN	*iShares DJ US Home Cons Idx	ITB	B+	21.16	A+ / 9.7	69.50 / 99	21.15 / 91	9.55 / 67	0.48	C+ / 6.4	-4.68	N/A
IN	*PowerShares Dynamic Bldg & Cons	PKB	B+	17.41	A / 9.4	41.98 / 97	18.58 / 84	5.46 / 47	0.93	B- / 7.1	-3.06	-0.03
IN	*Powershares S&P 500 High Beta Po	SPHB	B+	21.92	A- / 9.1	14.61 / 47	--	--	1.69	B- / 7.2	-3.78	0.01
IN	*iShares FTSE NAREIT Retail Idx	RTL	B+	35.08	B+ / 8.7	27.54 / 88	22.92 / 94	6.92 / 54	4.79	B- / 7.7	-1.71	N/A
IN	*SPDR S&P Retail ETF	XRT	B+	62.38	B+ / 8.6	21.55 / 75	22.25 / 94	18.04 / 97	3.71	B / 8.0	-1.16	-0.01
IN	*Vanguard Consumer Discret ETF	VCR	B+	75.87	B+ / 8.5	23.94 / 82	19.81 / 88	12.24 / 78	1.52	B- / 7.9	-3.17	0.03
IN	*iShares FTSE NAREIT Residential	REZ	B+	48.47	B / 8.2	16.69 / 56	21.25 / 92	11.45 / 75	3.12	B- / 7.9	-1.98	0.02
IN	*iShares DJ US Consumer Services	IYC	B+	86.80	B / 8.1	24.62 / 83	18.50 / 84	11.05 / 73	3.11	B / 8.1	-3.04	N/A
IN	*Guggenheim S&P 500 Pure Value	RPV	B+	34.20	B / 8.0	23.82 / 81	14.15 / 69	7.52 / 57	1.71	B / 8.0	-3.01	-0.01
IN	Flaherty&Crumrine Preferred Income	PFD	B+	13.63	B / 7.9	10.13 / 35	21.07 / 91	13.44 / 83	18.49	B / 8.3	-0.37	14.48
IN	J Hancock Tax Advantage Div Income	HTD	B+	18.04	B / 7.6	12.77 / 41	20.29 / 89	12.42 / 78	6.55	B / 8.8	-10.69	-7.21
IN	J Hancock Preferred Income II	HPF	B+	21.66	B- / 7.4	16.78 / 57	18.26 / 84	11.85 / 76	7.76	B / 8.8	-2.08	2.90
IN	J Hancock Preferred Inc	HPI	B+	21.91	B- / 7.4	13.73 / 44	18.69 / 85	11.99 / 77	7.67	B / 8.9	-1.57	3.86
IN	Nuveen Quality Preferred Income	JTP	B+	8.67	B- / 7.3	18.54 / 65	18.00 / 83	4.08 / 38	6.92	B / 8.9	-5.04	-1.10
IN	John Hancock Premium Dividend	PDT	B+	13.57	B- / 7.2	9.51 / 34	19.76 / 88	15.80 / 92	6.12	B / 8.9	-6.02	-0.97
IN	*Market Vectors Biotech ETF	BBH	B	53.50	A+ / 9.8	42.75 / 98	--	--	0.03	C+ / 6.1	-5.73	0.05
IN	*Market Vectors Bank and Brokerag	RKH	B	45.73	A+ / 9.8	31.01 / 92	--	--	1.88	C+ / 6.0	-4.65	0.01
IN	*ProShares Ultra Real Estate	URE	B	69.09	A+ / 9.6	40.33 / 97	30.24 / 99	-9.85 / 5	0.50	C+ / 6.0	-5.37	-0.02
IN	*ProShares Ult Telecommunications	LTL	B	58.58	B+ / 8.8	37.61 / 96	19.59 / 88	0.21	0.21	C+ / 6.9	-5.23	0.16
IN	*ProShares Ultra Russell1000 Valu	UVG	B	35.35	B+ / 8.8	34.37 / 94	16.76 / 79	-3.05 / 11	0.35	C+ / 6.5	-8.35	-0.21
IN	*Guggenheim 2x S&P 500 ETF	RSU	B	51.45	B+ / 8.8	33.20 / 94	18.65 / 85	0.10 / 20	1.46	C+ / 6.5	-6.37	-0.09
IN	*PowerShares Dynamic Basic Materi	PYZ	B	40.45	B+ / 8.5	24.47 / 83	16.67 / 79	9.19 / 66	3.67	C+ / 6.8	-4.67	N/A
IN	Gabelli Equity Trust	GAB	B	5.58	B / 8.1	26.90 / 87	16.52 / 78	6.35 / 51	10.04	B- / 7.6	-4.29	0.55
IN	*PowerShares Dynamic Industrials	PRN	B	31.82	B / 7.8	18.81 / 66	15.30 / 74	5.81 / 48	4.61	B- / 7.4	-4.39	-0.13
IN	*iShares MSCI USA	EUSA	B	30.68	B / 7.7	16.85 / 57	--	--	2.71	B / 8.1	-3.10	-0.05
IN	*First Trust ISE Water Index Fund	FIW	B	26.02	B / 7.6	25.92 / 85	13.29 / 64	7.62 / 58	0.55	B- / 7.6	-3.49	-0.03
IN	*iShares FTSE NAREIT Real Estate	FTY	B	39.82	B- / 7.5	19.33 / 69	18.58 / 85	8.41 / 62	3.65	B- / 7.9	-2.59	0.01
IN	*iShares Cohen & Steers Realty Ma	ICF	B	78.54	B- / 7.5	16.69 / 56	18.87 / 86	6.79 / 53	3.39	B- / 7.6	-1.85	-0.01
IN	Nuveen Quality Preferred Income 2	JPS	B	9.46	B- / 7.2	24.95 / 84	16.83 / 79	5.71 / 47	6.98	B / 8.6	-2.17	-0.52
IN	Nuveen Quality Preferred Income 3	JHP	B	8.89	B- / 7.2	20.64 / 72	17.36 / 81	4.69 / 42	7.02	B / 8.5	-5.43	-0.53
IN	*PowerShares Dynamic Retail	PMR	B	25.22	B- / 7.2	14.43 / 46	18.09 / 83	13.79 / 85	7.47	B / 8.2	0.20	-0.04
IN	J Hancock Preferred Income III	HPS	B	18.75	C+ / 6.8	19.36 / 69	17.27 / 80	9.79 / 69	7.82	B / 8.8	-2.95	1.85
IN	*PowerShares CEF Inc Composite Po	PCEF	B	25.14	C+ / 6.7	16.55 / 55	--	--	7.83	B / 8.6	-3.38	0.09
IN	BlackRock Credit Alloc Inc Tr IV	BTZ	B	13.73	C+ / 6.6	22.18 / 77	14.60 / 71	5.89 / 48	7.43	B / 8.8	-10.90	-8.03
IN	*WisdomTree Dividend Ex-Financial	DTN	B	55.58	C+ / 6.6	13.44 / 43	15.88 / 76	6.85 / 54	4.97	B / 8.9	-2.71	0.07
IN	*TrimTabs Float Shrink ETF	TTFS	B	33.89	C+ / 6.5	15.40 / 49	--	--	0.63	B / 8.8	-3.99	-0.12

* Denotes ETF Fund, N/A denotes number is not available

VI. Top-Rated ETFs and Other Closed-End Funds: Loan Participation

99 Pct = Best
0 Pct = Worst

Fund Type	Fund Name	Ticker Symbol	Overall Investment Rating	Price As of 12/31/12	PERFORMANCE						RISK	VALUATION	
					Perform-ance Rating/Pts	Annualized Total Return Through 12/31/12			Dividend Yield %		Risk Rating/ Pts	Premium/Discount	
						1Yr/Pct	3Yr/Pct	5Yr/Pct				As of 12/31/12	1 Year Average
LP	Avenue Income Credit Strategies	ACP	A-	18.17	A+ / 9.6	25.54 / 85	--	--	7.93		B- / 7.3	-4.72	-3.24
LP	PIMCO Income Strategy Fund II	PFN	B+	11.05	B+ / 8.5	36.21 / 96	16.34 / 78	6.87 / 54	58.82		B / 8.1	3.46	4.88
LP	Apollo Senior Floating Rate Fd Inc	AFT	B+	18.77	B / 8.2	23.59 / 81	--	--	14.70		B- / 7.8	-1.16	-0.04
LP	Blackstone/GSO Sr Floating Rate Tr	BSL	B+	20.33	B / 7.8	16.98 / 58	--	--	6.49		B / 8.3	4.58	1.81
LP	PIMCO Income Strategy Fund	PFL	B	12.74	B+ / 8.3	35.82 / 96	15.40 / 74	8.40 / 62	32.65		B- / 7.6	3.41	7.15
LP	Eaton Vance Floating Rate Income T	EFT	B	17.04	B / 7.8	29.64 / 90	13.38 / 65	9.95 / 69	6.27		B / 8.1	5.77	2.68
LP	Invesco Van Kampen Senior Inc Tr	VVR	B	5.18	B- / 7.5	28.71 / 90	13.74 / 68	3.78 / 36	7.07		B / 8.3	0.97	-1.29
LP	First Tr Senior Floating Rte Inc I	FCT	B	15.17	B- / 7.1	18.93 / 67	15.41 / 74	7.30 / 56	6.92		B / 8.3	0.86	1.31
LP	Eaton Vance Senior Income Trust	EVF	B-	7.54	C+ / 6.6	26.89 / 87	12.43 / 60	9.18 / 66	9.23		B / 8.4	1.89	-0.16
LP	Blackstone / GSO Lng-Sht Credit In	BGX	B-	18.75	C+ / 6.5	16.94 / 58	--	--	6.91		B / 8.3	-2.14	-0.78
LP	LMP Corporate Loan Fund Inc	TLI	B-	12.92	C+ / 6.4	20.40 / 72	14.26 / 70	9.17 / 66	6.73		B / 8.4	-0.62	-1.31
LP	Nuveen Floating Rate Income Fund	JFR	C+	12.19	C+ / 6.5	22.55 / 78	13.40 / 66	9.94 / 69	7.85		B / 8.0	-0.49	-0.17
LP	ING Prime Rate Trust	PPR	C+	6.21	C+ / 6.3	27.65 / 88	10.54 / 50	7.61 / 58	6.55		B- / 8.0	3.85	-0.02
LP	Nuveen Floating Rate Income Opp	JRO	C+	12.25	C+ / 5.9	19.92 / 70	12.32 / 60	10.72 / 72	9.87		B- / 7.9	0.33	1.74
LP	Pioneer Floating Rate Trust	PHD	C+	13.27	C+ / 5.8	18.29 / 64	12.80 / 62	6.33 / 51	6.78		B / 8.1	0.76	1.27
LP	Invesco Van Kampen Dynamic Cred Op	VTA	C+	12.48	C+ / 5.7	27.92 / 88	9.80 / 46	6.61 / 52	7.21		B / 8.0	-4.59	-3.91
LP	BlackRock Defined Opp Credit Trust	BHL	C+	14.18	C / 5.3	18.06 / 63	11.28 / 54	--	8.17		B / 8.2	-1.46	-2.88
LP	Eaton Vance Senior Floating Rate	EFR	C	15.97	C+ / 5.7	20.69 / 73	10.35 / 49	9.61 / 68	6.99		B- / 7.5	1.40	2.43
LP	BlackRock Floating Rt Income	BGT	C	15.05	C+ / 5.6	22.71 / 79	11.23 / 54	8.89 / 65	16.94		B- / 7.6	2.94	1.94
LP	BlackRock Floating Rate Inc Strat	FRA	C	15.15	C / 5.1	22.18 / 77	9.41 / 45	8.47 / 62	6.61		B- / 7.5	-0.66	-0.79
LP	Nuveen Sr Inc	NSL	C	7.31	C / 5.0	20.65 / 72	9.68 / 46	9.03 / 65	4.41		B / 8.0	0.27	1.61
LP	*PowerShares Senior Loan	BKLN	C	24.98	C- / 3.7	9.36 / 33	--	--	4.68		B+ / 9.6	-0.64	0.40

* Denotes ETF Fund, N/A denotes number is not available

Fund Type	Fund Name	Ticker Symbol	Overall Investment Rating	Price As of 12/31/12	Perform-ance Rating/Pts	Annualized Total Return Through 12/31/12			Dividend Yield %	Risk Rating/ Pts	Premium/Discount	
						1Yr/Pct	3Yr/Pct	5Yr/Pct			As of 12/31/12	1 Year Average
MTG	Western Asset Mtge Defined Oppty	DMO	A+	24.21	A+ / 9.8	46.13 / 98	--	--	7.43	B / 8.5	-1.98	3.69
MTG	Nuveen Mortgage Opportunity Term 2	JMT	A+	27.18	A+ / 9.8	41.29 / 97	--	--	7.62	B / 8.3	-2.65	1.68
MTG	*Market Vectors Mtge REIT Income	MORT	A+	25.18	A- / 9.1	26.96 / 87	--	--	12.39	B / 8.8	-6.78	0.12
MTG	PCM Fund	PCM	A+	12.02	A- / 9.0	24.67 / 83	24.45 / 96	16.99 / 96	16.76	B / 8.8	3.89	8.27
MTG	Nuveen Mortgage Opportunity Term	JLS	B+	27.22	B+ / 8.3	39.78 / 97	13.86 / 68	--	7.60	B / 8.2	-1.45	2.77
MTG	American Income Fund	MRF	C+	8.37	C+ / 6.6	21.42 / 75	13.67 / 67	11.03 / 73	6.81	B- / 7.1	-3.46	-4.40
MTG	PIMCO Strategic Glob Gov Fund	RCS	C+	11.35	C+ / 5.9	15.59 / 50	14.63 / 71	16.21 / 94	32.64	B / 8.4	18.35	23.53
MTG	Helios Total Return Fund Inc	HTR	C	23.62	C+ / 5.6	16.15 / 53	15.06 / 72	7.84 / 59	9.65	B- / 7.0	-6.82	0.48
MTG	American Select Portfolio	SLA	C	10.93	C / 4.4	17.50 / 60	9.72 / 46	9.58 / 68	6.86	B / 8.2	-10.12	-10.34
MTG	American Strat Inc Portfolio	ASP	C	11.45	C- / 4.1	15.12 / 48	10.64 / 51	11.88 / 76	6.81	B / 8.1	-9.13	-8.53
MTG	BlackRock Income Trust	BKT	C	7.35	C- / 3.5	5.06 / 24	10.46 / 50	10.51 / 71	6.61	B+ / 9.6	-4.17	-4.76
MTG	American Strat Inc Portfolio II	BSP	C-	8.82	C- / 3.7	20.45 / 72	6.59 / 34	6.32 / 50	6.46	B- / 7.9	-14.12	-14.31
MTG	First Trust Mortgage Income Fund	FMY	C-	17.66	C- / 3.6	5.39 / 25	10.89 / 52	12.18 / 77	9.51	B- / 7.2	-1.51	9.41
MTG	American Strat Inc Portfolio III	CSP	C-	7.49	C- / 3.4	21.53 / 75	5.13 / 30	2.21 / 28	6.01	B- / 7.5	-7.99	-11.93
MTG	*iShares Barclays MBS Bond	MBB	C-	107.99	D / 2.2	1.71 / 17	4.12 / 26	4.88 / 43	1.03	B+ / 9.7	-0.09	0.06
MTG	*SPDR Barclays Mortg Backed Bond	MBG	C-	27.31	D / 2.1	1.76 / 18	3.71 / 25	--	0.22	B+ / 9.6	0.22	N/A
MTG	*Vanguard Mort-Backed Secs Idx ET	VMBS	C-	52.20	D / 2.1	1.73 / 17	4.10 / 26	--	0.51	B+ / 9.8	0.13	0.20

99 Pct = Best
0 Pct = Worst

* Denotes ETF Fund, N/A denotes number is not available

Fund Type	Fund Name	Ticker Symbol	Overall Investment Rating	Price As of 12/31/12	PERFORMANCE Perform-ance Rating/Pts	Annualized Total Return Through 12/31/12 1Yr/Pct	3Yr/Pct	5Yr/Pct	Dividend Yield %	RISK Risk Rating/ Pts	VALUATION Premium/Discount As of 12/31/12	1 Year Average
MUH	Pioneer Municipal High Income Trus	MHI	A+	15.79	A / 9.3	20.52 / 93	15.03 / 95	11.53 / 97	7.85	B / 8.4	6.33	8.47
MUH	Pioneer Municipal High Income Adv	MAV	A+	15.47	A / 9.3	18.62 / 90	16.94 / 98	11.36 / 97	7.37	B / 8.4	12.10	15.38
MUH	Nuveen Muni High Income Opport 2	NMD	A	13.42	A- / 9.1	25.58 / 97	12.94 / 88	6.55 / 70	6.48	B / 8.2	1.82	0.86
MUH	Nuveen Muni High Income Opport	NMZ	A-	14.10	B+ / 8.6	21.21 / 94	12.30 / 86	6.73 / 71	6.53	B / 8.1	3.75	3.52
MUH	MFS High Inc Muni Tr	CXE	B+	5.46	B / 8.1	13.57 / 73	13.30 / 89	8.67 / 83	5.93	B / 8.6	-1.97	6.00
MUH	MFS High Yield Muni Trust	CMU	B+	4.86	B / 7.8	13.58 / 73	12.54 / 87	8.82 / 84	5.93	B / 8.6	-2.80	6.45
MUH	*Market Vectors Hi-Yld Mun Idx ET	HYD	B	32.84	C+ / 6.1	14.47 / 77	8.70 / 66	--	5.30	B+/ 9.1	-0.67	0.21
MUH	Western Asset Municipal High Inc	MHF	C+	7.92	C / 5.4	10.45 / 53	9.21 / 69	8.45 / 81	5.00	B / 8.7	-3.53	2.68
MUH	*PowerShares VRDO Tax-Free Weekly	PVI	C-	24.99	D- / 1.4	0.13 / 14	0.33 / 16	1.08 / 25	0.05	B+/ 9.9	-0.04	-0.03

99 Pct = Best
0 Pct = Worst

* Denotes ETF Fund, N/A denotes number is not available

Fund Type	Fund Name	Ticker Symbol	Overall Investment Rating	Price As of 12/31/12	Perform-ance Rating/Pts	Annualized Total Return Through 12/31/12 1Yr/Pct	3Yr/Pct	5Yr/Pct	Dividend Yield %	Risk Rating/ Pts	Premium/Discount As of 12/31/12	1 Year Average
			99 Pct = Best *0 Pct = Worst*									
MUN	BlackRock MuniHoldings Fund	MHD	A+	18.36	A+ / 9.6	23.49 / 96	17.52 / 99	13.13 / 99	7.52	B / 8.7	1.60	3.24
MUN	BlackRock Municipal Income Quality	BYM	A+	16.20	A / 9.4	22.96 / 95	15.38 / 96	10.27 / 92	5.78	B / 8.2	0.25	1.44
MUN	BlackRock MuniYield Fund	MYD	A+	16.37	A / 9.4	21.19 / 94	16.92 / 98	11.05 / 96	7.21	B / 8.5	2.44	3.64
MUN	BlackRock MuniYield Quality Fund	MQY	A+	17.64	A / 9.4	20.98 / 93	15.80 / 96	12.39 / 99	5.47	B / 8.4	4.69	1.98
MUN	DWS Municipal Income Trust	KTF	A+	14.39	A / 9.3	18.72 / 90	16.63 / 98	14.72 / 99	5.84	B / 8.6	0.14	4.36
MUN	PIMCO Municipal Income Fund II	PML	A+	13.16	A- / 9.2	21.57 / 94	15.06 / 95	5.40 / 61	5.93	B / 8.5	5.45	6.77
MUN	BlackRock MuniVest Fund II	MVT	A+	17.51	A- / 9.2	20.33 / 92	16.07 / 97	12.83 / 96	6.60	B / 8.6	5.10	5.84
MUN	Western Asset Municipal Partners	MNP	A+	17.22	A- / 9.2	19.70 / 91	16.43 / 97	11.89 / 98	4.88	B / 8.7	2.07	1.92
MUN	BlackRock MuniVest Fund	MVF	A+	11.03	A- / 9.2	19.23 / 90	15.19 / 95	11.68 / 97	6.42	B / 8.8	2.80	4.59
MUN	BlackRock Strategic Municipal Tr	BSD	A+	14.84	A- / 9.2	18.55 / 89	16.32 / 97	8.17 / 79	5.98	B / 8.5	-2.69	0.66
MUN	BlackRock MuniHoldings Fund II	MUH	A+	16.64	A- / 9.2	18.29 / 89	16.54 / 97	12.35 / 99	9.27	B / 8.5	-1.42	1.38
MUN	Eaton Vance Municipal Inc Tr	EVN	A+	13.77	A- / 9.1	20.45 / 93	15.65 / 96	9.22 / 86	6.82	B / 8.5	6.09	12.52
MUN	AllianceBernstein Nat Muni Inc Fun	AFB	A+	15.55	A- / 9.1	19.71 / 91	14.21 / 93	10.59 / 94	5.98	B / 8.8	2.30	3.24
MUN	BlackRock Municipal Bond Trust	BBK	A+	17.00	A- / 9.1	18.70 / 90	15.95 / 97	10.67 / 94	6.05	B / 8.4	0.29	3.74
MUN	PIMCO Municipal Income Fund	PMF	A+	15.70	A- / 9.1	17.24 / 86	16.64 / 98	8.87 / 84	6.21	B / 8.5	13.60	17.21
MUN	BlackRock Muni Interm Duration	MUI	A+	16.63	A- / 9.1	15.74 / 82	15.93 / 97	10.75 / 95	6.01	B / 8.8	0.24	1.64
MUN	Dreyfus Strategic Muni Bond Fund	DSM	A+	9.36	A- / 9.0	18.76 / 90	14.99 / 95	10.67 / 94	6.09	B / 8.7	3.20	3.98
MUN	BlackRock Municipal Income Trust I	BLE	A+	16.21	A- / 9.0	18.50 / 89	15.19 / 95	10.06 / 91	6.93	B / 8.4	-0.18	3.15
MUN	Western Asset Managed Municipals	MMU	A+	14.37	B+ / 8.9	18.73 / 90	14.08 / 92	13.66 / 99	5.43	B / 8.7	-0.62	3.21
MUN	PIMCO Municipal Income Fund III	PMX	A+	12.33	B+ / 8.9	18.28 / 88	15.31 / 95	5.17 / 59	6.81	B / 8.8	9.80	15.53
MUN	*Market Vectors CEF Muni Inc ETF	XMPT	A+	28.30	B+ / 8.6	15.31 / 81	--	--	6.11	B+ / 9.2	-4.59	0.11
MUN	Neuberger Berman Intermediate Muni	NBH	A+	16.18	B+ / 8.4	13.07 / 71	13.89 / 92	11.10 / 96	5.19	B+ / 9.1	0.87	3.81
MUN	Eaton Vance Tx Adv Bd&Option Str	EXD	A	17.67	A- / 9.2	18.88 / 90	--	--	9.62	B / 8.0	-3.07	-4.11
MUN	Putnam Managed Muni Inc Tr	PMM	A	8.06	A- / 9.0	19.05 / 90	15.20 / 95	10.54 / 94	5.79	B / 8.4	-0.98	1.23
MUN	BlackRock Long Term Muni Adv	BTA	A	12.59	A- / 9.0	18.14 / 88	15.62 / 96	8.54 / 82	5.92	B / 8.3	-1.95	1.67
MUN	BlackRock MuniHoldings Quality II	MUE	A	15.08	A- / 9.0	16.37 / 84	14.55 / 94	11.96 / 98	5.67	B / 8.3	-2.01	-0.21
MUN	BlackRock MuniYield Quality III	MYI	A	15.30	A- / 9.0	16.08 / 83	15.23 / 95	10.18 / 92	5.87	B / 8.4	-0.97	0.38
MUN	American Municipal Income Portfoli	XAA	A	15.77	B+ / 8.9	21.48 / 94	13.00 / 89	12.11 / 98	5.90	B / 8.5	-0.57	1.79
MUN	Invesco Municipal Income Opp Tr	OIA	A	7.32	B+ / 8.9	19.81 / 91	14.08 / 92	7.47 / 75	5.74	B / 8.5	-2.66	-1.00
MUN	BlackRock MuniYield Quality Fund I	MQT	A	14.44	B+ / 8.9	15.56 / 81	15.29 / 95	11.57 / 97	5.78	B / 8.4	-1.57	0.13
MUN	Dreyfus Strategic Municipals	LEO	A	9.55	B+ / 8.8	16.97 / 86	14.00 / 92	10.68 / 94	6.16	B / 8.4	2.36	4.29
MUN	BlackRock Investment Qual Muni Tr	BKN	A	16.34	B+ / 8.7	14.87 / 79	14.89 / 94	9.36 / 88	6.20	B / 8.4	0.31	3.89
MUN	BlackRock Municipal Income Trust	BFK	A	15.52	B+ / 8.6	17.48 / 87	14.71 / 94	9.51 / 89	6.28	B / 8.4	1.04	3.88
MUN	Nuveen Prem Inc Muni 4	NPT	A	14.11	B+ / 8.6	16.10 / 83	13.56 / 91	11.15 / 96	5.78	B / 8.6	-3.16	-0.95
MUN	Nuveen Investment Quality Muni Fun	NQM	A	16.03	B+ / 8.6	13.94 / 75	14.43 / 93	10.15 / 92	6.16	B / 8.6	-3.78	0.05
MUN	Nuveen New Jersey Municipal Value	NJV	A	17.14	B+ / 8.5	18.51 / 89	11.68 / 83	--	4.76	B / 8.6	1.30	-0.49
MUN	Nuveen Performance Plus Muni	NPP	A	16.17	B+ / 8.4	14.39 / 77	13.20 / 89	10.85 / 95	5.71	B / 8.7	-3.75	-1.72
MUN	BlackRock MuniHoldings Quality	MUS	A-	15.10	B+ / 8.6	16.30 / 84	14.33 / 93	11.63 / 97	5.88	B / 8.3	-2.01	1.13
MUN	Nuveen Div Adv Muni	NAD	A-	15.48	B+ / 8.4	15.89 / 83	12.99 / 88	9.99 / 91	6.07	B / 8.6	-4.39	-2.95
MUN	Dreyfus Municipal Income	DMF	A-	10.43	B+ / 8.4	15.70 / 82	14.53 / 94	12.03 / 98	6.04	B / 8.6	0.10	4.18
MUN	BlackRock MuniEnhanced Fund	MEN	A-	12.29	B+ / 8.4	15.42 / 81	13.68 / 91	10.28 / 92	5.66	B / 8.6	-2.61	-1.21
MUN	Putnam Muni Opp Tr	PMO	A-	12.95	B / 8.2	14.76 / 79	13.04 / 89	10.30 / 93	5.18	B / 8.7	-4.71	-1.59
MUN	Invesco Van Kampen Adv Muni Inc II	VKI	A-	13.15	B / 8.2	14.35 / 77	13.30 / 89	8.56 / 82	6.48	B / 8.7	0.61	3.44
MUN	DWS Strategic Municipal Inc Tr	KSM	A-	14.55	B / 8.2	14.13 / 76	13.95 / 92	14.88 / 99	6.35	B / 8.6	2.18	8.40
MUN	BlackRock MuniAssets Fund	MUA	A-	13.92	B / 8.1	17.37 / 86	10.97 / 79	8.04 / 78	7.69	B / 8.6	-1.90	-1.34
MUN	Nuveen Prem Inc Muni	NPI	A-	14.97	B / 8.1	14.30 / 76	12.66 / 87	9.30 / 87	5.77	B / 8.8	-3.42	-1.36
MUN	Nuveen Prem Inc Muni Oppty	NPX	A-	14.27	B / 8.0	13.91 / 75	12.08 / 84	9.69 / 90	5.21	B / 8.7	-4.29	-2.29
MUN	Delaware Inv Nat Muni Inc	VFL	A-	14.03	B / 7.9	16.37 / 84	10.79 / 78	7.55 / 75	4.70	B+ / 9.0	-7.76	-5.44
MUN	Managed Duration Investment Grd Mu	MZF	B+	15.30	B / 8.1	13.41 / 72	13.55 / 91	11.97 / 98	6.08	B / 8.5	-0.58	3.19
MUN	Invesco Van Kampen Tr Fr Inv Gr Mu	VGM	B+	15.22	B / 7.9	13.01 / 71	12.61 / 87	9.11 / 85	6.54	B / 8.8	0.13	3.14
MUN	Nuveen Premium Income Muni 2	NPM	B+	15.20	B / 7.8	12.05 / 65	12.30 / 86	9.23 / 86	5.76	B / 8.8	-5.06	-2.55
MUN	Western Asset Intermediate Muni	SBI	B+	10.58	B- / 7.5	14.89 / 79	11.27 / 81	9.32 / 88	4.54	B+ / 9.1	0.47	0.57

* Denotes ETF Fund, N/A denotes number is not available

www.thestreetratings.com

VI. Top-Rated ETFs and Other Closed-End Funds: Municipal - Single State

99 Pct = Best
0 Pct = Worst

Fund Type	Fund Name	Ticker Symbol	Overall Investment Rating	Price As of 12/31/12	PERFORMANCE Perform-ance Rating/Pts	Annualized Total Return Through 12/31/12 1Yr/Pct	3Yr/Pct	5Yr/Pct	Dividend Yield %	RISK Risk Rating/Pts	VALUATION Premium/Discount As of 12/31/12	1 Year Average
MUS	Eaton Vance CA Muni Bond II	EIA	A+	14.10	A+ / 9.6	27.57 / 97	16.50 / 97	9.23 / 87	5.46	B / 8.2	3.91	1.85
MUS	PIMCO CA Municipal Income Fund	PCQ	A+	15.93	A+ / 9.6	24.29 / 96	17.46 / 98	8.79 / 84	5.80	B / 8.3	9.11	8.32
MUS	BlackRock MuniYield Invt Fund	MYF	A+	16.87	A+ / 9.6	22.37 / 95	17.94 / 99	12.79 / 99	5.62	B / 8.8	2.12	1.78
MUS	Nuveen CA Quality Inc Muni	NUC	A+	17.35	A+ / 9.6	20.94 / 93	17.52 / 99	12.56 / 99	5.88	B / 8.4	4.27	3.28
MUS	Nuveen CA Muni Market Opportunity	NCO	A+	16.34	A / 9.5	23.30 / 96	16.96 / 98	11.26 / 97	5.88	B / 8.7	-1.09	0.53
MUS	BlackRock CA Municipal Income Trus	BFZ	A+	16.34	A / 9.5	22.89 / 95	16.94 / 98	9.14 / 86	5.71	B / 8.4	-1.15	-0.21
MUS	BlackRock MuniYield California Qly	MCA	A+	16.43	A / 9.5	21.56 / 94	17.78 / 99	11.33 / 97	5.55	B / 8.6	-1.73	-2.52
MUS	BlackRock MuniHoldings CA Qly	MUC	A+	16.34	A / 9.5	18.55 / 89	17.93 / 99	11.85 / 98	5.80	B / 8.6	-0.91	-0.64
MUS	Nuveen CA Select Quality Muni	NVC	A+	16.64	A / 9.4	20.28 / 92	16.55 / 98	12.54 / 99	5.99	B / 8.4	0.12	2.43
MUS	Nuveen CA Div Adv Muni	NAC	A+	16.10	A / 9.4	19.95 / 92	17.04 / 98	10.81 / 95	5.52	B / 8.5	1.51	-0.43
MUS	BlackRock MuniYield CA Fund	MYC	A+	16.93	A / 9.4	18.07 / 88	17.83 / 99	11.78 / 98	5.60	B / 8.7	-1.23	-0.95
MUS	Nuveen CA Performance Plus Muni	NCP	A+	16.26	A / 9.4	16.94 / 85	17.51 / 98	11.06 / 96	5.83	B / 8.6	1.37	1.23
MUS	Nuveen OH Quality Inc Muni	NUO	A+	19.05	A / 9.3	23.39 / 96	14.25 / 93	12.75 / 99	5.04	B / 8.8	7.81	4.66
MUS	PIMCO CA Municipal Income Fund II	PCK	A+	10.59	A / 9.3	21.87 / 94	16.47 / 97	3.12 / 43	7.08	B / 8.7	15.86	19.12
MUS	PIMCO CA Municipal Income Fund III	PZC	A+	11.28	A- / 9.2	22.38 / 95	16.10 / 97	3.45 / 46	6.38	B / 8.6	8.88	9.33
MUS	BlackRock MuniHoldings Inv Quality	MFL	A+	16.10	A- / 9.2	20.17 / 92	15.59 / 96	12.22 / 98	5.70	B / 8.5	-0.43	-0.23
MUS	Nuveen CA Prem Inc Muni	NCU	A+	15.46	A- / 9.2	16.22 / 84	16.97 / 98	10.72 / 95	5.43	B / 8.7	-3.07	-1.56
MUS	BlackRock MuniYield Inv Quality	MFT	A+	15.70	A- / 9.1	19.34 / 91	15.41 / 96	11.74 / 98	5.43	B / 8.7	-1.81	-1.02
MUS	Eaton Vance NY Muni Inc Tr	EVY	A+	15.64	A- / 9.1	18.28 / 88	14.38 / 93	9.26 / 87	5.82	B / 8.6	3.64	3.14
MUS	Invesco Van Kampen PA Val Muni Inc	VPV	A+	15.30	A- / 9.0	18.95 / 90	14.54 / 94	10.50 / 93	5.88	B / 8.5	-1.54	0.36
MUS	BlackRock Muni Bond Invt Trust	BIE	A+	17.18	A- / 9.0	17.68 / 87	15.80 / 96	9.07 / 85	5.45	B / 8.6	0.53	-0.12
MUS	PIMCO NY Municipal Income Fund II	PNI	A+	12.78	B+ / 8.9	21.17 / 94	14.50 / 94	5.72 / 64	6.23	B / 8.5	8.67	11.24
MUS	BlackRock MuniYield Michigan Qly	MIY	A+	15.65	B+ / 8.9	16.13 / 83	15.07 / 95	10.68 / 95	5.87	B / 8.6	-3.69	-1.60
MUS	Nuveen NJ Prem Inc Muni	NNJ	A+	16.53	B+ / 8.8	18.59 / 89	14.32 / 93	10.92 / 96	5.15	B / 8.6	1.29	1.32
MUS	BlackRock Muni NY Interm Duration	MNE	A+	15.44	B+ / 8.8	15.95 / 83	14.72 / 94	9.46 / 89	4.86	B+ / 9.1	-3.38	-2.24
MUS	BlackRock MuniHoldings NJ Qly	MUJ	A+	16.67	B+ / 8.7	15.67 / 82	13.38 / 90	10.71 / 95	5.33	B / 8.7	0.60	-1.72
MUS	Delaware Inv MN Muni Inc Fund II	VMM	A+	15.22	B+ / 8.5	18.67 / 90	12.84 / 88	8.25 / 79	4.53	B+ / 9.4	-1.55	-2.68
MUS	BlackRock Municipal Income Invt Tr	BBF	A	15.87	A- / 9.1	20.61 / 93	15.43 / 96	9.30 / 87	5.47	B / 8.2	-1.55	0.04
MUS	BlackRock PA Strategic Muni Tr	BPS	A	15.21	A- / 9.1	15.53 / 81	15.45 / 96	8.56 / 82	6.53	B / 8.2	-2.00	0.29
MUS	Eaton Vance OH Muni Inc Tr	EVO	A	16.45	A- / 9.0	21.03 / 94	14.20 / 92	10.99 / 96	5.06	B / 8.2	6.89	3.34
MUS	BlackRock NJ Municipal Income Trus	BNJ	A	17.05	A- / 9.0	19.94 / 92	15.55 / 96	7.65 / 76	5.71	B / 8.3	4.92	7.48
MUS	BlackRock MuniYield New York Qly	MYN	A	15.10	B+ / 8.9	14.52 / 78	15.35 / 96	9.69 / 90	5.64	B / 8.4	0.53	-0.85
MUS	Nuveen CA Inv Quality Muni	NQC	A	15.68	B+ / 8.8	16.49 / 84	15.90 / 97	10.90 / 95	5.89	B / 8.6	-2.91	1.87
MUS	Invesco Van Kampen Tr Fr Inv NY Mu	VTN	A	16.59	B+ / 8.7	17.09 / 86	13.31 / 90	10.25 / 92	6.08	B / 8.8	4.14	3.28
MUS	BlackRock MuniHoldings New York Ql	MHN	A	16.15	B+ / 8.7	14.81 / 79	13.80 / 91	11.23 / 96	5.73	B / 8.4	3.46	2.00
MUS	BlackRock MuniYield AZ Fund	MZA	A	15.34	B+ / 8.6	17.05 / 86	14.29 / 93	9.23 / 87	5.44	B / 8.7	0.66	1.30
MUS	BlackRock MuniYield NJ Fund	MYJ	A	16.60	B+ / 8.5	17.84 / 87	13.90 / 92	10.51 / 94	5.66	B / 8.7	-2.18	-0.43
MUS	Nuveen OH Div Adv Muni	NXI	A	16.31	B+ / 8.5	15.85 / 83	12.45 / 87	10.68 / 95	4.78	B / 8.6	0.25	0.36
MUS	Nuveen PA Prem Inc Muni 2	NPY	A	15.08	B+ / 8.5	15.55 / 81	13.78 / 91	10.33 / 93	5.57	B / 8.8	-2.65	-3.58
MUS	BlackRock New York Muni Inc Qly	BSE	A	16.11	B+ / 8.5	15.21 / 80	14.22 / 93	8.71 / 83	5.33	B / 8.5	3.53	2.94
MUS	Eaton Vance MI Muni Inc Tr	EMI	A	13.80	B+ / 8.5	14.79 / 79	13.32 / 90	8.95 / 85	5.57	B / 8.7	-7.44	-5.69
MUS	Nuveen NY Performance Plus Muni	NNP	A	16.47	B+ / 8.5	14.67 / 78	13.34 / 90	10.26 / 92	5.37	B+ / 9.0	-1.50	-1.20
MUS	BlackRock MuniYield PA Qly	MPA	A	16.35	B+ / 8.4	9.29 / 46	14.12 / 92	10.06 / 91	5.43	B / 8.7	-2.10	-2.04
MUS	PIMCO NY Municipal Income Fund III	PYN	A	10.63	B+ / 8.3	16.44 / 84	12.91 / 88	2.09 / 33	5.93	B / 8.7	9.47	8.80
MUS	Nuveen PA Investment Quality Muni	NQP	A	15.64	B / 8.2	11.78 / 63	13.66 / 91	10.29 / 93	5.68	B / 8.9	-3.69	-1.01
MUS	Nuveen NJ Div Adv Muni Fund 2	NUJ	A-	16.34	B+ / 8.8	20.32 / 92	13.81 / 91	10.35 / 93	4.41	B / 8.2	4.01	3.43
MUS	PIMCO NY Muni Income Fund	PNF	A-	12.28	B+ / 8.3	15.24 / 80	13.36 / 90	6.34 / 68	5.57	B / 8.6	1.74	4.85
MUS	BlackRock MuniYield New Jersey Qly	MJI	A-	16.23	B+ / 8.3	14.92 / 79	14.00 / 92	10.67 / 94	5.84	B / 8.6	-0.92	0.93
MUS	BlackRock MuniYield Michigan Qly I	MYM	A-	14.35	B+ / 8.3	7.37 / 37	14.48 / 94	9.69 / 90	5.77	B / 8.6	-5.59	-2.34
MUS	Nuveen CA Div Adv Muni 2	NVX	A-	15.61	B / 8.2	13.60 / 73	13.41 / 90	10.27 / 92	5.77	B / 8.7	-4.53	-1.04
MUS	Nuveen MI Quality Inc Muni	NUM	A-	15.31	B / 8.1	13.83 / 74	13.65 / 91	9.64 / 90	5.80	B / 8.9	-6.42	-3.19
MUS	Nuveen AZ Div Adv Muni Fund 3	NXE	A-	14.77	B / 8.0	16.56 / 85	12.02 / 84	8.10 / 78	4.71	B+ / 9.0	-3.46	-3.82

* Denotes ETF Fund, N/A denotes number is not available

99 Pct = Best
0 Pct = Worst

Fund Type	Fund Name	Ticker Symbol	Overall Investment Rating	Price As of 12/31/12	Perform-ance Rating/Pts	Annualized Total Return Through 12/31/12			Dividend Yield %	Risk Rating/ Pts	Premium/Discount As of 12/31/12	1 Year Average
						1Yr/Pct	3Yr/Pct	5Yr/Pct				
PM	*ETFS Physical Palladium Shares	PALL	C+	69.22	B / 8.1	9.27 / 33	--	--	0.00	C+ / 6.4	1.63	0.11
PM	*First Trust ISE Global Copper Id	CU	C	30.32	B+ / 8.4	3.02 / 21	--	--	1.32	C / 4.6	-4.98	-0.22
PM	*Global X Copper Miners ETF	COPX	C	13.02	B+ / 8.3	2.17 / 19	--	--	3.29	C / 4.4	-5.38	-0.11
PM	*UBS E-TRACS S&P 500 Gold Hedged	SPGH	C	50.99	B / 7.9	17.25 / 59	--	--	0.00	C / 4.8	-4.05	-0.10
PM	*iShares MSCI ACWI ex US Mtls Ind	AXMT	C	54.92	B- / 7.4	5.84 / 25	--	--	1.90	C+ / 5.9	-1.51	-0.69
PM	*ProShares Ultra Gold	UGL	C	85.26	B- / 7.0	-2.60 / 12	20.99 / 91	--	0.00	C+ / 5.9	2.00	0.24
PM	*SPDR Gold Shares	GLD	C	162.02	C / 4.3	1.13 / 16	13.26 / 64	13.00 / 81	0.00	B / 8.1	0.95	0.14
PM	*ETFS Physical Swiss Gold Shares	SGOL	C	165.16	C / 4.3	1.10 / 16	13.26 / 64	--	0.00	B / 8.1	0.95	0.15
PM	*PowerShares DB Gold Double Lg ET	DGP	C-	52.03	B- / 7.5	-1.29 / 13	22.20 / 93	--	0.00	C- / 3.9	1.62	0.02
PM	*iShares Silver Trust	SLV	C-	29.37	C+ / 6.3	2.29 / 19	17.77 / 82	12.96 / 80	0.00	C / 4.9	-1.01	0.51
PM	Central Fund of Canada	CEF	C-	21.03	C / 4.8	1.86 / 18	14.14 / 69	13.52 / 84	0.05	B- / 7.0	2.59	4.19
PM	*ETFS Physical Platinum Shares	PPLT	C-	151.36	C / 4.6	8.82 / 32	--	--	0.00	C+ / 6.9	-5.21	0.25
PM	*PowerShares DB Precious Metals F	DBP	C-	57.09	C- / 4.2	0.21 / 14	13.05 / 63	11.82 / 76	0.00	B- / 7.5	0.63	N/A
PM	*PowerShares DB Gold Fund	DGL	C-	57.35	C- / 3.8	-0.02 / 14	12.06 / 58	11.55 / 75	0.00	B / 8.1	0.81	0.01
PM	Central Gold-Trust	GTU	C-	62.78	C- / 3.7	-0.57 / 13	11.87 / 57	13.34 / 83	0.00	B- / 7.7	2.25	3.23
PM	*PowerShares DB Silver Fund	DBS	D+	52.35	C+ / 5.8	1.53 / 17	16.82 / 79	11.87 / 76	0.00	C / 4.8	0.13	0.04
PM	*Global X Silver Miners ETF	SIL	D+	22.65	C / 4.4	2.33 / 19	--	--	0.89	C / 5.2	1.12	-0.01
PM	*ETFS Physical Asian Gold Shares	AGOL	D+	166.25	D / 1.8	2.19 / 19	--	--	0.00	B / 8.0	1.09	-0.14
PM	*ETFS Physical WM Basket Shares	WITE	D	50.76	C- / 3.0	4.99 / 24	--	--	0.00	C / 5.4	-2.05	0.37
PM	GAMCO Global Gold Nat ResandIncome	GGN	D	12.80	D / 2.1	-0.15 / 14	3.25 / 23	-3.39 / 10	11.25	C+ / 6.2	-4.55	4.09
PM	*ETFS Physical PM Basket Shares	GLTR	D	92.81	D / 2.0	2.22 / 19	--	--	0.00	C+ / 6.8	-0.08	0.27
PM	*iShares Gold Trust	IAU	D-	16.28	C / 4.3	1.25 / 16	13.37 / 65	13.04 / 81	0.00	D / 1.9	0.99	0.15
PM	*Market Vectors Gold Miners ETF	GDX	D-	46.39	D- / 1.1	-15.17 / 6	-0.80 / 13	-0.82 / 17	1.00	C / 5.1	2.27	-0.03
PM	*First Trust ISE Global Platinum	PLTM	E+	14.77	D / 1.9	-16.60 / 6	--	--	0.23	C- / 3.6	-6.22	-0.02
PM	*PowerShares Glb Gold & Precious	PSAU	E+	37.08	D- / 1.1	-12.62 / 7	-1.00 / 13	--	0.52	C / 4.7	2.66	-0.17
PM	*PowerShares DB Base Metals Sht E	BOS	E+	20.34	D- / 1.0	-2.92 / 11	-2.79 / 11	--	0.00	C- / 3.9	0.05	-0.27
PM	*Market Vectors Junior Gold Mnrs	GDXJ	E+	19.80	E+ / 0.9	-20.49 / 5	-4.17 / 10	--	3.79	C- / 4.1	-1.93	0.17
PM	*Global X Pure Gold Miners ETF	GGGG	E+	10.48	E / 0.4	-20.59 / 5	--	--	0.13	C / 5.3	2.34	0.38
PM	*FactorShares Gold Bull S&P 500 B	FSG	E+	20.88	E- / 0.2	-32.13 / 3	--	--	0.00	C / 4.4	10.59	-0.05
PM	*Direxion Daily Gold Miners Bear	DUST	E	31.50	D / 1.8	-5.88 / 10	--	--	0.00	D / 2.2	-10.36	0.23
PM	ASA Gold & Precious Metals Ltd	ASA	E	21.53	E+ / 0.9	-17.80 / 5	-3.98 / 10	-0.22 / 18	6.50	D+ / 2.8	-8.89	-7.98
PM	*PowerShares DB Gold Short ETN	DGZ	E	11.81	E+ / 0.6	-3.34 / 11	-14.98 / 6	--	0.00	C- / 3.0	-0.76	-0.04
PM	*PowerShares DB Base Mtls Dbl Sh	BOM	E-	11.87	E+ / 0.7	-7.88 / 9	-8.93 / 7	--	0.00	D / 2.2	-3.02	-0.19
PM	*PowerShares DB Base Mtls Dbl Lg	BDD	E-	10.82	E+ / 0.7	-10.92 / 8	-15.22 / 5	--	0.00	D+ / 2.4	2.08	-0.07
PM	*PowerShares DB Gold Double Sht E	DZZ	E-	4.47	E / 0.4	-8.11 / 9	-29.85 / 3	--	0.00	D / 1.9	-1.76	-0.07
PM	*Direxion Daily Gold Miners Bull	NUGT	E-	11.00	E- / 0.1	-54.60 / 1	--	--	0.00	D / 1.9	7.63	-0.03

* Denotes ETF Fund, N/A denotes number is not available

www.thestreetratings.com

					PERFORMANCE						RISK	VALUATION	
												Premium/Discount	
99 Pct = Best / 0 Pct = Worst					Perform-	Annualized Total Return Through 12/31/12					Risk		
Fund Type	Fund Name	Ticker Symbol	Overall Investment Rating	Price As of 12/31/12	ance Rating/Pts	1Yr/Pct	3Yr/Pct	5Yr/Pct	Dividend Yield %		Rating/ Pts	As of 12/31/12	1 Year Average
USA	*Direxion Daily 7-10 Yr Trs Bull	TYD	B+	85.82	B+ / 8.7	6.67 / 27	27.23 / 99	--	0.00		B- / 7.8	1.68	-0.02
USA	*Direxion Daily 20+ Yr Treas Bull	TMF	C+	71.81	A- / 9.2	-1.79 / 12	33.30 / 99	--	0.10		C / 5.3	3.52	-0.02
USA	*PIMCO 25+ Year Zero Coupon US Tr	ZROZ	C+	109.12	C+ / 6.5	0.81 / 15	20.20 / 89	--	3.96		B- / 7.1	1.92	-0.20
USA	*Vanguard Extnd Durtn Trea Idx ET	EDV	C+	116.00	C+ / 6.4	1.38 / 17	19.69 / 88	10.82 / 72	4.13		B- / 7.7	2.10	0.27
USA	*PIMCO 15 Plus Year US TIPS Idx E	LTPZ	C+	71.65	C / 5.3	9.54 / 34	14.46 / 71	--	0.98		B+ / 9.1	0.58	0.01
USA	*PowerShares Build America Bond	BAB	C+	30.24	C / 4.6	9.09 / 33	12.68 / 62	--	4.73		B+ / 9.3	0.47	0.10
USA	*iShares Barclays 20+Yr Treasury	TLT	C	121.18	C- / 4.2	1.84 / 18	13.66 / 67	8.72 / 64	2.66		B / 8.4	1.47	0.12
USA	*SPDR Barclays LongTerm Treasury	TLO	C	70.11	C- / 3.9	1.83 / 18	12.50 / 61	8.57 / 63	2.57		B / 8.7	1.17	0.05
USA	*Vanguard Long-Term Govt Bd Idx E	VGLT	C	75.30	C- / 3.8	2.03 / 18	12.28 / 59	--	2.73		B / 8.7	1.06	0.09
USA	*iShares Barclays 10-20 Yr Treasu	TLH	C	134.86	C- / 3.4	2.83 / 20	10.48 / 50	7.90 / 59	2.11		B+ / 9.1	0.96	0.07
USA	*SPDR Barclays TIPS ETF	IPE	C	60.72	C- / 3.3	6.31 / 27	8.92 / 43	6.56 / 52	0.31		B+ / 9.7	0.36	0.01
USA	*PowerShares 1-30 Laddered Treasu	PLW	C	32.60	C- / 3.2	2.02 / 18	9.61 / 45	7.06 / 55	3.10		B+ / 9.2	0.77	0.06
USA	*PIMCO Broad US TIPS Index ETF	TIPZ	C	61.20	C- / 3.1	5.62 / 25	8.52 / 41	--	1.25		B+ / 9.7	0.33	N/A
USA	*iShares Barclays TIPS Bond	TIP	C	121.41	C- / 3.1	5.46 / 25	8.13 / 39	6.19 / 50	0.05		B+ / 9.7	0.18	0.10
USA	*iShares Barclays 7-10Yr Treasury	IEF	C	107.49	C- / 3.1	3.01 / 20	8.67 / 41	6.88 / 54	1.68		B+ / 9.5	0.68	0.05
USA	*PIMCO 7-15 Year US Treasury Idx	TENZ	C	86.82	C- / 3.0	2.51 / 19	8.64 / 41	--	1.52		B+ / 9.3	0.92	-0.02
USA	Western Asset/Claymore Inf-Link O&	WIW	C	13.20	D+ / 2.9	7.11 / 28	7.16 / 36	6.62 / 52	2.79		B+ / 9.6	-11.41	-10.83
USA	*iShares Barclays Govt/Credit Bd	GBF	C	114.87	D+ / 2.5	3.29 / 21	5.81 / 32	5.42 / 47	2.15		B+ / 9.7	-0.01	0.33
USA	*FlexShs iB 5Y Tgt Dur TIPS Idx	TDTF	C	26.30	D+ / 2.3	5.31 / 24	--	--	0.75		B+ / 9.9	0.54	0.12
USA	*iShares Barclays 3-7 Yr Treasury	IEI	C	123.22	D+ / 2.3	1.58 / 17	5.05 / 29	4.89 / 43	0.61		B+ / 9.7	0.14	0.04
USA	*PIMCO Build America Bond ETF	BABZ	C-	55.00	D+ / 2.8	8.46 / 31	--	--	4.15		B+ / 9.3	0.60	-0.01
USA	Western Asset/Claymore Inf-Link S&	WIA	C-	13.11	D+ / 2.5	6.30 / 27	5.33 / 31	5.81 / 48	2.68		B+ / 9.5	-10.82	-10.58
USA	*Vanguard Intm-Term Govt Bd Idx E	VGIT	C-	65.41	D+ / 2.4	1.96 / 18	5.80 / 32	--	1.45		B+ / 9.6	0.17	0.05
USA	BlackRock Enhanced Government	EGF	C-	15.63	D+ / 2.3	7.24 / 29	3.33 / 24	5.72 / 47	4.99		B+ / 9.1	-2.50	-4.97
USA	*PIMCO 3-7 Year US Treasury Idx E	FIVZ	C-	81.36	D+ / 2.3	1.53 / 17	4.99 / 29	--	1.37		B+ / 9.7	0.17	-0.03
USA	*PIMCO 1-5 Year US TIPS Index ETF	STPZ	C-	54.06	D / 2.1	2.01 / 18	3.32 / 24	--	0.55		B+ / 9.9	0.02	-0.01
USA	*SPDR Barclays Int Tr Treas ETF	ITE	C-	60.72	D / 2.1	1.31 / 17	3.91 / 26	4.00 / 37	1.54		B+ / 9.8	0.03	-0.06
USA	*iShares Barclays Agency Bond	AGZ	C-	113.30	D / 2.0	1.29 / 17	3.17 / 23	--	1.12		B+ / 9.9	-0.04	0.12
USA	*FlexShs iB 3Y Tgt Dur TIPS Idx	TDTT	C-	25.52	D / 1.9	2.94 / 20	--	--	0.56		B+ / 9.9	0.28	0.23
USA	*iShares Barclays 0-5 Year TIPS B	STIP	C-	103.08	D / 1.7	1.79 / 18	--	--	0.71		B+ / 9.9	0.00	0.11
USA	*Schwab Intmdt-Term US Treasury E	SCHR	C-	54.08	D / 1.6	1.96 / 18	--	--	0.94		B+ / 9.7	0.20	N/A
USA	*Vanguard Short-Term Gvt Bd Idx E	VGSH	C-	60.89	D / 1.6	0.46 / 15	1.16 / 18	--	0.24		B+ / 9.9	0.03	0.03
USA	*PIMCO 1-3 Year US Treasury Idx E	TUZ	C-	50.85	D / 1.6	0.28 / 14	1.20 / 18	--	0.32		B+ / 9.9	-0.10	-0.02
USA	*iShares Barclays 1-3Yr Treasury	SHY	C-	84.42	D / 1.6	0.25 / 14	1.14 / 18	1.91 / 26	0.30		B+ / 9.9	0.00	0.02
USA	*SPDR Barclays Sht Trm Treasury E	SST	C-	30.17	D- / 1.5	0.77 / 15	--	--	0.74		B+ / 9.9	0.10	0.02
USA	*PIMCO Broad US Treasury Index ET	TRSY	C-	106.66	D- / 1.4	1.64 / 17	--	--	1.46		B+ / 9.6	2.17	0.21
USA	*Schwab Short-Term US Treas ETF	SCHO	C-	50.49	D- / 1.4	0.25 / 14	--	--	0.29		B+ / 9.9	-0.08	N/A
USA	*iShares Barclays Short Treasury	SHV	C-	110.26	D- / 1.3	0.02 / 14	0.07 / 15	0.55 / 21	0.01		B+ / 9.9	0.04	0.01
USA	*SPDR Barclays 1-3 Month T-Bill E	BIL	C-	45.81	D- / 1.3	-0.04 / 14	-0.03 / 15	0.27 / 20	0.00		B+ / 9.9	0.00	N/A
USA	*PowerShares DB US Inflation ETN	INFL	D	51.33	D+ / 2.4	4.32 / 23	--	--	0.00		C+ / 5.7	0.14	0.19
USA	Federated Enhanced Treasury Income	FTT	D	14.18	D / 2.1	2.73 / 19	--	--	6.18		B- / 7.5	-10.31	-9.76
USA	*iPath US Treas 10Yr Bull ETN	DTYL	D-	71.70	D / 1.7	4.87 / 23	--	--	0.00		C / 5.1	1.44	-0.02
USA	*iPath US Treas Flattener ETN	FLAT	D-	62.48	D- / 1.5	4.88 / 24	--	--	0.00		C / 5.2	1.15	N/A
USA	*iPath US Treas Lng Bd Bull ETN	DLBL	D-	70.33	D- / 1.2	2.89 / 20	--	--	0.00		C / 5.0	2.61	-0.24
USA	*PowerShares DB US Deflation ETN	DEFL	D-	46.77	E+ / 0.9	-7.51 / 9	--	--	0.00		C+ / 5.6	0.32	0.01
USA	*ProShares Short 20+ Year Treas	TBF	D-	29.38	E+ / 0.6	-5.00 / 10	-15.89 / 5	--	0.00		C+ / 5.9	-1.28	-0.11
USA	*ProShares Ultra 7-10 Year Treasu	UST	E+	56.75	D / 1.6	4.73 / 23	--	--	0.02		C / 4.3	1.30	0.09
USA	*iPath US Treas 2Yr Bear ETN	DTUS	E+	40.51	D- / 1.2	-1.39 / 13	--	--	0.00		C / 4.7	0.50	0.09
USA	*iPath ETN US Treasury 5Yr Bear E	DFVS	E+	38.26	E+ / 0.9	-6.79 / 10	--	--	0.00		C / 4.8	-0.62	0.44
USA	*ProShares Ultra 20+ Year Treasur	UBT	E+	69.53	E+ / 0.8	0.39 / 15	--	--	0.07		C / 4.4	3.30	0.19
USA	*PowerShares DB 3x Lg 25+ Yr Tr E	LBND	E+	47.22	E+ / 0.7	0.62 / 15	--	--	0.00		C / 4.8	4.22	0.01
USA	*Direxion Daily 7-10 Yr Trs Bear	TYO	E+	22.98	E / 0.4	-13.93 / 7	-27.46 / 3	--	0.00		C / 4.4	-1.29	0.02

* Denotes ETF Fund, N/A denotes number is not available

Fund Type	Fund Name	Ticker Symbol	Overall Investment Rating	Price As of 12/31/12	Performance Rating/Pts	1Yr/Pct	3Yr/Pct	5Yr/Pct	Dividend Yield %	Risk Rating/Pts	Premium/Discount As of 12/31/12	1 Year Average
UT	*SPDR S&P Transportation ETF	XTN	B+	53.78	A / 9.4	21.40 / 75	--	--	2.16	B- / 7.1	-5.30	-0.08
UT	Cohen&Steers Infrastructure Fund	UTF	B+	18.75	B / 8.0	26.40 / 86	15.68 / 76	3.54 / 35	7.68	B / 8.3	-10.84	-8.85
UT	Reaves Utility Income Trust	UTG	C+	23.82	C+ / 5.8	3.95 / 22	17.13 / 80	9.57 / 68	6.61	B / 8.7	-4.83	2.54
UT	*ProShares Ultra Utilities	UPW	C+	54.01	C / 5.3	8.98 / 32	15.55 / 75	-2.78 / 12	2.17	B / 8.3	-3.86	-0.15
UT	*Guggenheim S&P 500 Eq Wght Util	RYU	C+	57.47	C / 4.7	14.01 / 45	12.63 / 61	5.28 / 45	4.01	B+ / 9.2	-2.79	-0.04
UT	*PowerShares Dynamic Utilities	PUI	C	17.31	C- / 3.7	12.42 / 40	9.34 / 44	2.87 / 31	3.69	B / 8.8	-2.42	-0.16
UT	*Vanguard Utilities Index ETF	VPU	C	75.30	C- / 3.4	6.67 / 27	9.62 / 45	2.42 / 29	4.24	B+ / 9.2	-1.49	0.02
UT	Gabelli Global Utility&Income Trus	GLU	C	20.88	C- / 3.3	9.13 / 33	8.06 / 39	5.80 / 48	5.75	B+ / 9.0	0.24	2.12
UT	*iShares DJ US Utilities	IDU	C	86.36	C- / 3.2	5.85 / 25	9.28 / 44	1.79 / 25	3.04	B+ / 9.2	-1.51	-0.01
UT	*First Trust Utilities AlphaDEX	FXU	C	17.98	C- / 3.1	5.84 / 25	8.47 / 40	3.98 / 37	2.74	B+ / 9.0	-1.10	-0.02
UT	*Utilities Select Sector SPDR	XLU	C	34.92	C- / 3.1	5.64 / 25	8.99 / 43	1.84 / 26	4.58	B+ / 9.1	-1.33	-0.02
UT	DNP Select Income Fund Inc	DNP	C-	9.47	C- / 3.6	-3.42 / 11	12.13 / 59	7.50 / 57	8.24	B / 8.1	12.07	26.18
UT	*iShares MSCI ACWI ex US Utl Sct	AXUT	D+	41.26	D+ / 2.8	3.85 / 22	--	--	2.89	B- / 7.0	-2.50	0.13
UT	Duff & Phelps Global Utility Incom	DPG	D+	16.87	D / 1.9	4.66 / 23	--	--	8.30	B- / 7.9	-13.13	-4.55
UT	*iShares S&P Global Utilities	JXI	D+	41.23	D- / 1.4	5.86 / 26	-0.62 / 14	-5.05 / 9	3.56	B / 8.4	-0.22	0.16
UT	*EGShares Utilities GEMS ETF	UGEM	D	17.13	D+ / 2.6	7.59 / 29	--	--	1.68	C+ / 6.9	-0.87	-0.32
UT	*WisdomTree Global ex-US Utilitie	DBU	D	18.40	D- / 1.5	8.64 / 32	-1.76 / 12	-6.53 / 7	2.82	B- / 7.5	-0.43	0.05
UT	Wells Fargo Avtg Utilities&High In	ERH	D	11.18	D- / 1.3	5.97 / 26	-1.60 / 12	-6.74 / 7	8.05	C+ / 6.5	-6.29	-0.11
UT	Gabelli Utility Trust	GUT	D	6.16	D- / 1.2	-4.99 / 10	1.11 / 17	4.90 / 43	9.95	C+ / 6.6	10.39	33.95
UT	*SPDR SP Intl Utils Sector ETF	IPU	D	16.73	D- / 1.1	8.09 / 30	-5.75 / 8	--	3.38	B- / 7.2	0.36	0.36
UT	*ProShares UltraShort Utilities	SDP	D-	29.74	E / 0.4	-15.41 / 6	-22.97 / 4	-17.34 / 3	0.00	C+ / 5.8	4.76	0.02

99 Pct = Best
0 Pct = Worst

* Denotes ETF Fund, N/A denotes number is not available

www.thestreetratings.com

Appendix

What is a Mutual Fund?

Picking individual stocks is difficult and buying individual bonds can be expensive. Mutual funds were introduced to allow the small investor to participate in the stock and bond market for just a small initial investment. Mutual funds are pools of stocks or bonds that are managed by investment professionals.First, an investment company organizes the fund and collects the money from investors. The company then takes that money and pays a portfolio manager to invest it in stocks, bonds, money market instruments and other types of securities.

Most funds fit within one of two main categories, open-end funds or closed-end funds. Open-end funds issue new shares when investors put in money and redeem shares when investors withdraw money. The price of a share is determined by dividing the total net assets of the fund by the number of shares outstanding.

On the other hand, closed-end funds issue a fixed number of shares in an initial public offering, trading thereafter in the open market like a stock. Thus by their very nature, closed-end funds are unique in that they do not always trade at their net asset value (NAV). Unlike their open-end counterparts, closed-end funds trade on an exchange at market prices that are independent of their NAV. If the price is above the fund's NAV, the fund is said to be trading at a premium. If the price is lower than the fund's NAV, the fund trades at a discount. Investing in either class of funds means you own a share of the portfolio, so you participate in the fund's gains and losses.

Exchange traded funds are an increasingly popular subset of closed-end funds. Their portfolios are predefined "baskets" of investments (usually stocks or bonds, but sometimes commodity-related vehicles). Because they are passively managed, their expense ratios are generally much lower than actively managed open-end and closed-end funds. ETFs also incorporate an arbitrage process that keeps their market prices during the trading day extremely close to their respective net asset per share values. So unlike traditional closed-end funds, which frequently trade at premiums or discounts of several percentage points from their respective NAVs, ETFs normally remain within a fraction of a percent of NAV.

There are more than 20,000 different mutual funds, each with a stated investment objective. Here are descriptions for five of the most popular types of funds:

Stock funds: A mutual fund which invests mainly in stocks. These funds are more actively traded than other more conservative funds. The stocks chosen may vary widely according to the fund's investment strategy.

Bond funds: A mutual fund which invests in bonds, in an effort to provide stable income while preserving principal as much as possible. These funds invest in medium- to long-term bonds issued by corporations and governments.

Index funds: A mutual fund that aims to match the performance of a specific index, such as the S&P 500. Index funds tend to have fewer expenses than other funds because portfolio decisions are automatic and transactions are infrequent.

Balanced funds: A mutual fund that buys a combination of stocks and bonds, in order to supply both income and capital growth while ensuring a minimal amount of risk for investors.

Money market funds: An open-end mutual fund which invests only in stable, short-term securities. The fund seeks to preserve its value at a constant $1 per share. Money market funds are not insured by the FDIC, however may be covered by SIPC insurance. Investors should contact the firm administering their investment account to determine the insurance coverage of the funds or contact the FDIC and/or the SIPC directly.

Investing in a mutual fund has several advantages over owning a single stock or bond. For example, funds offer instant portfolio diversification by giving you ownership of many stocks or bonds simultaneously. This diversification protects you in case a part of your investment takes a sudden downturn. You also get the benefit of having a professional handling your investment, though a management fee is charged for these services, typically 1% or 2% a year. You should be aware that the fund may also levy other fees and that you will likely have to pay a commission to purchase the fund through a brokerage firm.

The fund manager's strategy is laid out in the fund's prospectus, which is the official name for the legal document that contains financial information about the fund, including its history, its officers and its performance. Mutual fund investments are fully liquid so you can easily get in or out by just placing an order through a broker.

How Do Open-End and Exchange-Traded Funds Differ?

Similarities:

Both open-end and ETFs…
- may be invested in stocks, bonds, derivatives, commodity-related instruments or a combination thereof.
- provide benefits of diversification by holding a basket of stocks, bonds, derivatives and/or commodity-related instruments.

Differences:

Open-End	Exchange-Traded Funds*
• Open-end funds are more popular. There are around 24,000 open-end funds available. The general term "mutual funds" typically refers to the much more common, open-end mutual funds.	• Exchange-traded funds are lesser known, and there are significantly fewer in existence.*
• Fund companies may require an initial minimum amount that must be invested.	• There is no minimum initial investment required. *
• Investors cannot utilize limit and stop orders.	• Investors may utilize limit and stop orders. *
• 12b-1 fees are used to pay for marketing the fund.	• 12b-1 fees are not charged. *
• All transactions occur at the end of each business day based upon the movement in the value of the fund's portfolio of securities.	• Shares are traded on an exchange throughout the day. *

* These attributes also apply to traditional closed-end funds. See next page for more information on traditional closed-end funds.

How do "Exchange-Traded Funds" (ETFs) and Traditional Closed-End Funds Differ?

ETFs are an increasingly popular subset of closed-end funds. The funds' portfolios represent "baskets" of securities or commodities, frequently representing components of popular indices such as the S&P 500 or the NASDAQ 100. They differ from traditional closed-end funds in several ways

A traditional closed-end fund issues a set number of shares. The shares outstanding rarely changes and only when approved by a vote of shareholders. ETFs, however, allow an arbitrage process whereby shares are frequently added and redeemed. The arbitrage tends to impact the price of the ETF fund as well as the prices of the individual investments in its portfolio.

While it is not uncommon for investor demand to drive traditional closed-end fund prices to premiums or discounts of several percentage points above or below their respective net asset values per share, the ETF arbitrage process normally keeps the market price of an ETF extremely close to its net asset per share value. ETFs normally trade within a small fraction of 1% above or below net asset value per share.

Only investment organizations pre-approved by an ETF's management company may engage in the normal arbitrage process involving shares of that fund. For a fee, a pre-approved arbitrageur may exchange a fund's shares for a "redemption unit" of actual shares in the component stocks, bonds and/or commodities of the fund's "basket" of securities or commodities. Conversely, the arbitrageur has the option of delivering to the ETF a predefined "basket" of securities or commodities known as a "creation unit." The arbitrage firm then receives in exchange a predetermined number shares in the fund.

How Do Open-End and Traditional Closed-End Funds Differ?

Similarities:

Both open-end and traditional (non-ETF) closed-end mutual funds…

- employ a fund manager or management team to invest assets in various types of securities according to the fund's stated objectives and policies.
- may be invested in stocks, bonds, commodities or a combination thereof.
- provide benefits of diversification by holding a basket of stocks, bonds and/or commodities.

Differences:

Open-End	Traditional Closed-End
• The mutual fund company issues and redeems shares on demand, whenever investors put money into the fund or take it out.	• The mutual fund company issues a set number of shares in an initial public offering and the shares then trade on an exchange.
• There is no limit to the number of shares the fund can issue.	• The fund offers a fixed number of shares.
• The share price is determined by the total value of the assets it holds.	• The share price is determined by investor demand for the fund.
• Fund shares trade at net asset value (NAV).	• Fund shares generally trade at a premium (above NAV) or discount (below NAV).

Performance Benchmark

The following benchmarks represent the average performance for all mutual funds within each ETF and closed-end fund category as of December 31, 2012. Investment returns are averages for all closed-end funds, which include ETFs. Comparing an individual mutual fund's returns to these benchmarks is yet another way to assess its performance. For the top performing funds within each of the following categories, turn to Section VI, Top-Rated ETFs and Other Closed-End Funds by Fund Type, beginning on page 732.

		3 Month Total Return %	1 Year Total Return %	Refer to page:
COH	Corporate - High Yield	2.49%	17.41%	732
COI	Corporate - Investment Grade	0.64%	7.25%	733
EM	Emerging Market Income	6.91%	15.57%	734
EN	Energy/Natural Res	1.10%	0.73%	735
FO	Non-US Equity	8.15%	15.61%	737
FS	Financial Services	7.03%	21.10%	736
GEI	General Bond - Investment Grade	-0.02%	6.29%	738
GEN	Multi-Sector Bond	1.66%	17.05%	739
GI	Growth & Income	2.50%	14.28%	742
GL	Global	3.73%	12.82%	740
GR	Growth - Domestic	3.45%	9.20%	741
HL	Health	5.18%	23.48%	743
IN	Equity Income	3.33%	12.07%	744
LP	Loan Participation	4.71%	23.17%	745
MTG	General Mortgage	1.35%	18.96%	746
MUH	Municipal - High Yield	2.82%	15.35%	747
MUN	Municipal - National	2.04%	13.20%	748
MUS	Municipal Single State	1.97%	14.07%	749
PM	Precious Metals	-2.84%	-4.62%	750
USA	Government Bond	-0.39%	0.74%	751
UT	Utilities	0.57%	6.72%	752

Exchange-Traded Funds Summary Data

ETF SUMMARY BY INVESTMENT OBJECTIVE *

INVESTMENT OBJECTIVE	NO. OF ETFs	TOTAL NET ASSETS ($MIL.)
Corporate - High Yield	14	31,161.3
Corporate - Investment Grade	38	61,132.1
Emerging Market Equity	55	120,158.2
Emerging Market Income	9	11,769.8
Equity Income	214	139,807.3
General Bd - Investment Grade	32	52,951.6
General Mortgage	4	6,922.1
Global Equity	112	20,843.2
Global Income	37	9,743.9
Government Bond	56	54,911.1
Growth & Income	86	33,488.5
Growth - Domestic	265	422,568.6
Loan Participation	2	1,531.3
Multi-Sector Bond	1	388.0
Municipal - High Yield	2	1,319.0
Municipal - National	18	9,596.2
Municipal Single State	2	410.1
Non-US Equity	227	165,009.1
Sector - Energy/Natural Res	99	34,053.3
Sector - Financial Services	31	19,081.3
Sector - Health/Biotechnology	25	13,343.8
Sector - Precious Metals	38	111,679.6
Sector - Utilities	14	7,982.4
TOTALS	1381	1,329,851.9

* ETFs only (traditional closed-end funds not included).

FUND GROUP	ETFs #	NET ASSETS ($MIL.)	FUND GROUP	ETFs #	NET ASSETS ($MIL.)
AdvisorShares Investments	16	604.2	Guggenheim Investments	34	6,907.7
ALPS Advisors Inc	26	5,537.0	Huntington Asset Advisors	2	16.1
Arrow Investment Advisors	1	26.9	IndexIQ Advisors LLC	11	580.0
Bank of New York Mellon	6	41,446.7	Invesco Powershares Cap Mgmt	122	27,725.5
Barclays Bank PLC	65	6,204.5	JP Morgan	2	4,869.1
BlackRock Fund Advisors	279	556,654.2	Morgan Stanley Inv Mgmt	4	66.9
BNP Paribas Quantitative Strat	1	17.8	Northern Trust Investments Inc	7	1,910.4
Charles Schwab Inv Mgmt	15	8,552.6	Nuveen Commodities Asset Mg	1	197.1
Citi Fund Management Inc	1	-	Pax World Management LLC	2	25.2
Columbia Management Inv Adv	4	22.6	PIMCO	18	8,883.7
Credit Suisse	21	1,187.1	Precidian Funds LLC	1	192.9
DB Commodity Services	22	11,553.2	ProShare Advisors LLC	134	21,163.9
DBX Advisors LLC	5	32.4	Pyxis Capital LP	1	31.9
DBX Strategic Advisors LLC	5	108.5	Rafferty Asset Mgmt LLC	45	5,927.2
Deutsche Bank AG (London)	18	312.3	Royal Bank of Scotland	11	141.2
Emerging Global Advisors LLC	1	2.0	Russell Investment Mgmt Co	1	2.9
ETF Securities USA LLC	7	4,072.0	SSgA Funds Management Inc	111	184,460.0
Exchange Traded Concepts	3	102.1	State Street Bank and Trust Co	2	133,924.3
Factor Capital Management	4	11.2	Swedish Export Credit Co	6	942.6
FFCM LLC	4	27.3	Teucrium Trading LLC	7	56.8
Fidelity Management & Res Co	1	178.4	UBS Global Asset Mgmt	31	1,281.9
First Trust Advisors LP	71	8,129.8	United States Commodity Funds	12	3,139.7
Global X Management Co	31	1,511.3	Van Eck Associates Corp	50	27,048.4
Goldman Sachs & Co/GSAM	1	-	Vanguard Group Inc	63	230,022.1
Greenhaven Commodity Svcs	1	474.6	VTL Associates LLC	6	421.7
Guggenheim Funds Inv Adv	42	4,858.6	WisdomTree Asset Mgmt	46	18,285.3
* ETFs only (traditional closed-end funds excluded)			**TOTALS**	**1381**	**1,329,851.9**

Fund Type Descriptions

<u>COH - Corporate - High Yield</u> - Seeks high current income by investing a minimum of 65% of its assets in generally low-quality corporate debt issues.

<u>COI - Corporate - Investment Grade</u> - Seeks current income by investing a minimum of 65% in investment grade corporate debt issues. Investment grade securities must be BBB or higher, as rated by Standard & Poor's.

<u>EM - Emerging Market</u> - Seeks long term capital appreciation and/or income by investing primarily in emerging market equity and/or income producing securities.

<u>EN - Energy/Natural Resources</u> - Invests primarily in equity securities of companies involved in the exploration, distribution, or processing of natural resources.

<u>FS - Financial</u> - Seeks capital appreciation by investing in equity securities of companies engaged in providing financial services. Typically, securities are from commercial banks, S&Ls, finance companies, securities brokerages, investment managers, insurance companies, and leasing companies.

<u>FO - Foreign</u> - Invests primarily in non-U.S. equity securities of any market capitalization. Income is usually incidental.

<u>GEI - General - Investment Grade</u> - Seeks income by investing in investment grade domestic or foreign corporate debt, government debt and preferred securities.

<u>GEN - General Bond</u> - Seeks income by investing without geographic boundary in corporate debt, government debt or preferred securities. Investments are not tied to any specific maturity or duration.

<u>GL - Global</u> - Invests primarily in domestic and foreign equity securities of any market capitalization and/or fixed income securities issued by domestic and/or foreign governments.

<u>GR - Growth</u> - Seeks long term capital appreciation by investing primarily in equity securities of any market capitalization. Income is usually incidental.

<u>GI - Growth and Income</u> - Seeks both capital appreciation and income primarily by investing in equities with a level or rising dividend stream.

<u>HL - Health</u> - Seeks capital appreciation by investing primarily in equities of companies engaged in the design, manufacture, or sale of products or services connected with health care or medicine.

<u>IN - Income</u> - Seeks current income by investing a minimum of 65% of its assets in income-producing equity securities.

<u>LP - Loan Participation</u> - Invests a minimum of 65% of its assets in loan interests.

<u>MTG - Mortgage</u> - Invests a minimum of 65% of its assets in a broad range of mortgage or mortgage-related securities, including those issued by the U.S. government and by government related and private organizations.

<u>MUH - Municipal - High Yield</u> - Seeks tax-free income by investing a minimum of 65% of its assets in generally low-quality issues from any state municipality.

<u>MUN - Municipal - National</u> - Seeks federally tax-free income by investing at least 65% in issues from any state municipality.

<u>MUS - Municipal - Single State</u> - Seeks tax-free income by investing in issues which are exempt from federal and the taxation of a specified state.

<u>PM - Precious Metals</u> - Seeks capital appreciation by investing primarily in equity securities of companies involved in mining, distribution, processing, or dealing in gold, silver, platinum, diamonds, or other precious metals and minerals.

<u>USA - U.S. Government - Agency</u> - Invests a minimum of 65% in securities issued or guaranteed by the Government, its agencies or instrumentalities. Investments are not tied to any specific maturity or duration.

<u>UT - Utilities</u> - Seeks a high level of current income by investing primarily in the equity securities of utility companies.